SO-AJH-876

Business Communication

Business Communication

Principles and Processes

Mary Cullinan
California State University—Hayward

Holt, Rinehart and Winston, Inc.
Fort Worth   Chicago   San Francisco   Philadelphia
Montreal   Toronto   London   Sydney   Tokyo

Publisher, Humanities: *Charlyce Jones Owen*
Developmental Editors: *Kate Morgan, Susan Alkana*
Assistant Editor: *Tod Gross*
Senior Project Editor: *Lester A. Sheinis*
Production Manager: *Annette Mayeski*
Design Supervisor: *Gloria Gentile*
Text and Cover Design: *Caliber Design Planning, Inc.*

Library of Congress Cataloging-in-Publication Data

Cullinan, Mary.
   Business communication : principles and processes / Mary Cullinan.
     p.   cm.
   Bibliography: p.
   Includes index.
    1. Business communication.   2. Commercial correspondence.
3. Commercial correspondence.   4. Word processing.   I. Title.
HF5718.C85   1989
651.7—dc19   88–32218
                                   CIP

ISBN 0-03-011869-7

Printed in the United States of America

9 0 1 2   015   9 8 7 6 5 4 3 2 1

Holt, Rinehart and Winston, Inc.
The Dryden Press
Saunders College Publishing

Credits

1 "Pursuant to Your Request, A Story on Bad Business Writing," by Eric Best. From *The San Francisco Examiner*, 1/24/88. Copyright © *The San Francisco Examiner* 1988. Reprinted with permission.

2 Excerpts pp. 12 and 16–17 from *The Technical Writer* by Ann Stuart, copyright © 1988 by Holt, Rinehart and Winston, Inc., reprinted by permission of the publisher.

3 Drawing by C. Barsotti; copyright © 1984 *The New Yorker Magazine, Inc.* From *The New Yorker Magazine*, 11/26/84.

4 Drawing by Lorenz; copyright © 1984 *The New Yorker Magazine, Inc.* From *The New Yorker Magazine*, 12/24/84.

5 Drawing by Weber; copyright © 1985 *The New Yorker Magazine, Inc.* From *The New Yorker Magazine*, 2/4/85.

6 Drawing by Dana Fradon; copyright © 1986 *The New Yorker Magazine, Inc.* From *The New Yorker Magazine*.

7 Drawing by Maslin; copyright © 1987 *The New Yorker Magazine, Inc.* From *The New Yorker Magazine*, 9/17/87.

8 "In This Futuristic Office, Intimacy Exists Between Workers Separated by 500 Miles," by Michael Miller. From *The Wall Street Journal*, 6/27/86. Reprinted by permission of *The Wall Street Journal*, © Dow Jones & Company, Inc. 1986. All rights reserved.

9 Drawing by Gerard. From *The Wall Street Journal*—Permission, Cartoon Features Syndicate.

(Credits continue on page 733.)

To the Instructor

Business Communication: Principles and Processes is a comprehensive business communication text that students will find exciting, practical, lucid, and informative. It combines thorough coverage of written and oral communication with cases that enable students to apply communication strategies to a wide range of business situations and problems. Interviews with business people highlight techniques and approaches that have been successful in small and large companies and in nonprofit organizations. Articles from journals and magazines focus on real-life communication problems and solutions. The Business Writer's Handbook at the end of the text provides an overview of grammar, punctuation, and mechanics accompanied by exercises to help students review writing fundamentals.

The *process* of communication is a major focus of this text. The chapters on oral communication involve students in a process approach to speaking and listening. The chapters on business writing stress the importance of brainstorming, audience analysis, and other prewriting activities, as well as strategies for drafting and revising. Since computers are an integral part of modern business communication and an invaluable aid for writers, a chapter on word processing encourages students to use computers for each step of the writing process.

Four chapters are devoted to employment strategies. These chapters will help students both to decide what type of job they want and to be successful in their job search. Also, because business is becoming increasingly global in nature, a section on intercultural communication outlines concepts and strategies vital to success in a multicultural business environment.

Business Communication: Principles and Processes is a dynamic and practical classroom text. It is also a reference book that students can turn to for advice on writing and speaking for other classes and for their jobs. The text is divided into nine parts, the Business Writer's Handbook, two appendixes, and a glossary of business terms. Part 1, "Communication Principles and Process," introduces students to the communication process and to ways in which communication problems can be solved. Part 2, "Writing and Revising Business Documents," concentrates on how the writing process can be used to develop business documents and how computers can facilitate the process. Part 3, "Business Letters," examines the importance of external business communication and focuses on informational as well as persuasive letters. Part 4, "Memorandums," discusses the unique features of memos and techniques for developing them effectively. Part 5, "Reports," examines short reports, proposals, formal reports, and report graphics. Part 6, "Employment Communication Principles and Processes," discusses both job-search and interview strategies and techniques for developing effective resumes, application letters, and other documents related to employment. Part 7, "Oral Communication Principles and Processes," provides guidelines for listening and speaking effectively in meetings, in interviews, in front of groups, and on the telephone. Part 8, "Intercultural Communication," introduces students to the types of problems they may encounter when working with people of other cultures and to strategies for avoiding these problems.

At the end of each chapter on business writing are word processing exercises designed to help students increase their knowledge of word processing and improve their skills. Mini-cases enable students to apply concepts learned in each section of the text. Part 9, "Cases," includes ten additional cases that may be used for oral and written assignments as well as for class discussion.

The Business Writer's Handbook is a guide to grammar, punctuation, and mechanics that focuses on the most common problems encountered by students and business writers. The handbook includes a glossary of grammatical terms and exercises students can use to test their skills as they study. Appendix A, "Legal Aspects of Business Writers," discusses some of the legal problems business writers need to be aware of. Appendix B, "Business Letter Parts and Formats," is a useful reference for letter writers. The "Glossary of Business Terms" enables students to look up key terms with ease.

A comprehensive ancillary package of teaching and learning aids complements the text:

- *Study Guide* by Mary Cullinan. This workbook provides students with a chapter-by-chapter review of the text, including chapter pretests, post-tests, and vocabulary quizzes, as well as supplemental cases and exercises. The workbook enables students to practice writing and revising sentences, paragraphs, and business documents and to reinforce their understanding of business communication concepts discussed in the text.
- *The Russell and Associates Papers: A Casebook of Business Writing* by J. Stephen Russell. This unique casebook contains 100 letters, memos, and reports that illustrate the concepts and skills of business communication. The "papers," which reflect one year in the business life of a company, include assignments that ask students to write documents responding to real-life business situations. The casebook includes analyses of the papers from the point of view of style and effectiveness.
- *Instructor's Manual.* This resource manual includes detailed information on teaching writing, an annotated bibliography, articles on teaching busi-

ness communication, and answers to the exercises in the text, in the study guide, and in the casebook.

- *Transparency Acetates.* These 32 overhead transparencies highlight major concepts in the text.
- *Test Bank.* The Test Bank includes 2,000 carefully constructed items to assist instructors in creating objective tests and essay questions.
- *Computerized Test Bank.* This test-generation program, which contains the items from the printed *Test Bank,* provides an option for developing alternate test versions that are specific to an instructor's needs. The program is available for IBM, Apple, and Macintosh computers.
- *ProcessWriter.* This exciting new word processing program has been designed to allow writers to transfer writing process techniques to the computer. The program includes an on-line handbook of grammar and usage. The program comes with a User's Guide and is available for IBM and Macintosh computers. A supplementary disk contains exercises and writing assignments from *Business Communication: Principles and Processes* so that students can practice writing and revising using ProcessWriter.
- *ProcessWriter Guide to Writing* by Deborah Holdstein. This writing workbook, which includes exercises that supplement *ProcessWriter,* has been designed to teach students about using features of *ProcessWriter* to explore the writing process.
- *A Guide to Computer Aided Instruction* by David Roberts. This instructor's manual accompanying *ProcessWriter* provides advice on teaching both with computers in general and with this software in particular. The manual includes an annotated bibliography of important articles on computer aided instruction.
- *The Business Writing Tutor.* This eight-disk interactive software program provides a tutorial and exercises for 36 grammar and writing topics, including parts of speech, sentence errors, style, mechanics, and punctuation. The program is available for IBM, Apple, and Macintosh computers.

For an examination copy of any of these ancillaries, please write to: English Editor, Holt, Rinehart and Winston, Inc., 301 Commerce Street, Fort Worth, TX 76102.

Acknowledgments

I would like to thank the following people at Holt: Charlyce Jones Owen, Publisher Humanities, who supported the book from the beginning; Kate Morgan, Developmental Editor, and Tod Gross, Assistant Editor, who contributed to every phase of the project; Susan Alkana, Developmental Editor, whose hard work and creativity are evident in every chapter; Lester Sheinis, Senior Project Editor, Gloria Gentile, Design Supervisor, and Annette Mayeski, Production Manager, who have contributed their special talents to the book's design and production. Finally, I thank the many reviewers who provided valuable insights and suggestions at every stage of the manuscript: Pat Allen, Northeastern State University; Mary Sexton Barrett, Edgecombe Community College; Della Bates, Highland Park Community College; Arthur Bell, University of Southern California; Jane Bergman, St. Louis Community College at Meremac; Anna Burford, Middle Tennessee State University; Beth Camp, Linn-Benton Community College; John Comeau, Indiana Vocational Technical College; Carol David, Iowa State University; Patricia Evanson, Northcentral Technical College; Sallyanne Fitzgerald, University of Missouri–St. Louis; Patricia Hinchey, The Pennsylvania State University; Betty Hughes, Beaufort County Community College; Ruth Keller, Indiana Vocational Technical College; Shelby Kipplen, Owens Technical College; Alexandra Linnett, Delaware Technical and Community College; Thomas Means, Louisiana Tech University; Carol Pemberton, Normandale Community College; Joanne Rathburne, Northeastern Wisconsin Technical Institute; Patricia Rochelt, Western Wisconsin Technical College; Michael Rossi, Merrimack College; Robert Scattergood, Belmont Technical College; Bill Stiffler, Harford Community College; Dene Kay Thomas, University of Idaho; Thomas Trzyna, Seattle Pacific University; Ted Valvoda, Lakeland Community College; and Jane Vire, Ivy Tech Southwest.

M.C.

To the Student

Business Communication: Principles and Processes is designed to help you develop skills that you will use throughout your life, no matter what your background, interests, or career goals. Addressing questions and problems that students have voiced over and over in business communication classes, this text provides a comprehensive guide to spoken and written business communication. It will help you in a wide range of situations, from writing a memo to getting a job, from attending a meeting to giving a speech.

Business Communication: Principles and Processes is not only a comprehensive guide to spoken and written business communication: It also provides examples of communication strategies that work in the real world. Interviews with business people provide insights into communication problems and practical ways in which they can be solved. Articles from magazines and newspapers highlight both recent trends in communication and actual problems faced by managers and employees. Cases and exercises give you opportunities to develop your own strategies for handling a myriad of situations requiring business communication skills.

While emphasizing fundamentals of communication theory and practice, *Business Communication: Principles and Processes* also advocates creative approaches to problem-solving that will help you while you are in college and throughout every phase of your career.

A Sampling of Features

- A *case* at the opening of each chapter introduces you to concepts covered in the chapter and is then discussed at the end of the chapter.
- *Mini-cases* at the end of each section and longer cases at the end of the text provide springboards for class discussion and assignments.
- *Interviews* with businesspeople from a variety of industries stress communication strategies they use in the real world.

- Chapter objectives, checklists, marginal notes, summaries, terms to remember, questions for review and discussion, and exercises help you preview and review the subject matter in each chapter.
- *Word processing exercises* will help you use computers for writing and revising.
- *Glossaries* of word processing terms, business terms, and grammatical terms provide a reference for important terminology.
- *Boxed material* in each chapter highlights and supplements key concepts.
- Chapters on *writing and revising business prose* as well as on the writing process itself introduce important techniques for writing.
- *Detailed discussions* highlight the many types of letters, memorandums, and reports used in business.
- The chapters on *oral communication* provide strategies useful for both entry-level employees and managers.
- A thorough section on *employment* focuses on self-appraisal, research, and practical strategies for successful job-hunting.
- A *business writer's handbook* summarizes guidelines for grammar, punctuation, and mechanics and contains numerous exercises that will enable you to check your mastery of the material.

The following supplements to the text are also available:

- The *Study Guide* will help you review and test yourself on each chapter of the text and give you more practice in drafting and revising business documents.
- *The Casebook of Business Writing* provides additional opportunities for you to apply principles of effective communication to business situations.
- *The Business Writing Tutor,* software that supplements both the Handbook for Business Writers in your text and the Study Guide, provides interactive exercises to help you review and master elements of grammar, mechanics, and style essential for writing business documents.
- *ProcessWriter,* an exciting and unique word processing program, enables you to transfer writing process techniques to the computer.

Contents

Part Three
Business Letters   148

Part Four

Memorandums 276

Part Five

Reports 322

Part Six

Employment Communications   432

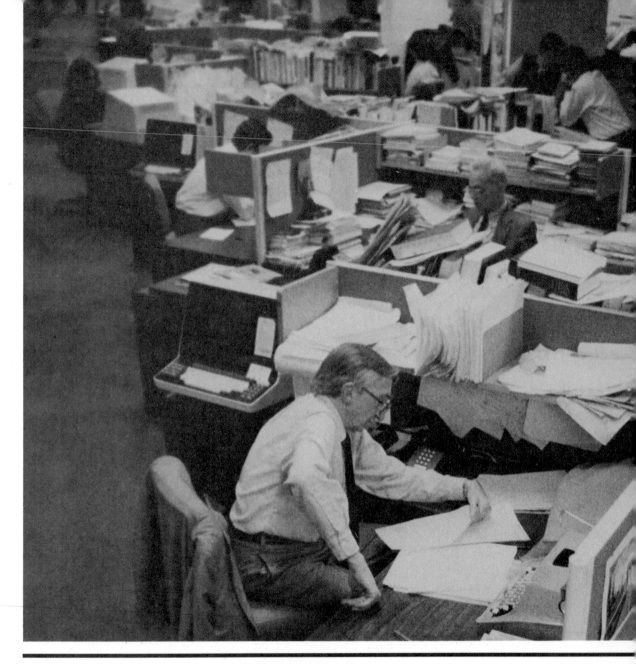

Communication
Principles and Processes

Part
One

The Communication Process

- Defining commu-
  nication
- Using a communi-
  cation model
- Developing the
  you-attitude
- Recognizing the
  communication
  process
- Communicating
  with words
- Communicating
  without words
- Sending uninten-
  tional messages
- Sending external
  and internal mes-
  sages

Objectives

To understand how
the communication
process works

To recognize the
importance of the
you-attitude

To learn the forms
of communication
within an organiza-
tion

1

Tom Milner and the Typing Pool

Tom Milner is a young executive working his way to the top of Z-Tone Chemical Corporation. He has a friendly, almost exuberant manner and a knack for remembering people's names.

He also has a knack for getting special favors. For example, the typists in the typing pool are supposed to have three days' lead time to finish a project over five pages long. However, Tom often asks one of them to put his drafts on a word processor "right away."

"How are you, Karen?" he asks in his booming voice one day.

"I've got a cold," she answers. "It's this rainy weather."

"Fine, fine," he replies without really hearing her. "Do you think you could get this done right away? I'm running behind schedule this week."

After giving Karen the work to do, he jokes for a moment with other members of the clerical staff and leaves people smiling after him.

"That guy's going to make vice-president," says Jim Slade, one of the typing pool staff. "He knows everybody."

Karen corrects him. "He remembers names. He doesn't *know* any of us."

"You're right," comments another staff member. "He doesn't hear anything you tell him. He didn't even hear you say you have a cold."

"The man talks," says Karen, "but he doesn't communicate at all."

Points to Consider

- Does Tom Milner have a communication problem? If so, what could he do to improve his communication skills?
- Is talking different from communicating?

Defining Communication

Most people believe they know what communication is. Students asked to define communication usually have no trouble describing its various aspects. Managers asked to point out a "communication problem" in their organization are quick to find one—or several.

Communication occurs in innumerable ways. It may take place face-to-face or on the telephone; by means of interviews, meetings, conferences, classes, or lectures; through letters, reports, or memoranda; through the use of computers, movies, television, billboards, newspapers, magazines, or other media.

Communication is an ongoing process in our lives.

The types and means of communication, in fact, are too numerous to list. In general, however, the major goal remains the same: to convey a message to someone else. The word comes from a Latin word *communis* meaning *common*: it includes everything you have, or try to have, *in common* with someone else.

Communication involves conveying a message to someone else.

Although you spend a large portion of every day communicating, you probably do not often stop to consider exactly what happens during the communication process. Whether you are speaking on the telephone, writing a postcard, exchanging glances with a friend, or waiting at a bus stop, you are communicating. But what elements are common to all these situations?

Using a Communication Model

To perceive the elements of the communication process, visualize it as a loop with five major components: a sender, a message, a channel, a receiver, and feedback (Figure 1–1).

The Sender

Internal and external variables affect the sender of a message.

As the sender or *source* of a message, you are affected by the environment surrounding you. Perceptions, attitudes, values, opinions, cultural and educational background, and a whole spectrum of internal variables affect the way you process stimuli coming from outside.

Consider Meg Woods, a student sitting in an American history class. As she listens to her classmates discuss World War II, she finds herself disagreeing with some of their opinions. Having spent her childhood in France, she has a different perspective from some of the other students in the class. The discussion around her and her own perceptions lead her to raise her hand and state her point of view.

The Message

The *sender* encodes ideas for a receiver.

In order to communicate, you must transform your ideas into a form that someone else can comprehend. This process, called *encoding*, occurs as you select and put together ideas and then translate them into words, pictures, numbers, gestures, or other symbols that someone else can understand.

Meg Woods, for instance, raises her hand to indicate that she wishes to speak in class. Then she uses spoken words to convey her opinion about the war.

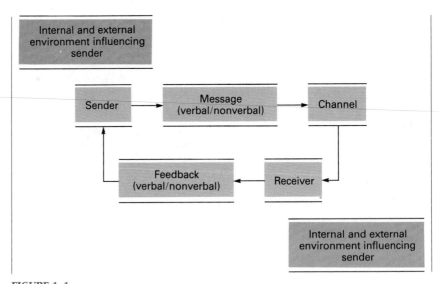

FIGURE 1–1
A communication model

The Channel

As the sender of a message, you need to choose an appropriate channel through which to transmit the message. The possible channels are innumerable. Messages may be conveyed through print, touch, sound, smell, and many other media. The channel may be a letter, a telephone call, a meeting, a speech, or an interview; it may be a newspaper, a magazine, a billboard, a radio, television, or computer message.

Meg Woods speaks directly to her classmates and instructor. Later on in the semester, she will incorporate her ideas into a written report.

The Receiver

The receiver of the message is the focus of the communication process. If this person does not understand the message, the whole process has been a failure. The receiver deciphers or *decodes* the message by methods such as listening, reading, and watching. The receiver's environment, attitudes, social skills, perceptions, and other variables affect the decoding of the message just as the sender's environment influences the encoding.

To send a message successfully, you need to adapt your message especially to the receiver. Meg Woods must adapt her comments to both her instructor and her classmates.

Feedback

Although not always present, feedback is an important element of communication because it completes the process. It allows the sender to understand how the receiver responded to the message. When feedback occurs, the

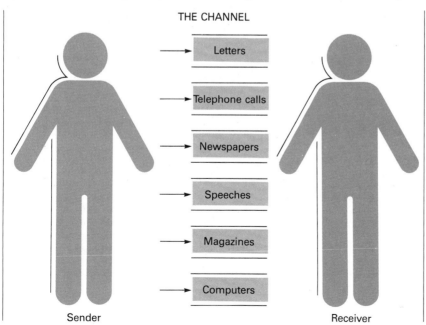

THE CHANNEL

Letters

Telephone calls

Newspapers

Speeches

Magazines

Computers

Sender

Receiver

"To be a good communicator you have to create an environment that helps other people to be free and comfortable to communicate their problems and concerns," says Eileen Grizer, Northeast Regional Director for National Consumer Affairs for Maxicare Health Plans. *"I see myself as the mortar between the bricks, the facilitator, who helps others put forth a good product."* In this case, the product is good health care under the Maxicare HMO (health maintenance organization). Eileen defines a HMO as *"a person or group of persons who enter into an arrangement to provide health service. The HMO arranges for the provision of these services (both on an ambulatory care and inpatient basis) through agreements with physicians, hospitals, and other providers."*

Eileen practices her communication skills daily as she travels around the Northeast, meeting with the administrators of consumer affairs departments within each Maxicare HMO. She "consults with them about operational problems, helps them establish objectives for efficient functioning, and reminds them of their goals: public relations, problem solving and advocacy for members, and educating members about how the system works."

Eileen says, "Consumer advocates talk to members of Maxicare over the phone, where they must be responsive and convey a sense of caring. They must use their tone of voice, supportive statements, and affirmations to establish a sense of rapport and convey the message, 'We care.' They must also know what questions to ask and how to answer questions in a way that will lay the groundwork for a resolution of the member's problem.

"Letters are the second, and a most important, step," says Eileen. A follow-up letter is the more formalized response to the member's difficulty. Often this is a standard letter, contained in the word processor, which the consumer advocates modify and individualize. "The follow-up letter confirms the oral interactions and suggests a recourse for the member."

Eileen says the most important attributes in consumer advocacy are "interpersonal skills, a positive attitude, excellent communications skills, and the ability to be a team player. A person can be productive, but if she or he doesn't know how to work as part of a team, the person can't be effective in this work. The finished product is the result of negotiation, the exchange of ideas, and compromise."

A good example of team playing takes place in grievance hearings, which Eileen occasionally attends to advise the executive directors of individual Maxicare HMOs. Here patients, consumer advocates, medical directors, and executive directors meet to work out a patient's complaint in face-to-face question and answer interactions. "One woman had been told by a marketing representative that a particular benefit, an artificial eye, would be covered under the Maxicare plan. It isn't covered ordinarily, but because the woman had been told, however informally, that it would be, Maxicare directors accepted that a verbal commitment had been made, and they agreed to cover it." Maxicare then sent a letter, a written document, to confirm the decision.

Eileen says, "We can teach many skills to newcomers. We can train them in policies and procedure, but they must have basic communication skills. They must know how to adapt what they have to communicate to each person they deal with. They must sense what that person needs to hear to accept the message. They must ask themselves, 'How do I phrase this idea so the other person will understand and accept it?'"

Communication tips from Eileen:

- Adapt your communications to the particular person you are dealing with.
- Phrase your communications so the person will accept your message.
- Use a warm, positive tone of voice.
- Be as supportive as possible.
- Individualize standard letters.

receiver becomes the sender of a message, but that message is a response to a former message. When you press the switch on a lamp and the light comes on, you have received instant feedback. If the light does not come on, you have received a message as well—that the lamp is broken or the bulb burned out.

Feedback takes many forms. It may appear as a sudden rise in sales after a commercial has been aired, or it may be manifested in a person's voice quality over the telephone; it may take the form of a nod, a smile, or a fleeting expression of anger or distaste.

Feedback is an essential element of the communication process because it helps the sender know how the message was received or *if* it was received. If the sender perceives that the message was misinterpreted or misunderstood, he or she can choose to retransmit or modify the message. Moreover, feedback often leads into a new message: the receiver of the first message becomes a sender, and the whole process continues. For example, notice what happens in the following dialogue:

> JAN: I saw Doug yesterday.
> TED: So did I. He's leaving for Aspen on Wednesday.
> JAN: Great! I am too.

Jan initiates a message in this dialogue; then, when Ted responds, he sends a message back to her. Next, Jan provides feedback—and a new message. Similarly, Meg Woods' comments in her history class lead to a discussion involving the students, the instructor, and Meg herself.

Most communication, then, can be envisioned as a loop, a continuous process actively involving both senders and receivers. Strategies for successfully relaying messages, transmitting and understanding feedback, and appropriately modifying messages will be the focus for your study of business communication.

Developing the You-Attitude

Whatever message or channel you choose, one aspect of communication remains the same: to be successful, your message must be tailored to the receiver.

The you-attitude is crucial to effective communication.

If the receiver cannot understand, or *misunderstands*, the message, your efforts have been wasted. If your receiver understands but responds negatively to your message, your communication may be equally futile. At the core of any communication, then, is what has been termed the *you-attitude*: an approach to communication in which the sender adapts the message to the receiver's interests and needs. This approach requires putting yourself in someone else's shoes.

Notice what happens in the following conversations.

> DANA: Fix the grammar in this letter, Phil. I found some dangling participles.
> PHIL: Dangling participles?
> DANA: Three of them. Don't let Hank see the letter till it's correct.

Are You a Good Communicator?

Which reaction to these situations best describes how you would respond?

1. An instructor has given you three weeks to write a report on a topic you know little about—the rise of labor unions in Japan after World War II.
   a. You ask the instructor to recommend some articles so you can begin researching the topic.
   b. You begin frantically writing and revising drafts of the report.
   c. You do nothing until the night before the report is due.
2. The person at Smith & Company who interviewed you calls to say you did not get the job you applied for.
   a. You politely say how sorry you are and hang up.
   b. You ask the interviewer what areas you need to improve.
   c. You hang up angrily.
3. Your supervisor at work requests that you call a meeting for the three people working on the project you are in charge of.
   a. You send an announcement of the meeting to the three people.
   b. You call up the people and tell them about the meeting.
   c. You find out when each person is free during the following week and then send an announcement of the meeting.
4. One of the people working on a team project with you did not finish part of the work allocated to him or her.
   a. You complain about the person's behavior during the next team meeting.
   b. You speak to the person privately and try to find out what the problem is.
   c. You tell the other team members that the person should be expelled from the group.
5. You are taking an important course taught by a dull instructor.
   a. You "tune out" and wait for each class to be over.
   b. You write down everything that is said in each class.
   c. You summarize key points in your notes and ask questions when you are confused.

Discussion

Good communication usually requires a two-way flow of information. Rather than just soaking in information or simply delivering messages, work on creating a flow of messages and feedback.

1. Talk with your instructor before beginning a big project. Best answer: a
2. Find out from the interviewer why you were not hired. Best answer: b
3. Talk to colleagues before sending a written announcement. Best answer: c
4. Find out if the problem can be solved before embarrassing someone. Best answer: b
5. Listen actively and participate so you will learn the material and lessen your boredom. Best answer: c

JIM: I need those reports from Accounting by 3 p.m.
JILL: Kate says they won't be available until 4:30.
JIM: They *have* to be available.
JILL: But—
JIM: Don't argue. That's all there is to it.

In the first dialogue, Phil's feedback indicates that he does not know what dangling participles are. Dana does not define the term, so she may not get the action from Phil that she wants. In the second dialogue, Jim refuses to listen to Jill's response. Jim's self-centered attitude could hurt his working relationship with Jill—and it probably will not help him get the reports by 3 o'clock.

No communication can be transmitted perfectly. However, you can learn to avoid the worst pitfalls. The you-attitude is particularly useful in solving a great number of communication problems that you will encounter both at your job and in your day-to-day life.

Using the You-Attitude

Compare the following examples of the I-attitude and the you-attitude. Note that examples of the I-attitude do not always contain the word *I*.

I-Attitude	*You-Attitude*
I believe your company could use an efficient programmer like me. I enclose my resume.	If your company is looking for an efficient programmer, please consider the enclosed resume.
Company management requests that employees attend the driver's education course on June 12.	To upgrade your safe driving skills, you are invited to attend the driver's education course on June 12.
After the research team reviewed the information, I summarized it in the following report.	The following report summarizes the information reviewed by the research team.
Student Volunteers is an organization founded to help children with learning disabilities. As we need your support, we are inviting you to a meeting on October 4.	If you are interested in using your skills to help children with learning disabilities, please attend our meeting on October 4.
Dan's Stationer's is having a half-price sale on school supplies this Saturday.	Enjoy 50% off school supplies at Dan's Stationer's this Saturday.
I wrote this story with your experiences in my mind.	This story is based on your experiences.

Recognizing the Communication Process

Communication, of course, is not an isolated incident. It is a complex, on-going process involving words, sensory stimuli, emotions, actions, and reactions.

When you meet someone at a party, for example, both you and the other person begin interpreting facial expressions, voice tones, physical appearance, and gestures as well as words. You decode and encode messages through your language, cultural backgrounds, values, and social situations. You are both affected by internal and external stimuli.

Communication is a dynamic process that involves many related activities working together. Although a memo from you to a fellow employee may seem like a simple one-way unit of communication, it is actually only part

Communication is an ongoing process involving far more than words and actions.

of a whole process. What prompted you to write the memo? Why did you write a memo instead of telephoning? Why did you choose the words you chose? What response will the reader make to the memo? The stimuli that caused you to write and send the memo are highly complex, as are the messages you will receive from your reader.

Moreover, that memo is only one element in an ongoing communication process between you and other employees. And it is only a small part of a communication process that runs through your entire organization and through the whole society.

In order to understand business communication more thoroughly, you need to identify different forms of communication. In general, communication may be verbal and nonverbal, intentional and unintentional, and internal and external.

Communicating with Words

A verbal message may be written or spoken.

A message transmitted by words is a *verbal* communication. Letters, memos, reports, telephone conversations, telegrams, television commercials, and meetings all require some form of verbal communication.

Oral messages are conveyed through speech.

Written messages are usually conveyed on paper or by computer.

Words, however, may be either spoken or written. The two major types of verbal communication are distinguished by the words *oral* and *written*. Oral communication consists of formal presentations, speeches, meetings, television and radio commercials, telephone conversations, informal discussions, and so on. Written communication includes memos, letters, reports, resumes, scripts, newspapers, and many other types of documents.

Both types of verbal communication have strengths and weaknesses. Each is useful and appropriate for certain situations. Oral communication, for example, is usually faster than written. Because oral communication often receives almost instantaneous feedback from the receiver, a speaker may be able to alter the message, if need be, in order to make sure it is understood.

On the other hand, because oral communication is usually linked with many sensory variables, the receiver may not hear a message correctly. For example, in a noisy room you may think someone has said he was *fired* when actually he has said he was *tired*. Or, because you were distracted when an instructor was telling the class about an upcoming exam, you might think it is scheduled for the fifteenth of May when actually it is scheduled for the fifth of May.

Oral messages are conveyed quickly, but they may be confusing or imprecise.

If the exam date is written on the course syllabus, on the other hand, you can check it any time you want. Written communications take longer to transmit and do not usually result in rapid feedback, but they may also be more carefully analyzed. A written contract, for example, may contain hundreds of pieces of information that readers can digest slowly.

As the sender of a written message, you must rely solely on the words on the page. Therefore, precision is extremely important. When speaking, you can make corrections: "Did I say that sales *exceeded* last year's? I meant they *equaled* last year's." When you write, your error stays on the page and cannot be so easily corrected.

Written messages can easily convey complicated information.

Both types of verbal communication require the use of language. Although the spoken and the written language are similar in many ways, they also have many significant differences (Figure 1–2). To be an effective communicator, become aware of these differences and learn to use both written and spoken language as channels for your messages.

Communicating Without Words

Nonverbal communication includes a multitude of cues that people use to accompany and sometimes to replace their words. Nonverbal communication includes the way you furrow your brow, tap your feet, smile, frown, or use your voice. It includes the way you dress, stand, and walk.

Messages can be conveyed without words.

Imagine seeing a fellow student walk into a classroom on the first day of class. Even though you have never seen her before, you pick up some non-

	Spoken	*Written*
Uses words	x	x
Communicates very quickly	x	
Can receive instant feedback	x	
Can be quickly retransmitted	x	
Involves many sensory variables	x	
Can be easily analyzed		x
Can be easily saved		x

FIGURE 1–2

Two types of verbal communication

Nonverbal messages may support or contradict the verbal messages accompanying them.

verbal messages. She smiles as she sees some people she knows; she walks with confidence; she wears an outfit that has been carefully put together. You decide, even before she speaks, that she is self-assured, outgoing, and organized.

Sometimes nonverbal messages contradict rather than enhance verbal communication. The words themselves may be harmless and friendly, for instance, but their tone and other subtle nonverbal elements can transmit negative feelings. Interestingly, people tend to believe the nonverbal more than the verbal messages.

Nonverbal messages, however, do not always transmit the truth. Upon getting to know the woman who walked into class the first day, you might find she is shy, self-conscious, and disorganized. Perhaps your initial perceptions were wrong, or perhaps the woman had learned to use a nonverbal language that disguised her weaknesses. No communication transmits totally reliable messages.

Sending Unintentional Messages

People frequently send messages they do not intend to convey.

You have undoubtedly had the experience of sending a message you did not plan to send. Perhaps, while you sat in a job interview, your feet jiggled nervously; while giving an oral report in class, you stammered. These unintentional messages may have directly contradicted your oral messages of self-assurance or pleasure at being in the situation.

No one can help sending some unintentional messages. You cannot totally control your eyes, gestures, and tone of voice. However, you can increase your awareness and control over these unintentional nonverbal messages. You can improve your performance in job interviews and oral presentations, for example, by minimizing the audience's awareness of your discomfort or insecurity.

Being aware of unintentional messages can enhance your management skills.

You can also increase your own awareness of the messages sent out by others. When working in an organization, watch for the unintentional communication sent out by both superiors and subordinates. Just as a doctor can often diagnose patients' problems from the way they walk or hold themselves, a manager may be able to detect morale problems simply by noticing the way people sit at their desks or walk in each morning.

No matter what else they are doing, people are almost always communicating. Being able to decode unspoken messages is a skill you will find useful in any field or career you enter.

Sending External and Internal Messages

All companies rely upon both external and internal communication. External messages are those that flow in and out of an organization. These may take such forms as advertisements, telephone conversations with vendors, letters to customers, and meetings with clients.

External communications are essential to almost every business. Organizations take great care that their letterhead, offices, and other attributes reflect appropriate images and values to the world outside.

External messages form an important part of a company's image.

Similarly, salespeople, customer service representatives, and other employees who work with the public are chosen carefully. Being able to write a good business letter and to speak effectively on the telephone are skills that employers look for in job candidates. No matter how good a company's services or products, poor external communication can ruin an organization.

Internal communication takes up far more of most people's time than do external messages. These messages that flow within an organization range from policy manuals and corporate magazines to bulletin boards, memos, and reports to meetings, casual conversations, and gossip. A well-managed company has well-organized methods for selecting and conveying internal messages, but every company should constantly monitor the efficiency and effectiveness of its communication flow.

Communication flows constantly within a company.

Within organizations, messages flow upward, downward, and laterally (Figure 1-3). The majority of messages flow downward: that is, they are sent to subordinates. Downward messages may take the form of memos, annual reports, directives, orders, policies, in-house magazines, interviews, group presentations, bulletin boards, and computer-generated mail.

Most messages flow from superiors to subordinates.

In many organizations, the communication is almost all downward. The people at the top rarely receive feedback or new messages from their subordinates. In some companies, suggestion boxes help move communication from subordinates to supervisors. Other companies use quality control circles—small groups that meet to discuss issues and make recommendations to management. But many organizations have no formal methods of upward communication. Employees, moreover, are often reluctant to speak their minds.

In well-managed companies, messages flow easily throughout the organization.

Lateral communication, messages flowing between people of equal rank in an organization, is often even less efficient than the upward flow of information. Caught up in their own concerns, department heads may communicate with each other infrequently, or they may receive such a flood of information from other departments that they do not take the time to assimilate it. In either situation, problems can result.

Lateral communication occurs when messages flow between people of equal rank in an organization.

In every organization, information also moves through an informal communication channel known as the grapevine. Gossip, anecdotes, and rumors travel through the grapevine, but so does a wealth of information important to managers and employees. Fast-moving, spontaneous, and "off the record," information received through the grapevine is usually a vital part of an organization's communication system. The grapevine is not totally reliable, but

The grapevine is a dynamic but sometimes unreliable source of information.

Upward communication	Reports Quality control circles Suggestion boxes Meetings
Downward communication	Meetings Speeches Classes Job instructions Memos Handbooks Bulletin boards Electronic mail Manuals Personnel evaluations Bulletins Newsletters Company magazines
Lateral communication	Electronic mail Memos Meetings Bulletin boards

FIGURE 1–3
Formal communication channels commonly used in organizations

it often functions more quickly than formal communication processes such as meetings and memoranda, and it often carries personal information not transmitted by formal channels.

Summary

Human beings spend a large part of each day communicating: in words and actions, through facial expressions and gestures as well as through the way they dress, walk, write, and speak. The most efficient communication is two-way: a sender conveys a message, and a receiver responds with feedback and perhaps a new message.

Communication flows both in and out of every organization and through its every level. Every message is part of a continuous system reaching throughout the organization. A memo sent from one person to another is not a unique incident: it is part of a much larger communication network that reaches every individual within the organization.

A successful organization usually has effective channels for two-way internal and external communication. Understanding and using these channels effectively should be a goal for every businessperson.

What Would You Do?

Wanda Carson is the owner of Wanda's Apparel, a chain of 15 clothes stores in the Midwest. Having seen her sales flatten in recent months, Wanda is thinking about changing her approach. She talks about the changes with Carlos Anders, a friend who is also a management consultant.

"I'd like to focus primarily on the tall woman," she tells him. "It seems like women over 5 feet 8 inches haven't yet been fully discovered by retailers."

"Have you discussed your ideas with anyone?" Carlos asks.

"I wrote each of the store managers a letter about the plan. No one's written back. I figure they'll tell me if they don't like it."

"Don't you want to meet with them?"

"They're scattered from Nebraska to Ohio. I can't possibly meet with them all. I visit the stores periodically, but I can't meet with them every time I make some changes."

"What about your customers? How do you know they'll go for this change?"

"I've talked to the salespeople in my store here in Chicago. They think the Chicago customers will love the idea. I expect customers in other places will be just as enthusiastic."

Carlos does not respond to this comment right away, but he continues to give it some thought. After a couple of days, he decides to write a letter to Wanda: he feels she will take a letter more seriously than she would take his spoken comments.

As Carlos Anders, write a letter to Wanda Carson. Tactfully tell her that she should communicate with her managers, salespeople, and customers before she makes any drastic changes in her stores. Emphasize the importance of a two-way communication flow in a successful business.

Address the letter to:

> Ms. Wanda Carson, President
> Wanda's Apparel
> 3245 Rainey Avenue
> Chicago, IL 60892

Summary Discussion: Tom Milner and the Typing Pool from Case in Point, p. 3

Generally, the best communication results when people both send and receive messages. Tom Milner sends out messages but does not listen to people's responses. He *is* communicating, but he lacks the you-attitude. The component missing from his conversation is feedback: he does not listen when Karen speaks to him, and so he does not respond to her message about her health. If he improved his listening skills, he would become a better communicator.

Communication Process Checklist

Communication Process

- To convey messages effectively,

  _____ encode messages so people will understand them

  _____ send messages through an appropriate channel

  _____ use the you-attitude

  _____ pay attention to feedback or new messages

  _____ watch for nonverbal as well as verbal messages

- To receive messages effectively,

  _____ decode messages carefully

  _____ pay attention to verbal and nonverbal cues

  _____ send appropriate feedback

Verbal Communication

- Use speech to communicate when

  _____ you want to communicate quickly

  _____ you want instant responses from listeners

  _____ sensory variables will not interfere too much with the message

  _____ you do not need to save the message

- Use writing to communicate when

  _____ speed is not a primary concern

  _____ you do not need instant feedback

  _____ you want readers to analyze the information

  _____ you want the message saved

Organizational Communication

• Within an organization,

_____ encourage upward, downward, and lateral communication flow

_____ use external communication to enhance company image as well as to exchange verbal messages

_____ use the grapevine as a positive communication network

Terms to Remember

Channel: the mode through which a message is sent. A letter or speech, for example, is a communication channel.

Communication: the process by which a message is sent from one person to another

Decode: the process by which a receiver deciphers a message

Downward communication: messages flowing to subordinates in an organization

Encode: the process by which a sender transforms an idea into a message someone can understand

External communication: messages flowing into and out of an organization

Feedback: a message responding to an earlier message

Grapevine: the informal communication channel in an organization

Intentional communication: a message the sender means to convey

Internal communication: message flowing within an organization

Lateral communication: message flowing between people of equal status or rank in an organization

Nonverbal communication: messages sent without the use of words

Quality control circle: group that meets to discuss issues and make recommendations to management

Receiver: the person such as a listener or reader to whom a message is conveyed

Sender: the source of a message, such as a speaker or writer

Unintentional communication: message, often nonverbal, that the sender does not mean to convey

Upward communication: messages flowing to people of higher rank in the organization

Verbal communication: messages sent through spoken or written words

You-attitude: an approach to communication in which the sender adapts the message to the receiver's interests and needs

Questions for Review and Discussion

1. Define what is meant by the communication *process.*
2. Describe a situation in which someone's educational background might interfere with the effective transmission of a message.
3. Describe a situation in which a message was poorly transmitted because the wrong channel was chosen.
4. When a company advertises on television, how does it receive feedback regarding its commercial messages?

5. Describe some differences between oral and written language.
6. What are some of the strengths of written communication? What are some weaknesses?
7. People often believe a nonverbal message more easily than a verbal one. Why?
8. Describe some ways in which external messages may differ from internal messages.

9. Why is upward communication often so difficult to implement in a company?
10. Give examples of *encoding* and *decoding*.
11. What characteristics should an effective business communicator possess?
12. Upper management often receives distorted messages from subordinates in the organization. Why does this happen?

Exercises

1. Carefully examine an office in which you or someone else works. What nonverbal messages do you think are transmitted through the office arrangement and decor?
2. Examine a piece of "junk mail" that has been delivered to your home. What nonverbal messages do you think the company is sending out about itself through its written communication? Are these nonverbal messages consistent with its verbal messages?
3. Remember an instructor from a previous semester. Describe some of the nonverbal messages the person transmitted to the students on the first day of class. Were these messages consistent with the person's verbal messages?
4. Consider a place where you have worked in the past or are presently employed. Describe the channels for upward and downward communication. Outline some methods that could be implemented to increase two-way communication flow.
5. Describe a situation in which language formed barriers to your communication with someone else.
6. Describe a situation from your experience in which the sender of a message did not use the you-attitude when transmitting a message.
7. Describe a situation in which you unintentionally communicated information that you did not want someone to know.
8. In the following situations, what would be the most effective communication channel? Explain your answers.
   a. You are a manager firing an employee
   b. You are inviting good friends to a party
   c. You are a salesperson telling your best customers about a special sale
   d. You are a department head summarizing sales data for management
   e. You are telling fellow employees about a company softball game
9. Describe a situation in which a person's nonverbal message contradicted his or her verbal message.
10. Describe a class you have taken in the past in which information moved downward (from the instructor to the students) but not upward. Outline some techniques the instructor could have used to increase upward and lateral communication.
11. Write a letter to your instructor outlining your major goals for this class. Describe specific areas of communication that you believe will be most useful to you in your work and day-to-day life.
12. The grapevine is an important communication channel for students as well as business people. What types of information do you learn informally rather than through formal channels such as the school catalog and meetings with advisers?
13. Interview a manager in a local business concerning the internal communication in his or her organization. In three or four paragraphs, describe the formal channels for upward, downward, and lateral communication in that organization.

Solving Common Business Communication Problems

- **Defining communication goals**
- **Recognizing barriers to effective communication**
- **Examining barriers in the world around you**
- **Examining barriers inside you**
- **Examining barriers between people**
- **Examining barriers made by words**
- **Solving communication problems**
- **Improving communication through change**

Objectives

To recognize the barriers that impede communication

To solve common communication problems

2

Peter Fairmont's Telephone Conversation

Catherine Westerly, division manager, has been traveling extensively for the past three weeks. Every day around 4 p.m. she telephones the assistant manager, Peter Fairmont. This is the most hectic time in Peter's day, but he has not found an appropriate moment to ask her to telephone in the mornings. This afternoon, Peter is particularly busy when Catherine calls.

"What's all that noise in the background?" she asks.

"The painters are coming in tomorrow," Peter answers glumly. "I'll have to work in Alan's office. Sam's moving my desk now. You'll have to speak up. I'm having trouble hearing you."

"Too bad we lost the Gridley account today," Catherine says in a louder voice. "I just heard."

"It's been a miserable day," Peter says. "And I'm going to be here until 7 tonight." His comment indicates that he'd like to get off the telephone and start working now, but Catherine does not respond to his hint.

"I've got those stats on our competitors, Peter. They don't look too good for us. Both Simpson's and USG have an 8 percent return on investment—while we've got only 3 percent. Simpson's got a 45 percent debt ratio, and ours is almost 70 percent. We better start making some changes."

Peter doodles on his memo pad, hardly listening.

"You better call Marty Sterne sometime soon, Peter. He needs those figures on the Barnes account."

"Will do, Catherine."

"Oh, one more thing. That report to Weston better go out by early next week. Is Alice working on it?"

"Yes, she's almost finished. Excuse me, Catherine—" Peter gives some instructions to the man moving his desk and papers. "I better go now, Catherine. Sam has some questions."

Six days later, when Catherine returns to the office, she goes in to see Peter.

"Peter, didn't you call Marty like I asked? He's furious about not getting those figures."

Peter stares at her. Dimly, he remembers her saying something about calling Marty.

"I didn't know it was urgent, Catherine," he said lamely.

"I said to call him *soon*. That meant right away, not next month. This could mean losing another account. Now you better do some fast talking when you call him."

She turns angrily and goes out. Peter wonders why he always runs into these communication problems with Catherine.

Points to Consider

- What nonverbal barriers impeded Catherine and Peter's telephone conversation?
- What language problems impeded their telephone conversation?
- What could Peter have done to improve the situation?
- What could Catherine have done to improve the situation?

Defining Communication Goals

Communication is always somewhat imprecise.

Although there are many ways to convey a message, every method is limited. Messages often do not reach the person for whom they are intended. When they do reach the person, they are often misinterpreted or misunderstood. In fact, both verbal and nonverbal communication is imperfect: no one but you can ever know exactly what goes on in your mind, no matter how sophisticated your communication methods may be.

While communication can never be perfect, it can be improved. Overcoming the imperfections of communication has always been a human am-

Executives' Ranking of the Five Most Serious Communication Problems	
Ranking	*Problem*
1	Lack of clarity
2	Poor listening skills
3	Lack of conciseness
4	Poor speaking ability
5	Poor analytical skills

bition. Our society has created amazing devices to communicate across the world, underwater, even in space, yet even these tools remain limited. People still cannot convey *everything* exactly, so they are continually striving to improve their communication methods and their understanding of communication itself.

In Chapter 1, you read about the primary goal of communication: to transmit a message to someone else. This goal is closely related to two other objectives: to bring about a specific response to the message and to attain or keep the good will of the receiver.

None of these goals is as simple to attain as it might seem. At every step of the process, potential problems or barriers can prevent a communicator from reaching one or more of these objectives. Consider these paragraphs from two memos:

> As you might already know, I would like to see some substantial alterations made in the reporting processes between department heads, so if you have some ideas on the subject, please get in touch with me as soon as you can.

> Ted, I was shocked to see the way you dressed for work yesterday. You knew we were meeting with Harbison at nine. How could you choose that day of all days to show up without a tie? And before you meet with James next week, think about getting a haircut. You're an account executive, not a rock musician.

Communication goals include
- conveying a message to someone else
- bringing about a specific response
- attaining the goodwill of the receiver

GOALS OF COMMUNICATION

To transmit a message

To receive a specific response and goodwill

IBM

400 Parson's Pond Drive
Franklin Lakes, NJ 07417

"Seventy-five percent of my communicating is done on the computer," says Evelyn Miller, Development Manager for Invoice Applications at IBM. Her department consists of programmers who provide administrative functions for invoicing all of IBM's customers. "In a given month I might have 50 to 60 thousand bits of communication data coming in or going out."

Most of Evelyn's job consists of communicating with her unit managers, project leaders, team leaders, and team members. Most communication takes place over the computer system through electronic notes. People are notified that there is a message on their computer, and she receives an acknowledgment when the communication has been read. She also uses verbal communications: she may need to know a piece of information right away, or there may be an emergency. She communicates over the phone to IBM branches in other states. Evelyn receives written status reports once a week from each staff member on her or his area, and she writes personnel and management reports to her manager. Memos in her office are not formal; Evelyn uses a routing slip to pass along pertinent documents and information such as guidelines for working and personnel information. She uses letters to document agreements or make inquiries within IBM.

Evelyn also holds a monthly staff meeting to transmit personnel information and to receive feedback from the staff about problems and concerns. At these meetings she presents a mind-set, "a sense of urgency about a project; how it might benefit the corporation—why it is needed." She also presents level-sets: "The staff have to understand my point of view and the reasons behind my point of view."

Throughout this communicating, Evelyn pinpoints "timeliness and accuracy" as central to communications. "For example, we have a new release going into production next week. Last Friday I set up a meeting with the staff to identify the primary and backup teams and to assign first and second shifts, since 24-hour coverage will be necessary. Don't wait until the last minute to tell your staff what you need from them," she advises.

Evelyn uses an authoritative tone "only when nothing else works." She likes to rely on cooperation and understanding and to adapt her messages to the personality of the person she is dealing with. She is coming to the conclusion, reluctantly, that folksiness, a style natural to her, doesn't work.

Her tips for entering a business situation are:

- Listen attentively—"make sure you understand what's being said."
- Document critical and important agreements and problems.
- Use a good distribution list—make sure information gets to the right people.
- Follow up and follow through. "Make sure people get your correspondence and reply. Add to your note, 'If I don't hear from you, such and such will happen.'"
- When you are communicating problems, give the cause and solutions. Also include dependencies, things you need to implement the solution, and exposures, what will happen if the solution is implemented and what will happen if the solution isn't implemented.

In the first paragraph, the writer does not manage to convey a clear message. She does not explain what problems presently exist in the reporting process, what exactly she wants the reader to do, or when she wants it done. Whatever message she has in mind is not on the page and, thus, cannot reach the reader.

In the second paragraph, the writer makes his point, but he may well have lost the goodwill of his reader. Ted may now wear a tie and get a haircut, but his attitude and morale may be badly affected by the memo. The writer has chosen the wrong tone and also the wrong communication channel: he has used a memo when a personal conversation would have been more appropriate.

Recognizing Barriers to Effective Communication

Recognizing the most common barriers to effective business communication can help you prevent them from occurring. These barriers, also called "noise," can occur at any stage of the communication process. They may take place as the sender selects material to be communicated, during the passage of the message through its channel, or as the receiver gets the message. Similar problems can occur if the receiver sends feedback to the sender.

    Some of these barriers are verbal, while others are nonverbal. Some exist in the environment. Others are inside the people sending and receiving the messages.

Noise is anything that interferes with the message being transmitted.

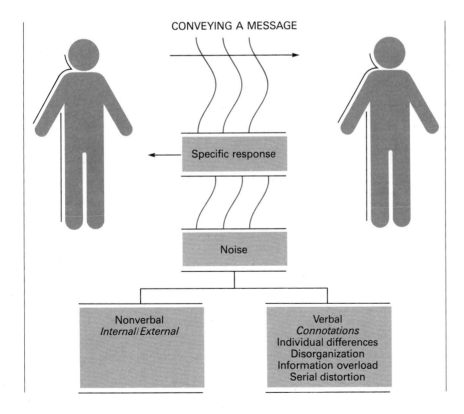

CONVEYING A MESSAGE

Specific response

Noise

| Nonverbal
Internal/External | Verbal
Connotations
Individual differences
Disorganization
Information overload
Serial distortion |

Examining Barriers in the World Around You

Innumerable barriers to effective communication exist in the world around you. Distractions, problems of space and distance, poor physical appearance, or the use of a wrong communication channel can impede the free flow of messages.

Distractions

Many distractions constantly compete for our attention.

Many things distract people: noise, bright colors, sudden movements. Noisy offices, for example, seriously impede day-to-day communication in numerous organizations: transmitting and hearing messages in such settings become arduous tasks.

Sending or receiving messages may also be difficult in some environments because so many other things are competing for attention. Perhaps telephones are ringing; customers are asking for help; people are hurrying to and fro.

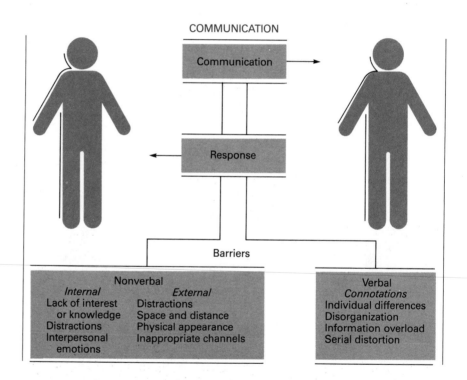

COMMUNICATION

Communication

Response

Barriers

Nonverbal		Verbal
Internal	*External*	*Connotations*
Lack of interest or knowledge	Distractions	Individual differences
Distractions	Space and distance	Disorganization
Interpersonal emotions	Physical appearance	Information overload
	Inappropriate channels	Serial distortion

Space and Distance

Space and distance affect our ability to transmit and receive messages.

Where people sit or stand can be an important factor in their receiving and transmitting messages. If you have ever sat in a classroom with people blocking your view of the instructor, you may remember how difficult it was to concentrate on what was happening in class. Some spatial arrangements facilitate communication while others impede it.

Of course, the distance between sender and receiver also affects their communication. A telephone conversation is less direct and immediate than a face-to-face conversation. Because you are only hearing a voice, not seeing an entire person, you may find it more difficult to understand or remember a telephone conversation.

Physical Appearance

If you have ever watched a movie when the sound was bad or the reel had to be stopped, you know how irritating the experience is. The effect of the film is lost because you are annoyed. An advertisement with too much small print or confusing graphics can prevent potential consumers from reading it: the appearance is as important as the content of the ad.

The appearance of a document or person has a strong effect on a reader or listener.

Similarly, a letter that is typed poorly or contains typographical errors may be irritating and distracting to a reader. Using a correct format for a letter, report, or memo is an important part of business communication; so is good grammar, spelling, punctuation, and word usage.

Many times, also, the appearance of the person sending or receiving the message has an effect on the transmission of the message.

Inappropriate Channel

Another factor in poor communication can be the choice of an inappropriate channel to transmit a message. In some cases, a personal conversation will be more appropriate than a memo. At other times, a letter will be more effective than a telephone call.

Choosing an appropriate channel is a vital element of good communication.

The memo to Ted that we looked at on page 21 is ineffective partially because the writer should have chosen to speak personally to Ted, not berate him in a memo.

The Right Kind of Listening

When Jerry Rogoway took over as president of Mode O'Day, he had serious problems to solve. The company's 460 franchised women's clothing stores were in towns that were too small for major department stores or shopping malls. But the previous management had decided to change the emphasis of the clothing lines to the low-priced end.

That reduced the chain's investment in merchandise—which it owns and consigns to store owners—but displeased the customers.

Rogoway, president since early this year of the Los Angeles-based chain, listened both to franchisees—all of whom are women—and customers.

"We have been doing a lot of listening," Rogoway says. "The customer has told us that she wants value and is willing to pay for it."

As a result, Rogoway says, the company has learned that it should be getting back to basics by serving the customer with a full range of clothing in all sizes as it had when it was founded: "We have shifted back to what it was that made this company grow."

As part of listening, says Rogoway, the company has tried to make its franchisees part of the decision making process. "I have an open line. I talk to anyone, I answer all their letters, and I require that everybody take time with franchisees so that we hear their side of the story."

The franchisees are telling the home office what kinds of merchandise they need. "When you're dealing with a chain our size," Rogoway says, "you have to be aware of geographical and economic differences. You don't send the same things to Phoenix that you send to Minneapolis."

Examining Barriers Inside You

Naturally, your state of mind has a strong effect on your ability to send or receive a message. No doubt you have noticed that digesting information is easier on some days than on others. You may find yourself not *listening* or paying attention for one reason or another.

Lack of Interest or Knowledge

Boredom can dramatically affect our ability to receive messages.

If you are bored by a topic being discussed, you may simply tune it out. Almost every student learns to do this in some classes, and most employees do too.

Sometimes the tuning out may be the result of confusion rather than lack of interest. You might well have trouble concentrating in class on a subject you know nothing about. Other times, you might stop paying attention because the material is *too* familiar or is being presented in a way that does not catch your attention. You do have control over your wandering attention, but you need to concentrate, to keep yourself focused on the material.

Internal Distractions

Everyone thinks and listens at the same time.

Just as frequently, you may receive messages poorly because you have other things on your mind. You can think much faster than you can speak; therefore, you have lots of time as a listener to think about other things while still catching the gist of what someone is saying. At any moment, however, your internal distraction may take precedence over the speaker's message. At that point, communication breaks down.

Examining Barriers Between People

Anger, depression, excitement, and other emotions can interfere with the communication process.

Often communication problems occur simply because people do not like each other, are afraid of each other, or have some preconceptions about each other that get in the way of the message.

These preconceptions often affect upward communication: employees may be reluctant to speak their minds to some managers for rear of reprisals, or employees may adjust the message so it is in keeping with what they think a manager wants to hear.

A common internal barrier is the emotional state of the sender or receiver. If you have ever quarreled with someone, you know that misunderstandings occur when people are angry or upset.

Even less extreme emotions, however, can interfere with the transmission of messages. If you are slightly depressed or annoyed, you may send or receive messages ineffectively; similarly, if you are extremely happy, you may well ignore feedback from others.

Test Your Skills

Do You Know These Terms?

Match each example of a communication problem with an appropriate definition.

1. Serial distortion

2. Improper channel

3. Error in denotation

4. Information overload

5. Error in connotation

a. Jan says the problem has been *alleviated* when she means it has gotten worse.

b. By the time rumors of Arnold's lottery win come back to him, he finds people think he's won $200,000, not $2,000.

c. Roger explains three complex theories about bioengineering to a confused group of company managers.

d. The health club employee offends a potential member by saying she is *fat* rather than *overweight*.

e. Fran sends an assistant of six years a memo saying she is fired.

Answers: 1b, 2e, 3a, 4c, 5d

Examining Barriers Made by Words

How many times have you found yourself saying, "What I *meant* to say was—" or "I *thought* you meant—"? Sometimes these language problems are trivial, but they can also be very serious. In both speaking and writing, the biggest pitfall awaiting the sender and receiver is language itself.

These problems occur primarily because language is composed of symbols: words stand for certain things in our minds. In fact, often a word stands for several things simultaneously. "Do you mean *funny* weird or *funny* ha-ha?" we have to ask, since the word *funny* has several meanings.

Moreover, not only do most words have more than one meaning (or *denotation*), but they also have *connotations*, the associations the words arouse. Although *beautiful*, *attractive*, *pretty*, and *handsome* have similar denotations, people have different emotions about each word. Thus, you have to be careful which one you use in different contexts.

Words are imprecise and may have many meanings.

A dictionary definition does not always capture the emotions that a word arouses in us.

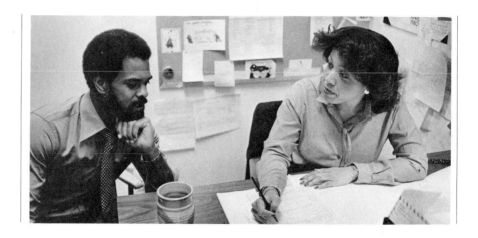

What Are Your Strongest Communication Skills?

To chart some of your skills as a communicator, rate yourself 4 (almost always), 3 (most of the time), 2 (sometimes), or 1 (rarely) for each of the following points.

1. Speak effectively in front of a group   4 3 2 1
2. Speak effectively on the telephone   4 3 2 1
3. Choose my words carefully when speaking   4 3 2 1
4. Am aware of my body language as I speak   4 3 2 1
5. Try to set up environments for good interpersonal communication   4 3 2 1
6. Have a clear writing style   4 3 2 1
7. Organize my thoughts effectively   4 3 2 1
8. Make sure my written documents have a good appearance   4 3 2 1
9. Am aware of my readers' feelings   4 3 2 1
10. Consider what words my readers are familiar with   4 3 2 1
11. Encourage people to communicate with me   4 3 2 1
12. Follow directions accurately   4 3 2 1
13. Read carefully   4 3 2 1
14. Am a good listener   4 3 2 1
15. Am attentive to how people look when they speak   4 3 2 1
16. Avoid making judgments before hearing or reading a whole message   4 3 2 1
17. Try to establish environments where I can read and listen without distractions   4 3 2 1
18. Let people know if I don't understand what they're saying   4 3 2 1
19. Let people know if I do understand what they're saying   4 3 2 1
20. Ask questions to clarify issues   4 3 2 1

Discussion

Add up your scores and rate yourself:

65–80 excellent
49–64 good
33–48 fair
20–32 poor

From the chart you probably see specific areas in which you excel and others in which you need to improve. Numbers 1–10 focus on your skills as a sender of messages, numbers 11–17 on your skills as a receiver, and numbers 18–20 on your ability to provide feedback.

Rate yourself again when you have completed this course. You should see substantial improvements!

Individual Differences

People use words in different ways. Associations with various words may vary from person to person: the word *conservative*, for example, evokes different reactions in different people. In fact, every person's language differs slightly from everyone else's. No one else has exactly your vocabulary or emotional associations with specific words. The differences between people's use of language can cause serious communication problems.

These language problems are most evident when the people communicating are from different geographic areas, ethnic backgrounds, or even professions. Someone unacquainted with computers might not know what a *byte* is, just as a person who has not studied law might not know what a *tort* is.

A New Hampshire native might not be familiar with the expression *a pig in a poke*, whereas a Texan might not know what a *bubbler* is. (A *poke* is a bag in parts of the South; a *bubbler* is a drinking fountain in parts of the Midwest.)

These problems can become even more pronounced when people deal with non-native speakers or try to communicate in a foreign language. American companies have learned the problems of translation at great expense. In West Germany, for example, the phrase "Come Alive with Pepsi" was translated as "Come Out of the Grave with Pepsi." In Latin America, the translation of "Use Parker Pen, Avoid Embarrassment" appeared as "Use Parker Pen, Avoid Pregnancy." (For more information on intercultural communication, see Chapter 26).

Each person uses language in a unique way.

Translation problems highlight the complexity of every language.

Disorganization

Another potential communication barrier is disorganization. When a message is disorganized, the major points become lost or the receiver becomes too confused to understand the message. When writing or speaking, you will find careful planning will greatly increase the effectiveness of your message.

A disorganized message can confuse a reader or listener.

Information Overload

Information overload is yet another common communication problem. People can take in only so much information at once. That is one reason why college courses are usually divided into one- or two-hour classes, not four- or five-hour ones. When the sender overloads a message with too much information, a sizable portion is inevitably going to be lost on the receiver.

Too much information overloads a listener or reader.

Serial Distortion

If you have ever played the game "telephone," you know about serial distortion. It means that a message becomes distorted as it passes from person to person. Everyone perceives, selects, and transmits messages differently. As a result, when information is passed through several people, the original message will inevitably be altered.

A message usually changes as it is conveyed from one person to another.

Walter Kechel III

Manage by wandering around. Share your vision of the company's future. Act more like the Japanese—keep workers informed, encourage them to speak up, listen to what they have to say. Get out there and be a leader, not just a manager.

Splendid advice. The only problem: it isn't happening, at least not in the practice of most executives. For all the rhetoric in books like *In Search of Excellence* or *Reinventing the Corporation*, employee surveys indicate that the troops think management is doing a poorer job communicating with them than it did five years ago. From a report based on surveys of 48,000 employees by Opinion Research Corp., an arm of the Arthur D. Little consulting company: "Downward communication, measured by employees' ratings of their companies on letting them know what is going on, is rated favorably by fewer than half of employees in all groups."

If the brass don't wake up soon, they stand to get their sleepy little heads handed to them by the competition. Virtually everyone who has studied the problem—executives, consultants, business school professors—agrees that you have to share lots of information with employees if you hope to elicit their commitment. Commitment, the latest emerging buzzword, means high productivity, low turnover, and a better chance of avoiding corporate death at the hands of the Japanese.

Top executives at Tandem Computers, a California-based computer manufacturer, work at communications. Last year the company staged some 600 hours of meetings in which honchos from the different disciplines—marketing, finance, manufacturing—explained the corporation's strategy to employees. The chief executive or another heavyweight presides over televised monthly confabs beamed to all the company's U.S. facilities, with telephone hookups to take questions. There are also junkets for high performers from the ranks that combine taking in some exotic scenery with still more briefing from executives on the company's plans. Tandem has, it claims, one of the lowest turnover rates in Silicon Valley, as well as high productivy.

Dialogue also works at GM's Packard Electric plant in Brookhaven, Mississippi. Besides providing a hefty dose of conventional communications—a monthly newspaper, frequent meetings of employee teams, an electronic news display in the cafeteria—management at the unionized facility puts on a quarterly meeting for all employees. Says plant manager J. Edward Zuga, "We share with our people all the pertinent information—financial performance, future plans, quality performance . . . anything of significance to them and the company." An open discussion follows the presentation. According to Zuga, the openness has helped keep turnover low and productivity high. Eugene Edwards, president of the union local at the plant, agrees: "There's more communication between management and labor here than I've seen in any other plant. It's a good atmosphere. No one wants to quit his job."

Solving Communication Problems

The following list touches on some solutions to communication problems. You will study all of these in greater detail later on in this text.

Create an Effective Environment

You can create an environment that enhances communication.

Too often people forget the importance of their physical environment to communication. Cutting down on noise and other distractions and arranging the physical space effectively can make sending and receiving messages more pleasant and more efficient.

Consider Physical Appearance

The appearance of your message often determines how it is received. Make sure your written communications are error-free as well as neat and easy to read. If you are communicating in person, consider your own appearance. The way you look is an intrinsic part of your message.

Choose the Correct Channel

Before transmitting a message, carefully consider the best way to send it: in person, by telephone, on paper, by computer mail, or by some other means. In some situations, your choices will be limited, but, in others, you will have to consider both your audience and your message before choosing the channel.

Know Your Audience

Your audience may be your most important consideration. The you-attitude is a vital component of effective communication. Who are your readers or listeners? Are they your peers? Your subordinates? Your superiors? What are their interests and concerns? What motivates them? How will they react to your message?

Audience analysis is a vital part of effective communication.

Before communicating, analyze your readers or listeners.

Choose Your Words Carefully

Choosing correct words in speaking and writing will help overcome numerous problems related to verbal communication. If you have a good sense

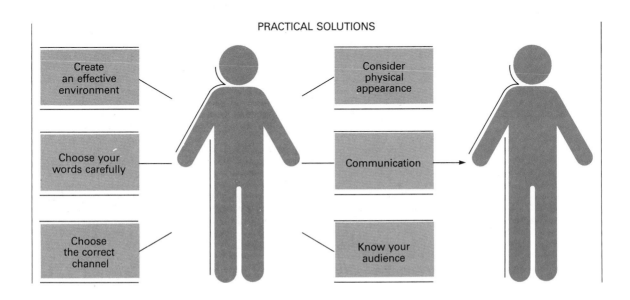

PRACTICAL SOLUTIONS

Create an effective environment

Consider physical appearance

Choose your words carefully

Communication

Choose the correct channel

Know your audience

of whom you are addressing, you will be better able to choose words that the receiver both understands and responds to appropriately.

You should pay particular attention to weeding out technical jargon, obscure or difficult words, and regionalisms that your reader or listener may not understand.

Organize Your Thoughts

Whether you are speaking or writing, organize the components of your message so the receiver knows what to expect and recognizes the major points. A major concept, for instance, should not get lost in the middle of less important material.

To emphasize a major point in a written communication, you may use several approaches:

1. Tell your readers that the point is important.
2. Repeat your point several times for emphasis.
3. Put the point at the beginning or end of a paragraph.
4. Use a short paragraph to attract the reader's attention.
5. Highlight the point in a list (like this one).
6. Use underlining, CAPITAL LETTERS, or **boldface** to make the point look important.
7. Use headings and subheadings as we do in this text.

Make sure, too, that you include sufficient material so that an uninformed receiver will have no trouble following your message. On the other hand, delete material that your receiver does not need. Your audience analysis will help you figure out how much your listeners or readers already know and what they need to know.

What Would You Do?

Ed Barlow is the new sales manager for a computer software company. A new MBA with good credentials, he has little actual experience in sales. Now, since he has been hired, he finds sales are slipping; the salespeople under him seem to be losing their motivation.

In order to find out what is going on, he knows he has to communicate directly with the salespeople. He drafts a memo to go to each salesperson:

In order to reverse the escalating downward trend of CXS software sales, functional changes must be effectuated and policy decisions must be made. If you have an interest in participating in the initiation and implementation of sales-incentive or other programs, please contact me immediately.

He shows this draft to you and asks for comments. You tell him it is confusing. Revise the memo for him using more effective language.

Focus on a Topic

Focusing your topic is related to organization. To avoid information overload, isolate one major point and highlight the important supporting data in your presentation. Give the receiver pointers that indicate something is important.

Limit Communication Channels

To avoid serial distortion, avoid letting your message pass through too many people. A company president who relies on six or seven intermediaries to pass information to employees may well find the message has been distorted by the time it reaches them.

Encourage Feedback

One-way communication is often ineffective because the sender cannot tell whether the three communication goals have been achieved. Has the message been received? Will the receiver respond appropriately? Has the goodwill of the receiver been retained?

Work on creating two-way communication.

To facilitate effective communication, set up two-way communication channels. Make it easy for receivers to respond to your messages. And, then, pay attention to the feedback and respond as necessary. Remember: communication is a loop, not a line.

Improving Communication Through Change

Realizing the importance of good communication, large numbers of companies are hiring communication consultants and sending their employees to communication seminars. Consultants and seminar leaders alone, however, do not improve communication. The solutions that they recommend work only if management and employees are willing to change their present methods for transmitting and receiving messages.

Some simple changes in the physical environment and in people's communication techniques often reap more advantages to an organization than much of the expensive gadgetry that companies buy to facilitate internal and external communication.

Summary

In order to communicate effectively, be aware of the potential barriers to communication. These include external distractions such as noise and distance as well as internal barriers such as emotions and biases. Even language itself can act as a barrier to good communication.

To overcome these potential problems, consider both your message and your audience while organizing ideas, choosing words, deciding on an appropriate channel, and creating an effective external environment.

Communication Problem and Solution Checklist

Communication Goals

• As a communicator, present your messages so they

_____ clearly transmit information

_____ bring about a specific response in the receiver

_____ attain or keep the goodwill of the receiver

Communication Barriers

• To reduce miscommunication, be aware of possible external communication barriers such as

_____ a noisy or otherwise distracting environment

_____ the distance between sender and receiver

_____ the spatial arrangements of sender and receiver

_____ the physical appearance of the message or the sender

_____ the use of an inappropriate channel

• Watch also for internal and verbal barriers such as

_____ the receiver's lack of interest in or knowledge about the topic

_____ the receiver's internal distractions

_____ personality problems between sender and receiver

_____ the emotions of the sender or receiver

_____ individual differences in language usage

_____ disorganized messages

_____ information overload

_____ serial distortion

Solutions

- To overcome potential problems, work on

  _____ creating an external environment with minimal distractions

  _____ paying attention to the physical appearance of the message

  _____ considering your own personal appearance

  _____ choosing the correct communication channel

  _____ knowing your audience

  _____ choosing words carefully

  _____ organizing and focusing your message

  _____ limiting the number of communication channels

  _____ establishing two-way communication

Summary Discussion: Peter Fairmont's Telephone Conversation from Case in Point, p. 20

Peter and Catherine's conversation is impeded by the noise and confusion in Peter's office, Peter's tiredness, and Catherine's preoccupation with her own interests. Speaking on the telephone, too, creates more barriers than face-to-face conversation.

The word *soon* also becomes a problem: Peter assumes the word means *sometime in the near future*, but Catherine means *immediately*.

Peter could have improved the situation by telling Catherine to call at a less hectic time or by taking the call in another office. Catherine should have realized that she was not getting through to Peter. If she had emphasized her concern about Marty, Peter would have responded more promptly.

Terms to Remember

Audience analysis: defining listeners' or readers' characteristics, needs, and interests in order to communicate effectively

Connotation: the associations connected to a word

Denotation: the definition of a word

Information overload: an excessive amount of data that prevents the receiver from deciphering the complete message being sent

Serial distortion: the alteration of a message as it passes through several people

Questions for Review and Discussion

1. Why is maintaining goodwill such an important part of the communicator's goals?
2. Have you ever found your reception of a message impeded by the appearance of the sender? Describe the situation.
3. Have you ever encountered a communication problem that resulted from two people's different interpretations of a word? Describe the situation.
4. What is information overload? Give an example.
5. Have you ever experienced serial distortion? Describe the experience.
6. Have you ever encountered a communication problem that resulted from personal biases? Describe the situation.

Exercises

1. Rewrite the two paragraphs from memos on page 21. You may add and delete information as necessary.
2. Write down the emotional associations you have with the following words. (Be honest!) Then compare your associations with those of the other people in your class.

   revolutionary   technical
   perfectionist   football

3. Examine the environment you are in as you read this sentence. Is it conducive to your receiving the messages? Explain why or why not.
4. Describe a communication problem that you experienced at school or work. What specific barriers helped to create the problem? How could the problem have been solved?
5. Listening is an important part of being a good communicator. What methods can you use to improve your listening skills?
6. Go back to the chart on page 8 where you rated your abilities as a communicator. What did you perceive as your weakest point as a communicator? List some ways you could improve in that area.
7. The words *schlep* and *gum band* are regionalisms used only in certain parts of the United States. Do you know of any regionalisms used in your part of the country that are unfamiliar to Americans in other areas? List three regionalisms that you have encountered in your own area or in parts of the country where you have traveled. Then write definitions for each of these words or phrases.
8. Assume you are going to write a sales letter to the people in your class or to members of a club to which you belong. List as many *characteristics* of your prospective audience as you can. Include information such as age and income levels as well as any details you might know about their values, opinions, and beliefs.
9. You are setting up a new department with employees from over ten foreign countries as well as from different parts of the United States. You want to implement strategies that will eliminate communication problems as much as possible. In two or three paragraphs, describe some methods that could help keep communication flowing easily and accurately.
10. The following memo confused the employees for whom it was intended. What communication barriers make it confusing? Revise it so the message is clearer.

    TO: All Employees
    FROM: A. Whyte
    SUBJECT: Procedure Change
    DATE: September 3, 19xx

    Last month we ordered twelve reams of paper, but we actually needed another three reams before the end of the month. Whereas we could have ordered all fifteen for $60, we ended up paying $73 for paper by the end of the month. This seems like a small problem, but it adds up after awhile. So, from now on, I am going to ask each of you to put in your requests for supplies by the 15th of each month. Give your requests to Katherine. If necessary, estimate your purchases a little high: we are better off buying more in bulk and saving money the following month. I do not want anyone placing small orders during the month. Katherine will tally everyone's orders. Let's try this procedure for six months and see how the costs work out. Don't bother estimating supplies for the IBM copier—I'll do that myself. Use the supply request forms on Katherine's desk for your monthly orders. Thanks.

11. Communication barriers can occur at every stage of the communication process. Describe situations in which the following problems occur:
   a. The sender's external environment negatively affects his or her message.
   b. The sender does not send the message she or he meant to convey.
   c. The sender uses an inappropriate channel to convey the message.
   d. The receiver receives the wrong message.
   e. The receiver's external environment negatively affects his or her reception of the message.
   f. The receiver sends incorrect feedback to the sender.

12. Revise the following sentences to make them more you-oriented.
   a. From now on employees will be allowed to smoke only in the employee lounges.
   b. I am recruiting people to collect money for the Multiple Sclerosis Foundation. I hope you will sign up.
   c. I haven't heard from you in two weeks, so I thought I'd write again to ask you for a letter of recommendation. I need it by June 1.
   d. Our new hedge-trimmer is terrific. It will help gardeners like you trim and prune hedges in half the time it usually takes.
   e. I am having a dinner party next Saturday night, and I hope you can attend.

13. Examine a brochure, sales letter, or other piece of "junk mail." What techniques have the writers and printers used to make important information stand out on the page? Write two or three paragraphs describing these strategies; attach the promotional piece to your analysis.

The New Technology

- **Communicating before the twentieth century**
- **Working in the pre-electronic office**
- **Adapting to the electronic office**
- **Using microcomputers**
- **Using computers for desktop publishing**
- **Locating information through database services**
- **Communicating instantly by electronic mail**
- **Networking with computers**
- **Conducting meetings by video**
- **Overcoming problems with technology**

Objectives

To use technology effectively for communication

To recognize strengths and weaknesses of electronic communication

3

Karen Alsop's Suggestions

Litener, Hubbard, and Kimble is a five-attorney law firm in an Ohio community of 150,000 people. The firm employs five legal secretaries, a paralegal assistant, a bookkeeper, and an office manager. Each secretary works at an IBM typewriter. Until recently, the only innovation in the office since 1978 had been the introduction of dictating machines. Rather than dictating to a secretary, the attorneys dictated into a machine, and the secretaries typed the dictation from cassette tapes.

After one of the partners left the firm, the attorney hired to replace him was surprised to find that every document generated by the firm was typed from scratch. Even wills, leases, and other standard agreements were typed over and over again with only minor changes.

The new attorney, Karen Alsop, urged that the firm invest in microcomputers. She estimated that the firm was spending over $8,000 a month for secretaries to retype documents unnecessarily. Moreover, the accounting software available for law firms could cut the bookkeeper's work in half. The firm would recover the cost of its investment in less than six months.

But everyone objected to Karen's proposal. The attorneys did not want to spend the money. The secretaries did not want to learn new techniques. Besides, they were afraid their jobs were in jeopardy.

Finally, a compromise was reached. The firm bought two microcomputers and one printer. The six secretaries still have typewriters at their work stations, but they can use the word processing equipment if they want to. However, only one secretary can print documents at a time.

Since no secretary can use the computer on a full-time basis, most of them continue to type (and retype) on their typewriters. The computers remain unused 40 percent of the time. No accounting software was purchased, so the bookkeeper still uses notepads and an adding machine to compute every telephone call, letter, and hour that each attorney bills each client.

At one office meeting, someone did suggest buying a second printer, but the suggestion was vetoed. Even Karen vetoed it. However, her reason was different from the others'. "This office needs a computer *system*," she said. "Every secretary should have a fully equipped work station. How can I bill a client for the time it takes my secretary to retype a document three times? Buying another printer doesn't solve anything." But no one wanted to invest in that much equipment.

Soon after that, Karen resigned. The firm's attitude toward an electronic law office, she decided, indicated an overall nearsightedness that she found too frustrating to deal with.

Points to Consider
- Why do the secretaries use the communal microcomputers less than they would if there was a computer in each work station?
- What other electronic equipment might be useful to a law firm (or any company) of this size?

Communicating Before the Twentieth Century

Prehistoric peoples communicated by means of sign language and simple sounds. This system must have led to countless misunderstandings. To communicate more effectively, more complicated symbols were needed. Spoken language became more complex.

No matter how sophisticated spoken language became, however, it still had obvious limitations. First, a person could communicate only with people in hearing range: spoken language was definitely limited by distance. Second, once it was spoken, a message could not be saved: a person could not retain a message except in memory. Eventually messengers were sent to convey people's words beyond the reach of a speaker's voice. However, the second problem remained. The messenger and then the listener had to rely on memory alone.

The messenger, moreover, could take weeks, even months, to deliver a message. By the time the messenger arrived, the message might be worthless.

Writing, of course, solved the first two problems. People learned to translate their thoughts into written symbols that could be saved and even transported far beyond the reach of their voices. Like speech, writing had limitations—misunderstandings still occurred—but a great stride had been taken in human communication.

Writing, however, was painstaking work. Many people spent their lives scrupulously copying precious documents. And a time problem remained. Not only did copying take time, but a messenger carrying a letter took just as long as a messenger with oral information. Until very recent times, a message could be transported only as fast as a horse and rider could carry it.

Not until the fifteenth century did the printing press begin to relieve the tedium of hand copying. Only then did books and manuscripts become available to more than a very few people. However, even at the end of the 1800s, offices still employed *scriveners* who hand-copied documents, and messages still traveled at a horse's pace.

The twentieth century brought more changes in communication than had occurred in the previous three thousand years. Typewriters, telegraphs, telephones, carbon paper, duplicating machines: every day seemed to bring changes. Not only was hand copying a thing of the past, but messages could travel faster than a horse or even an automobile. Letters could be sent by air and arrive overnight. Telegrams and voice messages could arrive at their destination moments after they were transmitted.

Writing enables a message to be saved and transported.

Technology enables messages to be sent anywhere in the world almost instantly.

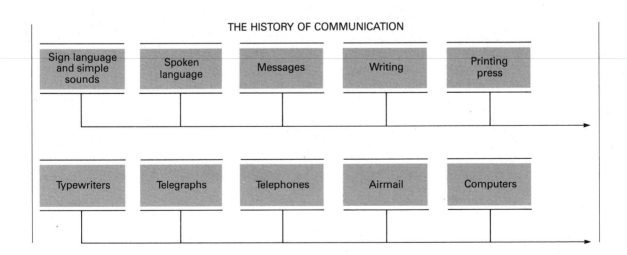

THE HISTORY OF COMMUNICATION

Sign language and simple sounds — Spoken language — Messages — Writing — Printing press

Typewriters — Telegraphs — Telephones — Airmail — Computers

Working in the Pre-Electronic Office

What people think of as the "traditional" office actually came into being only a few decades ago. Now, while it still exists, it is quickly disappearing.

In this traditional pre-electronic office, oral communication is handled through telephone and intercom systems. Written communication is managed in much the same way as in the law firm described at the opening of this chapter. Memos and letters are dictated either directly to a secretary or into a dictaphone. The secretary then transcribes the dictation, types the document, and gives it back to be proofread.

After changes have been made, the document is retyped. Copies are made by a copy machine; one or more copies are filed in file cabinets, and one or more copies are sent out to readers. Documents sent through the mail system arrive at their destination in two or three days. At the receiver's office, then, the document may be copied once more, sent to other people within the company, and filed again.

To carry out the multitude of tasks associated with internal and external communications, the office secretary has erasers, pens, liquid paper, typewriter ribbons, typing paper, dictionaries, file folders, stacks of forms, address books, and other reference materials. The office itself is lined with file cabinets and cupboards filled with paper.

In a traditional office, employees spend a great deal of time typing, copying, and filing documents.

Michael W. Miller

For a year, in rooms filled with computers, cameras, microphones and xylophones, Xerox Corp. scientists in cities 500 miles apart have been collaborating as if they were in the same building.

The scientists hope to achieve an electronic "office of the future" that goes well beyond such temporary and awkward methods as picture phones and teleconferences. To study the daunting sociological and technological challenges of such an office, the company has put labs in Palo Alto, Calif., and Portland, Ore., in constant communication, using an assortment of commercially available devices.

The workers watch and talk to each other via video and speaker-phone connections that are always open. They exchange documents over a network that links the computers on their desks.

By examining life in this environment, Xerox hopes to learn how to combine the disparate links into one super work station that functions as both a computer and a TV monitor, running programs, projecting images from other offices and storing paper work and video images.

Some strange things may appear in such files. Last National Secretaries Day, for example, researchers in the two cities gathered in a "circle" to belt out a pastiche of "Seventy-Six Trombones." The circle's halves were joined by cameras, speaker phones and a computer network.

Yet far more is at stake than a better way for widely dispersed colleagues to make dubious music together. Corporate executives have long complained that poor coordination between far-flung operations hurts productivity. Moreover, as the rise of two-career marriages makes many professionals more reluctant to relocate, companies are trying harder to link offices electronically rather than uproot employees.

So far the products available commercially for such linking are piecemeal and designed chiefly for formal, not informal, communications. Offices can swap electronic mail, using computers or facsimile machines. Executives in different cities can hold teleconferences.

Rival Projects

With a few new offerings, they can go a little further. Optel Communications Inc., New York, sells a system that lets personal-computer users instantly send words and pictures over phone lines to PC screens. Luma Telecom Inc. of Santa Clara, Calif., and PicTel Corp. of Peabody, Mass., among others, seek to ignite the soggy market for picture phones, with cheaper and simpler models.

But offices still can't buy pictures, voice and personal computing in a single device as easy to use as a telephone. "Commercial systems that lash all these things together just aren't there yet," says Robert Johansen, the director of telecommunications and computing at Institute for the Future, a Menlo Park, Calif., think tank.

Today a handful of projects are trying to change that. Bolt Beranek & Newman, for example, a Cambridge, Mass., consulting firm, is developing a multimedia communications link under a Defense Department contract. And scientists at Massachusetts Institute of Technology are studying the special technical problems of such links, such as how to design software that many users can share simultaneously.

Xerox's project is one of the most promising, largely because the Palo Alto facility has a record of spawning innovative systems. In the 1970s its scientists developed a futuristic tool for moving information between machines, the now-widespread Ethernet network endorsed by Digital Equipment Corp., among others. The center also originated a computer design that involved breaking the screen into "windows" and entering commands by moving a cursor. That became the popular format for Apple Computer Inc.'s Macintosh.

Now the linked-office experiment is under way. Tinkering with all the gear is a band of irreverent young researchers in sneakers and corduroys, whose ranks include a physicist, a psychologist and two architects as well as computer types.

Xerox has assembled an eclectic group for the project because it is investigating the sociology of office communications as well as the technology. "There's more to working with people than just sitting down and having meetings," says George Goodman, a cognitive psychologist in the Portland office. "There's the sense of being able to walk up to someone's office, lean on the door and say something random."

The all-day video and audio connections make a big difference, letting the offices interrelate casually as well as formally. The main links connect the common areas at the center of both labs, each of which has a camera, a big-screen video monitor and a speaker phone. Everyone typically passes under those cameras' gaze several times a day. And a few workers have cameras and monitors in their own offices.

On a recent day, a scientist in Portland strolled into the common area, noticed an engineer in Palo Alto, and shouted a quick question about a technical problem with a camera. People in both cities regularly eat lunch on camera, chatting with one another on the screens. And one Palo Alto researcher recently took a break to teach a colleague in Portland to juggle.

But the team has also discovered that its hookup requires new rules of etiquette and new technologies. In Portland, Mark Abel joins a circle of researchers conferring with their boss in Palo Alto, but his chair is out of range of the Portland camera. The boss can't see him, so he quickly pipes up: "I don't want to be video-rude—I'm here listening to you too."

Getting someone's attention over the video link takes ingenuity; even shouting into a phone doesn't always work. So Xerox has put a xylophone in each office and has assigned every researcher a personal melody. Now, when people in Portland want to page Randall Smith, a physicist in Palo Alto, they tap out the start of the theme song from TV's "The Jetsons." When a Palo Alto researcher plays the first notes of "Tomorrow," Tom Merrow pokes his head out of his Portland office to see who's summoning him.

Awkward Moments

Being on display like this around the clock makes life awkward at times. "One of the cameras used to point right into my office, and every so often I'd stop and worry, 'Oh boy, am I sitting up straight?' " says Jane Laursen a member of the Portland group.

Still unsolved are some of the most difficult problems. For instance, the researchers hope to use their video links to accumulate a taped record of their work, but they don't want to wind up mired in so much tape that they couldn't easily retrieve a picture or event. So one researcher is trying to develop ways for a computer to search through videos for a specific image, just as a computer can search through a document for a word.

The group also intends to install cameras and microphones in every office, a plan that threatens privacy. So in Portland Mr. Abel is designing easy ways to switch off the electronic eyes and ears.

"In our research there's a real potential for Big Brotherism," he says. "It's great to have a camera in every office, but you better damn well have a way of putting a lens cap on it."

FIRST NATIONAL

TELLER

"I'm a little embarrassed about being overdrawn. Is there a machine I can talk to?"

Adapting to the Electronic Office

The microprocessor chip has radically altered business communication.

Offices started to become "electronic" as soon as they were equipped with telephones and radios. Now the microprocessor chip has carried electronics into every aspect of business communication and significantly altered message production, transmission, and storage.

Change in communication capabilities has become such an integral part of our lives that people accept it almost without noticing. In an earlier generation, people would have remembered the first time they ever heard of a radio or a television. Do you remember the first time you ever heard of a videocassette recorder? A laser printer? A compact disk? A cellular telephone? Such items seem to appear in homes, offices, and even automobiles every day, and yet each has been a minor revolution in our ability to transmit and receive information.

In the next part of this chapter, you will examine a few of these revolutions, discuss how they affect our ability to communicate in business, and learn some strategies for improving communication in this setting.

Using Microcomputers

The microcomputer has rapidly become a fixture in homes as well as in offices. Equipped with a keyboard, a video display screen, one or more disk drives, and appropriate software, the microcomputer can perform hundreds of functions, from handling payroll to maintaining mailing lists to storing telephone numbers.

As a word processor, the microcomputer can relieve you of many unpleasant and painstaking duties. The computer screen lets you see a document before it is printed onto a piece of paper. You may make corrections, add, delete, and move words, sentences, and paragraphs, realign margins, center text, and reformat a page by simply pressing a few keys (Figure 3-1). The computer can even check your documents against its own dictionary to

A microcomputer can help create and edit documents, handle accounting, manage and store data, and produce graphics.

SAMPLE USES OF THE COMPUTER

Microcomputer
(Word processor)
  Composing
  Proofreading
  Producing graphics
  Printing
  Storing
  Accessing data
  Filing
  Calculating
  Training
Database
(Library research)
  Storing and accessing information
  Subscribing to bibliographies

Electronic mail (Digital network)
  Sending messages, scanning documents
  Making purchases and payments
  Sending bills
  Performing banking activities
  Decentralizing work force
Networking
  Communicating within organizations
  Exchanging information
  Sending documents back and forth
  Working jointly on projects
Teleconferencing (Meetings)

FIGURE 3–1
A sampling of word processing capabilities

spot most spelling and typographical errors. The computer, moreover, is not limited simply to written text: it can produce tables, charts, and other graphics to supplement written or oral presentations.

After being saved on a hard or floppy disk, the document may be printed out in a "hard" copy or simply kept on a disk for future reference. Not only does the computer greatly reduce the toil of typing, but it also reduces the amount of storage space needed for documents: hundreds of pages can be saved on a 5¼-inch floppy disk. (See Chapter 7 for an extended look at word processing.)

A document may be printed out as well as kept on a disk.

Computers, in fact, act as facilities for storing and accessing data. Real estate agents can check to see what houses are available in certain locations and price ranges. Store managers can keep track of their inventory. And computers can also be used as calculators to generate financial projections, calculate interest payments, and accomplish many other painstaking tasks.

In the electronics office, the microcomputer may replace the typewriter, filing cabinets, adding machines, calculators, mailing lists, reams of paper covered with data, and piles of supplies such as correction tape, liquid paper, and reference volumes. The work station is less cluttered, more compact, and much more efficient.

Computers, too, can be used as trainers. You may have already worked with software that supplemented your coursework in accounting, economics, algebra, or other subjects. Companies are using computers to train employees at all levels, from mechanics to executives.

Computers are often used successfully for training.

Using Computers for Desktop Publishing

Computers can calso be used to create documents that look like they were professionally printed. These machines can handle documents hundreds of pages long, and they can format and design them in numerous ways. Book-length documents can be created in many different typefaces, with colorful graphics and other enhancements.

Desktop publishing creates documents that look as if they were professionally printed.

As the price of desktop publishing is rapidly decreasing, it will shortly be within the means of individuals as well as businesses.

Locating Information Through Database Services

Because computers can store vast quantities of information and make it easily accessible, they are being used to replace laborious library research. With appropriate software, you can set up your own database, putting in information you can access later. Moreover, thousands of database services now provide current and detailed information on a wide range of topics for personal computer users.

A database is a body of information entered into a computer in an organized fashion.

Using a modem and a terminal, subscribers to database services have access to bibliographies in specialized areas, stock quotations, information on companies, texts of newspaper and periodical articles, and much more. The Dow Jones News/Retrieval Service, for example, provides extensive in-

Computers Talk Their Way Out of the Laboratory

A middle manager at the Cleveland headquarters of TRW, Inc. needs a dozen new calculators for his department. No problem. He simply dials the talking computer that TRW's purchasing department recently bought from the Votan Co. of Fremont, California.

"How many units do you need?" an electronic voice asks. "When would you like delivery? Which brand or vendor do you prefer?" There are no requisitions in triplicate; no delays by interoffice mail; no need to repeat instructions to personnel. Seconds after this brief tête-à-tête between man and machine, a high-speed printer zips the order to a purchasing clerk for swift execution.

Advances in voice-recognition and voice-response technology have now brought conversational computers out of the sci-fi realm. Like many human beings, they tend to talk better than they listen. But they are learning quickly, and they are fast and accurate. "The technology is just now getting to the point where it can be taken out of the laboratory and into the working environment," says Vincent Prehen, a vice president at PROTEO Technology Corp. in Valley Forge, Pennsylvania.

A closely related marvel is the voice-operated typewriter. Experts say a breakthrough is likely as early as next year, either by IBM or by Xerox and others who are working on talking typewriters. "Near term you will see a voice-generated system in which the user talks into a PC or a PC-based typewriter, and his words are automatically converted to digital form and displayed on the screen," predicts New York-based technology analyst F.G. "Ted" Withington.

"With a cursor the user can correct any errors directly on the screen and then have the message typed or printed out."

Withington says the speech/spelling software needed for voice-operated typewriters has already been developed. He says it can spell in context up to 97% of the words dictated into it—distinguishing, for example, between such like-sounding words as "here" and "hear" and "through" and "threw."

As for message-sending applications, a number of companies now make voice-conversion circuit boards that users can slip directly into their PCs. Signal-processing chips built into the circuit boards convert voice signals to digital form and then, via speech synthesis, turn the digital signals into human-sounding voice signals. This enables the user to enter verbal messages by telephone into an electronic mail system and retrieve them either on a computer screen or over the phone.

This technology is now relatively cheap. National Microsystems of Natick, Massachusetts, for example, makes a voice-response board, called the Watson, that includes both a digital signal-processing chip and a modem and sells for about $500. The company says it has sold about 15,000 units since introducing the Watson several years ago, mostly to business and professional customers. With enhancements, says National, the board can read files from a company's database.

Microlog Corp. of Germantown, Maryland, also offers circuit boards, plus voice-response software called VCS-3000, which sell for $2,200. The company has had the most success selling the equipment to customers who want to deliver a large volume of computer-generated voice messages for telemarketing purposes.

vestment information as well as the full text of *The Wall Street Journal*, while Lexis/Nexis provides the full text of law-related articles.

With database services, businesspeople have at their fingertips an enormous amount of information useful for doing market research, assessing competitors, projecting industry trends, and making a wide assortment of decisions.

Communicating Instantly by Electronic Mail

For years, Telex, TWX, Western Union, and other companies have been sending written messages electronically. Now computers make it possible for businesses to send written messages anywhere in the world in a matter of moments. Using a modem and telecommunication software, someone at a computer terminal in London can type a message that is sent over telephone lines to a computer in San Francisco. Whole documents can be scanned, too, and sent to a compatible machine.

Sending messages electronically by telephone outside a local area involves paying long-distance telephone rates, but usually those will be less than the cost of an overnight mail service; moreover, the message arrives at its destination within moments.

As a result of the ease and relative low cost of electronic mail, many businesses are doing the majority of their transactions by computer. They can make purchases and payments, send bills, and perform banking activities without using the U.S. Postal Service. Electronic mail is also enabling more and more people to work at home—or wherever they choose—and send their work to their offices in moments.

Within a few years, the public telephone system may have an integrated digital network in place that will increase the speed of data flow and reduce costs even more.

Electronic mail enables users to send messages from one computer to another.

Networking with Computers

Businesses are also using computers to communicate within the organization. Using workstations connected to each other with high-speed cable connections, users can exchange information and send documents back and forth. With electronic "mailboxes" people can exchange messages and ideas without leaving their desks. Computers are replacing bulletin boards in some organizations.

An internal computer network also helps employees work together on reports and other projects. Someone developing a departmental budget can send the figures to a colleague in another office for review; groups can work together writing and revising documents before they are printed.

In many companies, computers have helped substantially to reduce the flow of paper for both internal and external communication.

People in organizations send computer messages to each other.

Conducting Meetings by Video

Meetings are now being conducted by means of video equipment. Television equipment is set up in two or more meeting rooms so that participants can see and hear each other without actually traveling to each other's offices. Videocassette tapes of the meeting can also be saved and viewed later.

Now you can attend a meeting in another city without leaving your desk.

The equipment for this process, which is called *teleconferencing*, has been in existence for some time, but costs have been prohibitive. Now, however, an investment in appropriate video equipment can greatly reduce a company's expenditures on airfares, hotel rooms, and other travel costs.

Overcoming Problems with Technology

Naturally, these changes in the traditional office can create problems. People do not always react positively toward innovation. Given a choice, many people would choose to keep things the way they are rather than face the problems that changes bring. Furthermore, these electronic devices *do* create some problems that cannot be ignored. But the electronic office is definitely here to stay, so it is important to face the problems associated with it.

Fear of the Unknown

Often managers are reluctant to spend money on equipment they do not understand. Employees are often nervous that the equipment could jeopardize their jobs.

Not only are people afraid of buying and using high-tech equipment, but they are also afraid the equipment will jeopardize their jobs.

These fears are legitimate in some ways. People should not buy equipment without knowing what they are doing. Every potential buyer should thoroughly research equipment and costs. However, a little time spent researching options usually results in long-term savings of time and money.

Fears about losing jobs have more validity. Throughout the nineteenth and twentieth centuries, people have lost jobs as automation replaced them. The solution to the problem, however, is not to resist automation. The only way to survive the changes is to learn new skills, to adapt.

Secretaries who do not develop microcomputer skills, for example, will find they are unable to compete even with high school students for clerical positions.

Managers and executives must learn to adapt as well. Many managers who formerly thought that typing was "secretaries' work" are learning about the convenience of having a terminal on their desks. Now they can write and send messages themselves as well as access information in moments. They have had to learn that using a keyboard is not demeaning: it is an essential skill for most businesspeople.

Information Overload

Computers can generate an overwhelming amount of data.

Another problem generated by the electronic office is information overload. Databases can provide people with so much information that they may feel overwhelmed by it all. Thousands of technical articles, for example, are printed every day—and now they are easily available to us. Who could possibly assimilate all the information at our fingertips?

Learning to use database services effectively has become an art in itself, as has distilling the most relevant information for specific uses. Reading and research skills are even more important than they used to be for a business-person interested in keeping up with industry changes and trends.

The flood of information can be a problem even within one organization. Both transmitting and reproducing messages have become so easy that many people are inundated with messages. This problem began in earnest when the photocopy machine made generating copies so easy. Rather than deciding who really needed a piece of information, people were making hundreds of copies of *everything* and sending them to everyone.

Now, writing, storing, and retrieving data electronically make this situation even more acute. How can people make sure the messages they send are not lost in the flood? Computers themselves can help by reducing information to graphs and charts so it can be perceived more quickly. But people also have to develop strategies of their own that reduce the overload problem.

Some of the most effective of these strategies involve effective writing. Rather than reducing the need for good writing skills, the electronic office actually increases it. One of the best ways to make messages visible and memorable, for example, is to use effective outlining, organizing, and high-lighting techniques so a reader can grasp and digest the ideas easily and quickly. Moreover, deleting excess words and using a clear writing style will encourage a reader to finish reading a message.

Computers have increased the need for effective writing skills.

What Would You Do?

Philip and Vera Tremaine run a hotel resort in New England. Built in the nineteenth century, the hotel has a hundred elegant rooms overlooking woods and lakes.

One key element of the Tremaines' success has been their personal touch: a bottle of champagne awaits each new visitor, a Godiva chocolate sits on each pillow in the evenings.

Although the Tremaines have bought a computer system to help with reservations and billing, they always answer written inquiries about the hotel with handwritten notes on expensive stationery. When someone makes a reservation, he or she receives a handwritten letter confirming the reservation.

As the Tremaines' hotel has become more popular, writing these notes has become a tremendous burden. To save precious time, Philip believes they should use their computer for routine correspondence. Vera, however, believes that the handwritten notes help draw many new visitors to the hotel each year. Visitors, she maintains, come to this hotel for personal attention: a computerized letter would drive them somewhere else.

How do you think they should resolve their difference of opinion? Write the Tremaines a letter outlining a solution. Address it to:

Mr. and Mrs. Philip Tremaine
The Hotel Nottingham
Alta Ridge, VT 03492

Computer Unfriendliness

You have heard commercials touting computers or software as *user-friendly*. The phrase is meant to help people overcome the fears discussed earlier in this chapter.

While most computers are becoming more "friendly" to their users, you are probably familiar with the frustrations that can develop when you are at the receiving end of a computer message. If you have ever been the victim of a "computer error," you understand the problem: the computer sends you an incorrect bill; you write the company and receive another incorrect computerized bill; you call the company and hear a computerized voice giving you information you do not need.

You may have gotten used to dealing with a machine instead of a human bank teller. You may even buy gas from a machine instead of an attendant. However, businesses are still run by people; computers should not be used in ways that destroy the personal element in dealings with clients, customers, vendors, and employees.

Teleconferencing, for example, has proved disappointing in some companies. Watching people on a screen cannot replace actually sitting and working with them in person. Electronic gadgetry cannot replace human warmth and friendliness.

Communication should be oriented toward people, not toward machines.

Similarly, your writing style should not reflect the impersonality of a computer. Even though computers may be used to produce and transmit our messages, the messages are still being sent from human beings to other human beings. The basic goals of communication remain the same as they were 30,000 years ago. Make sure that you use computers and other electronic devices to help bring about rather than hinder those goals.

Summary

Business communication has changed in the last fifty years as offices have become computerized. Electronic equipment has changed the way people get information, the way they write and produce documents, and the way they convey messages to others.

While remaining open to the great advantages of electronic communication, remember that the electronic revolution does not, and cannot, alter the basic precepts of communication. Technology cannot replace the human elements of communication. Learn to use machines as tools to improve the communication process, not to damage it.

New Technology Checklist

Working in a High-Tech Office

• In a high-tech office, you can use a microcomputer to

_____ write, revise, and print documents

_____ produce book-length manuscripts with the quality of printed pages

_____ produce graphics

_____ store and access data

_____ train employees

- You can subscribe to database services in order to have access to data such as

  _____ specialized bibliographies

  _____ up-to-date investment information

  _____ full texts of newspapers and articles

- You may choose to communicate electronically by means of

  _____ electronic mail

  _____ networking

  _____ teleconferencing

- When introducing high-tech equipment to an organization, take pains to avoid problems such as

  _____ the employees' fear of the unknown and worries about loss of jobs

  _____ information overload brought about by too much raw data

  _____ impersonal modes of communicating that reduce empathy with people receiving messages

Summary Discussion: Karen Alsop's Suggestions from Case in Point, p. 39

If a computer were installed at each work station, the secretaries could use their machines full-time. They would use them for the majority of their typing tasks without ever having to wait to use a machine. With full-time use of a computer, too, each secretary would develop competence on the machine and could set up an individual work station that was suitable and efficient for his or her individual needs.

Even a small company such as this one could benefit from modems to allow computer communication by telephone lines. Database services such as Lexis/Nexis might also prove very useful. Teleconferencing equipment could be worthwhile if meetings with people in different geographical areas need to be set up with some frequency.

Terms to Remember

Database service: service that provides subscribing computer users with data

Desktop publishing: using a computer to create documents that look professionally printed

Electronic mail: messages sent between computers on telephone lines

Microcomputer: a complete computer system to be used by one person at a time

Modem: a device that allows computer signals to be transmitted by telephone

Networking: transmitting data between two or more computer systems

Teleconferencing: conducting meetings with people in different geographic locations by means of television equipment

Questions for Review and Discussion

1. What limitations of spoken language led people to develop written communication?
2. Why is experience with a computer as important for managers as it is for clerical workers?
3. Describe the strengths and weaknesses of electronic mail.
4. Describe the strengths and weaknesses of teleconferencing.
5. What is an online database service? What are its strengths and weaknesses?
6. Computer companies are aware that many people are still afraid of using computers. What advertising strategies have companies used to reduce people's fears?
7. This chapter mentioned a few reasons why people are reluctant to accept changes in their office procedures and equipment. What other reason may make people reluctant to make changes?
8. Computer programs are being refined so that they can help writers locate errors in grammar and punctuation as well as in spelling. Ultimately, computers may be able to put together meaningful business correspondence, but this goal still seems quite far away. Why is it so hard to teach computers how to write?

Exercises

1. Assume that you are interested in buying a personal computer for yourself or your office. Make a list of the features you are interested in and then visit a computer store. Which brand and model meets your needs most effectively? Why?

   To arrive at a decision, you might want to use the following criteria:
   a. Cost
   b. Types of programs (such as word processing, accounting, and graphics) the machine can run
   c. Features of specific programs you are interested in
   d. Available memory
   e. Number of disk drives
   f. Compatibility with other equipment such as printers and modems

2. If you already have a personal computer of your own, describe what you feel are its strong and weak points with regard to your needs. If you were to upgrade your present equipment, what features would you be interested in adding? Explain.

3. Visit a nearby company and explain that you are doing a project on communication equipment. Find out what types of equipment the business uses for internal and external communication. Be prepared to discuss the strengths and weaknesses of the equipment the company has chosen.

   You might want to find out, for example, whether the company's present equipment is suitable for its needs. Can the equipment be expanded if the company grows? Is the equipment compatible with that of other companies?

4. Godfrey's Office Equipment Company is concerned about the costs of sending salespeople to thousands of offices around the country each year. To reduce these costs, some members of upper management want the company to develop a videotape of salespeople demonstrating and discussing the equipment.

   If prospective customers watched the tape, they could actually see some of the equipment in action, and the company would not have to pay for the salespeople's travel expenses.

   You have been asked to help decide whether the project would be worthwhile.

Draw up a list of the project's strong and weak points. Should the company reduce its personal selling efforts and send videotapes to interested customers? Why or why not?

5. Research some of the newest changes in electronic equipment by looking through recent issues of personal computer magazines. Which of the most recent breakthroughs do you think will be most useful to businesses in the next few years? Explain.

6. You have undoubtedly been affected by the "electronic revolution" in the past decade. What changes have occurred in your own home? In your office? In what ways has your ability to create, transmit, or receive messages been affected by these changes?

7. Visit your public library or school library to find out what online database services are available for people in the field you are in or are planning to enter. (You will probably want to start with database directories in the library reference section.) Be prepared to explain to your class what kinds of information are available and the approximate costs for using the services.

Part 1 Mini-Cases

1–1. Len Johnson sets up a meeting of department heads every Friday afternoon during lunch. He arranges for sandwiches and coffee to be served in the conference room while the meeting is going on. In this way, he feels, the atmosphere is informal and sociable; business gets done in a relatively painless fashion.

However, some problems are resulting from these informal meetings. On several occasions, someone has been assigned a task and then forgotten all about it.

"I didn't write it down at the meeting," one of the department heads explains to Len. "I can't take notes and eat lunch at the same time."

Similarly, a few important decisions have gone unnoticed by some of the people at the meeting.

"We decided *that?*" someone asks. "I didn't know we'd made a final decision on that issue. I thought those lunch meetings were just informal get-togethers."

Len realizes that some communication barriers have arisen from his lunch-meeting system. Describe the barriers and offer some solutions to his problem.

1–2. This letter was sent to students of Hartmann College during their summer vacation.

July 18, 19xx

Dear Students:

   Welcome back to Hartmann. We hope the upcoming year will be an exciting and challenging one for all of us. I know you will be pleased to see the changes that have taken place in the Student Union: now you will have a choice of excellent luncheon dishes in the cafeteria as well as a smorgasbord of good food in the new cafe.

By the way, the college swimming pool is open during the summer from 9 a.m. until 5 p.m., so drop by for a swim if you're in the area!

To make your lives easier this year, we have developed an alternative procedure for fall registration. Now, instead of standing in line in September, you can register in advance for most classes if you choose to do so. To arrange for early registration materials to be sent to you, be sure to let us know by August 1. Otherwise, just come to registration as usual on September 12.

We know this will be a terrific year at Hartmann. I look forward to seeing you in September!

Sincerely,

Erin Hart

Erin Hart
Student Service Center

College administrators were surprised when very few students requested early registration materials. Someone suggested that maybe the message about the new option had not been communicated effectively to the students.

a. Why do you think so few students responded to this letter?

b. Revise the letter from Erin Hart so that the major message is more effectively conveyed. You may add or delete information as you wish.

1–3. Charlie Gregers is vice-president of the marketing division of Simms Corporation. Although he sends memos almost daily to the supervisors in his division, he receives very little information from them through formal channels: their monthly reports and an occasional meeting are the only formal methods he has for getting messages about his division.

However, Charlie receives a lot of information through the grapevine. On a sample day, for instance, he overheard employees talking at lunch; he chatted in the elevator with two secretaries; he had a brief conversation with the supervisor of the market research group; and he had a cup of coffee with the vice-president of finance. From these encounters he learned the following pieces of information about his division:

a. Katie Lee just had a baby boy

b. Some employees are griping about the air conditioning system

c. Ron Carruthers had trouble with his computer terminal that morning

d. Patricia Hennley worked extremely hard on the Worth project

e. Some employees are pleased with the new office chairs; others find them too small

f. Jack Lehrer got back from Barbados last night

g. Katie Lee just had twins

From these messages and your own intuition, write two or three paragraphs describing some of the characteristics of information received through the grapevine.

1–4. Review the results of the questionnaire on communication skills that you took while reading Chapter 2 (p. 8). Now assume that the results you found were typical for employees in Fremont Corporation.

You are in charge of developing a one-day communication seminar specifically for Fremont employees: you want the seminar to help employees overcome their weakest areas. Write two or three paragraphs describing an ideal seminar targeting specific communication areas. What areas of communication should receive the most attention? What types of activities would be of greatest benefit to the employees participating in the seminar? How much time would you allot to the different topic areas in the seminar?

1–5. Assume that you are a salesperson who makes presentations concerning computer equipment to company employees and management. Typically, you make three presentations in large companies:

1. To managers with little knowledge of computers who will not actually be using the equipment but who will make the ultimate buying decisions

2. To computer programmers who will influence the decision made by management

3. To employees with little technical knowledge who will actually be using the equipment and whose opinions will carry weight with management

For each of your presentations, you want to adjust your message to the specific audience. For each group, write a paragraph or two outlining your approach. You might answer the following questions:

a. What are my listeners' major concerns?

b. How much do they already know about my products?

c. What kind of word choices should I make?

d. What *motivates* my listeners?

1–6. Johanna Dilsey has loved working with computers since she was a child. Now that she is setting up her own office, she longs to achieve a "paperless office"—one in which all internal communications and almost all external ones are done electronically.

Each employee in her Tucson and Denver offices has a terminal that can communicate with each of the others. Moreover, her customers can connect their personal computers with the mainframe in her Denver office.

However, Johanna soon finds that electronic communications are not as effective as paper in some situations. Although the computers are useful for writing and revising all the company documents, she has to admit that some situations require hard copy for the finished materials. Paper is more efficient and more appropriate for letters reminding customers of late payments, sales information to customers, product descriptions for sales representatives, memos related to sensitive problem areas, legal documents, and a number of other types of written communications.

Describe the general advantages of paper over electronic communications for some types of documents.

1–7. Niteline Inc. recently altered the work situations for neary fifty employees: they now "telecommute," working at home on personal computers and sending their work over the telephone lines to the company's main computer. At first, this change pleased most of the telecommuting employees. They enjoyed making their own hours and being their own bosses. Without the distractions of the office, the productivity of most of the telecommuting employees rose immediately after the change was made.

After a few months, however, some problems surfaced. Without the stimulus of being around their colleagues, some of the telecommuting employees' work began to lack creativity.

"I feel like I'm in a vacuum," one said. "I'm running out of ideas."

"I'm losing my enthusiasm for this job," another one said. "I hate to say it, but I'm lonely!"

Write two or three paragraphs offering suggestions to the managers in charge of these employees. What can they do to increase the morale of the telecommuting employees and make them feel more integrated with the company?

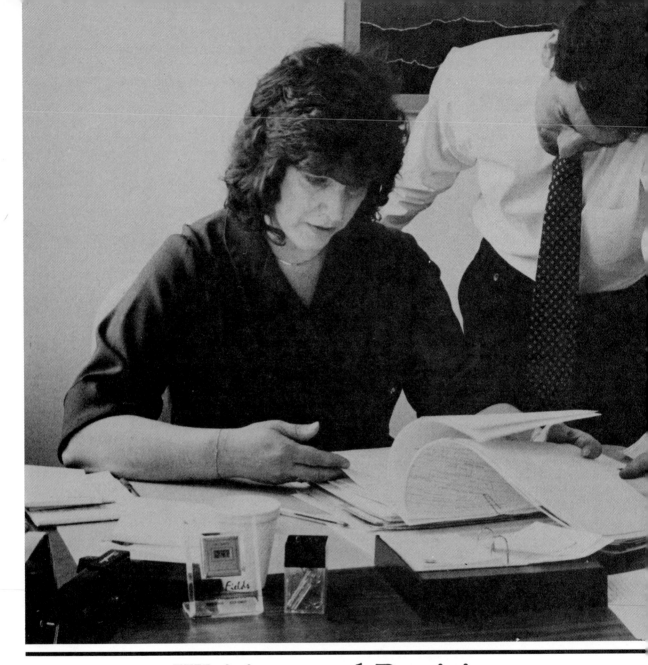

Writing and Revising
Business Documents

Part Two

Introduction to Business Writing

- **Communicating through business documents**
- **Recognizing the qualities and goals of business writing**
- **Writing for an audience**
- **Avoiding biased language**
- **Identifying legal issues**
- **Writing under pressure**
- **Identifying the writing process**

Objectives

To identify the unique qualities of business writing

To orient business writing to the needs and interests of readers

To create effective documents under pressure

4

Frank Harmon's Business Letter

Frank Harmon was one of OmniData's best salespeople. When customers came to the company's retail outlet, he could find out their needs efficiently and talk to them enthusiastically. His jokes and personable manner were complemented by a wealth of information about OmniData's personal computers and accessories.

Because he was so good on the sales floor, management asked Frank to draft the letter for a direct-mail package.

"Put some of your sales charm on paper for us," the store manager told him. "We're trying to get more business customers interested in our portable Omni-Z model. Right now, we're mainly selling it to students."

Frank created a letter that began like this:

How many times have you been lying on the warm, white sand of Waikiki and suddenly remembered that you needed to write to your branch managers in Lapland? This is it, ladies and germs: the personal computer you can take to the beach! With the Omni-Z, you can do just that *without getting off your towel!*

The OmniData manager read the letter in horror. "You've missed the whole point, Frank. We're trying to sell machines to businesses. We can't come across like comedians."

"But this is just the sort of thing I always say to customers when I first meet them," Frank replied. "I make them laugh. They love it."

"They're not going to love this, Frank. They're going to read the opening lines and throw away the letter. And they're going to wonder whether OmniData is a legitimate computer company."

Reluctantly, Frank sat down to try another approach.

Points to Consider

- From Frank's experience, what differences do you perceive between spoken and written communication?
- What points should Frank consider before he revises his letter?

Communicating Through Business Documents

Business writing includes every type of writing used to further the goals of a business or to communicate between members of the public and businesses. The brochures you receive from Time/Life Books and the letters you receive from United Way are pieces of business writing; so are the resumes you send off in response to want ads and the letter you write renewing your subscription to *Sports Illustrated*.

Although the principles of good writing remain fairly constant, you will find that written business communication differs significantly from the writing you have been doing as student.

As a business writer, for instance, you will not always receive guidelines such as those you receive from a college instructor regarding page length and content. You may have more freedom than you had in school, but you may also feel more uncertain about what your colleagues and supervisors are looking for. Although most companies use standard formats for letters, memos, and reports, you will probably have to gauge appropriate guidelines for yourself: most companies do not have writing instruction manuals.

Many companies do not provide guidelines for writing business documents.

Another aspect of business writing is that many documents are written by one person and signed by another. Someone may tell you, "Just write up

You may have to write business documents for other people in your organization.

Business documents are frequently developed by several people.

those results in a letter to Joe. I'll sign the letter when you're done." Moreover, much business writing is done in a group—your whole marketing team may have to write up a marketing report, for example.

As a result of these differences, you may change some of the writing habits you developed when you were writing in the privacy of your room for instructors who gave you specific assignments and detailed outlines on what they expected.

Recognizing the Qualities and Goals of Business Writing

"I write the way I speak," many people claim. "What's wrong with that?" Although writing and speaking have many points in common, business documents need more careful development and construction than do conversations.

Unlike a spoken sentence, business writing cannot usually be changed once it is sent to a reader. A confusing, inaccurate, or offensive letter can damage your relationship with the reader and even lead to legal problems. As a business writer, you need to review your documents carefully before sending them out.

Business documents must be written carefully.

One of the assets of business writing is that it can be sent to different people in different places, but writers have to make sure that their approach works for those different people. Moreover, while written communications are more permanent than spoken ones—the words do not disappear into the air—they must be able to withstand the test of being read and reread.

Business documents are often read and reread by more than one person.

What Is Unique About Business Writing?

You can see that writing differs from speaking. But how does business writing differ from other types of writing? "Writing is writing," some students maintain. "I got a B in Freshman English. My writing is fine."

Actually, in many ways, these students are correct. The similarities between business prose and other types of writing are more obvious than their differences. The writing process is similar for most types of written communication. The differences, however, are significant. Writing a movie script is not quite the same as developing a marketing report, and thanking your Uncle Eddie for the red mittens is not exactly like writing a sales letter.

From the Desk of ...

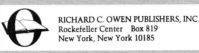

RICHARD C. OWEN PUBLISHERS, INC.
Rockefeller Center   Box 819
New York, New York 10185

"Good communication is the key to persuading authors to sign with my company," states Richard Owen, President and Publisher of Richard C. Owen Publishers, Inc. *"When I am talking on the phone, I can find out what a person is concerned about; I can receive an instantaneous response; the exchange is synergistic. We each give our ideas and often a third cluster of ideas is the result."*

Richard's company has developed quickly. He began by reissuing out-of-print college textbooks and professional books with a focus on reading and other language arts. He has now moved into the elementary education field. His list attracted the interest of the New Zealand government, and he has become the U.S. publisher of *Ready to Read,* the national "whole language" reading program of New Zealand. He is also publishing school-level materials produced by Whole Language consultants of Winnipeg, Canada.

Richard says the major communication task of the first two years of his business was to persuade potential authors that his company would survive. Despite twenty years of experience in college publishing, he says, "it takes time to develop visibility when you are on your own." The second task was to show authors that he could market their books, "get the word out." The third task, often the hardest he says, is to help authors accept changes in editorial content and structure that are needed.

"We are dealing with people who have pretty strong opinions. We want them to take our advice without being forced, so we do a lot of describing and explaining." Richard thinks that in many cases the telephone is the best channel for these exchanges.

Richard's use of direct mail marketing brochures points to the need for writers to identify the audience they wish to reach. When Richard is advertising college-level or professional books, markets not dominated by sales representatives, his brochures are different from when he is advertising school-level books that will be sold by sales representatives. In the first instance a marketing brochure will be his single opportunity to sell a book, so "I tend to include far more substantive material. My goal is to inform and persuade. I want the reader to order the book.

"When I write a marketing brochure for school-level books, I want to generate interest and a response. I want the potential buyer to pick up the phone or send us a note. The design and layout become more important. I use fewer words, touch lightly on points. Once the brochure's reader has contacted us, we can send a sales rep to discuss the content of the books in face-to-face conversation."

In all communication, Richard suggests the key is to state your point simply and clearly. "It will carry more weight than flowery or effusive prose."

A final tip from Richard on writing: use the word processor. "With the word processor you can try things out. It gives you freedom. If you don't like what you've written, you can delete it or move it around. Once you learn the mechanics, it's faster. You'll be a better writer."

Four qualities set business writing apart from many other types of writing:

1. A company is represented.
2. The writing is usually persuasive.
3. The writing has serious goals.
4. The style should be invisible.

A Company Is Represented

When you write to thank Uncle Eddie, you write as yourself. When you write a sales letter or other business document, you represent a company. Not only do you act as an agent for the company, but also your letter becomes part of the company's image. Rather than commending or criticizing the writer of such a letter, readers are apt to say, "That company does a quality job on its letters" or "That company seems confused and disorganized."

The documents you write as a company employee become part of that company's image.

Most Business Writing Is Persuasive

Whereas a novel may have entertainment as a key goal and your letter to Uncle Eddie may be an expression of duty or appreciation, most business letters, memos, and reports are ultimately designed to persuade.

A sales letter is meant to persuade its readers to buy a product or support a service or organization. But even year-end reports and simple memos have a similar underlying function: the writers are attempting to persuade readers to support a proposal, agree to a recommendation, attend a meeting, adhere to a policy, or invest in the company's stock. Most business writers hope to gain their readers' cooperation and support, no matter what their more obvious message may be.

Most business writing is persuasive in nature.

Business Writing Has Serious Goals

Some business writers have a pleasant and breezy style that contrasts with many of their colleagues' dreary business prose. But even the funniest memos usually have a serious purpose. After all, running a business is essentially a serious undertaking.

While a fiction writer might write a short story with the primary goal of making people laugh, a business writer has different motives: he or she may try to make people laugh so that they will feel positively about a proposal or agree to a recommendation. In fact, humor in business writing is usually

FRANK AND ERNEST ©by Bob Thaves

HERE'S WHERE THE MAGIC OF EDITING COMES IN.

a persuasive technique used for a serious purpose. And, of course, most business writing is not humorous at all.

Business Writing Style Is Invisible

Writing *style* is the way ideas are expressed. Writing can be ornate or simple, personal or impersonal, succinct and direct, or wordy and roundabout.

The content of a business document should be more apparent than its style.

Most people maintain that content is more important than style in business writing. In a sense, this is true. Business writers do not emulate fiction writers whose style may be more apparent than their story lines.

However, business writing does have a style; certain identifiable characteristics recur in most business documents. And this style has changed considerably in the past forty years.

In the first part of this century, business writing style was much more formal and impersonal than it is now; simple letters sometimes sounded more like legal documents than personal communications between individuals. Quasilegal phrases such as "Hereinwith enclosed" and "Per our agreement" appeared frequently in letters and memos. Business writers tended to avoid personal pronouns such as *I* and *you* (Figure 4-1).

In recent decades, business writers have come to understand the importance of the personal elements of communication: they recognize that the receiver of a message is a vital component of the communication process. As a result, most business writers now write in a style that is more natural and personal, less cold and legalistic. Clarity, conciseness, and an appropriate, effective tone are perceived as essential ingredients for good business writing.

Business writing style is less formal and more personal than it used to be.

Now business writers work to achieve a style that subtly complements the content. The "style," in fact, is almost invisible. The strokes of a good tennis player or swimmer look effortless; similarly, the best business writing appears to have been written easily, without strain.

Herb Caen, columnist for the *San Francisco Chronicle*, once remarked that he knows he has been successful when people tell him what an easy life he has—just putting out that breezy column every day. His goal is making that column *look* easy to write. As a business writer, you should have a similar goal. Your memos and letters should look like they flowed onto your page without effort. Of course, creating that effortless effect takes a lot of effort!

Old Style	*New Style*
Pursuant to your request, this letter acknowledges receipt of Order #324.	We have received your Order #324.
Enclosed herewith are the terms of the aforementioned lease.	I have enclosed the terms of your lease.
On May 29, this department made inquiry into the events subsequent to your presentation.	On May 29, Henry Johnson and I asked about the events that followed your presentation.

FIGURE 4–1

A comparison of business writing styles

Writing for an Audience

Focus on your reader as well as on your message.

When you are creating business documents, remember that you are writing *to* and *for* your readers. The style, the organization, and even the words should be chosen with your audience in mind: the you-attitude is a key to effective communication.

As a student, you may have found yourself analyzing your instructor as you write reports, homework assignments, or essay questions: "This instructor likes lots of detail," you might tell yourself, or "That instructor prefers short answers that get right to the point."

As a business writer, you will not always know your readers personally. When writing a report to upper management, a sales letter to credit card customers, a memo to hundreds of staff members, or a job application letter to someone you have never met, you will not be able to analyze your readers so easily. You can learn, however, to organize and present material so it will convey information effectively to a diverse audience or to a reader with particular interests.

As you study this text and practice writing business documents, you will find yourself becoming more skillful in analyzing your readers. With experience, you can fine-tune your writing so it is appropriate for the type of document you are writing, the information you are conveying, and the audience you are addressing.

The following guidelines can help you establish a positive relationship with your reader while you communicate the messages you want to convey.

Your business writing should be appropriate for
- the type of document you are creating
- the message you are conveying
- the readers you are addressing

1. *Consider why your readers are going to read your message.* When you know the readers' goals, you will find it easier to present information in a way they will find helpful.
2. *Consider what the readers already know—and what they need to know.* You do not want to bore readers with information they already have, but you do not want to confuse them by discussing issues they are not familiar with. Analysis can help you provide information that is useful and relevant.
3. *Orient information to the readers' needs.* The you-attitude can help you organize and present material so readers understand why it is beneficial to them.

> Our new finger-paints are water-soluble. [I-attitude]
>
> Our new finger-paints will quickly wash off your child's hands. [you-attitude]

4. *Remain calm and polite.* A calm, polite tone emphasizes your professionalism and enhances your credibility. If you write anything when you are upset, angry, or exhausted, do not send it off right away. When you reread it a few hours later, you can revise it in a way that will maintain the reader's goodwill while still conveying a message.

> If you are interested in keeping your job, come see me today about your lousy attendance record. [rude]
>
> Ann, you have missed five out of the last fourteen work days. What's wrong? Please come see me today. [calm]

Avoiding Biased Language

To communicate effectively with your readers, choose words that do not offend them. Keep your tone objective and professional and your word choices free of bias. Avoid swear words, off-color humor, and language that discriminates against a person's race, ethnic background, sex, age, or disability.

The following hints can help you keep your writing free of bias.

Business writing should be professional and un-biased.

Avoid terms that indicate a bias concerning
• sex
• race or ethnic background
• age
• disability

Avoid Using Male Pronouns to Refer to Men and Women

Traditionally, writers have used *he, him, his,* and *himself* to refer to singular nouns representing men and women. These pronouns can easily be changed so the writing does not appear biased in favor of men.

Each customer showed his receipt. [biased]
Each customer showed a receipt. [unbiased]
All customers showed their receipts. [unbiased]

A manager may wish to add topics to his agenda. [biased]
A manager may wish to add topics to his/her agenda. [unbiased]
Managers may wish to add topics to their agendas. [unbiased]

Avoid Using the Word *Man* to Refer to Men and Women

In the past, the words *man, men,* and *mankind* were used to refer to all of humanity. Replace such terms with words such as *people* and *humanity* that do not reflect a bias toward one gender.

Henryson wrote about communication among mankind. [biased]
Henryson wrote about human communication. [unbiased]

Man owes much of his understanding of astronomy to Galileo. [biased]
People owe much of their understanding of astronomy to Galileo. [unbiased]
We owe much of our understanding of astronomy to Galileo. [unbiased]

Dr. Jenson, chairman of this department, is retiring. [biased]
Dr. Jenson, chair of this department, is retiring. [unbiased]

Avoid Stereotyping Professions

Avoid implying that members of a certain profession are usually male or usually female.

Doctors often spend little time with their wives and children. [biased]
Doctors often spend little time with their families. [unbiased]

Jack Smith, a male nurse, works here. [biased]
Jack Smith, a nurse, works here. [unbiased]

(See Figures 4-2 and 4-3.)

```
                    MEMORANDUM
   TO:        All Employees
   FROM:      D. Struthers
   SUBJECT:   Sick Days
   DATE:      November 23, 19xx

   Please remember that each employee has eight sick
   days allotted to him each year. However, after an
   employee has taken three sick days, he must get
   verification from his doctor before the company
   will pay for time away from work. Employees should
   make sure their doctor signs his name to a note and
   indicates the nature of the illness.

   Thanks for your cooperation.
```

FIGURE 4–2 _____

This memorandum uses masculine pronouns for both the employees and the doctor. See
Figure 4-3 for a revision.

```
                    MEMORANDUM
   TO:        All Employees
   FROM:      D. Struthers
   SUBJECT:   Sick Days
   DATE:      November 23, 19xx

   Please remember that you have eight sick days
   allotted to you each year. However, after you have
   taken three sick days, you must get verification
   from your doctor before the company will pay for
   time away from work. Make sure your doctor signs a
   note addressed to your supervisor indicating the
   nature of your illness.

   Thanks for your cooperation.
```

FIGURE 4–3 _____

This memo contains no sexual biases. Also, the second-person pronouns (*you* and *your*)
make this memo more personal than the first version.

Avoid Racial/Ethnic Bias

Indicate someone's race only if it is relevant to the context of your writing.

> Jan Smith, a black employee of this company, won the award. [biased]
> Jan Smith, a company employee, won the award. [unbiased]

> Bill Lee, an Asian-American, is running for Congress. [biased]
> Bill Lee is running for Congress. [unbiased]

Avoid Age Bias

Refer to someone's age only if it is relevant to your context. When you do so, avoid subjective terms such as *old*.

> This law will not help old people. [biased]
> This law will not help people over 65. [unbiased]

Avoid Disability Bias

Refer to a disability only if it is relevant and, once again, keep your wording objective.

> Last year the company hired two handicapped people who are deaf. [biased]
> Last year the company hired two hearing-impaired employees. [unbiased]

Identifying Legal Issues

Legislation has substantially affected major areas of business communication. People in business should be aware of laws and regulations affecting them as consumers and as advertisers, as job applicants, as employees and employers, as lenders and creditors. Many companies employ full-time legal counsel to help them through the maze of legal issues pertaining to mergers, discrimination, credit practices, personnel policies, consumer protection, copyrights, and other areas.

When studying chapters on credit and collection letters and on employment in this text, you will focus on specific legal issues. Because the laws are numerous and complex, however, most people in business cannot master the fine points of all relevant legislation. As a business communicator, be aware of the legal environment surrounding you and become familiar with the legislation that directly affects your field and organization.

If you are in doubt about a legal question, remember that the price of consulting with an attorney is far less than the cost of a lawsuit. (For more information on legal aspects of business writing, see Appendix A.)

Pay attention to the legal issues affecting areas such as personnel, credit, and consumer protection.

Writing Under Pressure

Pressure is often part of the business environment. Unexpected deadlines and sudden increases in workloads are frequent occurrences. As a student,

What Would You Do?

To be an effective communicator, learn to write well under pressure.

you may have had time to prepare assignments weeks in advance or to do research over an entire semester. In a job, such luxuries often disappear. You may, instead, have to write a 10-page proposal by tomorrow or send a memo to fifty employees this afternoon.

Writing under pressure is an art you will learn with experience. However, some guidelines can help you overcome nervousness about deadlines and pressured writing situations.

Stay Calm

Nothing can be accomplished by panic. If you are faced with a seemingly impossible writing assignment, take a deep breath and begin examining it logically. Things are usually less complicated than they appear. If time is short, you will have to decide what areas are most vital and what areas you can delete or cover less thoroughly. To make these types of decisions, however, you have to remain calm.

Eliminate Distractions

When you do sit down to write, make sure that your environment is conducive to concentration. If you can get away from noise, telephones, and other distractions, do so. If you cannot move to a totally calm environment, reduce distractions as much as possible. Inform co-workers that you cannot be disturbed for two hours; have someone field your calls for you.

Assemble Your Materials

When under pressure, you may begin writing before you are ready. Then you have to stop every few minutes to get more paper, find a new cartridge for your typewriter, or locate a dictionary.

Instead, set up your work environment so the writing tools you need are always accessible. Before you write, run through a checklist of things you will need—and get them *before* you begin putting words to paper.

Set Up a Schedule

When you work under pressure, time seems to go by more quickly than usual. Set up a schedule before you begin writing. Allocate time for research, outlining, drafting, typing, and proofreading. Remember that sometimes the

Test Your Skills

How Do You Respond to Pressure?

Check the answer that best describes the way you would respond to the following situations.

1. Your instructor gives you two difficult essay questions on the exam.
   a. You become so tense that you can hardly write anything at all as you watch the minutes ticking by.
   b. You write a thorough answer for the first essay and never begin the second essay.
   c. You allocate time to each essay and plan a concise answer for each.
2. Your supervisor hands you a messy list of statistics and tells you to write up a summary of the figures *now*.
   a. You begin organizing your work but find yourself constantly interrupted by telephone calls and inquiries from fellow workers.
   b. You have your calls answered by someone else and work single-mindedly on the summary.
   c. You explain to your supervisor that the summary cannot be finished until the next day.
3. You have an important 15-page report due in three days. You want to spend the mornings working on it, but you have committee meetings scheduled every day at 10 a.m.
   a. You explain to the committee chairs that you must work on the report and miss the meetings.
   b. You attend the meetings and work on the report in the afternoons when the office is busy and filled with distractions.
   c. You take the work home with you and work on it all night when you are groggy and exhausted.

Discussion

The best approaches to these situations are described in 1-c, 2-b, and 3-a.

1. If you have more work than you expected in a limited time period, panic will just reduce your ability to do a good job. You will have to cut out some detail. Do not eliminate planning and outlining, but do work on writing concise, straightforward prose.
2. Distractions are a problem for many writers. If telephone calls and conversations interrupt you when you are working on an important piece of writing, take your work somewhere less distracting or make sure the distractions are reduced or eliminated.
3. Learn to prioritize your responsibilities. If a piece of writing is more important than a meeting, the meeting should be sacrificed. Staying up all night or working in a distracting environment will lead to a less effective piece of writing—and will just put more pressure on you.

final appearance of your document can be almost as important as the content: avoid spending so much time on the writing that you have no time for accurate typing and proofreading.

Work at Your Best Time of Day

Most people write best at certain times of the day. You probably know, for example, if you are a "morning person" or a "night person." During the hours when you are most alert and efficient, writing will be much easier for you. If at all possible, schedule your writing for those hours. A "morning person" can often accomplish more in three morning hours than in eight hours of staying up all night.

Use a Word Processor to Save Time

A word processor will help you write more efficiently.

A word processor can save you many hours of work. If you do not already use a word processor—or if you have only a little experience—take the time to become proficient. Then, when working under tight deadlines, you will have the skills that will considerably reduce the time you need for planning, drafting, writing, revising, and proofreading.

Identifying the Writing Process

Writing involves a series of tasks that have been called the *writing process.*

Creating a business document is not a one-step task. It involves a series of steps that transform ideas into words and transform a blank page or video screen into a medium that conveys messages. These steps are often called the writing *process.*

The word *process* has several meanings, but the one we are most concerned with here is "a series of operations." The word also conveys an important aspect of writing: that it is ongoing, work in progress. Nothing that you write has to be left the way it is, and no piece of writing is ever really "finished."

The process of writing is satisfying and exhilarating. When you watch your widely scattered, half-formed ideas emerge into a letter, memo, or report, you will probably be amazed at your own skills. Your writing may seem to take on a life of its own. "Did I really write that?" you might ask yourself weeks later.

The seven-step writing process we recommend (Figure 4–4) is outlined in the next two chapters. As you work, you will probably find yourself altering the process described here: you will go back and forth between steps and do some steps more than once. However, it is important to go through the major steps as you create a document. Using this process will help reduce the stress you may feel about writing. It will also assist you in planning and

1. Brainstorming
2. Defining your goals and your audience
3. Doing necessary research
4. Making a plan
5. Drafting
6. Revising
7. Proofreading

FIGURE 4-4

The seven-step writing process

drafting a document that conveys information effectively and addresses your specific audience.

Summary

Business writing is a key function in most organizations, and it can be a key to your success in whatever career you choose. Whether you are an accountant or a secretary, a programmer or an engineer, a stockbroker or a medical technician, you are probably going to spend a significant portion of your time writing. As you progress in your career, moreover, the percentage of time spent writing will increase.

Using the writing process described in the following chapters can help make your writing time more productive and your finished documents more effective. Before beginning to write, brainstorm ideas, sketch out your goals, analyze your audience, and do any necessary research. Then you can begin organizing your material and making a draft. When you have a draft, you can begin revising and finally proofreading your material.

Summary Discussion: Frank Harmon's Business Letter from Case in Point, p. 61

Frank's experience reveals some essential differences between written and spoken communication. His humorous style worked well in person when he could immediately gauge people's reactions and change his approach if it was not appreciated. The humor did not work when he used it in a letter that would be read by hundreds of business customers. Because the letter will be part of the company's image, it should convey the professionalism and credibility that business customers buying computer equipment are looking for. Some humor might be appropriate, but not in the heavy doses Frank was using.

Before revising his letter, Frank needs to work out an approach that will both respond to the customers' interests and needs and make customers want the product. The letter should also enhance the professional image of the company.

Business Writing Checklist

Qualities of Business Writing

- When writing most business documents, remember that

  _____ you are representing a company

  _____ you are trying to be persuasive

  _____ your underlying purpose is serious

  _____ your writing style should be invisible

- As you plan, write, and revise, work on

  _____ writing with your readers' needs in mind

  _____ making your writing readable and clear

  _____ being concise and accurate

  _____ establishing your credibility

  _____ making sure the final document has an appropriate format

  _____ proofreading for errors

Audience

- In analyzing your audience,

  _____ consider why your readers will read your message

  _____ consider what the readers know and what they need to know

  _____ orient information to the readers' needs

  _____ remain calm and polite

- To maintain a professional tone and establish the goodwill of your reader, avoid

  _____ swear words

  _____ off-color humor

  _____ language that discriminates against race, ethnic background, sex, age, or disability

Legal Issues

- To avoid legal problems, become familiar with legislation affecting the field in which you work.

- Pay particular attention to laws and regulations regarding

  _____ consumers' rights

  _____ personnel policies

  _____ lending policies

  _____ credit practices

  _____ discrimination

  _____ privacy

  _____ copyrights

Pressure

- To write effectively under pressure,

  _____ stay calm

  _____ eliminate distractions

  _____ assemble necessary materials

  _____ set up a time schedule

  _____ work at your best time of day

  _____ use a word processor to save time

Terms to Remember

Biased language: language that indicates prejudice

Writing process: a series of operations that leads from thoughts to a polished document

Writing style: the way in which writers express their ideas

1. Describe ways in which the following pieces of business writing can actually be persuasive:
   a. a memo informing employees about a new no-smoking policy in the company offices
   b. a letter informing people about a Neighborhood Watch (crime prevention) program
   c. a report outlining possible investment strategies for the company
   d. a memo informing employees about an upcoming stress seminar.

2. Describe at least three different writing styles that you have encountered in your reading: you might, for example, examine an article in a popular magazine, a page in a computer manual, and a letter from a charity organization. What characterizes these different styles? Do you see different types of words? Different types of sentences and paragraphs?

3. What do we mean by an "invisible" writing style? Why should business writing style be essentially "invisible"?

4. What types of business writing have you already done? What types do you think you will be doing most often in the future?

5. Do you think the *appearance* of homework assignments in most of your classes has an effect on the grades the assignments receive? Why or why not? Do you think appearance *should* have an effect?

6. Define *credibility*. Give an example of a situation in which you doubted the credibility of a speaker or writer. Why did you doubt it?

7. Describe a situation in which you had to write under pressure. What did you do to reduce the pressure and write effectively?

1. Interview a manager in a local company to find out what types of business writing he or she does most commonly. What types of problems does the person encounter most frequently in the memos and letters written by co-workers, clients, and customers? Write a memo to your instructor summarizing your findings.

2. Collect samples of junk mail delivered to your home. Find an example of what you consider poor business writing. In a paragraph or two, describe the weaknesses of the poor piece of writing. You may look at style, clarity, conciseness, you-attitude, physical appearance, and other qualities.

   Compare the piece of junk mail you have chosen with a more effective piece of business writing. What are the major differences between them? Write a page or two summarizing your findings.

3. Find two advertisements that effectively convey qualities about a *company* as well as about a product. How do the ads manage to create a company image while informing readers about the qualities of the product? Write a page or two summarizing your findings.

4. Write a letter to a friend describing some of the qualities of business writing that make it different from doing *one* of the following types of writing:
   a. Diary entries
   b. Short stories
   c. Magazine articles
   d. Essays for college classes

5. Revise the following memo so it is concise, clear, and professional.

```
                MEMORANDUM
TO:        All Clerical Staff
FROM:      H. Johnson
SUBJECT:   Monthly Meeting
DATE:      June 12, 19xx
```

As you know, the clerical staff members of
this organization meet once a month to
exchange ideas and discuss problems.
Usually everyone meets in the Employee
Lounge of Building A. This month
management has agreed to pay for a
luncheon meeting at Henderson's Restaurant
in Millwood. This restaurant specializes
in steaks, but it also serves Diet Plates
for you ladies who are watching your
weight. The luncheon will run from 12 noon
until 1:30 p.m. on Monday, June 24.
Although the luncheon will be a nice break
from the working day, each staff member
should bring her own notebook and writing
materials as some important points will be
covered before lunch is served. If a staff
member cannot attend, she should let me
know in writing or telephone me at Ext.
7434 as soon as possible.

The Business Writing Process: Planning

- Getting ready to write
- Setting up a suitable working environment
- Brainstorming
- Defining your goals and your audience
- Doing necessary research
- Improving research skills
- Reading actively
- Making a plan

Objectives

To establish an environment suitable for writing

To prepare thoroughly before drafting a business document

To improve writing and research skills

To organize ideas effectively

5

Chuck Mason's Memo

"We're having a meeting to evaluate the new accounting software next month," Chuck Mason's boss told him. "Write a memo telling the staff about it. They should review the software beforehand. Here's the basic information."

Chuck glumly took the notes that his boss had jotted down. He hated writing projects. He could happily talk to people for hours, but writing two paragraphs was sheer misery. At least his boss had told him to get the memo out within the week. He still had three days.

Friday came more quickly than usual, and Chuck still had not written the memo. He set aside an hour for his task. Having straightened his desk, piled yellow tablets in front of him, and lined up three pens along his blotter, he started to write.

Or, rather, he started to write words and promptly cross them out. Nothing came out the way he wanted it to. He could not get past the first paragraph—or even the first sentence. After two hours he had a wastebasket filled with crumpled yellow paper.

"I just wasn't made to be a writer," he told himself. "I can't do this."

Points to Consider
- What steps could Chuck have taken before trying to write his first sentence?
- What could Chuck do to improve his attitude toward the project?

Getting Ready to Write

You may have noticed a significant feature about the seven-step writing process outlined at the end of Chapter 4: four steps precede the first drafting stage. Getting ready to write a first draft is an important part of writing. Without proper preparation, you will waste time and energy and may well end up without a document that you are proud of.

Before even beginning the initial step of the writing process, try to rid yourself of any fears, doubts, and preconceptions you may have about writing. One reason some people panic when faced with a blank page is that they have already convinced themselves that they "can't write." If you believe you cannot write, you will undoubtedly prove yourself correct. So, have faith in your own abilities!

Face your writing task calmly.

Do not let the following myths prevent you from becoming a good business writer.

Myth #1. Writers Are Born, Not Made. False. Some people have an interest in language and writing, but they do not write well "naturally" any more than they play the guitar or program computers "naturally." Being good at something takes work.

Myth #2. Other People Write More Quickly Than I Do. True, some people do write quickly, but chances are they have already gone through the first steps of the writing process: they have done some initial brainstorming and planning. Good writing takes time and thought. Do not be impressed

Good writing takes time and effort.

by people who wrote their reports in two hours; be impressed by the people who left themselves enough time to do a good job.

Myth #3. Writing Requires Inspiration. False. The adage about genius applies to writing as well: it's 10 percent inspiration and 90 percent perspiration. Good business writing might even be 95 percent perspiration.

Myth #4. Other People Don't Get As Upset About Writing As I Do. False, again. Facing a blank page or empty computer screen frightens most people. Famous writers may even be more scared than you are, since their whole careers and reputations rest on their writing. Athletes are often frightened before they compete; stage actors are terrified before the curtain goes up. To be successful, these people learn to control their fears. You can, too, if you do not let your fears control you.

Setting Up a Suitable Working Environment

A good working environment can help you write effectively.

When many people are faced with a writing project, they begin by procrastinating. They sharpen pencils, rearrange their desks, dust their typewriter, and perform numerous other tasks that help them feel productive without actually making them write.

There is nothing wrong with establishing an environment that helps you work comfortably, but you should set it up permanently. Create a space in your office or home that enables you to think and write with a minimum of distractions. Keep on hand all the writing supplies you will need. You should have a dictionary, pens, pencils, and pads of paper, for instance.

Then establish a writing process that works for you. The seven steps we recommend are guidelines; you will develop a slightly different set of procedures for each project and situation.

Brainstorming

Linda Redovian, assistant to the head of the Parks and Recreation Department, has been given a writing assignment.

"We're having a seminar on pesticide safety next month," the department head told her. "Write a memo telling all department employees about it. I really want them to attend, but I can't make it mandatory. Try to get them interested."

Linda took the information the department head had gathered for her and sat down with it. Her first task, she knew, was to begin brainstorming.

Before you write, think about your project.

Brainstorming means letting your mind roam freely on a topic. Many people faced with a writing project such as a memo, letter, or even exam question, simply begin writing without any real thinking. They count on the thoughts to come while they write. Instead, begin by jotting down ideas as they come to you. If doodling helps to release your thoughts, doodle on your notepad. Do not try to organize your ideas. This process should be fun.

Thinking and jotting down ideas about the project beforehand not only help you gather ideas but also help release some of the tension you may feel about the writing task. You will begin to get ideas because you are not experiencing the pressure of writing—you are just brainstorming.

When Linda Redovian began brainstorming, she created a page that looked like Figure 5-1. Her second page of brainstorming (Figure 5-2) was more organized.

FIGURE 5–1

Brainstorming—first effort

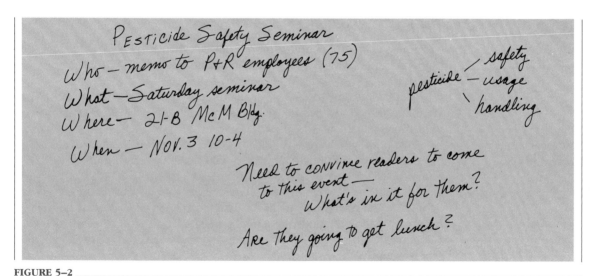

FIGURE 5–2

Brainstorming—second effort

Defining Your Goals and Your Audience

Once you have brainstormed, you have taken one tremendous step forward. You are no longer facing an empty page. But now you need to focus on two important questions:

Why am I writing?
Who is my audience?

Why Am I Writing?

You may think the answer to this question is obvious. You know, for instance, why you are writing a job application letter or a periodic report. Linda Redovian knew she had to write an informative memo telling employees about a pesticide safety seminar.

Usually, however, your reasons for writing will be more complex than you might think. For example, you probably have personal goals as well as company goals. You may be trying to impress your boss with your writing ability or to convince readers that a new program will be successful. You may want to convince your reader that you are a good employee.

When Linda Redovian evaluated her reasons for writing, they looked like this:

I need to inform employees about the pesticide seminar
I need to *convince* employees to attend the seminar
I want my boss to like my work

Reviewing her list, Linda saw that she was actually getting ready to write a persuasive memo, not just an informative one.

Who Is My Audience?

The second question is also more complex than it seems. "Of course, I'm writing to park employees," Linda Redovian might say. "What's so complex about that?"

The complexity comes from really understanding those employees. What is their attitude toward the memo going to be? What is their background? What interests them? What motivates them?

The reader is the focus of your message.

As you know, the receiver (in this case, the reader) is the focus of your message. If you do not really grasp who that person is, your whole communication effort could fail.

Sometimes you will not have all the answers about your readers. You may not know the reader personally, or, like Linda Redovian, you may be writing to many people at once. You might need to do some research on your audience. On the other hand, you may find that you already know a lot about these people.

When Linda asked herself about the audience for her memo, she discovered she knew some vital points about them:

They were all employees of the Parks and Recreation Department

Most had at least a high school education

They were between 18 and 59 years old

About one-quarter of them routinely had to handle pesticides

All of them lived and worked near pesticides

Office workers were going to think the seminar was irrelevant for them; the outside workers would respond more favorably

No one would want to attend a seminar on Saturday.

In general, a writer should know basic *demographic* and *psychographic* information about an audience. Demographic information includes external characteristics such as age, gender, marital status, race, religion, income, and location. Psychographic information is harder to determine accurately; it includes interests, opinions, values, beliefs, and other intangible variables that affect people's behavior.

> Demographic data include external characteristics.
>
> Psychographic data include ideas, values, and interests.

Naturally, the nature of your writing project will determine how extensively you need to analyze your audience. Linda Redovian just needed to *think* about her readers before writing them a memo; an advertising copywriter might need to research a particular audience for several months before creating the final draft of a magazine advertisement.

In many cases, you may find that you are writing for two or more audiences. Linda is writing for her boss as well as for the park employees. The advertising copywriter is writing for the ad agency's client as well as for the magazine readers. Knowing that you have different readers may well affect the decisions you make regarding the organization, word choice, and tone of your finished document.

> Consider every reader, not just one.

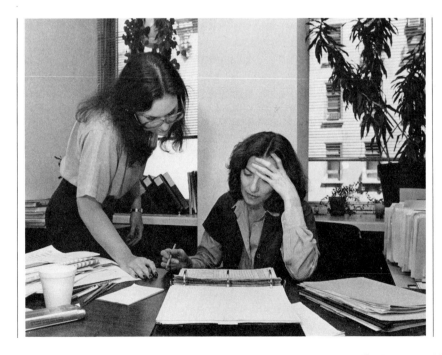

Doing Necessary Research

Research is a formidable word that sounds like hours in the library. For a formal report, you may have to do some library research, but most of the time your business writing will demand a different approach. You may have to ask people questions, go back through company files, work some projections up on the computer, or read previous reports.

You might want to collect file cards or keep a notebook during this stage of your writing, but in many cases much of your research will be internal. That is, you will go through your own mind for the data you need and the approach you will take.

For her research, Linda Redovian wrote down the information that had to be incorporated into her memo:

Pesticide Safety Seminar
Date: Nov. 3
Time: 10 a.m. to 4 p.m.
Sponsored by Dept. of Parks and Recreation
Main topics: handling pesticides, pesticide poisoning, pesticide spills, pesticide usage.
Place: Room 21-B, McMillan Building
Lunch?
Comp time?
Why should they bother attending?

She had gotten most of the information she needed from her boss's notes, but she needed to know whether lunch would be served and whether attendees would be compensated for attending. To get those questions answered, she made some telephone calls. Yes, lunch would be served from 12 until 1. Yes, employees could get compensation time for attending, or they could choose to be paid time-and-a-half.

Her other question concerned *why* people would choose to give up their Saturday for this event. To make points with their supervisors? To enhance their resumes? When she talked the matter over with her own boss, Linda learned that attendance at work-related seminars was always considered when employees went up for promotions. (Suddenly Linda realized that attending a Saturday seminar on pesticides was not such a bad idea after all.)

When she had all the information she needed, Linda could begin to organize it.

Improving Research Skills

Often your research will not require reading. Linda Redovian, writing a memo about a pesticide safety seminar, needed to make a telephone call or two. Many times, however, your writing project will require extensive reading. You may have to go through hundreds of pages of statistics, journal articles, company correspondence, reports, and industry data. Learning to read well will definitely help your writing.

College graduates usually believe they are good readers. After all, they have mastered science and business texts, read an array of novels and stories for English classes, analyzed articles in professional journals, gathered research materials from newspapers, magazines, and books.

Often, however, these graduates learn that their research and study skills do not carry over particularly well when they start working. The auditor scanning company reports, the personnel manager assessing employee files, the office worker reviewing computer documentation, the investment counselor analyzing market trends—these people need to read in different ways than they did as students.

Auditors, for instance, do not have to prepare for multiple choice tests as they may have done as accounting majors. But auditors spend considerable time reading in order to make presentations and write reports.

Business people do not always perceive the fundamental connections between reading and writing, nor do they always realize that their reading habits should be molded to specific tasks dictated by their jobs.

Reading effectively will help you to see what works and does not work in business writing; it will enable you to envision how other writers put the writing process to work for them; it will show you the possibilities of language and style in the types of business writing particular to your field; and it will enable you to effectively do research for your own writing.

Reading Actively

Many readers are a little like airplane passengers who sit passively while the pilot takes them to their destination. They do not know how the airplane works or what exactly they are flying into or over. To increase your reading and research skills while reducing the time you spend on these tasks, work on becoming an active reader.

The reading process requires active participation.

How do you read actively? Like writing, reading should be a process rather than an isolated activity. Going through the reading process (which in many ways mirrors the writing process) will change you from a reading "passenger" to a pilot.

The Reading Process
- Brainstorming
- Defining goals and audience
- Scanning your material
- Making a reading plan
- Keeping an annotated bibliography
- Discussing your findings
- Evaluating the material

Brainstorming Before You Start

If you have a big research project ahead of you, think about the type of assignment facing you, the kinds of sources you will find most helpful, the

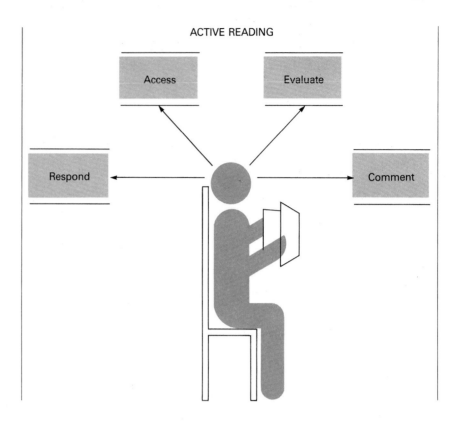

ACTIVE READING

Access

Evaluate

Respond

Comment

order in which you should read the material, and the kinds of information you need to derive from the reading.

Blake Martin, for instance, was faced with a major project: he had to write a report on company sales trends over the past three years. He knew he had to go through letters from customers, salespeople's monthly reports, the company's annual reports, computer data, and articles about the industry in general.

Before he actually began reading, Blake thought about the type of information he was looking for and jotted down general ideas for sources he would have to investigate.

Defining Goals and Audience

Establishing goals before you begin reading will save you time and effort. Are you looking for material you can use in a presentation? Data to put in a financial report? Supporting evidence for a recommendation you want to make? The more carefully you define your objectives, the less time you will waste in the long run.

Blake Martin summarized a few crucial goals before he began reading his piles of letters, memos, reports, and clippings.

1. Find information for a national sales overview
2. Look for regional sales patterns for last three years

3. Characterize industry trends nationally and regionally
4. Look for unexpected information regarding consumer responses, sales strategies, and regional differences

Blake was writing his report for upper management; he knew he would have to back up all his information and make it clear where he found the data he used.

Knowing what he was looking for and who was going to read the final product helped him focus on important data and move quickly through less relevant material.

Scanning Your Material

Scan the material quickly. You might want to know who the author is, when the material was written, what context it was written in, and how much information in it seems relevant to your goals.

You may also want to categorize the material. Blake Martin arranged his material under one of his four major goals. Then, he put all the material regarding industry trends, for example, in one pile *before* he began reading each document thoroughly.

> Outline your goals before beginning a project.

Making a Reading Plan

After you see what you have to read and know why you are reading it, make a plan of attack. Answering a few questions is useful here:

Do I need to summarize major points?
Do I need to analyze major points?
Am I looking for details or a broad overview?
Will I need to locate the source of my information later on?

> Writing a summary helps you to remember and analyze the material you read.

The answers to questions such as these can help you decide what active reading technique will be most useful.

Remember that, as an active reader, you are a participant. Do not just passively write down what was said. Instead, evaluate, argue, question, doubt. Ask yourself whether the writer was objective or biased. What else should have been said? What might have been deleted? Which points are logical and which are not? Which points are valid and which are not? (See Figure 5–3 for some tools that can help you with this process.) You will quickly discover that most pieces of writing are far from perfect—and your discoveries will help you improve your own writing.

> Never take a writer's opinions for granted: argue, question, and analyze as you read.

Keeping an Annotated Bibliography

If you are doing ongoing work in a certain field, start an annotated bibliography of all the relevant materials you read. Rather than simply listing your sources, as you would do in a regular bibliography, include a sentence or two describing or evaluating them. Then, when you take on a similar project, you will not have to go back over the same ground. An annotated bibliog-

> An annotated bibliography will help you locate materials you have found useful in the past.

The following tools can help your active reading process. The first two require that you mark the document as you read. The last four tools are useful for library materials and other items you do not wish to mark up.

Highlighting Pens. Brightly colored highlighting pens allow you to make important items stand out so you can easily locate them later.

Marginal Notes. Making marginal notes helps you be an active reader. You can ask questions, make comments, or star important material.

Post-It Notes. Post-It Notes are a wonderful aid for readers. You can jot ideas or comments on a yellow sheet and stick it onto the page of a book. Then you can remove the note later without having damaged the book.

Note Cards. Using note cards to outline the important points of a document helps you remember the information. The cards will then be useful references if you need the information later on.

Summaries. Writing a summary forces you to pull together the major ideas. You may want to use note cards for your summary or simply write it at the end of the document itself. The former method is useful if you are going to use the information in a piece of writing of your own; the second method is more useful if you are going to return to the document later on in order to review the major points.

Before writing a summary, try answering questions like these:

What is the writer's most important idea here?
What type of data supports the writer's views?
How relevant is the information to me?
Is the writing well researched?

Photocopying. If you make copies of important materials, you can mark them up and reread them later on. You can also carry them with you to your office or home—or wherever you plan to do your research.

FIGURE 5–3 _____
Tools for active reading

raphy should contain all the information you need to find the materials again as well as a brief note on the contents and usefulness of the materials.

> Reichek, Morton A. "The Year's 10 Best Books on Business and Economics." *Business Week*, 15 September 1986, pp. 10–13. Concise reviews of David Halberstam's *The Reckoning* and Robert Lacey's *Ford: The Men and the Machine*.

Discussing Your Findings

Discuss the material with a friend or colleague. Nothing helps you remember and evaluate a piece of writing more than talking about it. You may even find that talking into a tape recorder after you read something will help you both to remember the document and to generate ideas of your own.

Evaluating the Material

Actually, you have been evaluating the piece of writing ever since you first looked at it. But, now that you have read it actively, you should assess it again. Not only will your evaluation be more valid now, but it will also help you evaluate and revise your own business documents.

You might ask yourself the following questions:

Is it clear? Did the writer have a defined point of view? Did he or she clearly state recommendations and provide evidence?

Is it accurate? Are there flaws in the logic? Are the figures correct? Are parts missing from the analysis?

Is it credible? Where did the writer get these figures? How old are they? What type of sample was used? Was the writer biased?

Making a Plan

When your research is well underway, you can begin step 4 of the writing process, planning your project. Most of the time, you will face fairly specific projects as a business writer: a memo about company policy, a sales report, a personnel evaluation. These projects often have standard formats, and many have general organizational patterns that you can use as a basis for your project. (You will be studying a number of these specific approaches in later chapters.)

Although at this stage you will begin ordering some of the information you have collected, remember that nothing you are doing now needs to be permanent. Just get a plan on paper so you can look at it and think about it. You can go back to your plan at any time during the writing process.

If you are using index cards, this is a good time to organize them in piles. If you write notes on legal pads, you can begin cutting up the sheets or marking them for different sections of your project.

As you make a plan, keep your readers in mind.

What do they know already?
What questions will they ask?
What background information should I include?
What kinds of material will they find convincing?
How detailed do they want the material to be?
Do they already believe this material or do I have to convince them?

Often you can use a standard organizational pattern to form the basis of your plan:

Chronological order: useful if you wish to emphasize movement from past to present or from present to past
Comparison/contrast: useful if you wish to show similarities and differences between two things or ideas
Deductive order: useful if you wish to present conclusions before providing supporting details
Inductive order: useful if you need to convince a reader by presenting supporting details before you present a conclusion
Problem/solution order: useful if you wish to recommend ways to solve problems

(These and other patterns are discussed at length in Chapters 12 and 14.)

However you decide to organize your material, make sure to include everything the readers need to know and to arrange it in an order that will make sense to the reader.

When she was writing her memo on the pesticide safety seminar, Linda Redovian decided on these general headings and listed major points under each one.

1. Time and date of seminar
2. Topics covered
3. Reasons for attending
4. Comp time info
5. Registration info

For his report on sales trends, Blake Martin put together a more detailed outline.

I. General background on industry trends
   A. National trends
   B. Regional trends
II. Analysis of sales and profit figures
   A. 1987
   B. 1988
   C. 1989
III. Analysis of market share
   A. 1987
   B. 1988
   C. 1989
IV. Analysis of marketing strategies
   A. National strategies
   B. Regional strategies
V. Conclusions and recommendations

With much of their thinking, research, and planning done and their readers' needs in mind, both Linda and Blake were ready to begin writing and revising.

What Would You Do?

A friend of yours has signed up for a course that you have already taken. The course demands a lot of reading besides the text, and the tests include essay questions that require students to have an overview of the assigned books and journal articles. Your friend has asked you for some tips before the course begins.

In a memo to your friend, write up a series of steps that she or he should take in order to handle the reading assignments effectively. Refer specifically to subject areas covered in the course.

Planning Checklist

Brainstorming

- when facing a writing project, begin by

  _____ letting your mind roam freely on the topic

  _____ jotting down ideas as they come to you

Defining Your Goals and Your Audience

- After brainstorming, ask yourself,

  _____ Why am I writing?

  _____ Who is my audience?

- Define your personal goals as well as company goals

- Analyze your readers' needs and interests. Consider

  _____ demographic data such as their age and gender

  _____ psychographic data such as their values and opinions

Doing Necessary Research

- Go through your own mind for the data you will need and the approach you will take

- Actively read any documents you need to research for the project

  _____ Summarize your reading goals.

  _____ Scan material quickly at first.

  _____ Mark important material or summarize data.

  _____ Keep an annotated bibliography if necessary.

  _____ Discuss your findings with colleagues.

  _____ Evaluate the material you research.

Making a Plan

- Order the information you have collected. Consider

    _____ what your readers already know

    _____ what questions they will ask

    _____ what background information you need to include

    _____ what types of data readers will find convincing

    _____ how detailed the information should be

    _____ whether readers need to be convinced of your position

Summary

The writing process begins before you begin writing. Even for short or seemingly simple projects, you will save time and effort in the long run by first thinking about your message, your purpose in writing, and your readers. Then, if necessary, you can begin actively reading, researching the information you need. When you have a good grasp on the material you will be using, you can begin making a plan, organizing the material in a way that will be logical and useful to your readers.

Summary Discussion: Chuck Mason's Memo from Case in Point, p. 79

Chuck makes his task harder for himself by starting out writing and revising right away. Brainstorming first would reduce his anxiety and get his thoughts flowing. Then he could begin defining his goals and his readers, researching material, and making a general plan.

To improve his attitude, Chuck needs to stop saying that he "can't" write. Writing takes work, but it does not take genius. A calm approach and use of the writing process should help him overcome much of his frustration.

Terms to Remember

Active reading: participating in the reading process rather than simply taking in information.

Annotated bibliography: list of sources that includes a summary or analysis of each book or article

1. Is the process approach to business writing discussed in this text different from the approach you have taken in the past when faced with a writing assignment? If so, describe the differences.
2. Describe a situation in which your efforts at communication failed because you analyzed an audience incorrectly.
3. What type of environment do you usually write in at home? Is it conducive to writing effectively? What changes would improve the environment?
4. What steps of the active reading process do you usually follow? What problems have you encountered in the way you currently read?
5. What types of documents, books, or articles do you read most frequently in school or at work? How will active reading help you tackle your reading assignments more effectively?
6. Has reading helped you to improve your writing? Explain.
7. What nonfiction books or publications have you found most readable and enjoyable as well as informative? Did you learn techniques from them that you could use in your own writing? Explain.

Exercises

1. Consider a project you are working on for school or at work. Actively read at least two articles or text chapters that could be useful to the project. Summarize the major topics presented in each. Then write one or two paragraphs evaluating the strengths and weaknesses of the material in terms of your specific needs. You might consider some of these questions:

   • How relevant was the subject matter to the project you are working on?
   • Was the material presented clearly?
   • Did the writer use strong arguments to back up major points?
   • Did the writer cite sources for the material that increased the credibility of the article or chapter?
   • Did the writer use any techniques to make the material interesting as well as informative? Describe them.

2. Begin an annotated bibliography for a project you are working on or for a class you are taking. Use either index cards or a database management program on a computer. Set up the bibliography so you can update it and find items easily.

3. Assume a colleague has asked you for help in reading *one* type of document that you tackle frequently at your job. Write a page describing some active reading techniques that will increase the person's efficiency. (You might choose to describe techniques for reading and assessing documents such as personnel files, sales reports, or computer-generated data.)
4. You have been asked to write a letter urging your class members to join a campus organization. Having decided which organization to represent, jot down some characteristics of your proposed readers that could be useful to your approach. Explain how those characteristics could affect the way you write the letter.
5. You have been asked to write an editorial for the campus newspaper urging freshmen and sophomores to consider majoring in your field. You will be writing for both the editor of the newspaper and the students. How will your goals differ for these two audiences? What points should you consider when writing for the editor? For the students?
6. Exchange a page or two of writing with another student. Interview him or her regarding the goals for the piece of writing, the audience for whom the writing is intended, and the way

the material is organized. Then discuss with the student some ways he or she could revise the writing. Do not proofread the piece of writing.

You might ask the student questions such as these:

What topic are you writing on? Is this the answer to an essay question or to a specific assignment?

Who will be reading this—your instructor? Other students? People at work?

How much information does the reader already have about this material? Do you need to provide a lot of background material, or will the reader know that already?

What method have you used to organize your ideas? Do you think this is the best order in which to present this information?

7. Find three advertisements from three different publications. From each ad you should be able to tell what type of audience the ad is trying to attract. Write a brief analysis of the *audience* at which you think each ad is aimed. Consider the audience's age, income level, gender, and other demographic characteristics. Also consider what you imagine the audience's basic values and lifestyle might be.

The Business Writing Process: Drafting and Revising

- **Drafting business documents**
- **Organizing your material logically**
- **Developing paragraphs that highlight ideas**
- **Writing readable sentences**
- **Maintaining a professional tone**
- **Clichés**
- **Proofreading**

Objectives

To organize material you have drafted

To develop logical paragraphs

To write clear, concise sentences

To establish a tone appropriate to your message and your audience

To proofread documents accurately

6

Peggy McCormick's Memo

As an assistant supervisor in the Training Department, Peggy McCormick frequently writes memos to employees in different departments. On this occasion, her boss, Frank Lau, tells her that a recent memo has brought in complaints from several readers.

"What's wrong with it?" Peggy asks. "All the information is correct."

"It's confusing," Frank replies. "Before you send it to the Production Department, I suggest you revise it."

Peggy rereads the memo.

```
TO:        All Employees
FROM:      Peggy McCormick
SUBJECT:   Customer Analysis
DATE:      June 12, 19xx
```

```
All of us know that there is an economic
importance to coming to a realization
of our customers' demographic and
psychographic parameters, so that we can
assess their respective wants and be
responsive to their individual needs as
well as target identifiable groups for
future promotional efforts. This area
that has been so very vital to the
aggregate success of Spenser Products
has been very greatly and positively
affected by the outstanding efforts of
Mrs. Kathleen Lanahan, a respected
market research specialist and expert on
consumer behavior and analysis, who has
contributed greatly to our collective
and individual comprehension through
learned books and articles as well as
through personal presentations such as
the one she will be making at Spenser
Products on June 21. Mrs. Lanahan's
expertise will be brought right to our
doorstep by the seminar, which has been
developed for all our benefit by Jeremy
Fitch and Heather Perason and which will
be held in the Conference Room on Floor
B-21. It will start at 11:00 a.m. It
will last two hours. Doughnuts and
coffee will be served.
```

Points to Consider

- Is Peggy's memo confusing? Why or why not?
- Do you find any problems with the paragraphing? If so, what problems do you see?
- Do you find any problems with the sentences? If so, what problems do you see?

Drafting Business Documents

The writing process discussed in this text includes four steps before the writer begins drafting and revising: brainstorming, defining goals and audience, doing necessary research, and making a plan. Writing, however, is not a linear process. You will almost always find yourself moving back and forth between steps, going back to adjust your plan, doing some additional research, or redefining your goals. In general, however, it is important to prepare carefully before you begin drafting. In the long run, your preparations will save you time and probably lead to a more effective piece of writing.

Write your first draft without stopping to revise it.

So, once you are ready, begin drafting. *Drafting* is an important word. It does not mean "make a perfect piece of writing." It means "sketch" or "make a preliminary version." When drafting, follow a few guidelines.

1. Write quickly. Do NOT stop to edit. Once you begin to get your thoughts down, do not edit them. That part of the process comes later.
2. Double- or triple-space. Whether using a pen, pencil, or keyboard, leave lots of space on your page so you can make notes later on.
3. Let your ideas flow. Do not be afraid of writing too much. You can always cut later, but you cannot always retrieve a good idea that you failed to jot down.

Revising

The revision stage of the writing process is one of the most interesting and vital. Many times when people say they cannot write, they actually mean they cannot revise. Because the sixth step in the writing process is so important, this chapter focuses almost entirely on revision.

As you revise, keep in mind the questions you asked when you were defining your goals and your audience. How close are you to achieving those goals? How close does this document come to meeting your readers' interests and needs?

Many writers spend hours during the revision stage flipping through dictionaries and other reference books, trying to find the exact word they want. This word hunt can be another form of procrastination—like cleaning off your desk. Save the details of word choice until after you have evaluated and revised your organization, paragraphs, and sentences. By then, you will have a much better sense of which words you really need to change.

Another pitfall at this stage is to begin proofreading. You will be tempted to fix typographical errors and check your spelling. Working on these details can make you lose your perspective on the whole document. Work on larger issues first and leave proofreading until the very end of the writing process.

Proofread only at the end of the writing process.

Organizing Your Material Logically

In Step 4 of the writing process, you developed a plan for presenting the information in your document. This plan gave you some guidance when you were drafting. However, most plans change as ideas develop. Do not feel bound to your original organizational structure. As you revise, read your document objectively and rearrange material as necessary. You may even want to develop new outlines to order your thoughts as you progress.

Answering some questions can help you organize your document.

How Will Readers React to My Material?

This question is crucial. If you are conveying information that your readers will be happy to read—or will feel neutral about—a direct organizational plan will be most effective: your introduction will state your major purpose and perhaps even your conclusions.

Use a direct plan if you are conveying information to which your readers will respond positively.

Eric Best

A major oil company had to reinvent a pesticide one of its researchers discovered five years earlier but buried on page 25 of a hopelessly wordy report. No one had read it thoroughly enough to find the crucial information.

In another instance, a Stanford Business School student wrote: "Love Canal has been catapulted by the media into a nexus of a dense web with filaments splayed from the continent and through more than three decades."

And in another, the chairman of a major West Coast firm told his stockholders in an annual report: "Our results were not benefited by the impact of the strike that closed operations for six weeks during the prior year, lowering costs."

From the board room to the business school, such untoward prose is under renewed attack for the damage it can do to good business. More and more companies are recognizing the real costs of dangling modifiers, impenetrable wordiness and syntactical labyrinths that strangle an idea before it's born.

The case of the lost pesticide, for example, is not all that rare.

"That's a typical problem in business, that someone who has important information to convey, instead of coming right out with it, comes out with a report so wordy that the information would be missed by most readers," says Gary Blake, a New York writing consultant who runs The Communication Workshop.

The costs of poor prose are found not just in reports that don't work, but in the labored work of those trying to report.

"The larger issue is not the humorous disaster but the silent bleeding that all companies go through when an employee spends all morning trying to write a memo," Blake says. His clients include the Teachers Insurance and Annuity Association of America, Chase Manhattan Bank, Hughes Aircraft Co. and New York's City Department of Sanitation.

He believes the problem for business has worsened in recent years because colleges have enrolled people unprepared in basic writing skills and allowed them to choose many of their own courses. Students then graduate to the business world suffering the effects of a culture that continues to devalue reading with TV.

"People are just not reading as much, so they don't have as good a sense of what constitutes good writing," Blake says.

Joyce Pharris, who runs the management communication skills workshop at Stanford University, often hears from executives wrestling with bad writing, and not always their own.

One called her recently to ask how to deal with two managers whose poor writing kept embarrassing him.

Her advice: Send the managers to a workshop or individual tutoring on how to write more appropriately for a business setting.

Several basic errors clutter and confuse business prose, Pharris says in a recent article she wrote for the Stanford Business School Magazine about how well MBAs can—or can't—write.

The errors: thinking aloud on paper, ignoring the reader and adopting the "Prevalent Business Style."

She says, "The result is that much executive writing sounds dreadfully similar—stilted, overly formal, obscure and inflated—whether the subject is the quarterly earnings report or a commendation to an employee for 25 years of faithful service."

Many business school students, she finds, have adopted this numbing prose style much as they have adopted dress codes and other elements of corporate culture. One such memo began:

"It has come to my attention that the introduction of the Ittol by 870 line as planned is anticipated to require an increase in advertising support of approximately 27 percent so as to achieve required levels of expectation."

Such ponderous declarations are on a collision course with clarity.

Abigail Shaw, a writing expert for Rothschild Consultants of San Francisco, taught business writing to UC-Berkeley business students before taking her skills into business herself. She recently won a "bad-technical-writing" contest conducted by the Palo Alto author of a coming book entitled, "The Manager's Guide to Optical Storage."

Entries had to be sensible to experts but impossible for ordinary business managers.

Based on her recent experience trying to explain the use of computer disks to store graphic information, Shaw wrote:

"Cheap RAM for big buffers in the nodes on a network has changed image encoding in the tiling environment by using PROMs and PALs to pipeline parallel board sets in the work station itself, reducing contention by using local optical storage and, when centralized storage is unavoidable, by using sophisticated collision detection algorithms."

Translation: Engineers can now use their own computers to create and revise engineering drawings and they can store the drawings in their computer or in a central drawing file.

Such deadly TechnoSpeak is a natural byproduct of modern computer engineering and attempts to market new products, Shaw says, adding that it often produces prose which, "If it's not too jargon-infested it's just too vague."

"It's just a gorgeous vineyard of bad writing," she said—then laughed aloud at her own "messy metaphor."

If your readers will be unhappy about your material, an indirect plan is usually more appropriate. Begin with material that they do feel positively about or present reasons for your position before actually stating it. (For more information on direct/indirect approaches, see Chapter 12.)

Use an indirect plan to convey information to which your readers might respond negatively.

Linda Redovian, writing a memo to inform Park Department employees about a pesticide safety seminar, realized that her readers would be resistant to attending a seminar on Saturday. When she made notes on her first draft (Figure 6–1), she reminded herself to open with an explanation oriented to her readers.

Are Central Paragraphs Organized Logically?

Go back again to your readers and their needs. Check through your document to see that all your readers' questions will be answered. Then see if the information is arranged in an order useful for the readers. Are similar ideas grouped together? Is there a logical progression of ideas?

Good organization is crucial to effective business writing.

There will be a seminar on pesticide safety for all Park Department

All Park personel have been requested by the Parks and Recreation department management to attend a pesticide safety seminar that will be held on Sat. Nov. 3, from the hours of 10 until 4. Some of the topics to be covered will include safe pesticide handling, knowing various warning signs of pesticide poisoning, safe application techniques, how to avoid pesticide spills, and pesticide application. As participants in this seminar, you will learn safe techniques and gain current knowledge about pesticides, which will help you upgrade your professional expertise. By attending the seminar, you will find that you will enhanse your career opportunities. The seminar will be held in Room 20-B of the McMillan Building. Lunch will be served from 12 until 1. You can choose to get six hours of comp time or time-and-a-half pay for the six hour seminar. The seminar begins promptly at 10, so all Park Personnel are requested to be prompt. Call Ext. 5512 if you plan to attend.

FIGURE 6–1
First draft with notes

Is There Any Unnecessary Information?

You will probably find that your first drafts contain more information than your readers need. You may well wander off the main point or include material the readers already know.

You will lose your readers quickly if they find themselves bored by familiar or irrelevant information. As you reorganize, cut out unnecessary material.

Does My Conclusion Pull the Document Together?

When your readers come to the end of your document, they should *know* that they are at the end. A conclusion usually summarizes key points, makes recommendations, or suggests future action. Avoid introducing unrelated ideas in the conclusion: the last paragraph or so should pull things together, not open up new topics.

Developing Paragraphs that Highlight Ideas

Like the document as a whole, every paragraph should be carefully constructed with no unnecessary parts. Good paragraphs usually introduce, clarify, and reinforce the ideas you want your readers to note and remember.

Short paragraphs help to make business documents more readable.

Paragraphs serve to make your writing more readable by breaking thoughts into chunks a reader can easily understand and by creating visual markers on the page. In business writing, paragraphs are usually short, often with fewer than eight lines. One-sentence paragraphs are common. (While making notes on her first draft, Linda Redovian tells herself to shorten her paragraphs.)

To revise your paragraphs, consider the following pointers:

- Check for topic sentences.
- Make sure every sentence in the paragraph
    is related to the topic sentence.
- Use transitions between ideas.
- Use a variety of paragraph lengths.

Check for Topic Sentences

Most paragraphs contain a sentence that summarizes the point of the paragraphs or pulls together the major ideas. Often a topic sentence appears at the opening of a paragraph, as it does in this one. However, topic sentences may appear at the conclusion or, occasionally, in the middle of a paragraph.

If you cannot find topic sentences in your paragraphs, the paragraphs may be loose and incoherent. Or you may be packing too many ideas into one paragraph.

Make Sure Every Sentence in the Paragraph Is Related to the Topic Sentence

The sentences in a paragraph should be related to each other and to the topic sentence. They may provide more detail or present opposing points of view, but they should not deviate from the core idea.

Every paragraph should focus on a core idea.

In her second draft (Figure 6–2), Linda broke the memo into three paragraphs, each of which had an opening topic sentence. However, the last sentence, she saw, was not about topics being covered, so she created a fourth paragraph.

TO:	All Park Department Personel	Date: October 12, 19xx
FROM:	Linda Redovian	
SUBJECT:	Pesticide Safety Seminar	

To increase your knowledge and understanding of pesticides, a Pesticide Safety seminar will be held by the Parks and Recreation department.

wordy
passive

Your professional status and expertise and your resume will be enhansed by this six-hour seminar, and you'll get paid for attending. You may either take six hours of comp time or request time-and-a-half pay for the time. (You'll even get a free lunch!)

too many and's

too chatty

The seminar will cover topics of interest to everyone who works and lives around pesticides—and that includes all of us. Topics to be covered include handling pesticides safely, knowing warning signs of pesticide poisoning, and applying pesticides safely. If you plan to attend, call Dan at Ext 5512.

ands

passive
new paragraph

Date:	Saterday, November 3
Time:	10 a.m.–4 p.m. (lunch from 12–1 p.m.)
Place:	Room 20-B McMillan Building

FIGURE 6–2
Second draft with notes

Use Transitions Between Ideas

Transitions are links between ideas. A piece of writing that "flows" moves smoothly from one concept to the next without surprising the reader. Transitions are road signs that tell your reader you are adding material, providing a different perspective, moving on in time, or giving examples.

Transitional words such as *additionally, as well as, moreover, however, on the other hand, for example, therefore, so,* and *in other words* help your reader to understand the relationship between various sentences in a paragraph and between different paragraphs.

You can also make transitions between sentences and paragraphs by referring to preceding words or phrases. Pronouns and echoing words help to make transitions smooth.

> The interviews with the employees raised their morale. *They* now seem more eager to help the company reach its goals. [Pronoun works as transition.]

> The new banking machines are convenient. *Convenience,* however, does not always make up for personalized service. [Echoing word works as transition.]

A Sampling of Transitional Words and Phrases

To add material: *additionally, also, as well as, besides, moreover, furthermore*
To show contrast: *although, but, on the other hand, however, whereas, yet*
To show examples: *such as, for example, that is*
To summarize: *in short, in other words, in summary*
To show cause and effect: *because, since, therefore, thus, so*

Put Major Ideas at the Opening and Closing of Paragraphs

Readers tend to remember information at the beginning and ending of paragraphs, just as they remember information at the beginning and ending of sentences. If central concepts are embedded in the middle of a paragraph, your reader may never realize their importance.

Use a Variety of Paragraph Lengths

Because paragraphs are important for their visual qualities as well as for their content, a variety of paragraph lengths makes your writing more interesting and readable. A series of one-sentence paragraphs is as deadly as a paragraph stretching over a full page. Like lists and illustrations, varied paragraphs heighten interest and readability.

Writing Readable Sentences

When you have a logical overall organization and your paragraphs are set up effectively, you can begin revising your sentences. Linda Redovian's early drafts (Figures 6–1 through 6–3) reveal some of the common problems with sentences: wordiness, passive sentences, an excess of *and*'s, and lack of clarity.

Make your revisions with your reader and your message in mind. A formal report written to an educated reader may contain more complicated sentences than a memo to employees that is meant to be read quickly by diverse readers. In general, however, readers are looking for sentences that make points quickly and clearly. Excess words and roundabout phrasing will bore, confuse, and irritate your readers.

To revise sentences so they are readable and clear, watch particularly for embedded ideas, excessive length, wordiness, passive sentences, choppiness, and lack of variety.

> Always check your sentences to make sure they are clear.

Embedded Ideas

Most sentences should have a subject (the doer of an action) near the beginning and the verb (the action itself) immediately afterward. Keeping to this subject + verb format will help you simplify your sentences and even straighten out your own thoughts. To emphasize major points, put them at the beginning or end of your sentences.

> Having written and edited the company newsletter, which is rapidly becoming one of the best publications of its kind, Janet Ryder is training two assistants to help her. [roundabout]

TO: All Park Department Personel Date: October 12, 19xx	*sp*
FROM: Linda Redovian	
SUBJECT: Pesticide Safety Seminar	
To increase your understanding of pesticides, the Parks and Recreation department is sponsoring a Pesticide Safety Seminar.	*no caps*
This six-hour seminar will not only enhanse your professional expertise and your resume, but you will also get paid for attending and enjoy a complimentary lunch. You may either take six hours of comp time or request time-and-a-half pay for the time.	*sp* *long sentence* *punc* *confusing*
The seminar will cover topics of interest to everyone who works or lives around pesticides—and that includes all of us:	
• Handling pesticides safely • Recognizing warning signs of pesticide poisoning • Applying pesticides safely	
If you plan to atend, call Dan at Ext 5512.	
Date: Saterday, November 3 Time: 10 a.m.–4 p.m. (lunch from 12–1 p.m.) Place: Room 20-B McMillan Building	*sp*

FIGURE 6-3 _____
Third draft with notes

Janet Ryder is training two assistants to help her write and edit the company newsletter, which is rapidly becoming one of the best publications of its kind. [better]

John Anderson, because of problems in the Purchasing Department due to late orders received, has revised the ordering policy. [Poor: subject separated from verb]

John Anderson has revised the ordering policy because of late orders received by the Purchasing Department. [better]

Make sure, too, that the subject of your sentence is actually the person, place, or thing doing the action.

The idea for company training would improve morale as well as performance. [Poor: the *idea* will not do those things]

Company training would improve morale as well as performance. [better]

Our investigation of data processing has shortened turnaround time. [Poor: *investigation* did not shorten it]

Data processing has shortened turnaround time. [better]

Our investigation of data processing shows it would shorten turnaround time. [better]

Excessive Length

No sentence length is ideal for all readers and all contexts, but short sentences are generally easier to read than long ones. Your fundamental goal as a business writer is to convey a message, so most of your sentences should be fairly simple and convey one major thought.

Compare the difference between the following sentences:

Construction costs, because they are variable and always subject to fluctuations, especially in spring months when the weather is variable, are certain to cause us the most problem, despite our continual monitoring and reevaluation of the budget terms specified in the contract with Dagget Inc., so we should meet with Mrs. James as soon as possible to discuss potential problems and ways of solving them.

Because construction costs fluctuate in the spring, we have been continually monitoring the budget specified in the Dagget contract. We should meet with Mrs. James as soon as possible to discuss possible budget changes.

Most early drafts are overly complicated.

In the first example, all the ideas are crushed into one sentence. In the second example, the major thoughts are separated into two sentences and many unnecessary words have been deleted. To check for excessive sentence length, try reading your sentences out loud: you will often "hear" a problem. Also, check sentences for a central concept. What are you trying to say? If you discover that you are trying to make two or three major points in one sentence, break the sentence up.

As you revise, watch for these warning signals:

And's. Too many *and*'s in a sentence will be tedious for your reader. They may also indicate excessive length. Watch particularly for using *and* as a link between main clauses. Often, sentences will be improved by more logical transitions.

> We are hoping to meet with Mr. Farley in April and we have requested that his assistant call us next week and let us know when the meeting could be arranged. [poor]

> As we are hoping to meet with Mr. Farley in April, we have requested that his assistant call us next week to let us know when the meeting could be arranged. [better: logical transitions have replaced *and*'s]

Excessive Commas. A lot of commas in a sentence may indicate that you are trying to put too many unrelated thoughts in one sentence or that you need to put logical components next to one another.

> Mrs. Kellhere, author of the personnel manual, has requested that we, the marketing staff, read her new version of the manual, which she has recently completed, to see if she should make further changes. [poor]

> Mrs. Kellhere has asked that the marketing staff read the version of the personnel manual, which she recently completed, to see if she should make further changes. [better]

> Although the university has suffered from decreases in student enrollment in recent years, the programs being planned, which should bring in returning students and night students, would help to keep enrollment steady, but, if the number of students remains below 8,000 in the next two years, the school may have to reduce program offerings. [poor]

> The university has suffered from decreases in student enrollment in recent years, but the programs being planned should help keep enrollment steady by bringing in returning students and night students. However, if the number of enrolled students remains below 8,000 in the next two years, the school may have to reduce program offerings. [Better: main ideas are separated into two sentences. Six commas have been reduced to three.]

Wordiness

The preceding examples have shown you some ways to reduce wordiness as well as to create more effective sentences. If you can delete the unnecessary words from your sentences, you will find your writing is sharper, easier to read, and more persuasive.

The most persuasive documents are concise.

Remember, with every moment someone takes to finish your piece of writing, the more apt she or he is to throw it away or forget about it. To be persuasive and effective, be brief.

The following hints are useful for reducing wordiness:

Eliminate redundancies.
Use strong verbs.
Delete delayed openings.
Delete unnecessary phrases and clauses.
Delete unnecessary modifiers.

Eliminate Redundancies. A number of phrases common to our language actually say the same thing two or more times. Think about what your words mean and delete the ones you do not need.

Redundant	Concise
advance planning	planning
blue in color	blue
basic fundamentals	fundamentals
consensus of opinion	consensus
descended down	descended
desirable benefits	benefits
gathered together	gathered
important essentials	essentials
merge together	merge
mutual cooperation	cooperation
past history	history
true facts	facts

Despite their mutual cooperation, the two departments have not merged together. [poor]
Despite their cooperation, the two departments have not merged. [better]

Use Strong Verbs. The verb is usually the focal point of a sentence. Avoid relying too heavily on handy but dull verbs such as *to be, to do, to have,* and *to make.* Also, try not to put long nouns after these dull verbs. Instead, turn the nouns themselves into interesting, strong verbs.

Boring Verbs	Strong Verbs
are in agreement	agree
bring about an improvement in	improve
bring to a conclusion	conclude
give an indication of	indicate
is suggestive of	suggests
made an experiment	experimented

Hank will soon make a decision about the proposals. [poor]
Hank will soon decide about the proposals. [better]

We are in agreement that these signs are indicative of change. [poor]
We agree that these signs indicate change. [better]

Avoid Delayed Openings. Avoid putting "filler" at the opening of your sentences. Delayed openings include *There is/are, The fact that, It is clear that, I feel,* and other such phrases. Delete them.

The fact that the costs increased affected sales. [poor]
The increased costs affected sales. [better]

There seems to an argument developing in the conference room. [poor]
An argument is developing in the conference room. [better]

It is clear that demand is low. [poor]
Demand is low. [better]

Delete Unnecessary Phrases and Clauses. Try to reduce phrases and clauses to adverbs or adjectives. Even deleting unnecessary *that*'s from your sentences can make them more effective.

David spoke with enthusiasm in a loud voice. [poor]
David spoke loudly and enthusiastically. [better]

The company that is buying the property will see that tenants have all the information that they need. [poor]
The company buying the property will see that tenants have all the information they need. [better]

Delete Unnecessary Modifiers. Check to make sure you need all the adverbs and adjectives in your sentences. Modifiers such as *quite, really,* and *very* can often be deleted.

We are very concerned and quite worried about his health. [poor]
We are concerned and worried about his health. [better]

Many times, the sense of your sentence will make modifiers unnecessary.

Sharon bought an expensive house for $350,000. [poor]
Sharon bought a house for $350,000. [better]

Passive Sentences

Passive sentences are often tedious as well as wordy. Check to make sure most of your sentences are active rather than passive.

In an active sentence, the subject is the doer of the action: *Jim revised the memo.* In a passive sentence, however, this logical order is altered: *The memo was revised by Jim.* When a sentence is passive, the *logical* subject either disappears or is tacked onto the end in a prepositional phrase; the actual subject of a passive sentence is being acted upon rather than doing an action.

I evaluated the employees. [active]
The employees were evaluated by me. [passive]
The employees were evaluated. [passive]

Sometimes you will need a passive sentence. You may not know who did an action, or you may want to emphasize the person or thing being acted upon rather than the doer of the action. However, too many passive sentences are tedious. They take the life out of your writing.

> Make sure the majority of your sentences are active, not passive.

Choppiness

Choppy sentences may remind you of the "See Spot run" type of sentences encountered in children's reading books. In themselves, choppy sentences are readable, but their abruptness and childish sound are distracting and annoying. Moreover, choppy sentences are often wordy because they repeat words needlessly.

You can often spot choppy sentences by checking the subjects. If the subjects of two or more consecutive sentences are the same, the effect can be choppy.

Karen is a new employee. Karen used to work for Speedway Inc. She is an experienced accountant. [choppy]

An experienced accountant, Karen is a new employee who used to work for Speedway, Inc. [better]

> Short, choppy sentences can actually be wordy.

Our new employee, Karen, is an experienced accountant who used to work for Speedway, Inc. [better]

Sometimes, too, if the opening of a sentence uses a word or phrase that appeared at the end of the previous sentence, the effect can be choppy.

We have hired a clown for the occasion. The occasion should be a happy one. [choppy]

We have hired a clown for the occasion, which should be a happy one. [better]

Lack of Variety

Avoid falling into writing "ruts": keep your writing varied.

Variety will make your sentences more readable and interesting. Avoid using the same sentence structures over and over again. Vary your active sentences with an occasional passive one; open some sentences with dependent clauses, others with independent clauses; make some sentences short, some long; use a variety of transitional words rather than relying on *and*.

Your readers will probably never know the thought you have put into creating concise, varied, interesting sentences, but they will find your writing effective and persuasive.

Test Your Skills

Check Your Knowledge of Words Commonly Confused

Writers often confuse the meanings of words that sound similar. In the following sentences, which word choice is correct?

1. Maureen Thompson is one of the most [imminent eminent] economists in our state.
2. The committee has been [apprised appraised] of the problems and is working toward some solutions.
3. Although the champagne is [complimentary complementary], we will have to pay for the mixed drinks.
4. We are hoping that the salary increases will have an [effect affect] on morale.
5. So far the truth of the situation has [alluded eluded] the managers.
6. The [principle principal] reasons for the bankruptcy are listed in this document.
7. Norman Tillotson's technique is to [illicit elicit] comments from the audience.
8. We will [proceed precede] with the meeting in ten minutes.
9. [Alot A lot] of our supporters have given up the struggle.
10. Please ask the staff to order more blue [stationery stationary].

Answers

1. eminent 2. apprised 3. complimentary 4. effect 5. eluded 6. principal 7. elicit 8. proceed 9. A lot 10. stationery

Maintaining a Professional Tone

Can you define the difference between these two sentences?

It will be impossible for me to assist you until Tuesday morning.
I will be happy to assist you on Tuesday morning.

Although quite close in meaning, the two sentences convey a different *tone:* the first is negative and cold, while the second is positive and personal.

We are all aware of the importance of tone in spoken communication. In fact, we usually believe people's tone more than we believe their actual words. "She claimed she was happy for me," we might say, "but her tone showed her real feelings." In writing, however, we sometimes forget that tone is equally important.

During the last phases of the revision process, check whether you have chosen an appropriate tone for the message you are sending, the channel you are using, and the audience to whom you are writing.

Persuasive documents are often phrased positively.

The Message

The nature of your message should help you determine an appropriate tone. The tone of a sales letter will vary from that of a collection letter; the tone of a memo conveying bad news will vary from that of a memo praising the reader. However, remember that, in general, you are hoping for cooperation from your readers: an angry, threatening collection letter sent to a slightly forgetful reader could lose you a customer. Give your readers the benefit of the doubt—and maintain your own credibility as a reasonable person.

Apparently you have forgotten that you still owe $50 on the brochures you ordered from us. [snide tone]

When you ordered brochures from us on May 2, you agreed to pay $75 down and $50 when the work was completed. You picked up the brochures on May 15, and now the remaining $50 is due. [professional tone]

The Channel

The tone of your message will change according to the type of writing you are doing: you do not use the same tone writing a personal note to a friend that you use writing a research paper for a class. Similarly, the tone of an informal memo will be different from that of a formal report. The memo will probably contain personal pronouns such as *I* and *you,* for example, whereas the formal report may not.

For the most part, however, your business writing should appear objective and rational. Rather than using vague, subjective words, back up your statements with objective detail.

Business documents usually contain specific, concrete details.

The new procedure has had a *terrific impact* on production. [vague, subjective]
The new procedure has increased production by 50 percent. [specific, objective]

Some Tips on Tone	
Do	**Don't**
stay calm	lose your temper
state a grievance politely	whine
make a request	beg
maintain objectivity	see everything from your own viewpoint
back up conclusions with data	make irrational statements or personal attacks
state ideas positively	emphasize negatives
sound human	sound pretentious and condescending

The Audience

A third variable affecting the tone of your business writing is the audience. How well do you know your readers? Are they your subordinates or superiors? A memo to the company president whom you know slightly will be different than one to your assistant with whom you work every day.

> Give me a call when you get a chance. [a memo to a colleague]
> I would appreciate your calling me when you have time. [a memo to a superior]

Effective business writing should sound professional. Avoid using words that are too informal or that are pompous or hackneyed.

Slang

Words are always changing. Some words drop out of sight, while new ones suddenly make their way into the language. Some words that came into English as slang (*kudos, foul play*) have now become part of our standard vocabularies; other slang words, however, (*guy, nerd, booze*) remain slang.

While some informal language may be appropriate in a memo to a fellow

Instead of This	Try This
according to our records	we find
at this point in time	now
it has come to my attention	[delete]
it is incumbent on me	I must
make inquiry	ask
prior to	before
subsequent to	after
utilize	use

worker, generally keep your business writing free of slang, nonstandard words, regionalisms, and other informal word choices. Usually your dictionary will note when words are colloquial or slang.

Pompous Language

To avoid sounding too informal, you may find yourself using words that are pompous or inflated. When revising, give yourself the "speech test": ask yourself if you would ever *say* the words you have written.

Please advise me upon receipt of the aforementioned document.
Please let me know when you receive my letter.

The first of these sentences fails the speech test; the second is clearer and more natural.

The best word choices are neither pompous nor overly informal.

Clichés

Clichés are hackneyed expressions that can make your writing seem trite and dull. The following list contains terms that are overused in business writing. Delete them whenever you can.

aired their grievances	kindly advise
attached please find	maximize
ballpark figure	optimize
bottom line	parameter
came on board	prioritize
cost effective	receipt is hereby acknowledged
each and every one of you	state of the art
foreseeable future	straitened circumstances
herewith enclosed	viable alternative

Proofreading

This is the least creative step of the writing process, but it is important. A carelessly proofread piece of writing will make a bad impression, even if it is otherwise accurate and well written. Typographical errors and careless mistakes make the writer appear unprofessional.

To proofread effectively, leave your piece of writing alone for a few hours or even a few days so you can see it with "new eyes." Check the spelling of every word you are even slightly unsure of; keep a writing handbook nearby to check punctuation and usage rules. Do quotation marks go outside the period? How many *m*'s are in *accommodate?* If you are not sure, check. Do not guess! Figure 6-4 shows you Linda Redovian's proofread manuscript.

Leave yourself ample time to proofread.

```
TO:        All Park Department Personnel
DATE:      October 12, 19xx
FROM:      Linda Redovian
SUBJECT:   Pesticide Safety Seminar
```

You-oriented opening

To increase your understanding of pesticides, the Parks and Recreation Department is sponsoring a pesticide safety seminar.

Details to motivate readers

This six-hour seminar will enhance your professional expertise and your resume. You will also get paid for attending and enjoy a complimentary lunch. If you attend, you may either take six hours of comp time or request time-and-a-half pay.

Topics listed for easy reading

The seminar will cover topics of interest to everyone who works or lives around pesticides—and that includes all of us:

• Handling pesticides safely
• Recognizing warning signs of pesticide poisoning
• Applying pesticides safely.

If you plan to attend, call Dan at Ext 5512.

Key information listed at end

```
Date:   Saturday, November 3
Time:   10 a.m.—4 p.m. (lunch from 12—1 p.m.)
Place:  Room 20-B McMillan Building
```

FIGURE 6-4
Final draft

Test Your Skills

How Well Do You Proofread?

Read through the following paragraph. How many typographical errors can you find?

One crucial dimension of leadership style is is the degree of control exerted on the behavior of others. How much latitude is given to others to make their own decisions? How much infomration is shared with them? How free are are they to question orders, or to initiiate ideas? Are they constantly watched, or is their performance checked only periodically? In short, are they encoraged to try to influence the way things are done?

Answers

One crucial dimension of leadership style is is the degree of control exerted on the behavior of others. How much latitude is given to others to make their own decisions? How much infomration is shared with them? How free are are they to question orders, or to initiiate ideas? Are they constantly watched, or is their performance checked only periodically? In short, are they encoraged to try to influence the way things are done?

What Would You Do?

After Dan Watson had sent the following memo to the employees in his department, he was shocked when several people told him they had been offended by it. Revise the memo for Dan.

MEMORANDUM

TO: All Employees, Shipping Department
FROM: Dan Watson, Assistant Manager
SUBJECT: Prohibited Usage of Freight Elevator
DATE: June 2, 19xx

As many of you have been continuously utilizing the freight
elevator despite my explicit verbal instructions, it is
incumbent on me to precede with a written policy on the
matter.
   1. The elevator is to be used by employees carrying pallets
or pushing carts. No employees capable of climbing a flight
of stairs may utilize the freight elevator simply to get
themselves up to the second floor.
   2. If you think this policy does not apply to you because
of your advanced age or some handicap, come see me.
   3. This regulation has been made because of our insurance
liability as well as the heavy usage of the elevator for
legitimate purposes. I am NOT simply acting like a turkey
about the situation.

"Well, little Susan is not so little now. She's married,
and she's in a field that's rife with jargon."

Drawing by C. Barsotti; © 1984 The New Yorker Magazine, Inc.

Summary

Using the writing process to create business documents will not make writing easy. Writing effectively is never easy. However, using a process approach will reduce much of the anxiety you may feel about writing. You will find that the process actually reduces the time it takes to reach an effective draft. You will waste less time procrastinating and working in circles. And you may even find you are enjoying yourself!

Summary Discussion: Peggy McCormick's Memo from Case in Point, p. 96

Peggy McCormick's memo is wordy, pompous, and confusing. The memo is actually announcing an upcoming seminar, but some readers would never figure that out. When she revises, Peggy should orient the memo to the readers, whom she hopes will attend the seminar. The subject line of the memo, for instance, should tell the readers what the memo is about. Peggy should avoid jargon and unnecessarily difficult words (*parameters, aggregate*) and shorten her sentences so that readers can quickly understand the main idea in each. Her final draft should have shorter paragraphs that make the memo more accessible at first glance.

Terms to Remember

Drafting: making a preliminary version of a document

Modifier: a word that describes another word in a sentence (*red* dress)

Passive sentence: a sentence in which the subject is acted upon: *The book was read by Jan.*

Redundancy: a word or phrase such as *past history* that says the same thing more than once

Tone: the attitude or emotion expressed in a piece of writing

Topic sentence: a sentence that states major point of a paragraph

Transition: a word or phrase that establishes connections between sentences and paragraphs

Drafting and Revising Checklist

Drafting

• When you draft,

_____ write quickly without making changes

_____ leave lots of space on the page for making revisions later on

Organizing Material

• As you organize your ideas,

_____ use a direct approach if readers will react positively to your material

_____ use an indirect approach if readers will initially react negatively to your material

_____ organize your ideas in a sequence that will make sense to your readers

_____ delete any information readers do not need

_____ add anything that will help your readers follow your ideas

_____ develop a conclusion that pulls the document together

Paragraphs

• As you revise paragraphs, check for

_____ topic sentences

_____ details that support the topic sentence

_____ transitions between ideas

_____ a variety of paragraph lengths

Sentences

- As you revise sentences, make sure that

   _____ major ideas are stated clearly

   _____ excess words have been deleted

   _____ verbs are varied and active

   _____ openings are direct

   _____ ideas flow smoothly

Tone

- Adapt the tone of your document to

   _____ the nature of your message

   _____ the type of document you are writing

   _____ your specific readers

- To maintain a professional tone, work on

   _____ staying calm and polite

   _____ remaining objective

   _____ stating ideas positively

   _____ avoiding slang, pompous language, and cliches

Questions for Review and Discussion

1. Why is it important to retain a professional tone in business writing?
2. Why should writers usually delete slang from their business writing?
3. What are *transitions?* Why are they important in business writing?
4. What is the "speech test" described in this chapter? When is it useful?
5. What tips can you give someone who wants to improve his or her proofreading skills?
6. Why should business writers try to reduce wordiness in their sentences?
7. Why are active sentences usually more effective than passive ones? Give examples.
8. Give an example of a cliché. Why should you usually try to delete clichés from business writing?
9. What are redundancies? Give three examples.

1. Revise Peggy McCormick's memo at the opening of this chapter.

2. Choose two paragraphs from a magazine or newspaper article. Locate the topic sentences. What is the function of the other sentences in each paragraph? Do they contribute to the topic sentence? Do they employ transitional devices? If so, what are they?

3. Find an article in a popular magazine such as *People* or *Sports Illustrated.* Are there any word choices in the article that you would not use in a report or other business document? List the words that you think would be inappropriate and be prepared to discuss why you would not use them in a report or business letter.

4. The following sentences convey an unpleasant, negative tone. Revise them using more positive word choices.
   a. Dan, your analysis in this report is wrong; check you faulty figures.
   b. Mrs. Deerborn, your child is deficient in mathematics this term.
   c. The work in this department has been mediocre. The staff had better shape up.
   d. I am writing to complain about the lousy service I have been receiving from your service department.
   e. If you are derelict in your duties, the whole department will suffer.

5. Revise the following memo:

Memorandum

```
TO:      All Staff
FROM:    Al Kelley
TOPIC:   Slipshod Work Habits
DATE:    February 12,19xx
```

A lot of our clients have been complaining
recently about our filthy offices and
slipshod work habits. Needless to say, we
are supposed to be running a professional
office here, not a pigsty. Let's stop
acting like retarded pigs and get moving.
Here are some suggestions.
1. Don't eat at your desks. We don't need
to smell putrid tuna fish sandwiches
around here all day.

2. Try to keep your coffee inside your
cups. Half our paperwork has unsightly
coffee stains on it.
3. See if you can put off listening to
idiotic radio shows till you drive home.
Thanks for your attention.

6. Revise the following memo:

Memorandum

```
TO:       All Staff
FROM:     Carol Guardino
SUBJECT:  R & D Funds
DATE:     September 3, 19xx
```

Pursuant to the policy outlined in your
policy and procedures manual, R & D funds
are available to those staff members who
came on board this company prior to 1987
and who will be doing appropriate research
work in the foreseeable future. Attached
herewith are relevant paragraphs from the
aforementioned manual for your perusal and
review. To facilitate applications for
such funds, several proposals have been
made available in the staff library.

7. Revise the following sentences:
   a. Mike Toomey, although he is always reluctant to admit his weaknesses, has finally admitted that he has had the flu for two weeks, and he has given his top project to me.
   b. Because of the large number of materials that have been gathered together for our review and consideration, we have failed to arrive at a general consensus of opinion.
   c. There should be some answers to the problem in the long report that Marsha Donald has written.
   d. Our branch office, which is located in Des Moines, Iowa, and which has been in operation since 1981, is sponsoring a bicycle race which is designed to raise money for the homeless.
   e. I enclose my resume. My resume summarizes my work experience and coursework. I look forward to hearing from you. Please call me next week. My telephone number is 508-892-9022.

8. Revise the following memo:

TO: Patricia Hawthorne
FROM: Larry Charleston
SUBJECT: Sales Personnel Shortage
DATE: March 2, 19xx

The Kalamazoo branch performed well
this year. We won 210 new customers. We
increased profits by 20 percent. We hope
to do even better this year. We need your
help.

In April three of our key salespeople were
relocated to the Norman, Oklahoma, office.
We now have only six salespeople left.
This number is not sufficient to service
our present customers. And we cannot try
to win new accounts.

It is impossible for us to maintain
customer loyalty with only six
salespeople. And we have to spend money to
make money. Please authorize three new
salespeople for this office. Perhaps you
can transfer them from the Ann Arbor
branch. I hear that branch is cutting
staff. Thank you.

Using a Word Processor

Objectives

To identify the components of a word processing system

To learn how word processing can help you plan, write, and revise

To assess the advantages and disadvantages of word processing

7

Charlie Grainger's Typing Task

For the eighteen months it has been in business, USA Consulting has been doing contract work for state agencies. The small company bids on projects by writing proposals that run from 100 to 200 pages. The proposals, usually developed by a four-person team, must be submitted by specific deadlines. No matter how well the team members plan a proposal, they always end up finishing the project in a last-minute panic.

Their current project, a proposal to the State Department of Transportation, must be finished today so it can reach its destination by overnight mail. The team members are typing and handwriting their sections of the proposal and giving them to Charlie Grainger, the typist, as they finish. Ann Foreman is reading through each page as Charlie finishes it.

"Steve's redoing the budget," Ann tells Charlie. "Don't type the version he gave you."

"I've already typed it. You mean I have to type it again?"

"It's all wrong. He calculated the overhead incorrectly. Oops, you'll need to white-out this word. *Questionnaire* has two *n*'s."

"Greg wrote it with one *n*. I'm a typist, not Noah Webster."

"It's still wrong. I'll white it out if you can type it in again."

Hal Fine came into the office. "I have to revise the introduction, Charlie. Give me back the version you typed."

"It's 2 o'clock, Hal. Can't we break for lunch?"

"Forget food, Charlie. We've got to get this done. Have you typed the staffing section yet? Steve needs to make some changes."

"This company's operating in the dark ages," Charlie grumbled. "If you'd cough up the money for a word processor, you'd save yourselves a lot of headaches. You might even find a typist who'd stay at this place for more than six weeks."

"We should each have a word processor," Ann agreed. "Then you could put the proposal together from data on our different disks. We could do charts and graphs on the machine, too."

"You could store a lot of these data and use them over and over," Steve added. "I'd have to type this information only once."

"If we win this contract, we'll buy a word processor," Hal promised Charlie. "Oh no, look at this, Ann. We're going to have to rewrite the evaluation section."

Points to Consider
- How would a word processor make Charlie's life easier?
- How would word processors help the USA Consulting staff even in the early stages of the writing process?

Writing with a Computer

You have probably already had some experience with computers. You may have played video games at home, worked on simulation games in your classes, or used spreadsheet programs. If you have not experimented with word processing programs, now is the time to begin. Even if you write only a few pages a week, using a word processor will make your writing easier. If you write *more* than a few pages a week, a word processor will change your life.

What makes the word processor so wonderful? You will not appreciate its joys until you work on one yourself, but here are some of its advantages.

Making Changes Is Almost Effortless

When you use a word processor, your decisions are *reversible:* deleting, adding, and moving material require hitting only a couple of keys. You can see your changes displayed immediately on the video screen—without cutting or pasting. You no longer have to face messy drafts. All your changes are typed neatly, without cross-outs, arrows directing you to the back of the page, or illegible notes scribbled in the margin. Your word processor cannot edit your writing for you, but it can do almost everything else.

Word processing lets you experiment with minimal effort.

A Note to Beginning Users

Frustration is a part of learning word processing. If you throw up your hands and quit after the first 15 minutes or the first attempt to create a document, you will not give the program or yourself a fair chance. One of the greatest frustrations is the loss of text. It is important to know that if you do not "save," you will not have a record of what you have written. You can avoid this disappointment by enacting the "SAVE" command frequently as you create text and absolutely when you finish a document. It is also a good idea to make a printed copy of drafts or originals that you reformat. If you do not and decide that you liked the original better, you may have no record of the original and may not be able to reconstruct it.

Early in your learning, practice using features such as indenting, tabbing, and hard spacing because these actions can produce something different from what you had in mind and be a bother when you are ready to edit.

Do not be a quitter. Do not pay to have your paper typed by someone who has been patient enough to learn word processing. Stay with it, and find out that soon you will master the details that are the source of frustration.

Source: Ann Stuart, *The Technical Writer* (New York: Holt, Rinehart and Winston, 1988), pp. 16–17.

You Type Only New Material

When you do make changes, you do not have to retype the material that stays the same.

You Can Experiment

You think you might like the last paragraph at the opening? Move it and see how it works. You do not have to retype anything.

You Can Change Individual Words

You want to change the word *profits* to *savings* throughout your report? Your word processing program can locate *profits* each time it is used and automatically make the change for you.

You Can Check Your Spelling

With a spelling program, you can check your document for spelling errors. (Some programs can even help with grammar and punctuation.)

You Can Make Your Documents Attractive

You can adjust and justify margins, center headings, put words in **boldface,** underline words—all with the touch of a button. With many systems, you can also use different print styles.

You Can Make Copies

You need two or three copies of that letter? Print out more copies.

You Can Communicate with Other People

With a modem and compatible equipment, you can send and receive messages on your machine. Now you can write at home, send your document electronically to someone else, and get it back with suggestions and changes.

You Can Work Quietly

Typewriters click, clatter, and clang. Word processors hum softly. Many printers are noisy, but they are not usually run as frequently as word processors. In general, offices and homes become more enjoyable places to work when the typewriter noises stop.

You Do Not Have to Understand Computers to Use Word Processing

You can use word processing without knowing how to program or how a computer works. Word processing *IS* a program, and if you can turn the computer on, load the program into it, and know how to use the program's functions, you *can* write using word processing.

You may become an avid user of a computer for technical communication and never use it for anything else. That is what I do. People often assume that because I write books about computers and writing I know a lot about computers. I do not. My present needs do not require that I program, know computer languages, or understand the technical workings of a computer. If my needs change, I shall learn what is necessary to pursue my new interests. You can adopt the same attitude.

Source: Ann Stuart, *The Technical Writer* (New York: Holt, Rinehart and Winston, 1988), pp. 16–17.

Identifying the Equipment

Technology has spawned a lot of new vocabulary in the past twenty years. You have probably encountered all the terms described in this section, but if computers are new to you, this section and the Glossary of Computer Terms at the end of this chapter may prove helpful.

What is a word processor? Basically, it is a computer composed of a group of components, like a stereo system's, that may vary from one system to another. Many people use personal computers, also called microcomputers, for their word processing; however, any size computer may be used for word processing.

Figure 7-1 shows a typical personal computer. The equipment includes a keyboard, a terminal, a printer, and the word processor itself.

Keyboard

A keyboard (Figure 7-2) is used to enter data (called *input*) into the word processor. The keyboard looks much like a typewriter keyboard, but it has several extra keys. Often a set of "function keys" appears on the left of the keyboard, while a numeric keypad is on the right.

The function keys differ from one system to the next, but they perform such tasks as moving to the beginning or end of a text, setting margins, and creating special effects such as underlining.

The numeric keypad is useful when you want to enter numeric data, but

Function keys enable you to perform complex tasks with a single keystroke.

FIGURE 7–1
Personal computer

FIGURE 7–2
Keyboard

also it usually has keys with arrows on them that help you move to different parts of the screen and to move back and forth through your document.

Video Screen

The video screen, which looks like a television screen, displays the characters (the *output*) that you type in on the keyboard. The characters you type appear on the screen, usually in green or orange lettering. The characters are also stored in the computer's memory and then on your floppy disk.

Printer

Hard copy is printed on sheets of paper.

A printer enables you to transform output onto paper—also called *hard copy*. Good quality printers are quickly coming down in price, so you may want to invest in a new printer in a few years when one that you like has become more affordable. Right now, most people must choose between dot matrix and letter quality printers.

Letter quality printers produce nice-looking pages, but the printers cost more and work more slowly than dot matrix printers. As laser printers become less expensive, they may well replace all other types as they produce beautiful pages and work quietly and quickly.

Word Processor

The actual word processor itself is a computer that controls the keyboard, terminal, and printer. The circuitry inside the word processor transmits information to the other parts of the system.

ROM operates the computer system; RAM holds data temporarily.

The computer has two types of memory, read-only memory (called *ROM*) and random access memory (called *RAM*). ROM operates the system, while RAM saves your input as you work on it. The data in RAM are temporary, so you must save your input on a hard disk or floppy disk.

Sampling of Word Processing Capabilities

Moving to the beginning and end of a text
Moving to a specified page in a text
Moving to different points on the screen
Inserting characters into the text
Deleting characters from the text
Deleting words, lines, and blocks of text
Copying blocks of text
Moving blocks of text to different parts of a document
Moving blocks of texts to other files
Searching for specified words or characters in a text
Automatically changing a word or character throughout a text
Setting margins
Justifying right-hand margins
Adjusting line spaces
Creating tabs
Making footnotes
Numbering pages
Underlining
Printing in boldface

Disk Drives

The disk drives, located in the front of the computer, are boxes into which you slip floppy disks or "diskettes." The disks are as important to your computer as your cassettes are to your tape recorder. They should be carefully handled and clearly labeled.

Software

To make your system work, you need software or *programs*. Some computers have word processing programs built in, but most programs come separately on floppy disks. Word processing programs differ widely, so experiment with different programs before you buy one. Almost all, however, have the capabilities that we will refer to in this text.

Streamlining the Writing Process

Because each computer system and program works differently, we cannot provide "instructions" for word processing. You will have to study the manuals accompanying your machine and software and get advice from colleagues. You may even want to join a "user group," people with similar machines who meet to discuss problems and ideas. Personal computing magazines, also, contain articles you will find useful.

What we can do here is show you how word processing can streamline every facet of the writing process, and we can give you examples and exercises you may find helpful as you get used to writing electronically. (See Figures 7-3 to 7-9 for illustrations of the writing process on a computer.)

Jack Gee has been asked to write a short report on the computer skills that employees in his company need and on ways their skills could be upgraded. The following figures illustrate the development of Jack's report on his word processor.

---

accounting/word processing/ database mgt
how many terminals? Who uses them? how to teach skills? college courses? in-house training? manuals? develop a special course for this company? do we need programing courses? what's most important? learning how computers work? solving problems we face every day? how much money can we spend on this project? should computer knowledge be mandatory? how much time can we ask employees to spend upgrading skills? better talk to Jim Watson— consider an employee questionnaire?

FIGURE 7–3 _____
Brainstorming

What am I writing? Proposal. Come up with a plan. Make recommendations based on solid information.
Major purpose: Convince management to implement computer training

Who is my audience? Karen Blackwood asked me to write this, but everyone in management is going to see it. Some of them are the people who need the computer experience. They won't know technical computer terms. They will know about money and time allocations.
All the managers are over 30 yrs old.
They are all college educated.
They all use computerized information from our data bank.
Most of them have access to terminals which they're not using to their fullest capability.
None of them currently do any writing on computers. They hand write stuff for the secretaries to put on disks. Some of the managers do spreadsheet analysis, etc. But most ask for the print-outs and just work with those.

Why am I writing? I'd like company employees to be computer-literate. I want to show management how important our computer system really is. I am trying to convince people with rational argument and financial data.
I want Karen B. to know that I write effectively.

FIGURE 7–4 _____
Defining goals and audience

1. Talk to Henry Folsom, Francine Waters, and Hilda Fredericks.
2. Go through weekly work sheets. How much time do employees spend at their terminals?
3. Interview employees. What would they like to be capable of doing? What kinds of problems have they run into?
4. *Think.* What possibilities do we have?
   In-house training
   College courses
   Home-study with manuals
   Work up pros and cons of those three options.
5. Check costs, time, benefits. Get catalog for Henley Community College for information. Call about costs and programs put out by computer consulting companies.
6. Call other companies. Find out what they've been doing.

FIGURE 7–5
Doing necessary research

1. Introduction. Who asked for this report? What is my purpose? Give stats on number of employees, number of terminals, and how much usage we get from our system.
2. State need for improved computer training. Mention people spoken with, what companies I called.
3. Give options: college courses
   home study training
   in-house training
4. Give benefits and weaknesses of each option.
   Cost
   Time
   Relevance of material
   Overall effectiveness
5. Give proposal: In-house training is the best option. Costs more but will bring us exactly what we need.

FIGURE 7–6
Making a plan

Brainstorming

You may find the first step of the writing process to be so personal that you do not want to use a computer: you may feel more comfortable with scratch pads. But do consider the advantages of a computer.

Brainstorming on the computer is fast. You can make your words appear on the screen so quickly and clearly that often you will find sentences and even paragraphs forming before you know it. If your brainstorming seems to be getting away from you, do not stop the flow! Revising your ideas will

Even slow typists find it useful to brainstorm on a computer.

Do You Know How to Prevent Word Processing Disasters?

Which description best fits the way you work?

1. You have finished a term paper on a word processor. You print the paper and do a final proofreading. Now you
   a. delete the file that held the text of the paper and turn off the machine
   b. keep the file and turn off the machine
   c. copy the file onto a second disk and keep both files before turning off the machine
2. You need several diskettes nearby while working on a large project. What do you do with the diskettes not actually in use? You
   a. keep them in diskette envelopes beside your printer.
   b. keep them in their envelopes a little away from your work area.
   c. keep them nearby without their envelopes so you can reach them easily when you need them.
3. You are writing a report that will run to over ten pages. You
   a. interrupt your thoughts every fifteen minutes by stopping to save the material in the file you are working on.

   b. work intensely without stopping and save the material right before printing it out.
   c. save the material when you take your hourly breaks.

Discussion

1. To be extra careful of your material, save it on a backup disk as well as on the original disk. Do not delete files until you are sure you will never need them again. Best answer: C.
2. To preserve your diskettes, keep them in their envelopes when they are not in the disk drives. They are safer a little away from your work area where they will not be accidentally damaged. Avoid leaving diskettes near a printer when it is working (or near a telephone) as the magnetic field could damage the data on the disk. Best answer: B.
3. Save your data frequently. If you are typing in new material, you should stop every 15 minutes or so to save the data: otherwise, a surge of current or other problem could cause you to lose a lot of data. Best answer: A.

be easy on the computer, so whatever you write even at this early stage may well be useful later on.

Unless you have specialized software, you will not be able to doodle as you brainstorm. If you need to doodle as you think, keep a pad beside your keyboard.

Defining Your Goals and Your Audience

Defining your goals and audience is often done more easily on a computer than on a pad of paper once you get the knack. You might try typing a series of questions about your project and your readers as quickly as you can think of them. Then go back and answer them with some careful thought.

With a word processing program, you can easily skip backward and forward through the ideas and questions you have typed in; you can move material so concepts are grouped logically; you can delete material that seems irrelevant—or just move it to another file in case you want to look at it later on.

Karen Blackwood has requested that I put together a brief report summarizing the need this company has for computer-literate employees and options we have for upgrading employees' computer skills. I interviewed twenty of our thirty-five employees and five managers to find out the level of their computer literacy and the needs they have for computers on a daily basis.

Then I gathered information on the equipment we have and how much it gets used. Each of our clerical staff members has an IBM terminal and printer. They use word processing, but do not know all the capabilities of the programs and equipment they use. The manager of each of our six departments has a terminal hooked up to our big computer. There are also five "rotating" personal computers that people can use if they want. None of them gets used more than three hours a day. Most of the managers simply request information from the computer but do not know how to access it themselves.

It became apparent that we are underusing our computer equipment and that almost everyone could use quite a lot more training in word processing, database management, and spreadsheets. I spoke with Mr. Henry Folsom at Theyer Corporation and Ms. Francoine Waters at C & F Consulting. They have both implemented several types of computer training at their companies and were familiar with training done by other companies. This training consisted of college courses for employees, home-study training, and in-house training.

Each of these options has strengths and weaknesses.

College Courses. Some comanies pay their employees' tuition while they take night courses at a local community college. Tuition comes to about $300 per course. Employees can learn programming in different languages and hands-on techniques for business applications. They can also take classes without missing any time from work. The problem is, they may end up taking courses that aren't really useful for their needs at this company.

Home Study Training. Some companies simply give employees manuals to study from at home. Then employees can learn how to use a word processing program or whatever on their own time—and experiment with it when they get back to their terminals. This is a cheap method but not very practical as employees waste a lot of time and unmotivated employees don't really learn from the manuals.

In-house Training. This can be expensive as trainers usually receive a substantial fee to come into a company and work with the employees. The trainers I spoke with and heard about conduct a three-hour seminar during a workday and then work with people in small groups who have similar needs such as wanting to work with spreadsheets. The method takes up more work time for employees than the other methods, but is usually time well spent. Moreover, in the long run this method costs less than funding tuition.

Within two weeks, inhouyse seminars could increase productivity in this corporation and substantially increase the flexibility and skills of employees and managers.

wide margins for making notes
add headings throughout
put in methods section
cut excess words
separate methods from results

reorganize this paragraph

vague
mention Hilda Fredericks

put this information in methods section

what could we do with more computer expertise?

put strengths and weaknesses of each option in subsection

put in conclusions section

FIGURE 7–7
A first draft with notations

center internal headings

put conclusions at beginning

wordy

number methods and indent them

how it is used.

these sentences are too I-oriented; rephrase

capitalize subtitles

Their computer-related work often interferes with the tasks outlined in their job descriptions

PURPOSE *SUMMARY*

In response to Karen Blackwood's request, this report summarizes our company's needs for computer-literate employees and describes options for upgrading our employee and managers' computer skills.

METHODS

To prepare this report, I interviewed twenty of our thirty-five employees and the managers of our five departments to find out the level of their computer literacy and their computer needs.

With the assistance of Hilda Fredericks, I gathered information on the computre *sp /* equipment owned by this company and the uses to which it is put.

I also spoke with Mr. Henry Folsom at Theyer Corporation and Ms. Francine Waters at C & F Consulting as they are familiar with the different types of computer training available and respective costs. *the /*

RESULTS OF RESEARCH

Equipment Each of our clerical staff staff members has an IBM terminal and printer. The five department managers have terminals hooked up to our main computer. There are also five "rotating" personal computers that anyone may use.

Uses The clerical staff members use word processing programs but do not *and Skills* know all the capabilities of the programs and equipment they use. Four of the *All* managers simply request request information from the computer but do not know how to access it themselves.

The most knowledgeable person in our company with regard to computers is Hilda Fredericks. She and her assistant, James Kearny, handle almost all the computer-related tasks in the company.

NEEDS

There is no doubt that we are underutilizing our computer equipment and taking too much time for routine tasks that a computer could do efficiently. With more computer-literate employees and managers for example we could *tr*
1. Put together and use a database for compiling industry statistics and trends
2. Use spreadsheets for efficiently compiling financial information
3. Computerize billing procedures

FIGURE 7-8

A second draft with notations

Doing Necessary Research

The computer is an excellent research tool. With the right equipment, you can communicate with other people by electronic mail to get the information you need. You can also go back through documents and other data stored on floppy disks or on a hard disk.

Many companies, libraries, and individual writers subscribe to database and search facilities that provide lists of books and articles on a certain topic, information about organizations, and other specialized data. Journalists, doctors, lawyers, and financial analysts commonly subscribe to such services. *The New York Times* Information Service, the Dow Jones Information Service,

4. Hook up ~~with~~ [to] online database services nationwide
5. Develop specialized programs for our own needs
6. Troubleshoot problems ~~with~~our computer system. *without relying solely on Hilda Fredericks and James Kearny.*

OPTIONS

We have three options: standard college courses, home study training, and in-house training. Each option has strengths and weaknesses. *trs*

organize options from worst to best

2. 1. COLLEGE COURSES. Some companies pay their employee's tuition while they take night courses. Tuition ~~at a community college~~ comes to about $500 per course.

STRENGTHS. Employees [would] learn programming languages and hands-on techniques for business applications. They ~~do~~ not miss time from work. *would*

WEAKNESSES. Courses ~~are~~ not tailored to their (or our) needs. Tuition is expensive. *would be /* *would / be*

1. 2. HOME STUDY. Some companies give employees manuals to study at home. Then employees practice on their computers at work when they have time. *move to position 1*

STRENGTH. This would be the least expensive method.

WEAKNESSES. Employees waste time trying to teach themselves. Unmotivated employees would never really learn from the manuals.

3. IN-HOUSE TRAINING. Trainers come to the company, conduct a three-hour seminar during a workday, and then work with small groups of people with similar needs.

STRENGTH. This approach would ensure that [our] employees ~~would~~ learn what they need to learn. *sp*

WEAKNESSES. This methoid would take up the most company time and could cost as much as $3,000.

CONCLUSIONS

Despite its cost, the in-house seminars are the best option for this company. Within two weeks, our employees and managers would be substantially more productive and would have acquired skills they can use and develop whle doing their jobs. *sp*

Despite the initial cost and loss of work time, this company would benefit from in-house computer training.

---

and The Source provide news, financial data, and a wide range of information for the student and businessperson.

Many new services are being created all the time, so find out what is currently available in your areas of interest. Your library's reference section will provide you with current information regarding on-line databases. (These database services are often expensive, so find out about costs as you research the options available.)

It may well be worth your time to set up a database of your own if you are going to be writing and researching in one field. If you want to organize

Even expensive on-line databases may end up saving you money in the long run.

REPORT

TO: All Managers
FROM: Jack Gee
SUBJECT: Computer Training
DATE: June 12, 19xx

SUMMARY

In response to Karen Blackwood's request, this
report summarizes our company's needs for computer-
literate employees and describes options for
upgrading our employees' and managers' computer
skills.

Having researched our equipment, our needs, and our
employees' skill levels, I recommend that the
company invest in in-house computer training.

METHODS

To prepare this report, I used four major sources
of information.

1. Interviews with twenty of our thirty-five
   employees and five department managers to find
   out the level of their computer literacy and
   their computer needs.

2. Interviews with Hilda Fredericks and other
   computer users in the company to find out what
   equipment the company owns and how it is used.

3. Conversations with Mr. Henry Folsom at Theyer
   Corporation and Ms. Francine Waters at C & F
   Consulting as they are familiar with the
   different types of computer training available
   and the respective costs.

RESULTS OF RESEARCH

EQUIPMENT. Each clerical staff member has an IBM
terminal and printer. The five department managers
have terminals hooked up to our main computer.
There are also five ''rotating'' personal computers
that anyone may use.

USES AND SKILLS. The clerical staff members use
word processing programs but do not know all the
capabilities of the programs and equipment they
use. All the managers simply request information
from the computer but do not know how to access it
themselves.

The most knowledgeable person in our company with
regard to computers is Hilda Fredericks. She and
her assistant, James Kearny, handle almost all the

FIGURE 7-9 _____
A third draft

computer-related tasks in the company. Their computer-related work often interferes with the tasks outlined in their job descriptions.

NEEDS

There is no doubt that we are underutilizing our computer equipment and taking too much time for routine tasks that a computer could do efficiently. With more computer-literate employees and managers, we could, for example,

1. put together and use a database for compiling industry statistics and trends

2. use spreadsheets for efficiently compiling financial information

3. computerize billing procedures

4. hook up to on-line database services nationwide

5. develop specialized programs for our own needs

6. troubleshoot problems with our computer system without relying solely on Hilda Fredericks and James Kearny

OPTIONS

We have three options: home study, standard college courses, and in-house training. Each option has strengths and weaknesses.

1. HOME STUDY. Some companies give employees manuals to study at home. Then employees practice on their computers at work when they have time.

STRENGTH. This would be the least expensive method.

WEAKNESSES. Employees would waste time trying to teach themselves. Unmotivated employees would never really learn from the manuals.

2. COLLEGE COURSES. Some companies pay their employees' tuition while they take night courses. Tuition at a community college comes to about $300 per course.

STRENGTHS. Employees would learn programming languages and hands-on techniques for business applications. They would not miss time from work.

WEAKNESSES. Courses would not be tailored to their (or our) needs. Tuition would be expensive.

3. IN-HOUSE TRAINING. Trainers would come to the company, conduct a three-hour seminar during a workday, and then work with small groups of people with similar needs.

STRENGTH. This approach would ensure that our employees learn what they need to learn.

(continued on next page)

```
        WEAKNESSES. This method would take up the most
        company time and could cost as much as $3,000.
                        CONCLUSIONS
        Despite its cost, the in-house seminars are the
        best option for this company. Within two weeks, our
        employees and managers would be substantially more
        productive and would have acquired skills they can
        use and develop while doing their jobs.

        Despite the initial cost and loss of work time,
        this company would benefit most from in-house
        computer training.
```

and access a lot of information, you may want to buy a database management system or file management system specifically suited to your needs. However you set up your system, you can begin to categorize and type in information as you write, think, and read.

Taking Notes

Learning to take notes on your word processor as you read may prove a difficult art to master, but it can be a profitable component of active reading and research. For instance, if you are reading a book that you may refer to in a report, you can type the bibliographic details. You will not need to retype that information when you write the bibliography for your report; simply copy the information onto the file containing your report.

Similarly, you can type in notes as you read. If you like working with index cards, you can print out your notes later on and cut them into note-card sizes.

Make sure you do not use other people's words or ideas without giving them credit.

When you do any type of research, of course, you must be careful about plagiarism—using someone else's words or ideas without giving the person credit for them. (For information about documenting your sources, see Chapter 16.) As you do your research, make sure you keep track of where you came across major ideas as well as key phrases and quotations.

Making a Plan

If you have taken notes on your computer, you need to organize them into coherent sections. You may find it useful to print out all your notes and look through them before organizing them into categories.

You also want to make an outline or plan at this point. Some programs, such as ThinkTank, have been created to help writers create outlines. ThinkTank helps you evolve a list of ideas into numbered and structured sections. Other programs are geared to help you outline specific types of projects.

You will probably not find these types of programs as helpful as formats that you design for your own needs. For example, if you frequently write similar letters for ordering materials, you should develop a format and even some basic wording that you can modify for each letter.

Companies like USA Consulting, the small business that appears at the opening of this chapter, usually develop formats for the proposals they send out. Whole chunks of text can be modified and reused for each proposal. Descriptions of company staff, equipment, and experience, for example, will change only slightly for each proposal. Budgets can be formatted so that only the figures have to be inserted for each project.

Drafting

Your computer can really transform the drafting process. In the past, you may have been reluctant to write your first draft quickly. Maybe you were afraid to create so much material that you would probably never use or would have to revise drastically. Maybe you were discouraged by how messy your drafts became. As a result, you wrote the first draft painfully, slowly, revising each sentence as you wrote it. After hours of work, you had only a few paragraphs or even sentences to show for your labors.

Your computer can liberate you from the frustrations of drafting. Just let yourself go. Type as quickly as you can. Later on you will be able to move sentences, correct spelling, add and delete material.

To keep yourself from revising at this point, comment on your draft as you go along. Comments like [this sounds awkward] or [check references] can be put in parentheses or brackets to jog your memory later on. Some programs allow you to add notes to yourself that will not appear when you print out the text.

Revising

Revision is the word processor's most important function. Here you really get the most out of the program's features for adding, deleting, moving, searching and replacing, and formatting. Be daring. Experiment.

You can write notes to yourself on a computer just as you do when using pen and paper.

No matter how experienced you become revising on the screen, you will still want to check the hard copy periodically. As you revise, print out different versions and number them. You may want to use something that you have deleted or to try different organizational patterns. If you are going to delete something important, write the material onto a separate file so you can retrieve it later if necessary.

Style checkers such as Word Plus and Writer's Workbench may prove useful as you revise for style and readability, but you will have to rely primarily on your own skills as you turn confusing, disorganized, overly complex, or monotonous drafts into effective business documents.

Proofreading

After looking at a document through all these stages, you will probably find it quite difficult to notice typing errors. (Also, because the copy *looks* so tidy when it has been written on a word processor, you may be lulled into thinking you have not made any errors.)

Spelling programs are a great help in the final stage of your writing process. Some of them are slow, especially if they must scan a long document, but they will bring any words to your attention that do not appear in their dictionaries. These programs, however, cannot catch all your errors. If you write *their* when you meant *there,* the program will not catch the error since *their* does appear in its dictionary.

Proofreading should be done both on the screen and on hard copy. Plan on printing out one more draft before you get to the final draft. You will be able to make formatting changes at this point, perhaps changing the document from double-spaced to single-spaced or reducing the wide margins that you used throughout the writing process.

The visual aspect of any business document is important, so experiment with centering headings, justifying right-hand margins, underlining, indenting, and using boldface and various print styles.

Too many enhancements, however, can actually detract from readability. Review your documents after printing them out. Are so many words underlined that none really stands out? Have you combined underlining and boldface so that the page looks cluttered? Have you added so many headings that the reader will have trouble following the flow of your ideas?

Recognizing the Disadvantages of Word Processing

So, what are the disadvantages to writing with a computer? There are a few, but they are easily outweighed by the advantages.

You Have to Invest in the Equipment

Computers are expensive, but they are getting less expensive *and* more flexible and easy to use every year. The company described in the case at the opening of this chapter has allocated its funds poorly: a word processor should have been one of its first investments.

As a student, you probably have access to word processing equipment on your campus. Take advantage of it! Most college computer laboratories are staffed by people who are happy to show you how to get started.

You Have No Keyboarding Experience

You have resisted typing classes for years, and now you just do not have time to learn. This reasoning is as poor as USA Consulting's allocation of funds.

No computer program can thoroughly edit a document.

A word processor can help make your documents visually attractive and readable.

Now is the time to learn keyboarding skills.

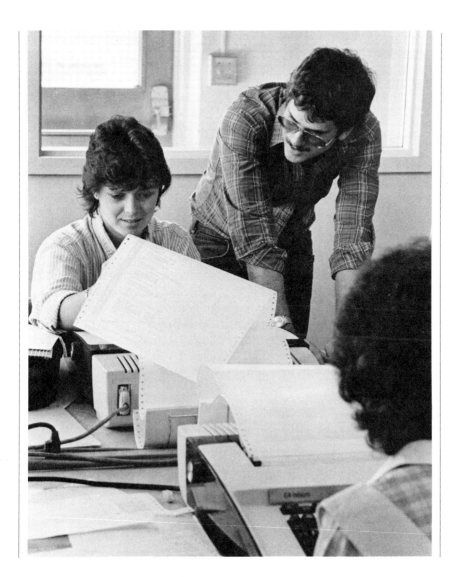

What Would You Do?

A friend of yours is planning to take a script-writing course that requires each student to write and revise a 30-page play or movie script. Your friend knows how to type and has always worked on an electric typewriter, but now might be a good time for him to learn word processing. He writes to you for advice.

He has three weeks before the class begins. Should he learn a word processing program? If so, which one? He does not have the money to buy the equipment. Can he work at a computer terminal on campus?

Write a letter to your friend advising him either to stay with his typewriter for now *or* to change to word processing. Back up your advice with solid reasons one way or the other.

If you are hiring typists and cajoling your friends to type for you, you are wasting time and money. Even if you use a hunt-and-peck typing technique, you will produce pages more quickly and easily on a computer than if you write by hand.

Typing Is Clerical Work

If you think you will always have a secretary to type for you, remember the situation at USA Consulting. Many executives are learning that using a keyboard is profitable and even enjoyable, not tedious "secretary's work."

You Hate Writing on a Screen

Using a computer does eliminate that tactile thrill of writing on a brand-new pad of paper. However, writers who initially feel their computer screen is cold and impersonal usually come to feel more comfortable with it than they did with their pads of paper or their trusty Remington typewriters. Writing on a computer is so easy, so much like talking, that most writers quickly develop a rapport with their machines. And, of course, you can always print out a file to see how the document looks on paper.

You Cannot See an Entire Document on the Screen

Never lose sight of the document as a whole.

Most computer screens show less than one full page of text. Thus, you have to scroll through a file to see most documents in their entirety. This limitation can make it hard to spot large-scale problems—problems that require moving sections of text or adding transitional material. Some writers find that they concentrate on sentence-level editing, fixing wordiness or awkward phrasing rather than reorganizing a whole document.

To get a good sense of an entire document, print it out every once in a while to look at it. You can even print out several versions and compare them. Then, when you do see an organizational problem, you can easily move, add, and delete blocks of text.

You Are Afraid of Losing Material

Back-ups can help save you from computer disasters.

Yes, computers can break down. Some programs have "bugs" in them. Electrical problems can cause you to lose data. Disks can become damaged. However, computers and their software are becoming more reliable all the time. If you save your data periodically, make backup copies, keep backup floppy disks in safe spots, and take good care of your disks and equipment, your material is quite safe.

Summary

Word processing has so many advantages for writers that systems now appear in almost every office and in millions of homes as well. Although a computer cannot write business documents for you, it can simplify and streamline every phase of the writing process. If you take the time to become familiar with different types of equipment and to experiment with different word processing programs, your efforts will be well rewarded.

Summary Discussion: Charlie Grainger's Typing Task from Case in Point, p. 120

As a typist who needs to create professional-looking documents under severe time constraints, Charlie desperately needs a word processor. He would no longer have to retype entire pages with only small errors on them, and he could reuse material from similar documents without having to type it again.

The USA Consulting staff could use computers of their own for brainstorming and the other phases of the writing process. They could store data and use it again for other projects. If they used computers that could communicate with each other, staff writers could also exchange ideas and data without leaving their terminals.

Word Processing Checklist

Word Processing Capabilities

- When using a word processor, you can

  _____ easily make changes in the text of documents without retyping correct material

  _____ experiment with different organizational approaches and word choices

  _____ use enhancements to make documents attractive and easy to read

  _____ print additional copies of documents

  _____ communicate with people using other computers

- With most word processing programs, you can

  _____ move quickly to any point in your text

  _____ move quickly to different points on your screen

  _____ insert, move, and delete characters, words, lines, and blocks of text

  _____ search for and change specified words or characters throughout a text

  _____ adjust margins and spacing

  _____ number pages

  _____ enhance text with boldface, underlining, and capitalization

  _____ create subscripts and superscripts

Additional Software

- To supplement word processing programs, you can also use programs to

  _____ check your spelling

  _____ give you access to a thesaurus

  _____ create graphics

_____ help with outlining

_____ assist with style and grammar

_____ generate mass mailings

Questions for Review and Discussion

1. For what purposes have you used computers before now? How are they going to be of help to you in your career?
2. If you currently use a word processor, what steps of the writing process do you use it for?
3. If you have worked for a company in which employees use word processors, describe whether the machines are used effectively. Could the company develop a process to make the creation of business documents even more efficient?

Exercises

1. Report orally to your class on the word processing equipment, programs, and types of assistance available to students on your campus.
2. Check your library to find out what on-line database facilities could be useful to business writers or students.
3. Interview a salesperson in a computer store to find out what word processing program would be the most useful for the type of writing you do now or will be doing. Then write a report summarizing your findings.

   You might ask the salesperson questions like these:

   - How much does the program cost?
   - Is it compatible with other equipment?
   - How easy is it to add and delete material?
   - How easy is it to mark and move blocks of text?
   - How easy is it to adjust pagination, margins, and spacing?
   - Does the program allow you to see on screen exactly what will be printed on the page?
   - Does the program allow for subscripts and superscripts?

   - What type of text enhancements such as boldface and underlining can be done with the program?
   - How easy is it to use tabs for creating tables?
   - Does the program have a windowing feature?
   - Does the program allow you to replace material you have deleted by accident?
   - Is there a built-in spell checker program?
   - Is there a built-in mail merge program?

4. If you currently use a word processor, interview someone who works on a word processing program other than the one you use. Compare the two programs, listing the strengths and weaknesses of both. You may want to use the questions in Exercise 3 as guidelines for your comparison. Write a report on your findings.
5. If you currently use a word processor, write a paragraph or two describing how it has altered your writing habits, writing style, and the process by which you create, organize, and revise documents.
6. Interview someone who does not use a computer for writing. Find out why the person does not use it. Then write two or three para-

graphs responding to the person's reasons and persuading him or her to experiment with a word processing program.

7. Write a short report on two or three ways in which businesses will be using computers in the coming decade. You may want to read current computer magazines and journals or talk to programmers interested in business applications for computers.

Word Processing Exercises: Learning Basic Commands

Because knowing the basics of word processing is important for everyone in business, word processing exercises are included in this text after every chapter related to business writing. By doing the following exercise, you will become familiar with basic operations for writing, revising, and saving text.

1. To begin, you will have to learn how to start your computer. Read the manual carefully before inserting disks. You should learn how to handle and care for your disks as well as how to format blank disks for your computer. You manual will tell you how to start up your word processing program.

2. Enter the command to get into your word processing program. You will be presented with a *menu* of options, a list of commands to enable you to perform different functions. Press the command that will enable you to *edit* a document. You will be asked to name the file that you wish to edit. Type in LIST for the name of the file and press the return key. You will have a new file, called LIST, to begin writing and revising.

3. You can now begin typing very much as you would on a typewriter. The *cursor,* a blinking line or square on your keyboard, tells you where the characters will appear on the screen when you begin typing. You may use arrow keys to move the cursor to different parts of the screen.

4. Your first exercise is designed to help you learn the basic commands you will need to use your word processing program. That is, you will learn what keys to press to perform different processes. For example, in the WordStar word processing program, you simultaneously press the CONTROL key and the letter *g* if you want to delete the letter under the cursor. Rather than typing the word *control,* you may use the $^\wedge$ mark on your keyboard:

To delete a character $^\wedge$ g

Using your computer manual as a reference, you will create a list of commands that you can refer to until you know your program thoroughly. You may even want to tape the printed list beside your keyboard for easy reference and update it as you learn more commands.

5. Begin by giving your list a heading, LIST OF COMMANDS. Then start the list, putting one command on each line. Press the RETURN key to move to the next line. Your list should contain the commands for at least the following basic functions, but add any others that you want to learn right away:

Function	Command
Edit a file	
Insert a character	
Delete a character	
Delete a word	
Delete a line	
Move to the next word	
Move to the previous word	
Move to the beginning of the line	
Move to the top of the screen	
Move to the beginning of the file	
Move to the end of the file	
Move to the beginning of a line	
Save a file	
Exit from file	
Print a file	

6. As you prepare this list, practice the commands you are learning: try deleting words, moving back and forth along the lines, moving to the beginning and end of the file, and fixing typographical errors.

7. When you have completed a useful list, SAVE the file and EXIT from the file. Look at the names of the files now on your disk directory. The file LIST should be there. Many programs automatically create a backup file: if your program does this, the filename LIST.BAK will also appear on your screen.

8. Now you will have to learn how to turn on your printer and adjust the paper. Then give the command for printing the file LIST that you just created.

9. When you see the "hard copy" of your file, you may find that you would like to make some changes. You can go back into the file and add, delete, and change as much as you want. Then print the file again.

As you begin doing more complicated functions on your computer, you may want to expand your list of commands. You can always go back to your LIST file and add more items to the list.

10. When you are finished using the computer, check the manual for the procedures for turning off the equipment.

Note: As you work on the word processing exercises in this text, you will be asked to create files such as LIST. Keep one copy of these files for exercises later on.

Glossary of Word Processing Terms

Application software: programs that help users do specific tasks such as word processing and graphics

Bit: an abbreviation for *binary digit,* this is a basic unit of computer machine code. Usually eight bits make up one *byte.*

Block: a unit of text in a word processing program that is marked so it may be moved or deleted

Block move: an editing technique that enables users to move a section of text to another place in a file or to another file

Buffer: a temporary computer storage space. Useful for holding sections of text that will later be inserted in a draft.

Byte: a tiny, computer-readable unit. Represents one character—a letter, symbol, number, or space. The internal memory of a computer is measured in bytes.

Central processing unit (CPU): the part of the computer that controls and performs instructions

Command: a signal that tells a computer what operation to perform. In some programs, for example, striking the CONTROL key and the X key simultaneously is a command to leave the program.

Computer assisted instruction (CAI): programs that help users to learn material, usually by presenting a question-and-answer format that requires feedback from the user

Computer memory: the device that holds information in the computer. A computer's power is determined in part by its memory, which is often measured in bytes. Different programs require different amounts of memory.

Configure: adjusting software so it meets the requirements of the hardware on which it is run

Cursor: a blinking light on the video display screen that shows where characters will appear when they are typed in

Cursor control key: also called an *arrow key*, it moves the cursor up, down, or sideways on the screen

Database: a collection of information entered into the computer in an organized format. A program can be used to add, delete, sort, merge, and update data.

Dedicated word processor: a computer set up to be used only for word processing

Default setting: command automatically given to a computer by a program because it is used frequently. For example, standard margins are usually given default settings in word processing programs. Users can choose to change these settings.

Directory: a list of files on a diskette or hard disk

Disk drive: a device that holds a diskette and transfers information between the diskette and the computer. Most computers have one or two disk drives.

Diskette: also called a *floppy disk*. A flat, thin object coated with magnetically sensitive material that is inserted into a disk drive. A diskette is used to store information and transfer it to a computer.

Dot matrix printer: uses dots to create letters, numbers, symbols, and designs. The quality of print is not as good as that of a letter-quality printer.

Error message: tells users that the computer cannot carry out an instruction. For example, an error message may appear when a diskette has become too full to hold more data.

Filename: the name you give a file when you create it to type in a document. To access the file again, you must use this exact name.

Font: a type style such as Times Roman

Format: a computer function that prepares a disk to receive data

Formatting: the process by which computer-created text is prepared to be printed on paper

Function key: often on the left-hand side of a personal computer keyboard, function keys enable users to perform operations with a minumum of commands. For example, one function key may be used to set a new left-hand margin.

Hard copy: the printed version of a document

Hard disk: a storage device capable of storing large quantities of information. More expensive than diskettes, hard disks hold more information.

Hardware: the physical components of the computer system such as printers, motors, and integrated circuitry

Justification: alignment of text that produces straight right and left margins

Keyboard: the device that allows a user to put information into the computer. Most computer keyboards are similar to those of a typewriter but have keys such as function and cursor control keys as well as the standard typewriter keys.

Laser printer: a high-quality printer that produces a quality of print rivaling that of professional publishers

Letter-quality printer: a printer that produces clear type similar to that of a high-quality electric typewriter

Mail merging: an accessory to word processing programs that facilitates the production of personalized form letters

Mainframe: a large computer that may support many users simultaneously

Menu: a list of commands that allows users to choose the part of a program they want. In some programs, for example, users choose to edit a document in a word processing program by typing the command E.

Microcomputer: a complete computer system to be used by one person at a time. Microcomputers are less powerful than minicomputers.

Minicomputers: a computer that can support more than one user at a time. Typically, minicomputers support fewer users at a time than do mainframes.

Modem: a device that allows computer signals to be transmitted by telephone

Monitor: a cathode ray tube (CRT) that looks like a television screen and displays data input

Network: connection of two or more computers that enables users to transmit data across systems

Operating system: program that controls operations of the computer

Peripheral: machine that operates with the computer but is not part of the main computer. Modems and printers are peripherals.

Program: a set of instructions for carrying out specific tasks. Programs may be referred to as *software*.

RAM: random access memory in a computer saves input as the user works. RAM is temporary memory.

ROM: read-only memory operates the computer system

SAVE command: command that instructs computer to put information on a permanent storage medium such as a diskette

Scrolling: moving backward or forward through the text as though it were on a scroll

SEARCH command: an operation that allows a user to find a certain string of letters or numbers in a text

SEARCH AND REPLACE command: an operation that replaces one string of letters or numbers in a text with another string. For example, a user may choose to replace the word *men* with the word *people* throughout a document.

Software: computer programs that can be used to carry out a variety of activities such as word processing or accounting

Template: a program that provides formats for documents such as letters. Mail merge programs are templates.

Terminal: computer hardware consisting of a keyboard, video display screen, and computer operating system

Timesharing: use of a single computer system by more than one user

User: a person using a computer

Windowing: feature that allows users to split a screen into two or more sections and to view data from different files, from different sections of a file, or from different programs

Word processing program: a program designed primarily to allow users to write, edit, format, and print texts

Word wrapping: a feature of word processing programs that moves text automatically to the beginning of the next line

2-1. Germaine Jones is the assistant to the president of a small nonprofit organization that coordinates theater programs in upstate New York. Much of the work done by the organization involves fundraising activities: getting people in various communities to support theater by contributing money and attending performances.

The organization has two IBM-compatible personal computers hooked up to dot matrix printers. These printers are easy to use, reliable, and fast. However, the quality of the print is not as good as that of a high-quality electric typewriter. The mailings the organization sends to prospective patrons are crucial to its success, but Germaine believes the relatively poor appearance of the documents has a bad effect on the organization's image—and its fundraising efforts.

Germaine wants to write a memo to the president of the organization and the board of directors to convince them to invest in a laser printer. Her readers are educated, but they are conservative about expenditures and have little knowledge of computers and word processing. Most of them are wealthy patrons of the arts.

a. Using a word processor or paper and pen, brainstorm some ideas for Germaine to include in her memo. Then define her goals and audience as thoroughly as you can.

b. Research the cost of a laser printer as well as some of its capabilities and advantages. (Choose a brand that could be used easily with IBM-compatible equipment.) Compile a list of costs and benefits that Germaine could include in her memo.

c. Develop a plan or outline of major points Germaine should cover in the memo. Include as much detail as you can.

2-2. Joshua Parker is in charge of setting up offices for the six consultants in MACRODATE Corporation. The consultants come from fields as varied as engineering, biology, and city planning; however, their tasks are essentially similar: each will spend up to twenty hours a week writing proposals and reports. They will often be working together on projects as well as writing independently.

a. In a paragraph or two, describe a good working situation for these business writers. For example,

you might consider spatial arrangements: should each consultant be in a separate office, should there simply be room dividers between desks, or should all the desks be together in a large, open office? What type of lighting would be best? What atmosphere would be most conducive to productive writing?

b. Having done some research on available equipment, write a paragraph or two convincing Joshua to choose either separate personal computers or a networking system for the consultants. Assume the corporation has sufficient funds to make intelligent equipment purchases, but it does not want to spend more than necessary. Your research should be based on:

• Costs
• Possibilities for updating the equipment later on
• Available software options
• Speed and ease of use for the consultants' purposes

2-3. Assume that you have been put in charge of creating a reference room for the business for which you work—or a business for which you would eventually like to work. The room will contain professional publications as well as items such as company and industry newsletters, annual reports, and copies of reports written by company managers.

a. One major task is to decide which magazines, newspapers, and periodicals would be useful for the people using the reference room. Using your library for assistance, create an *annotated* list of at least ten publications to which the company should subscribe. Each annotation, which should be two or three sentences long, should contain a reason why the subscription would be worthwhile.

b. Through the reference room, the organization will also subscribe to at least one on-line database service. Using a terminal in the reference room, employees can access information from a national service. In a paragraph or two, describe the service you think would be most useful for this organization and why it is the best choice for the company.

2-4. You are in charge of a department that hires new college graduates each year. At the end of twelve months, most of these employees are moved on to other departments and you train yet another group of graduates. After a few years of saying the same things over and over to these trainees, you have decided to write a training manual that will help the new hires with the major skills they must acquire. (For this case, you may choose any type of organization with which you are familiar.)

In their first months with the company, the trainees must learn how to read newspapers, magazines, and other publications to spot articles and information relevant to the organization. (If they worked for an accounting firm, for example, they might note articles about competing accounting firms, investment trends, tax-related legislation, and so on.) Then they write up weekly summaries of the information they have discovered and cite the sources for their data.

a. Write a page or two for the training manual emphasizing reading techniques that will help the new employees cover the material efficiently and thoroughly. Refer specifically to the types of material they will actually be reading.

b. Write a page or two for the manual outlining a process that will help the trainees write clear, thorough, relevant, and concise summaries of their reading. You may want to outline a format for these summaries or provide questions the employees should answer while compiling each summary.

2-5. You are assistant to Reggie Banks, president of the local Heart Association. Reggie likes to draft correspondence himself, but you are in charge of editing it before it is sent out.

This week, Reggie is working on a promotional letter that will be sent to hundreds of well-to-do people who have contributed time or money to the organization in the past. The letter will invite readers to the annual Valentine's Day Ball, the event that traditionally raises many thousands of dollars for the organization. At $100 per person, the event is not cheap: the letter should appeal to the readers' desire for a wonderful evening and make them feel part of the organization as a whole.

When you read Reggie's effort, you see it needs a lot of work. It is wordy, dull, writer-oriented, and impersonal. Revise the letter so it will motivate readers to attend the gala event.

Dear Patron:

We here at the Heart Association would like to take this opportunity to extend a personal invitation to our friends who have supported us in our work throughout the year. We would like to invite you to our annual Valentine's Day Ball.

The annual Valentine's Day Ball, which will take place on Saturday, February 14, provides us with an opportunity to show our appreciation for your personal assistance. The Ball also helps us continue our vital research on heart diseases.

The Ball will be held at the Hyatt Regency and will be a black-tie affair starting at 7 p.m. Dinner, which will be served at 8 p.m., will follow no-host cocktails. Dancing will follow dinner. Music by the Theodore Smith Orchestra will be playing for your listening and dancing pleasure.

A tax-deductible $100-per-person check can be enclosed in the attached envelope. Please return the envelope with your check by February 8.

We look forward to a most enjoyable evening and hope you can join us on the 14th from 7 p.m. until 1 a.m.

Sincerely yours,

Reginald Banks

Reginald Banks
President

Business Letters

Part
Three

Communicating Through Letters

- **Developing external communications**
- **Writing letters when record-keeping is important**
- **Using letters to communicate inexpensively**
- **Representing yourself and your company**
- **Determining costs and benefits of writing letters**
- **Using an appropriate tone: the four *p*'s**
- **Using the writing process**
- **Conveying accurate and concrete information**
- **Using mechanics correctly**

Objectives

To determine when business letters are an appropriate communication channel

To learn guidelines for creating an effective tone

To use the writing process for creating business letters

To use correct formats for business letters

8

Don Nickels's Business Letter

Don Nickels is the founder and manager of an office supply store in Cleveland. His income is derived principally from a steady flow of regular customers, so he feels it is important to keep in touch with them through regular mailings. Recently he put together the following form letter for the customers who had not ordered any supplies in the past eight months. (His secretary typed in each customer's name and address.)

```
            NICKELS OFFICE SUPPLY
               900 Broad Street
              Cleveland, OH 54890


November 17, 19xx

Mrs. Daniel Gobel, Manager
Wilcon Products
6290 Fair Oaks Avenue
Cleveland, OH 54987

Dear Customer:

You haven't ordered any copier or
computer supplies from us in over eight
months, so we are writing to see if we
can be of assistance to you.

We hope that you have not found our
products to be unsatisfactory as we
pride ourselves on offering the best
prices and the best quality in the area.
```

```
As a matter of fact, one major reason
I am writing to you is that we are
currently having an end-of-the-year sale
on copier and computer paper. You can
get all available sizes and colors for
nearly 50% off if you order more
than $50 worth of supplies before
December 10.

A brochure has been enclosed in this
letter. Would you be interested in
having our sales representative call
your office to discuss these products?
Call us and let us know.

                       Sincerely,

                       Don Nickels

                       Don Nickels,
                       Manager
```

Points to Consider

- What are the major weaknesses in this letter?
- Is anything wrong with the opening? With the closing? Describe the problems.
- Is any information missing? What would you add to the letter?
- What would you delete from this letter?
- What is the major message in this letter?
- How does this letter deviate from a standard business letter format?

Developing External Communications

Despite the importance of telephone and electronic communications in today's businesses, letters are used extensively for external communications. Letters flow between a company and customers, vendors, suppliers, government agencies, other companies, and a host of other readers.

Rather than becoming less vital to our high-tech offices, letters are actually gaining importance. The computer has made mass mailings more efficient and more personalized. Increasingly, too, companies need to communicate with huge numbers of people over a wide geographical area: one-to-one contact on the telephone and in person can become impossibly expensive and time-consuming.

Letters are becoming increasingly important to business communication.

Letters are particularly useful when record-keeping and costs are important concerns.

Writing Letters When Record-Keeping Is Important

Letters provide tangible records for oral agreements.

Many businesspeople have learned the disasters that may result from "doing business on a handshake." Any time you want a tangible record of items such as transactions, agreements, and financial terms, they should be recorded in a letter. You will often find it useful to send a letter verifying whatever was decided during a telephone conversation or in a meeting; you should definitely send a letter confirming the terms of any oral agreement. Orders, bills, terms of insurance policies, employment agreements, and any financial transactions should be recorded in a letter or other document.

Using Letters to Communicate Inexpensively

Letters are useful when you want to
- communicate with large numbers of people
- communicate with people far away
- send routine messages

Letters may often be the least expensive way to communicate effectively. Telephone calls or personal meetings may not be efficient, financially feasible, or even possible.

You will want to send letters:

- When you need to communicate the same message to large numbers of people. Computers have helped to combine the cost savings of mass mailings with the personalized touches of individualized letters.
- When you need to communicate with people in distant parts of the country and the world. You can waste both time and money making long-distance telephone calls; often a letter will be simpler and much less expensive. In fact, a letter may also be more effective as the receiver can focus on your message and even reread it without the distractions that can occur during a conversation.
- When you are communicating a routine message that can most efficiently be transmitted in a letter. Orders, bills, subscriptions, insurance claims, and so on can often be handled through standard business documents or preprinted form letters.

Representing Yourself and Your Company

Letters are promotional tools.

Your letters have a dual function: they are a personal message from you, but they also represent your company. A promotional letter from a magazine publisher, for example, may be signed by the company president, but readers see the letter as being from *Time* or *Psychology Today.* Similarly, readers

From the Desk of . . .

CITY OF DALLAS

"I like writing letters. It forces me to bring my thoughts together logically," says Patrick O'Brien, Director, Dallas Public Library System. "I challenge myself to get across my message in less than a page. I hate to read long letters."

O'Brien reads many letters a day: complimentary letters, complaints, surveys, suggestions, inquiries, and sales correspondence. He and his staff respond to each one or pass it along to the proper department. They also initiate formal letters, such as reapplying to the state for accreditation; letters that solicit funds, such as when they needed a video tape projector for the children's center; and letters asking for support for programs, such as the adult literacy program.

O'Brien prefers responding by letter. "A letter is logical. It has a beginning, a middle, and an end. Phone calls are quick and slipshod. You cover a lot over the phone. Then, when you hang up, unless you have a superb memory, it's gone." He also prefers to have people write to him. He takes letters more seriously than phone calls because "when people take the time to sit down and write a letter, something untoward has probably happened." When letters compliment or complain about a department or staff person, O'Brien sends a copy of the letter he received, along with his response, to the party involved.

How does O'Brien deal with complaints? His motto as a public servant is similar to that of business owners: "The customer is always right." He says he is quick to apologize.

O'Brien is adamant about the importance of the impression that a letter gives. "I make pretty quick judgments about what a person is willing to sign his or her name to. If I see a good letter, I say to myself, 'This is an organized person and one who cares.' It shows respect for the person reading it. Remember, a letter is the record a person has of you."

When O'Brien went back to school to get his MBA, he says he was horrified to find 40-year-old students who couldn't "string two sentences together." He feels that "business schools don't pay enough attention to business correspondence."

What does O'Brien notice when he reads a letter?

- Physical presentation. "Original letters shouldn't be penciled over or whited out."
- How ideas are phrased.
- Whether the person gets right to the point.
- Whether the letter is succinct or padded with meaningless phrases.
- Whether the thoughts are organized.

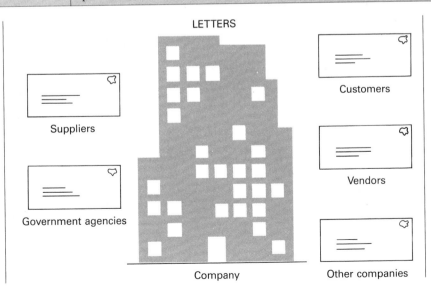

	Strengths	**Weaknesses**
Business Letters	• Message can be saved	• Feedback is delayed
	• Message can reach many people inexpensively	• Message may seem impersonal
Telephone Calls	• Feedback is immediate	• Message cannot be saved easily
	• Message is personal	• May be expensive

will automatically associate characteristics of your letters with your company: inaccuracy, mechanical errors, or a poor tone will affect their view of the company itself. A well-written, personal letter, on the other hand, can make a reader a lifetime supporter of an organization. A good business letter is good promotion for a company.

Determining Costs and Benefits of Writing Letters

A well-written letter will ultimately cost less than a poorly written one.

Business letters may be more efficient and less expensive than some other means of communication, but they are not cheap. Sending out one business letter may cost a company over $10—including the writer's time, typist's time, stationery, and postage. With the number of letters flowing from most companies every day, business correspondence becomes a sizable expense.

A poorly written letter, moreover, will cost even more than an effective letter. Not only can a poor business letter lead to further costly correspondence, but it can cost the company a client or customer's goodwill. In the long run, it pays to send out high-quality business correspondence.

Using an Appropriate Tone: the Four *P*'s

A business letter, in some ways, is like a conversation: usually it is a brief, personal communication. Business writers, however, often lose sight of the interpersonal communication elements fundamental to business letters. Check to see that your letters are personal, positive, polite, and professional.

Send Letters to
• communicate the same message to a large number of people: mass mailings
• communicate with people in distant parts of the country and the world
• communicate a routine message in a form letter: orders, bills, subscriptions, insurance claims, and so forth

The Four P*'s of Business Letters*
✓ Is it personal?
✓ Is it positive?
✓ Is it polite?
✓ Is it professional?

Be Personal

Remember you are addressing a human being, not a piece of paper. Use personal pronouns (*I* and *we* and *you*) and active verbs. Avoid the pompous language discussed in Chapter 6.

Be Professional

Specialists in any field may find themselves assuming a superior tone that will irritate, not impress, their readers. If you must use technical or unusual terms in your letter, for instance, go ahead and define them. Just avoid adding comments that could sound condescending. Treat your reader as an equal.

Never talk down to your readers.

> Not being an economist, Mrs. Watson, you may never have heard the term *return on investment*. The concept, however, is simple enough for any layperson to understand. [condescending]

> For our purposes here, let's define *return on investment* in this way . . . [professional tone]

Even if you have to write unpleasant messages such as collection letters and letters of resignation, keep your tone professional. Your business letter should not be an escape valve for your emotions; it should convey a message.

No matter how upsetting the circumstances, avoid losing your temper. Anger is not often an effective persuasive tactic. You may convey your dissatisfaction or the urgency of a situation, but remember again that you are representing your company as well as yourself. Your tone can be urgent without breaching your professionalism.

Be Polite

Getting your message across is a prime concern, but your reader's reaction to the message is equally important. When you delete unnecessary words, remember to leave in some courtesy words. Including *please* and *thank you* will not interfere with a concise, clear presentation. Even form letters can be polite.

> Respond by March 14. [abrupt]
> We would appreciate your response by March 14. [courteous]
> Please respond by March 14. [courteous]

Be Positive

> The glass is half-empty.
> The glass is half-full.

These two sentences describe identical situations, but they convey quite different images to a reader. A simple turn of phrase can radically alter your letter's effect on a reader. Whenever possible, phrase your sentences from a positive veiwpoint.

> Your order cannot be delivered without your signed authorization. [negative]
>
> With your signed authorization, we can deliver your order immediately. [positive]

Using the Writing Process

Use the writing process even for what seems to be simple correspondence.

The steps of the writing process will help you create well-organized, effective business letters. You will undoubtedly adapt the steps to your needs, going back to do more research after you have made a draft or revising after you have done some proofreading. You may also find that you can streamline the process as you gain experience. Adapt the process to your needs, but use the steps to direct and focus your work.

In Figure 8-1, for example, the writer loses sight of the information the reader needs the most—the list of items being ordered. With some thought about his own goals and his reader's needs, the writer could have made a simple plan and revised the letter to make it clearer and more effective. (Figure 8-2 shows a revision of the letter.)

Brainstorming	Making a plan
Defining your goals and	Drafting
your audience	Revising
Doing necessary research	Proofreading

```
                    DARIEN ENGINEERING
                    2099 BAYLOR AVENUE
                    BELLVIEW, OH 56980

  June 12, 19xx

  Mr. Don Nickels
  Nickels Office Supply
  900 Broad Street
  Cleveland, OH 54890

  Dear Mr. Nickels:

  We are going to hire two more staff members soon,
  so we are going to be renting two more offices. If
  you have any catalogs or brochures on the office
  furniture you carry, I'd appreciate your sending
  them to us. This month we need to order three dozen
  boxes of your fine-point black Pilot pens. We also
  need a dozen boxes of white computer paper. I am
  returning the electric stapler we ordered last
  month. It seems to jam when stapling more than
  three pages at once. Please credit our account with
  the $34.57.
  We also need four dozen boxes of Post-It Notes
  (small size).


  Thanks for your help.

  Sincerely,

  Glenn Brown

  Glenn Brown
  Manager
```

FIGURE 8-1

Disorganized Letter. This letter's poor organization makes the reader work too hard. Glenn has put unrelated elements in his first paragraph. He has also opened the letter with material that detracts from his major focus—the items he is ordering.

Can You Identify the Parts of a Business Letter?

Match these samples from a business letter with their correct names.

1. Dear Evelyn Miller:
2. Sincerely,
3. cc Dean Forbes
4. POLICY 202-34-67123
5. HB:rn

a. Reference initials
b. Salutation
c. Complimentary close
d. Copy notation
e. Subject line

Answers: 1b, 2c, 3d, 4e, 5a
For more information on the parts and formats of business letters, see Appendix B, Business Letter Parts and Formats.

Conveying Accurate and Concrete Information

Figure 8-2 illustrates yet another important aspect of a good business letter: accurate and concrete information. If you have ever received a letter that is missing a vital piece of information, you know how frustrating the experience can be.

When brainstorming and defining your goals, jot down the questions your readers will have and make sure you answer them. What date? What time? Where? Who? How much? How many? Why? Compare

Try out our summer sportswear at great sale prices.

with

Try out our summer sportswear—at half price!

- Women's tennis shoes $9.99
- Men's running shorts $5.98
- ALL T-shirts $1.99

Avoid letting time constraints affect the accuracy of your details.

Make sure, too, that all your information is accurate. (Quoting the *wrong* sale price could be disastrous!) It will be well worth your while to double-check all your facts before your letter goes in the mail.

Using Mechanics Correctly

Typos reflect badly on the company as well as on the writer.

We have already emphasized the importance of good grammar, spelling, and punctuation in any business document. In external communications, these assume great importance because, again, a letter is a reflection of a company. Typographical errors or grammatical problems make the organization as well as the writer appear sloppy, uncaring, or inept.

```
                    DARIEN ENGINEERING
                    2099 BAYLOR AVENUE
                    BELLVIEW, OH 56980

         June 12, 19xx

         Mr. Don Nickels
         Nickels Office Supply
         900 Broad Street
         Cleveland, OH 54890

         Dear Mr. Nickels:

         Please send me the following items:
             1. 36 boxes of fine-point black Pilot pens
             2. 12 boxes of white computer paper
             3. 48 boxes of Post-It Notes (small size)

         I am returning the electric stapler we ordered
         from you last month as it tends to jam. You should
         receive the package this week. Please credit our
         account with $34.57.

         If you have a catalog or other information on the
         office furniture you carry, I would appreciate your
         sending it to us.

         Thanks for your help.

         Sincerely,

         Glenn Brown

         Glenn Brown
         Manager
```

FIGURE 8-2

Organized Letter. In this revision, the order is in list form at the opening. Separate items are in separate paragraphs following the order. The letter moves from the most important to the least important information.

In the final stages of the writing process, use the handbook at the end of this text for problems you encounter with grammar and punctuation. Guidelines in Appendix B will also help you correctly format business letters.

To avert errors, you may find these three suggestions helpful:

1. Know the rules. The best way to avoid errors is to have a good grasp of the conventions of grammar, punctuation, and mechanics.
2. Try not to send off letters in a hurry. Letters sent in haste (to alter a familiar phrase) may be repented at leisure. Leaving time for revision will lead to a more effective and error-free letter.

3. Have a second person proofread any important documents. You probably know how hard it is to spot your own errors; a second set of eyes can catch typographical errors and other problems that the writer or typist has missed.

What Would You Do?

As assistant to a new department manager, you are in charge of editing the correspondence she writes to customers. Your first assignment is the following letter:

```
                         DUBOIS GLASSWARE
                         900 Chelsea Court
                         Ryder, NY 12458

August 3, 19xx

Mrs. Arnold Hacker
9821 Kaye Drive
Seaport, NY 12456

SUBJECT: DAMAGED PRODUCT POLICY

I am sorry to inform you that we cannot offer a warranty on
any glassware product after it has been delivered to your
home. Glassware is easily broken. We cannot be responsible
for breakage after we have delivered it.

PATRICIA WEINSTOCK
MANAGER
CUSTOMER SERVICE DEPARTMENT
```

You believe the format as well as the content of the letter would benefit from revision. Revise the letter. Check Appendix B for information on business letter formats.

Summary

Business letters are a primary form of external communication for most businesses. Because letters reflect the image of a company and because they are expensive to create and send out, they should be developed carefully. Attention to appearance and format as well as to content, grammar, and punctuation is essential.

As you draft and revise business letters, remember that you are communicating with *people,* readers who should be able to understand your letters easily and who you hope will respond positively to your messages.

Business Letter Checklist

Communication Channel

- Choose a business letter as your communication channel if at least one of the following criteria is applicable:

  _____ You want a written record of a message, transaction, or agreement.

  _____ You need to communicate basically the same message to large numbers of people outside your company.

  _____ You need to communicate with people in distant parts of the country or the world.

  _____ You are communicating a routine message that can be efficiently transmitted in a preprinted form letter.

Effective Letters

- To write effective business letters,

  _____ remember that letters represent your company or organization as well as yourself

  _____ check to see that the tone of your business letter is personal, positive, polite, and professional

  _____ review your business letters for accuracy and concreteness as well as for correct grammar, punctuation, and mechanics

  _____ correctly use the parts of a business letter and the different business letter formats

Term to Remember

Business letter: document used primarily for external communication

Summary Discussion: Don Nickels's Business Letter from Case in Point, p. 151

Don Nickels's letter has problems with tone, content, and format. The tone is predominantly negative. He hopes the reader has *not* found his products *unsatisfactory;* he should hope the reader *has* found them *satisfactory.* Similarly, he gets his letter off to a poor start by mentioning that the reader has not ordered anything from him in a long time.

Don did not really understand that he was writing a sales letter: his letter sounds more like a complaint. When revising his draft, he should have eliminated everything unrelated to his special offer and added more concrete details about the offer. Moreover, at the end of the letter, he could simply have told the reader that a sales representative would call.

His letter, also, deviates from a standard format: he uses a full-block style until he gets to the complimentary close and signature. Also, he follows his typewritten name with a comma even though his title is on the following line. These departures from the norm are small, but Don's readers, used to standard formats, may view the letter (and thus the business it represents) as unprofessional.

Questions for Review and Discussion

1. How has the increased use of computers made significant changes in business letters?
2. Why might correct writing mechanics and format be more important in an external communication than in an interoffice memo?
3. Losing your temper in a letter can have a disastrous effect on your relationship with the reader. Describe a situation from your experience in which an angry letter led to problems.
4. What are two good reasons for having a second person read your business letters before they are sent?
5. Why do you think the appearance of business letters is so formalized? Would it be more efficient simply to get the message across and forget about aspects of format such as spacing, correct placement of words, and so on? Explain.

Exercises

1. Rewrite Don Nickels's letter in the Case in Point at the opening of this chapter.
2. Revise the following sentences so they are phrased positively.
   a. You will not be able to apply for credit at Webley's until you are 18 years old.
   b. I hope you are not unhappy with this alternative plan.
   c. The report has one error, but it is a fairly small one.
   d. The book is for parents like you whose children are unsuccessful in school.

e. I am too busy to see you on Friday. Is Monday inconvenient for you?`

3. Revise the following sentences so the tone is professional.

   a. The calculator that you told me you were sending in December still isn't here. I would appreciate an update on its "status" before the spring thaw.

   b. If your check isn't here on Monday, I'll be talking to you in small claims court.

   c. If you had bothered to read my last letter, you would see that I ordered *six* boxes, not *five*.

4. You have just concluded a telephone conversation in which Mr. Lowell Dunn suggested that you and he join the resources of your two firms to bid on a federal contract to conduct business communication seminars for small businesses in the Seattle area. He has the capital to set up the seminars, but he lacks the expertise that you and your colleagues have in teaching business communication strategies.

   He mentioned a meeting date two weeks in the future. Write him a letter repeating your interest in his idea and confirming the meeting time and date. Use the full block letter style.

   Address the letter to:

   ```
   Mr. Lowell Dunn, President
   SDR Inc.
   2300 Ridell Road
   Seattle, WA 98567
   ```

5. You have received this memo from your assistant, who handled your telephone calls while you were at lunch.

   > Orion Summers called to say "Congratulations!" She loved your article and will be including it in the June issue of *Business Day*. She just wants to talk with you about a few changes. She will be out of town until the 12th but hopes to set up a meeting with you after that. You might let her know the days you are free to meet with her.

   Write a letter to Orion that confirms her acceptance of your article and suggests a meeting time at the end of the month. Write to:

   ```
   Ms. Orion Summers, Editor
   Business Day Magazine
   900 Bullton Avenue
   Hyattville, CO 98356
   ```

6. You are making arrangements to attend a convention in Chicago with two co-workers. Write a letter to the Hotel Winslow confirming the reservation dates, number of rooms, check-in times, rates, and any other information you discussed on the telephone with the reservation clerk. Use the simplified letter style.

   Write to:

   ```
   Alan Silva, Reservations
   Hotel Winslow
   800 Rogers Boulevard
   Chicago, IL 60645
   ```

7. Revise the following letter so it is more professional and effective. Check the *format* for a business letter as well as the content.

```
Roger Kent
Dormitory A
Tennyson University
Tennyson, NC 34671

Professor Jill Harter
Department of English
Tennyson University
Tennyson, NC 34671

October 14, 19xx

Dear Professor Harter:

    I have telephoned your office several
times but haven't been able to reach you.
I am interested in discussing with you the
reason why I received a C in the Modern
British Authors course you taught during
the summer semester when I received almost
all A's and B's on the papers I handed in.
I also attended almost every class. Did I
bomb on the final exam? I would like to
meet with you in the next week or two to
discuss this issue.
    If you get a chance, call me at Ext.
6732. I will also continue to keep trying
your office. Thanks.

                          Sincerely,

                          Roger Kent

                          Roger Kent
```

8. Revise the following letter so it is more effective.

672 A Street
Madison, OH 34689
March 18, 19xx

Mr. Owen Candless
Trinity Music Camp
Trinity, CA 98674

Dear Mr. Candless:

I have played the guitar for several years and have hopes of getting a graduate degree in music after I finish college. I play in a classical music group at my college (I am a sophomore) and also work as an entertainer in folk music clubs in town. Anyway, I have heard a lot about your wonderful music camp where musicians come to study with famous musicians and perform at colleges in northern California during the summer. Is there a chance that I could be admitted this summer? Please send me any information or application forms you may have. Thanks!

Sincerely,

Ann Rodgers

Ann Rodgers

Word Processing Exercises: Formatting Documents

This exercise will give you some more experience with basic word processing operations and help you learn how to format documents so they look the way you want them to look.

To format documents, you need to know how to

- adjust spacing of lines
- reform a paragraph
- justify right-hand margins
- adjust left- and right-hand margins

Before learning how to perform these formatting procedures, find out whether the word processing program you use shows the text on the screen looking the same way it will look when it is printed on paper. The best programs do this: they show your document double-spaced on the screen, for example, if you choose to have it double-spaced on paper. However, some programs do not show you exactly what will be printed, and you will have to learn what to expect if you are using one of these programs.

1. CREATE a file named BUSCOM.
2. When you are in the file, type out three or four sentences describing the topics covered in your business communication course. Your course might cover memos, letters, reports, and job interviews, for example. Include the title of the course and the major goals of the class.

The first draft of your paragraph may look something like this:

> Business Communication 3200 is a course designed to help studetns learn al the basics of bsuiness writing and oral communication. We spend 60 percent of the course on writting and 40 percent on speaking skills. The goals of the class isto improve students' abilties to write business documents, make speeches, and perform effectively in jod interviews.

3. Now, using commands to INSERT and DELETE words and characters, fix the typos and other errors in your short paragraph. Note that you insert and delete spaces just as you do individual characters. (Some programs allow you to retrieve characters that you have deleted by mistake; this would be a good opportunity to check whether your program has such a function. If not, be careful not to delete items carelessly!)
4. You may have to REFORM your paragraph. That is, while you are editing, some lines may get too long. The REFORM (or ALIGN) command fixes the lines so they are the correct length. Your program may ask you if you wish to hyphenate a word that does not fit easily on one line; if you hyphenate the word, the spacing between words remains more even. However, remember that words may be hyphenated only at syllable breaks.

Your edited paragraph may look like this:

Business Communication 3200 is a course designed to help students learn all the basics of business writing and oral communication. We spend 60 percent of the course on writing and 40 percent on speaking skills. The goal of the class is to improve students' abilities to write business documents, make speeches, and perform effectively in job interviews.

5. Now learn to adjust the spacing of the lines in a document. Most programs automatically single-space documents unless you give instructions to do otherwise. Double- and triple-spacing are useful for drafts of documents as you can easily make notes and changes on the hard copy. Double-spacing is appropriate, too, for many reports and other documents.

   Give the command to double-space your BUSCOM file. Now reform, save, and print out the file. It should look something like this:

   Business Communication 3200 is a course de-

   signed to help students learn all the basics of

   business writing and oral communication. We

   spend 60 percent of the course on writing and

   40 percent on speaking skills. The goal of the

   class is to improve students' abilities to write

   business documents, make speeches, and per-

   form effectively in job interviews.

6. Most word processing programs automatically JUSTIFY the right-hand margin of documents: the right-hand margin is straight, like the left margin. However, you may choose not to have the right-hand margins justified; then they will look much the way they did when you were using a typewriter. A "ragged" right margin eliminates odd spacing between words and the excessive use of hyphenated words.

   Most justification commands are *toggles:* that is, you press them once to turn them on; when you press them again, they go off.

Change the right-hand margins of your BUSCOM document to ragged right. Reform, save, and print the file. The paragraph should look something like this:

Business Communication 3200 is a course

designed to help students learn all the basics

of business writing and oral communication. We

spend 60 percent of the course on writing and

40 percent on speaking skills. The goal of the

class is to improve students' abilities to write

business documents, make speeches, and

perform effectively in job interviews.

7. While learning about margins, learn how to make the right- and left-hand margins narrower and wider. Most programs automatically set up standard margins of about 1 inch; however, you may want to format documents with margins of different widths.

   Assume you would like to increase both margins. Learn the commands and adjust the margins of the BUSCOM document at approximately 2 inches. Reform the document, save it, and print it. It should look like this:

   Business Communication 3200 is a

   course designed to help students learn

   all the basics of business writing and

   oral communication. We spend 60

   percent of the course on writing and 40

   percent on speaking skills. The goal of

   the class is to improve students' abilities

   to write business documents, make

   speeches, and perform effectively in job

   interviews.

Inquiries, Requests, Orders, Letters of Recommendation, and Special Letters

- Developing effective business correspondence
- Writing letters that ask for information
- Writing letters that make requests
- Conveying good news: positive responses to inquiries and requests
- Conveying bad news: negative responses to inquiries and requests
- Avoiding common errors in bad news letters
- Placing and acknowledging orders
- Writing letters of recommendation
- Writing letters of appreciation, congratulation, and condolence

Objectives

To make inquiries and requests that get the results you want

To write responses to inquiries and requests that maintain the reader's goodwill

To place and acknowledge orders accurately and efficiently

To write effective letters of recommendation

To write special letters that are sincere and personal

9

Nancy Taylor's Request

1908 Ridge Avenue
Gillian, MI 56909
February 27, 19XX

Dr. Harvey Olsen
Chair, Department of Geology
Whelan College
Baytown, MI 56903

Dear Dr. Olsen:

We were all so delighted to hear that a former resident of Gillian had received a prestigious prize for work in geology. Your work on discovering the age of ancient rocks must be simply fascinating.

The Cultural Society of Gillian is having a luncheon on Sunday, April 1, and we hope you can attend. We will have lunch in the Historical Museum cafeteria and then watch a short slide show on the museum, which was built in 1880, as you might already know. (There should be about 55 members in attendance.) Then we were hoping that you might give us a few words on your geological research.

Nothing too long—maybe thirty minutes or so—on what you've been doing.

It is important that you let us know by March 15 if you can attend our luncheon. We need enough time to send out the invitations to our members.

I hope we get an affirmative answer:

Sincerely,

Nancy Taylor

Nancy Taylor
Secretary
Cultural Society of Gillian

Points to Consider

- What is the main point of this letter?
- What do you think should be included in the opening paragraph of the letter?
- Is anything missing from the letter? Explain.
- Should anything be deleted? Explain.
- Has the writer used the you-attitude? Explain.

Developing Effective Business Correspondence

Letters concerning inquiries, requests, and orders make up a large percentage of business correspondence. Writing and responding to these letters may take up a significant portion of your working hours.

You can learn to effectively streamline the writing process.

If you often write the same types of letters to the same types of readers, you will find that you can significantly decrease the time you spend on various steps of the writing process. Once you have accurately defined your goals and researched your audience while creating a letter of inquiry, for example, you will not need to spend time on those tasks each time you prepare a similar letter for similar readers.

Also, when you recognize the type of letter you are composing, you will find that the organizational patterns discussed in this chapter will help you plan your letter so it is both useful and tactful. In fact, you may sometimes be able to use *boilerplate* paragraphs—paragraphs that you can incorporate again and again, with minor alterations, into letters with basically the same

Boilerplate material can be reused in different documents.

message. (A word processor is a great help for creating individual letters from boilerplate paragraphs.)

With experience, you can create accurate and readable business correspondence without spending inordinate amounts of time writing and revising. However, do not let time-saving efforts decrease the goodwill you wish to maintain with your readers. Your readers, remember, are the key to your success. As in any communication effort, a routine letter that emphasizes the writer and ignores the reader can lead to poor results.

Occasionally, you will also have to write special letters that require tact and a personal touch. Letters of recommendation, appreciation, congratulation, and condolence are not routine: for these, you will need to pay particular attention to the emotions as well as the needs of your readers.

Writing Letters That Ask for Information

Inquiry letters ask for information. To make sure you receive the information you want, organize your letter carefully. Be as specific as you can and explain why you need the information. Your letter should get to the point quickly and make it easy for the reader to respond. (Compare Figure 9-1 with Figure 9-2.)

Make it easy for your reader to respond to your inquiry.

Enclosing a preaddressed stamped envelope or a postcard for the reader's response will increase your chances of receiving the information you need.

Answer every question your reader may have.

Probably the biggest pitfall for a writer of inquiry letters is vagueness. In Figure 9-1, for example, Bud Allen does not say when he took the instructor's class or even what class it was: the reader may well have no idea what articles were mentioned "several years ago."

Sample Outline for Letters of Inquiry
1. Open with request for information.
2. State reason for inquiry.
3. Ask specific questions in a list format.
4. Thank reader and state date by which the information is needed.

Writing Letters That Make Requests

Requests are often persuasive in nature.

Request letters usually demand more of their readers than inquiries. Not just asking for information, request letters ask for action. When writing a request letter, you are actually trying to persuade the reader to do something. You will want to provide concrete detail that makes your request seem reasonable and end with a clear, action-oriented sentence or paragraph to help the reader see exactly what you want done.

If your request is relatively simple or pleasant for the reader to accomplish, then open the letter with your request. Make sure it is clear and specific (Figure 9-3).

```
                              Zircon Industries
                              2965 J Street
                              Sacramento, CA 95816
                              August 3, 19XX

Dr. Philip Gregory
Department of Management
Paulson College
Bakersfield, CA 96789

Dear Dr. Gregory:

    You may not remember me, but I am a former
student of yours. I took an introductory management
course with you several years ago. Now I am working
for Zircon Industries, a high-tech firm in
Bakersfield.
    I remember when I took your class you mentioned
several times a series of articles that had focused
on managerial problems in computer firms. I have
been asked to compile a bibliography of relevant
materials for trainers to use in our personnel
development seminars, and I thought those articles
could be useful. I would appreciate it if you could
send me the information pertaining to those
articles: I believe you said they were in a major
magazine—was it Business Week? I would also
appreciate the names of any other books or articles
you think would be useful.
    Thanks for your help. I really enjoyed your
class.

                              Sincerely,

                              Bud Allen

                              Bud Allen
```

FIGURE 9-1

Ineffective inquiry. This letter is roundabout and vague. If the writer wants a prompt and helpful response, he should say when he took the reader's class and the date by which he needs the information. He should specify all the information he needs regarding the articles and delete all irrelevant material. To make his inquiry more you-oriented, the writer could also reduce the I-focus in his letter. See Figure 9-2 for a revision of this letter.

```
                                        Zircon Industries
                                        2965 J Street
                                        Sacramento, CA 95816
                                        August 3, 19XX

                    Dr. Phillip Gregory
                    Department of Management
                    Paulson College
                    Bakersfield, CA 96789

                    Dear Dr. Gregory:

                       In the Management 4589 class that you taught
                    during the fall of 1987, you described a series of
                    articles outlining managerial problems in computer
                    firms. You mentioned that they had recently
                    appeared in a national magazine. Could you tell me
                    where and when those articles appeared? I am
                    preparing a bibliography for trainers leading
                    personnel development seminars in our company.
                       If you know of other articles or books that
                    discuss the special management problems of high-
                    tech companies, I would greatly appreciate your
                    listing them for me. My bibliography is scheduled
                    to be completed by September 15.
                       A stamped, addressed envelope is enclosed. Thanks
                    for your help. I really enjoyed your class.

                                        Sincerely,

                                        Bud Allen

                                        Bud Allen
```

Request is clearly stated

Reason for request

Date by which
he needs materials
Appreciation ⟶
Pleasant ending ⟶

FIGURE 9-2 _____

Revised inquiry. In this revised letter, Bud's inquiry is clearer and more concrete. He gives the reader a date by which he needs the information and encloses an envelope for the reader's convenience.

```
                              Carson Corporation
                              666 Alta Avenue
                              Dallas, TX 56902
                              October 23, 19XX

Mr. Blake Sims
Marketing Department
Barrows Corporation
Dallas, TX 56901

Dear Mr. Sims:

    As you may know, Carson Corporation is planning a
convention in January that will bring together
software companies from all over the Southwest. We
would be delighted if you would lead one of the
hour seminars scheduled for January 24.
    The convention, which will focus on developing
and marketing software for industry, will feature
talks and demonstrations from well-known figures in
the academic and business sectors. Since your
recent research on software marketing strategies is
tremendously interesting to our participants, we
know you would have a large, enthusiastic audience.
    We have not yet completed our final timetable,
but the seminar is tentatively set for 3 p.m.
    We are able to offer you a $150 honorarium for
participating in the convention, and we would be
pleased if you and your wife joined us for the
cocktail party and dinner following the day's
activities.
    If you are interested in participating, please
call me at 783-9011, Extension 3567, before
November 15. By then I should have more information
concerning the time, number of participants, and so
on. I very much hope you will be able to join us.

                         Sincerely,

                         Tony Andorra

                         Tony Andorra
                         Special Events Coordinator
```

FIGURE 9-3

Effective request. This letter includes the writer's request in the opening paragraph. As the financial reimbursement is minimal, Tony must appeal to the reader's self-esteem and also his interest in the event. Note the specific information and request for action in the concluding paragraph.

```
Dear Mr. Simmonds:

    I am interested in joining the Connecticut
Historical Society. Please send me a membership
application and the most recent issue of the
society's newsletter.

                              Sincerely,

                              John Gavin

                              John Gavin
```

If your request requires some special effort or cooperation from the reader, use a more tactful approach. In the following letter, Don Irving is too abrupt.

```
Dear Mr. Phillips:

    I want to change Order 3467. I asked for 250
typewriter ribbons, but now I want only 150. Be
sure to adjust the shipment before it goes out.

                              Sincerely,

                              Don Irving

                              Don Irving
```

Don's request, combined with his harsh and authoritative tone, will annoy the reader. Mr. Phillips might not bother cooperating. To get the results he wants, Don should have tried a more friendly approach. An opening "buffer" that establishes a pleasant tone can help to ensure goodwill.

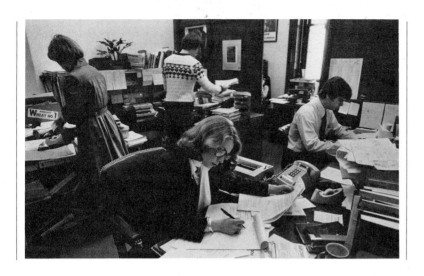

Dear Mr. Phillips:

   I appreciate your help in filling our
clerical supply orders in the past.
   Last week when we typed our order #548,
we incorrectly requested 250 rather than
150 typewriter ribbons.
   If you can correct the order before the
shipment goes out, I would appreciate it
very much. Thank you.

               Sincerely,

               Don Irving

               Don Irving

This letter is more friendly. Reminding the reader that the writer is a return customer gives more weight to the request. (Compare Figure 9-4 with Figure 9-5.)

Sample Outline for a Difficult or Unpleasant Request	*Sample Outline for Pleasant Request*
1. Open pleasantly.	1. State request.
2. Give a reason for the request.	2. Add any information the reader might need.
3. Make the request itself.	3. Thank reader.
4. Thank the reader and end positively.	

```
                                        239 Mountain Road
                                        Carson City, NV 95689
                                        March 19, 19XX

George Monihan
Larrson Appliances
Service Center
3490 Whyler Blvd.
Beatty, NV 98560

Mr. Monihan:

    The Newpoint toaster oven I purchased on December
11 does not get hot anymore. I am sure the three-
month warranty must have a few extra days added to
it for emergencies like these, so I am sending the
oven back to you for servicing under the warranty
agreement.
    The necessary paperwork is in the box with the
toaster.

                                    Sincerely,

                                    Jim Healy

                                    Jim Healy
```

FIGURE 9-4 _____

Ineffective request. Jim Healy is assuming that the reader of this letter will do him a favor: add a few extra days to the warranty. The writer would have a greater chance of success if he _requested_ the special extension. See Figure 9-5 for a revision of this letter.

239 Mountain Road
Carson City, NV 95689
March 19, 19XX

George Monihan
Larrson Appliances
Service Center
3490 Whyler Blvd.
Beatty, NV 98560

Dear Mr. Monihan:

My Hotpoint toaster oven was purchased on December 11, 19XX. Today, eight days after the warranty expired, the toaster seems to have expired as well: it will not get hot. (Yes, it was plugged in.)

As I have been a faithful Larrson customer for many years and as the warranty expired so recently, I thought you might consider extending the warranty provisions to cover this problem. I am sending the oven, with the necessary paperwork, for your attention. If you cannot extend the warranty, please let me know how much repairs will cost.

Thank you very much for considering this situation.

Sincerely,

Jim Healy

Jim Healy

FIGURE 9-5

Revised request. This letter presents the problem fairly. Jim does not *demand* special attention, but he does request it in a friendly way—with reasons for the request.

```
Dear Marjorie:

   Please put together a list of all the people who
have requested promotions in the past year. When I
visit your office on Monday, I'd like to see the
complete list.

                                        Thanks,

                                        Bob

                                        Bob
```

This letter requests that the reader perform what may appear a meaning-less task. If Bob wants cooperation, he should provide a rationale and some guidelines.

```
Dear Marjorie:

   As you may know, I have been preparing a special
personnel report for the board of directors. Last
week, Michael Dolan asked me to add a section that
summarizes statistics on employees of all branches
who have requested promotions in the past eighteen
months.
   I would appreciate it very much if you could
compile the following data for the Citrus City
branch:
   1. The name of each applicant for a promotion
since June of last year.
   2. The position for which each applicant applied.
   3. The decision we reached regarding the
promotion.
   Thanks for your help. I look forward to touring
the branch on Monday!

                                        Sincerely,

                                        Bob

                                        Bob
```

The key, then, to conveying information and insuring cooperation is to be personal, clear, and detailed. Remember that your readers are not your opponents; whether they are your clients or vendors, lenders or borrowers, they are still vital components of your business. If you address them in a spirit of cooperation, they will usually respond in the same spirit.

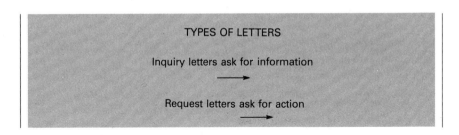

TYPES OF LETTERS

Inquiry letters ask for information

Request letters ask for action

Conveying Good News: Positive Responses to Inquiries and Requests

When you convey good news, get right to the point. A positive reply to an inquiry or request should be direct and well organized. Avoid any implication that you are cooperating grudgingly or unwillingly. (Compare Figure 9-6 with Figure 9-7.)

Get to the point right away when responding positively to requests.

Dear Bud:

   The articles you are interested in appeared in the June, July, and August 1987, issues of *Business Trends*. They were entitled "Managing the High-Tech Company."
   You might also want to look at George Ulrich's *Technocracy Revised*. New York: Paul Publishers, 1987.
   Good luck compiling the bibliography.

                                    Sincerely,

                                    Phillip Gregory

                                    Phillip Gregory

```
                    Barrows Corporation
                 896 Industrial Boulevard
                    Dallas, TX 56901
                                     November 1, 19XX

        Mr. Tony Andorra
        Special Events Coordinator
        Carson Corporation
        666 Alta Avenue
        Dallas, TX 56902

        Dear Mr. Andorra:

           Thank you for your letter of October 23 regarding
        the upcoming convention being coordinated by Carson
        Corporation. I believe the innovative marketing
        campaign recently developed by Barrows could be of
        interest to your participants.
           I will be in Houston until January 23 but would
        be able to lead the seminar on January 24 as you
        requested. Please let me know when the details are
        finalized.

                                     Sincerely,

                                     Blake Sims

                                     Blake Sims
```

FIGURE 9-6

Ineffective reply. In this reply to a request (see Figure 9-3), the writer delays accepting the invitation until the second paragraph. Rather than being enthusiastic, he implies that he has a busy schedule. He does not mention the cocktail party and dinner to which Tony invited him.

```
                    Barrows Corporation
                 896 Industrial Boulevard
                    Dallas, TX 56901

                                   November 1, 19XX

Mr. Tony Andorra
Special Events Coordinator
Carson Corporation
666 Alta Avenue
Dallas, TX 56902

Dear Mr. Andorra:

   I am happy to accept your invitation to lead a
seminar at your convention on January 24. Barrows
has recently launched an innovative marketing
program that I am sure your participants will be
interested in.
   Some of my material is on videotape. I would
appreciate your letting me know if a VCR will be
available for the seminar. Also, please send me the
timetable of convention events when they are
completed.
   My wife Sharon and I will be happy to join you at
the cocktail party and dinner on the evening of
January 24.

                            Sincerely,

                            Blake Sims

                            Blake Sims
```

FIGURE 9-7

Revised positive reply. This reply opens with good news and supplies some specific details
helpful to the reader. Blake also accepts the invitation for that evening.

Conveying Bad News: Negative Responses to Inquiries and Requests

Saying "no" can be difficult. We tend either to emphasize the negative to such an extent that the reader is upset or to hide the message in a confused effort to be polite and friendly.

A refusal letter should be personal, not cold and abrupt.

Dear Mr. Santos:

We cannot offer you the secretarial position for which you applied. Many qualified candidates were reviewed, and we have chosen someone with more technical expertise.

Sincerely,

Foster Harris

Foster Harris

In the preceding letter, Foster Harris was too impersonal. In his revision, however, he obscured his main point:

Dear Mr. Santos:

We were delighted to meet you last week and review your outstanding qualifications for the secretarial position. Your education and professional experience will be a great help to you in your future success. We will be happy to call if we have an opening suited to your excellent abilities and background.

Sincerely,

Foster Harris

Foster Harris

In the preceding letter, Mr. Santos must read between the lines of this letter to see that he is being rejected for the job he wanted. Moreover, when he does understand the message, he may feel cheated: if he is so outstanding, why wasn't he hired?

The most effective refusal letters usually follow a format similar to that of a letter requesting something unpleasant:

- Start with a positive or neutral "buffer."
- Provide reasons for the refusal.
- Make the refusal.
- End with something positive.

(Compare Figures 9-8 and 9-10 with Figure 9-9.)

In general, a reader is most affected by material at the opening or close of a piece of writing; thus, the positive or neutral information acts as buffer to soften the blow of the bad news. Then, if the reader *understands* the decision before reading it, he or she is apt to be less upset.

Positive or neutral information acts as a buffer at the beginning of a letter that may be unpleasant for the reader.

Dear Mr. Santos:

    Both Larry Sawyer and I enjoyed speaking with you on Thursday afternoon. Your qualifications for a secretarial position are certainly very good.
    Because ACI is a computer software firm, we need a staff experienced in the technical materials and language associated with our work. Our clerical staff must be able to interpret computer manuals and use a range of programs.
    Since you have no computer experience at this time, we will not be able to hire you for this position. If you take some introductory computer classes in the near future, however, you might consider re-activating your application.

                 Sincerely,

                 Foster Harris

In this letter, Foster Harris opens with a positive note, but he does not give the reader false hopes. The second paragraph immediately emphasizes what the company needs in a secretary, so the reader is prepared for the refusal in the following paragraph. The ending, moreover, gives him specific information on how he might alter the situation in the future.

```
                                          348 White Road
                                          Providence, RI 10093
                                          April 3, 19XX

Leanne Renwick
President, Home and Garden Society
Washington, D.C. Chapter
2199 45th Street
Washington, D.C. 20014

Dear Mrs. Renwick:

   Thank you so much for inviting me to speak at
your annual awards banquet on June 10. It will be a
memorable occasion.
   However, I am scheduled to lead a series of
seminars at Pembroke College every weekend in June
and will not be able to attend the banquet.
   Thank you again for the invitation. Perhaps we
will see each other at the October meeting.

                                 Sincerely,

                                 Catherine Morris

                                 Catherine Morris
```

FIGURE 9-8

Effective refusal. This letter is personal and polite. Catherine opens with a positive statement, provides a reason for her refusal, and returns to a positive statement at the end.

```
                              Office of the Dean
                              Galway College
                              12 North Park Road
                              Galway, MN 60893
                              July 2, 19XX

Stephen Bernard
7621 Rosefield Street
St. Paul, MN 60459

Dear Mr. Bernard:

    We are sorry to inform you that you will not be
admitted to Galway College this September. We wish
you the best in your decision to return to college.

                         Sincerely,

                         Peter Lacey

                         Peter Lacey
                         Dean of Admissions
```

FIGURE 9-9 _____

Poor refusal letter. This letter is impersonal and does not offer a reason for the rejection. In an effort to maintain goodwill, the writer should develop a form letter that is both friendly and helpful. (See Figure 9-10.)

```
                              Office of the Dean
                              Galway College
                              12 North Park Road
                              Galway, MN 60893
                              July 2, 19XX

Stephen Bernard
7621 Rosefield Street
St. Paul, MN 60459

Dear Mr. Bernard:

    I enjoyed speaking with you in June regarding
your application to Galway College as a re-entry
student.
    As you know, our Admissions Committee has agreed
that our re-entry students must receive a score of
500 or better on our Re-Entry Student Test and
Writing Sample. Since your test score was below
500, we will not be able to admit you for the fall
semester.
    If you would like to take the exam again in
August and apply for winter semester, we will be
happy to reconsider your application. Paula Gold in
the Testing Office (Ext. 324) can send you
information on the test. I enclose a copy of your
test scores.
    Thank you again for applying to Galway College.

                              Sincerely,

                              Peter Lacey

                              Peter Lacey
                              Dean of Admissions
```

FIGURE 9-10

Effective refusal letter. This is a form letter, but it is friendly and offers the prospective student both an explanation and an alternative.

Avoiding Common Errors in Bad News Letters

Try to avoid the errors that appear frequently in refusal letters.

Provide Good Explanations

Provide a reason for your refusal that makes sense to the reader. If possible, orient the reason toward the reader, not toward the company. For example, do not use company policy as an excuse. Most readers will resent this approach. (Compare Figure 9-11 with Figure 9-12.)

Try to orient your refusal letter to the reader, not to your own needs.

> We would be glad to give you the promotion, but the hiring policy of this company maintains no employee can be promoted more than once every eighteen months. [poor excuse]

> To enable employees to adjust to new positions and to thoroughly learn their job duties, we promote employees only after they have worked at one job for at least eighteen months. [reader-oriented explanation]

Emphasize Positives

Do not emphasize the reader's disappointment or reasons for wanting whatever he or she requested. You want the reader to feel better, not worse.

> I know how disappointed you must be: no doubt our Easy-On pliers would appeal to hundreds of your customers, but we just won't be able to fill your order for eight months. [negative emphasis]

> We know our Easy-On pliers are very popular items; you can assure your customers that you will have a large supply of them by May 1. [positive emphasis]

Stick to Related Topics

An unrelated topic may confuse your reader; do not inject unrelated information simply to add an upbeat tone to the letter.

Do not confuse your reader by getting too far from your central topic.

> We are happy to tell you that over the past six months ARP has had one of its best sales records in history. We will not be able, however, to lower the price on our styrofoam containers. [disjointed]

> We make every effort to support American-made products, even though they are sometimes a few cents higher than our competitors' products. We cannot lower the price of our styrofoam containers, but we hope you will appreciate their durability and versatility. [unified and convincing]

```
                                    PLW Accounting
                                    982 Jefferson Avenue
                                    Oldtown, WV 32456
                                    May 12, 19XX

       Mr. Robert McPherson
       P.O. Box 23
       Langland, WV 32455

       Dear Bob:

       Company policy prevents us from hiring your son
       Henry as a summer intern. I wish him well in his
       search for a summer position.

       Thanks for your letter. I look forward to seeing
       you at the Board of Directors meeting in June.

                                    Sincerely,

                                    Don Hughes

                                    Don Hughes
```

FIGURE 9-11

Ineffective refusal letter. This letter is abrupt and vague. Don Hughes refers to company policy without explaining what it is, and he offers nothing to break the blow of the refusal. (See Figure 9-12 for an improved version.)

```
                              PLW Accounting
                              982 Jefferson Avenue
                              Oldtown, WV 32456
                              May 12, 19XX

Mr. Robert McPherson
P.O. Box 23
Langland, WV 32455

Dear Bob:

I was glad to receive your note telling me of your
son Henry's accomplishments. He will surely make a
fine accountant.

Because we are such a small company, we do not hire
students for the summer. Our present staff can
handle the workload between May and February; we
do, however, occasionally hire temporary workers
during tax season.

Although we cannot hire Henry for the summer, we
will be happy to review his application for part-
time work in the spring. Also, he could be
considered for a full-time position when he
graduates. If he is interested in either
alternative, please have him call me. I will be
happy to talk with him about working for PLW.

Thank you again for your letter. I look forward to
seeing you at the June Board meeting.

                              Sincerely,

                              Don Hughes

                              Don Hughes
```

FIGURE 9-12

Revised refusal. This letter explains the company policy and offers some alternatives to the son. Don also encourages the son to call him: Don would rather not have the father as intermediary. Note, also, that Don does not make a commitment to hiring the son: he simply offers to consider the application.

Trust the Reader

Avoid using language that throws doubt on the reader's truthfulness or implies that he or she is to blame for what has occurred.

Although we thoroughly check every package before mailing, you maintain that the train set was defective before you attempted to set it up. [implies reader is lying]

We thoroughly check every package that we mail, but the train set may have been damaged in transit. [offers an explanation that does not blame either the reader or the writer]

What Would You Do?

As president of a large corporation, you are often asked to contribute to charitable events. This year, however, an organization that raises money for scholarships has made a special request. The organization wants to use your large conference room, which seats 500 people, for a fundraising luncheon.

The luncheon is to be held on a Wednesday afternoon in September, the busiest time of year for your company. Although the organization's representative maintains that the huge luncheon will not interfere with your company's operation, you know it will. You simply cannot agree to the organization's request.

Write the organization's president a letter refusing the request. Address it to:

Ms. Phyllis Emery
President, Orion Educational Association
459 Somerset Way
Lyme, Connecticut 02134

Placing and Acknowledging Orders

Most companies use a standard form for placing orders. If you do place an order by letter, remember to include all the information necessary to have it completed efficiently (Figure 9-13).

Standard Information for Letters Placing Orders
1. A first sentence with a phrase such as "Please send me" or "please ship"
2. Quantity of each item
3. Price of each item
4. Size, color, and other identifying characteristics
5. Catalog numbers
6. Total price, including tax, handling charges, and so on
7. Shipping method
8. Name of receiver and shipping address
9. Method of payment (check, money order, credit card, COD)
10. Date by which delivery must be made
11. Special instructions regarding substitutions, delays, and so on

```
                              784 Floral Court
                              Portland, OR 92378
                              June 12, 19XX

Mr. Thomas Dormer
Hiker's Paradise
1200 Brittany Boulevard
Seattle, WA 93217

Dear Mr. Dormer:

Please send me the following items from your spring
catalog:

   2 Star Down sleeping bags    (# 234-67)    $142.00
   1 pair of Klondike boots
        size 10 medium          (# 456-99)      68.00
   Total                                      $210.00
   Tax                                          12.60
   Handling charge                              4.00
   Amount due                                 $226.60

My check for the full amount is enclosed. As I need
these items by July 15, please call me at (908)
456-2786 if you foresee a delay in the delivery.

Thank you.

                         Sincerely,

                         Robin Hale

                         Robin Hale
```

FIGURE 9-13 _____

Order. This letter first states the writer's purpose for writing and then includes all pertinent
information in list form. The final paragraph states a date by which Robin needs the camping
gear and mentions the method of payment.

Accuracy and complete-
ness are vital to letters
placing orders.

Double-check every order to make sure it is complete and accurate. Listing the wrong item number, total price, or item description can lead to frustration and delays for both seller and buyer.

Acknowledging Orders

In most cases, sellers write letters acknowledging orders only if problems or delays are anticipated. To create goodwill, some companies may write to special or first-time customers; other companies (Figure 9-14) might use a letter of acknowledgement as an opportunity to make a further sale.

When problems do arise, however, you should respond quickly either by letter or with a telephone call.

Errors in the Order Form

Be tactful when a cus-
tomer is at fault.

If a customer has requested an item in a color or size not listed in the catalog (Figure 9-15), you should be tactful: do not point out the customer's error. Simply list the available options and request clarification.

Delays

Provide alternatives to
keep the customer
satisfied.

If an item is out of stock or back-ordered, inform the reader of the problem and list alternatives.

Dear Mrs. Pine:

We have received your order #761-23 for three ceramic planters. Unfortunately, the planters cannot be shipped to our warehouse until April 26. We would then be able to rush them to you by May 1.

If you need planters before May 1, you may want to order our smaller ceramic planters (item #23-56 in our catalog).

Please fill out and return the enclosed postcard if you want to cancel or change your order. If we do not hear from you within ten days, we will ship the planters on April 27.

Thank you for your cooperation and understanding.

Sincerely,

Patricia Fellowes

Patricia Fellowes
Customer Service

```
                    Hiker's Paradise
               1200 Brittany Boulevard
                  Seattle, WA 93217
                   (800) 347-9221
                                        June 15, 19XX

Ms. Robin Hale
784 Floral Court
Portland, OR 92378

Dear Ms. Hale:

   Thank you for your order, which arrived
yesterday. The merchandise will be shipped this
week by UPS.
   I enclose a sheet listing our summer sale items.
If you order anything from this list before July 1,
the shipment will reach you before July 15.

                          Sincerely,

                          Thomas Dormer

                          Thomas Dormer
                          Customer Service
```

FIGURE 9-14

Positive reply to an order. In this reply, Thomas assures the customer that the order will be delivered on time. He also takes the opportunity to send her a list of items on sale.

```
                    Hiker's Paradise
                 1200 Brittany Boulevard
                   Seattle, WA 93217
                    (800) 347-9221
                                            July 16, 19XX
     Mr. and Mrs. Henry Miller
     56 Holly Court
     Isleton, WA 93216

     Dear Mr. and Mrs. Miller:

        Thank you for your order, which arrived today. We
     will ship all but the backpack by UPS next week.
        Unfortunately, we do not carry the backpack you
     ordered (Item 534-78) in royal blue. We do carry it
     in red and forest green.
        If you would like to order the pack in one of
     those colors, or if you want another style
     backpack, please call our toll-free number to place
     your order. If we hear from you by July 20, we will
     be able to ship a backpack with your initial order.
        I look forward to hearing from you.

                                  Sincerely,

                                  Thomas Dormer

                                  Thomas Dormer
                                  Customer Service
```

FIGURE 9-15

Response to an order with a problem. In this letter, the writer acknowledges an order but has to explain he cannot fill the entire order. (Note that he does not blame the customer for ordering an item in a color not described in the catalog.) He also offers the customer an easy plan for altering the order.

In general, responses to orders should be tactful, polite, and personal: even form letters can use active verbs and personal pronouns. Remember, while you want to convey information, you also want to keep your reader happy. When written well, even the simplest letter can impress readers enough to make them continue doing business with your company.

Writing Letters of Recommendation

Letters of recommendation convey information about a job candidate or about someone applying to a college or university. These letters tend to fall into one of two categories: character references and experience references. The former speak primarily to the applicant's personal qualities and reputation; the latter, more frequently used, discuss the applicant's skills and performance at a job or in school.

If you are asked to write a letter of recommendation, consider the request carefully. Agree to write letters only for candidates whom you feel you can honestly recommend. Your letter should make clear to the reader how well you know the applicant and in what context you know him or her. In general, avoid writing letters for people you know only slightly or with whose work you are unfamiliar.

In 1974, federal legislation gave parents and students over eighteen years old the right to review files in public schools and colleges. Job seekers can now view these letters unless they waive their right to do so. As a result, some employers do not value them as highly as they once did since they know that candidates can check their files and remove negative letters.

Writers of letters of recommendation, moreover, are more reluctant now to include any negative information. A number of employers have been sued by former employees because their letters of recommendation contained libelous material—false and malicious statements that could injure the person's character or reputation.

> Letters of recommendation can lead to legal problems for the writer.

If you have any qualification about the person requesting the letter, carefully consider whether you should agree to write the letter. You might even discuss with the candidate any reservations you have: "I only worked with you on that one brief project, Kim. I can't comment on anything beyond that" or "I only gave you a B− in that class, Joe. I'll have to include that information in my letter."

In a letter of recommendation, include specific information:

> Include specific details in letters of recommendation.

- The type of position for which you are recommending the applicant

- In what context you know the applicant (as friend, co-worker, instructor, and so on)

- For how long you have known the candidate

- How well you know the candidate

- The candidate's major strengths in relation to the position he or she is seeking

- Any concrete data that can help a reader make a decision regarding the candidate

Be careful to present your information fairly. While you do not want to understate the job applicant's abilities, you also do not want to write a glowing report that will mislead the reader.

Make sure, too, that you send accurate information. Do not include rumors or pieces of information you have heard from others. Avoid including irrelevant information: provide data directly related to the position the person is seeking.

Letters for Excellent Candidates

Writing a letter about someone with excellent qualifications is usually a pleasant experience. Your most difficult task is to make your praise convincing by adding concrete detail.

In Figure 9-16, for example, Michael McGuire states that he gave the job applicant an A in two marketing courses. He also mentions that the applicant worked successfully as a group leader in class. Both of those pieces of information will be useful for someone considering the applicant for a marketing assistant position.

Details about any relevant skills or personal qualities can also be useful to the reader:

In 1986, Ms. Hudson won two awards for top sales, and she was partly responsible for our store's making higher sales than any other Tops 'n Jeans outlet in this area.

Mike always received top marks from the employees who trained with him. In 1988, he received two citations from management regarding his excellent training programs.

Letters for Less Outstanding Candidates

If you believe that, to be honest, a negative note must appear in the letter, be very careful not to write anything that could be construed as libelous. You may choose either to ignore any negative areas completely or to tactfully subordinate the negative. In Figure 9-17, for example, the writer mentions

```
                          Department of Marketing
                          Wheeler University
                          Pittstown, Missouri 34671
                          August 12, 19XX

To Prospective Employers:

I am happy to recommend Felipe Hernandez for a
marketing assistant position.

Mr. Hernandez took both my Marketing Management and
Marketing Research classes during the academic year
1987-88. In both classes, he showed an ability to
work hard and creatively. He received an A in both
classes.

As a group leader in Marketing Management, he
worked on a marketing plan for a small business. He
and his group developed a plan for a local shoe
store that the company owners were most
enthusiastic about. Mr. Hernandez also did an
excellent oral presentation on the project. Using
slides and charts, he presented information lucidly
and calmly in front of fifty people.

Mr. Hernandez speaks and writes well. He has been a
successful student, and I feel certain he will be a
strong candidate for a marketing assistant position
that requires creativity, dedication, and
communication skills.

                Sincerely,

                Michael McGuire

                Michael McGuire
                Professor of Marketing
```

FIGURE 9-16 _____

Letter of recommendation. This letter provides specific information on when the writer knew
the prospective employee and in what context. The third paragraph contains more concrete
information about Felipe's performance in class, and the conclusion sums up the writer's
opinion.

```
                              TRC Engineering Consultants
                              5621 West End Boulevard
                              Denver, Colorado 89762
                              April 19, 19XX

Dear Prospective Employer:

I am pleased to recommend Ms. Erika Grey for an
assistant editor position.

Ms. Grey worked as a copywriter for TRC Consultants
for two years while she was enrolled in school.
Writing and editing documents for a wide variety of
projects, she demonstrated a good sense of language
and was able to work independently. Although Ms.
Grey does not have a strong technical background,
she learned quickly and responded well to
constructive criticism. In fact, she received
several commendations from our technical writers
for her editing of their work.

I found Ms. Grey to be creative, intelligent, and
personable. She would be an asset to any company.

Sincerely,

Jacob Hall

Jacob Hall
Manager, Advertising Department
```

FIGURE 9-17 —————————————————————————————
Letter of recommendation. In this letter, the writer warmly recommends the candidate. He subordinates the candidate's weakness and emphasizes her overall strengths.

that Ms. Grey does not have a technical background. However, he puts that information in a dependent clause and counters it with the comment that she showed improvement and received commendations from technical writers on the staff.

Writing Letters of Appreciation, Congratulation, and Condolence

Sometimes you will have to write letters thanking people, offering congratulations, or expressing sorrow regarding someone's death. These letters require tact and a personal touch.

Letters of Appreciation

A sincere letter of appreciation may be remembered warmly for a long time afterward. If someone has helped you on a project, sent you information, worked overtime, or made a difficult deadline, take the time to write a brief letter. Don't delay: the sooner you write, the more pleased your reader will be.

```
Dear Paul:

Everyone here appreciates the great job you did
designing our promotional flyers. You transformed
our wild ideas into a highly professional and
effective piece of advertising. Thanks so much.


                              Bob
```

Keep letters of appreciation short and sincere. Avoid clichés such as "Thank you from the bottom of my heart." In Figure 9-18, Anna thanks the reader for making a presentation to department heads. Her letter is only three sentences long, but it effectively conveys her appreciation.

Letters of Congratulation

Like letters of appreciation, letters of congratulation should be written promptly. When someone is promoted, elected or appointed to a position, gets engaged or married, or becomes a parent, a letter of congratulation is in order (Figure 9-19).

> The news of your promotion has just reached Atlanta. Everyone in the office here wishes you great success in your new position.

> Congratulations on your election to the board of supervisors. I know you will do an excellent job for our community.

Letters of Condolence

These are always difficult letters to write. If you did not know the person who died, you will have to make sure your letter does not sound perfunctory. If you did know the person, you should try to express your sorrow without sounding maudlin or insincere. A letter of condolence, which is often hand-written, is usually brief. If you knew the person well, you might add a sentence or two highlighting the personal relationship.

> I was very grieved to hear of Ben's death. He was one of the most patient, kind, and conscientious men I have ever known.

> Those summers we spent at Camp of the Wolf with you and Ben have made some of my fondest memories. Please accept my sincerest sympathy.

```
                              Anders Corporation
                              4591 Willows Avenue
                              Iowa City, Iowa 56902
                              April 29, 19XX

Mr. Henry Young
Anchor Investments
78 Pierce Street
Iowa City, Iowa 56905


Dear Mr. Young:

Thank you for speaking to our department heads last
Thursday. I know everyone found your discussion of
the bond market extremely exciting as well as
informative.

We all appreciate your taking time from your busy
schedule to speak to us.

Sincerely,

Anna Orringer

Anna Orringer
Vice-President
```

FIGURE 9-18

Letter of appreciation. This letter thanking a speaker is brief but enthusiastic.

```
                                    Martin's Fashion Shoes
                                    8900 Royale Boulevard
                                    Orion, Georgia 36982
                                    March 27, 19XX

Mrs. Jessica Danvers
Keller, Smith & Rowan Legal Services
9871 Fish Ranch Road
Penn Valley, Georgia 36732


Dear Mrs. Danvers:

I was pleased to read in this morning's Penn Valley
Gazette that you are now a partner with Keller,
Smith & Rowan Legal Services. Everyone here at
Martin's wishes you the best.

We all appreciate the time and effort you have
spent working with us over the past two years. I am
glad to see such outstanding work being recognized.

Best wishes,

Larry Sellers

Larry Sellers
Manager
```

FIGURE 9-19

Letter of congratulation. This letter opens with congratulations and then thanks the reader for her professional help over the years.

Summary

To maintain and increase the good will of your readers, pay particular attention to how they are apt to respond to your message: use a direct approach if they will respond favorably to the letter, but develop an indirect approach if they are probably going to react negatively to your message.

Writing and responding to routine business letters can take up a lot of your working time. To minimize time spent on these letters, determine your goals and then use standard organizational patterns to help you organize your material.

Letters of recommendation and other special letters such as those expressing appreciation, congratulations, and condolence should sound sincere. Write letters of recommendation only if you can honestly recommend the person for the position. Letters of appreciation, congratulation, and condolence require a personal touch. Avoid delays in writing these letters.

Checklist for Routine and Special Letters

Inquiry Letters

- Develop a direct approach when writing inquiry letters to request information:

  _____ Open with request for information.

  _____ State reason for inquiry.

  _____ Ask specific questions in list format.

  _____ Thank reader and state date by which the information is needed.

Request Letters

- Use a request letter to ask for action.

- If a request is pleasant or routine for the reader, use a direct approach:

  _____ State request.

  _____ Add any information the reader might need.

  _____ Thank reader.

- If the request is difficult or unpleasant, use an opening "buffer":

  _____ Open pleasantly.

  _____ Add a reason for the request.

  _____ Make the request itself.

  _____ Thank the reader and end positively.

Responses Conveying Good News

- Use a direct opening for a positive response to an inquiry or request:

  _____ Open with the positive response.

  _____ Add specific details pertaining to inquiry or request.

Responses Conveying Bad News

- Open a negative response to an inquiry or request with a "buffer":

  _____ Open with neutral or pleasant statement.

  _____ Include a reason for the refusal.

  _____ End with refusal itself.

  _____ Return to a positive note.

- To promote the reader's goodwill, be careful when phrasing negative replies:

  _____ Provide you-oriented explanations.

  _____ Emphasize positives whenever possible.

  _____ Stick to related topics.

  _____ Use language that implies trust in the reader.

Orders

- When placing orders, include all necessary information and use a direct approach:

  _____ Place order.

  _____ Include all information related to order.

  _____ List any special instructions.

Acknowledging Orders

- Acknowledge orders when you want to:

  _____ Create goodwill with special or first-time customers.

  _____ Mention errors in the order form.

  _____ Inform customer of delays.

Letters of Recommendation

- Agree to write a letter of recommendation only if your letter can truthfully be positive.

- Include specific information rather than generalizations.

- If you must include a negative note, deemphasize it in the letter.

  _____ State type of position for which you are recommending the candidate.

  _____ State how well, how long, and in what context you have known the applicant.

  _____ Describe specific details on the candidate's strengths and skills.

  _____ Reiterate support for candidate.

Letters of Appreciation

- Use letters of appreciation to thank people or show appreciation for their work.

- Write the letter promptly.

- Keep letter brief and sincere.

  _____ Thank reader for specific actions.

  _____ Add any material that will convey your sincerity and appreciation.

Letters of Congratulation

- Write letters of congratulation if someone is promoted, elected or appointed to a position, gets engaged or married, or becomes a parent.

  _____ Congratulate reader on specific event.

  _____ Add details to convey your sincerity.

Letters of Condolence

- Write a letter of condolence if you knew the person who has died or if you know a close friend or relative of the person who has died.

  _____ State your sorrow to hear of the death of the reader's family member or friend.

  _____ Include a sentence or two referring to the deceased's good qualities or your memories of the person.

Summary Discussion: Nancy Taylor's Request from Case in Point, p. 167

Nancy Taylor's letter is not a simple invitation to a luncheon: it is a request that Dr. Olsen speak at a luncheon. Because the request could be a nuisance for him, an upbeat opening is in order. However, the request itself should be placed more prominently in the letter: it should not get lost at the end of the second paragraph.

The letter lacks the you-attitude. Ms. Taylor forgets to tell Dr. Olsen the time of the luncheon—and she hints that he should not speak too long. Moreover, she adds information such as the date the museum was built that is irrelevant to the letter as a whole. Her reason for wanting to hear from him by March 15 is oriented to her needs, not his.

Terms to Remember

Letter of appreciation: a letter thanking a person, particularly for a special effort or job well done

Buffer: a positive or neutral opening that encourages the reader's goodwill

Letter of condolence: a letter of sympathy to family member or friend of someone who has died

Letter of congratulation: a letter conveying your happiness at an event in the reader's life such as a promotion

Letter of inquiry: a letter used to request information

Letter of recommendation: a letter to prospective employers outlining the candidate's qualifications for a position

Letter of request: a letter used to request action

Questions for Review and Discussion

1. What is the difference between an inquiry and a request?
2. Why is it a good idea to open a letter conveying bad news with a buffer?
3. Why is it useful to include a reason for your request in your letter?
4. Why is it often best to avoid relying on company policy when responding negatively?
5. What items are usually included in an order?
6. Why should a writer of a recommendation letter mention the type of job for which he or she is recommending the applicant?
7. Why do you think a letter of appreciation or congratulation can be more effective at times than a telephone call?
8. Why are letters of condolence often handwritten?

1. Revise the following refusal letter. Add or delete information as necessary.

Dear George:

We aren't going to be able to relocate you in Greensborough after all. Loretta and I know how much you want to go there since your children are in college nearby and you've already picked out a house, but it just won't be possible this year.

Have you had any success with the Lynch account yet? Let me know as soon as you've made some progress. And give me a call if you have questions about the relocation.

Yours truly,

Constance LaFarge

Constance LaFarge

2. Rewrite the following request, adding or deleting information as necessary.

Dear Mrs. Fenton:

Our chapter of American College Women will not be meeting this Wednesday, February 21, as scheduled. Our next meeting will be on March 13, so we have rescheduled your talk and slide show for that evening. Please let us know if you cannot be there that night.

Yours truly,

Kathryn Johnson

Kathryn Johnson

3. Revise Nancy Taylor's letter at the opening of this chapter.

4. You are the owner of Jason's Discount Mail Order. In the past you have sent a free catalogue to anyone who requested one. Now you have changed your policy: you will send free catalogues only to customers who did $200 worth of business with you last year. Everyone else must pay $5 for the catalogue. Loren Garrison has written asking for a free catalogue. You must tell him the catalogue will cost $5 as he bought only $120 worth of goods from you last year. He is a long-time customer, so you do not want to lose his business.

5. You are Janet Furniss, a salesperson for TRC Corporation. You have been accepted into a graduate business program at the University of Massachusetts and hope to work part-time while in school. Write to Gayle Hopkins, head of sales in the company's corporate headquarters, requesting a temporary change to part-time status.

6. You are Gayle Hopkins, head of sales at TRC Corporation (see Exercise 5). You have approved Janet's request to work part-time, but you do insist that she maintain a certain productivity level while she is in school.

7. James Roby has written to you in the corporate headquarters of TRC Corporation requesting a transfer from the West Coast to the East Coast. He is a very good accountant whom you do not want to lose, but you have no openings for him on the East Coast. Write a letter refusing the request.

8. In March, you bought a home computer from Techton Computer Company. Your agreement included five hours of free assistance in setting up and training. The five hours are now completed, but you are still having problems. The software seems to be full of bugs. Write a letter to the computer company requesting one more free hour of assistance to check out the problems.

9. You are manager of the Techton Computer Company (see Exercise 8). Explain that your technical assistant cannot make another free visit to the customer's home; you can, however, inspect the software and give the buyer some tips if the disks are mailed or brought into your store. Your technical assistant is available for personal instruction, but the charge is $45 per hour.

10. Your company has small retail outlets all over the country. Right now, you are suffering some financial losses that may mean closing two or three of these outlets. To keep from closing any, you are first going to request a hiring and wage freeze for three months. You are writing the managers of each shop to request their participation and cooperation.

11. Write a letter ordering five books that Haynes Academic Publishers advertised in a magazine. You have lost the order form, so make sure you include all the necessary information for your order to be successfully completed.

12. As a sales representative from Haynes Academic Publishers, acknowledge the order made in Exercise 11. Explain, however, that one of the books is out of stock and there will be at least a three-month delay before it will be available.

13. Write a letter refusing the following request:

A team of managers from all over the world is coming to our city this week to visit successful businesses. We would appreciate your taking the time to let the team tour your production facilities from 2 to 4 p.m. on Thursday, April 8.

14. Write to a mail-order company that specializes in dried fruit and candy giftwrapped for holidays. You are ordering three gifts, each to be sent to a different person. Include all pertinent information.

15. You are president of a campus organization that sets up social functions with students and prospective employers in the community. Write a letter to a company representative inviting him or her to attend a wine-and-cheese event on campus.

16. You are a recruiter for a large accounting firm. You have received an invitation to attend a campus event (see Exercise 15). Although you do plan to interview students on that campus, you cannot attend this event. Write a letter refusing the invitation.

17. You are the owner of a boutique. You have heard that a company in Laredo, Texas, imports Mexican clothing and sells it to retailers nationwide. Write a letter to the company owners requesting information on what they

import, what their price range is, how long it takes to receive an order, and what payment method they prefer. Send the letter to:

Mr. and Mrs. Paul Stephens
TexMex Imports
3491 Bollson Boulevard
Laredo, TX 89721

18. You are the customer service representative for a company that sells shoes and boots through a catalog. A customer has requested a pair of men's leather dress shoes in size 12 C. Write to the customer explaining that the largest size for that particular shoe is 11 C.

19. Revise the following letter.

Dear Helen:

    Congratulations on your promotion to manager of the Sales Department in Beloit. That job has had a high casualty list over the years—at least five people had held it since 1985. But I'm sure you can handle the stress! Your success as a product manager should guarantee your success in Beloit.

Best wishes,
Sharon Munz
Sharon Munz

20. Revise the following letter.

Dear Mrs. Gridley:

Words fail me when I try to write how sorrowful I felt when I saw your husband Tom had passed away after so many months of illness. I am sure you must feel that, in some sense, his death was "for the best," but those of us who remember him from the company picnics and other events will always remember his cheerful face and great sense of humor.

                    Sadly,
                    C. R. Archer
                    Charles R. Archer

21. Looking for a house in Chicago took nearly six months. You worked daily with your real estate agent before he found you the perfect place. His commission can never pay for the time he spent with you. Write a letter thanking him for his efforts.

22. A former instructor wrote a letter of recommendation that proved to be a major asset in your job search. Now that you have landed the job you wanted, write a letter thanking the instructor.

23. You just saw in the newspaper that the mother of a friend of yours died in an automobile accident. Write a letter of condolence to the friend.

24. One of the employees under your supervision has applied for a transfer. While you hate to lose a good employee, you are happy to write a good letter of recommendation for him. You have worked with him for two years and approved a major promotion for him last year.

25. Your company has organized a summer training session in London for certain qualified personnel. Only five people were accepted, and you were not one of them. An acquaintance in your department, however, was chosen from among the 75 candidates. Write a congratulatory letter to her.

26. The husband of one of your co-workers has died. You never met him, but you want to write the wife a personal message. Write the letter of condolence.

27. You underestimated the number of stuffed bears that your customers would order during the Christmas season. Flooded with orders, you begged the company that manufactures the bears to rush you 300 more. Despite the Christmas rush, the manufacturer sent you the bears within a week. Write a letter to the sales representative thanking her and her company.

28. You are a physical education instructor at a junior college. One of your students is applying for jobs as a swimming and tennis instructor at summer camps throughout the northeast. He wants you to write a letter of recommendation. You think the student would make an excellent instructor for beginning and intermediate levels, but his tennis and swimming are not strong enough for him to teach advanced students. Your letter should reflect this qualification.

29. An instructor that you had in high school is being considered for a prestigious teaching award. Write a letter recommending the instructor to the award committee.

30. Tim Lynch and Molly Dennison have been campaigning against each other for student body president at your college. The contest has been marred by unpleasantness on both sides. Both candidates' supporters put up posters and banners that insulted the other contestant, and some angry hecklers disturbed both candidates' speeches.

   Although neither candidate was directly responsible for these incidents, the two are not on particularly friendly terms. Election day was highly emotional. After a tense count and recount of the votes, Tim was declared the winner.

   Molly knows she should write a letter sincerely congratulating Tim, but she can't write anything appropriate. She asks you for help. Write the letter for Molly.

Word Processing Exercises: Backups

At some point in your word processing experience, you will probably run into problems. An electrical blackout, a faulty disk, or a bug in a program can cause you to lose precious data. As you work on a file, make sure you SAVE the material every fifteen minutes or so. Then you can be sure you will not lose too much if the machine goes down.

People often start out being overly confident about the safety of their files. It takes only one mishap—an energy surge, for example—to teach them to save their work. Be sure to make backups for all important files and keep printed copies as well. Keeping your disks in their envelopes when not in use will also help to prevent disasters.

If you are just starting to use a word processor,

you may be doing all your work on one or two disks. For the sake of both safety and convenience, invest in a box of disks and use different disks for different types of documents. For instance, you might use one disk solely for personal correspondence and another for papers you are writing for school. Mark each disk label with a felt-tip pen.

We recommend using one disk for the exercises in this text. Save the files you create while doing these exercises—at least until the course is over!

Be sure to copy all important files onto another disk and keep your backup disks separate from the ones you usually use. (You may even want to keep them in a separate room for safety.)

By doing these exercises, you will learn to

- make backup copies of files
- copy files onto another disk
- copy disks.

1. Enter a file you have already created. We will assume it is BUSCOM. Make any revisions you want.

2. Save the file and exit from it. If your program makes an automatic backup file, you now have both the file BUSCOM and BUSCOM.BAK.

3. To make a backup of your own, use the command to COPY a file. The program will ask you what file you want to copy (BUSCOM) and what you want to name the copy. Call the copy BUSCOM2. When you press return, you will have two identical files. Exit from the word processing program.

4. Now learn the procedure for copying a file onto a second formatted disk. This is an essential practice if you want to protect important data: if you are working on important files, get in the habit of making your backup files at the end of each work session.

   Copy BUSCOM onto a second disk that you have marked as a backup disk. Call the backup file BUSCOM as well.

5. You also need to know how to copy an entire disk onto a new formatted disk. This procedure is somewhat tedious if you have only one disk drive, but it is simple with two drives. Learn the commands for copying all the BUSCOM disk onto a second disk by referring to your manual. Check the directories of both disks to see that they are the same. (Your directory will also tell you how much space is left on your disk; get in the habit of checking it fairly often so you do not run out of room.)

Review Exercises

These exercises will help you to practice some of the word processing commands and techniques you have been learning.

1. Create a file named REV. Without stopping to fix typos, type in the following paragraphs. Single-space the text, but double-space between paragraphs.

   The keyboard on your word personal computer is almost identical to your typewriter keyboard. As you enter text using a word processing program, you will be typing much as you do on your typewriter.

   Several keys such as ESCAPE and CONTROL, as well as the arrow keys, may be new to you. With practice, you will become as familiar with these keys as you are with standard letters, numbers, and punctuation marks.

   You will find the arrow keys particularly helpful. Pressing the different arrow keys moves your cursor to selected locations in your text. The cursor moves in the direction shown on the key. (The cursor is the light-colored rectangle that shows where the character you type next will appear.)

2. Now go back and edit the paragraphs you typed by adding and deleting characters and reforming (or aligning) text as necessary. Your paragraphs should be identical to those in this text.

3. When you have edited the paragraphs, save the file and print it.

4. Change the right-hand margin to ragged right. Save and print the file again. It should look like this:

The keyboard on your word personal computer is almost identical to your typewriter keyboard. As you enter text using a word processing program, you will be typing much as you do on your typewriter.

Several keys such as ESCAPE and CONTROL, as well as the arrow keys, may be new to you. With practice, you will become as familiar with these keys as you are with standard letters, numbers, and punctuation marks.

You will find the arrow keys particularly helpful. Pressing the different arrow keys moves your cursor to selected locations in your text. The cursor moves in the direction shown on the key. (The cursor is the light-colored rectangle that shows where the character you type next will appear.)

5. Go back to the beginning of the file REV. Justify the right-hand margins again. Now change the spacing from single-spaced to double-spaced. Leave the double-spacing between paragraphs. PRINT the file: it should look like this:

The keyboard on your word personal computer

is almost identical to your typewriter keyboard.

As you enter text using a word processing pro-

gram, you will be typing much as you do on your

typewriter.

Several keys such as ESCAPE and CONTROL, as

well as the arrow keys, may be new to you. With

practice, you will become as familiar with these

keys as you are with standard letters, numbers,

and punctuation marks.

You will find the arrow keys particularly helpful.

Pressing the different arrow keys moves your

cursor to selected locations in your text. The

cursor moves in the direction shown on the key.

(The cursor is the light-colored rectangle that shows where the character you type next will appear.)

6. Return to single-spacing but change the left- and right-hand margins of REV so they are 2-inches wide. PRINT the file. It should look like this:

The keyboard on your word personal computer is almost identical to your typewriter keyboard. As you enter text using a word processing program, you will be typing much as you do on your typewriter.

Several keys such as ESCAPE and CONTROL, as well as the arrow keys, may be new to you. With practice, you will become as familiar with these keys as you are with standard letters, numbers, and punctuation marks.

You will find the arrow keys particularly helpful. Pressing the different arrow keys moves your cursor to selected locations in your text. The cursor moves in the direction shown on the key. (The cursor is the light-colored rectangle that shows where the character you type next will appear.)

7. Go to the end of the file REV. Type in two more paragraphs of your own that give information to someone learning about word processing. You might choose to discuss

- the three commands you find most useful
- the uses of the HELP command in your word processing program
- the uses of the FUNCTION keys in your system.

8. Edit the paragraphs you have just written. Then save and print out the entire file. If you see any errors, go back and edit the paragraphs again. If you have a spell-check program, use it on the file REV to help you catch typographical errors.

9. Print the final version of REV. Save the file for later exercises.

Sales and Promotional Letters

- **Communicating persuasively**
- **Knowing your readers**
- **Motivating your readers**
- **Knowing your product**
- **Developing rational and emotional approaches**
- **Creating a persuasive style and theme**
- **Making a plan for a sales letter**
- **Drafting and revising promotional letters**
- **Solving common problems with promotional letters**

Objectives

To learn strategies for persuasive writing

To write sales and promotional letters that motivate readers

10

Martin DeVries's Sales Letter

CDS Management Services
101 Georgia Street
San Francisco, CA 94521
(415) 678-2390
August 3, 19XX

Mr. Frederick Benson
Carnes-Lowe Technologies
12793 Perrot Drive
Los Gatos, CA 95683

Dear Sir:

We have a wide range of services to offer your company. CDS Management Services can make your company more productive. Undoubtedly, your company has some time management, paper flow, or employee morale problems: we can help you solve them. Our trainers can organize management seminars to help your managers be more efficient and proficient. Our unique classes on new approaches in labor relations, productivity, flextime, benefits, and stress can make you and your managers see your operation in a whole new light! Our staff is composed of professional consultants from a wide variety of fields—all of whom are up-to-the-minute with new management methods and concepts.

So give CDS a call. We'll be glad to talk to you. And *you'll* be glad you talked to us.

Sincerely,

Martin DeVries

Martin DeVries
Vice President, CDS

Points to Consider

- What problems do you see in this letter?
- Summarize what the letter is selling. How effective is the sales pitch?
- What do you think should be added to this letter? Explain.
- Is there anything you would delete? Explain.
- If you were looking for services like these, would this letter make you want to call CDS? Why or why not?

Communicating Persuasively

The art of persuasion is fundamental to business.

Advertising is so specialized these days that most large and even mid-size companies either hire an agency to develop advertising materials or maintain an advertising staff within the company. Despite this specialization, however, many businesspeople are called upon to write sales and promotional letters.

Frequently, employees of small businesses and nonprofit organizations must develop sales letters, flyers, or brochures for their organizations, and they often do so at great expense without understanding the principles involved. Also, businesspeople who become involved in raising money for community projects often find themselves writing fundraising materials without the expertise to do so effectively.

Besides being useful for sales and promotional letters, the art of persuasion is important to almost every type of writing. Even when writers seem to be simply conveying facts, they usually are trying to convince their readers in some way.

Because persuasion is fundamental to business and to life in general, you will find the following hints useful for any type of persuasive writing.

Keep Your Reader Interested

Writers are often so wrapped up in delivering information that they forget to *sell* their product or service. Their letters are verbally and visually boring. You cannot expect your product to "sell itself"; you have to catch your readers' attention and make them want to read on.

Avoid boring your readers.

From the Desk of . . .

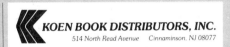

KOEN BOOK DISTRIBUTORS, INC.
514 North Read Avenue   Cinnaminson, NJ 08077

"Make your sales letters fun to read," says John Shaw, Advertising and Sales Coordinator for Koen Books. Koen Books is a wholesaler that purchases books from publishers and sells them to retailers. For the larger publishers, Koen Books complements their own distribution system; for the smaller publishers, Koen offers a complete package of distribution and marketing.

John "works both sides of the street," writing to both publishers and retail customers. He says, "The main problem is that people have so much to read that it's hard to get and keep their attention." He compares his approach to that of writing news copy. "It's important to make the letter brief and to the point. Figure out what the message is and say it up front." Often the letter is a cover letter, sent along with a package of forms and more detailed information. "The purpose of the letter is to stimulate interest and get the reader to call you." John emphasizes that when you are writing a letter "usually you are writing to a position, not to a person. Letters should be more formal and restrained than conversation."

"It's important to find a device to sell your product, whether it's a book or a service. Tell the customer what you are offering that is different, unique." In the following opening to a letter, John uses Koen Books' interest in regional publishing to interest this small publisher in Maine. He also catches the publisher's attention by appealing for her help: "Thank you for your interest in advertising with Koen. We have undertaken an ambitious project in becoming a comprehensive supplier of regional titles and need the help of publishers to get things going."

He then goes on to explain the programs, referring the publisher to the enclosed information and forms. He concludes with, "Don't hesitate to call or write if you have any questions about the enclosed materials," inviting action on the part of the reader.

John says that before he started doing this kind of work he was less concerned with the appearance of written material, but now he sees that form "can counteract what I'm saying, or, conversely, support it."

- His tip to students is to be aware of the difference between writing for a college course and writing for business. He contrasts writing an essay with writing a letter: "There's a different set of priorities. When you're writing in college, you're encouraged to be comprehensive and exhaustive. When you're writing a sales or promotional letter, you want to hit the essential points. Use short sentences and paragraphs. Most important—make your point, then stop writing."

SNAFU® by Bruce Beattie

"The truth-in-advertising people want us to call it: Dimethyl-Isoglyceride."

Selling your product

Make the Presentation Relevant to the Reader

Emphasize the benefits your reader will receive.

If a letter is not relevant to readers, they will not believe they *need* the product or service. As a persuasive writer, you must show readers that they will indeed benefit from whatever you are offering. (To do this, you have to know who your readers are so you can appeal directly to them.)

Maintain an Appropriate Tone

Create a tone appropriate to
- *your reader*
- *your product or service*
- *your organization*

An effective letter selling computer software to a business will differ in tone as well as message from a letter selling cassette tapes to teenagers. Make sure your tone is appropriate for your reader, your product or service, and the image of the organization you represent.

Focus on Action

As a persuasive writer, focus on getting your reader to *do* something: to call you, come to your store, request a free sample, send you a check, or just look forward to your telephone call. If your letter does not make a reader want to act, it has not accomplished its major goal.

Knowing Your Readers

If you have ever subscribed to a magazine, ordered a product through the mail, used a credit card, or listed your address in a telephone directory, you probably receive several sales letters a week. Companies all over the country are constantly attempting to categorize you by your demographic and psychographic characteristics (Figure 10-1).

Demographic variables include data about characteristics such as people's age, gender, and race as well as their income, profession, marital status, and

Demographic

Variable	Example
Sex	Female, male
Age	Under 5, 5–13, 14–17, 18–24, 25–34, 35–44, 45–54, 55–64, 65+
Income	Under $8,000, $8,000–9,999, $10,000–14,999, $15,000–24,999, $25,000–34,999, $35,000–49,999, $50,000–74,000, $75,000+
Household type	Single, married without dependent children, married with children, divorced husband without children, divorced wife without children, divorced husband with children, divorced wife with children, widowed single
Religion	Catholic, Protestant, Jewish, Mormon, Moslem
Race	Black, white, Asian, Indian, Hispanic
Education	Grade school or less, high school, college, postgraduate

Psychographic

Variable	Example
Activities	Indoor work, outdoor work, sports, cultural events, travel, shopping
Personality	Extrovert, introvert, high energy, competitive, easygoing
Interests	Family, job, fitness, food, education, gardening, status, fashion

FIGURE 10-1

A sampling of demographic and psychographic variables

living situation. Psychographic variables include data about people's personalities, values, lifestyles, interests, and opinions.

When marketers know your demographic and psychographic characteristics, they prepare sales approaches they hope you will find persuasive (Figure 10-2).

Age and Sex	Radio Preferences
Men under 25	Album rock
Teenagers and women under 30	Contemporary hits
Women 25–44	Light rock/less talk
	Easy oldies
Men over 45	Big band/nostalgia
Women over 45	Adult contemporary
Men and women over 55	Beautiful music, News and talk

Data from "Radio's Lifestyles," *American Demographics*, February 1986, pp. 32–35.

FIGURE 10-2

Sampling of radio station preferences based on demographic variables

Targeted Advertising

Companies have long targeted their products at different demographic segments of the population. S. J. Johnson & Son, maker of Raid, conducts heavy roach-killer promotions in roach-infested cities such as Houston and New Orleans. The company spends more money on ads for flea sprays in flea-ridden Tampa and Birmingham.

Campbell Soup's subsidiary, Vlasic Pickles, targets its Zesty Pickles at northeasterners, who prefer their pickles more sour than do people in other parts of the country.

Northeasterners and midwesterners prefer chicken noodle soup and tomato soup; Californians prefer cream of mushroom. Promotional campaigns are adjusted accordingly.[1]

As advertising becomes more sophisticated, however, companies are using more and more psychographic indicators to supplement demographic data. While Miller Lite targets blue-collar but upscale young men who do not want a "diet" beer, Old Milwaukee aims for cost-conscious but funloving men who enjoy activities such as stone crab fishing in the Gulf of Mexico.[2]

[1]Thomas Moore, "Different Folks, Different Strokes." *Fortune*, September 16, 1985, pp. 65, 68.
[2]Robert Reed, "Satisfying a Thirst for Images," *Advertising Age*, January 16, 1984, pp. M9–M11.

Finding Out About Your Audience

The first commandment of any sales or marketing effort is to know the audience. Thus, the second and third steps of the writing process, defining goals and audience and doing necessary research, are of paramount importance. Companies spend millions of dollars every year in efforts to figure out whether consumers nationwide choose price over taste or speed over dependability. Then their product design and advertising are slanted accordingly.

Avoid assuming that your reader is similar to you.

To write persuasively, bear in mind that your readers' age, gender, ethnic background, education, values, beliefs, cultural associations, needs, sense of humor, and many other characteristics may well differ radically from your own. Write for your audience, not for yourself.

Researching your readers can be a complex process involving thousands of dollars and hours of effort, or it can be a simple task involving a brief survey. Once again, large companies employ market research specialists to analyze the markets toward which a product is being targeted.

If you are doing market analysis on your own, you will have to consider whether to use *primary* or *secondary* data for your information. Primary data are collected specifically for the project at hand. You might develop oral or written questionnaires, for example, or simply observe your potential buyers.

Questionnaires and observation are useful for collecting primary data.

Secondary data have already been collected for purposes other than your

> Market research sometimes discovers surprising preferences in consumers. Extensive research at Nabisco Brands, Inc., led the company to put forty-two Oreo cookies in a package rather than forty or forty-five—customers clearly preferred packages with forty-two cookies. Oscar Mayer & Company receives frequent complaints from customers who want eight to twelve hot dogs in a pack to match the number of buns in a bag. However, when the company sells hot dogs in those quantities, sales immediately go down.
>
> > Data from John Koten, "Why Do Hot Dogs Come in Packs of 10 and Buns in 8s or 12s?" *The Wall Street Journal,* September 21, 1984 (pp. 1, 15).

project. Secondary data are less expensive and time-consuming to acquire, but the information is not targeted specifically to your needs. You may gather secondary data from sources such as government publications, market studies done by other companies, articles forecasting market trends, and company sales histories.

Company records, government publications, and other documents are useful for collecting secondary data.

Orienting Your Material to Your Readers

When you have acquired information about your readers, sift through the material you have acquired and organize it so it is useful to you. You might want to put together a sample profile of one reader: writing to someone you know and understand can help make your letter compelling and effective.

Of course, sending your sales letter to a localized or specially chosen group is much easier than sending it to thousands of people across the country. If your letter is directed only to people who have recently bought farm equipment or maternity dresses, you can tailor your approach to their interests and needs.

Tailor your approach to your readers' interests and needs.

When Roger Baptista was drafting a sales letter for his home insulation service, for example, he put together a mailing list of homeowners who lived in certain middle-class neighborhoods in his midwestern city. From some simple market research he composed this profile of a typical household:

- It contains a married couple.
- They are each over forty years old.
- They finished high school and some college.
- They have children under twenty.
- They own a house over five years old.
- They make between $20,000 and $35,000 a year.
- They plan to stay in this home for at least seven more years.
- The man does most of the household repairs.
- They spend $50 per month on house and garden upkeep.
- They spend five evenings a week at home.

With this broad profile, Roger could begin considering what factors would motivate his audience.

Motivating Your Readers

Maslow's hierarchy of needs can help writers focus on areas that will motivate their readers.

Just knowing what your readers are like is not sufficient for a good sales letter: you also have to know what will motivate them. The famous hierarchy of needs developed by Abraham Maslow is often cited as a good jumping-off place for understanding how to motivate an audience.

1. Physiological needs: hunger, thirst, shelter
2. Safety needs: protection, stability
3. Love needs: affection, friendship
4. Esteem needs: prestige, success
5. Self-actualization needs: self-fulfillment

Maslow's hierarchy begins with lower-order physiological needs and moves to needs for safety, love, esteem, and self-actualization. You can appeal to people's needs for esteem and self-actualization only if their lower-order needs, such as hunger and thirst, have been satisfied.

Understanding the powerful motivators identified by Maslow can help you find a central sales theme. As you develop your approach, ask yourself whether your product

- saves time
- saves or makes money
- is long-lasting, durable
- is safe
- is easy to use
- is fun to use
- is educational
- is attractive
- makes people more comfortable
- tastes, smells, sounds, or looks good
- makes people smell or look good
- makes people healthier
- makes people more secure
- makes people appear fashionable
- makes people appear wealthy
- appeals to people's interests (art, religion, sports, gardening, and so on)
- appeals to people's desires for recreation, entertainment
- appeals to people's desires to help others or improve the world.

Most people will be motivated by some of these factors, but no one will be motivated by them all. Your task is to assess the factors that will motivate your readers in particular—and to link those factors with your product.

Knowing Your Product

It is vital to know everything about your product: where it is made, what it is made of, how much it costs, how long it lasts, who uses it, why they use it, what features it has, what components it contains, what warranty is included, what colors and sizes it comes in, what its upkeep costs are, what competition it has, what competing prices are.

Before writing a sales letter, find out everything you can about your product or service.

You will not use all this information in your sales letter, but it will help you link the product with your audience's needs and interests.

While organizing his sales approach, Roger Baptista listed some of the strong points of his home insulation service.

- Saves homeowner's fuel bills
- Saves homeowner's time
- Makes home more comfortable
- Is done quickly and easily
- Can be paid in monthly installments
- Offers more options than most services
- Includes free diagnostic visit
- Is performed by trained professionals
- Can make home more attractive
- Includes ten-year warranty
- Promotes health of home inhabitants

Ten Tips for Selling Your Product

1. Know who your readers are
2. Know what motivates your readers
3. Use the you-attitude
4. Know your product thoroughly
5. Decide on a rational or emotional approach
6. Catch your readers' attention
7. Make your readers desire the product
8. Make the price seem desirable
9. Show your good faith
10. Encourage your readers to *act*

Now Roger had a profile of his service and his readers as well as a good sense of what would motivate them. Because many of his readers were middle-income owners of older homes who would not be moving in the near future, he figured he would focus on the long-term benefits of his service as well as on lower fuel bills and the immediate comforts of a well-insulated house (Figure 10-3).

Developing Rational and Emotional Approaches

When you have analyzed who makes up your audience and how readers will respond to certain sales stimuli, you can decide on the nature of your approach. Consider whether your appeal is going to be rational or emotional.

Rational Approach

Rational approaches focus on concrete features.

A rational approach appeals to the reader's logic. Most sales letters addressed to business professionals, for example, use this approach. So do letters for services or products, such as Roger Baptista's insulation service, that are useful or cost-efficient rather than glamorous.

A rational sales letter emphasizes concrete details about a product: its features, uses, durability, warranty, and accessories. The letter answers obvious questions and provides valid, persuasive arguments for buying the product.

The tone of a rational sales letter is factual, although it can still be dynamic, aggressive, and perhaps even humorous.

Emotional Approach

Emotional approaches are useful for products your readers do not actually need.

An emotional sales letter is effective for products that appeal to a reader's desire for luxury or wish to be attractive, sexy, or fashionable. Such a letter works for products that your readers do not *need*—but that you can convince them to want: perfume, aftershave lotion, gourmet kitchen utensils, vacations, designer clothing, automobile accessories.

Because you are appealing to a reader's extravagant, impulsive side, your language should be more emotional. You will not sell aftershave lotion by listing its ingredients—you have to describe how it will make the reader feel and how others will feel when they smell it (Figure 10-4).

You may, of course, combine the rational and emotional appeals: offering free cosmetic samples with a purchase of a new perfume may appeal to your readers' love of a bargain as well as their desire to be glamorous or sensual.

Developing a Persuasive Style and Theme

Most sales letters have a personal tone.

Whatever your approach, your style should be human and readable. Sound like yourself, not like the voice of your company. Do not be afraid to use

```
                    Baptista's Home Insulation Service
                    645 Mendota Boulevard
                    Clear Lake, WI 54678
                    (608) 456-9011
                    September 23, 19xx

Mr. and Mrs. Richard Cobbs
34 River Road
Clear Lake, WI 54679

Dear Mr. and Mrs. Cobbs:

     Are your heating bills going up every year? Is
your house damp, cold, drafty? Are some rooms cold
while others are warm? Baptista's Home Insulation
Service can help. Call us for a free appraisal.
     We do far more than insulate your home. Working
with your budget and needs in mind, we develop a
winterizing plan tailored for your individual
house. And whatever we do—weatherstrip the windows,
insulate the roof, install energy-efficient
windows, or put in radiant heaters—you can count
on:

• lower fuel bills
• a warmer, more evenly heated home
• a ten-year warranty
• a free follow-up visit
• payments that won't break your budget
• knowledgeable, professional workers

     An investment in our services will help make you
and your family warmer and healthier this winter—
and for years to come.
     So don't shiver through another winter. Give us a
call. We'll be glad to diagnose your winterizing
needs. And our first visit won't cost you a penny!

                              Sincerely yours,

                              Roger Baptista

                              Roger Baptista
```

FIGURE 10-3

Effective rational sales letter. This letter emphasizes the rational reasons for calling Baptista's. Since the free appraisal is one of Roger's best selling points, he mentions it at the beginning and the end. His central list provides concrete detail focusing on money as well as comfort and professional service.

```
                                        Dubois Cosmetics
                                        7863 43rd Street
                                        Newark, NJ 19324
                                        December 1, 19xx

        Ms. Kate Reilly
        298 Stonewall Avenue
        Blair, WA 98467

        Dear Ms. Reilly:

           In 1785, Marie Antoinette paid the equivalent of
        $25,000 for five jars of facial cream.
           This rich moisturizer, rightfully called "L'Or
        des Reines"—the Queens' Gold—was made of herbs and
        precious oils brought from the West Indies and the
        Orient. Fragrant and rich, it made a woman's face
        look fresh, ageless, radiant.
           Now you can try L'Or des Reines. Open the packet
        we've enclosed. Rub a little cream on your
        forehead, under your eyes. Swirl it on your cheeks.
        Immediately you will feel the warmth, the magic of
        L'Or des Reines. In eight hours, you will look and
        feel younger, more beautiful.
           L'Or des Reines, made from a formula jealously
        prized by French royalty for over 200 years, is
        only now available to discriminating American
        women. Still expensive—yes. But just the thinnest
        film is all you need for softer, younger skin.
           So ask for L'Or des Reines at any major
        department store. Pamper your skin. It deserves to
        be treated like a queen.

                                        Sincerely,

                                        Adele Dubois

                                        Adele Dubois
```

FIGURE 10-4 _____

Effective emotional sales letter. This letter accompanying a sample of face cream is aimed at women willing to pay high prices for cosmetics. The story of Marie Antoinette, the emphasis on expense and royalty, and the suggestion that the cream is new on the American market should appeal to a reader who wants to pamper herself.

the word *I*. Readers respond better to individuals than they do to organizations. When you revise your letter for style,

- use strong action verbs
- avoid passive sentences
- include every pertinent detail
- keep sentences and paragraphs short
- use a personal tone

In effective sales letters, a persuasive style is often combined with a theme. This theme helps readers keep reading and makes it easier for them to understand the message. Your theme might be simply a phrase or slogan that will stay in the reader's mind. Don't overdo the theme—it can interfere with your selling points—but don't let it drop. You may find it particularly useful in your closing paragraph.

The sales letter for Tom Mead running shorts, for example (Figure 10-5), opens and closes with the concept of "meeting" Tom Mead, while the letter selling perfume (see Figure 10-4) develops a theme of royalty centered on Marie Antoinette.

Beneath these overt themes, however, the major thesis of every sales letter is the same: buying the service or product is in the reader's best interest. However you say it—that is your ultimate point.

When you have a sense of the approach and style you are going to use, you can begin planning, drafting, and revising your sales letter. In the planning stage, decide what will appear in the opening, body, and conclusion of the letter.

Making a Plan for a Sales Letter

The fourth step of the writing process, making a plan, will help you organize your material so that you keep your readers interested and motivate them to act. One of your prime goals is to keep your audience *reading*: once someone puts down a sales letter without having finished it, you may well have lost a customer.

Openings That Attract Readers

An effective opening can be the key to an effective letter. Within moments, your reader is going to decide whether to keep reading or to throw the letter away. A good opening attracts the reader's interest.

Having done your homework on your audience and your product, you should let your imagination take over: come up with an opening that is dynamic, original, and, above all, interesting.

Today's audiences are hit so hard with advertising of every type that you will have to be creative if you want to get their attention. Television commercials can rely at times on familiar or trite phrasing because they can capture a viewer's eyes with pictures on a screen. Writing copy for a sales letter is more difficult, even if you have color photos of your product.

A good opening can be the key to an effective sales letter.

```
                              TM Corporation
                              87451 Laguna Blvd.
                              Los Angeles, CA 92378
                              April 25, 19xx

Mr. Morris Collins, Manager
Running Wild
Daisy Court Shopping Center
Fort Lauderdale, FL 37892

Dear Morris:

   We would like to introduce your customers to Tom
Mead. Tom Mead running shorts, that is.
   Here are some of the reasons why your customers
will love our shorts:

• Incredible, tailored fit
• New light and versatile fabric
• Sizes from extra small to extra large
• Comfortable built-in briefs
• Unique inside pocket
• A price 15% below that of major brands

   Our new blended fabric breathes more easily than
nylon—keeps a runner dry and cool. And our shorts
are available in checks, solids, and flower prints.
   TM running shorts are functional yet stylish,
comfortable but attractive. And they cost less than
you expect.
   So please examine our TM catalogue. Our
representative will call you within a week to
answer your questions and set up a time for showing
you some samples.
   Believe me. Your customers will be glad to meet
Tom Mead. We've already won the race for the
perfect running shorts!

                              Sincerely,

                              Bob Rudell

                              Bob Rudell
                              Marketing Manager
```

FIGURE 10-5 _____

Effective sales letter. As it accompanies a catalogue, this letter to a store manager simply highlights the major features of the product and informs the reader what will happen next—the
sales representative will call next week. The catchy opening, list format, and short paragraphs
make the letter appealing and easy to read.

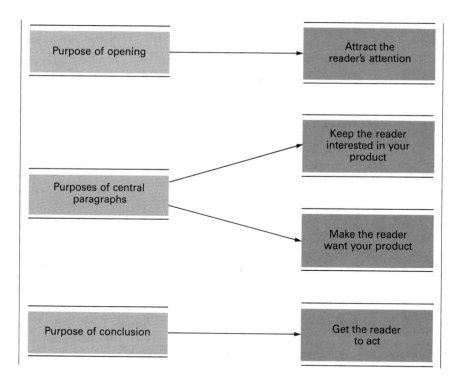

When composing the opening of your sales letter, ask yourself these questions:

- Is it oriented to the reader?
- Is it short and dynamic?
- Does it present an interesting idea or question?
- Does it have *action*?
- Does it introduce a theme?
- Is it relevant to the rest of the letter?
- Will it make someone want to read on?

A good opening gets the reader involved.

Your opening may not fulfill all these criteria, but it should fulfill most of them.

When writing your opening, of course, you will have to make sure it is appropriate in tone and theme to your product and your audience and to the rest of your letter. In fact, you will probably end up rewriting your opening after you have finished the rest of the letter.

Central Paragraphs That Increase Readers' Interest

The main paragraphs of your sales letter should achieve two goals:

- Keep the reader interested in your product
- Make the reader want your product

Do not give your reader a chance to *stop* reading.

Focus every sentence on these goals. In a rational sales letter, you will provide the reader with facts about the product that appeal to his or her

Openings to Consider

The following are some ideas for good openings. You will probably be able to think of others.

Interesting Question

Do you know where the Grenadines are? Not many people do—and that's why you might like to take your next vacation at our secluded beach resort.

Interesting Fact

Your nervous system is made up of billions of nerve cells—each one affected by a single cup of coffee.

Interesting Anecdote

In 1960, Henry Corporation started designing a computer larger than a livingroom. We've been very busy ever since. Today, Henry Corporation's personal computer

Openings to Avoid

These types of openings are usually dull or irritating.

Boring Descriptions or Statistics

The new Regal TV is 24 inches tall and weighs 12 pounds.
In February the temperature averaged 32 degrees in downtown Milwaukee.

Both of these ideas could be useful in a sales letter, but not in the way they are presented here. First of all, the facts themselves are not earthshaking enough for an opening sentence. And, second, the facts have no context. Is the Regal television particularly light or particularly tall? Was it colder or warmer than usual in Milwaukee? These sentences don't give us anything to compare.

Writer-Oriented Statements

Amtron Products has just developed a new detergent.
Pacific Corporation is opening a new branch in Detroit.

These openings are very dull—but their main problem is their writer-viewpoint. Upon reading an opening sentence like this, your readers are apt to say, "Who cares?" Once they react like that, your letter is wasted.

Irritating Openers

What would happen to us if the world suddenly stopped moving? We can't tell you that, but we can tell you about Amtron's great new detergent.

Often these openings are intended to catch the readers' attention, to lead is smaller than a typewriter. It's a hundred times more powerful than the company's first creation. And it's one-tenth the price.

Bargain

Believe it or not: now you can paint your whole house—for the price it used to cost to paint one room.

Variant of a Cliché or Familiar Saying

The way to a man's heart is through his boots.
A penny saved, nowadays, is a penny taxed.

Interesting Comparison

Is your phone system like a brachiosaurus—extinct?

---

them on to the rest of the letter. But when the readers see that the opening was just a bluff, they may be too annoyed to keep reading.

Unpleasant or Negative Concepts

Are you too heavy to fit into last year's clothes?
Is your company going broke?

People prefer reading a pleasant or positive letter rather than an unpleasant or negative one. Also, they are apt to answer "No" to questions like these—and immediately put down your letter. Try a more upbeat angle:

Would you like to lose five pounds in a week?
Would you like to have the edge on your competition?

Try to get your reader to say, "Yes."

If you get your readers to answer "Yes," they will be more likely to keep reading.

Clichés

Hall's Superstore is offering you the most fantastic deal you've ever seen.
Every cloud has a silver lining.

Getting a reader's attention requires fresh ideas, not old, tired ones. Words like *fantastic* and *fabulous* have been overdone to such an extent that they mean very little anymore. And trite sayings are not going to make many readers want to read on. A *variation* of a trite saying, however, can be effective.

desire for efficiency, cost savings, profits, safety, comfort, or health. In an emotional letter, you will appeal to the reader's desire for beauty, luxury, excitement, culture, status, and other intangibles. In either case, provide evidence about your product.

Do not make false or unbelievable claims: "With a U-Form Lounge Chair, you'll never have a backache again." You may run into legal problems while also losing credibility with your audience (See Appendix A, Legal Aspects of Business Communication). But do offer details or testimonials supporting your claims.

> Researchers at the University of Connecticut worked for five years to design the unique support system of the U-Form Lounge Chair.

> Dr. Lawrence Reed of Massachusetts City Hospital writes us: "I have recommended the U-Form Lounge Chair to over a hundred patients with chronic back pain. All of them rest easier now."

The key to effective detail is *concreteness*. Facts and figures will bolster your credibility and the appeal of your product. You might say how many thousands of people have used your product, how many years it was tested, what ingredients it contains, what your staff members' credentials are. Be precise, not vague.

> For only a small amount of money every month, you will enjoy our informative magazine. [vague]

> For only $2.75 a month, you will enjoy over 200 pages of text and pictures taken by world-famous photographers such as Ansel Adams. [concrete]

With an emotional appeal, you can take more liberties with your facts, but even your most gullible readers will probably not believe that:

> Your new hairstyle from Francine's Salon will make you the most beautiful woman in Los Angeles.

On the other hand, they might well believe:

> Your new hairstyle from Francine's Salon will release the new you—the prettier, sexier, more glamorous you.

Making the Price Desirable

The price is usually the least desirable element of a service or product. You will have to decide when and how to deal with it. In most cases, you will not put it at the beginning of the letter; you will make your readers *want* the product before they know how much it costs.

Unless you are selling to an audience that cares little about cost, you will probably want to show either how the product saves or makes money for the buyer or how the product is less expensive or of better quality than competing products. You may also want to minimize costs by showing how much the item costs per month or how much it costs over the long run.

Make the price appear to be a positive aspect of the product.

> For $25 a month, you can have a machine that washes twice as many clothes with half the hot water of your present machine.
>
> Since most people keep their Hobcat Hand Tools for over ten years, you end up paying less than a penny a day for the most efficient tools on the market.

Showing Your Good Faith

Some advertisers are certain that "there's a sucker born every minute." That adage may have some truth to it, but you still will have many readers who are reluctant to respond to sales pitches without some sign of credibility or good faith on the writer's part.

The following list itemizes some methods for reducing your readers' skepticism and increasing the appeal of your product.

Money-Back Guarantees. Include a clear policy on how and when readers can get their money back if they are not satisfied with the product. Your sales letter is, in a sense, a legal document: you are bound to follow through on what you promise. Your readers will have increased confidence knowing they will not be buying a product they cannot use.

Free Trials. You may offer the product to your customer on a free-trial basis: "After ten days, you may return your Tame Hairdryer if you aren't completely satisfied."

Warranties and Service. Make it clear to your readers that the warranty accompanying your product is comprehensive and your follow-up services extensive. For many people, a good warranty and service are as important as the product itself.

Free Samples. Including a sample of your product with your letter can increase your readers' trust and help them remember your product. Even if they do not read your letter, they may well use your product and then continue to buy it in their stores.

Endings that Motivate

The conclusion of a sales letter should lead to action.

Your conclusion has one major purpose: get your readers to *act*. Now that you have succeeded in making readers desire your product, you want them to be able to respond easily and quickly.

Your ending should

1. tie the whole letter together
2. provide clear instructions on what the readers should do
3. give readers an incentive to act quickly

Depending on your audience and your product, you will have to choose between an aggressive, "hard sell" conclusion and a more tactful, low-key ending. Whichever approach you use, make sure to provide details on how to respond—and make it easy for the readers. Tell them to call your toll-free number, mail in the enclosed card, come to your sale, or put a check in the mail.

At the same time, impart a sense of urgency to your ending. You want readers to respond right away. You can say that the offer is limited to this

Revising Sales Letters

Sales letters require careful revision. The following list of questions can help you as you revise your drafts.

- What am I really selling?
- Why will people want to buy my product?
- Who will want this product?
- What have I used to motivate my readers?
- Is my rational (or emotional) approach appropriate?
- Is my style persuasive?
- Have I developed an effective theme?
- Is the opening dynamic?
- Do the central paragraphs add information that will motivate my readers?
- Is the ending action-oriented?

Remember: the best sales letters look like they were put together spontaneously, but only hard work makes them look effortless.

month, that prices go up on August 1, or that the supply of your product is limited. However you do it, convince readers that they will benefit from acting immediately. (See Figure 10-6 for a summary of sales letter strategies that have been successful for some companies.)

Envelope	To imitate personal correspondence, envelopes may be handwritten or individually typed. Colorful stamps and "teaser copy" (You May Have Already Won!) encourage readers to open envelopes. Plastic windows showing part of the offer inside are used to increase readers' curiosity.
Letter	Good quality stationery is used to promote a good image. The reader's name is often inserted in the text, and a conversational style establishes a personal tone. Short sentences and paragraphs are combined with lots of white space on the page to enhance readability. Catchy headlines summarize major ideas. Handwritten signature heightens personal touch. Postscript is used to attract reader's eye.
Enclosures	Colorful brochures and folders are enclosed to attract visual attention. Order forms and discount coupons are designed to get immediate response. Samples encourage readers to try product. Extra slips are enclosed with a personal word from the seller. Gimmicks such as "yes" and "no" stickers to paste on and boxes to check for additional prizes are added to get the reader actively involved.

FIGURE 10-6 —————————————————
Some popular strategies for sales letters

Drafting and Revising Promotional Letters

Similar to sales letters, promotional letters urge readers to attend an event, support a cause, or donate money rather than to buy a product or service.

Successful promotional letters work on nearly the same principles as sales letters. You still need to

1. capture the readers' interest
2. tell them about your situation, service or cause
3. motivate them to act

As you draft and revise, work on a theme and an approach that will motivate your particular readers and achieve the goals you have in mind.

Promotional letters operate on principles similar to sales letters.

Solving Common Problems with Promotional Letters

Unsuccessful promotional letters are often I-oriented.

Writers of promotional letters often make two serious errors: they overestimate their readers' interest in or sympathy with the cause, and they underestimate readers' knowledge about the cause.

Avoid Abrupt Openings

Because writers often assume that the readers will be interested in their cause, they do not bother to create a dynamic opening. Many request letters open too abruptly or abrasively.

> Franklin Childcare Center needs $10,000.
> Senior Citizens' Hotline is looking for volunteers.
> As a Democrat, you will want to support Thomas Hayes.

Seeing that it is asking for money or time, many people will toss out the letter right away—particularly if they have never heard of Franklin Childcare Center, the Senior Citizens' Hotline, or Thomas Hayes.

Add Reader-Oriented Information

Promotional letter writers are often so wrapped up in the needs and concerns of their cause or organization that they never consider the readers' feelings or motivations. The letters become bogged down in the organization's history or in descriptions of the people who contribute their time or money. (Compare Figure 10-7 with Figure 10-8.)

Use the You-Attitude

The you-attitude is an essential component of any persuasive communication: do not let your zeal for a cause diminish your attention to your audience. In general, regard your promotional letter in light of a sales letter: like Roger Baptista with his insulation service, examine who your readers are, what motivates them, and what reward they will attain from supporting the cause or organization.

Promotional letters often use intangible rewards to motivate readers.

Often a careful combination of rational and emotional appeals will be most effective. Many times the rewards from such support will be intangible: the readers will derive pleasure from helping others, feel they are helping society, or believe they are joining an elite group of sponsors. But if there are more tangible rewards—tax deductions, gold plaques, monogrammed tote bags, or membership advantages—the writer should sell those as well. (Compare Figure 10-9 with Figure 10-10.)

The following are some tips for good promotions.

```
                    Children's Counseling Center
                    867 Rodgers Ave.
                    Wayne City, WA 98465
                    October 5, 19xx

Dear Fellow Wayne City Resident:

    I am writing you today asking for your help in
making certain that mental health services remain
available for disturbed children in our community.
The Children's Counseling Center has been in
operation for the past seven years. The staff has
seen over 1,500 children during that time. Now the
program desperately needs your help to stay in
operation.
    The budget cuts of the past two years have taken
their toll. The CCC has had to drastically reduce
services and today the waiting list for services is
over six months long. For a child's growth and
development, six months is a very long time.
    The CCC serves children referred by schools and
churches. It charges fees on an ability-to-pay
basis. But now that revenues have dropped over 75%
due to federal budget cuts, nine staff members have
been laid off and three others are working part-
time in an agency that once had fifteen full-time
therapists and teachers.
    Your help is desperately needed TODAY. This is a
request from a program that serves you and your
neighbors—not from an agency you can't see. To help
us, please send your tax-deductible contributions
to CCC. Help us save a child's future.

                         Sincerely,

                         Carla Gardiner

                         Carla Gardiner
```

FIGURE 10-7

Poor promotional letter. This letter is wordy and roundabout. It discusses budget cuts before it tells what the organization does. Even when the writer finally does describe the organization, she keeps the description general and impersonal.

Because the writer never makes the reader feel special, sets a goal for the reader, or says what a donation might really accomplish, the letter never really grips the reader. See Figure 10-8 for a revised version of this letter.

```
                        Children's Counseling Center
                        867 Rodgers Ave.
                        Wayne City, WA 98465
                        October 5, 19xx

Dear Wayne City Resident:

    Six-year-old Sam needs your help. For two months
he has been crying in school, unable to concentrate
in class or even to talk with his schoolmates.
    His teacher referred him to us: the Children's
Counseling Center. In the past, we could have
treated Sam—and hundreds of other children—within a
week. Now he and his family must wait six months
before one of our therapists can see him.
    CCC is a unique program in Wayne City. We open
our doors to any child between 2 and 14 whose
family cannot afford a regular therapist. Our fully
accredited staff of doctors, psychologists,
counselors, and teachers has treated over 1,500
children since 19xx. In the March issue of Parent
and Child Magazine, Dr. Marion Block wrote: "CCC's
astonishingly successful program shows a unique
combination of skill, creativity, and dedication."
    Today, however, state and federal budget cuts put
our program in peril. Since January, nine staff
members have been laid off and three others are
working part-time. Children like Sam now must wait
six months for our help. And, in a child's life,
six months can be crucial.
    CCC is a program of neighbor helping neighbor.
But we cannot continue without funds. Please help
us before the year is out. Send your tax-deductible
contribution in the enclosed postage-paid envelope.
    The children are waiting.

                        Sincerely,

                        Carla Gardiner

                        Carla Gardiner
```

FIGURE 10-8 _____

Revised promotional letter. This letter opens with an emotional appeal: the plight of one child. Carla then goes on to describe the organization in terms a reader can relate to—showing a track record, reputable staff, and an enthusiastic tribute. In the conclusion, she emphasizes the necessity of giving before the end of the year. Her ending repeats the theme of waiting introduced by the story of Sam.

```
                        Friends of the City Library
                        14 Mayfair Avenue
                        Fair Oaks, PA 19643
                        April 21, 19xx

Mrs. Harry Norton
1984 Cobalt Avenue
Fair Oaks, PA 19642

Dear Mrs. Norton:

   Fifty years ago this month, Friends of the City
Library was founded to help support our city's
public libraries. Since then, we have worked in a
variety of capacities: raising money through
booksales, volunteering as storytellers and
docents, and contributing many interesting books to
the four city library branches.
   To celebrate our fiftieth anniversary, a buffet
dinner will be held at McClellan Hall, 201 Flower
Street, on Saturday, May 7. The event will run from
5 pm until 9 pm. Wine and hors d'oeuvres will be
served from 5 until 6, and many books will be on
view. Alice Floyd, who contributes valuable hours
every week to coordinating volunteers, will give us
a few words at 6 p.m.
   So please join us. Fill out the enclosed card and
send it with your $25 contribution. Your money will
help our city libraries continue to provide top
service to the residents of Fair Oaks. If you have
any questions, don't hesitate to call me at 221-
5673. I look forward to seeing you on May 7!

                        Sincerely,

                        Teresa Howard

                        Teresa Howard
                        Secretary
```

FIGURE 10-9

Poor promotional letter. This letter is clearly writer-oriented. It also lacks enthusiasm and detail. The letter should get the reader to send money for the event and then to attend. The invitation, however, does not appear until the end of the second paragraph—and even then the reader is never clearly *invited*.

Moreover, the description of the organization's responsibilities will hold little interest for the reader, and the passive voice makes this letter impersonal and even ungrammatical. (Note the dangling modifer at the opening to the second paragraph. *Who* is celebrating?)

Teresa does not describe the dinner or even the books on view. Her vagueness makes the letter uninspiring. Even dedicated library users may not want to donate to this cause. And most readers will want to miss Alice Floyd's "few words."

See Figure 10-10 for an improved version of this letter.

Friends of the City Library
14 Mayfair Avenue
Fair Oaks, PA 19643
April 21, 19xx

Mrs. Harry Norton
1984 Cobalt Avenue
Fair Oaks, PA 19642

Dear Mrs. Norton:

Help us celebrate our fiftieth birthday! On Saturday, May 7, the Friends of the City Library will be celebrating our fiftieth year in Fair Oaks. We hope you will join us for wine and hors d'oeuvres and then a sumptuous buffet dinner catered by Chef Louis.

Since 19xx, the Friends of the City Library has worked to make our library more useful and enjoyable for adults and children, professionals and hobbyists, teachers and students—for everyone in Fair Oaks. We introduce new residents to the library, organize reading hours for children, work at the Information Desk, and set up meetings and film viewing in the library meeting rooms.

In the past decade, we have also raised over $100,000 for the library through book sales and auctions!

Join us for our fiftieth birthday. You will taste some unusual European wines and an elegant array of Spanish and French dishes. You will also enjoy our display of early Pennsylvania diaries, collected by local historian Ed Copley, which is about to go on tour of northeastern public libraries.

Your contribution to our fiftieth anniversary celebration will go directly to the city library for replacement of lost and damaged books. So please fill out the enclosed card and return it with your tax-deductible contribution by May 1. We will hold your tickets at the door. Each ticket is $25 apiece or $45 a couple.

Do come celebrate with us! Our fiftieth birthday will be our best ever.

Sincerely,

Teresa Howard

Teresa Howard
Secretary

Place: McClellan Hall, 201 Flower Street
Date: May 7
Time: 6–9 p.m.
Dress: Informal

Provide Details

Provide details on your organization or cause—its purpose, track record, major supporters—in reader-oriented terms.

> Parents Partnership acts as a liaison between governmental agencies and foster homes. [poor: description is writer-oriented]

> Last year, Parents Partnership found homes for over three hundred homeless children in our city. [good: reader-oriented]

> The Art Society of Sacramento was founded in 1900 to bring European talent to California. [dull: writer-oriented]

> For over eighty years the Art Society of Sacramento has been bringing the best talent in the world to our city. Anna Pavlova, Maria Callas, Arthur Rubinstein, Luciano Pavarotti—all came to perform for Sacramento audiences through the efforts of the Art Society. [good: concrete, reader-oriented]

Personalize Your Needs

Most people prefer to donate to something particular: a new museum building, specific medical equipment, an individual's political campaign. People want to feel special; they prefer helping one child to supporting an organization's operating expenses. The more human and personal your approach, the more successful your request is apt to be.

> The American Eye Clinic needs $200 every day just to keep its doors open. Please help us. [general, impersonal]

> With our help, a hundred people a week can see clearly again. With your $10, these two needy children can be fitted with glasses. Please help them. [specific personal]

Add Interesting Information

If you are sponsoring an event, make it sound interesting. Many organizations assume that the readers' innate desire to help will bring them to the charity ball, the wine and cheese event, or the 1950s fashion show. Most people on charitable mailing lists, however, are inundated with requests: you will have to persuade them that this event is worth their time.

Charitable events should sound exciting.

Once again, highlight the strong points of your event: the free drinks, the celebrity entertainment, the dinner cooked by Chef Louis. Give details that will make your readers excited.

◄ **FIGURE 10-10** ——————————————————————————————

Revised promotional letter. This letter conveys more enthusiasm than the first version. Teresa now opens with the invitation and makes the event sound appealing. Then her concrete description of the organization's activities makes them sound worthwhile.

Concrete detail makes this letter come alive: the dinner sounds worth eating, the book display sounds worth seeing. By the time we reach the end, the $25 contribution doesn't sound too bad. (Now Teresa also tells us how our money will be spent.)

The summary at the end makes it easy for the reader to check on essential information.

What Would You Do?

The Counseling Center on your campus is starting a telephone hotline for students who are considering suicide, have a drug or alcohol problem, or need emergency counseling for other reasons. Myrna Tracey has been asked to write a letter that will go to both instructors and students to tell them about the hotline and urge students to use it if they need help.

After a week, Myrna hasn't been able to write a letter that satisfies her. She wants a letter that provides basic information on the service but also appeals emotionally to students in trouble who are afraid to ask for help.

Draft the letter for Myrna.

Moreover, make sure you include *all* necessary details: do not forget to mention the type of attire required or the time the dinner begins. Many thousands of dollars have been lost due to careless errors like this.

Establish an Effective Tone

Remember to adapt your tone to your readers and your cause.

Adapt your tone to your audience and your cause. A sophisticated, well-to-do reader may not respond well to a folksy, "Hi, Friend" at the beginning of your invitation to an expensive luncheon. On the other hand, a formal invitation to a charity barbeque may look and sound absurd.

In conclusion, the major rule for all persuasive writing is the fundamental rule of effective communication: consider your reader, not yourself. Your ultimate aim is to link your reader with your goal, whatever it is. Never lose sight of your audience or your goal.

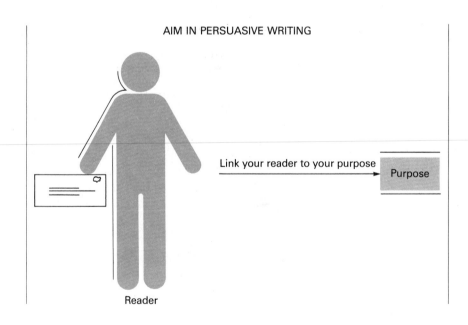

AIM IN PERSUASIVE WRITING

Link your reader to your purpose

Purpose

Reader

Summary

Sales and promotional letters require that a writer learn to be persuasive. The content and appearance of these letters should be focused on getting specific readers to *act*. What motivates these readers? What do they want? What do they need?

Analyzing your audience and doing necessary research are essential steps to the creation of good sales and promotional letters. A key to effective persuasive writing is remembering that your readers are not like you: find out what they are like and then develop your letters accordingly.

Summary Discussion: Martin DeVries's Sales Letter from Case in Point, p. 212

Martin DeVries's letter is both dull and vague. The impersonal salutation, long opening paragraph, and lifeless sentences discourage a reader from finishing the letter. The letter also has a negative emphasis: the writer *assumes* the reader's company has problems.

As Martin is addressing professional people concerned with getting quality services, the letter should establish the credibility of CDS Management Services. Specific details would be more impressive than general statements about "unique classes" and "professional consultants from a wide variety of fields."

The ending is writer-oriented and lacks dynamism. Nothing in the letter motivates a reader to call right away.

Checklist for Sales and Promotional Letters

Goals and Audience

• Make your presentation relevant to the reader.

• Maintain a tone appropriate to

_____ your company

_____ your product

_____ your audience

• Focus on getting the reader to *act*.

• Know what motivates your reader.

• Know your product thoroughly.

Approach and Style

• Determine whether a rational or persuasive approach will be more effective.

• Use a persuasive style that features

_____ active verbs

_____ short sentences and paragraphs

_____ a personal tone

• Develop a theme to unify the letter.

Organization

• Write an opening that will make the reader want to read on.

• Develop central paragraphs that

_____ provide information

_____ maintain the reader's interest

_____ maintain your credibility with the reader

- Develop an ending that

  _____ ties the letter together

  _____ urges the reader to act quickly

Promotional Letters

- Develop promotional letters that

  _____ provide reader-oriented details

  _____ make the reader feel special

- Adapt your tone to your audience and your cause.

Terms to Remember

Credibility: the extent to which your reader believes in you, your product, and your organization

Demographic variables: external characteristics such as people's age, sex, race, income, job type, and education

Emotional approach: an approach to persuasive writing that stresses things people want rather than need

Maslow's hierarchy of needs: a theory of motivation based on the concept that lower-order needs such as hunger and thirst must be satisfied before higher-order needs such as a desire for prestige can emerge

Primary data: information collected specifically for the project at hand. A questionnaire, for example, might be used to collect primary data.

Promotional letter: a letter urging readers to support a cause

Psychographic variables: internal characteristics such as people's personality types, values, lifestyles, interests, and opinions

Rational approach: an approach to persuasive writing that appeals to a reader's logic. A rational approach emphasizes factual data.

Sales letter: a letter selling a product or service

Secondary data: information collected for purposes other than your project. Magazine articles might be a source for secondary data.

Questions for Review and Discussion

1. What communication techniques can you learn from studying sales letters?
2. What are four common barriers to effective persuasive writing?
3. What characteristics of an audience do you think are most important to a writer of sales letters? Why?
4. What is an advantage of using secondary data when you research your audience?
5. Name five products best sold through an emotional approach. Name five items best sold through a rational approach.
6. Why do sales letters often have a theme running through them?

7. What is the purpose of the opening to a sales letter?
8. What should be included in the central sections of a sales letter?
9. How can you make the price of an item appear appealing to a reader?
10. How could a writer improve the credibility of a letter selling a magazine subscription?
11. How is a promotional letter different from a sales letter?
12. What characteristics of a promotional letter are similar to those of a sales letter?

Exercises

1. Which of the following opening statements do you think would be effective for a sales letter?
   a. [for exercise equipment] Are you worried about adipose tissue?
   b. [for a business magazine] Would you invest ten dollars to make a hundred? We bet you would. That's why *Business World* is making you this offer.
   c. [for a mail-order jewelry outlet] Did you know that some clouds have *golden* linings?
   d. [for a group of dentists] Many people are afraid to go to a dentist. They assume their teeth are all right if they don't hurt.
   e. [for a mail order clothing outlet] If you love beautiful clothes but hate to shop, take a walk through our catalogue.
   Describe why some of these openings seemed to work while others didn't. Now write better openings for the items you found ineffective.
2. What problems do you see in the following paragraph from a sales letter? Revise the paragraph, adding or deleting information as necessary.

   While your neighbors are sweating behind their lawnmowers, you will be sitting in luxury on your Green-Gro's plush leather seat. And your tall grass and weeds will be disappearing like magic! For only a little over $300, you will have the best lawnmower ever made, the one lawnmower that takes care of *all* your grass and weed problems.

3. Revise the following paragraph from a promotional letter to make it more interesting. You may add details if necessary.

   The annual Seniors' Day Concert should be a lot of fun this year. The Hillsdale Pops Symphony will play selections from well-known musicals. We will hand out sheets with lyrics for some of the most popular tunes, so we can all sing along. At intermission, refreshments will be available.

4. Revise this sales letter to make it more effective.

   ```
                          A-1 Athletics Company
                          1723 Holly Drive
                          Greenstown, TX 54590
                          February 12, 19xx

   Mr. Joel Brumer
   237 Adell Lane
   Honig, PA 19589

   Dear Mr. Brumer:

      As a health club member, you will be
   interested in the Martin Rowing Machine.
   Experts claim that Olympic rowers are the
   most fit athletes in the games. Rowing is
   very intense and dynamic. It involves the
   whole body in an aerobics workout. Rowing
   can also help take care of some of your
   muscle-strength imbalances. And rowing
   works the legs as well as the upper body.
      A Martin Rowing Machine will fit your
   body—whatever size you are. Its stable and
   heavy frame is strong enough for the
   biggest man—but is easily handled by the
   smallest woman. The hydraulic, gas-filled
   shocks on our machine will last for years,
   and the pivoting oars work a wide range of
   muscles. The rowing team at the University
   of Connecticut uses Martin machines
   exclusively, and they will attest to its
   superiority: "The machine simulates the
   rowing motion very well," asserts Coach
   Greg Freed.
      So read our enclosed brochure. If you
   ```

like what you see, send in the enclosed
postcard and try a Martin free for 30
days. If not completely satisfied, you can
send it back to us anytime before 30 days
are up. If you are satisfied—and we know
you will be—you pay only $350. So for less
than your health club membership, you can
have total fitness!

Sincerely,

Sam Waters

Sam Waters
President
A-1 Athletics Company

5. When you have read the following letter, list
problem areas you have spotted in the
writer's approach. Does the letter have any
strong points? Revise the letter.

GRUBER'S GARDENING SERVICES

4119 Rosetown Highway •
Rosetown, PA 19845 • 657-9000

March 12, 19xx

Mr. and Mrs. Richard Biddle
34 Timothy Court
Rosetown, PA 19846

Dear Mr. and Mrs. Biddle:

Is your front yard a mess? Do you lie
awake at night worrying whether your
shrubs have been fertilized? Then you
should call us, Gruber's Gardening
Service. We'll make sure the job is done
on time—and done right. For $60 a month we
can also mow your lawn and weed your
gardens. For a low, low $80 a month, we
will also trim your bushes and trees. We
can install sprinkling systems, too, and
advise you about when to plant—and where.

So now that it's spring planting time,
call us. Gruber's Gardening Service will
make you sleep better at night.

Sincerely,

Bob Gruber

Bob Gruber

6. Revise Martin DeVries's sales leter at the
opening of this chapter (p. 212).

7. A small group of people is opening a new
sandwich shop on campus. Write a letter to
students and faculty promoting the new place
and offering a one-week sandwich deal: two
for the price of one.

8. The local animal shelter is badly in need of
funds. Write a letter to former supporters
urging them to help keep the shelter open.

9. A new travel agency is opening in a suburban
area. Write a letter to local residents—mostly
people with young families—promoting the
agency's services.

10. A cooking school is starting a series of classes.
Write a letter to former students—mostly
women between 20 and 50—promoting the
classes. (Choose a specialized topic for the
class such as tofu, wine, chocolate, or pastry.)

11. You are setting up your own gardening or
housekeeping service. To promote your
services, write a letter that will go to a
hundred homes in your area.

12. Your campus organization is starting an informational newsletter that will list upcoming
events sponsored by the organization, job
openings, and other items of interest to all
students. Write a letter to all students asking
them to read and contribute to this newsletter.

13. You are organizing an athletic event to raise
money for the homeless in your city. Write a
letter to the owners of local businesses asking
them to donate funds or equipment for the
event.

14. You are organizing a one-day clinic for students who want to upgrade their skills with
the Lotus 1-2-3 computer program. Write a
letter to business majors explaining why they
should attend and providing all pertinent details about the clinic.

15. A friend of yours has opened a small shop
that carries artifacts from the 1950s: hula
hoops, comic books, Eisenhower campaign
buttons, and so on. Your friend has bought a
mailing list of people in your area who listen
to an "oldies" radio station. Write a sales letter about the store to the people on the list.

16. You are the head of an organization that
raises money to send children to summer
camps. This year you are organizing a gala
dinner-dance. Write a letter promoting the
event to people who often donate to charity.

Most word processing programs enable you to MARK a block of text within a file so it can be copied, deleted, or moved. The programs we find most preferable indicate the marked blocks by highlighting them in reverse video on the screen: that is, you will see black characters on a green background, for instance, instead of green characters on a black background.

Learning to work with blocks of text is vital to good editing. Revising requires more than simply fixing individual sentences; often it requires shifting paragraphs to different parts of a document, moving sentences from the beginning to the end of a paragraph, and deleting sections that do not contribute to your major points. Word processing techniques are valuable for all these situations.

By doing the following exercises, you will learn to

- mark blocks of text
- copy the blocks
- delete the blocks
- move the blocks

1. Create a file named BLOCK and type in the following paragraphs.

> It is easy to see why word processing has been called the greatest advance in written composition since the typewriter. Word processing is the answer to every writer's dream, and writers especially appreciate its editing capabilities.

> With our powerful word processing program, you can use your personal computer as a word processor. Whether you are typing a memo, a ten-page report, or a complicated table, text entry is quick and easy. Because you can correct or revise a document on the screen—before it is printed—you can save yourself time and effort.

2. Now learn the commands for MARKING a block of text. You will have to put a marker at the beginning and at the end of the words, sentences, or paragraphs you want to mark. Put a marker at the beginning of paragraph 1 of the file BLOCK (before *It*) and after the end of the paragraph (after *capabilities*). If your program highlights marked text, you will now see this paragraph in reverse video.

3. Marked text may be copied to any part of your file: just move the cursor to the place you want the text to appear and enter the necessary command. Move the cursor to the end of the file and COPY the marked text. Then enter the command to delete the block markers. Your file should now look like this:

> It is easy to see why word processing has been called the greatest advance in written composition since the typewriter. Word processing is the answer to every writer's dream, and writers especially appreciate its editing capabilities.

> With our powerful word processing program, you can use your personal computer as a word processor. Whether you are typing a memo, a ten-page report, or a complicated table, text entry is quick and easy. Because you can correct or revise a document on the screen—before it is printed—you can save yourself time and effort.

> It is easy to see why word processing has been called the greatest advance in written composition since the typewriter. Word processing is the answer to every writer's dream, and writers especially appreciate its editing capabilities.

4. Go back and mark the first paragraph the same way you did in Step 3. This time enter the command to delete the marked text. Your new file should look like this:

> With our powerful word processing program, you can use your personal computer as a word processor. Whether you are typing a memo, a ten-page report, or a complicated table, text entry is quick and easy. Because you can correct or revise a document on the screen—before it is printed—you can save yourself time and effort.

> It is easy to see why word processing has been called the greatest advance in written composition since the typewriter. Word

processing is the answer to every writer's dream, and writers especially appreciate its editing capabilities.

5. Now mark the first paragraph again—one marker before *With* and one after *effort*. This time MOVE the marked text so the first paragraph follows the second one. Your file should look like this:

It is easy to see why word processing has been called the greatest advance in written composition since the typewriter. Word processing is the answer to every writer's dream, and writers especially appreciate its editing capabilities.

With our powerful word processing program, you can use your personal computer as a word processor. Whether you are typing a memo, a ten-page report, or a complicated table, text entry is quick and easy. Because you can correct or revise a document on the screen—before it is printed—you can save yourself time and effort.

Practice these block techniques until you are comfortable with them. You will find them invaluable aids to your revision of business writing: you can experiment with different effects, quickly delete data you do not want in your finished document, and copy phrases, headings, or paragraphs that you use repeatedly in a document without having to retype them.

WRITE and READ Commands

The WRITE command enables you to select a portion of a file and move it to a new file. Thus, if you want to save certain paragraphs or data and use them again, you can do so.

The READ command enables you to insert another file into the one you are working on. For example, you can save paragraphs from one letter and use them again in a new letter simply by READING in the file containing the paragraphs.

WRITE and READ commands are particularly useful if you use similar material over and over for letters and reports: you do not have to retype the material once you have written it.

1. Create a file named SMITH. Type in the following letter:

```
Mr. Henry Smith, Editor
Hardwoods Magazine
1200 Lakeshore Drive
Atlas, KS 78943

Dear Mr. Smith:

As the owner of a new business that
specializes in woodworking tools, I am
interested in your publication.

Please send me the following information
regarding your magazine:
```

- Subscription rates
- Advertising rates
- Average monthly circulation

```
Thank you for your assistance.

Sincerely,
```

Mary Anne Macomb

```
Mary Anne Macomb
Owner
```

2. Now mark a block of text beginning with the first sentence (before the word *As*) and ending with the last word of the file (*Owner*).

3. Learn the procedure for WRITING text to a new file. Enter the command. When asked to name the file you want the text written to, give the name MAG.

4. When the text has been written to the new file, delete the block markers. Save the file SMITH and exit from it. Your file directory should now list both SMITH and MAG.

5. Open a new file named JONES. Type in the following return address and salutation:

Mrs. Terri Jones, Editor
Woodworking Today
982 Millstone Road
Janesville, WI 64537

Dear Mrs. Jones:

6. Learn the commands for READING in a file. Then put the cursor under the salutation of the letter and READ in the file MAG. Your letter should now look like this:

Mrs. Terri Jones, Editor
Woodworking Today
982 Millstone Road
Janesville, WI 64537

Dear Mrs. Jones:

As the owner of a new business that specializes in woodworking tools, I am interested in your publication.

Please send me the following information regarding your magazine:

• Subscription rates
• Advertising rates
• Average monthly circulation

Thank you for your assistance.

Sincerely,

Mary Anne Macomb

Mary Anne Macomb
Owner

7. Save the SMITH and JONES files.

Credit, Claim, and Collection Letters

Objectives

To write effective letters granting and denying credit

To write claim letters that persuade the reader to respond positively

To respond negatively to claims without losing the reader's goodwill

To create a series of collection letters that persuade readers to make payments

11

Deana Gilroy's Claim Letter

Technical Research, Inc.
5211 Ohleyer Road
St. Paul, MN 65328
(603) 666-1212
May 12, 19xx

Mrs. Jackie Webster
Vericom Office Systems
2289 Rose Boulevard
Minneapolis, MN 65329

Dear Mrs. Webster:

We are extremely unhappy with the copier
we bought a few weeks ago from your
company. Although the machine was
reconditioned rather than new, we were
assured the drum and all other parts
were as good as new. Needless to say, we
followed all instructions carefully.
Within a few days, however, the copies
became pale and blurred.

Your company has already sent one person
out here to repair the machine, but
now the problem is happening again. We
simply do not have time to deal with
a copier that will always be breaking
down. I am sure you will agree that an
adjustment should be made regarding this
machine.

Sincerely yours,

Deana Gilroy

Deana Gilroy
Senior Consultant

Points to Consider

- What is Deana's major purpose in writing this letter?
- What do you recommend adding to this letter?
- What do you recommend deleting from the letter?
- What is the biggest communication problem in this letter?

Communicating About Credit, Claims, and Collections

Credit, claim, and collection letters often convey unpleasant messages.

Credit, claim, and collection letters have several qualities in common. Such letters are concerned principally with money, and often they convey unpleasant messages to the reader. As a writer of these letters, be aware of legal as

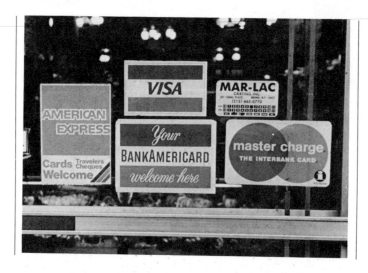

well as business and interpersonal considerations. To accomplish your communication goals in these situations, work on creating letters that are tactful as well as accurate and persuasive.

These letters involve a number of communication problems, so they can all be quite difficult to write. To increase efficiency, many large companies use form letters that may be adapted to various credit, claim, and collection situations. Having standard formats for routine situations is a useful practice.

Even these standard letters, however, can be personal and you-oriented. In many cases, taking the time to add personal touches to your standard letters will lead to significantly better responses from your readers.

Even form letters can be you-oriented.

Writing Good and Bad News Letters Concerning Credit

Buying on credit has become part of almost everyone's life; department stores, restaurants, gas stations—thousands of businesses flourish by offering credit. Even supermarkets are winning customers by letting them pay with plastic rather than cash.

Credit customers are valuable to a business. Although charge accounts cost a business money, credit customers often buy more liberally and return more frequently than cash customers. On the other hand, credit customers who do not pay their bills can ruin a company. Knowing the importance of having credit customers who will pay their bills regularly, companies are developing ever more sophisticated techniques for assessing the people to whom they will grant credit.

If you are going to be writing letters about credit, you need to observe the legal restrictions. An attorney skilled in this area can save you many problems in the long run. You should become familiar with both federal laws and your state laws regarding credit. Federal laws such as the Consumer Credit Protection Act, the Equal Credit Opportunity Act, the Fair Credit Billing Act, and the Fair Credit Reporting Act are all important to businesspeople who grant and deny credit. (For more information on these laws and on legal restrictions regarding credit, see Appendix A, Legal Aspects of Business Communication.)

Many laws govern credit policies.

Good News Letters: Approving Credit Requests

Letters approving credit have several goals:

Credit approvals should get to the point right away.

1. To inform customers that their credit has been approved
2. To provide all legally required information concerning credit policies
3. To encourage readers to buy your products or use your services over the long term

Letters approving requests for credit should be concise and clear. Put the good news in the opening paragraph.

Dear Ms. Hill:
    We are pleased to tell you that you are now one of Janyce Clothier's credit customers.

Companies must fully disclose their credit policies.

Companies are required by law to disclose information regarding their credit policies. Such information includes how much credit the customer has been given, when payments are due, what the interest charges are, and whom the customer should talk to if problems come up. With the letter granting credit, many companies enclose a brochure outlining this important information. If you do not enclose a brochure, summarize these terms in the letter itself.

Keep the tone friendly and you-oriented throughout this section. Compare

If you do not pay your bill by the 15th of the month, we will charge you 1.5 percent interest on your balance.

with

If you pay your bill by the 15th of each month, you pay only the amount of your purchase. Any balance remaining after the 15th will incur a 1.5 percent monthly interest charge.

Keep the wording simple and clear in this section of the letter.

You may now make up to $1,500 worth of credit purchases at any of Janyce's outlets. Each month we will mail you a statement listing purchases made during the previous month. If you pay the balance by the 21st of the month, no interest will accrue. You may choose to pay as little as $10 a month on your purchases; we will add a 1.65 percent monthly interest charge to the next billing.

The enclosed brochure provides you with complete information on our credit terms. Please call us at (302) 356-9000 if you have questions.

To encourage customers to use their new credit, you may want to add details about sales or services that will appeal to them.

With your Janyce's credit card, getting ready for a winter holiday is a breeze. Our new line of Canal Cruisewear is on sale through December—and parking is free in our newly completed garage.

Bad News Letters: Refusing Credit

Credit refusals can lead to bad feelings and even lawsuits, so be very careful to avoid errors. Once again, you may well want to work with an attorney if you are setting up a credit policy.

Letters denying a credit request are more difficult to write than those granting credit. Not only do you want to convey the bad news, but you also want to retain your reader's goodwill and avoid legal complications: your goal is to keep the reader as a cash customer.

> Dear Mrs. Malthaus:
> We are sorry to inform you that we cannot extend you credit at this time.

Even when you have refused credit, you want to keep the reader as a cash customer.

Many companies use a direct refusal similar to the preceding letter. This approach, however, is bound to lose some cash customers. Figure 11-1 shows

```
                    P. B. Hahn's Home Supplies
                    23 East Street
                    Oklahoma City, OK 73498
                    (405) 339-7000
                    October 18, 19xx



Mr. Clarence Frye
9876 Danson Court, Apt. 2B
Oklahoma City, OK 73968


Dear Mr. Frye:

    Thank you for your request for a charge account
at Hahn's Home Supplies.
    We have reviewed your credit references and found
them very favorable. However, your present balances
on several charge accounts are high in proportion
to your monthly income. We will be happy to serve
you on a cash basis, but we cannot grant you credit
at this time. If your outstanding balances are
lower at the end of six months, you may reapply for
credit at that time.
    I have enclosed our Christmas catalog for your
information. Thank you again for your interest in
Hahn's.

                    Sincerely,

                    Betty Hollenhoff

                    Betty Hollenhoff
                    Credit Supervisor
```

Opening acts as buffer

Explanation precedes refusal

Refusal is clear

Ending is pleasant

Sentence encourages cash purchases

FIGURE 11–1 ———————————————
Letter refusing credit. This letter is polite but firm. The upbeat opening and conclusion soften the bad news.

a more effective approach: a pleasant opening acts as a buffer, and reasons for the refusal precede the actual refusal.

To encourage cash purchases, you may want to describe some advantages to doing business on a cash basis:

Paying with cash will help to ease the strain of those end-of-the-month bills.

You probably know how unpleasant monthly bills can be; knowing you paid cash for your equipment and tools can be highly satisfying. And you avoid accruing interest charges, too.

After refusing the request, you might mention when the reader should consider reapplying.

Until your financial condition improves, we will not be able to grant your credit request. We would welcome your application in six months, however, if your financial situation has become more stable.

We cannot issue credit cards to customers under eighteen years old. After your eighteenth birthday, however, we will be happy to reactivate your application.

In general, a courteous, tactful, but honest approach will convey your bad news effectively without losing the goodwill of the customer.

Writing Letters Regarding Claims

Claim letters should be written promptly.

Claim letters and letters responding to claims are some of the most common business correspondence. Both consumers and companies often buy products that turn out to be defective or order products that arrive late or are in the wrong color, size, or quantity. And most companies respond frequently to customer complaints. On both sides, the letters should be written promptly, and they should be well organized, accurate, and complete. (See Figure 11–2.)

Claim Letters

Many people tell "horror tales" about endless controversies they have had with companies regarding routine claims. Sometimes a simple request to exchange a damaged product can lead to months of frustration with customer service representatives, billing departments, computers, and salespeople.

```
                    Omega Industries
                    3467 Simpson Lane
                    Beachtown, FL 33245

                                        April 9, 19xx

        Mr. Frederick Jansen
        Customer Service Manager
        TTT Computers
        8992 Atlantic Boulevard
        Miami, FL 33456

        Dear Mr. Jensen:

           On November 1, I bought a TTT Personal Computer
        from your Beachtown dealership. Since then, the
        machine has caused immense problems for the two
        file clerks for whom I bought it.
             1. The machine does not automatically make a
        back-up copy when a file is saved.
             2. If a disk is more than half-full, an error
        reading appears on the screen, and often the
        material not yet saved is lost.
           In December, the dealership repairman worked on
        the machine while I used a "loaner" machine. The
        problems, however, remain. The repairman assures me
        the problem lies in the machine, not the software;
        he just can't locate the problem. (See the enclosed
        copy of his report.)
           This machine has cost my company time and money.
        I know TTT has an excellent reputation for quality
        and service, but this machine is definitely a
        "lemon." Please give me a replacement machine or
        refund the $867.

                            Sincerely,

                            Kaye Abbott

                            Kaye Abbott
                            Manager, Purchasing Department
```

Opening states product type, date of purchase, and location of purchase

List summarizes problems

Paragraph summarizes situation so far

Paragraph persuades reader to act

Conclusion contains request for action

FIGURE 11–2

Claim letter. This letter politely states all the necessary information: the date and location of the original purchase, the exact problem, and the efforts the writer has made to fix the problem. Her letter is persuasive without being angry.

In general, however, most claims are settled simply and equably. As a buyer, you can follow certain steps that will facilitate the process.

1. Contact the seller as soon as you recognize a problem. The longer you wait, the harder it may be to resolve the situation.

2. Put everything in writing. You may choose to begin the process by telephoning the salesperson whom you originally dealt with. But even if you do speak with the person, follow up with a letter. You may need to document the situation later on.

> On Monday, May 4, I spoke with you regarding the defective heater in the Toyota Corolla that I bought from you on April 18. You told me to bring the car in to the Toyota repair shop in Kenosha and to send a copy of the repair bill to you.

3. Be polite. Legitimate, reasonable claim letters usually receive positive responses; you will gain nothing by writing an angry letter.
4. Be specific. Include any information pertinent to the transaction: order number, catalog number, date of sale, place of sale, item number, description of item, and so on.
5. Keep copies of all letters, invoices, checks, receipts, and other material relevant to the transaction. Having this information accessible will help you write clear, accurate letters; the documents will also back up your claim if you run into a legal controversy. (In some situations, you may also want to photograph a damaged item.)

> Claim letters should contain all the information pertinent to the transaction and the problem.

Good and Bad News Letters Responding to Claims

> Most companies grant the majority of claims.

Companies, like consumers, have an interest in resolving problems quickly. Companies also want to maintain goodwill with their customers. Many companies will grant even fairly questionable claims if the customer does not have a history of complaints or if he or she is a long-term or valuable customer.

If you are responding to claims, consider the following points to facilitate the process:

1. Respond quickly to any customer complaint.
2. Avoid stating or even implying that the customer is ignorant or lying. Avoid phrases such as "You claim that."

You claim that the bookends were incorrectly packaged.
You seem to believe that your washing machine is defective.

3. Keep your tone gracious and positive, no matter what decision you make regarding the claim. Nothing can be gained from a condescending or discourteous approach. (Compare Figure 11-3 with Figure 11-4.)
4. Make your responses personal. Use individually typed letters rather than preprinted forms.

Figgins Furniture
Onstott Mall
Eastern Highway
Ridgefield, NJ 02346
April 17, 19xx

Mr. Peter Darryl
1944 Loy Avenue
Milltown, NY 01256

Dear Mr. Darryl:

We have received your request that we either replace the upholstery on two of the Hampton diningroom chairs delivered to your house on March 5 or pick up the whole diningroom set and credit your account with $2,100.

It is difficult for me to see how those chairs could have been stained in our warehouse or on the delivery truck. However, as our furniture specialist who visited your home on April 5 asserts that the stains cannot be removed, we will agree to replace the two chairs.

Our delivery company will be in touch with you within two weeks to set up a time for delivering two new chairs and picking up the damaged ones.

Sincerely yours,

Angus Munch

Angus Munch

FIGURE 11–3

Poor letter granting a claim. This letter implies that the reader damaged the chairs and grants the claim reluctantly. Even though the company has granted the claim, it may well lose the customer. See Figure 11–4 for a revision of this letter.

Letters Granting Claims—Seller at Fault

Your letter granting a claim should help maintain the reader's trust in your company.

Responding to a situation in which your company made a mistake can be an exercise in diplomacy. You must accept responsibility for the error but still make sure the buyer retains confidence in your company.

Although it is unreasonable to maintain that such mistakes will never happen again, you can reaffirm your company's commitment to quality and service. In order to help maintain the customer's faith in your company, avoid implying that a specific individual or department was responsible for the mistake.

As with most letters bearing good news, open with the information that the claim has been granted. Keep your tone professional; do not apologize profusely.

> Dear Mr. Craig:
>
> As you requested on September 5, we are sending you a new Fletcher Raincoat lined with lambswool.
>
> I know you must have been disappointed to find the lining missing from the first raincoat we sent you. Our items are all handsewn, as you know, and sometimes errors like this can occur.
>
> Thank you for returning the raincoat so promptly. Please accept the enclosed Scottish tartan scarf as a gift from all of us at Fletcher's.

When necessary, include a full explanation of financial data or other pertinent information.

> Your previous invoice, dated September 12, listed these purchases:
>
> | | |
> |---|---|
> | 2 prs. Lyons' wool socks | $14,98 |
> | 1 Tryon umbrella | 9.99 |
> | 1 leather belt | 10.67 |
> | Total | $35.64 |
>
> Now that we have credited your account for the price of the umbrella, your new balance is $24.97.

Sample Outline for Letter Granting Credit—Seller at Fault
1. Grant claim.
2. Explain error without being unprofessional or overly apologetic.
3. Summarize pertinent financial information or other necessary details.
4. End pleasantly to help maintain goodwill.

Letters Granting Claims—Buyer at Fault

Sometimes you will have to consider a questionable claim when customers return items that they themselves were responsible for damaging. If you decide keeping the customer's business is worth granting the claim, your letter should tactfully let the customer know he or she is at fault.

Word your explanation carefully so it will not offend the reader. Avoid using words such as "error" and "mistake."

Even though this type of letter conveys good news, you may want to lead up to your decision with a tactful explanation. In this way, you ensure that the buyer understands what he or she did wrong. The following letter is organized in a way that you may find useful:

When the buyer is at fault, tactfully explain what was done wrong.

```
Dear Mrs. O'Connor:

We received your letter requesting that we credit
your account for $65.98.

We were sorry to read that the Crowne knit dress
you bought from us on April 12 stretched out of
shape after the first washing and is unwearable.

Please remember that our knit dresses must be
handwashed in cold water and dried flat to prevent
just such a problem occurring. If you follow these
instructions, you will have many years of enjoyment
from your Crowne knits.

We will credit your account with the $65.98 as soon
as we receive the dress from you. We look forward
to serving you in the future.
```

The preceding letter lets the reader know that she made a mistake but does not overtly tell her she was wrong. If you do not tell buyers that they were in error, you may have to deal with repeated claims for the same problem; telling them they were wrong, however, requires tact.

Even though the washing instructions are clearly attached inside the neckline of the dress, we are granting your request anyway. [condescending]

We aren't responsible for the mistakes our customers make; however, we have decided to credit your account this time. [rude]

Knowing that even the most careful customer can sometimes make a mistake, we are happy to credit your account. [better]

Sample Outline for Letter Granting Claim—Buyer at Fault
1. Acknowledge claim.
2. Describe situation.
3. Explain how situation could have been avoided.
4. Grant the claim.
5. End pleasantly.

Figgins Furniture
Onstott Mall
Eastern Highway
Ridgefield, NJ 02346
April 17, 19xx

Mr. Peter Darryl
1944 Loy Avenue
Milltown, NY 01256

Dear Mr. Darryl:

We were sorry to learn that two of your Hampton
diningroom chairs had been stained. We will be
happy to pick up the two chairs and replace them
with new ones.

Our delivery company will call you within the next
two weeks to set up a convenient time for pick-up
and delivery of the chairs.

Your Hampton diningroom set will be a beautiful
asset to your home. If you are interested in other
items in our line of Hampton furniture, please come
see us or call us at 800-213-2376.

Sincerely,

Angus Munch

Angus Munch

FIGURE 11–4

Revised letter granting a claim. This letter graciously delivers the good news and sets up a plan of action. The letter also encourages the reader to continue doing business with the store.

Letters Denying Claims

Denying a claim requires an indirect approach and a clear explanation. Once again, you do not want to lose your customer's business (Figure 11-5).

The explanation for the refusal is a crucial aspect of a letter denying a claim. You must make it clear why the claim is denied without apologizing profusely or making accusations. If possible, follow the denial with an option available to the customer: for example, he or she may be able to replace the item at a discount or try other stores in the area.

Avoid profuse apologies.

Once again, end the letter in a pleasant manner that will soften the blow of the bad news.

```
                    Crazy Tommy Athletic Outfitters
                    6723 41st Street
                    York, TN 56892
                    January 12, 19xx

Mr. and Mrs. E. R. Scheriner
3626 Stevenson Place
Nashville, TN 56895

Dear Mr. and Mrs. Scheriner:

We received your package with our J & T jogging
shoes and your request for a refund. We were sorry
to read that the shoes do not fit your niece.

The shoes, however, were marked as a sale item that
may not be exchanged after purchase. We must return
the jogging shoes to you.

We would be happy to help your niece find a pair of
shoes if you bring her in for a fitting.

                         Sincerely,

                         Ursula George

                         Ursula George
                         Customer Service
```

FIGURE 11–5 _____

Letter denying a claim. This letter politely acknowledges the returned item and provides a reason for denying the customer's request. The denial is indirect, and the friendly ending offers a reasonable course of action to the customer.

What Would You Do?

You work for a company that sells fairly expensive clothes through a catalog. Your job is to respond to customer requests and complaints. Today you receive a letter from a customer requesting that you credit her account for $123. The enclosed dress, she maintains, does not fit.

Upon inspecting the dress, you can see that it has been worn—maybe more than once. In fact, there is a small stain on the collar.

Write a letter responding to the customer's request.

Developing a Collection Letter Series

When Bill Towne first set up his printing business, he had not considered when and how he would send out collection letters. As soon as one of his first customers was a month delinquent, Bill wrote the following letter:

Dear Mr. Mathers:

You owe Towne Printshop $159 for the brochures we printed for you in March. Send our check immediately if you want to avoid going to court.

Collection letters should be persuasive documents.

Mr. Mathers, who had lost the original bill and forgotten about it, was annoyed by the letter. He paid the bill but afterward took his business to another printer. Bill won in the short run, but not in the long run.

Collection letters must incorporate elements of persuasion as well as clear information. Like sales letters, collection letters urge readers to *act*. However, collection letters have legal restrictions. Be aware of legal considerations such as those laid out in the Fair Debt Collection Practices Act, which prohibits harrassment and abusive language as well as threats to take action that the writer does not actually intend to take. (For more information, see Appendix A.)

How Would You Handle These Situations?

Choose the answer that best fits the way you would handle these problems.

1. You own a small business that imports Scottish woolens and sells them through a catalog to customers in the United States. Mrs. Laney, one of your most loyal customers recently bought $300 worth of sweaters right before Christmas. However, she sent back one $75 sweater that had obviously been worn, saying it was the wrong size and requesting her money back.
   a. You return the sweater to her with a polite note saying that only unworn goods may be returned.
   b. You return her money with a note thanking her for doing business with your company.
   c. You write her an angry letter saying she is trying to rip off your business.
2. For five years, Mr. Hobbes has been buying woodworking tools directly from your factory and selling them in his retail store. He has been a good customer, but now he is having cash-flow problems. In January, he bought $5,000 worth of equipment and made a $2,500 down-payment. Since the remaining money was due by February 15, you sent him a bill on February 1. It is now March 1 and no money has arrived.
   a. You write him an urgent letter requesting the money by the end of the week.
   b. You send a second copy of the bill with the words PAYMENT OVERDUE stamped across it.
   c. You call him to discuss rescheduling his payment.

Discussion

In both of these situations, give the loyal customers the benefit of the doubt: their continued business is worth losing some time and money. Send Mrs. Laney her refund with a simple thank-you. Call Mr. Hobbes and discuss rescheduling his payment. If these problems persist, you will have to alter your tactics. At this point, the best answers are 1b and 2c.

The tone and content of the letters should be appropriate to the amount owed and to the length of time the bill is overdue.

Most companies develop a series of collection letters that move from reminders to friendly letters to increasingly firm requests for payment.

> Most companies develop a series of collection letters that become increasingly urgent.

Reminder

A reminder might be simply a copy of the original bill with a heading such as Second Notice. Many customers, like Tom Mathers, will respond after the first reminder.

Friendly Letter

The first letter, following one or two reminders, should maintain a friendly and personal touch. You might encourage the customer to speak with you concerning the bill if he or she cannot pay in full; do not imply that you will lower the amount owed, but do offer to work with the reader on the problem.

Your friendly letter might be structured like this:

Dear Mrs. Wilson:

Have you ever lent money to a friend? If you have, you probably expected to get it back after a reasonable amount of time. That's exactly how we feel. By extending you credit, we are in a sense making you a loan. And now we need to hear from you.

We have not received your check for the Sony clock radio we sold you on August 12. With accumulating finance charges, your bill of $95 has now increased to $104.

As you have been a valued TRC customer for many years, we feel some special problem must have occurred to delay your payment. If you cannot mail your check for the whole amount, please call me at Ext. 321. We may be able to work out a payment schedule for you.

I need to either receive your check or speak with you by the end of this week, Mrs. Wilson. Please do not delay.

The friendly reminder has a personal touch (the writer refers to her as a valued customer and then uses her name in the final paragraph), but the tone is still strong and the message clear (Figure 11-6).

Sample Outline for a Friendly Reminder
1. Get the reader's attention.
2. List a summary of charges.
3. Offer to discuss the problem.
4. Urge reader to contact the writer.

Urgent Appeal

Your tone must get stronger as the situation worsens. You may want to appeal to the customers' pride, sense of justice, or fear of reprisals. Remember, though, that your first goal is still to get the money; do not let your anger overpower your judgment. Having recourse to legal action or a collection agency will significantly decrease the amount of money you actually receive (Figure 11-7).

Dear Mr. Kariotis:

You know how important it is for a business to maintain its cash flow; it is equally important for a business person like yourself to retain his good credit rating. Paying your delinquent bill of $678 will help both of us.

We do not wish to hand your account to a collection agency, but we will have to do just that on Friday, April 25, if we do not receive your check for the full amount by that time.

```
                    Mann's Advertising
                    287 Ridge Road
                    Chevy Chase, MD 20345
                    July 15, 19xx

Mr. Marvin Snyder
Rockville Children's Center
20089 Matson Road
Rockville, MD 20854

Dear Mr. Snyder:

   On June 2, you signed an agreement for three
promotional brochures at a cost of $1500. At that
time you paid $500 and agreed to pay the remainder
upon your acceptance of the photographs and copy.
We finished the work on June 25, but you have not
returned our calls.
   We need to meet with you immediately so that you
can approve the materials and pay the remaining
amount.
   Please call us by the end of the week to set up a
meeting. If a problem has come up concerning the
project, we can discuss it then.
   I look forward to hearing from you by Friday,
July 19.

                    Sincerely yours,

                    Cecilia Blair

                    Cecilia Blair
```

Opening summarizes situation and gets reader's attention

One central paragraph persuasively requests payment

Paragraph offers to discuss problem
Ending is pleasant

FIGURE 11–6

Friendly collection letter. This letter politely summarizes the situation before requesting payment. The writer also emphasizes why she needs the money and sets up a clear line of action for the reader.

Sample Outline for Urgent Appeals
1. Stress urgency of situation.
2. Summarize amount owed.
3. State firmly when amount is due before drastic action is taken.
4. Stress problems that will result for customer if he or she does not pay.

```
                              ABC Wood Suppliers
                              56 Lee Boulevard
                              Clear Lake, KY 45892
                              February 1, 19xx

          Mr. Herbert Flynn
          Manager, Garam's Building Supplies
          7821 Brandywine Terrace
          Clear Lake, KY 45893

          Dear Mr. Flynn:

          On November 12 of last year, you charged a load of
          oak and pine louvered doors worth $432.89 to your
          store account. As you have not responded to our
          three previous letters, we must now urgently
          request your payment.

          If we do not receive your check for the full amount
          within five days of the date you receive this
          letter, we will have to put your account in the
          hands of a collection agency. Since this action
          will cost us money and will seriously damage your
          company's credit rating, we hope to receive your
          payment.

                              Sincerely,

                              John Bacardi

                              John Bacardi
                              Credit Department
```

Summarizes situation

Urgently requests payment

Summarizes consequences of not paying

FIGURE 11–7

Urgent collection letter. This letter offers the customer a final opportunity to pay and reminds him of the consequences of not paying. While the letter is courteous, it has an urgent tone.

It is illegal to send abusive collection letters.

Unless you have such a large volume of delinquent customers that you cannot personalize your letters, you will find a human approach, such as that in the preceding letter, more effective than form letters. Most people will respond better, also, to calm, persuasive appeals than to angry words. Moreover, abusive letters are illegal. If you do have to go to court over the matter, a series of rational and clear appeals will strengthen your position.

Summary

Granting and refusing credit, handling claims, and collecting money are some of the most common tasks for people in business. These tasks require persuasive and informative writing skills as well as tact, the you-attitude, and knowledge of relevant laws. If written effectively, credit, claim, and collection letters can enhance your organization's image, create customer goodwill, and effectively persuade your readers to act as you request.

Credit, Claim, and Collection Letter Checklist

Credit, Claims, and Collections

• Observe legal restrictions as well as effective communication strategies.

• Try to maintain customer goodwill even when communicating bad news.

Letters Approving Credit

• Remember that letters approving credit have three goals:

_____ To inform customers of credit approval

_____ To provide necessary credit information

_____ To encourage customers to use their credit

• Keep the tone of the letter pleasant, orient information to the reader, and enclose all financial information required by law.

_____ Inform reader that credit has been granted.

_____ Outline credit terms.

_____ Promote your company's products or services.

_____ End on a friendly note.

Letters Refusing Credit

• Work on achieving three goals with letters refusing credit:

_____ To convey the bad news to the reader

_____ To maintain reader's goodwill

_____ To avoid legal complications

• Use an indirect organizational pattern:

_____ Acknowledge credit request.

_____ Explain why credit was denied.

_____ State the refusal clearly.

_____ Encourage cash purchases.

Letters Making Claims

- If you need to make a claim, contact the seller immediately.

- Document every stage of the claim process.

- Keep your letters polite and specific; make copies of all important documents involved.

  _____ State date and location of purchase, product type, order number, and other pertinent information.

  _____ Clearly describe problems.

  _____ Summarize action taken so far.

  _____ Include persuasive detail.

  _____ Request reader to act.

Letters Granting Claims—Seller at Fault

- Accept responsibility for error but try to maintain readers' trust in your company or product.

  _____ Grant claim.

  _____ Explain error without being overly apologetic.

  _____ Summarize pertinent financial information or other data.

  _____ Conclude on a pleasant note.

Letters Granting Claim—Buyer at Fault

- Let readers know they are at fault without directly accusing them.

  _____ Acknowledge claim.

  _____ Describe situation.

  _____ Mention how situation might have been avoided.

  _____ Grant claim.

  _____ End pleasantly.

Letters Denying Claims

- Make sure to explain why claim was denied without making accusations:

  _____ Acknowledge claim.

  _____ Indicate understanding of problem.

  _____ Explain reasons for refusal.

  _____ Clearly deny claim.

  _____ Offer alternative to reader if possible.

  _____ End pleasantly to encourage future sales.

Collection Letter Series

- Create a series of collection letters moving from reminders to friendly letters to urgent appeals.

- Make sure your collection letters do not violate state or federal laws.

- Use copies of the original bills as reminders of late payments.

- When the reminders fail, send a friendly, persuasive letter:

  _____ Get reader's attention.

  _____ List charges.

  _____ Offer to discuss problem.

  _____ Urge reader to contact you.

- Use an urgent appeal when the situation worsens:

  _____ Stress urgency of situation.

  _____ Summarize amount owed.

  _____ State firmly what is owed before drastic action is taken.

  _____ Stress problems customer will have if amount is not paid.

Terms to Remember

Claim: demand for payment or other retribution

Collection letter series: increasingly urgent letters developed to persuade people to pay their bills. Series often includes a reminder, a friendly letter, and an urgent request for payment.

Credit customer: customer who has made an agreement with a seller to pay for products or services at a later date

Credit laws: laws such as the Fair Credit Billing Act that help to protect customers from unfair credit practices

Summary Discussion: Deana Gilroy's Claim Letter from Case in Point, p. 248

Deana Gilroy's letter is vague and poorly organized. She does not mention exactly when she bought the copier, what type of copier it is, and other pertinent information. Her summary of action taken so far does not mention when the repair person worked on the machine.

Deana's letter is particularly inefficient because it does not request any specific action. Does she want to exchange the machine? Get her money back? Her letter should end with a definite request.

Questions for Review and Discussion

1. Why are credit customers valuable to a company?
2. Why are credit customers expensive for a company?
3. What are two major objectives in a letter denying credit?
4. What information should be included in a letter requesting a claim?
5. Why should a company approve a claim when the buyer is at fault?
6. Why should a letter refusing a claim include an explanation?
7. What are the advantages of writing several times to a late-paying customer instead of immediately turning the account over to a collection agency?

Exercises

1. Revise the following "friendly collection letter" to make it more effective.

Dear Ms. Jackson:

Please send us a check for $300 immediately. We sold you two DGH stereo speakers on March 3 and now, six weeks later, have received no payment. We cannot afford to give away our merchandise. If we do not hear from you by the end of this week, we will turn your account over to a collection agency.

2. Revise the following bad news letter.

Mr. Tom Hagarty
5389 C Street
Veraville, LA 70021

Dear Mr. Hagarty:

Unfortunately, we will not be able to fix
your clock radio free of charge. Since you
purchased it over a year ago, the warranty
has expired, and you are responsible for
repairs. We do have a repair service here
at Pioneer Designs, so you should feel
free to send the clock to us or bring it
in. We will repair it for a small fee and
get it back to you quite quickly. Call us
if you want additional information on our
services.

You might want to check the batteries on
your model. We have found that with that
particular brand the batteries slip out of
place sometimes. If they're not correctly
packed, they could be causing your
problem.

Thanks for contacting us about your broken
radio.

Sincerely,

Dan Diver

Dan Diver
Customer Service Representative

3. Revise Deana Gilroy's letter from the Case in Point at the beginning of this chapter (p. 248).

4. You are credit manager for a small clothes store. A teenage girl has requested a credit card, but you cannot issue her one until she is eighteen. Write a letter explaining the situation and refusing her request.

5. When Ruth Holley bought a refrigerator from your store in January, she arranged to pay $100 per month for eight months. When her April payment did not arrive, you sent her a second bill. Now her May payment is two weeks overdue. Write a friendly but firm letter requesting $200.

6. You are a building supply wholesaler. You receive an order from Daisy Hardware for a large order of light fixtures. Since the store already owes you $1,200, this order puts the account over the store's credit limit of $1,500. You must refuse the order until a part of the former bill has been paid—but you do not want to lose the store's business.

7. Review the friendly collection letter in Figure 11-6. Then, assuming the writer still has heard nothing from the delinquent client, compose a more forceful letter regarding the $1,000.

8. Write a more urgent letter to Ms. Jackson (see Exercise 1). As she did not respond to your friendly appeal, her bill is now ten weeks overdue.

9. Harrold's Department Store delivered a sofa to your house. Upon inspecting it, you found a deep scratch on one of the mahogany arms. Write a letter to Colleen Wagner, the salesperson you dealt with at Harrold's; request that the store replace the damaged sofa.

10. Colleen Wagner, salesperson at Harrold's (see preceding exercise), is responding to the customer who received the damaged sofa. Harrold's policy is to send someone to inspect the damage and see if it can be repaired. If the damage is irreparable, Harrold's will replace the sofa or grant a refund. Write the letter to the customer for Ms. Wagner.

11. You are the office manager for Donald's Audio Store. You ordered 160 stereo receivers from the manufacturer's warehouse; today, 145 receivers arrived on the truck, but you were billed for the entire 160 units. Write a letter to the manufacturer explaining the situation and offering a solution.

12. You are the head of an advertising agency. Last month your staff developed a magazine advertisement for Lustrous Shampoo. The ad was approved by the head of the marketing department at Lustrous, Inc. Now, however, the company has decided that another approach in the ad would be more effective; the management wants your staff to redo the ad for free. You write back explaining that your staff did not make an error—the Lustrous staff did. You are willing to do a second ad, but you will charge your usual rates.

13. Write to a store or company explaining that the product you purchased was broken or spoiled. Ask for your money back. You may choose to complain about items such as

a. spoiled milk

b. a defective bicycle pump

c. stale bread

d. a book with pages missing

e. a broken lamp

f. "slightly flawed" pantyhose that are un-wearable

g. an audio cassette that broke on first usage

Word Processing Exercises: Text Enhancements

Using a word processor makes it easy to enhance your text with features such as centering, bold-face, and underlining.

1. Create a file named CLUB. Then type in the following text:

> DO YOU WANT TO BELONG?
> Join the Student Outdoors Club!
> The Student Outdoors Club will take you skiing in winter and hiking in summer—as well as scuba diving, fishing, and even skydiving.
>
> Sound like fun? Come to our gala membership get-together next week. Enjoy pizza and beer and meet some new friends who like to get away from it all in the outdoors. You'll also get to see the films some club members took over the summer while backpacking in the Tetons!
>
> WHERE: Student Union Room 236
> WHEN: Tuesday, September 18, 4 p.m.

2. Learn the command for CENTERING text. Now CENTER the first two lines and last two lines of the text.

3. Use the boldface command to highlight the word *BELONG* at the beginning of the text and the words *WHERE* and *WHEN* at the end.

4. Use the UNDERLINING command to underline the words *membership get-together* and *pizza and beer*.

5. PRINT the file. Your text should look like this.

> DO YOU WANT TO **BELONG**?
> Join the Student Outdoors Club!
> The Student Outdoors Club will take you skiing in winter and hiking in summer—as well as scuba diving, fishing, and even skydiving.
>
> Sound like fun? Come to our gala <u>membership get-together</u> next week. Enjoy <u>pizza and beer</u> and meet some new friends who like to get away from it all in the outdoors. You'll also get to see the films some club members took over the summer while backpacking in the Tetons!
>
> **WHERE**: Student Union, Room 236
> **WHEN**: Tuesday, September 18, 4 p.m.

Word Processing Exercises: Search and Replace

The SEARCH and REPLACE commands are extremely useful in many situations. The SEARCH command may be used to locate a specific word or section of a document. It is most useful for documents longer than a page.

If you have typed in a few pages and need to locate a sentence somewhere in the document, you can ask the computer to search for a string of letters or numbers within that sentence. If you want to locate the report heading PART 4, for example, you might search for the distinctive characters *RT 4*. This technique saves you from scroll-ing through the entire document for the section you want.

The SEARCH AND REPLACE command may be used if you want to substitute one *string*—a word or set of characters—for another. You may choose to make one substitution or a "global" change: that is, you can choose to make the substitution throughout the file.

If you have written a report assuming a build-ing is five stories high and then discover it is three stories high, you can have the computer auto-matically replace the word *five* with the word *three* wherever necessary. Most programs will reformat your text as the changes are made. Of course, the computer will take you to *every* occurrence of the word *five*: you can signal the computer not to make a change if it is inappropriate.

1. Enter a file over two pages long that you have already created and copy it so you can use it to experiment with commands in this exercise.

    Now read the instructions in your manual for using the SEARCH (or FIND) command. When you have entered the SEARCH command, request the computer to find the word *the* (or another common word in your file). The cursor will go to the first occurrence of *the* in your text.

Check the instructions for continuing the search. Enter the command to search for the next occurrence of *the*.

2. Go back to the beginning of the file. This time experiment with the SEARCH AND REPLACE command.

    Assume you want to change the word *to* to the word *for* throughout your file. You may have to indicate that you want only the word *to* changed so that the computer does not take you to words such as *tonight* and *into* that simply contain the letters *to*.

    Enter the SEARCH AND REPLACE commands and make the changes.

Optional Programs

Many optional programs are available to help you write and revise on the computer. These optional accessories include dictionaries, thesauruses, spell checkers, and style checkers. None of these will do your writing and revising for you, but each one has advantages that may be useful for you.

Dictionaries

A dictionary is indispensable for every writer. Unless your computer has a lot of memory, most on-line dictionaries take up too much space to be useful; you will probably need to keep a traditional bound dictionary on your desk. However, some companies have developed good dictionaries, and more are being developed every year. A dictionary program may be something you want to investigate and perhaps eventually invest in.

Thesauruses

A thesaurus is another useful tool as it helps you find words with similar meanings (synonyms). Thesaurus programs have been set up so that you do not need to leave your word processing program in order to see a selected list of synonyms.

In some cases, you may simply indicate which synonym you prefer, and it will be automatically inserted into your text.

Spell Checkers

Some word processing programs contain spell-check programs, but they may also be purchased separately. A spell checker compares the words in your document with its own dictionary and lists any items it does not find. Thus, it lists misspelled words as well as proper names or words not in its dictionary. You may then choose to change the misspelled words; most programs will automatically replace the incorrect word with the correct one. With some programs, you may add words to the spell-checker dictionary.

Naturally, a spell checker cannot recognize whether you have used a word incorrectly: if you typed *affect* but meant *effect*, the spell checker will not signal the error. However, a spell checker is still a valuable tool for business writers.

Style Checkers

Many programs have been designed to help you improve the style and readability of your writing. Some programs check for jargon, sexist language, clichés, and awkward phrases; others detect passive sentences and analyze sentences for readability.

These programs are becoming more sophisticated all the time. They cannot replace your own good editing, but they can be useful, especially if you are just learning the basics of good revision techniques.

1. Do some research on *one* of the four types of optional programs we have just described. If possible, try out one or more of the programs yourself. Your research should include:
   a. the names of at least four available programs of that type
   b. the type of equipment needed to run them
   c. the cost of each program
   d. the amount of memory needed for each program
   e. the strengths and weaknesses of each program
2. Using a word processing program, create a file named OPT and prepare a written summary of your findings. Explain why you think one program is superior to the others for your own uses.

   At the end of your summary, state the name of the word processing program and the type of computer you used to prepare your summary.

Part 3 Mini-Cases

3-1. Ardway Incorporated is a consulting firm in Evanston, Illinois, that specializes in developing training programs and organizing seminars and conferences for companies. Ardway has just won a contract with Hudson Dairy Products, a large firm in Chicago, to put on a training program. The three-day program, which will focus on developing the interpersonal communication skills of Hudson management and employees, will take place in four months.

The training program, for which Ardway will be paid $5,000, will take place in the Hudson conference facilities. The fee will cover the salaries of the Ardway personnel who will develop the program, the expenses of a speaker from out of town, and miscellaneous costs such as postage, telephone, training materials, and equipment rentals.

a. You are George Barnes, president of Ardway. Write a letter to the president of Hudson Dairy Products, Mrs. John Porter. Tell her you are happy that Ardway has won the contract and repeat its key points: the time, dates, location of the training program, the fee agreed upon, and any other information you would like documented before work begins on the contract.

The letter should be sent to:

Mrs. John Porter
President
Hudson Dairy Products
9800 Rogers Road
Chicago, IL 60432

Your return address is:

Ardway Incorporated
14 Loggins Street
Evanston, IL 60456

b. You are Corinne Schumacher, a senior consultant at Ardway and now project leader for the Hudson training program. You are in charge of developing an agenda for the three days, arranging for the guest speaker, having training materials written and printed, and taking care of a multitude of other tasks. Write a letter to Mr. Edward Lely, head of the Personnel Department at Hudson. He is the person you will be working with closely over the next four months.

Ask him to send you a list of any particular areas that he especially wants to see the training program focus on. Let him know that you usually use an overhead projector and video equipment in your programs and ask what equipment is already available at the Hudson facility. Also, ask how many people he expects to attend the training session each day.

c. You are Edward Lely. Write back to Corinne Schumacher telling her that approximately 100 people will attend the training session each day. Hudson has none of the equipment Corinne wants. The major areas he wants the program to focus on are communicating in meetings, communicating with difficult clients, handling problems over the telephone, and dealing with employee-management conflicts.

d. As Corinne Schumacher, write to Ms. Pauline DeVille, Professor of Business Communications at New Hampshire University. Ask her to be a speaker at the Hudson training program as she is nationally known for her work in employee-management communication problems.

Give her all the information she needs to know. You will be able to pay her transportation, hotel, and meals for two days; she will receive a $250 honorarium for her participation. Her speech will run an hour, and she should be available to answer questions for at least 30 minutes afterward.

Also, if she is interested in leading one of the training "modules" you are developing, you would be delighted.

Address the letter to:

Professor Pauline DeVille
School of Business
New Hampshire University
Durham, NH 12675

e. You are Pauline DeVille. Write to Corinne that you will be able to speak at the conference. You can stay only one day, however, and will not have time to lead a module. You would like Corinne to make a reservation for you at the Hamilton Hotel; you will arrive the night before the conference and then head to the airport after your speech. You have another conference to attend the following day. Also, you would appreciate it if Corinne could arrange for a slide projector to be in the room for your speech.

f. You are Corinne Schumacher. One of your staff is writing the agenda for the training session and developing some training materials. These will be printed and bound together for the participants and trainers. A local printer, Ripley's Instant Press, has agreed to do the job for $350.

Write a letter to Frank Wheeler, the manager of Ripley's confirming the agreement you made over the telephone. Tell him that you need 150 copies of the materials bound in cardboard covers with spiral bindings. The work must be done at least a week before the session is scheduled to begin.

Address the letter to:

Mr. Frank Wheeler
Manager
Ripley's Instant Press
800 Carlton Boulevard
Evanston, IL 60532

g. You are Pauline DeVille. You will not be able to attend the training session as you have broken your leg and cannot travel. You have telephoned Corinne Schumacher but had to leave the message with her secretary. Now write Corinne to explain the situation.

h. You are Corinne Schumacher. You arranged for Professor Richard Quinn to take Pauline's place at the conference. He spoke on handling employee-client conflicts and did an excellent job on very short notice. Now that the training session is over, write him a letter of appreciation for his help. Address the letter to:

Professor Richard Quinn
Management Department
Hallsburg College
Hallsburg, MA 32453

3-2. Mr. Martin Lancers is a recent graduate of Lebow University in Vermont and has just begun working as an assistant manager at Arlington Automotive in Burlington. He is single, 23 years old, and has a good credit history.

a. Martin is setting up an apartment in Burlington, so he needs to purchase housewares and small appliances. He has applied for credit at Woodward's Home Store. You are David Jergins, Credit Manager at Woodward's. Write a letter granting Martin credit up to $1,000. Send the letter to:

Mr. Martin Lancers
2987 Floral Way, Apt. 2
Burlington, VT 02134

Your return address is:

Woodward's Home Store
700 Bland Boulevard
Burlington, VT 02143

b. You are Martin Lancers. You have recently bought a large, heavy-duty, nonstick griddle from Woodward's as you plan to make pancakes for yourself every morning. After using it twice, however, the surface of the griddle is a mess: the nonstick material is coming off. You put the griddle in a box and send it back. The griddle, you point out, has a year's warranty. Write a letter to Ms. Dora Collier, the salesperson who sold you the griddle, explaining the situation and asking for a new griddle.

c. Ms. Collier has passed Martin's letter along to you, Mrs. Janet Renstrom, Customer Service Representative. You explain that the year's warranty for the griddle applies only if the customer follows the directions on the box: only a plastic spatula can be used on the griddle. Martin, you explain, has clearly used a metal spatula on the griddle. You must return the griddle to him.

d. It is three weeks since Martin has received the letter from Janet Renstrom. He has also received the bill for the griddle, but he has not, however, received the griddle. Write a letter to Janet explaining that you are not going to pay the $34.95 until you have the griddle.

e. Martin has not received the griddle after six weeks. The Billing Department at Woodward's knows nothing of the griddle dilemma, so, as Martin

has not paid his bill, the department must send him a friendly collection letter. As Mr. Herb Greene, write a letter reminding Martin that he owes $34.95 plus interest.

f. Martin is irate at receiving the letter, but he calms down enough to write Herb the complete story. As Martin, explain the situation in detail and make it clear that you will not pay for merchandise you do not have. You are also sending a copy of Herb's letter and your letter to Janet Renstrom.

g. Janet Renstrom has done some checking and found that Martin's griddle never left the store's mailroom. Knowing how upset Martin is at the whole episode, she decides to send him a new griddle to make up for his frustration. Write a letter explaining that Martin will not be billed interest charges. Remind him to use the griddle properly.

3-3. Wes Bennet is the owner of a bookshop in Chicago that specializes in hard-to-find books. He has a loyal group of customers interested in rare editions and out-of-print books. As he himself is a murder mystery and spy novel fan, he stocks a wide assortment of English and American books of those types as well as general fiction and nonfiction.

a. Wes Bennet has bought several boxes of old spy novels from a collector. He has decided to send out a letter to 100 of his customers who have bought spy novels in the past to tell them about his interesting new acquisitions. He wants to mention several of these books that specialize in codes and ciphers: Dennison Haley Clift's *Spy in the Room* (1944), Alex Gordon's *The Cipher* (1961), Edward D. Hoch's *The Spy and the Thief* (1971), and James L. Johnson's *Code Name Sebastian* (1967).

Write a letter for Wes persuading the customers to come in and examine these and other books of interest to them. (If you wish, you may add information about spy novels with which you are familiar to pique the readers' interest and enthusiasm.)

The return address for his letter is:

Everyman's Bookshop
198 Alton Place
Chicago, IL 60678

b. Three months ago, Ms. Maureen Paley asked Wes to find her hardback copies of three crime novels: *The Crime in Dutch Garden* by Herbert Adams, *Murder in the Maze* by J.J. Connington, and *The Wizard of Death* by Richard Forrest. She has not heard from him. Write a letter of inquiry for her. Her return address is:

256 East Dayton Street
Madison, WI 64578

c. Wes wants to tell Maureen Paley that two of the books she requested have arrived: *The Crime in Dutch Garden* ($12.95) and *Murder in the Maze* ($10.50). He has not been able to find *The Wizard of Death*. He will send her the two books right away and let her know if he finds the third. He will charge her a $2.50 mailing and handling charge as well as the cost of the books.

Write a letter for Wes that conveys the preceding information and clearly outlines the amount Maureen should send him.

d. Maureen Paley, a graduate student at the University of Wisconsin, is writing a paper on detective stories involving trains, such as Agatha Christie's *Murder on the Orient Express*, John Creasey's *Murder on the Line*, Michael Crichton's *The Great Train Robbery*, and Ethel Lina White's *The Lady Vanishes*. She is putting together a bibliography of such books and hopes that Wes can send her the names and authors of some of them.

Write a letter from Maureen to Wes thanking him for the two books he sent her and sending him the required amount. Also request any help he can give on the bibliography she is doing. If he has some train mysteries in stock at a reasonable price, she would be interested in knowing what books he has and how much they cost.

Memorandums

Part
Four

Communicating Through Memos

- **Developing internal communications**
- **Considering whether a memo is necessary**
- **Reviewing parts of a memo**
- **Defining your goals and your audience**
- **Making a plan**
- **Revising for appearance, tone, and accuracy**

Objectives

To create memos that are relevant and useful for readers

To learn the standard parts of a memo

To organize memos effectively

12

Bernice Lum's Memo

As Department Supervisor, Bernice Lum was concerned about poor record keeping and possible thefts from the department's petty cash box. She decided to alter procedures for disbursing petty cash and wrote the following memo:

```
    TO:    All Sales Department Employees
  FROM:    Bernice Lum, Department
           Supervisor
SUBJECT:   Problems with Petty Cash
  DATE:    May 2, 19xx

I have noticed that discrepancies in the
petty cash have been increasing lately.
While we have often had $1 or $2
discrepancies, losses in March and April
came to over $25. I do not know whether
theft or carelessness is operating here,
but the losses must stop. They are
affecting our department's high
efficiency rating and could reduce our
employee incentive pay bonuses.

In the past, the petty cash box was open
to almost everyone. This led to abuses.
Employees have been using the petty cash
for bus fare and other expenses
unrelated to running this office. In
order to correct these abuses and ensure
that our books balance each month, I
have decided to change the procedures.

Robert Wynn and I will now be the only
persons with authorized access to the
petty cash box. Requests for petty cash
should be made to either of us. For
employees to receive petty cash, the
petty cash sheet must be signed and
filled out. After a purchase has been
made, the receipt for the purchase must
be stapled to the sheet.

Your cooperation is appreciated.
```

Points to Consider

- What problems do you see in this memo?
- Is the subject line accurate? Explain.
- Does Bernice use the you-attitude here? Explain.
- Are there any organizational problems? Problems with emphasis? Describe them.
- What questions does Bernice leave unanswered?
- Is the memo as visually effective as it might be? How could it be improved?

TABLE 12-1

Business Communication Forms Used by Executives

Form	Respondents Using Currently (percent)	Respondents Using in 1970 (percent)
Letter	100	86
Oral presentation	98	100
Memorandum	98	94
Informational report	91	86
Analytical report	91	80
Other	13	17

Developing Internal Communications

In studying business letters, you examined primarily *external* communications, correspondence to people outside a company. Now you turn to internal communications, the documents that flow within every organization, large and small.

Memos are the most common form of internal correspondence.

Memos are often less formal than letters.

Memorandums (memos) are the most common type of written communication in business. Although they are similar to letters, memos have their own format and are used for different purposes.

While a letter is typically sent to one reader, a memo is apt to be sent to several readers simultaneously. In general, memos are used for less formal situations than letters are. A memo, for instance, could be as informal as a few words scrawled on a message pad, whereas a formal message, such as a notice of resignation, would probably be written in a letter.

Whether they work in marketing, financial planning, auditing, personnel, production, or almost any other area, business people often find they spend much of their work day writing memos. Despite the proliferation of memos on almost every office desk in the world, however, people are rarely trained to write them effectively. In many companies, a random sampling of these documents reveals the majority of memos to be incomplete, unclear, verbose, offensively worded, or unnecessary.

Using the writing process and following a few guidelines will help make your memos more readable and worthwhile.

Considering Whether a Memo Is Necessary

Paper flow has become a big problem in some organizations. The computer printer and copy machine seem to propagate endless reams of paper that pile up on every desk. As a result, people barely glance at most memos. A busy employee is apt to throw a memo in the wastebasket and then ask his neighbor, "Anything in that memo from Accounting?"

Before you even begin the brainstorming step of the memo-writing process, ask yourself:

How many people need the information in this?
Is the information simple or complicated?
Do we need a written record of this information?

If only two or three people really need the information and the facts are simple, a phone call might be more efficient than a memo. For example, you could call up your three fellow committee members and inform them of an upcoming meeting instead of writing a memo about it.

If you want the information kept on file, however, a memo is preferable. For example, if you are announcing a change in policy or making a monthly tally of office costs, the information should be on paper or on a disk.

A computer mail system can alleviate the paper problem in offices where employees have access to terminals. On the other hand, an informational bulletin board can be just as effective in a small company, and it can cut paper and copying costs to an astonishing extent.

Computer mail systems have reduced the need for memos on paper.

Reviewing Parts of a Memo

Like other types of business documents, memorandums have standard formats. Although these formats vary from one organization to another, most have several points in common. Some printed memo forms do not have a subject line, but many companies have memo forms with headings that look like this:

```
     TO:
   FROM:
SUBJECT:
   DATE:
```

Sometimes the headings are arranged in two columns:

```
TO:                        FROM:
SUBJECT:                   DATE:
```

Sometimes the date is at the top left of the memo, and sometimes it is on the right:

```
TO:                        DATE:
FROM:
SUBJECT:
```

Although filling out the appropriate information seems simple, consider a few points.

"To" and "From"

Limit your readers to those who need the information and use names if you are sending the memo to a small number of people.

In some cases, you may want to include the reader's title after his or her name: *To: Harry Von Gelder, Sales Manager.* Use this format particularly if you do not know the reader well or if the memo is going to be kept on file.

If you put the reader's title, also put your own: *From: Charlene Carlson, Sales Representative.* Usually a memo writer initials the line on which his or her name is typed (see Figure 12-2).

Be consistent, also, with first and last names: do not put your reader's first name and then your first *and* last names. In some companies, courtesy titles such as *Mr., Mrs., Ms.,* and *Dr.* are used in memo headings. If you use a courtesy title for your reader, use one for yourself:

```
TO:     Mr. Harry Von Gelder
FROM:   Ms. Charlene Carlson
```

Subject

Because readers should grasp the gist of a memo within moments, the most effective subject lines are informative and specific. The subject line should also make readers want to read the memo. Avoid upsetting your readers before they have even started reading!

A clear subject line can be a guide to a focused memo.

Make sure that your memo titles are clear and straightforward. Avoid jargon like "Implementation of Cost-Efficient Regulations" when you mean "How to Lower Our Electricity Costs."

Defining Your Goals and Your Audience

The second step of the writing process is essential to good memo-writing. Many memos are fuzzy or difficult to read because the writer either is unclear what the message is or has more than one message to convey. In general, try to condense the focus of your memo into the subject line at the top of your memo. If you cannot come up with a clear, meaningful subject, you may not have one: you may have two or more subjects—or none at all.

Goals

Tim Gardiner struggled for hours trying to put together a memo that both summarized the events of a recent meeting and outlined the findings of a company survey. He discovered his problem only when he tried to write a title for his memo: he was not comfortable with any of his variations on "Hiring Committee Meeting and Employee Survey Results." He finally determined that he had two separate goals: he was trying to condense two major ideas into one memo. Tim then included the results of the employee survey in a recommendation report to the Personnel Department and wrote a memo to department supervisors entitled "Minutes of Hiring Committee Meeting."

Figures 12-1 and 12-2 show how Ben Swift turned a vague, wordy draft into a brief, well-planned memo. Having written a first draft without brainstorming, defining his goals, doing necessary research, or making a plan,

Ben found he had a rambling memo that most of his readers would probably never finish, much less act upon. His revision is much more effective, but he wasted time and effort by not using the writing process from the start.

Audience

Some writers send most of their memos to all employees. This procedure seems simpler because the writer does not have to look up a list of names of take the time to consider who actually needs the information. As a result, everyone's desk is flooded with unnecessary information.

Your memo will be much more effective if you send it only to people affected by the information. If the production staff does not need to know about the new software available for the accounting personnel, then do not send the memo to the Production Department.

If your memo is being sent to only a small group, you can often get a better response by listing individual names. If a memo is personally addressed, the recipient is more apt to read it. Compare:

Send a memo only to the people who need it.

From the Desk of . . .

345 Park Avenue
New York, New York 10154

"In my writing I have to get information across accurately and clearly," says Karen Amico, Senior Financial Analyst at Clairol. Karen was hired as a business analyst in Clairol's Personal Care Division and subsequently was promoted. She now does profit planning and analysis for the corporation. Karen attributes her promotion to her good communications skills. "If written and oral communications are consistently good, then supervisors recognize what you've done—you've documented it. Otherwise, if your work is not communicated to others, you can do some really good work, but it will probably go unnoticed."

Karen uses oral communications at meetings and reviews of profit analyses. "Written documents go into a file that can be read for years. The documents confirm and report for the corporation the results of their operations." Clairol is a wholly owned subsidiary of Bristol-Meyers so, "a lot of what we do is passed on to Bristol-

Meyers. We have to be accurate and clear."

The purposes of the communications are varied: "explanations of analyses, for example, how to account for certain sales, or, are we going to make a key sale in a certain place." Karen says it's important to send copies of written work to the right people starting, of course, with your boss.

Although Karen has always written fairly easily, the content and form of what she writes have changed since she has been doing business writing. Her tips for students?

In written communications:

- Be concise.
- Use summary paragraphs so the reader knows in a few sentences whether she or he needs to read the report.
- Make sure the body of the text follows the summary closely.
- Use bullets to highlight your points.
- Use key terminology that people in your field will understand.

In oral communications:

- Make sure your message is clear.
- Use clear pronunciation.
- Use a calm and controlled tone.
- Use eye contact.
- Be aware of body language.

To: All Supervisors

with

To: Karen Jones, Henry Korning, Bill Lawson,
Jill Pointer, Patricia Wong

Most people will respond more positively to a personalized memo, just as they will respond better to a letter addressed to them by name rather than to "Occupant."

You will also find that having a small, well-defined audience will help you write a better memo. You can usually convey information more efficiently to a smaller audience because your audience analysis is so much easier: you know exactly who the readers are, what they already know, and what they need to know.

```
TO:    All Managers   DATE:    August 3, 19xx
FROM:  Ben Swift      SUBJECT:  Lunch

Lunch is a very important time for most of us. We
have been sitting at our desks for three hours, and
we desperately need a sandwich or maybe even a hot
meal to get us through the rest of the day. People
tell me breakfast is the most important meal, but I
am convinced it is lunch.

We are not allowed to eat lunch at our desks, which
could be a good policy since we are tired of
sitting there anyway. Besides, who wants to work on
a desk covered with crumbs? We are supposed to eat
in the cafeteria or else head out to Sam's or one
of the fast food places nearby. Most of us don't
want fast food, and Sam's food isn't worth a
special trip for, anyway. So we are stuck with the
cafeteria.

That means over a hundred people are waiting in
line at noon for their lunch. Nearly half our lunch
time is spent standing in line. And if we are the
front of the line, we have to eat quickly so the
others can have our seats. A staggered lunch hour
would take care of all these problems: have
different groups eat between 11:30 a.m. and 1 p.m.

A few more tables in the cafeteria wouldn't hurt,
either. Thanks for any attention you can give this
problem.
```

FIGURE 12-1 ───

Ineffective memo. This memo is long-winded and roundabout. The subject line is vague; central points are lost in the middle of the last paragraph; and the final request is vague. See Figure 12-2 for a revision of this memo.

If you must send a memo to a large audience, make sure you research your readers, assessing their needs and considering what motivates them.

Making a Plan

Disorganization is one of the biggest problems with memos. People write them so fast and so frequently that the results are jumbled. If your information is worth putting in written form, it is worth expressing clearly. So, once you have defined your goals and done any research necessary, you can develop a strong plan. Standard organizational patterns will often help you construct an effective plan.

Most memos have three main parts:

1. An introduction stating the purpose of the memo
2. A central portion, often in list form, providing the specifics of the topic
3. A conclusion informing the readers what action they should take or expect

This is the basic pattern Ben Swift uses in Figure 12-2.

Direct and Indirect Openings

Like letters, memos are usually organized around either a direct or an indirect approach. Knowing how your audience will respond to your message will help you determine which approach will be more successful.

In memos that convey positive or neutral information, the opening sen-

```
TO:    All Managers   DATE:     August 3, 19xx
FROM:  Ben Swift       SUBJECT:  Staggered
                                 Lunch Hours

We have all been suffering from the crowded
cafeteria and from a lack of seating space to eat
lunch. I have two suggestions:
    1. Stagger lunch hours between 11:30 a.m. and
    1 p.m. so each department starts for lunch at a
    different time;
    2. Add two more tables with eight chairs apiece
    to the cafeteria (there is plenty of room).

I plan to bring this idea up at the managers'
meeting on August 17. If you have some questions or
thoughts on how we would implement the plan, let me
know before then.
```

FIGURE 12-2 ——————————————————————————————
Revised memo. This memo is concise. The subject line and opening paragraph give the reader specific information. Ben uses short paragraphs and a list so his readers can see his points at a glance. The ending provides a plan for future action.

tences should get directly to the point, expanding the subject line of the heading and giving a strong sense of the memo as a whole.

The best opening paragraphs are appropriate to the subject matter: a memo about a serious problem should not open with a joke; a memo on a pleasant topic—like the company picnic—should not have a dull, heavy-handed beginning.

The following openings are clear, readable, and appropriate:

```
SUBJECT: Trade Show Budget

The accounting staff has finished evaluating the
projected budget for the trade show. Although we
found most of the figures reasonable, we questioned
two areas.

  Subject: Market Research Classes
Since many of our new staff members have expressed
an interest in learning the fundamentals of market
research, Leonard Gold will be offering a series of
lunchtime classes on the principles and techniques
used by market researchers in our industry.

  Subject: Convention Committee Meeting
The Convention Committee will be meeting on
Thursday, April 19, at 3:00 in Room 34-B.
```

```
SUBJECT: Overtime Schedules

We are all pleased that we won the Newton Bakeries
contract—it will be very exciting work for all of
us. Before beginning work on that contract,
however, we must finish up the ones we are working
on. To keep on schedule, some overtime will
probably be necessary in the next two weeks.
```

(For more examples, look ahead to Figures 13-1 and 13-2.)

If the memo holds unpleasant news, the opening sentences can be slightly off the main point although still linked to the main theme.

Checklist for Memo Openings

- Is my opening paragraph linked to both my subject line and the rest of the memo?
- Is my opening going to interest my readers? Does it make someone want to read on?
- Is my opening suitable for the subject matter as a whole?

If you answer yes to these questions, you probably have a good beginning.

Central Paragraphs

Because your central message should be logical and easy to follow, the key task here is organization. Once again, an outline can be useful. After listing your major points, order them in a way that will be most helpful to the reader—or most effective at presenting your point. You may want to consider one of four standard organizational methods: chronological steps, logical narration, order of increasing or decreasing importance, and comparison/contrast (Figure 12-3).

Chronological Steps. If you are telling your readers about a new procedure or illustrating how something works, a step-by-step description is usually most useful (Figure 12-4).

If you use this method, make sure your steps *are* chronological. You would not want to describe starting a car, for instance, with a list like this:

1. Insert key.
2. Turn key to the right until engine comes on.
3. Press accelerator.
4. Make sure car is in Park before you insert the key.

Chronological organization is useful for procedural memos.

Instead, arrange your list this way:

1. Make sure car is in Park before you insert the key.
2. Insert key.
3. Turn key to the right until engine come on.
4. Press accelerator.

Logical Narration. In a memo based on logical narration, the writer organizes material in a manner useful for the reader; often the writer answers unspoken questions in the order they would naturally come to the reader's mind (Figure 12-5).

Order of Increasing or Decreasing Importance. A list of items or points should have some sort of internal logic. One of the easiest and most effective

FIGURE 12-3 _____
Organizational strategies for memos

Strategy	Frequent Uses
Chronological steps	Procedural memos
	Informative memos
Logical narration	Informative memos
Order of increasing or decreasing importance	Persuasive memos
Comparison/contrast	Persuasive memos

```
TO:       All Staff
FROM:     Hank Lanier
SUBJECT:  Copy Card Procedures
DATE:     April 4, 19xx

On April 7, our copiers will be replaced by new
copiers that require a copy card. Use the following
procedures when you wish to make copies:
    1. Pick up a copy card from either Rita Kerry or
       Sam Vaughn.
    2. Sign your name and put the date on the list
       posted beside each copier.
    3. Insert copy card in slot beside copier.
    4. Make copies as usual.
    5. Mark number of copies you made beside your
       name on the sheet.
    6. Return copy card to Rita or Sam.
    The new machines are fast and versatile. They
should make our copying chores much less arduous.
```

FIGURE 12-4 _____
Memo using chronological steps

The order of increasing importance builds to a climax.

The order of decreasing importance is designed to catch the reader's attention right away.

organizing devices is to move the reader from the least important points to the most important ones (see Figure 12-6.)

In the memo report discussed in Chapter 7 (see pp. 132–134), Jack Gee uses a variation on this approach by moving from the least desirable option to the most desirable.

The order of decreasing importance is useful if you want to get your reader's attention with the most important information at the beginning and then move toward less vital details (Figure 12-7).

```
TO:       All Employees
FROM:     Latrice Frye
SUBJECT:  New Library
DATE:     January 12, 19xx

On Monday, January 20, our new company library will
be opening in Room 213 of Building C. The books,
journals, newspaper, and company materials on file
there will be useful for all of us.

The library, which will be staffed by a full-time
secretary, will be open from 9 a.m. until 5 p.m.
every week day.

Please join Marsha Higgins and me at 1:30 p.m. on
January 20 if you are interested in a tour of the
new facility.
```

FIGURE 12-5
Memo using logical narration

```
TO:       David Guilder
FROM:     Ann Howe
SUBJECT:  Hiring Temporary Assistants
DATE:     July 26, 19xx

Please consider authorizing my department to hire
two temporary clerical assistants for August and
September.

The whole staff has been working overtime almost
every evening and weekend, and many of them are
exhausted from the extra hours. Additional part-
time staff would reduce anxiety and raise morale in
the department. Having some assistants will also
enable us to do an outstanding job on the Bartson
project, which is an important one for the whole
company.

Most important, given our recent cash-flow
problems, I estimate we will save approximately
$200 a week by hiring part-time assistants instead
of paying overtime.

Please let me know by Friday whether we can hire
the part-time assistants. Thank you!
```

FIGURE 12-6
Memo using order of increasing importance

```
TO:        George Fairwell
FROM:      Tom Flores
SUBJECT:   New Sales Department Manager
DATE:      December 12, 19xx

I recommend that we seriously consider Amie Wong
for the sales department manager position. I have
interviewed the four candidates we discussed, and
Ms. Wong is clearly the outstanding candidate.

As you can see from the enclosed materials,
Ms. Wong's background is excellent: she has ten
years' experience in the sales department at Vital
Services. This experience alone makes her ideal for
the job here.

Ms. Wong has also received very good
recommendations from her colleagues at Vital
Services, and her academic credentials include a
Masters in Business.

I have arranged for Ms. Wong to visit our offices
on Monday afternoon. Let me know by this Friday if
you will be available to meet with her.
```

FIGURE 12-7 _____

Memo using order of decreasing importance

Comparison/Contrast. This method is most useful in a persuasive memo in which options are described. You may want to establish such contrasts as advantages versus disadvantages or costs versus benefits.

To be persuasive, you must answer your readers' questions and doubts: avoid stressing the good points of an option without delineating the costs or the weaknesses. By comparing and contrasting options, you actually end up with a more persuasive piece of writing (Figure 12-8).

Effective Endings

Usually the final paragraph accomplishes one or more of the following tasks:

The ending of a memo can be used to motivate readers and to summarize key points.

- Summarizes the information from the central paragraphs
- Requests the reader to act
- Returns the memo to an upbeat point made at the opening
- Summarizes the writer's recommendations

The last paragraph should provide a definite ending; do not leave your readers in midair. (They should not have to turn the page to see if you wrote more.) Also make sure you include nothing *new* in the ending: restate points—do not introduce entirely new topics.

Sometimes a simple list at the end will catch a reader's eye and help her

```
TO:       Francine Barker
FROM:     Ted Sealts
SUBJECT:  Gardening Services
DATE:     May 12, 19xx

I researched the two local services that specialize
in plant care for companies. Although it is a
little more expensive, I find Green-Gro superior to
Hanson's Garden Service in terms of staff and
services.

COST: Green-Gro will give us a month-to-month
contract for $130 per month. Hanson's will accept
only a six-month contract, but the monthly average
is only $115.

STAFF: Green-Gro's staff impressed me with its
professionalism and knowledge. Only full-time,
experienced gardeners would be working with our
plants. Although the head of Hanson's is
experienced, he often sends part-time workers to
care for the clients' plants.

SERVICES: Green-Gro offers both indoor and outdoor
gardening services. While we do not yet have
outdoor plantings, we may be putting them in next
year: Green-Gro's expertise would be useful.
Hanson's works only on indoor plants.

In summary, although Hanson's is a larger company
and offers a somewhat lower price, it seems clear
we should hire Green-Gro on a month-to-month
contract. Please let me know this week if you want
Green-Gro to start on June 1.
```

FIGURE 12-8

Memo using comparison/contrast

or him remember your most important points. The key information regarding an upcoming meeting, for example, could be summarized at the end of the memo:

Time: 3 p.m.
Date: Wednesday, July 8
Place: Conference Room

Revising for Appearance, Tone, and Accuracy

When revising, remember that the appearance of a memo often determines whether people read or do not read it, while the tone has a direct impact on the way readers respond to your message.

A reader should be able to scan a memo easily.

Appearance

Lists can often convey information clearly and concisely.

Short paragraphs, wide margins, and lists help to make a memo easy to glance at. A list, also, can help you make sure your thoughts are organized logically.

Some memos, like reports, benefit from tables, graphs, and charts. (Graphic aids are discussed in detail in Chapter 17.) Bear in mind that often a visual representation will save you and your readers time and effort. A graphic representation of the costs and benefits of your recommendations, for example, could allow your reader to glance over the data before reading the entire memo.

Rather than describing recent sales figures, show them on a bar graph. Rather than detailing proposed salary increases, illustrate them with a chart.

Tone

The tone of a memo opening should be consistent with the central message.

Whatever its main purpose, the memo should not intimidate or alienate your readers. Remember that your memo should sound like it came from *you*, not from a robot or computer. Avoid tired phrases such as "It has come to my attention," "per your request," and "upon receipt of." (Go back to Chapter 6 if you want to review some pointers on effective tone.)

As you revise your memo, ask yourself questions like these:

Make sure that most sentences in a memo are active.

- Have I written to my readers in much the same way I would speak to them?
- Have I kept a pleasant and positive tone?
- Have I used the passive voice too often?
- Have I used too much business jargon?

Conciseness and Accuracy

Design your memos to convey information concisely.

While revising your memo for tone, you will naturally be revising also for conciseness, word choice, sentence structure, and other points discussed in Chapter 6. Deleting excess words should always be part of your editing process, but it is particularly important with memos since they are meant for efficient communication. Check every sentence for unnecessary words and phrases.

Also, delete information irrelevant to your reader or your message. You may not have to summarize an entire telephone call, for example, before responding to one point discussed during the conversation. Or you might not have to provide all the background of a problem if you are certain your readers know the situation.

On the other hand, if you are not sure what your readers know about a situation, give them all the details. Make sure, too, that every detail is accurate: errors of fact in a memo can have unpleasant, even disastrous, consequences.

Ask yourself these questions as you review your draft:

- Have I provided unnecessary or irrelevant information?
- Have I delayed getting to my major points?
- Could I make my points more concisely?
- Is there any information *missing*?
- Is every point accurate?

How Effective Are Your Memo-Writing Skills?

Your company has recently developed a direct-deposit payroll system, so employees may choose to have their paychecks deposited directly into their bank accounts. This precedure saves employees time and trouble, but initially they have to fill out forms from your office to authorize the change.

You write a memo to all employees to inform them of the new procedures. Which answers most closely fit the way you would write this memo?

1. You title the memo
   a. New Payroll System
   b. Forms 456-56
   c. Direct Deposit Paychecks

2. The opening of your memo is the following:
   a. Tired of waiting in line at the bank to deposit your paycheck? Our new system saves you time and effort.
   b. Fill out Forms 456-56 by May 15 if you want your paycheck deposited directly into your bank account.
   c. The Personnel Department, in conjunction with Accounting, has developed a new system that will save you time and effort.

Discussion

The most specific memo title is the most effective: a new payroll system does not necessarily affect the employees personally—a direct deposit system does. Best answer: 1c.

Filling out forms is distasteful to most people, so that aspect of the procedure should be mentioned *after* people are convinced that they want to participate in the new system. Telling readers who developed the system is I-oriented rather than reader-oriented. To encourage readers to participate in the program, the opening of the memo should appeal to readers' needs and interests. Best answer: 2a.

Solving Problems with Memos

Problem	Solution
The information is not relevant to the person reading it	Send memo only to people who need the information. Orient the information to the readers' needs and interests.
The information is not comprehensible to all readers	Analyze your audience. Define technical terms. Provide necessary background details.
The information is disorganized	Follow a logical plan. Use headings and lists to organize material. Know your purpose for writing.
The memo cannot be quickly scanned	Leave white space on the page. Summarize major points at the beginning or end. Delete excess words. Use lists.
The tone is inappropriate	Consider who your readers are and how they will react to your message.
The information is inaccurate or sketchy	Revise and proofread carefully. Double-check your sources of information. Provide necessary details.

What Would You Do?

You are a student assistant working at Howell Corporation for the summer. Your immediate boss has admitted to you privately that he hates writing and puts off writing memos and letters whenever possible. He is delighted that now he can give his rough drafts to you for revision.

Your first task is to revise the following memo.

```
    TO:  Gerald Abercomb                    Date: June 23, 19xx
  FROM:  Matt Fischer
SUBJECT:  Employee Survey


I have personally interviewed our 102 employees regarding
their complaints with regard to our Leitner Laboratory
facilities. Over 75 percent of these employees work at night,
and 90 percent of that group believes that the outdoor
lighting at the lab is insufficient. The lighting on the
walkway between the parking lot and the front door is
particularly bad, and several people have almost fallen on
the steps. So far we have been fortunate that no crimes have
occurred out there, but our luck may be running out. I
feel the lack of good lighting should be brought to your
attention. Hopefully, you will consider some alternative
lighting systems that we can discuss at the meeting of all
department heads next month. With high utility rates, the
company may have a problem providing safe lighting. We know
cuts must be made, but should it be the lighting? The trend
today is toward the use of high-pressure sodium or mercury
lighting because it creates more light for less money.
```

Summary

Memos are the most common form of internal written communication in businesses. Because memos are meant for conveying data efficiently, construct them carefully so that readers can glance quickly at major points, and send them only to readers who actually need the information.

Despite the informality of many memos, they deserve your careful writing and editing skills. Well-written memos are invaluable aids to both employees and managers since, in most businesses, they are essential components of internal communication. To heighten the effectiveness of your memos, work on creating a personal tone, organizing material in a manner helpful to your readers, and editing for conciseness and accuracy.

Memo Checklist

- Choose a memo as your communication channel if at least one of the following criteria is applicable:

  _____ You are writing a fairly informal message to someone within your organization

  _____ More than one person in the organization needs the information

  _____ The information is too complicated for a telephone call

  _____ You want a written record of the information

- Make sure the memo goes only to people who need it.

Opening of Memo

- Use a standard memo format:

  _____ *To/From* lines should be consistent.

  _____ *From* line should be initialed.

  _____ *Subject* line should be informative and specific.

- Choose a direct opening if you are writing a positive or neutral message.

- Choose an indirect opening if your message is negative or unpleasant.

- Make sure your opening is

  _____ linked to the subject line and the rest of the memo

  _____ of interest to your reader

  _____ suitable for the subject matter

Body of Memo

- Organize central material in a useful pattern:

  _____ Chronological steps are useful for descriptions of procedures.

  _____ Logical narration is useful for conveying information.

_____ Order of increasing or decreasing importance and comparison/contrast are useful for persuasive memos.

• Use short paragraphs, white space, lists, and graphics aids to heighten readability.

• Make sure the tone is appropriate to your message and your readers.

Ending of Memo

• Create an ending that performs at least one of these functions:

_____ Summarizes central paragraphs

_____ Requests reader to act

_____ Returns to upbeat note made at the opening

_____ Summarizes recommendations

Terms to Remember

Chronological organization: step-by-step description of procedure or activity
Comparison/contrast organization: establishes strengths and weaknesses of two or more items
Logical narration: information arranged in a manner that makes sense to readers and answers their probable questions as they arise

Order of decreasing importance: saves reader time by making more important points at first
Order of increasing importance: uses crescendo method to keep reader interested

Summary Discussion: Bernice Lum's Memo from Case in Point, p. 279

Bernice loses sight of her main point: she intended to write a memo outlining procedures, but she began her memo with a complaint. Thus, the new procedure seems like a punishment. She needs a more positive subject line and opening.

Moreover, the memo is wordy and hard to read. The procedures should be more specifically worded and then numbered for easy reference. Her memo could have been outlined like this:

1. Reader-oriented reason for change in procedures
2. List of procedures employees should follow
3. Request for cooperation with the new system

Questions for Review and Discussion

1. Why are internal communications often more informal than external communications?
2. Name three ways in which memos can hurt effective communication

3. What is a good method for determining the major point of your memo?
4. Why is an appropriate tone important to a memo?

Exercises

1. Visit an office in your college or in a local business. Ask if you may copy at least two memos for use in your business communication class. Then in a page or two analyze both memos for effectiveness:

   • Are they well organized?
   • Can you identify an organizational plan?
   • Are they wordy or concise? Give examples.
   • Are they visually effective? Explain.
   • Can you easily summarize their major points? What are they?

2. Interview a manager in a local business. How many memos does he or she write each week? How many does he or she read? What problems does this manager encounter while writing and reading memos?

3. Many companies now use computer mail in place of hard-copy memos. What are the strengths and weaknesses of having memos on paper rather than on a screen?

4. An instructor in one of your classes has asked your help in developing a new course that would benefit students in your major. You have a number of ideas that you want to present in memo form. While developing the memo, keep each page you use as you go through the writing process (or save the material on a disk).

   a. Brainstorm ideas for the course.
   b. Define your goals. Consider what you are writing, who your audience is (it may include more than the instructor), and your reasons for writing.
   c. Do necessary research. You may want to read syllabuses for other courses, for instance.
   d. Make a plan. Identify which organizational approach you will find most useful.
   e. Draft, revise, and proofread.

5. Revise the following memo so it is more effective. You may reorganize, add, and delete material as you wish.

```
TO:        Mary Jackson, Personnel Manager
FROM:      Steve Olney, Marketing Manager
SUBJECT:   Student Applicants
DATE:      February 3, 19xx
```

I know you have begun looking at the applications of graduating students for our entry-level marketing slots. The following are some points that you should cover in the screening interviews with them.

First, ask if they have any experience with graphics and layout. Also, you might try to find out how creatively they might respond to consumer products similar to ours. Check to make sure they have some market research background, and see if they have any experience with a big company. It would be nice, too, if you made sure they have taken a copywriting class.

I'd also like you to gauge how aggressive they are and check their time management skills as well as their writing and speaking skills. Will you be able to tell me how long they would stay with us if we hired them? And find out if they have taken any mass communication classes.

6. Revise the following memo. Delete, add, or reorganize as you wish.

```
TO:        All Staff        December 1, 19xx
FROM:      George Ho
SUBJECT:   Holiday Party


I'm sure you're as glad as I am to see
this year come to an end, so I know you'll
want to join me at the holiday party on
December 21, at the Fulton Hotel, 1679 B
Street. I've invited some folks from
Tritech, too, as we've been working with
them so hard this year, and they need a
```

```
lift of spirits as much as we do. The
tickets cost $5 apiece, which isn't much
considering you get all the appetizers you
can eat and a glass of champagne. After
that the champagne will cost you 50 cents
a glass, but that's almost free these
days, isn't it? And there will be dancing
too, once things get rolling after 9 or
so. Let me know by Friday if you can come
as I have to let the caterers know. The
event starts at 7 p.m. and will go to
midnight.
```

7. Revise Bernice Lum's memo at the opening of this chapter.

Word Processing Exercises: Pagination

One of the joys of word processing programs is their ability to number pages automatically. If you type in a 12-page report and then add another page somewhere in the report, the computer will repaginate correctly when you print out the document again.

Programs differ in the way they handle pagination. Some programs automatically start every file with page 1 unless you give them other directions; some programs leave pages unnumbered unless you specify otherwise. While doing the following exercises, you will learn the pagination techniques for your word processing program. Specifically, you will learn to

- start paginating with page numbers other than 1
- suppress pagination
- move page numbers
- insert page breaks

1. COPY any file you have created so far that is at least two pages long. (If you do not have such a file, then type in a least 500 words of double-spaced text from a book of your choice.) Call the new file PAGE.

2. If your word processing program does not automatically number pages when you print out a file, then enter the command for paginating. PRINT the file to see if the pagination is correct: the first page of your text should be number 1, the second page number 2, and so on.

3. Now learn how to begin paginating with a number other than 1. If you are writing a long report, for example, you may want to put each section of it in a different file. If the first section of the report is 20 pages, then you will want to begin the second file at page 21.

Enter the command to begin your file PAGE at page 12 rather than page 1. PRINT the file to see that it has paginated correctly.

4. Sometimes you will not want a page number on a page. A one-page letter or memo, for example, should not be numbered. This time, enter the command for SUPPRESSING pagination. PRINT the file PAGE to make sure no page numbers appear.

5. Sometimes you will have to create a document according to a specific format. Some companies, for example, require that the page numbers of reports appear in a specific location on the page such as the upper-right-hand corner. Many word processing programs automatically put numbers at the bottom of the page; some put them in the corner. You should learn the commands for altering the automatic (or DEFAULT) pagination.

If your program automatically puts page numbers at the bottom of the page, enter the commands for moving the numbers to the upper-right-hand corner. PRINT the file to see if the page numbers are correctly placed.

If your program automatically puts page numbers at the top of the page, enter the commands for moving them to the bottom of the page. PRINT the file to check for correct placement.

6. Your word processor has a default setting for page breaks: each page of text contains the same number of lines unless you request another format.

You will want to add page breaks in many situations. For example, you might want to start a new section of a long memo on a new page; or you might want to keep a list together on one page. Sometimes a section heading will appear as the last line of a page; you can have the page break occur *before* the heading so it will appear at the top of the next page.

Look up the command for creating a page break. Insert that command at the end of the second paragraph of the file PAGE. Now PRINT the file again to see if the second page begins with the third paragraph.

Informational, Procedural, and Persuasive Memos

- **Establishing the purpose of the memo**
- **Writing memos that convey information**
- **Writing memos that outline procedures**
- **Writing memos to convince a reader**

Objectives

To write memos that convey facts clearly and succinctly

To develop memos that accurately outline each step of a procedure

To create memos that convince the reader of a particular viewpoint

13

Henry Morton's Memo

```
TO:         All Employees
FROM:       Henry Morton, President
SUBJECT:    Upcoming Changes
DATE:       September 14, 19XX
```

As you well know, our company has had considerable difficulty this year with various labor difficulties and problems with new products. Also, some of our departments have been growing and shrinking for no logical reasons, and before this occasion we had not really examined our goals and how we were meeting them. Instead, we were patching things up here and there, making short-term decisions that were not in keeping with long-term goals.

This situation has forced management to assess the company and its operations with a view to finding a better way to set it up and improve profits as well as efficiency. As a result, we are making the following changes, effective October 1.

We will be merging the Department of Product Research with the Research and Development Department. The new R & D Department will be headed by Laura DeMont. Ian Moore, presently head of the Department of Product Research, will become Vice-President of Operations. Maryanne Newell, presently head of R & D, will become head of Planning. Nobody's job will be eliminated, but some of you will be reassigned. Your cooperation through the transition period will be greatly appreciated.

Points to Consider

- What is the major idea in this memo?
- Is the memo informational, procedural, or persuasive?
- Does the memo perform its function effectively? Explain.
- What would be a more effective subject line?
- What information should be in the opening paragraph?
- How could the memo be more you-oriented?

Establishing the Purpose of the Memo

Defining your goals simplifies and speeds up the memo-writing process. Knowing your primary aims will not only help you develop a workable plan, but also help you establish an effective tone and select appropriate data for your particular audience.

Most memos are primarily informational, procedural, or persuasive. So, as you define your goals, ask yourself, "Am I conveying information? Am I explaining a procedure? Am I trying to convince someone?" When you have identified the primary purpose of your memo, you will find that making a plan and following the other steps of the writing process become much easier.

Most memos are designed to convey information, describe a procedure, or persuade the reader.

Writing Memos that Convey Information

Informational memos are some of the most common in any company. They may announce a policy change, summarize the minutes of a meeting, outline

Informational memos are designed to relay facts.

a problem or situation, or describe proceedings. Informational memos may be as short as one or two sentences (Figure 13-1) or several pages long.

Since your major concern in an informational memo is to convey facts, focus on clarity, concrete data, and effective organization (Figure 13-2).

Because a memo is similar in many ways to a letter, you will usually find that the communication strategies outlined in Part 3 are also applicable to memos. Remember to consider how your reader is going to view your memo. If you are giving pleasant or neutral information, start with it: "I am pleased to announce that management has agreed to our request for a 10 percent pay raise." You do not need a preface to the good news.

If your news is less agreeable, start with a delaying sentence or two. (Compare the effectiveness of the memos in Figures 13-3 and 13-5 with that of the memo in Figure 13-4.) You might also choose to incorporate explanations before you pass on the news.

TYPES OF MEMOS

Informational   Procedural   Persuasive

```
TO:    All Employees     SUBJECT: New Executive
FROM:  E. M. Parris,               Vice-President
       President          DATE:    November 3, 19XX


I am pleased to inform you that Marilyn Almon has
accepted our offer to become Executive Vice-
President of Parson's Corporation. She will assume
her position on January 1.
```

FIGURE 13-1 _____

Memo conveying pleasant or neutral information. This brief memo makes the point quickly and efficiently. The writer does not confuse the memo with irrelevant information.

```
TO:        All Employees
FROM:      Douglas Quinn, Personnel Development
           Director
SUBJECT:   Telephone Skills Seminar
DATE:      September 23, 19XX

Those of you interested in improving your
interpersonal communication skills will want to
attend the seminar we have scheduled for next
Thursday.

You'll have to get up earlier in the morning, but
we'll compensate you for your time. And you'll find
the payoffs from the seminar will be well worth
your effort.

Entitled "Improving Telephone Techniques," the
seminar will focus on helping us become better
communicators over the telephone. Robert Mitford,
nationally known telemarketing specialist, will
lead the seminar.

I highly recommend this seminar for all our
salespeople and customer service representatives.
The seminar is limited to 20 participants, so sign
up early.
                    SEMINAR SPECIFICS
WHERE:      Library, 2nd Floor
WHEN:       Thursday, October 2
TIME:       7-9 a.m.
TO ENROLL:  Sign the sheet beside the 2nd floor
            elevators
```

FIGURE 13-2 ⎯⎯⎯⎯⎯⎯⎯⎯⎯⎯⎯⎯⎯⎯⎯⎯⎯⎯⎯⎯⎯⎯⎯⎯⎯⎯

Memo conveying pleasant or neutral information. Like many memos, this incorporates persuasive techniques with the information it conveys. The writer emphasizes the benefits to attending the seminar and presents the information so it is appealing to employees.

```
TO:   Mr. Connoll Girton    SUBJECT: Survey Results
FROM: Mr. Lee D'Amico       DATE:      April 19, 19XX

The survey you requested was filled out by 30
employees. Although most employees enjoy working at
Top Hat Restaurant, many are upset by low wages and
certain working conditions.

Employee complaints are listed below in order of
decreasing importance.

1. Top Hat wages are competitive with those of
comparable restaurants only for entry-level
employees. After six months of experience,
employees do not begin getting raises commensurate
with those of other companies. Thus, we have lost
many experienced employees to competitors.
2. Work schedules are constantly changing.
Employees find it difficult to adjust their work
and schedules when they never know from one week to
the next the hours and times they will be working.
3. The work area near the oven is cramped and hot.
During peak hours, temperatures approach 95
degrees, and as many as seven people may be trying
to work in the small space. The situation leads to
tension and loss of efficiency.


             PROBLEMS CITED BY EMPLOYEES
       (Employees could cite more than one problem.)

                  0   5   10  15  20  25  30

WAGES             _____
SCHEDULES         _____
WORKING
CONDITIONS        _____
OTHER             _____


           DEGREE OF EMPLOYEE SATISFACTION
       (Employees could mark only one category.)

                  0   5   10  15  20  25  30

VERY SATISFIED    _____
SATISFIED         _____
DISSATISFIED      _____

Clearly, we need to concentrate our efforts on
improving the three areas that are leading to
employee dissatisfaction. A small expenditure of
money and effort should considerably reduce
employee turnover and increase the number of highly
satisfied employees.
```

FIGURE 13-3 _____

Informational memo. This memo conveys some unpleasant news, so the writer includes
upbeat information at the beginning and end. He also puts his relevant data in graphic form
so the reader can see the information at a glance.

```
TO:       Ms. Wilma Brown
FROM:     Mr. Ned Thornedyke
SUBJECT:  Personnel Problem
DATE:     March 2, 19XX

Management has been seeing some very poor work
coming out of your department, and most of it is
initialed by Jack Patterson. He used to be pretty
good—what happened? Now he's sending us incomplete
and inaccurate data, and his last report was two
days overdue.

This situation is hurting the efficiency rating of
your department, Wilma—and it's hurting the whole
company. I can't afford to personally check every
piece of data from your employees.
```

FIGURE 13-4

Ineffective memo conveying bad news. The writer used this memo to let off steam rather than to constructively convey unpleasant information. His information is vague, and he does not provide a specific line of action. Moreover, he is actually criticizing Wilma as much as he is complaining about Jack; to enlist her help, he should address her more positively.

```
TO:       Ms. Wilma Brown
FROM:     Mr. Ned Thornedyke
SUBJECT:  Employee Evaluation
DATE:     March 2, 19XX

This memo is a follow-up to our conversation of
March 1. As we discussed, your department has
always achieved high ratings for accuracy and
efficiency. Recently, however, management has been
seeing some work initialed by Jack Patterson that
is considerably below your department's usual
standards.
     1. The cost report dated February 10 did not
     include publication costs.
     2. The data on PRO Industries was sent to the
     Chief Engineer instead of to the Controller.
     3. The information on materials that we needed
     for our bid last week was two days late. The
     delay could have caused us to lose the bid.

Jack Patterson used to be a dependable employee,
but his work has been declining seriously since
December. Now the situation is urgent. Please issue
him a warning that his work must improve over the
next month if he is to stay with our company.

If he has a personal problem that is affecting his
work, ask him to speak to me. I want to resolve
this situation with a minimum of bad feeling.
```

FIGURE 13-5

Revised informational memo conveying bad news. Although the message is urgent, this memo is objective in tone and conveys specific points useful to the reader. The improved subject line also makes the memo more palatable to the reader.

EQUITABLE CAPITAL

*"A good memo clearly describes the issue,"
says Robert Connolly, a Vice-President of
Equitable Capital Management Corporation, an investment bank/merchant bank
subsidiary of The Equitable Life Assurance
Society of the United States, which arranges deals and investments for Equitable and other clients. "A memo should be
well thought-out and cover all the topics.
The reader shouldn't come away from it
with questions."*

Robert frequently writes memos for
members of senior management who
have substantial demands placed on their
time. To assist these senior executives in
reviewing materials, lengthy memos will
be accompanied by a brief covering
memo which outlines the main topics
being discussed, usually using bullet
points to highlight significant points.

Robert emphasizes that you should be
aware of your audience. "Somebody
wrote a highly technical memo that was
correct in technical terms, but didn't describe its practical applications for a lay
person. The writer didn't say, 'What this
means is tomorrow when you do X, Y, and
Z, consider this.' As a result the person
who received the memo didn't understand it and didn't apply it to a situation
where it would have helped."

Robert also suggests that in writing
memos you should pose possible solutions to problems, as well as the problems
themselves. "Don't just isolate a problem;
give solutions or reasons for or against
particular solutions," so the reader can
assess the problem and develop a plan of
action for dealing with the problem.

In addition, think through the implications of the problem so that you can see
if it applies to a particular situation. For
example, "Sometimes you'll structure a
transaction to cause a certain tax result. If
you are putting together a deal, it can be
either to the buyer's advantage or disadvantage that the company being considered has substantial assets that can be de-
preciated. If I'm a buyer and have little
income, but lots of net losses, I don't get
any economic benefit from buying a company with the potential for tax depreciation. On the other hand, if I am rich in
taxable income, I will benefit from a company that will generate tax depreciation
deductions. In other words, when presenting an issue, you must analyze it in the
light of the specifics of the situation you're
involved in."

A memo should also be organized, not
rambling. "When you are reading one section, all the information should be there.
You shouldn't find something related to it
tucked away in another section."

Robert considers a memo well-written
if it:

- is well thought out from many angles
- clearly describes the issue
- covers the topic thoroughly
- presents possible solutions, not just
  problems
- keeps the audience in mind

Writing Memos that Outline Procedures

A procedural memo is a specialized type of informational memo that usually
takes a reader through a set of chronological instructions.

Many jokes have been made about the frustrated parent trying to assemble
a child's toy on Christmas morning by following instructions such as "Insert
module C into aperture 2-P." But, if you have ever been irritated while
running a computer program or filling out your IRS forms, you know that
poorly written procedures or instructions are not amusing.

Memos delineating new policies or procedures are deceptive: they appear to be easy to write, and yet writers often find pitfalls awaiting them. Because the writer already *knows* the procedures, he or she often finds it difficult to clarify items to a less knowledgeable reader. (See Figure 13-6 for a list of problems and solutions related to procedural memos. Figures 13-7 through 13-10 illustrate some of these problems and their solutions.)

As you make a plan, break down the procedures into a chronological list of actions; then, when you draft and revise, start each item on the list with an active verb describing what the reader should do. Do not assume the reader can fill in any gaps in the instructions. If your instructions are overly simple, no one will complain; if they are too complex, all types of problems may result.

Avoid s
a proce

If your memo is describing particularly important or complex procedures, ask someone to follow your instructions step by step before you write your final draft. A "trial run" can often help you discover muddled language or missing steps

Sample Outline for Procedural Memo
1. Open with you-oriented reason for procedure:
2. Organize the body of memo using a numbered list of steps, each of which begins with an active verb.

Problem	*Solution*
The writer forgets the audience. As a result, the memo outlines procedures irrelevant to the reader.	Make sure each action outlined in the memo is something the reader will actually be doing.
The procedures being described are unpleasant or incomprehensible to the reader.	Begin with a you-oriented explanation that can help to break down the reader's initial resistance.
The memo gets off the point.	Stick to your initial goals and plan.
The writer forgets a vital step or describes procedures vaguely.	Have someone go through the procedure using your directions. Include any details the reader might find useful.

FIGURE 13-6

Solving problems with procedural memos

```
TO:       Clerical Employees
FROM:     Patrick Thurber
SUBJECT:  Incoming Mail
DATE:     March 22, 19XX

Beginning next month, our corporate office will
observe a new procedure for distributing and filing
incoming correspondence. The new system will handle
our increased workload more efficiently.

In the past, the receptionist dated and distributed
incoming mail. As of April 1, the Mail Room will
handle this mail. After the postal delivery, the
Mail Room staff will date-stamp each envelope and
place it in a departmental mail box in the Mail
Room. Your mail should be in the boxes between 1
and 2 p.m. The mail will not be opened.

In most cases, the incoming mail box will be the
same as the department's inter-office mail box. If
your department receives a large quantity of mail,
your department may have been given a larger
mailbox. Please check the Mail Room floor plan to
see if your box has been relocated.

Within each department, the contents of the letters
will be date-stamped. Staple the letters to their
envelopes and distribute them to the addressees.
Any envelopes marked personal should be delivered
unopened to the addressee.

Thank you for following these new procedures.
```

FIGURE 13-7 _____

Ineffective procedural memo. This memo is visually ineffective: it needs a list format to increase readability. The memo also suffers from a focus problem. As a procedural memo, it should inform clerical employees what they should do, not what other employees will be doing. The clerical staff's role in the new procedures is unclear.

```
TO:        Clerical Employees
FROM:      Patrick Thurber
SUBJECT:   Incoming Mail
DATE:      March 22, 19XX

Beginning April 1, we will observe new procedures
for picking up and distributing incoming
correspondence.

Each department manager will appoint a clerical
staff member to handle the department's mail. That
person should follow these procedures:

1. Check the Mail Room floor plan to see if your
departmental mailbox has been relocated.
2. Pick up your department's mail from your
departmental mailbox between 1 and 2 p.m. each day.
Each envelope will already be date-stamped.
3. Open the envelopes and staple the letters to
their envelopes.
4. Date-stamp the contents and distribute them to
the addressees.
5. Do not open any letters marked personal; simply
deliver them to the addressees.
```

FIGURE 13-8

Revised procedural memo. This memo effectively tells the readers in a logical way exactly what they should do. It does not explain what the former procedure was or what other employees will be doing with regard to the mail. Note that each step begins with an active verb.

```
TO:        All Supervisors
FROM:      Carl Houghton, Director of Human
           Resources
SUBJECT:   Procedures for Facilitating Transfers
DATE:      August 17, 19XX

When employees request transfers to other
departments, you should meet with the employees
and, while you shouldn't discourage them, you
should make sure they are aware of anything that
could disqualify them. Then the employees should
complete the application for transfer. Add your
comments and attach a copy of each employee's
latest Performance Evaluation to the pink copy of
the form.

Send the pink copy to me. Keep the yellow copy for
your reference.
```

FIGURE 13-9

Ineffective procedural memo. This memo doesn't take the reader through the procedure step by step. The writer is unclear regarding where the supervisor should write comments and never mentions how long the employees must wait before knowing whether their request was approved.

Writing Memos to Convince a Reader

In some ways every memo is persuasive. As a business writer, you are always attempting at some level to convince your reader. While explaining the steps of a new procedure, you may also be saying implicitly, "These steps will make life easier for us" or "This new procedure will save us money." While telling your reader about an upcoming convention or meeting, you might also be convincing the reader that the event is worthwhile.

Moreover, you could also argue that any memo that conveys facts is informational. Distinctions among the three categories of memos covered in this chapter often become blurred. Some memos, however, are very similar to sales letters. The writer is basically trying to win a reader over to a certain position or to get the reader to act in a certain way. These memos are labeled *persuasive* to highlight their primary purpose.

```
TO:        All Supervisors
FROM:      Carl Houghton, Director of Human
           Resources
SUBJECT:   Procedures for Facilitating Transfers
DATE:      August 17, 19XX

When employees request transfers to other
departments, you should follow these procedures:

1. Meet individually with the employees to discuss
their qualifications for the new position. Make
sure they are aware of anything that could
disqualify them.
2. Do not discourage the request; our company
policy is to help employees find the jobs they
want.
3. Give Form 34-12, Application for Transfer, to
the employees requesting transfers.
4. When employees have completed Sections I—V of
the form, you should fill out Section VI,
Supervisor's Comments, at the bottom of the form.
5. Attach a copy of each employee's latest
Performance Evaluation to the pink copy of the
form.
6. Send the pink copy to me. Keep the yellow copy
for your reference.
7. Employees should know the outcome of their
application within three weeks. At that time, they
may review the documents pertaining to the transfer
and discuss the decision with you.
```

FIGURE 13-10 _____

Procedural memo. This procedural memo is concise and logical. Each step is clearly outlined for the reader.

What Would You Do?

Jenny Harbison, a department manager, wrote the following memo to Ed Neely. While Ed is a department manager too, he is also the chair of a special committee that dispenses tuition reimbursement funds to company employees.

```
TO:        Ed Neely
FROM:      Jenny Harbison
SUBJECT:   Tuition Reimbursement Problems
DATE:      November 29, 19XX
```

```
I've been hearing a lot of complaints recently about the
criteria your committee uses for reimbursing employees. No
one seems to understand who gets reimbursed or why some do
and some don't. Last year Wally Gleason was reimbursed and
this year he hasn't been. Why? Now hourly employees are
asking why they can't be reimbursed too. If your committee is
playing fair, what are the rules you are playing by?
```

Not surprisingly, Ed Neely did not care for the tone or approach in this memo. His angry response answered none of Jenny's questions.

Write a more effective memo for Jenny.

Like a sales letter, a persuasive memo requires knowledge of the audience. Usually *evidence* or data will also be vital. You may need to bolster your arguments and recommendations with specific examples, benefits, or financial information (Figures 13–11 and 13–12). A persuasive memo may also weigh advantages and disadvantages. The central sections of persuasive memos are often organized in comparison/contrast terms or in an order of increasing or decreasing importance.

Persuasive memos usually include specific, concrete details.

Like an informational or procedural memo, a persuasive memo should vary in terms of how resistant the reader is to the subject. If the reader will be difficult to persuade, you might begin with your supporting data and delay the central point. But, whatever your strategy, maintain a factual, objective, and upbeat tone, so your reader does not feel that he or she is being pressured.

Sample Outline for Persuasive Memo
1. Describe a problem or situation.
2. State your purpose.
3. Describe strong and weak points of various options.
4. Make a recommendation and indicate specific action you want the reader to take.

```
       TO:  William Tierson, Acting Chief, Psychiatry
            Service
     FROM:  Lisa Gower, Coordinator, Westwood Clinic
  SUBJECT:  Staffing
     DATE:  May 12, 19XX
```

I hope you will support my request to the Board
that we add two additional clinicians to the
Westwood staff. All of us have been carrying much
heavier caseloads than our contracts specify;
overwork has led to a steady increase in the staff
turnover rate and a subsequent decline in patient
services. The numbers speak for themselves:

    1. Based on our staffing level, the county
    established that our clinic caseload should be
    22,000 patient visits per year.
    2. If each staff member maintained the former
    personal caseload limits of 128 patients, our
    yearly patient visits would have come to over
    31,000. Such an overload strains every aspect of
    our patient care program.

To raise staff morale, I lowered individual
caseload limits to 120 patients, but this reduction
lowers our yearly patient visits only to 26,000.

As a result of the reduction, we have had to
establish a patient waiting list. For the first
four months of this fiscal year, the average wait
for treatment has been 2 months after intake. This
waiting time can be disastrous for many patients
needing psychiatric help.

Adding two more staff members is crucial to our
continuing a high level of service at the Westwood
Clinic. With your support, I hope, the Board will
approve funds to hire additional staff.

FIGURE 13-11 ————

Persuasive memo. In this persuasive memo, the writer provides good reasons for her position. While remaining calm and backing up her argument with figures, she makes a strong case for needing the additional staff.

TO: Mr. James Boduin, Vice-President
FROM: Ms. Kari White, Assistant Manager,
           Production
SUBJECT: Lockers
DATE: November 5, 19XX

Employees are delighted with the new exercise room
and the early morning aerobic dance lessons. Every
day this month, at least 50 employees have attended
the lessons, and the exercise equipment is also
being heavily used.

The popularity of our exercise program, however,
has led to a problem: employees have no place to
store their gear while they are working or their
work outfits while they are exercising. They pile
their belongings on benches near the showers, but
they are afraid of theft—and of getting their
clothes ruined.

I recommend the company buy 30 lockers for the
men's locker room and 30 for the women's. There is
ample space for them.

Lockers would
    1. encourage more employees to take part in our
    exercise program,
    2. help to keep the offices more tidy—without
    leotards and exercise shoes piled everywhere, and
    3. deter petty theft

Lockers would be a small investment after all the
company has spent to set up our excellent exercise
program. With your authorization, I will be happy
to research costs and options.

FIGURE 13-12

Persuasive memo. This persuasive memo argues logically for an investment in lockers. The writer's praise for the present exercise program and her upbeat tone make her request more appealing. Her numbered list of reasons is easy to glance at, and her last paragraph outlines a clear course of action.

"Loved your last memo, Ted. You're beginning to find your own voice."

Drawing by Lorenz; © 1984 The New Yorker Magazine, Inc.

Summary

When you are writing memos, knowing your goals and your audience is a particularly important step of the writing process. Establishing clear communication objectives will help you organize and revise your memos so they act as efficient and effective communication channels for your readers.

Informational, Procedural, and Persuasive Memo Checklist

Informational Memo

• Use an informational memo when you want to

_____ announce a policy change

_____ summarize minutes of a meeting

_____ outline a problem or situation

_____ describe proceedings

• Use a direct approach when you write a memo conveying pleasant or neutral information:

_____ Opening states major point

_____ Central paragraphs add more information

_____ Ending provides summary or request for action

• Use an indirect approach when you write a memo conveying bad news:

_____ Opening sets pleasant or neutral tone

_____ Second paragraph provides explanation for bad news

_____ Central paragraphs state the bad news

_____ Ending is pleasant or neutral

Procedural Memo

• Use a procedural memo to explain set of instructions to a reader.

• Make sure your procedural memo is you-oriented, focused on major points, complete, and clear.

• In most cases, organize a procedural memo so it contains a you-oriented explanation for the procedure as well as a list of steps beginning with an active verb.

Persuasive Memo

• Develop persuasive memos when you wish to convince a reader of a specific point of view.

• In most cases, organize your persuasive memo so that

_____ the opening describes a problem or situation

_____ the second paragraph contains a statement of purpose

_____ the central paragraphs describe solutions and recommendations

_____ the conclusion summarizes the point and indicates specific action you want the reader to take

Summary Discussion: Henry Morton's Memo from Case in Point, p. 301

This memo opens with negative information that sets an unpleasant tone to the whole communication. Henry is writing a memo conveying basically neutral information: no one is losing a job, but everyone will have to face some changes. After a you-oriented opening, Henry should get right to his point and explain what the changes are. A more precise subject line and a list format in the body of the memo would make it easier to scan quickly. He should stress the advantages to these changes, not the problems that have brought them about.

Questions for Review and Discussion

1. Why are procedural memos often difficult to write?

2. Why is knowing your audience particularly important for writing persuasive memos?

3. What arguments can you give for the statement "All memos are persuasive memos"?

Exercises

1. The following openings to informative memos could be revised or eliminated if the writer had thought of a good subject line. Turn the relevant material in each opening into a subject line. Then revise the opening sentences.

a. We need to know how our customers feel about Pro-Tem Products. This memo summarizes the data we acquired from the 3,000 questionnaires we sent to our customers last June.

b. You indicated that you would be interested in seeing how our market share has varied over the past decade. The following memo is a summary and analysis of the variations.

c. Just as we did last year, the College Accounting Association is starting the school year with an orientation session. We hope you'll attend.

2. Reorganize and revise the following memo to make it more effective.

As you know, we are badly in need of more offices now that we increased our staff by 24. However, we have been uncertain whether to rent offices for a year or two or whether to begin building offices right away. My research on obtaining more office space indicates that we should rent rather than build additional offices. The below points are relevant to my conclusion:

1. We can move into offices much sooner.
2. Renting will cost us $45,000 less this year than will building; until our income stabilizes, this cost difference is crucial.
3. There are seven offices for rent right across the street from our Barton Complex.
4. Renting will give us time to find out exactly what our needs will be over the next decade.
5. The Barton Complex management is eager to lease space, so we could get a good rental agreement.
6. We will need more space before July if we make a successful bid on the GICO project.

Renting has drawbacks, but it still seems to make sense in this situation.

3. Revise the following memo:

TO: All Employees
FROM: Les Forbes
SUBJECT: Timesharing Vacations
DATE: November 4, 19XX

I know November seems like an absurd time to be thinking about summer vacations, but all of you know the importance of advance planning. Some of you always go to the beach in the summer; some go to the mountains. I'd like to inform you of another possibility: renting a condo on Maui for two weeks. Sound too expensive? It may not be if you take part in a new program available to QRT employees. This program would enable us all to buy into a condominium and then use it for our separate vacations all year long. If enough employees join the program, our vacations could cost less than they ever have—and they'll be a lot more exciting.

Anyway, read the brochure I'm sending around to each of you. If the idea appeals to enough people, we'll begin to discuss details.

4. Revise the following memo.

TO: All Employees
FROM: Kara Charles
SUBJECT: Procedures for Receiving
             Compensatory Pay
DATE: June 13, 19XX

There has been some confusion recently concerning how you get paid if you work overtime. The procedure simply involves getting a comp-time form from Joe Herschel (Room 2098) and filling it out completely each time you work overtime.

If you work on a weekend, you will receive time-and-a-half pay, but overtime during the week will be the same as your hourly wage. Make sure you give both the times you worked and the actual number of hours to make things easier for the payroll staff.

Make sure, however, before you work overtime, that you check with your supervisor to make sure he or she wants you to work the extra hours. Your supervisor must approve each comp-time request, so if you work extra hours without giving notice, you may find you worked for free.

5. Revise the following memo.

                GORILLA SANDWICHES TO GO
TO: All Employees
FROM: Max Duffy
SUBJECT: Stealing
DATE: August 1, 19XX

There have been some differences between the amount of salami and pastrami I have been ordering and the number of sandwiches being sold. Either I'm going crazy or employees are eating free lunches and inviting their friends to join them.

I seem to be acting sanely otherwise, so I suspect employees are stealing luncheon meats. I am not accusing anyone, but I am issuing a warning. Anyone found enjoying a free lunch will be treated in the same way as they would be if they were found stealing money. You will be discharged immediately. If you want a gorilla sandwich for lunch, use your 40% discount. Your friends, however, must pay the full price.

6. Revise Henry Morton's informational memo (p. 301).

7. Write a procedural memo explaining to new students at your school how to enroll for the classes they want.

8. Write a memo to your department chair that argues for a curriculum change in your major. You might suggest adding or deleting a required course or altering certain prerequisites.

9. Write a memo to the employees of a company informing them that they must now punch a time clock when they arrive in the morning and leave in the afternoon. This new policy will be upsetting to the employees, so be tactful.

10. As head of a large word processing department, you have had to hire temporary workers whenever the workload becomes too heavy. Now it seems the workload is *always* heavy. Persuade management that you need an additional full-time worker instead of a constant flow of temporary workers. Include data to substantiate your request.

11. As a summer employee at Hank's Beefburger restaurant, you have been asked to assess the brief questionnaires that are left on the tables for customers to fill out. The questionnaire has only three questions:

    1. How would rate the service you received at Hank's today?

1	2	3
poor	good	terrific

    2. How would you rate the food you ate at Hank's today?

1	2	3
poor	good	terrific

    3. Do you have any suggestions for us?

    You have collected 300 of these questionnaires and found the results are positive but not outstanding. Tabulate the data for Hank, the owner, and write a memo explaining your findings.

12. Write an informational memo to members of a college club telling them of some group airfare rates now available to them for winter and spring vacations. Give specific information concerning airlines, destinations, times, and fares.

13. Some employees in your company have requested that their paychecks be automatically deposited in their bank accounts each month. Write a memo explaining the steps employees must take if they want the automatic deposit.

14. Your company has just installed a new telephone system. Write a memo explaining how to transfer outside calls to a different extension.

15. Write a memo persuading employees to attend the annual Awards Dinner, an event that has been poorly attended in the past.

16. You are an undergraduate who also works as a secretarial assistant in the School of Engineering office. Usually you work 20 hours a week, but you realize that you will have to cut back your hours during exam week. Write a memo to your supervisor explaining when you can work and convincing the reader that you are unable to maintain your usual schedule.

Word Processing Exercises: Review

1. Enter a file called MEMO. Type in a brief memo such as that illustrated in Figure 13-1.

2. SUPPRESS pagination so no page number will appear when you print the file.

3. Write in the word Memorandum at the top of the page; center it and underline it.

4. Increase the left and right margins to approximately 2 inches.

5. Add blank lines above the text so the memo will be centered on the page.

6. PRINT the file MEMO. Check for correct format.

4-1. CGF Outdoor Equipment Company, located in Concord, Massachusetts, specializes in high-quality equipment for backpackers, mountain climbers, and cross-country skiers. The majority of products are designed and manufactured by CGF employees and then marketed through a catalogue. The equipment is expensive and appeals to a limited but well-to-do market segment. The company has grown quickly in its five years of operation; at present it has 125 employees, and its sales have almost doubled every year for the past three years.

The three people who founded the company, Charles Collins, Catherine Gough, and Dan Ferguson, were young and inexperienced: they knew the product but not the business. They have learned quickly. The company's future looks promising.

One change that has come about from the company's fast growth has been an increase in written communication. Whereas the employees used to work together in three rooms, now they are spread throughout a four-story office building and a smaller production facility. Memos are becoming more common and somewhat more formal. In fact, as the day-to-day pace of the company increases, memos are becoming a major medium for upward, downward, and lateral communication.

a. A major trade show for the outdoor equipment industry is held in San Diego every year. Formerly, the three founders used to leave Massachusetts every December to attend, but this year they have decided to send department heads.

You are Dan Ferguson, one of the founders. Write a memo to four department heads informing them of the upcoming show. Give them pertinent information concerning dates and location. Let them know that the company can afford to send only two representatives; those who are interested in going should get back to you as soon as possible. The memo should be addressed to Darlene Thompson, Head of Production; Gail Lawes, Head of Marketing; Jack Winters, Head of Planning; and Ed Simons, Head of Research and Design.

b. You are Darlene Thompson, Head of Production. You have volunteered to attend the San Diego trade show, but you have discovered that the company has no specific guidelines for handling employee reimbursement for such trips. You would like

to know whether you are entitled to rent a car in San Diego, whether you would be paid a certain daily amount for meals and lodging.

As you might be making contacts with important new customers and associates, you want to know whether you will be reimbursed for entertainment expenses. Also, can you get an advance on some of this money or must you wait until January to be reimbursed?

Write a memo to Dan Ferguson saying you are happy to attend the trade show but need some more information.

c. Dan Ferguson has forwarded Darlene Thompson's memo to Herbert Zawalsky in Accounting. As the company has no guidelines for employee reimbursement on such a large scale, Dan would like Herb to write up some reasonable procedures. Herb should then send the procedures to the three founders for their approval.

You are Herbert Zawalsky. You would like to implement a procedure that has worked well in other companies: anyone representing the company at conventions, trade shows, and similar events can be reimbursed, up to $150 per day, for transportation, meals, and lodging. Airfare is not included in that amount. Employees may receive up to $200 in advance of the trip. To be reimbursed, they must submit receipts for each expenditure.

As Herbert, write a memo outlining reimbursement procedures for employees.

d. As it happens, three of the department heads to whom Dan Ferguson originally wrote want to attend the show; only Ed Simons expressed no interest. As head of marketing, Gail Lawes feels she should attend the show along with Darlene Thompson. Gail believes a marketing person should attend the show, especially as the company is concentrating on expanding its marketing efforts in southern California. Gail argues that having Jack Winters, head of planning, at the show will be less useful for the company.

You are Gail Lawes. Write a memo to the three founders persuading them that you should be a company representative at the trade show. Your memo must be tactful as well as persuasive: you do not want to make an enemy of Jack Winters.

e. You are Catherine Gough, one of the founders.

While thinking over the importance of the San Diego trade show, you have decided you should take the time away from the office to attend: potential customers really prefer making contact with the principals of a company. As you agree that a marketing expert should also attend, you have approved Gail Lawes's request.

Write Jack Winters and Darlene Thompson with the news that neither of them will be able to attend the trade show. They may, perhaps, be interested in attending a similar event scheduled for July in Seattle. Try not to hurt anyone's feelings.

4-2. Anita's Toy Company, founded in 1985, has been growing slowly but surely. Anita and Gregory Farmer, the company's founders, have focused on a segment of the toy market that many companies have been disregarding: old-fashioned dolls of all sizes with attractive and fairly expensive accessories. Many of the dolls are made in Anita's production facility.

This year, however, an unfortunate event occurred that upset the whole company. A four-year-old child, playing with one of the company's miniature dolls, managed to swallow the whole thing. The child survived, but Anita's Toy Company received some unpleasant publicity. Now some of the managers feel that the miniature dolls should be dropped from Anita's product line.

a. You are Gregory Farmer, cofounder of the company. Write a memo to all department heads informing them of an upcoming meeting to discuss Anita's Minis, the miniature dolls. Tell the readers where and when the meeting will be. Let them know the topic of the meeting. Everyone should come with any information they have that will help make a decision about keeping or dropping this line of dolls. Stress the urgency of the meeting.

b. You are Roberta Tauber, head of Financial Planning. You will be out of town on the day of the meeting, so you are writing this memo to Anita and Gregory Farmer as well as to all managers. You feel they should have this information before deciding whether to drop Anita's Minis.

Your data are as follows: Anita's Minis have brought in $150,000 in profits for each of the last two years; they are outsold only by Anita's Rag Dolls; sales have not declined appreciably this quarter since the swallowing incident. The figures indicate that the company should not drop Anita's Minis.

c. The meeting regarding Anita's Minis was not as productive as the Farmers had hoped. Despite the financial information indicating that Anita's sales had not been unduly affected by the swallowing incident, some managers felt it would be best to drop the line anyway to retain customer goodwill. Others felt that, since Anita's Minis were no more dangerous than any other small toy, the line should be retained. Finally, the group decided to conduct a market survey of consumers' opinions.

You are Mike Thomas, market research analyst. You conducted a mail survey of 1,000 people who had bought toys from Anita's in the past. The survey looked like this:

1. Do you advise that Anita's Toy Company
   a. Stop selling Anita's Minis line of dolls? _____
   b. Keep on selling Anita's Minis? _____
2. Have you bought a Mini in the past? _____
3. Would you buy a Mini again? _____
4. Please add your own comments regarding Anita's Minis.

Nearly 500 people responded. Sixty percent believed that the Mini line should be kept, but 215 of these respondents commented that a warning should be on the box telling parents the dolls are intended for children over five years old.

Write the memo from Mike. Provide the figures you obtained from the survey.

d. As Anita Farmer, write a memo to Roland Lee, Head of Production. Tell him that Anita's Minis will be retained. The only change will be a warning on the box. The new box will be redesigned within a week, and production can continue as usual after that time.

Reports

Part
Five

The Report-Writing Process

- **Communicating through reports**
- **Choosing a report format**
- **Using the report-writing process**
- **Brainstorming**
- **Defining your goals and your audience**
- **Gathering data**
- **Making a plan**
- **Completing the report-writing process**

Objectives

To write reports useful for internal and external communication

To use the report-writing process to create readable, accurate, timely reports

To gather and analyze primary and secondary data

To organize reports logically and readably

14

Andrea Nelson's Report

Andrea Nelson has recently been hired as a junior consultant at KLF Accounting, a firm that specializes in helping small businesses set up their books and handle financial problems. With a BS in accounting and a good background in general business, Andrea is excited about working directly with companies that need assistance.

Her first solo assignment is with The Roof Company, which specializes in repairing roofs of private homes. Andrea's task is to analyze the company's accounting procedures and write a report recommending changes.

Rita Berenson, Andrea's boss, emphasizes the importance of Andrea's report to the company. "Companies pay us for the report, something tangible they can hold on to," she tells Andrea. "Your report should summarize how The Roof Company is handling its accounting procedures and how it *should* be handling them."

Andrea feels confident she can provide The Roof Company with effective assistance, but she dreads writing the report. After two weeks of reviewing the company's bookkeeping systems, meeting with the company managers, and interviewing the company bookkeeper, who knows more about roofs than about accounting, Andrea has pages of information and recommendations. But she still does not have a coherent report.

"It's all in pieces," she tells Rita. "I've got too much information here."

"Your draft has more problems than that," Rita says when she reads the sheets Andrea has given her. "I can see you've done a lot of work, but you need to organize your information effectively. And you need to write so the managers and employees can use your information. They're not accountants—that's why they need you. Use these pages as your notes and start again. And don't take forever. In this job, you're only as good as your report."

Points to Consider

- How is Andrea's task different from writing a letter or memo? How is it similar?
- What are the elements of a good report that she should consider before she starts to write?
- What sort of communication barriers should she be careful to avoid?

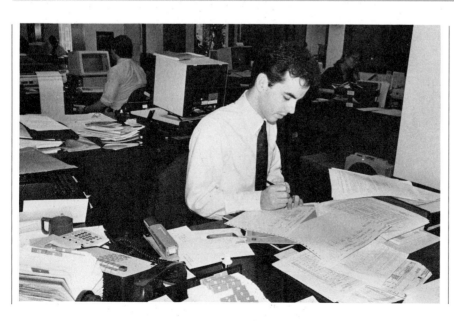

Communicating Through Reports

Reports are some of the most commonly used written communications in business. They may range from one page to book-length, from a letter or memo to a bound, formal document. They may be written for one reader or for thousands, for an audience internal or external to an organization. However, reports usually have a few characteristics in common: they are objective, orderly documents that organize information for a reader.

Reports are objective, orderly documents.

In most cases, reports are written for someone higher in authority: subordinates in an organization prepare reports to keep people above them aware of issues, trends, and problems. However, reports on policies and procedures often move from upper management to middle management to employees. Moreover, a large number of reports are written for clients, customers, shareholders, and other people external to an organization (Figure 14-1).

Reports have numerous functions: they are used to convey information, make recommendations, evaluate personnel, propose projects, analyze issues, and help in decision making. Although not written as frequently as business letters and memos, reports are vital to the communication flow in most organizations and serve as permanent records of company activity.

Reports serve as permanent records.

Figure 14-2 summarizes some of the most common types of reports. As you can see, the various types overlap: an annual report, for example, may also be termed a periodic report or an informational report. A proposal could also be a recommendation report.

Whatever its function, an effective report has the following characteristics. It is

- accurate
- objective
- complete
- logical
- easy to read

- well organized
- free of writing errors
- on time
- professional looking
- useful for the reader(s)

TABLE 14–1

Internal and External Business Communication Forms Used in Business in the 1980s

Form	Frequently Used (percent)	Sometimes Used (percent)	Seldom Used (percent)
Memorandum	95.6	4.4	0.0
Letter	95.6	2.2	2.2
Oral presentations	82.1	12.8	5.1
Analytical report	80.4	15.2	4.4
Informational report	71.8	21.7	6.5
Computer networks	53.3	31.1	15.6
Audio teleconferencing	34.8	30.4	34.8
Video teleconferencing	11.3	27.3	61.4

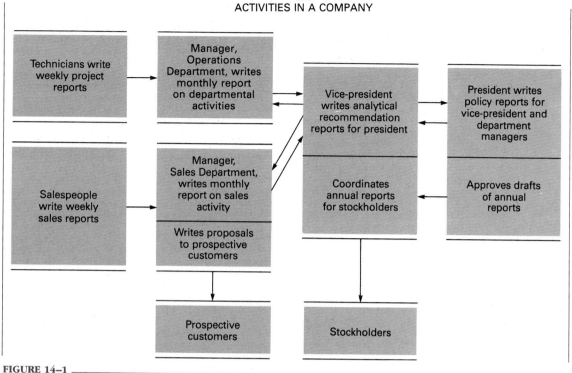

SELECTED REPORT-WRITING
and
ACTIVITIES IN A COMPANY

FIGURE 14-1

Sampling of report-writing activities in a company

Choosing a Report Format

Many times the choice of a report format will be made for you. Reports are usually requested by someone higher in an organization who also designates a specific format. Often, too, company policy dictates a format for documents such as sales reports and proposals. In general, three general formats are available to you:

1. Memorandum reports
2. Letter reports
3. Formal reports

Memorandum Reports

Memorandum reports, usually used for internal reporting, have the same basic format discussed in Chapter 13. Memo reports are also apt to have headings, subheadings, footnotes, graphics, and other components to help a reader assimilate information and to document data. (See Figure 15–2 for an example of a memo report.)

Memorandum reports are usually used for internal reporting.

Annual report [informational/analytical/ persuasive]	A formal report on a publicly held company's activities that includes sections on a company's finances, personnel, and achievements. Published every year for shareholders as well as for employees, the annual report is often an attractive, bound document.
Periodic report [informational]	A report prepared daily, weekly, monthly, or yearly that usually moves upward in an organization. A periodic report generally contains a summary of activities covered in the designated time period and an explanation of any unusual data. Many companies use standard forms or computer printouts as the basis for periodic reports
Informational report [informational]	A report designed to present information in an objective and organized manner. Informational reports are sometimes called *research* reports.
Recommendation report [analytical/persuasive]	A report that examines a situation and concludes with specific recommendations. Recommendation reports are sometimes called *analytical* reports.
Proposal [analytical/persuasive]	Reports written to convince a reader that a need exists and that specific action should be taken to remedy the need. Proposals, which are often informational and analytical as well as persuasive, are written to seek funding or support for projects and to bid on government contracts. Proposals may also be written to management or committee members within an organization

FIGURE 14–2 _____

Common types of reports

Letter Reports

Letter reports, like regular business letters, are used primarily for reports going outside a company. Letter reports have all the basic components of a business letter, but they may also have headings, subheadings, footnotes, graphics, and other components. (See Figure 15-4 for an example of a letter report.)

Letter reports are usually used for external reporting.

Formal Reports

In general, as reports become longer, they become more formal. Additional components such as a title page and table of contents are required to help organize larger quantities of information. Also, longer reports are often written for upper management, so increased formality is necessary. Formal reports usually run longer than eight pages, and they require careful organizing and formatting. (See Chapter 16 for more on formal reports.)

Formal reports should be carefully formatted.

Using the Report-Writing Process

Reports often require amassing and organizing large quantities of information, so they appear more difficult to write than a brief memo or letter. However, using the writing process will provide significant help in creating reports that are readable, accurate, and useful to your readers. In fact, the longer and more complex your report-writing task, the more you need the organizing tools provided by the writing process.

The Writing Process
Brainstorming
Defining your goals and your audience
Doing necessary research
Making a plan
Drafting
Revising
Proofreading

Brainstorming

As always, begin with informal jottings to help you get started. You may want to glance at similar reports to get some ideas, but do not get involved in research too early.

As you jot down ideas, remember that reports are objective, orderly documents that organize information for a particular purpose and a particular audience. No matter what your subject matter, your report should be objective, logical, well documented, and orderly.

Objective

The style of a report is often less personal than that of other business documents.

To be objective, you will have to report information without showing a bias. Your style may well be less personal in a report than in a letter or memo since you are focusing on transmitting accurate data in a logical, unbiased way.

Logical

The longer and more complex a piece of writing, the harder it is to move logically from one thought to the next. As a report writer, make sure your reasoning is clear, your transitions smooth, and your conclusions valid.

Well Documented

A report should be based, not on hunches or beliefs, but on documented evidence. You need to support your statements with data from reliable sources. Some of this documentation may take the form of footnotes, bibliographies, and appendixes. Step 3 of the writing process (doing necessary research) will probably be more extensive for a report than for other types of business documents.

Orderly

Reports should be organized for maximum efficiency.

Your report must be organized so the information in it is readily accessible to the reader. Long reports have tables of contents, summaries, headings, and subheadings to help readers locate the information they need right away. Even short reports should be organized for maximum efficiency. You will find that organizing your data is crucial to the overall effectiveness of the report.

Refine your outline as you develop the report.

Since reports can be complicated to put together, begin developing a plan as you begin defining your goals and doing research. Start with a rough outline and refine it as you acquire more insight and information.

When Ben Corino was hired as a consultant to evaluate marketing options for Jackson Inspection Services, a company that inspects houses for prospective homebuyers, he did not look forward to gathering and organizing all the information needed for a good report. However, he found that adjusting the writing process to his specific needs reduced his frustration and increased his efficiency.

Ben knew he had to cover certain areas in his report. He spent half an hour brainstorming at his computer, typing out ideas and questions. The results are shown on page 331.

Marketing Report: Jackson Inspection Services
—weaknesses of company. How strong is its competition?
    What legal problems might it have?
    Finances? Are they a problem?
    Could the management techniques be better?
  (Do research on the competition.)
—current marketing strategy
    description of service
    pricing
    promotion
    distribution
—strengths of company
    ??
    good service—price? timely—accurate?
    (interview customers, managers, employees)
—recommended strategies
—overview

Defining Your Goals and Your Audience

Before collecting the data that will form the basis for your report, consider the needs of your readers and the purpose of the report. With this information in mind, you will find it easier to begin shaping your report and to decide what types of research you need to do.

Answering the following questions can help you at this point in the report-writing process:

1. *What do my readers already know?* Do not include a lot of information

with which your readers are already familiar. On the other hand, do not leave out essential data.

2. *What are my readers' biases?* If you think your readers will resist some of your recommendations, you may want to present documentation and logical analysis before actually making your point. Remember, you will have to maintain an unbiased, objective tone throughout the report to maintain your readers' credibility and trust.

   If your readers are going to respond positively to your report, use a direct approach that quickly conveys the most important points.

3. *What do I want my readers to remember?* Important points should be placed at the beginning and ending of your report. Headings will help to emphasize major points as will the actual number of paragraphs or pages you allocate to the topic.

4. *What ordering principles will convey the bulk of my information most effectively?* Examining both the nature of your information and the needs of your audience, decide on a logical method for organizing your material. (Some structural patterns are outlined in Figure 14-3.)

Reports are often written for multiple audiences.

Ben Corino knew he was writing a report to the owners of Jackson Inspection Services regarding present and future marketing strategies. But he was also writing for his own colleagues at his consulting company, KLF Enterprises: his report had to include information useful to them as well. Moreover, the report would be kept on file for people to read in the future. A good report would be the basis for other reports on similar firms. A poor report could be an embarrassment for years to come.

Having a multiple audience meant that Ben had to provide adequate background about the company to make the report understandable to his colleagues: at the same time, he had to collect and organize the comprehensive information Jackson Inspection Services had paid his company to provide. To insure his own credibility, he had to document his data and recommendations.

Structuring Patterns

In your preliminary work, you will find it useful to consider the organizational patterns you can use to structure your report and organize the material so it is useful for your readers. If you work out a preliminary outline for your material, you will find it much easier to organize your data as you do your research. Some of the organizational patterns you studied in Chapter 12 are also useful in reports.

Consider, for example, whether your readers would benefit from seeing data organized in a chronological sequence in which you move from present to past, from past to present, or from present to the future. If your report will be written to present solutions to problems, a problem-to-solution order may be effective. If you have two or more recommendations or solutions, you may want to move from the least important to the most important—or vice versa.

If you know your readers will be receptive to your ideas, you may want to use a deductive order and state your conclusions or recommendations at

Pattern	Description	Sample Use
Deductive order	The writer presents a conclusion and then gives explanations and details.	Useful if reader is receptive to information
Inductive order	The writer presents the explanations and supporting data and then presents conclusions.	Useful if reader is resistant to information
Chronological order	The writer arranges events according to the time at which they occurred.	Used for minutes of meetings, police reports, and so on
Step-by-step order	The writer organizes instructions, processes, or procedures according to the order in which they should be done.	Used for reports on policies, procedures
Order of decreasing importance	The writer begins with the most important points and then moves to less important ones. Useful in reports that analyze two or more options.	Useful for a busy reader
Order of increasing importance	The writer builds toward the most important points. Also called the *crescendo* approach. Useful when analyzing two or more options.	Useful for persuading a reader
Problem/solution order	The writer presents problems and then offers one or more solutions.	Useful for proposals, recommendations
Comparison/ contrast	Shows similarities and differences between two or more ideas or entities	Useful for persuasive and analytical reports
Logical categories	Breaks subject areas down into distinct components	Useful for many types of analysis

FIGURE 14–3

Common structural patterns for reports

the beginning; for a more resistant audience, an inductive order may be more persuasive.

For his marketing report, Ben Corino realized that he would be discussing both the present situation of Jackson Inspection Services and ways it could alter its situation in the future, so at least part of his report would be chronological. He also knew that his busy readers would appreciate a deductive order: he would state his major findings in the opening section and then move to supporting details. For much of the report, he would also be examining various facets of the client company such as its advertising and pricing, so he would have to use logical categories in his report as well.

Working at his computer, he made a copy of his earlier brainstorming efforts and began molding them into a rough outline (Figure 14–4).

Gathering Data

Gathering data is a vital component of most reports. When you have figured out who your audience is, you can figure out what your readers need to know. From there, you can begin gathering relevant materials and data. Inevitably, you will gather more information than you need. While planning and drafting your report, you will have to dispense with the material that is less directly related to your project or is of less interest to your reader.

A computer can be a useful tool at this stage of the writing process. Not only can you use it to access information, but you can also use it to keep your own "notes" as you do your research.

Index cards are useful tools for report research.

Many people, however, prefer using an index card system to keep track of their research. If you gather information on cards, make sure you list pertinent bibliographic information. You will have to document the sources of your information, remember, when you write the report.

Marketing Report
Jackson Inspection Services

—General recommendations   overall deductive order
—Overview of company
  History
  Present situation   } from past to present
—Current marketing strategy
  Description of service
  Pricing
  Promotion
  Distribution   } Logical categories
—Weaknesses of company
  Competition?
  Legal problems?
  Finances?
  Management?   } Logical categories
—Strengths of company
  Product
  Management?
  Client base?   } Logical categories
—Recommended strategies
  Immediate strategies
  Future strategies   } From present to future

FIGURE 14-4
Rough outline

If you have already set up a rough outline for yourself, you can begin marking the index cards and arranging them according to the section of the report to which they refer. Figure 14-5 illustrates sample index cards for references Ben Corino found useful.

Research is commonly divided into two types, *primary* and *secondary*. Your particular project will determine which type you rely on most heavily and which type you tackle first.

Researching and Evaluating Secondary Sources

Secondary research involves gathering information that has already been put together for a use other than your own project. For some projects, you will want to begin with secondary sources; after all, there is no point in redoing the work someone else has done for you. Then, when you know what has already been done, you can assess how much you need to do on your own.

Kenneth P. Uhl and Gregory D. Upah. "The Marketing of Services: How and Why Is It Different?" in *Marketing Management: A Comprehensive Reader,* eds. Jagdish N. Sheth and Dennis E. Garrett. Cincinnati: South-Western Publishing Co., 1986, pp. 999–1026.

Provides excellent bibliography on marketing of services. Discusses ways to market an "intangible" product [like home inspections]. "Four principal production capabilities are available to service organizations to attract customers. They are the facilities and equipment, people, methods, and overall organization used to provide services" (p. 1008). Useful for introduction to report.

Thomas V. Bonoma. "Making Your Marketing Strategy Work," *Harvard Business Review,* March–April 1984, pp. 68–76.

Good overview of the characteristics of companies with effective marketing strategies. Emphasizes that *creativity* and *commitment* to the customer or client can increase market share. Bonoma's research findings may be useful for documenting suggestions I make in the recommendations section of report.

FIGURE 14-5

Sample index cards

Secondary sources can
include letters, memos,
and reports.

Often your research-gathering will begin with internal secondary sources such as company reports, invoices, correspondence, and sales statistics. Then your research may take you to atlases, almanacs, dictionaries, periodicals, newspapers, trade publications, government publications, computerized information systems, and a host of other external resources. (Figure 14-6 lists some common secondary reference sources.)

When gathering material from secondary sources, remember that data vary in terms of validity. You are depending on other people for your information, so you need to examine the material carefully before including it in your report. In assessing your secondary data, ask yourself these questions.

Who Collected the Data? The data may have been collected by an individual or organization that was biased, more interested in proving a point than in gathering or presenting accurate data. Look carefully, for example, at the reputation of an organization that has sponsored a study before accepting the results as valid.

Why Were the Data Collected Initially? The purpose of the original study may have been different from yours, and so the material may not be as appropriate to your needs as it appears.

How Were the Data Gathered? Research methods vary widely, and problems with methodology discredit many studies. Before accepting the results of a study, check the methods that were used to obtain the data.

Government Publications
Directory of Government Document Collections and Librarians
Government Reference Books
Statistical Abstracts of the United States

Periodicals and Books
American Book Publishing Record
Business and Economics Books and Serials in Print
Business Periodicals Index
Encyclopedia of Associations
Reader's Guide to Periodical Literature
Standard and Poor's Industry Surveys
Statistical Abstract of the United States
Ulrich's International Periodicals Directory

Commercial Data
A.C. Nielsen Company
Market Research Corporation of America
Moody's Manuals

FIGURE 14-6
Sampling of secondary sources

One study, for example, showed that students who took speed reading courses performed significantly better in college than those who did not take speed reading. When the methodology was examined, however, it was found that students from the two groups had not been chosen randomly, as the researchers had claimed. The results of the study, thus, were discredited.

What Groups Were Studied? Data may have been collected for one geographical area, such as a county or state. For example, the results of a study on the age group that drinks the most diet soft drinks per year may seem to fit your needs exactly; however, on closer examination, you see that the study pertains only to people in Texas. You cannot assume that the study is valid nationwide.

When Were the Data Collected? Conditions change rapidly, and studies can quickly become outdated. Before using the data, find out when the study was conducted. Then consider how much population changes or other fluctuations could affect the validity of the study over time.

Ben Corino began his research for Jackson Inspection Services by studying home-buying and demographic trends in the area as well as the competitive and legal variables affecting the company. He read a series of articles in *Real Estate Today* magazine, reviewed articles on the marketing of services, found a list of all the home inspection services in the United States, and read the text of a recent court decision affecting home inspections.

Obtaining Primary Data

Primary research, which usually takes the form of observation, experimentation, or personal interviews and surveys, involves gathering data specifically for your project. As Figure 14-7 indicates, primary research is often more accurate than secondary research, but it can be expensive and time-consuming. For example, the data collected by the U.S. Census Bureau may not be keyed to your exact needs, but you probably do not have the resources or the time to conduct interviews on a national scale. Therefore, you rely on the data already provided.

Moreover, since doing primary research may require training in areas such as statistics and questionnaire development, you may find that using secondary data is more practical for your purposes.

On the other hand, for many types of reports, businesspeople rely almost solely on primary research: they speak with the people involved in a project, inspect earlier reports and correspondence, review computer data, and make personal observations.

For his marketing report, Ben Corino used observation as part of his primary research. Observational research entails watching people or situations. Ben observed the home inspectors as they worked and watched how the office staff interacted with present and potential clients.

Observational research entails watching people or situations.

	Strengths	*Weaknesses*
Primary	Relevant to project	Expensive
	Accurate	Time-consuming
	Trustworthy	Possibly difficult to obtain
	Likely to be current	
Secondary	Inexpensive	Possibly irrelevant
	Convenient	Possibly inaccurate
	Usually simple to obtain	

FIGURE 14-7 _____

Primary versus secondary research

Experimentation allows
a researcher to judge
cause and effect.

The second type of primary research, experimentation, was not useful for Ben's purposes. Experimentation allows a researcher to judge cause and effect. By altering the price of a product in one area and not in another, for instance, a researcher may be able to infer whether a higher or lower price will affect sales of the product.

Ben did use the third type of primary research, personal interviews and surveys. Interviews may be informal conversations or formal, structured question-and-answer sessions. Surveys may be done in person, by telephone, or through the mail. (Figure 14-8 outlines some strengths and weaknesses of each method.) They, too, may be formal or informal, structured or unstructured.

Surveys are usually
done in person, by tele-
phone, or through the
mail.

Ben collected much of the information for his report through informal, personal interviews with company management and staff. He also gained information from past and present clients of Jackson Inspection Services through a mail survey (Figure 14-9).

In general, questionnaires should be short, simple, easy to read, relevant to your purpose, and well organized. To achieve these goals, you need to understand exactly what information you are looking for and what form you want it in. Closed-ended questions, which ask for a response from a set of alternatives, allow you to tabulate data easily. However, you may miss interesting pieces of information that would appear as answers to open-ended questions.

Make sure question-
naires are clear and easy
to fill out.

Open-Ended Question

What are your short-term goals?

_____

Closed-Ended Question

How old are you?

_____ 20 or under

_____ 21–40

_____ 41–60

_____ 61 or over

In developing your questionnaire, remember that you have to motivate your respondents. Give them sufficient space on the page to answer your questions and move from easy to more difficult questions. Test your questionnaire before sending it out: you may be surprised to find your questions are ambiguous, confusing, or even offensive. Figure 14-10 illustrates some pitfalls common to questionnaires.

	Mail	Telephone	Personal
Time	Slow	Fast	Medium
Cost	Low	Low	High
Response rate	Low	High	High
Complexity of data	Medium	Low	High
Flexibility	Low	Medium	High

FIGURE 14-8
Survey methods

Jackson Inspection Services
Evaluation Form

1. How would you rate our service overall?
   _____ Excellent _____ Good _____ Average _____ Poor

2. How would you rate the following?

	Excellent	Good	Average	Poor
Thoroughness of our report	_____	_____	_____	_____
Speed of process from inspection through final report	_____	_____	_____	_____
Efficiency of our inspectors	_____	_____	_____	_____
Cooperation/efficiency of office staff	_____	_____	_____	_____
Value of service for price paid	_____	_____	_____	_____

3. If you marked any item in #2 as Average or Poor, please explain why you were not perfectly pleased.

   _____

4. If any aspects of our service were outstanding, please let us know what they were.

   _____

5. How did you learn about our service?
   _____ Real estate agent
   _____ Friend, relative, or colleague
   _____ Newspaper advertisement
   _____ Telephone directory
   _____ Brochure
   _____ Other _____

FIGURE 14-9
Sample questionnaire

Pitfall	Sample Question	Problem
Combination question	Have you eaten in Chinese and Japanese restaurants? ____ YES ____ NO	What do you answer if you have eaten in one but not the other?
Leading question	Why do you prefer driving an American-made automobile to driving an import?	You are led to answer positively about American-made cars.
Unclear question	Do you frequently travel on business?	What is meant by *frequently?*
Overlapping answers	What is your income? ____ Under $20,000 ____ $20,000–$30,000 ____ $30,000 and over	What do you answer if your income is $30,000?
Offensive question	When was the last time you drove a car while under the influence of alcohol or drugs?	Question assumes respondent has driven under the influence—and more than once.

FIGURE 14-10 _____

Questionnaire pitfalls

Test Your Skills

Which Survey Method Would You Use?

Choose the answer that best fits the type of survey you would use.

1. You want to get immediate feedback from 100 possible buyers about a new product you are testing. You
   a. put samples of the product and questionnaires in the mail
   b. send people samples and telephone them later for their responses
   c. ask people in a shopping mall to try the product right there and discuss it

2. You are doing a long-term study on people's eating habits and health. You want to track 200 people statewide over a ten-year period. You
   a. mail them a three-page questionnaire every six months and ask them to fill it out and return it
   b. telephone them every six months and speak to them for about thirty minutes
   c. visit their homes and speak to them personally

Discussion

Sampling. To choose respondents for a survey, researchers use a process called *sampling*. Often you will not be able to survey every person in a given population. With probability sampling techniques, however, you can survey a part of the population that is representative of the whole: every individual in the sample has a known probability of being selected. Nonprobability sampling, on the other hand, is based somewhat on your judgment as researcher: the probability of each person being included in the sample is unknown. Figure 14-11 outlines several probability and nonprobability sampling methods.

Sampling enables researchers to survey part of a population.

For his marketing report, Ben Corino sent questionnaires to the total population of Jackson Inspection Services' present and former clients. He used convenience sampling to interview by telephone fifty real estate agents about home inspection services. And he used his judgment to determine which company managers and employees would provide the most useful information about the company in personal interviews.

Interpreting Data. When you have collected your information, you still face the task of analyzing and interpreting the data. You will face problems, of course, if your questionnaire was poorly constructed or your sample too small, unrepresentative, or biased.

And, even if your data collection techniques were impeccable, you still must work on being unbiased and logical in your analyses. Too often, researchers ruin their own work by allowing their biases to affect their interpretation of results or by failing to consider other variables.

Bias can hurt even the most careful research.

The Coca-Cola Company fell into this latter trap when researching consumer response to its recipe for New Coke. The majority of people surveyed clearly preferred the taste of New Coke; however, the company did not consider the loyalty consumers would have to the old formula.

Figure 14-12 outlines steps in the report research process.

	Probability Sampling
Random	Random sampling gives each member of a population a known and equal chance of being chosen.
Stratified	Researchers divide the population into mutually exclusive groups and then draw random samples from each group.
Area	Researchers divide the population into mutually exclusive geographic areas and then draw a sample from each group.
	Nonprobability Sampling
Convenience	Researchers interview the people most easily accessible.
Quota	Researchers predetermine mutually exclusive categories from which to select interviewees. Then researchers interview a prescribed number of people from each group.
Judgment	Researchers use their judgment to determine good prospects for interviewing.

FIGURE 14-11
Examples of sampling methods

1. Outline research objectives. *What do I need to know? What do my readers need to know?*

2. Determine sources of information. *What type of data is available? What type of research will be most feasible and useful?*

3. Research and evaluate secondary sources. *What internal documents, books, articles, and other publications will give me the information I need? Are these data valid for my purposes?*

4. Do necessary primary research. *What types of observation, experimentation, or interviews and surveys will give me the data I need?*

5. Develop data collection instruments. *What type of questions will be most useful? What information do I actually want? How am I going to evaluate responses? How can I motivate people to answer questions?*

6. Determine sampling procedure. *What methods can I use to survey a representative group?*

7. Collect data. *How can I get a maximum number of valid responses in a timely and cost-effective fashion?*

8. Process data. *How can I effectively organize research results?*

9. Interpret research results. *How can I make sure my results are valid and unbiased?*

FIGURE 14-12
Steps in the report research process

Making a Plan

A good plan is essential to a good report. Even in the earliest stages of the report-writing process, begin putting a rough outline together. Browsing through reports of a similar nature will help you see the general type of plan with which you will be working. Then amend a rough outline as you do your research.

Some people prefer to work with formal outlines. A formal outline is particularly useful when a group of people is working together on a report—a very common situation. Clear delineation of each section enables people to work independently on their allotted areas.

A formal outline is particularly useful when people work together on a report.

If you are working alone on a lengthy report, you will probably want to begin with an informal outline that becomes more detailed as you progress. You can create a formal outline during the final revision stages to check the overall logic and organization; this outline can then be used as a basis for a table of contents when you have completed the body of the report.

Whether you use an informal or a formal outline, it should be *written*. You need to see the overall design as it emerges. Writing pages and pages and *then* trying to make a plan will cost you unnecessary time and frustration. However, avoid letting your outline lock you into an approach that does not work. You may well find as you write that your outline simply does not allow you to present material logically and effectively: then feel free to revise your plan.

An outline should be flexible.

A formal outline is usually set up with either a phrase or a sentence format (Figures 14-13 and 14-14). Use a parallel construction for whichever approach you use. The headings and subheadings should indicate the order in which your material will appear and what information will be used to support major ideas.

Sections of formal reports are identified by numbers and letters that delineate the relative importance and relationship of the sections to each other.

- Roman numerals indicate major headings.
- Capital letters indicate secondary headings.
- Arabic numerals indicate general supporting details.
- Lower-case letters indicate specific supporting details.

To develop the formal outline for his marketing report (Figure 14-15), Ben Corino expanded the rough outline he had made earlier (see Figure 14-4). He made one major organizational change, moving the section on the weaknesses of the company so it followed, rather than preceded, a section on the company's strengths. With this change, he could make a smooth transition from the problem areas to the changes he was recommending in Part V.

Completing the Report-Writing Process

Drafting

When you have your research and outline done, you can begin writing. Move quickly through the first draft and leave lots of white space on each page for

Title: Relocation Site for French's Hardware Store

Introduction: Our research shows that the suburban location, 1990 Orchard Street, Harbor Hills, is the better relocation site for French's Hardware Store.

I. Criteria for relocation site
  A. Easy access and parking
  B. Highly visible
  C. No nearby direct competitors
  D. Adequate size
  E. Reasonable rent and long-term lease option

II. Freeway location
  A. Assets
    1. Easy access and parking
      a. Near freeway exit
      b. Lot for fifty cars
    2. Good visibility from freeway
    3. Nearest hardware store 3 miles away
    4. Adequate size
  B. Possible Problems
    1. No foot traffic
    2. High rent; no long-term lease option

III. Suburban location
  A. Assets
    1. Easy access and parking
      a. Corner location
      b. Lot for forty-five cars
    2. Good visibility from major road
    3. Walk-in and drive-in trade
    4. Adequate size
    5. Five-year lease available
  B. Possible Problems
    1. Competing hardware store 1.5 miles away
    2. Rent higher than desired

IV. Conclusion: Suburban location better choice
  A. Higher rent compensated by higher sales volume
  B. Competition not a problem in high-growth area

FIGURE 14-13

Sample report outline—phrase format

Title: Report on Internal Theft Investigation for Carter Stores

Introduction: Dawson Corporation has completed the investigation authorized on December 1, 19xx. A high percentage of Carter Stores' losses is due to employee theft. The company can guard against employee theft by following three procedures.

I. Internal security in a store must address many areas of concern.
   A. Merchandise may leave through the front door.
   B. Cash receipts may be reported inaccurately.
   C. Inventory may disappear from the stockrooms.

II. We used generally accepted methods to study Carter Stores' problem.
   A. We observed and recorded arrival and departure times of employees.
   B. We noted which employees spend their unstructured time together during the day.
   C. We introduced one of our investigators into the workforce to monitor employee conversations.
   D. We audited inventory reports and cash receipts.

III. Carter Stores is losing cash and inventory in a variety of ways.
   A. Employees are undercharging their friends.
      1. Cite examples
      2. Estimate losses
   B. Employees are ringing up sales for less than the amount of cash received.
      1. Cite examples
      2. Estimate losses
   C. Employees are condoning shoplifting by customers.
      1. Cite examples
      2. Estimate losses
   D. Employees are under-reporting inventory received into stock areas.
      1. Cite examples
      2. Estimate losses

IV. The following procedures will help control losses.
   A. Institute a computerized inventory system that will enable merchandise to be priced with a bar coder.
      1. Estimate costs
      2. Estimate savings
   B. Attach tags to merchandise that will set off an alarm at exits if they are not removed.
      1. Estimate costs
      2. Estimate savings
   C. Employ two people to process incoming shipments and act as a check on each other.
      1. Estimate costs
      2. Estimate savings

Conclusion: These three procedures will significantly reduce Carter Stores' losses and reduce internal theft as well as shoplifting.

Figure 14–14 _____

Sample report outline—sentence format

Title: Marketing Report for Jackson Inspection Services

I. Introduction, major recommendations

II. Company background
   A. History
   B. Management structure
   C. Goals

II. Present marketing strategy
   A. Description of service
   B. Pricing
   C. Promotional materials
   D. Geographic area covered

III. Company assets
   A. Management
   B. Growing population
   C. Legislative changes

IV. Company weaknesses
   A. Slow delivery of service
      1. Comments from customer questionnaires
      2. Comments from telephone interviews with agents
   B. Priced above competition
   C. Fragmented promotion

V. Proposed marketing strategy
   A. Streamlined service delivery
   B. Competitive pricing
   C. Strong, unified promotional program

FIGURE 14-15 _____
Ben Corino's outline

making notes and corrections. As you draft, identify areas where you will want to include graphic supports such as charts.

Revising

Your revisions should follow the principles outlined in earlier sections on business writing. Although reports going to upper management or to people outside your company require a more formal style than a standard memo or business letter, avoid writing in stilted, awkward prose. Never forget that you are writing *for* a reader: dull, long, or choppy sentences, awkward constructions, passives, and tedious repetitions are as unpalatable in a report as they are in other business documents.

In many reports, information can be effectively relayed in charts, graphs, and other visual media. Chapter 17 provides more information on report graphics.

See Figure 14-16 for some ways to revise common problems in reports.

Charts and graphs can often relay information effectively.

Problem	Solution
Wording is overly difficult	Define technical terms
	Use concise, clear sentences
Material is hard to understand	Keep sentences and paragraphs short
	Limit the amount of data in each section
	Use graphics to illustrate data
	Use headings and subheadings to ease readability
Organization is poor	Use an organizational pattern your reader can identify
	Outline your draft to check for logic and parallel constructions
	Put supporting material in appendices rather than in the report body
Documentation is poor	Identify both opinions and facts
	List sources for primary and secondary data
Report appears biased	Keep your wording objective
	Show both sides of issues

FIGURE 14–16

Handling common problems in reports

Proofreading

Even if you have a typist prepare the final version of a report, make sure you proofread it yourself. Factual and typographical errors can ruin the credibility of even the most carefully prepared document.

Summary

Reports are objective, orderly business documents that may move horizontally or laterally in an organization. A report may be written as a memo, a letter, or a formal report. Because reports organize information and often help in decision making, the researching and planning steps of the writing process are particularly important to report writing. Both the types of data gathered and the way they are presented should be determined by your reader's needs as well as by the type of report you are writing.

Report Checklist

- Write reports when you need to convey information, make recommendations, evaluate personnel, propose projects, request support or funding for a project, analyze issues, or help in decision making.

Report Formats

- Use a letter format for a report primarily if

  _____ you are sending it to someone outside your organization and

  _____ the document is less than about eight pages long

- Use a memo format for a report primarily if

  _____ you are sending it to someone inside your organization

  _____ the reader is not many steps above you in the organization

  _____ the document is less than about eight pages long.

- Use a formal report format if

  _____ the document is over eight pages long or

  _____ the document is intended for readers more than a few steps higher than you in the organization

Report Goals

- As you define your goals for a report, remember that the final draft should be

  _____ objective

  _____ logical

  _____ well documented

  _____ orderly

Research

- Use secondary sources for your data if

  _____ they will provide adequate documentation for your report

_____ the expense and time spent gathering primary data offset the use-fulness of these data

_____ the secondary data are accurate and relevant to your project

- Use primary sources for your data if

  _____ observation, experimentation, or surveys will bring you the relevant material you need

  _____ you have the time and money to implement primary research

  _____ the person doing the research has the required expertise to gather valid and reliable data

- If you choose to do a survey, you may conduct it

  _____ by mail

  _____ by telephone

  _____ in person

- In developing questionnaires, keep them

  _____ as short and simple as possible

  _____ relevant to your purpose

  _____ clear, unambiguous, and inoffensive

- If you cannot survey an entire population, you may use a sampling procedure in which you survey a representative portion of the population or use your judgment to choose interviewees.

Organization

- As you plan the report, use an informal or formal written outline that develops as the project goes on.

- Develop a formal report outline if

  _____ you are working with a group and need to designate sections for each writer

  _____ you find that you can organize your data more easily with a formal plan

_____ you are developing a final draft and want to use the outline as a basis for the table of contents

- Choose an organizational pattern appropriate to the type of report you are writing and to the needs and attitudes of your readers; you may want to combine two or more structural patterns.

- Choose a deductive organizational pattern if

  _____ you are writing an informational report

  _____ your reader will be receptive to the material

- Choose an inductive organizational pattern if

  _____ you are writing an informational or persuasive report

  _____ your reader may be resistant to the material

- Choose chronological order to report events that occurred in a certain order.

- Choose step-by-step order for reports detailing procedures.

- Choose an order of decreasing importance if you wish to convey important material as quickly as possible.

- Choose an order of increasing importance if you wish to persuade resistant readers or keep readers interested throughout the report.

- Choose a problem/solution order for proposals and analytical reports.

Terms to Remember

Deductive organization: organizational pattern in which the conclusions precede the explanatory data

Inductive organization: organizational pattern in which the supporting data precede the conclusions

Nonprobability sampling: method of choosing interviewees in which the probability of a person being included in the sample is unknown

Primary data: research data collected specifically for the project at hand. Most primary data are drawn from surveys, observation, and experimentation.

Probability sampling: sampling procedure in which each individual has a known probability of being selected

Secondary data: research data that have already been put together for a use other than the project at hand

Summary Discussion: Andrea Nelson's Report from Case in Point, p. 325

Andrea Nelson's report is going to be more complex and more formal than most letters or memos. She will be writing for both the managers of The Roof Company and her own boss. Also, the report will remain on file with both the client company and her own. She will have to incorporate background about the client company and carefully document her findings and the bases for her recommendations.

Andrea may well use a letter format for her report if she can keep the report under eight or nine pages. She should, however, use headings, subheadings, and footnotes to aid readability and document her information.

In this report, Andrea should be particularly careful in her word choice: she must avoid technical jargon and define accounting terms without condescending to her readers. She must also be careful to avoid obvious criticism of the client company: although the managers have requested her help, she should make her analyses and recommendations tactfully.

Questions for Review and Discussion

1. What are the strengths and weaknesses of secondary research?
2. You have decided to interview the first ten people who enter your store in the morning. What sampling method are you using?
3. You want some information on how customers are responding to your company's new skin care products. You decide to ask a hundred people two questions each, and you want the answers quickly. What survey method would you choose? Why?
4. You are conducting a study of thirty-five people's eating habits that requires asking them over fifty questions, some of them fairly complicated. What survey method would you use? Why?
5. Why is secondary research often done before primary research?
6. You are writing a report telling upper management about the successful changes that have taken place in your department. What organizational method would you use for the report. Why?
7. What are the strengths and weaknesses of closed-ended survey questions?

Exercises

1. Explain why each of the following questions is or is not appropriate for a questionnaire. Revise any questions that you find inappropriate.
   a. Do you enjoy discussion classes more than lectures?
   b. Wouldn't you rather have your tax money spent on human services than on military spending?
   c. Have you ever visited France, Germany, and Italy?
   d. Rate your department supervisor on his time management skills: 1. Excellent 2. Very good 3. Good 4. Poor
   e. How old are you?_____years
2. Choose an article from a publication such as *Newsweek* or *Time*. Can you tell what types of

research the writer used to get information? What sources did the writer use? How does the type of source affect the credibility of the article?

3. You have been asked to write a report on the career goals of your classmates in one class and draw some conclusions from your findings. Using the steps of the writing process as a guide, outline the steps you would take to prepare the report. Include specific information on the research methods you would use.

4. Assume you have decided to use a questionnaire for the report described in Question 3. Develop a questionnaire with at least four questions.

5. Create an outline for the report that you discussed in Exercise 3.

6. You have been asked to report on career possibilities for students graduating in your major. Go to the library and locate at least five recent articles or books that provide information you could use in the report.

7. To write the report described in Exercise 6, prepare six to seven interview questions for each of two interviews. You may decide, for example, to interview someone at the career counseling office, a professional in the field, or a student.

8. What source in the library could provide you with the following information?

    a. The number of unemployed people in the United States
    b. The standard interest rates charged by most banks
    c. The worth of the Japanese yen compared to the dollar in 1988
    d. Data on the newest word processing software
    e. The background of the Iran/Iraq war

9. Develop a research report on a topic of your choice. This project will involve several phases.

    a. Jot down ideas and isolate a few possible ideas.
    b. Write a brief summary of your initial ideas that includes
       —the topic and a possible title
       —the reasons you are writing the report
       —the types of readers you will be writing for
       —the types of research you will need to do
       —a rough outline
    c. After completing your research, write a summary of the methodology you used and the results you obtained. Describe any problems or limitations to your research. Then create a more detailed formal outline.
    d. Draft the report. For more information on appropriate formats for different types of reports, see Chapters 15 and 16. If you decide to include graphics in the report, see Chapter 17.

Word Processing Exercises: Printing Techniques

I. You have been using a printer ever since you began working with word processing, but you may not have learned all of your printer's capabilities. By doing these exercises, you will learn to

- suspend a print job
- print selected pages
- pause for paper changes

Suspending a print job can save you time. You may be printing out a document when you see that you have made an error. Rather than waiting for the whole document to be printed, you can stop the print job midway. Then you can choose to continue printing or to stop the print job altogether.

You will often want only some pages of a document printed. You should learn how to command the printer to print only the pages you select. And if you want to use sheets of paper rather than a continuous roll of paper, you must tell the printer to pause as you insert each sheet.

1. Check your manual for the procedures for sus-

pending a print job. Choose to print a file such as JONES that has two or more pages. Partway through page 1, command the printer to stop.

2. The computer may now ask you whether you wish to stop printing altogether or to resume. Enter the command to continue the job.

3. Stop the printing again in the middle of page 2. This time, stop the print job altogether.

4. Print the file again, but this time command the computer to begin with page 2 rather than page 1. If you are asked where you want the computer to *stop* printing, command it to stop at the end of page 2.

5. Now try printing the file with individual sheets of paper. (You will find this technique useful when you write formal business letters and perhaps reports as well.) You will have to command the computer to pause at the end of each page for paper changes.

Invisible Notes

Many word processing programs have a command that enables you to make notes to yourself on the screen as you write. These notes do not appear on the hard copy. As you write early drafts, these "invisible notes" are useful: you can make comments to yourself as you write, jotting down questions and ideas without stopping the writing process.

You might, for example, simply mark questionable word choices with a symbol such as * or ??— or write yourself a note such as "Fix this later!"

1. Find out if the word processing program you are using has the capacity to make notes to yourself on the screen. (If it does not have this capacity, you will have to skip this exercise!)

2. Enter the file OPT2 that you created for an earlier exercise. Using the invisible note command, put ** to mark any poor word choices or typos in the text.

3. PRINT the file to make sure your invisible notes do not appear on the page.

4. Use the SEARCH command to find each ** in your text. Make appropriate changes for every problem area that you marked.

5. DELETE the invisible notes.

6. PRINT the file. Check the text to make sure it is correct and coherent.

Short Reports and Proposals

- **Writing effective short reports**
- **Defining the purpose of a report**
- **Conveying information in reports**
- **Writing progress reports**
- **Evaluating employees**
- **Combining persuasive and informational elements**
- **Writing recommendation reports**
- **Developing proposals**

Objectives

To learn the common types of short reports

To draft and revise effective informa-

tional and persuasive reports

To develop and organize persuasive proposals

15

Susan Schultz's Recommendation Report

Susan Schultz is the assistant to the owner of a restaurant, The Big Hat Cafe. The owner, Larry DeRobbia, has asked Susan to write a recommendation report on a study of employee turnover that they have discussed. When she finished the memorandum report, Susan was dissatisfied with it.

```
           MEMORANDUM REPORT
TO:        Larry DeRobbia
FROM:      Susan Schultz
SUBJECT:   Employee Turnover Study
DATE:      April 12, 19xx
```

A certain amount of turnover is standard in any industry. However, the sudden turnover rate The Big Hat Cafe is experiencing is alarming. After our discussion on March 15, 19xx, I returned to the office to outline plans necessary to evaluate the restaurant's situation.

The best place to initiate such a study is with employees. Management, nonmanagement, and former employees were interviewed in an attempt to discover the basis for the turnover problem. It is not uncommon when one interviews several people for a wide range of answers to result. Such was the case here. When asked about the strengths and weaknesses of the restaurant, a number of managers mentioned the restaurant's future growth prospects as a strength and its disorganization as a weakness. Nonmanagement employees were apt to say that wages were a strength but ineffective management was a weakness. Former employees often stated that

stable employment was a strength but unrealistic demands were a weakness.

Observation provides an objective opinion and allows one to confirm or reevaluate interview results. During observations on five separate occasions, one significant factor was revealed: disorganization. During one lunch hour, three customers received the wrong orders, and two returned steaks that were undercooked. The staff was too overworked and disorganized to handle a large crowd of customers.

The Big Hat Cafe's rapid success has created unrealistic demands on managers and nonmanagers. The pressures due to an overworked and disorganized staff build up until employees quit. To resolve the problem, I recommend enlarging the workforce during peak hours, establishing more reasonable work schedules, setting up better communication between kitchen and diningroom staff, and providing more effective training. I hope my recommendations will help the employee turnover problem.

Points to Consider

- What information is missing from Susan's short report?
- Should she delete anything from the report?
- What could she do to make the report more persuasive?
- What could she do to make the report more readable?

Writing Effective Short Reports

Most short reports move upward in an organization. Through short reports, subordinates inform their superiors of progress and problems, make recommendations, evaluate employees and programs, record decisions and agreements, and, in general, keep management up-to-date on the daily activities of the organization.

Some short reports, however, move laterally and downward. The head of the marketing department might send an employee evaluation report to the head of the personnel department; a division manager might send an informational report to each department head in the division.

Most short reports convey information in a compact format.

A short report is meant to convey information in an efficient, compact format. Like any report, it should be accurate, complete, well organized, unbiased, and logical as well as geared to the needs of the reader.

While a short report may not have as many graphic aids as a formal report, it will often benefit from lists, headings, charts, and white space to heighten readability and emphasize major points. Figure 15-1 lists some hints for writing effective short reports.

Defining the Purpose of a Report

- Your supervisor asks you to report every Monday on the work you did during the previous week.
- You are in charge of taking notes during meetings and writing up what took place.
- You must summarize the progress you are making on a project.
- You want to justify the expense of buying new office equipment.
- You have researched a problem and wish to make recommendations for solving it.
- You want to propose that management authorize you to complete a project you have in mind.

All the preceding situations could require you to write a short report. The first three situations require primarily informative reports, while the last three require more persuasive elements.

Most business writing, as we have seen, is persuasive in some way. However, some reports are principally intended to inform, while others are principally intended to persuade. Both general groups include a wide assortment

1. Use headings and subheadings to highlight and organize material effectively.

2. Use white space, short paragraphs, and adequate margins to make the report accessible to the reader.

3. Get to your major points quickly. Short reports should inform or persuade a reader with a minimum of delay.

4. Use graphs, charts, numbered or lettered lists, and other visual aids to simplify and clarify information.

5. Use active sentences and personal pronouns, but keep your writing as factual and objective as possible.

FIGURE 15-1
Hints for effective short reports

of report types, too many to discuss or even list in this chapter. However, while highlighting features common to most short reports, we will discuss some common types of primarily informational and primarily persuasive reports.

Common Informational Reports		Common Persuasive Reports
Accident reports	Itineraries	Justification reports
Agendas	Minutes of meetings	Proposals
Audits	Periodic reports	Recommendation reports
Employee evaluations	Progress reports	

Conveying Information in Reports

When you convey information in a report, your basic goals are to include all the information the readers will need and to organize it so that they can easily grasp the material. When you analyze the readers, carefully consider exactly what they already know, what they need to know, and how they will respond to the information. Then choose an organizational pattern that will most effectively convey the data they need.

Often a direct, deductive pattern will be most useful for an informational report: summarize the major point of the report and then supply supporting data. Minutes, agendas, itineraries, and progress reports will probably require a chronological structure as well; procedures may require step-by-step explanations.

Direct organizational patterns are common in informational reports.

THE WILDLIFE CENTER

76 Albert Park Lane P.O. Box 957 San Rafael, CA 94915
Administration (415) 454-6965 Animal Care (415) 454-6961

"Proposals should both persuade and inform the reader," says Marsha Mather-Thrift, Executive Director of The Wildlife Center in Marin County, California. Marsha is the administrator, public relations person, and fundraiser for the Center. *"In a small, nonprofit organization, everyone wears a lot of hats."* She writes many proposals to obtain grant money. *"Each foundation has a different format for applying, but in every case I must persuade the foundation that our organization is stable, strong, and well managed."*

The major function of The Wildlife Center is as a hospital for wildlife. Although the Center needs money to cover hospital costs such as food for animals, foundations often want to fund particular projects, especially those that educate children. "People think that animals are less important than humans. They would rather include a picture of a smiling child in their annual report, than one of a healed bear walking into the woods."

The first thing Marsha does when she is writing a proposal is to do research. She needs to target those foundations interested in the areas where she needs funding. She researches general guidelines of the foundation she is applying to, checking on what kinds of projects they are funding and how much money they are giving. Marsha gets a lot of her information from the foundation's annual report and from telephone discussions with foundation staff. She also checks with other directors to see which foundations are funding projects similar to hers. Her most recent proposal, sent to the California Coastal Conservancy, is for a trail project that is part of an effort to conserve the California coastline.

The initial contact with a foundation is through a two-page case statement. It begins with a short summary paragraph that tells what the proposal is for and how much money she is requesting. The case statement also gives, "a brief outline of the project, the history of the organization, its leadership and board of directors, how its financial affairs are conducted, a statement of need that explains why your organization is worthwhile (the need it fills that no other organization does), and its operations—its staffing and programs."

When it comes to writing the actual proposal, Marsha expands each section in the case statement, making sure, however, not to exceed ten pages. "Beyond that amount, you repeat yourself, and people will go to sleep." If the foundation asks specific questions, it's often useful to provide brief answers using the questions as headings.

Marsha's tips on the physical presentation of a proposal:

- List the contact person and his or her phone number at the top of the proposal.
- Use subheadings. "They are crucial as guideposts. People can flip through the proposal to find points they want to read."
- Use a space and a half between lines. "It's easier to read."
- Create a neat, professional appearance, but if you work for a small organization, don't go out of your way to use fancy binders. "The foundation will think you are wasting money."

The following sections on progress reports and employee evaluations provide suggestions that you may find useful for many types of informational reports.

Writing Progress Reports

Progress reports (Figure 15-2) help managers to see the details of a project as it unfolds. Because managers must often supervise a number of projects simultaneously, progress reports help them to evaluate whether each one is progressing effectively, note possible changes in costs, and forestall problems before they get out of hand.

Most progress reports include

1. the activities that took place during the time period being described
2. any problems that were encountered
3. an overall appraisal of work
4. a statement regarding the work to be described in the next progress report
5. a statement of key action needed to be done by the reader or a compelling reason for reader to continue supporting the project

Progress reports help managers supervise on-going projects.

Many companies use standardized report forms for the most common progress reports.

In the first report you write on a project, summarize the project's goals and scope; after that, begin with an overview of the activities covered in the report. If you know you will be writing a series of progress reports, set up a format you can use for each report. This format will make organizing the material easier for you and will help the reader assimilate the information you provide for each segment of the project. However, do not let a comfortable format lead you away from an honest evaluation of the project's progress.

Evaluating Employees

Most companies have a system for regularly evaluating employees, and most have developed a standard form appropriate to the company and various job categories in the organization. Generally, employee evaluations include subject areas such as the employee's reliability, knowledge of job, quality of work, attitude, and promotability.

Evaluations of performance are important documents for both employees and managers. These reports have a number of functions: they

1. help to identify employees who should be promoted, demoted, or transferred, and those who should receive warnings, awards, raises, or bonuses
2. provide incentives for employee performance

Sample Outline for Progress Report
- The opening of the first report contains an overview of the project.
- The opening of subsequent reports contains an introductory statement summarizing activities covered in the report.
- Central sections provide details on major activities and describe any problems encountered.
- Conclusions explain what will be done next.

TO: John Forster   DATE: February 29, 19xx
FROM: James McCloud
       Dorothy Hubbard
       Chuck Hanford

SUBJECT: Site Visit, San Antonio, Texas

The evaluation team visited the two San Antonio schools on January 13, 14, and 15. The following progress report summarizes particular circumstances pertaining to the site, difficulties with questionnaires and interviewing, status of quality control and coding integrity, and our general impressions.

I. PARTICULAR CIRCUMSTANCES PERTAINING TO THE SITE
The Control School had tested all children the week before the evaluation team arrived. In order to determine the uniformity across testing sites, the team interviewed all teachers on test administration practices.

A. We found that tests were administered exclusively at grade level: that is, children known to read below grade level were not given an easier test. We found that (contrary to our instructions) the Experimental School had followed the same procedure.

B. Children who were obviously frustrated by the test were *not* pulled out from the testing situation at the Control School as they were at the Experimental School.

C. One teacher at the Control School took the tests home with her overnight. All other teachers reported that the Reading Specialists had secured the tests overnight.

II. DIFFICULTIES WITH QUESTIONNAIRES AND INTERVIEWING
We encountered two problems with the questionnaires and the interviewing process.

A. At the Experimental School, almost all teachers answered that the teacher and the Reading Specialist had equivalent responsibilities in the classroom. However, the team's assessment is that the Reading Specialists have a primary role and the teachers reinforce their instruction.

B. At the Control School, volunteer parents play a major role in classroom instruction. As our questionnaires did not allow us to code for this information, we have included Attachment A to our analysis of questionnaire results.

III. STATUS OF QUALITY CONTROL AND CODING INTEGRITY
The project secretary at the San Antonio site, Ms.
Sherry Thompson, has proved to be a careful,
accurate coder. She has carefully tracked each test
and questionnaire. We encountered no problems with
quality control or coding.

IV. GENERAL IMPRESSIONS
Two conditions set the San Antonio site apart from
other sites in the study.
    A. There is noticeable competition between the
    Control and Experimental Schools which does not
    exist at the other sites.
    B. The staff of the two schools repeatedly
    complained about the evaluation team sent to the
    schools two years ago.
        The poor relations between the staff and the
    team may have affected earlier data collection
    efforts. Fortunately, the present team did not
    encounter a similar problem.

For your files, we have attached to this report the
following documents:
    1. The Control School principal's questionnaire
    2. A teacher questionnaire
    3. All the single-sheet questionnaires
    4. A list of all students tested out-of-level

On May 1, 19xx, we will begin our evaluation of the
Baton Rouge, Louisiana, site. If you have
suggestions on ways we can handle the problems
identified at that site two years ago (see attached
report), please let us know as soon as possible.

FIGURE 15-2 _____
Progress report in memo form

3. assess the extent to which employees take part in decision making within the organization.
4. identify areas that employees need to improve and areas in which they excel.
5. help to determine whether employees need counseling or other types of assistance.
6. help to provide criteria for developing training programs and other personnel development programs.
7. provide supporting data when disputes arise regarding issues such as raises and promotions.
8. serve to encourage supervisors to observe employees
9. help to insure that employees receive consistent types of ratings throughout the organization

Employee evaluations have personal, professional, and legal implications.

As the writer of an employee evaluation, be aware of both the personal impact of the report and its legal implications. Employee evaluations can increase employee morale and motivation, but they can also cause anger and frustration. Biased evaluations, furthermore, may lead to lawsuits. Since employee evaluations must meet standards for validity and reliability, you may want to obtain Equal Employment Opportunity (EEO) guidelines for employee selection and appraisal.

If you are going to be writing such reports, make sure that employees have clearly outlined job descriptions; then orient your report strictly to the job-related specifications. Keep your wording objective. Document your information whenever possible.

> Ms. Kelley received three letters of appreciation from clients in a two-month period. (See attached letters.)

> As the enclosed transcript indicates, Henry Gordon has maintained an A average at Cooper Community College while working full-time.

Be as specific as you can. Compare:

> Mr. Smith appears unmotivated.

> Mr. Smith was 30 minutes late for work on September 2, 5, and 12.

An indirect organizational pattern is often used for employee evaluations.

Employee evaluations are often organized on an inductive pattern: the evidence is presented and then recommendations are made. Evaluations contain the following types of information:

- Employee's job title
- Overall assessment of performance
- Specific details on projects completed
- Summaries of statements from peers or supervisors
- Comparisons with other employees
- Information on coursework or training employee has completed
- Recommendation based on foregoing information

Many companies require that employees be evaluated on a standard rating scale. Employees are measured from 1 to 10 or from Poor to Excellent on factors such as communication skills, attitude, reliability, quality of work, motivation, and overall performance. If you use these forms, make sure you can support and document the ratings you assign. Be as objective as possible as you rate each area.

Sample Outline for an Employee Evaluation Report
- Identify type of evaluation.
- State employee's name and job title as well as the time period covered in the evaluation.
- Provide details on employee's performance. Refer, if necessary, to attached documents that provide evidence for evaluative statements.
- Make recommendations.

See Figure 15–3 for an example of an employee evaluation.

Combining Persuasive and Informational Elements

As soon as you begin drawing conclusions and making recommendations, you move away from a purely informational document to one that is persuasive. If you state what an employee accomplished during a certain time period, you are simply conveying information. However, as soon as you conclude, based on the data just presented, that an employee should be retained or promoted, you are implicitly trying to *convince* your reader of your position.

Thus, although employee evaluations are primarily informational, they usually contain persuasive elements. Often an inductive organizational method increases the persuasive qualities: the writer presents the data first so that the reader will agree with recommendations made later on.

Evaluations contain informational and persuasive elements.

Writing Recommendation Reports

Recommendation reports are written when the writer wishes to recommend a course of action to the reader. Many recommendation reports include the following information:

- Reason for report
- Summary of recommendations
- Data supporting the recommendations
- Methodology for implementing the recommendations
- Costs and benefits of recommendations

NAME OF EMPLOYEE: Franklin Ames   DATE: 4/3/xx

DEPARTMENT: Accounting   JOB TITLE: Data
                                    Processing
                                    Clerk

NAME OF EVALUATOR: J. Carling

TYPE OF REVIEW

New Employee _____

Transfer Employee _____

Annual Review ___√___

PERFORMANCE

In the two years that Mr. Ames has worked for this company, he has proved himself a hard worker who is eager to learn and to take on more responsibility. He is well liked by his fellow employees, who nominated him "Most Congenial Co-worker" at a recent departmental dinner. He has helped to reorganize the computer filing system in the Accounting Department and has researched several new software programs that the department is planning to acquire.

Mr. Ames is a mature employee who has been late only once during this evaluation period; he consistently finishes projects on time and has been commended by the assistant manager of the department, Karen Wilkinson, as "one of the most productive employees in this department."

STRONG POINTS

Mr. Ames is a motivated employee who has proven himself knowledgeable in the data processing needs of the Accounting Department. Mature, responsible, and eager to advance in the organization, he hopes to move to a supervisory position when one becomes available.

AREAS TO IMPROVE

Although willing to learn, Mr. Ames has no supervisory experience at present and is still completing courses in business at Mountain Community College.

EVALUATOR'S SUMMARY AND RECOMMENDATIONS

When Mr. Ames has received his A.S. degree in June, he should be considered for a position that would provide him with broader experience and help him acquire supervisory skills.

FIGURE 15-3 _____

Sample employee evaluation

Before deciding on your approach, analyze your readers' needs and probable responses to your recommendations. If your readers are going to benefit from getting to key information right away or if they are going to view your recommendations favorably, a direct or deductive approach may work best. However, if you feel you are going to have to prove your points to your readers, an indirect or inductive approach may be more successful.

Figure 15-4, which illustrates the first page of a recommendation report in letter format, opens with a *buffer*, positive information that assures the reader of his organization's overall success. The writer then tactfully introduces her suggestions by saying they are "inexpensive" and will increase

Audience analysis can help you decide how to organize a recommendation report.

NORTHWOOD ATHLETIC CLUB
23 Rim Road
Northwood, WA 98432

November 3, 19xx

Mr. Otto G. Johnson
Owner, Northwood Athletic Club
2349 Thornapple Road
Ferndale, WA 98321

Dear Mr. Johnson:

This report presents recommendations for Northwood Athletic Club after one year of operation. The club is doing exceptionally well despite intense competition from neighboring clubs. Our promotional campaign has successfully brought membership to our maximum capacity of 1,000 members.

Although most of our members are delighted with our facilities and services, we could improve their satisfaction with a few inexpensive changes. Surveys and observations have led to the following recommendations:

1. Add activities between 7 and 10 a.m. for nonworking women
2. Increase communication between club management and members through monthly meetings
3. Hire a cleaning service to work every night

BACKGROUND
On September 1, 19xx, I mailed a questionnaire to all 1,000 members (see Attachment A) with their monthly bill. By October 15, I had received 67 percent of the completed questionnaires and began coding the responses. During that same six-week period, I also spoke informally with employees and recorded the number of people using the facilities during different periods of each day.

FIGURE 15-4
Excerpt from recommendation report in letter format

customer satisfaction. Her recommendations are documented by surveys and observation (not included here). She avoids simply stating her opinions and keeps her wording objective.

Developing Proposals

Proposals are a special type of report that may vary in length from one page to several volumes. Companies competing for government contracts often submit proposals in response to a request for a proposal (RFP). Individuals seeking funding for projects write proposals to government agencies, research organizations, and universities, while people within an organization often submit proposals for projects to management or to committees within the organization.

Proposals are persuasive reports.

In general, proposals are persuasive reports that outline a problem or need and attempt to convince the reader that certain courses of action will meet the need or solve the problem. Many RFPs outline specific guidelines that writers must follow while developing the proposal. In other situations, writers have more flexibility in format and organization.

Many proposals follow a basic approach similar to the table of contents reproduced in Figure 15-5: the document moves from a statement of the problem to a general approach to the solution (see Figures 15-6 and 15-7). From there, the proposal outlines specific methodology, tasks in chronological order (see Figure 15-8), personnel, and costs. Proposals often end with a capability statement and resumes.

Because your proposals may face competition, underline your own or your company's competence and experience in the proposal. Provide concrete detail concerning every phase of a project, including timetables, hours of work involved, and actual personnel working on each task.

Proposals are often competitive.

The appearance of a proposal is important to its success.

To be persuasive, also, make sure your proposals are attractively presented. The type should be crisp and black, the charts professional looking, the photocopies as clear as the original. Long proposals are usually bound and presented in a heavy paper or plastic cover. Figure 15-9 lists some hints for creating effective proposals.

CONTENTS

FIGURE 15-5

Table of contents for a proposal to provide technical assistance to contractors

---

PROPOSAL TO FACILITATE A ONE-DAY CONFERENCE ON FOSTER CARE

INTRODUCTION

Rowlandson Consultants is pleased to submit this proposal in response to RFP No. 120-78-0032, issued by the Department of Health and Human Services, Regional Office, Chicago.

Rowlandson Consultants proposes to assist in planning, organizing, and facilitating a one-day conference on foster care during the week of November 3, 19xx. This conference will accomplish the following goals:

1. Provide participants with information on external monitoring of the foster care system, particularly on the review systems currently operating in Illinois
2. Provide a forum for an exchange of ideas on external review systems in foster care
3. Explore the long-term effects of the systems in Illinois

Rowlandson Consultants is well suited to perform the tasks of this project. Our experience with conferences and workshops as well as with training and evaluation provides strong credentials for our effectiveness and efficiency. Our track record and satisfied clients attest that our services are timely and of the highest quality.

FIGURE 15-6

Excerpt from a proposal to facilitate a conference

II. CONCEPTUAL APPROACH

Our conceptual approach to this compendium is based on four objectives. Our goals are to develop a document which is

    A. *comprehensive* as a single source of information
    B. *standardized* in its organization and visual format
    C. *modular* in its data structure and
    D. *flexible* in construction

A. COMPREHENSIVE

The anticipated target readership of our document will consist of plant and facilities managers of large commercial/industrial operations who are investigating the potential of cogeneration systems. Our compendium must be sufficiently detailed to assist research and decision making with regard to the technical, environmental, and economic feasibility of specific cogeneration systems.

The document must provide sufficient detail, for example, for an engineer to determine the resource energy consumption of a diesel engine in response to demands for primary output energy and secondary recoverable heat.

B. STANDARDIZED

An effective compendium of equipment must be more than a collection of independent manufacturers' source materials. Our compendium will standardize the display of the different manufacturers' performance descriptions and also present the listed as well as hidden operating costs

C. MODULAR

The basic building block of the compendium will be a module corresponding to one particular manufacturer's model at a rated capacity. A numbering system will be developed to identify each module. This method will facilitate readers' survey efforts, provide sufficient detail to conduct a definitive study of the options, and aid subsequent revisions.

D. FLEXIBLE

To be useful, our compendium must respond to changing technologies. The data structure we develop will allow us to revise easily as more innovative central plant components are developed in the near future. Our computerized database and word processing systems will enable us to update the compendium at minimal expense.

FIGURE 15-7

Excerpt from a proposal to assess available cogeneration equipment

---

Hints for effective proposals (opposite page)

FIGURE 15–9 ➤

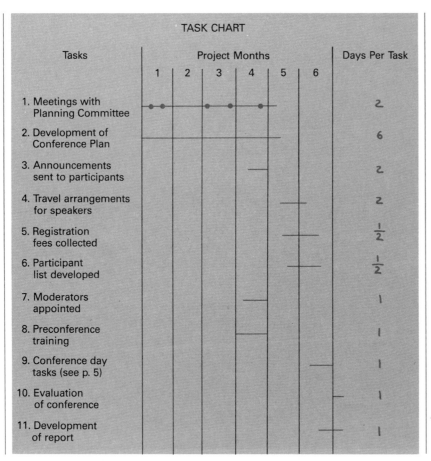

TASK CHART

Tasks	Project Months 1	2	3	4	5	6	Days Per Task
1. Meetings with Planning Committee							2
2. Development of Conference Plan							6
3. Announcements sent to participants							2
4. Travel arrangements for speakers							2
5. Registration fees collected							$\frac{1}{2}$
6. Participant list developed							$\frac{1}{2}$
7. Moderators appointed							1
8. Preconference training							1
9. Conference day tasks (see p. 5)							1
10. Evaluation of conference							1
11. Development of report							1

FIGURE 15–8

Sample task chart for proposal to facilitate a conference

1. Open with an overview of the whole situation. The introduction should summarize your approach and why you or your organization should do the work you propose.
2. Include a methodology section that not only outlines what you will do but also convinces the reader that this approach is the best one for the situation.
3. Outline specific tasks and dates as well as costs and personnel involved. Be as realistic as possible: your proposal will act as a legal document if it is accepted.
4. Include an organizational chart of people involved in the project so that the reader will know who is in charge of what facets.
5. Include any information about your company and staff that will increase the credibility of your proposal. Information such as the years the company has been in business, its resources in terms of staff and equipment, its previous clients, and its success with similar projects is particularly valuable.
6. If you must meet a proposal deadline, give yourself enough time to do a good job. Many proposals suffer from being written in haste. RFPs often specify not only a date but a time of day by which the proposal must be received: that deadline is not negotiable, so plan your writing time carefully.

What Would You Do?

Dale Randall has been brainstorming with a group of fellow students about setting up a newsletter in their college that will focus on issues relevant to students in their area of interest. This newsletter would contain features such as faculty profiles, job information, scholarships, upcoming lectures, films, or workshops, and student awards.

To get funding for this project, Dale must write a proposal to the dean. Write a formal outline for Dale that specifies what information should be included in the proposal.

Summary

Short reports are meant to convey information in an efficient, compact format; most short reports are written in letter or memorandum form. Knowing why you are writing the report, who your readers will be, and how they will react will help you organize your approach and choose effective wording.

Progress reports, minutes, agendas, and other primarily informational reports are often organized deductively. Recommendation reports, proposals, and other primarily persuasive documents are often set up inductively. Proposals are frequently set up according to strict guidelines and submitted by a specific time and date.

Whatever their purpose, reports usually benefit from effective use of headings, white space, charts, and lists, as well as you-oriented word choices and clear organization.

Short Report Checklist

Format

- To increase persuasiveness and readability in short reports

  _____ adhere to your organization's guidelines for different types of reports

  _____ use headings and subheadings

  _____ be generous with margins and white space

  _____ present key information graphically or in lists

  _____ use an appropriate organizational plan

  _____ gear your word choices to your readers

Progress Reports

- Use progress reports to summarize activities that took place during a specified time period.

- Keep a consistent format for each progress report on a particular project.

- Use a deductive organizational plan:

  _____ Open first progress report with overview of project.

  _____ Open subsequent progress reports with summary of activities covered during specified time period.

  _____ Provide details on major activities and any problems encountered.

  _____ Explain what will be done next.

Employee Evaluations

- Consider personal and legal implications of employee evaluations as well as the factual material.

- Document your information and keep your tone objective.

- Unless using a preprinted appraisal form or following company guidelines, you might organize the evaluation in this way:

  _____ a title that specifies the type of evaluation being done (monthly, annual, etc.)

_____ an opening that states employee's name, job title, and time period covered in evaluation

_____ central sections that contain details on employee's performance, attitudes, motivation, skills, training, leadership, and related areas

_____ an ending that contains recommendations concerning items such as for further training, promotions, transfers, and counseling

Recommendation Reports

- Use recommendation reports to persuade a reader to take a particular course of action.

- To be persuasive, make sure recommendation reports contain data supporting your recommendations.

  _____ Open with an introduction providing an overview and a list of recommendations.

  _____ Provide a section outlining the background of the situation and how data were obtained.

  _____ Include a section summarizing research findings.

  _____ Summarize costs and benefits.

  _____ Include a persuasive conclusion repeating recommendations.

Proposals

- Use proposals to outline a problem or need and to offer solutions.

- Because proposals often compete with other proposals, prepare them carefully in accordance with any guidelines provided and submit them by any deadline required.

- Consider the following subject areas when organizing a proposal:

  _____ an introduction stating the problem and offering a solution

  _____ a background section summarizing the project and summarizing the offeror's qualifications

  _____ a body describing methods for carrying out the project, specific tasks and time schedules, personnel, facilities, and equipment

  _____ a budget with specific costs

  _____ a conclusion summarizing the importance of the project and the qualifications of the offeror

Terms to Remember

Employee evaluation: report or form that includes an appraisal of the work an employee has been doing over a specified time period, the employee's qualifications, and the writer's recommendations for the employee

Offeror: a person, group, or organization writing a proposal, particularly in response to a request for a proposal

Progress report: report providing information on work done on a project during a particular time period

Proposal: persuasive report outlining a problem and urging that particular steps be taken to solve it

Recommendation report: report recommending that the reader take a particular course of action

Request for a proposal (RFP): formal request from a company or government agency stating a need and asking that individuals or organizations develop proposals responding to the need

Short report: document under eight pages long used for conveying information. Presented in letter or memorandum form, a short report is usually sent vertically in an organization, often to people only a few steps higher than the writer.

Summary Discussion: Susan Schultz's Recommendation Report from Case in Point, p. 355

Susan Schultz's report does not present complete information. She does not even mention the actual rate of employee turnover or the extent it has increased in recent months. Her questionnaire results, also, are unclear: How many of each group did she interview? What proportion of each group gave the answers she records?

Susan needs to cut a lot of wordy sentences that delay the reader from getting to the major ideas in the report. Phrases such as "Nonmanagement employees were apt to say" are vague; she should replace them with figures.

To revise, Susan should set up a plan that includes headings to increase readability and charts to highlight data. Her report should include details on her research methods as well as her results. She might open with a positive sentence that will encourage the owner to read the whole report: she should end with definite recommendations in list form.

Questions for Review and Discussion

1. Describe a situation in which a progress report might be necessary.
2. What information is usually included in an employee evaluation?
3. What organizational method is usually used for proposals?
4. Discuss some techniques that can enhance the persuasiveness of a proposal.
5. What is so important about the use of white space in a report?
6. Why do many recommendation reports require a section outlining the writer's methodology for obtaining data?

1. Develop a questionnaire that Susan Schultz could use to survey both managers and non-managers on the strengths and weaknesses of The Big Hat Cafe. (See Case in Point, p. 355)
2. Revise Susan Schultz's report.
3. Assume that you have been asked to recommend a change in the undergraduate curriculum at your school. Write a report recommending that a certain class be added to or deleted from the core requirements. Make sure you back up your report with reasoning and data appropriate for your audience—the administrators of your school.
4. Your instructor has assigned a term project to be completed later in the term. Write a proposal to the instructor concerning the topic you hope to undertake for the project. Include persuasive information on why you think the project is relevant and useful, why you are the right person to undertake the project, and why the project is appropriate for the course.
5. Your instructor has assigned a project that is due toward the end of the term. Before the project is due, write a progress report outlining what you have done so far and outlining the timeframe you have set up for the remaining tasks.
6. Your college has been acquiring personal computers (PCs) for the students to use, but there are still not enough computers to meet the demands of the students. Write a report to the school administration proposing that more computers be purchased. In your report include information such as:
   a. the number of students who use the PC lab every day
   b. the percentage of students using PCs for (1) spreadsheets, (2) word processing, (3) programming, (4) simulation games, (5) other uses
   c. the average length of time students must wait for the lab during peak periods
   d. specific recommendations on the number

and type of machines to be purchased.
7. Your campus is very dark at night. Write a short report proposing that additional lights be put along key walkways and in parking lots. Back up your report with concrete information on costs and benefits.
8. Your company has been hiring people from outside rather than training present employees for more advanced jobs. Write a report summarizing how this hiring practice has affected morale and raised costs for the company. Propose a training program that could help employees move vertically in the organization.
9. Your neighborhood is adjacent to a major road that is getting more and more heavy use. Turning from your residential street, Sharon Lane, onto Highway 20 is becoming increasingly difficult and dangerous. Three accidents occurred at that intersection last month alone. Write a short report to your local office of the Department of Transportation. Recommend that a traffic light be placed at the intersection of Sharon and Highway 20.
10. You are the head of a department in a company. You must write a report evaluating one of your clerical staff who has worked for the company only six months. Write a paragraph or two for each section of the evaluation. Keep your wording fair and back up your statements wherever possible.
   Employee evaluations in your organization are set up like this:

```
          PERFORMANCE APPRAISAL
Employee Name:                    Date:
Position Held:
Date of Hiring:
Review Period:

1. Accomplishments
2. Significant Changes Since Last Review
   Period
3. Potential for Advancement
4. Overall Performance Appraisal
```

11. Write the proposal for a college newsletter described on p. 370.

Many reports that you write for school and for work must be documented: that is, you need to cite the sources of your information. A standard method for marking footnotes is to use superscripts—numbers slightly raised above the line:

This research was verified by C. P. Hall in 1987.[1]
As George Arms writes, "This action was the final blow."[2]

Both superscripts and subscripts, numbers or letters put slightly below the line, are used in chemical and mathematical notation:

H_2O
$a^2 + b^2 = c^2$

1. Find out if your word processing program has the capability for creating subscripts and superscripts. If it does, learn the commands and continue with this exercise.

2. Create a file SCRIPT and type in the following paragraphs.

a. The final step in the analysis was to compute a price that maximizes profit. We can do this by first computing total revenue (TR):

$$TR = pq = 12{,}480p - 224p^2$$

Then, profit (P) equals TR − TC:

$$\begin{aligned} P &= 12{,}480p - 224p^2 - 21{,}000 - 20q \\ &= 12{,}480p - 224p^2 - 20{,}000 - \\ &\quad 20(12{,}480 - 224p) \\ &= -224p^2 + 16{,}960p - 249{,}600 \end{aligned}$$

b. Let us examine the conditions faced by a two-firm oligopoly (i.e., a duopoly). For simplicity, we assume that the two firms have the same MR function and face demand D. However, firm A has higher marginal costs than does Firm B (i.e., $MC_A > MC_B$). Under these conditions, Firm A will prefer to set its price at P_A, while Firm B will desire to set its price at P_B.

3. Print SCRIPT and check to see that the superscripts and subscripts have been printed correctly.

Formal Reports

Objectives

To organize and present material clearly and objectively

To write formal reports in a style that is appropriate for the content and the readers

To learn the standard components of a formal report

To use conventional formats for report layout and documentation

16

Tim Baskins's Formal Report

Tim Baskins is a research assistant with Arnell Associates, a company that specializes in performing studies and evaluations for other businesses. Tim has a broad background in statistics, problem analysis, and general business strategies, but he has never written a formal report; he has been responsible only for researching and analyzing information other people needed for their reports.

Now he is in charge of his first project, which includes a formal report that will be read by upper management of both the client company and his own organization. Although he and his team have done an excellent job of designing a study and evaluating the problem, Tim panics at the thought of doing a good report.

"I don't even know what the major parts of a report are," he tells his friend Jill Monahan. "What should the final document *look* like? What should it *sound* like?"

"Looks don't matter, I'm sure," Jill tells him. "Just write up your results. You're a good writer. Use your usual style. The company managers will love it when they see what you've done."

Points to Consider

- Is Jill right that "looks don't matter" in a formal report?
- What writing style is appropriate for a formal report?
- What should Tim do next?

Developing Formal Reports

Most formal reports describe and analyze problems and situations; most are over eight pages long and are written for upper management. The subjects of formal reports can include any topic that requires distillation and analysis. Accounting, sales, marketing, management—every area of a business may be a basis for a formal report.

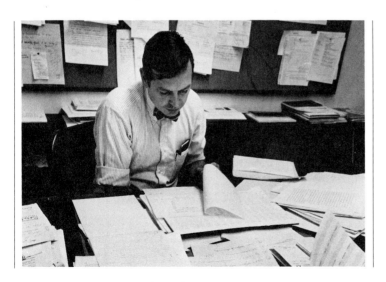

Formal reports have a
number of components
that must be carefully
organized.

Formal reports are written far less frequently than short reports, but they are an important part of the communication flow in most companies. They are often read by a number of people and kept on file for years. Because formal reports may contribute significantly to a company's image, their appearance and format are designed to reflect professionalism as well as to enhance readability. Because reports often present large quantities of complex material, their components are organized to help a reader locate key data and assimilate them efficiently.

Before you write a formal report, your research should include, not just information on the topic of the report, but also on the conventions for formal reports used in your organization. Your readers will expect to encounter a specific writing style and format.

Using an Appropriate Style

When writing a formal report, some people revert to unwieldy sentences and unnatural word choices. However, the conventions of effective writing do not change for report writing. *No* business writing should contain awkward sentences or stilted word choices.

In fact, the guidelines for good writing that we have discussed throughout this text apply here: your first task is to convey information clearly, accurately, and concisely. The revision stage of the writing process should be similar for all business writing.

Formal reports should
have a readable but ob-
jective style.

However, because a formal report is usually intended for more than one reader, for readers you do not know personally, and for people several steps higher than you in the organization, your style will probably be more formal than in other business documents. To enhance the credibility of your report, moreover, you should be even more careful than usual to be objective and to convey information accurately.

The following pointers can help you develop an objective but readable style.

Avoid Using *I* and *Me*

The readers of your report should not be thinking about *you* but about the information you are conveying. In general, first-person singular pronouns (*I, me, mine, myself*) are not acceptable in formal reports. To avoid confusing the reader and using awkward constructions, however, you may use *we, us, our research team*, and similar words (see the formal report excerpted in Figures 16-4 through 16-6.) In some cases, particularly when the report has been written by a team, report writers refer to themselves in the third person:

> As Project Director, I evaluated the reports before I sent them to the vice-president. [first person]

> The Project Director evaluated the reports before sending them to the vice-president. [third person]

Distinguish Between Documented Information and Opinions

Your readers should always be able to tell when you are reporting information that you can prove and when you are conveying interpretations or analyses.

State the sources for your statements.

> The three site engineers have stated their belief that the problem will not recur. [opinion]
>
> The Personnel Department reports a 20 pecent employee turnover rate for 1988. [fact]

Make sure, also, to provide documentation (footnotes, sources) when you

- quote someone else's written or spoken words
- paraphrase someone else's words
- summarize someone else's ideas
- refer to the results of a study
- use a chart or other graphic developed by someone else

For more information on documentation, see pages 396–399.

Use Objective and Concrete Language

Objective and concrete language will enhance the credibility of your report. Present facts rather than subjective interpretations. Use figures and provable data instead of vague adjectives and adverbs.

> Most managers find the new system terrific. [subjective, vague]
>
> Fifteen managers maintain that the new system has helped increase productivity by 15 percent. [objective, concrete]
>
> In the near future the department will issue a follow-up report. [subjective, vague]
>
> By July 1 the department will issue a follow-up report. [objective, concrete]

Watch for Passive Sentences

In order to avoid using personal pronouns, you may find yourself writing more passive sentences than usual. Be careful: Passive sentences are as deadly to read in reports as they are in other types of writing. Check to make sure that each passive sentence has a purpose.

> The research team was supervised by Caroline Freeman. [passive]
>
> Caroline Freeman supervised the research team. [active]

Use Words Your Reader Will Understand

The guidelines for word choice that you studied in Part 2 of this text apply to formal reports as well as to other types of business writing. Do not let your efforts to be more formal lead you into technical jargon or other types of words with which your reader may not be familiar. Define any necessary technical terms. You may even choose to include a glossary.

Provide a glossary if the report contains terms unfamiliar to the readers.

Use Meaningful Headings to Guide Your Reader

Readers should be able to spot areas of particular interest by glancing at your headings and subheadings. Make your report headings meaningful.

Headings should be useful to the reader.

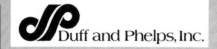

Duff and Phelps, Inc.

"Say it up front," says Philip D. Goodman, Vice-President of Duff and Phelps, a financial analysis and consulting firm in Chicago. Duff and Phelps' worldwide list of clients consists of banks, brokerage houses, insurance companies, investment advisors, and private investors. "No matter what kind of report you're writing, put the vital information first. The people reading it are busy. They have lots to read and may not be reading it in prime time: they're probably reading it on a train or in an easy chair after dinner. Give them your conclusion first. For example, 'X Company's earnings in the last quarter were much worse than we expected them to be.' Then follow up with the details."

As a security analyst covering electronics companies such as Hewlett Packard, Motorola, and Texas Instruments, Philip writes a number of different kinds of reports including Stock Sheets, "Scoop" Articles, and Basic Analyses.

Duff and Phelps' Stock Sheets are brief two-page company summaries that are written for busy portfolio managers. They consist of brief investment opinions, earnings estimates, and fundamentals, as well as stock and financial tables—all crammed onto two pages. "Every word must count; space is at a premium!" Stock Sheets are updated quarterly.

Scoop is an electronic mail service that clients pick on their computer terminals. Scoop articles are more timely and less structured than Stock Sheets. "Our analysts might write a Scoop article on how the latest events in the Near East could impact on oil company earnings or on how import restrictions could affect the semiconductor industry."

Basic Reports are fifteen- to thirty-five-page analyses of a company. They include a long-term investment opinion, a corporate profile, a discussion of management and strategy, a list of strengths and weaknesses, and a five-year earnings and balance sheet forecast.

What if he has to write an unfavorable report on a company he follows regularly? "If I do it with integrity, there's no problem," says Philip. "There may be times when it's better to avoid a particular stock."

He reads a wide variety of trade and industry publications in order to keep up with the industry. In reading quarterly and annual reports, his advice is, "Look at the fine print. Read through to the end: the beginning tends to be public relations. Make sure the company is telling you what you want to know. See what accounting methods they use to present data."

Philip says the financial and public relations reports he receives from companies are well written. "The writers probably took a journalism or business communications course." On the other hand, "many business majors never learned to write."

His advice to students? Reports should be written in the same style as newspaper journalism.

- Put the important information first; then go on to support it.
- Be clear.
- Be direct.
- Be concise.
- Keep the readers in mind. Think about what they want to know.
- Use language the readers will understand. "Sometimes analysts with technical expertise will go off the deep end and lose their readers."

Identifying a new section with simply a Roman numeral, for example, does not provide a reader with enough information. A heading such as *Data from Employee Surveys* gives the reader more information than *Research Results*.

Present Information Visually as Well as Verbally

Most reports contain information that can be clearly represented in tables and charts. To help your reader grasp the data in your report, consider using graphic aids. (See Chapter 17 for more information on report graphics.) However, make sure every piece of information you present visually is also included in the written text.

Style Checklist for Formal Reports

—DO use a variety of words and sentence structures.

—DO avoid using *I, me,* and related personal pronouns.

—DO document your sources.

—DO remove jargon and stilted word choices.

—DO define any words your reader may not understand.

—DO maintain an objective, rational approach.

—DO use meaningful headings to guide the reader.

—DO use white space, lists, and visual aids to increase readability.

—DON'T rely on passive sentences.

—DON'T move abruptly from one idea to the next.

—DON'T forget that you are writing for a reader.

Organizing the Components of a Formal Report

Formal reports are usually set up to facilitate easy access to key information. As a result, a certain redundancy is often built into their structure: main points, for example, may be covered in the summary, the introduction, and the conclusion as well as highlighted graphically in a chart.

Most formal reports have standard components that readers expect to see. These components vary in accordance with their purpose, the information they contain, and the individual conventions of an organization. The following chart outlines standard components that appear in the prefatory material, body, and addenda of a formal report. (Most formal reports will not contain all of these components.)

Formal report components have been developed to help the reader locate and understand key information.

Standard Parts of a Formal Report

Prefatory Material	*Body*	*Addenda*
Cover	Introduction	Glossary
Letter of transmittal	Analysis of findings	Appendices
Title fly	Conclusions	Tables/figures
Title page	Recommendations	Bibliography
Letter of authorization		Index
Letter of acceptance		
Table of contents		
List of tables		
Abstract or summary		

Developing Prefatory Material

The prefatory material of formal reports sets them apart from other business documents: standard components have been developed to help the reader both to locate key points and to grasp the nature, source, and purpose of the report.

Cover

The report cover establishes an image.

Most long reports have a heavy paper or leather cover. Because it establishes an image right away, the cover should be consistent with the nature of the report and the organization it represents. Most report covers contain the title and the author's name as well as the name and perhaps the logo of the company. Like the report as a whole, the title should be informative and clear.

Letter of Transmittal

The letter of transmittal (Figure 16-1) may come before or after the title page. The letter lets the readers know why and for whom the report was written. The letter may also summarize or highlight the most important findings in the report.

Title Fly

The title fly, also called the flyleaf, precedes the title page and contains only the title of the report. This component is generally used only with the most formal of reports.

Place the title a little above the center of the page, center all lines, and double space if the title is longer than one line. The title should be in capital letters.

Title Page

The title page (Figure 16-2) contains the report title, usually in capital letters, as well as the name, title, and company of the author and the recipient of the report. The title page also contains the date the report was submitted.

Center the lines and arrange on the page as illustrated in Figure 16-2.

Letter of Authorization

The person authorizing the report may have written a letter or memo specifying the scope of the project and financial and time limitations. If so, you may choose to include a copy of the letter after the title page of the report. Such a letter or memo is more common in government reports than in business reports.

```
                    ARNELL ASSOCIATES
                   3411 Mission Boulevard
                     Houston, TX 70023

December 12, 19xx

Ms. Carla David
Vice-President, Western Sales Area
Paulsen Corporation
9000 Rockridge Avenue
Dallas, TX 70023

Dear Ms. David:

The attached report contains the results of the
analysis we performed on discounts in Commercial
Market Area A since October 19xx. Our team
investigated the excessive use of sales discounts
in that area and identified five key factors
for attention from an original list of over 30
behaviors and attitudes. The information in this
report should help you to increase profits in
Commercial Market Area A.

Thank you for the opportunity to complete this
project for Paulsen Corporation. We hope you will
find that our analysis meets your needs.

Sincerely,



Mr. Timothy Baskins  Ms. Lynn Calder    Mr. Peter Forbes
Research Assistant    Research Assistant  Research Assistant



enc.
```

Figure 16-1
Sample letter of transmittal

Letter of Acceptance

The letter of acceptance is a reply that confirms the terms in the letter of
authorization. The letter of acceptance may also lay out any changes made
in the original agreement. Letters of acceptance are included in formal reports even less frequently than are letters of transmittal.

```
┌─────────────────────────────────────────────────────────┐
│                                                           │
│        ANALYSIS OF DISCOUNTS IN COMMERCIAL MARKET AREA A  │
│                                                           │
│                        Prepared for                       │
│                                                           │
│                     Ms. Carla David                       │
│             Vice-President, Western Sales Area            │
│                    Paulson Corporation                    │
│                                                           │
│                                                           │
│                        Prepared by                        │
│                                                           │
│            Mr. Timothy Baskins, Ms. Lynn Calder,          │
│                      Mr. Peter Forbes                     │
│                     Research Assistants                   │
│                      Arnell Associates                    │
│                                                           │
│                                                           │
│                     December 12, 19xx                     │
│                                                           │
└─────────────────────────────────────────────────────────┘
```

Figure 16-2

Title page for a formal report

Table of Contents

Prepare the table of contents when the report is in its final form.

The table of contents (Figure 16-3) should be typed after the rest of the report is completed. As it lists all first-, second-, and third-level section headings and their page numbers, the table of contents helps the reader to see the overall organization of the report. Usually the section titles are connected to the page numbers by a series of spaced dots.

```
                                                          Page
   Abstract  ............................................   ii
   I. INTRODUCTION  .....................................    1
          A. Statement of the Problem  ..................    1
          B. Scope of the Report  ......................     2
          C. Methods of Data Collection  ...............     3
                 1. Questionnaires  ....................     3
                 2. Observation  .......................     5
```

The table of contents should list any prefatory material that follows it; it should also include tables, charts, and graphs unless they are listed separately. Double-space between all first-level headings. You may choose to double-space or single-space between second- and third-level headings.

Table of Illustrations

The table of illustrations may also be entitled "Table of Figures," "List of Illustrations and Charts," or other appropriate heading. The table of illustrations (Figure 16-3) provides the reader with the type, number, title, and page of each illustration. The title of each illustration should be consistent with the title actually used in the report.

CONTENTS

TABLE OF ILLUSTRATIONS

FIGURE 16-3
Sample table of contents

Abstract or Executive Summary

An abstract, executive summary, precis, or synopsis describes the major findings in the report. Begin writing it only after the report is completed. Because the abstract is meant to help a busy reader, it should be brief. Many abstracts are about a page in length, but they may be as long as 10 percent of the report as a whole: for a hundred-page report, you may need a ten-page abstract.

An abstract should summarize key information for the reader.

Abstracts are either informative or descriptive. The majority of abstracts in formal reports are informative because they are more useful to a reader: they summarize the purpose, findings, and recommendations in the report. Descriptive abstracts simply provide a preview of major topics to be discussed; they are useful for researchers searching for reports relevant to their needs.

Figure 16-4 presents an informative abstract. A descriptive abstract for the same report might run as follows:

Formal Reports   385

This report covers the investigation of the use of sales discount in Commercial Market Area A of Paulsen Corporation. The report includes analysis of the research results and identifies factors in the discount performance of Area A.

SUMMARY

In September 19xx, a research team was brought in from Arnell Associates to investigate the excessive use of sales discount in Commercial Market Area A of Paulsen Corporation. The purpose of the investigation was to provide information about the attitudes and behaviors of the sales force that management could use while developing a strategy to reduce discount.

The team researched, planned, implemented, and analyzed a survey of all Area A sales representatives. Analysis of the results identified five key areas for attention out of an original list of over thirty behaviors and attitudes.

Our research team identified the following key factors in the discount performance of Area A:

1. Sales representatives' statement of a reasonable target discount level is 40 percent higher than the area's budgeted level.
2. Although 80 percent of proposals are written at list price, less than 40 percent are finally sold at list.
3. Nearly three-quarters of the lowest-tenure sales representatives appeared in the highest discount category.
4. The largest single factor in sales discount, accounting for nearly one-third of total points, was the belief that competitive products were identical.
5. The second largest single factor was the use of sales discount to speed buying: this factor is related to pressure to attain month-end quotas.

FIGURE 16-4 _____
Informative abstract

Organizing the Body of the Report

The body of a report may be set up in a number of different ways. Usually the introduction provides the background, purpose, methodology, and scope of the report, while central sections analyze findings. The final sections of text usually offer conclusions and recommendations.

Note again the redundancy built into the format of a formal report. As you can see from Figures 16-1 through 16-5, the letter of transmittal, abstract, and introduction may repeat key details, such as the purpose of the report and the major findings. Conclusions may be summarized in the abstract and at the end of the report. This redundancy insures that readers can easily grasp the most important information without studying every page of the report.

Repetition of key points helps readers who do not study the whole report.

Introduction

You may choose to divide the introduction of a report into subsections, or you may keep it to one section as the writer has done in Figure 16-5. In general, the introduction should quickly inform the readers of the report's major purpose and subtly persuade them that the report is worth their attention.

```
                    I. INTRODUCTION

    This project was initiated in September 19xx, by
Carla David, Vice-President, Western Sales Area
(Commercial Market Area A). The project was
initiated for two reasons:

    1. Area A would have achieved sales quota in 19xx
       if the Area had kept sales discount dollars
       below the budgeted amount.
    2. The sales discount percentage figure for Area
       A exceeded the nationwide average. This
       deficiency blocked Area A's stated objective
       of achieving top ranking in comprehensive
       sales performance.

    The goal of this project was to identify a set of
individual characteristics and motivating factors
that would differentiate high-discount performers
from low-discount performers in the sales force.
This information would help management decide which
goals, guidelines, or training should be adjusted
to improve overall discount performance.

    Because the discount issue was interrelated
with virtually all aspects of the business (i.e.,
equipment, system design, installation, management
attitude, training), the project required
consultants with experience in sales, service, and
training.
```

FIGURE 16-5
Sample introduction

II. PRELIMINARY INVESTIGATION

The first stage of the project was to establish a list of all the potential causes for sales discount. After a brainstorming session, the team members tested the completeness of an initial list by reviewing it with local sales representatives.

The review was conducted as a modified Delphi process composed of the following steps:

1. The research team arranged an initial list in random order and presented it to three sales representatives known for high discount levels. The sales representatives were then asked to add any items that affected sales discounts and delete items that did not.
2. The team modified the list, ignoring deletions but including additions listed by the sales representatives.
3. The research team selected three sales representatives known for low discount levels and presented the modified list to them for additions and deletions.
4. The team compiled a second modified list by keeping all items except those deleted by both groups.
5. The team reviewed and combined items in the second modified list to create a final list of ten discount factors.

As a result of this process, the final list of factors represented not only the ideas of the research team but also the unbiased comments of active sales representatives. This list became the foundation for the discount survey and all subsequent analysis.

III. SURVEY PROCEDURE

The next stage of the project was to measure the relative strength among the sales force of each of the ten discount factors and correlate this with other demographic and behavioral material. Because the subject population was only 150 sales representatives under direct control of management, we chose to conduct an areawide written survey of the entire population.

The survey was designed to be brief, self-explanatory, anonymous, and easy to analyze. (See Appendix A for a copy of the survey form.) To promote a candid response, each form was identified by a preprinted region number but was otherwise anonymous.

Figure 16-6 (*continues*)

```
        Questions 1 through 4 provided information about
    the representative's actual discount performance
    and about his or her attitude towards discount.
    Question 5, combined with the preprinted region
    number, provided demographic information. The most
    complex question was number 6, dealing with all ten
    discount motivational factors. Question 4 was
    specifically constructed in a similar style to
    serve as a warm-up question for number 6.

        The surveys were distributed through the regional
    managers (see Appendix B). The requested return
    date allowed about one week for response. However,
    to allow for stragglers, the analysis did not
    actually begin until two weeks after the return
    date.

                    IV. DATA REDUCTION

        The overall response rate was 78 percent at the
    beginning of the analysis but rose to 85 percent
    by the time the final analyses were performed.
    Attachment C is a chart of the response rate by
    Region, showing a range from 58 percent to 100
    percent.
```

FIGURE 16-6
Sample excerpt from report body

Purpose. Why have you written this report? Let your readers know your purpose right away. You may want to outline a problem, as the writer has done in Figure 16-6, and state its significance.

Background. Present a perspective that will help your readers understand the report within a larger context. You may have to explain the history of a situation in the company or in the industry at large.

Scope. How extensive was your study? How many people did you survey? Over what period of time did your study take place? The scope of the report is its size and complexity.

Limitations. Your study was probably limited by time, budget, or other conditions. Mentioning these toward the beginning of the report will enhance its credibility as well as its accuracy. (If you wish to mention weaknesses in your procedures, you may choose to put this section after the part of the report in which you discuss data collection.)

A statement of the limitations of your work actually enhances its credibility.

Methods of Data Collection. How did you get your information? How valid and reliable is it? Most reports contain a section explaining what primary and secondary sources were used and the rationale for any sampling that was done.

Definition of Terms. Once again, remember your readers. If they may not know some of the key words you use in the report, define them. You may want to include definitions in a separate section, in footnotes, or in a glossary at the end of the report. (See the Glossary of Word Processing Terms at the end Chapter 7 for examples of definitions.)

Analysis of Findings

The analysis section is the focus of the whole report.

Usually the longest section of the report, the analysis section describes the data you found. Be careful here to indicate how you derived your information. Tables and figures (Figure 16-7) are often useful for presenting complex information. The organizational patterns discussed in Chapter 14 can help you organize material effectively.

Conclusions

Make sure you draw logical conclusions from your data.

The last sections of your report text may include a summary, if you did not put one at the opening of the report, as well as the conclusions you have drawn from your data analysis. Your conclusions should answer the questions or solve the problems presented at the opening of the report.

Make sure you draw your conclusions carefully from the data you analyzed; specious reasoning will undermine the credibility of the whole report.

Table D. Analysis of Item Six for Zero to Two-Year Tenure

Factor	Number of Responses	Number of Points	Normalized Percentage
A. Identical Product	31	988	32
B. Coverage	7	90	1
C. Automatic	23	375	9
D. Corrections	16	220	4
E. Installation	19	431	9
F. Value	16	287	5
G. Features	11	258	3
H. Competitive Product	14	300	4
I. Competitive Tactics	13	212	3
J. Decide Quickly	34	849	30

FIGURE 16-7
Sample table

Recommendations

In some situations, you will have to make recommendations based upon your conclusions; however, do not make recommendations unless you have been specifically asked to do so. In general, align your recommendations with your conclusions. That is, if one conclusion is that errors are becoming increasingly common in the purchasing process, then you should make specific recommendations to solve that problem.

The more specific and action-oriented your recommendations are, the more useful they will be to your readers.

Organizing Addenda

The last sections of your report may include materials that you mentioned in the text but chose to leave out of the report body. These materials may be only indirectly related to the main parts of the report, or they may be so long that they would interfere with the readability of the report.

Glossary

As mentioned earlier, you may want to include a glossary defining terms unfamiliar to the reader. Use a glossary if you have more than five or six items to define. These items should be listed alphabetically. (Sometimes, if a glossary is particularly important, it appears at the beginning of the report, immediately after the table of contents. This placement is also useful if the reader will not be knowledgeable about the terms in the report.)

Appendixes

Appendixes may include tables and figures, maps, questionnaires, correspondence (Figure 16-8), computer printouts of data, and so on. Include only items related to the report that could be useful references for the reader.

List different types of material in separate appendixes (see Figure 16-3), and label each appendix with a capital letter and a title: "Appendix A. Map of Frostburg." Mention each appendix in the body of the report.

Appendixes provide additional information or supporting material for the report.

Tables/Figures

In general, as we will discuss in Chapter 17, visual aids should be placed in the text where a reader can refer to them easily. If they will interfere with the readability of the report or are not vital to a reader's understanding of the report, you may choose to place tables and figures in an appendix or in a separate section at the end of the report.

Each visual aid should be numbered and titled.

Figure 1. Equipment Purchases in 1988.

Table 2. Employee Salaries

Reading Between the Lines of an Annual Report

Gary Weiss

"To our shareholders." An innocent enough beginning, but what follows those three words can try the patience of the most savvy investor. Sure, reading a corporate annual report is easy—but extracting the most value from the experience is something else again.

At the beginning there is a "message from the chairman" that doesn't always give a brutally frank version of the year's events. Ignore it for now. Part of the challenge is learning how to translate this verbiage—as we've done in the accompanying illustrations on these pages.

In their quest for higher earnings, more companies are resorting to accounting changes, pension-plan terminations, and other controversial techniques. "There are lots of tricks to make things less obvious in annual reports," observes Douglas W. Kurz, a partner at accountants Coopers & Lybrand.

You needn't be an accountant to do a solid analysis of a company's report. With the tips that follow, you can sift out enough facts to decide whether a company is a good or a shaky investment.

Revealing Glance. A general rule: Look at the back pages of the report first. That's where you find the opinion of the independent auditor that the company hires. Even a glance can be revealing. "Generally the auditor's statement is two paragraphs. Anything longer can be significant," notes Norman Strauss, regional director of accountants Ernst & Whinney in New York. So if the statement's long, better take time to read it.

It's possible that an extra paragraph or two may simply be a note that the company has changed its accounting practices in some minor way. But the additional material also may focus on serious stuff. In Texaco's 1985 annual report, for instance, the auditors at Arthur Andersen added a paragraph mentioning the $11.1 billion judgment against the company in a suit brought by Pennzoil. It noted that the "ultimate outcome of this litigation is not presently determinable." Andersen could endorse the financial statement only "subject to the effect . . . of such adjustments, if any, that might have been required had the outcome of the litigation . . . been

known." (It still isn't, although one Texas court has shaved $2 billion from the judgment.)

That kind of cautionary note—or "qualified opinion"—rarely tells the observant stockholder anything that's terribly surprising. Indeed, the initial Pennzoil judgment was old news when the annual report came out. But to skip the auditor's statement risks overlooking a bombshell. At least, it can confirm earlier hints of trouble.

Next, look for the section labeled "Management Discussion and Analysis of Financial Condition and Results of Operations." Undoubtedly, management does a considerable amount of discussing and analyzing throughout the report. But this section has to meet standards set by the Securities & Exchange Commission and the Financial Accounting Standards Board. "The auditors review it to make sure that it's factually consistent with the financial statement," notes Kurz.

Straight Talk. You can expect the section to present a reasonably straightforward analysis of the company's operations. Let's say that the report says earnings went up, and you wonder why. In U.S. Shoe's 1985 annual report, for instance, readers learned that the company's specialty retailing operations were "dramatically ahead of last year's depressed results." Note that word "depressed." It's significant. If the prior year hadn't been so weak, 1985 wouldn't have looked so good.

For more details, turn to the footnotes to the report. Among them, you'll find a breakdown of the company's lines of business, and how much each unit contributes to sales and earnings. You can also learn if the company has been making heavy use of tax benefits. The new tax law wipes out many such provisions, including the investment tax credit for equipment purchases, so the future might not be as bright.

The footnotes also indicate the health of the company's pension plan. If it's underfunded, coming up with the money to meet future pension liabilities could be a strain. But if the plan is overfunded, the company may be able to terminate the plan and institute a new one, shifting the excess into its own coffers. As an example, knowledgeable readers of the 1985 annual report of U.S. Steel (now USX) were pleased to see that the company's pension plan held 26% more assets—about $2 billion—than would be required to pay its pensioners in the future. Exactly how much the pension plan is overfunded is a matter of controversy, but the footnote was an indication that the amount may be considerable, and could be a possible source of future cash for the corporation.

Your next step: Examine the report's income statement and balance sheet. The income statement tells you how the company has been doing recently. It shows revenues, costs, and earnings for the past three years. Here you can see if the company has been able to sustain or increase the market for its products and services, and you can also gauge the company's ability to control its costs. Further down is the proverbial "bottom line"—earnings per share based on the average number of common shares outstanding during the year. If the company has issued bonds convertible into stock, or if executives have a lot of stock options yet to be exercised, the statement will show the earnings per share "fully diluted"—as if all the potential shares were in existence.

If earnings per share have been increasing steadily, stockholders have reason to be happy. But don't rejoice if the statement shows that significant income has been derived from one-time events, such as selling off the corporate headquarters. Similarly, don't be too apprehensive if the company's earnings have been penalized during the year by the cost of shutting down facilities. Earnings may benefit in the long run.

Ripe for Raids? Then there's the balance sheet, a snapshot of the company's capital structure. It shows the assets, liabilities, and the common shareholders' equity in the company at the end of the year. That's the same as net worth, or book value: the amount that the common stockholders would get, at least in theory, if the company were liquidated. The balance sheet also tells you how much cash the company has

on hand. Too little, and it may have trouble expanding; too much, and it may tempt a raider to move in—which could be bad for management but good for the stock's price. You'll also see the degree to which the company relies on borrowed funds to finance its operations. A heavy debt isn't always bad, if the company's rate of return on its assets is above the cost of borrowing.

With the balance sheet and earnings statement before you, pull out your calculator. Divide common shareholder equity by the number of shares outstanding to get book value per share. If the company's shares are selling at book value or less, they may be a bargain. Generally, shares sell well above book value.

To measure how well the company is using its resources, divide net income by the company's assets, taking the year's average instead of the yearend figure. What you get is the percentage return on assets. And divide net income by average equity to see how well the company is doing for its stockholders. Is there adequate cash? You can find out by dividing the current assets by current liabilities. That's the current ratio.

By deriving these ratios for the previous and current years, you can tell if the company's financial position is improving or worsening. It also helps to compare your results with the numbers prevailing in the particular industry. A profit margin, of course, is the difference between the price a company gets for its products and the cost of producing them. But retailers commonly have margins as low as 1% or 2%, while 15% isn't unusual among newspaper publishers.

Have you mused over the earnings statement and balance sheet? And crunched numbers to your heart's content? Now, finally, you can read what the chairman has to say (or, more precisely, what the chairman's public relations person has to say). You may get some valuable insight into the company's condition. . . . If the chairman's words jibe with your analysis of the data in the annual report, you will feel more confident as an investor. If not, you may be happier owning stock in a company where rhetoric matches results.

```
         Appendix B. Regional Managers' Notification Memo

                          MEMORANDUM

    TO:       Bill Barker          DATE: April 21, 19xx
              Sam Carlson
              Mary Hodges
              Kate Jawarsky
              Linda May

    FROM:     Timothy Baskins

    SUBJECT: Discount Project


    Ms. Carla David has requested that Lynn Carter,
    Peter Forbes, and I design and implement a project
    to identify and control the general causes of
    discount in your area. We have produced the
    attached brief survey to help us identify and focus
    on specific issues in the area.

    Please distribute copies of the survey to your
    sales representatives and encourage them to
    complete it quickly. The completed questionnaires
    should be returned directly to me by April 29. As
    stated on the survey, results will not be tracked
    by individual.

    Thank you for your help. Please call me at Ext. 367
    if you have questions.
```

FIGURE 16-8
Sample appendix

Documentation

You must list the sources you have used while preparing the report. To prepare a documentation section, use a standard format such as the one we discuss at the end of this chapter or use a format specified by your organization.

Index

Usually an index is included only in published reports. Your report index should include alphabetized cross-references to the major subject areas and names in the report and the pages on which they are found. (See the index at the end of this text for an example.)

Designing the Report Layout

The appearance of your report is an important part of its message and effectiveness. Like the components of a report, its layout has become formalized. The following guides for laying out pages, spacing and indenting, typing headings, and numbering pages are standard for many organizations.

Formal guidelines usually govern the layout of a report.

Page Layout

The type on report pages should be centered, with approximately one-inch margins on the sides, top, and bottom. As most formal reports are bound, leave an extra half-inch or so on the left if the report will be bound on the left or on the top if it will be bound on the top.

If you are typing the report on a word processor, you may choose to have the right margins justified; then your right-hand margins will be uniform, as your left-hand margins are. If you are using a typewriter or if you choose ragged-right margins, base the right-hand margin on the average length of your lines. Avoid widely divergent line lengths.

Some pages of the report, such as the title page and table of contents, have special layouts discussed earlier in this chapter. Letters and memos included in the report should be typed in their traditional forms.

Before typing a report, find out if it will be bound on the top or on the left.

Spacing and Indenting

Reports may be either single- or double-spaced. Double-spacing increases readability, but single-spacing reduces printing and copying costs. When typing double-spaced reports, indent each paragraph five spaces. If you choose to single-space the report, do not indent paragraphs; simply double-space between paragraphs.

Headings

Headings (also called *captions*) should be a major aid to readers looking for information in a report. Their type and position on the page show their relative importance, as do the headings throughout this text.

Figure 16-9 shows a conventional approach for headings. With this approach, first-level headings are centered on the page and are in all uppercase (capital) letters. Second-level headings, then, are also centered, but they are underscored and printed in both upper- and lowercase. Third-level headings are typed like the second-level ones but begin at the left margin.

The form and location of report headings indicate their relative importance.

You may choose other formats for your headings, but make sure your choices are consistent throughout the report.

Make sure that centered headings are arranged to look centered on a *bound* page; if the report will be left-bound, move the headings to right of center so they will look centered after the report is bound.

Numbering Pages

Two systems are used to number report pages. Lowercase Roman numerals are used for the pages preceding the text. Although the title page is counted, it is not numbered: the second page of prefatory material begins with ii. The first page of text should be numbered 1.

For left-bound reports, place the numbers in the top right-hand corner in line with the right-hand margin, one inch from the top edge of the page. For top-bound reports, center numbers at the bottom of the page.

Providing Documentation

Documentation makes your report more credible and allows interested readers to go to the source for more information. It also ensures that people you quote or paraphrase receive credit for what they have said or written. Documentation may be used to support your own viewpoint or to cite other people's viewpoints as well as to refer readers to peripheral issues you do not discuss fully in the report.

Usually you will not need footnotes and bibliography for primary sources since your primary research such as surveys and observation will be discussed within the text of the report. When you quote or refer to a secondary

```
                    REPORT-WRITING STRATEGIES

   xxxxxxxxxxxxxxxxxxxxxxxxxxxxxxxxxxxxxxxxxxxxxxxxxxxxxxxx
   xxxxxxxxxxxxxxxxxxxxxxxxxxxxxxxxxxxxxxxxxxxxxxxxxxxxxxxx
   xxxxxxxxxxxxxxxxxxxxxxxxxxxxxxxxxxxxxxxxxxxxxxxxxxxxxxxx

                    Persuasive Techniques

   xxxxxxxxxxxxxxxxxxxxxxxxxxxxxxxxxxxxxxxxxxxxxxxxxxxxxxxx
   xxxxxxxxxxxxxxxxxxxxxxxxxxxxxxxxxxxxxxxxxxxxxxxxxxxxxxxx
   xxxxxxxxxxxxxxxxxxxxxxxxxxxxxxxxxxxxxxxxxxxxxxxxxxxxxxxx

   Concrete Details

   xxxxxxxxxxxxxxxxxxxxxxxxxxxxxxxxxxxxxxxxxxxxxxxxxxxxxxxx
   xxxxxxxxxxxxxxxxxxxxxxxxxxxxxxxxxxxxxxxxxxxxxxxxxxxxxxxx
```

FIGURE 16-9
First-, second-, and third-level headings

Abbreviation	Meaning
cf.	"compare." Do not use to mean "see."
ch., chs.	chapter, chapters
ed., eds.	edited by, editor, editors
e.g.	"for example"
et al.	"and others"
f., ff.	and the following page(s) or lines(s)
ibid.	"in the same place." Use to refer to a title in a note immediately preceding. You may choose to use the author's name and a short title instead.
i.e.	"that is"
ms. mss	manuscript(s)
n., nn.	note(s)
N.B.	"take notice"
n.d.	no date
no., nos.	number(s)
op. cit.	"in the work cited." Used to refer when citing a passage on another page. Avoid using. Better to use the author's name and a short title.
p., pp.	page(s)
vol., vols.	volume(s)

FIGURE 16-10 _____

Abbreviations commonly used in documentation

source in a report, however, you must tell your readers where you found the information. If you do not document your sources, you will be plagiarizing someone's work. Remember to provide documentation for ideas and opinions as well as for direct quotations.

There are a number of standard ways to document secondary sources in a report. One standard approach is described here, the Modern Language Association (MLA) style, but your school or organization may prefer another approach. Be consistent in whatever documentation style you use.

Also, make sure you are accurate: check each entry for correctness and completeness. Double-check the spelling of the authors' names, the page and volume numbers, dates of publication, and titles (Figure 16–10).

Documentation should be accurate and complete.

MLA Documentation

The following methods for documentation are outlined in the *MLA Handbook for Writers of Research Papers* published by the Modern Language Association of America.

1. Parenthetical References in the Text. If you use MLA documentation, references are inserted in parentheses in the text. Often the author's last name and a page number provide sufficient information. (A list of works cited appears at the end of the paper or report.)

In 1987, these findings were disproved (Harrison, 452).

If you refer to more than one title by the same author, include a shortened form of the title within the parenthetical reference.

> In 1987, these findings were disproved (Harrison, <u>Market Research</u> 452).

If the author or title is mentioned in the text, do not include it in the parenthetical reference.

> In 1987, Harrison disproved these findings in his book <u>Market Research</u> (452).

If the work cited has two or three authors, list them in the parenthetical reference.

> These are the key factors identified for sales success (Baier and Dugan, 38).
>
> The methodology has been questioned for several reasons (Danus, Smith, and Barnes, 231).

For works written by more than three authors, list the first author and follow it with *et al.* (*and others*).

> "The most practical model has five principal functions" (Franck et al., 45).

A reference list contains items cited in the text.

2. List of Works Cited All your sources should appear alphabetically at the end of your paper in a section entitled "Works Cited." The following examples illustrate the format for some of the most common types of references.

A Book by a Single Author

> Barker, Roger G. <u>Ecological Psychology</u>. Stanford: Stanford UP, 1968.
>
> Lawrence, D. H. <u>Selected Poems</u>. New York: Viking, 1972.

If you cite more than one entry by the same author, use three hyphens instead of repeating the author's name.

> Lewis, C. S. <u>Out of the Silent Planet</u>. New York: Macmillan, 1965.
>
> ---. <u>That Hideous Strength</u>. New York: Macmillan, 1975.

A Book by Two or More Authors

> Lange, Oskar, and Fred M. Taylor. <u>On the Economic Theory of Socialism</u>. New York: McGraw, 1975.
>
> Nie, Norman H., et al. <u>Statistical Packages for the Social Sciences</u>. New York: McGraw, 1975.

An Edited Work

> Robert Ferber, ed. <u>Research Methods in Economics and Business</u>. New York: Macmillan, 1962.

A Multivolume Work

Hansen, M. H., et al. Sample Survey Methods and Theory.
    2 vols. New York: John Wiley, 1953. Vol. 1.

The Foreword, Preface, or Afterword of a Book

Rosenthal, M. L. Foreword. <u>Selected Poems and Two Plays of</u>
    <u>William Butler Yeats</u>. New York: Macmillan, 1962, v–vi.

An Article in a Scholarly Journal

Belk, Russell W. "Situational Variables and Consumer Behavior."
    <u>Journal of Consumer Research</u>, 40 (1975): 302–309.

An Article in a Magazine

Bordewich, Fergus M. "Education: Mortal Fears." <u>The Atlantic</u>
    Feb. 1988: 30–34.

A Newspaper Article

Smith, Stan. "Fast Growth, Bad Management." <u>Washington Post</u>
    12 Dec. 1985, late ed.: B32.

A Lecture

Rothstein, Kathleen. "How to Lie With Statistics." Statistics
    Seminar, Department of Statistics, Carlman College,
    12 Nov. 1988

A Radio or Television Program

Stanford, Frederick. <u>Evening Editorial</u>. KPFO, Berkeley,
    12 June 1987.

A Film

"Where the Whales Are." <u>Discovery</u>. Dir. Freida Michaels.
    Prod. J. K. Long. A Merrimount Film. KGA, Seattle.
    6 Aug. 1972.

3. Explanatory Notes. If you wish to comment on your sources or add information that is somewhat peripheral to your paper or report, use a raised number (superscript) in your text to tell your reader that there is a note regarding the material.

> Footnotes may appear at the end of the text or the bottom of a page.

We cannot discuss discriminate analysis at length in this
paper.[1]

The notes themselves appear on a separate numbered page following the text and preceding the list of works cited. This page should be entitled "Notes." Each note should be preceded by a superscript.

[1]For more information, see Conover 198–250.

What Would You Do?

The president of Hartford College has asked that James Silverman, Director of the Athletic Office, to report on the swimming program at the college. The president believes that the administration, faculty, and students should be more aware of the team's wins and losses over the last five years, the background of the coach, assistant coach, and best swimmers, as well as of other key information regarding the team.

The president would also like the report to include recommendations from swimmers and coaches as to how the swimming program at the college could be improved.

James does not know how to go about writing this formal report. Write him a memo outlining procedures you think he should perform before writing a first draft of the report.

Summary

Formal reports are an important part of the communication flow in most organizations. While any subject area may be the basis for formal reports, they are most commonly written to describe and analyze problems and situations.

The writing style of formal reports is less personal than that of many other business documents. Formal report components and documentation are generally organized and presented according to standard guidelines.

Terms to Remember

Addendum (plural **addenda**): material at the back of a document, following the body

Appendix: additional material such as correspondence or survey data put at the back of a document so it will not interfere with the flow of text in the report body

Bibliography: list of secondary research materials alphabetized by author (or by title if the document is anonymous)

Documentation: information on the sources used in the creation of a document. Footnotes, bibliographies, and reference lists provide documentation in many reports

Footnote: a numbered note, corresponding with a superscript number in the text, that provides additional information or documentation

Glossary: alphabetized list of words and definitions

Prefatory material: the cover, title page, table of contents, and other materials preceding the body of the text

Reference list: documentation method used in many business reports. The list, alphabetized by author, includes every secondary source referred to in the text of the report.

Formal Report Checklist

Writing Style

- Use a straightforward, lucid writing style for formal reports.

    _____ Avoid using first-person pronouns.

    _____ Use concrete language.

    _____ Back up analyses with provable data.

    _____ Avoid passive sentences and roundabout constructions.

    _____ Use readings and graphic aids to help your reader locate and understand key points.

Prefatory Material

- Put the report title, author's name, and company name on the report cover.

- Use a title fly with only the report title in very formal reports.

- If you choose to insert a letter of transmittal, put it before or after the title page.

- Include the title page with the report title, author's name and title as well as the recipient's name and title.

- Include copies of letters of transmittal and acceptance for government reports and some business reports.

- Develop a table of contents and perhaps also a table of illustrations after writing the whole report.

- After writing the report, develop an abstract summarizing the key points of the report.

Report Body

- Introduce the report with information on the purpose, scope, and limitations of the report.

- Include an analysis section describing data you found.

- Put conclusions and recommendations (if any) at the end of the report body.

Addenda

- Include in addenda any lengthy documents or materials only indirectly related to main points of the report.

- Add an alphabetized glossary if the report contains many words a reader might not understand.

- Put maps, questionnaires, tables, correspondence, and so on in appendixes.

- Document secondary sources in reference sections.

- Add an alphabetized index only for lengthy reports and for those that will be published.

Typing

- Center type on the page with one-inch margins all around.

- If report is to be bound on the left leave an extra half-inch margin on the left; if it is to be bound on the top, leave an extra half-inch on the top.

- Use a standard layout for the title page and table of contents.

- If report is double-spaced, indent each paragraph five spaces.

- If report is single-spaced, do not indent each paragraph but double-space between paragraphs.

- Use conventional methods for distinguishing first-, second-, and third-level headings.

Pagination

- Use lowercase Roman numerals for pages preceding the text of the report.

- Do not paginate the title page but begin the next page with ii.

- Use Arabic numbers beginning with 1 for the body of the report.

- For left-bound reports, put numbers in the top right-hand corner in line with right-hand margin.

- For top-bound reports, center numbers at the bottom of the page.

Documentation

- Use documentation to give credit to secondary sources and to provide credibility for your report.

- For most business reports and business journals, use a documentation method in which references are inserted into the body of the text and an alphabetized list of references used appears at the end of the report.

Summary Discussion: Tim Baskins' Formal Report from Case in Point, p. 377

Tim should not listen to his friend Jill. The looks of a formal report do matter: he should research formal report guidelines before he begins writing about his project.

His final draft should be written in a fairly formal, impersonal style since he is writing for the upper management of two companies. While describing his project, he should retain an objective and logical tone but choose words his readers will understand. It is important that he distinguish between fact and opinion, document any secondary sources he has used, and include any primary data that will be useful to the readers.

Before making final copies of the report, Tim should make sure the typing is in accordance with report conventions and that the final product is readable, attractive, and professional looking.

Questions for Review and Discussion

1. Why is it important to follow the standard conventions for writing formal reports?
2. Why is there so much repetition of key material in many formal reports?
3. Why is an impersonal style popular in formal reports?
4. Why do you think the use of in-text references has become so popular in business reports?
5. Why are both footnotes and bibliographies required for some business reports and other types of writing?

Exercises

1. Request a copy of a formal report from a local business. Then write an analysis of the report that answers the following questions:
   a. What are the components of the report?
   b. What is the scope and purpose of the report?
   c. For what audience was the report intended?
   d. How effective is the physical presentation (layout, cover, printing, and so on)?
   e. How effective is the writing in the report?
   f. Is there anything that you feel is missing from the report?
2. Plan a report assessing the attitudes of students, instructors, and administrators toward one course in your school. The report will be written for the information of all three groups.
   a. Write a brief proposal outlining your methodology for the report. You may include
      (1) Reasons for choosing this one course to write about
      (2) A questionnaire you have developed for each group
      (3) Your plans for sampling the populations involved
      (4) Any sources for secondary research
      (5) A sample outline
   b. Write a formal report to convey the information you derived from your research
3. Using primary and secondary sources, write a formal report on one of the following general

topics. (You may narrow the topic as you work on it.)

a. A marketing plan for your college
b. The rise or decline of crime in your local area
c. The use of computers to improve business writing
d. The forecast for homebuying in your city
e. A plan to increase student participation in campus activities
f. A comparison of the grading systems used by your college and that of a nearby school
g. An analysis of the employment situation of recent graduates from your school
h. An analysis of two major texts used in an introductory accounting, business communication, or economics course in your school
i. A comparison of the campus housing at your college and at a similar college
j. A comparison of two word processing programs in terms of their usefulness for business writing
k. An evaluation of employee turnover at a company where you work or have worked
l. Recommendations to lower shoplifting in a store where you work
m. An analysis of the most common communication problems encountered by employees and managers in a company
n. An analysis of problems most frequently encountered by incoming freshmen at your college

4. Write the report that the college president requested James Silverman to write (see page 400). Use your own college or university swimming team for the project.

Word Processing Exercises: Tabs and Windows

I. Tabs have many uses, but they are particularly helpful for typing tables as they allow you to set up columns on your page.

1. Check your manual for the commands to set tabs. Now create a file called TABLE.
2. Type in this table using the following directions:

```
        TABLE 1. ITEMS ORDERED
ITEM    DESCRIPTION    PRICE    QUANTITY
145     pens           2.95        15
235     disks          5.90        25
654     pads           2.00        30
567     tape           1.97        34
```

3. UNDERLINE and CENTER the title.
4. Set tabs in columns 1, 8, 35, and 42. (With most programs, columns are marked at the top of the screen.)
5. Type in the four headings. Use the TAB command to move the cursor to each column.
6. Type in each line of the chart using the TAB command.
7. SAVE the file and PRINT it.
8. If the table has been typed correctly, enter the command to clear the tabs you created.

II. Some word processing programs have a WINDOWING or SPLIT SCREEN capability that enables you to see a file other than the one you are editing. Thus, you can check the data in one memo while writing another or scroll through the file containing your report while you are writing the report summary.

By doing this exercise, you will learn to create a table of contents for a report by using a window. (We have assumed that you have already written a report and saved it on a disk.)

1. Create a file named TOC. This will contain your table of contents.
2. SPLIT your screen so one window shows you the text of the report you have already written.
3. SCROLL through the report. As you come to major and minor headings in the report, type them into the table of contents. Use the same wording for the headings that you used in the report.
4. Once you have printed both the report and the table of contents, check to make sure the table accurately lists each section of the report and gives the correct page number.

Report Graphics

Objectives

To learn the uses of graphics in reports

To choose appropriate graphics for your data and purpose

To develop effective tables, graphs, and charts

17

Roy Corell's Report Graphics

In his first job out of college, Roy Corell began working as an assistant to the marketing director of a toy manufacturing company, JRT Incorporated, in Columbus, Ohio. One of Roy's first assignments was to draft a report from data supplied by his boss, Hal Brighton.

In one section of the report, Roy wanted to compare sales figures for two products his firm has been manufacturing since 1984—Muscleman Robot and Huggable Honey Bear. The first draft of one paragraph read like this:

In 1984, when Muscleman Robot and Huggable
Honey Bear first came out, we sold almost equal
numbers of both: 4,000 of each toy. The next year,
we sold many more Muscleman Robots: 6,500 of
them and only 2,300 Huggable Honey Bears.
We doubled production of the robots and sold 8,000
in 1986, but sales of Huggable Honey Bears
dropped to 1,500. We decided to increase advertising
for the Honey Bears in 1987: that year we sold over

4,000 of them. Sales for Muscleman Robots came
to only 6,500 in 1987.

When Roy showed this section of the report to his boss, Hal laughed.

"You're wasting your readers' time, Roy. Don't *write* about all those figures. Put them in a graph or table of some kind."

"But I don't know what type of visual aid to use. And how can I make it accurate and professional looking?"

"Get Linda to help you," Hal told him. "She's great with graphics."

Points to Consider
- Why should Roy's information be presented visually?
- What type of graphic would work best for Roy's data?
- How can he make the visual aid professional looking?

Communicating Through Graphics

When you first sit down to read a book with drawings or photographs scattered through the text, you may find yourself flipping through to glance at the illustrations before you read the words. We are drawn to pictures, as every reader of a newspaper's comic strips will tell you. Graphics play a major part in many types of business writing because they interest readers— and because they are extremely versatile media for conveying many types of data.

Ranging from tables and graphs to charts, photographs, drawings, diagrams, and computer-generated images, graphics serve a multitude of uses in business writing.

Graphics are also gaining in popularity. As increasing amounts of information come across the desks of managers, they are finding graphic summaries increasingly helpful. And now that generating graphics on computers has become easier, even the least artistic of report writers can produce effective and useful graphic aids.

Graphics Increase Interest and Readability

Graphics break up the text of a report or other piece of writing, creating a visual impact. Graphics are useful when you want to add interest to the written page. (Note how frequently graphics are used in business publications such as *Business Week*.)

Moreover, graphics enhance readability. Whereas paragraphs full of figures may be painful to read, for example, a graph with the same figures may actually be enjoyable to look at.

Test Your Skills

Which Graphic Would You Choose?

Choose the answer that best fits the type of graphic you would choose.

1. You are writing a report for upper management on the effects of changing oil prices on your company's sales. To show the trends in sales over the past six years, you use
   a. a pie graph
   b. a chart
   c. a line graph

2. You are writing a story about imported car sales for a popular magazine. To show the dramatic increase in imports from 1960 to the present, you use

   a. a pictogram with symbols of cars stacked on one another
   b. a segmented bar graph
   c. a flow chart

Discussion

1. A pie graph shows proportions, not trends. A chart simply lists data, so readers have to work out trends for themselves. A line graph depicts trends effectively. Best answer: 1c.

2. A segmented bar graph is not appropriate when you are illustrating only one variable, and a flow chart cannot show sales trends. Pictograms are effective in stories such as this one for a magazine. Best answer: 2a.

Graphics Emphasize and Support Major Concepts

Graphics are versatile tools for summarizing data.

If you glance through your college texts, you will probably find that many of the most important concepts are highlighted in tables, graphs, illustrations, or even cartoons. Because readers tend to remember data that is presented visually, both textbook authors and business writers find graphics useful for highlighting central points.

Graphics are also useful for providing support for major points. A graph depicting sales decreases may illustrate the industry slump a writer is describing; a table summarizing employees' answers to a questionnaire may support a writer's statement concerning employee morale.

Graphics Condense and Simplify Data

Graphics often make a report easier to read.

Probably the most important function of visual aids is their ability to present complex data in a simple, organized, and coherent manner. Whereas a writer might spend three pages summarizing employees' answers to each item on a questionnaire, a chart can summarize the results in a few square inches of space.

Graphics such as blueprints, diagrams, maps, and photographs enable readers to visualize physical objects, while graphics such as charts and graphs enable readers to visualize concepts and relationships.

Generating Graphics

To be effective, graphics must look professional.

Graphics not only add interest to a report but they also add a touch of professionalism: effective graphics help a report to look impressive. Shoddily drawn or poorly conceived graphics, however, will profoundly damage the overall impact of your work. If you cannot create a professional-looking graphic, you are better off staying solely with words.

Many companies employ graphic artists to create the visuals for reports, brochures, manuals, and other business documents. Even nonartists, however, can design effective graphics with materials from office supply and art stores: a ruler and compass, press-on numbers and letters, and graph paper can help you create many visual effects.

While computer-aided graphics used to be an area understood only by computer professionals, many graphics programs are now readily available for use on personal computers. These programs, which can design line graphs, pie graphs, bar charts, as well as other types of graphics (see four-color insert), can generate them simply from quantitative data fed in by the business writer. With computers, you can also create a wide variety of illustrations in many colors and sizes.

Placing, Identifying, and Documenting Graphics

Refer to graphics before they appear in the text.

Every graphic aid that appears in your report should be mentioned in the text. You may tell your reader to "see Figure 2" or you may simply write, "as shown in Figure 2." Refer to the graphic aid *before* its appearance in the text.

Where should your graphics appear in a report? Ideally, a graphic aid should appear as close as possible to the place in the text where it is mentioned. However, the graphic should not interfere with the flow of the text. It should be an aid, not an impediment, to the reader.

If you are using a graphic aid that takes up a half-page or less in the report, place it on the page in which it is mentioned. (But avoid making your graphic aid too small—your reader will have trouble deciphering it.) If the aid takes up a full page, place it on the page after it is mentioned. If your graphics are only of peripheral importance to your report, you may place them in an appendix.

Wherever you place your graphics, give them a heading or *caption:* a number and a title that identifies their contents. You may use consecutive Roman or Arabic numerals to number your graphics. Some writers choose to separate tables from other illustrations: they use Roman numerals for tables (Table I, Table II) and Arabic numbers for other figures (Figure 1, Figure 2).

Provide a caption for every graphic aid.

You may put captions either above or below the graphic, but be consistent throughout your report.

If you have developed the visual aid from your own data, you do not need to document the source. However, if you used any type of secondary source, it must be documented.

Source: Pfeiffer, John. "How Not to Lose the Trade Wars by Cultural Gaffes." *Smithsonian* Jan. 1988:145–156

Source: Mosher, G. *Kyoto: A Contemplative Guide*. Rutland, VT: Charles E. Tuttle Company, 208–209

This information usually appears at the bottom of the graphic aid or under the caption.

Choosing Appropriate Graphics

Tables and graphs are some of the most commonly used visual aids in reports. Before deciding which to use, consider which type will work most effectively for your readers and for the type of data you wish to convey.

Tables are more precise but less exciting than graphs.

Tables display words or numerical data in columns and rows, while graphs usually depict trends or relationships. Tables are more precise than graphs, but they are less dynamic: while a pie graph may let readers gain an overview, a table presents exact information.

If your readers want to know the average clerical worker's salary at HBG Corporation in 1986, a table will give them the answer. But if they want to know whether professional or technical employees are being paid proportionately more each year, a graph will show them the answer more effectively.

The pie graph and table depicted in Figure 17-1, for example, both illustrate the types of books sold by a small bookstore in a particular month. The pie graph shows the percentage of each type: you can see at a glance that

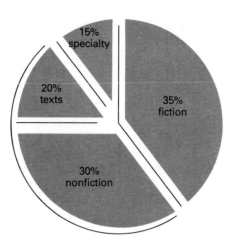

Types of books sold by
Jillie Book Company
in August 1988

Fiction	Nonfiction	Texts	Specialty
175	150	100	75

Book Sales for Jillie Book
Company, August 1988

FIGURE 17-1
Pie graph and table

specialty books make up only a small fraction of sales. The table tells you exactly how many books of each type were sold, but you have to work out the sales trends on your own.

Tables are less exciting than graphs; they are also easier to create, convey complex information clearly, and are less apt to deceive a reader. Graphs may make a report more exciting, but you have to construct them carefully so they convey the data accurately.

Checklist for Graphs and Tables

- Use a table to convey exact figures.
- Use a table to convey complex information.
- Use a table if you do not have enough time or resources to create effective graphs.
- Use a graph to convey relationships and trends.
- Use a graph if you want to convey data in an exciting way.
- Use a graph if you have the time and resources to create one that is professional-looking and accurate.

Using Tables to Summarize Data

Tables may be either informal or formal. Informal tables are incorporated right into the text of the report.

From 1985 to 1987, Denmore Corporation earned substantial profits:

1985	$2.1
1986	3.5
1987	2.8
(in millions)	

Formal tables (see Figure 17-2) are separated from the body of the text. They present more complex information than informal tables.

To set up a table, follow these procedures:

1. Make each column the same width.
2. Label each row and column. If necessary, state the units being used (i.e., *millions*).
3. If data are missing for an entry, use an em-dash (—) to fill the space.
4. If using numerical data, align the right margins of each column. If using words, align the left margins.

Mike Paulson	$43.00
Jan Franks	3.52
Timothy Whitson	123.93

5. Use vertical and horizontal lines if they will enhance readability.

TABLE 17–1 ————————————————————— ← Table number and title

Average Salaries, HBG Corporation ←

Year	Professional	Technical	Clerical	← Column headings
1986	$43,000	$35,000	$24,000	
1987	46,500	38,000	25,400	
1988	49,000	40,000	26,500	

Source: primary. ← Documentation

FIGURE 17-2 ————————————————————
Sample table

Using Graphs to Depict Relationships

When you have decided that a graph will best communicate the type of information you want to convey to your readers, you will have to decide which type of graph will be most effective. Your decision once again should be based on the type of data you have, the purpose of the graph, and your readers' needs.

Bar graphs are easy to read.

Bar graphs, pie graphs, and line graphs are some of the most common types of visual aids. Bar graphs are rectangular boxes used to show relationships over time. Line graphs reflect trends over time. Pie graphs illustrate percentages of a whole (the pie).

Bar Graphs

Bar graphs may be drawn vertically (Figure 17-3) or horizontally (Figure 17-4). They are some of the easiest graphs to understand. To avoid misrepresenting data, make sure that you mark equal intervals on your scale and that you make every bar the same width. If you group two or more bars

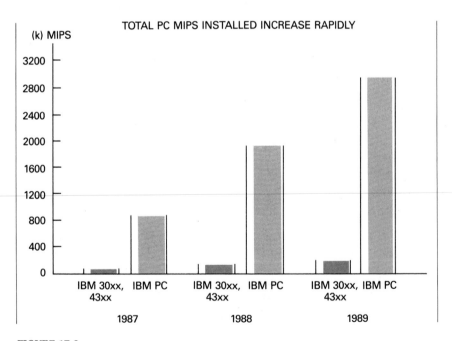

FIGURE 17-3 _____

Vertical bar graph

together, as shown in Figure 17-3, use shading, cross-hatching, or colors to differentiate the bars.

To add variety to your graphics, you may want to create a three-dimensional bar graph (Figure 17-5).

Segmented Bar Graphs

Segmented bar graphs (Figure 17-6) show various sections that make up an entity. Once again, use shading, cross-hatching, or colors to differentiate the sections of each bar. Make sure you identify each segment.

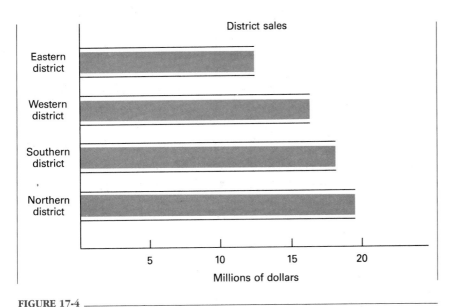

FIGURE 17-4
Horizontal bar graph

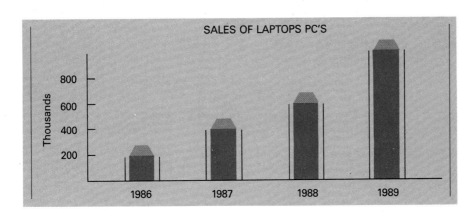

FIGURE 17-5
Three-dimensional bar graph

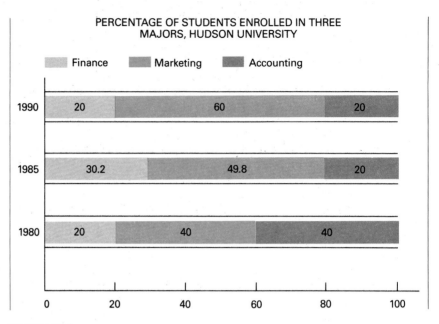

PERCENTAGE OF STUDENTS ENROLLED IN THREE MAJORS, HUDSON UNIVERSITY

FIGURE 17-6 ——————————————————————————
Segmented bar graph

A one-column segmented bar graph (Figure 17-7) may be useful if you wish to show the percentage breakdown of one item.

If you want to show negative as well as positive quantities, use a bar graph that has positive and negative values (Figure 17-8).

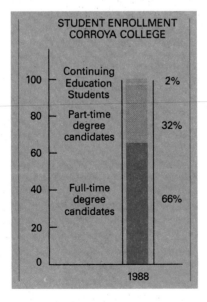

FIGURE 17-7 ——————————————————————————
One-column segmented bar graph

© A. M. Rosario, The Image Bank.

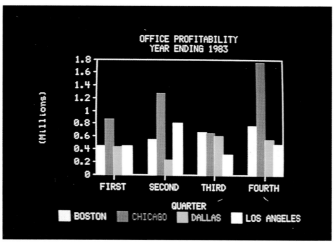

© 1983 Walter Bibikow, The Image Bank.

© A. M. Rosario, The Image Bank.

Computers may be used to generate standard two-dimensional graphs with the enhancements of colors or icons to differentiate the various functions.

© 1980 Nicholas Foster, The Image Bank.

© Luis Veiga, The Image Bank.

The computer allows the user to make a greater impact with certain graphs by giving them a three-dimensional or nonlinear form.

© 1983 Walter Bibikow, The Image Bank.

© 1985 Bill Varie, The Image Bank.

© Michael Tcherevkoff, The Image Bank.

© 1986 Bill Varie, The Image Bank.

Computer-aided design software allows the user either to translate data into visual images or actually to "draw" on the screen with a stylus and touch sensitive pad.

© Robert Kristofik, The Image Bank.

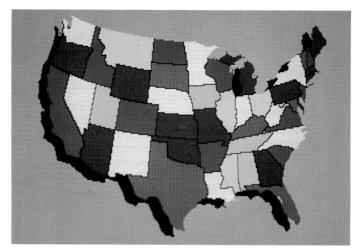

© A. M. Rosario, The Image Bank.

Possibilities for the
business writer using
computers include maps,
visual representations
of nonvisual events
(such as a heartbeat),
and a variety of design
options (such as logos).

© A. M. Rosario, The Image Bank.

DATACORP'S PROFITS AND LOSSES
(IN MILLIONS)

FIGURE 17-8 _____

Bar graph with positive and negative values

Line Graphs

Line graphs are particularly useful for showing changes over time (See Figure 17-9). Units of time are usually shown on the horizontal axis, while dollar amounts or other data are shown on the vertical axis.

Line graphs show changes over time.

To make an effective line graph, you may want to use graph paper—paper marked with boxes of equal size. Start the vertical axis at zero and mark off equal intervals in appropriate units.

Be sure to choose units that will effectively suit the data being presented. In Figure 17-10, for example, two graphs present the same data on different scales. Since the yearly employee turnover never exceeded 100, the top graph does not represent the proportional changes as accurately as the bottom one.

Like bar graphs, line graphs may be set up to present positive and negative values (Figure 17-11).

Multiple Line Graphs

Multiple line graphs (Figure 17-12) compare two or more items over the same time period. To differentiate the entities, use different colors or solid and broken lines. Avoid using too many lines: you will end up confusing your readers instead of assisting them.

Pie Graphs

Pie graphs are useful when you want to represent the parts of a whole at one point in time (Figure 17-13). Usually pie charts begin at the 12 o'clock position and move clockwise, with the first slice being the largest and the rest appearing in descending order. Make sure to label each slice.

Pie graphs show parts of a whole at one point in time.

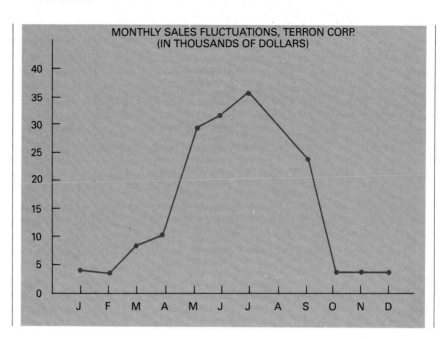

FIGURE 17-9
Line graph

Developing Charts and Miscellaneous Graphic Aids

Tables and graphs make up only a portion of the visual aids used in business reports. You may find that your report would benefit from organizational charts, flow charts, floor plans, pictograms, photographs, maps, or a wide variety of other graphics.

Organizational Charts

Organizational charts depict the hierarchy of authority within an organization or part of an organization (Figure 17-14). Organizational charts are set up with the highest authority at the top. Solid lines indicate direct lines of authority; dashed lines indicate advisory status.

Flow Charts

Flow charts usually illustrate procedures.

Flow charts are used primarily to illustrate procedures. They may "flow" from top to bottom (Figure 17-15) or from left to right (Figure 17-16).

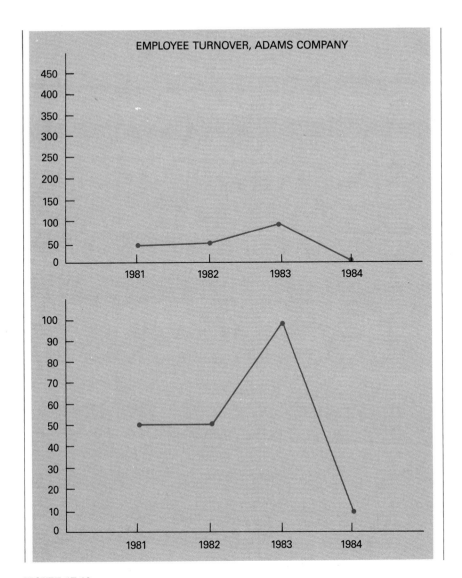

FIGURE 17-10 _____

Two line graphs showing the same information on different scales

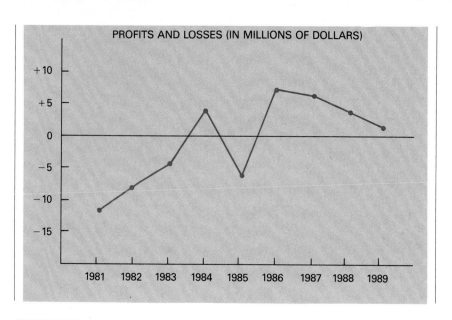

FIGURE 17-11

Positive/negative line graph

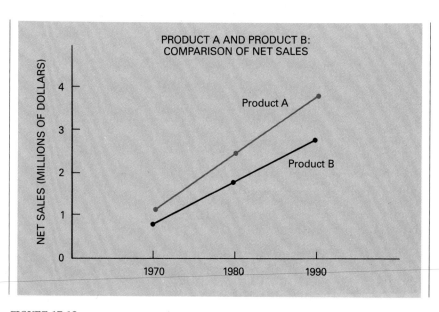

FIGURE 17-12

Multiple line graph

FIGURE 17-13
Pie graphs

FIGURE 17-14
Organizational chart

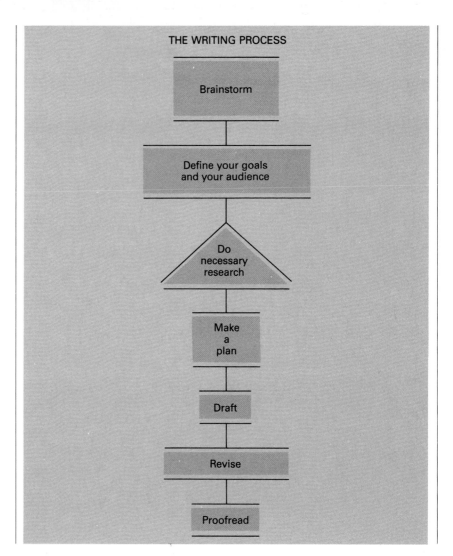

FIGURE 17-15
Flow chart

Floor Plans

Floor plans are maps showing the interior of a building or part of a building (Figure 17-17). Floor plans should show the shape of each major room or section and the relationship of one part to another. Depending on the circumstances, information such as room sizes, electrical outlets, and furniture placement is indicated in a floor plan.

Pictograms

In a pictogram, symbols are used to represent numbers of people or items. Drawings of shoes are used to indicate the number of shoes manufactured,

FIGURE 17-16
Flow chart

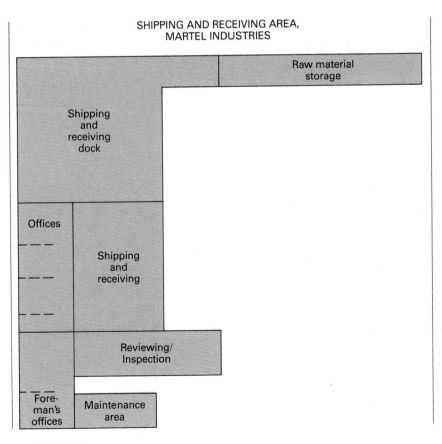

FIGURE 17-17
Floor plan

for example. Quantities are indicated by the numbers of symbols used (Figure 17-18).

Sometimes graphic artists use a larger size item to indicate a larger quantity, but this approach can seriously distort the data.

Pictograms are used more frequently in magazines than in reports.

Pictograms should be used to present fairly simple information to readers who want an overview rather than exact data. Because they are designed to attract the reader's attention, pictograms are used extensively in magazine and newspaper articles. They are less useful in reports.

Photographs

Photographs provide readers with pictures of people and things "as they really are." Now that high-quality copiers can reproduce photographs with increasing effectiveness, photographs are being used more frequently in business documents.

Maps

Maps are useful for illustrating a variety of geographical information. Areas can be highlighted in different colors, and captions or drawings may be superimposed on various parts of the map. For example, a map of the United States might have pictures of agricultural products superimposed on farming areas and pictures of factories on industrial areas.

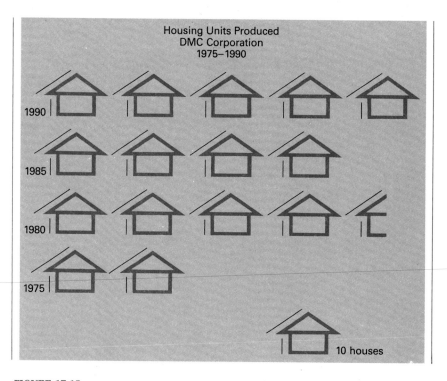

FIGURE 17-18
Pictogram

What Would You Do?

Brian Jenner has tabulated Tarey Hardware's sales for small appliances, housewares, and gardening equipment over a five-year period.

	Small Appliances	Housewares	Gardening equipment
1989	$100,000	$64,000	$16,000
1988	92,000	65,000	17,000
1987	89,000	62,000	18,500
1986	79,500	61,000	19,000
1985	75,000	56,000	22,500

Now Brian wants to show sales trends over these years. Design an effective graphic aid for him.

Overcoming Problems with Graphics

Graphics are a useful addition to many reports. However, graphics can also be distracting, confusing, and even deceptive. Consider these questions before incorporating a graphic aid in your business document.

- Does the graphic enhance, document, or clarify the written text? Avoid using graphics simply to make your report look more impressive or professional; if they do not serve a useful function, they will be irritating rather than appealing to your reader.
- Does the graphic simplify the written text? Avoid packing too much information into one graph or chart. A line graph with six lines, for instance, may be more confusing than a written explanation.
- Does the graphic represent the data fairly? As you saw in Figure 17-10, the same data can look quite different when presented on different scales: in the top graph, the changes in employee turnover appear minimal, whereas in the bottom graph, there appears to have been a drastic change in 1983 and 1984.

To avoid deception, make sure your vertical axis on graphs begins at zero (unless it is a positive and negative graph). Construct pie graphs so that the slices correctly depict the correct percentage of the whole, and make sure the width of each bar in a bar graph is the same.

Keep graphics simple and present data fairly.

Summary

Graphics can aid readability and add professionalism to business reports. However, they should be created with care so they highlight rather than distort data. They should be identified with captions and documented.

Tables and graphs, the most common types of report graphics, are used for different purposes. Tables provide the reader with exact data but do not summarize trends or relationships. Graphs, which do show trends and relationships, are more dynamic but less precise.

A whole range of graphics, including maps, photographs, and various types of charts, may also emphasize, support, and highlight concepts in a report.

Report Graphic Checklist

- Use graphics to increase interest and readability in your reports as well as to highlight and condense key information.

- Make sure your graphics are accurate and professional-looking.

- Mention each graphic in the text of the report.

Placement, Identification, Documentation

- Place each important graphic as close as possible to the place in the text where it is mentioned; place less relevant graphics in an appendix.

- Identify graphic aids with a number and a heading.

- Document every graphic aid obtained from a secondary source.

Tables

- Use tables when

  _____ you need to display precise data or complex data

  _____ you do not have the time or resources to create other professional-looking graphics

  _____ an eyecatching graphic is not essential

- To create a table, do the following:

  _____ Set up columns of equal width across the page.

  _____ Divide the columns into as many rows as you need.

  _____ Label each row and column.

  _____ For numbers, align the right margin of each column.

  _____ For words, align the left margin of each column.

- Incorporate an informal table into your text if the information is fairly simple. Informal tables should not be labeled.

- Set off formal tables from the body of your text.

_____ Use vertical and horizontal lines in tables to enhance readability.

_____ Provide a number and heading for each table.

Graphs

• Use graphs when you

_____ want to illustrate relationships and trends rather than precise data

_____ want to convey data in an exciting way

_____ have the time and resources to create professional-looking graphs

Bar Graphs

• Use bar graphs to show relationships over time.

• Make sure each bar is the same width.

• If bars are drawn together, use colors or cross-hatching to differentiate them.

• Use segmented bar graphs to illustrate the parts that make up an entity. Colors or cross-hatching should differentiate the sections of each bar.

• Label each bar and segment.

Line Graphs

• Use line graphs to show changes over time.

• To create a line graph.

_____ draw lines indicating horizontal and vertical axes

_____ start vertical axis at zero and mark off units of equal size

_____ if necessary, mark off negative as well as positive values

_____ use horizontal axis to represent equal units of time

_____ choose units that effectively represent the data you are illustrating

_____ draw lines indicating the changes over time

_____ to avoid confusion, limit the number of lines on each line graph

_____ label each line

Pie Graphs

- Use pie graphs to represent parts of a whole.
- Develop pie graphs clockwise with the largest slice at 12 o'clock.
- Label each slice.

Pictograms

- Develop pictograms for simple information that you want to convey in an interesting manner.
- Use relevant symbols to indicate quantities of people or items.
- Use different numbers of these symbols to indicate the respective quantities being described.

Charts and Other Graphic Aids

- Use organizational charts to show the hierarchy of authority in an organization.
- Use flow charts to illustrate the movement of people or things.
- Use floor plans to illustrate the interior of a building.
- Use photographs to depict people and things as they really are.
- Use maps to illustrate a variety of geographical data.

Terms to Remember

Bar graph: diagram designed so that the height or length of rectangular boxes shows relationships over time. The boxes may be set up vertically or horizontally on a page.

Flow chart: diagram of the movement of people or things. Flow charts may depict a set of procedures, for example.

Graph: diagram showing the relationship between two variables. Usually each variable is measured along one of a pair of axes at right angles to one another.

Line graph: diagram in which lines indicate changes. Usually the horizontal axis depicts time while the horizontal axis depicts dollar amounts or other data.

Organizational chart: diagram depicting the hierarchy of authority within an organization

Pictogram: diagram in which symbols such as stick figures or dollar signs are used to represent numbers of people or items

Pie graph: circle graph in which an entire "pie" represents a whole entity, and "slices" show the respective size of each part at one point in time

Segmented bar graph: diagram in which each bar is divided into sections illustrating various parts of an entire entity. Colors or cross-hatching differentiate the different sections.

Table: list of numbers or facts systematically arranged in columns and rows

Summary Discussion: Roy Corell's Report Graphics from Case in Point, p. 406

Graphics would simplify the sales information that Roy is putting into his report. Graphics would also help to make sense out of the figures. Right now, he merely lists figures; we cannot easily see trends or relationships. Roy should still *analyze* the sales figures in words, but he need not list all the sales figures in sentences.

His choice of a table or graph will depend on the point of his report and his readers' interests. He may choose to summarize sales information in two ways: a table giving exact sales figures from 1984 to the present and a graph showing the sales trends for the two items over the years.

A professional-looking table can be created on a typewriter or word processor. An experienced graphic artist can create a professional-looking graph. However, a computer graphics program could also create a graph easily from the data Roy provides.

Questions for Review and Discussion

1. When would a pie graph be more useful than a line graph? Why?
2. If you have a graphic aid that takes up less than half a page, where should it be placed in your report?
3. If you are creating a line graph to illustrate sales figures over a period of three years, which axis should be used for the sales figures?
4. How can a graphic aid be deceptive?
5. Why are pictograms used more frequently in magazines than in reports?
6. What graphic aid would you use to illustrate the following information? Why?

a. The hierarchy of authority in a hospital
b. The fluctuations in the average price of houses in your area over the past ten years
c. the number of students who have dropped out of your college each year since 1985
d. The procedures for applying for a government-funded student loan
e. The sales of textbooks versus the sales of general trade books of one publishing company over three years
f. The percentage of textbooks, general trade hardback books, and general trade paperback books of one publishing company at one point in time

1. Create a graph to illustrate the data in Roy Corell's paragraph at the beginning of this chapter. Then create a table showing the same data.

2. Create a visual aid that depicts the following data:

   In 1984, we purchased 100 heaters and 50 air conditioners, while in 1983 we purchased only 75 heaters and 25 air conditioners. In 1986, 130 heaters were purchased, but only 20 air conditioners were purchased. In 1987 and 1988, we purchased 125 air conditioners each year and 150 heaters.

3. Create a visual aid depicting the following data:

   Mr. Simmons, vice-president, reports directly to Pat Forbes, president of ACI. Under Mr. Simmons are four division managers: Alice Kehoe, Division A; Gerry Warton, Division B; Ilda Greene, Division C; and Fred Varen, Division D.

4. This year, Herborn Corporation estimates that it will sell a million dollars worth of its products. Of this amount, 50 percent will come from sales of small appliances; 12 percent will come from sales of office supplies; 20 percent will come from sales of large appliances. The remaining sales will be from miscellaneous products. Construct a graphic aid that effectively depicts this information.

5. Greg Reimer wants to create a visual aid to compare his average monthly expenses this year and last year. Create the graphic aid for him.

   Greg knows that he spent $400 per month for rent this year and $350 per month last year. His food costs rose from $200 a month last year to $275 this year. His utilities remained steady at $55 per month. His gasoline costs dropped from $50 last year to $45 this year, but his entertainment costs rose from $65 last year to $90 this year. Clothing and other expenses came to $95 this year but only $55 last year.

6. The following chart shows the yearly sales figures achieved by four salespeople from 1982 to 1985:

	1982	1983	1984	1985
Henry	$20,000	$25,000	$34,000	$29,000
Gail	19,000	27,000	33,000	34,000
Freida	23,000	31,000	40,000	35,000
Fran	17,000	23,000	23,000	29,000

   Prepare a graph depicting the same data.

7. Prepare a graph or chart that effectively depicts the following data:

   In the graduating class from Thompson College, 44 percent of the students are humanities majors; 25 percent are social science majors: 15 percent are business majors; 10 percent are science majors. The remaining percentage have individual majors.

8. Prepare a graphic aid that effectively depicts one of the following:
   a. How to change a tire on an automobile
   b. The floor plan of your house or apartment
   c. The levels of authority in the company for which you work

9. Write a short informational report on the computer programs currently available that would be most practical for creating report graphics. You will want to focus on specific criteria such as

   • Program costs
   • The types of graphics that can be generated
   • Ease of use
   • Types of computers with which they can be used
   • The quality of the graphics produced

Write a short informational report to a colleague who plans to use the same word processing program and equipment that you use. Assume that the reader will be writing letters, memos, and reports and that he or she has a basic understanding of terms such as disk, printer, and video screen and of the major keys on the keyboard.

The report should cover these areas:

1. An overview of the strong points of this word processing system.

2. A summary of any weaknesses you have encountered.

3. A description of at least four of the word processing capabilities you have found particularly useful. You might describe, for example, the benefits of windowing, search and replace commands, block moves, and subscripts and superscripts.

Your report should be formatted according to these guidelines:

1. Make a title page according to the format described on page 382 of this text. Center the title. Do not number the title page.

2. Begin paginating with the first page of the report body: this page should be page 1. Put the numbers at the top right-hand corner of each page.

3. Double-space the body of the report. Indent each paragraph. Justify the right-hand margins.

4. Include at least one footnote in the report. (For example, you might quote from your computer manual.) Use superscripts for footnote notation. Include footnote references on a separate sheet at the end of the report.

5. Include at least three major headings. Underline these headings and center them.

6. When you have edited the report, run it through a spell-check program if one is available.

7. Print the report on continuous form paper.

8. Edit and proofread one more time.

9. Print the report on individual sheets of paper.

Part 5 Mini-Cases

5-1. Paula Levinson founded her company, Amber Skin Products, in 1981. Specializing in creams created from natural products for both men and women, the company has always catered to college-educated people between 25 and 45 years old who live in the New England area. While not exactly a household word, Amber Skin Products developed a small, staunch following. The products were sold in health-food stores, through a small sales brochure, and door-to-door.

Paula Levinson started out working on the principle that good products would bring good customers; she never developed much advertising, ventured out of her New England locale, or worked on varying her initial product line. Nonetheless, her business grew steadily. Now the situation is changing. With both small and major cosmetic companies getting into natural products, Amber's sales have been increasing only slightly.

Total Sales for Amber Skin Products

1985	$1,790,000	1988	$2,925,000
1986	2,230,000	1989	2,935,000
1987	2,910,000		

Some of Paula's managers at Amber feel some changes must be made.

a. As head of the Research and Development team at Amber, you feel certain that the company's limited product line is having a negative effect on sales. At this point, Amber sells only six products:

Herbal Facial Scrub	Apricot Soap
Citrus-Aloe Cleanser	Sesame Talc
Natural Skin Toner	Peppermint Moisturizer

You write a proposal addressed to Paula Levinson, President, recommending that current and past customers be surveyed on whether they would like to see a fuller line of Amber products. At the same time, find out what they like and do not like about Amber products as they are now.

Surveys would be sent to customers who have ordered products through Amber's mail-order and door-to-door services. Approximately 5,000 surveys would be sent out.

Your proposal should explain the background to the situation, describe why mail surveys would be the best way to get customer data, and estimate costs of the project. Include a graph of sales trends and a sample questionnaire.

b. As one of the salespeople for Amber Skin Products, you believe that the company should be targeting a bigger group of people. Particularly, you feel, women and men under 25 would be attracted to the products, which are comparable in price to standard brands sold in drug stores but have natural ingredients and intriguing textures and scents.

From your experience, however, few people under 25 have ever heard of Amber products. You are worried that Amber products are not going to younger people who could become lifelong users. Moreover, Amber is missing out on a large segment of the population that tends to be attracted to unusual products.

Write a recommendation report to the head of the marketing department, Randy Connor, suggesting that the company consider marketing the products to women and men aged 18 to 25 years. Base your report on demographic data on the number of people in your proposed age range and their income levels. If possible, include psychographic data on the trends followed by that group in recent years.

To back up your assertions about Amber Skin Products, summarize an informal survey you conducted over a six-week period while selling Amber Products door-to-door. Of the 600 people you spoke with, 200 were under 25. Of those, only 45 had ever heard of Amber. Of the 400 people over 25, nearly 300 had heard of Amber.

c. As a result of the surveys sent to past and present Amber customers (see 5-1a, above), the product development team has come out with a line requested by thousands of those surveyed: Amber Sun Screens. These natural products range from a light protecting cream to one that almost fully blocks harmful rays from the skin.

As head of the marketing team, you would like top management to approve an intensive research effort to decide how and where this new line of products should be marketed. Write a report recommending a two-part research effort:

1. A primary research effort in which people from different age groups who use natural products would be brought together in focus groups: informal gatherings in which they would talk about

what they are looking for in summer skincare products and the types of promotion that appeal to them.

2. A secondary research effort in which researchers would compile data on the promotional efforts of similar companies and, as much as possible, track their sales trends and target buyers.

Your report should include a timeframe for these efforts and summarize major costs. To be persuasive, you may want to mention the company's growing problems with competition and sales.

d. As head of the marketing team, you have been working on the research project (see 5-1c, above) approved by top management. The team has conducted two out of five projected focus groups and has begun the secondary research.

Write a progress report to Germaine Guill, vice-president of Amber, explaining what has been accomplished so far, what trends you are seeing, what you plan to do next, and when you expect to have the project completed.

The ten people in the first group, who were aged 18 to 24, wanted products that would protect their skin while also letting them get a basic light tan. Ingredients and price were less important than the colors and scents. Product packaging and innovative product ideas were important to them. They tended to buy products they saw advertised on television.

The ten men and women in the second group, aged 25 to 45, were concerned about keeping their skin young-looking. A tan was less important to them. Price was not terribly important, but the ingredients were. They tended to buy products advertised in magazines.

In your report, make sure you do not make recommendations or jump to conclusions; just provide information for your reader. Develop at least one graphic aid illustrating the trends your team spotted during the first two focus groups.

5-2. You are the executive director of a nonprofit organization, Dramatic Action, that coordinates most of the theater groups in your city. The organization is supported by grants from local businesses and donations from individuals.

Every six months, you have to develop a formal report for the board of directors, fifteen influential people who support the arts in your area. The report summarizes

1. The activities that have taken place in the six-month period
2. The personnel changes that have happened or are needed

3. Problems that have arisen
4. Plans for the next six months

For this report, you want to inform the readers that your organization has coordinated publicity for four productions:

Natural Graces by the Women's Theater Group
Towing the Line: A Comedy by Mel Ray's Acting Troupe
Life in a Northern Suburb by Thorne
Winning the Lottery by RT Mime Group

Your staff developed flyers for these productions, advertised them in the bulletin published by your organization, and sent announcements to public radio and television stations.

You are pleased to announce that all the productions were successful. Three of them are still running after five months. *Life in a Northern Suburb* closed after a two-month run.

The only staffing problem you have encountered is with your clerical assistant, who has decided to return to college. You will be advertising for a new assistant.

Right now you can have only a part-time clerical assistant who is paid minimum wage. To get and retain a good worker, you would like to have a full-time assistant who is paid an adequate salary. In the next grant proposal that you send to local businesses, you would like to include that staffing change. You hope the board of directors will approve the change.

The only real problem that has evolved in the last six months has been a leak in the roof of your facility, which is a renovated theater. So far the leak has been patched at minimal cost. However, the rains could make a new roof necessary. In the next six months, you hope to meet with the board to decide whether to add a new roof or move to a more modern and convenient facility.

In the next six months, too, you will be developing a major fundraising effort. This will involve developing proposals to be sent to twenty organizations in the area and setting up the yearly Dramatic Action White Elephant Sale, which usually brings in over $6,000 in one weekend.

Your report should be written in a formal style and have the following components:

1. A title page
2. A table of contents
3. A summary
4. An introduction
5. A body with at least three sections
6. At least one graphic aid
7. A conclusion

Add any other information or details you think would make the report more effective.

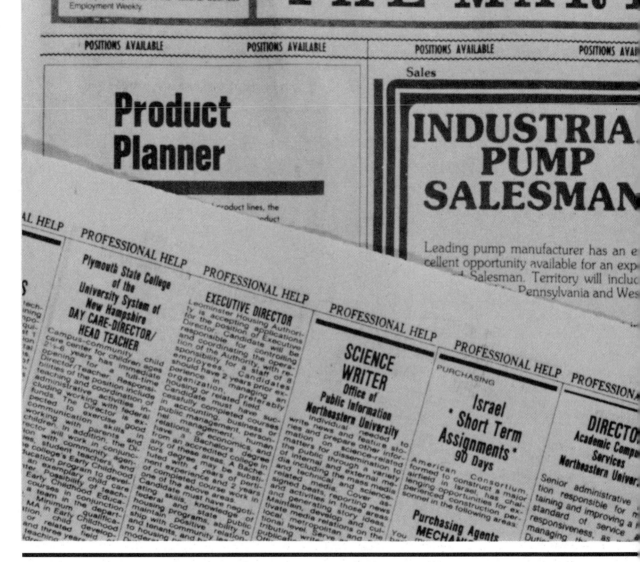

CLASSIFIED ADVERTISIN

THE MART

POSITIONS AVAILABLE   POSITIONS AVAILABLE   POSITIONS AVAILABLE   POSITIONS AVAI

Product Planner

'roduct lines, the
duct

Sales

INDUSTRIA
PUMP
SALESMAN

Leading pump manufacturer has an e
cellent opportunity available for an exp
Salesman. Territory will includ
Pennsylvania and Wes

AL HELP   PROFESSIONAL HELP   PROFESSIONAL HELP   PROFESSIONAL HELP   PROFESSIONAL HELP   PROFESSION

Plymouth State College of the University System of New Hampshire DAY CARE-DIRECTOR/HEAD TEACHER

EXECUTIVE DIRECTOR

SCIENCE WRITER Office of Public Information Northeastern University

PURCHASING
Israel * Short Term Assignments * 90 Days

Purchasing Agents MECHA

DIRECTOR Academic Comp Services Northeastern Univer

Employment
Communications

Part Six

The Employment Process

- **Looking for the perfect job**
- **Understanding the process**
- **Using a wide range of communication skills**
- **Analyzing yourself**
- **Researching career fields and job opportunities**
- **Organizing your materials**
- **Knowing what employers are looking for**
- **Keeping a good perspective**

Objectives

To learn how to apply all your communication skills to the job search

To identify methods for analyzing yourself and your employment options

To organize and carry out an effective job search

18

Barbara Ratcher's Job Search

On June 18, Barbara Ratcher graduated with a degree in business administration. Usually she worked as a waitress at Denny's Restaurant during the summers, but this year, she realized, would be different: she would not be returning to school in the fall. She needed to look for a permanent position.

Starting in the middle of May, Barbara began reading newspaper want ads. With her business coursework, she felt qualified for a management position, so she composed a basic letter that she sent to twenty-five of the jobs listed in the paper.

```
Dear Sirs:

    My business degree qualifies me for
the job described in today's Morning
News. I am hardworking and enthusiastic,
and I feel sure I would be a great asset
as a manager in your company.
    If you are interested in interviewing
me, please call me at (402) 378-9521
between 9 a.m. and noon on weekdays.

                    Sincerely,

                    Barbara Ratcher
                    Barbara Ratcher
```

To her astonishment, no one responded to these letters. On June 15, she was forced to ask her former supervisor at Denny's if he would consider her for yet another summer. He told her the position had already been filled.

On June 16, Barbara applied for a job serving hamburgers at MacDonald's and was told she would know in two weeks if she had the job. She was so upset by her job-hunting experiences that she decided not to attend her graduation ceremonies.

Points to Consider
- What did Barbara do wrong?
- How much time should she have allowed for her job hunt?
- What sort of goals should she have set for herself?
- Where else should she have looked for job openings?
- What should she do now?

Looking for the Perfect Job

The job-search process has a bad reputation. Looking for a job, people will tell you, is an unnatural process that requires being aggressive, facing constant rejection, and making unpleasant compromises. In actuality, the process can be both exciting and productive. But making the search a positive experience takes careful planning and a thorough assessment of your goals, abilities, and opportunities.

Planning is essential to the job search process.

A successful job search also requires the full use of verbal and nonverbal communication skills: it demands not only competency in one-on-one interviewing and group interaction, but also effective persuasive writing and marketing abilities.

A job search requires a wide range of communication skills.

The job search, in fact, may require more extensive—and *intensive*—use of your business communication skills than some of the jobs you have held. Moreover, it will actually help you develop skills and prepare you for your career in many ways that your educational and work experiences cannot.

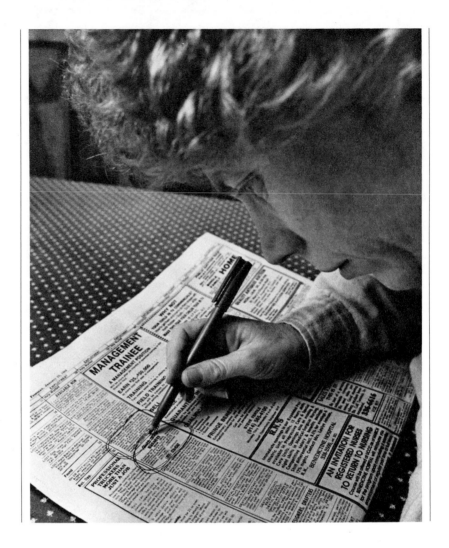

Whether or not you have applied for a career position in the past, this chapter and the three that follow can help you gain an overall sense of how the employment process works and what you can do to find the job that best suits you. Remember, it is never too soon to begin some aspects of job-search preparation.

Understanding the Process

When Jane Martinelli accepted a job as financial analyst at H & R Corporation, an international manufacturing company, her friends congratulated her on her luck at being offered just the type of job she had wanted. She said it hadn't been luck at all: she'd been planning for this job for ten years. Ever since she discovered her quantitative skills in junior high school, she had been talking to people about the careers that might be open to her.

In the business classes she took in high school, she'd found that finance and computer programming interested her the most. Talking with her parents' friends had convinced her that an international corporation would offer her the opportunities she was looking for.

In college, she worked with an adviser to set up a well-rounded program of liberal arts, communications, computer science, and business classes to complement her finance major. Because she was interested in international business, she continued with the Spanish classes she had begun in high school. She also joined the College Business Association and began attending informational meetings about job opportunities with various companies. Through the CBA, she heard of a summer internship with H & R Corporation. Her success at that internship eventually helped her win the position she wanted after graduation.

Jane's success story began while she was in her teens, but do not feel dismayed if you are not as focused as she was. Many people are not sure where they want to go or what they need to do to get there. To a certain extent, such uncertainty can be an asset: exploring different fields and discovering new talents can be exciting and productive.

Right now you should begin thinking about your goals, values, and expectations. Figure out what you are good at, what you *like* doing, what part of the world you want to live in, what sort of work environment you would like best.

Joining clubs, talking to people, reading journals and newspapers, working as a volunteer, going on informational interviews — all these can help you to discover what is available, what you enjoy doing, and what goals you want to attain. This kind of preparation can never begin too soon.

Once you have some idea of your goals and the sort of environment you want to work in, you can begin making yourself a desirable and knowledgeable candidate. Taking appropriate classes, developing particular skills, researching the field, and working as a volunteer or intern will all contribute substantially to your status as a candidate.

As you can see, forethought and self-analysis are vital to a successful job search. They will not only help focus your search, saving you time and effort, but also contribute to your strengths as a job candidate. Poor planning and hasty decisions have always plagued inexperienced job searchers. You can avoid making the same mistakes.

> Establish career goals for yourself.

> You can make yourself a good job candidate.

Using a Wide Range of Communication Skills

The actual job search is a diverse process that requires integrating and applying a wide range of communication skills. As a job researcher, you need to speak with people, listen, read, and assess the data you acquire. As a candidate, you need to use interpersonal skills as well as organizing and writing skills. These demands can be challenging and exciting. If you leave yourself enough time, organize your search, and set realistic goals, you will find your communication skills developing and the search itself rewarding.

Just remember: unless you inherit a fortune or win a state lottery, you'll probably have to hold jobs for a good part of your life. They should be the ones you want!

Analyzing Yourself

Every day, people make poor decisions about their careers. Some are jolted into facing reality; others wait out their years until retirement, imagining that then they can begin to "live." More and more people, however, are changing careers in mid-life, going back to school, developing new skills, and realizing they can do the things they always wanted to do. And college students are realizing more than ever that they are in control of their lives, that they can make the career decisions right for them.

Searching for and getting the right job should be a long-term process. Begin, not with the want ads, but with brainstorming—honest self-analysis—and research. Then, when you have narrowed your field and established some goals, you can begin tailoring your search and your self-presentation to whatever employers in that field are looking for.

Self-assessment should be the first step in your job search. Consider what you want to do, what you do well, and how you want to live. Try to separate those things from what other people want for you. You will find it helpful to talk to friends, relatives, advisers, and teachers regarding their opinions of you. You may also want to work with a career counselor who can give you comprehensive tests to identify possible career fields. Ultimately, however, only you can know what kind of person you are and what you want to do.

Your self-analysis can be broken down into four areas: (1) personality, (2) values and goals, (3) skills, and (4) preferred work environment.

Personality

Jot down some thoughts on your personality. Don't think about employment at this point; just consider your own character traits. (The questions in Figure 18-1 should prove helpful.)

While assessing yourself, remember that there are no *right* answers: it's not better to be a leader than a follower, for example, or to be more logical than creative. It *is* important to see yourself realistically.

Values and Goals

Knowing your own values will help you make career decisions.

Closely related to your personality are your values and goals. Your values are the things you find most important; your goals are the external and internal achievements you are aiming for. Your job satisfaction will probably depend on the similarity of your values and goals to those of your company or your fellow workers; consequently, your self-analysis as well as your later research and job interviews should focus on these areas.

STEPS IN JOB SEARCH

Looking for a job

Organizing your job search

Researching career fields

Self-analysis

1. Am I outgoing and talkative or shy and quiet?
2. Do I like working or studying with people, or do I work better alone?
3. Do I work well under supervision, or am I essentially an independent worker?
4. Am I a go-getter? Energetic?
5. Am I always thinking up new ideas or do I prefer following other people's systems?
6. Do I thrive on schedules? Am I well organized? Do I stick to deadlines?
7. Do I always set definite goals for myself?
8. If I do set goals, what type are they? Financial? Personal? Long-term or short-term?
9. How flexible am I? Do I like change, or do I prefer security?
10. How competitive am I? Do I always try to do things better or faster than other people?
11. Do I like being a leader, or do I prefer being a team member?
12. Am I a good speaker? Am I good at persuading people?
13. Am I a good listener? Do people come to me for advice?
14. Would I rather figure out a quantitative problem with a definite answer or work on an analytical problem that might have several answers?
15. Am I usually contented with my situation, or am I always looking for something more challenging, more enjoyable, or more profitable?
16. Do I prefer designing and researching or physically producing something?
17. Do I consider myself imaginative or logical?
18. Do I prefer working with machines or ideas?
19. Do I prefer making decisions about people or about things?
20. Do I prefer working out broad concepts or individual details?

FIGURE 18-1
Personality quiz

To help understand your value system, number the following items in order of decreasing importance. (Add any other items that are important to you.)

___ Money   ___ Personal integrity
___ Intellectual challenge   ___ Responsibility
___ Power/influence   ___ Security
___ Independence   ___ Interpersonal contact
___ Creative expression   ___ Improving society
___ Helping people   ___ Working with a team
___ Free time   ___ Dressing the way I want

Your honest value decisions should play an important role in your career decisions. For example, if helping people, improving society, and being independent are more important to you than money and security, you may want to consider teaching or working with nonprofit organizations. If working as a team is an important value, you will want to look for organizations that stress teamwork over individual efforts.

Your goals will be a direct result of your values and personality. These are the personal and career achievements you are aiming for. To determine some of your goals, ask yourself questions such as: How much money do I want to be making five years from now? How important are promotions going to be? What would I like to be doing at my job in five years? Where do I want to live? What would I consider a major accomplishment for myself? (These questions will be vital to your job interviews as well as to your self-analysis, so start thinking about them well before your first interview.)

By the time you have answered questions regarding your personality, values, and goals, you should have a good idea of some consistent trends. Jobs that force you to deviate widely from these aspects of your character could make you unhappy. But, naturally, you also have to mesh these personal components with your skills and the opportunities available to you.

Skills

Your personality analysis will tell you a lot about the kinds of work you would enjoy and excel in. Understanding your personal qualities will also help you see what type of skills will be useful for you. For example, if you know you are a logical person with strong quantitative and analytical skills who enjoys working with machines, you may excel at computer programming. If you haven't taken a programming course, now might be the time to sign up for one! On the other hand, if you are a computer science major who prefers communicating with people to working with machines, you might want to apply for an internship or summer job in a marketing firm or retail outlet before you make a career decision.

Begin your skills analysis with two lists: SKILLS I HAVE NOW and SKILLS I SHOULD HAVE. The first list can serve as a basis for the job-search materials discussed in Chapters 19 and 20; the second list can help you set goals for yourself. Both lists will help you decide the type of job you're able to do and would like to do. (See Figure 18-2 for some examples of skills.)

Check the skills you have; then make a list of any skills you need to reach your goals.

- Solve problems easily
- Write well
- Am a self-starter
- Type accurately
- Have worked with computers
- Am detail-oriented
- Have technical expertise
- Have accounting skills
- Can sell anything
- Have had multicultural experiences
- Can work with numbers
- Have athletic ability
- Have time management skills
- Can meet deadlines
- Work well in a team

- Get along with people
- Can speak in front of groups
- Can organize anything
- Can use office machines
- Have a facility for foreign languages
- Work well with machinery
- Do effective research
- Have supervisory skills
- Can adapt to new environments
- Am a fast learner
- Have artistic or musical ability
- Can work with my hands
- Work well under pressure
- Am a good trainer/instructor
- Am creative

FIGURE 18-2
Skills checklist

Work Environment

In some ways, this area of your analysis may seem the simplest, especially if you have a good understanding of your personal attributes and skills. However, the work environment actually includes far more than simply the size of your office or the number of people in your department. To assess the work environment you would find most satisfactory, consider questions such as these:

- Do I prefer working indoors or outdoors?
- Do I prefer working at night or during the day?
- Do I like to travel a lot?
- Do I want to work in a certain part of this country or in a foreign country?
- Do I prefer a city or a rural environment?
- Do I want a big organization or a small one?
- Do I want a highly structured organization?
- Do I prefer an industrial setting?
- Do I want a company focused on services, on products, or on ideas?
- Do I want a company with high-technology equipment?
- Do I want a very pressured environment?
- Do I want a salary, hourly wage, or commission?
- What type of fellow employees would I like to work with?
- What type of customer/clients would I like?
- Do I want opportunities to become an owner or manager?

What kind of work setting do you find congenial?

The more precise you can be in your appraisal of an ideal work environment, the more you'll be able to identify the type of job or even a specific company that will be right for you.

Researching Career Fields and Job Opportunities

When you have a good sense of yourself and your preferences, you can begin examining actual career areas and job opportunities. If you have not already chosen a career area, start reading articles about future employment trends.

Hiring trends change from year to year.

Demand for most jobs is cyclical: for a few years there will be great opportunities for oil geologists, for example, and so thousands of students will major in geology. Then the field will be glutted with graduates, and some other field will open up. Engineers, attorneys, and computer programmers were in demand in the 1980s, but some forecasters predict that liberal arts graduates will be needed in the 1990s. To make long-range plans, keep an eye on these hiring trends.

What Would You Do?

Margaret Sanchez knows she has good communication skills and leadership qualities. She is energetic and competitive, and she works well with people. Her interest in high-fashion clothes led her to work for retail stores when she was in college, and now that she has a degree in management she wants a career in retail management.

Here is her problem. She has been offered a position as assistant store manager in the clothes store in her home town. The store is prestigious in the town, and the job pays well. Margaret would have a lot of freedom to make decisions, and she could eventually become a part owner.

However, she has also been offered a management trainee position with a national retail chain. This position pays less than the other position, but in the long run the salary will exceed anything her local store could offer. Working for the national chain will force her to relocate and travel. She will also have to work as part of a team and will not have a chance to enter upper management unless she works aggressively and successfully for a number of years.

To help make her decision, Margaret listed some of her values and preferences in order of decreasing importance.

1. Challenge
2. Power/influence
3. High-pressure environment
4. Money
5. Dynamic fellow workers
6. Security

What do you think she should do? Write her a memo giving her some advice.

Networking

Networking, which can be valuable for both researching careers and looking for a specific job, involves talking with friends, friends of friends, family, colleagues, advisers, and instructors. Speak with company representatives who come to your campus; keep in touch with friends who have career positions.

Do not hesitate to ask people questions: What are the opportunities in this field today? What educational background is helpful for such a position? What kinds of future positions would be available? What type of work environment does this job entail? What companies are the leaders in this field?

Also, consider scheduling informational interviews with people working in fields that interest you. These interviews can help you gain firsthand information about careers and companies while also enabling you to meet people who might want to hire you later on.

Other networking sources include national organizations and local clubs or associations. Your school may have campus clubs for students interested in fields such as accounting, marketing, data processing, and engineering. If not, write the national organizations related to these fields and request information about job opportunities. Job fairs are another source of contacts and information. You should check to see if any are going to be in your area.

As you speak with people, remember your self-analysis. Keep checking whether your personality, values, goals, and skills are compatible with the jobs you are looking at. If you know that working independently of supervisors is essential to your success or that you will be happy only if your job changes constantly, you will be able to eliminate some options and focus on others.

Reading

The first steps of your career research should also involve general reading in a number of broad areas. Most candidates do not even know what types of jobs may be available. Students often make flat statements based on hearsay rather than on research: "There aren't any journalism jobs out there any more" or "No one wants to hire anthropology majors." Before eliminating something you're interested in, find out about some or all of the options available!

Avoid making career decisions based on hearsay.

To research general career fields, check your library and bookstore for publications that describe jobs and forecast hiring needs. Publications such as the *Wall Street Journal, Business Week,* and your local newspapers will often have articles about employment opportunities, hiring trends, and companies that are looking for certain types of job candidates. Newsletters or journals published by organizations in specific fields offer good information about careers and even about actual jobs available.

From the Desk of ...

executive recruitment, inc.
14 E 60 st nyc 10022   PL 92942

"If you act professional and confident, know what your goals are, and express yourself well, you are likely to find the position you want," says Susan Gordon, personnel recruiter for the Lynne Palmer Agency.

Susan interviews hundreds of candidates for every level in publishing, from students fresh out of college, to people who change jobs every few years, to managers who have been in the same position for 20 years and now want a change. She must match the right person with the right position. As well as looking at skills, she must look at personalities. "Ordinarily, I don't want to place someone who hates paperwork into a large corporation." People from companies call to tell her about job openings. She interviews candidates, helps them decide on career paths, sets up appointments for them, and does follow-up, giving candidates feedback on their interviews.

What candidates are likely to be successful in getting a position? The right skills are important, but so is conveying a good attitude through body language. Susan says she recently interviewed an entry-level candidate who slouched in his chair, dressed in jeans, then leaned back, holding his head in his hands. "I spend time advising a person like that. How you're viewed is very important. The company you are interviewing with may not give you a second chance. Going on an interview in jeans, for instance, shows the company you may not have good judgment and the right attitude."

Susan suggests that candidates for positions should "give direct answers to questions." They should be honest. "If there's a question you don't understand, say so." Finally, they should ask good questions on an interview, for instance, "If I start as an assistant editor, how would I get to position A or B?"

Susan emphasizes that students should research their potential field. "Many students don't know the resources available to them. Go to the library. Take vacation time to set up exploratory interviews. Talk to alumni in the field you're interested in. Work on the college newspaper if you're interested in publishing. That shows me and a potential employer that you had enough interest to spend three or four hours a week in the field."

Susan suggests you "gear the resume to the industry you're interested in." Put education on top for an entry-level position. Make sure that the resume has a neat physical appearance with no typos. "This is your first presentation to me and presumably your best work. If it looks sloppy, I'm going to say to myself, 'If that's your *best* effort, what will your everyday work be like?'"

Summer employment, particularly internships, is important on resumes. Extracurricular activities are important. Also, "fit your resume onto one page. If you have room, at the bottom add skills such as typing, and in today's market, word processing and computer skills."

What is most important for a person interviewing? "Everything," says Susan, but particularly:

- A professional, confident presence
- Verbal skills
- Nonverbal skills such as eye contact, appearance, and appropriate dress
- A good, eager attitude
- A neat, correct resume

Useful References for Career Search

Business Periodicals Index
The Dictionary of Occupational Titles
Occupational Outlook for College Graduates (Government Printing Office)
The College Placement Annual
The Encyclopedia of Associations

Many publications list job openings. The newspaper want ads are the most obvious, but they may also be the least helpful as the information in the advertisement is often limited: you may waste time applying for a job for which you are under- or overqualified or that does not suit your needs.

You will probably find job advertisements in trade journals, specialized magazines, and campus publications more useful than those in newspapers. Also check your newsstand for the *National Business Employment Weekly,* job listings published each week by *The Wall Street Journal.*

College Placement Center

If your school has a placement center, become acquainted with its facilities. Many placement centers have advisers to discuss job opportunities with you, and most centers have information about companies as well as actual job listings.

College placement offices also will help you put together job application materials and will send them to prospective employers on request.

Look for the job-search facilities available on your campus.

On-Campus Interviews

Many companies recruit from college campuses. Find out when company recruiters are coming to campus and sign up for interviews. If company representatives are appearing at a club meeting or social function, be sure to attend—and wear your interview attire.

Employment Agencies

Employment agencies are natural sources for jobs. Many of them are specialized in fields such as data processing and clerical work, and many receive information from all over the country.

Some employment agencies, however, will not be suited to the kind of jobs you are looking for, and some require that you pay a hefty sum for their services: make sure you check into any agencies before deciding to sign up.

Direct Applications

Simply applying for positions with companies will probably be an important part of your job search. Before applying, research the company's work environment, goals, and opportunities; again, your placement center often has copies of annual reports and other information about companies. Then send a letter and resume or application form. In some cases, telephoning the personnel department or a department in which you are interested can lead to an interview right away.

Organizing Your Materials

Looking for a job requires good organizational as well as good communi-

Gather the materials employers will want to see.

cation skills. Once you know what you are looking for, get your application materials in order and provide yourself with a few essentials.

Resume

You need an effective, current resume. See Chapter 19 for more details.

Application Letter

If you are applying by mail, you will need a cover letter to complement your resume. See Chapter 20 for more details.

References

You should have at least three people who can act as references for you. Provide these people with your resume and with some idea of what jobs you are applying for. These people may have to write letters of recommendation vouching for you, or they may have to speak with prospective employers on the telephone. Make sure employers have these people's correct titles, addresses, and telephone numbers.

Transcripts

Some companies will want to see your college transcripts. These can be kept on file with letters of reference and other application materials in your college placement office.

Portfolio

In some fields, you will need to provide samples of your work. For jobs requiring graphic art or writing skills, you should compile a portfolio that will show an employer your skills and versatility.

Marketing majors, for example, might put together a portfolio of marketing cases they have written; technical writers could include manuals they have written at previous jobs or projects they have worked on in classes; graphic artists should have a selection of their best work. A professional presentation can be a key aspect of your successful job search.

Interview Attire

For most jobs, you will have to invest in an outfit or two for interviewing. For both men and women, a suit is ideal for most professional positions. You may find that your interviewers in some professions (advertising, education) dress quite casually, but you should still dress professionally for an interview.

Organizational Chart

If you are doing an extensive job search, a chart can help you get organized and prevent you from forgetting important dates or tasks. You should record what companies (and individuals) you have written to, what companies you have heard from, what interview dates have been set up. Make sure you keep copies of the letters you write and any correspondence you receive from companies.

Figure 18-3 shows how you might set up an organizational chart.

Knowing What Employers Are Looking For

Naturally, each employer is different, but in general you can assume that employers are looking for specific skills, commitment, industriousness, personality, and certain values and goals.

Skills

Your research into career areas and specific jobs should help you identify the skills employers are looking for. Naturally, some areas require technical

Letters Sent		
Company/ Contact Person/ Date	Response	Action
IBM Henry Lim 12/2	1/23 No openings now	Call in June
Apple Vera Fletcher 12/3	2/3	Interview: 2/12
Fortune Manny Brown 12/3	—	Call in Feb. if I don't hear from him
Interviews		
Company/ Interviewer/ Date	Response	Action/Comments
G & T William Juarez 12/13	1/10 Don't fit their needs	—
AmTech Gloria James 12/20	1/23 Candidate must have BS	Call her in June
Sears 2/23 Karen Richmond		Bring writing sample

FIGURE 18-3 —————————————————————
Job search organizational chart

expertise: you will have trouble getting a position as an accountant if you have no accounting skills.

On the other hand, employers know that many jobs can be learned within a few months. They would prefer to hire candidates whose personal characteristics, values, and goals are in keeping with those of the organization. The way you come across in an interview or in an application letter may be more important to your success than having the "right" major or attending the "right" school.

One thing you can be sure of is that employers will value a candidate's ability to communicate. Communication, as we have seen, is an integral part of every aspect of life. Even the most technical fields demand good writing and speaking skills. Your application letter and interview should demonstrate your ability to communicate effectively.

Employers look for strong communication skills.

Commitment

Employers know that training new employees is costly and time-consuming. If you appear to have a long-term commitment to a company, you will rank high with interviewers.

Industriousness

Every employer wants employees who will work hard. Your resume, letter, and interview should demonstrate that you have this quality.

Personality

Personality conflicts can cause expensive problems in organizations. Employers evaluate whether candidates will get along with other employees. You should demonstrate your ability to work well with all types of people.

Values and Goals

As we have seen, your values and goals should be similar to those of the company. Employers are as concerned as you are that these elements mesh.

You should know what values and goals a company emphasizes: does it value creativity or conformity? Independence or teamwork? Aggressive individual competition or group unity?

Corporate newsletters, annual reports, brochures, and personal contacts can give you clues about company values and goals. When you know you are right for the company, emphasize the appropriate areas in your application letter and interview.

Keeping a Good Perspective

Once you have established the career area you want, your actual job search may take anywhere from a month to a year. Start early. You don't want to end up accepting something out of desperation.

To avoid getting discouraged, keep the following pointers in mind:

- Be realistic. You simply are not going to be qualified for a lot of positions. Apply for jobs that mesh with your qualifications. If a job description specifies that candidates must have a doctorate, for example, you are probably wasting your time by applying with only a BS.
- Go to every interview you can. Interviews will help you meet people and find out about companies and jobs. You will also develop interviewing skills. And you never know—the most unlikely interview may lead to the best offer.
- Revise your approach and materials. If no one is answering your application letters or if your interviews are not leading to offers, you may need to reassess your approach and your materials.

  On the other hand, you may need to alter your job goals: companies may not be hiring in that particular field or your skills may be inappropriate. If possible, get feedback from interviewers to find out what you are doing wrong.

  Get feedback from interviewers whenever possible.

- Don't panic. No one wants to hire a desperate candidate. Stay calm, organized, and optimistic. With the right strategies and good application materials, you will find the opportunities are there. You just need to find them!

Summary

Looking for the right job demands diverse communication skills as well as careful planning and self-assessment. Knowing your options and your own skills and interests will help you narrow your search and present yourself as a focused, dynamic candidate.

Employment Process Checklist

Research and Analysis

- Before you begin applying for jobs, analyze your own

  _____ personality

  _____ values

  _____ goals

  _____ skills

- When you know some of your preferences, begin researching fields of interest by

  _____ networking with friends and colleagues

  _____ reading trade journals, reference books, business publications, and newspapers

Applying for Jobs

- As you begin applying for jobs, find out about opportunities by

  _____ networking

  _____ reading advertisements in newspapers and journals

  _____ using your college placement center

  _____ going through on-campus interviews

  _____ checking with employment agencies

  _____ writing or telephoning companies directly

Organizing Materials

- When you begin job-hunting, make sure you have

  _____ a resume

  _____ application letters

_____ references

_____ transcripts

_____ a portfolio if necessary

_____ interview attire

_____ a checklist of interviews and applications

Terms to Remember

Interview attire: outfit appropriate for an interview. A two- or three-piece suit is often the best choice for men and women.

Summary Discussion: Barbara Ratcher's Job Search from Case in Point, p. 435

Barbara Ratcher's most obvious error was to wait too long to begin researching job options. Although about to graduate, she did not give any real thought to what she wanted to do or what career options were available. She should have begun early in her senior year analyzing herself and the job market as well as gathering her job-application materials.

When she did begin applying for jobs, Barbara limited her applications to newspaper want ads and sent out a vague letter that did nothing to sell her skills as a manager. She could have gone to her college placement office, spoken with friends, instructors, and colleagues, gone to an employment agency, or telephoned the personnel offices of businesses in her area.

Perhaps Barbara's worst error was to avoid analyzing herself and outlining specific goals. Even if she takes the MacDonald's job to tide her over, she should begin the brainstorming and research process that she failed to do during the school year.

Questions for Review and Discussion

1. Why should the job search process be a long-term effort?
2. How can you begin right now improving your position as a potential job candidate?
3. Why do you think knowing your own values is important to a job search?

4. Why are the communication components of the job search so complex?
5. List three of your personal values that should mesh with those of a company you work for.
6. What are your most important short- and long-term goals? What are you doing now to attain them?
7. What skills do you think will be essential to the type of job you want? What are you doing now to improve them?
8. What are the components of your ideal work environment?

9. What publications will be most useful to your job search?
10. What is networking?
11. Would an employment agency be useful in your job search? Why or why not?
12. Would a portfolio be useful to your job search? Why or why not?
13. What three qualities do you think employers in your field are most interested in seeing in their candidates?

Exercises

1. Choose a position for which you might be applying in the near future. Write a page or two evaluating your personality, values and goals, skills, education, and job experience in terms of the position you would like. What skills and background will the job require? What will be the strengths of your application? What will be the weaknesses?
2. Write a few paragraphs analyzing Margaret Sanchez' situation (p. 442). With the limited information you have, what do you suggest she should do?
3. John Tenniel is a college junior majoring in business administration. He is deciding between getting an MBA and going to law school. Write a memo advising him on what he should do in order to make up his mind.
4. Marcia Czajkowski is studying computer science, but she is also a writer with one published book. She wants a job working with computers that will give her some free time to write. Write two or three paragraphs explaining where she could start researching such positions and what kinds of jobs might be available.
5. You are the owner of a large hardware store. You are looking for a manager who can handle the varied responsibilities of the store but who also could work with you on planning a new store in a nearby suburb. What kinds of personal qualities would you want in your ideal candidate for the position? What type of educational background or experience would you want the person to have? Discuss.
6. You are interviewing candidates for a clerical position in a large organization. The candidates have been screened, so you see only those with good skills. What personal qualities, values, and goals would you want to see in a candidate? Discuss.
7. Write a short report on the career resources available on your campus. Include information on library resources as well as on the campus placement center and other facilities.

Resumes

- Developing a resume that works for you
- Avoiding common errors
- Brainstorming
- Tailoring your resume to the job
- Identifying resume types
- Making a good impression
- Organizing resume components
- Handling special problems

Objective

To develop an effective resume appropriate to your background and goals

19

Andrew Poole's Resume

Andrew Poole was a college sophomore interested in finding a summer job. He had worked as a grocery store clerk in previous summers, but now he wanted a job with more career potential.

Realizing that he had no experience related to his interest in communications, he hoped to work for a local radio station during the summer. Although the positions available were primarily clerical, he felt he could derive some important experience from them. He put together the following resume.

```
Andrew Poole
9801 Eastwood Way
Baltimore, MD 21134
(212) 347-4598

QUALIFICATIONS. I feel that I am
qualified to assume the responsibilities
required of me as an employee of your
radio station. I am confident that my
background, knowledge, and variety of
work experiences will assist me in
handling these responsibilities.

EDUCATION. I have completed two (2)
years of college and plan to graduate
with a B.A. in Communications. GPA 2.9
in major.

EXPERIENCE. For the last three (3)
summers I have been a checkout clerk at
```

```
Safe way. I work well with people and
have a good eye for detail.

MEMBERSHIP. I am an active member of the
college chess team.

PERSONAL. Single 5'10" 168 lbs.

PERSONAL
REFERENCE. Mr. Frederick Pintero
          Minister, All Souls Church
          765 Southard Street
          Baltimore, MD 21136
```

Andrew mailed this resume to seven radio stations and received no answer from them. Finally, he called one of the program directors to whom he had written. The program director replied that the resume did not indicate Andrew to be a good candidate for an internship.

Points to Consider
- Do you see any problems with the physical appearance of Andrew's resume? Explain.
- Is there anything on the resume that you suggest deleting?
- What type of information would you include on this resume?
- Do you see any typographical errors on the resume? Where?
- Would you alter the reference section? Explain.

Developing a Resume That Works for You

The resume may be one of the most important documents you ever write. Not only is it essential to the job-hunting process, but it may prove useful throughout your career. Many companies keep employees' resumes on file, insert them in corporate capability statements, and include them in proposals for grants or government contracts. Your resume may be examined when internal promotions are discussed or when management teams are being organized.

Keep your resume
up-to-date.

Because resumes are used so frequently and for so many reasons, it is important to keep yours updated and ready for viewing.

Resume styles are as varied as the people who write them, but the best are clear, precise, and professional. Written in phrases rather than sentences,

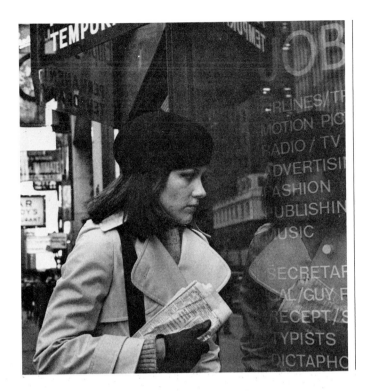

they focus on objective aspects of your experience, not on descriptions of your personal qualities. For example, most prospective employers expect to see some information on where you went to school rather than statements like, "I am well versed in all aspects of business."

A resume is not a life history. The word *resume* comes from a French word meaning *to summarize*. It is an outline meant to be glanced at: a prospective employer might look at your resume for less than 30 seconds before putting it in the *yes* or *no* pile. Make sure the best things about yourself can be spotted quickly!

A resume is a summary.

One of the most important things to remember about a resume is that it is *yours*. The format should be adapted to your particular goals, experience, and strengths. Nothing negative should appear on the page.

Also, remember, your resume is not meant to impress a reader with your charm or enthusiasm. It should be factual and straightforward; leave the enthusiastic tone to your cover letters and interviews.

A resume should be objective.

Do look at your friends' resumes and at the examples in this book: but, ultimately, you will have to design a format that best suits you and your needs. (See Figure 19-1 for a sample resume format.)

Focus your resume on the position you want.

Before you start, bear in mind a few pointers:

- Keep it short—no more than two pages.
- Make it easy on the eye—easy to *glance* at.
- Include only positive aspects of yourself.
- Put the most important information toward the beginning—most people glance at a resume from top to bottom.

Put the most important information toward the beginning of the resume.

Name→

Address→

Telephone Number→

Job objective→

Degree, major, school (reverse
chronological order)

DANIELLE LAMONT

803 Mead Drive   (921) 490-2331
Conway, WA 98456

CAREER OBJECTIVES: Junior Accountant
                     CMA Certification

EDUCATION: B.S., Business
1988   Administration, Accounting
                     Marsden College, Seattle, WA
                     GPA 3.5

1986–88   A.A., General Studies
                     Westfield Junior College
                     Conway, WA
                     GPA 3.6, Honors

HONORS   National Dean's List
                     AAUW Scholarship

ACTIVITIES   Secretary,
                     Accounting Association
                     Marsden College
                     Schedule meetings, prepare
                     agendas, handle correspondence

EXPERIENCE: Office Manager/Bookkeeper
                     Gregory Lim, M.D., Seattle, WA

1986–present   Handle accounts receivable and
                     payable, prepare payroll,
                     schedule staff, write letters
                     and reports

                     Receptionist
                     Dart Communication
                     Services, 1986–88
                     Conway, WA

1985–86   Handled heavy telephones,
                     scheduled client appointments,
                     handled correspondence, dealt
                     with the public

INTERESTS: Water skiing, coin collecting

REFERENCES: Dr. Gregroy Nguyen
                     235 Elton Street
                     Seattle, WA 98745
                     (967) 337-2376

                     Mrs. George Hale
                     Dart Communication Services
                     Conway, WA 98324
                     (921) 455-1200

                     Professor Frederick Wiley
                     Department of Accounting
                     Marsden College
                     Seattle, WA 98324

Avoiding Common Errors

Make sure to steer clear of errors that will prevent your resume from being effective.

Too Little White Space

An effective use of white space on the page is essential for readability. If you have too much material on the page, delete some information or use a two-page format.

Too Much White Space

On the other hand, your resume should not look too brief or cramped in one part of the page. (Figure 19-2 illustrates this problem. Figure 19-3 shows an improved version.) Expand your information or reformat to fill most of the page.

Poor Format

Your resume should have blocks of information that a reader can scan quickly. Some resumes demand too much attention from the reader. (Figure 19-4 illustrates this problem. Figure 19-5 illustrates an improved version.) Avoid sentences, long lines, and large paragraphs.

Inconsistent Format

You must decide how to set up your headings, entries, dates, and so on. Once you have a design, keep it simple and consistent. If you start underlining job titles, then underline all of them. If some major headings are in capital letters, make sure all of them are capitalized.

Irrelevant Material

Your resume should have a focus. If you are aiming at a sales position, for example, as much of the information as possible should be appropriate for that position. An entry on your abilities as a baseball player should not be placed as prominently as your experience in retail work.

◄ FIGURE 19-1 ————————————————————————————————
Sample resume format. This is a standard format for a chronological resume. Danielle has some experience related to the job she wants; her degree and activities are relevant to the job. The resume format is uncluttered, and the entries are easy to read.

```
                         RESUME

GEORGE AMALFI                        (504) 329-0021
5001 Lampe Avenue
Carnsdale, IL 60983

     OBJECTIVE:          Commercial Loan Officer

     WORK EXPERIENCE:    Commercial Credit Analyst
     1986—present        Biggs Bank, Carnsdale, IL

     EDUCATION:          MBA, Finance
     June 1987           Crandell University,
                         Chicago, IL

     June 1983           BS, Business Administration
                         University of Wisconsin,
                         Madison, WI

     INTERESTS:          Triathlete training,
                         photography

     REFERENCES:         Available on request
```

FIGURE 19-2 _____

Ineffective resume. George has an excellent background for the job he wants, but his resume would benefit from more relevant detail and a more effective format. Although a resume need not fill up a page, white space should be used effectively. This resume is crowded toward the top of the page. See Figure 19-3 for George's revision.

Vague Entries

Your entries should be specific. When you can, quantify your information. Rather than saying you had a lot of responsibility, say you supervised six employees. Rather than saying you dealt with the public, say you waited on 190 customers a day.

Inaccurate Entries

Your resume should highlight your strong points, but you must be careful not to include any inaccurate or dishonest information.

Brainstorming

If you have already developed a list of skills useful to the job you want, it can serve as a beginning for your resume brainstorming session. Jot down, too, the factual details about your education and experience.

```
                    GEORGE AMALFI
                   5001 Lampe Avenue
                  Carnsdale, IL 60983
                   (504) 329-0021

OBJECTIVE:          Commercial Loan Officer

WORK EXPERIENCE:    Commercial Credit Analyst
1986—present        Biggs Bank, Carnsdale, IL

                    • Analyze and structure
                      commercial loan packages
                    • Develop new business
                      prospects
                    • Manage and train junior loan
                      officers
                    • Work with domestic and
                      international clients

EDUCATION:          MBA, Finance
                    Crandell University
June 1987           Chicago, IL
                    GPA 3.59

June 1983           BS, Business Administration
                    University of Wisconsin
                    Madison, WI
                    GPA 3.59

COURSEWORK:         • Financial management of
                      banking institutions
                    • Money and banking
                    • Decision support systems
                    • Managerial writing
                    • Quantitative business
                      methods
                    • Marketing management
                    • International business

HONORS:             Crandell University
                    Fellowship

FOREIGN LANGUAGE:   Fluent in German

INTERESTS:          Triathlete training,
                    photography

REFERENCES:         Available on request
```

FIGURE 19-3

Revised resume. George's revised resume has details about his work experience and course-work that will strengthen his application for a position. The revised format looks more professional.

PERSONNEL

NOTICE THE PAINSTAKING ATTENTION TO DETAIL ON THE RESUMÉ.. LIKE THE CURLYCUES ON "LAID OFF" AND "NO FIXED ADDRESS".

© 1987 by NEA, Inc. THAVES 9-28

Also consider who will be reading this resume and remember what employers are looking for. An accountant will be reading resumes in a different way than a marketing manager. Someone hiring a salesperson will be looking for different qualities than the person searching for an entry-level programmer.

Tailoring Your Resume to the Job

Naturally, one vital component to this brainstorming process is figuring out what you want the resume for: you should have a good sense of your goals so you can highlight the appropriate skills and experience. You may, in fact, end up having to write two or more resumes if you are applying for different kinds of positions.

If you are going to apply for two types of summer jobs, for example—as a lifeguard and as a salesperson—you may want to develop two resumes. One would highlight your swimming and sports experience while the other would emphasize your experience and skill in sales. Both would emphasize your skills with people.

A grasp of your own strengths and weaknesses will help you determine the format and content of your resume: you will be highlighting your strengths, of course, and deemphasizing your weaknesses.

When Timothy Chu was looking for a management trainee position, part of his first brainstorming list looked like this:

Positive	*Negative*
BS in management	Took 6 years to get my BS
Have held two full-time jobs	Took 3 years off from school
Supervised six people	30 years old (good or bad?)
High GPA	Not willing to relocate
Have computer programming skills	Paid jobs were clerical
Have managerial experience	

Timothy believed that many companies hiring trainees would not like his apparent lack of direction: he had taken time off from school, worked at clerical jobs, and gone slowly through college. Employers, he figured, might

```
Resume of:
Theodore Compton
                      PERSONAL

Born in NYC, 1960. Height 6', wt. 196 lbs.
Married, three children
Health: good
Hobbies: bowling, dancing, football (spectator)
                EMPLOYMENT HIGHLIGHTS

1980–82
Edwards County Community Action Agency
Directed six full-time employees; trained staff;
participated in solving employee grievances;
assisted in performance reviews of personnel.

1982 (summer)
Superintendent of Schools, Edwards County
Developed orientation program.

1982–84
Community College District, Edwards County
Program was funded for twelve months. It was an in-
school program. I evaluated participants' career
goals and gained experience communicating with all
nationalities.

1984–88
United Council of Educational Organizations,
Newark, NJ
Responsibilities include recruitment of students
from local high schools to participate in
educational talent search. I assist students with
educational plans for higher education. I
disseminate information on college admissions and
financial aid procedures. Also conduct group
presentations for students, parents, and community
organizations.
                      EDUCATION

1987–present
Working toward a School Counseling Credential and
Community College Counselor Credential, Farwood
College.
                               9871 E. Street
                               Basil, NJ 09122
                               (201) 389-2299
```

FIGURE 19-4 _____

Ineffective resume. Theodore's resume is confusing and hard to read. He has put personal information first and has used a chronological listing of his work experience that shows the most recent employer at the end. He does not indicate what positions he held. His address and telephone number should be at the top of the page. The long lines and occasional sentences add to the ineffectiveness of this resume. See Figure 19-5 for a revision of this resume.

```
                    THEODORE COMPTON
                    9871 E. Street
                    Basil, NJ 09122
                    (201) 389-2299

OBJECTIVE:          Student Counselor

QUALIFICATIONS:     School Counseling Credential
                    Community College Counseling
                    Credential
                    Coursework in Educational
                    Psychology
                    Eight years' related work
                    experience

EMPLOYMENT          Counselor, United Council of
1984-88             Educational Organizations,
                    Newark, NJ. Recruit students from
                    local high schools to participate
                    in educational talent search.
                    Assist students with educational
                    plans for higher education.
                    Disseminate information on
                    college admissions and financial
                    aid procedures. Conduct group
                    presentations for students,
                    parents, and community
                    organizations

1982-84             Counselor, Community College
                    District, Edwards County, MS.
                    Evaluated participants' career
                    goals and gained experience
                    communicating with all
                    nationalities

1982 (summer)       Program Coordinator,
                    Superintendent of Schools,
                    Edwards County, MS. Developed
                    orientation programs for
                    supervisors and new workers

1980-82             Equal Opportunity Counselor,
                    Community Action Agency, Edwards
                    County, MS. Directed six full-
                    time employees; trained staff;
                    participated in solving employee
                    grievances; assisted in
                    performance reviews of personnel

EDUCATION
1988                School Counseling Credential
                    Community College Counselor
                    Credential

1985-87             Coursework in Educational
                    Psychology, Farwood College

HOBBIES:            Bowling, dancing, watching
                    football

REFERENCES:         On request
```

not be as interested in a 30-year-old as they were in 22-year-olds who had devoted themselves to management since high school.

Timothy's major strengths, on the other hand, were his degree, his good grades, and the skills he had developed as a clerical worker and as a volunteer. He developed a resume that played down dates and highlighted his education and skills. (For his resume, see Figure 19-6. Figure 19-7 also illustrates a resume that deemphasizes dates.)

Identifying Resume Types

Traditionally, resumes have fallen into two formats: the chronological and the functional (or skills) resume. The first type takes a reader from the present to the past (Figures 19-1, 19-3, 19-5, 19-9, and 19-11). It mentions job titles, employers, and dates.

A chronological resume moves from present to past.

The second type, as the name implies, highlights skills. It does not state what you were doing when, but what you *can* do. Rather than saying you took an advanced programming seminar in 1984, it states that you have developed accounting software for a small business—not mentioning that the software was a special project for the seminar. Timothy Chu's resume (Figure 19-6) is a functional or skills resume.

A functional resume highlights skills.

Until recently, almost everyone used a chronological resume. More and more, however, as people began changing careers more frequently and older people began returning to the workforce, the functional resume has gained in popularity.

Also, people are now combining the two types: a combined form enables a potential employer to see both your work history and your skills (Figures 19-8 and 19-10).

Basically, the key to a good resume is how effectively it displays your strong points and links you with the position or goal you have in mind.

Making a Good Impression

The resume must look *perfect:* no typos, faded print, misaligned margins, or misspellings. Check all your information: someone seeing *Sear's* instead of *Sears* or *Arthur Anderson* instead of *Arthur Andersen* might decide not to read your resume any further.

Because the reader of a resume usually has only a piece of paper with which to judge your ability, you want that paper to be attractive as well as informative. Arrange your information with an artistic eye. You may want to have the resume typeset; at least have it typed on a good typewriter and photocopied neatly and clearly. A computer is a great tool for writing a

Make your resume attractive as well as readable.

◄ FIGURE 19-5 _____

Revised resume. This revised resume shows Theodore's goal and qualifications. He has included his job titles and used a reverse chronological format. Personal information, except for hobbies, is deleted.

```
                        TIMOTHY CHU
                      309 Fleury Street
                      St. Paul, MN 50456
          (605) 299-1256 (daytime)   (605) 988-1578 (evenings)

                          EDUCATION

June 1988           BS, Management,
                    University of Minnesota
                    GPA 3.75

                          OBJECTIVE

                    Management Trainee

                           SKILLS

Managerial:         • Planned fundraising activities
                      for nonprofit corporation.
                    • Supervised a staff of six
                      clerical workers
                    • Organized and facilitated
                      clerical planning group to
                      improve work environment
                    • Organized and conducted financial
                      aid workshops

Technical:          • Handled managerial accounts,
                      accounts payable, and payroll for
                      small company
                    • Estimated data patterns using
                      diverse forecasting methods
                    • Have experience with cost benefit
                      analysis
                    • Program in IFPS, MINITAB, and
                      BASIC

Analytical:         • Conducted research project on
                      recidivism rate among mentally
                      ill in St. Paul

Communication:      • Implemented project to improve
                      communication between management
                      and clerical staff
                    • Created system to improve data
                      collection for reports to
                      management

                          PERSONAL

                    Willing to relocate

                    References on request
```

FIGURE 19-6 _____

Functional resume. Timothy's skills have been derived primarily from clerical positions and from volunteer work. As he is looking for a position as a management trainee, he puts his managerial skills first.

```
                    TERESA WESTBANK

3786 Durant Avenue              (415) 347-9888 (w)
Dublin, CA 94568                (415) 899-2301 (h)


                      OBJECTIVE

               Personnel Administrator

            PROFESSIONAL BACKGROUND


Personnel Administrator, Carey Corporation, Oakland,
CA (1987—present).

• Recruit and interview exempt and nonexempt
  personnel
• Administer self-insured employee health insurance
  programs
• Administer union employee pension and health
  insurance programs
• Design personnel policies and procedures
• Develop employee handbooks for salaried and hourly
  employees
• Monitor workers' compensation and unemployment
  insurance claims
• Supervise four clerical workers


Personnel Representative, Business Consultants
Corporation, Oakland, CA (1985—86).

• Orient new employees
• Evaluate performance appraisals
• Compile statistical information
• Administer employee health insurance programs


                      EDUCATION

MBA, Personnel Administration/Industrial Relations,
California State University, San Francisco (1988).

BS, Social Welfare, California State University,
Sacramento (1985).


             References on request
```

FIGURE 19-7

Resume deemphasizing dates. This chronological resume deemphasizes dates and highlights
the duties Teresa has had at her jobs. Because her work experience is even more relevant
than her education, she has placed her professional experience first.

```
                        ARTHUR TOWNE
                        478 Coy Drive
                        Hanes, NH 32456
                        (303) 230-1296

    JOB OBJECTIVE       Computer Programmer/Analyst

    QUALIFICATIONS      • BS, Management Information
                          Systems
                        • 2 years' full-time programming
                          experience

    EXPERIENCE          Programmer, Computerland,
                        Boston, MA
                        Designed an integrated sales
                        order/purchase order system.
                        Designed and implemented accounts
                        receivable system and utilities
                        to work with point-of-sale
                        software. Also worked in sales,
                        customer support, and technical
                        service. (1987-89)

    EDUCATION           BS, Computer Science,
                        Boston College.
                        Mathematics minor (June 1989).

    COMPUTER SKILLS     Have worked on IBM PC/XT, IMSAI
                        8080, Northstar Horizon,
                        HP-2000F, CDC Cyber 170 720-2.

                        Familiar with UNIX, PC-DOS,
                        Primos, CP/M, NOS.

                        Can program in C, PASCAL, BASIC,
                        Fortran, PL/1, COBOL.

    COURSEWORK          Information Systems
                        Administration
                        Management Information Systems
                        Technical Writing
                        Business Calculus

    MEMBERSHIP          Data Processing Management
                        Association

    REFERENCES          On request
```

FIGURE 19-8 _____

Combination form resume. This resume combines skills with chronological information. Arthur puts his academic and professional qualifications at the beginning of the resume and deemphasizes dates. He includes a computer skills section that will be useful for an employer interested in hiring a programmer or analyst.

_____ **FIGURE 19-9** ►

Effective resume. This resume includes a specific career objective and relevant details about Marianne's preceptorship experience. The resume also lists names, addresses, and telephone numbers of three references. See Figure 21-8 for application letter accompanying this resume.

```
                              Marianne Ramirez
                              3789 M Street
                              Washington, DC 20016
                              (202) 298-2888

CAREER OBJECTIVE      Registered Nurse in an
                      intensive care nursery

EDUCATION             Bachelor of Science, Nursing,
   1989               George Washington University
                      Washington, DC

CLINICAL EXPERIENCE   PRECEPTORSHIP, Samuels
   1988               Medical Center, Bethesda, MD.
                      Attended deliveries;
                      stabilized and admitted
                      infants to ICN; performed
                      arterial and venous
                      punctures; assisted
                      physicians with UA, UV, and
                      percutaneous central line
                      placement, lumbar structures,
                      and intubation; assisted in
                      transfer of neonates to
                      tertiary centers. Completed
                      300 hours.

EMPLOYMENT            STOCK CLERK, Cornell
   1986—88            Pharmacy, Fairfax, VA.
                      Organized merchandise and
                      filled orders.

ORGANIZATIONS         Student Nurses Association

HONORS                Award of Recognition, Student
                      Nurses Association

                      Dean's List, George
                      Washington University

REFERENCES            Dr. Patricia Armand
                      Samuels Medical Center
                      10021 Manville Road
                      Bethesda, MD 20018
                      (202) 298-1290, ext. 246

                      Professor Gregory Hinsdale
                      School of Nursing
                      George Washington University
                      Washington, DC 20012
                      (202) 450-9212

                      Florence Miller, RN
                      Samuels Medical Center
                      10021 Manville Road
                      Bethesda, MD 20018
                      (202) 298-1290, ext. 235
```

```
                    ANITA NASMITH
                   170 E. 20th Street
                 New York City, NY 10013
                    (212) 347-4598
```

OBJECTIVE: Internship with a newspaper

EDUCATION: B.S., Communications and Journalism,
                expected June 1990, Brooklyn College

COURSEWORK: Interpersonal Communication
                Business Administration
                Feature Writing
                Introduction to Journalistic Writing
                Principles of Speech Communication

PROJECT   Wrote a research paper entitled
                "Newspapers or TV—Which Will Dominate
                the 1990s?"

EXPERIENCE: Clerk, Greene's Deli, New York City
                (summers, 1986—present)

                • Serve over 300 customers daily
                • Handle detail work effectively

AWARDS   Good Customer Service Awards, 1986
                and 1987

SKILLS: • Have good writing and speaking
                  skills
                • Am familiar with Wordstar and other
                  word processing programs
                • Type 60 wpm
                • Manage time effectively
                • Have extensive experience with the
                  public
                • Have strong analytical and problem-
                  solving skills

MEMBERSHIPS   College Debating Team
                College chess team

REFERENCES   Mr. Howard Charles   Dr. Marion Herrera
                Manager, Safeway   Communication Dept.
                412 East Avenue   Conway College
                Baltimore, MD 21135   12 Albemarle Street
                (301) 348-0923   Baltimore, MD 21134
                                        (301) 982-4477
```

**FIGURE 19-10** ───────────────────────────────────────────

Effective resume. This resume highlights the applicant's education and skills. Because the internships for which she is applying may involve clerical duties, she emphasizes office-related experience as well as communication skills.
```

```
                        RESUME
John Lehmann
90 Rose Court
Albany, GA
(216) 897-3881

GOAL:              Regional District
                   Superintendent

EXPERIENCE:        Albany Services District,
                   Albany, GA

4/85—present       Park Maintenance Superintendent
                   Duties: Handle maintenance of
                   park, swimming pool,
                   recreational and administrative
                   facilities. Administer $1.5
                   million budget. Supervise
                   personnel in Recreation
                   Department. Report to General
                   Manager.

7/82–3/85          Park Maintenance Worker
                   Duties: Handled landscape
                   maintenance and construction.
                   Communicated with superiors
                   regarding yearly budget needs.
                   Operated light and heavy
                   equipment.

6/81–7/82          Gardener's Assistant
                   Duties: Handled landscaping
                   duties. Worked with light and
                   heavy equipment.

EDUCATION:         BA, Business Administration,
6/86               Marysville College, Albany, GA

6/84               AS, Biological Sciences,
                   Beckford Junior College,
                   Beckford, GA

TRAINING COURSES:  Pest Management
                   Plant Disease Management
                   Urban Wildlife Management
                   Landscape Horticulture

MEMBERSHIPS:       • Park and Recreation Society
                   • Georgia Agricultural Pest
                       Control Advisers
                   • Landscape Superviors Forum

REFERENCES:        On request
```

FIGURE 19-11

Resume showing promotions. John Lehmann has worked for only one employer, but this resume shows the progress he made in his career. Dates in the margin show he has been continuously employed. Memberships and training courses as well as academic degrees show John's dedication to his career.

resume since you can easily update it. But do use a good printer and quality paper for the final copy.

If you are applying for a job, use that same quality paper for your cover letter and envelope. In essence, you are designing a marketing package for yourself. The appearance of that package can be almost as important as the contents.

Resume Format

Your resume should be typed in black or maybe brown ink on 8½ × 11 inch paper. The paper should be white or, at its wildest, beige. Your resume should stand out because of its quality, not because it is printed on turquoise paper.

The general arrangement of entries is more or less up to you: you may want to center your titles and print them in boldface, or underline them and put them in the margin. You may choose to set off your entries with stars, bullets, or dashes.

Whatever your artistic choices, make sure you leave a sizeable amount of white space on the page, so entries may be read easily. Avoid using fancy print that will slow down a reader.

Consistency

If you choose to write your graduation date as *6/85,* do not write out the month (*April 1984*) elsewhere in the resume. Do not underline one heading and then put another in boldface. Do not provide dates for one job but not for another.

Active Verbs

To make your resume as dynamic as possible, use verbs that highlight action. Avoid sluggish phrases such as "Helped new employees learn their job duties" when you can say, "Trained new employees."

Parallel Structure

Your entries should be consistent not only in their appearance on the page but also in their word usage. Most descriptions of job duties, for example, should start with verbs such as those in the list on page 471. Avoid complete sentences.

Duties: I was responsible for supervising six waiters. [wordy and ineffective]

Duties: Supervised six watiers. [direct and effective]

Keep to the same verb tense and format throughout each entry.

Duties: Supervised six waiters; handling customer complaints; telephones. [poor: not parallel]

Duties: Supervised six waiters; handled customer complaints; answered telephones. [good]

Duties: Supervising six waiters; handling customer complaints; answering telephones. [good]

Similarly, a list of skills should be in the same grammatical form.

Not Parallel	Parallel
Good writing skills	Write effectively
Am proficient in BASIC	Can program in BASIC
Type 75 wpm	Type 75 wpm
Time management	Manage time effectively

Strong Verbs

Consider using some of these action-oriented verbs in your resume:

Achieved	Formulated	Produced
Administered	Hired	Programmed
Analyzed	Implemented	Promoted
Assessed	Initiated	Recruited
Audited	Instructed	Revised
Centralized	Interviewed	Scheduled
Composed	Introduced	Staffed
Conducted	Launched	Streamlined
Created	Maintained	Supervised
Demonstrated	Marketed	Surveyed
Determined	Monitored	Tested
Developed	Negotiated	Tracked
Directed	Operated	Trained
Established	Organized	
Expedited	Planned	

Organizing Resume Components

Heading

Some resumes are titled *RESUME*. This heading is purely optional: most people will recognize what it is without being told. If you are short of space, omit the heading. (Note: the French word *résumé* has an accent over each *e*. In English, it is perfectly acceptable to omit the accents, especially as they are usually not included on English keyboards.)

Name, Address, Telephone Number

You must put your name, address, and telephone number at the top of your resume. You may include both a permanent address and a school address, a home and a business telephone number, but avoid cluttering the resume with too many addresses and numbers. You want an address where you will definitely receive your mail, and you want a phone number that will be answered consistently by you or by a friend, family member, answering service, or machine.

Your resume should not look cluttered.

Design the top of your resume to make it attractive and appealing to the eye.

Job Objective

Many resumes have an objective or job goal toward the top. This entry is optional, but useful. If you have a clear goal, such as Computer Programmer or Travel Agent, then include it. If you have Programmer as your objective, of course, you cannot send the resume in response to an ad for a Bank Teller. If you plan to apply for several kinds of jobs, either delete this entry or design more than one resume.

Remember, a reader glancing down the page wants to know what you are applying for. If you do not have a clear objective, omit the entry. (Make sure, however, that your cover letter states clearly what position you are seeking.) Avoid vague, verbose descriptions that fill up space on the page and tell the reader nothing.

> Job Objective: Seeking a position with management potential which will enable me to advance. Ideally, this would be a position in which an individual of ability and initiative would continue to grow professionally and obtain personal satisfaction. [verbose, vague]

> Job Objective: Interested in a public-oriented position, preferably where business knowledge would be applied and developed. [vague]

> Job Objective: Management Trainee [precise, clear]

Qualified By

If you have several strong points that you want your reader to spot right away, you might summarize your qualifications toward the top of your re-sume. For instance, if you have several years of work experience and a Masters degree, you could put this information under one heading. Do not go into a lot of detail here; simply pique your reader's interest and make him or her want to read further (see Figure 19-8). Again, avoid, long, fuzzy descriptions.

> Qualified by: A Masters in Business Administration from George Washington University and four years' full-time work experience with United Airlines. [good entry]

Skills

In a functional resume, the skills section is the most important. And, as noted earlier, you may want to include a skills section even in a chronological resume. In either case, brainstorming is probably in order. Jot down lots of skills, then organize them: organizational, computer, communication, accounting, marketing, and so on.

Starting with the skills most relevant to the job you want, list them in a way the reader will easily understand. Accountants would start with accounting skills, programmers with computer skills. You may be surprised at how many skills you have!

Remember, you do not have to explain when or where you acquired or used these skills.

Education

Many recent graduates will put education toward the top of their resume. If your work experience is more impressive, however, put that first. The education entry usually includes the degree, the major, the name and location of the school, and the date of graduation. (If you are deemphasizing dates, you do not need to include when you started the program, and you may even delete the graduation date. Include only what will speak *in your favor*.)

All items in your education and work experience entries should be arranged in *reverse* chronological order: start with the most recent items and move backwards in time.

If you attended several schools, you need not mention them all. Do mention where you got your degree(s) and include any impressive or unusual programs. Include your GPA if it is very good; do not include an even marginally good GPA.

You might also want to include awards, citations, fellowships, and so on in this section. You can also give them a separate section (see Figure 19-9).

Coursework

Do NOT list all your classes. If you have taken some unusual or particularly impressive courses, put them down. Computer programmers might want to list all the computer language courses they have taken; accountants need not mention that they took Principles of Accounting, but they might want to mention a tax or auditing class. (Figure 19-10 illustrates a resume in which coursework is highlighted.)

High School

Include high school information only if you did not graduate too long ago and if the information is particularly relevant to the job you want.

The farther you get from high school, the less relevant it becomes. Even entries about being yearbook editor or senior class president look a little strained fifteen years later.

Work Experience

Education and Work Experience are usually the focal points of a resume. Once again, decide how your format will best highlight your strong points.

(Figures 19-3 and 19-7 present you with some interesting variations on the work experience entries.) You do NOT need to include

- all your jobs
- all your duties
- the name of your supervisor
- the full address of the places you worked

And you should NEVER include

- why you left
- your salary

Keep to a consistent format throughout the resume.

Do put each entry in a consistent format: if you begin with the name of the company in capitals, then use that format throughout. Avoid listing too many duties; try to highlight the most relevant ones. For example, if you are looking for an accounting position, put any accounting-related duties first— even if you did them less frequently than, say, answering the telephone or working a cash register.

Memberships

Make sure you list any memberships in community or school organizations and any positions you have held (see Figures 19-1 and 19-11). For some people, memberships and activities may be more important than work experience.

Languages

Include foreign languages that you can read or speak and any computer languages with which you are familiar.

Other Entries

Include licenses, special abilities, training courses, technical skills (see Figure 19-11).

Interests

This entry is optional. You may want to include some hobbies or activities if you have room on your resume. Be concrete rather than vague: *Varsity Swimming* is more impressive than *Sports*, for instance. Put down any particularly relevant interests: someone interested in advertising might want to mention an interest in photography or graphics.

Personal Data

In years past, many resumes began with information about the writer's age, place of birth, marital status, and health. Now none of this information is mandatory; employers cannot legally ask questions about several of these areas, and most people consider applicant's eye color, weight, and height irrelevant to most jobs.

Either delete these data or put a few selected details at the *end* of the resume. Timothy Chu (Figure 19-6), for example, included his willingness to relocate.

References

You may list references on the resume, add a separate sheet of references, or tell the reader that they are available on request. If your resume is crowded, you could delete the entry altogether and mention references in your cover letter. When you do list them on the resume, make sure you have more than one and no more than four. Put the full name, title, address, and telephone number of each reference (see Figures 19-9 and 19-10).

Include complete information for each reference.

What Would You Do?

Kyle Thorpe was looking for a managerial position, so he went to a resume service advertised in his college newspaper. The service produced the following resume.

```
THE CONFIDENTIAL RESUME OF: Kyle P. Thorpe

2893 T Street                        Personal: single
Washington, DC 20016                 willing to travel
(202) 235-8924                       6' 2", 210 lbs.

Objective: A management position that will give me an
opportunity to utilize my financial and "people" skills.
Education: BA, Mathematics (University of Maryland)
           MBA, Operations Research (University of Maryland)
Experience: I worked as a sixth grade mathematics teacher in
Baltimore, Maryland before returning to school for my MBA.
While in graduate school, I worked as a Teaching Assistant in
Mathematics.
For the past six years, I have worked for Grey Brothers
Corporation (Baltimore) as a Financial Clerk and then as
Budgets Accountant.
My skills include: basic accounting and programming
```

Shocked at how poorly this resume reflected his experience and skills, Kyle refused to pay the $50 the service charged. When he went home that night, however, he could not figure out how to improve the version produced by the service.

Design a more effective resume for him.

Handling Special Problems

Most people worry that they have deficiencies in their backgrounds that will hurt their chances of getting the job they want. Some of the most common problems, however, can be handled with an effective resume format. The following questions are some of the ones job applicants ask most frequently.

None of my work experience is relevant. What should I do? Highlight your education and skills. You may want to design a functional resume.

My only experience is in the military. Should I include it? Yes. Military experience is relevant to many positions. List your branch of service, rank, dates of induction and discharge, and duties most relevant to the job you want.

I've done volunteer work but never held a paying job. What should I put on my resume? Your abilities are more important than whether you were paid. You can list your volunteer work under Experience or develop a functional resume.

How do I keep employers from seeing I'm older than the other applicants? You may not have as much of a problem as you think; many employers prefer more mature employees. However, you can design a resume without dates, or you can deemphasize dates. Also, you do not have to include information going back to your earliest jobs.

I have the wrong major for the job. What do I do? You can put your education entry toward the bottom of the resume. If you have an academic degree and have taken coursework related to the job, emphasize them. (The longer you have been out of school, the less important your major will become.)

I was fired from a job. How do I handle that? You don't. The resume should not indicate why you left a position. You do not even have to mention that job on the resume. Be prepared, however, to discuss the problem in an interview if the subject comes up.

Should I mention that I am unwilling to travel or relocate? No, just mention if you *are* willing.

What if I haven't been working for a some time? You do not have to account for every month of your time on the resume.

What if some of my jobs were relevant and some were not? You do not have to list every job you held—or every school you attended. The resume should list only *highlights* of your career.

Should I mention salary on the resume? No. Save discussion of salary until you get an interview or, even better, an actual job offer.

I am physically disabled. Should I mention my handicap on my resume? Usually an interview is the proper place to discuss a disability. Do not feel obligated to mention it on the resume.

I don't know anyone to ask for letters of recommendation. You can ask any instructor, supervisor, or even coworker. In the future, ask for letters of reference before you leave a job or a school.

Summary

Your resume should highlight your unique skills and background. Whatever format you choose, the resume should be easy to read and should contain specific details relevant to the type of position you are interested in. Make sure the headings are consistent and the entries accurate. Proofread carefully.

You will find it worthwhile to keep your resume updated, since it can be useful even when you are not actively looking for a job.

Resume Checklist

Format

- In developing a resume format,

  _____ use white space on the page effectively

  _____ set up consistent headings and entries

  _____ delete irrelevant material

  _____ include only positive information

  _____ make entries as specific as possible

  _____ check that entries are accurate and objective

  _____ use active verbs whenever possible

  _____ use black or brown ink on white or beige paper

  _____ check carefully for typographical errors

- Considering using a chronological format when you want

  _____ to emphasize dates

  _____ to highlight relevant previous jobs

- Consider using a functional or skills format when you want

  _____ to deemphasize dates

  _____ to highlight skills rather than jobs

Terms to Remember

Chronological resume: resume set up to indicate what you were doing during specified years

Functional or skills resume: resume set up to show what skills you possess

Summary Discussion: Andrew Poole's Resume from Case in Point, p. 454

The long lines of Andrew Poole's resume make it difficult to read. Nothing of importance stands out on the page. To revise the resume, Andrew should reduce sentences to phrases and use lists to highlight important information. (And he should change *Safe way* to *Safeway*.)

Andrew would be better off deleting both the personal data entry and the GPA. However, he could add coursework and skills to link himself more closely with the type of job he wants. In general, the resume needs more concrete detail.

The resume would benefit from a focused job objective entry. Work- and school-related references would be more useful to prospective employers than this one personal reference.

Questions for Review and Discussion

1. When is a chronological resume more effective than a functional one? When is a functional resume more effective?
2. Why should a resume be only one or two pages long?
3. When should you put a job objective on your resume?
4. Should you list every school you have attended? Why or why not?
5. Should you list high school activities? Why or why not?
6. Should your grade point average be on the resume? Why or not?
7. What personal data are appropriate?
8. Should you list references? If so, how many?
9. Why is "white space" important to the resume format?
10. Should your salary history be on the resume? Why or why not?

Exercises

1. Revise the following sluggish descriptions from resumes. Write in phrases, not complete sentences; remove personal pronouns.
   a. When the company needed a new manual on personnel procedures, I helped to organize and write it.
   b. Was instructed to draw the illustrations for the company's newspaper advertisements.
   c. Showed clerical employees how to operate new computer hardware.
   d. When job applicants telephoned, I would talk to them before scheduling their interviews with department managers
   e. When the supervisor was out of town, I made sure the office ran smoothly
2. Design an effective resume for Andrew Poole

   (see p. 454).
3. Develop a list of your strong and weak points. Make sure you consider these points from *an employer's* viewpoint. Then write a paragraph or two explaining what your resume strategy should be: given your particular job goals, what should you highlight? What should you deemphasize? Should you use a chronological or functional resume—or a composite of the two? Why?
4. Develop a resume for a full-time, part-time, or summer job.
5. Exchange resumes with a fellow classmate. Each of you should evaluate the other's resume for appearance and content. Write comments directly on the resume sheet.

Word processing techniques are particularly useful for resumes since you can try different formats without having to retype each version. The following exercise draws on some of the techniques you learned in earlier exercises.

Create a standard chronological resume on the word processor. (See the resume at the end of the exercise for an example.) Use the following format guidelines:

1. Put your name in all capital letters in boldface at the top of the page. Center your name.
2. Center your address and telephone number under your name.
3. Underline all major headings and put them in all capital letters. Headings should include *OBJECTIVE, EXPERIENCE, EDUCATION,* and *COURSEWORK.* You may include other headings as well. Put dates in left-hand margin.
4. Use a tab to begin all entries approximately 2 inches from the left-hand side of the page.
5. Make ragged right-hand margins.
6. Single-space entries, but double-space between each section.
7. Put job titles in boldface.
8. Center copy so top and bottom margins are of similar width.
9. Enter the command to eliminate page numbers on the resume.
10. Print the resume and edit the hard copy. Then print it on an individual sheet of paper.

JAMES G. SAICHOW
3478 Mill Drive
Oakwood, VT 21347
(812) 492-1276

<u>OBJECTIVE</u>	Freelance Writer
<u>EDUCATION</u> 1988	BA, Journalism, Handlin University, Paige, VT, GPA 3.45
1982	AA, General Studies, Cabot Junior College, Westland, VT
<u>COURSEWORK</u>	Newspaper Reporting Expository Writing Copywriting Business Communication Advertising
<u>EXPERIENCE</u> 1988	**Editor,** <u>The Pennysaver,</u> Oakwood, VT. Wrote and edited articles for neighborhood newspaper.
1987	**Reporter,** <u>Oakwood Times,</u> Oakwood, VT. Wrote articles on local high school sports for newspaper.
1985–86	**Courier,** <u>Oakwood Times,</u> Oakwood, VT. Delivered newspapers.

Application Letters and Other Employment Communications

- Writing letters regarding employment
- Creating an employer-oriented application letter
- Writing job inquiry letters
- Filling out application forms
- Requesting letters of recommendation
- Writing follow-up letters
- Writing thank-you letters
- Accepting a position
- Refusing a position
- Requesting more time
- Resigning from a position

Objectives

To create job application letters that get the results you want

To write effective letters for all facets of the employment process

20

Jonathan Lee's Application Letter

When Jonathan Lee saw this advertisement in his local newspaper, he was excited at the prospect of making some extra money.

BUSINESS MAJORS. EARN EXTRA $$$$ IN SALES

Major Publishing Company is looking for energetic business majors to work as sales representatives during the school year. You should have some knowledge of accounting and economics and some sales experience. Interested students, mail a resume and application letter to Hoover Publishers, 231 Annandale Blvd., Peterson, VA 21134. Equal Opportunity Employer.

Jonathan immediately wrote the following letter.

```
                         378 Lorie Street,
                         Apt. B
                         Peterson, VA 21136
                         August 8, 19xx

Hoover Publishers
231 Annandale Boulevard
Peterson, VA 21134
```

```
Dear Sirs:

    If you want to hire an aggressive
college student, I'm the man for you.
Although I have not yet taken an
economics class, I have a lot of
appropriate skills, and I can persuade
anyone of anything!
    When my resume enclosed herewith has
been reviewed, call me at the number
listed. I know you'll find I'm perfect
for your company.

                         Sincerely,

                         Jonathan Lee

                         Jonathan Lee
```

To his dismay, Jonathan never heard from Hoover Publishers or from several other firms to which he sent similar letters.

Points to Consider
• What information is missing from this letter?
• What do you suggest deleting from this letter?
• Do you think the letter is effective? Explain.

Writing Letters Regarding Employment

Creating an effective resume is a major part of the employment process, but it is still only a part. As a job candidate, you will probably have to write letters of inquiry and application as well as thank-you letters and letters accepting or refusing positions. You may also have to resign from a position you already hold.

All of these communications require tact and a reader–oriented attitude. However, for a number of them, you will be able to use one general format repeatedly: when you develop a format you like, you will not have to start from scratch every time you write a letter with a similar purpose.

The job-search process requires letter-writing skills.

Creating an Employer-Oriented Application Letter

The application letter is a vital component of your application. Not only does it interpret and humanize your resume, but it reveals your abilities as a communicator—and even as a salesperson. Because they are difficult to write,

Your application letter humanizes your resume.

application letters give a prospective employer insights into your abilities that she or he cannot receive from the resume alone or even from an interview.

The letter also allows you to demonstrate interest and excitement in the job as well as to highlight the skills and experience directly linking you with the position and the firm. And, perhaps most importantly, the letter enables you to request an interview.

To get you that interview, your application letter must be flawlessly written and attractively presented. In fact, like your resume, it must be perfect.

The You-Attitude

The application letter is very similar to a sales letter. It must be persuasive, and it must relate to the reader even though it is describing the writer.

To focus your letter on the needs of a prospective employer, remember the list in Chapter 18 (pp. 447–448) of the qualities an employer is looking for: specific job-related skills, communication skills, commitment, industriousness, personality, and appropriate values and goals. Your letter should reflect these qualities as well as an interest in the position.

Specific Skills

One goal of the application letter is to highlight skills useful to the position you are applying for. If you are applying for a type of position you have held in the past, this aspect of your letter will be fairly easy; knowing the company

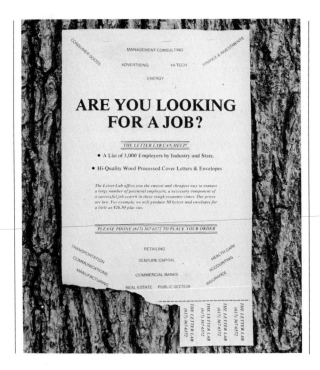

is looking for someone who can program in Cobol, you can describe your expertise and the successful work you accomplished either in school or at another company.

If the position is different from what you have held in the past, you will have to show how your skills and coursework make you a good candidate (Figures 20-1 and 20-2).

For example, if you are applying for a position in Personnel, you can accentuate how your academic background will be useful and then perhaps highlight relevant aspects of former jobs, such as hiring, supervising, counseling, or training.

To indicate capability, also, you will want to demonstrate your success in school, at work, and even in sports or hobbies. Most employers know that exact knowledge of a job is often less important than the success applicants have demonstrated throughout their lives.

Commitment

Training employees takes time and money. Most employers are looking for someone who will want to stay with the firm for some time. Even employers looking for part-time or summer employees want applicants with a stable work history and an interest in the job.

If you have held one or more jobs for a long time, emphasize your loyalty. Never criticize a company or job in any way. If you have held many jobs for short durations, indicate your enthusiasm for the job you are applying for and your interest in a career with the firm.

Avoid any negative comments in your application letter.

At times you may have to use some tact. Most employers, for example, will not be happy to learn that you are hoping to start your own company some day. While your successful leadership and fascination with entrepreneurship may strike you as your most positive qualities, you will have to reveal them in some other way. If you want to continue your education, do not indicate that you will be leaving the job in order to go back to school.

A little research can help you. Some firms encourage employee education. Some even fund it. Others would rather have the undivided attention of their workforce. By announcing your educational plans, you might think you are showing your ambition and assertiveness, while actually you are insuring that you do not get an interview. Before revealing your plans, try to find out the company's attitudes or policies.

One of the best ways to demonstrate your potential loyalty is to show knowledge about the firm itself. Tailor the letter to the firm as well as to the job so the reader will sense that you really do care about the company. A sentence or two can go a long way to assuring an employer that you will be a dedicated employee.

Indicate your enthusiasm for the particular company to which you are applying.

Industriousness

Most employers, of course, want employees who will work hard and manage their time successfully. Without bragging, establish these qualities in your letter (Figure 20–3).

```
                                        1928 Arbor Avenue
                                        Detroit, MI 57892
                                        May 1, 19xx

    Mr. Craig Reuben
    Derbin Accounting Corporation
    390 Wilson Boulevard
    Detroit, MI 57823

    Dear Mr. Reuben:

       Thank you for taking the time to speak with me
    at the University Job Fair regarding entry-level
    positions at Derbin Accounting Corporation. As you
    suggested, I am enclosing a resume for your
    consideration.
       Both coursework and experience qualify me
    for an entry-level accounting position. As an
    undergraduate at Wilson University, I have taken
    courses in intermediate accounting, cost
    accounting, auditing, and auditing research
    methods. Coursework in business law, management
    information sciences, and economic forecasting has
    contributed to my well-rounded business background.
       Positions as a salesperson and as a property
    manager have also given me valuable practical
    experience. Excellent communication and time-
    management skills, combined with experience with
    small businesses, will also be an asset to my work
    with Derbin Accounting Corporation's numerous small
    business clients.
       Please consider my application to become part
    of Derbin Accounting Corporation's excellent
    accounting staff. As my graduation date is June 30,
    I could begin work early in July. I will telephone
    your office on Monday, May 8 to see if we can set
    up an interview.

                                        Sincerely,

                                        Marina LaGuardia

                                        Marina LaGuardia

    enclosure
```

FIGURE 20-1

Application letter. This effective application letter is polite and professional. Marina relates
her experience directly to the job she is interested in and includes relevant, concrete information.

```
                              165 Wildberry Drive
                              Valley Hill, NH 02345
                              July 3, 19xx

Mr. Gregory Jamison
Personnel Manager
C and T Stores
235 Union Plaza
Fairfield, NH 02347

Dear Mr. Jamison:

   Please consider my application for the Assistant
Personnel Manager position advertised in the Valley
Hill College Placement Center. My education and
background qualify me for the position.
   As a personnel major at Valley Hill College,
I have taken classes in personnel evaluation,
compensation, and collective bargaining and labor
law. While taking a full load of courses and
working 30 hours a week, I have maintained a 3.4
grade point average and participated actively in
student organizations. (See my enclosed resume.)
   Extensive work with the Personnel Administration
Club on campus has increased my interest in
practical aspects of the field and has given me
additional experience dealing with individuals
and groups.
   Having long known the company's reputation for
excellent employee relations and customer service,
I am very enthusiastic about a career with C & T
Stores. I would be able to start work full-time on
December 1. Please call me at 343-4677 if you are
interested in my application. Thank you for your
consideration.

                         Sincerely,

                         Philip O'Brien

                         Philip O'Brien
```

FIGURE 20-2 _____

Application letter. This application letter highlights Philip's academic experience as he has no
work experience. Note that he does not apologize about his lack of experience; he simply
outlines his strong points.

```
                                        2391 Lexington Avenue
                                        Millburn, OH 34970
                                        April 3, 19xx

Ms. Laura Bazzani
District Manager
PARTCO Corporation
231 Jane Drive
Millburn, OH 34971

Dear Ms. Bazzani:

   Please consider my application for the summer
sales position advertised in today's Daily News.
Having discussed opportunities at PARTCO with your
sales representative, John Healy, I am very
interested in working as a salesperson in the
business forms industry.
   Presently completing my sophomore year at Ohio
State University, I am majoring in business
administration. My classes in marketing and retail
sales, combined with my experience as a sales
clerk, will be an asset to the sales position.
   As a sales clerk at Gerri's Boutique last summer,
I quickly acquired a loyal clientele and won two
monthly Top Sales Awards. In fact, my sales figures
for the summer were higher than those of any other
temporary employee.
   I am a highly motivated, energetic, and
persuasive person eager to handle the independence
and challenge of a position in industrial sales.
   The enclosed resume highlights my academic
background and work experience. I will telephone
you next week to see if we can set up an interview.

                              Sincerely,

                              Terry Inouye

                              Terry Inouye
```

FIGURE 20-3 _____

Application letter. This application for a summer job effectively ties Terry's work and educational background to the job and emphasizes the qualities needed in a sales position. By mentioning her sales awards, Terry offers specific evidence of her sales abilities.

To show your industriousness, you must provide facts. Simply claiming "I work hard" does not carry much impact. By mentioning that you work part-time while going to school full-time or that you have maintained a high GPA with a double major, you *show* that you can work. When you tell a prospective employer that you have been promoted—or that you were offered a full-time position after finishing a summer job—you are letting him or her know in the best possible way that you are a good worker.

Note: *Never* indicate in a letter or an interview that you have trouble managing your time or that you changed jobs or majors because you were overworked.

Personality

Probably the hardest part of writing an application letter is conveying a pleasant personality. Many times letters are pompous, assertive, groveling, or overly remote and formal. Yet an employer is often more concerned about the personality of an applicant than about his or her skills: after all, most people can be trained to perform a job, but if they do not get along with their co-workers, everyone will suffer.

Work on creating a pleasant, professional tone.

The key to a good application letter is a pleasant, enthusiastic, but professional tone that will make the reader want to meet you.

Values and Goals

As you know, employers are often interested in finding employees whose values and goals are similar to those of the company. Again, research can help you find out whether you and the company mesh. If the company's literature mentions social or environmental commitment, for example, you might insert your similar values in your letter. If you know the company values a willingness to travel in its new employees, mention your own willingness.

Avoiding Major Pitfalls

Before starting to develop an effective letter, be aware of some major pitfalls.

- *Copying from Books*. Write your own letter rather than relying on examples from books. Your letter should not sound like someone else wrote it.
- *Clichés*. Use natural word choices. Avoid clichés and common formulas of application letters such as "Thank you in advance for your time."
- *Bragging*. Use objective language to highlight your strengths. Avoid telling the employer how much he or she needs you.
- *Criticism*. Never find fault with your present employer, fellow workers, or supervisor.
- *Long-windedness*. A few concrete details will say far more than pages of autobiography.
- *Groveling*. Speak to the employer as one professional to another, not as slave to master.
- *Self-deprecation*. Present your background in the best possible light. Do not include ANY negative details about yourself.
- *Pompous Language*. Like the resume, the letter should be easy to read. The reader is more apt to be annoyed than impressed by ponderous words.
- *Passive Voice*. Be personal. Use active verbs. Compare "An interview with you at your convenience would be much appreciated" with "I look forward to meeting you."

(Figures 20-4, 20-5, 20-6, and 20-7 show examples of poor application letters and revisions.)

```
                                        389 Alsop Street
                                        Houston, TX 98445
                                        January 23, 19xx

         Ms. Theresa Schumacher
         Personnel Department
         Bechtel Corporation
         50 Beale Street
         San Francisco, CA 92106

         Dear Ms. Schumacher:

            In the past, I have worked with numerous large
         companies with a wide diversity of information
         systems. I realize that accurate and timely
         information is vital. I foresee the widespread
         installation and use of small desk-top computers
         tied into mainframes. This transformation, when
         complete, will make information readily available
         to all who need it. I will be in a good position to
         make this transition as smooth as possible for
         Bechtel as I have experience with both small and
         larger machines.
            The level of professionalism at Bechtel has
         always impressed me, and I would be happy to work
         with you on a permanent basis. When I have a job to
         do, I cannot rest until it is done right. I know I
         can exhibit this professional work ethic as an
         assistant systems analyst working at Bechtel. I
         spent a summer working with Bechtel overseas and
         would appreciate an interview for a full-time
         position.
            Would you please inform me if an interview can be
         arranged? Thank you.

                                        Sincerely,

                                        Gayle Lyons

                                        Gayle Lyons
```

FIGURE 20-4 _____

Poor application letter. This application letter is long-winded without containing much useful information. The long paragraphs make the letter difficult to scan, and the roundabout format deters the reader from discovering the point of the letter. The major points—the job she is applying for and her experience with the company—are lost in the clutter.

See Figure 20-5 for a revision of this letter.

```
                              389 Alsop Street
                              Houston, TX 98445
                              January 23, 19xx

Ms. Theresa Schumacher
Personnel Department
Bechtel Corporation
50 Beale Street
San Francisco, CA 92106

Dear Ms. Schumacher:

   Please consider me an applicant for the assistant
analyst position advertised in the Wall Street
Journal on January 21. My double major in business
administration and computer science, coupled with
my experience working with Bechtel overseas, should
make me an excellent candidate for the position.
   As you can see from the enclosed resume, I have
worked both on a mainframe and on personal
computers. As assistant programmer for Stores
Unlimited, I maintain batch jobs and on-line jobs
while developing new on-line and batch jobs for
users. As student tutor in the computer laboratory
at Houston University, I have worked with a wide
range of programs and programming styles.
   Experience as an intern clerk with Bechtel's
offices in Saudi Arabia convinced me that I want
the excitement and dynamism of a Bechtel career.
As I will be in San Francisco in February, I will
telephone you next week to see if we can set up an
interview. Thank you for considering my
application.

                              Sincerely,

                              Gayle Lyons

                              Gayle Lyons
```

FIGURE 20-5 _____

Revised application letter. In this letter, Gayle demonstrates her enthusiasm for Bechtel as well as some concrete skills relevant to the position she wants. Her revision is also much less I-oriented than the original version.

```
                                        56830 Byrd Drive
                                        Winton, WY 45908
                                        September 12, 19xx

        Mr. James Dubois
        Assistant Treasurer
        Hart Communications
        9325 Mitten Avenue
        Winton, WY 45909

        Dear Mr. Dubois:

           The recent article in Business Week on troubles
        in the communication industry mentioned that,
        although Hart Communications is making profits, it
        could use some troubleshooters with new ideas. As a
        financial analyst in your company, I could be just
        that type of troubleshooter.
           My MBA in Finance has enabled me to gain an
        extensive understanding of all the operations
        necessary to a company like yours. I can perform
        financial analyses, and I have enormous experience
        in capital budgeting, cash flow analysis, and
        security valuation.
           I know Hart Communications would benefit from a
        young, enthusiastic go-getter like me on your team.
        Please call me any weekday between 9 a.m. and 1
        p.m. for an interview. My resume is enclosed.

                                        Sincerely,

                                        Todd Pilson

                                        Todd Pilson
```

FIGURE 20-6 _____

Poor application letter. This application letter is brash and reader-oriented. Rather than linking himself professionally with the position, Todd boasts about his abilities. His letter also
implicitly criticizes the company. In this letter, Todd has forgotten a cardinal rule of persuasive writing: do not criticize or patronize the reader.

See Figure 20-7 for a revision of this letter.

```
                                        56890 Byrd Drive
                                        Winton, WY 45908
                                        September 12, 19xx

Mr. James Dubois
Assistant Treasurer
Hart Communications
9325 Mitten Avenue
Winton, WY 45909

Dear Mr. Dubois:

    The recent Business Week article on the
communication industry showed that Hart
Communications is one of the strongest companies in
the field. As a financial analyst, I could
contribute to Hart's continuing success.
    My MBA coursework in finance and my experience as
a purchasing agent with Spring Communications make
me an ideal candidate for a financial analyst
position. As a buyer, I have performed cost
analyses on capital equipment purchases and have
become familiar with the company's operations.
    Coursework at the University of Wyoming has
enhanced my skills in capital budgeting, cash flow
analysis, and security valuation. Much of what I
have learned will be valuable to my work at Hart.
    I am particularly interested in working for a
company that is growing as quickly as Hart, and one
that is competing so successfully with larger
companies.
    I will call your office next week to arrange an
interview at your convenience.

                                        Sincerely,

                                        Todd Pilson

                                        Todd Pilson
```

FIGURE 20-7

Revised application letter. This letter puts the company in a good light and presents Todd's skills positively but realistically. Without using a lot of words, Todd reveals both his knowledge about the company and his own relevant background.

Sending Solicited and Unsolicited Application Letters

A solicited letter is sent in response to a job announcement.

A solicited letter is sent in response to an advertised job opening or a personal request for your application. An unsolicited letter is sent when no job has been announced or advertised.

Whether solicited or unsolicited, most application letters have the same basic outline and information. In the opening paragraph of a solicited letter, however, indicate how you know about the position:

Mrs. Ralph Henderson on your accounting staff recommended that I apply for the entry-level accounting position advertised in the *Dallas Sun*.

I am applying for the programmer position you listed in the Bolt College Placement Center.

An unsolicited letter is sent when no position has been announced.

An unsolicited letter can be more difficult to write because you do not have any job description to use as a basis for your qualifications. Moreover, you may not know to whom you should address the application.

You can address the letter to the manager of the personnel department, but you might want to telephone the company before writing and ask where to send your application letter. From the telephone conversation, also, you may learn that the company wants applicants to fill out a standard application form.

Organizing Components of Application Letters

The sections of an application letter are similar to those of a sales letter; in fact, an application letter *is* a sales letter of a very special sort. (Thinking of yourself as a product, by the way, may help you create an effective letter.) As in a sales letter, you need to

1. Get the attention of the reader
2. Create interest through concrete information
3. Provide the reader with a plan of action

Attention. Most application letters open with a sentence such as, "I am responding to your advertisement in the *Sunday Post*." This is similar to a sales letter beginning, "We found your name on a list of magazine subscribers." Such an opening would not make anyone's pulse quicken with excitement.

Your application letter should make the reader want to read on.

Remember that your application letter may well receive about the same attention as a piece of junk mail unless you get the reader's attention from the start. How do you do this? Applicants should have individual methods that suit their own needs and personality. Lines copied from a book are as boring as television reruns. However, consider some techniques that have worked for applicants in the past.

Summarize Your Qualifications. Often you can capture your reader's attention by stating your strong points in the opening sentence—particularly if they mesh with requirements listed in the job description.

As a recent graduate with a BS in finance and two years' experience with Ohio National Bank, I am applying for the assistant analyst position advertised in this morning's *Post*.

My degrees in both marketing and journalism, coupled with strong communication skills, should make me a strong candidate for a copywriter position with your firm.

Mention Meeting or Speaking with Your Reader. If you have met your reader even briefly, mention the meeting in the opening of your letter. Even if you only heard him or her speak at a conference, make that contact right away: the personal note will set your letter apart from the others.

> If you can, introduce a personal element to your letter.

When you spoke to the Balboa Accounting Association last spring, you mentioned that your company is always looking for intelligent and hardworking accounting majors.

If you spoke to the reader, definitely remind her or him of that occasion. If the person recommended that you apply for a job, be especially sure to jog the person's memory.

Thank you again for taking the time to speak with me about Harrison Corporation at the Marketing Symposium last April. At that time you recommended that I consider a career with your firm when I finished my bachelor degree. Now that I have graduated from the University of Alabama, I would very much like to apply for a management trainee position with your firm.

Mention Personal Recommendations. In a similar vein, if an employee of the firm, preferably someone who knows your reader, has recommended that you apply, then mention him or her in the opening sentence.

Ms. Patricia Hooper recommended that I apply for an entry-level accounting position with FJI.

Refer to the Company's Needs. Another attention-getter is a sentence that reveals your knowledge and interest while also indicating the company's need for your skills.

The recent *Wall Street Journal* article on your firm's expansion to West Virginia interested me very much. As the article indicated that you may be looking for computer programmers in this area, I am enclosing my resume for your consideration.

Refer to the Advertisement. Another approach is to refer to relevant lines of the job description and apply them to yourself.

Your advertisement for an assistant personnel manager requests that applicants have an undergraduate business degree and at least two years' experience with a retail outlet. I have those qualifications.

Concrete Evidence. After getting your reader's attention, you have to keep him or her interested with strong sentences filled with concrete detail concerning your skills and background. Remember, however, to link that experience with the job you are applying for: do not just list items randomly.

Relevant Background. Many application letters catalogue the writer's work history like this:

> After graduating from high school, I worked at Hock's Hardware as a salesclerk and continued there part-time after I started college. I presently work part-time as a cashier and bookkeeper at Toy World and tutor students in algebra in the university Math Laboratory.

This writer actually has some good experience, but she has not developed it successfully in the letter. In fact, she has only repeated information on her resume. Her *interpretation* of that information should depend on the type of job she is applying for.

If she is applying for a personnel position, for example, she could highlight her work with people.

> As a bookkeeper/cashier at Toy World, I deal with over a hundred customers a day; I also train new cashiers to work the computerized cash registers and assist the Manager with payroll procedures. As a clerk at Hock's Hardware, I received the Employee of the Month Award for maintaining good relations with customers.

> While tutoring in the Math Laboratory, I work closely with ten students a semester: since many of them come to me with a "mental block" about algebra, I am happy to say that all of them have finished the course with a B− or better.

In a subsequent paragraph, she should also emphasize that she works at two jobs while attending school full-time.

If the same applicant were applying for an entry-level accounting position, she would interpret her experience differently.

> As a bookkeeper/cashier at Toy World, I work with the manager on payroll procedures and input accounts payable information on the IBM computer system. While a clerk at Hock's Hardware, I helped the manager to choose the best accounting software available for a store of that size and type.

> My strong quantitative and personal skills have helped me work effectively with students in the university Math Laboratory. I am happy to say that all my students have received a B− or better in their algebra classes.

Notice that this applicant does not keep saying, "I am a hard worker" or "I am successful." She simply *shows* her success and the trust her employers have put in her.

Most students' application letters will have one or two strong paragraphs on their education and one or two on their experience. Do not write too much, but do make sure you include important information such as your degree and where you work at present (Figure 20-8).

Avoid long lists. Do not mention *every* accounting or computer class you have taken or every duty you had at a certain job. Your sentences, like those in a sales letter, should be crisp and clear—and not too long. Remember, you are constantly in danger of losing your reader's interest. Keep things moving.

Links with Company/Position. Do not assume that your reader can read between the lines of a resume to find your skills. State clearly the connections

```
                                        3789 M Street
                                        Washington, DC 20016
                                        February 2, 1989

Mrs. Henry Liu
Coordinator, Nurse Recruitment
Harrison Hospital
Nursing Administration, Room 245
Washington, DC 20018

Dear Mrs. Liu:

    I am interested in pursuing a career as a
registered nurse in the Intensive Care Nursery at
Harrison Hospital.
    A recent graduate of George Washington
University, I have also completed a preceptorship
at Samuels Medical Center. My responsibilities
included attending deliveries, stabilizing and
admitting infants, assessing the newborn, and
implementing appropriate nursing interventions.
    Harrison Hospital has outstanding facilities and
offers many opportunities for a new graduate. The
Harrison Hospital Intensive Care Nursery has a
national reputation for excellence. I hope you will
seriously consider my application.
    Enclosed you will find my resume, clinical skills
inventory list, transcripts, and letters of
reference. Please let me know if you need further
information.
    I will telephone you on February 12 to arrange an
appointment.

                            Sincerely,

                            Marianne Ramirez

                            Marianne Ramirez
```

FIGURE 20-8 _____

Application letter. This application letter, which accompanies the resume in Figure 19-9, concisely presents the writer's background and enthusiasm for the position she wants.

between your skills and the position. For example, in the application for an accounting position described on page 494, the applicant should include specific references to the job and the company while detailing her experience.

Avoid general statements such as, "I know my skills will be an asset to your company." Instead, try sentences such as

I know my experience with customers and students will be helpful in a firm like yours, which has such a wide variety of small business clients.

or

Having gone to school full-time while working at Toy World through the Christmas season, I know I will be able to handle the long hours and pressure of the tax season with your firm. In fact, I look forward to the challenge.

Emphasize qualities you will bring to that specific company and position.

As we mentioned earlier, the reader of an application letter is not interested just in *you*: he or she wants to know how you relate to the job and the firm. The more information you have about the company, the better you will be able to provide links between yourself and the job. (This information will become even more important when you get an interview.)

If you are really interested in the position, do some of the research discussed in Chapter 18. Read *The Wall Street Journal*, company newsletters, annual reports, Standard & Poor's *Register of Corporations, Directors and Executives*, and business magazines. If you are applying to small companies, try telephoning for some information. You can at least learn how many employees and offices the company has—and you may pick up some other worthwhile information.

If you are looking for programming work, find out what systems the firm uses. If you are looking for sales work, find out about the products. Concrete details will make your letter stand out from the rest.

While on the tennis team at Ohio State University, I found Nike tennis shoes to be the most durable and comfortable product on the market. I know I could convince retailers of Nike's superiority and give them useful information to pass on to salespeople and customers.

Of course, if you are writing to a box number in a newspaper ad, you cannot do this type of research; but, in other situations, you should do your homework. A good job is worth some effort!

Conclusion. The beginning and ending are the most important parts of any sales writing, and an application letter is no exception. Many writers become overly assertive or overly formal at the end; many are afraid to get to the point. Work on being direct and clear. Avoid cliches and roundabout expressions.

Your goal is to get an interview.

The point of this letter is to get an interview. Do not avoid the issue with statements like, "May I hear from you soon?" When is soon? "Please contact me at your convenience" is also a poor ending. What do you mean by *contact?* Letter? Telephone? Carrier pigeon? Do not leave things so open-ended.

On the other hand, avoid being obnoxious. Most employers will flinch at endings like this:

You need my skills at AMB. Call me at 234-8971 for an interview. You'll be glad you did!

A businessperson hoping to set up an appointment with another businessperson will be direct, clear, and polite. If you are going to follow up your letter with a telephone call, tell the reader your plan:

In order to discuss this position with you as soon as possible, I will call your office next week to set up an appointment.

If you plan to wait for a response from the reader, let him or her know the best way to reach you.

If my qualifications interest you, please call me at home in the evenings (657-0922) or write me at the above address.

Handling Special Problems

Job candidates frequently ask the following questions about application letters.

Some people tell me they never look at an application letter—they go straight to the resume. Do you think a letter is really that important?
Yes. If the resume interests the reader, she or he will go back to the letter. The letter can be the document that insures you get an interview.

Doesn't an application letter just repeat information from the resume?
No. The letter interprets that information so it is significant to a particular job and company. You should avoid repeating phrases from the resume in your letter.

What do I do if I don't have a name to write to? Do I say "To Whom It May Concern"?
"To Whom It May Concern" is acceptable, as is "Ladies and Gentlemen" and "Dear Sir/Madam." However, when you are writing to a company's personnel department, it is preferable to address the reader as "Dear Personnel Manager." If possible, address your letter to *someone*. Telephone the company, for example, and ask for the name of the personnel manager or the manager of the department you are interested in.

How do I address a woman employer in my letter?
Once again, a telephone call can often answer this question for you. You may ask a receptionist, for example, whether the personnel manager prefers to be addressed as *Ms. Winters* or as *Mrs. Winters*. If you know her name is Carol Winters, you may write "Dear Carol Winters."

Should I mention that my father or other relative works for the company?
Some companies encourage family members to apply, while other companies discourage the practice, so you should discuss this problem with the relative before you write the letter. In general, personal contact with the company will be an asset to your application.

Should I mention someone in the company if I met him or her only briefly?
Yes. Do not say the person *recommended* you, however, if he or she did not.

What if I don't want my present employer to know I'm job hunting?
You may request confidentiality in your application letter and ask that a prospective employer contact you at home.

Should I interject any humor into my letter?

Probably not. Usually humor in an application will look unprofessional, and often it will be neither effective nor funny. If you can successfully interject humor in an interview, save it for then.

Should I mention my spouse?

Employers should not ask you about your marital status, and you certainly need not mention you are married. If you know your marital status is an asset to your application and you want to mention it, you may do so in the letter or the interview.

Writing Job Inquiry Letters

Job-inquiry letters should be short.

The purpose of the job inquiry letter is to request an application form or find out what a company's application procedures are. These letters should be short and direct: they are basically letters of inquiry (see Chapter 9). However, you may want to include a few specific details about yourself to encourage a response.

> Please send me an application form for a secretarial position with your company. As a recent graduate of Patterson Business College, I have excellent typing, word processing, and shorthand skills.

> Could you please send me an application form for a proofreader position with your company? I have two years' experience as a proofreader with a New York publisher.

Whenever possible, however, visit the company to pick up application materials. You will get a sense of the company while you are there, and you may gain some worthwhile information from the people you meet. Do not dress too informally when you visit the company: sometimes personal visits lead to on-the-spot interviews!

Filling Out Application Forms

Many companies require that job applicants fill out standard application forms. These forms request information on your education, employment, and salary history; addresses of jobs and schools; names, addresses, and telephone numbers of supervisors; why you left each job; and other details.

Before filling out such a form, collect and write down all this information and have it with you. Few things are more irritating than trying to remember it all over and over again.

Here are some tips for application forms:

Be patient when filling out application forms.

• Don't get frustrated. Most applications allow far too little space for the information required. Preparing the information in advance will keep you from making errors and from having to erase or cross out lines. If you definitely need more space, attach a separate sheet.

- You do not have to write down the salary you want. Rather than indicating a salary range, write "salary negotiable." You will do better discussing salary in person with an interviewer.
- Ask whether you may include a resume with the application form; your resume will convey your skills far more accurately and effectively than the application form.
- Employers may not discriminate on the basis of race, ancestral descent, religion, marital status, height, weight, gender, number of children, physical disability unrelated to job performance, and so on. If you do not want to answer questions related to these areas, either leave the spaces on the form blank or write "not applicable."

Requesting Letters of Recommendation

If you have not kept up contact with a former employer or instructor, you may want to write her or him to request a letter of recommendation. The letter serves to jog the person's memory regarding your abilities and may be used as a basis for the letter of recommendation. You should include a resume with the letter and follow up with a telephone call.

This is a request letter, so get to the point quickly. Open with the request and then include a few sentences of pertinent detail regarding your qualifications and the jobs you are applying for.

```
Dear Dr. Framers:

    I would greatly appreciate your writing a letter
of recommendation for me. In the fall semester of
1987, I received an A— in your Business
Communication class.
    As you can see from my enclosed resume, I
graduated last June and am now looking for a
position in marketing. Writing and speaking skills,
as well as a broad business background, are
essential to the jobs for which I am applying.
    I will telephone you next week to discuss the
letter in more detail. Thank you so much.
```

Of course, you may telephone first rather than writing; in that case, however, you should follow up with a letter providing more detail.

You may want to telephone potential references before writing to them.

Dear Dr. Miller:

    Thank you for agreeing to write a letter of
recommendation for me. I enclose my resume as you
requested.
    Since the jobs for which I am applying require
excellent public speaking skills, I know your class
will prove a great asset to my application.
    Please send the letter of recommendation to the
campus placement office, Oates Hall, Room 9001.
Thank you again.

Writing Follow-up Letters

Follow-up letters indicate your continued interest in the job.

If you do not receive a response to your job application after four to six weeks, you may want to telephone the company to make sure your application was received. However, write a follow-up letter as well.

The letter will become a permanent part of your file at the company and will serve as a tangible record of your interest in the position—and of your good business correspondence skills. An organizational chart such as the one illustrated in Chapter 18 (p. 447) can help to remind you when sufficient time has passed for you to write a follow-up letter.

A follow-up letter should be positive rather than accusatory or complaining. You may include some new information pertinent to your application and request that your file be kept active.

> I applied for the secretarial position advertised in the *Daily News* on August 10. Since first writing to you, I have completed courses in word processing and basic accounting.

> Please keep my file active and let me know if you have an opening for a secretary or administrative assistant.

If you have received a letter telling you that your materials will be kept on file, follow up after three or four months. You can again demonstrate your interest in the firm and remind the reader of your qualifications.

> Upon my applying for an accountant position with your company in February, you wrote to say the company had no openings at that time. I am still very interested in working for Hanton Industries, so please let me know if any openings occur.

> As I will be graduating this semester with a BS in accounting, I will be available to work full-time after June 12.

Writing Thank-You Letters

Every time you have an interview, follow up immediately with a letter of thanks—even if you feel relatively certain you will not get the job or would not take the job if it were offered. The thank-you letter indicates common politeness on your part; it can also help maintain contact with people and generate their goodwill.

Always write to thank an interviewer.

If you are interested in the job, the thank-you letter allows you to reiterate your interest in the position and include any information omitted during the interview.

> Thank you so much for taking the time to meet with me on Monday regarding the sales position. Your insights into successful sales techniques were fascinating!
>
> If you need to reach me before April 9, please call me at (908) 328-8754.

If your interviewer let you know that you were deficient in a vital area, you can indicate your willingness to improve your candidacy.

> Thank you for your analysis of my strengths and weaknesses as a candidate. I will definitely enroll in an accounting course next semester so I can obtain the skills you mentioned.

Checklist for Thank-You Letters

Do
- Remember your interviewer's name and position; if possible, get his or her card.
- Include, if you can, a particular point from the interview that will remind your reader of the interviewer and your qualifications.
- Keep the letter short; this is not another application letter. One or two paragraphs are sufficient.

Don't
- Apologize for anything that occurred in the interview.
- Be too chatty or informal, even if the interview was informal.
- Repeat information from your resume or application letter.

Accepting a Position

Writing a letter to accept a position is usually a pleasant experience. The acceptance letter, however, is more than just a courtesy: it serves as a written agreement to your taking the position and can include information you want to have in writing regarding your starting date, salary, and so on.

An effective job-acceptance letter helps establish good will.

Get to your point quickly and add a sentence or two that will enhance the reader's goodwill.

I am happy to accept the product manager position offered to me on May 12, and look forward to working with you and Mike. I will see you both on June 1.

Your job-acceptance letter might also cover details related to the new position.

I enclose the medical forms you requested as well as the personnel documents you asked me to fill out. As I mentioned on the phone, I will be able to start work on December 1.

Job-refusal letters should be tactful.

Refusing a Position

As a job refusal is in some ways a bad-news letter, take an indirect approach. Keep your letter short, but do provide a concrete reason for your refusal. Keep your tone positive and pleasant.

Thank you for offering me the position of assistant manager. Although I would be proud to work for Hanover Corporation, I have decided to accept a job in Denver where my wife has also been offered a position.

Thank you again for your interest and time.

Requesting More Time

You may receive an offer while you are still waiting to hear from other companies. You are in a delicate situation: you would like additional time to make up your mind, but you do not want to lose your chance at the job offered. Your letter must be tactful; as it is in some way a bad-news letter, broach the subject indirectly.

After requesting additional time, ask that the reader let you know immediately whether your request can be granted.

Thank you for offering me the market researcher position. I am proud that Gateway Incorporated has offered me such an exciting opportunity.

However, I would appreciate your granting me an extra two weeks before I reply to your offer. Prior to hearing from you, I had told another company that I would consider an offer from them before accepting another position.

If you need my answer immediately, please let me know. Otherwise, thank you for allowing me the extra time to answer your offer.

What Would You Do?

Rose Callahan has been offered a job as a personnel analyst at WSA Corporation. In her job interview, she told her interviewer, Maurice LeBlanc, that she would not be able to start work until June 15 when she graduated. The letter offering her the position, however, stipulates that she must be in Los Angeles from June 3 until June 10 for a training session.

Rose wants the job with WSA, but she must stay in Kansas City until school ends in the middle of June. She is afraid that she'll lose the job if she tells Mr. LeBlanc about the confusion.

Your task: write a letter for her. Address it to:

Mr. Maurice LeBlanc
Personnel Department
WSA Corporation
662 Compton Boulevard
San Bernardino, CA 98567

Resigning from a Position

A resignation is a bad-news letter that requires tact and specific detail. You must make your position clear while minimizing bad feelings. Include some pleasant information about the job you are leaving as well as your reasons for resigning.

> My two years as assistant manager have been very challenging and exciting. I want to thank you for teaching me so much.
>
> I had hoped, however, to be able to assume the position of manager after graduating from college. As that possibility has not worked out, I have accepted an office manager position at Railway House.
>
> Although my work here will terminate on July 1, I will be happy to work extra hours between now and then to train the new assistant manager.
>
> Thank you again for your help during the past two years.

Avoid writing angry letters of resignation.

Summary

You may not have to write many employement-related letters during your career. However, when you do, they will be important. Maintaining the you-attitude and a warm, personal tone will help make your readers respond positively to your messages. Remember that a polite approach is as important in a job refusal or resignation letter as it is in a job acceptance or application letter.

Employment Communication Checklist

Application Letters

• When you write an application letter, focus on

  _____ specific skills

  _____ commitment

  _____ industriousness

  _____ values and goals

• As you organize the contents of an application letter,

  _____ develop an opening that will attract the reader's attention

  _____ provide concrete evidence about your skills and background

  _____ relate your skills to the specific job you want

  _____ express enthusiasm for the organization

  _____ conclude with a request for an interview

• As you revise the style and tone of your letter,

  _____ delete clichés

  _____ keep your approach objective but enthusiastic

  _____ include only positive information about yourself

  _____ use a natural tone rather than stilted language

Job Inquiry Letters

• When writing to request information about application procedures,

  _____ keep the letter short and direct

  _____ include a sentence about yourself to encourage a response

Application Forms

• As you fill out application forms,

_____ keep your answers clear and short

_____ append a resume if necessary

Requests for Letters of Recommendation

• When you write former instructors or employers requesting letters of recommendation,

_____ get to the point quickly

_____ give readers details on when you were in their classes or worked with them

_____ include information on your skills and the job you are applying for

Follow-up Letters

• If you do not hear from a company after an interview, write a follow-up letter that

_____ expresses your continued interest in the position

_____ reminds readers of your qualifications

Thank-You Letters

• After an interview, write a letter to the interviewer that

_____ thanks the interviewer for the interview

_____ reiterates your interest in the position

_____ includes any information omitted during the interview

Job Acceptance Letters

• If you are offered a job you want to accept, write a letter that

_____ formally accepts the position

_____ covers details such as the starting date that are related to the position

Job Refusal Letters

• if you are offered a job you want to refuse,

_____ keep the letter short

_____ provide a reason for the refusal

_____ maintain a pleasant tone

Requesting More Time

• If you need more time to make up your mind about an offer,

_____ broach the subject indirectly

_____ ask the reader to let you know if your request can be granted

Resigning from a Position

• When you formally resign from a position,

_____ include pleasant information about the job you are leaving

_____ mention reasons for resigning

Terms to Remember

Application form: a data sheet to be filled out by job applicants

Follow-up letter: a letter of inquiry that should be sent if an applicant does not hear from a company after an interview

Job inquiry letter: a request for job application forms or for information regarding positions available within an organization

Summary Discussion: Jonathan Lee's Application Letter from Case in Point, p. 481

Jonathan Lee should revise the letter completely. His present tone, first of all, is unprofessional: the "I'm the man for you" approach is overly assertive. Second, he should add concrete information concerning his experience as well as his interest in the job. Why does he want to work for a publishing company? Why is he qualified?

Jonathan should avoid mentioning that he has not taken an economics course, but he could describe relevant courses that he has taken. Also, his letter will be improved when he removes passive sentences and stilted phrases such as "my resume herewith enclosed."

Questions for Review and Discussion

1. What is the purpose of an application letter?
2. How can you demonstrate that you have appropriate skills if you have not worked for a job similar to the one you are applying for?
3. What is the difference between a solicited and unsolicited application?
4. What are the major components of an application letter?
5. How can you make the opening to your letter catch the reader's attention?
6. What should be the focus of the last paragraph of your letter?
7. Why shouldn't you use a "standard" letter adapted from a textbook?
8. Some people send a form letter with their resume. Why is this a poor practice?
9. What are some values or goals you might incorporate into a letter you would write?
10. Why should a job inquiry letter be short and direct rather than long and persuasive?
11. What types of questions should you consider *not* answering on an application form?
12. Why write a follow-up letter to someone who has agreed in person to write a letter of recommendation for you?
13. If you have not received a reply from a company regarding your application, why is it a good idea to write a follow-up letter as well as to telephone the company?
14. Why should you write a thank-you letter after an interview that clearly will not lead to a job offer?
15. Why shouldn't you be chatty and informal in a thank-you letter following an interview that was friendly and informal?
16. Why write a job acceptance letter if you have already accepted an offer in person?
17. If you are rejecting a job, why should you bother writing a pleasant letter with an explanation for your decision?
18. What elements should be included in a job requesting more time to accept a job offer?
19. What elements should you include in a letter of resignation?

Exercises

1. Revise Jonathan Lee's letter at the opening of this chapter. He is a business major who has taken some courses in marketing and accounting but not economics. He has also worked as a clerk in the Acme grocery store. You may add other relevant details.

2. Revise the following opening paragraph of an application letter to make it more effective.

   > Although I have no actual experience working with children, I think I would be a real asset to your children's counseling center. I have a degree in counseling and have worked as assistant to our college counsellor for some time now. The assistant counselor position described in your ad sounds perfect for me.

3. Revise the following application letter.

Mr. William Byron
Personnel Department
AA Real Estate
986 Marsdale Avenue
New York, NY 12459

Dear Mr. Byron:

   Your advertisement in the <u>Times</u> interested me a lot. I have always wanted to work for a small company like yours, and I know quite a bit about the kinds of problems you must be having.
   My background is most interesting. I grew up in Europe and learned to speak French and Spanish as well as English. I attended college in Italy before attending the University of Michigan, where I'll be graduating from in June. My BS in business and various real estate courses should be

useful to your company, which specializes in business properties.

I have some excellent business experience that should be useful to the real estate agent position as well. I have sold cars at Datsun Used and New and have worked as a clerk at Charlie's Deli in Brooklyn. I also have some good office skills. My mother used to work as a real estate agent in Connecticut, so I learned about the business from her before I began taking classes in the field.

If you think I'd be an "asset" to AA Real Estate, give me a call. I'm home during the day: (212) 345-0932.

Sincerely,

M. Rodriguez

M. Rodriguez

4. Write an application letter to accompany your resume. If you are not interested in a full-time position right now, apply for a part-time or summer job.

5. Exchange an application letter with a fellow student. Write your comments directly on the student's letter while he or she does the same with yours.

6. Write a leter in response to the following advertisement. You may use your own background or a fictional one (300–350 words).

> WANTED: Student assistant to work in the university personnel office 10–15 hours per week. Must have good typing skills and have worked on a word processor. Should be organized and detail-oriented. Write a letter outlining your background and why you are interested in this position. Do *not* enclose a resume.

7. Write an application letter to accompany the resume in Figure 19-7, 19-8, or 19-10.

8. Revise the following thank-you letter.

Mrs. Henry Abbott
Personnel Department
James Dice Incorporated
23 Avon Street
Conway, IA 56789

Dear Mrs. Abbott:

Now that I have talked to you and seen your offices, I am more convinced than

ever that I am the perfect analyst for your company. Your company clearly needs someone with strong technical skills like mine to help you compete with more established companies.

Thanks very much for interviewing me last week. I will be home in the evenings all this week if you want to get in touch with me.

Sincerely,

Nancy Mac Namara

Nancy MacNamara

9. You worked at Iowa Feed Company for two summers while you were in high school. Your supervisor was Mr. James Fine. You have not seen him in over three years, but now you want him to be a reference for you. Write a letter reminding him of the work you did and requesting that he write a letter of recommendation for your placement file.

10. At the end of your junior year of college, you interviewed at Hi-Tech Jeans, a retail store, for a part-time sales position. The interviewer told you he would have hired you if you had been able to work weekends. Now, in the middle of your senior year, you have time to work weekends. Write to the interviewer: remind him of the interview and explain your new schedule.

11. You interviewed for a copywriter position with G & G Advertising Corporation six weeks ago. You thought the interview went very well; the interviewer said he would definitely contact you within the month regarding the company's decision. Write the interviewer a follow-up letter. Address it to:

Mr. Nathaniel Murdock
G & G Advertising
Boston, MA 32897

12. You have been offered a job waiting on tables at the well-known Albany Restaurant—a job coveted by many of your fellow college students. The day after your interview with the Albany, however, you interviewed for an assistant manager position for another restaurant. Now you have an offer for the assistant manager position; although the restaurant is

less prestigious than the Albany, you feel the additional responsibilities will be a good opportunity for you. Write to your interviewer at the Albany declining her offer. Write to:

Mrs. Frank Ferrara
Manager
The Albany Restaurant
491 Westside Boulevard
Alpine, CO 89321

13. You have interviewed with six accounting firms. Your top choice is Patterson & Draper, but you have not received word from that company yet. Meanwhile, you have received an offer from Halford, Belson, and Forbes. Write a letter to your interviewer at Halford requesting extra time to make your decision. Write to:

Mr. James McElroy
Halford, Belson, and Forbes
7213 Washington Avenue
Harter, PA 94126

Word Processing Exercises: Application Letter Techniques

Word processing allows you to create a "boilerplate" application letter and then tailor it to each job that you apply for.

1. Create a file named JOB. Write a job application letter for a job you would like to have this summer or after graduation. Use the format for a personal business letter (see Appendix B).
    Your letter should include

- The name of the job you are applying for
- At least two reasons why you are a good candidate for the job
- At least two reasons why you want this job
- Information on when you could begin work and when the reader will hear from you next

2. Single-space except between paragraphs. Use ragged-right margins. Omit page numbers.

3. PRINT the file JOB. Edit it again.

4. Put block markers around the central paragraphs of the letter. Do not mark the reader's address, the salutation, or the date. Now WRITE the block of text to a file named BOIL. This will be your boilerplate text for whenever you write a job application letter.

5. Create a file named JOB2. Type in a new reader's address, salutation, and date. Then READ in the file named BOIL.

6. Edit JOB2, tailoring the information in the letter to the new application.

7. PRINT JOB2 on a single sheet of paper.

Job Interviews

Objectives

To prepare for job interviews

To perform effectively as a job applicant in interviews

21

John Wilkins's Job Interview

In two months, John Wilkins will graduate from a state university with a Bachelor of Science in business administration. He has held several part-time jobs while in school. His first interview for a full-time position was with a company that manufactures household cleansers and related products. The following dialogue is part of his interview with Pamela Bailey, a recruiter for the company's management training program.

PAMELA: Tell me a little about yourself—some of the things that aren't on your resume.

JOHN: Well, I was born in Janesville, and I've lived in Wisconsin all my life. I enjoy sports, particularly cross-country skiing. I'm really looking forward to getting out of school!

PAMELA: I see you changed schools two years ago. Why did you leave Moore College?

JOHN: I was tired of living so near my home town. I wanted to move to a bigger city. Besides, the state university offered a lot more classes in business, and I knew that was what I wanted.

PAMELA: Several of our company's branch offices are in smaller cities. Would you have a problem relocating to one of them?

JOHN: I'd prefer living in Milwaukee, but I suppose I would go to a smaller place for a year or so.

PAMELA: You haven't held a full-time job in the past?

JOHN: No.

PAMELA: Why did you want to interview with our company?

JOHN: The description in the Placement Office said you had opportunities for business graduates.

PAMELA: What else do you know about our company?

JOHN: Well, that's about it, actually.

PAMELA: Can you tell me why we should hire you for our program rather than one of the other graduating seniors we've been interviewing?

JOHN: I'm a hard worker. I get along with people. And I've taken a lot of courses that should be useful.

PAMELA: Why did you major in business?

JOHN: I started out in botany, but business seemed to offer more job opportunities.

PAMELA: Your resume indicates that you've worked in sales.

JOHN: Yes, I worked for Kay Drug Store and for a lumberyard, selling to different types of customers. I usually work twenty hours a week while I'm in school.

PAMELA: That's a lot of hours. Do you find that working so much interferes with your schoolwork?

JOHN: Not really. I'm pretty good at managing my time. I'm usually on the Dean's List. I don't have much time for clubs or anything like that, though.

PAMELA: Could you tell me what your goals are?

JOHN: Right now my major goal is to graduate. I can't see much further ahead than June 12!

Points to Consider

- How effective was John in this interview? How do you think he will be evaluated by the interviewer?
- What are John's major strengths as a job candidate? What are his weaknesses?
- How could John have highlighted his strengths more effectively?
- Which of John's answers was the most effective? Why?
- Which answer was the least effective? Why?
- Why did the interviewer ask John what he knew about the company?
- What *should* John have known about the company?
- Why did the interviewer ask John about his transfer to the state university? Should he have answered in a different way? Explain.
- How effective was John's answer to the relocation question? Explain.

Preparing for Different Types of Job Interviews

If your background is appropriate and your application materials are effective, you will receive offers for interviews. Having proven on paper that you fit some of the basic criteria employers have established, you will have to convince them in person that you are right for the job. This persuasive process involves skills in both verbal and nonverbal communication.

Prepare carefully for job interviews.

Job interviews take many shapes and forms. They range from highly formal to casual, from structured to free-flowing, from amiable to stressful. Sometimes candidates are interviewed by a panel rather than a single interviewer; sometimes several candidates are interviewed together. Most interviewing techniques remain the same, regardless of the location, format, or tone, but be aware of some general principles and patterns.

Your initial preparation should involve the self-analysis and career research discussed in Chapter 18. When you have an interview scheduled, you will feel more confident if you are organized.

- Find out about the company (see Figure 21-1) and figure out how you and your skills are suited to the job and the company.

- If you are being interviewed at the company, make sure you know how to get there, where to park, and what office to go to.

- Find out, if you can, the interviewer's name. Address the interviewer by name and pronounce the name correctly.

- Make sure your interview suit is clean and ready to be worn.

- Organize any materials you plan to bring with you. Always bring a resume. You might also need a transcript, portfolio, or writing sample. Check with the company if you are unsure what might be needed.

- Leave yourself enough time to get to the interview a little early.

- Where the company has headquarters and branches
- How many employees the company has
- What the company's main products or services are
- What the company's mission and goals are
- How the company divisions are organized
- What the company's earnings and market share have been for the past two to three years
- When the company was founded
- What specific job title you are applying for
- What salary range is typical for that job
- What major qualifications the job demands
- Where such a job usually leads an employee in his or her career

FIGURE 21-1
What you should know about a company and a job

Many companies interviewing student candidates use a three-step interview process: (1) on-campus interview, (2) office visit, and (3) second office interview. Any one of these may be structured or unstructured, a stress interview, or a panel interview.

On-Campus Interview

Companies that recruit college students may interview on campuses each year. Students sign up to meet with a company interviewer for thirty minutes or so. These interviewers screen candidates, often deciding which applicants should be asked to visit the company for a second interview.

On-campus interviews can prepare you for office interviews.

If you are going to be job-hunting sometime soon, sign up for a number of campus interviews. You will meet representatives of various companies and hone your interviewing skills in an environment that is less threatening than a corporate office.

Often, too, you will receive feedback from the campus interviewers on the strong and weak points of your interview: you may learn, for example, that you scored well on skills but not on appearance. In the future, then, you can improve your weak area. (See Figure 21-2, Sample Interviewer Rating Chart.)

Here are some tips for on-campus interviewing:

- Sign up for campus interviews as soon as possible. These interviews will help you learn about companies and develop interview skills, so do not wait until the last months of your senior year to sign up.
- Sign up for as many campus interviews as you can. Preparing for the interviews will help you learn about various companies—and you never know when an interesting opportunity will arise.
- Do not get discouraged if you are not invited for office visits. Some companies interview on campuses just to have an updated file of candidates

```
Interviewee:          _____

Rating Scale: 1 (Outstanding)   2 (Strong) 3 (Average)
              4 (Below Average) 5 (Poor)   6 (no rating)

_____ a. Interview preparation
_____ b. Clarity of career objectives
_____ c. Appropriate academic preparation
_____ d. Personal appearance
_____ e. Communicative ability
_____ f. Emotional maturity
_____ g. Self-confidence
_____ h. Ambition
_____ i. Intelligence

Overall Rating of Interviewee: _____

Additional Comments: _____
_____

Interest in Candidate:

_____ Particularly high
_____ Interest with further consideration
_____ Prefer not to make an offer
```

FIGURE 21-2 ————————————————————————————
Sample interviewer rating chart

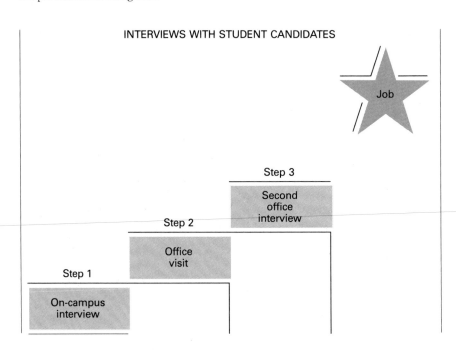

INTERVIEWS WITH STUDENT CANDIDATES

Job

Step 3

Second
office
interview

Step 2

Office
visit

Step 1

On-campus
interview

"Good. In this business you <u>have</u> to be crazy."

Drawing by Weber; © 1985 The New Yorker Magazine, Inc.

even though no positions are currently available. And, even if you are not offered a second interview, you will have made one contact to whom you may want to write later on if you are sending out resumes and application letters.
- Remember to write a thank-you letter (see Chapter 20) after every interview.

Office Visits

If your on-campus interview was successful, you may be invited to visit the company for a second interview. This often takes the form of a single interview with someone in the personnel department or the department to which you are applying. The office visit, however, may also consist of half-day or all-day meetings with your potential managers and co-workers. You may be invited to lunch with some of these people.

Do not schedule another interview or another important appointment for the same day as an office visit; if things are going well, or if one of your interviewers is delayed or late, you may find yourself at the company far longer than you expected.

Second Office Visits

In some cases, especially if you met only one or two people on your first visit, a second office visit will entail all-day meetings and lunch.

If you are invited for a second visit, you are undoubtedly among a small group of candidates for the position. Your interviewers are looking specifically for the person with whom they want to work and who will work most effectively with the company. You could even receive an offer at this time—be prepared!

Structured Versus Unstructured Interviews

Structured interviews are based on prepared questions.

Some on-campus interviews and office visits will be structured interviews: that is, your interviewer will go through a list of questions with you. Often she or he will be taking notes as you respond. Only at the end will the interviewer ask if you have any questions.

In some ways, structured interviews are frustrating because the script is so apparent and applicants know they are overtly being compared with other candidates who answered the same questions. On the other hand, structured interviews are easier than unstructured ones because the interviewer usually asks standard questions, and problems with a quiet or talkative interviewer are less apt to occur.

Unstructured interviews are similar to conversations.

Many first interviews, however—and almost all subsequent interviews—are unstructured. Interviewers and applicants speak in a conversational format. Applicants usually have more opportunity to sell themselves effectively in an unstructured interview, but they also face more pitfalls.

Stress Interviews

In an attempt to make their hiring decisions more precise, some companies use stress interviews as part of the selection process. Some interviewers are trained to pressure candidates with difficult questions or with comments that could upset or anger the candidates. Sometimes candidates are subjected to a difficult examination in their field; sometimes interviewers make negative comments about an applicant's appearance or background.

Companies may request that candidates take a written examination before or after the interview, while other companies may have candidates participate in role-playing, acting out stressful situations.

The stress interview is intended to put you on the defensive, to see if you become angry or upset when faced with a stressful situation. Whatever format or approach a company uses, you can be successful if you remain calm and professional.

Opinions differ on the effectiveness of stress interviews for selecting successful job candidates. Many personnel specialists maintain that the standard interview process is stressful enough as it is. Moreover, these interviews tend to leave interviewees with a poor view of the company.

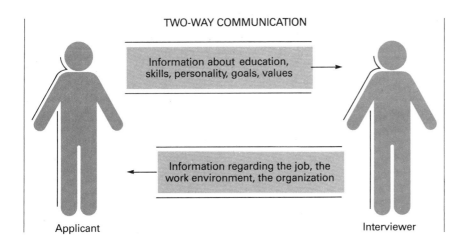

TWO-WAY COMMUNICATION

Information about education, skills, personality, goals, values

Information regarding the job, the work environment, the organization

Applicant

Interviewer

Panel Interviews

Sometimes you will be interviewed by a panel instead of one person. These panels are set up so that several members of the organization can meet a candidate in a minimum amount of time, and so they can all see the candidate under similar circumstances.

This type of interview can be intimidating as you must respond to different types of people and different types of questions. These guidelines for panel interviews can help you:

- Look each panel member in the eye as you speak so that you communicate with each interviewer.
- Listen carefully to each question and respond as you would to one interviewer.
- Do not let any members of the panel rattle you.
- Avoid answering any one question at length since other panel members are waiting to ask their questions.

Establishing Two-Way Communication with Interviewers

One of the most important things to remember about a job interview is that it is a two-way process. The applicant should not merely be sending information to the interviewer regarding education and skills; he or she should also be receiving information regarding the job, the work environment, the organization, and other factors of interest.

Much of the factual information interviewers are interested in can be obtained from your application documents; the interview will reveal the key personal elements that set you apart from other candidates. After all, most employers are looking for candidates who will look and act professionally,

Interviews reveal personal elements about job candidates.

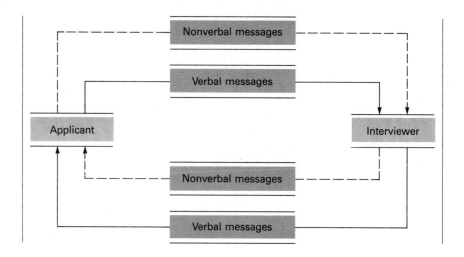

who can interact successfully with other people. If you appear unduly nervous or unprofessional in an interview, employers fear you will not work well with clients, customers, or co-workers.

Just remember that, as a candidate, you should be amassing information too. Given what you know about your personality, skills, values and goals, and work environment preferences, how will this job suit you? Many candidates lack the self-confidence to evaluate whether the job is right for them; they are too busy trying to make a good impression on the interviewers.

Having the self-confidence to assess each employment situation will actually enhance your position as a candidate. Employers like to see applicants who can make professional assessments; few employers are looking for employees who lack self-esteem and confidence.

Developing Verbal and Nonverbal Communication

The two-way communication process in a job interview requires verbal and nonverbal communication.

In many ways, the nonverbal cues received by both applicant and interviewer are more memorable and powerful than the actual words passing between the two people. The importance of nonverbal communication is significant to you as a job applicant for two reasons: (1) you must not only listen to interviewers but also pick up on more subtle nonverbal cues and (2) you must be careful to send off appropriate nonverbal information while speaking with the interviewer.

Overcoming Communication Barriers in Interviews

Given the complexity of the communication process in an interview, many types of problems can lead to miscommunication. As an applicant, watch for two major pitfalls and work on avoiding them.

Interviewer Inattention

Interviewers sometimes sit in an office for hours on end interviewing candidates. Being human, interviewers lose their concentration as they get more tired. As a job candidate, you will usually do better if you schedule interviews early in the day, before lunch if possible. To avoid meeting an interviewer before he or she is fully awake, try to set up mid-morning interviews.

New paragraph: If you see your interviewer is having trouble concentrating, try asking some questions. Responding to questions can bring back his or her attention. Or your lengthy monologues may be boring your listener; make sure you do not talk too much. Express interest in the company, the job, or the interviewer so you do not appear self-absorbed.

Make sure your interviewer is paying attention.

Applicant Inattention

Being nervous can interfere badly with your communication. Rather than listening to your interviewer, you may find yourself wondering how well you are doing or what you should say next. This inattention can irritate your interviewer: you will appear uninterested or bored.

New paragraph: The only solution to this problem is to listen intently. Forget about the impression you are making and think about your interviewer. Do not worry about a response until you have heard what the interviewer has to say: after all, you are having a conversation, not taking an examination. If you pay attention, your face and body movements will convey encouragement and enthusiasm to the interviewer.

Listening is an important interview skill.

Sending and Receiving Nonverbal Messages

Nonverbal messages may be conveyed in physical appearance, posture, hand gestures, eye contact, voice qualities, and a host of other ways.

New paragraph: These messages or cues combine to form an overall impression that strikes a viewer within moments. As every politician, actor, and public figure knows, the way a person comes across—the qualities he or she emits—will often make more of an impression on an audience than the actual words being spoken. "I don't like all his ideas," some voters will say about a candidate they have voted for, "but he has charm, charisma. I know he'll do a good job."

Appearance

The most obvious nonverbal cue you send to an interviewer is your general appearance. Your interview suit, shoes, haircut, and briefcase if you carry one should be appropriate: professional, low-key, not trendy.

Your appearance affects your self-confidence.

Remember that being a shade too conservative in your appearance is safer than being too informal. Do not worry if you arrive in a navy blue suit and find your interviewer in jeans. Employers expect candidates to dress in suits.

General appearance is one of the easiest nonverbal areas to control, so leave enough time before an interview to make sure you look the way you want to look. If you know you are dressed right, many of the other nonverbal cues will fall into place because your self-confidence will be high.

Posture

The way someone stands, walks, and sits says a lot about a person. Being nervous or shy, some job candidates hunch over, walk awkwardly, or sit ramrod straight. If you are relaxed about the interview, you will present yourself naturally; but you should work on your walk and sitting posture if you tend to slouch or sit too straight.

You might even practice while wearing your interview attire: sitting in a suit is quite different than sitting in jeans!

Handshake

If the interviewer is behind a desk or does not stand up, you may not be able to shake hands; however, if you are in a position to reach out a hand, do not hesitate. The handshake expresses your professionalism and self-confidence. That one cue may establish you as a professional in your interviewer's mind.

Gestures

Sometimes candidates feel as though they have an extra pair of hands when they are in an interview: they wonder whether to sit on their hands, grip the chair arms, or clasp their hands in their laps.

In general, again, be natural. If you use hand gestures when you talk, use them to some extent in an interview. But do avoid nervous habits like finger tapping. For the most part, you will look professional and natural with your hands in your lap or on the arms of the chair.

Make sure you do not have anything in your hands that you can play with nervously. Avoid smoking cigarettes or accepting a cup of coffee. Both can actually enhance your nervousness and can lead to irritating hand movements.

As you know, smoking is a controversial issue in the workplace; even if the interviewer is a chain smoker, the applicant should abstain from smoking. (One of the oldest tricks of a stress interview is to offer an applicant a cigarette but no ashtray and see if the person has the courage to ask for one!)

Eye Contact

Look your interviewer in the eye when you enter the room. After that, maintain normal eye contact, just as you would speaking to a friend. You do not want to stare the person down, but be careful not to stare at the ceiling or floor when trying to formulate a sentence. Good eye contact will show your self-confidence and help imprint your personality on the interviewer's mind.

Maintain eye contact with your interviewer.

Voice

You have probably heard your voice on a tape recorder. If you have not, you might want to record yourself before you start interviewing. There are some elements of your voice that you cannot control, but with practice you can improve several aspects of your voice. Watch especially the volume and speed; keep your voice at a moderate volume and avoid speaking so quickly that your interviewer has trouble understanding you. Work on keeping your voice enthusiastic.

Interviewer's Nonverbal Messages

While your interviewer is evaluating your nonverbal messages, be aware of the interviewer's. Noticing some simple cues can help you modify your presentation to your best advantage. Also, you can learn a lot about the company by perceiving cues in the work environment.

Pay attention to the nonverbal cues in the work environment.

1. *Note How Your Interviewer Is Dressed.* Noticing how formally or casually an interviewer is dressed can tell you about the person and about the company. If a certain type of atmosphere or image is important to you, a glance at an interviewer's outfit can give you some firsthand information about the company.
2. *Notice the Interviewer's Office.* If you are being interviewed in the interviewer's office, you can derive information from the setting: plaques, photographs, books, sports trophies. These items can help you through some conversation ("I see you play racquetball. That's a favorite sport of mine, too"), and they may help you understand the qualities an interviewer is looking for.
3. *Watch for Signs of Emotions.* Facial expressions can often tell whether someone is listening to, interested in, or understanding what you are saying. Do not get so absorbed in what you are saying that you forget to see how well your words are being received.

If your interviewer seems to have stopped listening, you need to change your approach. Shorten your answers, maybe, or ask a question that will bring the interviewer back to you.

If the interviewer seems impatient or glances at a clock after twenty or twenty-five minutes have passed, then help to bring the interview to an end. You do not want to annoy the interviewer by going on too long. If you still have a vital question, make sure you ask it.

If you see a positive response in the interviewer's face, figure out *what* led to that response. Was the person pleased by your enthusiasm? Your intelligent grasp of the question? Your humor? If you know what the person likes, you have a key to handling the rest of the interview.

Similarly, if you see a negative reaction, try to isolate the cause and deemphasize that quality for the rest of the interview.

These responses to nonverbal cues are fundamental aspects of any person-to-person communication, but job applicants often forget them because they are concentrating on their own presentation. You will find that an intelligent perception of the other person's cues will enhance your performance in an interview—and in any one-on-one situation.

Sending and Receiving Verbal Cues

Verbal responses are the aspects of an interview that we think of most readily. What shall I *say?* we wonder. What should I have *told* the interviewer? Naturally, your words are essential to a good interview; just do not forget that the way you say them may be equally important.

To help your oral presentation in an interview, review the following tips:

Be Positive

Nothing in your interview should have a negative ring to it. Do not complain. Do not criticize an instructor, supervisor, or co-worker. Even if you are hoping to leave your present company, avoid making negative comments about it.

> INTERVIEWER: But your job at Barlowe's is similar to what you are applying for here. Why do you want to leave Barlowe's?
> APPLICANT: There are more opportunities for me with your company. Also, I am interested in working with corporate clients, and your company will give me a chance to do that.

Be Direct

Provide information in as straightforward a manner as you can. Do not digress or answer at length.

Do Not Answer in Monosyllables

Avoid simply answering "yes" or, even worse, "no" to a question. Interviewers are not usually just verifying information; they are providing stepping-off places for you.

> INTERVIEWER: I see you went to the University of Iowa.
> APPLICANT: Yes.
> INTERVIEWER: You liked it there?
> APPLICANT: Yes.

Compare the preceding dialogue with one in which the applicant "runs with the ball."

INTERVIEWER: I see you went to the University of Iowa.
APPLICANT: Yes. I graduated last June with a BS in finance. Iowa has an excellent business program.
INTERVIEWER: You liked it there?
APPLICANT: Definitely. It was a great experience. I learned a lot and had a good time, too.

If you must answer "no" to a question, then make sure you follow up with something positive.

INTERVIEWER: You haven't held a full-time job in the past?
APPLICANT: No, I've been working part-time and going to school part-time for five years now. Even in the summers, I take two courses and work 30-hour weeks.

Be Specific

Whenever possible, include specific, concrete information in your answers. As in your application letters, avoid generalizations. Simply saying, "I am a good salesperson" will not carry the weight of specific figures: "I have been in the top 10 percent of my sales team for two years now. Last month I sold over $200,000 worth of computer equipment."

Compare the answers of two applicants to the following question. It is easy to see which answer is the more persuasive.

> Give complete but concise answers in interviews.

INTERVIEWER: Can you tell me why we should hire you rather than one of the other graduating seniors we've been interviewing?
APPLICANT 1: I have taken the right courses. And I have great skills.
APPLICANT 2: I've taken courses in management, accounting, and marketing that should be useful to a management trainee. And I've maintained an A− average in my major while working twenty to thirty hours a week. Also, my sales experience has allowed me to develop good persuasive skills that will be useful to me as a manager.

Know About the Job and the Company

Doing your homework on a company is a key aspect of any interview. Some students sign up for a slate of on-campus interviews and then do not remember what they signed up for: this carelessness can be fatal.

> Be knowledgeable about the company to which you are applying.

For every interview, find out some key facts about the company. Not only will this information help you present yourself intelligently and professionally to the interviewer, but it will help you evaluate the company and the job with regard to your personality, skills, values, goals, and work environment preferences.

Your placement center, college library, public library, and personal contacts should provide you with most of the necessary information (see sources discussed in Chapter 18).

How Would You Handle These Interview Situations?

Choose the answer that best fits the way you would handle these job interview situations.

1. Your interviewer is mechanically checking off questions and appears bored with the whole interview.
   a. You try to catch the interviewer's attention with a witty remark.
   b. You patiently answer the interviewer's questions as best you can.
   c. You begin asking the interviewer questions about the company and the job.
2. Your interviewer is interrupted by telephone calls every time you try to converse.
   a. You ask the interviewer if you can come back another time when he or she is less busy.
   b. You ask the interviewer if he or she could have

the calls held until after the interview.
   c. You become irritated and end the interview abruptly.

Discussion

If interviewers seem bored in a job interview, you can often revive their interest by asking questions. Witty remarks can backfire, and patient answers may not leave any impression on interviewers' minds. Best answer: 1c.

This problem is difficult to handle. Although you should not appear irritated, politely asking to reschedule the interview may be effective: the interviewer might either reschedule or ask to have calls held. However, *asking* interviewers to have their calls held would be offensive. Best answer: 2a.

Relate Yourself to the Job and the Company

When you go into an interview with some key information, you can tailor your presentation to the job and the company. If you do not know anything about the company you are interviewing with, you will not come across as a committed or enthusiastic candidate.

Note the specific details in this candidate's responses.

INTERVIEWER: Why did you want to interview with our company?

APPLICANT: I've always wanted to work for a manufacturing company with a strong regional emphasis like yours. You have a reputation for making excellent products, and your focus on the Southeastern states has made you the number one manufacturer of household products in that area. I know you're committed to your customers and your employees.

INTERVIEWER: What else do you know about our company?

APPLICANT: I know you've been in business since 1956—and you've increased your earnings every year since then. People have told me that working for Premium offers the kind of challenge and rewards I'm looking for.

If you know what the job entails, then you can consistently link yourself to those qualifications. Compare these two responses:

INTERVIEWER: What are your strengths?

APPLICANT 1: My business background. And I have good communication skills.

APPLICANT 2: I have the accounting background the job requires. But my writing and speaking skills will eventually be even more important than my technical abilities. I know Premium stresses strong communication skills for its managers.

Prepare for Standard Questions

Many questions come up routinely in interviews. Outlining some strong, positive answers in advance will help to ease the strain of the interview (Figure 21-3). Prepare answers for questions such as these:

- How has your education prepared you for this job?
- What job experience do you have?
- What relevant skills do you have to perform this job effectively?
- Why are you a good candidate for the job?
- What are your career goals?

Ask Questions

Many job applicants are too shy or nervous to ask questions. They simply sit passively, like students taking an oral examination, waiting to answer the next question. To show you are dynamic and enthusiastic, you must turn the oral exam into a conversation. Take some control of the situation. Remember—the communication flow should be two-way.

Take some control of your job interview.

The more you know about a company or a job, the more intelligent your questions will be. Do not ask about salary or vacations, but do ask about travel, career possibilities, and company projects or products.

- I've been reading about your new aerobic dancing shoe. Will that be on the market this year?
- Now that you have opened an international division, how likely is it that employees from your New York branch will be able to transfer overseas?

You might ask, too, what qualifications the interviewer is looking for in these interviewers; then you can tailor your responses to those qualifications. And, at the end of the interview, ask when you can expect to hear from the interviewer—or whether you should call him or her in a couple of weeks if you do not hear.

General Background and Qualities
- Tell me a little about yourself.
- How would a friend describe you?
- What motivates you?
- What type of person are you?
- What are your personal goals?
- What are your strengths and weaknesses?

Education
- Why did you major in — — —?
- Why did you go to the college you attended?
- Why did you change schools?
- What do you look for in an instructor?
- What classes did you like best?
- What classes did you dislike?
- What would you do differently if you were starting college again?

Past Jobs
- How has your work experience prepared you for this job?
- What type of skills have you acquired at your previous jobs?
- What kind of environment do you like working in?
- What type of manager do you like working with?
- Why weren't you working during this time period?

This Job
- Why do you want this job?
- How did you find out about this job?
- Why do you want to work for this company?
- What do you know about this company?
- What do you think this job entails?
- Where do you want to be in five years?
- Are you willing to travel? To relocate?
- How important is salary to you?
- Describe the qualities a person in this job should have.
- Why should we hire you?
- Here's a problem that came up recently in our company. How would you have handled it?

Interests
- What do you do in your spare time?
- Do you belong to clubs or other organizations?
- What extracurricular activities did you have in college?

FIGURE 21-3 _____
Questions often asked in interviews

Illegal Questions

Illegal interview questions are those that focus on issues of race, color, religion, sex, national origin, handicap, or age without bearing on job performance. Interviewers are prohibited, for example, from asking questions about a candidate's maiden name, birthplace, or ethnic origin; the church a candidate attends; a candidate's marital status or childbearing plans; or a candidate's physical disabilities if they are not related to job performance.

Interviewers who ask a candidate illegal questions and then do not hire the person may find themselves facing a legal complaint.

As a job candidate, you may choose to answer an illegal question, but you may also remind the interviewer tactfully that the question has no bearing on the job for which you are applying.

Sometimes illegal questions are used as a stress technique. Interviewers may be trained to be obnoxious so candidates will show their self-confidence and assertiveness. Responses such as "I'm not sure why you're asking me this" or "How is that question related to my qualifications as a job candidate?" may turn out to be the answers the interviewer wants to hear.

If the interviewer is being rude or discriminatory, you may have a good clue that this company is not for you. You may always let the interviewer know that the question is illegal or irrelevant to the job and decline to answer it. If you feel you have been discriminated against in the hiring process, you may file a complaint with the Equal Employment Opportunity Commission.

(See also Appendix A, Legal Aspects of Business Communication.)

Handling Problems and Difficult Questions

What do I do if my interviewer never stops talking? How do I show my strengths without being rude?
Pick up on whatever the interviewer is saying and ask appropriate questions: "What are you looking for in a job candidate?" "Can you tell me something about the company's new marketing program?" "How many college graduates did the company hire last year?" You may have to be even more aggressive and say such things as, "I'd like to tell you a little about my qualifications."

What if my interviewer is too quiet?
You are responsible for keeping things moving if the interviewer is shy, unprepared, or simply quiet. Ask questions and provide information about yourself. You may find that asking the interviewer about himself or herself can break the ice: "How long have you worked for ABC?" "Have you found ABC an exciting place to work?" Remember, if the interview lasts only ten minutes, it is your loss more than the interviewer's. Be prepared.

What if the interviewer keeps answering the telephone and letting other interruptions occur?
This is an unpleasant situation that you may not be able to control. You can

say, "You seem awfully busy. Would you like me to come back another day?" The interruptions, however, may be stress techniques aimed at upsetting you, so remain pleasant and patient.

What if the interviewer asks about my salary expectations?
Avoid talking about money until you receive an offer. You should, however, know the general salary range appropriate to such a position, just in case you are pressured into discussing figures. Often you can simply say, "I know ABC offers very competitive salaries. Shouldn't we talk about money after you decide whether I'm right for the job?"

How do I answer that question "Tell me a little about yourself"?
Use this question as a way of showing off your strengths. Do not give your life history; instead, relate your background and skills as closely as possible to the job you want. (Make sure you do not go on too *long* answering this question.)

How do I answer that question about my greatest weaknesses?
This is a good question to be prepared for. You should have one or two weaknesses—otherwise, you look arrogant or insincere. But the weaknesses should be unrelated to the job you want. The standard answer is to say, "My weakness is that I work too hard. I'm a workaholic." That one has been overused, so try something more original.

One approach to this question is to mention a weakness you *used* to have but are working on or have gotten rid of. "I used to be uncomfortable speaking before a group, but now that I've joined Toastmaster's my public speaking skills are improving."

(Note: Do NOT use that example if the job is going to entail public speaking!)

Turn your weaknesses into strengths.

What do I say if asked about my low grade point average?
You should try to turn every weakness into a strength. You may explain to the interviewer that, at the expense of your GPA, you purposely took challenging courses in very different areas to broaden your skills. Or perhaps you were supporting yourself while in school or participating in a demanding athletic activity.

Emphasize the importance of your successes in other areas and of the actual skills you have demonstrated.

I don't know where I want to be in five years. How can I answer that question?
You should figure out some goals before going into the interview. Your research into the company can help you find out the possibilities. In general, you want to let the interviewer know that you plan to stay with the company and move on to increasingly responsible positions.

How do I answer that question about which class did I hate most in school?
This is a loaded question. You should not say you hated *any* classes. Tell the interviewer which classes you liked the most—and show how they helped you acquire skills useful to job. If pressed, you could mention a class unrelated to your career that you found less interesting than the others.

People tell me to take control of an interview. How can I do that without being obnoxious?

There is a thin line between being assertive and being overly aggressive. By asking intelligent questions, you can lead the interview into areas that show your strengths. This approach will appear professional, not obnoxious.

What if I'm asked a question I can't answer?

Don't bluff. If you clearly do not know the answer, say so. However, if you think you may have misunderstood the question, ask the interviewer to rephrase it. The question may be quite different from what you thought it was. Asking for a restatement of the question will also give you a few moments to think about your response.

What Would You Do?

Deborah Strasburg was asked to interview for a position as an entry-level computer programmer with a large company. She had taken the computer classes mentioned in the company's job description, and she had experience working as a tutor in her college computer laboratory. She felt confident of her abilities and, from her research, this company seemed ideal for her.

Arriving on time, she met her interviewer, Mr. Albert Gardener. Immediately she sensed something was wrong. He replied gruffly to her greeting and had trouble looking her in the eye. He began a structured interview, reading from a list of questions.

Deborah responded as well as she could to each standard question regarding her education and experience, but she felt distinctly uncomfortable. She sensed that the interviewer disliked her on sight—for no apparent reason. Finally, he stopped looking at his list of questions.

"Why do you want to work here, Miss—er—"

"Deborah Strasburg," she said firmly. "I want to work in a nationally known firm, and I am very interested in your innovative—"

"I see. Well, we've never hired a woman programmer here. They don't stick around a company like men do."

Suddenly Deborah was irate. His rude manner had finally gotten to her. "If you've never hired one, how do you know they 'don't stick around?' " she asked. Then she stood up. "On the other hand, don't answer that. I know why." With that, she walked out.

Describe how you would have handled the situation.

Summary

Job interviews provide both job applicants and prospective employers with information. While an employer is learning about an applicant's skills, personality, and goals, the applicant should be finding out about the company and the position.

As an applicant, work on sending appropriate verbal and nonverbal cues to interviewers while also paying attention to the signals interviewers are sending out. With good preparation and organization, you can reduce your anxiety and increase your chances of performing well in interviews.

Interview Checklist

Preparation

- Before going to an interview,

    _____ find out as much as you can about the company and the job

    _____ find out the interviewer's name

    _____ organize the materials you plan to bring with you

    _____ make sure your attire and general appearance are appropriate

    _____ prepare for standard interview questions

    _____ leave enough time to arrive a few minutes early

Interview

- While in an interview,

    _____ work on keeping the interviewer's interest

    _____ look the interviewer in the eye

    _____ pay attention to the interviewer's verbal and nonverbal cues

    _____ stay calm

- As you speak,

    _____ keep your comments and answers positive

    _____ keep your answers concrete and direct

    _____ avoid answering in monosyllables

    _____ relate your skills to the job and the company

    _____ convey enthusiasm for the job

    _____ ask questions about the company and the job

Terms to Remember

Panel interview: an interview at which a candidate meets with a group of people

Stress interview: interview designed to test a candidate's ability to handle tense situations

Structured interview: an interview at which the interviewer asks the candidate prearranged questions

Unstructured interview: an interview at which the interviewer and candidate speak in conversational fashion

Summary Discussion: John Wilkins's Job Interview from Case in Point, p. 511

John's interview suffers from lack of preparation: he knows nothing about the job or the company. His answers tend to be negative—he apparently does not like school or his home town, and he is reluctant to work anywhere except Milwaukee.

John has had some good experience, but he does not highlight it or his academic background. He has been on the Dean's List while working twenty hours a week, but he does not expand on his strong points or relate them to the job he is applying for.

John needs to accentuate his enjoyment of business-related classes and his desire to work for this company. He should be more enthusiastic: if he *is* willing to work in a small community, for example, he should say so with conviction, not with obvious hesitation.

Questions for Review and Discussion

1. Why is it helpful to know your interviewer's name before the interview?
2. How does an applicant benefit from a structured interview? How does an applicant suffer from a structured interview?
3. Have you ever experienced a stress interview? Describe it.
4. What information should you know about the company before you go into an interview?
5. What kinds of questions should a candidate ask in an interview?

Exercises

1. Write a "script" for John Wilkins (see p. 511). Using the questions in the case, write more effective answers for him.
2. Prepare answers that you might use if the following questions came up in an interview.
   a. What skills can you bring to this job?
   b. Why should we hire you?
   c. How competitive are you?
   d. Do you work well under stress? Give an example.
   e. Why did you leave your last job?
3. What do you think is your greatest liability in terms of getting the job you want? (Your unrelated work experience? Your degree in the wrong field? Your low grades? Your time out of school?) Write a question addressing that

weakness and then answer it in a way that would turn the liability into an asset.

4. What three aspects of yourself would you particularly want an interviewer to know about? Why?

5. What information about a job or a company would you particularly want to find out in an interview? Why?

6. Speak to a local businessperson about his or her techniques for interviewing job candidates. What is he or she looking for in a candidate? What types of questions does he or she ask? What nonverbal cues are important? Report to the class on your findings.

Part 6 Mini-Cases

6-1. Suzanne Aaronson, 43 years old, is just finishing a Bachelor of Science degree in business administration with an emphasis in accounting. Now she is looking for an entry-level position with a Big Eight accounting firm. Her grades have been excellent, but she is worried about her unconventional background.

At eighteen, Suzanne had left high school to work in a cannery near her home town. At twenty, she got married and had two children. She worked at the cannery until her husband, who was in the army, was transferred to a big city. At that point she stopped working and began going to school to get her teacher's credentials.

When she was 30, her marriage fell apart. Having to support and take care of her two children, she dropped out of school and went to work as a secretary. Now, 13 years later, her children are on their own, and Suzanne is remarried. She has returned to college and will be finishing her degree in three months.

Suzanne knows she has good academic preparation, and some of her office experience will be useful in an accounting position. She has not, however, participated in campus organizations; working part-time and going to school take up all her time.

In general, Suzanne is worried that she will be less appealing to a Big Eight interviewer than her many competitors—22-year-olds fresh from college.

To prepare for her interview, she put together a list of questions for which she wanted to have solid answers.

a. Why should we hire you instead of someone else in your graduating class?

b. What do you do in your spare time?

c. Why did you change from an education major to an accounting major?

d. Do you think your work experience makes you a good candidate for this job? Why?

e. Do you think you can handle an entry-level position? [meaning *at your age*]

f. Will you mind having a younger person for a supervisor?

Write answers for Suzanne that will show an interviewer she is an excellent candidate.

6-2. Albert Oliveto had sent out dozens of resumes and application letters, and he had been to three interviews. He had not received any offers, but he also had not received any rejections. He decided to send follow-up letters to the companies that had not responded to his initial application.

The basic format of his follow-up letter looked like this:

Dear Personnel Manager:

I have not heard from you regarding my application three months ago for a management trainee position with your company. If you have forgotten about me or decided that my qualifications were not appropriate, I hope you will reconsider: I have a BS in management from Louisiana State University, and I have been assistant manager of a retail store in Baton Rouge.

I really want to work in New Orleans. Now that I have graduated and am unemployed, I have a lot of free time to come down for an interview.

I look forward to hearing from you.

Sincerely,

Albert Oliveto

Albert Oliveto

a. Discuss the strengths and weaknesses of Albert's letter.

b. Revise the letter.

6-3. Gerry Frasier is applying for a full-time sales clerk position in a department store. She is a college junior taking classes during the day, so she is looking for a job she can work at night and on weekends. As she has no sales experience, she has designed her resume like this.

```
                GERALDINE FRASIER
                 9811 Oakes Drive
               Los Gatos, CA 94567
                  (415) 569-0022

OBJECTIVE      Sales Clerk

EDUCATION      BS, Business Administration,
               Hobart College, Los Gatos,
               CA. Graduation date: 6/12/90

COURSEWORK     Sales Personnel Development
               Business Communications
               Principles of Marketing
               Organizational Behavior
               Accounting

HONORS         Dean's List every semester

SKILLS         Am familiar with sales and
               marketing strategies
               Have worked with computerized
               cash registers
               Have good communication
               skills

EXPERIENCE     Receptionist, Forbes Lumber
               Company, San Jose, CA
               Handled telephones, typed
               business documents, filed
               contracts, scheduled
               appointments (6/86-8/88)

               Secretary, Mason Hall
               Corporation, San Jose, CA
               Managed office procedures,
               wrote correspondence,
               organized meetings
               (5/85-5/86)

REFERENCES     On request
```

Gerry wants to send this resume to Macy's as the store is soliciting sales clerk applications for several women's clothing departments. The ads state that clerks should be able to work evenings and weekends. Her application should be addressed to Manager, Macy's, Southridge Mall, San Jose, CA 94576.

Write an application letter for her.

6-4. Curt Czarnowski is about to graduate from a state university and has been looking for a management trainee position with a major department store in Chicago. A business major who focused on management and marketing, Curt finds several stores seem interested in him. Although he has not been a brilliant student, he has taken relevant classes and has acquired good experience working as an assistant manager for Carl's Jr. while in school.

a. Curt has just had an interview for a position with Thurman's Department Store. The interview went fairly well, but the interviewer wanted to see a transcript of Curt's grades. Write a letter for Curt thanking the interviewer for the interview and explaining that your grades have been improving each year since your freshman year. Enclose a transcript. Address the letter to:

Mrs. Henry Dahlberg
Personnel Department
Thurmans' Department Store
8300 Lake Boulevard
Chicago, IL 60463

b. Curt has received an offer from Thurman's Department Store, but he would prefer working for Harold's Department Store. Harold's managers have not yet decided whom they want to hire. Write a letter to Thurman's requesting more time to consider the offer.

c. Thurman's tells him that he cannot have a time extension regarding the offer. Now he must appeal to Harold's; write a letter asking for an answer within a week. Write to:

Mr. Kelly Walters
Personnel Department
Harold's Department Store
2130 Gleason Avenue
Chicago, IL 60467

d. Harold's Department Store has made Curt an offer that he wants to accept; write a letter of acceptance and thank the interviewer who made the offer.

e. Write a letter to Curt's interviewer at Thurman's rejecting her offer.

f. Now that Curt is going to work for Harold's Department Store, he must resign from his present position at Carl's Jr. Write a letter of resignation to:

Mr. Ted DuBois
Manager
Carl's Jr.
782 Alcott Avenue
Chicago, IL 60437

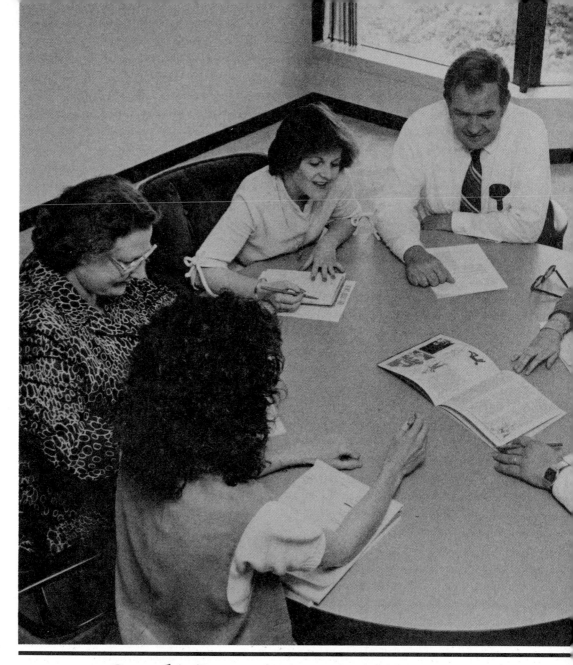

Oral Communication
Principles and Processes

Part Seven

The Oral Communication Process: Speaking and Listening

- **Learning to speak and listen effectively**
- **Recognizing unique qualities of oral communication**
- **Identifying strategies for effective communication**
- **Using listening skills to communicate**
- **Using the telephone effectively**
- **Establishing personal qualities that promote communication**
- **Overcoming barriers to effective oral communication**

Objectives

To communicate effectively through the spoken word

To develop active listening skills

To promote active listening skills in others

22

Mark Lowenthal's Meeting

David Lowenthal had run Lowenthal Corporation for twenty years when he died suddenly at the age of 56. His son Mark was now president of the company. At 32, Mark had spent most of his life in school and had recently received a doctorate in economics. He had not worked extensively with the business, but he felt confident that he could handle the responsibilities and improve the company's profits, which had not increased for five years.

A few weeks after his father's death, Mark called a meeting of top management. Rather than holding it in the conference room where such meetings had traditionally been held, he set it up in the company lounge filled with couches and overstuffed chairs. The managers, dressed in their dark suits, looked at each other doubtfully; Mark had appeared wearing a shirt and corduroys.

"I know you are shocked at meeting here and seeing me like this," Mark said. "But I'm not totally crazy. I wanted to meet you in this room to show that some changes are going to happen at Lowenthal. And I'm wearing a shirt to show you that I intend to roll up my sleeves and work hard for the corporation.

"Everyone here has done an excellent job of creating the fine image of Lowenthal menswear throughout the country. But we're not growing, not changing. I'm not talking about changing our product, which is terrific. I'm talking about marketing and management."

"We have a very traditional image," said one vice-president. "We can't start coming across like a blue jeans manufacturer."

Mark did not really listen to the vice-president's comment. Instead, he went on to outline some sensible changes that he had discussed with his father in previous months. By then, however, Mark's audience was not listening to him. Seeing him in his shirtsleeves, perched on a coffee table in the lounge, they imagined the conservative company was being turned upside-down.

The next day, two vice-presidents resigned. Only then did Mark realize that he had badly miscalculated his first attempt to communicate with management.

Points to Consider
- How did the environment and Mark's appearance interfere with his communication?
- Given Mark's background, what might have been a better way for him to approach his first meeting?
- What personal qualities should Mark have emphasized to facilitate communication with top management?
- What clues might have told him during the meeting that his message was not being heard?
- How could effective listening skills have improved communication at the meeting?
- What should Mark do now?

Learning to Speak and Listen Effectively

John Masoud is a student intern at EMI, a company that develops training materials for organizations. In a typical day at EMI, John must

- take telephone messages from clients and potential clients
- make routine telephone calls to clients
- summarize these messages for his supervisor and other company managers
- meet with his supervisor to set up his tasks for each day
- attend meetings that his supervisor cannot attend and summarize what went on in the meeting
- speak with fellow interns on several projects they are working on together
- speak casually with managers and other employees

These speaking and listening activities make up only a part of the oral communication that John participates in every day. Not only does he spend over half his work time speaking and listening, but he also spends an even higher percentage of time communicating orally at school and at home.

Regardless of the job you are hired to do, a majority of your time will probably be spent communicating orally—in groups and one-on-one, in person and over the telephone. Of course, having been speaking and listening for years, you are proficient in many elements that contribute to effective oral communication.

On the other hand, communicating effectively on the job requires some special skills that you may not have acquired in school or in your communications with family and friends.

No matter how skillful you are in accounting, programming, engineering, law, or whatever your field, you will have to develop expertise in speaking and listening in order to perform your job well and advance successfully. Developing these skills, moreover, will almost certainly increase your self-confidence, reduce frustration and conflict in your relationships, and enhance your performance at work.

The discussion of job interviews in Chapter 21 introduced some of the strategies essential to effective oral communication. This chapter and the ones that follow examine similarities and differences between oral and written communication and highlight techniques that will improve your effectiveness in a wide range of situations.

Much of your time is probably spent communicating orally.

Recognizing Unique Qualities of Oral Communication

In order to master strategies for effective oral communication, consider the qualities that set oral language apart from written language:

1. The speaker is part of the message.
2. The message cannot be saved easily.
3. Feedback may be immediate.
4. The listener must participate as actively as the speaker.

Oral messages are constructed and presented differently than written ones, and the communication channel is different. In oral communication, your appearance, personal attributes, voice, physical environment, and other factors affect the actual words being spoken.

Even on the telephone, you transmit far more than words. Just think of the impressions you receive when you speak on the telephone to someone you have never seen: you can usually guess the sex and approximate age of the other person, and you can also tell whether the person is friendly and enthusiastic or uninterested and bored.

To make oral communication effective, consider your body language, spatial arrangements, and other nonverbal elements as well as word choice, tone, and organization.

Speakers transmit messages through many channels.

Another basic quality of spoken communication is that, once you have spoken a word, it is gone. Unless it is captured on tape, a spoken word lasts only an instant. Receivers cannot reread an oral message. If you phrase a message in unfamiliar terms, listeners cannot pause to check their dictionaries.

Although the oral message is more fleeting than a written one, you can say it again if your receiver does not understand it. In most situations, you can receive almost instantaneous feedback from your listeners and can tailor your messages to their responses.

For example, when you speak, your listener may say, "What did you say? I didn't hear you" or "What do you mean by that?" When speaking to a group, you can tell if your listeners look enthusiastic, puzzled, or bored. Even on the telephone, you can respond to feedback: your listeners' tone of voice or even their silences may serve as feedback. So, even though your oral message can be lost more easily than a written one, it can often be repeated or rephrased to ensure that the receivers understand it and react to it the way you had intended.

In fact, if oral communication is to be a dynamic process, both sender and receiver must participate. If the receiver does not send feedback to the sender, the sender cannot know if the message was received or understood. The communication loop is never completed.

Identifying Strategies for Effective Communication

Identifying your reason for speaking and the characteristics of your listeners is an essential part of the oral communication process. Equally important is your control over nonverbal elements: your environment, body, and voice.

Oral communication is usually a two-way process.

Knowing Why You Are Speaking

You have probably gone to meetings and come away wondering, "What was

Identify a purpose for
business conversations
as well as for speeches.

that all about?" Or perhaps you have listened to someone giving a speech and wondered the same thing. To be an effective communicator, set yourself the task of identifying the major point of your message. If you do not focus on a central idea or theme, you will probably not convey a solid message to your listeners.

Naturally, having a central message is particularly important when you give a speech or deliver a presentation. However, telephone calls, meetings, and even conversations will be more effective if you know their underlying purpose. Telephone company commercials are constantly reminding us that some of the most important business conversations are personal, but few people in business are going to respond well to a seemingly pointless telephone call. Moreover, given the enormous amount of time many business-people spend in meetings, most will tell you how much they appreciate a meeting that is run efficiently and has a clear focus.

Knowing Your Audience

The importance of your audience cannot be overestimated. After all, your listeners are the people interpreting and responding to your message. If you misunderstand your audience, you might have a well-defined message but never accomplish your goals as a communicator.

Before speaking to a group, ask yourself questions about your audience. Defining the basic demographic material regarding your listeners can be important. In some cases, too, identifying values, political commitment, religious beliefs, and opinions can help you focus your message.

Identify tangible and in-
tangible characteristics
of your audience.

In many situations, your audience's characteristics will already be familiar, but you will also want to consider how many listeners you will have, the reasons they will be listening to you, and the attitudes they will probably have about your message. The *feelings* of your listeners can be major barriers to your message: you must try to assess these intangible factors as you develop your message.

Checklist for Analyzing Your Listeners

- What do my listeners feel about me?
- How do these listeners usually react to ideas like mine?
- What benefits will these listeners derive from the ideas I am expressing?
- What do my listeners already know about the material I am presenting?
- How do they feel about the material?
- What points will the listeners be least resistant to?
- What will they be most resistant to?
- How can I dress and arrange a setting that will be most comfortable for my listeners?

Controlling Your Environment

The environment around them is vital to people's emotions, state of mind, and productivity. A room that is too cold or too hot, too brightly lit or too dim, too noisy or too crowded can keep listeners from paying attention or responding favorably to what is said.

As a speaker, work on preparing an environment that will be conducive to listening. Consider the seating arrangements, lighting, and room temperature. Another important aspect of the physical environment is the distance between you and the person or people listening to you. Sitting or standing close can make you appear warm and friendly, but getting *too* close will make other people uncomfortable. With some experience, you will be able to establish a physical proximity that enhances rather than detracts from your message.

Using Your Body to Communicate

Your body speaks as eloquently as your words. Every gesture, facial expression, and movement can contain a message. The more you learn to control your body language, the more precisely you can learn to use it as a complement to your spoken messages.

In general, your body language should reinforce your listeners' confidence in you. People who are not telling the truth or who dislike the person they are addressing often drop their eyes. Meeting your listeners' eyes will increase their sense of your credibility and competence. Similarly, leaning toward someone tends to show that you feel positively toward that person.

Sitting with your arms folded, on the other hand, can make you appear cold or distant. Random hand movements can make you appear nervous, but a rigid posture can send the message that you are hostile or angry. Work on using your hands to make your points and avoid letting nervousness turn your body into a mass of frozen bone and tissue.

Your facial expressions, of course, are also very important. You have seen evil characters in movies who maintain disconcertingly blank expressions, never registering an emotion. Sometimes a speaker's nervousness or preoccupation can create the same effect and put up a major barrier between the speaker and the audience. While you do not want to paint a perpetual smile on your face, you do want to make sure your expressions help to generate positive emotions between you and your listeners.

Using Your Voice Effectively

You may believe that you have very little control over your voice. While you probably cannot turn your tenor voice into a bass or your contralto into a soprano, you can adjust the rate, volume, and inflections of your voice, just as you can adjust the way you pronounce words.

Make sure you speak at a rate that is slow enough to be understood and fast enough to save your listeners from boredom. You do not need to fill up every moment with words. Pauses can actually be dramatic. (If you get a chance to watch one of the old *Burns and Allen* television shows, notice how long George Burns holds his audience while he is lighting his cigar.) Avoid filling up empty moments with *uhms, ahs,* and *you knows.*

Pay attention to the volume of your voice.

Adjust the volume of your voice so your listeners can hear but are not overwhelmed by the decibels. Speaking too softly may show you are shy or not assertive enough, but too loud a voice can irritate your listeners.

With experience, you will be able to adjust your voice easily to the size and shape of the room and the number and proximity of your listeners.

If you speak in a monotone, work on adding more inflection to your voice. Let your voice register emotions. Listen to yourself on tape and ask your friends for assistance. Few people are born with a perfect "radio announcer's" voice, but everyone can dramatically improve voice quality.

Using Listening Skills to Communicate

Like the communication process itself, oral communication is usually a dynamic process that demands both speaking and listening. Most of the time, you are speaking *and* listening—sending messages, receiving feedback and more messages, sending feedback and more messages, and so on. Even when speaking to a crowd, you receive feedback from the audience's expressions, postures, and noises. To communicate effectively with that crowd, you must watch and listen as well as speak.

Good listening skills are vital to effective business communication. Following orders, handling personnel problems, making sales pitches, dealing with customers—almost every aspect of business relies on listening skills. If you are a counselor, psychiatrist, attorney—or student—you may spend most of your day listening. Even accountants, programmers, and office workers spend up to one-third of their working days listening to supervisors, customers, clients, suppliers, and fellow-workers.

Despite the vital importance of good listening, many people in business have never developed listening skills. Managers are frequently reluctant to pay attention to what employees and clients are saying, while employees often miss essential messages from supervisors and fellow-workers. Good listening can save time and money, improve morale, and promote upward, downward, and lateral communication.

In the famous Nero Wolfe detective stories, Nero Wolfe's assistant Archie Goodwin has near-perfect listening abilities. He can recount long, complex conversations verbatim. You can probably never attain Archie's superb (and fictional) listening abilities, but you can significantly improve your present skill levels. Moreover, you can work on making listening an intrinsic part of daily life. You can make it become natural for you, not something you "turn on" when you feel it is appropriate.

Do you think you are a good listener? Try testing yourself: listen to one of your instructors lecture for an hour and then try to summarize all the major points that were touched on. Or listen to a newscast for an hour. How many details about each news story can you remember?

In each of these situations, since you are *trying* to listen well, you will do better than you ordinarily would have. Yet you will probably be shocked at how little you remember of what was said. (How much would you remember if you had to take a surprise quiz on a lecture or newscast?)

To improve your listening skills, work on listening actively, take time to hear what people are saying, and use techniques that encourage people to speak openly.

Listening Actively

Like reading, listening should not be a passive activity. Active listening includes far more than simply *hearing*. It requires not only assimilating certain pieces of information but also perceiving nonverbal messages and evaluating what was said and what was *not* said.

Active listening requires more than hearing.

Consider, for example, the following dialogue between a supervisor, Angela, and an employee, Fred.

> ANGELA: Are you about done with that report?
> FRED: Just about. I've been working on it all morning. I didn't even take a coffee break.
> ANGELA: You know it has to go out today.
> FRED: Yes, it's too bad I didn't get it until this morning.
> ANGELA: Don't forget about those changes we discussed.

In this dialogue, Angela is not really listening. When Fred says he has been working all morning, he is letting her know that he is a dedicated worker who is getting the job done. Angela could have responded with feedback that complimented or motivated him; instead, she proceeds with her one-way communication.

In response to her lack of sensitivity, Fred sends a message with a note of complaint: he tells her she was at fault for waiting so long to give the report to him. But, again, Angela ignores the unspoken message and continues with the problem on her mind. She is hearing Fred, but she is not listening.

Taking Time to Listen

Active listening can appear time-consuming. It often seems faster and easier to issue directives and make assumptions without listening to other people's viewpoints. When you make active listening a part of your life, however, you will end up saving time: mistakes will be averted; clients, customers, employees, and supervisors will be more satisfied; and operations will move more smoothly.

Of course, sometimes direct action will be more appropriate than listening. As a manager, for instance, you may have to make decisions quickly, before you have heard everyone's point of view. There will be moments when you do not have time to listen to people's problems. You will have to use your judgment, balancing the importance of listening with other concerns.

Are You an Active Listener?

How would you respond to the following situations?

1. A supervisor speaks to you about problems with your work. Do you
   a. immediately defend yourself?
   b. feel so anxious that you do not hear the exact problems being defined?
   c. concentrate on the problems being defined so you can respond appropriately?
2. An instructor explains complex information that you have trouble understanding. Do you
   a. keep telling yourself that you will never grasp this material?
   b. keep worrying that the instructor will think you are stupid?
   c. sort out the ideas being presented and ask questions on areas that confuse you?
3. You sit in a meeting on Friday afternoon. Do you
   a. find yourself thinking about the weekend ahead?
   b. watch the people around you instead of hearing what they say?
   c. listen to other people, ask questions, and add information as necessary?
4. You sit in a class. Do you
   a. find yourself thinking about the person next to you, the temperature of the room, and your uncomfortable chair?
   b. write down everything the instructor says without trying to understand it?
   c. listen for main ideas and summarize key concepts?
5. A friend discusses a problem with you. Do you
   a. interrupt and discuss your own problems?
   b. jump to conclusions and begin giving advice immediately?
   c. pay attention to verbal and nonverbal cues that would help you understand and respond to the problem?

Discussion

If you would respond in ways described by the *c* answers, you are already an active listener. Most people, however, tend to let personal concerns, emotions, anxieties, and external distractions interfere with the active listening process—at least some of the time.

Responding to Speakers

Part of listening involves responding effectively to what someone is saying. Sometimes your natural response will be to start talking yourself, giving *your* point of view. This approach often cuts off the flow of real communication. Instead, try to provide positive responses that encourage rather than interrupt the speaker.

Silent Responses. You do not have to speak in order to respond. Nods, smiles, and gestures can help a speaker to continue. You do not have to indicate that you agree with the person, but you can indicate that you are listening and are interested in what is being said.

Probes. An occasional probing question or statement can also encourage a speaker to continue and help you understand what the person really wants to convey. These questions will subtly help to focus the speaker on key issues.

STUDENT: I just can't write the paper you assigned. I'm too confused.
INSTRUCTOR: You're confused about the topic?

In the preceding dialogue, the instructor rephrases the student's words to encourage her to explain what she means by *confused*. The best probes are indirect. Compare these two responses:

EMPLOYEE: I guess you're wondering why I've been late to work this week.
SUPERVISOR: Have you been staying out late—partying?

EMPLOYEE: I guess you're wondering why I've been late to work this week.
SUPERVISOR: Maybe you should tell me about it.

In the first dialogue, the supervisor's response could make the employee defensive or angry, even if the question is phrased jokingly. The second response is unbiased and indirect, encouraging the employee to speak out.

Summaries. A similar helpful response is to summarize a speaker's point every once in a while. Brief summaries indicate you are listening and help to ensure that you are understanding what is being said.

SUPERVISOR: Are you saying that you think the procedure could be streamlined?
EMPLOYEE: Yes, that's what I meant—

Both probes and summaries can help you to get an accurate idea of what the speaker is saying while they provide feedback helpful for the speaker.

Remaining Unbiased

You have probably tried speaking to people who have their minds made up before you spoke to them. You knew that nothing you said was going to make your listeners change their positions.

As a listener, suspend your judgment until you have listened carefully. If you make up your mind *before* someone has finished speaking, you will not really hear what is being said. Avoid arguing or stating your point of view until you have a sense of the whole picture. Your objectivity will encourage rather than stifle effective communication.

Using the Telephone Effectively

For many people, telephones are a primary channel for making sales, dealing with customers and clients, solving problems, and exchanging ideas. As a businessperson, you may find that placing, receiving, and waiting for calls take up a large percentage of your time. Telephones can enable you to communicate quickly and personally with people all over the world, but making and receiving calls can be frustrating and time-consuming. Since you cannot see the person with whom you are speaking, pay careful attention to both your speaking and listening skills.

Many people use the telephone for most of their daily communication.

The following guidelines can help you use the telephone more effectively.

Guidelines for Telephone Usage

Answering Calls
- Answer the telephone promptly: waiting while the telephone rings can annoy the caller before the conversation even begins.

- Identify yourself or your organization when you answer: "Hello, Aaronson Auto" or "Hello, Bob Masterson speaking."
- Screen calls before transfering them. "Yes, Mrs. Rescino is here. May I tell her who is calling?"
- Transfer calls correctly. Few things irritate a caller more than being disconnected while being transfered.
- Repeat major ideas. "I will have Mike call you. Your number is 765-2134?"
- If a call is for someone else, write down a complete message with name of caller, time and date of call, nature of message, and telephone number.

Placing Calls
- Clearly state your name and organization.
- If you want your call returned, say so.
- Make sure the person answering the telephone has your correct name and telephone number.
- Indicate a time and date when the call can be returned.

Conversing
- Prepare a list of major points beforehand so you can be thorough and accurate during the conversation.
- Hold the receiver an inch or so away from your mouth so your words are not muffled.
- Speak slowly and a little more loudly than usual.
- Get to your point quickly: most people appreciate a minimum of chatter.
- Maintain a friendly, personal tone.
- Pick up verbal cues: if the other person sounds busy or impatient, for example, ask whether you should return the call later on.
- Get feedback on ideas or plans: "Do you think a meeting on Monday would be worthwhile?" "Are you interested in pursuing these ideas further? Maybe we should have lunch tomorrow."
- Make sure you understand any agreements: "You would like to see samples of the R-23?" "You want to go ahead with the Morris deal?"
- At the end of the call, summarize major ideas or plans: "Okay, we'll meet on Monday at 9 a.m. here in my office." "Right, I'll call Wendy Norris and see if she can work on the contract this week."

Establishing Personal Qualities That Promote Communication

Personal qualities affect the oral communication process.

You are part of the message you transmit, so it is important to establish personal qualities that will facilitate the communication process—whether you are communicating by telephone or in person. Sincerity, openness, objectivity, and competence are some of the most important of these qualities.

E. F. HUTTON

William Morgan

"I spend 90 percent of my day on the phone," says William Morgan, First Vice-President of E. F. Hutton. "I buy securities and package them into unit investment trusts, so the small investor can participate in professionally managed products."

"I get many more phone calls than I make, mostly from salesmen at institutions such as banks and brokerage firms, people who want to sell me securities." Each firm assigns a salesman for institutional accounts. What salesmen will William do business with? First of all, "You have to have something to sell. Second, you should make me feel that you have my best interests at heart. I have to see you as knowledgeable, ethical, direct and professional. If I ask the question, 'What's the rating?' and you call to someone and say, 'Joe, what's the rating?' I'll say, 'Put Joe on.' Don't waste my time. Use my time effectively."

William says people at major firms tend to be well-trained. They have to have at least a college degree, usually an MBA. "They have to pay their dues to get into the business. Beyond that, personality is important. The person should be convincing, effervescent, aggressive, able to look you in the eye." These people also have to be able to accept rejection and handle pressure.

"There's a lot of psychology in the business," William says. "People can talk a market up or down." In addition, you're selling an intangible. "It's not like selling a car, where the buyer says, 'I like the color' or 'I like the bucket seats.'"

In the securities business, native intelligence is important. There are always new products being introduced. "The salesperson isn't the final source on the details, but he or she does have to have an overview."

How does William, faced with all these people trying to sell him securities, make a decision on what to buy? He says he's developed instincts. He listens to vibes. He can say quickly, "This is of value." "Then," he says, "you have to live with your trading position."

William's tips for students making persuasive calls?

- Be direct.
- Take as little time as possible.
- Be knowledgeable.
- Show that you know what the person at the other end of the line wants.
- Be professional.

Sincerity

If you come across sincerely, you have a good chance of being well regarded by people speaking and listening to you. Sincerity will not automatically establish your credibility, but it will help. If people trust you, they will be more likely to respond positively to you and to speak openly with you.

Openness

Openness is closely related to sincerity. If you can establish an atmosphere of openness, people will be more apt to speak to you and give you feedback regarding your messages. They will trust that you will listen to them and respond appropriately even if you disagree with their opinions.

Objectivity

Objectivity can also be a key ingredient to your success as a communicator. You will find that acknowledging both sides of an issue will show both your understanding of the situation and your openness to people who disagree with you.

As a speaker, work on emphasizing facts rather than opinions and on keeping your language free from obvious bias. As a listener, keep an open mind until you understand every side of an issue.

Competence

Competence and credibility are closely entwined. If you demonstrate your ability to perform, your credibility will be enhanced. As a speaker, you will also reassure your listeners if you back up your assertions with solid information. Avoid hyperbole and illogical conclusions.

Prepare carefully for a meeting, interview, speech, or even an important conversation. Make sure of your facts and organize them carefully. Rephrase and summarize so other people will be able to follow your reasoning.

Overcoming Barriers to Effective Oral Communication

Recognizing some of the main barriers to oral communication can help you overcome them both as a speaker and as a listener. Some of the most common barriers are external and internal distractions, biases, and language differences.

External Distractions

External distractions often interfere with the oral communication process. Noise, heat, cold, and other factors can severely reduce our attentiveness and retentiveness. If you have ever sat in a movie theater next to someone who fidgets, coughs, or talks, you know how such distractions can destroy your concentration even though you can still hear the movie dialogue.

The work environment you create influences the way you communicate.

As a speaker, try to set up environments conducive to good communication. You may be able to set up an office, meeting room, lecture hall, or classroom so that external distractions are minimized. As a listener, practice concentrating: if you actively weigh the speaker's words, review key points, and focus on the communication process, you will be able to shut out at least some external distractions.

Internal Distractions

We are capable of hearing much faster than we are capable of speaking. Thus, as listeners, we have a lot of spare time. We can listen to a friend talk about his car and his girlfriend and also think about what to have for lunch and what to wear on Saturday night. We can nod attentively in economics class and also worry about an upcoming statistics test. Worries, emotions, memories, tensions—thousands of distractions are competing with the messages people send.

As a speaker, be aware that you are constantly competing with your listeners' internal distractions. Keep watching to see if you have lost their attention. If possible, use visual aids, tell anecdotes, emphasize information relevant to the listeners, and employ other techniques to help focus their attention on your words.

As a listener, use the speed of your thoughts to your advantage. You have time to listen to what is being said, analyze, ask mental questions, and "read between the lines." Avoid using part of your brain to daydream; instead, use as much of your brain as possible to assimilate and remember what is being said.

A speaker is always competing with a listener's internal distractions.

Biases

Biases can prevent people from really hearing what is being said. If you do not like a person, you may not listen to him or her. If you are set in your views, you may not listen to opposing ones.

You may tell yourselves that someone "never has anything worthwhile to say" or that a person "is just droning on and on." At that point, you may shut down mentally and turn your attention to something else—just as you might switch a channel on a television set to something more worthwhile.

To overcome biases is a difficult but not impossible process. Avoid jumping to conclusions about people. Objectively review what they are saying instead of being distracted by what they look like, how they talk, or what they have said in the past.

To help your listeners overcome biases about you, work on conveying your sincerity, objectivity, and competence. Positive personal qualities can help your listeners realize that you have something worthwhile to say.

Language Differences

Naturally, you are not able to listen to people if you do not understand their language. Even if they are speaking a language with which you are familiar, you may have trouble following them if they use words you do not understand or speak in an accent with which you are unfamiliar.

If you have traveled to England or even to some parts of the United States, you may have encountered people whose English was almost impossible for you to understand. Both their vocabulary and their accent differed radically from your own. You may even have had trouble understanding someone whose vocabulary in a technical field left you wondering what was being said.

As a listener, you can often let speakers know when you cannot follow what they are saying. Ask them to define words, to speak more slowly, or to review key concepts. After all, speakers *want* you to understand them: usually they will be happy to increase their own clarity.

As a speaker, be aware of possible language problems. If you are not a native speaker of the language you are using, make sure you speak slowly and ask listeners for feedback.

Similarly, if you are unsure whether your listeners are familiar with the vocabulary you are going to use, ask them to let you know if they are confused. Provide them with definitions or even a glossary. Many times visual aids such as handouts or charts with key words on them can help listeners follow your presentation more easily.

Checklist for Improving Your Active Listening Skills

- If possible, establish an environment with a minimum of external distractions.
- Listen for key words and ideas.
- Rather than daydreaming, stay alert by rephrasing and summarizing the speaker's concepts.
- Look the speaker in the eyes.
- Listen for emotions as well as facts.
- Listen for what is being implied rather than just what is being said.
- Watch the speaker's body language.
- Be aware of your own biases; try to listen objectively.
- Focus on positive aspects of the speaker's presentation rather than on poor delivery or other negative qualities.
- Ask questions if you do not understand.

Checklist for Encouraging Good Listening in Others

- Maintain eye contact with your listeners.
- Summarize and rephrase so listeners follow your main ideas.
- Define key terms.
- Use visual aids to add interest and simplify your points.
- Use body language to reinforce your points.
- Speak slowly enough so people can follow you.
- Get to your point quickly; avoid getting sidetracked.
- Keep your voice interesting.
- Use vivid words.
- Remind the listeners of the benefits they will receive from listening.
- Ask listeners to give you feedback on what you have said.

What Would You Do?

Hugh Borjes is head of the Computer Department at BELCO Corporation. Having worked for the corporation for two years, he knows that many members of upper management know little about computers, and some even resisted setting up a computer department in the first place.

This week, Hugh has been asked to give a one-hour presentation to management on his department's accomplishments and goals. Hugh would also like to take this opportunity to request some additional equipment.

Hugh is concerned, however, that most of his audience will be there in body only—they will not be listening to him. Their biases against computers will keep them from really hearing what he has to say.

If you were Hugh Borjes, what steps would you take to help this audience listen actively? Write him a memo outlining some procedures he could use.

Summary

No matter what career you are in or plan to enter, you will find that good listening and speaking skills are essential to your success. The two activities reinforce and depend on each other. Both demand that you pay attention to verbal and nonverbal messages. Both activities also require that you consider other people's needs as well as your own. While learning to speak effectively, learn also to listen actively—and work on helping others to do the same.

Oral Communication Checklist

Oral Communication Process

- Remember that oral communication differs in some ways from written communication:

    _____ The speaker is an intrinsic part of the message.

    _____ A spoken word lasts only an instant, so the message cannot be "re-read" like a written message.

    _____ A speaker usually receives instant feedback from a listener.

    _____ A listener should participate as actively as a speaker.

Good Speakers

- To improve your spoken communication skills,

    _____ identify your message

    _____ analyze your audience

    _____ set up a physical environment that will minimize distractions and encourage listening and participation

    _____ use body language that reinforces your listeners' confidence in you

    _____ speak slowly enough to be understood

    _____ keep your voice interesting

    _____ encourage active listening

Poor Listeners

- To avoid being a poor listener, work on reducing these tendencies:

    _____ focusing on the speaker's negative attributes rather than on positive qualities

    _____ being more interested in making your own point than in listening to someone else's

    _____ letting your emotions interfere with objective listening

_____ allowing the external environment to distract you

_____ writing down every word instead of listening for key concepts

Active Listeners

- To increase your active listening skills,

  _____ take the time to listen carefully

  _____ try to keep your emotions and biases from interfering with the communication process

  _____ screen out external distractions

  _____ stop worrying about how the speaker feels about you

  _____ ask probing questions to clarify points

  _____ analyze and summarize major ideas

Telephone Usage

- To increase effective telephone communication,

  _____ take accurate messages

  _____ repeat and emphasize major ideas

  _____ make sure your voice is clear and audible

  _____ listen for verbal cues from the other person

Terms to Remember

Active listening: participating in the oral communication process rather than merely hearing what is said

Probes: indirect questions or statements that encourage people to speak openly

Summary Discussion: Mark Lowenthal's Meeting from Case in Point, p. 537

Mark Lowenthal set up a casual environment to make some serious points to his listeners. However, he did not realize the extent to which his listeners' biases and emotions would interfere with the communication process.

Despite the apparently casual atmosphere, too, Mark did not listen to the other people or make it easy for them to respond. He did not ask for feedback or appear interested in their responses. Because he did not listen actively to them, he did not perceive his listeners' dismay and outrage.

Before calling his first meeting, he should have analyzed his purpose and his audience. At the meeting, he could have worked on establishing his competence and credibility with top management. His dramatic effects in terms of setting and personal appearance might have worked later on, when his credibility had been established.

To make up for a bad start, Mark might try meeting individually with some top managers to reduce their panic. They might be able to listen to him more easily one-to-one. He could also summarize some key ideas in a letter or report highlighting his goals for the company. Then he should hold a more traditional meeting and prepare for it carefully.

Questions for Review and Discussion

1. What are the similarities between the spoken and oral communication processes?
2. Describe some communication barriers that occur with spoken messages that do not occur with written messages.
3. Explain why feedback is even more important to oral communication than it is to written communication.
4. Name someone whom you think is a successful speaker. What personal qualities does that person demonstrate?
5. In a classroom, what external elements do you find help the communication process going on. What elements hinder that process?
6. Why do you think the distance between a speaker and listener can be important? Give an example.
7. Why do you think eye contact is so important to both speakers and listeners?
8. How do biases affect our ability to listen? Give an example.
9. What techniques do you use to help you listen more carefully?

Exercises

1. Describe a situation in which you took an immediate dislike to a person based on his or her appearance. Did your initial reaction prevent you from listening carefully to what the person was saying to you? Explain.
2. Watch a television program with the sound turned off. As you watch, note the types of nonverbal behavior you perceive. Describe the

personality of the characters, as you see them, through their appearance and nonverbal behavior.

3. Describe a communication problem that could have been solved easily if one of the people involved had given feedback to someone else.

4. Watch a television actor or actress for at least thirty minutes. What body language did the person use to communicate? Were some gestures more effective than others? Be specific and cite a few examples.

5. Working with a partner, exchange the class notes you each took during one specified class. Discuss in what ways the notes differed and in what ways they were the same. What brought about the differences?

6. Keep a list of your listening activities during an average day at school or work. Whom were you listening to? What percentage of your day did you spend listening?

7. Break into groups of three or four. Ask one person in the group to recount an incident that occurred sometime recently. The story should go on for a minute or so. Afterward, each group member (including the speaker) will write a description of the incident using as many of the speaker's words and phrases as possible. Compare versions of the story.

8. Identify a well-known figure who acts as a spokesperson for a product or company. What characteristics of that person make him or her a good or poor spokesperson? Discuss personal qualities as well as body language and voice.

9. Contact a college instructor or local businessperson who often speaks to business or community groups. Ask the person to identify some of the techniques he or she uses to help the audience listen and retain what has been said.

Interviews

- **Recognizing unique features of interviews**
- **Planning the interview process**
- **Conducting the interview**
- **Identifying types of interviews**

Objectives

To plan and conduct interviews success-fully

To identify and achieve major goals

for each interview

To recognize different types of interviews

23

Sondra German's Interview

Sondra German is in charge of collecting data from supervisors in three departments concerning the performance of employees in their sections. Every six months she is supposed to meet with each employee, review the person's performance, and determine some goals for the following appraisal period.

Sondra dreads these interviews since employees tend to be resentful, complaining about their supervisors and co-workers and making excuses for their own performance. As a result of her reluctance to set up these interviews, Sondra puts them off until the last minute and schedules them in twenty-minute periods over a period of several days.

In the middle of the second day of interviews, Sondra is running behind schedule. Her interviewee, Phyllis Bolourchi, a typist in the typing pool, has been waiting for twenty-five minutes when Sondra finally calls her in. Sondra gets right to business.

"Well, Phyllis, you've kept a consistent rating from last time. You get a good rating on attitude, but you're only doing fair on output."

"I don't understand why I didn't get a better rating," Phyllis replies. "I do a lot more work than some of the others do. In fact, I'm always helping the others out when they get behind."

"Maybe you should make that clear to George, Phyllis. He doesn't know if you do extra work."

"I really think the old system we had there was better," Phyllis says. "Last year, George handed out our work to each of us, so—"

Sondra glances at her watch. She's gotten so far behind schedule that she's going to have to set up another whole day's worth of interviews. "Phyllis, I don't really have time to discuss the system in the typing pool right now. Take it up with George."

Phyllis turns red. "You and I are supposed to have a *discussion* in these interviews. That's what the personnel manual says. But I don't get a chance to discuss. It's not right that I get a fair rating when I do more work than half the others."

Phyllis leaves in tears. Sondra feels a headache coming on. She knows she has mishandled the situation, but she just does not have time to resolve the problem with Phyllis.

Points to Consider

- How could Sondra have started this interview more effectively?
- What could Sondra do to make these interviews less strenuous and more productive for herself and the interviewees?
- What should Sondra have done when she realized Phyllis was upset?
- What goals should Sondra have during these interviews?

Recognizing Unique Features of Interviews

Chapter 21 discussed job interviews from the perspective of a job candidate. Once you have a job, however, your experience with interviews will not end. Interviews are a common type of two-way communication in organizational settings. They are used, not just in hiring, but also in appraising, disciplining, and firing employees, in isolating and solving problems, in counseling, in selling, and in a myriad of other situations.

Many types of interviews are common in organizations.

In this chapter, you will focus primarily on the role of the interviewer who must plan and conduct interviews. However, you will also consider the interviewee, who must use planning, speaking, and listening skills to participate effectively in interviews.

You may think of interviews as being similar to a conversation: two people sit down to discuss a problem or exchange information. Interviews, however, differ from conversations in several important ways.

Interviews Have Goals

A conversation may meander through several topics, but an interview has definite goals. It has been set up for a purpose such as helping to select job candidates, appraise an employee's performance, or resolve conflicts.

As an interviewer, establish clear goals for each interview and make sure the person you are interviewing understands precisely why the interview is taking place.

Interviews Have Guidelines

Both conducting and participating in an interview demand perceptiveness and attentiveness as well as good listening and speaking skills. Because interviewing is a complex process, you will probably find it useful as an interviewer to follow guidelines for different types of interviews. Being familiar with these guidelines will also help you as an interviewee to understand why the interview is taking place and how the interviewer is approaching the process.

Interviewers Are in Charge

No matter how informal an interview may be, the interviewer has a leadership role. Having established the goals and guidelines and often the setting and time of the interview, the interviewer usually initiates topics, asks questions, and establishes the tone of the interview.

Both the interviewer and interviewee should participate actively in an interview.

The leadership aspect of interviews makes them quite different from conversations. As an interviewer, you will be observing and listening closely to the interviewee. You will be making decisions on the directions the interview should take and perhaps making notes on issues that arise.

As in job interviews, however, the interviewee should not be entirely passive. Whether you are the interviewee or the interviewer, remember that communication should be two-way, no matter what type of interview is taking place.

Interviews Are Usually Imprecise

Like conversations, interviews may cover several topics, and they may reveal unexpected information or take unexpected twists. This lack of precision is usually a positive element; exploratory elements can help to make an interview worthwhile. When interviews are too structured, they can lose some of their usefulness.

Planning the Interview Process

An interview consists of more than simply the minutes in which two (or more) people speak with each other. Most interviews are planned beforehand and evaluated afterwards.

Planning the Interview

As an interviewer, you are in charge of setting the goals and establishing the direction of the interview. You are also in charge of establishing tone and atmosphere. To help ensure a successful interview, review some key areas before the interview begins.

Determine goals for the interview. Make sure you know exactly why the interview is about to take place. In many cases, you will have primary and secondary goals. If you are screening job applicants, for instance, your primary goal might be to establish if a candidate has the necessary skills to do the job properly. Your secondary goal might be to find out if the person has the aggressive personality or energy the job requires.

Review key questions and content areas. You may find it helpful to write these out and refer to them occasionally during the interview. You may want to draw upon questions you have used successfully in similar interviews, but remember that this particular interview may vary in some significant ways. Be prepared to adapt your questions as the interview proceeds.

Consider the approaches or strategies that will best achieve your goals. These considerations involve evaluating the interviewee's needs, goals, and interests as well as your own. You should consider, for instance, whether you are conveying bad news or looking for information, whether you are going to have a resistant interviewee or a helpful one.

Choose between closed and open-ended questions. A major consideration in many instances will be whether to use closed or open-ended questions. Closed questions limit the data that the interviewee will provide:

When did you begin working for DarCo?

Are you familiar with the Audex System?

Open-ended questions give the interviewee a chance to bring up unexpected information:

Closed questions lead to a limited range of answers.

Open-ended questions may produce unexpected information.

Open-Ended Questions

Advantages:
- They can help an interviewee to feel relaxed
- They can help the interviewer discover unexpected information
- The interviewer can gain insights into the interviewee

Disadvantages:
- The interviewee's vague or irrelevant responses may waste time
- The interviewer has to be able to ascertain the key points of an interviewee's responses
- The interviewer may have trouble comparing and evaluating responses from two or more interviewees

Closed Questions

Advantages:
- The interviewer can easily obtain and assess information
- The interviewer stays in control of the interview
- Little time is lost

Disadvantages:
- The interviewer obtains no additional information
- The interview may seem impersonal or boring
- Interchanges of emotions rarely take place

What are your goals?

Has anything about this job been bothering you?

Do you have any suggestions for improving this project?

Both types of questions have advantages and disadvantages, and both are useful in various interview situations. Most interviewers, in fact, use a combination of closed and open-ended questions.

Establish an atmosphere in keeping with your goals. You must decide not only on a tone but also on the physical environment that will be most suitable and effective.

For a formal job interview, for example, you may choose to remain in your office. For a less formal counseling or informational exchange interview, you may want to move to a lounge or even a restaurant so the interviewee will be more at ease.

At times you may choose to conduct an interview that tests an interviewee's ability to handle pressure and stress. Called *stress interviews* (see also p. 516), these may be set up in a variety of ways. They differ from the majority of interviews in that, rather than making the interviewee feel relaxed, the interviewer creates an atmosphere and develops situations that make the interviewee feel pressured.

Conducting the Interview

How you actually conduct an interview will be determined by your goals and personal style. However, some guidelines are useful for almost any type of interview.

Establish a pleasant atmosphere. Unless you are conducting a stress interview, you can establish a rapport with your interviewee by greeting the person pleasantly and briefly talking about matters unrelated to the interview. Do not let this warm-up period go for too long: the interviewee will become *less* relaxed, wondering why he or she has been called in and why you are delaying getting to the point.

Atmosphere is an important component of an interview.

Review the agenda. Usually it is a good idea to begin the business part of the interview by summarizing the purpose of the meeting.

Avoid leading questions. Whether you use closed or open-ended questions, avoid questions that reveal a bias: "Don't you think the new manual is terrific?" "How do you like those great improvements Jake has been making in production?" Questions like these make it hard for an interviewee to respond honestly.

Leading questions presume the interviewee will answer in a certain way.

Remember to listen. Active listening is essential. Do not become so absorbed in your goals for the interview that you forget to listen attentively. Use verbal and nonverbal cues to encourage the interviewee to talk.

Be aware of the interviewee's nonverbal as well as verbal communication. Signs of fear, evasion, discomfort, nervousness, excitement, enthusiasm, or boredom can give you as much information as the interviewee's words.

Watch for turning points in the interview. At certain crucial moments, the time may be right to alter the direction of the interview or reach key decisions.

Clarify actions to be taken after the interview. Let interviewees know what will happen next. Whether you are going to write a report, telephone the interviewee, pass the interviewee's ideas to someone else, or wait for the interviewee to complete certain tasks, make sure that he or she understands what to expect. You may even set up a schedule for future actions.

Summarize future actions at the end of the interview.

End the interview cordially. Make sure you have scheduled sufficient time for the interview so it is not rushed—and then leave time to bring things to an end smoothly and pleasantly.

Evaluating the Interview

When the interview is over, take time to evaluate what occurred. You may want to jot down your thoughts or reactions. Note any significant decisions that were made and any schedule that has been set up for future meetings or actions.

In many cases, you will want to follow up with a memo to the interviewee summarizing key points and conveying additional information. In other cases, you will need to write an informational report to your superiors on the major issues covered in the interview.

Identifying Types of Interviews

Although interviews have many characteristics in common, each type takes place for a different purpose. When planning, conducting, and evaluating interviews, keep in mind their specific goals.

Checklist for Interviewees

- Be prepared for issues, problems, or questions the interviewer might raise.
- Go to the interview with a positive outlook.
- Know what you want to achieve in the interview.
- Stay calm even if the interview is stressful; try not to become defensive.
- Watch the interviewer's nonverbal cues.
- Listen actively: What is really being said here? What are the interviewer's real goals?
- Answer questions with sufficient detail but avoid overlong responses.
- Ask the interviewer to review key points whenever necessary.
- Before leaving the interview, clarify any action that will be taken next.
- Remain cordial throughout the interview

Employment Interviews

In employment interviews, both people are interested in obtaining information. As interviewer, you want to assess the job candidate's interpersonal skills and gain relevant information not evident from the applicant's resume.

You also want to give the applicant information about the position and the company. This information is vital to the applicant's decision-making process. Moreover, the applicant's reactions to this information can help you decide whether the person is right for the job and the company.

Exit Interviews

Exit interviews take place when employees are leaving a company.

Many companies make it a practice to conduct exit interviews when an employee leaves the organization. Once again, these should entail mutual exchanges of information. As an interviewer, you want to obtain information concerning why the employee is leaving. These data may help the company improve management techniques and lower turnover rate in the future. Remember, though, that the information received in an exit interview is not always accurate. A departing employee may be interested in getting good references from a supervisor and so will hesitate to speak frankly. On the other hand, an employee may be too angry or resentful to offer rational reasons for the departure.

Another goal for an exit interview is to provide the employee with information about severance pay, necessary forms, and other materials. Many times you as the interviewer may be able to use the exit interview as a way of helping the departing employee feel more positive about the company. If possible, make the employee's last impressions of the company as pleasant as possible.

Appraisal Interviews

Like a job interview, a performance appraisal interview should involve the mutual exchange of information. Both the employee and the interviewer should evaluate the employee's performance and set future goals.

These interviews can be stressful for employees, so, as an interviewer, try to create an atmosphere that promotes rather than stifles two-way communication. Because many employees complain that evaluations of their work are based on subjective or vague guidelines, establish clear criteria for evaluation. Make sure, too, that you get feedback from the employee: give the person opportunities to respond.

Appraisal interviews focus on an employee's performance.

Disciplinary Interviews

Disciplinary interviews may result when an employee has been chronically late or absent, has failed to follow regulations, or has an attitude problem.

Disciplinary interviews are intended to persuade employees to alter their behavior.

To conduct a successful disciplinary interview, do not lose sight of the three primary communication goals. While you must convey a message to the employee, try to persuade that person to act differently in the future and maintain goodwill between yourself and the employee. Achieving these goals, however, may not be easy.

Before the interview, make sure that you know all the facts of the situation and are familiar with relevant company policies. During the interview, remain unemotional. Address your criticism to the employee's actions, not to the employee. Try to find any underlying reasons for his or her behavior. Active listening is essential: use probing questions and nonverbal cues to encourage the interviewee to talk.

If disciplinary measures must be taken, make it clear that you are acting impartially, in keeping with company regulations.

> "Terry, company policy is quite clear about this. If you are late for work more than three days in a thirty-day period, you must be given a written warning. If you are late within the next thirty days, your pay will be docked."

Remember to keep a clear written account of the employee's actions and the interview itself.

Counseling Interviews

Managers frequently find themselves in the position of counselors, a role for which they may not have been trained. You may find that employees come to you for advice on personal matters as well as on job-related topics. These interviews may be awkward and ineffective if they are not handled skillfully.

Avoid taking on the role of a counselor unless you are trained to do so.

If the employee comes to you for help with a job-related problem, establish a friendly atmosphere and then work with the employee on isolating the reasons for the problem and outlining some possible solutions.

If the employee comes to you with personal problems concerning marriage, alcohol, drugs, or other matters, do not try to help if you are not a trained counselor; you may end up doing more harm than good. You may also be legally liable if you provide counseling without the training or authority to do so. If someone needs professional counseling, work with the person to find a counselor who is right for his or her particular needs.

On Promises Kept and Deadlines Met

Michael H. Mescon, Ph.D.

Timothy S. Mescon, Ph.D.

It was a 7 a.m. undergraduate course. The subject was management. For almost all of the students, it was their first exposure to the subject. The professor, in explaining his expectations, indicated that the class would begin at 7 a.m. sharp, and tardy students would not be allowed to enter. He further explained that he would repeat this announcement for three straight classes, giving each student an opportunity to weather the shock, adjust, or simply make other arrangements. In presenting his rationale, the professor stated the class would be studying management, and managers should not expect others to do what they won't or can't do themselves. Simply stated, the manager is a role model whose behavior is watched and often emulated. The manager should lead by deed.

To many of the students, the on-time or no-admittance policy was perceived as being unfair, unproper, un-American, or just plain crazy. Some indicated they lived long distances from campus. The professor suggested they leave home earlier. Others stated they were working, or had families with whom to contend. This generated even less sympathy, since the average age of the undergraduate student in the class was 28, and 85 percent worked either full- or part-time.

Still, a few felt compelled to test the on-time or no-admittance policy and were left out, looking in. Some of the younger students had parents call the professor to find out why, if they were paying tuition, their children couldn't enter class whenever they arrived. To these parents, the professor explained not only the nature of the course, but his desire to make certain their children developed a winning and responsible habit. Not one parent contested the policy after that explanation.

Actually, after the first three warnings, not only was tardiness *not* a problem, but attendance was unusually high and very few students dropped the class.

Now, the real shock was the view expressed by many of the students that this was the very first time they were ever held accountable in this fashion. Remember, 85 percent were employed, and yet promises-kept-and-deadlines-met behavior was not only initially considered off-the-wall, but out-of-this-world. However, once they understood the rationale, virtually all students showed up and succeeded—further demonstrating that most of us do exactly

Interviewer's Goals

Job interview	Obtain information about applicant; bring about exchange of information concerning job and company
Exit interview	Determine employee's assessment of the job and the company; give employee any necessary forms, financial information, and so on
Appraisal interview	Exchange information concerning employee's performance; establish clear goals for future performance
Disciplinary interview	Discuss employee's actions and attempt to determine a cause for them; provide information on any disciplinary action; try to improve employee's attitude
Counseling interview	Discuss employee's problem; try to determine an underlying cause; establish whether employee needs professional help

what we want to do, have time for those things we want to have time for, and remember what we truly consider to be important. Of course, there are factors we can't control. Happily, they seldom affect productivity, quality, and attitudinal issues. When they do, folks are generally both sympathetic and empathetic.

Symptoms, Not Causes

"The problem is lack of communication." In classroom-case analysis and in the "real" world, lack of communication is cited as the villain more often than any other factor. In reality, lack of communication is more often symptomatic of factors deeply (and sometimes not so deeply) buried in the organization.

Dr. Keith Davis, a legendary communication guru, argues that one of the greatest obstacles to effective communication is our gross inability to listen ... to stop talking. Our commitment to effective communication must start with a belief, from the highest levels of the organization, that customers, employees, and suppliers have valuable insights to offer. Davis argues that nature gave people two ears, but only one tongue— a gentle hint that we should listen more than talk. The listening is a reflection

that the people within the firm care about you and your ideas or concerns. In a similar vein, tardiness (or the repair person who promises but doesn't appear) is often merely a symptom of something else. The something else may be either rooted in the organization or in the individual. Whichever, the results are the same—the alienation of some other human being and the resulting loss of sales.

The failure to show is symptomatic of the belief that you don't matter. The failure to show, or to show up late, is a reflection of an ethos, a belief that the company doesn't care.

Domino's Pizza has revolutionized the food-delivery business by simply committing itself to the philosophy that each and every customer, regardless of position, status, or standing, will receive his pizza within 30 minutes ... guaranteed. This simple policy communicates to the public at large that each individual order, with or without anchovies, is important to the health and welfare of the company. This two-way communication sends an important message to everyone coming in contact with the organization: the company listens to its customers.

Interviewee's Goals

Job interview	Obtain information about the job and company; demonstrate competence and interest in the job
Exit interview	Politely explain reason for leaving; obtain any necessary forms or information
Appraisal interview	Actively listen to appraisal. Discuss problems and future goals. Try to obtain specific information on how your performance can improve.
Disciplinary interview	Let interviewer know why problems have occurred. Discuss how the situation can be improved.
Counseling interview	Speak to interviewer on topics with which he or she is qualified to offer assistance. If appropriate, ask for advice on obtaining specialized professional counseling.

What Would You Do?

Tom Kaiser is vice-president of marketing at Greengrow Foods. One of the product managers, Jim Dana, has been performing poorly during the last six months. He has been absent frequently and has had trouble dealing with employees.

Concerned that something is wrong, Tom calls Jim into his office.

"Hi, Jim, nice to see you. How are things going?"

"Okay, Tom," Jim says without enthusiasm. "Same as ever, I guess. Why do you want to see me?"

"Nothing in particular, really. It's just—you haven't been yourself recently, Jim. I thought something might be wrong. That bad back of yours still troubling you?"

"Nope, that's fine. I've had a little hay fever this fall. That's about it."

"Any trouble with that Fresh and New commercial?"

"It's just fine, Tom. So, if you don't have anything special to go over with me, I better get back to work."

Tom feels stymied. He knows Jim as a problem or is worried about something. What approach might get Jim to open up? Write a memo to Tom giving him some ideas on how to handle the situation.

Summary

Common in most organizational settings, interviews require that both interviewer and interviewee use active listening and speaking skills to obtain effective two-way communication. As an interviewer, plan each interview carefully, considering your goals for the interview and the personal traits and concerns of the interviewee. Make sure that the interviewee understands the goals of the interview, and plan to handle any special problems or questions.

Both interview participants should leave an interview with an understanding of what has occurred and what will happen next.

Interview Checklist

Interviewer Guidelines

- In planning an interview,

  _____ determine specific goals

  _____ review key questions and content areas

  _____ consider the needs and interests of the interviewee

  _____ develop strategies to achieve goals

  _____ outline appropriate closed and open-ended questions

- In conducting an interview,

  _____ establish a positive tone and atmosphere

  _____ review the agenda with the interviewee

  _____ listen actively

  _____ keep control of the movement of the interview

  _____ clarify what will happen after the interview

  _____ end cordially

- In evaluating an interview,

  _____ note significant actions or decisions

  _____ if appropriate, follow up with memo to interviewee

  _____ if appropriate, follow up with report to superiors

Interviewee Guidelines

- In planning the interview,

  _____ prepare for problems or questions that might arise

  _____ maintain a positive outlook

  _____ establish goals for the interview

      _____ remember the needs and interests of the interviewer

- While participating in an interview,

      _____ stay calm even if the situation is stressful

      _____ listen actively

      _____ watch for verbal and nonverbal cues

      _____ answer questions with appropriate detail

      _____ ask questions if necessary

      _____ avoid distractions; keep the interview on track if necessary

      _____ make sure you understand what will happen when the interview is over

- In evaluating the interview,

      _____ review key issues and ideas

      _____ if necessary, follow up with a memo to the interviewer clarifying issues or adding more information

Employment Interviews

- As interviewer,

      _____ obtain information on candidate's background, character, and goals

      _____ convey information about the job and organization

      _____ assess candidate's qualifications

- As interviewee,

      _____ obtain information about the job and organization

      _____ demonstrate competence and qualifications

Exit Interviews

- As interviewer,

      _____ find out why the employee is leaving

_____ obtain employee's assessment of the job and organization

_____ give interviewee necessary forms and information

- As interviewee,

  _____ explain reasons for leaving

  _____ obtain necessary forms and information

Appraisal Interview

- As interviewer,

  _____ summarize employee's performance ratings

  _____ establish clear goals for the next appraisal period

  _____ maintain a positive tone

- As interviewee,

  _____ listen actively to appraisal

  _____ discuss any problems

  _____ understand goals for next appraisal period

Disciplinary Interview

- As interviewer,

  _____ review employee's problems and try to identify causes

  _____ explain any disciplinary action

  _____ try to improve employee's attitude

- As interviewee,

  _____ listen actively to the problems described

  _____ provide any reasons for the problems

  _____ discuss ways to improve situation

Counseling Interview

- As interviewer,

  _____ listen actively to employee's problem

  _____ provide counseling or referral if necessary

- As interviewee,

  _____ outline problems and possible causes

  _____ request the interviewer's direct assistance or a referral to a professional counselor

Terms to Remember

Appraisal interview: a meeting in which an interviewer critiques the performance of an employee

Counseling interview: a meeting in which an interviewer gives advice to an interviewee on personal or job-related topics

Disciplinary interview: a meeting in which an interviewer and an employee discuss the employee's attitude problem or infraction of rules

Exit interview: a meeting in which an employee talks with a supervisor or personnel representative before ending employment at an organization

Summary Discussion: Sondra German's Interview from Case in Point, p. 557

Having put off the appraisal interviews, Sondra planned her time badly and made the situation unpleasant for herself and her interviewee. She should have allowed more time for Phyllis's interview and opened with some conversation to break the ice. She should have not only listened carefully to the problems Phyllis outlined but also offered some positive assistance.

Sondra was too distracted and rushed to exchange any information with her interviewee. Moreover, her abrupt manner and lack of empathy increased the stress of an already stressful situation. When she saw Phyllis was upset, she should have taken more time with her and scheduled subsequent interviews.

In the future, Sondra should plan the interviews carefully, conduct them over several days, listen empathetically, and respond constructively to each interviewee.

Questions for Review and Discussion

1. What significant information can an interviewer learn during an exit interview?
2. Some interviewers read questions to every job applicant they interview. What are the strengths and weaknesses of this approach?
3. What can an interviewer learn from an employment interview that he or she cannot learn from resumes, application letters, and personal references?
4. What qualities do you think an interviewer should have to conduct an effective counseling interview?
5. What are leading questions? Describe a time when they might be useful in an interview.
6. If you have ever been an interviewer, explain the process you went through preparing, conducting, and evaluating a typical interview.

Exercises

1. You are preparing for a disciplinary interview with Randy Winters. Randy has been taking extended lunch hours and leaving early in the evenings. What should you do to prepare for this interview?
2. Describe an interview you have participated in that was successful for both interviewer and interviewee. Describe the elements that made it successful.
3. Describe an interview you have participated in that was unsuccessful. What elements contributed to the failure?
4. Choose a partner from among the students in your class. Arrange an interview with that person outside of class time. Assume that one of you is appraising the other's performance in class. Tape record the interview and write up an evaluation of the strengths and weaknesses of the interview; hand in both the tape and the evaluation.
5. Contact someone at a local company who interviews job candidates. Arrange a time to meet with that person to discuss the strategies he or she uses to conduct employment interviews. Write an informational report on what you learned.
6. You have been asked by your department head to help interview job candidates in your area of specialization. Prepare ten questions that you think would help discover the candidates' capabilities in your field. Orient the questions to a specific position.

Meetings

- **Conducting business in meetings**
- **Developing democratic processes**
- **Planning productive meetings**
- **Developing strategies for meetings**
- **Overcoming common problems**
- **Evaluating meetings and distributing minutes**

Objectives

To establish appropriate goals and strategies for meetings

To conduct productive, useful meetings

To overcome common problems with meetings

To provide adequate follow-up

24

Robert Redondo's Meeting

Robert Redondo is the head of the Recruitment Committee, a group that designs and implements strategies for bringing talented new employees into the company. Robert calls a meeting every Tuesday morning at 9:30, and the ten committee members brainstorm new ideas and report on their individual efforts during the previous week.

Robert has encountered a major problem in these meetings: one committee member, Barbara Sidlerson, continually gets the meeting off-track by monopolizing the conversation with her own pet idea—to encourage vertical movement inside the company rather than to recruit heavily from outside. A typical incident in the meetings goes like this:

ROBERT: I'm glad to hear your efforts in Kansas City were so successful, Ruth. Thanks for the report.

BARBARA: I don't know why you want to bring programmers in from Kansas City in the first place. We've got tons of people right here in this company interested in developing those skills.

RUTH: Barbara, we've *been* encouraging the employees to get a programming degree—

BARBARA: The degree isn't important. We just need

people who have the skills—

ROBERT: Aren't we getting off-track here? We aren't concerned with promotions or training. We're—

BARBARA: But *shouldn't* we be? Morale in this company would be a whole lot higher—

Robert keeps trying to bring the discussion back to relevant topics, but Barbara seems to be sabotaging his efforts. The meetings go on too long and accomplish less than he had anticipated. Several committee members spend the time doodling on their notepads, and two members have been conspicuously absent for the last two meetings.

Robert knows he has a problem, but he cannot figure out how to solve it. He is considering resigning as committee chair.

Points to Consider
- How could planning help Robert solve his problem?
- What techniques during the meetings could keep the conversation going in productive directions?
- What could Robert do outside the meeting to solve his problem?

Conducting Business in Meetings

No matter what your job, meetings will probably play a major part in your life. Sales meetings, staff meetings, committee meetings, management meetings—they can all take up a large percentage of your time.

Unfortunately, a large percentage of meetings are dull, frustrating, unproductive, even counterproductive. They are often viewed as time-wasting processes that interrupt rather than contribute to the real work being done in an organization.

Meetings, however, are vital to the well-being of an organization. They should be forums where information is shared, problems are solved, and decisions are made. In fact, planned and handled correctly, meetings are synergistic: they can lead to ideas and create an energy that would never have developed without the dynamics of the group working together.

Meetings are full of potential, but that potential is developed far less often than it should be. With forethought and good leadership, meetings can be exciting and productive channels of communication.

Meetings should be
synergistic.

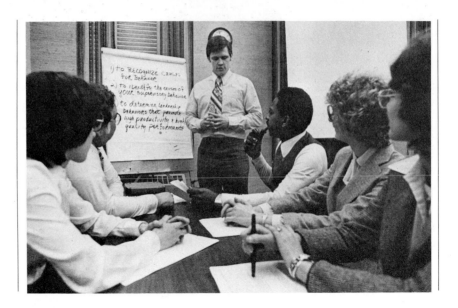

Developing Democratic Processes

One component essential to a good meeting is the underlying concept that everyone in the meeting has a voice. Meetings are meant to be forums, not lectures. As the leader of a meeting, you should recognize that these occasions are worthwhile only when people feel they can ask questions, try out ideas, and discuss problems.

If you routinely call meetings simply to tell people what they should be doing or to inform them of what you have been doing, you will be misusing the potential of the meeting as a dynamic forum for group communication.

Good meetings are usually handled democratically.

On the other hand, you must be able to handle the group so it stays in control. An effective meeting is democratic, not anarchic.

Planning Productive Meetings

Careful planning will help make your meetings more productive and less time consuming. Consider the following points before calling a meeting.

Determine the Goals

Every meeting should have a purpose or goal. Making your group meet every week, for example, may be a waste of time. Instead of holding a meeting every week, wait until there is a need to meet.

Ask yourself if the predominant point of the meeting is to share information, solve problems, provide training, or brainstorm. Then you can focus the meeting on concrete goals.

Choose the Right Meeting Room

The place in which you choose to meet should be the right size for the group and should provide the appropriate seating arrangements. If you plan a meeting at which people will be viewing a screen, for instance, you might want to set up classroom-type seating. If you want to encourage participation, seat people around a conference table.

The meeting place and atmosphere are important to the effectiveness of meetings.

You may also want to consider the atmosphere that will be most productive for the type of meeting you are planning. Some meetings will be more productive over lunch, while others will go more smoothly in a conference room or office.

As president and CEO of Bendix Corporation, William M. Agee replaced the boardroom table with comfortable chairs and a $30,000 oriental rug. He thought the new atmosphere encouraged communication and was pleased with the results of the change.

Choose the Right Participants

You may have heard complaints such as, "George asked me to go to that meeting about the Toledo office this afternoon. I don't know why he wants me there. I haven't had anything to do with the Toledo project."

Many times, people have to attend meetings on topics about which they have no interest or information. When planning a meeting, select participants who can contribute and are concerned with the issues involved.

If you find yourself inviting participants just to let them know what is happening in certain areas, reconsider your approach. You can easily keep them informed in less time-consuming ways.

Distribute an Agenda

An agenda (Figure 24-1) is an essential item for a well-planned meeting. An agenda will help you define your objectives for the meeting. Distributing it to the participants beforehand will help them prepare for specific issues. Moreover, an agenda helps keep the meeting on a time schedule: you can allow yourself so much time to cover each agenda item.

An agenda is a list of items to be covered in a meeting.

Gather Appropriate Materials

Using the agenda for a guide will also help you gather all the information and materials you will need for the meeting. Having everything at hand will save delays during the meeting and help you feel organized and well prepared.

```
                    MEMORANDUM
    TO:         Members, Special Events Committee
    FROM:       Henry Hill, Committee Chair
    SUBJECT:    Committee meeting
    DATE:       October 15, 19xx

    The Special Events Committee will meet from 9 a.m.
    until 10:30 a.m. on Monday, November 1 in the
    Conference Room. If you cannot attend, please let
    me know as soon as possible.

                    AGENDA

    Goal: To discuss funding possibilities for 19xx

    Old business: Approval of minutes of previous
    meeting

    New business: Informational items

        Summary by Henry Hill of funding for events
    scheduled for next year

        Report from Alicia Mathers on the status of the
    grant from the Ellis Institute

        Report from Roger Quan on our application to the
    Ford Foundation

    Discusion item: New sources of funding. Where to go
    now.
```

FIGURE 24-1 _____
Meeting agenda

Do Call a Meeting
- When you want people to generate new ideas
- When you need to disseminate complex material
- When you want feedback from the group
- When you want to create strong bonds within the group

Do Not Call a Meeting
- If you could disseminate information more efficiently in a memo or in person
- Simply to get the group together on a regular basis
- If you have no clear objectives or goals

GUMPERTZ

J & R
COMMUNIKATIONS

Gentlemen, this company is going downhill
and we've got to find out why

Developing Strategies for Meetings

As with most types of communication, a little planning can go a long way toward making meetings a productive part of the communication flow in an organization rather than a waste of time.

Know the Type of Meeting and the Participants

Preparing will be easier if you consider the type of meeting you are planning. The goals, format, setting, and number and type of participants should all contribute to the approach and structure of the meeting. There are many types of meetings, but two of the most common are information-exchanging and problem-solving.

Information-Exchanging Meetings Symposiums and conferences are meetings whose primary purpose is to exchange information. Many staff, management, and team meetings also have the exchange of information as a primary goal.

As the leader of an information-exchanging meeting, make clear to the participants why they need to know the information: keep them involved in the exchange process. Participants will remain interested and involved in the meeting if they understand how the information will benefit them.

If you are conveying the information, make sure that the other participants are understanding it. Stop to summarize at appropriate points and provide visual aids if necessary to clarify your points.

If someone else is conveying information, you may have to stop the person occasionally if you see that participants are confused. You may also have to remind the person of the time schedule of the meeting if he or she speaks too long.

Sample Outline for an Information-Exchanging Meeting

- Describe the nature of the information to be exchanged.
- Explain why the information is relevant to the participants.
- Convey the information clearly and logically.
- Ask for questions and feedback.

If you are conveying complicated concepts, or ones that may be interpreted in different ways, you may want to ask the participants questions related to the information. "Now that you have heard these guidelines on confidentiality, Dan, what would you do if you suspected one of our employees had leaked information to an employee of another company?" Such questions will encourage active listening in the meeting participants. However, try not to make the meeting seem like an oral exam; use such questions to help formulate ideas, not to "test" the participants.

Problem-Solving Meetings. Problem-solving meetings are more difficult to lead. They require an atmosphere conducive to the flow of ideas. As a leader, encourage brainstorming without losing sight of your agenda and time schedule.

The larger your group, the less manageable a problem-solving meeting will be. To get feedback from all participants, limit the size of the group to at most a dozen people. To generate the synergism of the group, react positively to ideas while still encouraging objective evaluation of each suggestion.

Sample Outline for a Problem-Solving Meeting

- Define the problem.
- Encourage participants to analyze the problem in detail.
- Ask for suggested solutions.
- Evaluate the suggestions.
- Choose the most effective solution.

Start and End Meetings on Time

Meetings are often delayed because participants straggle in ten or fifteen minutes late. "These meetings never begin on time," people say, "so why should I sit there waiting?" Waiting for latecomers delays the start of the meeting—and people become even more irritated because the meeting then goes on longer than anticipated.

As the leader of a meeting, make sure it starts on time. When people realize you are serious about starting on time, they will be prompt. When you call the meeting, also, indicate the time it will *end*. Then keep to your schedule as you move through the agenda.

Knowing that you will keep to your time schedule will help people plan their day and help them feel more positive about the meeting itself.

Start the Meeting Appropriately

Open the meeting in a manner that will establish an open, friendly atmosphere but will also clarify the goals you have set for the meeting. If the participants do not know one another, introduce them. You may want to begin with some informal conversation before getting down to work, but do not let too much time go by before you get the meeting started.

Make sure everyone has an agenda and any other necessary materials or documents.

Establish Your Role As Leader

As the leader of a meeting, maintain control without dominating the participants. While encouraging people to discuss their ideas on subjects related to items on your agenda, you must firmly prevent discussion from wandering.

To be a good leader, work on your sense of authority and self-confidence. Listen to others and watch their nonverbal signals. If you see the participants are bored, irritated, impatient, or confused, it is your responsibility to change the pace, intercede in the discussion, or summarize points being made. Avoid becoming impatient. No matter what happens, remain poised and in control.

Give the Meeting Direction

While keeping to your agenda and the timeframe you laid out for the meeting, make sure you also summarize decisions and restate important points as the meeting progresses. Participants should have a good sense of the progress being made in the meeting.

Keep a Record of the Meeting

Someone in the meeting (not the leader) should take notes. You may choose to bring in a secretary to take notes and then transcribe them into minutes of the meeting, or you may ask a participant to perform the function. Whoever records the notes should be accurate and impartial.

The format for minutes is usually similar to that of a memo. Information can be arranged with headings, subheadings, and lists to make reading easier (Figure 24-2).

The minutes of a meeting should include the following information:

- The date and time the meeting took place
- The names of people who attended (and often the names of people who were invited but were unable to attend)
- Any motions and the names of the people who made and seconded them
- A summary of agenda items covered, general responses to each item and any recommendations or decisions that were made as well as the names of people who made significant contributions
- Any items that will be covered at future meetings

End with Brief Summary

Summarize major points and decisions in meetings.

Participants should leave the meeting with a sense of accomplishment. In the last few minutes, summarize the major decisions or issues and emphasize any actions that must now take place. Encourage participants to feel positive about the whole meeting process.

Overcoming Common Problems

Some problems are common in many types of meetings. Learn to forestall them if possible and be able to handle them appropriately if they do occur.

Groupthink

Groupthink occurs when members become reluctant to disagree with their colleagues or leader. Participants tend to accept to ideas put forth in the group without considering them carefully, and those who disagree are inhibited from expressing their views.

As leader of a group, you can help to avoid groupthink by remaining unbiased, impartial. Avoid opening the meeting with a statement such as, "I

Kitchen Bazaars

Sherman Shapiro

"Too many people are afraid to speak up at meetings," says Sherman Shapiro, a retail business consultant who founded Kitchen Bazaars, a group of stores based in Washington, DC, that carries one of the most extensive lines of high-end cook- and serveware. Sherm managed the merchandising, advertising, and public relations areas of the Kitchen Bazaars stores.

"Communication is the most important thing I do," says Sherm. On a typical day, he looks over sales figures, meets with buyers, interviews salespeople about new merchandise, and receives a report from the director of public relations and the advertising manager.

He holds meetings for both the headquarters staff and for the store managers. At the headquarters meeting the staff discusses, among other things, what they want to bring up at the next biweekly managers' meeting. "For example, we're going to have a tent sale in one of our stores. We have to arrange to rent a tent and have it set up. We have to decide where, when, and how we will do our advertising and public relations. We have to make sure the managers reserve space in the parking lot, set up the displays properly, stock the displays, and schedule the help we need. The warehouse manager must arrange for a timely flow of goods to that particular store. The managers know ahead of time what will be discussed at the meetings, because we send out an agenda.

What problems does Sherman find when he runs meetings? "Sometimes a person brings up a topic that should be handled confidentially. I smooth things over at the meeting, then speak to him or her privately and tell the person to come to me first. There are things I don't want spread throughout the organization or would like them presented in a different light. Or sometimes a manager will get up and say, 'You sent me this cookbook and it was terrible.' The buyer is insulted and it affects morale. On the other hand, a manager will say at a meeting, 'We've sold hundreds of copies of this book' and this remark will, of course, generate enthusiasm."

Other barriers Sherm finds is that people don't know how to express themselves or they're reluctant to speak up, for fear of saying the wrong thing. Sherman encourages them to be less reticent. He never criticizes someone at a meeting unless the person embarrasses someone else.

What are the purposes of the meetings? "Informational certainly," says Sherm, "but we could send memos to convey the information. A major purpose is to generate enthusiasm. Show the managers a new chafing dish. Say, 'Isn't this great? How many do you think you can sell?' "

What kind of people does he want to hire? "I look for people who have a spark of imagination and originality, people who are daring and have an entrepreneurial spirit."

Sherm's advice on running a meeting?

- Get people involved.
- Encourage people to speak up and participate.
- Improve morale.
- Create enthusiasm.
- Smooth over difficulties at the meeting, then speak privately to the individuals involved.

think we should promote George Smith. What do the rest of you think?" Also, invite differing views, ask for criticism, and put forth a variety of options for the group to consider.

Hidden Agendas

Sometimes participants have personal "programs" that disrupt the flow of a meeting. Or participants may have personal grudges or problems that lead them to dominate or interfere with the meeting.

You may want to deal with such a person outside the meeting. Identifying the underlying cause of the person's actions may help you solve the problem.

```
                    MBR CONSULTING COMPANY

         FROM:    Francis Gaynor, Senior Consultant

         DATE:    June 12, 19xx

         TO:      All Department Heads

         SUBJECT: Minutes of meeting
                  June 10, 19xx, 11 a.m.
                  Meeting Room 4

         Attendance

            F. Gaynor, P. Lorenzini, H. Kantor, B. Lenz,
         K.T. Murdoch, A. Tenniel

         Old Business:

            P. Lorenzini moved and A. Tenniel seconded that
         the minutes of the meeting on May 12, 19xx be
         approved. Motion passed unanimously.

         New Business:

            Fountain Co. Project. B. Lenz reported on the
         status of the project so far. The computer system
         has been chosen and installed, but it is not yet
         being used by employees.

         Delays in the project were discussed. A. Tenniel
         reported that the delays in training employees have
         been caused by scheduling problems: the Fountain
         Company managers have not been cooperating in
         scheduling their employees for the necessary
         training. F. Gaynor suggested that we ask Gregory
         Gould, vice-president of Fountain, to act as
         liaison between us and Fountain management.

         Action Items:

            1. F. Gaynor will contact Gregory Gould by
         June 14.

            2. H. Kanter will draft a letter to Dana Fendel,
         president of Fountain, explaining the delay and
         revising our time schedule for the project.

                                    Submitted by

                                    Barry Lenz
```

FIGURE 24-2

Minutes of a meeting

If disruptions occur during a meeting, deal with them authoritatively: "Jim, we just don't have time to discuss that situation right now. We need to move on to Item 3."

As leader, you are responsible for establishing the "rules" of your meeting.

If you make it clear that private conversations, personal ridicule, and other disruptive behavior are unacceptable in your meetings, you will find that the group accepts the norms you have established.

As leader, you can establish guidelines for the meeting.

Interpersonal Conflicts

Some personalities just naturally jar on other personalities. Personal conflict in a meeting, however, can be disastrous. Establishing the norms discussed in the preceding section will help to deflect open conflict.

You may also want to work toward a group cohesiveness so that personal conflict is submerged in the group's unified goals. Clarify the benefits the group will derive from the meeting and reaffirm the group's commitment to specific objectives. When group members realize the rewards derived from participating positively in the meetings, they will be more apt to submerge their personal feelings toward other group members.

Tasks of a Meeting Leader

- Determine a need and goals for the meeting.
- Limit participants to those who need to be there.
- Decide on an appropriate meeting place and time.
- Give participants ample advance notice of the meeting.
- Develop and distribute an agenda.
- Develop and gather all necessary materials.
- Make sure any audiovisual or other equipment is available.
- Have someone take notes.
- Begin and end the meeting on time.
- Keep to the agenda.
- Sum up key points.
- Listen carefully and watch for nonverbal behavior of participants.
- Control disruptive behavior but encourage participation from everyone.
- Evaluate the effectiveness of the meeting.
- Distribute minutes to participants and absent members.

Tasks of a Meeting Participant

- Review any materials provided before the meeting.
- Arrive promptly.
- Bring any necessary materials to the meeting.
- Pay attention to what is being said; do not start up conversations on the side.
- Avoid creating distractions.
- Maintain a positive attitude; avoid looking bored or angry.
- Participate when you can make a positive contribution.
- Ask questions to clarify issues.
- Give meeting leader feedback after the meeting if it is appropriate.

What Would You Do?

Rosalie Bradford has recently been brought in from another company to be the head of the Payroll Department of Jefferson Industries. This is a big job, but one for which she is eminently qualified. Despite her competence, she has encountered problems at Jefferson simply because she is an attractive woman. The supervisors under her, all male, cannot believe that Rosalie can be both attractive and intelligent. Her worst problems have occurred at meetings with the department supervisors.

After a month at the job, she called a meeting and delivered a report outlining some decisions that needed to be made.

"Does anyone have any questions?" she asked, when she had presented the report.

"None I'm going to ask *you*," someone snickered.

Several people laughed. Rosalie knew that, to preserve her authority, she had to do something.

If you were Rosalie, what would you do? Write Rosalie a memo advising her on how to handle this situation.

Evaluating Meetings and Distributing Minutes

When the meeting is over, you have two tasks: to evaluate the meeting and to distribute minutes.

Take some time after a meeting to evaluate whether your goals had been met and whether the group process had been effective. Consider what you could have done to improve the meeting and how you should plan for even more successful subsequent ones.

Make sure, too, that every participant—and any group member who was absent—receives a summary of the meeting as soon as possible. The minutes provide a written record of key decisions, plans, votes, and ideas. The minutes also remind participants of any responsibilities they have assumed or actions that need to be taken.

Minutes provide a written record of a meeting.

Summary

Meetings can be an efficient way to disseminate information and solve problems. When run well, meetings encourage communication and help maintain morale. A leader who combines democratic processes with clear goals, good planning, a strong sense of the participants' needs and interests, and a firm but flexible leadership style can help to make meetings productive and beneficial to the whole organization.

Meeting Checklist

Before a Meeting

- To decide whether a meeting is necessary, determine whether you need to

  _____ generate ideas

  _____ disseminate complex material

  _____ get feedback from a group

  _____ help build strong bonds within a group

- While planning a meeting,

  _____ determine its goals

  _____ choose the right location and time

  _____ choose appropriate participants

  _____ plan an agenda that can be covered in the time alloted

  _____ gather necessary materials and equipment

During a Meeting

- As the leader of a meeting,

  _____ start and end it on time

  _____ establish a positive atmosphere

  _____ recognize the type of meeting you are leading

  _____ establish your position as leader

  _____ reduce tendencies toward groupthink by remaining as unbiased as possible and rewarding new ideas

  _____ avoid disruptive behavior and conflicts by firm assertion of leadership

  _____ keep the meeting focused on the agenda

_____ emphasize the benefits participants will derive from the meeting

_____ keep a record of the meeting

_____ summarize major points at the end

Follow-up

• When the meeting is over, follow up by

_____ evaluating its effectiveness

_____ distributing minutes to all participants and absentees

Terms to Remember

Agenda: list of items to be covered in a meeting
Groupthink: situation that occurs when people are reluctant to disagree with their colleagues or leader

Hidden agenda: personal programs that differ from the official agenda of a meeting
Minutes: summary of motions, decisions, and other activities in a meeting

Summary Discussion: Robert Redondo's Meeting from Case in Point, p. 573

Robert Redondo seems unable to keep committee members focused on the problems at hand. He does not maintain enough control over his participants. Feeling threatened, he loses his authority as a leader.

Better planning and a firmer approach could have kept the meeting from going off in unproductive directions. Also, Robert might consider calling meetings less frequently; the weekly meetings may not be useful enough.

Knowing that Barbara Sidlerson is fundamentally opposed to the whole concept of the Recruitment Committee, Robert might speak to her privately to see if she should remain on the committee or join another group.

Questions for Review and Discussion

1. Why are problem-solving meetings often more difficult to lead than informational meetings?
2. Describe a situation in which it would be inappropriate to call a meeting.
3. Describe a situation you have encountered in which the wrong participants had been asked to a meeting.
4. Explain why an agenda is essential to an effective meeting.
5. Why is the prompt distribution of minutes so important?
6. What qualities do you think a meeting leader should have?

Exercises

1. Consider one of your classes as a meeting. Take notes during class and then write up your notes as "minutes" of the meeting.
2. You are planning a meeting for an organization to which you belong. Make a list of all the preparations you need to make for a group that size. Now plan an agenda for the meeting.
3. Ask the members of a student organization if you can attend a meeting and assess its effectiveness. During the meeting, take notes regarding group interaction, the qualities shown by the leader, the format of the meeting, the use of time, and the effectiveness of participants in achieving their goals. Write a memo on your findings.
4. You are the head of an informal planning group in your company. You need to meet with the four people who are currently working on a special project. Your supervisor has to be kept informed of your group's progress, but his or her presence at meetings inhibits the other participants. As the supervisor is not actually involved in the forecasting project, you would prefer he or she did not attend. What should you do? Discuss your ideas in class.
5. You are the head of a committee to organize orientation programs for incoming freshmen.

Unfortunately, your group members do not seem interested in working or able to generate ideas. You find yourself doing all the work and most of the talking in meetings. What strategies could you use to increase participation of group members? Write a memo discussing your ideas.

6. Select a topic of concern to your college or to local residents. You might focus on problems regarding crime on campus, the homeless in your city, or even the quality of food in your campus cafeteria. You will lead your class in an information-exchanging or problem-solving meeting. Perform the tasks of a meeting leader:

   distribute an agenda at least a day in advance
   gather any data that might be useful and prepare copies of materials if necessary
   develop an approach appropriate for your goals, your topic, and the number and type of participants
   assign someone to take minutes
   conduct the meeting democratically but maintain your role as leader
   distribute minutes no more than a week after the meeting

Speeches and Oral Presentations

- **Speaking in front of a group**
- **Overcoming stage fright**
- **Identifying types of speeches**
- **Analyzing the audience and situation**
- **Organizing data**
- **Presenting the material**
- **Handling questions and answers**
- **Using visual and audiovisual aids**
- **Using your body and voice for effective delivery**

Objectives

To overcome fears of public speaking

To develop and organize material appropriate for the audience and situation

To use visual aids and body language to enhance speeches and oral presentations

25

Henry Armour's Presentation

Henry Armour was recently hired as project leader in a large research laboratory. He and his group immediately began making good progress on the plant cell experiments they were working on. After he had been on the job a month, Henry and the other project leaders were asked to attend a general staff meeting and give 15-minute briefings on their work.

"Just give us an overview, Henry," said Dr. Monzack, the scientist in charge of Henry's research unit. "Nothing formal."

Henry was proud that his group had accomplished so much in such a short time, but he was terrified of speaking in front of a group. He wrote out his presentation carefully, including every detail that would help his listeners understand what his group had been doing. Then he read through his speech dozens of times until he almost knew it by heart.

Three project leaders preceded Henry at the meeting. All of them gave succinct, extemporaneous talks and used slides to show exactly what they had accomplished. Henry began to panic. He had not prepared any slides, and he could not speak to this group without reading his prepared speech. His palms began to sweat. Perspiration trickled down his spine.

When Henry got up to give his presentation, he clutched the lectern for support. Then be began to read. Fifteen minutes passed. He was only halfway through. He tried to read more quickly. People began shuffling papers and clearing their throats.

After twenty minutes, Dr. Monzack interrupted him. "I'm sorry, Henry, but we have to leave time for everyone else. Can you summarize?"

Henry stumbled over his words and made his way unhappily back to his seat. His first appearance in front of his colleagues had been a disaster.

Points to Consider
- What kind of preparation should Henry have done before the presentation?
- What types of notes should Henry have made for himself?
- How would rehearsing have helped his performance?

Speaking in Front of a Group

At some point in your career, you will have to speak in front of a group. As they advance in their careers, people in business find they are called upon more and more often to speak at meetings, conferences, seminars, and banquets. For some, these occasions are dynamic, exciting events. For others, the minutes spent in front of an audience are sheer agony. In our society, fear of public speaking exceeds almost all other phobias—including fear of snakes and heights.

Many people whose stomachs turn to jelly when they address a group look enviously at other speakers. "How come Joe is so self-confident?" they ask. "Why isn't Marilyn nervous about this?" Joe and Marilyn may actually be extremely nervous, but they have learned to prepare themselves effectively so that they appear calm and cool. They may even have learned to use their nervousness as a source of positive energy.

Most businesspeople have to speak in front of groups.

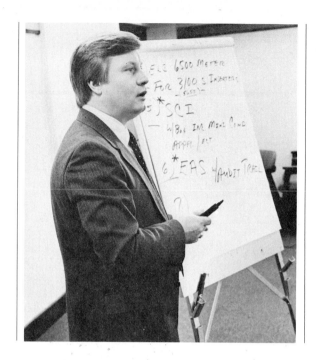

Three Myths About Public Speaking

To begin your progress toward effective public speaking, consider some popular misconceptions that can inhibit your powers as a speaker.

Myth #1. Speakers Are Born, Not Made. False. Nervous speakers often think that other people are "just naturally" good speakers. But, as you learned while studying business writing, nothing replaces hard work. The simplest, clearest memo may have taken the most time to write. Similarly, the best speeches do not occur at a moment's notice.

Most of the world's greatest speakers—people like Winston Churchill and John F. Kennedy—consciously decided to develop strong speaking skills. They knew their future success lay in powerful speaking skills. The Greek orator Demosthenes is said to have trained himself for years in elocution and delivery.

Myth #2. The Best Speeches Are Spontaneous. False. Many of the best speeches may *appear* spontaneous, but they are undoubtedly the result of hard work and practice. Great speeches, like Martin Luther King, Jr.'s, famous "I have a dream" speech were carefully crafted.

Myth #3. Good Speakers Have Overcome Their Nervousness. False again. Most speakers will admit that they will experience "butterflies" as they step in front of an audience. However, their nervousness does not cause them to freeze, panic, or stumble. It simply gets their adrenalin pumping and stimulates them to produce an effective presentation.

Overcoming Stage Fright

Fear is such a problem for many speakers that we need to address the subject before we go any further. While it may be comforting to know that other people are experiencing butterflies, how can you keep them from ruining your performance? Try the following approaches.

Figure Out Why You Are Afraid

Getting at the root of the problem may help you overcome it. Are you afraid that people will laugh at you? Afraid that you will appear unprofessional or unprepared?

Good preparation can help reduce nervousness.

If you are afraid of losing status or appearing unprofessional, make sure that you prepare your speech thoroughly. Then you will be an expert, knowing more about the subject than anyone else. If you are simply afraid to appear nervous, preparation will help, too. The more confident you are that you prepared thoroughly, the more confident you will appear to your listeners.

Remember That You Look Less Nervous Than You Feel

Your heart may be beating fast and your mouth may be dry, but your listeners see only your normal, unperturbed self. Students and businesspeople are often reluctant to have their speeches videotaped, but they are usually amazed afterward when they see how calm they actually looked. If you keep your voice and hands steady, no one will know about your fears.

Focus on the Speech and the Audience, Not on Yourself

Speakers often let their nervousness overwhelm them because they are focusing so intently on themselves. Try not to let your own feelings preoccupy you. Instead, focus on presenting your material effectively and communicating with your listeners. Consider their needs, not yours.

Remember Most Audiences Are Friendly

In most circumstances, your listeners *want* you to do a good job. They want to be informed, entertained, or persuaded. Knowing that public speaking is a strenuous task, your listeners will be rooting for you, not hoping you will stumble.

Identifying Types of Speeches

To prepare, organize, and rehearse your speech effectively, you need to consider the type of speech you will be delivering. The early stages of the speech-preparation process will be easier when you know what speeches like yours are usually like.

"I should now like to say something quotable."

Drawing by Dana Fradon; © 1986 The New Yorker Magazine, Inc.

The following list includes some of the most common types of speeches. (Some types overlap with others.)

Briefings

Many organizations use briefings to keep management and colleagues abreast of projects. Briefings are intended to inform people or teach them something. In either case, briefings must indeed be brief. Visual aids are often useful to help your audience understand and retain key concepts.

Informative Talks

Audience analysis is essential for informative talks.

Informative talks are often addressed to people who are unfamiliar with the topic being presented. You may be asked to tell employees about new policies, for example, or to orient new employees to company procedures. In these situations, you need to find out what the audience already knows. You do not want to bore them with old information or to bewilder them with too much new information.

Visual aids can be effective additions to an informative talk as well as to a briefing.

Introductions

Some of the most painful moments in public speaking can occur when an unprepared speaker introduces someone. If your job is to introduce a speaker, remember that the audience wants to hear the speaker, not you: be brief. If possible, ask the speaker in advance what he or she wants you to say. You may want to clarify links between the audience and the speaker so people will be motivated to hear the person's speech.

After-Dinner Talks

After a meal, most people have little patience for long or serious presentations. After-dinner speakers often use a lively and humorous style to keep their listeners' interest. If you are addressing a group on a serious topic, consider a flip chart or other visual aids to help retain the attention of your audience.

After-dinner talks are usually lively.

Long Presentations

Long presentations are like formal reports: they require thorough planning and organization. You may be asked to make a long sales presentation to clients, report on marketing strategies to top management, or present an overview of company objectives to stockholders. Whatever its purpose, a long presentation is apt to involve complicated ideas, visual aids, and an interchange with the audience.

Like written reports, long oral presentations always retain persuasive elements even when their purpose is primarily informative.

Analyzing the Audience and Situation

Analyzing your audience and situation is vital to preparing an effective speech. Both the content and tone of a speech in front of the Kiwanis Club will differ from those of a speech in front of your company's board of directors. Other variables such as the size and mood of the audience, the time of day, location, physical setup, and remainder of the program will also determine the way you prepare, organize, and present your material.

From the Desk of . . .

USPAACC

UNITED STATES PAN ASIAN
AMERICAN CHAMBER OF COMMERCE

"If you prepare a wonderful speech but do not deliver it well, your audience may not understand it and your message is lost," says Susan Au Allen, President of the U.S. Pan Asian American Chamber of Commerce. *The Chamber is a national organization founded in 1984 to promote economic growth and social independence for Asian businesses and professionals. It provides opportunities for Asian-Americans to network with each other; it also serves as a link between American and Asian businesses in the Pacific Basin.*

A lawyer by profession, Ms. Allen gives speeches to such diversified groups as officials of the Small Business Administration, the Society for International Development, the National Association of Professional Asian American Women, the National Institute for Women of Color, the Asian American Civil Rights Alliance, and the Washington International School. As a lawyer, she must also give presentations to her clients.

Ms. Allen suggests that students tape some of their speeches in preparation for giving them, saying, "It's very revealing and humbling." She also recommends speaking in front of a mirror to overcome self-consciousness. "Watch yourself talk in front of a mirror to see if your lips are moving. If they aren't, you aren't projecting your voice and chances are that you will not be heard or understood by an audience who has never heard you before."

However, according to Ms. Allen, the best cure for stage fright is preparing yourself well. "Find out about the organization who invites you to talk. Get to know who the audience is and their interests. Determine the purpose of the meeting, the size of the audience and its level: Will there be professionals, managers or technicians? Would they prefer a reflective analytical speech or one that sketches the basic nuts and bolts? Once that is determined, decide on a theme—the thought and mood of your message. Once a central message is identified, research well so you know what you are talking about."

Ms. Allen's speeches are well structured. Her opening summarizes what she is going to tell the audience. She goes on to the specifics, limiting them to three to four points. "Listeners retain less than 25 percent of what they hear," cautions Ms. Allen. "Repeat your message over and over. The conclusion should reiterate the central message with conviction, in an authoritative manner."

Ms. Allen starts with an outline, which is her "map for preparing the speech," she says. "Check to see if you have tied the

As you analyze your listeners, consider not only their main characteristics and interests but also their attitudes toward you and your subject matter. Ask yourself:

- How do they feel about my subject matter? Will they be hostile, mildly opposed, uninterested, interested, positive, excited?
- What do they already know about my subject matter? How much background do they need?
- What do my listeners think of me? Do they consider me an expert or do I have to prove my expertise? Do they already have positive or negative feelings about me or my position?
- What is their status compared to mine in this organization?
- How old are they? What parts of the country or the world are they from? What are their occupations? Their economic and educational backgrounds?
- How many people will be in the audience?
- What special interests do they represent or support?
- What mood will they be in when I get up to speak?

points together in a logical sequence," she continues and proposes starting with the easy points first, then moving on to the more complex ones.

Ms. Allen writes her speeches out, then rewrites and edits them, shortening the sentences, and using simple, clear and brisk expressions that are easy to pronounce. Her final draft is in typewritten form and she leaves lots of space in between paragraphs so it is easy for her to cut short her speech when she runs overtime, without losing the flow of her message.

"What listeners retain depends not only on the message, but on the speaker and how the speaker presents the materials. Look at the audience deliberately. Eye contact provides feedback, and it will give you confidence. It also conveys a sense of your seriousness to the audience." Before she utters her first words, she usually takes a deep breath, surveys the audience and picks a few warm and friendly faces. Then she starts talking to these faces and slowly moves her eyes across the room to reach out to others.

She suggests using a lot of pauses. "The audience welcomes them. The pauses give the audience a chance to digest what you have just said, give them breathing space, and prepare them to follow the rest of your speech."

Ms. Allen stands straight with her feet about six inches apart. "That shows the audience that you are sincere and serious." She also carries a pen, so she can write down questions during the question-and-answer period. "Don't worry about this part. Think ahead of time about the questions your talk is likely to stimulate and be prepared with the answers. Remember, the answers are often embedded in your speech. If you do not have an immediate answer to a question, tell the questioner to see you at the end of the session. Don't apologize for not having an answer."

Ms. Allen's tips for students:

- Prepare well. "Know your audience, your subject, your opening remarks and your closing statements cold."
- Concentrate on how you are speaking. "Speak slowly and deliberately."
- Make sure you reach out to the audience by making eye contact and by giving easy warm smiles.
- Be yourself. "Talk as if you are talking in your living room."
- Believe in what you are saying. "Your commitment to the principle of your message will generate enthusiasm, radiate confidence, and build credibility."
- Never apologize. "You are invited to speak because you are special. You have accepted the challenge because you are willing to prepare for the occasion. When you speak, you will have researched the subject well and are fully prepared. Enjoy the occasion and let the audience know it."

- What will interest them about my topic?
- What types of approaches will convince them of my position?

Knowing your audience will help you make numerous decisions about issues such as

- the use of a direct or indirect approach
- the length and complexity of your material
- the type of visual aids to use
- the word choices to make
- the type of material that will motivate and persuade.

While considering the situation in which you will be speaking, remember that people's moods help to determine their receptiveness to a speaker. Try to predict whether your audience will be feeling benign, bored, tired, impatient, excited, or enthusiastic. Ask yourself:

- What is the purpose of the gathering? To provide entertainment? Solve problems? Sell an idea or product?

- When is your speech scheduled? Early morning when listeners are sleepy? Late morning when they are hungry? After dinner when they are convivial?
- What will the setting be like? A large hall? An intimate conference room? A restaurant?
- What else will be on the program? Other speakers? Films? Music?
- Where will you appear on the program? At the beginning, where you will set the mood for the whole program? At the end when only a little time is left?

Find out what will be on the program besides your speech.

Correctly assessing your situation can help you create a presentation that is appropriate for the setting, appropriately lighthearted or serious, and an appropriate length. Situation analysis can also help you foresee and forestall problems that might come up, such as a severe time shortage.

Organizing Data

Like a piece of writing, a speech must have a beginning, middle, and end. Once you have focused on a topic, done some brainstorming, defined your goals and audience, and at least started any necessary research, you will need to organize the material you have. Many of the tips on persuasive and organizational strategies that you studied in the business writing chapters of this text are also useful for oral presentations.

Remember, though, that you have to overcome your listeners' external and internal distractions as you speak. Clarity, conciseness, and a strong organizational pattern will help your audience listen actively. Smooth transitions and some repetition will help your listeners understand where you are going in your speech—and why.

Identify Key Issues

Listeners can take in only a limited amount of information at a time, so you will usually end up limiting yourself to a few key areas. How many? The topic of your speech, the audience, and the situation will help you determine how much material you can present. You would probably be shocked, for example, if a guest speaker in your European history class announced that she was going to spend the hour presenting fifty reasons for the fall of the Roman Empire. Even fifteen reasons would be too many for listeners to assimilate.

For many speeches, three or four main points provide sufficient material and a narrow enough focus for an effective presentation. As you organize your ideas, then, you will have to discard some that are of only peripheral interest or are too complex to be communicated orally.

Identify Subpoints for Each Key Issue

While organizing, remember that you want this material to *convince* your listeners: back up your points with illustrations, examples, statistics, logical explanations, or other supporting material.

In order to create a sense of balance in your speech, support each key issue with approximately the same number and type of subpoints. If you support one major point with statistical analyses and another major point with a light anecdote, your speech may well appear imbalanced or illogical.

Develop an Outline

An outline is essential for almost every type of speech. Your outline does not have to be formal, but it should reflect your key points, subpoints, and the general organizational pattern you are using. Developing an outline will help you focus your ideas and sort them into patterns your readers will understand.

As you organize your ideas in an outline, too, you can often see that some ideas need to be discarded while others need to be given more support or moved to another section of the speech.

In choosing a general organizational pattern for your speech, you may want to work with one or more of the patterns discussed in Chapters 12 and 14. Chronological and spatial order, logical narration, order of increasing or decreasing importance, and inductive and deductive patterns can all be useful.

Suzanne Ringrose, organizing a speech to management, wished to convince her listeners to set up an in-house market research team rather than continuing to use a market research company. She developed a problem/solution organizational pattern combined with an inductive approach: knowing that her listeners were resistant to spending more money on market research, she wanted to give them convincing details and *then* present them with her conclusions and recommendations.

Figure 25-1 illustrates the formal sentence outline she used to organize her ideas.

Provide Repetition and Make Transitions Between Thoughts

Repetition in speeches serves a useful purpose. Since listeners cannot assimilate as much material as a reader can, they are more apt to get lost, confused, or disoriented. Summaries and reviews of major points that might seem repetitious in a piece of writing come as a relief to people listening to a speech. Visual aids can often be used to provide "instant replays" of points that you have just covered orally.

Clear transitions also help to keep listeners on the right path. Tell your listeners how many major points you plan to cover, when you are shifting topics, and when you are discussing information most important to them. Organize your speech so that listeners know where you are at every turn.

Make sure your listeners know where your speech is going.

Create an Opening That Makes People Listen

An effective opening sets an appropriate tone and establishes good feelings between you and your listeners. Give your listeners a general idea of your topic even though you may not want to take a stand on an issue this early in the speech.

Do not apologize about your speech.

Purpose: To convince management to set up an in-house market research team.

I. We need to expand our market research efforts.
   A. The low sales of our Accusystem software resulted from insufficient information about our target market.
      1. Our limited research showed us that our targeted buyers would buy the least expensive option. In actuality, they were more swayed by quality and a familiar brand name
      2. Our research indicated that buyers would be willing to change brands. In the marketplace, they showed themselves to be brand loyal
   B. Our survival depends on accurate and up-to-date information about competition, trends, and consumers.
      1. X-Ton Corporation and Ficher, Inc. have taken over 3 percent of our market share since they increased their market research budget.
      2. Industrywide data reveal positive correlation between market research expenditures and increased sales.
II. We have two options: expand the services of Market Knowledge, Inc., the market research company we presently use, or develop an in-house market research team.
   A. Market Knowledge, Inc. can offer us more complete information if we are willing to pay for it.
      1. The benefits of expanding MKI's services include the following:
         a. The company is set up to acquire exactly the type of information we need.
         b. We will know in advance the cost of the services we contract for.
      2. The drawbacks to using MKI have already been evident to us.
         a. The yearly cost is high and will get higher.
         b. MKI does not have our company's interests as its sole or prime concern.
   B. We can develop our own market research team.
      1. The benefits of this approach include:
         a. We will know that employees are working solely for our company's interests.
         b. Our company will be more self-sufficient.
         c. Eventually this option will be less expensive.
      2. This option has definite drawbacks.
         a. Start-up costs will be high.
         b. We may lose precious time setting up the team.
III. Recommendation: This company should begin hiring and training its own market research experts and retain MKI's present level of service one more year.
   A. This option will cost more only at first.
   B. The long-term benefits will be significant.

FIGURE 25-1
Sample speech outline

One key element of your opening should be to capture the attention and interest of your audience. You also want to win your listeners' respect. Do not apologize about your speaking abilities or indicate you are not fully prepared on the issues. Make your opening concise, clear, and relevant.

Some Ideas for Speech Openings

- An anecdote that involves listeners in the material to come
- Interesting data that lead into the key points of the speech
- A relevant quotation
- A preview of the main points in the speech
- Questions that arouse listeners' interest
- A visual aid that catches the listeners' attention

Create a Conclusion That Impresses Your Listeners

The conclusion may leave the most lasting impression on your listeners, so it should be strong and well thought out. Avoid wandering off at the end with lines such as, "I guess that's about it." As in a piece of writing, an effective ending summarizes, calls for action, or restates recommendations. Do not introduce material on a new topic or alter the tone you have established.

Make sure, by the way, that you leave yourself enough time to make your ending effective. Rushing through the last part of a speech can ruin the effect of the whole presentation.

Some Ideas for Speech Endings

- A summary that pulls together major ideas or recommendations
- A reference to future events or trends related to your topic
- A reference to an anecdote, data, or visual aid used in the opening
- A motivating statement to get listeners to act

Preventing Common Problems with Speeches

Problem	Solution
Speech is long-winded	Time your rehearsals. Do not exceed time limit. Use repetition only to clarify. Cut mercilessly as you revise.
Tone is apologetic	Be positive about yourself or your topic. Do not admit to inexperience or lack of preparation. Do not say the material is difficult or uninteresting.
Material is dull	Keep your tone lively. Use visual aids to enhance major points. Emphasize relevance of material to listeners.
Material is complex	Summarize major points. Tell listeners what data mean. Use clear visual aids.
Parts seem irrelevant	Stick to your topic. Explain significance of each part of your speech. Outline the speech on a visual aid.

Presenting the Material

Having analyzed the type of presentation, the audience, the situation, and the material, you can decide how you will present your speech. Methods of presentation range from reading a prepared manuscript to speaking extemporaneously. In general, avoid memorizing your speech word for word: it will not sound spontaneous, and you may well forget something vital.

Reading a Manuscript

Reading a manuscript may be necessary in a formal gathering where you are presenting complex material. Listening to someone read can be a painful experience. If you choose this method, make sure you work on speaking clearly and varying your pace and inflections.

Type your speech with lots of white space on the page and add "stage directions" in the margins: *pause, change slide, smile.*

Using Note Cards

Many speakers use note cards.

For most long presentations, and for many short ones, using note cards is the most practical method of presentation. Index cards are less conspicuous than sheets of paper, and you can carry them with you easily if you move away from the lectern or podium.

Make sure you do not write out entire sentences: you will find yourself reading them. Instead, put key words or an outline of your speech on the cards. Include any exact figures or quotations you will be using. Number your cards clearly and make sure they are in the right order before you get up to speak.

Referring to Visual Aids

To give the appearance of speaking without notes, you might want to develop visual aids that will help you as well as your listeners. You can design slides, overhead transparencies, or charts that list major points and key figures.

Visual aids can take the place of notes.

If you use this mode of presentation, however, you must make sure you do not face the visual aids instead of your listeners. Just glance at your "notes" and then return to your audience.

Speaking Without Notes

Speaking without notes is often an effective mode of presentation, but it requires careful preparation. For a short speech in a casual situation, this approach may work the best. But, until you feel fairly comfortable in front of people, you may want to use note cards.

Ten Hints for Rehearsing Your Speech

1. Rehearse after preparing outline and materials.
2. Memorize only sequence of ideas and quotations, statistics, and so on.
3. Rehearse silently at first and then deliver the speech orally.
4. If you make mistakes while rehearsing orally, do not stop: keep going until the end.
5. Rehearse at least a day before the speech.
6. If possible, space rehearsals over a couple of days; avoid packing all rehearsal time into one long session.
7. Tape your rehearsal. As you listen to the tape, take notes on where and how delivery could be improved.
8. Try to have one rehearsal in front of a full-length mirror where you can watch your gestures, expressions, movements.
9. Try to rehearse once in the room where you will actually be speaking. Check seating arrangements, acoustics, lectern, lighting. If you are going to use a microphone, practice with it.
10. Work on varying your presentation as you rehearse. Change inflections, pauses, gestures, so your speech sounds spontaneous, not "canned."

Which Visual Aid Would You Choose?

Choose the answers that best fit the types of visual aid you would choose.

1. You are preparing a speech on tax changes and need to show fairly complex data to over 200 people. You use
   a. a flip chart
   b. transparencies and an overhead projector
   c. a blackboard
2. You are speaking to a crowd of 30 about the different health plans available to them. You cannot cover all the financial and medical data in your speech, but you want them to have it. You use
   a. handouts
   b. slides
   c. transparencies and an overhead projector
3. You are speaking to a group of top 35 high school seniors, telling them about your college and urging them to apply. To give them a sense of the college's beautiful campus, you use
   a. transparencies and an overhead projector
   b. posters
   c. slides

Discussion

A large group will not be able to see data on a flip chart or blackboard. They can, however, see material projected on a screen. Best answer: 1b.

If you want people to have access to a lot of material that you cannot cover during the presentation, give it to them to take home. Best answer: 2a.

To really give people a sense of what something looks like, slides (or videotape) work better than posters or transparencies. Despite your having to darken the room and use the equipment, the presentation will benefit from the slides. Best answer: 3c.

Humor Checklist

Before using humor in your speech, check the following list of pointers.

- Make sure the humor is relevant to your goals in the speech.
- Do not use humor in questionable taste.
- Avoid telling jokes that your listeners may have already heard.
- Keep your humor brief. Fast-moving humor works best.
- Poke fun at yourself rather than at other people.
- Use anecdotes from your own experience; they will be less familiar to your listeners.
- Use a variety of humorous forms; do not rely on standard jokes.
- Use humor only if you are confident you can do it well.

Handling Questions and Answers

Prepare for questions your listeners may ask.

Most long presentations will include interaction with the audience. You may respond to questions during your speech or have a question-and-answer session afterward. The former method interrupts the flow of your talk and can distract the audience from the main issues. The latter method may detract from the strong impression that you made at the conclusion of your talk.

As an alternative, you may choose to take questions toward the end of your talk and then conclude with a strong summary of key points.

However you choose to handle questions, keep a few pointers in mind.

1. Consider in advance what questions might be asked. A little preparation can greatly increase the effectiveness of your answers.

2. Stay calm. Never let someone make you angry. If someone is antagonistic, respond rationally. Do not become involved in a personal conflict or let a heckler get you away from your main points.,

3. Do not let one person monopolize the session. If someone uses a question as a platform for his or her own ideas, you may have to interrupt calmly and explain that time is short and that others want to speak. You may offer to speak with the person after the presentation.

4. If you do not know the answer to a question, admit that you do not know. Avoid hedging or guessing. You can always say, "I don't have that information at hand right now, but I'll be happy to get it for you."

Using Visual and Audiovisual Aids

Using visual or audiovisual aids can make your speech more effective and more memorable. As with graphic aids in written communication, however, you must choose the right medium to convey your ideas and handle that medium effectively in front of your audience (Figures 25-2 and 25-3).

In general, keep your visual aids simple. Your audience should not have to read long columns of figures or decipher complex graphs. Also, your listeners should be able to read the visual aids easily. Make them large and clear enough for everyone in the room to see.

Keep visual aids simple.

Your visual aids will be more effective if you show them to the audience only when you are discussing ideas related to them. If you expose the visual aids too early, people will focus on them, not you.

Handouts

The simplest visual aid is the handout. You may want to pass out an outline of your speech or other information the audience will find useful. Avoid giving people too much material to read, however; they will read it instead of listening to you. If you like, you can hand out material at the end of your speech so that interested listeners can read it at their leisure.

Chalkboards

Chalkboards are useful if you wish to highlight words or illustrate points as you move through your presentation. Chalkboards are particularly useful if you need to illustrate answers to questions. However, you do not want to spend much time writing on the board, so use another medium for graphs, charts, and complex formulas.

	Inexpensive	Convenient/ easy to handle	Require special equipment	Professional looking	Can be visible to large audience	Can handle complex material
Handouts	usually	✓		sometimes	✓	✓
Chalk-boards	✓	✓				
Flip charts	✓	✓		sometimes		
Posters	✓	✓				
Overhead transparencies	✓		✓	sometimes	✓	✓
Slides			✓	✓	✓	✓
Video-tapes			✓	✓	✓	✓

FIGURE 25-2 _____
Visual aids at a glance

Flip Charts

Flip charts are large tablets of paper attached to an easel. You flip the pages of the tablet over the top of the easel as you move from one point to the next. These can serve as your own "notes" while helping your listeners follow your major points.

Flip charts can be a nuisance to carry around before the speech, but they are easy to use once they are set up.

Posters

You may simply want to use large pieces of posterboard for your visual aids. These come in many sizes and colors and can be colorful additions to your speech. Make sure that you bring tape or tacks to attach them securely to a wall.

Overhead Transparencies

Handwritten, typed, or printed materials may be transferred to a transparency and then projected onto a screen by an overhead projector. If you want to highlight certain points as you speak, you may even write on a transparency with a special pen as you speak.

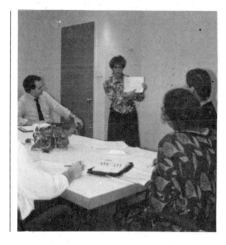

The visual aid is too small.

The speaker blocks the view.

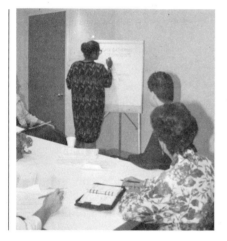

The speaker addresses the visual aid.

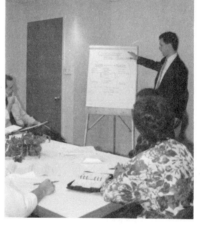

The visual aid is too complex.

FIGURE 25-3
Visual aid pitfalls

Slides

Slides can be an effective adjunct to your presentation, but they require that the room be darkened. Slide shows are prone to mishaps, so make sure you place the slides carefully in the carousel and practice with the projector beforehand.

Slides are most effective in a darkened room.

Audiovisual Aids

Some presentations may require videotaped materials, filmstrips, cassette tapes, and other aids. Just be sure you are adept at handling whatever equipment is necessary, or have an assistant work with you during your presentation.

Visual Aid Checklist

- Use visual aids that the audience can see easily.
- Prepare them before the presentation.
- Make them look as professional as possible.
- Keep them clear and easy to read.
- Practice using them as you rehearse.
- Make sure they are relevant to the presentation.
- Refer to each visual aid that you show.
- Remove visual aids from view when you have discussed them.

Using Your Body and Voice for Effective Delivery

Your body and voice are almost as important as the content of your speech. Your listeners perceive you and your speech as a whole, a unit. Every motion and intonation conveys a message, so make sure your nonverbal messages enhance the content of your speech.

Eye Contact

Eye contact helps listeners feel that they are important to you and, thus, helps them to feel positively about you and to keep listening to you.

Also, maintaining eye contact with your listeners helps you keep track of their reactions. By noting how people are responding, you can modify your presentation if you see signs of boredom or confusion. When you see people responding positively, on the other hand, you will find your confidence and energy increase significantly.

If you are shy about public speaking, maintaining eye contact may be difficult at first. Try not to stare intensely at one or two people, but do keep your eyes from wandering down to your notes or up to the ceiling. Instead, look briefly at people in every section of the room. Make contact with people, just as you do when speaking with someone one to one.

Speak to your listeners, not to your notes.

Posture

Your posture is an important part of your image as a speaker. Try to stand comfortably without looking rigid and without slumping. Do not use your podium or lectern for support, and avoid shifting from one foot to the other.

Gestures

Your gestures should be meaningful. While you should not stand motionless like a statue, avoid pointless gestures that indicate nervousness. Fidgeting, playing with a pen or note cards, and similar activities will distract your listeners and detract from what you are saying—especially if you are using a microphone.

As you rehearse your speech, work on emphatic gestures to highlight major points or descriptive gestures to indicate size, distance, or direction.

Do not let your gestures appear mechanical. As you rehearse, vary your gestures until they seem comfortable and natural.

Voice

Your voice is the major channel of your oral message. It can make people want to listen to you, but it can also irritate, bore, and annoy them. An inaudible voice or poor enunciation can prevent your listeners from understanding you at all.

We have all experienced that sign of nervousness, the "tightening" of the throat. This tension can produce squeaks, breathiness, and harsh, unpleasant noises. Some speech instructors recommend neck exercises to reduce this tension, and many recommend breathing exercises as well.

When speaking to a group, slow down your rate of delivery and increase your volume. Work particularly on varying your pitch and adding animation to your voice. Listening to a monotone is a painful experience you do not want to inflict on your audience.

If you are going to use a microphone, practice with it beforehand. Microphones are so sensitive that they pick up noises such as papers rustling and fingers tapping. Make sure to keep such noises to a minimum. Try to keep your mouth more or less the same distance from the microphone, too, so your voice does not suddenly increase or decrease in volume.

Project your voice to your listeners and speak more slowly than usual.

What Would You Do?

Patricia Koltenik has been asked to give a speech at the regional convention of data processing professionals. While the convention-goers drink coffee after a three-course luncheon, she will speak to them from a lectern at one end of the large banquet room.

The convention coordinator who asked Patricia to speak was quite vague about the length and nature of Patricia's speech.

"You're so well known in the field," she told Patricia, "that I'm sure you will give us a fascinating presentation. After you give your talk, John Lewis and Belle Cantrip will speak as well. We're looking forward to hearing you all."

Patricia is perplexed. She does not know how long, how formal, or how complex her speech should be.

What guidelines can you give her? Write Patricia a memo outlining some suggestions.

Summary

Speaking before a group is difficult for many people. However, careful preparation and practice can help reduce anxiety and overcome possible problems. Knowing why you will be speaking, who the audience will be, and what the situation will be like can help you to organize your material and choose an appropriate method of presentation. Well-designed visual aids, also, can significantly help the effectiveness of your presentation.

Speech and Oral Presentation Checklist

Stage Fright

• To overcome stage fright,

_____ figure out why you are afraid

_____ remember you look less nervous than you feel

_____ focus on the speech and audience, not on yourself

_____ remember most audiences are friendly

_____ prepare your material carefully

Audience and Situation Analysis

• To analyze your audience, consider

_____ their ages, backgrounds, educational levels, status

_____ their attitudes toward you and your material

_____ what motivates and persuades them

_____ their probable mood at the time of the presentation

• To analyze the situation, consider

_____ why the group has gathered

_____ what time of day or night you will be speaking

_____ when your presentation appears on the program

_____ other components of the program

Organization

• To create an effective opening,

_____ catch the listeners' attention and interest

_____ avoid apologies

_____ make it relevant to the rest of the speech

- To organize the body,

  _____ use a logical organizational pattern

  _____ focus on a limited number of key points

  _____ tell your listeners when you move to a new section

  _____ if appropriate, use visual aids to support and highlight ideas

- To conclude effectively,

  _____ end with a memorable statement

  _____ avoid rushing the last sentences

  _____ tie together the whole speech

Presentation Techniques

- To make your presentation effective, you may want to

  _____ read the manuscript for some formal gatherings

  _____ use note cards for most long presentations

  _____ use visual aids instead of notes if you can avoid looking at the visual aids too frequently

  _____ speak without notes if you can do so comfortably and effectively

Visual Aids

- Use visual aids that listeners can see and understand.

- Practice with visual aids so they enhance rather than detract from your presentation.

- Choose a type of visual aid that

  _____ is appropriate for the size of the room and the audience

  _____ you can handle easily

  _____ you can afford and have time to prepare

  _____ highlights your particular material

Terms to Remember

Briefing: short talk to inform or teach listeners

Flip chart: large tablet of paper attached to an easel

Overhead transparency: clear piece of plastic on which handwritten, typed, or printed material may be imprinted and then projected onto a screen

Summary Discussion: Henry Armour's Presentation from Case in Point, p. 589

If Henry Armour had asked other project leaders about briefings before trying to prepare one, he would have learned the importance of brevity and the usefulness of visual aids.

Despite his nervousness, Henry should have put a few notes on cards instead of writing out his presentation. Then, by rehearsing carefully to increase his self-confidence and mastery of the material, he could have effectively briefed his listeners on his group's achievements.

Questions for Review and Discussion

1. Discuss any methods you have used in the past to help overcome stage fright.
2. Describe a speech that you found difficult to listen to or understand. What qualities affected your ability to enjoy and concentrate on the speech?
3. What are the drawbacks to giving handouts to your listeners before your speech? What are the drawbacks to using a chalkboard as you speak?
4. What can you do as a speaker if someone takes over a question-and-answer session with long or complex questions?
5. What types of messages can your voice quality convey to an audience?
6. How does a briefing differ from an informative speech?
7. You have been asked to visit a high school in a nearby city to tell students about your college or university. What types of preparation should you do before the day of your presentation?
8. You have been asked to inform fellow students about the general education courses they need to graduate. Would you use any visual aids for this presentation? If so, what types would you choose?

1. You have been asked to introduce a fellow student to the rest of the class. Interview the student so you will have accurate and interesting information to give the class.

2. Now that you have interviewed your fellow classmate (see Exercise 1), prepare the introductory speech. What techniques can you use to keep your listeners' attention and leave a positive impression of you and your classmate on your audience? Deliver the speech to the class.

3. You have been asked to address a group of business owners on the good and bad aspects of testing employees for drugs in the workplace: your speech is to be informative, not persuasive. List all the preparations you should make before you deliver the speech.

4. Outline the major points you would cover in the speech described in Exercise 3.

5. You are the president of a campus organization. Prepare a speech to persuade your classmates to join the organization.

6. Give a five- to ten-minute speech to your fellow employees on the new fire regulations in your building. Use any visual aids that will make your major points easier to understand.

7. Assume you are a salesperson making a presentation to a group of company managers. Give a five- to ten-minute speech on the benefits of the product or service you are selling.

8. You have been asked to give an after-dinner speech to a group of executives. Write a speech using humor to keep their attention while you cover two or three points of interest to your listeners.

9. Deliver a five-minute briefing to new students on the major areas covered in your communication class.

10. You are an executive with North-South Airline. East-West Airline has just decided to lower fares on your most popular route, and many of your colleagues want to lower North-South's fares as well. Convince them the fares should remain the same.

11. Parking has become a problem since your company expanded a few years ago. Employees are fighting over spaces, and managers with reserved spots have received threatening letters about having their own parking spots. Your company is buying a lot next door, but there will not be additional parking for at least another year. Persuade employees that you have some answers to this problem.

12. An ingredient in your company's chocolate chip cookies *may* cause cancer in laboratory rats. You want to convince employees and management not to panic and to keep producing cookies until more tests have been made.

13. Employees in your company have been calling for childcare service in the company building. You must convince them that this idea is impractical and offer some alternatives.

14. Salespeople in your store are paid on commission and can be very competitive about customers. Some customers have complained about being followed around by salespeople, and some salespeople have "stolen" clients from the others. Customers have occasionally heard salespeople arguing about who was responsible for making a sale. Convince your sales staff that their commissions will actually rise if they work together professionally.

15. You are a manager in a conservative computer or accounting firm. Top management wants to keep promoting the company in traditional ways, but the company is losing market share in this competitive environment. You want to convince management that a flamboyant promotional scheme will help the company attract new clients. Outline such a plan in a speech to top management.

16. Your locally made beer could be gulped down by Budweiser in a takeover scheme. Speak to your stockholders, urging them to hold out against the potential buyers.

17. When you were hired as sales manager of this

toy company three years ago, you promised to increase sales by 25 percent. In fact, sales have dropped. Your job is on the line. Address management, explaining how the situation has not been due to your mismanagement.

18. Salespeople in your company have been making good money by selling large computer systems to businesses. Some of these companies, however, have found that they do not need such powerful machines: they need only a few personal computers. Persuade the salespeople that selling more expensive equipment will not necessarily be best for them or the company in the long run.

19. The convenience store that you manage presently stocks mostly nonperishable and packaged goods: canned food, beer, sodas, cleaning products. To compete with chain convenience stores and with local grocery stores, you want to persuade the store owners to stock fruit and vegetables. You are convinced that unusual quality and selection will draw new customers to the store.

20. Your company manufactures athletic shoes of various types. You recently came out with a shoe that has some unusual qualities, but it has sold poorly. Management wants to reduce the price and sell the remaining shoes at a loss. As marketing manager, you propose *raising* the price and promoting the shoe as a top-of-the-market product.

21. Your company is opening an office in Brazil. You do not want to hire managers from outside the company until the office has been opened and Brazilian managers have been trained. Therefore, you want a substantial number of managers from the main office to move to Brazil for at most two years. Persuade the managers that this temporary move will be worthwhile.

22. Top management is urging that lie detector tests be used as part of the employee hiring process; top candidates would have to submit to such a test. As a personnel manager, persuade management that such tests would be detrimental to the company.

23. You own a small technical company with a number of very talented technical employees. As yet, the company is not making great profits, but the future looks good. However, headhunters are constantly trying to lure your employees away. Speak to your employees, urging them to stay with this company rather than leave for a more established organization.

24. Employees in the company you work for are unhappy about the small pay increases they have been receiving. Higher salaries are out of the question right now. You want to convince management that allowing employees to buy stock in the company would be helpful for both the employees and the company itself.

25. A can of Fruit 'n Cola has been found contaminated with poison. Some managers of CRT Products, which manufactures Fruit 'n Cola, want to discontinue the product altogether. As vice-president of the company, convince top management that new packaging and good promotion will keep sales from plummeting.

7-1. You are the owner of Uptown Books, a bookstore that opened five years ago in Westwood, an urban mall. Before signing a lease for mall space, the store owners agreed to abide by the mall owner's decisions regarding upkeep of the mall, decorating, parking, and so on. However, the mall owner, Hal Nardi, realizes that he has to discuss such topics with the store owners if he is going to keep his tenants happy.

Until recently, things have gone smoothly; the mall has been kept up well and is attracting more and more customers. However, now Hal wants to have all the mall stores open seven days a week — presently they are all closed on Sundays. He also wants to extend hours until 10 every night — presently all the stores close at 6:30.

You are concerned that these changes will not be for the better. Hal has called a meeting of store owners in two weeks, but you are afraid that everyone will simply agree with him without thinking about the consequences of the changes.

You decide to meet first with your own employees to find out their opinions. They are against the changes; they say that mall security probably would not be sufficient for night hours, that the sales made during those extra hours might not make up for the extra wages being paid, and that they would all like a rest on Sundays.

a. You send out an announcement to all the store owners informing them of a meeting that week to discuss the issues. Write a memo to the owners that provides details about the meeting and outlines an agenda.

b. At the meeting, you find that only the restaurants are in favor of the later hours and Sundays; 15 of the 20 owners are against the changes. You agree to make a presentation to Hal at the upcoming meeting with him.

Prepare a detailed outline for a persuasive five- to ten-minute presentation. Use estimates on costs and sales to back up your position.

c. Prepare two visual aids to highlight major points in your presentation.

7-2. You are in charge of seven personnel trainees in a large company. These trainees meet with clerical employees every six months to review their performance. The trainees base their evaluations on written reports from supervisors, commendations and complaints received, and the appraisal interview themselves.

You realize that your subordinates are conducting these interviews in different ways. As you would like to minimize differences, you put together a set of guidelines that remind the trainees how to prepare for each interview and what specific questions they should ask each interviewee.

Write these guidelines in memo form for the trainees. Avoid a lecturing tone.

a. One of your personnel trainees informs you that Thea Brandt, a clerical assistant, has been receiving bad reviews from her supervisor. Thea has been repeatedly late for work and does not always complete her assignments. Up until the last appraisal period, Thea was doing well. Apparently something has happened. The trainee has been unable to get much information out of Thea; she is sullen and angry. You agree to meet with her yourself.

In a role play with one of your classmates, interview Thea and attempt to get at the root of the problem.

b. The head of the accounting department is looking for a clerical assistant who could eventually become a bookkeeper. You and your trainees are in charge of interviewing the applicants for the position. You want the interviewers to know the criteria the department head has in mind: someone with at least a community college degree or a business background who has word processing and spreadsheet skills as well as basic telephone and filing skills.

Develop ten questions that you want each trainee to ask the applicants during the interview.

c. One of the trainees, Randy Siegel, has decided to leave this company and go to another job. Although Randy has not complained to you, you have heard rumors that Randy has been unhappy with the personnel training program.

Prepare to conduct an exit interview with Randy by outlining three goals you would like to achieve in the interview and three questions or techniques you can use to achieve those goals.

d. Conduct a mock exit interview with a fellow student acting the part of Randy. Use the questions or techniques developed in 7-2c.

e. After the interview with Randy, write a memo to the head of your department. Summarize what happened in the interview and, if possible, make recommendations based on the information gained from the interview.

Intercultural
Communication

Part
Eight

Communicating Across Cultures

- **Acknowledging the globalization of business**
- **Overcoming ethnocentrism**
- **Examining myths of intercultural communication**
- **Overcoming barriers to intercultural communication**
- **Increasing your chances of success**
- **Getting help**

Objectives

To communicate successfully with businesspeople of other cultures

To learn how to prepare for business trips to other countries

26

Jim Janssen's Swedish Dinner

Jim Janssen is an American marketing executive who has traveled extensively in South America. In his business and social experiences in those countries, Jim had learned that people have a different sense of time than he does. Once, having been invited to dinner in Caracas, Venezuela, at 7:30 p.m., he had arrived on time only to find that his host and hostess were not even dressed. The other guests did not arrive until an hour later.

Jim was not so concerned about making such a social *faux pas,* however, when he was planning a trip to Sweden some months later. Jim himself had a Swedish grandmother. He had a sense that Swedes and Americans were basically the same, despite language differences.

In Stockholm, then, Jim was not disturbed to find himself running slightly behind schedule for a dinner party at the home of a Swedish executive. But when Jim arrived 25 minutes late, the host and host-ess looked upset; the other guests were already hovering near the dining room. When Jim apologized for being late, people politely told him that they understood he had been delayed. However, Jim knew he had blundered.

He relayed his experience to a friend the next day.

"Swedish people are very punctual about such things," his friend told him. "You probably caused a panic in your hostess' kitchen. You can make amends by sending her some flowers—but do it today!"

Points to Consider

- What areas should Jim have researched before he traveled to Sweden?
- Where could Jim have gone for information before traveling to Sweden?

Acknowledging the Globalization of Business

Thirty years ago, Peter Drucker issued a warning to American businesses: "We have to accept the fact that leadership is not ours by right, but must be earned. We have to accept the fact that we are going to be increasingly dependent on the international economy, while the international economy is likely to be less dependent on us."[1]

American businesspeople, however, responded slowly to this warning and to the evidence for it that lay before their eyes. Only recently have many businesses begun to move quickly and profitably into an international economy that has been growing at astonishing speed for the past few decades.

Now the situation is clear to everyone. The economy has become essentially a global one. Most American companies find that they must deal with foreign competitors, customers, vendors, or subsidiaries. Moreover, the percentage of non-native employees and managers in American companies has risen substantially: The American workplace is a heterogeneous environment where different languages and cultures intermingle.

The American workplace is a heterogeneous environment.

Why have Americans been so slow to adapt to these changes? Although our nation was settled by people from many cultures, its size set it apart

[1]Drucker, Peter F. "Realities of Our World Position." *Harvard Business Review* 37 (1959): 45.

from other countries. Unlike citizens of countries like Switzerland, for instance, who have learned to deal with different languages and cultures on a daily basis, Americans tended to remain insular. Most never mastered a second language; many never dealt with other cultures except occasionally as tourists.

Upon entering into international trade, business people realized that they had to consider areas such as tariffs, import/export regulations, and international laws, but they often forgot to consider the cultural differences that can lead to communication breakdowns.

Overcoming Ethnocentrism

Ethnocentrism has led to expensive blunders.

When American businesses did begin to penetrate foreign markets, they made expensive and embarrassing errors. American *ethnocentrism*—a tendency to believe that the rest of the world revolves around and is dependent upon Americans—led many businesspeople to forget basic maxims of good business such as finding out about a new market and communicating effectively with customers, vendors, employees, and colleagues.

There are hundreds of tales of American blunders abroad. American appliance companies, for example, tried to sell American-size appliances in Japan, where most people's houses had no space for large washing machines and refrigerators. Some companies never thought to translate their instruction manuals: they assumed everyone could read English.

Language differences have also created marketing fiascos. Ford learned belatedly that its *Fiera* brand meant "ugly old woman" in Spanish. The Hertz ad, "Hertz puts you in the driver's seat," meant "let Hertz make you a chauffeur" when it was translated into German.

Nuances of different cultures have also escaped American businesspeople. After creating an advertising campaign in France, the makers of Cue toothpaste discovered that Cue is the name of a French pornographic magazine. The Marlboro cowboy had to be removed from British advertisements since British regulations prohibit using heroic figures in cigarette ads.

American businesspeople have made errors in personal as well as corporate areas. Failures to understand social norms and language subtleties have ruined hundreds of potentially positive business and social relationships abroad. Jim Janssen's experiences in Caracas and Stockholm, described in the case at the beginning of this chapter, are indicative of just some of these problems.

Errors involving cultural misunderstandings, moreover, are not confined to Americans doing business overseas. They occur frequently in the modern American workplace, which is frequently filled with employees and managers from all over the world.

Examining Myths of Intercultural Communication

Many of the errors made by native American businesspeople dealing with non-natives both in the United States and abroad are derived from the Americans' belief in certain myths. These myths have prevented them from perceiving the need to understand and adapt to foreign cultures.

Myth #1. We're All the Same Under the Skin

Many people were raised to believe that human nature is basically the same all over the world. Perhaps there are some constants in human behavior, but for the most part we are products of our individual families, cultures, and societies. The belief that "we're all basically the same" has led many Americans to think people of other cultures will act and respond the way we do—even though they clearly do not.

Myth #2. People of One Culture Are Basically the Same

A similar error is to believe in stereotypes, to assume that "all Arabs are like this" or "all Chinese believe that." Not only do cultural, regional, and religious differences exist among people of countries other than ours, but people everywhere also have individual differences.

You may be annoyed or amused when you hear someone in another country say something like, "All Americans are impatient." But, unless you are careful, you may immediately make the same type of error about people of other cultures.

Myth #3. If They Can Speak English, We Can Communicate with Them

Many people believe that language is the primary barrier between people of different cultures. Relieved to find that a foreign client or colleague speaks English, an American may assume that the two of them are communicating clearly.

One obvious error in this belief is evident to anyone who has studied a foreign language: a person may speak fairly well but still not *understand* everything other people are saying. Also, each language has subtleties that become apparent to speakers only after having mastered it quite thoroughly.

Moreover, as Jim Janssen discovered, nonverbal communication is as important as language. Misreading cultural cues can be as damaging as misunderstanding spoken or written words.

Communication involves more than having some words in common.

Myth #4. America Is Everybody's Ideal

Ethnocentrism has led Americans to believe that they are idealized by people of other cultures. This may be far from the truth. Seeing teenagers in Beijing wearing blue jeans and listening to rock music, you may conclude that Chinese young people are becoming "Westernized" and want to be more so.

To explode this myth, all you have to do is ask yourself how "Easternized" Americans have become from eating chow mein and driving Hondas.

Overcoming Barriers to Intercultural Communication

Because every culture is unique and diverse, this text can barely scrape the surface of intercultural communication. The following general areas, however, are ones to consider when traveling outside this country or dealing with people from cultures other than your own. (Figure 26-1 illustrates a sampling of cultural differences between Japanese and American managers.)

Time

People in different cultures have different attitudes toward time.

In the case at the opening of this chapter, Jim Janssen discovered that different cultures have different attitudes towards time. Americans are well known for being in a hurry, for making deadlines, and for being "on time." In most parts of the world, however, life is more leisurely, and rushing is considered rude.

In many countries, important decisions are given the time they deserve to be talked over and thought about. Americans may think a Saudi Arabian is intentionally delaying negotiations, for instance, when the person may actually be giving it the greatest attention. Many Japanese have learned that delaying tactics drive Americans to distraction. To get what they want, Japanese negotiators may choose simply to wait until the Americans give in to their demands.

Japanese	*North Americans*
Often employ ambiguous, indirect references	Prefer making points clearly
Believe important decisions should be made slowly	Want to move quickly, get negotiations over with
Place value on rituals and politeness	Tend to be informal
Emphasize importance of family, company, group	Emphasize importance of the individual
Drink tea and eat meals as part of serious business relationship	Eat and drink as informal social activities
Tend to be employed with same company for lifetime	Move from company to company as opportunities occur
Avoid self-praise	Want to establish superiority of product or idea

FIGURE 26-1

Sampling of cultural differences: Japanese versus North American managers

Even the basic times for doing business change from country to country. In some countries, offices close during the heat of the afternoon and then reopen later on, staying open much later than American offices. In other countries, business hours begin as early as 7:30 a.m. and end at 4:00 p.m.

Personal Space and Touching

The amount of space normally left between yourself and another person is an intangible cultural element that is more important than you might imagine. Americans are used to leaving a couple of feet between people as they talk; if a colleague steps too close or touches them, Americans tend to back away. On a bus, Americans tend to sit in empty two-person seats; they do not sit next to each other until the empty two-person seats are all taken.

In many other cultures, people naturally sit and stand closer to each other than Americans do. When Americans back away from them, they feel they are being rejected.

Similarly, in America, businesspeople are apt to shake hands but otherwise stay away from touching each other; they are often surprised when foreign businesspeople embrace or kiss them. On the other hand, people in Thailand do not touch in public. The makers of Listerine learned this only after finding that commercials showing a boy touching a girl and advising her about bad breath were considered unacceptable in Thailand.

Another cultural difference regarding space is visible within offices. Americans allocate more space to people with more authority in an organization: a supervisor will often have a private office. In France, Japan, and many other countries, however, the people in charge sit in the midst of the workers. An American who imagines that someone working in an office full of people is without authority can be very wrong indeed.

Attitudes toward personal space differ in different cultures.

Etiquette

The rules of etiquette in a culture can be complex and difficult to learn. However, mastering them may be the key to success in a foreign culture. Mentioning a businessman's children, for example, is considered ill-mannered in Saudi Arabia. Refusing coffee in Arab countries is also a breach of etiquette.

Exchanging business cards is an important preliminary to Japanese negotiations, and bowing is an essential part of a greeting. (In fact, the depth and numbers of bows Japanese people give someone provide intricate messages about that person's status.) Too often, Americans give offense or miss vital social cues because they do not pay attention to the nonverbal communication around them.

Individualism

Whereas Americans place a lot of emphasis on individualism, many cultures emphasize the good of the group over that of the individual. People in other cultures often see American individualism as destructive of essential units such as the family, tribe, or community.

People of other cultures also emphasize long-term relationships over new ones. They see American friendliness as superficial. Rather than making a long-term friendship, Americans want to make a deal and go home. One major reason that Americans have had trouble penetrating certain foreign markets has been their inability to focus on the long-term benefits of ongoing relationships.

Americans, too, want to dispense with the formalities of coffee-drinking or other social amenities—and yet these are key components to building a relationship, becoming a part of the other person's group or community.

Gender Roles

Gender roles can create problems for both male and female Americans doing business abroad. Many cultures, such as that of the Arabs, are dominated by men, and American women may have difficulty establishing professional relationships. However, because American companies are often reluctant to send American women abroad, foreign businesspeople may have little experience dealing with them. Thus, the same problems repeat themselves.

Women in some countries hold higher positions than they normally do in the United States.

American women can be expected to receive different treatment than their male counterparts in foreign countries. But even in countries where the local women hold an inferior status, American businesswomen may not be considered inferior. Women should try not to take offense; they may find they receive preferential treatment that is actually helpful to their business dealings.

In many areas, too—Eastern Europe, China, and the Philippines, for example—women hold high-ranking positions and work in jobs that, even in America, are often reserved primarily for men.

From the Desk of ...

Christopher P. Brown

Licensed Customs House Broker

"When you're working with people in other cultures, use your normal standards of courtesy," says Christopher P. Brown, Licensed Customs House Broker. When an importer has commercial goods, such as electronics, appliances, car parts, chemicals, fabric, or other items arriving in the United States, customs house brokers take care of U.S. Government formalities, dealing primarily with the U.S. Customs Service, but also with the Food and Drug Administration, the Environmental Protection Agency (EPA), the Department of Agriculture, the State Department, and others. They also arrange for the transfer of goods to their final destinations. About 90 percent of their business with clients takes place over the phone. Also, "ninety percent of my business is done in English," says Chris, "since the government requires that all paperwork be done in English." Chris has learned some basic Japanese phrases that he uses as a courtesy: hello, goodbye, how are you, how can I help you. He says he can understand Japanese to a certain extent, but he says, "If I speak in Japanese, the Japanese will reply in English."

The major problem Chris runs into when working with the Japanese is the time pressure: "They need the shipment yesterday. They have paid $2,000 to ship a 500-pound carton. They know when the airline will arrive, but they have no idea of the time it takes to get goods through customs. The Japanese keep low inventories on hand for their factories. They must constantly resupply their businesses or the assembly line stops, so there's an urgency about their deadlines."

Has Chris been involved in the Japanese formality we have all heard about? He thinks they are "more inclined to be formal among themselves, rather than when they are dealing with Americans. As a matter of fact often when Japanese people first come to the United States, after they have finished with what they are saying over the phone, there's a click. No goodbye at all. After a few weeks, they've adjusted to our phone manners."

Chris says that the Japanese culture is more reserved when it comes to business lunches. "It may be a lunch, but there's a purpose for the lunch." He finds the Japanese inquisitive about his personal life, but Chris attributes this to the fact that the Japanese are on foreign soil. "If I were in Japan, the situation would be reversed."

Chris says he feels the Japanese are less individualistic, more company- and society-oriented. "A Japanese friend of mine had lived here for 17 years, his kids were born here and were American citizens, but when he received a telegram from his company telling him to go back to Japan, he shrugged his shoulders and went back."

According to Chris, the women find it harder to leave. They enjoy the freedom of the United States. Chris deals with very few Japanese women managers. "The managers are usually men."

Chris's advice for working with people from other cultures:

- Be courteous.
- Use a low-key, conservative look.
- Be warm and cheerful.
- Be formal initially.
- Stay calm in situations of extreme pressure.

Increasing Your Chances of Success

Successful intercultural communication cannot be achieved by superficial efforts. Some American companies are realizing now that the costs of educating their employees in cultural differences and preparing them for culture shock will reap great rewards in the long run. Like the companies of other countries, American companies are beginning to see the advantages of planning for the long-term rather than for the instant return.

To be successful with people of different cultural backgrounds, you will find that a simple awareness of cultural differences will help you avoid and recover from blunders of various types. As you gain experience, you will find it easier to perceive nonverbal messages and social nuances—and you will be more aware of your own cultural biases.

Two major efforts on your part will considerably increase your chances of success in communicating with people of other cultures: learn the language and analyze the environments you will be encountering.

Learn the Language

There is no substitute for learning the language. Simply having made the effort will please your foreign hosts—and knowledge of the language will eliminate many of the dilemmas most travelers encounter in other countries. Knowledge of the language, moreover, will give you great insight into the culture itself.

Even travelers to English-speaking countries should do a little research on the local language. If you have traveled to England, Scotland, or Australia, you will know that people not only speak in dialects we find difficult to understand but also use words in quite different ways.

If you do not have time to learn a foreign language before doing business abroad, make sure you have a good translator. In fact, before completing an important transaction or signing documents you cannot read, you might want *two* translators to ensure that messages have been sent and received accurately.

Whether speaking directly to a non-native English speaker or using a translator, remember to keep your messages short and clear. Avoid speaking too fast or using idiomatic phrases that could confuse your listener. Try to get feedback from the other person as you speak—and provide him or her with feedback as well.

Analyze the Environments

As a businessperson in a foreign culture, you are apt to be interacting with four overlapping environments (Figure 26-2): the political/legal, economic, technological, and social/cultural.

The political/legal environment, which includes a country's laws and regulations as well as its political structures, will have a major impact on almost any international negotiations. Understanding import and export regulations, price controls, local laws, and many other political and legal factors can save you and your company money and time.

Closely intertwined with law and politics is the economic environment: Is the economy in an inflationary state? Are there problems with resource or energy shortages? What percentage of the population is unemployed? How much disposable income do the people have?

The technological environment is intertwined with the economy. What technological advances have occurred in the country? Is it fully industrialized or just emerging technologically?

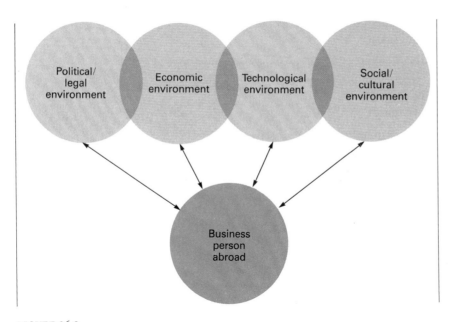

FIGURE 26-2

Overlapping environments affecting a businessperson abroad

The fourth environment, the social/cultural, may hold the most surprises for business travelers. Whereas companies may brief their employees fairly thoroughly on the first three environments, they may neglect vital social and cultural factors. Before doing business abroad, find out when and how the people do business, what types of social situations you might encounter, and what various verbal and nonverbal messages can mean. Find out about religious practices, dress codes, power structures, and even eating habits.

The more you know, the fewer unpleasant surprises you will have—and the greater your chances of success, both professional and personal.

Getting Help

A number of organizations, films, and books are available to help you improve your intercultural communication. The *Going International* film series provides particularly useful guides for international travelers. To find out more about these films, write to:

Copeland Briggs Productions
411 15th Avenue
San Francisco, CA 94118

Transnational Managers as Intercultural Communicators is also a useful film. It is part of the *International Management Productivity Series* put out by Gulf Publishing Company:

Gulf Publishing Company
P.O. Box 2608
Houston, TX 77252

For information on individual countries, you may write the following organizations:

American Society for Training and Development
1630 Duke Street
Box 1443
Alexandria, VA 22313

Intercultural Communications, Inc.
P.O. Box 14358
University Station
Minneapolis, MN 55414

Intercultural Press, Inc.
P.O. Box 768
Yarmouth, ME 04096

International Association of Business Communication
870 Market St., Suite 940
San Francisco, CA 94102

Society for Intercultural Education, Training, and Research International
1414-22nd Street
Washington, DC 20037

World Information Sources
130 North Road
Vershire, VT 05079

Some books of interest include:

Do's and Taboos Around the World. New York: The Benjamin Company, Inc., 1985. (Put together by the Parker Pen Co.)

Harris, Philip R., and Robert T. Moran. *Managing Cultural Differences.* Houston: Gulf, 1979.

Ricks, David A., Marilyn Y. C. Fu, and Jeffrey S. Arpan. *International Business Blunders,* Columbus: Grid, Inc., 1974.

Terpstra, Vern, and Kenneth David. *The Cultural Environment of International Business.* New York: Pantheon Books, 1983.

Summary

To be successful, American businesspeople must be aware that modern business is becoming increasingly heterogeneous and international. Relying on people of other cultures to accommodate to our language, customs, and needs has caused many expensive and long-term problems for American companies. Awareness of and openness to cultural differences can help avert problems and increase our success at many levels.

Intercultural Communication Checklist

- To increase your success when communicating with people of other cultures,

  _____ be aware of individual and cultural differences

  _____ remember that a common spoken language does not ensure good communication

  _____ research the political/legal, economic, technological, and social/cultural environments

  _____ learn the language when possible

- When analyzing differences between cultures, be aware of different

  _____ perceptions of time

  _____ attitudes toward personal space and touching

  _____ rules of etiquette

  _____ attitudes toward the individual and the group

  _____ gender roles

Terms to Remember

American ethnocentrism: American tendency to believe the world revolves around America.

Globalization: the increasingly worldwide nature of business

Summary Discussion: Jim Janssen's Swedish Dinner from Case in Point, p. 617

Jim should have researched the various environments of Sweden as thoroughly as he might have researched those of a more unfamiliar country: he should not have assumed basic similarities between himself and his Swedish hosts. Since time is often a crucial cultural element, he should have been particularly careful to find out Swedish attitudes toward time. To gain information, he could have contacted any of the organizations listed in this chapter.

Exercises

1. Give an example of *ethnocentrism* from your personal experience.
2. What are stereotypes? Give an example.
3. Describe how *globalization* has affected local businesses such as grocery stores.
4. How can different attitudes toward personal space affect business negotiations? Give examples.
5. What are idioms? Give some examples of idioms in English that a foreign speaker might have trouble understanding or using correctly. If you know a language other than English, cite some examples of idioms in that language that English speakers learning the language should be aware of.
6. Why is knowledge of communication principles so important to an international businessperson? Explain.
7. Describe how you might apply concepts of active listening to an intercultural situation.
8. If you were a female manager or professional person being sent abroad, what information or training might you find useful in addition to that given your male colleagues?
9. Describe a cross-cultural mistake you have made.

Questions for Review and Discussion

1. Research the culture of one country. Present a report to the class that summarizes your findings. Give details on the attitudes of that culture regarding time, etiquette, male and female roles, religion, and other areas. Give your listeners hints on how to prepare for a business trip to that country.
2. Interview a student or businessperson from China, Japan, Korea, or Vietnam on nonverbal communication in his or her country. What gestures, facial expressions, and other nonverbal behaviors differ from those familiar to Americans?
3. What are the characteristics of your own culture? Describe attitudes toward work, personal space, time, sex, education, and other major areas.
4. Assume a person from India was planning a business trip to the United States. This person speaks English learned in school but has little sense of what to expect in your area of the United States. Put together a report summarizing important information this person would be interested in. (To make the report useful, you should find out some cultural characteristics that the visitor from India might have in contrast to those of North Americans.)
5. Research an American company or product that failed in another country. Prepare a report on what happened—and why.
6. Report on a trip you have taken to another part of the United States. Describe at least two or three cultural differences you noticed in that area. What did you do, if anything, to change your behavior?
7. Assume you are a manager of a department company with both native-born and foreign-born employees from many parts of the world. Prepare a brief report on techniques you might use to increase communication in your department.
8. Assume you are preparing someone for a business trip to a country of your choice. Choose one of the four "environments" described in this chapter and develop a useful report for that person on *one* of the environments.
9. Work with a team of students in your class to research sources of information on one culture. Prepare a bibliography that a business traveler to that culture would find useful: you might include magazine and newspaper articles as well as books and films.
10. When you were in another country, what generalizations did you encounter regarding Americans? Do you agree or disagree with these generalizations?

11. (For non-native students) What generalizations have you found Americans make about your culture? Do you agree or disagree with these generalizations?

12. (For non-native students) You are writing or speaking to people in your native country, preparing them for a trip to the United States for business, school, or vacation. What cultural differences should they be particularly aware of?

13. Describe several taboos in a foreign culture that American visitors should be aware of.

14. Consider a product that is sold in both the United States and another country. Describe the different ways the product is marketed in the two countries.

15. Describe how the same nonverbal elements convey different messages in the United States and in another country.

16. Choose a foreign country and research how a person's status is conveyed in companies of that country. Compare these with ways an individual's status is conveyed in American companies.

Part 8 Mini-Cases

8-1. VHJ Manufacturing is an American firm with a plant near Birmingham, England. The workers are primarily English, but management is 50 percent American, 50 percent English. The relationships among the managers and between management and employees are cordial but not enthusiastic.

The English plant badly needs to be updated, so management has been exchanging ideas and budgets with the American headquarters to arrive at a workable and affordable renovation plan. The Americans in England want to move quickly and implement changes that have been successful in their Indiana site. They feel the English managers are stalling the operation.

The English managers believe they understand what changes would be in keeping with local ordinances and customs as well as the needs of the English workers. However, they feel the American managers have all the clout with the American headquarters: the English managers believe their expertise is being ignored. The Americans, on the other hand, believe the English managers resent the affluence and aggressiveness of Americans and are trying to thwart efforts to make the business grow.

a. Assume you are Fred McCall, an American manager at the English VHJ plant. After doing research on the cultural characteristics of the English, write a short report to American headquarters outlining some cultural differences between the American and English managers that could be a problem.

b. Assume you are Alan Gregory, an English man-ager at the English VHJ site. Write a report to all the managers at this site outlining the problems between the two cultural groups and summarizing some suggestions for improving the situation.

8-2. Denise DiPietro is an executive with a New York advertising company. Her company has recently agreed to send her to Nigeria to meet with a client. Denise knows that the country is divided between Muslims and Christians, but she has no time to learn the language or to research essential points about the country before she goes there.

She has asked you to prepare a "briefing report" for her: a report on political, economic, and cultural factors that will help her to meet successfully with businesspeople in Nigeria.

8-3. You are in charge of winning a contract for your company with a firm in a Middle Eastern country.

One day you are approached by a man who holds an important position in the country's government. He assures you that he has the influence to win the contract for you, but his efforts will cost $25,000. Your company would be willing to spend that much to win the contract if the expenses were legitimate; however, the company has specific regulations prohibiting the payment of bribes. The $25,000 would most certainly be seen as a bribe.

Write a brief report summarizing how you would handle this situation—and why you would handle it this way.

Cases

Part Nine

The Alison Weaver Case

Upon graduating from college, Alison Weaver started work as assistant to the fundraiser of a nonprofit corporation. Her duties included writing grant proposals to government agencies and private corporations and developing marketing materials. With a major in marketing and minor in English, Alison was sure this job would draw upon and improve her good writing skills and knowledge about business practices.

During her first week on the job, her boss, Pat Bagrowski, told her to track down some information from various agencies in Washington, D.C. After three fruitless hours of long-distance calls, Alison had unearthed none of the information Pat wanted.

"You're not dealing with those bureaucrats in the right way," Pat told her. "You'll have to learn how to approach them."

Alison nodded but didn't ask *how* she was going to learn.

The following week, Pat said she would be in Dallas for three days. "We have to let the staff know what progress we've made on our proposals," she told Alison. "At the meeting on Wednesday, you'll have to do a presentation. Here are the major items you should cover. Let me know if you have any questions."

Alison went home that night in a state of panic. She had never made a presentation at a meeting. She was terrified to speak in front of groups. Besides, she did not understand a good portion of the material Pat had covered with her that afternoon. She had been too afraid to ask questions about the proposals.

During the week Pat was scheduled to be away, moreover, Alison would have to handle all the telephone calls and the communication between her office and the rest of the organization.

Alison seriously considered resigning. This job demanded expertise in areas with which she had almost no experience. It demanded excellent communication skills for dealing with people on the telephone, in person, and in groups. After having been successful throughout her academic career, Alison believed she was doomed to fail at work because she couldn't communicate with people.

Assignments

1. In class, discuss ways in which Alison could have improved her communication with Pat Bagrowski. What could Alison do to begin overcoming her stage fright? What steps could she take to improve her oral communication skills?

2. Discuss what Pat could have done to improve communication with Alison.

3. What should Alison do next?

The Century Cereal Company Case

Century Cereal Company, with headquarters in Kalamazoo, Michigan, is a small company with a few popular cereal brands. These cereals, marketed primarily in the Midwest, are targeted for children aged three to twelve years old. The best-selling brand in recent months has been HoneyBees, a wheat cereal shaped like tiny bees.

To target young consumers, CCC has been following standard marketing practice in the industry by advertising HoneyBees on Saturday morning cartoon shows. The commercials feature animated characters who come to breakfast with kids and introduce them to HoneyBees. With milk, toast, and orange juice, the characters tell the children, HoneyBees provide all the nutrients kids need for their morning meal.

Although these commercials are not substantially different from those of larger cereal companies, CCC has been receiving protest letters from parents. HoneyBees cereal, they say, contains too much sugar for their children. The company is morally irresponsible, these parents claim: it should be promoting good nutritional habits in the children, not hooking them on sugary garbage for breakfast. Some newspapers have taken up the issue, so the company has decided to respond to the criticism.

The company is going to revise the commercials slightly, but it will not drop them from Saturday morning television. Its new commercials will emphasize the importance of well-balanced nutritious meals throughout every child's day.

The company, however, feels that these changes may not end the criticism levied against it. As head of marketing for CCC, Marlene Mendelson has been asked to decide if the company should respond directly to the accusations—and how.

Her research shows that the protests have had only a minimal effect on sales; in fact, the publicity may have actually heightened people's recognition of the company's name. But the company's goodwill is also at stake. She wonders whether a direct response would help people feel confident that CCC has their children's interests at heart.

Now that the company is slightly altering the commercials, Marlene must decide whether she should appear on television talkshows to discuss the matter, send a letter to each protester who has written the company, or simply ignore the protesters and let the controversy die down.

Assignments

1. In class, discuss what communication channel (if any) Marlene should use. What are the strengths and weaknesses of each approach?
2. Assume Marlene has decided to write a letter to each person who has written to criticize the commercials. As Marlene, write a letter describing the company's new commercials and its concern for the children who are viewing the commercials and eating HoneyBees cereal.
3. As Marlene, write a short report to company management outlining the way in which you want to handle the situation—and why.

Turner's Office Equipment Case

Carol Flores has been hired as head of accounting for Turner's Office Equipment, a business with over three hundred employees. One of her initial concerns has been the way petty cash is handled in the company.

A cash box is always left on the office manager's desk, and people who need emergency money for supplies or other work-related expenses are expected to fill out a form, take the money they need, and leave a receipt once they have purchased the necessary items.

Carol has found, however, that people are borrowing money for bus fare and other personal expenses. Moreover, they are not always filling out a form or returning the money they borrow: every month shows discrepancies of $20 to $30 in the cash box. Over a period of a year, $350 is unaccounted for.

Carol finds the whole situation disturbing. On the one hand, the amounts missing each month are fairly small. On the other hand, company money is being misused. Moreover, the situation creates serious accounting problems.

Carol would like to implement the method for obtaining petty cash that had been used in the company she worked for previously. At that company, money was kept in a locked box, and everyone making a request for cash had to speak to the person in charge of the box before filling out a form. There had never been any discrepancies at the end of the month.

Having worked at Turner's for only six weeks, Carol is reluctant to set up a new system. When she discussed her ideas with the vice-president, he told her to go ahead. But she is afraid that people will think she is accusing them of theft and throwing her weight around to impress top management.

She has considered simply getting a locked box, appointing someone to handle the funds, and sending a memo informing employees of a new policy. Now she is reconsidering: maybe she should get people together and make an informal presentation to explain the new system. Perhaps a more personal approach would lower people's resistance. But getting people together would give them an opportunity to complain about the new system.

Assignments

1. In class, discuss which communication channel would work most effectively for Carol.
2. Discuss the concerns Carol should have about doing a presentation. What sort of preparations should she make? What information should she emphasize in her presentation? What should she deemphasize?
3. Assume Carol has decided a memo would be more effective. As Carol, write a memo to all employees that explains the new policy.

The Tim Dawes Case

For six months, Tim Dawes had worked as manager of the Delivery Department of Hardwicke & Company. He was surprised when James Elshani, the vice-president, called him in for a talk, but Tim thought that this might be a good opportunity to discuss some of the cost-saving changes he had implemented in his department.

James Elshani, sitting behind his large mahogany desk, was on the telephone when Tim came in. James waved Tim to a seat, a straight-back chair. Tim sat there uncomfortably while James continued talking about a tennis tournament he was playing in the following weekend.

"Sorry, George," James said after a few minutes, "Gotta go. I'm in an important meeting." He winked at Tim. Tim got the joke: the "meeting" wasn't important at all.

Finally James was off the telephone. The friendly tone he had used with George was gone. Now he was businesslike.

"Well, Mr. Dawes," he said. "I've got some bad news." he paused to let the message sink in. Tim clenched his hands in his lap. Was he being fired?

Rather than looking at him, James examined some papers on his desk. "Profits aren't what they should be," he went on. "We're going to be economizing in every department."

Tim shifted in his seat. His new procedures in the Delivery Department had already cut costs by 10 percent, but now he didn't have the nerve to say anything. James still wasn't looking him in the eye.

"I see you had a customer complaint last week," James continued. "Your delivery to C & G was three days late."

Tim gulped. What did that have to do with cutting costs? "That wasn't our fault, sir—" he began.

"It never is, is it?" James responded coldly. "But it could've lost a major account. Make sure it doesn't happen again."

The telephone rang. James reached for it and nodded at Tim. Tim knew he was supposed to leave. He left, shaking. He felt like a child who had just been spanked. But he didn't deserve it. C & G had filled out the order form incorrectly—*that* was why the delivery was late. Elshani hadn't given Tim a moment to explain. And why had Elshani called him in, anyway?

The more Tim thought about the experience, the angrier he became. But he could think of nothing to do about it—and his frustration made him even angrier.

Assignments

1. In class, discuss what elements other than words communicated messages in this situation? What messages did James transmit intentionally? Did he transmit any unintentional messages? What were they? What role did the physical setting play in the conversation? What messages did Tim transmit (intentionally and unintentionally) to James? In what important ways did communication fail in this situation?

2. Discuss what Tim should do now. Should he ignore the encounter? Should he ask James for another meeting? Should he write a memo to James?

3. Assume Tim has decided to write a memo to James. As Tim, write a memo explaining that you have implemented cost-cutting procedures in your department. Mention the C & G complaint as well.

The WLB Broadcasting Company Case

The WLB Broadcasting Company operates a medium-power AM radio broadcast station in Beale, Pennsylvania, a semirural community of 15,000. WLB has carved out a niche in the local radio market, despite competition from high-power metropolitan stations in Philadelphia, by emphasizing local events and fostering a trustworthy, neighborly image.

As advertising manager, Margie Fine is responsible for setting rates, managing the sales staff, and coordinating the airtime schedule. Her regular sales staff consists of only two full-time sales representatives, but three of her disk jockeys also sell advertising on a part-time basis. She reports directly to the station manager, who is also the owner.

As part of a promotional effort for the live broadcast of the local high-school basketball season, Margie has established special rates for customers who buy one 60-second "spot" for each game. Instead of $100 per spot, the customer can buy a "strip" of all 14 games for only $1,000, paid in advance. The special offer has proven popular, especially since the team expects a strong season, and all of the available advertising time has been booked since before the season began.

Last week, at the final home game, a foul-up occurred between the studio and the remote sportscaster at the gymnasium: the 60-second strip spot for Big Daddy Dog, a local hot dog stand, was missed. The owner of the stand, who was listening, was upset because his postgame business was off even though the local team won. Blaming his loss of business on the radio station, he called the owner and threatened to sue for lost business.

Assignment

The owner of the station has asked Margie to write a letter to Michael Dwyer, the owner of Big Daddy Dog. Margie is willing to make some concessions to make Mr. Dwyer happy, but she would prefer to grant advertising credit rather than issue a refund. She certainly wants to avoid the trouble and expense of a lawsuit.

As Margie, write a letter to Mr. Dwyer. Address it to:

Mr. Michael Dwyer, Owner
Big Daddy Dog
32 March Street
Beale, PA 19123

Employee Relocation Case

Western America Bank has had branches throughout northern and southern California for over thirty years. At this point, however, financial difficulties have caused the bank to face major changes. To retrench, the corporate management in Los Angeles has decided to close most of its northern California branches and to concentrate on its branches in the Los Angeles area, which are all doing fairly well.

As Personnel Director for the corporation, George Neri has a difficult job.

He discovers that a number of the southern California managers and employees are giving notice simply because they see the company has some serious troubles: they want to get out now.

Ordinarily, George would want to hire new employees who live near the branches where they would work. However, at this point, over a hundred northern California managers and employees are distressed about losing their jobs. George wants to keep as many of these knowledgeable, responsible employees as he can. But most of them are from northern California communities of under 150,000 people. How effectively would they relocate to the Los Angeles area?

George discusses the problem with his assistant, Sam Meyerson.

"We have to examine all the files of interested applicants," George says. "But most of our decisions will be based on personal interviews."

"Jack Geer came down here from Sonoma," Sam says. "Remember how he hated it? We kept him for six months. Now he's back in the country somewhere."

"We'll have to find people who thrive on the energy and excitement of a big city," George agrees. "We don't want employees to move here just to avoid looking for another job. I want to hire people who love big metropolitan areas. We should find out where they grew up, where they've lived before.

"And we'll really need to pinpoint their goals. These candidates should be go-getters. They should be excited about being close to the corporate headquarters because their long-term goals are with Western America."

"We'll have to give our interviewers some guidelines," Sam says. "Maybe they can even screen some candidates on the telephone. I'll think up some approaches our interviewers can use."

"That's just what I wanted you to do," George says.

Assignments

1. As Sam, write a memo to the Personnel Department staff. Explain the situation to them and outline some questions the interviewers may be able to use to screen candidates who say they are interested in relocation.
2. Assume you are a bank employee or manager who wants to move to a Los Angeles branch. Write a letter that explains why you want to keep working for Western America Bank and why relocating to Los Angeles will be a good move for you. Address the letter to: Mr. George Neri, Director of Personnel, Western America Bank, Los Angeles, CA 92346.

The AMTO Industries Case

Thad Sorenson has been working for AMTO Industries for two years. His boss, Jack Chan, has been supportive and helpful while Thad learned his way in the large company. In recent months, however, Jack has become withdrawn, preoccupied. Thad knows Jack has had some personal problems, but understanding the situation does not help the day-to-day problems at work.

Thad is particularly concerned about some changes that have been occurring in their department: productivity has fallen, and employee turnover is on the rise. Jack, however, hardly seems to notice the changes. Thad finally goes to Jack with some figures he has been working on.

"Say, Jack, this is our worst month so far. Look at these production figures."

Jack takes the papers but does not really look at them. "I'll get to these later on today, Thad. I'm busy now."

"This situation is pretty urgent, Jack. We better talk about it right away."

Jack shuffles through the papers. "I'll get to them as soon as I can, Thad," he says.

Despondent, Thad leaves the office. He can't make the necessary decisions without Jack's approval. But these figures indicate a crucial problem for the whole company. He simply *must* break through to Jack and get some feedback from him. But how?

He considers some alternatives. He could talk the problem over with Madge Dorset, a manager in another department who does not work directly with either Jack or himself. She knows Jack quite well and might have some ideas. On the other hand, Thad does not know her at all; she might consider that Jack is being presumptuous and offensive by wanting to discuss his boss with her.

Thad also considers going to Jack's immediate boss, Ann Bakman, the Vice-President of Research and Development. Ann is directly concerned with the department's productivity. However, Jack might resent Thad's going over his head to discuss anything with Ann. Besides, Ann will not be able to counsel Jack the way Madge might be able to; Ann might even decide to fire Jack.

Thad figures he has three options: (1) write an urgent memo to Jack saying he will have to talk with upper management about the department unless Jack will take the time to discuss it with him; (2) meet with Madge to see if she can help him find out what is bothering Jack and help him solve the communication problems he is having with Thad; and (3) meet with Ann to outline the problems in the department.

Assignments

1. In class, discuss the communication channel that Thad should use.
2. Assume Thad has decided to write a memo to Jack repeating the concerns that he mentioned in person the day before. He will send a copy of the memo to Ann. Write the memo for Thad.

The Employee Education Case

TechData Corporation was founded three years ago by a team of engineers with plans for some dynamic and innovative computer-related products. In three years the company has grown to two hundred employees and is filling up a sprawling building outside of Phoenix, Arizona. The company has thrived on the introduction of reliable new products produced on schedule.

Now that the company has so many employees, Janice Sotto, head of the Personnel Department, is putting together a manual on policy and procedures; until now, most personnel decisions have been made erratically.

One question that has come up repeatedly concerns employee education. Should the company compensate employees who wish to further their education? Should the company give employees more flexible schedules if they wish to take classes? Should the company finance its own in-house classes? Or should the company wait until it is in a stronger financial position to do anything about employee education?

Janice decides to call a meeting to discuss management's opinions on this subject. The meeting includes John Ficarra, President; Pat Ford, Vice-President; and Ted Rolfes, Head of Production. At the meeting, Janice is surprised to find strong feelings on both sides of the subject. Pat favors employee education, while Ted is dead set against it.

"We have to compete with a lot of high-tech firms," Pat maintains. "Our employees have to stay up-to-date in their various specialties. We're not in a position to rest on our laurels."

"You're right about that," says Ted. "We've got nearly impossible deadlines to meet between now and August. Even with all our employees working full-time, we will be lucky to keep to our schedule. And this company's reputation rests on meeting deadlines—we mustn't lose that edge. We can't have employees off taking classes. We need them here, giving us over a hundred percent of themselves."

"They'll do that only for so long," Pat says. "Then they'll see that other companies let their employees get ahead by working toward advanced degrees and taking specialized seminars. We'll find our turnover rate going sky-high."

"I'm already hearing complaints," Janice says quietly.

Finally John Ficarra, the president, stops the discussion. "I see both of your viewpoints. We do need to set up a policy about this. I'll write a memo this week outlining a tentative plan. You can give me your thoughts on it when you've read the memo."

Assignments

1. As John Ficarra, write a memo outlining a fair policy on employee education. Make sure you explain your rationale for the policy you have chosen.

2. Assume John Ficarra has suggested a policy that the company will pay employees' tuition if they take evening courses related to their area of work. As Ted Rolfes, write a memo to John Ficara explaining why you feel evening classes would interfere with the company's de-

manding production schedule over the next eight months.

3. Assume John Ficarra has suggested a policy that the company will not encourage employee education for another year. Then management will reassess the situation. As Pat Ford, write a memo explaining why this policy would be detrimental to the company's short- and long-term success.

Lenore's Ristorante Case

Lenore's Ristorante has been a well-known eating place in downtown Indianapolis since 1953. Located on a busy street, the restaurant has always attracted groups of businesspeople for lunch and families for dinner.

The owners, John and Lenore Cortese, no longer work in the kitchen, but the restaurant still features their original creations. Huge tureens of minestrone, crusty bread, and a lavish salad precede each main course. The entrees are served family style: veal parmesan, ravioli, chicken baked in tomato sauce, and, of course, spaghetti. As Lenore's loyal patrons know, customers receive quality food at astonishingly low prices.

They also receive quantity. In fact, hardly any group of customers can finish all the food delivered to their table.

Since 1986, George Bernard has been the manager of Lenore's. James and Lenore, now in their 60's, do not come into the restaurant every day, but they maintain a firm hand on all aspects of the business. They screen job applicants, go over the books, check the restaurant for cleanliness, and make sure the waiters and waitresses are polite and helpful. Their son Jack is a part-owner as well, but he works as an accountant for a large firm in Gary and does not participate actively in the day-to-day operations of Lenore's.

George Bernard has a good working relationship with John and Lenore, but he finds them old-fashioned and resistant to change. When George has suggested redecorating the restaurant or slightly altering the menu, they have not agreed with his ideas.

Now, however, George is seeing some real changes that must be addressed: the lunch crowd has been falling off significantly. Customers, he notices, are asking for lighter meals: they do not want the soup, or they want the soup but no entree. When they find that they must pay for soup, salad, and an entree, many of them leave. Fast food restaurants, some with salad bars, are opening in the neighborhood, and businesspeople are heading to them for fast, lighter meals.

George sees that Lenore's is just not responding to people's needs. Soon, he feels sure, the dinner crowd will begin diminishing as well. All Lenore's has to do is become more flexible: offer lighter meals and more a la carte items. Not only will business pick up again, but less food will be thrown out at the end of every day.

But how can George get Lenore and John to listen to his ideas? They have resisted even less radical ideas than this in the past. Their whole concept for the restaurant has been based on large, family-style Italian feasts. Perhaps, George thinks, he should involve their son Jack in the decision making. Jack is more open to change—and he is very interested in making a profit from his share in the business. On the other hand, John and Lenore will not like feeling that the young men are teamed up against them. Besides, Jack is an unknown quantity: he could side with his parents. George will have to be very tactful.

Assignments

1. In class, discuss the communication channel George should use. Should he call for a meeting with Jack, Lenore, and John? Should he first talk with Jack? Should he meet with Lenore and John alone? Or should he put his concerns in a short report addressed to all three?

2. If George decides on a meeting with all three people, what kinds of preparations should he make? Should he try to approach Jack as an ally before the meeting? What kinds of strategies should George use in the meeting? Should George work toward a compromise with the owners?

3. Assume that George has decided to write a letter to Jack inviting him to the meeting and outlining some of his concerns. Write the letter for George. It should be addressed to Mr. Jack Cortese, 3499 Broad Street, Gary, Indiana 89762

4. Assume that George has decided to write a short report to the three members of the Cortese family. Write a recommendation report for George that will tactfully inform them of the customers' needs and persuade the owners to make some changes.

The Clothes Incorporated Case

Ken Guttierrez is in charge of coordinating a new retail outlet being planned by Clothes Incorporated (CI). The new store will be designed in part by a team of architects from Japan who are arriving this week. An American architect will work with the visitors throughout the planning stages—making sure that their ideas stay within budget and that the concepts will work in an American shopping mall.

First, though, Ken must meet with the Japanese visitors in an all-day orientation session during which he will introduce them to the project and to CI's particular needs. He will have to describe American shopping malls to them, outline CI's basic image and customer type, and explain some of the cultural differences the visitors will encounter when working with Americans on the project.

Ken dreads this session. A translator will solve only some of the potential problems. There will be myriads of communication barriers he has not even thought of yet.

To work out a plan for this orientation, he goes to you for help.

Assignments

1. In class, discuss the kinds of communication problems that Ken should be prepared for— besides basic language problems.

2. Where can Ken go to get some information on Japan and its culture so he can be better prepared to deal effectively with the visitors?

3. Write a memo to Ken giving him some pertinent information on where he should hold this orientation session and what sort of materials he should provide the Japanese visitors. Be sure to add any communication hints that you think will make his meeting with the visitors more successful.

Business Writer's
Handbook

Contents

Knowing the principles of good sentence construction, basic grammar, and standard usage is essential to creating effective business documents. This handbook provides an easy reference for many of the problems you may encounter as you revise your writing.

As you study the principles in this handbook, test yourself on the Check Your Knowledge exercises. Answers to these exercises are at the end of the handbook. If you are unfamiliar with grammatical terms, you will find definitions in the Terms to Remember at the end of each section. More extensive definitions, as well as examples, are listed in the Glossary of Grammatical Terms.

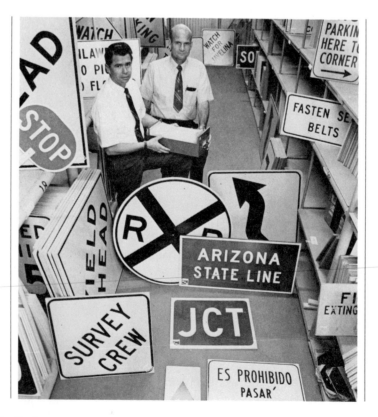

Section 1. Creating Sentences

Sentences are the building blocks of writing. To communicate effectively, writers need to recognize the components of complete and correct sentences. This section will help you to recognize three major pitfalls in sentence construction: fragments, run-on sentences, and comma splices.

Test Your Skills

Can You Name These Grammatical Errors?

Choose the answer that most closely fits the grammatical errors illustrated in the following sentences.

1. I am sure of the results, I checked with both Dana Smith and the group leader.
   a. Parallelism error
   b. Comma splice
   c. Modifier error
2. When you are through reading the report, give it to Tom Higgins or I.
   a. Pronoun case error
   b. Comma splice
   c. Modifier error
3. Having been given the promotion, Henry's salary went up considerably.
   a. Modifier error
   b. Comma splice
   c. Parallelism error

Answers

1b, 2a, 3a

1a. Writing in Complete Sentences

You probably remember this definition: "A sentence is a group of words that contains a subject and verb and expresses a complete thought." To create a complete sentence, then, all you need is a subject (usually someone or something doing an action), a verb (the action), and a complete idea.

   s   v
Jill swims.

(1) *Additional Sentence Components*
   Of course, most sentences are more complicated than just a subject and verb; they may contain a variety of descriptive words and related ideas:

Although she works 10 hours a day, Jill swims energetically every afternoon.

At the core of this sentence, however, are still a subject and verb; without them, a group of words is not a sentence.

(2) *Commands*
   One exception to the standard sentence we have just described is a command or request in which the subject is understood to be *you*, the reader or listener. The command *Sit!* actually means *You, sit!*

(3) *Multiple Subjects and Verbs*
   Many sentences contain more than one subject and verb.

s   s

Jill and Sam correspond with the salespeople every day.

      v   v

Sam reads and revises each report.

Moreover, many verbs are made up of both a main verb (m.v.) and a helping verb (h.v.).

  h.v.   m.v.

I have established the truthfulness of his statement.

      h.v.   m.v.   h.v.   m.v.

The company is investigating the matter and will determine the alternatives.

(4) Questions

In sentences that ask questions, the usual subject + verb order is often changed. The verb may precede the subject.

  v   s

Are you the new president?

  v s

Is this Mike's final decision?

"Sorry, but I'm going to have to issue you a summons for reckless grammar and driving without an apostrophe."

Drawing by Maslin; © 1987 The New Yorker Magazine, Inc.

When a question contains both a helping verb and main verb, the subject often comes between them.

h.v.   s   m.v.
Have you met Norm Pinkerton?

h.v.   s   m.v.
Does the solution meet your approval?

Exercise 1-1. Check Your Knowledge of Subjects and Verbs

Put one line under the subjects of the following sentences. Put two lines under the verbs.

Example: Joseph sees the document.

1. Mr. Freedman has won the sales award.
2. Although dull, the lectures were worthwhile.
3. Please hand me the tape.
4. Will you read the letter to us?
5. The man just won the state lottery.
6. At the end of the hall, Barbara and I saw Mrs. Loomis.
7. Greg changed the tire and then drove to Nashville.
8. The staff has requested a meeting.
9. Has the city condemned the building?
10. Notify me if he calls.

1b. Identifying and Revising Sentence Fragments

A *sentence fragment* is punctuated to look like a sentence, but it is missing at least one of the vital components of a sentence.

(1) *Missing Verb*

Johann Benson, one of the newly hired managers. [fragment]

In the preceding fragment, we have a person's name and a description, but we have no verb, no action. What did Johann Benson *do?*

Johann Benson, one of the newly hired managers, *wrote the report.* [correct]

(2) *Missing Subjects and Verbs*

To ensure a thorough approach. [fragment]

This fragment is a *phrase,* a group of words that has no subject or verb. To revise, add an independent clause, a group of words containing a subject and verb that could stand alone as a sentence.

To ensure a thorough approach, *Mrs. Smith revised the report.* [correct]

(3) *Participles*

Quickly evaluating the applicants. [fragment]

This fragment is also a phrase. The word *evaluating* looks like a verb, but the *ing* tells you that it is not; it is actually a type of verbal called a *participle.* Without helping verbs such as *is, are, will be, has been,* and *should be,* words ending in *ing* are not verbs.

To revise this phrase, you may add an independent clause.

Quickly evaluating the applicants, *I read their application letters.* [correct]

You could also choose to add a subject and a helping verb:

I am quickly evaluating the applicants. [correct]

Gayle, having directed the program. [fragment]

Once again we have a problem with a word ending in *ing*. *Having directed the program* is a participial phrase, so the subject *Gayle* still needs a verb.

Gayle, having directed the program, *resigned*. [sample revision]

Rather than separating the subject and verb, you might want to put the phrase at the beginning of the sentence:

Having directed the program, Gayle resigned. [sample revision]

(4) *Dependent Clauses*

Although the requests have not been processed. [fragment]

This fragment looks suspiciously like a sentence since there is a subject (*requests*), a helping verb (*have been*), and a main verb (*processed*). The problem is the word *Although*. This word, called a subordinate conjunction, prevents the group of words from being a complete thought. When you read the group of words, you want to know something more.

Subordinate conjunctions introduce *dependent clauses,* groups of words that have subjects and verbs but cannot stand on their own as sentences. To revise, you need to add an independent clause.

We are writing the letters although the requests have not been processed. [correct]

Although the requests have not been processed, *they have been evaluated.* [correct]

Some Subordinate Conjunctions

after	although	as	as if
because	before	how	if
in order that	since	though	unless
when	where	while	

Put an *S* after each sentence, an *F* after each fragment. Then revise each fragment so it is a complete sentence.

1. Peter is hiring Dana Williams.
2. Gretchen, speaking on the telephone.
3. Let me know when you find out.
4. Unless you hear from me, I will be in New York.
5. Eliminating the excess paperwork was difficult.
6. To review these documents carefully.
7. If you cannot meet with Fred this morning.
8. Our best client, Henry Forbison.
9. When she arrives, call me.
10. To enjoy the music, Edna raised the volume.

1c. Identifying and Revising Run-On Sentences

A run-on sentence is composed of two or more independent clauses run together without any punctuation.

I saw the error Jane retyped the page. [run-on]

I saw the error is one independent clause, while *Jane retyped the page* is another.

To revise run-on sentences, you have a number of choices. Using different techniques will add variety to your writing.

(1) *A period between the clauses.*

Because an independent clause may stand alone as a sentence, you may separate independent clauses with periods.

The company is bankrupt we are looking for new jobs. [run-on]
The company is bankrupt. We are looking for new jobs. [correct]

(2) *A semicolon between the clauses.*

A semicolon may also be used between independent clauses.

Lance fired the employee now he is interviewing candidates. [run-on]
Lance fired the employee; now he is interviewing candidates. [correct]

(3) *A comma and a coordinate conjunction between the clauses.*

A comma followed by *and, but, so, for, or, nor,* or *yet* may separate independent clauses.

Sales are declining morale is still good. [run-on]

Sales are declining, but morale is still good. [correct]

I am disappointed John is angry. [run-on]

I am disappointed, and John is angry. [correct]

(4) *Dependent and independent clauses*

To revise run-on sentences, you may also turn one of the independent clauses into a dependent clause.

The contract has been signed some decisions have not been made. [run-on]

Although the contract has been signed, some decisions have not been made. [correct]

The contract has been signed even though some decisions have not been made. [correct]

Exercise 1-3. Check Your Knowledge of Run-On Sentences

I. Write *R* after a run-on sentence; write *S* after a correct sentence.

1. Come to lunch if you can the sandwiches are terrific.
2. When I heard the news, I called Fran.
3. The store will open today all the salespeople have been notified.
4. Answer the letter this afternoon it is urgent.
5. Lawrence Mills is the executor contact him if you have questions.

II. Now revise in *two ways* each of the run-on sentences that you marked in Part I of this exercise.

1d. Identifying and Revising Comma Splices

If you can recognize run-on sentences, you should not fall into the trap of creating comma splices.

(1) *Identifying Comma Splices*
Comma splices occur when independent clauses are connected to each other with commas.

Peter Dawes spoke about nuclear power, the crowd applauded. [comma splice]

The word processor is defective, I have been losing files. [comma splice]

(2) *Revising Comma Splices*
To revise comma splices, use the same choices discussed for run-on sentences.

Jane won the award, she also won a week's vacation. [comma splice]

Jane won the award. She also won a week's vacation. [revision with a period after the first clause]

Jane won the award; she also won a week's vacation. [revision with a semicolon after the first clause]

Jane won the award, and she also won a week's vacation. [revision with a comma and a coordinate conjunction after the first clause]

Since Jane won the award, she also won a week's vacation. [revision with a dependent and an independent clause]

(3) *Transitional Words*
Transitional words such as *however* and *therefore* may not be used with commas to connect independent clauses. If you do, you create a comma splice.

I will leave in February, however, I will be back in June. [comma splice]

I will be back in February; however, I will be back in June. [correct]

Exercise 1-4. Check Your Knowledge of Comma Splices

Put a *C* after each comma splice. Put an *S* after each correct sentence. Then revise each comma splice so it is a correct sentence.

1. FCD Corporation is expanding, but it is not diversifying.
2. I voted for Gertrude Hammer, she was not elected.
3. This department, however, will stay open on Christmas Day.
4. Give me a call, I will be here tomorrow.
5. When Jim arrives, send him into the library.
6. Jane has resigned, therefore, I will be working for Karen.
7. Until noon, we will be working in the factory.
8. Having arranged the meeting, Ed cancelled it.
9. The company has changed direction, so we are writing new personnel manuals.
10. At the end of the seminar, speak to the participants, they will want to hear from you.

Terms to Remember

Comma splice: two independent clauses connected only by a comma

Coordinate conjunction: *and, but, nor, for, or, so,* and *yet.* May be used with a comma to separate two independent clauses.

Dependent clause: group of words that contains a subject and verb but cannot stand alone as a sentence

Fragment: group of words that is punctuated to look like a sentence but is missing at least one of the vital components of a sentence

Participle: word formed from a verb that acts as a descriptive word rather than an action. Cannot be used alone as a verb.

Phrase: group of related words that does not contain a subject and verb

Run-on sentence: two or more independent clauses run together without punctuation

Sentence: group of words that contains a subject and verb and expresses a complete thought

Subordinate conjunction: words such as *although, because, if,* and *when* that usually introduce dependent clauses

Questions for Review and Discussion

1. Why should a writer pay attention to the conventions of sentence construction?
2. Describe three methods a writer can use to separate independent clauses.

1. Examine each of the following groups of words punctuated to look like sentences. Write *S* after each correct sentence; *F* after each sentence fragment; *R* after each run-on sentence; and *C* after each comma splice.
   a. I am sure that Jane is the culprit.
   b. Kelley is here, where is Sam?
   c. The company is changing profits are rising.
   d. Let me speak to Sara.
   e. Is there a chance we can be on time?
   f. I know the problem, we are losing interest in the case.
   g. Bill, having finished his dinner.
   h. The new computer is down Pam is working on it.
   i. Because the temperature is dropping below zero tonight.
   j. My brother, who recently joined the army.

2. Correct the fragments, run-ons, and comma splices you identified in Exercise 1.

3. Revise any sentence errors in the following memo. Do not change correct sentences.

TO: All Staff
FROM: Alyce Meredith
SUBJECT: Staff Meetings
DATE: February 3, 19xx

As you know, we have been meeting every Wednesday to discuss our successes and our problems with products. These meetings have been productive, however, they are taking up more time than we can spare. From now on we will meet every three weeks this schedule should keep us in touch with each other without slowing down our work. And without hurting our sales efforts.

Our next meeting will be at 9:30 a.m. on Monday, February 24.

Section 2. Writing Grammatically

Grammatical writing heightens your credibility with your reader and also makes your message clearer and sharper. Most grammar rules were devised to reduce ambiguity and confusion in written and spoken messages, not to create problems for unwary writers.

Studying the grammar hints in the following pages will help you avoid some of the pitfalls awaiting the business writer. This section, however, provides only highlights of English grammar. For a more thorough examination of grammar conventions, refer to a comprehensive writing handbook or grammar text.

2a. Subject/Verb Agreement

In grammatical sentences, subjects *agree* with verbs. Verbs must agree with their subjects in number (singular or plural) and person (first, second, or third). A regular verb has only two forms in the present tense:

	Singular	*Plural*
First person	I swim	we swim
Second person	you swim	you swim
Third person	*he, she, it swims*	they swim

In the present tense, third-person singular verbs end in *s*; *is, has, does, wins*. When revising and proofreading, you need to check the number and person of your subject; if it is third-person singular and the corresponding main or helping verb is in the present tense, then that verb must end in *s*.

> Larry delivers messages. [not *Larry deliver*]
>
> Larry has delivered the message. [not *Larry have delivered*]

We say and write most verbs correctly most of the time. Problems occur most commonly in the following situations.

(1) *Separation of Subject and Verb*.

Your subject may be some distance from your verb; check to make sure you are agreeing the verb with the correct word.

> One of these details confuse me. [incorrect: The subject is *one*, not details.]
>
> One of these details confuses me. [correct]

> The efficiency of the procedures have been increased. [incorrect: The subject is *efficiency*, not *procedures*.]
>
> The efficiency of the procedure has been increased. [correct]

(2) *Reversal of Subject and Verb*

We expect the subject to precede the verb, but sometimes the usual order is reversed. Watch particularly for sentences beginning with *There*.

> There has been several problems with the pipes. [incorrect: The subject is *problems*.]

There have been several problems with the pipes. [correct]

At the end of the week comes two important meetings. [incorrect: The subject is *meetings.*]

At the end of the week come two important meetings. [correct]

(3) *Titles and Collective Nouns*

Collective nouns refer to groups of people or things: *management, corporation, army, group.* Usually these words are singular.

The company is going bankrupt. [not *are going*]

Similarly, the names of companies, books, records, and so on are singular.

Greyson and Herries, Inc. has opened a new office. [not *have opened*]

The University of Colorado have hired new faculty. [incorrect]

The University of Colorado has hired new faculty. [correct]

(4) *Indefinite Pronouns*

Some indefinite pronouns are singular, while others are plural; some change according to their meaning.

Some Indefinite Pronouns

Singular		Plural	Singular/Plural
anybody	neither	both	all
each	nobody	few	any
everybody	no one	many	more
either	one	others	most
everyone	someone	several	none

If a singular indefinite pronoun is the subject of your sentence, make sure the verb is singular.

Each of the women have a computer. [incorrect: The subject is *each.*]
Each of the women has a computer. [correct]

If your subject is an indefinite pronoun that may be either singular or plural, you must check to see what the pronoun is describing.

Most of the papers *have* gone. [*papers* is plural]
Most of the initiative *has* gone. [*initiative* is singular]

(5) *AND Sentences*

When subjects are connected by *and*, they require a plural verb.

Honesty and effort *are* his strong points.

(6) *OR/NOR Sentences*

When subjects are connected by *or* or *nor*, the verb will agree with the subject closest to the verb.

> Either Ellen or Thad *is* planning the reception.
>
> Neither Randy nor his friends *are* going to attend.
>
> My brothers or my sister *has developed* this plan.

Exercise 2-1. Check Your Knowledge of Subject/Verb Agreement

Correct any subject/verb agreement errors in the following sentences by changing the verbs.

1. Neither one of the applicants have given me a resume.
2. There goes Mr. and Mrs. Rennells.
3. Both David and Patricia agree on these points.
4. Do any of these employees have the file?
5. Bedford, James, & Dowson are a top investment firm.
6. Greg and his friend Jim have the answer for you.
7. In the middle of the book comes some surprises.
8. Each of the variables need to be considered.
9. Are either of the secretaries applying for the promotion?
10. The convenience of these new products are outstanding.

2b. Pronoun Agreement

Many pronouns are words used to replace nouns. Although pronouns are useful parts of speech, they must be handled carefully. Your readers must easily recognize the *antecedent* of the pronoun, the noun each pronoun is replacing; moreover, you must make sure the pronoun agrees with the antecedent in number, person, and gender (masculine, feminine, or neuter).

Noun	*Qualities*	*Pronoun*
woman	singlar, third person, feminine	she, her
father	singular, third person, masculine	he, him
management	singular, third person, neuter	it
uncles	plural, third person, masculine	they, them
sisters	plural, third person, feminine	they, them
desks	plural, third person, neuter	they, them

(1) *Agreement of Number*

The most common pronoun agreement problems occur when writers switch from singular nouns or pronouns to plural pronouns.

> When I saw my instructor today, *they* gave me the textbook. [incorrect: *instructor* is singular, so the pronoun must be *he* or *she*, depending on the gender of the instructor.]

If a singular indefinite pronoun is the subject of your sentence, the pronouns referring to it must also be singular.

Each of the men gave me their opinion. [incorrect: *Each* is singular, but *their* is plural.]

Each of the men gave me his opinion. [correct: the pronoun is singular and masculine.]

If a subject is a collective noun, the pronouns referring to the subject are usually singular.

The company is expanding their territory. [incorrect: *company* is singular, but *their* is plural.]

The company is expanding its territory. [correct]

(2) *Agreement of Person*

If a noun or pronoun is in the third person, you cannot replace it with *you,* a second-person pronoun.

Everyone here can get your lunch at the counter. [incorrect: *Everyone* is a third-person pronoun, but *your* is a second-person pronoun.]

Everyone here can get his or her lunch at the counter. [correct]

You can get your lunch at the counter. [correct]

(3) *Agreement of Gender*

In the example in the preceding section, the subject *everyone* is singular but has no gender. The singular pronoun that follows *everyone,* however, must indicate gender. In the past, writers used the masculine singular pronouns even when the group referred to was both male and female. To avoid sexist references, that approach has been largely replaced by pronouns that use both genders: *his or her, he and she, he/she, him/her,* and *s/he.*

All of these options are somewhat unwieldy. To simplify your sentences, you may want to use plural subject pronouns more frequently. Instead of writing, *Each of the students brought in his/her projects,* you can write, *All of the students brought in their projects.*

If you refer to a specific individual, however, you will have to designate the person's gender.

When I asked the manager for help, he/she refused. [incorrect: The manager must be either male or female, so *he/she* must be changed to either *he* or *she.*]

Exercise 2-2. Check Your Knowledge of Agreement

Correct any errors you see in the following sentences.

1. When department heads meet this week, they will decide the issue.
2. If you see either of the new employees, give them this message.
3. When my supervisor returns from Japan, he will meet with the assistant manager.
4. Neither of the attorneys has brought their own lunch.
5. Each senior should attend this lecture before you graduate.

6. Every one of the secretaries has given me his/her resume.

7. Len and Marie have given me his/her approval.

8. At the end of the president's tour, he/she met with upper management.

9. All the appendices have been replaced in their folders.

10. The corporation is opening their new offices.

2c. Making Clear Pronoun References

Pronoun reference is one of the most common problems that plague unwary writers.

(1) *Pronoun Reference*

Because pronouns take the place of nouns in a sentence, make sure your reader knows which noun is being replaced.

> Hank gave Bill his notebook. [confusing: *his* could refer to either Hank or Bill.]
>
> Hank returned Bill's book to him. [clear]

(2) *Relative and Demonstrative Pronouns*

Pronouns such as *which, this, these, those,* and *that* also need to be clearly defined in your writing. Make sure each of them replaces a particular noun.

> The car skidded on the highway and almost hit a trailer. This terrified Patricia. [confusing: Did the skid or almost hitting the trailer terrify her?]
>
> The car skidded on the highway and almost hit a trailer, which terrified Patricia. [confusing: Did the *trailer* terrify her?]
>
> The car skidded on the highway and almost hit a trailer. The near-accident terrified Patricia. [clear]
>
> When her car skidded on the highway and almost hit a trailer, Patricia was terrified. [clear]

2d. Using the Correct Pronoun Case

Unlike nouns, pronouns change form depending on their function in a sentence. You need to know whether a pronoun is functioning as a subject or object.

Subject Pronouns	Object Pronouns
I	me
you	you
he	him
she	her
it	it
we	us
they	them
who	whom

(1) *Compound Subjects and Objects*

Do not get confused if your sentence has more than one subject or object: the form of the pronoun remains the same regardless of other subjects or objects.

Karen and him have been elected. [incorrect]

Karen and he have been elected. [correct: *he* is part of the subject.]

The Garrahers are visiting Maryanne and I. [incorrect]

The Garrahers are visiting Maryanne and me. [correct: *me* is part of the direct object.]

Give the book to Ursula and I. [incorrect]

Give the book to Ursula and me. [correct: *me* is an object of the preposition *to.*]

(2) *Comparisons with THAN and AS.*

Than and *as* often introduce new clauses that require a subject pronoun.

Helena is taller than me. [incorrect]

Helena is taller than I. [correct: *than* actually introduces a clause in which the verb *am* is understood.]

Helena is taller than I am. [correct]

Jack is as capable as them. [incorrect]

Jack is as capable as they. [correct]

Jack is as capable as they are. [correct]

(3) *Appositives*

An appositive is a description following a noun or pronoun. If an appositive is a pronoun, it should be in the same case as the noun it follows.

My friends—Tom and him—are arriving today. [incorrect]

My friends—Tom and he—are arriving today. [correct: *he* is part of the description of the subject.]

They were welcoming the guests—Kim and I. [incorrect]

They were welcoming the guests—Kim and me. [correct: *me* is part of the description of the object.]

(4) *WHO and WHOM*

Who and *whom* function in the same way as *he* and *him* and *she* and *her*. Use *who* for the subjects of clauses and *whom* for objects.

Who is our chairperson? [*Who* is the subject]

Whom did we elect? [*Whom* is the direct object: *we* is the subject.]

Whom is the gift for? [*Whom* is the object of the preposition *for.* You could write, *For whom is the gift?*]

Let me speak to whoever has the information. [*Whoever* is the subject of the verb *has.*]

Let me speak to whomever you recommend. [*Whomever* is the object of the verb *recommend.*]

Correct any pronoun errors in the following sentences.

1. Between you and I, this problem is getting worse.
2. Who will we send to Washington this spring?
3. She is more creative than me, but she is less reliable.
4. When the boat docked at the pier, it was on fire.
5. Let Henry and I know when you decide.
6. Felicia and him are the nominees.
7. We have bought a new building, which we are redecorating.
8. Neither Janice nor I have the answer.
9. Renee will applaud anyone who speaks to us.
10. The managers—Pete and her—are late for work today.

2e. Using Modifiers

Modifiers are descriptive words, phrases, and clauses.

We bought expensive wallpaper. [*Expensive* is an adjective modifying *wallpaper.*]

The supervisor worked energetically. [*Energetically* is an adverb modifying *worked.*]

We wrote a proposal to raise funds. [*To raise funds* is a phrase modifying *proposal.*]

Reading quickly, Sam spotted the error. [*Reading quickly* is a phrase modifying *Sam.*]

The man who is wearing a hat is my cousin. [*Who is wearing a hat* is a clause modifying *man.*]

(1) Adjectives and Adverbs

Adjectives modify nouns; do not use them to describe other parts of your sentence. Adverbs (which often end in *ly*) are used to describe verbs, adjectives, and other adverbs.

He speaks quick. [incorrect]

He speaks quickly. [correct: *quickly* modifies the verb *speaks.*]

She is real enthusiastic. [incorrect]

She is really enthusiastic. [correct: *really* is an adverb modifying the adjective *enthusiastic.*]

(2) Misplaced Modifiers

Place modifiers as close as possible to the words they describe. Do not make your reader do your work for you.

James Gallagher decided to head downtown for some office supplies quickly. [unclear: Did he decide quickly or decide to head downtown quickly?]

James Gallagher quickly decided to head downtown for some office supplies. [clear]

James Gallagher decided to head downtown quickly for some office supplies. [clear]

Misplaced modifiers can be ridiculous as well as ungrammatical.

Francine walked her dog wearing a raincoat. [poor]

Wearing a raincoat, Francine walked her dog. [correct]

Covered with peanut butter, I ate the toast. [poor]

I ate the toast that was covered with peanut butter. [correct]

(3) Dangling Modifers

In sentences with dangling modifiers, the word being described never actually appears in the sentence. Usually dangling modifiers are stuck onto the beginning or ending of a sentence.

Writing quickly, the report was finished in two days. [incorrect: *Who* was writing quickly?]

Writing quickly, we finished the report in two days. [correct: The modifier describes the subject, *we.*]

Note that dangling modifiers cannot be fixed simply by moving them:

The report was finished in two days, writing quickly. [incorrect]

To revise a dangling modifier, you must either change the modifier or change the rest of the sentence.

Heading for Texas, the weather got warmer. [incorrect]

While we were heading for Texas, the weather got warmer. [correct: *we* is now the subject of the dependent clause.]

Heading for Texas, we experienced warmer weather. [correct: *we* is now the subject of the independent clause.]

The modifier must describe a subject or object, not a possessive noun or pronoun.

Having graduated, Nora's job began. [incorrect: Her *job* did not graduate.]

When Nora graduated, her job began. [correct]

Having graduated, Nora began her job. [correct]

Exercise 2-4. Check Your Knowledge of Modifiers

Revise any modifier errors in the following sentences. (There may be more than one way to revise.)

1. The blue carpet with red binding has been rolled up in the corridor.
2. Running quickly, my briefcase dropped.
3. Lenore is not real happy with the change in procedures that Greg has developed.
4. As a new employee, this sheet is important to you.
5. Let me know when you want to go to Dallas as soon as possible.
6. Having finished the memo, Darlene drafted a brief letter.
7. After making copies of the brochure, several mistakes were found in the copy.
8. His views are realistic, but his speeches are quite dull.
9. When you finish lunch, come to my office.
10. He spoke to the crowd using a microphone.

2f. Creating Parallel Sentences

If you balance two or more items in a sentence, each item should be in the same grammatical form.

We are interested in swimming, jogging, and to play tennis. [incorrect]

We are interested in swimming, jogging, and playing tennis. [correct]

We like to swim, jog, and play tennis. [correct]

Please send this memo to the clerical staff, new employees, and to your supervisor. [incorrect]

Please send this memo to the clerical staff, to new employees, and to your supervisor. [correct]

Please send this memo to the clerical staff, new employees, and your supervisor. [correct]

(1) Lists

If you use a list in a memo, letter, or report, each item in the list should be parallel.

At the end of the day, follow these procedures:
1. Shut off the air conditioning.
2. Lock the back doors.
3. The lights should be turned off. [incorrect]

At the end of the day, follow these procedures:
1. Shut off the air conditioning.
2. Lock the back doors.
3. Turn off the lights. [correct]

At the end of the day, check the following items:
1. air conditioning
2. back doors
3. turn off lights [incorrect]

At the end of the day, check the following items:
1. air conditioning
2. back doors
3. lights [correct]

(2) Correlative Conjunctions

When you have conjunction pairs such as *either . . . or, neither . . . nor, both . . . and*, and *not only . . . but also*, the words following the second part of the pair should be in the same grammatical form as those following the first part.

We have both tomatoes and we have lettuce. [incorrect]

We have both tomatoes and lettuce. [correct: Nouns follow each part of the conjunction pair.]

They have not only graduated from college but also they have published books. [incorrect]

They have not only graduated from college but also published books. [correct: A main verb follows each conjunction.]

They not only have graduated from college but also have published books. [correct: A helping verb and main verb follow each conjunction.]

Exercise 2-5. Check Your Knowledge of Parallelism

Fix any parallelism errors in the following sentences. There may be more than one way to revise.

1. Please let me know if you have any answers, suggestions, or if you have ideas.
2. This is the first time that we have both introduced a new product and a new product line.
3. She is both capable and intelligent.
4. To enter the program:
   1. Push the POWER button to ON.
   2. Insert diskette in Drive A.
   3. Type GO.

5. Organizing the staff, meeting the managers, and learning the procedures have exhausted Gregory.
6. We will either move to New York or will stay in Milwaukee.
7. Let me know if you want to meet someone or to ask a question.
8. Both Lollie and her cousins are working for IBM and taking yoga lessons.
9. Either this company will expand or go bankrupt.
10. The lessons we learned were expensive, obvious, and they were painful.

Terms to Remember

Adjective: word describing a noun or pronoun

Adverb: word describing a verb, adjective, adverb, or clause

Antecedent: the word or group of words replaced by a pronoun.

Appositive: description following a noun or pronoun

Case: the form of a noun or pronoun that indicates the function of that word in the sentence

Correlative conjunctions: paired conjunctions that require a grammatical balance in the sentence

Dangling modifier: modifier that does not describe any element in the sentence in which it appears

Gender: the aspect of a noun or pronoun that indicates whether it is masculine, feminine, or neuter

Indefinite pronoun: pronoun such as *each* and *everyone* that makes general rather than specific references to people or things

Misplaced modifier: modifier placed next to an element that it does not describe

Modifier: descriptive word or group of words

Number: the aspect of a noun, pronoun, or verb that indicates whether it is singular or plural

Objective case: form of pronouns used for direct objects, indirect objects, objects of prepositions, and appositives describing objects

Parallelism: a grammatical balance of two or more items in a sentence

Person: the aspect of a noun, pronoun, or verb that indicates whether it refers to the person speaking (first person), the person spoken to (second person), or the person, place, or thing spoken about (third person)

Possessive case: form of nouns and pronouns used to indicate ownership

Pronoun references: clear correspondence between pronouns and antecedents

Subjective case: form of pronouns used for the subjects of clauses, for complements, and for appositives describing subjects

Subject/verb agreement: correspondence between verbs and subjects in number and person

Questions for Review and Discussion

1. Most of us do not speak perfectly grammatical English all the time. Why is good grammar more important on the written page than in the spoken language?
2. Give three examples of singular indefinite pronouns. Why should we remember these pronouns?
3. Give three examples of correlative conjunctions. Why should we remember these conjunctions?

Exercises

1. Review a piece of writing you have done for another class. Now that you have studied this section of *Business Writer's Handbook*, can you spot any errors in that piece of writing? Write out the sentences that contain an error; then write a revised version of each sentence.
2. Check the underlined words in each of the following sentences. If an underlined word is correct, put a C over the word. If an underlined word is incorrect, cross it out and replace it with a correct form.
    a. Each of the men <u>have</u> brought <u>their</u> own books.
    b. <u>Is</u> either of your friends expected today?
    c. Both Jim and Mark <u>do</u> have exams this week.
    d. There <u>appears</u> to be some errors in the report.
    e. The new management <u>has</u> exceeded <u>their</u> budget.
    f. <u>Do</u> you accountants know the correct answer?
    g. At the end of the street <u>stands</u> two policemen.
    h. The success of our projects <u>lie</u> solely with you and <u>I</u>.
    i. Neither of us <u>have</u> examined the problem.
    j. <u>Has</u> either of the students graduated?
3. Fix any grammatical errors in the following sentences. Do not change correct sentences.
    a. The recommendations made by Mr. Peters has not yet been implemented.
    b. My father is taller than me, but he weighs less.
    c. I am real pleased to be here today with you both.
    d. Have either of the marketing majors seen this film?
    e. I have been promised a raise, it is long overdue.
    f. Gerri is neither as tired nor is she as bored as we are.
    g. While interviewing these candidates, we discovered some interesting information.
    h. Evaluating and implementing these programs has been successful so far.
    i. Who do you think should be our next supervisor?
    j. Please give a questionnaire to each student who has decided on their major.
4. Fix any grammatical errors in the following memo. Do not change correct sentences.

```
TO:       All Staff
FROM:     Charlie Burch
SUBJECT:  Customer Service
DATE:     April 8, 19xx
```

While evaluating customer correspondence from the past three months, there seems to be several problem areas we should face. The following list contains some hints for improving customer service.

1. If a customer is browsing and does not want to be helped, leave them alone. Several customers have complained that they are being "badgered" by employees.
2. If the store is crowded, tell each customer waiting for service that you will be with them as soon as you can. If possible, ask Susan or I for assistance.
3. When customers return items without receipts, come to me immediately, I will handle the situation.
4. When writing up sales, sales prices

should be checked carefully. Customers have complained that salespeople are trying to cheat them out of their discounts.

Thanks for your attention, I am sure our customer complaints will decrease from now on.

5. After working for three months as head of the Women's Clothing Department at Garrison's Department Store, Denise Murchison saw the sales staff had some problems handling telephone orders. To make the process more accurate and efficient, she instituted some changes that she summed up in a memo.

Revise the memo so it is free of grammatical and sentence errors.

```
TO:      All Sales Staff
FROM:    Denise Murchison
SUBJECT: Telephone Orders
DATE:    July 6, 19xx
```

Since beginning work in this department in April, several problems have cropped up with regard to orders that are late and not received. To facilitate the ordering process, I have established the following new procedures. Each of you are responsible for both learning these procedures and for implementing them.

1. When you take an order from a customer, make sure you get their correct address and telephone number. Repeat all pertinent information back to them, write it clearly on a duplicate order form.
2. If a customer has questions you cannot answer, refer the person to Fran Charleton or I for more information.
3. Having placed a telephone order, a post card should be sent to the customer repeating all details of the transaction.
4. If a customer does not receive an item by the time specified, check with not only the supplier but also with the Shipping Department before referring the problem to me.

Thanks for your cooperation.

Section 3. Punctuating Business Writing

Punctuation marks are an important part of business writing. They not only act as signposts to make your writing easier to understand but also help to reduce ambiguity and to emphasize major points. Adhering to the conventions of punctuation will increase the credibility and readability of your business prose.

As a reader, you expect correctly punctuated writing; as a writer, you should make sure you have a good grasp of the most common conventions of punctuation outlined in the following pages. Like Part 2 of this handbook, however, this section is only a review. For a complete guide to punctuation, refer to a comprehensive writing handbook.

3a. Using Periods

Periods are used to indicate the end of most sentences and to mark most abbreviations.

(1) *Declarative Sentences*
   Put periods at the end of sentences that make a statement.

   The company was founded in 1982.

   Jane said, "The coffee is here."

(2) *Requests*
   Put periods at the end of sentences that make a request.

   Please file these papers.

   Come to the hotel at noon.

(3) *Indirect Questions*
   Put periods at the end of sentences that state questions indirectly.

   I wondered if the company had gone bankrupt.

   He asked if the profit and loss statement was complete.

(4) *Abbreviations*
   Put periods after most abbreviations.

   Dr. Michaels is in town.

   Carleton, Inc. is a huge multinational company.

   If a sentence ends with an abbreviation, use only one period.

   We will leave at 2 p.m.

3b. Using Question Marks

Use question marks to ask direct questions.

   Do you want to defer your payments?

   Hank asked, "Have you met Mrs. Greeley?"

Note the difference between direct questions and the indirect questions illustrated in 3a(3).

3c. Using Exclamation Points

Use exclamation points to show emotion.

> Boy! We had a great day!
> Hello! I am so surprised to see you.

Exclamation points are used infrequently in business writing.

Exercise 3-1. Check Your Knowledge of Periods, Question Marks, and Exclamation Points

Correct any punctuation errors in the following sentences. Some sentences may be correct.

1. I would like to request an interview at your convenience.
2. Frederick asked if we would consider lowering our prices?
3. "Yes," shouted the crowd enthusiastically.
4. Please let me know if you will consider my request?
5. This is the company's first venture in the U.S..

3d. Using Commas

Commas, which usually indicate a brief pause in a sentence, help readers to recognize relationships among sentence elements. Comma usage is governed for the most part by specific conventions with which business writers should be familiar.

(1) *With Conjunctions Between Main Clauses*
Use a comma before a coordinating conjunction connecting two main clauses.

> Roy has bought the estate, but I will continue to manage it.
> The corporation is expanding, so we are opening an office in LaPorte.

Note: Remember that the conjunction after the comma is necessary. If you separate two main clauses with only a comma, you create a comma splice (see 1d).

(2) *Introductory Dependent Clauses*
Use a comma after a dependent clause at the opening of a sentence.

> When I arrived, the meeting began.
> After you return the book, give me a call.

(3) *Long Introductory Prepositional Phrases*
Put a comma after an introductory prepositional phrase of more than four words.

> Of all the people surveyed, Henry was the only one who answered this question.
> At the turn of the century, this company was founded.

(4) *Introductory Verbal Phrases*

Put a comma after an introductory phrase that begins with a verb.

Typing quickly, I finished the report in two hours.

To get here on time, take the shuttle bus.

(5) *Items in Series*

Put a comma after each item in a series.

We have ordered typing paper, staples, and floppy disks.

Greg ate ham and cheese sandwiches, pickles, and potato chips.

(6) *Modifiers*

Use commas between modifiers describing the same word or words.

He is an intelligent, creative employee. [*Intelligent* and *creative* are modifying *employee.*]

The clean, neat, and attractive office belongs to Kim. [*Clean*, *neat*, and *attractive* modify *office.*]

Do *not* use commas if modifiers are not describing the same word.

I bought a *bright orange* dress.

In the preceding example, *bright* is modifying *orange*, so no comma comes between the two modifiers.

(7) *Appositives*

Put commas on both sides of appositives, descriptions of words set beside nouns to describe them.

Mr. Bingley, an accountant, works upstairs.

Albany, the capital of New York, is two hundred miles from here.

(8) *Direct Address*

When you address a person in a sentence, use commas to set off the direct address.

Please, Mrs. King, let me explain the situation.

Mr. Rowley, I hope you will meet with me on Tuesday.

(9) *Nonessential Descriptive Clauses*

Use commas on both sides of descriptive clauses beginning with *which* or *who* that are not essential to the main point of the sentence.

My attorney, who used to be a football player, wrote the letter.

The report, which has a red cover, is on the table.

(10) *Days of the Week*

Put a comma after the day of the week when it is followed by the date.

Our appointment was set for Tuesday, February 12.

(11) *Dates*

Use a comma after the date when it is followed by the year.

I will graduate on June 6, 1990.

Put a comma after the year when it is preceded by the date.

She was born on Monday, March 31, 1987, at 11 a.m.

(12) Addresses

Put a comma after the city when it is followed by the state; put a comma after a city when it is followed by a county or country.

He is a native of Albany, New York.

We moved the convention to London, England.

Put a comma after the state or country when it is preceded by the city.

I believe that El Paso, Texas, should be our choice.

Ted lived in Paris, France, for eighteen years.

(13) Numbers

Use commas to break up long numbers. Counting from the right, put a comma after every three digits.

We have bought 3,267 bushels of potatoes.

I estimate the company could gain $34,000,000.

(14) Direct Quotations

Use commas to set off the exact words someone has written or spoken.

I asked, "Which lever do I pull?"

"Please listen carefully," said Greta.

"This is the end," said Chris, "of the whole problem."

(15) Compound Subjects, Verbs, and Direct Objects

Do *not* use commas between two subjects, two verbs, or two direct objects.

Jerry and Fran went sailing on Tuesday. [compound subjects]

Hilda read the report and edited it. [compound verbs]

The department has encouraged education and teamwork. [compound direct objects]

(16) THAT Clauses

Do *not* use a comma before a clause beginning with *that*.

This is the problem that we are facing.

I know that you have the answer.

(17) Short Internal Phrases

Do *not* use commas to set off short prepositional phrases in the middle or at the end of sentences.

I hope to bring the equipment with me from Tokyo in the spring.

My office is in the east wing at the end of the hall.

Fix any punctuation errors in the following sentences. Some sentences may be correct.

1. Des Moines, Iowa is building a beautiful convention center.
2. Our company which is facing bankruptcy has terminated over a hundred employees.
3. "I have not seen the data," explained Dave, "but I understand the concepts."
4. I began work here on January 23, 1923 at 9:30 a.m.
5. Mike Tanner, an engineer, and Karen Smith, a geologist, have designed, and implemented this plan.
6. "At the end of the fall semester I will receive my degree in economics," said Cathy.
7. Please tell me if this is the report, that Fred Perry recommended we read.
8. Rummaging through his desk Mike found old credit cards, golf balls, and thumb tacks.
9. "George Chalmers, my assistant, is on vacation but you may speak with Ed Timms," said Margaret Wasserman.
10. When we moved into this office in November we had to paint all the walls, and refinish the floors.

3e. Using Semicolons

Semicolons indicate a weaker break in a sentence than a period but a stronger break than a comma. Semicolons are usually used between two independent clauses or, at times, between items in a series.

(1) *Between Independent Clauses*
As discussed in 1c(2), semicolons may separate two independent clauses.

Greg is my friend; Frank is my cousin.

This is the train to Green Bay; that is the train to Eau Claire.

(2) *Listed Items*
Semicolons are used to reduce confusion in lists when the listed items contain commas.

We wrote to people in Paris, France; Munich, Germany; and London, England.

The vice-president commanded James Slaney, Head Programmer; Annette Carlson, Manager; and Lynne Bache, Assistant Controller.

(3) *Items of Unequal Grammatical Rank*
Do *not* use semicolons to separate dissimilar grammatical elements such as independent and dependent clauses.

When I am finished with the memo; I will go to lunch [incorrect]

When I am finished with the memo, I will go to lunch. [correct]

Do *not* use semicolons between clauses and phrases.

I am working for the accounting department; not for the production department [incorrect]

I am working for the accounting department, not for the production department. [correct]

3f. Using Colons

Colons usually introduce and highlight the words that follow them.

(1) *Salutations*
Use colons after salutations in business letters.

Dear Mr. Smith:
Dear Editor:

(2) *Explanations and Series*
Colons often precede explanations and series.

I left the job for one reason: low pay.
The memo focuses on three areas: employees, clients, and vendors.

(3) *Long Quotations*
Colons precede long quotations.

At his farewell dinner, Mark Erenhart said: "I have long been aware that this company needs to expand operations, to bring greater innovation and variety to its products and management. I hope the new generation of managers I see here tonight will not be afraid to make some changes and to plan for the future."

3g. Using Apostrophes

Apostrophes are used to indicate ownership, some plurals, and contractions.

(1) *Possessive Case of Nouns*
Use an apostrophe to indicate the possessive case of nouns. Note that an apostrophe + *s* follows singular and plural nouns that do not end in *s*. The apostrophe alone follows plural nouns that end in *s*.

The company bought Mary Foster's apartment building after her father's death in 1987. [*Foster* and *father* do not end in *s*.]

The children's outfits were designed by my brother John's wife. [*Children* and *John* do not end in *s*.]

The secretaries' luncheon has been postponed. [*Secretaries* is a plural noun that ends in *s*.]

If the singular form of a noun ends in *s*, add an apostrophe + *s* unless the second *s* makes pronunciation difficult.

Janet Hanks's address was changed this week. [*Hanks* ends in *s* in the singular form.]

Aristophanes' plays are still performed. [The addition of *s* after the apostrophe would make pronunciation difficult.]

(2) *Indefinite Pronouns*
Use apostrophes to indicate the possessive case of indefinite pronouns.

I use everybody's telephone.
This matter is no one's business.

Do *not* use apostrophes to indicate the possessive case of personal pronouns.

> The boat is ours, not theirs.
>
> Have you put the book in its place?

(3) *Plurals of Letters and Numbers*
Use apostrophes to form the plural of letters and numbers.

> The typist has missed the 3's and the *b*'s in this paragraph.
>
> We are hoping the Oakland A's will win the game.

(4) *Plurals of Abbreviations*
If you choose, you may use apostrophes to form the plural of abbreviated words.

> The CPA's [or CPAs] are meeting in Chicago.
>
> We are hiring three MBA's [or MBAs].

(5) *Contractions*
Use apostrophes to form contractions.

> She can't use the extra equipment.
>
> I shouldn't be telling you this.

Note: Contractions are too informal for some business writing. Delete contractions from reports, job application letters, and other formal correspondence.

3h. Using Dashes

While dashes set off nonessential material, they also draw attention to the material and highlight it.

(1) *Changes in thought*
Use dashes to indicate sudden changes in thought.

> I was going to remind you—but I am sure you will remember.
>
> This sandwich—I wish I had two of them—is delicious.

(2) *Examples*
Use dashes to emphasize examples.

> This is one of our best ads—for Wink Lotion.

(3) *Parenthetical Information*
Use dashes to highlight parenthetical information.

> Susan Armstrong—my oldest friend—won the award.

Note: Since most keyboards do not have dashes, use two hyphens to indicate a dash. There should be no space preceding or following dashes.

3i. Using Hyphens

Hyphens allow a typist to break a word into two lines. Hyphens are also used in numbers and compound words.

(1) *At the End of Lines*

If you cannot fit a word of more than one syllable on one line, you may put a hyphen between syllables and continue the word on the next line.

> Now the team must face the awesome challenge of inter-
> national competition.

Do *not* break up one-syllable words or leave single letters at the end or beginning of lines.

> The garage may be reached by going thr-
> ough the basement. [incorrect]

> The garage may be reached by going through
> the basement. [correct]

> Karen and Gregory have acquired an immense bo-
> a constrictor. [incorrect]

> Karen and Gregory have acquired an immense boa
> constrictor. [correct]

(2) *Numbers over Twenty*

Use hyphens when writing out numbers over twenty.

> Thirty-two people have arrived already.

> Almost one hundred forty-nine letters have been sent.

(3) *Compound Words*

Use hyphens to break up some compound words. Check your dictionary if you are unsure whether a compound requires a hyphen.

> Georgia is my mother-in-law.

> Theresa found the office topsy-turvy.

Some words formed from a prefix and a root word require a hyphen.

> He is a self-centered person.

> Hilary calls herself a quasi-intellectual.

Compound adjectives formed from a number and a noun require a hyphen.

> Henry bought a two-pound bag of potatoes.

> I need a three-inch piece of pipe.

Exercise 3-3. Check Your Knowledge of Semicolons, Colons, Apostrophes, Dashes, and Hyphens

Fix any punctuation errors in the following sentences. Some sentences may be correct.

1. The mens department is being redecorated to make more room for suits and overcoats; not to make more room for sweatsuits.

2. I am leaving this company for the following reasons; low wages, poor management, and high pressure.

3. If you have seen Harrys report—it's on my desk—you'll understand why I am upset.

4. We gave our grandson a Jack in the box for Christmas, but he was terrified of it: however, he wasn't afraid of the Godzilla monster his father gave him.

5. By the end of the twenty first century, the United State's economy could be beyond help.

3j. Using Quotation Marks

Quotation marks are used in pairs to set off direct quotations and some titles.

(1) *Direct Quotations*
Use quotation marks around the exact words someone has spoken or written.

"This is the truth," said Harold.

Janet Forbes writes, "Do not underestimate the power of the past."

(2) *Titles*
Use quotation marks around titles of articles, stories, chapters, or other printed material that appears within a larger volume.

Please read the article entitled "Estimating Market Share."

Susan walked down the hall whistling the song "Secret Agent Man."

Use quotation marks with the titles of speeches.

Martin Luther King, Jr.'s most famous speech was entitled "I Have a Dream."

3k. Using Italics and Underlining

Italics, a distinctive, sloping typeface, are used to highlight certain words. Since most keyboards do not allow for italics, we must underline words to indicate they are italicized.

(1) *Titles*
Ue italics or underlining for the titles of record albums, books, magazines, journals, newspapers, and other publications that appear on their own.

We subscribe to *Time* and to *Savvy.*

We are putting out an album titled *Comic Songs of the 1960s.*

Our instructor recommended that we read *Writing for the Media.*

(2) *Foreign Words*
Use italics or underlining for foreign words that are not commonly used in English.

Miss Piggy refers to herself as *moi.*

In vino veritas is his favorite slogan.

(3) *Single Letters*
Use italics or underlining when referring to a single letter of the alphabet.

There is only one *r* in my name.

My printer is not producing a clear capital *S*.

3l. Using Parentheses

Parentheses are used in pairs to deemphasize the words they surround.

(1) *References*

Use parentheses to cite a reference in a report or research paper.

Import quotas need to be reexamined (Ruckers, *Imports and Quotas,* p. 234).

(2) *Nonessential Material*

Use parentheses when referring to material that is not clearly related to the main topic of a sentence or paragraph. Parentheses deemphasize the material they set off.

Training costs (like most things today) are high.

Please keep my dictionary (I have two) on your desk.

3m. Using Brackets

Brackets are used primarily within quotations when you want to add material or clarify information. The brackets show that the words they enclose are yours, not those of the person you are quoting.

"Profits declined this year [1988]," stated Terrence Kelleher.

"Even at this point I cannot trust his [Albert Holman's] judgment," wrote Brenda Gee.

3n. Using Ellipses

Ellipses are three spaced dots used to indicate that words have been deleted from a quotation or sentence. If the ellipses appear at the end of a sentence, use a fourth dot to indicate the period.

(1) *Quoted Material*

Use ellipses to show that material has been deleted from a direct quotation. Do not alter the writer's original meaning.

According to Gleason's article, "These estimates ... have not been verified."

(2) *Pauses and Unfinished Thoughts*

Use ellipses to indicate a pause or a thought left unfinished. (This use of ellipses is fairly uncommon in business writing.)

"I know ... let's adjourn to the library," suggested Dave.

I have told you the answer.... Now what was your question?

Quick Reference for Quotation Marks and Parentheses

1. Periods and commas always go inside quotation marks.

   "These are my estimates," said Jane, "for the repairs."

2. Semicolons and colons go outside quotation marks.

   Tim calls himself a "go-fer": he is really a clerical assistant.

3. Question marks and exclamation points go inside quotation marks if they are part of the material being quoted.

   "Hey!" shouted Karen. "Can you hear me?"

4. Question marks and exclamation points go outside the quotation marks if they are not part of the material being quoted.

   Have you studied the chapter entitled "Punctuating Business Writing"?

5. If a quotation is in parentheses, quotation marks go inside the parentheses.

   Our slogan ("Keep the Peace") has been successful.

6. If a full sentence is in parentheses and is not inside another sentence, put the punctuation inside the parentheses.

   I am voting for Pearson. (He has always been my choice.)

7. If a full sentence enclosed in parentheses appears inside another sentence, do not capitalize the opening or put a period after the enclosed sentence.

   Jerry's resolution (he makes one very week) is to exercise daily.

   If the enclosed sentence ends with a question mark or exclamation point, put the punctuation inside the parentheses.

   The two new desks (have you seen them?) will help improve our productivity.

8. If a sentence in parentheses appears at the end of an unenclosed sentence, put the period outside the parentheses.

   I have ordered two new chairs (they will arrive tomorrow).

Exercise 3-4. Check Your Knowledge of Quotation Marks, Italics, Parentheses, Brackets, and Ellipses

Fix any punctuation errors in the following sentences. Some sentences may be correct.

1. When you have read the original screenplay for "Arsenic and Old Lace," let me know what you think of it.
2. This program [We just started it in May] should help reduce monthly expenses
3. Governor Morris said yesterday that "he would not reconsider. . . the highway bill."
4. My secretary—a former Marine, is highly organized and conscientious.
5. Greg's appointment (which he worked hard to get) may not last more than two months.

Terms to Remember

Abbreviation: shortened form of a word. Usually followed by a period.

Apostrophe [']: mark used to indicate the possessive case of nouns, to form contractions, and to indicate the plurals of abbreviations, letters, and numbers

Brackets [ ]: marks used to add information or clarification within a quotation

Colon [:]: mark used after salutations in business letters and before explanations, series, and long quotations

Comma [,]: mark used to indicate pauses within sentences; used with coordinate conjunctions to separate independent clauses; used to separate introductory dependent clauses and phrases from the main part of a sentence; used to set off parenthetical material such as nonrestrictive clauses, appositives, and direct address

Dash [—]: mark used to show sudden changes of thought and parenthetical information

Ellipses [. . .]: marks used to indicate material deleted from a direct quotation

Exclamation point [!]: mark used after words or sentences showing extreme excitement or emotion

Hyphen [-]: mark used to break a word onto two lines; also used in numbers over twenty and some compound words

Italics [often indicated by <u>underlining</u>]: typeface used to indicate titles of publications such as magazines and books; also used to indicate foreign words and single letters

Parentheses [( )]: marks used to set off and deemphasize the words they surround

Period [.]: mark used at ends of declarative sentences, requests, and indirect questions and after most abbreviations

Question mark [?]: mark used at the end of direct questions

Quotation marks [" "]: marks used to surround the exact words someone has spoken or written; also used with titles of chapters, articles, and other pieces that appear in a larger volume; used with titles of speeches

Semicolon [;]: mark used to separate closely related independent clauses and listed items that contain commas

Questions for Review and Discussion

1. Why is it important to learn standard conventions for punctuation?
2. Punctuation can radically alter the meaning of sentences. What is the difference in meaning between the following sets of sentences?
   a. Teenagers who are bad drivers go to traffic school.
   b. Teenagers, who are bad drivers, go to traffic school.

   a. Please call me Mike.
   b. Please call me, Mike.

   a. We went to *Oklahoma!* this week.
   b. We went to Oklahoma this week.

Exercises

1. Fix any punctuation errors in the following sentences.
   a. In May, 1945 Michael Davidson published his little-known book "The Rewards of Crime."
   b. "Have you ever wondered," asked Greg "whether we should invest in stocks."
   c. The answers to these problems (at least to most of the problems,) are being studied by Gerry Zimmerman and Pat Woolf emi-

nent financial analysts.

d. No, I do not agree with these hypotheses; they are illogical, and inconsistent.

e. I have often wondered what is meant by "real property".

2. Correctly punctuate the following paragraph:

The chalkboard—which many people still think of as a blackboard regardless of its color, can be of great help to speakers, who are attempting to make their messages clear. A chalkboard is usually readily available, and is relatively simple to use. The chalkboard is, especially, useful in presenting procedures, or a flow diagram, that depicts successive phases in a process.

3. Correctly punctuate the following paragraph:

Frequently people ask me "How much time should I spend preparing my speech?". This is a hard question to answer. Some say little preparation is needed, however others claim that preparing a speech is a long arduous task. People argue frequently, for instance on how much time Abraham Lincoln took to prepare *The Gettysburg Address* which he delivered in less than five minutes. Lincoln scholars now assure us, that the speech was far more than an overnight production—it represented the thought of a man, who had devoted his lifetime to the study of government, and politics.

4. Judith Hekemian was shocked when her supervisor sent back the draft of a report that she had sent him. "Fix the punctuation!" he had scribbled on the cover.

Revise the punctuation errors in the following paragraphs from that report.

```
Our study has shown, that 43 percent of
our companys recent applicants, and 25
percent of our newly hired employees are
non-native Americans.

These figures may seem surprisingly
high, however, data collected from our
Personnal Department, and Research
Department support the information
printed in a recent issue of "Tech World",
an industry trade journal. In an article
entitled Applicants from the Pacific Rim
Mr Lawrence Whitman writes, "Our
industry should expect to see ever-
increasing numbers of trained dedicated
job applicants coming from Pacific Rim
nations. The high tech industry has
developed one of the most culturally
diverse workplaces the melting pot of
America has ever seen".
```

Section 4. Using Words Correctly

To communicate effectively, you need to use words correctly. Keep a dictionary by your side as you read so you can keep expanding your vocabulary.

A dictionary, however, will not always tell you how words are actually used. Some words are appropriate only for informal writing; others are too technical for some readers. Active reading and listening will help you use words accurately and effectively.

Be particularly careful of homophones, words that sound alike but are spelled differently and have different meanings (*fair* and *fare, pear, pair,* and *pare*). Some words, too, (*accept, except*) are not exactly homophones but sound so similar that they are easily confused.

The following list of words commonly confused can help you as you revise your business writing. We suggest you become familiar with the words in this list and then begin a list of your own. Also, keep *using* the words you have trouble with; if you avoid them, you will never learn them.

TO ACCEPT: *to receive* or *to approve: Mrs. Reilley accepted the terms of the contract.*

TO EXCEPT: *to make an exception. Except* is also a preposition. *Jack bought all the furniture except this.*

TO ADAPT: *to alter or remodel: We adapted the constitution of the former organization.*

TO ADOPT: *to take as one's own: The supervisor adopted an aggressive managerial style.*

ALOT OF: Colloquial. Do not use.

A LOT OF: Even this form is slightly colloquial. In formal business writing, use *many* or a similar word. *We have acquired a lot of new computers* is less acceptable than *We have acquired many new computers.*

TO AFFECT: *to influence: The rain affected our spirits.*

TO EFFECT: *to bring about: His research effected a cure.* (It did not simply influence a cure—it brought it into existence.)

TO ALLUDE: *to refer to: Greg alluded to Einstein's theories.*

TO ELUDE: *to escape from: The convict eluded the authorities.*

ALREADY: *by a certain time: The ships were already on the bay by noon.*

ALL READY: *completely ready: Are you all ready for the performance?*

AMOUNT: should be used when referring to singular nouns: *The warehouse stores a large amount of sugar.* (*Sugar* is singular.)

NUMBER: should refer to plural nouns: *A large number of reporters converged on the courtroom.* (*Reporters* is plural.)

TO APPRAISE: *to set a value on: The jeweler appraised the gold watch.*

TO APPRISE: *to inform: We have been apprised of the current situation.*

TO COMPLEMENT: *to go with or accompany: The colors complement her face.*

TO COMPLIMENT: *to say something favorable: He complimented the candidate on his experience.* (A *complimentary* item is a free item.)

CONTINUAL: *recurring at intervals: The volcano has erupted continually over a thousand years.*

CONTINUOUS: *without interruption: Warren has spoken continuously for three hours.*

DISINTERESTED: *impartial: The panel chose seven disinterested judges.*

UNINTERESTED: *without interest: Doug is uninterested in politics.*

ELICIT: *to bring out: The speaker elicited a cheer from the crowd.*

ILLICIT: *illegal: The bookkeeper had developed some illicit procedures.*

EMINENT: *distinguished: Alice is an eminent psychologist.*

IMMINENT: *soon: The bankruptcy proceedings are imminent.*

EXPLICIT: *expressed directly: The reporter explicitly accuses the man by referring to him as "the arsonist."*

IMPLICIT: *expressed indirectly: The wording is vague, but the implicit message is alarming.*

FEWER: should be used with plural nouns: *This company employs fewer programmers than that company.* (*Programmers* is plural.)

LESS: should be used with singular nouns: *I have less enthusiasm for the project than you do.* (*Enthusiasm* is singular.)

TO FLOUNDER: *to move awkwardly: Without his notes, the speaker floundered.*

TO FOUNDER: *to sink or to fall apart: The ship foundered on the sunken rocks.*

FORMER and **LATTER:** should be used when referring to two items: *Of these two ideas, the former is too expensive and the latter is too uncertain.*

FIRST and **LAST:** should be used when referring to more than two items: *Of all the items on my grocery list, I forgot only the first and the last.*

IRREGARDLESS is substandard. Do not use. Use REGARDLESS.

TO LIE: *to recline.* This verb does not take a direct object. The past tense is *lay*; the past participle is *lain*; the progressive form is *lying. Ted lies in the sun every day. Ted lay in the sun for an hour. Ted has lain in the sun for six hours. Ted is lying in the sun right now.*

TO LAY: *to put down.* This verb does take a direct object. The past tense and the past participle are *laid*; the progressive form is *laying. Jill lays the books on the table. Jill laid the books on the table yesterday. Jill has laid the books on the table every afternoon. Jill is laying the books on the table right now.*

TO PRECEDE: *to go before: Wild speculation preceded the stock market crash.*

TO PROCEED: *to go ahead: The company proceeded with its plans.*

PRINCIPAL: an adjective meaning *chief: Profits are their principal concern. Principal* is also a noun referring to an administrator and to a sum of money: *The school principal is retiring. The principal has grown by ten percent.*

PRINCIPLE: a *belief: Alex is a man of strong principles.*

STATIONARY: *not movable: The stationary bicycle was bolted to the floor.*

STATIONERY: *letter-paper and envelopes.*

THAN: is used in comparison: *Quincy is taller than Harry.*

THEN: refers to time: *Only then will we decide on the merger.*

WOULD OF: Often confused with the helping verbs *would have: I would have helped if I had known.* Do not use *would of.*

Exercise 4-1. Using Words Correctly

Correct any word usage problems in the following sentences.

1. I would of seen the problem earlier if I had spent more time on the calculations.
2. Mr. Simpson often eludes to a number of people he met in New York.
3. The stationary we have ordered has illicited some controversy from the staff.
4. The principals in the personnel handbook have already been adopted by the new company.
5. There are less people in this department now that we have a computerized system.
6. John never mentioned the employees' morale problem when he appraised the Board of the financial situation.
7. Please do not except this job offer unless you are willing to work alot of hours.
8. The imminent attorney Leonard Flagg has all ready addressed the group.
9. A large amount of secretaries are complaining of nervous tension.
10. I believe we will survive longer then many other companies our size.

Term to Remember

Homophones: words that sound alike but are spelled differently and have different meanings (*to, too,* and *two*)

Questions for Review and Discussion

1. Suggest two methods people can use to successfully expand their vocabulary.
2. Provide an example of two words (not discussed in this section) that you often confuse.

If you have found a way to remember the meaning of each word, explain your method to the class.

Exercises

1. Cross out the words used incorrectly and write in the appropriate counterpart to each. Some sentences may be correct.
   a. For your convenience, we have set up a special lane for people with less than ten items.
   b. Before the trial began, everyone believed that the defendant had tried to allude the authorities.
   c. Because George Martin is a man of strong principles, I knew he would of been an excellent representative of our cause.
   d. The menu states explicitly that the champagne is complementary irregardless of the price of one's entree.
   e. The large amount of news stories have convinced us that the issue is important to the public.
   f. Of the three issues at stake, the former is most vital.
   g. Many disinterested observers have informed us that a strike is eminent.
   h. I hope your opinion has not been effected by this lone incident.
   i. According to a large number of commuters, these trains are continuously late.
   j. These marketing experts are working on implicit messages that filter into the subconscious minds of the readers.

2. Fill in the blanks with correct forms of *to lie* and *to lay*.
   a. When my back went out last week, I _____ on the bed for fifteen hours.
   b. Sam carefully _____ the vase on the table before unwrapping it.
   c. Now that she has heard the evidence, she realizes that the truth _____ somewhere between the two versions of the story.
   d. By _____ newspapers on the kitchen floor, Marty soaked up most of the spilled stew.
   e. Harry had _____ in the bathtub an hour by the time he woke up.
   f. The busboy was _____ glasses on the cart when the customer called for help.
   g. Patsy _____ in the sun every morning when she is on vacation.
   h. I have been _____ tile this way for six years even though I realize there are simpler methods.
   i. The coat had been _____ there for days before someone claimed it.
   j. Jack had just _____ the watch in the store window when Marilyn spotted it.

3. Using a dictionary, write a brief definition for the following words. Then use each in a sentence.

   a. All together
      Altogether
   b. Imaginary
      Imaginative
   c. Incidence
      Incidents
   d. Conscious
      Conscience
   e. Censure
      Censor
   f. Incredible
      Incredulous
   g. Condole
      Condone
   h. Detract
      Distract
   i. Elemental
      Elementary
   j. Populace
      Populous

Section 5. Capitalizing Words

The conventions of capitalization in English are simpler than in many other languages. In general, avoid capitalizing words in business writing unless they fall into one of the categories described in this section.

5a. Capitalizing the First Word of a Sentence

Capitalize the first word of a sentence.

> Hand the book to Henry.
>
> Did you vote this morning?

5b. Capitalizing Directly Quoted Speech

Capitalize the first word of directly quoted speech.

> Karen said, "Give me the answer."
>
> "These are the statistics," admitted Gary.

Do not capitalize the second part of an interrupted sentence in quotation.

> "I will have the report," said Joan, "at nine."

5c. Capitalizing Sentences in Parentheses

Capitalize the first word of a sentence in parentheses that is separate from other sentences.

> I saw the parade. (It was a disaster.)

Do not capitalize the first word of a sentence in parentheses if it comes inside another sentence.

> If you see Teddy (he has been here recently), give him the message.

5d. Capitalizing Proper Nouns

Capitalize proper nouns. Proper nouns include such things as the names of individual people, countries, continents, states, counties, cities, regions, languages, historical periods, political parties, companies, colleges, government and company departments, product brands, days of the week, months of the year, and holidays.

> George Ferman is from England, but he lives in Colorado.
>
> We are taking a poll of Alameda County, California, including the cities of Oakland and San Leandro.
>
> Carrie was born in the Midwest.
>
> Jim learned Latin in order to study manuscripts of the Middle Ages.
>
> One of his parents was a Democrat; the other was a Republican.

Janice applied for a job at IBM and at Macy's after she graduated from Georgetown University.

Len has been working in the Design Department for five years; recently he was responsible for designing a new package for Irish Spring soap.

Peter was elected on Tuesday, September 2, right after the Labor Day weekend.

5e. Capitalizing Proper Adjectives

Capitalize adjectives derived from proper nouns.

David is a German scholar.

I studied Keynesian economics.

5f. Capitalizing Official Titles

Capitalize a person's official title if it precedes his or her name.

I hope Governor Jones will be present at the dinner.

We attended a documentary on Princess Margaret.

Do not capitalize terms that follow a person's name or that are not actually proper titles.

Frederick Jones, who is the governor of Nevada, will be present.

Paula is a supervisor in this department.

Sam Wellins, a vice-president for six years, is retiring.

5g. Capitalizing Academic Degrees

Capitalize academic degrees.

H. Thatcher, Ph.D., was awarded the prize.

Rosemary Travis, Attorney at Law, attended the conference.

5h. Capitalizing Academic Courses

Capitalize the names of specific academic courses.

The brothers signed up for Management 3200.

I am taking a course titled Business Communication.

Do not capitalize a general academic subject area unless it is the name of a language.

Jim is majoring in accounting.

I am studying anthropology.

These students are taking English and French courses.

5i. Capitalizing Titles of Movies, Songs, and Publications

Capitalize the major words of movie, song, record, report, book, magazine, article, play, and poem titles. Do not capitalize *a*, *an*, *the*, short prepositions, or conjunctions unless they are the first word of the title.

> While I was reading *War and Peace*, Ken was practicing "Dixie" on the piano.
>
> Jack went to see *Night of the Living Dead*.
>
> My article, titled "Writing Hints for Accountants," will appear in *Working with Words*.

5j. Capitalizing Abbreviations

Capitalize abbreviations derived from capitalized words.

> He is working for IBM. [International Business Machines]
>
> I sailed on the HMS Liberty. [Her Majesty's Ship]

Exercise 5-1. Check Your Knowledge of Capitalization

Fix any capitalization errors in the following sentences. Some sentences may be correct.

1. On our Vacation, we visited Prince George's County, maryland.
2. Although president Henryson has a degree in spanish, she is more interested in Business.
3. Tim Udell worked for nasa for ten years before beginning a new career as an Accountant.
4. "Let me know your ideas," said Kate, "Before the end of the day. We need to decide by friday."
5. The Beatles' album *Abbey road* has become a Classic.

Term to Remember

Capitalization: use of uppercase letters to signal the beginnings of sentences and direct quotations and to signify the importance of proper names and titles

Questions for Review and Discussion

1. Before the twentieth century, writers frequently used capital letters to highlight important words in a sentence: the rules for capitalization were not so carefully laid out. Is the present system more useful—or less useful?
2. Why do you think the personal pronoun *I* is the only pronoun that is always capitalized?

Exercises

1. Choose three paragraphs from a recent issue of *Time* or *Newsweek*. Write out a rule for each of the capital letters in those paragraphs.
2. Correctly capitalize the following sentences.
   a. While attending the University, Winn took a number of courses in the Economics Department; he particularly liked the course on Macroeconomics.
   b. "I hope to finish the hiring process by monday," Ken said. "It has been a difficult task

as we had a lot of qualified Candidates."

c. The new Mayor of this town has decided to establish a local Holiday on April 3.

d. The japanese manager has introduced numerous innovative management techniques into the Company.

e. Having set up his offices, doctor Raymond notified each of his Patients of the change of address.

3. Write a sentence using each of the following words. Do *not* begin a sentence with any of these words.

a. Senator
senator

b. Thanksgiving
thanksgiving

c. Anthropology
anthropology

d. College
college

e. Doctor
doctor

4. Fix capitalization errors in the following paragraphs.

Jan Mulhern, who won decorations from two countries for his work as a Foreign Correspondent during the war, worked at Hillyard, inc. for many years after the war. He was one of five Executives to receive awards from the university of Connecticut this month.

"During the war, we all cared about the integrity of our news coverage," he told a crowd gathered at the University. "Our goal," he added, "was to maintain honest and effective reporting."

5. In brief sentences, explain why you made each change in Exercise 4.

6. Fix capitalization errors in the following paragraphs.

Norman b. Jamison is an american karate expert. He recently attended a Neighborhood martial-arts event in a Bowling Alley in newark, New Jersey. In the first minute before the crowd, he tore a deck of cards and its box in half with a single seesaw of his wrists.

"I have no special secrets," he told me after he had accomplished a number of astonishing feats, "it's all in the training."

Jamison has worked with a number of trainers (He has studied intensively with chinese teachers), but now works principally by himself. he maintains a daily Training Schedule that requires an iron will and dedication.

7. Fix the capitalization errors in the following business letter.

2636 fessenden street
Washington, dc 20012
April 6, 19xx

Professor Charlotte Haynes, chair
Department of Marketing
Twin City college
St. Paul, MN 60123

Dear professor Haynes:

I recently attended a fascinating lecture that you gave in Silver Spring, maryland, on marketing for nonprofit Organizations.

During the lecture, you mentioned that you have published an article entitled "Marketing The Arts." As I work for an art gallery here in Washington, I would appreciate your sending the name of the publication in which your Article appeared. I enclose a stamped post card for your convenience.

Thank you for your assistance. I look forward to reading the article.

Sincerely,

Arthur Czerny

Arthur Czerny

Section 6. Writing Numbers

When writing numbers, you have to choose between using words (*two hundred*) and using figures (*200*). As figures are usually easier to read and comprehend, they are used more frequently in business writing.

The following section outlines some general conventions for writing numbers, but you will have to use your own judgment in some situations. Consistency and readability should be your goals.

6a. Spelling Out Numbers Ten and Under

Spell out numbers ten and under.

> They have six employees.
>
> This is my fourth application letter.

6b. Writing Complicated Numbers

Use figures for complicated numbers.

> The city has 2.9 million inhabitants.
>
> The city has 2,900,000 inhabitants.

6c. Putting Numbers at the Beginning of Sentences

Spell out numbers at the beginning of sentences.

> Two hundred managers attended the convention.
>
> A thousand dinners were prepared.

6d. Writing About Time

Spell out times using *o'clock*.

> We began at three o'clock.

Use numbers for times with *a.m.* and *p.m.*

> The movie began at 6 p.m.

6e. Using Numbers in Lists

Be consistent with lists of numbers.

> I used 12 reams of paper, 15 pens, and 4 cartridges.
>
> Sharon hired two programmers, one clerk, and three engineers.

6f. Writing Addresses and Telephone Numbers

Use figures for addresses and telephone numbers.

2323 Garrison Street
Hilltown, VT 16789
(213) 676-7888

6g. Writing Dates

Use figures for dates.

> We arrived on September 3, 1988.
> The report is dated 12/3/75.

6h. Using Figures for Percentages, Decimals, and Money

Use figures for percentages, decimals, and money.

> She won 13 percent of the vote.
> The answer is 4.5.
> The sale price is $567.90.

Even amounts of money are written without a decimal point and zeros.

> I owe you $150 for the dress.

6i. Using Figures for Statistics and Scores

Use figures for statistics and scores.

> The odds on Courageous Runner are 4 to 1.
> The Cougars won 12 to 7.

6j. Using Figures for Page and Volume Numbers

Use figures for page and volume numbers.

> You will find the answer in Volume 2, page 34.

6k. Using Figures for Dimensions and Distances

Use figures for dimensions and distances.

> The room is 10 feet long.
> Dana moved 6 miles from here.
> Sam and Wendy ran 10 kilometers.

Exercise 6-1. Check Your Knowledge of Numbers

Fix any errors in the following sentences.

1. 1,200 employees went on strike today.
2. I am leaving at three o'clock.
3. The corporation owes the staff twelve dollars and thirty-two cents.
4. On page four of the manual, you will see the directions for starting the equipment.
5. I will let you know by February 12 if I can send the four hundred cartons and 345 reams of paper on time.

Questions for Review and Discussion

1. Why are numbers written more frequently as figures in business and technical writing than in many other types of writing?
2. Clip out an article with at least five references to numbers from *Business Week* or another business-oriented publication. Explain why the writer has chosen words or figures to express the numbers in the article.

Exercises

1. Fix any errors involving numbers in the following sentences. Some sentences may be correct.
   a. The new room is twenty feet long and 10 feet wide.
   b. Georgette lives at three hundred Bayview Avenue.
   c. Although profits went up twelve percent this year, we are still one million five hundred thousand dollars in debt.
   d. When the managers arrived at six p.m., all the employees were leaving.
   e. By the end of the inning, the Brewers were ahead five to two.
2. In brief sentences, explain why you made each change in Exercise 1.
3. Fix any errors involving numbers in the following paragraph.

   We administered surveys to one hundred fifty-nine employees over the course of 6 days. The employees, who work in nine divisions of the company, were given from noon until two p.m. to finish the survey. Of these employees, fifty-one percent stated that they were unhappy with their salaries; forty percent stated they were satisfied; only nine percent stated they were really happy with their salaries.

4. Fix any errors involving numbers in the following paragraph.

   Hired on December third, 1958, Violet Moore worked as an accountant for this company until she became a manager in 1969. In 1970, Ms. Moore established a salary pool concept that has been in operation ever since. With this concept, a fixed five percent of company profits is set aside for promotions and merit increases. In 1988, this amount came to a hundred thousand dollars.

Section 7. Using Abbreviations

Abbreviations can be useful, but they can be confusing as well. As a business writer, use abbreviations sparingly. If you are unsure whether your reader will understand an abbreviation, identify it in parentheses after the first usage.

7a. Abbreviating Titles

A few titles are almost always abbreviated when they precede or follow a person's name.

Mr. and Mrs. John Harrison and Ms. Klein

Dr. Smithers

St. Patrick's Cathedral

Pat Linmore, Sr. and Ken Westerly, Jr.

Carol Turlock, Ph.D.

In business writing, avoid abbreviating most titles.

Reverend James Monahan [not *Rev.*]

Major Jane Antonioni [not *Maj.*]

Senator Albert Hutchison [not *Sen.*]

President Forchet [not *Pres.*]

7b. Abbreviating State Names

In the text of letters, memos, and reports, the full names of streets, cities, states, and countries should be used. On the envelope, return address, and inside address of business correspondence, however, it is permissible to use the standard abbreviations for the states (see p. 690). Note that the abbreviations are not followed by periods.

7c. Abbreviating Organizations and Government Agencies

Many organizations and government agencies are commonly known by abbreviated names (FBI, FDA, CIA, NASA). Less familiar abbreviations should be identified after their first usage in a business document.

Thad Maynard presented a paper at the MLA (Modern Language Association) convention.

I am member of the AMA (American Marketing Association).

Avoid abbreviating words such as *company*, *corporation*, and *incorporated* unless the abbreviation is part of an organization's official name.

We work for BankAmerica Corp. [incorrect]

We work for BankAmerica Corporation. [correct]

Note that an ampersand (&) should not be used as an abbreviation for *and* unless it appears as part of the official name of a company.

Alabama	AL	Montana	MT
Alaska	AK	Nebraska	NE
Arizona	AZ	Nevada	NV
Arkansas	AR	New Hampshire	NH
California	CA	New Jersey	NJ
Canal Zone	CZ	New Mexico	NM
Colorado	CO	New York	NY
Connecticut	CT	North Carolina	NC
Delaware	DE	North Dakota	ND
District of Columbia	DC	Ohio	OH
Florida	FL	Oklahoma	OK
Georgia	GA	Oregon	OR
Guam	GU	Pennsylvania	PA
Hawaii	HI	Puerto Rico	PR
Idaho	ID	Rhode Island	RI
Illinois	IL	South Carolina	SC
Indiana	IN	South Dakota	SD
Iowa	IA	Tennessee	TN
Kansas	KS	Texas	TX
Kentucky	KY	Trust Territories	TT
Louisiana	LA	Utah	UT
Maine	ME	Vermont	VT
Maryland	MD	Virgin Islands	VI
Massachusetts	MA	Virginia	VA
Michigan	MI	Washington	WA
Minnesota	MN	West Virginia	WV
Mississippi	MS	Wisconsin	WI
Missouri	MO	Wyoming	WY

American Telephone & Telegraph Company (AT&T) [correct]

Merrill Lynch, Pierce, Fenner & Smith, Inc. [correct]

7d. Abbreviating Dates, Times, and Temperatures

Standard abbreviations are associated with dates, times, and temperatures. These may be used in even the most formal business writing.

The history begins in 34 B.C.

The king's reign began in A.D. 980.

The meeting begins at 5 p.m. (or P.M.)

We arrived at 9 a.m. (or A.M.)

The recorded temperature was 15°C.

The recorded temperature was 98°F.

Note that *a.m.* and *p.m.* may be used following a specified time: they should not be used alone as abbreviations for *morning* and *afternoon*.

> I met Jim in the p.m. [incorrect]
>
> I met Jim at 6 p.m. [correct]

Exercise 7-1. Check Your Knowledge of Abbreviations

Correct any errors involving abbreviations in the following sentences.

1. Roberta Costner, the well-known dr., arrived at 9:30 a.m.
2. Mr. Frederick Hobbes lives at 2334 Jackson St. in Fair Oaks.
3. The corp. has expanded its operations to Albany, NY.
4. Jack & Rita were introduced to Ken Meyer, Jr.
5. Sen. Michael Thompson spoke to the crowd.

Questions for Review and Discussion

1. Abbreviations make life easier for writers. How can abbreviations actually benefit readers?
2. Name at least two abbreviations commonly used in your field of interest. What type of reader would recognize them without an explanation?

Exercises

1. Correct any errors involving abbreviations in the following sentences.
   a. I know that Gen. Wilkins will be pleased to meet with you this a.m.
   b. Ms. Patricia Tillotson was born in Dallas, TX, in 1977.
   c. After working for IBM, I began a job with a computer firm in N.Y.
   d. We visited St. Thomas in the Virgin Islands before flying to Puerto Rico.
   e. I am taking an excellent course from Prof. Aaronson in the Mathematics Dept.
2. In brief sentences, explain why you made each change in Exercise 1.
3. Correct any errors involving abbreviations in the following business letter.

```
                                    2134 A St.
                                    Derby, Penn. 91457
                                    Sept. 12, 19xx

Doctor Phyllis Ortega
7700 Venter Ave.
Hunter, Tex. 78934

Dear Doctor Ortega:

I am writing to confirm our meeting on
Sept. 23 at 3 p.m. in the corp. offices. I
appreciate your taking the time to meet
with me.

                          Sincerely yrs.,


                          Allen Canter
```

Glossary of Grammatical Terms

ADJECTIVE. A word used to describe or limit a noun or pronoun. (see MODIFIER.)

Article: a, an, and *the. A* is used before consonant sounds; *an* is used before vowel sounds.

A table is for sale.

An elephant is carrying us.

The report is incomplete.

Common Adjective: describes a noun or pronoun.

The *unstable* economy is causing *many* problems.

Demonstrative Adjective: this, that, these, those. Points to the noun it precedes.

That man is an engineer with *this* company.

Interrogative Adjective: precedes noun in a question.

Which pizza did you order?

Whose hat is on the chair?

Proper Adjective: formed from proper nouns (see NOUN). Proper adjectives are usually capitalized.

A *European* holiday could be expensive.

ADVERB. A word that describes or limits a verb, an ADJECTIVE, another adverb, a VERBAL, a PHRASE, a CLAUSE, or a SENTENCE. (See also MODIFIER.)

I ran *quickly.* [Adverb modifies verb *ran.*]

He is *quite* small. [Adverb modifies adjective *small.*]

The company grew *particularly* fast. [Adverb modifies adverb *fast.*]

He lost weight by exercising *vigorously.* [Adverb modifies verbal *exercising.*]

Accurately solving problems is his specialty. [Adverb modifies phrase *solving problems.*]

Therefore, we will adjourn. [Adverb modifies independent clause.]

AGREEMENT. The correspondence between SUBJECT and VERB or between NOUN and PRONOUN with regard to PERSON, NUMBER, or GENDER.

Person: First person refers to the speaker; *second person* refers to the person spoken to; *third person* refers to the person, place, or thing spoken about.

I sold *my* bike. [*I* and *my* are both first-person pronouns.]

You gave me *your* desk. [*You* and *your* are both second-person pronouns.]

If *Pete* works hard, *he* will succeed. [*He* is a third-person pronoun referring to Pete.]

Number: Nouns, pronouns, and verbs may be either singular or plural.

Bill and Fred are visiting their parents. [The plural pronoun *their* agrees with the plural ANTECEDENT, *Bill and Fred; are visiting,* the plural form of the verb, agrees with the plural subject, *Bill and Fred.*

Gender: Nouns and pronouns may be masculine, feminine, or neuter.

Peter saw *his* chance. [*Peter* and *his* are both masculine.]

I gave my *mother her* gift. [*Mother* and *her* are both feminine.]

This *mug* has *its* own shelf. [*Mug* and *its* are both neuter.]

ANTECEDENT. The noun or group of words to which a PRONOUN refers:

John Schultz bought the hammer before he left the store. [*John Schultz* is the antecedent of the pronoun *he.*]

APPOSITIVE. A NOUN or noun substitute set beside a noun or noun substitute to describe, identify, or explain it.

My brother, *an accountant,* will speak to us. [*An accountant* describes *My brother.*]

AUXILIARY VERB. See HELPING VERB.

CASE. The form a noun or pronoun takes to indicate its relationship to other words in a sentence. The three cases in English are subjective (also called *nominative*), objective (also called *accusative*), and possessive (also called *genitive*).

Subjective Case: used for SUBJECTS and COMPLEMENTS.

He and *she* are the winners. [Pronouns are subjects.]

That must be *they.* [Pronoun is a complement.]

Objective Case: used for DIRECT OBJECTS, INDIRECT OBJECTS, and objects of PREPOSITIONS.

I like *him* and *her.* [Pronouns are direct objects.]

Please give *him* and *her* the awards. [Pronouns are indirect objects.]

Hand the reports to *him* and *her.* [Pronouns are objects of a preposition.]

Possessive Case: used to show ownership.

The prize is *yours* and *ours.* [Pronouns show possession.]

The possessive is the only case in which nouns change:

Have you checked the *company's* records?

CLAUSE. A group of related words that contains a SUBJECT and a PREDICATE and that functions as part of a SENTENCE. Clauses are either independent (*main*) or dependent (*subordinate*).

A main clause may stand by itself as a sentence.

The company raised wages.

Two or more main clauses may be connected by a coordinate CONJUNC-TION and a comma or by a semicolon.

The company raised wages, and the strike ended.

The company raised wages; the strike ended.

A dependent clause must be attached to an independent clause. A dependent clause usually begins with a subordinate CONJUNCTION or a relative PRONOUN.

Because the company raised wages, the strike ended.

We toasted the man *who* bought the building.

Dependent clauses may function as NOUNS, ADJECTIVES, or ADVERBS.

Whoever bought the building is a millionaire. [Noun clause acts as noun and as SUBJECT of the sentence.]

The building *that we bought* cost a fortune. [Adjective clause modifies *building.*]

Because he wanted a bargain, Sam bought the building. [Adverb clause modifies *bought.*]

COMMA SPLICE. A grammatical error in which a comma is used without a coordinate CONJUNCTION to connect two independent CLAUSES.

Nancy Hill is studying archeology, Bill Mason is studying economics. [comma splice]

Nancy Hill is studying archeology. Bill Mason is studying economics. [correct]

Nancy Hill is studying archeology, and Bill Mason is studying economics. [correct]

Nancy Hill is studying archeology; Bill Mason is studying economics. [correct]

COMPARISON. The forms of an ADJECTIVE or ADVERB that show degree. Forms of comparison are positive, comparative, and superlative.

Positive Form: describes without comparing.

The boy is *tall.*

Karen is *creative.*

Comparative Form: compares two people or things.

This boy is *taller* than that boy.

Karen is *more creative* than Joe.

Karen is *less creative* than Joe.

Superlative Form: compares three or more people or things.

The boy is the *tallest* in the class.

Karen is the *most creative* student in the class.

Karen is the *least creative* student in the class.

COMPLEMENT. A NOUN, PRONOUN, or ADJECTIVE that follows a LINKING VERB and renames or describes the SUBJECT.

Tom is our *manager.* [noun complement]

This must be *he*. [pronoun complement]

David is *efficient*. [adjective complement]

CONJUNCTION. A connecting word that joins words, PHRASES, SENTENCES, or CLAUSES. Conjunctions are coordinate, correlative, or subordinate.

Coordinate Conjunctions: and, but, for, nor, or, so. Coordinate conjunctions connect words or groups of words that have similar functions in a sentence:

Jaime went to Spain *and* to France. [Conjunctions connect PHRASES.]

I will go, *but* I may not return. [Conjunctions link independent CLAUSES.]

Correlative Conjunctions: both . . . and; either . . . or; neither . . . nor; not only . . . but also; whether . . . or. Correlative conjunctions are used in pairs. Like coordinate conjunctions, they connect words or groups of words that have similar functions in a sentence.

I am *not only* hungry *but also* thirsty. [Conjunctions link adjective complements.]

Either I will travel *or* I will stay home. [Conjunctions link independent clauses.]

Subordinate Conjunctions: words such as *because, while, even though*, and *if*. They mark the beginning of a dependent CLAUSE and connect a dependent clause to an independent clause.

Because I was hungry, I ate some sandwiches.

I was hungry *even though* I ate some sandwiches.

DIRECT ADDRESS. A word or phrase naming the person or thing addressed. Commas separate these words or phrases from the rest of the sentence.

Rover, sit!

Here, *Mrs. Herman*, are the reports.

DIRECT OBJECT. A noun or noun substitute influenced by an action VERB. To locate a direct object, ask WHOM? or WHAT? after the verb.

The car hit a tree. [Hit WHAT? *tree*]

Joanne married Fred. [Married WHOM? *Fred.*]

A PRONOUN used as a direct object will be in the objective CASE.

Tanya hit *him*.

Henry married *her*.

DIRECT QUOTATION. The exact words written or spoken by others. A direct quotation is set off with quotation marks.

"Please call the meeting to order," said Mrs. Lerner.

An indirect quotation is a paraphrase of words actually spoken or written.

The manager said he was happy to see us.

FRAGMENT. A word or group of words, written as a sentence, that is not a sentence.

> Because of the problem.

> Running for help.

GENDER. The aspect of a noun or pronoun that indicates whether it is masculine (*uncle, he*), feminine (*mother, she*), or neuter (*house, it*). (See AGREEMENT)

GERUND. See VERBAL and PHRASE.

HELPING (or AUXILIARY) **VERB.** One or more verbs used with a main verb to indicate TENSE, VOICE, MOOD, PERSON, NUMBER. Common helping verbs are formed from *be, do,* and *have.* See VERB.

> The helping verbs *be* and *have* indicate the tense and voice of the main verb.

> I *have* eaten.

> He *has* completed the job.

> You *were* running.

> The helping verb *do* is used for emphasis, for negative statements, and for questions.

> I *do* have an answer.

> She *does* not have the book.

> *Does* Henry have the report?

> Other helping verbs such as *could, can, may, might, must, should* and *would* indicate necessity, possibility, and ability.

> I *must* finish the report.

> I *might* finish the report.

> I *could* finish the report.

INDIRECT OBJECT. A noun or noun substitute that states to whom or for whom the action of the verb is done. Indirect objects must precede direct objects.

> I lent *George* a book.

> Fred owes the *company* fifty dollars.

> We sent *Peter* the book.

Pronouns that are indirect objects will be in the objective case.

> Give *them* the book.

INDIRECT QUOTATION. See DIRECT QUOTATION.

INFINITIVE. See VERBAL and PHRASE.

INTERJECTION. A word or words expressing emotion. An interjection is followed by a comma or exclamation mark.

"Hey!" cried Dan.

"Oh, that's an error," said Felicia.

IRREGULAR VERB. A verb that does not form its past TENSE and past PARTICIPLE in the standard fashion (by adding *d* or *ed*).

Allen has *run* the race.

We have *lain* in the sun since noon.

LINKING VERB. Verbs such as *be, seem,* and *appear* that express a state of being rather than an action. Linking verbs have COMPLEMENTS rather than DIRECT OBJECTS.

He *seems* enthusiastic.

That *is* she at the door.

MODIFIER. A word, PHRASE, or CLAUSE that limits or describes another word or group of words. Modifiers should be placed close to the word or words they are modifying. Problems with modifiers include dangling modifiers, misplaced modifiers, and squinting modifiers.

Dangling Modifier: a modifier that does not clearly modify a word or group of words in the sentence.

Flying home, the plane crashed. [dangling modifier]

While they were flying home, the plan crashed. [correct]

Misplaced Modifier: a modifier placed incorrectly in the sentence.

I gave a speech to the students *using my notes.* [misplaced modifier]

Using my notes, I gave a speech to the students. [correct]

Squinting Modifier: a modifier that describes either of two items in a sentence.

Being beaten *thoroughly* disgusted us. [squinting modifier]

Being thoroughly beaten disgusted us. [correct]

Being beaten disgusted us thoroughly. [correct]

MOOD. The form of a VERB that indicated the attitude of the writer. The three moods are indicative, imperative, and subjunctive.

Indicative Mood: used for making statements and asking questions.

The director *interviews* the candidates.

Does the director *interview* the candidates?

Imperative Mood: used for commands or requests. The subject is often understood to be *you.*

(You) Run!

Please revise this memo.

Subjunctive Mood: used to express wishes and hypothetical conditions.

I wish I *were* president.

I request that this matter *be* settled.

NONRESTRICTIVE CLAUSE. A CLAUSE that is not essential to the meaning of the sentence.

> These employees, *who are all in the accounting department,* are being promoted.

NOUN. A part of speech that names a person, place, thing, or idea.
Common Noun: names a class of people, places, or things.

> The *man* is carrying a *briefcase.*

> Have you taken a *photograph?*

Proper Noun: names a particular person, place, or thing. Proper nouns are always capitalized.

> *Caroline* visited *Europe.*

> *President Lincoln* was assassinated.

Collective Noun: refers to a group of people, places, or things as a unit.

> The *army* is stationed near the *university.*

NUMBER. The aspect of a noun, pronoun, or verb that indicates if it is singular or plural. (See AGREEMENT.)

PARTICIPLE. See VERBAL and PHRASE.

PARTS OF SPEECH. The eight basic components of a SENTENCE: NOUNS, VERBS, PRONOUNS, ADJECTIVES, ADVERBS, PREPOSITIONS, CONJUNCTIONS, and INTERJECTIONS.

PERSON. The aspect of a noun, pronoun, or verb that indicates whether one is speaking (first person), spoken to (second person), or spoken about (third person). See also AGREEMENT.

> *I am* a violinist. [first person]

> *You are* a violinist. [second person]

> *He is* a violinist. [third person]

PHRASE. A group of related words that acts as unit but does not contain both a subject and verb.
Gerund Phrase: a phrase containing a gerund and acting as a noun. (See VERBAL.)

> *Climbing mountains* can be dangerous.

> I like *running this machine.*

Infinitive Phrase: group of words containing an infinitive and acting as a noun, adjective, or adverb. (See VERBAL.)

> *To win this race* requires time and effort. [Phrase acts as a noun.]

> The movie *to see tonight* is listed here. [Phrase acts as an adjective.]

> *To sleep better,* try these ear plugs. [Phrase acts as an adverb.]

Participial Phrase: group of words containing a participle and acting as an adjective. (See VERBAL.)

The desk *piled with books* is mine.

A report *filled with errors* is unacceptable.

Prepositional Phrase: group of words beginning with a preposition and containing a noun or pronoun that is the object of the preposition. Prepositional phrases usually act as adjectives or adverbs.

The company is located *near a shopping center.* [Phrase acts as an adjective.]

In the morning, we departed. [Phrase acts as an adverb.]

Verb Phrase: group of words containing a verb and showing the action of a subject.

The company *should have negotiated.*

I *did insist* on the proper format.

PREDICATE. The word or words in a sentence that tell or ask something about the SUBJECT. A predicate always contains a VERB.

The manager *has organized the reception.*

Has the building been *painted?*

PREPOSITION. A word that links a word or group of words (prepositional PHRASE) to another word or words in the sentence. Common prepositions: *about, to, with, for, in, on, out, from, over, near.*

He spoke *with* excitement *about* the project scheduled *for* the autumn.

PRONOUN. A word used in place of a noun.

Demonstrative Pronoun: points out one or more people or things.

This is an outdated program.

These are my boots.

Indefinite Pronoun: refers to one or more people or things in general.

Each of us has decided to join.

Is *either* of the people here?

Intensive Pronoun: ends in *-self* or *-selves.* Emphasizes a noun or pronoun.

I *myself* believe in humanity.

Pete *himself* voted for Johnson and Walters.

Interrogative Pronoun: introduces a question.

Who is there?

Which do you want?

Personal Pronoun: takes the place of a common or proper noun.

He approves of the speech.

I live in France; *it* is my favorite country.

Reflexive Pronoun: ends in *-self* or *-selves.* Refers to a subject.

She bought *herself* a new scarf.

They saw *themselves* in the mirror.

Relative Pronoun: introduces a dependent clause.

I bought the house *that* I liked.

This is the man *who* spoke to me.

RESTRICTIVE CLAUSE. A CLAUSE essential to the meaning of the sentence.

The pupils *who left school early* were punished.

This is the only book *that was on sale.*

RUN-ON (or FUSED) **SENTENCE.** Two or more independent CLAUSES that are not separated by appropriate punctuation or a coordinate CONJUNCTION and a comma.

I saw the proposal it was finished. [run-on]

I saw the proposal. It was finished. [correct]

I saw the proposal; it was finished. [correct]

I saw the proposal, and it was finished. [correct]

SENTENCE. A group of words containing a SUBJECT and PREDICATE that can stand by itself as a complete thought. Sentences are classified according to their *purpose:* they may be declarative, imperative, interrogative, or exclamatory.

Declarative Sentence: makes a statement.

I like string beans.

Imperative Sentence: makes a request or command.

Go to the file cabinet.

Interrogative Sentence: asks a question.

Will you assist me?

Exclamatory Sentence: expresses emotion.

We're going home!

Sentences are also classified according to their *form.* Sentences may be simple, compound, complex, or compound-complex.

Simple Sentence: contains one independent clause.

We won the award.

Compound Sentence: contains two or more independent clauses.

We won the award, but they won the publicity.

Complex Sentence: contains at least one independent clause and at least one dependent clause.

Although we won the award, they won the publicity.

Compound-Complex Sentence: contains at least two independent clauses and at least one dependent clause.

Although we won the award, they won the publicity; we all went home happy.

SUBJECT. The word or words about which something is asserted or asked in a sentence.

The *man* made a request.

Are *you* going home?

TENSE. The aspect of a verb that indicates when an action took place or a condition occurred.

Simple Tenses

Past: I *rode* home.
Present: I *ride* home.
Future: I *will ride* home.

Perfect Tenses

Perfect tenses are formed by combining *have, has,* or *had* with the past PARTICIPLE of the verb.

The *past perfect tense* shows an action completed by a certain time in the past. The past perfect tense is formed by combining *had* + the past participle of a verb.

Past Perfect: I *had ridden* home by noon.

The *present perfect tense* shows an action begun in the past but continuing to the present, being completed in the present, or being completed just before the present.

Present Perfect: Henry *has realized* the truth since Tuesday.
                  I *have written* the proposal.
                  Jill *has* just *finished* the book.

The *future perfect tense* is formed by combining *will have* + the past participle of the verb. The future perfect tense shows that action will have been completed before some time in the future.

Future Perfect: By September, we *will have finished* the house.

Progressive Tenses

Progressive tenses show ongoing action. All of the six tenses described above have progressive forms. Progressive tenses are formed by combining a form of the verb *be* with the present participle of a verb.

Past Progressive: was or *were* + present participle

Jim *was writing* the report.

Present Progressive: is, am, or *are* + present participle

Jim *is writing* the report.

Future Progressive: will be + present participle

Jim *will be writing* the report tomorrow.

Past Perfect Progressive: had been + present participle

Jim *had been writing* the report when he got hungry.

Present Perfect Progressive: have been or *has been* + present participle

Jim *has been* writing the report all day.

Future Perfect Progressive: will have been + present participle

By noon Jim *will have been writing* the report for six hours.

Emphatic Tenses

Past and present tenses have emphatic forms. These are formed by combining *does, do,* or *did* and the ROOT of the verb.

I *did finish* the report.

I *do state* the truth.

He *does state* the truth.

VERB. A word or group of words that express an action or state of being. Main verbs may be combined with helping verbs to form verb PHRASES.

    h.v.   m.v.
I have developed a program.

A *transitive verb* is an action verb that has a DIRECT OBJECT.

        v.   d.o.
David wrote the report.

A *transitive verb* may also have an INDIRECT OBJECT.

      v.   i.o.   d.o.
Jim gave Helen the papers.

An *intransitive verb* may be an action verb that does not have a direct object.

The glass *broke.* [intransitive verb].

An *intransitive verb* may also be a LINKING VERB.

Jim *seems* happy.

VERBAL. A word or words derived from a verb that are used as a noun, adjective, or adverb. Gerunds, infinitives, and participles are verbals. Verbals may have COMPLEMENTS, OBJECTS, MODIFIERS, and sometimes SUBJECTS. (See also PHRASE.)

Gerunds: end in *-ing* and act as nouns.

Training was essential to the job. [gerund subject]

Infinitives: formed from *to* + the root of a verb.

To help was his goal. [infinitive used as noun/subject]

This is the car *to buy.* [infinitive used as adjective]

He plays *to win.* [infinitive used as adverb]

Past Infinitives: formed from *to* + *have* + the past participle of a verb.

To have finished the reports this afternoon was our goal.

Present Participles: verb forms ending in *-ing* that act as adjectives.

Running, he caught the ball. [present participle acting as adjective]

Past Participles: end in *-d* or *-ed* if they are formed from regular verbs. Past participles of irregular verbs have a variety of forms.

Heated, the casserole became almost edible. [regular past participle]

The fish *caught* in the net was struggling. [irregular past participle]

Combined with HELPING VERBS, participles also function as part of verb PHRASES.

The car *is stalling.*

The car *has stalled.*

VOICE. The aspect of a verb that determines whether a subject is doing the action or being acted upon.

Active Voice: The subject performs the action.

Karen *wrote* the book.

Passive Voice: The grammatical object becomes the subject of the sentence. The doer of the action either does not appear or appears in a prepositional phrase.

The book *was written.*

The book *was written* by Karen.

Passive verbs are created by combining a form of the verb *be* and the past participle of a verb. Writers should use passive verbs only when they serve a clear purpose.

Answers to *Check Your Knowledge* Exercises

Ex. 1-1. (1) sub: Mr. Freedman; verb: has won (2) sub: lectures; verb: were (3) sub: (You); verb: hand (4) sub: you; verb: will read (5) sub: man; verb: won (6) sub: Barbara, I; verb: saw (7) sub: Greg; verb: changed, drove (8) sub: staff; verb: has requested (9) sub: city; verb: has condemned (10) sub: (You); verb: notify

Ex. 1-2 (1) sentence (2) fragment (3) sentence (4) sentence (5) sentence (6) fragment (7) fragment (8) fragment (9) sentence (10) sentence

Ex. 1-3. (1) run-on (2) sentence (3) run-on (4) run-on (5) run-on

Ex. 1-4. (1) sentence (2) comma splice (3) sentence (4) comma splice (5) sentence (6) comma splice (7) sentence (8) sentence (9) sentence (10) comma splice

Ex. 2-1. (1) has given (2) go (3) correct (4) Does (5) is (6) correct (7) come (8) needs (9) Is (10) is

Ex. 2-2. (1) correct (2) If you see either of the new employees, give him or her this message. (3) correct (4) Neither of the attorneys has brought his or her own lunch. (5) Each senior should attend this lecture before he or she graduates. (6) correct (7) Len and Marie have given me their approval. (8) At the end of the president's tour, she met with upper management. (9) correct (10) The corporation is opening its new offices.

Ex. 2-3 (1) Between you and me, this problem is getting worse. (2) Whom will we send to Washington this spring? (3) She is more creative than I, but she is less reliable. (4) When it docked at the pier, the boat was on fire. (5) Let Henry and me know when you decide. (6) Felicia and he are the nominees. (7) correct (8) correct (9) correct (10) The managers—Pete and she—are late for work today.

Ex. 2-4. (1) correct (2) While I was running quickly, my briefcase dropped. (3) Lenore is not really happy with the change in procedures that Greg has developed. (4) As a new employee, you will find this sheet is important. (5) Let me know as soon as possible when you want to go to Dallas. (6) correct (7) After making copies of the brochure, we found several mistakes in the copy. (8) correct (9) correct (10) Using a microphone, he spoke to the crowd.

Ex. 2-5. (1) Please let me know if you have any answers, suggestions, or ideas. (2) This is the first time that we have introduced both a new product and a new product line. (3) correct (4) correct (5) correct (6) We will either move to New York or stay in Milwaukee. (7) correct (8) correct (9) Either this company will expand or it will go bankrupt. (10) The lessons we learned were expensive, obvious, and painful.

Ex. 3-1. (1) correct (2) prices. (3) "Yes!" shouted (4) request. (5) U.S.

Ex. 3-2. (1) Des Moines, Iowa, (2) company, which is facing bankruptcy, (3) correct (4) January 23, 1923, (5) have designed and implemented (6) "At the end of the fall semester, I will (7) this is the report that Fred (8) Rummaging through his desk, Mike (9) on vacation, but you (10) When we moved into this office in November, we had to paint all the walls and refinish the floors.

Ex. 3-3. (1) The men's department is being redecorated to make more room for suits and overcoats, not to make more room for sweatsuits. (2) for the following reasons: (3) Harry's (4) Jack-in-the-box (5) twenty-first century, the United States'

Ex. 3-4. (1) Arsenic and Old Lace, (2) (we just started it in May) (3) that he would not reconsider . . . the highway bill. (4) secretary—a former Marine— (5) correct

Ex. 4-1. (1) would have seen (2) alludes (3) stationery, elicited (4) principles (5) fewer (6) apprised (7) accept, a lot (8) eminent, already (9) number of secretaries (10) than many other

Ex. 5-1. (1) vacation, Maryland (2) President Henryson, Spanish, business (3) NASA, accountant (4) before, Friday (5) Abbey Road, classic

Ex. 6-1. (1) One thousand two hundred (2) correct (3) $12.32 (4) page 4 (5) 400 cartons

Ex. 7-1. (1) doctor (2) Jackson Street (3) corporation, New York (4) Jack and Rita (5) Senator

Legal Aspects
of Business
Communication

Appendix A

Federal and state laws have an impact upon almost every aspect of business, from taxes to employee hiring and safety, to product liability. Despite the complexity of the legal environment surrounding businesses, many business people go to an attorney only when they are in trouble. This is a risky approach. Most businesses benefit from a program of "preventative legal advice" in which managers and attorneys work together on an ongoing basis to avert problems before they occur.

As a businessperson, you should not attempt to do your own legal work, but you should have some knowledge of the federal and state laws that affect advertising, credit and collection policies, employment, and other areas crucial to your business.

The following summary of relevant federal legislation is intended simply to make you aware of the legal environment surrounding a few key aspects of business. Since state laws vary and new legislation is always being passed, get advice from an attorney if you need information concerning specific problems in these areas—or in others such as health and safety regulations, labor practices, and product liability.

Advertising

In 1963, President John F. Kennedy issued an address on the "Consumer's Bill of Rights." One of the major rights he discussed was that a consumer should be accurately and adequately informed about products. The consumer should be protected against fraud and deceit, including misleading advertising and deceptive labeling.

To protect the consumer, hundreds of local and federal laws have been created to regulate advertising and promotional activities. The Federal Trade Commission (FTC) has powers to regulate unfair and deceptive trade practices, including false advertising.

If you are writing copy or designing promotions of any kind, avoid making claims that may be considered unfair or deceptive. The line between exaggeration and deception may be a fine one, but it is one to watch carefully. One FTC action, for instance, was taken against a company advertising a "permanent" hair dye. As the dye was not actually permanent, the advertisement was judged deceptive.[1]

In another case, the FTC issued a "cease and desist" order against a soup manufacturer that allegedly advertised soup in a deceptive manner by placing marbles at the bottom of the bowl: the marbles forced the vegetables upward and made the soup look richer on television.[2]

All aspects of marketing, including pricing, labeling and packaging, warranties, and direct mail promotions are regulated by state and federal laws. The following list is only a sampling of legislation pertinent to this area.

Sampling of Pertinent Legislation

Wheeler-Lea Act (1938) Amends the Federal Trade Commission Act (1914). Gives the Federal Trade Commission power to protect consumers against false and misleading advertising.

Fair Packaging and Labeling Act (1966) Regulates language that can be used on labels and provides for voluntary adoption of uniform packaging standards. The purpose of the act is to enable consumers to obtain accurate information from labels and packages that will help them make value comparisons between products.

Magnuson-Moss Warranty/Federal Trade Commission Improvement Act (1975) Gives the FTC the power to make rules for consumer-product warranties and increases FTC powers to make rules regarding unfair or deceptive acts and practices. The purpose of the act is to increase information available to customers, prevent deception, improve competition in the marketing of consumer products, and establish rules required in the written warranty of products.[3]

Credit and Collection Policies

If your company extends credit to customers, you should have a basic understanding of laws governing credit and collection.

Legislation has been passed to ensure that consumers are fully aware of a company's credit policies and that companies issue credit without biases. As a businessperson, make sure that your credit data on customers are reliable and that the statements you make concerning someone's credit are related only to the specific data you have: avoid jumping to conclusions or altering the facts in any way.

When evaluating credit applications, for example, a creditor cannot do the following:[4]

1. Assign a value to sex or marital status
2. Assign a value to the existence of a telephone listing
3. Request or use information about birth control practices or childbearing capability
4. Require reapplication or change terms based solely on change of name or marital status
5. Discount all or part of the income of the applicant or applicant's spouse
6. Use prohibited information
7. Prohibit an applicant from using any particular name
8. Fail to act or unreasonably delay action

Both federal and state laws have also been passed to protect consumers from being harassed by companies to which they owe money. False and misleading representations and other unfair practices are also prohibited. A creditor is forbidden to communicate with the debtor at unusual places and times, to use threats of force or violence, and to use obscene language. In California, state law forbids a creditor from intentionally inflicting emotional distress on a debtor.

State laws are used in cases involving blackmail, slander, libel, and fraud. In general, however, when sending collection letters, be careful to avoid referring to a person in terms usually considered libelous, such as *cheat, criminal,* and *liar.* In your state, it may also be illegal to threaten criminal prosecution.

Sampling of Pertinent Legislation

Truth-in-Lending Act (1969) Requires full disclosure of terms and conditions of finance charges in consumer credit transactions.

Fair Credit Reporting Act (1970) Requires that businesses correctly communicate credit information and regulates use of credit information.

Fair Credit Billing Act (1975) Sets up mechanisms for consumers to correct errors in their credit reports. Sets time limits for communications sent by businesses to consumers.

Equal Credit Opportunity Act (1976) Prohibits credit discrimination on the basis of sex, marital status, age, race, color, or religious origin.

Fair Debt Collection Act (1980) Makes it illegal to harrass or abuse debtors. It also prohibits the use of falsehoods and other unfair methods to collect a debt.

Employment

Since parents and students over 18 now have access to the students' files held by public schools and colleges, they may view the letters of recommendation in those files; this legislation has affected the way such letters are written. Writers must take great care to avoid potentially libelous language in their letters.

Numerous federal and state laws have been passed to prohibit discrimination on the basis of race, color, religion, sex, national origin, handicap, or age. Employers may not discriminate when advertising for job applicants, making preemployment inquiries, or testing applicants. Employers are required to keep records on employees in each job category and to demonstrate fairness in personnel policies.

It is usually a good idea to go through your company's applications forms carefully to see what information is really necessary: many application forms in the past asked for information that did not relate to the applicants' skills or the positions for which they were applying.

In interviewing job candidates, be careful not to ask questions that may be considered illegal. Keep your questions strictly related to the position for which the candidate is applying. For example, avoid questions regarding the maiden name of a female applicant, childcare practices, and the applicant's religious preference or ethnic background.

As an employer, make sure that various groups are represented at different job levels and scales and that employees are given adequate preparation to move upward.

Sampling of Pertinent Legislation

Equal Pay Act (1963) Rules that women should be paid the same as men if they are doing equivalent jobs with equivalent skills under similar working conditions.

Civil Rights Act, Title VII (1964) Prohibits discrimination on the basis of race, color, religion, national origin, and sex in the hiring, firing, pay, promotion, training, or dismissal of employees. The Act creates the Equal Employment Opportunity Commission (EEOC), which has the power and responsibility to file actions, investigate all charges of discrimination, attempt to compromise violations, and issue guidelines and regulations.

Age Discrimination in Employment Act (1967) Prohibits discrimination against people 40 to 70 years in terms of hiring, retirement, and conditions of employment.

Rehabilitation Act (1973) Attempts to assist the handicapped to obtain employment, rehabilitation training, and access to public facilities.

Family Education Rights and Privacy Act (1974) Permits parents and students over 18 years old to have access to their public school and college files.

Notes

[1]Data have been adapted from Choudhury, Pravat. "FTC Interpretation of Deception Giving Advertisers New Latitude." *Marketing News* 27 April 1984: 11.

[2]Posch, Robert J., Jr. *What Every Manager Needs to Know About Marketing and the Law,* New York: McGraw-Hill, 1984. 271.

[3]Data from Paust, Jordan L., Robert D. Upp, and John E. H. Sherry. *Business Law.* 4th ed., St. Paul, MN, West Publishing, 1984. 467.

[4]Data from Paust, Upp, and Sherry. 464–465.

Business Letter Parts and Formats

Appendix B

The appearance and layout of a business letter are important to the image you are conveying. Like good mechanics, the appropriate appearance of a letter enhances your credibility and professionalism as well as that of the organization you represent.

Most companies have their own stationery and a standard letter format so that their correspondence is consistent in appearance. You should, however, be familiar with the parts of a letter and the conventions that accompany them.

Heading

The heading usually consists of printed letterhead on business stationery. If you are not using letterhead stationery, the heading consists of your address. Do not type your name over the address.

Date

Type the month, day, and year. Do not abbreviate the month or add *nd, st,* or *th* to the day.

September 2, 19xx

or

2 September 19xx

Inside Address

The inside address consists of the name of the person to whom the letter is being sent, that person's official title (such as Director or Chair), the name of the company or organization, and the complete address. Also include a courtesy title such as Mr., Mrs., Miss, Ms., or Dr.

Spell out words such as *Street* and *Boulevard*. (In fact, most words in business correspondence should be written out, not abbreviated.) You may use the official abbreviations for states in the inside address. Remember to include the ZIP code after the state.

The official title may appear on the same line as the name (separated by a comma) or on the line below (with no comma).

Mr. Herbert Tryon   Ms. Helen Brady, Manager
Director of Personnel   Dartmouth Clothes
Flare Corporation   2967 D Street
2378 Forest Road   Raines, MI 42378
Bell, TX 78912

Attention Line

Attention: Customer Service Department

An attention line is optional. You may use an attention line to direct your letter to a certain person or department. The attention line appears below the inside address. Usually you will not use a salutation if you use an attention line.

If you use an attention line, the first line of your inside address should be the name of a company or organization, not the name of an individual. When you use an attention line, put it on the envelope as well as on the letter.

Salutation

The salutation usually coincides with the first line of the inside address. Thus, if your inside address reads *Mr. George Blake,* your salutation would read *Dear Mr. Blake.* The salutation is usually followed by a colon. To avoid having to use *Mr., Mrs.* and *Ms.,* many business writers simply use the reader's full name as a salutation: *Dear Marion Smith.*

If the first line of your inside address is the name of a company, you will have to decide on a suitable salutation. Traditionally, business writers have used *Dear Sirs* or *Gentlemen* as salutations. Then, in an effort to eliminate sexist language, writers began using *Ladies and Gentlemen* or *Dear Sir or Madam.* These terms now sound old-fashioned, so some writers use the simplified letter style that does not require a salutation. Also, salutations such as *Dear Editor* and *Dear Treasurer* are becoming more popular.

Subject Line

SUBJECT: ACCOUNT NUMBER 234-56-9110

The subject line, which is often capitalized, is an option you may use to indicate the purpose, subject, and urgency of your message. Written for your primary reader, the subject line is also used for filing materials.

Usually the subject line opens with the word *Subject* followed by a colon and a heading or title. The subject line usually appears below the salutation, but occasionally it appears above the salutation.

In the simplified letter style, a subject line is used in place of a salutation and attention line. This format simplifies typing but decreases the personal elements of the letter.

Body

The message in your letter begins below the salutation or subject line. Single-space the body; double-space between paragraphs. Most letters are typed single-spaced, with double spaces between paragraphs, before and after the salutation, and before the complimentary close.

Complimentary Close

The complimentary close, which appears two lines after the end of the body, is usually followed by a comma. Only the first word is capitalized: *Sincerely yours.*

Company Name

The name of the company, often in capital letters, is sometimes inserted under the complimentary close. This format is used particularly when the writer is acting as a legal agent for the company.

Sincerely,
J. N. TAYLOR, INC.

Thomas Yarley

Thomas Yarley
Vice-President

Signature

Sign your name above your typed name and title. Do not give yourself a courtesy title.

Writer's Typewritten Name and Title

Your name and title should be typed below the handwritten signature. Women writers often put a courtesy title in parentheses before their typed name to avoid confusion for the person responding to the letter.

(Ms.) Beryl Jones, Manager
Research Department

(Mrs.) Karen Johnson
Vice-President

Reference Initials

Reference initials are those of the writer (capitalized) and the typist (small letters) separated by a colon or dash. Sometimes the typist's initials appear alone in small letters.

BH:ed   BH/ed   ed

Enclosure Line

If you have included enclosures with your letter, you may write *Enclosure, Enclosures,* or *Enc.* below the reference initials. You may also describe the enclosure: *Enclosure: Resume.*

Copy Line

cc	Dr. Lawrence Kelleher	Copy: Professor Marion Small
c:	Ms. Nancy Ashby	C Nancy Ashby
	Mr. David Chatham	

If copies of the letter are being sent to other readers, a copy line is used to list readers other than the person to whom the letter is addressed. (Readers are usually listed in alphabetical order.) Nowadays, *c, copy,* or *copies* may be used instead of *cc,* which stands for *carbon copy,* since most copies now are not made with carbon paper. The colon is optional.

The notation *bcc* means *blind carbon copy.*

bcc: Mrs. Jane Fredericks

This notation is used on the copy being sent to Mrs. Fredericks, but not on the original letter.

Unless a postscript is used, the copy line is the last line of the business letter page.

Postscript

If you wish to include a postscript, make it the last item on your page. Begin it at the left margin two lines below the preceding section. You may begin the postscript with P.S. or PS if you like.

Avoid using postscripts too frequently; they may indicate poor planning.

Second Page of Letter

At the top of the second page of a business letter, put the name of the person addressed, the page number, and the date. You may put the information vertically or horizontally.

or

Mr. Benjamin Howard
December 5, 19xx
Page 2

```
                                    600 Finch Street
                                    Peterson, KY 78934
                                    April 15, 19xx

Ms. Harriet Forbes
Customer Service
Tom's Hardware Store
921 Beeson Road
Arbour, KY 78654

Dear Ms. Forbes:

Thank you very much for helping me locate new lawn
chairs to replace the two chairs that were broken
in transit. I appreciate the time and personal
attention you gave to a difficult situation.

The new chairs arrived in perfect condition and
perfectly match the rest of my set.

                                    Sincerely,

                                    Garth Newton

                                    Garth Newton
```

Personal Business Letter. Because this writer does not use a letterhead, he begins the letter with his address, not his name. He uses standard punctuation and allows about three spaces for his signature.

V & H CONSULTANTS
6789 Felton Avenue
Seal Harbor, SC 23678

May 23, 19xx

Mr. George Bortz
Assistant Manager
Nobbley's Department Store
1298 N. Deerfield Avenue
Merriman, SC 29766

Dear Mr. Bortz:

Subject: Research on Improved Security System

During our telephone conversation on Wednesday,
April 23, Ms. Charlene Simpson informed me that
Nobbley's Department Store has been experiencing
increased shoplifting problems in the last year.
She asked me whether V & H Consultants could
research the problem and provide some
recommendations on how Nobbley's could effectively
increase security.

We are very interested in the project and would
like to discuss it with you in more detail. Then we
will develop a proposal outlining our methodology,
budget, and timeframe. I enclose our company
brochure.

I will call Nobbley's next week to set up a meeting
at your convenience.

Sincerely yours,

Beryl Jones

Beryl Jones, Manager
Research Department

BJ/af

Enclosure

cc Mr. John Radner
   Dr. Laura Turner

P.S. Congratulations on opening your new store in
Bayfair Mall.

Full block letter style. With the full block letter style, every line begins at the left margin.
Because it is easy to type, this format is gaining in popularity. The subject line may be
underlined or printed in capital letters.
    This letter shows the standard punctuation for business letters.

```
                    V & H CONSULTANTS
                    6789 Felton Avenue
                    Seal Harbor, SC 23678

                              May 23, 19xx

Ms. Charlene Simpson, Manager
Nobbley's Department Store
1298 Deerfield Avenue
Merriman, SC 29766

Dear Ms. Simpson:

     SUBJECT: RESEARCH ON IMPROVED SECURITY SYSTEM

   During our telephone conversation on Wednesday,
April 23, you informed me that Nobbley's Department
Store has been experiencing increased shoplifting
problems in the last year. You asked me whether CCC
Consulting Services could research the problem and
provide some recommendations on how Nobbley's could
effectively increase security.

   We are very interested in the project and would
like to discuss it with you in more detail. Then we
will develop a proposal outlining our methodology,
budget, and timeframe. I enclose our company
brochure.

   I will call you next week to set up a meeting at
your convenience.

                         Sincerely yours,

                         Beryl Jones

                         Beryl Jones, Manager
                         Research Department

BJ/af

Enc: brochure

c: Mr. John Radner
   Dr. Laura Turner
```

Semiblock letter style. With the semiblock letter style, each paragraph either is indented five spaces, as we see here, or begins at the left margin. The date, complimentary close, and signature begin at the center of page or to the right of the center. The subject line may be indented or, as in this example, centered. The subject line in this example is also capitalized.

You may use the standard punctuation that is used here, or you may use the open style of punctuation. With open punctuation, no colon or comma appears after the salutation, and no comma appears after the complimentary close.

The semiblock letter style is the format most commonly used in business correspondence.

```
                    V & H CONSULTANTS
                    6789 Felton Avenue
                  Seal Harbor, SC 23678

May 23, 19xx

Ms. Charlene Simpson
Manager
Nobbley's Department Store
1298 N. Deerfield Avenue
Merriman, SC 29766

RESEARCH ON IMPROVED SECURITY SYSTEM

During our telephone conversation on Wednesday,
April 23, you informed me that Nobbley's Department
Store has been experiencing increased shoplifting
problems in the last year. You asked me whether CCC
Consulting Services could research the problem and
provide some recommendations on how Nobbley's could
effectively increase security.

We are very interested in the project and would
like to discuss it with you in more detail. Then we
will develop a proposal outlining our methodology,
budget, and timeframe. I enclose our company
brochure.

I will call you next week to set up a meeting at
your convenience.

Beryl Jones

BERYL JONES
MANAGER
RESEARCH DEPARTMENT

af
```

Simplified letter style. This is the least common format for business letters. Although it is easy to type, it lacks a personal touch. The lines begin at the left margin, as they do with the full-block style, but neither a salutation nor a complimentary close is used. The subject line and signature section are capitalized.

Glossary of
Business Terms

AGENDA. List of items to be covered in a meeting.

APPLICATION FORM. A data sheet to be filled out by job applicants.

APPLICATION LETTER. Letter persuading a prospective employer to interview a job candidate.

APPRAISAL INTERVIEW. A meeting in which an interviewer critiques the performance of an employee.

BAR GRAPH. Diagram designed so that the height or length of rectangular boxes shows relationships over time.

BRIEFING. Short talk to inform or teach listeners.

BUSINESS LETTER. Document used primarily for external communication.

CHRONOLOGICAL RESUME. Resume set up to indicate what a person was doing during specified years.

CLAIM. Demand for payment or other retribution.

COLLECTION LETTER SERIES. Increasingly urgent letters developed to persuade people to pay their bills. A series often includes a reminder, a friendly letter, and an urgent request for payment.

COUNSELING INTERVIEW. A meeting in which an interviewer gives advice to an interviewee on personal or job-related topics.

CREDIT CUSTOMER. Customer who has made an arrangement with a seller to pay for products or services at a later date.

CREDIT LAWS. Laws such as the Fair Credit Billing Act that help to protect customers from unfair credit practices.

DATABASE SERVICE. Service that provides subscribing computer users with data.

DEMOGRAPHIC VARIABLES. External characteristics such as people's age, sex, race, income, job type, and education.

DISCIPLINARY INTERVIEW. A meeting in which an interviewer and an employee discuss the employee's attitude problem or infraction of rules.

DOWNWARD COMMUNICATION. Messages flowing to subordinates in an organization.

EMPLOYEE EVALUATION. Report or form that includes an appraisal of the work an employee has been doing over a specified time period, the employee's qualifications, and the writer's recommendations for the employee.

EXIT INTERVIEW. A meeting in which an employee talks with a supervisor or personnel representative before ending employment in an organization.

EXTERNAL COMMUNICATION. Messages flowing into and out of an organization.

FLIP CHART. Large tablet of paper attached to an easel.

FLOW CHART. Diagram of the movement of people or things.

FOLLOW-UP LETTER. A letter of inquiry sent when an applicant does not hear from a company after an interview.

FORMAL REPORT. A report usually over eight pages long used to describe and analyze problems. Formal reports are often written and designed according to precise guidelines for content, organization, and appearance.

FUNCTIONAL RESUME. Resume set up to highlight someone's skills and capabilities. Also called a *skills resume*.

GLOBALIZATION. The increasingly worldwide nature of business.

GRAPH. Diagram showing the relationship between two variables. Usually each variable is measured along one of a pair of axes at right angles to one another.

GRAPEVINE. The informal communication channel in an organization.

GROUPTHINK. Situation that occurs when people are reluctant to disagree with their colleagues or leader.

HIDDEN AGENDA. Personal programs that differ from the official agenda of a meeting.

JOB INQUIRY LETTER. A request for job application forms or for information regarding positions available within an organization.

LATERAL COMMUNICATION. Messages flowing between people of equal status or rank in an organization.

LETTER OF APPRECIATION. Letter thanking a person, particularly for a special effort or a job well done.

LETTER OF CONDOLENCE. Letter of sympathy to a family member or friend of someone who has died.

LETTER OF CONGRATULATION. Letter conveying happiness at an event in the reader's life such as a promotion.

LETTER OF INQUIRY. Letter used to request information.

LETTER OF RECOMMENDATION. Letter to prospective employers regarding the candidate's qualifications for a position.

LETTER OF REQUEST. Letter used to request action.

LINE GRAPH. Diagram in which lines indicate changes. Usually the horizontal axis depicts time while the horizontal axis depicts dollar amounts or other data.

MASLOW'S HIERARCHY OF NEEDS. Theory of motivation based on the concept that lower-order needs such as hunger and thirst must be satisfied before higher-order needs such as a desire for prestige can emerge.

MEMORANDUM (MEMO). A written communication used primarily within an organization to convey information, explain procedures, or persuade readers to act.

MINUTES. Summary of motions, decisions, and other activities at a meeting.

NONPROBABILITY SAMPLING. Method of choosing interviewees in which the probability of a person being included in the sample is unknown.

OFFEROR. A person, group, or organization writing a proposal in response to a request for a proposal (RFP).

ORGANIZATIONAL CHART. Diagram depicting the hierarchy of authority within an organization.

OVERHEAD TRANSPARENCY. Clear piece of plastic on which handwritten, typed, or printed material may be imprinted and then projected onto a screen.

PANEL INTERVIEW. An interview at which a candidate meets with a group of people.

PICTOGRAM. Diagram in which symbols such as stick figures or dollar signs are used to represent people or items.

PIE GRAPH. Circle graph in which an entire "pie" represents a whole entity, and "slices" show the respective size of each part at one point in time.

PRIMARY DATA. Information collected specifically for the project at hand.

A questionnaire, for example, might be used to collect primary data.

PROBABILITY SAMPLING. Sampling procedure in which each individual has a known probability of being selected.

PROGRESS REPORT. A report providing information on work done on a project during a particular time.

PROPOSAL. A persuasive report outlining a problem and urging that particular steps be taken to solve it.

PROMOTIONAL LETTER. Letter urging readers to support a cause.

PSYCHOGRAPHIC VARIABLES. Internal characteristics such as people's personality types, values, lifestyles, interests, and opinions.

QUALITY CONTROL CIRCLE. Group that meets to discuss issues and make recommendations to management.

RECOMMENDATION REPORT. A report recommending that the reader take a particular course of action.

REQUEST FOR A PROPOSAL (RFP). A formal request from a company or government agency stating a need and asking that individuals or organizations develop proposals responding to the need.

SALES LETTER. Letter selling a product or service.

SECONDARY DATA. Information collected for purposes other than the project at hand. Magazine articles might be a source for secondary data.

SEGMENTED BAR GRAPH. Diagram in which each bar is divided into sections illustrating various parts of an entire entity. Colors or cross-hatching differentiates the different sections.

SHORT REPORT. A document under eight pages long used for conveying information. Presented in letter or memorandum form, a short report is usually sent vertically in an organization, often to people only a few steps higher than the writer.

STRESS INTERVIEW. An interview designed to test a candidate's ability to handle tense situations.

STRUCTURED INTERVIEW. An interview at which the interviewer asks the candidate prearranged questions.

TABLE. List of numbers or facts systematically arranged in columns and rows.

TELECONFERENCING. Conducting meetings with people in different locations by means of television equipment.

UNSTRUCTURED INTERVIEW. An interview at which the interviewer and candidate speak in conversational fashion.

UPWARD COMMUNICATION. Messages flowing to people of higher rank in an organization.

Index

Credits (continued from p. iv)

Correction Symbols

ab	abbreviation	689
agr	agreement	653, 655, 692
amb	ambiguous	
awk	awkward	
cap	capital letter	682
cl	cliché	111
coh	coherence	
colloq	colloquialism	110
cs	comma splice	650, 694
dm	dangling modifier	660, 697
d	diction	
frag	fragment	647
id	idiomatic expression	
ital	italics	673
lc	lowercase letter	682
mm	misplaced modifier	659, 697
p	punctuation	665
pl	plural	653, 655, 698
ref	reference of pronoun	657
ro	run-on sentence	649
sp	spelling	
u	unity	
vb	verb form	701, 702
w	wordiness	105
ww	wrong word	678
ℰ	delete	
∧	omission	
‖	parallelism	661
¶	paragraph	100
⋏	comma	666
⋏̟	semicolon	669
⋎	apostrophe	670
⋎/⋎	quotation marks	673, 675
⋏	colon	670
—⊥ₘ	em dash	671
—⊥ₙ	en dash	672
-	hyphen	672
( )	parentheses	674, 675
[ ]	brackets	674
...	ellipses	674

CONTEMPORARY DRAMA
FIFTEEN PLAYS

Contemporary Drama

FIFTEEN PLAYS

AMERICAN
ENGLISH AND IRISH
EUROPEAN

Selected and Edited by

E. Bradlee Watson

DARTMOUTH COLLEGE

and Benfield Pressey

DARTMOUTH COLLEGE

CHARLES SCRIBNER'S SONS

NEW YORK

ACKNOWLEDGMENTS

Page vii constitutes an extension of the copyright page.

Uncle Vanya reprinted from *Plays* by Anton P. Chekhov, translated by Marian Fell (1912). Used by permission of Charles Scribner's Sons.

Murder in the Cathedral by T. S. Eliot, copyright 1935, by Harcourt, Brace & World, Inc.; renewal copyright © 1963, by T. S. Eliot.

Look Homeward, Angel by Ketti Frings. Used by permission of Edward C. Aswell on behalf of the Thomas Wolfe Estate, and Ketti Frings. © 1958 Edward C. Aswell as Administrator C.T.A. of the Estate of Thomas Wolfe and/or Fred W. Wolfe and Ketti Frings.

FOREWORD

This collection should meet the needs of two kinds of teachers: those who wish to introduce students to modern drama by means of an adequate number of great plays, but do not require that these plays be placed in time or theatrical history; and those who do wish to give a minimum conception of how dramatic technique has changed and varieties widened since the rejuvenation of drama began with Ibsen. To be found here are plays by the greatest authors of the modern period whose work is complete: Ibsen, Shaw, O'Neill, Chekhov, Pirandello, Synge, Strindberg, Wilde, Lorca. No historical study of the modern drama can omit any of these. But many of the plays here are by authors from whom much can still be expected: Eliot, Wilder, O'Casey, Miller, Inge, Frings. Three of the plays are from the decade of the 1950's, and one has been most recently awarded the Pulitzer Prize at the time of publication. We have tried hard in this collection to make a workable compromise between history and up-to-dateness, and we think we have succeeded.

The teacher who is privileged to give a semester course in the drama since Ibsen, however, will not find this volume alone adequate. We hope such a teacher will consider combining this volume with our Nine-Play and Eleven-Play volumes in the CONTEMPORARY DRAMA series. In the Nine-Play volume he will find dramas by Rostand, Barrie, Galsworthy, Čapek, Maugham, O'Neill, Rice, Howard and Sherwood; in the Eleven-Play volume, by Shaw, Saroyan, Connelly, Wilder, Coward, Anouilh, Tennessee Williams, Giraudoux, Hellman, Miller, and Fry. We believe the three volumes together would make a very illuminating survey of the modern drama, with four plays from the decade of the 1890's; four from the first decade of the twentieth century; two from the decade of the First World War; five from the 1920's; seven from the 1930's; ten from the 1940's; and three from the 1950's. Of these thirty-five plays, fifteen are American, eleven English or Irish, and nine European.

Three texts in this volume perhaps call for comment. *Purple Dust* follows the form in which it was played in New York, according to Mr. O'Casey's wish. By the kind permission of Mr. Eliot, part II of *Murder in the Cathedral* begins with both Chorus and Priests, as in the latest English editions. *Man and Superman* is presented complete, as Bernard Shaw wished it to be read, with Epistle Dedicatory, the third act, known in separate presentation as *Don Juan in Hell*, and The Revolutionist's Handbook, as well as the play as customarily acted.

In making this volume, we did not need to try for variety in either theme or technique, for it comes without trying in any collection of modern drama. We found it easy to think of and try to obtain for this collection works of intellectual distinction, for the modern period is rich in them. We have tried to include works that hold the stage or seem likely to. All these plays are theatrical in the sense that theatricality is demanded in plays. The modern drama is delightful to teach and to study, and we hope that teachers and students who use this volume will enjoy it.

E.B.W.

B.P.

CONTENTS

CONTEMPORARY DRAMA
FIFTEEN PLAYS

HEDDA GABLER*

By

HENRIK IBSEN

Translated by EDMUND GOSSE *and* WILLIAM ARCHER

IBSEN WROTE OF "HEDDA GABLER": "MY intention in giving it this name was to indicate that Hedda, as a personality, is to be regarded rather as her father's daughter than as her husband's wife. It was not my desire to deal in this play with so-called problems. What I principally wanted to do was to depict human beings, human emotions, and human destinies, upon a groundwork of certain of the social conditions and principles of the present day."

The strange qualities of the Ibsen mind and soul emerge amusingly and pathetically in the encounter that gave rise to *Hedda Gabler* and *The Master Builder*. In the autumn of 1889 Ibsen met Emilie Bardach, a miss of eighteen. He was sixty, married, a parent, and famous; she was pretty, gay, and a head-hunter. She came from Austria to meet and captivate him, and by smiling at him from a park bench as he passed on his walks, she aroused his timid interest. Thereafter they had long talks, always in public places, for Ibsen was careful. Yet he was impressed; one can imagine that short stiff figure, with the aureole of white fringe about the face and the spectacles glittering in the light, turned attentively toward the slight vivacious girl, chattering and posing for him —in the lobby of a hotel. She seems to have thought herself a "new" woman, an "Ibsen woman," in fact; and he must have been both fascinated and repelled at this embodiment of his influence. Here, in a way, was posterity, the judge to which every artist appeals, and it was already impregnated with what it thought were his ideas. Here he found the courage in action that he himself had always lacked and wished for, but it was directed and reenforced by a flippant ruthlessness. Emilie professed to wish never to marry; she would capture other women's husbands. Yet she strangely invited boredom: she was clever, she had talent for music and painting, but she would do noth-

ing with them. She preferred to pose as mysterious, tired, aloof. Ibsen once wrote to her, sadly, "You and the Christmas season do not quite fit together."

But she fired his imagination. Since *The Wild Duck* the use of the symbol as substitute for actuality had been a growing habit with him. He had always used life itself as his material, but in his shyness and seclusion he had tended to take it second or third hand, and compensate for lack of closely observed outline by lending depth and shadow. Emilie Bardach, so closely listened to and studied, gave him actuality first hand. At least, she gave him a character, or rather many characters, for it may be guessed that she was the prototype not only of Hedda, but also of Hilda Wangel and even of Kaia Fosli. With his hard mind and stern artistic eye, he lifted from the living girl those qualities she had displayed in their variety to charm him, and poured each into its appropriate mold. She gave him no incident, to be sure; at eighteen, what incident could there be? But fortunately he heard, at about the same time, of a brilliant but dissipated young professor who lost a manuscript; of the wife of a composer who in jealousy burned her husband's just completed symphony; and of another wife who tempted her husband, cured of alcoholism, by leaving brandy in his room. Then came the fusion, and *Hedda Gabler*. As soon as he began work on the play, early in 1890, Ibsen forbade Emilie to write to him or see him. But he remembered her, and sent her a copy of *Hedda Gabler* as a Christmas gift.

Hedda Gabler was the last of the plays in which Ibsen's mind moved outward, upon "the social conditions and principles of the present day." Thereafter he was to write four more plays, but each of them seems to move inward, to explore the geography and climate of a soul rather than of a society. And they are great plays, plays such as only a master could write, but they are not plays which would have brought an Emilie Bardach

* Used by permission of Charles Scribner's Sons.

3

from Vienna. For the inventor of the "Ibsen woman" and the "founder of modern drama" made his impact upon society and the theatre through plays which seemed to advocate a new morality, or at least a firmer one, such plays as *Pillars of Society* (1877), *A Doll's House* (1879), *Ghosts* (1881), and *An Enemy of the People* (1882). This new morality seemed liberating, based on clear insights, especially to the young of the 1880's and 1890's, and it was presented in masterly concreteness and impressive dramaturgy, in settings all could recognize, by people like those one could meet on the street. Here was truth, new truth, and Emilie Bardach was far from alone in embracing it. It demanded candor, acceptance and confession of defect or wickedness, brave confidence in the self and its judgments, vigorous espousal of causes seen to be socially desirable, defiance of mere convention. Many a bright-faced liberal has professed this code since Ibsen, and a few, of course, before him, but none more persuasively than he in the "social" plays which made his world reputation.

But he himself was not persuaded. In *The Wild Duck* (1884) the code was questioned, and in a fashion deeply moving; again, with more poetry, perhaps, in *Rosmersholm* (1886); in *The Lady from the Sea* (1888) it scarcely seems to enter—the play's conflict cannot be resolved by any code. But Hedda Gabler professes the code, at least by implication, and she is not liberated but destroyed, and destroys others.

Perhaps Ibsen left us only with the doctrine: "The Golden Rule is that there is no Golden Rule." But the mind and spirit rebel at regarding such a blank as the product of Ibsen's life and labor. Here is one of the half-dozen of the world's greatest dramatists; he may not have given us one single message, but many; his work may picture a life lived into art which changes as the life changes, as all lives change. Unity lies not in the said but in the saying.

In this saying is Ibsenism. Modern drama, as a historical development, is surely partly created by Ibsenism. And Ibsenism is not so much a system as an attitude: thoughtfulness, seriousness, and especially searching characterization. All these and high art are to be found in *Hedda Gabler*.

HENRIK IBSEN

Born 1828, Skien, Norway.

1843–1850, Apprenticed to an apothecary in Grimstad.

1850–1851, Attended the University of Christiania (Oslo).

1851–1856, "Theatre-poet" at Bergen. For a few months before assuming this post, he traveled in Denmark and Germany studying theatrical production.

1857–1862, Manager and artistic advisor of theatres in Christiania.

1858, Married. One son.

1864, Began self-imposed exile in resentment at hostile criticism, failure of his theatre, and the state's refusal of an adequate pension. Angered by Norwegian indifference to the Prusso-Danish War, he decided not to return. Lived in Italy and Germany.

1891, Returned to Norway.

1899, Apoplexy. Unable to work thereafter.

Died 1906.

PLAYS

1850 *Catiline.* 1850 *The Viking's Barrow.* 1853 *St. John's Night.* 1855 *Lady Inger of Ostrat.* 1856 *The Feast of Solhaug.* 1857 *Olaf Liljekrans.* 1858 *Vikings of Helgeland.* 1862 *Love's Comedy.* 1864 *The Pretenders.* 1866 *Brand.* 1867 *Peer Gynt.* 1869 *The League of Youth.* 1873 *Emperor and Galilean.* 1877 *Pillars of Society.* 1879 *A Doll's House.* 1881 *Ghosts.* 1882 *An Enemy of the People.* 1884 *The Wild Duck.* 1886 *Rosmersholm.* 1888 *The Lady from the Sea.* 1890 *Hedda Gabler.* 1892 *The Master Builder.* 1894 *Little Eyolf.* 1896 *John Gabriel Borkman.* 1899 *When We Dead Awaken.*

WRITINGS ON DRAMA

See *From Ibsen's Workshop,* 1912.

HEDDA GABLER

Characters

GEORGE TESMAN.[1]
HEDDA TESMAN, *his wife.*
MISS JULIANA TESMAN, *his aunt.*
MRS. ELVSTED.
JUDGE [2] BRACK.

EILERT LÖVBORG.
BERTA, *servant at the Tesmans.*

The scene of the action is Tesman's villa, in the west end of Christiania.

ACT FIRST

A spacious, handsome, and tastefully furnished drawing-room, decorated in dark colors. In the back, a wide doorway with curtains drawn back, leading into a smaller room decorated in the same style as the drawing-room. In the right-hand wall of the front room, a folding door leading out to the hall. In the opposite wall, on the left, a glass door, also with curtains drawn back. Through the panes can be seen part of a veranda outside, and trees covered with autumn foliage. An oval table, with a cover on it, and surrounded by chairs, stands well forward. In front, by the wall on the right, a wide stove of dark porcelain, a high-backed arm-chair, a cushioned foot-rest, and two footstools. A settee, with a small round table in front of it, fills the upper right-hand corner. In front, on the left, a little way from the wall, a sofa. Further back than the glass door, a piano. On either side of the doorway at the back a whatnot with terra-cotta and majolica ornaments.—Against the back wall of the inner room a sofa, with a table, and one or two chairs. Over the sofa hangs a portrait of a handsome elderly man in a General's uniform. Over the table a hanging lamp, with an opal glass shade.—A number of bouquets are arranged about the drawing-room, in vases and glasses. Others lie upon the tables. The floors in both rooms are covered with thick carpets.—Morning light. The sun shines in through the glass door.

[MISS JULIANA TESMAN, with her bon-net on and carrying a parasol, comes in from the hall, followed by BERTA, who carries a bouquet wrapped in paper. MISS TESMAN is a comely and pleasant-looking lady of about sixty-five. She is nicely but simply dressed in a gray walking-costume. BERTA is a middle-aged woman of plain and rather countrified appearance.]

Miss Tesman. [Stops close to the door, listens, and says softly.] Upon my word, I don't believe they are stirring yet!

Berta. [Also softly.] I told you so, Miss. Remember how late the steamboat got in last night. And then, when they got home!—good Lord, what a lot the young mistress had to unpack before she could get to bed.

Miss Tesman. Well, well—let them have their sleep out. But let us see that they get a good breath of the fresh morning air when they do appear.

[She goes to the glass door and throws it open.]

Berta. [Beside the table, at a loss what to do with the bouquet in her hand.] I declare there isn't a bit of room left. I think I'll put it down there, Miss.

[She places it on the piano.]

Miss Tesman. So you've got a new mistress now, my dear Berta. Heaven knows it was a wrench to me to part with you.

Berta. [On the point of weeping.] And do you think it wasn't hard for me too, Miss? After all the blessed years I've been with you and Miss Rina.[1]

Miss Tesman. We must make the best of it, Berta. There was nothing else to be done.

---

[1] Tesman, whose Christian name in the original is "Jörgen," is described as "stipendiat i kulturhistorie" —that is to say, the holder of a scholarship for purposes of research into the History of Civilization.
[2] In the original "Assessor."

[1] Pronounce *Reena* (All notes to *Hedda Gabler* are by the translators).

George can't do without you, you see—he absolutely can't. He has had you to look after him ever since he was a little boy.

Berta. Ah, but, Miss Julia, I can't help thinking of Miss Rina lying helpless at home there, poor thing. And with only that new girl too! She'll never learn to take proper care of an invalid.

Miss Tesman. Oh, I shall manage to train her. And of course, you know, I shall take most of it upon myself. You needn't be uneasy about my poor sister, my dear Berta.

Berta. Well, but there's another thing, Miss. I'm so mortally afraid I shan't be able to suit the young mistress.

Miss Tesman. Oh, well—just at first there may be one or two things——

Berta. Most like she'll be terrible grand in her ways.

Miss Tesman. Well, you can't wonder at that—General Gabler's daughter! Think of the sort of life she was accustomed to in her father's time. Don't you remember how we used to see her riding down the road along with the General? In that long black habit—and with feathers in her hat?

Berta. Yes, indeed—I remember well enough!—But, good Lord, I should never have dreamt in those days that she and Master George would make a match of it.

Miss Tesman. Nor I.—But by-the-bye, Berta—while I think of it: in future you mustn't say Master George. You must say Dr. Tesman.

Berta. Yes, the young mistress spoke of that too—last night—the moment they set foot in the house. Is it true then, Miss?

Miss Tesman. Yes, indeed it is. Only think, Berta—some foreign university has made him a doctor—while he has been abroad, you understand. I hadn't heard a word about it, until he told me himself upon the pier.

Berta. Well, well he's clever enough for anything, he is. But I didn't think he'd have gone in for doctoring people, too.

Miss Tesman. No, no, it's not that sort of doctor he is. [*Nods significantly.*] But let me tell you, we may have to call him something still grander before long.

Berta. You don't say so! What can that be, Miss?

Miss Tesman. [*Smiling.*] H'm—wouldn't you like to know! [*With emotion.*] Ah, dear, dear—if my poor brother could only look up from his grave now, and see what his little boy has grown into! [*Looks around.*] But bless me, Berta—why have you done this? Taken the chintz covers off all the furniture?

Berta. The mistress told me to. She can't abide covers on the chairs, she says.

Miss Tesman. Are they going to make this their everyday sitting-room then?

Berta. Yes, that's what I understood—from the mistress. Master George—the doctor—he said nothing.

[GEORGE TESMAN *comes from the right into the inner room, humming to himself, and carrying an unstrapped empty portmanteau. He is a middle-sized, young-looking man of thirty-three, rather stout, with a round, open, cheerful face, fair hair and beard. He wears spectacles, and is somewhat carelessly dressed in comfortable indoor clothes.*]

Miss Tesman. Good morning, good morning, George.

Tesman. [*In the doorway between the rooms.*] Aunt Julia! Dear Aunt Julia! [*Goes up to her and shakes hands warmly.*] Come all this way—so early! Eh?

Miss Tesman. Why, of course I had to come and see how you were getting on.

Tesman. In spite of your having had no proper night's rest?

Miss Tesman. Oh, that makes no difference to me.

Tesman. Well, I suppose you got home all right from the pier? Eh?

Miss Tesman. Yes, quite safely, thank goodness. Judge Brack was good enough to see me right to my door.

Tesman. We were so sorry we couldn't give you a seat in the carriage. But you saw what a pile of boxes Hedda had to bring with her.

Miss Tesman. Yes, she had certainly plenty of boxes.

Berta. [*To* TESMAN.] Shall I go in and see if there's anything I can do for the mistress?

Tesman. No, thank you, Berta—you needn't. She said she would ring if she wanted anything.

Berta. [*Going towards the right.*] Very well.

Tesman. But look here—take this portmanteau with you.

Berta. [*Taking it.*] I'll put it in the attic.
[*She goes out by the hall door.*]

Tesman. Fancy, Auntie—I had the whole of that portmanteau chock full of copies of documents. You wouldn't believe how much I have picked up from all the archives I have been examining—curious old details that no one has had any idea of——

Miss Tesman. Yes, you don't seem to have wasted your time on your wedding trip, George.

Tesman. No, that I haven't. But do take

off your bonnet, Auntie. Look here! Let me untie the strings—eh?

Miss Tesman. [*While he does so.*] Well, well—this is just as if you were still at home with us.

Tesman. [*With the bonnet in his hand, looks at it from all sides.*] Why, what a gorgeous bonnet you've been investing in!

Miss Tesman. I bought it on Hedda's account.

Tesman. On Hedda's account? Eh?

Miss Tesman. Yes, so that Hedda needn't be ashamed of me if we happened to go out together.

Tesman. [*Patting her cheek.*] You always think of everything, Aunt Julia. [*Lays the bonnet on a chair beside the table.*] And now, look here—suppose we sit comfortably on the sofa and have a little chat, till Hedda comes.

[*They seat themselves. She places her parasol in the corner of the sofa.*]

Miss Tesman. [*Takes both his hands and looks at him.*] What a delight it is to have you again, as large as life, before my very eyes, George! My George—my poor brother's own boy!

Tesman. And it's a delight for me, too, to see you again, Aunt Julia! You, who have been father and mother in one to me.

Miss Tesman. Oh yes, I know you will always keep a place in your heart for your old aunts.

Tesman. And what about Aunt Rina? No improvement—eh?

Miss Tesman. Oh no—we can scarcely look for any improvement in her case, poor thing. There she lies, helpless, as she has lain for all these years. But heaven grant I may not lose her yet a while! For if I did, I don't know what I should make of my life, George—especially now that I haven't you to look after any more.

Tesman. [*Patting her back.*] There, there, there——!

Miss Tesman. [*Suddenly changing her tone.*] And to think that here are you a married man, George!—And that you should be the one to carry off Hedda Gabler—the beautiful Hedda Gabler! Only think of it—she, that was so beset with admirers!

Tesman. [*Hums a little and smiles complacently.*] Yes, I fancy I have several good friends about town who would like to stand in my shoes—eh?

Miss Tesman. And then this fine long wedding-tour you have had! More than five—nearly six months——

Tesman. Well, for me it has been a sort of tour of research as well. I have had to do much grubbing among old records—and to read no end of books too, Auntie.

Miss Tesman. Oh yes, I suppose so. [*More confidentially, and lowering her voice a little.*] But listen now, George—have you nothing—nothing special to tell me?

Tesman. As to our journey?

Miss Tesman. Yes.

Tesman. No, I don't know of anything except what I have told you in my letters. I had a doctor's degree conferred on me—but that I told you yesterday.

Miss Tesman. Yes, yes, you did. But what I mean is—haven't you any—any—expectations——?

Tesman. Expectations?

Miss Tesman. Why, you know, George—I'm your old auntie!

Tesman. Why, of course I have expectations.

Miss Tesman. Ah!

Tesman. I have every expectation of being a professor one of these days.

Miss Tesman. Oh yes, a professor——

Tesman. Indeed, I may say I am certain of it. But my dear Auntie—you know all about that already!

Miss Tesman. [*Laughing to herself.*] Yes, of course I do. You are quite right there. [*Changing the subject.*] But we were talking about your journey. It must have cost a great deal of money, George?

Tesman. Well, you see—my handsome traveling-scholarship went a good way.

Miss Tesman. But I can't understand how you can have made it go far enough for two.

Tesman. No, that's not so easy to understand—eh?

Miss Tesman. And especially traveling with a lady—they tell me that makes it ever so much more expensive.

Tesman. Yes, of course—it makes it a little more expensive. But Hedda had to have this trip, Auntie. She really had to. Nothing else would have done.

Miss Tesman. No, no, I suppose not. A wedding-tour seems to be quite indispensable nowadays.—But tell me now—have you gone thoroughly over the house yet?

Tesman. Yes, you may be sure I have. I have been afoot ever since daylight.

Miss Tesman. And what do you think of it all?

Tesman. I'm delighted! Quite delighted! Only I can't think what we are to do with the two empty rooms between this inner parlor and Hedda's bedroom.

Miss Tesman. [*Laughing.*] Oh, my dear George, I daresay you may find some use for them—in the course of time.

Tesman. Why of course, you are quite right, Aunt Julia! You mean as my library increases—eh?

Miss Tesman. Yes, quite so, my dear boy. It was your library I was thinking of.

Tesman. I am especially pleased on Hedda's account. Often and often, before we were engaged, she said that she would never care to live anywhere but in Secretary Falk's villa.[1]

Miss Tesman. Yes, it was lucky that this very house should come into the market, just after you had started.

Tesman. Yes, Aunt Julia, the luck was on our side, wasn't it—eh?

Miss Tesman. But the expense, my dear George! You will find it very expensive, all this.

Tesman. [*Looks at her, a little cast down.*] Yes, I suppose I shall, Aunt!

Miss Tesman. Oh, frightfully!

Tesman. How much do you think? In round numbers?—Eh?

Miss Tesman. Oh, I can't even guess until all the accounts come in.

Tesman. Well, fortunately, Judge Brack has secured the most favorable terms for me —so he said in a letter to Hedda.

Miss Tesman. Yes, don't be uneasy, my dear boy.—Besides, I have given security for the furniture and all the carpets.

Tesman. Security? You? My dear Aunt Julia—what sort of security could you give?

Miss Tesman. I have given a mortgage on our annuity.

Tesman. [*Jumps up.*] What! On your— and Aunt Rina's annuity!

Miss Tesman. Yes, I knew of no other plan, you see.

Tesman. [*Placing himself before her.*] Have you gone out of your senses, Auntie? Your annuity—it's all that you and Aunt Rina have to live upon.

Miss Tesman. Well, well—don't get so excited about it. It's only a matter of form, you know—Judge Brack assured me of that. It was he that was kind enough to arrange the whole affair for me. A mere matter of form, he said.

Tesman. Yes, that may be all very well. But nevertheless——

Miss Tesman. You will have your own salary to depend upon now. And, good heavens, even if we did have to pay up a little——! To eke things out a bit at the start——! Why, it would be nothing but a pleasure to us.

[1] In the original, "Statsrådinde Falks villa"—showing that it had belonged to the widow of a cabinet minister.

Tesman. Oh Auntie—will you never be tired of making sacrifices for me!

Miss Tesman. [*Rises and lays her hand on his shoulder.*] Have I any other happiness in this world except to smooth your way for you, my dear boy? You, who have had neither father nor mother to depend on. And now we have reached the goal, George! Things have looked black enough for us, sometimes; but, thank heaven, now you have nothing to fear.

Tesman. Yes, it is really marvelous how everything has turned out for the best.

Miss Tesman. And the people who opposed you—who wanted to bar the way for you—now you have them at your feet. They have fallen, George. Your most dangerous rival—his fall was the worst.—And now he has to lie on the bed he has made for himself —poor misguided creature.

Tesman. Have you heard anything of Eilert? Since I went away, I mean.

Miss Tesman. Only that he is said to have published a new book.

Tesman. What! Eilert Lövborg! Recently—eh?

Miss Tesman. Yes, so they say. Heaven knows whether it can be worth anything! Ah, when your new book appears—that will be another story, George! What is it to be about?

Tesman. It will deal with the domestic industries of Brabant during the Middle Ages.

Miss Tesman. Fancy—to be able to write on such a subject as that!

Tesman. However, it may be some time before the book is ready. I have all these collections to arrange first, you see.

Miss Tesman. Yes, collecting and arranging—no one can beat you at that. There you are my poor brother's own son.

Tesman. I am looking forward eagerly to setting to work at it; especially now that I have my own delightful home to work in.

Miss Tesman. And, most of all, now that you have got the wife of your heart, my dear George.

Tesman. [*Embracing her.*] Oh yes, yes, Aunt Julia! Hedda—she is the best part of it all! [*Looks toward the doorway.*] I believe I hear her coming—eh?

[HEDDA *enters from the left through the inner room. She is a woman of nine-and-twenty. Her face and figure show refinement and distinction. Her complexion is pale and opaque. Her steel-gray eyes express a cold, unruffled repose. Her hair is of an agreeable medium brown, but not particularly abundant. She is dressed in a tasteful, somewhat loose-fitting morning gown.*]

Miss Tesman. [*Going to meet* HEDDA.] Good morning, my dear Hedda! Good morning, and a hearty welcome.

Hedda. [*Holds out her hand.*] Good morning, dear Miss Tesman! So early a call! That is kind of you.

Miss Tesman. [*With some embarrassment.*] Well—has the bride slept well in her new home?

Hedda. Oh yes, thanks. Passably.

Tesman. [*Laughing.*] Passably! Come, that's good, Hedda! You were sleeping like a stone when I got up.

Hedda. Fortunately. Of course one has always to accustom one's self to new surroundings, Miss Tesman—little by little. [*Looking toward the left.*] Oh—there the servant has gone and opened the veranda door, and let in a whole flood of sunshine.

Miss Tesman. [*Going toward the door.*] Well, then we will shut it.

Hedda. No, no, not that! Tesman, please draw the curtains. That will give a softer light.

Tesman. [*At the door.*] All right—all right.—There now, Hedda, now you have both shade and fresh air.

Hedda. Yes, fresh air we certainly must have, with all these stacks of flowers——. But —won't you sit down, Miss Tesman?

Miss Tesman. No, thank you. Now that I have seen that everything is all right here— thank heaven!—I must be getting home again. My sister is lying longing for me, poor thing.

Tesman. Give her my very best love, Auntie; and say I shall look in and see her later in the day.

Miss Tesman. Yes, yes, I'll be sure to tell her. But by-the-bye, George— [*Feeling in her dress pocket.*] —I had almost forgotten —I have something for you here.

Tesman. What is it, Auntie? Eh?

Miss Tesman. [*Produces a flat parcel wrapped in newspaper and hands it to him.*] Look here, my dear boy.

Tesman. [*Opening the parcel.*] Well, I declare!—Have you really saved them for me, Aunt Julia! Hedda! isn't this touching— eh?

Hedda. [*Beside the whatnot on the right.*] Well, what is it?

Tesman. My old morning-shoes! My slippers.

Hedda. Indeed. I remember you often spoke of them while we were abroad.

Tesman. Yes, I missed them terribly.

[*Goes up to her.*] Now you shall see them, Hedda!

Hedda. [*Going toward the stove.*] Thanks, I really don't care about it.

Tesman. [*Following her.*] Only think—ill as she was, Aunt Rina embroidered these for me. Oh, you can't think how many associations cling to them.

Hedda. [*At the table.*] Scarcely for me.

Miss Tesman. Of course not for Hedda, George.

Tesman. Well, but now that she belongs to the family, I thought——

Hedda. [*Interrupting.*] We shall never get on with this servant, Tesman.

Miss Tesman. Not get on with Berta?

Tesman. Why, dear, what puts that in your head? Eh?

Hedda. [*Pointing.*] Look there! She has left her old bonnet lying about on a chair.

Tesman. [*In consternation, drops the slippers on the floor.*] Why, Hedda——

Hedda. Just fancy, if anyone should come in and see it!

Tesman. But Hedda—that's Aunt Julia's bonnet.

Hedda. Is it!

Miss Tesman. [*Taking up the bonnet.*] Yes, indeed it's mine. And, what's more, it's not old, Madam Hedda.

Hedda. I really did not look closely at it, Miss Tesman.

Miss Tesman. [*Tying on the bonnet.*] Let me tell you it's the first time I have worn it —the very first time.

Tesman. And a very nice bonnet it is too —quite a beauty!

Miss Tesman. Oh, it's no such great thing, George. [*Looks around her.*] My parasol ——? Ah, here. [*Takes it.*] For this is mine too— [*Mutters.*] —not Berta's.

Tesman. A new bonnet and a new parasol! Only think, Hedda!

Hedda. Very handsome indeed.

Tesman. Yes, isn't it? Eh? But Auntie, take a good look at Hedda before you go! See how handsome she is!

Miss Tesman. Oh, my dear boy, there's nothing new in that. Hedda was always lovely. [*She nods and goes toward the right.*]

Tesman. [*Following.*] Yes, but have you noticed what splendid condition she is in? How she has filled out on the journey?

Hedda. [*Crossing the room.*] Oh, do be quiet——!

Miss Tesman. [*Who has stopped and turned.*] Filled out?

Tesman. Of course you don't notice it so much now that she has that dress on. But I, who can see——

Hedda. [*At the glass door, impatiently.*] Oh, you can't see anything.

Tesman. It must be the mountain air in the Tyrol——

Hedda. [*Curtly, interrupting.*] I am exactly as I was when I started.

Tesman. So you insist; but I'm quite certain you are not. Don't you agree with me, Auntie?

Miss Tesman. [*Who has been gazing at her with folded hands.*] Hedda is lovely—lovely—lovely. [*Goes up to her, takes her head between both hands, draws it downward, and kisses her hair.*] God bless and preserve Hedda Tesman—for George's sake.

Hedda. [*Gently freeing herself.*] Oh—! Let me go.

Miss Tesman. [*In quiet emotion.*] I shall not let a day pass without coming to see you.

Tesman. No, you won't, will you, Auntie? Eh?

Miss Tesman. Good-by—good-by!

[*She goes out by the hall door.* TESMAN *accompanies her. The door remains half open.* TESMAN *can be heard repeating his message to Aunt Rina and his thanks for the slippers.*

In the meantime, HEDDA *walks about the room, raising her arms and clenching her hands as if in desperation. Then she flings back the curtains from the glass door, and stands there looking out.*

Presently TESMAN *returns and closes the door behind him.*]

Tesman. [*Picks up the slippers from the floor.*] What are you looking at, Hedda?

Hedda. [*Once more calm and mistress of herself.*] I am only looking at the leaves. They are so yellow—so withered.

Tesman. [*Wraps up the slippers and lays them on the table.*] Well, you see, we are well into September now.

Hedda. [*Again restless.*] Yes, to think of it!—Already in—in September.

Tesman. Don't you think Aunt Julia's manner was strange, dear? Almost solemn? Can you imagine what was the matter with her? Eh?

Hedda. I scarcely know her, you see. Is she not often like that?

Tesman. No, not as she was today.

Hedda. [*Leaving the glass door.*] Do you think she was annoyed about the bonnet?

Tesman. Oh, scarcely at all. Perhaps a little, just at the moment——

Hedda. But what an idea, to pitch her bonnet about in the drawing-room! No one does that sort of thing.

Tesman. Well, you may be sure Aunt Julia won't do it again.

Hedda. In any case, I shall manage to make my peace with her.

Tesman. Yes, my dear, good Hedda, if you only would.

Hedda. When you call this afternoon, you might invite her to spend the evening here.

Tesman. Yes, that I will. And there's one thing more you could do that would delight her heart.

Hedda. What is it?

Tesman. If you could only prevail on yourself to say *du* [1] to her. For my sake, Hedda? Eh?

Hedda. No, no, Tesman—you really mustn't ask that of me. I have told you so already. I shall try to call her "Aunt"; and you must be satisfied with that.

Tesman. Well, well. Only I think now that you belong to the family, you——

Hedda. H'm—I can't in the least see why——

[*She goes up toward the middle doorway.*]

Tesman. [*After a pause.*] Is there anything the matter with you, Hedda? Eh?

Hedda. I'm only looking at my old piano. It doesn't go at all well with all the other things.

Tesman. The first time I draw my salary, we'll see about exchanging it.

Hedda. No, no—no exchanging. I don't want to part with it. Suppose we put it there in the inner room, and then get another here in its place. When it's convenient, I mean.

Tesman. [*A little taken aback.*] Yes—of course we could do that.

Hedda. [*Takes up the bouquet from the piano.*] These flowers were not here last night when we arrived.

Tesman. Aunt Julia must have brought them for you.

Hedda. [*Examining the bouquet.*] A visiting-card. [*Takes it out and reads.*] "Shall return later in the day." Can you guess whose card it is?

Tesman. No. Whose? Eh?

Hedda. The name is "Mrs. Elvsted."

Tesman. Is it really? Sheriff Elvsted's wife? Miss Rysing that was.

Hedda. Exactly. The girl with the irritating hair, that she was always showing off. An old flame of yours, I've been told.

Tesman. [*Laughing.*] Oh, that didn't last long; and it was before I knew you, Hedda. But fancy her being in town!

Hedda. It's odd that she should call upon us. I have scarcely seen her since we left school.

---

[1] *Du* = thou; Tesman means, "If you could persuade yourself to *tutoyer* her."

Tesman. I haven't seen her either for—heaven knows how long. I wonder how she can endure to live in such an out-of-the-way hole—eh?

Hedda. [*After a moment's thought, says suddenly.*] Tell me, Tesman—isn't it somewhere near there that he—that—Eilert Lövborg is living?

Tesman. Yes, he is somewhere in that part of the country.

[BERTA *enters by the hall door.*]

Berta. That lady, ma'am, that brought some flowers a little while ago, is here again. [*Pointing.*] The flowers you have in your hand, ma'am.

Hedda. Ah, is she? Well, please show her in.

[BERTA *opens the door for* MRS. ELVSTED, *and goes out herself.*—MRS. ELVSTED *is a woman of fragile figure, with pretty, soft features. Her eyes are light blue, large, round, and somewhat prominent, with a startled, inquiring expression. Her hair is remarkably light, almost flaxen, and unusually abundant and wavy. She is a couple of years younger than* HEDDA. *She wears a dark visiting dress, tasteful, but not quite in the latest fashion.*]

Hedda. [*Receives her warmly.*] How do you do, my dear Mrs. Elvsted? It's delightful to see you again.

Mrs. Elvsted. [*Nervously, struggling for self-control.*] Yes, it's a very long time since we met.

Tesman. [*Gives her his hand.*] And we too—eh?

Hedda. Thanks for your lovely flowers——

Mrs. Elvsted. Oh, not at all——. I would have come straight here yesterday afternoon; but I heard that you were away——

Tesman. Have you just come to town? Eh?

Mrs. Elvsted. I arrived yesterday, about midday. Oh, I was quite in despair when I heard that you were not at home.

Hedda. In despair? How so?

Tesman. Why, my dear Mrs. Rysing—I mean Mrs. Elvsted——

Hedda. I hope that you are not in any trouble?

Mrs. Elvsted. Yes, I am. And I don't know another living creature here that I can turn to.

Hedda. [*Laying the bouquet on the table.*] Come—let us sit here on the sofa——

Mrs. Elvsted. Oh, I am too restless to sit down.

Hedda. Oh no, you're not. Come here.

[*She draws* MRS. ELVSTED *down upon the sofa and sits at her side.*]

Tesman. Well? What is it, Mrs. Elvsted——?

Hedda. Has anything particular happened to you at home?

Mrs. Elvsted. Yes—and no. Oh—I am so anxious you should not misunderstand me——

Hedda. Then your best plan is to tell us the whole story, Mrs. Elvsted.

Tesman. I suppose that's what you have come for—eh?

Mrs. Elvsted. Yes, yes—of course it is. Well then, I must tell you—if you don't already know—that Eilert Lövborg is in town, too.

Hedda. Lövborg——!

Tesman. What! Has Eilert Lövborg come back? Fancy that, Hedda!

Hedda. Well, well—I hear it.

Mrs. Elvsted. He has been here a week already. Just fancy—a whole week! In this terrible town, alone! With so many temptations on all sides.

Hedda. But, my dear Mrs. Elvsted—how does *he* concern you so much?

Mrs. Elvsted. [*Looks at her with a startled air, and says rapidly.*] He was the children's tutor.

Hedda. Your children's?

Mrs. Elvsted. My husband's. I have none.

Hedda. Your step-children's, then?

Mrs. Elvsted. Yes.

Tesman. [*Somewhat hesitatingly.*] Then was he—I don't know how to express it—was he—regular enough in his habits to be fit for the post? Eh?

Mrs. Elvsted. For the last two years his conduct has been irreproachable.

Tesman. Has it indeed? Fancy that, Hedda!

Hedda. I hear it.

Mrs. Elvsted. Perfectly irreproachable, I assure you! In every respect. But all the same—now that I know he is here—in this great town—and with a large sum of money in his hands—I can't help being in mortal fear for him.

Tesman. Why did he not remain where he was? With you and your husband? Eh?

Mrs. Elvsted. After his book was published he was too restless and unsettled to remain with us.

Tesman. Yes, by-the-bye, Aunt Julia told me he had published a new book.

Mrs. Elvsted. Yes, a big book, dealing with the march of civilization—in broad outline, as it were. It came out about a fortnight ago. And since it has sold so well, and been so much read—and made such a sensation——

Tesman. Has it indeed? It must be something he has had lying by since his better days.

Mrs. Elvsted. Long ago, you mean?

Tesman. Yes.

Mrs. Elvsted. No, he has written it all since he has been with us—within the last year.

Tesman. Isn't that good news, Hedda? Think of that!

Mrs. Elvsted. Ah yes, if only it would last!

Hedda. Have you seen him here in town?

Mrs. Elvsted. No, not yet. I have had the greatest difficulty in finding out his address. But this morning I discovered it at last.

Hedda. [*Looks searchingly at her.*] Do you know, it seems to me a little odd of your husband—h'm——

Mrs. Elvsted. [*Starting nervously.*] Of my husband! What!

Hedda. That he should send *you* to town on such an errand—that he does not come himself and look after his friend.

Mrs. Elvsted. Oh no, no—my husband has no time. And besides, I—I had some shopping to do.

Hedda. [*With a slight smile.*] Ah, that is a different matter.

Mrs. Elvsted. [*Rising quickly and uneasily.*] And now I beg and implore you, Mr. Tesman—receive Eilert Lövborg kindly if he comes to you! And that he is sure to do. You see you were such great friends in the old days. And then you are interested in the same studies—the same branch of science— so far as I can understand.

Tesman. We used to be, at any rate.

Mrs. Elvsted. That is why I beg so earnestly that you—you too—will keep a sharp eye upon him. Oh, you will promise me that, Mr. Tesman—won't you?

Tesman. With the greatest of pleasure, Mrs. Rysing——

Hedda. Elvsted.

Tesman. I assure you I shall do all I possibly can for Eilert. You may rely upon me.

Mrs. Elvsted. Oh, how very, very kind of you! [*Presses his hands.*] Thanks, thanks, thanks! [*Frightened.*] You see, my husband is so very fond of him!

Hedda. [*Rising.*] You ought to write to him, Tesman. Perhaps he may not care to come to you of his own accord.

Tesman. Well, perhaps it would be the right thing to do, Hedda? Eh?

Hedda. And the sooner the better. Why not at once?

Mrs. Elvsted. [*Imploringly.*] Oh, if you only would!

Tesman. I'll write this moment. Have you his address, Mrs.—Mrs. Elvsted?

Mrs. Elvsted. Yes. [*Takes a slip of paper from her pocket and hands it to him.*] Here it is.

Tesman. Good, good. Then I'll go in—— [*Looks about him.*] By-the-bye—my slippers? Oh, here.

[*Takes the packet, and is about to go.*]

Hedda. Be sure you write him a cordial, friendly letter. And a good long one, too.

Tesman. Yes, I will.

Mrs. Elvsted. But please, please don't say a word to show that I have suggested it.

Tesman. No, how could you think I would? Eh?

[*He goes out to the right, through the inner room.*]

Hedda. [*Goes up to* Mrs. Elvsted, *smiles, and says in a low voice.*] There! We have killed two birds with one stone.

Mrs. Elvsted. What do you mean?

Hedda. Could you not see that I wanted him to go?

Mrs. Elvsted. Yes, to write the letter——

Hedda. And that I might speak to you alone.

Mrs. Elvsted. [*Confused.*] About the same thing?

Hedda. Precisely.

Mrs. Elvsted. [*Apprehensively.*] But there is nothing more, Mrs. Tesman! Absolutely nothing!

Hedda. Oh yes, but there is. There is a great deal more—I can see that. Sit here— and we'll have a cozy, confidential chat.

[*She forces* Mrs. Elvsted *to sit in the easy-chair beside the stove, and seats herself on one of the footstools.*]

Mrs. Elvsted. [*Anxiously, looking at her watch.*] But, my dear Mrs. Tesman—I was really on the point of going.

Hedda. Oh, you can't be in such a hurry. —Well? Now tell me something about your life at home.

Mrs. Elvsted. Oh, that is just what I care least to speak about.

Hedda. But to me, dear——? Why, weren't we schoolfellows?

Mrs. Elvsted. Yes, but you were in the class above me. Oh, how dreadfully afraid of you I was then!

Hedda. Afraid of me?

Mrs. Elvsted. Yes, dreadfully. For when we met on the stairs you used always to pull my hair.

Hedda. Did I, really?

Mrs. Elvsted. Yes, and once you said you would burn it off my head.

Hedda. Oh, that was all nonsense, of course.

Mrs. Elvsted. Yes, but I was so silly in those days.—And since then, too—we have drifted so far—far apart from each other. Our circles have been so entirely different.

Hedda. Well then, we must try to drift together again. Now listen! At school we said *du* to each other; and we called each other by our Christian names——

Mrs. Elvsted. No, I am sure you must be mistaken.

Hedda. No, not at all! I can remember quite distinctly. So now we are going to renew our old friendship. [*Draws the footstool close to* Mrs. Elvsted.] There now! [*Kisses her cheek.*] You must say *du* to me and call me Hedda.

Mrs. Elvsted. [*Presses and pats her hands.*] Oh, how good and kind you are! I am not used to such kindness.

Hedda. There, there, there! And I shall say *du* to you, as in the old days, and call you my dear Thora.

Mrs. Elvsted. My name is Thea.[1]

Hedda. Why, of course! I meant Thea. [*Looks at her compassionately.*] So you are not accustomed to goodness and kindness, Thea? Not in your own home?

Mrs. Elvsted. Oh, if I only had a home! But I haven't any; I have never had a home.

Hedda. [*Looks at her for a moment.*] I almost suspected as much.

Mrs. Elvsted. [*Gazing helplessly before her.*] Yes—yes—yes.

Hedda. I don't quite remember—was it not as housekeeper that you first went to Mr. Elvsted's?

Mrs. Elvsted. I really went as governess. But his wife—his late wife—was an invalid—and rarely left her room. So I had to look after the housekeeping as well.

Hedda. And then—at last—you became mistress of the house.

Mrs. Elvsted. [*Sadly.*] Yes, I did.

Hedda. Let me see—about how long ago was that?

Mrs. Elvsted. My marriage?

Hedda. Yes.

Mrs. Elvsted. Five years ago.

Hedda. To be sure; it must be that.

Mrs. Elvsted. Oh, those five years——! Or at all events the last two or three of them! Oh, if you[2] could only imagine——

Hedda. [*Giving her a little slap on the hand.*] *De?* Fie, Thea!

Mrs. Elvsted. Yes, yes, I will try—— Well, if—you could only imagine and understand——

Hedda. [*Lightly.*] Eilert Lövborg has been in your neighborhood about three years, hasn't he?

Mrs. Elvsted. [*Looks at her doubtfully.*] Eilert Lövborg? Yes—he has.

Hedda. Had you known him before, in town here?

Mrs. Elvsted. Scarcely at all. I mean—I knew him by name, of course.

Hedda. But you saw a good deal of him in the country?

Mrs. Elvsted. Yes, he came to us every day. You see, he gave the children lessons; for in the long run I couldn't manage it all myself.

Hedda. No, that's clear.—And your husband——? I suppose he is often away from home?

Mrs. Elvsted. Yes. Being sheriff, you know, he has to travel about a good deal in his district.

Hedda. [*Leaning against the arm of the chair.*] Thea—my poor, sweet Thea—now you must tell me everything—exactly as it stands.

Mrs. Elvsted. Well then, you must question me.

Hedda. What sort of a man is your husband, Thea? I mean—you know—in everyday life. Is he kind to you?

Mrs. Elvsted. [*Evasively.*] I am sure he means well in everything.

Hedda. I should think he must be altogether too old for you. There is at least twenty years' difference between you, is there not?

Mrs. Elvsted. [*Irritably.*] Yes, that is true, too. Everything about him is repellent to me! We have not a thought in common. We have no single point of sympathy—he and I.

Hedda. But is he not fond of you all the same? In his own way?

Mrs. Elvsted. Oh, I really don't know. I think he regards me simply as a useful property. And then it doesn't cost much to keep me. I am not expensive.

Hedda. That is stupid of you.

Mrs. Elvsted. [*Shakes her head.*] It cannot be otherwise—not with him. I don't think he really cares for anyone but himself—and perhaps a little for the children.

Hedda. And for Eilert Lövborg, Thea.

Mrs. Elvsted. [*Looking at her.*] For

---

[1] Pronounce *Tora* and *Taya.*

[2] Mrs. Elvsted here uses the formal pronoun *De,* whereupon Hedda rebukes her. In her next speech Mrs. Elvsted says *du.*

Eilert Lövborg? What puts that into your head?

Hedda. Well, my dear—I should say, when he sends you after him all the way to town —— [*Smiling almost imperceptibly.*] And besides, you said so yourself, to Tesman.

Mrs. Elvsted. [*With a little nervous twitch.*] Did I? Yes, I suppose I did. [*Vehemently, but not loudly.*] No—I may just as well make a clean breast of it at once! For it must all come out in any case.

Hedda. Why, my dear Thea——?

Mrs. Elvsted. Well, to make a long story short: My husband did not know that I was coming.

Hedda. What! Your husband didn't know it!

Mrs. Elvsted. No, of course not. For that matter, he was away from home himself—he was traveling. Oh, I could bear it no longer, Hedda! I couldn't, indeed—so utterly alone as I should have been in the future.

Hedda. Well? And then?

Mrs. Elvsted. So I put together some of my things—what I needed most—as quietly as possible. And then I left the house.

Hedda. Without a word?

Mrs. Elvsted. Yes—and took the train straight to town.

Hedda. Why, my dear, good Thea—to think of you daring to do it!

Mrs. Elvsted. [*Rises and moves about the room.*] What else could I possibly do?

Hedda. But what do you think your husband will say when you go home again?

Mrs. Elvsted. [*At the table, looks at her.*] Back to *him*?

Hedda. Of course.

Mrs. Elvsted. I shall never go back to him again.

Hedda. [*Rising and going toward her.*] Then you have left your home—for good and all?

Mrs. Elvsted. Yes. There was nothing else to be done.

Hedda. But then—to take flight so openly.

Mrs. Elvsted. Oh, it's impossible to keep things of that sort secret.

Hedda. But what do you think people will say of you, Thea?

Mrs. Elvsted. They may say what they like, for aught *I* care. [*Seats herself wearily and sadly on the sofa.*] I have done nothing but what I *had* to do.

Hedda. [*After a short silence.*] And what are your plans now? What do you think of doing?

Mrs. Elvsted. I don't know yet. I only know this, that I must live here, where Eilert Lövborg is—if I am to live at all.

Hedda. [*Takes a chair from the table, seats herself beside her, and strokes her hands.*] My dear Thea—how did this—this friendship—between you and Eilert Lövborg come about?

Mrs. Elvsted. Oh, it grew up gradually. I gained a sort of influence over him.

Hedda. Indeed?

Mrs. Elvsted. He gave up his old habits. Not because I asked him to, for I never dared do that. But of course he saw how repulsive they were to me; and so he dropped them.

Hedda. [*Concealing an involuntary smile of scorn.*] Then you have reclaimed him—as the saying goes—my little Thea.

Mrs. Elvsted. So he says himself, at any rate. And he, on his side, has made a real human being of me—taught me to think, and to understand so many things.

Hedda. Did he give *you* lessons too, then?

Mrs. Elvsted. No, not exactly lessons. But he talked to me—talked about such an infinity of things. And then came the lovely, happy time when I began to share in his work—when he allowed me to help him!

Hedda. Oh, he did, did he?

Mrs. Elvsted. Yes! He never wrote anything without my assistance.

Hedda. You were two good comrades, in fact?

Mrs. Elvsted. [*Eagerly.*] Comrades! Yes, fancy, Hedda—that is the very word he used! Oh, I ought to feel perfectly happy; and yet I cannot; for I don't know how long it will last.

Hedda. Are you no surer of him than that?

Mrs. Elvsted. [*Gloomily.*] A woman's shadow stands between Eilert Lövborg and me.

Hedda. [*Looks at her anxiously.*] Who can *that* be?

Mrs. Elvsted. I don't know. Someone he knew in his—in his past. Someone he has never been able wholly to forget.

Hedda. What has he told you—about this?

Mrs. Elvsted. He has only once—quite vaguely—alluded to it.

Hedda. Well! And what did he say?

Mrs. Elvsted. He said that when they parted, she threatened to shoot him with a pistol.

Hedda. [*With cold composure.*] Oh nonsense! No one does that sort of thing here.

Mrs. Elvsted. No. And that is why I think it must have been that red-haired singing-woman whom he once——

Hedda. Yes, very likely.

Mrs. Elvsted. For I remember they used to say of her that she carried loaded firearms.

Hedda. Oh—then of course it must have been she.

Mrs. Elvsted. [*Wringing her hands.*] And now just fancy, Hedda—I hear that this singing-woman—that she is in town again! Oh, I don't know what to do——

Hedda. [*Glancing toward the inner room.*] Hush! Here comes Tesman. [*Rises and whispers.*] Thea—all this must remain between you and me.

Mrs. Elvsted. [*Springing up.*] Oh yes—yes! For heaven's sake——!

[GEORGE TESMAN, *with a letter in his hand, comes from the right through the inner room.*]

Tesman. There now—the epistle is finished.

Hedda. That's right. And now Mrs. Elvsted is just going. Wait a moment—I'll go with you to the garden gate.

Tesman. Do you think Berta could post the letter, Hedda dear?

Hedda. [*Takes it.*] I will tell her to.

[BERTA *enters from the hall.*]

Berta. Judge Brack wishes to know if Mrs. Tesman will receive him.

Hedda. Yes, ask Judge Brack to come in. And look here—put this letter in the post.

Berta. [*Taking the letter.*] Yes, ma'am.

[*She opens the door for* JUDGE BRACK *and goes out herself.* BRACK *is a man of forty-five; thick-set, but well-built and elastic in his movements. His face is roundish with an aristocratic profile. His hair is short, still almost black, and carefully dressed. His eyes are lively and sparkling. His eyebrows thick. His moustaches are also thick, with short-cut ends. He wears a well-cut walking-suit, a little too youthful for his age. He uses an eye-glass, which he now and then lets drop.*]

Judge Brack. [*With his hat in his hand, bowing.*] May one venture to call so early in the day?

Hedda. Of course one may.

Tesman. [*Presses his hand.*] You are welcome at any time. [*Introducing him.*] Judge Brack—Miss Rysing——

Hedda. Oh——!

Brack. [*Bowing.*] Ah—delighted——

Hedda. [*Looks at him and laughs.*] It's nice to have a look at you by daylight, Judge!

Brack. Do you find me—altered?

Hedda. A little younger, I think.

Brack. Thank you so much.

Tesman. But what do you think of Hedda —eh? Doesn't she look flourishing? She has actually——

Hedda. Oh, do leave me alone. You haven't thanked Judge Brack for all the trouble he has taken——

Brack. Oh, nonsense—it was a pleasure to me——

Hedda. Yes, you are a friend indeed. But here stands Thea all impatience to be off—so *au revoir*, Judge. I shall be back again presently.

[*Mutual salutations.* MRS. ELVSTED *and* HEDDA *go out by the hall door.*]

Brack. Well—is your wife tolerably satisfied——

Tesman. Yes, we can't thank you sufficiently. Of course she talks of a little rearrangement here and there; and one or two things are still wanting. We shall have to buy some additional trifles.

Brack. Indeed!

Tesman. But we won't trouble you about these things. Hedda says she herself will look after what is wanting.—Shan't we sit down? Eh?

Brack. Thanks, for a moment. [*Seats himself beside the table.*] There is something I wanted to speak to you about, my dear Tesman.

Tesman. Indeed? Ah, I understand! [*Seating himself.*] I suppose it's the serious part of the frolic that is coming now. Eh?

Brack. Oh, the money question is not so very pressing; though, for that matter, I wish we had gone a little more economically to work.

Tesman. But that would never have done, you know! Think of Hedda, my dear fellow! You, who know her so well——. I couldn't possibly ask her to put up with a shabby style of living!

Brack. No, no—that is just the difficulty.

Tesman. And then—fortunately—it can't be long before I receive my appointment.

Brack. Well, you see—such things are often apt to hang fire for a time.

Tesman. Have you heard anything definite? Eh?

Brack. Nothing exactly definite——. [*Interrupting himself.*] But by-the-bye—I have one piece of news for you.

Tesman. Well?

Brack. Your old friend, Eilert Lövborg, has returned to town.

Tesman. I know that already.

Brack. Indeed! How did you learn it?

Tesman. From that lady who went out with Hedda.

Brack. Really? What was her name? I didn't quite catch it.

Tesman. Mrs. Elvsted.

Brack. Aha—Sheriff Elvsted's wife? Of

course—he has been living up in their regions.

Tesman. And fancy—I'm delighted to hear that he is quite a reformed character!

Brack. So they say.

Tesman. And then he has published a new book—eh?

Brack. Yes, indeed he has.

Tesman. And I hear it has made some sensation!

Brack. Quite an unusual sensation.

Tesman. Fancy—isn't that good news! A man of such extraordinary talents——. I felt so grieved to think that he had gone irretrievably to ruin.

Brack. That was what everybody thought.

Tesman. But I cannot imagine what he will take to now! How in the world will he be able to make his living? Eh?

[*During the last words,* HEDDA *has entered by the hall door.*]

Hedda. [*To* BRACK, *laughing with a touch of scorn.*] Tesman is forever worrying about how people are to make their living.

Tesman. Well, you see, dear—we were talking about poor Eilert Lövborg.

Hedda. [*Glancing at him rapidly.*] Oh, indeed? [*Seats herself in the arm-chair beside the stove and asks indifferently.*] What is the matter with *him?*

Tesman. Well—no doubt he has run through all his property long ago; and he can scarcely write a new book every year—eh? So I really can't see what is to become of him.

Brack. Perhaps I can give you some information on that point.

Tesman. Indeed!

Brack. You must remember that his relations have a good deal of influence.

Tesman. Oh, his relations, unfortunately, have entirely washed their hands of him.

Brack. At one time they called him the hope of the family.

Tesman. At one time, yes! But he has put an end to all that.

Hedda. Who knows? [*With a slight smile.*] I hear they have reclaimed him up at Sheriff Elvsted's——

Brack. And then this book that he has published——

Tesman. Well, well, I hope to goodness they may find something for him to do. I have just written to him. I asked him to come and see us this evening, Hedda dear.

Brack. But my dear fellow, you are booked for my bachelors' party this evening. You promised on the pier last night.

Hedda. Had you forgotten, Tesman?

Tesman. Yes, I had utterly forgotten.

Brack. But it doesn't matter, for you may be sure he won't come.

Tesman. What makes you think that? Eh?

Brack. [*With a little hesitation, rising and resting his hands on the back of his chair.*] My dear Tesman—and you too, Mrs. Tesman—I think I ought not to keep you in the dark about something that—that——

Tesman. That concerns Eilert——?

Brack. Both you and him.

Tesman. Well, my dear Judge, out with it.

Brack. You must be prepared to find your appointment deferred longer than you desired or expected.

Tesman. [*Jumping up uneasily.*] Is there some hitch about it? Eh?

Brack. The nomination may perhaps be made conditional on the result of a competition——

Tesman. Competition! Think of that, Hedda!

Hedda. [*Leans further back in the chair.*] Aha—aha!

Tesman. But who can my competitor be? Surely not——?

Brack. Yes, precisely—Eilert Lövborg.

Tesman. [*Clasping his hands.*] No, no—it's quite inconceivable! Quite impossible! Eh?

Brack. H'm—that is what it may come to, all the same.

Tesman. Well but, Judge Brack—it would show the most incredible lack of consideration for me. [*Gesticulates with his arms.*] For—just think—I'm a married man! We have married on the strength of these prospects, Hedda and I; and run deep into debt; and borrowed money from Aunt Julia too. Good heavens, they had as good as promised me the appointment. Eh?

Brack. Well, well, well—no doubt you will get it in the end; only after a contest.

Hedda. [*Immovable in her arm-chair.*] Fancy, Tesman, there will be a sort of sporting interest in that.

Tesman. Why, my dearest Hedda, how can you be so indifferent about it?

Hedda. [*As before.*] I am not at all indifferent. I am most eager to see who wins.

Brack. In any case, Mrs. Tesman, it is best that you should know how matters stand. I mean—before you set about the little purchases I hear you are threatening.

Hedda. This can make no difference.

Brack. Indeed! Then I have no more to say. Good-by! [*To* TESMAN.] I shall look in on my way back from my afternoon walk, and take you home with me.

Tesman. Oh yes, yes—your news has quite upset me.

Hedda. [*Reclining, holds out her hand.*] Good-by, Judge; and be sure you call in the afternoon.

Brack. Many thanks. Good-by, good-by!

Tesman. [*Accompanying him to the door.*] Good-by, my dear Judge! You must really excuse me——

[JUDGE BRACK *goes out by the hall door.*]

Tesman. [*Crosses the room.*] Oh Hedda —one should never rush into adventures. Eh?

Hedda. [*Looks at him, smiling.*] Do *you* do *that?*

Tesman. Yes, dear—there is no denying—it *was* adventurous to go and marry and set up house upon mere expectations.

Hedda. Perhaps you are right there.

Tesman. Well—at all events, we have our delightful home, Hedda! Fancy, the home we both dreamed of—the home we were in love with, I may almost say. Eh?

Hedda. [*Rising slowly and wearily.*] It was part of our compact that we were to go into society—to keep open house.

Tesman. Yes, if you only knew how I had been looking forward to it! Fancy—to see you as hostess—in a select circle! Eh? Well, well, well—for the present we shall have to get on without society, Hedda—only to invite Aunt Julie now and then.—Oh, I intended you to lead such an utterly different life, dear——!

Hedda. Of course I cannot have my man in livery just yet.

Tesman. Oh no, unfortunately. It would be out of the question for us to keep a footman, you know.

Hedda. And the saddle-horse I was to have had——

Tesman. [*Aghast.*] The saddle-horse!

Hedda. ——I suppose I must not think of that now.

Tesman. Good heavens, no!—that's as clear as daylight.

Hedda. [*Goes up the room.*] Well, I shall have one thing at least to kill time with in the meanwhile.

Tesman. [*Beaming.*] Oh, thank heaven for that! What is it, Hedda? Eh?

Hedda. [*In the middle doorway, looks at him with covert scorn.*] My pistols, George.

Tesman. [*In alarm.*] Your pistols!

Hedda. [*With cold eyes.*] General Gabler's pistols.

[*She goes out through the inner room, to the left.*]

Tesman. [*Rushes up to the middle doorway and calls after her.*] No, for heaven's sake, Hedda darling—don't touch those dangerous things! For my sake, Hedda! Eh?

CURTAIN

ACT SECOND

The room at the Tesmans' as in the First Act, except that the piano has been removed, and an elegant little writing-table with book-shelves put in its place. A smaller table stands near the sofa on the left. Most of the bouquets have been taken away. MRS. ELVSTED'S bouquet is upon the large table in front.— It is afternoon.

[HEDDA, *dressed to receive callers, is alone in the room. She stands by the open glass door, loading a revolver. The fellow to it lies in an open pistol-case on the writing-table.*]

Hedda. [*Looks down the garden, and calls.*] So you are here again, Judge!

Brack. [*Is heard calling from a distance.*] As you see, Mrs. Tesman!

Hedda. [*Raises the pistol and points.*] Now I'll shoot you, Judge Brack!

Brack. [*Calling unseen.*] No, no, no! Don't stand aiming at me!

Hedda. This is what comes of sneaking in by the back way.[1] [*She fires.*]

Brack. [*Nearer.*] Are you out of your senses——?

Hedda. Dear me—did I happen to hit you?

Brack. [*Still outside.*] I wish you would let these pranks alone!

Hedda. Come in then, Judge.

[JUDGE BRACK, *dressed as though for a men's party, enters by the glass door. He carries a light overcoat over his arm.*]

Brack. What the deuce—haven't you tired of that sport, yet? What are you shooting at?

Hedda. Oh, I am only firing in the air.

---

[1] "Bagveje" means both "back ways" and "underhand courses."

Brack. [*Gently takes the pistol out of her hand.*] Allow me, Madam! [*Looks at it.*] Ah—I know this pistol well! [*Looks around.*] Where is the case? Ah, here it is. [*Lays the pistol in it, and shuts it.*] Now we won't play at that game any more today.

Hedda. Then what in heaven's name would you have me do with myself?

Brack. Have you had no visitors?

Hedda. [*Closing the glass door.*] Not one. I suppose all our set are still out of town.

Brack. And is Tesman not at home either?

Hedda. [*At the writing-table, putting the pistol-case in a drawer which she shuts.*] No. He rushed off to his aunt's directly after lunch; he didn't expect you so early.

Brack. H'm—how stupid of me not to have thought of that!

Hedda. [*Turning her head to look at him.*] Why stupid?

Brack. Because if I had thought of it I should have come a little—earlier.

Hedda. [*Crossing the room.*] Then you would have found no one to receive you; for I have been in my room changing my dress ever since lunch.

Brack. And is there no sort of little chink that we could hold a parley through?

Hedda. You have forgotten to arrange one.

Brack. That was another piece of stupidity.

Hedda. Well, we must just settle down here—and wait. Tesman is not likely to be back for some time yet.

Brack. Never mind; I shall not be impatient.

[HEDDA *seats herself in the corner of the sofa.* BRACK *lays his overcoat over the back of the nearest chair, and sits down, but keeps his hat in his hand. A short silence. They look at each other.*]

Hedda. Well?

Brack. [*In the same tone.*] Well?

Hedda. I spoke first.

Brack. [*Bending a little forward.*] Come, let us have a cosy little chat, Mrs. Hedda.[1]

Hedda. [*Leaning further back in the sofa.*] Does it not seem like a whole eternity since our last talk? Of course I don't count those few words yesterday evening and this morning.

Brack. You mean since our last confidential talk? Our last *tête-à-tête*?

Hedda. Well, yes—since you put it so.

Brack. Not a day has passed but I have wished that you were home again.

Hedda. And I have done nothing but wish the same thing.

Brack. You? Really, Mrs. Hedda? And I thought you had been enjoying your tour so much!

Hedda. Oh yes, you may be sure of that!

Brack. But Tesman's letters spoke of nothing but happiness.

Hedda. Oh, Tesman! You see, he thinks nothing so delightful as grubbing in libraries and making copies of old parchments, or whatever you can call them.

Brack. [*With a spice of malice.*] Well, that is his vocation in life—or part of it at any rate.

Hedda. Yes, of course; and no doubt when it's your vocation——. But *I*! Oh, my dear Mr. Brack, how mortally bored I have been.

Brack. [*Sympathetically.*] Do you really say so? In downright earnest?

Hedda. Yes, you can surely understand it——! To go for six whole months without meeting a soul that knew anything of our circle, or could talk about the things we are interested in.

Brack. Yes, yes—I too should feel that a deprivation.

Hedda. And then, what I found most intolerable of all——

Brack. Well?

Hedda. ——was being everlastingly in the company of—one and the same person——

Brack. [*With a nod of assent.*] Morning, noon, and night, yes—at all possible times and seasons.

Hedda. I said "everlastingly."

Brack. Just so. But I should have thought, with our excellent Tesman, one could——

Hedda. Tesman is—a specialist, my dear Judge.

Brack. Undeniably.

Hedda. And specialists are not at all amusing to travel with. Not in the long run at any rate.

Brack. Not even—the specialist one happens to *love*?

Hedda. Faugh—don't use that sickening word!

Brack. [*Taken aback.*] What do you say Mrs. Hedda?

Hedda. [*Half laughing, half irritated.*] You should just try it! To hear of nothing but the history of civilization, morning, noon and night——

Brack. Everlastingly.

Hedda. Yes, yes, yes! And then all this about the domestic industry of the middle

---

[1] As this form of address is contrary to English usage, and as the note of familiarity would be lacking in "Mrs. Tesman," Brack may, in stage representation, say "Miss Hedda," thus ignoring her marriage and reverting to the form of address no doubt customary between them of old.

ges——! That's the most disgusting part of it!

Brack. [*Looks searchingly at her.*] But tell me—in that case, how am I to understand your——? H'm——

Hedda. My accepting George Tesman, you mean?

Brack. Well, let us put it so.

Hedda. Good heavens, do you see anything so wonderful in that?

Brack. Yes and no—Mrs. Hedda.

Hedda. I had positively danced myself tired, my dear Judge. My day was done—— [*With a slight shudder.*] Oh no—I won't say that; nor think it either!

Brack. You have assuredly no reason to.

Hedda. Oh, reasons—— [*Watching him closely.*] And George Tesman—after all, you must admit that he is correctness itself.

Brack. His correctness and respectability are beyond all question.

Hedda. And I don't see anything absolutely ridiculous about him.—Do you?

Brack. Ridiculous? N-no—I shouldn't exactly say so——

Hedda. Well—and his powers of research, at all events, are untiring.—I see no reason why he should not one day come to the front, after all.

Brack. [*Looks at her hesitatingly.*] I thought that you, like every one else, expected him to attain the highest distinction.

Hedda. [*With an expression of fatigue.*] Yes, so I did.—And then, since he was bent, at all hazards, on being allowed to provide for me—I really don't know why I should not have accepted his offer.

Brack. No—if you look at it in *that* light——

Hedda. It was more than any other adorers were prepared to do for me, my dear Judge.

Brack. [*Laughing.*] Well, I can't answer for all the rest; but as for myself, you know quite well that I have always entertained a—certain respect for the marriage tie—for marriage as an institution, Mrs. Hedda.

Hedda. [*Jestingly.*] Oh, I assure you I have never cherished any hopes with respect to *you.*

Brack. All I require is a pleasant and intimate interior, where I can make myself useful in every way, and am free to come and go as—as a trusted friend——

Hedda. Of the master of the house, do you mean?

Brack. [*Bowing.*] Frankly—of the mistress first of all; but of course of the master too, in the second place. Such a triangular friendship—if I may call it so—is really a great convenience for all parties, let me tell you.

Hedda. Yes, I have many a time longed for someone to make a third on our travels. Oh—those railway-carriage *tête-à-têtes*——!

Brack. Fortunately your wedding journey is over now.

Hedda. [*Shaking her head.*] Not by a long —long way. I have only arrived at a station on the line.

Brack. Well, then the passengers jump out and move about a little, Mrs. Hedda.

Hedda. I never jump out.

Brack. Really?

Hedda. No—because there is always someone standing by to——

Brack. [*Laughing.*] To look at your ankles, do you mean?

Hedda. Precisely.

Brack. Well, but, dear me——

Hedda. [*With a gesture of repulsion.*] I won't have it. I would rather keep my seat where I happen to be—and continue the *tête-à-tête.*

Brack. But suppose a third person were to jump in and join the couple.

Hedda. Ah—that is quite another matter!

Brack. A trusted, sympathetic friend——

Hedda. ——with a fund of conversation on all sorts of lively topics——

Brack. ——and not the least bit of a specialist!

Hedda. [*With an audible sigh.*] Yes, that would be a relief indeed.

Brack. [*Hears the front door open, and glances in that direction.*] The triangle is completed.

Hedda. [*Half aloud.*] And on goes the train.

[GEORGE TESMAN, *in a gray walking-suit, with a soft felt hat, enters from the hall. He has a number of unbound books under his arm and in his pockets.*]

Tesman. [*Goes up to the table beside the corner settee.*] Ouf—what a load for a warm day—all these books. [*Lays them on the table.*] I'm positively perspiring, Hedda. Hallo—are you there already, my dear Judge? Eh? Berta didn't tell me.

Brack. [*Rising.*] I came in through the garden.

Hedda. What books have you got there?

Tesman. [*Stands looking them through.*] Some new books on my special subjects— quite indispensable to me.

Hedda. Your special subjects?

Brack. Yes, books on his special subjects, Mrs. Tesman.

[BRACK *and* HEDDA *exchange a confidential smile.*]

Hedda. Do you need still more books on your special subjects?

Tesman. Yes, my dear Hedda, one can never have too many of them. Of course one must keep up with all that is written and published.

Hedda. Yes, I suppose one must.

Tesman. [*Searching among his books.*] And look here—I have got hold of Eilert Lövborg's new book too. [*Offering it to her.*] Perhaps you would like to glance through it, Hedda? Eh?

Hedda. No, thank you. Or rather—afterwards perhaps.

Tesman. I looked into it a little on the way home.

Brack. Well, what do you think of it—as a specialist?

Tesman. I think it shows quite remarkable soundness of judgment. He never wrote like that before. [*Putting the books together.*] Now I shall take all these into my study. I'm longing to cut the leaves——! And then I must change my clothes. [*To* Brack.] I suppose we needn't start just yet? Eh?

Brack. Oh, dear no—there is not the slightest hurry.

Tesman. Well then, I will take my time. [*Is going with his books, but stops in the doorway and turns.*] By-the-bye, Hedda—Aunt Julia is not coming this evening.

Hedda. Not coming? Is it that affair of the bonnet that keeps her away?

Tesman. Oh, not at all. How could you think such a thing of Aunt Julia? Just fancy——! The fact is Aunt Rina is very ill.

Hedda. She always is.

Tesman. Yes, but today she is much worse than usual, poor dear.

Hedda. Oh, then it's only natural that her sister should remain with her. I must bear my disappointment.

Tesman. And you can't imagine, dear, how delighted Aunt Julia seemed to be—because you had come home looking so flourishing!

Hedda. [*Half aloud, rising.*] Oh, those everlasting Aunts!

Tesman. What?

Hedda. [*Going to the glass door.*] Nothing.

Tesman. Oh, all right.

[*He goes through the inner room, out to the right.*]

Brack. What bonnet were you talking about?

Hedda. Oh, it was a little episode with Miss Tesman this morning. She had laid down her bonnet on the chair there—[*Looks at him and smiles.*]—and I pretended to think it was the servant's.

Brack. [*Shaking his head.*] Now my dear Mrs. Hedda, how could you do such a thing? To that excellent old lady, too!

Hedda. [*Nervously crossing the room.*] Well, you see—these impulses come over me all of a sudden; and I cannot resist them. [*Throws herself down in the easy-chair by the stove.*] Oh, I don't know how to explain it.

Brack. [*Behind the easy-chair.*] You are not really happy—that is at the bottom of it.

Hedda. [*Looking straight before her.*] I know of no reason why I should be—happy. Perhaps you can give me one?

Brack. Well—amongst other things, because you have got exactly the home you had set your heart on.

Hedda. [*Looks up at him and laughs.*] Do you too believe in that legend?

Brack. Is there nothing in it, then?

Hedda. Oh yes, there is *something* in it.

Brack. Well?

Hedda. There is this in it, that I made use of Tesman to see me home from evening parties last summer——

Brack. I, unfortunately, had to go quite a different way.

Hedda. That's true. I know you were going a different way last summer.

Brack. [*Laughing.*] Oh fie, Mrs. Hedda! Well, then—you and Tesman——?

Hedda. Well, we happened to pass here one evening; Tesman, poor fellow, was writhing in the agony of having to find conversation; so I took pity on the learned man——

Brack. [*Smiles doubtfully.*] You took pity? H'm——

Hedda. Yes, I really did. And so—to help him out of his torment—I happened to say, in pure thoughtlessness, that I should like to live in this villa.

Brack. No more than that?

Hedda. Not *that* evening.

Brack. But afterwards?

Hedda. Yes, my thoughtlessness had consequences, my dear Judge.

Brack. Unfortunately that too often happens, Mrs. Hedda.

Hedda. Thanks! So you see it was this enthusiasm for Secretary Falk's villa that first constituted a bond of sympathy between George Tesman and me. From that came our engagement and our marriage, and our wedding journey, and all the rest of it. Well well, my dear Judge—as you make your bed so you must lie, I could almost say.

Brack. This is exquisite! And you really cared not a rap about it all the time?

Hedda. No, heaven knows I didn't.

Brack. But now? Now that we have made it so homelike for you?

Hedda. Uh—the rooms all seem to smell of lavender and dried rose-leaves.— But perhaps it's Aunt Julia that has brought that scent with her.

Brack. [*Laughing.*] No, I think it must be a legacy from the late Mrs. Secretary Falk.

Hedda. Yes, there is an odor of mortality about it. It reminds me of a bouquet—the day after the ball. [*Clasps her hands behind her head, leans back in her chair and looks at him.*] Oh, my dear Judge—you cannot imagine how horribly I shall bore myself here.

Brack. Why should not you, too, find some sort of vocation in life, Mrs. Hedda?

Hedda. A vocation—that should attract me?

Brack. If possible, of course.

Hedda. Heaven knows what sort of a vocation that could be. I often wonder whether—— [*Breaking off.*] But that would never do either.

Brack. Who can tell? Let me hear what it is.

Hedda. Whether I might not get Tesman to go into politics, I mean.

Brack. [*Laughing.*] Tesman? No, really now, political life is not the thing for him—not at all in his line.

Hedda. No, I daresay not.—But if I could get him into it all the same?

Brack. Why—what satisfaction could you find in that? If he is not fitted for that sort of thing, why should you want to drive him into it?

Hedda. Because I am bored, I tell you! [*After a pause.*] So you think it quite out of the question that Tesman should ever get into the ministry?

Brack. H'm—you see, my dear Mrs. Hedda,—to get into the ministry, he would have to be a tolerably rich man.

Hedda. [*Rising impatiently.*] Yes, there we have it! It is this genteel poverty I have managed to drop into——! [*Crosses the room.*] That is what makes life so pitiable! So utterly ludicrous!—For that's what it is.

Brack. Now *I* should say the fault lay elsewhere.

Hedda. Where, then?

Brack. You have never gone through any really stimulating experience.

Hedda. Anything serious, you mean?

Brack. Yes, you may call it so. But now you may perhaps have one in store.

Hedda. [*Tossing her head.*] Oh, you're thinking of the annoyances about this wretched professorship! But that must be Tesman's own affair. I assure you I shall not waste a thought upon it.

Brack. No, no, I daresay not. But suppose now that what people call—in elegant language—a solemn responsibility were to come upon you? [*Smiling.*] A new responsibility, Mrs. Hedda?

Hedda. [*Angrily.*] Be quiet! Nothing of that sort will ever happen.

Brack. [*Warily.*] We will speak of this again a year hence—at the very outside.

Hedda. [*Curtly.*] I have no turn for anything of the sort, Judge Brack. No responsibilities for me!

Brack. Are you so unlike the generality of women as to have no turn for duties which——?

Hedda. [*Beside the glass door.*] Oh, be quiet, I tell you!—I often think there is only one thing in the world I have any turn for.

Brack. [*Drawing near to her.*] And what is that, if I may ask?

Hedda. [*Stands looking out.*] Boring myself to death. Now you know it. [*Turns, looks toward the inner room, and laughs.*] Yes, as I thought! Here comes the Professor.

Brack. [*Softly, in a tone of warning.*] Come, come, come, Mrs. Hedda!

[GEORGE TESMAN, *dressed for the party, with his gloves and hat in his hand, enters from the right through the inner room.*]

Tesman. Hedda, has no message come from Eilert Lövborg? Eh?

Hedda. No.

Tesman. Then you'll see he'll be here presently.

Brack. Do you really think he will come?

Tesman. Yes, I am almost sure of it. For what you were telling us this morning must have been a mere floating rumor.

Brack. You think so?

Tesman. At any rate, Aunt Julia said she did not believe for a moment that he would ever stand in my way again. Fancy that!

Brack. Well then, that's all right.

Tesman. [*Placing his hat and gloves on a chair on the right.*] Yes, but you must really let me wait for him as long as possible.

Brack. We have plenty of time yet. None of my guests will arrive before seven or half-past.

Tesman. Then meanwhile we can keep Hedda company, and see what happens. Eh?

Hedda. [*Placing* BRACK'S *hat and overcoat upon the corner settee.*] And at the worst Mr. Lövborg can remain here with me.

Brack. [*Offering to take his things.*] Oh,

allow me, Mrs. Tesman!— What do you mean by "at the worst"?

Hedda. If he won't go with you and Tesman.

Tesman. [*Looks dubiously at her.*] But, Hedda dear—do you think it would quite do for him to remain with you? Eh? Remember, Aunt Julia can't come.

Hedda. No, but Mrs. Elvsted is coming. We three can have a cup of tea together.

Tesman. Oh yes, *that* will be all right.

Brack. [*Smiling.*] And that would perhaps be the safest plan for him.

Hedda. Why so?

Brack. Well, you know, Mrs. Tesman, how you used to gird at my little bachelor parties. You declared they were adapted only for men of the strictest principles.

Hedda. But no doubt Mr. Lövborg's principles are strict enough now. A converted sinner——

[BERTA *appears at the hall door.*]

Berta. There's a gentleman asking if you are at home, ma'am——

Hedda. Well, show him in.

Tesman. [*Softly.*] I'm sure it is he! Fancy that!

[EILERT LÖVBORG *enters from the hall. He is slim and lean; of the same age as* TESMAN, *but looks older and somewhat worn-out. His hair and beard are of a blackish brown, his face long and pale, but with patches of color on the cheekbones. He is dressed in a well-cut black visiting suit, quite new. He has dark gloves and a silk hat. He stops near the door, and makes a rapid bow, seeming somewhat embarrassed.*]

Tesman. [*Goes up to him and shakes him warmly by the hand.*] Well, my dear Eilert—so at last we meet again!

Lövborg. [*Speaks in a subdued voice.*] Thanks for your letter, Tesman. [*Approaching* HEDDA.] Will you too shake hands with me, Mrs. Tesman?

Hedda. [*Taking his hand.*] I am glad to see you, Mr. Lövborg. [*With a motion of her hand.*] I don't know whether you two gentlemen——?

Lövborg. [*Bowing slightly.*] Judge Brack, I think.

Brack. [*Doing likewise.*] Oh yes—in the old days——

Tesman. [*To* LÖVBORG, *with his hands on his shoulders.*] And now you must make yourself entirely at home, Eilert! Mustn't he, Hedda?—For I hear you are going to settle in town again? Eh?

Lövborg. Yes, I am.

Tesman. Quite right, quite right. Let me

tell you, I have got hold of your new book; but I haven't had time to read it yet.

Lövborg. You may spare yourself the trouble.

Tesman. Why so?

Lövborg. Because there is very little in it.

Tesman. Just fancy—how can you say so?

Brack. But it has been very much praised, I hear.

Lövborg. That was what I wanted; so I put nothing into the book but what every one would agree with.

Brack. Very wise of you.

Tesman. Well, but, my dear Eilert——!

Lövborg. For now I mean to win myself a position again—to make a fresh start.

Tesman. [*A little embarrassed.*] Ah, that is what you wish to do? Eh?

Lövborg. [*Smiling, lays down his hat, and draws a packet, wrapped in paper, from his coat pocket.*] But when this one appears, George Tesman, you will have to read it. For *this* is the real book—the book I have put my true self into.

Tesman. Indeed? And what is it?

Lövborg. It is the continuation.

Tesman. The continuation? Of what?

Lövborg. Of the book.

Tesman. Of the new book?

Lövborg. Of course.

Tesman. Why, my dear Eilert—does it not come down to our own days?

Lövborg. Yes, it does; and this one deals with the future.

Tesman. With the future! But, good heavens, we know nothing of the future!

Lövborg. No; but there is a thing or two to be said about it all the same. [*Opens the packet.*] Look here——

Tesman. Why, that's not your handwriting.

Lövborg. I dictated it. [*Turning over the pages.*] It falls into two sections. The first deals with the civilizing forces of the future. And here is the second— [*Running through the pages toward the end.*] forecasting the probable line of development.

Tesman. How odd now! I should never have thought of writing anything of that sort.

Hedda. [*At the glass door, drumming on the pane.*] H'm——. I daresay not.

Lövborg. [*Replacing the manuscript in its paper and laying the packet on the table.*] I brought it, thinking I might read you a little of it this evening.

Tesman. That was very good of you, Eilert. But this evening——? [*Looking at* BRACK.] I don't quite see how we can manage it——

Lövborg. Well then, some other time. There is no hurry.

Brack. I must tell you, Mr. Lövborg—there is a little gathering at my house this evening—mainly in honor of Tesman, you know——

Lövborg. [*Looking for his hat.*] Oh—then I won't detain you——

Brack. No, but listen—will you not do me the favor of joining us?

Lövborg. [*Curtly and decidedly.*] No, I can't—thank you very much.

Brack. Oh, nonsense—do! We shall be quite a select little circle. And I assure you we shall have a "lively time" as Mrs. Hed—as Mrs. Tesman says.

Lövborg. I have no doubt of it. But nevertheless——

Brack. And then you might bring your manuscript with you, and read it to Tesman at my house. I could give you a room to yourselves.

Tesman. Yes, think of that, Eilert—why shouldn't you? Eh?

Hedda. [*Interposing.*] But, Tesman, if Mr. Lövborg would really rather not! I am sure Mr. Lövborg is much more inclined to remain here and have supper with me.

Lövborg. [*Looking at her.*] With you, Mrs. Tesman?

Hedda. And with Mrs. Elvsted.

Lövborg. Ah—— [*Lightly.*] I saw her for a moment this morning.

Hedda. Did you? Well, she is coming this evening. So you see you are almost bound to remain, Mr. Lövborg, or she will have no one to see her home.

Lövborg. That's true. Many thanks, Mrs. Tesman—in that case I will remain.

Hedda. Then I have one or two orders to give the servant——

[*She goes to the hall door and rings. BERTA enters. HEDDA talks to her in a whisper, and points toward the inner room. BERTA nods and goes out again.*]

Tesman. [*At the same time, to LÖVBORG.*] Tell me, Eilert—is it this new subject—the future—that you are going to lecture about?

Lövborg. Yes.

Tesman. They told me at the bookseller's that you are going to deliver a course of lectures this autumn.

Lövborg. That is my intention. I hope you won't take it ill, Tesman.

Tesman. Oh no, not in the least! But——?

Lövborg. I can quite understand that it must be disagreeable to you.

Tesman. [*Cast down.*] Oh, I can't expect you, out of consideration for me, to——

Lövborg. But I shall wait till you have received your appointment.

Tesman. Will you wait? Yes, but—yes, but—are you not going to compete with me? Eh?

Lövborg. No; it is only the moral victory I care for.

Tesman. Why, bless me—then Aunt Julia was right after all! Oh yes—I knew it! Hedda! Just fancy—Eilert Lövborg is not going to stand in our way!

Hedda. [*Curtly.*] Our way? Pray leave *me* out of the question.

[*She goes up toward the inner room, where BERTA is placing a tray with decanters and glasses on the table. HEDDA nods approval, and comes forward again. BERTA goes out.*]

Tesman. [*At the same time.*] And you, Judge Brack—what do you say to this? Eh?

Brack. Well, I say that a moral victory—h'm—may be all very fine——

Tesman. Yes, certainly. But all the same——

Hedda. [*Looking at TESMAN with a cold smile.*] You stand there looking as if you were thunderstruck——

Tesman. Yes—so I am—I almost think——

Brack. Don't you see, Mrs. Tesman, a thunderstorm has just passed over?

Hedda. [*Pointing toward the inner room.*] Will you not take a glass of cold punch, gentlemen?

Brack. [*Looking at his watch.*] A stirrup cup? Yes, it wouldn't come amiss.

Tesman. A capital idea, Hedda! Just the thing! Now that the weight has been taken off my mind——

Hedda. Will you not join them, Mr. Lövborg?

Lövborg. [*With a gesture of refusal.*] No, thank you. Nothing for me.

Brack. Why bless me—cold punch is surely not poison.

Lövborg. Perhaps not for everyone.

Hedda. I will keep Mr. Lövborg company in the meantime.

Tesman. Yes, yes, Hedda dear, do.

[*He and BRACK go into the inner room, seat themselves, drink punch, smoke cigarettes, and carry on a lively conversation during what follows. EILERT LÖVBORG remains standing beside the stove. HEDDA goes to the writing-table.*]

Hedda. [*Raising her voice a little.*] Do you care to look at some photographs, Mr. Lövborg? You know Tesman and I made a tour in the Tyrol on our way home?

[*She takes up an album and places it on*

the table beside the sofa in the further corner of which she seats herself. EILERT LÖVBORG *approaches, stops and looks at her. Then he takes a chair and seats himself to her left, with his back toward the inner room.*]

Hedda. [*Opening the album.*] Do you see this range of mountains, Mr. Lövborg? It's the Ortler group. Tesman has written the name underneath. Here it is: "The Ortler group near Meran."

Lövborg. [*Who has never taken his eyes off her, says softly and slowly.*] Hedda—Gabler!

Hedda. [*Glancing hastily at him.*] Ah! Hush!

Lövborg. [*Repeats softly.*] Hedda Gabler!

Hedda. [*Looking at the album.*] That was my name in the old days—when we two knew each other.

Lövborg. And I must teach myself never to say Hedda Gabler again—never, as long as I live.

Hedda. [*Still turning over the pages.*] Yes, you must. And I think you ought to practice in time. The sooner the better, I should say.

Lövborg. [*In a tone of indignation.*] Hedda Gabler married! And married to—George Tesman!

Hedda. Yes—so the world goes.

Lövborg. Oh, Hedda, Hedda—how could you [1] throw yourself away!

Hedda. [*Looks sharply at him.*] What? I can't allow this!

Lövborg. What do you mean?

[TESMAN *comes into the room and goes toward the sofa.*]

Hedda. [*Hears him coming and says in an indifferent tone.*] And this is a view from the Val d'Ampezo, Mr. Lövborg. Just look at these peaks! [*Looks affectionately up at* TESMAN.] What's the name of these curious peaks, dear?

Tesman. Let me see. Oh, those are the Dolomites.

Hedda. Yes, that's it!—Those are the Dolomites, Mr. Lövborg.

Tesman. Hedda dear—I only wanted to ask whether I shouldn't bring you a little punch after all? For yourself at any rate—eh?

Hedda. Yes, do, please; and perhaps a few biscuits.

Tesman. No cigarettes?

Hedda. No.

Tesman. Very well.

[*He goes into the inner room and ou. to the right.* BRACK *sits in the inner room, and keeps an eye from time to time on* HEDDA *and* LÖVBORG.]

Lövborg. [*Softly, as before.*] Answer me Hedda—how could you go and do this?

Hedda. [*Apparently absorbed in the album.*] If you continue to say *du* to me I won't talk to you.

Lövborg. May I not say *du* even when we are alone?

Hedda. No. You may think it; but you mustn't say it.

Lövborg. Ah, I understand it. It is an offense against George Tesman, whom you [1] —love.

Hedda. [*Glances at him and smiles.*] Love? What an idea!

Lövborg. You don't love him then!

Hedda. But I won't hear of any sort of unfaithfulness. Remember that.

Lövborg. Hedda—answer me one thing——

Hedda. Hush!

[TESMAN *enters with a small tray from the inner room.*]

Tesman. Here you are! Isn't this tempting? [*He puts the tray on the table.*]

Hedda. Why do you bring it yourself?

Tesman. [*Filling the glasses.*] Because I think it's such fun to wait upon you, Hedda.

Hedda. But you have poured out two glasses. Mr. Lövborg said he wouldn't have any——

Tesman. No, but Mrs. Elvsted will soon be here, won't she?

Hedda. Yes, by-the-bye—Mrs. Elvsted ——

Tesman. Had you forgotten her? Eh?

Hedda. We were so absorbed in these photographs. [*Shows him a picture.*] Do you remember this little village?

Tesman. Oh, it's that one just below the Brenner Pass. It was there we passed the night——

Hedda. ——and met that lively party of tourists.

Tesman. Yes, that was the place. Fancy—if we could only have had *you* with us, Eilert! Eh?

[*He returns to the inner room and sits beside* BRACK.]

Lövborg. Answer me this one thing, Hedda——

Hedda. Well?

Lövborg. Was there no love in your friendship for *me* either? Not a spark—not a tinge of love in it?

<hr>

[1] He uses the familiar *du.*

[1] From this point onward Lövborg uses the formal *De.*

Hedda. I wonder if there was? To me it seems as though we were two good comrades —two thoroughly intimate friends. [*Smilingly.*] You especially were frankness itself.

Lövborg. It was you that made me so.

Hedda. As I look back upon it all, I think there was really something beautiful, something fascinating—something daring—in—in that secret intimacy—that comradeship which no living creature so much as dreamed of.

Lövborg. Yes, yes, Hedda! Was there not?—When I used to come to your father's in the afternoon—and the General sat over at the window reading his papers—with his back toward us——

Hedda. And we two on the corner sofa——

Lövborg. Always with the same illustrated paper before us——

Hedda. For want of an album, yes.

Lövborg. Yes, Hedda, and when I made my confessions to you—told you about myself, things that at that time no one else knew! There I would sit and tell you of my escapades—my days and nights of devilment. Oh, Hedda—what was the power in you that forced me to confess these things?

Hedda. Do you think it was any power in me?

Lövborg. How else can I explain it? And all those—those roundabout questions you used to put to me——

Hedda. Which you understood so particularly well——

Lövborg. How could you sit and question me like that? Question me quite frankly——

Hedda. In roundabout terms, please observe.

Lövborg. Yes, but frankly nevertheless. Cross-question me about—all that sort of thing?

Hedda. And how could you answer, Mr. Lövborg?

Lövborg. Yes, that is just what I can't understand—in looking back upon it. But tell me now, Hedda—was there not love at the bottom of our friendship? On your side, did you not feel as though you might purge my stains away—if I made you my confessor? Was it not so?

Hedda. No, not quite.

Lövborg. What was your motive, then?

Hedda. Do you think it quite incomprehensible that a young girl—when it can be done—without anyone knowing——

Lövborg. Well?

Hedda. ——should be glad to have a peep, now and then, into a world which——

Lövborg. Which——?

Hedda. ——which she is forbidden to know anything about?

Lövborg. So *that* was it?

Hedda. Partly. Partly—I almost think.

Lövborg. Comradeship in the thirst for life. But why should not *that,* at any rate, have continued?

Hedda. The fault was yours.

Lövborg. It was you that broke with me.

Hedda. Yes, when our friendship threatened to develop into something more serious. Shame upon you, Eilert Lövborg! How could you think of wronging your—your frank comrade?

Lövborg. [*Clenching his hands.*] Oh, why did you not carry out your threat? Why did you not shoot me down?

Hedda. Because I have such a dread of scandal.

Lövborg. Yes, Hedda, you are a coward at heart.

Hedda. A terrible coward. [*Changing her tone.*] But it was a lucky thing for you. And now you have found ample consolation at the Elvsteds'.

Lövborg. I know what Thea has confided to you.

Hedda. And perhaps you have confided to her something about us?

Lövborg. Not a word. She is too stupid to understand anything of that sort.

Hedda. Stupid?

Lövborg. She is stupid about matters of that sort.

Hedda. And I am cowardly. [*Bends over toward him, without looking him in the face, and says more softly.*] But now I will confide something to *you.*

Lövborg. [*Eagerly.*] Well?

Hedda. The fact that I dared not shoot you down——

Lövborg. Yes!

Hedda. ——that was not my most arrant cowardice—that evening.

Lövborg. [*Looks at her a moment, understands, and whispers passionately.*] Oh, Hedda! Hedda Gabler! Now I begin to see a hidden reason beneath our comradeship! You [1] and I——! After all, then it was your craving for life——

Hedda. [*Softly, with a sharp glance.*] Take care! Believe nothing of the sort!

[*Twilight has begun to fall. The hall door is opened from without by* BERTA.]

Hedda. [*Closes the album with a bang and calls smilingly.*] Ah, at last! My darling Thea—come along!

---

[1] In this speech he once more says *du.* Hedda addresses him throughout as *De.*

[MRS. ELVSTED *enters from the hall. She is in evening dress. The door is closed behind her.*]

Hedda. [*On the sofa, stretches out her arms toward her.*] My sweet Thea—you can't think how I have been longing for you!

[MRS. ELVSTED, *in passing, exchanges slight salutations with the gentlemen in the inner room, then goes up to the table and gives* HEDDA *her hand.* EILERT LÖVBORG *has risen. He and* MRS. ELVSTED *greet each other with a silent nod.*]

Mrs. Elvsted. Ought I to go in and talk to your husband for a moment?

Hedda. Oh, not at all. Leave those two alone. They will soon be going.

Mrs. Elvsted. Are they going out?

Hedda. Yes, to a supper-party.

Mrs. Elvsted. [*Quickly, to* LÖVBORG.] Not *you?*

Lövborg. No.

Hedda. Mr. Lövborg remains with us.

Mrs. Elvsted. [*Takes a chair and is about to seat herself at his side.*] Oh, how nice it is here!

Hedda. No, thank you, my little Thea! Not *there!* You'll be good enough to come over here to me. I will sit between you.

Mrs. Elvsted. Yes, just as you please.

[*She goes round the table and seats herself on the sofa on* HEDDA'S *right.* LÖVBORG *reseats himself on his chair.*]

Lövborg. [*After a short pause, to* HEDDA.] Is not she lovely to look at?

Hedda. [*Lightly stroking her hair.*] Only to look at?

Lövborg. Yes. For *we* two—she and I— we are two real comrades. We have absolute faith in each other; so we can sit and talk with perfect frankness——

Hedda. Not roundabout, Mr. Lövborg?

Lövborg. Well——

Mrs. Elvsted. [*Softly clinging close to* HEDDA.] Oh, how happy I am, Hedda! For, only think, he says I have inspired him too.

Hedda. [*Looks at her with a smile.*] Ah! Does he say that, dear?

Lövborg. And then she is so brave, Mrs. Tesman!

Mrs. Elvsted. Good heavens—am I brave?

Lövborg. Exceedingly—where your comrade is concerned.

Hedda. Ah yes—courage! If one only had *that!*

Lövborg. What then? What do you mean?

Hedda. Then life would perhaps be livable, after all. [*With a sudden change of tone.*] But now, my dearest Thea, you really must have a glass of cold punch.

Mrs. Elvsted. No, thanks—I never take anything of that kind.

Hedda. Well then, *you,* Mr. Lövborg.

Lövborg. Nor I, thank you.

Mrs. Elvsted. No, he doesn't either.

Hedda. [*Looks fixedly at him.*] But if I say you *shall?*

Lövborg. It would be no use.

Hedda. [*Laughing.*] Then I, poor creature, have no sort of power over you?

Lövborg. Not in *that* respect.

Hedda. But seriously, I think you ought to—for your own sake.

Mrs. Elvsted. Why, Hedda——!

Lövborg. How so?

Hedda. Or rather on account of other people.

Lövborg. Indeed?

Hedda. Otherwise people might be apt to suspect that—in your heart of hearts—you did not feel quite secure—quite confident in yourself.

Mrs. Elvsted. [*Softly.*] Oh please, Hedda——

Lövborg. People may suspect what they like—for the present.

Mrs. Elvsted. [*Joyfully.*] Yes, let them!

Hedda. I saw it plainly in Judge Brack's face a moment ago.

Lövborg. What did you see?

Hedda. His contemptuous smile, when you dared not go with them into the inner room.

Lövborg. Dared not? Of course I preferred to stop here and talk to *you.*

Mrs. Elvsted. What could be more natural, Hedda?

Hedda. But the Judge could not guess that. And I saw, too, the way he smiled and glanced at Tesman when you dared not accept his invitation to this wretched little supper-party of his.

Lövborg. Dared not! Do you say I dared not?

Hedda. *I* don't say so. But that was how Judge Brack understood it.

Lövborg. Well, let him.

Hedda. Then you are not going with them?

Lövborg. I will stay here with you and Thea.

Mrs. Elvsted. Yes, Hedda—how can you doubt that?

Hedda. [*Smiles and nods approvingly to* LÖVBORG.] Firm as a rock! Faithful to your principles, now and forever! Ah, that is how a man should be! [*Turns to* MRS. ELVSTED *and caresses her.*] Well now, what did I tell you, when you came to us this morning in such a state of distraction——

Lövborg. [*Surprised.*] Distraction!

Mrs. Elvsted. [*Terrified.*] Hedda—oh Hedda——!

Hedda. You can see for yourself! You haven't the slightest reason to be in such mortal terror——. [*Interrupting herself.*] There! Now we can all three enjoy ourselves!

Lövborg. [*Who has given a start.*] Ah—what is all this, Mrs. Tesman?

Mrs. Elvsted. Oh, my God, Hedda! What are you saying? What are you doing?

Hedda. Don't get excited! That horrid Judge Brack is sitting watching you.

Lövborg. So she was in mortal terror! On my account!

Mrs. Elvsted. [*Softly and piteously.*] Oh, Hedda—now you have ruined everything!

Lövborg. [*Looks fixedly at her for a moment. His face is distorted.*] So *that* was my comrade's frank confidence in me?

Mrs. Elvsted. [*Imploringly.*] Oh, my dearest friend—only let me tell you——

Lövborg. [*Takes one of the glasses of punch, raises it to his lips, and says in a low, husky voice.*] Your health, Thea!

[*He empties the glass, puts it down, and takes the second.*]

Mrs. Elvsted. [*Softly.*] Oh, Hedda, Hedda —how *could* you do this?

Hedda. *I* do it? *I?* Are you crazy?

Lövborg. Here's to your health too, Mrs. Tesman. Thanks for the truth. Hurrah for the truth!

[*He empties the glass and is about to refill it.*]

Hedda. [*Lays her hand on his arm.*] Come, come—no more for the present. Remember you are going out to supper.

Mrs. Elvsted. No, no, no!

Hedda. Hush! They are sitting watching you.

Lövborg. [*Putting down the glass.*] Now, Thea—tell me the truth——

Mrs. Elvsted. Yes.

Lövborg. Did your husband know that you had come after me?

Mrs. Elvsted. [*Wringing her hands.*] Oh, Hedda—do you hear what he is asking?

Lövborg. Was it arranged between you and him that you were to come to town and look after me? Perhaps it was the Sheriff himself that urged you to come? Aha, my dear—no doubt he wanted my help in his office! Or was it at the card-table that he missed me?

Mrs. Elvsted. [*Softly, in agony.*] Oh, Lövborg, Lövborg——!

Lövborg. [*Seizes a glass and is on the point of filling it.*] Here's a glass for the old Sheriff too!

Hedda. [*Preventing him.*] No more just now. Remember, you have to read your manuscript to Tesman.

Lövborg. [*Calmly, putting down the glass.*] It was stupid of me, all this, Thea—to take it in this way, I mean. Don't be angry with me, my dear, dear comrade. You shall see—both you and the others—that if I was fallen once—now I have risen again! Thanks to *you*, Thea.

Mrs. Elvsted. [*Radiant with joy.*] Oh, heaven be praised——!

[BRACK *has in the meantime looked at his watch. He and* TESMAN *rise and come into the drawing-room.*]

Brack. [*Takes his hat and overcoat.*] Well, Mrs. Tesman, our time has come.

Hedda. I suppose it has.

Lövborg. [*Rising.*] Mine too, Judge Brack.

Mrs. Elvsted. [*Softly and imploringly.*] Oh, Lövborg, don't do it!

Hedda. [*Pinching her arm.*] They can hear you!

Mrs. Elvsted. [*With a suppressed shriek.*] Ow!

Lövborg. [*To* BRACK.] You were good enough to invite me.

Brack. Well, are you coming after all?

Lövborg. Yes, many thanks.

Brack. I'm delighted——

Lövborg. [*To* TESMAN, *putting the parcel of manuscript in his pocket.*] I should like to show you one or two things before I send it to the printer's.

Tesman. Fancy—that will be delightful. But, Hedda dear, how is Mrs. Elvsted to get home? Eh?

Hedda. Oh, that can be managed somehow.

Lövborg. [*Looking toward the ladies.*] Mrs. Elvsted? Of course, I'll come again and fetch her. [*Approaching.*] At ten or thereabouts, Mrs. Tesman? Will that do?

Hedda. Certainly. That will do capitally.

Tesman. Well, then, that's all right. But you must not expect *me* so early, Hedda.

Hedda. Oh, you may stop as long—as long as ever you please.

Mrs. Elvsted. [*Trying to conceal her anxiety.*] Well then, Mr. Lövborg—I shall remain here until you come.

Lövborg. [*With his hat in his hand.*] Pray do, Mrs. Elvsted.

Brack. And now off goes the excursion train, gentlemen! I hope we shall have a lively time, as a certain fair lady puts it.

Hedda. Ah, if only the fair lady could be present unseen——!

Brack. Why unseen?

Hedda. In order to hear a little of your liveliness at first hand, Judge Brack.

Brack. [*Laughing.*] I should not advise the fair lady to try it.

Tesman. [*Also laughing.*] Come, you're a nice one, Hedda! Fancy that!

Brack. Well, good-by, good-by, ladies.

Lövborg. [*Bowing.*] About ten o'clock, then.

[BRACK, LÖVBORG, *and* TESMAN *go out by the hall door. At the same time,* BERTA *enters from the inner room with a lighted lamp, which she places on the drawing-room table; she goes out by the way she came.*]

Mrs. Elvsted. [*Who has risen and is wandering restlessly about the room.*] Hedda—Hedda—what will come of all this?

Hedda. At ten o'clock—he will be here. I can see him already—with vine-leaves in his hair—flushed and fearless——

Mrs. Elvsted. Oh, I hope he may.

Hedda. And then, you see—then he will have regained control over himself. Then he will be a free man for all his days.

Mrs. Elvsted. Oh God!—if he would only come as you see him now!

Hedda. He will come as I see him—so, and not otherwise! [*Rises and approaches* THEA.] You may doubt him as long as you please; *I* believe in him. And now we will try——

Mrs. Elvsted. You have some hidden motive in this, Hedda!

Hedda. Yes, I have. I want for once in my life to have power to mold a human destiny.

Mrs. Elvsted. Have you not the power?

Hedda. I have not—and have never had it.

Mrs. Elvsted. Not your husband's?

Hedda. Do you think *that* is worth the trouble? Oh, if you could only understand how poor I am. And fate has made you so rich! [*Clasps her passionately in her arms.*] I think I must burn your hair off, after all.

Mrs. Elvsted. Let me go! Let me go! I am afraid of you, Hedda!

Berta. [*In the middle doorway.*] Tea is laid in the dining-room, ma'am.

Hedda. Very well. We are coming.

Mrs. Elvsted. No, no, no! I would rather go home alone! At once!

Hedda. Nonsense! First you shall have a cup of tea, you little stupid. And then—at ten o'clock—Eilert Lövborg will be here—with vine-leaves in his hair.

[*She drags* MRS. ELVSTED *almost by force toward the middle doorway.*]

CURTAIN

ACT THIRD

The room at the Tesmans'. The curtains are drawn over the middle doorway, and also over the glass door. The lamp, half turned down, and with a shade over it, is burning on the table. In the stove, the door of which stands open, there has been a fire, which is now nearly burnt out.

[MRS. ELVSTED, *wrapped in a large shawl, and with her feet upon a footrest, sits close to the stove, sunk back in the arm-chair.* HEDDA, *fully dressed, lies sleeping upon the sofa, with a sofa-blanket over her.*]

Mrs. Elvsted. [*After a pause, suddenly sits up in her chair, and listens eagerly. Then she sinks back again wearily, moaning to herself.*] Oh God—oh God—not yet!

[BERTA *slips cautiously in by the hall door. She has a letter in her hand.*]

Mrs. Elvsted. [*Turns and whispers eagerly.*] Well—has any one come?

Berta. [*Softly.*] Yes, a girl has just brought this letter.

Mrs. Elvsted. [*Quickly, holding out her hand.*] A letter! Give it to me!

Berta. No, it's for Dr. Tesman, ma'am.

Mrs. Elvsted. Oh, indeed.

Berta. It was Miss Tesman's servant that brought it. I'll lay it here on the table.

Mrs. Elvsted. Yes, do.

Berta. [*Laying down the letter.*] I think I had better put out the lamp. It's smoking.

Mrs. Elvsted. Yes, put it out. It must soon be daylight now.

Berta. [*Putting out the lamp.*] It is daylight already, ma'am.

Mrs. Elvsted. Yes, broad day! And no one come back yet——!

Berta. Lord bless you, ma'am—I guessed how it would be.

Mrs. Elvsted. You guessed?

Berta. Yes, when I saw that a certain person had come back to town—and that he went off with them. For we've heard enough about that gentleman before now.

Mrs. Elvsted. Don't speak so loud. You will waken Mrs. Tesman.

Berta. [*Looks toward the sofa and sighs.*] No, no—let her sleep, poor thing. Shan't I put some wood on the fire?

Mrs. Elvsted. Thanks, not for me.

Berta. Oh, very well.

[*She goes softly out by the hall door.*]

Hedda. [*Is wakened by the shutting of the door, and looks up.*] What's that——?

Mrs. Elvsted. It was only the servant——

Hedda. [*Looking about her.*] Oh, we're here——! Yes, now I remember. [*Sits erect upon the sofa, stretches herself, and rubs her eyes.*] What o'clock is it, Thea?

Mrs. Elvsted. [*Looks at her watch.*] It's past seven.

Hedda. When did Tesman come home?

Mrs. Elvsted. He has not come.

Hedda. Not come home yet?

Mrs. Elvsted. [*Rising.*] No one has come.

Hedda. Think of our watching and waiting here till four in the morning——

Mrs. Elvsted. [*Wringing her hands.*] And how I watched and waited for him!

Hedda. [*Yawns, and says with her hand before her mouth.*] Well, well—we might have spared ourselves the trouble.

Mrs. Elvsted. Did you get a little sleep?

Hedda. Oh yes; I believe I have slept pretty well. Have you not?

Mrs. Elvsted. Not for a moment. I couldn't, Hedda!—not to save my life.

Hedda. [*Rises and goes toward her.*] There, there, there! There's nothing to be so alarmed about. I understand quite well what has happened.

Mrs. Elvsted. Well, what do you think? Won't you tell me?

Hedda. Why, of course it has been a very late affair at Judge Brack's——

Mrs. Elvsted. Yes, yes—that is clear enough. But all the same——

Hedda. And then, you see, Tesman hasn't cared to come home and ring us up in the middle of the night. [*Laughing.*] Perhaps he wasn't inclined to show himself either—immediately after a jollification.

Mrs. Elvsted. But in that case—where can he have gone?

Hedda. Of course he has gone to his Aunts' and slept there. They have his old room ready for him.

Mrs. Elvsted. No, he can't be with *them;* for a letter has just come for him from Miss Tesman. There it lies.

Hedda. Indeed? [*Looks at the address.*] Why yes, it's addressed in Aunt Julia's own hand. Well then, he has remained at Judge Brack's. And as for Eilert Lövborg—he is sitting, with vine-leaves in his hair, reading his manuscript.

Mrs. Elvsted. Oh Hedda, you are just saying things you don't believe a bit.

Hedda. You really are a little blockhead Thea.

Mrs. Elvsted. Oh yes, I suppose I am.

Hedda. And how mortally tired you look

Mrs. Elvsted. Yes, I am mortally tired

Hedda. Well then, you must do as I tell you. You must go into my room and lie down for a little while.

Mrs. Elvsted. Oh no, no—I shouldn't be able to sleep.

Hedda. I am sure you would.

Mrs. Elvsted. Well, but your husband is certain to come soon now; and then I want to know at once——

Hedda. I shall take care to let you know when he comes.

Mrs. Elvsted. Do you promise me, Hedda?

Hedda. Yes, rely upon me. Just you go in and have a sleep in the meantime.

Mrs. Elvsted. Thanks; then I'll try to.

[*She goes off through the inner room.*]

[HEDDA *goes up to the glass door and draws back the curtains. The broad daylight streams into the room. Then she takes a little hand-glass from the writing-table, looks at herself in it, and arranges her hair. Next she goes to the hall door and presses the bell-button.* BERTA *presently appears at the hall door.*]

Berta. Did you want anything, ma'am?

Hedda. Yes; you must put some more wood in the stove. I am shivering.

Berta. Bless me—I'll make up the fire at once. [*She rakes the embers together and lays a piece of wood upon them; then stops and listens.*] That was a ring at the front door, ma'am.

Hedda. Then go to the door. I will look after the fire.

Berta. It'll soon burn up.

[*She goes out by the hall door.*]

[HEDDA *kneels on the foot-rest and lays some more pieces of wood in the stove. After a short pause,* GEORGE TESMAN *enters from the hall. He looks tired and rather serious. He steals on tiptoe toward the middle doorway and is about to slip through the curtains.*]

Hedda. [*At the stove, without looking up.*] Good morning.

Tesman. [*Turns.*] Hedda! [*Approaching her.*] Good heavens—are you up so early? Eh?

Hedda. Yes. I am up very early this morning.

Tesman. And I never doubted you were still sound asleep. Fancy that, Hedda!

Hedda. Don't speak so loud. Mrs. Elvsted is resting in my room.

Tesman. Has Mrs. Elvsted been here all night?

Hedda. Yes, since no one came to fetch her.

Tesman. Ah, to be sure.

Hedda. [*Closes the door of the stove and rises.*] Well, did you enjoy yourselves at Judge Brack's?

Tesman. Have you been anxious about me? Eh?

Hedda. No, I should never think of being anxious. But I asked if you had enjoyed yourself.

Tesman. Oh yes—for once in a way. Especially the beginning of the evening; for then Eilert read me part of his book. We arrived more than an hour too early—fancy that! And Brack had all sorts of arrangements to make—so Eilert read to me.

Hedda. [*Seating herself by the table on the right.*] Well? Tell me, then——

Tesman. [*Sitting on a footstool near the stove.*] Oh Hedda, you can't conceive what a book that is going to be! I believe it is one of the most remarkable things that have ever been written. Fancy that!

Hedda. Yes, yes; I don't care about that——

Tesman. I must make a confession to you, Hedda. When he had finished reading—a horrid feeling came over me.

Hedda. A horrid feeling?

Tesman. I felt jealous of Eilert for having had it in him to write such a book. Only think, Hedda!

Hedda. Yes, yes, I am thinking!

Tesman. And then how pitiful to think that he—with all his gifts—should be irreclaimable, after all.

Hedda. I suppose you mean that he has more courage than the rest?

Tesman. No, not at all—I mean that he is incapable of taking his pleasures in moderation.

Hedda. And what came of it all—in the end?

Tesman. Well, to tell the truth, I think it might best be described as an orgy, Hedda.

Hedda. Had he vine-leaves in his hair?

Tesman. Vine-leaves? No, I saw nothing of the sort. But he made a long, rambling speech in honor of the woman who had inspired him in his work—that was the phrase he used.

Hedda. Did he name her?

Tesman. No, he didn't; but I can't help thinking he meant Mrs. Elvsted. You may be sure he did.

Hedda. Well—where did you part from him?

Tesman. On the way to town. We broke up—the last of us at any rate—all together; and Brack came with us to get a breath of fresh air. And then, you see, we agreed to take Eilert home; for he had had far more than was good for him.

Hedda. I daresay.

Tesman. But now comes the strange part of it, Hedda; or, I should rather say, the melancholy part of it. I declare I am almost ashamed on Eilert's account—to tell you ——

Hedda. Oh, go on——!

Tesman. Well, as we were getting near town, you see, I happened to drop a little behind the others. Only for a minute or two—fancy that!

Hedda. Yes, yes, yes, but——?

Tesman. And then, as I hurried after them —what do you think I found by the wayside? Eh?

Hedda. Oh, how should I know!

Tesman. You mustn't speak of it to a soul, Hedda! Do you hear? Promise me, for Eilert's sake. [*Draws a parcel, wrapped in paper, from his coat pocket.*] Fancy, dear— I found this.

Hedda. Is not that the parcel he had with him yesterday?

Tesman. Yes, it is the whole of his precious, irreplaceable manuscript! And he had gone and lost it, and knew nothing about it. Only fancy, Hedda! So deplorably——

Hedda. But why did you not give him back the parcel at once?

Tesman. I didn't dare to—in the state he was then in——

Hedda. Did you not tell any of the others that you had found it?

Tesman. Oh, far from it! You can surely understand that, for Eilert's sake, I wouldn't do that.

Hedda. So no one knows that Eilert Lövborg's manuscript is in your possession?

Tesman. No. And no one *must* know it.

Hedda. Then what did you say to him afterwards?

Tesman. I didn't talk to him again at all; for when we got in among the streets, he and two or three of the others gave us the slip and disappeared. Fancy that!

Hedda. Indeed! They must have taken him home then.

Tesman. Yes, so it would appear. And Brack, too, left us.

Hedda. And what have you been doing with yourself since?

Tesman. Well, I and some of the others went home with one of the party, a jolly fellow, and took our morning coffee with him; or perhaps I should rather call it our night coffee—eh? But now, when I have rested a little, and given Eilert, poor fellow, time to have his sleep out, I must take this back to him.

Hedda. [*Holds out her hand for the packet.*] No—don't give it to him! Not in such a hurry, I mean. Let me read it first.

Tesman. No, my dearest Hedda, I mustn't, I really mustn't.

Hedda. You must not?

Tesman. No—for you can imagine what a state of despair he will be in when he wakens and misses the manuscript. He has no copy of it, you must know! He told me so.

Hedda. [*Looking searchingly at him.*] Can such a thing not be reproduced? Written over again?

Tesman. No, I don't think that would be possible. For the inspiration, you see——

Hedda. Yes, yes—I suppose it depends on that—— [*Lightly.*] But, by-the-bye—here is a letter for you.

Tesman. Fancy——!

Hedda. [*Handing it to him.*] It came early this morning.

Tesman. It's from Aunt Julia! What can it be? [*He lays the packet on the other footstool, opens the letter, runs his eye through it, and jumps up.*] Oh, Hedda—she says that poor Aunt Rina is dying!

Hedda. Well, we were prepared for that.

Tesman. And that if I want to see her again, I must make haste. I'll run in to them at once.

Hedda. [*Suppressing a smile.*] Will you run?

Tesman. Oh, my dearest Hedda—if you could only make up your mind to come with me! Just think!

Hedda. [*Rises and says wearily, repelling the idea.*] No, no, don't ask me. I *will* not look upon sickness and death. I loathe all sorts of ugliness.

Tesman. Well, well, then——! [*Bustling around.*] My hat——? My overcoat——? Oh, in the hall——. I do hope I mayn't come too late, Hedda. Eh?

Hedda. Oh, if you run——

[BERTA *appears at the hall door.*]

Berta. Judge Brack is at the door, and wishes to know if he may come in.

Tesman. At this time! No, I can't possibly see him.

Hedda. But I can. [*To* BERTA.] Ask Judge Brack to come in. [BERTA *goes out.*]

Hedda. [*Quickly, whispering.*] The parcel, Tesman!

[*She snatches it up from the stool.*]

Tesman. Yes, give it to me!

Hedda. No, no, I will keep it till you come back.

[*She goes to the writing-table and places it in the bookcase.* TESMAN *stands in a flurry of haste, and cannot get his gloves on.* JUDGE BRACK *enters from the hall.*]

Hedda. [*Nodding to him.*] You are an early bird, I must say.

Brack. Yes, don't you think so? [*To* TESMAN.] Are you on the move, too?

Tesman. Yes, I *must* rush off to my aunts'. Fancy—the invalid one is lying at death's door, poor creature.

Brack. Dear me, is she indeed? Then on no account let me detain you. At such a critical moment——

Tesman. Yes, I must really rush—— Good-by! Good-by!

[*He hastens out by the hall door.*]

Hedda. [*Approaching.*] You seem to have made a particularly lively night of it at your rooms, Judge Brack.

Brack. I assure you I have not had my clothes off, Mrs. Hedda.

Hedda. Not you, either?

Brack. No, as you may see. But what has Tesman been telling you of the night's adventures?

Hedda. Oh, some tiresome story. Only that they went and had coffee somewhere or other.

Brack. I have heard about that coffee-party already. Eilert Lövborg was not with them, I fancy?

Hedda. No, they had taken him home before that.

Brack. Tesman too?

Hedda. No, but some of the others, he said.

Brack. [*Smiling.*] George Tesman is really an ingenuous creature, Mrs. Hedda.

Hedda. Yes, heaven knows he is. Then is there something behind all this?

Brack. Yes, perhaps there may be.

Hedda. Well then, sit down, my dear Judge, and tell your story in comfort.

[*She seats herself to the left of the table.* BRACK *sits near her, at the long side of the table.*]

Hedda. Now then?

Brack. I had special reasons for keeping

track of my guests—or rather of some of my guests—last night.

Hedda. Of Eilert Lövborg among the rest, perhaps.

Brack. Frankly—yes.

Hedda. Now you make me really curious——

Brack. Do you know where he and one or two of the others finished the night, Mrs. Hedda?

Hedda. If it is not quite unmentionable, tell me.

Brack. Oh no, it's not at all unmentionable. Well, they put in an appearance at a particularly animated soirée.

Hedda. Of the lively kind?

Brack. Of the very liveliest——

Hedda. Tell me more of this, Judge Brack——

Brack. Lövberg, as well as the others, had been invited in advance. I knew all about it. But he had declined the invitation; for now, as you know, he has become a new man.

Hedda. Up at the Elvsteds', yes. But he went after all, then?

Brack. Well, you see, Mrs. Hedda—unhappily the spirit moved him at my rooms last evening——

Hedda. Yes, I hear he found inspiration.

Brack. Pretty violent inspiration. Well, I fancy that altered his purpose; for we menfolk are unfortunately not always so firm in our principles as we ought to be.

Hedda. Oh, I am sure *you* are an exception, Judge Brack. But as to Lövborg——?

Brack. To make a long story short—he landed at last in Mademoiselle Diana's rooms.

Hedda. Mademoiselle Diana's?

Brack. It was Mademoiselle Diana that was giving the soirée, to a select circle of her admirers and her lady friends.

Hedda. Is she a red-haired woman?

Brack. Precisely.

Hedda. A sort of a—singer?

Brack. Oh yes—in her leisure moments. And moreover a mighty huntress—of men— Mrs. Hedda. You have no doubt heard of her. Eilert Lövborg was one of her most enthusiastic protectors—in the days of his glory.

Hedda. And how did all this end?

Brack. Far from amicably, it appears. After a most tender meeting, they seem to have come to blows——

Hedda. Lövborg and she?

Brack. Yes. He accused her or her friends of having robbed him. He declared that his pocket-book had disappeared—and other

things as well. In short, he seems to have made a furious disturbance.

Hedda. And what came of it all?

Brack. It came to a general scrimmage, in which the ladies as well as the gentlemen took part. Fortunately the police at last appeared on the scene.

Hedda. The police too?

Brack. Yes. I fancy it will prove a costly frolic for Eilert Lövborg, crazy being that he is.

Hedda. How so?

Brack. He seems to have made a violent resistance—to have hit one of the constables on the head and torn the coat off his back. So they had to march him off to the police station with the rest.

Hedda. How have you learnt all this?

Brack. From the police themselves.

Hedda. [*Gazing straight before her.*] So that is what happened. Then he had no vine-leaves in his hair.

Brack. Vine-leaves, Mrs. Hedda?

Hedda. [*Changing her tone.*] But tell me now, Judge—what is your real reason for tracking out Eilert Lövborg's movements so carefully?

Brack. In the first place, it could not be entirely indifferent to me if it should appear in the police-court that he came straight from my house.

Hedda. Will the matter come into court, then?

Brack. Of course. However, I should scarcely have troubled so much about that. But I thought that, as a friend of the family, it was my duty to supply you and Tesman with a full account of his nocturnal exploits.

Hedda. Why so, Judge Brack?

Brack. Why, because I have a shrewd suspicion that he intends to use you as a sort of blind.

Hedda. Oh, how can you think such a thing?

Brack. Good heavens, Mrs. Hedda—we have eyes in our head. Mark my words! This Mrs. Elvsted will be in no hurry to leave town again.

Hedda. Well, even if there should be anything between them, I suppose there are plenty of other places where they could meet.

Brack. Not a single *home*. Henceforth, as before, every respectable house will be closed against Eilert Lövborg.

Hedda. And so ought mine to be, you mean?

Brack. Yes. I confess it would be more than painful to me if this personage were to be made free of your house. How superfluous, how intrusive, he would be, if he were to force his way into——

Hedda. ——into the triangle?

Brack. Precisely. It would simply mean that I should find myself homeless.

Hedda. [*Looks at him with a smile.*] So you want to be the one cock in the basket [1]— that is your aim.

Brack. [*Nods slowly and lowers his voice.*] Yes, that is my aim. And for that I will fight—with every weapon I can command.

Hedda. [*Her smiling vanishing.*] I see you are a dangerous person—when it comes to the point.

Brack. Do you think so?

Hedda. I am beginning to think so. And I am exceedingly glad to think—that you have no sort of hold over me.

Brack. [*Laughing equivocally.*] Well, well, Mrs. Hedda—perhaps you are right there. If I had, who knows what I might be capable of!

Hedda. Come, come now, Judge Brack! That sounds almost like a threat.

Brack. [*Rising.*] Oh, not at all! The triangle, you know, ought, if possible, to be spontaneously constructed.

Hedda. There I agree with you.

Brack. Well, now I have said all I had to say; and I had better be getting back to town. Good-by, Mrs. Hedda.

[*He goes toward the glass door.*]

Hedda. [*Rising.*] Are you going through the garden?

Brack. Yes, it's a short cut for me.

Hedda. And then it is a back way, too.

Brack. Quite so. I have no objection to back ways. They may be piquant enough at times.

Hedda. When there is ball practice going on, you mean?

Brack. [*In the doorway, laughing to her.*] Oh, people don't shoot their tame poultry, I fancy.

Hedda. [*Also laughing.*] Oh no, when there is only one cock in the basket——

[*They exchange laughing nods of farewell. He goes. She closes the door behind him.*]

[HEDDA, *who has become quite serious, stands for a moment looking out. Presently she goes and peeps through the curtain over the middle doorway. Then she goes to the writing-table, takes* LÖVBORG'S *packet out of the bookcase, and is on the point of looking through its contents.* BERTA *is heard speaking*

loudly in the hall. HEDDA *turns and listens. Then she hastily locks up the packet in the drawer, and lays the key on the inkstand.*]

[EILERT LÖVBORG, *with his greatcoat on and his hat in his hand, tears open the hall door. He looks somewhat confused and irritated.*]

Lövborg. [*Looking toward the hall.*] And I tell you I must and will come in! There!

[*He closes the door, turns, sees* HEDDA, *at once regains his self-control, and bows.*]

Hedda. [*At the writing-table.*] Well, Mr. Lövborg, this is rather a late hour to call for Thea.

Lövborg. You mean rather an early hour to call on you. Pray pardon me.

Hedda. How do you know that she is still here?

Lövborg. They told me at her lodgings that she had been out all night.

Hedda. [*Going to the oval table.*] Did you notice anything about the people of the house when they said that?

Lövborg. [*Looks inquiringly at her.*] Notice anything about them?

Hedda. I mean, did they seem to think it odd?

Lövborg. [*Suddenly understanding.*] Oh, yes, of course! I am dragging her down with me! However, I didn't notice anything.—I suppose Tesman is not up yet?

Hedda. No—I think not——

Lövborg. When did he come home?

Hedda. Very late.

Lövborg. Did he tell you anything?

Hedda. Yes, I gathered that you had had an exceedingly jolly evening at Judge Brack's.

Lövborg. Nothing more?

Hedda. I don't think so. However, I was so dreadfully sleepy——

[MRS. ELVSTED *enters through the curtains of the middle doorway.*]

Mrs. Elvsted. [*Going toward him.*] Ah, Lövborg! At last——!

Lövborg. Yes, at last. And too late!

Mrs. Elvsted. [*Looks anxiously at him.*] What is too late?

Lövborg. Everything is too late now. It is all over with me.

Mrs. Elvsted. Oh no, no—don't say that!

Lövborg. You will say the same when you hear——

Mrs. Elvsted. I won't hear anything!

Hedda. Perhaps you would prefer to talk to her alone? If so, I will leave you.

Lövborg. No, stay—you too. I beg you to stay.

---

[1] "Eneste hane i kurven"—a proverbial saying.

Mrs. Elvsted. Yes, but I won't hear anything, I tell you.

Lövborg. It is not last night's adventures that I want to talk about.

Mrs. Elvsted. What is it then——?

Lövborg. I want to say that now our ways must part.

Mrs. Elvsted. Part!

Hedda. [*Involuntarily.*] I knew it!

Lövborg. You can be of no more service to me, Thea.

Mrs. Elvsted. How can you stand there and say that! No more service to you! Am I not to help you now, as before? Are we not to go on working together?

Lövborg. Henceforward I shall do no work.

Mrs. Elvsted. [*Despairingly.*] Then what am I to do with my life?

Lövborg. You must try to live your life as if you had never known me.

Mrs. Elvsted. But you know I cannot do that!

Lövborg. Try if you cannot, Thea. You must go home again——

Mrs. Elvsted. [*In vehement protest.*] Never in this world! Where you are, there will I be also! I will not let myself be driven away like this! I will remain here! I will be with you when the book appears.

Hedda. [*Half aloud, in suspense.*] Ah yes —the book!

Lövborg. [*Looks at her.*] My book and Thea's; for *that* is what it is.

Mrs. Elvsted. Yes, I feel that it is. And that is why I have a right to be with you when it appears! I will see with my own eyes how respect and honor pour in upon you afresh. And the happiness—the happiness— oh, I must share it with you!

Lövborg. Thea—our book will never appear.

Hedda. Ah!

Mrs. Elvsted. Never appear!

Lövborg. Can never appear.

Mrs. Elvsted. [*In agonized foreboding.*] Lövborg—what have you done with the manuscript?

Hedda. [*Looks anxiously at him.*] Yes, the manuscript——?

Mrs. Elvsted. Where is it?

Lövborg. Oh, Thea—don't ask me about it!

Mrs. Elvsted. Yes, yes, I *will* know. I demand to be told at once.

Lövborg. The manuscript——. Well then —I have torn the manuscript into a thousand pieces.

Mrs. Elvsted. [*Shrieks.*] Oh no, no——!

Hedda. [*Involuntarily.*] But that's not——

Lövborg. [*Looks at her.*] Not true, you think?

Hedda. [*Collecting herself.*] Oh well, of course—since you say so. But it sounded so improbable——

Lövborg. It is true, all the same.

Mrs. Elvsted. [*Wringing her hands.*] Oh God—oh God, Hedda—torn his own work to pieces!

Lövborg. I have torn my own life to pieces. So why should I not tear my life-work too——?

Mrs. Elvsted. And you did this last night?

Lövborg. Yes, I tell you! Tore it into a thousand pieces—and scattered them on the fiord—far out. There, there is cool sea-water at any rate—let them drift upon it—drift with the current and the wind. And then presently they will sink—deeper and deeper —as I shall, Thea.

Mrs. Elvsted. Do you know, Lövborg, that what you have done with the book—I shall think of it to my dying day as though you had killed a little child.

Lövborg. Yes, you are right. It is a sort of child-murder.

Mrs. Elvsted. How could you, then——! Did not the child belong to me too?

Hedda. [*Almost inaudibly.*] Ah, the child——

Mrs. Elvsted. [*Breathing heavily.*] It is all over, then. Well, well, now I will go, Hedda.

Hedda. But you are not going away from town?

Mrs. Elvsted. Oh, I don't know what I shall do. I see nothing but darkness before me.   [*She goes out by the hall door.*]

Hedda. [*Stands waiting for a moment.*] So you are not going to see her home, Mr. Lövborg?

Lövborg. I? Through the streets? Would you have people see her walking with me?

Hedda. Of course I don't know what else may have happened last night. But is it so utterly irretrievable?

Lövborg. It will not end with last night —I know that perfectly well. And the thing is that now I have no taste for that sort of life either. I won't begin it anew. She has broken my courage and my power of braving life out.

Hedda. [*Looking straight before her.*] So that pretty little fool has had her fingers in a man's destiny. [*Looks at him.*] But all the same, how could you treat her so heartlessly?

Lövborg. Oh, don't say that it was heartless!

Hedda. To go and destroy what has filled

her whole soul for months and years! You do not call that heartless!

Lövborg. To you I can tell the truth, Hedda.

Hedda. The truth?

Lövborg. First promise me—give me your word—that what I now confide to you Thea shall never know.

Hedda. I give you my word.

Lövborg. Good. Then let me tell you that what I said just now was untrue.

Hedda. About the manuscript?

Lövborg. Yes. I have not torn it to pieces —nor thrown it into the fiord.

Hedda. No, no——. But—where is it, then?

Lövborg. I have destroyed it none the less —utterly destroyed it, Hedda!

Hedda. I don't understand.

Lövborg. Thea said that what I had done seemed to her like a child-murder.

Hedda. Yes, so she said.

Lövborg. But to kill his child—that is not the worst thing a father can do to it.

Hedda. Not the worst?

Lövborg. No. I wanted to spare Thea from hearing the worst.

Hedda. Then what is the worst?

Lövborg. Suppose now, Hedda, that a man —in the small hours of the morning—came home to his child's mother after a night of riot and debauchery, and said: "Listen—I have been here and there—in this place and in that. And I have taken our child with me —to this place and to that. And I have lost the child—utterly lost it. The devil knows into what hands it may have fallen—who may have had their clutches on it."

Hedda. Well—but when all is said and done, you know—this was only a book——

Lövborg. Thea's pure soul was in that book.

Hedda. Yes, so I understand.

Lövborg. And you can understand, too, that for her and me together no future is possible.

Hedda. What path do you mean to take, then?

Lövborg. None. I will only try to make an end of it all—the sooner the better.

Hedda. [*A step nearer him.*] Eilert Lövborg—listen to me.—Will you not try to—to do it beautifully?

Lövborg. Beautifully? [*Smiling.*] With vine-leaves in my hair, as you used to dream in the old days——?

Hedda. No, no. I have lost my faith in the vine-leaves. But beautifully nevertheless! For once in a way!—Good-by! You must go now—and do not come here any more.

Lövborg. Good-by, Mrs. Tesman. And give George Tesman my love.

[*He is on the point of going.*]

Hedda. No, wait! I must give you a memento to take with you.

[*She goes to the writing-table and opens the drawer and the pistol-case; then returns to* LÖVBORG *with one of the pistols.*]

Lövborg. [*Looks at her.*] This? Is *this* the memento?

Hedda. [*Nodding slowly.*] Do you recognize it? It was aimed at you once.

Lövborg. You should have used it then.

Hedda. Take it—and do *you* use it now.

Lövborg. [*Puts the pistol in his breast pocket.*] Thanks!

Hedda. And beautifully, Eilert Lövborg. Promise me that!

Lövborg. Good-by, Hedda Gabler.

[*He goes by the hall door.*]

[HEDDA *listens for a moment at the door. Then she goes up to the writing-table, takes out the packet of manuscript, peeps under the cover, draws a few of the sheets half out, and looks at them. Next she goes over and seats herself in the arm-chair beside the stove, with the packet in her lap. Presently she opens the stove door, and then the packet.*]

Hedda. [*Throws one of the quires into the fire and whispers to herself.*] Now I am burning your child, Thea!—Burning it, curly-locks! [*Throwing one or two more quires into the stove.*] Your child and Eilert Lövborg's. [*Throws the rest in.*] I am burning —I am burning your child.

CURTAIN

ACT FOURTH

The same rooms at the Tesmans'. It is evening. The drawing-room is in darkness. The back room is lighted by the hanging lamp over the table. The curtains over the glass door are drawn close.

[HEDDA, *dressed in black, walks to and*

fro in the dark room. Then she goes into the back room and disappears for a moment to the left. She is heard to strike a few chords on the piano. Presently she comes in sight again, and returns to the drawing-room.

BERTA *enters from the right, through the inner room, with a lighted lamp, which she places on the table in front of the corner settee in the drawing-room. Her eyes are red with weeping, and she has black ribbons in her cap. She goes quietly and circumspectly out to the right.* HEDDA *goes up to the glass door, lifts the curtain a little aside, and looks out into the darkness.*

Shortly afterwards, MISS TESMAN, *in mourning, with a bonnet and veil on, comes in from the hall.* HEDDA *goes toward her and holds out her hand.*]

Miss Tesman. Yes, Hedda, here I am, in mourning and forlorn; for now my poor sister has at last found peace.

Hedda. I have heard the news already, as you see. Tesman sent me a card.

Miss Tesman. Yes, he promised me he would. But nevertheless I thought that to Hedda—here in the house of life—I ought myself to bring the tidings of death.

Hedda. That was very kind of you.

Miss Tesman. Ah, Rina ought not to have left us just *now*. This is not the time for Hedda's house to be a house of mourning.

Hedda. [*Changing the subject.*] She died quite peacefully, did she not, Miss Tesman?

Miss Tesman. Oh, her end was so calm, so beautiful. And then she had the unspeakable happiness of seeing George once more —and bidding him good-by.—Has he not come home yet?

Hedda. No. He wrote that he might be detained. But won't you sit down?

Miss Tesman. No, thank you, my dear, dear Hedda. I should like to, but I have so much to do. I must prepare my dear one for her rest as well as I can. She shall go to her grave looking her best.

Hedda. Can I not help you in any way?

Miss Tesman. Oh, you must not think of it! Hedda Tesman must have no hand in such mournful work. Nor let her thoughts dwell on it either—not at this time.

Hedda. One is not always mistress of one's thoughts——

Miss Tesman. [*Continuing.*] Ah, yes, it is the way of the world. At home we shall be sewing a shroud; and here there will soon be sewing too, I suppose—but of another sort, thank God!

[GEORGE TESMAN *enters by the hall door.*]

Hedda. Ah, you have come at last!

Tesman. You here, Aunt Julia? With Hedda? Fancy that!

Miss Tesman. I was just going, my dear boy. Well, have you done all you promised?

Tesman. No; I'm really afraid I have forgotten half of it. I must come to you again tomorrow. Today my brain is all in a whirl. I can't keep my thoughts together.

Miss Tesman. Why, my dear George, you mustn't take it in this way.

Tesman. Mustn't——? How do you mean?

Miss Tesman. Even in your sorrow you must rejoice, as I do—rejoice that she is at rest.

Tesman. Oh yes, yes—you are thinking of Aunt Rina.

Hedda. You will feel lonely now, Miss Tesman.

Miss Tesman. Just at first, yes. But that will not last very long, I hope. I daresay I shall soon find an occupant for poor Rina's little room.

Tesman. Indeed? Who do you think will take it? Eh?

Miss Tesman. Oh, there's always some poor invalid or other in want of nursing, unfortunately.

Hedda. Would you really take such a burden upon you again?

Miss Tesman. A burden! Heaven forgive you, child—it has been no burden to me.

Hedda. But suppose you had a total stranger on your hands——

Miss Tesman. Oh, one soon makes friends with sick folk; and it's such an absolute necessity for me to have someone to live for. Well, heaven be praised, there may soon be something in this house, too, to keep an old aunt busy.

Hedda. Oh, don't trouble about anything here.

Tesman. Yes, just fancy what a nice time we three might have together, if——?

Hedda. If——?

Tesman. [*Uneasily.*] Oh, nothing. It will all come right. Let us hope so—eh?

Miss Tesman. Well, well, I daresay you two want to talk to each other. [*Smiling.*] And perhaps Hedda may have something to tell you too, George. Good-by! I must go home to Rina. [*Turning at the door.*] How strange it is to think that now Rina is with me and with my poor brother as well!

Tesman. Yes, fancy that, Aunt Julia! Eh?

[MISS TESMAN *goes out by the hall door.*]

Hedda. [*Follows* TESMAN *coldly and searchingly with her eyes.*] I almost believe your Aunt Rina's death affects *you* more than it does your Aunt Julia.

Tesman. Oh, it's not that alone. It's Eilert I am so terribly uneasy about.

Hedda. [*Quickly.*] Is there anything new about him?

Tesman. I looked in at his rooms this afternoon, intending to tell him the manuscript was in safe keeping.

Hedda. Well, did you not find him?

Tesman. No. He wasn't at home. But afterwards I met Mrs. Elvsted, and she told me that he had been here early this morning.

Hedda. Yes, directly after you had gone.

Tesman. And he said that he had torn his manuscript to pieces—eh?

Hedda. Yes, so he declared.

Tesman. Why, good heavens, he must have been completely out of his mind! And I suppose you thought it best not to give it back to him, Hedda?

Hedda. No, he did not get it.

Tesman. But of course you told him that we had it?

Hedda. No. [*Quickly.*] Did you tell Mrs. Elvsted?

Tesman. No; I thought I had better not. But you ought to have told him. Fancy, if, in desperation, he should go and do himself some injury! Let me have the manuscript, Hedda! I will take it to him at once. Where is it?

Hedda. [*Cold and immovable, leaning on the arm-chair.*] I have not got it.

Tesman. Have not got it? What in the world do you mean?

Hedda. I have burnt it—every line of it.

Tesman. [*With a violent movement of terror.*] Burnt! Burnt Eilert's manuscript!

Hedda. Don't scream so. The servant might hear you.

Tesman. Burnt! Why, good God——! No, no, no! It's impossible!

Hedda. It is so, nevertheless.

Tesman. Do you know what you have done, Hedda? It's unlawful appropriation of lost property. Fancy that! Just ask Judge Brack, and he'll tell you what it is.

Hedda. I advise you not to speak of it—either to Judge Brack, or to anyone else.

Tesman. But how could you do anything so unheard-of? What put it into your head? What possessed you? Answer me that—eh?

Hedda. [*Suppressing an almost imperceptible smile.*] I did it for your sake, George.

Tesman. For my sake!

Hedda. This morning, when you told me about what he had read to you——

Tesman. Yes, yes—what then?

Hedda. You acknowledged that you envied him his work.

Tesman. Oh, of course I didn't mean that literally.

Hedda. No matter—I could not bear the idea that anyone should throw you into the shade.

Tesman. [*In an outburst of mingled doubt and joy.*] Hedda! Oh, is this true? But—but—I never knew you to show your love like that before. Fancy that!

Hedda. Well, I may as well tell you that—just at this time—— [*Impatiently, breaking off.*] No, no; you can ask Aunt Julia. *She* will tell you, fast enough.

Tesman. Oh, I almost think I understand you, Hedda! [*Clasps his hands together.*] Great heavens! do you really mean it! Eh?

Hedda. Don't shout so. The servant might hear.

Tesman. [*Laughing in irrepressible glee.*] The servant! Why, how absurd you are, Hedda. It's only my old Berta! Why, I'll tell Berta myself.

Hedda. [*Clenching her hands together in desperation.*] Oh, it is killing me—it is killing me, all this!

Tesman. What is, Hedda? Eh?

Hedda. [*Coldly, controlling herself.*] All this—absurdity—George.

Tesman. Absurdity! Do you see anything absurd in my being overjoyed at the news! But after all—perhaps I had better not say anything to Berta.

Hedda. Oh——why not that too?

Tesman. No, no, not yet! But I must certainly tell Aunt Julia. And then that you have begun to call me George too! Fancy that! Oh, Aunt Julia will be so happy—so happy!

Hedda. When she hears that I have burnt Eilert Lövborg's manuscript—for your sake?

Tesman. No, by-the-bye—that affair of the manuscript—of course nobody must know about that. But that you love me so much,[1] Hedda—Aunt Julia must really share my joy in that! I wonder, now, whether this sort of thing is usual in young wives? Eh?

Hedda. I think you had better ask Aunt Julia that question too.

Tesman. I will indeed, some time or other. [*Looks uneasy and downcast again.*] And yet the manuscript—the manuscript! Good God! it is terrible to think what will become of poor Eilert now.

[MRS. ELVSTED, *dressed as in the First*

---

[1] Literally, "That you burn for me."

Act, with hat and cloak, enters by the hall door.]

Mrs. Elvsted. [*Greets them hurriedly, and says in evident agitation.*] Oh, dear Hedda, forgive my coming again.

Hedda. What is the matter with you, Thea?

Tesman. Something about Eilert Lövborg again—eh?

Mrs. Elvsted. Yes! I am dreadfully afraid some misfortune has happened to him.

Hedda. [*Seizes her arm.*] Ah—do you think so?

Tesman. Why, good Lord—what makes you think that, Mrs. Elvsted?

Mrs. Elvsted. I heard them talking of him at my boarding-house—just as I came in. Oh, the most incredible rumors are afloat about him today.

Tesman. Yes, fancy, so I heard too! And I can bear witness that he went straight home to bed last night. Fancy that!

Hedda. Well, what did they say at the boarding-house?

Mrs. Elvsted. Oh, I couldn't make out anything clearly. Either they knew nothing definite, or else——. They stopped talking when they saw me; and I did not dare to ask.

Tesman. [*Moving about uneasily.*] We must hope—we must hope that you misunderstood them, Mrs. Elvsted.

Mrs. Elvsted. No, no; I am sure it was of him they were talking. And I heard something about the hospital or——

Tesman. The hospital?

Hedda. No—surely that cannot be!

Mrs. Elvsted. Oh, I was in such mortal terror! I went to his lodgings and asked for him there.

Hedda. You could make up your mind to that, Thea!

Mrs. Elvsted. What else could I do? I really could bear the suspense no longer.

Tesman. But you didn't find him either—eh?

Mrs. Elvsted. No. And the people knew nothing about him. He hadn't been home since yesterday afternoon, they said.

Tesman. Yesterday. Fancy, how could they say that?

Mrs. Elvsted. Oh, I am sure something terrible must have happened to him.

Tesman. Hedda, dear—how would it be if I were to go and make inquiries——?

Hedda. No, no—don't you mix yourself up in this affair.

[JUDGE BRACK, *with his hat in his hand, enters by the hall door, which* BERTA *opens, and closes behind him. He looks grave and bows in silence.*]

Tesman. Oh, is that you, my dear Judge? Eh?

Brack. Yes. It was imperative I should see you this evening.

Tesman. I can see you have heard the news about Aunt Rina.

Brack. Yes, that among other things.

Tesman. Isn't it sad—eh?

Brack. Well, my dear Tesman, that depends on how you look at it.

Tesman. [*Looks doubtfully at him.*] Has anything else happened?

Brack. Yes.

Hedda. [*In suspense.*] Anything sad, Judge Brack?

Brack. That, too, depends on how you look at it, Mrs. Tesman.

Mrs. Elvsted. [*Unable to restrain her anxiety.*] Oh! it is something about Eilert Lövborg!

Brack. [*With a glance at her.*] What makes you think that, Madam? Perhaps you have already heard something——?

Mrs. Elvsted. [*In confusion.*] No, nothing at all, but——

Tesman. Oh, for heaven's sake, tell us!

Brack. [*Shrugging his shoulders.*] Well, I regret to say Eilert Lövborg has been taken to the hospital. He is lying at the point of death.

Mrs. Elvsted. [*Shrieks.*] Oh God! oh God——!

Tesman. To the hospital! And at the point of death!

Hedda. [*Involuntarily.*] So soon then

Mrs. Elvsted. [*Wailing.*] And we parted in anger, Hedda!

Hedda. [*Whispers.*] Thea—Thea—be careful!

Mrs. Elvsted. [*Not heeding her.*] I must go to him! I must see him alive!

Brack. It is useless, Madam. No one will be admitted.

Mrs. Elvsted. Oh, at least tell me what has happened to him. What is it?

Tesman. You don't mean to say that he has himself——. Eh?

Hedda. Yes, I am sure he has.

Tesman. Hedda, how can you——?

Brack. [*Keeping his eyes fixed upon her.*] Unfortunately you have guessed quite correctly, Mrs. Tesman.

Mrs. Elvsted. Oh, how horrible!

Tesman. Himself, then! Fancy that!

Hedda. Shot himself!

Brack. Rightly guessed again, Mrs. Tesman.

Mrs. Elvsted. [*With an effort at self-control.*] When did it happen, Mr. Brack?

Brack. This afternoon—between three and four.

Tesman. But, good Lord, where did he do it? Eh?

Brack. [*With some hesitation.*] Where? Well—I suppose at his lodgings.

Mrs. Elvsted. No, that cannot be; for I was there between six and seven.

Brack. Well then, somewhere else. I don't know exactly. I only know that he was found——. He had shot himself—in the breast.

Mrs. Elvsted. Oh, how terrible! That he should die like that!

Hedda. [*To* BRACK.] Was it in the breast?

Brack. Yes—as I told you.

Hedda. Not in the temple?

Brack. In the breast, Mrs. Tesman.

Hedda. Well, well—the breast is a good place, too.

Brack. How do you mean, Mrs. Tesman?

Hedda. [*Evasively.*] Oh, nothing—nothing.

Tesman. And the wound is dangerous, you say—eh?

Brack. Absolutely mortal. The end has probably come by this time.

Mrs. Elvsted. Yes, yes, I feel it. The end! The end! Oh, Hedda——!

Tesman. But tell me, how have you learnt all this?

Brack. [*Curtly.*] Through one of the police. A man I had some business with.

Hedda. [*In a clear voice.*] At last a deed worth doing!

Tesman. [*Terrified.*] Good heavens, Hedda! what are you saying?

Hedda. I say there is beauty in this.

Brack. H'm, Mrs. Tesman——

Tesman. Beauty! Fancy that!

Mrs. Elvsted. Oh, Hedda, how can you talk of beauty in such an act!

Hedda. Eilert Lövborg has himself made up his account with life. He has had the courage to do—the one right thing.

Mrs. Elvsted. No, you must never think *that* was how it happened! It must have been in delirium that he did it.

Tesman. In despair!

Hedda. That he did not. I am certain of that.

Mrs. Elvsted. Yes, yes! In delirium! Just as when he tore up our manuscript.

Brack. [*Starting.*] The manuscript? Has he torn that up?

Mrs. Elvsted. Yes, last night.

Tesman. [*Whispers softly.*] Oh, Hedda, we shall never get over this.

Brack. H'm, very extraordinary.

Tesman. [*Moving about the room.*] To think of Eilert going out of the world in this way! And not leaving behind him the book that would have immortalized his name——

Mrs. Elvsted. Oh, if only it could be put together again!

Tesman. Yes, if it only could! I don't know what I would not give——

Mrs. Elvsted. Perhaps it can, Mr. Tesman.

Tesman. What do you mean?

Mrs. Elvsted. [*Searches in the pocket of her dress.*] Look here. I have kept all the loose notes he used to dictate from.

Hedda. [*A step forward.*] Ah——!

Tesman. You have kept them, Mrs. Elvsted! Eh?

Mrs. Elvsted. Yes, I have them here. I put them in my pocket when I left home. Here they still are——

Tesman. Oh, do let me see them!

Mrs. Elvsted. [*Hands him a bundle of papers.*] But they are in such disorder—all mixed up.

Tesman. Fancy, if we could make something out of them, after all! Perhaps if we two put our heads together——

Mrs. Elvsted. Oh yes, at least let us try——

Tesman. We *will* manage it! We *must!* I will dedicate my life to this task.

Hedda. You, George? Your life?

Tesman. Yes, or rather all the time I can spare. My own collections must wait in the meantime. Hedda—you understand, eh? I owe this to Eilert's memory.

Hedda. Perhaps.

Tesman. And so, my dear Mrs. Elvsted, we will give our whole minds to it. There is no use in brooding over what can't be undone —eh? We must try to control our grief as much as possible, and——

Mrs. Elvsted. Yes, yes, Mr. Tesman, I will do the best I can.

Tesman. Well then, come here. I can't rest until we have looked through the notes. Where shall we sit? Here? No, in there, in the back room. Excuse me, my dear Judge. Come with me, Mrs. Elvsted.

Mrs. Elvsted. Oh, if only it were possible!

[TESMAN *and* MRS. ELVSTED *go into the back room. She takes off her hat and cloak. They both sit at the table under the hanging lamp, and are soon deep in an eager examination of the papers.* HEDDA *crosses to the stove and sits in the arm-chair. Presently* BRACK *goes up to her.*]

Hedda. [*In a low voice.*] Oh, what a sense of freedom it gives one, this act of Eilert Lövborg's.

Brack. Freedom, Mrs. Hedda? Well, of course, it is a release for him——

Hedda. I mean for me. It gives me a sense of freedom to know that a deed of deliberate courage is still possible in this world —a deed of spontaneous beauty.

Brack. [*Smiling.*] H'm—my dear Mrs. Hedda——

Hedda. Oh, I know what you are going to say. For you are a kind of specialist too, like—you know!

Brack. [*Looking hard at her.*] Eilert Lövborg was more to you than perhaps you are willing to admit to yourself. Am I wrong?

Hedda. I don't answer such questions. I only know that Eilert Lövborg has had the courage to live his life after his own fashion. And then—the last great act, with its beauty! Ah! that he should have the will and the strength to turn away from the banquet of life—so early.

Brack. I am sorry, Mrs. Hedda—but I fear I must dispel an amiable illusion.

Hedda. Illusion?

Brack. Which could not have lasted long in any case.

Hedda. What do you mean?

Brack. Eilert Lövborg did not shoot himself—voluntarily.

Hedda. Not voluntarily?

Brack. No. The thing did not happen exactly as I told it.

Hedda. [*In suspense.*] Have you concealed something? What is it?

Brack. For poor Mrs. Elvsted's sake I idealized the facts a little.

Hedda. What are the facts?

Brack. First, that he is already dead.

Hedda. At the hospital?

Brack. Yes—without regaining consciousness.

Hedda. What more have you concealed?

Brack. This—the event did not happen at his lodgings.

Hedda. Oh, that can make no difference.

Brack. Perhaps it may. For I must tell you—Eilert Lövborg was found shot in—in Mademoiselle Diana's boudoir.

Hedda. [*Makes a motion as if to rise, but sinks back again.*] That is impossible, Judge Brack! He cannot have been *there* again to-day.

Brack. He was there this afternoon. He went there, he said, to demand the return of something which they had taken from him. Talked wildly about a lost child——

Hedda. Ah—so that was why——

Brack. I thought probably he meant his manuscript; but now I hear he destroyed that himself. So I suppose it must have been his pocket-book.

Hedda. Yes, no doubt. And there—there he was found?

Brack. Yes, there. With a pistol in his breast-pocket, discharged. The ball had lodged in a vital part.

Hedda. In the breast—yes.

Brack. No—in the bowels.

Hedda. [*Looks up at him with an expression of loathing.*] That too! Oh, what curse is it that makes everything I touch turn ludicrous and mean?

Brack. There is one point more, Mrs. Hedda—another disagreeable feature in the affair.

Hedda. And what is that?

Brack. The pistol he carried——

Hedda. [*Breathless.*] Well? What of it?

Brack. He must have stolen it.

Hedda. [*Leaps up.*] Stolen it? That is not true! He did not steal it!

Brack. No other explanation is possible. He *must* have stolen it——. Hush!

[TESMAN *and* MRS. ELVSTED *have risen from the table in the back room, and come into the drawing-room.*]

Tesman. [*With the papers in both his hands.*] Hedda, dear, it is almost impossible to see under that lamp. Think of that!

Hedda. Yes, I am thinking.

Tesman. Would you mind our sitting at your writing-table—eh?

Hedda. If you like. [*Quickly.*] No, wait! Let me clear it first!

Tesman. Oh, you needn't trouble, Hedda. There is plenty of room.

Hedda. No, no, let me clear it, I say! I will take these things in and put them on the piano. There!

[*She has drawn out an object, covered with sheet music, from under the bookcase, places several other pieces of music upon it, and carries the whole into the inner room, to the left.* TESMAN *lays the scraps of paper on the writing-table, and moves the lamp there from the corner table. He and* MRS. ELVSTED *sit down and proceed with their work.* HEDDA *returns.*]

Hedda. [*Behind* MRS. ELVSTED'S *chair, gently ruffling her hair.*] Well, my sweet Thea—how goes it with Eilert Lövborg's monument?

Mrs. Elvsted. [*Looks dispiritedly up at her.*] Oh, it will be terribly hard to put in order.

Tesman. We *must* manage it. I am determined. And arranging other people's papers is just the work for me.

[HEDDA *goes over to the stove, and seats herself on one of the footstools.* BRACK *stands over her, leaning on the arm-chair.*]

Hedda. [*Whispers.*] What did you say about the pistol?

Brack. [*Softly.*] That he must have stolen it.

Hedda. Why stolen it?

Brack. Because every other explanation *ought* to be impossible, Mrs. Hedda.

Hedda. Indeed?

Brack. [*Glances at her.*] Of course Eilert Lövborg was here this morning. Was he not?

Hedda. Yes.

Brack. Were you alone with him?

Hedda. Part of the time.

Brack. Did you not leave the room whilst he was here?

Hedda. No.

Brack. Try to recollect. Were you not out of the room a moment?

Hedda. Yes, perhaps just a moment—out in the hall.

Brack. And where was your pistol-case during that time?

Hedda. I had it locked up in——

Brack. Well, Mrs. Hedda?

Hedda. The case stood there on the writing-table.

Brack. Have you looked since, to see whether both the pistols are there?

Hedda. No.

Brack. Well, you need not. I saw the pistol found in Lövborg's pocket, and I knew it at once as the one I had seen yesterday—and before, too.

Hedda. Have you it with you?

Brack. No; the police have it.

Hedda. What will the police do with it?

Brack. Search till they find the owner.

Hedda. Do you think they will succeed?

Brack. [*Bends over her and whispers.*] No, Hedda Gabler—not so long as I say nothing.

Hedda. [*Looks frightened at him.*] And if you do *not* say nothing—what then?

Brack. [*Shrugs his shoulders.*] There is always the possibility that the pistol was stolen.

Hedda. [*Firmly.*] Death rather than that.

Brack. [*Smiling.*] People say such things —but they don't *do* them.

Hedda. [*Without replying.*] And supposing the pistol was not stolen, and the owner is discovered? What then?

Brack. Well, Hedda—then comes the scandal.

Hedda. The scandal!

Brack. Yes, the scandal—of which you are so mortally afraid. You will, of course, be brought before the court—both you and Mademoiselle Diana. She will have to explain how the thing happened—whether it was an accidental shot or murder. Did the pistol go off as he was trying to take it out of his pocket, to threaten her with? Or did she tear the pistol out of his hand, shoot him, and push it back into his pocket? That would be quite like her; for she is an able-bodied young person, this same Mademoiselle Diana.

Hedda. But *I* have nothing to do with all this repulsive business.

Brack. No. But you will have to answer the question: Why did you give Eilert Lövborg the pistol? And what conclusions will people draw from the fact that you did give it to him?

Hedda. [*Lets her head sink.*] That is true. I did not think of that.

Brack. Well, fortunately, there is no danger, so long as I say nothing.

Hedda. [*Looks up at him.*] So I am in your power, Judge Brack. You have me at your beck and call, from this time forward.

Brack. [*Whispers softly.*] Dearest Hedda—believe me—I shall not abuse my advantage.

Hedda. I am in your power none the less. Subject to your will and your demands. A slave, a slave then! [*Rises impetuously.*] No, I cannot endure the thought of that! Never!

Brack. [*Looks half-mockingly at her.*] People generally get used to the inevitable.

Hedda. [*Returns his look.*] Yes, perhaps. [*She crosses to the writing-table. Suppressing an involuntary smile, she imitates* TESMAN'S *intonations.*] Well? Are you getting on, George? Eh?

Tesman. Heaven knows, dear. In any case it will be the work of months.

Hedda. [*As before.*] Fancy that! [*Passes her hands softly through* MRS. ELVSTED'S *hair.*] Doesn't it seem strange to you, Thea? Here are you sitting with Tesman—just as you used to sit with Eilert Lövborg.

Mrs. Elvsted. Ah, if I could only inspire your husband in the same way!

Hedda. Oh, that will come too—in time.

Tesman. Yes, do you know, Hedda—I really think I begin to feel something of the sort. But won't you go and sit with Brack again?

Hedda. Is there nothing I can do to help you two?

Tesman. No, nothing in the world. [*Turn-*

ing his head.] I trust to you to keep Hedda company, my dear Brack.

Brack. [*With a glance at* HEDDA.] With the very greatest of pleasure.

Hedda. Thanks. But I am tired this evening. I will go in and lie down a little on the sofa.

Tesman. Yes, do, dear—eh?

[HEDDA *goes into the back room and draws the curtains. A short pause. Suddenly she is heard playing a wild dance on the piano.*]

Mrs. Elvsted. [*Starts from her chair.*] Oh —what is that?

Tesman. [*Runs to the doorway.*] Why, my dearest Hedda—don't play dance-music tonight! Just think of Aunt Rina! And of Eilert too!

Hedda. [*Puts her head out between the curtains.*] And of Aunt Julia. And of all the rest of them.—After this, I will be quiet.

[*Closes the curtains again.*]

Tesman. [*At the writing-table.*] It's not good for her to see us at this distressing work. I'll tell you what, Mrs. Elvsted—you shall take the empty room at Aunt Julia's, and then I will come over in the evenings, and we can sit and work *there*—eh?

Hedda. [*In the inner room.*] I hear what you are saying, Tesman. But how am *I* to get through the evenings out here?

Tesman. [*Turning over the papers.*] Oh, I daresay Judge Brack will be so kind as to look in now and then, even though I am out.

Brack. [*In the arm-chair, calls out gaily.*] Every blessed evening, with all the pleasure in life, Mrs. Tesman! We shall get on capitally together, we two!

Hedda. [*Speaking loud and clear.*] Yes, don't you flatter yourself we will, Judge Brack? Now that you are the one cock in the basket——

[*A shot is heard within.* TESMAN, MRS. ELVSTED, *and* BRACK *leap to their feet.*]

Tesman. Oh, now she is playing with those pistols again.

[*He throws back the curtains and runs in, followed by* MRS. ELVSTED. HEDDA *lies stretched on the sofa, lifeless. Confusion and cries.* BERTA *enters in alarm from the right.*]

Tesman. [*Shrieks to* BRACK.] Shot herself! Shot herself in the temple! Fancy that!

Brack. [*Half-fainting in the arm-chair.*] Good God!—people don't do such things!

CURTAIN

THE IMPORTANCE
OF BEING EARNEST

By

OSCAR WILDE

BEYOND DOUBT, THE THREE FORCES which revivified the drama and made it "modern" were, first, Ibsenism, or the intellectual integrity and energy brought to the theatre by the Ibsen plays; second, naturalism, or the scientific imitation by playwrights of the surfaces of observed reality, which made earlier plays too often seem merely entertaining artificiality; and third, the Free Theatre movement, or the dedication by both theatre-workers and audiences to art independent of commerce. These three forces made the mainstream of progressive drama from the rise of Ibsenism and naturalism in the 1870's and the rapid spread of the Free Theatre movement following Antoine's in 1887. But great plays could appear outside the mainstream, and did. One such is Rostand's *Cyrano de Bergerac* (1897), and another is certainly Wilde's *The Importance of Being Earnest.*

Probably no masterpiece was ever more casually achieved or catastrophically accompanied than *The Importance of Being Earnest.* It was written in three weeks, apparently very easily, at Worthing, which supplied the name of a character, for George Alexander, the actor-manager who had put himself in the forefront of the 1890's brand of British dramatic modernity by producing Pinero's *The Second Mrs. Tanqueray* in 1893. He had earlier produced Wilde's *Lady Windermere's Fan.* When Wilde had delivered *The Importance of Being Earnest* in four acts, and Alexander had had it reduced to three, Wilde became bothered by doubts. He thought Alexander was too romantic an actor for the part of Worthing, and the whole play too insubstantial for the company Alexander had gathered, even if—and Wilde showed no doubts of this—the play won popular success. So Wilde dashed off the scenario of another play, one more in the pattern of *Lady Windermere's Fan,* and promised Alexander to complete it after the run of *The Importance.* But when *The Importance* had finished its run, Oscar Wilde was in prison; his name had been erased from programs and billboards, and he clearly could never again appear before the British public as a playwright. Even the scenario he had given Alexander was used five years later by another writer without immediate acknowledgment to him.

A reporter asked Wilde before the first night if he thought *The Importance of Being Earnest* would be as successful as his earlier plays. Wilde answered, "The play *is* a success. The only question is whether the audience will be a success." The first-night and later audiences were delighted with the play, and it is to this day as alive in the theatre as any play of its day, even though the 1890's was a decade unusually productive of lasting plays, and even though it demands a very high quality of acting. Essential, of course, is the utmost gravity and seriousness among the cast. They must behave as though all they do and say is not merely natural but ordinary and reasonable. They will find then that Wilde has provided them both with plot to direct their action and character to create their interaction. Lady Bracknell, in particular, is a character rich in acting possibilities and in audience impact in every scene in which she appears. She epitomizes the never-recurring climate of culture which made the play possible: she is the perfectly secure personage in a perfectly secure society, immune to loss of any kind, adequate to any emergency. The play may be much more easily regarded as the wish-fulfillment of Victorian society at its ripest and most assured than as satire upon it, though some critics detect satire. But neither those who believe Wilde admired his society or those who think he despised it will agree that the play is merely nonsense. It is like no other farce: it does not use slapstick, violence, excessive rapidity, or bawdiness, but it has to be called farce because it imposes on its audiences an illusion so fantastic that it leaves mere comedy on the earth while it flies off to its own region.

The original production took place in February 1895. The play has been repeatedly revived in both Britain and the United States. Distinguished actors and actresses have appeared in its leading roles in the commercial theatre, and it is still a favorite choice for production in the academic and local theatres.

OSCAR WILDE

Born 1854, Dublin, Ireland.

Educated at Trinity College, Dublin, and Magdalen College, Oxford.

1878, Won double first honors in Classical Moderations and *Literae Humaniores* and Newdigate Prize for Poetry at Oxford.

1884, Married. Two sons.

1895, Sentenced to two years' imprisonment for sexual perversion.

1900, Died in Paris.

Writer of fiction, poetry, and criticism.

PLAYS

1880 *Vera, or The Nihilists.* 1883 *The Duchess of Padua.* 1892 *Lady Windermere's Fan.* 1893 *Salomé* (one act; written in French, translated by various persons, not including the author). 1893 *A Woman of No Importance.* 1895 *An Ideal Husband.* 1895 *The Importance of Being Earnest.* 1906 *A Florentine Tragedy* (incomplete). 1908 *La Sainte Courtisane* (incomplete, written in English). 1922 *For Love of the King,* a Burmese Masque.

WRITINGS ON DRAMA

"The Truth of Masks," in *Intentions,* 1891, and random comment elsewhere in that volume. "Shakespeare on Scenery" (1885), "*Henry the Fourth* at Oxford" (1885), "*The Cenci*" (1886), "Ben Jonson" (1886), reprinted in volume 12 of Patrons' edition of *The Complete Works of Oscar Wilde,* 1923.

THE IMPORTANCE
OF BEING EARNEST

The Persons of the Play

JOHN WORTHING, J. P.
ALGERNON MONCRIEFF.
REV. CANON CHASUBLE, D.D.
MERRIMAN, *Butler.*
LANE, *Manservant.*
LADY BRACKNELL.
HON. GWENDOLEN FAIRFAX.
CECILY CARDEW.
MISS PRISM, *Governess.*

THE SCENES OF THE PLAY

ACT I. *Algernon Moncrieff's Flat in Half-Moon Street, W.*
ACT II. *The Garden at the Manor House, Woolton.*
ACT III. *Drawing-room at the Manor House, Woolton.*
TIME. *The Present.*

FIRST ACT

Morning-room in ALGERNON'S *flat in Half-Moon Street. The room is luxuriously and artistically furnished. The sound of a piano is heard in the adjoining room.* [LANE *is arranging afternoon tea on the table, and after the music has ceased,* ALGERNON *enters.*]

Algernon. Did you hear what I was playing, Lane?[1]

Lane. I didn't think it polite to listen, sir.

Algernon. I'm sorry for that, for your sake. I don't play accurately—any one can play accurately—but I play with wonderful expression. As far as the piano is concerned, sentiment is my forte. I keep science for Life.

Lane. Yes, sir.

Algernon. And, speaking of the science of Life, have you got the cucumber sandwiches cut for Lady Bracknell?

Lane. Yes, sir. [*Hands them on a salver.*]

Algernon. [*Inspects them, takes two, and sits down on the sofa.*] Oh! . . . by the way, Lane, I see from your book that on Thursday night, when Lord Shoreman and Mr[2] Worthing were dining with me, eight bottles of champagne are entered as having been consumed.

Lane. Yes, sir; eight bottles and a pint.

Algernon. Why is it that at a bachelor's establishment the servants invariably drink the champagne? I ask merely for information.

Lane. I attribute it to the superior quality of the wine, sir. I have often observed that in married households the champagne is rarely of a first-rate brand.

Algernon. Good heavens! Is marriage so demoralizing as that?

Lane. I believe it *is* a very pleasant state, sir. I have had very little experience of it myself up to the present. I have only been married once. That was in consequence of a misunderstanding between myself and a young person.

Algernon. [*Languidly.*] I don't know that I am much interested in your family life, Lane.

Lane. No, sir; it is not a very interesting subject. I never think of it myself.

Algernon. Very natural, I am sure. That will do, Lane, thank you.

Lane. Thank you, sir. [*Goes out.*]

Algernon. Lane's views on marriage seem somewhat lax. Really, if the lower orders don't set us a good example, what on earth is the use of them? They seem, as a class, to have absolutely no sense of moral responsibility. [*Enter* LANE.]

Lane. Mr Ernest Worthing.

[*Enter* JACK. LANE *goes out.*]

Algernon. How are you, my dear Ernest? What brings you up to town?

Jack. Oh, pleasure, pleasure! What else should bring one anywhere? Eating as usual, I see, Algy!

Algernon. [*Stiffly.*] I believe it is cus-

---

[1] Lane was named for John Lane, Wilde's publisher, whom Wilde disliked.
[2] This play follows such British spelling as "Mr". "Dr", "candour."

45

tomary in good society to take some slight refreshment at five o'clock. Where have you been since last Thursday?

Jack. [*Sitting down on the sofa.*] In the country.

Algernon. What on earth do you do there?

Jack. [*Pulling off his gloves.*] When one is in town one amuses oneself. When one is in the country one amuses other people. It is excessively boring.

Algernon. And who are the people you amuse?

Jack. [*Airily.*] Oh, neighbours, neighbours.

Algernon. Got nice neighbours in your part of Shropshire?

Jack. Perfectly horrid! Never speak to one of them.

Algernon. How immensely you must amuse them! [*Goes over and takes sandwich.*] By the way, Shropshire is your county, is it not?

Jack. Eh? Shropshire? Yes, of course. Hallo! Why all these cups? Why cucumber sandwiches? Why such reckless extravagance in one so young? Who is coming to tea?

Algernon. Oh! merely Aunt Augusta and Gwendolen.

Jack. How perfectly delightful!

Algernon. Yes, that is all very well; but I am afraid Aunt Augusta won't quite approve of your being here.

Jack. May I ask why?

Algernon. My dear fellow, the way you flirt with Gwendolen is perfectly disgraceful. It is almost as bad as the way Gwendolen flirts with you.

Jack. I am in love with Gwendolen. I have come up to town expressly to propose to her.

Algernon. I thought you had come up for pleasure? . . . I call that business.

Jack. How utterly unromantic you are!

Algernon. I really don't see anything romantic in proposing. It is very romantic to be in love. But there is nothing romantic about a definite proposal. Why, one may be accepted. One usually is, I believe. Then the excitement is all over. The very essence of romance is uncertainty. If ever I get married, I'll certainly try to forget the fact.

Jack. I have no doubt about that, dear Algy. The Divorce Court was specially invented for people whose memories are so curiously constituted.

Algernon. Oh! there is no use speculating on that subject. Divorces are made in Heaven— [*Jack puts out his hand to take a sandwich.* Algernon *at once interferes.*]

Please don't touch the cucumber sandwiches. They are ordered specially for Aunt Augusta. [*Takes one and eats it.*]

Jack. Well, you have been eating them all the time.

Algernon. That is quite a different matter. She is my aunt. [*Takes plate from below.*] Have some bread and butter. The bread and butter is for Gwendolen. Gwendolen is devoted to bread and butter.

Jack. [*Advancing to table and helping himself.*] And very good bread and butter it is too.

Algernon. Well, my dear fellow, you need not eat as if you were going to eat it all. You behave as if you were married to her already. You are not married to her already, and I don't think you ever will be.

Jack. Why on earth do you say that?

Algernon. Well, in the first place, girls never marry the men they flirt with. Girls don't think it right.

Jack. Oh, that is nonsense!

Algernon. It isn't. It is a great truth. It accounts for the extraordinary number of bachelors that one sees all over the place. In the second place, I don't give my consent.

Jack. Your consent!

Algernon. My dear fellow, Gwendolen is my first cousin. And before I allow you to marry her, you will have to clear up the whole question of Cecily. [*Rings bell.*]

Jack. Cecily! What on earth do you mean? What do you mean, Algy, by Cecily? I don't know any one of the name of Cecily. [*Enter* LANE.]

Algernon. Bring me that cigarette case Mr Worthing left in the smoking-room the last time he dined here.

Lane. Yes, sir. [*Goes out.*]

Jack. Do you mean to say you have had my cigarette case all this time? I wish to goodness you had let me know. I have been writing frantic letters to Scotland Yard about it. I was very nearly offering a large reward.

Algernon. Well, I wish you would offer one. I happen to be more than usually hard up.

Jack. There is no good offering a large reward now that the thing is found.

[*Enter* LANE *with the cigarette case on a salver.* ALGERNON *takes it at once.* LANE *goes out.*]

Algernon. I think that is rather mean of you, Ernest, I must say. [*Opens case and examines it.*] However, it makes no matter, for, now that I look at the inscription inside, I find that the thing isn't yours after all.

Jack. Of course it's mine. [*Moving to him.*] You have seen me with it a hundred times, and you have no right whatsoever to read what is written inside. It is a very ungentlemanly thing to read a private cigarette case.

Algernon. Oh! it is absurd to have a hard and fast rule about what one should read and what one shouldn't. More than half of modern culture depends on what one shouldn't read.

Jack. I am quite aware of the fact, and I don't propose to discuss modern culture. It isn't the sort of thing one should talk of in private. I simply want my cigarette case back.

Algernon. Yes; but this isn't your cigarette case. This cigarette case is a present from someone of the name of Cecily, and you said you didn't know anyone of that name.

Jack. Well, if you want to know, Cecily happens to be my aunt.

Algernon. Your aunt!

Jack. Yes. Charming old lady she is, too. Lives at Tunbridge Wells. Just give it back to me, Algy.

Algernon. [*Retreating to back of sofa.*] But why does she call herself little Cecily if she is your aunt and lives at Tunbridge Wells? [*Reading.*] 'From little Cecily with her fondest love.'

Jack. [*Moving to sofa and kneeling upon it.*] My dear fellow, what on earth is there in that? Some aunts are tall, some aunts are not tall. That is a matter that surely an aunt may be allowed to decide for herself. You seem to think that every aunt should be exactly like your aunt! That is absurd. For Heaven's sake give me back my cigarette case. [*Follows* ALGERNON *round the room.*]

Algernon. Yes. But why does your aunt call you her uncle? 'From little Cecily, with her fondest love to her dear Uncle Jack.' There is no objection, I admit, to an aunt being a small aunt, but why an aunt, no matter what her size may be, should call her own nephew her uncle, I can't quite make out. Besides, your name isn't Jack at all; it is Ernest.

Jack. It isn't Ernest; it's Jack.

Algernon. You have always told me it was Ernest. I have introduced you to every one as Ernest. You answer to the name of Ernest. You look as if your name was Ernest. You are the most earnest-looking person I ever saw in my life. It is perfectly absurd your saying that your name isn't Ernest. It's on your cards. Here is one of them. [*Taking it from case.*] 'Mr Ernest Worthing, B.4, The Albany.' I'll keep this as a proof that your name is Ernest if ever

you attempt to deny it to me, or to Gwendolen, or to any one else.

[*Puts the card in his pocket.*]

Jack. Well, my name is Ernest in town and Jack in the country, and the cigarette case was given to me in the country.

Algernon. Yes, but that does not account for the fact that your small Aunt Cecily, who lives at Tunbridge Wells, calls you her dear uncle. Come, old boy, you had much better have the thing out at once.

Jack. My dear Algy, you talk exactly as if you were a dentist. It is very vulgar to talk like a dentist when one isn't a dentist. It produces a false impression.

Algernon. Well, that is exactly what dentists always do. Now, go on! Tell me the whole thing. I may mention that I have always suspected you of being a confirmed and secret Bunburyist; and I am quite sure of it now.

Jack. Bunburyist? What on earth do you mean by a Bunburyist?

Algernon. I'll reveal to you the meaning of that incomparable expression as soon as you are kind enough to inform me why you are Ernest in town and Jack in the country.

Jack. Well, produce my cigarette case first.

Algernon. Here it is. [*Hands cigarette case.*] Now produce your explanation, and pray make it improbable. [*Sits on sofa.*]

Jack. My dear fellow, there is nothing improbable about my explanation at all. In fact it's perfectly ordinary. Old Mr Thomas Cardew, who adopted me when I was a little boy, made me in his will guardian to his granddaughter, Miss Cecily Cardew. Cecily, who addresses me as her uncle from motives of respect that you could not possibly appreciate, lives at my place in the country under the charge of her admirable governess, Miss Prism.

Algernon. Where is that place in the country, by the way?

Jack. That is nothing to you, dear boy. You are not going to be invited. . . . I may tell you candidly that the place is not in Shropshire.

Algernon. I suspected that, my dear fellow! I have Bunburyed all over Shropshire on two separate occasions. Now, go on. Why are you Ernest in town and Jack in the country?

Jack. My dear Algy, I don't know whether you will be able to understand my real motives. You are hardly serious enough. When one is placed in the position of guardian, one has to adopt a very high moral tone on all subjects. It's one's duty to do so. And as a high moral tone can hardly be said to conduce very much to either one's health or one's happiness, in order to get up to town I have always pretended to have a younger brother of the name of Ernest, who lives in the Albany, and gets into the most dreadful scrapes. That, my dear Algy, is the whole truth pure and simple.

Algernon. The truth is rarely pure and never simple. Modern life would be very tedious if it were either, and modern literature a complete impossibility!

Jack. That wouldn't be at all a bad thing.

Algernon. Literary criticism is not your forte, my dear fellow. Don't try it. You should leave that to people who haven't been at a University. They do it so well in the daily papers. What you really are is a Bunburyist. I was quite right in saying you were a Bunburyist. You are one of the most advanced Bunburyists I know.

Jack. What on earth do you mean?

Algernon. You have invented a very useful younger brother called Ernest, in order that you may be able to come up to town as often as you like. I have invented an invaluable permanent invalid called Bunbury, in order that I may be able to go down into the country whenever I choose. Bunbury is perfectly invaluable. If it wasn't for Bunbury's extraordinary bad health, for instance, I wouldn't be able to dine with you at Willis's to-night, for I have been really engaged to Aunt Augusta for more than a week.

Jack. I haven't asked you to dine with me anywhere to-night.

Algernon. I know. You are absurdly careless about sending out invitations. It is very foolish of you. Nothing annoys people so much as not receiving invitations.

Jack. You had much better dine with your Aunt Augusta.

Algernon. I haven't the smallest intention of doing anything of the kind. To begin with, I dined there on Monday, and once a week is quite enough to dine with one's own relations. In the second place, whenever I do dine there I am always treated as a member of the family, and sent down with either no woman at all, or two. In the third place, I know perfectly well whom she will place me next to, to-night. She will place me next Mary Farquhar, who always flirts with her own husband across the dinner-table. That is not very pleasant. Indeed, it is not even decent . . . and that sort of thing is enormously on the increase. The amount of women in London who flirt with their own husbands is perfectly scandalous. It looks so bad. It is simply washing one's clean linen

in public. Besides, now that I know you to be a confirmed Bunburyist I naturally want to talk to you about Bunburying. I want to tell you the rules.

Jack. I'm not a Bunburyist at all. If Gwendolen accepts me, I am going to kill my brother; indeed I think I'll kill him in any case. Cecily is a little too much interested in him. It is rather a bore. So I am going to get rid of Ernest. And I strongly advise you to do the same with Mr . . . with your invalid friend who has the absurd name.

Algernon. Nothing will induce me to part with Bunbury, and if you ever get married, which seems to me extremely problematic, you will be very glad to know Bunbury. A man who marries without knowing Bunbury has a very tedious time of it.

Jack. That is nonsense. If I marry a charming girl like Gwendolen, and she is the only girl I ever saw in my life that I would marry, I certainly won't want to know Bunbury.

Algernon. Then your wife will. You don't seem to realize that in married life three is company and two is none.

Jack. [*Sententiously.*] That, my dear young friend, is the theory that the corrupt French Drama has been propounding for the last fifty years.

Algernon. Yes; and that the happy English home has proved in half the time.

Jack. For heaven's sake, don't try to be cynical. It's perfectly easy to be cynical.

Algernon. My dear fellow, it isn't easy to be anything nowadays. There's such a lot of beastly competition about. [*The sound of an electric bell is heard.*] Ah! that must be Aunt Augusta. Only relatives, or creditors, ever ring in that Wagnerian manner. Now, if I get her out of the way for ten minutes, so that you can have an opportunity for proposing to Gwendolen, may I dine with you to-night at Willis's?

Jack. I suppose so, if you want to.

Algernon. Yes, but you must be serious about it. I hate people who are not serious about meals. It is so shallow of them.

[*Enter* LANE.]

Lane. Lady Bracknell and Miss Fairfax.

[ALGERNON *goes forward to meet them. Enter* LADY BRACKNELL *and* GWENDOLEN.]

Lady Bracknell. Good afternoon, dear Algernon. I hope you are behaving very well.

Algernon. I'm feeling very well, Aunt Augusta.

Lady Bracknell. That's not quite the same

thing. In fact the two things rarely go to-gether.

[*Sees* JACK *and bows to him with icy coldness.*]

Algernon. [*To* GWENDOLEN.] Dear me, you are smart!

Gwendolen. I am always smart! Am I not, Mr Worthing?

Jack. You're quite perfect, Miss Fairfax.

Gwendolen. Oh! I hope I am not that. It would leave no room for developments, and I intend to develop in many directions.

[GWENDOLEN *and* JACK *sit down together in the corner.*]

Lady Bracknell. I'm sorry if we are a little late, Algernon, but I was obliged to call on dear Lady Harbury. I hadn't been there since her poor husband's death. I never saw a woman so altered; she looks quite twenty years younger. And now I'll have a cup of tea, and one of those nice cucumber sandwiches you promised me.

Algernon. Certainly, Aunt Augusta.

[*Goes over to tea-table.*]

Lady Bracknell. Won't you come and sit here, Gwendolen?

Gwendolen. Thanks, mamma, I'm quite comfortable where I am.

Algernon. [*Picking up empty plate in horror.*] Good heavens! Lane! Why are there no cucumber sandwiches? I ordered them specially.

Lane. [*Gravely.*] There were no cu-cumbers in the market this morning, sir. I went down twice.

Algernon. No cucumbers!

Lane. No, sir. Not even for ready money.

Algernon. That will do, Lane, thank you.

Lane. Thank you, sir.   [*Goes out.*]

Algernon. I am greatly distressed, Aunt Augusta, about there being no cucumbers, not even for ready money.

Lady Bracknell. It really makes no mat-ter, Algernon. I had some crumpets with Lady Harbury, who seems to me to be living entirely for pleasure now.

Algernon. I hear her hair has turned quite gold from grief.

Lady Bracknell. It certainly has changed its colour. From what cause I, of course, cannot say. [ALGERNON *crosses and hands tea.*] Thank you. I've quite a treat for you to-night, Algernon. I am going to send you down with Mary Farquhar. She is such a nice woman, and so attentive to her husband. It's delightful to watch them.

Algernon. I am afraid, Aunt Augusta, I shall have to give up the pleasure of dining with you to-night after all.

Lady Bracknell. [*Frowning.*] I hope not, Algernon. It would put my table completely out. Your uncle would have to dine up-stairs. Fortunately he is accustomed to that.

Algernon. It is a great bore, and, I need hardly say, a terrible disappointment to me, but the fact is I have just had a telegram to say that my poor friend Bunbury is very ill again. [*Exchanges glances with* JACK.] They seem to think I should be with him.

Lady Bracknell. It is very strange. This Mr Bunbury seems to suffer from curiously bad health.

Algernon. Yes; poor Bunbury is a dread-ful invalid.

Lady Bracknell. Well, I must say, Alger-non, that I think it is high time that Mr Bunbury made up his mind whether he was going to live or to die. This shilly-shallying with the question is absurd. Nor do I in any way approve of the modern sympathy with invalids. I consider it morbid. Illness of any kind is hardly a thing to be encouraged in others. Health is the primary duty of life. I am always telling that to your poor uncle, but he never seems to take much notice . . . as far as any improvement in his ailment goes. I should be much obliged if you would ask Mr Bunbury, from me, to be kind enough not to have a relapse on Saturday, for I rely on you to arrange my music for me. It is my last reception, and one wants something that will encourage conversation, particularly at the end of the season when every one has practically said whatever they had to say, which, in most cases, was probably not much.

Algernon. I'll speak to Bunbury, Aunt Augusta, if he is still conscious, and I think I can promise you he'll be all right by Satur-day. Of course the music is a great difficulty. You see, if one plays good music, people don't listen, and if one plays bad music peo-ple don't talk. But I'll run over the pro-gramme I've drawn out, if you will kindly come into the next room for a moment.

Lady Bracknell. Thank you, Algernon. It is very thoughtful of you. [*Rising, and fol-lowing* ALGERNON.] I'm sure the programme will be delightful, after a few expurgations. French songs I cannot possibly allow. Peo-ple always seem to think that they are im-proper, and either look shocked, which is vulgar, or laugh, which is worse. But Ger-man sounds a thoroughly respectable lan-guage, and, indeed, I believe is so. Gwen-dolen, you will accompany me.

Gwendolen. Certainly, mamma.

[LADY BRACKNELL *and* ALGERNON *go into the music-room*, GWENDOLEN *re-mains behind.*]

Jack. Charming day it has been, Miss Fairfax.

Gwendolen. Pray don't talk to me about the weather, Mr Worthing. Whenever people talk to me about the weather, I always feel quite certain that they mean something else. And that makes me so nervous.

Jack. I do mean something else.

Gwendolen. I thought so. In fact, I am never wrong.

Jack. And I would like to be allowed to take advantage of Lady Bracknell's temporary absence. . . .

Gwendolen. I would certainly advise you to do so. Mamma has a way of coming back suddenly into a room that I have often had to speak to her about.

Jack. [*Nervously.*] Miss Fairfax, ever since I met you I have admired you more than any girl . . . I have ever met since . . . I met you.

Gwendolen. Yes, I am quite well aware of the fact. And I often wish that in public, at any rate, you had been more demonstrative. For me you have always had an irresistible fascination. Even before I met you I was far from indifferent to you. [JACK *looks at her in amazement.*] We live, as I hope you know, Mr Worthing, in an age of ideals. The fact is constantly mentioned in the more expensive monthly magazines, and has reached the provincial pulpits, I am told; and my ideal has always been to love some one of the name of Ernest. There is something in that name that inspires absolute confidence. The moment Algernon first mentioned to me that he had a friend called Ernest, I knew I was destined to love you.

Jack. You really love me, Gwendolen?

Gwendolen. Passionately!

Jack. Darling! You don't know how happy you've made me.

Gwendolen. My own Ernest!

Jack. But you don't really mean to say that you couldn't love me if my name wasn't Ernest?

Gwendolen. But your name is Ernest.

Jack. Yes, I know it is. But supposing it was something else? Do you mean to say you couldn't love me then?

Gwendolen. [*Glibly.*] Ah! that is clearly a metaphysical speculation, and like most metaphysical speculations has very little reference at all to the actual facts of real life, as we know them.

Jack. Personally, darling, to speak quite candidly, I don't much care about the name of Ernest. . . . I don't think the name suits me at all.

Gwendolen. It suits you perfectly. It is a divine name. It has music of its own. It produces vibrations.

Jack. Well, really, Gwendolen, I must say that I think there are lots of other much nicer names. I think Jack, for instance, a charming name.

Gwendolen. Jack? . . . No, there is very little music in the name Jack, if any at all, indeed. It does not thrill. It produces absolutely no vibrations. . . . I have known several Jacks, and they all, without exception, were more than usually plain. Besides, Jack is a notorious domesticity for John! And I pity any woman who is married to a man called John. She would probably never be allowed to know the entrancing pleasure of a single moment's solitude. The only really safe name is Ernest.

Jack. Gwendolen, I must get christened at once—I mean we must get married at once. There is no time to be lost.

Gwendolen. Married, Mr Worthing?

Jack. [*Astounded.*] Well . . . surely. You know that I love you, and you led me to believe, Miss Fairfax, that you were not absolutely indifferent to me.

Gwendolen. I adore you. But you haven't proposed to me yet. Nothing has been said at all about marriage. The subject has not even been touched on.

Jack. Well . . . may I propose to you now?

Gwendolen. I think it would be an admirable opportunity. And to spare you any possible disappointment, Mr Worthing, I think it only fair to tell you quite frankly beforehand that I am fully determined to accept you.

Jack. Gwendolen!

Gwendolen. Yes, Mr Worthing, what have you got to say to me?

Jack. You know what I have got to say to you.

Gwendolen. Yes, but you don't say it.

Jack. Gwendolen, will you marry me?
                                    [*Goes on his knees.*]

Gwendolen. Of course I will, darling. How long you have been about it! I am afraid you have had very little experience in how to propose.

Jack. My own one, I have never loved any one in the world but you.

Gwendolen. Yes, but men often propose for practice. I know my brother Gerald does. All my girl-friends tell me so. What wonderfully blue eyes you have, Ernest! They are quite, quite blue. I hope you will always look at me just like that, especially when there are other people present.
                                    [*Enter* LADY BRACKNELL.]

Lady Bracknell. Mr Worthing! Rise, sir,

'rom this semi-recumbent posture. It is most
ndecorous.

Gwendolen. Mamma! [*He tries to rise;
she restrains him.*] I must beg you to re-
ire. This is no place for you. Besides, Mr
Worthing has not quite finished yet.

Lady Bracknell. Finished what, may I ask?

Gwendolen. I am engaged to Mr Worth-
ng, mamma.   [*They rise together.*]

Lady Bracknell. Pardon me, you are not
engaged to any one. When you do become
engaged to some one, I, or your father,
should his health permit him, will inform you
of the fact. An engagement should come on
a young girl as a surprise, pleasant or unpleasant, as the case may be. It is hardly a
matter that she could be allowed to arrange
for herself. . . . And now I have a few
questions to put to you, Mr Worthing. While
I am making these inquiries, you, Gwendolen, will wait for me below in the carriage.

Gwendolen. [*Reproachfully.*] Mamma!

Lady Bracknell. In the carriage, Gwendolen! [GWENDOLEN *goes to the door. She
and* JACK *blow kisses to each other behind*
LADY BRACKNELL's *back.* LADY BRACKNELL
*looks vaguely about as if she could not un-
derstand what the noise was. Finally turns
round.*] Gwendolen, the carriage!

Gwendolen. Yes, mamma.

[*Goes out, looking back at* JACK.]

Lady Bracknell. [*Sitting down.*] You can
take a seat, Mr Worthing.

[*Looks in her pocket for note-book and
pencil.*]

Jack. Thank you, Lady Bracknell, I prefer
standing.

Lady Bracknell. [*Pencil and note-book in
hand.*] I feel bound to tell you that you are
not down on my list of eligible young men,
although I have the same list as the dear
Duchess of Bolton has. We work together,
in fact. However, I am quite ready to enter
your name, should your answers be what
a really affectionate mother requires. Do
you smoke?

Jack. Well, yes, I must admit I smoke.

Lady Bracknell. I am glad to hear it. A
man should always have an occupation of
some kind. There are far too many idle men
in London as it is. How old are you?

Jack. Twenty-nine.

Lady Bracknell. A very good age to be
married at. I have always been of opinion
that a man who desires to get married should
know either everything or nothing. Which do
you know?

Jack. [*After some hesitation.*] I know
nothing, Lady Bracknell.

Lady Bracknell. I am pleased to hear it.

I do not approve of anything that tampers
with natural ignorance. Ignorance is like a
delicate exotic fruit; touch it and the bloom
is gone. The whole theory of modern education is radically unsound. Fortunately in
England, at any rate, education produces no
effect whatsoever. If it did, it would prove
a serious danger to the upper classes, and
probably lead to acts of violence in Grosvenor Square. What is your income?

Jack. Between seven and eight thousand a
year.

Lady Bracknell. [*Makes a note in her
book.*] In land, or in investments?

Jack. In investments, chiefly.

Lady Bracknell. That is satisfactory.
What between the duties expected of one
during one's lifetime, and the duties exacted
from one after one's death, land has ceased
to be either a profit or a pleasure. It gives
one position, and prevents one from keeping
it up. That's all that can be said about land.

Jack. I have a country house with some
land, of course, attached to it, about fifteen
hundred acres, I believe; but I don't depend
on that for my real income. In fact, as far as
I can make out, the poachers are the only
people who make anything out of it.

Lady Bracknell. A country house! How
many bedrooms? Well, that point can be
cleared up afterwards. You have a town
house, I hope? A girl with a simple, un-
spoiled nature, like Gwendolen, could hardly
be expected to reside in the country.

Jack. Well, I own a house in Belgrave
Square, but it is let by the year to Lady
Bloxham. Of course, I can get it back when-
ever I like, at six months' notice.

Lady Bracknell. Lady Bloxham? I don't
know her.

Jack. Oh, she goes about very little. She
is a lady considerably advanced in years.

Lady Bracknell. Ah, nowadays that is no
guarantee of respectability of character.
What number in Belgrave Square?

Jack. 149.

Lady Bracknell. [*Shaking her head.*] The
unfashionable side. I thought there was
something. However, that could easily be
altered.

Jack. Do you mean the fashion, or the
side?

Lady Bracknell. [*Sternly.*] Both, if necessary, I presume. What are your politics?

Jack. Well, I am afraid I really have none.
I am a Liberal Unionist.[1]

Lady Bracknell. Oh, they count as Tories.
They dine with us. Or come in the eve-

---

[1] Those who left the Liberal Party when its leader,
W. E. Gladstone, advocated Home Rule for Ireland
in 1885–6.

ning, at any rate. Now to minor matters. Are your parents living?

Jack. I have lost both my parents.

Lady Bracknell. To lose one parent, Mr Worthing, may be regarded as a misfortune; to lose both looks like carelessness. Who was your father? He was evidently a man of some wealth. Was he born in what the Radical papers call the purple of commerce, or did he rise from the ranks of the aristocracy?

Jack. I am afraid I really don't know. The fact is, Lady Bracknell, I said I had lost my parents. It would be nearer the truth to say that my parents seem to have lost me. . . . I don't actually know who I am by birth. I was . . . well, I was found.

Lady Bracknell. Found!

Jack. The late Mr Thomas Cardew, an old gentleman of a very charitable and kindly disposition, found me, and gave me the name of Worthing, because he happened to have a first-class ticket for Worthing in his pocket at the time. Worthing is a place in Sussex. It is a seaside resort.

Lady Bracknell. Where did the charitable gentleman who had a first-class ticket for this seaside resort find you?

Jack. [*Gravely.*] In a hand-bag.

Lady Bracknell. A hand-bag?

Jack. [*Very seriously.*] Yes, Lady Bracknell. I was in a hand-bag—a somewhat large, black leather hand-bag, with handles to it—an ordinary hand-bag in fact.

Lady Bracknell. In what locality did this Mr James, or Thomas, Cardew come across this ordinary hand-bag?

Jack. In the cloak-room at Victoria Station. It was given to him in mistake for his own.

Lady Bracknell. The cloak-room at Victoria Station?

Jack. Yes. The Brighton line.

Lady Bracknell. The line is immaterial. Mr Worthing, I confess I feel somewhat bewildered by what you have just told me. To be born, or at any rate bred, in a hand-bag, whether it had handles or not, seems to me to display a contempt for the ordinary decencies of family life that reminds one of the worst excesses of the French Revolution. And I presume you know what that unfortunate movement led to? As for the particular locality in which the hand-bag was found, a cloak-room at a railway station might serve to conceal a social indiscretion—has probably, indeed, been used for that purpose before now—but it could hardly be regarded as an assured basis for a recognized position in good society.

Jack. May I ask you then what you would

advise me to do? I need hardly say I would do anything in the world to ensure Gwendolen's happiness.

Lady Bracknell. I would strongly advise you, Mr Worthing, to try and acquire some relations as soon as possible, and to make a definite effort to produce at any rate one parent, of either sex, before the season is quite over.

Jack. Well, I don't see how I could possibly manage to do that. I can produce the hand-bag at any moment. It is in my dressing-room at home. I really think that should satisfy you, Lady Bracknell.

Lady Bracknell. Me, sir! What has it to do with me? You can hardly imagine that I and Lord Bracknell would dream of allowing our only daughter—a girl brought up with the utmost care—to marry into a cloakroom, and form an alliance with a parcel. Good morning, Mr Worthing!

[*She sweeps out in majestic indignation.*]

Jack. Good morning! [ALGERNON, *from the other room, strikes up the Wedding March.* JACK *looks perfectly furious, and goes to the door.*] For goodness' sake don't play that ghastly tune, Algy! How idiotic you are!

[*The music stops and* ALGERNON *enters cheerily.*]

Algernon. Didn't it go off all right, old boy? You don't mean to say Gwendolen refused you? I know it is a way she has. She is always refusing people. I think it is most ill-natured of her.

Jack. Oh, Gwendolen is as right as a trivet. As far as she is concerned, we are engaged. Her mother is perfectly unbearable. Never met such a Gorgon. . . . I don't really know what a Gorgon is like, but I am quite sure that Lady Bracknell is one. In any case, she is a monster, without being a myth, which is rather unfair. . . . I beg your pardon, Algy, I suppose I shouldn't talk about your own aunt in that way before you.

Algernon. My dear boy, I love hearing my relations abused. It is the only thing that makes me put up with them at all. Relations are simply a tedious pack of people who haven't got the remotest knowledge of how to live, nor the smallest instinct about when to die.

Jack. Oh, that is nonsense!

Algernon. It isn't!

Jack. Well, I won't argue about the matter. You always want to argue about things.

Algernon. That is exactly what things were originally made for.

Jack. Upon my word, if I thought that,

I'd shoot myself. . . . [*A pause.*] You don't think there is any chance of Gwendolen becoming like her mother in about a hundred and fifty years, do you, Algy?

Algernon. All women become like their mothers. That is their tragedy. No man does. That's his.

Jack. Is that clever?

Algernon. It is perfectly phrased! and quite as true as any observation in civilized life should be.

Jack. I am sick to death of cleverness. Everybody is clever nowadays. You can't go anywhere without meeting clever people. The thing has become an absolute public nuisance. I wish to goodness we had a few fools left.

Algernon. We have.

Jack. I should extremely like to meet them. What do they talk about?

Algernon. The fools? Oh! about the clever people, of course.

Jack. What fools!

Algernon. By the way, did you tell Gwendolen the truth about your being Ernest in town, and Jack in the country?

Jack. [*In a very patronizing manner.*] My dear fellow, the truth isn't quite the sort of thing one tells to a nice, sweet, refined girl. What extraordinary ideas you have about the way to behave to a woman!

Algernon. The only way to behave to a woman is to make love to her, if she is pretty, and to someone else, if she is plain.

Jack. Oh, that is nonsense.

Algernon. What about your brother? What about the profligate Ernest?

Jack. Oh, before the end of the week I shall have got rid of him. I'll say he died in Paris of apoplexy. Lots of people die of apoplexy, quite suddenly, don't they?

Algernon. Yes, but it's hereditary, my dear fellow. It's a sort of thing that runs in families. You had much better say a severe chill.

Jack. You are sure a severe chill isn't hereditary, or anything of that kind?

Algernon. Of course it isn't!

Jack. Very well, then. My poor brother Ernest is carried off suddenly, in Paris, by a severe chill. That gets rid of him.

Algernon. But I thought you said that . . . Miss Cardew was a little too much interested in your poor brother Ernest? Won't she feel his loss a good deal?

Jack. Oh, that is all right. Cecily is not a silly romantic girl, I am glad to say. She has got a capital appetite, goes long walks, and pays no attention at all to her lessons.

Algernon. I would rather like to see Cecily.

Jack. I will take very good care you never do. She is excessively pretty, and she is only just eighteen.

Algernon. Have you told Gwendolen yet that you have an excessively pretty ward who is only just eighteen?

Jack. Oh! one doesn't blurt these things out to people. Cecily and Gwendolen are perfectly certain to be extremely great friends. I'll bet you anything you like that half an hour after they have met they will be calling each other sister.

Algernon. Women only do that when they have called each other a lot of other things first. Now, my dear boy, if we want to get a good table at Willis's, we really must go and dress. Do you know it is nearly seven?

Jack. [*Irritably.*] Oh! it always is nearly seven.

Algernon. I'm hungry.

Jack. I never knew you when you weren't. . . .

Algernon. What shall we do after dinner? Go to a theatre?

Jack. Oh no! I loathe listening.

Algernon. Well, let us go to the Club?

Jack. Oh, no! I hate talking.

Algernon. Well, we might trot round to the Empire at ten?

Jack. Oh, no! I can't bear looking at things. It is so silly.

Algernon. Well, what shall we do?

Jack. Nothing!

Algernon. It is awfully hard work doing nothing. However, I don't mind hard work where there is no definite object of any kind.   [*Enter* LANE.]

Lane. Miss Fairfax.

[*Enter* GWENDOLEN. LANE *goes out.*]

Algernon. Gwendolen, upon my word!

Gwendolen. Algy, kindly turn your back. I have something very particular to say to Mr Worthing.

Algernon. Really, Gwendolen, I don't think I can allow this at all.

Gwendolen. Algy, you always adopt a strictly immoral attitude towards life. You are not quite old enough to do that.

[ALGERNON *retires to the fire-place.*]

Jack. My own darling!

Gwendolen. Ernest, we may never be married. From the expression on mamma's face I fear we never shall. Few parents nowadays pay any regard to what their children say to them. The old-fashioned respect for the young is fast dying out. Whatever influence I ever had over mamma, I lost at the age of three. But although she may prevent us from becoming man and wife, and I may marry someone else, and marry often, nothing that she can possibly do can alter my eternal devotion to you.

Jack. Dear Gwendolen!

Gwendolen. The story of your romantic origin, as related to me by mamma, with unpleasing comments, has naturally stirred the deeper fibres of my nature. Your Christian name has an irresistible fascination. The simplicity of your character makes you exquisitely incomprehensible to me. Your town address at the Albany I have. What is your address in the country?

Jack. The Manor House, Woolton, Hertfordshire.

[ALGERNON, *who has been carefully listening, smiles to himself, and writes the address on his shirt-cuff. Then picks up the Railway Guide.*]

Gwendolen. There is a good postal service, I suppose? It may be necessary to do something desperate. That of course will require serious consideration. I will communicate with you daily.

Jack. My own one!

Gwendolen. How long do you remain in town?

Jack. Till Monday.

Gwendolen. Good! Algy, you may turn round now.

Algernon. Thanks, I've turned round already.

Gwendolen. You may also ring the bell.

Jack. You will let me see you to your carriage, my own darling?

Gwendolen. Certainly.

Jack. [To LANE, *who now enters.*] I will see Miss Fairfax out.

Lane. Yes, sir.

[JACK *and* GWENDOLEN *go off.*]
[LANE *presents several letters on a salver to* ALGERNON. *It is to be surmised that they are bills, as* ALGERNON, *after looking at the envelopes, tears them up.*]

Algernon. A glass of sherry, Lane.

Lane. Yes, sir.

Algernon. To-morrow, Lane, I'm going Bunburying.

Lane. Yes, sir.

Algernon. I shall probably not be back till Monday. You can put up my dress clothes, my smoking jacket, and all the Bunbury suits . . .

Lane. Yes, sir.   [*Handing sherry.*]

Algernon. I hope to-morrow will be a fine day, Lane.

Lane. It never is, sir.

Algernon. Lane, you're a perfect pessimist.

Lane. I do my best to give satisfaction, sir.   [*Enter* JACK. LANE *goes off.*]

Jack. There's a sensible, intellectual girl! the only girl I ever cared for in my life. [ALGERNON *is laughing immoderately.*] What on earth are you so amused at?

Algernon. Oh, I'm a little anxious about poor Bunbury, that is all.

Jack. If you don't take care, your friend Bunbury will get you into a serious scrape some day.

Algernon. I love scrapes. They are the only things that are never serious.

Jack. Oh, that's nonsense, Algy. You never talk anything but nonsense.

Algernon. Nobody ever does.

[JACK *looks indignantly at him, and leaves the room.* ALGERNON *lights a cigarette, reads his shirt-cuff, and smiles.*]

CURTAIN

SECOND ACT

Garden at the Manor House. A flight of grey stone steps leads up to the house. The garden, an old-fashioned one, full of roses. Time of year, July. Basket chairs, and a table covered with books, are set under a large yew-tree.
[MISS PRISM *discovered seated at the table.* CECILY *is at the back, watering flowers.*]

Miss Prism. [*Calling.*] Cecily, Cecily! Surely such a utilitarian occupation as the watering of flowers is rather Moulton's duty than yours? Especially at a moment when intellectual pleasures await you. Your German grammar is on the table. Pray open it at page fifteen. We will repeat yesterday's lesson.

Cecily. [*Coming over very slowly.*] But I don't like German. It isn't at all a becoming language. I know perfectly well that I look quite plain after my German lesson.

Miss Prism. Child, you know how anxious your guardian is that you should improve yourself in every way. He laid particular stress on your German, as he was leaving for town yesterday. Indeed, he always lays stress on your German when he is leaving for town.

Cecily. Dear Uncle Jack is so very serious! Sometimes he is so serious that I think he cannot be quite well.

Miss Prism. [*Drawing herself up.*] Your guardian enjoys the best of health, and his gravity of demeanour is especially to be commended in one so comparatively young as he is. I know no one who has a higher sense of duty and responsibility.

Cecily. I suppose that is why he often looks a little bored when we three are together.

Miss Prism. Cecily! I am surprised at you. Mr Worthing has many troubles in his life. Idle merriment and triviality would be out of place in his conversation. You must remember his constant anxiety about that unfortunate young man his brother.

Cecily. I wish Uncle Jack would allow that unfortunate young man, his brother, to come down here sometimes. We might have a good influence over him, Miss Prism. I am sure you certainly would. You know German, and geology, and things of that kind influence a man very much.

[CECILY *begins to write in her diary.*]

Miss Prism. [*Shaking her head.*] I do not think that even I could produce any effect on a character that according to his own brother's admission is irretrievably weak and vacillating. Indeed I am not sure that I would desire to reclaim him. I am not in favor of this modern mania for turning bad people into good people at a moment's notice. As a man sows so let him reap. You must put away your diary, Cecily. I really don't see why you should keep a diary at all.

Cecily. I keep a diary in order to enter the wonderful secrets of my life. If I didn't write them down, I should probably forget all about them.

Miss Prism. Memory, my dear Cecily, is the diary that we all carry about with us.

Cecily. Yes, but it usually chronicles the things that have never happened, and couldn't possibly have happened. I believe that Memory is responsible for nearly all the three-volume novels that Mudie [1] sends us.

Miss Prism. Do not speak slightingly of the three-volume novel, Cecily. I wrote one myself in earlier days.

[1] Mudie's Lending Library, a very popular and successful Victorian institution.

Cecily. Did you really, Miss Prism? How wonderfully clever you are! I hope it did not end happily. I don't like novels that end happily. They depress me so much.

Miss Prism. The good ended happily, and the bad unhappily. That is what Fiction means.

Cecily. I suppose so. But it seems very unfair. And was your novel ever published?

Miss Prism. Alas! no. The manuscript unfortunately was abandoned. [CECILY *starts.*] I used the word in the sense of lost or mislaid. To your work, child, these speculations are profitless.

Cecily. [*Smiling.*] But I see dear Dr Chasuble coming up through the garden.

Miss Prism. [*Rising and advancing.*] Dr Chasuble! This is indeed a pleasure.

[*Enter* CANON CHASUBLE.]

Chasuble. And how are we this morning? Miss Prism, you are, I trust, well?

Cecily. Miss Prism has just been complaining of a slight headache. I think it would do her so much good to have a short stroll with you in the Park, Dr Chasuble.

Miss Prism. Cecily, I have not mentioned anything about a headache.

Cecily. No, dear Miss Prism, I know that, but I felt instinctively that you had a headache. Indeed I was thinking about that, and not about my German lesson, when the Rector came in.

Chasuble. I hope, Cecily, you are not inattentive.

Cecily. Oh, I am afraid I am.

Chasuble. That is strange. Were I fortunate enough to be Miss Prism's pupil, I would hang upon her lips. [MISS PRISM *glares.*] I spoke metaphorically.—My metaphor was drawn from bees. Ahem! Mr Worthing, I suppose, has not returned from town yet?

Miss Prism. We do not expect him till Monday afternoon.

Chasuble. Ah yes, he usually likes to spend his Sunday in London. He is not one of those whose sole aim is enjoyment, as, by all accounts, that unfortunate young man his brother seems to be. But I must not disturb Egeria and her pupil any longer.

Miss Prism. Egeria? My name is Laetitia, Doctor.

Chasuble. [*Bowing.*] A classical allusion merely, drawn from the Pagan authors. I shall see you both no doubt at Evensong?

Miss Prism. I think, dear Doctor, I will have a stroll with you. I find I have a headache after all, and a walk might do it good.

Chasuble. With pleasure, Miss Prism, with

pleasure. We might go as far as the schools and back.

Miss Prism. That would be delightful. Cecily, you will read your Political Economy in my absence. The chapter on the Fall of the Rupee you may omit. It is somewhat too sensational. Even these metallic problems have their melodramatic side.

[*Goes down the garden with* DR CHASUBLE.]

Cecily. [*Picks up books and throws them back on table.*] Horrid Political Economy! Horrid Geography! Horrid, horrid German!

[*Enter* MERRIMAN *with a card on a salver.*]

Merriman. Mr Ernest Worthing has just driven over from the station. He has brought his luggage with him.

Cecily. [*Takes the card and reads it.*] 'Mr Ernest Worthing, B.4, The Albany, W.' Uncle Jack's brother! Did you tell him Mr Worthing was in town?

Merriman. Yes, Miss. He seemed very much disappointed. I mentioned that you and Miss Prism were in the garden. He said he was anxious to speak to you privately for a moment.

Cecily. Ask Mr Ernest Worthing to come here. I suppose you had better talk to the housekeeper about a room for him.

Merriman. Yes, Miss.

[MERRIMAN *goes off.*]

Cecily. I have never met any really wicked person before. I feel rather frightened. I am so afraid he will look just like every one else. [*Enter* ALGERNON, *very gay and debonair.*] He does!

Algernon. [*Raising his hat.*] You are my little cousin Cecily, I'm sure.

Cecily. You are under some strange mistake. I am not little. In fact, I believe I am more than usually tall for my age. [AL-GERNON *is rather taken aback.*] But I am your cousin Cecily. You, I see from your card, are Uncle Jack's brother, my cousin Ernest, my wicked cousin Ernest.

Algernon. Oh! I am not really wicked at all, cousin Cecily. You mustn't think that I am wicked.

Cecily. If you are not, then you have certainly been deceiving us all in a very inexcusable manner. I hope you have not been leading a double life, pretending to be wicked and being really good all the time. That would be hypocrisy.

Algernon. [*Looks at her in amazement.*] Oh! Of course I have been rather reckless.

Cecily. I am glad to hear it.

Algernon. In fact, now you mention the subject, I have been very bad in my own small way.

Cecily. I don't think you should be so proud of that, though I am sure it must have been very pleasant.

Algernon. It is much pleasanter being here with you.

Cecily. I can't understand how you are here at all. Uncle Jack won't be back till Monday afternoon.

Algernon. That is a great disappointment. I am obliged to go up by the first train on Monday morning. I have a business appointment that I am anxious . . . to miss!

Cecily. Couldn't you miss it anywhere but in London?

Algernon. No: the appointment is in London.

Cecily. Well, I know, of course, how important it is not to keep a business engagement, if one wants to retain any sense of the beauty of life, but still I think you had better wait till Uncle Jack arrives. I know he wants to speak to you about your emigrating.

Algernon. About my what?

Cecily. Your emigrating. He has gone up to buy your outfit.

Algernon. I certainly wouldn't let Jack buy my outfit. He has no taste in neckties at all.

Cecily. I don't think you will require neckties. Uncle Jack is sending you to Australia.

Algernon. Australia! I'd sooner die.

Cecily. Well, he said at dinner on Wednesday night, that you would have to choose between this world, the next world, and Australia.

Algernon. Oh, well! The accounts I have received of Australia and the next world are not particularly encouraging. This world is good enough for me, cousin Cecily.

Cecily. Yes, but are you good enough for it?

Algernon. I'm afraid I'm not that. That is why I want you to reform me. You might make that your mission, if you don't mind, cousin Cecily.

Cecily. I'm afraid I've no time, this afternoon.

Algernon. Well, would you mind my reforming myself this afternoon?

Cecily. It is rather Quixotic of you. But I think you should try.

Algernon. I will. I feel better already.

Cecily. You are looking a little worse.

Algernon. That is because I am hungry.

Cecily. How thoughtless of me. I should have remembered that when one is going to lead an entirely new life, one requires regular and wholesome meals. Won't you come in?

Algernon. Thank you. Might I have a buttonhole first. I have never any appetite unless I have a buttonhole first.

Cecily. A Maréchal Niel?

[*Picks up scissors.*]

Algernon. No, I'd sooner have a pink rose.

Cecily. Why? [*Cuts a flower.*]

Algernon. Because you are like a pink rose, cousin Cecily.

Cecily. I don't think it can be right for you to talk to me like that. Miss Prism never says such things to me.

Algernon. Then Miss Prism is a short-sighted old lady. [CECILY *puts the rose in his buttonhole.*] You are the prettiest girl I ever saw.

Cecily. Miss Prism says that all good looks are a snare.

Algernon. They are a snare that every sensible man would like to be caught in.

Cecily. Oh, I don't think I would care to catch a sensible man. I shouldn't know what to talk to him about.

[*They pass into the house.* MISS PRISM *and* DR CHASUBLE *return.*]

Miss Prism. You are too much alone, dear Dr Chasuble. You should get married. A misanthrope I can understand—a woman-thrope, never!

Chasuble. [*With a scholar's shudder.*] Believe me, I do not deserve so neologistic a phrase. The precept as well as the practice of the Primitive Church was distinctly against matrimony.

Miss Prism. [*Sententiously.*] That is obviously the reason why the Primitive Church has not lasted up to the present day. And you do not seem to realize, dear Doctor, that by persistently remaining single, a man converts himself into a permanent public temptation. Men should be more careful; this very celibacy leads weaker vessels astray.

Chasuble. But is a man not equally attractive when married?

Miss Prism. No married man is ever attractive except to his wife.

Chasuble. And often, I've been told, not even to her.

Miss Prism. That depends on the intellectual sympathies of the woman. Maturity can always be depended on. Ripeness can be trusted. Young women are green. [DR CHASUBLE *starts.*] I spoke horticulturally. My metaphor was drawn from fruits. But where is Cecily?

Chasuble. Perhaps she followed us to the schools.

[*Enter* JACK *slowly from the back of the*

garden. *He is dressed in the deepest mourning, with crepe hatband and black gloves.*]

Miss Prism. Mr Worthing!

Chasuble. Mr Worthing?

Miss Prism. This is indeed a surprise. We did not look for you till Monday afternoon.

Jack. [*Shakes* MISS PRISM'S *hand in a tragic manner.*] I have returned sooner than I expected. Dr Chasuble, I hope you are well?

Chasuble. Dear Mr Worthing, I trust this garb of woe does not betoken some terrible calamity?

Jack. My brother.

Miss Prism. More shameful debts and extravagance?

Chasuble. Still leading his life of pleasure?

Jack. [*Shaking his head.*] Dead!

Chasuble. Your brother Ernest dead?

Jack. Quite dead.

Miss Prism. What a lesson for him! I trust he will profit by it.

Chasuble. Mr Worthing, I offer you my sincere condolence. You have at least the consolation of knowing that you were always the most generous and forgiving of brothers.

Jack. Poor Ernest! He had many faults, but it is a sad, sad blow.

Chasuble. Very sad indeed. Were you with him at the end?

Jack. No. He died abroad; in Paris, in fact. I had a telegram last night from the manager of the Grand Hotel.

Chasuble. Was the cause of death mentioned?

Jack. A severe chill, it seems.

Miss Prism. As a man sows, so shall he reap.

Chasuble. [*Raising his hand.*] Charity, dear Miss Prism, charity! None of us are perfect. I myself am peculiarly susceptible to draughts. Will the interment take place here?

Jack. No. He seems to have expressed a desire to be buried in Paris.

Chasuble. In Paris! [*Shakes his head.*] I fear that hardly points to any very serious state of mind at the last. You would no doubt wish me to make some slight allusion to this tragic domestic affliction next Sunday. [JACK *presses his hand convulsively.*] My sermon on the meaning of the manna in the wilderness can be adapted to almost any occasion, joyful, or, as in the present case, distressing. [*All sigh.*] I have preached it at harvest celebrations, christenings, confirmations, on days of humiliation and festal days. The last time I delivered it was in the Cathedral, as a charity sermon on behalf of the Society for the Prevention of Discontent among the Upper Orders. The Bishop, who was present, was much struck by some of the analogies I drew.

Jack. Ah! that reminds me, you mentioned christenings, I think, Dr Chasuble? I suppose you know how to christen all right? [DR CHASUBLE *looks astounded.*] I mean, of course, you are continually christening, aren't you?

Miss Prism. It is, I regret to say, one of the Rector's most constant duties in this parish. I have often spoken to the poorer classes on the subject. But they don't seem to know what thrift is.

Chasuble. But is there any particular infant in whom you are interested, Mr Worthing? Your brother was, I believe, unmarried, was he not?

Jack. Oh yes.

Miss Prism. [*Bitterly.*] People who live entirely for pleasure usually are.

Jack. But it is not for any child, dear Doctor. I am very fond of children. No! the fact is, I would like to be christened myself, this afternoon, if you have nothing better to do.

Chasuble. But surely, Mr Worthing, you have been christened already?

Jack. I don't remember anything about it.

Chasuble. But have you any grave doubts on the subject?

Jack. I certainly intend to have. Of course I don't know if the thing would bother you in any way, or if you think I am a little too old now.

Chasuble. Not at all. The sprinkling, and, indeed, the immersion of adults is a perfectly canonical practice.

Jack. Immersion!

Chasuble. You need have no apprehensions. Sprinkling is all that is necessary, or indeed I think advisable. Our weather is so changeable. At what hour would you wish the ceremony performed?

Jack. Oh, I might trot round about five if that would suit you.

Chasuble. Perfectly, perfectly! In fact, I have two similar ceremonies to perform at that time. A case of twins that occurred recently in one of the outlying cottages on your own estate. Poor Jenkins the carter, a most hard-working man.

Jack. Oh! I don't see much fun in being christened along with other babies. It would be childish. Would half-past five do?

Chasuble. Admirably! Admirably! [*Takes out watch.*] And now, dear Mr Worthing, I will not intrude any longer into a house of sorrow. I would merely beg you not to be too much bowed down by grief. What seem to us bitter trials are often blessings in disguise.

Miss Prism. This seems to me a blessing of an extremely obvious kind.

[*Enter* CECILY *from the house.*]

Cecily. Uncle Jack! Oh, I am pleased to see you back. But what horrid clothes you have got on. Do go and change them.

Miss Prism. Cecily!

Chasuble. My child! my child!

[CECILY *goes toward* JACK; *he kisses her brow in a melancholy manner.*]

Cecily. What is the matter, Uncle Jack? Do look happy! You look as if you had a toothache, and I have got such a surprise for you. Who do you think is in the dining-room? Your brother!

Jack. Who?

Cecily. Your brother Ernest. He arrived about half an hour ago.

Jack. What nonsense! I haven't got a brother.

Cecily. Oh, don't say that. However badly he may have behaved to you in the past he is still your brother. You couldn't be so heartless as to disown him. I'll tell him to come out. And you will shake hands with him, won't you, Uncle Jack?

[*Runs back into the house.*]

Chasuble. These are very joyful tidings.

Miss Prism. After we had all been resigned to his loss, his sudden return seems to me peculiarly distressing.

Jack. My brother is in the dining-room? I don't know what it all means. I think it is perfectly absurd.

[*Enter* ALGERNON *and* CECILY *hand in hand. They come slowly up to* JACK.]

Jack. Good heavens!

[*Motions* ALGERNON *away.*]

Algernon. Brother John, I have come down from town to tell you that I am very sorry for all the trouble I have given you, and that I intend to lead a better life in the future.

[JACK *glares at him and does not take his hand.*]

Cecily. Uncle Jack, you are not going to refuse your own brother's hand?

Jack. Nothing will induce me to take his hand. I think his coming down here disgraceful. He knows perfectly well why.

Cecily. Uncle Jack, do be nice. There is some good in everyone. Ernest has just been telling me about his poor invalid friend, Mr Bunbury, whom he goes to visit so often. And surely there must be much good in one who is kind to an invalid, and leaves the pleasures of London to sit by a bed of pain.

Jack. Oh! he has been talking about Bunbury, has he?

Cecily. Yes, he has told me all about poor Mr Bunbury, and his terrible state of health.

Jack. Bunbury! Well, I won't have him talk to you about Bunbury or about anything else. It is enough to drive one perfectly frantic.

Algernon. Of course I admit that the faults were all on my side. But I must say that I think that Brother John's coldness to me is peculiarly painful. I expected a more enthusiastic welcome, especially considering it is the first time I have come here.

Cecily. Uncle Jack, if you don't shake hands with Ernest I will never forgive you.

Jack. Never forgive me?

Cecily. Never, never, never!

Jack. Well, this is the last time I shall ever do it.

[*Shakes hands with* ALGERNON *and glares.*]

Chasuble. It's pleasant, is it not, to see so perfect a reconciliation? I think we might leave the two brothers together.

Miss Prism. Cecily, you will come with us.

Cecily. Certainly, Miss Prism. My little task of reconciliation is over.

Chasuble. You have done a beautiful action to-day, dear child.

Miss Prism. We must not be premature in our judgements.

Cecily. I feel very happy.

[*They all go off except* JACK *and* ALGERNON.]

Jack. You young scoundrel, Algy, you must get out of this place as soon as possible. I don't allow any Bunburying here.

[*Enter* MERRIMAN.]

Merriman. I have put Mr Ernest's things in the room next to yours, sir. I suppose that is all right?

Jack. What?

Merriman. Mr Ernest's luggage sir. I have unpacked it and put it in the room next to your own.

Jack. His luggage?

Merriman. Yes, sir. Three portmanteaus, a dressing-case, two hat-boxes, and a large luncheon-basket.

Algernon. I am afraid I can't stay more than a week this time.

Jack. Merriman, order the dog-cart at once. Mr Ernest has been suddenly called back to town.

Merriman. Yes, sir.

[*Goes back into the house.*]

Algernon. What a fearful liar you are, Jack. I have not been called back to town at all.

Jack. Yes, you have.

Algernon. I haven't heard any one call me.

Jack. Your duty as a gentleman calls you back.

Algernon. My duty as a gentleman has never interfered with my pleasures in the smallest degree.

Jack. I can quite understand that.

Algernon. Well, Cecily is a darling.

Jack. You are not to talk of Miss Cardew like that. I don't like it.

Algernon. Well, I don't like your clothes. You look perfectly ridiculous in them. Why on earth don't you go up and change? It is perfectly childish to be in deep mourning for a man who is actually staying for a whole week with you in your house as a guest. I call it grotesque.

Jack. You are certainly not staying with me for a whole week as a guest or anything else. You have got to leave . . . by the four-five train.

Algernon. I certainly won't leave you so long as you are in mourning. It would be most unfriendly. If I were in mourning you would stay with me, I suppose. I should think it very unkind if you didn't.

Jack. Well, will you go if I change my clothes?

Algernon. Yes, if you are not too long. I never saw anybody take so long to dress, and with such little result.

Jack. Well, at any rate, that is better than being always over-dressed as you are.

Algernon. If I am occasionally a little over-dressed, I make up for it by being always immensely over-educated.

Jack. Your vanity is ridiculous, your conduct an outrage, and your presence in my garden utterly absurd. However, you have got to catch the four-five, and I hope you will have a pleasant journey back to town. This Bunburying, as you call it, has not been a great success for you.

[*Goes into the house.*]

Algernon. I think it has been a great success. I'm in love with Cecily, and that is everything. [*Enter* CECILY *at the back of the garden. She picks up the can and begins to water the flowers.*] But I must see her before I go, and make arrangements for another Bunbury. Ah, there she is.

Cecily. Oh, I merely came back to water the roses. I thought you were with Uncle Jack.

Algernon. He's gone to order the dog-cart for me.

Cecily. Oh, is he going to take you for a nice drive?

Algernon. He's going to send me away.

Cecily. Then have we got to part?

Algernon. I am afraid so. It's a very painful parting.

Cecily. It is always painful to part from people whom one has known for a very brief space of time. The absence of old friends one can endure with equanimity. But even a momentary separation from any one to whom one has just been introduced is almost unbearable.

Algernon. Thank you.

[*Enter* MERRIMAN.]

Merriman. The dog-cart is at the door, sir.

[ALGERNON *looks appealingly at* CECILY.]

Cecily. It can wait, Merriman . . . for . . . five minutes.

Merriman. Yes, miss. [*Exit* MERRIMAN.]

Algernon. I hope, Cecily, I shall not offend you if I state quite frankly and openly that you seem to me to be in every way the visible personification of absolute perfection.

Cecily. I think your frankness does you great credit, Ernest. If you will allow me, I will copy your remarks into my diary.

[*Goes over to table and begins writing in diary.*]

Algernon. Do you really keep a diary? I'd give anything to look at it. May I?

Cecily. Oh no. [*Puts her hand over it.*] You see, it is simply a very young girl's record of her own thoughts and impressions, and consequently meant for publication. When it appears in volume form I hope you will order a copy. But pray, Ernest, don't stop. I delight in taking down from dictation. I have reached 'absolute perfection.' You can go on. I am quite ready for more.

Algernon. [*Somewhat taken aback.*] Ahem! Ahem!

Cecily. Oh, don't cough, Ernest. When one is dictating one should speak fluently and not cough. Besides, I don't know how to spell a cough.

[*Writes as* ALGERNON *speaks.*]

Algernon. [*Speaking very rapidly.*] Cecily, ever since I first looked upon your wonderful and incomparable beauty, I have dared to love you wildly, passionately, devotedly, hopelessly.

Cecily. I don't think that you should tell me that you love me wildly, passionately, devotedly, hopelessly. Hopelessly doesn't seem to make much sense, does it?

Algernon. Cecily. [*Enter* MERRIMAN.]

Merriman. The dog-cart is waiting, sir.

Algernon. Tell it to come round next week, at the same hour.

Merriman. [*Looks at* CECILY, *who makes no sign.*] Yes, sir. [MERRIMAN *retires.*]

Cecily. Uncle Jack would be very much annoyed if he knew you were staying on till next week, at the same hour.

Algernon. Oh, I don't care about Jack. I don't care for anybody in the whole world but you. I love you, Cecily. You will marry me, won't you?

Cecily. You silly boy! Of course. Why, we have been engaged for the last three months.

Algernon. For the last three months?

Cecily. Yes, it will be exactly three months on Thursday.

Algernon. But how did we become engaged?

Cecily. Well, ever since dear Uncle Jack first confessed to us that he had a younger brother who was very wicked and bad, you of course have formed the chief topic of conversation between myself and Miss Prism. And of course a man who is much talked about is always very attractive. One feels there must be something in him, after all. I daresay it was foolish of me, but I fell in love with you, Ernest.

Algernon. Darling. And when was the engagement actually settled?

Cecily. On the 14th of February last. Worn out by your entire ignorance of my existence, I determined to end the matter one way or the other, and after a long struggle with myself I accepted you under this dear old tree here. The next day I bought this little ring in your name, and this is the little bangle with the true lover's knot I promised you always to wear.

Algernon. Did I give you this? It's very pretty, isn't it?

Cecily. Yes, you've wonderfully good taste, Ernest. It's the excuse I've always given for your leading such a bad life. And this is the box in which I keep all your dear letters.

[*Kneels at table, opens box, and produces letters tied up with blue ribbon.*]

Algernon. My letters! But, my own sweet Cecily, I have never written you any letters.

Cecily. You need hardly remind me of that, Ernest. I remember only too well that I was forced to write your letters for you. I wrote always three times a week, and sometimes oftener.

Algernon. Oh, do let me read them, Cecily?

Cecily. Oh, I couldn't possibly. They would make you far too conceited. [*Replaces* box.] The three you wrote me after I had broken off the engagement are so beautiful, and so badly spelled, that even now I can hardly read them without crying a little.

Algernon. But was our engagement ever broken off?

Cecily. Of course it was. On the 22nd of last March. You can see the entry if you like. [*Shows diary.*] 'To-day I broke off my engagement with Ernest. I feel it is better to do so. The weather still continues charming.'

Algernon. But why on earth did you break it off? What had I done? I had done nothing at all. Cecily, I am very much hurt indeed to hear you broke it off. Particularly when the weather was so charming.

Cecily. It would hardly have been a really serious engagement if it hadn't been broken off at least once. But I forgave you before the week was out.

Algernon. [*Crossing to her, and kneeling.*] What a perfect angel you are, Cecily.

Cecily. You dear romantic boy. [*He kisses her, she puts her fingers through his hair.*] I hope your hair curls naturally, does it?

Algernon. Yes, darling, with a little help from others.

Cecily. I am so glad.

Algernon. You'll never break off our engagement again, Cecily?

Cecily. I don't think I could break it off now that I have actually met you. Besides, of course, there is the question of your name.

Algernon. Yes, of course. [*Nervously.*]

Cecily. You must not laugh at me, darling, but it had always been a girlish dream of mine to love some one whose name was Ernest. [ALGERNON *rises*, CECILY *also*.] There is something in that name that seems to inspire absolute confidence. I pity any poor married woman whose husband is not called Ernest.

Algernon. But, my dear child, do you mean to say you could not love me if I had some other name?

Cecily. But what name?

Algernon. Oh, any name you like—Algernon—for instance . . .

Cecily. But I don't like the name of Algernon.

Algernon. Well, my own dear, sweet, loving little darling, I really can't see why you should object to the name of Algernon. It is not at all a bad name. In fact, it is rather an aristocratic name. Half of the chaps who get into the Bankruptcy Court are called Algernon. But seriously, Cecily . . .

[*Moving to her.*] if my name was Algy, couldn't you love me?

Cecily. [*Rising.*] I might respect you, Ernest, I might admire your character, but I fear that I should not be able to give you my undivided attention.

Algernon. Ahem! Cecily! [*Picking up hat.*] Your Rector here is, I suppose, thoroughly experienced in the practice of all the rites and ceremonials of the Church?

Cecily. Oh, yes. Dr Chasuble is a most learned man. He has never written a single book, so you can imagine how much he knows.

Algernon. I must see him at once on a most important christening—I mean on most important business.

Cecily. Oh!

Algernon. I shan't be away more than half an hour.

Cecily. Considering that we have been engaged since February the 14th, and that I only met you to-day for the first time, I think it is rather hard that you should leave me for so long a period as half an hour. Couldn't you make it twenty minutes?

Algernon. I'll be back in no time.

[*Kisses her and rushes down the garden.*]

Cecily. What an impetuous boy he is! I like his hair so much. I must enter his proposal in my diary. — [*Enter* MERRIMAN.]

Merriman. A Miss Fairfax has just called to see Mr Worthing. On very important business, Miss Fairfax states.

Cecily. Isn't Mr Worthing in his library?

Merriman. Mr Worthing went over in the direction of the Rectory some time ago.

Cecily. Pray ask the lady to come out here; Mr Worthing is sure to be back soon. And you can bring tea.

Merriman. Yes, Miss. [*Goes out.*]

Cecily. Miss Fairfax! I suppose one of the many good elderly women who are associated with Uncle Jack in some of his philanthropic work in London. I don't quite like women who are interested in philanthropic work. I think it is so forward of them.

[*Enter* MERRIMAN.]

Merriman. Miss Fairfax.

[*Enter* GWENDOLEN. *Exit* MERRIMAN.]

Cecily. [*Advancing to meet her.*] Pray let me introduce myself to you. My name is Cecily Cardew.

Gwendolen. Cecily Cardew? [*Moving to her and shaking hands.*] What a very sweet name! Something tells me that we are going to be great friends. I like you already more than I can say. My first impressions of people are never wrong.

Cecily. How nice of you to like me so much after we have known each other such a comparatively short time. Pray sit down.

Gwendolen. [*Still standing up.*] I may call you Cecily, may I not?

Cecily. With pleasure!

Gwendolen. And you will always call me Gwendolen, won't you?

Cecily. If you wish.

Gwendolen. Then that is all quite settled, is it not?

Cecily. I hope so.

[*A pause. They both sit down together.*]

Gwendolen. Perhaps this might be a favorable opportunity for my mentioning who I am. My father is Lord Bracknell. You have never heard of papa, I suppose?

Cecily. I don't think so.

Gwendolen. Outside the family circle, papa, I am glad to say, is entirely unknown. I think that is quite as it should be. The home seems to me to be the proper sphere for the man. And certainly once a man begins to neglect his domestic duties he becomes painfully effeminate, does he not? And I don't like that. It makes men so very attractive. Cecily, mamma, whose views on education are remarkably strict, has brought me up to be extremely shortsighted; it is part of her system; so do you mind my looking at you through my glasses?

Cecily. Oh! Not at all, Gwendolen. I am very fond of being looked at.

Gwendolen. [*After examining* CECILY *carefully through a lorgnette.*] You are here on a short visit, I suppose.

Cecily. Oh no! I live here.

Gwendolen. [*Severely.*] Really? Your mother, no doubt, or some female relative of advanced years, resides here also?

Cecily. Oh no! I have no mother, nor, in fact, any relations.

Gwendolen. Indeed?

Cecily. My dear guardian, with the assistance of Miss Prism, has the arduous task of looking after me.

Gwendolen. Your guardian?

Cecily. Yes, I am Mr Worthing's ward.

Gwendolen. Oh! It is strange he never mentioned to me that he had a ward. How secretive of him! He grows more interesting hourly. I am not sure, however, that the news inspires me with feelings of unmixed delight. [*Rising and going to her.*] I am very fond of you, Cecily; I have liked you ever since I met you! But I am bound to state that now that I know that you are Mr Worthing's ward, I cannot help expressing a wish you were—well, just a little older than you seem to be—and not quite so very alluring in appearance. In fact, if I may speak candidly——

Cecily. Pray do! I think that whenever one has anything unpleasant to say, one should always be quite candid.

Gwendolen. Well, to speak with perfect candour, Cecily, I wish that you were fully forty-two, and more than usually plain for your age. Ernest has a strong upright nature. He is the very soul of truth and honour. Disloyalty would be as impossible to him as deception. But even men of the noblest possible moral character are extremely susceptible to the influence of the physical charms of others. Modern, no less than Ancient History, supplies us with many most painful examples of what I refer to. If it were not so, indeed, History would be quite unreadable.

Cecily. I beg your pardon, Gwendolen, did you say Ernest?

Gwendolen. Yes.

Cecily. Oh, but it is not Mr Ernest Worthing who is my guardian. It is his brother—his elder brother.

Gwendolen. [*Sitting down again.*] Ernest never mentioned to me that he had a brother.

Cecily. I am sorry to say they have not been on good terms for a long time.

Gwendolen. Ah! that accounts for it. And now that I think of it I have never heard any man mention his brother. The subject seems distasteful to most men. Cecily, you have lifted a load from my mind. I was growing almost anxious. It would have been terrible if any cloud had come across a friendship like ours, would it not? Of course you are quite, quite sure that it is not Mr Ernest Worthing who is your guardian?

Cecily. Quite sure. [*A pause.*] In fact, I am going to be his.

Gwendolen. [*Inquiringly.*] I beg your pardon?

Cecily. [*Rather shy and confidingly.*] Dearest Gwendolen, there is no reason why I should make a secret of it to you. Our little county newspaper is sure to chronicle the fact next week. Mr Ernest Worthing and I are engaged to be married.

Gwendolen. [*Quite politely, rising.*] My darling Cecily, I think there must be some slight error. Mr Ernest Worthing is engaged to me. The announcement will appear in the *Morning Post* on Saturday at the latest.

Cecily. [*Very politely, rising.*] I am afraid you must be under some misconception. Ernest proposed to me exactly ten minutes ago. [*Shows diary.*]

Gwendolen. [*Examines diary through her lorgnette carefully.*] It is very curious, for he asked me to be his wife yesterday afternoon at 5.30. If you would care to verify the incident, pray do so. [*Produces diary of her own.*] I never travel without my diary. One should always have something sensational to read in the train. I am so sorry, dear Cecily, if it is any disappointment to you, but I am afraid I have the prior claim.

Cecily. It would distress me more than I can tell you, dear Gwendolen, if it caused you any mental or physical anguish, but I feel bound to point out that since Ernest proposed to you he clearly has changed his mind.

Gwendolen. [*Meditatively.*] If the poor fellow has been entrapped into any foolish promise I shall consider it my duty to rescue him at once, and with a firm hand.

Cecily. [*Thoughtfully and sadly.*] Whatever unfortunate entanglement my dear boy may have got into, I will never reproach him with it after we are married.

Gwendolen. Do you allude to me, Miss Cardew, as an entanglement? You are presumptuous. On an occasion of this kind it becomes more than a moral duty to speak one's mind. It becomes a pleasure.

Cecily. Do you suggest, Miss Fairfax, that I entrapped Ernest into an engagement? How dare you? This is no time for wearing the shallow mask of manners. When I see a spade I call it a spade.

Gwendolen. [*Satirically.*] I am glad to say that I have never seen a spade. It is obvious that our social spheres have been widely different.

[*Enter* MERRIMAN, *followed by the footman. He carries a salver, table cloth, and plate stand.* CECILY *is about to retort. The presence of the servants exercises a restraining influence, under which both girls chafe.*]

Merriman. Shall I lay tea here as usual, Miss?

Cecily. [*Sternly, in a calm voice.*] Yes, as usual.

[MERRIMAN *begins to clear table and lay cloth. A long pause.* CECILY *and* GWENDOLEN *glare at each other.*]

Gwendolen. Are there many interesting walks in the vicinity, Miss Cardew?

Cecily. Oh, yes! a great many. From the top of one of the hills quite close one can see five counties.

Gwendolen. Five counties! I don't think I should like that; I hate crowds.

Cecily. [*Sweetly.*] I suppose that is why you live in town?

[GWENDOLEN *bites her lip, and beats her foot nervously with her parasol.*]

Gwendolen. [*Looking round.*] Quite a well-kept garden this is, Miss Cardew.

Cecily. So glad you like it, Miss Fairfax.

Gwendolen. I had no idea there were any flowers in the country.

Cecily. Oh, flowers are as common here, Miss Fairfax, as people are in London.

Gwendolen. Personally I cannot understand how anybody manages to exist in the country, if anybody who is anybody does. The country always bores me to death.

Cecily. Ah! This is what the newspapers call agricultural depression, is it not? I believe the aristocracy are suffering very much from it just at present. It is almost an epidemic amongst them, I have been told. May I offer you some tea, Miss Fairfax?

Gwendolen. [*With elaborate politeness.*] Thank you. [*Aside.*] Detestable girl! But I require tea!

Cecily. [*Sweetly.*] Sugar?

Gwendolen. [*Superciliously.*] No, thank you. Sugar is not fashionable any more.

[CECILY *looks angrily at her, takes up the tongs and puts four lumps of sugar into the cup.*]

Cecily. [*Severely.*] Cake or bread and butter?

Gwendolen. [*In a bored manner.*] Bread and butter, please. Cake is rarely seen at the best houses nowadays.

Cecily. [*Cuts a very large slice of cake and puts it on the tray.*] Hand that to Miss Fairfax.

[MERRIMAN *does so, and goes out with footman.* GWENDOLEN *drinks the tea and makes a grimace. Puts down cup at once, reaches out her hand to the bread and butter, looks at it, and finds it is cake. Rises in indignation.*]

Gwendolen. You have filled my tea with lumps of sugar, and though I asked most distinctly for bread and butter, you have given me cake. I am known for the gentleness of my disposition, and the extraordinary sweetness of my nature, but I warn you, Miss Cardew, you may go too far.

Cecily. [*Rising.*] To save my poor, innocent, trusting boy from the machinations of any other girl there are no lengths to which I would not go.

Gwendolen. From the moment I saw you I distrusted you. I felt that you were false and deceitful. I am never deceived in such matters. My first impressions of people are invariably right.

Cecily. It seems to me, Miss Fairfax, that I am trespassing on your valuable time. No doubt you have many other calls of a similar character to make in the neighborhood. [*Enter* JACK.]

Gwendolen. [*Catching sight of him.*] Ernest! My own Ernest!

Jack. Gwendolen! Darling!

[*Offers to kiss her.*]

Gwendolen. [*Drawing back.*] A moment! May I ask if you are engaged to be married to this young lady? [*Points to* CECILY.]

Jack. [*Laughing.*] To dear little Cecily! Of course not! What could have put such an idea into your pretty little head?

Gwendolen. Thank you. You may!

[*Offers her cheek.*]

Cecily. [*Very sweetly.*] I knew there must be some misunderstanding, Miss Fairfax. The gentleman whose arm is at present round your waist is my guardian, Mr John Worthing.

Gwendolen. I beg your pardon?

Cecily. This is Uncle Jack!

Gwendolen. [*Receding.*] Jack! Oh!

[*Enter* ALGERNON.]

Cecily. Here is Ernest!

Algernon. [*Goes straight over to* CECILY *without noticing anyone else.*] My own love! [*Offers to kiss her.*]

Cecily. [*Drawing back.*] A moment, Ernest! May I ask you—are you engaged to be married to this young lady?

Algernon. [*Looking round.*] To what young lady? Good heavens! Gwendolen!

Cecily. Yes: to good heavens, Gwendolen, I mean to Gwendolen.

Algernon. [*Laughing.*] Of course not! What could have put such an idea into your pretty little head?

Cecily. Thank you. [*Presenting her cheek to be kissed.*] You may.

[ALGERNON *kisses her.*]

Gwendolen. I felt there was some slight error, Miss Cardew. The gentleman who is now embracing you is my cousin, Mr Algernon Moncrieff.

Cecily. [*Breaking away from* ALGERNON.] Algernon Moncrieff! Oh!

[*The two girls move towards each other and put their arms round each other's waists as if for protection.*]

Cecily. Are you called Algernon?

Algernon. I cannot deny it.

Cecily. Oh!

Gwendolen. Is your name really John?

Jack. [*Standing rather proudly.*] I could deny it if I liked. I could deny anything if I liked. But my name certainly is John. It has been John for years.

Cecily. [*To* GWENDOLEN.] A gross deception has been practised on both of us.

Gwendolen. My poor wounded Cecily!

Cecily. My sweet wronged Gwendolen!

Gwendolen. [*Slowly and seriously.*] You will call me sister, will you not?

[*They embrace.* JACK *and* ALGERNON *groan and walk up and down.*]

Cecily. [*Rather brightly.*] There is just one question I would like to be allowed to ask my guardian.

Gwendolen. An admirable idea! Mr Worthing, there is just one question I would like to be permitted to put to you. Where is your brother Ernest? We are both engaged to be married to your brother Ernest, so it is a matter of some importance to us to know where your brother Ernest is at present.

Jack. [*Slowly and hesitatingly.*] Gwendolen—Cecily—it is very painful for me to be forced to speak the truth. It is the first time in my life that I have ever been reduced to such a painful position, and I am really quite inexperienced in doing anything of the kind. However, I will tell you quite frankly that I have no brother Ernest. I have no brother at all. I never had a brother in my life, and I certainly have not the smallest intention of ever having one in the future.

Cecily. [*Surprised.*] No brother at all?

Jack. [*Cheerily.*] None!

Gwendolen. [*Severely.*] Had you never a brother of any kind?

Jack. [*Pleasantly.*] Never. Not even of any kind.

Gwendolen. I am afraid it is quite clear, Cecily, that neither of us is engaged to be married to anyone.

Cecily. It is not a very pleasant position for a young girl suddenly to find herself in. Is it?

Gwendolen. Let us go into the house. They will hardly venture to come after us there.

Cecily. No, men are so cowardly, aren't they?

[*They retire into the house with scornful looks.*]

Jack. This ghastly state of things is what you call Bunburying, I suppose?

Algernon. Yes, and a perfectly wonderful Bunbury it is. The most wonderful Bunbury I have ever had in my life.

Jack. Well, you've no right whatsoever to Bunbury here.

Algernon. That is absurd. One has a right to Bunbury anywhere one chooses. Every serious Bunburyist knows that.

Jack. Serious Bunburyist? Good heavens!

Algernon. Well, one must be serious about something, if one wants to have any amusement in life. I happen to be serious about

Bunburying. What on earth you are serious about I haven't got the remotest idea. About everything, I should fancy. You have such an absolutely trivial nature.

Jack. Well, the only small satisfaction I have in the whole of this wretched business is that your friend Bunbury is quite exploded. You won't be able to run down to the country quite so often as you used to do, dear Algy. And a very good thing too.

Algernon. Your brother is a little off colour, isn't he, dear Jack? You won't be able to disappear to London quite so frequently as your wicked custom was. And not a bad thing either.

Jack. As for your conduct towards Miss Cardew, I must say that your taking in a sweet, simple, innocent girl like that is quite inexcusable. To say nothing of the fact that she is my ward.

Algernon. I can see no possible defence at all for your deceiving a brilliant, clever, thoroughly experienced young lady like Miss Fairfax. To say nothing of the fact that she is my cousin.

Jack. I wanted to be engaged to Gwendolen, that is all. I love her.

Algernon. Well, I simply wanted to be engaged to Cecily. I adore her.

Jack. There is certainly no chance of your marrying Miss Cardew.

Algernon. I don't think there is much likelihood, Jack, of you and Miss Fairfax being united.

Jack. Well, that is no business of yours.

Algernon. If it was my business, I wouldn't talk about it. [*Begins to eat muffins.*] It is very vulgar to talk about one's business. Only people like stockbrokers do that, and then merely at dinner parties.

Jack. How you can sit there, calmly eating muffins when we are in this horrible trouble, I can't make out. You seem to me to be perfectly heartless.

Algernon. Well, I can't eat muffins in an agitated manner. The butter would probably get on my cuffs. One should always eat muffins quite calmly. It is the only way to eat them.

Jack. I say it's perfectly heartless your eating muffins at all, under the circumstances.

Algernon. When I am in trouble, eating is the only thing that consoles me. Indeed, when I am in really great trouble, as any one who knows me intimately will tell you, I refuse everything except food and drink. At the present moment I am eating muffins because I am unhappy. Besides, I am particularly fond of muffins. [*Rising.*]

Jack. [*Rising.*] Well, there is no reason why you should eat them all in that greedy way. [*Takes muffins from* ALGERNON.]

Algernon. [*Offering tea-cake.*] I wish you would have tea-cake instead. I don't like tea-cake.

Jack. Good heavens! I suppose a man may eat his own muffins in his own garden.

Algernon. But you have just said it was perfectly heartless to eat muffins.

Jack. I said it was perfectly heartless of you, under the circumstances. That is a very different thing.

Algernon. That may be. But the muffins are the same.

[*He seizes the muffin-dish from* JACK.]

Jack. Algy, I wish to goodness you would go.

Algernon. You can't possibly ask me to go without having some dinner. It's absurd. I never go without my dinner. No one ever does, except vegetarians and people like that. Besides I have just made arrangements with Dr Chasuble to be christened at a quarter to six under the name of Ernest.

Jack. My dear fellow, the sooner you give up that nonsense the better. I made arrangements this morning with Dr Chasuble to be christened myself at 5.30, and I naturally will take the name of Ernest. Gwendolen would wish it. We can't both be christened Ernest. It's absurd. Besides, I have a perfect right to be christened if I like. There is no evidence at all that I have ever been christened by anybody. I should think it extremely probable I never was, and so does Dr Chasuble. It is entirely different in your case. You have been christened already.

Algernon. Yes, but I have not been christened for years.

Jack. Yes, but you have been christened. That is the important thing.

Algernon. Quite so. So I know my constitution can stand it. If you are not quite sure about your ever having been christened, I must say I think it rather dangerous your venturing on it now. It might make you very unwell. You can hardly have forgotten that someone very closely connected with you was very nearly carried off this week in Paris by a severe chill.

Jack. Yes, but you said yourself that a severe chill was not hereditary.

Algernon. It usen't to be, I know—but I daresay it is now. Science is always making wonderful improvements in things.

Jack. [*Picking up the muffin-dish.*] Oh, that is nonsense; you are always talking nonsense.

Algernon. Jack, you are at the muffins

again! I wish you wouldn't. There are only two left. [*Takes them.*] I told you I was particularly fond of muffins.

Jack. But I hate tea-cake.

Algernon. Why on earth then do you allow tea-cake to be served up for your guests? What ideas you have of hospitality!

Jack. Algernon! I have already told you to go. I don't want you here. Why don't you go!

Algernon. I haven't quite finished my tea yet! and there is still one muffin left.

[JACK *groans, and sinks into a chair.* ALGERNON *continues eating.*]

CURTAIN

THIRD ACT

Drawing-room at the Manor House.
[GWENDOLEN *and* CECILY *are at the window, looking out into the garden.*]

Gwendolen. The fact that they did not follow us at once into the house, as any one else would have done, seems to me to show that they have some sense of shame left.

Cecily. They have been eating muffins. That looks like repentance.

Gwendolen. [*After a pause.*] They don't seem to notice us at all. Couldn't you cough?

Cecily. But I haven't got a cough.

Gwendolen. They're looking at us. What effrontery!

Cecily. They're approaching. That's very forward of them.

Gwendolen. Let us preserve a dignified silence.

Cecily. Certainly. It's the only thing to do now.

[*Enter* JACK *followed by* ALGERNON. *They whistle some dreadful popular air from a British Opera.*]

Gwendolen. This dignified silence seems to produce an unpleasant effect.

Cecily. A most distasteful one.

Gwendolen. But we will not be the first to speak.

Cecily. Certainly not.

Gwendolen. Mr Worthing, I have something very particular to ask you. Much depends on your reply.

Cecily. Gwendolen, your common sense is invaluable. Mr Moncrieff, kindly answer me the following question. Why did you pretend to be my guardian's brother?

Algernon. In order that I might have an opportunity of meeting you.

Cecily. [*To* GWENDOLEN.] That certainly seems a satisfactory explanation, does it not?

Gwendolen. Yes, dear, if you can believe him.

Cecily. I don't. But that does not affect the wonderful beauty of his answer.

Gwendolen. True. In matters of grave importance, style, not sincerity, is the vital thing. Mr Worthing, what explanation can you offer to me for pretending to have a brother? Was it in order that you might have an opportunity of coming up to town to see me as often as possible?

Jack. Can you doubt it, Miss Fairfax?

Gwendolen. I have the gravest doubts upon the subject. But I intend to crush them. This is not the moment for German scepticism. [*Moving to* CECILY.] Their explanations appear to be quite satisfactory, especially Mr Worthing's. That seems to me to have the stamp of truth upon it.

Cecily. I am more than content with what Mr Moncrieff said. His voice alone inspires one with absolute credulity.

Gwendolen. Then you think we should forgive them?

Cecily. Yes. I mean no.

Gwendolen. True! I had forgotten. There are principles at stake that one cannot surrender. Which of us should tell them? The task is not a pleasant one.

Cecily. Could we not both speak at the same time?

Gwendolen. An excellent idea! I nearly always speak at the same time as other people. Will you take the time from me?

Cecily. Certainly.

[GWENDOLEN *beats time with uplifted finger.*]

Gwendolen and Cecily. [*Speaking together.*] Your Christian names are still an insuperable barrier. That is all!

Jack and Algernon. [*Speaking together.*] Our Christian names! Is that all? But we are going to be christened this afternoon.

Gwendolen. [*To* JACK.] For my sake you are prepared to do this terrible thing?

Jack. I am.

Cecily. [*To* ALGERNON.] To please me you are ready to face this fearful ordeal?

Algernon. I am!

Gwendolen. How absurd to talk of the equality of the sexes! Where questions of self-sacrifice are concerned, men are infinitely beyond us.

Jack. We are.

[*Clasps hands with* ALGERNON.]

Cecily. They have moments of physical courage of which we women know absolutely nothing.

Gwendolen. [*To* JACK.] Darling!

Algernon. [*To* CECILY.] Darling!

[*They fall into each other's arms.*]
[*Enter* MERRIMAN. *When he enters he coughs loudly, seeing the situation.*]

Merriman. Ahem! Ahem! Lady Bracknell.

Jack. Good heavens!

[*Enter* LADY BRACKNELL. *The couples separate in alarm. Exit* MERRIMAN.]

Lady Bracknell. Gwendolen! What does this mean?

Gwendolen. Merely that I am engaged to be married to Mr Worthing, mamma.

Lady Bracknell. Come here. Sit down. Sit down immediately. Hesitation of any kind is a sign of mental decay in the young, of physical weakness in the old. [*Turns to* JACK.] Apprised, sir, of my daughter's sudden flight by her trusty maid, whose confidence I purchased by means of a small coin, I followed her at once by a luggage train. Her unhappy father is, I am glad to say, under the impression that she is attending a more than usually lengthy lecture by the University Extension Scheme on the Influence of a Permanent Income on Thought. I do not propose to undeceive him. Indeed I have never undeceived him on any question. I would consider it wrong. But of course, you will clearly understand that all communication between yourself and my daughter must cease immediately from this moment. On this point, as indeed on all points, I am firm.

Jack. I am engaged to be married to Gwendolen, Lady Bracknell!

Lady Bracknell. You are nothing of the kind, sir. And now as regards Algernon! . . . Algernon!

Algernon. Yes, Aunt Augusta.

Lady Bracknell. May I ask if it is in this house that your invalid friend Mr Bunbury resides?

Algernon. [*Stammering.*] Oh! No! Bunbury doesn't live here. Bunbury is somewhere else at present. In fact, Bunbury is dead.

Lady Bracknell. Dead! When did Mr Bunbury die? His death must have been extremely sudden.

Algernon. [*Airily.*] Oh! I killed Bunbury this afternoon. I mean poor Bunbury died this afternoon.

Lady Bracknell. What did he die of?

Algernon. Bunbury? Oh, he was quite exploded.

Lady Bracknell. Exploded! Was he the victim of a revolutionary outrage? I was not aware that Mr Bunbury was interested in social legislation. If so, he is well punished for his morbidity.

Algernon. My dear Aunt Augusta, I mean he was found out! The doctors found out that Bunbury could not live, that is what I mean—so Bunbury died.

Lady Bracknell. He seems to have had great confidence in the opinion of his physicians. I am glad, however, that he made up his mind at the last to some definite course of action, and acted under proper medical advice. And now that we have finally got rid of this Mr Bunbury, may I ask, Mr Worthing, who is that young person whose hand my nephew Algernon is now holding in what seems to me a peculiarly unnecessary manner?

Jack. That lady is Miss Cecily Cardew, my ward.

[LADY BRACKNELL *bows coldly to* CECILY.]

Algernon. I am engaged to be married to Cecily, Aunt Augusta.

Lady Bracknell. I beg your pardon?

Cecily. Mr Moncrieff and I are engaged to be married, Lady Bracknell.

Lady Bracknell. [*With a shiver, crossing to the sofa and sitting down.*] I do not know whether there is anything peculiarly exciting in the air of this particular part of Hertfordshire, but the number of engagements that go on seems to me considerably above the proper average that statistics have laid down for our guidance. I think some preliminary inquiry on my part would not be out of place. Mr Worthing, is Miss Cardew at all connected with any of the larger railway stations in London? I merely desire information. Until yesterday I had no idea that there were any families or persons whose origin was a Terminus.

[JACK *looks perfectly furious, but restrains himself.*]

Jack. [*In a cold, clear voice.*] Miss Cardew is the granddaughter of the late Mr Thomas Cardew of 149 Belgrave Square, S.W.; Gervase Park, Dorking, Surrey; and the Sporran, Fifeshire, North Britain.

Lady Bracknell. That sounds not unsatisfactory. Three addresses always inspire confidence, even in tradesmen. But what proof have I of their authenticity?

Jack. I have carefully preserved the Court Guides of the period. They are open to your inspection, Lady Bracknell.

Lady Bracknell. [*Grimly.*] I have known strange errors in that publication.

Jack. Miss Cardew's family solicitors are Messrs Markby, Markby, and Markby.

Lady Bracknell. Markby, Markby, and Markby? A firm of the very highest position in their profession. Indeed I am told that one of the Mr Markbys is occasionally to be seen at dinner parties. So far I am satisfied.

Jack. [*Very irritably.*] How extremely kind of you, Lady Bracknell! I have also in my possession, you will be pleased to hear, certificates of Miss Cardew's birth, baptism, whooping cough, registration, vaccination, confirmation, and the measles; both the German and the English variety.

Lady Bracknell. Ah! A life crowded with incident, I see; though perhaps somewhat too exciting for a young girl. I am not myself in favour of premature experiences. [*Rises, looks at her watch.*] Gwendolen! the time approaches for our departure. We have not a moment to lose. As a matter of form, Mr Worthing, I had better ask you if Miss Cardew has any little fortune?

Jack. Oh! about a hundred and thirty thousand pounds in the Funds. That is all. Good-bye, Lady Bracknell. So pleased to have seen you.

Lady Bracknell. [*Sitting down again.*] A moment, Mr Worthing. A hundred and thirty thousand pounds! And in the Funds! Miss Cardew seems to me a most attractive young lady, now that I look at her. Few girls of the present day have any really solid qualities, any of the qualities that last, and improve with time. We live, I regret to say, in an age of surfaces. [*To* CECILY.] Come over here, dear. [CECILY *goes across.*] Pretty child! your dress is sadly simple, and your hair seems almost as Nature might have left it. But we can soon alter all that. A thoroughly experienced French maid produces a really marvellous result in a very brief space of time. I remember recommending one to young Lady Lancing, and after three months her own husband did not know her.

Jack. And after six months nobody knew her.

Lady Bracknell. [*Glares at* JACK *for a few moments. Then bends, with a practised smile, to* CECILY.] Kindly turn round, sweet child. [CECILY *turns completely round.*] No, the side view is what I want. [CECILY *presents her profile.*] Yes, quite as I expected. There are distinct social possibilities in your profile. The two weak points in our age are its want of principle and its want of profile. The chin a little higher, dear. Style largely depends on the way the chin is worn. They are worn very high, just at present. Algernon!

Algernon. Yes, Aunt Augusta!

Lady Bracknell. There are distinct social possibilities in Miss Cardew's profile.

Algernon. Cecily is the sweetest, dearest, prettiest girl in the whole world. And I don't care twopence about social possibilities.

Lady Bracknell. Never speak disrespectfully of Society, Algernon. Only people who can't get into it do that. [*To* CECILY.] Dear child, of course you know that Algernon has nothing but his debts to depend upon. But I do not approve of mercenary marriages. When I married Lord Bracknell I had no fortune of any kind. But I never dreamed for a moment of allowing that to stand in my way. Well, I suppose I must give my consent.

Algernon. Thank you, Aunt Augusta.

Lady Bracknell. Cecily, you may kiss me!

Cecily. [*Kisses her.*] Thank you, Lady Bracknell.

Lady Bracknell. You may also address me as Aunt Augusta for the future.

Cecily. Thank you, Aunt Augusta.

Lady Bracknell. The marriage, I think, had better take place quite soon.

Algernon. Thank you, Aunt Augusta.

Cecily. Thank you, Aunt Augusta.

Lady Bracknell. To speak frankly, I am not in favour of long engagements. They give people the opportunity of finding out each other's character before marriage, which I think is never advisable.

Jack. I beg your pardon for interrupting you, Lady Bracknell, but this engagement is quite out of the question. I am Miss Cardew's guardian, and she cannot marry without my consent until she comes of age. That consent I absolutely decline to give.

Lady Bracknell. Upon what grounds, may I ask? Algernon is an extremely, I may almost say an ostentatiously, eligible young man. He has nothing, but he looks everything. What more can one desire?

Jack. It pains me very much to have to speak frankly to you, Lady Bracknell, about your nephew, but the fact is that I do not approve at all of his moral character. I suspect him of being untruthful.

[ALGERNON *and* CECILY *look at him in indignant amazement.*]

Lady Bracknell. Untruthful! My nephew Algernon? Impossible! He is an Oxonian.

Jack. I fear there can be no possible doubt about the matter. This afternoon during my temporary absence in London on an important question of romance, he obtained admission to my house by means of the false pretence of being my brother. Under an assumed name he drank, I've just been informed by my butler, an entire pint bottle of my Perrier-Jouet, Brut, '89; wine I was specially reserving for myself. Continuing his disgraceful deception, he succeeded in the course of the afternoon in alienating the affections of my only ward. He subsequently stayed to tea, and devoured every single muffin. And what makes his conduct all the more heartless is that he was perfectly well aware from the first that I have no brother, that I never had a brother, and that I don't intend to have a brother, not even of any kind. I distinctly told him so myself yesterday afternoon.

Lady Bracknell. Ahem! Mr Worthing, after careful consideration I have decided entirely to overlook my nephew's conduct to you.

Jack. That is very generous of you, Lady Bracknell. My own decision, however, is unalterable. I decline to give my consent.

Lady Bracknell. [*To* CECILY.] Come here, sweet child. [CECILY *goes over.*] How old are you, dear?

Cecily. Well, I am really only eighteen, but I always admit to twenty when I go to evening parties.

Lady Bracknell. You are perfectly right in making some slight alteration. Indeed, no woman should ever be quite accurate about her age. It looks so calculating. . . . [*In a meditative manner.*] Eighteen, but admitting to twenty at evening parties. Well, it will not be very long before you are of age and free from the restraints of tutelage. So I don't think your guardian's consent is, after all, a matter of any importance.

Jack. Pray excuse me, Lady Bracknell, for interrupting you again, but it is only fair to tell you that according to the terms of her grandfather's will Miss Cardew does not come legally of age till she is thirty-five.

Lady Bracknell. That does not seem to me to be a grave objection. Thirty-five is a very attractive age. London society is full of women of the very highest birth who have, of their own free choice, remained thirty-five for years. Lady Dumbleton is an instance in point. To my own knowledge she has been thirty-five ever since she arrived at the age of forty, which was many years ago now. I see no reason why our dear Cecily should not be even still more attractive at the age you mention than she is at present. There will be a large accumulation of property.

Cecily. Algy, could you wait for me till I was thirty-five?

Algernon. Of course I could, Cecily. You know I could.

Cecily. Yes, I felt it instinctively, but I couldn't wait all that time. I hate waiting even five minutes for anybody. It always makes me rather cross. I am not punctual myself, I know, but I do like punctuality in others, and waiting, even to be married, is quite out of the question.

Algernon. Then what is to be done, Cecily?

Cecily. I don't know, Mr Moncrieff.

Lady Bracknell. My dear Mr Worthing, as Miss Cardew states positively that she cannot wait till she is thirty-five—a remark which I am bound to say seems to me to show a somewhat impatient nature—I would beg of you to reconsider your decision.

Jack. But my dear Lady Bracknell, the matter is entirely in your own hands. The moment you consent to my marriage with Gwendolen, I will most gladly allow your nephew to form an alliance with my ward.

Lady Bracknell. [*Rising and drawing herself up.*] You must be quite aware that what you propose is out of the question.

Jack. Then a passionate celibacy is all that any of us can look forward to.

Lady Bracknell. That is not the destiny I propose for Gwendolen. Algernon, of course, can choose for himself. [*Pulls out her watch.*] Come, dear, [GWENDOLEN *rises.*] we have already missed five, if not six, trains. To miss any more might expose us to comment on the platform.

[*Enter* DR CHASUBLE.]

Chasuble. Everything is quite ready for the christenings.

Lady Bracknell. The christenings, sir! Is not that somewhat premature?

Chasuble. [*Looking rather puzzled, and pointing to* JACK *and* ALGERNON.] Both these gentlemen have expressed a desire for immediate baptism.

Lady Bracknell. At their age? The idea is grotesque and irreligious! Algernon, I forbid you to be baptized. I will not hear of such excesses. Lord Bracknell would be highly displeased if he learned that that was the way in which you wasted your time and money.

Chasuble. Am I to understand then that there are to be no christenings at all this afternoon?

Jack. I don't think that, as things are now, it would be of much practical value to either of us, Dr Chasuble.

Chasuble. I am grieved to hear such sentiments from you, Mr Worthing. They savour of the heretical views of the Anabaptists, views that I have completely refuted in four of my unpublished sermons. However, as your present mood seems to be one peculiarly secular, I will return to the church at once. Indeed, I have just been informed by the pew-opener that for the last hour and a half Miss Prism has been waiting for me in the vestry.

Lady Bracknell. [*Starting.*] Miss Prism! Did I hear you mention a Miss Prism?

Chasuble. Yes, Lady Bracknell. I am on my way to join her.

Lady Bracknell. Pray allow me to detain you for a moment. This matter may prove to be one of vital importance to Lord Bracknell and myself. Is this Miss Prism a female of repellent aspect, remotely connected with education?

Chasuble. [*Somewhat indignantly.*] She is the most cultivated of ladies, and the very picture of respectability.

Lady Bracknell. It is obviously the same person. May I ask what position she holds in your household?

Chasuble. [*Severely.*] I am a celibate, madam.

Jack. [*Interposing.*] Miss Prism, Lady Bracknell, has been for the last three years Miss Cardew's esteemed governess and valued companion.

Lady Bracknell. In spite of what I hear of her, I must see her at once. Let her be sent for.

Chasuble. [*Looking off.*] She approaches; she is nigh. [*Enter* MISS PRISM *hurriedly.*]

Miss Prism. I was told you expected me in the vestry, dear Canon. I have been waiting for you there for an hour and three-quarters.

[*Catches sight of* LADY BRACKNELL, *who has fixed her with a stony glare.* MISS PRISM *grows pale and quails. She looks anxiously round as if desirous to escape.*]

Lady Bracknell. [*In a severe, judicial voice.*] Prism! [MISS PRISM *bows her head in shame.*] Come here, Prism! [MISS PRISM *approaches in a humble manner.*] Prism! Where is that baby? [*General consternation.* THE CANON *starts back in horror.* ALGERNON *and* JACK *pretend to be anxious to shield* CECILY *and* GWENDOLEN *from hearing the details of a terrible public scandal.*] Twenty-eight years ago, Prism, you left Lord Bracknell's house, Number 104, Upper Grosvenor Square, in charge of a perambulator that contained a baby of the male sex. You never returned. A few weeks later, through the elaborate investigations of the Metropolitan police, the perambulator was discovered at midnight standing by itself in a remote corner of Bayswater. It contained the manuscript of a three-volume novel of more than usually revolting sentimentality. [MISS PRISM *starts in involuntary indignation.*] But the baby was not there. [*Every one looks at* MISS PRISM.] Prism! Where is that baby? [*A pause.*]

Miss Prism. Lady Bracknell, I admit with shame that I do not know. I only wish I did. The plain facts of the case are these. On the morning of the day you mention, a day that is for ever branded on my memory, I prepared as usual to take the baby out in its perambulator. I had also with me a somewhat old, but capacious hand-bag in which I had intended to place the manuscript of a work of fiction that I had written during my few unoccupied hours. In a moment of mental abstraction, for which I can never forgive myself, I deposited the manuscript in the bassinette and placed the baby in the hand-bag.

Jack. [*Who has been listening attentively.*] But where did you deposit the hand-bag?

Miss Prism. Do not ask me, Mr Worthing.

Jack. Miss Prism, this is a matter of no small importance to me. I insist on knowing where you deposited the hand-bag that contained that infant.

Miss Prism. I left it in the cloak-room of one of the larger railway stations in London.

Jack. What railway station?

Miss Prism. [*Quite crushed.*] Victoria. The Brighton line. [*Sinks into a chair.*]

Jack. I must retire to my room for a moment. Gwendolen, wait here for me.

Gwendolen. If you are not too long, I will wait here for you all my life.

[*Exit* JACK *in great excitement.*]

Chasuble. What do you think this means, Lady Bracknell?

Lady Bracknell. I dare not even suspect, Dr Chasuble. I need hardly tell you that in families of high position strange coincidences are not supposed to occur. They are hardly considered the thing.

[*Noises heard overhead as if some one was throwing trunks about. Every one looks up.*]

Cecily. Uncle Jack seems strangely agitated.

Chasuble. Your guardian has a very emotional nature.

Lady Bracknell. This noise is extremely unpleasant. It sounds as if he was having an argument. I dislike arguments of any kind. They are always vulgar, and often convincing.

Chasuble. [*Looking up.*] It has stopped now. [*The noise is redoubled.*]

Lady Bracknell. I wish he would arrive at some conclusion.

Gwendolen. This suspense is terrible. I hope it will last.

[*Enter* JACK *with a hand-bag of black leather in his hand.*]

Jack. [*Rushing over to* MISS PRISM.] Is this the hand-bag, Miss Prism? Examine it carefully before you speak. The happiness of more than one life depends on your answer.

Miss Prism. [*Calmly.*] It seems to be mine. Yes, here is the injury it received through the upsetting of a Gower Street omnibus in younger and happier days. Here is the stain on the lining caused by the explosion of a temperance beverage, an incident that occurred at Leamington. And here, on the lock, are my initials. I had forgotten that in an extravagant mood I had had them placed there. The bag is undoubtedly mine. I am delighted to have it so unexpectedly restored to me. It has been a great inconvenience being without it all these years.

Jack. [*In a pathetic voice.*] Miss Prism, more is restored to you than this hand-bag. I was the baby you placed in it.

Miss Prism. [*Amazed.*] You?

Jack. [*Embracing her.*] Yes . . . mother!

Miss Prism. [*Recoiling in indignant astonishment.*] Mr Worthing. I am unmarried!

Jack. Unmarried! I do not deny that is a serious blow. But after all, who has the right to cast a stone against one who has suffered? Cannot repentance wipe out an act of folly? Why should there be one law for men, and another for women? Mother, I forgive you. [*Tries to embrace her again.*]

Miss Prism. [*Still more indignant.*] Mr Worthing, there is some error. [*Pointing to* LADY BRACKNELL.] There is the lady who can tell you who you really are.

Jack. [*After a pause.*] Lady Bracknell, I hate to seem inquisitive, but would you kindly inform me who I am?

Lady Bracknell. I am afraid that the news I have to give you will not altogether please you. You are the son of my poor sister, Mrs Moncrieff, and consequently Algernon's elder brother.

Jack. Algy's elder brother! Then I have a brother after all. I knew I had a brother! I always said I had a brother! Cecily—how could you have ever doubted that I had a brother? [*Seizes hold of* ALGERNON.] Dr Chasuble, my unfortunate brother. Miss Prism, my unfortunate brother. Gwendolen, my unfortunate brother. Algy, you young scoundrel, you will have to treat me with more respect in the future. You have never behaved to me like a brother in all your life.

Algernon. Well, not till to-day, old boy, I admit. I did my best, however, though I was out of practice. [*Shakes hands.*]

Gwendolen. [*To* JACK.] My own! But what own are you? What is your Christian name, now that you have become some one else?

Jack. Good heavens! . . . I had quite forgotten that point. Your decision on the subject of my name is irrevocable, I suppose?

Gwendolen. I never change, except in my affections.

Cecily. What a noble nature you have, Gwendolen!

Jack. Then the question had better be cleared up at once. Aunt Augusta, a moment. At the time when Miss Prism left me in the hand-bag, had I been christened already?

Lady Bracknell. Every luxury that money could buy, including christening, had been lavished on you by your fond and doting parents.

Jack. Then I was christened! That is settled. Now, what name was I given? Let me know the worst.

Lady Bracknell. Being the eldest son you were naturally christened after your father.

Jack. [*Irritably.*] Yes, but what was my father's Christian name?

Lady Bracknell. [*Meditatively.*] I cannot at the present moment recall what the General's Christian name was. But I have no doubt he had one. He was eccentric, I admit. But only in later years. And that was the result of the Indian climate, and marriage, and indigestion, and other things of that kind.

Jack. Algy! Can't you recollect what our father's Christian name was?

Algernon. My dear boy, we were never even on speaking terms. He died before I was a year old.

Jack. His name would appear in the Army Lists of the period, I suppose, Aunt Augusta?

Lady Bracknell. The General was essentially a man of peace, except in his domestic life. But I have no doubt his name would appear in any military directory.

Jack. The Army Lists of the last forty years are here. These delightful records should have been my constant study. [*Rushes to bookcase and tears the books out.*] M. Generals . . . Mallam, Maxbohm, Magley—what ghastly names they have—Markby, Migsby, Mobbs, Moncrieff! Lieutenant 1840, Captain, Lieutenant-Colonel, Colonel, General 1869, Christian names, Ernest John. [*Puts book very quietly down and speaks quite calmly.*] I always told you, Gwendolen, my name was Ernest, didn't I? Well, it is Ernest after all. I mean it naturally is Ernest.

Lady Bracknell. Yes, I remember now that the General was called Ernest. I knew I had some particular reason for disliking the name.

Gwendolen. Ernest! My own Ernest! I felt from the first that you could have no other name!

Jack. Gwendolen, it is a terrible thing for a man to find out suddenly that all his life he has been speaking nothing but the truth. Can you forgive me?

Gwendolen. I can. For I feel that you are sure to change.

Jack. My own one!

Chasuble. [*To* MISS PRISM.] Laetitia! [*Embraces her.*]

Miss Prism. [*Enthusiastically.*] Frederick! At last!

Algernon. Cecily! [*Embraces her.*] At last!

Jack. Gwendolen! [*Embraces her.*] At last!

Lady Bracknell. My nephew, you seem to be displaying signs of triviality.

Jack. On the contrary, Aunt Augusta, I've now realized for the first time in my life the vital Importance of Being Earnest.

CURTAIN

UNCLE VANYA*

Scenes from Country Life

By

ANTON P. CHEKHOV

Translated by MARIAN FELL

CHEKHOV'S FEELING TOWARD THE THE-atre and playwriting was curious. He seems always to have felt distrust of them, in relation at least to his own work. Though he began writing plays as early as he began to write at all, he usually destroyed his work. As late as September, 1887, he wrote, "I will not write any play. I have absolutely no interest in the theatre, nor in humanity." But, persuaded by his friends, and by the opportunity for making money, he wrote *Ivanov*, his first full-length play, in two weeks during October, 1887. Then he had fits of nervousness lest the play should be inadequately mounted and acted. He could only with difficulty be persuaded that in performance it had been a marked success. These fears, the counterpart, no doubt, of the highest hopes, became habitual with him in regard to all his plays. By his short stories he had early won reputation, and he thought of his work in that form with more confidence, but he said, "The novel is a lawful wife, but the stage is a noisy, flashy, and insolent mistress."

Uncle Vanya, in its original form, was Chekhov's second full-length play. Planned by him in collaboration with A. S. Suvorin, who withdrew, it was entitled *The Wood Demon*, and occupied Chekhov from October, 1888, to October, 1889. He seems at first to have thought well of it, but, when it was not favorably received on performance, to have become quite discouraged. *The Wood Demon* was therefore not printed during his lifetime. But he seems to have kept the manuscript by him, and to have worked over it from time to time, so that in 1897, when an edition of his plays was being published, he decided to include with the already produced *Sea Gull* and *Ivanov* what he called "the universally

unknown *Uncle Vanya*." By means of this publication the play became known, and was frequently played in the provincial theatres of Russia during 1898, and by the Moscow Art Theatre in 1899.

The steps in the development of *Uncle Vanya* from synopsis through *The Wood Demon* to the form in which we now have it may be fairly easily traced, by reference to Chekhov's letters and the still extant early play. Through them it may be seen how consistently Chekhov moved toward economy and force: by elimination of unnecessary characters, by tautening emotion, by subtilizing action, by giving the whole an allegorical value. The early play has thirteen speaking characters, the revision only nine; in *The Wood Demon* the quarrel between the professor and his brother-in-law is broken into by the entrance of extraneous people, in *Uncle Vanya* it continues with rising tensity to the attempted murder; and in *The Wood Demon* there is no parallel to the beautiful speech of Sonia which closes *Uncle Vanya*.

Chekhov wrote of his naturalistic technique: "The action goes on quietly and peacefully, and then I give the audience a blow. All my energy is spent on a few really brisk, forceful climaxes; but the bridges joining these are insignificant, loose, not startling."

Chekhov's repute as a playwright is indissolubly connected with the Moscow Art Theatre, and it with him. His plays failed —or seemed to him to fail—until the Moscow Art Theatre produced them. Stanislavsky, whose standing as the greatest twentieth-century director and teacher of actors rests on his work with the Moscow Art Theatre, learned, from his struggle to plumb the depths of Chekhov's plays, the power of trifles, the ways of extracting from slender hints the remoter yet more individual-

---

* Used by permission of Charles Scribner's Sons.

73

izing qualities of character. Yet Stanislavsky, if he had had his way in the beginning, would not have produced Chekhov.

The Moscow Art Theatre resulted from an eighteen-hour talk between Nemirovich-Danchenko, an established novelist and playwright, and Stanislavsky, a wealthy amateur of acting and directing, in the spring of 1897. They felt that the existing theatres of Russia, either state-subsidized or private-commercial, were not doing what ought to be done for theatrical art. Stanislavsky and Nemirovich-Danchenko aimed, through the Moscow Art Theatre, to bring acting, directing, lighting, scenic design, movement, music, all the arts of the theatre, to the highest possible refinement. The division of labor between them was hazy, but as they phrased it at first, Stanislavsky was to have charge of form, Nemirovich-Danchenko of content. It was Nemirovich-Danchenko, therefore, who chose Chekhov's *The Sea Gull* for the Moscow Art Theatre and who kept Stanislavsky at the job of directing the play despite his early objections. But Stanislavsky soon came to like the quiet but profound Chekhov method, and remained one of the dramatist's devoted admirers and disciples during the six years Chekhov lived after the production of *The Sea Gull*.

Uncle Vanya was the second Chekhov play the Moscow Art Theatre produced. The Moscow Art Theatre is a repertory theatre; plays are not given in continuous run but at intervals during a season, as operas appear on the programs of opera houses. The company is a permanent company, not one organized for a single play. This organization, which compelled every member to make himself part of an ensemble but at the same time develop himself so as to bring the ensemble individually valuable qualities, created what during the first quarter of this century was undoubtedly the world's most distinguished acting company. And it was fitting that one of the four or five greatest dramatists of the modern period should have contributed his finest plays to that theatre.

The movement to reorganize the theatre by redefining its aims and by freshening it with new talent appeared in Moscow, therefore, as it had earlier in Paris, in Berlin, in London. As Antoine in Paris had found new French playwrights and had brought Ibsen and Tolstoy to French attention, or Brahm in Berlin had given Hauptmann his start, or Grein in London had discovered Bernard Shaw's playwriting ability, so in Moscow the Art Theatre, non-commercial like the others, brought Gorki into the theatre and gave Andreyev his first production. But the Moscow Art Theatre was also a theatre of the classics, and its audiences could be sure of presentations varied in age, mood, and manner. It was not committed, as other Free Theatres tended to be, to naturalism, though it inevitably felt and responded to the naturalistic tendencies of the age. It did not rely, as the other Free Theatres had to, upon the subscription method of financing, which tries to create a pledged and sympathetic audience in advance, and sometimes succeeds. The Moscow Art Theatre was financed in the early and difficult years by a millionaire patron, Morozov. Perhaps that is why it has outlasted all the other Free Theatres. It imposed upon its company and even upon its audience a discipline unmatched elsewhere in severity and dedication. Tardiness was forbidden either actor or patron; applause and curtain calls were not allowed; there was no interval music. But this discipline persists to this day, not only in Russia, but abroad, in the "Stanislavsky Method," which trains actors' minds, conscious and unconscious, as well as their bodies, to promote their creativity. This widely used method has been perhaps the most famous product of the combination of the Moscow Art Theatre and Chekhov.

ANTON PAVLOVITCH CHEKHOV

Born 1860, Taganrog, Russia.
M.D., University of Moscow, 1884.
1886, First volume of short stories published.
1888, Awarded Pushkin prize.
1898, Began association with the Moscow Art Theatre.
1904, Died of tuberculosis.
Journalist and short-story writer.

PLAYS

1884 *On the High Road* (one act, also translated as *On the Highway*). 1887 *Ivanov*. 1888 *The Tragedian in Spite of Himself* (one act, also translated as *An Unwilling Martyr*). 1888 *The Bear* (one act, also translated as *The Boor*). 1889 *The Wood Demon*. 1889 *That Worthless Fellow Platonov* (unfinished). 1889 *Tatyana Riepin* (one act, continuation of A. S. Suvorin's play of same name). 1889 *The Swan Song* (one act). 1889 *The Proposal* (one act, also translated as *A Marriage Proposal*). 1896 *The Sea Gull*. 1897 *Uncle Vanya* (revision of *The Wood Demon*). 1900 *The Three Sisters*. 1903 *The Jubilee* (one act, also translated as *The Anniversary*). 1903 *The Wedding* (one act). 1904 *The Cherry Orchard* (also translated as *The Cherry Garden*).

WRITINGS ON DRAMA

Chekhov wrote a good deal about the drama and theatre, but it is scattered through his letters. See *Letters on the Short Story, the Drama, and Other Literary Topics, by Chekhov*, edited by Louis S. Friedlander, 1924, especially pp. 113–202; *The Life and Letters of Anton Tchekhov*, edited by S. S. Koteliansky and Philip Tomlinson, n.d.; *Selected Letters of Anton Chekhov*, edited by Lillian Hellman, 1955.

UNCLE VANYA

Characters

ALEXANDER SEREBRAKOFF, *a retired professor.*
HELENA, *his wife, twenty-seven years old.*
SONIA, *his daughter by a former marriage.*
MME. VOITSKAYA, *widow of a privy councilor, and mother of Serebrakoff's first wife.*
IVAN (VANYA) (JEAN) VOITSKI, *her son.*

MICHAEL ASTROFF, *a doctor.*
ILIA (WAFFLES) TELEGIN, *an impoverished landowner.*
MARINA, *an old nurse.*
A WORKMAN.
The scene is laid on SEREBRAKOFF'S *country place.*

ACT FIRST

A country house on a terrace. In front of it a garden. In an avenue of trees, under an old poplar, stands a table set for tea, with a samovar, etc. Some benches and chairs stand near the table. On one of them is lying a guitar. A hammock is swung near the table. It is three o'clock in the afternoon of a cloudy day.
[MARINA, *a quiet, gray-haired, little old woman, is sitting at the table knitting a stocking.* ASTROFF *is walking up and down near her.*]

Marina. [*Pouring some tea into a glass.*] Take a little tea, my son.
Astroff. [*Takes the glass from her unwillingly.*] Somehow, I don't seem to want any.
Marina. Then will you have a little vodka instead?
Astroff. No, I don't drink vodka every day, and besides, it is too hot now. [*A pause.*] Tell me, nurse, how long have we known each other?
Marina. [*Thoughtfully.*] Let me see, how long is it? Lord—help me to remember. You first came here, into our parts—let me think—when was it? Sonia's mother was still alive—it was two winters before she died; that was eleven years ago— [*Thoughtfully.*] perhaps more.
Astroff. Have I changed much since then?
Marina. Oh, yes. You were handsome and young then, and now you are an old man and not handsome any more. You drink, too.
Astroff. Yes, ten years have made me another man. And why? Because I am overworked. Nurse, I am on my feet from dawn till dusk. I know no rest; at night I tremble under my blankets for fear of being dragged

out to visit some one who is sick; I have toiled without repose or a day's freedom since I have known you; could I help growing old? And then, existence is tedious, anyway; it is a senseless, dirty business, this life, and goes heavily. Every one about here is silly, and after living with them for two or three years one grows silly oneself. It is inevitable. [*Twisting his mustache.*] See what a long mustache I have grown. A foolish, long mustache. Yes, I am as silly as the rest, nurse, but not as stupid; no, I have not grown stupid. Thank God, my brain is not addled yet, though my feelings have grown numb. I ask nothing, I need nothing, I love no one, unless it is yourself alone. [*He kisses her head.*] I had a nurse just like you when I was a child.
Marina. Don't you want a bite of something to eat?
Astroff. No. During the third week of Lent I went to the epidemic at Malitskoi. It was eruptive typhoid. The peasants were all lying side by side in their huts, and the calves and pigs were running about the floor among the sick. Such dirt there was, and smoke! Unspeakable! I slaved among these people all day, not a crumb passed my lips, but when I got home there was still no rest for me; a switchman was carried in from the railroad; I laid him on the operating table and he went and died in my arms under chloroform, and then my feelings that should have been deadened awoke again, my conscience tortured me as if I had killed the man. I sat down and closed my eyes—like this—and thought: will our descendants two hundred years from now, for whom we are breaking the road, remember to give us a

76

:ind word? No, nurse, they will forget.

Marina. Man is forgetful, but God re-
nembers.

Astroff. Thank you for that. You have
poken the truth.

[*Enter* VOITSKI *from the house. He has
been asleep after dinner and looks rather
disheveled. He sits down on the bench
and straightens his collar.*]

Voitski. H'm. Yes. [*A pause.*] Yes.

Astroff. Have you been asleep?

Voitski. Yes, very much so. [*He yawns.*]
Ever since the professor and his wife have
come, our daily life seems to have jumped
the track. I sleep at the wrong time, drink
wine, and eat all sorts of messes for luncheon
and dinner. It isn't wholesome. Sonia and I
used to work together and never had an idle
moment, but now Sonia works alone and I
only eat and drink and sleep. Something is
wrong.

Marina. [*Shakes her head.*] Such a confusion in the house! The professor gets up
at twelve, the samovar is kept boiling all the
morning, and everything has to wait for him.
Before they came we used to have dinner at
one o'clock, like everybody else, but now we
have it at seven. The professor sits up all
night writing and reading, and suddenly, at
two o'clock, there goes the bell! Heavens,
what is that? The professor wants some tea!
Wake the servants, light the samovar! Lord,
what disorder!

Astroff. Will they be here long?

Voitski. A hundred years! The professor
has decided to make his home here.

Marina. Look at this now! The samovar
has been on the table for two hours, and they
are all out walking!

Voitski. All right, don't get excited; here
they come.

[*Voices are heard approaching.* SERE-
BRAKOFF, HELENA, SONIA, *and* TELEGIN
come in from the depths of the garden,
returning from their walk.*]

Serebrakoff. Superb! Superb! What beautiful views!

Telegin. They are wonderful, your Excellency.

Sonia. Tomorrow we shall go into the
woods, shall we, papa?

Voitski. Ladies and gentlemen, tea is
ready.

Serebrakoff. Won't you please be good
enough to send my tea into the library? I
still have some work to finish.

Sonia. I am sure you will love the woods.

[HELENA, SEREBRAKOFF, *and* SONIA *go
into the house.* TELEGIN *sits down at
the table beside* MARINA.]

Voitski. There goes our learned scholar
on a hot, sultry day like this, in his overcoat
and galoshes and carrying an umbrella!

Astroff. He is trying to take good care of
his health.

Voitski. How lovely she is! How lovely!
I have never in my life seen a more beautiful
woman.

Telegin. Do you know, Marina, that as I
walk in the fields or in the shady garden, as
I look at this table here, my heart swells with
unbounded happiness. The weather is enchanting, the birds are singing, we are all living in peace and contentment—what more
could the soul desire? [*Takes a glass of tea.*]

Voitski. [*Dreaming.*] Such eyes—a
glorious woman!

Astroff. Come, Ivan, tell us something.

Voitski. [*Indolently.*] What shall I tell
you?

Astroff. Haven't you any news for us?

Voitski. No, it is all stale. I am just the
same as usual, or perhaps worse, because I
have become lazy. I don't do anything now
but croak like an old raven. My mother,
the old magpie, is still chattering about the
emancipation of woman, with one eye on her
grave and the other on her learned books, in
which she is always looking for the dawn of
a new life.

Astroff. And the professor?

Voitski. The professor sits in his library
from morning till night, as usual——

"Straining the mind, wrinkling the brow,
We write, write, write,
Without respite
Or hope of praise in the future or now." [1]

Poor paper! He ought to write his autobiography; he would make a really splendid subject for a book! Imagine it, the life of a
retired professor, as stale as a piece of hard-
tack, tortured by gout, headaches, and rheumatism, his liver bursting with jealousy and
envy, living on the estate of his first wife,
although he hates it, because he can't afford
to live in town. He is everlastingly whining
about his hard lot, though, as a matter of
fact, he is extraordinarily lucky. He is the
son of a common deacon and has attained
the professor's chair, become the son-in-law
of a senator, is called "your Excellency,"
and so on. But I'll tell you something; the
man has been writing on art for twenty-five
years, and he doesn't know the very first
thing about it. For twenty-five years he has
been chewing on other men's thoughts about
realism, naturalism, and all such foolishness;
for twenty-five years he has been reading and

---

[1] Quotation from Dmitriev (1794).

writing things that clever men have long known and stupid ones are not interested in; for twenty-five years he has been making his imaginary mountains out of molehills. And just think of the man's self-conceit and presumption all this time! For twenty-five years he has been masquerading in false clothes and has now retired, absolutely unknown to any living soul; and yet see him! Stalking across the earth like a demi-god!

Astroff. I believe you envy him.

Voitsky. Yes, I do. Look at the success he has had with women! Don Juan himself was not more favored. His first wife, who was my sister, was a beautiful, gentle being, as pure as the blue heaven there above us, noble, great-hearted, with more admirers than he has pupils, and she loved him as only beings of angelic purity can love those who are as pure and beautiful as themselves. His mother-in-law, my mother, adores him to this day, and he still inspires a sort of worshipful awe in her. His second wife is, as you see, a brilliant beauty; she married him in his old age and has surrendered all the glory of her beauty and freedom to him. Why? What for?

Astroff. Is she faithful to him?

Voitski. Yes, unfortunately she is.

Astroff. Why "unfortunately"?

Voitski. Because such fidelity is false and unnatural, root and branch. It sounds well, but there is no logic in it. It is thought immoral for a woman to deceive an old husband whom she hates, but quite moral for her to strangle her poor youth in her breast and banish every vital desire from her heart.

Telegin. [*In a tearful voice.*] Vanya, I don't like to hear you talk so. Listen, Vanya; every one who betrays husband or wife is faithless, and could also betray his country.

Voitski. [*Crossly.*] Turn off the tap, Waffles.

Telegin. No, allow me, Vanya. My wife ran away with a lover on the day after our wedding, because my exterior was unprepossessing. I have never failed in my duty since then. I love her and am true to her to this day. I help her all I can and have given my fortune to educate the daughter of herself and her lover. I have forfeited my happiness, but I have kept my pride. And she? Her youth has fled, her beauty has faded according to the laws of nature, and her lover is dead. What has she kept?

[HELENA *and* SONIA *come in; after them comes* MME. VOITSKAYA *carrying a book. She sits down and begins to read. Some one hands her a glass of tea, which she drinks without looking up.*]

Sonia. [*Hurriedly, to the* NURSE.] There are some peasants waiting out there. Go and see what they want. I shall pour the tea. [*Pours out some glasses of tea.*]

[MARINA *goes out.* HELENA *takes a glass and sits drinking in the hammock.*]

Astroff. I have come to see your husband. You wrote me that he had rheumatism and I know not what else, and that he was very ill, but he appears to be as lively as a cricket.

Helena. He had a fit of the blues yesterday evening and complained of pains in his legs, but he seems all right again today.

Astroff. And I galloped over here twenty miles at breakneck speed! No matter, though, it is not the first time. Once here, however, I am going to stay until tomorrow, and at any rate sleep *quantum satis.*

Sonia. Oh, splendid! You so seldom spend the night with us. Have you had dinner yet?

Astroff. No.

Sonia. Good. So you will have it with us. We dine at seven now. [*Drinks her tea.*] This tea is cold!

Telegin. Yes, the samovar has grown cold.

Helena. Don't mind, Monsieur Ivan, we will drink cold tea, then.

Telegin. I beg your pardon, my name is not Ivan, but Ilia, ma'am—Ilia Telegin, or Waffles, as I am sometimes called an account of my pock-marked face. I am Sonia's godfather, and his Excellency, your husband, knows me very well. I now live with you, ma'am, on this estate, and perhaps you will be so good as to notice that I dine with you every day.

Sonia. He is our great help, our right-hand man. [*Tenderly.*] Dear godfather, let me pour you some tea.

Mme. Voitskaya. Oh! Oh!

Sonia. What is it, grandmother?

Mme. Voitskaya. I forgot to tell Alexander—I have lost my memory—I received a letter today from Paul Alexevitch in Kharkoff. He has sent me a new pamphlet.

Astroff. Is it interesting?

Mme. Voitskaya. Yes, but strange. He refutes the very theories which he defended seven years ago. It is appalling!

Voitski. There is nothing appalling about it. Drink your tea, mamma.

Mme. Voitskaya. It seems you never want to listen to what I have to say. Pardon me, Jean, but you have changed so in the last year that I hardly know you. You used to be a man of settled convictions and had an illuminating personality——

Voitski. Oh, yes. I had an illuminating personality, which illuminated no one. [*A pause.*] I had an illuminating personality!

You couldn't say anything more biting. I am forty-seven years old. Until last year I endeavored, as you do now, to blind my eyes by your pedantry to the truths of life. But now— Oh, if you only knew! If you knew how I lie awake at night, heartsick and angry, to think how stupidly I have wasted my time when I might have been winning from life everything which my old age now forbids.

Sonia. Uncle Vanya, how dreary!

Mme. Voitskaya. [*To her* Son.] You speak as if your former convictions were somehow to blame, but you yourself, not they, were at fault. You have forgotten that a conviction, in itself, is nothing but a dead letter. You should have done something.

Voitski. Done something! Not every man is capable of being a writer *perpetuum mobile* like your Herr Professor.

Mme. Voitskaya. What do you mean by that?

Sonia. [*Imploringly.*] Mother! Uncle Vanya! I entreat you!

Voitski. I am silent. I apologize and am silent. [*A pause.*]

Helena. What a fine day! Not too hot. [*A pause.*]

Voitski. A fine day to hang oneself.

[Telegin *tunes the guitar.* Marina *appears near the house, calling the chickens.*]

Marina. Chick, chick, chick!

Sonia. What did the peasants want, nurse?

Marina. The same old thing, the same old nonsense. Chick, chick, chick!

Sonia. Why are you calling the chickens?

Marina. The speckled hen has disappeared with her chicks. I am afraid the crows have got her.

[Telegin *plays a polka. All listen in silence. Enter* Workman.]

Workman. Is the doctor here? [*To* Astroff.] Excuse me, sir, but I have been sent to fetch you.

Astroff. Where are you from?

Workman. The factory.

Astroff. [*Annoyed.*] Thank you. There is nothing for it, then, but to go. [*Looking around him for his cap.*] Damn it, this is annoying!

Sonia. Yes, it is too bad, really. You must come back to dinner from the factory.

Astroff. No, I won't be able to do that. It will be too late. Now where, where— [*To the* Workman.] Look here, my man, get me a glass of vodka, will you? [*The* Workman *goes out.*] Where—where— [*Finds his cap.*] One of the characters in Ostroff's plays is a man with a long mustache and short wits, like me. However, let me bid you good-bye, ladies and gentleman. [*To* Helena.] I should be really delighted if you would come to see me some day with Miss Sonia. My estate is small, but if you are interested in such things I should like to show you a nursery and seed-bed whose like you will not find within a thousand miles of here. My place is surrounded by government forests. The forester is old and always ailing, so I superintend almost all the work myself.

Helena. I have always heard that you were very fond of the woods. Of course one can do a great deal of good by helping to preserve them, but does not that work interfere with your real calling?

Astroff. God alone knows what a man's real calling is.

Helena. And do you find it interesting?

Astroff. Yes, very.

Voitski. [*Sarcastically.*] Oh, extremely!

Helena. You are still young, not over thirty-six or seven, I should say, and I suspect that the woods do not interest you as much as you say they do. I should think you would find them monotonous.

Sonia. No, the work is thrilling. Dr. Astroff watches over the old woods and sets out new plantations every year, and he has already received a diploma and a bronze medal. If you will listen to what he can tell you, you will agree with him entirely. He says that forests are the ornaments of the earth, that they teach mankind to understand beauty and attune his mind to lofty sentiments. Forests temper a stern climate, and in countries where the climate is milder, less strength is wasted in the battle with nature, and the people are kind and gentle. The inhabitants of such countries are handsome, tractable, sensitive, graceful in speech and gesture. Their philosophy is joyous, art and science blossom among them, their treatment of women is full of exquisite nobility——

Voitski. [*Laughing.*] Bravo! Bravo! All that is very pretty, but it is also unconvincing. So my friend [*To* Astroff.], you must let me go on burning firewood in my stoves and building my sheds of planks.

Astroff. You can burn peat in your stoves and build your sheds of stone. Oh, I don't object, of course, to cutting wood from necessity, but why destroy the forests? The woods of Russia are trembling under the blows of the axe. Millions of trees have perished. The homes of the wild animals and birds have been desolated; the rivers are shrinking, and many beautiful landscapes are gone forever. And why? Because men are too lazy and stupid to stoop down and pick up their fuel from the ground. [*To* Helena.]

Am I not right, Madame? Who but a stupid barbarian could burn so much beauty in his stove and destroy that which he cannot make? Man is endowed with reason and the power to create, so that he may increase that which has been given him, but until now he had not created, but demolished. The forests are disappearing, the rivers are running dry, the game is exterminated, the climate is spoiled, and the earth becomes poorer and uglier every day. [*To* Voitski.] I read irony in your eye; you do not take what I am saying seriously, and—and—after all, it may very well be nonsense. But when I pass peasant-forests that I have preserved from the axe, or hear the rustling of the young plantations set out with my own hands, I feel as if I had had some small share in improving the climate, and that if mankind is happy a thousand years from now I will have been a little bit responsible for their happiness. When I plant a little birch tree and then see it budding into young green and swaying in the wind, my heart swells with pride and I— [*Sees the* Workman, *who is bringing him a glass of vodka on a tray.*] However— [*He drinks.*] I must be off. Probably it is all nonsense, anyway. Good-bye.

[*He goes toward the house.* Sonia *takes his arm and goes with him.*]

Sonia. When are you coming to see us again?

Astroff. I can't say.

Sonia. In a month?

[Astroff *and* Sonia *go into the house.* Helena *and* Voitski *walk over to the terrace.*]

Helena. You have behaved shockingly again. Ivan, what sense was there in teasing your mother and talking about *perpetuum mobile?* And at breakfast you quarreled with Alexander again. Really, your behavior is too petty.

Voitski. But if I hate him?

Helena. You hate Alexander without reason; he is like every one else, and no worse than you are.

Voitski. If you could only see your face, your gestures! Oh, how tedious your life must be.

Helena. It is tedious, yes, and dreary! You all abuse my husband and look on me with compassion; you think, "Poor woman, she is married to an old man." How well I understand your compassion! As Astroff said just now, see how you thoughtlessly destroy the forests, so that there will soon be none left. So you also destroy mankind, and soon fidelity and purity and self-sacrifice will have vanished with the woods. Why cannot you look calmly at a woman unless she is yours? Because, the doctor was right, you are all possessed by a devil of destruction; you have no mercy on the woods or the birds or on women or on one another.

Voitski. I don't like your philosophy.

Helena. That doctor has a sensitive, weary face—an interesting face. Sonia evidently likes him, and she is in love with him, and I can understand it. This is the third time he has been here since I have come, and I have not had a real talk with him yet or made much of him. He thinks I am disagreeable. Do you know, Ivan, the reason you and I are such friends? I think it is because we are both lonely and unfortunate. Yes, unfortunate. Don't look at me in that way, I don't like it.

Voitski. How can I look at you otherwise when I love you? You are my joy, my life, and my youth. I know that my chances of being loved in return are infinitely small, do not exist, but I ask nothing of you. Only let me look at you, listen to your voice——

Helena. Hush, some one will overhear you.

[*They go toward the house.*]

Voitski. [*Following her.*] Let me speak to you of my love, do not drive me away, and this alone will be my greatest happiness!

Helena. Ah! This is agony!

[Telegin *strikes the strings of his guitar and plays a polka.* Mme. Voits- kaya *writes something on the leaves of her pamphlet.*]

THE CURTAIN FALLS

ACT SECOND

The dining-room of Serebrakoff's *house.* [*It is night. The tapping of the* Watch- man's *rattle is heard in the garden.* Serebrakoff *is dozing in an armchair by an open window and* Helena *is sit- ting beside him, also half asleep.*]

Serebrakoff. [*Rousing himself.*] Who is here? Is it you, Sonia?

Helena. It is I.

Serebrakoff. Oh, it is you, Nelly. This pain is intolerable.

Helena. Your shawl has slipped down.

[*She wraps up his legs in the shawl.*] Let me shut the window.

Serebrakoff. No, leave it open; I am suffocating. I dreamt just now that my left leg belonged to some one else, and it hurt so that I woke. I don't believe this is gout, it is more like rheumatism. What time is it?

Helena. Half-past twelve. [*A pause.*]

Serebrakoff. I want you to look for Batushka's works in the library tomorrow. I think we have him.

Helena. What is that?

Serebrakoff. Look for Batushka tomorrow morning; we used to have him, I remember. Why do I find it so hard to breathe?

Helena. You are tired; this is the second night you have had no sleep.

Serebrakoff. They say that Turgenieff got angina of the heart from gout. I am afraid I am getting angina too. Oh, damn this horrible, accursed old age! Ever since I have been old I have been hateful to myself, and I am sure, hateful to you all as well.

Helena. You speak as if we were to blame for your being old.

Serebrakoff. I am more hateful to you than to any one.

[HELENA *gets up and walks away from him, sitting down at a distance.*]

Serebrakoff. You are quite right, of course. I am not an idiot; I can understand you. You are young and healthy and beautiful, and longing for life, and I am an old dotard, almost a dead man already. Don't I know it? Of course I see that it is foolish for me to live so long, but wait! I shall soon set you all free. My life cannot drag on much longer.

Helena. You are overtaxing my powers of endurance. Be quiet, for God's sake!

Serebrakoff. It appears that, thanks to me, everybody's power of endurance is being overtaxed; everybody is miserable, only I am blissfully triumphant. Oh, yes, of course!

Helena. Be quiet! You are torturing me.

Serebrakoff. I torture everybody. Of course.

Helena. [*Weeping.*] This is unbearable! Tell me, what is it you want me to do?

Serebrakoff. Nothing.

Helena. Then be quiet, please.

Serebrakoff. It is funny that everybody listens to Ivan and his old idiot of a mother, but the moment I open my lips you all begin to feel ill-treated. You can't even stand the sound of my voice. Even if I am hateful, even if I am a selfish tyrant, haven't I the right to be one at my age? Haven't I deserved it? Haven't I, I ask you, the right to be respected, now that I am old?

Helena. No one is disputing your rights. [*The window slams in the wind.*] The wind is rising, I must shut the window. [*She shuts it.*] We shall have rain in a moment. Your rights have never been questioned by anybody.

[*The* WATCHMAN *in the garden sounds his rattle.*]

Serebrakoff. I have spent my life working in the interests of learning. I am used to my library and the lecture hall and to the esteem and admiration of my colleagues. Now I suddenly find myself plunged in this wilderness, condemned to see the same stupid people from morning till night and listen to their futile conversation. I want to live; I long for success and fame and the stir of the world, and here I am in exile! Oh, it is dreadful to spend every moment grieving for the lost past, to see the success of others and sit here with nothing to do but to fear death. I cannot stand it! It is more than I can bear. And you will not even forgive me for being old!

Helena. Wait, have patience; I shall be old myself in four or five years.

[SONIA *comes in.*]

Sonia. Father, you sent for Dr. Astroff, and now when he comes you refuse to see him. It is not nice to give a man so much trouble for nothing.

Serebrakoff. What do I care about your Astroff? He understands medicine about as well as I understand astronomy.

Sonia. We can't send for the whole medical faculty, can we, to treat your gout?

Serebrakoff. I won't talk to that madman!

Sonia. Do as you please. It's all the same to me. [*She sits down.*]

Serebrakoff. What time is it?

Helena. One o'clock.

Serebrakoff. It is stifling in here. Sonia, hand me that bottle on the table.

Sonia. Here it is.

[*She hands him a bottle of medicine.*]

Serebrakoff. [*Crossly.*] No, not that one! Can't you understand me? Can't I ask you to do a thing?

Sonia. Please don't be captious with me. Some people may like it, but you must spare me, if you please, because I don't. Besides, I haven't the time; we are cutting the hay tomorrow and I must get up early.

[VOITSKI *comes in dressed in a long gown and carrying a candle.*]

Voitski. A thunderstorm is coming up. [*The lightning flashes.*] There it is! Go to bed, Helena and Sonia. I have come to take your place.

Serebrakoff. [*Frightened.*] No, no, no!

Don't leave me alone with him! Oh, don't. He will begin to lecture me.

Voitski. But you must give them a little rest. They have not slept for two nights.

Serebrakoff. Then let them go to bed, but you go away too! Thank you. I implore you to go. For the sake of our former friendship do not protest against going. We will talk some other time——

Voitski. Our former friendship! Our former——

Sonia. Hush, Uncle Vanya!

Serebrakoff. [*To his* WIFE.] My darling, don't leave me alone with him. He will begin to lecture me.

Voitski. This is ridiculous.

[MARINA *comes in carrying a candle.*]

Sonia. You must go to bed, nurse, it is late.

Marina. I haven't cleared away the tea things. Can't go to bed yet.

Serebrakoff. No one can go to bed. They are all worn out, only I enjoy perfect happiness.

Marina. [*Goes up to* SEREBRAKOFF *and speaks tenderly.*] What's the matter, master? Does it hurt? My own legs are aching too, oh, so badly. [*Arranges his shawl about his legs.*] You have had this illness such a long time. Sonia's dead mother used to stay awake with you too, and wear herself out for you. She loved you dearly. [*A pause.*] Old people want to be pitied as much as young ones, but nobody cares about them, somehow. [*She kisses* SEREBRAKOFF'S *shoulder.*] Come, master, let me give you some linden-tea and warm your poor feet for you. I shall pray to God for you.

Serebrakoff. [*Touched.*] Let us go, Marina.

Marina. My own feet are aching so badly, oh, so badly! [*She and* SONIA *lead* SEREBRAKOFF *out.*] Sonia's mother used to wear herself out with sorrow and weeping. You were still little and foolish then, Sonia. Come, come, master.

[SEREBRAKOFF, SONIA, *and* MARINA *go out.*]

Helena. I am absolutely exhausted by him, and can hardly stand.

Voitski. You are exhausted by him, and I am exhausted by my own self. I have not slept for three nights.

Helena. Something is wrong in this house. Your mother hates everything but her pamphlets and the professor; the professor is vexed, he won't trust me, and fears you; Sonia is angry with her father, and with me, and hasn't spoken to me for two weeks! I am at the end of my strength, and have come near bursting into tears at least twenty times today. Something is wrong in this house.

Voitski. Leave speculating alone.

Helena. You are cultured and intelligent, Ivan, and you surely understand that the world is not destroyed by villains and conflagrations, but by hate and malice and all this spiteful tattling. It is your duty to make peace, and not to growl at everything.

Voitski. Help me first to make peace with myself. My darling! [*Seizes her hand.*]

Helena. Let go! [*She drags her hand away.*] Go away!

Voitski. Soon the rain will be over, and all nature will sigh and awake refreshed. Only I am not refreshed by the storm. Day and night the thought haunts me like a fiend, that my life is lost forever. My past does not count, because I frittered it away on trifles, and the present has so terribly miscarried! What shall I do with my life and my love? What is to become of them? This wonderful feeling of mine will be wasted and lost as a ray of sunlight is lost that falls into a dark chasm, and my life will go with it.

Helena. I am as it were benumbed when you speak to me of your love, and I don't know how to answer you. Forgive me, I have nothing to say to you. [*She tries to go out.*] Good night!

Voitski. [*Barring the way.*] If you only knew how I am tortured by the thought that beside me in this house is another life that is being lost forever—it is yours! What are you waiting for? What accursed philosophy stands in your way? Oh, understand, understand——

Helena. [*Looking at him intently.*] Ivan, you are drunk!

Voitski. Perhaps. Perhaps.

Helena. Where is the doctor?

Voitski. In there, spending the night with me. Perhaps I am drunk, perhaps I am; nothing is impossible.

Helena. Have you just been drinking together? Why do you do that?

Voitski. Because in that way I get a taste of life. Let me do it, Helena!

Helena. You never used to drink, and you never used to talk so much. Go to bed, I am tired of you.

Voitski. [*Falling on his knees before her.*] My sweetheart, my beautiful one——

Helena. [*Angrily.*] Leave me alone! Really, this has become too disagreeable.

[HELENA *goes out. A pause.*]

Voitski. [*Alone.*] She is gone! I met her first ten years ago, at her sister's house, when she was seventeen and I was thirty-seven. Why did I not fall in love with her then and ropose to her? It would have been so easy! And now she would have been my wife. Yes, we would both have been waked tonight by the thunderstorm, and she would have been frightened, but I would have held her in my arms and whispered: "Don't be afraid! I am here." Oh, enchanting dream, so sweet that I laugh to think of it. [*He laughs.*] But my God! My head reels! Why am I so old? Why won't she understand me? I hate all that rhetoric of hers, that morality of insolence, that absurd talk about the destruction of the world—— [*A pause.*] Oh, how I have been deceived! For years I have worshiped that miserable gout-ridden professor. Sonia and I have squeezed this estate dry for his sake. We have bartered our butter and curds and peas like misers, and have never kept a morsel for ourselves, so that we could scrape enough pennies together to send to him. I was proud of him and of his learning; I received all his words and writings as inspired, and now? Now he has retired, and what is the total of his life? A blank! He is absolutely unknown, and his fame has burst like a soap-bubble. I have been deceived; I see that now, basely deceived.

[ASTROFF *comes in. He has his coat on, but is without his waistcoat or collar, and is slightly drunk.* TELEGIN *follows him, carrying a guitar.*]

Astroff. Play!

Telegin. But every one is asleep.

Astroff. Play!

[TELEGIN *begins to play softly.*]

Astroff. Are you alone here? No women about? [*Sings with his arms akimbo.*] "The hut is cold, the fire is dead; Where shall the master lay his head?" The thunderstorm woke me. It was a heavy shower. What time is it?

Voitski. The devil only knows.

Astroff. I thought I heard Helena's voice.

Voitski. She was here a moment ago.

Astroff. What a beautiful woman! [*Looking at the medicine bottles on the table.*] Medicine, is it? What a variety we have; prescriptions from Moscow, from Kharkoff, from Tula! Why, he has been pestering all the towns of Russia with his gout! Is he ill, or simply shamming?

Voitski. He is really ill.

Astroff. What is the matter with you tonight? You seem sad. Is it because you are sorry for the professor?

Voitski. Leave me alone.

Astroff. Or in love with the professor's wife?

Voitski. She is my friend.

Astroff. Already?

Voitski. What do you mean by "already"?

Astroff. A woman can only become a man's friend after having first been his acquaintance and then his beloved—then she becomes his friend.

Voitski. What vulgar philosophy!

Astroff. What do you mean? Yes, I must confess I am getting vulgar, but then, you see, I am drunk. I usually only drink like this once a month. At such times my audacity and temerity know no bounds. I feel capable of anything. I attempt the most difficult operations and do them magnificently. The most brilliant plans for the future take shape in my head. I am no longer a poor fool of a doctor, but mankind's greatest benefactor. I evolve my own system of philosophy and all of you seem to crawl at my feet like so many insects or microbes. [*To* TELEGIN.] Play, Waffles!

Telegin. My dear boy, I would with all my heart, but do listen to reason; everybody in the house is asleep.

Astroff. Play! [TELEGIN *plays softly.*]

Astroff. I want a drink. Come, we still have some brandy left. And then, as soon as it is day, you will come home with me.

[*He sees* SONIA, *who comes in at that moment.*]

Astroff. I beg your pardon, I have no collar on.

[*He goes out quickly, followed by* TELEGIN.]

Sonia. Uncle Vanya, you and the doctor have been drinking! The good fellows have been getting together! It is all very well for him, he has always done it, but why do you follow his example? It looks dreadful at your age.

Voitski. Age has nothing to do with it. When real life is wanting one must create an illusion. It is better than nothing.

Sonia. Our hay is all cut and rotting in these daily rains, and here you are busy creating illusions! You have given up the farm altogether. I have done all the work alone until I am at the end of my strength— [*Frightened.*] Uncle! Your eyes are full of tears!

Voitski. Tears? Nonsense, there are no tears in my eyes. You looked at me then just as your dead mother used to, my darling —— [*He eagerly kisses her face and hands.*] My sister, my dearest sister, where are you now? Ah, if you only knew, if you only knew!

Sonia. If she only knew what, Uncle?

Voitski. My heart is bursting. It is awful. No matter, though. I must go.

[*He goes out.*]

Sonia. [*Knocks at the door.*] Dr. Astroff! Are you awake? Please come here for a minute.

Astroff. [*Behind the door.*] In a moment.

[*He appears in a few seconds. He has put on his collar and waistcoat.*]

Astroff. What do you want?

Sonia. Drink as much as you please yourself, if you don't find it revolting, but I implore you not to let my uncle do it. It is bad for him.

Astroff. Very well; we won't drink any more. I am going home at once. That is settled. It will be dawn by the time the horses are harnessed.

Sonia. It is still raining; wait till morning.

Astroff. The storm is blowing over. This is only the edge of it. I must go. And please don't ask me to come and see your father any more. I tell him he has gout, and he says it is rheumatism. I tell him to lie down, and he sits up. Today he refused to see me at all.

Sonia. He has been spoilt. [*She looks in the sideboard.*] Won't you have a bite to eat?

Astroff. Yes, please. I believe I will.

Sonia. I love to eat at night. I am sure we shall find something in here. They say that he has made a great many conquests in his life, and that the women have spoiled him. Here is some cheese for you.

[*They stand eating by the sideboard.*]

Astroff. I haven't eaten anything today. Your father has a very difficult nature. [*He takes a bottle out of the sideboard.*] May I? [*He pours himself a glass of vodka.*] We are alone here, and I can speak frankly. Do you know, I could not stand living in this house for even a month? This atmosphere would stifle me. There is your father, entirely absorbed in his books, and his gout; there is your Uncle Vanya with his hypochondria, your grandmother, and finally, your stepmother——

Sonia. What about her?

Astroff. A human being should be entirely beautiful: the face, the clothes, the mind, the thoughts. Your step-mother is, of course, beautiful to look at, but don't you see? She does nothing but sleep and eat and walk and bewitch us, and that is all. She has no responsibilities, everything is done for her—am I not right? And an idle life can never be a pure one. [*A pause.*] However, I may be judging her too severely. Like your Uncle Vanya, I am discontented, and so we are both grumblers.

Sonia. Aren't you satisfied with life?

Astroff. I like life as life, but I hate and despise it in a little Russian country village, and as far as my own personal life goes, by heaven! there is absolutely no redeeming feature about it. Haven't you noticed if you are riding through a dark wood at night and see a little light shining ahead, how you forget your fatigue and the darkness and the sharp twigs that whip your face? I work— that you know—as no one else in the country works. Fate beats me on without rest; at times I suffer unendurably and I see no light ahead. I have no hope; I do not like people. It is long since I have loved any one.

Sonia. You love no one?

Astroff. Not a soul. I only feel a sort of tenderness for your old nurse for old-times' sake. The peasants are all alike; they are stupid and live in dirt, and the educated people are hard to get along with. One gets tired of them. All our good friends are petty and shallow and see no farther than their own noses; in one word, they are dull. Those that have brains are hysterical, devoured with a mania for self-analysis. They whine, they hate, they pick faults everywhere with unhealthy sharpness. They sneak up to me sideways, look at me out of a corner of the eye, and say: "That man is a lunatic," "That man is a wind-bag." Or, if they don't know what else to label me with, they say I am strange. I like the woods; that is strange. I don't eat meat; that is strange, too. Simple, natural relations between man and man or man and nature do not exist.

[*He tries to go out;* Sonia *prevents him.*]

Sonia. I beg you, I implore you, not to drink any more!

Astroff. Why not?

Sonia. It is so unworthy of you. You are well-bred, your voice is sweet, you are even —more than any one I know—handsome. Why do you want to resemble the common people that drink and play cards? Oh, don't, I beg you! You always say that people do not create anything, but only destroy what heaven has given them. Why, oh why, do you destroy yourself? Oh, don't, I implore you not to! I entreat you!

Astroff. [*Gives her his hand.*] I won't drink any more.

Sonia. Promise me.

Astroff. I give you my word of honor.

Sonia. [*Squeezing his hand.*] Thank you.

Astroff. I have done with it. You see, I

m perfectly sober again, and so I shall stay
till the end of my life. [*He looks at his
watch.*] But, as I was saying, life holds nothing for me; my race is run. I am old, I am
tired, I am trivial; my sensibilities are dead.
I could never attach myself to any one again.
I love no one, and—never shall! Beauty
alone has the power to touch me still. I am
deeply moved by it. Helena could turn my
head in a day if she wanted to, but that is
not love, that is not affection——

[*He shudders and covers his face with
his hands.*]

Sonia. What is it?

Astroff. Nothing. During Lent one of my
patients died under chloroform.

Sonia. It is time to forget that. [*A pause.*]
Tell me, doctor, if I had a friend or a
younger sister, and if you knew that she, well
—loved you, what would you do?

Astroff. [*Shrugging his shoulders.*] I
don't know. I don't think I should do anything. I should make her understand that I
could not return her love—however, my
mind is not bothered about those things now.
I must start at once if I am ever to get off.
Good-bye, my dear girl. At this rate we shall
stand here talking till morning. [*He shakes
hands with her.*] I shall go out through the
sitting-room, because I am afraid your uncle
might detain me. [*He goes out.*]

Sonia. [*Alone.*] Not a word! His heart
and soul are still locked from me, and yet
for some reason I am strangely happy. I
wonder why? [*She laughs with pleasure.*] I
told him that he was well-bred and handsome
and that his voice was sweet. Was that a
mistake? I can still feel his voice vibrating
in the air; it caresses me. [*Wringing her
hands.*] Oh! how terrible it is to be plain!
I am plain, I know it. As I came out of
church last Sunday I overheard a woman say,
"She is a dear, noble girl, but what a pity
she is so ugly!" So ugly!

[HELENA *comes in and throws open the
window.*]

Helena. The storm is over. What de-
licious air! [*A pause.*] Where is the doctor?

Sonia. He has gone. [*A pause.*]

Helena. Sonia!

Sonia. Yes?

Helena. How much longer are you going
to sulk at me? We have not hurt each
other. Why not be friends? We have had
enough of this.

Sonia. I myself— [*She embraces* HEL-
ENA.] Let us make peace.

Helena. With all my heart.

[*They are both moved.*]

Sonia. Has papa gone to bed?

Helena. No, he is sitting up in the drawing-room. Heaven knows what reason you
and I had for not speaking to each other for
weeks. [*Sees the open sideboard.*] Who left
the sideboard open?

Sonia. Dr. Astroff has just had supper.

Helena. There is some wine. Let us seal
our friendship.

Sonia. Yes, let us.

Helena. Out of one glass. [*She fills a
wine-glass.*] So, we are friends, are we?

Sonia. Yes. [*They drink and kiss each
other.*] I have long wanted to make friends,
but somehow, I was ashamed to.

[*She weeps.*]

Helena. Why are you crying?

Sonia. I don't know. It is nothing.

Helena. There, there, don't cry. [*She
weeps.*] Silly! Now I am crying too. [*A
pause.*] You are angry with me because I
seem to have married your father for his
money, but don't believe the gossip you hear.
I swear to you I married him for love. I was
fascinated by his fame and learning. I know
now that it was not real love, but it seemed
real at the time. I am innocent, and yet your
clever, suspicious eyes have been punishing
me for an imaginary crime ever since my
marriage.

Sonia. Peace, peace! Let us forget the
past.

Helena. You must not look so at people.
It is not becoming to you. You must trust
people, or life becomes impossible.

Sonia. Tell me truly, as a friend, are you
happy?

Helena. Truly, no.

Sonia. I knew it. One more question: do
you wish your husband were young?

Helena. What a child you are! Of course
I do. Go on, ask something else.

Sonia. Do you like the doctor?

Helena. Yes, very much indeed.

Sonia. [*Laughing.*] I have a stupid face,
haven't I? He has just gone out, and his
voice is still in my ears; I hear his step; I see
his face in the dark window. Let me say all
I have in my heart! But no, I cannot speak
of it so loudly. I am ashamed. Come to my
room and let me tell you there. I seem
foolish to you, don't I? Talk to me of him.

Helena. What can I say?

Sonia. He is clever. He can do everything.
He can cure the sick, and plant woods.

Helena. It is not a question of medicine
and woods, my dear; he is a man of genius.
Do you know what that means? It means he
is brave, profound, and of clear insight. He
plants a tree and his mind travels a thousand

years into the future, and he sees visions of the happiness of the human race. People like him are rare and should be loved. What if he does drink and act roughly at times? A man of genius cannot be a saint in Russia. There he lives, cut off from the world by cold and storm and endless roads of bottomless mud, surrounded by a rough people who are crushed by poverty and disease, his life one continuous struggle, with never a day's respite; how can a man live like that for forty years and keep himself sober and unspotted? [*Kissing* SONIA.] I wish you happiness with all my heart; you deserve it. [*She gets up.*] As for me, I am a worthless, futile woman. I have always been futile; in music, in love, in my husband's house—in a word, in everything. When you come to think of it, Sonia, I am really very, very unhappy. [*Walks excitedly up and down.*] Happiness can never exist for me in this world. Never. Why do you laugh?

Sonia. [*Laughing and covering her face*

with her hands.] I am so happy, so happy!

Helena. I want to hear music. I might play a little.

Sonia. Oh, do, do! [*She embraces her.*] I could not possibly go to sleep now. Do play!

Helena. Yes, I will. Your father is still awake. Music irritates him when he is ill, but if he says I may, then I shall play a little. Go, Sonia, and ask him.

Sonia. Very well.

[*She goes out. The* WATCHMAN'S *rattle is heard in the garden.*]

Helena. It is long since I have heard music. And now, I shall sit and play, and weep like a fool. [*Speaking out of the window.*] Is that you rattling out there, Ephim?

Voice of the Watchman. It is I.

Helena. Don't make such a noise. Your master is ill.

Voice of the Watchman. I am going away this minute.   [*Whistles a tune.*]

Sonia. [*Comes back.*] He says no.

THE CURTAIN FALLS

ACT THIRD

The drawing-room of SEREBRAKOFF'S *house.* [*There are three doors: one to the right, one to the left, and one in the center of the room.* VOITSKI *and* SONIA *are sitting down.* HELENA *is walking up and down, absorbed in thought.*]

Voitski. We were asked by the professor to be here at one o'clock. [*Looks at his watch.*] It is now a quarter to one. It seems he has some communication to make to the world.

Helena. Probably a matter of business.

Voitski. He never had any business. He writes twaddle, grumbles, and eats his heart out with jealousy; that's all he does.

Sonia. [*Reproachfully.*] Uncle!

Voitski. All right. I beg your pardon. [*He points to* HELENA.] Look at her. Wandering up and down from sheer idleness. A sweet picture, really.

Helena. I wonder you are not bored, droning on in the same key from morning till night. [*Despairingly.*] I am dying of this tedium. What shall I do?

Sonia. [*Shrugging her shoulders.*] There is plenty to do if you would.

Helena. For instance?

Sonia. You could help run this place,

teach the children, care for the sick—isn't that enough? Before you and papa came, Uncle Vanya and I used to go to market ourselves to deal in flour.

Helena. I don't know anything about such things, and besides, they don't interest me. It is only in novels that women go out and teach and heal the peasants; how can I suddenly begin to do it?

Sonia. How can you live here and not do it? Wait awhile, you will get used to it all. [*Embraces her.*] Don't be sad, dearest. [*Laughing.*] You feel miserable and restless, and can't seem to fit into this life, and your restlessness is catching. Look at Uncle Vanya, he does nothing now but haunt you like a shadow, and I have left my work to-day to come here and talk with you. I am getting lazy, and don't want to go on with it. Dr. Astroff hardly ever used to come here; it was all we could do to persuade him to visit us once a month, and now he has abandoned his forestry and his practice, and comes every day. You must be a witch.

Voitski. Why should you languish here? Come, my dearest, my beauty, be sensible! The blood of a nixie runs in your veins. Oh, won't you let yourself be one? Give your nature the reins for once in your life; fall

ead over ears in love with some other water
prite and plunge down head first into a deep
ool, so that the Herr Professor and all of us
may have our hands free again.

Helena. [*Angrily.*] Leave me alone! How
ruel you are! [*She tries to go out.*]

Voitski. [*Preventing her.*] There, there,
my beauty, I apologize. [*He kisses her
and.*] Forgive me.

Helena. Confess that you would try the
patience of an angel.

Voitski. As a peace offering I am going to
etch some flowers which I picked for you
his morning: some autumn roses, beautiful,
sorrowful roses. [*He goes out.*]

Sonia. Autumn roses, beautiful, sorrowful
roses!

[*She and* HELENA *stand looking out of
the window.*]

Helena. September already! How shall we
live through the long winter here? [*A
pause.*] Where is the doctor?

Sonia. He is writing in Uncle Vanya's
room. I am glad Uncle Vanya has gone out,
I want to talk to you about something.

Helena. About what?

Sonia. About what?

[*She lays her head on* HELENA'S *breast.*]

Helena. [*Stroking her hair.*] There, there,
that will do. Don't, Sonia.

Sonia. I am ugly!

Helena. You have lovely hair.

Sonia. Don't say that! [*She turns to look
at herself in the glass.*] No, when a woman
is ugly they always say she has beautiful hair
or eyes. I have loved him now for six years;
I have loved him more than one loves one's
mother. I seem to hear him beside me every
moment of the day. I feel the pressure of
his hand on mine. If I look up, I seem to see
him coming, and as you see, I run to you to
talk of him. He is here every day now, but
he never looks at me, he does not notice my
presence. It is agony. I have absolutely no
hope; no, no hope. Oh, my God! Give me
strength to endure. I prayed all last night.
I often go up to him and speak to him and
look into his eyes. My pride is gone. I am
not mistress of myself. Yesterday I told
Uncle Vanya. I couldn't control myself, and
all the servants know it. Every one knows
that I love him.

Helena. Does he?

Sonia. No, he never notices me.

Helena. [*Thoughtfully.*] He is a strange
man. Listen, Sonia, will you allow me to
speak to him? I shall be careful, only hint.
[*A pause.*] Really, to be in uncertainty all
these years! Let me do it!

[SONIA *nods an affirmative.*]

Helena. Splendid! It will be easy to find
out whether he loves you or not. Don't be
ashamed, sweetheart, don't worry. I shall be
careful; he will not notice a thing. We only
want to find out whether it is yes or no, don't
we? [*A pause.*] And if it is no, then he
must keep away from here, is that so?

[SONIA *nods.*]

Helena. It will be easier not to see him
any more. We won't put off the examination an instant. He said he had a sketch to
show me. Go and tell him at once that I
want to see him.

Sonia. [*In great excitement.*] Will you
tell me the whole truth?

Helena. Of course I will. I am sure that
no matter what it is, it will be easier for you
to bear than this uncertainty. Trust to me,
dearest.

Sonia. Yes, yes. I shall say that you want
to see his sketch. [*She starts out, but stops
near the door and looks back.*] No, it is
better not to know—and yet—there may be
hope.

Helena. What do you say?

Sonia. Nothing. [*She goes out.*]

Helena. [*Alone.*] There is no greater sorrow than to know another's secret when you
cannot help them. [*In deep thought.*] He is
obviously not in love with her, but why
shouldn't he marry her? She is not pretty,
but she is so clever and pure and good, she
would make a splendid wife for a country
doctor of his years. [*A pause.*] I can understand how the poor child feels. She lives
here in this desperate loneliness with no one
around her except these colorless shadows
that go mooning about talking nonsense and
knowing nothing except that they eat, drink,
and sleep. Among them appears from time
to time this Dr. Astroff, so different, so handsome, so interesting, so charming. It is like
seeing the moon rise on a dark night. Oh, to
surrender oneself to his embrace! To lose
oneself in his arms! I am a little in love with
him myself! Yes, I am lonely without him,
and when I think of him I smile. That Uncle
Vanya says I have the blood of a nixie in
my veins: "Give rein to your nature for once
in your life!" Perhaps it is right that I
should. Oh, to be free as a bird, to fly away
from all your sleepy faces and your talk and
forget that you have existed at all! But I am
a coward, I am afraid; my conscience torments me. He comes here every day now. I
can guess why, and feel guilty already; I
should like to fall on my knees at Sonia's feet
and beg her forgiveness, and weep.

[ASTROFF *comes in carrying a portfolio.*]

Astroff. How do you do? [*Shakes hands*

with her.] Do you want to see my sketch?

Helena. Yes, you promised to show me what you had been doing. Have you time now?

Astroff. Of course I have!

[*He lays the portfolio on the table, takes out the sketch and fastens it to the table with thumbtacks.*]

Astroff. Where were you born?

Helena. [*Helping him.*] In St. Petersburg.

Astroff. And educated?

Helena. At the Conservatory there.

Astroff. You don't find this life very interesting, I dare say?

Helena. Oh, why not? It is true I don't know the country very well, but I have read a great deal about it.

Astroff. I have my own desk there in Ivan's room. When I am absolutely too exhausted to go on I drop everything and rush over here to forget myself in this work for an hour or two. Ivan and Miss Sonia sit rattling at their counting-boards, the cricket chirps, and I sit beside them and paint, feeling warm and peaceful. But I don't permit myself this luxury very often, only once a month. [*Pointing to the picture.*] Look there! That is a map of our country as it was fifty years ago. The green tints, both dark and light, represent forests. Half the map, as you see, is covered with it. Where the green is striped with red the forests were inhabited by elk and wild goats. Here on this lake lived great flocks of swans and geese and ducks; as the old men say, there was a power of birds of every kind. Now they have vanished like a cloud. Beside the hamlets and villages, you see, I have dotted down here and there the various settlements, farms, hermit's caves, and water-mills. This country carried a great many cattle and horses, as you can see by the quantity of blue paint. For instance, see how thickly it lies in this part; there were great herds of them here, an average of three horses to every house. [*A pause.*] Now, look lower down. This is the country as it was twenty-five years ago. Only a third of the map is green now with forests. There are no goats left and no elk. The blue paint is lighter, and so on, and so on. Now we come to the third part; our country as it appears today. We still see spots of green, but not much. The elk, the swans, the black-cock have disappeared. It is, on the whole, the picture of a regular and slow decline which it will evidently only take about ten or fifteen more years to complete. You may perhaps object that it is the march of progress, that the old order must give place to the new, and you might be right if roads had been run through these ruined woods, or if factories and schools had taken their place. The people then would have become better educated and healthier and richer, but as it is, we have nothing of the sort. We have the same swamps and mosquitoes; the same disease and want; the typhoid, the diphtheria, the burning villages. We are confronted by the degradation of our country, brought on by the fierce struggle for existence of the human race. It is the consequence of the ignorance and unconsciousness of starving, shivering sick humanity that, to save its children, instinctively snatches at everything that can warm it and still its hunger. So it destroys everything it can lay its hands on, without a thought for the morrow. And almost everything has gone, and nothing has been created to take its place. [*Coldly.*] But I see by your face that I am not interesting you.

Helena. I know so little about such things!

Astroff. There is nothing to know. It simply isn't interesting, that's all.

Helena. Frankly, my thoughts were elsewhere. Forgive me! I want to submit you to a little examination, but I am embarrassed and don't know how to begin.

Astroff. An examination?

Helena. Yes, but quite an innocent one. Sit down. [*They sit down.*] It is about a certain young girl I know. Let us discuss it like honest people, like friends, and then forget what has passed between us, shall we?

Astroff. Very well.

Helena. It is about my step-daughter, Sonia. Do you like her?

Astroff. Yes, I respect her.

Helena. Do you like her—as a woman?

Astroff. [*Slowly.*] No.

Helena. One more word, and that will be the last. You have not noticed anything?

Astroff. No, nothing.

Helena. [*Taking his hand.*] You do not love her. I see that in your eyes. She is suffering. You must realize that, and not come here any more.

Astroff. My sun has set, yes; and then I haven't the time. [*Shrugging his shoulders.*] Where shall I find time for such things?

[*He is embarrassed.*]

Helena. Bah! What an unpleasant conversation! I am as out of breath as if I had been running three miles uphill. Thank heaven, that is over! Now let us forget everything as if nothing had been said. You are sensible. You understand. [*A pause.*] I am actually blushing.

Astroff. If you had spoken a month ago I might perhaps have considered it, but now—

He shrugs his shoulders.] Of course, if she ᵴ suffering—but I cannot understand why ᵒu had to put me through this examination. *He searches her face with his eyes, and ᵸakes his finger at her.*] Oho, you are ᵣily!

Helena. What does this mean?

Astroff. [*Laughing.*] You are a wily one! admit that Sonia is suffering, but what ᵈoes this examination of yours mean? [*He ᵣevents her from retorting, and goes on ᵧuickly.*] Please don't put on such a look of ᵤrprise; you know perfectly well why I ᵒme here every day. Yes, you know per- ᵉctly why and for whose sake I come! Oh, ᵐy sweet tigress! don't look at me in that ᵥay! I am an old bird!

Helena. [*Perplexed.*] A tigress? I don't ᵤnderstand you.

Astroff. Beautiful, sleek tigress, you must ᵸave your victims! For a whole month I ᵸave done nothing but seek you eagerly. I ᵸave thrown over everything for you, and ᵧou love to see it. Now then, I am sure you ᵏnew all this without putting me through ᵧour examination. [*Crossing his arms and ᵇowing his head.*] I surrender. Here you ᵸave me—now, eat me.

Helena. You have gone mad!

Astroff. You are afraid!

Helena. I am a better and stronger woman than you think me. Good-bye.

[*She tries to leave the room.*]

Astroff. Why good-bye? Don't say good- bye, don't waste words. Oh, how lovely you are—what hands! [*He kisses her hands.*]

Helena. Enough of this! [*She frees her hands.*] Leave the room! You have forgot- ten yourself.

Astroff. Tell me, tell me, where can we meet tomorrow? [*He puts his arm around her.*] Don't you see that we must meet, that it is inevitable?

[*He kisses her.* VOITSKI *comes in carry- ing a bunch of roses; and stops in the doorway.*]

Helena. [*Without seeing* VOITSKI.] Have pity! Leave me. [*Lays her head on* AS- TROFF'S *shoulder.*] Don't!

[*She tries to break away from him.*]

Astroff. [*Holding her by the waist.*] Be in the forest tomorrow at two o'clock. Will you? Will you?

Helena. [*Sees* VOITSKI.] Let me go! [*Goes to the window, deeply embarrassed.*] This is appalling!

Voitski. [*Throws the flowers on a chair, and speaks in great excitement, wiping his face with his handkerchief.*] Nothing—yes, yes, nothing.

Astroff. The weather is fine today, my dear Ivan; the morning was overcast and looked like rain, but now the sun is shining again. Honestly, we have had a very fine autumn, and the wheat is looking fairly well. [*Puts his map back into the portfolio.*] But the days are growing short. [*Exit.*]

Helena. [*Goes quickly up to* VOITSKI.] You must do your best; you must use all your power to get my husband and myself away from here today! Do you hear? I say, this very day!

Voitski. [*Wiping his face.*] Oh! Ah! Oh! All right! I—Helena, I saw everything!

Helena. [*In great agitation.*] Do you hear me? I must leave here this very day.

[SEREBRAKOFF, SONIA, MARINA, *and* TELEGIN *come in.*]

Telegin. I am not very well myself, your Excellency. I have been limping for two days, and my head——

Serebrakoff. Where are the others? I hate this house. It is a regular labyrinth. Every one is always scattered through the twenty- six enormous rooms; one never can find a soul. [*Rings.*] Ask my wife and Madame Voitskaya to come here!

Helena. I am here already.

Serebrakoff. Please, all of you, sit down.

Sonia. [*Goes up to* HELENA *and asks anxiously.*] What did he say?

Helena. I'll tell you later.

Sonia. You are moved. [*Looking quickly and inquiringly into her face.*] I understand; he said he would not come here any more. [*A pause.*] Tell me, did he?

[HELENA *nods*].

Serebrakoff. [*To* TELEGIN.] One can, after all, become reconciled to being an invalid, but not to this country life. The ways of it stick in my throat and I feel exactly as if I had been whirled off the earth and landed on a strange planet. Please be seated, ladies and gentlemen. Sonia! [SONIA *does not hear. She is standing with her head bowed sadly forward on her breast.*] Sonia! [*A pause.*] She does not hear me. [*To* MARINA.] Sit down too, nurse. [MARINA *sits down and be- gins to knit her stocking.*] I crave your in- dulgence, ladies and gentlemen; hang your ears, if I may say so, on the peg of attention. [*He laughs.*]

Voitski. [*Agitated.*] Perhaps you do not need me—may I be excused?

Serebrakoff. No, you are needed now more than any one.

Voitski. What is it you want of me?

Serebrakoff. You—but what are you angry about? If it is anything I have done, I ask you to forgive me.

Voitski. Oh, drop that and come to business; what do you want?

[MME. VOITSKAYA *comes in.*]

Serebrakoff. Here is mother. Ladies and gentlemen, I shall begin. I have asked you to assemble here, my friends, in order to discuss a very important matter. I want to ask you for your assistance and advice, and knowing your unfailing amiability I think I can count on both. I am a book-worm and a scholar, and am unfamiliar with practical affairs. I cannot, I find, dispense with the help of well-informed people such as you, Ivan, and you, Telegin, and you, mother. The truth is, *manet omnes una nox,* that is to say, our lives are in the hands of God, and as I am old and ill, I realize that the time has come for me to dispose of my property in regard to the interests of my family. My life is nearly over, and I am not thinking of myself, but I have a young wife and daughter. [*A pause.*] I cannot continue to live in the country; we were not made for country life, and yet we cannot afford to live in town on the income derived from this estate. We might sell the woods, but that would be an expedient we could not resort to every year. We must find some means of guaranteeing to ourselves a certain more or less fixed yearly income. With this object in view, a plan has occurred to me which I now have the honor of presenting to you for your consideration. I shall only give you a rough outline, avoiding all details. Our estate does not pay on an average more than two per cent on the money invested in it. I propose to sell it. If we then invest our capital in bonds, it will earn us four to five per cent, and we should probably have a surplus over of several thousand roubles, with which we could buy a summer cottage in Finland——

Voitski. Hold on! Repeat what you just said; I don't think I heard you quite right.

Serebrakoff. I said we would invest the money in bonds and buy a cottage in Finland with the surplus.

Voitski. No, not Finland—you said something else.

Serebrakoff. I propose to sell this place.

Voitski. Aha! That was it! So you are going to sell the place? Splendid. The idea is a rich one. And what do you propose to do with my old mother and me and with Sonia here?

Serebrakoff. That will be decided in due time. We can't do everything at once.

Voitski. Wait! It is clear that until this moment I have never had a grain of sense in my head. I have always been stupid enough to think that the estate belonged to Sonia. My father bought it as a wedding present for my sister, and I foolishly imagined that as our laws were made for Russians and not Turks, my sister's estate would come down to her child.

Serebrakoff. Of course it is Sonia's. Has any one denied it? I don't want to sell it without Sonia's consent; on the contrary, what I am doing is for Sonia's good.

Voitski. This is absolutely incomprehensible. Either I have gone mad or—or——

Mme. Voitskaya. Jean, don't contradict Alexander. Trust to him; he knows better than we do what is right and what is wrong.

Voitski. I shan't. Give me some water. [*He drinks.*] Go ahead! Say anything you please—anything!

Serebrakoff. I can't imagine why you are so upset. I don't pretend that my scheme is an ideal one, and if you all object to it I shall not insist. [*A pause.*]

Telegin. [*With embarrassment.*] I not only nourish feelings of respect toward learning, your Excellency, but I am also drawn to it by family ties. My brother Gregory's wife's brother, whom you may know; his name is Constantine Lakedemonoff, and he used to be a magistrate——

Voitski. Stop, Waffles. This is business; wait a bit, we will talk of that later. [*To* SEREBRAKOFF.] There now, ask him what he thinks; this estate was bought from his uncle.

Serebrakoff. Ah! Why should I ask questions? What good would it do?

Voitski. The price was ninety-five thousand roubles. My father paid seventy and left a debt of twenty-five. Now listen! This place could never have been bought had I not renounced my inheritance in favor of my sister, whom I deeply loved—and what is more, I worked for ten years like an ox, and paid off the debt.

Serebrakoff. I regret ever having started this conversation.

Voitski. Thanks entirely to my own personal efforts, the place is entirely clear of debts, and now, when I have grown old, you want to throw me out, neck and crop!

Serebrakoff. I can't imagine what you are driving at.

Voitski. For twenty-five years I have managed this place, and have sent you the returns from it like the most honest of servants, and you have never given me one single word of thanks for my work, not one—neither in my youth nor now. You allowed me a meager salary of five hundred roubles a year, a beggar's pittance, and have never even thought of adding a rouble to it.

Serebrakoff. What did I know about such

hings, Ivan? I am not a practical man and lon't understand them. You might have ɨelped yourself to all you wanted.

Voitski. Yes, why did I not steal? Don't ʏou all despise me for not stealing, when it ʍould have been only justice? And I should ɩot now have been a beggar!

Mme. Voitskaya. [*Sternly.*] Jean!

Telegin. [*Agitated.*] Vanya, old man, lon't talk in that way. Why spoil such pleasɪnt relations? [*He embraces him.*] Do stop!

Voitski. For twenty-five years I have been ɜitting here with my mother like a mole in a ɓurrow. Our every thought and hope was ʏours and yours only. By day we talked with pride of you and your work, and spoke your ɳame with veneration; our nights we wasted ɼeading the books and papers which my soul ɳow loathes.

Telegin. Don't, Vanya, don't. I can't stand ɪt.

Serebrakoff. [*Wrathfully.*] What under heaven do you want, anyway?

Voitski. We used to think of you as almost superhuman, but now the scales have fallen from my eyes and I see you as you are! You write on art without knowing anything about it. Those books of yours which I used to admire are not worth one copper kopeck. You are a hoax!

Serebrakoff. Can't any one make him stop? I am going!

Helena. Ivan, I command you to stop this instant! Do you hear me?

Voitski. I refuse! [SEREBRAKOFF *tries to get out of the room, but* VOITSKI *bars the way.*] Wait! I have not done yet! You have wrecked my life. I have never lived. My best years have gone for nothing, have been ruined, thanks to you. You are my most bitter enemy!

Telegin. I can't stand it; I can't stand it. I am going.

[*He goes out in great excitement.*]

Serebrakoff. But what do you want? What earthly right have you to use such language to me? Ruination! If this estate is yours, then take it, and let me be ruined!

Helena. I am going away out of this hell this minute. [*Shrieks.*] This is too much!

Voitski. My life has been a failure. I am clever and brave and strong. If I had lived a normal life I might have become another Schopenhauer or Dostoievski. I am losing my head! I am going crazy! Mother, I am in despair! Oh, mother!

Mme. Voitskaya. [*Sternly.*] Listen, Alexander!

[SONIA *falls on her knees beside the* NURSE *and nestles against her.*]

Sonia. Oh, nurse, nurse!

Voitski. Mother! What shall I do? But no, don't speak! I know what to do. [*To* SEREBRAKOFF.] And you will understand me!

[*He goes out through the door in the center of the room and* MME. VOITSKAYA *follows him.*]

Serebrakoff. Tell me, what on earth is the matter? Take this lunatic out of my sight! I cannot possibly live under the same roof with him. His room [*He points to the center door.*] is almost next door to mine. Let him take himself off into the village or into the wing of the house, or I shall leave here at once. I cannot stay in the same house with him.

Helena. [*To her* HUSBAND.] We are leaving today; we must get ready at once for our departure.

Serebrakoff. What a perfectly dreadful man!

Sonia. [*On her knees beside the* NURSE *and turning to her* FATHER. *She speaks with emotion.*] You must be kind to us, papa. Uncle Vanya and I are so unhappy! [*Controlling her despair.*] Have pity on us. Remember how Uncle Vanya and Granny used to copy and translate your books for you every night—every, every night. Uncle Vanya has toiled without rest; he would never spend a penny on us, we sent it all to you. We have not eaten the bread of idleness. I am not saying this as I should like to, but you must understand us, papa, you must be merciful to us.

Helena. [*Very excited, to her* HUSBAND.] For heaven's sake, Alexander, go and have a talk with him—explain!

Serebrakoff. Very well, I shall have a talk with him, but I won't apologize for a thing. I am not angry with him, but you must confess that his behavior has been strange, to say the least. Excuse me, I shall go to him.

[*He goes out through the center door.*]

Helena. Be gentle with him; try to quiet him. [*She follows him out.*]

Sonia. [*Nestling nearer to* MARINA.] Nurse, oh, nurse!

Marina. It's all right, my baby. When the geese have cackled they will be still again. First they cackle and then they stop.

Sonia. Nurse!

Marina. You are trembling all over, as if you were freezing. There, there, little orphan baby, God is merciful. A little linden-tea, and it will all pass away. Don't cry, my sweetest. [*Looking angrily at the door in the center of the room.*] See, the geese have all gone now. The devil take them!

[*A shot is heard.* HELENA *screams behind the scenes.* SONIA *shudders.*]

Marina. Bang! What's that?

Serebrakoff. [*Comes in reeling with terror.*] Hold him! hold him! He has gone mad!

[HELENA *and* VOITSKI *are seen struggling in the doorway.*]

Helena. [*Trying to wrest the revolver from him.*] Give it to me; give it to me, I tell you!

Voitski. Let me go, Helena, let me go! [*He frees himself and rushes in, looking everywhere for* SEREBRAKOFF.] Where is he?

Ah, there he is! [*He shoots at him. A pause.*] I didn't get him? I missed again? [*Furiously.*] Damnation! Damnation! To hell with him!

[*He flings the revolver on the floor, and drops helpless into a chair.* SEREBRAKOFF *stands as if stupefied.* HELENA *leans against the wall, almost fainting.*]

Helena. Take me away! Take me away! I can't stay here—I can't!

Voitski. [*In despair.*] Oh, what shall I do? What shall I do?

Sonia. [*Softly.*] Oh, nurse, nurse!

THE CURTAIN FALLS

ACT FOURTH

VOITSKI'S *bedroom, which is also his office. A table stands near the window; on it are ledgers, letter scales, and papers of every description. Near by stands a smaller table belonging to* ASTROFF, *with his paints and drawing materials. On the wall hangs a cage containing a starling. There is also a map of Africa on the wall, obviously of no use to anybody. There is a large sofa covered with buckram. A door to the left leads into an inner room; one to the right leads into the front hall, and before this door lies a mat for the peasants with their muddy boots to stand on. It is an autumn evening. The silence is profound.*

[TELEGIN *and* MARINA *are sitting facing one another, winding wool.*]

Telegin. Be quick, Marina, or we shall be called away to say good-bye before you have finished. The carriage has already been ordered.

Marina. [*Trying to wind more quickly.*] I am a little tired.

Telegin. They are going to Kharkoff to live.

Marina. They do well to go.

Telegin. They have been frightened. The professor's wife won't stay here an hour longer. "If we are going at all, let's be off," says she, "we shall go to Kharkoff and look about us, and then we can send for our things." They are traveling light. It seems, Marina, that fate has decreed for them not to live here.

Marina. And quite rightly. What a storm they have just raised! It was shameful!

Telegin. It was indeed. The scene was worthy of the brush of Aibazofski.

Marina. I wish I'd never laid eyes on them. [*A pause.*] Now we shall have things as they were again: tea at eight, dinner at one, and supper in the evening; everything in order as decent folks, as Christians like to have it. [*Sighs.*] It is a long time since I have eaten noodles.

Telegin. Yes, we haven't had noodles for ages. [*A pause.*] Not for ages. As I was going through the village this morning, Marina, one of the shop-keepers called after me, "Hi! you hanger-on!" I felt it bitterly.

Marina. Don't pay the least attention to them, master; we are all dependents on God. You and Sonia and all of us. Every one must work, no one can sit idle. Where is Sonia?

Telegin. In the garden with the doctor, looking for Ivan. They fear he may lay violent hands on himself.

Marina. Where is his pistol?

Telegin. [*Whispers.*] I hid it in the cellar.

[VOITSKI *and* ASTROFF *come in.*]

Voitski. Leave me alone! [*To* MARINA *and* TELEGIN.] Go away! Go away and leave me to myself, if but for an hour. I won't have you watching me like this!

Telegin. Yes, yes, Vanya.

[*He goes out on tiptoe.*]

Marina. The gander cackles; ho! ho! ho!

[*She gathers up her wool and goes out.*]

Voitski. Leave me by myself!

Astroff. I would, with the greatest pleasure. I ought to have gone long ago, but I shan't leave you until you have returned what you took from me.

Voitski. I took nothing from you.

Astroff. I am not jesting, don't detain me, I really must go.

Voitski. I took nothing of yours.

Astroff. You didn't? Very well, I shall have to wait a little longer, and then you will have to forgive me if I resort to force. We shall have to bind you and search you. I mean what I say.

Voitski. Do as you please. [*A pause.*] Oh, to make such a fool of myself! To shoot twice and miss him both times! I shall never forgive myself.

Astroff. When the impulse came to shoot, it would have been as well had you put a bullet through your own head.

Voitski. [*Shrugging his shoulders.*] Strange! I attempted murder, and am not going to be arrested or brought to trial. That means they think me mad. [*With a bitter laugh.*] Me! I am mad, and those who hide their worthlessness, their dullness, their crying heartlessness behind a professor's mask, are sane! Those who marry old men and then deceive them under the noses of all, are sane! I saw you kiss her; I saw you in each other's arms!

Astroff. Yes, sir, I did kiss her; so there. [*He puts his thumb to his nose.*]

Voitski. [*His eyes on the door.*] No, it is the earth that is mad, because she still bears us on her breast.

Astroff. That is nonsense.

Voitski. Well? Am I not a madman, and therefore irresponsible? Haven't I the right to talk nonsense?

Astroff. This is a farce! You are not mad; you are simply a ridiculous fool. I used to think every fool was out of his senses, but now I see that lack of sense is a man's normal state, and you are perfectly normal.

Voitski. [*Covers his face with his hands.*] Oh! If you knew how ashamed I am! These piercing pangs of shame are like nothing on earth. [*In an agonized voice.*] I can't endure them! [*He leans against the table.*] What can I do? What can I do?

Astroff. Nothing.

Voitski. You must tell me something! Oh, my God! I am forty-seven years old. I may live to sixty; I still have thirteen years before me; an eternity! How shall I be able to endure life for thirteen years? What shall I do? How can I fill them? Oh, don't you see? [*He presses* Astroff's *hand convulsively.*] Don't you see, if only I could live the rest of my life in some new way! If I could only wake some still, bright morning and feel that life had begun again; that the past was forgotten and had vanished like smoke. [*He weeps.*] Oh, to begin life anew! Tell me, tell me how to begin.

Astroff. [*Crossly.*] What nonsense! What sort of a new life can you and I look forward to? We can have no hope.

Voitski. None?

Astroff. None. Of that I am convinced.

Voitski. Tell me what to do. [*He puts his hand to his heart.*] I feel such a burning pain here.

Astroff. [*Shouts angrily.*] Stop! [*Then, more gently.*] It may be that posterity, which will despise us for our blind and stupid lives, will find some road to happiness; but we—you and I—have but one hope, the hope that we may be visited by visions, perhaps by pleasant ones, as we lie resting in our graves. [*Sighing.*] Yes, brother, there were only two respectable, intelligent men in this county, you and I. Ten years or so of this life of ours, this miserable life, have sucked us under, and we have become as contemptible and petty as the rest. But don't try to talk me out of my purpose! Give me what you took from me, will you?

Voitski. I took nothing from you.

Astroff. You took a little bottle of morphine out of my medicine-case. [*A pause.*] Listen! If you are positively determined to make an end to yourself, go into the woods and shoot yourself there. Give up the morphine, or there will be a lot of talk and guess-work; people will think I gave it to you. I don't fancy having to perform a post-mortem on you. Do you think I should find it interesting? [Sonia *comes in.*]

Voitski. Leave me alone.

Astroff. [*To* Sonia.] Sonia, your uncle has stolen a bottle of morphine out of my medicine-case and won't give it up. Tell him that his behavior is—well, unwise. I haven't time, I must be going.

Sonia. Uncle Vanya, did you take the morphine?

Astroff. Yes, he took it. [*A pause.*] I am absolutely sure.

Sonia. Give it up! Why do you want to frighten us? [*Tenderly.*] Give it up, Uncle Vanya! My misfortune is perhaps even greater than yours, but I am not plunged in despair. I endure my sorrow, and shall endure it until my life comes to a natural end. You must endure yours, too. [*A pause.*] Give it up! Dear, darling Uncle Vanya. Give it up! [*She weeps.*] You are so good, I am sure you will have pity on us and give it up. You must endure your sorrow, Uncle Vanya; you must endure it.

[Voitski *takes a bottle from the drawer of the table and hands it to* Astroff.]

Voitski. There it is! [*To* SONIA.] And now, we must get to work at once; we must do something, or else I shall not be able to endure it.

Sonia. Yes, yes, to work! As soon as we have seen them off we shall go to work. [*She nervously straightens out the papers on the table.*] Everything is in a muddle!

Astroff. [*Putting the bottle in his case, which he straps together.*] Now I can be off.

[HELENA *comes in.*]

Helena. Are you here, Ivan? We are starting in a moment. Go to Alexander, he wants to speak to you.

Sonia. Go, Uncle Vanya. [*She takes* VOITSKI's *arm.*] Come, you and papa must make peace; that is absolutely necessary.

[SONIA *and* VOITSKI *go out.*]

Helena. I am going away. [*She gives* ASTROFF *her hand.*] Good-bye.

Astroff. So soon?

Helena. The carriage is waiting.

Astroff. Good-bye.

Helena. You promised me you would go away yourself today.

Astroff. I have not forgotten. I am going at once. [*A pause.*] Were you frightened? Was it so terrible?

Helena. Yes.

Astroff. Couldn't you stay? Couldn't you? Tomorrow—in the forest——

Helena. No. It is all settled, and that is why I can look you so bravely in the face. Our departure is fixed. One thing I must ask of you: don't think too badly of me; I should like you to respect me.

Astroff. Ah! [*With an impatient gesture.*] Stay, I implore you! Confess that there is nothing for you to do in this world. You have no object in life; there is nothing to occupy your attention, and sooner or later your feelings must master you. It is inevitable. It would be better if it happened not in Kharkoff or in Kursk, but here, in nature's lap. It would then at least be poetical, even beautiful. Here you have the forests, the houses half in ruins that Turgenieff writes of.

Helena. How comical you are! I am angry with you and yet I shall always remember you with pleasure. You are interesting and original. You and I will never meet again, and so I shall tell you—why should I conceal it?—that I am just a little in love with you. Come, one more last pressure of our hands, and then let us part good friends. Let us not bear each other any ill will.

Astroff. [*Pressing her hand.*] Yes, go. [*Thoughtfully.*] You seem to be sincere and good, and yet there is something strangely disquieting about all your personality. No sooner did you arrive here with your husband than every one whom you found busy and actively creating something was forced to drop his work and give himself up for the whole summer to your husband's gout and yourself. You and he have infected us with your idleness. I have been swept off my feet; I have not put my hand to a thing for weeks, during which sickness has been running its course unchecked among the people, and the peasants have been pasturing their cattle in my woods and young plantations. Go where you will, you and your husband will always carry destruction in your train. I am joking, of course, and yet I am strangely sure that had you stayed here we should have been overtaken by the most immense desolation. I would have gone to my ruin, and you—you would not have prospered. So go! È finita la commèdia!

Helena. [*Snatching a pencil off* ASTROFF's *table, and hiding it with a quick movement.*] I shall take this pencil for memory!

Astroff. How strange it is. We meet, and then suddenly it seems that we must part forever. That is the way in this world. As long as we are alone, before Uncle Vanya comes in with a bouquet—allow me—to kiss you good-bye—may I? [*He kisses her on the cheek.*] So! Splendid!

Helena. I wish you every happiness. [*She glances about her.*] For once in my life, I shall! and scorn the consequences! [*She kisses him impetuously, and they quickly part.*] I must go.

Astroff. Yes, go. If the carriage is there, then start at once. [*They stand listening.*]

Astroff. È finita!

[VOITSKI, SEREBRAKOFF, MME. VOITSKAYA *with her book,* TELEGIN, *and* SONIA *come in.*]

Serebrakoff. [*To* VOITSKI.] Shame on him who bears malice for the past. I have gone through so much in the last few hours that I feel capable of writing a whole treatise on the conduct of life for the instruction of posterity. I gladly accept your apology, and myself ask your forgiveness.

[*He kisses* VOITSKI *three times.* HELENA *embraces* SONIA.]

Serebrakoff. [*Kissing* MME. VOITSKAYA's *hand.*] Mother!

Mme. Voitskaya. [*Kissing him.*] Have your picture taken, Alexander, and send me one. You know how dear you are to me.

Telegin. Good-bye, your Excellency. Don't forget us.

Serebrakoff. [*Kissing his* DAUGHTER.] Good-bye, good-bye all. [*Shaking hands with*

ASTROFF.] Many thanks for your pleasant company. I have a deep regard for your opinions and your enthusiasm, but let me, as an old man, give one word of advice at parting: do something, my friend! Work! Do something! [*They all bow.*] Good luck to you all.

[*He goes out, followed by* MME. VOITSKAYA *and* SONIA.]

Voitski. [*Kissing* HELENA'S *hand fervently.*] Good-bye—forgive me. I shall never see you again!

Helena. [*Touched.*] Good-bye, dear boy. [*She lightly kisses his head as he bends over her hand, and goes out.*]

Astroff. Tell them to bring my carriage around too, Waffles.

Telegin. All right, old man.

[ASTROFF *and* VOITSKI *are left behind alone.* ASTROFF *collects his paints and drawing materials on the table and packs them away in a box.*]

Astroff. Why don't you go to see them off?

Voitski. Let them go! I—I can't go out there. I feel too sad. I must go to work on something at once. To work! To work!

[*He rummages through his papers on the table. A pause. The tinkling of bells is heard as the horses trot away.*]

Astroff. They have gone! The professor, I suppose, is glad to go. He couldn't be tempted back now by a fortune.

[MARINA *comes in.*]

Marina. They have gone.

[*She sits down in an armchair and knits her stocking.*]

[SONIA *comes in wiping her eyes.*]

Sonia. They have gone. God be with them. [*To her* UNCLE.] And now, Uncle Vanya, let us do something!

Voitski. To work! To work!

Sonia. It is long, long, since you and I have sat together at this table. [*She lights a lamp on the table.*] No ink! [*She takes the inkstand to the cupboard and fills it from an inkbottle.*] How sad it is to see them go!

[MME. VOITSKAYA *comes slowly in.*]

Mme. Voitskaya. They have gone.

[*She sits down and at once becomes absorbed in her book.*]

[SONIA *sits down at the table and looks through an account book.*]

Sonia. First, Uncle Vanya, let us write up the accounts. They are in a dreadful state. Come, begin. You take one and I will take the other.

Voitski. In account with——

[*They sit silently writing.*]

Marina. [*Yawning.*] The sand-man has come.

Astroff. How still it is. Their pens scratch; the cricket sings; it is so warm and comfortable. I hate to go.

[*The tinkling of bells is heard.*]

Astroff. My carriage has come. There now remains but to say good-bye to you, my friends, and to my table here, and then—away!

[*He puts the map into the portfolio.*]

Marina. Don't hurry away; sit a little longer with us.

Astroff. Impossible.

Voitski. [*Writing.*] And carry forward from the old debt two seventy-five——

[WORKMAN *comes in.*]

Workman. Your carriage is waiting, sir.

Astroff. All right. [*He hands the* WORKMAN *his medicine-case, portfolio, and box.*] Look out, don't crush the portfolio!

Workman. Very well, sir. [*Exit.*]

Sonia. When shall we see you again?

Astroff. Hardly before next summer. Probably not this winter; though, of course, if anything should happen you will let me know. [*He shakes hands with them.*] Thank you for your kindness, for your hospitality, for everything! [*He goes up to* MARINA *and kisses her head.*] Good-bye, old nurse!

Marina. Are you going without your tea?

Astroff. I don't want any, nurse.

Marina. Won't you have a drop of vodka?

Astroff. [*Hesitatingly.*] Yes, I might.

[MARINA *goes out.*]

Astroff. [*After a pause.*] My off-wheeler [1] has gone lame for some reason. I noticed it yesterday when Peter was taking him to water.

Voitski. You should have him re-shod.

Astroff. I shall have to go around by the blacksmith's on my way home. It can't be avoided. [*He stands looking up at the map of Africa hanging on the wall.*] I suppose it is roasting hot in Africa now.

Voitski. Yes, I suppose it is.

[MARINA *comes back carrying a tray on which are a glass of vodka and a piece of bread.*]

Marina. Help yourself. [ASTROFF *drinks.*]

Marina. To your good health! [*She bows deeply.*] Eat your bread with it.

Astroff. No, I like it so. And now, good-bye. [*To* MARINA.] You needn't come out to see me off, nurse.

[*He goes out.* SONIA *follows him with a candle to light him to the carriage.* MARINA *sits down in her armchair.*]

Voitski. [*Writing.*] On the 2d of February, twenty pounds of butter; on the 16th,

---

[1] The outer horse of a *troika.*

twenty pounds of butter again. Buckwheat flour——

[*A pause. Bells are heard tinkling.*]
Marina. He has gone.   [*A pause.*]
[SONIA *comes in and sets the candle-stick on the table.*]
Sonia. He has gone.
Voitski. [*Adding and writing*]. Total, fifteen—twenty-five——
[SONIA *sits down and begins to write.*]
Marina. [*Yawning.*] Oh, ho! The Lord have mercy.
[TELEGIN *comes in on tiptoe, sits down near the door, and begins to tune his guitar.*]
Voitski. [*To* SONIA, *stroking her hair.*] Oh, my child, I am so miserable; if you only knew how miserable I am!
Sonia. What can we do? We must live our lives. [*A pause.*] Yes, we shall live, Uncle Vanya. We shall live through the long procession of days before us, and through the long evenings; we shall patiently bear the trials that fate imposes on us; we shall work for others without rest, both now and when we are old; and when our last hour comes we shall meet it humbly, and there, beyond the grave, we shall say that we have suffered and wept, that our life was bitter, and God will have pity on us. Ah, then, dear, dear Uncle, we shall see that bright and beautiful life; we shall rejoice and look back upon our sorrow here; a tender smile—and—we shall rest. I have faith, Uncle, fervent, passionate faith. [SONIA *kneels down before her* UNCLE *and lays her head on his hands. She speaks in a weary voice.*] We shall rest. [TELEGIN *plays softly on the guitar.*] We shall rest. We shall hear the angels. We shall see heaven shining like a jewel. We shall see all evil and all our pain sink away in the great compassion that shall enfold the world. Our life will be as peaceful and tender and sweet as a caress. I have faith; I have faith. [*She wipes away her tears.*] My poor, poor Uncle Vanya, you are crying! [*Weeping.*] You have never known what happiness was, but wait, Uncle Vanya, wait! We shall rest. [*She embraces him.*] We shall rest. [*The* WATCHMAN'S *rattle is heard in the garden;* TELEGIN *plays softly;* MME. VOITSKAYA *writes something on the margin of her pamphlet;* MARINA *knits her stocking.*] We shall rest.

THE CURTAIN SLOWLY FALLS

THE DREAM PLAY *

By

AUGUST STRINDBERG

Translated by EDWIN BJÖRKMAN

LIKE IBSEN, AUGUST STRINDBERG HAS CAST the shadow of his genius athwart the modern theater. If the Ibsen shadow has receded with time, Strindberg's has advanced and, as many believe, will long continue to do so. Like Ibsen he first wrote for the theater of naturalism and later, far more significantly than Ibsen, he wrote for the theater of symbols. As a naturalist—that is, as a realist who observes life with scientific insight into its causal relations—Strindberg was more penetrating than Ibsen. He laid bare recesses of the mind that Ibsen left veiled. Conflicts which Ibsen presented as moral issues, Strindberg treated as the clashes of mental states which were as complex as the experience and the heritage of the individuals involved.

His daring self-revelation in the novel form, especially in the two parts of *Marriage* and the three parts of *The Bondwoman's Son,* made his name anathema to his own countrymen, but gained him in Paris a cordial welcome to the newly formed circle of the naturalists. His play *The Father* was published in translation with a preface by Zola in 1887, just as Antoine was opening his *Théâtre-Libre.* He was inspired to write for Antoine's theater the plays *Lady Julie, Comrades, Creditors,* and *The Stronger.* And so, as a chief apostle of the naturalist movement, he took his place among the foremost dramatists of our age. Except as the author of these early plays, he remains almost unknown on the English-speaking stage. These have won him a scant popularity and have left him an enigma. His vitalizing characterization and the bold experiments in play structure of his later period have, however, profoundly influenced such modernists as O'Neill and they therefore deserve more general study than they have received. His Anglo-Saxon readers have been inclined to

rule him out of the theater as a morbid and unamiable writer, labeling him a woman-hater, a neurotic, a misanthrope, a disorderly liver, a visionary, and a sensationalist. On the contrary, he was more than orderly, and was tragically devoted to women. He was a clear-minded observer, and except for a few years of almost insane preoccupation with futile scientific experiments, his intellectual life was more than usually self-possessed. He was an ardent but inept reformer, who had to create a Utopia in which only he himself was at home. To many, however, he still remains repulsively frank and egoistic in his reactions to love and life.

His immense influence upon dramatic style and form is due to the focus of his intense and analytical mind upon the springs of action, and particularly upon the inner reality of thought and impulse, both conscious and unconscious. His has been called "the shadow drama of the soul." It is his relentless disclosure of deeply hidden motives—happily hidden, perhaps—that keeps his work still abreast of our psychologizing dramatists. At this point, chiefly, he took exception to Ibsen, whose insistence upon moral reality in character and action blinded him to forces of the mind that seemed to Strindberg still more decisive. Ibsen, for instance, on moral principles, demanded social and moral equality for woman, and made the independent woman his protagonist. Strindberg found this attitude toward woman revoltingly sentimental. He, on the other hand, invoked biological and psychological facts as well as ethics and logic, and in this light revealed woman as needing no such aid. He saw in her mother-mentality a terrible force, cosmic and insatiable, against which man, as bread-winner, was at a hopeless, tragic disadvantage. Even her charm, to which Strindberg owned himself a slave, made her doubly dangerous. The revolt of man against the domination of the creation instinct in woman

---

* Used by permission of Charles Scribner's Sons.

became as prominent in Strindberg's work for the stage as the reverse situation in Ibsen's.

This belief was by no means academic. Strindberg had seen his quiet, cultured father dominated by a servant-girl wife, his own mother, to whom he also was passionately devoted. Against this wife-and-mother tyranny he waged a life-long battle. He met it again in his wives, and made it the basic motive in many of his feminine characters. This attitude was not, however, one of personal dislike. So long as woman remained in her own sphere and did not offer rivalry or domination in man's, Strindberg professed to admire and even to worship her. He was ready to grant her full equality before the law. He even advocated votes for women. It was intellectual and spiritual domination that he protested against. In both respects he believed woman man's inferior. Her aggressive invasion of man's own vocations and mental life he regarded as a menace to the race. She should remain the home-maker. When she assumed a larger influence, the horrors set forth in *The Father* might be expected; the husband might then become merely an instrument to help her fulfil her racial purpose, to be cast off or, perhaps, driven insane. Biassed and lacking in a sense of humor as Strindberg seems to have been when dealing with this aspect of the sex war, he has, nevertheless, enlisted a host of followers from Shaw to O'Neill.

Although his contributions to the naturalist theater were of first importance, those he made to the more recent theater of varied symbolic expression have made him a living influence in the theater of today and tomorrow. The mystic was always latent in him. In his last Stockholm period the writings of Maeterlinck and Swedenborg aroused this dormant side of his nature. Beginning with *To Damascus* (1898) and continuing through *The Dream Play* and *The Spook Sonata*, he set on foot those tendencies that have disrupted the old dramatic forms and are now known as expressionistic. This much debated and vague term, first used by the *Sturm* school of German artists and literary revolters of about 1915, has come to be applied in the theater to all those methods, whether of playwriting or of staging, which aim to give expression by means of stage symbols to a state of mind or an emotion. For our present purpose it suffices to consider the dream as such a state. To make concrete in the theater the dream consciousness of the writer or of his characters is to be expressionistic in one sense of that term. The old surfaces of life are broken as in a dream and the photographic method of representation is frankly abandoned. Symbol personages walk abroad regardless of time or the three dimensions. Personalities break into their component aspects, each becoming symbolic rather than individual.

The Dream Play affords a pleasant example of this method, which has obviously influenced recent American writers like O'Neill, as well as writers for the German and Russian theaters. Strindberg described the process in a memorandum prefixed to his play:

"In this *Dream Play,* as in the previous *To Damascus,* the author has sought to imitate the disconnected, but apparently logical, form of the dream. Anything may happen; everything is possible and probable. Time and space do not exist; on an insignificant background of reality imagination spins threads and weaves new patterns: a mixture of memories, experiences, free fancies, absurdities, and improvisations. The characters split, double, multiply, evaporate, solidify, diffuse, clarify. But one consciousness reigns above them all—that of the dreamer; it knows no secrets, no incongruities, no scruples, no law."

Other comments of Strindberg regarding playwriting and presentation have been so influential in the modern theater that they are appended:

On the function of tragedy: "People clamor for the joy of life, and theatrical managers order farces, as though the joy of life consisted in being foolish. . . . I find the joy of life in the powerful, cruel struggle of life, and my enjoyment is in discovering something, in learning something." Preface to *Lady Julie.*

On the true and false naturalism: "This [literary photography] is realism, a method latterly exalted to an art, a little art which cannot see the wood for the trees. This is the false naturalism, which believed that art consisted merely in sketching a piece of nature in a natural manner; but the true naturalism is that which seeks out those points in life where the great conflicts occur, which loves to see that which cannot be seen every day, rejoices in the battle of elemental powers, whether they be called love or hatred, revolt or sociability; which cares not whether a subject be beautiful or ugly, if only it is great." *On Modern Drama and the Modern Theatre.*

On character analysis and complexity of personality: [Strindberg's insistence on hidden motivation and many-sided personality is still productive of results in our own theater.]

"An event in life—and this is a comparatively new discovery—is generally produced by a whole series of more or less deep-seated motives, but the spectator chooses for the most part the one which is easiest for him to grasp. . . ." [He cites as illustration commonly assigned causes for a suicide and continues.] "It is possible that the motives lay in all of these causes, or in none, and that the dead man hid the real one by putting forward another which has thrown a more favorable light on his memory.

"I have drawn my characters vacillating, broken, mixtures of old and new. . . . My souls are conglomerations of past and present stages of culture, scraps of books and newspapers, fragments of men and women, torn shreds of Sunday attire that are now rags such as go to make up a soul.

"I do not, therefore, believe in simple theatrical characters, and the summary judgments which authors pass on human beings, such as: this one is stupid; that one is brutal; he is jealous; he is mean, etc., should be refuted by naturalists who know the rich complexity of the soul, and realize that vice has an obverse which shows a considerable likeness to virtue." Preface to *Lady Julie*.

Of Strindberg's modern ideas about staging, the following have been largely influential:

1. Footlights should be suppressed and side lights and borders used.

2. No more scenery should be used than is necessary. "With the aid of a table and two chairs, the strongest conflicts which life offers could be presented." Not a whole room, but an impressionist suggestion of one corner with its furniture is enough. Simple draperies were used by him at a later period.

3. Actors should be taught to play for the public and not at it. They may even turn their backs to it, and they should use a minimum of make-up.

4. The orchestra should be concealed.

5. The house should be small and intimate. Strindberg's own theater, opened in 1907, seated only 200 persons. The Künstler Theater in Munich is said to reflect his ideas.

AUGUST STRINDBERG

Born 1849, Stockholm.

1867–1872, University of Upsala.

1872, First Version of *Master Olof*, inspired by Ibsen's *Brand*, was unsuccessful. In 1880 the fifth version was successfully produced.

1877–1891, First and most influential of three marriages.

1883–1897, Lived mainly on the Continent.

1887, *The Father*, his first naturalistic play. In Paris he wrote for Antoine's *Théâtre-Libre* his plays, *Lady Julie, Comrades, The Stronger,* and *Creditors*.

1894–1897, Period of scientific activity and mental aberration.

1897–1912, Return to Stockholm. Historical plays and plays of symbolism.

1907, The Intimate Theatre, devoted to Strindberg's plays, opened in Stockholm.

1912, Popular triumph and death.

PLAYS

1869 *The Free Thinker.* 1869 *Hermione.* 1870 *In Rome.* 1871 *The Outlaw.* 1872 *The Heretic* (rewritten and published as *Master Olof*). 1880 *Master Olof* (fifth version). 1880 *The Secret of the Guild.* 1881 *The Year Forty-Eight.* 1881 *The Wanderings of Lucky-Per.* 1882 *Sir Bengt's Lady.* 1887 *The Father.* 1888 *Comrades.* 1888 *Lady Julie.* 1889 *Hemsö Folk.* 1890 *Creditors.* 1890 *Pariah.* 1890 *Samum.* 1890 *The*

Stronger. 1892 *The Keys of Heaven.* 1893 *Facing Death.* 1893 *The First Warning.* 1893 *Debit and Credit.* 1893 *Mother Love.* 1893 *Playing with Fire.* 1893 *The Link.* 1898 *To Damascus* (Parts I and II). 1899 *There Are Crimes and Crimes.* 1899 *Advent.* 1899 *Gustavus Vasa.* 1899 *Eric XIV.* 1899 *The Saga of the Folkungs.* 1900 *Gustavus Adolphus.* 1901 *Caspar's Shrove Tuesday.* 1901 *Easter.* 1901 *Midsummer.* 1901 *The Dance of Death* (Parts I and II). 1901 *Engelbrecht.* 1901 *Charles XII.* 1902 *The Bridal Crown.* 1902 *Swanwhite.* 1902 *The Dream Play.* 1903 *Christina.* 1903 *Gustavus III.* 1904 *The Nightingale of Wittenberg* (Martin Luther). 1904 *To Damascus* (Part III). 1907 *Storm.* 1907 *The Burned Lot.* 1907 *The Spook Sonata.* 1907 *The Pelican.* 1908 *The Slippers of Abou Casem.*

1908 *The Last Knight.* 1909 *The National Director.* 1909 *The Earl of Bjalbo.* 1909 *The Black Glove.* 1909 *The Great Highway.* 1909 *The Tooth.* 1917 *Moses.* 1918 *Greece or Socrates.* 1918 *The Lamb and the Wild Beast; or Christ.*

WRITINGS ON DRAMA

1887 Author's Preface to *Lady Julie.* 1889 *On Modern Drama and the Modern Theatre.* 1908 *Memorandum to the Members of the Intimate Theatre.* 1909 *An Open Letter to the Intimate Theatre.* 1911 *Dramaturgie* (translated into German by E. Schering). 1914 *Dramatische Charakteristiken* (translated into German by E. Schering).

THE DREAM PLAY

PROLOGUE

The background represents cloud banks that resemble corroding slate cliffs with ruins of castles and fortresses.
The constellations of Leo, Virgo, and Libra are visible, and from their midst the planet Jupiter is shining with a strong light.
[THE DAUGHTER OF INDRA [1] *stands on the topmost cloud.*]

The Voice of Indra. [*From above.*]
Where are you, daughter, where?
The Daughter.
Here, father, here.
The Voice.
You've lost your way, my child—beware,
    you sink—
How got you there?
The Daughter.
I followed from ethereal heights the ray
Of lightning, and for a car a cloud I took—
It sank, and now my journey downward
    tends.
O, noble father, Indra, tell what realms
I now draw near? The air is here so close,
And breathing difficult.
The Voice.
Behind you lies the second world; the
    third
Is where you stand. From Cukra, morning
    star,
You have withdrawn yourself to enter
    soon
The vapory circle of the earth. For mark,
The Seventh House you take. It's Libra
    called:
There stands the day-star in the balanced
    hour
When Fall gives equal weight to night and
    day.
The Daughter.
You named the earth—is that the ponder-
    ous world
And dark, that from the moon must take
    its light?
The Voice.
It is the heaviest and densest sphere
Of all that travel through the space.

The Daughter.
And is it never brightened by the sun?
The Voice.
Of course, the sun does reach it—now and
    then——
The Daughter.
There is a rift, and downward goes my
    glance——
The Voice.
What sees my child?
The Daughter.
I see—O beautiful!—with forests green,
With waters blue, white peaks, and yellow
    fields——
The Voice.
But still more beautiful it was of yore,
Yes, beautiful as all that Brahma made—
In primal morn of ages. Then occurred
Some strange mishap; the orbit was dis-
    turbed;
Rebellion led to crime that called for
    check——
The Daughter.
Now from below I hear some sounds
    arise—
What sort of race is dwelling there?
The Voice.
See for yourself—Of Brahma's work no ill
    I say: but what you hear, it is their speech.
The Daughter.
It sounds as if—it has no happy ring!
The Voice.
I fear me not—for even their mother-
    tongue
Is named complaint. A race most hard to
    please,
And thankless, are the dwellers on the
    earth——
The Daughter.
O, say not so—for I hear cries of joy,
Hear noise and thunder, see the lightnings
    flash——
Now bells are ringing, fires are lit,
And thousand upon thousand tongues
Sing praise and thanks unto the heavens
    on high——
Too harshly, father, you are judging them.
The Voice.
Descend, that you may see and hear, and
    then
Return and let me know if their com-
    plaints

[1] In Hindu mythology Indra, the god of the heavens, corresponded to Zeus of the Greeks and Jupiter of the Romans. Brahma was the god of creation.

And wailings have some reasonable ground——

The Daughter.

Well then, I go; but, father, come with me.

The Voice.

No, there below I cannot breathe——

The Daughter.

Now sinks the cloud—what sultriness—I choke!

I am not breathing air, but smoke and steam—

With heavy weight it drags me down, And I can feel already how it rolls—

Indeed, the best of worlds is not the third——

The Voice.

The best I cannot call it, nor the worst.

Its name is Dust; and like them all, it rolls:

And therefore dizzy sometimes grows the race,

And seems to be half foolish and half mad—

Take courage, child—a trial, that is all!

The Daughter.

[*Kneeling as the cloud sinks downward.*] I sink!

CURTAIN

THE PLAY

The background represents a forest of gigantic hollyhocks in bloom. They are white, pink, crimson, sulphurous, violet; and above their tops is seen the gilded roof of a castle, the apex of which is formed by a bud resembling a crown. At the foot of the castle walls stand a number of straw ricks, and around these stable litter is scattered. The side-scenes, which remain unchanged throughout the play, show conventionalized frescoes, suggesting at once internal decoration, architecture, and landscape.

[*Enter* THE GLAZIER *and* THE DAUGHTER.]

The Daughter. The castle is growing higher and higher above the ground. Do you see how much it has grown since last year?

The Glazier. [*To himself.*] I have never seen this castle before—have never heard of a castle that grew, but— [*To* THE DAUGHTER, *with firm conviction.*] Yes, it has grown two yards, but that is because they have manured it—and if you notice, it has put out a wing on the sunny side.

The Daughter. Ought it not to be blooming soon, as we are already past midsummer?

The Glazier. Don't you see the flower up there?

The Daughter. Yes, I see! [*Claps her hands.*] Say, father, why do flowers grow out of dirt?

The Glazier. [*Simply.*] Because they do not feel at home in the dirt, and so they make haste to get up into the light in order to blossom and die.

The Daughter. Do you know who lives in that castle?

The Glazier. I have known it, but cannot remember.

The Daughter. I believe a prisoner is kept there—and he must be waiting for me to set him free.

The Glazier. And what is he to pay for it?

The Daughter. One does not bargain about one's duty. Let us go into the castle.

The Glazier. Yes, let us go in.

[*They go toward the background, which opens and slowly disappears to either side.*]

[*The stage shows now a humble, bare room, containing only a table and a few chairs. On one of the chairs sits an* OFFICER, *dressed in a very unusual yet modern uniform. He is tilting the chair backward and beating the table with his sabre.*]

The Daughter. [*Goes to* THE OFFICER, *from whose hand she gently takes the sabre.*] Don't! Don't!

The Officer. Oh, Agnes dear, let me keep the sabre.

The Daughter. No, you break the table. [*To* THE GLAZIER.] Now you go down to the harness-room and fix that window pane. We'll meet later. [THE GLAZIER *goes out.*]

The Daughter. You are imprisoned in your own rooms—I have come to set you free.

The Officer. I have been waiting for you, but I was not sure you were willing to do it.

The Daughter. The castle is strongly built; it has seven walls, but—it can be done! —Do you want it, or do you not?

The Officer. Frankly speaking, I cannot tell—for in either case I shall suffer pain.

Every joy that life brings has to be paid for with twice its measure of sorrow. It is hard to stay where I am, but if I buy the sweets of freedom, then I shall have to suffer twice as much—Agnes, I'd rather endure it as it is, if I can only see you.

The Daughter. What do you see in me?

The Officer. Beauty, which is the harmony of the universe—There are lines of your body which are nowhere to be found, except in the orbits of the solar system, in strings that are singing softly, or in the vibrations of light—You are a child of heaven——

The Daughter. So are you.

The Officer. Why must I then keep horses, tend stable, and cart straw?

The Daughter. So that you may long to get away from here.

The Officer. I am longing, but it is so hard to find one's way out.

The Daughter. But it is a duty to seek freedom in the light.

The Officer. Duty? Life has never recognized any duties toward me.

The Daughter. You feel yourself wronged by life?

The Officer. Yes, it has been unjust——

[*Now voices are heard from behind a partition, which a moment later is pulled away.* THE OFFICER *and* THE DAUGHTER *look in that direction and stop as if paralyzed in the midst of a gesture.*]

[*At a table sits* THE MOTHER, *looking very sick. In front of her a tallow candle is burning, and every little while she trims it with a pair of snuffers. The table is piled with new-made shirts, and these she is marking with a quill and ink. To the left stands a brown-colored wardrobe.* THE FATHER *holds out a silk mantilla toward* THE MOTHER.]

The Father. [*Gently.*] You don't want it?

The Mother. A silk mantilla for me, my dear—of what use would that be when I am going to die shortly?

The Father. Do you believe what the doctor says?

The Mother. Yes, I believe what he says, but still more what the voice says in here.

The Father. [*Sadly.*] It is true then?— And you are thinking of your children first and last.

The Mother. That has been my life and my reason for living—my joy and my sorrow——

The Father. Christine, forgive me—everything!

The Mother. What have I to forgive? Dearest, you forgive *me!* We have been

tormenting each other. Why? That we may not know. We couldn't do anything else— However, here is the new linen for the children. See that they change twice a week— Wednesdays and Sundays—and that Louise washes them—their whole bodies—Are you going out?

The Father. I have to be in the Department at eleven o'clock.

The Mother. Ask Alfred to come in before you go.

The Father. [*Pointing to* THE OFFICER.] Why, he is standing right there, dear heart.

The Mother. So my eyes are failing, too— Yes, it is turning dark. [*Trims the candle.*] Come here, Alfred.

[THE FATHER *goes out through the middle of the wall, nodding good-bye as he leaves.* THE OFFICER *goes over to* THE MOTHER.]

The Mother. Who is that girl?

The Officer. [*Whispers.*] It is Agnes.

The Mother. Oh, is that Agnes?—Do you know what they say?—That she is a daughter of the god Indra who has asked leave to descend to the earth in order that she may find out what the conditions of men are— But don't say anything about it.

The Officer. A child of the gods, indeed!

The Mother. [*Aloud.*] My Alfred, I must soon part from you and from the other children—But let me first speak a word to you that bears on all the rest of your life.

The Officer. [*Sadly.*] Speak, mother.

The Mother. Only a word: don't quarrel with God!

The Officer. What do you mean, mother?

The Mother. Don't go around feeling that life has wronged you.

The Officer. But when I am treated unjustly——

The Mother. You are thinking of the time when you were unjustly punished for having taken a penny that later turned up?

The Officer. Yes, and that one wrong gave a false twist to my whole life——

The Mother. Perhaps. But please take a look into that wardrobe now——

The Officer. [*Embarrassed.*] You know, then? It is——

The Mother. "The Swiss Family Robinson"—for which——

The Officer. Don't say any more!

The Mother. For which your brother was punished—and which you had torn and hidden away.

The Officer. Just think that the old wardrobe is still standing there after twenty years—— We have moved so many times, and my mother died ten years ago.

The Mother. Yes, and what of it? You are always asking all sorts of questions, and in that way you spoil the better part of your life—There is Lena, now.

Lena. [*Enter.*] Thank you very much, ma'am, but I can't go to the baptism.

The Mother. And why not, my girl?

Lena. I have nothing to put on.

The Mother. I'll let you use my mantilla here.

Lena. Oh, no, ma'am, that wouldn't do!

The Mother. Why not?—It is not likely that I'll go to any more parties.

The Officer. And what will father say? It is a present from him——

The Mother. What small minds——

The Father. [*Puts his head through the wall.*] Are you going to lend my present to the servant girl?

The Mother. Don't talk that way! Can you not remember that I was a servant girl also? Why should you offend one who has done nothing?

The Father. Why should you offend me, your husband?

The Mother. Oh, this life! If you do anything nice, there is always somebody who finds it nasty. If you act kindly to one, it hurts another. Oh, this life!

[*She trims the candle so that it goes out. The stage turns dark and the partition is pushed back to its former position.*]

The Daughter. Men are to be pitied.

The Officer. You think so?

The Daughter. Yes, life is hard—but love overcomes everything. You shall see for yourself. [*They go toward the background.*]

[*The background is raised and a new one revealed, showing an old, dilapidated party-wall. In the center of it is a gate closing a passageway. This opens upon a green, sunlit space, where is seen a tremendous blue monk's-hood (aconite). To the left of the gate sits* THE POR-TRESS. *Her head and shoulders are covered by a shawl, and she is crocheting at a bedspread with a starlike pattern. To the right of the gate is a billboard, which* THE BILLPOSTER *is cleaning. Beside him stands a dipnet with a green pole. Further to the right is a door that has an air-hole shaped like a four-leaved clover. To the left of the gate stands a small linden tree with coal-black trunk and a few pale-green leaves. Near it is a small air-hole leading into a cellar.*[1]]

---

[1] Though the author says nothing about it here, subsequent stage directions indicate a door and a window behind the place occupied by THE PORTRESS. Both lead into her room or lodge, which contains a telephone.

The Daughter. [*Going to* THE PORTRESS.] Is the spread not done yet?

The Portress. No, dear. Twenty-six years on such a piece of work is not much.

The Daughter. And your lover never came back?

The Portress. No, but it was not his fault. He had to go—poor thing! That was thirty years ago now.

The Daughter. [*To* THE BILLPOSTER.] She belonged to the ballet? Up there in the opera-house?

The Billposter. She was number one—but when *he* went, it was as if her dancing had gone with him—and so she didn't get any more parts.

The Daughter. Everybody complains—with their eyes, at least, and often with words also——

The Billposter. I don't complain very much—not now, since I have a dipnet and a green cauf[1]——

The Daughter. And that can make you happy?

The Billposter. Oh, I'm so happy, so—It was the dream of my youth, and now it has come true. Of course, I have grown to be fifty years——

The Daughter. Fifty years for a dipnet and a cauf——

The Billposter. A *green* cauf—mind you, green——

The Daughter. [*To* THE PORTRESS.] Let me have the shawl now, and I shall sit here and watch the human children. But you must stand behind me and tell me about everything.

[*She takes the shawl and sits down at the gate.*]

The Portress. This is the last day, and the house will be closed up for the season. This is the day when they learn whether their contracts are to be renewed.

The Daughter. And those that fail of engagement——

The Portress. O, Lord have mercy! I pull the shawl over my head not to see them.

The Daughter. Poor human creatures!

The Portress. Look, here comes one—She's not one of the chosen. See, how she cries.

[THE SINGER *enters from the right; rushes through the gate with her handkerchief to her eyes; stops for a moment in the passageway beyond the gate and leans her head against the wall; then out quickly.*]

The Daughter. Men are to be pitied!

---

[1] A floating wooden box with holes in it used to hold fish.

The Portress. But look at this one. That's the way a happy person looks.

[THE OFFICER *enters through the passageway, dressed in Prince Albert coat and high hat, and carrying a bunch of roses in one hand; he is radiantly happy.*]

The Portress. He is going to marry Miss Victoria.

The Officer. [*Far down on the stage, looks up and sings.*] Victoria!

The Portress. The young lady will be coming in a moment.

The Officer. Good! The carriage is waiting, the table is set, the wine is on ice—— Oh, permit me to embrace you, ladies! [*He embraces* THE PORTRESS *and* THE DAUGHTER. *Sings.*] Victoria!

A Woman's Voice from Above. [*Sings.*] I am here!

The Daughter. Do you know me?

The Officer. No, I know one woman only —Victoria. Seven years I have come here to wait for her—at noon, when the sun touched the chimneys, and at night, when it was growing dark. Look at the asphalt here, and you will see the path worn by the steps of a faithful lover. Hooray! She is mine. [*Sings.*] Victoria. [*There is no reply.*] Well, she is dressing, I suppose. [*To* THE BILLPOSTER.] There is the dipnet, I see. Everybody belonging to the opera is crazy about dipnets— or rather about fishes—because the fishes are dumb and cannot sing!—What is the price of a thing like that?

The Billposter. It is rather expensive.

The Officer. [*Sings.*] Victoria! [*Shakes the linden tree.*] Look, it is turning green once more. For the eighth time. [*Sings.*] Victoria!—Now she is fixing her hair. [*To* THE DAUGHTER.] Look here, Madam, could I not go up and get my bride?

The Portress. Nobody is allowed on the stage.

The Officer. Seven years I have been coming here. Seven times three hundred and sixty-five makes two thousand five hundred and fifty-five. [*Stops and pokes at the door with the four-leaved clover hole.*] And I have been looking two thousand five hundred and fifty-five times at that door without discovering where it leads. And that clover leaf which is to let in light—for whom is the light meant? Is there anybody within? Does anybody live there?

The Portress. I don't know. I have never seen it opened.

The Officer. It looks like a pantry door which I saw once when I was only four years old and went visiting with the maid on a Sunday afternoon. We called at several houses—on other maids—but I did not get beyond the kitchen anywhere, and I had to sit between the water barrel and the salt box. I have seen so many kitchens in my days; and the pantry was always just outside, with small round holes bored in the door, and one big hole like a clover leaf—— But there cannot be any pantry in the opera-house as they have no kitchen. [*Sings.*] Victoria!—Tell me, Madam, could she have gone out any other way?

The Portress. No, there is no other way.

The Officer. Well, then, I shall see her here.

[STAGE PEOPLE *rush out and are closely watched by* THE OFFICER *as they pass.*]

The Officer. Now she must soon be coming—Madam, that blue monk's-hood outside —I have seen it since I was a child. Is it the same?—I remember it from a country rectory where I stopped when I was seven years old—— There are two doves, two blue doves, under the hood—but that time a bee came flying and went into the hood. Then I thought: now I have you! And I grabbed hold of the flower. But the sting of the bee went through it, and I cried—but then the rector's wife came and put damp dirt on the sting—and we had strawberries and cream for dinner—— I think it is getting dark already. [*To* THE BILLPOSTER.] Where are you going?

The Billposter. Home for supper.

The Officer. [*Draws his hand across his eyes.*] Evening? At this time?—O, please, may I go in and telephone to the Growing Castle?

The Daughter. What do you want there?

The Officer. I am going to tell the Glazier to put in double windows, for it will soon be winter, and I am feeling horribly cold.

[*Goes into the gatekeeper's lodge.*]

The Daughter. Who is Miss Victoria?

The Portress. His sweetheart.

The Daughter. Right said! What she is to us and others matters nothing to him. And what she is to him, that alone is her real self.

[*It is suddenly turning dark.*]

The Portress. [*Lights a lantern.*] It is growing dark early today.

The Daughter. To the gods a year is as a minute.

The Portress. And to men a minute may be as long as a year.

The Officer. [*Enters again, looking dusty; the roses are withered.*] She has not come yet?

The Portress. No.

The Officer. But she will come—— She

will come! [*Walks up and down.*] But come to think of it, perhaps I had better call off the dinner after all—as it is late? Yes, I will do that.

[*Goes back into the lodge and telephones.*]

The Portress. [*To* THE DAUGHTER.] Can I have my shawl back now?

The Daughter. No, dear, be free a while. I shall attend to your duties—for I want to study men and life, and see whether things really are as bad as they say.

The Portress. But it won't do to fall asleep here—never sleep night or day——

The Daughter. No sleep at night?

The Portress. Yes, if you are able to get it, but only with the bell string tied around the wrist—for there are night watchmen on the stage, and they have to be relieved every third hour.

The Daughter. But that is torture!

The Portress. So you think, but people like us are glad enough to get such a job, and if you only knew how envied I am——

The Daughter. Envied?—Envy for the tortured?

The Portress. Yes—— But I can tell you what is harder than all drudging and keeping awake nights, harder to bear than draught and cold and dampness—it is to receive the confidences of all the unhappy people up there—— They all come to me. Why? Perhaps they read in the wrinkles of my face some runes that are graved by suffering and that invite confessions—— In that shawl, dear, lie hidden thirty years of my own and other people's agonies.

The Daughter. It is heavy, and it burns like nettles.

The Portress. As it is your wish, you may wear it. When it grows too burdensome, call me, and I shall relieve you.

The Daughter. Good-bye. What can be done by you ought not to surpass my strength.

The Portress. We shall see!—But be kind to my poor friends, and don't grow impatient of their complaints.

[*She disappears through the passageway.*]

[*Complete darkness covers the stage, and while it lasts the scene is changed so that the linden tree appears stripped of all its leaves. Soon the blue monk's-hood is withered, and when the light returns, the verdure in the open space beyond the passageway has changed into autumnal brown.*]

The Officer. [*Enters when it is light again. He has gray hair and a gray beard. His clothes are shabby, his collar is soiled and wrinkled. Nothing but the bare stems remain of the bunch of roses. He walks to and fro.*] To judge by all signs, Summer is gone and Fall has come. The linden shows it, and the monk's-hood also. [*Walks.*] But the Fall is *my* Spring, for then the opera begins again, and then she must come. Please, Madam, may I sit down a little on this chair?

The Daughter. Yes, sit down, friend—I am able to stand.

The Officer. [*Sits down.*] If I could only get some sleep, then I should feel better— [*He falls asleep for a few moments. Then he jumps up and walks back and forth again. Stops at last in front of the door with the clover leaf and pokes at it.*] This door here will not leave me any peace—what is behind it? There must be something. [*Faint dance music is heard from above.*] Oh, now the rehearsals have begun. [*The light goes out and flares up again, repeating this rhythmically as the rays of a lighthouse come and go.*] What does this mean? [*Speaking in time with the blinkings of the light.*] Light and dark—light and dark?

The Daughter. [*Imitating him.*] Night and day—night and day! A merciful Providence wants to shorten your wait. Therefore the days are flying in hot pursuit of the nights.

[*The light shines unbrokenly once more.*]

[THE BILLPOSTER *enters with his dipnet and his implements.*]

The Officer. There is the Billposter with his dipnet. Was the fishing good?

The Billposter. I should say so. The Summer was hot and a little long—the net turned out pretty good, but not as I had expected.

The Officer. [*With emphasis.*] Not as I had expected!—That is well said. Nothing ever was as I expected it to be—because the thought is more than the deed, more than the thing.

[*Walks to and fro, striking at the wall with the rose stems so that the last few leaves fall off.*]

The Billposter. Has she not come down yet?

The Officer. Not yet, but she will soon be here—Do you know what is behind that door, Billposter?

The Billposter. No, I have never seen that door open yet.

The Officer. I am going to telephone for a locksmith to come and open it.

[*Goes into the lodge.*]

[THE BILLPOSTER *posts a bill and goes toward the right.*]

The Daughter. What is the matter with the dipnet?

The Billposter. Matter? Well, I don't know as there is anything the matter with it —but it just didn't turn out as I had expected, and the pleasure of it was not so much after all.

The Daughter. How did you expect it to be?

The Billposter. How?—Well, I couldn't tell exactly——

The Daughter. I can tell you! You had expected it to be what it was not. It had to be green, but not that kind of green.

The Billposter. You have it, Madam. You understand it all—and that is why everybody goes to you with his worries. If you would only listen to me a little also——

The Daughter. Of course, I will!—Come in to me and pour out your heart.

[*She goes into the lodge.*]
[THE BILLPOSTER *remains outside, speaking to her.*]
[*The stage is darkened again. When the light is turned on, the tree has resumed its leaves, the monk's-hood is blooming once more, and the sun is shining on the green space beyond the passageway.*]
[THE OFFICER *enters. Now he is old and white-haired, ragged, and wearing worn-out shoes. He carries the bare remnants of the rose stems. Walks to and fro slowly, with the gait of an aged man. Reads on the posted bill.*]
[*A* BALLET GIRL *comes in from the right.*]

The Officer. Is Miss Victoria gone?

The Ballet Girl. No, she has not gone yet.

The Officer. Then I shall wait. She will be coming soon, don't you think?

The Ballet Girl. Oh, yes, I am sure.

The Officer. Don't go away now, for I have sent word to the locksmith, so you will soon see what is behind that door.

The Ballet Girl. Oh, it will be awfully interesting to see that door opened. That door, there, and the Growing Castle—have you heard of the Growing Castle?

The Officer. Have I?—I have been a prisoner in it.

The Ballet Girl. No, was that you? But why do they keep such a lot of horses there?

The Officer. Because it is a stable castle, don't you know.

The Ballet Girl. [*With confusion.*] How stupid of me not to guess that!

[*A* MALE CHORUS SINGER *enters from the right.*]

The Officer. Has Miss Victoria gone yet?

The Chorus Singer. [*Earnestly.*] No, she has not. She never goes away.

The Officer. That is because she loves me—— See here, don't go before the locksmith comes to open the door here.

The Chorus Singer. No, is the door going to be opened? Well, that will be fun!—I just want to ask the Portress something.

[THE PROMPTER *enters from the right.*]

The Officer. Is Miss Victoria gone yet?

The Prompter. Not that I know of.

The Officer. Now, didn't I tell you she was waiting for me?—Don't go away, for the door is going to be opened.

The Prompter. Which door?

The Officer. Is there more than one door?

The Prompter. Oh, I know—that one with the clover leaf. Well, then, I have got to stay—— I am only going to have a word with the Portress.

[THE BALLET GIRL, THE CHORUS SINGER, *and* THE PROMPTER *gather beside* THE BILLPOSTER *in front of the lodge window and talk by turns to* THE DAUGHTER.]
[THE GLAZIER *enters through the gate.*]

The Officer. Are you the locksmith?

The Glazier. No, the locksmith had visitors, and a glazier will do just as well.

The Officer. Yes, of course, of course—but did you bring your diamond along?

The Glazier. Why, certainly!—A glazier without his diamond, what would that be?

The Officer. Nothing at all!—Let us get to work then.

[*Claps his hands together. All gather in a ring around the door.* MALE MEMBERS *of the chorus dressed as Master Singers and* BALLET GIRLS *in costumes from the opera "Aïda" enter from the right and join the rest.*]

The Officer. Locksmith—or glazier—do your duty!

[THE GLAZIER *goes up to the door with the diamond in his hand.*]

The Officer. A moment like this will not occur twice in a man's life. For this reason, my friends, I ask you—please consider carefully——

A Policeman. [*Enters.*] In the name of the law, I forbid the opening of that door!

The Officer. Oh, Lord! What a fuss there is as soon as anybody wants to do anything new or great. But we will take the matter into court—let us go to the Lawyer. Then we shall see whether the laws still exist or not—— Come along to the Lawyer.

[*Without lowering of the curtain, the stage changes to a lawyer's office, and in this manner: The gate remains, but as a wicket in the railing running clear across the stage. The gatekeeper's lodge turns into the private enclosure of* THE LAW-YER, *and it is now entirely open to the front. The linden, leafless, becomes a hat tree. The billboard is covered with legal notices and court decisions. The door with the four-leaved clover hole forms part of a document chest.*]

[THE LAWYER, *in evening dress and white necktie, is found sitting to the left, inside the gate, and in front of him stands a desk covered with papers. His appearance indicates enormous suffer-ings. His face is chalk-white and full of wrinkles, and its shadows have a purple effect. He is ugly, and his features seem to reflect all the crimes and vices with which he has been forced by his profes-sion to come into contact. Of his two* CLERKS, *one has lost an arm, the other an eye.*]

[*The* PEOPLE *gathered to witness "the opening of the door" remain as before, but they appear now to be waiting for an audience with* THE LAWYER. *Judging by their atttitudes, one would think they had been standing there forever.*]

[THE DAUGHTER, *still wearing the shawl, and* THE OFFICER *are near the foot-lights.*]

The Lawyer. [*Goes over to* THE DAUGH-TER.] Tell me, sister, can I have that shawl? I shall keep it here until I have a fire in my grate, and then I shall burn it with all its miseries and sorrows.

The Daughter. Not yet, brother. I want it to hold all it possibly can, and I want it above all to take up your agonies—all the confidences you have received about crime, vice, robbery, slander, abuse——

The Lawyer. My dear girl, for such a pur-pose your shawl would prove totally insuffi-cient. Look at these walls. Does it not look as if the wall-paper itself had been soiled by every conceivable sin? Look at these docu-ments into which I write tales of wrong. Look at myself—— No smiling man ever comes here; nothing is to be seen here but angry glances, snarling lips, clenched fists— And everybody pours his anger, his envy, his suspicions, upon me. Look—my hands are black, and no washing will clean them. See how they are chapped and bleeding—— I can never wear my clothes more than a few days because they smell of other people's crimes— At times I have the place fumigated with sulphur, but it does not help. I sleep near by, and I dream of nothing but crimes—— Just now I have a murder case in court—oh, I can

stand that, but do you know what is worse than anything else?—That is to separate married people! Then it is as if something cried way down in the earth and up there in the sky—as if it cried treason against the primal force, against the source of all good, against love—— And do you know, when reams of paper have been filled with mutual accusations, and at last a sympathetic person takes one of the two apart and asks, with a pinch of the ear or a smile, the simple ques-tion: what have you really got against your husband?—or your wife?—then he, or she, stands perplexed and cannot give the cause. Once—well, I think a lettuce salad was the principal issue; another time it was just a word—mostly it is nothing at all. But the tortures, the sufferings—these I have to bear —See how I look! Do you think I could ever win a woman's love with this countenance so like a criminal's? Do you think anybody dares to be friendly with me, who have to collect all the debts, all the money obliga-tions, of the whole city?—It is a misery to be man!

The Daughter. Men are to be pitied!

The Lawyer. They are. And what people are living on puzzles me. They marry on an income of two thousand, when they need four thousand. They borrow, of course— everybody borrows. In some sort of happy-go-lucky fashion, by the skin of their teeth, they manage to pull through—and thus it continues to the end, when the estate is found to be bankrupt. Who pays for it at last no one can tell.

The Daughter. Perhaps He who feeds the birds.

The Lawyer. Perhaps. But if He who feeds the birds would only pay a visit to this earth of His and see for Himself how the poor human creatures fare—then His heart would surely fill with compassion.

The Daughter. Men are to be pitied!

The Lawyer. Yes, that is the truth!— [*To* THE OFFICER.] What do you want?

The Officer. I just wanted to ask if Miss Victoria has gone yet.

The Lawyer. No, she has not; you can be sure of it—— Why are you poking at my chest over there?

The Officer. I thought the door of it looked exactly——

The Lawyer. Not at all! Not at all!

[*All the church bells begin to ring.*]

The Officer. Is there going to be a fu-neral?

The Lawyer. No, it is graduation day—a number of degrees will be conferred, and I am going to be made a Doctor of Laws. Perhaps you would also like to be graduated and receive a laurel wreath?

The Officer. Yes, why not? That would be a diversion, at least.

The Lawyer. Perhaps then we may begin upon this solemn function at once—— But you had better go home and change your clothes.   [THE OFFICER *goes out.*]

[*The stage is darkened and the following changes are made. The railing stays, but it encloses now the chancel of a church. The billboard displays hymn numbers. The linden hat tree becomes a candelabrum.* THE LAWYER'S *desk is turned into the desk of the presiding functionary, and the door with the clover leaf leads to the vestry.*]

[*The chorus of* MASTER SINGERS *become heralds with staffs, and the* BALLET GIRLS *carry laurel wreaths. The rest of the* PEOPLE *act as spectators.*]

[*The background is raised, and the new one thus discovered represents a large church organ, with the keyboards below and the organist's mirror above.*]

[*Music is heard. At the sides stand figures symbolizing the four academic faculties: Philosophy, Theology, Medicine, and Jurisprudence.*]

[*At first the stage is empty for a few moments.*]

[HERALDS *enter from the right.* BALLET GIRLS *follow with laurel wreaths carried high before them.* THREE GRADUATES *appear one after another from the left, receive their wreaths from the* BALLET GIRLS, *and go out to the right.* THE LAWYER *steps forward to get his wreath. The* BALLET GIRLS *turn away from him and refuse to place the wreath on his head. Then they withdraw from the stage.* THE LAWYER, *shocked, leans against a column. All the others withdraw gradually until only* THE LAWYER *remains on the stage.*]

The Daughter. [*Enters, her head and shoulders covered by a white veil.*] Do you see, I have washed the shawl! But why are you standing there? Did you get your wreath?

The Lawyer. No, I was not held worthy.

The Daughter. Why? Because you have defended the poor, put in a good word for the wrong-doers, made the burden easier for the guilty, obtained a respite for the condemned? Woe upon men: they are not angels —but they are to be pitied!

The Lawyer. Say nothing evil of men— for after all it is my task to voice their side.

The Daughter. [*Leaning against the organ.*] Why do they strike their friends in the face?

The Lawyer. They know no better.

The Daughter. Let us enlighten them. Will you try? Together with me?

The Lawyer. They do not accept enlightenment—— Oh, that our plaint might reach the gods of heaven!

The Daughter. It shall reach the throne— [*Turns toward the organ.*] Do you know what I see in this mirror?—The world turned the right way!—Yes indeed, for naturally we see it upside down.

The Lawyer. How did it come to be turned the wrong way?

The Daughter. When the copy was taken——

The Lawyer. You have said it! The copy—I have always had the feeling that it was a spoiled copy. And when I began to recall the original images, I grew dissatisfied with everything. But men called it soreheadedness, looking at the world through the devil's eyes, and other such things.

The Daughter. It is certainly a crazy world! Look at the four faculties here. The government, to which has fallen the task of preserving society, supports all four of them. Theology, the science of God, is constantly attacked and ridiculed by philosophy, which declares itself to be the sum of all wisdom. And medicine is always challenging philosophy, while refusing entirely to count theology a science and even insisting on calling it a mere superstition. And they belong to a common Academic Council, which has been set to teach the young respect—for the university. It is a bedlam. And woe unto him who first recovers his reason!

The Lawyer. Those who find it out first are the theologians. As a preparatory study, they take philosophy, which teaches them that theology is nonsense. Later they learn from theology that philosophy is nonsense. Madmen, I should say!

The Daughter. And then there is jurisprudence which serves all but the servants.

The Lawyer. Justice, which, when it wants to do right, becomes the undoing of men. Equity, which so often turns into iniquity!

The Daughter. What a mess you have made of it, you man-children. Children, indeed!—Come here, and I will give you a wreath—one that is more becoming to you. [*Puts a crown of thorns on his head.*] And now I will play for you.

[*She sits down at the keyboards, but instead of organ-notes human voices are heard.*]

Voices of Children. O Lord everlasting!
[*Last note sustained.*]
Voices of Women. Have mercy upon us!
[*Last note sustained.*]
Voices of Men. [*Tenors.*] Save us for Thy mercy's sake!
[*Last note sustained.*]
Voices of Men. [*Basses.*] Spare Thy Children, O Lord, and deliver us from Thy wrath!
All. Have mercy upon us! Hear us! Have pity upon the mortals!—O Lord eternal, why art Thou afar?—Out of the depths we call unto Thee: Make not the burden of Thy children too heavy! Hear us! Hear us!

[*The stage turns dark. The* DAUGHTER *rises and draws close to* THE LAWYER. *By a change of light, the organ becomes Fingal's Cave. The ground-swell of the ocean, which can be seen rising and falling between the columns of basalt, produces a deep harmony that blends the music of winds and waves.*]

The Lawyer. Where are we, sister?
The Daughter. What do you hear?
The Lawyer. I hear drops falling——
The Daughter. Those are the tears that men are weeping—— What more do you hear?
The Lawyer. There is sighing—and whining—and wailing——
The Daughter. Hither the plaint of the mortals has reached—and no farther. But why this never-ending wailing? Is there then nothing in life to rejoice at?
The Lawyer. Yes, what is most sweet, and what is also most bitter—love—wife and home—the highest and the lowest!
The Daughter. May I try it?
The Lawyer. With me?
The Daughter. With you—— You know the rocks, the stumbling-stones. Let us avoid them.
The Lawyer. I am so poor.
The Daughter. What does that matter if we only love each other? And a little beauty costs nothing.
The Lawyer. I have dislikes which may prove your likes.
The Daughter. They can be adjusted.
The Lawyer. And if we tire of it?
The Daughter. Then come the children and bring with them a diversion that remains for ever new.
The Lawyer. You, you will take me, poor and ugly, scorned and rejected?
The Daughter. Yes—let us unite our destinies.
The Lawyer. So be it then!

CURTAIN

An extremely plain room inside THE LAWYER'S *office. To the right, a big double bed covered by a canopy and curtained in. Next to it, a window. To the left, an iron heater with cooking utensils on top of it.*
[CHRISTINE *is pasting paper strips along the cracks of the double windows. In the background, an open door to the office. Through the door are visible a number of poor* CLIENTS *waiting for admission.*]

Christine. I paste, I paste.
The Daughter. [*Pale and emaciated, sits by the stove.*] You shut out all the air. I choke!
Christine. Now there is only one little crack left.
The Daughter. Air, air—I cannot breathe!
Christine. I paste, I paste.
The Lawyer. That's right, Christine! Heat is expensive.
The Daughter. Oh, it feels as if my lips were being glued together.
The Lawyer. [*Standing in the doorway, with a paper in his hand.*] Is the child asleep?
The Daughter. Yes, at last.
The Lawyer. [*Gently.*] All this crying scares away my clients.
The Daughter. [*Pleasantly.*] What can be done about it?
The Lawyer. Nothing.
The Daughter. We shall have to get a larger place.
The Lawyer. We have no money for it.
The Daughter. May I open the window—this bad air is suffocating.
The Lawyer. Then the heat escapes, and we shall be cold.
The Daughter. It is horrible!—May we clean up out there?
The Lawyer. You have not the strength to do any cleaning, nor have I; and Christine must paste. She must put strips through the whole house, on every crack, in the ceiling, in the floor, in the walls.
The Daughter. Poverty I was prepared for, but not for dirt.
The Lawyer. Poverty is always dirty, relatively speaking.
The Daughter. This is worse than I dreamed!
The Lawyer. We are not the worst off by far. There is still food in the pot.
The Daughter. But what sort of food?
The Lawyer. Cabbage is cheap, nourishing, and good to eat.
The Daughter. For those who like cabbage—to me it is repulsive.
The Lawyer. Why didn't you say so?

The Daughter. Because I loved you, I wanted to sacrifice my own taste.

The Lawyer. Then I must sacrifice my taste for cabbage to you—for sacrifices must be mutual.

The Daughter. What are we to eat, then? Fish? But you hate fish.

The Lawyer. And it is expensive.

The Daughter. This is worse than I thought it!

The Lawyer. [*Kindly.*] Yes, you see how hard it is—— And the child that was to become a link and a blessing—it becomes our ruin.

The Daughter. Dearest, I die in this air, in this room, with its backyard view, with its baby cries and endless hours of sleeplessness, with those people out there, and their whinings, and bickerings, and incriminations—— I shall die here!

The Lawyer. My poor little flower, that has no light and no air——

The Daughter. And you say that people exist who are still worse off?

The Lawyer. I belong with the envied ones in this locality.

The Daughter. Everything else might be borne, if I could only have some beauty in my home.

The Lawyer. I know you are thinking of flowers—and especially of heliotropes—but a plant costs half a dollar, which will buy us six quarts of milk or a peck of potatoes.

The Daughter. I could gladly get along without food, if I could only have some flowers.

The Lawyer. There is a kind of beauty that costs nothing—but the absence of it in the home is worse than any other torture to a man with a sense for the beautiful.

The Daughter. What is it?

The Lawyer. If I tell, you will get angry.

The Daughter. We have agreed not to get angry.

The Lawyer. We have agreed—— Everything can be overcome, Agnes, except the short, sharp accents—— Do you know them? Not yet!

The Daughter. They will never be heard between us.

The Lawyer. Not as far as it lies in me!

The Daughter. Tell me now.

The Lawyer. Well—when I come into a room, I look first of all at the curtains— [*Goes over to the window and straightens out the curtains.*] If they hang like ropes or rags, then I leave soon. And next I take a glance at the chairs—if they stand straight along the wall, then I stay. [*Puts a chair back against the wall.*] Finally I look at the candles in their sticks—if they point this way and that, then the whole house is askew. [*Straightens up a candle on the chest of drawers.*] This is the kind of beauty, dear heart, that costs nothing.

The Daughter. [*With bent head.*] Beware of the short accents, Axel!

The Lawyer. They were not short.

The Daughter. Yes, they were.

The Lawyer. Well, I'll be——

The Daughter. What kind of language is that?

The Lawyer. Pardon me, Agnes! But I have suffered as much from your lack of orderliness as you have suffered from dirt. And I have not dared to set things right myself, for when I do so, you get as angry as if I were reproaching you—ugh! Hadn't we better quit now?

The Daughter. It is very difficult to be married—it is more difficult than anything else. One has to be an angel, I think!

The Lawyer. I think so, too.

The Daughter. I fear I shall begin to hate you after this!

The Lawyer. Woe to us then!—But let us forestall hatred. I promise never again to speak of any untidiness—although it is torture to me!

The Daughter. And I shall eat cabbage though it means agony to me.

The Lawyer. A life of common suffering, then! One's pleasure, the other one's pain!

The Daughter. Men are to be pitied!

The Lawyer. You see that?

The Daughter. Yes, but for heaven's sake, let us avoid the rocks, now when we know them so well.

The Lawyer. Let us try! Are we not decent and intelligent persons? Able to forbear and forgive?

The Daughter. Why not smile at mere trifles?

The Lawyer. We—only we—can do so. Do you know, I read this morning—by the bye, where is the newspaper?

The Daughter. [*Embarrassed.*] Which newspaper?

The Lawyer. [*Sharply.*] Do I keep more than one?

The Daughter. Smile now, and don't speak sharply—I used your paper to make the fire with——

The Lawyer. [*Violently.*] Well, I'll be damned!

The Daughter. Why don't you smile?—I burned it because it ridiculed what is holy to me.

The Lawyer. Which is unholy to me! Yah! [*Strikes one clenched fist against the open palm of the other hand.*] I smile, I smile so that my wisdom teeth show—— Of course, I am to be nice, and I am to swallow my own opinions, and say yes to everything, and cringe and dissemble! [*Tidies the curtains around the bed.*] That's it! Now I am going to fix things until you get angry again—Agnes, this is simply impossible!

The Daughter. Of course it is!

The Lawyer. And yet we must endure—not for the sake of our promises, but for the sake of the child!

The Daughter. You are right—for the sake of the child. Oh, oh—we have to endure!

The Lawyer. And now I must go out to my clients. Listen to them—how they growl with impatience to tear each other, to get each other fined and jailed——Lost souls!

The Daughter. Poor, poor people! And this pasting!

[*She drops her head forward in dumb despair.*]

Christine. I paste, I paste.

[THE LAWYER *stands at the door, twisting the doorknob nervously.*]

The Daughter. How that knob squeaks! It is as if you were twisting my heartstrings——

The Lawyer. I twist, I twist!

The Daughter. Don't!

The Lawyer. I twist!

The Daughter. No!

The Lawyer. I——

The Officer. [*In the office, on the other side of the door, takes hold of the knob.*] Will you permit me?

The Lawyer. [*Lets go his hold.*] By all means. Seeing that you have your degree!

The Officer. Now all life belongs to me. Every road lies open. I have mounted Parnassus. The laurel is won. Immortality, fame, all is mine!

The Lawyer. And what are you going to live on?

The Officer. Live on?

The Lawyer. You must have a home, clothes, food——

The Officer. Oh, that will come—if you can only find somebody to love you!

The Lawyer. You don't say so!—You don't—— Paste, Christine, paste until they cannot breathe!

[*Goes out backward, nodding.*]

Christine. I paste, I paste—until they cannot breathe.

The Officer. Will you come with me now?

The Daughter. At once! But where?

The Officer. To Fairhaven. There it is summer; there the sun is shining; there we find youth, children, and flowers, singing and dancing, feasting and frolicking.

The Daughter. Then I will go there.

The Officer. Come!

The Lawyer. [*Enters again.*] Now I go back to my first hell—this was the second and greater. The sweeter the hell, the greater—— And look here, now she has been dropping hair-pins on the floor again.

[*He picks up some hair-pins.*]

The Officer. My! but he has discovered the pins also.

The Lawyer. Also?—Look at this one. You see two prongs, but it is only one pin. It is two, yet only one. If I bend it open, it is a single piece. If I bend it back, there are two, but they remain one for all that. It means: these two are one. But if I break—like this!—then they become two.

[*Breaks the pin and throws the pieces away.*]

The Officer. All that he has seen!—But before breaking, the prongs must diverge. If they point together, then it holds.

The Lawyer. And if they are parallel, then they will never meet—and it neither breaks nor holds.

The Officer. The hair-pin is the most perfect of all created things. A straight line which equals two parallel ones.

The Lawyer. A lock that shuts when it is open.

The Officer. And thus shuts in a braid of hair that opens up when the lock shuts.

The Lawyer. It is like this door. When I close it, then I open—the way out—for you, Agnes!

[*Withdraws and closes the door behind him.*]

The Daughter. Well then?

[*The stage changes. The bed with its curtains becomes a tent. The stove stays as it was. The background is raised. To the right, in the foreground, are seen hills stripped of their trees by fire, and red heather growing between the blackened tree stumps. Red-painted pig-sties and outhouses. Beyond these, in the open, apparatus for mechanical gymnastics, where sick persons are being treated on machines resembling instruments of torture. To the left, in the foreground, the quarantine station, consisting of open sheds, with ovens, furnaces, and pipe coils. In the middle distance, a narrow strait. The background shows a beautiful wooded shore. Flags are flying on its piers, where ride white sailboats, some with sails set and some without. Little Italian villas, pavilions, arbors,*] *marble statues are glimpsed through the foliage along the shore.*]

[THE MASTER OF QUARANTINE, *made up like a blackamoor, is walking along the shore.*]

The Officer. [*Meets him and they shake hands.*] Why Ordström![1] Have you landed here?

Master of Q. Yes, here I am.

The Officer. Is this Fairhaven?

Master of Q. No, that is on the other side. This is Foulstrand.

The Officer. Then we have lost our way.

Master of Q. We?—Won't you introduce me?

The Officer. No, that wouldn't do. [*In a lowered voice.*] It is Indra's own daughter.

Master of Q. Indra's? And I was thinking of Varuna[2] himself—— Well, are you not surprised to find me black in the face?

The Officer. I am past fifty, my boy, and at that age one has ceased to be surprised. I concluded at once that you were bound for some fancy ball this afternoon.

Master of Q. Right you were! And I hope both of you will come along.

The Officer. Why, yes—for I must say —the place does not look very tempting. What kind of people live here anyhow?

Master of Q. Here you find the sick; over there, the healthy.

The Officer. Nothing but poor folk on this side, I suppose.

Master of Q. No, my boy, it is here you find the rich. Look at that one on the rack. He has stuffed himself with *paté de foie gras* and truffles and Burgundy until his feet have grown knotted.

The Officer. Knotted?

Master of Q. Yes, he has a case of knotted feet. And that one who lies under the guillotine—he has swilled brandy so that his backbone has to be put through the mangle.

The Officer. There is always something amiss!

Master of Q. Moreover, everybody living on this side has some kind of canker to hide. Look at the fellow coming here, for instance.

[*An old DANDY is pushed on the stage in a wheel-chair. He is accompanied by a gaunt and grisly COQUETTE in the sixties, to whom THE FRIEND, a man of about forty, is paying court.*]

The Officer. It is the major—our schoolmate!

---

[1] Means literally "wordspout."
[2] The Hindu god of the ocean.

Master of Q. Don Juan. Can you see that he is still enamored of that old spectre beside him? He does not notice that she has grown old, or that she is ugly, faithless, cruel.

The Officer. Why, that is love! And I couldn't have dreamt that a fickle fellow like him would prove capable of loving so deeply and so earnestly.

Master of Q. That is a mighty decent way of looking at it.

The Officer. I have been in love with Victoria myself—in fact I am still waiting for her in the passageway——

Master of Q. Oh, you are the fellow who is waiting in the passageway?

The Officer. I am the man.

Master of Q. Well, have you got that door opened yet?

The Officer. No, the case is still in court —— The Billposter is out with his dipnet, of course, so that the taking of evidence is always being put off—and in the meantime the Glazier has mended all the window panes in the castle, which has grown half a story higher—— This has been an uncommonly good year—warm and wet——

Master of Q. But just the same you have had no heat comparing with what I have here.

The Officer. How much do you have in your ovens?

Master of Q. When we fumigate cholera suspects, we run it up to one hundred and forty degrees.

The Officer. Is the cholera going again?

Master of Q. Don't you know that?

The Officer. Of course, I know it, but I forget so often what I know.

Master of Q. I wish often that I could forget—especially myself. That is why I go in for masquerades and carnivals and amateur theatricals.

The Officer. What have you been up to, then?

Master of Q. If I told, they would say that I was boasting; and if I don't tell, then they call me a hypocrite.

The Officer. That is why you blackened your face?

Master of Q. Exactly—making myself a shade blacker than I am.

The Officer. Who is coming here?

Master of Q. Oh, a poet who is going to have his mud bath.

[THE POET *enters with his eyes raised toward the sky and carrying a pail of mud in one hand.*]

The Officer. Why, he ought to be having light baths and air baths.

Master of Q. No, he is roaming about the higher region so much that he gets homesick for the mud—and wallowing in the mire makes the skin callous like that of a pig. Then he cannot feel the stings of the wasps.

The Officer. This is a queer world, full of contradictions.

The Poet. [*Ecstatically.*] Man was created by the god Phtah out of clay on a potter's wheel, or a lathe— [*Sceptically.*] or any damned old thing! [*Ecstatically.*] Out of clay does the sculptor create his more or less immortal masterpieces— [*Sceptically.*] which mostly are pure rot. [*Ecstatically.*] Out of clay they make those utensils which are so indispensable in the pantry and which generically are named pots and plates— [*Sceptically.*] but what in thunder does it matter to me what they are called anyhow? [*Esctatically.*] Such is the clay! When clay becomes fluid, it is called mud—— *C'est mon affaire!*— [*Shouts.*] Lena!

[LENA *enters with a pail in her hand.*]

The Poet. Lena, show yourself to Miss Agnes—— She knew you ten years ago, when you were a young, happy and, let us say, pretty girl—— Behold how she looks now. Five children, drudgery, baby-cries, hunger, ill-treatment. See how beauty has perished and joy vanished in the fulfilment of duties which should have brought that inner satisfaction which makes each line in the face harmonious and fills the eye with a quiet glow.

Master of Q. [*Covering* THE POET'S *mouth with his hand.*] Shut up! Shut up!

The Poet. That is what they all say. And if you keep silent, then they cry: speak! Oh, restless humanity!

The Daughter. [*Goes to* LENA.] Tell me your troubles.

Lena. No, I dare not, for then they will be made worse.

The Daughter. Who could be so cruel?

Lena. I dare not tell, for if I do, I shall be spanked.

The Poet. That is just what will happen. But I will speak, even though the blackamoor knock out all my teeth—I will tell that justice is not always done—Agnes, daughter of the gods, do you hear music and dancing on the hill over there?—Well, it is Lena's sister who has come home from the city where she went astray—you understand? Now they are killing the fatted calf; but Lena, who stayed at home, has to carry slop pails and feed the pigs.

The Daughter. There is rejoicing at home because the stray has left the paths of evil, and not merely because she has come back. Bear that in mind.

The Poet. But then they should give a ball and banquet every night for the spotless worker that never strayed into paths of error—— Yet they do nothing of the kind, but when Lena has a free moment, she is sent to prayer-meetings where she has to hear reproaches for not being perfect. Is this justice?

The Daughter. Your question is so difficult to answer because—— There are so many unforeseen cases——

The Poet. That much the Caliph, Haroun the Just, came to understand. He was sitting on his throne, and from its height he could never make out what happened below. At last complaints penetrated to his exalted ears. And then, one fine day, he disguised himself and descended unobserved among the crowds to find out what kind of justice they were getting.

The Daughter. I hope you don't take me for Haroun the Just!

The Officer. Let us talk of something else —— Here come visitors.

[*A white boat, shaped like a viking ship, with a dragon for figure-head, with a pale-blue silken sail on a gilded yard, and with a rose-red standard flying from the top of a gilded mast, glides through the strait from the left.* HE *and* SHE *are seated in the stern with their arms around each other.*]

The Officer. Behold perfect happiness, bliss without limits, young love's rejoicing!
[*The stage grows brighter.*]

He. [*Stands up in the boat and sings.*]

Hail, beautiful haven,
Where the Springs of my youth were spent,
Where my first sweet dreams were dreamt—
To thee I return
But lonely no longer!

Ye hills and groves,
Thou sky o'erhead,
Thou mirroring sea,
Give greeting to her:
My love, my bride,
My light and my life!

[*The flags at the landings of Fairhaven are dipped in salute; white handkerchiefs are waved from verandahs and boats, and the air is filled with tender chords from harps and violins.*]

The Poet. See the light that surrounds

them! Hear how the air is ringing with music!—Eros!

The Officer. It is Victoria.

Master of Q. Well, what of it?

The Officer. It is his Victoria—— My own is still mine. And nobody can see her—— Now you hoist the quarantine flag, and I shall pull in the net.

[THE MASTER OF QUARANTINE *waves a yellow flag.*]

The Officer. [*Pulling a rope that turns the boat toward Foulstrand.*] Hold on there!

[HE *and* SHE *become aware of the hideous view and give vent to their horror.*]

Master of Q. Yes, it comes hard. But here every one must stop who hails from plague-stricken places.

The Poet. The idea of speaking in such manner, or acting in such a way, in the presence of two human beings united in love! Touch them not! Lay not hands on love! It is treason—— Woe to us! Everything beautiful must now be dragged down—dragged into the mud!

[HE *and* SHE *step ashore, looking sad and shamefaced.*]

He. Woe to us! What have we done?

Master of Q. It is not necessary to have done anything in order to encounter life's little pricks.

She. So short-lived are joy and happiness!

He. How long must we stay here?

Master of Q. Forty days and nights.

She. Then rather into the water!

He. To live here—among blackened hills and pig-sties?

The Poet. Love overcomes all, even sulphur fumes and carbolic acid.

Master of Q. [*Starts a fire in the stove; blue, sulphurous flames break forth.*] Now I set the sulphur going. Will you please step in?

She. Oh, my blue dress will fade.

Master of Q. And become white. So your roses will also turn white in time.

He. Even your cheeks—in forty days!

She. [*To* THE OFFICER.] That will please you.

The Officer. No, it will not!—Of course, your happiness was the cause of my suffering, but—it doesn't matter—for I am graduated and have obtained a position over there —heigh-ho and alas! And in the Fall I shall be teaching school—teaching boys the same lessons I myself learned during my childhood and youth—the same lessons throughout my manhood and, finally, in my old age —the self-same lessons! What does twice two make? How many times can four be evenly divided by two?—Until I get a pen-sion and can do nothing at all—just wait around for meals and the newspapers—until at last I am carted to the crematorium and burned to ashes—— Have you nobody here who is entitled to a pension? Barring twice two makes four, it is probably the worst thing of all—to begin school all over again when one already is graduated; to ask the same questions until death comes——

[*An* ELDERLY MAN *goes by, with his hands folded behind his back.*]

The Officer. There is a pensioner now, waiting for himself to die. I think he must be a captain who missed the rank of major; or an assistant judge who was not made a chief justice. Many are called but few are chosen—— He is waiting for his breakfast now.

The Pensioner. No, for the newspaper— the morning paper.

The Officer. And he is only fifty-four years old. He may spend twenty-five more years waiting for meals and newspapers—is it not dreadful?

The Pensioner. What is not dreadful? Tell me, tell me!

The Officer. Tell that who can!—Now I shall have to teach boys that twice two makes four. And how many times four can be evenly divided by two. [*He clutches his head in despair.*] And Victoria, whom I loved and therefore wished all the happiness life can give—now she has her happiness, the greatest one known to her, and for this reason I suffer—suffer, suffer!

She. Do you think I can be happy when I see you suffering? How can you think it? Perhaps it will soothe your pains that I am to be imprisoned here for forty days and nights? Tell me, does it soothe your pains?

The Officer. Yes and no. How can I enjoy seeing you suffer? Oh!

She. And do you think my happiness can be founded on your torments?

The Officer. We are to be pitied—all of us!

All. [*Raise their arms toward the sky and utter a cry of anguish that sounds like a dissonant chord.*] Oh!

The Daughter. Everlasting One, hear them! Life is evil! Men are to be pitied!

All. [*As before.*] Oh!

[*For a moment the stage is completely darkened, and during that moment* EVERYBODY *withdraws or takes up a new position. When the light is turned on again, Foulstrand is seen in the background, lying in deep shadow. The strait is in the middle distance and Fairhaven in the foreground, both steeped*

in light. To the right, a corner of the Casino, where DANCING COUPLES *are visible through the open windows.* THREE SERVANT MAIDS *are standing outside on top of an empty box, with arms around each other, staring at the dancers within. On the verandah of the Casino stands a bench, where* "PLAIN" EDITH *is sitting. She is bareheaded, with an abundance of tousled hair, and looks sad. In front of her is an open piano. To the left, a frame house painted yellow.* TWO CHILDREN *in light dresses are playing ball outside. In the centre of the middle distance, a pier with white sailboats tied to it, and flag poles with hoisted flags. In the strait is anchored a naval vessel, brig-rigged, with gun ports. But the entire landscape is in winter dress, with snow on the ground and on the bare trees.]*
*[*THE DAUGHTER *and* THE OFFICER *enter.]*

The Daughter. Here is peace, and happiness, and leisure. No more toil; every day a holiday; everybody dressed up in his best; dancing and music in the early morning. *[To* THE MAIDS.*]* Why don't you go in and have a dance, girls?

The Maids. We?

The Officer. They are servants, don't you see!

The Daughter. Of course!—But why is Edith sitting there instead of dancing?

*[*EDITH *buries her face in her hands.]*

The Officer. Don't question her! She has been sitting there three hours without being asked for a dance.

[Goes into the yellow house on the left.]

The Daughter. What a cruel form of amusement!

The Mother. *[In a low-necked dress, enters from the Casino and goes up to* EDITH.*]* Why don't you go in as I told you?

Edith. Because—I cannot throw myself at them. That I am ugly I know, and I know that nobody wants to dance with me, but I might be spared from being reminded of it.

[Begins to play on the piano a Toccata con fuga by Sebastian Bach.]

[The waltz music from within is heard faintly at first. Then it grows in strength, as if to compete with the Bach Toccata. EDITH *prevails over it and brings it to silence.* DANCERS *appear in the doorway to hear her play.* EVERYBODY *on the stage stands still and listens reverently.]*

A Naval Officer. *[Takes* ALICE, *one of the dancers, around the waist and drags her toward the pier.]* Come quick!

*[*EDITH *breaks off abruptly, rises and stares at the* COUPLE *with an expression of utter despair; stands as if turned to stone.]*

[Now the front wall of the yellow house disappears, revealing three benches full of SCHOOLBOYS. *Among these* THE OFFICER *is seen, looking worried and depressed. In front of the* BOYS *stands* THE TEACHER, *bespectacled and holding a piece of chalk in one hand, a rattan cane in the other.]*

The Teacher. *[To* THE OFFICER.*]* Well, my boy, can you tell me what twice two makes?

*[*THE OFFICER *remains seated while he racks his mind without finding an answer.]*

The Teacher. You must rise when I ask you a question.

The Officer. *[Harassed, rises.]* Two—twice—let me see. That makes two-two.

The Teacher. I see! You have not studied your lesson.

The Officer. *[Ashamed.]* Yes, I have, but —I know the answer, but I cannot tell it——

The Teacher. You want to wriggle out of it, of course. You know it, but you cannot tell. Perhaps I may help you.

[Pulls his hair.]

The Officer. Oh, it is dreadful, it is dreadful!

The Teacher. Yes, it is dreadful that such a big boy lacks all ambition——

The Officer. *[Hurt.]* Big boy—yes, I am big—bigger than all these others—I am full-grown, I am done with school—— *[As if waking up.]* I have graduated—why am I then sitting here? Have I not received my doctor's degree?

The Teacher. Certainly, but you are to sit here and mature, you know. You have to mature—isn't that so?

The Officer. *[Feels his forehead.]* Yes, that is right, one must mature—— Twice two—makes two—and this I can demonstrate by analogy, which is the highest form of all reasoning. Listen!—Once one makes one; consequently twice two must make two. For what applies in one case must also apply in another.

The Teacher. Your conclusion is based on good logic, but your answer is wrong.

The Officer. What is logical cannot be wrong. Let us test it. One divided by one gives one, so that two divided by two must give two.

The Teacher. Correct according to analogy. But how much does once three make?

The Officer. Three, of course.

The Teacher. Consequently twice three must also make three.

The Officer. [*Pondering.*] No, that cannot be right—it cannot—or else—— [*Sits down dejectedly.*] No, I am not mature yet.

The Teacher. No, indeed, you are far from mature.

The Officer. But how long am I to sit here, then?

The Teacher. Here—how long? Do you believe that time and space exist?—Suppose that time does exist, then you should be able to say what time is. What is time?

The Officer. Time— [*Thinks.*] I cannot tell, but I know what it is. Consequently I may also know that twice two is without being able to tell it. And teacher, can you tell what time is?

The Teacher. Of course I can.

All the Boys. Tell us then!

The Teacher. Time—let me see. [*Stands immovable with one finger on his nose.*] While we are talking, time flies. Consequently time is something that flies while we talk.

A Boy. [*Rising.*] Now you are talking, teacher, and while you are talking, I fly: consequently I am time. [*Runs out.*]

The Teacher. That accords completely with the laws of logic.

The Officer. Then the laws of logic are silly, for Nils, who ran away, cannot be time.

The Teacher. That is also good logic, although it is silly.

The Officer. Then logic itself is silly.

The Teacher. So it seems. But if logic is silly, then all the world is silly—and then the devil himself wouldn't stay here to teach you more silliness. If anybody treats me to a drink, we'll go and take a bath.

The Officer. That is a *posterus prius,* or the world turned upside down, for it is customary to bathe first and have a drink afterward. Old fogy!

The Teacher. Beware of a swelled head, doctor!

The Officer. Call me captain, if you please. I am an officer, and I cannot understand why I should be sitting here to get scolded like a schoolboy——

The Teacher. [*With raised index finger.*] We were to mature!

Master of Q. [*Enters.*] The quarantine begins.

The Officer. Oh, there you are. Just think of it, this fellow makes me sit among the boys although I am graduated.

Master of Q. Well, why don't you go away?

The Officer. Heaven knows!—Go away? Why, that is no easy thing to do.

The Teacher. I guess not—just try!

The Officer. [*To* MASTER OF QUARANTINE.] Save me! Save me from his eye!

Master of Q. Come on. Come and help us dance—— We have to dance before the plague breaks out. We must!

The Officer. Is the brig leaving?

Master of Q. Yes, first of all the brig must leave—— Then there will be a lot of tears shed, of course.

The Officer. Always tears; when she comes and when she goes—— Let us get out of here.

[*They go out.* THE TEACHER *continues his lesson in silence.*]

[THE MAIDS *that were staring through the window of the dance hall walk sadly down to the pier.* EDITH, *who has been standing like a statue at the piano, follows them.*]

The Daughter. [*To* THE OFFICER.] Is there not one happy person to be found in this paradise?

The Officer. Yes, there is a newly married couple. Just watch them.

[THE NEWLY MARRIED COUPLE *enter.*]

Husband. [*To his* WIFE.] My joy has no limits, and I could now wish to die——

Wife. Why die?

Husband. Because at the heart of happiness grows the seed of disaster. Happiness devours itself like a flame—it cannot burn for ever, but must go out some time. And this presentiment of the coming end destroys joy in the very hour of its culmination.

Wife. Let us then die together—this moment!

Husband. Die? All right! For I fear happiness—that cheat!

[*They go toward the water.*]

The Daughter. Life is evil! Men are to be pitied!

The Officer. Look at this fellow. He is the most envied mortal in this neighborhood.

[THE BLIND MAN *is led in.*]

The Officer. He is the owner of these hundred or more Italian villas. He owns all these bays, straits, shores, forests, together with the fishes in the water, the birds in the air, the game in the woods. These thousand or more people are his tenants. The sun rises upon his sea and sets upon his land——

The Daughter. Well—is he complaining also?

The Officer. Yes, and with right, for he cannot see.

Master of Q. He is blind.

The Daughter. The most envied of all!

The Officer. Now he has come to see the brig depart with his son on board.

The Blind Man. I cannot see, but I hear. I hear the anchor bill claw the clay bottom as when the hook is torn out of a fish and brings up the heart with it through the neck—— My son, my only child, is going to journey across the wide sea to foreign lands, and I can follow him only in my thought! Now I hear the clanking of the chain—and —there is something that snaps and cracks like clothes drying on a line—wet handkerchiefs perhaps. And I hear it blubber and snivel as when people are weeping—maybe the splashing of the wavelets among the seines—or maybe girls along the shore, deserted and disconsolate—— Once I asked a child why the ocean is salt, and the child, who had a father on a long trip across the high seas, said immediately: the ocean is salt because the sailors shed so many tears into it. And why do the sailors cry so much then?—Because they are always going away, replied the child; and that is why they are always drying their handkerchiefs in the rigging—— And why does man weep when he is sad? I asked at last—— Because the glass in the eyes must be washed now and then, so that we can see clearly, said the child.

[*The brig has set sail and is gliding off.* THE GIRLS *along the shore are alternately waving their handkerchiefs and wiping off their tears with them. Then a signal is set on the foremast—a red ball in a white field, meaning "yes." In response to it* ALICE *waves her handkerchief triumphantly.*]

The Daughter. [*To* THE OFFICER.] What is the meaning of that flag?

The Officer. It means "yes." It is the lieutenant's troth—red as the red blood of the arteries, set against the blue cloth of the sky.

The Daughter. And how does "no" look?

The Officer. It is blue as the spoiled blood in the veins—but look, how jubilant Alice is.

The Daughter. And how Edith cries.

The Blind Man. Meet and part. Part and meet. That is life. I met his mother. And then she went away from me. He was left to me; and now he goes.

The Daughter. But he will come back.

The Blind Man. Who is speaking to me? I have heard that voice before—in my dreams; in my youth, when vacation began; in the early years of my marriage, when my child was born. Every time life smiled at me, I heard that voice, like a whisper of the south wind, like a chord of harps from above, like what I feel the angels' greeting must be in the Holy Night——

[THE LAWYER *enters and goes up to whisper something into* THE BLIND MAN'S *ear.*]

The Blind Man. Is that so?

The Lawyer. That's the truth. [*Goes to* THE DAUGHTER.] Now you have seen most of it, but you have not yet tried the worst of it.

The Daughter. What can that be?

The Lawyer. Repetition—recurrence. To retrace one's own tracks; to be sent back to the task once finished—come!

The Daughter. Where?

The Lawyer. To your duties.

The Daughter. What does that mean?

The Lawyer. Everything you dread. Everything you do not want but must. It means to forego, to give up, to do without, to lack—it means everything that is unpleasant, repulsive, painful.

The Daughter. Are there no pleasant duties?

The Lawyer. They become pleasant when they are done.

The Daughter. When they have ceased to exist—Duty is then something unpleasant. What is pleasant then?

The Lawyer. What is pleasant is sin.

The Daughter. Sin?

The Lawyer. Yes, something that has to be punished. If I have had a pleasant day or night, then I suffer infernal pangs and a bad conscience the next day.

The Daughter. How strange!

The Lawyer. I wake up in the morning with a headache; and then the repetitions begin, but so that everything becomes perverted. What the night before was pretty, agreeable, witty, is presented by memory in the morning as ugly, distasteful, stupid. Pleasure seems to decay, and all joy goes to pieces. What men call success serves always as a basis for their next failure. My own successes have brought ruin upon me. For men view the fortune of others with an instinctive dread. They regard it unjust that fate should favor any one man, and so they try to restore balance by piling rocks on the road. To have talent is to be in danger of one's life, for then one may easily starve to death!—However, you will have to return to your duties, or I shall bring suit against you, and we shall pass through every court up to the highest—one, two, three!

The Daughter. Return?—To the iron

stove, and the cabbage pot, and the baby clothes——

The Lawyer. Exactly! We have a big wash today, for we must wash all the handkerchiefs——

The Daughter. Oh, must I do it all over again?

The Lawyer. All life is nothing but doing things over again. Look at the teacher in there—— He received his doctor's degree yesterday, was laureled and saluted, climbed Parnassus and was embraced by the monarch —and today he starts school all over again, asks how much twice two makes, and will continue to do so until his death—— However, you must come back to your home!

The Daughter. I would rather die!

The Lawyer. Die?—That is not allowed. First of all, it is a disgrace—so much so that even the dead body is subjected to insults; and secondly, one goes to hell—it is a mortal sin!

The Daughter. It is not easy to be human!

All. Hear!

The Daughter. I shall not go back with you to humiliation and dirt—— I am longing for the heights whence I came—but first the door must be opened so that I may learn the secret—— It is my will that the door be opened!

The Lawyer. Then you must retrace your own steps, cover the road you have already traveled, suffer all annoyances, repetitions, tautologies, recopyings, that a suit will bring with it——

The Daughter. May it come then—— But first I must go into the solitude and the wilderness to recover my own self. We shall meet again! [*To* THE POET.] Follow me.

[*Cries of anguish are heard from a distance:* Woe! Woe! Woe!]

The Daughter. What is that?

The Lawyer. The lost souls at Foulstrand.

The Daughter. Why do they wail more loudly than usual today?

The Lawyer. Because the sun is shining here; because here we have music, dancing, youth. And it makes them feel their own sufferings more keenly.

The Daughter. We must set them free.

The Lawyer. Try it! Once a liberator appeared, and he was nailed to a cross.

The Daughter. By whom?

The Lawyer. By all the right-minded.

The Daughter. Who are they?

The Lawyer. Are you not acquainted with all the right-minded? Then you must learn to know them.

The Daughter. Were they the ones that prevented your graduation?

The Lawyer. Yes.

The Daughter. Then I know them!

CURTAIN

On the shores of the Mediterranean. To the left, in the foreground, a white wall, and above it branches of an orange tree with ripe fruit on them. In the background, villas and a Casino placed on a terrace. To the right, a huge pile of coal and two wheelbarrows. In the background, to the right, a corner of blue sea.

[TWO COALHEAVERS, *naked to the waist, their faces, hands, and bodies blackened by coal dust, are seated on the wheelbarrows. Their expressions show intense despair.*]

[THE DAUGHTER *and* THE LAWYER *in the background.*]

The Daughter. This is paradise!

First Coalheaver. This is hell!

Second Coalheaver. One hundred and twenty degrees in the shadow.

First Heaver. Let's have a bath.

Second Heaver. The police won't let us. No bathing here.

First Heaver. Couldn't we pick some fruit off that tree?

Second Heaver. Then the police would get after us.

First Heaver. But I cannot do a thing in this heat—I'll just chuck the job——

Second Heaver. Then the police will get you for sure!— [*Pause.*] And you wouldn't have anything to eat anyhow.

First Heaver. Nothing to eat? We, who work hardest, get least food; and the rich, who do nothing, get most. Might one not —without disregard of truth—assert that this is injustice?—What has the daughter of the gods to say about it?

The Daughter. I can say nothing at all—— But tell me, what have you done that makes you so black and your lot so hard?

First Heaver. What have we done? We have been born of poor and perhaps not very good parents—— Maybe we have been punished a couple of times.

The Daughter. Punished?

First Heaver. Yes, the unpunished hang out in the Casino up there and dine on eight courses with wine.

The Daughter. [*To* THE LAWYER.] Can that be true?

The Lawyer. On the whole, yes.

The Daughter. You mean to say that

every man at some time has deserved to go to prison?

The Lawyer. Yes.

The Daughter. You, too?

The Lawyer. Yes.

The Daughter. Is it true that the poor cannot bathe in the sea?

The Lawyer. Yes. Not even with their clothes on. None but those who intend to take their own lives escape being fined. And those are said to get a good drubbing at the police station.

The Daughter. But can they not go outside of the city, out into the country, and bathe there?

The Lawyer. There is no place for them —all the land is fenced in.

The Daughter. But I mean in the free, open country.

The Lawyer. There is no such thing—it all belongs to somebody.

The Daughter. Even the sea, the great, vast sea——

The Lawyer. Even that! You cannot sail the sea in a boat and land anywhere without having it put down in writing and charged for. It is lovely!

The Daughter. This is not paradise.

The Lawyer. I should say not!

The Daughter. Why don't men do something to improve their lot?

The Lawyer. Oh, they try, of course, but all the improvers end in prison or in the madhouse——

The Daughter. Who puts them in prison?

The Lawyer. All the right-minded, all the respectable——

The Daughter. Who sends them to the madhouse?

The Lawyer. Their own despair when they grasp the hopelessness of their efforts.

The Daughter. Has the thought not occurred to anybody, that for secret reasons it must be as it is?

The Lawyer. Yes, those who are well off always think so.

The Daughter. That it is all right as it is?

First Heaver. And yet we are the foundations of society. If the coal is not unloaded, then there will be no fire in the kitchen stove, in the parlor grate, or in the factory furnace; then the light will go out in streets and shops and homes; then darkness and cold will descend upon you—and, therefore, we have to sweat as in hell so that the black coals may be had—— And what do you do for us in return?

The Lawyer. [*To* THE DAUGHTER.] Help them!— [*Pause.*] That conditions cannot be

quite the same for everybody, I understand, but why should they differ so widely?

[A GENTLEMAN *and* A LADY *pass across the stage.*]

The Lady. Will you come and play a game with us?

The Gentleman. No, I must take a walk so I can eat something for dinner.

First Heaver. So that he *can* eat something?

Second Heaver. So that he *can*——?

[CHILDREN *enter and cry with horror when they catch sight of the grimy* WORKERS.]

First Heaver. They cry when they see us. They cry——

Second Heaver. Damn it all!—I guess we'll have to pull out the scaffolds soon and begin to operate on this rotten body——

First Heaver. Damn it, I say, too! [*Spits.*]

The Lawyer. [*To* THE DAUGHTER.] Yes, it is all wrong. And men are not so very bad—but——

The Daughter. But——?

The Lawyer. But the government——

The Daughter. [*Goes out, hiding her face in her hands.*] This is not paradise.

Coalheavers. No, hell, that's what it is!

CURTAIN

Fingal's Cave. Long green waves are rolling slowly into the cave. In the foreground, a siren buoy is swaying to and fro in time with the waves, but without sounding except at the indicated moment. Music of the winds. Music of the waves. [THE DAUGHTER *and* THE POET *enter.*]

The Poet. Where are you leading me?

The Daughter. Far away from the noise and lament of the man-children, to the utmost end of the ocean, to the cave that we name Indra's Ear because it is the place where the king of the heavens is said to listen to the complaints of the mortals.

The Poet. What? In this place?

The Daughter. Do you see how this cave is built like a shell? Yes, you can see it. Do you know that your ear, too, is built in the form of a shell? You know it, but have not thought of it. [*She picks up a shell from the beach.*] Have you not as a child held such a shell to your ear and listened—and heard the ripple of your heart-blood, the humming of your thoughts in the brain, the snapping of a thousand little worn-out

threads in the tissues of your body? All that
you hear in this small shell. Imagine then
what may be heard in this larger one!

The Poet. [*Listening.*] I hear nothing
but the whispering of the wind.

The Daughter. Then I shall interpret it
for you. Listen. The wail of the winds.
[*Recites to subdued music.*]

Born beneath the clouds of heaven,
Driven we were by the lightnings of Indra
Down to the sand-covered earth.
Straw from the harvested fields soiled our
   feet;
Dust from the high-roads,
Smoke from the cities,
Foul-smelling breaths,
Fumes from cellars and kitchens,
All we endured.
Then to the open sea we fled,
Filling our lungs with air,
Shaking our wings,
And laving our feet.

Indra, Lord of the Heavens,
Hear us!
Hear our sighing!
Unclean is the earth;
Evil is life;
Neither good nor bad
Can men be deemed.
As they can, they live,
One day at a time.
Sons of dust, through dust they journey;
Born out of dust, to dust they return.
Given they were, for trudging,
Feet, not wings for flying.
Dusty they grow—
Lies the fault then with them,
Or with Thee?

The Poet. Thus I heard it once——
The Daughter. Hush! The winds are still
singing.   [*Recites to subdued music.*]

We, winds that wander,
We, the air's offspring,
Bear with us men's lament
Heard us you have
During gloom-filled Fall nights,
In chimneys and pipes,
In key-holes and door cracks,
When the rain wept on the roof:
Heard us you have
In the snowclad pine woods
Midst wintry gloom:
Heard us you have,
Crooning and moaning
In ropes and rigging
On the high-heaving sea.

It was we, the winds,
Offspring of the air,
Who learned how to grieve
Within human breasts
Through which we passed—
In sick-rooms, on battle-fields,
But mostly where the newborn
Whimpered and wailed
At the pain of living.

We, we the winds,
We are whining and whistling:
Woe! Woe! Woe!

The Poet. It seems to me that I have
already——
The Daughter. Hush! Now the waves
are singing.   [*Recites to subdued music.*]

We, we waves,
That are rocking the winds
To rest—
Green cradles, we waves!
Wet are we, and salty;
Leap like flames of fire—
Wet flames are we:
Burning, extinguishing;
Cleansing, replenishing;
Bearing, engendering.

We, we waves,
That are rocking the winds
To rest!

The Daughter. False waves and faithless!
Everything on earth that is not burned, is
drowned—by the waves. Look at this.
[*Pointing to pile of débris.*] See what the
sea has taken and spoiled! Nothing but the
figure-heads remain of the sunken ships—
and the names: *Justice, Friendship, Golden
Peace, Hope*—this is all that is left of *Hope*
—of fickle *Hope*—railings, tholes, bails! And
lo: the life buoy—which saved itself and let
distressed men perish.

The Poet. [*Searching in the pile.*] Here
is the name-board of the ship *Justice*. That
was the one which left Fairhaven with the
Blind Man's son on board. It is lost then!
And with it are gone the lover of Alice, the
hopeless love of Edith.

The Daughter. The blind man? Fairhaven? I must have been dreaming of them.
And the lover of Alice, "Plain" Edith, Foulstrand and the Quarantine, sulphur and carbolic acid, the graduation in the church, the
Lawyer's office, the passageway and Victoria, the Growing Castle and the Officer——
All this I have been dreaming——

The Poet. It was in one of my poems.

The Daughter. You know then what poetry is——

The Poet. I know then what dreaming is—— But what is poetry?

The Daughter. Not reality, but more than reality—not dreaming, but daylight dreams

The Poet. And the man-children think that we poets are only playing—that we invent and make believe.

The Daughter. And fortunate it is, my friend, for otherwise the world would lie fallow for lack of ministration. Everybody would be stretched on his back, staring into the sky. Nobody would be touching plough or spade, hammer or plane.

The Poet. And you say this, Indra's daughter, you who belong in part up there

The Daughter. You do right in reproaching me. Too long have I stayed down here taking mud baths like you—— My thoughts have lost their power of flight; there is clay on their wings—mire on their feet—and I myself— [*Raising her arms.*] I sink, I sink— Help me, father, Lord of the Heavens! [*Silence.*] I can no longer hear his answer. The ether no longer carries the sound from his lips to my ear's shell—the silvery thread has snapped—— Woe is me, I am earthbound!

The Poet. Do you mean to ascend—soon?

The Daughter. As soon as I have consigned this mortal shape to the flames—for even the waters of the ocean cannot cleanse me. Why do you question me thus?

The Poet. Because I have a prayer——

The Daughter. What kind of prayer?

The Poet. A written supplication from humanity to the ruler of the universe, formulated by a dreamer.

The Daughter. To be presented by whom?

The Poet. By Indra's daughter.

The Daughter. Can you repeat what you have written?

The Poet. I can.

The Daughter. Speak it then.

The Poet. Better that you do it.

The Daughter. Where can I read it?

The Poet. In my mind—or here.

[*Hands her a roll of paper.*]

The Daughter. [*Receives the roll, but reads without looking at it.*] Well, by me it shall be spoken then:

"Why must you be born in anguish?
Why, O man-child, must you always
Wring your mother's heart with torture
When you bring her joy maternal,
Highest happiness yet known?

Why to life must you awaken,
Why to light give natal greeting,
With a cry of anger and of pain?
Why not meet it smiling, man-child,
When the gift of life is counted
In itself a boon unmatched?
Why like beasts should we be coming,
We of race divine and human?
Better garment craves the spirit,
Than one made of filth and blood!
Need a god his teeth be changing——"

—Silence, rash one! Is it seemly
For the work to blame its maker?
No one yet has solved life's riddle.
"Thus begins the human journey
O'er a road of thorns and thistles;
If a beaten path be offered,
It is named at once forbidden;
If a flower you covet, straightway
You are told it is another's;
If a field should bar your progress,
And you dare to break across it,
You destroy your neighbor's harvest;
Others then your own will trample,
That the measure may be evened!
Every moment of enjoyment
Brings to some one else a sorrow,
But your sorrow gladdens no one,
For from sorrow naught but sorrow springs.

"Thus you journey till you die,
And your death brings others' bread."

—Is it thus that you approach,
Son of Dust, the One Most High?

The Poet.
Could the son of dust discover
Words so pure and bright and simple
That to heaven they might ascend——?

Child of gods, wilt thou interpret
Mankind's grievance in some language
That immortals understand?

The Daughter. I will.

The Poet. [*Pointing to the buoy.*] What is that floating there?—A buoy?

The Daughter. Yes.

The Poet. It looks like a lung with a windpipe.

The Daughter. It is the watchman of the seas. When danger is abroad, it sings.

The Poet. It seems to me as if the sea were rising and the waves growing larger——

The Daughter. Not unlikely.

The Poet. Woe! What do I see? A ship bearing down upon the reef.

The Daughter. What ship can that be?

The Poet. The ghost ship of the seas, I think.

The Daughter. What ship is that?

The Poet. The *Flying Dutchman.*

The Daughter. Oh, that one. Why is he punished so hard, and why does he not seek harbor?

The Poet. Because he has seven faithless wives.

The Daughter. And for this he should be punished?

The Poet. Yes, all the right-minded condemned him——

The Daughter. Strange world, this!— How can he then be freed from his curse?

The Poet. Freed?—Oh, they take good care that none is set free.

The Daughter. Why?

The Poet. Because—— No, it is not the *Dutchman!* It is an ordinary ship in distress. Why does not the buoy cry out now? Look, how the sea is rising—how high the waves are—soon we shall be unable to get out of the cave! Now the ship's bell is ringing— Soon we shall have another figurehead. Cry out, buoy! Do your duty, watchman! [*The buoy sounds a four-voice chord of fifths and sixths, reminding one of fog horns.*] The crew is signaling to us—but we are doomed ourselves.

The Daughter. Do you not wish to be set free?

The Poet. Yes, of course—of course, I wish it—but not just now, and not by water.

The Crew. [*Sings in quartet.*] Christ Kyrie!

The Poet. Now they are crying aloud, and so is the sea, but no one gives ear.

The Crew. [*As before.*] Christ Kyrie!

The Daughter. Who is coming there?

The Poet. Walking on the waters? There is only one who does that—and it is not Peter, the Rock, for he sank like a stone——

[*A white light is seen shining over the water at some distance.*]

The Crew. Christ Kyrie!

The Daughter. Can this be He?

The Poet. It is He, the crucified——

The Daughter. Why—tell me—why was He crucified?

The Poet. Because He wanted to set free——

The Daughter. Who was it—I have forgotten—that crucified Him?

The Poet. All the right-minded.

The Daughter. What a strange world!

The Poet. The sea is rising. Darkness is closing in upon us. The storm is growing——

[*The* CREW *set up a wild outcry.*]

The Poet. The crew scream with horror at the sight of their Saviour—and now— they are leaping overboard for fear of the Redeemer——

[*The* CREW *utter another cry.*]

The Poet. Now they are crying because they must die. Crying when they are born, and crying when they pass away!

[*The rising waves threaten to engulf the* TWO *in the cave.*]

The Daughter. If I could only be sure that it is a ship——

The Poet. Really—I don't think it is a ship—— It is a two-storied house with trees in front of it—and—a telephone tower—a tower that reaches up into the skies—— It is the modern Tower of Babel sending wires to the upper regions—to communicate with those above——

The Daughter. Child, the human thought needs no wires to make a way for itself— the prayers of the pious penetrate the universe. It cannot be a Tower of Babel, for if you want to assail the heavens, you must do so with prayer.

The Poet. No, it is no house—no telephone tower—don't you see?

The Daughter. What are you seeing?

The Poet. I see an open space covered with snow—a drill ground—— The winter sun is shining from behind a church on a hill, and the tower is casting its long shadow on the snow—— Now a troop of soldiers come marching across the grounds. They march up along the tower, up the spire. Now they have reached the cross, but I have a feeling that the first one who steps on the gilded weathercock at the top must die. Now they are near it—a corporal is leading them— ha-ha! There comes a cloud sweeping across the open space, and right in front of the sun, of course—now everything is gone—the water in the cloud put out the sun's fire!— The light of the sun created the shadow picture of the tower, but the shadow picture of the cloud swallowed the shadow picture of the tower——

[*While* THE POET *is still speaking, the stage is changed and shows once more the passageway outside the opera-house.*]

The Daughter. [*To* THE PORTRESS.] Has the Lord Chancellor arrived yet?

The Portress. No.

The Daughter. And the Deans of the Faculties?

The Portress. No.

The Daughter. Call them at once, then, for the door is to be opened——

The Portress. Is it so very pressing?

The Daughter. Yes, it is. For there is a suspicion that the solution of the world-riddle may be hidden behind it. Call the Lord Chancellor, and the Deans of the Four Faculties also.

[THE PORTRESS *blows a whistle.*]

The Daughter. And do not forget the Glazier and his diamond, for without them nothing can be done.

[STAGE PEOPLE *enter from the left as in the earlier scene.*]

The Officer. [*Enters from the background, in Prince Albert and high hat, with a bunch of roses in his hand, looking radiantly happy.*] Victoria!

The Portress. The young lady will be coming in a moment.

The Officer. Good! The carriage is waiting, the table is set, the wine is on ice— Permit me to embrace you, Madam! [*Embraces* THE PORTRESS.] Victoria!

A Woman's Voice from above. [*Sings.*] I am here!

The Officer. [*Begins to walk to and fro.*] Good! I am waiting.

The Poet. It seems to me that all this has happened before——

The Daughter. So it seems to me also.

The Poet. Perhaps I have dreamt it.

The Daughter. Or put it in a poem, perhaps.

The Poet. Or put it in a poem.

The Daughter. Then you know what poetry is.

The Poet. Then I know what dreaming is.

The Daughter. It seems to me that we have said all this to each other before, in some other place.

The Poet. Then you may soon figure out what reality is.

The Daughter. Or dreaming!

The Poet. Or poetry!

[*Enter the* LORD CHANCELLOR *and the* DEANS *of the* THEOLOGICAL, PHILOSOPHICAL, MEDICAL, *and* LEGAL FACULTIES.]

Lord Chancellor. It is about the opening of that door, of course—— What does the Dean of the Theological Faculty think of it?

Dean of Theology. I do not think—I believe—Credo——

Dean of Philosophy. I hold——

Dean of Medicine. I know——

Dean of Jurisprudence. I doubt until I have evidence and witnesses.

Lord Chancellor. Now they are fighting again!—Well, what does Theology believe?

Theology. I believe that this door must not be opened, because it hides dangerous truths——

Philosophy. Truth is never dangerous.

Medicine. What is truth?

Jurisprudence. What can be proved by two witnesses.

Theology. Anything can be proved by two false witnesses—thinks the pettifogger.

Philosophy. Truth is wisdom; and wisdom, knowledge, is philosophy itself— Philosophy is the science of sciences, the knowledge of knowing, and all other sciences are its servants.

Medicine. Natural science is the only true science—and philosophy is no science at all. It is nothing but empty speculation.

Theology. Good!

Philosophy. [*To* THEOLOGY.] Good, you say! And what are you, then? You are the arch-enemy of all knowledge; you are the very antithesis of knowledge; you are ignorance and obscurantism——

Medicine. Good!

Theology. [*To* MEDICINE.] You cry "good," you, who cannot see beyond the length of your own nose in the magnifying glass; who believe in nothing but your own unreliable senses—in your vision, for instance, which may be far-sighted, near-sighted, blind, purblind, cross-eyed, one-eyed, color-blind, red-blind, green-blind——

Medicine. Idiot!

Theology. Ass!   [*They fight.*]

Lord Chancellor. Peace! One crow does not peck out the other's eye.

Philosophy. If I had to choose between those two, Theology and Medicine, I should choose—neither!

Jurisprudence. And if I had to sit in judgment on all three of you, I should find—all guilty! You cannot agree on a single point, and you never could. Let us get back to the case in court. What is the opinion of the Lord Chancellor as to this door and its opening?

Lord Chancellor. Opinion? I have no opinion whatever. I am merely appointed by the government to see that you don't break each other's arms and legs in the Council— while you are educating the young! Opinion? Why, I take mighty good care to avoid everything of the kind. Once I had one or two, but they were refuted at once. Opinions are always refuted—by their opponents, of course—— But perhaps we might open the door now, even with the risk of finding some dangerous truths behind it?

Jurisprudence. What is truth? What is truth?

Theology. I am the truth and the life——

Philosophy. I am the science of sciences——

Medicine. I am the only exact science——

Jurisprudence. I doubt—— [*They fight.*]

The Daughter. Instructors of the young, take shame!

Jurisprudence. Lord Chancellor, as representative of the government, as head of the corps of instructors, you must prosecute this woman's offence. She has told all of you to take shame, which is an insult; and she has —in a sneering, ironical sense—called you instructors of the young, which is a slanderous speech.

The Daughter. Poor youth!

Jurisprudence. She pities the young, which is to accuse us. Lord Chancellor, you must prosecute the offence.

The Daughter. Yes, I accuse you—you in a body—of sowing doubt and discord in the minds of the young.

Jurisprudence. Listen to her—she herself is making the young question our authority, and then she charges us with sowing doubt. Is it not a criminal act, I ask all the right-minded?

All Right-Minded. Yes, it is criminal.

Jurisprudence. All the right-minded have condemned you. Leave in peace with your lucre, or else——

The Daughter. My lucre? Or else? What else?

Jurisprudence. Else you will be stoned.

The Poet. Or crucified.

The Daughter. I leave. Follow me, and you shall learn the riddle.

The Poet. Which riddle?

The Daughter. What did he mean by "my lucre?"

The Poet. Probably nothing at all. That kind of thing we call talk. He was just talking.

The Daughter. But it was what hurt me more than anything else!

The Poet. That is why he said it, I suppose—— Men are that way.

All Right-Minded. Hooray! The door is open.

Lord Chancellor. What was behind the door?

The Glazier. I can see nothing.

Lord Chancellor. He cannot see anything —of course, he cannot! Deans of the Faculties: what was behind that door?

Theology. Nothing! That is the solution of the world-riddle. In the beginning God created heaven and earth out of nothing——

Philosophy. Out of nothing comes nothing.

Medicine. Yes, bosh—which is nothing!

Jurisprudence. I doubt. And this is a case of deception. I appeal to all the right-minded.

The Daughter. [*To* THE POET.] Who are the right-minded?

The Poet. Who can tell? Frequently all the right-minded consist of a single person. Today it is me and mine; tomorrow it is you and yours. To that position you are appointed—or rather, you appoint yourself to it.

All Right-Minded. We have been deceived.

Lord Chancellor. Who has deceived you?

All Right-Minded. The Daughter!

Lord Chancellor. Will the Daughter please tell us what she meant by having this door opened?

The Daughter. No, friends. If I did, you would not believe me.

Medicine. Why, then, there is nothing there.

The Daughter. You have said it—but you have not understood.

Medicine. It is bosh, what she says!

All. Bosh!

The Daughter. [*To* THE POET.] They are to be pitied.

The Poet. Are you in earnest?

The Daughter. Always in earnest.

The Poet. Do you think the right-minded are to be pitied also?

The Daughter. They most of all, perhaps.

The Poet. And the four faculties, too?

The Daughter. They also, and not the least. Four heads, four minds, and one body. Who made that monster?

All. She has not answered!

Lord Chancellor. Stone her then!

The Daughter. I have answered.

Lord Chancellor. Hear—she answers.

All. Stone her! She answers!

The Daughter. Whether she answer or do not answer, stone her! Come, prophet, and I shall tell you the riddle—but far away from here—out in the desert, where no one can hear us, no one see us, for——

The Lawyer. [*Enters and takes* THE DAUGHTER *by the arm.*] Have you forgotten your duties?

The Daughter. Oh, heavens, no! But I have higher duties.

The Lawyer. And your child?

The Daughter. My child—what of it?

The Lawyer. Your child is crying for you.

The Daughter. My child! Woe, I am earthbound! And this pain in my breast, this anguish—what is it?

The Lawyer. Don't you know?

The Daughter. No.

The Lawyer. It is remorse.

The Daughter. Is that remorse?

The Lawyer. Yes, and it follows every

neglected duty; every pleasure, even the most innocent, if innocent pleasures exist, which seems doubtful; and every suffering inflicted upon one's fellow beings.

The Daughter. And there is no remedy?

The Lawyer. Yes, but only one. It consists in doing your duty at once——

The Daughter. You look like a demon when you speak that word duty—— And when, as in my case, there are two duties to be met?

The Lawyer. Meet one first, and then the other.

The Daughter. The highest first—therefore, you look after my child, and I shall do my duty——

The Lawyer. Your child suffers because it misses you—can you bear to know that a human being is suffering for your sake?

The Daughter. Now strife has entered my soul—it is rent in two, and the halves are being pulled in opposite directions!

The Lawyer. Such, you know, are life's little discords.

The Daughter. Oh, how it is pulling!

The Poet. If you could only know how I have spread sorrow and ruin around me by the exercise of my calling—and note that I say *calling,* which carries with it the highest duty of all—then you would not even touch my hand.

The Daughter. What do you mean?

The Poet. I had a father who put his whole hope on me as his only son, destined to continue his enterprise. I ran away from the business college. My father grieved himself to death. My mother wanted me to be religious, and I could not do what she wanted—and she disowned me. I had a friend who assisted me through trying days of need—and that friend acted as a tyrant against those on whose behalf I was speaking and writing. And I had to strike down my friend and benefactor in order to save my soul. Since then I have had no peace. Men call me devoid of honor, infamous—and it does not help that my conscience says, "You have done right," for in the next moment it is saying, "You have done wrong." Such is life.

The Daughter. Come with me into the desert.

The Lawyer. Your child!

The Daughter. [*Indicating all those present.*] Here are my children. By themselves they are good, but if they only come together, then they quarrel and turn into demons—Farewell!

[*Outside the castle. The same scenery as in the first scene of the first act. But now the ground in front of the castle wall is covered with flowers—blue monk's-hood or aconite. On the roof of the castle, at the very top of its lantern, there is a chrysanthemum bud ready to open. The castle windows are illuminated with candles.*]

[THE DAUGHTER *and* THE POET *enter.*]

The Daughter. The hour is not distant when, with the help of the flames, I shall once more ascend to the ether. It is what you call to die, and what you approach in fear.

The Poet. Fear of the unkown.

The Daughter. Which is known to you.

The Poet. Who knows it?

The Daughter. All! Why do you not believe your prophets.

The Poet. Prophets have always been disbelieved. Why is that so? And "if God has spoken, why will men not believe then?" His convincing power ought to be irresistible.

The Daughter. Have you always doubted?

The Poet. No. I have had certainty many times. But after a while it passed away, like a dream when you wake up.

The Daughter. It is not easy to be human!

The Poet. You see and admit it?

The Daughter. I do.

The Poet. Listen! Was it not Indra that once sent his son down here to receive the complaints of mankind?

The Daughter. Thus it happened—and how was he received?

The Poet. How did he fill his mission?—to answer with another question.

The Daughter. And if I may reply with still another—was not man's position bettered by his visit to the earth? Answer truly!

The Poet. Bettered?—Yes, a little. A very little—— But instead of asking questions —will you not tell the riddle?

The Daughter. Yes. But to what use? You will not believe me.

The Poet. In you I shall believe, for I know who you are.

The Daughter. Then I shall tell! In the morning of the ages, before the sun was shining, Brahma, the divine primal force, let himself be persuaded by Maya, the world-mother, to propagate himself. This meeting of the divine primal matter with the earth-matter was the fall of heaven into sin. Thus the world, existence, mankind, are nothing but a phantom, an appearance, a dream-image—

The Poet. My dream!

The Daughter. A dream of truth! But in

order to free themselves from the earth-matter, the offspring of Brahma seek privation and suffering. There you have suffering as a liberator. But this craving for suffering comes into conflict with the craving for enjoyment, or love—do you now understand what love is, with its utmost joys merged into its utmost sufferings, with its mixture of what is most sweet and most bitter? Can you now grasp what woman is? Woman, through whom sin and death found their way into life?

The Poet. I understand!—And the end?

The Daughter. You know it: conflict between the pain of enjoyment and the pleasure of suffering—between the pangs of the penitent and the joys of the prodigal——

The Poet. A conflict it is then?

The Daughter. Conflict between opposites produces energy, as fire and water give the power of steam——

The Poet. But peace? Rest?

The Daughter. Hush! You must ask no more, and I can no longer answer. The altar is already adorned for the sacrifice—the flowers are standing guard—the candles are lit—there are white sheets in the windows—spruce boughs have been spread in the gateway——

The Poet. And you say this as calmly as if for you suffering did not exist!

The Daughter. You think so? I have suffered all your sufferings, but in a hundredfold degree, for my sensations were so much more acute——

The Poet. Relate your sorrow!

The Daughter. Poet, could you tell yours so that not one word went too far? Could your word at any time approach your thought?

The Poet. No, you are right! To myself I appeared like one struck dumb, and when the mass listened admiringly to my song, I found it mere noise—— For this reason, you see, I have always felt ashamed when they praised me.

The Daughter. And then you ask me—Look me straight in the eye!

The Poet. I cannot bear your glance——

The Daughter. How could you bear my word then, were I to speak in your tongue?

The Poet. But tell me at least before you go: from what did you suffer most of all down here?

The Daughter. From—being: to feel my vision weakened by an eye, my hearing blunted by an ear, and my thought, my bright and buoyant thought, bound in labyrinthine coils of fat. You have seen a brain—what roundabout and sneaking paths——

The Poet. Well, that is because all the right-minded think crookedly!

The Daughter. Malicious, always malicious, all of you!

The Poet. How could one possibly be otherwise?

The Daughter. First of all I now shake the dust from my feet—the dirt and the clay——

[*Takes off her shoes and puts them into the fire.*]

The Portress. [*Puts her shawl into the fire.*] Perhaps I may burn my shawl at the same time? [*Goes out.*]

The Officer. [*Enters.*] And I my roses, of which only the thorns are left. [*Goes out.*]

The Billposter. [*Enters.*] My bills may go, but never the dipnet! [*Goes out.*]

The Glazier. [*Enters.*] The diamond that opened the door—good-bye! [*Goes out.*]

The Lawyer. [*Enters.*] The minutes of the great process concerning the pope's beard or the water loss in the sources of the Ganges. [*Goes out.*]

Master of Quarantine. [*Enters.*] A small contribution in shape of the black mask that made me a blackamoor against my will! [*Goes out.*]

Victoria. [*Enters.*] My beauty, my sorrow! [*Goes out.*]

Edith. [*Enters.*] My plainness, my sorrow! [*Goes out.*]

The Blind Man. [*Enters; puts his hand into the fire.*] I give my hand for my eye. [*Goes out.*]

[Don Juan *in his wheel-chair;* She *and* The Friend.]

Don Juan. Hurry up! Hurry up! Life is short! [*Leaves with the* Other Two.]

The Poet. I have read that when the end of life draws near, everything and everybody rushes by in continuous review—— Is this the end?

The Daughter. Yes, it is my end. Farewell!

The Poet. Give us a parting word.

The Daughter. No, I cannot. Do you believe that your words can express our thoughts?

Dean of Theology. [*Enters in a rage.*] I am cast off by God and persecuted by man; I am deserted by the government and scorned by my colleagues! How am I to believe when nobody else believes? How am I to defend a god that does not defend his own? Bosh, that's what it is!

[*Throws a book on the fire and goes out.*]

The Poet. [*Snatches the book out of the fire.*] Do you know what it is? A martyrology, a calender with a martyr for each day of the year.

The Daughter. Martyr?

The Poet. Yes, one that has been tortured and killed on account of his faith! Tell me, why?—Do you think that all who are tortured suffer, and that all who are killed feel pain? Suffering is said to be salvation, and death a liberation.

Christine. [*With slips of paper.*] I paste, I paste until there is nothing more to paste——

The Poet. And if heaven should split in twain, you would try to paste it together— Away!

Christine. Are there no double windows in this castle?

The Poet. Not one, I tell you.

Christine. Well, then I'll go. [*Goes out.*]

The Daughter.

The parting hour has come, the end draws near.
And now farewell, thou dreaming child of man,
Thou singer, who alone know'st how to live!
When from thy winged flight above the earth
At times thou sweepest downward to the dust,
It is to touch it only, not to stay!

And as I go—how, in the parting hour,
As one must leave for e'er a friend, a place
The heart with longing swells for what one loves,
And with regret for all wherein one failed!

O, now the pangs of life in all their force
I feel: I know at last the lot of man——
Regretfully one views what once was scorned;
For sins one never sinned remorse is felt;
To stay one craves, but equally to leave:
As if to horses tied that pull apart,
One's heart is split in twain, one's feelings rent,
By indecision, contrast, and discord.

Farewell! To all thy fellow-men make known
That where I go I shall forget them not;
And in thy name their grievance shall be placed
Before the throne. Farewell!
[*She goes into the castle. Music is heard. The background is lit up by the burning castle and reveals a wall of human faces, questioning, grieving, despairing. As the castle breaks into flames, the bud on the roof opens into a gigantic chrysanthemum flower.*]

CURTAIN

MAN AND SUPERMAN*

A Comedy and a Philosophy

By

BERNARD SHAW

[Since Shaw has furnished *Man and Superman* with so brilliant a preface in the "Epistle Dedicatory," the editors have limited themselves to annotation of his highly allusive text. Moreover, Shaw forbad introductions and annotations to his work during his lifetime; though we annotate, we still obey him in not introducing.]

EPISTLE DEDICATORY

TO ARTHUR BINGHAM WALKLEY [1]

MY DEAR WALKLEY

You once asked me why I did not write a Don Juan play. The levity with which you assumed this frightful responsibility has probably by this time enabled you to forget it; but the day of reckoning has arrived: here is your play! I say your play, because *qui facit per alium facit per se*.[2] Its profits, like its labor, belong to me: its morals, its manners, its philosophy, its influence on the young, are for you to justify. You were of mature age when you made the suggestion; and you knew your man. It is hardly fifteen years since, as twin pioneers of the New Journalism of that time, we two, cradled in the same new sheets, began an epoch in the criticism of the theatre and the opera house by making it the pretext for a propaganda of our own views of life. So you cannot plead ignorance of the character of the force you set in motion. You meant me to *épater le bourgeois;*[3] and if he protests, I hereby refer him to you as the accountable party.

I warn you that if you attempt to repudiate your responsibility, I shall suspect you of finding the play too decorous for your taste. The fifteen years have made me older and graver. In you I can detect no such becoming change. Your levities and audacities are like the loves and comforts prayed for by Desdemona: they increase, even as your days do grow. No mere pioneering journal dares meddle with them now: the stately *Times* itself is alone sufficiently above suspicion to act as your chaperone; and even *The Times* must sometimes thank its stars that new plays are not produced every day, since after each such event its gravity is comprised, its platitude turned to epigram, its portentousness to wit, its propriety to elegance, and even its decorum into naughtiness by criticisms which the traditions of the paper do not allow you to sign at the end, but which you take care to sign with the most extravagant flourishes between the lines. I am not sure that this is not a portent of Revolution. In eighteenth century France the end was at hand when men bought the *Encyclopedia* and found Diderot there. When I buy *The Times* and find you there, my prophetic ear catches a rattle of twentieth century tumbrils.

However, that is not my present anxiety. The question is, will you not be disappointed with a Don Juan play in which not one of that hero's *mille e tre*[1] adventures is brought upon the stage? To propitiate you, let me explain myself. You will still retort that I never do anything else: it is your favorite jibe at me that what I call drama is nothing but explanation. But you must not expect me to adopt your inexplicable, fantastic, petulant,

---

* Used by arrangement with Dodd, Mead and Company, Inc.
[1] In 1903 dramatic critic of the London *Times*. Walkley always insisted that Shaw's comedies were not plays. He was noted for applying the principles stated in Aristotle's *Poetics* to modern plays. He is the original of Trotter in *Fanny's First Play*.
[2] "Whoever creates through another creates through himself." Shaw adapts a sentence from a decree of Pope Boniface VIII.
[3] "Shock the ordinary citizen."

[1] Leporello, in Mozart's *Don Giovanni,* asserts that the Don has had "one thousand and three" love affairs in Spain alone.

fastidious ways: you must take me as I am, a reasonable, patient, consistent, apologetic, laborious person, with the temperament of a school master and the pursuits of a vestryman. No doubt that literary knack of mine which happens to amuse the British public distracts attention from my character; but the character is there none the less, solid as bricks. I have a conscience; and conscience is always anxiously explanatory. You, on the contrary, feel that a man who discusses his conscience is much like a woman who discusses her modesty. The only moral force you condescend to parade is the force of your wit: the only demand you make in public is the demand of your artistic temperament for symmetry, elegance, style, grace, refinement, and the cleanliness which comes next to godliness if not before it. But my conscience is the genuine pulpit article: it annoys me to see people comfortable when they ought to be uncomfortable; and I insist on making them think in order to bring them to conviction of sin. If you don't like my preaching you must lump it. I really cannot help it.

In the preface to my *Plays for Puritans* I explained the predicament of our contemporary English drama, forced to deal almost exclusively with cases of sexual attraction, and yet forbidden to exhibit the incidents of that attraction or even to discuss its nature. Your suggestion that I should write a Don Juan play was virtually a challenge to me to treat this subject myself dramatically. The challenge was difficult enough to be worth accepting, because, when you come to think of it, though we have plenty of dramas with heroes and heroines who are in love and must accordingly marry or perish at the end of the play, or about people whose relations with one another have been complicated by the marriage laws, not to mention the looser sort of plays which trade on the tradition that illicit love affairs are at once vicious and delightful, we have no modern English plays in which the natural attraction of the sexes for one another is made the mainspring of the action. That is why we insist on beauty in our performers, differing herein from the countries our friend William Archer [1] holds up as examples of seriousness to our childish theatres. There the Juliets and Isoldes, the Romeos and Tristans, might be our mothers and fathers. Not so the English actress. The heroine she impersonates is not allowed to discuss the elemental relations of men and women: all

her romantic twaddle about novelet-made love, all her purely legal dilemmas as to whether she was married or "betrayed," quite miss our hearts and worry our minds. To console ourselves we must just look at her. We do so; and her beauty feeds our starving emotions. Sometimes we grumble ungallantly at the lady because she does not act as well as she looks. But in a drama which, with all its preoccupation with sex, is really void of sexual interest, good looks are more desired than histrionic skill.

Let me press this point on you, since you are too clever to raise the fool's cry of paradox whenever I take hold of a stick by the right end instead of the wrong end. Why are our occasional attempts to deal with the sex problem on the stage so repulsive and dreary that even those who are most determined that sex questions shall be held open and their discussion kept free, cannot pretend to relish these joyless attempts at social sanitation? Is it not because at bottom they are utterly sexless? What is the usual formula for such plays? A woman has, on some past occasion, been brought into conflict with the law which regulates the relations of the sexes. A man, by falling in love with her, or marrying her, is brought into conflict with the social convention which discountenances the woman. Now the conflicts of individuals with law and convention can be dramatized like all other human conflicts; but they are purely judicial; and the fact that we are much more curious about the suppressed relations between the man and the woman than about the relations between both and our courts of law and private juries of matrons, produces that sensation of evasion, of dissatisfaction, of fundamental irrelevance, of shallowness, of useless disagreeableness, of total failure to edify and partial failure to interest, which is as familiar to you in the theatres as it was to me when I, too, frequented those uncomfortable buildings, and found our popular playwrights in the mind to (as they thought) emulate Ibsen.

I take it that when you asked me for a Don Juan play you did not want that sort of thing. Nobody does: the successes such plays sometimes obtain are due to the incidental conventional melodrama with which the experienced popular author instinctively saves himself from failure. But what did you want? Owing to your unfortunate habit —you now, I hope, feel its inconvenience— of not explaining yourself, I have had to discover this for myself. First, then, I have had to ask myself, what is a Don Juan?

---

[1] Dramatic critic and translator of Ibsen. He admired the French and Scandinavian theatres.

Vulgarly, a libertine. But your dislike of vulgarity is pushed to the length of a defect (universality of character is impossible without a share of vulgarity); and even if you could acquire the taste, you would find yourself overfed from ordinary sources without troubling me. So I took it that you demanded a Don Juan in the philosophic sense.

Philosophically, Don Juàn is a man who, though gifted enough to be exceptionally capable of distinguishing between good and evil, follows his own instincts without regard to the common, statute, or canon law; and therefore, whilst gaining the ardent sympathy of our rebellious instincts (which are flattered by the brilliancies with which Don Juan associates them) finds himself in mortal conflict with existing institutions, and defends himself by fraud and force as unscrupulously as a farmer defends his crops by the same means against vermin. The prototypic Don Juan, invented early in the seventeenth century by a Spanish monk,[1] was presented, according to the ideas of that time, as the enemy of God, the approach of whose vengeance is felt throughout the drama, growing in menace from minute to minute. No anxiety is caused on Don Juan's account by any minor antagonist: he easily eludes the police, temporal and spiritual; and when an indignant father seeks private redress with the sword, Don Juan kills him without an effort. Not until the slain father returns from heaven as the agent of God, in the form of his own statue, does he prevail against his slayer and cast him into hell. The moral is a monkish one: repent and reform now; for tomorrow it may be too late. This is really the only point on which Don Juan is sceptical; for he is a devout believer in an ultimate hell, and risks damnation only because, as he is young, it seems so far off that repentance can be postponed until he has amused himself to his heart's content.

But the lesson intended by an author is hardly ever the lesson the world chooses to learn from his book. What attracts and impresses us in *El Burlador de Sevilla* is not the immediate urgency of repentance, but the heroism of daring to be the enemy of God. From Prometheus to my own Devil's Disciple, such enemies have always been popular. Don Juan became such a pet that the world could not bear his damnation. It reconciled him sentimentally to God in a second version, and clamored for his canonization for a whole century, thus treating

him as English journalism has treated that comic foe of the gods, Punch. Molière's Don Juan casts back to the original in point of impenitence; but in piety he falls off greatly. True, he also proposes to repent; but in what terms! "Oui, ma foi! il faut s'amender. Encore vingt ou trente ans de cette vie-ci, et puis nous songerons à nous."[1] After Molière comes the artist-enchanter, the master beloved by masters, Mozart, revealing the hero's spirit in magical harmonies, elfin tones, and elate darting rhythms as of summer lightning made audible. Here you have freedom in love and in morality mocking exquisitely at slavery to them, and interesting you, attracting you, tempting you, inexplicably forcing you to range the hero with his enemy the statue on a transcendent plane, leaving the prudish daughter and her priggish lover on a crockery shelf below to live piously ever after.

After these completed works Byron's fragment[2] does not count for much philosophically. Our vagabound libertines are no more interesting from that point of view than the sailor who has a wife in every port; and Byron's hero is, after all, only a vagabond libertine. And he is dumb: he does not discuss himself with a Sganarelle-Leporello[3] or with the fathers or brothers of his mistresses: he does not even, like Casanova,[4] tell his own story. In fact he is not a true Don Juan at all; for he is no more an enemy of God than any romantic and adventurous young sower of wild oats. Had you and I been in his place at his age, who knows whether we might not have done as he did, unless indeed your fastidiousness had saved you from the empress Catherine.[5] Byron was as little of a philosopher as Peter the Great: both were instances of that rare and useful, but unedifying variation, an energetic genius born without the prejudices or superstitions of his contemporaries. The resultant unscrupulous freedom of thought made Byron a bolder poet than Wordsworth just as it made Peter a bolder king than George III; but as it was, after all, only a negative qualification, it did not prevent Peter from being an appalling blackguard and an arrant poltroon, nor did it enable Byron to become a

---

[1] Tirso de Molina (1571–1648), author of *El Burlador de Sevilla*.

[1] "Yes, indeed I must reform. Give me twenty or thirty more years of life like this and then I will think about it."
[2] *Don Juan*, sixteen cantos and some stanzas of the 17th.
[3] Sganarelle is Don Juan's servant in Molière's *Don Juan*; Leporello in Mozart's *Don Giovanni*.
[4] Giovanni Jacopo Casanova de Seingalt, author of *Mémoires* (1826), notorious for their recital of amours.
[5] Byron's canto 9 tells of his Juan's affair with Catherine the Great.

religious force like Shelley. Let us, then, leave Byron's Don Juan out of account. Mozart's is the last of the true Don Juans; for by the time he was of age, his cousin Faust had, in the hands of Goethe, taken his place and carried both his warfare and his reconciliation with the gods far beyond mere love-making into politics, high art, schemes for reclaiming new continents from the ocean, and recognition of an eternal womanly principle in the universe. Goethe's Faust and Mozart's Don Juan were the last words of the XVIII century on the subject; and by the time the polite critics of the XIX century, ignoring William Blake as superficially as the XVIII had ignored Hogarth or the XVII Bunyan, had got past the Dickens-Macaulay Dumas-Guizot stage and the Stendhal-Meredith-Turgenieff stage, and were confronted with philosophic fiction by such pens as Ibsen's and Tolstoy's, Don Juan had changed his sex and become Doña Juana, breaking out of the Doll's House and asserting herself as an individual instead of a mere item in a moral pageant.

Now it is all very well for you at the beginning of the XX century to ask me for a Don Juan play; but you will see from the foregoing survey that Don Juan is a full century out of date for you and for me; and if there are millions of less literate people who are still in the eighteenth century, have they not Molière and Mozart, upon whose art no human hand can improve? You would laugh at me if at this time of day I dealt in duels and ghosts and "womanly" women. As to mere libertinism, you would be the first to remind me that the *Festin de Pierre* [1] of Molière is not a play for amorists, and that one bar of the voluptuous sentimentality of Gounod or Bizet would appear as a licentious stain on the score of *Don Giovanni*. Even the more abstract parts of the Don Juan play are dilapidated past use: for instance, Don Juan's supernatural antagonist hurled those who refuse to repent into lakes of burning brimstone, there to be tormented by devils with horns and tails. Of that antagonist, and of that conception of repentance, how much is left that could be used in a play by me dedicated to you? On the other hand, those forces of middle class public opinion which hardly existed for a Spanish nobleman in the days of the first Don Juan, are now triumphant everywhere. Civilized society is one huge bourgeoisie: no nobleman dares now shock his greengrocer. The women, "mar-

chesane, principesse, cameriere, cittadine" [1] and all, are become equally dangerous: the sex is aggressive, powerful: when women are wronged they do not group themselves pathetically to sing "Protegga il giusto cielo": [2] they grasp formidable legal and social weapons, and retaliate. Political parties are wrecked and public careers undone by a single indiscretion. A man had better have all the statues in London to supper with him, ugly as they are, than be brought to the bar of the Nonconformist Conscience by Donna Elvira.[3] Excommunication has become almost as serious a business as it was in the tenth century.

As a result, Man is no longer, like Don Juan, victor in the duel of sex. Whether he has ever really been may be doubted: at all events the enormous superiority of Woman's natural position in this matter is telling with greater and greater force. As to pulling the Nonconformist Conscience by the beard as Don Juan plucked the beard of the Commandant's statue in the convent of San Francisco, that is out of the question nowadays: prudence and good manners alike forbid it to a hero with any mind. Besides, for it is Don Juan's own beard that is in danger of plucking. Far from relapsing into hypocrisy, as Sganarelle feared, he has unexpectedly discovered a moral in his immorality. The growing recognition of his new point of view is heaping responsibility on him. His former jests he has had to take as seriously as I have had to take some of the jests of Mr W. S. Gilbert.[4] His scepticism, once his least tolerated quality, has now triumphed so completely that he can no longer assert himself by witty negations, and must, to save himself from cipherdom, find an affirmative position. His thousand and three affairs of gallantry, after becoming, at most, two immature intrigues leading to sordid and prolonged complications and humiliations, have been discarded altogether as unworthy of his philosophic dignity and compromising to his newly acknowledged position as the founder of a school. Instead of pretending to read Ovid he does actually read Schopenhauer and Nietzsche, studies Westermarck,[5] and is con-

---

[1] "Marquises, princesses, chambermaids, citizens' wives"—so Leporello in *Don Giovanni* lists the Don's victims.
[2] "May just Heaven protect . . ." from a trio sung in scene 4, Act I, of *Don Giovanni*.
[3] Old love deserted by Don Giovanni.
[4] Collaborator with Sir Arthur Sullivan in the famous operettas. Shaw is thinking of the line of succession in comedy.
[5] Books representing this change might be: Ovid's *Ars Amoris*, Schopenhauer's *The World as Will and Idea*, Nietzsche's *Beyond Good and Evil*, Westermarck's *History of Human Marriage*.

cerned for the future of the race instead of for the freedom of his own instincts. Thus his profligacy and his dare-devil airs have gone the way of his sword and mandoline into the rag shop of anachronisms and superstitions. In fact, he is now more Hamlet than Don Juan; for though the lines put into the actor's mouth to indicate to the pit that Hamlet is a philosopher are for the most part mere harmonious platitude which, with a little debasement of the word-music, would be properer to Pecksniff,[1] yet if you separate the real hero, inarticulate and unintelligible to himself except in flashes of inspiration, from the performer who has to talk at any cost through five acts; and if you also do what you must always do in Shakespear's tragedies: that is, dissect out the absurd sensational incidents and physical violences of the borrowed story from the genuine Shakespearian tissue, you will get a true Promethean foe of the gods, whose instinctive attitude towards women much resembles that to which Don Juan is now driven. From this point of view Hamlet was a developed Don Juan whom Shakespear palmed off as a reputable man just as he palmed poor Macbeth off as a murderer. Today the palming off is no longer necessary (at least on your plane and mine) because Don Juanism is no longer misunderstood as mere Casanovism. Don Juan himself is almost ascetic in his desire to avoid that misunderstanding; and so my attempt to bring him up to date by launching him as a modern Englishman into a modern English environment has produced a figure superficially quite unlike the hero of Mozart.

And yet I have not the heart to disappoint you wholly of another glimpse of the Mozartian *dissoluto punito* [2] and his antagonist the statue. I feel sure you would like to know more of that statue—to draw him out when he is off duty, so to speak. To gratify you, I have resorted to the trick of the strolling theatrical manager who advertizes the pantomime of Sinbad the Sailor with a stock of second-hand picture posters designed for Ali Baba. He simply thrusts a few oil jars into the valley of diamonds, and so fulfils the promise held out by the hoardings to the public eye. I have adapted this easy device to our occasion by thrusting into my perfectly modern three-act play a totally extraneous act in which my hero, enchanted by the air of the Sierra, has a dream in which his Mozartian ancestor appears and philosophizes at great length in a Shavio-Socratic dialogue

with the lady, the statue, and the devil.

But this pleasantry is not the essence of the play. Over this essence I have no control. You propound a certain social substance, sexual attraction to wit, for dramatic distillation; and I distil it for you. I do not adulterate the product with aphrodisiacs nor dilute it with romance and water; for I am merely executing your commission, not producing a popular play for the market. You must therefore (unless, like most wise men, you read the play first and the preface afterwards) prepare yourself to face a trumpery story of modern London life, a life in which, as you know, the ordinary man's main business is to get means to keep up the position and habits of a gentleman, and the ordinary woman's business is to get married. In 9,999 cases out of 10,000, you can count on their doing nothing, whether noble or base, that conflicts with these ends; and that assurance is what you rely on as their religion, their morality, their principles, their patriotism, their reputation, their honor and so forth.

On the whole, this is a sensible and satisfactory foundation for society. Money means nourishment and marriage means children; and that men should put nourishment first and women children first is, broadly speaking, the law of Nature and not the dictate of personal ambition. The secret of the prosaic man's success, such as it is, is the simplicity with which he pursues these ends: the secret of the artistic man's failure, such as that is, is the versatility with which he strays in all directions after secondary ideals. The artist is either a poet or a scallawag: as poet, he cannot see, as the prosaic man does, that chivalry is at bottom only romantic suicide: as scallawag, he cannot see that it does not pay to spunge and beg and lie and brag and neglect his person. Therefore do not misunderstand my plain statement of the fundamental constitution of London society as an Irishman's reproach to your nation. From the day I first set foot on this foreign soil I knew the value of the prosaic qualities of which Irishmen teach Englishmen to be ashamed as well as I knew the vanity of the poetic qualities of which Englishmen teach Irishmen to be proud. For the Irishman instinctively disparages the quality which makes the Englishman dangerous to him; and the Englishman instinctively flatters the fault that makes the Irishman harmless and amusing to him. What is wrong with the prosaic Englishman is what is wrong with the prosaic men of all countries: stupidity. The vitality which places nourishment and children first, heaven and hell a somewhat

---

[1] Hypocritical moralizer in Dickens' *Martin Chuzzlewit.*
[2] "Punished libertine."

remote second, and the health of society as an organic whole nowhere, may muddle successfully through the comparatively tribal stages of gregariousness; but in nineteenth century nations and twentieth century commonwealths the resolve of every man to be rich at all costs, and of every woman to be married at all costs, must, without a highly scientific social organization, produce a ruinous development of poverty, celibacy, prostitution, infant mortality, adult degeneracy, and everything that wise men most dread. In short, there is no future for men, however brimming with crude vitality, who are neither intelligent nor politically educated enough to be Socialists. So do not misunderstand me in the other direction either: if I appreciate the vital qualities of the Englishman as I appreciate the vital qualities of the bee, I do not guarantee the Englishman against being, like the bee (or the Canaanite) smoked out and unloaded of his honey by beings inferior to himself in simple acquisitiveness, combativeness, and fecundity, but superior to him in imagination and cunning.

The Don Juan play, however, is to deal with sexual attraction, and not with nutrition, and to deal with it in a society in which the serious business of sex is left by men to women, as the serious business of nutrition is left by women to men. That the men, to protect themselves against a too aggressive prosecution of the women's business, have set up a feeble romantic convention that the initiative in sex business must always come from the man, is true; but the pretence is so shallow that even in the theatre, that last sanctuary of unreality, it imposes only on the inexperienced. In Shakespear's plays the woman always takes the initiative. In his problem plays and his popular plays alike the love interest is the interest of seeing the woman hunt the man down. She may do it by charming him, like Rosalind, or by stratagem, like Mariana; but in every case the relation between the woman and the man is the same: she is the pursuer and contriver, he the pursued and disposed of. When she is baffled, like Ophelia, she goes mad and commits suicide; and the man goes straight from her funeral to a fencing match. No doubt Nature, with very young creatures, may save the woman the trouble of scheming; Prospero knows that he has only to throw Ferdinand and Miranda together and they will mate like a pair of doves; and there is no need for Perdita to capture Florizel as the lady doctor in *All's Well That Ends Well* (an early Ibsenite heroine) captures Bertram. But the mature cases all illustrate the Shake-

spearian law. The one apparent exception, Petruchio, is not a real one: he is most carefully characterized as a purely commercial matrimonial adventurer. Once he is assured that Katharine has money, he undertakes to marry her before he has seen her. In real life we find not only Petruchios, but Mantalinis [1] and Dobbins [2] who pursue women with appeals to their pity or jealousy or vanity, or cling to them in a romantically infatuated way. Such effeminates do not count in the world scheme: even Bunsby dropping like a fascinated bird into the jaws of Mrs MacStinger [3] is by comparison a true tragic object of pity and terror. I find in my own plays that Woman, projecting herself dramatically by my hands (a process over which I assure you I have no more real control than I have over my wife), behaves just as Woman did in the plays of Shakespear.

And so your Don Juan has come to birth as a stage projection of the tragi-comic love chase of the man by the woman; and my Don Juan is the quarry instead of the huntsman. Yet he is a true Don Juan, with a sense of reality that disables convention, defying to the last the fate which finally overtakes him. The woman's need of him to enable her to carry on Nature's most urgent work does not prevail against him until his resistance gathers her energy to a climax at which she dares to throw away her customary exploitations of the conventional affectionate and dutiful poses, and claim him by natural right for a purpose that far transcends their mortal personal purposes.

Among the friends to whom I have read this play in manuscript are some of our own sex who are shocked at the "unscrupulousness," meaning the utter disregard of masculine fastidiousness, with which the woman pursues her purpose. It does not occur to them that if women were as fastidious as men, morally or physically, there would be an end of the race. Is there anything meaner than to throw necessary work upon other people and then disparage it as unworthy and indelicate? We laugh at the haughty American nation because it makes the negro clean its boots and then proves the moral and physical inferiority of the negro by the fact that he is a shoeblack; but we ourselves throw the whole drudgery of creation on one sex, and then imply that no female of any womanliness or delicacy would initiate any effort in that direction. There are no limits to male hypocrisy in this matter. No doubt

[1] In Dickens' *Nicholas Nickleby*.
[2] In Thackeray's *Vanity Fair*.
[3] In Dickens' *Dombey and Son*.

there are moments when man's sexual immunities are made acutely humiliating to him. When the terrible moment of birth arrives, its supreme importance and its superhuman effort and peril, in which the father has no part, dwarf him into the meanest insignificance: he slinks out of the way of the humblest petticoat, happy if he be poor enough to be pushed out of the house to outface his ignominy by drunken rejoicings. But when the crisis is over he takes his revenge, swaggering as the breadwinner, and speaking of Woman's "sphere" with condescension, even with chivalry, as if the kitchen and the nursery were less important than the office in the city. When his swagger is exhausted he drivels into erotic poetry or sentimental uxoriousness; and the Tennysonian King Arthur posing at Guinevere [1] becomes Don Quixote grovelling before Dulcinea.[2] You must admit that here Nature beats Comedy out of the field: the wildest hominist or feminist farce is insipid after the most commonplace "slice of life." The pretence that women do not take the initiative is part of the farce. Why, the whole world is strewn with snares, traps, gins, and pitfalls for the capture of men by women. Give women the vote, and in five years there will be a crushing tax on bachelors. Men, on the other hand, attach penalties to marriage, depriving women of property, of the franchise, of the free use of their limbs, of that ancient symbol of immortality, the right to make oneself at home in the house of God by taking off the hat, of everything that he can force Woman to dispense with without compelling himself to dispense with her. All in vain. Woman must marry because the race must perish without her travail: if the risk of death and the certainty of pain, danger, and unutterable discomforts cannot deter her, slavery and swaddled ankles will not. And yet we assume that the force that carries women through all these perils and hardships stops abashed before the primnesses of our behavior for young ladies. It is assumed that the woman must wait, motionless, until she is wooed. Nay, she often does wait motionless. That is how the spider waits for the fly. But the spider spins her web. And if the fly, like my hero, shews a strength that promises to extricate him, how swiftly does she abandon her pretence of passiveness, and openly fling coil after coil about him until he is secured for ever!

If the really impressive books and other art-works of the world were produced by ordinary men, they would express more fear of women's pursuit than love of their illusory beauty. But ordinary men cannot produce really impressive art-works. Those who can are men of genius: that is, men selected by Nature to carry on the work of building up an intellectual consciousness of her own instinctive purpose. Accordingly, we observe in the man of genius all the unscrupulousness and all the "self-sacrifice" (the two things are the same) of Woman. He will risk the stake and the cross; starve, when necessary, in a garret all his life; study women and live on their work and care as Darwin studied worms and lived upon sheep; work his nerves into rags without payment, a sublime altruist in his disregard of himself, an atrocious egotist in his disregard of others. Here Woman meets a purpose as impersonal, as irresistible as her own; and the clash is sometimes tragic. When it is complicated by the genius being a woman, then the game is one for a king of critics: your George Sand becomes a mother to gain experience for the novelist and to develop her, and gobbles up men of genius, Chopins, Mussets and the like, as mere hors d'œuvres.

I state the extreme case, of course; but what is true of the great man who incarnates the philosophic consciousness of Life and the woman who incarnates its fecundity, is true in some degree of all geniuses and all women. Hence it is that the world's books get written, its pictures painted, its statues modelled, its symphonies composed, by people who are free from the otherwise universal dominion of the tyranny of sex. Which leads us to the conclusion, astonishing to the vulgar, that art, instead of being before all things the expression of the normal sexual situation, is really the only department in which sex is a superseded and secondary power, with its consciousness so confused and its purpose so perverted, that its ideas are mere fantasy to common men. Whether the artist becomes poet or philosopher, moralist or founder of a religion, his sexual doctrine is nothing but a barren special pleading for pleasure, excitement, and knowledge when he is young, and for contemplative tranquility when he is old and satiated. Romance and Asceticism, Amorism and Puritanism are equally unreal in the great Philistine world. The world shewn us in books, whether the books be confessed epics or professed gospels, or in codes, or in political orations, or in philosophic systems, is not the main world at all: it is only the self-consciousness of certain abnormal people who have the specific artistic talent and temperament. A serious

---

[1] See *Guinevere* in *Idylls of the King.*
[2] See chapter 10 of Part II of *Don Quixote.*

matter this for you and me, because the man whose consciousness does not correspond to that of the majority is a madman; and the old habit of worshipping madmen is giving way to the new habit of locking them up. And since what we call education and culture is for the most part nothing but the substitution of reading for experience, of literature for life, of the obsolete fictitious for the contemporary real, education, as you no doubt observed at Oxford, destroys, by supplantation, every mind that is not strong enough to see through the imposture and to use the great Masters of Arts as what they really are and no more: that is, patentees of highly questionable methods of thinking, and manufacturers of highly questionable, and for the majority but half valid, representations of life. The schoolboy who uses his Homer to throw at his fellow's head makes perhaps the safest and most rational use of him; and I observe with reassurance that you occasionally do the same, in your prime, with your Aristotle.

Fortunately for us, whose minds have been so overwhelmingly sophisticated by literature, what produces all these treatises and poems and scriptures of one sort or another is the struggle of Life to become divinely conscious of itself instead of blindly stumbling hither and thither in the line of least resistance. Hence there is a driving towards truth in all books on matters where the writer, though exceptionally gifted, is normally constituted, and has no private axe to grind. Copernicus had no motive for misleading his fellowmen as to the place of the sun in the solar system: he looked for it as honestly as a shepherd seeks his path in a mist. But Copernicus would not have written love stories scientifically. When it comes to sex relations, the man of genius does not share the common man's danger of capture, nor the woman of genius the common woman's overwhelming specialization. And that is why our scriptures and other art works, when they deal with love, turn from honest attempts at science in physics to romantic nonsense, erotic ecstasy, or the stern asceticism of satiety ("the road of excess leads to the palace of wisdom" said William Blake; for "you never know what is enough unless you know what is more than enough").

There is a political aspect of this sex question which is too big for my comedy, and too momentous to be passed over without culpable frivolity. It is impossible to demonstrate that the initiative in sex transactions remains with Woman, and has been confirmed to her, so far, more and more by the suppression of rapine and discouragement of importunity, without being driven to very serious reflections on the fact that this initiative is politically the most important of all the initiatives, because our political experiment of democracy, the last refuge of cheap misgovernment, will ruin us if our citizens are ill bred.

When we two were born,[1] this country was still dominated by a selected class bred by political marriages. The commercial class had not then completed the first twenty-five years of its new share of political power; and it was itself selected by money qualification, and bred, if not by political marriage, at least by a pretty rigorous class marriage. Aristocracy and plutocracy still furnish the figureheads of politics; but they are now dependent on the votes of the promiscuously bred masses. And this, if you please, at the very moment when the political problem, having suddenly ceased to mean a very limited and occasional interference, mostly by way of jobbing public appointments, in the mismanagement of a tight but parochial little island, with occasional meaningless prosecution of dynastic wars, has become the industrial reorganization of Britain, the construction of a practically international Commonwealth, and the partition of the whole of Africa and perhaps the whole of Asia by the civilized Powers. Can you believe that the people whose conceptions of society and conduct, whose power of attention and scope of interest, are measured by the British theatre as you know it today, can either handle this colossal task themselves, or understand and support the sort of mind and character that is (at least comparatively) capable of handling it? For remember: what our voters are in the pit and gallery they are also in the polling booth. We are all now under what Burke called "the hoofs of the swinish multitude." Burke's language gave great offence because the implied exceptions to its universal application made it a class insult; and it certainly was not for the pot to call the kettle black. The aristocracy he defended, in spite of the political marriages by which it tried to secure breeding for itself, had its mind undertrained by silly school-masters and governesses, its character corrupted by gratuitous luxury, its self-respect adulterated to complete spuriousness by flattery and flunkeyism. It is no better today and never will be any better: our very peasants have something morally hardier in them that culminates occasionally in a Bunyan, a Burns,

---

[1] Walkley was born in 1855; Shaw in 1856.

or a Carlyle. But observe, this aristocracy, which was overpowered from 1832 to 1885 by the middle class, has come back to power by the votes of "the swinish multitude." Tom Paine has triumphed over Edmund Burke; and the swine are now courted electors. How many of their own class have these electors sent to parliament? Hardly a dozen out of 670, and these only under the persuasion of conspicuous personal qualifications and popular eloquence. The multitude thus pronounces judgment on its own units: it admits itself unfit to govern, and will vote only for a man morphologically and generically transfigured by palatial residence and equipage, by transcendent tailoring, by the glamor of aristocratic kinship. Well, we two know these transfigured persons, these college passmen, these well groomed monocular Algys and Bobbies, these cricketers to whom age brings golf instead of wisdom, these plutocratic products of "the nail and sarspan business as he got his money by." Do you know whether to laugh or cry at the notion that they, poor devils! will drive a team of continents as they drive a four-in-hand; turn a jostling anarchy of casual trade and speculation into an ordered productivity; and federate our colonies into a world-Power of the first magnitude? Give these people the most perfect political constitution and the soundest political program that benevolent omniscience can devise for them, and they will interpret it into mere fashionable folly or canting charity as infallibly as a savage converts the philosophical theology of a Scotch missionary into crude African idolatry.

I do not know whether you have any illusions left on the subject of education, progress, and so forth. I have none. Any pamphleteer can shew the way to better things; but when there is no will there is no way. My nurse was fond of remarking that you cannot make a silk purse out of a sow's ear; and the more I see of the efforts of our churches and universities and literary sages to raise the mass above its own level, the more convinced I am that my nurse was right. Progress can do nothing but make the most of us all as we are, and that most would clearly not be enough even if those who are already raised out of the lowest abysses would allow the others a chance. The bubble of Heredity has been pricked: the certainty that acquirements are negligible as elements in practical heredity has demolished the hopes of the educationists as well as the terrors of the degeneracy mongers; and we know now that there is no hereditary "governing class" any more than a hereditary hooliganism. We must either breed political capacity or be ruined by Democ-racy, which was forced on us by the failure of the older alternatives. Yet if Despotism failed only for want of a capable benevolent despot, what chance has Democracy, which requires a whole population of capable voters: that is, of political critics who, if they cannot govern in person for lack of spare energy or specific talent for administration, can at least recognize and appreciate capacity and benevolence in others, and so govern through capably benevolent representatives? Where are such voters to be found today? Nowhere. Plutocratic inbreeding has produced a weakness of character that is too timid to face the full stringency of a thoroughly competitive struggle for existence and too lazy and petty to organize the commonwealth co-operatively. Being cowards, we defeat natural selection under cover of philanthropy: being sluggards, we neglect artificial selection under cover of delicacy and morality!

Yet we must get an electorate of capable critics or collapse as Rome and Egypt collapsed. At this moment the Roman decadent phase of *panem et circenses* [1] is being inaugurated under our eyes. Our newspapers and melodramas are blustering about our imperial destiny; but our eyes and hearts turn eagerly to the American millionaire. As his hand goes down to his pocket, our fingers go up to the brims of our hats by instinct. Our ideal prosperity is not the prosperity of the industrial north, but the prosperity of the Isle of Wight, of Folkestone and Ramsgate, of Nice and Monte Carlo.[2] That is the only prosperity you see on the stage, where the workers are all footmen, parlormaids, comic lodging-letters, and fashionable professional men, whilst the heroes and heroines are miraculously provided with unlimited dividends and eat gratuitously, like the knights in Don Quixote's books of chivalry. The city papers prate of the competition of Bombay with Manchester and the like. The real competition is the competition of Regent Street with the Rue de Rivoli, of Brighton and the south coast with the Riviera, for the spending money of the American Trusts. What is all this growing love of pageantry, this effusive loyalty, this officious rising and uncovering at a wave from a flag or a blast from a brass band? Imperialism? Not a bit of it. Obsequiousness, servility, cupidity roused by the prevailing smell of

[1] "Bread and circuses."
[2] British and European seaside resorts.

money. When Mr Carnegie rattled his millions in his pockets all England became one rapacious cringe. Only, when Rhodes (who had probably been reading my *Socialism for Millionaires*) left word that no idler was to inherit his estate, the bent backs straightened mistrustfully for a moment. Could it be that the Diamond King was no gentleman after all? However, it was easy to ignore a rich man's solecism. The ungentlemanly clause was not mentioned again; and the backs soon bowed themselves back into their natural shape.

But I hear you asking me in alarm whether I have actually put all this tub thumping into a Don Juan comedy. I have not. I have only made my Don Juan a political pamphleteer, and given you his pamphlet in full by way of appendix. You will find it at the end of the book. I am sorry to say that it is a common practice with romancers to announce their hero as a man of extraordinary genius, and then leave his works entirely to the reader's imagination; so that at the end of the book you whisper to yourself ruefully that but for the author's solemn preliminary assurance you should hardly have given the gentleman credit for ordinary good sense. You cannot accuse me of this pitiable barrenness, this feeble evasion. I not only tell you that my hero wrote a revolutionists' handbook: I give you the handbook at full length for your edification if you care to read it. And in that handbook you will find the politics of the sex question as I conceive Don Juan's descendant to understand them. Not that I disclaim the fullest responsibility for his opinions and for those of all my characters, pleasant and unpleasant. They are all right from their several points of view; and their points of view are, for the dramatic moment, mine also. This may puzzle the people who believe that there is such a thing as an absolutely right point of view, usually their own. It may seem to them that nobody who doubts this can be in a state of grace. However that may be, it is certainly true that nobody who agrees with them can possibly be a dramatist, or indeed anything else that turns upon a knowledge of mankind. Hence it has been pointed out that Shakespear had no conscience. Neither have I, in that sense.

You may, however, remind me that this digression of mine into politics was preceded by a very convincing demonstration that the artist never catches the point of view of the common man on the question of sex, because he is not in the same predicament. I first prove that anything I write on the relation of the sexes is sure to be misleading; and

then I proceed to write a Don Juan play. Well, if you insist on asking me why I behave in this absurd way, I can only reply that you asked me to, and that in any case my treatment of the subject may be valid for the artist, amusing to the amateur, and at least intelligible and therefore possibly suggestive to the Philistine. Every man who records his illusions is providing data for the genuinely scientific psychology which the world still waits for. I plank down my view of the existing relations of men to women in the most highly civilized society for what it is worth. It is a view like any other view and no more, neither true nor false, but, I hope, a way of looking at the subject which throws into the familiar order of cause and effect a sufficient body of fact and experience to be interesting to you, if not to the play-going public of London. I have certainly shewn little consideration for that public in this enterprise; but I know that it has the friendliest disposition towards you and me as far as it has any consciousness of our existence, and quite understands that what I write for you must pass at a considerable height over its simple romantic head. It will take my books as read and my genius for granted, trusting me to put forth work of such quality as shall bear out its verdict. So we may disport ourselves on our own plane to the top of our bent; and if any gentleman points out that neither this epistle dedicatory nor the dream of Don Juan in the third act of the ensuing comedy is suitable for immediate production at a popular theatre we need not contradict him. Napoleon provided Talma [1] with a pit of kings, with what effect on Talma's acting is not recorded. As for me, what I have always wanted is a pit of philosophers; and this is a play for such a pit.

I should make formal acknowledgment to the authors whom I have pillaged in the following pages if I could recollect them all. The theft of the brigand-poetaster from Sir Arthur Conan Doyle is deliberate; [2] and the metamorphosis of Leporello into Enry Straker, motor engineer and New Man, is an intentional dramatic sketch of the contemporary embryo of Mr H. G. Wells's anticipation of the efficient engineering class which will, he hopes, finally sweep the jabberers out of the way of civilization. Mr Barrie has also, whilst I am correcting my proofs, delighted London with a servant who knows

---

[1] French actor, 1763–1826.
[2] In "How the Brigadier Held the King," a story in Conan Doyle's *Exploits of Brigadier Gerard* (1895), a brigand called El Cuchillo writes poetry, but no samples of it appear.

more than his masters.[1] The conception of Mendoza Limited I trace back to a certain West Indian colonial secretary,[2] who, at a period when he and I and Mr Sidney Webb were sowing our political wild oats as a sort of Fabian Three Musketeers, without any prevision of the surprising respectability of the crop that followed, recommended Webb, the encyclopedic and inexhaustible, to form himself into a company for the benefit of the shareholders. Octavius I take over unaltered from Mozart; and I hereby authorize any actor who impersonates him, to sing "Dalla sua pace"[3] (if he can) at any convenient moment during the representation. Ann was suggested to me by the fifteenth-century Dutch morality called *Everyman,* which Mr William Poel has lately resuscitated so triumphantly. I trust he will work that vein further, and recognize that Elizabethan Renascence fustian is no more bearable after medieval poesy than Scribe after Ibsen. As I sat watching *Everyman* at the Charterhouse,[4] I said to myself Why not Everywoman? Ann was the result: every woman is not Ann; but Ann is Everywoman.

That the author of *Everyman* was no mere artist, but an artist-philosopher, and that the artist-philosophers are the only sort of artists I take quite seriously, will be no news to you. Even Plato and Boswell, as the dramatists who invented Socrates and Dr Johnson, impress me more deeply than the romantic playwrights. Ever since, as a boy, I first breathed the air of transcendental regions at a performance of Mozart's *Zauberflöte,*[5] I have been proof against the garish splendors and alcoholic excitements of the ordinary stage combinations of Tappertitian[6] romance with the police intelligence. Bunyan, Blake, Hogarth, and Turner (these four apart and above all the English classics), Goethe, Shelley, Schopenhauer, Wagner, Ibsen, Morris, Tolstoy, and Nietzsche are among the writers whose peculiar sense of the world I recognize as more or less akin to my own. Mark the word peculiar. I read Dickens and Shakespear without shame or stint; but their pregnant observations and demonstrations of life are not co-ordinated into any philosophy or religion: on the contrary, Dickens's sentimental assumptions are violently contradicted by his observations; and Shakespear's pessimism is only his wounded humanity. Both have the specific genius of the fictionist and the common sympathies of human feeling and thought in pre-eminent degree. They are often saner and shrewder than the philosophers just as Sancho Panza was often saner and shrewder than Don Quixote. They clear away vast masses of oppressive gravity by their sense of the ridiculous, which is at bottom a combination of sound moral judgment with light-hearted good humor. But they are concerned with the diversities of the world instead of with its unities: they are so irreligious that they exploit popular religion for professional purposes without delicacy or scruple (for example, Sydney Carton[1] and the ghost in Hamlet!): they are anarchical, and cannot balance their exposures of Angelo and Dogberry, Sir Leicester Dedlock[2] and Mr Tite Barnacle,[3] with any portrait of a prophet or a worthy leader: they have no constructive ideas: they regard those who have them as dangerous fanatics: in all their fictions there is no leading thought or inspiration for which any man could conceivably risk the spoiling of his hat in a shower, much less his life. Both are alike forced to borrow motives for the more strenuous actions of their personages from the common stockpot of melodramatic plots; so that Hamlet has to be stimulated by the prejudices of a policeman and Macbeth by the cupidities of a bushranger. Dickens, without the excuse of having to manufacture motives for Hamlets and Macbeths, superfluously punts his crew down the stream of his monthly parts by mechanical devices which I leave you to describe, my own memory being quite baffled by the simplest question as to Monks in *Oliver Twist,* or the long lost parentage of Smike,[4] or the relations between the Dorrit and Clennam families so inopportunely discovered by Monsieur Rigaud Blandois.[5] The truth is, the world was to Shakespear a great "stage of fools" on which he was utterly bewildered. He could see no sort of sense in living at all; and Dickens saved himself from the despair of the dream in *The Chimes* by taking the world for granted and busying himself with its details. Neither of them could do anything with a serious positive character: they could place a human figure before you with perfect verisimilitude; but when the moment came for making it live and move, they found, unless it made them

---

[1] *The Admirable Crichton.*
[2] Sydney Olivier, later Lord Olivier.
[3] Don Ottavio's aria in Act I of *Don Giovanni:* "My peace depends on hers."
[4] Poel's revival was played in the courtyard of the medieval almshouse, Charterhouse, in 1901.
[5] *The Magic Flute.*
[6] Tappertit is an apprentice in Dickens' *Barnaby Rudge.*

[1] In *A Tale of Two Cities.*
[2] In *Bleak House.*
[3] In *Little Dorrit.*
[4] In *Nicholas Nickleby.*
[5] In *Little Dorrit.*

laugh, that they had a puppet on their hands, and had to invent some artificial external stimulus to make it work. This is what is the matter with Hamlet all through: he has no will except in his bursts of temper. Foolish Bardolaters make a virtue of this after their fashion: they declare that the play is the tragedy of irresolution; but all Shakespear's projections of the deepest humanity he knew have the same defect: their characters and manners are lifelike; but their actions are forced on them from without, and the external force is grotesquely inappropriate except when it is quite conventional, as in the case of Henry V. Falstaff is more vivid than any of these serious reflective characters, because he is self-acting: his motives are his own appetites and instincts and humors. Richard III, too, is delightful as the whimsical comedian who stops a funeral to make love to the corpse's son's widow; but when, in the next act, he is replaced by a stage villain who smothers babies and offs with people's heads, we are revolted at the imposture and repudiate the changeling. Faulconbridge, Coriolanus, Leontes are admirable descriptions of instinctive temperaments: indeed the play of Coriolanus is the greatest of Shakespear's comedies; but description is not philosophy; and comedy neither compromises the author nor reveals him. He must be judged by those characters into which he puts what he knows of himself, his Hamlets and Macbeths and Lears and Prosperos. If these characters are agonizing in a void about factitious melodramatic murders and revenges and the like, whilst the comic characters walk with their feet on solid ground, vivid and amusing, you know that the author has much to shew and nothing to teach. The comparison between Falstaff and Prospero is like the comparison between Micawber and David Copperfield. At the end of the book you know Micawber, whereas you only know what has happened to David, and are not interested enough in him to wonder what his politics or religion might be if anything so stupendous as a religious or political idea, or a general idea of any sort, were to occur to him. He is tolerable as a child; but he never becomes a man, and might be left out of his own biography altogether but for his usefulness as a stage confidant, a Horatio or "Charles his friend": what they call on the stage a feeder.

Now you cannot say this of the works of the artist-philosophers. You cannot say it, for instance, of *The Pilgrim's Progress.* Put your Shakespearian hero and coward, Henry V and Pistol or Parolles, beside Mr Valiant

and Mr Fearing, and you have a sudden revelation of the abyss that lies between the fashionable author who could see nothing in the world but personal aims and the tragedy of their disappointment or the comedy of their incongruity, and the field preacher who achieved virtue and courage by identifying himself with the purpose of the world as he understood it. The contrast is enormous: Bunyan's coward stirs your blood more than Shakespear's hero, who actually leaves you cold and secretly hostile. You suddenly see that Shakespear, with all his flashes and divinations, never understood virtue and courage, never conceived how any man who was not a fool could, like Bunyan's hero, look back from the brink of the river of death over the strife and labor of his pilgrimage, and say "yet do I not repent me"; or, with the panache of a millionaire, bequeath "my sword to him that shall succeed me in my pilgrimage, and my courage and skill to him that can get it." This is the true joy in life, the being used for a purpose recognized by yourself as a mighty one; the being thoroughly worn out before you are thrown on the scrap heap; the being a force of Nature instead of a feverish selfish little clod of ailments and grievances complaining that the world will not devote itself to making you happy. And also the only real tragedy in life is the being used by personally minded men for purposes which you recognize to be base. All the rest is at worst mere misfortune or mortality: this alone is misery, slavery, hell on earth; and the revolt against it is the only force that offers a man's work to the poor artist, whom our personally minded rich people would so willingly employ as pandar, buffoon, beauty monger, sentimentalizer and the like.

It may seem a long step from Bunyan to Nietzsche; but the difference between their conclusion is merely formal. Bunyan's perception that righteousness is filthy rags, his scorn for Mr Legality in the village of Morality, his defiance of the Church as the supplanter of religion, his insistence on courage as the virtue of virtues, his estimate of the career of the conventionally respectable and sensible Worldly Wiseman as no better at bottom than the life and death of Mr Badman: all this, expressed by Bunyan in the terms of a tinker's theology, is what Nietzsche has expressed in terms of post-Darwin, post-Schopenhauer philosophy; Wagner in terms of polytheistic mythology; and Ibsen in terms of mid-XIX century Parisian dramaturgy. Nothing is new in these matters except their novelties: for instance, it is a novelty to call Justification by Faith "Wille," and Justification by Works "Vorstellung." The sole use of the novelty is that you and I buy and read Schopenhauer's treatise on Will and Representation when we should not dream of buying a set of sermons on Faith versus Works. At bottom the controversy is the same, and the dramatic results are the same. Bunyan makes no attempt to present his pilgrims as more sensible or better conducted than Mr Worldly Wiseman. Mr W. W.'s worst enemies, Mr Embezzler, Mr Never-go-to-Church-on-Sunday, Mr Bad Form, Mr Murderer, Mr Burglar, Mr Corespondent, Mr Blackmailer, Mr Cad, Mr Drunkard, Mr Labor Agitator and so forth, can read *The Pilgrim's Progress* without finding a word said against them; whereas the respectable people who snub them and put them in prison, such as Mr W. W. himself and his young friend Civility; Formalist and Hypocrisy; Wildhead, Inconsiderate, and Pragmatick (who were clearly young university men of good family and high feeding); that brisk lad Ignorance, Talkative, By-ends of Fairspeech and his mother-in-law Lady Feigning, and other reputable gentlemen and citizens, catch it very severely. Even Little Faith, though he gets to heaven at last, is given to understand that it served him right to be mobbed by the brothers Faint Heart, Mistrust, and Guilt, all three recognized members of respectable society and veritable pillars of the law. The whole allegory is a consistent attack on morality and respectability, without a word that one can remember against vice and crime. Exactly what is complained of in Nietzsche and Ibsen, is it not? And also exactly what would be complained of in all the literature which is great enough and old enough to have attained canonical rank, officially or unofficially, were it not that books are admitted to the canon by a compact which confesses their greatness in consideration of abrogating their meaning; so that the reverend rector can agree with the prophet Micah as to his inspired style without being committed to any complicity in Micah's furiously Radical opinions. Why, even I, as I force myself, pen in hand, into recognition and civility, find all the force of my onslaught destroyed by a simple policy of nonresistance. In vain do I redouble the violence of the language in which I proclaim my heterodoxies. I rail at the theistic credulity of Voltaire, the amoristic superstition of Shelley, the revival of tribal soothsaying and idolatrous rites which Huxley called Science and mistook for an advance on the Pentateuch, no less than at the welter

of ecclesiastical and professional humbug which saves the face of the stupid system of violence and robbery which we call Law and Industry. Even atheists reproach me with infidelity and anarchists with nihilism because I cannot endure their moral tirades. And yet, instead of exclaiming "Send this inconceivable Satanist to the stake," the respectable newspapers pith me by announcing "another book by this brilliant and thoughtful writer." And the ordinary citizen, knowing that an author who is well spoken of by a respectable newspaper must be all right, reads me, as he reads Micah, with undisturbed edification from his own point of view. It is narrated that in the eighteenseventies an old lady, a very devout Methodist, moved from Colchester to a house in the neighborhood of the City Road, in London, where, mistaking the Hall of Science for a chapel, she sat at the feet of Charles Bradlaugh for many years, entranced by his eloquence, without questioning his orthodoxy or moulting a feather of her faith. I fear I shall be defrauded of my just martyrdom in the same way.

However, I am digressing, as a man with a grievance always does. And, after all, the main thing in determining the artistic quality of a book is not the opinions it propagates, but the fact that the writer has opinions. The old lady from Colchester was right to sun her simple soul in the energetic radiance of Bradlaugh's genuine beliefs and disbeliefs rather than in the chill of such mere painting of light and heat as elocution and convention can achieve. My contempt for *belles lettres,* and for amateurs who become the heroes of the fanciers of literary virtuosity, is not founded on any illusion of mine as to the permanence of those forms of thought (call them opinions) by which I strive to communicate my bent to my fellows. To younger men they are already outmoded; for though they have no more lost their logic than an eighteenth-century pastel has lost its drawing or its color, yet, like the pastel, they grow indefinably shabby, and will grow shabbier until they cease to count at all, when my books will either perish, or, if the world is still poor enough to want them, will have to stand, with Bunyan's, by quite amorphous qualities of temper and energy. With this conviction I cannot be a bellettrist. No doubt I must recognize, even as the Ancient Mariner did, that I must tell my story entertainingly if I am to hold the wedding guest spellbound in spite of the siren sounds of the loud bassoon. But "for art's sake" alone I would not face the toil of writing a single sentence. I know that there are men who, having nothing to say and nothing to write, are nevertheless so in love with oratory and with literature that they delight in repeating as much as they can understand of what others have said or written aforetime. I know that the leisurely tricks which their want of conviction leaves them free to play with the diluted and misapprehended message supply them with a pleasant parlor game which they call style. I can pity their dotage and even sympathize with their fancy. But a true original style is never achieved for its own sake: a man may pay from a shilling to a guinea, according to his means, to see, hear, or read another man's act of genius; but he will not pay with his whole life and soul to become a mere virtuoso in literature, exhibiting an accomplishment which will not even make money for him, like fiddle playing. Effectiveness of assertion is the Alpha and Omega of style. He who has nothing to assert has no style and can have none: he who has something to assert will go as far in power of style as its momentousness and his conviction will carry him. Disprove his assertion after it is made, yet its style remains. Darwin has no more destroyed the style of Job nor of Handel than Martin Luther destroyed the style of Giotto. All the assertions get disproved sooner or later; and so we find the world full of a magnificent débris of artistic fossils, with the matter-of-fact credibility gone clean out of them, but the form still splendid. And that is why the old masters play the deuce with our mere susceptibles. Your Royal Academician thinks he can get the style of Giotto without Giotto's beliefs, and correct his perspective into the bargain. Your man of letters thinks he can get Bunyan's or Shakespear's style without Bunyan's conviction or Shakespear's apprehension, especially if he takes care not to split his infinitives. And so with your Doctors of Music, who, with their collections of discords duly prepared and resolved or retarded or anticipated in the manner of the great composers, think they can learn the art of Palestrina from Cherubini's treatise.[1] All this academic art is far worse than the trade in sham antique furniture; for the man who sells me an oaken chest which he swears was made in the XIII century, though as a matter of fact he made it himself only yesterday, at least does not pretend that there are any modern ideas in it; whereas your academic copier of fossils offers them to you as the latest outpouring of the human

spirit, and, worst of all, kidnaps young people as pupils and persuades them that his limitations are rules, his observances dexterities, his timidities good taste, and his emptiness purities. And when he declares that art should not be didactic, all the people who have nothing to teach and all the people who don't want to learn agree with him emphatically.

I pride myself on not being one of these susceptibles. If you study the electric light with which I supply you in that Bumbledonian public capacity [1] of mine over which you make merry from time to time, you will find that your house contains a great quantity of highly susceptible copper wire which gorges itself with electricity and gives you no light whatever. But here and there occurs a scrap of intensely insusceptible, intensely resistant material; and that stubborn scrap grapples with the current and will not let it through until it has made itself useful to you as those two vital qualities of literature, light and heat. Now if I am to be no mere copper wire amateur but a luminous author, I must also be a most intensely refractory person, liable to go out and to go wrong at inconvenient moments, and with incendiary possibilities. These are the faults of my qualities; and I assure you that I sometimes dislike myself so much that when some irritable reviewer chances at that moment to pitch into me with zest, I feel unspeakably relieved and obliged. But I never dream of reforming, knowing that I must take myself as I am and get what work I can out of myself. All this you will understand; for there is community of material between us: we are both critics of life as well as of art; and you have perhaps said to yourself when I have passed your windows "There, but for the grace of God, go I." An awful and chastening reflection, which shall be the closing cadence of this immoderately long letter from yours faithfully,

        G. BERNARD SHAW.

WOKING, 1903

P.S.—Amid unprecedented critical cerebration over this book of ours—alas! that your own voice should be dedicated to silence!— I find myself warned to prepare a new edition. I take the opportunity to correct a slip or two. You may have noticed (nobody else has, by the way) that I fitted you with a quotation from *Othello*, and then unconsciously referred it to *A Winter's Tale*. I

---

[1] In 1903 Shaw was a Borough Councilor for St. Pancras, London. Bumble is a domineering beadle in Dickens' *Oliver Twist*.

correct this with regret; for half its appropriateness goes with Florizel and Perdita: still, one must not trifle with Shakespear; so I have given Desdemona back her property.[1]

On the whole, the book has done very well. The strong critics are impressed; the weak intimidated; the connoisseurs tickled by my literary bravura (put in to please you): the humorists alone, oddly enough, sermonize me, scared out of their profession into the quaintest tumults of conscience. Not all my reviewers have understood me: like Englishmen in France, confidently uttering their own island diphthongs as good French vowels, many of them offer, as samples of the Shavian philosophy, the likest article from their own stock. Others are the victims of

[1] This refers to the fourth sentence of the second paragraph of the *Epistle Dedicatory*.

association of ideas: they call me Pessimist because my remarks wound their self-complacency, and Renegade because I would have my mob all Cæsars instead of Toms, Dicks, and Harrys. Worst of all, I have been accused of preaching a Final Ethical Superman: no other, in fact, than our old friend the Just Man made Perfect! This misunderstanding is so galling that I lay down my pen without another word lest I should be tempted to make the postscript longer even than the letter.

POSTSCRIPT 1933. The evolutionary theme of the third act of Man and Superman was resumed by me twenty years later in the preface to *Back to Methuselah*, where it developed as the basis of the religion of the near future.

GEORGE BERNARD SHAW

Born 1856, Dublin, Ireland.

1871–1876, Clerk and cashier in Dublin Land Agency.

1876, Moved to London. For nine years earned almost nothing, but read widely and practiced writing and public speaking.

1879–1883, Wrote five novels, but none published till 1884.

1884, Joined the Fabian Society and immediately became a leader in it.

1885, Began to have regular employment as a literary, music, and art critic for various London journals, and became self-supporting again.

1891, *The Quintessence of Ibsenism* published.

1892, First play, *Widowers' Houses,* produced by The Independent Theatre.

1894, *Arms and the Man,* a commercial failure in London, but a small success in New York.

1895–1898, Dramatic critic for *The Saturday Review.* These criticisms collected in *Our Theatres in the Nineties,* 1932.

1897, *The Devil's Disciple,* produced in New York, his first dramatic financial success, enabled him to quit journalism.

1898, Married Charlotte Payne-Townshend.

1904–1907, The Barker-Vedrenne repertory management at the Court Theatre established Shaw's reputation in London as it had been earlier established in New York.

1925, Awarded the Nobel Prize for Literature.

Died 1950. His will provided that the residue of his large estate should be used to propagandize for the reform of the English Alphabet, but the courts held this to be contrary to the public interest and the funds were divided among the British Museum, The National Gallery of Ireland, and the Royal Academy of Dramatic Art.[1]

PLAYS

(Date of completion precedes title; date of production is in italics; date of publication follows in roman.) 1892 *Widowers' Houses, 1892,* 1893. 1893 *The Philanderer, 1898,* 1898. 1893 *Mrs. Warren's Profession, 1902,* 1898. 1894 *Arms and the Man, 1894,* 1898. 1894 *Candida, 1895,* 1898. 1895 *The Man of Destiny, 1897,* 1898. 1896 *You Never Can Tell, 1898,* 1898. 1896 *The Devil's Disciple, 1897,* 1901. 1898 *Caesar and Cleopatra, 1899,* 1901. 1899 *Captain Brassbound's Conversion, 1899,* 1901. 1901 *The Admirable Bashville, 1902,* 1909 (dramatization in verse of Shaw's novel *Cashel Byron's Profession.* Productions under the title *Cashel Byron's Profession* are of dramatizations not made by Shaw). 1903 *Man and Superman, 1903,* 1903. 1904 *John Bull's Other Island, 1904,* 1907. 1904 *How He Lied to Her Husband, 1904,* 1907 (one act). 1905 *Major Barbara, 1905,* 1907. 1905 *Passion, Poison, and Petrifaction, or, The Fatal Gazogene, 1905,* 1926 (one act). 1906 *The Doctor's Dilemma, 1906,* 1911. 1907 *The Interlude at the Playhouse, 1907,* 1907 (one act). 1908 *Getting Married 1908,* 1911. 1909 *The Shewing-up of Blanco Posnet, 1909,* 1911 (one act). 1909 *Press Cuttings, 1909,* 1926 (one act). 1909 *The Fascinating Foundling, 1909,* 1926 (one act). 1909 *The Glimpse of Reality, 1927,* 1926 (one act). 1910 *Misalliance, 1910,* 1914. 1910 *The Dark Lady of the Sonnets, 1910,* 1914 (one act). 1911 *Fanny's First Play, 1911,* 1914. 1912 *Androcles and the Lion, 1912,* 1916. 1912 *Overruled, 1912,* 1916 (one act). 1912 *Pygmalion, 1913,* 1916. 1913 *Great Catherine, 1913,* 1919. 1913 *The Music Cure, 1914,* 1926 (one act). 1915 *O'Flaherty, V.C., 1917,* 1919 (one act). 1916 *The Inca of Perusalem, 1916,* 1919 (one act). 1916 *Augustus Does His Bit, 1917,* 1919 (one act). 1917 *Annajanska, the Bolshevik Empress, 1918,* 1919 (one act). 1919 *Heartbreak House, 1920,* 1919. 1920 *Back to Methuselah, 1922,* 1921 (a play cycle in five parts: I, *In the Beginning,* B.C. 4004; II, *The Gospel of the Brothers Barnabas,* A.D. 1920; III, *The Thing Happens,* A.D. 2170; IV, *The Tragedy of an Elderly Gentleman,* A.D. 3000; V,

As Far as Thought Can Reach, A.D. 31920). 1922 *Jitta's Atonement, 1923,* 1926 ("translation" of *Frau Gitta's Sühne,* by Siegfried Trebitsch). 1923 *Saint Joan, 1923,* 1924. 1929 *The Apple Cart, 1929,* 1931. 1931 *Too True to Be Good, 1932,* 1934. 1933 *Village Wooing, 1934,* 1934. 1933 *On the Rocks, 1933,* 1934. 1934 *The Simpleton of the Unexpected Isles, 1935,* 1936. 1934 *The Six of Calais, 1934,* 1936 (one act). 1935 *The Millionairess, 1936,* 1936. 1937 *Cymbeline Refinished, 1937,* 1947 (Shaw's substitute for the fifth act of Shakespeare's *Cymbeline,* in verse). 1938 *Geneva, 1938,* 1939 (This play was much rewritten after first publication, and subsequent editions differ). 1939 *In Good King Charles's Golden Days, 1939,* 1939. 1948 *Buoyant Billions, 1948,* 1950. 1949 *Shakes versus Shav, 1949,* 1951 (a puppet play, one act). 1950 *Farfetched Fables, 1950,* 1951. 1950 *Why She Would Not,* (unfinished, unproduced), 1956.

SCREENWRITING

1938 *Pygmalion.* 1941 *Major Barbara.* 1945 *Caesar and Cleopatra.*

WRITINGS ON DRAMA

The Quintessence of Ibsenism, 1891, 1913. *Dramatic Opinions and Essays,* selected by James Huneker, 1906; re-edited and expanded by Shaw as *Our Theatres in the Nineties,* 1932, 1948, from his contributions as dramatic critic to *The Saturday Review,* 1895–1898. Prefaces to: *Widowers' Houses,* 1893; *Plays Pleasant,* 1898; *Plays Unpleasant,* 1898; *Mrs. Warren's Profession,* 1902, 1930; *Three Plays for Puritans,* 1901; *Man and Superman,* 1903; *The Shewing-up of Blanco Posnet,* 1911; *Overruled,* 1916; *Great Catherine,* 1919; *Heartbreak House,* 1919; *Back to Methuselah,* 1921. Preface to *Three Plays* by Brieux, 1911. Preface to *Three Plays* by William Archer, 1927. *The Art of Rehearsal,* 1928. *Ellen Terry and Bernard Shaw: a Correspondence,* ed. by Christopher St. John, 1931. *Bernard Shaw and Mrs. Patrick Campbell, Their Correspondence,* 1952. *Advice to a Young Critic,* 1955. See also *Shaw on Theatre,* edited by E. J. West, 1958. Various fugitive pieces in periodicals.

[1] See *Contemporary Drama 11 Plays,* for a more extended summary of Shaw's career.

MAN AND SUPERMAN

ACT I

ROEBUCK RAMSDEN *is in his study, opening the morning's letters. The study, handsomely and solidly furnished, proclaims the man of means. Not a speck of dust is visible: it is clear that there are at least two housemaids and a parlormaid downstairs, and a housekeeper upstairs who does not let them spare elbow-grease. Even the top of* ROEBUCK'S *head is polished: on a sunshiny day he could heliograph his orders to distant camps by merely nodding. In no other respect, however, does he suggest the military man. It is in active civil life that men get his broad air of importance, his dignified expectation of deference, his determinate mouth disarmed and refined since the hour of his success by the withdrawal of opposition and the concession of comfort and precedence and power. He is more than a highly respectable man: he is marked out as a president of highly respectable men, a chairman among directors, an alderman among councillors, a mayor among aldermen. Four tufts of iron-grey hair, which will soon be as white as isinglass, and are in other respects not at all unlike it, grow in two symmetrical pairs above his ears and at the angles of his spreading jaws. He wears a black frock coat, a white waistcoat (it is bright spring weather), and trousers, neither black nor perceptibly blue, of one of those indefinitely mixed hues which the modern clothier has produced to harmonize with the religions of respectable men. He has not been out of doors yet today; so he still wears his slippers, his boots being ready for him on the hearthrug. Surmising that he has no valet, and seeing that he has no secretary with a shorthand notebook and a typewriter, one meditates on how little our great burgess domesticity has been disturbed by new fashions and methods, or by the enterprise of the railway and hotel companies which sell you a Saturday to Monday of life at Folkestone as a real gentleman for two guineas, first class fares both ways included.*

How old is ROEBUCK? *The question is important on the threshold of a drama of ideas; for under such circumstances everything depends on whether his adolescence belonged to the sixties or to the eighties. He was born, as a matter of fact, in 1839, and was a Unitarian and Free Trader from his boyhood, and an Evolutionist from the publication of the* Origin of Species. *Consequently he has always classed himself as an advanced thinker and fearlessly outspoken reformer.*

Sitting at his writing table, he has on his right the windows giving on Portland Place. Through these, as through a proscenium, the curious spectator may contemplate his profile as well as the blinds will permit. On his left is the inner wall, with a stately bookcase, and the door not quite in the middle, but somewhat further from him. Against the wall opposite him are two busts on pillars: one, to his left, of John Bright; the other, to his right, of Mr[1] Herbert Spencer. Between them hang an engraved portrait of Richard Cobden; enlarged photographs of Martineau, Huxley, and George Eliot;[2] autotypes of allegories by Mr G. F. Watts (for ROEBUCK *believes in the fine arts with all the earnestness of a man who does not understand them), and an impression of Dupont's engraving of Delaroche's Beaux Arts hemicycle, representing the great men of all ages. On the wall behind him, above the mantelshelf, is a family portrait of impenetrable obscurity.*

A chair stands near the writing table for the convenience of business visitors. Two other chairs are against the wall between the busts.

[*A* PARLORMAID *enters with a visitor's card.* ROEBUCK *takes it, and nods, pleased. Evidently a welcome caller.*]

Ramsden. Shew him in.

[*The* PARLORMAID *goes out and returns with the visitor.*]

---

[1] The play follows Shaw's spellings.
[2] These six were leaders of "advanced" thought in the third quarter of the 19th century.

The Maid. Mr Robinson.

[MR ROBINSON *is really an uncommonly nice looking young fellow. He must, one thinks, be the jeune premier; for it is not in reason to suppose that a second such attractive male figure should appear in one story. The slim, shapely frame, the elegant suit of new mourning, the small head and regular features, the pretty little moustache, the frank clear eyes, the wholesome bloom on the youthful complexion, the well brushed glossy hair, not curly, but of fine texture and good dark color, the arch of good nature in the eyebrows, the erect forehead and neatly pointed chin, all announce the man who will love and suffer later on. And that he will not do so without sympathy is guaranteed by an engaging sincerity and eager modest serviceableness which stamp him as a man of amiable nature. The moment he appears,* RAMSDEN'S *face expands into fatherly liking and welcome, an expression which drops into one of decorous grief as the young man approaches him with sorrow in his face as well as in his black clothes.* RAMSDEN *seems to know the nature of the bereavement. As the visitor advances silently to the writing table, the old man rises and shakes his hand across it without a word: a long, affectionate shake which tells the story of a recent sorrow common to both.*]

Ramsden. [*Concluding the handshake and cheering up.*] Well, well, Octavius, it's the common lot. We must all face it some day. Sit down.

[OCTAVIUS *takes the visitor's chair.* RAMSDEN *replaces himself in his own.*]

Octavius. Yes: we must face it, Mr Ramsden. But I owed him a great deal. He did everything for me that my father could have done if he had lived.

Ramsden. He had no son of his own, you see.

Octavius. But he had daughters; and yet he was as good to my sister as to me. And his death was so sudden! I always intended to thank him—to let him know that I had not taken all his care of me as a matter of course, as any boy takes his father's care. But I waited for an opportunity; and now he is dead—dropped without a moment's warning. He will never know what I felt.

[*He takes out his handkerchief and cries unaffectedly.*]

Ramsden. How do we know that, Octavius? He may know it: we cannot tell.

Come! dont grieve. [OCTAVIUS *masters himself and puts up his handkerchief.*] That's right. Now let me tell you something to console you. The last time I saw him—it was in this very room—he said to me: "Tavy is a generous lad and the soul of honor; and when I see how little consideration other men get from their sons, I realize how much better than a son he's been to me." There! Doesnt that do you good?

Octavius. Mr Ramsden: he used to say to me that he had met only one man in the world who was the soul of honor, and that was Roebuck Ramsden.

Ramsden. Oh, that was his partiality: we were very old friends, you know. But there was something else he used to say about you. I wonder whether I ought to tell you or not!

Octavius. You know best.

Ramsden. It was something about his daughter.

Octavius. [*Eagerly.*] About Ann! Oh, do tell me that, Mr Ramsden.

Ramsden. Well, he said he was glad, after all, you were not his son, because he thought that someday Annie and you—— [OCTAVIUS *blushes vividly.*] Well, perhaps I shouldnt have told you. But he was in earnest.

Octavius. Oh, if only I thought I had a chance! You know, Mr Ramsden, I dont care about money or about what people call position; and I cant bring myself to take an interest in the business of struggling for them. Well, Ann has a most exquisite nature; but she is so accustomed to be in the thick of that sort of thing that she thinks a man's character incomplete if he is not ambitious. She knows that if she married me she would have to reason herself out of being ashamed of me for not being a big success of some kind.

Ramsden. [*Getting up and planting himself with his back to the fireplace.*] Nonsense, my boy, nonsense! Youre too modest. What does she know about the real value of men at her age? [*More seriously.*] Besides, she's a wonderfully dutiful girl. Her father's wish would be sacred to her. Do you know that since she grew up to years of discretion, I dont believe she has ever once given her own wish as a reason for doing anything or not doing it. It's always "Father wishes me to," or "Mother wouldnt like it." It's really almost a fault in her. I have often told her she must learn to think for herself.

Octavius. [*Shaking his head.*] I couldnt ask her to marry me because her father wished it, Mr Ramsden.

Ramsden. Well, perhaps not. No: of

course not. I see that. No: you certainly couldnt. But when you win her on your own merits, it will be a great happiness to her to fulfil her father's desire as well as her own. Eh? Come! youll ask her, won't you?

Octavius. [*With sad gaiety.*] At all events I promise you I shall never ask anyone else.

Ramsden. Oh, you shant need to. She'll accept you, my boy—although [*Here he suddenly becomes very serious indeed.*] you have one great drawback.

Octavius. [*Anxiously.*] What drawback is that, Mr Ramsden? I should rather say which of my many drawbacks?

Ramsden. I'll tell you, Octavius. [*He takes from the table a book bound in red cloth.*] I have in my hand a copy of the most infamous, the most scandalous, the most mischievous, the most blackguardly book that ever escaped burning at the hands of the common hangman. I have not read it: I would not soil my mind with such filth; but I have read what the papers say of it. The title is quite enough for me. [*He reads it.*] The Revolutionist's Handbook and Pocket Companion. By John Tanner, M.I.R.C., Member of the Idle Rich Class.

Octavius. [*Smiling.*] But Jack——

Ramsden. [*Testily.*] For goodness' sake, dont call him Jack under my roof. [*He throws the book violently down on the table. Then, somewhat relieved, he comes past the table to* OCTAVIUS, *and addresses him at close quarters with impressive gravity.*] Now, Octavius, I know that my dead friend was right when he said you were a generous lad. I know that this man was your schoolfellow, and that you feel bound to stand by him because there was a boyish friendship between you. But I ask you to consider the altered circumstances. You were treated as a son in my friend's house. You lived there; and your friends could not be turned from the door. This man Tanner was in and out there on your account almost from his childhood. He addresses Annie by her Christian name as freely as you do. Well, while her father was alive, that was her father's business, not mine. This man Tanner was only a boy to him: his opinions were something to be laughed at, like a man's hat on a child's head. But now Tanner is a grown man and Annie a grown woman. And her father is gone. We dont as yet know the exact terms of his will; but he often talked it over with me; and I have no more doubt than I have that youre sitting there that the will appoints me Annie's trustee and guardian. [*Forcibly.*] Now I tell you, once for all, I cant and I

wont have Annie placed in such a position that she must, out of regard for you, suffer the intimacy of this fellow Tanner. It's not fair: it's not right: it's not kind. What are you going to do about it?

Octavius. But Ann herself has told Jack that whatever his opinions are, he will always be welcome because he knew her dear father.

Ramsden. [*Out of patience.*] That girl's mad about her duty to her parents. [*He starts off like a goaded ox in the direction of John Bright, in whose expression there is no sympathy for him. As he speaks he fumes down to Herbert Spencer, who receives him still more coldly.*] Excuse me, Octavius; but there are limits to social toleration. You know that I am not a bigoted or prejudiced man. You know that I am plain Roebuck Ramsden when other men who have done less have got handles to their names, because I have stood for equality and liberty of conscience while they were truckling to the Church and to the aristocracy. Whitefield and I lost chance after chance through our advanced opinions. But I draw the line at Anarchism and Free Love and that sort of thing. If I am to be Annie's guardian, she will have to learn that she has a duty to me. I wont have it: I will not have it. She must forbid John Tanner the house; and so must you.

[*The* PARLORMAID *returns.*]

Octavius. But——

Ramsden. [*Calling his attention to the* SERVANT.] Sssh! Well?

The Maid. Mr Tanner wishes to see you, sir.

Ramsden. Mr Tanner!

Octavius. Jack!

Ramsden. How dare Mr Tanner call on me! Say I cannot see him.

Octavius. [*Hurt.*] I am sorry you are turning my friend from your door like that.

The Maid. [*Calmly.*] He's not at the door, sir. He's upstairs in the drawing room with Miss Ramsden. He came with Mrs Whitefield and Miss Ann and Miss Robinson, sir.

[RAMSDEN's *feelings are beyond words.*]

Octavius. [*Grinning.*] Thats very like Jack, Mr Ramsden. You must see him, even if it's only to turn him out.

Ramsden. [*Hammering out his words with suppressed fury.*] Go upstairs and ask Mr Tanner to be good enough to step down here. [*The* PARLORMAID *goes out; and* RAMSDEN *returns to the fireplace, as to a fortified position.*] I must say that of all the confounded pieces of impertinence—well, if these are

Anarchist manners, I hope you like them. And Annie with him! Annie! A——
[*He chokes.*]

Octavius. Yes: thats what surprises me. He's so desperately afraid of Ann. There must be something the matter.

[MR JOHN TANNER *suddenly opens the door and enters. He is too young to be described simply as a big man with a beard. But it is already plain that middle life will find him in that category. He has still some of the slimness of youth; but youthfulness is not the effect he aims at: his frock coat would befit a prime minister; and a certain high chested carriage of the shoulders, a lofty pose of the head, and the Olympian majesty with which a mane, or rather a huge wisp, of hazel colored hair is thrown back from an imposing brow, suggest Jupiter rather than Apollo. He is prodigiously fluent of speech, restless, excitable (mark the snorting nostril and the restless blue eye, just the thirty-secondth of an inch too wide open), possibly a little mad. He is carefully dressed, not from the vanity that cannot resist finery, but from a sense of the importance of everything he does which leads him to make as much of paying a call as other men do of getting married or laying a foundation stone. A sensitive, susceptible, exaggerative, earnest man: a megalomaniac, who would be lost without a sense of humor.*[1]
Just at present the sense of humor is in abeyance. To say that he is excited is nothing: all his moods are phases of excitement. He is now in the panic-stricken phase; and he walks straight up to RAMSDEN *as if with the fixed intention of shooting him on his own hearthrug. But what he pulls from his breast pocket is not a pistol, but a foolscap document which he thrusts under the indignant nose of* RAMSDEN *as he exclaims.*]

Tanner. Ramsden: do you know what this is?

Ramsden. [*Loftily.*] No, sir.

Tanner. It's a copy of Whitefield's will. Ann got it this morning.

Ramsden. When you say Ann, you mean, I presume, Miss Whitefield.

Tanner. I mean our Ann, your Ann, Tavy's Ann, and now, Heaven help me, my Ann!

---

[1] At the Court Theatre production of *Man and Superman* in 1905, Harley Granville Barker, playing Tanner, was made up to look like Shaw.

Octavius. [*Rising, very pale.*] What do you mean?

Tanner. Mean! [*He holds up the will.*] Do you know who is appointed Ann's guardian by this will?

Ramsden. [*Coolly.*] I believe I am.

. *Tanner.* You! You and I, man. I! I!! I!!! Both of us!
[*He flings the will down on the writing table.*]

Ramsden. You! Impossible.

Tanner. It's only too hideously true. [*He throws himself into* OCTAVIUS'S *chair.*] Ramsden: get me out of it somehow. You don't know Ann as well as I do. She'll commit every crime a respectable woman can; and she'll justify every one of them by saying that it was the wish of her guardians. She'll put everything on us; and we shall have no more control over her than a couple of mice over a cat.

Octavius. Jack: I wish you wouldnt talk like that about Ann.

Tanner. This chap's in love with her: thats another complication. Well, she'll either jilt him and say I didnt approve of him, or marry him and say you ordered her to. I tell you, this is the most staggering blow that has ever fallen on a man of my age and temperament.

Ramsden. Let me see that will, sir. [*He goes to the writing table and picks it up.*] I cannot believe that my old friend Whitefield would have shewn such a want of confidence in me as to associate me with——
[*His countenance falls as he reads.*]

Tanner. It's all my own doing: thats the horrible irony of it. He told me one day that you were to be Ann's guardian; and like a fool I began arguing with him about the folly of leaving a young woman under the control of an old man with obsolete ideas.

Ramsden. [*Stupent.*] My ideas obsolete!!!!!!!

Tanner. Totally. I had just finished an essay called Down with Government by the Greyhaired; and I was full of arguments and illustrations. I said the proper thing was to combine the experience of an old hand with the vitality of a young one. Hang me if he didnt take me at my word and alter his will—it's dated only a fortnight after that conversation—appointing me as joint guardian with you!

Ramsden. [*Pale and determined.*] I shall refuse to act.

Tanner. Whats the good of that? Ive been refusing all the way from Richmond: but Ann keeps on saying that of course she's only an orphan; and that she cant expect the people who were glad to come to the house in her father's time to trouble much about her now. Thats the latest game. An orphan! It's like hearing an ironclad talk about being at the mercy of the wind and waves.

Octavius. This is not fair, Jack. She is an orphan. And you ought to stand by her.

Tanner. Stand by her! What danger is she in? She has the law on her side; she has popular sentiment on her side; she has plenty of money and no conscience. All she wants with me is to load up all her moral responsibilities on me, and do as she likes at the expense of my character. I cant control her; and she can compromise me as much as she likes. I might as well be her husband.

Ramsden. You can refuse to accept the guardianship. *I* shall certainly refuse to hold it jointly with you.

Tanner. Yes; and what will she say to that? what does she say to it? Just that her father's wishes are sacred to her, and that she shall always look up to me as her guardian whether I care to face the responsibility or not. Refuse! You might as well refuse to accept the embraces of a boa constrictor when once it gets round your neck.

Octavius. This sort of talk is not kind to me, Jack.

Tanner. [*Rising and going to* OCTAVIUS *to console him, but still lamenting.*] If he wanted a young guardian, why didn't he appoint Tavy?

Ramsden. Ah! why indeed?

Octavius. I will tell you. He sounded me about it; but I refused the trust because I loved her. I had no right to let myself be forced on her as a guardian by her father. He spoke to her about it; and she said I was right. You know I love her, Mr Ramsden; and Jack knows it too. If Jack loved a woman, I would not compare her to a boa constrictor in his presence, however much I might dislike her.

[*He sits down between the busts and turns his face to the wall.*]

Ramsden. I do not believe that Whitefield was in his right senses when he made that will. You have admitted that he made it under your influence.

Tanner. You ought to be pretty well obliged to me for my influence. He leaves you two thousand five hundred for your trouble. He leaves Tavy a dowry for his sister and five thousand for himself.

Octavius. [*His tears flowing afresh.*] Oh, I cant take it. He was too good to us.

Tanner. You wont get it, my boy, if Ramsden upsets the will.

Ramsden. Ha! I see. You have got me in a cleft stick.

Tanner. He leaves me nothing but the charge of Ann's morals, on the ground that I have already more money than is good for me. That shews that he had his wits about him, doesnt it?

Ramsden. [*Grimly.*] I admit that.

Octavius. [*Rising and coming from his refuge by the wall.*] Mr Ramsden: I think you are prejudiced against Jack. He is a man of honor, and incapable of abusing——

Tanner. Dont, Tavy: you'll make me ill. I am not a man of honor: I am a man struck down by a dead hand. Tavy: you must marry her after all and take her off my hands. And I had set my heart on saving you from her!

Octavius. Oh, Jack, you talk of saving me from my highest happiness.

Tanner. Yes, a lifetime of happiness. If it were only the first half hour's happiness, Tavy, I would buy it for you with my last penny. But a lifetime of happiness! No man alive could bear it: it would be hell on earth.

Ramsden. [*Violently.*] Stuff, sir. Talk sense; or else go and waste someone else's time: I have something better to do than listen to your fooleries.

[*He positively kicks his way to his table and resumes his seat.*]

Tanner. You hear him, Tavy! Not an idea in his head later than eighteensixty. We cant leave Ann with no other guardian to turn to.

Ramsden. I am proud of your contempt for my character and opinions, sir. Your own are set forth in that book, I believe.

Tanner. [*Eagerly going to the table.*] What! Youve got my book! What do you think of it?

Ramsden. Do you suppose I would read such a book, sir?

Tanner. Then why did you buy it?

Ramsden. I did not buy it, sir. It has been sent me by some foolish lady who seems to admire your views. I was about to dispose of it when Octavius interrupted me. I shall do so now, with your permission.

[*He throws the book into the wastepaper basket with such vehemence that* TANNER *recoils under the impression that it is being thrown at his head.*]

Tanner. You have no more manners than I have myself. However, that saves ceremony between us. [*He sits down again.*] What do you intend to do about this will?

Octavius. May I make a suggestion?

Ramsden. Certainly, Octavius.

Octavius. Arnt we forgetting that Ann

herself may have some wishes in this matter?

Ramsden. I quite intend that Annie's wishes shall be consulted in every reasonable way. But she is only a woman, and a young and inexperienced woman at that.

Tanner. Ramsden: I begin to pity you.

Ramsden. [*Hotly.*] I dont want to know how you feel towards me, Mr Tanner.

Tanner. Ann will do just exactly what she likes. And whats more, she'll force us to advise her to do it; and she'll put the blame on us if it turns out badly. So, as Tavy is longing to see her——

Octavius. [*Shyly.*] I am not, Jack.

Tanner. You lie, Tavy: you are. So lets have her down from the drawing room and ask her what she intends us to do. Off with you, Tavy, and fetch her. [*Tavy turns to go.*] And dont be long; for the strained relations between myself and Ramsden will make the interval rather painful.

[*Ramsden compresses his lips, but says nothing.*]

Octavius. Never mind him, Mr Ramsden. He's not serious.   [*He goes out.*]

Ramsden. [*Very deliberately.*] Mr Tanner: you are the most impudent person I have ever met.

Tanner. [*Seriously.*] I know it, Ramsden. Yet even I cannot wholly conquer shame. We live in an atmosphere of shame. We are ashamed of everything that is real about us; ashamed of ourselves, of our relatives, of our incomes, of our accents, of our opinions, of our experience, just as we are ashamed of our naked skins. Good Lord, my dear Ramsden, we are ashamed to walk, ashamed to ride in an omnibus, ashamed to hire a hansom instead of keeping a carriage, ashamed of keeping one horse instead of two and a groom-gardener instead of a coachman and footman. The more things a man is ashamed of, the more respectable he is. Why, youre ashamed to buy my book, ashamed to read it: the only thing youre not ashamed of is to judge me for it without having read it; and even that only means that youre ashamed to have heterodox opinions. Look at the effect I produce because my fairy godmother withheld from me this gift of shame. I have every possible virtue that a man can have except——

Ramsden. I am glad you think so well of yourself.

Tanner. All you mean by that is that you think I ought to be ashamed of talking about my virtues. You dont mean that I havnt got them: you know perfectly well that I am as sober and honest a citizen as yourself, as truthful personally, and much more truthful politically and morally.

Ramsden. [*Touched on his most sensitive point.*] I deny that. I will not allow you or any man to treat me as if I were a mere member of the British public. I detest its prejudices; I scorn its narrowness; I demand the right to think for myself. You pose as an advanced man. Let me tell you that I was an advanced man before you were born.

Tanner. I knew it was a long time ago.

Ramsden. I am as advanced as ever I was. I defy you to prove that I have ever hauled down the flag. I am more advanced than ever I was. I grow more advanced every day.

Tanner. More advanced in years, Polonius.

Ramsden. Polonius! So you are Hamlet, I suppose.

Tanner. No: I am only the most impudent person youve ever met. Thats your notion of a thoroughly bad character. When you want to give me a piece of your mind, you ask yourself, as a just and upright man, what is the worst you can fairly say of me. Thief, liar, forger, adulterer, perjurer, glutton, drunkard? Not one of these names fit me. You have to fall back on my deficiency in shame. Well, I admit it. I even congratulate myself; for if I were ashamed of my real self, I should cut as stupid a figure as any of the rest of you. Cultivate a little impudence, Ramsden; and you will become quite a remarkable man.

Ramsden. I have no——

Tanner. You have no desire for that sort of notoriety. Bless you, I knew that answer would come as well as I know that a box of matches will come out of an automatic machine when I put a penny in the slot: you would be ashamed to say anything else.

[*The crushing retort for which* Mr Ramsden *has been visibly collecting his forces is lost for ever; for at this point* Octavius *returns with* Miss Ann Whitefield *and her* Mother; *and* Ramsden *springs up and hurries to the door to receive them. Whether* Ann *is good-looking or not depends upon your taste; also and perhaps chiefly on your age and sex. To* Octavius *she is an enchantingly beautiful woman, in whose presence the world becomes transfigured, and the puny limits of individual consciousness are suddenly made infinite by a mystic memory of the whole life of the race to its beginnings in the east, or even back to the paradise from which it fell. She is to him the reality of ro-*

mance, the inner good sense of nonsense, the unveiling of his eyes, the freeing of his soul, the abolition of time, place, and circumstance, the etherealization of his blood into rapturous rivers of the very water of life itself, the revelation of all the mysteries and the sanctification of all the dogmas. To her MOTHER *she is, to put it as moderately as possible, nothing whatever of the kind. Not that* OCTAVIUS'S *admiration is in any way ridiculous or discreditable.* ANN *is a well formed creature, as far as that goes; and she is perfectly ladylike, graceful, and comely, with ensnaring eyes and hair. Besides, instead of making herself an eyesore, like her mother, she has devised a mourning costume of black and violet silk which does honor to her late father and reveals the family tradition of brave unconventionality by which* RAMSDEN *sets such store.*

But all this is beside the point as an explanation of ANN'S *charm. Turn up her nose, give a cast to her eye, replace her black and violet confection by the apron and feathers of a flower girl, strike all the aitches out of her speech, and* ANN *would still make men dream. Vitality is as common as humanity; but, like humanity, it sometimes rises to genius; and* ANN *is one of the vital geniuses. Not at all, if you please, an oversexed person: that is a vital defect, not a true excess. She is a perfectly respectable, perfectly self-controlled woman, and looks it; though her pose is fashionably frank and impulsive. She inspires confidence as a person who will do nothing she does not mean to do; also some fear, perhaps, as a woman who will probably do everything she means to do without taking more account of other people than may be necessary and what she calls right. In short, what the weaker of her own sex sometimes call a cat.*

Nothing can be more decorous than her entry and her reception by RAMSDEN, *whom she kisses. The late Mr Whitefield would be gratified almost to impatience by the long faces of the men (except* TANNER, *who is fidgety), the silent handgrasps, the sympathetic placing of chairs, the sniffing of the widow, and the liquid eye of the daughter, whose heart, apparently, will not let her control her tongue to speech.* RAMSDEN *and* OCTAVIUS *take the two chairs from the wall, and place them for the two ladies;*

but ANN *comes to* TANNER *and takes his chair, which he offers with a brusque gesture, subsequently relieving his irritation by sitting down on the corner of the writing table with studied indecorum.* OCTAVIUS *gives* MRS WHITEFIELD *a chair next* ANN, *and himself takes the vacant one which* RAMSDEN *has placed under the nose of the effigy of Mr Herbert Spencer.*

MRS WHITEFIELD, *by the way, is a little woman, whose faded flaxen hair looks like straw on an egg. She has an expression of muddled shrewdness, a squeak of protest in her voice, and an odd air of continually elbowing away some larger person who is crushing her into a corner. One guesses her as one of those women who are conscious of being treated as silly and negligible, and who, without having strength enough to assert themselves effectually, at any rate never submit to their fate. There is a touch of chivalry in* OCTAVIUS'S *scrupulous attention to her, even whilst his whole soul is absorbed by* ANN.

RAMSDEN *goes solemnly back to his magisterial seat at the writing table, ignoring* TANNER, *and opens the proceedings.]*

Ramsden. I am sorry, Annie, to force business on you at a sad time like the present. But your poor dear father's will has raised a very serious question. You have read it, I believe? [ANN *assents with a nod and a catch of her breath, too much affected to speak.*] I must say I am surprised to find Mr Tanner named as joint guardian and trustee with myself of you and Rhoda. [*A pause. They all look portentous; but have nothing to say.* RAMSDEN, *a little ruffled by the lack of any response, continues.*] I dont know that I can consent to act under such conditions. Mr Tanner has, I understand, some objection also; but I do not profess to understand its nature: he will no doubt speak for himself. But we are agreed that we can decide nothing until we know your views. I am afraid I shall have to ask you to choose between my sole guardianship and that of Mr Tanner; for I fear it is impossible for us to undertake a joint arrangement.

Ann. [*In a low musical voice.*] Mamma——

Mrs Whitefield. [*Hastily.*] Now, Ann, I do beg you not to put it on me. I have no opinion on the subject; and if I had, it would probably not be attended to. I am quite content with whatever you three think best.

[TANNER *turns his head and looks fix-edly at* RAMSDEN, *who angrily refuses to receive this mute communication.*]

Ann. [*Resuming in the same gentle voice, ignoring her* MOTHER'S *bad taste.*] Mamma knows that she is not strong enough to bear the whole responsibility for me and Rhoda without some help and advice. Rhoda must have a guardian; and though I am older, I do not think any young unmarried woman should be left quite to her own guidance. I hope you agree with me, Granny?

Tanner. [*Starting.*] Granny! Do you intend to call your guardians Granny?

Ann. Dont be foolish, Jack. Mr Ramsden has always been Grandpapa Roebuck to me: I am Granny's Annie; and he is Annie's Granny. I christened him so when I first learned to speak.

Ramsden. [*Sarcastically.*] I hope you are satisfied, Mr Tanner. Go on, Annie: I quite agree with you.

Ann. Well, if I am to have a guardian, can I set aside anybody whom my dear father appointed for me?

Ramsden. [*Biting his lip.*] You approve of your father's choice, then?

Ann. It is not for me to approve or disapprove. I accept it. My father loved me and knew best what was good for me.

Ramsden. Of course I understand your feeling, Annie. It is what I should have expected of you; and it does you credit. But it does not settle the question so completely as you think. Let me put a case to you. Suppose you were to discover that I had been guilty of some disgraceful action—that I was not the man your poor dear father took me for! Would you still consider it right that I should be Rhoda's guardian?

Ann. I cant imagine you doing anything disgraceful, Granny.

Tanner. [*To* RAMSDEN.] You havnt done anything of the sort, have you?

Ramsden. [*Indignantly.*] No, sir.

Mrs Whitefield. [*Placidly.*] Well, then, why suppose it?

Ann. You see, Granny, Mamma would not like me to suppose it.

Ramsden. [*Much perplexed.*] You are both so full of natural and affectionate feeling in these family matters that it is very hard to put the situation fairly before you.

Tanner. Besides, my friend, you are not putting the situation fairly before them.

Ramsden. [*Sulkily.*] Put it yourself, then.

Tanner. I will. Ann: Ramsden thinks I am not fit to be your guardian; and I quite agree with him. He considers that if your father had read my book, he wouldnt have appointed me. That book is the disgraceful action he has been talking about. He thinks it's your duty for Rhoda's sake to ask him to act alone and to make me withdraw. Say the word; and I will.

Ann. But I havnt read your book, Jack.

Tanner. [*Diving at the waste-paper basket and fishing the book out for her.*] Then read it at once and decide.

Ramsden. [*Vehemently.*] If I am to be your guardian, I positively forbid you to read that book, Annie.

[*He smites the table with his fist and rises.*]

Ann. Of course not if you dont wish it.

[*She puts the book on the table.*]

Tanner. If one guardian is to forbid you to read the other guardian's book, how are we to settle it? Suppose I order you to read it! What about your duty to me?

Ann. [*Gently.*] I am sure you would never purposely force me into a painful dilemma, Jack.

Ramsden. [*Irritably.*] Yes, yes, Annie: this is all very well, and, as I said, quite natural and becoming. But you must make a choice one way or the other. We are as much in a dilemma as you.

Ann. I feel that I am too young, too inexperienced, to decide. My father's wishes are sacred to me.

Mrs Whitefield. If you two men wont carry them out I must say it is rather hard that you should put the responsibility on Ann. It seems to me that people are always putting things on other people in this world.

Ramsden. I am sorry you take it in that way.

Ann. [*Touchingly.*] Do you refuse to accept me as your ward, Granny?

Ramsden. No: I never said that. I greatly object to act with Mr Tanner: thats all.

Mrs Whitefield. Why? What's the matter with poor Jack?

Tanner. My views are too advanced for him.

Ramsden. [*Indignantly.*] They are not. I deny it.

Ann. Of course not. What nonsense! Nobody is more advanced than Granny. I am sure it is Jack himself who has made all the difficulty. Come, Jack! be kind to me in my sorrow. You dont refuse to accept me as your ward, do you?

Tanner. [*Gloomily.*] No. I let myself in for it; so I suppose I must face it.

[*He turns away to the bookcase, and stands there, moodily studying the titles of the volumes.*]

Ann. [*Rising and expanding with subdued but gushing delight.*] Then we are all agreed;

and my dear father's will is to be carried out. You dont know what a joy that is to me and to my mother! [*She goes to* RAMSDEN *and presses both his hands, saying.*] And I shall have my dear Granny to help and advise me. [*She casts a glance at* TANNER *over her shoulder.*] And Jack the Giant Killer. [*She goes past her* MOTHER *to* OCTAVIUS.] And Jack's inseparable friend Ricky-ticky-tavy. [*He blushes and looks inexpressibly foolish.*]

Mrs Whitefield. [*Rising and shaking her widow's weeds straight.*] Now that you are Ann's guardian, Mr Ramsden, I wish you would speak to her about her habit of giving people nicknames. They cant be expected to like it.   [*She moves towards the door.*]

Ann. How can you say such a thing, Mamma! [*Glowing with affectionate remorse.*] Oh, I wonder can you be right! Have I been inconsiderate? [*She turns to* OCTAVIUS, *who is sitting astride his chair with his elbows on the back of it. Putting her hand on his forehead she turns his face up suddenly.*] Do you want to be treated like a grown-up man? Must I call you Mr Robinson in future?

Octavius. [*Earnestly.*] Oh please call me Ricky-ticky-tavy. "Mr Robinson" would hurt me cruelly.

Ann. [*Laughs and pats his cheek with her finger; then comes back to* RAMSDEN.] You know I'm beginning to think that Granny is rather a piece of impertinence. But I never dreamt of its hurting you.

Ramsden. [*Breezily, as he pats her affectionately on the back.*] My dear Annie, nonsense. I insist on Granny. I wont answer to any other name than Annie's Granny.

Ann. [*Gratefully.*] You all spoil me, except Jack.

Tanner. [*Over his shoulder, from the bookcase.*] I think you ought to call me Mr Tanner.

Ann. [*Gently.*] No you dont, Jack. Thats like the things you say on purpose to shock people: those who know you pay no attention to them. But, if you like, I'll call you after your famous ancestor Don Juan.

Ramsden. Don Juan!

Ann. [*Innocently.*] Oh, is there any harm in it? I didnt know. Then I certainly wont call you that. May I call you Jack until I can think of something else?

Tanner. Oh, for Heaven's sake dont try to invent anything worse. I capitulate. I consent to Jack. I embrace Jack. Here endeth my first and last attempt to assert my authority.

Ann. You see, Mamma, they all really like to have pet names.

Mrs Whitefield. Well, I think you might at least drop them until we are out of mourning.

Ann. [*Reproachfully, stricken to the soul.*] Oh, how could you remind me, mother?

[*She hastily leaves the room to conceal her emotion.*]

Mrs Whitefield. Of course. My fault as usual!   [*She follows* ANN.]

Tanner. [*Coming from the bookcase.*] Ramsden: we're beaten—smashed—nonentitized, like her mother.

Ramsden. Stuff, sir.

[*He follows* MRS WHITEFIELD *out of the room.*]

Tanner. [*Left alone with* OCTAVIUS, *stares whimsically at him.*] Tavy: do you want to count for something in the world?

Octavius. I want to count for something as a poet: I want to write a great play.

Tanner. With Ann as the heroine?

Octavius. Yes: I confess it.

Tanner. Take care, Tavy. The play with Ann as the heroine is all right; but if youre not very careful, by Heaven she'll marry you.

Octavius. [*Sighing.*] No such luck, Jack!

Tanner. Why, man, your head is in the lioness's mouth: you are half swallowed already—in three bites—Bite One, Ricky; Bite Two, Ticky; Bite Three, Tavy; and down you go.

Octavius. She is the same to everybody, Jack: you know her ways.

Tanner. Yes: she breaks everybody's back with the stroke of her paw; but the question is, which of us will she eat? My own opinion is that she means to eat us.

Octavius. [*Rising, pettishly.*] It's horrible to talk like that about her when she is upstairs crying for her father. But I do so want her to eat me that I can bear your brutalities because they give me hope.

Tanner. Tavy: thats the devilish side of a woman's fascination: she makes you will your own destruction.

Octavius. But it's not destruction: it's fulfilment.

Tanner. Yes, of her purpose; and that purpose is neither her happiness nor yours. but Nature's. Vitality in a woman is a blind fury of creation. She sacrifices herself to it: do you think she will hesitate to sacrifice you?

Octavius. Why, it is just because she is self-sacrificing that she will not sacrifice those she loves.

Tanner. That is the profoundest of mistakes, Tavy. It is the self-sacrificing women that sacrifice others most recklessly. Because they are unselfish, they are kind in little things. Because they have a purpose which is not their own purpose, but that of the whole universe, a man is nothing to them but an instrument of that purpose.

Octavius. Dont be ungenerous, Jack. They take the tenderest care of us.

Tanner. Yes, as a soldier takes care of his rifle or a musician of his violin. But do they allow us any purpose of freedom of our own? Will they lend us to one another? Can the strongest man escape from them when once he is appropriated? They tremble when we are in danger, and weep when we die; but the tears are not for us, but for a father wasted, a son's breeding thrown away. They accuse us of treating them as a mere means to our pleasure; but how can so feeble and transient a folly as a man's selfish pleasure enslave a woman as the whole purpose of Nature embodied in a woman can enslave a man?

Octavius. What matter, if the slavery makes us happy?

Tanner. No matter at all if you have no purpose of your own, and are, like most men, a mere breadwinner. But you, Tavy, are an artist: that is, you have a purpose as absorbing and as unscrupulous as a woman's purpose.

Octavius. Not unscrupulous.

Tanner. Quite unscrupulous. The true artist will let his wife starve, his children go barefoot, his mother drudge for his living at seventy, sooner than work at anything but his art. To women he is half vivisector, half vampire. He gets into intimate relations with them to study them, to strip the mask of convention from them, to surprise their inmost secrets, knowing that they have the power to rouse his deepest creative energies, to rescue him from his cold reason, to make him see visions and dream dreams, to inspire him, as he calls it. He persuades women that they may do this for their own purpose whilst he really means them to do it for his. He steals the mother's milk and blackens it to make printer's ink to scoff at her and glorify ideal women with. He pretends to spare her the pangs of child-bearing so that he may have for himself the tenderness and fostering that belong of right to her children. Since marriage began, the great artist has been known as a bad husband. But he is worse: he is a child-robber, a blood-sucker, a hypocrite, and a cheat. Perish the race and wither a thousand women if only the sacrifice of them enable him to act Hamlet better, to paint a finer picture, to write a deeper poem, a greater play, a profounder philosophy! For mark you, Tavy, the artist's work is to shew us ourselves as we really are. Our minds are nothing but this knowledge of ourselves; and he who adds a jot to such knowledge creates new mind as surely as any woman creates new men. In the rage of that creation he is as ruthless as the woman, as dangerous to her as she to him, and as horribly fascinating. Of all human struggles there is none so treacherous and remorseless as the struggle between the artist man and the mother woman. Which shall use up the other? that is the issue between them. And it is all the deadlier because, in your romanticist cant, they love one another.

Octavius. Even if it were so—and I dont admit it for a moment—it is out of the deadliest struggles that we get the noblest characters.

Tanner. Remember that the next time you meet a grizzly bear or a Bengal tiger, Tavy.

Octavius. I meant where there is love, Jack.

Tanner. Oh, the tiger will love you. There is no love sincerer than the love of food. I think Ann loves you that way: she patted your cheek as if it were a nicely underdone chop.

Octavius. You know, Jack, I should have to run away from you if I did not make it a fixed rule not to mind anything you say. You come out with perfectly revolting things sometimes.

[RAMSDEN *returns, followed by* ANN. *They come in quickly, with their former leisurely air of decorous grief changed to one of genuine concern, and, on* RAMSDEN'S *part, of worry. He comes between the two men, intending to address* OCTAVIUS, *but pulls himself up abruptly as he sees* TANNER.]

Ramsden. I hardly expected to find you still here, Mr Tanner.

Tanner. Am I in the way? Good morning, fellow guardian.

[*He goes towards the door.*]

Ann. Stop, Jack. Granny: he must know, sooner or later.

Ramsden. Octavius: I have a very serious piece of news for you. It is of the most private and delicate nature—of the most painful nature too, I am sorry to say. Do you wish Mr Tanner to be present whilst I explain?

Octavius. [*Turning pale.*] I have no secrets from Jack.

Ramsden. Before you decide that finally,

let me say that the news concerns your sister, and that it is terrible news.

Octavius. Violet! What has happened? Is she—dead?

Ramsden. I am not sure that it is not even worse than that.

Octavius. Is she badly hurt? Has there been an accident?

Ramsden. No: nothing of that sort.

Tanner. Ann: will you have the common humanity to tell us what the matter is?

Ann. [*Half whispering.*] I cant. Violet has done something dreadful. We shall have to get her away somewhere.

[*She flutters to the writing table and sits in* RAMSDEN'S *chair, leaving the three men to fight it out between them.*]

Octavius. [*Enlightened.*] Is that what you meant, Mr Ramsden?

Ramsden. Yes. [OCTAVIUS *sinks upon a chair, crushed.*] I am afraid there is no doubt that Violet did not really go to Eastbourne three weeks ago when we thought she was with the Parry Whitefields. And she called on a strange doctor yesterday with a wedding ring on her finger. Mrs Parry Whitefield met her there by chance; and so the whole thing came out.

Octavius. [*Rising with his fists clenched.*] Who is the scoundrel?

Ann. She wont tell us.

Octavius. [*Collapsing into the chair again.*] What a frightful thing!

Tanner. [*With angry sarcasm.*] Dreadful. Appalling. Worse than death, as Ramsden says. [*He comes to* OCTAVIUS.] What would you not give, Tavy, to turn it into a railway accident, with all her bones broken, or something equally respectable and deserving of sympathy?

Octavius. Dont be brutal, Jack.

Tanner. Brutal! Good Heavens, man, what are you crying for? Here is a woman we all supposed to be making bad watercolor sketches, practising Grieg and Brahms, gadding about to concerts and parties, wasting her life and her money. We suddenly learn that she has turned from these sillinesses to the fulfilment of her highest purpose and greatest function—to increase, multiply, and replenish the earth. And instead of admiring her courage and rejoicing in her instinct; instead of crowning the completed womanhood and raising the triumphal strain of "Unto us a child is born: unto us a son is given," here you are—you who have been as merry as grigs in your mourning for the dead—all pulling long faces and looking as ashamed and disgraced as if the girl had committed the vilest of crimes.

Ramsden. [*Roaring with rage.*] I will not have these abominations uttered in my house.

[*He smites the writing table with his fist.*]

Tanner. Look here: if you insult me again I'll take you at your word and leave your house. Ann: where is Violet now?

Ann. Why? Are you going to her?

Tanner. Of course I am going to her. She wants help; she wants money; she wants respect and congratulation; she wants every chance for her child. She does not seem likely to get it from you: she shall from me. Where is she?

Ann. Dont be so headstrong, Jack. She's upstairs.

Tanner. What! Under Ramsden's sacred roof! Go and do your miserable duty, Ramsden. Hunt her out into the street. Cleanse your threshold from her contamination. Vindicate the purity of your English home. I'll go for a cab.

Ann. [*Alarmed.*] Oh, Granny, you mustnt do that.

Octavius. [*Broken-heartedly, rising.*] I'll take her away, Mr Ramsden. She had no right to come to your house.

Ramsden. [*Indignantly.*] But I am only too anxious to help her. [*Turning on* TANNER.] How dare you, sir, impute such monstrous intentions to me? I protest against it. I am ready to put down my last penny to save her from being driven to run to you for protection.

Tanner. [*Subsiding.*] It's all right, then. He's not going to act up to his principles. It's agreed that we all stand by Violet.

Octavius. But who is the man? He can make reparation by marrying her; and he shall, or he shall answer for it to me.

Ramsden. He shall, Octavius. There you speak like a man.

Tanner. Then you dont think him a scoundrel, after all?

Octavius. Not a scoundrel! He is a heartless scoundrel.

Ramsden. A damned scoundrel. I beg your pardon, Annie; but I can say no less.

Tanner. So we are to marry your sister to a damned scoundrel by way of reforming her character? On my soul, I think you are all mad.

Ann. Dont be absurd, Jack. Of course you are quite right, Tavy; but we dont know who he is: Violet wont tell us.

Tanner. What on earth does it matter who he is? He's done his part; and Violet must do the rest.

Ramsden. [*Beside himself.*] Stuff! lunacy! There is a rascal in our midst, a libertine, a villain worse than a murderer; and we are not to learn who he is! In our ignorance we are to shake him by the hand; to introduce him into our homes; to trust our daughters with him; to—to——

Ann. [*Coaxingly.*] There, Granny, dont talk so loud. It's most shocking: we must all admit that; but if Violet wont tell us, what can we do? Nothing. Simply nothing.

Ramsden. Hmph! I'm not so sure of that. If any man has paid Violet any special attention, we can easily find that out. If there is any man of notoriously loose principles among us——

Tanner. Ahem!

Ramsden. [*Raising his voice.*] Yes, sir, I repeat, if there is any man of notoriously loose principles among us——

Tanner. Or any man notoriously lacking in self-control.

Ramsden. [*Aghast.*] Do you dare to suggest that *I* am capable of such an act?

Tanner. My dear Ramsden, this is an act of which every man is capable. That is what comes of getting at cross purposes with Nature. The suspicion you have just flung at me clings to us all. It's a sort of mud that sticks to the judge's ermine or the cardinal's robe as fast as to the rags of the tramp. Come, Tavy! dont look so bewildered: it might have been me: it might have been Ramsden; just as it might have been anybody. If it had, what could we do but lie and protest—as Ramsden is going to protest.

Ramsden. [*Choking.*] I—I—I——

Tanner. Guilt itself could not stammer more confusedly. And yet you know perfectly well he's innocent, Tavy.

Ramsden. [*Exhausted.*] I am glad you admit that, sir. I admit, myself, that there is an element of truth in what you say, grossly as you may distort it to gratify your malicious humor. I hope, Octavius, no suspicion of me is possible in your mind.

Octavius. Of you? No, not for a moment.

Tanner. [*Drily.*] I think he suspects me just a little.

Octavius. Jack: you couldnt—you wouldnt——

Tanner. Why not?

Octavius. [*Appalled.*] Why not!

Tanner. Oh, well, I'll tell you why not. First, you would feel bound to quarrel with me. Second, Violet doesnt like me. Third, if I had the honor of being the father of Violet's child, I should boast of it instead of denying it. So be easy: our friendship is not in danger.

Octavius. I should have put away the suspicion with horror if only you would think and feel naturally about it. I beg your pardon.

Tanner. My pardon! nonsense! And now lets sit down and have a family council. [*He sits down. The rest follow his example, more or less under protest.*] Violet is going to do the State a service; consequently she must be packed abroad like a criminal until it's over. Whats happening upstairs?

Ann. Violet is in the housekeeper's room—by herself, of course.

Tanner. Why not in the drawing room?

Ann. Don't be absurd, Jack. Miss Ramsden is in the drawing room with my mother, considering what to do.

Tanner. Oh! the housekeeper's room is the penitentiary, I suppose; and the prisoner is waiting to be brought before her judges. The old cats!

Ann. Oh, Jack!

Ramsden. You are at present a guest beneath the roof of one of the old cats, sir. My sister is the mistress of this house.

Tanner. She would put me in the housekeeper's room, too, if she dared, Ramsden. However, I withdraw cats. Cats would have more sense. Ann: as your guardian, I order you to go to Violet at once and be particularly kind to her.

Ann. I have seen her, Jack. And I am sorry to say I am afraid she is going to be rather obstinate about going abroad. I think Tavy ought to speak to her about it.

Octavius. How can I speak to her about such a thing? [*He breaks down.*]

Ann. Don't break down, Ricky. Try to bear it for all our sakes.

Ramsden. Life is not all plays and poems, Octavius. Come! face it like a man.

Tanner. [*Chafing again.*] Poor dear brother! Poor dear friends of the family! Poor dear Tabbies and Grimalkins! Poor dear everybody except the woman who is going to risk her life to create another life! Tavy: dont you be a selfish ass. Away with you and talk to Violet; and bring her down here if she cares to come. [OCTAVIUS *rises.*] Tell her we'll stand by her.

Ramsden. [*Rising.*] No, sir——

Tanner. [*Rising also and interrupting him.*] Oh, we understand: it's against your conscience; but still youll do it.

Octavius. I assure you all, on my word, I never meant to be selfish. It's so hard to know what to do when one wishes earnestly to do right.

Tanner. My dear Tavy, your pious English habit of regarding the world as a moral gymnasium built expressly to strengthen your character in, occasionally leads you to think about your own confounded principles when you should be thinking about other people's necessities. The need of the present hour is a happy mother and a healthy baby. Bend your energies on that; and you will see your way clearly enough.

[OCTAVIUS, *much perplexed, goes out.*]

Ramsden. [*Facing* TANNER *impressively.*] And morality, sir? What is to become of that?

Tanner. Meaning a weeping Magdalen and an innocent child branded with her shame. Not in our circle, thank you. Morality can go to its father the devil.

Ramsden. I thought so, sir. Morality sent to the devil to please our libertines, male and female. That is to be the future of England, is it?

Tanner. Oh, England will survive your disapproval. Meanwhile, I understand that you agree with me as to the practical course we are to take?

Ramsden. Not in your spirit, sir. Not for your reasons.

Tanner. You can explain that if anybody calls you to account, here or hereafter.

[*He turns away and plants himself in front of Mr Herbert Spencer, at whom he stares gloomily.*]

Ann. [*Rising and coming to* RAMSDEN.] Granny: hadnt you better go up to the drawing room and tell them what we intend to do?

Ramsden. [*Looking pointedly at* TANNER.] I hardly like to leave you alone with this gentleman. Will you not come with me?

Ann. Miss Ramsden would not like to speak about it before me, Granny. I ought not to be present.

Ramsden. You are right: I should have thought of that. You are a good girl, Annie.

[*He pats her on the shoulder. She looks up at him with beaming eyes; and he goes out, much moved. Having disposed of him, she looks at* TANNER. *His back being turned to her, she gives a moment's attention to her personal appearance, then softly goes to him and speaks almost into his ear.*]

Ann. Jack [*He turns with a start.*], are you glad that you are my guardian? You dont mind being made responsible for me, I hope.

Tanner. The latest edition to your collection of scapegoats, eh?

Ann. Oh, that stupid old joke of yours about me! Do please drop it. Why do you say things that you know must pain me? I do my best to please you, Jack: I suppose I may tell you so now that you are my guardian. You will make me so unhappy if you refuse to be friends with me.

Tanner. [*Studying her as gloomily as he studied the bust.*] You need not go begging for my regard. How unreal our moral judgments are! You seem to me to have absolutely no conscience—only hypocrisy; and you cant see the difference—yet there is a sort of fascination about you. I always attend to you, somehow. I should miss you if I lost you.

Ann. [*Tranquilly slipping her arm into his and walking about with him.*] But isnt that only natural, Jack? We have known each other since we were children. Do you remember——

Tanner. [*Abruptly breaking loose.*] Stop! I remember everything.

Ann. Oh, I daresay we were often very silly; but——

Tanner. I wont have it, Ann. I am no more that schoolboy now than I am the dotard of ninety I shall grow into if I live long enough. It is over: let me forget it.

Ann. Wasnt it a happy time?

[*She attempts to take his arm again.*]

Tanner. Sit down and behave yourself. [*He makes her sit down in the chair next the writing table.*] No doubt it was a happy time for you. You were a good girl and never compromised yourself. And yet the wickedest child that ever was slapped could hardly have had a better time. I can understand the success with which you bullied the other girls: your virtue imposed on them. But tell me this: did you ever know a good boy?

Ann. Of course. All boys are foolish sometimes; but Tavy was always a really good boy.

Tanner. [*Struck by this.*] Yes: youre right. For some reason you never tempted Tavy.

Ann. Tempted! Jack!

Tanner. Yes, my dear Lady Mephistopheles, tempted. You were insatiably curious as to what a boy might be capable of, and diabolically clever at getting through his guard and surprising his inmost secrets.

Ann. What nonsense! All because you used to tell me long stories of the wicked things you had done—silly boy's tricks! And you call such things inmost secrets! Boy's secrets are just like men's; and you know what they are!

Tanner. [*Obstinately.*] No, I dont. What are they, pray?

Ann. Why, the things they tell everybody, of course.

Tanner. Now I swear I told you things I told no one else. You lured me into a compact by which we were to have no secrets from one another. We were to tell one another everything. I didnt notice that you never told me anything.

Ann. You didnt want to talk about me, Jack. You wanted to talk about yourself.

Tanner. Ah, true, horribly true. But what a devil of a child you must have been to know that weakness and to play on it for the satisfaction of your own curiosity! I wanted to brag to you, to make myself interesting. And I found myself doing all sorts of mischievous things simply to have something to tell you about. I fought with boys I didnt hate; I lied about things I might just as well have told the truth about; I stole things I didnt want; I kissed little girls I didnt care for. It was all bravado: passionless and therefore unreal.

Ann. I never told on you, Jack.

Tanner. No; but if you had wanted to stop me you would have told on me. You wanted me to go on.

Ann. [*Flashing out.*] Oh, thats not true: it's not true, Jack. I never wanted you to do those dull, disappointing, brutal, stupid, vulgar things. I always hoped that it would be something really heroic at last. [*Recovering herself.*] Excuse me, Jack; but the things you did were never a bit like the things I wanted you to do. They often gave me great uneasiness; but I could not tell on you and get you into trouble. And you were only a boy. I knew you would grow out of them. Perhaps I was wrong.

Tanner. [*Sardonically.*] Do not give way to remorse, Ann. At least nineteen twentieths of the exploits I confessed to you were pure lies. I soon noticed that you didnt like the true stories.

Ann. Of course I knew that some of the things couldnt have happened. But——

Tanner. You are going to remind me that some of the most disgraceful ones did.

Ann. [*Fondly, to his great terror.*] I dont want to remind you of anything. But I knew the people they happened to, and heard about them.

Tanner. Yes; but even the true stories were touched up for telling. A sensitive boy's humiliations may be very good fun for ordinary thickskinned grown-ups; but to the boy himself they are so acute, so ignominious, that he cannot confess them—cannot but deny them passionately. However, perhaps it was as well for me that I romanced a bit; for, on the one occasion when I told you the truth, you threatened to tell on me.

Ann. Oh, never. Never once.

Tanner. Yes, you did. Do you remember a dark-eyed girl named Rachel Rosetree? [ANN's *brows contract for an instant involuntarily.*] I got up a love affair with her; and we met one night in the garden and walked about very uncomfortably with our arms round one another, and kissed at parting, and were most conscientiously romantic. If that love affair had gone on, it would have bored me to death; but it didnt go on; for the next thing that happened was that Rachel cut me because she found out that I had told you. How did she find it out? From you. You went to her and held the guilty secret over her head, leading her a life of abject terror and humiliation by threatening to tell on her.

Ann. And a very good thing for her, too. It was my duty to stop her misconduct; and she is thankful to me for it now.

Tanner. Is she?

Ann. She ought to be, at all events.

Tanner. It was not your duty to stop my misconduct, I suppose.

Ann. I did stop it by stopping her.

Tanner. Are you sure of that? You stopped my telling you about my adventures; but how do you know that you stopped the adventures?

Ann. Do you mean to say that you went on in the same way with other girls?

Tanner. No. I had enough of that sort of romantic tomfoolery with Rachel.

Ann. [*Unconvinced.*] Then why did you break off our confidences and become quite strange to me?

Tanner. [*Enigmatically.*] It happened just then that I got something that I wanted to keep all to myself instead of sharing it with you.

Ann. I am sure I shouldnt have asked for any of it if you had grudged it.

Tanner. It wasnt a box of sweets, Ann. It was something youd never have let me call my own.

Ann. [*Incredulously.*] What?

Tanner. My soul.

Ann. Oh, do be sensible, Jack. You know youre talking nonsense.

Tanner. The most solemn earnest, Ann. You didnt notice at that time that you were getting a soul too. But you were. It was not for nothing that you suddenly found you had a moral duty to chastise and reform Rachel. Up to that time you had traded pretty extensively in being a good child; but you had never set up a sense of duty to others. Well, I set one up too. Up to that time I had played the boy buccaneer with no more conscience than a fox in a poultry farm. But now I began to have scruples, to feel obligations, to find that veracity and honor were no longer goody-goody expressions in the mouths of grown-up people, but compelling principle in myself.

Ann. [*Quietly.*] Yes, I suppose youre right. You were beginning to be a man, and I to be a woman.

Tanner. Are you sure it was not that we were beginning to be something more? What does the beginning of manhood and womanhood mean in most people's mouths? You know: it means the beginning of love. But love began long before that for me. Love played its part in the earliest dreams and follies and romances I can remember—may I say the earliest follies and romances we can remember?—though we did not understand it at the time. No: the change that came to me was the birth in me of moral passion; and I declare that according to my experience moral passion is the only real passion.

Ann. All passions ought to be moral, Jack.

Tanner. Ought! Do you think that anything is strong enough to impose oughts on a passion except a stronger passion still?

Ann. Our moral sense controls passion, Jack. Dont be stupid.

Tanner. Our moral sense! And is that not a passion? Is the devil to have all the passions as well as all the good tunes? If it were not a passion—if it were not the mightiest of the passions, all the other passions would sweep it away like a leaf before a hurricane. It is the birth of that passion that turns a child into a man.

Ann. There are other passions, Jack. Very strong ones.

Tanner. All the other passions were in me before; but they were idle and aimless —mere childish greediness and cruelties, curiosities and fancies, habits and superstitions, grotesque and ridiculous to the mature intelligence. When they suddenly began to shine like newly lit flames it was by no light of their own, but by the radiance of the dawning moral passion. That passion dignified them, gave them conscience and meaning, found them a mob of appetites and organized them into an army of purposes and principles. My soul was born of that passion.

Ann. I noticed that you got more sense. You were a dreadfully destructive boy before that.

Tanner. Destructive! Stuff! I was only mischievous.

Ann. Oh, Jack, you were very destructive. You ruined all the young fir trees by chopping off their leaders with a wooden sword. You broke all the cucumber frames with your catapult. You set fire to the common: the police arrested Tavy for it because he ran away when he couldnt stop you. You——

Tanner. Pooh! pooh! pooh! these were battles, bombardments, stratagems to save our scalps from the red Indians. You have no imagination, Ann. I am ten times more destructive now than I was then. The moral passion has taken my destructiveness in hand and directed it to moral ends. I have become a reformer, and, like all reformers, an iconoclast. I no longer break cucumber frames and burn gorse bushes: I shatter creeds and demolish idols.

Ann. [*Bored.*] I am afraid I am too feminine to see any sense in destruction. Destruction can only destroy.

Tanner. Yes. That is why it is so useful. Construction cumbers the ground with institutions made by busybodies. Destruction clears it and gives us breathing space and liberty.

Ann. It's no use, Jack. No woman will agree with you there.

Tanner. Thats because you confuse construction and destruction with creation and murder. Theyre quite different: I adore creation and abhor murder. Yes: I adore it in tree and flower, in bird and beast, even in you. [*A flash of interest and delight suddenly chases the growing perplexity and boredom from her face.*] It was the creative instinct that led you to attach me to you by bonds that have left their mark on me to this day. Yes, Ann: the old childish compact between us was an unconscious love compact——

Ann. Jack!

Tanner. Oh, dont be alarmed——

Ann. I am not alarmed.

Tanner. [*Whimsically.*] Then you ought to be: where are your principles?

Ann. Jack: are you serious or are you not?

Tanner. Do you mean about the moral passion?

Ann. No, no: the other one. [*Confused.*] Oh! you are so silly: one never knows how to take you.

Tanner. You must take me quite seriously. I am your guardian; and it is my duty to improve your mind.

Ann. The love compact is over, then, is it? I suppose you grew tired of me?

Tanner. No; but the moral passion made our childish relations impossible. A jealous sense of my new individuality arose in me——

Ann. You hated to be treated as a boy any longer. Poor Jack!

Tanner. Yes, because to be treated as a boy was to be taken on the old footing. I had become a new person; and those who knew the old person laughed at me. The only man who behaved sensibly was my tailor: he took my measure anew every time he saw me, whilst all the rest went on with their old measurements and expected them to fit me.

Ann. You became frightfully self-conscious.

Tanner. When you go to heaven, Ann, you will be frightfully conscious of your wings for the first year or so. When you meet your relatives there, and they persist in treating you as if you were still a mortal, you will not be able to bear them. You will try to get into a circle which has never known you except as an angel.

Ann. So it was only your vanity that made you run away from us after all?

Tanner. Yes, only my vanity, as you call it.

Ann. You need not have kept away from me on that account.

Tanner. From you above all others. You fought harder than anybody against my emancipation.

Ann. [*Earnestly.*] Oh, how wrong you are! I would have done anything for you.

Tanner. Anything except let me get loose from you. Even then you had acquired by instinct that damnable woman's trick of heaping obligations on a man, of placing yourself so entirely and helplessly at his mercy that at last he dare not take a step without running to you for leave. I know a poor wretch whose one desire in life is to run away from his wife. She prevents him by threatening to throw herself in front of the engine of the train he leaves her in. That is what all women do. If we try to go where you do not want us to go there is no law to prevent us; but when we take the first step your breasts are under our foot as it descends: your bodies are under our wheels as we start. No woman shall ever enslave me in that way.

Ann. But, Jack, you cannot get through life without considering other people a little.

Tanner. Ay; but what other people? It is this consideration of other people—or rather this cowardly fear of them which we call consideration—that makes us the sentimental slaves we are. To consider you, as you call it, is to substitute your will for my own. How if it be a baser will than mine? Are women taught better than men or worse? Worse, of course, in both cases. And then what sort of world are you going to get, with its public men considering its voting mobs, and its private men considering their wives? What does Church and State mean nowadays? The Woman and the Rate-payer.

Ann. [*Placidly.*] I am so glad you understand politics, Jack: it will be most useful to you if you go into parliament. [*He collapses like a pricked bladder.*] But I am sorry you thought my influence a bad one.

Tanner. I didn't say it was a bad one. But bad or good, I didnt choose to be cut to your measure. And I wont be cut to it.

Ann. Nobody wants you to, Jack. I assure you—really on my word—I dont mind your queer opinions one little bit. You know we have all been brought up to have advanced opinions. Why do you persist in thinking me so narrow minded?

Tanner. Thats the danger of it. I know you dont mind, because youve found out that is doesnt matter. The boa constrictor doesnt mind the opinions of a stag one little bit when once she has got her coils round it.

Ann. [*Rising in sudden enlightenment.*] O-o-o-o-oh! now I understand why you warned Tavy that I am a boa constrictor. Granny told me. [*She laughs and throws her boa round his neck.*] Doesnt it feel nice and soft, Jack?

Tanner. [*In the toils.*] You scandalous woman, will you throw away even your hypocrisy?

Ann. I am never hypocritical with you, Jack. Are you angry? [*She withdraws the boa and throws it on a chair.*] Perhaps I shouldnt have done that.

Tanner. [*Contemptuously.*] Pooh, prudery! Why should you not, if it amuses you?

Ann. [*Shyly.*] Well, because—because I suppose what you really meant by the boa constrictor was this.

[*She puts her arms round his neck.*]

Tanner. [*Staring at her.*] Magnificent audacity! [*She laughs and pats his cheeks.*] Now just to think that if I mentioned this episode not a soul would believe me except the people who would cut me for telling, whilst if you accused me of it nobody would believe my denial!

Ann. [*Taking her arms away with perfect*

dignity.] You are incorrigible, Jack. But you should not jest about our affection for one another. Nobody could possibly misunderstand it. You do not misunderstand it, I hope.

Tanner. My blood interprets for me, Ann. Poor Ricky Ticky Tavy!

Ann. [*Looking quickly at him as if this were a new light.*] Surely you are not so absurd as to be jealous of Tavy.

Tanner. Jealous! Why should I be? But I dont wonder at your grip of him. I feel the coils tightening round my very self, though you are only playing with me.

Ann. Do you think I have designs on Tavy?

Tanner. I know you have.

Ann. [*Earnestly.*] Take care, Jack. You may make Tavy very unhappy if you mislead him about me.

Tanner. Never fear: he will not escape you.

Ann. I wonder are you really a clever man!

Tanner. Why this sudden misgiving on the subject?

Ann. You seem to understand all the things I dont understand; but you are a perfect baby in the things I do understand.

Tanner. I understand how Tavy feels for you, Ann: you may depend on that, at all events.

Ann. And you think you understand how I feel for Tavy, don't you?

Tanner. I know only too well what is going to happen to poor Tavy.

Ann. I should laugh at you, Jack, if it were not for poor papa's death. Mind! Tavy will be very unhappy.

Tanner. Yes; but he wont know it, poor devil. He is a thousand times too good for you. Thats why he is going to make the mistake of his life about you.

Ann. I think men make more mistakes by being too clever than by being too good. [*She sits down, with a trace of contempt for the whole male sex in the elegant carriage of her shoulders.*]

Tanner. Oh, I know you dont care very much about Tavy. But there is always one who kisses and one who only allows the kiss. Tavy will kiss; and you will only turn the cheek. And you will throw him over if anybody better turns up.

Ann. [*Offended.*] You have no right to say such things, Jack. They are not true, and not delicate. If you and Tavy choose to be stupid about me, that is not my fault.

Tanner. [*Remorsefully.*] Forgive my bru-

talities, Ann. They are levelled at this wicked world, not at you. [*She looks up at him, pleased and forgiving. He becomes cautious at once.*] All the same, I wish Ramsden would come back. I never feel safe with you: there is a devilish charm—or no: not a charm, a subtle interest. [*She laughs.*] —Just so: you know it; and you triumph in it. Openly and shamelessly triumph in it!

Ann. What a shocking flirt you are, Jack!

Tanner. A flirt!! I!!!

Ann. Yes, a flirt. You are always abusing and offending people; but you never really mean to let go your hold of them.

Tanner. I will ring the bell. This conversation has already gone further than I intended.

[RAMSDEN *and* OCTAVIUS *come back with* MISS RAMSDEN, *a hard-hearted old maiden lady in a plain brown silk gown, with enough rings, chains, and brooches to shew that her plainness of dress is a matter of principle, not of poverty. She comes into the room very determinedly: the two* MEN, *perplexed and downcast, following her.* ANN *rises and goes eagerly to meet her.* TANNER *retreats to the wall between the busts and pretends to study the pictures.* RAMSDEN *goes to his table as usual; and* OCTAVIUS *clings to the neighborhood of* TANNER.]

Miss Ramsden. [*Almost pushing* ANN *aside as she comes to* MRS WHITEFIELD'S *chair and plants herself there resolutely.*] I wash my hands of the whole affair.

Octavius. [*Very wretched.*] I know you wish me to take Violet away, Miss Ramsden. I will. [*He turns irresolutely to the door.*]

Ramsden. No, no——

Miss Ramsden. What is the use of saying no, Roebuck? Octavius knows that I would not turn any truly contrite and repentant woman from your doors. But when a woman is not only wicked, but intends to go on being wicked, she and I part company.

Ann. Oh, Miss Ramsden, what do you mean? What has Violet said?

Ramsden. Violet is certainly very obstinate. She wont leave London. I dont understand her.

Miss Ramsden. I do. It's as plain as the nose on your face, Roebuck, that she wont go because she doesnt want to be separated from this man, whoever he is.

Ann. Oh, surely, surely! Octavius: did you speak to her?

Octavius. She wont tell us anything. She wont make any arrangement until she has consulted somebody. It cant be anybody else than the scoundrel who has betrayed her.

Tanner. [*To* OCTAVIUS.] Well, let her consult him. He will be glad enough to have her sent abroad. Where is the difficulty?

Miss Ramsden. [*Taking the answer out of* OCTAVIUS'S *mouth.*] The difficulty, Mr Jack, is that when I offered to help her I didn't offer to become her accomplice in her wickedness. She either pledges her word never to see that man again, or else she finds some new friends; and the sooner the better.

[*The* PARLORMAID *appears at the door.* ANN *hastily resumes her seat, and looks as unconcerned as possible.* OCTAVIUS *instinctively imitates her.*]

The Maid. The cab is at the door, maam.

Miss Ramsden. What cab?

The Maid. For Miss Robinson.

Miss Ramsden. Oh! [*Recovering herself.*] All right. [*The* MAID *withdraws.*] She has sent for a cab.

Tanner. *I* wanted to send for that cab half an hour ago.

Miss Ramsden. I am glad she understands the position she has placed herself in.

Ramsden. I dont like her going away in this fashion, Susan. We had better not do anything harsh.

Octavius. No: thank you again and again; but Miss Ramsden is quite right. Violet cannot expect to stay.

Ann. Hadnt you better go with her, Tavy?

Octavius. She wont have me.

Miss Ramsden. Of course she wont. She's going straight to that man.

Tanner. As a natural result of her virtuous reception here.

Ramsden. [*Much troubled.*] There, Susan! You hear! and theres some truth in it. I wish you could reconcile it with your principles to be a little patient with this poor girl. She's very young; and theres a time for everything.

Miss Ramsden. Oh, she will get all the sympathy she wants from the men. I'm surprised at you, Roebuck.

Tanner. So am I, Ramsden, most favorably.

[VIOLET *appears at the door. She is as impenitent and self-possessed a young lady as one would desire to see among the best behaved of her sex. Her small head and tiny resolute mouth and chin; her haughty crispness of speech and trimness of carriage; the ruthless elegance of her equipment, which includes a very smart hat with a dead bird in it, mark a personality which is as for-midable as it is exquisitely pretty. She is not a siren, like* ANN: *admiration comes to her without any compulsion or even interest on her part; besides, there is some fun in* ANN, *but in this woman none, perhaps no mercy either: if anything restrains her, it is intelligence and pride, not compassion. Her voice might be the voice of a schoolmistress addressing a class of girls who had disgraced themselves, as she proceeds with complete composure and some disgust to say what she has come to say.*]

Violet. I have only looked in to tell Miss Ramsden that she will find her birthday present to me, the filagree bracelet, in the housekeeper's room.

Tanner. Do come in, Violet; and talk to us sensibly.

Violet. Thank you: I have had quite enough of the family conversation this morning. So has your mother, Ann: she has gone home crying. But at all events, I have found out what some of my pretended friends are worth. Goodbye.

Tanner. No, no: one moment. I have something to say which I beg you to hear. [*She looks at him without the slightest curiosity, but waits, apparently as much to finish getting her glove on as to hear what he has to say.*] I am altogether on your side in this matter. I congratulate you, with the sincerest respect, on having the courage to do what you have done. You are entirely in the right; and the family is entirely in the wrong.

[*Sensation.* ANN *and* MISS RAMSDEN *rise and turn towards the two.* VIOLET, *more surprised than any of the others, forgets her glove, and comes forward into the middle of the room, both puzzled and displeased.* OCTAVIUS *alone does not move nor raise his head: he is overwhelmed with shame.*]

Ann. [*Pleading to* TANNER *to be sensible.*] Jack!

Miss Ramsden. [*Outraged.*] Well, I must say!

Violet. [*Sharply to* TANNER.] Who told you?

Tanner. Why, Ramsden and Tavy of course. Why should they not?

Violet. But they dont know.

Tanner. Dont know what?

Violet. They dont know that I am in the right, I mean.

Tanner. Oh, they know it in their hearts, though they think themselves bound to blame you by their silly superstitions about morality and propriety and so forth. But I know, and the whole world really knows, though it dare not say so, that you were right to follow your instinct; that vitality and bravery are the greatest qualities a woman can have, and motherhood her solemn initiation into womanhood; and that the fact of your not being legally married matters not one scrap either to your own worth or to our real regard for you.

Violet. [*Flushing with indignation.*] Oh! you think me a wicked woman, like the rest. You think I have not only been vile, but that I share your abominable opinions. Miss Ramsden: I have borne your hard words because I knew you would be sorry for them when you found out the truth. But I wont bear such a horrible insult as to be complimented by Jack on being one of the wretches of whom he approves. I have kept my marriage a secret for my husband's sake. But now I claim my right as a married woman not to be insulted.

Octavius. [*Raising his head with inexpressible relief.*] You are married!

Violet. Yes; and I think you might have guessed it. What business had you all to take it for granted that I had no right to wear my wedding ring? Not one of you even asked me: I cannot forget that.

Tanner. [*In ruins.*] I am utterly crushed. I meant well. I apologize—abjectly apologize.

Violet. I hope you will be more careful in future about the things you say. Of course one does not take them seriously; but they are very disagreeable, and rather in bad taste, I think.

Tanner. [*Bowing to the storm.*] I have no defence: I shall know better in future than to take any woman's part. We have all disgraced ourselves in your eyes, I am afraid, except Ann. She befriended you. For Ann's sake, forgive us.

Violet. Yes: Ann has been kind; but then Ann knew.

Tanner. [*With a desperate gesture.*] Oh!!! Unfathomable deceit! Double crossed!

Miss Ramsden. [*Stiffly.*] And who, pray, is the gentleman who does not acknowledge his wife?

Violet. [*Promptly.*] That is my business, Miss Ramsden, and not yours. I have my reasons for keeping my marriage a secret for the present.

Ramsden. All I can say is that we are extremely sorry, Violet. I am shocked to think of how we have treated you.

Octavius. [*Awkwardly.*] I beg your pardon, Violet. I can say no more.

Miss Ramsden. [*Still loth to surrender.*] Of course what you say puts a very different complexion on the matter. All the same, I owe it to myself——

Violet. [*Cutting her short.*] You owe me an apology, Miss Ramsden: thats what you owe both to yourself and to me. If you were a married woman you would not like sitting in the housekeeper's room and being treated like a naughty child by young girls and old ladies without any serious duties and responsibilities.

Tanner. Dont hit us when we're down, Violet. We seem to have made fools of ourselves; but really it was you who made fools of us.

Violet. It was no business of yours, Jack, in any case.

Tanner. No business of mine! Why, Ramsden as good as accused me of being the unknown gentleman.

[RAMSDEN *makes a frantic demonstration; but* VIOLET'S *cool keen anger extinguishes it.*]

Violet. You! Oh, how infamous! how abominable! how disgracefully you have all been talking about me! If my husband knew it he would never let me speak to any of you again. [*To* RAMSDEN.] I think you might have spared me that, at least.

Ramsden. But I assure you I never—at least it is a monstrous perversion of something I said that——

Miss Ramsden. You neednt apologize, Roebuck. She brought it all on herself. It is for her to apologize for having deceived us.

Violet. I can make allowances for you, Miss Ramsden: you cannot understand how I feel on this subject, though I should have expected rather better taste from people of greater experience. However, I quite feel that you have placed yourselves in a very painful position; and the most truly considerate thing for me to do is to go at once. Good morning.

[*She goes, leaving them staring.*]

Miss Ramsden. Well, I must say!

Ramsden. [*Plaintively.*] I dont think she is quite fair to us.

Tanner. You must cower before the wedding ring like the rest of us, Ramsden. The cup of our ignominy is full.

ACT II

On the carriage drive in the park of a country house near Richmond an open touring car has broken down. It stands in front of a clump of trees round which the drive sweeps to the house, which is partly visible through them: indeed TANNER, *standing in the drive with his back to us, could get an unobstructed view of the west corner of the house on his left were he not far too interested in a pair of supine legs in dungaree overalls which protrude from beneath the machine. He is watching them intently with bent back and hands supported on his knees. His leathern overcoat and peaked cap proclaim him one of the dismounted passengers.*

The legs. Aha! I got him.
Tanner. All right now?
The legs. Aw rawt nah.

[TANNER *stoops and takes the legs by the ankles, drawing their owner forth like a wheelbarrow, walking on his hands, with a hammer in his mouth. He is a young man in a neat suit of blue serge, clean shaven, dark eyed, square fingered, with short well brushed black hair and rather irregular sceptically turned eyebrows. When he is manipulating the car his movements are swift and sudden, yet attentive and deliberate. With* TANNER *and* TANNER'S *friends his manner is not in the least deferential, but cool and reticent, keeping them quite effectually at a distance whilst giving them no excuse for complaining of him. Nevertheless he has a vigilant eye on them always, and that, too, rather cynically, like a man who knows the world well from its seamy side. He speaks slowly and with a touch of sarcasm; and as he does not at all affect the gentleman in his speech, it may be inferred that his smart appearance is a mark of respect to himself and his own class, not to that which employs him.*

He now gets into the car to stow away his tools and divest himself of his overalls. TANNER *takes off his leathern overcoat and pitches it into the car with a sigh of relief, glad to be rid of it. The* CHAUFFEUR, *noting this, tosses his head contemptuously, and surveys his employer sardonically.*]

The Chauffeur. Had enough of it, eh?

Tanner. I may as well walk to the house and stretch my legs and calm my nerves a little. [*Looking at his watch.*] I suppose you know that we have come from Hyde Park Corner to Richmond in twenty-one minutes.

The Chauffeur. I'd ha done it under fifteen if I'd had a clear road all the way.

Tanner. Why do you do it? Is it for love of sport or for the fun of terrifying your unfortunate employer?

The Chauffeur. What are you afraid of?

Tanner. The police, and breaking my neck.

The Chauffeur. Well, if you like easy going, you can take the bus, you know. It's cheaper. You pay me to save your time and give you the value of what you paid for the car. [*He sits down calmly.*]

Tanner. I am the slave of that car and of you too. I dream of the accursed thing at night.

The Chauffeur. Youll get over that all right. If youre going up to the house, may I ask how long youre going to stay? Because if you mean to put in the whole morning in there talking to the ladies, I'll put the car in the garage and make myself agreeable with a view to lunching here. If not, I'll keep the car on the go about here till you come.

Tanner. Better wait here. We shant be long. Theres a young American gentleman, a Mr Malone, who is driving Mr Robinson down in his new American steam car.

The Chauffeur. [*Springing up and coming hastily out of the car to* TANNER.] American steam car! Wot! racin us dahn from London!

Tanner. Perhaps they're here already.

The Chauffeur. If I'd known it! [*With deep reproach.*] Why didnt you tell me, Mr Tanner?

Tanner. Because Ive been told that this car is capable of 84 miles an hour; and I already know what you are capable of when there is a rival car on the road. No, Henry: there are things it is not good for you to know; and this was one of them. However, cheer up: we are going to have a day after your own heart. The American is to take Mr Robinson and his sister and Miss Whitefield. We are to take Miss Rhoda.

The Chauffeur. [*Consoled, and musing on another matter.*] Thats Miss Whitefield's sister, isnt it?

Tanner. Yes.

The Chauffeur. And Miss Whitefield herself is goin in the other car? Not with you?

Tanner. Why the devil should she come with me? Mr Robinson will be in the other car. [*The* CHAUFFEUR *looks at* TANNER *with cool incredulity, and turns to the car, whistling a popular air softly to himself.* TANNER, *a little annoyed, is about to pursue the subject, when he hears the footsteps of* OCTAVIUS *on the gravel.* OCTAVIUS *is coming from the house, dressed for motoring, but without his overcoat.*] Weve lost the race, thank Heaven: heres Mr Robinson. Well, Tavy, is the steam car a success?

Octavius. I think so. We came from Hyde Park Corner here in seventeen minutes. [*The* CHAUFFEUR, *furious, kicks the car with a groan of vexation.*] How long were you?

Tanner. Oh, about three quarters of an hour or so.

The Chauffeur. [*Remonstrating.*] Now, now, Mr Tanner, come now! We could ha done it easy under fifteen.

Tanner. By the way, let me introduce you. Mr Octavius Robinson: Mr Enry Straker.

Straker. Pleased to meet you, sir. Mr Tanner is gittin at you with is Enry Straker, you know. You call it Henery. But I dont mind, bless you!

Tanner. You think it's simply bad taste in me to chaff him, Tavy. But youre wrong. This man takes more trouble to drop his aitches than ever his father did to pick them up. It's a mark of caste to him. I have never met anybody more swollen with the pride of class than Enry is.

Straker. Easy, easy! A little moderation, Mr Tanner.

Tanner. A little moderation, Tavy, you observe. You would tell me to draw it mild. But this chap has been educated. Whats more, he knows that he havnt. What was that Board School of yours, Straker?

Straker. Sherbrooke Road.

Tanner. Sherbrooke Road! Would any of us say Rugby! Harrow! Eton! in that tone of intellectual snobbery? Sherbrooke Road is a place where boys learn something! Eton is a boy farm where we are sent because we are nuisances at home, and because in after life, whenever a Duke is mentioned, we can claim him as an old school-fellow.

Straker. You dont know nothing about it, Mr Tanner. It's not the Board School that does it: it's the Polytechnic.

Tanner. His university, Octavius. Not Oxford, Cambridge, Durham, Dublin, or Glasgow. Not even those Nonconformist holes in Wales. No, Tavy. Regent Street! Chelsea! the Borough!—I dont know half

their confounded names: these are his universities, not mere shops for selling class limitations like ours. You despise Oxford, Enry, dont you?

Straker. No, I dont. Very nice sort of place, Oxford, I should think, for people that like that sort of place. They teach you to be a gentleman there. In the Polytechnic they teach you to be an engineer or such like. See?

Tanner. Sarcasm, Tavy, sarcasm! Oh, if you could only see into Enry's soul, the depth of his contempt for a gentleman, the arrogance of his pride in being an engineer, would appal you. He positively likes the car to break down because it brings out my gentlemanly helplessness and his workmanlike skill and resource.

Straker. Never you mind him, Mr Robinson. He likes to talk. We know him, dont we?

Octavius. [*Earnestly.*] But theres a great truth at the bottom of what he says. I believe most intensely in the dignity of labor.

Straker. [*Unimpressed.*] Thats because you never done any, Mr Robinson. My business is to do away with labor. Youll get more out of me and a machine than you will out of twenty laborers, and not so much to drink either.

Tanner. For Heaven's sake, Tavy, dont start him on political economy. He knows all about it; and we dont. Youre only a poetic Socialist, Tavy: he's a scientific one.

Straker. [*Unperturbed.*] Yes. Well, this conversation is very improvin; but Ive got to look after the car; and you two want to talk about your ladies. *I* know.

[*He pretends to busy himself about the car, but presently saunters off to indulge in a cigaret.*]

Tanner. Thats a very momentous social phenomenon.

Octavius. What is?

Tanner. Straker is. Here have we literary and cultured persons been for years setting up a cry of the New Woman whenever some unusually old fashioned female came along, and never noticing the advent of the New Man. Straker's the New Man.

Octavius. I see nothing new about him, except your way of chaffing him. But I dont want to talk about him just now. I want to speak to you about Ann.

Tanner. Straker knew even that. He learnt it at the Polytechnic, probably. Well, what about Ann? Have you proposed to her?

Octavius. [*Self-reproachfully.*] I was brute enough to do so last night.

Tanner. Brute enough! What do you mean?

Octavius. [*Dithyrambically.*] Jack: we men are all coarse: we never understand how exquisite a woman's sensibilities are. How could I have done such a thing!

Tanner. Done what, you maudlin idiot?

Octavius. Yes, I am an idiot. Jack: if you had heard her voice! if you had seen her tears! I have lain awake all night thinking of them. If she had reproached me, I could have borne it better.

Tanner. Tears! thats dangerous. What did she say?

Octavius. She asked me how she could think of anything now but her dear father. She stifled a sob—— [*He breaks down*].

Tanner. [*Patting him on the back.*] Bear it like a man, Tavy, even if you feel it like an ass. It's the old game: she's not tired of playing with you yet.

Octavius. [*Impatiently.*] Oh, dont be a fool, Jack. Do you suppose this eternal shallow cynicism of yours has any real bearing on a nature like hers?

Tanner. Hm! Did she say anything else?

Octavius. Yes; and that is why I expose myself and her to your ridicule by telling you what passed.

Tanner. [*Remorsefully.*] No, dear Tavy, not ridicule, on my honor! However, no matter. Go on.

Octavius. Her sense of duty is so devout, so perfect, so——

Tanner. Yes: I know. Go on.

Octavius. You see, under this new arrangement, you and Ramsden are her guardians; and she considers that all her duty to her father is now transferred to you. She said she thought I ought to have spoken to you both in the first instance. Of course she is right; but somehow it seems rather absurd that I am to come to you and formally ask to be received as a suitor for your ward's hand.

Tanner. I am glad that love has not totally extinguished your sense of humor, Tavy.

Octavius. That answer wont satisfy her.

Tanner. My official answer is, obviously, Bless you, my children: may you be happy!

Octavius. I wish you would stop playing the fool about this. If it is not serious to you, it is to me, and to her.

Tanner. You know very well that she is as free to choose as you are.

Octavius. She does not think so.

Tanner. Oh, doesnt she! just! However, say what you want me to do?

Octavius. I want you to tell her sincerely and earnestly what you think about me. I want you to tell her that you can trust her to me—that is, if you feel you can.

Tanner. I have no doubt that I can trust her to you. What worries me is the idea of trusting you to her. Have you read Maeterlinck's book about the bee? [1]

Octavius. [*Keeping his temper with difficulty.*] I am not discussing literature at present.

Tanner. Be just a little patient with me. I am not discussing literature: the book about the bee is natural history. It's an awful lesson to mankind. You think that you are Ann's suitor; that you are the pursuer and she the pursued; that it is your part to woo, to persuade, to prevail, to overcome. Fool: it is you who are the pursued, the marked down quarry, the destined prey. You need not sit looking longingly at the bait through the wires of the trap: the door is open, and will remain so until it shuts behind you for ever.

Octavius. I wish I could believe that, vilely as you put it.

Tanner. Why, man, what other work has she in life but to get a husband? It is a woman's business to get married as soon as possible, and a man's to keep unmarried as long as he can. You have your poems and your tragedies to work at: Ann has nothing.

Octavius. I cannot write without inspiration. And nobody can give me that except Ann.

Tanner. Well, hadnt you better get it from her at a safe distance? Petrarch didnt see half as much of Laura, nor Dante of Beatrice, as you see of Ann now; and yet they wrote first-rate poetry—at least so I'm told. They never exposed their idolatry to the test of domestic familiarity; and it lasted them to their graves. Marry Ann; and at the end of a week youll find no more inspiration in her than in a plate of muffins.

Octavius. You think I shall tire of her!

Tanner. Not at all: you dont get tired of muffins. But you dont find inspiration in them; and you wont in her when she ceases to be a poet's dream and becomes a solid eleven stone wife. Youll be forced to dream about somebody else; and then there will be a row.

Octavius. This sort of talk is no use, Jack. You dont understand. You have never been in love.

Tanner. I! I have never been out of it. Why, I am in love even with Ann. But I am neither the slave of love nor its dupe. Go to the bee, thou poet: consider her ways and be

---

[1] *The Life of the Bee,* by Maurice Maeterlinck (1901).

wise.[1] By Heaven, Tavy, if women could do without our work, and we ate their children's bread instead of making it, they would kill us as the spider kills her mate or as the bees kill the drone. And they would be right if we were good for nothing but love.

Octavius. Ah, if we were only good enough for Love! There is nothing like Love: there is nothing else but Love: without it the world would be a dream of sordid horror.

Tanner. And this—this is the man who asks me to give him the hand of my ward! Tavy: I believe we were changed in our cradles, and that you are the real descendant of Don Juan.

Octavius. I beg you not to say anything like that to Ann.

Tanner. Dont be afraid. She has marked you for her own; and nothing will stop her now. You are doomed. [STRAKER *comes back with a newspaper.*] Here comes the New Man, demoralizing himself with a halfpenny paper as usual.

Straker. Now would you believe it, Mr Robinson, when we're out motoring we take in two papers: the *Times* for him, the *Leader* or the *Echo* for me. And do you think I ever see my paper? Not much. He grabs the *Leader* and leaves me to stodge myself with his *Times*.

Octavius. Are there no winners in the *Times?*

Tanner. Enry dont old with bettin, Tavy. Motor records are his weakness. Whats the latest?

Straker. Paris to Biskra at forty mile an hour average, not countin the Mediterranean.

Tanner. How many killed?

Straker. Two silly sheep. What does it matter? Sheep dont cost such a lot: they were glad to ave the price without the trouble o sellin em to the butcher. All the same, d'y'see, therell be a clamor agin it presently; and then the French Government'll stop it; an our chance'll be gone, see? Thats what makes me fairly mad: Mr Tanner wont do a good run while he can.

Tanner. Tavy: do you remember my Uncle James?

Octavius. Yes. Why?

Tanner. Uncle James had a first rate cook: he couldnt digest anything except what she cooked. Well, the poor man was shy and hated society. But his cook was proud of her skill, and wanted to serve up dinners to princes and ambassadors. To prevent her from leaving him, that poor old man had to give a big dinner twice a month, and suffer

agonies of awkwardness. Now here am I; and here is this chap Enry Straker, the New Man. I loathe travelling; but I rather like Enry. He cares for nothing but tearing along in a leather coat and goggles, with two inches of dust all over him, at sixty miles an hour and the risk of his life and mine. Except, of course, when he is lying on his back in the mud under the machine trying to find out where it has given way. Well, if I dont give him a thousand mile run at least once a fortnight I shall lose him. He will give me the sack and go to some American millionaire; and I shall have to put up with a nice respectful groom-gardener-amateur, who will touch his hat and know his place. I am Enry's slave, just as Uncle James was his cook's slave.

Straker. [*Exasperated.*] Garn! I wish I had a car that would go as fast as you can talk, Mr Tanner. What I say is that you lose money by a motor car unless you keep it workin. Might as well ave a pram and a nussmaid to wheel you out in it as that car and me if you dont git the last inch out of us both.

Tanner. [*Soothingly.*] All right, Henry, all right. We'll go out for half an hour presently.

Straker. [*In disgust.*] Arf an ahr!

[*He returns to his machine; seats himself in it; and turns up a fresh page of his paper in search of more news.*]

Octavius. Oh, that reminds me. I have a note for you from Rhoda.

[*He gives* TANNER *a note.*]

Tanner. [*Opening it.*] I rather think Rhoda is heading for a row with Ann. As a rule there is only one person an English girl hates more than she hates her eldest sister; and thats her mother. But Rhoda positively prefers her mother to Ann. She—— [*Indignantly.*] Oh, I say!

Octavius. Whats the matter?

Tanner. Rhoda was to have come with me for a ride in the motor car. She says Ann has forbidden her to go out with me.

[STRAKER *suddenly begins whistling his favorite air with remarkable deliberation. Surprised by this burst of larklike melody, and jarred by a sardonic note in its cheerfulness, they turn and look inquiringly at him. But he is busy with his paper; and nothing comes of their movement.*]

Octavius. [*Recovering himself.*] Does she give any reason?

Tanner. Reason! An insult is not a reason. Ann forbids her to be alone with me on any occasion. Says I am not a fit person for

---

[1] Go to the ant, thou sluggard; consider her ways and be wise. *Proverbs*, VI, 6.

a young girl to be with. What do you think of your paragon now?

Octavius. You must remember that she has a very heavy responsibility now that her father is dead. Mrs Whitefield is too weak to control Rhoda.

Tanner. [*Staring at him.*] In short, you agree with Ann.

Octavius. No; but I think I understand her. You must admit that your views are hardly suited for the formation of a young girl's mind and character.

Tanner. I admit nothing of the sort. I admit that the formation of a young lady's mind and character usually consists in telling her lies; but I object to the particular lie that I am in the habit of abusing the confidence of girls.

Octavius. Ann doesnt say that, Jack.

Tanner. What else does she mean?

Straker. [*Catching sight of* ANN *coming from the house.*] Miss Whitefield, gentlemen.

[*He dismounts and strolls away down the avenue with the air of a man who knows he is no longer wanted.*]

Ann. [*Coming between* OCTAVIUS *and* TANNER.] Good morning, Jack. I have come to tell you that poor Rhoda has got one of her headaches and cannot go out with you today in the car. It is a cruel disappointment to her, poor child!

Tanner. What do you say now, Tavy?

Octavius. Surely you cannot misunderstand, Jack. Ann is shewing you the kindest consideration, even at the cost of deceiving you.

Ann. What do you mean?

Tanner. Would you like to cure Rhoda's headache, Ann?

Ann. Of course.

Tanner. Then tell her what you said just now; and add that you arrived about two minutes after I had received her letter and read it.

Ann. Rhoda has written to you!

Tanner. With full particulars.

Octavius. Never mind him, Ann. You were right—quite right. Ann was only doing her duty, Jack; and you know it. Doing it in the kindest way, too.

Ann. [*Going to* OCTAVIUS.] How kind you are, Tavy! How helpful! How well you understand!   [OCTAVIUS *beams.*]

Tanner. Ay: tighten the coils. You love her, Tavy, dont you?

Octavius. She knows I do.

Ann. Hush. For shame, Tavy!

Tanner. Oh, I give you leave. I am your

guardian; and I commit you to Tavy's care for the next hour. I am off for a turn in the car.

Ann. No, Jack. I must speak to you about Rhoda. Ricky: will you go back to the house and entertain your American friend. He's rather on Mamma's hands so early in the morning. She wants to finish her housekeeping.

Octavius. I fly, dearest Ann.

[*He kisses her hand.*]

Ann. [*Tenderly.*] Ricky Ticky Tavy!

[*He looks at her with an eloquent blush, and runs off.*]

Tanner. [*Bluntly.*] Now look here, Ann. This time youve landed yourself; and if Tavy were not in love with you past all salvation he'd have found out what an incorrigible liar you are.

Ann. You misunderstand, Jack. I didnt dare tell Tavy the truth.

Tanner. No: your daring is generally in the opposite direction. What the devil do you mean by telling Rhoda that I am too vicious to associate with her? How can I ever have any human or decent relations with her again, now that you have poisoned her mind in that abominable way?

Ann. I know you are incapable of behaving badly——

Tanner. Then why did you lie to her?

Ann. I had to.

Tanner. Had to!

Ann. Mother made me.

Tanner. [*His eye flashing.*] Ha! I might have known it. The mother! Always the mother!

Ann. It was that dreadful book of yours. You know how timid mother is. All timid women are conventional: We must be conventional, Jack, or we are so cruelly, so vilely misunderstood. Even you, who are a man, cannot say what you think without being misunderstood and vilified—yes: I admit it: I have had to vilify you. Do you want to have poor Rhoda misunderstood and vilified in the same way? Would it be right for mother to let her expose herself to such treatment before she is old enough to judge for herself?

Tanner. In short, the way to avoid misunderstanding is for everybody to lie and slander and insinuate and pretend as hard as they can. That is what obeying your mother comes to.

Ann. I love my mother, Jack.

Tanner. [*Working himself up into a sociological rage.*] Is that any reason why you are not to call your soul your own? Oh, I protest against this vile abjection of youth to age! Look at fashionable society as you know it. What does it pretend to be? An exquisite dance of nymphs. What is it? A horrible procession of wretched girls, each in the claws of a cynical, cunning, avaricious, disillusioned, ignorantly experienced, foulminded old woman whom she calls mother, and whose duty it is to corrupt her mind and sell her to the highest bidder. Why do these unhappy slaves marry anybody, however old and vile, sooner than not marry at all? Because marriage is their only means of escape from these decrepit fiends who hide their selfish ambitions, their jealous hatreds of the young rivals who have supplanted them, under the mask of maternal duty and family affection. Such things are abominable: the voice of nature proclaims for the daughter a father's care and for the son a mother's. The law for father and son and mother and daughter is not the law of love: it is the law of revolution, of emancipation, of final supersession of the old and worn-out by the young and capable. I tell you, the first duty of manhood and womanhood is a Declaration of Independence: the man who pleads his father's authority is no man: the woman who pleads her mother's authority is unfit to bear citizens to a free people.

Ann. [*Watching him with quiet curiosity.*] I suppose you will go in seriously for politics some day, Jack.

Tanner. [*Heavily let down.*] Eh? What? Wh—? [*Collecting his scattered wits.*] What has that got to do with what I have been saying?

Ann. You talk so well.

Tanner. Talk! Talk! It means nothing to you but talk. Well, go back to your mother, and help her to poison Rhoda's imagination as she has poisoned yours. It is the tame elephants who enjoy capturing the wild ones.

Ann. I am getting on. Yesterday I was a boa constrictor: today I am an elephant.

Tanner. Yes. So pack your trunk and begone: I have no more to say to you.

Ann. You are so utterly unreasonable and impracticable. What can I do?

Tanner. Do! Break your chains. Go your way according to your own conscience and not according to your mother's. Get your mind clean and vigorous; and learn to enjoy a fast ride in a motor car instead of seeing nothing in it but an excuse for a detestable intrigue. Come with me to Marseilles and across to Algiers and Biskra, at sixty miles an hour. Come right down to the Cape if you like. That will be a Declaration of Independence with a vengeance. You can write a book about it afterwards. That will finish your mother and make a woman of you.

Ann. [*Thoughtfully.*] I dont think there would be any harm in that, Jack. You are my guardian: you stand in my father's place, by his own wish. Nobody could say a word against our travelling together. It would be delightful: thank you a thousand times, Jack. I'll come.

Tanner. [*Aghast.*] Youll come!!!

Ann. Of course.

Tanner. But—— [*He stops, utterly appalled; then resumes feebly.*] No: look here, Ann: if theres no harm in it theres no point in doing it.

Ann. How absurd you are! You dont want to compromise me, do you?

Tanner. Yes: thats the whole sense of my proposal.

Ann. You are talking the greatest nonsense; and you know it. You would never do anything to hurt me.

Tanner. Well, if you dont want to be compromised, dont come.

Ann. [*With simple earnestness.*] Yes, I will come, Jack, since you wish it. You are my guardian; and I think we ought to see more of one another and come to know one another better. [*Gratefully.*] It's very thoughtful and very kind of you, Jack, to offer me this lovely holiday, especially after what I said about Rhoda. You really are good—much better than you think. When do we start?

Tanner. But——

[*The conversation is interrupted by the arrival of* MRS WHITEFIELD *from the house. She is accompanied by the* AMERICAN GENTLEMAN, *and followed by* RAMSDEN *and* OCTAVIUS.

HECTOR MALONE *is an Eastern American; but he is not at all ashamed of his nationality. This makes English people of fashion think well of him, as a young fellow who is manly enough to confess to an obvious disadvantage without any attempt to conceal or extenuate it. They feel that he ought not to be made to suffer for what is clearly not his fault, and make a point of being specially kind to him. His chivalrous manners to women, and his elevated moral sentiments, being both gratuitous and unusual, strike them as perhaps a little unfortunate; and though they find his vein of easy humor rather amusing when it has ceased to puzzle them (as it does at first), they*] *have had to make him understand that he really must not tell anecdotes unless they are strictly personal and scandalous, and also that oratory is an accomplishment which belongs to a cruder stage of civilization than that in which his migration has landed him. On these points* HECTOR *is not quite convinced: he still thinks that the British are apt to make merits of their stupidities, and to represent their various incapacities as points of good breeding. English life seems to him to suffer from a lack of edifying rhetoric (which he calls moral tone); English behavior to shew a want of respect for womanhood; English pronunciation to fail very vulgarly in tackling such words as world, girl, bird, etc.; English society to be plain spoken to an extent which stretches occasionally to intolerable coarseness; and English intercourse to need enlivening by games and stories and other pastimes; so he does not feel called upon to acquire these defects after taking great pains to cultivate himself in a first rate manner before venturing across the Atlantic. To this culture he finds English people either totally indifferent, as they very commonly are to all culture, or else politely evasive, the truth being that* HECTOR'S *culture is nothing but a state of saturation with our literary exports of thirty years ago, reimported by him to be unpacked at a moment's notice and hurled at the head of English literature, science, and art, at every conversational opportunity. The dismay set up by these sallies encourages him in his belief that he is helping to educate England. When he finds people chattering harmlessly about Anatole France and Nietzsche, he devastates them with Matthew Arnold, the* Autocrat of the Breakfast Table, *and even Macaulay; and as he is devoutly religious at bottom, he first leads the unwary, by humorous irreverence, to leave popular theology out of account in discussing moral questions with him, and then scatters them in confusion by demanding whether the carrying out of his ideals of conduct was not the manifest object of God Almighty in creating honest men and pure women. The engaging freshness of his personality and the dumbfounding staleness of his culture make it extremely difficult to decide whether he is worth knowing; for whilst his company is undeniably pleasant and enlivening, there is intellectually nothing new to be got out of him, especially as he despises politics, and is careful not to talk commercial shop, in which department he is probably much in advance of his English capitalist friends. He gets on best with romantic Christians of the amoristic sect: hence the friendship which has sprung up between him and* OCTAVIUS.

In appearance HECTOR *is a neatly built young man of twenty-four, with a short, smartly trimmed black beard, clear, well shaped eyes, and an ingratiating vivacity of expression. He is, from the fashionable point of view, faultlessly dressed. As he comes along the drive from the house with* MRS WHITEFIELD *he is sedulously making himself agreeable and entertaining, and thereby placing on her slender wit a burden it is unable to bear. An Englishman would let her alone, accepting boredom and indifference as their common lot; and the poor lady wants to be either let alone or let prattle about the things that interest her.]*

*[*RAMSDEN *strolls over to inspect the motor car.* OCTAVIUS *joins* HECTOR.]*

Ann. [*Pouncing on her* MOTHER *joyously.*] Oh, mamma, what do you think? Jack is going to take me to Nice in his motor car. Isnt it lovely? I am the happiest person in London.

Tanner. [*Desperately.*] Mrs Whitefield objects. I am sure she objects. Doesnt she, Ramsden?

Ramsden. I should think it very likely indeed.

Ann. You dont object, do you, mother?

Mrs Whitefield. I object! Why should I? I think it will do you good, Ann. [*Trotting over to* TANNER.] I meant to ask you to take Rhoda out for a run occasionally: she is too much in the house; but it will do when you come back.

Tanner. Abyss beneath abyss of perfidy!

Ann. [*Hastily, to distract attention from this outburst.*] Oh, I forgot; you have not met Mr Malone. Mr Tanner, my guardian: Mr Hector Malone.

Hector. Pleased to meet you, Mr Tanner. I should like to suggest an extension of the travelling party to Nice, if I may.

Ann. Oh, we're all coming. Thats understood, isnt it?

Hector. I also am the mawdest possessor of a motor car. If Miss Rawbnsn will allow me the privilege of taking her, my car is at her service.

Octavius. Violet! [*General constraint.*]

Ann. [*Subduedly.*] Come, mother: we

must leave them to talk over the arrangements. I must see to my travelling kit.

[Mrs Whitefield *looks bewildered; but* Ann *draws her discreetly away; and they disappear round the corner towards the house.*]

Hector. I think I may go so far as to say that I can depend on Miss Rawbnsn's consent.   [*Continued embarrassment.*]

Octavius. I'm afraid we must leave Violet behind. There are circumstances which make it impossible for her to come on such an expedition.

Hector. [*Amused and not at all convinced.*] Too American, eh? Must the young lady have a chaperone?

Octavius. It's not that, Malone—at least not altogether.

Hector. Indeed! May I ask what other objection applies?

Tanner. [*Impatiently.*] Oh, tell him, tell him. We shall never be able to keep the secret unless everybody knows what it is. Mr Malone: if you go to Nice with Violet, you go with another man's wife. She is married.

Hector. [*Thunderstruck.*] You dont tell me so!

Tanner. We do. In confidence.

Ramsden. [*With an air of importance, lest* Malone *should suspect a misalliance.*] Her marriage has not yet been made known: she desires that it shall not be mentioned for the present.

Hector. I shall respect the lady's wishes. Would it be indiscreet to ask who her husband is, in case I should have an opportunity of cawnsulting him about this trip?

Tanner. We dont know who he is.

Hector. [*Retiring into his shell in a very marked manner.*] In that case, I have no more to say.

[*They become more embarrassed than ever.*]

Octavius. You must think this very strange.

Hector. A little singular. Pardn mee for saying so.

Ramsden. [*Half apologetic, half huffy.*] The young lady was married secretly; and her husband has forbidden her, it seems, to declare his name. It is only right to tell you, since you are interested in Miss—er—in Violet.

Octavius. [*Sympathetically.*] I hope this is not a disappointment to you.

Hector. [*Softened, coming out of his shell again.*] Well: it is a blow. I can hardly understand how a man can leave his wife in such a position. Surely it's not custoMary. It's not manly. It's not considerate.

Octavius. We feel that, as you may imagine, pretty deeply.

Ramsden. [*Testily.*] It is some young fool who has not enough experience to know what mystifications of this kind lead to.

Hector. [*With strong symptoms of moral repugnance.*] I hope so. A man need be very young and pretty foolish too to be excused for such conduct. You take a very lenient view, Mr Ramsden. Too lenient to my mind. Surely marriage should ennoble a man.

Tanner. [*Sardonically.*] Ha!

Hector. Am I to gather from that cachinnation that you dont agree with me, Mr Tanner?

Tanner. [*Drily.*] Get married and try. You may find it delightful for a while: you certainly wont find it ennobling. The greatest common measure of a man and a woman is not necessarily greater than the man's single measure.

Hector. Well, we think in America that a woman's morl number is higher than a man's, and that the purer nature of a woman lifts a man right out of himself, and makes him better than he was.

Octavius. [*With conviction.*] So it does.

Tanner. No wonder American women prefer to live in Europe! It's more comfortable than standing all their lives on an altar to be worshipped. Anyhow, Violet's husband has not been ennobled. So whats to be done?

Hector. [*Shaking his head.*] I cant dismiss that man's cawnduct as lightly as you do, Mr Tanner. However, I'll say no more. Whoever he is, he's Miss Rawbnsn's husband; and I should be glad for her sake to think better of him.

Octavius. [*Touched; for he divines a secret sorrow.*] I'm very sorry, Malone. Very sorry.

Hector. [*Gratefully.*] Youre a good fellow, Rawbnsn. Thank you.

Tanner. Talk about something else. Violet's coming from the house.

Hector. I should esteem it a very great favor, gentlemen, if you would take the opportunity to let me have a few words with the lady alone. I shall have to cry off this trip; and it's rather a dullicate——

Ramsden. [*Glad to escape.*] Say no more. Come, Tanner. Come, Tavy.

[*He strolls away into the park with* Octavius *and* Tanner, *past the motor car.* Violet *comes down the avenue to* Hector.]

Violet. Are they looking?

Hector. No.   [*She kisses him.*]

Violet. Have you been telling lies for my sake?

Hector. Lying! Lying hardly describes it. I overdo it. I get carried away in an ecstasy of mendacity. Violet: I wish youd let me own up.

Violet. [*Instantly becoming serious and resolute.*] No, no, Hector: you promised me not to.

Hector. I'll keep my prawmis until you release me from it. But I feel mean, lying to those men, and denying my wife. Just dastardly.

Violet. I wish your father were not so unreasonable.

Hector. He's not unreasonable. He's right from his point of view. He has a prejudice against the English middle class.

Violet. It's too ridiculous. You know how I dislike saying such things to you, Hector; but if I were to—oh, well, no matter.

Hector. I know. If you were to marry the son of an English manufacturer of awffice furniture, your friends would consider it a misalliance. And here's my silly old dad, who is the biggest awffice furniture man in the world, would shew me the door for marrying the most perfect lady in England merely because she has no handle to her name. Of course it's just absurd. But I tell you, Violet, I don't like deceiving him. I feel as if I was stealing his money. Why wont you let me own up?

Violet. We cant afford it. You can be as romantic as you please about love, Hector; but you mustnt be romantic about money.

Hector. [*Divided between his uxoriousness and his habitual elevation of moral sentiment.*] Thats very English. [*Appealing to her impulsively.*] Violet: dad's bound to find us out someday.

Violet. Oh yes, later on of course. But dont lets go over this every time we meet, dear. You promised——

Hector. All right, all right, I——

Violet. [*Not to be silenced.*] It is I and not you who suffer by this concealment; and as to facing a struggle and poverty and all that sort of thing I simply will not do it. It's too silly.

Hector. You shall not. I'll sort of borrow the money from my dad until I get on my own feet; and then I can own up and pay up at the same time.

Violet. [*Alarmed and indignant.*] Do you mean to work? Do you want to spoil our marriage?

Hector. Well, I dont mean to let marriage spoil my character. Your friend Mr Tanner has got the laugh on me a bit already about that; and——

Violet. The beast! I hate Jack Tanner.

Hector. [*Magnanimously.*] Oh, hee's all right: he only needs the love of a good woman to ennoble him. Besides, he's proposed a motoring trip to Nice; and I'm going to take you.

Violet. How jolly!

Hector. Yes; but how are we going to manage? You see, theyve warned me off going with you, so to speak. Theyve told me in cawnfidnce that youre married. Thats just the most overwhelming cawnfidnce Ive ever been honored with.

[TANNER *returns with* STRAKER, *who goes to his car.*]

Tanner. Your car is a great success, Mr Malone. Your engineer is showing it off to Mr Ramsden.

Hector. [*Eagerly—forgetting himself.*] Lets come, Vi.

Violet. [*Coldly, warning him with her eyes.*] I beg your pardon, Mr Malone: I did not quite catch——

Hector. [*Recollecting himself.*] I ask to be allowed the pleasure of shewing you my little American steam car, Miss Rawbnsn.

Violet. I shall be very pleased.

[*They go off together down the avenue.*]

Tanner. About this trip, Straker.

Straker. [*Preoccupied with the car.*] Yes?

Tanner. Miss Whitefield is supposed to be coming with me.

Straker. So I gather.

Tanner. Mr Robinson is to be one of the party.

Straker. Yes.

Tanner. Well, if you can manage so as to be a good deal occupied with me, and leave Mr Robinson a good deal occupied with Miss Whitefield, he will be deeply grateful to you.

Straker. [*Looking round at him.*] Evidently.

Tanner. "Evidently"! Your grandfather would have simply winked.

Straker. My grandfather would have touched his at.

Tanner. And I should have given your good nice respectful grandfather a sovereign.

Straker. Five shillings, more likely. [*He leaves the car and approaches* TANNER.] What about the lady's views?

Tanner. She is just as willing to be left to Mr Robinson as Mr Robinson is to be left to her. [STRAKER *looks at his principal with cool scepticism; then turns to the car whistling his favorite air.*] Stop that aggravating noise. What do you mean by it? [STRAKER *calmly resumes the melody and finishes it.* TANNER *politely hears it out before he again addresses* STRAKER, *this time with elaborate seriousness.*] Enry: I have ever been a warm advocate of the spread of music among the masses; but I object to your obliging the company whenever Miss Whitefield's name is mentioned. You did it this morning, too.

Straker. [*Obstinately.*] It's not a bit o use. Mr Robinson may as well give it up first as last.

Tanner. Why?

Straker. Garn! You know why. Course it's not my business; but you neednt start kiddin me about it.

Tanner. I am not kidding. I dont know why.

Straker. [*Cheerfully sulky.*] Oh, very well. All right. It aint my business.

Tanner. [*Impressively.*] I trust, Enry, that, as between employer and engineer, I shall always know how to keep my proper distance, and not intrude my private affairs on you. Even our business arrangements are subject to the approval of your Trade Union. But dont abuse your advantages. Let me remind you that Voltaire said that what was too silly to be said could be sung.

Straker. It wasnt Voltaire: it was Bow Mar Shay.

Tanner. I stand corrected: Beaumarchais of course. Now you seem to think that what is too delicate to be said can be whistled. Unfortunately your whistling, though melodious, is unintelligible. Come! theres nobody listening: neither my genteel relatives nor the secretary of your confounded Union. As man to man, Enry, why do you think that my friend has no chance with Miss Whitefield?

Straker. Cause she's arter summun else.

Tanner. Bosh! who else?

Straker. You.

Tanner. Me!!!

Straker. Mean to tell me you didnt know? Oh, come, Mr Tanner!

Tanner. [*In fierce earnest.*] Are you playing the fool, or do you mean it?

Straker. [*With a flash of temper.*] I'm not playin no fool. [*More coolly.*] Why, it's

as plain as the nose on your face. If you aint spotted that, you dont know much about these sort of things. [*Serene again.*] Ex-cuse me, you know, Mr Tanner; but you asked me as man to man; and I told you as man to man.

Tanner. [*Wildly appealing to the heavens.*] Then I—*I* am the bee, the spider, the marked down victim, the destined prey.

Straker. I dunno about the bee and the spider. But the marked down victim, thats what you are and no mistake; and a jolly good job for you, too, I should say.

Tanner. [*Momentously.*] Henry Straker: the golden moment of your life has arrived.

Straker. What d'y'mean?

Tanner. That record to Biskra.

Straker. [*Eagerly.*] Yes?

Tanner. Break it.

Straker. [*Rising to the height of his destiny.*] D'y'mean it?

Tanner. I do.

Straker. When?

Tanner. Now. Is that machine ready to start?

Straker. [*Quailing.*] But you cant——

Tanner. [*Cutting him short by getting into the car.*] Off we go. First to the bank for money; then to my rooms for my kit; then to your rooms for your kit; then break the record from London to Dover or Folkestone; then across the Channel and away like mad to Marseilles, Gibraltar, Genoa, any port from which we can sail to a Mahometan country where men are protected from women.

Straker. Garn! youre kiddin.

Tanner. [*Resolutely.*] Stay behind then. If you wont come I'll do it alone.

[*He starts the motor.*]

Straker. [*Running after him.*] Here! Mister! arf a mo! steady on!

[*He scrambles in as the car plunges forward.*]

ACT III

Evening in the Sierra Nevada. Rolling slopes of brown with olive trees instead of apple trees in the cultivated patches, and occasional prickly pears instead of gorse and bracken in the wilds. Higher up, tall stone peaks and precipices, all handsome and dignified. No wild nature here: rather a most aristocratic mountain landscape made by a fastidious artist-creator. No vulgar profusion of vegetation: even a touch of aridity in the frequent patches of stones: Spanish magnificence and Spanish economy everywhere.

Not very far north of a spot at which the high road over one of the passes crosses a tunnel on the railway from Malaga to Granada, is one of the moun-

tain amphitheatres of the Sierra. Looking at it from the wide end of the horseshoe, one sees, a little to the right, in the face of the cliff, a romantic cave which is really an abandoned quarry, and towards the left a little hill, commanding a view of the road, which skirts the amphitheatre on the left, maintaining its higher level on embankments and an occasional stone arch. On the hill, watching the road, is a MAN *who is either a Spaniard or a Scotchman. Probably a Spaniard, since he wears the dress of a Spanish goatherd and seems at home in the Sierra Nevada, but very like a Scotchman for all that. In the hollow, on the slope leading to the quarry-cave, are about a* DOZEN MEN *who, as they recline at their ease round a heap of smouldering white ashes of dead leaf and brushwood, have an air of being conscious of themselves as picturesque scoundrels honoring the Sierra by using it as an effective pictorial background. As a matter of artistic fact they are not picturesque; and the mountains tolerate them as lions tolerate lice. An English policeman or Poor Law Guardian would recognize them as a selected band of tramps and ablebodied paupers. This description of them is not wholly contemptuous. Whoever has intelligently observed the tramp, or visited the ablebodied ward of a workhouse will admit that our social failures are not all drunkards and weaklings. Some of them are men who do not fit the class they were born into. Precisely the same qualities that make the educated gentleman an artist may make an uneducated manual laborer an ablebodied pauper. There are men who fall helplessly into the workhouse because they are good for nothing; but there are also men who are there because they are strongminded enough to disregard the social convention (obviously not a disinterested one on the part of the ratepayer) which bids a man live by heavy and badly paid drudgery when he has the alternative of walking into the workhouse, announcing himself as a destitute person, and legally compelling the Guardians to feed, clothe, and house him better than he could feed, clothe, and house himself without great exertion. When a man who is born a poet refuses a stool in a stockbroker's office, and starves in a garret, sponging on a poor landlady or on his friends and relatives sooner than work against his grain; or when a lady, because she is a lady, will face any extremity of parasitic dependence rather than take a situation as cook or parlormaid, we make large allowances for them. To such allowances the ablebodied pauper and his nomadic variant the tramp are equally entitled.*

Further, the imaginative man, if his life is to be tolerable to him, must have leisure to tell himself stories, and a position which lends itself to imaginative decoration. The ranks of unskilled labor offer no such positions. We misuse our laborers horribly; and when a man refuses to be misused, we have no right to say that he is refusing honest work. Let us be frank in this matter before we go on with our play; so that we may enjoy it without hypocrisy. If we were reasoning, far-sighted people, four fifths of us would go straight to the Guardians for relief, and knock the whole social system to pieces with most beneficial reconstructive results. The reason we do not do this is because we work like bees or ants, by instinct or habit, not reasoning about the matter at all. Therefore when a man comes along who can and does reason, and who, applying the Kantian test to his conduct, can truly say to us, If everybody did as I do, the world would be compelled to reform itself industrially, and abolish slavery and squalor, which exist only because everybody does as you do, let us honor that man and seriously consider the advisability of following his example. Such a man is the ablebodied, ableminded pauper. Were he a gentleman doing his best to get a pension or a sinecure instead of sweeping a crossing, nobody would blame him for deciding that so long as the alternative lies between living mainly at the expense of the community and allowing the community to live mainly at his, it would be folly to accept what is to him personally the greater of the two evils.

We may therefore contemplate the tramps of the Sierra without prejudice, admitting cheerfully that our objects— briefly, to be gentlemen of fortune— are much the same as theirs, and the difference in our position and methods merely accidental. One or two of them, perhaps, it would be wiser to kill without malice in a friendly and frank manner; for there are bipeds, just as there are quadrupeds, who are too dangerous to be left unchained and unmuzzled; and these cannot fairly expect to have other men's lives wasted in the work of watching them. But as society has not the courage to kill them, and, when it catches them, simply wreaks on them some superstitious expiatory rites of torture and degradation, and then lets them loose with heightened qualifications for mischief, it is just as well that they are at large in the Sierra, and in the hands of a CHIEF *who looks as if he might possibly, on provocation, order them to be shot.*

This CHIEF, *seated in the centre of the group on a squared block of stone from the quarry, is a tall strong man, with a striking cockatoo nose, glossy black hair, pointed beard, upturned moustache, and a Mephistophelean affectation which is fairly imposing, perhaps because the scenery admits of a larger swagger than Piccadilly, perhaps because of a certain sentimentality in the man which gives him that touch of grace which alone can excuse deliberate picturesqueness. His eyes and mouth are by no means rascally; he has a fine voice and a ready wit; and whether he is really the strongest man in the party or not, he looks it. He is certainly the best fed, the best dressed, and the best trained. The fact that he speaks English is not unexpected, in spite of the Spanish landscape; for with the exception of one man who might be guessed as a bullfighter ruined by drink, and one unmistakeable Frenchman, they are all cockney or American; therefore, in a land of cloaks and sombreros, they mostly wear seedy overcoats, woollen mufflers, hard hemispherical hats, and dirty brown gloves. Only a very few dress after their leader, whose broad sombrero with a cock's feather in the band, and voluminous cloak descending to his high boots, are as un-English as possible. None of them are armed; and the ungloved ones keep their hands in their pockets because it is their national belief that it must be dangerously cold in the open air with the night coming on. (It is as warm an evening as any reasonable man could desire.)*

Except the bullfighting inebriate there is only one person in the company who looks more than, say, thirty-three. He is a SMALL MAN *with reddish whiskers, weak eyes, and the anxious look of a small tradesman in difficulties. He wears the only tall hat visible: it shines in the sunset with the sticky glow of some sixpenny patent hat reviver, often applied and constantly tending to produce a worse state of the original surface than the ruin it was applied to remedy. He has a collar and cuffs of celluloid; and his brown Chesterfield overcoat, with velvet collar, is still presentable. He is preeminently the respectable man of the party, and is certainly over forty, possibly over fifty. He is the corner man on the leader's right, opposite* THREE MEN *in scarlet ties on his left. One of these three is the* FRENCHMAN. *Of the remaining* TWO, *who are both English, one is argumentative, solemn, and obstinate; the other rowdy and mischievous.*

[The CHIEF, *with a magnificent fling of the end of his cloak across his left shoulder, rises to address them. The applause which greets him shews that he is a favorite orator.]*

The Chief. Friends and fellow brigands. I have a proposal to make to this meeting. We have now spent three evenings in discussing the question Have Anarchists or Social-Democrats the most personal courage? We have gone into the principles of Anarchism and Social-Democracy at great length. The cause of Anarchy has been ably represented by our one Anarchist, who doesnt know what Anarchism means. [*Laughter.*]

The Anarchist. [*Rising.*] A point of order, Mendoza——

Mendoza. [*Forcibly.*] No, by thunder: your last point of order took half an hour. Besides, Anarchists dont believe in order.

The Anarchist. [*Mild, polite but persistent: he is, in fact, the respectable-looking elderly man in the celluloid collar and cuffs.*] That is a vulgar error. I can prove——

Mendoza. Order, order.

The Others. [*Shouting.*] Order, order. Sit down. Chair! Shut up.

[The ANARCHIST *is suppressed.]*

Mendoza. On the other hand we have three Social-Democrats among us. They are not on speaking terms; and they have put before us three distinct and incompatible views of Social-Democracy.

The Three Men in Scarlet Ties. 1. Mr Chairman, I protest. A personal explanation. 2. It's a lie. I never said so. Be fair, Mendoza. 3. Je demande la parole. C'est ab-

solument faux.[1] C'est faux! faux!! faux!!!
Assas-s-s-s-sin!!!!!!

Mendoza. Order, order.

The Others. Order, order, order! Chair!
[*The* SOCIAL-DEMOCRATS *are suppressed.*]

Mendoza. Now, we tolerate all opinions
here. But after all, comrades, the vast
majority of us are neither Anarchists nor
Socialists, but gentlemen and Christians.

The Majority. [*Shouting assent.*] Hear,
hear! So we are. Right.

The Rowdy Social-Democrat. [*Smarting
under suppression.*] You aint no Christian.
Youre a Sheeny, you are.

Mendoza. [*With crushing magnanimity.*]
My friend: *I* am an exception to all rules.
It is true that I have the honor to be a
Jew; and when the Zionists need a leader to
reassemble our race on its historic soil of
Palestine, Mendoza will not be the last to
volunteer. [*Sympathetic applause—Hear,
Hear, &c.*] But I am not a slave to any
superstition. I have swallowed all the formulas, even that of Socialism; though,
in a sense, once a Socialist, always a Socialist.

The Social-Democrats. Hear, hear!

Mendoza. But I am well aware that the
ordinary man—even the ordinary brigand,
who can scarcely be called an ordinary man
[*Hear, hear!*] —is not a philosopher. Common sense is good enough for him; and in
our business affairs common sense is good
enough for me. Well, what is our business
here in the Sierra Nevada, chosen by the
Moors as the fairest spot in Spain? Is it to
discuss abstruse questions of political economy? No: it is to hold up motor cars
and secure a more equitable distribution of
wealth.

The Sulky Social-Democrat. All made by
labor, mind you.

Mendoza. [*Urbanely.*] Undoubtedly. All
made by labor, and on its way to be squandered by wealthy vagabonds in the dens of
vice that disfigure the sunny shores of the
Mediterranean. We intercept that wealth.
We restore it to circulation among the class
that produced it and that chiefly needs it:
the working class. We do this at the risk of
our lives and liberties, by the exercise of the
virtues of courage, endurance, foresight, and
abstinence—especially abstinence. I myself
have eaten nothing but prickly pears and
broiled rabbit for three days.

The Sulky Social-Democrat. [*Stubbornly.*] No more aint we.

Mendoza. [*Indignantly.*] Have I taken
more than my share?

The Sulky Social-Democrat. [*Unmoved.*]
Why should you?

The Anarchist. Why should he not? To
each according to his needs: from each according to his means.

The Frenchman. [*Shaking his fist at the*
ANARCHIST.] Fumiste![1]

Mendoza. [*Diplomatically.*] I agree with
both of you.

The Genuinely English Brigands. Hear,
hear! Bravo, Mendoza!

Mendoza. What I say is, let us treat one
another as gentlemen, and strive to excel in
personal courage only when we take the
field.

The Rowdy Social-Democrat. [*Deri-
sively.*] Shikespear.

[*A whistle comes from the* GOATHERD
*on the hill. He springs up and points
excitedly forward along the road to the
north.*]

The Goatherd. Automobile! Automobile!
[*He rushes down the hill and joins the
rest, who all scramble to their feet.*]

Mendoza. [*In ringing tones.*] To arms!
Who has the gun?

The Sulky Social-Democrat. [*Handing a
rifle to* MENDOZA.] Here.

Mendoza. Have the nails been strewn in
the road?

The Rowdy Social-Democrat. Two ahnces
of em.

Mendoza. Good! [*To the* FRENCHMAN.]
With me, Duval. If the nails fail, puncture
their tires with a bullet.

[*He gives the rifle to* DUVAL, *who follows him up the hill.* MENDOZA *produces an opera glass. The others hurry
across to the road and disappear to the
north.*]

Mendoza. [*On the hill, using his glass.*]
Two only, a capitalist and his chauffeur.
They look English.

Duval. Angliche! Aoh yess. Cochons!
[*Handling the rifle.*] Faut tirer, n'est-ce-
pas?[2]

Mendoza. No: the nails have gone home.
Their tire is down: they stop.

Duval. [*Shouting to the others.*] Fondez
sur eux, nom de Dieu![3]

Mendoza. [*Rebuking his excitement.*] Du
calme, Duval: keep your hair on. They take
it quietly. Let us descend and receive them.

[MENDOZA *descends, passing behind the*

---

[1] "Humbug!"
[2] Swine! Let's pull the trigger, eh?
[3] Pounce on them, for God's sake!

fire and coming forward, whilst TANNER *and* STRAKER, *in their motoring goggles, leather coats, and caps, are led in from the road by the* BRIGANDS.]

Tanner. Is this the gentleman you describe as your boss? Does he speak English?

The Rowdy Social-Democrat. Course e daz. Y' downt suppowz we Hinglishmen luts ahrselves be bossed by a bloomin Spenniard, do you?

Mendoza. [*With dignity.*] Allow me to introduce myself: Mendoza, President of the League of the Sierra! [*Posing loftily.*] I am a brigand: I live by robbing the rich.

Tanner. [*Promptly.*] I am a gentleman: I live by robbing the poor. Shake hands.

The English Social-Democrats. Hear, hear!

[*General laughter and good humor.* TANNER *and* MENDOZA *shake hands. The* BRIGANDS *drop into their former places.*]

Straker. Ere! where do I come in?

Tanner. [*Introducing.*] My friend and chauffeur.

The Sulky Social-Democrat. [*Suspiciously.*] Well, which is he? friend or showfoor? It makes all the difference, you know.

Mendoza. [*Explaining.*] We should expect ransom for a friend. A professional chauffeur is free of the mountains. He even takes a trifling percentage of his principal's ransom if he will honor us by accepting it.

Straker. I see. Just to encourage me to come this way again. Well, I'll think about it.

Duval. [*Impulsively rushing across to* STRAKER.] Mon frère!

[*He embraces him rapturously and kisses him on both cheeks.*]

Straker. [*Disgusted.*] Ere, git aht: dont be silly. Who are you, pray?

Duval. Duval: Social-Democrat.

Straker. Oh, youre a Social-Democrat, are you?

The Anarchist. He means that he has sold out to the parliamentary humbugs and the bourgeoisie. Compromise! that is his faith.

Duval. [*Furiously.*] I understand what he say. He say Bourgeois. He say Compromise. Jamais de la vie! Misérable menteur—— [1]

Straker. See here, Captain Mendoza, ah mach o this sort o thing do you put up with here? Are we avin a pleasure trip in the mountains, or are we at a Socialist meetin?

The Majority. Hear, hear! Shut up. Chuck it. Sit down, &c. &c.

---
[1] Never in my life! Miserable liar.

[*The* SOCIAL-DEMOCRATS *and the* AN-ARCHIST *are hustled into the background.* STRAKER, *after superintending this proceeding with satisfaction, places himself on* MENDOZA's *left,* TANNER *being on his right.*]

Mendoza. Can we offer you anything? Broiled rabbit and prickly pears——

Tanner. Thank you: we have dined.

Mendoza. [*To his followers.*] Gentlemen: business is over for the day. Go as you please until morning.

[*The* BRIGANDS *disperse into groups lazily. Some go into the cave. Others sit down or lie down to sleep in the open. A few produce a pack of cards and move off towards the road; for it is now starlight, and they know that motor cars have lamps which can be turned to account for lighting a card party.*]

Straker. [*Calling after them.*] Dont none of you go fooling with that car, d'ye hear?

Mendoza. No fear, Monsieur le Chauffeur. The first one we captured cured us of that.

Straker. [*Interested.*] What did it do?

Mendoza. It carried three brave comrades of ours, who did not know how to stop it, into Granada, and capsized them opposite the police station. Since then we never touch one without sending for the chauffeur. Shall we chat at our ease?

Tanner. By all means.

[TANNER, MENDOZA, *and* STRAKER *sit down on the turf by the fire.* MENDOZA *delicately waives his presidential dignity, of which the right to sit on the squared stone block is the appanage, by sitting on the ground like his guests, and using the stone only as a support for his back.*]

Mendoza. It is the custom in Spain always to put off business until tomorrow. In fact, you have arrived out of office hours. However, if you would prefer to settle the question of ransom at once, I am at your service.

Tanner. Tomorrow will do for me. I am rich enough to pay anything in reason.

Mendoza. [*Respectfully, much struck by this admission.*] You are a remarkable man, sir. Our guests usually describe themselves as miserably poor.

Tanner. Pooh! Miserably poor people dont own motor cars.

Mendoza. Precisely what we say to them.

Tanner. Treat us well: we shall not prove ungrateful.

Straker. No prickly pears and broiled rabbits, you know. Dont tell me you cant do us a bit better than that if you like.

Mendoza. Wine, kids, milk, cheese, and bread can be procured for ready money.

Straker. [*Graciously.*] Now youre talkin.

Tanner. Are you all Socialists here, may I ask?

Mendoza. [*Repudiating this humiliating misconception.*] Oh no, no, no: nothing of the kind, I assure you. We naturally have modern views as to the injustice of the existing distribution of wealth: otherwise we should lose our self-respect. But nothing that you could take exception to, except two or three faddists.

Tanner. I had no intention of suggesting anything discreditable. In fact, I am a bit of a Socialist myself.

Straker. [*Drily.*] Most rich men are, I notice.

Mendoza. Quite so. It has reached us, I admit. It is in the air of the century.

Straker. Socialism must be lookin up a bit if your chaps are taking to it.

Mendoza. That is true, sir. A movement which is confined to philosophers and honest men can never exercise any real political influence: there are too few of them. Until a movement shews itself capable of spreading among brigands, it can never hope for a political majority.

Tanner. But are your brigands any less honest than ordinary citizens?

Mendoza. Sir: I will be frank with you. Brigandage is abnormal. Abnormal professions attract two classes: those who are not good enough for ordinary bourgeois life and those who are too good for it. We are dregs and scum, sir: the dregs very filthy, the scum very superior.

Straker. Take care! some o the dregs'll hear you.

Mendoza. It does not matter: each brigand thinks himself scum, and likes to hear the others called dregs.

Tanner. Come! you are a wit. [MENDOZA *inclines his head, flattered.*] May one ask you a blunt question?

Mendoza. As blunt as you please.

Tanner. How does it pay a man of your talent to shepherd such a flock as this on broiled rabbit and prickly pears? I have seen men less gifted, and I'll swear less honest, supping at the Savoy on foie gras and champagne.

Mendoza. Pooh! they have all had their turn at the broiled rabbit, just as I shall have my turn at the Savoy. Indeed, I have had a turn there already—as waiter.

Tanner. A waiter! You astonish me!

Mendoza. [*Reflectively.*] Yes: I, Mendoza of the Sierra, was a waiter. Hence, perhaps, my cosmopolitanism. [*With sudden intensity.*] Shall I tell you the story of my life?

Straker. [*Apprehensively.*] If it aint too long, old chap——

Tanner. [*Interrupting him.*] Tsh-sh: you are a Philistine, Henry: you have no romance in you. [*To* MENDOZA.] You interest me extremely, President. Never mind Henry: he can go to sleep.

Mendoza. The woman I loved——

Straker. Oh, this is a love story, is it? Right you are. Go on: I was only afraid you were going to talk about yourself.

Mendoza. Myself! I have thrown myself away for her sake: that is why I am here. No matter: I count the world well lost for her. She had, I pledge you my word, the most magnificent head of hair I ever saw. She had humor; she had intellect; she could cook to perfection; and her highly strung temperament made her uncertain, incalculable, variable, capricious, cruel, in a word enchanting.

Straker. A six shillin novel sort o woman, all but the cookin. Er name was Lady Gladys Plantagenet, wasnt it?

Mendoza. No, sir: she was not an earl's daughter. Photography, reproduced by the half-tone process, has made me familiar with the appearance of the daughters of the English peerage; and I can honestly say that I would have sold the lot, faces, dowries, clothes, titles, and all, for a smile from this woman. Yet she was a woman of the people, a worker: otherwise—let me reciprocate your bluntness—I should have scorned her.

Tanner. Very properly. And did she respond to your love?

Mendoza. Should I be here if she did? She objected to marrying a Jew.

Tanner. On religious grounds?

Mendoza. No: she was a freethinker. She said that every Jew considers in his heart that English people are dirty in their habits.

Tanner. [*Surprised.*] Dirty!

Mendoza. It shewed her extraordinary knowledge of the world; for it is undoubtedly true. Our elaborate sanitary code makes us unduly contemptuous of the Gentile.

Tanner. Did you ever hear that, Henry?

Straker. Ive heard my sister say so. She was cook in a Jewish family once.

Mendoza. I could not deny it; neither could I eradicate the impression it made on her mind. I could have got round any other objection; but no woman can stand a suspicion of indelicacy as to her person. My entreaties were in vain: she always retorted that she wasnt good enough for me, and recommended me to marry an accursed barmaid named Rebecca Lazarus, whom I loathed. I talked of suicide: she offered me a packet of beetle poison to do it with. I hinted at murder: she went into hysterics; and as I am a living man I went to America so that she might sleep without dreaming that I was stealing upstairs to cut her throat. In America I went out west and fell in with a man who was wanted by the police for holding up trains. It was he who had the idea of holding up motor cars in the South of Europe: a welcome idea to a desperate and disappointed man. He gave me some valuable introductions to capitalists of the right sort. I formed a syndicate; and the present enterprise is the result. I became leader, as the Jew always becomes leader, by his brains and imagination. But with all my pride of race I would give everything I possess to be an Englishman. I am like a boy: I cut her name on the trees and her initials on the sod. When I am alone I lie down and tear my wretched hair and cry Louisa——

Straker. [*Startled.*] Louisa!

Mendoza. It is her name—Louisa—Louisa Straker——

Tanner. Straker!

Straker. [*Scrambling up on his knees most indignantly.*] Look here: Louisa Straker is my sister, see? Wot do you mean by gassin about her like this? Wotshe got to do with you?

Mendoza. A dramatic coincidence! You are Enry, her favorite brother!

Straker. Oo are you callin Enry? What call have you to take a liberty with my name or with hers? For two pins I'd punch your fat edd, so I would.

Mendoza. [*With grandiose calm.*] If I let you do it, will you promise to brag of it afterwards to her? She will be reminded of her Mendoza: that is all I desire.

Tanner. This is genuine devotion, Henry. You should respect it.

Straker. [*Fiercely.*] Funk, more likely.

Mendoza. [*Springing to his feet.*] Funk! Young man: I come of a famous family of fighters; and as your sister well knows, you would have as much chance against me as a perambulator against your motor car.

Straker. [*Secretly daunted, but rising from his knees with an air of reckless pugnacity.*] I aint afraid of you. With your Louisa! Louisa! Miss Straker is good enough for you, I should think.

Mendoza. I wish you could persuade her to think so.

Straker. [*Exasperated.*] Here——

Tanner. [*Rising quickly and interposing.*] Oh come, Henry: even if you could fight the President you cant fight the whole League of the Sierra. Sit down again and be friendly. A cat may look at a king; and even a President of brigands may look at your sister. All this family pride is really very old fashioned.

Straker. [*Subdued, but grumbling.*] Let him look at her. But wot does he mean by making out that she ever looked at im? [*Reluctantly resuming his couch on the turf.*] Ear him talk, one ud think she was keepin company with him.

[*He turns his back on them and composes himself to sleep.*]

Mendoza. [*To* TANNER, *becoming more confidential as he finds himself virtually alone with a sympathetic listener in the still starlight of the mountains; for all the rest are asleep by this time.*] It was just so with her, sir. Her intellect reached forward into the twentieth century: her social prejudices and family affections reached back into the dark ages. Ah, sir, how the words of Shakespear seem to fit every crisis in our emotions!

> I loved Louisa: 40,000 brothers
> Could not with all their quantity of love
> Make up my sum.[1]

And so on. I forget the rest. Call it madness if you will—infatuation. I am an able man, a strong man: in ten years I should have owned a first-class hotel. I met her; and—you see!—I am a brigand, an outcast. Even Shakespear cannot do justice to what I feel for Louisa. Let me read you some lines that I have written about her myself. However slight their literary merit may be, they express what I feel better than any casual words can.

[*He produces a packet of hotel bills scrawled with manuscript, and kneels at the fire to decipher them, poking it with a stick to make it glow.*]

Tanner. [*Slapping him rudely on the shoulder.*] Put them in the fire, President.

Mendoza. [*Startled.*] Eh?

Tanner. You are sacrificing your career to a monomania.

Mendoza. I know it.

Tanner. No you dont. No man would commit such a crime against himself if he really knew what he was doing. How can you look round at these august hills, look up at this divine sky, taste this finely tempered air, and then talk like a literary hack on a second floor in Bloomsbury?

---

[1] See *Hamlet*, V. 1. 292–294.

Mendoza. [*Shaking his head.*] The Sierra is no better than Bloomsbury when once the novelty has worn off. Besides, these mountains make you dream of women—of women with magnificent hair.

Tanner. Of Louisa, in short. They will not make me dream of women, my friend: I am heartwhole.

Mendoza. Do not boast until morning, sir. This is a strange country for dreams.

Tanner. Well, we shall see. Goodnight. [*He lies down and composes himself to sleep.*]

[MENDOZA, *with a sigh, follows his example; and for a few moments there is peace in the Sierra. Then* MENDOZA *sits up suddenly and says pleadingly to* TANNER.]

Mendoza. Just allow me to read a few lines before you go to sleep. I should really like your opinion of them.

Tanner. [*Drowsily.*] Go on. I am listening.

Mendoza. I saw thee first in Whitsun week
Louisa, Louisa——

Tanner. [*Rousing himself.*] My dear President, Louisa is a very pretty name; but it really doesnt rhyme well to Whitsun week.

Mendoza. Of course not. Louisa is not the rhyme, but the refrain.

Tanner. [*Subsiding.*] Ah, the refrain. I beg your pardon. Go on.

Mendoza. Perhaps you do not care for that one: I think you will like this better. [*He recites, in rich soft tones, and in slow time.*]

Louisa, I love thee.
I love thee, Louisa.
Louisa, Louisa, Louisa, I love thee.
One name and one phrase make my music,
    Louisa.
Louisa, Louisa, Louisa, I love thee.

Mendoza thy lover,
Thy lover, Mendoza,
Mendoza adoringly lives for Louisa.
Theres nothing but that in the world for
    Mendoza.
Louisa, Louisa, Mendoza adores thee.

[*Affected.*] There is no merit in producing beautiful lines upon such a name. Louisa is an exquisite name, is it not? [TANNER, *all but asleep, responds with a faint groan.*]

O wert thou, Louisa,
The wife of Mendoza,
Mendoza's Louisa, Louisa Mendoza,
How blest were the life of Louisa's Mendoza!
How painless his longing of love for Louisa!

That is real poetry—from the heart—from the heart of hearts. Dont you think it will move her? [*No answer. Resignedly.*] Asleep, as usual. Doggrel to all the world: heavenly music to me! Idiot that I am to wear my heart on my sleeve! [*He composes himself to sleep, murmuring.*] Louisa, I love thee; I love thee, Louisa; Louisa, Louisa, Louisa, I——

[STRAKER *snores; rolls over on his side; and relapses into sleep. Stillness settles on the Sierra; and the darkness deepens. The fire has again buried itself in white ash and ceased to glow. The peaks shew unfathomably dark against the starry firmament; but now the stars dim and vanish; and the sky seems to steal away out of the universe. Instead of the Sierra there is nothing: omnipresent nothing. No sky, no peaks, no light, no sound, no time nor space, utter void. Then somewhere the beginning of a pallor, and with it a faint throbbing buzz as of a ghostly violoncello palpitating on the same note endlessly. A couple of ghostly violins presently take advantage of this bass*]

and therewith the pallor reveals a MAN *in the void, an incorporeal but visible* MAN, *seated, absurdly enough, on nothing. For a moment he raises his head as the music passes him by. Then, with a heavy sigh, he drops in utter dejection; and the violins, discouraged, retrace their melody in despair and at last give it up, extinguished by wailings from uncanny wind instruments, thus:——*

It is all very odd. One recognizes the Mozartian strain; and on this hint, and by the aid of certain sparkles of violet light in the pallor, the MAN's *costume explains itself as that of a Spanish noble-*

---

[1] From the overture to Mozart's *Don Giovanni*, measures 31–38.
[2] Measures 201–204 of the same overture.

man of the XV–XVI century. DON JUAN, *of course; but where? why? how? Besides, in the brief lifting of his face, now hidden by his hat brim, there was a curious suggestion of* TANNER. *A more critical, fastidious, handsome face, paler and colder, without* TANNER'S *impetuous credulity and enthusiasm, and without a touch of his modern plutocratic vulgarity, but still a resemblance, even an identity. The name too:* DON JUAN TENORIO, JOHN TANNER. *Where on earth— or elsewhere—have we got to from the XX century and the Sierra? Another pallor in the void, this time not violet, but a disagreeable smoky yellow. With it, the whisper of a ghostly clarionet turning this tune into infinite sadness:*

1

The yellowish pallor moves: there is an OLD CRONE *wandering in the void, bent and toothless; draped, as well as one can guess, in the coarse brown frock of some religious order.*[2] *She wanders and wanders in her slow hopeless way, much as a wasp flies in its rapid busy way, until she blunders against the thing she seeks: companionship. With a sob of relief the poor old creature clutches at the presence of the* MAN *and addresses him in her dry unlovely voice, which can still express pride and resolution as well as suffering.*]

The Old Woman. Excuse me; but I am so lonely; and this place is so awful.

Don Juan. A new comer?

The Old Woman. Yes: I suppose I died this morning. I confessed; I had extreme unction; I was in bed with my family about me and my eyes fixed on the cross. Then it grew dark; and when the light came back it was this light by which I walk seeing nothing. I have wandered for hours in horrible loneliness.

Don Juan. [*Sighing.*] Ah! you have not yet lost the sense of time. One soon does, in eternity.

The Old Woman. Where are we?

Don Juan. In hell.

[1] From Donna Anna's aria in Act II of *Don Giovanni,* "Non mi dir."

[2] The career given Ana after her marriage to Don Ottavio: twelve children, widowhood, membership in a religious order until her death, is not derived from any of the variations of the Don Juan legend cited in the *Epistle Dedicatory.* Apparently Shaw thought this a typical career of a seventeenth-century Spanish noblewoman.

The Old Woman. [*Proudly.*] Hell! I in hell! How dare you?

Don Juan. [*Unimpressed.*] Why not, Señora?

The Old Woman. You do not know to whom you are speaking. I am a lady, and a faithful daughter of the Church.

Don Juan. I do not doubt it.

The Old Woman. But how then can I be in hell? Purgatory, perhaps: I have not been perfect: who has? But hell! oh, you are lying.

Don Juan. Hell, Señora, I assure you; hell at its best: that is, its most solitary—though perhaps you would prefer company.

The Old Woman. But I have sincerely repented; I have confessed——

Don Juan. How much?

The Old Woman. More sins than I really committed. I loved confession.

Don Juan. Ah, that is perhaps as bad as confessing too little. At all events, Señora, whether by oversight or intention, you are certainly damned, like myself; and there is nothing for it now but to make the best of it.

The Old Woman. [*Indignantly.*] Oh! and I might have been so much wickeder! All my good deeds wasted! It is unjust.

Don Juan. No: you were fully and clearly warned. For your bad deeds, vicarious atonement, mercy without justice. For your good deeds, justice without mercy. We have many good people here.

The Old Woman. Were you a good man?

Don Juan. I was a murderer.

The Old Woman. A murderer! Oh, how dare they send me to herd with murderers! I was not as bad as that: I was a good woman. There is some mistake: where can I have it set right?

Don Juan. I do not know whether mistakes can be corrected here. Probably they will not admit a mistake even if they have made one.

The Old Woman. But whom can I ask?

Don Juan. I should ask the Devil, Señora: he understands the ways of this place, which is more than I ever could.

The Old Woman. The Devil! *I* speak to the Devil!

Don Juan. In hell, Señora, the Devil is the leader of the best society.

The Old Woman. I tell you, wretch, I know I am not in hell.

Don Juan. How do you know?

The Old Woman. Because I feel no pain.

Don Juan. Oh, then there is no mistake: you are intentionally damned.

The Old Woman. Why do you say that?

Don Juan. Because hell, Señora, is a place for the wicked. The wicked are quite comfortable in it: it was made for them. You tell me you feel no pain. I conclude you are one of those for whom Hell exists.

The Old Woman. Do you feel no pain?

Don Juan. I am not one of the wicked, Señora; therefore it bores me, bores me beyond description, beyond belief.

The Old Woman. Not one of the wicked! You said you were a murderer.

Don Juan. Only a duel. I ran my sword through an old man who was trying to run his through me.

The Old Woman. If you were a gentleman, that was not a murder.

Don Juan. The old man called it murder, because he was, he said, defending his daughter's honor. By this he means that because I foolishly fell in love with her and told her so, she screamed; and he tried to assassinate me after calling me insulting names.

The Old Woman. You were like all men. Libertines and murderers all, all, all!

Don Juan. And yet we meet here, dear lady.

The Old Woman. Listen to me. My father was slain by just such a wretch as you, in just such a duel, for just such a cause. I screamed: it was my duty. My father drew on my assailant: his honor demanded it. He fell: that was the reward of honor. I am here: in hell, you tell me: that is the reward of duty. Is there justice in heaven?

Don Juan. No; but there is justice in hell: heaven is far above such idle human personalities. You will be welcome in hell, Señora. Hell is the home of honor, duty, justice, and the rest of the seven deadly virtues. All the wickedness on earth is done in their name: where else but in hell should they have their reward? Have I not told you that the truly damned are those who are happy in hell?

The Old Woman. And are you happy here?

Don Juan. [*Springing to his feet.*] No; and that is the enigma on which I ponder in darkness. Why am I here? I, who repudiated all duty, trampled honor underfoot, and laughed at justice!

The Old Woman. Oh, what do I care why you are here? Why am *I* here? I, who sacrificed all my inclinations to womanly virtue and propriety!

Don Juan. Patience, lady: you will be perfectly happy and at home here. As saith the poet, "Hell is a city much like Seville." [1]

---

[1] "Hell is a city much like London."—Shelley.

The Old Woman. Happy! here! where I am nothing! where I am nobody!

Don Juan. Not at all: you are a lady; and wherever ladies are is hell. Do not be surprised or terrified: you will find everything here that a lady can desire, including devils who will serve you from sheer love of servitude, and magnify your importance for the sake of dignifying their service—the best of servants.

The Old Woman. My servants will be devils!

Don Juan. Have you ever had servants who were not devils?

The Old Woman. Never: they were devils, perfect devils, all of them. But that is only a manner of speaking. I thought you meant that my servants here would be real devils.

Don Juan. No more real devils than you will be a real lady. Nothing is real here. That is the horror of damnation.

The Old Woman. Oh, this is all madness. This is worse than fire and the worm.

Don Juan. For you, perhaps, there are consolations. For instance: how old were you when you changed from time to eternity?

The Old Woman. Do not ask me how old I was—as if I were a thing of the past. I am 77.

Don Juan. A ripe age, Señora. But in hell old age is not tolerated. It is too real. Here we worship Love and Beauty. Our souls being entirely damned, we cultivate our hearts. As a lady of 77, you would not have a single acquaintance in hell.

The Old Woman. How can I help my age, man?

Don Juan. You forget that you have left your age behind you in the realm of time. You are no more 77 than you are 7 or 17 or 27.

The Old Woman. Nonsense!

Don Juan. Consider, Señora: was not this true even when you lived on earth? When you were 70, were you really older underneath your wrinkles and your grey hairs than when you were 30?

The Old Woman. No, younger: at 30 I was a fool. But of what use is it to feel younger and look older?

Don Juan. You see, Señora, the look was only an illusion. Your wrinkles lied, just as the plump smooth skin of many a stupid girl of 17, with heavy spirits and decrepit ideas, lies about her age! Well, here we have no bodies: we see each other as bodies only because we learnt to think about one another under that aspect when we were alive; and we still think in that way, knowing no other. But we can appear to one another at what age we choose. You have but to will any of your old looks back, and back they will come.

The Old Woman. It cannot be true.

Don Juan. Try.

The Old Woman. Seventeen!

Don Juan. Stop. Before you decide, I had better tell you that these things are a matter of fashion. Occasionally we have a rage for 17; but it does not last long. Just at present the fashionable age is 40—or say 37; but there are signs of a change. If you were at all good-looking at 27, I should suggest your trying that, and setting a new fashion.

The Old Woman. I do not believe a word you are saying. However, 27 be it.

[*Whisk! the* OLD WOMAN *becomes a young one, magnificently attired, and so handsome that in the radiance into which her dull yellow halo has suddenly lightened one might almost mistake her for* ANN WHITEFIELD.]

Don Juan. Doña Ana de Ulloa!

Ana. What? You know me!

Don Juan. And you forget me!

Ana. I cannot see your face. [*He raises his hat.*] Don Juan Tenorio! Monster! You who slew my father! Even here you pursue me.

Don Juan. I protest I do not pursue you. Allow me to withdraw.   [*Going.*]

Ana. [*Seizing his arm.*] You shall not leave me alone in this dreadful place.

Don Juan. Provided my staying be not interpreted as pursuit.

Ana. [*Releasing him.*] You may well wonder how I can endure your presence. My dear, dear father!

Don Juan. Would you like to see him?

Ana. My father here!!!

Don Juan. No: he is in heaven.

Ana. I knew it. My noble father! He is looking down on us now. What must he feel to see his daughter in this place, and in conversation with his murderer!

Don Juan. By the way, if we should meet him——

Ana. How can we meet him? He is in heaven.

Don Juan. He condescends to look in upon us here from time to time. Heaven bores him. So let me warn you that if you meet him he will be mortally offended if you speak of me as his murderer! He maintains that he was a much better swordsman than I, and that if his foot had not slipped he would have killed me. No doubt he is right: I was not a good fencer. I never dispute the point; so we are excellent friends.

Ana. It is no dishonor to a soldier to be proud of his skill in arms.

Don Juan. You would rather not meet him, probably.

Ana. How dare you say that?

Don Juan. Oh, that is the usual feeling here. You may remember that on earth—though of course we never confessed it—the death of anyone we knew, even those we liked best, was always mingled with a certain satisfaction at being finally done with them.

Ana. Monster! Never, never.

Don Juan. [*Placidly.*] I see you recognize the feeling. Yes: a funeral was always a festivity in black, especially the funeral of a relative. At all events, family ties are rarely kept up here. Your father is quite accustomed to this: he will not expect any devotion from you.

Ana. Wretch: I wore mourning for him all my life.

Don Juan. Yes: it became you. But a life of mourning is one thing: an eternity of it quite another. Besides, here you are as dead as he. Can anything be more ridiculous than one dead person mourning for another? Do not look shocked, my dear Ana; and do not be alarmed: there is plenty of humbug in hell (indeed there is hardly anything else); but the humbug of death and age and change is dropped because here we are all dead and all eternal. You will pick up our ways soon.

Ana. And will all the men call me their dear Ana?

Don Juan. No. That was a slip of the tongue. I beg your pardon.

Ana. [*Almost tenderly.*] Juan: did you really love me when you behaved so disgracefully to me?

Don Juan. [*Impatiently.*] Oh, I beg you not to begin talking about love. Here they talk of nothing else but love: its beauty, its holiness, its spirituality, its devil knows what—excuse me; but it does so bore me. They dont know what theyre talking about: I do. They think they have achieved the perfection of love because they have no bodies. Sheer imaginative debauchery! Faugh!

Ana. Has even death failed to refine your soul, Juan? Has the terrible judgment of which my father's statue was the minister taught you no reverence?

Don Juan. How is that very flattering statue, by the way? Does it still come to supper with naughty people and cast them into this bottomless pit?

Ana. It has been a great expense to me. The boys in the monastery school would not let it alone: the mischievous ones broke it; and the studious ones wrote their names on it. Three new noses in two years, and fingers without end. I had to leave it to its fate at last; and now I fear it is shockingly mutilated. My poor father!

Don Juan. Listen! [*Two great chords rolling on syncopated waves of sound break forth. D minor and its dominant: a sound of dreadful joy to all musicians.*] Ha! Mozart's statue music. It is your father. You had better disappear until I prepare him.

[*She vanishes. From the void comes a living* STATUE *of white marble, designed to represent a majestic old man. But he waives his majesty with infinite grace; walks with a feather-like step; and makes every wrinkle in his war worn visage brim over with holiday joyousness. To his sculptor he owes a perfectly trained figure, which he carries erect and trim; and the ends of his moustache curl up, elastic as watchsprings, giving him an air which, but for its Spanish dignity, would be called jaunty. He is on the pleasantest terms with* DON JUAN. *His voice, save for a much more distinguished intonation, is so like the voice of* ROEBUCK RAMSDEN *that it calls attention to the fact that they are not unlike one another in spite of their very different fashions of shaving.*]

Don Juan. Ah, here you are, my friend. Why dont you learn to sing the splendid music Mozart has written for you?

The Statue. Unluckily he has written it for a bass voice. Mine is a countertenor. Well: have you repented yet?

Don Juan. I have too much consideration for you to repent, Don Gonzalo. If I did, you would have no excuse for coming from heaven to argue with me.

The Statue. True. Remain obdurate, my boy. I wish I had killed you, as I should have done but for an accident. Then I should have come here; and you would have had a statue and a reputation for piety to live up to. Any news?

Don Juan. Yes: your daughter is dead.

The Statue. [*Puzzled.*] My daughter? [*Recollecting.*] Oh! the one you were taken with. Let me see: what was her name?

Don Juan. Ana.

The Statue. To be sure: Ana. A goodlooking girl, if I recollect aright. Have you warned Whatshisname, her husband?

Don Juan. My friend Ottavio? No: I have not seen him since Ana arrived.

[ANA *comes indignantly to light.*]

Ana. What does this mean? Ottavio here and your friend! And you, father, have forgotten my name. You are indeed turned to stone.

The Statue. My dear: I am so much more admired in marble than I ever was in my own person that I have retained the shape the sculptor gave me. He was one of the first men of his day: you must acknowledge that.

Ana. Father! Vanity! personal vanity! from you!

The Statue. Ah, you outlived that weakness, my daughter: you must be nearly 80 by this time. I was cut off (by an accident) in my 64th year, and am considerably your junior in consequence. Besides, my child, in this place, what our libertine friend here would call the farce of parental wisdom is dropped. Regard me, I beg, as a fellow creature, not as a father.

Ana. You speak as this villain speaks.

The Statue. Juan is a sound thinker, Ana. A bad fencer, but a sound thinker.

Ana. [*Horror creeping upon her.*] I begin to understand. These are devils, mocking me. I had better pray.

The Statue. [*Consoling her.*] No, no, no, my child: do not pray. If you do, you will throw away the main advantage of this place. Written over the gate here are the words "Leave every hope behind, ye who enter." Only think what a relief that is! For what is hope? A form of moral responsibility. Here there is no hope, and consequently no duty, no work, nothing to be gained by praying, nothing to be lost by doing what you like. Hell, in short, is a place where you have nothing to do but amuse yourself. [DON JUAN *sighs deeply.*] You sigh, friend Juan; but if you dwelt in heaven, as I do, you would realize your advantages.

Don Juan. You are in good spirits today, Commander. You are positively brilliant. What is the matter?

The Statue. I have come to a momentous decision, my boy. But first, where is our friend the Devil? I must consult him in the matter. And Ana would like to make his acquaintance, no doubt.

Ana. You are preparing some torment for me.

Don Juan. All that is superstition, Ana. Reassure yourself. Remember: the devil is not so black as he is painted.

The Statue. Let us give him a call.

[*At the wave of* THE STATUE'S *hand the great chords roll out again; but this time Mozart's music gets grotesquely adulterated with Gounod's. A scarlet halo begins to glow; and into it* THE DEVIL *rises, very Mephistophelean, and not at all unlike* MENDOZA, *though not so interesting. He looks older; is getting prematurely bald; and, in spite of an*] *effusion of good-nature and friendliness, is peevish and sensitive when his advances are not reciprocated. He does not inspire much confidence in his powers of hard work or endurance, and is, on the whole, a disagreeably self-indulgent looking person; but he is clever and plausible, though perceptibly less well bred than the* TWO OTHER MEN, *and enormously less vital than the* WOMAN.]

The Devil. [*Heartily.*] Have I the pleasure of again receiving a visit from the illustrious Commander of Calatrava? [*Coldly.*] Don Juan, your servant. [*Politely.*] And a strange lady? My respects, Señora.

Ana. Are you——

The Devil. [*Bowing.*] Lucifer, at your service.

Ana. I shall go mad.

The Devil. [*Gallantly.*] Ah, Señora, do not be anxious. You come to us from earth, full of the prejudices and terrors of that priest-ridden place. You have heard me ill spoken of; and yet, believe me, I have hosts of friends there.

Ana. Yes: you reign in their hearts.

The Devil. [*Shaking his head.*] You flatter me, Señora; but you are mistaken. It is true that the world cannot get on without me; but it never gives me credit for that: in its heart it mistrusts and hates me. Its sympathies are all with misery, with poverty, with starvation of the body, and of the heart. I call on it to sympathize with joy, with love, with happiness, with beauty——

Don Juan. [*Nauseated.*] Excuse me: I am going. You know I cannot stand this.

The Devil. [*Angrily.*] Yes: I know that you are no friend of mine.

The Statue. What harm is he doing you, Juan? It seems to me that he was talking excellent sense when you interrupted him.

The Devil. [*Warmly patting* THE STATUE'S *hand.*] Thank you, my friend: thank you. You have always understood me: he has always disparaged and avoided me.

Don Juan. I have treated you with perfect courtesy.

The Devil. Courtesy! What is courtesy? I care nothing for mere courtesy. Give me warmth of heart, true sincerity, the bond of sympathy with love and joy——

Don Juan. You are making me ill.

The Devil. There! [*Appealing to* THE STATUE.] You hear, sir! Oh, by what irony of fate was this cold selfish egotist sent to my kingdom, and you taken to the icy mansions of the sky?

The Statue. I can't complain. I was a hypocrite; and it served me right to be sent to heaven.

The Devil. Why, sir, do you not join us, and leave a sphere for which your temperament is too sympathetic, your heart too warm, your capacity for enjoyment too generous?

The Statue. I have this day resolved to do so. In future, excellent Son of the Morning, I am yours. I have left heaven for ever.

The Devil. [*Again touching the marble hand.*] Ah, what an honor! what a triumph for our cause! Thank you, thank you. And now, my friend—I may call you so at last—could you not persuade him to take the place you have left vacant above?

The Statue. [*Shaking his head.*] I cannot conscientiously recommend anybody with whom I am on friendly terms to deliberately make himself dull and uncomfortable.

The Devil. Of course not; but are you sure he would be uncomfortable? Of course you know best: you brought him here originally; and we had the greatest hopes of him. His sentiments were in the best taste of our best people. You remember how he sang? [*He begins to sing in a nasal operatic baritone, tremulous from an eternity of misuse in the French manner.*]

Vivan le femmine!
Viva il buon vino!

The Statue. [*Taking up the tune an octave higher in his countertenor.*]

Sostegno e gloria
D'umanità.[1]

The Devil. Precisely. Well, he never sings for us now.

Don Juan. Do you complain of that? Hell is full of musical amateurs: music is the brandy of the damned. May not one lost soul be permitted to abstain?

The Devil. You dare blaspheme against the sublimest of the arts!

Don Juan. [*With cold disgust.*] You talk like a hysterical woman fawning on a fiddler.

The Devil. I am not angry. I merely pity you. You have no soul; and you are unconscious of all that you lose. Now you, Señor Commander, are a born musician. How well you sing! Mozart would be delighted if he were still here; but he moped and went to heaven. Curious how these clever men, whom you would have supposed born to be

[1] "Long live women! Long live wine, Prop and glory Of humanity." Sung by Don Giovanni late in Act II. just before the Statue knocks at his door.

popular here, have turned out social failures, like Don Juan!

Don Juan. I am really very sorry to be a social failure.

The Devil. Not that we dont admire your intellect, you know. We do. But I look at the matter from your own point of view. You dont get on with us. The place doesnt suit you. The truth is, you have—I wont say no heart; for we know that beneath all your affected cynicism you have a warm one——

Don Juan. [*Shrinking.*] Dont, please dont.

The Devil. [*Nettled.*] Well, youve no capacity for enjoyment. Will that satisfy you?

Don Juan. It is a somewhat less insufferable form of cant than the other. But if youll allow me, I'll take refuge, as usual, in solitude.

The Devil. Why not take refuge in heaven? Thats the proper place for you. [*To* ANA.] Come, Señora! could you not persuade him for his own good to try change of air?

Ana. But can he go to heaven if he wants to?

The Devil. Whats to prevent him?

Ana. Can anybody—can *I* go to heaven if I want to?

The Devil. [*Rather contemptuously.*] Certainly, if your taste lies that way.

Ana. But why doesnt everybody go to heaven, then?

The Statue. [*Chuckling.*] I can tell you that, my dear. It's because heaven is the most angelically dull place in all creation: thats why.

The Devil. His excellency the Commander puts it with military bluntness; but the strain of living in heaven is intolerable. There is a notion that I was turned out of it; but as a matter of fact nothing could have induced me to stay there. I simply left it and organized this place.

The Statue. I dont wonder at it. Nobody could stand an eternity of heaven.

The Devil. Oh, it suits some people. Let us be just, Commander: it is a question of temperament. I dont admire the heavenly temperament: I dont understand it: I dont know that I particularly want to understand it; but it takes all sorts to make a universe. There is no accounting for tastes: there are people who like it. I think Don Juan would like it.

Don Juan. But—pardon my frankness— could you really go back there if you desired to; or are the grapes sour?

The Devil. Back there! I often go back there. Have you never read the book of Job?

Have you any canonical authority for assuming that there is any barrier between our circle and the other one?

Ana. But surely there is a great gulf fixed.

The Devil. Dear lady: a parable must not be taken literally. The gulf is the difference between the angelic and the diabolic temperament. What more impassable gulf could you have? Think of what you have seen on earth. There is no physical gulf between the philosopher's class room and the bull ring; but the bull fighters do not come to the class room for all that. Have you ever been in the country where I have the largest following, England? There they have great racecourses, and also concert rooms where they play the classical compositions of his Excellency's friend Mozart. Those who go to the racecourses can stay away from them and go to the classical concerts instead if they like: there is no law against it; for Englishmen never will be slaves: they are free to do whatever the Government and public opinion allow them to do. And the classical concert is admitted to be a higher, more cultivated, poetic, intellectual, ennobling place than the racecourse. But do the lovers of racing desert their sport and flock to the concert room? Not they. They would suffer there all the weariness the Commander has suffered in heaven. This is the great gulf of the parable between the two places. A mere physical gulf they could bridge; or at least I could bridge it for them (the earth is full of Devil's Bridges); but the gulf of dislike is impassable and eternal. And that is the only gulf that separates my friends here from those who are invidiously called the blest.

Ana. I shall go to heaven at once.

The Statue. My child: one word of warning first. Let me complete my friend Lucifer's similitude of the classical concert. At every one of these concerts in England you will find rows of weary people who are there, not because they really like classical music, but because they think they ought to like it. Well, there is the same thing in heaven. A number of people sit there in glory, not because they are happy, but because they think they owe it to their position to be in heaven. They are almost all English.

The Devil. Yes, the Southerners give it up and join me just as you have done. But the English really do not seem to know when they are thoroughly miserable. An Englishman thinks he is moral when he is only uncomfortable.

The Statue. In short, my daughter, if you go to heaven without being naturally qualified for it, you will not enjoy yourself there.

Ana. And who dares say that I am not naturally qualified for it? The most distinguished princes of the Church have never questioned it. I owe it to myself to leave this place at once.

The Devil. [*Offended.*] As you please, Señora. I should have expected better taste from you.

Ana. Father: I shall expect you to come with me. You cannot stay here. What will people say?

The Statue. People! Why, the best people are here—princes of the Church and all. So few go to heaven, and so many come here, that the blest, once called a heavenly host, are a continually dwindling minority. The saints, the fathers, the elect of long ago are the cranks, the faddists, the outsiders of today.

The Devil. It is true. From the beginning of my career I knew that I should win in the long run by sheer weight of public opinion, in spite of the long campaign of misrepresentation and calumny against me. At the bottom the universe is a constitutional one; and with such a majority as mine I cannot be kept permanently out of office.

Don Juan. I think, Ana, you had better stay here.

Ana. [*Jealously.*] You do not want me to go with you.

Don Juan. Surely you do not want to enter heaven in the company of a reprobate like me.

Ana. All souls are equally precious. You repent, do you not?

Don Juan. My dear Ana, you are silly. Do you suppose heaven is like earth, where people persuade themselves that what is done can be undone by repentance; that what is spoken can be unspoken by withdrawing it; that what is true can be annihilated by a general agreement to give it the lie? No: heaven is the home of the masters of reality: that is why I am going thither.

Ana. Thank you: I am going to heaven for happiness. I have had quite enough of reality on earth.

Don Juan. Then you must stay here; for hell is the home of the unreal and of the seekers for happiness. It is the only refuge from heaven, which is, as I tell you, the home of the masters of reality, and from earth, which is the home of the slaves of reality. The earth is a nursery in which men and women play at being heroes and heroines, saints and sinners; but they are dragged down from their fool's paradise by their bodies: hunger and cold and thirst, age and decay and disease, death above all, make them slaves of reality: thrice a day meals must be eaten and digested: thrice a century a new generation must be engendered: ages of faith, of romance, and of science are all driven at last to have but one prayer: "Make me a healthy animal." But here you escape this tyranny of the flesh; for here you are not an animal at all: you are a ghost, an appearance, an illusion, a convention, deathless, ageless: in a word, bodiless. There are no social questions here, no political questions, no religious questions, best of all, perhaps, no sanitary questions. Here you call your appearance beauty, your emotions love, your sentiments heroism, your aspirations virtue, just as you did on earth; but here there are no hard facts to contradict you, no ironic contrast of your needs with your pretensions, no human comedy, nothing but a perpetual romance, a universal melodrama. As our German friend put it in his poem, "the poetically nonsensical here is good sense; and the Eternal Feminine draws us ever upward and on" [1]—without getting us a step farther. And yet you want to leave this paradise!

Ana. But if hell be so beautiful as this, how glorious must heaven be!

[THE DEVIL, THE STATUE, *and* DON JUAN *all begin to speak at once in violent protest; then stop, abashed.*]

Don Juan. I beg your pardon.

The Devil. Not at all. I interrupted you.

The Statue. You were going to say something.

Don Juan. After you, gentlemen.

The Devil. [*To* DON JUAN.] You have been so eloquent on the advantages of my dominions that I leave you to do equal justice to the drawbacks of the alternative establishment.

Don Juan. In heaven, as I picture it, dear lady, you live and work instead of playing and pretending. You face things as they are; you escape nothing but glamor; and your steadfastness and your peril are your glory. If the play still goes on here and on earth, and all the world is a stage, heaven is at least behind the scenes. But heaven cannot be described by metaphor. Thither I shall go presently, because there I hope to escape at last from lies and from the tedious, vulgar pursuit of happiness, to spend my eons in contemplation——

The Statue. Ugh!

Don Juan. Señor Commander: I do not blame your disgust: a picture gallery is a dull

---

[1] The concluding lines of Goethe's *Faust II*. Shaw's own translation?

place for a blind man. But even as you enjoy the contemplation of such romantic mirages as beauty and pleasure; so would I enjoy the contemplation of that which interests me above all things: namely, Life: the force that ever strives to attain greater power of contemplating itself. What made this brain of mine, do you think? Not the need to move my limbs; for a rat with half my brain moves as well as I. Not merely the need to do, but the need to know what I do, lest in my blind efforts to live I should be slaying myself.

The Statue. You would have slain yourself in your blind efforts to fence but for my foot slipping, my friend.

Don Juan. Audacious ribald: your laughter will finish in hideous boredom before morning.

The Statue. Ha ha! Do you remember how I frightened you when I said something like that to you from my pedestal in Seville?[1] It sounds rather flat without my trombones.

Don Juan. They tell me it generally sounds flat with them, Commander.

Ana. Oh, do not interrupt with these frivolities, father. Is there nothing in heaven but contemplation, Juan?

Don Juan. In the heaven I seek, no other joy. But there is the work of helping Life in its struggle upward. Think of how it wastes and scatters itself, how it raises up obstacles to itself and destroys itself in its ignorance and blindness. It needs a brain, this irresistible force, lest in its ignorance it should resist itself. What a piece of work is man! says the poet. Yes; but what a blunderer! Here is the highest miracle of organization yet attained by life, the most intensely alive thing that exists, the most conscious of all the organisms; and yet, how wretched are his brains! Stupidity made sordid and cruel by the realities learnt from toil and poverty: Imagination resolved to starve sooner than face these realities, piling up illusions to hide them, and calling itself cleverness, genius! And each accusing the other of its own defect: Stupidity accusing Imagination of folly, and Imagination accusing Stupidity of ignorance: whereas, alas! Stupidity has all the knowledge, and Imagination all the intelligence.

The Devil. And a pretty kettle of fish they make of it between them. Did I not say, when I was arranging that affair of Faust's, that all Man's reason has done for him is to make him beastlier than any beast?[2] One

splendid body is worth the brains of a hundred dyspeptic, flatulent philosophers.

Don Juan. You forget that brainless magnificence of body has been tried. Things immeasurably greater than man in every respect but brain have existed and perished. The megatherium, the ichthyosaurus have paced the earth with seven-league steps and hidden the day with cloud-vast wings. Where are they now? Fossils in museums, and so few and imperfect at that, that a knuckle bone or a tooth of one of them is prized beyond the lives of a thousand soldiers. These things lived and wanted to live; but for lack of brains they did not know how to carry out their purpose, and so destroyed themselves.

The Devil. And is Man any the less destroying himself for all this boasted brain of his? Have you walked up and down upon the earth lately?[1] I have; and I have examined Man's wonderful inventions. And I tell you that in the arts of life man invents nothing; but in the arts of death he outdoes Nature herself, and produces by chemistry and machinery all the slaughter of plague, pestilence, and famine. The peasant I tempt today eats and drinks what was eaten and drunk by the peasants of ten thousand years ago; and the house he lives in has not altered as much in a thousand centuries as the fashion of a lady's bonnet in a score of weeks. But when he goes out to slay, he carries a marvel of mechanism that lets loose at the touch of his finger all the hidden molecular energies, and leaves the javelin, the arrow, the blowpipe of his fathers far behind. In the arts of peace Man is a bungler. I have seen his cotton factories and the like, with machinery that a greedy dog could have invented if it had wanted money instead of food. I know his clumsy typewriters and bungling locomotives and tedious bicycles: they are toys compared to the Maxim gun, the submarine torpedo boat. There is nothing in Man's industrial machinery but his greed and sloth: his heart is in his weapons. This marvellous force of Life of which you boast is a force of Death: Man measures his strength by his destructiveness. What is his religion? An excuse for hating me. What is his law? An excuse for hanging you. What is his morality? Gentility! an excuse for consuming without producing. What is his art? An excuse for gloating over pictures of slaughter. What are his politics? Either the worship of a despot because a despot can kill, or parliamentary cock-fighting. I spent

---

[1] In *Don Giovanni* the first words the Statue sings are: "Your laughter will end before morning."
[2] See Mephistopheles' first speech in Goethe's *Faust.*

[1] See *Job* 1:7.

an evening lately in a certain celebrated legislature, and heard the pot lecturing the kettle for its blackness, and ministers answering questions. When I left I chalked up on the door the old nursery saying "Ask no questions and you will be told no lies." I bought a sixpenny family magazine, and found it full of pictures of young men shooting and stabbing one another. I saw a man die: he was a London bricklayer's laborer with seven children. He left seventeen pounds club money; and his wife spent it all on his funeral and went into the workhouse with the children next day. She would not have spent sevenpence on her children's schooling: the law had to force her to let them be taught gratuitously; but on death she spent all she had. Their imagination glows, their energies rise up at the idea of death, these people: they love it; and the more horrible it is the more they enjoy it. Hell is a place far above their comprehension: they derive their notion of it from two of the greatest fools that ever lived, an Italian and an Englishman.[1] The Italian described it as a place of mud, frost, filth, fire, and venomous serpents: all torture. This ass, when he was not lying about me, was maundering about some woman whom he saw once in the street. The Englishman described me as being expelled from heaven by cannons and gunpowder; and to this day every Briton believes that the whole of his silly story is in the Bible. What else he says I do not know; for it is all in a long poem which neither I nor anyone else ever succeeded in wading through. It is the same in everything. The highest form of literature is the tragedy, a play in which everybody is murdered at the end. In the old chronicles you read of earthquakes and pestilences, and are told that these shewed the power and majesty of God and the littleness of Man. Nowadays the chronicles describe battles. In a battle two bodies of men shoot at one another with bullets and explosive shells until one body runs away, when the others chase the fugitives on horseback and cut them to pieces as they fly. And this, the chronicle concludes, shews the greatness and majesty of empires, and the littleness of the vanquished. Over such battles the people run about the streets yelling with delight, and egg their Governments on to spend hundreds of millions of money in the slaughter, whilst the strongest Ministers dare not spend an extra penny in the pound against the poverty and pestilence through which they themselves

---

[1] Dante and Milton.

daily walk. I could give you a thousand instances; but they all come to the same thing: the power that governs the earth is not the power of Life but of Death; and the inner need that has nerved Life to the effort of organising itself into the human being is not the need for higher life but for a more efficient engine of destruction. The plague, the famine, the earthquake, the tempest were too spasmodic in their action; the tiger and crocodile were too easily satiated and not cruel enough: something more constantly, more ruthlessly, more ingeniously destructive was needed; and that something was Man, the inventor of the rack, the stake, the gallows, the electric chair; of sword and gun and poison gas: above all, of justice, duty, patriotism, and all the other isms by which even those who are clever enough to be humanely disposed are persuaded to become the most destructive of all the destroyers.

Don Juan. Pshaw! all this is old. Your weak side, my diabolic friend, is that you have always been a gull: you take Man at his own valuation. Nothing would flatter him more than your opinion of him. He loves to think of himself as bold and bad. He is neither one nor the other: he is only a coward. Call him tyrant, murderer, pirate, bully; and he will adore you, and swagger about with the consciousness of having the blood of the old sea kings in his veins. Call him liar and thief; and he will only take an action against you for libel. But call him coward; and he will go mad with rage: he will face death to outface that stinging truth. Man gives every reason for his conduct save one, every excuse for his crimes save one, every plea for his safety save one; and that one is his cowardice. Yet all his civilization is founded on his cowardice, on his abject tameness, which he calls his respectability. There are limits to what a mule or an ass will stand; but Man will suffer himself to be degraded until his vileness becomes so loathsome to his oppressors that they themselves are forced to reform it.

The Devil. Precisely. And these are the creatures in whom you discover what you call a Life Force!

Don Juan. Yes; for now comes the most surprising part of the whole business.

The Statue. What's that?

Don Juan. Why, that you can make any of these cowards brave by simply putting an idea into his head.

The Statue. Stuff! As an old soldier I admit the cowardice: it's as universal as sea sickness, and matters just as little. But that about putting an idea into a man's head is stuff and nonsense. In a battle all you need to make you fight is a little hot blood and the knowledge that it's more dangerous to lose than to win.

Don Juan. That is perhaps why battles are so useless. But men never really overcome fear until they imagine they are fighting to further a universal purpose—fighting for an idea, as they call it. Why was the Crusader braver than the pirate? Because he fought, not for himself, but for the Cross. What force was it that met him with a valor as reckless as his own? The force of men who fought, not for themselves, but for Islam. They took Spain from us, though we were fighting for our very hearths and homes; but when we, too, fought for that mighty idea, a Catholic Church, we swept them back to Africa.

The Devil. [*Ironically.*] What! you a Catholic, Señor Don Juan! A devotee! My congratulations.

The Statue. [*Seriously.*] Come, come! as a soldier, I can listen to nothing against the Church.

Don Juan. Have no fear, Commander: this idea of a Catholic Church will survive Islam, will survive the Cross, will survive even that vulgar pageant of incompetent schoolboyish gladiators which you call the Army.

The Statue. Juan: you will force me to call you to account for this.

Don Juan. Useless: I cannot fence. Every idea for which Man will die will be a Catholic idea. When the Spaniard learns at last that he is no better than the Saracen, and his prophet no better than Mahomet, he will arise, more Catholic than ever, and die on a barricade across the filthy slum he starves in, for a universal liberty and equality.

The Statue. Bosh!

Don Juan. What you call bosh is the only thing men dare die for. Later on, Liberty will not be Catholic enough: men will die for human perfection, to which they will sacrifice all their liberty gladly.

The Devil. Ay: they will never be at a loss for an excuse for killing one another.

Don Juan. What of that? It is not death that matters, but the fear of death. It is not killing and dying that degrades us, but base living, and accepting the wages and profits of degradation. Better ten dead men than one live slave or his master. Men shall yet rise up, father against son and brother against brother, and kill one another for the great Catholic idea of abolishing slavery.

The Devil. Yes, when the Liberty and Equality of which you prate shall have made free white Christians cheaper in the labor market than black heathen slaves sold by auction at the block.

Don Juan. Never fear! the white laborer shall have his turn too. But I am not now defending the illusory forms the great ideas take. I am giving you examples of the fact that this creature Man, who in his own selfish affairs is a coward to the backbone, will fight for an idea like a hero. He may be abject as a citizen; but he is dangerous as a fanatic. He can only be enslaved whilst he is spiritually weak enough to listen to reason. I tell you, gentlemen, if you can shew a man a piece of what he now calls God's work to do, and what he will later on call by many new names, you can make him entirely reckless of the consequences to himself personally.

Ana. Yes: he shirks all his responsibilities, and leaves his wife to grapple with them.

The Statue. Well said, daughter. Do not let him talk you out of your common sense.

The Devil. Alas! Señor Commander, now that we have got on to the subject of Woman, he will talk more than ever. However, I confess it is for me the one supremely interesting subject.

Don Juan. To a woman, Señora, man's duties and responsibilities begin and end with the task of getting bread for her children. To her, Man is only a means to the end of getting children and rearing them.

Ana. Is that your idea of a woman's mind? I call it cynical and disgusting animalism.

Don Juan. Pardon me, Ana: I said nothing about a woman's whole mind. I spoke of her view of Man as a separate sex. It is no more cynical than her view of herself as above all things a Mother. Sexually, Woman is Nature's contrivance for perpetuating its highest achievement. Sexually, Man is Woman's contrivance for fulfilling Nature's behest in the most economical way. She knows by instinct that far back in the evolutionary process she invented him, differentiated him, created him in order to produce something better than the single-sexed process can produce. Whilst he fulfils the purpose for which she made him, he is welcome to his dreams, his follies, his ideals, his heroisms, provided that the keystone of them all is the worship of woman, of motherhood, of the family, of the hearth. But how rash and dangerous it was to invent a separate creature whose sole function was her own impregnation! For mark what has happened. First, Man has multiplied on her hands until there are as many men as women; so that she has been unable to employ for her purposes more than a fraction of the immense energy she has left at his disposal by saving him the exhausting labor of gestation. This superfluous energy has gone to his brain and to his muscle. He has become too strong to be controlled by her bodily, and too imaginative and mentally vigorous to be content with mere self-reproduction. He has created civilization without consulting her, taking her domestic labor for granted as the foundation of it.

Ana. That is true, at all events.

The Devil. Yes; and this civilization! what is it, after all?

Don Juan. After all, an excellent peg to hang your cynical commonplaces on; but before all, it is an attempt on Man's part to make himself something more than the mere instrument of Woman's purpose. So far, the result of Life's continual effort, not only to maintain itself, but to achieve higher and higher organization and completer self-consciousness, is only, at best, a doubtful campaign between its forces and those of Death and Degeneration. The battles in this campaign are mere blunders, mostly won, like actual military battles, in spite of the commanders.

The Statue. That is a dig at me. No matter: go on, go on.

Don Juan. It is a dig at a much higher power than you, Commander. Still, you must have noticed in your profession that even a stupid general can win battles when the enemy's general is a little stupider.

The Statue. [*Very seriously.*] Most true, Juan, most true. Some donkeys have amazing luck.

Don Juan. Well, the Life Force is stupid; but it is not so stupid as the forces of Death and Degeneration. Besides, these are in its pay all the time. And so Life wins, after a fashion. What mere copiousness of fecundity can supply and mere greed preserve, we possess. The survival of whatever form of civilization can produce the best rifle and the best fed riflemen is assured.

The Devil. Exactly! the survival, not of the most effective means of Life but of the most effective means of Death. You always come back to my point, in spite of your wrigglings and evasions and sophistries, not to mention the intolerable length of your speeches.

Don Juan. Oh, come! who began making long speeches? However, if I overtax your intellect, you can leave us and seek the society of love and beauty and the rest of your favorite boredoms.

The Devil. [*Much offended.*] This is not fair, Don Juan, and not civil. I am also on the intellectual plane. Nobody can appreciate it more than I do. I am arguing fairly with you, and, I think, successfully refuting you. Let us go on for another hour if you like.

Don Juan. Good: let us.

The Statue. Not that I see any prospect of your coming to any point in particular, Juan. Still, since in this place, instead of merely killing time we have to kill eternity, go ahead by all means.

Don Juan. [*Somewhat impatiently.*] My point, you marble-headed old masterpiece, is only a step ahead of you. Are we agreed that Life is a force which has made innumerable experiments in organizing itself; that the mammoth and the man, the mouse and the megatherium, the flies and the fleas and the Fathers of the Church, are all more or less successful attempts to build up that raw force into higher and higher individuals, the ideal individual being omnipotent, omniscient, infallible, and withal completely, unilludedly self-conscious: in short, a god?

The Devil. I agree, for the sake of argument.

The Statue. I agree, for the sake of avoiding argument.

Ana. I most emphatically disagree as regards the Fathers of the Church; and I must beg you not to drag them into the argument.

Don Juan. I did so purely for the sake of alliteration, Ana; and I shall make no further allusion to them. And now, since we are, with that exception, agreed so far, will you not agree with me further that Life has not measured the success of its attempts at godhead by the beauty or bodily perfection of the result, since in both these respects the birds, as our friend Aristophanes long ago pointed out, are so extraordinarily superior, with their power of flight and their lovely plumage, and, may I add, the touching poetry of their loves and nestings, that it is inconceivable that Life, having once produced them, should, if love and beauty were her object, start off on another line and labor at the clumsy elephant and the hideous ape, whose grandchildren we are?

Ana. Aristophanes was a heathen; and you, Juan, I am afraid, are very little better.

The Devil. You conclude, then, that Life was driving at clumsiness and ugliness?

Don Juan. No, perverse devil that you are, a thousand times no. Life was driving at brains—at its darling object: an organ by which it can attain not only self-consciousness but self-understanding.

The Statue. This is metaphysics, Juan.

Why the devil should—— [*To* THE DEVIL.] I beg your pardon.

The Devil. Pray dont mention it. I have always regarded the use of my name to secure additional emphasis as a high compliment to me. It is quite at your service, Commander.

The Statue. Thank you: thats very good of you. Even in heaven, I never quite got out of my old military habits of speech. What I was going to ask Juan was why Life should bother itself about getting a brain. Why should it want to understand itself? Why not be content to enjoy itself?

Don Juan. Without a brain, Commander, you would enjoy yourself without knowing it, and so lose all the fun.

The Statue. True, most true. But I am quite content with brain enough to know that I'm enjoying myself. I dont want to understand why. In fact, I'd rather not. My experience is that one's pleasures dont bear thinking about.

Don Juan. That is why intellect is so unpopular. But to Life, the force behind the Man, intellect is a necessity, because without it he blunders into death. Just as Life, after ages of struggle, evolved that wonderful bodily organ the eye, so that the living organism could see where it was going and what was coming to help or threaten it, and thus avoid a thousand dangers that formerly slew it, so it is evolving today a mind's eye that shall see, not the physical world, but the purpose of life, and thereby enable the individual to work for that purpose instead of thwarting and baffling it by setting up shortsighted personal aims as at present. Even as it is, only one sort of man has ever been happy, has ever been universally respected among all the conflicts of interests and illusions.

The Statue. You mean the military man.

Don Juan. Commander: I do not mean the military man. When the military man approaches, the world locks up its spoons and packs off its womankind. No: I sing not arms and the hero, but the philosophic man: he who seeks in contemplation to discover the inner will of the world, in invention to discover the means of fulfilling that will, and in action to do that will by the so-discovered means. Of all other sorts of men I declare myself tired. They are tedious failures. When I was on earth, professors of all sorts prowled round me feeling for an unhealthy spot in me on which they could fasten. The doctors of medicine bade me consider what I must do to save my body,

and offered me quack cures for imaginary diseases. I replied that I was not a hypochondriac; so they called me Ignoramus and went their way. The doctors of divinity bade me consider what I must do to save my soul; but I was not a spiritual hypochondriac any more than a bodily one, and would not trouble myself about that either; so they called me Atheist and went their way. After them came the politician, who said there was only one purpose in nature, and that was to get him into parliament. I told him I did not care whether he got into parliament or not; so he called me Mugwump and went his way. Then came the romantic man, the Artist, with his love songs and his paintings and his poems; and with him I had great delight for many years, and some profit; for I cultivated my senses for his sake; and his songs taught me to hear better, his paintings to see better, and his poems to feel more deeply. But he led me at last into the worship of Woman.

Ana. Juan!

Don Juan. Yes: I came to believe that in her voice was all the music of the song, in her face all the beauty of the painting, and in her soul all the emotion of the poem.

Ana. And you were disappointed, I suppose. Well, was it her fault that you attributed all these perfections to her?

Don Juan. Yes, partly. For with a wonderful instinctive cunning, she kept silent and allowed me to glorify her: to mistake my own visions, thoughts, and feelings for hers. Now my friend the romantic man was often too poor or too timid to approach those women who were beautiful or refined enough to seem to realize his ideal; and so he went to his grave believing in his dream. But I was more favored by nature and circumstance. I was of noble birth and rich; and when my person did not please, my conversation flattered, though I generally found myself fortunate in both.

The Statue. Coxcomb!

Don Juan. Yes; but even my coxcombry pleased. Well, I found that when I had touched a woman's imagination, she would allow me to persuade myself that she loved me; but when my suit was granted she never said "I am happy; my love is satisfied": she always said, first, "At last, the barriers are down," and second, "When will you come again?"

Ana. That is exactly what men say.

Don Juan. I protest I never said it. But all women say it. Well, these two speeches always alarmed me; for the first meant that the lady's impulse had been solely to throw down my fortifications and gain my citadel; and the second openly announced that henceforth she regarded me as her property, and counted my time as already wholly at her disposal.

The Devil. That is where your want of heart came in.

The Statue. [*Shaking his head.*] You shouldnt repeat what a woman says, Juan.

Ana. [*Severely.*] It should be sacred to you.

The Statue. Still, they certainly do say it. I never minded the barriers; but there was always a slight shock about the other, unless one was very hard hit indeed.

Don Juan. Then the lady, who had been happy and idle enough before, became anxious, preoccupied with me, always intriguing, conspiring, pursuing, watching, waiting, bent wholly on making sure of her prey: I being the prey, you understand. Now this was not what I had bargained for. It may have been very proper and very natural; but it was not music, painting, poetry, and joy incarnated in a beautiful woman. I ran away from it. I ran away from it very often: in fact, I became famous for running away from it.

Ana. Infamous, you mean.

Don Juan. I did not run away from you. Do you blame me for running away from the others?

Ana. Nonsense, man. You are talking to a woman of 77 now. If you had had the chance, you would have run away from me too—if I had let you. You would not have found it so easy with me as with some of the others. If men will not be faithful to their home and their duties, they must be made to be. I daresay you all want to marry lovely incarnations of music and painting and poetry. Well, you cant have them, because they dont exist. If flesh and blood is not good enough for you, you must go without: thats all. Women have to put up with flesh-and-blood husbands—and little enough of that too, sometimes; and you will have to put up with flesh-and-blood wives. [THE DEVIL *looks dubious.* THE STATUE *makes a wry face.*] I see you dont like that, any of you; but it's true, for all that; so if you dont like it you can lump it.

Don Juan. My dear lady, you have put my whole case against romance into a few sentences. That is just why I turned my back on the romantic man with the artistic nature, as he called his infatuation. I thanked him for teaching me to use my eyes and ears; but I told him that his beauty worshipping and happiness hunting and women idealizing was not worth a dump as a philosophy of life; so he called me Philistine and went his way.

Ana. It seems that Woman taught you something, too, with all her defects.

Don Juan. She did more: she interpreted all the other teaching for me. Ah, my friends, when the barriers were down for the first time, what an astounding illumination! I had been prepared for infatuation, for intoxication, for all the illusions of love's young dream; and lo! never was my perception clearer, nor my criticism more ruthless. The most jealous rival of my mistress never saw every blemish in her more keenly than I. I was not duped: I took her without chloroform.

Ana. But you did take her.

Don Juan. That was the revelation. Up to that moment I had never lost the sense of being my own master; never consciously taken a single step until my reason had examined and approved it. I had come to believe that I was a purely rational creature: a thinker! I said, with the foolish philosopher,[1] "I think; therefore I am." It was Woman who taught me to say "I am; therefore I think." And also "I would think more; therefore I must be more."

The Statue. This is extremely abstract and metaphysical, Juan. If you would stick to the concrete, and put your discoveries in the form of entertaining anecdotes about your adventures with women, your conversation would be easier to follow.

Don Juan. Bah! what need I add? Do you not understand that when I stood face to face with Woman, every fibre in my clear critical brain warned me to spare her and save myself? My morals said No. My conscience said No. My chivalry and pity for her said No. My prudent regard for myself said No. My ear, practised on a thousand songs and symphonies; my eye, exercised on a thousand paintings; tore her voice, her features, her color to shreds. I caught all those tell-tale resemblances to her father and mother by which I knew what she would be like in thirty years' time. I noted the gleam of gold from a dead tooth in the laughing mouth: I made curious observations of the strange odors of the chemistry of the nerves. The visions of my romantic reveries, in which I had trod the plains of heaven with a deathless, ageless creature of coral and ivory, deserted me in that supreme hour. I re-

---

[1] Descartes.

membered them and desperately strove to recover their illusion; but they now seemed the emptiest of inventions: my judgment was not to be corrupted: my brain still said No on every issue. And whilst I was in the act of framing my excuse to the lady, Life seized me and threw me into her arms as a sailor throws a scrap of fish into the mouth of a seabird.

The Statue. You might as well have gone without thinking such a lot about it, Juan. You are like all the clever men: you have more brains than is good for you.

The Devil. And were you not the happier for the experience, Señor Don Juan?

Don Juan. The happier; not the wiser, yes. That moment introduced me for the first time to myself, and, through myself, to the world. I saw then how useless it is to attempt to impose conditions on the irresistible force of Life; to preach prudence, careful selection, virtue, honor, chastity——

Ana. Don Juan: a word against chastity is an insult to me.

Don Juan. I say nothing of your chastity, Señora, since it took the form of a husband and twelve children. What more could you have done had you been the most abandoned of women?

Ana. I could have had twelve husbands and no children: thats what I could have done, Juan. And let me tell you that that would have made all the difference to the earth which I replenished.

The Statue. Bravo Ana! Juan: you are floored, quelled, annihilated.

Don Juan. No: for though that difference is the true essential difference—Doña Ana has, I admit, gone straight to the real point—yet it is not a difference of love or chastity, or even constancy; for twelve children by twelve different husbands would have replenished the earth perhaps more effectively. Suppose my friend Ottavio had died when you were thirty, you would never have remained a widow: you were too beautiful. Suppose the successor of Ottavio had died when you were forty, you would still have been irresistible; and a woman who marries twice marries three times if she becomes free to do so. Twelve lawful children borne by one highly respectable lady to three different fathers is not impossible nor condemned by public opinion. That such a lady may be more law-abiding than the poor girl whom we used to spurn into the gutter for bearing one unlawful infant is no doubt true; but dare you say she is less self-indulgent?

Ana. She is more virtuous: that is enough for me.

Don Juan. In that case, what is virtue but the Trade Unionism of the married? Let us face the facts, dear Ana. The Life Force respects marriage only because marriage is a contrivance of its own to secure the greatest number of children and the closest care of them. For honor, chastity, and all the rest of your moral figments it cares not a rap. Marriage is the most licentious of human institutions——

Ana. Juan!

The Statue. [*Protesting.*] Really!——

Don Juan. [*Determinedly.*] I say the most licentious of human institutions: that is the secret of its popularity. And a woman seeking a husband is the most unscrupulous of all the beasts of prey. The confusion of marriage with morality has done more to destroy the conscience of the human race than any other single error. Come, Ana! do not look shocked: you know better than any of us that marriage is a mantrap baited with simulated accomplishments and delusive idealizations. When your sainted mother, by dint of scoldings and punishments, forced you to learn how to play half a dozen pieces on the spinet—which she hated as much as you did—had she any other purpose than to delude your suitors into the belief that your husband would have in his home an angel who would fill it with melody, or at least play him to sleep after dinner? You married my friend Ottavio: well, did you ever open the spinet from the hour when the Church united him to you?

Ana. You are a fool, Juan. A young married woman has something else to do than sit at the spinet without any support for her back; so she gets out of the habit of playing.

Don Juan. Not if she loves music. No: believe me, she only throws away the bait when the bird is in the net.

Ana. [*Bitterly.*] And men, I suppose, never throw off the mask when their bird is in the net. The husband never becomes negligent, selfish, brutal—oh, never!

Don Juan. What do these recriminations prove, Ana? Only that the hero is as gross an imposture as the heroine.

Ana. It is all nonsense: most marriages are perfectly comfortable.

Don Juan. "Perfectly" is a strong expression, Ana. What you mean is that sensible people make the best of one another. Send me to the galleys and chain me to the felon whose number happens to be next before mine; and I must accept the inevitable and make the best of the companionship. Many such companionships, they tell me, are touchingly affectionate; and most are at least tolerably friendly. But that does not make a chain a desirable ornament nor the galleys an abode of bliss. Those who talk most about the blessings of marriage and the constancy of its vows are the very people who declare that if the chain were broken and the prisoners left free to choose, the whole social fabric would fly asunder. You cannot have the argument both ways. If the prisoner is happy, why lock him in? If he is not, why pretend that he is?

Ana. At all events, let me take an old woman's privilege again, and tell you flatly that marriage peoples the world and debauchery does not.

Don Juan. How if a time come when this shall cease to be true? Do you not know that where there is a will there is a way? that whatever Man really wishes to do he will finally discover a means of doing? Well, you have done your best, you virtuous ladies, and others of your way of thinking, to bend Man's mind wholly towards honorable love as the highest good, and to understand by honorable love romance and beauty and happiness in the possession of beautiful, refined, delicate, affectionate women. You have taught women to value their own youth, health, shapeliness, and refinement above all things. Well, what place have squalling babies and household cares in this exquisite paradise of the senses and emotions? Is it not the inevitable end of it all that the human will shall say to the human brain: Invent me a means by which I can have love, beauty, romance, emotion, passion, without their wretched penalties, their expenses, their worries, their trials, their illnesses and agonies and risks of death, their retinue of servants and nurses and doctors and schoolmasters?

The Devil. All this, Señor Don Juan, is realized here in my realm.

Don Juan. Yes, at the cost of death. Man will not take it at that price: he demands the romantic delights of your hell whilst he is still on earth. Well, the means will be found: the brain will not fail when the will is in earnest. The day is coming when great nations will find their numbers dwindling from census to census; when the six-roomed villa will rise in price above the family mansion; when the viciously reckless poor and the stupidly pious rich will delay the extinction of the race only by degrading it; whilst the boldly prudent, the thriftily selfish and am-

bitious, the imaginative and poetic, the lovers of money and solid comfort, the worshippers of success, of art, and of love, will all oppose to the Force of Life the device of sterility.

The Statue. That is all very eloquent, my young friend; but if you had lived to Ana's age, or even to mine, you would have learned that the people who get rid of the fear of poverty and children and all the other family troubles, and devote themselves to having a good time of it, only leave their minds free for the fear of old age and ugliness and impotence and death. The childless laborer is more tormented by his wife's idleness and her constant demands for amusement and distraction than he could be by twenty children; and his wife is more wretched than he. I have had my share of vanity; for as a young man I was admired by women; and as a statue I am praised by art critics. But I confess that had I found nothing to do in the world but wallow in these delights I should have cut my throat. When I married Ana's mother—or perhaps, to be strictly correct, I should rather say when I at last gave in and allowed Ana's mother to marry me—I knew that I was planting thorns in my pillow, and that marriage for me, a swaggering young officer thitherto unvanquished, meant defeat and capture.

Ana. [*Scandalized.*] Father!

The Statue. I am sorry to shock you, my love; but since Juan has stripped every rag of decency from the discussion I may as well tell the frozen truth.

Ana. Hmf! I suppose I was one of the thorns.

The Statue. By no means: you were often a rose. You see, your mother had most of the trouble you gave.

Don Juan. Then may I ask, Commander, why you have left heaven to come here and wallow, as you express it, in sentimental beatitudes which you confess would once have driven you to cut your throat?

The Statue. [*Struck by this.*] Egad, thats true.

The Devil. [*Alarmed.*] What! You are going back from your word! [*To* DON JUAN.] And all your philosophizing has been nothing but a mask for proselytizing! [*To* THE STATUE.] Have you forgotten already the hideous dulness from which I am offering you a refuge here? [*To* DON JUAN.] And does your demonstration of the approaching sterilization and extinction of mankind lead to anything better than making the most of those pleasures of art and love which you yourself admit refined you, elevated you, developed you?

Don Juan. I never demonstrated the extinction of mankind. Life cannot will its own extinction either in its blind amorphous state or in any of the forms into which it has organized itself. I had not finished when His Excellency interrupted me.

The Statue. I begin to doubt whether you ever will finish, my friend. You are extremely fond of hearing yourself talk.

Don Juan. True; but since you have endured so much, you may as well endure to the end. Long before this sterilization which I described becomes more than a clearly foreseen possibility, the reaction will begin. The great central purpose of breeding the race: ay, breeding it to heights now deemed superhuman: that purpose which is now hidden in a mephitic cloud of love and romance and prudery and fastidiousness, will break through into clear sunlight as a purpose no longer to be confused with the gratification of personal fancies, the impossible realization of boys' and girls' dreams of bliss, or the need of older people for companionship or money. The plain-spoken marriage services of the vernacular Churches will no longer be abbreviated and half suppressed as indelicate. The sober decency, earnestness, and authority of their declaration of the real purpose of marriage will be honored and accepted, whilst their romantic vowings and pledgings and until-death-do-us-partings and the like will be expunged as unbearable frivolities. Do my sex the justice to admit, Señora, that we have always recognized that the sex relation is not a personal or friendly relation at all.

Ana. Not a personal or friendly relation! What relation is more personal? more sacred? more holy?

Don Juan. Sacred and holy, if you like, Ana, but not personally friendly. Your relation to God is sacred and holy: dare you call it personally friendly? In the sex relation the universal creative energy, of which the parties are both the helpless agents, overrides and sweeps away all personal considerations, and dispenses with all personal relations. The pair may be utter strangers to one another, speaking different languages, differing in race and color, in age and disposition, with no bond between them but a possibility of that fecundity for the sake of which the Life Force throws them into one another's arms at the exchange of a glance. Do we not recognize this by allowing marriages to be made by parents without con-

sulting the woman? Have you not often expressed your disgust at the immorality of the English nation, in which women and men of noble birth become acquainted and court each other like peasants? And how much does even the peasant know of his bride or she of him before he engages himself? Why, you would not make a man your lawyer or your family doctor on so slight an acquaintance as you would fall in love with and marry him!

Ana. Yes, Juan: we all know the libertine's philosophy. Always ignore the consequences to the woman.

Don Juan. The consequences, yes: they justify her fierce grip of the man. But surely you do not call that attachment a sentimental one. As well call the policeman's attachment to his prisoner a love relation.

Ana. You see you have to confess that marriage is necessary, though, according to you, love is the slightest of all human relations.

Don Juan. How do you know that it is not the greatest of all human relations? far too great to be a personal matter. Could your father have served his country if he had refused to kill an enemy of Spain unless he personally hated him? Can a woman serve her country if she refuses to marry any man she does not personally love? You know it is not so: the woman of noble birth marries as the man of noble birth fights, on political and family grounds, not on personal ones.

The Statue. [*Impressed.*] A very clever point that, Juan: I must think it over. You are really full of ideas. How did you come to think of this one?

Don Juan. I learnt it by experience. When I was on earth, and made those proposals to ladies which, though universally condemned, have made me so interesting a hero of legend, I was not infrequently met in some such way as this. The lady would say that she would countenance my advances, provided they were honorable. On inquiring what that proviso meant, I found that it meant that I proposed to get possession of her property if she had any, or to undertake her support for life if she had not; that I desired her continual companionship, counsel, and conversation to the end of my days, and would take a most solemn oath to be always enraptured by them: above all, that I would turn my back on all other women for ever for her sake. I did not object to these conditions because they were exorbitant and inhuman: it was their extraordinary irrelevance that prostrated me. I invariably replied with perfect frankness that I had never dreamt of any of these things; that unless the lady's character and intellect were equal or superior to my own, her conversation must degrade and her counsel mislead me; that her constant companionship might, for all I knew, become intolerably tedious to me; that I could not answer for my feelings for a week in advance, much less to the end of my life; that to cut me off from all natural and unconstrained intercourse with half my fellow-creatures would narrow and warp me if I submitted to it, and, if not, would bring me under the curse of clandestinity; that, finally, my proposals to her were wholly unconnected with any of these matters, and were the outcome of a perfectly simple impulse of my manhood towards her womanhood.

Ana. You mean that it was an immoral impulse.

Don Juan. Nature, my dear lady, is what you call immoral. I blush for it; but I cannot help it. Nature is a pandar, Time a wrecker, and Death a murderer. I have always preferred to stand up to those facts and build institutions on their recognition. You prefer to propitiate the three devils by proclaiming their chastity, their thrift, and their loving kindness; and to base your institutions on these flatteries. Is it any wonder that the institutions do not work smoothly?

The Statue. What used the ladies to say, Juan?

Don Juan. Oh, come! Confidence for confidence. First tell me what you used to say to the ladies.

The Statue. I! Oh, I swore that I would be faithful to the death; that I should die if they refused me; that no woman could ever be to me what she was——

Ana. She! Who?

The Statue. Whoever it happened to be at the time, my dear. I had certain things I always said. One of them was that even when I was eighty, one white hair of the woman I loved would make me tremble more than the thickest gold tress from the most beautiful young head.[1] Another was that I could not bear the thought of anyone else being the mother of my children.

Don Juan. [*Revolted.*] You old rascal!

The Statue. [*Stoutly.*] Not a bit; for I really believed it with all my soul at the moment. I had a heart: not like you. And it was this sincerity that made me successful.

Don Juan. Sincerity! To be fool enough to believe a ramping, stamping, thumping lie: that is what you call sincerity! To be so greedy for a woman that you deceive yourself in your eagerness to deceive her: sincerity, you call it!

The Statue. Oh, damn your sophistries! I was a man in love, not a lawyer. And the women loved me for it, bless them!

Don Juan. They made you think so. What will you say when I tell you that though I played the lawyer so callously, they made me think so too? I also had my moments of infatuation in which I gushed nonsense and believed it. Sometimes the desire to give pleasure by saying beautiful things so rose in me on the flood of emotion that I said them recklessly. At other times I argued against myself with a devilish coldness that drew tears. But I found it just as hard to escape when I was cruel as when I was kind. When the lady's instinct was set on me, there was nothing for it but lifelong servitude or flight.

Ana. You dare boast, before me and my father, that every woman found you irresistible.

Don Juan. Am I boasting? It seems to me that I cut the most pitiable of figures. Besides, I said "when the lady's instinct was set on me." It was not always so; and then, heavens! what transports of virtuous indignation! what overwhelming defiance to the dastardly seducer! what scenes of Imogen and Iachimo![1]

Ana. I made no scenes. I simply called my father.

Don Juan. And he came, sword in hand, to vindicate outraged honor and morality by murdering me.

The Statue. Murdering! What do you mean? Did I kill you or did you kill me?

Don Juan. Which of us was the better fencer?

The Statue. I was.

Don Juan. Of course you were. And yet you, the hero of those scandalous adventures you have just been relating to us, you had the effrontery to pose as the avenger of outraged morality and condemn me to death! You would have slain me but for an accident.

The Statue. I was expected to, Juan. That is how things were arranged on earth. I was not a social reformer; and I always did what it was customary for a gentleman to do.

Don Juan. That may account for your attacking me, but not for the revolting hypocrisy of your subsequent proceedings as a statue.

[1] See p. 210.

[1] In Shakespeare's *Cymbeline* Iachimo, scoffer at feminine virtue, attempts for a wager to seduce the innocent Imogen, wife of the exiled Posthumus.

The Statue. That all came of my going to heaven.

The Devil. I still fail to see, Señor Don Juan, that these episodes in your earthly career and in that of the Señor Commander in any way discredit my view of life. Here, I repeat, you have all that you sought without anything that you shrank from.

Don Juan. On the contrary, here I have everything that disappointed me without anything that I have not already tried and found wanting. I tell you that as long as I can conceive something better than myself I cannot be easy unless I am striving to bring it into existence or clearing the way for it. That is the law of my life. That is the working within me of Life's incessant aspiration to higher organization, wider, deeper, intenser self-consciousness, and clearer self-understanding. It was the supremacy of this purpose that reduced love for me to the mere pleasure of a moment, art for me to the mere schooling of my faculties, religion for me to a mere excuse for laziness, since it had set up a God who looked at the world and saw that it was good, against the instinct in me that looked through my eyes at the world and saw that it could be improved. I tell you that in the pursuit of my own pleasure, my own health, my own fortune, I have never known happiness. It was not love for Woman that delivered me into her hands: it was fatigue, exhaustion. When I was a child, and bruised my head against a stone, I ran to the nearest woman and cried away my pain against her apron. When I grew up, and bruised my soul against the brutalities and stupidities with which I had to strive, I did again just what I had done as a child. I have enjoyed, too, my rests, my recuperations, my breathing times, my very prostrations after strife; but rather would I be dragged through all the circles of the foolish Italian's Inferno than through the pleasures of Europe. That is what has made this place of eternal pleasures so deadly to me. It is the absence of this instinct in you that makes you that strange monster called a Devil. It is the success with which you have diverted the attention of men from their real purpose, which in one degree or another is the same as mine, to yours, that has earned you the name of The Tempter. It is the fact that they are doing your will, or rather drifting with your want of will, instead of doing their own, that makes them the uncomfortable, false, restless, artificial, petulant, wretched creatures they are.

The Devil. [*Mortified.*] Señor Don Juan: you are uncivil to my friends.

Don Juan. Pooh! why should I be civil to them or to you? In this Palace of Lies a truth or two will not hurt you. Your friends are all the dullest dogs I know. They are not beautiful: they are only decorated. They are not clean: they are only shaved and starched. They are not dignified: they are only fashionably dressed. They are not educated: they are only college passmen. They are not religious: they are only pewrenters. They are not moral: they are only conventional. They are not virtuous: they are only cowardly. They are not even vicious: they are only "frail." They are not artistic: they are only lascivious. They are not prosperous: they are only rich. They are not loyal, they are only servile; not dutiful, only sheepish; not public-spirited, only patriotic; not courageous, only quarrelsome; not determined, only obstinate; not masterful, only domineering; not self-controlled, only obtuse; not self-respecting, only vain; not kind, only sentimental; not social, only gregarious; not considerate, only polite; not intelligent, only opinionated; not progressive, only factious; not imaginative, only superstitious; not just, only vindictive; not generous, only propitiatory; not disciplined, only cowed; and not truthful at all: liars every one of them, to the very backbone of their souls.

The Statue. Your flow of words is simply amazing, Juan. How I wish I could have talked like that to my soldiers.

The Devil. It is mere talk, though. It has all been said before; but what change has it ever made? What notice has the world ever taken of it?

Don Juan. Yes, it is mere talk. But why is it mere talk? Because, my friend, beauty, purity, respectability, religion, morality, art, patriotism, bravery, and the rest are nothing but words which I or anyone else can turn inside out like a glove. Were they realities, you would have to plead guilty to my indictments; but fortunately for your self-respect, my diabolical friend, they are not realities. As you say, they are mere words, useful for duping barbarians into adopting civilization, or the civilized poor into submitting to be robbed and enslaved. That is the family secret of the governing caste; and if we who are of that caste aimed at more Life for the world instead of at more power and luxury for our miserable selves, that secret would make us great. Now, since I, being a nobleman, am in the secret too, think how tedious to me must be your unending cant about all these moralistic figments, and how squalidly disastrous your sacrifice of your lives to them! If you even believed in your moral game enough to play it fairly, it would be interesting to watch; but you dont: you cheat at every trick; and if your opponent outcheats you, you upset the table and try to murder him.

The Devil. On earth there may be some truth in this, because the people are uneducated and cannot appreciate my religion of love and beauty; but here——

Don Juan. Oh yes: I know. Here there is nothing but love and beauty. Ugh! it is like sitting for all eternity at the first act of a fashionable play, before the complications begin. Never in my worst moments of superstitious terror on earth did I dream that hell was so horrible. I live, like a hairdresser, in the continual contemplation of beauty, toying with silken tresses. I breathe an atmosphere of sweetness, like a confectioner's shopboy. Commander: are there any beautiful women in heaven?

The Statue. None. Absolutely none. All dowdies. Not two pennorth of jewellery among a dozen of them. They might be men of fifty.

Don Juan. I am impatient to get there. Is the word beauty ever mentioned; and are there any artistic people?

The Statue. I give you my word they wont admire a fine statue even when it walks past them.

Don Juan. I go.

The Devil. Don Juan: shall I be frank with you?

Don Juan. Were you not so before?

The Devil. As far as I went, yes. But I will now go further, and confess to you that men get tired of everything, of heaven no less than of hell; and that all history is nothing but a record of the oscillations of the world between these two extremes. An epoch is but a swing of the pendulum; and each generation thinks the world is progressing because it is always moving. But when you are as old as I am; when you have a thousand times wearied of heaven, like myself and the Commander, and a thousand times wearied of hell, as you are wearied now, you will no longer imagine that every swing from heaven to hell is an emancipation, every swing from hell to heaven an evolution. Where you now see reform, progress, fulfilment of upward tendency, continual ascent by Man on the stepping stones of his dead selves to higher things, you will see nothing but an infinite comedy of illusion. You will discover the profound truth of the saying of my friend Koheleth, that there is nothing new under the sun. Vanitas vanitatum——

Don Juan. [*Out of all patience.*] By Heaven, this is worse than your cant about love and beauty. Clever dolt that you are, is a man no better than a worm, or a dog than a wolf, because he gets tired of everything? Shall he give up eating because he destroys his appetite in the act of gratifying it? Is a field idle when it is fallow? Can the Commander expend his hellish energy here without accumulating heavenly energy for his next term of blessedness? Granted that the great Life Force has hit on the device of the clockmaker's pendulum, and uses the earth for its bob; that the history of each oscillation, which seems so novel to us the actors, is but the history of the last oscillation repeated; nay more, that in the unthinkable infinitude of time the sun throws off the earth and catches it again a thousand times as a circus rider throws up a ball, and that our agelong epochs are but the moments between the toss and the catch, has the colossal mechanism no purpose?

The Devil. None, my friend. You think, because you have a purpose, Nature must have one. You might as well expect it to have fingers and toes because you have them.

Don Juan. But I should not have them if they served no purpose. And I, my friend, am as much a part of Nature as my own finger is a part of me. If my finger is the organ by which I grasp the sword and the mandoline, my brain is the organ by which Nature strives to understand itself. My dog's brain serves only my dog's purposes; but my own brain labors at a knowledge which does nothing for me personally but make my body bitter to me and my decay and death a calamity. Were I not possessed with a purpose beyond my own I had better be a ploughman than a philosopher; for the ploughman lives as long as the philosopher, eats more, sleeps better, and rejoices in the wife of his bosom with less misgivings. This is because the philosopher is in the grip of the Life Force. This Life Force says to him "I have done a thousand wonderful things unconsciously by merely willing to live and following the line of least resistance: now I want to know myself and my destination, and choose my path; so I have made a special brain—a philosopher's brain—to grasp this knowledge for me as the husbandman's hand grasps the plough for me. And this" says the Life Force to the philosopher "must thou strive to do for me until thou diest, when I will make another brain and another philosopher to carry on the work."

The Devil. What is the use of knowing?

Don Juan. Why, to be able to choose the line of greatest advantage instead of yielding in the direction of the least resistance. Does a ship sail to its destination no better than a log drifts nowhither? The philosopher is Nature's pilot. And there you have our difference: to be in hell is to drift: to be in heaven is to steer.

The Devil. On the rocks, most likely.

Don Juan. Pooh! which ship goes oftenest on the rocks or to the bottom? the drifting ship or the ship with a pilot on board?

The Devil. Well, well, go your way, Señor Don Juan. I prefer to be my own master and not the tool of any blundering universal force. I know that beauty is good to look at; that music is good to hear; that love is good to feel; and that they are all good to think about and talk about. I know that to be well exercised in these sensations, emotions, and studies is to be a refined and cultivated being. Whatever they may say of me in churches on earth, I know that it is universally admitted in good society that the Prince of Darkness is a gentleman; and that is enough for me. As to your Life Force, which you think irresistible, it is the most resistible thing in the world for a person of any character. But if you are naturally vulgar and credulous, as all reformers are, it will thrust you first into religion, where you will sprinkle water on babies to save their souls from me; then it will drive you from religion into science, where you will snatch the babies from the water sprinkling and inoculate them with disease to save them from catching it accidentally; then you will take to politics, where you will become the catspaw of corrupt functionaries and the henchman of ambitious humbugs; and the end will be despair and decrepitude, broken nerve and shattered hopes, vain regrets for that worst and silliest of wastes and sacrifices, the waste and sacrifice of the power of enjoyment: in a word, the punishment of the fool who pursues the better before he has secured the good.

Don Juan. But at least I shall not be bored. The service of the Life Force has that advantage, at all events. So fare you well, Señor Satan.

The Devil. [*Amiably.*] Fare you well, Don Juan. I shall often think of our interesting chats about things in general. I wish you every happiness: heaven, as I said before, suits some people. But if you should change your mind, do not forget that the gates are always open here to the repentant prodigal. If you feel at any time that warmth of heart, sincere unforced affection, innocent enjoyment, and warm, breathing, palpitating reality——

Don Juan. Why not say flesh and blood at once, though we have left those two greasy commonplaces behind us?

The Devil. [*Angrily.*] You throw my friendly farewell back in my teeth, then, Don Juan?

Don Juan. By no means. But though there is much to be learnt from a cynical devil, I really cannot stand a sentimental one. Señor Commander: you know the way to the frontier of hell and heaven. Be good enough to direct me.

The Statue. Oh, the frontier is only the difference between two ways of looking at things. Any road will take you across it if you really want to get there.

Don Juan. Good. [*Saluting* DOÑA ANA.] Señora: your servant.

Ana. But I am going with you.

Don Juan. I can find my own way to heaven, Ana; not yours. [*He vanishes.*]

Ana. How annoying!

The Statue. [*Calling after him.*] Bon voyage, Juan! [*He wafts a final blast of his great rolling chords after him as a parting salute. A faint echo of the first ghostly melody comes back in acknowledgment.*] Ah! there he goes. [*Puffing a long breath out through his lips.*] Whew! How he does talk! They'll never stand it in heaven.

The Devil. [*Gloomily.*] His going is a political defeat. I cannot keep these Life Worshippers: they all go. This is the greatest loss I have had since that Dutch painter went: a fellow who would paint a hag of 70 with as much enjoyment as a Venus of 20.

The Statue. I remember: he came to heaven. Rembrandt.

The Devil. Ay, Rembrandt. There is something unnatural about these fellows. Do not listen to their gospel, Señor Commander: it is dangerous. Beware of the pursuit of the Superhuman: it leads to an indiscriminate contempt for the Human. To a man, horses and dogs and cats are mere species, outside the moral world. Well, to the Superman, men and women are a mere species too, also outside the moral world. This Don Juan was kind to women and courteous to men as your daughter here was kind to her pet cats and dogs; but such kindness is a denial of the exclusively human character of the soul.

The Statue. And who the deuce is the Superman?

The Devil. Oh, the latest fashion among the Life Force fanatics. Did you not meet in Heaven, among the new arrivals, that German Polish madman? what was his name? Nietzsche?

The Statue. Never heard of him.

The Devil. Well, he came here first, before he recovered his wits. I had some hopes of him; but he was a confirmed Life Force worshipper. It was he who raked up the Superman, who is as old as Prometheus; and the 20th century will run after this newest of the old crazes when it gets tired of the world, the flesh, and your humble servant.

The Statue. Superman is a good cry; and a good cry is half the battle. I should like to see this Nietzsche.

The Devil. Unfortunately he met Wagner here, and had a quarrel with him.

The Statue. Quite right, too. Mozart for me!

The Devil. Oh, it was not about music. Wagner once drifted into Life Force worship, and invented a Superman called Siegfried. But he came to his senses afterwards. So when they met here, Nietzsche denounced him as a renegade; and Wagner wrote a pamphlet to prove that Nietzsche was a Jew; and it ended in Nietzsche's going to heaven in a huff. And a good riddance too. And now, my friend, let us hasten to my palace and celebrate your arrival with a grand musical service.

The Statue. With pleasure: youre most kind.

The Devil. This way, Commander. We go down the old trap.

[*He places himself on the grave trap.*]

The Statue. Good. [*Reflectively.*] All the same, the Superman is a fine conception. There is something statuesque about it. [*He places himself on the grave trap beside* THE DEVIL. *It begins to descend slowly. Red glow from the abyss.*] Ah, this reminds me of old times.

The Devil. And me also.

Ana. Stop! [*The trap stops.*]

The Devil. You, Señora, cannot come this way. You will have an apotheosis. But you will be at the palace before us.

Ana. That is not what I stopped you for. Tell me: where can I find the Superman?

The Devil. He is not yet created, Señora.

The Statue. And never will be, probably. Let us proceed: the red fire will make me sneeze. [*They descend.*]

Ana. Not yet created! Then my work is not yet done. [*Crossing herself devoutly.*]

I believe in the Life to Come. [*Crying to the universe.*] A father! a father for the Superman!

[*She vanishes into the void; and again there is nothing: all existence seems suspended infinitely. Then, vaguely, there is a live human voice crying somewhere. One sees, with a shock, a mountain peak shewing faintly against a lighter background. The sky has returned from afar; and we suddenly remember where we were. The cry becomes distinct and urgent: it says* Automobile, Automobile. *The complete reality comes back with a rush: in a moment it is full morning in the Sierra; and the* BRIGANDS *are scrambling to their feet and making for the road as the goatherd runs down from the hill, warning them of the approach of another motor.* TANNER *and* MENDOZA *rise amazedly and stare at one another with scattered wits.* STRAKER *sits up to yawn for a moment before he gets on his feet, making it a point of honor not to shew any undue interest in the excitement of the* BANDITS. MENDOZA *gives a quick look to see that his followers are attending to the alarm; then exchanges a private word with* TANNER.]

Mendoza. Did you dream?

Tanner. Damnably. Did you?

Mendoza. Yes. I forget what. You were in it.

Tanner. So were you. Amazing!

Mendoza. I warned you. [*A shot is heard from the road.*] Dolts! they will play with that gun. [*The* BRIGANDS *come running back scared.*] Who fired that shot? [*To* DUVAL.] Was it you?

Duval. [*Breathless.*] I have not shoot. Dey shoot first.

Anarchist. I told you to begin by abolishing the State. Now we are all lost.

The Rowdy Social-Democrat. [*Stampeding across the amphitheatre.*] Run, everybody.

Mendoza. [*Collaring him; throwing him on his back; and drawing a knife.*] I stab the man who stirs. [*He blocks the way. The stampede is checked.*] What has happened?

The Sulky Social-Democrat. A motor——

The Anarchist. Three men——

Duval. Deux femmes——

Mendoza. Three men and two women! Why have you not brought them here? Are you afraid of them?

The Rowdy One. [*Getting up.*] Thyve a hescort. Ow, de-ooh luts ook it, Mendowza.

The Sulky One. Two armored cars full o soldiers at the ed o the valley.

Anarchist. The shot was fired in the air. It was a signal.

[STRAKER *whistles his favorite air, which falls on the ears of the* BRIGANDS *like a funeral march.*]

Tanner. It is not an escort, but an expedition to capture you. We were advised to wait for it; but I was in a hurry.

The Rowdy One. [*In an agony of apprehension.*] And Ow my good Lord, ere we are, wytin for em! Luts tike to the mahntns.

Mendoza. Idiot, what do you know about the mountains? Are you a Spaniard? You would be given up by the first shepherd you met. Besides, we are already within range of their rifles.

The Rowdy One. But——

Mendoza. Silence. Leave this to me. [*To* TANNER.] Comrade: you will not betray us.

Straker. Oo are you callin comrade?

Mendoza. Last night the advantage was with me. The robber of the poor was at the mercy of the robber of the rich. You offered your hand: I took it.

Tanner. I bring no charge against you, comrade. We have spent a pleasant evening with you: that is all.

Straker. I gev my and to nobody, see?

Mendoza. [*Turning on him impressively.*] Young man: if I am tried, I shall plead guilty, and explain what drove me from England, home, and duty. Do you wish to have the respectable name of Straker dragged through the mud of a Spanish criminal court? The police will search me. They will find Louisa's portrait. It will be published in the illustrated papers. You blench. It will be your doing, remember.

Straker. [*With baffled rage.*] I dont care about the court. It's avin our name mixed up with yours that I object to, you blackmailin swine, you.

Mendoza. Language unworthy of Louisa's brother! But no matter: you are muzzled: that is enough for us.

[*He turns to face his own* MEN, *who back uneasily across the amphitheatre towards the cave to take refuge behind him, as a fresh party, muffled for motoring, comes from the road in riotous spirits.* ANN, *who makes straight for* TANNER, *comes first; then* VIOLET, *helped over the rough ground by* HECTOR *holding her right hand and* RAMSDEN *her left.* MENDOZA *goes to his presidential block and seats himself calmly with his rank and file grouped behind him, and*

his STAFF, *consisting of* DUVAL *and the* ANARCHIST *on his right and the two* SOCIAL-DEMOCRATS *on his left, supporting him in flank.*]

Ann. It's Jack!

Tanner. Caught!

Hector. Why, certainly it is. I said it was you, Tanner. Weve just been stopped by a puncture: the road is full of nails.

Violet. What are you doing here with all these men?

Ann. Why did you leave us without a word of warning?

Hector. I wawnt that bunch of roses, Miss Whitefield. [*To* TANNER.] When we found you were gone, Miss Whitefield bet me a bunch of roses my car would not overtake yours before you reached Monte Carlo.

Tanner. But this is not the road to Monte Carlo.

Hector. No matter. Miss Whitefield tracked you at every stopping place: she is a regular Sherlock Holmes.

Tanner. The Life Force! I am lost.

Octavius. [*Bounding gaily down from the road into the amphitheatre, and coming between* TANNER *and* STRAKER.] I am so glad you are safe, old chap. We were afraid you had been captured by brigands.

Ramsden. [*Who has been staring at* MENDOZA.] I seem to remember the face of your friend here.

[MENDOZA *rises politely and advances with a smile between* ANN *and* RAMSDEN.]

Hector. Why, so do I.

Octavius. I know you perfectly well, sir; but I cant think where I have met you.

Mendoza. [*To* VIOLET.] Do you remember me, madam?

Violet. Oh, quite well; but I am so stupid about names.

Mendoza. It was at the Savoy Hotel. [*To* HECTOR.] You sir, used to come with this lady [VIOLET.] to lunch. [*To* OCTAVIUS.] You, sir, often brought this lady [ANN.] and her mother to dinner on your way to the Lyceum Theatre. [*To* RAMSDEN.] You, sir, used to come to supper, with [*Dropping his voice to a confidential but perfectly audible whisper.*] several different ladies.

Ramsden. [*Angrily.*] Well, what is that to you, pray?

Octavius. Why, Violet, I thought you hardly knew one another before this trip, you and Malone!

Violet. [*Vexed.*] I suppose this person was the manager.

Mendoza. The waiter, madam. I have a grateful recollection of you all. I gathered from the bountiful way in which you treated me that you all enjoyed your visits very much.

Violet. What impertinence!

[*She turns her back on him, and goes up the hill with* HECTOR.]

Ramsden. That will do, my friend. You do not expect these ladies to treat you as an acquaintance, I suppose, because you have waited on them at table.

Mendoza. Pardon me: it was you who claimed my acquaintance. The ladies followed your example. However, this display of the unfortunate manners of your class closes the incident. For the future, you will please address me with the respect due to a stranger and fellow traveller.

[*He turns haughtily away and resumes his presidential seat.*]

Tanner. There! I have found one man on my journey capable of reasonable conversation; and you all instinctively insult him. Even the New Man is as bad as any of you. Enry, you have behaved just like a miserable gentleman.

Straker. Gentleman! Not me.

Ramsden. Really, Tanner, this tone——

Ann. Dont mind him, Granny: you ought to know him by this time.

[*She takes his arm and coaxes him away to the hill to join* VIOLET *and* HECTOR. OCTAVIUS *follows her, doglike.*]

Violet. [*Calling from the hill.*] Here are the soldiers. They are getting out of their motors.

Duval. [*Panicstricken.*] Oh, nom de Dieu!

The Anarchist. Fools: the State is about to crush you because you spared it at the prompting of the political hangers-on of the bourgeoisie.

The Sulky Social-Democrat. [*Argumentative to the last.*] On the contrary, only by capturing the State machine——

The Anarchist. It is going to capture you.

The Rowdy Social-Democrat. [*His anguish culminating.*] Ow, chack it. Wot are we ere for? Wot are we wytin for?

Mendoza. [*Between his teeth.*] Go on. Talk politics, you idiots: nothing sounds more respectable. Keep it up. I tell you.

[*The* SOLDIERS *line the road, commanding the amphitheatre with their rifles. The* BRIGANDS, *struggling with an overwhelming impulse to hide behind one another, look as unconcerned as they can.* MENDOZA *rises superbly, with undaunted front. The* OFFICER *in command steps down from the road into the amphitheatre; looks hard at the* BRIGANDS; *and then inquiringly at* TANNER.]

The Officer. Who are these men, Señor Ingles?

Tanner. My escort.

[MENDOZA, *with a Mephistophelean smile, bows profoundly. An irrepressible grin runs from face to face among the* BRIGANDS. *They touch their hats, except the* ANARCHIST, *who defies the State with folded arms.*]

ACT IV

The garden of a villa in Granada. Whoever wishes to know what it is like must go to Granada to see. One may prosaically specify a group of hills dotted with villas, the Alhambra on the top of one of the hills, and a considerable town in the valley, approached by dusty white roads in which the children, no matter what they are doing or thinking about, automatically whine for halfpence and reach out little clutching brown palms for them; but there is nothing in this description except the Alhambra, the begging, and the color of the roads, that does not fit Surrey as well as Spain. The difference is that the Surrey hills are comparatively small and ugly, and should properly be called the Surrey Protuberances; but these Spanish hills are of mountain stock: the amenity which conceals their size does not compromise their dignity.

This particular garden is on a hill opposite the Alhambra; and the villa is as expensive and pretentious as a villa must be if it is to be let furnished by the week to opulent American and English visitors. If we stand on the lawn at the foot of the garden and look uphill, our horizon is the stone balustrade of a flagged platform on the edge of infinite space at the top of the hill. Between us and this platform is a flower garden with a circular basin and fountain in the centre, surrounded by geometrical flower beds, gravel paths, and clipped yew trees in the genteelest order. The garden is higher than our lawn; so we reach it by a few steps in the middle of its embankment. The platform is higher again than the garden, from which we mount a couple more steps to look over the balustrade at a fine view of the town up the valley and of the hills that stretch away beyond it to where, in the remotest distance, they become mountains. On our left is the villa, accessible by steps from the left hand corner of the garden. Returning from the platform through the garden and down again to the lawn (a movement which leaves the villa behind us on our right) we find evidence of literary interests on the part of the tenants in the fact that there is no tennis net nor set of croquet hoops, but, on our left, a little iron garden table with books on it, mostly yellow-backed, and a chair beside it. A chair on the right has also a couple of open books upon it. There are no newspapers, a circumstance which, with the absence of games, might lead an intelligent spectator to the most far-reaching conclusions as to the sort of people who live in the villa. Such speculations are checked, however, on this delightfully fine afternoon, by the appearance at a little gate in a paling on our left, of HENRY STRAKER *in his professional costume. He opens the gate for an* ELDERLY GENTLEMAN, *and follows him on to the lawn.*

This ELDERLY GENTLEMAN *defies the Spanish sun in a black frock coat, tall silk hat, trousers in which narrow stripes of dark grey and lilac blend into a highly respectable color, and a black necktie tied into a bow over spotless linen. Probably therefore a man whose social position needs constant and scrupulous affirmation without regard to climate: one who would dress thus for the middle of the Sahara or the top of Mont Blanc. And since he has not the stamp of the class which accepts as its life mission the advertizing and maintenance of first-rate tailoring and millinery, he looks vulgar in his finery, though in a working dress of any kind he would look dignified enough. He is a bullet-cheeked man with a red complexion, stubbly hair, smallish eyes, a hard mouth that folds down at the corners, and a dogged chin. The looseness of skin that comes with age has attacked his throat and the laps of his cheeks; but he is still hard as an apple above the mouth; so that the upper half of his face looks younger than the lower. He has the self-confidence of*

one who has made money, and something of the truculence of one who has made it in a brutalizing struggle, his civility having under it a perceptible menace that he has other methods in reserve if necessary. Withal, a man to be rather pitied when he is not to be feared; for there is something pathetic about him at times, as if the huge commercial machine which has worked him into his frock coat had allowed him very little of his own way and left his affections hungry and baffled. At the first word that falls from him it is clear that he is an Irishman whose native intonation has clung to him through many changes of place and rank. One can only guess that the original material of his speech was perhaps the surly Kerry brogue; but the degradation of speech that occurs in London, Glasgow, Dublin, and big cities generally has been at work on it so long that nobody but an arrant cockney would dream of calling it a brogue now; for its music is almost gone, though its surliness is still perceptible. STRAKER, *being a very obvious cockney, inspires him with implacable contempt, as a stupid Englishman who cannot even speak his own language properly.* STRAKER, *on the other hand, regards the* OLD GENTLEMAN'S *accent as a joke thoughtfully provided by Providence expressly for the amusement of the British race, and treats him normally with the indulgence due to an inferior and unlucky species, but occasionally with indignant alarm when the* OLD GENTLEMAN *shews signs of intending his Irish nonsense to be taken seriously.*

Straker. I'll go tell the young lady. She said youd prefer to stay here.

[*He turns to go up through the garden to the villa.*]

The Irishman. [*Who had been looking round him with lively curiosity.*] The young lady? Thats Miss Violet, eh?

Straker. [*Stopping on the steps with sudden suspicion.*] Well, you know, dont you?

The Irishman. Do I?

Straker. [*His temper rising.*] Well, do you or dont you?

The Irishman. What business is that of yours?

[STRAKER, *now highly indignant, comes back from the steps and confronts the* VISITOR.]

Straker. I'll tell you what business it is of mine. Miss Robinson——

The Irishman. [*Interrupting.*] Oh, her name is Robinson, is it? Thank you.

Straker. Why, you dont know even her name?

The Irishman. Yes I do, now that youve told me.

Straker. [*After a moment of stupefaction at the* OLD MAN'S *readiness in repartee.*] Look here; what do you mean by gittin into my car and lettin me bring you here if youre not the person I took that note to?

The Irishman. Who else did you take it to, pray?

Straker. I took it to Mr Ector Malone, at Miss Robinson's request, see? Miss Robinson is not my principal: I took it to oblige her. I know Mr. Malone; and he aint you, not by a long chalk. At the hotel they told me that your name is Ector Malone——

Malone. Hector Malone.

Straker. [*With calm superiority.*] Hector in your own country: thats what comes o livin in provincial places like Ireland and America. Over here youre Ector: if you avnt noticed it before, you soon will.

[*The growing strain of the conversation is here relieved by* VIOLET, *who has sallied from the villa and through the garden to the steps, which she now descends, coming very opportunely between* MALONE *and* STRAKER.]

Violet. [*To* STRAKER.] Did you take my message?

Straker. Yes, miss. I took it to the hotel and sent it up, expecting to see young Mr Malone. Then out walks this gent, and says it's all right and he'll come with me. So as the hotel people said he was Mr. Ector Malone, I fetched him. And now he goes back on what he said. But if he isnt the gentleman you meant, say the word: it's easy enough to fetch him back again.

Malone. I should esteem it a great favor if I might have a short conversation with you, madam. I am Hector's father, as this bright Britisher would have guessed in the course of another hour or so.

Straker. [*Coolly defiant.*] No, not in another year or so. When weve ad you as long to polish up as weve ad im, perhaps youll begin to look a little bit up to is mark. At present you fall a long way short. Youve got too many aitches, for one thing. [*To* VIOLET, *amiably.*] All right, Miss: you want to talk to him: I shant intrude.

[*He nods affably to* MALONE *and goes out through the little gate in the paling.*]

Violet. [*Very civilly.*] I am sorry, Mr Malone, if that man has been rude to you. But what can we do? He is our chauffeur.

Malone. Your hwat?

Violet. The driver of our automobile. He can drive a motor car at seventy miles an hour, and mend it when it breaks down. We are dependent on our motor cars; and our motor cars are dependent on him; so of course we are dependent on him.

Malone. Ive noticed, madam, that every thousand dollars an Englishman gets seems to add one to the number of people he's dependent on. However, you neednt apologize for your man: I made him talk on purpose. By doing so I learnt that youre staying here in Grannida with a party of English, including my son Hector.

Violet. [*Conversationally.*] Yes. We intended to go to Nice; but we had to follow a rather eccentric member of our party who started first and came here. Wont you sit down?

[*She clears the nearest chair of the two books on it.*]

Malone. [*Impressed by this attention.*] Thank you. [*He sits down, examining her curiously as she goes to the iron table to put down the books. When she turns to him again, he says.*] Miss Robinson, I believe?

Violet. [*Sitting down.*] Yes.

Malone. [*Taking a letter from his pocket.*] Your note to Hector runs as follows. [*VIOLET is unable to repress a start. He pauses quietly to take out and put on his spectacles, which have gold rims.*] "Dearest: they have all gone to the Alhambra for the afternoon. I have shammed headache and have the garden all to myself. Jump into Jack's motor: Straker will rattle you here in a jiffy. Quick, quick, quick. Your loving Violet." [*He looks at her; but by this time she has recovered, and meets his spectacles with perfect composure. He continues slowly.*] Now I dont know on hwat terms young people associate in English society; but in America that note would be considered to imply a very considerable degree of affectionate intimacy between the parties.

Violet. Yes: I know your son very well, Mr Malone. Have you any objection?

Malone. [*Somewhat taken aback.*] No, no objection exactly. Provided it is understood that my son is altogether dependent on me, and that I have to be consulted in any important step he may propose to take.

Violet. I am sure you would not be unreasonable with him, Mr Malone.

Malone. I hope not, Miss Robinson; but at your age you might think many things unreasonable that dont seem so to me.

Violet. [*With a little shrug.*] Oh, well, I suppose theres no use our playing at cross purposes, Mr Malone. Hector wants to marry me.

Malone. I inferred from your note that he might. Well, Miss Robinson, he is his own master; but if he marries you he shall not have a rap from me.

[*He takes off his spectacles and pockets them with the note.*]

Violet. [*With some severity.*] That is not very complimentary to me, Mr Malone.

Malone. I say nothing against you, Miss Robinson: I daresay you are an amiable and excellent young lady. But I have other views for Hector.

Violet. Hector may not have other views for himself, Mr Malone.

Malone. Possibly not. Then he does without me: thats all. I daresay you are prepared for that. When a young lady writes to a young man to come to her quick, quick, quick, money seems nothing and love seems everything.

Violet. [*Sharply.*] I beg your pardon, Mr Malone: I do not think anything so foolish. Hector must have money.

Malone. [*Staggered.*] Oh, very well, very well. No doubt he can work for it.

Violet. What is the use of having money if you have to work for it? [*She rises impatiently.*] It's all nonsense, Mr. Malone: you must enable your son to keep up his position. It is his right.

Malone. [*Grimly.*] I should not advise you to marry him on the strength of that right, Miss Robinson.

[VIOLET, *who has almost lost her temper, controls herself with an effort; unclenches her fingers; and resumes her seat with studied tranquillity and reasonableness.*]

Violet. What objection have you to me, pray? My social position is as good as Hector's, to say the least. He admits it.

Malone. [*Shrewdly.*] You tell him so from time to time, eh? Hector's social position in England, Miss Robinson, is just what I choose to buy for him. I have made him a fair offer. Let him pick out the most historic house, castle, or abbey that England contains. The very day he tells me he wants it for a wife worthy of its traditions, I buy it for him, and give him the means of keeping it up.

Violet. What do you mean by a wife worthy of its traditions? Cannot any well bred woman keep such a house for him?

Malone. No: she must be born to it.

Violet. Hector was not born to it, was he?

Malone. His granmother was a barefooted Irish girl that nursed me by a turf fire. Let him marry another such, and I will not stint her marriage portion. Let him raise himself socially with my money or raise somebody else: so long as there is a social profit somewhere, I'll regard my expenditure as justified. But there must be a profit for someone. A marriage with you would leave things just where they are.

Violet. Many of my relations would object very much to my marrying the grandson of a common woman, Mr Malone. That may be prejudice; but so is your desire to have him marry a title prejudice.

Malone. [*Rising, and approaching her with a scrutiny in which there is a good deal of reluctant respect.*] You seem a pretty straightforward downright sort of a young woman.

Violet. I do not see why I should be made miserably poor because I cannot make profits for you. Why do you want to make Hector unhappy?

Malone. He will get over it right enough. Men thrive better on disappointments in love than disappointments in money. I daresay you think that sordid; but I know what I'm talking about. Me father died of starvation in Ireland in the black 47. Maybe youve heard of it.

Violet. The Famine?

Malone. [*With smouldering passion.*] No, the starvation. When a country is full o food, and exporting it, there can be no famine. Me father was starved dead; and I was starved out to America in me mother's arms. English rule drove me and mine out of Ireland. Well, you can keep Ireland. Me and me like are coming back to buy England; and we'll buy the best of it. I want no middle-class properties and no middle-class women for Hector. Thats straightforward, isnt it, like yourself?

Violet. [*Icily pitying his sentimentality.*] Really, Mr. Malone, I am astonished to hear a man of your age and good sense talking in that romantic way. Do you suppose English noblemen will sell their places to you for the asking?

Malone. I have the refusal of two of the oldest family mansions in England. One historic owner cant afford to keep all the rooms dusted: the other cant afford the death duties. What do you say now?

Violet. Of course it is very scandalous; but surely you know that the Government will sooner or later put a stop to all these Socialistic attacks on property.

Malone. [*Grinning.*] D'y'think they'll be able to get that done before I buy the house —or rather the abbey? Theyre both abbeys.

Violet. [*Putting that aside rather impatiently.*] Oh, well, let us talk sense, Mr Malone. You must feel that we havnt been talking sense so far.

Malone. I cant say I do. I mean all I say.

Violet. Then you dont know Hector as I do. He is romantic and faddy—he gets it from you, I fancy—and he wants a certain sort of wife to take care of him. Not a faddy sort of person, you know.

Malone. Somebody like you, perhaps?

Violet. [*Quietly.*] Well, yes. But you cannot very well ask me to undertake this with absolutely no means of keeping up his position.

Malone. [*Alarmed.*] Stop a bit, stop a bit. Where are we getting to? I'm not aware that I'm asking you to undertake anything.

Violet. Of course, Mr Malone, you can make it very difficult for me to speak to you if you choose to misunderstand me.

Malone. [*Half bewildered.*] I dont wish to take any unfair advantage; but we seem to have got off the straight track somehow.

[STRAKER, *with the air of a man who has been making haste, opens the little gate, and admits* HECTOR, *who, snorting with indignation, comes upon the lawn, and is making for his* FATHER *when* VIOLET, *greatly dismayed, springs up and intercepts him.* STRAKER *does not wait; at least he does not remain visibly within earshot.*]

Violet. Oh, how unlucky! Now please, Hector, say nothing. Go away until I have finished speaking to your father.

Hector. [*Inexorably.*] No, Violet: I mean to have this thing out, right away. [*He puts her aside; passes her by; and faces his* FATHER, *whose cheeks darken as his Irish blood begins to simmer.*] Dad: youve not played this hand straight.

Malone. Hwat d'y'mean?

Hector. Youve opened a letter addressed to me. Youve impersonated me and stolen a march on this lady. Thats disawnerable.

Malone. [*Threateningly.*] Now you take care what youre saying, Hector. Take care, I tell you.

Hector. I have taken care. I am taking care. I'm taking care of my honor and my position in English society.

Malone. [*Hotly.*] Your position has been got by my money: do you know that?

Hector. Well, youve just spoiled it all by opening that letter. A letter from an English lady, not addressed to you—a cawnfidential letter! a dullicate letter! a private letter! opened by my father! Thats a sort of thing a man cant struggle against in England. The sooner we go back together the better.

[*He appeals mutely to the heavens to witness the shame and anguish of two outcasts.*]

Violet. [*Snubbing him with an instinctive dislike for scene making.*] Dont be unreasonable, Hector. It was quite natural for Mr Malone to open my letter: his name was on the envelope.

Malone. There! Youve no common sense, Hector. I thank you, Miss Robinson.

Hector. I thank you, too. It's very kind of you. My father knows no better.

Malone. [*Furiously clenching his fists.*] Hector——

Hector. [*With undaunted moral force.*] Oh, it's no use hectoring me. A private letter's a private letter, dad: you cant get over that.

Malone. [*Raising his voice.*] I wont be talked back to by you, d'y'hear?

Violet. Ssh! please, please. Here they all come.

[FATHER *and* SON, *checked, glare mutely at one another as* TANNER *comes in through the little gate with* RAMSDEN, *followed by* OCTAVIUS *and* ANN.]

Violet. Back already!

Tanner. The Alhambra is not open this afternoon.

Violet. What a sell.

[TANNER *passes on, and presently finds himself between* HECTOR *and a strange* ELDER, *both apparently on the verge of personal combat. He looks from one to the other for an explanation. They sulkily avoid his eye, and nurse their wrath in silence.*]

Ramsden. Is it wise for you to be out in the sunshine with such a headache, Violet?

Tanner. Have you recovered too, Malone?

Violet. Oh, I forgot. We have not all met before. Mr. Malone: wont you introduce your father?

Hector. [*With Roman firmness.*] No, I will not. He is no father of mine.

Malone. [*Very angry.*] You disown your dad before your English friends, do you?

Violet. Oh, please dont make a scene.

[ANN *and* OCTAVIUS, *lingering near the gate, exchange an astonished glance, and discreetly withdraw up the steps to the garden, where they can enjoy the disturbance without intruding. On their way to the steps* ANN *sends a little grimace of mute sympathy to* VIOLET, *who is standing with her back to the little table, looking on in helpless annoyance as her husband soars to higher and*

*higher moral eminences without the least
regard to the* OLD MAN's *millions.*]

Hector. I'm very sorry, Miss Rawbnsn;
but I'm contending for a principle. I am a
son, and I hope, a dutiful one; but before
everything I'm a Mahn!!! And when dad
treats my private letters as his own, and
takes it on himself to say that I shant marry
you if I am happy and fortunate enough to
gain your consent, then I just snap my fingers and go my own way.

Tanner. Marry Violet!

Ramsden. Are you in your senses?

Tanner. Do you forget what we told you?

Hector. [*Recklessly.*] I dont care what
you told me.

Ramsden. [*Scandalized.*] Tut tut, sir!
Monstrous!

[*He flings away towards the gate, his
elbows quivering with indigation.*]

Tanner. Another madman! These men in
love should be locked up.

[*He gives* HECTOR *up as hopeless, and
turns away towards the garden; but* MA-
LONE, *taking offence in a new direction,
follows him and compels him, by the
aggressiveness of his tone, to stop.*]

Malone. I don't understand this. Is
Hector not good enough for this lady, pray?

Tanner. My dear sir, the lady is married
already. Hector knows it; and yet he persists
in his infatuation. Take him home and lock
him up.

Malone. [*Bitterly.*] So this is the high-
born social tone Ive spoilt be me ignorant,
uncultivated behavior! Makin love to a
married woman! [*He comes angrily between*
HECTOR *and* VIOLET, *and almost bawls into*
HECTOR's *left ear.*] Youve picked up that
habit of the British aristocracy, have you?

Hector. Thats all right. Dont you trouble
yourself about that. I'll answer for the
morality of what I'm doing.

Tanner. [*Coming forward to* HECTOR's
right hand with flashing eyes.] Well said,
Malone! You also see that mere marriage
laws are not morality! I agree with you;
but unfortunately Violet does not.

Malone. I take leave to doubt that, sir.
[*Turning on* VIOLET.] Let me tell you, Mrs
Robinson, or whatever your right name is,
you had no right to send that letter to my
son when you were the wife of another man.

Hector. [*Outraged.*] This is the last
straw. Dad: you have insulted my wife.

Malone. Your wife!

Tanner. You the missing husband! Another moral impostor!

[*He smites his brow, and collapses into*
MALONE's *chair.*]

Malone. Youve married without my consent!

Ramsden. You have deliberately hum-
bugged us, sir!

Hector. Here: I have had just enough of
being badgered. Violet and I are married:
thats the long and short of it. Now what
have you got to say—any of you?

Malone. I know what Ive got to say.
She's married a beggar.

Hector. No: she's married a Worker.
[*His American pronunciation imparts an
overwhelming intensity to this simple and
unpopular word.*] I start to earn my own
living this very afternoon.

Malone. [*Sneering angrily.*] Yes: youre
very plucky now, because you got your remittance from me yesterday or this morning,
I reckon. Waitl it's spent. You wont be so
full of cheek then.

Hector. [*Producing a letter from his
pocketbook.*] Here it is. [*Thrusting it on
his* FATHER.] Now you just take your remittance and yourself out of my life. I'm
done with remittances; and I'm done with
you. I dont sell the privilege of insulting my
wife for a thousand dollars.

Malone. [*Deeply wounded and full of
concern.*] Hector: you dont know what poverty is.

Hector. [*Fervidly.*] Well, I wawnt to
know what it is. I wawnt'be a Mahn. Violet,
you come along with me, to your own home:
I'll see you through.

Octavius. [*Jumping down from the garden
to the lawn and running to* HECTOR's *left
hand.*] I hope youll shake hands with me
before you go, Hector. I admire and respect
you more than I can say.

[*He is affected almost to tears as they
shake hands.*]

Violet. [*Also almost in tears, but of vexation.*] Oh, dont be an idiot, Tavy. Hector's
about as fit to become a workman as you are.

Tanner. [*Rising from his chair on the
other side of* HECTOR.] Never fear: theres
no question of his becoming a navvy,[1] Mrs
Malone. [*To* HECTOR.] Theres really no
difficulty about capital to start with. Treat
me as a friend: draw on me.

Octavius. [*Impulsively.*] Or on me.

Malone. [*With fierce jealousy.*] Who
wants your durty money? Who should he
draw on but his own father? [TANNER *and*
OCTAVIUS *recoil,* OCTAVIUS *rather hurt,* TAN-
NER *consoled by the solution of the money
difficulty.* VIOLET *looks up hopefully.*]

---

[1] Common laborer.

Hector: dont be rash, my boy. I'm sorry for what I said: I never meant to insult Violet: I take it all back. She's just the wife you want: there!

Hector. [*Patting him on the shoulder.*] Well, thats all right, dad. Say no more: we're friends again. Only, I take no money from anybody.

Malone. [*Pleading abjectly.*] Dont be hard on me, Hector. I'd rather you quarrelled and took the money than made friends and starved. You dont know what the world is: I do.

Hector. No, no, NO. Thats fixed: thats not going to change. [*He passes his* FATHER *inexorably by, and goes to* VIOLET.] Come, Mrs Malone: youve got to move to the hotel with me, and take your proper place before the world.

Violet. But I must go in, dear, and tell Davis to pack. Wont you go on and make them give you a room overlooking the garden for me? I'll join you in half an hour.

Hector. Very well. Youll dine with us, dad, wont you?

Malone. [*Eager to conciliate him.*] Yes, yes.

Hector. See you all later.

[*He waves his hand to* ANN, *who has now been joined by* TANNER, OCTAVIUS, *and* RAMSDEN *in the garden, and goes out through the little gate, leaving his* FATHER *and* VIOLET *together on the lawn.*]

Malone. Youll try to bring him to his senses, Violet: I know you will.

Violet. I had no idea he could be so headstrong. If he goes on like that, what can I do?

Malone. Dont be discurridged: domestic pressure may be slow; but it's sure. Youll wear him down. Promise me you will.

Violet. I will do my best. Of course I think it's the greatest nonsense deliberately making us poor like that.

Malone. Of course it is.

Violet. [*After a moment's reflection.*] You had better give me the remittance. He will want it for his hotel bill. I'll see whether I can induce him to accept it. Not now, of course, but presently.

Malone. [*Eagerly.*] Yes, yes, yes: thats just the thing. [*He hands her the thousand dollar bill, and adds cunningly.*] Y'understand that this is only a bachelor allowance.

Violet. [*Coolly.*] Oh, quite. [*She takes it.*] Thank you. By the way, Mr. Malone, those two houses you mentioned—the abbeys.

Malone. Yes?

Violet. Dont take one of them until Ive seen it. One never knows what may be wrong with these places.

Malone. I wont. I'll do nothing without consulting you, never fear.

Violet. [*Politely, but without a ray of gratitude.*] Thanks: that will be much the best way.

[*She goes calmly back to the villa, escorted obsequiously by* MALONE *to the upper end of the garden.*]

Tanner. [*Drawing* RAMSDEN's *attention to* MALONE's *cringing attitude as he takes leave of* VIOLET.] And that poor devil is a billionaire! one of the master spirits of the age! Led in a string like a pug dog by the first girl who takes the trouble to despise him! I wonder will it ever come to that with me. [*He comes down to the lawn.*]

Ramsden. [*Following him.*] The sooner the better for you.

Malone. [*Slapping his hands as he returns through the garden.*] That'll be a grand woman for Hector. I wouldn't exchange her for ten duchesses.

[*He descends to the lawn and comes between* TANNER *and* RAMSDEN.]

Ramsden. [*Very civil to the* BILLIONAIRE.] It's an unexpected pleasure to find you in this corner of the world, Mr Malone. Have you come to buy up the Alhambra?

Malone. Well, I dont say I mightnt. I think I could do better with it than the Spanish government. But thats not what I came about. To tell you the truth, about a month ago I overheard a deal between two men over a bundle of shares. They differed about the price: they were young and greedy, and didnt know that if the shares were worth what was bid for them they must be worth what was asked, the margin being too small to be of any account, you see. To amuse meself, I cut in and bought the shares. Well, to this day I havnt found out what the business is. The office is in this town; and the name is Mendoza, Limited. Now whether Mendoza's a mine, or a steamboat line, or a bank, or a patent article——

Tanner. He's a man. I know him: his principles are thoroughly commercial. Let us take you round the town in our motor, Mr Malone, and call on him on the way.

Malone. If youll be so kind, yes. And may I ask who——

Tanner. Mr Roebuck Ramsden, a very old friend of your daughter-in-law.

Malone. Happy to meet you, Mr Ramsden.

Ramsden. Thank you. Mr Tanner is also one of our circle.

Malone. Glad to know you also, Mr Tanner.

Tanner. Thanks. [MALONE *and* RAMSDEN *go out very amicably through the little gate.* TANNER *calls to* OCTAVIUS, *who is wandering in the garden with* ANN.] Tavy! [TAVY *comes to the steps,* TANNER *whispers loudly to him.*] Violet's father-in-law is a financier of brigands.

[TANNER *hurries away to overtake* MALONE *and* RAMSDEN. ANN *strolls to the steps with an idle impulse to torment* OCTAVIUS.]

Ann. Wont you go with them, Tavy?

Octavius. [*Tears suddenly flushing his eyes.*] You cut me to the heart, Ann, by wanting me to go.

[*He comes down on the lawn to hide his face from her. She follows him caressingly.*]

Ann. Poor Ricky Ticky Tavy! Poor heart!

Octavius. It belongs to you, Ann. Forgive me: I must speak of it. I love you. You know I love you.

Ann. What's the good, Tavy? You know that my mother is determined that I shall marry Jack.

Octavius. [*Amazed.*] Jack!

Ann. It seems absurd, doesnt it?

Octavius. [*With growing resentment.*] Do you mean to say that Jack has been playing with me all this time? That he has been urging me not to marry you because he intends to marry you himself?

Ann. [*Alarmed.*] No, no: you mustnt lead him to believe that I said that. I dont for a moment think that Jack knows his own mind. But it's clear from my father's will that he wished me to marry Jack. And my mother is set on it.

Octavius. But you are not bound to sacrifice yourself always to the wishes of your parents.

Ann. My father loved me. My mother loves me. Surely their wishes are a better guide than my own selfishness.

Octavius. Oh, I know how unselfish you are, Ann. But believe me—though I know I am speaking in my own interest—there is another side to this question. Is it fair to Jack to marry him if you do not love him? Is it fair to destroy my happiness as well as your own if you can bring yourself to love me?

Ann. [*Looking at him with a faint impulse of pity.*] Tavy, my dear, you are a nice creature—a good boy.

Octavius. [*Humiliated.*] Is that all?

Ann. [*Mischievously in spite of her pity.*] Thats a great deal, I assure you. You would always worship the ground I trod on, wouldnt you?

Octavius. I do. It sounds ridiculous; but it's no exaggeration. I do; and I always shall.

Ann. Always is a long word, Tavy. You see, I shall have to live up always to your idea of my divinity; and I dont think I could do that if we were married. But if I marry Jack, youll never be disillusioned—at least not until I grow too old.

Octavius. I too shall grow old, Ann. And when I am eighty, one white hair of the woman I love will make me tremble more than the thickest gold tress from the most beautiful young head.[1]

Ann. [*Quite touched.*] Oh, thats poetry, Tavy, real poetry. It gives me that strange sudden sense of an echo from a former existence which always seems to me such a striking proof that we have immortal souls.

Octavius. Do you believe that it is true?

Ann. Tavy: if it is to come true, you must lose me as well as love me.

Octavius. Oh!

[*He hastily sits down at the little table and covers his face with his hands.*]

Ann. [*With conviction.*] Tavy: I wouldnt for worlds destroy your illusions. I can neither take you nor let you go. I can see exactly what will suit you. You must be a sentimental old bachelor for my sake.

Octavius. [*Desperately.*] Ann: I'll kill myself.

Ann. Oh no, you wont: that wouldnt be kind. You wont have a bad time. You will be very nice to women; and you will go a good deal to the opera. A broken heart is a very pleasant complaint for a man in London if he has a comfortable income.

Octavius. [*Considerably cooled, but believing that he is only recovering his self-control.*] I know you mean to be kind, Ann. Jack has persuaded you that cynicism is a good tonic for me.

[*He rises with quiet dignity.*]

Ann. [*Studying him slyly.*] You see, I'm disillusionizing you already. Thats what I dread.

Octavius. You do not dread disillusionizing Jack.

Ann. [*Her face lighting up with mischievous ecstasy—whispering.*] I cant: he has no illusions about me. I shall surprise Jack the other way. Getting over an unfavorable im-

[1] See p. 197.

ression is ever so much easier than living
up to an ideal. Oh, I shall enrapture Jack
sometimes!

Octavius. [*Resuming the calm phase of
despair, and beginning to enjoy his broken
heart and delicate attitude without knowing
it.*] I don't doubt that. You will enrapture
him always. And he—the fool!—thinks you
would make him wretched.

Ann. Yes: thats the difficulty, so far.

Octavius. [*Heroically.*] Shall *I* tell him
hat you love him?

Ann. [*Quickly.*] Oh no: he'd run away
again.

Octavius. [*Shocked.*] Ann: would you
marry an unwilling man?

Ann. What queer creature you are, Tavy!
Theres no such thing as a willing man when
you really go for him. [*She laughs naugh-
tily.*] I'm shocking you, I suppose. But you
know you are really getting a sort of satisfaction already in being out of danger yourself.

Octavius. [*Startled.*] Satisfaction! [*Reproachfully.*] You say that to me!

Ann. Well, if it were really agony, would
you ask for more of it?

Octavius. Have I asked for more of it?

Ann. You have offered to tell Jack that I
love him. That's self-sacrifice, I suppose; but
there must be some satisfaction in it. Perhaps it's because youre a poet. You are like
the bird that presses its breast against the
sharp thorn to make itself sing.

Octavius. It's quite simple. I love you;
and I want you to be happy. You dont love
me; so I cant make you happy myself; but I
can help another man to do it.

Ann. Yes: it seems quite simple. But I
doubt if we ever know why we do things.
The only really simple thing is to go straight
for what you want and grab it. I suppose I
dont love you, Tavy; but sometimes I feel as
if I should like to make a man of you somehow. You are very foolish about women.

Octavius. [*Almost coldly.*] I am content
to be what I am in that respect.

Ann. Then you must keep away from
them, and only dream about them. I wouldnt
marry you for worlds, Tavy.

Octavius. I have no hope, Ann: I accept
my ill luck. But I dont think you quite know
how much it hurts.

Ann. You are so softhearted! It's queer
that you should be so different from Violet.
Violet's as hard as nails.

Octavius. Oh no. I am sure Violet is
thoroughly womanly at heart.

Ann. [*With some impatience.*] Why do
you say that? Is it unwomanly to be

thoughtful and businesslike and sensible?
Do you want Violet to be an idiot—or something worse, like me?

Octavius. Something worse—like you!
What do you mean, Ann?

Ann. Oh well, I dont mean that, of course.
But I have a great respect for Violet. She
gets her own way always.

Octavius. [*Sighing.*] So do you.

Ann. Yes; but somehow she gets it without coaxing—without having to make people
sentimental about her.

Octavius. [*With brotherly callousness.*]
Nobody could get very sentimental about
Violet, I think, pretty as she is.

Ann. Oh yes they could, if she made them.

Octavius. But surely no really nice woman
would deliberately practice on men's instincts
in that way.

Ann. [*Throwing up her hands.*] Oh, Tavy,
Tavy, Ricky Ticky Tavy, heaven help the
woman who marries you!

Octavius. [*His passion reviving at the
name.*] Oh why, why, why do you say that?
Dont torment me. I dont understand.

Ann. Suppose she were to tell fibs, and lay
snares for men?

Octavius. Do you think *I* could marry
such a woman—I, who have known and loved
you?

Ann. Hm! Well, at all events, she wouldnt
let you if she were wise. So thats settled.
And now I cant talk any more. Say you forgive me, and that the subject is closed.

Octavius. I have nothing to forgive; and
the subject is closed. And if the wound is
open, at least you shall never see it bleed.

Ann. Poetic to the last, Tavy. Goodbye,
dear.

[*She pats his cheek; has an impulse to
kiss him and then another impulse of
distaste which prevents her; finally runs
away through the garden and into the
villa.* OCTAVIUS *again takes refuge at
the table, bowing his head on his arms
and sobbing softly.* MRS WHITEFIELD,
*who has been pottering round the Gra-
nada shops and has a net full of little
parcels in her hand, comes in through
the gate and sees him.*]

Mrs Whitefield. [*Running to him and lifting his head.*] What's the matter, Tavy?
Are you ill?

Octavius. No, nothing, nothing.

Mrs Whitefield. [*Still holding his head,
anxiously.*] But youre crying. Is it about
Violet's marriage?

Octavius. No, no. Who told you about
Violet?

Mrs Whitefield. [*Restoring the head to its

owner.] I met Roebuck and that awful old Irishman. Are you sure youre not ill? Whats the matter?

Octavius. [*Affectionately.*] It's nothing. Only a man's broken heart. Doesnt that sound ridiculous?

Mrs Whitefield. But what is it all about? Has Ann been doing anything to you?

Octavius. It's not Ann's fault. And dont think for a moment that I blame you.

Mrs Whitefield. [*Startled.*] For what?

Octavius. [*Pressing her hand consolingly.*] For nothing. I said I didn't blame you.

Mrs Whitefield. But I havnt done anything. Whats the matter?

Octavius. [*Smiling sadly.*] Cant you guess? I daresay you are right to prefer Jack to me as a husband for Ann; but I love Ann; and it hurts rather.

[*He rises and moves away from her towards the middle of the lawn.*]

Mrs Whitefield. [*Following him hastily.*] Does Ann say that I want her to marry Jack?

Octavius. Yes, she has told me.

Mrs Whitefield. [*Thoughtfully.*] Then I'm very sorry for you, Tavy. It's only her way of saying she wants to marry Jack. Little she cares what *I* say or what *I* want!

Octavius. But she would not say it unless she believed it. Surely you dont suspect Ann of—of deceit!!

Mrs Whitefield. Well, never mind, Tavy. I dont know which is best for a young man: to know too little, like you, or too much, like Jack.   [TANNER *returns.*]

Tanner. Well, Ive disposed of old Malone. Ive introduced him to Mendoza, Limited; and left the two brigands together to talk it out. Hullo, Tavy! anything wrong?

Octavius. I must go wash my face, I see. [*To* MRS WHITEFIELD.] Tell him what you wish. [*To* TANNER.] You may take it from me, Jack, that Ann approves of it.

Tanner. [*Puzzled by his manner.*] Approves of what?

Octavius. Of what Mrs Whitefield wishes.

[*He goes his way with sad dignity to the villa.*]

Tanner. [*To* MRS WHITEFIELD.] This is very mysterious. What is it you wish? It shall be done, whatever it is.

Mrs Whitefield. [*With snivelling gratitude.*] Thank you, Jack. [*She sits down.* TANNER *brings the other chair from the table and sits close to her with his elbows on his knees, giving her his whole attention.*] I dont know why it is that other people's children are so nice to me, and that my own have so little consideration of me. It's no wonder I dont seem able to care for Ann and Rhoda as I do for you and Tavy and Violet. It's a very queer world. It used to be so straightforward and simple; and now nobody seems to think and feel as they ought. Nothing has been right since that speech that Professor Tyndall made at Belfast.[1]

Tanner. Yes: life is more complicated than we used to think. But what am I to do for you?

Mrs Whitefield. Thats just what I want to tell you. Of course youll marry Ann whether I like it or not——

Tanner. [*Starting.*] It seems to me that I shall presently be married to Ann whether I like it myself or not.

Mrs Whitefield. [*Peacefully.*] Oh, very likely you will: you know what she is when she has set her mind on anything. But dont put it on me: thats all I ask. Tavy has just let out that she's been saying that I am making her marry you; and the poor boy is breaking his heart about it; for he is in love with her himself, though what he sees in her so wonderful, goodness knows: *I* dont. It's no use telling Tavy that Ann puts things into people's heads by telling them that I want them when the thought of them never crossed my mind. It only sets Tavy against me. But you know better than that. So if you marry her, dont put the blame on me.

Tanner. [*Emphatically.*] I havnt the slightest intention of marrying her.

Mrs Whitefield. [*Slyly.*] She'd suit you better than Tavy. She'd meet her match in you, Jack. I'd like to see her meet her match.

Tanner. No man is a match for a woman, except with a poker and a pair of hobnailed boots. Not always even then. Anyhow, *I* cant take the poker to her. I should be a mere slave.

Mrs Whitefield. No: she's afraid of you. At all events, you would tell her the truth about herself. She wouldnt be able to slip out of it as she does with me.

Tanner. Everybody would call me a brute if I told Ann the truth about herself in terms of her own moral code. To begin with, Ann says things that are not strictly true.

Mrs Whitefield. I'm glad somebody sees she is not an angel.

Tanner. In short—to put it as a husband would put it when exasperated to the point of speaking out—she is a liar. And since she has plunged Tavy head over ears in love with her without any intention of marrying him, she is a coquette, according to the

---

[1] As president of the British Association, John Tyndall spoke on science and religion in 1874.

standard definition of a coquette as a woman who rouses passions she has no intention of gratifying. And as she has now reduced you to the point of being willing to sacrifice me at the altar for the mere satisfaction of getting me to call her a liar to her face, I may conclude that she is a bully as well. She cant bully men as she bullies women; so she habitually and unscrupulously uses her personal fascination to make men give her whatever she wants. That makes her almost something for which I know no polite name.

Mrs Whitefield. [*In mild expostulation.*] Well, you cant expect perfection, Jack.

Tanner. I dont. But what annoys me is that Ann does. I know perfectly well that all this about her being a liar and a bully and a coquette and so forth is a trumped-up moral indictment which might be brought against anybody. We all lie; we all bully as much as we dare; we all bid for admiration without the least intention of earning it; we all get as much rent as we can out of our powers of fascination. If Ann would admit this I shouldnt quarrel with her. But she wont. If she has children she'll take advantage of their telling lies to amuse herself by whacking them. If another woman makes eyes at me, she'll refuse to know a coquette. She will do just what she likes herself whilst insisting on everybody else doing what the conventional code prescribes. In short, I can stand everything except her confounded hypocrisy. Thats what beats me.

Mrs Whitefield. [*Carried away by the relief of hearing her own opinion so eloquently expressed.*] Oh, she is a hypocrite. She is: she is. Isnt she?

Tanner. Then why do you want to marry me to her?

Mrs Whitefield. [*Querulously.*] There now! put it on me, of course. I never thought of it until Tavy told me she said I did. But, you know, I'm very fond of Tavy; he's a sort of son to me; and I dont want him to be trampled on and made wretched.

Tanner. Whereas I dont matter, I suppose.

Mrs Whitefield. Oh, you are different, somehow: you are able to take care of yourself. Youd serve her out. And anyhow, she must marry somebody.

Tanner. Aha! there speaks the life instinct. You detest her; but you feel that you must get her married.

Mrs Whitefield. [*Rising, shocked.*] Do you mean that I detest my own daughter? Surely you dont believe me to be so wicked and unnatural as that, merely because I see her faults.

Tanner. [*Cynically.*] You love her then?

Mrs Whitefield. Why, of course I do. What queer things you say, Jack! We cant help loving our own blood relations.

Tanner. Well, perhaps it saves unpleasantness to say so. But for my part, I suspect that the tables of consanguinity have a natural basis in a natural repugnance.

[*He rises.*]

Mrs Whitefield. You shouldnt say things like that, Jack. I hope you wont tell Ann that I have been speaking to you. I only wanted to set myself right with you and Tavy. I couldnt sit mumchance and have everything put on me.

Tanner. [*Politely.*] Quite so.

Mrs Whitefield. [*Dissatisfied.*] And now Ive only made matters worse. Tavy's angry with me because I dont worship Ann. And when it's been put into my head that Ann ought to marry you, what can I say except that it would serve her right?

Tanner. Thank you.

Mrs Whitefield. Now dont be silly and twist what I say into something I dont mean. I ought to have fair play——

[ANN *comes from the villa, followed presently by* VIOLET, *who is dressed for driving.*]

Ann. [*Coming to her* MOTHER'S *right hand with threatening suavity.*] Well, mamma darling, you seem to be having a delightful chat with Jack. We can hear you all over the place.

Mrs Whitefield. [*Appalled.*] Have you overheard——

Tanner. Never fear: Ann is only—well, we were discussing that habit of hers just now. She hasnt heard a word.

Mrs Whitefield. [*Stoutly.*] I dont care whether she has or not: I have a right to say what I please.

Violet. [*Arriving on the lawn and coming between* MRS WHITEFIELD *and* TANNER.] Ive come to say goodbye. I'm off for my honeymoon.

Mrs Whitefield. [*Crying.*] Oh, dont say that, Violet. And no wedding, no breakfast, no clothes, nor anything.

Violet. [*Petting her.*] It wont be for long.

Mrs Whitefield. Dont let him take you to America. Promise me that you wont.

Violet. [*Very decidedly.*] I should think not, indeed. Dont cry, dear: I'm only going to the hotel.

Mrs Whitefield. But going in that dress, with your luggage, makes one realize—— [*She chokes, and then breaks out again.*] How I wish you were my daughter, Violet!

Violet. [*Soothing her.*] There, there: so I am. Ann will be jealous.

Mrs Whitefield. Ann doesnt care a bit for me.

Ann. Fie, mother! Come, now: you mustnt cry any more: you know Violet doesnt like it.

[MRS WHITEFIELD *dries her eyes, and subsides.*]

Violet. Goodbye, Jack.

Tanner. Goodbye, Violet.

Violet. The sooner you get married too, the better. You will be much less misunderstood.

Tanner. [*Restively.*] I quite expect to get married in the course of the afternoon. You all seem to have set your minds on it.

Violet. You might do worse. [*To* MRS WHITEFIELD: *putting her arm round her.*] Let me take you to the hotel with me: the drive will do you good. Come in and get a wrap. [*She takes her towards the villa.*]

Mrs Whitefield. [*As they go up through the garden.*] I dont know what I shall do when you are gone, with no one but Ann in the house; and she always occupied with the men! It's not to be expected that your husband will care to be bothered with an old woman like me. Oh, you neednt tell me: politeness is all very well; but I know what people think——

[*She talks herself and* VIOLET *out of sight and hearing.* ANN, *alone with* TANNER, *watches him and waits. He makes an irresolute movement towards the gate; but some magnetism in her draws him to her, a broken man.*]

Ann. Violet is quite right. You ought to get married.

Tanner. [*Explosively.*] Ann: I will not marry you. Do you hear? I wont, wont, wont, wont, WONT marry you.

Ann. [*Placidly.*] Well, nobody axd you, sir she said, sir she said, sir she said. So thats settled.

Tanner. Yes, nobody has asked me; but everybody treats the thing as settled. It's in the air. When we meet, the others go away on absurd pretexts to leave us alone together. Ramsden no longer scowls at me: his eye beams, as if he were already giving you away to me in church. Tavy refers me to your mother and gives me his blessing. Straker openly treats you as his future employer: it was he who first told me of it.

Ann. Was that why you ran away?

Tanner. Yes, only to be stopped by a lovesick brigand and run down like a truant schoolboy.

Ann. Well, if you dont want to be married, you neednt be.

[*She turns away from him and sits down, much at her ease.*]

Tanner. [*Following her.*] Does any man want to be hanged? Yet men let themselves be hanged without a struggle for life, though they could at least give the chaplain a black eye. We do the world's will, not our own. I have a frightful feeling that I shall let myself be married because it is the world's will that you should have a husband.

Ann. I daresay I shall, someday.

Tanner. But why me? me of all men! Marriage is to me apostasy, profanation of the sanctuary of my soul, violation of my manhood, sale of my birthright, shameful surrender, ignominious capitulation, acceptance of defeat. I shall decay like a thing that has served its purpose and is done with; I shall change from a man with a future to a man with a past; I shall see in the greasy eyes of all the other husbands their relief at the arrival of a new prisoner to share their ignominy. The young men will scorn me as one who has sold out: to the women I, who have always been an enigma and a possibility, shall be merely somebody else's property —and damaged goods at that: a second-hand man at best.

Ann. Well, your wife can put on a cap and make herself ugly to keep you in countenance, like my grandmother.

Tanner. So that she may make her triumph more insolent by publicly throwing away the bait the moment the trap snaps on the victim!

Ann. After all, though, what difference would it make? Beauty is all very well at first sight; but who ever looks at it when it has been in the house three days? I thought our pictures very lovely when papa bought them; but I havnt looked at them for years. You never bother about my looks: you are too well used to me. I might be the umbrella stand.

Tanner. You lie, you vampire: you lie.

Ann. Flatterer. Why are you trying to fascinate me, Jack, if you dont want to marry me?

Tanner. The Life Force. I am in the grip of the Life Force.

Ann. I dont understand in the least: it sounds like the Life Guards.

Tanner. Why dont you marry Tavy? He is willing. Can you not be satisfied unless your prey struggles?

Ann. [*Turning to him as if to let him into a secret.*] Tavy will never marry.

Havnt you noticed that that sort of man never marries?

Tanner. What! a man who idolizes women! who sees nothing in nature but romantic scenery for love duets! Tavy, the chivalrous, the faithful, the tenderhearted and true! Tavy never marry! Why, he was born to be swept up by the first pair of blue eyes he meets in the street.

Ann. Yes, I know. All the same, Jack, men like that always live in comfortable bachelor lodgings with broken hearts, and are adored by their landladies, and never get married. Men like you always get married.

Tanner. [*Smiting his brow.*] How frightfully, horribly true! It has been staring me in the face all my life; and I never saw it before.

Ann. Oh, it's the same with women. The poetic temperament's a very nice temperament, very amiable, very harmless and poetic, I daresay; but it's an old maid's temperament.

Tanner. Barren. The Life Force passes it by.

Ann. If thats what you mean by the Life Force, yes.

Tanner. You dont care for Tavy?

Ann. [*Looking round carefully to make sure that* TAVY *is not within earshot.*] No.

Tanner. And you do care for me?

Ann. [*Rising quietly and shaking her finger at him.*] Now, Jack! Behave yourself.

Tanner. Infamous, abandoned woman! Devil!

Ann. Boa-constrictor! Elephant!

Tanner. Hypocrite!

Ann. [*Softly.*] I must be, for my future husband's sake.

Tanner. For mine! [*Correcting himself savagely.*] I mean for his.

Ann. [*Ignoring the correction.*] Yes, for yours. You had better marry what you call a hypocrite, Jack. Women who are not hypocrites go about in rational dress and are insulted and get into all sorts of hot water. And then their husbands get dragged in too, and live in continual dread of fresh complications. Wouldnt you prefer a wife you could depend on?

Tanner. No: a thousand times no: hot water is the revolutionist's element. You clean men as you clean milkpails, by scalding them.

Ann. Cold water has its uses too. It's healthy.

Tanner. [*Despairingly.*] Oh, you are witty: at the supreme moment the Life Force endows you with every quality. Well, I too can be a hypocrite. Your father's will appointed me your guardian, not your suitor. I shall be faithful to my trust.

Ann. [*In low siren tones.*] He asked me who I would have as my guardian before he made that will. I chose you!

Tanner. The will is yours then! The trap was laid from the beginning.

Ann. [*Concentrating all her magic.*] From the beginning—from our childhood—for both of us—by the Life Force.

Tanner. I will not marry you. I will not marry you.

Ann. Oh, you will, you will.

Tanner. I tell you, no, no, no.

Ann. I tell you, yes, yes, yes.

Tanner. No.

Ann. [*Coaxing—imploring—almost exhausted.*] Yes. Before it is too late for repentance. Yes.

Tanner. [*Struck by the echo from the past.*] When did all this happen to me before? Are we two dreaming?

Ann. [*Suddenly losing her courage, with an anguish that she does not conceal.*] No. We are awake; and you have said no: that is all.

Tanner. [*Brutally.*] Well?

Ann. Well, I made a mistake: you do not love me.

Tanner. [*Seizing her in his arms.*] It is false. I love you. The Life Force enchants me. I have the whole world in my arms when I clasp you. But I am fighting for my freedom, for my honor, for my self, one and indivisible.

Ann. Your happiness will be worth them all.

Tanner. You would sell freedom and honor and self for happiness?

Ann. It will not be all happiness for me. Perhaps death.

Tanner. [*Groaning.*] Oh, that clutch holds and hurts. What have you grasped in me? Is there a father's heart as well as a mother's?

Ann. Take care, Jack: if anyone comes while we are like this, you will have to marry me.

Tanner. If we two stood now on the edge of a precipice, I would hold you tight and jump.

Ann. [*Panting, failing more and more under the strain.*] Jack: let me go. I have dared so frightfully—it is lasting longer than I thought. Let me go: I cant bear it.

Tanner. Nor I. Let it kill us.

Ann. Yes: I don't care. I am at the end of my forces. I dont care. I think I am going to faint.

[*At this moment* VIOLET *and* OCTAVIUS *come from the villa with* MRS WHITE- FIELD, *who is wrapped up for driving. Simultaneously* MALONE *and* RAMSDEN, *followed by* MENDOZA *and* STRAKER, *come in through the little gate in the paling.* TANNER *shamefacedly releases* ANN, *who raises her hand giddily to her forehead.*]

Malone. Take care. Something's the matter with the lady.

Ramsden. What does this mean?

Violet. [*Running between* ANN *and* TAN- NER.] Are you ill?

Ann. [*Reeling, with a supreme effort.*] I have promised to marry Jack.

[*She swoons.* VIOLET *kneels by her and chafes her hand.* TANNER *runs round to her other hand, and tries to lift her head.* OCTAVIUS *goes to* VIOLET'S *assistance, but does not know what to do.* MRS WHITEFIELD *hurries back into the villa.* OCTAVIUS, MALONE, *and* RAMS- DEN *run to* ANN *and crowd round her, stooping to assist.* STRAKER *coolly comes to* ANN'S *feet, and* MENDOZA *to her head, both upright and self-possessed.*]

Straker. Now then, ladies and gentlemen: she dont want a crowd round her: she wants air—all the air she can git. If you please, gents—— [MALONE *and* RAMSDEN *allow him to drive them gently past* ANN *and up to the lawn towards the garden, where* OCTAVIUS, *who has already become conscious of his uselessness, joins them.* STRAKER, *following them up, pauses for a moment to instruct* TANNER.] Don't lift er ed, Mr Tanner: let it go flat so's the blood can run back into it.

Mendoza. He is right, Mr Tanner. Trust to the air of the Sierra.

[*He withdraws delicately to the garden steps.*]

Tanner. [*Rising.*] I yield to your superior knowledge of physiology, Henry.

[*He withdraws to the corner of the lawn; and* OCTAVIUS *immediately hurries down to him.*]

Tavy. [*Aside to* TANNER, *grasping his hand.*] Jack: be very happy.

Tanner. [*Aside to* TAVY.] I never asked her. It is a trap for me.

[*He goes up the lawn towards the garden.* OCTAVIUS *remains petrified.*]

Mendoza. [*Intercepting* MRS WHITE-

FIELD, *who comes from the villa with a glass of brandy.*] What is this, madam?

[*He takes it from her.*]

Mrs Whitefield. A little brandy.

Mendoza. The worst thing you could give her. Allow me. [*He swallows it.*] Trust to the air of the Sierra, madam.

[*For a moment the* MEN *all forget* ANN *and stare at* MENDOZA.]

Ann. [*In* VIOLET'S *ear, clutching her round the neck.*] Violet: did Jack say anything when I fainted?

Violet. No.

Ann. Ah!

[*With a sigh of intense relief she relapses.*]

Mrs Whitefield. Oh, she's fainted again.

[*They are about to rush back to her; but* MENDOZA *stops them with a warning gesture.*]

Ann. [*Supine.*] No, I havnt. I'm quite happy.

Tanner. [*Suddenly walking determinedly to her, and snatching her hand from* VIOLET *to feel her pulse.*] Why, her pulse is positively bounding. Come! get up. What nonsense! Up with you.

[*He hauls her up summarily.*]

Ann. Yes: I feel strong enough now. But you very nearly killed me, Jack, for all that.

Malone. A rough wooer, eh? Theyre the best sort, Miss Whitefield. I congratulate Mr Tanner; and I hope to meet you and him as frequent guests at the abbey.

Ann. Thank you. [*She goes past* MALONE *to* OCTAVIUS.] Ricky Ticky Tavy: congratulate me. [*Aside to him.*] I want to make you cry for the last time.

Tavy. [*Steadfastly.*] No more tears. I am happy in your happiness. And I believe in you in spite of everything.

Ramsden. [*Coming between* MALONE *and* TANNER.] You are a happy man, Jack Tanner. I envy you.

Mendoza. [*Advancing between* VIOLET *and* TANNER.] Sir: there are two tragedies in life. One is to lose your heart's desire. The other is to gain it.[1] Mine and yours, sir.

Tanner. Mr Mendoza: I have no heart's desires. Ramsden: it is very easy for you to call me a happy man: you are only a spectator. I am one of the principals; and I know better. Ann: stop tempting Tavy, and come back to me.

[1] "In this world there are only two tragedies. One is not getting what one wants, and the other is getting it." Dumby in Act III of Oscar Wilde's *Lady Winder- mere's Fan* (1892).

Ann. [*Complying.*] You are absurd, Jack.
[*She takes his offered arm.*]

Tanner. [*Continuing.*] I solemnly say that I am not a happy man. Ann looks happy; but she is only triumphant, successful, victorious. That is not happiness, but the price for which the strong sell their happiness. What we have both done this afternoon is to renounce happiness, renounce freedom, renounce tranquillity, above all, renounce the romantic possibilities of an unknown future, for the cares of a household and a family. I beg that no man may seize the occasion to get half drunk and utter imbecile speeches and coarse pleasantries at my expense. We propose to furnish our own house according to our own taste; and I hereby give notice that the seven or eight travelling clocks, the four or five dressing cases, the carvers and fish slicers, the copies of Patmore's *Angel In The House* in extra morocco, and the other articles you are preparing to heap upon us, will be instantly sold, and the proceeds devoted to circulating free copies of the *Revolutionist's Handbook*. The wedding will take place three days after our return to England, by special licence, at the office of the district superintendent registrar, in the presence of my solicitor and his clerk, who, like his clients, will be in ordinary walking dress——

Violet. [*With intense conviction.*] You are a brute, Jack.

Ann. [*Looking at him with fond pride and caressing his arm.*] Never mind her, dear. Go on talking.

Tanner. Talking! [*Universal laughter.*]

>>>>>>>>>>>>>>>>>>>>>>>>>><<<<<<<<<<<<<<<<<<<<<<<<<

THE REVOLUTIONIST'S HANDBOOK AND POCKET COMPANION

By

JOHN TANNER, M.I.R.C.

(*Member of the Idle Rich Class*)

PREFACE TO THE REVOLUTIONIST'S HANDBOOK

"No one can contemplate the present condition of the masses of the people without desiring something like a revolution for the better." SIR ROBERT GIFFEN: *Essays in Finance,* vol. ii. p. 393.

FOREWORD

A REVOLUTIONIST IS ONE WHO DESIRES to discard the existing social order and try another.

The constitution of England is revolutionary. To a Russian or Anglo-Indian bureaucrat, a general election is as much a revolution as a referendum or plebiscite in which the people fight instead of voting. The French Revolution overthrew one set of rulers and substituted another with different interests and different views. That is what a general election enables the people to do in England every seven years if they choose. Revolution is therefore a national institution in England; and its advocacy by an Englishman needs no apology.

Every man is a revolutionist concerning the thing he understands. For example, every person who has mastered a profession is a sceptic concerning it, and consequently a revolutionist.

Every genuine religious person is a heretic and therefore a revolutionist.

All who achieve real distinction in life begin as revolutionists. The most distinguished persons become more revolutionary as they grow older, though they are commonly supposed to become more conservative owing to their loss of faith in conventional methods of reform.

Any person under the age of thirty, who, having any knowledge of the existing social order, is not a revolutionist, is an inferior.

AND YET

Revolutions have never lightened the burden of tyranny: they have only shifted it to another shoulder.

JOHN TANNER.

THE REVOLUTIONIST'S HANDBOOK

I

ON GOOD BREEDING

IF THERE WERE NO GOD, SAID THE EIGHTeenth century Deist, it would be necessary to invent Him. Now this XVIII century god was *deus ex machina,* the god who helped those who could not help themselves, the god of the lazy and incapable. The nineteenth century decided that there is indeed no such god; and now Man must take in hand all the work that he used to shirk with an idle prayer. He must, in effect, change himself into the political Providence which he formerly conceived as god; and such change is not only possible, but the only sort of change that is real. The mere transfiguration of institutions, as from military and priestly dominance to commercial and scientific dominance, from commercial dominance to proletarian democracy, from slavery to serfdom, from serfdom to capitalism, from monarchy to republicanism,

218

from polytheism to monotheism, from monotheism to atheism, from atheism to pantheistic humanitarianism, from general illiteracy to general literacy, from romance to realism, from realism to mysticism, from metaphysics to physics, are all but changes from Tweedledum to Tweedledee: *plus ça change, plus c'est la même chose.*[1] But the changes from the crab apple to the pippin, from the wolf and fox to the house dog, from the charger of Henry V to the brewer's draught horse and the racehorse, are real; for here Man has played the god, subduing Nature to his intention, and ennobling or debasing Life for a set purpose. And what can be done with a wolf can be done with a man. If such monsters as the tramp and the gentleman can appear as mere by-products of Man's individual greed and folly, what might we not hope for as a main product of his universal aspiration?

This is no new conclusion. The despair of institutions, and the inexorable "ye must be born again," with Mrs Poyser's[2] stipulation, "and born different," recurs in every generation. The cry for the Superman did not begin with Nietzsche, nor will it end with his vogue. But it has always been silenced by the same question: what kind of person is this Superman to be? You ask, not for a super-apple, but for an eatable apple; not for a super-horse, but for a horse of greater draught or velocity. Neither is it of any use to ask for a Superman: you must furnish a specification of the sort of man you want. Unfortunately you do not know what sort of man you want. Some sort of good-looking philosopher-athlete, with a handsome healthy woman for his mate, perhaps.

Vague as this is, it is a great advance on the popular demand for a perfect gentleman and a perfect lady. And, after all, no market demand in the world takes the form of exact technical specification of the article required. Excellent poultry and potatoes are produced to satisfy the demand of housewives who do not know the technical differences between a tuber and a chicken. They will tell you that the proof of the pudding is in the eating; and they are right. The proof of the Superman will be in the living; and we shall find out how to produce him by the old method of trial and error, and not by waiting for a completely convincing prescription of his ingredients.

Certain common and obvious mistakes may be ruled out from the beginning. For example, we agree that we want superior mind; but we need not fall into the football club folly of counting on this as a product of superior body. Yet if we recoil so far as to conclude that superior mind consists in being the dupe of our ethical classifications of virtues and vices, in short, of conventional morality, we shall fall out of the frying-pan of the football club into the fire of the Sunday School. If we must choose between a race of athletes and a race of "good" men, let us have the athletes: better Samson and Milo[1] than Calvin and Robespierre. But neither alternative is worth changing for: Samson is no more a Superman than Calvin. What then are we to do?

II

PROPERTY AND MARRIAGE

Let us hurry over the obstacles set up by property and marriage. Revolutionists make too much of them. No doubt it is easy to demonstrate that property will destroy society unless society destroys it. No doubt, also, property has hitherto held its own and destroyed all the empires. But that was because the superficial objection to it (that it distributes social wealth and the social labor burden in a grotesquely inequitable manner) did not threaten the existence of the race, but only the individual happiness of its units, and finally the maintenance of some irrelevant political form or other, such as a nation, an empire, or the like. Now as happiness never matters to Nature, as she neither recognizes flags and frontiers nor cares a straw whether the economic system adopted by a society is feudal, capitalistic, or collectivist, provided it keeps the race afoot (the hive and the anthill being as acceptable to her as Utopia), the demonstrations of Socialists, though irrefutable, will never make any serious impressions on property. The knell of that overrated institution will not sound until it is felt to conflict with some more vital matter than mere personal inequities in industrial economy. No such conflict was perceived whilst society had not yet grown beyond national communities too small and simple to overtax Man's limited political capacity disastrously. But we have now reached the stage of international organization. Man's political capacity and magnanimity are clearly beaten by the vastness and complexity of the problems forced on him. And it is at this anxious mo-

---

[1] "The more it changes, the more it remains the same."

[2] In George Eliot's *Adam Bede.*

---

[1] Milo of Crotona, six times champion wrestler at the Olympic Games in the sixth century B. C.

ment that he finds, when he looks upward for a mightier mind to help him, that the heavens are empty. He will presently see that his discarded formula that Man is the Temple of the Holy Ghost happens to be precisely true, and that it is only through his own brain and hand that this Holy Ghost, formally the most nebulous person in the Trinity, and now become its sole survivor as it has always been its real Unity, can help him in any way. And so, if the Superman is to come, he must be born of Woman by Man's intentional and well-considered contrivance. Conviction of this will smash everything that opposes it. Even Property and Marriage, which laugh at the laborer's petty complaint that he is defrauded of "surplus value," and at the domestic miseries of the slaves of the wedding ring, will themselves be laughed aside as the lightest of trifles if they cross this conception when it becomes a fully realized vital purpose of the race.

That they must cross it becomes obvious the moment we acknowledge the futility of breeding men for special qualities as we breed cocks for game, greyhounds for speed, or sheep for mutton. What is really important in Man is the part of him that we do not yet understand. Of much of it we are not even conscious, just as we are not normally conscious of keeping up our circulation by our heart-pump, though if we neglect it we die. We are therefore driven to the conclusion that when we have carried selection as far as we can by rejecting from the list of eligible parents all persons who are uninteresting, unpromising, or blemished without any set-off, we shall still have to trust to the guidance of fancy (*alias* Voice of Nature), both in the breeders and the parents, for that superiority in the unconscious self which will be the true characteristic of the Superman.

At this point we perceive the importance of giving fancy the widest possible field. To cut humanity up into small cliques, and effectively limit the selection of the individual to his own clique, is to postpone the Superman for eons, if not forever. Not only should every person be nourished and trained as a possible parent, but there should be no possibility of such an obstacle to natural selection as the objection of a countess to a navvy or of a duke to a charwoman. Equality is essential to good breeding; and equality, as all economists know, is incompatible with property.

Besides, equality is an essential condition of bad breeding also; and bad breeding is indispensable to the weeding out of the human race. When the conception of heredity took hold of the scientific imagination in the middle of last century, its devotees announced that it was a crime to marry the lunatic to the lunatic or the consumptive to the consumptive. But pray are we to try to correct our diseased stocks by infecting our healthy stocks with them? Clearly the attraction which disease has for diseased people is beneficial to the race. If two really unhealthy people get married, they will, as likely as not, have a great number of children who will all die before they reach maturity. This is a far more satisfactory arrangement than the tragedy of a union between a healthy and an unhealthy person. Though more costly than sterilization of the unhealthy, it has the enormous advantage that in the event of our notions of health and unhealth being erroneous (which to some extent they most certainly are), the error will be corrected by experience instead of confirmed by evasion.

One fact must be faced resolutely, in spite of the shrieks of the romantic. There is no evidence that the best citizens are the offspring of congenial marriages, or that a conflict of temperament is not a highly important part of what breeders call crossing. On the contrary, it is quite sufficiently probable that good results may be obtained from parents who would be extremely unsuitable companions and partners, to make it certain that the experiment of mating them will sooner or later be tried purposely almost as often as it is now tried accidentally. But mating such couples must clearly not involve marrying them. In conjugation two complementary persons may supply one another's deficencies: in the domestic partnership of marriage they only feel them and suffer from them. Thus the son of a robust, cheerful, eupeptic British country squire, with the tastes and range of his class, and of a clever, imaginative, intellectual, highly civilized Jewess, might be very superior to both his parents; but it is not likely that the Jewess would find the squire an interesting companion, or his habits, his friends, his place and mode of life congenial to her. Therefore marriage, whilst it is made an indispensable condition of mating, will delay the advent of the Superman as effectually as Property, and will be modified by the impulse towards him just as effectually.

The practical abrogation of Property and Marriage as they exist at present will occur without being much noticed. To the mass of men, the intelligent abolition of property would mean nothing except an increase in the quantity of food, clothing, housing, and comfort at their personal disposal, as well as a greater control over their time and circumstances. Very few persons now make any distinction between virtually complete property and property held on such highly developed public conditions as to place its income on the same footing as that of a propertyless clergyman, officer, or civil servant. A landed proprietor may still drive men and women off his land, demolish their dwellings, and replace them with sheep or deer; and in the unregulated trades the private trader may still spunge on the regulated trades and sacrifice the life and health of the nation as lawlessly as the Manchester cotton manufacturers did at the beginning of last century. But though the Factory Code on the one hand, and Trade Union organization on the other, have, within the lifetime of men still living, converted the old unrestricted property of the cotton manufacturer in his mill and the cotton spinner in his labor into a mere permission to trade or work on stringent public or collective conditions, imposed in the interest of the general welfare without any regard for individual hard cases, people in Lancashire still speak of their "property" in the old terms, meaning nothing more by it than the things a thief can be punished for stealing. The total abolition of property, and the conversion of every citizen into a salaried functionary in the public service, would leave much more than 99 per cent of the nation quite unconscious of any greater change than now takes place when the son of a shipowner goes into the navy. They would still call their watches and umbrellas and back gardens their property.

Marriage also will persist as a name attached to a general custom long after the custom itself will have altered. For example, modern English marriage, as modified by divorce and by Married Women's Property Acts, differs more from early XIX century marriage than Byron's marriage did from Shakespear's. At the present moment marriage in England differs not only from marriage in France, but from marriage in Scotland. Marriage as modified by the divorce laws in South Dakota would be called mere promiscuity in Clapham. Yet the Americans, far from taking a profligate and cynical view of marriage, do homage to its ideals with a seriousness that seems old fashioned in Clapham. Neither in England nor America would a proposal to abolish marriage be tolerated for a moment; and yet nothing is more certain than that in both countries the progressive modification of the marriage contract will be continued until it is no more onerous nor irrevocable than any ordinary commercial deed of partnership. Were even this dispensed with, people would still call themselves husbands and wives; describe their companionships as marriages; and be for the most part unconscious that they were any less married than Henry VIII. For though a glance at the legal conditions of marriage in different Christian countries shews that marriage varies legally from frontier to frontier, domesticity varies so little that most people believe their own marriage laws to be universal. Consequently here again, as in the case of Property, the absolute confidence of the public in the stability of the institution's name, makes it all the easier to alter its substance.

However, it cannot be denied that one of the changes in public opinion demanded by the need for the Superman is a very unexpected one. It is nothing less than the dissolution of the present necessary association of marriage with conjugation, which most unmarried people regard as the very diagnostic of marriage. They are wrong, of course: it would be quite as near the truth to say that conjugation is the one purely accidental and incidental condition of marriage. Conjugation is essential to nothing but the propagation of the race; and the moment that paramount need is provided for otherwise than by marriage, conjugation, from Nature's creative point of view, ceases to be essential in marriage. But marriage does not thereupon cease to be so economical, convenient, and comfortable, that the Superman might safely bribe the matrimonomaniacs by offering to revive all the old inhuman stringency and irrevocability of marriage, to abolish divorce, to confirm the horrible bond which still chains decent people to drunkards, criminals, and wasters, provided only the complete extrication of conjugation from it were conceded to him. For if people could form domestic companionships on no easier terms than these, they would still marry. The Roman Catholic, forbidden by his Church to avail himself of the divorce laws, marries as freely as the South Dakotan Presbyterians who can change partners with a facility that scandalizes the old world; and were his Church to dare a further step towards Christianity and enjoin celibacy on its laity as well as on its clergy, marriages would still be contracted for the sake of domesticity by perfectly obedient sons and daughters of the Church. One need not further pursue these hypotheses: they are only suggested here to help the reader to analyse marriage into its two functions of regulating conjugation and supplying a form of domesticity. These two functions are quite separable; and domesticity is the only one of the two which is essential to the existence of marriage, because conjugation without domesticity is not marriage at all, whereas domesticity without conjugation is still marriage: in fact it is necessarily the actual condition of all fertile marriages during a great part of their duration, and of some marriages during the whole of it.

Taking it, then, that Property and Marriage, by destroying Equality and thus hampering sexual selection with irrelevant conditions, are hostile to the evolution of the Superman, it is easy to understand why the only generally known modern experiment in breeding the human race took place in a community which discarded both institutions.

III

The Perfectionist Experiment at Oneida Creek

In 1848 the Oneida Community was founded in America to carry out a resolution arrived at by a handful of Perfectionist Communists "that we will devote ourselves exclusively to the establishment of the Kingdom of God." Though the American nation declared that this sort of thing was not to be tolerated in a Christian country, the Oneida Community held its own for over thirty years, during which period it seems to have produced healthier children and done and suffered less evil than any Joint Stock Company on record. It was, however, a highly selected community; for a genuine communist (roughly definable as an intensely proud person who proposes to enrich the common fund instead of to spunge on it) is superior to an ordinary joint stock capitalist precisely as an ordinary joint stock capitalist is superior to a pirate. Further, the Perfectionists were mightily shepherded by their chief Noyes,[1] one of those chance attempts at the Superman which occur from time to time in spite of the interference of Man's blundering institutions. The existence of Noyes simplified the breeding problem for the Communists, the question as to what sort of man they should strive to breed being settled at once by the obvious desirability of breeding another Noyes.

[1] John Humphrey Noyes (1811–1886). See article in *The Dictionary of American Biography*.

But an experiment conducted by a handful of people, who, after thirty years of immunity from the unintentional child slaughter that goes on by ignorant parents in private homes, numbered only 300, could do very little except prove that Communists, under the guidance of a Superman "devoted exclusively to the establishment of the Kingdom of God," and caring no more for property and marriage than a Camberwell minister cares for Hindoo Caste or Suttee, might make a much better job of their lives than ordinary folk under the harrow of both these institutions. Yet their Superman himself admitted that this apparent success was only part of the abnormal phenomenon of his own occurrence; for when he came to the end of his powers through age, he himself guided and organized the voluntary relapse of the Communists into marriage, capitalism, and customary private life, thus admitting that the real social solution was not what a casual Superman could persuade a picked company to do for him, but what a whole community of Supermen would do spontaneously. If Noyes had had to organize, not a few dozen Perfectionists, but the whole United States, America would have beaten him as completely as England beat Oliver Cromwell, France Napoleon, or Rome Julius Cæsar. Cromwell learnt by bitter experience that God Himself cannot raise a people above its own level, and that even though you stir a nation to sacrifice all its appetites to its conscience, the result will still depend wholly on what sort of conscience the nation has got. Napoleon seems to have ended by regarding mankind as a troublesome pack of hounds only worth keeping for the sport of hunting with them. Cæsar's capacity for fighting without hatred or resentment was defeated by the determination of his soldiers to kill their enemies in the field instead of taking them prisoners to be spared by Cæsar; and his civil supremacy was purchased by colossal bribery of the citizens of Rome. What great rulers cannot do, codes and religions cannot do. Man reads his own nature into every ordinance: if you devise a superhuman commandment so cunningly that it cannot be misinterpreted in terms of his will, he will denounce it as seditious blasphemy, or else disregard it as either crazy or totally unintelligible. Parliaments and synods may tinker as much as they please with their codes and creeds as circumstances alter the balance of classes and their interests; and, as a result of the tinkering, there may be an occasional illusion of moral evolution, as when the victory of the commercial caste over the military caste leads to the substitution of social boycotting and pecuniary damages for duelling. At certain moments there may even be a considerable material advance, as when the conquest of political power by the working class produces a better distribution of wealth through the simple action of the selfishness of the new masters; but all this is mere readjustment and reformation: until the heart and mind of the people is changed the very greatest man will no more dare to govern on the assumption that all are as great as he than a drover dare leave his flock to find its way through the streets as he himself would. Until there is an England in which every man is a Cromwell, a France in which every man is a Napoleon, a Rome in which every man is a Cæsar, a Germany in which every man is a Luther plus a Goethe, the world will be no more improved by its heroes than a Brixton villa is improved by the pyramid of Cheops. The production of such nations is the only real change possible to us.

IV

MAN'S OBJECTION TO HIS OWN IMPROVEMENT

But would such a change be tolerated if Man must rise above himself to desire it? It would, through his misconception of its nature. Man does desire an ideal Superman with such energy as he can spare from his nutrition, and has in every age magnified the best living substitute for it he can find. His least incompetent general is set up as an Alexander; his king is the first gentleman in the world; his Pope is a saint. He is never without an array of human idols who are all nothing but sham Supermen. That the real Superman will snap his superfingers at all Man's present trumpery ideals of right, duty, honor, justice, religion, even decency, and accept moral obligations beyond present human endurance, is a thing that contemporary Man does not foresee: in fact he does not notice it when our casual Supermen do it in his very face. He actually does it himself every day without knowing it. He will therefore make no objection to the production of a race of what he calls Great Men or Heroes, because he will imagine them, not as true Supermen, but as himself endowed with infinite brains, infinite courage, and infinite money.

The most troublesome opposition will arise from the general fear of mankind that any interference with our conjugal customs will be an interference with our pleasures and our romance. This fear, by putting on airs of offended morality, has always intimidated people who have not measured its essential weakness; but it will prevail with those degenerates only in whom the instinct of fertility has faded into a mere itching for pleasure. The modern devices for combining pleasure with sterility, now universally known and accessible, enable these persons to weed themselves out of the race, a process already vigorously at work; and the consequent survival of the intelligently fertile means the survival of the partizans of the Superman; for what is proposed is nothing but the replacement of the old unintelligent, inevitable, almost unconscious fertility by an intelligently controlled, conscious fertility, and the elimination of the mere voluptuary from the evolutionary process.* Even if this selective agency had not been invented, the purpose of the race would still shatter the opposition of individual instincts. Not only do the bees and the ants satisfy their reproductive and parental instincts vicariously; but marriage itself successfully imposes celibacy on millions of unmarried normal men and women. In short, the individual instinct in this matter, overwhelming as it is thoughtlessly supposed to be, is really a finally negligible one.

V

THE POLITICAL NEED FOR THE SUPERMAN

The need for the Superman is, in its most imperative aspect, a political one. We have been driven to Proletarian Democracy by the failure of the alternative systems; for these depended on the existence of Supermen acting as despots or oligarchs; and not only were these Supermen not always or even often forthcoming at the right moment and in an eligible social position, but when they were forthcoming they could not, except for a short time and by morally suicidal coercive

---

* The part played in evolution by the voluptuary will be the same as that already played by the glutton. The glutton, as the man with the strongest motive for nourishing himself, will always take more pains than his fellows to get food. When food is so difficult to get that only great exertions can secure a sufficient supply of it, the glutton's appetite develops his cunning and enterprise to the utmost; and he becomes not only the best fed but the ablest man in the community. But in more hospitable climates, or where the social organization of the food supply makes it easy for a man to overeat, then the glutton eats himself out of health and finally out of existence. All other voluptuaries prosper and perish in the same way; and this is why the survival of the fittest means finally the survival of the self-controlled, because they alone can adapt themselves to the perpetual shifting of conditions produced by industrial progress.

methods, impose superhumanity on those whom they governed; so, by mere force of "human nature," government by consent of the governed has supplanted the old plan of governing the citizen as a public-schoolboy is governed.

Now we have yet to see the man who, having any practical experience of Proletarian Democracy, has any belief in its capacity for solving great political problems, or even for doing ordinary parochial work intelligently and economically. Only under despotisms and oligarchies has the Radical faith in "universal suffrage" as a political panacea arisen. It withers the moment it is exposed to practical trial, because Democracy cannot rise above the level of the human material of which its voters are made. Switzerland seems happy in comparison with Russia; but if Russia were as small as Switzerland, and had her social problems simplified in the same way by impregnable natural fortifications and a population educated by the same variety of intimacy of international intercourse, there might be little to choose between them. At all events Australia and Canada, which are virtually protected democratic republics, and France and the United States, which are avowedly independent democratic republics, are neither healthy, wealthy, nor wise; and they would be worse instead of better if their popular ministers were not experts in the art of dodging popular enthusiasms and duping popular ignorance. The politician who once had to learn how to flatter Kings has now to learn how to fascinate, amuse, coax, humbug, frighten, or otherwise strike the fancy of the electorate; and though in advanced modern States, where the artizan is better educated than the King, it takes a much bigger man to be a successful demagogue than to be a successful courtier, yet he who holds popular convictions with prodigious energy is the man for the mob, whilst the frailer sceptic who is cautiously feeling his way towards the next century has no chance unless he happens by accident to have the specific artistic talent of the mountebank as well, in which case it is as a mountebank that he catches votes, and not as a meliorist. Consequently the demagogue, though he professes (and fails) to readjust matters in the interests of the majority of the electors, yet stereotypes mediocrity, organizes intolerance, disparages exhibitions of uncommon qualities, and glorifies conspicuous exhibitions of common ones. He manages a small job well: he muddles rhetorically through a large one. When a great political movement takes place, it is not consciously led nor organized: the unconscious self in mankind breaks its way through the problem as an elephant breaks through a jungle; and the politicians make speeches about whatever happens in the process, which, with the best intentions, they do all in their power to prevent. Finally, when social aggregation arrives at a point demanding international organization before the demagogues and electorates have learnt how to manage even a country parish properly, much less internationalize Constantinople, the whole political business goes to smash; and presently we have Ruins of Empires, New Zealanders sitting on a broken arch of London Bridge,[1] and so forth.

To that recurrent catastrophe we shall certainly come again unless we can have a Democracy of Supermen; and the production of such a Democracy is the only change that is now hopeful enough to nerve us to the effort that Revolution demands.

VI

PRUDERY EXPLAINED

Why the bees should pamper their mothers whilst we pamper only our operatic prima donnas is a question worth reflecting on. Our notion of treating a mother is, not to increase her supply of food, but to cut it off by forbidding her to work in a factory for a month after her confinement. Everything that can make birth a misfortune to the parents as well as a danger to the mother is conscientiously done. When a great French writer, Émile Zola, alarmed at the sterilization of his nation, wrote an eloquent and powerful book to restore the prestige of parentage, it was at once assumed in England that a work of this character, with such a title as *Fecundity,* was too abominable to be translated, and that any attempt to deal with the relations of the sexes from any other than the voluptuary or romantic point of view must be sternly put down. Now if this assumption were really founded on public opinion, it would indicate an attitude of disgust and resentment towards the Life Force that could only arise in a diseased and moribund community in which Ibsen's Hedda Gabler would be the typical woman. But it has no vital foundation at all. The prudery of the newspapers is, like the prudery of the dinner table, a mere difficulty of education and lan-

---

[1] Macaulay, in his essay on Ranke's *History of the Popes,* said that the Church would still endure even when a New Zealander sat on a broken arch of London Bridge to sketch the ruins of St. Paul's.

guage. We are not taught to think decently on these subjects, and consequently we have no language for them except indecent language. We therefore have to declare them unfit for public discussion, because the only terms in which we can conduct the discussion are unfit for public use. Physiologists, who have a technical vocabulary at their disposal, find no difficulty; and masters of language who think decently can write popular stories like Zola's *Fecundity* or Tolstoy's *Resurrection* without giving the smallest offence to readers who can also think decently. But the ordinary modern journalist, who has never discussed such matters except in ribaldry, cannot write a simple comment on a divorce case without a conscious shamefulness or a furtive facetiousness that makes it impossible to read the comment aloud in company. All this ribaldry and prudery (the two are the same) does not mean that people do not feel decently on the subject: on the contrary, it is just the depth and seriousness of our feeling that makes its desecration by vile language and coarse humor intolerable; so that at last we cannot bear to have it spoken of at all because only one in a thousand can speak of it without wounding our self-respect, especially the self-respect of women. Add to the horrors of popular language the horrors of popular poverty. In crowded populations poverty destroys the possibility of cleanliness; and in the absence of cleanliness many of the natural conditions of life become offensive and noxious, with the result that at last the association of uncleanliness with these natural conditions becomes so overpowering that among civilized people (that is, people massed in the labyrinths of slums we call cities), half their bodily life becomes a guilty secret, unmentionable except to the doctor in emergencies; and Hedda Gabler shoots herself because maternity is so unladylike. In short, popular prudery is only a mere incident of popular squalor: the subjects which it taboos remain the most interesting and earnest of subjects in spite of it.

VII

Progress an Illusion

Unfortunately the earnest people get drawn off the track of evolution by the illusion of progress. Any Socialist can convince us easily that the difference between Man as he is and Man as he might become, without further evolution, under millennial conditions of nutrition, environment, and training, is enormous. He can shew that inequality and iniquitous distribution of wealth and allotment of labor have arisen through an unscientific economic system, and that Man, faulty as he is, is no more intended to establish any such ordered disorder than a moth intends to be burnt when it flies into a candle flame. He can shew that the difference between the grace and strength of the acrobat and the bent back of the rheumatic field laborer is a difference produced by conditions, not by nature. He can shew that many of the most detestable human vices are not radical, but are mere reactions of our institutions on our very virtues. The Anarchist, the Fabian, the Salvationist, the Vegetarian, the doctor, the lawyer, the parson, the professor of ethics, the gymnast, the soldier, the sportsman, the inventor, the political program-maker, all have some prescription for bettering us; and almost all their remedies are physically possible and aimed at admitted evils. To them the limit of progress is, at worst, the completion of all the suggested reforms and the levelling up of all men to the point attained already by the most highly nourished and cultivated in mind and body.

Here, then, as it seems to them, is an enormous field for the energy of the reformer. Here are many noble goals attainable by many of those paths up the Hill Difficulty along which great spirits love to aspire. Unhappily, the hill will never be climbed by Man as we know him. It need not be denied that if we all struggled bravely to the end of the reformers' paths we should improve the world prodigiously. But there is no more hope in that If than in the equally plausible assurance that if the sky falls we shall all catch larks. We are not going to tread those paths: we have not sufficient energy. We do not desire the end enough: indeed in most cases we do not effectively desire it at all. Ask any man would he like to be a better man; and he will say yes, most piously. Ask him would he like to have a million of money; and he will say yes, most sincerely. But the pious citizen who would like to be a better man goes on behaving just as he did before. And the tramp who would like the million does not take the trouble to earn ten shillings: multitudes of men and women, all eager to accept a legacy of a million, live and die without having ever possessed five pounds at one time, although beggars have died in rags on mattresses stuffed with gold which they accumulated because they desired it enough to nerve them to get it and keep it. The economists who discovered that demand created supply soon had to limit the proposition to "effective demand," which turned out, in the final analysis, to mean nothing more than supply itself; and this holds good in politics, morals, and all other departments as well: the actual supply is the measure of the effective demand; and the mere aspirations and professions produce nothing. No community has ever yet passed beyond the initial phases in which its pugnacity and fanaticism enabled it to found a nation, and its cupidity to establish and develop a commercial civilization. Even these stages have never been attained by public spirit, but always by tolerant wilfulness and brute force. Take the Reform Bill of 1832 as an example of a conflict between two sections of educated Englishmen concerning a political measure which was as obviously necessary and inevitable as any political measure has ever been or is ever likely to be. It was not passed until the gentlemen of Birmingham had made arrangements to cut the throats of the gentlemen of St James's parish in due military form. It would not have been passed to this day if there had been no force behind it except the logic and public conscience of the Utilitarians. A despotic ruler with as much sense as Queen Elizabeth would have done better than the mob of grown-up Eton boys who governed us then by privilege, and who, since the introduction of practically Manhood Suffrage in 1884, now govern us at the request of Proletarian Democracy.

At the present time we have, instead of the Utilitarians, the Fabian Society, with its peaceful, constitutional, moral, economical policy of Socialism, which needs nothing for its bloodless and benevolent realization except that the English people shall understand it and approve of it. But why are the Fabians well spoken of in circles where thirty years ago the word Socialist was understood as equivalent to cut-throat and incendiary? Not because the English have the smallest intention of studying or adopting the Fabian policy, but because they believe that the Fabians, by eliminating the element of intimidation from the Socialist agitation, have drawn the teeth of insurgent poverty and saved the existing order from the only method of attack it really fears. Of course, if the nation adopted the Fabian policy, it would be carried out by brute force exactly as our present property system is. It would become the law; and those who resisted it would be fined, sold up, knocked on the head by policemen, thrown into prison, and in the last resort "executed" just as they are when they break the present law. But as our

proprietary class has no fear of that conversion taking place, whereas it does fear sporadic cut-throats and gunpowder plots, and strives with all its might to hide the fact that there is no moral difference whatever between the methods by which it enforces its proprietary rights and the method by which the dynamitard asserts his conception of natural human rights, the Fabian Society is patted on the back just as the Christian Social Union is, whilst the Socialist who says bluntly that a Social revolution can be made only as all other revolutions have been made, by the people who want it killing, coercing, and intimidating the people who dont want it, is denounced as a misleader of the people, and imprisoned with hard labor to shew him how much sincerity there is in the objection of his captors to physical force.

Are we then to repudiate Fabian methods, and return to those of the barricader, or adopt those of the dynamitard and the assassin? On the contrary, we are to recognize that both are fundamentally futile. It seems easy for the dynamitard to say "Have you not just admitted that nothing is ever conceded except to physical force? Did not Gladstone admit that the Irish Church was disestablished, not by the spirit of Liberalism, but by the explosion which wrecked Clerkenwell prison?"[1] Well, we need not foolishly and timidly deny it. Let it be fully granted. Let us grant, further, that all this lies in the nature of things; that the most ardent Socialist, if he owns property, can by no means do otherwise than Conservative proprietors until property is forcibly abolished by the whole nation; nay, that ballots and parliamentary divisions, in spite of their vain ceremony of discussion, differ from battles only as the bloodless surrender of an outnumbered force in the field differs from Waterloo or Trafalgar. I make a present of all these admissions to the Fenian who collects money from thoughtless Irishmen in America to blow up Dublin Castle; to the detective who persuades foolish young workmen to order bombs from the nearest ironmonger and then delivers them up to penal servitude; to our military and naval commanders who believe, not in preaching, but in an ultimatum backed by plenty of lyddite; and, generally, to all whom it may concern. But of what use is it to substitute the way of the reckless and bloodyminded for the way of the cautious and humane? Is England any the better for

---

[1] Clerkenwell prison, near London, was blown up by Irish agitators in 1867. In 1869 Gladstone sponsored and Parliament passed the bill disestablishing the Anglican Church of Ireland.

the wreck of Clerkenwell prison, or Ireland for the disestablishment of the Irish Church? Is there the smallest reason to suppose that the nation which sheepishly let Charles and Laud and Strafford coerce it, gained anything because it afterwards, still more sheepishly, let a few strongminded Puritans, inflamed by the masterpieces of Jewish revolutionary literature, cut off the heads of the three? Suppose the Gunpowder plot had succeeded, and set a Fawkes dynasty permanently on the throne, would it have made any difference to the present state of the nation? The guillotine was used in France up to the limit of human endurance, both on Girondins and Jacobins. Fouquier-Tinville followed Marie Antoinette to the scaffold; and Marie Antoinette might have asked the crowd, just as pointedly as Fouquier did, whether their bread would be any cheaper when her head was off.[1] And what came of it all? The Imperial France of the Rougon-Macquart family,[2] and the Republican France of the Panama scandal[3] and the Dreyfus case.[4] Was the difference worth the guillotining of all those unlucky ladies and gentlemen, useless and mischievous as many of them were? Would any sane man guillotine a mouse to bring about such a result? Turn to Republican America. America has no Star Chamber, and no feudal barons. But it has Trusts; and it has millionaires whose factories, fenced in by live electric wires and defended by Pinkerton retainers with magazine rifles, would have made a Radical of Reginald Front de Bœuf.[5] Would Washington or Franklin have lifted a finger in the cause of American Independence if they had foreseen its reality?

No: what Cæsar, Cromwell, and Napoleon could not do with all the physical force and moral prestige of the State in their mighty hands, cannot be done by enthusiastic criminals and lunatics. Even the Jews, who, from Moses to Marx and Lasalle, have inspired all the revolutions, have had to confess that, after all, the dog will return to his vomit and the sow that was washed to her wallowing

in the mire; and we may as well make up our minds that Man will return to his idols and his cupidities, in spite of all "movements" and all revolutions, until his nature is changed. Until then, his early successes in building commercial civilizations (and such civilizations, Good Heavens!) are but preliminaries to the inevitable later stage, now threatening us, in which the passions which built the civilization became fatal instead of productive, just as the same qualities which make the lion king in the forest ensure his destruction when he enters a city. Nothing can save society then except the clear head and the wide purpose: war and competition, potent instruments of selection and evolution in one epoch, become ruinous instruments of degeneration in the next. In the breeding of animals and plants, varieties which have arisen by selection through many generations relapse precipitously into the wild type in a generation or two when selection ceases; and in the same way a civilization in which lusty pugnacity and greed have ceased to act as selective agents and have begun to obstruct and destroy, rushes downwards and backwards with a suddenness that enables an observer to see with consternation the upward steps of many centuries retraced in a single lifetime. This has often occurred even within the period covered by history; and in every instance the turning point has been reached long before the attainment, or even the general advocacy on paper, or the levelling-up of the mass to the highest point attainable by the best nourished and cultivated normal individuals.

We must therefore frankly give up the notion that Man as he exists is capable of net progress. There will always be an illusion of progress, because wherever we are conscious of an evil we remedy it, and therefore always seem to ourselves to be progressing, forgetting that most of the evils we see are the effects, finally become acute, of long-unnoticed retrogressions; that our compromising remedies seldom fully recover the lost ground; above all, that on the lines along which we are degenerating, good has become evil in our eyes, and is being undone in the name of progress precisely as evil is undone and replaced by good on the lines along which we are evolving. This is indeed the Illusion of Illusions; for it gives us infallible and appalling assurance that if our political ruin is to come, it will be effected by ardent reformers and supported by enthusiastic patriots as a series of necessary steps in our progress. Let the Reformer, the Progressive, the Meliorist then reconsider

---

[1] Fouquier-Tinville, prosecutor under the Terror, was told by the mob to "Go, join your victims." He answered, "Go, look for bread."
[2] Described by Zola in some twenty novels.
[3] In 1893 some directors of the French Panama Company, then trying to dig the Canal, were convicted of bribing members of the Chamber of Deputies in connection with government loans to the Company.
[4] In 1894 Capt. Alfred Dreyfus, a Jew, was accused of revealing French Army secrets to a foreign power (Germany was meant). Convicted on forged evidence and sentenced to harsh imprisonment on Devil's Island, he served five years before agitation led by Zola and Clemenceau resulted in new trials and complete exoneration in 1906.
[5] The stolid villain in Scott's *Ivanhoe*.

himself and his eternal ifs and ans which never become pots and pans. Whilst Man remains what he is, there can be no progress beyond the point already attained and fallen headlong from at every attempt at civilization; and since even that point is but a pinnacle to which a few people cling in giddy terror above an abyss of squalor, a mere progress should no longer charm us.

VIII

THE CONCEIT OF CIVILIZATION

After all, the progress illusion is not so very subtle. We begin by reading the satires of our fathers' contemporaries; and we conclude (usually quite ignorantly) that the abuses exposed by them are things of the past. We see also that reforms of crying evils are frequently produced by the sectional shifting of political power from oppressors to oppressed. The poor man is given a vote by the Liberals in the hope that he will cast it for his emancipators. The hope is not fulfilled; but the lifelong imprisonment of penniless men for debt ceases; Factory Acts are passed to mitigate sweating; schooling is made free and compulsory; sanitary by-laws are multiplied; public steps are taken to house the masses decently; the bare-footed get boots; rags become rare; and bathrooms and pianos, smart tweeds and starched collars, reach numbers of people who once, as "the unsoaped," played the Jew's harp or the accordion in moleskins and belchers.[1] Some of these changes are gains: some of them are losses. Some of them are not changes at all: all of them are merely the changes that money makes. Still, they produce an illusion of bustling progress; and the reading class infers from them that the abuses of the early Victorian period no longer exist except as amusing pages in the novels of Dickens. But the moment we look for a reform due to character and not to money, to statesmanship and not to interest or mutiny, we are disillusioned. For example, we remembered the maladministration and incompetence revealed by the Crimean war as part of a bygone state of things until the South African war shewed that the nation and the War Office, like those poor Bourbons who have been so impudently blamed for a universal characteristic, had learnt nothing and forgotten nothing. We had hardly recovered from the fruitless irritation of this discovery when it transpired that the officers' mess of

our most select regiment included a flogging club presided over by the senior subaltern. The disclosure provoked some disgust at the details of this schoolboyish debauchery, but no surprise at the apparent absence of any conception of manly honor and virtue, of personal courage and self-respect, in the front rank of our chivalry. In civil affairs we had assumed that the sycophancy and idolatry which encouraged Charles I to undervalue the Puritan revolt of the XVII century had been long outgrown; but it has needed nothing but favorable circumstances to revive, with added abjectness to compensate for its lost piety. We have relapsed into disputes about transubstantiation at the very moment when the discovery of the wide prevalence of theophagy as a tribal custom has deprived us of the last excuse for believing that our official religious rites differ in essentials from those of barbarians. The Christian doctrine of the uselessness of punishment and the wickedness of revenge has not, in spite of its simple common sense, found a single convert among the nations: Christianity means nothing to the masses but a sensational public execution which is made an excuse for other executions. In its name we take ten years of a thief's life minute by minute in the slow misery and degradation of modern reformed imprisonment with as little remorse as Laud and his Star Chamber clipped the ears of Bastwick and Burton. [1] We dug up and mutilated the remains of the Mahdi [2] the other day exactly as we dug up and mutilated the remains of Cromwell two centuries ago. We have demanded the decapitation of the Chinese Boxer princes as any Tartar would have done; and our military and naval expeditions to kill, burn, and destroy tribes and villages for knocking an Englishman on the head are so common a part of our Imperial routine that the last dozen of them has not called forth as much pity as can be counted on by any lady criminal. The judicial use of torture to extort confession is supposed to be a relic of darker ages; but whilst these pages are being written an English judge has sentenced a forger to twenty years' penal servitude with an open declaration that the sentence will be carried out in full unless he confesses where he has hidden the notes he forged. And no comment whatever is made either on this or on a telegram from the seat of war in Somaliland mentioning that certain

---

[1] Parti-colored neckerchiefs.

[1] Puritan agitators who accused Laud of favoring Roman Catholicism.
[2] Sudanese leader of rebellion against Egyptian-British authority 1881–1885. His body was exhumed, burned, and the ashes thrown into the Nile in 1898.

information has been given by a prisoner of war "under punishment." Even if these reports are false, the fact that they are accepted without protest as indicating a natural and proper course of public conduct shews that we are still as ready to resort to torture as Bacon was. As to vindictive cruelty, an incident in the South African war, when the relatives and friends of a prisoner were forced to witness his execution, betrayed a baseness of temper and character which hardly leaves us the right to plume ourselves on our superiority to Edward III at the surrender of Calais.[1] And the democratic American officer indulges in torture in the Philippines just as the aristocratic English officer did in South Africa. The incidents of the white invasion of Africa in search of ivory, gold, diamonds, and sport, have proved that the modern European is the same beast of prey that formerly marched to the conquest of new worlds under Alexander, Antony, and Pizarro. Parliaments and vestries are just what they were when Cromwell suppressed them and Dickens derided them. The democratic politician remains exactly as Plato described him; the physician is still the credulous impostor and petulant scientific coxcomb whom Molière ridiculed; the schoolmaster remains at best a pedantic child farmer and at worst a flagellomaniac; arbitrations are more dreaded by honest men than lawsuits; the philanthropist is still a parasite on misery as the doctor is on disease; the miracles of priestcraft are none the less fraudulent and mischievous because they are now called scientific experiments and conducted by professors; witchcraft, in the modern form of patent medicines and prophylactic inoculations, is rampant; the landowner who is no longer powerful enough to set the mantrap of Rhampsinitis[2] improves on it by barbed wire; the modern gentleman who is too lazy to daub his face with vermilion as a symbol of bravery employs a laundress to daub his shirt with starch as a symbol of cleanliness; we shake our heads at the dirt of the middle ages in cities made grimy with soot and foul and disgusting with shameless tobacco smoking; holy water, in its latest form of disinfectant fluid, is more widely used and believed in than ever; public health authorities deliberately go through incantations with burning sulphur (which they know to be useless) because the people believe in it as devoutly as the Italian peasant believes in the liquefaction of the blood of St Januarius; and straightforward public lying has reached gigantic developments, there being nothing to choose in this respect between the pickpocket at the police station and the minister on the treasury bench, the editor in the newspaper office, the city magnate advertizing bicycle tires that do not side-slip, the clergyman subscribing the thirty-nine articles, and the vivisector who pledges his knightly honor that no animal operated on in the physiological laboratory suffers the slightest pain. Hypocrisy is at its worst; for we not only persecute bigotedly but sincerely in the name of the cure-mongering witchcraft we do believe in, but callously and hypocritically in the name of the Evangelical creed that our rulers privately smile at as the Italian patricians in the fifth century smiled at Jupiter and Venus. Sport is, as it has always been, murderous excitement: the impulse to slaughter is universal; and museums are set up throughout the country to encourage little children and elderly gentlemen to make collections of corpses preserved in alcohol, and to steal birds' eggs and keep them as the red Indian used to keep scalps. Coercion with the lash is as natural to an Englishman as it was to Solomon spoiling Rehoboam:[1] indeed, the comparison is unfair to the Jews in view of the facts that the Mosaic law forbade more than forty lashes in the name of humanity, and that floggings of a thousand lashes were inflicted on English soldiers in the XVIII and XIX centuries, and would be inflicted still but for the change in the balance of political power between the military caste and the commercial classes and the proletariat. In spite of that change, flogging is still an institution in the public school, in the military prison, on the training ship, and in that school of littleness called the home. The lascivious clamor of the flagellomaniac for more of it, constant as the clamor for more insolence, more war, and lower rates, is tolerated and even gratified because, having no moral ends in view, we have sense enough to see that nothing but brute coercion can impose our selfish will on others. Cowardice is universal: patriotism, public opinion, parental duty, discipline, religion, morality, are only fine names for intimidation; and cruelty, gluttony, and credulity keep cowardice in countenance. We cut the throat of a calf and hang it up by the heels to bleed to death so that our veal cutlet may be white; we nail geese to a board and cram

---

[1] In 1934 Shaw dramatized this historical episode in one act, *The Six of Calais*.
[2] Rameses III of Egypt, who caught robbers of his treasury.

[1] The Bible reports no episode in which Solomon "spoils" Rehoboam.

them with food because we like the taste of liver disease; we tear birds to pieces to decorate our women's hats; we mutilate domestic animals for no reason at all except to follow an instinctively cruel fashion; and we connive at the most abominable tortures in the hope of discovering some magical cure for our own diseases by them.

Now please observe that these are not exceptional developments of our admitted vices, deplored and prayed against by all good men. Not a word has been said here of the excesses of our Neros, of whom we have the full usual percentage. With the exception of the few military examples, which are mentioned mainly to shew that the education and standing of a gentleman, reinforced by the strongest conventions of honor, *esprit de corps*, publicity and responsibility, afford no better guarantees of conduct than the passions of a mob, the illustrations given above are commonplaces taken from the daily practices of our best citizens, vehemently defended in our newspapers and in our pulpits. The very humanitarians who abhor them are stirred to murder by them: the dagger of Brutus and Ravaillac is still active in the hands of Caserio and Luccheni; and the pistol has come to its aid in the hands of Guiteau and Czolgosz.[1] Our remedies are still limited to endurance or assassination; and the assassin is still judicially assassinated on the principle that two blacks make a white. The only novelty is in our methods: through the discovery of dynamite the overloaded musket of Hamilton of Bothwellhaugh[2] has been superseded by the bomb; but Ravachol's[3] heart burns just as Hamilton's did. The world will not bear thinking of to those who know what it is, even with the largest discount for the restraints of poverty on the poor and cowardice on the rich.

All that can be said for us is that people must and do live and let live up to a certain point. Even the horse, with his docked tail and bitted jaw, finds his slavery mitigated by the fact that a total disregard of his need for food and rest would put his master to the expense of buying a new horse every second day; for you cannot work a horse to death and then pick up another one for nothing, as you can a laborer. But this natural check on inconsiderate selfishness is itself checked,

partly by our shortsightedness, and partly by deliberate calculation; so that beside the man who, to his own loss, will shorten his horse's life in mere stinginess, we have the tramway company which discovers actuarially that though a horse may live from 24 to 40 years, yet it pays better to work him to death in 4 and then replace him by a fresh victim. And human slavery, which has reached its worst recorded point within our own time in the form of free wage labor, has encountered the same personal and commercial limits to both its aggravation and its mitigation. Now that the freedom of wage labor has produced a scarcity of it, as in South Africa, the leading English newspaper and the leading English weekly review have openly and without apology demanded a return to compulsory labor: that is, to the methods by which, as we believe, the Egyptians built the pyramids. We know now that the crusade against chattel slavery in the XIX century succeeded solely because chattel slavery was neither the most effective nor the the the least humane method of labor exploitation; and the world is now feeling its way towards a still more effective system which shall abolish the freedom of the worker without again making his exploiter responsible for him.

Still, there is always some mitigation: there is the fear of revolt; and there are the effects of kindliness and affection. Let it be repeated therefore that no indictment is here laid against the world on the score of what its criminals and monsters do. The fires of Smithfield[1] and of the Inquisition were lighted by earnestly pious people, who were kind and good as kindness and goodness go. And when a negro is dipped in kerosene and set on fire in America at the present time, he is not a good man lynched by ruffians: he is a criminal lynched by crowds of respectable, charitable, virtuously indignant, high-minded citizens, who, though they act outside the law, are at least more merciful than the American legislators and judges who not so long ago condemned men to solitary confinement for periods, not of five months, as our own practice is, but of five years and more. The things that our moral monsters do may be left out of account with St. Bartholomew massacres[2] and other momentary outbursts of social disorder. Judge us by the admitted and respected practice of our most reputable circles; and, if you know the facts and are strong enough to look

[1] Ravaillac assassinated Henry IV of France; Caserio, Carnot; Luccheni, Queen Elizabeth of Austria; Guiteau, President Garfield; Czolgosz, President McKinley.
[2] Assassin of the Earl of Moray, regent of Scotland, 1570.
[3] Guillotined in 1893 for numerous dynamite murders. Claimed to be an anarchist.

[1] District in the City of London where executions took place, especially of religious recalcitrants under the Tudors.
[2] Massacre of Protestants in France, 1572.

n in the face, you must admit that unless we are replaced by a more highly evolved animal—in short, by the Superman—the world must remain a den of dangerous animals among whom our few accidental supermen, our Shakespears, Goethes, Shelleys, and their like, must live as precariously as lion tamers do, taking the humor of their situation, and the dignity of their superiority, as a set-off to the horror of the one and the loneliness of the other.

IX

The Verdict of History

It may be said that though the wild beast breaks out in Man and casts him back momentarily into barbarism under the excitement of war and crime, yet his normal life is higher than the normal life of his forefathers. This view is very acceptable to Englishmen, who always lean sincerely to virtue's side as long as it costs them nothing either in money or in thought. They feel deeply the injustice of foreigners, who allow them no credit for this conditional highmindedness. But there is no reason to suppose that our ancestors were less capable of it than we are. To all such claims for the existence of a progressive moral evolution operating visibly from grandfather to grandson, there is the conclusive reply that a thousand years of such evolution would have produced enormous social changes, of which the historical evidence would be overwhelming. But not Macaulay himself, the most confident of Whig meliorists, can produce any such evidence that will bear crossexamination. Compare our conduct and our codes with those mentioned contemporarily in such ancient scriptures and classics as have come down to us, and you will find no jot of ground for the belief that any moral progress whatever has been made in historic time, in spite of all the romantic attempts of historians to reconstruct the past on that assumption. Within that time it has happened to nations as to private families and individuals that they have flourished and decayed, repented and hardened their hearts, submitted and protested, acted and reacted, oscillated between natural and artificial sanitation (the oldest house in the world, unearthed the other day in Crete, has quite modern sanitary arrangements), and rung a thousand changes on the different scales of income and pressure of population, firmly believing all the time that mankind was advancing by leaps and bounds because men

were constantly busy. And the mere chapter of accidents has left a small accumulation of chance discoveries, such as the wheel, the arch, the safety pin, gunpowder, the magnet, the Voltaic pile and so forth: things which, unlike the gospels and philosophic treatises of the sages, can be usefully understood and applied by common men; so that steam locomotion is possible without a nation of Stephensons, although national Christianity is impossible without a nation of Christs. But does any man seriously believe that the *chauffeur* who drives a motor car from Paris to Berlin is a more highly evolved man than the charioteer of Achilles, or that a modern Prime Minister is a more enlightened ruler than Cæsar because he rides a tricycle, writes his dispatches by the electric light, and instructs his stockbroker through the telephone?

Enough, then, of this goose-cackle about Progress: Man, as he is, never will nor can add a cubit to his stature by any of its quackeries, political, scientific, educational, religious, or artistic. What is likely to happen when this conviction gets into the minds of the men whose present faith in these illusions is the cement of our social system, can be imagined only by those who know how suddenly a civilization which has long ceased to think (or in the old phrase, to watch and pray) can fall to pieces when the vulgar belief in its hypocrisies and impostures can no longer hold out against its failures and scandals. When religious and ethical formulæ become so obsolete that no man of strong mind can believe them, they have also reached the point at which no man of high character will profess them; and from that moment until they are formally disestablished, they stand at the door of every profession and every public office to keep out every able man who is not a sophist or a liar. A nation which revises its parish councils once in three years, but will not revise its articles of religion once in three hundred, even when those articles avowedly began as a political compromise dictated by Mr Facing-Both-Ways, is a nation that needs remaking.

Our only hope, then, is in evolution. We must replace the man by the superman. It is frightful for the citizen, as the years pass him, to see his own contemporaries so exactly reproduced by the younger generation, that his companions of thirty years ago have their counterparts in every city crowd, where he has to check himself repeatedly in the act of saluting as an old friend some young man to whom he is only an elderly stranger. All hope of advance dies in his bosom as he watches them: he knows that they will do just what their fathers did, and that the few voices which will still, as always before, exhort them to do something else and be something better, might as well spare their breath to cool their porridge (if they can get any). Men like Ruskin and Carlyle will preach to Smith and Brown for the sake of preaching, just as St Francis preached to the birds and St Anthony to the fishes. But Smith and Brown, like the fishes and birds, remain as they are; and poets who plan Utopias and prove that nothing is necessary for their realization but that Man should will them, perceive at last, like Richard Wagner, that the fact to be faced is that Man does not effectively will them. And he never will until he becomes Superman.

And so we arrive at the end of the Socialist's dream of "the socialization of the means of production and exchange," of the Positivist's dream of moralizing the capitalist, and of the ethical professor's, legislator's, educator's dream of putting commandments and codes and lessons and examination marks on a man as harness is put on a horse, ermine on a judge, pipe-clay on a soldier, or a wig on an actor, and pretending that his nature has been changed. The only fundamental and possible Socialism is the socialization of the selective breeding of Man: in other terms, of human evolution. We must eliminate the Yahoo, or his vote will wreck the commonwealth.

X

THE METHOD

As to the method, what can be said as yet except that where there is a will, there is a way? If there be no will, we are lost. That is a possibility for our crazy little empire, if not for the universe; and as such possibilities are not to be entertained without despair, we must, whilst we survive, proceed on the assumption that we have still energy enough to not only will to live, but to will to live better. That may mean that we must establish a State Department of Evolution, with a seat in the Cabinet for its chief, and a revenue to defray the cost of direct State experiments, and provide inducements to private persons to achieve successful results. It may mean a private society or a chartered company for the improvement of human live stock. But for the present it is far more likely to mean a blatant repudiation of such proposals as indecent and immoral, with,

nevertheless, a general secret pushing of human will in the repudiated direction; so that all sorts of institutions and public authorities will under some pretext or other feel their way furtively towards the Superman. Mr. Graham Wallas has already ventured to suggest, as Chairman of the School Management Committee of the London School Board, that the accepted policy of the Sterilization of the Schoolmistress, however administratively convenient, is open to criticism from the national stock-breeding point of view; and this is as good an example as any of the way in which the drift towards the Superman may operate in spite of all our hypocrisies. One thing at least is clear to begin with. If a woman can, by careful selection of a father, and nourishment of herself, produce a citizen with efficient senses, sound organs, and a good digestion, she should clearly be secured a sufficient reward for that natural service to make her willing to undertake and repeat it. Whether she be financed in the undertaking by herself, or by the father, or by a speculative capitalist, or by a new department of, say, the Royal Dublin Society, or (as at present) by the War Office maintaining her "on the strength" and authorizing a particular soldier to marry her, or by a local authority under a by-law directing that women may under certain circumstances have a year's leave of absence on full salary, or by the central government, does not matter provided the result be satisfactory.

It is a melancholy fact that as the vast majority of women and their husbands have, under exacting circumstances, not enough nourishment, no capital, no credit, and no knowledge of science or business, they would, if the State would pay for birth as it now pays for death, be exploited by joint stock companies for dividends, just as they are in ordinary industries. Even a joint stock human stud farm (piously disguised as a reformed Foundling Hospital or something of that sort) might well, under proper inspection and regulation, produce better results than our present reliance on promiscuous marriage. It may be objected that when an ordinary contractor produces stores for sale to the Government, and the Government rejects them as not up to the required standard, the condemned goods are either sold for what they will fetch or else scrapped: that is, treated as waste material whereas if the goods consisted of human beings, all that could be done would be to let them loose or send them to the nearest work house. But there is nothing new in privat enterprise throwing its human refuse on the cheap labor market and the workhouse; and the refuse of the new industry would presumably be better bred than the staple product of ordinary poverty. In our present happy-go-lucky industrial disorder, all the human products, successful or not, would have to be thrown on the labor market; but the unsuccessful ones would not entitle the company to a bounty and so would be a dead loss to it. The practical commercial difficulty would be the uncertainty and the cost in time and money of the first experiments. Purely commercial capital would not touch such heroic operations during the experimental stage; and in any case the strength of mind needed for so momentous a new departure could not be fairly expected from the Stock Exchange. It will have to be handled by statesmen with character enough to tell our democracy and plutocracy that statecraft does not consist in flattering their follies or applying their suburban standards of propriety to the affairs of four continents. The matter must be taken up either by the State or by some organization strong enough to impose respect upon the State.

The novelty of any such experiment, however, is only in the scale of it. In one conspicuous case, that of royalty, the State does already select the parents on purely political grounds; and in the peerage, though the heir to a dukedom is legally free to marry a dairymaid, yet the social pressure on him to confine his choice to politically and socially eligible mates is so overwhelming that he is really no more free to marry the dairymaid than George IV was to marry Mrs Fitzherbert; and such a marriage could only occur as a result of extraordinary strength of character on the part of the dairymaid acting upon extraordinary weakness on the part of the duke. Let those who think the whole conception of intelligent breeding absurd and scandalous ask themselves why George IV was not allowed to choose his own wife whilst any tinker could marry whom he pleased? Simply because it did not matter a rap politically whom the tinker married, whereas it mattered very much whom the king married. The way in which all considerations of the king's personal rights, of the claims of the heart, of the sanctity of the marriage oath, and of romantic morality crumpled up before this political need shews how negligible all these apparently irresistible prejudices are when they come into conflict with the demand for quality in our rulers. We learn the same lesson from the case of the soldier, whose marriage, when it is permitted at all, is despotically controlled with a view solely to military efficiency.

Well, nowadays it is not the King that rules, but the tinker. Dynastic wars are no longer feared, dynastic alliances no longer valued. Marriages in royal families are becoming rapidly less political, and more popular, domestic, and romantic. If all the kings in Europe were made as free tomorrow as King Cophetua,[1] nobody but their aunts and chamberlains would feel a moment's anxiety as to the consequences. On the other hand a sense of the social importance of the tinker's marriage has been steadily growing. We have made a public matter of his wife's health in the month after her confinement. We have taken the minds of his children out of his hands and put them into those of our State schoolmaster. We shall presently make their bodily nourishment independent of him. But they are still riff-raff; and to hand the country over to riff-raff is national suicide, since riff-raff can neither govern nor will let anyone else govern except the highest bidder of bread and circuses. There is no public enthusiast alive of twenty years' practical democratic experience who believes in the political adequacy of the electorate or of the bodies it elects. The overthrow of the aristocrat has created the necessity for the Superman.

Englishmen hate Liberty and Equality too much to understand them. But every Englishman loves and desires a pedigree. And in that he is right. King Demos must be bred like all other Kings; and with Must there is no arguing. It is idle for an individual writer to carry so great a matter further in a pamphlet. A conference on the subject is the next step needed. It will be attended by men and women who, no longer believing that they can live for ever, are seeking for some immortal work into which they can build the best of themselves before their refuse is thrown into that arch dust destructor, the cremation furnace.

MAXIMS FOR REVOLUTIONISTS

THE GOLDEN RULE

Do not do unto others as you would that they should do unto you. Their tastes may not be the same.

Never resist temptation: prove all things: hold fast that which is good.[2]

Do not love your neighbor as yourself. If

---

[1] Who married a beggar maid.
[2] See *I Thessalonians*, 5:21.

you are on good terms with yourself it is an impertinence: if on bad, an injury.

The golden rule is that there are no golden rules.

IDOLATRY

The art of government is the organization of idolatry.

The bureaucracy consists of functionaries; the aristocracy, of idols; the democracy, of idolaters.

The populace cannot understand the bureaucracy: it can only worship the national idols.

The savage bows down to idols of wood and stone: the civilized man to idols of flesh and blood.

A limited monarchy is a device for combining the inertia of a wooden idol with the credibility of a flesh and blood one.

When the wooden idol does not answer the peasant's prayer, he beats it: when the flesh and blood idol does not satisfy the civilized man, he cuts its head off.

He who slays a king and he who dies for him are alike idolaters.

ROYALTY

Kings are not born: they are made by artificial hallucination. When the process is interrupted by adversity at a critical age, as in the case of Charles II, the subject becomes sane and never completely recovers his kingliness.

The Court is the servant's hall of the sovereign.

Vulgarity in a king flatters the majority of the nation.

The flunkeyism propagated by the throne is the price we pay for its political convenience.

DEMOCRACY

If the lesser mind could measure the greater as a footrule can measure a pyramid, there would be finality in universal suffrage. As it is, the political problem remains unsolved.

Democracy substitutes selection by the incompetent many for appointment by the corrupt few.

Democratic republics can no more dispense with national idols than monarchies with public functionaries.

Government presents only one problem: the discovery of a trustworthy anthropometric method.

IMPERIALISM

Excess of insularity makes a Briton an Imperialist.

Excess of local self-assertion makes a colonist an Imperialist.

A colonial Imperialist is one who raises colonial troops, equips a colonial squadron, claims a Federal Parliament sending its measures to the Throne instead of to the Colonial Office, and, being finally brought by this means into insoluble conflict with the insular British Imperialist, "cuts the painter" and breaks up the Empire.

LIBERTY AND EQUALITY

He who confuses political liberty with freedom and political equality with similarity has never thought for five minutes about either.

Nothing can be unconditional: consequently nothing can be free.

Liberty means responsibility. That is why most men dread it.

The duke inquires contemptuously whether his gamekeeper is the equal of the Astronomer Royal; but he insists that they shall both be hanged equally if they murder him.

The notion that the colonel need be a better man than the private is as confused as the notion that the keystone need be stronger than the coping stone.

Where equality is undisputed, so also is subordination.

Equality is fundamental in every department of social organization.

The relation of superior to inferior excludes good manners.

EDUCATION

When a man teaches something he does not know to somebody else who has no aptitude for it, and gives him a certificate of proficiency, the latter has completed the education of a gentleman.

A fool's brain digests philosophy into folly, science into superstition, and art into pedantry. Hence University education.

The best brought-up children are those who have seen their parents as they are. Hypocrisy is not the parent's first duty.

The vilest abortionist is he who attempts to mould a child's character.

At the University every great treatise is postponed until its author attains impartial judgment and perfect knowledge. If a horse could wait as long for its shoes and would pay for them in advance, our blacksmiths would all be college dons.

He who can, does. He who cannot, teaches.

A learned man is an idler who kills time with study. Beware of his false knowledge: it is more dangerous than ignorance.

Activity is the only road to knowledge.

Every fool believes what his teachers tell him, and calls his credulity science or morality as confidently as his father called it divine revelation.

No man fully capable of his own language ever masters another.

No man can be a pure specialist without being in the strict sense an idiot.

Do not give your children moral and religious instruction unless you are quite sure they will not take it too seriously. Better be the mother of Henri Quatre and Nell Gwynne than of Robespierre and Queen Mary Tudor.

MARRIAGE

Marriage is popular because it combines the maximum of temptation with the maximum of opportunity.

Marriage is the only legal contract which abrogates as between the parties all the laws that safeguard the particular relation to which it refers.

The essential function of marriage is the continuance of the race, as stated in the Book of Common Prayer.[1]

The accidental function of marriage is the gratification of the amoristic sentiment of mankind.

The artificial sterilization of marriage makes it possible for marriage to fulfil its accidental function whilst neglecting its essential one.

The most revolutionary invention of the XIX century was the artificial sterilization of marriage.

Any marriage system which condemns a majority of the population to celibacy will be violently wrecked on the pretext that it outrages morality.

Polygamy, when tried under modern democratic conditions, as by the Mormons, is wrecked by the revolt of the mass of inferior men who are condemned to celibacy by it; for the maternal instinct leads a woman to prefer a tenth share in a first rate man to the exclusive possession of a third rate one. Polyandry has been tried under these conditions.

The minimum of national celibacy (ascertained by dividing the number of males in the community by the number of females,

and taking the quotient as the number of wives or husbands permitted to each person) is secured in England (where the quotient is 1) by the institution of monogamy.

The modern sentimental term for the national minimum of celibacy is Purity.

Marriage, or any other form of promiscuous amoristic monogamy, is fatal to large States because it puts its ban on the deliberate breeding of man as a political animal.

CRIME AND PUNISHMENT

All scoundrelism is summed up in the phrase "Que Messieurs les Assassins commencent!"[1]

The man who has graduated from the flogging block at Eton to the bench from which he sentences the garotter to be flogged is the same social product as the garotter who has been kicked by his father and cuffed by his mother until he has grown strong enough to throttle and rob the rich citizen whose money he desires.

Imprisonment is as irrevocable as death.

Criminals do not die by the hands of the law. They die by the hands of other men.

The assassin Czolgosz made President McKinley a hero by assassinating him. The United States of America made Czolgosz a hero by the same process.

Assassination on the scaffold is the worst form of assassination, because there it is invested with the approval of society.

It is the deed that teaches, not the name we give it. Murder and capital punishment are not opposites that cancel one another, but similars that breed their kind.

Crime is only the retail department of what, in wholesale, we call penal law.

When a man wants to murder a tiger he calls it sport: when the tiger wants to murder him he calls it ferocity. The distinction between Crime and Justice is no greater.

Whilst we have prisons it matters little which of us occupy the cells.

The most anxious man in a prison is the governor.

It is not necessary to replace a guillotined criminal: it is necessary to replace a guillotined social system.

TITLES

Titles distinguish the mediocre, embarrass the superior, and are disgraced by the inferior.

Great men refuse titles because they are jealous of them.

---

[1] The Prayer Book of the Church of England, but the Prayer Book of the Protestant Episcopal Church in the United States does not contain the statement.

[1] From an article published in January, 1849, by Alphonse Karr, defending capital punishment. He made the point that if it were desirable to abolish the death penalty, "Let the murderers begin!"

HONOR

There are no perfectly honorable men; but every true man has one main point of honor and a few minor ones.

You cannot believe in honor until you have achieved it. Better keep yourself clean and bright: you are the window through which you must see the world.

Your word can never be as good as your bond, because your memory can never be as trustworthy as your honor.

PROPERTY

Property, said Proudhon, is theft. This is the only perfect truism that has been uttered on the subject.

SERVANTS

When domestic servants are treated as human beings it is not worth while to keep them.

The relation of master and servant is advantageous only to masters who do not scruple to abuse their authority, and to servants who do not scruple to abuse their trust.

The perfect servant, when his master makes humane advances to him, feels that his existence is threatened, and hastens to change his place.

Masters and servants are both tyrannical; but the masters are the more dependent of the two.

A man enjoys what he uses, not what his servants use.

Man is the only animal which esteems itself rich in proportion to the number and voracity of its parasites.

Ladies and gentlemen are permitted to have friends in the kennel, but not in the kitchen.

Domestic servants, by making spoiled children of their masters, are forced to intimidate them in order to be able to live with them.

In a slave state, the slaves rule; in Mayfair, the tradesman rules.

HOW TO BEAT CHILDREN

If you strike a child, take care that you strike it in anger, even at the risk of maiming it for life. A blow in cold blood neither can nor should be forgiven.

If you beat children for pleasure, avow your object frankly, and play the game according to the rules, as a foxhunter does; and you will do comparatively little harm. No foxhunter is such a cad as to pretend that he hunts the fox to teach it not to steal chickens, or that he suffers more acutely than the fox at the death. Remember that even in childbeating there is the sportsman's way and the cad's way.

RELIGION

Beware of the man whose god is in the skies.

What a man believes may be ascertained, not from his creed, but from the assumptions on which he habitually acts.

VIRTUES AND VICES

No specific virtue or vice in a man implies the existence of any other specific virtue or vice in him, however closely the imagination may associate them.

Virtue consists, not in abstaining from vice, but in not desiring it.

Self-denial is not a virtue: it is only the effect of prudence on rascality.

Obedience simulates subordination as fear of the police simulates honesty.

Disobedience, the rarest and most courageous of the virtues, is seldom distinguished from neglect, the laziest and commonest of the vices.

Vice is waste of life. Poverty, obedience, and celibacy are the canonical vices.

Economy is the art of making the most of life.

The love of economy is the root of all virtue.

FAIRPLAY

The love of fairplay is a spectator's virtue, not a principal's.

GREATNESS

Greatness is only one of the sensations of littleness.

In heaven an angel is nobody in particular.

Greatness is the secular name for Divinity: both mean simply what lies beyond us.

If a great man could make us understand him, we should hang him.

We admit that when the divinity we worshipped made itself visible and comprehensible we crucified it.

To a mathematician the eleventh means only a single unit: to the bushman who cannot count further than his ten fingers it is an incalculable myriad.

The difference between the shallowest routineer and the deepest thinker appears, to the latter, trifling; to the former, infinite.

In a stupid nation the man of genius becomes a god: everybody worships him and nobody does his will.

BEAUTY AND HAPPINESS, ART AND RICHES

Happiness and Beauty are by-products.

Folly is the direct pursuit of Happiness and Beauty.

Riches and Art are spurious receipts for the production of Happiness and Beauty.

He who desires a lifetime of happiness with a beautiful woman desires to enjoy the taste of wine by keeping his mouth always full of it.

The most intolerable pain is produced by prolonging the keenest pleasure.

The man with toothache thinks everyone happy whose teeth are sound. The poverty-stricken man makes the same mistake about the rich man.

The more a man possesses over and above what he uses, the more careworn he becomes.

The tyranny that forbids you to make the road with pick and shovel is worse than that which prevents you from lolling along it in a carriage and pair.

In an ugly and unhappy world the richest man can purchase nothing but ugliness and unhappiness.

In his efforts to escape from ugliness and unhappiness the rich man intensifies both. Every new yard of West End creates a new acre of East End.[1]

The XIX century was the Age of Faith in Fine Art. The results are before us.

THE PERFECT GENTLEMAN

The fatal reservation of the gentleman is that he sacrifices everything to his honor except his gentility.

A gentleman of our days is one who has money enough to do what every fool would do if he could afford it: that is, consume without producing.

The true diagnostic of modern gentility is parasitism.

No elaboration of physical or moral accomplishment can atone for the sin of parasitism.

A modern gentleman is necessarily the enemy of his country. Even in war he does not fight to defend it, but to prevent his power of preying on it from passing to a foreigner. Such combatants are patriots in the same sense as two dogs fighting for a bone are lovers of animals.

The North American Indian was a type of the sportsman warrior gentleman. The Periclean Anthenian was a type of the intellectually and artistically cultivated gentleman. Both were political failures. The modern gentleman, without the hardihood of the one or the culture of the other, has the appetite of both put together. He will not succeed where they failed.

He who believes in education, criminal law, and sport, needs only property to make him a perfect modern gentleman.

MODERATION

Moderation is never applauded for its own sake.

A moderately honest man with a moderately faithful wife, moderate drinkers both, in a moderately healthy house: that is the true middle class unit.

THE UNCONSCIOUS SELF

The unconscious self is the real genius. Your breathing goes wrong the moment your conscious self meddles with it.

Except during the nine months before he draws his first breath, no man manages his affairs as well as a tree does.

REASON

The reasonable man adapts himself to the world: the unreasonable one persists in trying to adapt the world to himself. Therefore all progress depends on the unreasonable man.

The man who listens to Reason is lost: Reason enslaves all whose minds are not strong enough to master her.

DECENCY

Decency is Indecency's Conspiracy of Silence.

EXPERIENCE

Men are wise in proportion, not to their experience, but to their capacity for experience.

If we could learn from mere experience, the stones of London would be wiser than its wisest men.

TIME'S REVENGES

Those whom we call brutes had their revenge when Darwin shewed us that they are our cousins.

The thieves had their revenge when Marx convicted the bourgeoisie of theft.

GOOD INTENTIONS

Hell is paved with good intentions, not bad ones.

All men mean well.

---

[1] London's rich live in the West End; her poor in the East End.

NATURAL RIGHTS

The Master of Arts, by proving that no man has any natural rights, compels himself to take his own for granted.

The right to live is abused whenever it is not constantly challenged.

FAUTE DE MIEUX

In my childhood I demurred to the description of a certain young lady as "the pretty Miss So and So." My Aunt rebuked me by saying "Remember always that the least plain sister is the family beauty."

No age or condition is without its heroes. The least incapable general in a nation is its Cæsar, the least imbecile statesman its Solon, the least confused thinker its Socrates, the least commonplace poet its Shakespear.

CHARITY

Charity is the most mischievous sort of pruriency.

Those who minister to poverty and disease are accomplices in the two worst of all the crimes.

He who gives money he has not earned is generous with other people's labor.

Every genuinely benevolent person loathes almsgiving and mendicity.

FAME

Life levels all men: death reveals the eminent.

DISCIPLINE

Mutiny Acts are needed only by officers who command without authority. Divine right needs no whip.

WOMEN IN THE HOME

Home is the girl's prison and the woman's workhouse.

CIVILIZATION

Civilization is a disease produced by the practice of building societies with rotten material.

Those who admire modern civilization usually identify it with the steam engine and the electric telegraph.

Those who understand the steam engine and the electric telegraph spend their lives in trying to replace them with something better.

The imagination cannot conceive a viler criminal than he who should build another London like the present one, nor a greater benefactor than he who should destroy it.

GAMBLING

The most popular method of distributing wealth is the method of the roulette table.

The roulette table pays nobody except him that keeps it. Nevertheless a passion for gaming is common, though a passion for keeping roulette tables is unknown.

Gambling promises the poor what Property performs for the rich: that is why the bishops dare not denounce it fundamentally.

THE SOCIAL QUESTION

Do not waste your time on Social Questions. What is the matter with the poor is Poverty: what is the matter with the rich is Uselessness.

STRAY SAYINGS

We are told that when Jehovah created the world he saw that it was good. What would he say now?

The conversion of a savage to Christianity is the conversion of Christianity to savagery.

No man dares say so much of what he thinks as to appear to himself an extremist.

Mens sana in corpore sano is a foolish saying. The sound body is a product of the sound mind.

Decadence can find agents only when it wears the mask of progress.

In moments of progress the noble succeed because things are going their way: in moments of decadence the base succeed for the same reason: hence the world is never without the exhilaration of contemporary success.

The reformer for whom the world is not good enough finds himself shoulder to shoulder with him that is not good enough for the world.

Every man over forty is a scoundrel.

Youth, which is forgiven everything, forgives itself nothing: age, which forgives itself everything, is forgiven nothing.

When we learn to sing that Britons never will be masters we shall make an end of slavery.

Do not mistake your objection to defeat for an objection to fighting, your objection to being a slave for an objection to slavery, your objection to not being as rich as your neighbor for an objection to poverty. The cowardly, the insubordinate, and the envious share your objections.

Take care to get what you like or you will be forced to like what you get. Where there is no ventilation fresh air is declared unwholesome. Where there is no religion hypocrisy becomes good taste. Where there is no knowledge ignorance calls itself science.

If the wicked flourish and the fittest survive, Nature must be the God of rascals.

If history repeats itself, and the unexpected always happens, how incapable must Man be of learning from experience!

Compassion is the fellow-feeling of the unsound.

Those who understand evil pardon it: those who resent it destroy it.

Acquired notions of propriety are stronger than natural instincts. It is easier to recruit for monasteries and convents than to induce an Arab woman to uncover her mouth in public, or a British officer to walk through Bond Street in a golfing cap on an afternoon in May.

It is dangerous to be sincere unless you are also stupid.

The Chinese tame fowls by clipping their wings, and women by deforming their feet. A petticoat round the ankles serves equally well.

Political Economy and Social Economy are amusing intellectual games; but Vital Economy is the Philosopher's Stone.

When a heretic wishes to avoid martyrdom he speaks of "Orthodoxy, True and False" and demonstrates that the True is his heresy.

Beware of the man who does not return your blow: he neither forgives you nor allows you to forgive yourself.

If you injure your neighbor, better not do it by halves.

Sentimentality is the error of supposing that quarter can be given or taken in moral conflicts.

Two starving men cannot be twice as hungry as one; but two rascals can be ten times as vicious as one.

Make your cross your crutch; but when you see another man do it, beware of him.

SELF-SACRIFICE

Self-sacrifice enables us to sacrifice other people without blushing.

If you begin by sacrificing yourself to those you love, you will end by hating those to whom you have sacrificed yourself.

THE END

RIDERS TO THE SEA[*]

By

JOHN MILLINGTON SYNGE

"HE BELONGED TO THOSE WHO, LIKE Wordsworth, like Coleridge, like Goldsmith, like Keats, have little personality, as far as the casual eye can see, little personal will, but fiery brooding imagination." These words, from Synge's closest friend, W. B. Yeats, give the clue to the character and work of this almost unknowable dramatist.

At first sight, a play by Synge appears to be the work of an unschooled and primitive observer who reports, as if by chance, with the instinct of genius for the significant. Synge, on the contrary, was almost moribund with education and culture before he discovered the true bent of his faculties. He had become proficient in music, well-read in four languages, and classically inclined to the point of composing a worshipful study of Racine, when Yeats "discovered" him in a Paris garret. The previous year, however, Synge had come under the spell of life in the Aran Islands. Yeats had little difficulty in winning him from his "literary" pursuits to join the young Irish renaissance and to return to the Aran Islands for his material.

Few dramatists have come to their task with a wider background or set about it in a more workmanlike manner. First, he observed and made copious notes, then selected and compressed, and finally shaped with unerring craftsmanship. In method, he seems never to have experimented, but to have created with perfect mastery from the beginning.

In 1902, John Masefield found him in London at work on his first plays, probably *The Tinker's Wedding, In the Shadow of the Glen,* and *Riders to the Sea.* The English poet described him as "a strange personality," with a face "dark from gravity," as though "the man behind were forever listening to life's case before passing judgment." His voice had "a kind of lively bitterness in it." This dour exterior was offset by "a humorous mouth, the kindling in the eyes

and something robust in his build." In conversation, though always polite, "he offered nothing of his own." His interest was "in life, not in ideas." He composed slowly on a typewriter and rewrote each play several times. Friends gathered to hear his first plays read, and from their verdict "Synge learned his métier that night."

In the Shadow of the Glen was given by the newly organized Irish National Theatre Company on October 8, 1903. In 1904, this company moved into its now famous home, the Abbey Theatre, and appointed Synge to cooperate with W. B. Yeats and Lady Gregory as adviser. He gave the rest of his life to this enterprise. His *Riders to the Sea* was produced that year. The hostility that Synge's work created is now difficult to understand, but it proved to be excellent publicity, and, what was more important, it fired the workers for the Theatre with loyalty to their artistic standards and with the fighting spirit. *In the Shadow of the Glen* had profaned the romantic conception of Ireland's womanhood and *The Playboy of the Western World* (1907) had spoiled the idyllic belief in the Irish peasant's unsullied virtue. Synge was astonished at the turmoil he had unsuspectingly aroused and his already weakened constitution was severely strained. He had counted too much on the Irish sense of humor. The loyalty of W. B. Yeats and Lady Gregory and their faith in his ultimate triumph are among the brightest records of modern drama. A futile operation cut short his life before his sixth play, *Deirdre of the Sorrows,* had been completed. He died in a nursing home on March 24, 1909.

In Synge's plays, the poetic and dramatic insight of the reader is subjected to a searching test. They depend hardly at all on the unessential—theatricality, exploitation of ideas, moralizing, and sentimentality. They are rather the work of the true poet-dramatist who substitutes for theatrical mechanism the reality of life itself, reporting it not photographically, but with a sensitive discernment for dramatic values, for color,

* Reprinted by permission of Random House, Inc.

hythm, and form, and, above all, for psycho-ogical reality. It is, therefore, easy to fall nto George Moore's rather snobbish error of pronouncing *Riders to the Sea,* for in-stance, essentially undramatic because of he absence of obvious theatrical conflict. If, however, the dramatic greatness of *Edipus, Hamlet, Faustus,* and *The Misan-hrope* lies not in their externals but in their presentation of a progressive spiritual reac-tion to an inscrutable destiny, by means of perfectly conceived characters and dialogue truthfully colored, then *Riders to the Sea* is the masterpiece it has been pronounced. One must, however, read all of Synge to appre-ciate his breadth and versatility. The wild riot of humor in *The Playboy* and *The Tinker's Wedding* is, perhaps, truer to his mentality than the tragic beauty of *Riders to the Sea.*

He wrote comparatively little about him-self and was not inclined to abstract think-ing even about his art. What he wrote was, nevertheless, highly significant and true to the best critical standards.

COMMENTS CONCERNING DRAMA

"The drama is made serious, in the French sense of the word, not by the degree in which it is taken up with problems that are serious in themselves, but by the degree in which it gives the nourishment, not very easy to de-fine, on which our imaginations live. . . . In these days, the playhouse is too often stocked with the drugs of many seedy problems, or with the absinthe or vermouth of the last musical comedy. Of the things that nourish the imagination, humor is one of the most needful."

"The drama, like the symphony, does not teach or prove anything. Analysts with their problems, and teachers with their systems, are soon as old-fashioned as the pharmaco-poeia of Galen—look at Ibsen and the Ger-mans—but the best plays of Ben Jonson and Molière can no more go out of fashion than the blackberries on the hedges."

Preface to *The Tinker's Wedding.*

"In writing *The Playboy of the Western World,* as in my other plays, I have used one or two words only that I have not heard among the country people of Ireland, or spoken in my own nursery before I could read the newspapers. . . . I am glad to acknowledge how much I owe to the folk imagination of these fine people."

"All art is a collaboration, and there is little doubt that in the happy ages of litera-ture, striking and beautiful phrases were as ready to the story-teller's or the playwright's hand, as the rich cloaks and dresses of his time. I got more aid than any learning could have given me from a chink in the floor of the old Wicklow house where I was staying, that let me hear what was being said by the servant girls in the kitchen."

"On the stage, one must have reality and one must have joy, and that is why the in-tellectual modern drama has failed . . . the joy found only in what is superb and wild in reality. In a good play every speech should be as fully flavored as a nut or apple, and such speeches cannot be written by any-one who works among people who have shut their lips on poetry. In Ireland, for a few years more, we have a popular imagination that is fiery, and magnificent, and tender."

Preface to *The Playboy of the Western World.*

PRODUCTION

Synge's *In the Shadow of the Glen* was presented in a small and badly adapted hall on October 8, 1903, as one of the first offer-ings of the newly formed Irish National Theatre Company, and *Riders to the Sea* was produced by the same company in 1904 after the opening of their Abbey Theatre. This Theatre, now among the most famous of modern playhouses, and the first government subsidized theatre in the English-speaking world, was presented outright for a period of five years by Miss A. E. F. Horniman, who had been deeply impressed by the work of the Irish players when they appeared the previous year at Queen's Gate Hall in Lon-don. The auditorium, dating from 1820, seated 562 persons, and was in the horseshoe form with one balcony. The stage was only fifteen feet deep. The curtain was black with gold stripes and the signal for its rising was a deep-toned gong. Original lighting, by no means elaborate, produced a glow, rather than a glare, giving an artistic effect that was perhaps not calculated.

The style of acting which the company developed was something new in the theatre of its period and was immediately recog-nized as artistically superior to anything known in the professional theatre. The brothers Fay, who headed the work of pro-duction, contributed a professional but not conventional tone to the work of this un-paid and amateur troup. Frank Fay, skilled in speech production, insisted from the be-ginning upon a musical and vigorous de-livery that has always distinguished the work of the company. It imparted to prose, es-pecially that of Synge, the rhythm and tonality of poetry, as was clearly the author's intention, but never to the extent of losing its simple naturalism. Of one of Synge's plays given at this theater George Moore wrote: "I would call attention to the abundance of the beauty of the dialogue, to the fact that one listened to it as one listens to music, charmed by the inevitableness of the words and the ease with which phrase is linked with phrase. . . . Mr. Synge has also discovered great literature in barbarous idiom as gold is discovered in quartz."

When the company played in London, inviting direct comparison with the expert acting of the reigning naturalistic school, the London critics were even more impressed. A. B. Walkley, of the *Times,* found the effect produced "quite outside the range of anything which those houses (the public theaters) have to offer." He noted especially their naturalness that appeared artless, although in reality it was carefully studied. "They stand stock still," he wrote; "the speaker of the moment is the only one who is allowed a little gesture. . . . The listeners do not distract one's attention with fussy stage business; they just stay where they are and listen."

A writer in the *Manchester Guardian* caught the significance of the new art. "These Irish actors have contrived to reach back past most of the futilities that have grown upon the ordinary theater of commerce and get a fresh, clean hold on their craft in its elements. They know how to let things alone, how to stand still when nothing is to be done . . . how to save up the voice and gesture for rare and brief passages of real poignancy, how to fade into the background."

JOHN MILLINGTON SYNGE

Born 1871, Newton Little, near Dublin.
Son of a thrifty landowner.
Studied music and prepared with tutors for Trinity College, Dublin.
1892, Degree of A.B., Trinity College. Prize in harmony and counterpoint at the Royal Irish Academy.
1893, Continued study of music in Germany.
1894, Abandoned music for a literary career in Paris.
1896, Toured Italy.
1898, Visited the Aran Islands.
1899, Discovered in Paris by W. B. Yeats, who advised him to abandon literary criticism for a life of creative writing, and to return to the Aran Islands for his material.
1902, Worked on his first plays in London.
1903, *In the Shadow of the Glen* produced by the Irish National Theatre Company.
1904, Made adviser of this company in their new Abbey Theatre.
1909, Died after an operation for a cancerous growth.

PLAYS

1903 *In the Shadow of the Glen.* 1904 *Riders to the Sea.* 1905 *The Well of the Saints.* 1907 *The Playboy of the Western World.* 1909 *The Tinker's Wedding* (published, but written earlier). 1910 *Deirdre of the Sorrows* (published).

WRITINGS ON DRAMA

Preface to *The Playboy of the Western World,* 1907. Preface to *The Tinker's Wedding,* 1909.

RIDERS TO THE SEA

Characters

MAURYA, *an old woman.*
BARTLEY, *her son.*

CATHLEEN, *her daughter.*
NORA, *a younger daughter.*
MEN *and* WOMEN.

SCENE: *An island off the West of Ireland.
Cottage kitchen, with nets, oilskins,
spinning-wheel, some new boards standing by the wall, etc.* CATHLEEN, *a girl
of about twenty, finishes kneading cake,
and puts it down in the pot-oven by the
fire; then wipes her hands, and begins
to spin at the wheel.* NORA, *a young
girl, puts her head in at the door.*

Nora. [*In a low voice.*] Where is she?
Cathleen. She's lying down, God help her,
and may be sleeping, if she's able.

[NORA *comes in softly, and takes a
bundle from under her shawl.*]
Cathleen. [*Spinning the wheel rapidly.*]
What is it you have?
Nora. The young priest is after bringing
them. It's a shirt and a plain stocking were
got off a drowned man in Donegal.

[CATHLEEN *stops her wheel with a sudden movement, and leans out to listen.*]
Nora. We're to find out if it's Michael's
they are, some time herself will be down
looking by the sea.
Cathleen. How would they be Michael's,
Nora? How would he go the length of that
way to the far north?
Nora. The young priest says he's known
the like of it. "If it's Michael's they are,"
says he, "you can tell herself he's got a clean
burial by the grace of God, and if they're
not his, let no one say a word about them,
for she'll be getting her death," says he,
"with crying and lamenting."

[*The door which* NORA *half closed is
blown open by a gust of wind.*]
Cathleen. [*Looking out anxiously.*] Did
you ask him would he stop Bartley going this
day with the horses to the Galway fair?
Nora. "I won't stop him," says he, "but
let you not be afraid. Herself does be saying
prayers half through the night, and the
Almighty God won't leave her destitute,"
says he, "with no son living."
Cathleen. Is the sea bad by the white
rocks, Nora?

Nora. Middling bad, God help us. There's
a great roaring in the west, and it's worse
it'll be getting when the tide's turned to the
wind. [*She goes over to the table with the
bundle.*] Shall I open it now?
Cathleen. Maybe she'd wake up on us,
and come in before we'd done. [*Coming to
the table.*] It's a long time we'll be, and the
two of us crying.
Nora. [*Goes to the inner door and listens.*] She's moving about on the bed. She'll
be coming in a minute.
Cathleen. Give me the ladder, and I'll put
them up in the turf-loft, the way she won't
know of them at all, and maybe when the
tide turns she'll be going down to see would
he be floating from the east.

[*They put the ladder against the gable
of the chimney;* CATHLEEN *goes up a
few steps and hides the bundle in the
turf-loft.* MAURYA *comes in from the
inner room.*]
Maurya. [*Looking up at* CATHLEEN *and
speaking querulously.*] Isn't it turf enough
you have for this day and evening?
Cathleen. There's a cake baking at the
fire for a short space [*Throwing down the
turf.*] and Bartley will want it when the tide
turns if he goes to Connemara.

[NORA *picks up the turf and puts it
round the pot-oven.*]
Maurya. [*Sitting down on a stool at the
fire.*] He won't go this day with the wind
rising from the south and west. He won't
go this day, for the young priest will stop
him surely.
Nora. He'll not stop him, Mother, and I
heard Eamon Simon and Stephen Pheety and
Colum Shawn saying he would go.
Maurya. Where is it itself?
Nora. He went down to see would there
be another boat sailing in the week, and I'm
thinking it won't be long till he's here now,
for the tide's turning at the green head, and
the hooker's tacking from the east.
Cathleen. I hear some one passing the
big stones.

Nora. [*Looking out.*] He's coming now, and he in a hurry.

Bartley. [*Comes in and looks round the room. Speaking sadly and quietly.*] Where is the bit of new rope, Cathleen, was bought in Connemara?

Cathleen. [*Coming down.*] Give it to him, Nora; it's on a nail by the white boards. I hung it up this morning, for the pig with the black feet was eating it.

Nora. [*Giving him a rope.*] Is that it, Bartley?

Maurya. You'd do right to leave that rope, Bartley, hanging by the boards. [BARTLEY *takes the rope.*] It will be wanting in this place, I'm telling you, if Michael is washed up tomorrow morning, or the next morning, or any morning in the week, for it's a deep grave we'll make him by the grace of God.

Bartley. [*Beginning to work with the rope.*] I've no halter the way I can ride down on the mare, and I must go now quickly. This is the one boat going for two weeks or beyond it, and the fair will be a good fair for horses. I heard them saying below.

Maurya. It's a hard thing they'll be saying below if the body is washed up and there's no man in it to make the coffin, and I after giving a big price for the finest white boards you'd find in Connemara.

[*She looks around at the boards.*]

Bartley. How would it be washed up, and we after looking each day for nine days, and a strong wind blowing a while back from the west and south?

Maurya. If it wasn't found itself, that wind is raising the sea, and there was a star up against the moon, and it rising in the night. If it was a hundred horses, or a thousand horses you had itself, what is the price of a thousand horses against a son where there is one son only?

Bartley. [*Working at the halter, to* CATHLEEN.] Let you go down each day, and see the sheep aren't jumping in on the rye, and if the jobber comes you can sell the pig with the black feet if there is a good price going.

Maurya. How would the like of her get a good price for a pig?

Bartley. [*To* CATHLEEN.] If the west wind holds with the last bit of the moon let you and Nora get up weed enough for another cock for the kelp. It's hard set we'll be from this day with no one in it but one man to work.

Maurya. It's hard set we'll be surely the day you're drownd'd with the rest. What way will I live and the girls with me, and I an old woman looking for the grave?

[BARTLEY *lays down the halter, takes off his old coat, and puts on a newer one of the same flannel.*]

Bartley. [*To* NORA.] Is she coming to the pier?

Nora. [*Looking out.*] She's passing the green head and letting fall her sails.

Bartley. [*Getting his purse and tobacco.*] I'll have half an hour to go down, and you'll see me coming again in two days, or in three days, or maybe in four days if the wind is bad.

Maurya. [*Turning around to the fire, and putting her shawl over her head.*] Isn't it a hard and cruel man won't hear a word from an old woman, and she holding him from the sea?

Cathleen. It's the life of a young man to be going on the sea, and who would listen to an old woman with one thing and she saying it over?

Bartley. [*Taking the halter.*] I must go now quickly. I'll ride down on the red mare, and the gray pony'll run behind me. . . . The blessing of God on you.

[*He goes out.*]

Maurya. [*Crying out as he is in the door.*] He's gone now, God spare us, and we'll not see him again. He's gone now, and when the black night is falling I'll have no son left me in the world.

Cathleen. Why wouldn't you give him your blessing and he looking round in the door? Isn't it sorrow enough is on every one in this house without your sending him out with an unlucky word behind him, and a hard word in his ear?

[MAURYA *takes up the tongs and begins raking the fire aimlessly without looking around.*]

Nora. [*Turning toward her.*] You're taking away the turf from the cake.

Cathleen. [*Crying out.*] The Son of God forgive us, Nora, we're after forgetting his bit of bread. [*She comes over to the fire.*]

Nora. And it's destroyed he'll be going till dark night, and he after eating nothing since the sun went up.

Cathleen. [*Turning the cake out of the oven.*] It's destroyed he'll be, surely. There's no sense left in any person in a house where an old woman will be talking forever.

[MAURYA *sways herself on her stool.*]

Cathleen. [*Cutting off some of the bread and rolling it in a cloth; to* MAURYA.] Let you go down now to the spring well and give him this and he passing. You'll see him then and the dark word will be broken, and you can say "God speed you," the way he'll be easy in his mind.

Maurya. [*Taking the bread.*] Will I be in it as soon as himself?

Cathleen. If you go now quickly.

Maurya. [*Standing up unsteadily.*] It's hard set I am to walk.

Cathleen. [*Looking at her anxiously.*] Give her the stick, Nora, or maybe she'll slip on the big stones.

Nora. What stick?

Cathleen. The stick Michael brought from Connemara.

Maurya. [*Taking a stick* NORA *gives her.*] In the big world the old people do be leaving things after them for their sons and children, but in this place it is the young men do be leaving things behind for them that do be old.

[*She goes out slowly.* NORA *goes over to the ladder.*]

Cathleen. Wait, Nora, maybe she'd turn back quickly. She's that sorry, God help her, you wouldn't know the thing she'd do.

Nora. Is she gone round by the bush?

Cathleen. [*Looking out.*] She's gone now. Throw it down quickly, for the Lord knows when she'll be out of it again.

Nora. [*Getting the bundle from the left.*] The young priest said he'd be passing to-morrow, and we might go down and speak to him below if it's Michael's they are surely.

Cathleen. [*Taking the bundle.*] Did he say what way they were found?

Nora. [*Coming down.*] "There were two men," says he, "and they rowing round with poteen before the cocks crowed, and the oar of one of them caught the body, and they passing the black cliffs of the north."

Cathleen. [*Trying to open the bundle.*] Give me a knife, Nora, the string's perished with the salt water, and here's a black knot on it you wouldn't loosen in a week.

Nora. [*Giving her a knife.*] I've heard tell it was a long way to Donegal.

Cathleen. [*Cutting the string.*] It is surely. There was a man in here a while ago—the man sold us that knife—and he said if you set off walking from the rocks beyond, it would be seven days you'd be in Donegal.

Nora. And what time would a man take, and he floating?

[CATHLEEN *opens the bundle and takes out a bit of stocking. They look at them eagerly.*]

Cathleen. [*In a low voice.*] The Lord spare us, Nora! Isn't it a queer hard thing to say if it's his they are surely?

Nora. I'll get his shirt off the hook the way we can put the one flannel on the other. [*She looks through some clothes hanging in the corner.*] It's not with them, Cathleen, and where will it be?

Cathleen. I'm thinking Bartley put it on him in the morning, for his own shirt was heavy with the salt in it. [*Pointing to the corner.*] There's a bit of a sleeve was of the same stuff. Give me that and it will do.

[NORA *brings it to her and they compare the flannel.*]

Cathleen. It's the same stuff, Nora; but if it is itself aren't there great rolls of it in the shops of Galway, and isn't it many another man may have a shirt of it as well as Michael himself?

Nora. [*Who has taken up the stocking and counted the stitches, crying out.*] It's Michael, Cathleen, it's Michael; God spare his soul, and what will herself say when she hears this story, and Bartley on the sea?

Cathleen. [*Taking the stocking.*] It's a plain stocking.

Nora. It's the second one of the third pair I knitted, and I put up three score stitches, and I dropped four of them.

Cathleen. [*Counts the stitches.*] It's that number is in it. [*Crying out.*] Ah, Nora, isn't it a bitter thing to think of him floating that way to the far north, and no one to keen him but the black hags that do be flying on the sea?

Nora. [*Swinging herself around, and throwing out her arms on the clothes.*] And isn't it a pitiful thing when there is nothing left of a man who was a great rower and fisher, but a bit of an old shirt and a plain stocking?

Cathleen. [*After an instant.*] Tell me, is herself coming, Nora? I hear a little sound on the path.

Nora. [*Looking out.*] She is, Cathleen. She's coming up to the door.

Cathleen. Put these things away before she'll come in. Maybe it's easier she'll be after giving her blessing to Bartley, and we won't let on we've heard anything the time he's on the sea.

Nora. [*Helping* CATHLEEN *to close the bundle.*] We'll put them here in the corner.

[*They put them into a hole in the chimney corner.* CATHLEEN *goes back to the spinning-wheel.*]

Nora. Will she see it was crying I was?

Cathleen. Keep your back to the door the way the light'll not be on you.

[NORA *sits down at the chimney corner, with her back to the door.* MAURYA *comes in very slowly, without looking at the girls, and goes over to her stool at the other side of the fire. The cloth with the bread is still in her hand. The girls look at each other, and* Nora *points to the bundle of bread.*]

Cathleen. [*After spinning for a moment.*] You didn't give him his bit of bread?

[Maurya *begins to keen softly, without turning around.*]

Cathleen. Did you see him riding down?

[Maurya *goes on keening.*]

Cathleen. [*A little impatiently.*] God forgive you; isn't it a better thing to raise your voice and tell what you seen, than to be making lamentation for a thing that's done? Did you see Bartley, I'm saying to you.

Maurya. [*With a weak voice.*] My heart's broken from this day.

Cathleen. [*As before.*] Did you see Bartley?

Maurya. I seen the fearfulest thing.

Cathleen. [*Leaves her wheel and looks out.*] God forgive you; he's riding the mare now over the green head, and the gray pony behind him.

Maurya. [*Starts, so that her shawl falls back from her head and shows her white tossed hair. With a frightened voice.*] The gray pony behind him.

Cathleen. [*Coming to the fire.*] What is it ails you, at all?

Maurya. [*Speaking very slowly.*] I've seen the fearfulest thing any person has seen, since the day Bride Dara seen the dead man with the child in his arms.

Cathleen and Nora. Uah.

[*They crouch down in front of the old woman at the fire.*]

Nora. Tell us what it is you seen.

Maurya. I went down to the spring well, and I stood there saying a prayer to myself. Then Bartley came along, and he riding on the red mare with the gray pony behind him. [*She puts up her hands, as if to hide something from her eyes.*] The Son of God spare us, Nora!

Cathleen. What is it you seen?

Maurya. I seen Michael himself.

Cathleen. [*Speaking softly.*] You did not, Mother. It wasn't Michael you seen, for his body is after being found in the far north, and he's got a clean burial by the grace of God.

Maurya. [*A little defiantly.*] I'm after seeing him this day, and he riding and galloping. Bartley came first on the red mare; and I tried to say "God speed you," but something choked the words in my throat. He went by quickly; and "the blessing of God on you," says he, and I could say nothing. I looked up then, and I crying, at the gray pony, and there was Michael upon it—with fine clothes on him, and new shoes on his feet.

Cathleen. [*Begins to keen.*] It's destroyed we are from this day. It's destroyed, surely.

Nora. Didn't the young priest say the Almighty God wouldn't leave her destitute with no son living?

Maurya. [*In a low voice, but clearly.*] It's little the like of him knows of the sea. . . . Bartley will be lost now, and let you call in Eamon and make me a good coffin out of the white boards, for I won't live after them. I've had a husband, and a husband's father, and six sons in this house—six fine men, though it was a hard birth I had with every one of them and they coming to the world— and some of them were found and some of them were not found, but they're gone now, the lot of them. . . . There were Stephen, and Shawn, were lost in the great wind, and found after in the Bay of Gregory of the Golden Mouth, and carried up the two of them on the one plank, and in by that door.

[*She pauses for a moment. The* Girls *start as if they heard something through the door that is half open behind them.*]

Nora. [*In a whisper.*] Did you hear that, Cathleen? Did you hear a noise in the northeast?

Cathleen. [*In a whisper.*] There's some one after crying out by the seashore.

Maurya. [*Continues without hearing anything.*] There was Sheamus and his father, and his own father again, were lost in a dark night, and not a stick or sign was seen of them when the sun went up. There was Patch after was drowned out of a curagh that turned over. I was sitting here with Bartley, and he a baby, lying on my two knees, and I seen two women, and three women, and four women coming in, and they crossing themselves, and not saying a word. I looked out then, and there were men coming after them, and they holding a thing in the half of a red sail, and water dripping out of it—it was a dry day, Nora—and leaving a track to the door.

[*She pauses again with her hand stretched out toward the door. It opens softly and* Old Women *begin to come in, crossing themselves on the threshold, and kneeling down in front of the stage with red petticoats over their heads.*]

Maurya. [*Half in a dream, to* Cathleen.] Is it Patch, or Michael, or what is it at all?

Cathleen. Michael is after being found in the far north, and when he is found there how could he be here in this place?

Maurya. There does be a power of young

men floating round in the sea, and what way would they know if it was Michael they had, or another man like him, for when a man is nine days in the sea, and the wind blowing, it's hard set his own mother would be to say what man was it.

Cathleen. It's Michael, God spare him, for they're after sending us a bit of clothes from the far north.

[*She reaches out and hands* MAURYA *the clothes that belong to* MICHAEL. MAURYA *stands up slowly, and takes them in her hands.* NORA *looks out.*]

Nora. They're carrying a thing among them and there's water dripping out of it and leaving a track by the big stones.

Cathleen. [*In a whisper to the* WOMEN *who have come in.*] Is it Bartley it is?

One of the Women. It is surely, God rest his soul.

[*Two* YOUNGER WOMEN *come in and pull out the table. Then* MEN *carry in the body of* BARTLEY, *laid on a plank, with a bit of a sail over it, and lay it on the table.*]

Cathleen. [*To the* WOMEN, *as they are doing so.*] What way was he drowned?

One of the Women. The gray pony knocked him into the sea, and he was washed out where there is a great surf on the white rocks.

[MAURYA *has gone over and knelt down at the head of the table. The* WOMEN *are keening softly and swaying themselves with a slow movement.* CATHLEEN *and* NORA *kneel at the other end of the table. The* MEN *kneel near the door.*]

Maurya. [*Raising her head and speaking as if she did not see the people around her.*] They're all gone now, and there isn't anything more the sea can do to me. . . . I'll have no call now to be up crying and praying when the wind breaks from the south, and you can hear the surf is in the east, and the surf is in the west, making a great stir with the two noises, and they hitting one on the other. I'll have no call now to be going down and getting Holy Water in the dark nights after Samhain, and I won't care what way the sea is when the other women will be keening. [*To* NORA.] Give me the Holy Water, Nora, there's a small sup still on the dresser. [NORA *gives it to her.*]

Maurya. [*Drops* MICHAEL'S *clothes across* BARTLEY'S *feet, and sprinkles the Holy Water over him.*] It isn't that I haven't prayed for you, Bartley, to the Almighty God. It isn't that I haven't said prayers in the dark night till you wouldn't know what I'd be saying; but it's a great rest I'll have

now, and it's time surely. It's a great rest I'll have now, and great sleeping in the long nights after Samhain, if it's only a bit of wet flour we do have to eat, and maybe a fish that would be stinking.

[*She kneels down again, crossing herself, and saying prayers under her breath.*]

Cathleen. [*To an* OLD MAN.] Maybe yourself and Eamon would make a coffin when the sun rises. We have fine white boards herself bought, God help her, thinking Michael would be found, and I have a new cake you can eat while you'll be working.

The Old Man. [*Looking at the boards.*] Are there nails with them?

Cathleen. There are not, Colum; we didn't think of the nails.

Another Man. It's a great wonder she wouldn't think of the nails, and all the coffins she's seen made already.

Cathleen. It's getting old she is, and broken.

[MAURYA *stands up again very slowly and spreads out the pieces of* MICHAEL'S *clothes beside the body, sprinkling them with the last of the Holy Water.*]

Nora. [*In a whisper to* CATHLEEN.] She's quiet now, and easy; but the day Michael was drowned you could hear her crying out from this to the spring well. It's fonder she was of Michael, and would any one have thought that?

Cathleen. [*Slowly and clearly.*] An old woman will be soon tired with anything she will do, and isn't it nine days herself is after crying and keening, and making great sorrow in the house?

Maurya. [*Puts the empty cup mouth downwards on the table, and lays her hands together on* BARTLEY'S *feet.*] They're all together this time, and the end is come. May the Almighty God have mercy on Bartley's soul, and on Michael's soul, and on the souls of Sheamus and Patch, and Stephen and Shawn. [*Bending her head.*] And may He have mercy on my soul, Nora, and on the soul of every one is left living in the world.

[*She pauses, and the keen rises a little more loudly from the* WOMEN, *then sinks away.*]

Maurya. [*Continuing.*] Michael has a clean burial in the far north, by the grace of the Almighty God. Bartley will have a fine coffin out of the white boards, and a deep grave surely. What more can we want than that? No man at all can be living forever, and we must be satisfied.

[*She kneels down again and the* CURTAIN *falls slowly.*]

"HENRY IV" *

[Enrico Quarto]

By

LUIGI PIRANDELLO

Translated by EDWARD STORER

PIRANDELLO SAID:
"There are authors who write for the pleasure they take in writing alone and who look for no other satisfaction. Such writers might be described as historical. But there are others who, in addition to deriving the pleasure I have described, feel a spiritual need that will not permit them to use characters, events, or scenes which are not impregnated, so to speak, with a special sense of life that gives them a universal significance or value. Such writers are, properly speaking, philosophical. And to this latter group I have the misfortune to belong."

Pirandello stands, therefore, among the intellectual dramatists, such as Ibsen, Shaw, Granville-Barker, and a few others, whose purpose is frankly and finally to make their audiences think. For this purpose they will arouse laughter or tears, but they do not consider laughter or tears the end of drama. Rather it is the stimulation of the intellect through the dramatic conflict of opinions and habits of thought. But whereas Ibsen and Shaw and the other philosophical dramatists were concerned with the problems of conduct confronting the individual in society, Pirandello was concerned with a problem he thought deeper and more puzzling, namely, what *is* the individual?

He said:
"When a man lives, he lives and does not see himself. Well, put a mirror before him and make him see himself in the act of living, under the sway of his passions: either he remains astonished and dumbfounded at his own appearance, or else he turns away his eyes so as not to see himself, or else in disgust he spits at his image, or again he clenches his fist to break it; and if he had been weeping, he can weep no more; if he

had been laughing, he can laugh no more, and so on. In a word, there arises a crisis, and that crisis is my theater."

And he makes the Father in *Six Characters* state the aspect of the problem of personality which he used in so many of his plays, including *"Henry IV"*:

"With different persons, we may be a quite different individual. We cling, however, to the illusion that we remain identical for all persons and every situation. Nothing could be more false than this illusion, as we realize when suddenly surprised in the midst of some particular action. We know that we are not wholly committed and expressed in this action, and that it would be a cruel injustice if a man were judged solely upon the strength of it, pinned down perpetually to this particular moment as if the whole of his life were thereby summarized and made manifest."

Pirandello saw that, though personality is fluid and dynamic, we live as though it were solid and static. Out of that conflict arise the plays. In *"Henry IV"* a personality is artificially made solid and static, and he is mad; when he becomes sane again, the lapse of time prevents his resuming life, since life and time have flowed past him; during the play he attempts action, only to be fixed forever in the attitude of madness.

In order to show a man "under the sway of his passions," Pirandello chose ordinarily a plot whose events are violent and sensational. But he rarely showed these events on stage; he preferred to employ the retrospective technique whereby they are gradually revealed to the audience as explanation of the peculiarities of the characters. The formula—and Pirandello used the same plan so often it may be called a formula—has this obvious defect, that we say to ourselves, "These things could never happen to us." But it was probably not Pirandello's inten-

* From *Three Plays* by Luigi Pirandello. Reprinted by permission of E. P. Dutton & Co.

tion to tell us they could; he wished to tell us rather that we cannot certainly know human beings; that the individual is and must remain eternally a puzzle. Perhaps that is why Pirandello called every volume of his collected plays *Maschere Nude—Naked Masks*.

Pirandello was late in turning to the drama, writing his first play when he was forty-six years old. But before then he had published numerous short stories, six volumes of poetry, and four novels, besides some critical works. In the novels his interest in the analysis of personality can be clearly perceived, while in the short stories he showed his flair for the dramatic, which he himself took account of by turning many of them into plays. Until he turned to drama he was not given much critical attention, but it came to him rapidly thereafter. With *Six Characters* in 1921 his reputation became world-wide.

"Henry IV" was produced in New York in 1924 as *The Living Mask*. In 1925 the play was offered in London under the original title, and revived in 1929 as *The Mock Emperor*.

HISTORICAL NOTE

Henry IV (1050-1106), King of Italy, Germany, and Burgundy, and later Emperor of the Holy Roman Empire, refused to obey a decree of Gregory VII (Hildebrand), pope 1073-1085, forbidding lay investiture, that is, the appointment by lay princes of bishops and other church officers. Henry was excommunicated by Gregory in January 1076, and in January 1077 made his famous submission at Canossa. He is reported to have stood for three days and two nights in the snow of the castle courtyard, unarmed and unattended, dressed in penitent's sackcloth, awaiting the pope's willingness to receive him. He seems to have made his submission in order to strengthen his cause against the rebellious Saxon nobles, who had nominated an antiking. In this he succeeded, but he had given dramatic evidence of the power of the pope's weapon of excommunication.

LUIGI PIRANDELLO

Born 1867, Girgenti, Sicily.
Ph.D., University of Bonn, Germany.
1899–1923, Teacher of Italian Literature in Normal College for Women in Rome.
1925, Formed his own Art Theatre in Rome.
1934, Awarded Nobel Prize for literature.
Novelist, short story writer, and poet.
Died 1936.

PLAYS

1913 *La Morsa* (one act, translated as *The Vise*). 1913 *Lumìe di Sicilia* (one act, translated as *Sicilian Limes*). The following three plays cannot be accurately dated, except that they are later than La Morsa: *Il Dovere del Medico* (one act, translated as *The Doctor's Duty*). *Cecè* (one act, translated as *Chee-Chee*). *L'Imbecille* (one act, translated as *The Imbecile*). 1915 *Se non Così* (first form of *La Ragione degli Altri*). 1916 *Liolà* (translated). 1916 *Pensaci, Giacomino!* (translated as *Think It Over, Jimmy*). 1916 *Così È (se vi pare)* (translated as *Right You Are! (If You Think So)*, and as *And That's the Truth!*). 1916 *All' Uscita* (one act, translated as *At the Gate*). 1917 *Il Berretto a Sonagli*. 1917 *Il Piacere dell' Onestà* (translated as *The Pleasure of Honesty*). 1917

L'Innesto. 1918 *Il Giuoco delle Parti* (translated as *The Game as He Played It*, and as *Playing the Game*). 1918 *Ma non è una Cosa Seria* (translated as *He Didn't Mean It*). 1919 *L'Uomo, La Bestia e la Virtù* (translated as *Man, Beast, and Virtue*, and as *Say It with Flowers*). 1920 *Tutto per Bene*. 1920 *Come Prima Meglio di Prima* (adapted as *Floriani's Wife*). 1920 *La Signora Morli Una e Due* (revised, 1926, with the title *Due in Una*). 1920 *La Patente* (one act, translated as *By Judgment of Court*, and as *Legal Title*). 1921 *La Ragione degli Altri* (second form of *Se non Così*). 1921 *Sei Personaggi in cerca d'Autore* (translated as *Six Characters in Search of an Author*). 1922 *Enrico Quarto* (translated as *"Henry IV"*). 1922 *Vestire gli Ignudi* (translated as *Naked*). 1923 *La Vita che ti Diedi* (translated as *The Life I Gave to Thee*, and as *The Mother*).

1923 *L'Uomo dal Fiore in Bocco* (one act, translated as *The Man with the Flower in His Mouth*). 1924 *Ciascuno a Suo Modo* (translated as *Each in His Own Way*). 1925 *L'Altro Figlio* (one act, translated as *The House with the Column*). 1925 *La Giara* (one act, translated as *The Jar*). 1925 *La Sagra del Signor della Nave* (one act, translated as *Our Lord of the Ship*). 1926 *Diana e la Tuda*. 1927 *L'Amica delle Mogli*. 1928 *La Nuova Colonia* (translated as *The New Colony*). 1929 *O di Uno o di Nessuno*. 1929 *Lazzaro* (translated as *Lazarus*, and as *Though One Rose*). 1930 *Come Tu Mi Vuoi* (translated as *As You Desire Me*). 1930 *Questa Sera si recita a Soggetto* (translated as *Tonight We Improvise*). 1932 *Trovarsi*. 1933 *Quando se è Qualcuno*. 1934 *La Favola del Figlio Combiato* (libretto for music of Malipiero). 1935 *Non Si Sa Come*. 1947 *I Giganti della Montagna* (unfinished).

WRITINGS ON DRAMA

"Comment et pourquoi j'ai écrit Six personnages en quête d'auteur," *Revue de Paris*, IV, 332 (July 15, 1925).

"HENRY IV"

Characters

"Henry IV."
The Marchioness Matilda Spina.
Her Daughter Frida.
The Young Marquis Charles Di Nolli.
Baron Tito Belcredi.
Doctor Dionysius Genoni.

The Four Private Counsellors:
Harold (Frank).
Landolph (Lolo).
Ordulph (Momo).
Berthold (Fino).
John, the Old Waiter.

The Two Valets in Costume.

A Solitary Villa in Italy in Our Own Time.

ACT I

Salon in the villa, furnished and decorated so as to look exactly like the throne room of Henry IV in the royal residence at Goslar. Among the antique decorations there are two modern life-size portraits in oil painting. They are placed against the back wall, and mounted in a wooden stand that runs the whole length of the wall. (It is wide and protrudes, so that it is like a large bench.) One of the paintings is on the right; the other on the left of the throne, which is in the middle of the wall and divides the stand.
The Imperial chair and baldachin.
The two portraits represent a lady and a gentleman, both young, dressed up in carnival costumes: one as "Henry IV," the other as the "Marchioness Matilda of Tuscany." Exits to right and left, two on each side.
[When the curtain goes up, the two Valets *jump down, as if surprised, from the stand on which they have been lying, and go and take their positions, as rigid as statues, on either side below the Throne with their halberds in their hands. Soon after, from the second exit, right, enter* Harold, Landolph, Ordulph *and* Berthold, *young men employed by the* Marquis Charles Di Nolli *to play the part of "Secret Counsellors" at the court of "*Henry IV." *They are, therefore, dressed like German knights of the XIth century.* Berthold, *nick-named* Fino, *is just entering on his duties for the first time. His companions are telling him what he has to do and* amusing themselves at his expense. The scene is to be played rapidly and vivaciously.]*

Landolph. [To Berthold *as if explaining.]* And this is the throne room.
Harold. At Goslar.
Ordulph. Or at the castle in the Hartz, if you prefer.
Harold. Or at Wurms.
Landolph. According as to what's doing, it jumps about with us, now here, now there.
Ordulph. In Saxony.
Harold. In Lombardy.
Landolph. On the Rhine.
One of the Valets. [Without moving, just opening his lips.] I say . . .
Harold. [Turning round.] What is it?
First Valet. [Like a statue.] Is he coming in or not? *[He alludes to* Henry IV.]
Ordulph. No, no, he's asleep. You needn't worry.
Second Valet. [Releasing his pose, taking a long breath and going to lie down again on the stand.] You might have told us at once.
First Valet. [Going over to Harold.] Have you got a match, please?
Landolph. What? You can't smoke a pipe here, you know.
First Valet. [While Harold *offers him a light.]* No; a cigarette.
[Lights his cigarette and lies down again on the stand.]
Berthold. [Who has been looking on in amazement, walking round the room, regarding the costumes of the others.] I say . . . this room . . . these costumes . . . Which

251

Henry IV is it? I don't quite get it. Is he Henry IV of France or not?

[*At this* LANDOLPH, HAROLD, *and* ORDULPH *burst out laughing.*]

Landolph. [*Still laughing; and pointing to* BERTHOLD *as if inviting the others to make fun of him.*] Henry of France he says: ha! ha!

Ordulph. He thought it was the king of France!

Harold. Henry IV of Germany, my boy: the Salian dynasty!

Ordulph. The great and tragic Emperor!

Landolph. He of Canossa. Every day we carry on here the terrible war between Church and State, by Jove.

Ordulph. The Empire against the Papacy!

Harold. Antipopes against the Pope!

Landolph. Kings against antikings!

Ordulph. War on the Saxons!

Harold. And all the rebel Princes!

Landolph. Against the Emperor's own sons!

Berthold. [*Covering his head with his hands to protect himself against this avalanche of information.*] I understand! I understand! Naturally, I didn't get the idea at first. I'm right then: these aren't costumes of the XVIth century?

Harold. XVIth century! Not much!

Ordulph. We're somewhere between a thousand and eleven hundred.

Landolph. Work it out for yourself: if we are before Canossa on the 25th of January, 1077 . . .

Berthold. [*More confused than ever.*] Oh my God! What a mess I've made of it!

Ordulph. Well, just slightly, if you supposed you were at the French court.

Berthold. All that historical stuff I've crammed!

Landolph. My dear boy, it's four hundred years earlier.

Berthold. [*Getting angry.*] Good Heavens! You ought to have told me it was Germany and not France. I can't tell you how many books I've read in the last fifteen days.

Harold. But I say, surely you knew that poor Tito was Adalbert of Bremen,[1] here?

Berthold. Not a damned bit!

Landolph. Well, don't you see how it is? When Tito died, the Marquis Di Nolli : . .

Berthold. Oh, it was he, was it? He might have told me.

Harold. Perhaps he thought you knew.

Landolph. He didn't want to engage anyone else in substitution. He thought the remaining three of us would do. But *he* began to cry out: "With Adalbert driven away . . .": because, you see, he didn't imagine poor Tito was dead; but that, as Bishop Adalbert, the rival bishops of Cologne and Mayence had driven him off . . .

Berthold. [*Taking his head in his hand.*] But I don't know a word of what you're talking about.

Ordulph. So much the worse for you, my boy!

Harold. But the trouble is that not even we know who you are.

Berthold. What? Not even you? You don't know who I'm supposed to be?

Ordulph. Hum! "Berthold."

Berthold. But which Berthold? And why Berthold?

Landolph. [*Solemnly imitating* HENRY IV.] "They've driven Adalbert away from me. Well then, I want Berthold! I want Berthold!" That's what he said.

Harold. We three looked one another in the eyes: who's got to be Berthold?

Ordulph. And so here you are, "Berthold," my dear fellow!

Landolph. I'm afraid you will make a bit of a mess of it.

Berthold. [*Indignant, getting ready to go.*] Ah, no! Thanks very much, but I'm off! I'm out of this!

Harold. [*Restraining him with the other two, amid laughter.*] Steady now! Don't get excited!

Landolph. Cheer up, my dear fellow! We don't any of us know who we are really. He's Harold; he's Ordulph; I'm Landolph! That's the way he calls us. We've got used to it. But who are we? Names of the period! Yours, too, is a name of the period: Berthold! Only one of us, poor Tito, has got a really decent part, as you can read in history: that of the Bishop of Bremen. He was just like a real bishop. Tito did it awfully well, poor chap!

Harold. Look at the study he put into it!

Landolph. Why, he even ordered his Majesty about, opposed his views, guided and counselled him. We're "secret counsellors" —in a manner of speaking only; because it is written in history that Henry IV was hated by the upper aristocracy for surrounding himself at court with young men of the bourgeoisie.

Ordulph. Us, that is.

Landolph. Yes, small devoted vassals, a bit dissolute and very gay . . .

Berthold. So I've got to be gay as well?

---

[1] Adalbert, Archbishop of Bremen, was Henry IV's *patronus* or tutor; he was driven from court in 1066 by the jealousy of other bishops; he returned in 1069 and died in 1072.

Harold. I should say so! Same as we are!

Ordulph. And it isn't too easy, you know.

Landolph. It's a pity; because the way we're got up, we could do a fine historical reconstruction. There's any amount of material in the story of Henry IV. But, as a matter of fact, we do nothing. We have the form without the content. We're worse than the real secret counsellors of Henry IV; because certainly no one had given them a part to play—at any rate, they didn't feel they had a part to play. It was their life. They looked after their own interests at the expense of others, sold investitures and—what not! We stop here in this magnificent court—for what?—Just doing nothing. We're like so many puppets hung on the wall, waiting for some one to come and move us or make us talk.

Harold. Ah no, old sport, not quite that! We've got to give the proper answer, you know. There's trouble if he asks you something and you don't chip in with the cue.

Landolph. Yes, that's true.

Berthold. Don't rub it in too hard! How the devil am I to give him the proper answer, if I've crammed Henry IV of France, and now he turns out to be Henry IV of Germany? [*The other three laugh.*]

Harold. You'd better start and prepare yourself at once.

Ordulph. We'll help you out.

Harold. We've got any amount of books on the subject. A brief run through the main points will do to begin with.

Ordulph. At any rate, you must have got some sort of general idea.

Harold. Look here! [*Turns him around and shows him the portrait of the* MARCHION-ESS MATILDA *on the wall.*] Who's that?

Berthold. [*Looking at it.*] That? Well, the thing seems to me somewhat out of place, anyway: two modern paintings in the midst of all this respectable antiquity!

Harold. You're right! They weren't there in the beginning. There are two niches there behind the pictures. They were going to put up two statues in the style of the period. Then the places were covered with those canvases there.

Landolph. [*Interrupting and continuing.*] They would certainly be out of place if they really were paintings!

Berthold. What are they, if they aren't paintings?

Landolph. Go and touch them! Pictures all right . . . but for him! [*Makes a mysterious gesture to the right, alluding to* HENRY IV.] . . . who never touches them! . . .

Berthold. No? What are they for him?

Landolph. Well, I'm only supposing, you know; but I imagine I'm about right. They're images such as . . . well—such as a mirror might throw back. Do you understand? That one there represents himself, as he is in this throne room, which is all in the style of the period. What's there to marvel at? If we put you before a mirror, won't you see yourself, alive, but dressed up in ancient costume? Well, it's as if there were two mirrors there, which cast back living images in the midst of a world which, as you will see, when you have lived with us, comes to life too.

Berthold. I say, look here . . . I've no particular desire to go mad here.

Harold. Go mad, be hanged! You'll have a fine time!

Berthold. Tell me this: how have you all managed to become so learned?

Landolph. My dear fellow, you can't go back over 800 years of history without picking up a bit of experience.

Harold. Come on! come on! You'll see how quickly you get into it!

Ordulph. You'll learn wisdom, too, at this school.

Berthold. Well, for Heaven's sake, help me a bit! Give me the main lines, anyway.

Harold. Leave it to us. We'll do it all between us.

Landolph. We'll put your wires on you and fix you up like a first class marionette. Come along!

[*They take him by the arm to lead him away.*]

Berthold. [*Stopping and looking at the portrait on the wall.*] Wait a minute! You haven't told me who that is. The Emperor's wife?

Harold. No! The Emperor's wife is Bertha of Susa, the sister of Amadeus II of Savoy.

Ordulph. And the Emperor, who wants to be young with us, can't stand her, and wants to put her away.

Landolph. That is his most ferocious enemy: Matilda, Marchioness of Tuscany.[1]

Berthold. Ah, I've got it: the one who gave hospitality to the Pope!

Landolph. Exactly: at Canossa!

Ordulph. Pope Gregory VII!

Harold. Our *bête noir!* Come on! come on!

[*All four move toward the right to go out, when, from the left, the old servant* JOHN *enters in evening dress.*]

---

[1] Lived 1046–1115. Always a vigorous supporter of the papacy. Her estates, which included Canossa, were the richest in Italy.

John. [*Quickly, anxiously.*] Hss! Hss! Frank! Lolo!

Harold. [*Turning round.*] What is it?

Berthold. [*Marvelling at seeing a man in modern clothes enter the throne room.*] Oh! I say, this is a bit too much, this chap here!

Landolph. A man of the XXth century, here! Oh, go away!

[*They run over to him, pretending to menace him and throw him out.*]

Ordulph. [*Heroically.*] Messenger of Gregory VII, away!

Harold. Away! Away!

John. [*Annoyed, defending himself.*] Oh, stop it! Stop it, I tell you!

Ordulph. No, you can't set foot here!

Harold. Out with him!

Landolph. [*To* BERTHOLD]. Magic, you know! He's a demon conjured up by the Wizard of Rome! Out with your swords!

[*Makes as if to draw a sword.*]

John. [*Shouting.*] Stop it, will you? Don't play the fool with me! The Marquis has arrived with some friends. . . .

Landolph. Good! Good! Are there ladies too?

Ordulph. Old or young?

John. There are two gentlemen.

Harold. But the ladies, the ladies, who are they?

John. The Marchioness and her daughter.

Landolph. [*Surprised.*] What do you say?

Ordulph. The Marchioness?

John. The Marchioness! The Marchioness!

Harold. Who are the gentlemen?

John. I don't know.

Harold. [*To* BERTHOLD.] They're coming to bring us a message from the Pope, do you see?

Ordulph. All messengers of Gregory VII! What fun!

John. Will you let me speak, or not?

Harold. Go on, then!

John. One of the two gentlemen is a doctor, I fancy.

Landolph. Oh, I see, one of the usual doctors.

Harold. Bravo, Berthold, you'll bring us luck!

Landolph. You wait and see how we'll manage this doctor!

Berthold. It looks as if I were going to get into a nice mess right away.

John. If the gentlemen would allow me to speak . . . they want to come here into the throne room.

Landolph. [*Surprised.*] What? She? The Marchioness here?

Harold. Then this is something quite different! No play-acting this time!

Landolph. We'll have a real tragedy: that's what!

Berthold. [*Curious.*] Why? Why?

Ordulph. [*Pointing to the portrait.*] She is that person there, don't you understand?

Landolph. The daughter is the fiancée of the Marquis. But what have they come for, I should like to know?

Ordulph. If he sees her, there'll be trouble.

Landolph. Perhaps he won't recognize her any more.

John. You must keep him there, if he should wake up . . .

Ordulph. Easier said than done, by Jove!

Harold. You know what he's like!

John. Even by force, if necessary! Those are my orders. Go on! Go on!

Harold. Yes, because who knows if he hasn't already waked up?

Ordulph. Come on then!

Landolph. [*Going toward* JOHN *with the others.*] You'll tell us later what it all means.

[*Exit the* FOUR COUNSELLORS.]

John. [*Shouting after them.*] Close the door there, and hide the key! That other door too.

[*Pointing to the other door on right.*]

John. [*To the two* VALETS.] Be off, you two! There! [*Pointing to exit right.*] Close the door after you, and hide the key!

[*The two* VALETS *go out by the first door on right.* JOHN *moves over to the left to show in:* DONNA MATILDA SPINA, *the young* MARCHIONESS FRIDA, DR. DIONYSIUS GENONI, *the* BARON TITO BELCREDI *and the young* MARQUIS CHARLES DI NOLLI, *who, as master of the house, enters last.*]

DONNA MATILDA SPINA *is about 45, still handsome, although there are too patent signs of her attempts to remedy the ravages of time with make-up. Her head is thus rather like a Walkyrie's. This facial make-up contrasts with her beautiful sad mouth. A widow for many years, she now has as her friend the* BARON TITO BELCREDI, *whom neither she nor anyone else takes seriously—at least so it would appear.*

What TITO BELCREDI *really is for her at bottom, he alone knows; and he is, therefore, entitled to laugh, if his friend feels the need of pretending not to know. He can always laugh at the jests which the beautiful* MARCHIONESS *makes with the others at his expense.*

He is slim, prematurely gray, and younger than she is. His head is bird-like in shape. He would be a very vivacious person, if his ductile agility (which among other things makes him a redoubtable swordsman) were not enclosed in a sheath of Arab-like laziness, which is revealed in his strange, nasal drawn-out voice.

FRIDA, *the daughter of the* MARCHION-ESS, *is 19. She is sad, because her imperious and too beautiful mother puts her in the shade, and provokes facile gossip against her daughter as well as against herself. Fortunately for her, she is engaged to the* MARQUIS CHARLES DI NOLLI.

CHARLES DI NOLLI *is a stiff young man, very indulgent toward others, but sure of himself for what he amounts to in the world. He is worried about all the responsibilities which he believes weigh on him. He is dressed in deep mourning for the recent death of his mother.*

DR. DIONYSIUS GENONI *has a bold, rubicund, Satyr-like face, prominent eyes, a pointed beard (which is silvery and shiny), and elegant manners. He is nearly bald. All enter in a state of perturbation, almost as if afraid, and all (except* DI NOLLI) *looking curiously about the room. At first, they speak sotto voce.*]

Di Nolli. [*To* JOHN.] Have you given the orders properly?

John. Yes, my Lord; don't be anxious about that.

Belcredi. Ah, magnificent! magnificent!

Doctor. How extremely interesting! Even in the surroundings his raving madness—has been perfectly taken into account!

Donna Matilda. [*Glancing round for her portrait, discovers it, and goes up close to it.*] Ah! Here it is! [*Going back to admire it, while mixed emotions stir within her.*] Yes . . . yes . . . [*Calls her daughter* FRIDA.]

Frida. Ah, your portrait!

Donna Matilda. No, no . . . look again; it's you, not I, there!

Di Nolli. Yes, it's quite true. I told you so, I . . .

Donna Matilda. But I would never have believed it! [*Shaking as if with a chill.*] What a strange feeling it gives one! [*Then looking at her* DAUGHTER.] Frida, what's the matter? [*She pulls her to her side, and slips an arm round her waist.*] Come; don't you see yourself in me there?

Frida. Well, I really . . .

Donna Matilda. Don't you think so? Don't you, really? [*Turning to* BELCREDI.] Look at it, Tito! Speak up, man!

Belcredi. [*Without looking.*] Ah, no! I shan't look at it. For me, *a priori*, certainly not!

Donna Matilda. Stupid! You think you are paying me a compliment! [*Turning to* DOCTOR GENONI.] What do you say, Doctor? Do say something, please!

[DOCTOR *makes a movement to go near to the picture.*]

Belcredi. [*With his back turned, pretending to attract his attention secretly.*] Hss! No, Doctor! For the love of Heaven, have nothing to do with it!

Doctor. [*Getting bewildered and smiling.*] And why shouldn't I?

Donna Matilda. Don't listen to him! Come here! He's insufferable!

Frida. He acts the fool by profession, didn't you know that?

Belcredi. [*To the* DOCTOR, *seeing him go over.*] Look to your feet, Doctor! Mind where you're going!

Doctor. Why?

Belcredi. Be careful you don't put your foot in it!

Doctor. [*Laughing feebly.*] No, no. After all, it seems to me there's no reason to be astonished at the fact that a daughter should resemble her mother!

Belcredi. Hullo! Hullo! He's done it now; he's said it.

Donna Matilda. [*With exaggerated anger, advancing toward* BELCREDI.] What's the matter? What has he said? What has he done?

Doctor. [*Candidly.*] Well, isn't it so?

Belcredi. [*Answering the* MARCHIONESS.] I said there was nothing to be astounded at —and you are astounded! And why so, then, if the thing is so simple and natural for you now?

Donna Matilda. [*Still more angry.*] Fool! fool! It's just because it is so natural! Just because it isn't my daughter who is there. [*Pointing to the canvas.*] That is my portrait; and to find my daughter there instead of me fills me with astonishment, an astonishment which, I beg you to believe, is sincere. I forbid you to cast doubts on it.

Frida. [*Slowly and wearily.*] My God! It's always like this . . . rows over nothing. . . .

Belcredi. [*Also slowly, looking dejected, in accents of apology.*] I cast no doubt on anything! I noticed from the beginning that you haven't shared your mother's astonishment; or, if something did astonish you, it was because the likeness between you and the portrait seemed so strong.

Donna Matilda. Naturally! She cannot recognize herself in me as I was at her age; while I, there, can very well recognize myself in her as she is now!

Doctor. Quite right! Because a portrait is always there fixed in the twinkling of an eye: for the young lady something far away and without memories, while, for the Marchioness, it can bring back everything: movements, gestures, looks, smiles, a whole heap of things. . . .

Donna Matilda. Exactly!

Doctor. [*Continuing, turning toward her.*] Naturally enough, you can live all these old sensations again in your daughter.

Donna Matilda. He always spoils every innocent pleasure for me, every touch I have of spontaneous sentiment! He does it merely to annoy me.

Doctor. [*Frightened at the disturbance he has caused, adopts a professorial tone.*] Likeness, dear Baron, is often the result of imponderable things. So one explains that . . .

Belcredi. [*Interrupting the discourse.*] Somebody will soon be finding a likeness between you and me, my dear professor!

Di Nolli. Oh! let's finish with this, please! [*Points to the two doors on the right, as a warning that there is someone there who may be listening.*] We've wasted too much time as it is!

Frida. As one might expect when *he's* present. [*Alludes to* BELCREDI.]

Di Nolli. Enough! The Doctor is here; and we have come for a very serious purpose which you all know is important for me.

Doctor. Yes, that is so! But now, first of all, let's try to get some points down exactly. Excuse me, Marchioness, will you tell me why your portrait is here? Did you present it to him then?

Donna Matilda. No, not at all. How could I have given it to him? I was just like Frida then—and not even engaged. I gave it to him three or four years after the accident. I gave it to him because his mother wished it so much. . . . [*Points to* DI NOLLI.]

Doctor. She was his sister? [*Alludes to* HENRY IV.]

Di Nolli. Yes, Doctor; and our coming here is a debt we pay to my mother, who has been dead for more than a month. Instead of being here, she and I [*Indicating* FRIDA.] ought to be traveling together. . . .

Doctor. . . . Taking a cure of quite a different kind!

Di Nolli. H'm! Mother died in the firm conviction that her adored brother was just about to be cured.

Doctor. And can't you tell me, if you please, how she inferred this?

Di Nolli. The conviction would appear to have derived from certain strange remarks which he made, a little before mother died.

Doctor. Oh, remarks! . . . Ah! . . . It would be extremely useful for me to have those remarks, word for word, if possible.

Di Nolli. I can't remember them. I know that mother returned awfully upset from her last visit with him. On her death-bed, she made me promise that I would never neglect him, that I would have doctors see him, and examine him.

Doctor. Um! Um! Let me see! let me see! Sometimes very small reasons determine . . . and this portrait here then? . . .

Donna Matilda. For Heaven's sake, Doctor, don't attach excessive importance to this. It made an impression on me because I had not seen it for so many years!

Doctor. If you please, quietly, quietly . . .

Di Nolli. Well, yes, it must be about fifteen years ago.

Donna Matilda. More, more: eighteen!

Doctor. Forgive me, but you don't quite know what I'm trying to get at. I attach a very great importance to these two portraits. . . . They were painted, naturally, prior to the famous—and most regrettable pageant, weren't they?

Donna Matilda. Of course!

Doctor. That is . . . when he was quite in his right mind—that's what I've been trying to say. Was it his suggestion that they should be painted?

Donna Matilda. Lots of the people who took part in the pageant had theirs done as a souvenir . . .

Belcredi. I had mine done—as "Charles of Anjou!"

Donna Matilda. . . . as soon as the costumes were ready.

Belcredi. As a matter of fact, it was proposed that the whole lot of us should be hung together in a gallery of the villa where the pageant took place. But in the end, everybody wanted to keep his own portrait.

Donna Matilda. And I gave him this portrait of me without very much regret . . . since his mother . . . [*Indicates* DI NOLLI.]

Doctor. You don't remember if it was he who asked for it?

Donna Matilda. Ah, that I don't remem-

ber . . . Maybe it was his sister, wanting
to help out . . .

Doctor. One other thing: was it his idea,
this pageant?

Belcredi. [*At once.*] No, no, it was mine!

Doctor. If you please . . .

Donna Matilda. Don't listen to him! It
was poor Belassi's idea.

Belcredi. Belassi! What had he got to do
with it?

Donna Matilda. Count Belassi, who died,
poor fellow, two or three months after . . .

Belcredi. But if Belassi wasn't there
when . . .

Di Nolli. Excuse me, Doctor; but is it
really necessary to establish whose the original idea was?

Doctor. It would help me, certainly!

Belcredi. I tell you the idea was mine!
There's nothing to be proud of in it, seeing
what the result's been. Look here, Doctor,
it was like this. One evening, in the first
days of November, I was looking at an illustrated German review in the club. I was
merely glancing at the pictures, because I
can't read German. There was a picture of
the Kaiser, at some university town where
he had been a student . . . I don't remember which.

Doctor. Bonn, Bonn!

Belcredi. You are right! Bonn! He was
on horseback, dressed up in one of those
ancient German student guild-costumes, followed by a procession of noble students, also
in costume. The picture gave me the idea.
Already some one at the club had spoken of
a pageant for the forthcoming carnival. So
I had the notion that each of us should
choose for this Tower of Babel pageant to
represent some character: a king, an emperor, a prince, with his queen, empress, or
lady, alongside of him—and all on horseback. The suggestion was at once accepted.

Donna Matilda. I had my invitation from
Belassi.

Belcredi. Well, he wasn't speaking the
truth! That's all I can say, if he told you
the idea was his. He wasn't even at the club
the evening I made the suggestion, just as
he [*Meaning* HENRY IV.] wasn't there either.

Doctor. So he chose the character of
Henry IV?

Donna Matilda. Because I . . . thinking
of my name, and not giving the choice any
importance, said I would be the Marchioness
Matilda of Tuscany.

Doctor. I . . . don't understand the relation between the two.

Donna Matilda. Neither did I, to begin
with, when he said that in that case he would

be at my feet like Henry IV of Canossa. I
had heard of Canossa of course; but to tell
the truth, I'd forgotten most of the story;
and I remember I received a curious impression when I had to get up my part, and
found that I was the faithful and zealous
friend of Pope Gregory VII in deadly enmity with the Emperor of Germany. Then
I understood why, since I had chosen to
represent his implacable enemy, he wanted
to be near me in the pageant as Henry IV.

Doctor. Ah, perhaps because . . .

Belcredi. Good Heavens, Doctor, because
he was then paying furious court to her!
[*Indicates the* MARCHIONESS.] And she,
naturally . . .

Donna Matilda. Naturally? Not naturally at all . . .

Belcredi. [*Pointing to her.*] She couldn't
stand him . . .

Donna Matilda. No, that isn't true! I
didn't dislike him. Not at all! But for me,
when a man begins to want to be taken seriously, well . . .

Belcredi. [*Continuing for her.*] He gives
you the clearest proof of his stupidity.

Donna Matilda. No, dear; not in this
case; because he was never a fool like you.

Belcredi. Anyway, I've never asked you
to take me seriously.

Donna Matilda. Yes, I know. But with
him one couldn't joke. [*Changing her tone
and speaking to the* DOCTOR.] One of the
many misfortunes which happen to us
women, Doctor, is to see before us every
now and again a pair of eyes glaring at us
with a contained intense promise of eternal
devotion. [*Bursts out laughing.*] There is
nothing quite so funny. If men could only
see themselves with that eternal fidelity look
in their faces! I've always thought it comic;
then more even than now. But I want to
make a confession—I can do so after twenty
years or more. When I laughed at him then,
it was partly out of fear. One might have
almost believed a promise from those eyes of
his. But it would have been very dangerous.

Doctor. [*With lively interest.*] Ah! ah!
This is most interesting! Very dangerous,
you say?

Donna Matilda. Yes, because he was very
different from the others. And then, I am
. . . well . . . what shall I say? . . . a little impatient of all that is pondered, or
tedious. But I was too young then, and a
woman. I had the bit between my teeth. It
would have required more courage than I
felt I possessed. So, I laughed at him too—
with remorse, to spite myself, indeed; since
I saw that my own laugh mingled with those

of all the others—the other fools—who made fun of him.

Belcredi. My own case, more or less!

Donna Matilda. You make people laugh at you, my dear, with your trick of always humiliating yourself. It was quite a different affair with him. There's a vast difference. And you—you know—people laugh in your face!

Belcredi. Well, that's better than behind one's back!

Doctor. Let's get to the facts. He was then already somewhat exalted, if I understand rightly.

Belcredi. Yes, but in a curious fashion, Doctor.

Doctor. How?

Belcredi. Well, cold-bloodedly, so to speak.

Donna Matilda. Not at all! It was like this, Doctor! He was a bit strange, certainly; but only because he was fond of life: eccentric, there!

Belcredi. I don't say he simulated exaltation. On the contrary, he was often genuinely exalted. But I could swear, Doctor, that he saw himself at once in his own exaltation. Moreover, I'm certain it made him suffer. Sometimes he had the most comical fits of rage against himself.

Doctor. Yes?

Donna Matilda. That is true.

Belcredi. [*To* Donna Matilda.] And why? [*To the* Doctor.] Evidently, because that immediate lucidity that comes from acting, assuming a part, at once put him out of key with his own feelings, which seemed to him not exactly false, but like something he was obliged to valorize there and then as—what shall I say?—as an act of intelligence, to make up for that sincere cordial warmth he felt lacking. So he improvised, exaggerated, let himself go, so as to distract and forget himself. He appeared inconstant, fatuous, and—yes—even ridiculous, sometimes.

Doctor. And may we say unsociable?

Belcredi. No, not at all. He was famous for getting up things: *tableaux vivants,* dances, theatrical performances for charity: all for the fun of the thing, of course. He was a jolly good actor, you know!

Di Nolli. Madness has made a superb actor of him.

Belcredi. Why, so he was even in the old days. When the accident happened, after the horse fell . . .

Doctor. Hit the back of his head, didn't he?

Donna Matilda. Oh, it was horrible! He was beside me! I saw him between the horse's hoofs! It was rearing!

Belcredi. None of us thought it was anything serious at first. There was a stop in the pageant, a bit of disorder. People wanted to know what had happened. But they'd already taken him off to the villa.

Donna Matilda. There wasn't the least sign of a wound, not a drop of blood.

Belcredi. We thought he had merely fainted.

Donna Matilda. But two hours afterwards . . .

Belcredi. He reappeared in the drawing-room of the villa . . . that is what I wanted to say . . .

Donna Matilda. My God! What a face he had! I saw the whole thing at once!

Belcredi. No, no! that isn't true. Nobody saw it, Doctor, believe me!

Donna Matilda. Doubtless, because you were all like mad folk.

Belcredi. Everybody was pretending to act his part for a joke. It was a regular Babel.

Donna Matilda. And you can imagine, Doctor, what terror struck into us when we understood that he, on the contrary, was playing his part in deadly earnest . . .

Doctor. Oh, he was there too, was he?

Belcredi. Of course! He came straight into the midst of us. We thought he'd quite recovered, and was pretending, fooling, like all the rest of us . . . only doing it rather better; because, as I say, he knew how to act.

Donna Matilda. Some of them began to hit him with their whips and fans and sticks.

Belcredi. And then—as a king, he was armed, of course—he drew out his sword and menaced two or three of us . . . It was a terrible moment, I can assure you!

Donna Matilda. I shall never forget that scene—all our masked faces hideous and terrified gazing at him, at that terrible mask of his face, which was no longer a mask, but madness, madness personified.

Belcredi. He was Henry IV, Henry IV in person, in a moment of fury.

Donna Matilda. He'd got into it all the detail and minute preparation of a month's careful study. And it all burned and blazed there in the terrible obsession which lit his face.

Doctor. Yes, that is quite natural, of course. The momentary obsession of a dilettante became fixed, owing to the fall and the damage to the brain.

Belcredi. [*To* Frida *and* Di Nolli.] You see the kind of jokes life can play on us.

[*To* DI NOLLI.] You were four or five years old. [*To* FRIDA.] Your mother imagines you've taken her place there in that portrait; when, at the time, she had not the remotest idea that she would bring you into the world. My hair is already gray; and he —look at him—— [*Points to the portrait.*] ha! A smack on the head, and he never moves again: Henry IV for ever!

Doctor. [*Seeking to draw the attention of the others, looking learned and imposing.*] Well, well, then it comes, we may say, to this . . .

[*Suddenly the first exit to right, the one nearest footlights, opens, and* BERTHOLD *enters all excited.*]

Berthold. [*Rushing in.*] I say! I say!

[*Stops for a moment, arrested by the astonishment which his appearance has caused in the others.*]

Frida. [*Running away terrified.*] Oh dear! oh dear! it's he, it's . . .

Donna Matilda. [*Covering her face with her hands so as not to see.*] Is it, is it he?

Di Nolli. No, no, what are you talking about? Be calm!

Doctor. Who is it then?

Belcredi. One of our masqueraders.

Di Nolli. He is one of the four youths we keep here to help him out in his madness . . .

Berthold. I beg your pardon, Marquis . . .

Di Nolli. Pardon be damned! I gave orders that the doors were to be closed, and that nobody should be allowed to enter.

Berthold. Yes, sir, but I can't stand it any longer, and I ask you to let me go away this very minute.

Di Nolli. Oh, you're the new valet, are you? You were supposed to begin this morning, weren't you?

Berthold. Yes, sir, and I can't stand it, I can't bear it.

Donna Matilda. [*To* DI NOLLI *excitedly.*] What? Then he's not so calm as you said?

Berthold. [*Quickly.*] No, no, my lady, it isn't he; it's my companions. You say, "help him out with his madness," Marquis; but they don't do anything of the kind. They're the real madmen. I come here for the first time, and instead of helping me . . .

[LANDOLPH *and* HAROLD *come in from the same door, but hesitate on the threshold.*]

Landolph. Excuse me.

Harold. May I come in, my Lord?

Di Nolli. Come in! What's the matter? What are you all doing?

Frida. Oh God! I'm frightened! I'm going to run away.

[*Makes toward exit at left.*]

Di Nolli. [*Restraining her at once.*] No, no, Frida!

Landolph. My Lord, this fool here . . .

[*Indicates* BERTHOLD.]

Berthold. [*Protesting.*] Ah, no thanks, my friends, no thanks! I'm not stopping here! I'm off!

Landolph. What do you mean—you're not stopping here?

Harold. He's ruined everything, my Lord, running away in here!

Landolph. He's made him quite mad. We can't keep him in there any longer. He's given orders that he's to be arrested; and he wants to "judge" him at once from the throne. What is to be done?

Di Nolli. Shut the door, man! Shut the door! Go and close that door!

[LANDOLPH *goes over to close it.*]

Harold. Ordulph, alone, won't be able to keep him there.

Landolph. My Lord, perhaps if we could announce the visitors at once, it would turn his thoughts. Have the gentlemen thought under what pretext they will present themselves to him?

Di Nolli. It's all been arranged! [*To the* DOCTOR.] If you, Doctor, think it well to see him at once. . . .

Frida. I'm not coming! I'm not coming! I'll keep out of this. You too, mother, for Heaven's sake, come away with me!

Doctor. I say . . . I suppose he's not armed, is he?

Di Nolli. Nonsense! Of course not. [*To* FRIDA.] Frida, you know this is childish of you. You wanted to come!

Frida. I didn't at all. It was mother's idea.

Donna Matilda. And I'm quite ready to see him. What are we going to do?

Belcredi. Must we absolutely dress up in some fashion or other?

Landolph. Absolutely essential, indispensable, sir. Alas! as you see . . . [*Shows his costume.*], there'd be awful trouble if he saw you gentlemen in modern dress.

Harold. He would think it was some diabolical masquerade.

Di Nolli. As these men seem to be in costume to you, so we appear to be in costume to him, in these modern clothes of ours.

Landolph. It wouldn't matter so much if he wouldn't suppose it to be the work of his mortal enemy.

Belcredi. Pope Gregory VII?

Landolph. Precisely. He calls him "a pagan."

Belcredi. The Pope a pagan? Not bad that!

Landolph. Yes, sir—and a man who calls up the dead! He accuses him of all the diabolical arts. He's terribly afraid of him.

Doctor. Persecution mania!

Harold. He'd be simply furious.

Di Nolli. [*To* BELCREDI.] But there's no need for you to be there, you know. It's sufficient for the doctor to see him.

Doctor. What do you mean? . . . I? Alone?

Di Nolli. But they are there.

[*Indicates the three* YOUNG MEN.]

Doctor. I don't mean that . . . I mean if the Marchioness . . .

Donna Matilda. Of course. I mean to see him too, naturally. I want to see him again.

Frida. Oh, why, mother, why? Do come away with me, I implore you!

Donna Matilda. [*Imperiously.*] Let me do as I wish! I came here for this purpose! [*To* LANDOLPH.] I shall be "Adelaide," the mother.

Landolph. Excellent! The mother of the Empress Bertha. Good! It will be enough if her Ladyship wears the ducal crown and puts on a mantle that will hide her other clothes entirely. [*To* HAROLD.] Off you go, Harold!

Harold. Wait a moment! And this gentleman here? [*Alludes to the* DOCTOR.]

Doctor. Ah yes . . . we decided I was to be . . . the Bishop of Cluny, Hugh of Cluny!

Harold. The gentleman means the Abbot. Very good! Hugh of Cluny.

Landolph. He's often been here before!

Doctor. [*Amazed.*] What? Been here before?

Landolph. Don't be alarmed! I mean that it's an easily prepared disguise . . .

Harold. We've made use of it on other occasions, you see!

Doctor. But . . .

Landolph. Oh no, there's no risk of his remembering. He pays more attention to the dress than to the person.

Donna Matilda. That's fortunate for me, too.

Di Nolli. Frida, you and I'll get along. Come on, Tito!

Belcredi. Ah no. If she [*Indicates the* MARCHIONESS.] stops here, so do I!

Donna Matilda. But I don't need you at all.

Belcredi. You may not need me, but I should like to see him again myself. Mayn't I?

Landolph. Well, perhaps it would be better if there were three.

Harold. How is the gentleman to be dressed then?

Belcredi. Oh, try and find some easy costume for me.

Landolph. [*To* HAROLD.] Hum! Yes . . . he'd better be from Cluny too.

Belcredi. What do you mean—from Cluny?

Landolph. A Benedictine's habit of the Abbey of Cluny. He can be in attendance on Monsignor. [*To* HAROLD.] Off you go! [*To* BERTHOLD.] And you too get away and keep out of sight all today. No, wait a bit! [*To* BERTHOLD.] You bring here the costumes he will give you. [*To* HAROLD.] You go at once and announce the visit of the "Duchess Adelaide" and "Monsignor Hugh of Cluny." Do you understand?

[HAROLD *and* BERTHOLD *go off by the first door on the right.*]

Di Nolli. We'll retire now.

[*Goes off with* FRIDA, *left.*]

Doctor. Shall I be a *persona grata* to him, as Hugh of Cluny?

Landolph. Oh, rather! Don't worry about that! Monsignor has always been received here with great respect. You too, my Lady, he will be glad to see. He never forgets that it was owing to the intercession of you two that he was admitted to the Castle of Canossa and the presence of Gregory VII, who didn't want to receive him.

Belcredi. And what do I do?

Landolph. You stand a little apart respectfully: that's all.

Donna Matilda. [*Irritated, nervous.*] You would do well to go away, you know.

Belcredi. [*Slowly, spitefully.*] How upset you seem! . . .

Donna Matilda. [*Proudly.*] I am as I am. Leave me alone!

[BERTHOLD *comes in with the costumes.*]

Landolph. [*Seeing him enter.*] Ah, the costumes: here they are. This mantle is for the Marchioness . . .

Donna Matilda. Wait a minute! I'll take off my hat.

[*Does so and gives it to* BERTHOLD.]

Landolph. Put it down there! [*Then to the* MARCHIONESS, *while he offers to put the ducal crown on her head.*] Allow me!

Donna Matilda. Dear, dear! Isn't there a mirror here?

Landolph. Yes, there's one there. [*Points*

to the door on the left.] If the Marchioness would rather put it on herself . . .

Donna Matilda. Yes, yes, that will be better. Give it to me!

[*Takes up her hat and goes off with* Berthold, *who carries the cloak and the crown.*]

Belcredi. Well, I must say, I never thought I should be a Benedictine monk! By the way, this business must cost an awful lot of money.

The Doctor. Like any other fantasy, naturally!

Belcredi. Well, there's a fortune to go upon.

Landolph. We have got there a whole wardrobe of costumes of the period, copied to perfection from old models. This is my special job. I get them from the best theatrical costumers. They cost lots of money.

[Donna Matilda *reenters, wearing mantle and crown.*]

Belcredi. [*At once, in admiration.*] Oh, magnificent! Oh, truly regal!

Donna Matilda. [*Looking at* Belcredi *and bursting out into laughter.*] Oh no, no! Take it off! You're impossible. You look like an ostrich dressed up as a monk.

Belcredi. Well, how about the doctor?

The Doctor. I don't think I look so bad, do I?

Donna Matilda. No; the doctor's all right . . . but you are too funny for words.

The Doctor. Do you have many receptions here then?

Landolph. It depends. He often gives orders that such and such a person appear before him. Then we have to find someone who will take the part. Women too . . .

Donna Matilda. [*Hurt, but trying to hide the fact.*] Ah, women too?

Landolph. Oh, yes; many at first.

Belcredi. [*Laughing.*] Oh, that's great! In costume, like the Marchioness?

Landolph. Oh well, you know, women of the kind that lend themselves to . . .

Belcredi. Ah, I see! [*Perfidiously to the* Marchioness.] Look out, you know he's becoming dangerous for you.

[*The second door on the right opens, and* Harold *appears, making first of all a discreet sign that all conversation should cease.*]

Harold. His Majesty, the Emperor!

[*The two* Valets *enter first, and go and stand on either side of the throne. Then* Henry IV *comes in between* Ordulph *and* Harold, *who keep a little in the rear respectfully.*]

[Henry IV *is about 50 and very pale. The hair on the back of his head is already gray; over the temples and forehead it appears blond, owing to its having been tinted in an evident and puerile fashion. On his cheek bones he has two small, doll-like dabs of color that stand out prominently against the rest of his tragic pallor. He is wearing a penitent's sack over his regal habit, as at Canossa. His eyes have a fixed look which is dreadful to see, and this expression is in strained contrast with the sackcloth.* Ordulph *carries the imperial crown;* Harold, *the sceptre with the eagle, and the globe with the cross.*]

Henry IV. [*Bowing first to* Donna Matilda *and afterwards to the* Doctor.] My lady . . . Monsignor . . . [*Then he looks at* Belcredi *and seems about to greet him too; when, suddenly, he turns to* Landolph, *who has approached him, and asks him sotto voce and with diffidence.*] Is that Peter Damiani?[1]

Landolph. No, Sire. He is a monk from Cluny who is accompanying the Abbot.

Henry IV. [*Looks again at* Belcredi *with increasing mistrust, and then noticing that he appears embarrassed and keeps glancing at* Donna Matilda *and the* Doctor, *stands upright and cries out.*] No, it's Peter Damiani! It's no use, Father, your looking at the Duchess. [*Then turning quickly to* Donna Matilda *and the* Doctor *as though to ward off a danger.*] I swear it! I swear it that my heart is changed toward your daughter. I confess that if he [*Indicates* Belcredi.] hadn't come to forbid it in the name of Pope Alexander, I'd have repudiated her. Yes, yes, there were people ready to favor the repudiation: the bishop of Mayence would have done it for a matter of one hundred and twenty farms. [*Looks at* Landolph *a little perplexed and adds.*] But I mustn't speak ill of the bishops at this moment! [*More humbly to* Belcredi.] I am grateful to you, believe me, I am grateful to you for the hindrance you put in my way!—God knows, my life's been all made of humiliations: my mother, Adalbert, Tribur, Goslar![2] And now this sackcloth you see me wearing! [*Changes tone suddenly and speaks like one who goes over his part in a parenthesis of astuteness.*] It doesn't matter: clarity of ideas, perspicacity, firmness, and

---

[1] Cardinal Pietro Damiani had persuaded Henry IV in 1069 not to divorce his wife Bertha.
[2] Henry was separated from his mother and Adalbert against his will; at Tribur and Goslar he was forced to yield to rebellious Saxon nobles.

patience under adversity—that's the thing. [*Then turning to all and speaking solemnly.*] I know how to make amends for the mistakes I have made; and I can humiliate myself even before you, Peter Damiani. [*Bows profoundly to him and remains curved. Then a suspicion is born in him which he is obliged to utter in menacing tones, almost against his will.*] Was it not perhaps you who started that obscene rumor that my holy mother had illicit relations with the Bishop of Augusta?

Belcredi. [*Since* HENRY IV *has his finger pointed at him.*] No, no, it wasn't I . . .

Henry IV. [*Straightening up.*] Not true, not true? Infamy! [*Looks at him and then adds.*] I didn't think you capable of it! [*Goes to the* DOCTOR *and plucks his sleeve, while winking at him knowingly.*] Always the same, Monsignor, those bishops, always the same!

Harold. [*Softly, whispering as if to help out the* DOCTOR.] Yes, yes, the rapacious bishops!

The Doctor. [*To* HAROLD, *trying to keep it up.*] Ah, yes, those fellows . . . ah yes . . .

Henry IV. Nothing satisfies them! I was a little boy, Monsignor . . . One passes the time, playing even, when, without knowing it, one is a king.—I was six years old; and they tore me away from my mother, and made use of me against her without my knowing anything about it [1] . . . always profaning, always stealing, stealing! . . . One greedier than the other . . . Hanno worse than Stephen! [2] Stephen worse than Hanno!

Landolph. [*Sotto voce, persuasively, to call his attention.*] Majesty!

Henry IV. [*Turning round quickly.*] Ah yes . . . this isn't the moment to speak ill of the bishops. But this infamy against my mother, Monsignor, is too much. [*Looks at the* MARCHIONESS *and grows tender.*] And I can't even weep for her, Lady . . . I appeal to you who have a mother's heart! She came here to see me from her convent a month ago . . . They had told me she was dead! [*Sustained pause full of feeling. Then smiling sadly.*] I can't weep for her; because if you are here now, and I am like this [*Shows the sackcloth he is wearing.*], it means I am twenty-six years old!

Harold. And that she is therefore alive, Majesty! . . .

Ordulph. Still in her convent!

Henry IV. [*Looking at them.*] Ah yes! And I can postpone my grief to another time. [*Shows the* MARCHIONESS *almost with coquetry the tint he has given to his hair.*] Look! I am still fair . . . [*Then slowly as if in confidence.*] For you . . . there's no need! But little exterior details do help! A matter of time, Monsignor, do you understand me? [*Turns to the* MARCHIONESS *and notices her hair.*] Ah, but I see that you too, Duchess . . . Italian, eh? [*As much as to say "false"; but without any indignation, indeed rather with malicious admiration.*] Heaven forbid that I should show disgust or surprise! Nobody cares to recognize that obscure and fatal power which sets limits to our will. But I say, if one is born and one dies . . . Did you want to be born, Monsignor? I didn't! And in both cases, independently of our wills, so many things happen we would wish didn't happen, and to which we resign ourselves as best we can! . . .

Doctor. [*Merely to make a remark, while studying* HENRY IV *carefully.*] Alas! Yes, alas!

Henry IV. It's like this: When we are not resigned, out come our desires. A woman wants to be a man . . . an old man would be young again. Desires, ridiculous fixed ideas of course—But reflect! Monsignor, those other desires are not less ridiculous: I mean, those desires where the will is kept within the limits of the possible. Not one of us can lie or pretend. We're all fixed in good faith in a certain concept of ourselves. However, Monsignor, while you keep yourself in order, holding on with both your hands to your holy habit, there slips down from your sleeves, there peels off from you like . . . like a serpent . . . something you don't notice: life, Monsignor! [*Turns to the* MARCHIONESS.] Has it never happened to you, my Lady, to find a different self in yourself? Have you always been the same? My God! One day . . . how was it, how was it you were able to commit this or that action? [*Fixes her so intently in the eyes as almost to make her blanch.*] Yes, that particular action. That very one: we understand each other! But don't be afraid: I shall reveal it to none. And you, Peter Damiani, how could you be a friend of that man? . . .

Landolph. Majesty!

Henry IV. [*At once.*] No, I won't name him! [*Turning to* BELCREDI.] What did you think of him? But we all of us cling tight to our conceptions of ourselves, just as he

---

[1] In 1062, when Henry was 12, not 6, Archbishop Hanno of Cologne engineered a successful conspiracy to take the young king away from his mother, the empress-regent Agnes.

[2] Stephen IX, pope 1057–1058, who opposed Henry's election as King of Germany, Italy, and Burgundy.

who is growing old dyes his hair. What does it matter that this dyed hair of mine isn't a reality for you, if it *is*, to some extent, for me?—you, you, my Lady, certainly don't dye your hair to deceive the others, nor even yourself; but only to cheat your own image a little before the looking-glass. I do it for a joke! You do it seriously! But I assure you that you too, Madam, are in masquerade, though it be in all seriousness; and I am not speaking of the venerable crown on your brows or the ducal mantle. I am speaking only of the memory you wish to fix in yourself of your fair complexion one day when it pleased you—or of your dark complexion, if you were dark: the fading image of your youth! For you, Peter Damiani, on the contrary, the memory of what you have been, of what you have done, seems to you a recognition of past realities that remain within you like a dream. I'm in the same case too: with so many inexplicable memories—like dreams! Ah! . . . There''s nothing to marvel at in it, Peter Damiani! Tomorrow it will be the same thing with our life of today! [*Suddenly getting excited and taking hold of his sackcloth.*] This sackcloth here! . . . [*Beginning to take it off with a gesture of almost ferocious joy while the three* VALETS *run over to him, frightened, as if to prevent his doing so.*] Ah, my God! [*Draws back and throws off sackcloth.*] To-morrow, at Bressanone, twenty-seven German and Lombard bishops will sign with me the act of deposition of Gregory VII! No Pope at all! Just a false monk! [1]

Ordulph. [*With the other three.*] Majesty! Majesty! In God's name! . . .

Harold. [*Inviting him to put on the sackcloth again.*] Listen to what he says, Majesty!

Landolph. Monsignor is here with the Duchess to intercede in your favor.

[*Makes secret signs to the* DOCTOR *to say something at once.*]

Doctor. [*Foolishly.*] Ah yes . . . yes . . . we are here to intercede . . .

Henry IV. [*Repenting at once, almost terrified, allowing the three to put on the sackcloth again, and pulling it down over him with his own hands.*] Pardon . . . yes . . . yes . . . pardon, Monsignor: forgive me, my Lady . . . I swear to you I feel the whole weight of the anathema. [*Bends himself, takes his face between his hands, as though waiting for something to crush him. Then changing tone, but without moving, says softly to* LANDOLPH, HAROLD, *and* OR-

DULPH.] But I don't know why I cannot be humble before that man there!

[*Indicates* BELCREDI.]

Landolph. [*Sotto voce.*] But why, Majesty, do you insist on believing he is Peter Damiani, when he isn't, at all?

Henry IV. [*Looking at him timorously.*] He isn't Peter Damiani?

Harold. No, no, he is a poor monk, Majesty.

Henry IV. [*Sadly with a touch of exasperation.*] Ah! None of us can estimate what we do when we do it from instinct . . . You, perhaps, Madam, can understand me better than the others, since you are a woman and a Duchess. This is a solemn and decisive moment. I could, you know, accept the assistance of the Lombard bishops, arrest the Pope, lock him up here in the castle, run to Rome, and elect an anti-Pope; offer alliance to Robert Guiscard [1]—and Gregory VII would be lost! I resist the temptation; and, believe me, I am wise in doing so. I feel the atmosphere of our times and the majesty of one who knows how to be what he ought to be! a Pope! Do you feel inclined to laugh at me, seeing me like this? You would be foolish to do so; for you don't understand the political wisdom which makes this penitent's sack advisable. The parts may be changed tomorrow. What would you do then? Would you laugh to see the Pope a prisoner? No! It would come to the same thing: I dressed as a penitent to-day; he, as prisoner tomorrow! But woe to him who doesn't know how to wear his mask, be he king or Pope!—Perhaps he is a bit too cruel! No! Yes, yes, maybe!—— You remember, my Lady, how your daughter Bertha, for whom, I repeat, my feelings have changed [*Turns to* BELCREDI *and shouts to his face as if he were being contradicted by him.*] —yes, changed on account of the affection and devotion she showed me in that terrible moment . . . [*Then once again to the* MARCHIONESS.] you remember how she came with me, my Lady, followed me like a beggar, and passed two nights out in the open, in the snow? You are her mother! Doesn't this touch your mother's heart? Doesn't this urge you to pity, so that you will beg His Holiness for pardon, beg him to receive us?

Donna Matilda. [*Trembling, with feeble voice.*] Yes, yes, at once . . .

Doctor. It shall be done!

Henry IV. And one thing more! [*Draws them in to listen to him.*] It isn't enough

---

[1] These words were used by Henry in a letter to Gregory VII before the excommunication.

[1] Duke of Apulia, in control of southern Italy.

that he should receive me! You know he can do *everything—everything*, I tell you! He can even call up the dead. [*Touches his chest.*] Behold me! Do you see me? There is no magic art unknown to him. Well, Monsignor, my Lady, my torment is really this: that whether here or there [*Pointing to his portrait almost in fear.*] I can't free myself from this magic. I am a penitent now, you see; and I swear to you I shall remain so until he receives me. But you two, when the excommunication is taken off, must ask the Pope to do this thing he can so easily do: to take me away from that [*Indicating the portrait again.*]; and let me live wholly and freely my miserable life. A man can't always be twenty-six, my Lady. I ask this of you for your daughter's sake too; that I may love her as she deserves to be loved, well disposed as I am now, all tender toward her for her pity. There: it's all there! I am in your hands! [*Bows.*] My Lady! Monsignor!

> [*He goes off, bowing grandly, through the door by which he entered, leaving every one stupefied, and the MARCHIONESS so profoundly touched, that no sooner has he gone than she breaks out into sobs and sits down almost fainting.*]

CURTAIN

ACT II

Another room of the villa, adjoining the throne room. Its furniture is antique and severe. Principal exit at rear in the background. To the left, two windows looking on the garden. To the right, a door opening into the throne room.

Late afternoon of the same day.

[DONNA MATILDA, *the* DOCTOR, *and* BELCREDI *are on the stage engaged in conversation; but* DONNA MATILDA *stands on one side, evidently annoyed at what the other two are saying, although she cannot help listening, because, in her agitated state, everything interests her in spite of herself. The talk of the other two attracts her attention, because she instinctively feels the need for calm at the moment.*]

Belcredi. It may be as you say, Doctor, but that was my impression.

Doctor. I won't contradict you; but, believe me, it is only . . . an impression.

Belcredi. Pardon me, but he even said so, and quite clearly. [*Turning to the* MARCHIONESS.] Didn't he, Marchioness?

Donna Matilda. [*Turning round.*] What did he say? . . . [*Then not agreeing.*] Oh yes . . . but not for the reason you think!

Doctor. He was alluding to the costumes we had slipped on . . . Your cloak [*Indicating the* MARCHIONESS.], our Benedictine habits . . . But all this is childish!

Donna Matilda. [*Turning, quickly, indignant.*] Childish? What do you mean, Doctor?

Doctor. From one point of view, it is— I beg you to let me say so, Marchioness! Yet, on the other hand, it is much more complicated than you can imagine.

Donna Matilda. To me, on the contrary, it is perfectly clear!

Doctor. [*With the condescending smile of the competent person toward those who do not understand.*] We must take into account the peculiar psychology of madmen; which, you must know, enables us to be certain that they observe things and can, for instance, easily detect people who are disguised; can in fact recognize the disguise and yet believe in it; just as children do, for whom disguise is both play and reality. That is why I used the word childish. But the thing is extremely complicated, inasmuch as he must be perfectly aware of being an image to himself and for himself—that image there, in fact!

> [*Alluding to the portrait in the throne room, and pointing to the right.*]

Belcredi. That's what he said!

Doctor. Very well then—— An image before which other images, ours, have appeared: understand? Now he, in his acute and perfectly lucid delirium, was able to detect at once a difference between his image and ours: that is, he saw that ours were make-believes. So he suspected us; because all madmen are armed with a special diffidence. But that's all there is to it! Our make-believe, built up all round his, did not seem pitiful to him. While his seemed all the more tragic to us, in that he, as if in defiance —understand?—and induced by his suspicion, wanted to show us up merely as a joke. That was also partly the case with him, in coming before us with painted cheeks and hair, and saying he had done it on purpose for a jest.

Donna Matilda. [*Impatiently.*] No, it's not that, Doctor. It's not like that! It's not like that!

Doctor. Why isn't it, may I ask?

Donna Matilda. [*With decision but trembling.*] I am perfectly certain he recognized me!

Doctor. It's not possible . . . it's not possible!

Belcredi. [*At the same time.*] Of course not!

Donna Matilda. [*More than ever determined, almost convulsively.*] I tell you, he recognized me! When he came close up to speak to me—looking in my eyes, right into my eyes—he recognized me!

Belcredi. But he was talking of your daughter!

Donna Matilda. That's not true! He was talking of me! Of me!

Belcredi. Yes, perhaps, when he said . . .

Donna Matilda. [*Letting herself go.*] About my dyed hair! But didn't you notice that he added at once: "or the memory of your dark hair, if you were dark"? He remembered perfectly well that I was dark—then!

Belcredi. Nonsense! nonsense!

Donna Matilda. [*Not listening to him, turning to the* Doctor.] My hair, Doctor, is really dark—like my daughter's! That's why he spoke of her.

Belcredi. But he doesn't even know your daughter! He's never seen her!

Donna Matilda. Exactly! Oh, you never understand anything! By my daughter, stupid, he meant me—as I was then!

Belcredi. Oh, this is catching! This is catching, this madness!

Donna Matilda. [*Softly, with contempt.*] Fool!

Belcredi. Excuse me, were you ever his wife? Your daughter is his wife—in his delirium: Bertha of Susa.

Donna Matilda. Exactly! Because I, no longer dark—as he remembered me—but *fair*, introduced myself as "Adelaide," the mother. My daughter doesn't exist for him: he's never seen her—you said so yourself! So how can he know whether she's fair or dark?

Belcredi. But he said dark, speaking generally, just as anyone who wants to recall, whether fair or dark, a memory of youth in the color of the hair! And you, as usual, begin to imagine things! Doctor, you said I ought not to have come! It's she who ought not to have come!

Donna Matilda. [*Upset for a moment by* Belcredi's *remark, recovers herself. Then with a touch of anger, because doubtful.*] No, no . . . he spoke of me . . . He spoke all the time to me, with me, of me . . .

Belcredi. That's not bad! He didn't leave me a moment's breathing space; and you say he was talking all the time to you? Unless you think he was alluding to you too, when he was talking to Peter Damiani!

Donna Matilda. [*Defiantly, almost exceeding the limits of courteous discussion.*] Who knows? Can you tell me why, from the outset, he showed a strong dislike for you, for you alone?

[*From the tone of the question, the expected answer must almost explicitly be: "Because he understands you are my lover."* Belcredi *feels this so well that he remains silent and can say nothing.*]

Doctor. The reason may also be found in the fact that only the visit of the Duchess Adelaide and the Abbot of Cluny was announced to him. Finding a third person present, who had not been announced, at once his suspicion . . .

Belcredi. Yes, exactly! His suspicion made him see an enemy in me: Peter Damiani! But she's got it into her head that he recognized her . . .

Donna Matilda. There's no doubt about it! I could see it from his eyes, Doctor. You know, there's a way of looking that leaves no doubt whatever . . . Perhaps it was only for an instant, but I am sure!

Doctor. It is not impossible: a lucid moment . . .

Donna Matilda. Yes, perhaps . . . And then his speech seemed to me full of regret for his and my youth—for the horrible thing that happened to him, that has held him in that disguise from which he has never been able to free himself, and from which he longs to be free—he said so himself!

Belcredi. Yes, so as to be able to make love to your daughter, or you, as you believe —having been touched by your pity.

Donna Matilda. Which is very great, I would ask you to believe.

Belcredi. As one can see, Marchioness; so much so that a miracle-worker might expect a miracle from it!

Doctor. Will you let me speak? I don't work miracles, because I am a doctor and not a miracle-worker. I listened very intently to all he said; and I repeat that that certain analogical elasticity, common to all symptomatised delirium, is evidently with him much . . . what shall I say?—much relaxed! The elements, that is, of his delirium no longer hold together. It seems to me he has lost the equilibrium of his second personality and sudden recollections drag him—and this is very comforting—not from a state of incipient apathy, but rather from a morbid inclination to reflective melancholy, which shows a . . . very considerable cerebral activity. Very comforting, I repeat! Now if, by this violent trick we've planned . . .

Donna Matilda. [*Turning to the window, in the tone of a sick person complaining.*] But how is it that the motor has not returned? It's three hours and a half since . . .

Doctor. What do you say?

Donna Matilda. The motor, Doctor! It's more than three hours and a half . . .

Doctor. [*Taking out his watch and looking at it.*] Yes, more than four hours, by this!

Donna Matilda. It could have reached here an hour ago at least! But, as usual . . .

Belcredi. Perhaps they can't find the dress . . .

Donna Matilda. But I explained exactly where it was! [*Impatiently.*] And Frida . . . where is Frida?

Belcredi. [*Looking out of the window.*] Perhaps she is in the garden with Charles . . .

Doctor. He'll talk her out of her fright.

Belcredi. She's not afraid, Doctor; don't you believe it: the thing bores her rather . . .

Donna Matilda. Just don't ask anything of her! I know what she's like.

Doctor. Let's wait patiently. Anyhow, it will soon be over, and it has to be in the evening . . . It will only be the matter of a moment! If we can succeed in rousing him, as I was saying, and in breaking at one go the threads—already slack—which still bind him to this fiction of his, giving him back what he himself asks for—you remember, he said: "One cannot always be twenty-six years old, madam!"—if we can give him freedom from this torment, which even *he* feels is a torment, then if he is able to recover at one bound the sensation of the distance of time . . .

Belcredi. [*Quickly.*] He'll be cured! [*Then emphatically with irony.*] We'll pull him out of it all!

Doctor. Yes, we may hope to set him going again, like a watch which has stopped at a certain hour . . . just as if we had our watches in our hands and were waiting for that other watch to go again. A shake—so —and let's hope it'll tell the time again after its long stop.

[*At this point the* MARQUIS CHARLES DI NOLLI *enters from the principal entrance.*]

Donna Matilda. Oh, Charles! . . . And Frida? Where is she?

Di Nolli. She'll be here in a moment.

Doctor. Has the motor arrived?

Di Nolli. Yes.

Donna Matilda. Yes? Has the dress come?

Di Nolli. It's been here some time.

Doctor. Good! Good!

Donna Matilda. [*Trembling.*] Where is she? Where's Frida?

Di Nolli. [*Shrugging his shoulders and smiling sadly, like one lending himself unwillingly to an untimely joke.*] You'll see, you'll see! . . . [*Pointing toward the hall.*] Here she is! . . .

[BERTHOLD *appears at the threshold of the hall, and announces with solemnity.*]

Berthold. Her Highness the Countess Matilda of Canossa!

[FRIDA *enters, magnificent and beautiful, arrayed in the robes of her mother as "Countess Matilda of Tuscany," so that she is a living copy of the portrait in the throne room.*]

Frida. [*Passing* BERTHOLD, *who is bowing, says to him with disdain.*] Of Tuscany, of Tuscany! Canossa is just one of my castles!

Belcredi. [*In admiration.*] Look! Look! She seems another person. . . .

Donna Matilda. One would say it were I! Look!—Why, Frida, look! She's exactly my portrait, alive!

Doctor. Yes, yes . . . Perfect! Perfect! The portrait, to the life.

Belcredi. Yes, there's no question about it. She *is* the portrait! Magnificent!

Frida. Don't make me laugh, or I shall burst! I say, mother, what a tiny waist you had! I had to squeeze so to get into this!

Donna Matilda. [*Arranging her dress a little.*] Wait! . . . Keep still! . . . These pleats . . . is it really so tight?

Frida. I'm suffocating! I implore you to be quick!

Doctor. But we must wait till it's evening!

Frida. No, no, I can't hold out till evening!

Donna Matilda. Why did you put it on so soon?

Frida. The moment I saw it, the temptation was irresistible. . . .

Donna Matilda. At least you could have called me, or have had someone help you! It's still all crumpled.

Frida. So I saw, mother; but they are old creases; they won't come out.

Doctor. It doesn't matter, Marchioness! The illusion is perfect. [*Then coming near and asking her to come in front of her* DAUGHTER, *without hiding her.*] If you please, stay there, there . . . at a certain distance . . . now a little more forward . . .

Belcredi. For the feeling of the distance of time . . .

Donna Matilda. [*Slightly turning to him.*] Twenty years after! A disaster! A tragedy!

Belcredi. Now don't let's exaggerate!

Doctor. [*Embarrassed, trying to save the situation.*] No, no! I meant the dress . . . so as to see . . . You know . . .

Belcredi. [*Laughing.*] Oh, as for the dress, Doctor, it isn't a matter of twenty years! It's eight hundred! An abyss! Do you really want to shove him across it [*Pointing first to* FRIDA *and then to the* MARCHIONESS.] from there to here? But you'll have to pick him up in pieces with a basket! Just think now: for us it is a matter of twenty years, a couple of dresses, and a masquerade. But if, as you say, Doctor, time has stopped for and around him: if he lives there [*Pointing to* FRIDA.] with her, eight hundred years ago . . . I repeat: the giddiness of the jump will be such that finding himself suddenly among us . . . [*The* DOCTOR *shakes his head in dissent.*] You don't think so?

Doctor. No, because life, my dear baron, can take up its rhythms. This—our life—will at once become real also to him; and will pull him up directly, wresting from him suddenly the illusion, and showing him that the eight hundred years, as you say, are only twenty! It will be like one of those tricks, such as the leap into space, for instance, of the Masonic rite, which appears to be heaven knows how far, and is only a step down the stairs.

Belcredi. Ah! An idea! Yes! Look at Frida and the Marchioness, Doctor! Which is more advanced in time? We old people, Doctor? The young ones think they are more ahead; but it isn't true: we are more ahead, because time belongs to us more than to them.

Doctor. If the past didn't alienate us . . .

Belcredi. It doesn't matter at all! How does it alienate us? They [*Pointing to* FRIDA *and* DI NOLLI.] have still to do what we

have accomplished, Doctor: to grow old, doing the same foolish things, more or less, as we did . . . This is the illusion: that one comes forward through a door to life. It isn't so! As soon as one is born, one starts dying; therefore, he who started first is the most advanced of all. The youngest of us is father Adam! Look there: [*Pointing to* FRIDA.] eight hundred years younger than all of us—the Countess Matilda of Tuscany.

[*He makes her a deep bow.*]

Di Nolli. I say, Tito, don't start joking.

Belcredi. Oh, you think I am joking? . . .

Di Nolli. Of course, of course . . . all the time.

Belcredi. Impossible! I've even dressed up as a Benedictine . . .

Di Nolli. Yes, but for a serious purpose.

Belcredi. Well, exactly. If it had been serious for the others . . . for Frida, now, for instance. [*Then turning to the* DOCTOR.] I swear, Doctor, I don't understand what you want to do.

Doctor. [*Annoyed.*] You'll see! Let me do as I wish. . . . At present you see the Marchioness still dressed as . . .

Belcredi. Oh, she also . . . has to masquerade?

Doctor. Of course! of course! In another dress that's in there ready to be used when it comes into his head he sees the Countess Matilda of Canossa before him.

Frida. [*While talking quietly to* DI NOLLI *notices the* DOCTOR's *mistake.*] Of Tuscany, of Tuscany!

Doctor. It's all the same!

Belcredi. Oh, I see! He'll be faced by two of them . . .

Doctor. Two, precisely! And then . . .

Frida. [*Calling him aside.*] Come here, Doctor! Listen!

Doctor. Here I am.

[*Goes near the* TWO YOUNG PEOPLE *and pretends to give some explanations to them.*]

Belcredi. [*Softly to* DONNA MATILDA.] I say, this is getting rather strong, you know!

Donna Matilda. [*Looking him firmly in the face.*] What?

Belcredi. Does it really interest you as much as all that—to make you willing to take part in . . . ? For a woman, this is simply enormous! . . .

Donna Matilda. Yes, for an ordinary woman.

Belcredi. Oh, no, my dear, for all women —in a question like this! It's an abnegation.

Donna Matilda. I owe it to him.

Belcredi. Don't lie! You know well enough it's not hurting you!

Donna Matilda. Well then, where does the abnegation come in?

Belcredi. Just enough to prevent you losing caste in other people's eyes—and just enough to offend me! . . .

Donna Matilda. But who is worrying about you now?

Di Nolli. [*Coming forward.*] It's all right. It's all right. That's what we'll do! [*Turning toward* BERTHOLD.] Here you, go and call one of those fellows!

Berthold. At once! [*Exit.*]

Donna Matilda. But first of all we've got to pretend that we are going away.

Di Nolli. Exactly! I'll see to that . . . [*To* BELCREDI.] You don't mind staying here?

Belcredi. [*Ironically.*] Oh, no, I don't mind, I don't mind! . . .

Di Nolli. We must look out not to make him suspicious again, you know.

Belcredi. Oh, Lord! He doesn't amount to anything!

Doctor. He must believe absolutely that we've gone away.

[LANDOLPH *followed by* BERTHOLD *enters from the right.*]

Landolph. May I come in?

Di Nolli. Come in! Come in! I say—your name's Lolo, isn't it?

Landolph. Lolo, or Landolph, just as you like!

Di Nolli. Well, look here: the Doctor and the Marchioness are leaving, at once.

Landolph. Very well. All we've got to say is that they have been able to obtain the permission for the reception from His Holiness. He's in there in his own apartments repenting of all he said—and in an awful state to have the pardon! Would you mind coming a minute? . . . If you would, just for a minute . . . put on the dress again . . .

Doctor. Why, of course, with pleasure . . .

Landolph. Might I be allowed to make a suggestion? Why not add that the Marchioness of Tuscany has interceded with the Pope that he should be received?

Donna Matilda. You see, he has recognized me!

Landolph. Forgive me . . . I don't know my history very well. I am sure you gentlemen know it much better! But I thought it was believed that Henry IV had a secret passion for the Marchioness of Tuscany.

Donna Matilda. [*At once.*] Nothing of the kind! Nothing of the kind!

Landolph. That's what I thought! But he says he's loved her . . . he's always saying it . . . And now he fears that her indignation against this secret love of his will work him harm with the Pope.

Belcredi. We must let him understand that this aversion no longer exists.

Landolph. Exactly! Of course!

Donna Matilda. [*To* BELCREDI.] History says—I don't know whether you know it or not—that the Pope gave way to the supplications of the Marchioness Matilda and the Abbot of Cluny. And I may say, my dear Belcredi, that I intended to take advantage of this fact—at the time of the pageant—to show him my feelings were not so hostile to him as he supposed.

Belcredi. You are most faithful to history, Marchioness . . .

Landolph. Well then, the Marchioness could spare herself a double disguise and present herself with Monsignor [*Indicating the* DOCTOR.] as the Marchioness of Tuscany.

Doctor. [*Quickly, energetically.*] No, no! That won't do at all. It would ruin everything. The impression from the confrontation must be a sudden one, give a shock! No, no, Marchioness, you will appear again as the Duchess Adelaide, the mother of the Empress. And then we'll go away. This is most necessary: that he should know we've gone away. Come on! Don't let's waste any more time! There's a lot to prepare.

[*Exeunt the* DOCTOR, DONNA MATILDA, *and* LANDOLPH, *right.*]

Frida. I am beginning to feel afraid again.

Di Nolli. Again, Frida?

Frida. It would have been better if I had seen him before.

Di Nolli. There's nothing to be frightened of, really.

Frida. He isn't furious, is he?

Di Nolli. Of course not! He's quite calm.

Belcredi. [*With ironic sentimental affectation.*] Melancholy! Didn't you hear that he loves you?

Frida. Thanks! That's just why I am afraid.

Belcredi. He won't do you any harm.

Di Nolli. It'll only last a minute . . .

Frida. Yes, but there in the dark with him . . .

Di Nolli. Only for a moment; and I will be near you, and all the others behind the door ready to run in. As soon as you see your mother, your part will be finished . . .

Belcredi. I'm afraid of a different thing: that we're wasting our time . . .

Di Nolli. Don't begin again! The remedy seems a sound one to me.

Frida. I think so too! I feel it! I'm all trembling!

Belcredi. But, mad people, my dear friends—though they don't know it, alas—have this felicity which we don't take into account . . .

Di Nolli. [*Interrupting, annoyed.*] What felicity? Nonsense!

Belcredi. [*Forcefully.*] They don't reason!

Di Nolli. What's reasoning got to do with it, anyway?

Belcredi. Don't you call it reasoning that he will have to do—according to us—when he sees her [*Indicates* FRIDA.] and her mother? We've reasoned it all out, surely!

Di Nolli. Nothing of the kind: no reasoning at all! We put before him a double image of his own fantasy, or fiction, as the Doctor says.

Belcredi. [*Suddenly.*] I say, I've never understood why they take degrees in medicine.

Di Nolli. [*Amazed.*] Who?

Belcredi. The alienists!

Di Nolli. What ought they to take degrees in, then?

Frida. If they are alienists, in what else should they take degrees?

Belcredi. In law, of course! All a matter of talk! The more they talk, the more highly they are considered. "Analogous elasticity," "the sensation of distance in time"! And the first thing they tell you is that they don't work miracles—when a miracle's just what is wanted! But they know that the more they say they are not miracle-workers, the more folk believe in their seriousness!

Berthold. [*Who has been looking through the keyhole of the door on right.*] There they are! There they are! They're coming in here.

Di Nolli. Are they?

Berthold. He wants to come with them . . . Yes! . . . He's coming too!

Di Nolli. Let's get away, then! Let's get away, at once! [*To* BERTHOLD.] You stop here!

Berthold. Must I?

[*Without answering him,* DI NOLLI, FRIDA, *and* BELCREDI *go out by the main exit, leaving* BERTHOLD *surprised. The door on the right opens, and* LANDOLPH *enters first, bowing. Then* DONNA MATILDA *comes in, with mantle and ducal crown as in the first act; also the* DOCTOR *as the* ABBOT OF CLUNY. HENRY IV *is among them in royal dress.* ORDULPH *and* HAROLD *enter last of all.*]

Henry IV. [*Following up what he has been saying in the other room.*] And now I will ask you a question: how can I be astute, if you think me obstinate?

Doctor. No, no, not obstinate!

Henry IV. [*Smiling, pleased.*] Then you think me really astute?

Doctor. No, no, neither obstinate, nor astute.

Henry IV. [*With benevolent irony.*] Monsignor, if obstinacy is not a vice which can go with astuteness, I hoped that in denying me the former, you would at least allow me a little of the latter. I can assure you I have great need of it. But if you want to keep it all for yourself . . .

Doctor. I? I? Do I seem astute to you?

Henry IV. No, Monsignor! What do you say? Not in the least! Perhaps in this case, I may seem a little obstinate to you. [*Cutting short to speak to* DONNA MATILDA.] With your permission: a word in confidence to the Duchess. [*Leads her aside and asks her very earnestly.*] Is your daughter really dear to you?

Donna Matilda. [*Dismayed.*] Why, yes, certainly . . .

Henry IV. Do you wish me to compensate her with all my love, with all my devotion, for the grave wrongs I have done her —though you must not believe all the stories my enemies tell about my dissoluteness!

Donna Matilda. No, no, I don't believe them. I never have believed such stories.

Henry IV. Well then, are you willing?

Donna Matilda. [*Confused.*] What?

Henry IV. That I return to love your daughter again? [*Looks at her and adds, in a mysterious tone of warning.*] You mustn't be a friend of the Marchioness of Tuscany!

Donna Matilda. I tell you again that she has begged and tried not less than ourselves to obtain your pardon . . .

Henry IV. [*Softly, but excitedly.*] Don't tell me that! Don't say that to me! Don't you see the effect it has on me, my Lady?

Donna Matilda. [*Looks at him; then very softly as if in confidence.*] You love her still?

Henry IV. [*Puzzled.*] Still? Still, you say? You know, then? But nobody knows! Nobody must know!

Donna Matilda. But perhaps she knows, if she has begged so hard for you!

Henry IV. [*Looks at her and says.*] And you love your daughter. [*Brief pause. He turns to the* DOCTOR *with laughing accents.*] Ah, Monsignor, it's strange how little I think of my wife! It may be a sin, but I swear to you that I hardly feel her at all in my heart. What is stranger is that her own mother scarcely feels her in her heart. Confess, my Lady, that she amounts to very little for you. [*Turning to* DOCTOR.] She talks to me of that other woman, insistently, insistently, I don't know why! . . .

Landolph. [*Humbly.*] Maybe, Majesty, it is to disabuse you of some ideas you have had about the Marchioness of Tuscany. [*Then, dismayed at having allowed himself this observation, adds.*] I mean just now, of course . . .

Henry IV. You too maintain that she has been friendly to me?

Landolph. Yes, at the moment, Majesty.

Donna Matilda. Exactly! Exactly! . . .

Henry IV. I understand. That is to say, you don't believe I love her. I see! I see! Nobody's ever believed it, nobody's ever thought it. Better so, then! But enough, enough! [*Turns to the* DOCTOR *with changed expression.*] Monsignor, you see? The reasons the Pope has had for revoking the excommunication have got nothing at all to do with the reasons for which he excommunicated me originally. Tell Pope Gregory we shall meet again at Brixen. And you, Madam, should you chance to meet your daughter in the courtyard of the castle of your friend the Marchioness, ask her to visit me. We shall see if I succeed in keeping her close beside me as wife and Empress. Many women have presented themselves here already assuring me that they were she. But they all, even while they told me they came from Susa—I don't know why—began to laugh! And then in the bedroom . . . Well, a man is a man, and a woman is a woman. Undressed, we don't bother much about who we are. And one's dress is like a phantom that hovers always near me. Oh, Monsignor, phantoms in general are nothing more than trifling disorders of the spirit: images we cannot contain within the bounds of sleep. They reveal themselves even when we are awake, and they frighten us. I . . . ah . . . I am always afraid when, at night time, I see disordered images before me. Sometimes I am even afraid of my own blood pulsing loudly in my arteries in the silence of night, like the sound of a distant step in a lonely corridor! . . . But forgive me! I have kept you standing too long already. I thank you, my Lady, I thank you, Monsignor. [DONNA MATILDA *and the* DOCTOR *go off bowing. As soon as they have gone,* HENRY IV *suddenly changes his tone.*] Buffoons, buffoons! One can play any tune on them! And that other fellow . . . Pietro Damiani! . . . Caught him out perfectly! He's afraid to appear before me again. [*Moves up and down excitedly while saying this; then sees* BERTHOLD, *and points him out to the other three* VALETS.] Oh, look at this imbecile watching me with his mouth wide open. [*Shakes him.*] Don't you understand? Don't you see, idiot, how I treat them, how I play the fool with them, make them appear before me just as I wish? Miserable, frightened clowns that they are! And you [*Addressing the* VALETS.] are amazed that I tear off their ridiculous masks now, just as if it wasn't I who had made them mask themselves to satisfy this taste of mine for playing the madman!

Landolph—Harold—Ordulph. [*Bewildered, looking at one another.*] What? What does he say? What?

Henry IV. [*Answers them imperiously.*] Enough! enough! Let's stop it. I'm tired of it. [*Then as if the thought left him no peace.*] By God! The impudence! To come here along with her lover! . . . And pretending to do it out of pity! So as not to infuriate a poor devil already out of the world, out of time, out of life! If it hadn't been supposed to be done out of pity, one can well imagine that fellow wouldn't have allowed it. Those people expect others to behave as they wish all the time. And, of course, there's nothing arrogant in that! Oh, no! Oh, no! It's merely their way of thinking, of feeling, of seeing. Everybody has his own way of thinking; you fellows, too. Yours is that of a flock of sheep—miserable, feeble, uncertain . . . But those others take advantage of this and make you accept their way of thinking; or, at least, they suppose they do; because, after all, what do they succeed in imposing on you? Words, words which anyone can interpret in his own manner! That's the way public opinion is formed! And it's a bad lookout for a man who finds himself labeled one day with one of these words which everyone repeats; for example "madman," or "imbecile." Don't you think it rather hard for a man to keep quiet, when he knows that there is a fellow going about trying to persuade everybody that he is as he sees him, trying to fix him in other people's opinion as a "madman"—according to him? Now I am talking seriously! Before I hurt my head, falling from my horse . . . [*Stops suddenly, noticing the dismay of the four* YOUNG MEN.] What's the matter with you? [*Imitates their amazed looks.*] What? Am I, or am I not, mad? Oh, yes! I'm mad all right! [*He becomes terrible.*] Well then, by God, down on your knees, down on your knees! [*Makes them go down on their knees one by one.*] I order you to go down on your knees before me! And touch the ground three times with your foreheads! Down, down! That's the way you've got to be before madmen! [*Then annoyed with their facile humiliation.*] Get up, sheep! You obeyed me, didn't you? You might have put the strait jacket on me! . . . Crush a man with the weight of a word—it's nothing—a fly! all our life is crushed by the weight of words: the weight of the dead. Look at me here: can you really suppose that Henry IV is still alive? All the same, I speak, and order you live men about! Do you think it's a joke that the dead continue to live?—— Yes, *here* it's a joke! But get out into the live world!—— Ah, you say: what a beautiful sunrise—for us! All time is before us!—Dawn! We will do what we like with this day.—Ah, yes! To Hell with tradition, the old conventions! Well, go on! You will do nothing but repeat the old, old words, while you imagine you are living! [*Goes up to* BERTHOLD, *who has now become quite stupid.*] You don't understand a word of this, do you? What's your name?

Berthold. I? . . . What? . . . Berthold . . .

Henry IV. Poor Berthold! What's your name here?

Berthold. I . . . I . . . my name is Fino.

Henry IV. [*Feeling the warning and critical glances of the others, turns to them to reduce them to silence.*] Fino?

Berthold. Fino Pagliuca, sire.

Henry IV. [*Turning to* LANDOLPH.] I've heard you call each other by your nicknames often enough! Your name is Lolo, isn't it?

Landolph. Yes, sire . . . [*Then with a sense of immense joy.*] Oh, Lord! Oh, Lord! Then he is not mad . . .

Henry IV. [*Brusquely.*] What?

Landolph. [*Hesitating.*] No . . . I said . . .

Henry IV. Not mad, eh? We're having a joke on those that think I am mad! [*To* HAROLD.] I say, boy, your name's Franco . . . [*To* ORDULPH.] And yours . . .

Ordulph. Momo.

Henry IV. Momo, Momo . . . A nice name that!

Landolph. So he isn't . . .

Henry IV. What are you talking about? Of course not! Let's have a jolly, good laugh! . . . [*Laughs.*] Ah! . . . Ah! . . . Ah! . . .

Landolph—Harold—Ordulph. [*Looking at each other half happy and half dismayed.*] Then he's cured! . . . he's all right! . . .

Henry IV. Silence! Silence! . . . [*To* BERTHOLD.] Why don't you laugh? Are you offended? I didn't mean it especially for

you. It's convenient for everybody to insist that certain people are mad, so they can be shut up. Do you know why? Because it's impossible to hear them speak! What shall I say of these people who've just gone away? That one is a whore, another a libertine, another a swindler . . . don't you think so? You can't believe a word he says . . . don't you think so?—By the way, they all listen to me terrified. And why are they terrified, if what I say isn't true? Of course, you can't believe what madmen say—yet, at the same time, they stand there with their eyes wide open with terror!—Why? Tell me, tell me, why?—You see I'm quite calm now!

Berthold. But, perhaps, they think that . . .

Henry IV. No, no, my dear fellow! Look me well in the eyes! . . . I don't say that it's true—nothing is true, Berthold! But . . . look me in the eyes!

Berthold. Well . . .

Henry IV. You see? You see? . . . You have terror in your own eyes now because I seem mad to you! There's the proof of it! [*Laughs.*]

Landolph. [*Coming forward in the name of the others, exasperated.*] What proof?

Henry IV. Your being so dismayed because now I seem again mad to you. You have thought me mad up to now, haven't you? You feel that this dismay of yours can become terror too—something to dash away the ground from under your feet and deprive you of the air you breathe! Do you know what it means to find yourselves face to face with a madman—with one who shakes the foundations of all you have built up in yourselves, your logic, the logic of all your constructions? Madmen, lucky folk! construct without logic, or rather with a logic that flies like a feather. Voluble! Voluble! Today like this and tomorrow—who knows? You say: "This cannot be"; but for them everything can be. You say: "This isn't true!" And why? Because it doesn't seem true to you, or you, or you . . . [*Indicates the three of them in succession.*] . . . and to a hundred thousand others! One must see what seems true to these hundred thousand others who are not supposed to be mad! What a magnificent spectacle they afford when they reason! What flowers of logic they scatter! I know that when I was a child, I thought the moon in the pond was real. How many things I thought real! I believed everything I was told—and I was happy! Because it's a terrible thing if you don't hold on to that which seems true to you today—to that which will seem true to you tomorrow, even if it is the opposite of that which seemed true to you yesterday. I would never wish you to think, as I have done, on this horrible thing which really drives one mad: that if you were beside another and looking into his eyes—as I one day looked into somebody's eyes—you might as well be a beggar before a door never to be opened to you; for he who does enter there will never be you, but someone unknown to you with his own different and impenetrable world . . . [*Long pause. Darkness gathers in the room, increasing the sense of strangeness and consternation in which the four* YOUNG MEN *are involved.* HENRY IV *remains aloof, pondering on the misery which is not only his, but everybody's. Then he pulls himself up, and says in an ordinary tone.*] It's getting dark here . . .

Ordulph. Shall I go for a lamp?

Henry IV. [*Ironically.*] The lamp, yes, the lamp! . . . Do you suppose I don't know that as soon as I turn my back with my oil lamp to go to bed, you turn on the electric light for yourselves, here, and even there, in the throne room? I pretend not to see it!

Ordulph. Well, then, shall I turn it on now?

Henry IV. No, it would blind me! I want my lamp!

Ordulph. It's ready here behind the door. [*Goes to the main exit, opens the door, goes out for a moment, and returns with an ancient lamp, which is held by a ring at the top.*]

Henry IV. Ah, a little light! Sit there around the table, no, not like that; in an elegant, easy manner! . . . [*To* HAROLD.] Yes, you, like that! [*Poses him. Then to* BERTHOLD.] You, so! . . . and I, here! [*Sits opposite them.*] We could do with a little decorative moonlight. It's very useful for us, the moonlight. I feel a real necessity for it, and pass a lot of time looking up at the moon from my window. Who would think, to look at her, that she knows that eight hundred years have passed, and that I, seated at the window, cannot really be Henry IV gazing at the moon like any poor devil? But, look, look! See what a magnificent night scene we have here: the emperor surrounded by his faithful counsellors! . . . How do you like it?

Landolph. [*Softly to* HAROLD, *so as not to break the enchantment.*] And to think it wasn't true! . . .

Henry IV. True? What wasn't true?

Landolph. [*Timidly as if to excuse himself.*] No . . . I mean . . . I was saying this morning to him [*Indicates* BERTHOLD.]

—he has just entered on service here—I was saying: what a pity that dressed like this and with so many beautiful costumes in the wardrobe . . . and with a room like that . . . [*Indicates the throne room.*]

Henry IV. Well? what's the pity?

Landolph. Well . . . that we didn't know . . .

Henry IV. That it was all done in jest, this comedy?

Landolph. Because we thought that . . .

Harold. [*Coming to his assistance.*] Yes . . . that it was done seriously!

Henry IV. What do you say? Doesn't it seem serious to you?

Landolph. But if you say that . . .

Henry IV. I say that—you are fools! You ought to have known how to create a fantasy for yourselves, not to act it for me, or anyone coming to see me; but naturally, simply, day by day, before nobody, feeling yourselves alive in the history of the eleventh century, here at the court of your emperor, Henry IV! You, Ordulph [*Taking him by the arm.*], alive in the castle of Goslar, waking up in the morning, getting out of bed, and entering straightway into the dream, clothing yourself in the dream that would be no more a dream, because you would have lived it, felt it all alive in you. You would have drunk it in with the air you breathed; yet knowing all the time that it was a dream, so you could better enjoy the privilege afforded you of having to do nothing else but live this dream, this far-off and yet actual dream! And to think that at a distance of eight centuries from this remote age of ours, so colored and so sepulchral, the men of the twentieth century are torturing themselves in ceaseless anxiety to know how their fates and fortunes will work out! Whereas you are already in history with me . . .

Landolph. Yes, yes, very good!

Henry IV. . . . Everything determined, everything settled!

Ordulph. Yes, yes!

Henry IV. And sad as is my lot, hideous as some of the events are, bitter the struggles and troublous the time—still all history! All history that cannot change, understand? All fixed for ever! And you could have admired at your ease how every effect followed obediently its cause with perfect logic, how every event took place precisely and coherently in each minute particular! The pleasure, the pleasure of history, in fact, which is so great, was yours.

Landolph. Beautiful, beautiful!

Henry IV. Beautiful, but it's finished! Now that you know, I could not do it any

more! [*Takes his lamp to go to bed.*]
Neither could you, if up to now you haven't
understood the reason of it! I am sick of it
now. [*Almost to himself with violent contained rage.*] By God, I'll make her sorry
she came here! Dressed herself up as a
mother-in-law for me . . . ! And he as an
abbot. . . ! And they bring a doctor with
them to study me . . . ! Who knows if they
don't hope to cure me? . . . Clowns . . . !
I'd like to smack one of them at least in the
face; yes, that one—a famous swordsman,
they say! . . . He'll kill me . . . Well, we'll
see, we'll see! . . . [*A knock at the door.*]
Who is it?

The Voice of John. Deo gratias!

Harold. [*Very pleased at the chance for
another joke.*] Oh, it's John, it's old John,
who comes every night to play the monk.

Ordulph. [*Rubbing his hands.*] Yes, yes!
Let's make him do it!

Henry IV. [*At once, severely.*] Fool,
why? Just to play a joke on a poor old man
who does it for love of me?

Landolph. [*To* ORDULPH.] It has to be
as if it were true.

Henry IV. Exactly, as if true! Because,
only so, truth is not a jest. [*Opens the door
and admits* JOHN *dressed as a humble friar
with a roll of parchment under his arm.*]
Come in, come, Father! [*Then assuming
a tone of tragic gravity and deep resentment.*] All the documents of my life and
reign favorable to me were destroyed deliberately by my enemies. One only has escaped destruction, this, my life, written by
a humble monk who is devoted to me. And
you would laugh at him. [*Turns affectionately to* JOHN, *and invites him to sit
down at the table.*] Sit down, Father, sit
down! Have the lamp near you! [*Puts the
lamp near him.*] Write! Write!

John. [*Opens the parchment and prepares
to write from dictation.*] I am ready, your
Majesty!

Henry IV. [*Dictating.*] "The decree of
peace proclaimed at Mayence helped the
poor and humble, while it damaged the
wicked and the powerful. [*Curtain begins
to fall.*] It brought wealth to the former,
hunger and misery to the latter . . ."

CURTAIN

ACT III

*The throne room, so dark that the wall at the
bottom is hardly seen. The canvases of
the two portraits have been taken away;
and, within their frames,* FRIDA, *dressed
as the "Marchioness of Tuscany" and*
CHARLES DI NOLLI, *as "Henry IV,"
have taken the exact positions of the
portraits.*
[*For a moment, after the raising of curtain, the stage is empty. Then the door
on the left opens; and* HENRY IV, *holding the lamp by the ring on top of it,
enters. He looks back to speak to the
four* YOUNG MEN *who, with* JOHN, *are
presumedly in the adjoining hall, as at
the end of the second act.*]

Henry IV. No: stay where you are, stay
where you are. I shall manage all right by
myself. Good night!
[*Closes the door and walks, very sad
and tired, across the hall toward the
second door on the right, which leads
into his apartments.*]
Frida. [*As soon as she sees that he has
just passed the throne, whispers from the
niche like one who is on the point of fainting away with fright.*] Henry . . .

Henry IV. [*Stopping at the voice, as if
someone had stabbed him traitorously in the
back, turns a terror-stricken face toward the
wall at the bottom of the room; raising an
arm instinctively, as if to defend himself and
ward off a blow.*] Who is calling me?
[*It is not a question, but an exclamation vibrating with terror, which does
not expect a reply from the darkness
and the terrible silence of the hall,
which suddenly fills him with the suspicion that he is really mad.*]
Frida. [*At his shudder of terror, is herself
not less frightened at the part she is playing, and repeats a little more loudly.*]
Henry! . . .
[*But, although she wishes to act the
part as they have given it to her, she
stretches her head a little out of the
frame toward the other frame.* HENRY
IV *gives a dreadful cry; lets the lamp
fall from his hands to cover his head
with his arms, and makes a movement
as if to run away.*]

Frida. [*Jumping from the frame on to the stand and shouting like a mad woman.*] Henry! . . . Henry! . . . I'm afraid! . . . I'm terrified! . . .

[*And while* DI NOLLI *jumps in turn on to the stand and thence to the floor and runs to* FRIDA, *who, on the verge of fainting, continues to cry out, the* DOCTOR, DONNA MATILDA, *also dressed as "Matilda of Tuscany,"* TITO BELCREDI, LANDOLPH, BERTHOLD, HAROLD, *and* ORDULPH *enter the hall from the doors on the right and on the left. One of them turns on the light: a strange light coming from lamps hidden in the ceiling so that only the upper part of the stage is well lighted. The others, without taking notice of* HENRY IV, *who, after the moment of terror which still causes him to tremble, looks on astonished by the unexpected inrush, run anxiously to support and comfort the still shaking* FRIDA, *who is moaning in the arms of her fiancé. All are speaking at the same time.*]

Di Nolli. No, no, Frida . . . Here I am . . . I am beside you!

Doctor. [*Coming with the others.*] Enough! Enough! There's nothing more to be done! . . .

Donna Matilda. He is cured, Frida. Look! He is cured! Don't you see?

Di Nolli. [*Astonished.*] Cured?

Belcredi. It was only for fun! Be calm!

Frida. No! I am afraid! I am afraid!

Donna Matilda. Afraid of what? Look at him! He was never mad at all! . . .

Di Nolli. That isn't true! What are you saying? Cured?

Doctor. It appears so. I should say so . . .

Belcredi. Yes, yes! They have told us so. [*Pointing to the four* YOUNG MEN.]

Donna Matilda. Yes, for a long time! He has confided in them, told them the truth!

Di Nolli. [*Now more indignant than astonished.*] But what does it mean? If, up to a short time ago . . . ?

Belcredi. Hum! He was acting, to take you in and also us, who in good faith . . .

Di Nolli. Is it possible? To deceive his sister, also, right up to the time of her death?

Henry IV. [*Remains apart, peering at one and now at the other under the accusation and the mockery of what all believe to be a cruel joke of his, which is now revealed. He has shown by the flashing of his eyes that he is meditating a revenge, which his violent contempt prevents him from defining clearly,* as yet. Stung to the quick and with a clear idea of accepting the fiction they have insidiously worked up as true, he bursts forth at this point.*] Go on, I say! Go on!

Di Nolli. [*Astonished at the cry.*] Go on! What do you mean?

Henry IV. It isn't *your* sister only that is dead!

Di Nolli. My sister? Yours, I say, whom you compelled up to the last moment, to present herself here as your mother Agnes!

Henry IV. And was she not *your* mother?

Di Nolli. My mother? Certainly my mother!

Henry IV. But your mother is dead for me, *old and far away!* You have just got down from there. [*Pointing to the frame from which he jumped down.*] And how do you know whether I have not wept her long in secret, dressed even as I am?

Donna Matilda. [*Dismayed, looking at the others.*] What does he say? [*Much impressed, observing him.*] Quietly! quietly, for Heaven's sake!

Henry IV. What do I say? I ask all of you if Agnes was not the mother of Henry IV? [*Turns to* FRIDA *as if she were really the Marchioness of Tuscany.*] You, Marchioness, it seems to me, ought to know.

Frida. [*Still frightened, draws closer to* DI NOLLI.] No, no, I don't know. Not I!

Doctor. It's the madness returning. . . . Quiet now, everybody!

Belcredi. [*Indignant.*] Madness indeed, Doctor! He's acting again! . . .

Henry IV. [*Suddenly.*] I? You have emptied those two frames over there, and he stands before my eyes as Henry IV. . . .

Belcredi. We've had enough of this joke now.

Henry IV. Who said joke?

Doctor. [*Loudly to* BELCREDI.] Don't excite him, for the love of God!

Belcredi. [*Without lending an ear to him, but speaking louder.*] But they have said so— [*Pointing again to the four* YOUNG MEN.] they, they!

Henry IV. [*Turning round and looking at them.*] You? Did you say it was all a joke?

Landolph. [*Timid and embarrassed.*] No . . . really we said that you were cured.

Belcredi. Look here! Enough of this! [*To* DONNA MATILDA.] Doesn't it seem to you that the sight of him [*Pointing to* DI NOLLI.], Marchioness, and that of your daughter dressed so, is becoming an intolerable puerility?

Donna Matilda. Oh, be quiet! What does the dress matter, if he is cured?

Henry IV. Cured, yes! I am cured! [*To* BELCREDI.] Ah, but not to let it end this way all at once, as you suppose! [*Attacks him.*] Do you know that for twenty years nobody has ever dared to appear before me here like you and that gentleman?
[*Pointing to the* DOCTOR.]

Belcredi. Of course I know it. As a matter of fact, I too appeared before you this morning dressed . . .

Henry IV. As a monk, yes!

Belcredi. And you took me for Peter Damiani! And I didn't even laugh, believing, in fact, that . . .

Henry IV. That I was mad! Does it make you laugh seeing her like that, now that I am cured? And yet you might have remembered that in my eyes her appearance now . . . [*Interrupts himself with a gesture of contempt.*] Ah! [*Suddenly turns to the* DOCTOR.] You are a doctor, aren't you?

Doctor. Yes.

Henry IV. And you also took part in dressing her up as the Marchioness of Tuscany? To prepare a counter-joke for me here, eh?

Donna Matilda. [*Impetuously.*] No, no! What do you say? It was done for you! I did it for your sake.

Doctor. [*Quickly.*] To attempt, to try, not knowing . . .

Henry IV. [*Cutting him short.*] I understand. I say counter-joke, in his case [*Indicates* BELCREDI.], because he believes that I have been carrying on a jest . . .

Belcredi. But excuse me, what do you mean? You say yourself you are cured.

Henry IV. Let me speak. [*To the* DOCTOR.] Do you know, Doctor, that for a moment you ran the risk of making me mad again? By God, to make the portraits speak; to make them jump alive out of their frames . . .

Doctor. But you saw that all of us ran in at once, as soon as they told us . . .

Henry IV. Certainly. [*Contemplates* FRIDA *and* DI NOLLI, *and then looks at the* MARCHIONESS, *and finally at his own costume.*] The combination is very beautiful . . . Two couples . . . Very good, very good, Doctor! For a madman, not bad! . . . [*With a slight wave of his hand to* BELCREDI.] It seems to him now to be a carnival out of season, eh? [*Turns to look at him.*] We'll get rid now of this masquerade costume of mine, so that I may come away with you. What do you say?

Belcredi. With me? With us?

Henry IV. Where shall we go? To the Club? In dress coats and with white ties? Or shall both of us go to the Marchioness' house?

Belcredi. Whatever you like! Do you want to remain here still, to continue—alone —what was nothing but the unfortunate joke of a day of carnival? It is really incredible, incredible how you have been able to do all this, freed from the disaster that befell you!

Henry IV. Yes, you see how it was! The fact is that falling from my horse and striking my head as I did, I was really mad for I know not how long . . .

Doctor. Ah! Did it last long?

Henry IV. [*Very quickly to the* DOCTOR.] Yes, Doctor, a long time! I think it must have been about twelve years. [*Then suddenly turning to speak to* BELCREDI.] Thus I saw nothing, my dear fellow, of all that, after that day of carnival, happened for you but not for me: how things changed, how my friends deceived me, how my place was taken by another, and all the rest of it! And suppose my place had been taken in the heart of the woman I loved? . . . And how should I know who was dead or who had disappeared? . . . All this, you know, wasn't exactly a jest for me, as it seems to you . . .

Belcredi. No, no! I don't mean that, if you please. I mean after . . .

Henry IV. Ah, yes? After? One day [*Stops and addresses the* DOCTOR.] —A most interesting case, Doctor! Study me well! Study me carefully! [*Trembles while speaking.*] All by itself, who knows how, one day the trouble here [*Touches his forehead.*] mended. Little by little, I open my eyes, and at first I don't know whether I am asleep or awake. Then I know I am awake. I touch this thing and that; I see clearly again . . . Ah!—then, as *he* says [*Alludes to* BELCREDI.], away, away with this masquerade, this incubus! Let's open the windows, breathe life once again! Away! Away! Let's run out! [*Suddenly pulling himself up.*] But where? And to do what? To show myself to all, secretly, as Henry IV, not like this, but arm in arm with you, among my dear friends?

Belcredi. What are you saying?

Donna Matilda. Who could think it? It's not to be imagined. It was an accident.

Henry IV. They all said I was mad before. [*To* BELCREDI.] And you know it! You were more ferocious than any one against those who tried to defend me.

Belcredi. Oh, that was only a joke!

Henry IV. Look at my hair! [*Shows him the hair on the nape of his neck.*]

Belcredi. But mine is gray too!

Henry IV. Yes, with this difference: that mine went gray here, as Henry IV, do you understand? And I never knew it! I perceived it all of a sudden, one day, when I opened my eyes; and I was terrified because I understood at once that not only had my hair gone gray, but that I was all gray, inside; that everything had fallen to pieces, that everything was finished; and I was going to arrive, hungry as a wolf, at a banquet which had already been cleared away . . .

Belcredi. Yes, but what about the others? . . .

Henry IV. [*Quickly.*] Ah, yes, I know! They couldn't wait until I was cured, not even those, who, behind my back, pricked my saddled horse till it bled. . . .

Di Nolli. [*Agitated.*] What, what?

Henry IV. Yes, treacherously, to make it rear and cause me to fall.

Dona Matilda. [*Quickly, in horror.*] This is the first time I knew that.

Henry IV. That was also a joke, probably?

Donna Matilda. But who did it? Who was behind us, then?

Henry IV. It doesn't matter who it was. All those that went on feasting and were ready to leave me their scrapings, Marchioness, of miserable pity, or some dirty remnant of remorse in the filthy plate! Thanks! [*Turning quickly to the* DOCTOR.] Now, Doctor, the case must be absolutely new in the history of madness; I preferred to remain mad—since I found everything ready and at my disposal for this new exquisite fantasy. I would live it—this madness of mine—with the most lucid consciousness; and thus revenge myself on the brutality of a stone which had dented my head. The solitude—this solitude—squalid and empty as it appeared to me when I opened my eyes again—I determined to deck it out with all the colors and splendors of that far-off day of carnival, when you [*Looks at* DONNA MATILDA *and points* FRIDA *out to her.*], when you, Marchioness, triumphed. So I would oblige all those who were around me to follow, by God, at my orders that famous pageant which had been—for you and not for me—the jest of a day. I would make it become—for ever—no more a joke but a reality, the reality of a real madness: here, all in masquerade, with throne room, and these my four secret counsellors: secret and, of course, traitors. [*He turns quickly toward them.*] I should like to know what you have gained by revealing the fact that I was cured! If I am cured, there's no longer any need of you, and you will be discharged! To give anyone one's confidence . . . that is really the act of a madman. But now I accuse you in my turn! [*Turning to the others.*] Do you know? They thought [*Alludes to the* VALETS.] they could make fun of me too with you.

[*Bursts out laughing. The others laugh, but shamefacedly, except* DONNA MATILDA.]

Belcredi. [*To* DI NOLLI.] Well, imagine that . . . That's not bad . . .

Di Nolli. [*To the four* YOUNG MEN.] You?

Henry IV. We must pardon them. This dress [*Plucking his dress.*] which is for me the evident, involuntary caricature of that other continuous, everlasting masquerade, of which we are the involuntary puppets [*Indicates* BELCREDI.], when, without knowing it, we mask ourselves with that which we appear to be . . . ah, that dress of theirs, this masquerade of theirs, of course, we must forgive it them, since they do not yet see it is identical with themselves . . . [*Turning again to* BELCREDI.] You know, it is quite easy to get accustomed to it. One walks about as a tragic character, just as if it were nothing . . . [*Imitates the tragic manner.*] in a room like this . . . Look here, Doctor! I remember a priest, certainly Irish, a nice-looking priest, who was sleeping in the sun one November day, with his arm on the corner of the bench of a public garden. He was lost in the golden delight of the mild sunny air which must have seemed for him almost summery. One may be sure that in that moment he did not know any more that he was a priest, or even where he was. He was dreaming . . . A little boy passed with a flower in his hand. He touched the priest with it here on the neck. I saw him open his laughing eyes, while all his mouth smiled with the beauty of his dream. He was forgetful of everything . . . But all at once, he pulled himself together, and stretched out his priest's cassock; and there came back to his eyes the same seriousness which you have seen in mine; because the Irish priests defend the seriousness of their Catholic faith with the same zeal with which I defend the secret rights of hereditary monarchy! I am cured, gentlemen: because I can act the madman to perfection, here; and I do it very quietly. I'm only sorry for you that have to live your madness so agitatedly, without knowing it or seeing it.

Belcredi. It comes to this, then, that it is we who are mad. That's what it is!

Henry IV. [*Containing his irritation.*] But if you weren't mad, both you and she [*Indicating the* MARCHIONESS.], would you have come here to see me?

Belcredi. To tell the truth, I came here believing that you were the madman.

Henry IV. [*Suddenly indicating the* MARCHIONESS.] And she?

Belcredi. Ah, as for her . . . I can't say. I see she is all fascinated by your words, by this *conscious* madness of yours. [*Turns to her.*] Dressed as you are [*Speaking to her.*], you could even remain here to live it out, Marchioness.

Donna Matilda. You are insolent!

Henry IV. [*Conciliatingly.*] No, Marchioness, what he means to say is that the miracle would be complete, according to him, with you here, who—as the Marchioness of Tuscany, you well know,—could not be my friend, save, as at Canossa, to give me a little pity . . .

Belcredi. Or even more than a little! She said so herself!

Henry IV. [*To the* MARCHIONESS, *continuing.*] And even, shall we say, a little remorse. . . .

Belcredi. Yes, that too she has admitted.

Donna Matilda. [*Angry.*] Now look here . . .

Henry IV. [*Quickly, to placate her.*] Don't bother about him! Don't mind him! Let him go on infuriating me—though the Doctor's told him not to. [*Turns to* BELCREDI.] But do you suppose I am going to trouble myself any more about what happened between us—the share you had in my misfortune with her [*Indicates the* MARCHIONESS *to him and, pointing* BELCREDI *out to her.*], the part he has now in your life? This is my life! Quite a different thing from your life! Your life, the life in which you have grown old—I have not lived that life. [*To* DONNA MATILDA.] Was this what you wanted to show me with this sacrifice of yours, dressing yourself up like this, according to the Doctor's idea? Excellently done, Doctor! Oh, an excellent idea:—"As we were then, eh? and as we are now?" But I am not a madman according to your way of thinking, Doctor. I know very well that that man there [*Indicates* DI NOLLI.] cannot be me; because I am Henry IV, and have been, these twenty years, cast in this eternal masquerade. She has lived these years! [*Indicates the* MARCHIONESS.] She has enjoyed them and has become—look at her!—a woman I can no longer recognize. It is so

that I knew her! [*Points to* FRIDA *and draws near her.*] This is the Marchioness I know, always this one! . . . You seem a lot of children to be so easily frightened by me . . . [*To* FRIDA.] And you're frightened too, little girl, aren't you, by the jest that they made you take part in—though they didn't understand it wouldn't be the jest they meant it to be, for me? Oh miracle of miracles! Prodigy of prodigies! The dream alive in you! More than alive in you! It was an image that wavered there and they've made you come to life! Oh, mine! You're mine, mine, mine, in my own right! [*He holds her in his arms, laughing like a madman, while all stand still terrified. Then as they advance to tear* FRIDA *from his arms, he becomes furious, terrible, and cries imperiously to his* VALETS.] Hold them! Hold them! I order you to hold them!

[*The four* YOUNG MEN *amazed, yet fascinated, move to execute his orders, automatically, and seize* DI NOLLI, *the* DOCTOR, *and* BELCREDI.]

Belcredi. [*Freeing himself.*] Leave her alone! Leave her alone! You're no madman!

Henry IV. [*In a flash draws the sword from the side of* LANDOLPH, *who is close to him.*] I'm not mad, eh! Take that, you! . . .

[*Drives sword into him. A cry of horror goes up. All rush over to assist* BELCREDI, *crying out together.*]

Di Nolli. Has he wounded you?

Berthold. Yes, yes, seriously!

Doctor. I told you so!

Frida. Oh God, oh God!

Di Nolli. Frida, come here!

Donna Matilda. He's mad, mad!

Di Nolli. Hold him!

Belcredi. [*While they take him away by the left exit, he protests as he is borne out.*] No, no, you're not mad! You're not mad. He's not mad!

[*They go out by the left amid cries and excitement. After a moment, one hears a still sharper, more piercing cry from* DONNA MATILDA, *and then, silence.*]

Henry IV. [*Who has remained on the stage between* LANDOLPH, HAROLD, *and* ORDULPH, *with his eyes almost starting out of his head, terrified by the life of his own masquerade which has driven him to crime.*] Ah now . . . yes now . . . inevitably [*Calls his* VALETS *around him as if to protect him.*] here together . . . here together . . . for ever . . . for ever.

CURTAIN

AH, WILDERNESS!*

A Comedy of Recollection

By

EUGENE O'NEILL

"Weary am I of tumult, sick of the staring
  crowd,
Pining for wild sea places where the soul
  may think aloud."

THESE LINES FROM HIS YOUTHFUL poem "Free" were a revealing prologue to Eugene O'Neill's actual escapes and adventures when, after expulsion from Princeton at the age of twenty, he earned his way by land and sea through the Americas and as far as Durban on the East African coast, and ended up a derelict "on the beach" near Buenos Aires. Then finding life in a New York dive—the setting for his *Anna Christie*—even less friendly, he shipped once more as able seaman on a return voyage to Southampton. Home at last and penniless, he joined his father's troupe as actor in bit parts and as manager.

His empty purse, he later realized, was counterweighted by a playwright's wealth acquired during his otherwise luckless adventures: an intimate understanding of raw humanity, not without its glimpses of worth, of courage, and even of beauty hidden deep in his seamates' reality. Besides, though schooled as son of a declaimer of English at its best, he had also acquired a variety of seamen's dialects later to be used in masterly fashion in his earliest plays, much as O'Casey gives poetic beauty and dramatic force to dialogue of Gaelic flavor.

Those to whom this dramatic innovator of earlier decades seems a newcomer on the present Broadway stages may wish to know by what efforts so unpromising a youth made himself a creative force in world drama, for during the period preceding World War II O'Neill's plays, because of their unique vitality, were widely produced not alone in America but throughout Europe, including Russia, where his daring dramaturgy, similar to the Soviets' own, was greatly ad-

mired by the Reds. Even Bernard Shaw, addressing a London school of drama, advised his hearers to begin their study with O'Neill's innovating plays rather than his own of a passing theatre epoch.

During his all but homeless early life as the son of a traveling actor, Eugene had become aloof and introspective, but was aware of a driving force within, akin to the poet's, as he pictured himself in *A Long Day's Journey Into Night*. This latent talent he strove unrelentingly to cultivate, despite innate libertinism, tubercular weakness, alcoholism, and asocial recklessness, any one of which tendencies might have been the ruin of a less determined genius. Having failed at Princeton, Eugene became his own educator, like many of the theatre great from Shakespeare to Shaw and O'Casey. Barrett Clark quotes him as declaring: "I read about everything I could lay my hands on: the Greeks [note his *Mourning Becomes Electra*], the Elizabethans, practically all the classics, and, of course, all the moderns, Ibsen and Strindberg—especially Strindberg." His persistence as writer was even more remarkable. A Provincetown pal told how "he would wrap himself in a blanket, stick an oil-burner under him, and write hour after hour." Yet he could be agreeable, as Mrs. Edith Isaacs, former editor of *Theatre Arts*, has assured us: "With his close friends he was simple, lovable, open-hearted . . . but eternally perplexed, hard-working, and distinctly over-productive." As we know, he ruthlessly destroyed play after play that he felt bound to condemn.

Negatively, his year spent as a minor actor in his father's immensely popular production of *The Count of Monte Cristo* had important educational value, for it made him a sworn rebel against the outworn staginess of Victorian theatricality. Deserting the troupe, he found employment that has furnished matter for many other playwrights: that of reporter on the New London Tele-

---

* Reprinted by permission of Random House, Inc.

graph, the editor of which was model for his Nat Miller of *Ah, Wilderness!*

Aware that his few attempts at play building were faulty, he enrolled in Professor George Pierce Baker's playwriting course (47 Workshop) at Harvard. His disappointment in the class lectures covering much that O'Neill already knew was counterbalanced by the essential gift of a true teacher, regarding which student O'Neill testified: "Yes, I did get a great deal from Baker—personally. He encouraged me, made me feel it was worth while to go ahead. My personal association with him meant the devil of a lot to me." About this student, Baker commented: "He showed by the end of this year that he knew how to write well in the one-act form, but he could not yet manage the longer forms. I was eager that he should return for a second year of work." But financially a second year was impossible.

At this point good fortune intervened. During the summer of 1916 at Provincetown, Eugene found himself in the midst of a small troupe of drama reformers as eager as he himself. On the second bill of their curious little Wharf Theatre appeared *Bound East for Cardiff,* O'Neill's first play to be produced anywhere. Naming themselves the Provincetown Players, they invaded New York's Greenwich Village, which, chiefly because of O'Neill's many contributions, became the most important off-Broadway experimental center that it still is. During the following decade the Players produced most of O'Neill's early works; spreading his fame while he greatly increased their own.

In 1920–1921 his relatively conventional *Beyond the Horizon* and *Anna Christie* both received the Pulitzer prize, and *The Emperor Jones,* with Charles Gilpin and later Paul Robeson in the part became an hypnotic stage miracle in monologue that defied all theatre conventions. Its accelerating drum-beat measuring the negro's mounting terror electrified the audience and announced the advent of an American expressionist of great ingenuity. By 1927 O'Neill had risen to the distinction of the New York Theatre Guild's favored dramatist following their successful mounting of his lengthy (five-hour) *Strange Interlude,* which made new expressionistic use of the age-old aside, and added the hoped-for American variety of this European technique to their repertory of plays by Toller and other foreign experimenters. Hardly ever has a dramatist opened so widely and speedily the highly conventional stage medium to new styles and moods as did O'Neill in the ten years of his early, strenuous productivity.

No American playwright since the twenties could feel himself any longer confined to the "water-tight" and "four-walled" play form of Ibsen and other photographic naturalists.

But O'Neill's novelty was not merely defiance of convention; his more important aim was to find fresh and effective ways to project the mood and thought inherent in the characters and dramatic situations he chose to exploit. Freedom to choose means of expression and emphasis laid on what he called "the behind-life" of characters, were his really important and lasting "innovations"—not innovations at all, for they were the unwritten laws of drama from the times of its Egyptian and Greek origins, a study of which had increased O'Neill's urge to reclaim their freedoms and minimize the confinement of the picture-frame theatre. And to this same end, he insisted on apt and meaningful settings, whether radically symbolic, as in *The Hairy Ape,* or fittingly idealized, as in the Greek-inspired *Mourning Becomes Electra,* or realistically Victorian, as in *Ah, Wilderness!,* for what could better symbolize the moral stuffiness of this satirical comedy than the stuffiness of the Victorian theatre? The reader should not pass over lightly O'Neill's mood-creating stage directions.

But *Ah, Wilderness!,* outwardly a delightful, conventional comedy of manners, is by no means without suggestion of "behind-life." At the final curtain we sense the depth of family love; its perversions and hypocrisies that have produced Sid and pathetic Lily; the urge for mental independence— the dramatist's own—in Richard; the age-old parental, but threatened, severity of Nat, against which the characters variedly strive to be themselves—and all depicted in O'Neill's most genial vein of satire. His masterly exploitation of this always disarmingly enjoyable dramatic simplicity gives this play, if only as a period piece, a universality and very likely a more lasting stage value than his more drastic experiments in the earlier works. It should also persuade those who have decried O'Neill's claim to greatness, asserting that his plays, without the experimental novelties, were below such distinction, to concede that he is as versatile and substantial a dramatist as America has produced. Nevertheless, we must admit, as many of his admirers do, that as pure literature the plays contain little of lasting greatness; but such ambition was farthest from O'Neill's intent. His genius and his bent, as his devoted friend Nathan defined them, were: "to delve into and appraise character . . . his sweep and pulse and high resolve, his command of a stage . . . and his mastery of the intricacies of dramaturgy." And we may add: he had an infallible instinct as to what was fitting and dramatically effective to do or to say at any moment in a scene on stage.

The mounting of *Ah, Wilderness!* in the Theatre Guild's best manner, with the inspired selection of George M. Cohan for the part of Nat, that he appeared not to act but actually to be, was an unforgettable Broadway event. It was perhaps significant, after O'Neill's more sensational departures from convention had won him all the theatre freedom he could wish, that in *Ah, Wilderness!* and in his last great creation, *A Long Day's Journey into Night,* he found stage realism the most appropriate and most expressive medium he could adopt, when complete fidelity to life was his inevitable obligation. He and the audiences seem to have found it adequate and completely satisfying.

EUGENE GLADSTONE O'NEILL

Born 1888, New York City, son of actor James O'Neill.

1906–1907, Attended Princeton University; suspended for misbehavior.

1909–1911, Period of roaming, seamanship, and varied employments, including prospecting for gold in Central America and office jobs in the United States and South America.

1911–1912, Taken into his father's acting company, playing small roles and helping in business management. Later, a reporter and contributer of verse on staff of New London *Telegraph.*

1913–1914, Hospitalized for tubercular infection; during convalescence wrote his first play, *The Web.* At his father's expense, his first play collection published: *Thirst and Other One-Act Plays.*

1914–1915, Enrolled in Professor George Pierce Baker's playwriting course (47 Workshop) at Harvard.

1916, *Bound East for Cardiff,* his first play produced; staged by the company later known in New York as the Provincetown Players.

1920–1921, *Beyond the Horizon,* his first Broadway production; awarded two Pulitzer prizes, for this and *Anna Christie.* These successes, followed by *Emperor Jones,* established O'Neill's position as America's leading playwright.

1928, Won his third Pulitzer prize for *Strange Interlude.*

1936, Awarded the Nobel Prize in Literature.

His later years, aside from marital and family involvements, were spent creatively on a vast serialized drama of many full-length divisions treating American history under the title of "A Story of Possessors Dispossessed." Of this incompleted opus he himself destroyed much that he had written. His own family story covering his early life in Connecticut, entitled *A Long Day's Journey Into Night,* he left completed with the request that it should not be produced within twenty-five years after his death; but it has been a sensational Broadway success of 1957–1958 and, together with the impressive revival of *The Iceman Cometh*, has given the present generation of playgoers convincing evidence of O'Neill's right to be still considered America's foremost dramatist.

Died 1953.

PLAYS

1914 *Thirst and Other One-Act Plays* published (containing *Thirst, The Web, Warnings, Fog, Recklessness*). 1916 *Bound East for Cardiff*. 1916 *Before Breakfast*. 1917 *The Sniper* (not published). 1917 *In the Zone*. 1917 *The Long Voyage Home*. 1917 *Ile*. 1918 *The Rope*. 1918 *Where the Cross Is Made*. 1918 *The Moon of the Caribbees*. 1919 *The Dreamy Kid*. 1920 *Beyond the Horizon*. 1920 *Chris Christopherson* (rewritten as *Anna Christie*). 1920 *Exorcism* (not published). 1920 *The Emperor Jones*. 1920 *Diff'rent*. 1921 *Gold*. 1921 *Anna Christie*. 1921 *The Straw*. 1922 *The First Man*. 1922 *The Hairy Ape*. 1924 *Welded*. 1924 *The Ancient Mariner* (not published). 1924 *All God's Chillun Got Wings*. 1924 *Desire Under the Elms*. 1924 *S. S. Glencairn* (containing *The Moon of the Caribbees, The Long Voyage Home, In the Zone, Bound East for Cardiff*, united to form a single full-length play). 1925 *The Fountain*. 1926 *The Great God Brown*. 1927 *Marco Millions*. 1927 *Lazarus Laughed*. 1928 *Strange Interlude*. 1929 *Dynamo*. 1931 *Mourning Becomes Electra*. 1933 *Ah, Wilderness!* 1934 *Days Without End*. 1946 *The Iceman Cometh*. 1947 *A Moon for the Misbegotten*. 1950 *Lost Plays: Abortion, The Movie Man, The Sniper, Servitude, A Wife for a Life*.

1956 *A Long Day's Journey Into Night*. 1957 *A Touch of the Poet*. 1958 *Hughie* (one act).

WRITINGS ON DRAMA

(For extensive quotations from O'Neill, written or conversational, see Barrett H. Clark's *Eugene O'Neill; the Man and His Plays*, 1933. On page 12, O'Neill's first brief bit of autobiography is reprinted.)

Letter (about *Beyond the Horizon*) to *New York Times*, April 11, 1920. Letter (about *Anna Christie*) to *New York Times*, December 12, 1921, Sec. 6. Letter (about *The Great God Brown*) headlined "Eugene O'Neill Writes About His Latest Play," *New York Evening Post*, February 13, 1926, reprinted in other New York papers the following day. "O'Neill Talks About Beyond the Horizon," *New York Evening Post*, November 27, 1926. Letters from O'Neill to George Jean Nathan in "The Record of a Stimulating Correspondence" by Isaac Goldberg, *Boston Evening Transcript*, December 12, 1925, Sec. 6 (reprinted in Goldberg's *The Theatre of George Jean Nathan*, 1927). Foreword to B. De Casseres' *Anathema*, New York, 1928. "O'Neill's Own Story of 'Electra' in the Making," *New York Herald Tribune*, November 3, 1931.

AH, WILDERNESS!

Characters

NAT MILLER, *owner of the "Evening Globe."*
ESSIE, *his wife.*
ARTHUR, *their son.*
RICHARD, *their son.*
MILDRED, *their daughter.*
TOMMY, *their son.*
SID DAVIS, *Essie's brother.*
LILY MILLER, *Nat's sister.*

DAVID McCOMBER, *dry-goods merchant.*
MURIEL McCOMBER, *his daughter.*
WINT SELBY, *a classmate of Arthur's at Yale.*
BELLE.
NORA.
BARTENDER.
SALESMAN.

SCENES

ACT ONE

SCENE I

Sitting-room of the Miller home in a large small-town in Connecticut—about seven-thirty in the morning of July 4th, 1906. The room is fairly large, homely looking and cheerful in the morning sunlight, furnished with scrupulous medium-priced tastelessness of the period. Beneath the two windows, right, a sofa with silk and satin cushions stands against the wall. Above sofa, a bookcase with glass doors, filled with cheap sets, extends along the remaining length of wall. In the rear wall, right center, is a double doorway with sliding doors and portieres, leading into a dark, windowless back parlor. At left of this doorway another bookcase, this time a small, open one, crammed with boys' and girls' books and the best-selling novels of many past years—books the family really have read. To the left center is the mate of the double doorway at right center, with sliding doors and portieres, this one leading to a well-lighted front parlor. In the upper left wall, a screen door opens on a porch. Farther forward in this wall are two windows, with a writing desk and a chair above them. At right center is a big, round table with a green shaded reading lamp, the cord of the lamp running up to one of five sockets in the chandelier above. Four chairs are grouped around the table—two rockers at left, right, rear of it; two armchairs right and left in front. A medium-priced, inoffensive rug covers most of the floor. At left center an armchair; down left a rocker. The walls are papered white with a cheerful ugly blue design.

[VOICES *are heard in a conversational tone from the dining-room beyond the back parlor, where the family are just finishing breakfast. Then* MRS. MILLER'S *voice, raised commandingly:* "Tommy! Come back here and finish your milk!" *At the same moment,* TOMMY *appears in the doorway from the back parlor—a chubby, sun-burnt boy of eleven with dark eyes, blond hair wetted and plastered down in a part, and a shiny, good-natured face, a rim of milk visible about his lips. Bursting with bottled-up energy on the Fourth, he*

282

nevertheless has hesitated obediently at his MOTHER'S *call.*]

Tommy. [*Calls back pleadingly.*] Aw, I'm full, Ma. And I said "excuse me" and you said "all right." [*His* FATHER'S *voice is heard speaking to his* MOTHER. MILLER— "Oh, let him run about." *Then she calls:* "All right, Tommy!" *And* TOMMY *asks eagerly.*] Can I go out now?

Mother's Voice. [*Correctingly.*] May I!

Tommy. [*Fidgeting, but obediently.*] May I, Ma?

Mother's Voice. Yes.

[TOMMY *jumps for the screen door to the porch like a sprinter released by the starting shot.*]

Father's Voice. [*Shouts after him.*] But you set off your crackers away from the house, remember!

[*But* TOMMY *is already through the screen door, which he leaves open behind him.*]

[*A moment later the family appear from the back parlor, coming from the dining-room. First is* MILDRED. MILDRED *is fifteen, tall and slender, with big, irregular features, resembling her father to the complete effacing of any pretence at prettiness. But her big, gray eyes are beautiful. She has vivacity and a fetching smile, and everyone thinks of her as an attractive girl. She is dressed in shirtwaist and skirt in the fashion of the period.*]

[ARTHUR *enters after* MILDRED. *He is the eldest of the Miller children who are still living home; is nineteen. He is tall, heavy, barrel-chested and muscular, the type of football linesman of that period, with a square, stolid face, small blue eyes and thick, sandy hair. His manner is solemnly collegiate. He is dressed in the latest college fashion of that day, which has receded a bit from the extreme of preceding years, but still runs to padded shoulders and pants half pegged at the top and so small at their wide-cuffed bottoms that they cannot be taken off with shoes on.*]

Mildred. [*Inquisitively, as* ARTHUR *appears.*] Where are you going today, Art?

Arthur. [*With superior dignity.*] That's my business.

[*He ostentatiously takes from his pocket a tobacco pouch with a big Y and class numerals stamped on it, and a heavy bulldog briar pipe with silver Y and numerals, and starts filling the pipe.*]

Mildred. [*Teasingly.*] Bet I know, just the same! Want me to tell you her initials? E. R.!

[*She laughs.* ARTHUR *is pleased by this insinuation at his lady-killing activities, yet finds it beneath his dignity to reply. He lights his pipe and picks up the local morning paper and slouches back into armchair, beginning to whistle "Oh, Waltz Me Around Again, Willie," as he scans the headlines.* MILDRED *sits on the sofa at right front. Meanwhile their* MOTHER *and their* AUNT LILY, *their father's sister, have appeared, following them from back parlor.* MRS. MILLER *is around fifty, a short, stout woman with fading light-brown hair sprinkled with gray, who must have been decidedly pretty as a girl in a round-faced, cute, small-featured, wide-eyed fashion. She has big, brown eyes, soft and maternal—a bustling, mother-of-a-family manner. She is dressed in shirtwaist and skirt.* LILY MILLER, *her sister-in-law, is forty-two, tall, dark, thin. She conforms outwardly to the conventional type of old-maid school teacher, even to wearing glasses. But behind the glasses her gray eyes are gentle and tired, and her whole atmosphere is one of shy kindliness. Her voice presents the greatest contrast to her appearance—soft and full of sweetness. She, also, is dressed in a shirt-waist and skirt.*]

Mrs. Miller. [*As they appear.*] Getting milk down him is like—— [*Suddenly she is aware of the screen door standing half open.*] Goodness, look at that door he's left open! The house will be alive with flies! I've told him again—and again—and that's all the good it does! It's just a waste of breath! [*She slams the door shut, then crosses to table and gets a magazine, then crosses to rocking chair down left and fans herself with magazine as she talks.*]

Lily. [*Smiling.*] Well, you can't expect a boy to remember to shut doors—on the Fourth of July. [*She goes diffidently to the straight-backed chair before the desk at left, leaving the comfortable chairs to the* OTHERS.]

Mrs. Miller. That's you all over—Lily—always making excuses for him. You'll have him spoiled to death in spite of me. Phew, I'm hot, aren't you? This is going to be a scorcher. [*She begins to rock, fanning herself. Meanwhile, her* HUSBAND *and her* BROTHER *have appeared from back parlor, both smoking cigars.* NAT MIL-

LER *is in his late fifties, a tall, dark, spare man, a little stoop-shouldered, more than a little bald, dressed with an awkward attempt at sober respectability imposed upon an innate heedlessness of clothes. His long face has large, irregular, undistinguished features, but he has fine, shrewd, humorous gray eyes.* SID DAVIS, *his brother-in-law, is forty-five, short and fat, bald-headed, with the Puckish face of a Peck's Bad Boy who has never grown up. He is dressed in what had once been a very natty loud light suit but is now a shapeless and faded nondescript in cut and color.*]

Sid. [*As they appear.*] Oh, I like the job first rate, Nat. Waterbury's a nifty old town with the lid off, when you get to know the ropes. I rang in a joke in one of my stories that tickled the folks there pink. Water-wagon—Waterbury—Waterloo!

Miller. [*Grinning.*] Darn good!

Sid. [*Pleased.*] I thought it was pretty fair myself. [*Goes on a bit ruefully, as if oppressed by a secret sorrow.*] Yes, you can see life in Waterbury, all right—that is, if you're looking for life in Waterbury!

Mrs. Miller. What's this about Waterbury, Sid?

Sid. I was saying it's all right in its way —but there's no place like home.

[*As if to punctuate this remark, there begins a series of bangs from just beyond the porch outside, as* TOMMY *inaugurates his celebration by setting off a package of firecrackers. The assembled family jump in their chairs.* SID *chuckles.*]

Mrs. Miller. That boy! [*She rushes to the screen door up left and out on the porch, calling.*] Tommy! You mind what your Pa told you! You take your crackers out in the back yard, you hear me!

Tommy. [*Off stage.*] All right, Ma.

Arthur. [*Frowning scornfully.*] Fresh kid! He did it on purpose to scare us.

Miller. [*Grinning through his annoyance.*] Darned youngster! He'll have the house afire before the day's out.

Sid. [*Grins and sings.*] "Dunno what ter call 'im. But he's mighty like a Rose-velt." [*They* ALL *laugh.*]

Lily. Sid, you crazy!

[SID *beams at her.* MRS. MILLER *comes back from the porch, still fuming.*]

Mrs. Miller. Well, I've made him go out back at last. Now we'll have a little peace. [*As if to contradict this, the bang of firecrackers and torpedoes begins from* the rear of the house, left, and continues at intervals throughout the scene, not nearly so loud as the first explosion, but sufficiently emphatic to form a disturbing punctuation to the conversation.*]

Miller. Well, what's on the tappee for all of you today? Sid, you're coming to the Sachem Club picnic with me, of course.

Sid. [*A bit embarrassedly.*] You bet!— That is, if——

Mrs. Miller. [*Regarding her* BROTHER *with smiling suspicion.*] Hmmm! I know what that Sachem Club picnic's always meant!

Lily. [*Breaks in, in a forced joking tone that conceals a deep earnestness.*] No, not this time, Essie. Sid's a reformed character since he's been on the paper in Waterbury. At least, that's what he swore to me last night.

Sid. [*Avoiding her eyes, humiliated—joking it off.*] Pure as the driven snow, that's me. They're running me for president of the W.C.T.U.

[*They* ALL *laugh.* ARTHUR *laughs longest.*]

Mrs. Miller. Sid, you're a caution. You turn everything into a joke. But you be careful, you hear? We're going to have dinner in the evening tonight, you know—the best shore dinner you ever tasted and I don't want you coming home—well, not able to appreciate it.

Lily. Oh, I know he'll be careful today. Won't you, Sid?

Sid. [*More embarrassed than ever—joking it off melodramatically.*] Lily, I swear to you if any man offers me a drink, I'll kill him—that is, if he changes his mind!

[*They* ALL *laugh except* LILY, *who bites her lip and stiffens.*]

Mrs. Miller. No use talking to him, Lily. We can only hope for the best.

Miller. Now, you women stop picking on Sid. It's the Fourth of July and even a down-trodden newspaper man has a right to enjoy himself when he's on his holiday.

Mrs. Miller. I wasn't thinking only of Sid.

Miller. [*With a wink at the* OTHERS.] What, are you insinuating I ever——?

Mrs. Miller. Well, to do you justice, no, not what you'd really call—But I've known you to come back from this darned Sachem Club picnic—Well, I didn't need any little bird to whisper that you'd been some place besides to the well!

[*She smiles good-naturedly.* MILLER *chuckles.*]

Sid. [*After a furtive glance at the stiff and silent* LILY—*changes the subject abruptly by turning to* ARTHUR.] How are you spending the festive Fourth, Boola-Boola?

[ARTHUR *stiffens dignifiedly.*]

Mildred. [*Teasingly.*] I can tell you, if he won't.

Mrs. Miller. [*Smiling.*] Off to the Rands', I suppose.

Arthur. [*With dignity.*] I and Bert Turner are taking Elsie and Ethel Rand canoeing. We're going to have a picnic lunch on Strawberry Island. And this evening I'm staying at the Rands' for dinner.

Miller. What about you, Mid?

Mildred. I'm going to the beach to Anne Culver's.

Arthur. [*Sarcastically.*] Of course, there won't be any boys present! Johnny Dodd, for example?

Mildred. [*Giggles—then with a coquettish toss of her head.*] Pooh! What do I care for him? He's not the only pebble on the beach.

Miller. Stop your everlasting teasing, you two. How about you and Lily, Essie?

Mrs. Miller. I don't know. I haven't made any plans. Have you, Lily?

Lily. [*Quietly.*] No. Anything you want to do.

Mrs. Miller. Well, I thought we'd just sit around and rest and talk.

Miller. You can gossip any day. This is the Fourth. Now, I've got a better suggestion than that. What do you say to an automobile ride? I'll get out the Buick and we'll drive around town and out to the lighthouse and back. Then Sid and I will let you off here, or anywhere you say, and we'll go on to the picnic.

Mrs. Miller. I'd love to. Wouldn't you, Lily?

Lily. It would be nice.

Miller. Then, that's all settled.

Sid. [*Embarrassedly.*] Lily, want to come with me to the fireworks display at the beach tonight?

Mrs. Miller. That's right, Sid. You take her out. Poor Lily never has any fun, always sitting home with me.

Lily. [*Flustered and grateful.*] I—I'd like to, Sid. Thank you. [*Then an apprehensive look comes over her face.*] Only not if you come back—you know!

Sid. [*Again embarrassed and humiliated—again joking it off, solemnly.*] Evil-minded, I'm afraid, Nat. I hate to say it of your sister.

[*They* ALL *laugh. Even* LILY *cannot suppress a smile.*]

Arthur. [*With heavy jocularity.*] Listen, Uncle Sid. Don't let me catch you and Aunt Lily spooning on a bench tonight—or it'll be my duty to call a cop!

[SID *and* LILY *look painfully embarrassed at this. The joke falls flat, except for* MILDRED, *who can't restrain a giggle at the thought of these two ancients spooning.*]

Mrs. Miller. [*Rebukingly.*] Arthur!

Miller. [*Dryly.*] That'll do you! Kicking a football around Yale seems to have blunted your sense of humor!

Mrs. Miller. [*Suddenly—startledly.*] But where's Richard? We're forgetting all about him. Why, where is that boy? I thought he came in with us from breakfast.

Mildred. I'll bet he's off somewhere writing a poem to Muriel McComber, the silly! Or pretending to write one. I think he just copies——

Arthur. [*Looking back toward the dining-room.*] He's still in the dining-room, reading a book. [*Turning back—scornfully.*] Gosh, he's always reading now. It's not *my* idea of having a good time in vacation.

Miller. [*Caustically.*] He read his school books, too, strange as that may seem to you. That's why he came out top of his class. I'm hoping before you leave New Haven they'll find time to teach you reading is a good habit.

Mrs. Miller. [*Sharply.*] That reminds me, Nat. I've been meaning to speak to you about those awful books Richard is reading. You've got to give him a good talking to—[*Starts off.*] I'll go up and get them right now. I found them where he'd hid them on the shelf in his wardrobe. You just wait till you see what—— [*She bustles off.*]

Miller. [*Plainly not relishing whatever is coming—grumblingly—to* SID.] Seems to me she might wait until the Fourth is over before bringing up— [*Then with a grin.*] I know there's nothing to it, anyway. Gosh, when I think of the books I used to sneak out and read when I was a kid!

Sid. Me, too. I suppose Dick is deep in "Nick Carter" or "Old Cap Collier."

Miller. No, he passed that period long ago. Poetry's his red meat nowadays, I think —love poetry—and Socialism, too, I suspect, from some dire declarations he's made. [*Then briskly—with a grin.*] Well, might as well get him on the carpet. [*He calls.*] Richard. [*No answer. Louder.*] Richard. [*No answer—in a bellow.*] Richard.

Arthur. [*Shouting.*] Hey, Dick, wake up! Pa's calling you.

Richard's voice. [*From the dining room.*] All right. I'm coming.

Miller. Darn him! When he gets his nose in a book, the house could fall down and he'd never——

[RICHARD *appears in the doorway, the book he has been reading in one hand, a finger marking his place. He looks a bit startled still, reluctantly called back to earth from another world. He is sixteen, just out of high school. In appearance he is a perfect blend of father and mother, so much so that each is convinced he is the image of the other. He has his mother's light-brown hair, his father's gray eyes; his features are neither large nor small; he is of medium height, neither fat nor thin. One would not call him a handsome boy; neither is he homely. But he is definitely different from both of his parents, too. There is something of extreme sensitiveness added—a restless, apprehensive, defiant, shy, dreamy, self-conscious intelligence about him. In manner he is alternately plain, simple boy and a posey actor solemnly playing a role. He is dressed in prep. school reflection of the college style of* ARTHUR.]

Richard. Did you want me, Pa?

Miller. I'd hoped I'd made that plain. Come and sit down a while.

[*He points to chair.*]

Richard. [*Coming forward—seizing on the opportunity to play up his preoccupation —with apologetic superiority.*] I didn't hear you, Pa. I was off in another world.

[MILDRED *slyly shoves her foot out so that he trips over it, almost falling. She laughs gleefully. So does* ARTHUR.]

Arthur. Good for you, Mid! That'll wake him up!

Richard. [*Grins sheepishly—all boy now.*] Darn you, Mid! I'll show you!

[*He pushes her back on the sofa and tickles her with his free hand, still holding the book in the other. She shrieks.*]

Arthur. Give it to her, Dick!

Miller. That's enough now. No more roughhouse. You sit down here, Richard. [RICHARD *obediently sits in chair.*] What were you planning to do with yourself today? Going out to the beach with Mildred?

Richard. [*Scornfully superior.*] That silly skirt party! I should say not!

Mildred. He's not coming because Muriel isn't. I'll bet he's got a date with her somewheres.

Richard. [*Flushing bashfully.*] You shut up, Mid! [*Then to his* FATHER.] I thought I'd just stay home, Pa—this morning, anyway.

Miller. Help Tommy set off firecrackers, eh?

Richard. [*Drawing himself up—with dignity.*] I should say not. [*Then frowning portentously.*] I don't believe in this silly celebrating the Fourth of July—all this lying talk about liberty—when there is no liberty!

Miller. [*A twinkle in his eye.*] Hmmmm.

Richard. [*Getting warmed up.*] The land of the free and the home of the brave! Home of the slave is what they ought to call it—the wage slave ground under the heel of the capitalist class, starving, crying for bread for his children, and all he gets is a stone! The Fourth of July is a stupid farce!

Miller. [*Putting a hand to his mouth to conceal a grin.*] Hmm. Them are mighty strong words. You'd better not repeat such sentiments outside the bosom of the family or they'll have you in jail.

Sid. And throw away the key.

Richard. [*Darkly.*] Let them put me in jail. But how about the freedom of speech in the Constitution, then? That must be a farce, too. [*Then he adds grimly.*] No, you can celebrate your Fourth of July. I'll celebrate the day the people bring out the guillotine again and I see Pierpont Morgan being driven by in a tumbril!

[*His* FATHER *and* SID *are vastly amused.* LILY *is shocked but, taking her cue from them, smiles.* MILDRED *stares at him in puzzled wonderment, never having heard this particular line before. Only* ARTHUR *betrays the outraged reaction of a patriot.*]

Arthur. Aw, say, you fresh kid, tie that bull outside! You ought to get a punch in the nose for talking that way on the Fourth!

Miller. [*Solemnly.*] Son, if I didn't know it was you talking, I'd think we had Emma Goldman [1] with us.

Arthur. Never mind, Pa. Wait till we get him down to Yale. We'll take that out of him!

Richard. [*With high scorn.*] Oh, Yale! You think there's nothing in the world besides Yale. After all, what is Yale?

Arthur. You'll find out what!

Sid. [*Provocatively.*] Don't let them scare you, Dick. Give 'em hell!

Lily. [*Shocked.*] Sid! You shouldn't swear before——

Richard. What do you think I am, Aunt Lily—a baby? I've heard worse than anything Uncle Sid says.

---

[1] Russian-born American anarchist (1869–1940), whose sensational speeches advocating birth control, obstruction of the draft, and communism led to her deportation to Russia in 1917.

Mildred. And said worse himself, I bet!

Miller. [*With a comic air of resignation.*] Well, Richard, I've always found I've had to listen to at least one stump speech every Fourth. I only hope getting your extra strong one right after breakfast will let me off for the rest of the day.

[*They* ALL *laugh now, taking this as a cue.*]

Richard. [*Somberly.*] That's right, laugh! After you, the deluge, you think! But look out! Supposing it comes before? Why shouldn't the workers of the world unite and rise? They have nothing to lose but their chains! [*He recites threateningly.*] "The days grow hot, O Babylon! 'Tis cool beneath thy willow trees!"

Miller. Hmm. But where's the connection, exactly? Something from that book you're reading?

Richard. [*Superior.*] No. That's poetry. This is prose.

Miller. I've heard there was a difference between 'em. What is the book?

Richard. [*Importantly.*] Carlyle's French Revolution.

Miller. Hmm. So that's where you drove the tumbril from and piled poor old Pierpont in it. [*Then seriously.*] Glad you're reading it, Richard. It's a darn fine book.

Richard. [*With unflattering astonishment.*] What, have you read it?

Miller. Well, you see, even a newspaper owner can't get out of reading a book every now and again.

Richard. [*Abashed.*] I—I didn't mean— I know you— [*Then enthusiastically.*] Say, isn't it a great book, though—that part about Mirabeau—and about Marat and Robespierre——

Mrs. Miller. [*Appears from front parlor in a great state of flushed annoyance.*] Never you mind Robespierre, young man! You tell me this minute where you've hidden those books! They were on the shelf in your wardrobe and now you've gone and hid them somewheres else. You go right up and bring them to your father.

[RICHARD, *for a second, looks suddenly guilty and crushed. Then he bristles defensively.*]

Miller. Never mind his getting them now. We'll waste the whole morning over those darned books. And anyway, he has a right to keep his library to himself. [*Looks from* MRS. MILLER.] That is, if they're not too— What books are they, Richard?

Richard. [*Self-consciously hesitant.*] Well —there's——

Mrs. Miller. I'll tell you if he won't—and you give him a good talking too. [*Then, after a glance at* RICHARD.] Not that I blame Richard. There must be some boy he knows who's trying to show off as advanced and wicked, and he told him about——

Richard. No! I read about them myself in the papers and other books.

Mrs. Miller. Well, no matter how, there they were on his shelf. Two by that awful Oscar Wilde they put in jail for heaven knows what wickedness.

Arthur. [*Suddenly—solemnly authoritative.*] He committed bigamy. [*Then as* SID *smothers a burst of ribald laughter.*] What are you laughing at? I guess I ought to know. A fellow at college told me. His father was in England when this Wilde was pinched—and he said he remembered once his mother asked his father about it and he told her he'd committed bigamy.

Miller. [*Hiding a smile behind his hand.*] Well, then, that must be right, Arthur.

Mrs. Miller. I wouldn't put it past him, nor anything else. One book was called the Picture of something or other.

Richard. "The Picture of Dorian Gray." It's one of the greatest novels ever written.

Mrs. Miller. Looked to me like cheap trash. And the second book was poetry. "The Ballad" of I forget what.

Richard. [*Defiantly.*] "The Ballad of Reading Gaol," one of the greatest poems ever written.

[*He pronounces it "Reading Goal"—as in goalpost.*]

Mrs. Miller. All about someone who murdered his wife and got hung, as he richly deserved, as far as I could make out. And then there were two books by that Bernard Shaw——

Richard. The greatest playwright alive today!

Mrs. Miller. To hear him tell it, maybe! You know, Nat, the one who wrote a play —that was so vile they wouldn't even let it play in New York!

Miller. Hmmm. I remember.

Mrs. Miller. One was a book of his plays and the other had a long title I couldn't make head or tail of, only it wasn't a play.

Richard. [*Proudly.*] "The Quintessence of Ibsenism."

Mildred. Phew! Good gracious, what a name! What does it mean, Dick? I'll bet he doesn't know.

Richard. [*Outraged.*] I do, too, know! It's about Ibsen, the greatest playwright since Shakespeare.

Mrs. Miller. And there was a book of plays by that Ibsen there, too! And poems by Swin-something——

Richard. "Poems and Ballads by Swinburne," Ma. The greatest poet since Shelley! He tells the truth about real love!

Mrs. Miller. Love! Well, all I can say is, from reading here and there, that if he wasn't flung in jail along with Wilde, he should have been. Some of the things I simply couldn't read, they were so indecent. All about—well, I can't tell you before Lily and Mildred.

Sid. [*With a wink at* RICHARD, *jokingly.*] Remember, I'm next on that one, Dick. I feel the need of a little poetical education.

Lily. [*Scandalized, but laughing.*] Sid! aren't you ashamed?

Mrs. Miller. This is no laughing matter. And then there was Kipling's—but I suppose he's not so bad. And last there was a poem —a long one—the Rubay—What is it, Richard?

Richard. "The Rubaiyat of Omar Khayyam!" That's the best of all!

Miller. Oh, I've read that, Essie—got a copy down at the office now.

Sid. [*Enthusiastically.*] So have I. It's a pippin!

Lily. [*With shy excitement.*] I—I've read it, too—at the library. I like—some parts of it.

Mrs. Miller. [*Scandalized.*] Why, Lily!

Miller. Everybody's reading that now, Essie—and it don't seem to do them any harm. There's fine things in it, seems to me —true things.

Mrs. Miller. [*A bit bewildered and uncertain now.*] Why, Nat, I don't see how you —It looked terrible blasphemous—parts I read.

Sid. Remember this one: [*He quotes rhetorically.*] "Oh Thou, who didst with pitfall and with gin Beset the path I was to wander in—" Now, I've always noticed how beset my path was with gin—in the past, you understand!

[*He casts a joking side glance at* LILY. *The* OTHERS *laugh. But* LILY *is in a melancholy dream and hasn't heard him.*]

Mrs. Miller. [*Tartly, but evidently suppressing her usual smile where he is concerned.*] You would pick out the ones with liquor in them!

Lily. [*Suddenly—with a sad pathos, quotes awkwardly and shyly.*] I like—because it's true:
"The Moving Finger writes, and having writ,
Moves on: nor all your Piety nor Wit
Shall lure it back to cancel half a Line,
Nor all your Tears wash out a Word of it."

Mrs. Miller. [*Astonished, as are all the* OTHERS.*] Why, Lily, I never knew you to recite poetry before!

Lily. [*Immediately guilty and apologetic.*] I—it just stuck in my memory somehow.

Richard. [*Looking at her as if he had never seen her before.*] Good for you, Aunt Lily! [*Then enthusiastically.*] But that isn't the best. The best is:
"A Book of Verses underneath the Bough,
A Jug of Wine, a Loaf of Bread—and Thou
Beside me singing in the Wilderness—"

Arthur. [*Who, bored to death by all this poetry quoting, looks out window down right.*] Hey, look who's coming up the walk —Old Man McComber!

Miller. [*Irritably.*] Dave? Now what in thunder does that damned old—Sid, I can see where we never are going to get to that picnic.

Mrs. Miller. [*Vexatiously.*] He'll know we're in this early, too. No use lying. [*Then appalled by another thought.*] That Norah— she's that thick, she never can answer the front door right unless I tell her each time. Nat, you've got to talk to Dave. I'll have her show him in here. Lily, let's us run up the back stairs and get our things on. Nat, you get rid of him the first second you can! Whatever can the old fool want——

[*She and* LILY *hurry out.*]

Arthur. I'm going to beat it—just time to catch the eight-twenty trolley.

Mildred. I've got to catch that, too. Wait till I get my hat, Art!

[*She rushes into the back parlor.*]

Arthur. [*Shouts after her.*] I can't wait. You can catch up with me if you hurry. [*He turns at the back-parlor door with a grin.*] Dick! McComber may be coming to see if your intentions toward his daughter are dishonorable! You'd better beat it while your shoes are good!

[*He disappears through back-parlor door, laughing.*]

Richard. [*A bit shaken, but putting on a brave front.*] Think I'm scared of him?

Miller. [*Gazing at him—frowning.*] Can't imagine what—But it's to complain about something, I know that. I only wish I didn't have to be pleasant with the old buzzard— but he's about the most valuable advertiser I've got.

Sid. [*Sympathetically.*] I know. But tell him to go to hell, anyway. He needs that ad more than you.

[*The sound of the bell comes from the rear of the house off right from back parlor.*]

Miller. There he is. You clear out, Dick— but come right back as soon as he's gone, you hear? I'm not through with you, yet.

Richard. Yes, Pa.

Miller. You better clear out, too, Sid. You know Dave doesn't approve jokes.

Sid. And loves me like poison! Come on, Dick, we'll go out and help Tommy celebrate. [*He takes* RICHARD'S *arm and they also disappear through back-parlor door.* MILLER *glances through the front parlor toward the front door, then calls in a tone of strained heartiness.*]

Miller. Hello, Dave. Come right in here. What good wind blows you around on this glorious Fourth? [*A flat, brittle voice answers him: "Good morning," and a moment later* DAVID MCCOMBER *appears. He is a thin, dried-up little man with a head too large for his body perched on a scrawny neck, and a long solemn horse face with deep-set little black eyes, a blunt formless nose and a tiny slit of a mouth. He is about the same age as* MILLER *but is entirely bald, and looks ten years older. He is dressed with a prim neatness in shiny old black clothes.*] Here, sit down and make yourself comfortable. [*Taking cigar case from pocket.*] Have a cigar?

McComber. [*Acidly.*] You're forgetting. I never smoke.

Miller. [*Forcing a laugh at himself.*] That's so. So I was. Well, I'll smoke alone, then.

[*He bites off the end of the cigar viciously, as if he wished it were* MC-COMBER'S *head, and sits down on desk chair; faces* MCCOMBER.]

McComber. You asked me what brings me here, so I'll come to the point at once. I regret to say it's something disagreeable— disgraceful would be nearer the truth—and it concerns your son, Richard!

Miller. [*Beginning to bristle—but calmly.*] Oh, come, now, Dave. I'm sure Richard hasn't——

McComber. [*Sharply.*] And I'm positive he has. You're not accusing me of being a liar, I hope.

Miller. No one said anything about liar. I only meant you're surely mistaken if you think——

McComber. I'm not mistaken. I have proof of everything *in his own handwriting!*

Miller. Let's get down to brass tacks. Just what is it you're charging him with?

McComber. With being dissolute and blasphemous—with deliberately attempting to corrupt the morals of my young daughter, Muriel.

Miller. Then I'm afraid I'll have to call you a *liar,* Dave!

McComber. [*Without taking offense—in the same flat, brittle voice.*] I thought you'd get around to that, so I brought the proofs with me. [*He takes a wallet from his inside coat pocket, selects five or six slips of paper, and holds them out to* MILLER.] My wife discovered them in one of Muriel's bureau drawers, hidden under the underwear. They're all in his handwriting. You can't deny it. Anyway, Muriel's confessed to me he wrote them. You read them and then say I'm a liar. [MILLER *has taken the slips and is reading them frowningly.* MCCOMBER *talks on.*] Evidently you've been too busy to take the right care about Richard's bringing up or what he's allowed to read—though I can't see why his *mother* failed in her duty. But that's your misfortune, and none of my business. But Muriel is my business and I can't and I won't have her innocence exposed to the contamination of a young man whose mind, judging from his choice of reading matter, is as foul——

Miller. [*Has finished the last of the slips and is making a tremendous effort to control his temper.*] Why, you damned old fool! Can't you see Richard's only a fool kid who's just at the stage when he's out to rebel against all authority, and so he grabs at everything radical to read and wants to pass it on to his elders and his girl and boy friends to show off what a young hellion he is! Why, at heart you'd find Richard is just as innocent and as big a kid as your Muriel is! This stuff doesn't mean anything to me—If you believe this could corrupt Muriel, then you must believe she's easily corrupted! But I'll bet you'd find she knows a lot more about life than you give her credit for—and can guess a stork didn't bring her down your chimney!

McComber. Now you're insulting my daughter.

Miller. I'm not insulting her. I'm giving her credit for ordinary good sense. I'd say the same about my own Mildred, who's the same age.

McComber. I know nothing about your Mildred except that she's known all over as a flirt. [*Then more sharply.*] Well, I knew you'd prove obstinate, but I certainly never *dreamed* you'd have the impudence, after reading those papers, to claim your son was innocent of all wrong-doing!

Miller. Just what *did* you dream I'd do?

McComber. Do what it's your plain duty to do as a citizen to protect other people's children! Take and give him a hiding he'd remember to the last day of his life! You'd ought to do it for his sake, if you had any sense—unless you want him to end up in jail.

Miller. [*His fists clenched, leans toward* McComber.] Dave, I've stood all I can stand from you! You get out! And get out quick, if you don't want a kick in the rear to help you!

McComber. [*Again in his flat, brittle voice, slowly getting to his feet but evincing no particular fear.*] You needn't lose your temper. I'm only demanding you do your duty by your own as I've already done by mine. I'm punishing Muriel. She's not to be allowed out of the house for a month and she's to be in bed every night by eight sharp. And yet she's blameless, compared to that——

Miller. [*Crosses to him—belligerently.*] I said I'd had enough out of you, Dave!

McComber. You needn't lay hands on me. I'm going. But there's one thing more. [*He takes a letter from his wallet.*] Here's a letter from Muriel for your son. [*Hands* Miller *the letter.*] It makes clear, I think, how she's come to think about him, now that her eyes have been opened. I hope he heeds what's inside—for his own good and yours—because if I ever catch him hanging about my place again I'll have him arrested! And don't think I'm not going to make you regret the insults you've heaped on me. I'm taking the advertisement for my store out of your paper—and it won't go in again, I tell you, not unless you apologize in writing and promise to punish——

Miller. I'll see you in hell first! As for your damned old ad, take it out and go to hell!

McComber. That's plain bluff. You know how badly you need it. So do I. Well, good day.

[McComber *turns and starts stiffly for the door.*]

Miller. Here! Listen a minute! I'm just going to call *your* bluff and tell you that, whether you want to reconsider your decision or not, I'm going to refuse to print your damned ad after tomorrow! Put that in your pipe and smoke it! Furthermore, I'll start a campaign to encourage outside capital to open a dry-goods store in opposition to you that won't be the public swindle I can prove yours is!

McComber. [*A bit shaken by this threat—but in the same flat tone.*] I'll sue you for libel.

Miller. When I get through, there won't be a person in town will buy a dishrag in your place!

McComber. [*More shaken, his eyes shifting about furtively.*] That's all bluff. You wouldn't dare— [*Then finally he says uncertainly.*] Well, good day.

[*And exits through front parlor.* Miller *stands looking after him. Slowly the anger drains from his face and leaves him looking a bit sick and disgusted.* Sid *appears from back parlor. He is nursing a burn on his right hand, but his face is one broad grin of satisfaction.*]

Sid. I burned my hand with one of Tommy's damned firecrackers and came in to get some vaseline. I was listening to the last of your scrap. Good for you, Nat! You sure gave him hell!

Miller. [*Dully.*] Much good it'll do. He knows it was all talk.

Sid. That's just what he don't know, Nat. The old skinflint has a guilty conscience.

Miller. Well, anyone who knows me knows I wouldn't use my paper for a dirty spiteful trick like that—no matter what he did to me.

Sid. Yes, everyone knows you're an old sucker, Nat, too decent for your own good. But McComber never saw you like this before. I tell you you scared the pants off him. [*He chuckles.*]

Miller. [*Still dejectedly.*] I don't know what made me let go like that. The hell of skunks like McComber is that after being with them ten minutes you become as big skunks as they are.

Sid. [*Notices the slips of paper in* Miller's *hand.*] What's this? Something he brought?

Miller. [*Grimly.*] Samples of the new freedom— [*Gives* Sid *slips of paper.* Sid *reads them.*] —from those books Essie found —that Richard's been passing on to Muriel to educate her. They're what started the rumpus. [*Then frowning.*] I've got to do something about that young anarchist or he'll be getting me, and himself, in a peck of trouble. [*Then, pathetically helpless.*] But what can I do? Putting the curb bit on would make him worse. Then he'd have a harsh tyrant to defy. He'd love that, darn him!

Sid. [*Has been reading the slips, a broad grin on his face. Suddenly he whistles.*] Phew! This is a warm lulu for fair! [*He recites with a joking intensity.*]

"My life is bitter with thy love; thine eyes
Blind me, thy tresses burn me, thy sharp sighs
Divide my flesh and spirit with soft sound—"

Miller. [*With a grim smile.*] Hmm. I missed that one. That must be Mr. Swinburne's copy. I've never read him, but I've heard something like that was the matter with him.

Sid. Yes, it's labelled Swinburne—"Anac- toria." Whatever that is. But wait, watch and listen! The worst is yet to come! [*He recites with added comic intensity.*]

"That I could drink thy veins as wine, and eat
Thy breasts like honey, that from face to feet
Thy body were abolished and consumed,
And in my flesh thy very flesh entombed!"

Miller. [*An irrepressible boyish grin coming to his face.*] Hell and hallelujah! Just picture old Dave digesting that for the first time! Gosh, I'd give a lot to have seen his face! [*Then a trace of shocked reproof showing in his voice.*] But it's no joking matter. That stuff *is* warm—too damned warm, if you ask me! I don't like this a damned bit, Sid. That's no kind of thing to be sending a decent girl. [*More worriedly.*] I thought he was really stuck on her—as one gets stuck on a decent girl at his age—all moonshine and holding hands and a kiss now and again. But this looks—I wonder if he is hanging around her to see what he can get? [*Angrily.*] By God, if that's true, he deserves that licking McComber says it's my duty to give him! I've got to draw the line somewhere!

Sid. Yes, it won't do to have him getting any decent girl in trouble.

Miller. The only thing I can do is put it up to him straight. [*With pride.*] Richard'll stand up to his guns, no matter what. I've never known him to lie to me.

Sid. [*At a noise from the back parlor, looks that way—in a whisper.*] Then now's your chance. I'll beat it and leave you alone —see if the women folks are ready upstairs. We ought to get started soon—if we're ever going to make that picnic. [*He is halfway to the entrance to the front parlor as* RICHARD *enters very evidently nervous about* McCOMBER'S *call.*]

Richard. [*Adopting a forced, innocent tone.*] How's your hand, Uncle Sid?

Sid. All right, Dick, thanks—only hurts a little.

[*He disappears.* MILLER *watches his* SON *frowningly.* RICHARD *gives him a quick side glance and grows more guiltily self-conscious.*]

Richard. [*Forcing a snicker.*] Gee, Pa, Uncle Sid's a bigger kid than Tommy is. He was throwing firecrackers in the air and catching them on the back of his hand and throwing 'em off again just before they went off—and one came and he wasn't quick enough, and it went off almost on top of——

Miller. Never mind that. I've got some-thing else to talk to you about besides fire-crackers.

Richard. [*Apprehensively.*] What, Pa?

Miller. [*Suddenly puts both hands on his shoulders and looks into his eyes—quietly.*] Look here, son. I'm going to ask you a ques-tion, and I want an honest answer. I warn you beforehand if the answer is "yes" I'm going to punish you and punish you hard be-cause you'll have done something no boy of mine ought to do. But you've never lied to me before, I know, and I don't believe, even to save yourself punishment, you'd lie to me now, would you?

Richard. [*Impressed—with dignity.*] I won't lie, Pa.

Miller. Have you been trying to have something to do with Muriel—something you shouldn't—you know what I mean.

Richard. [*Stares at him for a moment, as if he couldn't comprehend—then, as he does, a look of righteous indignation comes over his face.*] No! What do you think I am, Pa? I never would! She's not that kind. Why I—I love her! I'm going to marry her —after I get out of college! She's said she would! We're engaged!

Miller. [*A great relief showing in his face.*] All right. That's all I want to know. We won't talk any more about it. [*He gives him an approving pat on the back.*]

Richard. I don't see how you could think —Did that old idiot McComber say that about me?

Miller. [*Joking now.*] Shouldn't call your future father-in-law names, should you? 'Tain't respectful. [*Then after a glance at* RICHARD'S *indignant face—he points to the slips of paper on the desk.*] Well, you can't exactly blame old Dave, can you, when you read through that literature you wished on his innocent daughter?

Richard. [*Sees the slips for the first time and is overcome by embarrassment, which he immediately tries to cover up with a supe-rior, airy carelessness.*] Oh, so that's why. He found those, did he? I told her to be careful—Well, it'll do him good to read the truth about life for once and get rid of his old-fogey ideas.

Miller. I'm afraid I've got to agree with him, though, that they're hardly fit reading for a young girl. [*Then with subtle flattery.*] They're all well enough, in their way, for you who're a man—but— Think it over, and see if you don't agree with me.

Richard. [*Embarrassedly.*] Aw, I only did it because I liked them—and I wanted her to face life as it is. She's so darned afraid of life—afraid of her Old Man—afraid of people saying this or that about her—afraid of being in love—afraid of everything. She's even afraid to let me kiss her. I thought, maybe, reading those things—they're beautiful, aren't they, Pa? I thought they would give her the spunk to lead her own life, and not be—always thinking of being afraid.

Miller. I see. Well, I'm afraid she's still afraid. [*Takes the letter from the table.*] Here's a letter from her he said to give you. [RICHARD *takes the letter from him uncertainly, his expression changing to one of apprehension.* MILLER *adds with a kindly smile.*] You better be prepared for a bit of a blow. But never mind, son. There's lots of other fish in the sea. [RICHARD *is not listening to him, but staring at the letter with a sort of fascinated dread.* MILLER *looks into his* SON'S *face a second, then turns away, troubled and embarrassed.*] Darn it! I better go upstairs and get rigged out or I never will get to that picnic.

[*He moves awkwardly and self-consciously off.* RICHARD *continues to stare at the letter for a moment—then girds up his courage and tears it open and begins to read swiftly. As he reads his face grows more and more wounded and tragic, until at the end his mouth draws down at the corners, as if he were about to break into tears. With an effort he forces them back and his face grows flushed with humiliation and wronged anger.*]

Richard. [*Blurts out to himself.*] The little coward! I hate her! She can't treat me like that! I'll show her!

[*At sound of voices from off,* RICHARD *quickly shoves the letter into the inside pocket of his coat and does his best to appear calm and indifferent, even attempting to whistle "Waiting at the Church." But the whistle peters out miserably as his* MOTHER, LILY *and* SID *enter. They are dressed in all the elaborate paraphernalia of motoring at that period—linen dusters, veils, goggles,* SID *in a snappy cap.*]

Mrs. Miller. Well, we're about ready to start at last, thank goodness! Let's hope no more callers are on the way. What did that McComber want, Richard, do you know? Sid couldn't tell us.

Richard. You can search me. Ask Pa.

Mrs. Miller. [*Immediately sensing something "down" in his manner—going to him worriedly.*] Why, whatever's the matter with you, Richard? You sound as if you'd lost your last friend! What is it?

Richard. [*Desperately.*] I—I don't feel so well—my stomach's sick.

Mrs. Miller. [*Immediately all sympathy, smoothing his hair back from his forehead.*] You poor boy! What a shame—on the Fourth, too, of all days! [*Turning to the* OTHERS.] Maybe I better stay home with him, if he's sick.

Lily. Yes, I'll stay, too. Poor boy!

Richard. [*More desperately.*] No! You go, Ma! I'm not really sick. I'll be all right. You go. I want to be alone! [*Then, as a louder bang comes from in back as* TOMMY *sets off a cannon cracker, he jumps to his feet.*] Darn Tommy and his darned firecrackers. You can't get any peace in this house with that darned kid around! Darn the Fourth of July anyway! I wish we still belonged to England!

[*He strides off in an indignant fury of misery through the front parlor.*]

Mrs. Miller. [*Stares after him worriedly—then sighs philosophically.*] Well, I guess he can't be so very sick—after that. [*She shakes her head.*] He's a queer boy. Sometimes I can't make head or tail of him.

Miller. [*Calls from the front door beyond the back parlor.*] Come along, folks. Let's get started.

Sid. We're coming, Nat.

[*He and the* TWO WOMEN *move off through the front parlor.*]

CURTAIN

ACT TWO

Dining-room of the Miller home—a little after six in the evening of the same day. The room is much too small for the medium-priced, formidable dining-room set, especially now when all the leaves of the table are in. At right, toward rear, is a double doorway with sliding doors and portieres leading into the back parlor. In the rear wall, right center, is the door to the pantry. At the left of door is the china closet with its display of the family cut glass and fancy china. In the left wall are two windows looking out on a side lawn. In front of the windows is a heavy, ugly side-board with three pieces of old silver on its top. In the right wall, down stage, is a screen door opening on a side porch. A dark rug covers most of the floor. The table, with a chair at each end, left and right, three chairs on the far side, facing front, and two on the near side, their backs to front, takes up most of the available space. The walls are papered in a sombre brown and dark-red design.

[MRS. MILLER *is supervising and helping the Second Girl,* NORAH, *in the setting of the table.* NORAH *is a clumsy, heavy-handed, heavy-footed, long-jawed, beamingly good-natured young Irish girl—a "greenhorn."*]

Mrs. Miller. I really think you better put on the lights, Norah. It's getting so cloudy out, and this pesky room is so dark anyway.

Norah. Yes, Mum. [*She stretches awkwardly over the table to reach the chandelier that is suspended from the middle of the ceiling and manages to turn one light on—scornfully.*] Arrah, the contraption!

Mrs. Miller. [*Worriedly.*] Careful!

Norah. [*Cheerfully.*] Careful as can be, Mum.

[*But in drawing back to move around to reach the next bulb she knocks against the table.*]

Mrs. Miller. There! I do wish you'd watch——!

Norah. [*A flustered appeal in her voice.*] Arrah, what have I done wrong now?

Mrs. Miller. [*Draws a deep breath—then sighs helplessly.*] Oh, nothing. Never mind the rest of the lights. You might as well go out in the kitchen and wait until I ring.

Norah. [*Relieved and cheerful again.*] Yes, Mum. [*She starts for the pantry.*]

Mrs. Miller. But there's one thing—no, two other things—things I've told you over and over. Don't pass the plates on the wrong side at dinner tonight, and do be careful not to let that pantry door slam behind you.

Norah. Yes, Mum.

[*She goes into the pantry and lets the door almost slam behind her, but catches it in time to prevent the slam. She grins a pleased smile at* MRS. MILLER *as she allows the door to close quietly.* MRS. MILLER *sighs and reaches up with*

difficulty; can't reach lights. As she is doing so,* LILY *enters.*]

Lily. Here, let me do that, Essie. I'm taller. [*She quickly turns on lights.*]

Mrs. Miller. [*Gratefully.*] Thank you, Lily.

Lily. But where's Norah? Why didn't she——?

Mrs. Miller. [*Exasperatedly.*] Oh, that girl! She'll be the death of me! She's that thick, you honestly wouldn't believe it possible.

Lily. Is there anything I can do, Essie?

Mrs. Miller. She's got the table all wrong. We'll have to reset it. But you're always helping me. It isn't fair to ask you—in your vacation. You need your rest after teaching a pack of wild Indian kids all year.

Lily. [*Beginning to help with the table.*] You know I love to help. It makes me feel I'm some use in this house instead of just sponging——

Mrs. Miller. [*Indignantly.*] Sponging! You pay, don't you?

Lily. Almost nothing. And you and Nat only take that little to make me feel better about living with you. [*Forcing a smile.*] I don't see how you stand me—having a cranky old maid around all the time.

Mrs. Miller. What nonsense you talk! As if Nat and I—weren't only too tickled to death to have you! Lily Miller, I've no patience with you when you go on like that. [*Then she changes the subject abruptly.*] What time's it getting to be?

Lily. [*Glances at her watch.*] Quarter past six.

Mrs. Miller. I do hope those men folks aren't going to be late for dinner—— [*She sighs.*] But I suppose with that darned Sachem Club picnic it's more likely than not. [*Lily looks sad and worried, and sighs.* MRS. MILLER *gives her a quick side glance.*] I see you've got your new dress on.

Lily. [*Embarrassedly.*] Yes, I thought—if Sid's taking me to the fireworks—I ought to spruce up a little.

Mrs. Miller. [*Looking away.*] Hmm. [*A pause. Then she says with an effort to be casual.*] You mustn't mind if Sid comes home feeling a bit—gay. I expect Nat to and we'll have to listen to all those old stories about when he was a boy. You know what those picnics are, and he'd be running into all his old friends.

Lily. [*Agitatedly.*] I don't think he will —this time—not after his promise.

Mrs. Miller. [*Avoiding looking at her.*] I know. But men are weak. [*Then quickly.*] That was a good notion of Nat's, getting Sid the job on the *Waterbury Standard*. All Sid's ever needed was to get away from the rut he was in here. He's the kind that's the victim of his friends. [LILY *keeps silent, her eyes downcast.* MRS. MILLER *goes on meaningly.*] He's making good money in Waterbury, too—thirty-five a week. He's in a better position to get married than he ever was.

Lily. [*Stiffly.*] Well, I hope he finds a woman who's willing—though after he's through with his betting on horse races, and dice, and playing Kelly pool, there won't be much left for a wife—even if there was nothing else he spent his money on.

Mrs. Miller. Oh, he'd give up all that—for the right woman. [*Suddenly she comes directly to the point.*] Lily, why don't you change your mind and marry Sid and reform him? You love him and always have——

Lily. [*Stiffly.*] I can't love a man who drinks.

Mrs. Miller. You can't fool me. I know darned well you love him. And he loves you and always has.

Lily. Never enough to stop drinking for. [*Cutting off* MRS. MILLER's *reply.*] No, it's no good in your talking, Essie. We've been over this a thousand times before and I'll always feel the same as long as Sid's the same. If he gave me proof he'd—but even then I don't believe I could. It's sixteen years since I broke off our engagement, but what made me break it off is as clear to me today as it was then—his taking up with bad women——

Mrs. Miller. [*Protests half-heartedly.*] But he's always sworn he got raked into that party and never had anything to do with those harlots.

Lily. Well, I don't believe him—didn't then and don't now. I don't believe he deliberately planned to, but—— Oh, it's no good talking, Essie. What's done is done. But you know how much I like Sid—in spite of everything. I know he was just born to be what he is—irresponsible. But don't talk to me about marrying him—because I never could.

Mrs. Miller. [*Angrily.*] He's a dumb fool. —a stupid dumb fool, that's what he is!

Lily. [*Quietly.*] No. He's just Sid.

Mrs. Miller. It's a shame for you—a measly shame—you that would have made such a wonderful wife for any man—that ought to have your own home and children!

Lily. [*Winces but puts her arm around her affectionately—gently.*] Now don't you go feeling sorry for me. I won't have that. Here I am, thanks to your and Nat's kindness, with the best home in the world; and as for the children, I feel the same love for yours as if they were mine, and I didn't have the pain of bearing them. And then there are all the boys and girls I teach every year. I like to feel I'm a sort of second mother to them and helping them to grow up to be good men and women. So I don't feel such a useless old maid, after all.

Mrs. Miller. [*Kisses her impulsively— her voice husky.*] You're a good woman, Lily—too good for the rest of us. [*She turns away, wiping a tear furtively—then abruptly changing the subject.*] Good gracious, if I'm not forgetting one of the most important things! I've got to warn that Tommy not to give me away to Nat about the fish. He knows, because I had to send him to market for it, and he's liable to burst out laughing——

Lily. About what?

Mrs. Miller. [*Guiltily.*] Well, I've never told you, but you know how Nat carries on about not being able to eat bluefish.

Lily. I know he says it poisons him.

Mrs. Miller. [*Chuckling.*] Poisons him, nothing! He's been eating bluefish for years —only I tell him each time it's weakfish. We're having it tonight.

Lily. [*Laughing.*] Aren't you ashamed, Essie?

Mrs. Miller. Not much, I'm not. I like bluefish. [*She laughs.*] Where is Tommy? In the sitting-room?

Lily. No, Richard's there alone. I think Tommy's out on the piazza with Mildred. [MRS. MILLER *bustles out. As soon as she is gone, the smile fades from* LILY's *lips. Her face grows sad and she again glances nervously at her watch.* RICHARD *appears from the back parlor, moving aimlessly. His face wears a set expression of bitter gloom; he exudes tragedy. For* RICHARD, *after his first outburst of grief and humiliation, has begun to take a masochistic satisfaction in his great sorrow, especially in the concern which it arouses in the family circle. On seeing his* AUNT, *he gives her a dark look and turns and is about to stalk back toward the sitting room when she speaks to him pityingly.*] Feel any better, Richard?

Richard. [*Somberly.*] I'm all right, Aunt Lily. You mustn't worry about me.

Lily. [*Going to him.*] But I do worry about you. I hate to see you so upset.

Richard. It doesn't matter. Nothing matters.

Lily. [*Puts her arm around him sympathetically.*] You really mustn't let yourself take it so seriously. You know, things like that come up, and we think there's no hope——

Richard. Things like what come up?

Lily. What's happened between you and Muriel.

Richard. [*With disdain.*] Oh, her! I wasn't even thinking about her. [*Impressively.*] I was thinking about life.

Lily. But then—if we really, really love —why, then something else is bound to happen soon that changes everything again, and it's all as it was before the misunderstanding, and everything works out all right in the end. That's the way it is with life.

Richard. [*With a tragic sneer.*] Life! Life is a joke! And everything works out all wrong in the end.

Lily. [*A little shocked.*] You mustn't talk that way. But I know you don't mean it.

Richard. I do too mean it! You can have your silly optimism, if you like, Aunt Lily. But don't ask me to be so blind. I'm a pessimist! [*Then with an air of cruel cynicism.*] As for Muriel, that's all dead and past. I was only kidding her, anyway, just to have a little fun, and she took it seriously, like a fool. [*Pauses. He forces a cruel smile to his lips.*] You know what they say about women and trolley cars, Aunt Lily: There's always another one along in a minute.

Lily. [*Really shocked this time.*] I don't like you when you say such horrible, cynical things. It isn't nice.

Richard. Nice! That's all you women think of! I'm proud to be a cynic. It's the only thing you can be when you really face life. I suppose you think I ought to be heartbroken about Muriel—a little coward that's afraid to say her soul's her own, and keeps tied to her father's apron strings! Well, not for mine! There's plenty of other fish in the sea!

[*As he is finishing,* MRS. MILLER *comes back.*]

Mrs. Miller. Why, hello. You here, Richard? Getting hungry, I suppose?

Richard. [*Indignantly.*] I'm not hungry a bit! That's all you think of, Ma—food!

Mrs. Miller. Well, I must say I've never noticed you to hang back at meal times. [*To* LILY.] What's that he was saying about fish in the sea?

Lily. [*Smiling.*] He says he's through with Muriel now.

Mrs. Miller. [*Tartly—giving her* SON *a rebuking look.*] She's through with him, he means! The idea of your sending a nice girl like her things out of those indecent books!

[*Deeply offended,* RICHARD *disdains to reply but stalks woundedly to the screen door at right front and puts a hand on the knob.*] Where are you going?

Richard. [*Quotes from "Candida" in a hollow voice.*] "Out, then, into the night with me!"

[*He stalks out, slamming the door behind him.*]

Mrs. Miller. [*Calls.*] Well, don't you go far, 'cause dinner'll be ready in a minute, and I'm not coming running after you! [*She turns to* LILY *with a chuckle.*] Goodness, that boy! He ought to be on the stage! [*She mimics.*] "Out—into the night"—and it isn't even dark yet! He got that out of one of those books, I suppose. Do you know, I'm actually grateful to old Dave McComber for putting an end to his nonsense with Muriel. I never did approve of Richard getting so interested in girls. He's not old enough for such silliness. Why, seems to me it was only yesterday he was still a baby. [*She sighs, then matter-of-factly.*] Well, nothing to do now till those men turn up. We might as well go in the sitting room and be comfortable.

Lily. [*The nervous, worried note in her voice again.*] Yes, we might as well.

[*They go out. They have no sooner disappeared than the screen door is opened cautiously and* RICHARD *comes back in the room.*]

Richard. [*Stands inside the door, looking after them—quotes bitterly.*] "They do not know the secret in the poet's heart." [*He comes nearer the table and surveys it, especially the cut-glass dish containing olives, with contempt and mutters disdainfully.*] Food!

[*But the dish of olives seems to fascinate him and presently he has approached nearer, and stealthily lifts a couple and crams them into his mouth. He is just reaching out for more when the pantry door is opened slightly and* NORAH *peers in.*]

Norah. Master Dick, you thief, lave them olives alone, or the missus'll be swearing it was me at them!

Richard. [*Draws back his hand as if he had been stung—too flustered to be anything but guilty boy for a second.*] I—I wasn't eating——

Norah. Oho, no, of course not, divil fear you, you was only feeling their pulse! [*Then warningly.*] Mind what I'm saying now, or I'll have to tell on you to protect me good name!

[*She draws back into the pantry, closing the door.* RICHARD *stands a prey to feelings of bitterest humiliation and seething revolt against everyone and everything. A low whistle comes from just outside the porch door. He starts. Then a masculine voice calls, "Hey, Dick." He goes over to the screen door grumpily. Then as he recognizes the owner of the voice, his own as he answers becomes respectful and admiring.*]

Richard. Oh, hello, Wint. Come on in. [*He opens the door and* WINT SELBY *enters and stands just inside the door.* WINT *is nineteen, a classmate of* ARTHUR's *at Yale. He is a typical, good-looking college boy of the period, not the athletic but the hell-raising sport type. He is tall, blond, dressed in extreme collegiate cut.*]

Wint. [*As he enters—warningly, in a low tone.*] Keep it quiet, kid. I don't want the folks to know I'm here. Tell Art I want to see him a second—on the Q.T.

Richard. Can't. He's up at the Rands'—won't be home before ten, anyway.

Wint. [*Irritably.*] Damn, I thought he'd be here for dinner. [*More irritably.*] Well, that gums the works for fair!

Richard. [*Ingratiatingly.*] What is it, Wint? Can't I help?

Wint. [*Gives him an appraising glance.*] I might tell you, if you can keep your face shut.

Richard. I can.

Wint. Well, I ran into a couple of swift babies from New Haven this afternoon and I dated them up for tonight, thinking I could catch Art—— But now it's too late to get anyone else and I'll have to pass it up. I'm nearly broke and I can't afford to blow them both to drinks.

Richard. [*With shy eagerness.*] I've got eleven dollars saved up. I could loan you some.

Wint. [*Surveys him appreciatively.*] Say, you're a good sport. [*Then shaking his head.*] Nix, Kid, I don't want to borrow your money. [*Then getting an idea.*] But say, have you got anything on for tonight?

Richard. [*Hesitates a moment—then determinedly.*] No.

Wint. Want to come along with me? [*Then quickly.*] I'm not trying to lead you astray, understand, but it'll be a help if you would just sit around with Belle and feed her a few drinks while I'm off with Edith. [*He winks.*] See what I mean? You don't have to do anything, not even take a glass of beer—unless you want to.

Richard. [*Boastfully.*] Aw, what do you think I am—a rube?

Wint. You mean you're game for anything that's doing?

Richard. Sure I am!

Wint. Ever been out with any girls—I mean—real swift ones that there's something doing with, not these dead Janes around here?

Richard. [*Lies boldly.*] Aw, what do you think? Sure I have!

Wint. Ever drink anything besides sodas?

Richard. Sure. Lots of times. Beer and sloe-gin fizz and—Manhattans.

Wint. [*Impressed.*] Hell, you know more than I thought. [*Then considering.*] Can you fix it so your folks won't get wise? You can get back by half-past ten or eleven, though, all right. Think you can cook up some lie to cover that? [*As* RICHARD *hesitates—encouraging him.*] Ought to be easy —on the Fourth.

Richard. Sure. Don't worry about that.

Wint. But you've got to keep your face closed about this, you hear? I tell you straight, I wouldn't ask you to come if I wasn't in a hole—and if I didn't know you were coming down to Yale next year, and didn't think you're giving me the straight goods about having been around before. I don't want to lead you astray.

Richard. [*Scornfully.*] Aw, I told you that was silly.

Wint. Well, you be at the Pleasant Beach House at half-past nine, then—— Come in the back room. And don't forget to grab some cloves to take the booze off your breath.

Richard. Aw, I know what to do.

Wint. See you later, then. [*He starts out and is just about to close the door when he thinks of something.*] And say, I'll say you're a Harvard freshman, and you back me up. They don't know a damn thing about Harvard. I don't want them thinking I'm travelling around with any high-school kid.

Richard. Sure. That's easy.

Wint. So long, then. You better beat it right after your dinner while you've got a chance—and hang around until it's time. Watch your step, kid.

Richard. So long. [*The door closes behind* WINT. RICHARD *stands for a moment, a look of bitter, defiant rebellion coming over his face, and mutters to himself.*] I'll show her she can't treat me the way she's done! I'll show them all!

Tommy. [*A moment later, rushes in.*]
Where's Ma?

Richard. [*Surlily.*] In the sitting-room.
Where do you think, Bonehead?

Tommy. Pa and Uncle Sid are coming.
Mid and I saw them from the front piazza.
Gee, I'm glad. I'm awful hungry, ain't you?
Ma! They're coming! Let's have dinner
quick! [*A moment later,* MRS. MILLER *appears.*] Gee, but I'm awful hungry, Ma!

Mrs. Miller. I know. You always are.
You've got a tapeworm, that's what I think.

Tommy. Have we got lobsters, Ma? Gee,
I love lobsters.

Mrs. Miller. Yes, we've got lobsters.
And fish. You remember what I told you
about that fish. [*He snickers.*] Now—do
be quiet, Tommy. [*Then with a teasing smile
at* RICHARD.] Well, I'm glad to see you've
got back out of the night, Richard. [*He
scowls and turns his back on her.* LILY *appears, nervous and apprehensive. As she does
so, from the front yard* SID'S *voice is heard
singing a bit maudlinly:* "I nearly died with
aggravation. Then she shook her head, looked
at me and said: 'Poor John! Poor John!'"
MRS. MILLER *shakes her head forebodingly
—but, so great is the comic spell for her,
even in her brother's voice, a humorous smile
hovers at the corners of her lips.*] Mmm!
Mmm! Lily, I'm afraid——

Lily. [*Bitterly.*] Yes, I might have
known!

Mildred. [*Runs in. She is laughing to herself a bit shamefacedly. She rushes to her*
MOTHER.] Ma, Uncle Sid's——
[*She whispers in her ear.*]

Mrs. Miller. Never mind! You shouldn't
notice such things—at your age! And don't
you encourage him by laughing at his foolishness, do you hear?

Tommy. You needn't whisper, Mid. Think
I don't know? Uncle Sid's soused again.

Mrs. Miller. [*Shakes him by the arm indignantly.*] You be quiet! Did I ever!
You're getting too smart! [*Gives him a
push.*] Sit right down and not another word
out of you!

Tommy. [*Aggrieved—rubbing his arm as
he goes to his place.*] Aw, Ma!

Mrs. Miller. Richard, you take your right
place, and Mildred, sit down. You better,
too, Lily. We'll get him right in here and get
some food in him. He'll be all right then.
[RICHARD, *preserving the pose of the bitter,
disillusioned pessimist, sits down in his place
in the chair at left of the two whose backs
face front.* MILDRED *takes the other chair
facing back, at his right.* TOMMY *has al-*

ready slid into the end chair at left of those
at the rear of table facing front. LILY *sits
in the one of those at right, by the head of
the table, leaving the middle one,* SID'S, *vacant. While they are doing this, the front
screen door is heard slamming and* MILLER'S
and SID'S *laughing voices, raised as they come
in and for a moment after, then suddenly
cautiously lowered.* MRS. MILLER *goes to
the entrance and calls peremptorily.*] You
come right in here! Don't stop to wash up or
anything. Dinner's coming right on the table.

Miller's Voice. [*Jovially.*] All right,
Essie. Here we are! Here we are!

Mrs. Miller. [*Goes to pantry door, opens
it and calls.*] All right, Norah. You can
bring in the soup.

Miller. [*Enters. He isn't drunk by any
means. He is just mellow and benignly
ripened. His face is one large, smiling, happy
beam of utter appreciation of life. All's right
with the world, so satisfyingly right that he
becomes sentimentally moved even to think
of it.*] Here we are, Essie! Right on the dot!
Here we are!
[*He pulls her to him and gives her a
smacking kiss on the ear as she jerks
her head away.* MILDRED *and* TOMMY
giggle. RICHARD *holds rigidly aloof and
disdainful, his brooding gaze fixed on his
plate.* LILY *sits stiff and severe.*]

Mrs. Miller. [*Pulling away—embarrassedly, almost blushing.*] Don't, you crazy!
[*Then recovering herself—tartly.*] So I see,
you're here! And if I didn't, you've told me
four times already!

Miller. [*Beamingly.*] Now, Essie, don't
be critical. Don't be carpingly critical. Good
news can stand repeating, can't it? 'Course
it can!
[*He slaps her jovially on her fat buttocks.* TOMMY *and* MILDRED *roar with
glee. And* NORAH, *who has just entered
from the pantry with a large tureen of
soup in her hands, almost drops it as she
explodes in a merry guffaw.*]

Mrs. Miller. [*Scandalized.*] Nat! Aren't
you ashamed?

Miller. Couldn't resist it! Just simply
couldn't resist it!
[NORAH, *still standing with the soup
tureen held out stiffly in front of her,
again guffaws.*]

Mrs. Miller. [*Turns on her with outraged
indignation.*] Norah! Bring that soup here
this minute!

Norah. [*Guiltily.*] Yes, Mum.
[*She brings the soup above table to*
MRS. MILLER.]

Miller. [*Jovially.*] Why, hello, Norah!

Mrs. Miller. Nat!

Norah. [*Rebuking him familiarly.*] Arrah now, don't be making me laugh and getting me into trouble!

Mrs. Miller. Norah!

Norah. [*A bit resentfully.*] Yes, Mum. Here I am.

[NORAH *puts soup tureen down with a thud in front of* MRS. MILLER *and then passes around to rear of table, squeezing with difficulty between the china closet and the backs of chairs at the rear of table.*]

Mrs. Miller. Tommy! Stop spinning your napkin ring! How often have I got to tell you? Mildred! Sit up straight in your chair! Do you want to grow up a humpback? Richard! Take your elbows off the table.

Miller. [*Coming to his place at the head of the table, rubbing his hands together genially.*] Well, well, well. Well, well, well. It's good to be home again.

[NORAH *exits and lets the door slam with a bang behind her.*]

Mrs. Miller. [*Jumps.*] Oh! [*Then exasperatedly.*] Nat, I do wish you wouldn't encourage that stupid girl by talking to her, when I'm doing my best to train——

Miller. [*Beamingly.*] All right, Essie. Your word is law! [*Then laughing.*] We did have the darndest fun today! And Sid was the life of that picnic! You ought to have heard him!

Mrs. Miller. [*As* NORAH *comes back with a dish of saltines—begins ladling soup into the stack of plates before her. She calls.*] Sid! You come right in here! [*Then to* NORAH, *handing her a soup plate.*] Here, Norah. [NORAH *begins passing soup.*] Sit down, Nat, for goodness sakes. Start eating, everybody. Don't wait for me. You know I've given up soup.

Miller. [*Sits but bends forward to call to his* WIFE *in a hoarse, confidential tone.*] Essie—Sid's sort of embarrassed about coming—— I mean, I'm afraid he's a little bit—not too much, you understand—but he met such a lot of friends and—well, you know. Don't pretend to notice, eh? And don't you kids, you hear! And don't you, Lily. He's scared of you. [NORAH *leaves.*]

Lily. [*With stiff meekness.*] Very well, Nat.

Miller. [*All beaming again—calls.*] All right, Sid. The coast's clear. [*He begins to absorb his soup ravenously.*] Good soup, Essie! Good soup!

Sid. [*A moment later, makes his entrance. He is in a condition that can best be described as blurry. He is not staggering but his movements have a hazy uncertainty about them. His shiny fat face is one broad, blurred, Puckish, naughty-boy grin; his eyes have a blurred, wondering vagueness. As he enters, he makes a solemnly intense effort to appear casual and dead, cold sober. He waves his hand aimlessly and says with a silly gravity.*] Good evening. [*They* ALL *answer "Good evening," their eyes on their plates. He makes his way vaguely toward his place, continuing his grave effort at conversation.*] Beautiful evening. I never remember seeing—more beau'ful sunset. [*He bumps vaguely into* LILY'S *chair as he attempts to pass behind her—immediately he is all grave politeness.*] Sorry—sorry, Lily—deeply sorry——

Lily. [*Her eyes on her plate—stiffly.*] It's all right.

Sid. [*Manages to get into his chair at last—mutters to himself.*] Wha' was I sayin'? Oh, sunsets. But why butt in? Hasn't sun—perfect right to set? Mind y'r own business. [*He pauses thoughtfully, considering this—then looks around from face to face, fixing each with a vague, blurred, wondering look, as if some deep puzzle were confronting him. Then suddenly he grins mistily and nods with satisfaction.*] And there you are! Am I right?

Miller. [*Humoring him.*] Right.

Sid. Right! [*He is silent, studying his soup plate as if it were some strange enigma. Finally he looks up and regards his* SISTER *and asks with wondering amazement.*] Soup?

Mrs. Miller. Of course it's soup. What did you think it was? And you hurry up and eat it.

Sid. [*Again regards his soup with astonishment.*] Well! [*Then suddenly.*] Well, all right then! Soup be it! [EVERYONE *is relieved when* SID *starts to eat. He picks up his spoon and begins to eat, but after two tries in which he finds it difficult to locate his mouth, he addresses the spoon plaintively.*] Spoon, is this any way to treat a pal? [*Then suddenly comically angry, putting the spoon down with a bang.*] Down with spoons! [*He declaims.*] "We'll drink to the dead already, and hurrah for the next who dies." [*Bowing solemnly to right and left.*] Your good health, ladies and gents.

[*Lifts his soup plate and starts drinking the soup.* MILLER *guffaws, and* MILDRED *and* TOMMY *explode with laughter. Even* RICHARD *forgets his melancholy and snickers, and* MRS. MILLER *conceals a smile. Only* LILY *remains stiff and silent.*]

Mrs. Miller. [*With forced severity.*] Sid!

Sid. [*Peers at her muzzily, lowering the soup plate a little from his lips.*] Eh?

Mrs. Miller. Oh, nothing. Never mind.

Sid. [*Solemnly offended.*] Are you publicly rebuking me before assembled——? Isn't soup liquid? Aren't liquids drunk? What if they are drunk? It's a good man's failing. [*Speaks to* TOMMY.] Am I right or wrong, Tommy?

Mrs. Miller. Hurry up and finish your soup, and stop talking nonsense!

Sid. [*Turning to her—again offendedly.*] Oh, no, Essie, if I ever so far forget myself as to drink a leg of lamb, then you might have some—excuse for—Just think of wasted effort eating soup with spoons—fifty gruelling lifts per plate—billions of soup-eaters on globe—why, it's simply staggering—— [*Then darkly to himself.*] No more spoons for me! If I want to develop my biceps, I'll buy Sandow Exerciser! [*He drinks the rest of his soup in a gulp and beams around at the company, suddenly all happiness again.*] Am I right, Nat?

Miller. [*Who has been choking with laughter.*] Haw, haw! You're right, Sid.

Sid. [*Peers at him blurredly and shakes his head sadly.*] Poor old Nat! Always wrong—and drunk again, I regret to note. Sister, my heart bleeds for you and your poor fatherless chicks!

Mrs. Miller. [*Restraining a giggle—severely.*] Sid! Do shut up for a minute! Pass me your soup plates, everybody. If we wait for that girl to take them, we'll be here all night.

[ALL *pass up their plates, which* MRS. MILLER *stacks up and then puts on the sideboard. As she is doing this,* NORAH *appears with a platter of broiled fish. She is just about to place these before* MILLER *when* SID *catches her eye mistily and rises to his feet.*]

Sid. [*Raptly.*] Ah, Sight for Sore eyes, my beautiful Macushla.

Mrs. Miller. Sid!

Norah. [*Immensely pleased—gives him an arch, flirtatious glance.*] Ah, sure, Mister Sid, it's you that have kissed the Blarney Stone, when you've a drop taken!

Sid. My star-eyed Mavourneen!

Mrs. Miller. [*Outraged.*] Norah! Put down that fish!

Norah. [*Flusteredly.*] Yes, Mum.

[*She attempts to put the fish down hastily before* MILLER, *but her eyes are fixed nervously on* MRS. MILLER *and she gives* MILLER *a nasty swipe on the side of the head with the edge of the dish.*]

Miller. Ouch!

[*The* CHILDREN, *even* RICHARD, *explode into laughter.*]

Norah. [*Almost lets the dish fall.*] Oh, glory be to God! Is it hurted you are?

Miller. [*Rubbing his head, good-naturedly.*] No, no harm done. Only careful, Norah, careful.

Norah. [*Gratefully.*] Yes, sorr.

[*She thumps down the dish in front of him with a sigh of relief.*]

Sid. [*Who is still standing—with drunken gravity.*] Careful, Mavourneen, careful! You might have hit him some place besides the head. Always aim at his head, remember —so as not to worry us.

[*Again the* CHILDREN *explode. Also* NORAH. *Even* LILY *suddenly lets out an hysterical giggle and is furious with herself for doing so.*]

Lily. I'm sorry, Nat. I didn't mean to laugh. [*Turning on* SID, *furiously.*] Will you please sit down and stop making a fool of yourself!

[SID *gives her a hurt, mournful look and then sinks meekly down on his chair.*]

Norah. [*Grinning cheerfully, gives* LILY *a reassuring pat on the back.*] Ah, Miss Lily, don't mind him. He's only under the influence. Sure, there's no harm in him at all!

Mrs. Miller. Norah!

[NORAH *exits hastily letting the door slam with a crash behind her. There is silence for a moment as* MILLER *serves the fish and it is passed around.* NORAH *comes back with the vegetables. Again the door slams behind her as she goes out.*]

Miller. [*Is about to take his first bite— stops suddenly and asks his* WIFE.] This isn't, by any chance, bluefish, is it, my dear?

Mrs. Miller. [*With a warning glance at* TOMMY.] Of course not. It's weakfish. You know we never have bluefish, on account of you——

Miller. [*Addressing the table now with the gravity of a man confessing his strange peculiarities.*] Yes, I regret to say, there's a certain peculiar oil in bluefish that invariably poisons me. [*At this,* TOMMY *cannot stand it any more but explodes into laughter.* MRS. MILLER, *after a helpless glance at him, follows suit; then* LILY *goes off into uncontrollable, hysterical laughter, and* RICHARD *and* MILDRED *are caught in the contagion.* MILLER *looks around at them with a weak smile, his dignity now ruffled a bit.*] Well, I must say I don't see what's so darned funny about my being poisoned.

Sid. [*Peers around him—then with*

drunken cunning.] Aha! Nat, I suspect—plot! This fish looks blue to me—very blue—in fact despondent, desperate, and——
[*He points his fork dramatically at* MRS. MILLER, *who starts to chuckle and then laughs.*] Look how guilty *she* looks—a veritable Lucretia Borgia! Can it be this woman has been slowly poisoning you all these years? And how well—you've stood it! What iron constitution! Even now, when you are invariably at death's door, I can't believe——
[EVERYONE *goes off into uncontrollable laughter.*]

Miller. [*Grumpily.*] Oh, give us a rest, you darned fool! A joke's a joke, but——
[*He addresses his* WIFE *in a wounded tone.*] Is this true, Essie?

Mrs. Miller. [*Wiping the tears from her eyes—defiantly.*] Yes, it is true, if you must know, and you'd never have suspected it if it weren't for that darned Tommy, and Sid poking his nose in. You've been eating bluefish for years and thrived on it and it's all nonsense about that peculiar oil——

Miller. [*Deeply offended.*] Kindly allow me to know my own constitution! Now I think of it, I've felt upset afterwards every damned time we've had fish! [*He pushes his plate away from him with proud renunciation.*] I can't eat this.

Mrs. Miller. [*Insultingly matter-of-fact.*] Well, don't, then. There's lots of lobster coming and you can fill up on that.
[RICHARD *suddenly bursts out laughing again.*]

Miller. [*Turns to him, caustically.*] You seem in a merry mood, Richard. Why, I thought you were the original of the Heart Bowed Down today.

Sid. [*With mock condolence.*] Never mind, Dick. Let them—scoff! What do they know about girls whose hair sizzchels, whose lips are fireworks, whose eyes are red-hot sparks——

Mildred. [*Laughing.*] Is that what you wrote to Muriel? [*Turning to* RICHARD.] You silly goat, you!

Richard. [*Surlily.*] Aw, shut up, Mid. What do I care about her? I'll show all of you how much I care!

Mrs. Miller. Pass your plates as soon as you're through, everybody. I've rung for the lobster. And that's all. You don't get any dessert or tea after lobster, you know.
[NORAH *appears, bearing a huge platter of cold boiled lobster which she sets before* MILLER, *and exits.*]

Tommy. Gee, I love lobster!
[MILLER *puts one on each plate, and they are passed around and* EVERYONE starts in pulling the cracked shells apart.*]

Miller. [*Determining to give the conversation another turn, says to his* DAUGHTER.] Have a good time at the beach, Mildred?

Mildred. Oh, fine, Pa, thanks. The water was wonderful and warm.

Miller. Swim far?

Mildred. Yes, for me. But that isn't so awful far.

Miller. Well, you ought to be a good swimmer, if you take after me. I used to be a regular water rat when I was a boy. I'll have to go down to the beach with you one of these days—though I'd be rusty, not having been in in all these years. [*The reminiscent look comes into his eyes of one about to embark on an oft-told tale of childhood adventure.*] You know, speaking of swimming, I never go down to that beach but what it calls to mind the day I and Red Sisk went in swimming there and I saved his life.
[*By this time the* FAMILY *are beginning to exchange amused, guilty glances. They* ALL *know what is coming.*]

Sid. [*With a sly, blurry wink around.*] Aha!

Miller. [*Turning on him.*] What's that?

Sid. Nothing—go on swimming—don't mind me.

Miller. [*Glares at him—but immediately is overcome by the reminiscent mood again.*] Well—Red Sisk—his father kept a blacksmith shop where the Union Market is now—we kids called him Red because he had the darndest reddest crop of hair——

Sid. [*As if he were talking to his plate.*] Remarkable!—the curious imagination—of little children.

Mrs. Miller. [*As she sees* MILLER *about to explode—interposes tactfully.*] Sid! Eat your lobster and shut up! Go on, Nat.

Miller. [*Gives* SID *a withering look—then is off again.*] Well, as I was saying, Red and I went swimming that day. Must have been—let me see—Red was fourteen, bigger and older than me. I was only twelve—forty-five years ago—Wasn't a single house down there then—but there was a stake out where the whistling buoy is now, about a mile out. [TOMMY, *who has been having difficulty restraining himself, lets out a stifled giggle.* MILLER *bends a frowning gaze on him.*] One laugh more out of you, young man, and you'll leave the table!

Mrs. Miller. [*Quickly interposing, trying to stave off the story.*] Do eat your lobster, Nat. You didn't have any fish, you know.

Miller. [*Not liking the reminder—pet-*

tishly.] Well, if I'm going to be interrupted every second anyway——

[*He turns to his lobster and chews in silence for a moment.*]

Mrs. Miller. [*Trying to switch the subject.*] How's Anne's mother's rheumatism, Mildred?

Mildred. Oh, she's much better, Ma. She was in wading today. She says salt water's the only thing that really helps her bunion.

Mrs. Miller. Mildred! Where are your manners? At the table's no place to speak of——

Miller. [*Fallen into the reminiscent obsession again.*] Well, as I was saying, there was I and Red, and he dared me to race him out to the stake and back. Well, I didn't let anyone dare me in those days. I was a spunky kid. So I said "all right" and we started out. We swam and swam and were pretty evenly matched; though, as I've said, he was bigger and older than me, but finally I drew ahead. I was going along easy, with lots in reserve, not a bit tired, when suddenly I heard a sort of gasp from behind me—like this—"help." [*He imitates.* EVERYONE'S *eyes are firmly fixed on their plates, except* SID'S.] And I turned and there was Red, his face all pinched and white, and he says weakly: "Help, Nat! I got a cramp in my leg!" Well, I don't mind telling you I got mighty scared. Then suddenly I thought of the pile. If I could pull him to that, I could hang on to him till someone'd notice us. But the pile was still—well, I calculate it must have been two hundred feet away.

Sid. Two hundred and fifty!

Miller. [*In confusion.*] What's that?

Sid. I've taken down the distance every time you've saved Red's life for thirty years and the mean average to that pile is two hundred and fifty feet! [*There is a burst of laughter from around the table.* SID *continues complainingly.*] Why didn't you let that Red drown, anyway, Nat? I never knew him but I know I'd never have liked him.

Miller. [*Really hurt, forces a feeble smile to his lips and pretends to be a good sport about it.*] Well, guess you're right, Sid. Guess I have told that one too many times and bored everyone. But it's a good true story for kids because it illustrates the danger of being foolhardy in the water——

Mrs. Miller. [*Sensing the hurt in his tone, comes to his rescue.*] Of course it's a good story—and you tell it whenever you've a mind to! And you, Sid, if you were in any responsible state, I'd give you a good piece of my mind for teasing Nat like that!

Miller. [*With a sad, self-pitying smile at*

his WIFE.] Getting old, I guess, Mother—getting to repeat myself. *Someone* ought to stop me.

Mrs. Miller. No such thing! You're as young as you ever were. [*She turns on* SID *again angrily.*] You eat your lobster and maybe it'll keep your mouth shut!

Sid. [*Irrepressibly.*] Lobster! Did you know, Tommy, your Uncle Sid is the man invented lobster? Fact! One day—took a day off and just dashed off lobster. He was biggern' older than me and had the darndest crop of red hair, but I dashed him off just the same! Am I right, Nat?

Mrs. Miller. Mercy sakes! Can't you shut up?

Sid. In this cage you see the lobster. You will not believe me, ladies and gents, but it's a fact that this interesting bivalve only makes love to his mate once in every thousand years—but, dearie me, how he does enjoy it!

[*The* CHILDREN *roar.* LILY *and* MRS. MILLER *laugh in spite of themselves—then look embarrassed.* MILLER *guffaws—then suddenly grows shocked.*]

Miller. Careful, Sid, careful. Remember you're at home.

Tommy. [*Suddenly in a hoarse whisper to his* MOTHER, *with an awed glance of admiration at his* UNCLE.] Ma! Look at him! He's eating that lobster, shells and all!

Mrs. Miller. [*Horrified.*] Sid, do you want to kill yourself? Put that down!

Sid. [*With great dignity.*] But I prefer the shells. All famous epicures prefer the shells—it's the same with clams. Unless I eat the shells there is a certain, peculiar oil that invariably poisons me! Am I right, Nat?

Miller. [*Good-naturedly.*] You seem to be getting a lot of fun kidding me. Go ahead, then. I don't mind.

Mrs. Miller. He better go right up to bed for a while, that's what he better do.

Sid. [*Considering this owlishly.*] Bed? Yes, maybe you're right. [*He gets to his feet.*] I am not at all well—in very delicate condition. We are praying for a boy. Am I right, Nattie? Nat, I kept telling you all day I was in delicate condition and yet you kept forcing demon chowder on me, although you knew full well—even if you were full!—that there is a certain peculiar oil in chowder that invariably——

[*They are again* ALL *laughing—*LILY *hysterically.*]

Mrs. Miller. Will you get to bed, you idiot!

Sid. [*Mutters graciously.*] Immediately—if not sooner. [*He passes rear of* LILY *and stops.*] But wait. There is still a duty I must perform. No day is complete without it. Lily, answer once and for all, will you marry me?

Lily. [*With an hysterical giggle.*] No, I won't—never!

Sid. [*Nodding his head.*] Right! And perhaps it's all for the best. For how could I forget the pre—hic—precepts taught me at mother's dying knee. "Sidney," she said, "Sidney, my boy! Never marry a woman who drinks! Lips that touch liquor shall never touch yours!" [*Gazing at her mournfully.*] Too bad! So fine a woman once—and now such a slave to rum! [*Turning to* NAT.] What can we do to save her, Nat? [*In a hoarse, confidential whisper.*] Better put her in an institution where she'll be removed from temptation! The mere smell of it seems to drive her frantic!

Mrs. Miller. [*Again struggling with her laughter.*] You leave Lily alone and go to bed!

Sid. Right! Good night, ladies—*and* gents —We will meet—by and by! [*He gives an imitation of a Salvation Army drum.*] Boom! Boom! Boom! Come and be saved, Brothers! [*He starts to sing the old Army hymn.*] "In the sweet—Boom! Boom! [*He turns and marches solemnly out, singing.*]
By and by—Boom! Boom!
We will meet on that beautiful shore. Boom! Boom!
Work and pray—Boom! Boom!
While you may. Boom! Boom!
We will meet in the sky by and by."

[MILLER *and his* WIFE *and the* KIDS *are all roaring with laughter.* LILY *giggles hysterically.*]

Miller. [*Subsiding at last.*] Haw, haw. He's a case, if ever there was one! Darned if you can help laughing at him—even when he's poking fun at you!

Mrs. Miller. Goodness, but he's a caution! Oh, my sides ache, I declare. But I suppose we really shouldn't. It only encourages him. But my lands——!

Lily. [*Suddenly gets up from her chair and stands rigidly, her face working—jerkily.*] That's just it—you shouldn't—even I laughed —it does encourage—that's been his downfall—everyone always laughing, everyone always saying what a card he is, what a case, what a caution—and he's gone on —and we're all responsible—making it easy for him—and all we do is laugh!

Miller. [*Worriedly.*] Now, Lily, now, you mustn't take on so! It isn't as serious as all that!

Lily. [*Bitterly.*] Maybe—it is—to me. Or was—once. [*Then she says contritely.*] I'm sorry, Nat. I'm sorry, Essie. I didn't mean to—I'm not feeling myself tonight. If you'll excuse me. I'll go in the front parlor and lie down on the sofa a while.

Mrs. Miller. Of course, Lily. You do whatever you've a mind to. [LILY *goes out.*]

Miller. [*Frowning—a little shamefaced.*] Hmm. I suppose she's right. Never knew Lily to come out with things that way before. Anything special happened, Essie?

Mrs. Miller. Nothing I know—except he'd promised to take her to the fireworks.

Miller. That's so. Well, supposing I take her. I don't want her to feel disappointed.

Mrs. Miller. [*Shaking her head.*] Wild horses couldn't drag her there now.

Miller. Hmm. I thought she'd got completely over her foolishness about him long ago.

Mrs. Miller. She never will.

Miller. She'd better. He's got fired out of that Waterbury job—Told me at the picnic after he'd got enough Dutch courage in him.

Mrs. Miller. Oh, dear—Isn't he the fool!

Miller. I knew something was wrong when he came back home. Well, I'll find a place for him on my paper again, of course. He always was the best news-getter this town ever had. But I'll tell him he's got to stop his damn nonsense.

Mrs. Miller. [*Doubtfully.*] Yes.

Miller. Well, no use sitting here mourning over spilt milk. [*He gets up, and* MILDRED, TOMMY *and* MRS. MILLER *follow his example. The* CHILDREN *quiet and a bit awed.*] You kids go out in the yard and try to keep quiet for a while, so's your Uncle Sid'll get to sleep and your Aunt Lily can rest.

Tommy. [*Mournfully.*] Ain't we going to set off the sky rockets and Roman candles, Pa?

Miller. Later, son, later. It isn't dark enough for them yet, anyway.

Mildred. Come on, Tommy. I'll see he keeps quiet, Pa.

[MILDRED *and* TOMMY *go out.*]

Miller. That's a good girl. [RICHARD *remains sitting, sunk in bitter, gloomy thoughts.* MILLER *glances at him;—then a bit irritably.*] Well, Melancholy Dane, what are you doing?

Richard. [*Darkly.*] I'm going out—— [*Then suddenly.*] Do you know what I think? It's Aunt Lily's fault Uncle Sid's going to ruin. It's all because he loves her, and she keeps him dangling after her, and eggs him on and ruins his life—like all women love to ruin men's lives! I don't blame him for drinking himself to death! What does he care if he dies, after the way she's treated him! I'd do the same thing myself if I were in his boots!

Mrs. Miller. [*Indignantly.*] Richard! You stop that talk!

Richard. [*Quotes bitterly.*]
"Drink! For you know not whence you come nor why.
Drink! For you know not why you go nor where!"

Miller. [*Losing his temper—harshly.*] Listen here, young man! I've had about all I can stand of your nonsense for one day! You're growing a lot too big for your size, seems to me! You keep that damn fool talk to yourself, you hear me—or you're going to regret it! Mind, now!

[*He strides angrily out.*]

Mrs. Miller. [*Still indignant.*] Richard, I'm ashamed of you, that's what I am.

[*She follows her* HUSBAND. RICHARD *is bitter, humiliated, wronged, even his father turned enemy, his face growing more and more rebellious.*]

Richard. Aw, what the hell do I care? I'll show them!

[*He turns and goes out.*]

CURTAIN

ACT THREE

SCENE I

The back room of a bar in a small hotel—a small, dingy room, dimly lighted by two fly-specked globes in two fly-specked wall brackets left and right of hall door left center. At right, front, is the swinging door leading to the bar. At rear of door, against the rear wall, is a nickel-in-the-slot player-piano. In the rear wall, left center, is a door leading to the "Family Entrance" and the stairway to the upstairs rooms. In the left wall is a window with closed shutters. Three tables with stained tops, three chairs around each table, are down right, against rear wall just left of piano, and up left.

The hideous saffron-colored wall-paper is blotched and spotted. It is about ten the same night.

[RICHARD *and* BELLE *are discovered sitting at table up left.* BELLE *in chair above table and* RICHARD *in chair left of table.*

BELLE *is twenty, a rather pretty peroxide blonde, a typical college "tart" of the period, and of the cheaper variety, dressed with tawdry flashiness. But she is a fairly recent recruit to the ranks, and is still a bit remorseful behind her make-up and defiantly careless manner.* BELLE *has an empty gin-rickey glass before her,* RICHARD *a half-empty glass of beer. He looks horribly timid, embarrassed and guilty, but at the same time thrilled and proud of at last min-*

gling with the pace that kills. The player-piano is grinding out "Bedelia." The BARTENDER, *a stocky young Irishman with a foxily cunning, stupid face and a cynically wise grin, stands just inside the bar entrance, watching them.*]

Belle. [*With an impatient glance at her escort—rattling the ice in her empty glass.*] Drink up your beer, why don't you? It's getting flat.

Richard. [*Embarrassedly.*] I let it get that way on purpose. I like it better when it's flat.

[*But he hastily gulps down the rest of his glass as if it were some nasty-tasting medicine. The* BARTENDER *chuckles audibly.* BELLE *glances at him.*]

Belle. [*Nodding at the player-piano scornfully.*] Say, George, is "Bedelia" the latest to hit this hick burg? Well, it's only a couple of years old! You'll catch up in time! Why don't you get a new roll for that old box?

Bartender. [*With a grin.*] Complain to the boss, not me. We're not used to having Candy Kiddoes like you around—or maybe we'd get up to date.

Belle. [*With a professionally arch grin at him.*] Don't kid me, please. I can't bear it. [*Then she sings to the music from the piano, her eyes now on* RICHARD.] "Bedelia, I'd like to feel yer." [*The* BARTENDER *laughs. She smirks at* RICHARD.] Ever hear those words to it, Kid?

Richard. [*Who has heard them but is shocked at hearing a girl say them—putting on a blasé air.*] Sure, lots of times. That's old.

Belle. [*With a meaning smirk, edging her chair closer and putting a hand over one of his.*] Then why don't you act as if you knew what they were all about?

Richard. [*Terribly flustered.*] Sure, I've heard that old parody lots of times. What do you think I am?

Belle. I don't know, Kid. Honest to God, you've got me guessing.

Bartender. [*With a mocking chuckle.*] He's a hot sport, can't you tell it? I never seen such a spender. My head's dizzy bringing you in drinks!

Belle. [*Laughs irritably—to* RICHARD.] Don't let him kid you. You show him. Loosen up and buy another drink, what say?

Richard. [*Humiliated—manfully.*] Sure. Excuse me. I was thinking of something else. Have anything you like. [*He turns to the* BARTENDER.] See what the lady will have —and have one on me yourself.

Bartender. [*Coming to the table—with a wink at* BELLE *as he picks up empty glasses.*] That's talking! Didn't I say you were a sport? I'll take a cigar on you. [*To* BELLE.] What's yours, Kiddo—the same?

Belle. Yes. And forget the house rules this time and remember a rickey is supposed to have gin in it.

Bartender. [*Grinning.*] I'll try to—seeing it's you. [*Then to* RICHARD.] What's yours —another beer?

Richard. [*Shyly.*] A small one, please. I'm not thirsty.

Belle. [*Calculatedly taunting.*] Say, honest, are things that slow up at Harvard? If they had you down at New Haven, they'd put you in a kindergarten! Don't be such a dead one! Filling up on beer will only make you sleepy. Have a man's drink!

Richard. [*Shamefaced—weakly.*] All right. I was going to. Bring me a sloe-gin fizz.

Belle. [*To* BARTENDER.] And make it a real one.

Bartender. [*With a wink.*] I get you. Something that'll warm him up, eh?

[*He goes into the bar.*]

Belle. [*Looks after* BARTENDER *irritably.*] Christ, what a dump! [RICHARD *is startled and shocked by the curse and looks down at the table.*] If this isn't the deadest burg I ever struck! Bet they take the sidewalks in after nine o'clock. [*Then turning on him.*] Say, honestly, Kid, does your mother know you're out?

Richard. [*Defensively.*] Aw, cut it out, why don't you—trying to kid me!

Belle. [*Glances at him—then resolves on a new tack—patting his hand.*] All right. I didn't mean to, dearie. Please don't get sore at me.

Richard. I'm not sore.

Belle. [*Seductively.*] You see, it's this way with me. I think you're one of the sweetest kids I've ever met—and I could like you such a lot—if you'd give me half a chance—instead of acting so cold and indifferent.

Richard. I'm not cold and indifferent. [*Then solemnly tragic.*] It's only that I've got—a weight on my mind.

Belle. [*Impatiently.*] Well, get it off your mind.

Bartender. [*Comes in, bringing the drinks; setting them down—with a wink at* BELLE.] This'll warm him up for you. Forty cents, that is—with the cigar.

Richard. [*Pulls out his roll and hands a dollar bill over—with exaggerated carelessness.*] Keep the change.

[BELLE *emits a gasp and seems about to protest, then thinks better of it. The* BARTENDER *cannot believe his luck for a moment—then pockets the bill hastily, as if afraid* RICHARD *will change his mind.*]

Bartender. [*Respect in his voice.*] Thank you very much, sir.

Richard. [*Grandly.*] Don't mention it.

Bartender. I hope you like the drink. I took special pains with it. [*The voice of the* SALESMAN, *who has just come in the bar, calls "Hey! Anybody here?" and a coin is rapped on the bar.*] I'm coming.

[*The* BARTENDER *goes out.*]

Belle. [*Remonstrating gently, a new appreciation for her escort's possibilities in her voice.*] You shouldn't be so generous, Dearie. Gets him in bad habits. A dime would have been plenty.

Richard. Ah, that's all right. I'm no tightwad.

Belle. That's the talk I like to hear. [*With a quick look toward the bar, she stealthily pulls up her dress—to* RICHARD'S *shocked fascination—and takes a package of cheap cigarettes from her stocking.*] Keep an eye out for that bartender, Kid, and tell me if you see him coming. Girls are only allowed to smoke upstairs in the rooms, he said.

Richard. [*Embarrassedly.*] All right. I'll watch.

Belle. [*Holds the package out to him.*] Have a Sweet? You *smoke*, don't you?

Richard. [*Taking one.*] Sure! I've been smoking for the last two years—on the sly.

[*She lights his cigarette, then her own and throws match on floor with elaborate nonchalance.*] But next year I'll be allowed—that is, pipes and cigars. [*He puffs but does not inhale—then, watching her with shocked concern as she inhales deeply.*] Say, you oughtn't to inhale like that! Smoking's awful bad for girls, anyway, even if they don't——

Belle. [*Cynically amused.*] Afraid it will stunt my growth? Gee, Kid, you are a scream! You'll grow up to be a minister yet! [RICHARD *looks shamefaced. She scans him impatiently—then pushes his drink toward him, and holds up her drink.*] Well, here's how! Bottoms up, now! Show me you really know how to drink. [RICHARD *follows her example and they both drink the whole contents of their glasses—*RICHARD *longest—without setting them down.*] There! That's something like! Feel better?

Richard. [*Proud of himself—with a shy smile.*] You bet.

Belle. Well, you'll feel still better in a minute—and then maybe you won't be so distant and unfriendly, eh?

Richard. I'm not.

Belle. Yes, you are. I think you just don't like me.

Richard. [*More manfully.*] I do too like you.

Belle. How much? A lot?

Richard. Yes, a lot.

Belle. Show me how much! [*Then, as he fidgets embarrassedly.*] Want me to come sit on your lap?

Richard. Yes—I——

[*She comes and sits on his lap. He looks desperately uncomfortable, but the gin is rising to his head and he feels proud of himself and devilish, too.*]

Belle. Why don't you put your arm around me? [*He does so awkwardly.*] No, not that dead way. Hold me tight. You needn't be afraid of hurting me. I like to be held tight, don't you?

Richard. Sure I do.

Belle. 'Specially when it's by a nice handsome kid like you. [*Ruffling his hair.*] Gee, you've got pretty hair, do you know it? Honest, I'm awfully strong for you! Why can't you be about me? I'm not so awfully ugly, am I?

Richard. No, you're—you're pretty.

Belle. You don't say it as if you meant it.

Richard. I do mean it—honest.

Belle. Then why don't you kiss me? [*She bends down her lips toward his. He hesitates, then kisses her a quick short peck.*] Call that kissing? Here. [*She holds his head and fastens her lips on his and holds them there. He starts and struggles, then jerks his head away. She laughs.*] What's the matter, Honey Boy? Haven't you ever kissed like that before?

Richard. Sure. Lots of times.

Belle. Then why did you jump—as if I'd bitten you? [*Squirming around on his lap.*] Gee, I'm getting just crazy about you! What shall we do about it, eh? Tell me.

Richard. I—don't know. [*Then boldly.*] I—I'm crazy about you, too.

Belle. [*Hugging him again.*] Just think of the wonderful time Edith and your friend, Wint, are having—while we sit down here like two dead ones! A room only costs two dollars. And, seeing I like you so much, I'd only take five dollars—from you. I'd do it for nothing—for you—only I've got to live and I owe my room rent in New Haven—and you know how it is. I get ten dollars from every one else. Honest! [*She kisses him again, then gets up from his lap—briskly.*] Come on. Go out and tell the bartender you want a room. And hurry. Honest, I'm so strong for you I can hardly wait to get you upstairs.

Richard. [*Starts automatically for door—then hesitates, a great struggle going on in his mind—timidity, disgust at the money element, shocked modesty, and the guilty thought of* MURIEL, *fighting it out with the growing tipsiness that makes him want to be a hell of a fellow and go in for all forbidden fruit, and makes this tart a romantic, evil vampire in his eyes. Finally, he stops and mutters in confusion.*] I can't.

Belle. [*Starts for bar door.*] What, are you too bashful to ask for a room? Let me do it, then.

Richard. [*Desperately.*] No—I don't want you to—I don't want to.

Belle. [*Surveying him, anger coming into her eyes.*] Well, if you aren't the lousiest cheap skate——

Richard. I'm not a cheap skate!

Belle. Keep me around here all night fooling with you when I might be out with some real live one—if there is such a thing in this burg!—and now you quit on me! Don't be such a piker! You've got five dollars! I seen it when you paid for the drinks, so don't hand me any lies!

Richard. I— Who said I hadn't? And I'm not a piker. If you need the five dollars so bad—you can have it without—I mean, I'll be glad to give—— [RICHARD *has been fumbling in his pocket and pulls out his nine-dollar roll and holds out the five to her.*]

Belle. [*Hardly able to believe her eyes,*

almost snatches it from his hand.] Thanks, Kid. [*Then laughs and immediately becomes sentimentally grateful.*] Gee— Oh, thanks— Gee, forgive me for losing my temper and bawling you out, will you? Gee, you're a regular peach! You're the nicest kid I've ever met!

[*She hugs him and he grins proudly, a hero to himself now on many counts.*]

Richard. [*Grandly—and quite tipsily.*] It's—nothing—only too glad.

Belle. Come on, let's have another drink —and this time I'll blow you just to show my appreciation. [*She calls.*] Hey, George! Bring us another round—the same!

Richard. [*A remnant of caution coming to him.*] I don't know as I ought to——

Belle. Oh, another won't hurt you. And I want to blow you, see.

Richard. [*Boldly draws his chair closer and puts an arm around her—tipsily.*] I like you a lot—now I'm getting to know you. You're a darned nice girl.

Belle. Nice is good! Tell me another! Well, if I'm so nice, why didn't you want to take me upstairs? That's what I don't get.

Richard. [*Lying boldly.*] I did want to— only I——— [*Then he adds solemnly.*] I've sworn off.

Bartender. [*Enters with the drinks. Setting them on table.*] Here's your pleasure. [*Then, regarding* RICHARD'S *arm about her waist.*] Ho-ho, we're coming on, I see.

[RICHARD *grins at him muzzily.*]

Belle. [*Digs into her purse and gives him right change plus a dime tip.*] Here. This is mine. [BARTENDER *goes out. She puts the five* RICHARD *has given her in her stocking and picks up her glass.*] Here's how—and thanks again.   [*She sips.*]

Richard. [*Boisterously.*] Bottoms up! Bottoms up! [*He drinks all of his down and sighs with exaggerated satisfaction.*] Gee, that's good stuff, all right.

Belle. [*Watches him finish his drink.*] What did you mean a minute ago when you said you'd sworn off?

Richard. [*Solemnly.*] I took an oath I'd be faithful.

Belle. [*Cynically.*] Till death do us part, eh? Who's the girl?

Richard. [*Shortly.*] Never mind.

Belle. [*Bristling.*] I'm not good enough to talk about her, I suppose?

Richard. I didn't mean that. You're all right—— [*Then with tipsy gravity.*] Only you oughtn't to lead this kind of life. It isn't right—for a nice girl like you. Why don't you reform?

Belle. [*Sharply.*] Nix on that line of talk—— Can it. You hear! You can do a lot with me for five dollars—but you can't reform me. See!

Richard. I—I didn't mean to hurt your feelings.

Belle. I know you didn't mean. You're only like a lot of people who mean well, to hear them tell it. [*Changing the subject bitterly.*] So you're faithful to your one love, eh? [*With an ugly smile, speaks nastily.*] And how about her? Bet you she's out with a guy under some bush this minute, giving him all he wants.

Richard. [*Starting up in his chair—angrily.*] Don't you say that! Don't you dare——!

Belle. [*Unimpressed—with a cynical shrug of her shoulders.*] All right. Have it your own way—and be a sucker! It cuts no ice with me.

Richard. You don't know her or——

Belle. [*Sharply.*] And don't want to. Shut up about her, can't you?

[*She stares before her bitterly.* RICHARD *subsides into scowling gloom. He is becoming perceptibly more intoxicated with each moment now. The* BARTENDER *and the* SALESMAN *appear just inside swinging door. The* BARTENDER *nods toward* BELLE, *giving the* SALESMAN *a wink. The* SALESMAN *grins and comes into the room, carrying his highball in his hand. He is a stout, jowly-faced man in his late thirties, dressed with cheap nattiness, with the professional breeziness and jocular kid-'em-along manner of his kind.* BELLE *looks up as he enters and he and she exchange glances of complete recognition. She knows his type by heart and he knows hers.*]

Salesman. [*Crosses to table at right, grinning genially—sits in chair right of table; speaks insinuatingly.*] Good evening.

Belle. [*Returning the smile and speaks with same inflection.*] Good evening.

Salesman. Hope I'm not butting in on your party—but my dogs were giving out standing at that bar.

Belle. All right with me. [*Giving* RICHARD *a rather contemptuous look.*] I've got no party on.

Salesman. That sounds hopeful.

Richard. [*Suddenly recites sentimentally.*] "But I wouldn't do such, 'cause I loved her too much, but I learned about women from her." [1] [RICHARD *looks with a scowl at the* SALESMAN, *then turns to* BELLE.] Let's have 'nother drink!

---

[1] From Kipling's *The Ladies.*

Belle. You've had enough.

[RICHARD *subsides, muttering to himself.*]

Salesman. What is it—a child poet or a child actor?

Belle. Don't know. Got me guessing.

Salesman. Well, if you could shake the cradle-robbing act, maybe we could do a little business.

Belle. That's easy. I just pull my freight. [*She then shakes* RICHARD *by the arm.*] Listen, Kid. Here's an old friend of mine, Mr. Smith of New Haven, just come in. I'm going over and sit at his table for a while, see? And you better go home.

Richard. [*Blinking at her and scowling.*] I'm never going home! I'll show them!

Belle. Have it your own way—only let me up. [*She takes his arm from around her and goes to sit by the* SALESMAN.]

Richard. [*Stares after her offendedly.*] Go on. What do I care about what you do? [*He recites scornfully.*] "For a woman's only a woman, but a good cigar's a smoke." [1]

Salesman. [*As* BELLE *sits beside him.*] Well, what kind of beer will you have, Sister?

Belle. Mine's a gin rickey.

Salesman. You've got extravagant tastes, I'm sorry to see.

Richard. [*Suddenly begins to recite sepulchrally.*] "Yet each man kills the thing he loves, By each let this be heard."

Salesman. [*Grinning.*] Say, this is rich! [*He calls encouragement to* RICHARD.] That's swell dope, young feller. Give us some more.

Richard. [*Ignoring him—goes on more rhetorically.*]

"Some do it with a bitter look,
Some with a flattering word,
The coward does it with a kiss,
The brave man with a sword!" [2]

[*He stares at* BELLE *gloomily and mutters tragically.*] I did it with a kiss! I'm a coward.

Salesman. That's the old stuff, Kid. You've got something on the ball, all right, all right! Give us another—right over the old pan, now!

Richard. [*Rises, faces them and raises arm.*] "Oho! They cried"——

Belle. [*Laughs.*] Get the hook!

Richard. [*Glowering at her. Tragically.*] "The world is wide, But fettered limbs go lame!"

And once, or twice,
To throw the dice
Is a gentlemanly game,
But he does not win who plays with Sin
In the Secret House of Shame!" [1]

Belle. [*Angrily.*] Aw, can it! Give us a rest from that bunk!

Salesman. [*Mockingly.*] This gal of yours don't appreciate poetry. She's a lowbrow. But I'm the kid that eats it up. My middle name is Kelly and Sheets! Give us some more of the same! Do you know "The Lobster and the Wise Guy?" [*Turns to* BELLE *seriously.*] No kidding, that's a peacherino. I heard a guy recite it at Poli's. Maybe this nut knows it. Do you, Kid?

[*But* RICHARD *only glowers at him gloomily without answering.*]

Belle. [*Surveying* RICHARD *contemptuously.*] He's copped a fine skinful—and gee, he's hardly had anything.

Richard. [*Suddenly—with a dire emphasis.*] "And then—at ten o'clock—Eilert Lovborg will come—with vine leaves in his hair!"

Belle. And bats in his belfry, if he's you!

Richard. [*Regards her bitterly—then suddenly starts to his feet bellicosely—to the* SALESMAN.] I don't believe you ever knew this lady in New Haven at all! You just picked her up now! You leave her alone, you hear! You won't do anything to her—not while I'm here to protect her!

Belle. [*Laughing.*] Oh, my God! Listen to it!

Salesman. Ssshh! This is a scream! Wait! [*He addresses* RICHARD *in tone of exaggerated mock melodrama.*] Curse you, Jack Dalton—if I won't unhand her, what then?

Richard. [*Threateningly.*] I'll give you a good punch in the snoot, that's what! [*He starts toward* SALESMAN.]

Salesman. [*With mock terror—screams in falsetto.*] Help! Help! [*The* BARTENDER *comes in irritably.*]

Bartender. Hey! Cut out the noise! What the hell's up with you?

Salesman. [*Laughing—winks at* BARTENDER.] He's going to murder me.

Richard. [*Tipsily.*] He's too damn fresh.

Salesman. [*Gets a bright idea for eliminating* RICHARD.] Say, George! [*Seriously to the* BARTENDER.] It's none of my business, Brother, but if I were in your boots I'd give this young souse the gate. He's under age; any fool can see that.

---

[1] From Kipling's *The Betrothed.*
[2] From Wilde's *The Ballad of Reading Gaol.*

[1] From *The Ballad of Reading Gaol.*

Bartender. [*Guiltily.*] He told me he was over eighteen.

Salesman. Yes, and I tell you I'm Teddy Roosevelt—but you don't have to believe me. If you're not looking for trouble, I'd advise you to get him started for some other gin mill and let them do the lying if anything comes up.

Bartender. Hmm. [*He turns to* RICHARD *and tries to get him to his feet.*] Come on, now. On your way! You'll start no trouble in here! Beat it, now!

Richard. I will not beat it!

Bartender. Oho, won't you?
                    [*He gives him a shove.*]

Belle. [*Callously.*] Give him the bum's rush! I'm sick of his bull!

[RICHARD *turns furiously and tries to punch the* BARTENDER.]

Bartender. [*Avoids the punch.*] Oho, you would, would you!

[*He grabs* RICHARD *by the back of the neck and the seat of the pants and marches him ignominiously toward the door.*]

Richard. Leggo of me, you dirty coward!

Bartender. Quiet now—or I'll pin a Mary Ann on your jaw that'll quiet you!

[*He rushes him through the door and a moment later the outer doors are heard swinging back and forth.*]

Salesman. [*With a chuckle.*] Hand it to me, Kid! How was that for a slick way of getting rid of him?

Belle. [*Suddenly sentimental.*] Poor kid. I hope he makes home all right. I liked him —before he got soused.

Salesman. Who is he?

Belle. The boy who's upstairs with my friend told me, but I didn't pay much attention. Name's Miller. His old man runs a paper in this one-horse burg, I think he said.

Salesman. [*Emits a whistle.*] Phew! He must be Nat Miller's kid, then.

Bartender. [*Coming back from the bar.*] Well, he's on his way—with a good boot in the tail to help him!

Salesman. [*With a malicious chuckle.*] Yes? Well, maybe that boot will cost you a job, Brother. Know Nat Miller who runs the *Globe?* That's his kid.

Bartender. [*His face falling.*] The hell it is! Who said so?

Salesman. This baby doll. Say, I'll go keep cases on him—see he gets on the trolley all right, anyway. Nat Miller's a good scout.
                    [*He hurries out.*]

Bartender. [*Viciously.*] Damn the luck! If he ever finds out I served his kid, he'll run me out of town. [*He turns on* BELLE *furiously.*] Why didn't you put me wise, you lousy tramp, you!

Belle. Hey! I don't stand for that kind of talk—not from no hick beer-squirter like you, see!

Bartender. [*Furiously.*] You don't, don't you! Who was it but you told me to hand him dynamite in that fizz? [*He gives her chair a push that almost throws her to the floor.*] Beat it, you—and beat it quick—or I'll call Sullivan from the corner and have you run in for street-walking! [*He gives her a push that lands her in family-entrance doorway.*] Get the hell out of here—and no long waits!

Belle. [*Turns in doorway and calls back viciously.*] I'll fix you for this, you thick Mick, if I have to go to jail for it.
                    [*She goes out and slams the door.*]

Bartender. [*Looks after her worriedly for a second—then shrugs his shoulders.*] That's only her bull. [*Then with a sigh as he picks up glasses from table.*] Them lousy tramps is always getting this dump in Dutch!

CURTAIN

ACT THREE

SCENE II

Same as Act One—sitting-room of the Miller home—about eleven o'clock the same night.

[MILLER *is sitting in his favorite rocking chair. He has discarded collar and tie, coat and shoes, for comfort's sake, and wears an old, worn, brown dressing-gown and disreputable-looking carpet* slippers. *He has his reading specs on and is running over items in a newspaper. But his mind is plainly preoccupied and worried, and he is not paying much attention to what he reads.*

MRS. MILLER *sits by table at right front. She also has on her specs. A sewing basket is on her lap and she is trying hard to keep her attention fixed on the doily she is doing. But, as in the case of her husband but much more apparently, her mind is preoccupied with another matter, and she is obviously on tenterhooks of nervous uneasiness.*

LILY *is sitting in the armchair. She is pretending to read a novel, but her attention wanders, too, and her expression is sad, although now it has lost all its bitterness and become submissive and resigned again.*

MILDRED *sits at the desk at left, writing two words over and over again, stopping each time to survey the result critically, biting her tongue, intensely concentrated on her work.*

TOMMY *sits at the front end of the sofa at right. He has had a hard day and is terribly sleepy but will not acknowledge it. His eyes blink shut on him; his head begins to nod, but he isn't giving up, and every time he senses any of the family glancing in his direction, he goads himself into a bright-eyed wakefulness.*]

Mildred. [*Finally surveys the two words she has been writing and is satisfied with them.*] There! [*She takes the paper over to her* MOTHER.] Look, Ma. I've been practising a new way of writing my name. Don't you think it's the real goods?

Mrs. Miller. [*Pulled out of her preoccupation.*] Don't talk that horrible slang. My goodness, if my mother'd ever heard me——

Mildred. Well, don't you think it's nice, then?

Mrs. Miller. [*Sinks back into preoccupation—scanning the paper—vaguely.*] Yes, very nice, Mildred—very nice, indeed.

[*Hands the paper back mechanically.*]

Mildred. [*Is a little piqued, but smiles.*] Absent-minded! I don't believe you even saw it!

[*Turns and shows it to* LILY. MILLER *gives an uneasy glance at his* WIFE *and then, as if afraid of meeting her eye, looks quickly back at his paper again.*]

Mrs. Miller. [*Staring before her—sighs worriedly.*] Oh, I do wish that Richard would come home!

Miller. There now, Essie. He'll be in any minute now. Don't you worry about him.

Mrs. Miller. But I do worry about him!

Lily. [*Surveying* MILDRED'S *handiwork—smiling.*] This is fine, Mildred. Your penmanship is improving wonderfully. But don't you think that maybe you've got a little too many flourishes?

Mildred. [*Disappointedly.*] But, Aunt Lily, that's just what I was practising hardest on.

Mrs. Miller. [*With another heavy sigh.*] What time is it now, Nat?

Miller. [*Adopting a joking tone.*] I'm going to buy a clock for in here. You have me reaching for my watch every couple of minutes. [*He has pulled his watch out of his vest pocket—with forced carelessness.*] Only a little past ten.

Mrs. Miller. Why, you said it was that an hour ago! Nat Miller, you're telling me a fib so's not to worry me. You let me see that watch!

Miller. [*Guiltily.*] Well, it's a quarter to eleven—but that's not so late—when you remember it's the Fourth of July.

Mrs. Miller. If you don't stop talking Fourth of July——!

Mildred. [*Has brought her paper around to her* FATHER *and now she shoves it under his nose.*] Look, Pa.

Miller. [*Seizes on this interruption with eager relief—scanning the paper.*] Let's see. Hmm. Seems to me you've been inventing a new signature each week lately. What are you in training for—writing checks? You must be planning to catch a rich husband.

Mildred. [*With an arch toss of her head.*] No wedding bells for me! But how do you like it, Pa?

Miller. It's overpowering—no other word for it, overpowering! You could put it on the Declaration of Independence and not feel ashamed!

[*He passes paper to* MILDRED. *Both laugh.*]

Mrs. Miller. [*Desolately, almost on the verge of tears.*] It's all right for you to laugh and joke with Mildred! I'm the only one in this house who seems to care——

[*Her lips tremble.*]

Mildred. [*A bit disgustedly.*] Ah, Ma, Dick only sneaked off to the fireworks at the beach, you wait and see.

Mrs. Miller. Those fireworks were over long ago. If he had, he'd be home.

Lily. [*Soothingly.*] He probably couldn't get a seat, the trolleys are so jammed, and he had to walk home.

Miller. [*Seizing on this with relief.*] Yes, I never thought of that, but I'll bet that's it.

Mildred. Ah, don't let him worry you, Ma. He just wants to show off he's heartbroken about that silly Muriel—and get everyone fussing over him and wondering if he hasn't drowned himself or something.

Mrs. Miller. [*Snappily.*] You be quiet! I really believe you're that hard-hearted you haven't got a heart in you! [*With an accusing glance at her* HUSBAND.] One thing I know, you don't get that from me!

[*He chuckles and resumes reading paper. She sniffs and looks away from him around the room.*]

Tommy. [*Who is nodding and blinking, is afraid her eye is on him. He straightens alertly and speaks in a voice that is, in spite of his effort, dripping with drowsiness.*] Let me see what you wrote, Mid.

Mildred. [*Cruelly mocking.*] You? You're so sleepy you couldn't see it!

Tommy. [*Valiantly.*] I am not sleepy!

Mrs. Miller. [*Has fixed her eye on him.*] My gracious, I was forgetting you were still up! You run up to bed this minute! It's hours past your bedtime!

Tommy. But it's the Fourth of July. Ain't it, Pa?

Mrs. Miller. [*Again gives her* HUSBAND *an accusing stare.*] There! You see what you've done? You might know he'd copy your excuses! [*Then sharply, to* TOMMY.] You heard what I said, Young Man!

Tommy. Aw, Ma, can't I stay up a *little* longer?

Mrs. Miller. I said no! You obey me and no more arguing about it!

Tommy. Aw! I should think I could stay up till Dick——

Miller. [*Kindly but firmly.*] You heard your Ma say no more arguing. When she says git, you better git.

Tommy. [*Accepts his fate resignedly and starts around kissing them all good night. Leans over table and kisses* LILY.] Good night, Aunt Lily.

Lily. [*Fondly.*] Good night, dear. Sleep well.

Tommy. [*Pecking at* MILDRED *but obviously not kissing her.*] Good night, you.

Mildred. Good night, you.

Tommy. [*Sitting on arm of* MILLER'S *chair, snuggles against him.*] Good night, Pa.

Miller. Good night, Son. [*Kisses him.*] Sleep tight.

Tommy. [*Kissing her.*] Good night, Ma.

Mrs. Miller. Good night. Here! You look feverish. [*She feels his brow with her left hand.*] No, you're all right. Hurry up, now. And don't forget your prayers.

Tommy. [*Goes slowly to the doorway, then turns suddenly, the discovery of another excuse lighting up his face.*] Here's another thing, Ma. When I was up to the water closet last——

Mrs. Miller. [*Sharply.*] When you were where?

Tommy. The bathroom.

Mrs. Miller. That's better.

Tommy. Uncle Sid was snoring like a fog

horn—and he's right next to my room. How can I ever get to sleep while he's——

[*He is overcome by a jaw-cracking yawn.*]

Mrs. Miller. I guess you'd get to sleep all right if you were inside a fog horn! You run along now! [*TOMMY gives up, grins sleepily and moves off to bed. As soon as he is off her mind, all her former uneasiness comes back on* MRS. MILLER *tenfold. She sighs, moves restlessly, then finally asks.*] What time is it now, Nat?

Miller. Now, Essie, I just told you a minute ago.

Mrs. Miller. [*Resentfully.*] I don't see how you can take it so calm! Here it's midnight, you might say, and our Richard still out, and we don't even know where he is.

Mildred. There's someone! Bet that's him now, Ma.

Mrs. Miller. [*Her anxiety immediately turning to relieved anger.*] You give him a good piece of your mind, Nat! You're too easy with him, that's the whole trouble!

[SOMEONE *whistling "March, March Down the Field." Yale Song.*]

Mildred. No, that isn't Dick. It's Art.

Mrs. Miller. [*Her face falling.*] Oh!

[*A moment later* ARTHUR *enters, whistling softly half under his breath, looking complacently pleased with himself.*]

Miller. [*Surveys him over his glasses, not with enthusiasm—shortly.*] So you're back, eh? We thought it was Richard.

Arthur. Is he still out? Where'd he go to?

Miller. That's just what we'd like to know. You didn't run into him anywhere, did you?

Arthur. No. I've been at the Rands' ever since dinner. I suppose he sneaked off to the beach to watch the fireworks.

Miller. [*Pretending an assurance he is far from feeling.*] Of course. That's what we've been trying to tell your mother, but she insists on worrying her head off.

Mrs. Miller. But if he knew he was going to the fireworks why wouldn't he say so? He knew we'd let him.

Arthur. [*With calm wisdom.*] That's easy, Ma. [*He grins superiorly.*] Didn't you hear him this morning showing off bawling out the Fourth like an anarchist? He wouldn't want to reneg on that to you— but he'd want to see the old fireworks just the same. [*He adds complacently.*] I know. He's at that foolish age.

Miller. [*Stares at* ARTHUR *with ill-concealed astonishment, then grins, jokingly.*] Well, Arthur, by gosh, you make me feel as if I owed you an apology when you talk horse sense like that! [*He turns to his*

WIFE, *greatly relieved.*] Arthur's hit the nail right on the head, I think, Essie. That's where he is——

Mrs. Miller. [*With a sigh.*] Well—— I wish he was home.

Arthur. [*Lights pipe with solemn gravity.*] He oughtn't to be allowed out this late at his age. I wasn't—Fourth or no Fourth —if I remember.

Miller. [*A twinkle in his eyes.*] Don't tax your memory trying to recall those ancient days of your youth.

[MILDRED *laughs and* ARTHUR *looks sheepish. But he soon regains his aplomb and changes the subject tactfully.*]

Arthur. [*Importantly.*] We had a corking dinner at the Rands'. We had sweetbreads on toast.

Mrs. Miller. [*Arousing momentarily from her depression.*] Just like the Rands to put on airs before you! I never could see anything to sweetbreads. Always taste like soap to me. And no real nourishment to them. I wouldn't have the pesky things on my table.

[ARTHUR *again feels sat upon.*]

Mildred. [*Teasingly.*] Did you kiss Elsie good night?

Arthur. Stop trying to be so darn funny all the time! You give me a pain in the ear!

Mildred. And that's where she gives me a pain, the stuck-up thing! Thinks she's the whole cheese!

Miller. [*Irritably.*] And it's where your everlasting wrangling gives me a pain, you two. Give us a rest!

[*There is silence for a moment.*]

Mrs. Miller. [*Sighs worriedly again.*] I do wish that boy would get home!

Miller. [*Glances at her uneasily, peeks surreptitiously at his watch—then has an inspiration and turns to* ARTHUR.] Arthur, what's this I hear about your having such a good singing voice? Rand was telling me he liked nothing better than to hear you sing —said you did every night you were up there. Why don't you ever give us folks at home here a treat?

Arthur. [*Pleased, but still nursing wounded dignity.*] I thought you'd only sit on me.

Mrs. Miller. [*Perking up—proudly.*] Arthur has a real nice voice. He practices when you're not at home. I didn't know you cared for singing, Nat.

Miller. Well, I do—nothing better—and when I was a boy I had a fine voice myself and folks used to say I'd ought—— [*Then abruptly, mindful of his painful experience with reminiscence at dinner, looking about*

him guiltily.] Hmm. But don't hide your light under a bushel, Arthur. Why not give us a song or two now? You can play for him, can't you, Mildred?

Mildred. [*With a toss of her head.*] I can play as well as Elsie Rand, at least!

Arthur. [*Ignoring her—clearing his throat importantly.*] I've been singing a lot tonight, Pa. I don't know if my voice——

Mildred. [*Forgetting her grudge, grabs her* BROTHER'S *hand and tugs at it.*] Come on. Don't play modest. You know you're just dying to show off!

[*This puts* ARTHUR *off it at once. He snatches his hand away from her angrily.*]

Arthur. Let go of me, you! [*Then with surly dignity.*] I don't feel like singing tonight, Pa. I will some other time.

Miller. [*Sharply.*] You let him alone, Mildred!

[*Then he winks at* ARTHUR, *indicating with his eyes and a nod of head* MRS. MILLER, *who has again sunk into worried brooding. He makes it plain by this pantomime that he wants him to sing to distract his* MOTHER'S *mind.*]

Arthur. [*Puts aside his pipe and gets up promptly.*] Oh—sure, I'll do the best I can.

[*He follows* MILDRED *off into the front parlor, where he switches on the lights.*]

Miller. [*To his* WIFE.] It won't keep Tommy awake. Nothing could. And Sid, he'd sleep through an earthquake. [*Then suddenly, looking through the front parlor— grumpily.*] Darn it, speak of the devil, here he comes. Well, he's had a good sleep and he'd ought to be sobered up. [LILY *gets up from her chair and looks around her huntedly, as if for a place to hide.* MILLER *says soothingly.*] Lily, you just sit down and read your book and don't pay any attention to him.

[*She sits down again and bends over her book tensely. From the front parlor comes the tinkling of a piano as* MILDRED *runs over the scales. In the midst of this,* SID *enters. All the effervescence of his jag has worn off and he is now suffering from a bad case of hangover —nervous, sick, a prey to gloomy remorse and bitter feelings of self-loathing and self-pity. His eyes are bloodshot and puffed, his baldness tousled and tufty. He sidles into the room guiltily, his eyes shifting about, avoiding looking at anyone.*]

Sid. [*Forcing a sickly twitching smile.*] Hello.

Miller. [*Considerately casual.*] Hello, Sid.

Had a good nap? [*Then, as* SID *swallows hard and is about to break into further speech,* MILDRED'S *voice comes from the front parlor,* "I haven't played that in ever so long, but I'll try," *and she starts an accompaniment.* MILLER *motions* SID *to be quiet.*] Ssshh! Arthur's going to sing for us. [SID *flattens himself against the edge of the bookcase at center, rear, miserably self-conscious and ill at ease there but nervously afraid to move anywhere else.* ARTHUR *begins to sing. He has a fairly decent voice but his method is untrained sentimentality to a dripping degree. He sings that old sentimental favorite,* "Then You'll Remember Me." *The effect on his audience is instant.* MILLER *gazes before him with a ruminating melancholy, his face seeming to become gently sorrowful and old.* MRS. MILLER *stares before her, her expression becoming more and more doleful.* LILY *forgets to pretend to read her book but looks over it, her face growing tragically sad. As for* SID, *he is moved to his remorseful, guilt-stricken depths. His mouth pulls down at the corners and he seems about to cry. The song comes to an end.* MILLER *starts, then claps his hands enthusiastically and calls.*] Well done, Arthur—well done! Why, you've a splendid voice! Give us some more! You liked that, didn't you, Essie?

Mrs. Miller. [*Dolefully.*] Yes—but it's sad—terrible sad.

Sid. [*After swallowing hard, suddenly blurts out.*] Essie. Nat and—and Lily—— I—I want to apologize—for coming home the way I did—there's no excuse—but I didn't mean——

Miller. [*Sympathetically.*] Of course, Sid. It's all forgotten.

Mrs. Miller. [*Rousing herself—affectionately pitying.*] Don't be a goose, Sid. We know how it is with picnics. You forget it.

[SID'S *face lights up a bit but his gaze shifts to* LILY *with a mute appeal, hoping for a word from her which is not forthcoming. Her eyes are fixed on her book, her body tense and rigid.*]

Sid. [*Finally blurts out desperately.*] Lily—I'm sorry—about the fireworks. Can you—forgive me?

[*But* LILY *remains implacably silent. A stricken look comes over* SID'S *face.*]

Miller. [*Comes to* SID'S *rescue.*] Ssshh! We're going to have another song. Sit down, Sid. [SID, *hanging his head, flees to the farthest corner, left front, and sits, facing front, hunched up, elbows on knees, face in hands, his round eyes childishly wounded and woe-begone.* ARTHUR *sings* "Dearie, my

Dearie, nothing's worth while but dreams of you—" *etc.—playing up its sentimental values for all he is worth. The effect on his audience is that of the previous song, intensified—especially upon* SID. *As he finishes,* MILLER *again starts and applauds.*] Mighty fine, Arthur! You sang that darned well. Didn't he, Essie?

Mrs. Miller. [*Dolefully.*] Yes—but I wish he wouldn't sing such sad songs. [*Then, her lips trembling.*] Richard's always whistling that.

Miller. [*Hastily calls.*] Give us something cheery, next one, Arthur—— You know, just for variety's sake——

Sid. [*Suddenly turns toward* LILY—*his voice husky and choked with tears—in a passion of self-denunciation.*] You're right, Lily!—right not to forgive me! I'm no good and never will be! You shouldn't even wipe your feet on me!—no good to myself or anybody else! If I had any guts I'd kill myself, and good riddance!—but I haven't! I'm yellow, too!—a yellow, drunken bum!

[*He hides his face in his hands and begins to sob like a sick little boy. This is too much for* LILY. *All her bitter hurt and steely resolve to ignore and punish him vanish in a flash, swamped by a pityingly love for him. She runs and puts her arm around him—even kisses him tenderly and impulsively on his bald head, and soothes him as if he were a little boy.* MRS. MILLER, *almost equally moved, has half risen to go to her* BROTHER, *too, but* MILLER *winks and shakes his head vigorously and motions her to sit down.*]

Lily. There! Don't cry, Sid! I can't bear it! Of course I forgive you. Haven't I always forgiven you? I know you're not to blame—so don't, Sid!

Sid. [*Lifts a tearful, humbly grateful, pathetic face to her—but a face that the dawn of a cleansed conscience is already beginning to restore to its natural Puckish expression.*] Do you really forgive me—I know I don't deserve it—— Can you really——?

Lily. [*Gently.*] I told you I did, Sid—and I do.

Sid. [*Kisses her hand humbly, like a big puppy licking it.*] Thanks, Lily. I can't tell you—— [*In the front parlor,* ARTHUR *begins to sing rollickingly,* "Waiting at the Church," *and after the first line or two* MILDRED *joins in.* SID'S *face lights up with appreciation and, automatically, he begins to tap one foot in time, still holding fast to* LILY'S *hand. When they come to* "sent around

a note, this is what he wrote," he can no longer resist, but joins in a shaky bawl.] "Can't get away to marry you today. My wife won't let me!"
[As the song finishes, the Two in the other room laugh. MILLER and SID laugh. LILY smiles at SID's laughter. Only MRS. MILLER remains dolefully preoccupied, as if she hadn't heard.]
Miller. That's fine, Arthur and Mildred. That's darned good.
Sid. [Turning to LILY enthusiastically.] You ought to hear Vesta Victoria sing that! Gosh, she's great! I heard her at Hammerstein's Victoria—— You remember that trip I made to New York.
Lily. [Her face suddenly grown tired and sad again—for her memory of certain aspects of that trip is the opposite from what he would like to recall at this moment—gently disengaging her hand from his—with a hopeless sigh.] Yes, I remember, Sid.
[He is overcome momentarily by guilty confusion. She goes quietly and sits. In the front parlor, MILDRED plays rather quietly. She and ARTHUR whistle softly.]
Mrs. Miller. [Suddenly.] What time is it now, Nat? [Then, without giving him a chance to answer.] Oh, I'm getting worried something dreadful, Nat! You don't know what might have happened to Richard! You read in the papers every day about boys getting run over by automobiles.
Lily. Oh, don't say that, Essie!
Miller. [Sharply, to conceal his own reawakened apprehension.] Don't get to imagining things, now!
Mrs. Miller. Well, why couldn't it happen, with everyone that owns one out tonight, and lots of those driving drunk? [On the verge of hysteria.] Oh, I know something dreadful's happened! And you can sit there listening to songs and laughing as if—— Why don't you do something? Why don't you go out and find him? [She bursts into tears.]
Lily. [Comes to her quickly and puts her arm around her.] Essie, you mustn't worry so! You'll make yourself sick!
Mildred. [Comes hurrying in from front parlor.] What's the trouble? [ARTHUR appears in the doorway beside her.] Ah, don't cry, Ma! Dick'll turn up in a minute or two, wait and see!
Arthur. Sure, he will.
Miller. [Gets to his feet, frowning—soberly.] I was going out to look—if he wasn't back by twelve sharp. But I'll go now, if it'll ease your mind. I'll take the auto and drive out the beach road—— [He is start-

ing to get his bathrobe off.] You better come with me, Arthur.
Arthur. Sure thing, Pa. [Suddenly he listens and says.] Shhh! That must be him now.
Mrs. Miller. Oh, thank God!
Miller. [With a sheepish smile.] Darn him! I'll give him hell for worrying us all like this!
[Then RICHARD lurches in violently. His eyes are glassy and wild. He leans with back against desk chair. The knees of his trousers are dirty, one of them torn from the sprawl on the sidewalk he has taken, following the BARTENDER's kick. They ALL gape at him, too paralyzed for a moment to say anything.]
Mrs. Miller. Richard! Oh, God, what's happened to him! He's gone crazy!
Sid. [The first to regain presence of mind.] Crazy, nothing. He's only soused!
Richard. [With a wild gesture of defiance, maudlinly dramatic.] "Yesterday this Day's Madness did prepare Tomorrow's Silence, Triumph, or Despair. Drink! for——" [1]
Miller. [His face grown stern and angry, takes a threatening step toward him.] Richard! How——!
Mrs. Miller. [Hysterically.] Don't you strike him, Nat! Don't you——
Sid. [Grabbing his arm.] Steady, Nat! The boy don't know what he's doing!
Richard. [Drunkenly glorying in the sensation he is creating—recites with heroic, dramatic emphasis.] "And then—at ten o'clock—I will come—with vine leaves in my hair!"
[He laughs dramatically with a double-dyed sardonicism.]
Mrs. Miller. [Staring at him as if she couldn't believe her eyes.] Richard! You're intoxicated——! You bad, wicked boy, you!
Richard. [Forces a wicked leer to his lips and quotes with ponderous mockery.] "Fancy that, Hedda!" [Then suddenly his whole expression changes. His pallor takes on a greenish, sea-sick tinge, his eyes seem to be turned inward uneasily—and all pose gone, he calls to his MOTHER appealingly, like a sick little boy.] Ma! I feel—rotten!
[MRS. MILLER gives a cry and starts to go to him, but SID interrupts her.]
Sid. You let me take care of him, Essie. I know this game backwards.
Miller. [Putting his arm around his WIFE.] Yes, you leave him to Sid.
Sid. [His arm around RICHARD—leading

---

[1] From the Rubaiyat.

him off through the front parlor.] Come on, Old Sport! Upstairs we go! Your old Uncle Sid'll fix you up. He's the kid that wrote the book!

Mrs. Miller. [*Staring after them—still aghast.*] Oh, it's too terrible! Imagine our Richard! And did you hear him talking about some Hedda? Oh, I know he's been with one of those bad women, I know he has —my Richard!

CURTAIN

ACT FOUR

SCENE I

SCENE: *The same—Sitting-room of the Miller home—about one in the afternoon of the following day.*
[*As the Curtain rises the family, with the exception of* RICHARD, *are discovered coming in through the back parlor from dinner in the dining-room.* MILLER *and his* WIFE *come first. His face is set in an expression of frowning severity.* MRS. MILLER'S *face is drawn and worried. She has evidently had no rest yet from a long, sleepless, tearful night.* SID *is himself again, his expression as innocent as if nothing had occurred the previous day to remotely concern him. And outside of eyes that are bloodshot and nerves that are shaky, he shows no after-effects except that he is terribly sleepy.* LILY *is gently sad and depressed.* MILDRED *and* TOMMY *are subdued and covertly watching their* FATHER. ARTHUR *is self-consciously a virtuous young man against whom nothing can be said. The atmosphere is as stiltedly grave as if they were attending a funeral service. Their eyes keep fixed on the head of the house, who has gone to the window at left and is staring out frowningly, savagely chewing a tooth- pick.*]

Miller. [*Finally—irritably.*] Damn it, I'd ought to be back at the office putting in some good licks! I've a whole pile of things that have got to be done today!
Mrs. Miller. [*Accusingly.*] You don't mean to tell me you're going back without seeing him!
Miller. [*Exasperatedly.*] 'Course I'm not! I wish you'd stop jumping to conclusions!

[*She hides her face on* MILLER'S *shoulder and sobs heart-brokenly.*]
Miller. [*A tired, harassed, deeply worried look on his face—soothing her.*] Now, now, you mustn't get to imagining such things! You mustn't, Essie!
[LILY *and* MILDRED *and* ARTHUR *are standing about awkwardly with awed, shocked faces.*]

What else did I come home for, I'd like to know?
[*He ends up very lamely and is irritably conscious of the fact.*]
Tommy. [*Who has been fidgeting rest- lessly—unable to bear the suspense a moment longer.*] What's Dick done? Why is every- one scared to tell me?
Miller. [*Seizes this as an escape valve— turns and fixes his* YOUNGEST SON *with a stern, forbidding eye.*] Young man, I've never spanked you yet, but that don't mean I never will! You keep your mouth shut till you're spoken to—or I warn you some- thing's going to happen!
Mrs. Miller. Yes, Tommy, you keep still and don't bother your Pa. [*Then warningly to her* HUSBAND.] Careful what you say, Nat. Little pitchers have big ears.
Miller. [*Peremptorily.*] You kids ske- daddle—all of you. Why are you always hanging around the house? Go out and play in the yard, or take a walk and get some fresh air! [MILDRED *takes* TOMMY'S *hand and leads him out.* ARTHUR *hangs back as if the designation "kids" couldn't possibly apply to him. His* FATHER *notices this— impatiently.*] Arthur!
[ARTHUR *goes out with a stiff, wounded dignity.*]
Lily. [*Tactfully.*] I think I'll go for a walk, too.
[*She goes out.* SID *makes a movement as if to follow her.*]
Miller. I'd like you to stay, Sid—for a while, anyway.
Sid. Sure. [*He sits down in the rocking chair at right, rear, of table and immediately yawns.*] Gosh, I'm dead. Don't know what's the matter with me today. Can't seem to keep awake.
Miller. [*With caustic sarcasm.*] Maybe

that demon chowder you drank at the picnic poisoned you! [SID *looks sheepish and forces a grin.* Then MILLER *turns to his* WIFE *with the air of one who determinedly faces the unpleasant.*] Where is Richard?

Mrs. Miller. [*Flusteredly.*] He's still in bed. I made him stay in bed to punish him —and I thought he ought to, anyway, after being so sick. But he says he feels all right.

Sid. [*With another yawn.*] 'Course he does. When you're young you can stand anything without it fazing you. Why, I remember when I could come down on the morning after fresh as a daisy and eat a breakfast of pork chops and fried onions and——
[*He stops guiltily.*]

Miller. [*Bitingly.*] I suppose that was before eating lobster shells had ruined your iron constitution!

Mrs. Miller. [*Regards her* BROTHER *severely.*] If I was in your shoes, I'd keep still! [*Then, turning to* MILLER.] Richard must be feeling better. He ate all the dinner I sent up, Norah says.

Miller. [*Accusingly.*] I thought you weren't going to give him any dinner—to punish him.

Mrs. Miller. [*Guiltily.*] Well—in his weakened condition—I thought it best—— [*Then defensively.*] But you needn't think I haven't punished him. I've given him pieces of my mind he won't forget in a hurry. And I've kept reminding him his real punishment was still to come—that you were coming home to dinner on purpose—and then he'd learn that you could be terrible stern when he did such awful things.

Miller. [*Stirs uncomfortably.*] Hmm!

Mrs. Miller. And that's just what it's your duty to do—punish him good and hard! [*Then hastily.*] But you be careful how you go about it, Nat. Remember he's like you inside—too sensitive for his own good. And he never would have done it, I know, if it hadn't been for that darned little dunce, Muriel, and her numbskull father—and then all of us teasing him and hurting his feelings all day—and then you lost your temper and were so sharp with him right after dinner before he went out.

Miller. [*Resentfully.*] I see this is going to work round to where it's all my fault!

Mrs. Miller. Now, I didn't say that—did I? And here's another thing. You know as well as I, Richard would never have done such a thing alone. Why, he wouldn't know how! He must have been influenced and led by someone!

Miller. Yes, I believe that. Did you worm out of him who it was? [*Then angrily.*] By God, I'll make whoever it was regret it!

Mrs. Miller. No, he wouldn't admit there was any one. [*Then triumphantly.*] But there is one thing I did worm out of him—and I can tell you it relieved my mind more'n anything! You know, I was afraid he'd been with one of those bad women. Well, turns out there wasn't any Hedda. She was just out of those books he's been reading. He swears he's never known a Hedda in his life. And I believe him. Why, he seemed disgusted with me for having such a notion. [*Then lamely.*] So somehow—I can't kind of feel it's all as bad as I thought it was. [*Then quickly and indignantly.*] But it's bad enough, goodness knows—— The idea of a boy of his age! Shall I go up now and tell him to get dressed, you want to see him?

Miller. [*Helplessly—and irritably.*] Yes! I can't waste all day listening to you——

Mrs. Miller. [*Worriedly.*] Now you keep your temper, Nat, remember!
[*She goes out.*]

Miller. Darn women, anyway! They always get you mixed up. Their minds simply don't know what logic is! [*Then he notices that* SID *is dozing. Sharply.*] Sid!

Sid. [*Blinking—mechanically.*] I'll take the same. [*Then hurriedly.*] What'd you say, Nat?

Miller. [*Caustically.*] What I didn't say was "what'll you have." [*Then irritably.*] Do you want to be of some help, or don't you? Then keep awake and try and use your brains! This is a damned sight more serious than Essie has any idea! She thinks there weren't any girls mixed up with Richard's spree last night—but I happen to know there were! [*He takes a letter from his pocket.*] Here's a note a woman left with one of the boys downstairs at the office this morning— didn't ask to see me, just said give me this. He'd never seen her before—said she looked like a tart. [*He has opened the letter and reads.*] "Your son got the booze he drank last night at the Pleasant Beach House. The bartender there knew he was under age but served him just the same. He thought it was a good joke to get him soused. If you have any guts you will run that bastard out of town." Well, what do you think of that? It's a woman's handwriting—not signed, of course.

Sid. She's one of the babies, all right— judging from her elegant language.

Miller. [*Handing him the letter.*] See if you recognize the handwriting.

Sid. [*With a reproachful look.*] Nat, I resent the implication that I correspond with all the tramps around this town. [*Then, looking at the letter.*] No, I don't know who this could be. [*Handing the letter back.*] But I deduce that the lady had a run-in with the barkeep and wants revenge.

Miller. [*Grimly.*] And I deduce that before that she must have picked up Richard—or how would she know who he was?—and took him to this dive.

Sid. Maybe. The Pleasant Beach House is nothing but a bed house—— [*Quickly.*] At least, so I've been told.

Miller. That's just the sort of damned fool thing he might do to spite Muriel, in the state of mind he was in—pick up some tart. And she'd try to get him drunk so——

Sid. Yes it might have happened like that —and it might not. How're we ever going to prove it? Every one at the Pleasant Beach will lie their heads off.

Miller. [*Simply and proudly.*] Richard won't lie.

Sid. Well, don't blame him if he don't remember everything that happened last night. [*Then sincerely concerned.*] I hope you're wrong, Nat. That kind of baby is dangerous for a kid like Dick—in more ways than one. You know what I mean.

Miller. [*Frowningly.*] Yep—and that's just what's got me worried. Damn it, I've got to have a straight talk with him—about women and all those things. I ought to have long ago.

Sid. Yes. You ought.

Miller. I've tried a couple of times—but, hell, I always get sort of ashamed of myself and can't get started right. You feel, in spite of all his bold talk out of books, that he's so darned innocent inside.

Sid. I know. I wouldn't like the job. [*Then after a pause—curiously.*] How were you figuring to punish him for his sins?

Miller. [*Frowning.*] To be honest with you, Sid, I'm damned if I know. It all depends on what I feel about what he feels when I first size him up—and even then it'll be like shooting in the dark.

Sid. If I didn't know you so well, I'd say don't be too hard on him. [*He smiles a little bitterly.*] If you remember, I was always getting punished—and see what a lot of good it did me!

Miller. [*Kindly.*] Oh, there's lots worse than you around, so don't take to boasting. [*Then at a sound from the front parlor—with a sigh.*] Well, here comes the bad man, I guess.

Sid. [*Getting up.*] I'll beat it.

[*But it is* MRS. MILLER *who appears, looking guilty and defensive.* SID *sits down again.*]

Mrs. Miller. I'm sorry, Nat—but he was sound asleep and I didn't have the heart to wake him.

Miller. [*Concealing a relief of which he is ashamed—exasperatedly.*] Well, I'll be double damned! If you're not the——

Mrs. Miller. [*Defensively aggressive.*] Now don't lose your temper at me, Nat Miller. You know as well as I do he needs all the sleep he can get today—after last night's ructions! Do you want him to be taken down sick? You can see him when you come home for supper, can't you? My goodness, you'd think you couldn't bear waiting to punish him!

Miller. [*Outraged.*] Well, I'll be eternally—— [*Then suddenly he laughs.*] No use talking, you certainly take the cake! But you know darned well I told you I'm not coming home to supper tonight. I've got a date with Jack Lawson that may mean a lot of new advertising and it's important.

Mrs. Miller. Then you can see him when you do come home.

Miller. [*Covering his evident relief at this respite with a fuming manner.*] All right! All right! I give up! I'm going back to the office. [*He starts for the front parlor.*] Bring a man all the way back here on a busy day and then you—— No consideration——

[*He disappears, and a moment later the front door is heard shutting behind him.*]

Mrs. Miller. Well! I never saw Nat so bad-tempered!

Sid. [*With a chuckle.*] He's so tickled to get out of it for a while he can't see straight!

Mrs. Miller. [*With a sniff.*] I hope I know him better than you. [*Then fussing about the room, setting this and that in place, while* SID *yawns drowsily and blinks his eyes.*] And there was Richard sleeping like a baby—so innocent-looking! You'd think butter wouldn't melt in his mouth! It all goes to show you never can tell by appearances—not even when it's your own child. The idea!

Sid. [*Drowsily.*] Oh, Dick's all right, Essie. Stop worrying.

Mrs. Miller. [*With a sniff.*] Of course, you'd say that. I suppose you'll have him out with you painting the town red the next thing!

[*As she is talking,* RICHARD *appears in the doorway. He shows no ill effects from his experience the night before. In fact, he looks surprisingly healthy. He is dressed in flannel undershirt, trousers, shoes, covered by heavy brown bathrobe. His expression is one of hang-dog guilt mingled with defensive defiance.*]

Richard. [*With self-conscious unconcern, ignoring his* MOTHER.] Hello, Uncle Sid.

Mrs. Miller. [*Whirls on him.*] What are you doing here, young man? I thought you were asleep! Seems to me you woke up pretty quick—just after your Pa left the house!

Richard. [*Sulkily.*] I wasn't asleep.

Mrs. Miller. [*Outraged.*] Do you mean to say you were deliberately deceiving?

Richard. I wasn't deceiving—— You didn't ask if I was asleep.

Mrs. Miller. It amounts to the same thing and you know it! It isn't enough your wickedness last night, but now you have to take to lying!

Richard. I wasn't lying, Ma. If you'd asked if I was asleep I'd have said no.

Mrs. Miller. I've a good mind to send you straight back to bed and make you stay there!

Richard. Ah, what for, Ma? It was only giving me a headache, lying there.

Mrs. Miller. If you've got a headache, I guess you know it doesn't come from that! And imagine me standing there, and feeling sorry for you, like a fool—— But you wait till your Pa comes back tonight. If you don't catch it——

Richard. [*Sulkily.*] I don't care.

Mrs. Miller. You don't care? You talk as if you weren't sorry for what you did last night!

Richard. [*Defiantly.*] I'm not sorry.

Mrs. Miller. Richard.

Richard. [*With bitter despondency.*] I'm not sorry because I don't care a darn what I did, or anything about anything! But I won't do it again——

Mrs. Miller. [*Seizing on this to relent a bit.*] Well, I'm glad to hear you say that, anyway!

Richard. But that's not because I think it was wicked or any such old-fogey moral notion, but because it wasn't any fun. It didn't make me happy and funny like it does Uncle Sid——

Sid. [*Drowsily.*] What's that? Who's funny?

Richard. [*Ignoring him.*] It only made me sadder—and sick—so I don't see any sense in it.

Mrs. Miller. Now you're talking sense! That's a good boy.

Richard. But I'm not sorry I tried it once—"curing the soul by means of the senses," as Oscar Wilde says. [*Then with despairing pessimism.*] But what does it matter what I do or don't do? Life is all a stupid farce! I'm through with it! [*With a sinister smile.*] It's lucky there aren't any of General Gabler's pistols around—or you'd see if I'd stand it much longer!

Mrs. Miller. [*Worriedly impressed by this threat—but pretending scorn.*] I don't know anything about General Gabler—I suppose that's more of those darned books—but you're a silly gabbler yourself when you talk that way!

Richard. [*Darkly.*] That's how little you know about me.

Mrs. Miller. [*Giving in to her worry.*] I wish you wouldn't say those terrible things—about life and pistols! You don't want to worry me to death, do you?

Richard. [*Reassuringly stoical now.*] You needn't worry, Ma. It was only my despair talking. But I'm not a coward. I'll face—my fate.

Mrs. Miller. [*Stands looking at him puzzledly—then gives it up with a sigh.*] Well, all I can say is you're the queerest boy I ever did hear of! [*Then solicitously, putting her hand on his forehead.*] How's your headache? Do you want me to get you some Bromo Seltzer?

Richard. [*Taken down—disgustedly.*] No, I don't! Aw, Ma, you don't understand anything!

Mrs. Miller. [*Practically.*] Well, I understand this much: It's your liver, that's what! You'll take a good dose of salts tomorrow morning, and no nonsense about it! [*Then suddenly.*] My goodness, I wonder what time it's getting to be. I've got to go up-street. [*She goes to the doorway as she speaks.*] You stay here, Richard, you hear? Remember you're not allowed out today—for a punishment.

[*She hurries away.* RICHARD *is sitting in tragic gloom.* SID, *without opening his eyes, speaks to him drowsily.*]

Sid. Well, how's my fellow Rum Pot? Got a head?

Richard. [*Startled—sheepishly.*] Aw, don't go dragging that up, Uncle Sid. I'm never going to be such a fool again, I tell you.

Sid. [*With drowsy cynicism—not unmixed with bitterness at the end.*] Never again, eh? Seems to me I've heard someone say that before. Who could it have been, I wonder? Why, if it wasn't Sid Davis! Yes, sir, I've heard him say that very thing a thousand times, must be. But then he's always fooling; you can't take a word he says seriously; he's a card, that Sid is!

Richard. [*Darkly.*] I was desperate, Uncle—even if she wasn't worth it. I was wounded to the heart.

Sid. I like "to the quick" better myself—more stylish! [*Then sadly.*] But you're right. Love is hell on a poor sucker. Don't I know it?

[SID's *chin sinks on his chest and he begins to breathe noisily, fast asleep. There is a sound of someone on the porch and the screen door is opened and* MILDRED *enters. She smiles on seeing her* UNCLE, *then gives a start on seeing* RICHARD.]

Mildred. Hello! Are you allowed up?

Richard. Of course, I'm allowed up.

Mildred. How did Pa punish you?

Richard. He didn't. He went back to the office without seeing me.

Mildred. Well, you'll catch it later. [*Then rebukingly.*] And you ought to. If you'd ever seen how awful you looked last night!

Richard. Aw, forget it, can't you?

Mildred. Well, are you ever going to do it again, that's what I want to know.

Richard. What's that to you?

Mildred. [*With suppressed excitement.*] Well, if you don't solemnly swear you won't —then I won't give you something I've got for you.

Richard. Don't try to kid me. You haven't got anything.

Mildred. I have, too.

Richard. What?

Mildred. Wouldn't you like to know! I'll give you three guesses.

Richard. Don't bother me. I'm in no mood to play riddles with kids!

Mildred. Oh, well, if you're going to get snippy! Anyway, you haven't promised yet.

Richard. [*A prey to keen curiosity now.*] I promise. What is it?

Mildred. What would you like best in the world?

Richard. I don't know. What?

Mildred. And you pretend to be in love! If I told Muriel that!

Richard. [*Breathlessly.*] Is it—from her?

Mildred. [*Laughing.*] Well, I guess it's a shame to keep you guessing. Yes. It is from her. I was walking past her place just now when I saw her waving from their parlor window, and I went up and she said "give this to Dick," and she didn't have a chance to say anything else because her mother called her and said she wasn't allowed to have company. So I took it—and here it is. [*She gives him a letter folded many times into a tiny square.* RICHARD *opens it with a trembling eagerness and reads.* MILDRED *watches him curiously —then sighs affectedly.*] Gee, it must be wonderful to be in love like you are—all with one person.

Richard. [*His eyes shining with joy.*] Gee, Mid, do you know what she says—that she didn't mean a word in that other letter. Her old man made her write it. And she loves me and only me and always will, no matter how they punish her!

Mildred. My! I'd never think she had that much spunk.

Richard. Huh! You don't know her! Think I could fall in love with a girl that was afraid to say her soul's her own? I should say not! [*Then more gleefully still.*] And she's going to try and sneak out and meet me tonight. She says she thinks she can do it. [*Then suddenly, feeling this enthusiasm before* MILDRED *is entirely the wrong note for a cynical pessimist—with an affected bitter laugh.*] Ha! I knew darned well she couldn't hold out—that she'd ask me again. [*He misquotes cynically.*] "Women never know when the curtain has fallen. They always want another act." [1]

Mildred. Is that so, smarty?

Richard. [*As if he were weighing the matter.*] I don't know whether I'll consent to keep this date or not.

Mildred. Well, *I* know! You're not allowed out, you silly! So you can't!

Richard. [*Dropping all pretenses—defiantly.*] Can't I, though! You wait and see if I can't! I'll see her tonight if it's the last thing I ever do! I don't care how I'm punished after!

Mildred. [*Admiringly.*] Goodness! I never thought you had such nerve!

Richard. You promise to keep your face shut, Mid, —until after I've left tonight— then you can tell Pa and Ma where I've gone —I mean, if they're worrying I'm off like last night.

Mildred. All right. Only you've got to do something for me when I ask.

Richard. Course I will. [*Excitedly.*] And say, Mid, right now's the best chance for me to get away—while everyone's out. Ma'll be coming back soon and she'll keep watching me like a cat. [*Starts for door.*] I'm going now—I'll beat it upstairs and get dressed.

Mildred. But what will you do till night time—it's ages to wait?

Richard. What do I care how long I wait! [*With passionate intensity.*] I'd wait a million years and never mind it—for her! [*To* MILDRED, *with superior scornful look.*] The trouble with you is—you don't understand what love means.   [*He exits.*]

---

[1] From Wilde's *The Picture of Dorian Gray.* Wilde wrote "a sixth" instead of "another."

CURTAIN

ACT FOUR

SCENE II

SCENE: *A strip of beach along the harbor. At right, a bank of dark earth, running half-diagonally back along the beach, rises abruptly like a step a foot high marking the line where the sand of the beach ends and fertile land begins. The top of the bank is grassy and the trailing boughs of willow trees extend out over it and over a part of the beach. At right center is a path leading up the bank, between the willows. On the beach, at just left of center, a white, flat-bottomed rowboat is drawn up, its bow about touching the bank, the painter trailing up the bank, evidently made fast to the trunk of a willow. The new moon casts a soft, mysterious, caressing light over everything. The last of the path is in very pale moonlight which increases toward the boat, which is the high spot of the moonlight. The sand of the beach shimmers palely. In the distance, the orchestra of a summer hotel can be heard very faintly at intervals.*

[*Richard is discovered sitting sideways on the gunwale of the rowboat near the stern. He is facing right, watching the path. He is in a great nervous state of anxious expectancy, squirming about uncomfortably on the narrow gunwale, kicking at the sand restlessly, twirling his straw hat, with a bright-colored band in stripes, around on his finger.*]

Richard. [*Thinking aloud.*] Gosh, that music from the hotel sounds wonderful. Must be nearly nine—— I can hear the Town Hall clock strike, it's so still to-night—— I'll catch hell when I get back, but it'll be worth it. If only Muriel turns up—— Am I sure she wrote nine? [*He puts the straw hat on the sand right of boat and pulls the folded letter out of his pocket and peers at it in the moonlight.*] Yes, it's nine, all right. [*He starts to put the note back in his pocket, then stops and kisses it—then shoves it away hastily, sheepishly, looking around him shamefacedly, as if afraid he were being observed.*] Aw, that's silly—no, it isn't either—not when you're really in love—— [*He jumps to his feet restlessly.*] Darn it, I wish she'd show up!—think of something else—that'll make the time pass quicker—— [*Sits again on boat.*] Last

night?—the Pleasant Beach House—Belle—ah, forget her!—now, when Muriel's coming—that's a fine time to think of——! But I didn't go upstairs with her—even if she was pretty—— Aw, she wasn't pretty—— She was just a whore—— She was everything dirty—— Muriel's a million times prettier, anyway—— Muriel and I will go upstairs—when we're married—but that will be beautiful—— But I oughtn't even to think of that yet—it's not right—— I'd never—now—but after we're married—— [*He gives a little shiver of passionate longing—then resolutely turns his mind away from these improper, almost desecrating thoughts.*] That damned barkeep kicking me—— I'll bet you if I hadn't been drunk I'd have given him one good punch in the nose—— [*Then with a shiver of shamefaced revulsion and self-disgust.*] Aw, you deserved a kick in the pants—making such a darned slob of yourself! You must have been a fine sight when you got home!—having to be put to bed and getting sick! Phaw! [*He squirms disgustedly.*] Think of something else, can't you? Recite something—— See if you remember——

"Nay, let us walk from fire unto fire,
From passionate pain to deadlier delight,
I am too young to live without desire,
Too young art thou to waste this summer
night——" [1]

Gee, that's a peach! I'll have to memorize the rest and recite it to Muriel the next time—— I wish I could write poetry—about her and me—— [*He sighs and stares around him at the night.*] Gee, it's beautiful to-night—as if it was a special night—for me and Muriel—— Gee, I love tonight—— I love the sand, and the trees, and the grass, and the water, and the sky, and the moon—— It's all in me and I'm in it—— God, it's so beautiful! [*He stares at the moon with a rapt face. From the distance the Town Hall clock begins to strike. It brings him back to earth with a start.*] There's nine now—— [*He peers at the path apprehensively.*] I don't see her—— She must have got caught. [*Almost tearfully.*] Gee, I hate to go home and catch hell—without having seen her! [*Then calling a manly cynicism to his aid.*] Aw, who ever heard of a woman being on time—— I ought to know enough about life by this time not to expect—— [*Then, with sudden excitement.*]

---

[1] From Wilde's *Panthea*.

There she comes now—— Gosh! [*He heaves a sigh of relief—then recites dramatically to himself, his eyes on the approaching figure.*]

"And lo, my love, mine own soul's heart, more dear
Than mine own soul, more beautiful than God,
Who hath my being between the hands of her——* [1]

[*Then hastily.*] Mustn't let her know I'm so tickled—— If women are too sure of you, they treat you like slaves. Let her suffer for a change——

[*He strolls around with exaggerated carelessness, turning his back on the path, hands in pockets, whistling with insouciance "Waiting at the Church." MURIEL McCOMBER enters from down the path. She is fifteen, going on sixteen. She is a pretty girl with a plump, graceful little figure, fluffy, light-brown hair, big naive wondering dark eyes, a round dimpled face, a soft melting drawly voice. Just now she is in a great thrilled state of timid adventurousness. She hesitates in the shadow at the foot of the path, waiting for RICHARD to see her, but he resolutely goes on whistling with back turned, and she has to call him.*]

Muriel. Oh, Dick.

Richard. [*Turns around with an elaborate simulation of being disturbed in the midst of profound meditation.*] Oh, hello. Is it nine already?

Muriel. [*Coming toward him as far as the edge of the shadow—disappointedly.*] I thought you'd be waiting right here at the end of the path. I'll bet you'd forgotten I was even coming.

Richard. [*Strolling a little toward her but not too far—carelessly.*] No, I hadn't forgotten, honest. But I got to thinking about life.

Muriel. You might think of me for a change. [*Hesitating timidly on the edge of the shadow.*] Dick! You come here to me. I'm afraid to go out there where anyone might see me.

Richard. [*Coming toward her—scornfully.*] Aw, there you go again—always scared of life!

Muriel. [*Indignantly.*] Dick Miller, I do think you've got an awful nerve to say that after all the risks I've run making this date and then sneaking out! You didn't take the trouble to sneak any letter to me, I notice!

Richard. No, because after your first letter, I thought everything was dead and past between us.

Muriel. And I'll bet you didn't care one little bit! [*On the verge of humiliated tears.*] Oh, I was a fool ever to come here! I've got a good notion to go right home and never speak to you again!

[*She half turns back toward the path.*]

Richard. [*Frightened—immediately becomes terribly sincere—grabbing her by the shoulders.*] Aw, don't go, Muriel! Please! I didn't mean anything like that, honest I didn't! Gee, if you knew how broken-hearted I was by that first letter, and how darned happy your second letter made me——!

Muriel. [*Happily relieved—but appreciates she has the upper hand now and doesn't relent at once.*] I don't believe you!

Richard. You ask Mid how happy I was. She can prove it.

Muriel. She'd say anything you told her to. I don't care anything about what she'd say. It's you. You've got to swear to me.

Richard. I swear!

Muriel. [*Demurely.*] Well, then, all right, I'll believe you.

Richard. [*His eyes on her face lovingly—genuine adoration in his voice.*] Gosh, you're pretty tonight, Muriel! It seems ages since we've been together. If you knew how I've suffered——!

Muriel. I did, too.

Richard. [*Unable to resist falling into his tragic literary pose for a moment.*] The despair in my soul—— [*He recites dramatically.*] "Something was dead in each of us, And what was dead was Hope!" [1] That was me! My hope of happiness was dead! [*Then with sincere boyish fervor.*] Gosh, Muriel, it sure is wonderful to be with you again!

[*He puts a timid hand on her shoulder, awkwardly.*]

Muriel. [*Shyly.*] I'm glad—it makes you happy. I'm happy, too.

Richard. Can't I—won't you let me kiss you—now? Please!

[*He bends his face toward hers.*]

Muriel. [*Ducking her head away—timidly.*] No! You mustn't. Don't——

Richard. Aw, why can't I?

Muriel. Because—I'm afraid.

Richard. [*Discomfited—taking his arm from around her—a bit sulky and impatient with her.*] Aw, that's what you always say!

---

[1] From Swinburne's *Laus Veneris.*

[1] From Wilde's *The Ballad of Reading Gaol.*

You're always so afraid! Aren't you ever going to let me?

Muriel. I will—sometime.

Richard. When?

Muriel. Soon, maybe.

Richard. Tonight, will you?

Muriel. [*Coyly.*] I'll see.

Richard. Promise?

Muriel. I promise—maybe.

Richard. All right. You remember you've promised. [*Then coaxingly.*] Aw, don't let's stand here. Come on out and we can sit down in the boat.

Muriel. [*Hesitantly.*] It's so bright out there.

Richard. No one'll see. You know there's never anyone around here at night.

Muriel. [*Illogically.*] I know there isn't. That's why I thought it would be the best place. But there might be someone.

Richard. [*Taking her hand and tugging at it gently.*] There isn't a soul. [MURIEL *steps out a little and looks up and down fearfully.* RICHARD *goes on insistently.*] Aw, what's the use of a moon if you can't see it?

Muriel. But it's only a new moon. That's not much to look at.

Richard. But I want to see you. I can't here in the shadow. I want to—drink in—all your beauty.

Muriel. [*Can't resist this.*] Well, all right—— [*She lets him lead her toward the boat. They sit on the left end.*] Only I can't stay only a few minutes.

Richard. [*Pleadingly.*] Aw, you can stay a little while, can't you? Please!

Muriel. A little while. But I've got to be home in bed again pretending to be asleep by ten o'clock.

Richard. But you'll have lots of time to do that.

Muriel. [*Excitedly.*] Dick, you have no idea what I went through to get here tonight! My, but it was exciting! I had to get all undressed and into bed and Ma came up, and I pretended to be asleep, and she went down again, and I got up and dressed in such a hurry—— I must look a sight, don't I?

Richard. You do not. You look wonderful.

Muriel. And then I sneaked down the back stairs. And the pesky old stairs squeaked, and my heart was in my mouth, I was so scared, and then I sneaked out through the back yard, keeping in the dark under the trees, and—— My, but it was exciting! Dick, you don't realize how I've been punished for your sake.

Richard. And you don't realize what I've been through for you—and what I'm in for

—for sneaking out tonight—and staying away all day—— [*Then darkly.*] And for what I did last night—what your letter made me do!

Muriel. [*Made terribly curious by his ominous tone.*] What did my letter make you do?

Richard. [*Beginning to glory in this.*] It's too long a story—and let the dead past bury its dead. [*Then with real feeling.*] Only it isn't past, I can tell you! What I'll catch when Pa gets hold of me!

Muriel. Tell me, Dick! Begin at the beginning and tell me!

Richard. [*Tragically.*] Well, after your old—your father left our place I caught holy hell from Pa.

Muriel. Dick! You mustn't swear!

Richard. [*Darkly.*] Hell is the only word that can describe it. And on top of that, to torture me more, he gave me your letter. After I'd read that I didn't want to live any more. Life seemed like a tragic farce.

Muriel. [*Touched.*] I'm so awful sorry, Dick—honest I am! But you might have known I'd never write that unless——

Richard. I thought your love for me was dead. I wanted to die. I sat and brooded about death. Finally I made up my mind I'd kill myself.

Muriel. [*Excitedly.*] Dick! You didn't!

Richard. I did, too! If there'd been one of Hedda Gabler's pistols around, you'd have seen if I wouldn't have done it beautifully. I thought, "When I'm dead, she'll be sorry she ruined my life!"

Muriel. [*Cuddling up a little to him.*] If you ever had! I'd have died, too! Honest, I would!

Richard. But suicide is the act of a coward. [*Then with a bitter change of tone.*] And anyway, I thought to myself, she isn't worth it!

Muriel. [*Huffily.*] That's a nice thing to say!

Richard. Well, if you meant what was in that letter you wouldn't have been worth it, would you?

Muriel. But I've told you, Pa——

Richard. So I said to myself, "I'm through with women; they're all alike——"

Muriel. I'm not.

Richard. And I thought, "What difference does it make what I do now; I might as well forget her and lead the pace that kills, and drown my sorrows!" You know, I had eleven dollars saved up to buy you something for your birthday, but I thought: "She's dead to me now and why shouldn't I throw it away?" [*Then hastily.*] I've still got almost five left, Muriel, and I can get you something nice with that.

Muriel. [*Excitedly.*] What do I care about your old presents? You tell me what you did!

Richard. [*Darkly again.*] After it was dark, I sneaked out and went to a low dive I know about.

Muriel. Dick Miller, I don't believe you ever——

Richard. You ask them at the Pleasant Beach House if I didn't! They won't forget me in a hurry!

Muriel. [*Impressed and horrified.*] Why, that's a terrible place! Pa says it ought to be closed by the police!

Richard. [*Darkly.*] I said it was a dive, didn't I? It's a "secret house of shame." And they let me into a secret room behind the barroom. There wasn't anyone there but a Princeton Senior I know—he belongs to Tiger Inn and he's fullback on the football team—and he had two chorus girls from New York with him, and they were all drinking champagne.

Muriel. [*Disturbed by the entrance of the chorus girls.*] Dick Miller! I hope you didn't notice——

Richard. [*Carelessly.*] I noticed one of the girls—the one that wasn't with him—looking at me. She had strange-looking eyes. And then she asked me if I wouldn't drink champagne with them and come and sit with her.

Muriel. She must have been a nice thing! [*Then a bit falteringly.*] And—did you?

Richard. [*With tragic bitterness.*] Why shouldn't I, when you'd told me in that letter you'd never see me again?

Muriel. [*Almost tearfully.*] But you ought to have known Pa made me——

Richard. I didn't know that then. [*Then rubbing it in.*] Her name was Belle. She had golden hair—the kind that burns and stings you.

Muriel. I'll bet it was dyed!

Richard. She kept smoking one cigarette after another—but that's nothing for a chorus girl.

Muriel. [*Indignantly.*] She was low and bad; that's what she was or she couldn't be a chorus girl; and her smoking cigarettes proves it! [*Then falteringly again.*] And then what happened?

Richard. [*Carelessly.*] Oh, we just kept drinking champagne—and then I had a fight with the barkeep and knocked him down because he'd insulted her.

Muriel. [*Huffily.*] I don't see how he could insult that kind! And why did you

fight for her? Why didn't the Princeton full-back——

Richard. [*Slightly hesitant.*] He was too drunk by that time.

Muriel. And were you drunk?

Richard. Only a little then. I was worse later. You ought to have seen me when I got home! I was on the verge of delirium tremens!

Muriel. I'm glad I didn't see you. I hate people who get drunk! I'd have hated you! [*Then faltering but fascinated.*] But what happened with that Belle—after—before you went home?

Richard. Oh, we kept drinking champagne and she came and sat on my lap and kissed me.

Muriel. [*Stiffening.*] Oh!

Richard. [*Quickly, afraid he has gone too far.*] But it was only all in fun.

Muriel. And did you kiss her?

Richard. No, I didn't.

Muriel. [*Distractedly.*] You did, too! You're lying and you know it. [*Then tearfully.*] And there I was, right at that time, lying in bed not able to sleep, wondering how I was ever going to see you again and crying my eyes out, while you——! [*She suddenly jumps to her feet in a tearful fury.*] I hate you! I wish you were dead! I never want to lay eyes on you again! And this time I mean it!

[*She tries to leave but he holds her back. All the pose has dropped from him now and he is in a terrible state of contrition and fear of losing her.*]

Richard. [*Imploringly.*] Muriel! Wait! Listen!

Muriel. I don't want to listen! Let me go! If you don't I'll bite your hand!

Richard. I won't let you go! You've got to let me explain! I never——! Ouch! [*For* Muriel *has bitten his hand and it hurts, and, stung by the pain, he lets go instinctively. She immediately starts running toward the path.* Richard *calls after her with bitter despair and hurt.*] All right! Go if you want to—if you haven't the decency to let me explain. I hate you, too! I'll go and see Belle!

Muriel. [*Stops at foot of the path, then turns on him.*] Well, go and see her—if that's the kind of girl you like! What do I care? [*Then as he only stares before him broodingly, sitting dejectedly in the stern of the boat, a pathetic figure of injured grief—she drifts a step toward him.*] You can't explain! What can you explain! You owned up you kissed her!

Richard. I did not. I said she kissed me.

Muriel. [*Scornfully.*] And I suppose you just sat and let yourself be kissed! Tell that to the Marines!

Richard. [*Injuredly.*] All right! If you're going to call me a liar every word I say——

Muriel. [*Drifting back another step.*] I didn't call you a liar. I only meant—it sounds fishy. Don't you know it does?

Richard. I don't know anything. I only know I wish I was dead!

Muriel. [*Gently reproving.*] You oughtn't to say that. It's wicked. [*Then after a pause.*] And I suppose you'll tell me you didn't fall in love with her?

Richard. [*Scornfully.*] I should say not! Fall in love with that kind of girl! What do you take me for?

Muriel. [*Practically.*] How do you know what you did if you drank so much champagne?

Richard. I kept my head—with her. I'm not a sucker, no matter what you think!

Muriel. [*Drifting nearer.*] Then you didn't—love her?

Richard. I hated her! She wasn't even pretty! And I had a fight with her before I left, she got so fresh. I told her I loved you and never could love anyone else, and for her to leave me alone.

Muriel. But you said just now you were going to see her——

Richard. That was only bluff. I wouldn't —unless you left me. Then I wouldn't care what I did—any more than I did last night. [*Then suddenly defiant.*] And what if I did kiss her once or twice? I only did it to get back at you!

Muriel. Dick!

Richard. You're a fine one to blame me —when it was all your fault! Didn't I think you were out of my life forever? Hadn't you written me you were? Answer me that!

Muriel. But I've told you a million times that Pa——

Richard. Why didn't you have more sense than to let him make you write it? Was it my fault you didn't?

Muriel. It was your fault for being so stupid! You ought to have known he stood right over me and told me each word to write. If I'd refused, it would only have made everything worse. I had to pretend, so I'd get a chance to see you. Don't you see, Silly? And I had sand enough to sneak out to meet you tonight, didn't I? [*He doesn't answer. She moves nearer.*] Still, I can see how you felt the way you did—and maybe I am to blame for that. So I'll forgive and forget, Dick—if you'll swear to me you didn't even think of loving that——

Richard. [*Eagerly.*] I didn't! I swear, Muriel. I couldn't. I love you!

Muriel. Well, then—I still love you.

Richard. Then come back here, why don't you?

Muriel. [*Comes back and sits down by him shyly.*] All right—only I'll have to go soon, Dick. [*He puts his arm around her waist. She cuddles up close to him.*] I'm sorry—I hurt your hand.

Richard. That was nothing. It felt wonderful even to have you bite.

Muriel. [*Impulsively she kisses his hand.*] There! That'll cure it.
[*She is overcome by confusion at her boldness.*]

Richard. You shouldn't—waste that—on my hand. [*Then tremblingly.*] You said—you'd let me——

Muriel. Will it wash off—her kisses—make you forget you ever—for always?

Richard. I should say so! I'd never remember anything but it—never want anything but it—ever again.

Muriel. [*Shyly lifting her lips.*] Then —all right—Dick. [*He kisses her tremblingly and for a moment their lips remain together. Then she lets her head sink on his shoulder and sighs softly.*] The moon is beautiful, isn't it?

Richard. [*Kissing her hair.*] Not as beautiful as you. Nothing is! [*Then after a pause.*] Won't it be wonderful when we're married?

Muriel. Yes—but it's so long to wait.

Richard. Perhaps I needn't go to Yale. Perhaps Pa will give me a job. Then I'd soon be making enough to——

Muriel. You better do what your Pa thinks best—and I'd like you to be at Yale. [*Then taking his hand.*] Poor you! Do you think he'll punish you awful?

Richard. [*With intense sincerity.*] I don't know and I don't care! Nothing would have kept me from seeing you tonight—not if I'd have to crawl over red-hot coals! [*Then falling back on Swinburne.*] You are "my love, mine own soul's heart, more dear than mine own soul, more beautiful than God!"

Muriel. [*Shocked and delighted.*] Ssshh! It's wrong to say that!

Richard. [*Adoringly.*] Gosh, but I love you! Gosh, I love you—Darling!

Muriel. I love you, too—Sweetheart! [*They kiss. Then she lets her head sink on his shoulder again and they both sit in rapt trance, staring at the moon. After a pause —dreamily.*] Where'll we go on our honeymoon, Dick? To Niagara Falls?

Richard. [*Scornfully.*] That dump where

all the silly fools go? I should say not! [*With passionate romanticism.*] No, we'll go to some far-off wonderful place! [*He calls on Kipling to help him.*] Somewhere out on the Long Trail—the trail that is always new—— On the road to Mandalay! We'll watch the dawn come up like thunder out of China!

Muriel. [*Hazily but happily.*] That'll be wonderful, won't it?

CURTAIN

ACT FOUR

SCENE III

SCENE: *The sitting-room of the Miller house again—around ten o'clock the same night.*

[MILLER *is sitting in his rocker at right, his* WIFE *in her rocker at left. Moonlight shines faintly through the screen door up left. Only the green-shaded reading lamp is lit and by its light,* MILLER, *his specs on, is reading a book while his* WIFE, *sewing basket in lap, is working industriously on a doily.* MRS. MILLER's *face wears an expression of unworried content.* MILLER's *face has also lost its look of harassed preoccupation, although he still is a prey to certain misgivings, when he allows himself to think of them. Several books are piled on the table by his elbow, the books that have been confiscated from* RICHARD.]

Miller. [*Chuckles at something he reads—then closes the book and puts it on the table.* MRS. MILLER *looks up from her sewing.*] This Shaw's a comical cuss—even if his ideas are so crazy they oughtn't to allow them to be printed. And that Swinburne's got a fine swing to his poetry—if he'd only choose some other subjects besides loose women.

Mrs. Miller. [*Smiling teasingly.*] I can see where you're becoming corrupted by those books, too—pretending to read them out of duty to Richard, when your nose has been glued to the page!

Miller. No, no—but I've got to be honest. There's something to them. That "Rubaiyat of Omar Khayyam," now. I read that over again and liked it even better than I had before——

Mrs. Miller. [*Has been busy with her own thoughts during this last—with a deep sigh of relief.*] My, but I'm glad Mildred told me where Richard's gone. I'd have worried my heart out if she hadn't. But now it's all right.

Miller. [*Frowning a little.*] I'd hardly go so far as to say that. Just because we know he's all right tonight doesn't mean last night is wiped out. He's still got to be punished for that.

Mrs. Miller. [*Defensively.*] Well, if you ask me, I think after the way I punished him all day, and the way I know he's punished himself, he's had about all he deserves. I've told you how sorry he was, and how he said he'd never touch liquor again. He hated the taste of it, and it didn't make him feel happy like Sid, but only sad and sick, so he didn't see anything in it for him.

Miller. Well, if he's really got that view of it driven into his skull, I don't know but I'm glad it all happened. That'll protect him more than a thousand lectures—just horse sense about himself. [*Then frowning again.*] Still, I can't let him do such things and go scot-free. And then, besides, there's another side to it—— [*He stops abruptly.*]

Mrs. Miller. [*Uneasily.*] What do you mean, another side?

Miller. [*Hastily.*] I mean discipline. There's got to be some discipline in a family. I don't want him to get the idea he's got a stuffed shirt at the head of the table. No, he's got to be punished, if only to make the lesson stick in his mind, and I'm going to tell him he can't go to Yale, seeing he's so undependable.

Mrs. Miller. [*Up in arms at once.*] Not go to Yale! I guess he can go to Yale! Every man of your means in town is sending his boys to college! What would folks think of you? You let Wilbur go, and you'd have let Lawrence, only he didn't want to, and you're letting Arthur! If our other children can get the benefit of a college education, you're not going to pick on Richard——

Miller. Hush up, for God's sake! If you'd let me finish, I said I'd *tell* him that now—bluff—then later on I'll change my mind, if he behaves himself.

Mrs. Miller. Oh, well, if that's all—— [*Then defensively again.*] But it's your duty to give him every benefit. He's got an exceptional brain, that boy has! He's proved it by the way he likes to read all those deep plays and poetry.

Miller. But I thought you——

[*He stops abruptly, grinning helplessly.*]

Mrs. Miller. You thought I what?

Miller. Never mind.

Mrs. Miller. [*Sniffs, but thinks it better to let this pass.*] You mark my words, that boy's going to turn out to be a great lawyer, or a great doctor, or a great writer, or——

Miller. [*Grinning.*] You agree he's going to be great, anyway.

Mrs. Miller. Yes, I most certainly have a lot of faith in Richard.

Miller. Well, so have I, as far as that goes.

Mrs. Miller. And as for his being in love with Muriel! I don't see but what it might work out real well. Richard could do worse.

Miller. But I thought you had no use for Muriel, thought she was stupid——

Mrs. Miller. Well, so I did, but if she's good for Richard and he wants her—— [*Then inconsequentially.*] Ma used to say you weren't over bright but she changed her mind when she saw I didn't care if you were or not.

Miller. [*Not exactly pleased by this.*] Well, I've been bright enough to——

Mrs. Miller. [*Going on as if he had not spoken.*] And Muriel's real cute-looking, I have to admit that. Takes after her mother. Alice Briggs was the prettiest girl before she married!

Miller. Yes, and Muriel will get big as a house after she's married, the same as her mother did. That's the trouble. A man never can tell what he's letting himself in——

[*He stops, feeling his* WIFE's *eyes fixed on him with indignant suspicion.*]

Mrs. Miller. [*Sharply.*] I'm not too fat and don't you say it!

Miller. Who was talking about you?

Mrs. Miller. And I'd rather have some flesh on my bones than be built like a string bean and bore a hole in a chair every time I sat down—like some people!

Miller. [*Ignoring the insult—flatteringly.*] Why, no one'd ever call you fat, Essie. You're only plump, like a good figure ought to be.

Mrs. Miller. [*Childishly pleased—gratefully giving tit for tat.*] Well, you're not skinny, either—only slender—and I think you've been putting on weight lately, too.

[*Having thus squared matters, she takes up her sewing again. A pause. Then* MILLER *asks incredulously.*]

Miller. You don't mean to tell me you're actually taking this Muriel crush of Richard's seriously, do you? I know it's a good thing to encourage right now but—pshaw, why, Richard'll probably forget all about her before he's away six months and she'll have forgotten him.

Mrs. Miller. Don't be so cynical. [*Then, after a pause, thoughtfully.*] Well, anyway, he'll always have it to remember—no matter what happens after—and that's something.

Miller. You bet that's something. [*Then with a grin.*] You surprise me at times with your deep wisdom!

Mrs. Miller. You don't give me credit for ever having common sense, that's why. [*She goes back to her sewing.*]

Miller. [*After a pause.*] Where'd you say Sid and Lily had gone off to?

Mrs. Miller. To the beach to listen to the band. [*She sighs sympathetically.*] Poor Lily! Sid'll never change, and she'll never marry him. But she seems to get some queer satisfaction out of fussing over him.

Miller. Arthur's up with Elsie Rand, I suppose?

Mrs. Miller. Of course.

Miller. Where's Mildred?

Mrs. Miller. Out walking with her latest. I've forgot who it is. I can't keep track of them. [*She smiles.*]

Miller. [*Smiling.*] Then, from all reports, we seem to be completely surrounded by love!

Mrs. Miller. Well, we've had our share, haven't we? We don't have to begrudge it to our children. [*Then has a sudden thought.*] But I've done all this talking about Muriel and Richard and clean forgot how old McComber was against it. But he'll get over that, I suppose.

Miller. [*With satisfaction.*] He has already. I ran into him upstreet this afternoon and he was meek as pie. He backed water and said he guessed I was right. Richard had just copied stuff out of books, and kids would be kids, and so on. So I came off my high horse a bit—but not too far—and I guess all that won't bother anyone any more. [*Then rubbing his hands together—with a boyish grin of pleasure.*] And I told you about getting that business from Lawson, didn't I? It's been a good day, Essie—a darned good day!

[*From off up left is heard the footsteps of someone coming around the piazza to the side door.* MRS. MILLER *looks up from her sewing, listening a moment.*]

Mrs. Miller. [*In a whisper.*] It's Richard.

Miller. [*Immediately assuming an expression of becoming gravity.*] Hmm.

[*He takes off his spectacles and puts them back in their case and straightens himself in his chair.* RICHARD *comes slowly in. He walks like one in a trance, his eyes shining with a dreamy happiness, his spirit still too exalted to be conscious of his surroundings, or to remember the threatened punishment. He carries his straw hat dangling in his hand, quite unaware of its existence.*]

Richard. [*Dreamily, like a ghost addressing fellow shadows.*] Hello.

Mrs. Miller. [*Staring at him worriedly.*] Hello, Richard.

Miller. [*Sizing him up shrewdly.*] Hello, Son.

[RICHARD *moves past his* MOTHER *and comes to the far corner, right front, where the light is dimmest, and sits down on the sofa, and stares before him, his hat dangling in his hand.*]

Mrs. Miller. [*With frightened suspicion now.*] Goodness, he acts queer! Nat, you don't suppose he's been——?

Miller. [*With a reassuring smile.*] No. It's love, not liquor, this time.

Mrs. Miller. [*Only partly reassured—sharply.*] Richard! What's the matter with you? [*He comes to himself with a start. She goes on scoldingly.*] How many times have I told you to hang up your hat in the hall when you come in! [*He looks at his hat as if he were surprised at its existence.*] Here, give it to me. I'll hang it up for you this once. And what are you sitting over here in the dark for? Don't forget your father's been waiting to talk to you!

[*She comes back to the table and he follows her, still half in a dream, and stands by his* FATHER'S *chair.* MRS. MILLER *starts for the hall with his hat.*]

Miller. [*Quietly but firmly now.*] You better leave Richard and me alone for a while, Essie.

Mrs. Miller. [*Turns to stare at him apprehensively.*] Well—all right—I'll go sit on the piazza. Call me if you want me. [*Then a bit pleadingly.*] But you'll remember all I've said, Nat, won't you?

[MILLER *nods reassuringly. She disappears.* RICHARD, *keenly conscious of himself as the about-to-be-sentenced criminal by this time, looks guilty and a bit defiant, searches his* FATHER'S *expressionless face with uneasy side glances, and steels himself for what is coming.*]

Miller. [*Casually, indicating* MRS. MILLER'S *chair.*] Sit down, Richard. [RICHARD *slumps awkwardly into the chair and sits in* a self-conscious, unnatural position. MILLER *sizes him up keenly—then suddenly smiles and asks with quiet mockery.*] Well, how are the vine leaves in your hair this evening?

Richard. [*Totally unprepared for this approach, shamefacedly mutters.*] I don't know, Pa.

Miller. Turned out to be poison ivy, didn't they? [*Then kindly.*] But you needn't look so alarmed. I'm not going to read you any temperance lecture. That'd bore me more than it would you. And, in spite of your damn foolishness last night, I'm still giving you credit for having brains. So I'm pretty sure anything I could say to you you've already said to yourself.

Richard. [*His head down—humbly.*] I know I was a darned fool.

Miller. [*Thinking it well to rub in this aspect—disgustedly.*] You sure were—not only a fool but a downright, stupid, disgusting fool! [RICHARD *squirms, his head still lower.*] It was bad enough for you to let me and Arthur see you, but to appear like that before your mother and Mildred——! And I wonder if Muriel would think you were so fine if she ever saw you as you looked and acted then. I think she'd give you your walking papers for keeps. And you couldn't blame her. No nice girl wants to give her love to a stupid drunk!

Richard. [*Writhing.*] I know, Pa.

Miller. [*After a pause—quietly.*] All right. Then that settles the booze end of it. [*He sizes* RICHARD *up searchingly—then suddenly speaks sharply.*] But there is another thing that's more serious. How about that tart you went to bed with at the Pleasant Beach House?

Richard. [*Flabbergasted—stammers.*] You know? But I didn't! If they've told you about her down there, they must have told you I didn't! I gave her the five dollars just so she'd let me out of it. She made everything seem rotten and dirty—and—I didn't want to do a thing like that to Muriel —no matter how bad I thought she'd treated me—even after I felt drunk, I didn't. Honest!

Miller. How'd you happen to meet this lady, anyway?

Richard. I can't tell that, Pa. I'd have to snitch on someone—and you wouldn't want me to do that.

Miller. [*A bit taken back.*] No, I suppose I wouldn't. Hmm. Well, I believe you —and I guess that settles that. [*Then, after a quick, furtive glance at* RICHARD, *he nerves himself for the ordeal and begins with a shamefaced, self-conscious solemnity.*] But listen here, Richard—hmm—it's about time you and I had a serious talk about—hmm—certain matters pertaining to—and now that the subject's come up of its own accord, it's a good time—I mean, there's no use in procrastinating further—so, here goes. [*But it doesn't go smoothly, and as he goes on he becomes more and more guiltily embarrassed and self-conscious and his expressions more stilted.* RICHARD *sedulously avoids even glancing at him, his own embarrassment made tenfold more painful by his* FATHER'S.] Richard—you have now come to the age when—well, you're a fully developed man, in a way—and it's only natural for you to have certain—hmm—desires of the flesh, to put it that way—I mean, pertaining to the opposite sex—hmm—certain natural feelings and temptations—that'll want to be gratified—and you'll want to gratify them. Hmm—well, human society being organized as it is, there's only one outlet for—unless you're a scoundrel and go around ruining decent girls,—which you're not, of course. Well, there are a certain class of women—always have been and always will be as long as human nature is what it is—— It's wrong, maybe, but what can you do about it? I mean, girls like that one you—girls there's something doing with —and lots of 'em are pretty, and it's human nature if you—— But that doesn't mean to ever get mixed up with them seriously! You just have what you want and pay 'em and forget it. I know that sounds hard and unfeeling, but we're talking facts and—— Don't think I'm encouraging you to—— If you can stay away from 'em, all the better—but—if why—hmm—— Here's what I'm driving at, Richard. They're apt to be whited sepulchres. I mean, your whole life might be ruined if—so, darn it, you've got to know how to—I mean, there are ways and means—— [*Suddenly he can go no farther and explodes helplessly.*] But, hell, I suppose you boys talk this over among yourselves and you know more about it than I do. I'll admit I'm no authority. I never had anything to do with such women, and it'll be a hell of a lot better for you if you never do!

Richard. [*Without looking at him.*] I'm never going to, Pa. [*Then shocked indignation coming into his voice.*] I don't see how you could think I could—now—when you know I love Muriel and am going to marry her. I'd die before I'd——

Miller. [*Immensely relieved—enthusiastically.*] That's the talk! By God, I'm proud of you when you talk like that! [*Then hastily.*] And now that's all of that. There's

nothing more to say and we'll forget it, eh?

Richard. [*After a pause.*] How are you going to punish me, Pa?

Miller. I *was* sort of forgetting that, wasn't I? Well, I'd thought of telling you you couldn't go to Yale——

Richard. [*Eagerly.*] Don't I have to go? Gee, that's great! Muriel thought you'd want me to go. I was telling her I'd rather you gave me a job on the paper because then she and I could get married sooner. [*Then with a boyish grin.*] Gee, Pa, you picked a lemon. That isn't any punishment. You'll have to do something besides that.

Miller. [*Grimly—but only half concealing an answering grin.*] Then you'll go to Yale and you'll stay there till you graduate, that's the answer to that! Muriel's got good sense and you haven't! [RICHARD *accepts this philosophically.*] And now we're finished. You better call your mother.

[RICHARD *calls "Ma," toward screen door, and a moment later she comes in. She glances quickly from* SON *to* HUSBAND *and immediately knows that all is well, and tactfully refrains from all questions.*]

Mrs. Miller. My, it's a beautiful night. The moon's way down low—almost setting. [*She sits in her chair and sighs contentedly.* RICHARD *remains standing by the door, staring out at the moon, his face pale in the moonlight.*]

Miller. [*With a nod at* RICHARD, *winking at his* WIFE.] Yes, I don't believe I've hardly ever seen such a beautiful night— with such a wonderful moon. Have you, Richard?

Richard. [*Turning to them—enthusiastically.*] No! It was wonderful—down at the beach——

[*He stops abruptly, smiling shyly.*]

Miller. [*Watching his* SON—*quietly.*] No, I can only remember a few nights that were as beautiful as this—and they were long ago when your mother and I were young and planning to get married.

Richard. [*Stares at them wonderingly for a moment, then quickly from his* FATHER *to his* MOTHER *and back again, strangely as if he'd never seen them before—but then suddenly his face is transfigured by a smile of understanding and sympathy. He speaks shyly.*] Yes, I'll bet those must have been wonderful nights, too. You sort of forget the moon was the same way back then— and everything.

Miller. [*A trifle huskily.*] You're all right, Richard!

Mrs. Miller. [*Fondly.*] You're a good boy, Richard.

[RICHARD *looks dreadfully shy and embarrassed at this. His* FATHER *comes to his rescue.*]

Miller. Better get to bed early tonight, Son, hadn't you?

Richard. I couldn't sleep. Can't I go out on the piazza and sit for a while—until the moon sets?

Miller. All right. Then you better say good night now. I don't know about your mother, but I'm going to bed right away. I'm dead tired.

Mrs. Miller. So am I.

Richard. [*Goes to her and kisses her.*] Good night, Ma.

Mrs. Miller. Good night. Don't you stay up till all hours now.

Richard. [*Comes to his* FATHER *and stands awkwardly before him.*] Good night, Pa.

Miller. [*Puts his arms around him and gives him a hug.*] Good night, Son. [RICHARD *turns impulsively and kisses him—then hurries out.* MILLER *stares after him, then says huskily.*] First time he's done that in years. I don't believe in kissing between fathers and sons after a certain age—seems mushy and silly—but that meant something! And I don't think we'll ever have to worry about his being safe—from himself—again. And I guess no matter what life will do to him, he can take care of it now. [*He sighs with satisfaction and, sitting down in his chair, begins to unlace his shoes.*] My darned feet are giving me fits!

Mrs. Miller. [*Laughing.*] Why do you bother unlacing your shoes now, you big goose—when we're going right up to bed?

Miller. [*As if he hadn't thought of that before, stops.*] Guess you're right. [*Then getting to his feet—with a grin.*] Mind if I don't say my prayers tonight, Essie? I'm certain God knows I'm too darned tired.

Mrs. Miller. Don't talk that way. It's real sinful. [*She gets up—then laughing fondly.*] If that isn't you all over! Always looking for an excuse to—— You're worse than Tommy! But all right. I suppose you needn't tonight. You've had a hard day. [*She puts her hand on the reading-lamp switch.*] I'm going to turn out the light. All ready?

Miller. Yep. Let her go, Gallagher. [*She turns out the lamp. In the ensuing darkness the faint moonlight shines full in through the screen door. Walking back together toward the front parlor they stand full in it for a moment, staring out.* MILLER *reaches out and puts his right arm around her and she puts her left arm around him. He says in a low voice, smilingly.*] There he is—like a statue of Love's Young Dream. [*Then he sighs and speaks with a gentle nostalgic melancholy.*] What's it that Rubaiyat says:
"Yet Ah, that Spring should vanish with the Rose!
That Youth's sweet-scented manuscript should close!"
[*Then throwing off his melancholy with a loving smile at her.*] Well, Spring isn't everything, is it, Essie? There's a lot to be said for Autumn. Autumn's got beauty, too. And Winter—if you're together!

Mrs. Miller. [*Simply.*] Yes, Nat.

[*She kisses him and then they move quietly out of the moonlight into the darkness of the front parlor.*]

CURTAIN

BLOOD WEDDING *

By
FEDERICO GARCÍA LORCA

Translated by James Graham-Lujan and Richard L. O'Connell

"BLOOD WEDDING" WILL ESTABLISH, TO any sensitive and informed reader or viewer, the heavy loss suffered by the too-early death of Federico García Lorca. In this play is sophistication, learning, modernity, high theatricality, mixed with naïveté, primitivism, savagery, and deeply human drama. In beginning and end, the play is The Mother's, the same mother as Maurya of *Riders to the Sea,* in a similar tension, suffering the same release. In between, the play is the haunted lovers', at first separate and distraught, then united as arcing wires unite, with the violence and pain and ultimately death. These are old themes, but who would call *Blood Wedding* old? García Lorca is supposed to have been inspired by a newspaper story of eloping lover and bride and pursuing bridegroom. But who sees the tawdry smudge of journalism in this play? It seems written out of assured and confident instinct for the dramatically and theatrically right, for the right word and intonation of the word, for the right gesture and gesture's shape, for the right colors in setting and light, for the right directness and the right obliquity. It is indelibly Spanish, yet it echoes and reflects not only the Irish of Synge but also the German of Gottfried von Strassbourg or Richard Wagner, the French of the symbolists, the arias and choruses of Italian opera. It is, in sum, a product of total Western culture. But its Spanishness and its firm roots are in the folk, in the feeling and in the values simple people keep. For the songs of *Blood Wedding* García Lorca wrote music, and that music sounds like folk song, as if it were anonymous.

Blood Wedding illustrates splendidly the theory lovers of the drama have always had: that drama at its highest moments needs poetry, poetry that both audience and actor recognize as poetry. Enough of *Blood Wedding* is naturalistic to mark the play as embedded in our nature-worshiping period of history. But when it moves out of nature and time into art and timelessness with the lullaby of Leonardo's Wife and Mother-in-law, and further with the Three Woodcutters, the Moon, and the Beggar-Woman, it shows what even naturalism can turn into and how it can be enriched. The method can be called paradoxical symbolism, perhaps. The women sing about the horse; he is not the over-driven horse who carries Leonardo to the Bride's country, but a horse bringing dreams and quiet sleep. Yet Leonardo's horse is in the song too; as the women sing they think of him and weep. The Moon stands for the light lovers like best, but this Moon longs for their blood to warm his chill. Imperious Death is a beggar, and the lonely woodcutters here know what has happened better than the gossipy women in the marketplace. These are the tiny surprises so needed in a drama whose course can be so easily foreseen, but how much they heighten the play! Though *Blood Wedding* is not the latest play in this collection, nor the only poetic one, it may be regarded, for its exploitation of this technique, as the most advanced. To what splendors García Lorca might have carried drama had the Spanish Civil War not occurred!

The play has been performed all over the world, made into a ballet, a motion picture, and an opera. It established itself as a classic modern play within a quarter-century of its appearance.

* Reprinted by permission of New Directions.

FEDERICO GARCÍA LORCA

Born 1899, Fuentevaqueros, Granada, Spain.
1918, Published his first book, *Impresiones y paisajes,* prose.
1923, Licentiate in Law, University of Granada.
1929, Traveled in Great Britain and the United States. Enrolled as student in Columbia University, New York City, from summer of 1929 to spring of 1930. Lectured at Columbia and at Vassar College.
1930, Lectured and traveled in Cuba. Returned to Spain in summer.
1932, Directed traveling university-theatre, "La Barraca," in Spain.
1933–1934, Traveled, lectured, and directed plays in Argentina, Uruguay, and Brazil.
1936, Killed by Falangists at Granada during the Spanish Civil War.
Poet, critic, artist, musician, and folklorist.

PLAYS

1920 *El maleficio de la mariposa* (translated under the Spanish title). 1923 *Los títeres de Cachiporra: La niña que riega la albahaca y el príncipe preguntón.* 1927 *Mariana Pineda.* 1928 *La doncella, el marinero y el estudiante.* 1928 *El paseo de Buster Keaton.* 1930 *La zapatera prodigiosa* (translated as *The Shoemaker's Prodigious Wife*). 1931 *Así que pasen cinco años* (translated as *If Five Years Pass*). 1933 *Amor de Don Perlimplín con Belisa en su jardín* (translated as *The Love of Don Perlimplín and Belisa in the Garden*). 1933 *Retablillo de Don Cristóbal.* 1933 *Bodas de sangre* (translated as *Bitter Oleander* and as *Blood Wedding*). 1934 *Yerma* (translated). 1934 *El Público* (incomplete). 1937 *Los títeres de Cachiporra: Tragicomedia de Don Cristóbal y la señá Rosita.* 1941 *Quimera.* 1945 *La casa de Bernarda Alba* (translated as *The House of Bernarda Alba*). Plays or parts of plays on which García Lorca is known to have worked may still come to light.

WRITINGS ON DRAMA

In *Obras Completas,* ed. Arturo del Hoyo (1955): "Charla sobre teatro," 33–36; "Mariana Pineda," 1533–1555; letters to Angel Ferrant, 1604–1605; interviews, 1619–1631, 1634–1636.

BLOOD WEDDING

Characters

THE MOTHER.
THE BRIDE.
THE MOTHER-IN-LAW.
LEONARDO'S WIFE.
THE SERVANT WOMAN.
THE NEIGHBOR WOMAN.
YOUNG GIRLS.

LEONARDO.
THE BRIDEGROOM.
THE BRIDE'S FATHER.
THE MOON.
DEATH (as a Beggar Woman).
WOODCUTTERS.
YOUNG MEN.

ACT ONE

SCENE I

A room painted yellow.
Bridegroom. [Entering.] Mother.
Mother. What?
Bridegroom. I'm going.
Mother. Where?
Bridegroom. To the vineyard.
                            [*He starts to go.*]
Mother. Wait.
Bridegroom. You want something?
Mother. Your breakfast, son.
Bridegroom. Forget it. I'll eat grapes. Give me the knife.
Mother. What for?
Bridegroom. [Laughing.] To cut the grapes with.
Mother. [Muttering as she looks for the knife.] Knives, knives. Cursed be all knives, and the scoundrel who invented them.
Bridegroom. Let's talk about something else.
Mother. And guns and pistols and the smallest little knife—and even hoes and pitchforks.
Bridegroom. All right.
Mother. Everything that can slice a man's body. A handsome man, full of young life, who goes out to the vineyards or to his own olive groves—his own because he's inherited them . . .
Bridegroom. [Lowering his head.] Be quiet.
Mother. . . . and then that man doesn't come back. Or if he does come back it's only for someone to cover him over with a palm leaf or a plate of rock salt so he won't bloat. I don't know how you dare carry a knife on your body—or how I let this serpent [*She takes a knife from a kitchen chest.*] stay in the chest.
Bridegroom. Have you had your say?
Mother. If I lived to be a hundred I'd talk of nothing else. First your father; to me he smelled like a carnation and I had him for barely three years. Then your brother. Oh, is it right—how can it be—that a small thing like a knife or a pistol can finish off a man—a bull of a man? No, I'll never be quiet. The months pass and the hopelessness of it stings in my eyes and even to the roots of my hair.
Bridegroom. [Forcefully.] Let's quit this talk!
Mother. No. No. Let's not quit this talk. Can anyone bring me your father back? Or your brother? Then there's the jail. What do they mean, jail? They eat there, smoke there, play music there! My dead men choking with weeds, silent, turning to dust. Two men like two beautiful flowers. The killers in jail, carefree, looking at the mountains.
Bridegroom. Do you want me to go kill them?
Mother. No . . . If I talk about it it's because . . . Oh, how can I help talking about it, seeing you go out that door? It's . . . I don't like you to carry a knife. It's just that . . . that I wish you wouldn't go out to the fields.
Bridegroom. [Laughing.] Oh, come now!
Mother. I'd like it if you were a woman. Then you wouldn't be going out to the arroyo now and we'd both of us embroider flounces and little woolly dogs.
Bridegroom. [He puts his arm around his MOTHER *and laughs.]* Mother, what if I should take you with me to the vineyards?

Mother. What would an old lady do in the vineyards? Were you going to put me down under the young vines?

Bridegroom. [*Lifting her in his arms.*] Old lady, old lady—you little old, little old lady!

Mother. Your father, he used to take me. That's the way with men of good stock; good blood. Your grandfather left a son on every corner. That's what I like. Men, men; wheat, wheat.

Bridegroom. And I, Mother?

Mother. You, what?

Bridegroom. Do I need to tell you again?

Mother. [*Seriously.*] Oh!

Bridegroom. Do you think it's bad?

Mother. No.

Bridegroom. Well, then?

Mother. I don't really know. Like this, suddenly, it always surprises me. I know the girl is good. Isn't she? Well behaved. Hard working. Kneads her bread, sews her skirts, but even so when I say her name I feel as though someone had hit me on the forehead with a rock.

Bridegroom. Foolishness.

Mother. More than foolishness. I'll be left alone. Now only you are left me—I hate to see you go.

Bridegroom. But you'll come with us.

Mother. No. I can't leave your father and brother here alone. I have to go to them every morning and if I go away it's possible one of the Félix family, one of the killers, might die—and they'd bury him next to ours. And that'll never happen! Oh, no! That'll never happen! Because I'd dig them out with my nails and, all by myself, crush them against the wall.

Bridegroom. [*Sternly.*] There you go again.

Mother. Forgive me. [*Pause.*] How long have you known her?

Bridegroom. Three years. I've been able to buy the vineyard.

Mother. Three years. She used to have another sweetheart, didn't she?

Bridegroom. I don't know. I don't think so. Girls have to look at what they'll marry.

Mother. Yes. I looked at nobody. I looked at your father, and when they killed him I looked at the wall in front of me. One woman with one man, and that's all.

Bridegroom. You know my girl's good.

Mother. I don't doubt it. All the same, I'm sorry not to have known what her mother was like.

Bridegroom. What difference does it make now?

Mother. [*Looking at him.*] Son.

Bridegroom. What is it?

Mother. That's true! You're right! When do you want me to ask for her?

Bridegroom. [*Happily.*] Does Sunday seem all right to you?

Mother. [*Seriously.*] I'll take her the bronze earrings, they're very old—and you buy her . . .

Bridegroom. You know more about that . . .

Mother. . . . you buy her some open-work stockings—and for you, two suits—three! I have no one but you now!

Bridegroom. I'm going. Tomorrow I'll go see her.

Mother. Yes, yes—and see if you can make me happy with six grandchildren—or as many as you want, since your father didn't live to give them to me.

Bridegroom. The first-born for you!

Mother. Yes, but have some girls. I want to embroider and make lace, and be at peace.

Bridegroom. I'm sure you'll love my wife.

Mother. I'll love her. [*She starts to kiss him but changes her mind.*] Go on. You're too big now for kisses. Give them to your wife. [*Pause. To herself.*] When she is your wife.

Bridegroom. I'm going.

Mother. And that land around the little mill—work it over. You've not taken good care of it.

Bridegroom. You're right. I will.

Mother. God keep you. [THE SON *goes out.* THE MOTHER *remains seated—her back to the door. A* NEIGHBOR WOMAN *with a 'kerchief on her head appears in the door.*] Come in.

Neighbor. How are you?

Mother. Just as you see me.

Neighbor. I came down to the store and stopped in to see you. We live so far away!

Mother. It's twenty years since I've been up to the top of the street.

Neighbor. You're looking well.

Mother. You think so?

Neighbor. Things happen. Two days ago they brought in my neighbor's son with both arms sliced off by the machine. [*She sits down.*]

Mother. Rafael?

Neighbor. Yes. And there you have him. Many times I've thought your son and mine are better off where they are—sleeping, resting—not running the risk of being left helpless.

Mother. Hush. That's all just something thought up—but no consolation.

Neighbor. [*Sighing.*] Ay!

Mother. [*Sighing.*] Ay!   [*Pause.*]

Neighbor. [*Sadly.*] Where's your son?
Mother. He went out.
Neighbor. He finally bought the vineyard!
Mother. He was lucky.
Neighbor. Now he'll get married.
Mother. [*As though reminded of something, she draws her chair near* THE NEIGHBOR.] Listen.
Neighbor. [*In a confidential manner.*] Yes. What is it?
Mother. You know my son's sweetheart?
Neighbor. A good girl!
Mother. Yes, but . . .
Neighbor. But who knows her really well? There's nobody. She lives out there alone with her father—so far away—fifteen miles from the nearest house. But she's a good girl. Used to being alone.
Mother. And her mother?
Neighbor. Her mother I *did* know. Beautiful. Her face glowed like a saint's— but *I* never liked her. She didn't love her husband.
Mother. [*Sternly.*] Well, what a lot of things certain people know!
Neighbor. I'm sorry. I didn't mean to offend—but it's true. Now, whether she was decent or not nobody said. That wasn't discussed. She was haughty.
Mother. There you go again!
Neighbor. You asked me.
Mother. I wish no one knew anything about them—either the live one or the dead one—that they were like two thistles no one even names but cuts off at the right moment.
Neighbor. You're right. Your son is worth a lot.
Mother. Yes—a lot. That's why I look after him. They told me the girl had a sweetheart some time ago.

Neighbor. She was about fifteen. He's been married two years now—to a cousin of hers, as a matter of fact. But nobody remembers about their engagement.
Mother. How do you remember it?
Neighbor. Oh, what questions you ask!
Mother. We like to know all about the things that hurt us. Who was the boy?
Neighbor. Leonardo.
Mother. What Leonardo?
Neighbor. Leonardo Félix.
Mother. Félix!
Neighbor. Yes, but—how is Leonardo to blame for anything? He was eight years old when those things happened.
Mother. That's true. But I hear that name—Félix—and it's all the same. [*Muttering.*] Félix, a slimy mouthful. [*She spits.*] It makes me spit—spit so I won't kill!
Neighbor. Control yourself. What good will it do?
Mother. No good. But you see how it is.
Neighbor. Don't get in the way of your son's happiness. Don't say anything to him. You're old. So am I. It's time for you and me to keep quiet.
Mother. I'll say nothing to him.
Neighbor. [*Kissing her.*] Nothing.
Mother. [*Calmly.*] Such things . . . !
Neighbor. I'm going. My men will soon be coming in from the fields.
Mother. Have you ever known such a hot sun?
Neighbor. The children carrying water out to the reapers are black with it. Goodbye, woman.
Mother. Goodbye.
[THE MOTHER *starts toward the door at the left. Halfway there she stops and slowly crosses herself.*]

CURTAIN

ACT ONE

SCENE II

A room painted rose with copperware and wreaths of common flowers. In the center of the room is a table with a tablecloth. It is morning.
[LEONARDO'S MOTHER-IN-LAW *sits in one corner holding a child in her arms and rocking it. His* WIFE *is in the other corner mending stockings.*]

Mother-in-law.
Lullaby, my baby
once there was a big horse
who didn't like water.
The water was black there
under the branches.
When it reached the bridge
it stopped and it sang.
Who can say, my baby,
what the stream holds

with its long tail
in its green parlor?
Wife. [*Softly.*]
Carnation, sleep and dream,
the horse won't drink from the stream.
Mother-in-law.
My rose, asleep now lie,
the horse is starting to cry.
His poor hooves were bleeding,
his long mane was frozen,
and deep in his eyes
stuck a silvery dagger.
Down he went to the river,
Oh, down he went down!
And his blood was running,
Oh, more than the water.
Wife.
Carnation, sleep and dream,
the horse won't drink from the stream.
Mother-in-law.
My rose, asleep now lie,
the horse is starting to cry.
Wife.
He never did touch
the dank river shore
though his muzzle was warm
and with silvery flies.
So, to the hard mountains
he could only whinny
just when the dead stream
covered his throat.
Ay-y-y, for the big horse
who didn't like water!
Ay-y-y, for the snow-wound,
big horse of the dawn!
Mother-in-law.
Don't come in! Stop him
and close up the window
with branches of dreams
and a dream of branches.
Wife.
My baby is sleeping.
Mother-in-law.
My baby is quiet.
Wife.
Look, horse, my baby
has him a pillow.
Mother-in-law.
His cradle is metal.
Wife.
His quilt a fine fabric.
Mother-in-law.
Lullaby, my baby.
Wife.
Ay-y-y, for the big horse
who didn't like water!
Mother-in-law.
Don't come near, don't come in!
Go away to the mountains
and through the grey valleys,
that's where your mare is.

Wife. [*Looking at the baby.*]
My baby is sleeping.
Mother-in-law.
My baby is resting.
Wife. [*Softly.*]
Carnation, sleep and dream,
The horse won't drink from the stream.
Mother-in-law. [*Getting up, very softly.*]
My rose, asleep now lie
for the horse is starting to cry.
[*She carries the child out.* LEONARDO
enters.]
Leonardo. Where's the baby?
Wife. He's sleeping.
Leonardo. Yesterday he wasn't well. He
cried during the night.
Wife. Today he's like a dahlia. And you?
Were you at the blacksmith's?
Leonardo. I've just come from there.
Would you believe it? For more than two
months he's been putting new shoes on the
horse and they're always coming off. As
far as I can see he pulls them off on the
stones.
Wife. Couldn't it just be that you use him
so much?
Leonardo. No. I almost never use him.
Wife. Yesterday the neighbors told me
they'd seen you on the far side of the plains.
Leonardo. Who said that?
Wife. The women who gather capers. It
certainly surprised me. Was it you?
Leonardo. No. What would I be doing
there, in that wasteland?
Wife. That's what I said. But the horse
was streaming sweat.
Leonardo. Did you see him?
Wife. No. Mother did.
Leonardo. Is she with the baby?
Wife. Yes. Do you want some lemonade?
Leonardo. With good cold water.
Wife. And then you didn't come to eat!
Leonardo. I was with the wheat weighers.
They always hold me up.
Wife. [*Very tenderly, while she makes
the lemonade.*] Did they pay you a good
price?
Leonardo. Fair.
Wife. I need a new dress and the baby a
bonnet with ribbons.
Leonardo. [*Getting up.*] I'm going to
take a look at him.
Wife. Be careful. He's asleep.
Mother-in-law. [*Coming in.*] Well! Who's
been racing the horse that way? He's down
there, worn out, his eyes popping from their
sockets as though he'd come from the ends
of the earth.
Leonardo. [*Acidly.*] I have.
Mother-in-law. Oh, excuse me! He's your
horse.

Wife. [*Timidly.*] He was at the wheat buyers.

Mother-in-law. He can burst for all of me!   [*She sits down. Pause.*]

Wife. Your drink. Is it cold?

Leonardo. Yes.

Wife. Did you hear they're going to ask for my cousin?

Leonardo. When?

Wife. Tomorrow. The wedding will be within a month. I hope they're going to invite us.

Leonardo. [*Gravely.*] I don't know.

Mother-in-law. His mother, I think, wasn't very happy about the match.

Leonardo. Well, she may be right. She's a girl to be careful with.

Wife. I don't like to have you thinking bad things about a good girl.

Mother-in-law. [*Meaningfully.*] If he does, it's because he knows her. Didn't you know he courted her for three years?

Leonardo. But I left her. [*To his* WIFE.] Are you going to cry now? Quit that! [*He brusquely pulls her hands away from her face.*] Let's go see the baby.

[*They go in with their arms around each other. A* GIRL *appears. She is happy. She enters running.*]

Girl. Señora.

Mother-in-law. What is it?

Girl. The groom came to the store and he's bought the best of everything they had.

Mother-in-law. Was he alone?

Girl. No. With his mother. Stern, tall. [*She imitates her.*] And such extravagance!

Mother-in-law. They have money.

Girl. And they bought some open-work stockings! Oh, such stockings! A woman's dream of stockings! Look: a swallow here, [*She points to her ankle.*] a ship here, [*She points to her calf.*] and here, [*She points to her thigh.*] a rose!

Mother-in-law. Child!

Girl. A rose with the seeds and the stem! Oh! All in silk.

Mother-in-law. Two rich families are being brought together.

[LEONARDO *and his* WIFE *appear.*]

Girl. I came to tell you what they're buying.

Leonardo. [*Loudly.*] We don't care.

Wife. Leave her alone.

Mother-in-law. Leonardo, it's not that important.

Girl. Please excuse me.
            [*She leaves, weeping.*]

Mother-in-law. Why do you always have to make trouble with people?

Leonardo. I didn't ask for your opinion.
            [*He sits down.*]

Mother-in-law. Very well.   [*Pause.*]

Wife. [*To* LEONARDO.] What's the matter with you? What idea've you got boiling there inside your head? Don't leave me like this, not knowing anything.

Leonardo. Stop that.

Wife. No. I want you to look at me and tell me.

Leonardo. Let me alone.   [*He rises.*]

Wife. Where are you going, love?

Leonardo. [*Sharply.*] Can't you shut up?

Mother-in-law. [*Energetically, to her* DAUGHTER.] Be quiet! [LEONARDO *goes out.*] The baby!

[*She goes into the bedroom and comes out again with the baby in her arms.* THE WIFE *has remained standing, unmoving.*]

Mother-in-law.
  His poor hooves were bleeding,
  his long mane was frozen,
  and deep in his eyes
  stuck a silvery dagger.
  Down he went to the river,
  Oh, down he went down!
  And his blood was running,
  Oh, more than the water.

Wife. [*Turning slowly, as though dreaming.*]
  Carnation, sleep and dream,
  the horse is drinking from the stream.

Mother-in-law.
  My rose, asleep now lie
  the horse is starting to cry.

Wife.
  Lullaby, my baby.

Mother-in-law.
  Ay-y-y, for the big horse
  who didn't like water!

Wife. [*Dramatically.*]
  Don't come near, don't come in!
  Go away to the mountains!
  Ay-y-y, for the snow-wound,
  big horse of the dawn!

Mother-in-law. [*Weeping.*]
  My baby is sleeping . . .

Wife. [*Weeping, as she slowly moves closer.*]
  My baby is resting . . .

Mother-in-law.
  Carnation, sleep and dream,
  the horse won't drink from the stream.

Wife. [*Weeping, and leaning on the table.*]
  My rose, asleep now lie,
  the horse is starting to cry.

CURTAIN

ACT ONE

SCENE III

Interior of the cave where THE BRIDE *lives. At the back is a cross of large rose-colored flowers. The rounded doors have lace curtains with rose-colored ties. Around the walls, which are of a white and hard material, are round fans, blue jars, and little mirrors.*

Servant. Come right in . . . [*She is very affable, full of humble hypocrisy.* THE BRIDEGROOM *and his* MOTHER *enter.* THE MOTHER *is dressed in black satin and wears a lace mantilla;* THE BRIDEGROOM *in black corduroy with a great golden chain.*] Won't you sit down? They'll be right here.

[*She leaves.* THE MOTHER *and* SON *are left sitting motionless as statues. Long pause.*]

Mother. Did you wear the watch?

Bridegroom. Yes.

    [*He takes it out and looks at it.*]

Mother. We have to be back on time. How far away these people live!

Bridegroom. But this is good land.

Mother. Good; but much too lonesome. A four-hour trip and not one house, not one tree.

Bridegroom. This is the wasteland.

Mother. Your father would have covered it with trees.

Bridegroom. Without water?

Mother. He would have found some. In the three years we were married he planted ten cherry trees, [*Remembering.*] those three walnut trees by the mill, a whole vineyard and a plant called Jupiter which had scarlet flowers—but it dried up.   [*Pause.*]

Bridegroom. [*Referring to* THE BRIDE.] She must be dressing.

[THE BRIDE'S FATHER *enters. He is very old, with shining white hair. His head is bowed.* THE MOTHER *and* THE BRIDEGROOM *rise. They shake hands in silence.*]

Father. Was it a long trip?

Mother. Four hours.   [*They sit down.*]

Father. You must have come the longest way.

Mother. I'm too old to come along the cliffs by the river.

Bridegroom. She gets dizzy.   [*Pause.*]

Father. A good hemp harvest.

Bridegroom. A really good one.

Father. When I was young this land didn't even grow hemp. We've had to punish it, even weep over it, to make it give us anything useful.

Mother. But now it does. Don't complain. I'm not here to ask you for anything.

Father. [*Smiling.*] You're richer than I. Your vineyards are worth a fortune. Each young vine a silver coin. But—do you know?—what bothers me is that our lands are separated. I like to have everything together. One thorn I have in my heart, and that's the little orchard there, stuck in between my fields—and they won't sell it to me for all the gold in the world.

Bridegroom. That's the way it always is.

Father. If we could just take twenty teams of oxen and move your vineyards over here, and put them down on that hillside, how happy I'd be!

Mother. But why?

Father. What's mine is hers and what's yours is his. That's why. Just to see it all together. How beautiful it is to bring things together!

Bridegroom. And it would be less work.

Mother. When I die, you could sell ours and buy here, right alongside.

Father. Sell, sell? Bah! Buy, my friend, buy everything. If I had had sons I would have bought all this mountainside right up to the part with the stream. It's not good land, but strong arms can make it good, and since no people pass by, they don't steal your fruit and you can sleep in peace.   [*Pause.*]

Mother. You know what I'm here for.

Father. Yes.

Mother. And?

Father. It seems all right to me. They have talked it over.

Mother. My son has money and knows how to manage it.

Father. My daughter too.

Mother. My son is handsome. He's never known a woman. His good name cleaner than a sheet spread out in the sun.

Father. No need to tell you about my daughter. At three, when the morning star shines, she prepares the bread. She never talks: soft as wool, she embroiders all kinds of fancy work and she can cut a strong cord with her teeth.

Mother. God bless her house.

Father. May God bless it.

[THE SERVANT *appears with two trays. One with drinks and the other with sweets.*]

Mother. [*To* THE SON.] When would you like the wedding?

Bridegroom. Next Thursday.

Father. The day on which she'll be exactly twenty-two years old.

Mother. Twenty-two! My oldest son would be that age if he were alive. Warm and manly as he was, he'd be living now if men hadn't invented knives.

Father. One mustn't think about that.

Mother. Every minute. Always a hand on your breast.

Father. Thursday, then? Is that right?

Bridegroom. That's right.

Father. You and I and the bridal couple will go in a carriage to the church which is very far from here; the wedding party on the carts and horses they'll bring with them.

Mother. Agreed.

[THE SERVANT *passes through.*]

Father. Tell her she may come in now. [*To* THE MOTHER.] I shall be much pleased if you like her.

[THE BRIDE *appears. Her hands fall in a modest pose and her head is bowed.*]

Mother. Come here. Are you happy?

Bride. Yes, señora.

Father. You shouldn't be so solemn. After all, she's going to be your mother.

Bride. I'm happy. I've said "yes" because I wanted to.

Mother. Naturally. [*She takes her by the chin.*] Look at me.

Father. She resembles my wife in every way.

Mother. Yes? What a beautiful glance! Do you know what it is to be married, child?

Bride. [*Seriously.*] I do.

Mother. A man, some children and a wall two yards thick for everything else.

Bridegroom. Is anything else needed?

Mother. No. Just that you all live—that's it! Live long!

Bride. I'll know how to keep my word.

Mother. Here are some gifts for you.

Bride. Thank you.

Father. Shall we have something?

Mother. Nothing for me. [*To* THE SON.] But you?

Bridegroom. Yes, thank you.

[*He takes one sweet,* THE BRIDE *another.*]

Father. [*To* THE BRIDEGROOM.] Wine?

Mother. He doesn't touch it.

Father. All the better.

[*Pause. All are standing.*]

Bridegroom. [*To* THE BRIDE.] I'll come tomorrow.

Bride. What time?

Bridegroom. Five.

Bride. I'll be waiting for you.

Bridegroom. When I leave your side I feel a great emptiness, and something like a knot in my throat.

Bride. When you are my husband you won't have it any more.

Bridegroom. That's what I tell myself.

Mother. Come. The sun doesn't wait. [*To* THE FATHER.] Are we agreed on everything?

Father. Agreed.

Mother. [*To* THE SERVANT.] Goodbye, woman.

Servant. God go with you!

[THE MOTHER *kisses* THE BRIDE *and they begin to leave in silence.*]

Mother. [*At the door.*] Goodbye, daughter.

[THE BRIDE *answers with her hand.*]

Father. I'll go out with you.

[*They leave.*]

Servant. I'm bursting to see the presents.

Bride. [*Sharply.*] Stop that!

Servant. Oh, child, show them to me.

Bride. I don't want to.

Servant. At least the stockings. They say they're all open work. Please!

Bride. I said no.

Servant. Well, my Lord. All right then. It looks as if you didn't want to get married.

Bride. [*Biting her hand in anger.*] Ay-y-y!

Servant. Child, child! What's the matter with you? Are you sorry to give up your queen's life? Don't think of bitter things. Have you any reason to? None. Let's look at the presents. [*She takes the box.*]

Bride. [*Holding her by the wrists.*] Let go.

Servant. Ay-y-y, girl!

Bride. Let go, I said.

Servant. You're stronger than a man.

Bride. Haven't I done a man's work? I wish I were.

Servant. Don't talk like that.

Bride. Quiet, I said. Let's talk about something else.

[*The light is fading from the stage. Long pause.*]

Servant. Did you hear a horse last night?

Bride. What time?

Servant. Three.

Bride. It might have been a stray horse— from the herd.

Servant. No. It carried a rider.

Bride. How do you know?

Servant. Because I saw him. He was standing by your window. It shocked me greatly.

Bride. Maybe it was my fiancé. Sometimes he comes by at that time.

Servant. No.

Bride. You saw him?
Servant. Yes.
Bride. Who was it?
Servant. It was Leonardo.
Bride. [Strongly.] Liar! You liar! Why should he come here?

Servant. He came.
Bride. Shut up! Shut your cursed mouth.
[The sound of a horse is heard.]
Servant. [At the window.] Look. Lean out. Was it Leonardo?
Bride. It was!

QUICK CURTAIN

ACT TWO

SCENE I

The entrance hall of THE BRIDE's house. A large door in the back. It is night.
[THE BRIDE enters wearing ruffled white petticoats full of laces and embroidered bands, and a sleeveless white bodice. THE SERVANT is dressed the same way.]

Servant. I'll finish combing your hair out here.
Bride. It's too warm to stay in there.
Servant. In this country it doesn't even cool off at dawn.
[THE BRIDE sits on a low chair and looks into a little hand mirror. THE SERVANT combs her hair.]
Bride. My mother came from a place with lots of trees—from a fertile country.
Servant. And she was so happy!
Bride. But she wasted away here.
Servant. Fate.
Bride. As we're all wasting away here. The very walls give off heat. Ay-y-y! Don't pull so hard.
Servant. I'm only trying to fix this wave better. I want it to fall over your forehead. [THE BRIDE looks at herself in the mirror.] How beautiful you are! Ay-y-y!
[She kisses her passionately.]
Bride. [Seriously.] Keep right on combing.
Servant. [Combing.] Oh, lucky you—going to put your arms around a man; and kiss him; and feel his weight.
Bride. Hush.
Servant. And the best part will be when you'll wake up and you'll feel him at your side and when he caresses your shoulders with his breath, like a little nightingale's feather.
Bride. [Sternly.] Will you be quiet?
Servant. But, child! What is a wedding? A wedding is just that and nothing more. Is it the sweets—or the bouquets of flowers?

No. It's a shining bed and a man and a woman.
Bride. But you shouldn't talk about it.
Servant. Oh, that's something else again. But fun enough too.
Bride. Or bitter enough.
Servant. I'm going to put the orange blossoms on from here to here, so the wreath will shine out on top of your hair.
[She tries on the sprigs of orange blossom.]
Bride. [Looking at herself in the mirror.] Give it to me.
[She takes the wreath, looks at it and lets her head fall in discouragement.]
Servant. Now what's the matter?
Bride. Leave me alone.
Servant. This is no time for you to start feeling sad. [Encouragingly.] Give me the wreath. [THE BRIDE takes the wreath and hurls it away.] Child! You're just asking God to punish you, throwing the wreath on the floor like that. Raise your head! Don't you want to get married? Say it. You can still withdraw.   [THE BRIDE rises.]
Bride. Storm clouds. A chill wind that cuts through my heart. Who hasn't felt it?
Servant. You love your sweetheart, don't you?
Bride. I love him.
Servant. Yes, yes. I'm sure you do.
Bride. But this is a very serious step.
Servant. You've got to take it.
Bride. I've already given my word.
Servant. I'll put on the wreath.
Bride. [She sits down.] Hurry. They should be arriving by now.
Servant. They've already been at least two hours on the way.
Bride. How far is it from here to the church?
Servant. Five leagues by the stream, but twice that by the road.
[THE BRIDE rises and THE SERVANT grows excited as she looks at her.]

Servant.
    Awake, O Bride, awaken,
    On your wedding morning waken!
    The world's rivers may all
    Bear along your bridal Crown!
Bride. [*Smiling.*] Come now.
Servant. [*Enthusiastically kissing her and dancing around her.*]
    Awake,
    with the fresh bouquet
    of flowering laurel.
    Awake,
    by the trunk and branch
    of the laurels!
    [*The banging of the front door latch is heard.*]
Bride. Open the door! That must be the first guests.
    [*She leaves.* THE SERVANT *opens the door.*]
Servant. [*In astonishment.*] You!
Leonardo. Yes, me. Good morning.
Servant. The first one!
Leonardo. Wasn't I invited?
Servant. Yes.
Leonardo. That's why I'm here.
Servant. Where's your wife?
Leonardo. I came on my horse. She's coming by the road.
Servant. Didn't you meet anyone?
Leonardo. I *passed* them on my horse.
Servant. You're going to kill that horse with so much racing.
Leonardo. When he dies, he's dead!
                                [*Pause.*]
Servant. Sit down. Nobody's up yet.
Leonardo. Where's the bride?
Servant. I'm just on my way to dress her.
Leonardo. The bride! She ought to be happy!
Servant. [*Changing the subject.*] How's the baby?
Leonardo. What baby?
Servant. Your son.
Leonardo. [*Remembering, as though in a dream.*] Ah!
Servant. Are they bringing him?
Leonardo. No.
                [*Pause. Voices sing distantly.*]
Voices.
    Awake, O Bride, awaken,
    On your wedding morning waken!
Leonardo.
    Awake, O Bride, awaken,
    On your wedding morning waken!
Servant. It's the guests. They're still quite a way off.
Leonardo. The bride's going to wear a big wreath, isn't she? But it ought not to be so large. One a little smaller would look better

on her. Has the groom already brought her the orange blossom that must be worn on the breast?
Bride. [*Appearing, still in petticoats and wearing the wreath.*] He brought it.
Servant. [*Sternly.*] Don't come out like that.
Bride. What does it matter? [*Seriously.*] Why do you ask if they brought the orange blossom? Do you have something in mind?
Leonardo. Nothing. What would I have in mind? [*Drawing near her.*] You, you know me; you know I don't. Tell me so. What have I ever meant to you? Open your memory, refresh it. But two oxen and an ugly little hut are almost nothing. That's the thorn.
Bride. What have you come here to do?
Leonardo. To see your wedding.
Bride. Just as I saw yours!
Leonardo. Tied up by you, done with your two hands. Oh, they can kill me but they can't spit on me. But even money, which shines so much, spits sometimes.
Bride. Liar!
Leonardo. I don't want to talk. I'm hot-blooded and I don't want to shout so all these hills will hear me.
Bride. My shouts would be louder.
Servant. You'll have to stop talking like this. [*To* THE BRIDE.] You don't have to talk about what's past.
    [THE SERVANT *looks around uneasily at the doors.*]
Bride. She's right. I shouldn't even talk to you. But it offends me to the soul that you come here to watch me, and spy on my wedding, and ask about the orange blossom with something on your mind. Go and wait for your wife at the door.
Leonardo. But can't you and I even talk?
Servant. [*With rage.*] No! No, you can't talk.
Leonardo. Ever since I got married I've been thinking night and day about whose fault it was, and every time I think about it, out comes a new fault to eat up the old one; but always there's a fault left!
Bride. A man with a horse knows a lot of things and can do a lot to ride roughshod over a girl stuck out in the desert. But I have my pride. And that's why I'm getting married. I'll lock myself in with my husband and then I'll have to love him above everyone else.
Leonardo. Pride won't help you a bit.
                    [*He draws near to her.*]
Bride. Don't come near me!
Leonardo. To burn with desire and keep

quiet about it is the greatest punishment we can bring on ourselves. What good was pride to me—and not seeing you, and letting you lie awake night after night? No good! It only served to bring the fire down on me! You think that time heals and walls hide things, but it isn't true, it isn't true! When things get that deep inside you there isn't anybody can change them.

Bride. [*Trembling.*] I can't listen to you. I can't listen to your voice. It's as though I'd drunk a bottle of anise and fallen asleep wrapped in a quilt of roses. It pulls me along, and I know I'm drowning—but I go on down.

Servant. [*Seizing* LEONARDO *by the lapels.*] You've got to go right now!

Leonardo. This is the last time I'll ever talk to her. Don't you be afraid of anything.

Bride. And I know I'm crazy and I know my breast rots with longing; but here I am—calmed by hearing him, by just seeing him move his arms.

Leonardo. I'd never be at peace if I didn't tell you these things. I got married. Now you get married.

Servant. But she *is* getting married!

[*Voices are heard singing, nearer.*]

Voices.
Awake, O Bride, awaken,
On your wedding morning waken!

Bride.
Awake, O Bride, awaken!

[*She goes out, running toward her room.*]

Servant. The people are here now. [*To* LEONARDO.] Don't you come near her again.

Leonardo. Don't worry.

[*He goes out to the left. Day begins to break.*]

First Girl. [*Entering.*]
Awake, O Bride, awaken,
the morning you're to marry;
sing round and dance round;
balconies a wreath must carry.

Voices.
Bride, awaken!

Servant. [*Creating enthusiasm.*]
Awake,
with the green bouquet
of love in flower.
Awake,
by the trunk and the branch
of the laurels!

Second Girl. [*Entering.*]
Awake,
with her long hair,
snowy sleeping gown,
patent leather boots with silver—
her forehead jasmines crown.

Servant.
Oh, shepherdess,
the moon begins to shine!

First Girl.
Oh, gallant,
leave your hat beneath the vine!

First Young Man. [*Entering, holding his hat on high.*]
Bride, awaken,
for over the fields
the wedding draws nigh
with trays heaped with dahlias
and cakes piled high.

Voices.
Bride, awaken!

Second Girl.
The bride
has set her white wreath in place
and the groom
ties it on with a golden lace.

Servant.
By the orange tree,
sleepless the bride will be.

Third Girl. [*Entering.*]
By the citron vine,
gifts from the groom will shine.
[*Three* GUESTS *come in.*]

First Youth.
Dove, awaken!
In the dawn
shadowy bells are shaken.

Guest.
The bride, the white bride
today a maiden,
tomorrow a wife.

First Girl.
Dark one, come down
trailing the train of your silken gown.

Guest.
Little dark one, come down,
cold morning wears a dewy crown.

First Youth.
Awaken, wife, awake,
orange blossoms the breezes shake.

Servant.
A tree I would embroider her
with garnet sashes wound,
And on each sash a cupid,
with "Long Live" all around.

Voices.
Bride, awaken.

First Youth.
The morning you're to marry!

Guest.
The morning you're to marry
how elegant you'll seem;
worthy, mountain flower,
of a captain's dream.

Father. [*Entering.*]
A captain's wife

the groom will marry.
He comes with his oxen the treasure to
   carry!
Third Girl.
The groom
is like a flower of gold.
When he walks,
blossoms at his feet unfold.
Servant.
Oh, my lucky girl!
Second Youth.
Bride, awaken.
Servant.
Oh, my elegant girl!
First Girl.
Through the windows
hear the wedding shout.
Second Girl.
Let the bride come out.
First Girl.
Come out, come out!
Servant.
Let the bells
ring and ring out clear!
First Youth.
For here she comes!
For now she's near!
Servant.
Like a bull, the wedding
is arising here!
[THE BRIDE *appears. She wears a black
dress in the style of 1900, with a bustle
and large train covered with pleated
gauzes and heavy laces. Upon her
hair, brushed in a wave over her fore-
head, she wears an orange blossom
wreath. Guitars sound. The* GIRLS *kiss*
THE BRIDE.]
Third Girl. What scent did you put on
your hair?
Bride. [*Laughing.*] None at all.
Second Girl. [*Looking at her dress.*] This
cloth is what you can't get.
First Youth. Here's the groom!
Bridegroom. Salud!
First Girl. [*Putting a flower behind his
ear.*]
The groom
is like a flower of gold.
Second Girl.
Quiet breezes
from his eyes unfold.
[THE GROOM *goes to* THE BRIDE.]
Bride. Why did you put on those
shoes?
Bridegroom. They're gayer than the black
ones.
Leonardo's Wife. [*Entering and kissing*
THE BRIDE.] Salud!
[*They all speak excitedly.*]

Leonardo. [*Entering as one who performs
a duty.*]
The morning you're to marry
We give you a wreath to wear.
Leonardo's Wife.
So the fields may be made happy
with the dew dropped from your hair!
Mother. [*To* THE FATHER.] Are those
people here, too?
Father. They're part of the family. To-
day is a day of forgiveness!
Mother. I'll put up with it, but I don't
forgive.
Bridegroom. With your wreath, it's a joy
to look at you!
Bride. Let's go to the church quickly.
Bridegroom. Are you in a hurry?
Bride. Yes. I want to be your wife right
now so that I can be with you alone, not
hearing any voice but yours.
Bridegroom. That's what I want!
Bride. And not seeing any eyes but yours.
And for you to hug me so hard that even
though my dead mother should call me I
wouldn't be able to draw away from you.
Bridegroom. My arms are strong. I'll hug
you for forty years without stopping.
Bride. [*Taking his arm, dramatically.*]
Forever!
Father. Quick now! Round up the teams
and carts! The sun's already out.
Mother. And go along carefully! Let's
hope nothing goes wrong.
[*The great door in the background
opens.*]
Servant. [*Weeping.*]
As you set out from your house,
oh, maiden white,
remember you leave shining
with a star's light.
First Girl.
Clean of body, clean of clothes
from her home to church she goes.
            [*They start leaving.*]
Second Girl.
Now you leave your home
for the church!
Servant.
The wind sets flowers
on the sands.
Third Girl.
Ah, the white maid!
Servant.
Dark winds are the lace
of her mantilla.
[*They leave. Guitars, castanets and
tambourines are heard.* LEONARDO *and
his* WIFE *are left alone.*]
Wife. Let's go.
Leonardo. Where?

Wife. To the church. But not on your horse. You're coming with me.

Leonardo. In the cart?

Wife. Is there anything else?

Leonardo. I'm not the kind of man to ride in a cart.

Wife. Nor I the wife to go to a wedding without her husband. I can't stand any more of this!

Leonardo. Neither can I!

Wife. And why do you look at me that way? With a thorn in each eye.

Leonardo. Let's go!

Wife. I don't know what's happening. But I think, and I don't want to think. One thing I do know. I'm already cast off by you. But I have a son. And another coming. And so it goes. My mother's fate was the same. Well, I'm not moving from here.

Voices. [*Outside.*]
    As you set out from your home
    and to the church go
    remember you leave shining
    with a star's glow.

Wife. [*Weeping.*]
    Remember you leave shining
    with a star's glow!
I left my house like that too. They could have stuffed the whole countryside in my mouth. I was that trusting.

Leonardo. [*Rising.*] Let's go!

Wife. But you with me!

Leonardo. Yes. [*Pause.*] Start moving!
                                [*They leave.*]

Voices.
    As you set out from your home
    and to the church go,
    remember you leave shining
    with a star's glow.

SLOW CURTAIN

ACT TWO

SCENE II

The exterior of THE BRIDE's *Cave Home, in white gray and cold blue tones. Large cactus trees. Shadowy and silver tones. Panoramas of light tan tablelands, everything hard like a landscape in popular ceramics.*

Servant. [*Arranging glasses and trays on a table.*]
    A-turning,
    the wheel was a-turning
    and the water was flowing,
    for the wedding night comes.
    May the branches part
    and the moon be arrayed
    at her white balcony rail.
[*In a loud voice.*] Set out the tablecloths!
                [*In a pathetic voice.*]
    A-singing,
    bride and groom were singing
    and the water was flowing
    for their wedding night comes.
    Oh, rime-frost, flash!—
    and almonds bitter
    fill with honey!
[*In a loud voice.*] Get the wine ready!
                [*In a poetic tone.*]
    Elegant girl,
    most elegant in the world,
    see the way the water is flowing,
    for your wedding night comes.
    Hold your skirts close in
    under the bridegroom's wing
    and never leave your house,
    for the Bridegroom is a dove
    with his breast a firebrand
    and the fields wait for the whisper
    of spurting blood.
    A-turning
    the wheel was a-turning
    and the water was flowing
    and your wedding night comes.
    Oh, water, sparkle!

Mother. [*Entering.*] At last!

Father. Are we the first ones?

Servant. No. Leonardo and his wife arrived a while ago. They drove like demons. His wife got here dead with fright. They made the trip as though they'd come on horseback.

Father. That one's looking for trouble. He's not of good blood.

Mother. What blood would you expect him to have? His whole family's blood. It comes down from his great-grandfather, who started in killing, and it goes on down through the whole evil breed of knife-wielding and false-smiling men.

Father. Let's leave it at that!

Servant. But how can she leave it at that?

Mother. It hurts me to the tips of my veins. On the forehead of all of them I see only the hand with which they killed what was mine. Can you really see me? Don't I seem mad to you? Well, it's the madness of not having shrieked out all my breast needs to. Always in my breast there's a shriek standing tiptoe that I have to beat down and hold in under my shawls. But the dead are carried off and one has to keep still. And then, people find fault.
[*She removes her shawl.*]
Father. Today's not the day for you to be remembering these things.
Mother. When the talk turns on it, I have to speak. And more so today. Because today I'm left alone in my house.
Father. But with the expectation of having someone with you.
Mother. That's my hope: grandchildren.
[*They sit down.*]
Father. I want them to have a lot of them. This land needs hands that aren't hired. There's a battle to be waged against weeds, the thistles, the big rocks that come from one doesn't know where. And those hands have to be the owner's, who chastises and dominates, who makes the seeds grow. Lots of sons are needed.
Mother. And some daughters! Men are like the wind! They're forced to handle weapons. Girls never go out into the street.
Father. [*Happily.*] I think they'll have both.
Mother. My son will cover her well. He's of good seed. His father could have had many sons with me.
Father. What I'd like is to have all this happen in a day. So that right away they'd have two or three boys.
Mother. But it's not like that. It takes a long time. That's why it's so terrible to see one's own blood spilled out on the ground. A fountain that spurts for a minute, but costs us years. When I got to my son, he lay fallen in the middle of the street. I wet my hands with his blood and licked them with my tongue—because it was my blood. You don't know what that's like. In a glass and topaz shrine I'd put the earth moistened by his blood.
Father. Now you must hope. My daughter is wide-hipped and your son is strong.
Mother. That's why I'm hoping.
[*They rise.*]
Father. Get the wheat trays ready!
Servant. They're all ready.
Leonardo's Wife. [*Entering.*] May it be for the best!

Mother. Thank you.
Leonardo. Is there going to be a celebration?
Father. A small one. People can't stay long.
Servant. Here they are!
[GUESTS *begin entering in gay groups.* THE BRIDE *and* GROOM *come in arm-in-arm.* LEONARDO *leaves.*]
Bridegroom. There's never been a wedding with so many people!
Bride. [*Sullen.*] Never.
Father. It was brilliant.
Mother. Whole branches of families came.
Bridegroom. People who never went out of the house.
Mother. Your father sowed well, and now you're reaping it.
Bridegroom. There were cousins of mine whom I no longer knew.
Mother. All the people from the seacoast.
Bridegroom. [*Happily.*] They were frightened of the horses. [*They talk.*]
Mother. [*To* THE BRIDE.] What are you thinking about?
Bride. I'm not thinking about anything.
Mother. Your blessings weigh heavily.
[*Guitars are heard.*]
Bride. Like lead.
Mother. [*Stern.*] But they shouldn't weigh so. Happy as a dove you ought to be.
Bride. Are you staying here tonight?
Mother. No. My house is empty.
Bride. You ought to stay!
Father. [*To* THE MOTHER.] Look at the dance they're forming. Dances of the far away seashore.
[LEONARDO *enters and sits down. His* WIFE *stands rigidly behind him.*]
Mother. They're my husband's cousins. Stiff as stones at dancing.
Father. It makes me happy to watch them. What a change for this house!
[*He leaves.*]
Bridegroom. [*To* THE BRIDE.] Did you like the orange blossom?
Bride. [*Looking at him fixedly.*] Yes.
Bridegroom. It's all of wax. It will last forever. I'd like you to have had them all over your dress.
Bride. No need of that.
[LEONARDO *goes off to the right.*]
First Girl. Let's go and take out your pins.
Bride. [*To* THE GROOM.] I'll be right back.
Leonardo's Wife. I hope you'll be happy with my cousin!
Bridegroom. I'm sure I will.
Leonardo's Wife. The two of you here;

never going out; building a home. I wish I could live far away like this, too!

Bridegroom. Why don't you buy land? The mountainside is cheap and children grow up better.

Leonardo's Wife. We don't have any money. And at the rate we're going . . . !

Bridegroom. Your husband is a good worker.

Leonardo's Wife. Yes, but he likes to fly around too much; from one thing to another. He's not a patient man.

Servant. Aren't you having anything? I'm going to wrap up some wine cakes for your mother. She likes them so much.

Bridegroom. Put up three dozen for her.

Leonardo's Wife. No, no. A half-dozen's enough for her!

Bridegroom. But today's a day!

Leonardo's Wife. [*To* THE SERVANT.] Where's Leonardo?

Bridegroom. He must be with the guests.

Leonardo's Wife. I'm going to go see.
                        [*She leaves.*]

Servant. [*Looking off at the dance.*] That's beautiful there.

Bridegroom. Aren't you dancing?

Servant. No one will ask me.

     [TWO GIRLS *pass across the back of the stage; during this whole scene the background should be an animated crossing of figures.*]

Bridegroom. [*Happily.*] They just don't know anything. Lively old girls like you dance better than the young ones.

Servant. Well! Are you tossing me a compliment, boy? What a family yours is! Men among men! As a little girl I saw your grandfather's wedding. What a figure! It seemed as if a mountain were getting married.

Bridegroom. I'm not as tall.

Servant. But there's the same twinkle in your eye. Where's the girl?

Bridegroom. Taking off her wreath.

Servant. Ah! Look. For midnight, since you won't be sleeping, I have prepared ham for you, and some large glasses of old wine. On the lower shelf of the cupboard. In case you need it.

Bridegroom. [*Smiling.*] I won't be eating at midnight.

Servant. [*Slyly.*] If not you, maybe the bride.   [*She leaves.*]

First Youth. [*Entering.*] You've got to come have a drink with us!

Bridegroom. I'm waiting for the bride.

Second Youth. You'll have her at dawn!

First Youth. That's when it's best!

Second Youth. Just for a minute.

Bridegroom. Let's go.

     [*They leave. Great excitement is heard.* THE BRIDE *enters. From the opposite side* TWO GIRLS *come running to meet her.*]

First Girl. To whom did you give the first pin; me or this one?

Bride. I don't remember.

First Girl. To me, you gave it to me here.

Second Girl. To me, in front of the altar.

Bride. [*Uneasily, with a great inner struggle.*] I don't know anything about it.

First Girl. It's just that I wish you'd . . .

Bride. [*Interrupting.*] Nor do I care. I have a lot to think about.

Second Girl. Your pardon.

     [LEONARDO *crosses at the rear of the stage.*]

Bride. [*She sees* LEONARDO.] And this is an upsetting time.

First Girl. We wouldn't know anything about that!

Bride. You'll know about it when your time comes. This step is a very hard one to take.

First Girl. Has she offended you?

Bride. No. You must pardon me.

Second Girl. What for? But *both* the pins are good for getting married, aren't they?

Bride. Both of them.

First Girl. Maybe now one will get married before the other.

Bride. Are you so eager?

Second Girl. [*Shyly.*] Yes.

Bride. Why?

First Girl. Well . . .

     [*She embraces* THE SECOND GIRL. *Both go running off.* THE GROOM *comes in very slowly and embraces* THE BRIDE *from behind.*]

Bride. [*In sudden fright.*] Let go of me!

Bridegroom. Are you frightened of me?

Bride. Ay-y-y! It's you?

Bridegroom. Who else would it be? [*Pause.*] Your father or me.

Bride. That's true!

Bridegroom. Of course, your father would have hugged you more gently.

Bride. [*Darkly.*] Of course!

Bridegroom. [*Embracing her strongly and a little bit brusquely.*] Because he's old.

Bride. [*Curtly.*] Let me go!

Bridegroom. Why?   [*He lets her go.*]

Bride. Well . . . the people. They can see us.

     [THE SERVANT *crosses at the back of the stage again without looking at* THE BRIDE *and* BRIDEGROOM.]

Bridegroom. What of it? It's consecrated now.

Bride. Yes, but let me be . . . Later.

Bridegroom. What's the matter with you? You look frightened!

Bride. I'm all right. Don't go.

Leonardo's Wife. [*Enters.*] I don't mean to intrude . . .

Bridegroom. What is it?

Leonardo's Wife. Did my husband come through here?

Bridegroom. No.

Leonardo's Wife. Because I can't find him, and his horse isn't in the stable either.

Bridegroom. [*Happily.*] He must be out racing it.

[THE WIFE *leaves, troubled.* THE SERVANT *enters.*]

Servant. Aren't you two proud and happy with so many good wishes?

Bridegroom. I wish it were over with. The bride is a little tired.

Servant. That's no way to act, child.

Bride. It's as though I'd been struck on the head.

Servant. A bride from these mountains must be strong. [*To* THE GROOM.] You're the only one who can cure her, because she's yours.   [*She goes running off.*]

Bridegroom. [*Embracing* THE BRIDE.] Let's go dance a little.   [*He kisses her.*]

Bride. [*Worried.*] No. I'd like to stretch out on my bed a little.

Bridegroom. I'll keep you company.

Bride. Never! With all these people here? What would they say? Let me be quiet for a moment.

Bridegroom. Whatever you say! But don't be like that tonight!

Bride. [*At the door.*] I'll be better tonight.

Bridegroom. That's what I want.

[THE MOTHER *appears.*]

Mother. Son.

Bridegroom. Where've you been?

Mother. Out there—in all that noise. Are you happy?

Bridegroom. Yes.

Mother. Where's your wife?

Bridegroom. Resting a little. It's a bad day for brides!

Mother. A bad day? The only good one. To me it was like coming into my own. [THE SERVANT *enters and goes toward* THE BRIDE'S *room.*] Like the breaking of new ground; the planting of new trees.

Bridegroom. Are you going to leave?

Mother. Yes. I ought to be at home.

Bridegroom. Alone.

Mother. Not alone. For my head is full of things: of men, and fights.

Bridegroom. But now the fights are no longer fights.

[THE SERVANT *enters quickly; she disappears at the rear of the stage, running.*]

Mother. While you live, you have to fight.

Bridegroom. I'll always obey you!

Mother. Try to be loving with your wife, and if you see she's acting foolish or touchy, caress her in a way that will hurt her a little: a strong hug, a bite and then a soft kiss. Not so she'll be angry, but just so she'll feel you're the man, the boss, the one who gives orders. I learned that from your father. And since you don't have him, I have to be the one to tell you about these strong defenses.

Bridegroom. I'll always do as you say.

Father. [*Entering.*] Where's my daughter?

Bridegroom. She's inside.

[THE FATHER *goes to look for her.*]

First Girl. Get the bride and groom! We're going to dance a round!

First Youth. [*To* THE BRIDEGROOM.] You're going to lead it.

Father. [*Entering.*] She's not there.

Bridegroom. No?

Father. She must have gone up to the railing.

Bridegroom. I'll go see!

[*He leaves. A hubbub of excitement and guitars is heard.*]

First Girl. They've started it already!
          [*She leaves.*]

Bridegroom. [*Entering.*] She isn't there.

Mother. [*Uneasily.*] Isn't she?

Father. But where could she have gone?

Servant. [*Entering.*] But where's the girl, where is she?

Mother. [*Seriously.*] That we don't know.

[THE BRIDEGROOM *leaves.* Three GUESTS *enter.*]

Father. [*Dramatically.*] But, isn't she in the dance?

Servant. She's not in the dance.

Father. [*With a start.*] There are a lot of people. Go look!

Servant. I've already looked.

Father. [*Tragically.*] Then where is she?

Bridegroom. [*Entering.*] Nowhere. Not anywhere.

Mother. [*To* THE FATHER.] What does this mean? Where is your daughter?

[LEONARDO'S WIFE *enters.*]

Leonardo's Wife. They've run away! They've run away! She and Leonardo. On the horse. With their arms around each other, they rode off like a shooting star!

Father. That's not true! Not my daughter!

Mother. Yes, your daughter! Spawn of

a wicked mother, and he, he too. But now she's my son's wife!

Bridegroom. Let's go after them! Who has a horse?

Mother. Who has a horse? Right away! Who has a horse? I'll give him all I have— my eyes, my tongue even. . . .

Voice. Here's one.

Mother. [*To* The Son.] Go! After them! [*He leaves with two* Young Men.] No. Don't go. Those people kill quickly and well . . . but yes, run, and I'll follow!

Father. It couldn't be my daughter. Perhaps she's thrown herself in the well.

Mother. Decent women throw themselves in water; not that one! But now she's my son's wife. Two groups. There are two groups here. [*They all enter.*] My family and yours. Everyone set out from here. Shake the dust from your heels! We'll help my son. [*The* People *separate into two groups.*] For he has his family: his cousins from the sea, and all who came from inland. Out of here! On all roads. The hour of blood has come again. Two groups! You with yours and I with mine. After them! After them!

CURTAIN

ACT THREE

SCENE I

A forest. It is nighttime. Great moist tree trunks. A dark atmosphere.

[*Two violins are heard.* Three Wood-cutters *enter.*]

First Woodcutter. And have they found them?

Second Woodcutter. No. But they're looking for them everywhere.

Third Woodcutter. They'll find them.

Second Woodcutter. Sh-h-h!

Third Woodcutter. What?

Second Woodcutter. They seem to be coming closer on all the roads at once.

First Woodcutter. When the moon comes out they'll see them.

Second Woodcutter. They ought to let them go.

First Woodcutter. The world is wide. Everybody can live in it.

Third Woodcutter. But they'll kill them.

Second Woodcutter. You have to follow your passion. They did right to run away.

First Woodcutter. They were deceiving themselves but at the last blood was stronger.

Third Woodcutter. Blood!

First Woodcutter. You have to follow the path of your blood.

Second Woodcutter. But blood that sees the light of day is drunk up by the earth.

First Woodcutter. What of it? Better dead with the blood drained away than alive with it rotting.

Third Woodcutter. Hush!

First Woodcutter. What? Do you hear something?

Third Woodcutter. I hear the crickets, the frogs, the night's ambush.

First Woodcutter. But not the horse.

Third Woodcutter. No.

First Woodcutter. By now he must be loving her.

Second Woodcutter. Her body for him; his body for her.

Third Woodcutter. They'll find them and they'll kill them.

First Woodcutter. But by then they'll have mingled their bloods. They'll be like two empty jars, like two dry arroyos.

Second Woodcutter. There are many clouds and it would be easy for the moon not to come out.

Third Woodcutter. The bridegroom will find them with or without the moon. I saw him set out. Like a raging star. His face the color of ashes. He looked the fate of all his clan.

First Woodcutter. His clan of dead men lying in the middle of the street.

Second Woodcutter. There you have it!

Third Woodcutter. You think they'll be able to break through the circle?

Second Woodcutter. It's hard to. There are knives and guns for ten leagues 'round.

Third Woodcutter. He's riding a good horse.

Second Woodcutter. But he's carrying a woman.

First Woodcutter. We're close by now.

Second Woodcutter. A tree with forty branches. We'll soon cut it down.

Third Woodcutter. The moon's coming out now. Let's hurry.

[*From the left shines a brightness.*]

First Woodcutter.

O rising moon!
Moon among the great leaves.

Second Woodcutter.
Cover the blood with jasmines!
First Woodcutter.
O lonely moon!
Moon among the great leaves.
Second Woodcutter.
Silver on the bride's face.
Third Woodcutter.
O evil moon!
Leave for their love a branch in shadow.
First Woodcutter.
O sorrowing moon!
Leave for their love a branch in shadow.
[*They go out.* THE MOON *appears through the shining brightness at the left.* THE MOON *is a young woodcutter with a white face. The stage takes on an intense blue radiance.*]
Moon.
Round swan in the river
and a cathedral's eye,
false dawn on the leaves,
they'll not escape; these things am I!
Who is hiding? And who sobs
in the thornbrakes of the valley?
The moon sets a knife
abandoned in the air
which being a leaden threat
yearns to be blood's pain.
Let me in! I come freezing
down to walls and windows!
Open roofs, open breasts
where I may warm myself!
I'm cold! My ashes
of somnolent metals
seek the fire's crest
on mountains and streets.
But the snow carries me
upon its mottled back
and pools soak me
in their water, hard and cold.
But this night there will be
red blood for my cheeks,
and for the reeds that cluster
at the wide feet of the wind.
Let there be neither shadow nor bower,
and then they can't get away!
O let me enter a breast
where I may get warm!
A heart for me!
Warm! That will spurt
over the mountains of my chest;
let me come in, oh let me!
[*To the branches.*]
I want no shadows. My rays
must get in everywhere,
even among the dark trunks I want
the whisper of gleaming lights,
so that this night there will be
sweet blood for my cheeks,
and for the reeds that cluster

at the wide feet of the wind.
Who is hiding? Out, I say!
No! They will not get away!
I will light up the horse
with a fever bright as diamonds.
[*He disappears among the trunks, and the stage goes back to its dark lighting. An* OLD WOMAN *comes out completely covered by thin green cloth. She is barefooted. Her face can barely be seen among the folds.*]
Beggar Woman.
That moon's going away, just when
they're near.
They won't get past here. The river's
whisper
and the whispering tree trunks will
muffle
the torn flight of their shrieks.
It has to be here, and soon. I'm worn
out.
The coffins are ready, and white sheets
wait on the floor of the bedroom
for heavy bodies with torn throats.
Let not one bird awake, let the breeze,
gathering their moans in her skirt,
fly with them over black tree tops
or bury them in soft mud.
[*Impatiently.*]
Oh, that moon! That moon!
[THE MOON *appears. The intense blue light returns.*]
Moon. They're coming. One band through the ravine and the other along the river. I'm going to light up the boulders. What do you need?
Beggar Woman. Nothing.
Moon. The wind blows hard now, with a double edge.
Beggar Woman. Light up the waistcoat and open the buttons; the knives will know the path after that.
Moon.
But let them be a long time a-dying.
So the blood
will slide its delicate hissing between my
fingers.
Look how my ashen valleys already are
waking
in longing for this fountain of shudder-
ing gushes!
Beggar Woman. Let's not let them past the arroyo. Silence!
Moon. There they come!
[*He goes. The stage is left dark.*]
Beggar Woman. Quick! Lots of light! Do you hear me? They can't get away!
[THE BRIDEGROOM *and* THE FIRST YOUTH *enter.* THE BEGGAR WOMAN *sits down and covers herself with her cloak.*]
Bridegroom. This way.

First Youth. You won't find them.

Bridegroom. [*Angrily.*] Yes, I'll find them.

First Youth. I think they've taken another path.

Bridegroom. No. Just a moment ago I felt the galloping.

First Youth. It could have been another horse.

Bridegroom. [*Intensely.*] Listen to me. There's only one horse in the whole world, and this one's it. Can't you understand that? If you're going to follow me, follow me without talking.

First Youth. It's only that I want to . . .

Bridegroom. Be quiet. I'm sure of meeting them there. Do you see this arm? Well, it's not my arm. It's my brother's arm, and my father's, and that of all the dead ones in my family. And it has so much strength that it can pull this tree up by the roots, if it wants to. And let's move on, because here I feel the clenched teeth of all my people in me so that I can't breathe easily.

Beggar Woman. [*Whining.*] Ay-y-y!

First Youth. Did you hear that?

Bridegroom. You go that way and then circle back.

First Youth. This is a hunt.

Bridegroom. A hunt. The greatest hunt there is.

[THE YOUTH *goes off.* THE BRIDE-GROOM *goes rapidly to the left and stumbles over* THE BEGGAR WOMAN, DEATH.]

Beggar Woman. Ay-y-y!

Bridegroom. What do you want?

Beggar Woman. I'm cold.

Bridegroom. Which way are you going?

Beggar Woman. [*Always whining like a beggar.*] Over there, far away . . .

Bridegroom. Where are you from?

Beggar Woman. Over there . . . very far away.

Bridegroom. Have you seen a man and a woman running away on a horse?

Beggar Woman. [*Awakening.*] Wait a minute . . . [*She looks at him.*] Handsome young man. [*She rises.*] But you'd be much handsomer sleeping.

Bridegroom. Tell me; answer me. Did you see them?

Beggar Woman. Wait a minute . . . What broad shoulders! How would you like to be laid out on them and not have to walk on the soles of your feet which are so small?

Bridegroom. [*Shaking her.*] I asked you if you saw them! Have they passed through here?

Beggar Woman. [*Energetically.*] No. They haven't passed; but they're coming from the hill. Don't you hear them?

Bridegroom. No.

Beggar Woman. Do you know the road?

Bridegroom. I'll go, whatever it's like!

Beggar Woman. I'll go along with you. I know this country.

Bridegroom. [*Impatiently.*] Well, let's go! Which way?

Beggar Woman. [*Dramatically.*] This way!

[*They go rapidly out. Two violins, which represent the forest, are heard distantly.* THE WOODCUTTERS *return. They have their axes on their shoulders. They move slowly among the tree trunks.*]

First Woodcutter.
O rising death!
Death among the great leaves.

Second Woodcutter.
Don't open the gush of blood!

First Woodcutter.
O lonely death!
Death among the dried leaves.

Third Woodcutter.
Don't lay flowers over the wedding!

Second Woodcutter.
O sad death!
Leave for their love a green branch.

First Woodcutter.
O evil death!
Leave for their love a branch of green!
[*They go out while they are talking.* LEONARDO *and* THE BRIDE *appear.*]

Leonardo.
Hush!

Bride.
From here I'll go on alone.
You go now! I want you to turn back.

Leonardo.
Hush, I said!

Bride.
With your teeth, with your hands, anyway you can,
take from my clean throat
the metal of this chain,
and let me live forgotten
back there in my house in the ground.
And if you don't want to kill me
as you would kill a tiny snake,
set in my hands, a bride's hands,
the barrel of your shotgun.
Oh, what lamenting, what fire,
sweeps upward through my head!
What glass splinters are stuck in my tongue!

Leonardo.
We've taken the step now; hush!
because they're close behind us,
and I must take you with me.

Bride.
Then it must be by force!

Leonardo.
By force? Who was it first
went down the stairway?

Bride.
I went down it.

Leonardo.
And who was it put
a new bridle on the horse?

Bride.
I myself did it. It's true.

Leonardo.
And whose were the hands
strapped spurs to my boots?

Bride.
The same hands, these that are yours,
but which when they see you would like
to break the blue branches
and sunder the purl of your veins.
I love you! I love you! But leave me!
For if I were able to kill you
I'd wrap you 'round in a shroud
with the edges bordered in violets.
Oh, what lamenting, what fire,
sweeps upward through my head!

Leonardo.
What glass splinters are stuck in my
tongue!
Because I tried to forget you
and put a wall of stone
between your house and mine.
It's true. You remember?
And when I saw you in the distance
I threw sand in my eyes.
But I was riding a horse
and the horse went straight to your
door.
And the silver pins of your wedding
turned my red blood black.
And in me our dream was choking
my flesh with its poisoned weeds.
Oh, it isn't my fault—
the fault is the earth's—
and this fragrance that you exhale
from your breasts and your braids.

Bride.
Oh, how untrue! I want
from you neither bed nor food,
yet there's not a minute each day
that I don't want to be with you,
because you drag me, and I come,
then you tell me to go back
and I follow you,
like chaff blown on the breeze.
I have left a good, honest man,
and all his people,
with the wedding feast half over
and wearing my bridal wreath.
But you are the one will be punished
and that I don't want to happen.

Leave me alone now! You run away!
There is no one who will defend you.

Leonardo.
The birds of early morning
are calling among the trees.
The night is dying
on the stone's ridge.
Let's go to a hidden corner
where I may love you forever,
for to me the people don't matter,
nor the venom they throw on us.
[*He embraces her strongly.*]

Bride.
And I'll sleep at your feet,
to watch over your dreams.
Naked, looking over the fields,
as though I were a bitch.
Because that's what I am! Oh, I look
at you
and your beauty sears me.

Leonardo.
Fire is stirred by fire.
The same tiny flame
will kill two wheat heads together.
Let's go!

Bride.
Where are you taking me?

Leonardo.
Where they cannot come,
these men who surround us.
Where I can look at you!

Bride. [*Sarcastically.*]
Carry me with you from fair to fair,
a shame to clean women,
so that people will see me
with my wedding sheets
on the breeze like banners.

Leonardo.
I, too, would want to leave you
if I thought as men should.
But wherever you go, I go.
You're the same. Take a step. Try.
Nails of moonlight have fused
my waist and your chains.
[*This whole scene is violent, full of
great sensuality.*]

Bride.
Listen!

Leonardo.
They're coming.

Bride.
Run!
It's fitting that I should die here,
with water over my feet,
with thorns upon my head.
And fitting the leaves should mourn me
a woman lost and virgin.

Leonardo.
Be quiet. Now they're appearing.

Bride.
Go now!

Leonardo.
   Quiet. Don't let them hear us.
                    [THE BRIDE *hesitates.*]
Bride.
   Both of us!
Leonardo. [*Embracing her.*]
                        Any way you want!
   If they separate us, it will be
   because I am dead.
Bride.
                        And I dead too.
   [*They go out in each other's arms.* THE

MOON *appears very slowly. The stage takes on a strong blue light. The two violins are heard. Suddenly two long, ear-splitting shrieks are heard, and the music of the two violins is cut short. At the second shriek* THE BEGGAR WOMAN *appears and stands with her back to the audience. She opens her cape and stands in the center of the stage like a great bird with immense wings.* THE MOON *halts. The curtain comes down in absolute silence.*]

CURTAIN

ACT THREE

SCENE II

The Final Scene

A white dwelling with arches and thick walls. To the right and left, are white stairs. At the back, a great arch and a wall of the same color. The floor also should be shining white. This simple dwelling should have the monumental feeling of a church. There should not be a single gray nor any shadow, not even what is necessary for perspective.
[TWO GIRLS *dressed in dark blue are winding a red skein.*]

First Girl.
   Wool, red wool,
   what would you make?
Second Girl.
   Oh, jasmine for dresses,
   fine wool like glass.
   At four o'clock born,
   at ten o'clock dead.
   A thread from this wool yarn,
   a chain 'round your feet
   a knot that will tighten
   the bitter white wreath.
Little Girl. [*Singing.*]
   Were you at the wedding?
First Girl.
   No.
Little Girl.
   Well, neither was I!
   What could have happened
   'midst the shoots of the vineyards?
   What could have happened
   'neath the branch of the olive?
   What really happened
   that no one came back?
   Were you at the wedding?

Second Girl.
   We told you once, no.
Little Girl. [*Leaving.*]
   Well, neither was I!
Second Girl.
   Wool, red wool,
   what would you sing?
First Girl.
   Their wounds turning waxen
   balm-myrtle for pain.
   Asleep in the morning,
   and watching at night.
Little Girl. [*In the doorway.*]
   And then, the thread stumbled
   on the flinty stones,
   but mountains, blue mountains,
   are letting it pass.
   Running, running, running,
   and finally to come
   to stick in a knife blade,
   to take back the bread. [*She goes out.*]
Second Girl.
   Wool, red wool,
   what would you tell?
First Girl.
   The lover is silent,
   crimson the groom,
   at the still shoreline
   I saw them laid out.
                [*She stops and looks at the skein.*]
Little Girl. [*Appearing in the doorway.*]
   Running, running, running,
   the thread runs to here.
   All covered with clay
   I feel them draw near.
   Bodies stretched stiffly
   in ivory sheets!
   [THE WIFE *and* MOTHER-IN-LAW *of* LEONARDO *appear. They are anguished.*]
First Girl. Are they coming yet?

Mother-in-law. [*Harshly.*] We don't know.

Second Girl. What can you tell us about the wedding?

First Girl. Yes, tell me.

Mother-in-law. [*Curtly.*] Nothing.

Leonardo's Wife. I want to go back and find out all about it.

Mother-in-law. [*Sternly.*]
You, back to your house.
Brave and alone in your house.
To grow old and to weep.
But behind closed doors.
Never again. Neither dead nor alive.
We'll nail up our windows
and let rains and nights
fall on the bitter weeds.

Leonardo's Wife. What could have happened?

Mother-in-law.
It doesn't matter what.
Put a veil over your face.
Your children are yours,
that's all. On the bed
put a cross of ashes
where his pillow was. [*They go out.*]

Beggar Woman. [*At the door.*] A crust of bread, little girls.

Little Girl. Go away!

[THE GIRLS *huddle close together.*]

Beggar Woman. Why?

Little Girl. Because you whine; go away!

First Girl. Child!

Beggar Woman.
I might have asked for your eyes! A cloud
of birds is following me. Will you have one?

Little Girl. I want to get away from here!

Second Girl. [*To* THE BEGGAR WOMAN.] Don't mind her!

First Girl. Did you come by the road through the arroyo?

Beggar Woman. I came that way!

First Girl. [*Timidly.*] Can I ask you something?

Beggar Woman.
I saw them: they'll be here soon; two torrents
still at last, among the great boulders,
two men at the horse's feet.
Two dead men in the night's splendor.
[*With pleasure.*]
Dead, yes, dead.

First Girl. Hush, old woman, hush!

Beggar Woman.
Crushed flowers for eyes, and their teeth
two fistfuls of hard-frozen snow.

Both of them fell, and the Bride returns
with bloodstains on her skirt and hair.
And they come covered with two sheets
carried on the shoulders of two tall boys.
That's how it was; nothing more. What
was fitting.
Over the golden flower, dirty sand.

[*She goes.* THE GIRLS *bow their heads and start going out rhythmically.*]

First Girl.
Dirty sand.

Second Girl.
Over the golden flower.

Little Girl.
Over the golden flower
they're bringing the dead from the arroyo.
Dark the one,
dark the other.
What shadowy nightingale flies and
weeps over the golden flower!

[*She goes. The stage is left empty.*
THE MOTHER *and a* NEIGHBOR WOMAN
appear. THE NEIGHBOR *is weeping.*]

Mother. Hush.

Neighbor. I can't.

Mother. Hush, I said. [*At the door.*] Is there nobody here? [*She puts her hands to her forehead.*] My son ought to answer me. But now my son is an armful of shrivelled flowers. My son is a fading voice beyond the mountains now. [*With rage, to* THE NEIGHBOR.] Will you shut up? I want no wailing in this house. Your tears are only tears from your eyes, but when I'm alone mine will come—from the soles of my feet, from my roots—burning more than blood.

Neighbor. You come to my house; don't you stay here.

Mother. I want to be here. Here. In peace. They're all dead now: and at midnight I'll sleep, sleep without terror of guns or knives. Other mothers will go to their windows, lashed by rain, to watch for their sons' faces. But not I. And of my dreams I'll make a cold ivory dove that will carry camellias of white frost to the graveyard. But no; not graveyard, not graveyard: the couch of earth, the bed that shelters them and rocks them in the sky. [*A* WOMAN *dressed in black enters, goes toward the right, and there kneels. To* THE NEIGHBOR.] Take your hands from your face. We have terrible days ahead. I want to see no one. The earth and I. My grief and I. And these four walls. Ay-y-y! Ay-y-y!

[*She sits down, overcome.*]

Neighbor. Take pity on yourself!

Mother. [*Pushing back her hair.*] I must be calm. [*She sits down.*] Because the neighbor women will come and I don't want them to see me so poor. So poor! A woman without even one son to hold to her lips.

[THE BRIDE *appears. She is without her wreath and wears a black shawl.*]

Neighbor. [*With rage, seeing* THE BRIDE.] Where are you going?

Bride. I'm coming here.

Mother. [*To* THE NEIGHBOR.] Who is it?

Neighbor. Don't you recognize her?

Mother. That's why I asked who it was. Because I don't want to recognize her, so I won't sink my teeth in her throat. You snake! [*She moves wrathfully on* THE BRIDE, *then stops. To* THE NEIGHBOR.] Look at her! There she is, and she's crying, while I stand here calmly and don't tear her eyes out. I don't understand myself. Can it be I didn't love my son? But where's his good name? Where is it now? Where is it? [*She beats* THE BRIDE *who drops to the floor.*]

Neighbor. For God's sake! [*She tries to separate them.*]

Bride. [*To* THE NEIGHBOR.] Let her; I came here so she'd kill me and they'd take me away with them. [*To* THE MOTHER.] But not with her hands; with grappling hooks, with a sickle—and with force—until they break on my bones. Let her! I want her to know I'm clean, that I may be crazy, but that they can bury me without a single man ever having seen himself in the whiteness of my breasts.

Mother. Shut up, shut up; what do I care about that?

Bride. Because I ran away with the other one; I ran away. [*With anguish.*] You would have gone, too. I was a woman burning with desire, full of sores inside and out, and your son was a little bit of water from which I hoped for children, land, health; but the other one was a dark river, choked with brush, that brought near me the undertone of its rushes and its whispered song. And I went along with your son who was like a little boy of cold water—and the other sent against me hundreds of birds who got in my way and left white frost on my wounds, my wounds of a poor withered woman, of a girl caressed by fire. I didn't want to; remember that! I didn't want to. Your son was my destiny and I have not betrayed him, but the other one's arm dragged me along like the pull of the sea, like the head toss of a mule, and he would have dragged me always, always, always—even if I were an old woman and all your son's sons held me by the hair! [*A* NEIGHBOR *enters.*]

Mother. She is not to blame; nor am I! [*Sarcastically.*] Who is, then? It's a delicate, lazy, sleepless woman who throws away an orange blossom wreath and goes looking for a piece of bed warmed by another woman!

Bride. Be still! Be still! Take your revenge on me; here I am! See how soft my throat is; it would be less work for you than cutting a dahlia in your garden. But never that! Clean, clean as a new-born little girl. And strong enough to prove it to you. Light the fire. Let's stick our hands in; you, for your son, I, for my body. *You'll* draw yours out first. [ANOTHER NEIGHBOR *enters.*]

Mother. But what does your good name matter to me? What does your death matter to me? What does anything about anything matter to me? Blesséd be the wheat stalks, because my sons are under them; blesséd be the rain, because it wets the face of the dead. Blesséd be God, who stretches us out together to rest. [ANOTHER NEIGHBOR *enters.*]

Bride. Let me weep with you.

Mother. Weep. But at the door. [*The* LITTLE GIRL *enters.* THE BRIDE *stays at the door.* THE MOTHER *is at the center of the stage.*]

Leonardo's Wife. [*Entering and going to the left.*]
He was a beautiful horseman,
now he's a heap of snow.
He rode to fairs and mountains
and women's arms.
Now, the night's dark moss
crowns his forehead.

Mother.
A sunflower to your mother,
a mirror of the earth.
Let them put on your breast
the cross of bitter rosebay;
and over you a sheet
of shining silk;
between your quiet hands
let water form its lament.

Wife.
Ay-y-y, four gallant boys
come with tired shoulders!

Bride.
Ay-y-y, four gallant boys
carry death on high!

Mother.
Neighbors.

Little Girl. [*At the door.*]
They're bringing them now.

Mother.
It's the same thing.
Always the cross, the cross.

Women.
Sweet nails,

cross adored,
sweet name
of Christ our Lord.
Bride. May the cross protect both the quick and the dead.

Mother.
Neighbors: with a knife,
with a little knife,
on their appointed day, between two and
three,
these two men killed each other for
love.
With a knife,
with a tiny knife
that barely fits the hand,
but that slides in clean
through the astonished flesh
and stops at the place
where trembles, enmeshed,
the dark root of a scream.

Bride.
And this is a knife,
a tiny knife
that barely fits the hand;
fish without scales, without river,
so that on their appointed day, between
two and three,
with this knife,
two men are left stiff,
with their lips turning yellow.

Mother.
And it barely fits the hand
but it slides in clean
through the astonished flesh
and stops there, at the place
where trembles enmeshed
the dark root of a scream.
[THE NEIGHBORS, *kneeling on the floor, sob.*]

CURTAIN

MURDER IN THE CATHEDRAL *

By

T. S. ELIOT

T. S. ELIOT'S COMMANDING POSITION among twentieth-century writers in English of poetry and literary criticism is not duplicated in the drama. By reason of his eminence in those other endeavors he has a following in the theatre, especially among the intellectuals and academics. But they are notoriously few and notoriously undependable in loyalty, though undoubtedly very influential. The theatre-going public at large has made a commercial success of only one of his plays, *The Cocktail Party,* and he himself is reported to have thought its success due to the title and the fad. Nevertheless, Eliot stands for something unique and admirable in contemporary drama, and a sympathetic study of his work should lead to the hope that he will continue to write for the theatre and will come to have an influence on it approaching his influence on the poetry of his day.

But Eliot, if he continues to write for the theatre, will not, apparently, seek to "bring poetry into" it. That is, he will not wish to make his audiences aware that they are hearing verse. Instead, he will try to write lines of such loose rhythm and cadence that they will sound like prose and be uttered by the actor like prose, yet have an unconscious effect upon both actor and audience which arises from the dramatic intensification poetry gives. But he believes this verse should never call attention to itself as poetry. The test of every line is not its poetry, but its dramatic relevance.

Murder in the Cathedral, clearly, is not written according to Eliot's program for his future plays. In his *Poetry and Drama,* Eliot writes of *Murder in the Cathedral* as if it were his first play and ignores *Sweeney Agonistes* and *The Rock.* He asserts that *Murder in the Cathedral* had advantages not found for most plays: a remote period, which allowed the characters to be repre-

sented as speaking verse; a special audience, since the play was written for the Canterbury Festival of 1935; and its religious occasion, which permitted a religious play. It had the disadvantage of a very limited plot: Becket returns to Canterbury, foreseeing that he will be murdered, and is murdered. By both advantage and disadvantage Eliot was led to rely heavily upon the use of the chorus, who could express the suffering caused by Becket's danger and martyrdom and thereby help lift the murder from a drab brutality to significance. But that significance should be given by a chorus rather than by the action itself came to seem wrong to Eliot, and though he used a chorus in his next play, *The Family Reunion,* he abandoned it thereafter.

Eliot claims that *The Family Reunion,* though he thinks it a failure, solved for him the problem of versification. The obvious poetry of *Murder in the Cathedral* is given up; the verse sounds like contemporary speech and the actor should try to speak it with the utmost naturalness.

Murder in the Cathedral is the only Eliot play he will allow to be anthologized, and yet, as his history in the theatre shows, he thinks it most unlike what he would wish to write for the theatre.

Nevertheless, *Murder in the Cathedral* will serve adequately to represent Eliot's realest virtue in the drama. That is not in his verse, or in chorus or no-chorus, or in any detail of technique. When we first read *Gerontion* or *Ash Wednesday* we probably did not understand it, but if we were sensitive at all we felt that Eliot had something fresh and important to say there and that it was said with power, even if all the power could not be felt immediately. Except perhaps for *Sweeney Agonistes* and *The Rock,* the same quality inheres in *Murder in the Cathedral* and in all Eliot's plays. They are important plays, not because Eiot is eminent, a poet, or the foremost living critic, but because of what they are and say.

Does Eliot have little confidence in his

* Reprinted by permission of Harcourt, Brace and Company.

354

powers of narrative construction? The plots of all his plays after *Murder in the Cathedral*, which is drawn from history, rely on Greek drama for considerable suggestion: *The Family Reunion* on the *Eumenides* of Aeschylus, *The Cocktail Party* on the *Alcestis* of Euripides, *The Confidential Clerk* on the *Ion* of Euripides. The question seems to raise a serious issue, but actually does not. Eliot himself has usually had to indicate his sources—they are not obvious to even the learned critic. What happens, apparently, is that Eliot broods on an ancient play or event, transforms it deliberately in his imagination into a new pattern of contemporary meaning. The richness and importance of what he says may derive from this process, which also creates what seems and is fresh.

Readers of *Murder in the Cathedral*, unless very familiar with the effects that can be produced by a verse-speaking choir, will have difficulty imagining how the choruses sound unless they listen carefully to the admirable recording of the play made by the Old Vic Theatre, London.

THOMAS STEARNS ELIOT

Born 1888, St. Louis, Missouri.

B.A., Harvard, 1910; M.A., 1911.

1910–1915, Graduate study in philosophy abroad and at Harvard, and some teaching.

1916–1925, Work in a bank, writing, and editing, in London.

1922, Publication of *The Waste Land* establishes his reputation as poet.

1925–   , Employed by Faber and Faber, London publishers.

1927, Becomes member of the Church of England and a British citizen.

1948, Awarded Nobel Prize for Literature and appointed to the Order of Merit.

PLAYS

1932 *Sweeney Agonistes: Fragments of an Aristophanic Melodrama.* 1934 *The Rock, a Pageant Play.* 1935 *Murder in the Cathedral.* 1939 *The Family Reunion.* 1950 *The Cocktail Party.* 1953 *The Confidential Clerk.* 1958 *The Elder Statesman.*

WRITINGS ON DRAMA

"Whether Rostand Had Something about Him," *Athenaeum*, No. 4656, July 25, 1919. "Swinburne and the Elizabethans," *Athenaeum*, No. 4664, Sept. 19, 1919. "The Comedy of Humours," *Athenaeum*, No. 4672, Nov. 14, 1919. From *The Sacred Wood*, 1920: "The Possibility of Poetic Drama"; "Euripides and Professor Murray"; "Rhetoric and Poetic Drama"; "Notes on the Blank Verse of Christopher Marlowe"; "Hamlet and His Problems"; "Ben Jonson"; Philip Massinger." "The Poetic Drama," *Athenaeum*, No. 4698, May 14, 1920. "The Old Comedy," *Athenaeum*, No. 4702, June 11, 1920. "Dramatis Personae," *The Criterion*, I (April 1923), 303–306. Review of *Mr. Shaw and 'The Maid,'* by J. M. Robertson, *The Criterion*, IV (April 1926), 389–390. Review of *All God's Chillun Got Wings*, *Desire under the Elms*, and *Welded*, by Eugene O'Neill, *The Criterion*, IV (April 1926), 395–396. 1927 *Shakespeare and the Stoicism of Seneca.* Review of *The Complete Works of John Webster*, edited by F. L. Lucas, *The Criterion*, VII (June 1928), 155–158. Review of *Ben Jonson*, edited by C. H. Herford and Percy Simpson, *The Dial*, LXXXV (July 1928), 65–68. From *For Lancelot Andrewes*, 1928: "Thomas Middleton." 1930 Introduction to *The Wheel of Fire*, by G. Wilson Knight. From *Selected Essays 1917–1932*, 1932 (not including those listed above): "A Dialogue on Dramatic Poetry"; "Seneca in Elizabethan Translation"; "Four Elizabethan Dramatists"; "Christopher Marlowe"; "Thomas Heywood"; "Cyril Tourneur"; "John Ford." *John Dryden, the*

Poet, the Dramatist, the Critic. 1934 A letter to the Editor of *The Spectator*, No. 5528, June 8, 1934, about *The Rock.* "Shakespearean Criticism from Dryden to Coleridge" in *A Companion to Shakespeare Studies,* ed. by Harley Granville-Barker and G. B. Harrison.

From *Elizabethan Essays* (not including those listed above): "John Marston." 1936 A review of *Shakespeare,* by J. M. Murry, *The Criterion,* XV (July 1936), 708–710. 1943 Introduction to *Shakespeare and the Popular Dramatic Tradition,* by S. L. Bethell. 1949 *The Aims of Poetic Drama,* revised and republished in 1951 as *Poetry and Drama.* 1953 *The Three Voices of Poetry.* 1953 Introduction to *Shakespeare,* by Henri Fluchére. 1954 *Religious Drama, Medieval and Modern.*

SCREENWRITING

1951 *Murder in the Cathedral.*

MURDER IN THE CATHEDRAL

PART I

Characters

A Chorus of Women of Canterbury.
Three Priests of the Cathedral.
A Herald.
Archbishop Thomas Becket.
Four Tempters.

Attendants.

The Scene is the Archbishop's Hall, on December 2nd, 1170.

Chorus. Here let us stand, close by the
cathedral. Here let us wait.
Are we drawn by danger? Is it the knowl-
edge of safety, that draws our feet
Towards the cathedral? What danger can
be
For us, the poor, the poor women of Can-
terbury? what tribulation
With which we are not already familiar?
There is no danger
For us, and there is no safety in the cathe-
dral. Some presage of an act
Which our eyes are compelled to witness,
has forced our feet
Towards the cathedral. We are forced to
bear witness.

Since golden October declined into sombre
November
And the apples were gathered and stored,
and the land became brown sharp
points of death in a waste of water
and mud,
The New Year waits, breathes, waits,
whispers in darkness.
While the labourer kicks off a muddy boot
and stretches his hand to the fire,
The New Year waits, destiny waits for the
coming.
Who has stretched out his hand to the fire
and remembered the Saints at All
Hallows,
Remembered the martyrs and saints who
wait? and who shall
Stretch out his hand to the fire, and deny
his master? who shall be warm
By the fire, and deny his master?

Seven years and the summer is over
Seven years since the Archbishop left us,

He who was always kind to his people.
But it would not be well if he should re-
turn.
King rules or barons rule;
We have suffered various oppression,
But mostly we are left to our own de-
vices,
And we are content if we are left alone.
We try to keep our households in order;
The merchant, shy and cautious, tries to
compile a little fortune,
And the labourer bends to his piece of
earth, earth-colour, his own colour,
Preferring to pass unobserved.
Now I fear disturbance of the quiet sea-
sons:
Winter shall come bringing death from the
sea,
Ruinous spring shall beat at our doors,
Root and shoot shall eat our eyes and our
ears,
Disastrous summer burn up the beds of
our streams
And the poor shall wait for another decay-
ing October.
Why should the summer bring consola-
tion
For autumn fires and winter fogs?
What shall we do in the heat of summer
But wait in barren orchards for another
October?
Some malady is coming upon us. We wait,
we wait,
And the saints and martyrs wait, for those
who shall be martyrs and saints.
Destiny waits in the hand of God, shap-
ing the still unshapen:
I have seen these things in a shaft of sun-
light.
Destiny waits in the hand of God, not in
the hands of statesmen

357

Who do, some well, some ill, planning and guessing,
Having their aims which turn in their hands in the pattern of time.
Come, happy December, who shall observe you, who shall preserve you?
Shall the Son of Man be born again in the litter of scorn?
For us, the poor, there is no action,
But only to wait and to witness.

[*Enter* PRIESTS.]

First Priest. Seven years and the summer is over.
Seven years since the Archbishop left us.

Second Priest. What does the Archbishop do, and our Sovereign Lord the Pope
With the stubborn King and the French King
In ceaseless intrigue, combinations,
In conference, meetings accepted, meetings refused,
Meetings unended or endless
At one place or another in France?

Third Priest. I see nothing quite conclusive in the art of temporal government,
But violence, duplicity and frequent malversation.
King rules or barons rule:
The strong man strongly and the weak man by caprice.
They have but one law, to seize the power and keep it,
And the steadfast can manipulate the greed and lust of others,
The feeble is devoured by his own.

First Priest.   Shall these things not end
Until the poor at the gate
Have forgotten their friend, their Father in God, have forgotten
That they had a friend?

[*Enter* HERALD.]

Herald. Servants of God, and watchers of the temple,
I am here to inform you, without circumlocution:
The Archbishop is in England, and is close outside the city.
I was sent before in haste
To give you notice of his coming, as much as was possible,
That you may prepare to meet him.

First Priest. What, is the exile ended, is our Lord Archbishop
Reunited with the King? what reconciliation
Of two proud men? what peace can be found
To grow between the hammer and the anvil? Tell us,

Are the old disputes at an end, is the wall of pride cast down
That divided them? Is it peace or war? Does he come
In full assurance, or only secure
In the power of Rome, the spiritual rule,
The assurance of right, and the love of the people,
Contemning the hatred and envy of barons?

Herald. You are right to express a certain incredulity.
He comes in pride and sorrow, affirming all his claims,
Assured, beyond doubt, of the devotion of the people,
Who receive him with scenes of frenzied enthusiasm.
Lining the road and throwing down their capes,
Strewing the way with leaves and late flowers of the season.
The streets of the city will be packed to suffocation,
And I think that his horse will be deprived of its tail,
A single hair of which becomes a precious relic.
He is at one with the Pope, and with the King of France,
Who indeed would have liked to detain him in his kingdom:
But as for our King, that is another matter.

First Priest. But again, is it war or peace?

Herald.   Peace, but not the kiss of peace.
A patched up affair, if you ask my opinion.
And if you ask me, I think the Lord Archbishop
Is not the man to cherish any illusions,
Or yet to diminish the least of his pretensions.
If you ask my opinion, I think that this peace
Is nothing like an end, or like a beginning.
It is common knowledge that when the Archbishop
Parted from the King, he said to the King,
My Lord, he said, I leave you as a man
Whom in this life I shall not see again.
I have this, I assure you, on the highest authority;
There are several opinions as to what he meant
But no one considers it a happy prognostic.   [*Exit.*]

First Priest. I fear for the Archbishop, I fear for the Church,

I know that the pride bred of sudden prosperity
Was but confirmed by bitter adversity.
I saw him as Chancellor, flattered by the King,
Liked or feared by courtiers, in their over-bearing fashion,
Despised and despising, always isolated,
Never one among them, always insecure;
His pride always feeding upon his own virtues,
Pride drawing sustenance from impartial-ity,
Pride drawing sustenance from gener-osity,
Loathing power given by temporal devolu-tion,
Wishing subjection to God alone.
Had the King been greater, or had he been weaker
Things had perhaps been different for Thomas.

Second Priest. Yet our lord is returned. Our lord has come back to his own again.
We have had enough of waiting, from De-cember to dismal December.
The Archbishop shall be at our head, dis-pelling dismay and doubt.
He will tell us what we are to do, he will give us our orders, instruct us.
Our Lord is at one with the Pope, and also the King of France.
We can lean on a rock, we can feel a firm foothold
Against the perpetual wash of tides of balance of forces of barons and land-holders.
The rock of God is beneath our feet. Let us meet the Archbishop with cordial thanksgiving:
Our lord, our Archbishop returns. And when the Archbishop returns
Our doubts are dispelled. Let us there-fore rejoice,
I say rejoice, and show a glad face for his welcome.
I am the Archbishop's man. Let us give the Archbishop welcome!

Third Priest. For good or ill, let the wheel turn.
The wheel has been still, these seven years, and no good.
For ill or good, let the wheel turn.
For who knows the end of good or evil?
Until the grinders cease
And the door shall be shut in the street,
And all the daughters of music shall be brought low.

Chorus. Here is no continuing city, here is no abiding stay.

Ill the wind, ill the time, uncertain the profit, certain the danger.
O late late late, late is the time, late too late, and rotten the year;
Evil the wind, and bitter the sea, and grey the sky, grey grey grey.
O Thomas, return, Archbishop; return, re-turn to France.
Return. Quickly. Quietly. Leave us to perish in quiet.
You come with applause, you come with rejoicing, but you come bringing death into Canterbury:
A doom on the house, a doom on yourself, a doom on the world.

We do not wish anything to happen.
Seven years we have lived quietly,
Succeeded in avoiding notice,
Living and partly living.
There have been oppression and luxury,
There have been poverty and licence,
There has been minor injustice.
Yet we have gone on living,
Living and partly living.
Sometimes the corn has failed us,
Sometimes the harvest is good,
One year is a year of rain,
Another a year of dryness,
One year the apples are abundant,
Another year the plums are lacking.
Yet we have gone on living,
Living and partly living.
We have kept the feasts, heard the masses,
We have brewed beer and cider,
Gathered wood against the winter,
Talked at the corner of the fire,
Talked at the corners of streets,
Talked not always in whispers,
Living and partly living.
We have seen births, deaths and marriages,
We have had various scandals,
We have been afflicted with taxes,
We have had laughter and gossip,
Several girls have disappeared
Unaccountably, and some not able to.
We have all had our private terrors,
Our particular shadows, our secret fears.
But now a great fear is upon us, a fear not of one but of many,
A fear like birth and death, when we see birth and death alone
In a void apart. We
Are afraid in a fear which we cannot know, which we cannot face, which none understands,
And our hearts are torn from us, our brains unskinned like the layers of an onion, our selves are lost lost

In a final fear which none understands. O
  Thomas Archbishop,
O Thomas our Lord, leave us and leave
  us be, in our humble and tarnished
  frame of existence, leave us; do not
  ask us
To stand to the doom on the house, the
  doom on the Archbishop, the doom
  on the world.
Archbishop, secure and assured of your
  fate, unafraid among the shades, do
  you realise what you ask, do you
  realise what it means
To the small folk drawn into the pattern
  of fate, the small folk who live among
  small things,
The strain on the brain of the small folk
  who stand to the doom of the house,
  the doom of their lord, the doom of
  the world?
O Thomas, Archbishop, leave us, leave us,
  leave sullen Dover, and set sail for
  France. Thomas our Archbishop still
  our Archbishop even in France.
  Thomas Archbishop, set the white sail
  between the grey sky and the bitter
  sea, leave us, leave us for France.
Second Priest. What a way to talk at such
  a juncture!
You are foolish, immodest and babbling
  women.
Do you not know that the good Archbishop
  Is likely to arrive at any moment?
The crowds in the streets will be cheering
  and cheering,
You go on croaking like frogs in the tree-
  tops:
But frogs at least can be cooked and
  eaten.
Whatever you are afraid of, in your
  craven apprehension,
Let me ask you at the least to put on
  pleasant faces,
And give a hearty welcome to our good
  Archbishop.
                              [*Enter* THOMAS.]
Thomas. Peace. And let them be, in their
  exaltation.
They speak better than they know, and be-
  yond your understanding.
They know and do not know, what it is to
  act or suffer.
They know and do not know, that acting
  is suffering
And suffering is action. Neither does the
  actor suffer
Nor the patient act. But both are fixed
In an eternal action, an eternal patience
To which all must consent that it may
  be willed

And which all must suffer that they may
  will it,
That the pattern may subsist, for the pat-
  tern is the action
And the suffering, that the wheel may turn
  and still
Be forever still.
Second Priest. O my Lord, forgive me, I did
  not see you coming,
Engrossed by the chatter of these foolish
  women.
Forgive us, my Lord, you would have had
  a better welcome
If we had been sooner prepared for the
  event.
But your Lordship knows that seven years
  of waiting,
Seven years of prayer, seven years of
  emptiness,
Have better prepared our hearts for your
  coming,
Than seven days could make ready Can-
  terbury.
However, I will have fires laid in all your
  rooms
To take the chill off our English De-
  cember,
Your Lordship now being used to a better
  climate.
Your Lordship will find your rooms in
  order as you left them.
Thomas. And will try to leave them in or-
  der as I find them.
I am more than grateful for all your kind
  attentions.
These are small matters. Little rest in
  Canterbury
With eager enemies restless about us.
Rebellious bishops, York, London, Salis-
  bury,
Would have intercepted our letters,
Filled the coast with spies and sent to
  meet me
Some who hold me in bitterest hate.
By God's grace aware of their prevision
I sent my letters on another day,
Had fair crossing, found at Sandwich
Broc, Warenne, and the Sheriff of Kent,
Those who had sworn to have my head
  from me.
Only John, the Dean of Salisbury,
Fearing for the King's name, warning
  against treason,
Made them hold their hands. So for the
  time
We are unmolested.
First Priest.   But do they follow after?
Thomas. For a little time the hungry hawk
  Will only soar and hover, circling lower,
  Waiting excuse, pretence, opportunity.

End will be simple, sudden, God-given.
Meanwhile the substance of our first act
Will be shadows, and the strife with
shadows.
Heavier the interval than the consumma-
tion.
All things prepare the event. Watch.
                    [*Enter* FIRST TEMPTER.]
First Tempter. You see, my Lord, I do not
    wait upon ceremony:
Here I have come, forgetting all acrimony,
Hoping that your present gravity
Will find excuse for my humble levity
Remembering all the good time past.
Your Lordship won't despise an old friend
    out of favour?
Old Tom, gay Tom, Becket of London,
Your Lordship won't forget that evening
    on the river
When the King, and you and I were all
    friends together?
Friendship should be more than biting
    Time can sever.
What, my Lord, now that you recover
Favour with the King, shall we say that
    summer's over
Or that the good time cannot last?
Fluting in the meadows, viols in the hall,
Laughter and apple-blossom floating on
    the water,
Singing at nightfall, whispering in cham-
    bers,
Fires devouring the winter season,
Eating up the darkness, with wit and wine
    and wisdom!
Now that the King and you are in amity,
Clergy and laity may return to gaiety,
Mirth and sportfulness need not walk
    warily.
Thomas. You talk of seasons that are past.
    I remember
Not worth forgetting.
Tempter.   And of the new season.
Spring has come in winter. Snow in the
    branches
Shall float as sweet as blossoms. Ice along
    the ditches
Mirror the sunlight. Love in the orchard
Send the sap shooting. Mirth matches
    melancholy.
Thomas. We do not know very much of the
    future
Except that from generation to genera-
    tion
The same things happen again and again.
Men learn little from others' experience.
But in the life of one man, never
The same time returns. Sever
The cord, shed the scale. Only
The fool, fixed in his folly, may think

He can turn the wheel on which he turns.
Tempter. My Lord, a nod is as good as a
    wink.
A man will often love what he spurns.
For the good times past, that are come
    again
I am your man.
Thomas.   Not in this train.
Look to your behaviour. You were safer
Think of penitence and follow your mas-
    ter.
Tempter.   Not at this gait!
If you go so fast, others may go faster.
Your Lordship is too proud!
The safest beast is not the one that roars
    most loud.
This was not the way of the King our
    master!
You were not used to be so hard upon
    sinners
When they were your friends. Be easy,
    man!
The easy man lives to eat the best din-
    ners.
Take a friend's advice. Leave well alone,
Or your goose may be cooked and eaten
    to the bone.
Thomas. You come twenty years too late.
Tempter.   Then I leave you to your fate.
I leave you to the pleasures of your higher
    vices,
Which will have to be paid for at higher
    prices.
Farewell, my Lord, I do not wait upon
    ceremony,
I leave as I came, forgetting all acrimony,
Hoping that your present gravity
Will find excuse for my humble levity.
If you will remember me, my Lord, at
    your prayers,
I'll remember you at kissing-time below
    the stairs.
Thomas. Leave-well-alone, the springtime
    fancy,
So one thought goes whistling down the
    wind.
The impossible is still temptation.
The impossible, the undesirable,
Voices under sleep, waking a dead world,
So that the mind may not be whole in the
    present.
                    [*Enter* SECOND TEMPTER.]
Second Tempter. Your Lordship has forgot-
    ten me, perhaps. I will remind you.
We met at Clarendon, at Northampton,
And last at Montmirail, in Maine. Now
    that I have recalled them,
Let us but set these not too pleasant
    memories
In balance against other, earlier

And weighter ones: those of the Chancel-
lorship.
See how the late ones rise! The master of
policy
Whom all acknowledged, should guide the
state again.
Thomas. Your meaning?
Tempter.   The Chancellorship that
you resigned
When you were made Archbishop—that
was a mistake
On your part—still may be regained.
Think, my Lord,
Power obtained grows to glory,
Life lasting, a permanent possession,
A templed tomb, monument of marble.
Rule over men reckon no madness.
Thomas. To the man of God what gladness?
Tempter.   Sadness
Only to those giving love to God alone.
Fare forward, shun two files of shadows:
Mirth merrymaking, melting strength in
sweetness,
Fiddling to feebleness, doomed to disdain;
And godlovers' longings, lost in God.
Shall he who held the solid substance
Wander waking with deceitful shadows?
Power is present. Holiness hereafter.
Thomas. Who then?
Tempter.   The Chancellor. King
and Chancellor.
King commands. Chancellor richly rules.
This is a sentence not taught in the
schools.
To set down the great, protect the poor,
Beneath the throne of God can man do
more?
Disarm the ruffian, strengthen the laws,
Rule for the good of the better cause,
Dispensing justice make all even,
Is thrive on earth, and perhaps in heaven.
Thomas. What means?
Tempter.   Real power
Is purchased at price of a certain submis-
sion.
Your spiritual power is earthly perdi-
tion.
Power is present, for him who will wield.
Thomas. Whose was it?
Tempter.   His who is gone.
Thomas. Who shall have it?
Tempter.   He who will come.
Thomas. What shall be the month?
Tempter.   The last from the first.
Thomas. What shall we give for it?
Tempter.   Pretence of priestly power.
Thomas. Why should we give it?
Tempter.   For the power and the glory.
Thomas. No!
Tempter. Yes! Or bravery will be broken,

Cabined in Canterbury, realmless ruler,
Self-bound servant of a powerless Pope,
The old stag, circled with hounds.
Thomas. No!
Tempter. Yes! men must manoeuvre. Mon-
archs also,
Waging war abroad, need fast friends at
home.
Private policy is public profit;
Dignity still shall be dressed with de-
corum.
Thomas.   You forget the bishops
Whom I have laid under excommunica-
tion.
Tempter.   Hungry hatred
Will not strive against intelligent self-
interest.
Thomas. You forget the barons. Who will
not forget
Constant curbing of pretty privilege.
Tempter.   Against the barons
Is King's cause, churl's cause, Chancel-
lor's cause.
Thomas.   No! shall I, who keep the keys
Of heaven and hell, supreme alone in Eng-
land,
Who bind and loose, with power from the
Pope,
Descend to desire a punier power?
Delegate to deal the doom of damnation,
To condemn kings, not serve among their
servants,
Is my open office. No! Go.
Tempter.   Then I leave you to your fate.
Your sin soars sunward, covering kings'
falcons.
Thomas. Temporal power, to build a good
world,
To keep order, as the world knows order.
Those who put their faith in worldly order
Not controlled by the order of God,
In confident ignorance, but arrest disorder,
Make it fast, breed fatal disease,
Degrade what they exalt. Power with the
King—
I *was* the King, his arm, his better reason.
But what was once exaltation
Would now be only mean descent.
              [*Enter* THIRD TEMPTER.]
Third Tempter. I am an unexpected visitor.
Thomas.   I expected you.
Tempter. But not in this guise, or for my
present purpose.
Thomas.   No purpose brings surprise.
Tempter.   Well, my Lord,
I am no trifler, and no politician.
To idle or intrigue at court
I have no skill. I am no courtier.
I know a horse, a dog, a wench;
I know how to hold my estates in order,

A country-keeping lord who minds his own
business.
It is we country lords who know the coun-
try
And we who know what the country needs.
It is our country. We care for the coun-
try.
We are the backbone of the nation.
We, not the plotting parasites
About the King. Excuse my bluntness:
I am a rough straightforward Englishman.
Thomas. Proceed straight forward.
Tempter.   Purpose is plain.
Endurance of friendship does not depend
Upon ourselves, but upon circumstance.
But circumstance is not undetermined.
Unreal friendship may turn to real;
But real friendship, once ended, cannot
be mended.
Sooner shall enmity turn to alliance.
The enmity that never knew friendship
Can sooner know accord.
Thomas.   For a countryman
You wrap your meaning in as dark gen-
erality
As any courtier.
Tempter.   This is the simple fact!
You have no hope of reconciliation
With Henry the King. You look only
To blind assertion in isolation.
That is a mistake.
Thomas.   O Henry, O my King!
Tempter.   Other friends
May be found in the present situation.
King in England is not all-powerful;
King is in France, squabbling in Anjou;
Round him waiting hungry sons.
We are for England. We are in England.
You and I, my Lord, are Normans.
England is a land for Norman
Sovereignty. Let the Angevin
Destroy himself, fighting in Anjou.
He does not understand us, the English
barons.
We are the people.
Thomas. To what does this lead?
Tempter.   To a happy coalition
Of intelligent interests.
Thomas.   But what have you——
If you do speak for barons——
Tempter.   For a powerful party
Which has turned its eyes in your direc-
tion——
To gain from you, your Lordship asks.
For us, Church favour would be an ad-
vantage,
Blessing of Pope powerful protection
In the fight for liberty. You, my Lord,
In being with us, would fight a good stroke
At once, for England and for Rome,

Ending the tyrannous jurisdiction
Of king's court over bishop's court,
Of king's court over baron's court.
Thomas. Which I helped to found.
Tempter.   Which you helped to found.
But time past is time forgotten.
We expect the rise of a new constellation.
Thomas. And if the Archbishop cannot trust
the King,
How can he trust those who work for
King's undoing?
Tempter. Kings will allow no power but
their own;
Church and people have good cause against
the throne.
Thomas. If the Archbishop cannot trust the
Throne,
He has good cause to trust none but God
alone.
It is not better to be thrown
To a thousand hungry appetites than to
one.
At a future time this may be shown.
I ruled once as Chancellor
And men like you were glad to wait at my
door.
Not only in the court, but in the field
And in the tilt-yard I made many yield.
Shall I who ruled like an eagle over doves
Now take the shape of a wolf among
wolves?
Pursue your treacheries as you have done
before:
No one shall say that I betrayed a king.
Tempter. Then, my Lord, I shall not wait at
your door;
And I well hope, before another spring
The King will show his regard for your
loyalty.
Thomas. To make, then break, this thought
has come before,
The desperate exercise of failing power.
Samson in Gaza did no more.
But if I break, I must break myself alone.
    [*Enter* FOURTH TEMPTER.]
Fourth Tempter. Well done, Thomas, your
will is hard to bend.
And with me beside you, you shall not lack
a friend.
Thomas. Who are you? I expected
Three visitors, not four.
Tempter. Do not be surprised to receive one
more.
Had I been expected, I had been here be-
fore.
I always precede expectation.
Thomas.   Who are you?
Tempter. As you do not know me, I do not
need a name,
And, as you know me, that is why I come.

You know me, but have never seen my face.
To meet before was never time or place.
Thomas. Say what you come to say.
Tempter.   It shall be said at last.
Hooks have been baited with morsels of the past.
Wantonness is weakness. As for the King,
His hardened hatred shall have no end.
You know truly, the King will never trust
Twice, the man who has been his friend.
Borrow use cautiously, employ
Your services as long as you have to lend.
You would wait for trap to snap
Having served your turn, broken and crushed.
As for barons, envy of lesser men
Is still more stubborn than king's anger.
Kings have public policy, barons private profit,
Jealousy raging possession of the fiend.
Barons are employable against each other;
Greater enemies must kings destroy.
Thomas. What is your counsel?
Tempter.   Fare forward to the end.
All other ways are closed to you
Except the way already chosen.
But what is pleasure, kingly rule,
Or rule of men beneath a king,
With craft in corners, stealthy stratagem,
To general grasp of spiritual power?
Man oppressed by sin, since Adam fell——
You hold the keys of heaven and hell.
Power to bind and loose: bind, Thomas, bind,
King and bishop under your heel.
King, emperor, bishop, baron, king:
Uncertain mastery of melting armies,
War, plague, and revolution,
New conspiracies, broken pacts;
To be master or servant within an hour,
This is the course of temporal power.
The Old King shall know it, when at last breath,
No sons, no empire, he bites broken teeth.
You hold the skein: wind, Thomas, wind
The thread of eternal life and death.
You hold this power, hold it.
Thomas.   Supreme, in this land?
Tempter. Supreme, but for one.
Thomas.   That I do not understand.
Tempter. It is not for me to tell you how this may be so;
I am only here, Thomas, to tell you what you know.
Thomas. How long shall this be?
Tempter. Save what you know already, ask nothing of me.
But think, Thomas, think of glory after death.

When king is dead, there's another king,
And one more king is another reign.
King is forgotten, when another shall come:
Saint and Martyr rule from the tomb.
Think, Thomas, think of enemies dismayed,
Creeping in penance, frightened of a shade;
Think of pilgrims, standing in line
Before the glittering jewelled shrine,
From generation to generation
Bending the knee in supplication.
Think of the miracles, by God's grace,
And think of your enemies, in another place.
Thomas. I have thought of these things.
Tempter.   That is why I tell you.
Your thoughts have more power than kings to compel you.
You have also thought, sometimes at your prayers,
Sometimes hesitating at the angles of of stairs,
And between sleep and waking, early in the morning,
When the bird cries, have thought of further scorning.
That nothing lasts, but the wheel turns,
The nest is rifled, and the bird mourns;
That the shrine shall be pillaged, and the gold spent,
The jewels gone for light ladies' ornament,
The sanctuary broken, and its stores
Swept into the laps of parasites and whores.
When miracles cease, and the faithful desert you,
And men shall only do their best to forget you.
And later is worse, when men will not hate you
Enough to defame or to execrate you,
But pondering the qualities that you lacked
Will only try to find the historical fact.
When men shall declare that there was no mystery
About this man who played a certain part in history.
Thomas. But what is there to do? What is left to be done?
Is there no enduring crown to be won?
Tempter. Yes, Thomas, yes; you have thought of that too.
What can compare with glory of Saints
Dwelling forever in presence of God?
What earthly glory, of king or emperor,
What earthly pride, that is not poverty
Compared with richness of heavenly grandeur?

Seek the way of martyrdom, make yourself
  the lowest
On earth, to be high in heaven.
And see far off below you, where the gulf
  is fixed,
Your persecutors, in timeless torment,
Parched passion, beyond expiation.

Thomas.   No!
Who are you, tempting with my own de-
  sires?
Others have come, temporal tempters,
With pleasure and power at palpable price.
What do you offer? What do you ask?

Tempter. I offer what you desire. I ask
What you have to give. Is it too much
For such a vision of eternal grandeur?

Thomas. Others offered real goods, worth-
  less
But real. You only offer
Dreams to damnation.

Tempter.   You have often dreamt them.

Thomas. Is there no way, in my soul's sick-
  ness,
Does not lead to damnation in pride?
I well know that these temptations
Mean present vanity and future torment.
Can sinful pride be driven out
Only by more sinful? Can I neither act
  nor suffer
Without perdition?

Tempter. You know and do not know, what
  it is to act or suffer.
You know and do not know, that acting
  is suffering,
And suffering action. Neither does the
  actor suffer
Nor the patient act. But both are fixed
In an eternal action, an eternal patience
To which all must consent that it may be
  willed
And which all must suffer that they may
  will it,
That the pattern may subsist, that the
  wheel may turn and still
Be forever still.

Chorus. There is no rest in the house. There
  is no rest in the street.
I hear restless movement of feet. And the
  air is heavy and thick.
Thick and heavy the sky. And the earth
  presses up beneath my feet.
What is the sickly smell, the vapour? the
  dark green light from a cloud on a
  withered tree? The earth is heaving
  to parturition of issue of hell. What
  is the sticky dew that forms on the
  back of my hand?

The Four Tempters. Man's life is a cheat
  and a disappointment;
All things are unreal,

Unreal or disappointing:
The Catherine wheel, the pantomime cat,
The prizes given at the children's party,
The prize awarded for the English Essay,
The scholar's degree, the statesman's
  decoration.
All things become less real, man passes
From unreality to unreality.
This man is obstinate, blind, intent
On self-destruction,
Passing from deception to deception,
From grandeur to grandeur to final illusion,
Lost in the wonder of his own greatness,
The enemy of society, enemy of himself.

The Three Priests. O Thomas my Lord, do
  not fight the intractable tide,
Do not sail the irresistible wind; in the
  storm,
Should we not wait for the sea to subside,
  in the night
Abide the coming of day, when the traveller may find his way,
The sailor lay course by the sun?

Chorus. Is it the owl that calls, or a signal
  between the trees?

Priests. Is the window-bar made fast, is the
  door under lock and bolt?

Tempters. Is it rain that taps at the window,
  is it wind that pokes at the door?

Chorus. Does the torch flame in the hall, the
  candle in the room?

Priests. Does the watchman walk by the
  wall?

Tempters. Does the mastiff prowl by the
  gate?

Chorus. Death has a hundred hands and
  walks by a thousand ways.

Priests. He may come in the sight of all,
  he may pass unseen unheard.

Tempters. Come whispering through the ear,
  or a sudden shock on the skull.

Chorus. A man may walk with a lamp at
  night, and yet be drowned in a ditch.

Priests. A man may climb the stair in the
  day, and slip on a broken step.

Tempters. A man may sit at meat, and feel
  the cold in his groin.

Chorus. We have not been happy, my Lord,
  we have not been too happy.
We are not ignorant women, we know
  what we must expect and not expect.
We know of oppression and torture,
We know of extortion and violence,
Destitution, disease,
The old without fire in winter,
The child without milk in summer,
Our labour taken away from us,
Our sins made heavier upon us.
We have seen the young man mutilated,
The torn girl trembling by the mill-stream.

And meanwhile we have gone on living,
Living and partly living,
Picking together the pieces,
Gathering faggots at nightfall,
Building a partial shelter,
For sleeping, and eating and drinking and
    laughter.

God gave us always some reason, some
    hope; but now a new terror has soiled
    us, which none can avert, none can
    avoid, flowing under our feet and
    over the sky;
Under doors and down chimneys, flowing
    in at the ear and the mouth and the
    eye.
God is leaving us, God is leaving us, more
    pang, more pain, than birth or death.
Sweet and cloying through the dark air
Falls the stifling scent of despair;
The forms take shape in the dark air:
Puss-purr of leopard, footfall of padding
    bear,
Palm-pat of nodding ape, square hyaena
    waiting
For laughter, laughter, laughter. The
    Lords of Hell are here.
They curl round you, lie at your feet, swing
    and wing through the dark air.
O Thomas Archbishop, save us, save us,
    save yourself that we may be saved;
Destroy yourself and we are destroyed.
Thomas. Now is my way clear, now is the
    meaning plain:
Temptation shall not come in this kind
    again.
The last temptation is the greatest treason:
To do the right deed for the wrong reason.
The natural vigour in the venial sin
Is the way in which our lives begin.
Thirty years ago, I searched all the ways
That lead to pleasure, advancement and
    praise.
Delight in sense, in learning and in thought,
Music and philosophy, curiosity,
The purple bullfinch in the lilac tree,
The tiltyard skill, the strategy of chess,

Love in the garden, singing to the instru-
    ment,
Were all things equally desirable.
Ambition comes when early force is spent
And when we find no longer all things
    possible.
Ambition comes behind and unobservable.
Sin grows with doing good. When I im-
    posed the King's law
In England, and waged war with him
    against Toulouse,
I beat the barons at their own game. I
Could then despise the men who thought
    me most contemptible,
The raw nobility, whose manners matched
    their fingernails.
While I ate out of the King's dish
To become servant of God was never my
    wish.
Servant of God has chance of greater sin
And sorrow, than the man who serves a
    king.
For those who serve the greater cause may
    make the cause serve them,
Still doing right: and striving with polit-
    ical men
May make that cause political, not by
    what they do
But by what they are. I know
What yet remains to show you of my his-
    tory
Will seem to most of you at best futility,
Senseless self-slaughter of a lunatic,
Arrogant passion of a fanatic.
I know that history at all times draws
The strangest consequence from remotest
    cause.
But for every evil, every sacrilege,
Crime, wrong, oppression and the axe's
    edge,
Indifference, exploitation, you, and you,
And you, must all be punished. So must
    you.
I shall no longer act or suffer, to the
    sword's end.
Now my good Angel, whom God appoints
To be my guardian, hover over the swords'
    points.

INTERLUDE

'Glory to God in the highest, and on earth peace, good will toward men.' *The fourteenth verse of the second chapter of the Gospel according to Saint Luke.* In the Name of the Father, and of the Son, and of the Holy Ghost. Amen.

Dear children of God, my sermon this morning will be a very short one. I wish only that you should ponder and meditate the deep meaning and mystery of our masses of Christmas Day. For whenever Mass is said, we re-enact the Passion and Death of Our Lord; and on this Christmas Day we do this in celebration of His Birth. So that at the same moment we rejoice in His coming for the salvation of men, and offer again to God His Body and Blood in sacrifice, oblation and satisfaction for the sins of the whole world. It was in this same night that has just passed, that a multitude of the heavenly host appeared before the shepherds at Bethlehem, saying, 'Glory to God in the highest, and on earth peace, good will toward men'; at this same time of all the year that we celebrate at once the Birth of Our Lord and His Passion and Death upon the Cross. Beloved, as the World sees, this is to behave in a strange fashion. For who in the World will both mourn and rejoice at once and for the same reason? For either joy will be overborne by mourning, or mourning will be cast out by joy; so it is only in these our Christian mysteries that we can rejoice and mourn at once for the same reason. But think for a while on the meaning of this word 'peace.' Does it seem strange to you that the angels should have announced Peace, when ceaselessly the world has been stricken with War and the fear of War? Does it seem to you that the angelic voices were mistaken, and that the promise was a disappointment and a cheat?

Reflect now, how Our Lord Himself spoke of Peace. He said to His disciples 'My peace I leave with you, my peace I give unto you.' Did He mean peace as we think of it: the kingdom of England at peace with its neighbours, the barons at peace with the King, the householder counting over his peaceful gains, the swept hearth, his best wine for a friend at the table, his wife singing to the children? Those men His disciples knew no such things: they went forth to journey afar, to suffer by land and sea, to know torture, imprisonment, disappointment, to suffer death by martyrdom. What then did He mean? If you ask that, remember then that He said also, 'Not as the world gives, give I unto you.' So then, He gave to His disciples peace, but not peace as the world gives.

Consider also one thing of which you have probably never thought. Not only do we at the feast of Christmas celebrate at once Our Lord's Birth and His Death: but on the next day we celebrate the martyrdom of His first martyr, the blessed Stephen. Is it an accident, do you think, that the day of the first martyr follows immediately the day of the Birth of Christ? By no means. Just as we rejoice and mourn at once, in the Birth and in the Passion of Our Lord; so also, in a smaller figure, we both rejoice and mourn in the death of martyrs. We mourn, for the sins of the world that has martyred them; we rejoice, that another soul is numbered among the Saints in Heaven, for the glory of God and for the salvation of men.

Beloved, we do not think of a martyr simply as a good Christian who has been killed because he is a Christian: for that would be solely to mourn. We do not think of him simply as a good Christian who has been elevated to the company of the Saints: for that would be simply to rejoice: and neither our mourning nor our rejoicing is as the world's is. A Christian martyrdom is no accident. Saints are not made by accident. Still less is a Christian martyrdom the effect of a man's will to become a Saint, as a man by willing and contriving may become a ruler of men. Ambition fortifies the will of man to become ruler over other men: it operates with deception, cajolery, and violence, it is the action of impurity upon impurity. Not so in Heaven. A martyr, a saint, is always made by the design of God, for His love of men, to warn them and to lead them, to bring them back to His ways. A martyrdom is never the design of man; for the true martyr is he who has become the instrument of God, who has lost his will in the will of God, not lost it but found it, for he has found freedom in submission to God. The martyr no longer desires anything for himself, not even the glory of martyrdom. So thus as on earth the Church mourns and rejoices at once, in a fashion that the world cannot understand; so in Heaven the Saints are most high, having made themselves most low, seeing themselves not as we see them, but in the light of the Godhead from which they draw their being.

I have spoken to you today, dear children of God, of the martyrs of the past, asking you to remember especially our martyr of Canterbury, the blessed Archbishop Elphege; because it is fitting, on Christ's birth day, to remember what is that Peace which He brought; and because, dear children, I do not think I shall ever preach to you again; and because it is possible that in a short time you may have yet another martyr, and that one perhaps not the last. I would have you keep in your hearts these words that I say, and think of them at another time. In the Name of the Father, and of the Son, and of the Holy Ghost. Amen.

PART II

Characters

THREE PRIESTS.
FOUR KNIGHTS.
ARCHBISHOP THOMAS BECKET.
CHORUS OF WOMEN OF CANTERBURY.
ATTENDANTS.

The first scene is in the Archbishop's Hall, the second scene is in the Cathedral, on December 29th, 1170.

Chorus. Does the bird sing in the South?
Only the sea-bird cries, driven inland by the storm.
What sign of the spring of the year?
Only the death of the old: not a stir, not a shoot, not a breath.
Do the days begin to lengthen?
Longer and darker the day, shorter and colder the night.
Still and stifling the air: but a wind is stored up in the East.
The starved crow sits in the field, attentive; and in the wood
The owl rehearses the hollow note of death.
What signs of a bitter spring?
The wind stored up in the East.
What, at the time of the birth of Our Lord, at Christmastide,
Is there not peace upon earth, goodwill among men?
The peace of this world is always uncertain, unless men keep the peace of God.
And war among men defiles this world, but death in the Lord renews it,
And the world must be cleaned in the winter, or we shall have only
A sour spring, a parched summer, an empty harvest.
Between Christmas and Easter what work shall be done?
The ploughman shall go out in March and turn the same earth
He has turned before, the bird shall sing the same song.
When the leaf is out on the tree, when the elder and may
Burst over the stream, and the air is clear and high,
And voices trill at windows, and children tumble in front of the door,
What work shall have been done, what wrong
Shall the bird's song cover, the green tree cover, what wrong
Shall the fresh earth cover? We wait, and the time is short
But waiting is long.
[*Enter the* FIRST PRIEST *with a banner of St. Stephen borne before him.*]
First Priest. Since Christmas a day: and the day of St. Stephen, First Martyr.
A day that was always most dear to the Archbishop Thomas.
And he kneeled down and cried with a loud voice:
Lord, lay not this sin to their charge.
[*Enter the* SECOND PRIEST, *with a banner of St. John the Apostle borne before him.*]
Second Priest. Since St. Stephen a day: and the day of St. John the Apostle.
That which was from the beginning, which we have heard,
Which we Have seen with our eyes, and our hands have handled
Of the word of life; that which we have seen and heard
Declare we unto you.
[*Enter the* THIRD PRIEST, *with a banner of the Holy Innocents borne before him.*]
Third Priest. Since St. John the Apostle a day; and the day of the Holy Innocents.
As the voice of many waters, of thunder, of harps,
They sung as it were a new song.
The blood of thy saints have they shed like water,
And there was no man to bury them. Avenge, O Lord,
The blood of thy saints. In Rama, a voice heard, weeping.
Out of the mouth of very babes, O God!
[THE PRIESTS *stand together with the banners behind them.*]

369

First Priest. Since the Holy Innocents a day: the fourth day from Christmas.
As for the people, so also for himself, he offereth for sins.
He lays down his life for the sheep. To-day?
Second Priest. Today, what is today? For the day is half gone.
First Priest. Today, what is today? but another day, the dusk of the year.
Second Priest. Today, what is today? Another night, and another dawn.
Third Priest. What day is the day that we know that we hope for or fear for?
Every day is the day we should fear from or hope from. One moment
Weighs like another. Only in retrospection, selection,
We say, that was the day. The critical moment
That is always now, and here. Even now, in sordid particulars
The eternal design may appear.

     [*Enter the* FOUR KNIGHTS.]

First Knight. Servants of the King.
First Priest.   And known to us.
You are welcome. Have you ridden far?
First Knight. Not far today, but matters urgent
Have brought us from France. We rode hard,
Took ship yesterday, landed last night,
Having business with the Archbishop.
Second Knight. Urgent business.
Third Knight.   From the King.
Fourth Knight. By the King's order.
First Knight.   Our men are outside.
First Priest. You know the Archbishop's hospitality.
We are about to go to dinner.
The good Archbishop would be vexed
If we did not offer you entertainment
Before your business. Please dine with us.
Your men shall be looked after also.
Dinner before business. Do you like roast pork?
First Knight. Business before dinner. We will roast your pork
First, and dine upon it after.
Second Knight. We must see the Archbishop.
Third Knight.   Go, tell the Archbishop
We have no need of his hospitality.
We will find our own dinner.
First Priest. [*To* ATTENDANT.] Go, tell His Lordship.
Fourth Knight.   How much longer will you keep us waiting?

       [*Enter* THOMAS.]

Thomas. [*To* PRIESTS.] However certain our expectation

The moment foreseen may be unexpected
When it arrives. It comes when we are
Engrossed with matters of other urgency.
On my table you will find
The papers in order, and the documents signed.

       [*To* KNIGHTS.]

You are welcome, whatever your business may be.
You say, from the King?
First Knight.   Most surely from the King.
We must speak with you alone.
Thomas. [*To* PRIESTS.]   Leave us then alone.
Now what is the matter?
First Knight   This is the matter.
The Four Knights. You are the Archbishop in revolt against the King; in rebellion to the King and the law of the land;
You are the Archbishop who was made by the King; whom he set in your place to carry out his command.
You are his servant, his tool, and his jack,
You wore his favours on your back,
You had your honours all from his hand; from him you had the power, the seal and the ring.
This is the man who was the tradesman's son: the backstairs brat who was born in Cheapside;
This is the creature that crawled upon the King; swollen with blood and swollen with pride.
Creeping out of the London dirt,
Crawling up like a louse on your shirt,
The man who cheated, swindled, lied; broke his oath and betrayed his King.
Thomas. This is not true.
Both before and after I received the ring
I have been a loyal vassal to the King.
Saving my order, I am at his command,
As his most faithful vassal in the land.
First Knight. Saving your order! let your order save you——
As I do not think it is like to do.
Saving your ambition is what you mean,
Saving your pride, envy and spleen.
Second Knight. Saving your insolence and greed.
Won't you ask us to pray to God for you, in your need?
Third Knight. Yes, we'll pray for you!
Fourth Knight.   Yes, we'll pray for you!
The Four Knights. Yes, we'll pray that God may help you!
Thomas. But, gentlemen, your business
Which you said so urgent, is it only
Scolding and blaspheming?

First Knight. That was only
Our indignation, as loyal subjects.
Thomas. Loyal? to whom?
First Knight. To the King!
Second Knight. The King!
Third Knight. The King!
Fourth Knight. God bless him!
Thomas. Then let your new coat of loyalty
be worn
Carefully, so it get not soiled or torn.
Have you something to say?
First Knight. By the King's command.
Shall we say it now?
Second Knight. Without delay,
Before the old fox is off and away.
Thomas. What you have to say
By the King's command—if it be the
King's command——
Should be said in public. If you make
charges,
Then in public I will refute them.
First Knight. No! here and now!
[*They make to attack him, but the
Priests and Attendants return and
quietly interpose themselves.*]
Thomas. Now and here!
First Knight. Of your earlier misdeeds I
shall make no mention.
They are too well known. But after dis-
sension
Had ended, in France, and you were en-
dued
With your former privilege, how did you
show your gratitude?
You had fled from England, not exiled
Or threatened, mind you; but in the hope
Of stirring up trouble in the French do-
minions.
You sowed strife abroad, you reviled
The King to the King of France, to the
Pope,
Raising up against him false opinions.
Second Knight. Yet the King, out of his
charity,
And urged by your friends, offered clem-
ency,
Made a pact of peace, and all dispute
ended
Sent you back to your See as you de-
manded.
Third Knight. And burying the memory of
your transgressions
Restored your honours and your pos-
sessions.
All was granted for which you sued:
Yet how, I repeat, did you show your
gratitude?
Fourth Knight. Suspending those who had
crowned the young prince,
Denying the legality of his coronation;

Binding with the chains of anathema,
Using every means in your power to
evince
The King's faithful servants, everyone
who transacts
His business in his absence, the business of
the nation.
First Knight. These are the facts.
Say therefore if you will be content
To answer in the King's presence. There-
fore were we sent.
Thomas. Never was it my wish
' To uncrown the King's son, or to diminish
His honour and power. Why should he
wish
To deprive my people of me and keep me
from my own
And bid me sit in Canterbury, alone?
I would wish him three crowns rather
than one,
And as for the bishops, it is not my yoke
That is laid upon them, or mine to revoke.
Let them go to the Pope. It was he who
condemned them.
First Knight. Through you they were sus-
pended.
Second Knight. By you be this amended.
Third Knight. Absolve them.
Fourth Knight. Absolve them.
Thomas. I do not deny
That this was done through me. But it is
not I
Who can loose whom the Pope has bound.
Let them go to him, upon whom redounds
Their contempt towards me, their con-
tempt towards the Church shown.
First Knight. Be that as it may, here is the
King's command:
That you and your servants depart from
this land.
Thomas. If that *is* the King's command, I
will be bold
To say: seven years were my people with-
out
My presence; seven years of misery and
pain.
Seven years a mendicant on foreign charity
I lingered abroad: seven years is no
brevity.
I shall not get those seven years back
again.
Never again, you must make no doubt,
Shall the sea run between the shepherd
and his fold.
First Knight. The King's justice, the King's
majesty,
You insult with gross indignity;
Insolent madman, whom nothing deters
From attainting his servants and ministers.
Thomas. It is not I who insult the King,

And there is higher than I or the King.
It is not I, Becket from Cheapside,
It is not against me, Becket, that you
strive.
It is not Becket who pronounces doom,
But the Law of Christ's Church, the judge-
ment of Rome.
Go then to Rome, or let Rome come
Here, to you, in the person of her most
unworthy son.
Petty politicians in your endless adventure!
Rome alone can absolve those who break
Christ's indenture.
First Knight. Priest, you have spoken in
peril of your life.
Second Knight. Priest, you have spoken in
danger of the knife.
Third Knight. Priest, you have spoken
treachery and treason.
Fourth Knight. Priest! traitor confirmed
in malfeasance.
Thomas. I submit my cause to the judge-
ment of Rome.
But if you kill me, I shall rise from my
tomb
To submit my cause before God's throne.
Knights. Priest! monk! and servant! take,
hold, detain,
Restrain this man, in the King's name;
Or answer with your bodies, if he escape
before we come,
We come for the King's justice, we come
again.
                                    [*Exeunt.*]
Thomas. Pursue those who flee, track down
those who evade;
Come for arrest, come with the sword,
Here, here, you shall find me ready, in the
battle of the Lord.
At whatsoever time you are ready to come,
You will find me still more ready for
martyrdom.
Chorus. I have smelt them, the death-
bringers, senses are quickened
By subtile forebodings; I have heard
Fluting in the nighttime, fluting and owls,
have seen at noon
Scaly wings slanting over, huge and ridic-
ulous. I have tasted
The savour of putrid flesh in the spoon.
I have felt
The heaving of earth at nightfall, restless,
absurd. I have heard
Laughter in the noises of beasts that make
strange noises: jackal, jackass, jack-
daw; the scurrying noise of mouse
and jerboa; the laugh of the loon, the
lunatic bird. I have seen
Grey necks twisting, rat tails twining, in
the thick light of dawn. I have eaten

Smooth creatures still living, with the
strong salt taste of living things under
sea; I have tasted
The living lobster, the crab, the oyster, the
whelk and the prawn; and they live
and spawn in my bowels, and my
bowels dissolve in the light of dawn.
I have smelt
Death in the rose, death in the hollyhock,
sweet pea, hyacinth, primrose and
cowslip. I have seen
Trunk and horn, tusk and hoof, in odd
places;
I have lain on the floor of the sea and
breathed with the breathing of the
sea-anemone, swallowed with ingurgi-
tation of the sponge. I have lain in
the soil and criticised the worm. In
the air
Flirted with the passage of the kite, I
have plunged with the kite and cow-
ered with the wren. I have felt
The horn of the beetle, the scale of the
viper, the mobile hard insensitive skin
of the elephant, the evasive flank of
the fish. I have smelt
Corruption in the dish, incense in the la-
trine, the sewer in the incense, the
smell of sweet soap in the woodpath,
a hellish sweet scent in the woodpath,
while the ground heaved. I have seen
Rings of light coiling downwards, leading
To the horror of the ape. Have I not
known, not known
What was coming to be? It was here, in
the kitchen, in the passage,
In the mews in the barn in the byre in the
market place
In our veins our bowels our skulls as well
As well as in the plottings of potentates
As well as in the consultations of powers.
What is woven on the loom of fate
What is woven in the councils of princes
Is woven also in our veins, our brains,
Is woven like a pattern of living worms
In the guts of the women of Canterbury.

I have smelt them, the death-bringers;
now is too late
For action, too soon for contrition.
Nothing is possible but the shamed swoon
Of those consenting to the last humiliation.
I have consented, Lord Archbishop, have
consented.
Am torn away, subdued, violated,
United to the spiritual flesh of nature,
Mastered by the animal powers of spirit,
Dominated by the lust of self-demolition.
By the final utter uttermost death of spirit,
By the final ecstasy of waste and shame,

O Lord Archbishop, O Thomas Archbishop,
  forgive us, forgive us, pray for us that
  we may pray for you, out of our
  shame.
Thomas. Peace, and be at peace with your
  thoughts and visions.
These things had to come to you and you
  to accept them.
This is your share of the eternal burden,
The perpetual glory. This is one moment,
But know that another
Shall pierce you with a sudden painful joy
When the figure of God's purpose is made
  complete.
You shall forget these things, toiling in
  the household,
You shall remember them, droning by the
  fire,
When age and forgetfulness sweeten
  memory
Only like a dream that has often been
  told
And often been changed in the telling.
  They will seem unreal.
Human kind cannot bear very much
  reality.
Priests. [*Severally.*] My Lord, you must
  not stop here. To the minster.
  Through the cloister. No time to
  waste. They are coming back, armed.
  To the altar, to the altar. They are
  here already. To the sanctuary.
  They are breaking in. We can bar-
  ricade the minster doors. You can-
  not stay here. Force him to come.
  Seize him.
Thomas. All my life they have been com-
  ing, these feet. All my life I have waited.
  Death will come only when I am worthy,
  And if I am worthy, there is no danger.
  I have therefore only to make perfect my
  will.
Priests. My Lord, they are coming. They
  will break through presently.
You will be killed. Come to the altar.
Thomas. Peace! be quiet! remember where
  you are, and what is happening;
No life here is sought for but mine,
And I am not in danger: only near to
  death.
Priests. Make haste, my Lord. Don't stop
  here talking. It is not right.
What shall become of us, my Lord, if you
  are killed; what shall become of us?
Thomas.   That again is another theme
To be developed and resolved in the pat-
  tern of time.
It is not for me to run from city to city;
To meet death gladly is only
The only way in which I can defend

The Law of God, the holy canons.
Priests. My Lord, to vespers! You must
  not be absent from vespers. You
  must not be absent from the divine
  office. To vespers. Into the cathedral!
Thomas. Go to vespers, remember me at
  your prayers.
They shall find the shepherd here; the
  flock shall be spared.
I have had a tremor of bliss, a wink of
  heaven, a whisper,
And I would no longer be denied; all
  things
Proceed to a joyful consummation.
Priests. Seize him! force him! drag him!
Thomas.   Keep your hands off!
Priests. To vespers! Take his feet! Up with
  him! Hurry.
  [*They drag him off. While the* CHORUS
  *speak, the scene is changed to the cathe-
  dral.*]
Chorus. [*While a* Dies Irae *is sung in Latin
  by a choir in the distance.*]
Numb the hand and dry the eyelid,
Still the horror, but more horror
Than when tearing in the belly.

Still the horror, but more horror
Than when twisting in the fingers,
Than when splitting in the skull.

More than footfall in the passage,
More than shadow in the doorway,
More than fury in the hall.

The agents of hell disappear, the human,
  they shrink and dissolve
Into dust on the wind, forgotten, un-
  memorable; only is here
The white flat face of Death, God's silent
  servant,
And behind the face of Death the Judge-
  ment
And behind the Judgement the Void, more
  horrid than active shapes of hell;
Emptiness, absence, separation from God;
The horror of the effortless journey, to
  the empty land
Which is no land, only emptiness, absence, the Void,
Where those who were men can no longer
  turn the mind
To distraction, delusion, escape into
  dream, pretence,
Where the soul is no longer deceived, for
  there are no objects, no tones,
No colours, no forms to distract, to divert
  the soul
From seeing itself, foully united forever,
  nothing with nothing,

Not what we call death, but what beyond
    death is not death,
We fear, we fear. Who shall then plead
    for me,
Who intercede for me, in my most need?

Dead upon the tree, my Saviour,
Let not be in vain Thy labour;
Help me, Lord, in my last fear.

Dust I am, to dust am bending,
From the final doom impending
Help me, Lord, for death is near.
    [*In the cathedral.* THOMAS *and*
    PRIESTS.]
Priests.   Bar the door. Bar the door.
The door is barred.
We are safe. We are safe.
The enemy may rage outside, he will tire
In vain. They cannot break in.
They dare not break in.
They cannot break in. They have not the
    force.
We are safe. We are safe.
Thomas. Unbar the doors! throw open the
    doors!
I will not have the house of prayer, the
    church of Christ,
The sanctuary, turned into a fortress.
The Church shall protect her own, in her
    own way, not
As oak and stone; stone and oak decay,
Give no stay, but the Church shall endure.
The church shall be open, even to our
    enemies. Open the door!
Priests. My Lord! these are not men, these
    come not as men come, but
Like maddened beasts. They come not
    like men, who
Respect the sanctuary, who kneel to the
    Body of Christ,
But like beasts. You would bar the door
Against the lion, the leopard, the wolf or
    the boar,
Why not more
Against beasts with the souls of damned
    men, against men
Who would damn themselves to beasts.
    My Lord! My Lord!
Thomas. Unbar the door!
You think me reckless, desperate and mad.
You argue by results, as this world does,
To settle if an act be good or bad.
You defer to the fact. For every life and
    every act
Consequence of good and evil can be
    shown.
And as in time results of many deeds are
    blended

So good and evil in the end become con-
    founded.
It is not in time that my death shall be
    known;
It is out of time that my decision is taken
If you call that decision
To which my whole being gives entire con-
    sent.
I give my life
To the Law of God above the Law of Man.
Those who do not the same
How should they know what I do?
How should you know what I do? Yet
    how much more
Should you know than these madmen
    · beating on the door.
Unbar the door! unbar the door!
We are not here to triumph by fighting, by
    stratagem, or by resistance,
Not to fight with beasts as men. We have
    fought the beast
And have conquered. We have only to
    conquer
Now, by suffering. This is the easier vic-
    tory.
Now is the triumph of the Cross, now
Open the door! I command it. OPEN THE
    DOOR!
    [*The door is opened. The* KNIGHTS *en-
    ter, slightly tipsy.*]
Priests. This way, my Lord! Quick. Up the
    stair. To the roof. To the crypt.
    Quick. Come. Force him.
Knights. [*One line each.*] Where is Becket,
    the traitor to the King?
    Where is Becket, the meddling priest?
Come down Daniel to the lions' den,
    Come down Daniel for the mark of the
    beast.

Are you washed in the blood of the Lamb?
    Are you marked with the mark of the
    beast?
Come down Daniel to the lions' den,
    Come down Daniel and join in the feast.

Where is Becket the Cheapside brat?
    Where is Becket the faithless priest?
Come down Daniel to the lions' den,
    Come down Daniel and join in the feast.

Thomas. It is the just man who
    Like a bold lion, should be without fear.
I am here.
No traitor to the King. I am a priest,
A Christian, saved by the blood of Christ,
Ready to suffer with my blood.
This is the sign of the Church always,
The sign of blood. Blood for blood.
His blood given to buy my life,

My blood given to pay for His death,
My death for His death.

Knights. Absolve all those you have excommunicated.

Resign the powers you have arrogated.

Restore to the King the money you appropriated.

Renew the obedience you have violated.

Thomas. For my Lord I am now ready to
die,

That His Church may have peace and
liberty.

Do with me as you will, to your hurt and
shame;

But none of my people, in God's name,

Whether layman or clerk, shall you touch.

This I forbid.

Knights. Traitor! traitor! traitor! traitor!

Thomas. You, Reginald, three times traitor
you:

Traitor to me as my temporal vassal,

Traitor to me as your spiritual lord,

Traitor to God in desecrating His Church.

First Knight. No faith do I owe to a renegade,

And what I owe shall now be paid.

Thomas. Now to Almighty God, to the
Blessed Mary ever Virgin, to the
blessed John the Baptist, the holy
apostles Peter and Paul, to the blessed
martyr Denys, and to all the Saints, I
commend my cause and that of the
Church.

[*While the* KNIGHTS *kill him, we hear
the* CHORUS.]

Chorus. Clear the air! clean the sky! wash
the wind! take stone from stone and
wash them.

The land is foul, the water is foul, our
beasts and ourselves defiled with
blood.

A rain of blood has blinded my eyes.
Where is England? where is Kent?
where is Canterbury?

O far far far far in the past; and I wander
in a land of barren boughs: if I break
them, they bleed; I wander in a land
of dry stones: if I touch them they
bleed.

How how can I ever return, to the soft
quiet seasons?

Night stay with us, stop sun, hold season,
let the day not come, let the spring
not come.

Can I look again at the day and its common things, and see them all smeared
with blood, through a curtain of falling blood?

We did not wish anything to happen.

We understood the private catastrophe,

The personal loss, the general misery,
Living and partly living;

The terror by night that ends in daily action,

The terror by day that ends in sleep;

But the talk in the market-place, the hand
on the broom,

The nighttime heaping of the ashes,

The fuel laid on the fire at daybreak,

These acts marked a limit to our suffering.

Every horror had its definition,

Every sorrow had a kind of end:

In life there is not time to grieve long.

But this, this is out of life, this is out of
time,

An instant eternity of evil and wrong.

We are soiled by a filth that we cannot
clean, united to supernatural vermin,

It is not we alone, it is not the house, it is
not the city that is defiled,

But the world that is wholly foul.

Clear the air! clean the sky! wash the
wind! take the stone from the stone,
take the skin from the arm, take the
muscle from the bone, and wash
them. Wash the stone, wash the bone,
wash the brain, wash the soul, wash
them wash them!

[*The* KNIGHTS, *having completed the
murder, advance to the front of the
stage and address the audience.*]

First Knight. We beg you to give us your
attention for a few moments. We know that
you may be disposed to judge unfavourably
of our action. You are Englishmen, and
therefore you believe in fair play: and when
you see one man being set upon by four, then
your sympathies are all with the under dog.
I respect such feelings, I share them. Nevertheless, I appeal to your sense of honour.
You are Englishmen, and therefore will not
judge anybody without hearing both sides
of the case. That is in accordance with our
long established principle of Trial by Jury.
I am not myself qualified to put our case to
you. I am a man of action and not of words.
For that reason I shall do no more than introduce the other speakers, who, with their
various abilities, and different points of view,
will be able to lay before you the merits of
this extremely complex problem. I shall call
upon our youngest member to speak first.
William de Traci.

Second Knight. I am afraid I am not anything like such an experienced speaker as
Reginald Fitz Urse would lead you to believe. But there is one thing I should like
to say, and I might as well say it at once. It
is this: in what we have done, and whatever
you may think of it, we have been perfectly

T. S. ELIOT

disinterested. [*The other* KNIGHTS: *'Hear!
hear!'.*] *We* are not getting anything out of
this. We have much more to lose than to
gain. We are four plain Englishmen who put
our country first. I dare say that we didn't
make a very good impression when we came
in. The fact is that we knew we had taken
on a pretty stiff job; I'll only speak for myself, but I had drunk a good deal—I am not
a drinking man ordinarily—to brace myself
up for it. When you come to the point, it
does go against the grain to kill an Archbishop, especially when you have been
brought up in good Church traditions. So if
we seemed a bit rowdy, you will understand
why it was; and for my part I am awfully
sorry about it. We realised that this was
our duty, but all the same we had to work
ourselves up to it. And, as I said, *we* are not
getting a penny out of this. We know perfectly well how things will turn out. King
Henry—God bless him—will have to say,
for reasons of state, that he never meant
this to happen; and there is going to be an
awful row; and at the best we shall have to
spend the rest of our lives abroad. And even
when reasonable people come to see that the
Archbishop *had* to be put out of the way—
and personally I had a tremendous admiration for him—you must have noticed what a
good show he put up at the end—they won't
give *us* any glory. No, we have done for
ourselves, there's no mistake about that. So,
as I said at the beginning, please give us at
least the credit for being completely disinterested in this business. I think that is
about all I have to say.

First Knight. I think we will all agree that
William de Traci has spoken well and has
made a very important point. The gist of his
argument is this: that we have been completely disinterested. But our act itself needs
more justification than that; and you must
hear our other speakers. I shall next call
upon Hugh de Morville.

Third Knight. I should like first to recur
to a point that was very well put by our
leader, Reginald Fitz Urse: that you are
Englishmen, and therefore your sympathies
are always with the under dog. It is the English spirit of fair play. Now the worthy
Archbishop, whose good qualities I very
much admired, has throughout been presented as the under dog. But is this really
the case? I am going to appeal not to your
emotions but to your reason. You are hard-
headed sensible people, as I can see, and not
to be taken in by emotional clap-trap. I
therefore ask you to consider soberly: what
were the Archbishop's aims? and what are

King Henry's aims? In the answer to these
questions lies the key to the problem.

The King's aim has been perfectly consistent. During the reign of the late Queen
Matilda and the irruption of the unhappy
usurper Stephen, the kingdom was very
much divided. Our King saw that the one
thing needful was to restore order: to curb
the excessive powers of local government,
which were usually exercised for selfish and
often for seditious ends, and to systematise
the judiciary. There was utter chaos: there
were three kinds of justice and three kinds
of court: that of the King, that of the
Bishops, and that of the baronage. I must
repeat one point that the last speaker has
made. While the late Archbishop was Chancellor, he wholeheartedly supported the
King's designs: this is an important point,
which if necessary, I can substantiate. Now
the King intended that Becket, who had
proved himself an extremely able administrator—no one denies that—should unite the
offices of Chancellor and Archbishop. No
one would have grudged him that; no one
than he was better qualified to fill at once
these two most important posts. Had Becket
concurred with the King's wishes, we should
have had an almost ideal State: a union of
spiritual and temporal administration, under
the central government. I knew Becket well,
in various official relations; and I may say
that I have never known a man so well
qualified for the highest rank of the Civil
Service. And what happened? The moment
that Becket, at the King's instance, had been
made Archbishop, he resigned the office of
Chancellor, he became more priestly than the
priests, he ostentatiously and offensively
adopted an ascetic manner of life, he openly
abandoned every policy that he had hereto-
fore supported; he affirmed immediately that
there was a higher order than that which our
King, and he as the King's servant, had for
so many years striven to establish; and that
—God knows why—the two orders were incompatible.

You will agree with me that such interference by an Archbishop offends the instincts of a people like ours. So far, I know
that I have your approval: I read it in your
faces. It is only with the measures we have
had to adopt, in order to set matters to
rights, that you take issue. No one regrets
the necessity for violence more than we do.
Unhappily, there are times when violence is
the only way in which social justice can be
secured. At another time, you would condemn an Archbishop by vote of Parliament
and execute him formally as a traitor, and

no one would have to bear the burden of being called murderer. And at a later time still, even such temperate measures as these would become unnecessary. But, if you have now arrived at a just subordination of the pretensions of the Church to the welfare of the State, remember that it is we who took the first step. We have been instrumental in bringing about the state of affairs that you approve. We have served your interests; we merit your applause; and if there is any guilt whatever in the matter, you must share it with us.

First Knight. Morville has given us a great deal to think about. It seems to me that he has said almost the last word, for those who have been able to follow his very subtle reasoning. We have, however, one more speaker, who has I think another point of view to express. If there are any who are still unconvinced, I think that Richard Brito will be able to convince them. Richard Brito.

Fourth Knight. The speakers who have preceded me, to say nothing of our leader, Reginald Fitz Urse, have all spoken very much to the point. I have nothing to add along their particular lines of argument. What I have to say may be put in the form of a question: *Who killed the Archbishop?* As you have been eye-witnesses of this lamentable scene, you may feel some surprise at my putting it in this way. But consider the course of events. I am obliged, very briefly, to go over the ground traversed by the last speaker. While the late Archbishop was Chancellor, no one, under the King, did more to weld the country together, to give it the unity, the stability, order, tranquillity, and justice that it so badly needed. From the moment he became Archbishop he completely reversed his policy; he showed himself to be utterly indifferent to the fate of the country, to be, in fact, a monster of egotism, a menace to society. This egotism grew upon him, until it became at last an undoubted mania. Every means that had been tried to conciliate him, to restore him to reason, had failed. Now I have unimpeachable evidence to the effect that before he left France he clearly prophesied, in the presence of numerous witnesses, that he had not long to live, and that he would be killed in England. He used every means of provocation; from his conduct, step by step, there can be no inference except that he had determined upon a death by martyrdom. This man, formerly a great public servant, had become a wrecker. Even at the last, he could have given us reason: you have seen how he evaded our questions. And when he had deliberately exasperated us beyond human endurance, he could still have easily escaped; he could have kept himself from us long enough to allow our righteous anger to cool. That was just what he did not wish to happen; he insisted, while we were still inflamed with wrath, that the doors should be opened. Need I say more? I think, with these facts before you, you will unhesitatingly render a verdict of Suicide while of Unsound Mind. It is the only charitable verdict you can give, upon one who was, after all, a great man.

First Knight. Thank you, Brito. I think that there is no more to be said; and I suggest that you now disperse quietly to your homes. Please be careful not to loiter in groups at street corners, and do nothing that might provoke any public outbreak.

[*Exeunt* KNIGHTS.]

First Priest. O father, father, gone from us, lost to us,
How shall we find you, from what far place
Do you look down on us? You now in Heaven,
Who shall now guide us, protect us, direct us?
After what journey through what further dread
Shall we recover your presence? when inherit
Your strength? The Church lies bereft,
Alone, desecrated, desolated, and the heathen shall build on the ruins
Their world without God. I see it. I see it.

Third Priest. No. For the Church is stronger for this action,
Triumphant in adversity. It is fortified
By persecution: supreme, so long as men will die for it.
Go, weak sad men, lost erring souls, homeless in earth or heaven.
Go where the sunset reddens the last grey rock
Of Brittany, or the Gates of Hercules.
Go venture shipwreck on the sullen coasts
Where blackamoors make captive Christian men;
Go to the northern seas confined with ice
Where the dead breath makes numb the hand, makes dull the brain;
Find an oasis in the desert sun,
Go seek alliance with the heathen Saracen,
To share his filthy rites, and try to snatch
Forgetfulness in his libidinous courts,
Oblivion in the fountain by the date-tree;
Or sit and bite your nails in Aquitaine.

In the small circle of pain within the skull
You still shall tramp and tread one end-
    less round
Of thought, to justify your action to your-
    selves,
Weaving a fiction which unravels as you
    weave,
Pacing forever in the hell of make-believe
Which never is belief: this is your fate on
    earth
And we must think no further of you.
    O my lord,
The glory of whose new state is hidden
    from us,
Pray for us of your charity; now in the
    sight of God
Conjoined with all the saints and martyrs
    gone before you,
Remember us. Let our thanks ascend
To God, who has given us another Saint
    in Canterbury.
Chorus. [*While a* Te Deum *is sung in Latin
    by a choir in the distance.*]
We praise Thee, O God, for Thy glory
    displayed in all the creatures of the
    earth,
In the snow, in the rain, in the wind, in
    the storm; in all of Thy creatures,
    both the hunters and the hunted.
For all things exist only as seen by Thee,
    only as known by Thee, all things
    exist
Only in Thy light, and Thy glory is de-
    clared even in that which denies
    Thee; the darkness declares the glory
    of light.
Those who deny Thee could not deny, if
    Thou didst not exist; and their denial
    is never complete, for if it were so,
    they would not exist.
They affirm Thee in living; all things af-
    firm Thee in living; the bird in the
    air, both the hawk and the finch; the
    beast on the earth, both the wolf and
    the lamb; the worm in the soil and
    the worm in the belly.
Therefore man, whom Thou hast made to
    be conscious of Thee, must con-
    sciously praise Thee, in thought and
    in word and in deed.
Even with the hand to the broom, the
    back bent in laying the fire, the knee
    bent in cleaning the hearth, we, the
    scrubbers and sweepers of Canter-
    bury,

The back bent under toil, the knee bent
    under sin, the hands to the face under
    fear, the head bent under grief,
Even in us the voices of seasons, the
    snuffle of winter, the song of spring,
    the drone of summer, the voices of
    beasts and of birds, praise Thee.
We thank Thee for Thy mercies of blood,
    for Thy redemption by blood. For
    the blood of Thy martyrs and saints
Shall enrich the earth, shall create the holy
    places.
For wherever a saint has dwelt, wherever
    a martyr has given his blood for the
    blood of Christ,
There is holy ground, and the sanctity shall
    not depart from it
Though armies trample over it, though
    sightseers come with guide-books
    looking over it;
From where the western seas gnaw at the
    coast of Iona,
To the death in the desert, the prayer in
    forgotten places by the broken im-
    perial column,
From such ground springs that which for-
    ever renews the earth
Though it is forever denied. Therefore, O
    God, we thank Thee
Who hast given such blessing to Canter-
    bury.
Forgive us, O Lord, we acknowledge our-
    selves as type of the common man,
Of the men and women who shut the door
    and sit by the fire;
Who fear the blessing of God, the loneli-
    ness of the night of God, the sur-
    render required, the deprivation in-
    flicted;
Who fear the injustice of men less than
    the justice of God;
Who fear the hand at the window, the fire
    in the thatch, the fist in the tavern,
    the push into the canal,
Less than we fear the love of God.
We acknowledge our trespass, our weak-
    ness, our fault; we acknowledge
That the sin of the world is upon our
    heads; that the blood of the martyrs
    and the agony of the saints
Is upon our heads.
Lord, have mercy upon us.
Christ, have mercy upon us.
Lord, have mercy upon us.
Blessed Thomas, pray for us.

PURPLE DUST *

By

SEAN O'CASEY

"Away from all mouldherin' ashes we row
Far away O!"

THIS EXULTANT RIME IS SUNG AT THE
end of *Purple Dust* by master-mason
O'Killigain as he flees from the Tudor
manor, symbol of ancient oppression and
decay, that he has been employed to restore.
This gothic relic will shortly be engulfed by
the rising river on which O'Killigain's barque
is speeding him and his abducted Irish bride
to a symbolic freedom. The lilting lines
serve us well as threefold epitome: of the
scant but meaningful dramatic action of this
allegorical comedy; of its author's own
abandonment of a free, turbulent, but, as he
tragically had found it, an unregenerate Ireland; and, lastly and more importantly, the
same simple lines throw into clear perspective the play's complex allegory in which
many farcically amusing characters embody
various types of insincerity and degeneracy,
each masked by a show of noble intent.
They have suddenly found themselves dere-
licts in the "purple dust" soon to be swept
away by a reawakened and genuine humanity,
symbolized by the rising river. To such re-
birth, whether that of his beloved Erin of
legend or that of all human enlightenment,
O'Casey long ago dedicated his acknowledged genius.

His masterpieces of the 1920's, *The
Shadow of a Gunman, Juno and the Paycock,*[1] *and The Plough and the Stars,* brought
to Dublin's Abbey Theatre a virtually new
type of reportorial tragedy based on the
sanguinary rioting of Sinn Feiners against
Black and Tans, as viewed with laudable de-
tachment by the dramatist and pictured with
unsurpassed realism in Irish dialect, which no
one has used more forcefully or with a keener
sense of its humor, its musical rhythm, and
its idiomatic imagery.
The sensational success, particularly of

the second of these plays, had abruptly
raised a hardly known writer of forty to
high rank among world dramatists, but the
last, *The Plough and the Stars,* because of
its detached candor, touched off the worst of
the Abbey Theatre riots, and throughout
nationalist Ireland O'Casey found himself a
victim of insult and abuse. Disillusioned
and embittered, he took refuge in London in
1927 and his *The Silver Tassie* submitted to
the Abbey management was denied production. In stubborn anger he refused to offer
that theatre another new play, and he has
never done so, although that company later
staged *The Silver Tassie* and other of his
plays. No ostensible reconciliation has yet
resulted.

More disturbing to his admirers everywhere has been O'Casey's abandonment, for
aesthetic reasons, of conventional play forms
and consistently realistic treatment of characters and story, which in the earlier work
had been the principal attraction. He now
turned to the newer techniques of symbolism
and allegory (as in *Purple Dust*), expressionism (as in *Within the Gates*), and pronounced
lyricism, not only in song but also in dialogue.
This dialogue abounds in outspoken ridicule
of religious and social beliefs and practices,
without any clearly defined ideology to offer,
except scorn for man-made codes and faith in
free and independent mentality like the author's own.

As with many other dramatists of literary
stature bent on dramatic liberation and reform, O'Casey seems to regard the stabilized
naturalism of a Gorky, a Chekhov, a Galsworthy, or of his own earlier self, much as
the foreman O'Killigain and the Second
Workman in this play, who are clearly
spokesmen for the dramatist, view the stately
Ormond Manor as once a thing of strength
and beauty but now "a heap of purple dust"
that "will vanish away with the flow of the
river."

* Used with the permission of The Macmillan Company.
[1] Included in *Contemporary Drama 37 Plays* and
Contemporary Drama 9 Plays.

379

How such changes in O'Casey's artistry will affect his standing has been a subject of futile debate. Favorable critics maintain that his genius has attained to such heights that today's playgoers, fed on frothy fare of stage and screen, cannot grasp, much less appreciate, this modernist outpouring of Celtic genius. Those with opposite views find his profusion of abstruse dialogue and his less consistent realism of character and story difficult and unexciting in the theatre. Obviously the later plays have had far less stage success than the earlier, and surely this falling off cannot be explained merely on the ground that they are less realistic and more imaginative in expression; such qualities have not barred Shakespeare from the theatre, and not many years ago, four highly poetic and unconventional dramas of Christopher Fry were successful in a single London season.

There are simpler and more obvious reasons for O'Casey's theatre decline: an overdependence on the charm of superbly phrased dialect and upon individually amusing episodes at the expense of engrossing interest in the action of the play as a whole: action, that is, in the truly dramatic sense and not merely stage business, of which there is abundance, whether serious or comic, in any O'Casey play. The gripping, climactic conflict so prominent in his first successes has been minimized where it is felt at all. In short, O'Casey has deliberately eviscerated his drama of the most essential element of theatre success and made of himself a chamber dramatist to be more enjoyed in the study than in the theatre.

Such a work, in fact, is *Purple Dust,* although it is somewhat more stageworthy than others, as George Jean Nathan believed it to be when upon its publication he expressed astonishment that it had attracted no producer. But in that year of 1940, apart from any other aspect it may have had, this play must have seemed repugnant to even a large-minded Britisher, for no patriot could have endured its belittling ridicule of the two silly and vicious settlers from London; and there is not very much in the characters and action to attract a sensitive Irish auditor, whether at home or abroad.

But this play deserves careful study and it is neither difficult nor uninteresting to read. And, as always with O'Casey, the rhythmic, witty dialect is immensely entertaining in itself. The comparison of its method with that of *Juno and the Paycock* is instructive. Its loosely connected scenes follow each other like numbers in a vaudeville, with but faint intimations of its symbolism until it becomes impressively apparent at the close. Nor is an awareness of the deeper dramatic motives underlying its burlesque lampooning strong at any time during the play: the age-old British-Irish antagonism; commercialism against mutual helpfulness; bartered affection versus genuine love; insular spirit defeating friendliness—and all like "clouds of dust" dimming a golden dawn. The characters tainted by the dust are obvious; those of the dawn—spiritual kindred of the dramatist—are foreman Jack and Second Workman Philib, whose reclamation of the commercially enslaved loveliness of Erin's Avril and Souhaun provides the directive action in which symbol and drama clearly merge.

But throughout, our greater pleasure has been "listenin'," as Souhaun says, "to a voice that's makin' gold embroidery out o' dancin' words." Indeed, this play is what its author once said drama should be: "a commentary on life itself."

SEAN O'CASEY

Born 1880, Dublin, Ireland.

Common laborer from the slums, a self-educated member of the Anglican Church, the Gaelic League, and various labor unions.

1913–1917, Organizer and secretary of the Irish Citizen Army.

1918, His first publication: *History of the Citizen Army.*

1923, His first production by the Abbey Theatre: *The Shadow of a Gunman.* (He had begun writing plays as early as 1901, and not, as commonly supposed, because of interest in the Abbey Theatre.)

1926, The production of *The Plough and the Stars* pre-
cipitated rioting in the Abbey and attacks on O'Casey.
1927, Took refuge in England where he has since lived.
1928, Broke relations with the Abbey Theatre management. Continued playwriting, and has published
many volumes, chiefly autobiographical. Avows communist ideology.

PLAYS

1918 *The Robe of Rosheen* (one-act play published in a Republican periodical). 1923 *The Shadow of a Gunman*. 1923 *Cathleen Listens In* (produced by the Abbey, not published). 1923 *The Cooing of the Doves* (one-act, later used as Act II of *The Plough and the Stars*). 1924 *Juno and the Paycock*. 1924 *Nannie's Night Out*. 1926 *The Plough and the Stars*. 1928 *The Silver Tassie*. 1933 *Within the Gates*. 1935 *The End of the Beginning*. 1940 *The Star Turns Red*. 1940 *Purple Dust*. 1942 *Red Roses for Me*. 1946 *Oak Leaves and Lavender*. 1947 *A Pound on Demand*. 1949 *Cock-a-Doodle-Dandy*. 1951 *Hall of Healing*. 1951 *Bedtime Story* (one-act). 1951 *Time to Go*. 1954 *The Bishop's Bonfire*. 1958 *The Drums of Father Ned* (first entitled *The Night is Whispering*).

WRITINGS ON DRAMA

The Flying Wasp, 1937. *The Green Crow*, 1956. *On Playwriting* and *Before Curtain Rise* (both prefaced to *Plays of Sean O'Casey*, 1954). Much comment and criticism in the autobiographical volumes: *I Knock at the Door*, 1939; *Pictures in the Hallway*, 1942; *Drums Under the Window*, 1946; *Inishfallen, Fare Thee Well*, 1949; *Rose and Crown*, 1952. *Sunset and Evening Star*, 1954. "The Plays of Sean O'Casey" in *The Nineteenth Century and After*, CLV, pp. 399–402, September, 1928.

PURPLE DUST

Cast of Characters

CYRIL POGES.
BASIL STOKE.
SOUHAUN, Cyril's Mistress.
AVRIL, Basil's Mistress.
BARNEY, Their Manservant.
CLOYNE, Their Maidservant.
O'KILLIGAIN, A Foreman Stonemason.
FIRST WORKMAN.

SECOND WORKMAN.
THIRD WORKMAN.
THE REVEREND GEORGE CANON CREEHEWEL,
   P.P. of Clune na Geera.
THE POSTMASTER.
YELLOW-BEARDED WORKMAN.
THE FIGURE.
THE BULL.

THE SCENES

ACT ONE. *A room in an Old Tudor Mansion in Clune na Geera.*
ACT TWO. *The same.*
ACT THREE. *The same.*
TIME. *The present.*

ACT ONE

SCENE: *A wide, deep, gloomy room that was once part of the assembly or living-room of a Tudor-Elizabethan Mansion. The floor is paved with broad black and dull red flagstones. The walls are timbered with oak beams, and beams of the same wood criss-cross each other, forming the roof, so that the room looks somewhat like a gigantic cage. The beams are painted alternately, black and white, so as to show they are there and to draw attention to their beauty; but the paint makes them too conspicuous, and therefore ugly. On the right is a huge open fireplace, overhung by a huge hood. In the centre of the fireplace, is a big iron arm, with a swinging cross-piece, thrust out like a crane; from this cross-piece hangs a thick chain to which a big, shining copper kettle is attached. At the back are two rather narrow arched doorways, one towards the right, the other towards the left. Between these are two long, deep, mullioned windows. At the left, nearly opposite the fireplace, is a wider arched doorway leading to the entrance hall. Near the fireplace are two straight-backed seats, like infantile church pews, each big enough only to hold one person. A small Elizabethan or Jacobean table is somewhere near the centre of the room.*

On this table is a vase in which are a collection of violets and primroses, mostly primroses.
It is about seven o'clock of an Autumn morning, fine, crisp, and fair.
[Three WORKMEN are seen in the room, two with shovels and one with a pickaxe. One with a shovel and the one with the pickaxe are standing near the archway leading to the entrance hall; the other, with a shovel, is beside the wide fireplace, looking curiously at it. The FIRST WORKMAN is a tall, lean man, with a foxy face; the SECOND WORKMAN is tall, too, and strongly built; he has a dreamy look, and has a dark, trim beard faintly touched with grey; the THIRD WORKMAN is stouter than the others, and not so tall. They're ALL roughly dressed in soiled clothes, and wear high rubber boots.]

First Workman. [*Near the fireplace.*] Well, of all the wondhers . . . A house that's half down an' it's waning over. Thrickin' th' rotten beams into a look of sturdiness with a coat of black an' white paint, an' they for long a dismal home even for the gnawin' beetle an' th' borin' worm.
Third Workman. [*With the pickaxe.*] They like that sort of thing.
First Workman. An' th' maid was tellin'

382

me they're goin' to invest in hins an' cows, an' make th' place self-supportin'.

Third Workman. An' th' two o' them business men, rollin' in money.

First Workman. Women you're not married to cost a lot to keep an' th' two with them'll dip deep into the oul' men's revenue. Goin' over to London done them a world o' good.

Third Workman. Irish, too, an' not a bit ashamed o' themselves.

First Workman. Ashamed is it? Isn't th' oulder one proclaimin' she's straight from th' Duke of Ormond?

Third Workman. An' we knowin' the two o' them well, as kids with patched petticoats an' broken shoes, runnin' round th' lanes o' Killnageera.

First Workman. God be good to her, anyway, for bringin' a bit o' th' doddherers' money to where it's needed.

Third Workman. Th' two poor English omadhauns won't have much when th' lassies decide it's time for partin'.

Second Workman. [*Who has been silently leaning on his shovel, looking dreamily ahead of him.*] That day'll hasten, for God is good. Our poets of old have said it often: time'll see th' Irish again with wine an' ale on th' table before them; an' th' English, barefoot, beggin' a crust in a lonely sthreet, an' th' weather frosty.

First Workman. Afther a reckless life, they need th' peace o' th' country.

Third Workman. [*Assuming a listening attitude.*] They're stirrin'.

[MR [1] CYRIL POGES, SOUHAUN, and BARNEY *come in by one entrance at the back;* AVRIL, BASIL STOKE, *and* CLOYNE *from the other; they dance in what they think to be a country style, and meet in the centre, throwing their legs about while they sing.* AVRIL *has a garland of moonfaced daisies around her neck and carries a dainty little shepherd's crook in her hand.* CYRIL POGES, *a little wooden rake with a gaily coloured handle;* SOUHAUN *has a little hoe, garlanded with ribbons;* CLOYNE, *a dainty little hayfork;* BARNEY *a little reaping-hook; and* BASIL STOKE *a slim-handled little spade. Each wears a white smock having on it the stylized picture of an animal: on* POGES' *a pig; on* BASIL'S *a hen; on* SOUHAUN'S *a cow; on* AVRIL'S *a duck; on* CLOYNE'S *a sheep; on* BARNEY'S *a cock.*

POGES *is a man of sixty-five years of age. He was, when young, a rather good-looking man, but age has altered him a lot. He is now inclined to be too stout, with a broad chest, and too prominent belly; his face is a little too broad, too ruddy, and there are perceptible bags of flesh under his eyes. He has a large head, getting bald in front, though behind and over his ears the hair is long, fairly thick, and tinged with grey. He has a fussy manner, all business over little things, wants his own way at all times, and persuades himself that whatever he thinks of doing must be for the best, and expects everyone else to agree with him. He is apt to lose his temper easily, and to shout in the belief that that is the only way to make other people fall in with his opinions. He has now persuaded himself that in the country peace and good-will are to be found, and expects that everyone else should find them there, too. Under the smock he is dressed in morning clothes, and wears a tall hat.*

BASIL STOKE *is a long, thin man of thirty, with a rather gloomy face which he thinks betokens dignity, made gloomier still by believing that he is something of a philosopher. His cheeks are thin and their upper bones are as sharp as a hatchet. He is clean-shaven, and the thin hair on his half-bald head is trimly brushed back from his forehead. His eyes are covered with a pair of large horn-rimmed glasses. Under the smock he is dressed in jacket, plus-fours, and a cap.*

SOUHAUN *is a woman of thirty-two years of age. She must have been a very handsome girl and she is still very good-looking, in a more matronly way. She has the fine figure of her young friend—* AVRIL, *but her arms and her legs have grown a little plumper. She is still attractive enough to find attention from a good many men, when her young friend is out of the way. She wears, under the smock, what a lady would usually wear in the morning.*

CLOYNE *is a stoutly-built, fine-looking girl of twenty-six or so, and wears the servant's cap and dress under her smock.* BARNEY *is a middle-aged man with a discontented face and a muttering manner. Under his smock he wears the usual dress of a butler.*

AVRIL *is dressed, under her smock, in gay pyjamas.*]

---

[1] This play follows such British spellings as "Mr", "Dr", "colour".

Poges. [*Singing.*]
  Deep in the country, we're all
    right,
  Man's delight,
  Day and night,
  Far from the city's frantic fight.
All. Here in the bosky countrie!
Souhaun. [*Singing.*]
  Rural scenes are now our joy:
  Farmer's boy,
  Milkmaid coy,
  Each like a newly-painted
    toy.
All. Deep in the bosky countrie!
Avril. [*Singing.*]
  By poor little man the town was
    made,
  To degrade
  Man and maid;
  God's green thought in a little
    green shade,
  Made the bosky countrie!
Chorus [*All.*]
  Hey, hey, the country's here,
  The country's there,
  It's everywhere!
  We'll have it, now, last thing at
    night,
  And the very first thing in the
    morning!
Basil. [*Singing.*]
  Our music, now, is the cow's sweet
    moo,
  The pigeon's coo,
  The lark's song, too,
  And the cock's shrill
    cock-a-doodle-doo.
All. [*Together.*]
  Trees and nuts and
    bramble flowers,
  Shady bowers,
  Sun and showers,
  Bees and birds and all are ours,
  Deep in the bosky countrie!
All. [*Chorus.*]
  Hey, hey, the country's here,
  The country's there,
  It's everywhere!
  We'll have it, now, last thing at
    night,
  And the very first thing in the
    morning!

[*As they are singing the last lines of the chorus for the second time, those who have come in by the left entrance go out by the right one; and those who have come in by the right entrance, go out by the left one.*
THE WORKMEN *stand silent for a few moments, watching the places where the singers disappeared.*]

First Workman. Well, God help the poor omadhauns! It's a bad sign to see people actin' like that, an' they sober.

Third Workman. A sthrange crowd they are, to come gallivantin' outa the city to a lonely an' inconsiderate place like this.

First Workman. At home, now, they'd be sinkin' into their first sleep; because they're in the counthry they think the thing to do is to get up at the crack o' dawn.

Third Workman. An' they killin' themselves thryin' to look as if the counthry loved them all their life.

First Workman. With the young heifer gaddin' round with next to nothin' on, goadin' the decency an' circumspection of the place.

Third Workman. An' her eyes wiltin' when she sees what she calls her husband, an' widenin' wondherfully whenever they happen to light on O'Killigain.

First Workman. A handsome, hefty young sthripling, with a big seam in his arm that he got from a bullet fired in Spain.

Third Workman. Forever fillin' the place with reckless talk against the composure of the Church in the midst of the way things are now.

Second Workman. Ay, an' right he is, if ears didn't shut when his mind was speakin'.

First Workman. [*To* SECOND WORKMAN.] If I was you, I'd be dumb as well, for Canon Creehewel's mad to dhrive him outa th' place, with all who hear him.

Second Workman. [*Fervently.*] There's ne'er another man to be found as thrue or as clever as him till you touch a city's centre, an' if he goes, I'll go, too.

First Workman. It's what but they're thryin' to be something else beside themselves.

Third Workman. They'd plunge through any hardship to make themselves believe they are what they never can become.

Second Workman. [*Dolorously.*] An' to think of two such soilifyin' females bein' born in Ireland, an' denizenin' themselves here among decent people!

Third Workman. Whissht; here's the boss, O'Killigain.

[O'KILLIGAN *comes in from the side entrance, with a short straight-edge in his hand. He is a tall, fair young man of twenty-five or twenty-six years. He has a rough, clearly-cut face, dogged-looking when he is roused, and handsome when he is in a good humour, which is often enough. He is clean-shaven, show-ing rather thick, but finely formed lips. His hair, though cut short, is thick and striking. When he speaks of something interesting him, his hands make graceful gestures. He has had a pretty rough life, which has given him a great confidence in himself; and wide reading has strengthened that confidence consider-ably. He is dressed in blue dungarees and wears a deep yellow muffler, marked with blue decoration, round his neck. He is humming a tune as he comes in, and goes over toward the* MEN.]

O'Killigain. 'Morra, boys.

All the Men. 'Morra, Jack.

O'Killigain. [*With a gesture pointing to where he thinks the people of the house may be.*] Up yet?

First Workman. Up, is it? Ay, an' dancin' all about the place.

O'Killigain. Bright colours, in cloth and paint, th' ladies want, they say; jazz pat-terns, if possible, say the two dear young ladies: well, they'll want pretty bright colours to cheer up this morgue.

Third Workman. It's a strange thing, now, that a man with money would like to live in a place, lonesome an' cold enough to send a shiver through a year-old dead man!

O'Killigain. Because they think it has what they call a history. Everything old is sacred in every country. Give a house a history, weave a legend round it, let some titled tom-fool live or die in it—and some fool-mind will see loveliness in rottenness and ruin.

First Workman. A nephew of the Duke of Ormond, they say, dhrank himself to death in it, and the supernumary wife of the older codger says she's a direct descendant of the nephew; and she says they've come from the darkness an' danger of England to set-tle down in what is really their proper home.

O'Killigain. And they're goin' to have the spoons and forks an' knives done with what they say is the Ormond crest; Ormond's motto will shine out from their notepaper; and this tumble-down oul' shack is to be christened Ormond Manor.

Second Workman. [*Savagely.*] The Eng-lish get hurryin' off with the ensign privilege of an Irish gentleman!

Third Workman. Isn't it sthrange how many'll fall for a mere name? Remember oul' Miss MacWilliam who used to faint with ecstasy the times she told the story of sittin' for a second in the King o' Denmark's chair; an' oul' Tom Mulligan who swag-gered round for years afther the son o' the

Earl of Shibereen had accidentally spit in his eye!

O'Killigain. Well, men, we'd better make a start.

First Workman. [*Warningly.*] Shush! Here's the flower o' Finea!

[AVRIL *comes in from the left entrance. She is a pretty girl of twenty-one or so, inclined, at times, to be a little roman-tic, and is very much aware of her good looks. She is far from being unintelli-gent, but does little and cares less about developing her natural talents. Her eyes are large and expressive, but sometimes sink into a hardened lustre. She is in-clined to think that every good-looking young fellow, rich or poor, should fall for her pretty face and figure, and is a little worried if one of them doesn't. She adopts a free and easy and very un-natural attitude when she is talking to workmen. She is dressed now in gay scarlet trousers, widening at the ends, and very tight around her hips and bot-tom; low-cut black silk bodice, slashed with crimson, half hidden by a red and white striped scarf thrown carelessly round her shoulders—and black shoes. She trips over in a slow dancing way to where the* WORKMEN *are standing, and as she comes in she lilts "Nora O'Neale," or "Rose of Tralee."*]

Avril. [*Close to the* WORKMEN.] Top o' the mornin', boys!

O'Killigain. [*Humouring her.*] Same to you, miss, an' many of them, each of them fairer an' finer than the finest of all that ever brought the soft light o' the dawn at the peep o' day into your openin' eyes.

Avril. It's meself that hopes you like the lovely house you're renovatin'?

O'Killigain. An' tell me who wouldn't like the lovely house we're renovatin'? It's a dark man he'd be, without a stim o' light, an' destitute o' feelin'.

First Workman. [*Enthusiastically.*] Sure, miss, it's dumb with many wondhers we've all been for years that no one o' the well-to-do laid hands suddenly on the house to give it the glory again that musta been here throughout the jewel'd days of the times gone by!

Avril. When it's thoroughly restored it'll be a pleasure an' a pride to the whole dis-trict.

O'Killigain. [*With just a touch of sar-casm in his voice.*] Sure, when we're done with it wouldn't it be fit for the shelther an' ayse an' comfort of Nuad of the Silver Hand, were he with us now, or of the great Fergus himself, of the bright bronze chariots?

Avril. Or even the nephew of Ormond's great Duke, the warlike ancestor of my very own cousin.

O'Killigain. An' all the people here who are anything'll be mad with envy that they hadn't seized holt of it to make it what it'll soon be shown to be!

[*Avril lilts a reel and dances lightly about the room. The* First *and* Third Workmen *join in the lilting of the air. As she is passing* O'Killigain *he catches her excitedly and whirls her recklessly round the room till she is breathless, while the two* Men *quicken the time of the lilting.*]

O'Killigain. [*To* Avril *while she stands breathlessly before him.*] Bow to your partner. [Avril *bows to him and he bows to her. Indicating the two* Men *who lilted the tune of the reel.*] Bow, bow to the bards.

[*She bows to the two* Men, *and when she has bent to the bow,* O'Killigan *gives her a sharp skelp on the behind. She straightens herself with a little squeal of pain and a sharp cry of indignation and faces him angrily.*]

Avril. [*Indignantly.*] You low fellow, what did you dare do that for! How dare you lay your dirty hands on a real lady! That's the danger of being friendly with a guttersnipe! Wait till you hear what Mr Basil Stoke'll say, when he hears what you've done. Get out of the room, get out of the house—go away, and never let your ugly face be seen here again!

O'Killigain. [*With some mockery in his voice.*] Sure, I meant no harm, miss; it was simply done in the excitement of the game. [*To* First Workman.] Wasn't it, now, Bill?

Third Workman. Ay, was it, miss. Sure, th' poor man lost his caution in the gaiety of the gay tune.

O'Killigain. I did it all in play; I thought you'd like it.

Avril. [*Sarcastically.*] Oh, did you? Well, I didn't like it, and I don't allow anyone to take advantage of any effort I make to treat workmen as human beings.

Second Workman. [*Maliciously.*] If I was asked anything, I'd say I saw a spark of pleasure in the flame of pain that came into her eyes when she was hot!

Avril. [*Furiously—to the* Men.] Be off, you, and let me speak alone to this young man! I don't require any explanation from such as you; so be off, and I'll deal with this fellow! [*The* Three Workmen *slide away out of the scene. With a gentler tone in her voice.*] Never, never do a thing like that again, young man.

O'Killigain. [*With mocking earnestness.*] Never again, young lady. Sure, you looked so handsome, gay, and young, that my thoughts became as jaunty an' hilarious as your little dancin' feet.

Avril. Never again, mind you—especially when others are here to stand and gape. [*She goes over and feels the muscle of his arm.*] There's too much power in that arm to give a safe and gentle blow to a poor young girl.

O'Killigain. Ashamed I am of the force that sent a hand to hit a girl of grace, fit to find herself walkin' beside all the beauty that ever shone before the eyes o' man since Helen, herself, unbound her thresses, to dance her wild an' willin' way through the sthreets o' Throy!

Avril. It's I that know the truth is only in the shine o' the words you shower on me, as ready to you as the wild flowers a love-shaken, innocent girl would pick, in a hurry, outa the hedges, an' she on her way to Mass.

O'Killigain. Is it afther tellin' me that that you are, an' your own words dancin' out as fair an' fine as the best o' mine?

Avril. An' why wouldn't they, now, an' me that sang me song, first runnin' me years in, and runnin' them out, in th' fields an' roads that skirted the threes an' hills o' Killnageera? But is there an Irishman goin' who hasn't a dint o' wondher in his talkin'?

O'Killigain. I never met many who had it; but some evening somewhere away from me mother, who [*Proudly.*] once won a grand gold medal at a Feis for a song of her own, put together between the times of bringin' up six children an' puttin' an odd flower on the grave of the one that died.

Avril. You must sing me a few of your songs, sometime.

O'Killigain. Now if you'd like to listen, an' you think that the time is handy.

Avril. Not now; we might be disturbed; but some evening, somewhere away from here.

O'Killigain. I will, an' welcome; some of them, too, that have been set in a little book, lookin' gay an' grand, for all the world to see. Come; listen— [*In a mocking whisper.*] —and brave the wrath of a gouty, doughty Basil Stoke.

Avril. [*With a toss of her head.*] That thing! [*With bitter contempt.*] A toddler thricking with a woman's legs; a thief without the power to thieve the thing he covets;

a louse burrowing in a young lioness's belly; a perjurer in passion; a gutted soldier bee whose job is done, and still hangs on to life!

O'Killigain. [*Embracing her tightly.*] To-night, or tomorrow night, then, beside the blasted Rowan three.

Avril. [*With fright in her voice.*] The blasted Rowan tree! Oh, not there, not there —for evil things sit high, sit low in its twisty branches; and lovers, long ago, who leaned against it, lost their love, or died, No, no, not there: a saint himself would shudder, if he had to pass it on a dusky night, with only a sly chit of a moon in the sky to show the way.

O'Killigain. Oh, foolish girl, there never can be evil things where love is living. Between the evil things an' us, we'll make the sign of the rosy cross, an' it's blossomin' again the dead an' dhry thing will be, an' fruit will follow.

[*They sing "The Ruin'd Rowan Tree" together.*]

THE RUINED ROWAN TREE

A sour-souled Cleric, passing near,
Saw lovers by a rowan tree.
He curs'd its branches, berries, bloom,
Through time and through eternity.
Now evil things are waiting where
Fond lovers once found joy.
And fear of love now crowns the thought,
Of frighten'd girl—, of frighten'd boy.

The rowan tree's black as black can be,
On Killnageera's lonely hill.
And where lovers whispers once were warm,
Now blows a wind both cold and shrill.
Oh would I had a lover brave,
Who'd mock away its power;
I'd lie there firm within his arms,
And fill with love one glorious hour.

Then branches bare would leaf again,
And twisted ones grow straight and true.
And lovers caught within its ken,
Would nothing fear and nothing rue;
Its bloom would form a bridal veil,
Till summer days were sped.
Then autumn berries red would fall,
Like rubies on each nesting head.

Avril. [*After a little hesitation.*] Undher the Rowan three, then, with you.

[*As the sound of voices are heard he holds her tight for a few moments, kisses her several times, then lets her go. He goes over and examines a wall,*

where a telephone is evidently being put in. AVRIL, *all demure, stands at the other end of the room, watching him.* SOUHAUN, *followed by* POGES *and* BASIL, *comes into the room. She is carrying a large, two-handled earthenware jug in her right hand, and two coloured cushions under her left arm.* CYRIL POGES *is carrying a large coloured picture of himself in a gold frame; and* BASIL STOKE, *too, is bearing a picture of himself in a silver frame; he has a hammer sticking out of his side pocket.* CLOYNE *follows them in with a six-step A-ladder.* POGES *and* STOKE *are wearing gum boots, reaching to their thighs, and bright scarves round their necks.* POGES *and* BASIL *rest the pictures against a wall.*]

Souhaun. [*To* AVRIL.] Oh, here you are, with Mr O'Killigain. We were wondering where you were. We've a lot to do, dear, before we can get the house comfortable; so don't keep Mr O'Killigain from his work. [*She leaves the jug down in a corner.*] Filled with gay flowers, Cyril, this jug'll be just the thing on your quatto-centro desk-bureau.

Poges. Lovely, darling. [*To* O'KILLIGAIN.] We've been for a run over the fields, O'Killigain; lovely; feel as fresh as a daisy after it. [*Indicating the boots.*] Great comfort, these boots, in the long damp grass. Saw a swarm of rabbits—quaint creatures. Such alacrity! Amazing way they jump.

Basil. With these and rubber hats and rubber coats, we'll be able to weather anything. I've got the hammer. Have you got the nails?

Poges. I forgot them. I'll get them now.

Basil. And I'll get the string.

[*One goes out left, and the other right.*]

Souhaun. [*To* CLOYNE.] Hold this curtain stuff end, Cloyne, till we see its width.

[CLOYNE *holds one end of the stuff, while* SOUHAUN *holds the other.* O'KILLIGAIN, *pretending to be interested, bends over* CLOYNE, *and stretching out a hand to handle the stuff, half puts his arm around* CLOYNE'S *neck, who is very well pleased.*]

O'Killigain. Finely woven as a plover's wing it is. No way odd it would look as a cloak for the lovely Emer; an', if it hung from th' sturdy shoulders of Queen Maev, herself, she'd find a second glory!

Souhaun. [*Displeased at his covert attention to* CLOYNE.] Over here, Cloyne, please; hold this end.

[SOUHAUN *and* CLOYNE *change places,*

and O'KILLIGAIN *bends over* SOUHAUN.]

Avril. [*To* O'KILLIGAIN.] I must have a chat with that man working for you who knows everything worth knowing about Ireland's past and present, Mr O'Killigain.

O'Killigain. [*Very seriously.*] And, please, miss, don't try to make fun of him. Touch him not with a jibe, for he's a wandherin' king holdin' th' ages be th' hand.

Souhaun. How could a common worker be a king, O'Killigain?

O'Killigain. Easier than for a king to be a common worker. Th' king o' a world that doesn't exist was a carpenter.

Avril. Where is the real world to be found, then?

O'Killigain. Where I have found it often, an' seek to find it still.

Avril. And where's that place to be found?

O'Killigain. With the bittherness an' joy blendin' in a pretty woman's hand; with the pity in her breast; in th' battlin' beauty of her claspin' arms; an' rest beside her when th' heart is tired.

Cloyne. Sure, it's only makin' fun of us all he is.

O'Killigain. Softer an' safer than St. Patrick's Breastplate is a woman's breast to save a man from the slings of life.

[*Singing softly, moving a little away. Slyly towards the* WOMEN.]

Come in, or go out, or just stay at the door,
With a girl on each arm an' who standin' before;
Sure, the more that I have, the more I adore,
For there's life with the lassies,
Says Rory O'More!

Oh, courtin's an illigant, gorgeous affray,
When it's done in the night, or just done in the day;
When joy has been spent, sure, there's joy still in store;
For there's life with the lassies,
Says Rory O'More!

When all has been done, though nothin' been said,
Deep in the green grass, or at home in the bed,
To ev'ry brave effort, we'll yield an encore;
For there's life with the lassies,
Says Rory O'More!

[*As he ends his song,* POGES *and* BASIL *return, the one with the nails, the other with the string-wire.*]

Poges. [*To* O'KILLIGAIN—*briskly.*] The garage is well in hands, isn't it, O'Killigain?

O'Killigain. [*Who has tapped the wall, and is shaking his head.*] Yes, well in hands.

Poges. [*Enthusiastically.*] Good, man; when it's done I'll get a first-class artist over from London to paint and make it exactly like a little Tudor dwelling, so that it won't in any way distort the beauty of the fine old house. What do you say, O'Killigain? [O'KILLIGAIN *is silent.*] Eh?

O'Killigain. I didn't speak.

Basil. [*Who has moved over, and is looking ecstatically up at an end wall.*] Early Tudor, I think; yes, early Tudor, I'll swear. A great period, a great period. Full of flow, energy, colour, power, imagination, and hilarity.

O'Killigain. [*Tapping the wall beside him—ironically.*] And this is middle Tudor—not a doubt about it.

Poges. [*Looking ecstatically at the other end wall.*] Late Tudor, this one, I'm sure. Ah, England had no equal then. Look at the Lionheart, eh? Smashed the infidel, smashed him out of Jerusalem into the desert places. What was his name, follower of the Prophet? You remember, Hegira, the white stone, or was it a black stone?—Oh, what was the bounder's name?

Souhaun. [*Helpfully.*] Tuttuttankamen, dear?

Poges. [*Scornfully.*] Tuttuttankamen! My God, woman, he was only the other day!

Avril. [*More helpfully.*] The Mahdi, dear?

Poges. [*More scornfully.*] The Mahdi! [*Plaintively.*] Is there no one here knows a line of the history of his country!

Basil. [*With complacent confidence.*] Ghenghis Khan.

Poges. [*Emphatically.*] Ghenghis Khan! That was the name of the bounder driven from Jerusalem by the Lionhearted Richard. And, maybe he was actually in this very house. It's all very moving. [*To* O'KILLIGAIN.] I imagine I hear the clank, clank, clank of armour when I walk the rooms, and see the banners and banneroles, with their quaint designs, fluttering from the walls! Don't you feel the lovely sensation of er—er—er, old, unhappy, far-off things, and battles long ago? [O'KILLIGAIN *is silent. Insistently.*] Don't you feel something of all that, O'Killigain, eh?

O'Killigain. [*Quietly.*] I let the dead bury their dead.

Souhaun. Oh, don't worry Mr O'Killigain, Cyril; he's a work-a-day worker, and neither understands nor takes an interest in these things.

Poges. Nonsense; O'Killigain's an intelligent man, and is only too glad to learn a little about the finer things of life; and to think of great things past and gone is good —isn't that so?

O'Killigain. Occasionally, perhaps; but not to live among them. Life as it is, and will be, moves me more.

Poges. Come, come; we mustn't be always brooding upon the present and the future. Life is too much with us, O'Killigain; late and soon, getting and spending, we lay waste our powers. But you've never read good old Wordsworth, I suppose?

O'Killigain. As a matter of fact, I have.

Poges. You have? Well, that promotes a fellowship between us, eh? Great man, great man; but a greater poet, eh?

O'Killigain. A tired-out oul' blatherer; a man who made a hiding-place of his own life; a bladder blown that sometimes gave a note of music; a poet who jailed the striving of man in a moral lullaby; a snail to whom God gave the gleam of the glowworm; a poet singing the song of safety first!

Poges. [*Irritated.*] Oh! Is that the result of the new schooling? I'm afraid very few will agree with you, my friend. Well, well, we've more to do than discuss the merit of a poet; so hasten on the work of building the garage, like a good man.

O'Killigain. [*Bowing ironically.*] I go, sir.
[*He goes out.*]

Poges. [*To the* OTHERS.] Isn't that a shocking example of bad taste and ignorance? [*To* SOUHAUN.] There's one of your fine countrymen for you, dear.

Souhaun. Well, Cyril dear, you know you were just trying to show off to him. A few little quotations, drummed into you at school, is all you know of Wordsworth. You're never tired of saying that poetry isn't your cup of tea.

Poges. [*Angry.*] Modern poetry, modern poetry isn't my cup of tea; and I don't care who knows it. But I don't deny the past. Tradition—that is our strength in time of trouble; tradition—keep as close as we can to the beauties of the past—the, the glory that was Rome and the grandeur that was Greece —Shakespeare knew what he was talking about when he said that.

Souhaun. But Shakespeare didn't say that, dear.

Basil. Well, by living in this old, historic house, we're keeping close to the old traditions.

Souhaun. [*Dubiously.*] It's beginning to feel a little cold and damp to me.

Poges. [*Indignantly.*] Cold? What are you talking about? Damp? Nonsense. Were

it warmer, it would begin to feel uncomfortable. What do you say, Cloyne?

Cloyne. [*Who has been dusting the walls with a long-handled duster.*] I feel quite cozy, sir; though there is a bit of breeze blowing down the chimney.

Poges. [*Shivering a little.*] Eh? Cozy, eh? Of course you do; we all do. Think, too, of the loveliness all round us; river, lake, valley, and hill. [*Lilting.*] Angels often pausing here, doubt if Eden were more fair. Here, we have the peace of Eden.

Souhaun. And you must admit, dear, that we Irish are a simple, hearty, honest, and obliging people.

Basil. [*Enthusiastically.*] They're dears. All I've met of them are dears; so quaint and charming—they are sweet. They need control, though; they need control.

Poges. I agree. All the Irish are the same. Bit backward, perhaps, like all primitive peoples, especially now, for they're missing the example and influence of the gentry; but delightful people, all the same. They need control, though; oh, yes, they need it badly.

Basil. We must get to really know the country; it's one thing to be sensitive about the country scene, and quite another to understand it. To be one with the green grass; to be, metaphorically, in the trees with the squirrels; to march with the seasons; processional and recessional: in short to speak to mother earth and let mother earth speak to us.

Poges. [*Heartily.*] Quite right, Basil, we must get to know the country so that everything in it is natural to us. [*Lilting.*] To play and to sow, to reap and to mow, and to be a farmer's boy-oy-oy. The different trees, for example, to call them by their names the instant we see them.

Avril. In winter or summer.

Poges. Quite. In the summer by their fruits.

Avril. Trees don't have fruits, Cyril.

Poges. Of course not. I mean barks and branches. It will be a joy to say to some ignorant visitor from the city: That tree? Oh, that's just an oak; and that one there by the river is a—a——

Avril. Gooseberry tree, Cyril.

Poges. A lilac, or something. [*To* AVRIL.] Don't be funny. This is a serious matter.

Cloyne. We mustn't forget the hens, either, sir.

Poges. Hens? Yes, of course—the hens. A fine idea. Yes, we'll have to have hens; a first-class strain, though; nothing else would be of any use.

Cloyne. A first-class strain, of course.

Poges. And a cow as well.

Avril. A cow might be dangerous.

Poges. Dangerous? Nonsense; if he was, then we'd simply have to keep him in a cage. [*He sets up a stepladder, mounts it, and holds up his picture against the wall.*] How does that look?

Souhaun. [*Taking no notice.*] First of all, we must get to know the nature and names of all the wild flowers of the district.

Poges. [*Letting the picture rest on the ground, leaning over it and turning towards the rest.*] Especially the wild flowers that Shakespeare loved, the, the—er—er— [*His eye catches sight of primroses in a little vase on the table.*] —the primrose for instance; you know—a primrose by the river's brim, a yellow primrose was to him, but it was nothing more; though we all actually know all there is to be known about the little primrose.

Basil. [*Letting his picture rest on the ground, and leaning over the top so that he at one end of the room, and* POGES *at the other, look like preachers in pulpits, panelled with their own portraits.*] That's just ignorant complacency. Of course, if we regard, assume, or look at the plant purely as a single entity, then a primrose is a primrose, and there's nothing more to be said about it.

Poges. Well, you can't assume that the primrose may be an elm tree, can you?

Basil. [*Quickly.*] Don't interrupt me for a minute, please. If we take the primrose, however, into our synthetical consideration, as a whole, or, a priori, as a part, with the rest of the whole or natural objects, or phenomena, then there is, or may be, or can be a possibility of thinking of the flower as of above the status, or substance, or quality of a fragment; and, consequently, correlating it with the whole, so that, to a rational thinker, or logical mind, the simple primrose is, or may become, what we may venture to call a universal. See?

Poges. [*Bewildered.*] Eh? Oh, yes; yes; no, no; yes, yes.

Souhaun. [*To* CLOYNE.] This discussion is a little too profound for you, Cloyne, so you'd better go and look after the fires in our room.   [CLOYNE *rises and goes out.*]

Poges. What the devil are you trying to say, man?

Avril. [*With triumphant mockery.*] Aha, Cyril, you're caught!

Poges. [*Indignantly.*] Caught? Who's caught? Me? Nonsense, girl. He has simply compounded a fact with a fallacy. Can I see? Have I eyes? Yes. Very well, then. I see a flower with a root, leaves, and a blossom; I

ask myself, what is it? I answer, a primrose.

Basil. [*With languid scorn.*] So you say, sir.

Poges. [*Vehemently.*] So everyone says, man!

Basil. [*Leaning forward towards* POGES.] And what is a flower?

Poges. [*Furiously.*] A flower? Good god, a plant; a contrivance springing out of the earth; a vegetating combination of root, leaves, and blossom, sir!

Souhaun. Calmly, calmly, Cyril.

Basil. [*Leaning back again, and closing his eyes wearily.*] I know you'd just say that, sir. Words; you're merely using words. As easy to explain what a flower is as to tell me the height of the church steeple we can see from the front door.

Poges. You tell us its height.

Basil. From the front door, the height of a common pin; a little nearer, that of a walking stick; beneath it, some would say a hundred feet.

Poges. Clever fellow! [*Plaintively.*] First a primrose, then a steeple. [*Vehemently.*] Any fool knows the height of the steeple would be the length of its measurement!

Basil. [*Coolly—leaning forward towards* POGES.] Now tell me what is measurement and what is height, sir.

Poges. [*Inviting and scornful.*] You tell us, sir, please. [*Raising his hand, solemnly.*] Silence all. [*With a shout.*] Let the learned gentleman speak!

Souhaun. Now, Cyril, dear, discuss things quietly—remember you're an Englishman.

Basil. [*Calmly and languidly, as if he had not heard the loud voice of* POGES.] Try to think, sir, of a primrose, not as a primrose, per se, or of a steeple as a steeple, per se; but as simple objects and as substances outside of yourself.

Poges. [*Half frantic.*] Damn it, man, don't I know that primroses and steeples aren't simple substances inside of myself! Tell us how a man's to think of a primrose except as a primrose. He can't think of it as the dear little, sweet little shamrock of Ireland, can he? It is, indeed, a pitiful humiliation to have to listen to a half-educated fool!

Basil. [*Angry at last—setting the picture aside and taking a threatening step forward,* AVRIL *stepping in front to restrain him.*] A fool? Do you say I am a fool, sir? Is a man versed in all the philosophies of the world to be called a fool?

Avril. Basil, dear!

Souhaun. [*Getting in front of* POGES.] Cyril, darling, do remember that we are just having a little friendly discussion about a common country flower!

Poges. [*Louder than ever.*] We came down here to get away from the world, and here we have the world thrust in front of us again. And a world, too, that tries to turn a primrose into a steeple!

Avril. [*Ironically.*] Basil is only trying to share his great knowledge with us.

Poges. He calls that knowledge, does he?

Souhaun. We must remember that Basil passed through Oxford, dear.

Poges. I don't care if he crept under it or flew over it; he's not going to punish me with what he picked up there.

Basil. [*A little tearfully.*] Considering that I have read every word written by Hume, Spinoza, Aristotle, Locke, Bacon, Plato, Socrates, and Kant, among others, I think my views ought to receive some respect from an ignorant man.

Poges. [*Boastfully.*] I was reared any old how; and here I am today, a money'd man, able to say to almost any man, come, and he cometh, and to almost any other man go, and he goeth—and quick, too; able to shake hands with lords and earls, and call them by their Christian names. This— [*He touches his forehead.*] —and these— [*He holds out his hands.*] —did it all, without an inherited penny to help! [*He looks balefully at* BASIL.] And that's more than some of them can say. And I never passed through Oxford!

Souhaun. [*Soothingly—to* BASIL.] Come, now, go away for a few minutes, till he's calm again.

Basil. [*Tearfully and wrathfully.*] Invincible ignorance, God forgive it. Souhaun and you can see, Avril, that the virtue of respect and ready veneration that every right-minded Englishman has for the classic colleges has gone completely out of him.

Souhaun. [*Gently pushing* BASIL *out of the room.*] There, go, dear, till you recover yourself.

Basil. Quisabit grunniodem expectio porcum—what can one expect from a pig but a grunt? [*Going out—loudly.*] Invincible ignorance!

Poges. [*With the picture against the wall.*] There, how does that look here? [*Pityingly.*] Poor fool; juvenile mind, Souhaun, juvenile mind. But snappy enough, when he likes, and I, by cunning investment, have doubled his income for him. Ingratitude. [*Impatiently.*] Well, how does this look here?

Souhaun. I think the opposite wall would be more suitable, dear.

Avril. Where it is is best, mother.

Poges. Make up your minds, make up your minds!

Souhaun. Where it is, dear.

Poges. How is it for height?

Souhaun. A little higher.

Avril. A little lower.

Poges. One of you, one of you!

Souhaun. A little to the right, now.

Avril. A little to the left, now.

Poges. [*Lowering the picture to the ground.*] Which is it? How is it? What is it?

[CLOYNE *comes in with a newspaper in her hand.*]

Cloyne. [*To* POGES.] Your newspaper, sir —the Financial Universe.

[*She leaves it on the table, and goes out again.* POGES *breaks open his paper, and is about to look at it when* BARNEY *appears at the left entrance. A sound of cackling is heard outside, and the loud lowing of a cow, and the crowing of cocks.*]

Poges. [*With the paper half-spread before him.*] What the hell's that?

Barney. There's a man outside wants to know if you want any entherprisin' hins?

Poges. Any what?

Barney. Any hins, entherprisin' hins?

Poges. [*Impatiently.*] What the devil would I want with hins enterprising or unenterprising?

Barney. He says it's all over the counthry that you're searchin' high an' low for entherprisin' hins.

Cloyne. [*Appearing at the right entrance.*] There's two men here wantin' to know if you'd buy some prime an' startlin' cocks, goin' cheap?

First Workman. [*Appearing beside* BARNEY, *and shoving him aside to get in front.*] Excuse me, sir, but there's a friend o' mine just arrived with a cow that ud do any man good to see; a baste with a skin on her as shiny an' soft as the down on a first-class angel's wing; an' uddhers that'll make any man hard put to it to fetch enough pails to get the milk she gives!

Poges. Hins, cocks, and cows! [*To* FIRST WORKMAN.] What the hell do you take me for—a farmer's boy, or what?

Souhaun. It's all out of what you said about having hens and a cow in the place. [*To* CLOYNE.] And you, you little fool, must have gossiped it all over the district!

Cloyne. The only one I mentioned it to was Mr O'Killigain.

First Workman. [*Coming over to* POGES.]

Listen, sir, whisper now: Sthrike for th' honour of St. Patrick, while the iron's hot, for the cow. An' whisper, don't, for the love o' God, have anything to do with the hins an' cocks they're thryin' to palm off on you—there isn't one o' them that isn't th' essence of a false pretendher!

Souhaun. [*Angrily to* CLOYNE.] I won't have you gossiping to O'Killigain, spending time with him you ought to give getting the house in shape! The idea of discussing our private affairs with O'Killigain! If you think that O'Killigain has taken a fancy to you, you never made a bigger mistake, my girl.

Cloyne. [*Indignantly.*] Indeed, ma'am? Well, if Mr O'Killigain bids me the time o' day, I'll do the same, without any permission from you, ma'am!

Barney. [*Impatiently.*] An' what am I goin' to say to the man who's brought th' entherprisin' hins?

Poges. [*Shouting.*] Pack him off about his business! [BARNEY *goes out. To* CLOYNE.] And you do the same to the man who brought the startling cocks!

Souhaun. [*To* CLOYNE.] And no more trespassing on the good nature of O'Killigain, either!

Cloyne. [*Turning and facing* SOUHAUN *swiftly as she is going out.*] There's a withering woman, not a hundred miles from where I am, who ought to take her own advice, an' keep from thryin' her well-faded thricks of charm on poor Mr O'Killigain herself!   [*She goes out.*]

Poges. [*Loudly and complainingly.*] Oh, stop these unseemly disputes in a house that ought to know only peace and dignity! Can't you try to act as the les grand dames and the les grander monseurs must have acted when they moved about here in this beautiful Tudor house? [*Angrily—to* FIRST WORKMAN, *who has been tugging at his sleeve for the last few moments.*] What the hell do you want, man?

First Workman. [*Earnestly, almost into* POGES' *ear.*] Listen, whisper, sir; take the bull be th' horns, an' get the cow, before she's gone. An' as for entherprisin' hins, or cocks that'll do you credit, leave it to me, sir, an' you'll go about with a hilarious look in your eyes!

Souhaun. [*Quickly—to* AVRIL *when* POGES *has disappeared round the entrance.*] Go on up, and flatter and comfort your old fool by ridiculing my old fool; and, when he's half himself again, wanting still more comfort and flattery, wheedle a cheque out of the old prattler.

Avril. [*Jumping up.*] Splendid idea!
                                [*She runs off out.*]

Souhaun. [*Calling after her.*] A fat one, mind you!

[POGES *comes back fuming, and brushing his coat where it touched the* FIRST WORKMAN.]

Poges. Are we to have no peace down here where peace was born? [*He takes up the paper again, and begins to read it.*] Uum. Ha, tin shares up again. Good. [*He buries his face in the paper.*] If it weren't for the damned taxes.

[FIRST *and* THIRD WORKMEN *peer around corner of the left entrance; then they come over quickly and smoothly to where* POGES *is buried in his paper, the* FIRST WORKMAN *standing on his left hand, and the* THIRD WORKMAN *on his right.*]

First Workman. [*Persuasively—toward* POGES' *paper.*] Listen here, sir: if it's genuine poulthry you want, that lay with pride an' animation, an' not poor, insignificant fowls that set about th' business o' layin' like a member of Doyle Eireann makin' his maiden speech, I have a sthrain o' pullets that'll give you eggs as if you were gettin' them be steam!

Poges. [*Angrily—glancing over the top of his paper.*] Go away, go away, man, and don't be driving me mad!

Third Workman. [*Toward* POGES' *paper.*] Oh, the lies that some can tell to gain their own ends! Sure, sir, everyone knows that his poor hins are harmless; only venturin' to lay when heavy thundher frightens them into a hasty sign o' life! But it's meself can give you what you want, with a few lively cocks thrown in, to help them on with the work of furnishing nourishmen: to the whole world.

Poges. Go away; when I want poultry, I'll get into touch with the experts in the Department of Agriculture.

First Workman. [*Horrified—partly to* POGES *and partly to the* THIRD WORKMAN.] Oh, listen to that, now! Didja hear that, ma'am? The Department of Agriculture, is it? Wisha, God help your innocence, sir. Sure, it's only a tiny time ago, that the same Department sent down a special sthrong covey o' cocks to improve the sthrain, an' only afther a short probation, didn't they give the hins hysterics!

Poges. Hysterics! Good God!

First Workman. Ah, an' hadn't the frightened farmers to bring guns to bear on the cocks when they found their hins scatthered over hill an' dale, lyin' on their backs with their legs in the air, givin' their last gasp, an' glad to get outa the world they knew so well! The few mighty ones who survived were that stunned, that there wasn't an egg in th' place for years!

Poges. [*Good humouredly catching the* MEN *by the arm, and leading them to the left entrance.*] Now, now, man, I'm busy; I've some very important business to think about, and can't be bothered with hins!

First Workman. [*As they go out.*] Another time, sir; but don't think of the Department in this important matter; they'll send you hins'll paralyse the cocks, or cocks that'll paralyse the hins! [*They go out.*]

Poges. [*Returning and reading the paper.*] Childlike people, the Irish, aren't they? Hysteric hins! Dr what's his name, the fellow who said all man is moved by streams of thought that never enter his head—well, he'd find something to study down here. Well, it's delightful to be in a lovely house, in a lovely country, with nothing to think of but hysteric hins! [*He suddenly concentrates on something in the paper.*] I must have some of those shares. [*He runs to the telephone, and joggles and shakes it.*] What can be the matter with this Exchange—I can't hear a sound! [*To* SOUHAUN.] Call one of the workmen, will you? I must get through to London at once.

[SOUHAUN *runs out to call a workman. In a moment or two, the* SECOND WORKMAN *comes into the room.*]

Second Workman. Is it me you want, sir?

Poges. Not you especially; I just want to know if you know, or anyone in the country knows why I can't connect with the Exchange?

Second Workman. Oh, is that all, sir?

Poges. [*Snappily.*] Is that all? Isn't it enough, fool?

Second Workman. [*Sharply.*] Who th' hell are you callin' a fool to?

Poges. [*Placatingly, but with some impatience.*] My good man, please let me know if you can say why the Exchange doesn't answer my call?

Second Workman. Ask anyone from one end o' the counthry to the other, or even O'Killigain, himself, if Philib O'Dempsey's a fool, an' see what they'll say. A sound mind, armed with firm education for seven long years in a steady school, an' now well fit to stand his ground in any argument, barrin' th' highest philosophies of the greatest minds mendin' th' world!

Poges. My good man, I only asked you a simple question.

Second Workman. [*Ignoring the remark.*] Comin' over here, thinkin' that all the glory an' grandeur of the world, an' all the might of man was stuffed into a bulgin' purse, an' stickin' their tongue out at a race that's oldher than themselves by a little like a thousand years, greather in their beginnin' than they are in their prime; with us speakin' with ayse all mighty languages o' the world when they could barely gurgle a few sounds, sayin' the rest in the movement of their fingers.

Poges. [*Shouting in rage.*] Go to the devil, man, and learn manners!

Second Workman. [*Going on vehemently, but moving slowly to one of the entrances.*] Hammerin' out handsome golden ornaments for flowin' cloak an' tidy tunic we were, while you were busy gatherin' dhried grass, an' dyin' it blue, to hide the consternation of your middle parts; decoratin' eminent books with glowin' colour, an' audacious beauty were we, as O'Killigain, himself, will tell you, when you were still a hundred score o' years away from even hearin' of the alphabet. [*Beside the entrance.*] Fool? It's yourself's the fool, I'm sayin', settlin' down in a place that's only fit for the housin' o' dead men! Settlin' here, are you? Wait till God sends the heavy rain, and the floods come! [*He goes out.*]

Poges. [*To* SOUHAUN.] There's Erin, the tear and the smile in her eye for you! The unmannerly ruffian! Cheeking me up to my very face. Venomous, too—wanting me to wait till the floods come!

Souhaun. Well, it's not a royal face, is it? You'll have to learn to be respectful to the people, if you want them to be respectful to you.

Poges. [*Sarcastically.*] I'll be most deferential in the future. [*Stormily—to* FIRST WORKMAN *appearing at the entrance.*] Well, what do you want?

First Workman. Excuse, but I sailed in, hearin' you were in a difficulty, an' I wanted to see if I could help.

Poges. Well, I want to know where's the man who is responsible for putting in this 'phone?

First Workman. Why, is there anything wrong with it, sir?

Poges. [*Stormily.*] Everything's wrong, man! I can't get on to the Exchange.

First Workman. Sure, that's aysily explained; it's not connected yet.

Poges. It was to be connected, first thing this morning. When will it be connected?

First Workman. [*Cautiously.*] Oh, now, that depends, sir.

Poges. Depends? Depends on what?

First Workman. On how long it'll take to

get the sthrame o' the sound from here flowin' safely to whatever other end there may be fixed for it to be heard in.

Poges. [*Impatiently.*] Get O'Killigain, get him to come here, at once.

First Workman. Sure, that's the postmaster's job—Mr O'Killigain has nothing to do with it.

Poges. [*Shouting.*] Then get me the man that has something to do with it.

Souhaun. [*Who has been looking at the coloured curtain stuff, and spreading it out.*] Now, Cyril, see what you think: Is the red with the green stripe or the green with the red stripe the most suitable to go with the walls?

[*The sound of horses trotting is heard outside, becoming plainer, till the sound ceases somewhere close to the house.*]

Poges. [*To* SOUHAUN—*with irritation.*] For goodness' sake, one thing at a time. [*To* FIRST WORKMAN.] Go and get the man that's doing this job.

First Workman. I'm afraid you'll have to thravel a long way, if you want to get him, sir; you see, he had to go to pay his last respects to a dead cousin; but never fear, he won't be gone beyond a couple of hours, unless something out o' the ordinary keeps him away the whole o' the evenin'.

[POGES *sinks down on one of the seats, silent and confounded.*]

Cloyne. [*Appearing at back entrance.*] Th' horses are here, now, sir.

Poges. [*Sitting up.*] Horses? What horses?

Cloyne. The horses Mr Basil an' Miss Avril ordhered to come here.

Souhaun. Basil and Avril are going out for a little canter, Cyril.

Poges. Canter! [*Mocking.*] A gentleman goes a trit-trot! [*Peevishly.*] But this is no time to be thinking of amusement; we have to get the house into shape. Ask O'Killigain to come here.

Souhaun. [*To* CLOYNE.] Yes, get O'Killigain, Cloyne; he has a good eye, and will be able to judge which of these curtain stuffs should go on the windows.

[CLOYNE *goes.* O'KILLIGAIN *appears at the left entrance, with an anxious look on his face.*]

O'Killigain. Who's going to ride these horses that are outside?

Souhaun. [*Haughtily.*] Miss Avril and her friend, Mr Basil Stoke, are going to ride them.

O'Killigain. I suppose you know these horses are mettlesome creatures, and need riders at home in the saddle?

Souhaun. [*More haughtily still.*] My friend and her friend learned the art in a London riding school and exercised frequently in Richmond Park; so your kind solicitude is unnecessary, sir.

O'Killigain. [*Viciously.*] Richmond Park isn't Clune na Geera, ma'am. The horses there are animals; the horses here are horses. [AVRIL *comes tripping in, dressed in jersey and jodhpurs, and is followed by* BASIL, *dressed in a dark green kind of hunting coat, buckskin breeches, and big gleaming top-boots, with spurs; he carries a whip in his hand, and a high, handsome, shining tall-hat on his head. With a frightened look at* BASIL.] Good God!

[*He turns on his heel, and walks out again.*]

Basil. [*With complacent conceit—to* SOUHAUN.] The old ways coming back again to the old house, Souhaun.

Souhaun. [*Rapturously.*] Isn't it grand, dear? Don't forget to go through the Village.

Avril. [*Joyously.*] Basil has been so kind, Souhaun, dear; he has given me a grand cheque.

Souhaun. [*Giving* BASIL *a kiss.*] Basil, you're a darling!

Poges. [*Grumpily.*] Be careful how you handle those horses.

Basil. [*Haughtily—to* POGES.] Did you say anything, sir?

Poges. [*With some heat.*] I said be careful how you handle those horses!

Basil. [*With a mocking bow.*] Thank you, sir; we'll do our best. [*To* AVRIL.] Come, darling.

[AVRIL *trips out, and* BASIL *follows her in a way that he deems to be stately.*]

Poges. I hope they'll do no damage, now.

Souhaun. Oh, never fear; Basil sits the saddle like a centaur.

[*The movement of horses' hooves is heard, then a trot, getting fainter till it dies away.*]

Poges. [*Exasperated.*] God send he doesn't frighten the horse—looking like the cock of the South. More decent of him had he remained here to get this telephone going. They all seem to be determined here to keep us away from every semblance of civilization! [*To* SOUHAUN—*stormily.*] Will you, for God's sake, try to get O'Killigain to do something to get this thing in order? [*He goes over to where* SOUHAUN *is busy with the curtains and pulls the curtains out of her hands, and flings them to the floor.*] D'ye hear, d'ye hear what I'm saying to you, woman?

Souhaun. [*Losing patience, and seizing him, and shaking him roughly.*] What d'ye think you're doing, you old dim-eyed old half-dead old fool? I'll disconnect you as well as the telephone, if you don't learn to behave yourself! You settled on coming here, and you'll put up with the annoyances!

Poges. [*Protestingly.*] Eh, eh, there! It was you who persuaded me to come to this god-forsaken hole!

Souhaun. [*Shaking him more fiercely.*] You're a liar, I didn't! It was you yourself who were always pinin' to see the little squirrels jigging about on the trees, and see the violets and primroses dreaming in the budding stir of spring! [*She pushes him violently from her.*] Another snarly sound out of you, and I'm off to live alone.

Poges. [*Gloomily.*] You can well afford to be independent now, since, like a fool, I settled five hundred a year on you.

[*During this contest,* CLOYNE *has appeared at the left entrance, and now gives a judicious cough.*]

Souhaun. [*Quickly—to cover dispute from* CLOYNE.] We'll decide on this stuff, then, for the curtains, Cyril, dear.

Poges. It'll look delightful, darling. [*Pretending to see* CLOYNE *for the first time.*] Oh, what do you want?

Cloyne. Canon Creehewel's outside, an' would like to have a few words with you, if you're not too busy.

Poges. [*Showing irritation.*] Oh, these priests! Thick as weeds in this poor country. Opposed to every decent thought that happens not to have come from them. Sealing with seven seals any book an intelligent human being would wish to read. Ever on guard to keep the people from growing out of infancy. No one should give them the slightest encouragement. Oh, if the misguided people would only go back to the veneration of the old Celtic gods, what a stir we'd have here! To the delightful, if legendary, loveliness of er, er, er,—what's his name, what's her name, what's their name? I have so often said it, so often in my mind, the chief, or one of the chief gods of the ancient Celts?

Souhaun. Was it Gog or Magog, dear?

Poges. [*With fierce scorn.*] Oh, no, no, no; try to think a little, if you really want to assist me. Can't you remember that Gog and Magog were two Philistinian giants killed by David, or Jonathan, or Joshua, or Joab, or Samson, or someone? It's the old Celtic god I have in mind, the one—what was his name?

Souhaun. Gulliver?

Poges. Oh, no; not Gulliver!

Souhaun. Well, I don't know the hell who it was.

Poges. [*Slapping his thigh exultantly.*] Brobdingnag! That was the fellow—the fellow that ate the nine nuts—or was it seven? —plucked from the tree hanging over the well near the world's end.

Cloyne. What am I to say to the Canon, sir?

Poges. What does he want; did you ask him what he wants?

Cloyne. He says he just wants to drop a word of thanks for the fifty pounds you sent him.

[*A murmur of voices is heard outside. It comes nearer, and the sound seems excited.*]

Poges. [*Listening.*] What's that, now?

First Workman's Voice. [*Outside.*] Keep his head up.

Third Workman's Voice. [*Outside.*] You're home, sir, you're home, now.

[*They come in supporting* BASIL *by the arms, followed by the* SECOND MAN, *holding* BASIL'S *coat-tail.* BASIL *is pale, and has a frightened look on his face. His lovely coat is spattered with mud, and, in some places, torn. The* FIRST MAN *is carrying the tall hat, now looking like a battered concertina.*]

Poges. [*Anxiously.*] What's this; what's happened?

First Workman. [*Soothingly.*] He's all right, sir; just a little shock. We seen him crawling towards the house, an' went to his help. His horse flung him.

Souhaun. [*Running to* BASIL.] Are you much hurt, Basil, dear?

Basil. [*Brokenly.*] Bruised, bruised from head to foot.

Poges. [*With irritation.*] Why, why the hell didn't you stay here and help me to get the telephone fixed?

Basil. Why didn't you hold me back by force? Oh, why did you let me go!

Souhaun. [*Anxiously.*] Where's Avril?

Basil. [*Ignoring her query.*] Oh, I should never have ventured up on an Irish horse! Irresponsible, irresponsible, like the people. When he wouldn't go, I gave him just a little jab with the spur— [*Moaningly.*] —and the brute behaved like a wild animal, just like a wild animal! A monster, a mastodon!

First Workman. [*Soothingly—to* SOUHAUN.] He's not hurt much, ma'am; came down in th' grass on his poor bum.

Souhaun. But where's Avril? [*Shaking* BASIL'S *shoulder.*] Where's Avril?

Basil. Gone!

Souhaun. Gone?

Basil. Away with O'Killigain. He came

bounding up to help Avril, and abused me for falling off. Then they cantered away together. [*Loudly and a little shrilly.*] Naked and unashamed, the vixen went away with O'Killigain!

[*A hole appears in the ceiling, almost directly over the fireplace; then a thin rope comes dangling down, followed by the face of a heavily* YELLOW-BEARDED MAN, *who thrusts his head as far as it can go through the hole.*]

Yellow-Bearded Man. [*To those below.*] Hey, hey, there; is this where yous want the light to go?

Poges. [*With a vexatious yell when he sees where the rope hangs.*] No, it isn't, no, it isn't, you fool! [*Indicating a place near the centre and towards the back.*] There, there's where it's wanted! Where my desk will be!

Yellow-Bearded Man. [*Soothingly.*] Don't worry; just a little mistake in measurement, sir.

[*He takes his head out of the hole, and disappears, leaving* POGES *furious.*]

Souhaun. [*To* POGES.] Here, help me in with poor Basil, till he drinks some brandy, and lies down for a little.

[POGES *takes one arm,* SOUHAUN *takes the other, and they lead* BASIL *out of the room.*]

Cloyne. [*As they pass.*] What am I to do with the Canon, sir?

Poges. [*Ferociously.*] Tell him I'll give him another cheque, if he gets the telephone fixed for me before the night is out!

[BASIL, SOUHAUN, *and* POGES *go out by the left entrance;* CLOYNE *by that on the right, leaving the* MEN *standing together in a corner of the room.*]

Second Workman. [*Pensively.*] Th' spirit of the Grey o' Macha's in our Irish horse yet!

First Workman. [*Excitedly.*] Did yous hear that, eh? Did yous hear what he just let dhrop? That the lassie o' th' house went off with O'Killigain riding naked through the locality!

Second Workman. Stark naked, she was, too. Didn't I know well be th' cut of her jib that she was a hop, step, an' lep of a lassie!

First Workman. Th' sight near left me eyes when I seen her go prancin' out without as much as a garter on her to keep her modesty from catchin' cold.

Third Workman. This'll denude the disthrict of all its self-denyin' decency.

First Workman. [*Excitedly jumping up on a seat to get nearer to the hole in the ceiling.*] Cornelius, eh, there, Cornelius!

[*The* YELLOW-BEARDED HEAD *is thrust through the hole again.*]

Yellow-Bearded Man. What's up?

First Workman. Didja hear th' terrible thing that's afther happenin'?

Yellow-Bearded Man. No; what terrible thing?

First Workman. The lassie o' th' house's gone careerin' all over th' counthry on horseback with only her skin as a coverin'!

Yellow-Bearded Man. [*Horrified.*] G'way! No, no; oh, no!

Third Workman. [*Up to him.*] Oh, but, oh yes. I'm tellin' you. An' th' poor men workin' in th' fields had to flee to th' ditches to save th' sight of their eyes from th' shock o' seein' her!

Yellow-Bearded Man. [*With aggravated anguish in his voice.*] It's like me to be up here outa sight o' the world with great things happenin'!

CURTAIN

ACT TWO

SCENE: *The same as in the preceding act. The two portraits, one of* STOKE, *the other of* POGES, *are now hanging on the wall at back, between the windows. Bright green curtains, broadly striped with red, are on the windows. A Jacobean armchair has been added to the two stiff pew-like seats beside the fireplace. The table is to the left, so that two mattresses, one beside the other, can be seen, with their heads against the* wall and their feet towards the front. On these, wrapped round with rugs and blankets, are POGES and STOKE. Some thick rolled-up floor rugs are lying against the wall. A bunch of pampas grass is in the earthenware jug standing on the table. The rejected crimson curtain stuff is lying over one of the pewlike seats. A walking-stick—BASIL's— is leaning against the wall, near to where he is lying.

It is about half-past seven on a cold and misty morning. A few misty beams of sunlight are coming in through the windows, paling the light of a lighted lantern standing between the two beds.

[*The two men are twisting about uneasily on the mattresses; when* POGES *twists to the right,* BASIL *twists to the left, and vice versa. Then* POGES, *wearing a blue beret, with a black bow at the side, lifts his head a little, and glances over at* BASIL. *He is in that drowsy state felt by a man who has spent long hours of the night trying to get to sleep, and failing to do so.*

Before the scene is disclosed, the hooting of owls is heard, first; then the faint lowing of cattle, grunting of swine, crowing of cocks, bleating of sheep; then, vigorously from various directions, the whistling of the chorus of "The Farmer's Boy."]

Poges. Did you hear that cock crowing? [*Imitating.*] Cockadoodle doo! And that cuckoo calling? [*He imitates the bird.*] Cuckoo! Cuckoo!

Basil. Deafening, aren't they? And the owls too! [*Imitating them.*] Too whit, too whit! All the night, jungle noises!

Poges. Good God, isn't it cold? [BASIL *is silent.*] Eh, how d' ya feel now?

Basil. [*With a faint groan.*] Stiff as hell still! It's a mercy I'm alive. And, on the top of it, Avril to make a laughing-stock of me by enjoying herself with O'Killigain.

Poges. [*Sympathetically.*] It was damned mean of her, Basil. She's inclined that way, I'm afraid. You'll have to keep a strong hand over her, my boy.

Basil. [*With a deep groan.*] I can't— now.

Poges. Why can't you, man?

Basil. A month before we came here, I did a very foolish thing.

Poges. Oh?

Basil. [*Mournfully.*] Settled five hundred a year on her for life.

Poges. Oh! [*A fairly long pause.*] Basil, Basil, I did the same to Souhaun!

Basil. We're done for, Cyril.

Poges. [*In a sprightly way.*] No, no; a month in the country'll make us young again. We'll be as lively as goats, in no time. Besides, we can always cautiously hint at an increase in the settlement.

Basil. [*Gloomily.*] With the workers always striking for higher wages, it'll have to remain a hint.

Poges. [*As gloomily.*] It's damnable.

Basil. If much more is given to them, how's a poor man to live? [*He sinks back on the mattress, and pulls the clothes over his head. Outside a cock crows loudly, followed by the call of a cuckoo. Clicking his tongue, exasperatedly—from under the clothes.*] Dtch dtch dtch! Isn't it a good thing those birds aren't in the house! [*The cock crows again, much louder this time, and the cuckoo calls again.*] Damn that cock and that cuckoo! Did you hear that cock crowing, Basil, and the cuckoo?

Basil. Deafening, isn't it? And the owls, too, all the night.

Poges. The country's not going to be so quiet as I thought. Still, I'm glad we came.

Basil. So am I, really. These sounds are just part of the country's attractions—pleasant and homely.

Poges. And stimulating, Basil, stimulating. Look at the sunlight coming in through the windows—another dawn, Basil; another life. Every day in the country brings another chance of living a new life.

Basil. [*Enthusiastically.*] And we're going to live it, eh, what, Cyril?

Poges. [*Enthusiastically.*] Oh, boy, ay!

[SOUHAUN *appears at the back entrance, left, and* AVRIL *at entrance to the right. Both are wearing fur coats over their nightdresses and shiver a little.*]

Souhaun. [*Plaintively.*] For goodness' sake, will you two men get up, and do something? Cloyne's fallen down in a dark passage and hurt her wrist, and she can't do much.

Poges. Oh?

Avril. And something will have to be done to heat the rooms—we were almost frozen last night.

Poges. Ah! Well, we weren't scorched with the heat either.

Souhaun. Well, stir yourselves, and you'll soon get warm. O'Killigain and his men are already at work, and will want to be coming in and out of here.

[*The cock crows louder than ever, and is joined by many more, a few of them at a great distance, so that the sounds are heard but faintly; these are mingled with the barking of dogs, the lowing of cattle, the bleating of sheep, the twittering of birds, the grunting of pigs, and the cackling of hens.*]

Avril. There, you hear; everything's alive but you two.

Poges. Well, we'll be in the midst of them all in a second. [*The two* WOMEN *withdraw.* BASIL *and* POGES, *with the clothes wrapped round them, sit up, and dive down again.*

After a second or two, they sit bolt upright again, and again dive down. Shivering.]
Ooooh, Basil, cold!

Basil. [*Shivering.*] Bitter, bitter!

[*They lie quiet for a short time.*]

Poges. There's nothing for it but to plunge out of the summer into the black and bitter winter.

Basil. You say the word.

Poges. Ready! Steady! Go! [*They climb laboriously out of the beds. When they get out, it can be seen that they have been fully dressed, even to their heavy topcoats and scarves wound round their necks. Blowing on his hands and rubbing them.*] Ooooh, crisp, isn't it? Healthy, though. Ooooh! Where the hell's that Barney, that he hasn't a fire lighted for us? Ooooh! One would want to be on his tail all day. [*Shouting.*] Barney, Barney! [BARNEY *comes in holding some logs in the crook of his right arm, and a lantern in his left hand.* CLOYNE *follows, with some paper and sticks. Her left wrist is bandaged.* BARNEY *is wearing a topcoat, and has a muffler round his neck.* CLOYNE, *too, is wearing a heavy coat. They both go over to the fireplace. As they come in.*] Ah, here we are. Bit nippy, Barney; sharp, but beneficial. [*To* CLOYNE.] You'll have to be more careful with the steps and passages. Mind your feet coming in, mind your head going out. Ooooh! [*To* BASIL.] You better slip off and give the others any help you can. [*As* BASIL *is going.*] What about your walking-stick?

Basil. [*Moving stiffly.*] I must try to do without it—about the house, anyway.

[*He takes the lantern that is beside his bed, and goes out.*]

Poges. [*To the other two.*] Well, what do the pair of you think of the country, eh? And the house? Better than any your old Kings of Tarara had, eh?

Cloyne. [*Effusively.*] I'm sure it'll be lovely, sir, when we settle down.

[POGES *has been jerking his arms about in an effort to drive the cold from his body.* CLOYNE *begins to fold the clothes on the beds, and tidy them up.*]

Poges. Of course it will. We'll enjoy it all; we'll feel younger; we will be younger. The air, fresh air, pure air, exhilarating air, will be able to get at us. [*He sucks in his breath and blows it out again.*] Oooh! Soon we won't know ourselves. We'll eat better, sleep better; flabby muscles will become firm, and we'll realize that we are alive, alive, alive—— Think of the walks we'll have; so much to see, so much to hear, so much to smell; and then to come back, nicely tired,

to such a lovely house. A life for the gods!

Cloyne. Wondherful, wondherful, sir.

Poges. Now, I must be off to swallow down a cup of tea, for there's a lot to be done, a lot to be done yet.

[*He hurries off out of the room.*]

Cloyne. The poor oul' codger!

Barney. Comin' down to this back o' God-speed place for rest an' quietness! After all that science has thried to do for us, goin' back to lantherns an' candles. Th' only electric light he'll allow in a Tudor house is one over his own desk! Runnin' in the face o' God Almighty's goodness—that's what it is.

Cloyne. They'll get tired of it before us.

Barney. I can tell you I'm tired of it already. Looka the place we're livin' in: doors everywhere shaped like doors o' dungeons; passages dark as hell when it was first formed; crackin' your head when you're goin' in, and breakin' your toe when you're goin' out; an' I'm tellin' you, it's only beginnin'.

Cloyne. It might be worse.

Barney. [*Striking a match to light the paper.*] We're goin' to be worse, I'm tellin' you.

Cloyne. We can't be worse than we are.

Barney. [*As the flames of the paper die down.*] There's no chance o' kindlin' here. Why did you say, then, that we might be worse?

Cloyne. Well, so, indeed an' we might.

Barney. How can we be worse, woman, when we're as bad as we can be?

Cloyne. Simply by bein' worse than we were.

Barney. How can we be worse than we were, when we're as bad as we can be, now?

Cloyne. You'll see we'll be worse, before we're better.

Barney. Damn these logs! Isn't that what I'm sthrivin' to dhrive into your head?

Cloyne. What are you sthrivin' to dhrive into me head?

Barney. That we'll be worse than we were, before we're as bad as we are now, an' in a week's time we'll be lookin' back with a sigh to a time, bad as it could be then, that was betther than the worse that was on top of us now.

[POGES *bustles in again. The heavy topcoat is gone, and he is now dressed in bright-blue shorts, emerald-green jersey, brown shoes, and the scarf is still round his neck. He has a cup of tea in his hand and he is sipping it as he comes into the room. He is miserably cold, but he puts on a brisk air, sorting it out in his mind that to be cold in the country is natural, to be ignored as far as possible, and to be countered by a smiling face, a brisk manner, and the wearing of brilliant clothes denoting freedom of movement and utter disregard of the common rules of convention. He is feeling far from comfortable, but thinks this shouldn't be shown; for the colder you are, and the more uncomfortable you feel, the brisker you must be, and the hardier you'll get.*]

Poges. Here we are again! Ready for anything now. [*Losing his gay attitude when he sees that the fire isn't lighted.*] Isn't the fire lighted yet? What are you doing, Barney? Being in the country's no reason why we should be frozen to death.

Barney. I can't get a spark out of it, afther all me sthrivin'.

Poges. [*Testily.*] You can't light logs with a bit of paper, man. Oh, use your brains, Barney, use your brains.

Barney. An' what else have I got to light them?

Poges. Small sticks, man; put some small sticks under them.

Barney. An' will you tell me where I'm goin' to get the small sticks? Where am I goin' to get small sticks? Isn't the nearest shop a dozen miles away?

Poges. Well, if there's no sticks, sprinkle a little paraffin on them.

Barney. An' where am I goin' to get the paraffin? An' where am I goin' to get the paraffin? There's no oil wells knockin' about here.

Poges. [*Severely.*] Don't be funny. You've got to remember you're in the country now.

Barney. Isn't it meself that's gettin' to know it well!

Poges. We've got to do things for ourselves: there's no chance of pushing a button to get things done here.

Barney. Sure, I'm beginnin' to think you're right.

Poges. Can't you see that those logs are too big?

Barney. I think I do, unless me sight's goin' curious.

Poges. [*Hotly.*] Well, then, why don't you do it?

Barney. Arra, do what?

Poges. [*Loudly.*] Make them smaller, man!

Barney. [*Calmly and sarcastically.*] An' how?

Poges. And how? Why, with an axe, of course. [*Bending down close to* BARNEY'S

ear—*with a shout.*] An axe, man, an axe!

Barney. [*Losing his temper—shouting back.*] An' where's the axe, an' where's the axe?

Poges. There must be an axe knocking about somewhere.

Barney. There's nothin' knockin' about here, but a bitther breeze whirlin' through the passages that ud numb the legs of a Mother Superior.

Cloyne. [*Trying to mollify things.*] Sure, the poor man's back-broken an' heart-broken thryin' to kindle it, sir.

Poges. [*Who has been waving his arms and stamping his feet while his teeth chatter—turning fiercely on* CLOYNE.] You mind your own business, girl! [*Seeing her putting the mattress by the wall.*] Have we got to sleep down here again tonight?

Cloyne. Ay, an' yous have. Th' other rooms are too damp still. Sure, Mr O'Killigain says that it'll take a month of fierce fires to dhry them out.

Poges. [*Testily.*] Mr O'Killigain says this, and Mr O'Killigain says that! I'm getting tired of what Mr O'Killigain says. If we have to sleep here, you or Barney'll have to stay up all night keeping the fire going, or we'll be frozen in our sleep. [*His eye catches sight of the telephone. He goes over to it, and lifts the receiver.*] Not a sound! No, oh no; not a bit of a hurry. [*Angrily, to* CLOYNE.] Go out, girl, and send in the boy who's working at this telephone. [*With a low moan.*] Ireland!

[CLOYNE *goes out by the doorway on the right leading to entrance hall. After a few seconds the loud lowing of a cow is heard, followed by a scream from* CLOYNE, *who rushes frantically back into the room, pale and trembling.*]

Cloyne. [*Breathlessly rushing back into the room, falling on the floor, and catching* POGES *wildly by the legs.*] Save me! Stuck his head into me face, th' minute I opened the door. Mother o' God, I'll never see th' light of another day with th' fright I got!

Poges. [*Alarmed.*] What is it, what is it, woman?

Cloyne. [*Almost incoherent.*] A bull, a wild bull, out in th' enthrance hall!

Barney. [*Frantically.*] A wild bull! We're all desthroyed!

Poges. [*Trying to release himself from* CLOYNE'S *hold.*] Let me go, girl! Let me go, or I can't defend myself. If he comes in here the whole of us'll be horned.

Cloyne. [*Frantically.*] Me legs have given undher me. Let me hold on to you, sir— it's me only hope!

Poges. [*To* BARNEY.] Put the table to the doorway, man, and a mattress, and help to bar him out—quick, quick, man! [*To* CLOYNE, *while* BARNEY *is pushing the table and a mattress to the door.*] Why didn't you clap the door in his face, you fool?

Cloyne. Wasn't he half into the hall before I'd the door half open! Oh, sir, what are we goin' to do? Oh, please go, sir, an' thry an' shove him out!

Poges. [*Half dead with panic.*] My God, woman, you can't shove bullocks about! [*Shouting.*] Souhaun, there's a wild bull in the house! Help, O'Killigain, help! [*To* BARNEY.] Run, run, man, and get Mr Stoke to bring down the gun. Oh, go quick, man! [BARNEY *runs off. Shouting.*] O'Killigain, help! Can't you let me go, girl?

Cloyne. [*Still clinging to him.*] Carry me off, sir, please. Don't leave me here to die alone! Maybe he won't be able to climb the stairs after us. Oh, when I came to th' counthry, I never thought there'd be wild animals on th' door-step!

[BASIL *appears at one of the entrances at the back; he moves forward stealthily, and extends a gun to* POGES.]

Basil. [*Nervous.*] What is it, what is it?

Poges. A bull, out in the hall.

Basil. Who let him? Damn it, such carelessness! You must be on guard in the country, you know. Here, take the gun, man.

Poges. [*Angrily—to* BASIL.] Come out, come out in the open, man, and be ready to use the gun, if he comes into the room! [*Shoving the gun from him.*] You use it, man; weren't you an A. R. P.[1] man?

Basil. [*Indignantly.*] I never did anything more than clay-pigeon shooting! Let whoever let the damned animal in let the damned animal out! [*He pokes* POGES *with the gun.*] Here, take this, and down him—you're nearer the bull than I am.

Poges. [*Angrily.*] I'm not a toreador, am I? And don't point, don't point the gun at me! D'ye want me to die two deaths at once? What's the advantage of your passing through Oxford, if you can't face a bull with a gun in your hand? Be a man, man, and not a mouse.

Basil. [*Keeping well in the passage, and only showing his nose.*] Telephone the police, the fire brigade, or something.

Poges. [*Violently.*] Don't you know the kind of a country we're in? There's no police, no fire brigade, no telephone! Come here, if you won't use the gun, and help me carry this girl away out of danger.

---

[1] Air Raid Precautions.

[*The* BULL *puts a stylised head with long curving horns over the barricade and lets out a loud bellow.* CLOYNE *spasmodically tugs the legs of* POGES, *making him lose his balance so that he topples to the floor, after a frantic effort to save himself.*]

Cloyne. Oooh, sir, save me!

Poges. [*With a wild shout as he is falling.*] My God, he's on top of us! We're done for! Help!

[BASIL *throws the gun into the room, and runs for his life.*]

Barney. [*In the far distance.*] Sing out, sir, if you want any assistance!

[*Someone is heard stirring outside where the animal is; this stir is followed by the voice of the* FIRST WORKMAN *shooing the cow out of the hall. After a few moments,* POGES *slowly sits up and listens.*]

First Workman. [*Shouting outside.*] Eh, oick, oick, eh, yeh get; ay, ay oick oick!

[POGES *gets up on his feet, shaking a little, and going over, picks up the gun, and steadying himself on it, stands over the prostrate* CLOYNE, *who is almost in a faint, bundled up on the floor, with her face hidden in her hands. Shortly after, the* FIRST WORKMAN *appears at the entrance, with a bucket of coal and some sticks. He looks over the table, astonished to see the prostrate* CLOYNE *and* POGES *standing near, with a gun in his hand.*]

Poges. [*Stormily.*] Where the hell did that bull come from? Who owns her? Who let that bull come tearing into a private house?

First Workman. Bull, sir? Oh, that wasn't a bull, sir. [*He pushes the table back to its place.*] Jest a harmless, innocent cow, sir. Frightened the poor girl, now, did it? [*Cunningly.*] But I see it didn't frighten you, sir.

Poges. [*Flattered.*] No, no, not me. [*To* CLOYNE.] Here, girl, get up on your feet. [*Loudly.*] It wasn't a bull; I knew it couldn't be a bull! and it's gone, so get up. [*With the help of the* FIRST WORKMAN *and* POGES, CLOYNE *gets up on her feet.*] There now, be off with you. Get Miss Avril to give you a stiff glass of whiskey, and you'll be all right. And bring this gun back to Mr Basil.

[*He picks up the gun, and hands it to the shaking* CLOYNE.]

Cloyne. Oh, sir, this place is worse than a jungle in th' desert!

Poges. Go on, go on! I thought you Irish were a brave people.

[*He is shaky himself, but he stiffens himself to conceal the tremors.*]

Cloyne. [*Going out with the gun.*] For ages now, it's bulls I'll be dhreamin' of, an' there's ne'er a lock on me door either!

Poges. Fainting, shouting, screaming, and running about for nothing! No nerves, no nerves, no spirit; no coolness in a crisis.

First Workman. [*Craftily.*] An' did they all think it was a bull, sir? An' you stood your ground. Looka that now; prepared for anything, sir.

Poges. [*Taking it all in.*] The other fellow, Mr Basil, ran for his life; think of that—ran for his life!

First Workman. Did he, now?

Poges. British, too, think of that; surprising and disappointing, very. [*Briskly and a little anxiously.*] Still, I must acquaint the police. I can't have cows or bulls wandering about the rooms of Tudor Manor.

First Workman. [*Who has started to light the fire.*] One o' th' ladies sent me in to light a fire for you. [*Placatingly.*] Sure, sir, she was only the cow me friend brought this mornin' so that, when you had a minute, you could run out an' look her over. A fine animal, sir. She got loose an' wandhered in when she found the door open. She's betther than th' best that was in th' cattle raid o' Cooley.

[*Souhaun comes running in from the back entrance, hurriedly and somewhat alarmed.*]

Souhaun. What on earth's all this commotion about a bull? We had to stop Basil from throwing himself out of a window. And Barney climbed out on the roof! What does it mean?

Poges. [*Nonchalantly.*] Oh, nothing at all. A stray cow got into the garden, and Basil lost his head and Cloyne lost her feet. Nervy!

Souhaun. But Barney when he was rushing past said that you were roaring for help.

First Workman. [*Gayly.*] Roarin' for help, is it? Indeed, an' he wasn't, for I can testify to that, miss, but standing here, he was, on me Bible oath, miss, cool as you like, waitin' for the rush of th' angry animal.

Souhaun. But I'm certain I heard him roaring myself.

First Workman. That was only him, miss, dhrivin' the wild animal out.

Souhaun. You'll have to learn to keep bulls in proper places—we can't have them running round the rooms. [*To Poges—throwing the overall to him.*] There's your overall to wear when you're working. [*To Workman.*] And no more bulls.

First Workman. No, miss; no more bulls.

Poges. We'll deal with them when they come; we'll deal with them.

[*During the discussion, the Workman has been attending to the fire, and Poges goes over to it as Souhaun goes out.*]

First Workman. [*To Poges as he warms his hands at the fire.*] There y're, sir: a fire that'll warm y'up an' make your mind easy.

Poges. Good, great, grand! Are you the workman who knows all the stories and legends of Ireland since the world began?

First Workman. No, no, not me, sir; it's Philib you mean—the powerful man with th' powerful beard. [*Touching his forehead.*] Some say he isn't all there, but a wonderherful man, ay, indeed, is Philib. Does a man good to talk to him.

Poges. I'll have a chat with him, the first chance I get.

First Workman. [*Looking around the room with a ravishing air.*] This is a wonderherful house, so it is. It's an honour to be workin' in it. Afther hundreds o' years standin' in frost, rain, an' snow, frontin' th' winds o' the world, it's a marvel it isn't flat on its face, furnishin' only an odd shelther for a sthray fox; but here it stands, an' we all waitin' for a windy winther ud stagger it an' send it tottherin' down.

Poges. [*Indignantly.*] Tottherin' down! What d'ye mean, tottherin' down? The place is as firm as a lighthouse. Tottherin' down, indeed!

First Workman. [*Repelling the idea that he thought of such a thing.*] Tottherin' down, is it? Now, who, in th' name o' God, save a sure an' safe fool, ud think it was tottherin' down? Not me, now; oh no, not me. Tottherin' down, me neck! Isn't th' grand oul' house goin' to show, soon an' sudden, a sign of what a fine residence it was when the quality harnessed their horses for a hunt be the risin' rim o' th' dawn or sat down in their silks an' satins to their evenin' meal, in the shadowy shine o' th' golden candles!

Poges. Purple nights and golden days, my friend. [*He sighs.*] Aah!

First Workman. [*With a long, deep, imitative sigh.*] Aah! We'll never set eyes on the like o' them again, sir; th' sparklin' carriages comin' an' goin', th' steeds throttin' nicely an' neatly, or movin' at a gallop, always elegant, on a visit to me lord here, or me lady there, with th' sky above in a fair swoon o' pride for th' fine things movin' about below; an' they full o' grace, an' decked out in the grandeur o' th' West Indies an' th' East Indies, sobered down a thrifle for use in a Christian counthry, the women's bosoms asway with jewels, like a tendher evenin' sky, alive with stars. An' the gentlemen, just a dim step down, but elegant too, in finery fair, with ruffles an' lace, with cutaway coats an' vests embroidhered, each holdin' a cane to keep them steady, an' all halo'd with scents to ring them round from th' smell o' th' poor an' dingier world at work or play!

Poges. [*Enthusiastically.*] Those were handsome days. [*He fixes a plume of pampas grass in his beret.*] When shall we look upon their like again? [*He folds the crimson curtain stuff round him as if it were a cavalier's cloak.*] The lawns and rampart still are here, and we shall be the men! [*He snatches up* BASIL'S *walking-stick.*] The plume in the hat, the velvet cloak over the shoulder, the tapering rapier in the hand! [*He makes a vicious lunge at the* FIRST WORKMAN *who narrowly dodges the pass.*] Die, varlet!

First Workman. [*Remonstratively.*] Eh, eh, there; careful, sir, be careful!

Poges. [*Leaning on the stick as if it were a sword—sorrowfully.*] Where are the kings and queens and warriors now? Gone with all their glory! The present day and present men? Paltry, mean, tight and tedious. [*Disgustedly.*] Bah!

First Workman. What are we now, what are we all, but a tired thribe thryin' to do nothin' in the shortest possible time: worn away we are, I'm sayin', to shreds and shaddas, mountin' machines to do everything for us. Tired, is it? Ay, tired an' thremblin' towards th' edge of th' end of a life hardly worth livin'!

Poges. [*Gloomily pacing up and down.*] Not worth living, not worth living.

First Workman. [*With greater energy.*] Time ago, an' we gave a ready ear to one speakin' his faith in God an' his neighbour; but now, there's so many gabbers goin' that there's hardly a listener left. Sure, that, in itself, is as sharp a punishment as a lease o' hell for a long vacation. It's meself is sayin' ourselves came late, but soon enough to see the finery fade to purple dust, an' the glow o' th' quality turn to murmurin' ashes.

Poges. [*Striking the attitude of a clumsy cavalier.*] We won't let them perish completely! We'll keep the stern old walls standing. We'll walk where they walked; sit where they sat; and sleep where they slept!

First Workman. An' talk as they talked, too.

Poges. [*Wildly.*] Our pride shall be their pride; our elegance their elegance, and the banner of the Tudors shall fly from the battlements again! The King, the King, God bless him!

First Workman. I wouldn't say too much about the King, sir; we're a little touchy about Kings in Clune na Geera.

[SOUHAUN *comes in again from entrance with a look of alarmed indignation on her face.*]

Souhaun. Who on earth thought of bringing a gun into this peaceful place?

Poges. [*Testily.*] I did, I did! Peaceful place! You can never tell what might be knocking about at night, and we have to be ready.

Souhaun. Well, let some take charge of it who knows how to use it, and not Basil.

Poges. Basil. What's that fermented fool doing with it?

Souhaun. He says you never know what may be knocking about at night and he ought to get used to it so's to be ready.

Poges. [*Furiously.*] And what could be knocking about here at night, woman! He's a nice lad to shoot wild animals! He'll send a bullet full-speed through somebody, if it isn't taken from him. [*To* FIRST WORKMAN.] Go you, and take it from him.

First Workman. [*Stricken.*] Me, sir? Me, sir, an' have the weapon goin' off bang with th' muzzle lessn' half an inch from me belly or me brain!

Poges. [*Furiously.*] You don't expect me to do it, do you? Go on, then, and get Miss Avril to take it from him! Go on, get Miss Avril to do it!

[*He pushes the* FIRST WORKMAN *impatiently out of the room.* CLOYNE *appears at entrance at back with a troubled look on her face.*]

Cloyne. Here, they've gone and dumped the garden tools an' the roller right in front of the hall door! And the roller's so close that when you want to go out or come in, you have to climb over it.

Poges. Tell whoever brought them to bring them to the back, and put them in the shed, fool!

Cloyne. How can I tell him when him an' the lorry's gone?

Poges. [*Furiously.*] And why didn't you tell him before he went?

Cloyne. An' didn't I now? He just said that the back was threnched be the workmen, an' he hadn't time to build pontoon bridges.

Poges. What a country! What a people! [*Viciously, to* SOUHAUN.] And you encourage them, because you and your friends are Irish, too!

Souhaun. If you ask me, you're not such a shining paragon of goodness yourself.

Poges. [*Explosively.*] I believe in efficiency! I demand efficiency from myself, from everyone. Do the thing thoroughly and do it well: that's English. The word given, and the word kept: that's English. [*Roaring.*] And I'm an Englishman!

Souhaun. You are, indeed, God help you!

Cloyne. An' what are we goin' to do about the garden tools an' th' roller?

Souhaun. [*In a bustling and dominant way, catching up the jazz-patterned overall and putting it on* POGES.] Here, if we waste any more time talking, the house will never be ready to live in. Put this on, and go and bring the roller from the front door through here, out of the way to the back. When you've done that, bring the garden tools to the back, too, and let us see your grand English efficiency at work while I and Avril do some of the hundred things remaining to be done.

[*She gives him a push from her, and hurries away out by one of the back entrances.*]

Cloyne. [*Warningly.*] It seems a heavy roller, sir, so mind you don't sthrain yourself when you're pullin' it.

Poges. [*Testily.*] Go away, go away, girl; I'm not an invalid. [CLOYNE *goes.* POGES *moves over to the blazing fire, and stretches out his hands to the flame. The* SECOND WORKMAN *comes in by left entrance at back, wheeling a barrow filled with bricks. He is a powerful man, of fifty, with gleaming eyes and wide and strong beard. As he comes nearer,* POGES *turns to give him greeting. Warmly.*] Good day, good sir; it's a cold day that's in it, surely.

Second Workman. [*Eyeing* POGES *curiously.*] Ay, is it, for them who has to brave it, an' can't stand all day in front of a sturdy fire like a kingly Pharaoh.

Poges. [*A little nonplussed.*] Quite, yes, yes, quite. Everyone tells me the place round here is a rich storehouse of history, legend, and myth.

Second Workman. [*With a little scorn in his voice.*] It's a little they know an' little they care about those things. But the place has her share o' history an' her share o' wondhers.

Poges. [*Flatteringly.*] And I'm told, you have a rare stock of them yourself.

Second Workman. Ay, indeed, I have me share o' wondhers, new an' old.

Poges. [*Trying to be Irish.*] Looka that, now, arra, whist, an' amnt I told it's strange stories you do be tellin' of the noble things done by your fathers in their days, and in the old time before them?

Second Workman. [*Sinking into a meditative mood.*] When less than a score of the Fianna brought back the King of England prisoner, invaded Hindostan, an' fixed as subjects the men of all counthries between our Bay o' Dublin and the Holy river that gave to holy John the holy water to baptise our Lord.

Poges. [*Astonished.*] I never heard that one before.

Second Workman. [*With murmuring scorn.*] And where would th' like o' you hear it, man? That was in the days o' Finn Mac Coole, before his hair was scarred with a hint o' grey; the mighty Finn, I'm sayin', who stood as still as a stone in the heart of a hill to hear the cry of a curlew over th' cliffs o' Erris, the song of the blackbird, the cry o' the hounds hotfoot afther a boundin' deer, the steady wail o' the waves tumblin' in on a lonely shore; the mighty Finn who'd surrendher an emperor's pomp for a place with the bards, and the gold o' the king o' Greece for a night asleep be the sthream of Assaroe!

Poges. [*Solemnly.*] A great man, a great man, surely; a great man gone forever.

Second Workman. [*Sharply.*] He's here forever! His halloo can be heard on the hills outside; his spear can be seen with its point in the stars; but not with an eye that can't see over the well-fashioned edge of a golden coin.

Poges. [*Moving back a step—a little awed.*] You see these things, do you?

Second Workman. I hear sthrange things be day, an' see sthrange things be night when I'm touched be the feel of the touch of the long-handed Lugh. When the Dagda makes a gong o' the moon, an' th' Sword o' Light shows the way to all who see it.

Poges. Aah!

Second Workman. Then every rib o' grass grows into a burnished fighter that throws his spear, or waves a sword, an' flings a shield before him. Then Ireland crinkles into a camp, an' kings an' sages, queens an' heroes, saints an' harpers stare me in the face, an' bow, an' pass, an' cry out blessing an' vict'ry, too, for Heber's children, with the branch of greatness waving in their hands!

Poges. And there it ends!

Second Workman. [*Giving* POGES *a drowsy glance.*] I'm thinkin' it might have been well for some if the end an' all was there; but it sthretches out to the sight of a big dim ship with a followin' fleet in the great dim distance, with a stern-fac'd man in the blue-gold coat of the French Armee, standin' alone on the bridge of the big dim ship, his eyes fixed fast on the shore that was fallin' undher the high-headed, rough-tumblin' waves o' the sea!

Poges. [*Awed into interest—murmuringly.*] A big dim ship and a following fleet, carrying a man in the blue-gold coat of the French Armee—who was he, and when was that now?

Second Workman. Yestherday.

Poges. Yesterday!

Second Workman. The man was there, but the fleet was a golden dhream, always comin' in an' ever goin' out o' th' Bay o' Banthry!

[O'KILLIGAIN *has come in at the commencement of the* SECOND WORKMAN'S *musing, unnoticed by the dreaming worker, and barely noticed by the interested* POGES, *listening intently to what is being said, and a little awed by the influence of the* SECOND WORKMAN. O'KILLIGAIN *comes softly over, and stands a little behind, but close to the dreaming* WORKMAN.]

Poges. [*Bending towards the* SECOND WORKMAN.] And who was the man in the blue-gold coat of the French Armee?

Second Workman. He was a great Irish soldier and a great Irish friend to the people of no property in Ireland.

O'Killigain. [*Very softly.*] And there are others.

Second Workman. [*Softly, too, but not so softly.*] And there are others; for through the roads of the four green fields goes Shane the Proud, with his fine head hidden, waving away his more venturesome friends from the horns of a bull, the hoofs of a horse, the snarl of a dog, an' th' smile of an Englishman.

Poges. [*Going back a step.*] The smile of an Englishman!

Second Workman. [*Unheeding the interruption.*] An' in the midst of them all, is Parnell standing still; unheeding he stands with a hand on his breast, his white face is fixed on the East, with his wine-coloured eyes flashin' hathred to England!

O'Killigain. [*Very softly.*] And there are others.

Second Workman. [*With a glance at* O'KILLIGAIN.] They came later, an' haven't wandhered fully back to where they cleared a way for a gropin' people, but they will come, an' stare us into the will to take our own again.

Poges. [*Detaching himself from the spell.*]

And do none other of those you know, good man, see the things that you see?

Second Workman. Barrin' a few an' O'Killigain there, they see these things only as a little cloud o' purple dust blown before the wind.

Poges. That's very sad.

Second Workman. Barrin' O'Killigain, there, an' a few, what is it all now but a bitther noise of cadgin' mercy from heaven, an' a sour handlin' o' life for a cushion'd seat in a corner? There is no shout in it; no sound of a slap of a spear in a body; no song; no sturdy wine-cup in a sturdy hand; no liftin' of a mighty arm to push back the tumblin' waters from a ship just sthrikin' a storm. Them that fight now, fight in a daze o' thradin'; for buyin' an' sellin' for whores an' holiness; for the image o' God on a golden coin; while th' men o' peace are little men, now, writin' dead words with their tiny pens, seekin' a tidy an' tendher way to the end. Respectable lodgers with life they are, behind solid doors with knockers on them, an' curtained glass to keep the stars from starin'!

[*The* SECOND WORKMAN *stoops, lifts the shafts of the barrow, and is about to go out.*]

Poges. [*To* SECOND WORKMAN—*placatingly.*] My own great-grandfather was Irish, I'm told, and my grandmother was a kind of a Scotswoman.

Second Workman. [*Going out, with the barrow, slowly.*] That's not such a lot, an' you're not sure of any of it, either.

Poges. What a strange, odd man! I couldn't get half of what he was trying to say. Are there many like him?

O'Killigain. Millions of them, though few of them have tongues so musical.

Poges. He rather took to me, I think, and looks upon me as a friend.

O'Killigain. He looks upon you as a fool gathering from the tree of life poor apples, gone bad, and useless, leaving the rosier ones behind, with golden apples, too, dangling down in the dark.

Poges. [*Stunned.*] Oh!

O'Killigain. Why don't you seek to build a house that will give a royal chance of bringing newer skill and a newer idea of life to the men who build it? Why don't you try to bring newer grace of form and line before the eyes of Clune na Geera? Why th' hell don't you try to do something worthwhile? [*Sardonically.*] He looks upon you as a friend? He regards you, man, as a rascal and a hot-pulsed hypocrite!

Poges. [*Indignantly.*] Good God, but that's pure ignorance. Where would the world be without us?

O'Killigain. The giddy globe would wobble, slow down, stand still and death would come quick to us all.

Poges. [*A little puzzled by this remark.*] Eh? Quite. Well, no, not so bad as that, you know, but near it, damned near it.

[SOUHAUN *runs in with a look of dark annoyance on her face.*]

Souhaun. Oh, look at you standing here still, and so much to be done, [*Her voice rises.*] —so much to be done, so much to be done! I asked you to get the roller away from the door an hour ago, and here's Barney after twisting his wrist, trying to climb over it standing in the same old place! [*She catches him by the overall.*] Come, for God's sake, and take the damn thing out of the way!

Poges. [*Pulling her hand away from the overall—angrily.*] Oh, have some decency, order, and dignity, woman! Can't you see I'm having a serious discussion with O'Killigain? [*He turns swiftly on* O'KILLIGAIN.] We, sir, are a liberty-loving people, and have always striven to preserve perfect—perfect, mind you—freedom of thought, not only in our own land, but throughout the whole world; but that anyone should be permitted to hold opinions such as are held by that lunatic, just gone out, and are apparently held by you, sir, too, is a perfect scandal and disgrace!

Souhaun. Oh, there's no use of you trying to ride your high horse here in Clune na Geera!

Poges. [*Stormily.*] I'm not trying to ride my high horse in Clune na Geera! What is said in Clune na Geera is a matter of very little importance indeed. But every right-minded man, the world over, knows or ought to know, that wherever we have gone, progress, civilization, truth, justice, honour, humanity, righteousness, and peace have followed at our heels. In the Press, in the Parliament, in the pulpit, or on the battlefield, no lie has ever been uttered by us; no false claim made, no right of man infringed, no law of God ignored, no human law, national or international, broken.

O'Killigain. [*Very quietly.*] Oh, for God's sake, man, don't be pratin' like a pantaloon priest!

Souhaun. [*Trying to push* POGES *from her, impatiently.*] Go out and get the garden roller!

Poges. [*Loudly.*] I say, sir, that Justice is England's old nurse; righteousness and peace sit together in her common-room, and the porter at her gate is truth!

O'Killigain. [*Quietly but sarcastically.*] An' God, Himself, is England's butler.

Poges. [*Roaring with rage.*] That's a vile slander, sir!

O'Killigain. Whether it is or no, doesn't matter much, for in a generation or so, the English Empire will be remembered only as a half-forgotten nursery rhyme!

Poges. [*Fiercely, as* SOUHAUN *is pushing him out.*] An opinion like that deserves the jail!

Souhaun. [*Giving him a last strong push out into one of the back entrances.*] Oh, go on! [*She goes over towards* O'KILLIGAIN, *and stands looking shyly and a little archly at him.*] What a mighty man you are to provoke him into such a tantrum!

O'Killigain. [*After a slight pause.*] Why doesn't he spend his time, money, and energy in building something new, something showing a new idea, leading our eyes to the future?

Souhaun. Oh, I don't know. You like your job here anyhow.

O'Killigain. A little.

Souhaun. A lot, because Avril is here.

O'Killigain. Just as O'Dempsey likes it because you are here.

[*As he is about to go,* O'DEMPSEY, *the* SECOND WORKMAN, *appears and speaks to* O'KILLIGAIN *while his gaze is fixed on* SOUHAUN.]

Second Workman. You're wanted on the roof, Jack.

O'Killigain. [*With a laconic laugh.*] More mending—like slappin' the back of a dyin' man!

[*He goes out while the* SECOND WORKMAN *continues to look shyly but firmly at* SOUHAUN.]

Souhaun. Well, Mr Man, do you find me pleasant to look at?

Second Workman. Yes, you are a fine-lookin' woman, and a fine-lookin' woman shows me a sign that God is smilin'.

Souhaun. [*A little bitterly.*] It's Avril you have in mind, good man, and not me.

Second Workman. When I look at you close, I see you a week or two oldher than your younger friend, and when you go as bright about the house, an' dress as gay as she does, you look like an earlier summer kissin' a tardier spring goodbye.

Souhaun. It's ridiculous for me to be with Poges. It's like a young bird I feel that has just got command of its wings. [*She pauses a moment.*] You do think me as a woman worthy to be looked on—you're not just teasing me, are you?

Second Workman. Not I. You are one of the fine sights of the world. [*He lilts.*]

There are many fair things in this world as it goes,
Th' blue skies of summer, the flushin' red rose;
But of all th' fair blossomin' things that men see,
A comely-built lass is the dearest to me!

And you are a comely lass.

Souhaun. [*Coming close to him.*] What's your name?

Second Workman. Me name? Why, O'Dempsey, of course.

Souhaun. No, no; your more familiar name; the name your girl would call you by.

Second Workman. Filib.

Souhaun. [*Lingering over it.*] Filib! What a dear name! What a dear name! [*She suddenly leans towards him and kisses his cheek.*] Filib!

[*She backs away from him a little frightened at what she has done. And bumps into* Poges *laboriously pulling a gigantic roller as high as he is tall. The heavy iron side discs are vividly painted in panels of red, white, green and yellow. The* First Workman *is pushing the roller from behind, and is followed by* O'Killigain *gazing with laughing amazement at the ponderous machine.*]

Poges. [*Angrily, as* Souhaun *bumps into him.*] Eh, eh, there, look where you are going, can't you?

Souhaun. [*Amazed at the size of the roller.*] God bless us, Cyril, what on earth's that you're carting into the house?

Poges. [*Petulantly.*] Can't you see what it is? The roller, the roller I bought to roll the lawn.

Souhaun. But it's too big, man.

Poges. No, it isn't too big. The man who sold it to me said that the bigger it was, the more effective it would be.

Souhaun. But you'll never be able to pull a mighty thing like that.

Poges. And what's to prevent me from pulling it? Amn't I pulling it now? A child of ten could pull it; well balanced, you know, the man said. Easy to pull, and easier to propel, the man said.

Souhaun. You've just been taken in, Cyril. The thing's altogether too big. [*To the* First Workman]. Isn't it?

First Workman. It looks a size too large to me, ma'am.

Poges. The grass in this district needed a special big roller to level it, the man said, and this was the roller to level it.

First Workman. Sure, that roller ud level a hill.

O'Killigain. The grass'll give way under that, right enough.

Souhaun. The cheek of declaring that a child of ten could pull it like a toy.

First Workman. G'way, ma'am, an' did he really say that now?

Poges. One pull over the lawn with that roller would be enough for the season, the man said.

O'Killigain. An', faith, so it would, an' for every season afther too.

First Workman. Sure, an' wouldn't a specially powerful horse, himself, wilt undher a thing like that! Whoever gave you that, man, musta taken it off an oul' steam-roller.

[*The* Third Workman *appears at entrance to right, and proceeds to take an enjoyable interest in what is happening.*]

Third Workman. Mother o' God, looka what he's after buyin' be th' name of a roller! Isn't it a shame, now, to have imposed on a poor simple inoffensive man with a vehicle like that.

Poges. [*Defiantly.*] It's a bargain, I know it's a bargain; the man said it's a bargain.

Souhaun. [*Mockingly.*] The man said, the man said—ay, and you swallowed everything the man said.

O'Killigain. [*To* First Workman.] Give Mr Poges a hand to take this machine out of the sight of mortal men.

Poges. [*Obstinately.*] I'll take it myself, thank you all. Once you got the knack of balancing it, the man said, you could turn it with your little finger, and I believe what the man said.

O'Killigain. [*To* Third Workman.] Here, you go on back to your work; go on, off you go.

[*He follows the* Third Workman *out of the room.* Poges *gives a mighty push to the roller, propelling it slowly to one of the entrances at the back. The* First Workman *goes over, and helps him to push it.*]

Poges. [*Fiercely, to* First Workman.] Let go, you! I'll manoeuvre it myself. Let go, I tell you!

First Workman. [*As fiercely, to* Poges.] Can't you see, man, the declivity runnin' down the passage, that'll lead you, if the roller once gets outa hand, into God knows where?

Poges. [*With a roar into the face of the* FIRST WORKMAN.] Let go! [*The* FIRST WORKMAN, *startled, suddenly lets go his hold of the roller, and the roller shoots forward down the declivity,* POGES *going with it, like a flash of lightning. Heard as he is careening down the passage—with anguish in his voice.*] Help!

[*There is a pause of a few moments, then a thud is heard, followed by a rumbling crash of falling bricks and mortar; then silence again. The* FIRST WORKMAN *fearfully and hastily blesses himself—makes the Sign of the Cross.*]

First Workman. [*As he blesses himself.*] Jesus, Mary, an' Joseph!

Souhaun. [*With vehement rage.*] The blasted fool! He has rocked the house and killed himself and hasn't made his will.

First Workman. [*Staring down the passage.*] Right through the wall, he's gone! [*He runs to where the hole is in the ceiling, gets a seat, and stands on it. Calling up to the hole.*] Eh, Cornelius, eh, quick!

[*The face of the* YELLOW-BEARDED MAN *appears at the hole, and he thrusts down his head as far as it will go.*]

Yellow-Bearded Man. Well, what's up now?

First Workman. [*Excitedly.*] The oul' man, the oul' fool, has gone right through the wall with the roller, an' shook the house—bang!

Yellow-Bearded Man. Didn't I think it was an earthquake? [*Testily.*] An' don't be tellin' me these things while I'm up here. Can't you wait till I'm down in th' world o' men, and can enjoy these things happenin'?

First Workman. [*Running out.*] Mr O'Killigain, Jack, eh, Jack!

[SOUHAUN *returns, followed by* CLOYNE *and* BARNEY *leading in the frightened* POGES, *powdered with the dust of the falling mortar.* SOUHAUN *arranges a mattress for him on which he squats, supported by pillows.*]

Souhaun. You were warned, you were warned, and you would have your own way. It's fortunate you are, indeed, that none of your bones is broken.

Poges. [*Moaningly.*] Brandy, get me some brandy. [BARNEY *goes out, and comes back with a glass, brandy and soda-water. He fills out a glassful and gives it to* POGES. *After he has drunk the brandy,—to* CLOYNE *and* BARNEY.] Go away, you two, and don't stand there gaping at me! [*They go. Musingly.*] What a rascal that man must be who sold me the roller! In this simple country, among a simple people, where the very air is

redolent with fairy lore, that such a dangerous and materialistic mind should be lurking!

Souhaun. For God's sake, man, talk sense.

Poges. [*Shaking his head sorrowfully.*] A gay and charming people, but irresponsible, utterly irresponsible.

[O'KILLIGAIN *appears at the right entrance with a cloudy look on his face.*]

O'Killigain. Look here, that Basil of yours is goin' about the grounds, carrying a fully-cocked gun at a dangerous angle. He'll do harm. Send someone to take it off him, or I'll twist it out of his hands myself! And you'll want to be more careful, yourself, or you'll have th' oul' house down!

Poges. [*Indignantly.*] Oh, what a conceited fool that fellow is—going about to do dangerous damage for want of a little commonsense and caution. I don't believe he ever fired a gun in his life. [*To* SOUHAUN.] Go out, dear, and take it off him, before he shoots somebody—and go quick! [SOUHAUN *runs out by the entrance on the right, and* O'KILLIGAIN *is following her when* POGES *speaks to him, and halts him at the entrance.*] Oh yes, Mr O'Killigain, a word please. [*He drinks some more brandy.*] Er, just a word. People are saying there's a rumor going about that you and—and Miss Avril are—are, well, seen together at times.

O'Killigain. Well?

Poges. Well? Damn it, man, she's a lady, Mr Stoke's a gentleman, and you're only a —a tradesman!

O'Killigain. Well?

Poges. Well? Oh, don't be welling me. The week she was away from here was bad enough, and very suspicious. She had the damned cheek to say she was with you.

O'Killigain. So she was.

Poges. So she was, was she? Well, it's dishonourable, and it will have to stop.

O'Killigain. And who'll stop it?

Poges. [*Firmly.*] I and Mr Stoke will stop it.

O'Killigain. [*Quietly.*] You pair of miserable, old hypocritical, wizened old gets, I'd like to see you trying!

Poges. [*Choking with rage.*] Get out of the house, and come here no more! I'll write to your parish priest! I'll— [*A shot rings out in the grounds outside.*] Good God, the fool has shot someone!

[O'KILLIGAIN *goes off in a hurry. There is a pause. Then the* YELLOW-BEARDED FACE *is thrust through the hole in the ceiling as far as it can go, and shouts down at* POGES *sitting like Buddha on the mattress.*]

Yellow-Bearded Man. [*To* POGES.] He's shot her, shot her dead, the poor, little, innocent creature!

Poges. [*Up to the* YELLOW-BEARDED MAN.] Shot who, shot who, man?

Yellow-Bearded Man. Without warnin' he done it, without a flicker of an eyelid, he sent her into the unknown!

Poges. [*Murmuring in agony.*] Avril! Oh, my God, little Avril. The curse of the Irish thorntree is on us!

Yellow-Bearded Man. [*Savagely.*] Twenty-five pounds, an' not a penny less, he'll pay for it, or I'll have the heavy law on him. I'd ha' let you have her at first for the twenty, but in some compensation for th' agony of seein' the poor thing sink down into death, I'll have to get the other five, or I'll have the heavy law on him!

Poges. What are you talking about, man?

Yellow-Bearded Man. Be th' way, you don't know that that lean, skulkin' friend o' yours has shot dead me poor little, innocent, poor little cow! [*Sarcastically.*] He thought it was a bull!

Poges. [*Bewildered.*] Oh, what a terrible country to have anything to do with! Reverence for a house with dignity in all its corners has been turned into ridicule; the respect due to myself has been blown away by a lout's laughter. A wall's demolished, and an innocent animal's shot dead: what an awful country to be living in. A no-man's land; a waste land; a wilderness.

CURTAIN

ACT THREE

Before the room appears, the sounds of falling rain and swishing wind are heard; and these go on at intervals throughout the scene.

SCENE: *The same as in the preceding act; but some more articles of furniture have been added to the room. Between the entrance to the right at the back, and the right wall, stands what is said to be a Jacobean China-cabinet, filled with old pieces of china. At each side of the larger entrance on the right stands an armoured figure, comical-looking things, with long sharp points protruding where the man's nose (if a man were inside the suit) would certainly be; each figure, standing stiff, holds a long halberd well out from his body. Over these are crossed pennons, green and blue, fixed on the wall. A blazing fire is in the fireplace. No one is in the room.*

[*After a moment,* POGES, *dressed in his jazz-patterned overall, with a paper in his hand, runs in, and rushes over to the telephone.*]

Poges. [*Into the mouthpiece—hurriedly.*] Get me—Oh, good evening, good evening. This is Mr Poges, Tudor Manor. Get me St. Paul, London: 123. The house is getting on all right, thank you. Be quick, please. [*Warmly.*] There's no seems in it; I am in a hurry. Oh, the ladies are quite well, sir. No, no, no; I don't want to go to an all-night dance to hear Irish songs sung! I want St. Paul! Eh? No, St. Peter won't do; please don't try to be funny! I am on very serious business. Get me the number I want at once! [*He takes the mouthpiece from his mouth, and gives vent to a roaring growl of anger.*] Whether it won't matter a hundred years from now, isn't the point, sir. [*Shouting.*] Damn it, get me St. Paul! [*Bursting with rage.*] No wonder I use bad language. Is this the way business is done here? No wonder this country's as it is. What's wrong with it? [*Roaring.*] Everything's wrong with it! You what? You hope my stay here will help to civilize me a little! [*He looks stupefied; then he slams the receiver on the hook. Almost instantly the 'phone rings. He whips off the receiver again, and puts it to his ear.*] What the hell does this—eh? Who are you? St. Paul? Good God! This is Poges, Bradford. Oh, it's an awful place. People helpless, superstitious, and ignorant. I want you to get me five hundred shares in the Welldonian Cement Co.; shares are bound to jump, the minute the bombing starts seriously. They have jumped? Ah. What, a fiver a share, now? Well, get me two fifty. What? Not one to be had? [*Clicking his tongue.*] Dtch dtch. Run on them, eh? One wouldn't imagine there'd be so many trying to cash in on splintered bodies. The world, the world, Bradford! Yes, yes, of course; if there's any going, snap them up. Righto, goodbye.

[BARNEY *appears at the entrance on the right.*]

Barney. Canon Creehewel would like to speak to you, sir.

Poges. Right; send the Canon in to me.

[BARNEY *goes; and, in a second or so, the* CANON *comes in. He is inclined to be portly, rather a hard face, nicely fitted clothes, head bald at the front, and bushy greying hair at the back of his head and over his ears. He is wearing a soft hat, sodden with rain, which he puts on the end of the table when he comes in; and a long dark cloak, glistening with rain, too. He comes over eager to* POGES, *with a smile on his face, and outstretched hand.*]

Canon. Ah, my dear friend, I'm so glad to have a chance of a word with you. How are you liking Clune na Geera?

Poges. Splendid, though the weather has been cold and very wet. Take your cloak off.

Canon. [*Taking off his cloak.*] Isn't it a nuisance? And we're in for more of it, by all accounts. If it goes on much more, the district will be a dismal swamp.

Poges. [*Indicating a seat.*] Sit down, Canon, sit down. Glass of sherry?

[*The* CANON *sits, and* POGES *sits, too, opposite the* CANON.]

Canon. No thanks. I drink rarely. [*Apologetically.*] Good example, you know. Well, welcome, my dear sir, to our district. You have a very beautiful house here. An old house, but a fine one. It is almost a sacred thing to keep an old thing from dying, sir; for whatsoever things are just, whatsoever things are honest, whatsoever things are pure, whatsoever things are lovely and of good report, are invariably found close to, and, sometimes, intimately enclosed in the life and being of ages that have passed, and in the life of men and women who have gone away before us.

Poges. [*Gratified.*] I wholeheartedly agree with you, reverend sir. I feel it, I know it.

Canon. With all its frills, its frivolities, its studied ceremonial, however gayly coloured its leisure may have been, the past had in it the core of virtue; while the present swirl of young life, I'm saying, with its feverish sthrut of pretended bravery, its tawdry carelessness about the relation and rule of religion to man, with all its frantic sthretching of pleasure into every second of life, contains within it a tawny core of fear, that is turning darker with every chime of the passing hours!

[*The rain and wind are plainly heard.*]

Poges. [*Leaning towards the* CANON—*eagerly.*] We must lengthen our arm back to the past and pluck back some of the good things that haven't gone away as far from us as the dead who knew them.

Canon. A worthy enterprise, dear sir, and I hope you and your good people will be a help to us here to bring some of the slow movement of the past into the reckless and Godless speed of the present. [*He leans over towards* POGES *till their heads nearly touch.*] You and yours can do much to assist the clergy to keep a sensible check on the lower inclinations of the people, a work which should be near the heart of every sensible and responsible person with a stake in the country.

Poges. I'll do all I can. [*Leans back with an air of business importance.*] From the practical point of view, how am I to help?

Canon. [*Dropping a little into the idiom of the district.*] Help us to curtail th' damned activity of the devilish dance halls! In a month or less, the innocent disthrict becomes worse than your Leicester Square in London, when the night has fallen, if the dance halls are allowed to go ahead without the control of the clergy an' responsible people.

Poges. [*Shocked.*] Good God! Such a condition of things among a simple, charming, and pastoral people amazes me.

Canon. [*Warming to it.*] Arra, wouldn't it sicken you, when the hot days come, to see fools of oul' men an' fools of oul' women, too, settin' a bad example, goin' about nearly naked, in their coloured shorts, an' brazen-faced lassies mixed among them in low-cut bodices, defiant short skirts, an' shorter trousers, murdherin' modesty with a restless an' a reckless hand!

Poges. A lamentable state of affairs, entirely, sir.

Canon. [*Rising and going over close to* POGES—*intensely.*] An' like Eden, sir, we've a snake in our garden, too!

Poges. Oh!

Canon. O'Killigain!

Poges. Ah!

[*The wind and the rain are plainly heard.*]

Canon. Guard your womenfolk from him, for no woman is safe with that man. He publicly defends the wearing of low-necked blouses by brazen hussies; he stands be the practice of courting couples walking the highways and byways be night; why, one moonlight night, meetin' my curate dhrivin' home a lasciviously-minded girl, O'Killigain tore the stock from the curate's hand, an' smashed it into pieces! A dangerous man, my dear sir, a most dangerous man.

Poges. [*A little nervously.*] I'm what

you'd call a foreigner down here, and so couldn't interfere with O'Killigain, personally; but what I can do to help you, I certainly will, in any other way.

Canon. Thank you—I guessed you would. Your fifty pounds have helped a lot already. And now I've taken up a lot of your time and must go. [*He takes up his hat.*] By the way, how's the workman I sent you getting along?

Poges. Which one?

Canon. The one doing your electric light —a yellow-bearded fellow. A most pious chap.

Poges. [*Emphatically.*] Oh, he's getting along splendidly!

Canon. I'm glad to hear it. A good fellow —a Knight of St. Columbus.

Poges. Well, now, I never knew Columbus was a Saint.

Canon. [*Smiling indulgently.*] Oh, yes indeed; a great Irish Saint.

Poges. I always thought he was an American.

Canon. An American; who?

Poges. Christopher Columbus.

Canon. [*Smiling.*] Oh, there were two Columbuses, one Irish and the other—er—American.

[*As the* CANON *is about to move away,* AVRIL, *followed by* SOUHAUN, *dances into the room from an entrance at the back. She is dressed in a low-cut blouse, short tailor-made skirt, and soft-leather high boots moulded to her calves, and reaching to just below her knees; and looks, indeed, a very tempting and desirable young hussy. She has a mackintosh over her arms.* SOUHAUN, *too, is dressed in very short shorts, of vivid crimson, and a black V-necked jersey, looking as enticing, in a more mature way, as young* AVRIL, *herself.* POGES *is a little embarrassed, but the good* CANON *does not flicker an eyelid.* SOUHAUN *whips off* POGES' *overall, and shows him in a green jersey and brown shorts.*]

Souhaun. You mustn't receive the Canon, dear, in an overall!

Avril. I say, Cyril, old boy, when are we going to get that damned bathroom? It's a bit thick trying to have a bath in a basin.

[*She sees the* CANON *and stops to gaze at him.*]

Poges. [*Introducing her.*] Mr Stoke's— er—wife—Miss Avril, Canon. [*Introducing* SOUHAUN.] My—er—wife, Miss Souhaun.

Canon. [*Bowing graciously—to* AVRIL.] My dear, young lady. [*To* SOUHAUN.] Madam, I'm very pleased to know you.

Avril. [*To* POGES.] Well, when are we going to have a decent bathroom, old cock o' th' walk?

Poges. [*Deprecatingly.*] The Canon's here, Avril.

Canon. [*Jovially.*] Youthful spirits, sir, youthful spirits.

Poges. We'll have a bathroom, if we can fit one in without injuring the harmony of the old house. The Tudor period never saw a bathroom. This generation's getting soft, Canon; we want hardening.

Avril. Bunkum!

Poges. [*Indignantly.*] It's anything but bunkum! Shakespeare had to do without one.

Souhaun. But, surely, dear, you must know that the Tudor people knew nothing about the use of steam?

[BASIL *now appears at an entrance at the back, and when he sees the company, he stays there and listens. He is dressed in a yellow jersey and black shorts. No one notices him.*]

Poges. [*Petulantly.*] Steam! We stand here, in the centre, not of a house, but of a great civilization, and you mention steam!

Souhaun. In the centre of a hot bath, dear, I can remain in the centre of your civilization.

Basil. [*Joining in—looking like a statue in the doorway.*] Not precisely, Souhaun, for it would require, or at least, postulate, a full and concentrated retirement through the avenues of thought back to the time of which the visible surroundings are vividly, but quiescently reminiscent, till thought and all its correlations become su-su-su-such a sapient and sensuous determinate of all seen, heard, and felt in the retrospective activities of the mind, and the civilization remembered, recognized, and enjoyed, becomes, consciously and sub-consciously, an immanent and integral part of the person, determining the conception of the conscious thought, interrelating with the, with the outward and inward action and reaction of all —or most of the bodily senses, incorporating the outward vision of sight with the inward vision of the inward conception of the—of the fragmentary stimuli—er—stimuli, into a perfect and harmonious whole; a thing, if I may be allowed to say so, if not impossible is, at least improbable, sitting down or indeed, even standing up in the middle of a hot bath.

Avril. [*With mock enthusiasm.*] Hooray!

Poges. [*To the* CANON.] Mr Stoke, Canon; cousin to the uncle of the K.G., and passed through Oxford.

Canon. Really, well, well, remarkable connections. [*In the far distance a faint clap of thunder is heard; the* CANON *cocks his ear to listen.*] I must be off. Bad sign. The soft rain that's falling may change to a downpour, and I've a long way to go.

[*Puts on his cloak.* BARNEY *and* CLOYNE *come in carrying a heavy Jacobean chair between them.*]

Souhaun. Ah, the Jacobin chair. [*Indicating the way.*] Out in the entrance hall, Barney.

Poges. Let's look at it a second. [BARNEY *and* CLOYNE *pause.*] Ah, Canon, old things take a lot of beating.

Canon. They do, they do, sir. Well, I must go now.

Poges. [*Halting him.*] One second, sir. [*He goes to the table, writes a cheque and hands it to the* CANON.] Another little trifle to keep things going, Canon.

Canon. Twenty-five pounds! Oh, thank you, and God bless you, my very dear sir.

Souhaun. You must come to dinner some night.

Canon. I will, I will, with pleasure; goodbye all.

[*Midst a murmur of goodbyes the* CANON *goes out.*]

Poges. [*Indignantly.*] Never showed the slightest interest in the Jacobin chair. Ignorance; Irish ignorance! [*Angrily—to* CLOYNE *and* BARNEY, *who are holding the chair like a salesman displaying a piece of silk.*] Bring the damned thing into the Entrance Hall, will you, and don't stand there like fools! [CLOYNE, *in her hurry, jerks the chair from* BARNEY'S *hold and it bumps to the floor.*] Oh, butter-fingers, d'ye want to destroy it? That's a Jacobin chair, man, a Jacobin chair.

Barney. [*With a yell as he carries out the chair with* CLOYNE.] Well, if I let a damned chair fall, I didn't knock a wall down!

Poges. Impudent rascal. The more you do for them, the less they think of you! [*He bustles into his overall again.*] Now to business. What'll we do first? The rugs?

Souhaun. There's no use of trying the rugs till you get your quatto-centro bureau in position. Then we'll be able to see if the colour of the rugs suits the bureau.

[AVRIL *has put on her mackintosh and sidled over to the entrance on right, leading to the Hall, and is about to slip out, when* BASIL *darts to her side and catches her arm.*]

Basil. Where are you slipping off to?

Avril. I'm going for a brisk walk along the bank of the brimming river. I'm fed up carrying things about to get this foolish old house in order.

Poges. In this weather? Nonsense!

Basil. A good idea; I'll go with you, darling.

Avril. [*With a malevolent look at him.*] Wouldn't you like to, eh? Take my advice and don't! [*To* POGES.] Ay, in this weather.

[*She goes quickly, leaving* BASIL, *undecided, looking after her.*]

Basil. [*Bitterly.*] She's going to go with O'Killigain!

Souhaun. Nonsense. She can't be out of your sight for a minute, but you imagine the girl's with O'Killigain. The rain'll soon send her back. [*To* POGES.] You see about locking the bureau, while I get the men to carry it in for you.

[POGES *goes by one of the entrances at back.*]

Basil. [*Going towards entrance at back.*] I tell you the jade's gone after O'Killigain.

Souhaun. [*Warningly.*] If I were you, Basil, I shouldn't press hard after little Avril; you are a little too consequential to please her always.

Basil. [*Maliciously—as he goes out.*] And you, me lady, are a lot too old to please O'Killigain at any time!

[SOUHAUN *stands stiff for a few moments; then she goes quickly to the entrance to the Hall and is seen beckoning for one of the* WORKMEN.]

Souhaun. [*Calling.*] One of you, come here, please. [*The* SECOND WORKMAN *comes into the room and stands near the entrance, looking quietly at* SOUHAUN.] Send Mr O'Killigain in to me, please.

Second-Workman. He's gone to the station to see after a wagonload o' bricks.

Souhaun. [*Slowly, after a pause.*] By himself?

Second Workman. [*After a pause.*] With th' handsome young woman. [*A pause.*] You're a handsome woman yourself; you're Irish too; an' y'ought to be sensible.

Souhaun. [*Slowly.*] Am I not sensible, good man?

Second Workman. [*Earnestly.*] Your shinin' eyes can always say you are; an' soon you'll tire o' nestin' in a dusty nook, with the hills outside an' th' roads for walkin'!

Souhaun. I will, will I?

Second Workman. [*With his eyes turned towards the ground.*] Ay, will you, an' dance away from a smoky bragger who thinks th' world spins round on th' rim of a coin; you'll hurry away from him, I'm sayin', an' it's a glad heart'll lighten th' journey to a one'll find a place for your little hand in th' white clouds, an' a place for your saucy head in th' blue o' the sky.

Souhaun. [*With a touch of mockery.*] Yourself, for instance?

Second Workman. It's waitin' warm, he'll be, to please you highly, an' show you wondhers of a manly manner.

Souhaun. [*Laughing, with a little catch in the laugh.*] A daughter of the Ormond with a workman!

Second Workman. [*Raising his head proudly and looking steadily at her.*] An oldher name is his, an' an oldher glory than the honour thrown to th' earl o' Ormond when he crouched for favour at the English feet!

[*The* SECOND WORKMAN *looks at* SOU-HAUN, *and* SOUHAUN *looks at the* SEC-OND WORKMAN *for a moment, then she turns and goes slowly out by right entrance at back.*]

Third Workman. [*Appearing at the back, left entrance.*] Here, Philib, what'r you doin'? You're to give us a hand to get in the oul' codger's bureau.

[*The two of them go out by the entrance to the left at back. After a second or two, the sound of scuffling and of voices is heard just outside the narrow entrance through which the two men have gone out, then* POGES *comes in with an anxious look on his face, turns and concentrates his gaze on the entrance. Presently the end of the big gilded bureau—it is really a big gilded chest—comes in sight round the corner, with the* THREE WORKMEN *puffing, pulling, pushing, and scuffling it along, each giving orders to the other two, to the concern of poor old* POGES. *When the bureau comes to the entrance, it can be seen to be a very tight fit.*]

First Workman. A little to the ayste, there, a little more to the ayste, can't yous!

Second Workman. No, west, west; can't yous see it'll jam if yous cant it to the ayste? To th' west, I'm tellin' yous!

Poges. [*Anxiously.*] Easy, boys, easy, now; take care, take care; that's a thing you won't meet every day, you know. I had an anxious time while it was coming over.

Third Workman. [*Taking no notice of* POGES.] Where th' hell are yous shovin'? Are yous blind, or wha'? No squirmin'll get it in that way. [*Recklessly.*] Here, throw th' thing up on its hind legs an' let her go!

Poges. [*Loudly and anxiously.*] Eh, there, eh; steady, steady. Careful, how you handle that. Don't dare to throw her up on her hind

legs! I can't have a precious thing like that scratched and mangled. That's a quatto-centro piece of furniture, and hasn't another piece like it in the world.

First Workman. [*To the* OTHERS.] Hear what the gentleman's sayin' to yous! Amnt I tired tellin' yous yous ud look long before yous ud find such a piece o' furniture in Cluna na Geera? Yous can't fling a thing like this about the way you'd fling about an oul' kitchen chair. [*To* POGES.] Amnt I right, sir?

Poges. Yes, yes; quite right, my man. Thousands of people would give a fortune to possess a thing like that bureau. So gently, boys, gently. The slightest scratch will do irreparable damage.

First Workman. See, boys, it's a quatto-centro lump o' furniture, an' so needs gentle handlin'. [*To* SECOND WORKMAN.] You, Philib, there, give it a sudden swing to the ayste, an' while she's swingin', we'll shoot her ahead.

Second Workman. [*Angrily.*] How am I goin' to give her a sudden swing to the ayste when there's no purchase to get a grip of her? Squatto-centro, or notto-centro, I'm not goin' to let it whip a slice outa my hand!

Third Workman. [*Thoughtfully.*] Th' only way to get it in proper, is to get a sledge-hammer an' knock down some o' th' archway.

Poges. [*Indignantly.*] Knock down some of the archway! You'll do no such thing! You'll be suggesting that the house should be knocked down next. There's no sledge-hammer to be brought within sight of this precious bureau. [*Leaning over towards the* MEN.] Listen: this is a piece of quatto-centro —understand that, the whole of you, please!

First Workman. [*To the* OTHERS.] There, now, what did I tell yous? Yous hear what the gentleman says.

Poges. It ought to go in easily, if you knew your job. The driver of the furniture-van looked at this entrance and told me not to worry; that the bureau would slide in without the slightest trouble.

First Workman. [*Scornfully.*] Is it Larry Lunigan said that, now, did he? Don't mind anything Larry Lunigan says, sir. If your head was split, he'd say it was only a scratch, to keep your heart up.

Third Workman. Even if you were dead, he'd tell your wife to wait, an' say you never could be sure of anything. An' we're not furniture shifters, sir.

Poges. Well, I'm sure of one thing; that bureau is coming into this room, and coming in without a scratch.

Third Workman. 'Course it is.

First Workman. Time an' patience'll do it.

Poges. [*Looking closely at the bureau—in anguish.*] Oh, my God, there's the stone wall eating into its edge! Get it away, pull it out, shove it in, you fools! [*As they shove.*] Wait, wait!

First Workman. [*Soothingly.*] I shouldn't worry, sir; a shavin' or two off is th' worst that can happen to it.

Poges. Wait, wait a second. I'll go and get some cushions and pillows to guard the sides from the wall. [*He runs out by the adjoining entrance for the cushions.*]

First Workman. J'ever see such an oul' fustherer in your life? You'd think the thing was on its way to the kingdom of heaven, th' way he's cryin' over it.

Third Workman. With a look on his ugly oul' gob, like the tune th' oul' cow died of.

First Workman. A quatto-centro, mind you, says he.

Third Workman. Seven hundred years an' more old, says he. Well, it's near time it met its death, anyhow.

First Workman. Here, let's get it in before he comes back billowin' with cushions. It's well able to take a knock or two.

Second Workman. Here's th' crowbar he wouldn't let us use. [*He lifts up a big crowbar.*] We'll inch it in be main strength. Now, boys, get your shoulders to the quatto-centro while I heave with th' bar! [*To* First Workman.] Start a shanty, Bill, to give us encouragement.

First Workman. [*Chanting quickly, while they all brace themselves.*]

What shall we do with th' dhrunken sailor,
What shall we do with th' dhrunken sailor,
What shall we do with th' dhrunken sailor,
Early in th' mornin'?

All. [*Together—shoving and tugging vehemently.*]

Pull away, an' up she rises,
Pull away, an' up she rises,
Pull away, an' up she rises,
Early in th' mornin'!

[*Poges* rushes in with some cushions in his arms. He is frantic when he sees what the Men are doing. As he rushes in he is accompanied by a peal of thunder, louder than the last, but still fairly faint. As he comes to a halt near the bureau, the peal ends.*]

Poges. [*Enraged.*] What, in the devil's name, are you trying to do? Do you want to burst it to bits? Oh, why did I ever bring my poor quatto-centro to a country like this? Shove it from the wall, shove it from the wall, till I put a cushion in!

First Workman. Sure, it won't go far enough away from the wall to fit a cushion, man.

Poges. [*Frantically.*] Do what you're told, do what you're told. [*He drops the cushions, seizes the edge of the bureau and tries to pull it from the wall.*] Here, somebody, help me! [*Before he is aware of it, the* First Workman *leaps on to the top of the bureau to cross over to him, his heavy hobnailed boots scraping the top of it. Shouting at him.*] Get down, get down, man!

First Workman. [*Astonished.*] Amnt I only comin' across to help you?

Poges. [*Yelling at him.*] That's a quatto-centro, that's a quatto-centro, man!

First Workman. Sure, I know it is.

Poges. Then get off it, get off it—sticking your hob-nailed boots through and through it!

First Workman. [*Lifting up a foot so that the sole of the boot can be seen.*] Is it that, sir? Sure, th' nails are worn so soft an' smooth, they wouldn't mark the wing of a buttherfly.

Poges. [*Roaring.*] Get down, get down at once!

[*The* First Workman *jumps off the bureau back among his mates.*]

Second Workman. [*Muttering loudly.*] It ud be a god-send to some I know if they opened their eyes to th' sights an' wondhers showin'.

Poges. Now, no talk; and don't do anything till I give the order.

Men. All right, sir; go ahead; we're waitin'.

Poges. When I say go, you swing it to the right, while I swing it to the left. Are you all ready?

First Workman. Ready an' waitin' an' willin'.

Poges. Go! [*They all swing to the left, and* Poges' *foot is caught between the bureau and the archway. He lets a squeal out of him. In anguish.*] Release my foot, my foot's caught! Why did you all swing left? Don't you know right from left?

Third Workman. You should have said ayste, sir.

Poges. Shove it off, shove it from my foot!

First Workman. [*Placing the crowbar between archway, against the column, and the bureau.*] Now, boys, all together—heave yo ho! [*There is a mighty heave from them, one with the bar, the others with their shoulders. The bureau moves slowly; a crack is heard; the column snaps with the push of the bar against it; and falls over the bureau,*] *which suddenly shoots forward right into the middle of the room, the* MEN *stumbling after it. The* MEN *look triumphantly at the bureau, the* FIRST WORKMAN *leaning on the crowbar, like a warrior leaning on his spear.* POGES *rubs his foot and contemplates the damage to the bureau and the entrance.*] There she is for you, now sir; right where you want her to be.

Third Workman. I knew well patience ud do it in the end.

Poges. Oh, look at the bureau and look at the entrance!

First Workman. [*Confidently.*] Oh, a spot o' cement an' a lick o' white paint'll make th' entrance look as young as ever again.

[BASIL *and* SOUHAUN *come in, followed by* CLOYNE *and* BARNEY, *who are carrying a rug between them. They leave it on the floor.* BASIL *is wearing very wide plus fours.*]

Souhaun. We're getting the house into some kind of order at last. [*She sees the damage.*] Oh, who's caused all the wreckage?

Poges. [*Sarcastically.*] Your very clever countrymen, dear.

Basil. [*Mockingly.*] And the high opinion they have of themselves.

Second Workman. There is sweet music in the land, but not for th' deaf; there is wisdom, too, but it is not in a desk it is; but out in th' hills, an' in the life of all things rovin' around, undher th' blue sky.

Poges. [*Angrily.*] Take this broken column away and be off to your work again.

[*The* WORKMEN *take away the column and go out by entrance leading to the Hall.*]

Souhaun. Let us try the rugs. [CLOYNE *and* BARNEY *spread on the floor a rug scattered over with brightly-coloured geometrical patterns.* CLOYNE *and* BARNEY *then go out; the rest stare at the rug.*] Rather gay-looking for the floor of a Tudor house, dear.

Basil. [*Decidedly.*] Too bright and too modern.

Poges. Where? How? Why?

Basil. The Tudors, my dear sir, were a sensible and sober people, and wouldn't tolerate anything that was vulgar, or, shall I say, conspicuous.

Souhaun. [*With some mockery.*] You see, darling, it was taste, and not steam that was everything in those days.

Basil. Quite, Souhaun; taste was the Tudor er—er—*monumentum aere perennius.*

Poges. I don't know everything, my dear sir; but I do know something about the period that this house—er—exemplifies; in fact, the period was so riotous in colour that the men's breeches had one leg blue and the other leg red, or vice versa.

Basil. [*With a patronizing laugh.*] Ah, old boy, that wasn't th' Tudor period.

Poges. What period was it then?

Souhaun. The Hiawatha period.

Poges. [*Indignantly—to* SOUHAUN.] This is no joke, please. [*To* BASIL.] What period was it, then?

Basil. [*Airily.*] Not the Tudor period, certainly; no, certainly not, old boy.

Poges. [*Contemptuously.*] Pshaw! You don't know it yourself. [*From an entrance at back the* SECOND WORKMAN *appears wheeling a barrow filled with bricks. Passing by the disputants, on his way to the Hall entrance, he wheels the barrow over the rug. Shouting at him.*] Where the hell are you going with your dirty barrow?

Second Workman. [*Dropping the shafts of the barrow, and turning to answer* POGES.] I'm bringin' a barrow o' bricks to O'Killigain, sir.

Basil. Oh, he's back, is he?

Poges. What the hell do you think you're doing, man?

Second Workman. Amnt I after tellin' you, I'm bringin' a barrow o' bricks to O'Killigain?

Poges. What d'ye mean, trundling your dirty barrow over a handsome rug, laid out for inspection?

Second Workman. What d'ye want me to do? Take th' barrow o' bricks up in me arms an' fly over it?

Basil. [*With great dignity.*] Take it away at once, sir, and don't show impertinence to your betters.

Second Workman. [*Eyeing* BASIL *with scorn.*] Jasus, looka what calls itself a betther man than me!

[O'KILLIGAIN *appears at the entrance leading to the Hall.*]

Poges. [*Earnestly—to the* SECOND WORKMAN.] My man, you're cheeking a cousin of a K.G. whose family goes back to—to—— [*Turning to* BASIL.] William the Conqueror, isn't it?

Basil. [*Stiffening—with proud complacency.*] Farther back, old boy—Alfred; the last man of the last family at the Battle of Hastings.

Poges. [*Impressively.*] There, you see.

Souhaun. [*With a sign of mockery in her voice.*] And the ancient gentleman passed through Oxford, too.

O'Killigain. [*From the archway.*] The city of dissolute might!

Second Workman. [*With mock defer-*

ence.] D'ye tell me that, now? Why didn't you make me aware of all that glory, before I began to speak? Isn't it an alarmin' thing to hear of the ancientology of a being that I took to be an ordinary man! An' what might be the ancient gentleman's ancient name?

Poges. Basil, Horatio Nelson, Kaiser Stoke and, on his mother's side, Churchill.

Second Workman. A right worthy name. It mayn't have a musical sound, but it has a steady one. There's no flightiness in that name. An' now, would you like to know mine?

Poges. [*Amusedly.*] Here, be off with you to your work; as if your name mattered much.

Second Workman. Me name's O'Dempsey, of the Clan that were lords of Offaly, ere his ancient highness here was a thousand years from bein' born; a Clan that shtretches back as far as the time before an Englishman thought of buildin' a weedy shelther; an' farther back to a day or two afther th' one when the sun, herself, was called upon to shine.

[*He takes hold of the shafts of the barrow, preparatory to starting off.*]

Poges. [*Contemptuously.*] You don't look it, my poor man!

Second Workman. [*As he wheels the barrow out.*] I feel it; an' th' river's risin'.

Poges. [*Severely, to* O'KILLIGAIN.] You really oughtn't to allow, much more encourage, this silly, ignorant and superstitious conceit among your men; it is something close to scandalous!

O'Killigain. [*Quoting.*] They go their own gait: looking carelessly in the faces of presidents and governors, as to say, *Who are you?*

Poges. [*Imperatively.*] Well, it's not going to be heard in this house! The bobtag and ragtail must be made to keep their free and easy manners at a distance. Dignity reigns here.

[*A loud peal of thunder is heard in the distance, and the room darkens a little.*]

O'Killigain. It's raining.

Poges. Eh?

O'Killigain. It's raining hard.

Souhaun. [*Shivering.*] And growing cold.

O'Killigain. And old things are perishing.

Second Workman. [*Appearing at entrance.*] We're knocking off, O'Killigain, for the rain is heavier, an' th' winds are keen.

O'Killigain. You do well to knock off, for it is waste of time to try to butthress up a tumbling house.

Souhaun. [*Over to the* SECOND WORK-MAN.] The house'll be lonesome without you.

Second Workman. Come, then, an' abide with the men o' th' wide wathers, who can go off in a tiny curragh o' thought to the New Island with th' outgoin' tide, an' come back be th' same tide sweepin' in again!

Poges. [*Mockingly—to* SOUHAUN, *clapping her on the back.*] There's a high and hearty invitation to you, me lady!

[AVRIL *comes in, and dances over to* BASIL.]

Souhaun. [*Gleefully poking* POGES *in the ribs—to* SECOND WORKMAN.] A long sail on the widening waters, no less; what gift is offered when the tide returns, good man?

Second Workman. With firm-fed men an' comely, cordial women, there'll be laughter round a red fire when the mists are risin', when th' roads an' fields are frosty, an' when th' night is still.

Souhaun. [*In a mocking voice—to* POGES.] There, now, dear, is there anything more in the world than these that you can give?

Poges. [*With pretended dismay.*] He has me beaten; what am I going to do, at all, at all!

Second Workman. A portion, too, with them who, ruddy-faced, were first in battle, with crimson cloak, white coat, an' silver belt studded with splendour by a cunning hand; a portion, too, with them of paler faces, an' dhressed in dimmer clothes, who, fearless, stepped a straight way to th' gallows, silent an' darin' in th' midst of a yelled-out Sassenach song!

Souhaun. [*Trying to speak mockingly, but developing a slight catch in her voice; for she has been moved by the* SECOND WORKMAN'S *words.*] Where is the lady who would be slow to give a man with such a coaxing way an invitation to her pillow?

Avril. [*Sees her friend is affected. She comes close to her, touches her on the arm.*] Souhaun, come an' show me your newest dhresses, an' don't stay listenin' to his thrancin' talk.

Souhaun. [*Shaking off* AVRIL'S *hand. Falling into the Irish idiom.*] Let me be, girl, for it's right an' lovely listening to a voice that's makin' gold embroidery out o' dancin' words.

Poges. [*Mockingly.*] Gold embroidery out of dancing words—we'll have to kiss the Blarney Stone, Basil.

O'Killigain. [*Ignoring* POGES.] An' you, young girl, sweet bud of an out-spreading three, graft yourself on to the living, and don't stay hidden any longer here. Come where the rain is heavy, where the frost frets, and where the sun is warm. Avril, pulse of my heart, listen to me, an' let longin' flood into your heart for the call of life. The ruined young rowan tree, withered away now, can awaken again, an' spread its fragrance around us. Spit out what's here an' come where love is fierce an' fond an' fruitful. Come, lass, where there's things to say an' things to do an' love at the endings!

Second Workman. Jack has spoken fair, an' there's no handsome hindrance near to stop yous. What's here but a creakin' grandeur an' poor witherin' talk; salt food without dhrink to go with it; an' a purple dhryness turnin' timidly to dust?

Basil. Salt food without drink; purple dryness turning to dust—did you hear, Cyril?

Poges. [*Mocking gaily.*] I'm fairly moidered, I am.

O'Killigain. [*Coming closer to* AVRIL.] Aren't me words a star in your ear, lass? Haven't you heard them? They've hit your young breast, lass. Come with me, I say; come away from where rich ignorance is a blessing and foolishness a gift of God! Come to th' house on th' hill: the door is open, the fire's alight on the hearth and the table's laid with a clean white cloth.

Second Workman. Go with him, lass, where the table is laid and the fire's alight.

Souhaun. Go lass, to the house on the hill, go while the door is open.

Avril. Let another go in by the door; let another eat at the table; let another sit by the fire. Why didn't you come for me, O'Killigain, before the young thorntree had shed its blossom, and before the stems began to die?

O'Killigain. I'd other things to do. While you were livin' your lesser life, an' singin' your dowdy songs, I was fightin' in Spain that you might go on singin' in safety an' peace. [*He grips her arm.*] I've come for you now, me love.

Avril. [*Emotionally and anxious.*] I cannot go where things are said and things are done, for love has had no voice in the beginning of them! [*She tries to free her arm.*] Oh, Jack, let me go—you're hurting me!

O'Killigain. It's O'Killigain gives the pressure of comfort and of care. D'ye mind th' hurt when th' hurt's th' hurt of love?

Avril. [*Passionately.*] Yes, I do! Oh, no, no; I don't, O'Killigain! I don't, I don't. Your pressure on my arm presses on my heart, too. Oh, go away an' leave me lonely!

[*She breaks away and runs to* SOUHAUN, *who puts an arm around her.*]

Poges. [*Angrily.*] You've had your answers, both of you. Get going now. Be off to hell!

O'Killigain. Avril, come out of th' guttherin' candlelight here, to where the wind can put a flush on th' face, ruffle th' hair, and bring a catch to th' breath: come to th' one you want; come to the man who needs you!

Second Workman. [*To* SOUHAUN.] An' you, Souhaun, sturdy lily o' Clune na Geera, come into the love that can fix or flutther the stars o' th' sky, and change th' shinin' moon into a lamp for two. Come to th' one you need; come to th' man who wants you!

Souhaun. [*Half joking, but wholly in earnest.*] If you only had a horse handy, I'd ride away with you!

Second Workman. [*Quietly.*] He's outside waitin'. A loan from Mr O'Killigain. A horse that can gallop glorious the live-long day undher th' sound of a steady voice an' the touch of a steady hand.

Souhaun. [*A little hysterical.*] No, no!

Second Workman. [*Firmly.*] Yes!

Basil. [*Rising out of his astonishment— to* POGES, *angrily.*] How long more are you going to stick this man? Send these impudent fellows away!

Poges. [*As if waking from a stupor—furiously to the two* MEN.] Get out, the two of you! We haven't lived long enough with you to be touched with your insanity! Get out!

Souhaun. [*To the* SECOND WORKMAN.] I see. I'll do whatever Avril advises, my friend. [*To* AVRIL.] Come, dear, till we think out a wonderful answer.

O'Killigain. [*To* AVRIL—*as she goes out.*] Be ready; I'll call and come to take you, Avril, when the river rises. [*He goes out.*]

Second Workman. [*To* SOUHAUN—*as she goes out.*] I'll wait outside by th' good, gallopin' horse, till th' snowy-breasted pearl comes to shimmer on me shouldher.

[*He goes out.*]

Poges. [*Furious and mocking.*] When the river rises! Come with me, and be my love! Come into the garden, Maud! Was ever fools more foolish!

Basil. And the fellow with the galloping horse outside! Boot, saddle, and away! I never expected to see or hear the like, even in this odd country. [*Slapping* POGES *on the back—jokingly.*] You'd better keep an eye on that woman of yours, and look out for the sound of a galloping horse!

Poges. [*Clapping* BASIL *on the back.*] And you keep an ear open for O'Killigain's

call when the river rises! [*In mock tragedy.*]
Beware of O'Killigain's call!

Basil. [*Mocking.*] Beware the sound of
the galloping horse! Did you hear that
vulgar fellow chatting about making the
moon do something or other?

[POGES *goes over to the bureau, opens
a drawer, takes some papers out of it,
looks at them, sits down at the bureau,
and arranges things to write a letter.*]

Poges. Poor crazy fool. They're all a bit
demented. Must be the climate. Most amusing.

Basil. Amusing, yes, up to a point; but
hardly reassuring; no. [*He comes closer to*
POGES.] I don't like it, Poges.

Poges. [*A little startled.*] Eh?

Basil. Well, it isn't exactly comfortable
to be living among a lot of crazy people, is
it? It may even become dangerous.

Poges. [*Sitting up straight.*] Dangerous?
That's a serious thought, Stoke. Now that
you mention it, I do feel the insidious influence of the place. We might become demented, too.

Basil. If they allowed us to live long
enough.

Poges. Good God, what a thought! I
must have a talk with you when I've written this letter.

Basil. You saw how the influence is even
affecting the girls.

Poges. The girls? Oh, no, not the girls,
man. They were just humouring the poor
fools. Nonsense; not the girls.

Basil. You watch. Come up to our room
when you're finished, will you?

Poges. At once. [BASIL *goes out;* POGES
*shaking his head slowly from side to side—
musingly.*] Erin the tear and the smile in
thine eye!

[*He clears his throat with a cough, and
settles down to write. The room becomes darker. He has hardly been
writing a minute, when a curious face
appears round the corner of the entrance leading to the Hall. It is the
stout little face of a little man, dressed
in neat black clothes covered with a
saturated fawn-coloured mackintosh.
Big spectacles cover his eyes. A huge,
fiery red beard spreads over his chest,
like a breastplate, reaching to his belly,
and extending out from his body, like
a fan turned downwards. He wears a
black jerry hat. When he speaks he is
found to have a little voice. He carries
a blackthorn stick in his hand. As he
peeps round he sees* POGES *at the bureau,
and pulls in his head again. He thrusts*

*it forward again, steps out, and comes
into full view. He pulls his coat straight
with a jerk and smoothes his trousers;
and then comes with a trot into the
room, right over to* POGES, *bends over
towards him, and greets him in a hearty
manner. He is the* SUB-POSTMASTER *of
the village.*]

Postmaster. An honour it is, sir, to meet
the owner of such a fine house. A house with
a history. A house where the genthry joined
themselves to merriment, and danced th'
stars to sleep! [*He dances clumsily round
the room, singing.*] See me dance the polka,
see me dance the polka, see me dance the
polka, as I have done before. [*He suddenly
stops and comes to* POGES.] I hope I see you
well, sir? I bear a message from the Postmaster.

Poges. [*Amazed.*] I am well, thank you;
and what is your message from the Postmaster?

Postmaster. When I was outside, an' heard
you coughin', it's well I knew be th' sound
of th' cough that the cough was th' cough of
a gentleman.

Poges. [*Impatiently.*] Yes, yes, but what
is your message?

Postmaster. Well, as a genuine gentleman,
you'll be th' first to agree that a Postmaster
with a small wife an' a large family, an'
hardly any salary—I near forgot to mention that—hardly any salary at all, if the
thruth was told, as a thrue gentleman, you'll
agree that a man like that is handicapped,
an' has a claim on a gentleman's sympathy.

Poges. But I can't make his wife bigger,
or his family smaller, can I?

Postmaster. Sure, I know you can't, an'
that's not what the Postmaster's complainin'
about. [*He leans over* POGES.] But th' poor
man needs sleep, he needs his share o' sleep.

Poges. [*Humouring him—thinking his
visitor is out of his mind.*] Yes, yes; of
course, the poor man needs sleep. We all
need sleep. That's a fine stick you have in
your hand, sir: can I see it?

Postmaster. [*Holding up the stick and
stretching it away from* POGES.] Ay, ay, a
fine blackthorn. There y'are; look at it as
long as you like; [*Warningly.*] —but don't
lay a finger on it. There's a stick could give
a crack a man ud remember!

Poges. [*Nervous.*] Oh? I can't see it well
from here; let me take it in my hand for a
moment.

Postmaster. Sorra second you're goin' to
have it in your hand. That stick has never
been outa me father's hand an' it has never
been outa mine. D'ye know why?

Poges. No, friend, I don't.

Postmaster. Guess, now, guess.

Poges. [*Smiling sweetly.*] I haven't the slightest idea, friend; I couldn't guess.

Postmaster. This's th' very stick that me oul' fella made a swipe at Parnell with—th' scandaliser of Ireland's holy name, a swipe that, had it got home, ud a laid Parnell up for a month o' Sundays! Now, as a thrue gentleman, wouldn't you say it was right?

Poges. Yes, yes; quite right.

Postmaster. Well, havin' settled that, let's settle th' other; amnt I right in sayin' that every man should have his share o' sleep?

Poges. Yes, yes; of course.

Postmaster. Well, then, amnt I right in sayin' that th' poor Postmaster should have his share o' sleep, too?

Poges. To be sure. [*Rising from his seat.*] Now, I must be going.

[*A fairly loud clap of thunder is heard, followed by the sound, first of a trotting horse, then of one going off at a gallop. They listen till the sounds die in the distance.*]

Postmaster. [*Waving him back with the stick.*] Wait a minute——. I'm not done yet. You've just said the poor Postmaster should have his share o' sleep—didn't you?

Poges. Yes, yes, friend.

Postmaster. I knew you'd say that. [*He stretches out his hand to* Poges.] Lave it there. [*He shakes hands with* Poges.] Now I won't have to be keepin' one eye open an' me ear glued to the bell, for fear of a toll call or a trunk call, afther ten o'clock at night, an' I settlin' down for a cozy sleep.

Poges. [*The truth dawning on him.*] Oh, so you're the Postmaster, are you? So it was you who delayed me when I wanted St. Paul?

Postmaster. Didn't you know that?

Poges. The telephonic system here is an all-night one, isn't it?

Postmaster. 'Course it is, but that says nothin'.

Poges. [*Decidedly.*] Look here, my man; I'm a business man, and have to make calls at all hours of the night; I can't be thinking of every man having an honest night's sleep.

Postmaster. 'Course you can't; it's only the poor Postmaster that you've got to keep in mind.

Poges. [*Severely.*] Look here, my man, as long as I pay for the service, the service will have to be supplied. Good day.

Postmaster. There isn't a gentleman in th' whole disthrict ud think, except in the case o' sudden death or disasther, of givin' a tinkle afther th' hand o' th' clock had passed the figure of half past nine o' night.

Poges. Take yourself and your stick away out of the house, man!

Postmaster. [*Mimicking him.*] Take yourself and your stick away outa the house, man. Is it comin' down here to teach us good manners an' feelin' y' are, an' you puttin' a surly gob on you when you're asked to fall in with the sensible an' thried institutions of the neighbourhood?

[*While they have been talking together, the room has darkened still more, and* Poges *sharply tugs the string that puts on the light; the wind has risen and can be heard occasionally blowing through the trees outside; and even shaking the old house.*]

Poges. [*In a rage.*] Go on, get out!

[*As he says this, a long, loud peal of thunder is heard.*]

Postmaster. D'ye hear that? There won't be many thrunk calls goin' for a while, an' th' poor Postmaster'll have a sweeter night's sleep than some I know. [*He bends towards* Poges.] When—the river—rises!

[*The room has darkened; the wind rises; the one light in the room flickers. The* Postmaster *and* Poges *watch it. Then the* Postmaster *turns to go, but halts when a* Figure *of a man is seen standing at the entrance leading to the Hall. He is dressed from head to foot in gleaming black oilskins, hooded over his head, just giving a glimpse of a blue mask, all illumined by the rays of flickering lightning, so that the* Figure *seems to look like the spirit of the turbulent waters of the rising river. The* Postmaster *goes back, startled, till he is beside* Poges, *and the two men stand and stare at the ominous* Figure. Basil, Barney *and* Cloyne *appear at the entrances at back, each holding a lighted lantern in his and her hand. They are very frightened. They, too, hold up their lanterns and stare at the* Figure.]

Basil. The river is rising!

Barney. Risin' high!

Cloyne. An' will overwhelm us all!

The Figure. [*In a deep voice.*] The river has broken her banks, and is rising high; high enough to come tumbling in on top of you. Cattle, sheep, and swine are moaning in the whirling flood. Trees of an ancient heritage, that looked down on all below them, are torn from the power of the place they were born in, and are tossing about in the foaming energy of the waters. Those who have lifted their eyes unto the hills are firm of foot, for in the hills is safety; but a trembling perch in the highest place on the highest house shall be the portion of those who dwell in the valleys below!

[*The lightning ceases for a moment; the entrance becomes dark; and the* FIGURE *disappears.*]

Poges. [*Frantic.*] What shall we do? What must we do? What can we do?

Basil. [*In anguish.*] We're lost!

Cloyne. [*Sinking down on her knees.*] King o' th' Angels, save us!

Barney. [*Clasping his hands.*] Amen! A nice pass we've come to when we have to call for help in a Tudor House!

Poges. [*Bawling.*] Souhaun, Souhaun! O'Killigain, help!

Basil. [*Roaring at* POGES.] You made us come down here!

Poges. [*Roaring at* BASIL.] You're a liar; it was you!

Postmaster. [*Bringing down the black-thorn stick with a bang on the quattro-cento bureau.*] Eh, order, order, law an' order there; steady! Measures o' safety to be taken. [*Thrusting his stick towards* POGES *—sharply.*] Has the highest room in the house a way to the roof—quick!

Poges. [*Answering at once.*] Yes.

Cloyne. [*In anguish.*] Th' roof—oh, my God!

Postmaster. [*Rapidly.*] Up with us all with bread and wine, with firewood and coal, and an axe. Up!

Poges. An axe?

Postmaster. To hack whatever suitable furniture we can get into a raft, if we're swirled off th' roof. [*Driving* CLOYNE *and* BARNEY *before him.*] Up!

Poges. [*Loudly.*] Souhaun, Souhaun, where's Souhaun?

Basil. [*Impatiently.*] Come on, and come up.

[AVRIL *comes in from one of the back entrances. She is covered with a green mackintosh, and a coloured scarf, peasant-wise, is over her head. She carries a small case. She passes between the two* MEN *without a word, and stands still near the Entrance leading to the Hall, looking out before her.*]

Poges. [*Staring at her.*] What are you doing here? What are you watching? [AVRIL *stands still and silent.*] Where's Souhaun, where's Souhaun?

Avril. [*Quietly—without looking round.*] She's gone.

Poges. Gone? How? Where?

Avril. [*Quietly—still not moving.*] Gone with the wind; gone with the waters; gone with the one man who alone saw something in her!

Poges. [*Raging.*] What, with that loud-mouthed, ignorant, superstitious, low-born, half-mad Irishman! Oh, she's nicely rooked me! She was with him on the galloping horse that galloped away, was she? Oh, she's nicely rooked a simple, honest, loving-hearted, foolish man! She's gone, is she?

Avril. An' well it would be if I was with her.

Poges. You damned slut, are you in your mind as bad as she is?

Avril. [*Indicating* BASIL.] The mind that went with him is as bad as the mind that went with you.

Basil. [*Sneeringly.*] You lost the chance you had to get away from it.

Avril. He said he'd come when the river rises.

O'Killigain. [*Outside—loudly.*] Avril.

Avril. [*With a start of joy.*] O'Killigain! O'Killigain!

[O'KILLIGAIN *appears, his trench coat drenched and his hair soaking, at the entrance.*]

O'Killigain. My barque is waiting, love; come!

[AVRIL *picks up the case and runs to* O'KILLIGAIN.]

Basil. Honest, decent woman, she carries the booty of her friends in her pack.

Avril. [*Quietly.*] I gave more than I got, you gilded monkey. It's winnowed of every touch of life I'd be if I stayed with th' waste of your mind much longer. [*She taps the case*]. Th' trinkets I wormed out of you are all here, an' here they stay, for th' wages were low for what was done for you.

Poges. [*Sneering.*] And gentleman O'Killigain will happier be with a harlot's fortune!

O'Killigain. [*Good-humouredly.*] Of course he will. Th' good things of this life are good for all, an' a pretty girl looks handsomer in my arms. You have had your day, like every dog. Your Tudors have had their day, and they are gone; and th' little heap o' purple dust they left behind them will vanish away in th' flow of the river. [*To* AVRIL.] Come, love, to my little house up on th' hill.

[*He goes out with* AVRIL. *After a moment the sound of oars is heard splashing the waters, and* O'KILLIGAIN *is heard singing. Singing, other voices outside join in the chorus.*]

Come from the dyin' an' fly from th' dead,
Faraway O!
An', now, with th' quick, make your home an' your bed,
With a will an' a way, away O!

[*During song,* BASIL *runs off; comes back with bags. Then rushes to* POGES.]

Then away, love, away,
Faraway O!
To live any life that is looming ahead,
With a will an' a way, away O!

Away from all mouldherin' ashes we row,
Faraway O!
Takin' th' splendour of livin' in tow,
With a will an' a way, away O!

Then away, love, away,
Faraway O!

Where th' lightning of life flashes vivid, we go,
With a will an' a way, away O!

[POGES *stands still, listening till the song fades away in the distance. Suddenly* BASIL *clutches his arm.*]

Basil. [*Frantically.*] Wake up, man; wake up! The waters are tumbling towards us. What shall we do? Wake up! Come to the roof! [BASIL *rushes off on the trail of the others who have fled to the roof. As he runs.*] The roof! The roof!

[POGES *stands still for a few moments, then he sees the quattro-cento chest. He stumbles over to it, raises the lid, and climbs clumsily into it.*]

Poges. [*Climbing in.*] My poor little quattro-cento be my ark in the midst of the flood of waters. Bring me back, bring me back to where I first saw the light. Bring me back to dear old England now that April's there.

[*He closes the lid on himself as the waters surge around. Water falls on the bureau as he descends.*]

CURTAIN

THE SKIN OF OUR TEETH *

By

THORNTON WILDER

IN HIS PREFACE TO "THREE PLAYS" (1957), Wilder explains how he came to write his kind of play. He says that toward the end of the twenties he found going to the theatre less and less pleasant, because he was losing belief in what he saw. He still believed the plays he read, but when he saw the same plays in the theatre they lacked bite or warmth. The explanation lay, he thought, in the 19th-century middle-class wish to avoid being disturbed in the theatre. The middle classes smothered the theatre's bite and warmth by means of the box set.

Wilder claims that the box set destroys belief in the theatre because it localizes what is universal in both place and time. The theatre, he believes, is by nature universal, a place where it is always "now," but the box set in the theatre makes it "then."

So Wilder began writing short plays impossible to do on box sets, plays in which time and space are treated so as to create the belief he wanted. In *The Happy Journey to Trenton and Camden* four chairs make an automobile and it goes seventy miles in twenty minutes. *The Long Christmas Dinner* spans ninety years. Then come longer plays: *Our Town* moves about the village of Grover's Corners and involves years of time; *The Merchant of Yonkers*, later revised as *The Matchmaker*, ridicules 19th-century plays; *The Skin of Our Teeth* compresses into one "now" thousands of years of human effort and endurance. *The Matchmaker* uses box sets, but perhaps Wilder does not care whether that play is believed. *A Life in the Sun*, also called *The Alcestiad*, was written for the open stage of the Assembly Hall at the Edinburgh Festival and when performed will apparently always appear on a similar stage. In sum, Wilder has done something, perhaps a great deal, to help banish box sets from the contemporary stage.

Wilder's audiences have become international, and surely no American playwright better represents America to non-Americans. But does Wilder's avoidance of box sets account for the convincingness of his plays? When the audience confronts the bare stage of *Our Town* or when the walls of the Antrobus home fly into the air, do Americans, Italians, Swiss, Germans say to themselves, "How true!"?

Maybe these methods gain belief in the theatre, but somehow it seems unlikely. Rather, Wilder's plays seem to place the responsibility for convincingness firmly upon the actor; they free him from setting, but they demand of him a prompt and assured authority, even such complicated and ambiguous authority as Sabina must exert at the beginning of *The Skin of Our Teeth*. If the audience feels that authority, it believes the play—in the only sense in which belief ever is found in the sophisticated audiences Wilder writes for: the willing acceptance of illusion. But surely those audiences, having accepted the illusion of Wilder's plays, do not refuse another author's illusion when they later meet it in a box set.

The Skin of Our Teeth had great difficulty finding a producer, but once produced it promptly succeeded, won a Pulitzer Prize for its author, and has remained one of the great plays of the American theatre, capable of frequent and always fresh revival. Wilder acknowledges that it owes a great deal to *Finnegans Wake,* by James Joyce, but since that book is perhaps the prime 20th-century instance of an unread classic, theatre audiences do not find *The Skin of Our Teeth's* theme, characterizations, or humor unbearably familiar.

* Reprinted by permission of Harper and Brothers.

THORNTON NIVEN WILDER

Born 1897, Madison, Wisconsin. Elementary education at
Berkeley and Ojai, California.
1906, Went with family to China, where his father served
eight years as Consul General in Hong Kong and
Shanghai. Attended school in Chefoo.
1915–1917, Attended Oberlin College.
1918, Corporal in Coast Artillery.
1920, A.B., Yale University.
1920–1921, Study in the American Academy in Rome,
Italy.
1921–1928, Teacher of French and housemaster at The
Lawrenceville School, New Jersey.
1925, M.A., Princeton University.
1927, His second novel, *The Bridge of San Luis Rey,*
awarded the Pulitzer Prize.
1930–1937, Teaching English at the University of Chicago.
1938, *Our Town* awarded the Pulitzer Prize.
1942, *The Skin of Our Teeth* awarded the Pulitzer Prize.
1942, Enlisted in Air Corps Intelligence; appointed Lieutenant-Colonel in 1944.
1950, Charles Eliot Norton Professor of Poetry at Harvard.

PLAYS

1919 *The Trumpet Shall Sound.* 1928 *The
Angel That Troubled the Waters,* sixteen
short plays. 1931 *The Long Christmas Dinner,* including besides the title play: *Queens
of France, Pullman Car Hiawatha, Such
Things Happen Only in Books, The Happy
Journey to Trenton and Camden, Love and
How to Cure It.* 1932 *Lucrece,* translated
from the French of Obey. 1938 *Our Town.*
1938 *The Merchant of Yonkers,* translated
and adapted from *Einen Jux will er sich
machen,* by Nestroy, based on *A Day Well
Spent* (1836), by John Oxenford. 1942 *The
Skin of Our Teeth.* 1947 *Our Century.* 1948
The Victors, translated from *Morts sans
sépulture,* by Jean-Paul Sartre. 1954 *The*

Matchmaker, revision of *The Merchant of
Yonkers.* 1955 *A Life in the Sun (The Al-
cestiad).* 1957 *The Drunken Sisters.* 1957
Bernice. 1957 *The Wreck of the 5:25.*

SCREENWRITING

1928 *The Bridge of San Luis Rey.*

WRITINGS ON DRAMA

"Some Thoughts on Playwriting," in *The
Intent of the Artist,* edited by Augusto Cen-
teno, 1941. Preface to *Three Plays,* 1957;
reprinted, slightly expanded, as "A Platform
and a Passion or Two," in *Harper's Magazine,* CCXV (Oct. 1957), 48–51.

THE SKIN OF OUR TEETH

Characters

(in the order of their appearance)

ANNOUNCER.
SABINA.
MR. FITZPATRICK.
MRS. ANTROBUS.
DINOSAUR.
MAMMOTH.
TELEGRAPH BOY.
GLADYS.
HENRY.
MR. ANTROBUS.
DOCTOR.
PROFESSOR.
JUDGE [MOSES].
HOMER.
MISS E. MUSE.
MISS T. MUSE.
MISS M. MUSE.

TWO USHERS.
TWO DRUM MAJORETTES.
FORTUNE TELLER.
TWO CHAIR PUSHERS.
SIX CONVEENERS.
BROADCAST OFFICIAL.
DEFEATED CANDIDATE.
MR. TREMAYNE.
HESTER.
IVY.
FRED BAILEY.

ACT I. *Home, Excelsior, New Jersey.*

ACT II. *Atlantic City Boardwalk.*

ACT III. *Home, Excelsior, New Jersey.*

ACT I

A projection screen in the middle of the curtain. The first lantern slide: the name of the theatre, and the words: NEWS EVENTS OF THE WORLD. An AN-NOUNCER'S voice is heard.

Announcer. The management takes pleasure in bringing to you—The News Events of the World. [*Slide of the sun appearing above the horizon.*]

    Freeport, Long Island:
    The sun rose this morning at 6:32 a.m. This gratifying event was first reported by Mrs. Dorothy Stetson of Freeport, Long Island, who promptly telephoned the Mayor.
    The Society for Affirming the End of the World at once went into a special session and postponed the arrival of that event for TWENTY-FOUR HOURS.
    All honor to Mrs. Stetson for her public spirit.

    New York City: [*Slide of the front doors of the theatre in which this play is playing; three cleaning WOMEN with mops and pails.*]

The X Theatre. During the daily cleaning of this theatre a number of lost objects were collected as usual by Mesdames Simpson, Pateslewski, and Moriarty.
    Among these objects found today was a wedding ring, inscribed: *To Eva from Adam. Genesis II: 18.*
    The ring will be restored to the owner or owners, if their credentials are satisfactory.

    Tippehatchee, Vermont: [*Slide representing a glacier.*] The unprecedented cold weather of this summer has produced a condition that has not yet been satisfactorily explained. There is a report that a wall of ice is moving southward across these counties. The disruption of communications by the cold wave now crossing the country has rendered exact information difficult, but little credence is given to the rumor that the ice had pushed the Cathedral of Montreal as far as St. Albans, Vermont.
    For further information see your daily papers.

423

Excelsior, New Jersey: [*Slide of a modest suburban home.*] The home of Mr. George Antrobus, the inventor of the wheel. The discovery of the wheel, following so closely on the discovery of the lever, has centered the attention of the country on Mr. Antrobus of this attractive suburban residence district. This is his home, a commodious seven-room house, conveniently situated near a public school, a Methodist church, and a firehouse; it is right handy to an A. and P. [*Slide of* MR. ANTROBUS *on his front steps, smiling and lifting his straw hat. He holds a wheel.*] Mr. Antrobus, himself. He comes of very old stock and has made his way up from next to nothing.

It is reported that he was once a gardener, but left that situation under circumstances that have been variously reported.

Mr. Antrobus is a veteran of foreign wars, and bears a number of scars, front and back. [*Slide of* MRS. ANTROBUS, *holding some roses.*] This is Mrs. Antrobus, the charming and gracious president of the Excelsior Mothers' Club.

Mrs. Antrobus is an excellent needlewoman; it is she who invented the apron on which so many interesting changes have been rung since. [*Slide of the* FAMILY *and* SABINA.] Here we see the Antrobuses with their two children, Henry and Gladys, and friend. The friend in the rear, is Lily Sabina, the maid.

I know we all want to congratulate this typical American family on its enterprise. We all wish Mr. Antrobus a successful future. Now the management takes you to the interior of this home for a brief visit.

[*Curtain rises. Living room of a commuter's home.* SABINA—*straw-blonde, over-rouged—is standing by the window back center, a feather duster under her elbow.*]

Sabina. Oh, oh, oh! Six o'clock and the master not home yet.

Pray God nothing serious has happened to him crossing the Hudson River. If anything happened to him, we would certainly be inconsolable and have to move into a less desirable residence district.

The fact is I don't know what'll become of us. Here it is the middle of August and the coldest day of the year. It's simply freezing; the dogs are sticking to the sidewalks; can anybody explain that? No.

But I'm not surprised. The whole world's at sixes and sevens, and why the house hasn't fallen down about our ears long ago is a miracle to me. [*A fragment of the right wall leans precariously over the stage.* SABINA *looks at it nervously and it slowly rights itself.*] Every night this same anxiety as to whether the master will get home safely: whether he'll bring home anything to eat. In the midst of life we are in the midst of death, a truer word was never said. [*The fragment of scenery flies up into the lofts.* SABINA *is struck dumb with surprise, shrugs her shoulders and starts dusting* MR. ANTROBUS' *chair, including the under side.*] Of course, Mr. Antrobus is a very fine man, an excellent husband and father, a pillar of the church, and has all the best interests of the community at heart. Of course, every muscle goes tight every time he passes a policeman; but what I think is that there are certain charges that ought not to be made, and I think I may add, ought not to be allowed to be made; we're all human; who isn't? [*She dusts* MRS. ANTROBUS' *rocking chair.*] Mrs. Antrobus is as fine a woman as you could hope to see. She lives only for her children; and if it would be any benefit to her children she'd see the rest of us stretched out dead at her feet without turning a hair,— that's the truth. If you want to know anything more about Mrs. Antrobus, just go and look at a tigress, and look hard.

As to the children——

Well, Henry Antrobus is a real, clean-cut American boy. He'll graduate from High School one of these days, if they make the alphabet any easier.—Henry, when he has a stone in his hand, has a perfect aim; he can hit anything from a bird to an older brother —Oh! I didn't mean to say that!—but it certainly was an unfortunate accident, and it was very hard getting the police out of the house.

Mr. and Mrs. Antrobus' daughter is named Gladys. She'll make some good man a good wife some day, if he'll just come down off the movie screen and ask her.

So here we are!

We've managed to survive for some time now, catch as catch can, the fat and the lean, and if the dinosaurs don't trample us to death, and if the grasshoppers don't eat up our garden, we'll all live to see better days, knock on wood.

Each new child that's born to the Antrobuses seems to them to be sufficient reason for the whole universe's being set in motion;

and each new child that dies seems to them to have been spared a whole world of sorrow, and what the end of it will be is still very much an open question.

We've rattled along, hot and cold, for some time now— [*A portion of the wall above the door, right, flies up into the air and disappears.*] —and my advice to you is not to inquire into why or whither, but just enjoy your ice cream while it's on your plate,—that's my philosophy.

Don't forget that a few years ago we came through the depression by the skin of our teeth! One more tight squeeze like that and where will we be?

[*This is a cue line.* SABINA *looks angrily at the kitchen door and repeats.*] . . . we came through the depression by the skin of our teeth; one more tight squeeze like that and where will we be?

[*Flustered, she looks through the opening in the right wall; then goes to the window and reopens the Act.*] Oh, oh, oh! Six o'clock and the master not home yet. Pray God nothing has happened to him crossing the Hudson. Here it is the middle of August and the coldest day of the year. It's simply freezing; the dogs are sticking. One more tight squeeze like that and where will we be?

Voice. [*Offstage.*] Make up something! Invent something!

Sabina. Well . . . uh . . . this certainly is a fine American home . . . and—uh . . . everybody's very happy . . . and—uh . . . [*Suddenly flings pretense to the winds and coming downstage says with indignation.*] I can't invent any words for this play, and I'm glad I can't. I hate this play and every word in it.

As for me, I don't understand a single word of it, anyway,—all about the troubles the human race has gone through, there's a subject for you.

Besides, the author hasn't made up his silly mind as to whether we're all living back in caves or in New Jersey today, and that's the way it is all the way through.

Oh—why can't we have plays like we used to have—*Peg o' My Heart*, and *Smilin' Thru*, and *The Bat*—good entertainment with a message you can take home with you?

I took this hateful job because I had to. For two years I've sat up in my room living on a sandwich and a cup of tea a day, waiting for better things in the theatre. And look at me now: I—I who've played *Rain* and *The Barretts of Wimpole Street* and *First Lady*—God in Heaven!

[*The* STAGE MANAGER *puts his head out from the hole in the scenery.*]

Mr. Fitzpatrick. Miss Somerset!! Miss Somerset!

Sabina. Oh! Anyway—nothing matters! It'll all be the same in a hundred years. [*Loudly.*] We came through the depression by the skin of our teeth,—that's true!—one more tight squeeze like that and where will we be? [*Enter* MRS. ANTROBUS, *a mother.*]

Mrs. Antrobus. Sabina, you've let the fire go out.

Sabina. [*In a lather.*] One-thing-and-another; don't-know-whether-my-wits-are-upside-or-down; might-as-well-be-dead-as-alive-in-a-house-all-sixes-and-sevens. . . .

Mrs. Antrobus. You've let the fire go out. Here it is the coldest day of the year right in the middle of August, and you've let the fire go out.

Sabina. Mrs. Antrobus, I'd like to give my two weeks' notice, Mrs. Antrobus. A girl like I can get a situation in a home where they're rich enough to have a fire in every room, Mrs. Antrobus, and a girl don't have to carry the responsibility of the whole house on her two shoulders. And a home without children, Mrs. Antrobus, because children are a thing only a parent can stand, and a truer word was never said; and a home, Mrs. Antrobus, where the master of the house don't pinch decent, self-respecting girls when he meets them in a dark corridor. I mention no names and make no charges. So you have my notice, Mrs. Antrobus. I hope that's perfectly clear.

Mrs. Antrobus. You've let the fire go out! —Have you milked the mammoth?

Sabina. I don't understand a word of this play.—Yes, I've milked the mammoth.

Mrs. Antrobus. Until Mr. Antrobus comes home we have no food and we have no fire. You'd better go over to the neighbors and borrow some fire.

Sabina. Mrs. Antrobus! I can't! I'd die on the way, you know I would. It's worse than January. The dogs are sticking to the sidewalks. I'd die.

Mrs. Antrobus. Very well, I'll go.

Sabina. [*Even more distraught, coming forward and sinking on her knees.*] You'd never come back alive; we'd all perish; if you weren't here, we'd just perish. How do we know Mr. Antrobus'll be back? We don't know. If you go out, I'll just kill myself.

Mrs. Antrobus. Get up, Sabina.

Sabina. Every night it's the same thing. Will he come back safe, or won't he? Will we starve to death, or freeze to death, or boil to death or will we be killed by burglars? I don't know why we go on living. I don't know why we go on living at all. It's easier being dead.

[*She flings her arms on the table and buries her head in them. In each of the succeeding speeches she flings her head up—and sometimes her hands—then quickly buries her head again.*]

Mrs. Antrobus. The same thing! Always throwing up the sponge, Sabina. Always announcing your own death. But give you a new hat—or a plate of ice cream—or a ticket to the movies, and you want to live forever.

Sabina. You don't care whether we live or die; all you care about is those children. If it would be any benefit to them you'd be glad to see us all stretched out dead.

Mrs. Antrobus. Well, maybe I would.

Sabina. And what do they care about? Themselves—that's all they care about. [*Shrilly.*] They make fun of you behind your back. Don't tell me: they're ashamed of you. Half the time, they pretend they're someone else's children. Little thanks you get from them.

Mrs. Antrobus. I'm not asking for any thanks.

Sabina. And Mr. Antrobus—you don't understand *him.* All that work he does—trying to discover the alphabet and the multiplication table. Whenever he tries to learn anything you fight against˙ it.

Mrs. Antrobus. Oh, Sabina, I know you.

When Mr. Antrobus raped you home from your Sabine hills, he did it to insult me.

He did it for your pretty face, and to insult me.

You were the new wife, weren't you?

For a year or two you lay on your bed all day and polished the nails on your hands and feet.

You made puff-balls of the combings of your hair and you blew them up to the ceiling.

And I washed your underclothes and I made you chicken broths.

I bore children and between my very groans I stirred the cream that you'd put on your face.

But I knew you wouldn't last.

You didn't last.

Sabina. But it was I who encouraged Mr. Antrobus to make the alphabet. I'm sorry to say it, Mrs. Antrobus, but you're not a beautiful woman, and you can never know what a man could do if he tried. It's girls like I who inspire the multiplication table.

I'm sorry to say it, but you're not a beau-

tiful woman, Mrs. Antrobus, and that's the God's truth.

Mrs. Antrobus. And you didn't last—you sank to the kitchen. And what do you do there? *You let the fire go out!*

No wonder to you it seems easier being dead.

Reading and writing and counting on your fingers is all very well in their way,—but I keep the home going.—There's that dinosaur on the front lawn again.—Shoo! Go away. Go away.

[*The baby* DINOSAUR *puts his head in the window.*]

Dinosaur. It's cold.

Mrs. Antrobus. You go around to the back of the house where you belong.

Dinosaur. It's cold.

[*The* DINOSAUR *disappears.* MRS. ANTROBUS *goes calmly out.* SABINA *slowly raises her head and speaks to the audience. The central portion of the center wall rises, pauses, and disappears into the loft.*]

Sabina. Now that you audience are listening to this, too, I understand it a little better.

I wish eleven o'clock were here; I don't want to be dragged through this whole play again. [*The* TELEGRAPH BOY *is seen entering along the back wall of the stage from the right. She catches sight of him and calls.*] Mrs. Antrobus! Mrs. Antrobus! Help! There's a strange man coming to the house. He's coming up the walk, help!

[*Enter* MRS. ANTROBUS *in alarm, but efficient.*]

Mrs. Antrobus. Help me quick! [*They barricade the door by piling the furniture against it.*] Who is it? What do you want?

Telegraph Boy. A telegram for Mrs. Antrobus from Mr. Antrobus in the city.

Sabina. Are you sure, are you sure? Maybe it's just a trap!

Mrs. Antrobus. I know his voice, Sabina. We can open the door. [*Enter the* TELEGRAPH BOY, *12 years old, in uniform. The* DINOSAUR *and* MAMMOTH *slip by him into the room and settle down front right.*] I'm sorry we kept you waiting. We have to be careful, you know. [*To the* ANIMALS.] Hm! . . . Will you be quiet?   [*They nod.*] Have you had your supper?   [*They nod.*] Are you *ready* to come in?   [*They nod.*] Young man, have you any fire with you? Then light the grate, will you?

[*He nods, produces something like a briquet; and kneels by the imagined fireplace, footlights center. Pause.*]

What are people saying about this cold weather? [*He makes a doubtful shrug with his shoulders.*] Sabina, take this stick and go and light the stove.

Sabina. Like I told you, Mrs. Antrobus; two weeks. That's the law. I hope that's perfectly clear. [*Exit.*]

Mrs. Antrobus. What about this cold weather?

Telegraph Boy. [*Lowered eyes.*] Of course, I don't know anything . . . but they say there's a wall of ice moving down from the North, that's what they say. We can't get Boston by telegraph, and they're burning pianos in Hartford.

. . . It moves everything in front of it, churches and post offices and city halls.

I live in Brooklyn myself.

Mrs. Antrobus. What are people doing about it?

Telegraph Boy. Well . . . uh . . . Talking, mostly.

Or just what you'd do a day in February. There are some that are trying to go South and the roads are crowded; but you can't take old people and children very far in a cold like this.

Mrs. Antrobus. What's this telegram you have for me?

Telegraph Boy. [*Fingertips to his forehead.*] If you wait just a minute; I've got to remember it. [*The* ANIMALS *have left their corner and are nosing him. Presently they take their places on either side of him, leaning against his hips, like heraldic beasts.*] This telegram was flashed from Murray Hill to University Heights! And then by puffs of smoke from University Heights to Staten Island. And then by lantern from Staten Island to Plainfield, New Jersey. What hath God wrought!

[*He clears his throat.*]

"To Mrs. Antrobus, Excelsior, New Jersey:

My dear wife, will be an hour late. Busy day at the office. Don't worry the children about the cold just keep them warm burn everything except Shakespeare." [*Pause.*]

Mrs. Antrobus. Men! —He knows I'd burn ten Shakespeares to prevent a child of mine from having one cold in the head. What does it say next? [*Enter* SABINA.]

Telegraph Boy. "Have made great discoveries today have separated em from en."

Sabina. I know what that is, that's the alphabet, yes it is. Mr. Antrobus is just the cleverest man. Why, when the alphabet's finished, we'll be able to tell the future and everything.

Telegraph Boy. Then listen to this: "Ten tens make a hundred semi-colon consequences far-reaching." [*Watches for effect.*]

Mrs. Antrobus. The earth's turning to ice, and all he can do is to make up new numbers.

Telegraph Boy. Well, Mrs. Antrobus, like the head man at our office said: a few more discoveries like that and we'll be worth freezing.

Mrs. Antrobus. What does he say next?

Telegraph Boy. I . . . I can't do this last part very well. [*He clears his throat and sings.*] "Happy w'dding ann'vers'ry to you, Happy ann'vers'ry to you——"

[*The* ANIMALS *begin to howl soulfully;* SABINA *screams with pleasure.*]

Mrs. Antrobus. Dolly! Frederick! Be quiet.

Telegraph Boy. [*Above the din.*] "Happy w'dding ann'vers'ry, dear Eva; happy w'dding ann'vers'ry to you."

Mrs. Antrobus. Is that in the telegram? Are they singing telegrams now? [*He nods.*] The earth's getting so silly no wonder the sun turns cold.

Sabina. Mrs. Antrobus, I want to take back the notice I gave you. Mrs. Antrobus, I don't want to leave a house that gets such interesting telegrams and I'm sorry for anything I said. I really am.

Mrs. Antrobus. Young man, I'd like to give you something for all this trouble; Mr. Antrobus isn't home yet and I have no money and no food in the house——

Telegraph Boy. Mrs. Antrobus . . . I don't like to . . . appear to . . . ask for anything, but . . .

Mrs. Antrobus. What is it you'd like?

Telegraph Boy. Do you happen to have an old needle you could spare? My wife just sits home all day thinking about needles.

Sabina. [*Shrilly.*] We only got two in the house. Mrs. Antrobus, you know we only got two in the house.

Mrs. Antrobus. [*After a look at* SABINA, *taking a needle from her collar.*] Why yes, I can spare this.

Telegraph Boy. [*Lowered eyes.*] Thank you, Mrs. Antrobus. Mrs. Antrobus, can I ask you something else? I have two sons of my own; if the cold gets worse, what should I do?

Sabina. I think we'll all perish, that's what I think. Cold like this in August is just the end of the whole world. [*Silence.*]

Mrs. Antrobus. I don't know. After all, what does one do about anything? Just keep as warm as you can. And don't let your wife and children see that you're worried.

Telegraph Boy. Yes. . . . Thank you, Mrs. Antrobus. We'll, I'd better be going. —Oh, I forgot! There's one more sentence in the telegram. "Three cheers have invented the wheel."

Mrs. Antrobus. A wheel? What's a wheel?

Telegraph Boy. I don't know. That's what it said. The sign for it is like this. Well, goodbye.

[*The* WOMEN *see him to the door, with goodbyes and injunctions to keep warm.*]

Sabina. [*Apron to her eyes, wailing.*] Mrs. Antrobus, it looks to me like all the nice men in the world are already married; I don't know why that is. [*Exit.*]

Mrs. Antrobus. [*Thoughtful; to the* ANIMALS.] Do you ever remember hearing tell of any cold like this in August? [*The* ANIMALS *shake their heads.*] From your grandmothers or anyone? [*They shake their heads.*] Have you any suggestions? [*They shake their heads. She pulls her shawl around, goes to the front door and opening it an inch calls.*] HENRY. GLADYS. CHILDREN. Come right in and get warm. No, no, when mama says a thing she means it. Henry! HENRY. Put down that stone. You know what happened last time. [*Shriek.*] HENRY! Put down that stone! Gladys! Put down your dress!! Try and be a lady.

[*The* CHILDREN *bound in and dash to the fire. They take off their winter things and leave them in heaps on the floor.*]

Gladys. Mama, I'm hungry. Mama, why is it so cold?

Henry. [*At the same time.*] Mama, why doesn't it snow? Mama, when's supper ready? Maybe it'll snow and we can make snowballs.

Gladys. Mama, it's so cold that in one more minute I just couldn't of stood it.

Mrs. Antrobus. Settle down, both of you, I want to talk to you. [*She draws up a hassock and sits front center over the orchestra pit before the imaginary fire. The* CHILDREN *stretch out on the floor, leaning against her lap. Tableau by Raphael. The* ANIMALS *edge up and complete the triangle.*] It's just a cold spell of some kind. Now listen to what I'm saying.

When your father comes home I want you to be extra quiet. He's had a hard day at the office and I don't know but what he may have one of his moods.

I just got a telegram from him very happy and excited, and you know what that means. Your father's temper's uneven; I guess you know that. [*Shriek.*] HENRY! HENRY!

Why—why can't you remember to keep your hair down over your forehead? You must keep that scar covered up. Don't you know that when your father sees it he loses

all control over himself? He goes crazy. He wants to die. [*After a moment's despair she collects herself decisively, wets the hem of her apron in her mouth and starts polishing his forehead vigorously.*] Lift your head up. Stop squirming. Blessed me, sometimes I think that it's going away—and then there it is: just as red as ever.

Henry. Mama, today at school two teachers forgot and called me by my old name. They forgot, Mama. You'd better write another letter to the principal, so that he'll tell them I've changed my name. Right out in class they called me: Cain.

Mrs. Antrobus. [*Putting her hand on his mouth, too late; hoarsely.*] Don't say it. [*Polishing feverishly.*] If you're good they'll forget it. Henry, you didn't hit anyone . . . today, did you?

Henry. Oh . . . no-o-o!

Mrs. Antrobus. [*Still working, not looking at* GLADYS.] And, Gladys, I want you to be especially nice to your father tonight. You know what he calls you when you're good— his little angel, his little star. Keep your dress down like a little lady. And keep your voice nice and low. Gladys Antrobus!! What's that red stuff you have on your face? [*Slaps her.*] You're a filthy detestable child! [*Rises in real, though temporary, repudiation and despair.*] Get away from me, both of you! I wish I'd never seen sight or sound of you! Let the cold come! I can't stand it. I don't want to go on.

[*She walks away.*]

Gladys. [*Weeping.*] All the girls at school do, Mama.

Mrs. Antrobus. [*Shrieking.*] I'm through with you, that's all!—Sabina! Sabina!— Don't you know your father'd go crazy if he saw that paint on your face? Don't you know your father thinks you're perfect? Don't you know he couldn't live if he didn't think you were perfect?—Sabina! [*Enter* SABINA.]

Sabina. Yes, Mrs. Antrobus!

Mrs. Antrobus. Take this girl out into the kitchen and wash her face with the scrubbing brush.

Mr. Antrobus. [*Outside, roaring.*] "I've been working on the railroad, all the livelong day . . ." etc.

[*The* ANIMALS *start running around in circles, bellowing.* SABINA *rushes to the window.*]

Mrs. Antrobus. Sabina, what's that noise outside?

Sabina. Oh, it's a drunken tramp. It's a giant, Mrs. Antrobus. We'll all be killed in our beds, I know it!

Mrs. Antrobus. Help me quick. Quick.

Everybody. [*Again they stack all the furniture against the door.* MR. ANTROBUS *pounds and bellows.*] Who is it? What do you want?—Sabina, have you any boiling water ready?—Who is it?

Mr. Antrobus. Broken-down camel of a pig's snout, open this door.

Mrs. Antrobus. God be praised! It's your father.—Just a minute, George!—Sabina, clear the door, quick. Gladys, come here while I clean your nasty face!

Mr. Antrobus. She-bitch of a goat's gizzard, I'll break every bone in your body. Let me in or I'll tear the whole house down.

Mrs. Antrobus. Just a minute, George, something's the matter with the lock.

Mr. Antrobus. Open the door or I'll tear your livers out. I'll smash your brains on the ceiling, and Devil take the hindmost.

Mrs. Antrobus. Now, you can open the door, Sabina. I'm ready.

[*The door is flung open. Silence.* MR. ANTROBUS—*face of a Keystone Comedy Cop—stands there in fur cap and blanket. His arms are full of parcels, including a large stone wheel with a center in it. One hand carries a railroad man's lantern. Suddenly he bursts into joyous roar.*]

Mr. Antrobus. Well, how's the whole crooked family? [*Relief. Laughter. Tears. Jumping up and down.* ANIMALS *cavorting.* ANTROBUS *throws the parcels on the ground. Hurls his cap and blanket after them. Heroic embraces. Melee of* HUMANS *and* ANIMALS, SABINA *included.*] I'll be scalded and tarred if a man can't get a little welcome when he comes home. Well, Maggie, you old gunnysack, how's the broken down old weather hen?—Sabina, old fishbait, old skunkpot.—And the children,—how've the little smellers been?

Gladys. Papa, Papa, Papa, Papa, Papa.

Mr. Antrobus. How've they been, Maggie?

Mrs. Antrobus. Well, I must say they've been as good as gold. I haven't had to raise my voice once. I don't know what's the matter with them.

Antrobus. [*Kneeling before* GLADYS.] Papa's little weasel, eh?—Sabina, there's some food for you.—Papa's little gopher?

Gladys. [*Her arm around his neck.*] Papa, you're always teasing me.

Antrobus. And Henry? Nothing rash today, I hope. Nothing rash?

Henry. No, Papa.

Antrobus. [*Roaring.*] Well that's good, that's good—I'll bet Sabina let the fire go out.

Sabina. Mr. Antrobus, I've given my no-

tice. I'm leaving two weeks from today. I'm sorry, but I'm leaving.

Antrobus. [*Roar.*] Well, if you leave now you'll freeze to death, so go and cook the dinner.

Sabina. Two weeks, that's the law. [*Exit.*]

Antrobus. Did you get my telegram?

Mrs. Antrobus. Yes.—What's a wheel? [*He indicates the wheel with a glance.* HENRY *is rolling it around the floor. Rapid, hoarse interchange:* MRS. ANTROBUS: *What does this cold weather mean? It's below freezing.* ANTROBUS: *Not before the children!* MRS. ANTROBUS: *Shouldn't we do something about it?—start off, move?* ANTROBUS: *Not before the children!!! He gives* HENRY *a sharp slap.*]

Henry. Papa, you hit me!

Antrobus. Well, remember it. That's to make you remember today. Today. The day the alphabet's finished; and the day that we *saw* the hundred—the hundred, the hundred, the hundred, the hundred, the hundred—there's no end to 'em.

I've had a day at the office!

Take a look at that wheel, Maggie—when I've got that to rights: you'll see a sight.

There's a reward there for all the walking you've done.

Mrs. Antrobus. How do you mean?

Antrobus. [*On the hassock looking into the fire; with awe.*] Maggie, we've reached the top of the wave. There's not much more to be done. We're there!

Mrs. Antrobus. [*Cutting across his mood sharply.*] And the ice?

Antrobus. The ice!

Henry. [*Playing with the wheel.*] Papa, you could put a chair on this.

Antrobus. [*Broodingly.*] Ye-e-s, any booby can fool with it now,—but I thought of it first.

Mrs. Antrobus. Children, go out in the kitchen. I want to talk to your father alone. [*The* CHILDREN *go out.* ANTROBUS *has moved his chair up left. He takes the goldfish bowl on his lap; pulls the canary cage down to the level of his face. Both the* ANIMALS *put their paws up on the arms of his chair.* MRS. ANTROBUS *faces him across the room, like a judge.*]

Mrs. Antrobus. Well?

Antrobus. [*Shortly.*] It's cold.—How things been, eh? Keck, keck, keck.—And you, Millicent?

Mrs. Antrobus. I know it's cold.

Antrobus. [*To the canary.*] No spilling of sunflower seed, eh? No singing after lights-out, y'know what I mean?

Mrs. Antrobus. You can try and prevent us freezing to death, can't you? You can do something? We can start moving. Or can we go on the animals' backs?

Antrobus. The best thing about animals is that they don't talk much.

Mammoth. It's cold.

Antrobus. Eh, eh, eh! Watch that!—

—By midnight we'd turn to ice. The roads are full of people now who can scarcely lift a foot from the ground. The grass out in front is like iron,—which reminds me, I have another needle for you.—The people up north—where are they? Frozen . . . crushed. . . .

Mrs. Antrobus. Is that what's going to happen to us?—Will you answer me?

Antrobus. I don't know. I don't know anything. Some say that the ice is going slower. Some say that it's stopped. The sun's growing cold. What can I do about that? Nothing we can do but burn everything in the house, and the fenceposts and the barn. Keep the fire going. When we have no more fire, we die.

Mrs. Antrobus. Well, why didn't you say so in the first place?

[*She is about to march off when she catches sight of two* REFUGEES, *men, who have appeared against the back wall of the stage and who are soon joined by others.*]

Refugees. Mr. Antrobus! Mr. Antrobus! Mr. An-nn-tro-bus!

Mrs. Antrobus. Who's that? Who's that calling you?

Antrobus. [*Clearing his throat guiltily.*] Hm—let me see.

[*Two* REFUGEES *come up to the window.*]

Refugee. Could we warm our hands for a moment, Mr. Antrobus? It's very cold, Mr. Antrobus.

Another Refugee. Mr. Antrobus, I wonder if you have a piece of bread or something that you could spare.

[*Silence. They wait humbly.* MRS. AN-TROBUS *stands rooted to the spot. Suddenly a knock at the door, then another hand knocking in short rapid blows.*]

Mrs. Antrobus. Who are these people? Why, they're all over the front yard. What have they come *here* for? [*Enter* SABINA.]

Sabina. Mrs. Antrobus! There are some tramps knocking at the back door.

Mrs. Antrobus. George, tell these people to go away. Tell them to move right along. I'll go and send them away from the back door. Sabina, come with me.

[*She goes out energetically.*]

Antrobus. Sabina! Stay here! I have something to say to you. [*He goes to the door and opens it a crack and talks through it.*] Ladies and gentlemen! I'll have to ask you to wait a few minutes longer. It'll be all right . . . while you're waiting you might each one pull up a stake of the fence. We'll need them all for the fireplace. There'll be coffee and sandwiches in a moment.

[SABINA *looks out door over his shoulder and suddenly extends her arm pointing, with a scream.*]

Sabina. Mr. Antrobus, what's that??—that big white thing? Mr. Antrobus, it's ICE. It's ICE!!

Antrobus. Sabina, I want you to go in the kitchen and make a lot of coffee. Make a whole pail full.

Sabina. Pail full!!

Antrobus. [*With gesture.*] And sandwiches . . . piles of them . . . like this.

Sabina. Mr. An . . . !! [*Suddenly she drops the play, and says in her own person as* MISS SOMERSET, *with surprise.*] Oh, *I* see what this part of the play means now! This means refugees. [*She starts to cross the proscenium.*] Oh, I don't like it. I don't like it.

[*She leans against the proscenium and bursts into tears.*]

Antrobus. Miss Somerset!

Voice of the Stage Manager. Miss Somerset!

Sabina. [*Energetically, to the audience.*] Ladies and gentlemen! Don't take this play serious. The world's not coming to an end. You know it's not. People exaggerate! Most people really have enough to eat and a roof over their heads. Nobody actually starves— you can always eat grass or something. That ice-business—why, it was a long, long time ago. Besides they were only savages. Savages don't love their families—not like we do.

Antrobus and Stage Manager. Miss Somerset!!

[*There is renewed knocking at the door.*]

Sabina. All right. I'll say the lines, but I won't think about the play.

[*Enter* MRS. ANTROBUS.]

Sabina. [*Parting thrust at the audience.*] And I advise *you* not to think about the play, either. [*Exit* SABINA.]

Mrs. Antrobus. George, these tramps say that you asked them to come to the house. What does this mean?

[*Knocking at the door.*]

Antrobus. Just . . . uh . . . These are a few friends, Maggie, I met on the road. Real nice, real useful people. . . .

Mrs. Antrobus. [*Back to the door.*] Now,

don't you ask them in! George Antrobus, not another soul comes in here over my dead body.

Antrobus. Maggie, there's a doctor there. Never hurts to have a good doctor in the house. We've lost a peck of children, one way and another. You can never tell when a child's throat will get stopped up. What you and I have seen——!!!

[*He puts his fingers on his throat, and imitates diphtheria.*]

Mrs. Antrobus. Well, just one person then, the Doctor. The others can go right along the road.

Antrobus. Maggie, there's an old man, particular friend of mine——

Mrs. Antrobus. I won't listen to you——

Antrobus. It was he that really started off the A.B.C.'s.

Mrs. Antrobus. I don't care if he perishes. We can do without reading or writing. We can't do without food.

Antrobus. Then let the ice come!! Drink your coffee!! I don't want any coffee if I can't drink it with some good people.

Mrs. Antrobus. Stop shouting. Who else is there trying to push us off the cliff?

Antrobus. Well, there's the man . . . who makes all the laws. Judge Moses!

Mrs. Antrobus. Judges can't help us now.

Antrobus. And if the ice melts? . . . and if we pull through? Have you and I been able to bring up Henry? What have we done?

Mrs. Antrobus. Who are those old women?

Antrobus. [*Coughs.*] Up in town there are nine sisters. There are three or four of them here. They're sort of music teachers . . . and one of them recites and one of them——

Mrs. Antrobus. That's the end. A singing troupe! Well, take your choice, live or die. Starve your own children before your face.

Antrobus. [*Gently.*] These people don't take much. They're used to starving. They'll sleep on the floor. Besides, Maggie, listen: no, listen: Who've we got in the house, but Sabina? Sabina's always afraid the worst will happen. Whose spirits can she keep up? Maggie, these people never give up. They think they'll live and work forever.

Mrs. Antrobus. [*Walks slowly to the middle of the room.*] All right, let them in. You're master here. [*Softly.*]—But these animals must go. Enough's enough. They'll soon be big enough to push the walls down, anyway. Take them away.

Antrobus. [*Sadly.*] All right. The dinosaur and mammoth——! Come on, baby, come on, Frederick. Come for a walk. That's a good little fellow.

Dinosaur. It's cold.

Antrobus. Yes, nice cold fresh air. Bracing. [*He holds the door open and the* ANIMALS *go out. He beckons to his friends. The* REFUGEES *are typical elderly out-of-works from the streets of New York today.* JUDGE MOSES *wears a skull cap.* HOMER *is a blind beggar with a guitar. The seedy crowd shuffles in and waits humbly and expectantly.* ANTROBUS *introduces them to his wife, who bows to each with a stately bend of her head.*] Make yourself at home. Maggie, this the doctor . . . m . . . Coffee'll be here in a minute. . . . Professor, this is my wife. . . . And: . . . Judge . . . Maggie, you know the Judge. [*An old blind man with a guitar.*] Maggie, you know. . . you know Homer?—Come right in, Judge.—Miss Muse —are some of your sisters here? Come right in. . . . Miss E. Muse; Miss T. Muse, Miss M. Muse.

Mrs. Antrobus. Pleased to meet you. Just . . . make yourself comfortable. Supper'll be ready in a minute.

[*She goes out, abruptly.*]

Antrobus. Make yourself at home, friends. I'll be right back.

[*He goes out. The* REFUGEES *stare about them in awe. Presently several voices start whispering "Homer! Homer!" All take it up.* HOMER *strikes a chord or two on his guitar, then starts to speak.*]

Homer.

Μῆνιν ἄειδε, θεά, Πηληϊάδεω Ἀχιλῆος,
οὐλομένην, ἣ μυρί' Ἀχαιοῖς ἄλγε' ἔθηκε,
πολλὰς δ' ἰφθίμους ψυχὰς—— [1]

[HOMER'S *face shows he is lost in thought and memory and the words die away on his lips. The* REFUGEES *likewise nod in dreamy recollection. Soon the whisper "Moses, Moses!" goes around. An aged Jew parts his beard and recites dramatically.*]

Moses.

בְּרֵאשִׁית בָּרָא אֱלֹהִים אֵת הַשָּׁמַיִם וְאֵת הָאָרֶץ׃
וְהָאָרֶץ הָיְתָה תֹהוּ וָבֹהוּ וְחֹשֶׁךְ עַל־פְּנֵי תְהוֹם
וְרוּחַ אֱלֹהִים מְרַחֶפֶת עַל־פְּנֵי הַמָּיִם׃ [2]

[*The same dying away of the words take place, and on the part of the* REFUGEES *the same retreat into recollection. Some*

---

[1] The first two and one-half lines of Homer's *Iliad*.
[2] "In the beginning God created the heaven and the earth. And the earth was without form and void, and darkness was upon the face of the deep. And the Spirit of God moved upon the face of the waters." *Genesis*, I, 2.

of them murmur, "Yes, yes." The mood is broken by the abrupt entrance of MR. *and* MRS. ANTROBUS *and* SABINA *bearing platters of sandwiches and a pail of coffee.* SABINA *stops and stares at the guests.*]

Mr. Antrobus. Sabina, pass the sandwiches.

Sabina. I thought I was working in a respectable house that had respectable guests. I'm giving my notice, Mr. Antrobus: two weeks, that's the law.

Mr. Antrobus. Sabina! Pass the sandwiches.

Sabina. Two weeks, that's the law.

Mr. Antrobus. There's the law. That's Moses.

Sabina. [*Stares.*] The Ten Commandments—FAUGH!!—[*To audience.*] That's the worst line I've ever had to say on any stage.

Antrobus. I think the best thing to do is just not to stand on ceremony, but pass the sandwiches around from left to right.— Judge, help yourself to one of these.

Mrs. Antrobus. The roads are crowded, I hear?

The Guests. [*All talking at once.*] Oh, ma'am, you can't imagine. . . . You can hardly put one foot before you . . . people are trampling one another.
[*Sudden silence.*]

Mrs. Antrobus. Well, you know what I think it is,—I think it's sun-spots!

The Guests. [*Discreet hubbub.*] Oh, you're right, Mrs. Antrobus . . . that's what it is. . . . That's what I was saying the other day.
[*Sudden silence.*]

Antrobus. Well, I don't believe the whole world's going to turn to ice. [*All eyes are fixed on him, waiting.*] I can't believe it, Judge! Have we worked for nothing? Professor! Have we just failed in the whole thing?

Mrs. Antrobus. It is certainly very strange —well fortunately on both sides of the family we come of very hearty stock.—Doctor, I want you to meet my children. They're eating their supper now. And of course I want them to meet you.

Miss M. Muse. How many children have you, Mrs. Antrobus?

Mrs. Antrobus. I have two,—a boy and a girl.

Moses. [*Softly.*] I understood you had two sons, Mrs. Antrobus.

Mrs. Antrobus. [*In blind suffering; she walks toward the footlights. In a low voice.*] Abel, Abel, my son, my son, Abel, my son, Abel, Abel, my son.

[*The* REFUGEES *move with few steps toward her as though in comfort, murmuring words in Greek, Hebrew, German, et cetera.*
A piercing shriek from the kitchen,— SABINA'S *voice. All heads turn.*]

Antrobus. What's that?

[SABINA *enters, bursting with indignation, pulling on her gloves.*]

Sabina. Mr. Antrobus—that son of yours, that boy Henry Antrobus—I don't stay in this house another moment!—He's not fit to live among respectable folks and that's a fact.

Mrs. Antrobus. Don't say another word, Sabina. I'll be right back.

[*Without waiting for an answer she goes past her into the kitchen.*]

Sabina. Mr. Antrobus, Henry has thrown a stone again and if he hasn't killed the boy that lives next door, I'm very much mistaken. He finished his supper and went out to play; and I heard such a fight; and then I saw it. I saw it with my own eyes. And it looked to me like stark murder.

[MRS. ANTROBUS *appears at the kitchen door, shielding* HENRY, *who follows her. When she steps aside, we see on* HENRY'S *forehead a large ochre and scarlet scar in the shape of a* C. MR. ANTROBUS *starts toward him. A pause.*]

Henry. [*Under his breath.*] He was going to take the wheel away from me. He started to throw a stone at me first.

Mrs. Antrobus. George, it was just a boyish impulse. Remember how young he is. [*Louder, in an urgent wail.*] George, he's only four thousand years old.

Sabina. And everything was going along so nicely!

[*Silence.* ANTROBUS *goes back to the fireplace.*]

Antrobus. Put out the fire! Put out all the fires. [*Violently.*] No wonder the sun grows cold. [*He starts stamping on the fireplace.*]

Mrs. Antrobus. Doctor! Judge! Help me!—George, have you lost your mind?

Antrobus. There is no mind. We'll not try to live. [*To the* GUESTS.] Give it up. Give up trying.   [MRS. ANTROBUS *seizes him.*]

Sabina. Mr. Antrobus! I'm downright ashamed of you.

Mrs. Antrobus. George, have some more coffee.—Gladys! Where's Gladys gone?

[GLADYS *steps in, frightened.*]

Gladys. Here I am, mama.

Mrs. Antrobus. Go upstairs and bring your father's slippers. How could you forget a thing like that, when you know how tired he is? [ANTROBUS *sits in his chair. He covers his face with his hands.* Mrs. Antrobus *turns to the* Refugees.] Can't some of you sing? It's your business in life to sing, isn't it? Sabina! [*Several of the women clear their throats tentatively, and with frightened faces gather around* Homer's *guitar. He establishes a few chords. Almost inaudibly they start singing, led by* Sabina: "Jingle Bells." Mrs. Antrobus *to* Antrobus *in a low voice, while taking off his shoes.*] George, remember all the other times. When the volcanoes came right up in the front yard.

And the time the grasshoppers ate every single leaf and blade of grass, and all the grain and spinach you'd grown with your own hands. And the summer there were earthquakes every night.

Antrobus. Henry! Henry! [*Puts his hand on his forehead.*] Myself. All of us, we're covered with blood.

Mrs. Antrobus. Then remember all the times you were pleased with him and when you were proud of yourself.—Henry! Henry! Come here and recite to your father the multiplication table that you do so nicely.

[Henry *kneels on one knee beside his father and starts whispering the multiplication table.*]

Henry. [*Finally.*] Two times six is twelve; three times six is eighteen—I don't think I know the sixes.

[*Enter* Gladys *with the slippers.* Mrs. Antrobus *makes stern gestures to her: Go in there and do your best. The* Guests *are now singing "Tenting Tonight."*]

Gladys. [*Putting slippers on his feet.*] Papa . . . papa . . . I was very good in school today. Miss Conover said right out in class that if all the girls had as good manners as Gladys Antrobus, that the world would be a very different place to live in.

Mrs. Antrobus. You recited a piece at assembly, didn't you? Recite it to your father.

Gladys. Papa, do you want to hear what I recited in class? [*Fierce directorial glance from her* mother.] "THE STAR" by Henry Wadsworth Longfellow.

Mrs. Antrobus. Wait!!! The fire's going out. There isn't enough wood! Henry, go upstairs and bring down the chairs and start breaking up the beds.

[*Exit* Henry. *The singers return to "Jingle Bells," still very softly.*]

Gladys. Look, Papa, here's my report card. Lookit. Conduct A! Look, Papa. Papa, do you want to hear "The Star," by Henry Wadsworth Longfellow? Papa, you're not mad at me, are you?—I know it'll get

warmer. Soon it'll be just like spring, and we can go to a picnic at the Hibernian Picnic Grounds like you always like to do, don't you remember? Papa, just look at me once.

[*Enter* Henry *with some chairs.*]

Antrobus. You recited in assembly, did you? [*She nods eagerly.*] You didn't forget it?

Gladys. No!!! I was perfect.

[*Pause. Then* Antrobus *rises, goes to the front door and opens it. The* Refugees *draw back timidly; the song stops; he peers out of the door, then closes it.*]

Antrobus. [*With decision, suddenly.*] Build up the fire. It's cold. Build up the fire. We'll do what we can. Sabina, get some more wood. Come around the fire, everybody. At least the young ones may pull through. Henry, have you eaten something?

Henry. Yes, Papa.

Antrobus. Gladys, have you had some supper?

Gladys. I ate in the kitchen, papa.

Antrobus. If you do come through this—what'll you be able to do? What do you know? Henry, did you take a good look at that wheel?

Henry. Yes, papa.

Antrobus. [*Sitting down in his chair.*] Six times two are——

Henry. —twelve; six times three are eighteen; six times four are—Papa, it's hot and cold. It makes my head all funny. It makes me sleepy.

Antrobus. [*Gives him a cuff.*] Wake up. I don't care if your head is sleepy. Six times four are twenty-four. Six times five are——

Henry. Thirty. Papa!

Antrobus. Maggie, put something into Gladys' head on the chance she can use it.

Mrs. Antrobus. What do you mean, George?

Antrobus. Six times six are thirty-six. Teach her the beginning of the Bible.

Gladys. But, mama, it's so cold and close.

[Henry *has all but drowsed off. His* Father *slaps him sharply and the lesson goes on.*]

Mrs. Antrobus. "In the beginning God created the heavens and the earth; and the earth was waste and void; and the darkness was upon the face of the deep——"

[*The singing starts up again louder.* Sabina *has returned with wood.*]

Sabina. [*After placing wood on the fireplace comes down to the footlights and addresses the audience.*] Will you please start handing up your chairs? We'll need everything for this fire. Save the human race.— Ushers, will you pass the chairs up here? Thank you.

Henry. Six times nine are fifty-four; six times ten are sixty.

[*In the back of the auditorium the sound of chairs being ripped up can be heard.* USHERS *rush down the aisles with chairs and hand them over.*]

Gladys. "And God called the light Day and the darkness he called Night."

Sabina. Pass up your chairs, everybody. Save the human race.

CURTAIN

ACT II

Toward the end of the intermission, though with the houselights still up, lantern slide projections begin to appear on the curtain. Timetables for trains leaving Pennsylvania Station for Atlantic City. Advertisements of Atlantic City hotels, drugstores, churches, rug merchants; fortune tellers, Bingo parlors.

When the houselights go down, the voice of an ANNOUNCER *is heard.*

Announcer. The Management now brings you the News Events of the World. Atlantic City, New Jersey:

[*Projection of a chrome postcard of the waterfront, trimmed in mica with the legend: FUN AT THE BEACH.*]

This great convention city is playing host this week to the anniversary convocation of that great fraternal order,— the Ancient and Honorable Order of Mammals, Subdivision Humans. This great fraternal, militant and burial society is celebrating on the Boardwalk, ladies and gentlemen, its six-hundred-thousandth Annual Convention. It has just elected its president for the ensuing term,— [*Projection of* MR. *and* MRS. ANTROBUS *posed as they will be shown a few moments later.*] Mr. George Antrobus of Excelsior, New Jersey. We show you President Antrobus and his gracious and charming wife, every inch a mammal. Mr. Antrobus has had a long and chequered career. Credit has been paid to him for many useful enterprises including the introduction of the lever, of the wheel, and the brewing of beer. Credit has been also extended to President Antrobus's gracious and charming wife for many practical suggestions, including the hem, the gore, and the gusset; and the novelty of the year,—frying in oil. Before we show you Mr. An-

trobus accepting the nomination, we have an important announcement to make. As many of you know, this great celebration of the Order of the Mammals has received delegations from the other rival Orders,—or shall we say: esteemed concurrent Orders: the WINGS, the FINS, the SHELLS, and so on. These Orders are holding their conventions also, in various parts of the world, and have sent representatives to our own, two of a kind.

Later in the day we will show you President Antrobus broadcasting his words of greeting and congratulation to the collected assemblies of the whole natural world.

Ladies and Gentlemen! We give you President Antrobus!

[*The screen becomes a Transparency.* MR. ANTROBUS *stands beside a pedestal;* MRS. ANTROBUS *is seated wearing a corsage of orchids.* ANTROBUS *wears an untidy Prince Albert; spats; from a red rosette in his buttonhole hangs a fine long purple ribbon of honor. He wears a gay lodge hat,—something between a fez and a legionnaire's cap.*]

Antrobus. Fellow-mammals, fellow-vertebrates, fellow-humans, I thank you. Little did my parents think,—when they told me to stand on my own two feet,—that I'd arrive at this place.

My friends, we have come a long way.

During this week of happy celebration it is perhaps not fitting that we dwell on some of the difficult times we have been through. The dinosaur is extinct— [*Applause.*] —the ice has retreated; and the common cold is being pursued by every means within our power. [MRS. ANTROBUS *sneezes, laughs prettily, and murmurs: "I beg your pardon."*] In our memorial service yesterday we did honor to all our friends and relatives who are no longer with us, by reason of cold, earth-quakes, plagues and . . . and [*Coughs.*] differences of opinion.

As our Bishop so ably said . . . uh . . . so ably said. . . .

Mrs. Antrobus. [*Closed lips.*] Gone, but not forgotten.

Antrobus. 'They are gone, but not forgotten.' I think I can say, I think I can prophesy with complete . . . uh . . . with complete. . . .

Mrs. Antrobus. Confidence.

Antrobus. Thank you, my dear.—With complete lack of confidence, that a new day of security is about to dawn. The watchword of the closing year was: Work. I give you the watchword for the future: Enjoy Your-selves.

Mrs. Antrobus. George, sit down!

Antrobus. Before I close, however, I wish to answer one of those unjust and malicious accusations that were brought against me during this last electoral campaign.

Ladies and gentlemen, the charge was made that at various points in my career I leaned toward joining some of the rival orders,—that's a lie.

As I told reporters of the *Atlantic City Herald*, I do not deny that a few months be-fore my birth I hesitated between . . . uh . . . between pinfeathers and gill-breathing, —and so did many of us here,—but for the last million years I have been viviparous, hairy, and diaphragmatic.

[*Applause. Cries of 'Good old Antro-bus,' 'The Prince chap!' 'Georgie,' etc.*]

Announcer. [*Off-stage.*] Thank you. Thank you very much, Mr. Antrobus. Now I know that our visitors will wish to hear a word from that gracious and charming mam-mal, Mrs. Antrobus, wife and mother,—Mrs. Antrobus!

Mrs. Antrobus. [*Rises, lays her program on her chair, bows and says.*] Dear friends, I don't really think I should say anything. After all, it was my husband who was elected and not I.

Perhaps, as president of the Women's Auxiliary Bed and Board Society,—I had some notes here, oh, yes, here they are:—I should give a short report from some of our committees that have been meeting in this beautiful city.

Perhaps it may interest you to know that it has at last been decided that the tomato is edible. Can you all hear me? The tomato *is* edible.

A delegate from across the sea reports that the thread woven by the silkworm gives a cloth . . . I have a sample of it here . . . can you see it? smooth, elastic. I should say that it's rather attractive,—though per-sonally I prefer less shiny surfaces. Should the windows of a sleeping apartment be open or shut? I know all mothers will follow our debates on this matter with close inter-est. I am sorry to say that the most expert authorities have not yet decided. It does seem to me that the night air would be bound to be unhealthy for our children, but there are many distinguished authorities on both sides. Well, I could go on talking for-ever,—as Shakespeare says: a woman's work is seldom done; but I think I'd better join my husband in saying thank you, and sit down. Thank you. [*She sits down.*]

Announcer. Oh, Mrs. Antrobus!

Mrs. Antrobus. Yes?

Announcer. We understand that you are about to celebrate a wedding anniversary. I know our listeners would like to extend their felicitations and hear a few words from you on that subject.

Mrs. Antrobus. I have been asked by this kind gentleman . . . yes, my friends, this Spring Mr. Antrobus and I will be celebrat-ing our five-thousandth wedding anniversary.

I don't know if I speak for my husband, but I can say that, as for me, I regret every moment of it. [*Laughter of confusion.*]

I beg your pardon. What I *mean* to say is that I do not regret one moment of it. I hope none of you catch my cold. We have two children. We've always had two children, though it hasn't always been the same two. But as I say, we have two fine children, and we're very grateful for that. Yes, Mr. Antro-bus and I have been married five-thousand years. Each wedding anniversary reminds me of the times when there were no weddings. We had to crusade for marriage. Perhaps there are some women within the sound of my voice who remember that crusade and those struggles; we fought for it, didn't we? We chained ourselves to lampposts and we made disturbances in the Senate,—anyway, at last we women got the ring.

A few men helped us, but I must say that most men blocked our way at every step: they said we were unfeminine.

I only bring up these unpleasant memories, because I see some signs of backsliding from that great victory.

Oh, my fellow mammals, keep hold of that.

My husband says that the watchword for the year is Enjoy Yourselves. I think that's very open to misunderstanding. My watchword for the year is: Save the family. It's held together for over five thousand years: Save it! Thank you.

Announcer. Thank you, Mrs. Antrobus. [*The transparency disappears.*] We had hoped to show you the Beauty Contest that took place here today. President Antrobus, an experienced judge of pretty girls, gave the title of Miss Atlantic City 1942, to Miss Lily-Sabina Fairweather, charming hostess of our Boardwalk Bingo Parlor. Unfortunately, however, our time is up, and I must take you to some views of the Convention City and conveeners,—enjoying themselves.

[*A burst of music; the curtain rises. The Boardwalk. The audience is sitting in the ocean. A handrail of scarlet cord stretches across the front of the stage. A ramp—also with scarlet hand rail— descends to the right corner of the orchestra pit where a great scarlet beach umbrella or a cabana stands. Front and right stage left are benches facing the sea; attached to each bench is a streetlamp. The only scenery is two cardboard cut-outs six feet high, representing shops at the back of the stage. Reading from left to right they are:* SALT WATER TAFFY; FORTUNE TELLER; *then the blank space;* BINGO PARLOR; TURKISH BATH. *They have practical doors, that of the Fortune Teller's being hung with bright gypsy curtains. By the left proscenium and rising from the orchestra pit is the weather signal; it is like the mast of a ship with cross bars. From time to time black discs are hung on it to indicate the storm and hurricane warnings. Three roller chairs, pushed by melancholy* NEGROES *file by empty. Throughout the act they traverse the stage in both directions. From time to time,* CONVEENERS, *dressed like* MR. ANTROBUS, *cross the stage. Some walk sedately by; others engage in inane horseplay. The old gypsy* FORTUNE TELLER *is seated at the door of her shop, smoking a corncob pipe. From the Bingo Parlor comes the voice of the* CALLER.]

Bingo Caller. A-Nine; A-Nine. C-Twenty-six; C-Twenty-six. A-Four; A-Four. B-Twelve.

Chorus. [*Backstage.*] Bingo!!!

[*The front of the Bingo Parlor shudders, rises a few feet in the air and returns to the ground trembling.*]

Fortune Teller. [*Mechanically, to the unconscious back of a passerby, pointing with her pipe.*] Bright's disease! Your partner's deceiving you in that Kansas City deal. You'll have six grandchildren. Avoid high places. [*She rises and shouts after another.*] Cirrhosis of the liver!

[SABINA *appears at the door of the Bingo Parlor. She hugs about her a blue raincoat that almost conceals her red bathing suit. She tries to catch the* FORTUNE TELLER'S *attention.*]

Sabina. Ssssst! Esmeralda! Ssssst!

Fortune Teller. Keck!

Sabina. Has President Antrobus come along yet?

Fortune Teller. No, no, no. Get back there. Hide yourself.

Sabina. I'm afraid I'll miss him. Oh, Esmeralda, if I fail in this, I'll die; I know I'll die. President Antrobus!!! And I'll be his wife! If it's the last thing I'll do, I'll be Mrs. George Antrobus.—Esmeralda, tell me my future.

Fortune Teller. Keck!

Sabina. All right, I'll tell *you* my future. [*Laughing dreamily and tracing it out with one finger on the palm of her hand.*] I've won the Beauty Contest in Atlantic City,— well. I'll win the Beauty Contest of the whole world. I'll take President Antrobus away from that wife of his. Then I'll take every man away from his wife. I'll turn the whole earth upside down.

Fortune Teller. Keck!

Sabina. When all those husbands just think about me they'll get dizzy. They'll faint in the streets. They'll have to lean against lampposts.—Esmeralda, who was Helen of Troy?

Fortune Teller. [*Furiously.*] Shut your foolish mouth. When Mr. Antrobus comes along you can see what you can do. Until then,—go away.

[SABINA *laughs. As she returns to the door of her Bingo Parlor a group of* CONVEENERS *rush over and smother her with attentions: "Oh, Miss Lily, you know me. You've known me for years."*]

Sabina. Go away, boys, go away. I'm after bigger fry than you are.—Why, Mr. Simpson!! How *dare* you!! I expect that even you nobodies must have girls to amuse you; but where you find them and what you do with them, is of absolutely no interest to me.

[*Exit. The* CONVEENERS *squeal with pleasure and stumble in after her. The* FORTUNE TELLER *rises, puts her pipe down on the stool, unfurls her voluminous skirts, gives a sharp wrench to her bodice and strolls towards the audience, swinging her hips like a young woman.*]

Fortune Teller. I tell the future. Keck. Nothing easier. Everybody's future is in their face. Nothing easier.

But who can tell your past,—eh? Nobody!

Your youth,—where did it go? It slipped away while you weren't looking. While you were asleep. While you were drunk. Puh! You're like our friends, Mr. and Mrs. Antrobus; you lie awake nights trying to know your past. What did it mean? What was it trying to say to you?

Think! Think! Split your heads. I can't tell the past and neither can you. If anybody tries to tell you the past, take my word for it, they're charlatans! Charlatans! But I can tell the future. [*She suddenly barks at a passing chair-pusher.*] Apoplexy! [*She returns to the audience.*] Nobody listens.—Keck! I see a face among you now— I won't embarrass him by pointing him out, but, listen, it may be you: Next year the watchsprings inside you will crumple up. Death by regret,—Type Y. It's in the corners of your mouth. You'll decide that you should have lived for pleasure, but that you missed it. Death by regret,—Type Y. . . . Avoid mirrors. You'll try to be angry,—but no!—no anger. [*Far forward, confidentially.*] And now what's the immediate future of our friends, the Antrobuses? Oh, you've seen it as well as I have, keck,—that dizziness of the head; that Great Man dizziness? The inventor of beer and gunpowder? The sudden fits of temper and then the long stretches of inertia? "I'm a sultan; let my slave-girls fan me?"

You know as well as I what's coming. Rain. Rain. Rain in floods. The deluge. But first you'll see shameful things— shameful things. Some of you will be saying: "Let him drown. He's not worth saving. Give the whole thing up." I can see it in your faces. But you're wrong. Keep your doubts and despairs to yourselves.

Again there'll be the narrow escape. The survival of a handful. From destruction,— total destruction. [*She points sweeping with her hand to the stage.*] Even of the animals, a few will be saved: two of a kind, male and female, two of a kind. [*The heads of* CONVEENERS *appear about the stage and in the orchestra pit, jeering at her.*]

Conveeners. Charlatan! Madam Kill-joy! Mrs. Jeremiah! Charlatan!

Fortune Teller. And *you!* Mark my words before it's too late. Where'll *you* be?

Conveeners. The croaking raven. Old dust and ashes. Rags, bottles, sacks.

Fortune Teller. Yes, stick out your tongues. You can't stick your tongues out far enough to lick the death-sweat from your foreheads. It's too late to work now—bail out the flood with your soup spoons. You've had your chance and you've lost.

Conveeners. Enjoy yourselves!!!

[*They disappear. The* FORTUNE TELLER *looks off left and puts her finger on her lip.*]

Fortune Teller. They're coming—the Antrobuses. Keck. Your hope. Your despair. Your selves.

[*Enter from the left,* MR. *and* MRS. ANTROBUS *and* GLADYS.]

Mrs. Antrobus. Gladys Antrobus, stick your stummick in.

Gladys. But it's easier this way.

Mrs. Antrobus. Well, it's too bad the new president has such a clumsy daughter, that's all I can say. Try and be a lady.

Fortune Teller. Aijah! That's been said a hundred billion times.

Mrs. Antrobus. Goodness! Where's Henry? He was here just a minute ago. Henry!

[*Sudden violent stir. A roller-chair appears from the left. About it are dancing in great excitement* HENRY *and a* NEGRO CHAIR-PUSHER.]

Henry. [*Slingshot in hand.*] I'll put your eye out. I'll make you yell, like you never yelled before.

Negro. [*At the same time.*] Now, I warns you. I warns you. If you make me mad, you'll get hurt.

Antrobus. Henry! What is this? Put down that slingshot.

Mrs. Antrobus. [*At the same time.*] Henry! HENRY! Behave yourself.

Fortune Teller. That's right, young man. There are too many people in the world as it is. Everybody's in the way, except one's self.

Henry. All I wanted to do was—have some fun.

Negro. Nobody can't touch my chair, nobody, without I allow 'em to. You get clean away from me and you get away fast.

[*He pushes his chair off, muttering.*]

Antrobus. What were you doing, Henry?

Henry. Everybody's always getting mad. Everybody's always trying to push you around. I'll make him sorry for this; I'll make him sorry.

Antrobus. Give me that slingshot.

Henry. I won't. I'm sorry I came to this place. I wish I weren't here. I wish I weren't anywhere.

Mrs. Antrobus. Now, Henry, don't get so

excited about nothing. I declare I don't know what we're going to do with you. Put your slingshot in your pocket, and don't try to take hold of things that don't belong to you.

Antrobus. After this you can stay home. I wash my hands of you.

Mrs. Antrobus. Come now, let's forget all about it. Everybody take a good breath of that sea air and calm down. [*A passing CONVEENER bows to ANTROBUS who nods to him.*] Who was that you spoke to, George?

Antrobus. Nobody, Maggie. Just the candidate who ran against me in the election.

Mrs. Antrobus. The man who ran against you in the election!! [*She turns and waves her umbrella after the disappearing CONVEENER.*] My husband didn't speak to you and he never will speak to you.

Antrobus. Now, Maggie.

Mrs. Atrobus. After those lies you told about him in your speeches! Lies, that's what they were.

Gladys and Henry. Mama, everybody's looking at you. Everybody's laughing at you.

Mrs. Antrobus. If you must know, my husband's a SAINT, a downright SAINT, and you're not fit to speak to him on the street.

Antrobus. Now, Maggie, now, Maggie, that's enough of that.

Mrs. Antrobus. George Antrobus, you're a perfect worm. If you won't stand up for yourself, I will.

Gladys. Mama, you just act awful in public.

Mrs. Antrobus. [*Laughing.*] Well, I must say I enjoyed it. I feel better. Wish his wife had been there to hear it. Children, what do you want to do?

Gladys. Papa, can we ride in one of those chairs? Mama, I want to ride in one of those chairs.

Mrs. Antrobus. No, sir. If you're tired you just sit where you are. We have no money to spend on foolishness.

Antrobus. I guess we have money enough for a thing like that. It's one of the things you do at Atlantic City.

Mrs. Antrobus. Oh, we have? I tell you it's a miracle my children have shoes to stand up in. I didn't think I'd ever live to see them pushed around in chairs.

Antrobus. We're on a vacation, aren't we? We have a right to some treats, I guess. Maggie, some day you're going to drive me crazy.

Mrs. Antrobus. All right, go. I'll just sit here and laugh at you. And you can give me my dollar right in my hand. Mark my words, a rainy day is coming. There's a rainy day

ahead of us. I feel it in my bones. Go on, throw your money around. I can starve. I've starved before. I know how.

[*A CONVEENER puts his head through Turkish Bath window, and says with raised eyebrows.*]

Conveener. Hello, George. How are ya? I see where you brought the *whole* family along.

Mrs. Antrobus. And what do you mean by that?

[*CONVEENER withdraws head and closes window.*]

Antrobus. Maggie, I tell you there's a limit to what I can stand. God's Heaven, haven't I worked *enough*? Don't I get *any* vacation? Can't I even give my children so much as a ride in a roller-chair?

Mrs. Antrobus. [*Putting out her hand for raindrops.*] Anyway, it's going to rain very soon and you have your broadcast to make.

Antrobus. Now, Maggie, I warn you. A man can stand a family only just so long. I'm warning you.

[*Enter SABINA from the Bingo-Parlor. She wears a flounced red silk bathing suit, 1905. Red stockings, shoes, parasol. She bows demurely to ANTROBUS and starts down the ramp. ANTROBUS and the CHILDREN stare at her. ANTROBUS bows gallantly.*]

Mrs. Antrobus. Why, George Antrobus, how can you say such a thing! You have the best family in the world.

Antrobus. Good morning, Miss Fairweather.

[*SABINA finally disappears behind the beach umbrella or in a cabana in the orchestra pit.*]

Mrs. Antrobus. Who on earth was that you spoke to, George?

Antrobus. [*Complacent; mock-modest.*] Hm . . . m . . . just a . . . solambaka keray.[1]

Mrs. Antrobus. What? I can't understand you.

Gladys. Mama, wasn't she beautiful?

Henry. Papa, introduce her to me.

Mrs. Antrobus. Children, will you be quiet while I ask your father a simple question?—Who did you say it was, George?

Antrobus. Why-uh . . . a friend of mine. Very nice refined girl.

Mrs. Antrobus. I'm waiting.

Antrobus. Maggie, that's the girl I gave the prize to in the beauty contest,—that's Miss Atlantic City 1942.[2]

---

[1] A portmanteau word, in imitation of those found in *Finnegans Wake.*
[2] This date is changed to the year of performance.

Mrs. Antrobus. Hm! She looked like Sabina to me.

Henry. [*At the railing.*] Mama, the lifeguard knows her, too. Mama, he knows her well.

Antrobus. Henry, come here.—She's a very nice girl in every way and the sole support of her aged mother.

Mrs. Antrobus. So was Sabina, so was Sabina; and it took a wall of ice to open your eyes about Sabina.—Henry, come over and sit down on this bench.

Antrobus. She's a very different matter from Sabina. Miss Fairweather is a college graduate, Phi Beta Kappa.

Mrs. Antrobus. Henry, you sit here by mama. Gladys——

Antrobus. [*Sitting.*] Reduced circumstances have required her taking a position as hostess in a Bingo Parlor; but there isn't a girl with higher principles in the country.

Mrs. Antrobus. Well, let's not talk about it.—Henry, I haven't seen a whale yet.

Antrobus. She speaks seven languages and has more culture in her little finger than you've acquired in a lifetime.

Mrs. Antrobus. [*Assumed amiability.*] All right, all right, George. I'm glad to know there are such superior girls in the Bingo Parlors.—Henry, what's that?

[*Pointing at the storm signal, which has one black disk.*]

Henry. What is it, papa?

Antrobus. What? Oh, that's the storm signal. One of those black disks means bad weather; two means storm; three means hurricane; and four means the end of the world.

[*As they watch it a second black disk rolls into place.*]

Mrs. Antrobus. Goodness! I'm going this very minute to buy you all some raincoats.

Gladys. [*Putting her cheek against her father's shoulder.*] Mama, don't go yet. I like sitting this way. And the ocean coming in and coming in. Papa, don't you like it?

Mrs. Antrobus. Well, there's only one thing I lack to make me a perfectly happy woman: I'd like to see a whale.

Henry. Mama, we saw two. Right out there. They're delegates to the convention. I'll find you one.

Gladys. Papa, ask me something. Ask me a question.

Antrobus. Well . . . how big's the ocean?

Gladys. Papa, you're teasing me. It's—three-hundred and sixty million square-miles—and—it—covers—three-fourths—of—the—earth's—surface—and—its—deepest—place—is—five—and—a—half—miles—deep—and—its—average—depth—is—twelve—thousand—feet. No, Papa, ask me something hard, real hard.

Mrs. Antrobus. [*Rising.*] Now I'm going off to buy those raincoats. I think that bad weather's going to get worse and worse. I hope it doesn't come before your broadcast. I should think we have about an hour or so.

Henry. I hope it comes and zzzzzz everything before it. I hope it——

Mrs. Antrobus. Henry!—George, I think . . . . maybe, it's one of those storms that are just as bad on land as on the sea. When you're just as safe and safer in a good stout boat.

Henry. There's a boat out at the end of the pier.

Mrs. Antrobus. Well, keep your eye on it. George, you shut your eyes and get a good rest before the broadcast.

Antrobus. Thundering Judas, do I have to be told when to open and shut my eyes? Go and buy your raincoats.

Mrs. Antrobus. Now, children, you have ten minutes to walk around. Ten minutes. And, Henry: control yourself. Gladys, stick by your brother and don't get lost.

[*They run off.*]

Mrs. Antrobus. Will you be all right, George?

[CONVEENERS *suddenly stick their heads out of the Bingo Parlor and Salt Water Taffy store, and voices rise from the orchestra pit.*]

Conveeners. George. Geo-r-r-rge! George! Leave the old hen-coop at home, George. Domes-ticated Georgie!

Mrs. Antrobus. [*Shaking her umbrella.*] Low common oafs! That's what they are. Guess a man has a right to bring his wife to a convention, if he wants to. [*She starts off.*] What's the matter with a family, I'd like to know. What else have they got to offer?

[*Exit.* ANTROBUS *has closed his eyes. The* FORTUNE TELLER *comes out of her shop and goes over to the left proscenium. She leans against it watching* SABINA *quizzically.*]

Fortune Teller. Heh! Here she comes!

Sabina. [*Loud whisper.*] What's he doing?

Fortune Teller. Oh, he's ready for you. Bite your lips, dear, take a long breath and come on up.

Sabina. I'm nervous. My whole future depends on this. I'm nervous.

Fortune Teller. Don't be a fool. What more could you want? He's forty-five. His head's a little dizzy. He's just been elected president. He's never known any other woman than his wife. Whenever he looks at her he realizes that she knows every foolish thing he's ever done.

Sabina. [*Still whispering.*] I don't know why it is, but every time I start one of these I'm nervous.

[*The* FORTUNE TELLER *stands in the center of the stage watching the following.*]

Fortune Teller. You make me tired.

Sabina. First tell me my fortune. [*The* FORTUNE TELLER *laughs drily and makes the gesture of brushing away a nonsensical question.* SABINA *coughs and says.*] Oh, Mr. Antrobus,—dare I speak to you for a moment?

Antrobus. What?—Oh, certainly, certainly, Miss Fairweather.

Sabina. Mr. Antrobus . . . I've been so unhappy. I've wanted . . . I've wanted to make sure that you don't think that I'm the kind of girl who goes out for beauty contests.

Fortune Teller. That's the way!

Antrobus. Oh, I understand. I understand perfectly.

Fortune Teller. Give it a little more. Lean on it.

Sabina. I knew you would. My mother said to me this morning: Lily, she said, that fine Mr. Antrobus gave you the prize because he saw at once that you weren't the kind of girl who'd go in for a thing like that. But, honestly, Mr. Antrobus, in this world, honestly, a good girl doesn't know where to turn.

Fortune Teller. Now you've gone too far.

Antrobus. My dear Miss Fairweather!

Sabina. You wouldn't know how hard it is. With that lovely wife and daughter you have. Oh, I think Mrs. Antrobus is the finest woman I ever saw. I wish I were like her.

Antrobus. There, there. There's . . . uh . . . room for all kinds of people in the world, Miss Fairweather.

Sabina. How wonderful of you to say that. How generous!—Mr. Antrobus, have you a moment free? . . . I'm afraid I may be a little conspicuous here . . . could you come down, for just a moment, to my beach cabana . . . ?

Antrobus. Why-uh . . . yes, certainly . . . for a moment . . . just for a moment.

Sabina. There's a deck chair there. Because: you know you *do* look tired. Just this morning my mother said to me: Lily, she said, I hope Mr. Antrobus is getting a good rest. His fine strong face has deep, deep lines in it. Now isn't it true, Mr. Antrobus: you work too hard?

Fortune Teller. Bingo!

[*She goes into her shop.*]

Sabina. Now you will just stretch out. No, I shan't say a word, not a word. I shall

just sit there,—privileged. That's what I am.

Antrobus. [*Taking her hand.*] Miss Fairweather . . . you'll . . . spoil me.

Sabina. Just a moment. I have something I wish to say to the audience.—Ladies and gentlemen. I'm not going to play this particular scene tonight. It's just a short scene and we're going to skip it. But I'll tell you what takes place and then we can continue the play from there on. Now in this scene—

Antrobus. [*Between his teeth.*] But, Miss Somerset!

Sabina. I'm sorry. I'm sorry. But I have to skip it. In this scene, I talk to Mr. Antrobus, and at the end of it he decides to leave his wife, get a divorce at Reno and marry me. That's all.

Antrobus. Fitz!—Fitz!

Sabina. So that now I've told you we can jump to the end of it,—where you say——

[*Enter in fury* MR. FITZPATRICK, *the stage manager.*]

Mr. Fitzpatrick. Miss Somerset, we insist on your playing this scene.

Sabina. I'm sorry, Mr. Fitzpatrick, but I can't and I won't. I've told the audience all they need to know and now we can go on.

[*Other* ACTORS *begin to appear on the stage, listening.*]

Mr. Fitzpatrick. And *why* can't you play it?

Sabina. Because there are some lines in that scene that would hurt some people's feelings and I don't think the theatre is a place where people's feelings ought to be hurt.

Mr. Fitzpatrick. Miss Somerset, you can pack up your things and go home. I shall call the understudy and I shall report you to Equity.

Sabina. I sent the understudy up to the corner for a cup of coffee and if Equity tries to penalize me I'll drag the case right up to the Supreme Court. Now listen, everybody, there's no need to get excited.

Mr. Fitzpatrick and Antrobus. Why can't you play it? . . . what's the matter with the scene?

Sabina. Well, if you must know, I have a personal guest in the audience tonight. Her life hasn't been exactly a happy one. I wouldn't have my friend hear some of these lines for the whole world. I don't suppose it occurred to the author that some other women might have gone through the experience of losing their husbands like this. Wild horses wouldn't drag from me the details of my friend's life . . . well, they'd been married twenty years, and before he got rich, why, she'd done the washing and everything.

Mr. Fitzpatrick. Miss Somerset, your friend will forgive you. We must play this scene.

Sabina. Nothing, nothing will make me say some of those lines . . . about "a man outgrows a wife every seven years" and . . . and that one about "the Mohammedans being the only people who looked the subject square in the face." Nothing.

Mr. Fitzpatrick. Miss Somerset! Go to your dressing room. I'll *read* your lines.

Sabina. Now everybody's nerves are on edge.

Mr. Antrobus. Skip the scene.

[MR. FITZPATRICK *and the other* ACTORS *go off*].

Sabina. Thank you. I knew you'd understand. We'll do just what I said. So Mr. Antrobus is going to divorce his wife and marry me. Mr. Antrobus, you say: "It won't be easy to lay all this before my wife."

[*The* ACTORS *withdraw.*]

Antrobus. [*Walks about, his hand to his forehead muttering.*] Wait a minute. I can't get back into it as easily as all that. "My wife is a very obstinate woman." Hm . . . then you say . . . hm . . . Miss Fairweather, I mean Lily, it won't be easy to lay all this before my wife. It'll hurt her feelings a little.

Sabina. Listen, George: *other* people haven't got feelings. Not in the same way that we have,—we who are presidents like you and prize-winners like me. Listen, other people haven't got feelings; they just imagine they have. Within two weeks they go back to playing bridge and going to the movies. Listen, dear: everybody in the world except a few people like you and me are just people of straw. Most people have no insides at all. Now that you're president you'll see that. Listen, darling, there's a kind of secret society at the top of the world,—like you and me,—that know this. The world was made for us. What's life anyway? Except for two things, pleasure and power, what is life? Boredom! Foolishness. You know it is. Except for those two things, life's nau-se-at-ing. So,—come here! [*She moves close. They kiss.*] So.

Now when your wife comes, it's really very simple; just tell her.

Antrobus. Lily, Lily: you're a wonderful woman.

Sabina. Of course I am.

[*They enter the cabana and it hides them from view. Distant roll of thunder. A third black disk appears on the weather signal. Distant thunder is heard.* MRS. ANTROBUS *appears carrying parcels. She looks about, seats herself on the bench left, and fans herself with her handkerchief. Enter* GLADYS *right, followed by two* CONVEENERS. *She is wearing red stockings.*]

Mrs. Antrobus. Gladys!

Gladys. Mama, here I am.

Mrs. Antrobus. Gladys Antrobus!!! Where did you get those dreadful things?

Gladys. Wha-a-t? Papa liked the color.

Mrs. Antrobus. You go back to the hotel this minute!

Gladys. I won't. I won't. Papa liked the color.

Mrs. Antrobus. All right. All right. You stay here. I've a good mind to let your father see you that way. You stay right here.

Gladys. I . . . I don't want to stay if . . . if you don't think he'd like it.

Mrs. Antrobus. Oh . . . it's all one to me. I don't care what happens. I don't care if the biggest storm in the whole world comes. Let it come. [*She folds her hands.*] Where's your brother?

Gladys. [*In a small voice.*] He'll be here.

Mrs. Antrobus. Will he? Well, let him get into trouble. I don't care. I don't know where your father is, I'm sure.

[*Laughter from the cabana.*]

Gladys. [*Leaning over the rail.*] I think he's . . . Mama, he's talking to the lady in the red dress.

Mrs. Antrobus. Is that so? [*Pause.*] We'll wait till he's through. Sit down here beside me and stop fidgeting . . . what are you crying about?

[*Distant thunder. She covers* GLADYS's *stockings with a raincoat.*]

Gladys. You don't like my stockings.

[*Two* CONVEENERS *rush in with a microphone on a standard and various paraphernalia. The* FORTUNE TELLER *appears at the door of her shop. Other characters gradually gather.*]

Broadcast Official. Mrs. Antrobus! Thank God we've found you at last. Where's Mr. Antrobus? We've been hunting everywhere for him. It's about time for the broadcast to the conventions of the world.

Mrs. Antrobus. [*Calm.*] I expect he'll be here in a minute.

Broadcast Official. Mrs. Antrobus, if he doesn't show up in time, I hope you will consent to broadcast in his place. It's the most important broadcast of the year.

[SABINA *enters from cabana followed by* ANTROBUS.]

Mrs. Antrobus. No, I shan't. I haven't one single thing to say.

Broadcast Official. Then won't you help us

find him, Mrs. Antrobus? A storm's coming up. A hurricane. A deluge!

Second Conveener. [*Who has sighted* ANTROBUS *over the rail.*] Joe! Joe! Here he is.

Broadcast Official. In the name of God, Mr. Antrobus, you're on the air in five minutes. Will you kindly please come and test the instrument? That's all we ask. If you just please begin the alphabet slowly.

[ANTROBUS, *with set face, comes ponderously up the ramp. He stops at the point where his waist is level with the stage and speaks authoritatively to the* OFFICIALS.]

Antrobus. I'll be ready when the time comes. Until then, move away. Go away. I have something I wish to say to my wife.

Broadcast Official. [*Whimpering.*] Mr. Antrobus! This is the most important broadcast of the year.

[*The* OFFICIALS *withdraw to the edge of the stage.* SABINA *glides up the ramp behind* ANTROBUS.]

Sabina. [*Whispering.*] Don't let her argue. Remember arguments have nothing to do with it.

Antrobus. Maggie, I'm moving out of the hotel. In fact, I'm moving out of everything. For good. I'm going to marry Miss Fairweather. I shall provide generously for you and the children. In a few years you'll be able to see that it's all for the best. That's all I have to say.

Broadcast Official. Mr. Antrobus! I hope you'll be ready. This is the most important broadcast of the year.

Bingo Announcer. A—nine; A—nine. D—forty-two; D-forty-two. C—thirty; C—thirty. B—seventeen; B—seventeen. C—forty; C—forty.

Gladys. What did Papa say, Mama? I didn't hear what papa said.

Chorus. Bingo!!

Broadcast Official. Mr. Antrobus. All we want to do is test your voice with the alphabet.

Antrobus. Go away. Clear out.

Mrs. Antrobus. [*Composedly with lowered eyes.*] George, I can't talk to you until you wipe those silly red marks off your face.

Antrobus. I think there's nothing to talk about. I've said what I have to say.

Sabina. Splendid!!

Antrobus. You're a fine woman, Maggie, but . . . but a man has his own life to lead in the world.

Mrs. Antrobus. Well, after living with you

for five thousand years I guess I have a right to a word or two, haven't I?

Antrobus. [*To* SABINA.] What can I answer to that?

Sabina. Tell her that conversation would only hurt her feelings. It's-kinder-in-the-long-run-to-do-it-short-and-quick.

Antrobus. I want to spare your feelings in every way I can, Maggie.

Broadcast Official. Mr. Antrobus, the hurricane signal's gone up. We could begin right now.

Mrs. Antrobus. [*Calmly, almost dreamily.*] I didn't marry you because you were perfect. I didn't even marry you because I loved you. I married you because you gave me a promise. [*She takes off her ring and looks at it.*] That promise made up for your faults. And the promise I gave you made up for mine. Two imperfect people got married and it was the promise that made the marriage.

Antrobus. Maggie, . . . I was only nineteen.

Mrs. Antrobus. [*She puts her ring back on her finger.*] And when our children were growing up, it wasn't a house that protected them; and it wasn't our love that protected them—it was that promise.

And when that promise is broken—this can happen!

[*With a sweep of the hand she removes the raincoat from* GLADYS'S *stockings.*]

Antrobus. [*Stretches out his arm, apoplectic.*] Gladys!! Have you gone crazy? Has everyone gone crazy? [*Turning on* SABINA.] You did this. You gave them to her.

Sabina. I never said a word to her.

Antrobus. [*To* GLADYS.] You go back to the hotel and take those horrible things off.

Gladys. [*Pert.*] Before I go, I've got something to tell you,—it's about Henry.

Mrs. Antrobus. [*Claps her hands peremptorily.*] Stop your noise,—I'm taking her back to the hotel, George. Before I go I have a letter. . . . I have a message to throw into the ocean. [*Fumbling in her handbag.*] Where is the plagued thing? Here it is. [*She flings something—invisible to us —far over the heads of the audience to the back of the auditorium.*] It's a bottle. And in the bottle's a letter. And in the letter is written all the things that a woman knows. It's never been told to any man and it's never been told to any woman, and if it finds its destination, a new time will come. We're not what books and plays say we are. We're not what advertisements say we are. We're not in the movies and we're not on the radio.

We're not what you're all told and what you think we are: We're ourselves. And if any man can find one of us he'll learn why the whole universe was set in motion. And if any man harm any one of us, his soul—the only soul he's got—had better be at the bottom of that ocean,—and that's the only way to put it. Gladys, come here. We're going back to the hotel.

[*She drags* GLADYS *firmly off by the hand, but* GLADYS *breaks away and comes down to speak to her father.*]

Sabina. Such goings-on. Don't give it a minute's thought.

Gladys. Anyway, I think you ought to know that Henry hit a man with a stone. He hit one of those colored men that push the chairs and the man's very sick. Henry ran away and hid and some policemen are looking for him very hard. And I don't care a bit if you don't want to have anything to do with mama and me, because I'll never like you again and I hope nobody ever likes you again,—so there!

[*She runs off.* ANTROBUS *starts after her.*]

Antrobus. I . . . I have to go and see what I can do about this.

Sabina. You stay right here. Don't you go now while you're excited. Gracious sakes, all these things will be forgotten in a hundred years. Come, now, you're on the air. Just say anything,—it doesn't matter what. Just a lot of birds and fishes and things.

Broadcast Official. Thank you, Miss Fairweather. Thank you very much. Ready, Mr. Antrobus.

Antrobus. [*Touching the microphone.*] What is it, what is it? Who am I talking to?

Broadcast Official. Why, Mr. Antrobus! To our order and to all the other orders.

Antrobus. [*Raising his head.*] What are all those birds doing?

Broadcast Official. Those are just a few of the birds. Those are the delegates to our convention,—two of a kind.

Antrobus. [*Pointing into the audience.*] Look at the water. Look at them all. Those fishes jumping. The children should see this!—There's Maggie's whales!! Here are your whales, Maggie!!

Broadcast Official. I hope you're ready, Mr. Antrobus.

Antrobus. And look on the beach! You didn't tell me these would be here!

Sabina. Yes, George. Those are the animals.

Broadcast Official. [*Busy with the apparatus.*] Yes, Mr. Antrobus, those are the vertebrates. We hope the lion will have a word to say when you're through. Step right

up, Mr. Antrobus, we're ready. We'll just have time before the storm. [*Pause. In a hoarse whisper.*] They're wait-ing.

[*It has grown dark. Soon after he speaks a high whistling noise begins. Strange veering lights start whirling about the stage. The other characters disappear from the stage.*]

Antrobus. Friends. Cousins. Four score and ten billion years ago our forefather brought forth upon this planet the spark of life,——

[*He is drowned out by thunder. When the thunder stops the* FORTUNE TELLER *is seen standing beside him.*]

Fortune Teller. Antrobus, there's not a minute to be lost. Don't you see the four disks on the weather signal? Take your family into that boat at the end of the pier.

Antrobus. My family? I have no family. Maggie! Maggie! They won't come.

Fortune Teller. They'll come.—Antrobus! Take these animals into that boat with you. All of them,—two of each kind.

Sabina. George, what's the matter with you? This is just a storm like any other storm.

Antrobus. Maggie!

Sabina. Stay with me, we'll go . . . [*Losing conviction.*] This is just another thunderstorm,—isn't it? Isn't it?

Antrobus. Maggie!!!

[MRS. ANTROBUS *appears beside him with* GLADYS.]

Mrs. Antrobus. [*Matter-of-fact.*] Here I am and here's Gladys.

Antrobus. Where've you been? Where have you been? Quick, we're going into that boat out there.

Mrs. Antrobus. I know we are. But I haven't found Henry.

[*She wanders off into the darkness calling "Henry!"*]

Sabina. [*Low urgent babbling, only occasionally raising her voice.*] I don't believe it. I don't believe it's anything at all. I've seen hundreds of storms like this.

Fortune Teller. There's no time to lose. Go. Push the animals along before you. Start a new world. Begin again.

Sabina. Esmeralda! George! Tell me,—is it really serious?

Antrobus. [*Suddenly very busy.*] Elephants first. Gently, gently.—Look where you're going.

Gladys. [*Leaning over the ramp and striking an animal on the back.*] Stop it or you'll be left behind!

Antrobus. Is the Kangaroo there? *There* you are! Take those turtles in your pouch, will you? [*To some other animals, pointing to his shoulder.*] Here! You jump up here. You'll be trampled on.

Gladys. [*To her father, pointing below.*] Papa, look,—the snakes!

Mrs. Antrobus. I can't find Henry. Hen-ry!

Antrobus. Go along. Go along. Climb on their backs.—Wolves! Jackals,—whatever you are,—tend to your own business!

Gladys. [*Pointing, tenderly.*] Papa,— look.

Sabina. Mr. Antrobus—take me with you. Don't leave me here. I'll work. I'll help. I'll do anything.

[THREE CONVEENERS *cross the stage, marching with a banner.*]

Conveeners. George! What are you scared of?—George! Fellas, it looks like rain.— "Maggie, where's my umbrella?"—George, setting up for Barnum and Bailey.

Antrobus. [*Again catching his wife's hand.*] Come on now, Maggie,—the pier's going to break any minute.

Mrs. Antrobus. I'm not going a step without Henry. Henry!

Gladys. [*On the ramp.*] Mama! Papa! Hurry. The pier's cracking, Mama. It's going to break.

Mrs. Antrobus. Henry! Cain! CAIN!

[HENRY *dashes onto the stage and joins his mother.*]

Henry. Here I am, mama.

Mrs. Antrobus. Thank God!—now come quick.

Henry. I didn't think you wanted me.

Mrs. Antrobus. Quick!

[*She pushes him down before her into the aisle.*]

Sabina. [*All the* ANTROBUSES *are now in the theatre aisle.* SABINA *stands at the top of the ramp.*] Mrs. Antrobus, take me. Don't you remember me? I'll work. I'll help. Don't leave me here!

Mrs. Antrobus. [*Impatiently, but as though it were of no importance.*] Yes, yes. There's a lot of work to be done. Only hurry.

Fortune Teller. [*Now dominating the stage. To* SABINA *with a grim smile.*] Yes, go—back to the kitchen with you.

Sabina. [*Half-down the ramp.* To FORTUNE TELLER.] I don't know why my life's always being interrupted—just when everything's going fine!! [*She dashes up the aisle.*]

[*Now the* CONVEENERS *emerge doing a serpentine dance on the stage. They jeer at the* FORTUNE TELLER.]

Conveeners. Get a canoe—there's not a minute to be lost! Tell me my future, Mrs. Croaker.

Fortune Teller. Paddle in the water, boys —enjoy yourselves.

Voice from the Bingo Parlor. A-nine; A-nine. C-Twenty-four. C-Twenty-four.

Conveeners. Rags, bottles, and sacks.

Fortune Teller. Go back and climb on your roofs. Put rags in the cracks under your doors.—Nothing will keep out the flood. You've had your chance. You've had your day. You've failed. You've lost.

Voice from the Bingo Parlor. B-Fifteen. B-Fifteen.

Fortune Teller. [*Shading her eyes and looking out to sea.*] They're safe. George Antrobus! Think it over! A new world to make.—Think it over!

CURTAIN

ACT III

Just before the curtain rises, two sounds are heard from the stage: a cracked bugle call.

The curtain rises on almost total darkness. Almost all the flats composing the walls of MR. ANTROBUS'S *house, as of Act I, are up, but they lean helter-skelter against one another, leaving irregular gaps. Among the flats missing are two in the back wall, leaving the frames of the window and door crazily out of line. Off stage, back right, some red Roman fire is burning. The bugle*

call is repeated. Enter SABINA *through the tilted door. She is dressed as a Napoleonic camp follower, "la fille du regiment," in begrimed reds and blues.*

Sabina. Mrs. Antrobus! Gladys! Where are you? The war's over. The war's over. You can come out. The peace treaty's been signed. Where are they?—Hmpf! Are they dead, too? Mrs. Annnntrobus! Glaaaadus! Mr. Antrobus'll be here this afternoon. I just saw him downtown. Huuuurry and put things in order. He says that now that the war's over we'll all have to settle down and be perfect.

[*Enter* MR. FITZPATRICK, *the stage manager, followed by the whole company, who stand waiting at the edges of the stage.* MR. FITZPATRICK *tries to interrupt* SABINA.]

Mr. Fitzpatrick. Miss Somerset, we have to stop a moment.

Sabina. They may be hiding out in the back—

Mr. Fitzpatrick. Miss Somerset! We have to stop a moment.

Sabina. What's the matter?

Mr. Fitzpatrick. There's an explanation we have to make to the audience.—Lights, please. [*To the actor who plays* MR. ANTROBUS.] Will you explain the matter to the audience?

[*The lights go up. We now see that a balcony or elevated runway has been erected at the back of the stage, back of the wall of the Antrobus house. From its extreme right and left ends ladderlike steps descend to the floor of the stage.*]

Antrobus. Ladies and gentlemen, an unfortunate accident has taken place back stage. Perhaps I should say *another* unfortunate accident.

Sabina. I'm sorry. I'm sorry.

Antrobus. The management feels, in fact, we all feel that you are due an apology. And now we have to ask your indulgence for the most serious mishap of all. Seven of our actors have . . . have been taken ill. Apparently, it was something they ate. I'm not exactly clear what happened. [*All the* ACTORS *start to talk at once.* ANTROBUS *raises his hand.*] Now, now—not all at once. Fitz, do you know what it was?

Mr. Fitzpatrick. Why, it's perfectly clear. These seven actors had dinner together, and they ate something that disagreed with them.

Sabina. Disagreed with them!!! They have ptomaine poisoning. They're in Bellevue Hospital this very minute in agony. They're having their stomachs pumped out this very minute, in perfect agony.

Antrobus. Fortunately, we've just heard they'll all recover.

Sabina. It'll be a miracle if they do, a downright miracle. It was the lemon meringue pie.

Actors. It was the fish . . . it was the canned tomatoes . . . it was the fish.

Sabina. It was the lemon meringue pie. I saw it with my own eyes; it had blue mould all over the bottom of it.

Antrobus. Whatever it was, they're in no condition to take part in this performance. Naturally, we haven't enough understudies to fill all those roles; but we do have a number of splendid volunteers who have kindly consented to help us out. These friends have watched our rehearsals, and they assure me that they know the lines and the business very well. Let me introduce them to you— my dresser, Mr. Tremayne,—himself a distinguished Shakespearean actor for many years; our wardrobe mistress, Hester; Miss Somerset's maid, Ivy; and Fred Bailey, captain of the ushers in this theatre. [*These persons bow modestly.* IVY *and* HESTER *are colored girls.*] Now this scene takes place near the end of the act. And I'm sorry to say we'll need a short rehearsal, just a short run-through. And as some of it takes place in the auditorium, we'll have to keep the curtain up. Those of you who wish can go out in the lobby and smoke some more. The rest of you can listen to us, or . . . or just talk quietly among yourselves, as you choose. Thank you. Now will you take it over, Mr. Fitzpatrick?

Mr. Fitzpatrick. Thank you.—Now for those of you who are listening perhaps I should explain that at the end of this act, the men have come back from the War and the family's settled down in the house. And the author wants to show the hours of the night passing by over their heads, and the planets crossing the sky . . . uh . . . over their heads. And he says—this is hard to explain—that each of the hours of the night is a philosopher, or a great thinker. Eleven o'clock, for instance, is Aristotle. And nine o'clock is Spinoza. Like that. I don't suppose it means anything. It's just a kind of poetic effect.

Sabina. Not mean anything! Why, it certainly does. Twelve o'clock goes by saying those wonderful things. I think it means that when people are asleep they have all those lovely thoughts, much better than when they're awake.

Ivy. Excuse me, I think it means,—excuse me, Mr. Fitzpatrick——

Sabina. What were you going to say, Ivy?

Ivy. Mr. Fitzpatrick, you let my father come to a rehearsal; and my father's a Baptist minister, and he said that the author meant that—just like the hours and stars go by over our heads at night, in the same way the ideas and thoughts of the great men are in the air around us all the time and they're working on us, even when we don't know it.

Mr. Fitzpatrick. Well, well, maybe that's it. Thank you, Ivy. Anyway,—the hours of the night are philosophers. My friends, are you ready? Ivy, can you be eleven o'clock? "This good estate of the mind possessing its object in energy we call divine." Aristotle.

Ivy. Yes, sir. I know that and I know twelve o'clock and I know nine o'clock.

Mr. Fitzpatrick. Twelve o'clock? Mr. Tremayne, the Bible.

Tremayne. Yes.

Mr. Fitzpatrick. Ten o'clock? Hester,— Plato? [*She nods eagerly.*] Nine o'clock, Spinoza,—Fred?

Bailey. Yes, sir.

[FRED BAILEY *picks up a great gilded cardboard numeral IX and starts up the steps to the platform.* MR. FITZPATRICK *strikes his forehead.*]

Mr. Fitzpatrick. The planets!! We forgot all about the planets.

Sabina. O my God! The planets! Are they sick too? [ACTORS *nod.*]

Mr. Fitzpatrick. Ladies and gentlemen, the planets are singers. Of course, we can't replace them, so you'll have to imagine them singing in this scene. Saturn sings from the orchestra pit down here. The Moon is way up there. And Mars with a red lantern in his hand, stands in the aisle over there— Tz-tz-tz. It's too bad; it all makes a very fine effect. However! Ready—nine o'clock: Spinoza.

Bailey. [*Walking slowly across the balcony, left to right.*] "After experience had taught me that the common occurrences of daily life are vain and futile——"

Fitzpatrick. Louder, Fred. "And I saw that all the objects of my desire and fear——"

Bailey. "And I saw that all the objects of my desire and fear were in themselves nothing good nor bad save insofar as the mind was affected by them——"

Fitzpatrick. Do you know the rest? All right. Ten o'clock. Hester. Plato.

Hester. "Then tell me, O Critias, how will a man choose the ruler that shall rule over him? Will he not——"

Fitzpatrick. Thank you. Skip to the end, Hester.

Hester. ". . . can be multiplied a thousand fold in its effects among the citizens."

Fitzpatrick. Thank you.—Aristotle, Ivy?

Ivy. "This good estate of the mind possessing its object in energy we call divine. This we mortals have occasionally and it is this energy which is pleasant and best. But God has it always. It is wonderful in us; but in Him how much more wonderful."

Fitzpatrick. Midnight. Midnight, Mr. Tremayne. That's right,—you've done it

before.—All right, everybody. You know what you have to do.—Lower the curtain. House lights up. Act Three of THE SKIN OF OUR TEETH. [*As the curtain descends he is heard saying.*] You volunteers, just wear what you have on. Don't try to put on the costumes today.

[*House lights go down. The Act begins again. The Bugle call. Curtain rises. Enter* SABINA.]

Sabina. Mrs. Antrobus! Gladys! Where are you?

The war's over.—You've heard all this— [*She gabbles the main points.*] Where—are —they? Are—they—dead, too, et cetera. I—just—saw—Mr.—Antrobus—down town, et cetera. [*Slowing up.*] He says that now the war's over we'll all have to settle down and be perfect. They may be hiding out in the back somewhere. Mrs. An-tro-bus.

[*She wanders off. It has grown lighter. A trapdoor is cautiously raised and* MRS. ANTROBUS *emerges waist-high and listens. She is disheveled and worn; she wears a tattered dress and a shawl half covers her head. She talks down through the trapdoor.*]

Mrs. Antrobus. It's getting light. There's something burning over there—Newark, or Jersey City. What? Yes, I could swear I heard someone moving about up here. But I can't see anybody. I say: I can't see anybody.

[*She starts to move about the stage.* GLADYS' *head appears at the trapdoor. She is holding a* BABY.]

Gladys. Oh, mama. Be careful.

Mrs. Antrobus. Now, Gladys, you stay out of sight.

Gladys. Well, let me stay here just a minute. I want the baby to get some of this fresh air.

Mrs. Antrobus. All right, but keep your eyes open. I'll see what I can find. I'll have a good hot plate of soup for you before you can say Jack Robinson. Gladys Antrobus! Do you know what I think I see? There's old Mr. Hawkins sweeping the sidewalk in front of his A. and P. store. Sweeping it with a broom. Why, he must have gone crazy, like the others! I see some other people moving about, too.

Gladys. Mama, come back, come back.

Mrs. Antrobus. [*Returns to the trapdoor and listens.*] Gladys, there's something in the air. Everybody's movement's sort of different. I see some women walking right out in the middle of the street.

Sabina's Voice. Mrs. An-tro-bus!

Mrs. Antrobus and Gladys. What's that?!!
Sabina's Voice. Glaaaadys! Mrs. An-tro-bus! [*Enter* SABINA.]
Mrs. Antrobus. Gladys, that's Sabina's voice as sure as I live.—Sabina! Sabina!—Are you *alive?!!*
Sabina. Of course, I'm alive. How've you girls been?—*Don't* try and kiss me. I never want to kiss another human being as long as I live. Sh-sh, there's nothing to get emotional about. Pull yourself together, the war's over. Take a deep breath,—the war's over.
Mrs. Antrobus. The war's over!! I don't believe you. I don't believe you. I can't believe you.
Gladys. Mama!
Sabina. Who's that?
Mrs. Antrobus. That's Gladys and her baby. I don't believe you. Gladys, Sabina says the war's over. Oh, Sabina.
Sabina. [*Leaning over the* BABY.] Goodness! Are there any babies left in the world? Can it *see?* And can it cry and everything?
Gladys. Yes, he can. He notices everything very well.
Sabina. Where on earth did you get it? Oh, I won't ask.—Lord, I've lived all these seven years around camp and I've forgotten how to behave.—Now we've got to think about the men coming home.—Mrs. Antrobus, go and wash your face, I'm ashamed of you. Put your best clothes on. Mr. Antrobus'll be here this afternoon. I just saw him downtown.
Mrs. Antrobus and Gladys. He's alive!! He'll be here!! Sabina, you're not joking?
Mrs. Antrobus. And Henry?
Sabina. [*Dryly.*] Yes, Henry's alive, too; that's what they say. Now don't stop to talk. Get yourselves fixed up. Gladys, you look terrible. Have you any decent clothes? [SABINA *has pushed them toward the trapdoor.*]
Mrs. Antrobus. [*Half down.*] Yes, I've something to wear just for this very day. But, Sabina,—who won the war?
Sabina. Don't stop now,—just wash your face. [*A whistle sounds in the distance.*] Oh, my God, what's that silly little noise?
Mrs. Antrobus. Why, it sounds like . . . it sounds like what used to be the noon whistle at the shoe-polish factory. [*Exit.*]
Sabina. That's what it is. Seems to me like peacetime's coming along pretty fast—shoe polish!
Gladys. [*Half down.*] Sabina, how soon after peacetime begins does the milkman start coming to the door?
Sabina. As soon as he catches a cow. Give him time to catch a cow, dear. [*Exit* GLADYS. SABINA *walks about a moment, thinking.*] Shoe polish! My, I'd forgotten what peacetime was like. [*She shakes her head, then sits down by the trapdoor and starts talking down the hole.*] Mrs. Antrobus, guess what I saw Mr. Antrobus doing this morning at dawn. He was tacking up a piece of paper on the door of the Town Hall. You'll die when you hear: it was a recipe for grass soup, for a grass soup that doesn't give you the diarrhea. Mr. Antrobus is still thinking up new things.—He told me to give you his love. He's got all sorts of ideas for peacetime, he says. No more laziness and idiocy, he says. And oh, yes! Where are his books? What? Well, pass them up. The first thing he wants to see are his books. He says if you've burnt those books, or if the rats have eaten them, he says it isn't worthwhile starting over again. Everybody's going to be beautiful, he says, and diligent, and very intelligent. [*A hand reaches up with two volumes.*] What language is that? Pu-u-gh,—mould! And he's got such plans for you, Mrs. Antrobus. You're going to study history and algebra—and so are Gladys and I—and philosophy. You should hear him talk. [*Taking two more volumes.*] Well, these are in English, anyway.—To hear him talk, seems like he expects you to be a combination, Mrs. Antrobus, of a saint and a college professor, and a dancehall hostess, if you know what I mean. [*Two more volumes.*] Ugh. German! [*She is lying on the floor; one elbow bent, her cheek on her hand, meditatively.*] Yes, peace will be here before we know it. In a week or two we'll be asking the Perkinses in for a quiet evening of bridge. We'll turn on the radio and hear how to be big successes with a new toothpaste. We'll trot down to the movies and see how girls with wax faces live—all *that* will begin again. Oh, Mrs. Antrobus, God forgive me but I enjoyed the war. Everybody's at their best in wartime. I'm sorry it's over. And, oh, I forgot! Mr. Antrobus sent you another message—can you hear me?— [*Enter* HENRY, *blackened and sullen. He is wearing torn overalls, but has one gaudy admiral's epaulette hanging by a thread from his right shoulder, and there are vestiges of gold and scarlet braid running down his left trouser leg. He stands listening.*] Listen! Henry's never to put foot in this house again, he says. He'll kill Henry on sight, if he sees him.

You don't know about Henry??? Well, where have you been? What? Well, Henry rose right to the top. Top of *what?* Listen, I'm telling you. Henry rose from corporal to captain, to major, to general.—I don't know how to say it, but the enemy is *Henry; Henry is* the enemy. Everybody knows that.

Henry. He'll kill me, will he?

Sabina. Who are *you?* I'm not afraid of you. The war's over.

Henry. I'll kill him so fast. I've spent seven years trying to find him; the others I killed were just substitutes.

Sabina. Goodness! It's Henry!— [*He makes an angry gesture.*] Oh, I'm not afraid of you. The war's over, Henry Antrobus, and you're not any more important than any other unemployed. You go away and hide yourself, until we calm your father down.

Henry. The first thing to do is to burn up those old books; it's the ideas he gets out of those old books that . . . that makes the whole world so you can't live in it.

[*He reels forward and starts kicking the books about, but suddenly falls down in a sitting position.*]

Sabina. You leave those books alone!! Mr. Antrobus is looking forward to them a-special.—Gracious sakes, Henry, you're so tired you can't stand up. Your mother and sister'll be here in a minute and we'll think what to do about you.

Henry. What did they ever care about me?

Sabina. There's that old whine again. All you people think you're not loved enough, nobody loves you. Well, you start being lovable and we'll love you.

Henry. [*Outraged.*] I don't want anybody to love me.

Sabina. Then stop talking about it all the time.

Henry. I *never* talk about it. The last thing I want is anybody to pay any attention to me.

Sabina. I can hear it behind every word you say.

Henry. I want everybody to hate me.

Sabina. Yes, you've decided that's second best, but it's still the same thing.—Mrs. Antrobus! Henry's here. He's so tired he can't stand up.

[MRS. ANTROBUS *and* GLADYS, *with her* BABY, *emerge. They are dressed as in Act I.* MRS. ANTROBUS *carries some objects in her apron, and* GLADYS *has a blanket over her shoulder.*]

Mrs. Antrobus and Gladys. Henry! Henry! Henry!

Henry. [*Glaring at them.*] Have you anything to eat?

Mrs. Antrobus. Yes, I have, Henry. I've been saving it for this very day,—two good baked potatoes. No! Henry! One of them's for your father. Henry!! Give me that other potato back this minute.

[SABINA *sidles up behind him and snatches the other potato away.*]

Sabina. He's so dog-tired he doesn't know what he's doing.

Mrs. Antrobus. Now you just rest there, Henry, until I can get your room ready. Eat that potato good and slow, so you can get all the nourishment out of it.

Henry. You all might as well know right now that I haven't come back here to live.

Mrs. Antrobus. Sh. . . . I'll put this coat over you. Your room's hardly damaged at all. Your football trophies are a little tarnished, but Sabina and I will polish them up tomorrow.

Henry. Did you hear me? I don't live here. I don't belong to anybody.

Mrs. Antrobus. Why, how can you say a thing like that! You certainly do belong right here. Where else would you want to go? Your forehead's feverish, Henry, seems to me. You'd better give me that gun, Henry. You won't need that any more.

Gladys. [*Whispering.*] Look, he's fallen asleep already, with his potato half-chewed.

Sabina. Puh! The terror of the world.

Mrs. Antrobus. Sabina, you mind your own business, and start putting the room to rights.

[HENRY *has turned his face to the back of the sofa.* MRS. ANTROBUS *gingerly puts the revolver in her apron pocket, then helps* SABINA. SABINA *has found a rope hanging from the ceiling. Grunting, she hangs all her weight on it, and as she pulls the walls begin to move into their right places.* MRS. ANTROBUS *brings the overturned tables, chairs, and hassock into the positions of Act I.*]

Sabina. That's all we do—always beginning again! Over and over again. Always beginning again. [*She pulls on the rope and a part of the wall moves into place. She stops. Meditatively.*] How do we know that it'll be any better than before? Why do we go on pretending? Some day the whole earth's going to have to turn cold anyway, and until that time all these other things'll be happening again: it will be more wars and more walls of ice and floods and earthquakes.

Mrs. Antrobus. Sabina!! Stop arguing and go on with your work.

Sabina. All right. I'll go on just out of *habit*, but I won't believe in it.

Mrs. Antrobus. [*Aroused.*] Now, Sabina. I've let you talk long enough. I don't want to hear any more of it. Do I have to explain to you what everybody knows,—everybody who keeps a home going? Do I have to say to you what nobody should ever *have* to say, because they can read it in each other's eyes? Now listen to me: [*Mrs. Antrobus takes hold of the rope.*] I could live for seventy years in a cellar and make soup out of grass and bark, without ever doubting that this world has a work to do and will do it. Do you hear me?

Sabina. [*Frightened.*] Yes, Mrs. Antrobus.

Mrs. Antrobus. Sabina, do you see this house,—216 Cedar Street,—do you see it?

Sabina. Yes, Mrs. Antrobus.

Mrs. Antrobus. Well, just to have known this house is to have seen the idea of what we can do someday if we keep our wits about us. Too many people have suffered and died for my children for us to start reneging now. So we'll start putting this house to rights. Now, Sabina, go and see what you can do in the kitchen.

Sabina. Kitchen! Why is it that however far I go away, I always find myself back in the kitchen?   [*Exit.*]

Mrs. Antrobus. [*Still thinking over her last speech, relaxes and says with a reminiscent smile.*] Goodness gracious, wouldn't you know that my father was a parson? It was just like I heard his own voice speaking and he's been dead five-thousand years. There! I've gone and almost waked Henry up.

Henry. [*Talking in his sleep, indistinctly.*] Fellows . . . what have they done for us? . . . Blocked our way at every step. Kept everything in their own hands. And you've stood it. When are you going to wake up?

Mrs. Antrobus. Sh, Henry. Go to sleep. Go to sleep. Go to sleep.—Well, that looks better. Now let's go and help Sabina.

Gladys. Mama, I'm going out in the backyard and hold the baby right up in the air. And show him that we don't have to be afraid any more.

[*Exit* GLADYS *to the kitchen.* MRS. ANTROBUS *glances at* HENRY, *exits into kitchen.* HENRY *thrashes about in his sleep. Enter* ANTROBUS, *his arms full of bundles, chewing the end of a carrot. He has a slight limp. Over the suit of Act I he is wearing an overcoat too long for him, its skirts trailing on the ground. He lets his bundles fall and stands looking about. Presently his attention is fixed on* HENRY, *whose words grow clearer.*]

Henry. All right! What have you got to lose? What have they done for us? That's right—nothing. Tear everything down. I don't care what you smash. We'll begin again and we'll show 'em. [ANTROBUS *takes out his revolver and holds it pointing downwards. With his back towards the audience he moves toward the footlights.* HENRY'S *voice grows louder and he wakes with a start. They stare at one another. Then* HENRY *sits up quickly. Throughout the following scene* HENRY *is played, not as a misunderstood or misguided young man, but as a representation of strong unreconciled evil.*] All right! Do something. [*Pause.*] Don't think I'm afraid of you, either. All right, do what you were going to do. Do it. [*Furiously.*] Shoot me, I tell you. You don't have to think I'm any relation of yours. I haven't got any father or any mother, or brothers or sisters. And I don't want any. And what's more I haven't got anybody over me; and I never will have. I'm alone, and that's all I want to be: alone. So you can shoot me.

Antrobus. You're the last person I wanted to see. The sight of you dries up all my plans and hopes. I wish I were back at war still, because it's easier to fight you than to live with you. War's a pleasure—do you hear me?—War's a pleasure compared to what faces us now: trying to build up a peacetime with you in the middle of it.

[ANTROBUS *walks up to the window.*]

Henry. I'm not going to be a part of any peacetime of yours. I'm going a long way from here and make my own world that's fit for man to live in. Where a man can be free, and have a chance, and do what he wants to do in his own way.

Antrobus. [*His attention arrested; thoughtfully. He throws the gun out of the window and turns with hope.*] . . . Henry, let's try again.

Henry. Try what? Living *here?*—Speaking polite downtown to all the old men like you? Standing like a sheep at the street corner until the red light turns to green? Being a good boy and a good sheep, like all the stinking ideas you get out of your books? Oh, no. I'll make a world, and I'll show you.

Antrobus. [*Hard.*] How can you make a world for people to live in, unless you've first put order in yourself? Mark my words: I shall continue fighting you until my last breath as long as you mix up your idea of liberty with your idea of hogging everything for yourself. I shall have no pity on you. I shall pursue you to the far corners of the earth. You and I want the same thing; but until you think of it as something that everyone has a right to, you are my deadly enemy and I will destroy you.—I hear your mother's voice in the kitchen. Have you seen her?

Henry. I have no mother. Get it into your head. I don't belong here. I have nothing to do here. I have no home.

Antrobus. Then why did you come here? With the whole world to choose from, why did you come to this one place: 216 Cedar Street, Excelsior, New Jersey. . . . Well?

Henry. What if I did? What if I wanted to look at it once more, to see if——

Antrobus. Oh, you're related, all right—When your mother comes in you must behave yourself. Do you hear me?

Henry. [*Wildly.*] What is this?—*must behave* yourself. Don't you say *must* to me.

Antrobus. Quiet.

[*Enter* MRS. ANTROBUS *and* SABINA.]

Henry. Nobody can say *must* to me. All my life everybody's been crossing me,—everybody, everything, all of you. I'm going to be free, even if I have to kill half the world for it. Right now, too. Let me get my hand on his throat. I'll show him.

[*He advances toward* ANTROBUS. *Suddenly,* SABINA *jumps between them and calls out in her own person.*]

Sabina. Stop! Stop! Don't play this scene. You know what happened last night. Stop the play. [*The men fall back, panting.* HENRY *covers his face with his hands.*] Last night you almost strangled him. You became a regular savage. Stop it!

Henry. It's true. I'm sorry. I don't know what comes over me. I have nothing against him personally. I respect him very much . . . I . . . I admire him. But something comes over me. It's like I become fifteen years old again. I . . . I . . . listen: my own father used to whip me and lock me up every Saturday night. I never had enough to eat. He never let me have enough money to buy decent clothes. I was ashamed to go downtown. I never could go to the dances. My father and my uncle put rules on top of everything I wanted to do. They tried to prevent my living at all.—I'm sorry. I'm sorry.

Mrs. Antrobus. [*Quickly.*] No, go on. Finish what you were saying. Say it all.

Henry. In this scene it's as though I were back in High School again. It's like I had some big emptiness inside me,—the emptiness of being hated and blocked at every turn. And the emptiness fills up with the one thought that you have to strike and fight and kill. Listen, it's as though you have to kill somebody else so as not to end up killing yourself.

Sabina. That's not true. I knew your father and your uncle and your mother. You imagined all that. Why, they did everything they could for you. How can you say things like that? They didn't lock you up.

Henry. They did. They did. They wished I hadn't been born.

Sabina. That's not true.

Antrobus. [*In his own person, with self-condemnation, but cold and proud.*] Wait a minute. I have something to say, too. It's not wholly his fault that he wants to strangle me in this scene. It's my fault, too. He wouldn't feel that way unless there were something in me that reminded him of all that. He talks about an emptiness. Well, there's an emptiness in me, too. Yes,—work, work, work,—that's all I do. I've ceased to *live*. No wonder he feels that anger coming over him.

Mrs. Antrobus. There! At last you've said it.

Sabina. We're all just as wicked as we can be, and that's the God's truth.

Mrs. Antrobus. [*Nods a moment, then comes forward; quietly.*] Come. Come and put your head under some cold water.

Sabina. [*In a whisper.*] I'll go with him. I've known him a long while. You have to go on with the play. Come with me.

[HENRY *starts out with* SABINA, *but turns at the exit and says to* ANTROBUS.]

Henry. Thanks. Thanks for what you said. I'll be all right tomorrow. I won't lose control in that place. I promise.

[*Exeunt* HENRY *and* SABINA. ANTROBUS *starts toward the front door, fastens it.* MRS. ANTROBUS *goes up stage and places the chair close to table.*]

Mrs. Antrobus. George, do I see you limping?

Antrobus. Yes, a little. My old wound from the other war started smarting again. I can manage.

Mrs. Antrobus. [*Looking out of the window.*] Some lights are coming on,—the first in seven years. People are walking up and down looking at them. Over in Hawkins' open lot they've built a bonfire to celebrate the peace. They're dancing around it like scarecrows.

Antrobus. A bonfire! As though they hadn't seen enough things burning.—Maggie, —the dog died?

Mrs. Antrobus. Oh, yes. Long ago. There are no dogs left in Excelsior.—You're back again! All these years. I gave up counting on letters. The few that arrived were anywhere from six months to a year late.

Antrobus. Yes, the ocean's full of letters, along with the other things.

Mrs. Antrobus. George, sit down, you're tired.

Antrobus. No, you sit down. I'm tired but I'm restless. [*Suddenly, as she comes forward.*] Maggie! I've lost it. I've lost it.

Mrs. Antrobus. What, George? What have you lost?

Antrobus. The most important thing of all: The desire to begin again, to start building.

Mrs. Antrobus. [*Sitting in the chair right of the table.*] Well, it will come back.

Antrobus. [*At the window.*] I've lost it. This minute I feel like all those people dancing around the bonfire—just relief. Just the desire to settle down; to slip into the old grooves and keep the neighbors from walking over my lawn.—Hm. But during the war,—in the middle of all that blood and dirt and hot and cold—every day and night, I'd have moments, Maggie, when I *saw* the things that we could do when it was over. When you're at war you think about a better life; when you're at peace you think about a more comfortable one. I've lost it. I feel sick and tired.

Mrs. Antrobus. Listen! The baby's crying. I hear Gladys talking. Probably she's quieting Henry again. George, while Gladys and I were living here—like moles, like rats, and when we were at our wits' end to save the baby's life—the only thought we clung to was that you were going to bring something good out of this suffering. In the night, in the dark, we'd whisper about it, starving and sick. —Oh, George, you'll have to get it back again. Think! What else kept us alive all these years? Even now, it's not comfort we want. We can suffer whatever's necessary; only give us back that promise.

[*Enter* SABINA *with a lighted lamp. She is dressed as in Act I.*]

Sabina. Mrs. Antrobus . . .

Mrs. Antrobus. Yes, Sabina?

Sabina. Will you need me?

Mrs. Antrobus. No, Sabina, you can go to bed.

Sabina. Mrs. Antrobus, if it's all right with you, I'd like to go to the bonfire and celebrate, seeing the war's over. And, Mrs. Antrobus, they've opened the Gem Movie Theatre and they're giving away a hand-painted soup tureen to every lady, and I thought one of us ought to go.

Antrobus. Well, Sabina, I haven't any money. I haven't seen any money for quite a while.

Sabina. Oh, you don't need money.

They're taking anything you can give them. And I have some . . . some . . . Mrs. Antrobus, promise you won't tell anyone. It's a little against the law. But I'll give you some, too.

Antrobus. What is it?

Sabina. I'll give you some, too. Yesterday I picked up a lot of . . . of beef-cubes!

Mrs. Antrobus. [*Turns and says calmly.*] But, Sabina, you know you ought to give that in to the Center downtown. They know who needs them most.

Sabina. [*Outburst.*] Mrs. Antrobus, I didn't make this war. I didn't ask for it. And, in my opinion, after anybody's gone through what we've gone through, they have a right to grab what they can find. You're a very nice man, Mr. Antrobus, but you'd have got on better in the world if you'd realize that dog-eat-dog was the rule in the beginning and always will be. And most of all now. [*In tears.*] Oh, the world's an awful place, and you know it is. I used to think something could be done about it; but I know better now. I hate it. I hate it. [*She comes forward slowly and brings six cubes from the bag.*] All right. All right. You can have them.

Antrobus. Thank you, Sabina.

Sabina. Can I have . . . can I have one to go to the movies? [ANTROBUS *in silence gives her one.*] Thank you.

Antrobus. Good night, Sabina.

Sabina. Mr. Antrobus, don't mind what I say. I'm just an ordinary girl, you know what I mean, I'm just an ordinary girl. But you're a bright man, you're a very bright man, and of course you invented the alphabet and the wheel, and, my God, a lot of things . . . and if you've got any other plans, my God, don't let me upset them. Only every now and then I've got to go to the movies. I mean my nerves can't stand it. But if you have any ideas about improving the crazy old world, I'm really with you. I really am. Because it's . . . it's . . . Good night.

[*She goes out.* ANTROBUS *starts laughing softly with exhilaration.*]

Antrobus. Now I remember what three things always went together when I was able to see things most clearly: three things. Three things: [*He points to where* SABINA *has gone out.*] The voice of the people in their confusion and their need. And the thought of you and the children and this house. . . . And . . . Maggie! I didn't dare ask you: my books! They haven't been lost, have they?

Mrs. Antrobus. No. There are some of them right here. Kind of tattered.

Antrobus. Yes.—Remember, Maggie, we almost lost them once before? And when we finally did collect a few torn copies out of old cellars they ran in everyone's head like a fever. They as good as rebuilt the world. [*Pauses, book in hand, and looks up.*] Oh, I've never forgotten for long at a time that living is struggle. I know that every good and excellent thing in the world stands moment by moment on the razor-edge of danger and must be fought for—whether it's a field, or a home, or a country. All I ask is the chance to build new worlds and God has always given us that. And has given us [*Opening the book.*] voices to guide us; and the memory of our mistakes to warn us. Maggie, you and I will remember in peace-time all the resolves that were so clear to us in the days of war. We've come a long ways. We've learned. We're learning. And the steps of our journey are marked for us here. [*He stands by the table turning the leaves of a book.*] Sometimes out there in the war,—standing all night on a hill—I'd try and remember some of the words in these books. Parts of them and phrases would come back to me. And after a while I used to gives names to the hours of the night. [*He sits, hunting for a passage in the book.*] Nine o'clock I used to call Spinoza. Where is it: "After experience had taught me——"

[*The back wall has disappeared, revealing the platform.* FRED BAILEY *carrying his numeral has started from left to right.* MRS. ANTROBUS *sits by the table sewing.*]

Bailey. "After experience had taught me that the common occurrences of daily life are vain and futile; and I saw that all the objects of my desire and fear were in themselves nothing good nor bad save insofar as the mind was affected by them; I at length determined to search out whether there was something truly good and communicable to man."

[*Almost without break* HESTER, *carrying a large Roman numeral ten, starts*

crossing the platform. GLADYS *appears at the kitchen door and moves towards her mother's chair.*]

Hester. "Then tell me, O Critias, how will a man choose the ruler that shall rule over him? Will he not choose a man who has first established order in himself, knowing that any decision that has its spring from anger or pride or vanity can be multiplied a thousand fold in its effect upon the citizens?"

[HESTER *disappears and* IVY, *as eleven o'clock, starts speaking.*]

Ivy. "This good estate of the mind possessing its object in energy we call divine. This we mortals have occasionally and it is this energy which is pleasantest and best. But God has it always. It is wonderful in us; but in Him how much more wonderful."

[*As* MR. TREMAYNE *starts to speak,* HENRY *appears at the edge of the scene, brooding and unreconciled, but present.*]

Tremayne. "In the beginning, God created the Heavens and the earth; And the Earth was waste and void; And the darkness was upon the face of the deep. And the Lord said let there be light and there was light."

[*Sudden black-out and silence, except for the last strokes of the midnight bell. Then just as suddenly the lights go up, and* SABINA *is standing at the window, as at the opening of the play.*]

Sabina. Oh, oh, oh. Six o'clock and the master not home yet. Pray God nothing serious has happened to him crossing the Hudson River. But I wouldn't be surprised. The whole world's at sixes and sevens, and why the house hasn't fallen down about our ears long ago is a miracle to me.

[*She comes down to the footlights.*]

This is where you came in. We have to go on for ages and ages yet.

You go home.

The end of the play isn't written yet.

Mr. and Mrs. Antrobus! Their heads are full of plans and they're as confident as the first day they began,—and they told me to tell you: good night.

CURTAIN.

COME BACK, LITTLE SHEBA*

By

WILLIAM INGE

FEW DRAMATISTS HAVE COME TO BROAD-
way so much a stranger and yet so long
a devotee of theatre arts in all their
variety as William Motter Inge (pronounced
Inj). Little wonder that the Theatre Guild
found it advisable to try out a play by this
thirty-six-year-old playwright at their summer playhouse before risking it on Broadway.
Come Back, Little Sheba was just one of
many submitted by an agent of play scripts.

Its workman-like quality, enhanced by the
acting of Shirley Booth as Lola, soon won
the "unknown" author the common opinion
that he was "Broadway's most promising
playwright"; and, in addition, two of the high
awards for the best play of 1950. There was
no longer any doubt that here was no novice,
but a competent craftsman in play structure,
the projection of character, and conveyance
of a moral, not by wordy preachment but by
powerful suggestion from life itself, made
awesomely fascinating. From the all but lost
victims of life-destroying habit there is also
made to emerge a fortitude and even beauty
of spirit, without the least glossing, that
makes the most hardened observer eager for
a happy ending. But the dramatist wisely
avoids the suggestion of finality in the alcoholic's struggle, however possible victory
may be. Instead, the play ends in a renewal
of hope, strengthened by reawakened love
and sympathy between man and wife and by
their determination to win by selfless cooperation—the basic requirement of Alcoholics Anonymous, to which Doc owes allegiance.

The repeated call of the title phrase, as if
drawn by a psychoanalyst from the well of a
woman's love almost buried under tragic
neurosis, is the most moving reminder of
the play's underlying beauty. It punctuates
the harrowing climax in a dramatic struggle
which has been shared by hundreds of thousands, including many of the world's best
citizens, whose brave persistence paralleled
that of Doc, resulting in an ultimate victory

thanks to one of the wisest and most genuine
reformational societies established in this
land and others. Of the persistent salvaging
by Alcoholics Anonymous this play is by no
means an exceptional case history.

Its manifest but unobtrusive psychothera-
peutical approach to sexual as well as alcoholic obsessions heightens the play's veracity
and intensifies its dramatic force and its
meaning for a perceptive auditor, without
submerging dialogue under technicalities—a
further indication of the writer's expertness.
His objectivity and avoidance of verbal exposition and lyric exuberance increase the
play's forthright rhythm of incidents, each of
which adds to the frightening suspense created by the essentially affectionate and loyal
relations of Doc and his Lola in their all but
hopeless involvements. The ending, by no
means cheerful, is an open door, comparable
to the indeterminate endings of many modern
plays. To all A.A.'s it means persistent coop-
erative effort, to which thousands have clung
as to a life-raft buoying them to a final
rescue. When charged with having written a
"depressing play," Inge insisted that its import was quite the reverse, meaning, no
doubt, that the renewed determination and
confidence faintly evident at the end were
means to final victory and lasting happiness.

Inge's theatrical adroitness was acquired in
a life-long devotion to theatre expression
during the conventional schooling and college
career of a Midwestern intellectual. His special theatrical absorption is said to have
begun at the age of seven as the result of
success in a speech delivered before his
classmates. An impulse for platform appearance was aroused, inducing young Inge to
lose no opportunity to act on his school and
college stages. He also availed himself of
every college course in the history and theory
of drama, and later, as teacher, he gave instruction in the art and coached its staging.
He gratefully recalls a professor who paid
no heed to Broadway but grounded his
students in classics from Shakespeare to
O'Casey. Inge deplores the tendency of

schools and colleges to encourage student-written musicals but to neglect the original work of student dramatists whose creative talents might prove a driving force towards dramatic progress.

Inge himself is, in fact, the latest to appear in a long and notable line of academically inspired yet practical playwrights from O'Neill to Thornton Wilder and Arthur Miller. Few others have done so much to open new vistas or to provide sincerity and excellence on the American stage. One might deplore the necessity that forced Inge at an early age to follow the academic career that he calls "the security of teaching." But this experience yielded Inge as a writer unforeseen results, among which was a purpose conspicuous in this play—to bring a more realistic understanding to bear on the problems that threaten American youth.

WILLIAM MOTTER INGE

Born 1913, Independence, Kansas.

1935, A.B., University of Kansas.

1937–1938, Teacher of English, Columbus, Kans., High School.

1938, M.A., Peabody Teachers College, Nashville, Tennessee.

1938–1943, Instructor at Stephens College for Women, Columbia, Missouri.

1943–1946, Critic of music and drama on *The Saint Louis Star-Times*.

1947, First play to be produced: *Farther Off from Heaven,* staged by Margo Jones, Dallas, Texas.

1946–1949, Instructor of English, Washington University, St. Louis.

1949–1950, *Come Back, Little Sheba,* his first Broadway production; first staged by The Theatre Guild at Westport; then in New York. Awarded the George Jean Nathan and *Theatre Time* prizes.

1953, *Picnic* awarded the Pulitzer and Drama Critics' prizes and the Donaldson Award.

PLAYS

1947 *Farther Off from Heaven.* 1949 *Come Back, Little Sheba.* 1953 *Picnic.* 1955 *Bus Stop.* 1957 *The Dark at the Top of the Stairs.*

WRITINGS ON DRAMA

"Forgotten Anger," *Theatre Arts,* XLII (Feb. 1958), 68–9. "One Man's Experience in Living," *The New York Times,* July 27, 1958, II.1.3.

COME BACK, LITTLE SHEBA

CAST

(in order of appearance)

Doc.
Marie.
Lola.
Turk.
Postman.
Mrs. Coffman.
Milkman.
Messenger.
Bruce.
Ed Anderson.
Elmo Huston.

THE SCENE

An old house in a run-down neighborhood of a Midwestern city.

ACT ONE

Scene I: *Morning in late spring.*
Scene II: *The same evening, after supper.*

ACT TWO

Scene   I: *The following morning.*
Scene II: *Late afternoon the same day.*
Scene III: *5:30 the next morning.*
Scene IV: *Morning, a week later.*

ACT ONE

SCENE I

The stage is empty.
It is the downstairs of an old house in one of those semi-respectable neighborhoods in a Midwestern city. The stage is divided into two rooms, the living room at right and the kitchen at left, with a stairway and a door between. At the foot of the stairway is a small table with a telephone on it. The time is about 8:00 A.M., a morning in the late spring.
At rise of Curtain the sun hasn't come out in full force and outside the atmosphere is a little grey. The house is extremely cluttered and even dirty. The living room somehow manages to convey the atmosphere of the twenties, decorated with cheap pretense at niceness and respectability. The general effect is one of fussy awkwardness. The furniture is all heavy and rounded-looking, the chairs and davenport being covered with a shiny mohair. The davenport is littered and there are lace antimacassars on all the chairs. In such areas, houses are so close together, they hide each other from the sunlight. What sun could come through the window, at right, is dimmed by the smoky glass curtains. In the
kitchen there is a table center. On it are piled dirty dishes from supper the night before. Woodwork in the kitchen is dark and grimy. No industry whatsoever has been spent in making it one of those white, cheerful rooms that we commonly think kitchens should be. There is no action on stage for several seconds.
[Doc *comes downstairs to kitchen. Coat on back of chair center. Straightens chair. Takes roll from bag on drainboard. Folds bag, tucks behind sink. Lights stove. To table, fills dishpan there and takes it to sink. Turns on water. Tucks towel in vest for apron. To center chair, says prayer. To stove, takes fry pan to sink. Turns on water.* Marie, *a young girl of 18 or 19 who rooms in the house, comes out of her bedroom (next to the living room), skipping airily into the kitchen. Her hair is piled in curls on top of her head and she wears a sheer dainty negligee and smart, feathery mules on her feet. She has the cheerfulness only youth can feel in the morning.*]

Marie. [*To chair right, opens pocketbook there.*] Hi!

455

Doc. Well, well, how is our star boarder this morning?

Marie. Fine.

Doc. Want your breakfast now?

Marie. Just my fruit juice. I'll drink it while I dress and have my breakfast later.

Doc. [*Two glasses to table.*] Up a little early, aren't you?

Marie. I have to get to the library and check out some books before anyone else gets them.

Doc. Yes, you want to study hard, Marie. Learn to be a fine artist some day. Paint lots of beautiful pictures. I remember a picture my mother had over the mantelpiece at home, a picture of a cathedral in a sunset, one of those big cathedrals in Europe somewhere. Made you feel religious just to look at it.

Marie. These books aren't for art, they're for biology. I have an exam.

Doc. Biology? Why do they make you take biology?

Marie. [*Laughs.*] It's required. Didn't you have to take biology when you were in college?

Doc. Well—yes, but I was preparing to study medicine, so of course I *had* to take biology and things like that. You see—I was going to be a real doctor then—only I left college my third year.

Marie. What's the matter? Didn't you like the pre-Med course?

Doc. Yes, of course—I had to give it up.

Marie. Why?

Doc. [*To stove with roll on plate. Evasive.*] I'll put your sweet roll in now, Marie, so it will be nice and warm for you when you want it.

Marie. Dr. Delaney, you're so nice to your wife, and you're so nice to me; as a matter of fact, you're so nice to everyone. I hope my husband is as nice as you are. Most husbands would never think of getting their own breakfast.

Doc. [*Very pleased with this.*]—uh—you might as well sit down now and—yes, sit here and I'll serve you your breakfast now, Marie, and we can eat it together, the two of us.

Marie. [*A light little laugh as she starts dancing away from him.*] No, I like to bathe first and feel that I'm all fresh and clean to start the day. I'm going to hop into the tub now. See you later.

[*She goes upstairs.*]

Doc. Yes, fresh and clean——

[*Doc shows disappointment but goes on in businesslike way setting his breakfast on the table.*]

Marie. [*Off upstairs.*] Mrs. Delaney.

Lola. [*Off upstairs.*] 'Mornin', Honey.

[*Then* LOLA *comes downstairs. Enter* LOLA. *She is a contrast to* DOC'S *neat cleanliness, and* MARIE'S. *Over a nightdress she wears a lumpy kimono. Her eyes are dim with a morning expression of disillusionment, as though she had had a beautiful dream during the night and found on waking none of it was true. On her feet are worn, dirty comfies.*]

Lola. [*With some self-pity.*] I can't sleep late like I used to. It used to be I could sleep till noon if I wanted to, but I can't any more. I don't know why.

Doc. Habits change. Here's your fruit juice.

Lola. [*Taking it.*] I oughta be gettin' your breakfast, Doc, instead of you gettin' mine.

Doc. I have to get up anyway, Baby.

Lola. [*Sadly.*] I had another dream last night.

Doc. [*Pours coffee.*] About Little Sheba?

Lola. [*With sudden animation.*] It was just as real. I dreamt I put her on a leash and we walked down town—to do some shopping. All the people on the street turned around to admire her, and I felt so proud. Then we started to walk, and the blocks started going by so fast that Little Sheba couldn't keep up with me. Suddenly, I looked around and Little Sheba was gone. Isn't that funny? I looked everywhere for her but I couldn't find her. And I stood there feeling sort of afraid. [*Pause.*] Do you suppose that means anything?

Doc. Dreams are funny.

Lola. Do you suppose it means Little Sheba is going to come back?

Doc. I don't know, Baby.

Lola. [*Petulant.*] I miss her so, Doc. She was such a cute little puppy. Wasn't she cute?

Doc. [*Smiles with the reminiscence.*] Yes, she was cute.

Lola. Remember how white and fluffy she used to be after I gave her a bath? And how her little hind-end wagged from side to side when she walked?

Doc. [*An appealing memory.*] I remember.

Lola. She was such a cute little puppy. I hated to see her grow old, didn't you, Doc?

Doc. Yah. Little Sheba should have stayed young forever. Some things should never grow old. That's what it amounts to, I guess.

Lola. She's been gone for such a long time. What do you suppose ever happened to her?

Doc. You can't ever tell.

Lola. [*With anxiety.*] Do you suppose she got run over by a car?—Or do you think that old Mrs. Coffman next door poisoned her? I wouldn't be a bit surprised.

Doc. No, Baby. She just disappeared. That's all we know.

Lola. [*Redundantly.*] Just vanished one day—vanished into thin air.

[*As though in a dream.*]

Doc. I told you I'd find you another one, Baby.

Lola. [*Pessimistically.*] You couldn't ever find another puppy as cute as Little Sheba.

Doc. [*Back to reality.*] Want an egg?

Lola. No. Just this coffee. [*He pours coffee. Suddenly.*] Have you said your prayer, Doc?

Doc. Yes, Baby.

Lola. And did you ask God to be with you —all through the day, and keep you strong?

Doc. Yes, Baby.

Lola. Then God will be with you, Docky. He's been with you almost a year now and I'm so proud of you.

Doc. [*Preening a little.*] Sometimes I feel sorta proud of myself.

Lola. Say your prayer, Doc. I like to hear it.

Doc. [*Matter-of-factly.*] God grant me the serenity to accept the things I cannot change, courage to change the things I can, and wisdom always to tell the difference.

Lola. That's nice. That's so pretty. When I think of the way you used to drink, always getting into fights, we had so much trouble. I was so scared! I never knew what was going to happen.

Doc. That was a long time ago, Baby.

Lola. I know it, Daddy. I know how you're going to be when you come home now.

[*She kisses him lightly.*]

Doc. I don't know what I would have done without you.

Lola. And now you've been sober almost a year.

Doc. Yep. A year next month.

[*He rises and goes to the sink with coffee cup and two glasses, rinsing them.*]

Lola. Do you have to go to the meeting tonight?

Doc. No. I can skip the meetings now for a while.

Lola. Oh, good! Then you can take me to a movie.

Doc. Sorry, Baby. I'm going out on some Twelfth Step work with Ed Anderson.

Lola. What's that?

Doc. [*Drying the glasses.*] I showed you that list of twelve steps the Alcoholics Anon-

ymous have to follow. This is the final one! After you learn to stay dry yourself, then you go out and help other guys that need it.

Lola. Oh!

Doc. [*To sink.*] When we help others, we help ourselves.

Lola. I know what you mean. Whenever I help Marie in some way, it makes me feel good.

Doc. Yah. [LOLA *gives her cup to* Doc. *Washing it.*] Yes but this is a lot different, Baby. When I go out to help some poor drunk, I have to give him courage—to stay sober like I've stayed sober. Most alcoholics are disappointed men—They need courage——

Lola. You weren't ever disappointed, were you, Daddy?

Doc. [*After a pause.*] The important thing is to forget the past and live for the present. And stay sober doing it.

Lola. Who do you have to help tonight?

Doc. Some guy they picked up on Skid Row last night. [*Gets his coat from back of chair.*] They got him at the City Hospital. I kinda dread it.

Lola. I thought you said it helped you.

Doc. [*Puts on coat.*] It does, if you can stand it. I did some Twelfth Step work down there once before. They put alcoholics right in with the crazy people. It's horrible—these men all twisted and shaking—eyes all foggy and full of pain. Some guy there with his fists clamped together, so he couldn't kill anyone. There was a young man, just a young man, had scratched his eyes out.

Lola. [*Cringing.*] Don't, Daddy. Seems a shame to take a man there just cause he got drunk.

Doc. Well, they'll sober a man up. That's the important thing. Let's not talk about it any more.

Lola. [*With relief.*] Rita Hayworth's on tonight, out at the Plaza. Don't you want to see it?

Doc. Maybe Marie will go with you.

Lola. Oh, no. She's probably going out with Turk tonight.

Doc. She's too nice a girl to be going out with a guy like Turk.

Lola. I don't know why, Daddy. Turk's nice. [*Cuts coffee cake.*]

Doc. A guy like that doesn't have any respect for *nice* young girls. You can tell that by looking at him.

Lola. I never saw Marie object to any of the love-making.

Doc. A big, brawny bozo like Turk, he probably forces her to kiss him.

Lola. Daddy, that's not so at all. I came

in the back way once when they were in the living room, and she was kissing him like he was Rudolph Valentino.

Doc. [*An angry denial.*] Marie is a nice girl.

Lola. I know she's nice. I just said she and Turk were doing some tall spooning. It wouldn't surprise me any if——

Doc. Honey, I don't want to hear any more about it.

Lola. You try to make out like every young girl is Jennifer Jones in the Song of Bernadette.

Doc. I do not. I just like to believe that young people like her are clean and decent——

Marie. [*Comes down stairs.*] Hi!

[*Gets cup and saucer from drain board.*]

Lola. [*At stove.*] There's an extra sweet roll for you this morning, Honey. I didn't want mine.

Marie. One's plenty, thank you.

Doc. How soon do you leave this morning?

Marie. [*Eating.*] As soon as I finish my breakfast.

Doc. Well, I'll wait and we can walk to the corner together.

Marie. Oh, I'm sorry, Doc. Turk's coming by. He has to go to the library, too.

Doc. Oh, well I'm not going to be competition with a football player. [*To Lola.*] It's a nice spring morning. Wanta walk to the office with me?

Lola. I look too terrible, Daddy. I ain't even dressed.

Doc. Kiss Daddy goodbye.

Lola. [*Gets up and kisses him softly.*] Bye, bye, Daddy. If you get hungry, come home and I'll have something for you.

Marie. [*Joking.*] Aren't you going to kiss me, Dr. Delaney?

[*LOLA eggs DOC to go ahead.*]

Doc. [*Startled. Hesitates. Forces himself to realize she is only joking and manages to answer.*] Can't spend my time kissing all the girls.

[*MARIE laughs. DOC goes into living room while LOLA and MARIE continue talking. MARIE's scarf is tossed over his hat on chair, so he picks it up, then looks at it fondly, holding it in the air, inspecting its delicate gracefulness. He drops it back on chair and starts out by front door.*]

Marie. I think Dr. Delaney is so nice.

Lola. [*She is by the closet now, where she keeps a few personal articles. She is getting into a more becoming smock.*] When did you say Turk was coming by?

Marie. Said he'd be here about 9:30. [*Doc exits—hearing the line about TURK.*] That's a pretty smock.

Lola. [*To table, sits center chair, changes shoes.*] It'll be better to work around the house in.

Marie. [*Not sounding exactly cheerful.*] Mrs. Delaney, I'm expecting a telegram this morning. Would you leave it on my dresser for me when it comes?

Lola. Sure, Honey. No bad news, I hope.

Marie. Oh no! It's from Bruce.

Lola. [*MARIE's boy friends are one of her liveliest interests.*] Oh, your boy friend in Cincinnati. Is he coming to see you?

Marie. I guess so.

Lola. I'm just dying to meet him.

Marie. [*Changing the subject.*] Really, Mrs. Delaney, you and Doc have been so nice to me. I just want you to know I appreciate it.

Lola. Thanks, Honey.

Marie. You've been like a father and mother to me. I appreciate it.

Lola. Thanks, Honey.

Marie. Turk was saying just the other night what good sports you both are.

Lola. [*Brushing hair.*] That so?

Marie. Honest. He said it was just as much fun being with you as with kids our own age.

Lola. [*Couldn't be more flattered.*] Oh, I like that Turk. He reminds me of a boy I used to know in High School, Dutch McCoy. Where did you ever meet him?

Marie. In art class.

Lola. Turk take art?

Marie. [*Laughs.*] No. It was in a life class. He was modeling. Lots of the athletes do that. It pays them a dollar an hour.

Lola. That's nice.

Marie. Mrs. Delaney? I've got some corrections to make in some of my drawings. Is it all right if I bring Turk home this morning to pose for me? It'll just take a few minutes.

Lola. Sure, Honey.

Marie. There's a contest on now. They're giving a prize for the best drawing to use for advertising the Spring Relays.

Lola. And you're going to do a picture of Turk? That's nice. [*A sudden thought. A little secretively.*] Doc's gonna be gone tonight. You and Turk can have the living room if you want to.

Marie. [*This is a temptation.*] O.K. Thanks.   [*Exits to bedroom.*]

Lola. Tell me more about Bruce.

[*Follows right to bedroom door.*]

Marie. [*Off in bedroom. Remembering*

her affinity.] Well, he comes from one of the best families in Cincinnati. And they have a great big house. And they have a maid, too. And he's got a wonderful personality. He makes $300 a month.

Lola. That so?

Marie. And he stays at the best hotels. His company insists on it.   [*Enters.*]

Lola. Do you like him as well as Turk?
          [*Buttons up back of* MARIE'S *blouse.*]

Marie. [*Evasive.*] Bruce is so dependable, and—he's a gentleman, too.

Lola. Are you goin' to marry him, Honey?

Marie. Maybe, after I graduate from college and he feels he can support a wife and children. I'm going to have lots and lots of children.

Lola. I wanted children, too. When I lost my baby and found out I couldn't have any more, I didn't know what to do with myself. I wanted to get a job, but Doc wouldn't hear of it.

Marie. Bruce is going to come into a lot of money some day. His uncle made a fortune in men's garters.   [*Exits into her room.*]

Lola. [*Leans on door frame.*] Doc was a rich boy when I married him. His mother left him $25,000 when she died. [*Disillusioned.*] It took him a lot to get his office started and everything—then, he got sick. [*She makes a futile gesture; then on the bright side.*] But Doc's always good to me—now.

Marie. [*Reenters.*] Oh, Doc's a peach.

Lola. I used to be pretty, something like you. [*She gets her picture from table left.*] I was Beauty Queen of the Senior Class in High School. My dad was awful strict, though. Once he caught me holding hands with that good-looking Dutch McCoy. Dad sent Dutch home, and wouldn't let me go out after supper for a whole month. Daddy would never let me go out with boys much. Just because I was pretty. He was afraid all the boys would get the wrong idea—*you* know. I never had any fun at all until I met Doc.

Marie. Sometimes I'm glad I didn't know my father. Mom always let me do pretty much as I please.

Lola. Doc was the first boy my dad ever let me go out with. We got married that spring.
          [*Replaces picture.* MARIE *sits davenport, puts on shoes and socks.*]

Marie. What did your father think of that?

Lola. We came right to the city then. And, well, Doc gave up his pre-Med course, and went to Chiropractor School instead.

Marie. You must have been married awful young.

Lola. Oh yes. Eighteen.

Marie. That must have made your father really mad.

Lola. Yes, it did. I never went home after that, but my mother comes down here from Green Valley to visit me sometimes.

Turk. [*Bursts into the front room from outside. He is a young, big, husky, good-looking boy, nineteen or twenty. He has the openness, the generosity, vigor and health of youth. He's had a little time in the service, but he is not what one would call disciplined. He wears faded dungarees and a T-shirt. He always enters unannounced. He hollers for* MARIE.] Hey, Marie! Ready?

Marie. [*Calling. Runs up center and exits bedroom, closing door.*] Just a minute, Turk.

Lola. [*Confidentially.*] I'll entertain him until you're ready. [*She is by nature coy and kittenish with an attractive man. Picks up papers—stuffs under table right.*] The house is such a mess, Turk! I'll bet you think I'm an awful housekeeper. Some day I'll surprise you. But you're like one of the family now. [*Pause.*] My, you're an early caller.

Turk. Gotta get to the library. Haven't cracked a book for a biology exam and Marie's gotta help me.

Lola. [*Unconsciously admiring his stature and physique and looking him over.*] My. I'd think you'd be chilly running around in just that thin little shirt.

Turk. Me? I go like this in the middle of winter.

Lola. Well, you're a big husky man.

Turk. [*Laughs.*] Oh, I'm a brute, *I* am.

Lola. You should be out in Hollywood making those Tarzan movies.

Turk. I had enough of that place when I was in the Navy.

Lola. That so?

Turk. [*Calling.*] Hey, Marie, hurry up.

Marie. [*Off.*] Oh, be patient, Turk.

Turk. [*To* LOLA.] She doesn't realize how busy I am. I'll only have a half hour to study at most. I gotta report to the coach at 10:30.

Lola. What are you in training for now?

Turk. Spring track. They got me throwing the javelin.

Lola. The javelin? What's that?

Turk. [*Laughs at her ignorance.*] It's a big, long lance. [*Assumes the magnificent position.*] You hold it like this, erect—then you let go and it goes singing through the air, and lands yards away, if you're any good at it, and sticks in the ground, quivering like an arrow. I won the State Championship last year.

Lola. [*She has watched as though fascinated.*] My!

Turk. [*Very generous.*] Get Marie to take you to the track field some afternoon, and you can watch me.

Lola. That would be thrilling.

Marie. [*Comes dancing in.*] Hi, Turk.

Turk. Hi, juicy.

Lola. [*As the* YOUNG COUPLE *move to the doorway.*] Remember, Marie, you and Turk can have the room tonight. All to yourselves. You can play the radio and dance and make a plate of fudge, or anything you want.

Marie. [*To* TURK.] O.K.?

Turk. [*With eagerness*]. Sure.

Marie. Let's go. [*Exits.*]

Lola. 'Bye, kids.

Turk. 'Bye, Mrs. Delaney. [*Gives her a chuck under the chin.*] You're a swell skirt.

[LOLA *couldn't be more flattered. For a moment she is breathless. They speed out the door and* LOLA *stands, sadly watching them depart. Then a sad, vacant look comes over her face. Her arms drop in a gesture of futility. Slowly she walks out on the front porch and calls.*]

Lola. Little Sheba! Come, Little She-ba. Come back—come back, Little Sheba! [*She waits for a few moments, then comes wearily back into the house, closing the door behind her. Now the morning has caught up with her. She goes to the kitchen, kicks off her pumps and gets back into comfies. The sight of the dishes on the drainboard depresses her. Clearly she is bored to death. Then the telephone rings with the promise of relieving her. She answers it.*] Hello—— Oh no, you've got the wrong number—— Oh, that's all right. [*Again it looks hopeless. She hears the* POSTMAN. *Now her spirits are lifted. She runs to the front door, opens it and awaits him. When he's within distance, she lets loose a barrage of welcome.*] 'Morning, Mr. Postman.

Postman. 'Morning, Ma'am.

Lola. You better have something for me today. Sometimes I think you don't even know I live here. You haven't left me anything for two whole weeks. If you can't do better than that, I'll just have to get a new postman.

Postman. [*On the porch.*] You'll have to get someone to write you some letters, Lady. Nope, nothing for you.

Lola. Well, I was only joking. You knew I was joking, didn't you? I'll bet you're thirsty. You come right in here and I'll bring you a glass of cold water. [*Enters living room.*] Come in and sit down for a few minutes and rest your feet a while.

Postman. I'll take you up on that, Lady. [*Coming in.*] I've worked up quite a thirst.

Lola. You sit down. I'll be back in just a minute.

[*Goes to kitchen, gets pitcher out of refrigerator and brings it back.*]

Postman. Spring is turnin' into summer awful soon.

Lola. You feel free to stop here and ask me for a drink of water any time you want to. [*Pouring drink.*] That's what we're all here for, isn't it? To make each other comfortable?

Postman. Thank you, Ma'am.

Lola. [*Clinging, not wanting to be left alone so soon; she hurries her conversation to hold him.*] You haven't been our postman very long, have you?

Postman. [*She hands him a glass of water, stands holding pitcher as he drinks.*] No.

Lola. You postmen have things pretty nice, don't you? I hear you get nice pensions after you been working for the government twenty years. I think that's dandy. It's a good job, too. [*Pours him a second glass.*] You may get tired but I think it's good for a man to be outside and get a lot of exercise. Keeps him strong and healthy. My husband, he's a doctor, a *chiro*practor; he has to stay inside his office all day long. The only exercise he gets is rubbin' people's backbones. [*They laugh.* LOLA *crosses left to table, leaves pitcher.*] It makes his hands strong. He's got the strongest hands you ever did see. But he's got a poor digestion. I keep tellin' him he oughta get some fresh air once in a while and some exercise. [POSTMAN *rises as if to go, and this hurries her into a more absorbing monologue.*] You know what? My husband is an Alcoholics Anonymous. He doesn't care if I tell you that 'cause he's proud of it. He hasn't touched a drop in almost a year. All that time we've had a quart of whiskey in the pantry for company and he hasn't even gone near it. Doesn't even want to. You know, alcoholics can't drink like ordinary people; they're *allergic* to it. It affects them different. They get started drinking and can't stop. Liquor transforms them. Sometimes they get mean and violent and wanta fight—but if they let liquor alone, they're perfectly all right, just like you and me. [POSTMAN *tries to leave.*] You should have seen Doc before he gave it up. He lost all his patients, wouldn't even go to the office; just wanted to stay drunk all day long and he'd come home at night and—— You just wouldn't believe it if you saw him now. He's got his patients all back, and he's just doing fine.

Postman. Sure I know Dr. Delaney. I deliver his office mail. He's a fine man.

Lola. Oh thanks. You don't ever drink, do you?

Postman. Oh, a few beers once in a while. [*He is ready to go.*]

Lola. Well, I guess that stuff doesn't do any of us any good.

Postman. No. [*Crosses down for mailbag on floor center.*] Well, good day, Ma'am.

Lola. Say, you got any kids?

Postman. Three grandchildren.

Lola. [*Getting it from table left.*] We don't have any kids, and we got this toy in a box of breakfast food. Why don't you take it home to them?

Postman. Why, that's very kind of you, Ma'am. [*He takes it, and goes.*]

Lola. Goodbye, Mr. Postman.

Postman. [*On porch.*] I'll see that you get a letter, if I have to write it myself.

Lola. Thanks. Goodbye. [*Left alone, she turns on radio. Then she goes to kitchen to start dishes, showing her boredom in the half-hearted way she washes them. Takes water back to ice box. Then she spies* Mrs. Coffman *hanging baby clothes on lines just outside kitchen door. Goes to door.*] My, you're a busy woman this morning, Mrs. Coffman.

Mrs. Coffman. [*German accent. She is outside, but sticks her head in for some of the following.*] Being busy is being happy.

Lola. I guess so.

Mrs. Coffman. I don't have it as easy as you. When you got seven kids to look after, you got no time to sit around the house, Mrs. Delaney.

Lola. I s'pose not.

Mrs. Coffman. But you don't hear me complain.

Lola. Oh, no. You never complain. [*Pause.*] I guess my little doggie's gone for good, Mrs. Coffman. I sure miss her.

Mrs. Coffman. The only way to keep from missing one dog is to get another.

Lola. [*To sink, turns off water.*] Oh, I never could find another doggy as cute as Little Sheba.

Mrs. Coffman. Did you put an ad in the paper?

Lola. For two whole weeks. No one answered it. It's just like she vanished—into thin air. [*She likes this metaphor.*] Every day, though, I go out on the porch and call her. You can't tell; she might be around. Don't you think?

Mrs. Coffman. You should get busy and forget her. You should get busy, Mrs. Delaney.

Lola. Yes, I'm going to. I'm going to start my spring house-cleaning one of these days real soon. Why don't you come in and have a cup of coffee with me, Mrs. Coffman, and we can chat a while?

Mrs. Coffman. I got work to do, Mrs. Delaney. I got work. [*Exits.*] [Lola *turns from the window, annoyed at her rejection. Is about to start in on the dishes when the* Milkman *arrives. She opens the back door and detains him.*]

Milkman. 'Morning, Mrs. Coffman.

Mrs. Coffman. 'Morning.

Lola. Hello there, Mr. Milkman. How are you today?

Milkman. 'Morning, Lady.

Lola. I think I'm going to want a few specials today. Can you come in a minute? [*To icebox.*]

Milkman. [*He probably is used to her. He is not a handsome man but husky and attractive in his uniform.*] What'll it be?

Lola. [*At icebox.*] Well, now, let's see. Have you got any cottage cheese?

Milkman. We always got cottage cheese, Lady. [*Showing her card.*] All you gotta do is check the items on the card and we leave 'em. Now I gotta go back to the truck.

Lola. Now, don't scold me. I always mean to do that but you're always here before I think of it. Now, I guess I'll need some coffee cream, too—half a pint.

Milkman. Coffee cream. O.K.

Lola. Now let me see—— Oh, yes, I want a quart of buttermilk. My husband has liked buttermilk ever since he stopped drinking. My husband's an alcoholic. Had to give it up. Did I ever tell you?

Milkman. Yes, Lady. [*Starts to go. She follows.*]

Lola. Now he can't get enough to eat. Eats six times a day. He comes home in the middle of the morning, and I fix him a snack. In the middle of the afternoon he has a malted milk with an egg in it. And then another snack before he goes to bed.

Milkman. What'd ya know?

Lola. Keeps his energy up.

Milkman. I'll bet. Anything else, Lady?

Lola. No, I guess not.

Milkman. [*Going out.*] Be back in a jiffy. [*Gives her slip. Exits.*]

Lola. I'm just so sorry I put you to so much extra work. [*He returns shortly with dairy products.*] After this I'm going to do my best to remember to check the card. I

don't think it's right to put people to extra work.   [*To icebox, puts things away.*]
Milkman. [*Smiles, is willing to forget.*] That's all right, Lady.
Lola. Maybe you'd like a piece of cake or a sandwich. Got some awfully good cold cuts in the icebox.
Milkman. No, thanks, Lady.   .
Lola. Or maybe you'd like a cup of coffee.
Milkman. No, thanks.
    [*He's checking the items, putting them on the bill.*]
Lola. You're just a young man. You oughta be going to college. I think everyone should have an education. Do you like your job?
Milkman. It's O.K.   [*Looks at* LOLA.]
Lola. You're a husky young man. You oughta be out in Hollywood making those Tarzan movies.
Milkman. [*Steps back. Feels a little flattered.*] When I first began on this job I didn't get enough exercise, so I started working out on the bar bell.
Lola. Bar bells?
Milkman. Keeps you in trim.
Lola. [*Fascinated.*] Yes, I imagine.
Milkman. I sent my picture in to Strength and Health last month. [*Proudly.*] It's a physique study! If they print it, I'll bring you a copy.
Lola. Oh, will you? I think we should all take better care of ourselves, don't you?
Milkman. If you ask me, Lady, that's what's wrong with the world today. We're not taking care of ourselves.
Lola. I wouldn't be surprised.
Milkman. Every morning I do forty push-ups before I eat my breakfast.
Lola. Push-ups?
Milkman. Like this. [*He spreads himself on the floor and demonstrates, doing three rapid push-ups.* LOLA *couldn't be more fascinated. Then he springs to his feet.*] That's good for shoulder development. Wanta feel my shoulders?
Lola. Why—why, yes. [*He makes one arm tense and puts her hand on his shoulder.*] Why, it's just like a rock.
Milkman. I can do seventy-nine without stopping.
Lola. Seventy-nine!
Milkman. Now feel my arm.
Lola. [*Does so.*] Goodness!
Milkman. You wouldn't believe what a puny kid I was. Sickly, no appetite.
Lola. Is that a fact? And, my! Look at you now.

Milkman. [*Very proud.*] Shucks, any man could do the same—if he just takes care of himself.
Lola. Oh sure, sure.
        [*A horn is heard offstage.*]
Milkman. There's my buddy. I gotta beat it. [*Picks up his things, shakes hands, leaves hurriedly.*] See you tomorrow, Lady.
Lola. 'Bye.
    [*She watches him from kitchen window until he gets out of sight. There is a look of some wonder on her face, an emptiness, as though she were unable to understand anything that ever happened to her. She looks at clock, runs into living room, turns on radio. A pulsating tom-tom is heard as a theme introduction. Then the* ANNOUNCER.]
Announcer. [*In dramatic voice.*] TA-BOOoooo! [*Now in a very soft, highly personalized voice.* LOLA *sits davenport, eats candy.*] It's Ta-boo, radio listeners, your fifteen minutes of temptation. [*An alluring voice.*] Won't you join me? [LOLA *swings feet up.*] Won't you leave behind your routine, the dull cares that make up your day-to-day existence, the little worries, the uncertainties, the confusions of the work-a-day world and follow me where pagan spirits hold sway, where lithe natives dance on a moon-enchanted isle, where palm trees sway with the restless ocean tide, restless surging on the white shore. Won't you come along? [*More tom-tom. Now in an oily voice.*] But remember, it's TA-BOOOOOooooo-OOO!
    [*Now the tom-tom again, going into a sensual, primitive rhythm melody.* LOLA *has been transfixed from the beginning of the program. She lies down on the davenport, listening. Then, slowly, growing more and more comfortable.*]
Western Union Boy. [*At door.*] Telegram for Miss Maria Buckholder.
Lola. She's not here.
Western Union Boy. Sign here.
    [LOLA *does, then she closes the door and brings the envelope into the house, looking at it wonderingly. This is a major temptation for her. She puts the envelope on the table down right, but can't resist looking at it. Finally she gives in and takes it to the kitchen to steam it open. Then* MARIE *and* TURK *burst into the room.* LOLA, *confused, wonders what to do with the telegram, then decides, just in the nick of time, to jam it in her apron pocket.*]
Marie. Mrs. Delaney! [*Turns off radio. At the sound of* MARIE's *voice,* LOLA, *embar-*

rassedly, runs in to greet them.] —mind if we turn your parlor into an art studio?

Lola. Sure, go right ahead. Hi, Turk.

[TURK *gives a wave of his arm.*]

Marie. [*To* TURK, *indicating her bedroom.*] You can change in there, Turk.

[TURK *goes into bedroom.*]

Lola. Change?

Marie. He's gotta take off his clothes.

Lola. Huh? [*Closes door.*]

Marie. These drawings are for my life class.

Lola. [*Consoled but still mystified.*] Oh.

Marie. [*Sits davenport.*] Turk's the best male model we've had all year. Lotsa athletes pose for us 'cause they've all got muscles. They're easier to draw.

Lola. You mean—he's gonna pose *naked?*

Marie. [*Laughs.*] No. The women do, but the men are always more proper. Turk's going to pose in his track suit.

Lola. Oh. [*Almost to herself.*] The women pose nude but the men don't. [*This strikes her as a startling inconsistency.*] If it's all right for a woman, it oughta be for a man.

Marie. [*Businesslike.*] The man always keeps covered. [*Calling to* TURK.] Hurry up, Turk.

Turk. [*With all his muscles in place, he comes out. He is not at all self-conscious about his semi-nudity. His body is something he takes very much for granted.* LOLA *is a little dazed by the spectacle of flesh.*] How do you want this lovely body? Same pose I took in Art Class?

Marie. Yah. Over there where I can get more light on you.

Turk. [*Opens door. Starts pose.*] Anything in the house I can use for a javelin?

Marie. Is there, Mrs. Delaney?

Lola. How about the broom?

Turk. O.K.

[LOLA *runs out to get it.* TURK *goes to her in kitchen, takes it, returns to living room and resumes pose.*]

Marie. [*From davenport, studying* TURK *in relation to her sketch-pad. Moves his leg.*] Your left foot a little more this way. [*Studying it.*] O.K., hold it.

[*Starts sketching rapidly and industriously.*]

Lola. [*Looks on, lingeringly. Starts unwillingly into kitchen, changes her mind and returns to the scene of action.* MARIE *and* TURK *are too busy to comment.* LOLA *looks at sketch, inspecting it.*] Well—that's real pretty, Marie. [*Marie is intent.* LOLA *moves closer to look at the drawing.*] It—it's real artistic. [*Pause.*] I wish *I* was artistic.

Turk. Baby, I can't hold this pose very long at a time.

Marie. Rest whenever you feel like it.

Turk. O.K.!

Marie. [*To* LOLA.] If I make a good drawing, they'll use it for the posters for the Spring Relays.

Lola. Ya. You told me.

Marie. [*To* TURK.] After I'm finished with these sketches I won't have to bother you any more.

Turk. No bother. [*Rubs his shoulder—he poses.*] Hard pose, though. Gets me in the shoulder.

[MARIE *pays no attention.* LOLA *peers at him so closely he becomes a little self-conscious and breaks pose. This also breaks* LOLA'S *concentration.*]

Lola. I'll heat you up some coffee.

[*Goes to kitchen.*]

Turk. [*Crosses to* MARIE. *Softly to* MARIE.] Hey, can't you keep her out of here? She makes me feel naked.

Marie. [*Laughs.*] I can't keep her out of her own house, can I?

Turk. Didn't she ever see a man before?

Marie. Not a big, beautiful man like you, Turky. [TURK *smiles, is flattered by any recognition of his physical worth, takes it as an immediate invitation to lovemaking. Pulling her up, he kisses her as* DOC *comes up on porch.* MARIE *pushes* TURK *away.*] Turk, get back in your corner.

Doc. [*Comes in from outside. Cheerily.*] Hi, everyone.

Marie. Hi.

Turk. Hi, Doc. [DOC *then sees* TURK, *feels immediate resentment. Goes into kitchen to* LOLA.] What's goin' on here?

Lola. [*Getting cups.*] Oh, hello, Daddy. Marie's doin' a drawin'.

Doc. [*Trying to size the situation up.* MARIE *and* TURK *are too busy to speak.*] Oh.

Lola. I've just heated up the coffee. Want some?

Doc. Yeah. What happened to Turk's clothes?

Lola. Marie's doing some drawings for her *life* classes, Doc.

Doc. Can't she draw him with his clothes on?

Lola. [*Crossing with coffee. Very professional now.*] No, Doc, it's not the same. See, it's a *life* class. They draw bodies. They all do it, right in the classroom.

Doc. Why, Marie's just a young girl; she shouldn't be drawing things like that. I don't care if they do teach it at college. It's not right.

Lola. [*Disclaiming responsibility.*] I don't know, Doc.

Turk. [*Turns.*] I'm tired.

Marie. [*Squats at his feet.*] Just let me finish the foot.

Doc. Why doesn't she draw something else—a bowl of flowers or a cathedral—or a sunset.

Lola. All she told me, Doc, was if she made a good drawing of Turk, they'd use it for the posters for the Spring Relay. [*Pause.*] So I guess they don't want sunsets.

Doc. What if someone walked into the house now? What would they think?

Lola. Daddy, Marie just asked me if it was all right if Turk came and posed for her. Now that's all she said, and I said O.K. But if you think it's wrong, I won't let them do it again.

Doc. I just don't like it.

Marie. Hold it a minute more.

Turk. O.K.

Lola. Well, then you speak to Marie about it if——

Doc. [*He'd never mention anything disapprovingly to* MARIE.] No, Baby. I couldn't do that.

Lola. Well then——

Doc. Besides, it's not her fault. If those college people make her do drawings like that, I suppose she has to do them. I just don't think it's right she should have to, that's all.

Lola. Well, if you think it's wrong——

Doc. [*Ready to dismiss it.*] Never mind.

Lola. I don't see any harm in it, Daddy.

Doc. Forget it.

Lola. [*To ice box.*] Would you like some buttermilk?

Doc. Thanks.

Marie. [*Finishes sketch.*] O.K. That's all I can do for today.

Turk. Is there anything I can do for *you?*

Marie. Yes—get your clothes on.

Turk. O.K., Coach.

[TURK *exits to bedroom.* MARIE *sits down right.*]

Lola. You know what Marie said, Doc? She said that the women posed naked, but the men don't.

Doc. Why, of course, Honey.

Lola. Why is that?

Doc. [*Stumped.*] —well——

Lola. If it's all right for a woman, it oughta be for a man. But the man always keeps covered. That's what she said.

Doc. Well, that's the way it should be, Honey. A man, after all, is a man, and he —well, he has to protect himself.

Lola. And a woman doesn't?

Doc. It's different, Honey.

Lola. Is it? I've got a secret, Doc. Bruce is comin'.

Doc. Is that so?

Lola. [*After a glum silence.*] You know —Marie's boy friend from Cincinnati. I promised Marie a long time ago, when her fiance came to town, dinner was on me. So I'm getting out the best china and cook the best meal you ever sat down to.

Doc. When did she get the news?

Lola. The telegram came this morning.

Doc. That's fine. That Bruce sounds to me like just the fellow for her. I think I'll go in and congratulate her.

Lola. [*Nervous.*] Not now, Doc.

Doc. Why not?

Lola. Well, Turk's there. It might make him feel embarrassed.

Doc. Well, why doesn't Turk clear out now that Bruce is coming? What's he hanging around for? She's engaged to marry Bruce, isn't she?

[TURK *enters from bedroom and goes to* MARIE, *starting to make advances.*]

Lola. Marie's just doing a picture of him, Doc.

Doc. You always stick up for him. You encourage him.

Lola. Shhh, Daddy. Don't get upset.

Doc. [*Very angrily.*] All right, but if anything happens to the girl I'll never forgive you.

[*Doc goes upstairs.* TURK *then grabs* MARIE, *kisses her passionately.*]

CURTAIN

SCENE II

The same evening, after supper. Outside it is dark. There has been an almost miraculous transformation of the entire house. LOLA, *apparently, has been working hard and fast all day. The rooms are spotlessly clean and there are such additions as new lampshades, fresh curtains, etc. In the kitchen all the enamel surfaces glisten, and piles of junk that have lain around for months have been disposed of.*

[LOLA *and* DOC *are in the kitchen, he washing up the dishes and she puttering around putting the finishing touches on her housecleaning.*]

Lola. [*At stove.*] There's still some beans left. Do you want them, Doc?

Doc. I had enough.

Lola. I hope you got enough to eat to-night, Daddy. I been so busy cleaning I didn't have time to fix you much.

Doc. I wasn't very hungry.

Lola. [*To table, cleaning up.*] You know what? Mrs. Coffman said I could come over and pick all the lilacs I wanted for my centerpiece tomorrow. Isn't that nice? I don't think she poisoned Little Sheba, do you?

Doc. I never did think so, Baby. Where'd you get the new curtains?

Lola. I went out and bought them this afternoon. Aren't they pretty? Be careful of the woodwork; it's been varnished.

Doc. How come, Honey?

Lola. [*Gets broom and dust pan from closet.*] Bruce is comin'. I figured I had to do my spring house-cleaning sometime.

Doc. You got all this done in one day? The house hasn't looked like this in years.

Lola. I can be a good housekeeper when I want to be, can't I, Doc?

Doc. [*Kneels, holding dustpan for* LOLA.] I never had any complaints. Where's Marie now?

Lola. I don't know, Doc. I haven't seen her since she left here this morning with Turk.

Doc. [*Rises. A look of disapproval.*] Marie's too good to be wasting her time with him.

Lola. Daddy, Marie can take care of herself. Don't worry. [*To closet—returns broom.*]

Doc. [*Goes into living room.*] 'Bout time for Fibber McGee and Molly.

Lola. [*Untying apron. To closet and then to back door.*] Daddy, I'm gonna run over to Mrs. Coffman's and see if she's got any silver polish. I'll be right back.

[Doc *goes to radio.* LOLA *exits. At the radio* Doc *starts twisting the dial. He rejects one noisy program after another, then very unexpectedly he comes across a rendition of Schubert's famous "Ave Maria," sung in a high soprano voice. Probably he has encountered the piece before somewhere, but it is now making its first impression on him. Gradually he is transported into a world of ethereal beauty which he never knew existed. He listens intently. The music has expressed some ideal of beauty he never fully realized and he is even a little mystified. Then* LOLA *comes in the back door, letting it slam, breaking the spell, and announcing in a loud, energetic voice.*]

Lola. Isn't it funny? I'm not a bit tired tonight. You'd think after working so hard all day I'd be pooped.

Doc. [*He cringes.*] Baby, don't use that word.

Lola. [*Sets silver polish down and joins* Doc *on davenport.*] I'm sorry, Doc. I hear Marie and Turk say it all the time, and I thought it was kinda cute.

Doc. It—it sounds vulgar.

Lola. [*Kisses* Doc.] I won't say it again, Daddy. Where's Fibber McGee?

Doc. Not quite time yet.

Lola. Let's get some peppy music.

Doc. [*Tuning in a sentimental dance band.*] That what you want?

Lola. That's O.K. [Doc *takes a pack of cards off radio, returns to davenport and starts shuffling them very deftly.*] I love to watch you shuffle cards, Daddy. You use your hands so gracefully. [*She watches closely.*] Do me one of your card tricks.

Doc. Baby, you've seen them all.

Lola. But I never get tired of them.

Doc. O.K. Take a card. [LOLA *does.*] Keep it now. Don't tell me what it is.

Lola. I won't.

Doc. [*Shuffling cards again.*] Now put it back in the deck. I won't look. [*He closes his eyes.*]

Lola. [*With childish delight.*] All right.

Doc. Put it back.

Lola. Uh-huh.

Doc. O.K. [*Shuffles cards again, cutting them, taking top half off, exposing* LOLA's *card, to her astonishment.*] That your card?

Lola. [*Unbelievingly.*] Daddy, how did you do it?

Doc. Baby, I've pulled that trick on you dozens of times.

Lola. But I never understand how you do it.

Doc. Very simple.

Lola. Docky, show me how you do that.

Doc. [*You can forgive him a harmless feeling of superiority.*] Try it for yourself.

Lola. Doc, you're clever. I never could do it.

Doc. Nothing to it.

Lola. There is *too.* Show me how you do it, Doc.

Doc. And give away all my secrets? It's a gift, Honey. A magic gift.

Lola. Can't you give it to me?

Doc. [*Picks up newspaper.*] A man has to keep some things to himself.

Lola. It's not a gift at all, it's just some trick you *learned.*

Doc. O.K., Baby, any way you want to look at it.

Lola. Let's have some music. How soon do you have to meet Ed Anderson?

Doc. [*Turns on radio.*] I still got a little time. [*Pleased.*]

Lola. Marie's going to be awfully happy when she sees the house all fixed up. She can entertain Bruce here when he comes, and maybe we could have a little party here and you can do your card tricks.

Doc. O.K.

Lola. I think a young girl should be able to bring her friends home.

Doc. Sure.

Lola. We never liked to sit around the house 'cause the folks always stayed there with us. [*Rises—starts dancing alone.*] Remember the dances we used to go to, Daddy?

Doc. Sure.

Lola. We had awful good times—for a while, didn't we?

Doc. Yes, Baby.

Lola. Remember the homecoming dance, when Charlie Kettlekamp and I won the Charleston Contest?

Doc. Yah. Please, Honey, I'm trying to read.

Lola. And you got mad at him 'cause he thought he should take me home afterwards.

Doc. I did not.

Lola. Yes, you did. Charlie was all right, Doc, really he was. You were just jealous.

Doc. I *wasn't* jealous.

Lola. [*She has become very coy and flirtatious now, an old dog playing old tricks.*] You got jealous. Every time we went out any place and I even looked at another boy. There was never anything between Charlie and me; there never was.

Doc. That was a long time ago——

Lola. Lots of other boys called me up for dates—Sammy Knight—Hand Biederman—Dutch McCoy.

Doc. Sure, Baby. You were the "it" girl.

Lola. [*Pleading for his attention now.*] But I saved all my dates for *you,* didn't I, Doc?

Doc. [*Trying to joke.*] As far as *I* know, Baby.

Lola. [*Hurt.*] Daddy, I did. You *got* to believe that. I never took a date with any other boy but you.

Doc. [*A little weary and impatient.*] That's all forgotten now. [*Turns off radio.*]

Lola. How can you talk that way, Doc? That was the happiest time of our lives. I'll never forget it.

Doc. [*Disapprovingly.*] Honey!

Lola. [*At the window.*] That was a nice spring. The trees were so heavy and green and the air smelled so sweet. Remember the

walks we used to take, down to the old chapel, where it was so quiet and still?

[*Sits davenport.*]

Doc. In the spring a young man's fancy turns—pretty fancy.

Lola. [*In the same tone of reverie.*] I was pretty then, wasn't I, Doc? Remember the first time you kissed me? You were scared as a young girl, I believe, Doc; you trembled so. [*She is being very soft and delicate. Caught in the reverie, he chokes a little and cannot answer.*] We'd been going together all year and you were always so shy. Then for the first time you grabbed me and kissed me. Tears came to your eyes, Doc, and you said you'd love me forever and ever. Remember? You said—if I didn't marry you, you wanted to die—I remember 'cause it scared me for anyone to say a thing like that.

Doc. [*In a repressed tone.*] Yes, Baby.

Lola. And when the evening came on, we stretched out on the cool grass and you kissed me all night long.

Doc. [*Opens door.*] Baby, you've got to forget those things. That was twenty years ago.

Lola. I'll soon be forty. Those years have just vanished—vanished into thin air.

Doc. Yes.

Lola. Just disappeared—like Little Sheba. [*Pause.*] Maybe you're sorry you married me now. You didn't know I was going to get old and fat and sloppy——

Doc. Oh, Baby!

Lola. It's the truth. That's what I am. But I didn't know it, either. Are you sorry you married me, Doc?

Doc. Of course not.

Lola. I mean, are you sorry you *had* to marry me?

Doc. [*Onto porch.*] We were never going to talk about that, Baby.

Lola. [*Following* Doc *out.*] You *were* the first one, Daddy, the *only* one. I'd just die if you didn't believe that.

Doc. [*Tenderly.*] I know, Baby.

Lola. You were so nice and so proper, Doc; I thought nothing we could do together could ever be wrong—or make us unhappy. Do you think we did wrong, Doc?

Doc. [*Consoling.*] No, Baby, of course I don't.

Lola. I don't think anyone knows about it except my folks, do you?

Doc. [*Crossing in to up right.*] Of course not, Baby.

Lola. [*Follows in.*] I wish the baby had lived, Doc. I don't think that woman knew her business, do you, Doc?

Doc. I guess not.

Lola. If we'd gone to a doctor, she would have lived, don't you think?

Doc. Perhaps.

Lola. A doctor wouldn't have known we'd just got married, would he? Why were we so afraid?

Doc. [*Sits davenport.*] We were just kids. Kids don't know how to look after things.

Lola. [*Sits davenport.*] If we'd had the baby she'd be a young girl now; then maybe you'd have *saved* your money, Doc, and she could be going to college—like Marie.

Doc. Baby, what's done is done.

Lola. It must make you feel bad at times to think you had to give up being a doctor and to think you don't have any money like you used to.

Doc. No—no, Baby. We should never feel bad about what's past. What's in the past can't be helped. You—you've got to forget it and live for the present. If you can't forget the past, you stay in it and never get out. I might be a big M.D. today, instead of a chiropractor; we might have had a family to raise and be with us now; I might still have a lot of money if I'd used my head and invested it carefully, instead of gettin' drunk every night. We might have a nice house, and comforts, and friends. But we don't have any of those things. So what! We gotta keep on living, don't we? I can't stop just 'cause I made a few mistakes. I gotta keep goin' —somehow.

Lola. Sure, Daddy.

Doc. [*Sighs and wipes brow.*] I—I wish you wouldn't ask me questions like that, Baby. Let's not talk about it any more. I gotta keep goin', and not let things upset me, or—or—*I* saw enough at the City Hospital to keep me sober for a long time.

Lola. I'm sorry, Doc. I didn't mean to upset you.

Doc. I'm not upset.

Lola. What time'll you be home tonight?

Doc. 'Bout eleven o'clock.

Lola. I wish you didn't have to go tonight. I feel kinda lonesome.

Doc. Ya, so do I, Baby, but sometime soon we'll go *out* together. I kinda hate to go to those night clubs and places since I stopped drinking, but some night I'll take you out to dinner.

Lola. Oh, will you, Daddy?

Doc. We'll get dressed up and go to the Windermere and have a fine dinner, and dance between courses.

Lola. [*Eagerly.*] Let's do, Daddy. I got a little money saved up. I got about forty dollars out in the kitchen. We can take that if you need it.

Doc. I'll have plenty of money the first of the month.

Lola. [*She has made a quick response to the change of mood, seeing a future evening of carefree fun.*] What are we sitting round here so serious for? [*To radio.*] Let's have some music. [*LOLA gets a lively foxtrot on the radio, dances with DOC. They begin dancing vigorously, as though to dispense with the sadness of the preceding dialogue, but slowly it winds them and leaves LOLA panting.*] We oughta go dancing—all the time, Docky—It'd be good for us. Maybe if I danced more often I'd lose—some of—this fat. I remember—I used to be able to dance like this—all night—and not even notice—it. [*LOLA breaks into a Charleston routine as of yore.*] Remember the Charleston, Daddy?

[*DOC is clapping his hands in rhythm. Then MARIE bursts in through the front door, the personification of the youth that LOLA is trying to recapture.*]

Doc. Hi, Marie!

Marie. What are you trying to do, a jig, Mrs. Delaney?

[*MARIE doesn't intend her remark to be cruel, but it wounds LOLA. LOLA stops abruptly in her dancing, losing all the fun she has been able to create for herself. She feels she might cry, so to hide her feelings she hurries quietly out to kitchen. DOC and MARIE do not notice.*]

Marie. [*Noticing the change in atmosphere.*] Hey, what's been happening around here?

Doc. Lola got to feeling industrious. You oughta see the kitchen.

Marie. [*Running to kitchen, where she is too observant of the changes to notice LOLA is weeping in corner. LOLA, of course, straightens up as soon as MARIE enters.*] What got into you, Mrs. Delaney? You've done wonders with the house. It looks marvellous.

Lola. [*Quietly.*] Thanks, Marie.

Marie. [*Darting back into living room.*] I can hardly believe I'm in the same place.

Doc. [*Meaning BRUCE.*] Think your boy friend'll like it?

Marie. [*Thinking of TURK.*] You know how men are. Turk never notices things like that.

[*Starts into her own room, blowing a kiss to DOC on her way. LOLA comes back in, dabbing at her eyes.*]

Doc. Turk? [*MARIE is gone; turning to LOLA.*] What's the matter, Honey?

Lola. I don't know.

Doc. Feel bad about something?

Lola. I didn't want her to see me dancing that way. Makes me feel sorta silly.

Doc. Why, you're a fine dancer.

Lola. I feel kinda silly.

Marie. [*Jumps back into the room with her telegram.*] My telegram's here. When did it come?

Lola. It came about an hour ago, Honey. [LOLA *looks nervously at* DOC. DOC *looks puzzled and a little sore.*]

Marie. Bruce is coming! "Arriving tomorrow 5:00 P.M. CST, Flight 22, Love, Bruce." When did the telegram come?

Doc. So it came an hour ago. [*Looks hopelessly at* LOLA, *then goes to kitchen.*]

Lola. [*Nervously.*] Isn't it nice I got the house all cleaned? Marie, you bring Bruce to dinner with us tomorrow night. It'll be a sort of wedding present.

Marie. That would be wonderful, Mrs. Delaney, but I don't want you to go to any trouble.

Lola. No trouble at all. Now I insist. [*Front doorbell rings.*] That must be Turk.

Marie. [*Whispers.*] Don't tell *him*. [*Goes to door.* LOLA *scampers to kitchen.*] Hi, Turk. Come on in.

Turk. [*Entering. Stalks her.*] Hi. [*Looks around to see if anyone is present, then takes her in his arms and starts to kiss her.*]

Lola. I'm sorry, Doc. I'm sorry about the telegram.

Doc. Baby, people don't do things like that. Don't you understand? *Nice* people don't.

Marie. Stop it!

Turk. What's the matter?

Marie. They're in the kitchen. [*Goes into bedroom.* TURK *sits with book.*]

Doc. Why didn't you give it to her when it came?

Lola. Well, Doc, Turk was posing for Marie this morning, and I couldn't give it to her while he was here. [TURK *listens at door.*]

Doc. Well, it just isn't nice to open other people's mail. [TURK *crosses up to* MARIE'S *door.*]

Lola. I guess I'm not nice, then. That what you mean?

Marie. Turk, will you get away from that door?

Doc. No, Baby, but——

Lola. I don't see any harm in it, Doc. I steamed it open and sealed it back. [TURK *at switch in living room.*] She'll never know

the difference. I don't see any harm in that, Doc.

Doc. [*Gives up.*] O.K., Baby, if you don't see any harm in it, I guess I can't explain it. [*Starts getting ready to go.*]

Lola. I'm sorry, Doc. Honest, I'll never do it again. Will you forgive me?

Doc. [*Giving her a peck of a kiss.*] I forgive you.

Marie. [*Comes back with book.*] Let's look like we're studying.

Turk. Biology? Hot dog!

Lola. [*After* MARIE *leaves her room.*] Now I feel better. Do you have to go now? [TURK *sits by* MARIE *on davenport.*]

Doc. Yah.

Lola. Before you go why don't you show your tricks to Marie.

Doc. [*Reluctantly.*] Not now.

Lola. Oh, please do. They'd be crazy about them.

Doc. [*With pride.*] O.K. [*Preens himself a little.*] If you think they'd enjoy them— [LOLA, *starting to living room, stops suddenly upon seeing* MARIE *and* TURK *spooning behind a book. A broad, pleased smile breaks on her face and she stands silently watching.* Doc, *at sink.*] Well—what's the matter, Baby?

Lola. [*Soft voice.*] Oh—nothing—nothing —Doc.

Doc. Well, do you want me to show 'em my tricks or don't you?

Lola. [*Coming back to center of kitchen; in a secretive voice with a little giggle.*] I guess they wouldn't be interested now.

Doc. [*With injured pride. A little sore.*] Oh, very well.

Lola. Come and look, Daddy.

Doc. [*Shocked and angry.*] No!

Lola. Just one little look. They're just kids, Daddy. It's sweet. [*Drags him by arm.*]

Doc. [*Jerking loose.*] Stop it, Baby. I won't do it. It's not decent to snoop around spying on people like that. It's cheap and mischievous and mean.

Lola. [*This had never occurred to her.*] Is it?

Doc. Of course it is.

Lola. I don't spy on Marie and Turk to be mischievous and mean.

Doc. Then why *do* you do it?

Lola. You watch young people make love in the movies, don't you, Doc? There's nothing wrong with that. And I *know* Marie and I like her, and Turk's nice, too. They're both so young and pretty. Why shouldn't I watch them?

Doc. I give up.

Lola. Well, why shouldn't I?

Doc. I don't know, Baby, but it's not nice. [TURK *kisses* MARIE'S *ear.*]

Lola. I think it's one of the nicest things I know. [*Plaintive.*]

Marie. Let's go out on the porch. [*They steal out.*]

Doc. It's not right for Marie to do that, particularly since Bruce is coming. We shouldn't allow it.

Lola. Oh, they don't do any harm, Doc. I think it's all right.

Doc. It's not all right. I don't know why you encourage that sort of thing.

Lola. I don't encourage it.

Doc. You do, too. You like that fellow Turk. You said so. And I say he's no good. Marie's sweet and innocent; she doesn't understand guys like him. I think I oughta run him outa the house.

Lola. Daddy, you wouldn't do that.

Doc. [*Very heated.*] Then you talk to her and tell her how we feel.

Lola. Hush, Daddy. They'll hear you.

Doc. I don't care if they do hear me.

Lola. [*To* DOC *at stove.*] Don't get upset, Daddy. Bruce is coming and Turk won't be around any longer. I promise you.

Doc. All right. I better go.

Lola. I'll go with you, Doc. Just let me run up and get a sweater. Now wait for me.

Doc. Hurry, Baby.

[LOLA *goes upstairs.* DOC *is at platform when he hears* TURK *laugh on the porch. He goes down left to cabinet—sees whiskey bottle. Reaches for it and hears* MARIE *giggle. Turns away as* TURK *laughs again. Turns back to the bottle and hears* LOLA'S *voice from upstairs.* MARIE *and* TURK *return to living room.* TURK *takes* LOLA'S *picture from shelf up right.*]

Lola. I'll be there in a minute, Doc. [*Enters downstairs.*] I'm all ready. [DOC *turns out kitchen lights and they go into living room.*] I'm walking Doc down to the bus. [DOC *sees* TURK *with* LOLA'S *picture. Takes it out of his hand, puts it on shelf up right as* LOLA *leads him out.* DOC *is off.*] Come on, Dad, here's your hat. Then I'll go for a long walk in the moonlight. Have a good time. [*She exits.*]

Marie. 'Bye, Mrs. Delaney.

Turk. He hates my guts. [*To front door.*]

Marie. Oh, he does not.

[*Follows* TURK, *blocks his exit in door.*]

Turk. Yes, he does. If you ask me, he's jealous.

Marie. Jealous?

Turk. I've always thought he had a crush on you.

Marie. Now, Turk, don't be silly. Doc is nice to me. It's just in a few little things he does, like fixing my breakfast, but he's nice to everyone.

Turk. He ever make a pass?

Marie. No. He'd never get fresh.

Turk. He better not.

Marie. Turk, don't be ridiculous. Doc's such a nice, quiet man; if he gets any fun out of being nice to me, why not?

Turk. He's got a wife of his own, hasn't he? Why doesn't he make a few passes at her?

Marie. Things like that are none of our business.

Turk. O.K. How about a snuggle, Lovely?

Marie. [*A little prim and businesslike.*] No more for tonight, Turk.

Turk. Why's tonight different from any other night?

Marie. I think we should make it a rule, every once in a while, just to sit and talk. [*Starts to sit davenport—crosses to chair down right.*]

Turk. [*Restless. Sits davenport.*] O.K. What'll we talk about?

Marie. Well—there's lotsa things.

Turk. O.K. Start in.

Marie. A person doesn't start a conversation that way.

Turk. Start it any way you want to.

Marie. Two people should have something to talk about, like politics or psychology or religion.

Turk. How 'bout sex?

Marie. Turk!

Turk. [*Chases her around davenport.*] Have you read the Kinsey report, Miss Buckholder?

Marie. I should say not.

Turk. How old were you when you had your first affair, Miss Buckholder?—and did you ever have relations with your grandfather?

Marie. Turk, stop it.

Turk. You wanted to talk about something; I was only trying to please. Let's have a kiss.

Marie. Not tonight.

Turk. Who you savin' it up for?

Marie. Don't talk that way.

Turk. [*Yawns—crosses to door.*] Well, thanks, Miss Buckholder, for a nice evening. It's been a most enjoyable talk.

Marie. [*Anxious.*] Turk, where are you going?

Turk. I guess I'm a man of action, Baby.

Marie. Turk, don't go.

Turk. Why not? I'm not doin' any good here.

Marie. Don't go.

Turk. [*Returns and she touches him.*] Now why didn't you think of this before? C'mon, let's get to work.

[*They sit on davenport.*]

Marie. Oh Turk, this is all we ever do.

Turk. Are you complaining?

Marie. [*Weakly.*] —no.

Turk. Then what do you want to put on such a front for?

Marie. —it's not a front.

Turk. What else is it? [*Mimicking.*] Oh, no, Turk. Not tonight, Turk. I want to talk about philosophy, Turk. [*Himself again.*] When all the time you know that if I went outa here without givin' you a good lovin' up you'd be sore as hell—— Wouldn't you?

Marie. [*She has to admit to herself it's true; she chuckles.*] Oh—Turk——

Turk. It's true, isn't it?

Marie. Maybe.

Turk. How about tonight, Lovely; going to be lonesome?

Marie. Turk, you have the Spring Relays.

Turk. What of it? I can throw that old javelin any old time, *any* old time. C'mon, Baby, we've got by with it before, haven't we?

Marie. I'm not so sure.

Turk. What do you mean?

Marie. Sometimes I think Mrs. Delaney knows.

Turk. Well, bring her along. I'll take care of her too, if it'll keep her quiet.

Marie. [*A pretense of being shocked.*] Turk!

Turk. What makes you think so?

Marie. Women just sense those things. She asks so many questions.

Turk. She ever *say* anything?

Marie. No.

Turk. Now *you're* imagining things.

Marie. Maybe.

Turk. Well, stop it.

Marie. O.K.

Turk. [*Rises—follows* MARIE.] Honey, I know I talk awful rough around you at times; I never was a very gentlemanly bastard, but you really don't mind it—do you? [*She only smiles mischievously.*] Anyway, you know I'm nuts about you.

Marie. [*Smug.*] Are you?

[*Now they engage in a little rough-house, he cuffing her like an affectionate bear, she responding with "Stop it," "Turk, that hurt," etc. And she slaps him playfully. Then they laugh together at their own pretense. Now* LOLA *enters the back way very quietly, tiptoeing through the dark kitchen, standing by the doorway where she can peek at them. There is a quiet, satisfied smile on her face. She watches every move they make, alertly.*]

Turk. Now, Miss Buckholder, what is your opinion of the psychodynamic pressure of living in the atomic age?

Marie. [*Playfully.*] Turk, don't make fun of me.

Turk. Tonight?

Marie. [*Her eyes dance as she puts him off just a little longer.*] —well.

Turk. Tonight will never come again. [*This is true. She smiles.*] O.K.?

Marie. Tonight will never come again— O.K. [*They embrace and start to dance.*] Let's go out somewhere first and have a few beers. We can't come back till they're asleep.

Turk. O.K.

[*They dance slowly out the door. Then* LOLA *moves quietly into the living room and out onto the porch. There she can be heard calling plaintively in a lost voice.*]

Lola. Little Sheba—come back—Come back, Little Sheba. Come back.

CURTAIN

ACT TWO

SCENE I

The next morning.

[LOLA *and* DOC *are at breakfast again.* LOLA *is rambling on while* DOC *sits meditatively, his head down, his face in his hands.*]

Lola. [*In a light, humorous way, as though the faults of youth were as blameless as the uncontrollable actions of a puppy. Chuckles.*] Then they danced for a while and went out together, arm in arm——

Doc. [*Left of table. Very nervous and tense.*] I don't wanta hear any more about it, Baby.

Lola. What's the matter, Docky?

Doc. Nothing.

Lola. You look like you didn't feel very good.

Doc. I didn't sleep well last night.

Lola. You didn't take any of those sleeping pills, did you?

Doc. No.

Lola. Well, don't. The doctors say they're terrible for you.

Doc. I'll feel better after a while.

Lola. Of course you will.

Doc. What time did Marie come in last night?

Lola. I don't know, Doc. I went to bed early and went right to sleep. Why?

Doc. Oh—nothing.

Lola. You musta slept if you didn't hear her.

Doc. I heard her; it was after midnight.

Lola. Then what did you ask me for?

Doc. I wasn't sure it was her.

Lola. What do you mean?

Doc. I thought I heard a man's voice.

Lola. Turk probably brought her inside the door.

Doc. [*Troubled.*] I thought I heard someone laughing. A man's laugh—I guess I was just hearing things.

Lola. Say your prayer?

Doc. [*Gets up.*] Yes.

Lola. Kiss me 'bye. [*He leans over and kisses her, then puts on his coat and starts to leave.*] Do you think you could get home a little early? I want you to help me entertain Bruce. Marie said he'd be here about 5:30. I'm going to have a lovely dinner: stuffed pork chops, twice-baked potatoes, and asparagus, and for dessert a big chocolate cake and maybe ice cream——

Doc. Sounds fine.

Lola. So you get home and help me.

Doc. O.K.

[*Doc leaves kitchen and goes into living room. Again on the chair down right is* MARIE's *scarf. He picks it up as before and fondles it. Then there is the sound of* TURK's *laughter, soft and barely audible. It sounds like the laugh of a sated Bacchus. Doc's body stiffens. It is a sickening fact he must face and it has been revealed to him in its ugliest light. The lyrical grace, the spiritual ideal of Ave Maria is shattered. He has been fighting the truth, maybe suspecting all along that he was deceiving himself. Now he looks as though he might vomit. All his blind confusion is inside him. With an immobile expression of blankness on his face, he stumbles*

into the table above the davenport.]

Lola. [*Still in kitchen.*] Haven't you gone yet, Docky?

Doc. [*Dazed.*] No—no, Baby.

Lola. [*Coming in doorway.*] Anything the matter?

Doc. No—no. I'm all right now. [*Drops scarf, takes hat. He has managed to sound perfectly natural. He braces himself and goes out.* LOLA *stands a moment, looking after him with a little curiosity. Then* MRS. COFFMAN *enters, sticks her head in back door.*]

Mrs. Coffman. Anybody home?

Lola. [*On platform.*] 'Morning, Mrs. Coffman.

Mrs. Coffman. [*Inspecting the kitchen's new look.*] So this is what you've been up to, Mrs. Delaney.

Lola. [*Proud.*] Yes, I been busy. [*MARIE's door opens and closes.* MARIE *sticks her head out of her bedroom door to see if the coast is clear, then sticks her head back in again to whisper to* TURK *that he can leave without being observed.*]

Mrs. Coffman. Busy? Good Lord, I never seen such activity. What got into you, Lady?

Lola. Company tonight. I thought I'd fix things up a little.

Mrs. Coffman. You mean you done all this in one day?

Lola. [*With simple pride.*] I said I been busy.

Mrs. Coffman. Dear God, you done your spring housecleaning all in one day.

[*TURK appears in living room.*]

Lola. [*Appreciating this.*] I fixed up the living room a little, too.

Mrs. Coffman. I must see it. [*Goes into living room.* TURK *apprehends her and ducks back into* MARIE's *room, shutting the door behind himself and* MARIE.] I declare! Overnight you turn the place into something really swanky.

Lola. Yes, and I bought a few new things, too.

Mrs. Coffman. Neat as a pin, and so warm and cozy. I take my hat off to you, Mrs. Delaney. I didn't know you had it in you. All these years, now, I been sayin' to myself, "That Mrs. Delaney is a good for nothing—sits around the house all day, and never so much as shakes a dust mop." I guess it just shows, we never really know what people are like.

Lola. I still got some coffee, Mrs. Coffman.

Mrs. Coffman. Not now, Mrs. Delaney. Seeing your house so clean makes me feel

ashamed. I gotta get home and get to work.
[*To kitchen.*]

Lola. [*Follows.*] I hafta get busy, too.
I got to get out all the silver and china. I
like to set the table early, so I can spend the
rest of the day looking at it.
[BOTH *laugh.*]

Mrs. Coffman. Good day, Mrs. Delaney.
[*Exits.*]

[*Hearing the screen door slam,* MARIE
guards the kitchen door and TURK *slips
out the front. But neither has counted
on* DOC's *reappearance. After seeing
that* TURK *is safe,* MARIE *blows a good-
bye kiss to him and joins* LOLA *in the
kitchen. But* DOC *is coming in the front
door just as* TURK *starts to go out.
There is a moment of blind embarrassment, during which* DOC *only looks
stupefied and* TURK, *after mumbling an
unintelligible apology, runs out. First*
DOC *is mystified, trying to figure it all
out. His face looks more and more troubled. Meanwhile,* MARIE *and* LOLA *are
talking in the kitchen.*]

Marie. Boo!
[*Sneaking up behind* LOLA *at back porch.*]

Lola. [*Jumping around.*] Heavens! You
scared me, Marie. You up already?

Marie. Yah.

Lola. This is Saturday. You could sleep
as late as you wanted.

Marie. I thought I'd get up early and help
you.   [*Pouring a cup of coffee.*]

Lola. Honey, I'd sure appreciate it. You
can put up the table in the living room, after
you've had your breakfast. That's where
we'll eat. Then you can help me set it.
[DOC *closes door.*]

Marie. O.K.

Lola. Want a sweet roll?

Marie. I don't think so. Turk and I had
so much beer last night. He got kinda tight.

Lola. He shouldn't do that, Marie.

Marie. [*Starts for living room.*] Just
keep the coffee hot for me. I'll want another
cup in a minute. [*Stops on seeing* DOC.]
Why, Dr. Delaney. I thought you'd gone.

Doc. [*In his usual manner.*] Good morning, Marie.   [*But not looking at her.*]

Marie. [*She immediately wonders.*] Why
—why—how long have you been here, Doc?

Doc. Just got here, just this minute.

Lola. That you, Daddy?   [*Comes in.*]

Doc. It's me.

Lola. What are you doing back?

Doc. I—I just thought I'd feel better—if
I took a glass of soda water——

Lola. I'm afraid you're not well, Daddy.

Doc. I'm all right.   [*Starts for kitchen.*]

Lola. [*Helping* MARIE *move table from
behind davenport to right center.*] The
soda's on the drain board.

[DOC *goes to kitchen, fixes some soda,
but stands a moment, just thinking.
Then he sits sipping the soda, as though
he were trying to make up his mind
about something.*]

Lola. Marie, would you help me move the
table? It'd be nice now if we had a dining
room, wouldn't it? But if we had a dining
room, I guess we wouldn't have you, Marie.
It was my idea to turn the dining room into
a bedroom and rent it. I thought of lots of
things to do for extra money—a few years
ago—when Doc was so—so sick.

[*They set up table.* LOLA *gets cloth
from cabinet up left.*]

Marie. This is a lovely tablecloth.

Lola. Irish linen. Doc's mother gave it to
us when we got married. She gave us all
our silver and china, too. The china's Have-
lin. I'm so proud of it. It's the most valuable possession we own. I just washed it—
Will you help me bring it in? [*Getting china
from kitchen.*] Doc was sortuva Mama's
boy. He was an only child and his mother
thought the sun rose and set in him. Didn't
she, Docky? She brought Doc up like a real
gentleman.

Marie. Where are the napkins?

Lola. Oh, I forgot them. They're so nice
I keep them in my bureau drawer with my
handkerchiefs. Come upstairs and we'll get
them.

[LOLA *and* MARIE *go upstairs. Then,*
DOC *listens to be sure* LOLA *and* MARIE
*are upstairs, looks cautiously at the
whiskey bottle on cabinet shelf, but
manages to resist several times. Finally
he gives in to temptation, grabs bottle
off shelf, then starts wondering how to
get past* LOLA *with it. Finally, it occurs
to him to wrap it inside his trench coat,
which he gets from closet and carries it
over his arm.* LOLA *and* MARIE *are heard
upstairs and they return to the living
room and continue setting table as* DOC
enters from kitchen on his way out.]

Lola. [*Coming downstairs.*] Did you ever
notice how nice he keeps his fingernails? Not
many men think of things like that. And he
used to take his mother to church every
Sunday.

Marie. [*At table.*] Oh, Doc's a real
gentleman.

Lola. Treats women like they were all
beautiful angels. We went together a whole
year before he even kissed me. [DOC *comes
through the living room with coat and bottle,*

going to front door.] On your way back to the office now, Docky?

Doc. [*His back to them.*] Yes.

Lola. Aren't you going to kiss me goodbye before you go, Daddy? [*She goes to him and kisses him.* MARIE *catches Doc's eye and smiles. Then she exits to her room, leaving door open.*] Get home early as you can. I'll need you. We gotta give Bruce a royal welcome.

Doc. Yes, Baby.

Lola. Feeling all right?

Doc. Yes.

Lola. [*In doorway. He is on porch.*] Take care of yourself.

Doc. [*Toneless voice.*] Goodbye.

[*He goes.*]

Lola. [*Coming back to table with pleased expression, which changes to a puzzled look. Calls to* MARIE.] Now that's funny. Why did Doc take his raincoat? It's a beautiful day. There isn't a cloud in sight.

CURTAIN

SCENE II

It is now 5:30.

[*The scene is the same as the preceding except that more finishing touches have been added and the* TWO WOMEN, *still primping the table, lighting the tapers, are dressed in their best.* LOLA *is arranging the centerpiece.*]

Lola. [*Above table, fixing flowers.*] I just love lilacs, don't you, Marie? [*Takes one and studies it.*] Mrs. Coffman was nice; she let me have all I wanted. [*Looks at it very closely.*] Aren't they pretty? And they smell so sweet. I think they're the nicest flower there is.

Marie. They don't last long.

Lola. [*Respectfully.*] No. Just a few days. Mrs. Coffman's started blooming just day before yesterday.

Marie. By the first of the week they'll all be gone.

Lola. Vanish—they'll vanish into thin air. [*Gayer now.*] Here, Honey, we have them to spare *now*. Put this in your hair. There. [MARIE *does.*] Mrs. Coffman's been so nice lately. I didn't use to like her. Now where could Doc be? He didn't even come home for lunch.

Marie. [*Gets two chairs from bedroom.*] Mrs. Delaney, you're a peach to go to all this trouble.

Lola. [*Gets salt and pepper.*] Shoot, I'm gettin' more fun out of it than you are. Do you think Bruce is going to like us?

Marie. If he doesn't, I'll never speak to him again.

Lola. [*Eagerly.*] I'm just dying to meet him. But I feel sorta bad I never got to do anything nice for Turk.

Marie. [*Carefully prying.*] Did—Doc ever say anything to you about Turk—and me?

Lola. About Turk and you? No, Honey. Why?

Marie. I just wondered.

Lola. What if Bruce finds out that you've been going with someone else?

Marie. Bruce and I had a very businesslike understanding before I left for school that we weren't going to sit around lonely just because we were separated.

Lola. Aren't you being kind of mean to Turk?

Marie. I don't think so.

Lola. How's he going to feel when Bruce comes?

Marie. He may be sore for a little while. He'll get over it.

Lola. Won't he feel bad?

Marie. He's had his eye on a pretty little Spanish girl in his history class for a long time. I like Turk, but he's not the marrying kind.

Lola. No! Really?

[LOLA, *with a look of sad wonder on her face, sits right arm of couch. It's been a serious disillusionment.*]

Marie. What's the matter?

Lola. I—I just felt kinda tired.

[*Sharp buzzing of doorbell.* MARIE *runs to answer it.*]

Marie. That must be Bruce. [*She skips to the mirror, then to door.*] Bruce!

Bruce. [*Entering.*] How are you, Sweetheart?

Marie. Wonderful.

Bruce. Did you get my wire?

Marie. Sure.

Bruce. You're looking swell.

Marie. Thanks. What took you so long to get here?

Bruce. Well, Honey, I had to go to my hotel and take a bath.

Marie. Bruce, this is Mrs. Delaney.

Bruce. [*Now he gets the cozy quality out of his voice.*] How do you do, Ma'am?

Lola. How d'ya do?

Bruce. Marie has said some very nice things about you in her letters.

Marie. Mrs. Delaney has fixed the grandest dinner for us.

Bruce. Now that was to be my treat. I

have a big expense account now, Honey. I thought we could all go down to the hotel and have dinner there, and celebrate first with a few cocktails.

Lola. Oh, we can have cocktails, too. Excuse me just a minute.

[*She hurries to the kitchen and starts looking for the whiskey.* BRUCE *kisses* MARIE. *Then she whispers.*]

Marie. Now, Bruce, she's been working on this dinner all day. She even cleaned the house for you.

Bruce. Did she?

Marie. And Doc's joining us. You'll like Doc.

Bruce. Honey, are we going to have to stay here the whole evening?

Marie. We just can't eat and run right away. We'll get away as soon as we can.

Bruce. I hope so. I got the raise, Sweetheart. They're giving me new territory.

[LOLA *is frantic in the kitchen, having found the bottle missing. She hurries back into the living room.*]

Lola. You kids are going to have to entertain yourselves a while 'cause I'm going to be busy in the kitchen. Why don't you turn on the radio, Màrie? Get some dance music. I'll shut the door so—so I won't disturb you. [LOLA *does so. Then goes to the telephone.*]

Marie. Come and see my room, Bruce. I've fixed it up just darling. And I've got your picture in the prettiest frame right on my dresser.

[*They exit and their voices are heard from the bedroom while* LOLA *is telephoning.*]

Lola. [*At the telephone.*] This is Mrs. Delaney. Is—Doc there? Well, then, is Ed Anderson there? Well, would you give me Ed Anderson's telephone number? You see, he sponsored Doc into the club and helped him—you know—and—and I was a little worried tonight— Oh, thanks. Yes, I've got it. [*She writes down number.*] Could you have Ed Anderson call me if he comes in? Thank you. [*She hangs up. On her face is a dismal expression of fear, anxiety, and doubt. She searches flour bin, icebox, closet. Then she goes into the living room, calling to* MARIE *and* BRUCE *as she comes.*] I—I guess we'll go ahead without Doc, Marie.

Marie. [*Enters from her room.*] What's the matter with Doc, Mrs. Delaney?

Lola. Well—he got held up at the office— just one of those things, you know. It's too bad. It would have to happen when I needed him most.

Marie. Sure you don't need any help?

Lola. Huh? Oh, no. I'll make out. Every-

thing's ready. I tell you what I'm going to do. Three's a crowd, so I'm going to be the butler and serve the dinner to you two young lovebirds— [*The telephone rings.* MARIE *goes into bedroom.*] Pardon me—pardon me just a minute. [*She rushes to telephone, closing the door behind her.*] Hello? Ed? Have you seen Doc? He went out this morning and hasn't come back. We're having company for dinner and he was supposed to be home early—— That's not all. This time we've had a quart of whiskey in the kitchen and Doc's never gone near it. I went to get it tonight. I was going to serve some cocktails. It was *gone.* Yes, I saw it there yesterday. No, I don't think so— He said this morning he had an upset stomach but— Oh would you?— Thank you, Mr. Anderson. Thank you a million times. And you let me know when you find out anything. Yes, I'll be here. Yes. [*Hangs up and crosses back to living room.*] Well, I guess we're all ready.

[*Their voices continue in bedroom.*]

Bruce. Aren't you going to look at your present?

Marie. Oh, sure; let's get some scissors. [*Enters with* BRUCE.] Mrs. Delaney, we think you should eat with us.

Lola. Oh, no, Honey. I'm not very hungry. Besides, this is the first time you've been together in months and I think you should be alone. Marie, why don't you light the candles, then we'll have just the right atmosphere.

[*She goes into kitchen, gets tomato juice glasses from ice box while* BRUCE *lights the candles.*]

Bruce. Do we have to eat by candlelight? I won't be able to see.

Lola. [*Returns.*] Now, Bruce, you sit here. [*He and* MARIE *sit.*] Isn't that going to be cozy? Dinner for two. Sorry we won't have time for cocktails. Let's have a little music.

[*She turns on the radio and a Viennese waltz swells up as the Curtain falls, with* LOLA *looking at the young people eating.*]

CURTAIN

SCENE III

Funeral atmosphere. It is about 5:30 the next morning. The sky is just beginning to get light outside. While inside the room the shadows still cling heavily to the corners. The remains of last night's dinner clutter the table in the living room. *The candles have guttered down to stubs amid the dirty dinner plates, and the lilacs in the centerpiece have wilted.* [LOLA *is sprawled on the davenport, sleeping. Slowly she awakens and regards the morning light. She gets up and looks about strangely, beginning to show despair for the situation she is in. She wears the same spiffy dress she had on the night before, but it is wrinkled now, and her marcelled coiffure is awry. One silk stocking has twisted loose and falls around her ankle. When she is sufficiently awake to realize her situation, she rushes to the telephone and dials a number.*]

Lola. [*At telephone. She sounds frantic.*] Mr. Anderson? Mr. Anderson, this is Mrs. Delaney again. I'm sorry to call you so early, but I just *had* to— Did you find Doc?—No, he's not home yet. I don't suppose he'll come home till he's drunk all he can hold and wants to sleep— I don't know what else to think, Mr. Anderson. I'm scared, Mr. Anderson. I'm awful scared. Will you come right over?—Thanks, Mr. Anderson. [*Hangs up and goes to kitchen to make coffee. She finds some left from the night before, so turns on the fire to warm it up. She wanders around vaguely, trying to get her thoughts in order, jumping at every sound. Pours herself a cup of coffee, then takes it to living room, sits down right and sips it. Very quietly* DOC *enters through the back way into the kitchen. He carries a big bottle of whiskey, which he carefully places back in the cabinet, not making a sound—hangs up overcoat, then puts suitcoat on back of chair. Starts to go upstairs. But* LOLA *speaks.*] Doc? That you, Doc?

[*Then* DOC *quietly walks in from kitchen. He is staggering drunk, but he is managing for a few minutes to appear as though he were perfectly sober and nothing had happened. His steps, however, are not too sure and his eyes are like blurred ink pots.* LOLA *is too frightened to talk. Her mouth is gaping and she is breathless with fear.*]

Doc. Good morning, Honey.

Lola. Doc! You all right?

Doc. The morning paper here? I wanta see the morning paper.

Lola. Doc, we don't get a morning paper. *You* know that.

Doc. Oh, then I suppose I'm drunk or something. That what you're trying to say?

Lola. No, Doc——

Doc. Then give me the morning paper.

Lola. [*Scampering to get last night's paper from table left.*] Sure, Doc. Here it is. Now you just sit there and be quiet.

Doc. [*Resistance rising.*] Why shouldn't I be quiet?

Lola. Nothin', Doc——

Doc. [*Has trouble unfolding paper. He places it before his face in order not to be seen. But he is too blind even to see. Mockingly.*] Nothing, Doc.

Lola. [*Cautiously, after a few minute's silence.*] Doc, are you all right?

Doc. Of course I'm all right. Why shouldn't I be all right?

Lola. Where you been?

Doc. What's it your business where I been? I been to London to see the Queen. What do you think of that? [*Apparently she doesn't know what to think of it.*] Just let me alone. That's all I ask. I'm all right.

Lola. [*Whimpering.*] Doc, what made you do it? You said you'd be home last night—'cause we were having company. Bruce was here and I had a big dinner fixed —and you never came. What was the matter, Doc?

Doc. [*Mockingly.*] We had a big dinner for *Bruce.*

Lola. Doc, it was for you, too.

Doc. Well—I don't want it.

Lola. Don't get mad, Doc.

Doc. [*Threateningly.*] Where's Marie?

Lola. I don't know, Doc. She didn't come in last night. She was out with Bruce.

Doc. [*Back to audience.*] I suppose you tucked them in bed together and peeked through the keyhole and applauded.

Lola. [*Sickened.*] Doc, don't talk that way. Bruce is a nice boy. They're gonna get married.

Doc. He probably *has* to marry her, the poor bastard. Just 'cause she's pretty and he got amorous one day— Just like I had to marry *you.*

Lola. Oh, Doc.

Doc. You and Marie are both a couple of sluts.

Lola. Doc, please don't talk like that.

Doc. What are you good for? You can't even get up in the morning and cook my breakfast.

Lola. [*Mumbling.*] I will, Doc. I will after this.

Doc. You won't even sweep the floors till some bozo comes along to make love to Marie, and then you fix things up like Buckingham Palace or a Chinese whorehouse with perfume on the lampbulbs, and flowers, and the gold-trimmed china *my mother* gave us. We're not going to use these any more. My mother didn't buy those dishes for whores to eat off of.

[*Jerks the cloth off the table, sending the dishes rattling to the floor.*]

Lola. Doc! Look what you done.

Doc. Look what I *did*, not *done*. I'm going to get me a drink. [*To kitchen.*]

Lola. [*Follows to platform.*] Oh no, Doc! You know what it does to you!

Doc. You're damn right I know what it does to me. It makes me willing to come home here and look at you, you two-ton old heifer. [*Gets bottle. Takes a long swallow.*] There! And pretty soon I'm going to have another, then another.

Lola. [*With dread.*] Oh, Doc! [LOLA *takes phone.* DOC *sees this, rushes for the butcher-knife in kitchen cabinet drawer. Not finding it, he gets a hatchet from the back porch.*] Mr. Anderson? Come quick, Mr. Anderson. He's back. He's *back!* He's got a hatchet!

Doc. God damn you! Get away from that telephone. [*He chases her into living room, where she gets the davenport between them.*] That's right, phone! Tell the world I'm drunk. Tell the whole damn world. Scream your head off, you fat slut. Holler till all the neighbors think I'm beatin' hell outuv you. Where's Bruce now—under Marie's bed? You got all fresh and pretty for him, didn't you? Combed your hair for once—— You even washed the back of your neck, and put on a girdle. You were willing to harness all that fat into one bundle.

Lola. [*About to faint under the weight of the crushing accusations.*] Doc, don't say any more—— I'd rather you hit me with an axe, Doc—— Honest I would. But I can't stand to hear you talk like that.

Doc. I oughta hack off all that fat, and then wait for Marie and chop off those pretty ankles she's always dancing around on— then start lookin' for Turk and fix him too.

Lola. Daddy, you're talking crazy!

Doc. I'm making sense for the first time in my life. You didn't know I knew about it, did you? But I saw him coming outa there. I saw him. You knew about it all the time and thought you were hidin' something——

Lola. Daddy, I didn't know anything about it at all. Honest, Daddy.

Doc. Then *you're* the one that's crazy, if you think I didn't know. You were running a regular house, weren't you? It's probably been going on for years, ever since we were married.

[*He lunges for her. She breaks for*

kitchen. *They struggle in front of sink.*]

Lola. Doc, it's not so; it's not so. You gotta believe me, Doc.

Doc. You're lyin'. But none a that's gonna happen any more. I'm gonna fix you now, once and for all——

Lola. Doc—don't do that to me. [LOLA, *in a frenzy of fear clutches him around the neck, holding arm with axe by his side.*] Remember, Doc. It's *me*, Lola! You said I was the prettiest girl you ever saw. Remember, Doc! It's *me!* Lola!

Doc. [*The memory has overpowered him. He collapses, slowly mumbling.*] Lola—my pretty Lola.

[*He passes out on the floor.* LOLA *stands, now, as though in a trance. Quietly* MRS. COFFMAN *comes creeping in through the back way.*]

Mrs. Coffman. [*Calling softly.*] Mrs. Delaney! [LOLA *doesn't even hear.* MRS. COFFMAN *comes on in.*] Mrs. Delaney!— Here you are, Lady. I heard screaming and I was frightened for you.

Lola. I—I'll be all right—some men are comin' pretty soon; everything'll be all right.

Mrs. Coffman. I'll stay until they get here.

Lola. [*Feeling a sudden need.*] Would you—would you *please*, Mrs. Coffman? [*Breaks into sobs.*]

Mrs. Coffman. Of course, Lady. [*Regarding* Doc.] The Doctor got "sick" again?

Lola. [*Mumbling.*] Some men—'ll be here pretty soon——

Mrs. Coffman. I'll try to straighten things up before they get here——

[*She rights chair, hangs up telephone and picks up the axe, which she is holding when* ED ANDERSON *and* ELMO HUSTON *enter front door unannounced. They are experienced AA's. Neatly dressed businessmen approaching middle-age.*]

Ed. Pardon us for walking right in, Mrs. Delaney, but I didn't want to waste a second. [*To kitchen. Kneels at* Doc.]

Lola. [*Weakly.*] —it's all right——

[*Both* MEN *observe* DOC *on the floor, and their expressions hold understanding mixed with a feeling of irony. There is even a slight smile of irony on* ED'S *face. They have developed the surgeon's objectivity.*]

Ed. Where is the hatchet? [*To* ELMO, *as though appraising* DOC's *condition.*] What do you think, Elmo?

Elmo. We can't leave him here if he's gonna play around with hatchets.

Ed. Give me a hand, Elmo. We'll get him to sit up and then try to talk some sense into him. [*They struggle with the lumpy body,* Doc *grunting his resistance.*] Come on, Doc, old boy. It's Ed and Elmo. We're going to take care of you.

[*They seat him at table.*]

Doc. [*Through a thick fog.*] Lemme alone.

Ed. Wake up. We're taking you away from here.

Doc. Lemme 'lone, God damn it.

[*Falls forward—head on table.*]

Elmo. [*To* Mrs. Coffman.] Is there any coffee?

Mrs. Coffman. I think so. I'll see.

[*To stove with cup from drainboard. Lights fire under coffee, and waits for it to get heated.*]

Ed. He's way beyond coffee.

Elmo. It'll help some. Get something hot into his stomach.

Ed. —if we could get him to eat. How 'bout some hot food, Doc?

[Doc *gestures and they don't push the matter.*]

Elmo. City hospital, Ed?

Ed. I guess that's what it will have to be.

Lola. Where are you going to take him?

[Elmo *goes to telephone—speaks quietly to City Hospital.*]

Ed. Don't know. Wanta talk to him first.

Mrs. Coffman. [*Coming with the coffee.*] Here's the coffee.

Ed. [*Taking cup.*] Hold him, Elmo, while I make him swallow this.

Elmo. Come on, Doc, drink your coffee.

Doc. [*He only blubbers. After the coffee is down.*] Uh—what—what's goin' on here?

Ed. It's me, Doc. Your old friend Ed. I got Elmo with me.

Doc. [*Twisting his face painfully.*] Get out, both of you. Lemme 'lone.

Ed. [*With certainty.*] We're takin' you with us, Doc.

Doc. Hell you are. I'm all right. I just had a little slip. We all have slips——

Ed. Sometimes, Doc, but we gotta get over 'em.

Doc. I'll be O.K. Just gimme a day to sober up. I'll be as good as new.

Ed. Remember the last time, Doc? You said you'd be all right in the morning and we found you with a broken collar bone. Come on.

Doc. Boys, I'll be all right. Now lemme alone.

Ed. How much has he had, Mrs. Delaney?

Lola. I don't know. He had a quart when

he left here yesterday and he didn't get home till now.

Ed. He's probably been through a *couple* of quarts. He's been dry for a long time. It's going to hit him pretty hard. Yah, he'll be a pretty sick man for a few days. [*Louder to* Doc, *as though he were talking to a deaf man.*] Wanta go to the City Hospital, Doc?

Doc. [*This has a sobering effect on him. He looks about him furtively for possible escape.*] No—no, boys. Don't take me there. That's a torture chamber. No, Ed. You wouldn't do that to me.

Ed. They'll sober you up.

Doc. Ed, I been there; I've seen the place. That's where they take the crazy people. You can't do that to me, Ed.

Ed. Well, *you're* crazy, aren't you? Goin' after your wife with a hatchet.

[*They lift* Doc *to his feet.* Doc *looks with dismal pleading in his eyes at* Lola, *who has her face in her hands.*]

Doc. [*So plaintive, a sob in his voice.*] Honey! Honey! [Lola *can't look at him. Now* Doc *tries to make a getaway, bolting blindly into the living room before the* Two Men *catch him and hold him in front of table.*] Honey, don't let 'em take me there. They'll believe *you.* Tell 'em you won't *let* me take a drink.

Lola. Isn't there any place else you could take him?

Ed. Private sanitariums cost a lotta dough.

Lola. I got forty dollars in the kitchen.

Ed. That won't be near enough.

Doc. I'll be at the meeting tomorrow night sober as you are now.

Ed. [*To* Lola.] All the king's horses couldn't keep him from takin' another drink now, Mrs. Delaney. He got himself into this; he's gotta sweat it out.

Doc. I won't go to the City Hospital. That's where they take the crazy people.

[*Stumbles into chair down right.*]

Ed. [*Using all his patience now.*] Look, Doc. Elmo and I are your friends. You know that. Now if you don't come along peacefully, we're going to call the cops and you'll have to wear off this jag in the cooler. How'd you like that? [Doc *is as though stunned.*] The important thing is for you to get sober.

Doc. I don't wanta go.

Ed. The City Hospital or the City Jail. Take your choice. We're not going to leave you here. Come on, Elmo.

[*They grab hold of him.*]

Doc. [*Has collected himself and now*

given in.] O.K., boys. Gimme another drink and I'll go.

Lola. Oh no, Doc.

Ed. Might as well humor him, Ma'am. Another few drinks couldn't make much difference now.

[MRS. COFFMAN *runs for bottle and glass in cabinet, comes right back with them, hands them to* LOLA.]

Ed. O.K., Doc, we're goin' to give you a drink. Take a good one; it's gonna be your last for a long time to come. [ED *takes the bottle, removes the cork and gives* DOC *a glass of whiskey.* DOC *takes his fill, straight, coming up once or twice for air. Then* ED *takes the bottle from him and hands it to* LOLA.] They'll keep him three or four days, Mrs. Delaney; then he'll be home again, good as new. [*Modestly.*] I—I don't want to pry into personal affairs, Ma'am—but he'll need you then, pretty bad——

Lola. I know.

Ed. Come on, Doc. Let's go.

[ED *has a hold of* DOC'S *coat sleeve, trying to maneuver him. A faraway look is in* DOC'S *eyes, a dazed look containing panic and fear. He gets to his feet.*]

Doc. [*Struggling to sound reasonable.*] Just a minute, boys——

Ed. What's the matter?

Doc. I—I wanta glass of water.

Ed. You'll get a glass of water later. Come on.

Doc. [*Beginning to twist a little in* ED'S *grasp.*] —a glass of water—that's all——

[*One furious, quick twist of his body and he eludes* ED.]

Ed. Quick, Elmo.

[ELMO *acts fast and they get* DOC *before he gets away. Then* DOC *struggles with all his might, kicking and screaming like a pampered child,* ED *and* ELMO *holding him tightly to usher him out.*]

Doc. [*As he is led out.*] Don't let 'em take me there. Don't take me there. Stop them, somebody. Stop them. That's where they take the crazy people. Oh God, stop them, somebody. Stop them.

[LOLA *looks on blankly while* ED *and* ELMO *depart with* DOC. *Sits down right. Now there are several moments of deep silence.*]

Mrs. Coffman. [*Clears up. Very softly.*] Is there anything more I can do for you now, Mrs. Delaney?

Lola. I guess not.

Mrs. Coffman. [*Puts a hand on* LOLA'S *shoulder.*] Get busy, Lady. Get busy and forget it.

Lola. Yes—I'll get busy right away. Thanks, Mrs. Coffman.

Mrs. Coffman. I better go. I've got to make breakfast for the children. If you want me for anything, let me know.

Lola. Yes—yes—— Goodbye, Mrs. Coffman.

[MRS. COFFMAN *exits back door.* LOLA *is too exhausted to move from the big chair. At first she can't even cry; then the tears come slowly, softly. In a few moments* BRUCE *and* MARIE *enter, bright and merry.* LOLA *turns her head slightly to regard them as creatures from another planet.*]

Marie. [*Springing into room.*] Congratulate me, Mrs. Delaney. [BRUCE *follows.*]

Lola. Huh?

Marie. We're going to be married.

Lola. Married? [*It barely registers.*]

Marie. [*Showing ring.*] Here it is. My engagement ring.

[MARIE *and* BRUCE *are too engrossed in their own happiness to notice* LOLA'S *stupor.*]

Lola. That's lovely—lovely.

Marie. We've had the most wonderful time. We danced all night and then drove out to the lake and saw the sun rise.

Lola. That's nice.

Marie. We've made all our plans. I'm quitting school and flying back to Cincinnati with Bruce this afternoon. His mother has invited me to visit them before I go home. Isn't that wonderful?

Lola. Yes—yes, indeed.

Marie. Going to miss me?

Lola. Yes, of course, Marie. We'll miss you very much—— Uh—congratulations.

Marie. Thanks, Mrs. Delaney. [*Crosses up to bedroom door.*] Come on, Bruce, help me get my stuff. Mrs. Delaney, would you throw everything into a big box and send it to me at home? We haven't had breakfast yet. We're going down to the hotel and celebrate.

Bruce. I'm sorry we're in such a hurry, but we've got a taxi waiting.

[*They go into bedroom.*]

Lola. [*To telephone, dials.*] Long Distance? I want to talk to Green Valley 223. Yes. This is Delmar 1887.

[*She hangs up, crosses down. As she gets below table,* MARIE *comes from bedroom, followed by* BRUCE, *who carries suitcase.*]

Marie. Mrs. Delaney, I sure hate to say

goodbye to you. You've been so wonderful to me. But Bruce says I can come and visit you once in a while, didn't you, Bruce ?

Bruce. Sure thing.

Lola. You're going?

Marie. We're going downtown and have our breakfast, then do a little shopping and catch our plane. And thanks for everything, Mrs. Delaney.

Bruce. It was very nice of you to have us to dinner.

Lola. Dinner? Oh, don't mention it.

Marie. [*To* LOLA.] There isn't much time for goodbye now, but I just want you to know Bruce and I wish you the best of everything. You and Doc both. Tell Doc goodbye for me, will you, and remember, I think you're both a coupla peaches.

Bruce. Hurry, Honey.

Marie. 'Bye, Mrs. Delaney!

[*She goes out door.*]

Bruce. 'Bye, Mrs. Delaney. Thanks for being nice to my girl.

[*He goes out and off porch with* MARIE.]

Lola. [*Waves. The telephone rings. She goes to it quickly.*] Hello. Hello, Mom. It's Lola, Mom. How are you? Mom, Doc's sick again. Do you think Dad would let me come home for a while? I'm awfully unhappy, Mom. Do you think—just till I made up my mind?—All right. No, I guess it wouldn't do any good for you to come here—— I—I'll let you know what I decide to do. That's all, Mom. Thanks. Tell Daddy hello. [*She hangs up.*]

CURTAIN

SCENE IV

It is morning, a week later. The house is neat again, as in Act One, Scene II.

[LOLA *is dusting in the living room as* MRS. COFFMAN *enters from back door.*]

Mrs. Coffman. Mrs. Delaney! Good morning, Mrs. Delaney.

Lola. Come in, Mrs. Coffman.

Mrs. Coffman. [*Coming in.*] It's a fine day for the games. I've got a box lunch ready, and I'm taking all the kids to the Stadium. My boy's got a ticket for you, too. You better get dressed and come with us.

Lola. Thanks, Mrs. Coffman, but I've got work to do.

Mrs. Coffman. But it's such a big day. The Spring Relays—— All the athletes from the colleges are supposed to be there.

Lola. Oh yes. You know that boy Turk who used to come here to see Marie—he's one of the big stars.

Mrs. Coffman. Is that so? Come on—do. We've got a ticket for you——

Lola. Oh no, I have to stay here and clean up the house. Doc may be coming home today. I talked to him on the phone. He wasn't sure what time they'd let him out, but I wanta have the place all nice for him.

Mrs. Coffman. Well, I'll tell you all about it when I come home. Everybody and his brother will be there.

Lola. Yes, do, and have a good time.

Mrs. Coffman. 'Bye, Mrs. Delaney.

Lola. 'Bye.

[MRS. COFFMAN *leaves, and* LOLA *goes into kitchen. The* MAILMAN *comes onto porch and leaves a letter, but* LOLA *doesn't even know he's there. Then the* MILKMAN *knocks on the back door.*]

Lola. Come in.

Milkman. [*Entering with arm full of bottles, etc.*] I see you checked the list, Lady. You've got a lot of extras.

Lola. Ya—I think my husband's coming home.

Milkman. [*He puts the supplies on table, then pulls out magazine.*] Remember, I told you my picture was going to appear in *Strength and Health.* [*Showing her magazine.*] Well, see that pile of muscles? That's me.

Lola. [*Totally without enthusiasm.*] My goodness. You got your picture in a magazine.

Milkman. Yes, Ma'am. See what it says about my chest development? For the greatest self-improvement in a three months' period.

Lola. Goodness sakes. You'll be famous, won't you?

Milkman. If I keep busy on these bar-bells. I'm working now for "muscular separation."

Lola. That's nice.

Milkman. [*Cheerily.*] Well, good day, Ma'am.

Lola. You forgot your magazine.

Milkman. That's for you. [*Exits.*]

[LOLA *puts away the supplies in the icebox. Then* DOC *comes in the front door carrying the little suitcase she previously packed for him.* DOC *is himself again. His quiet manner, his serious demeanor, are the same as before.* LOLA *is shocked by his sudden appearance. She jumps and can't help showing her fright.*]

Lola. Docky!

[*Without thinking, she assumes an at-*

titude of fear. Doc *observes this and it obviously pains him.*]

Doc. Good morning, Honey.   [*Pause.*]

Lola. [*On platform.*] Are—are you all right, Doc?

Doc. Yes, I'm all right. [*An awkward pause. Then* Doc *tries to reassure her.*] Honest, I'm all right, Honey. Please don't stand there like that—like I was gonna—gonna——

Lola. [*Tries to relax.*] I'm sorry, Doc.

Doc. How you been?

Lola. Oh, I been all right, Doc. Fine.

Doc. Any news?

Lola. I told you about Marie—over the phone.

Doc. Yah.

Lola. He was a very nice boy, Doc. Very nice.

Doc. That's good. I hope they'll be happy.

Lola. [*Trying to sound bright.*] She said —maybe she'd come back and visit us sometime. That's what she *said.*

Doc. [*Pause.*] It—it's good to be home.

Lola. Is it, Daddy?

Doc. Yah.

[*Beginning to choke up just a little.*]

Lola. Did everything go all right—— I mean—did they treat you well and——

Doc. [*Now loses control of his feelings. Tears in his eyes, he all but lunges at her, gripping her arms, drilling his head into her bosom.*] Honey, don't ever leave me. *Please* don't ever leave me. If you do, they'd have to keep me down at that place all the time. I don't know what I said to you or what I did. I can't remember hardly anything. But please forgive me—please—please—— And I'll try to make everything up.

Lola. [*There is surprise on her face and new contentment. She becomes almost angelic in demeanor. Tenderly she places a soft hand on his head.*] Daddy! Why, of course I'll never leave you. [*A smile of satisfaction.*] You're all I've got. You're all I ever had.

Doc. [*Collecting himself now. Very tenderly he kisses her.* Lola *sits beside* Doc.] I—I feel better—already.

Lola. [*Almost gay.*] So do I. Have you had your breakfast?

Doc. No. The food there was terrible. When they told me I could go this morning, I decided to wait and fix myself breakfast here.

Lola. [*Happily.*] Come on out in the kitchen and I'll get you a nice, big breakfast. I'll scramble some eggs and—— You see I've got the place all cleaned up just the way you like it. [Doc *goes to kitchen.*] Now you sit down here and I'll get your fruit juice.

[*He sits and she gets fruit juice from refrigerator.*] I've got bacon this morning, too. My, it's expensive now. And I'll light the oven and make you some toast, and here's some orange marmalade, and——

Doc. [*With a new feeling of control.*] Fruit juice. I'll need lots of it for a while. The doctor said it would restore the vitamins. You see, that damn whiskey kills all the vitamins in your system, eats up all the sugar in your kidneys. They came around every morning and shot vitamins in my arm. Oh, it didn't hurt. And the doctor told me to drink a quart of fruit juice every day. And you better get some candy bars for me at the grocery this morning. Doctor said to eat lots of candy, try to replace the sugar.

Lola. I'll do that, Doc. Here's another glass of this pineapple juice now. I'll get some candy bars first thing.

Doc. The doctor said I should have a hobby. Said I should go out more. That's all that's wrong with me. I thought maybe I'd go hunting once in a while.

Lola. Yes, Doc. And bring home lots of good things to eat.

Doc. I'll get a big bird dog, too. Would you like a sad-looking old bird dog around the house?

Lola. Of course I would. [*All her life and energy have been restored.*] You know what, Doc? I had another dream last night.

Doc. About Little Sheba?

Lola. Oh, it was about everyone and everything. [*In a raptured tone. She gets bacon from ice box and starts to cook it.*] Marie and I were going to the Olympics back in our old High School Stadium. There were thousands of people there. There was Turk out in the center of the field throwing the javelin. Every time he'd throw it, the crowd would roar—and you know who the man in charge was? It was my father. Isn't that funny?—but Turk kept changing into someone else all the time. And then my father disqualified him. So he had to sit on the sidelines—and guess who took his place, Daddy? You! You came trotting out there on the field just as big as you please——

Doc. [*Smilingly.*] How did I do, Baby?

Lola. Fine. You picked the javelin up real careful, like it was awful heavy. But you threw it, Daddy, clear, *clear* up into the sky. And it never came down again. [Doc *looks very pleased with himself.* Lola *goes on.*] Then it started to rain. And I couldn't find Little Sheba. I almost went crazy looking for her and there were so many people I didn't even know where to look. And you were waiting to take me home. And we walked and walked through the slush and mud, and people were hurrying all around us and—and—— [*Leaves stove and sits. Sentimental tears come to her eyes*.] But this part is sad, Daddy. All of a sudden I saw Little Sheba—she was lying in the middle of the field —dead—— It made me cry, Doc. No one paid any attention—— I cried and cried. It made me feel so bad, Doc. That sweet little puppy—her curly white fur all smeared with mud, and no one to stop and take care of her——

Doc. Why couldn't *you?*

Lola. I wanted to, but you wouldn't let me.

You kept saying, "We can't stay here, Honey; we gotta go on. We gotta go on." [*Pause*.] Now, isn't that strange?

Doc. Dreams are funny.

Lola. I don't think Little Sheba's ever coming back, Doc. I'm not going to call her any more.

Doc. Not much point in it, Baby. I guess she's gone for good.

Lola. I'll fix your eggs.

[*She gets up, embraces* Doc, *and goes to stove.* Doc *remains at table sipping his fruit juice. The Curtain comes slowly down.*]

>>>>>>>>>>>>>>>>>>>>>>>>>>>>>><<<<<<<<<<<<<<<<<<<<<<<<<<<<<

THE CRUCIBLE*

By

ARTHUR MILLER

THE TRADITION FOR HISTORY PLAYS, perhaps derived from Shakespeare, calls for poetic form and romantic treatment, with conventional, rather external characterization and "big" scenes. This tradition is well illustrated by Bulwer-Lytton's *Richelieu* in the nineteenth century and Maxwell Anderson's *Elizabeth the Queen* or *Mary of Scotland* in this century. Plainly, Eliot's *Murder in the Cathedral* is not totally outside this tradition. Rostand's *Cyrano de Bergerac* is perhaps its most brilliant exemplar in non-English literature.

But the modern drama has also developed another kind of history play. This concentrates on psychology and deeper characterization; it becomes a study of the hero in his time. One such is Shaw's *Saint Joan;* another is Sherwood's *Abe Lincoln in Illinois.* Compared with the traditional history play, these are less theatrical, demand less identification with protagonist, but they give greater intellectual satisfaction and they do more to enrich the understanding.

Arthur Miller's *The Crucible* has a bearing toward history not found in either of these classes, but it represents a kind of play our time has produced in profusion. The theory underlying such plays is that art is a weapon to direct the minds and emotions of audiences deliberately toward action the writer desires. *The Crucible* appeared when the United States public was much agitated over the investigation conducted by Senator Joseph R. McCarthy of Wisconsin into Communism in government and public affairs. Miller says in the preface to his *Collected Plays* that this investigation and the accompanying public excitement led to his writing

The Crucible, though the Salem witch trials had interested him for many years. He felt that the emotional state of the country in 1953 was like the emotional state of Salem Village in 1692, and that he could show the terrible consequences of that state by writing a vigorous play. He wanted *The Crucible,* in short, to be a weapon against a present evil in society. It aimed more at making its audiences repent their approval of "McCarthyism" or at intensifying their disapproval than at illuminating their understanding of history.

Probably *The Crucible* was not a successful weapon. Perhaps American audiences did not see much likeness between independent John Proctor and saintly Rebecca Nurse as sufferers from public hysteria and the rather indistinct victims of the McCarthy investigation. The vividness of Miller's historical art may have made his blows at the present less telling. Also, that witchcraft and Communism as threats to a society were equally unreal and imaginary was hard for any American audience to see. If *The Crucible* failed as a weapon, it probably deserved to fail. If it succeeded anywhere, it succeeded in the domain of art, not politics, despite Miller's wish for it. *The Crucible* has been played in London, in Paris, where it ran for more than a year, in West Germany, and in Italy. It was adapted for motion pictures in France by Jean-Paul Sartre. Some of the French enthusiasm for the play may have been anti-American, which would not be Miller's wish, but would be a striking instance of how art conceived as a weapon could become a boomerang.

Not as politics, therefore, but as art, whatever its author intended, *The Crucible* fails or succeeds. As art it transforms history, not into a moral lesson about a passing political excitement, but into a revelation of the strange ways of the human heart and mind. A child not yet born could grow up to read *The Crucible* and be horrified, though McCarthy and Communism and all the agitations of their day were less than dreams to him.

ARTHUR MILLER

Born 1915, New York City.

1938, B.A., University of Michigan. As an undergraduate, won the Avery Hopwood Prize for student playwriting in 1936, 1937, and the Theatre Guild National Award in 1938.

1938–1944, Writing, first for Federal Theatre Project, then for radio, then for motion pictures. Exempt from military service for physical disability.

1944, Published first book, *Situation Normal,* about the war.

1945, Published *Focus,* novel about anti-Semitism.

1947, *All My Sons* won New York Drama Critics' Award, Antoinette Perry Award, Donaldson Award.

1949, *Death of a Salesman* won Pulitzer Prize, New York Drama Critics' Award.

1956, Divorced first wife, married Marilyn Monroe, actress.

1957, Found in contempt of Congress for refusing to identify persons known to him as Communists, but conviction reversed on appeal, 1958.

PLAYS

1936 *The Grass Still Grows.* 1944 *That They May Win* (one act). 1944 *The Man Who Had All the Luck.* 1947 *All My Sons.* 1949 *Death of a Salesman.* 1950 Adaptation of Ibsen's *An Enemy of the People.* 1953 *The Crucible.* 1955 *A Memory of Two Mondays* (one act) and *A View from the Bridge* (one act). 1956 *A View from the Bridge* (full length version).

WRITINGS ON DRAMA

Preface to *Death of a Salesman,* 1949. "Journey to 'The Crucible'," *The New York Times,* Feb. 8, 1953, II.3.1. "Picking a Cast," *The New York Times,* Aug. 21, 1955, II.1.1. "American Theater," *Holiday,* XVII (Jan. 1955), 90–98. "A View of One-Acters," *The New York Times,* Sept. 25, 1955, II.1.6. "The Family in Modern Drama," *The Atlantic Monthly,* CXCVII (April 1956), 35–41. Preface to *A View from the Bridge,* 1956. "Concerning the Boom," in *International Theatre Annual,* I, ed. Harold Hobson, 1956. Preface to *Collected Plays,* 1957. "Brewed in 'The Crucible'," *The New York Times,* March 9, 1958, II.3.1. "The Shadows of the Gods," *Harper's Magazine,* CCXVII (August 1958), 35–43.

THE CRUCIBLE

A NOTE ON THE HISTORICAL ACCURACY
OF THIS PLAY

This play is not history in the sense in which the word is used by the academic historian. Dramatic purposes have sometimes required many characters to be fused into one; the number of girls involved in the "crying-out" has been reduced; Abigail's age has been raised; while there were several judges of almost equal authority, I have symbolized them all in Hathorne and Danforth. However, I believe that the reader will discover here the essential nature of one of the strangest and most awful chapters in human history. The fate of each character is exactly that of his historical model, and there is no one in the drama who did not play a similar—and in some cases exactly the same —role in history.

As for the characters of the persons, little is known about most of them excepting what may be surmised from a few letters, the trial record, certain broadsides written at the time, and references to their conduct in sources of varying reliability. They may therefore be taken as creations of my own, drawn to the best of my ability in conformity with their known behavior, except as indicated in the commentary I have written for this text.

ACT ONE
(AN OVERTURE)

A small upper bedroom in the home of REVEREND SAMUEL PARRIS, *Salem, Massachusetts, in the spring of the year 1692.*
There is a narrow window at the left. Through its leaded panes the morning sunlight streams. A candle still burns near the bed, which is at the right. A chest, a chair, and a small table are the other furnishings. At the back a door opens on the landing of the stairway to the ground floor. The room gives off an air of clean spareness. The roof rafters are exposed, and the wood colors are raw and unmellowed.
[As the curtain rises, REVEREND PARRIS *is discovered kneeling beside the bed, evidently in prayer. His daughter,* BETTY PARRIS, *aged ten, is lying on the bed, inert.]*
[At the time of these events PARRIS *was in his middle forties. In history he cut a villainous path, and there is very little good to be said for him. He believed he was being persecuted wherever he went, despite his best efforts to win people and God to his side. In meeting, he felt insulted if someone rose to shut the door without first asking his permission. He was a widower with no interest in children, or talent with them.*

He regarded them as young adults, and until this strange crisis he, like the rest of Salem, never conceived that the children were anything but thankful for being permitted to walk straight, eyes slightly lowered, arms at the sides, and mouths shut until bidden to speak.
His house stood in the "town"—but we today would hardly call it a village. The meeting house was nearby, and from this point outward—toward the bay or inland—there were a few small-windowed, dark houses snuggling against the raw Massachusetts winter. Salem had been established hardly forty years before. To the European world the whole province was a barbaric frontier inhabited by a sect of fanatics, who, nevertheless, were shipping out products of slowly increasing quantity and value. No one can really know what their lives were like. They had no novelists—and would not have permitted anyone to read a novel if one were handy. Their creed forbade anything resembling a theater or "vain enjoyment." They did not celebrate Christmas, and a holiday from work meant only that they must concentrate even more upon prayer.
Which is not to say that nothing broke into this strict and somber way

484

of life. When a new farmhouse was built, friends assembled to "raise the roof," and there would be special foods cooked and probably some potent cider passed around. There was a good supply of ne'er-do-wells in Salem, who dallied at the shovelboard in Bridget Bishop's tavern. Probably more than the creed, hard work kept the morals of the place from spoiling, for the people were forced to fight the land like heroes for every grain of corn, and no man had very much time for fooling around.

That there were some jokers, however, is indicated by the practice of appointing a two-man patrol whose duty was to "walk forth in the time of God's worship to take notice of such as either lye about the meeting house, without attending to the word and ordinances, or that lye at home or in the fields without giving good account thereof, and to take the names of such persons, and to present them to the magistrates, whereby they may be accordingly proceeded against." This predilection for minding other people's business was time-honored among the people of Salem, and it undoubtedly created many of the suspicions which were to feed the coming madness. It was also, in my opinion, one of the things that a JOHN PROCTOR would rebel against, for the time of the armed camp had almost passed, and since the country was reasonably—although not wholly—safe, the old disciplines were beginning to rankle. But, as in all such matters, the issue was not clear-cut, for danger was still a possibility, and in unity still lay the best promise of safety.

The edge of the wilderness was close by. The American continent stretched endlessly west, and it was full of mystery for them. It stood, dark and threatening, over their shoulders night and day, for out of it Indian tribes marauded from time to time, and REVEREND PARRIS had parishioners who had lost relatives to these heathen.

The parochial snobbery of these people was partly responsible for their failure to convert the Indians. Probably they also preferred to take land from heathens rather than from fellow Christians. At any rate, very few Indians were converted, and the Salem folk believed that the virgin forest was the Devil's last preserve, his home base

and the citadel of his final stand. To the best of their knowledge the American forest was the last place on earth that was not paying homage to God.

For these reasons, among others, they carried about an air of innate resistance, even of persecution. Their fathers had, of course, been persecuted in England. So now they and their church found it necessary to deny any other sect its freedom, lest their New Jerusalem be defiled and corrupted by wrong ways and deceitful ideas.

They believed, in short, that they held in their steady hands the candle that would light the world. We have inherited this belief, and it has helped and hurt us. It helped them with the discipline it gave them. They were a dedicated folk, by and large, and they had to be to survive the life they had chosen or been born into in this country. The proof of their belief's value to them may be taken from the opposite character of the first Jamestown settlement, farther south, in Virginia. The Englishmen who landed there were motivated mainly by a hunt for profit. They had thought to pick off the wealth of the new country and then return rich to England. They were a band of individualists, and a much more ingratiating group than the Massachusetts men. But Virginia destroyed them. Massachusetts tried to kill off the Puritans, but they combined; they set up a communal society which, in the beginning, was little more than an armed camp with an autocratic and very devoted leadership. It was, however, an autocracy by consent, for they were united from top to bottom by a commonly held ideology whose perpetuation was the reason and justification for all their sufferings. So their self-denial, their purposefulness, their suspicion of all vain pursuits, their hard-handed justice, were altogether perfect instruments for the conquest of this space so antagonistic to man.

But the people of Salem in 1692 were not quite the dedicated folk that arrived on the Mayflower. A vast differentiation had taken place, and in their own time a revolution had unseated the royal government and substituted a junta which was at this moment in power. The times, to their eyes, must have been out of joint, and to the common folk must have seemed as *insoluble and complicated as do ours to-day. It is not hard to see how easily many could have been led to believe that the time of confusion had been brought upon them by deep and dark-ling forces. No hint of such speculation appears on the court record, but social disorder in any age breeds such mystical suspicions, and when, as in Salem, won-ders are brought forth from below the social surface, it is too much to expect people to hold back very long from lay-ing on the victims with all the force of their frustrations.*

The Salem tragedy, which is about to begin in these pages, developed from a paradox. It is a paradox in whose grip we still live, and there is no prospect yet that we will discover its resolution. Simply, it was this: for good purposes, even high purposes, the people of Salem developed a theocracy, a combine of state and religious power whose function was to keep the community together, and to prevent any kind of disunity that might open it to destruction by ma-terial or ideological enemies. It was forged for a necessary purpose and ac-complished that purpose. But all or-ganization is and must be grounded on the idea of exclusion and prohibition, just as two objects cannot occupy the same space. Evidently the time came in New England when the repressions of order were heavier than seemed war-ranted by the dangers against which the order was organized. The witch-hunt was a perverse manifestation of the panic which set in among all classes when the balance began to turn toward greater individual freedom.

When one rises above the individual villainy displayed, one can only pity them all, just as we shall be pitied some-day. It is still impossible for man to organize his social life without repres-sions, and the balance has yet to be struck between order and freedom.

The witch-hunt was not, however, a mere repression. It was also, and as importantly, a long overdue opportunity for everyone so inclined to express pub-licly his guilt and sins, under the cover of accusations against the victims. It suddenly became possible—and patriotic and holy—for a man to say that MARTHA COREY *had come into his bed-room at night, and that, while his wife was sleeping at his side,* MARTHA *laid herself down on his chest and "nearly*

suffocated him." Of course it was her spirit only, but his satisfaction at con-fessing himself was no lighter than if it had been MARTHA *herself. One could not ordinarily speak such things in pub-lic.*

Long-held hatred of neighbors could now be openly expressed, and vengeance taken, despite the Bible's charitable in-junctions. Land-lust which had been expressed before by constant bickering over boundaries and deeds could now be elevated to the arena of morality; one could cry witch against one's neigh-bor and feel perfectly justified in the bargain. Old scores could be settled on a plane of heavenly combat between Lucifer and the Lord; suspicions and the envy of the miserable toward the happy could and did burst out in the general revenge.]

[REVEREND PARRIS *is praying now, and, though we cannot hear his words, a sense of his confusion hangs about him. He mumbles, then seems about to weep; then he weeps, then prays again; but his daughter does not stir on the bed.*

The door opens, and his Negro slave en-ters. TITUBA *is in her forties.* PARRIS *brought her with him from Barbados, where he spent some years as a merchant before entering the ministry. She enters as one does who can no longer bear to be barred from the sight of her beloved, but she is also very frightened because her slave sense has warned her that, as always, trouble in this house eventually lands on her back.]*

Tituba. [*Already taking a step backward.*] My Betty be hearty soon?

Parris. Out of here!

Tituba. [*Backing to the door.*] My Betty not goin' die . . .

Parris. [*Scrambling to his feet in a fury.*] Out of my sight! [*She is gone.*] Out of my—— [*He is overcome with sobs. He clamps his teeth against them and closes the door and leans against it, exhausted.*] Oh, my God! God help me! [*Quaking with fear, mumbling to himself through his sobs, he goes to the bed and gently takes* BETTY'*s hand.*] Betty. Child. Dear child. Will you wake, will you open up your eyes! Betty, little one . . .

[*He is bending to kneel again when his niece,* ABIGAIL WILLIAMS, *seventeen, enters—a strikingly beautiful girl, an orphan, with an endless capacity for dissembling. Now she is all worry and apprehension and propriety.*]

Abigail. Uncle? [*He looks to her.*] Susanna Walcott's here from Doctor Griggs.

Parris. Oh? Let her come, let her come.

Abigail. [*Leaning out the door to call to* SUSANNA, *who is down the hall a few steps.*] Come in, Susanna.

[SUSANNA WALCOTT, *a little younger than* ABIGAIL, *a nervous, hurried girl, enters.*]

Parris. [*Eagerly.*] What does the doctor say, child?

Susanna. [*Craning around* PARRIS *to get a look at* BETTY.] He bid me come and tell you, reverend sir, that he cannot discover no medicine for it in his books.

Parris. Then he must search on.

Susanna. Aye, sir, he have been searchin' his books since he left you, sir. But he bid me tell you, that you might look to unnatural things for the cause of it.

Parris. [*His eyes going wide.*] No—no. There be no unnatural cause here. Tell him I have sent for Reverend Hale of Beverly, and Mr. Hale will surely confirm that. Let him look to medicine and put out all thought of unnatural causes here. There be none.

Susanna. Aye, sir. He bid me tell you.
[*She turns to go.*]

Abigail. Speak nothin' of it in the village, Susanna.

Parris. Go directly home and speak nothing of unnatural causes.

Susanna. Aye, sir. I pray for her.
[*She goes out.*]

Abigail. Uncle, the rumor of witchcraft is all about; I think you'd best go down and deny it yourself. The parlor's packed with people, sir. I'll sit with her.

Parris. [*Pressed, turns on her.*] And what shall I say to them? That my daughter and my niece I discovered dancing like heathen in the forest?

Abigail. Uncle, we did dance; let you tell them I confessed it—and I'll be whipped if I must be. But they're speakin' of witchcraft. Betty's not witched.

Parris. Abigail, I cannot go before the congregation when I know you have not opened with me. What did you do with her in the forest?

Abigail. We did dance, uncle, and when you leaped out of the bush so suddenly, Betty was frightened and then she fainted. And there's the whole of it.

Parris. Child. Sit you down.

Abigail. [*Quavering, as she sits.*] I would never hurt Betty. I love her dearly.

Parris. Now look you, child, your punish-

ment will come in its time. But if you trafficked with spirits in the forest I must know it now, for surely my enemies will, and they will ruin me with it.

Abigail. But we never conjured spirits.

Parris. Then why can she not move herself since midnight? This child is desperate! [ABIGAIL *lowers her eyes.*] It must come out—my enemies will bring it out. Let me know what you done there. Abigail, do you understand that I have many enemies?

Abigail. I have heard of it, uncle.

Parris. There is a faction that is sworn to drive me from my pulpit. Do you understand that?

Abigail. I think so, sir.

Parris. Now then, in the midst of such disruption, my own household is discovered to be the very center of some obscene practice. Abominations are done in the forest——

Abigail. It were sport, uncle!

Parris. [*Pointing at* BETTY.] You call this sport? [*She lowers her eyes. He pleads.*] Abigail, if you know something that may help the doctor, for God's sake tell it to me. [*She is silent.*] I saw Tituba waving her arms over the fire when I came on you. Why was she doing that? And I heard a screeching and gibberish coming from her mouth. She were swaying like a dumb beast over that fire!

Abigail. She always sings her Barbados songs, and we dance.

Parris. I cannot blink what I saw, Abigail, for my enemies will not blink it. I saw a dress lying on the grass.

Abigail. [*Innocently.*] A dress?

Parris. [*It is very hard to say.*] Aye, a dress. And I thought I saw—someone naked running through the trees!

Abigail. [*In terror.*] No one was naked! You mistake yourself, uncle!

Parris. [*With anger.*] I saw it! [*He moves from her. Then, resolved.*] Now tell me true, Abigail. And I pray you feel the weight of truth upon you, for now my ministry's at stake, my ministry and perhaps your cousin's life. Whatever abomination you have done, give me all of it now, for I dare not be taken unaware when I go before them down there.

Abigail. There is nothin' more. I swear it, uncle.

Parris. [*Studies her, then nods, half convinced.*] Abigail, I have fought here three long years to bend these stiff-necked people to me, and now, just now when some good respect is rising for me in the parish, you compromise my very character. I have given you a home, child, I have put clothes upon your back—now give me upright answer. Your name in the town—it is entirely white, is it not?

Abigail. [*With an edge of resentment.*] Why, I am sure it is, sir. There be no blush about my name.

Parris. [*To the point.*] Abigail, is there any other cause than you have told me, for your being discharged from Goody Proctor's service? I have heard it said, and I tell you as I heard it, that she comes so rarely to the church this year for she will not sit so close to something soiled. What signified that remark?

Abigail. She hates me, uncle, she must, for I would not be her slave. It's a bitter woman, a lying, cold, sniveling woman, and I will not work for such a woman!

Parris. She may be. And yet it has troubled me that you are now seven month out of their house, and in all this time no other family has ever called for your service.

Abigail. They want slaves, not such as I. Let them send to Barbados for that. I will not black my face for any of them! [*With ill-concealed resentment at him.*] Do you begrudge my bed, uncle?

Parris. No—no.

Abigail. [*In a temper.*] My name is good in the village! I will not have it said my name is soiled! Goody Proctor is a gossiping liar!

[*Enter* MRS. ANN PUTNAM. *She is a twisted soul of forty-five, a death-ridden woman, haunted by dreams.*]

Parris. [*As soon as the door begins to open.*] No—no, I cannot have anyone. [*He sees her, and a certain deference springs into him, although his worry remains.*] Why, Goody Putnam, come in.

Mrs. Putnam. [*Full of breath, shiny-eyed.*] It is a marvel. It is surely a stroke of hell upon you.

Parris. No, Goody Putnam, it is——

Mrs. Putnam. [*Glancing at* BETTY.] How high did she fly, how high?

Parris. No, no, she never flew——

Mrs. Putnam. [*Very pleased with it.*] Why, it's sure she did. Mr. Collins saw her goin' over Ingersoll's barn, and come down light as bird, he says!

Parris. Now, look you, Goody Putnam, she never—— [*Enter* THOMAS PUTNAM, *a well-to-do, hard-handed landowner, near fifty.*] Oh, good morning, Mr. Putnam.

Putnam. It is a providence the thing is out now! It is a providence.

[*He goes directly to the bed.*]

Parris. What's out, sir, what's—?

[MRS. PUTNAM *goes to the bed.*]

Putnam. [*Looking down at* BETTY.] Why, her eyes is closed! Look you, Ann.

Mrs. Putnam. Why, that's strange. [*To* PARRIS.] Ours is open.

Parris. [*Shocked.*] Your Ruth is sick?

Mrs. Putnam. [*With vicious certainty.*] I'd not call it sick; the Devil's touch is heavier than sick. It's death, y'know, it's death drivin' into them, forked and hoofed.

Parris. Oh, pray not! Why, how does Ruth ail?

Mrs. Putnam. She ails as she must—she never waked this morning, but her eyes open and she walks, and hears naught, sees naught, and cannot eat. Her soul is taken, surely. [PARRIS *is struck.*]

Putnam. [*As though for further details.*] They say you've sent for Reverend Hale of Beverly?

Parris. [*With dwindling conviction now.*] A precaution only. He has much experience in all demonic arts, and I——

Mrs. Putnam. He has indeed; and found a witch in Beverly last year, and let you remember that.

Parris. Now, Goody Ann, they only thought that were a witch, and I am certain there be no element of witchcraft here.

Putnam. No witchcraft! Now look you, Mr. Parris——

Parris. Thomas, Thomas, I pray you, leap not to witchcraft. I know that you—you least of all, Thomas, would ever wish so disastrous a charge laid upon me. We cannot leap to witchcraft. They will howl me out of Salem for such corruption in my house.

[*A word about* THOMAS PUTNAM. *He was a man with many grievances, at least one of which appears justified. Some time before, his wife's brother-in-law, James Bayley, had been turned down as minister of Salem. Bayley had all the qualifications, and a two-thirds vote into the bargain, but a faction stopped his acceptance, for reasons that are not clear.*

THOMAS PUTNAM *was the eldest son of the richest man in the village. He had fought the Indians at Narragansett, and was deeply interested in parish affairs. He undoubtedly felt it poor payment that the village should so blatantly disregard his candidate for one of its more important offices, especially since he regarded himself as the intellectual superior of most of the people around him.*

His vindictive nature was demonstrated long before the witchcraft began. Another former Salem minister, George Burroughs, had had to borrow money to pay for his wife's funeral, and, since the parish was remiss in his salary, he was soon bankrupt. THOMAS *and his brother John had Burroughs jailed for debts the man did not owe. The incident is important only in that Burroughs succeeded in becoming minister where Bayley,* THOMAS PUTNAM'S *brother-in-law, had been rejected; the motif of resentment is clear here.* THOMAS PUTNAM *felt that his own name and the honor of his family had been smirched by the village, and he meant to right matters however he could.*

Another reason to believe him a deeply embittered man was his attempt to break his father's will, which left a disproportionate amount to a stepbrother. As with every other public cause in which he tried to force his way, he failed in this.

So it is not surprising to find that so many accusations against people are in the handwriting of THOMAS PUTNAM, *or that his name is so often found as a witness corroborating the supernatural testimony, or that his daughter led the crying-out at the most opportune junctures of the trials, especially when— But we'll speak of that when we come to it.]*

Putnam. [*At the moment he is intent upon getting* PARRIS, *for whom he has only contempt, to move toward the abyss.*] Mr. Parris, I have taken your part in all contention here, and I would continue; but I cannot if you hold back in this. There are hurtful, vengeful spirits layin' hands on these children.

Parris. But, Thomas, you cannot——

Putnam. Ann! Tell Mr. Parris what you have done.

Mrs. Putnam. Reverend Parris, I have laid seven babies unbaptized in the earth. Believe me, sir, you never saw more hearty babies born. And yet, each would wither in my arms the very night of their birth. I have spoke nothin', but my heart has clamored intimations. And now, this year, my Ruth, my only—I see her turning strange. A secret child she has become this year, and shrivels like a sucking mouth were pullin' on her life too. And so I thought to send her to your Tituba——

Parris. To Tituba! What may Tituba—?

Mrs. Putnam. Tituba knows how to speak to the dead, Mr. Parris.

Parris. Goody Ann, it is a formidable sin to conjure up the dead!

Mrs. Putnam. I take it on my soul, but who else may surely tell us what person murdered my babies?

Parris. [*Horrified.*] Woman!

Mrs. Putnam. They were murdered, Mr. Parris! And mark this proof! Mark it! Last night my Ruth were ever so close to their little spirits; I know it, sir. For how else is she struck dumb now except some power of darkness would stop her mouth? It is a marvelous sign, Mr. Parris!

Putnam. Don't you understand it, sir? There is a murdering witch among us, bound to keep herself in the dark. [PARRIS *turns to* BETTY, *a frantic terror rising in him.*] Let your enemies make of it what they will, you cannot blink it more.

Parris. [*To* ABIGAIL.] Then you were conjuring spirits last night.

Abigail. [*Whispering.*] Not I, sir— Tituba and Ruth.

Parris. [*Turns now, with new fear, and goes to* BETTY, *looks down at her, and then, gazing off.*] Oh, Abigail, what proper payment for my charity! Now I am undone.

Putnam. You are not undone! Let you take hold here. Wait for no one to charge you—declare it yourself. You have discovered witchcraft——

Parris. In my house? In my house, Thomas? They will topple me with this! They will make of it a——

[*Enter* MERCY LEWIS, *the Putnams' servant, a fat, sly, merciless girl of eighteen.*]

Mercy. Your pardons. I only thought to see how Betty is.

Putnam. Why aren't you home? Who's with Ruth?

Mercy. Her grandma come. She's improved a little, I think—she gave a powerful sneeze before.

Mrs. Putnam. Ah, there's a sign of life!

Mercy. I'd fear no more, Goody Putnam. It were a grand sneeze; another like it will shake her wits together, I'm sure. [*She goes to the bed to look.*]

Parris. Will you leave me now, Thomas? I would pray a while alone.

Abigail. Uncle, you've prayed since midnight. Why do you not go down and——

Parris. No—no. [*To* PUTNAM]. I have no answer for that crowd. I'll wait till Mr.

Hale arrives. [*To get* Mrs. Putnam *to leave.*] If you will, Goody Ann . . .

Putnam. Now look you, sir. Let you strike out against the Devil, and the village will bless you for it! Come down, speak to them—pray with them. They're thirsting for your word, Mister! Surely you'll pray with them.

Parris. [*Swayed.*] I'll lead them in a psalm, but let you say nothing of witchcraft yet. I will not discuss it. The cause is yet unknown. I have had enough contention since I came; I want no more.

Mrs. Putnam. Mercy, you go home to Ruth, d'y'hear?

Mercy. Aye, mum.

[Mrs. Putnam *goes out.*]

Parris. [*To* Abigail.] If she starts for the window, cry for me at once.

Abigail. I will, uncle.

Parris. [*To* Putnam.] There is a terrible power in her arms today.

[*He goes out with* Putnam.]

Abigail. [*With hushed trepidation.*] How is Ruth sick?

Mercy. It's weirdish, I know not—she seems to walk like a dead one since last night.

Abigail. [*Turns at once and goes to* Betty, *and now, with fear in her voice.*] Betty? [Betty *doesn't move. She shakes her.*] Now stop this! Betty! Sit up now!

[Betty *doesn't stir.* Mercy *comes over.*]

Mercy. Have you tried beatin' her? I gave Ruth a good one and it waked her for a minute. Here, let me have her.

Abigail. [*Holding* Mercy *back.*] No, he'll be comin' up. Listen, now; if they be questioning us, tell them we danced—I told him as much already.

Mercy. Aye. And what more?

Abigail. He knows Tituba conjured Ruth's sisters to come out of the grave.

Mercy. And what more?

Abigail. He saw you naked.

Mercy. [*Clapping her hands together with a frightened laugh.*] Oh, Jesus!

[*Enter* Mary Warren, *breathless. She is seventeen, a subservient, naive, lonely girl.*]

Mary Warren. What'll we do? The village is out! I just come from the farm; the whole country's talkin' witchcraft! They'll be callin' us witches, Abby!

Mercy. [*Pointing and looking at* Mary Warren.] She means to tell, I know it.

Mary Warren. Abby, we've got to tell. Witchery's a hangin' error, a hangin' like they done in Boston two year ago! We must

tell the truth, Abby! You'll only be whipped for dancin', and the other things!

Abigail. Oh, *we'll* be whipped!

Mary Warren. I never done none of it, Abby. I only looked!

Mercy. [*Moving menacingly toward* Mary.] Oh, you're a great one for lookin', aren't you, Mary Warren? What a grand peeping courage you have!

[Betty, *on the bed, whimpers.* Abigail *turns to her at once.*]

Abigail. Betty? [*She goes to* Betty.] Now, Betty, dear, wake up now. It's Abigail. [*She sits* Betty *up and furiously shakes her.*] I'll beat you, Betty! [Betty *whimpers.*] My, you seem improving. I talked to your papa and I told him everything. So there's nothing to——

Betty. [*Darts off the bed, frightened of* Abigail, *and flattens herself against the wall.*] I want my mama!

Abigail. [*With alarm, as she cautiously approaches* Betty.] What ails you, Betty? Your mama's dead and buried.

Betty. I'll fly to Mama. Let me fly! [*She raises her arms as though to fly, and streaks for the window, gets one leg out.*]

Abigail. [*Pulling her away from the window.*] I told him everything; he knows now, he knows everything we——

Betty. You drank blood, Abby! You didn't tell him that!

Abigail. Betty, you never say that again! You will never——

Betty. You did, you did! You drank a charm to kill John Proctor's wife! You drank a charm to kill Goody Proctor!

Abigail. [*Smashes her across the face.*] Shut it! Now shut it!

Betty. [*Collapsing on the bed.*] Mama, Mama! [*She dissolves into sobs.*]

Abigail. Now look you. All of you. We danced. And Tituba conjured Ruth Putnam's dead sisters. And that is all. And mark this. Let either of you breathe a word, or the edge of a word, about the other things, and I will come to you in the black of some terrible night and I will bring a pointy reckoning that will shudder you. And you know I can do it; I saw Indians smash my dear parents' heads on the pillow next to mine, and I have seen some reddish work done at night, and I can make you wish you had never seen the sun go down! [*She goes to* Betty *and roughly sits her up.*] Now you —sit up and stop this!

[*But* Betty *collapses in her hands and lies inert on the bed.*]

Mary Warren. [*With hysterical fright.*]

What's got her? [ABIGAIL *stares in fright at* BETTY.] Abby, she's going to die! It's a sin to conjure, and we——

Abigail. [*Starting for* MARY.] I say shut it, Mary Warren!

[*Enter* JOHN PROCTOR. *On seeing him,* MARY WARREN *leaps in fright.*]

[PROCTOR *was a farmer in his middle thirties. He need not have been a partisan of any faction in the town, but there is evidence to suggest that he had a sharp and biting way with hypocrites. He was the kind of man—powerful of body, even-tempered, and not easily led—who cannot refuse support to partisans without drawing their deepest resentment. In* PROCTOR'S *presence a fool felt his foolishness instantly—and a Proctor is always marked for calumny therefore. But as we shall see, the steady manner he displays does not spring from an untroubled soul. He is a sinner, a sinner not only against the moral fashion of the time, but against his own vision of decent conduct. These people had no ritual for the washing away of sins. It is another trait we inherited from them, and it has helped to discipline us as well as to breed hypocrisy among us.* PROCTOR, *respected and even feared in Salem, has come to regard himself as a kind of fraud. But no hint of this has yet appeared on the surface, and, as he enters from the crowded parlor below, it is a man in his prime we see, with a quiet confidence and an unexpressed, hidden force.* MARY WARREN, *his servant, can barely speak for embarrassment and fear.*]

Mary Warren. Oh! I'm just going home, Mr. Proctor.

Proctor. Be you foolish, Mary Warren? Be you deaf? I forbid you leave the house, did I not? Why shall I pay you? I am looking for you more often than my cows!

Mary Warren. I only come to see the great doings in the world.

Proctor. I'll show you a great doin' on your arse one of these days. Now get you home; my wife is waitin' with your work!

[*Trying to retain a shred of dignity, she goes slowly out.*]

Mercy Lewis. [*Both afraid of him and strangely titillated.*] I'd best be off. I have my Ruth to watch. Good morning, Mr. Proctor.

[MERCY *sidles out. Since* PROCTOR'S *entrance,* ABIGAIL *has stood as though on tiptoe, absorbing his presence, wide-eyed. He glances at her, then goes to* BETTY *on the bed.*]

Abigail. Gah! I'd almost forgot how strong you are, John Proctor!

Proctor. [*Looking at* ABIGAIL *now, the faintest suggestion of a knowing smile on his face.*] What's this mischief here?

Abigail. [*With a nervous laugh.*] Oh, she's only gone silly somehow.

Proctor. The road past my house is a pilgrimage to Salem all morning. The town's mumbling witchcraft.

Abigail. Oh, posh! [*Winningly she comes a little closer, with a confidential, wicked air.*] We were dancin' in the woods last night, and my uncle leaped in on us. She took fright, is all.

Proctor. [*His smile widening.*] Ah, you're wicked yet, aren't y'! [*A trill of expectant laughter escapes her, and she dares come closer, feverishly looking into his eyes.*] You'll be clapped in the stocks before you're twenty. [*He takes a step to go, and she springs into his path.*]

Abigail. Give me a word, John. A soft word. [*Her concentrated desire destroys his smile.*]

Proctor. No, no, Abby. That's done with.

Abigail. [*Tauntingly.*] You come five mile to see a silly girl fly? I know you better.

Proctor. [*Setting her firmly out of his path.*] I come to see what mischief your uncle's brewin' now. [*With final emphasis.*] Put it out of mind, Abby.

Abigail. [*Grasping his hand before he can release her.*] John—I am waitin' for you every night.

Proctor. Abby, I never give you hope to wait for me.

Abigail. [*Now beginning to anger—she can't believe it.*] I have something better than hope, I think!

Proctor. Abby, you'll put it out of mind. I'll not be comin' for you more.

Abigail. You're surely sportin' with me.

Proctor. You know me better.

Abigail. I know how you clutched my back behind your house and sweated like a stallion whenever I come near! Or did I dream that? It's she put me out, you cannot pretend it were you. I saw your face when she put me out, and you loved me then and you do now!

Proctor. Abby, that's a wild thing to say——

Abigail. A wild thing may say wild things. But not so wild, I think. I have seen you since she put me out; I have seen you nights.

Proctor. I have hardly stepped off my farm this seven month.

Abigail. I have a sense for heat, John, and yours has drawn me to my window, and I have seen you looking up, burning in your loneliness. Do you tell me you've never looked up at my window?

Proctor. I may have looked up.

Abigail. [*Now softening.*] And you must. You are no wintry man. I know you, John. I *know* you. [*She is weeping.*] I cannot sleep for dreamin'; I cannot dream but I wake and walk about the house as though I'd find you comin' through some door.

[*She clutches him desperately.*]

Proctor. [*Gently pressing her from him, with great sympathy but firmly.*] Child——

Abigail. [*With a flash of anger.*] How do you call me child!

Proctor. Abby, I may think of you softly from time to time. But I will cut off my hand before I'll ever reach for you again. Wipe it out of mind. We never touched, Abby.

Abigail. Aye, but we did.

Proctor. Aye, but we did not.

Abigail. [*With a bitter anger.*] Oh, I marvel how such a strong man may let such a sickly wife be——

Proctor. [*Angered—at himself as well.*] You'll speak nothin' of Elizabeth!

Abigail. She is blackening my name in the village! She is telling lies about me! She is a cold, sniveling woman, and you bend to her! Let her turn you like a——

Proctor. [*Shaking her.*] Do you look for whippin'?

[*A psalm is heard being sung below.*]

Abigail. [*In tears.*] I look for John Proctor that took me from my sleep and put knowledge in my heart! I never knew what pretense Salem was, I never knew the lying lessons I was taught by all these Christian women and their covenanted men! And now you bid me tear the light out of my eyes? I will not, I cannot! You loved me, John Proctor, and whatever sin it is, you love me yet! [*He turns abruptly to go out. She rushes to him.*] John, pity me, pity me!

[*The words "going up to Jesus" are heard in the psalm, and* BETTY *claps her ears suddenly and whines loudly.*]

Abigail. Betty?

[*She hurries to* BETTY, *who is now sitting up and screaming.* PROCTOR *goes to* BETTY *as* ABIGAIL *is trying to pull her hands down, calling "Betty!"*]

Proctor. [*Growing unnerved.*] What's she doing? Girl, what ails you? Stop that wailing!

[*The singing has stopped in the midst of this, and now* PARRIS *rushes in.*]

Parris. What happened? What are you doing to her? Betty!

[*He rushes to the bed, crying, "Betty, Betty!"* MRS. PUTNAM *enters, feverish with curiosity, and with her* THOMAS PUTNAM *and* MERCY LEWIS. PARRIS, *at the bed, keeps lightly slapping* BETTY'S *face, while she moans and tries to get up.*]

Abigail. She heard you singin' and suddenly she's up and screamin'.

Mrs. Putnam. The psalm! The psalm! She cannot bear to hear the Lord's name!

Parris. No, God forbid. Mercy, run to the doctor! Tell him what's happened here!

[MERCY LEWIS *rushes out.*]

Mrs. Putnam. Mark it for a sign, mark it!

[REBECCA NURSE, *seventy-two, enters. She is white-haired, leaning upon her walking-stick.*]

Putnam. [*Pointing at the whimpering* BETTY.] That is a notorious sign of witchcraft afoot, Goody Nurse, a prodigious sign!

Mrs. Putnam. My mother told me that! When they cannot bear to hear the name of——

Parris. [*Trembling.*] Rebecca, Rebecca, go to her, we're lost. She suddenly cannot bear to hear the Lord's——

[GILES COREY, *eighty-three, enters. He is knotted with muscle, canny, inquisitive, and still powerful.*]

Rebecca. There is hard sickness here, Giles Corey, so please to keep the quiet.

Giles. I've not said a word. No one here can testify I've said a word. Is she going to fly again? I hear she flies.

Putnam. Man, be quiet now!

[*Everything is quiet.* REBECCA *walks across the room to the bed. Gentleness exudes from her.* BETTY *is quietly whimpering, eyes shut.* REBECCA *simply stands over the child, who gradually quiets.*]

[*And while they are so absorbed, we may put a word in for* REBECCA. REBECCA *was the wife of* FRANCIS NURSE, *who, from all accounts, was one of those men for whom both sides of the argument had to have respect. He was called upon to arbitrate disputes as though he were an unofficial judge, and* REBECCA *also enjoyed the high opinion most people had for him. By the time of the delusion, they had three hundred acres, and their children were settled in separate homesteads within the same estate. However,* FRANCIS *had origi-*

nally rented the land, and one theory has it that, as he gradually paid for it and raised his social status, there were those who resented his rise.

Another suggestion to explain the systematic campaign against REBECCA, *and inferentially against* FRANCIS, *is the land war he fought with his neighbors, one of whom was a Putnam. This squabble grew to the proportions of a battle in the woods between partisans of both sides, and it is said to have lasted for two days. As for* REBECCA *herself, the general opinion of her character was so high that to explain how anyone dared cry her out for a witch—and more, how adults could bring themselves to lay hands on her—we must look to the fields and boundaries of that time.*

As we have seen, THOMAS PUTNAM'S *man for the Salem ministry was Bayley. The Nurse clan had been in the faction that prevented Bayley's taking office. In addition, certain families allied to the Nurses by blood or friendship, and whose farms were contiguous with the Nurse farm or close to it, combined to break away from the Salem town authority and set up Topsfield, a new and independent entity whose existence was resented by old Salemites.*

That the guiding hand behind the outcry was PUTNAM'S *is indicated by the fact that, as soon as it began, this Topsfield-Nurse faction absented themselves from church in protest and disbelief. It was Edward and Jonathan Putnam who signed the first complaint against* RE-BECCA; *and* THOMAS PUTNAM'S *little daughter was the one who fell into a fit at the hearing and pointed to* REBECCA *as her attacker. To top it all,* MRS. PUT-NAM—*who is now staring at the bewitched child on the bed—soon accused* REBECCA'S *spirit of "tempting her to iniquity," a charge that had more truth in it than* MRS. PUTNAM *could know.*]

Mrs. Putnam. [*Astonished.*] What have you done?

[REBECCA, *in thought, now leaves the bedside and sits.*]

Parris. [*Wondrous and relieved.*] What do you make of it, Rebecca?

Putnam. [*Eagerly.*] Goody Nurse, will you go to my Ruth and see if you can wake her?

Rebecca. [*Sitting.*] I think she'll wake in time. Pray calm yourselves. I have eleven children, and I am twenty-six times a grandma, and I have seen them all through

their silly seasons, and when it come on them they will run the Devil bowlegged keeping up with their mischief. I think she'll wake when she tires of it. A child's spirit is like a child, you can never catch it by running after it; you must stand still, and, for love, it will soon itself come back.

Proctor. Aye, that's the truth of it, Rebecca.

Mrs. Putnam. This is no silly season, Rebecca. My Ruth is bewildered, Rebecca; she cannot eat.

Rebecca. Perhaps she is not hungered yet. [*To* PARRIS.] I hope you are not decided to go in search of loose spirits, Mr. Parris. I've heard promise of that outside.

Parris. A wide opinion's running in the parish that the Devil may be among us, and I would satisfy them that they are wrong.

Proctor. Then let you come out and call them wrong. Did you consult the wardens before you called this minister to look for devils?

Parris. He is not coming to look for devils!

Proctor. Then what's he coming for?

Putnam. There be children dyin' in the village, Mister!

Proctor. I seen none dyin'. This society will not be a bag to swing around your head, Mr. Putnam. [*To* PARRIS.] Did you call a meeting before you——?

Putnam. I am sick of meetings; cannot the man turn his head without he have a meeting?

Proctor. He may turn his head, but not to Hell!

Rebecca. Pray, John, be calm. [*Pause. He defers to her.*] Mr. Parris, I think you'd best send Reverend Hale back as soon as he come. This will set us all to arguin' again in the society, and we thought to have peace this year. I think we ought rely on the doctor now, and good prayer.

Mrs. Putnam. Rebecca, the doctor's baffled!

Rebecca. If so he is, then let us go to God for the cause of it. There is prodigious danger in the seeking of loose spirits. I fear it, I fear it. Let us rather blame ourselves and——

Putnam. How may we blame ourselves? I am one of nine sons; the Putnam seed have peopled this province. And yet I have but one child left of eight—and now she shrivels!

Rebecca. I cannot fathom that.

Mrs. Putnam. [*With a growing edge of sarcasm.*] But I must! You think it God's work you should never lose a child, nor grandchild either, and I bury all but one? There are wheels within wheels in this village, and fires within fires!

Putnam. [*To* PARRIS.] When Reverend Hale comes, you will proceed to look for signs of witchcraft here.

Proctor. [*To* PUTNAM.] You cannot command Mr. Parris. We vote by name in this society, not by acreage.

Putnam. I never heard you worried so on this society, Mr. Proctor. I do not think I saw you at Sabbath meeting since snow flew.

Proctor. I have trouble enough without I come five mile to hear him preach only hellfire and bloody damnation. Take it to heart, Mr. Parris. There are many others who stay away from church these days because you hardly ever mention God any more.

Parris. [*Now aroused.*] Why, that's a drastic charge!

Rebecca. It's somewhat true; there are many that quail to bring their children——

Parris. I do not preach for children, Rebecca. It is not the children who are unmindful of their obligations toward this ministry.

Rebecca. Are there really those unmindful?

Parris. I should say the better half of Salem village——

Putnam. And more than that!

Parris. Where is my wood? My contract provides I be supplied with all my firewood. I am waiting since November for a stick, and even in November I had to show my frostbitten hands like some London beggar!

Giles. You are allowed six pound a year to buy your wood, Mr. Parris.

Parris. I regard that six pound as part of my salary. I am paid little enough without I spend six pound on firewood.

Proctor. Sixty, plus six for firewood——

Parris. The salary is sixty-six pound, Mr. Proctor! I am not some preaching farmer with a book under my arm; I am a graduate of Harvard College.

Giles. Aye, and well instructed in arithmetic!

Parris. Mr. Corey, you will look far for a man of my kind at sixty pound a year! I am not used to this poverty; I left a thrifty business in the Barbados to serve the Lord. I do not fathom it, why am I persecuted here? I cannot offer one proposition but there be a howling riot of argument. I have often wondered if the Devil be in it somewhere; I cannot understand you people otherwise.

Proctor. Mr. Parris, you are the first minister ever did demand the deed to this house——

Parris. Man! Don't a minister deserve a house to live in?

Proctor. To live in, yes. But to ask ownership is like you shall own the meeting house itself; the last meeting I were at you spoke so long on deeds and mortgages I thought it were an auction.

Parris. I want a mark of confidence, is all! I am your third preacher in seven years. I do not wish to be put out like the cat whenever some majority feels the whim. You people seem not to comprehend that a minister is the Lord's man in the parish; a minister is not to be so lightly crossed and contradicted——

Putnam. Aye!

Parris. There is either obedience or the church will burn like Hell is burning!

Proctor. Can you speak one minute without we land in Hell again? I am sick of Hell!

Parris. It is not for you to say what is good for you to hear!

Proctor. I may speak my heart, I think!

Parris. [*In a fury.*] What, are we Quakers? We are not Quakers here yet, Mr. Proctor. And you may tell that to your followers!

Proctor. My followers!

Parris. [*Now he's out with it.*] There is a party in this church. I am not blind; there is a faction and a party.

Proctor. Against you?

Putnam. Against him and all authority!

Proctor. Why, then I must find it and join it.   [*There is shock among the others.*]

Rebecca. He does not mean that.

Putnam. He confessed it now!

Proctor. I mean it solemnly, Rebecca; I like not the smell of this "authority."

Rebecca. No, you cannot break charity with your minister. You are another kind, John. Clasp his hand, make your peace.

Proctor. I have a crop to sow and lumber to drag home. [*He goes angrily to the door and turns to* COREY *with a smile.*] What say you, Giles, let's find the party. He says there's a party.

Giles. I've changed my opinion of this man, John. Mr. Parris, I beg your pardon. I never thought you had so much iron in you.

Parris. [*Surprised.*] Why, thank you, Giles!

Giles. It suggests to the mind what the trouble be among us all these years. [*To all.*] Think on it. Wherefore is everybody suing everybody else? Think on it now, it's a deep thing, and dark as a pit. I have been six time in court this year——

Proctor. [*Familiarly, with warmth, although he knows he is approaching the edge of* GILES' *tolerance with this.*] Is it the Devil's fault that a man cannot say you good morning without you clap him for defamation? You're old, Giles, and you're not hearin' so well as you did.

Giles. [*He cannot be crossed.*] John Proctor, I have only last month collected four pound damages for you publicly sayin' I burned the roof off your house, and I——

Proctor. [*Laughing.*] I never said no such thing, but I've paid you for it, so I hope I can call you deaf without charge. Now come along, Giles, and help me drag my lumber home.

Putnam. A moment, Mr. Proctor. What lumber is that you're draggin', if I may ask you?

Proctor. My lumber. From out my forest by the riverside.

Putnam. Why, we are surely gone wild this year. What anarchy is this? That tract is in my bounds, it's in my bounds, Mr. Proctor.

Proctor. In your bounds! [*Indicating* REBECCA.] I bought that tract from Goody Nurse's husband five months ago.

Putnam. He had no right to sell it. It stands clear in my grandfather's will that all the land between the river and——

Proctor. Your grandfather had a habit of willing land that never belonged to him, if I may say it plain.

Giles. That's God's truth; he nearly willed away my north pasture but he knew I'd break his fingers before he'd set his name to it. Let's get your lumber home, John. I feel a sudden will to work coming on.

Putnam. You load one oak of mine and you'll fight to drag it home!

Giles. Aye, and we'll win too, Putnam—this fool and I. Come on! [*He turns to* PROCTOR *and starts out.*]

Putnam. I'll have my men on you, Corey! I'll clap a writ on you!

[*Enter* REVEREND JOHN HALE *of Beverly.*]

[MR. HALE *is nearing forty, a tight-skinned, eager-eyed intellectual. This is a beloved errand for him; on being called here to ascertain witchcraft he felt the pride of the specialist whose unique knowledge has at last been publicly called for. Like almost all men of learning, he spent a good deal of his time pondering the invisible world, especially since he had himself encoun-*

tered a witch in his parish not long before. That woman, however, turned into a mere pest under his searching scrutiny, and the child she had allegedly been afflicting recovered her normal behavior after HALE had given her his kindness and a few days of rest in his own house. However, that experience never raised a doubt in his mind as to the reality of the underworld or the existence of Lucifer's many-faced lieutenants. And his belief is not to his discredit. Better minds than HALE's were—and still are—convinced that there is a society of spirits beyond our ken. One cannot help noting that one of his lines has never yet raised a laugh in any audience that has seen this play; it is his assurance that "We cannot look to superstition in this. The Devil is precise." Evidently we are not quite certain even now whether diabolism is holy and not to be scoffed at. And it is no accident that we should be so bemused.

Like REVEREND HALE and the others on this stage, we conceive the Devil as a necessary part of a respectable view of cosmology. Ours is a divided empire in which certain ideas and emotions and actions are of God, and their opposites are of Lucifer. It is as impossible for most men to conceive of a morality without sin as of an earth without "sky." Since 1692 a great but superficial change has wiped out God's beard and the Devil's horns, but the world is still gripped between two diametrically opposed absolutes. The concept of unity, in which positive and negative are attributes of the same force, in which good and evil are relative, ever-changing, and always joined to the same phenomenon—such a concept is still reserved to the physical sciences and to the few who have grasped the history of ideas. When it is recalled that until the Christian era the underworld was never regarded as a hostile area, that all gods were useful and essentially friendly to man despite occasional lapses; when we see the steady and methodical inculcation into humanity of the idea of man's worthlessness—until redeemed—the necessity of the Devil may become evident as a weapon, a weapon designed and used time and time again in every age to whip men into a surrender to a particular church or church-state.

Our difficulty in believing the—for want of a better word—political inspiration of the Devil is due in great part to the fact that he is called up and damned not only by our social antagonists but by our own side, whatever it may be. The Catholic Church, through its Inquisition, is famous for cultivating Lucifer as the arch-fiend, but the Church's enemies relied no less upon the Old Boy to keep the human mind enthralled. Luther was himself accused of alliance with Hell, and he in turn accused his enemies. To complicate matters further, he believed that he had had contact with the Devil and had argued theology with him. I am not surprised at this, for at my own university a professor of history—a Lutheran, by the way—used to assemble his graduate students, draw the shades, and commune in the classroom with Erasmus. He was never, to my knowledge, officially scoffed at for this, the reason being that the university officials, like most of us, are the children of a history which still sucks at the Devil's teats. At this writing, only England has held back before the temptations of contemporary diabolism. In the countries of the Communist ideology, all resistance of any import is linked to the totally malign capitalist succubi, and in America any man who is not reactionary in his views is open to the charge of alliance with the Red hell. Political opposition, thereby, is given an inhumane overlay which then justifies the abrogation of all normally applied customs of civilized intercourse. A political policy is equated with moral right, and opposition to it with diabolical malevolence. Once such an equation is effectively made, society becomes a congerie of plots and counterplots, and the main role of government changes from that of the arbiter to that of the scourge of God.

The results of this process are no different now from what they ever were, except sometimes in the degree of cruelty inflicted, and not always even in that department. Normally the actions and deeds of a man were all that society felt comfortable in judging. The secret intent of an action was left to the ministers, priests, and rabbis to deal with. When diabolism rises, however, actions are the least important manifests of the true nature of a man. The Devil, as REVEREND HALE said, is a wily one, and, until an hour before he fell, even God thought him beautiful in Heaven.

The analogy, however, seems to falter when one considers that, while there were no witches then, there are Communists and capitalists now, and in each camp there is certain proof that spies of each side are at work undermining the other. But this is a snobbish objection and not at all warranted by the facts. I have no doubt that people were communing with, and even worshiping, the Devil in Salem, and if the whole truth could be known in this case, as it is in others, we should discover a regular and conventionalized propitiation of the dark spirit. One certain evidence of this is the confession of TITUBA, the slave of REVEREND PARRIS, and another is the behavior of the children who were known to have indulged in sorceries with her.

There are accounts of similar klatches in Europe, where the daughters of the towns would assemble at night and, sometimes with fetishes, sometimes with a selected young man, give themselves to love, with some bastardly results. The Church, sharp-eyed as it must be when gods long dead are brought to life, condemned these orgies as witchcraft and interpreted them, rightly, as a resurgence of the Dionysiac forces it had crushed long before. Sex, sin, and the Devil were early linked, and so they continued to be in Salem, and are today. From all accounts there are no more puritanical mores in the world than those enforced by the Communists in Russia, where women's fashions, for instance, are as prudent and all-covering as any American Baptist would desire. The divorce laws lay a tremendous responsibility on the father for the care of his children. Even the laxity of divorce regulations in the early years of the revolution was undoubtedly a revulsion from the nineteenth-century Victorian immobility of marriage and the consequent hypocrisy that developed from it. If for no other reasons, a state so powerful, so jealous of the uniformity of its citizens, cannot long tolerate the atomization of the family. And yet, in American eyes at least, there remains the conviction that the Russian attitude toward women is lascivious. It is the Devil working again, just as he is work-

ing within the Slav who is shocked at the very idea of a woman's disrobing herself in a burlesque show. Our opposites are always robed in sexual sin, and it is from this unconscious conviction that demonology gains both its attractive sensuality and its capacity to infuriate and frighten.

Coming into Salem now, REVEREND HALE *conceives of himself much as a young doctor on his first call. His painfully acquired armory of symptoms, catchwords, and diagnostic procedures are now to be put to use at last. The road from Beverly is unusually busy this morning, and he has passed a hundred rumors that make him smile at the ignorance of the yeomanry in this most precise science. He feels himself allied with the best minds of Europe—kings, philosophers, scientists, and ecclesiasts of all churches. His goal is light, goodness and its preservation, and he knows the exaltation of the blessed whose intelligence, sharpened by minute examinations of enormous tracts, is finally called upon to face what may be a bloody fight with the Fiend himself.*]

[*He appears loaded down with half a dozen heavy books.*]

Hale. Pray you, someone take these!

Parris. [*Delighted.*] Mr. Hale! Oh! it's good to see you again! [*Taking some books.*] My, they're heavy!

Hale. [*Setting down his books.*] They must be; they are weighted with authority.

Parris. [*A little scared.*] Well, you do come prepared!

Hale. We shall need hard study if it comes to tracking down the Old Boy. [*Noticing* REBECCA.] You cannot be Rebecca Nurse?

Rebecca. I am, sir. Do you know me?

Hale. It's strange how I knew you, but I suppose you look as such a good soul should. We have all heard of your great charities in Beverly.

Parris. Do you know this gentleman? Mr. Thomas Putnam. And his good wife Ann.

Hale. Putnam! I had not expected such distinguished company, sir.

Putnam. [*Pleased.*] It does not seem to help us today, Mr. Hale. We look to you to come to our house and save our child.

Hale. Your child ails too?

Mrs. Putnam. Her soul, her soul seems flown away. She sleeps and yet she walks . . .

Putnam. She cannot eat.

Hale. Cannot eat! [*Thinks on it. Then, to* PROCTOR *and* GILES COREY.] Do you men have afflicted children?

Parris. No, no, these are farmers. John Proctor——

Giles Corey. He don't believe in witches.

Proctor. [*To* HALE.] I never spoke on witches one way or the other. Will you come, Giles?

Giles. No—no, John, I think not. I have some few queer questions of my own to ask this fellow.

Proctor. I've heard you to be a sensible man, Mr. Hale. I hope you'll leave some of it in Salem.

[PROCTOR *goes.* HALE *stands embarrassed for an instant.*]

Parris. [*Quickly.*] Will you look at my daughter, sir? [*Leads* HALE *to the bed.*] She has tried to leap out the window; we discovered her this morning on the highroad, waving her arms as though she'd fly.

Hale. [*Narrowing his eyes.*] Tries to fly.

Putnam. She cannot bear to hear the Lord's name, Mr. Hale; that's a sure sign of witchcraft afloat.

Hale. [*Holding up his hands.*] No, no. Now let me instruct you. We cannot look to superstition in this. The Devil is precise; the marks of his presence are definite as stone, and I must tell you all that I shall not proceed unless you are prepared to believe me if I should find no bruise of hell upon her.

Parris. It is agreed, sir—it is agreed—we will abide by your judgment.

Hale. Good then. [*He goes to the bed, looks down at* BETTY. *To* PARRIS.] Now, sir, what were your first warning of this strangeness?

Parris. Why, sir—I discovered her [*Indicating* ABIGAIL.] and my niece and ten or twelve of the other girls, dancing in the forest last night.

Hale. [*Surprised.*] You permit dancing?

Parris. No, no, it were secret——

Mrs. Putnam. [*Unable to wait.*] Mr. Parris's slave has knowledge of conjurin', sir.

Parris. [*To* MRS. PUTNAM.] We cannot be sure of that, Goody Ann——

Mrs. Putnam. [*Frightened, very softly.*] I know it, sir. I sent my child—she should learn from Tituba who murdered her sisters.

Rebecca. [*Horrified.*] Goody Ann! You sent a child to conjure up the dead?

Mrs. Putnam. Let God blame me, not you, not you, Rebecca! I'll not have you judging me any more! [*To* HALE.] Is it a natural work to lose seven children before they live a day?

Parris. Sssh!

[REBECCA, *with great pain, turns her face away. There is a pause.*]

Hale. Seven dead in childbirth.

Mrs. Putnam. [*Softly.*] Aye.

[*Her voice breaks; she looks up at him. Silence.* HALE *is impressed.* PARRIS *looks to him. He goes to his books, opens one, turn pages, then reads. All wait, avidly.*]

Parris. [*Hushed.*] What book is that?

Mrs. Putnam. What's there, sir?

Hale. [*With a tasty love of intellectual pursuit.*] Here is all the invisible world, caught, defined, and calculated. In these books the Devil stands stripped of all his brute disguises. Here are all your familiar spirits—your incubi and succubi; your witches that go by land, by air, and by sea; your wizards of the night and of the day. Have no fear now—we shall find him out if he has come among us, and I mean to crush him utterly if he has shown his face!

[*He starts for the bed.*]

Rebecca. Will it hurt the child, sir?

Hale. I cannot tell. If she is truly in the Devil's grip we may have to rip and tear to get her free.

Rebecca. I think I'll go, then. I am too old for this.   [*She rises.*]

Parris. [*Striving for conviction.*] Why, Rebecca, we may open up the boil of all our troubles today!

Rebecca. Let us hope for that. I go to God for you, sir.

Parris. [*With trepidation—and resentment.*] I hope you do not mean we go to Satan here!   [*Slight pause.*]

Rebecca. I wish I knew.

[*She goes out; they feel resentful of her note of moral superiority.*]

Putnam. [*Abruptly.*] Come, Mr. Hale, let's get on. Sit you here.

Giles. Mr. Hale, I have always wanted to ask a learned man—what signifies the readin' of strange books?

Hale. What books?

Giles. I cannot tell; she hides them.

Hale. Who does this?

Giles. Martha, my wife. I have waked at night many a time and found her in a corner, readin' of a book. Now what do you make of that?

Hale. Why, that's not necessarily——

Giles. It discomfits me! Last night— mark this—I tried and tried and could not say my prayers. And then she close her

book and walks out of the house, and suddenly—mark this—I could pray again!

[OLD GILES *must be spoken for, if only because his fate was to be so remarkable and so different from that of all the others. He was in his early eighties at this time, and was the most comical hero in the history. No man has ever been blamed for so much. If a cow was missed, the first thought was to look for her around* COREY'S *house; a fire blazing up at night brought suspicion of arson to his door. He didn't give a hoot for public opinion, and only in his last years—after he had married* MARTHA— *did he bother much with the church. That she stopped his prayer is very probable, but he forgot to say that he'd only recently learned any prayers and it didn't take much to make him stumble over them. He was a crank and a nuisance, but withal a deeply innocent and brave man. In court, once, he was asked if it were true that he had been frightened by the strange behavior of a hog and had then said he knew it to be the Devil in an animal's shape. "What frighted you?" he was asked. He forgot everything but the word "frighted," and instantly replied, "I do not know that I ever spoke that word in my life."*]

Hale. Ah. The stoppage of prayer—that is strange. I'll speak further on that with you.

Giles. I'm not sayin' she's touched the Devil, now, but I'd admire to know what books she reads and why she hides them. She'll not answer me, y' see.

Hale. Aye, we'll discuss it. [*To all.*] Now mark me, if the Devil is in her you will witness some frightful wonders in this room, so please to keep your wits about you. Mr. Putnam, stand close in case she flies. Now, Betty, dear, will you sit up? [PUTNAM *comes in closer, ready-handed.* HALE *sits* BETTY *up, but she hangs limp in his hands.*] Hmmm. [*He observes her carefully. The others watch breathlessly.*] Can you hear me? I am John Hale, minister of Beverly. I have come to help you, dear. Do you remember my two little girls in Beverly?

[*She does not stir in his hands.*]

Parris. [*In fright.*] How can it be the Devil? Why would he choose my house to strike? We have all manner of licentious people in the village!

Hale. What victory would the Devil have to win a soul already bad? It is the best the

Devil wants, and who is better than the minister?

Giles. That's deep, Mr. Parris, deep, deep!

Parris. [*With resolution now.*] Betty! Answer Mr. Hale! Betty!

Hale. Does someone afflict you, child? It need not be a woman, mind you, or a man. Perhaps some bird invisible to others comes to you—perhaps a pig, a mouse, or any beast at all. Is there some figure bids you fly? [THE CHILD *remains limp in his hands. In silence he lays her back on the pillow. Now, holding out his hands toward her, he intones.*] In nomine Domini Sabaoth sui filiique ite ad infernos. [*She does not stir. He turns to* ABIGAIL, *his eyes narrowing.*] Abigail, what sort of dancing were you doing with her in the forest?

Abigail. Why—common dancing is all.

Parris. I think I ought to say that I—I saw a kettle in the grass where they were dancing.

Abigail. That were only soup.

Hale. What sort of soup were in this kettle, Abigail?

Abigail. Why, it were beans—and lentils, I think, and——

Hale. Mr. Parris, you did not notice, did you, any living thing in the kettle? A mouse, perhaps, a spider, a frog——?

Parris. [*Fearfully.*] I—do believe there were some movement—in the soup.

Abigail. That jumped in, we never put it in!

Hale. [*Quickly.*] What jumped in?

Abigail. Why, a very little frog jumped——

Parris. A frog, Abby!

Hale. [*Grasping* ABIGAIL.] Abigail, it may be your cousin is dying. Did you call the Devil last night?

Abigail. I never called him! Tituba, Tituba . . .

Parris. [*Blanched.*] She called the Devil?

Hale. I should like to speak with Tituba.

Parris. Goody Ann, will you bring her up? [MRS. PUTNAM *exits.*]

Hale. How did she call him?

Abigail. I know not—she spoke Barbados.

Hale. Did you feel any strangeness when she called him? A sudden cold wind, perhaps? A trembling below the ground?

Abigail. I didn't see no Devil! [*Shaking* BETTY.] Betty, wake up. Betty! Betty!

Hale. You cannot evade me, Abigail. Did your cousin drink any of the brew in that kettle?

Abigail. She never drank it!

Hale. Did you drink it?

Abigail. No, sir!

Hale. Did Tituba ask you to drink it?

Abigail. She tried, but I refused.

Hale. Why are you concealing? Have you sold yourself to Lucifer?

Abigail. I never sold myself! I'm a good girl! I'm a proper girl!

[MRS. PUTNAM *enters with* TITUBA, *and instantly* ABIGAIL *points at* TITUBA.]

Abigail. She made me do it! She made Betty do it!

Tituba. [*Shocked and angry.*] Abby!

Abigail. She makes me drink blood!

Parris. Blood!!

Mrs. Putnam. My baby's blood?

Tituba. No, no, chicken blood. I give she chicken blood!

Hale. Woman, have you enlisted these children for the Devil?

Tituba. No, no, sir, I don't truck with no Devil!

Hale. Why can she not wake? Are you silencing this child?

Tituba. I love me Betty!

Hale. You have sent your spirit out upon this child, have you not? Are you gathering souls for the Devil?

Abigail. She sends her spirit on me in church; she makes me laugh at prayer!

Parris. She have often laughed at prayer!

Abigail. She comes to me every night to go and drink blood!

Tituba. You beg *me* to conjure! She beg *me* make charm——

Abigail. Don't lie! [*To* HALE.] She comes to me while I sleep; she's always making me dream corruptions!

Tituba. Why you say that, Abby?

Abigail. Sometimes I wake and find myself standing in the open doorway and not a stitch on my body! I always hear her laughing in my sleep. I hear her singing her Barbados songs and tempting me with——

Tituba. Mister Reverend, I never——

Hale. [*Resolved now.*] Tituba, I want you to wake this child.

Tituba. I have no power on this child, sir.

Hale. You most certainly do, and you will free her from it now! When did you compact with the Devil?

Tituba. I don't compact with no Devil!

Parris. You will confess yourself or I will take you out and whip you to your death, Tituba!

Putnam. This woman must be hanged! She must be taken and hanged!

Tituba. [*Terrified, falls to her knees.*] No, no, don't hang Tituba! I tell him I don't desire to work for him, sir.

Parris. The Devil?

Hale. Then you saw him! [TITUBA *weeps.*] Now Tituba, I know that when we bind ourselves to Hell it is very hard to break with it. We are going to help you tear yourself free——

Tituba. [*Frightened by the coming process.*] Mister Reverend, I do believe somebody else be witchin' these children.

Hale. Who?

Tituba. I don't know, sir, but the Devil got him numerous witches.

Hale. Does he! [*It is a clue.*] Tituba, look into my eyes. Come, look into me. [*She raises her eyes to his fearfully.*] You would be a good Christian woman, would you not, Tituba?

Tituba. Aye, sir, a good Christian woman.

Hale. And you love these little children?

Tituba. Oh, yes, sir, I don't desire to hurt little children.

Hale. And you love God, Tituba?

Tituba. I love God with all my bein'.

Hale. Now, in God's holy name——

Tituba. Bless Him. Bless Him.

[*She is rocking on her knees, sobbing in terror.*]

Hale. And to His glory——

Tituba. Eternal glory. Bless Him—bless God . . .

Hale. Open yourself, Tituba—open yourself and let God's holy light shine on you.

Tituba. Oh, bless the Lord.

Hale. When the Devil comes to you does he ever come—with another person? [*She stares up into his face.*] Perhaps another person in the village? Someone you know.

Parris. Who come with him?

Putnam. Sarah Good? Did you ever see Sarah Good with him? Or Osburn?

Parris. Was it man or woman came with him?

Tituba. Man or woman. Was—was woman.

Parris. What woman? A woman, you said. What woman?

Tituba. It was black dark, and I——

Parris. You could see him, why could you not see her?

Tituba. Well, they was always talking; they was always runnin' round and carryin' on——

Parris. You mean out of Salem? Salem witches?

Tituba. I believe so, yes, sir.

[*Now* HALE *takes her hand. She is surprised.*]

Hale. Tituba. You must have no fear to tell us who they are, do you understand? We will protect you. The Devil can never overcome a minister. You know that, do you not?

Tituba. [*Kisses* HALE'S *hand.*] Aye, sir, oh, I do.

Hale. You have confessed yourself to witchcraft, and that speaks a wish to come to Heaven's side. And we will bless you, Tituba.

Tituba. [*Deeply relieved.*] Oh, God bless you, Mr. Hale!

Hale. [*With rising exaltation.*] You are God's instrument put in our hands to discover the Devil's agents among us. You are selected, Tituba, you are chosen to help us cleanse our village. So speak utterly, Tituba; turn your back on him and face God—face God, Tituba, and God will protect you.

Tituba. [*Joining with him.*] Oh, God, protect Tituba!

Hale. [*Kindly.*] Who came to you with the Devil? Two? Three? Four? How many?

[TITUBA *pants, and begins rocking back and forth again, staring ahead.*]

Tituba. There was four. There was four.

Parris. [*Pressing in on her.*] Who? Who? Their names, their names!

Tituba. [*Suddenly bursting out.*] Oh, how many times he bid me kill you, Mr. Parris!

Parris. Kill me!

Tituba. [*In a fury.*] He say Mr. Parris must be kill! Mr. Parris no goodly man, Mr. Parris mean man and no gentle man, and he bid me rise out of my bed and cut your throat! [*They gasp.*] But I tell him "No! I don't hate that man. I don't want kill that man." But he say, "You work for me, Tituba, and I make you free! I give you pretty dress to wear, and put you way high up in the air, and you gone fly back to Barbados!" And I say, "You lie, Devil, you lie!" And then he come one stormy night to me, and he say, "Look! I have *white* people belong to me." And I look—and there was Goody Good.

Parris. Sarah Good!

Tituba. [*Rocking and weeping.*] Aye, sir, and Goody Osburn.

Mrs. Putnam. I knew it! Goody Osburn were midwife to me three times. I begged you, Thomas, did I not? I begged him not to call Osburn because I feared her. My babies always shriveled in her hands!

Hale. Take courage, you must give us all their names. How can you bear to see this child suffering? Look at her, Tituba. [*He is indicating* BETTY *on the bed.*] Look at her God-given innocence; her soul is so tender; we must protect her, Tituba; the Devil is out and preying on her like a beast upon the flesh of the pure lamb. God will bless you for your help.

Abigail. [*Rises, staring as though inspired, and cries out.*] I want to open myself! [*They turn to her, startled. She is enraptured, as though in a pearly light.*] I want the light of God, I want the sweet love of Jesus! I danced for the Devil; I saw him; I wrote in his book; I go back to Jesus; I kiss His hand. I saw Sarah Good with the Devil! I saw Goody Osburn with the Devil! I saw Bridget Bishop with the Devil!

[*As she is speaking,* BETTY *is rising from the bed, a fever in her eyes, and picks up the chant.*]

Betty. [*Staring too.*] I saw George Jacobs with the Devil! I saw Goody Howe with the Devil!

Parris. She speaks! [*He rushes to embrace* BETTY.] She speaks!

Hale. Glory to God! It is broken, they are free!

Betty. [*Calling out hysterically and with great relief.*] I saw Martha Bellows with the Devil!

Abigail. I saw Goody Sibber with the Devil! [*It is rising to a great glee.*]

Putnam. The marshal, I'll call the marshal!

[PARRIS *is shouting a prayer of thanksgiving.*]

Betty. I saw Alice Barrow with the Devil! [*The curtain begins to fall.*]

Hale. [*As* PUTNAM *goes out.*] Let the marshal bring irons!

Abigail. I saw Goody Hawkins with the Devil!

Betty. I saw Goody Bibber with the Devil!

Abigail. I saw Goody Booth with the Devil!

[*On their ecstatic cries* THE CURTAIN FALLS]

ACT TWO

The common room of PROCTOR'S *house, eight days later. At the right is a door opening on the fields outside. A fireplace is at the left, and behind it a stairway leading upstairs. It is the low, dark, and rather long living room of the time.*

[*As the curtain rises, the room is empty. From above,* ELIZABETH *is heard softly singing to the children. Presently the door opens and* JOHN PROCTOR *enters, carrying his gun. He glances about the room as he comes toward the fireplace, then halts for an instant as he hears her singing. He continues on to the fireplace, leans the gun against the wall as he swings a pot out of the fire and smells it. Then he lifts out the ladle and tastes. He is not quite pleased. He reaches to a cupboard, takes a pinch of salt, and drops it into the pot. As he is tasting again, her footsteps are heard on the stair. He swings the pot into the fireplace and goes to a basin and washes his hands and face.* ELIZABETH *enters.*]

Elizabeth. What keeps you so late? It's almost dark.

Proctor. I were planting far out to the forest edge.

Elizabeth. Oh, you're done then.

Proctor. Aye, the farm is seeded. The boys asleep?

Elizabeth. They will be soon.

[*And she goes to the fireplace, proceeds to ladle up stew in a dish.*]

Proctor. Pray now for a fair summer.

Elizabeth. Aye.

Proctor. Are you well today?

Elizabeth. I am. [*She brings the plate to the table, and, indicating the food.*] It is a rabbit.

Proctor. [*Going to the table.*] Oh, is it! In Jonathan's trap?

Elizabeth. No, she walked into the house this afternoon; I found her sittin' in the corner like she come to visit.

Proctor. Oh, that's a good sign walkin' in.

Elizabeth. Pray God. It hurt my heart to strip her, poor rabbit.

[*She sits and watches him taste it.*]

Proctor. It's well seasoned.

Elizabeth. [*Blushing with pleasure.*] I took great care. She's tender?

Proctor. Aye. [*He eats. She watches him.*] I think we'll see green fields soon.

It's warm as blood beneath the clods.
Elizabeth. That's well.
Proctor. [*Eats, then looks up.*] If the crop is good I'll buy George Jacob's heifer. How would that please you?
Elizabeth. Aye, it would.
Proctor. [*With a grin.*] I mean to please you, Elizabeth.
Elizabeth. [*It is hard to say.*] I know it, John.
  [*He gets up, goes to her, kisses her. She receives it. With a certain disappointment, he returns to the table.*]
Proctor. [*As gently as he can.*] Cider?
Elizabeth. [*With a sense of reprimanding herself for having forgot.*] Aye!
  [*She gets up and goes and pours a glass for him. He now arches his back.*]
Proctor. This farm's a continent when you go foot by foot droppin' seeds in it.
Elizabeth. [*Coming with the cider.*] It must be.
Proctor. [*Drinks a long draught, then, putting the glass down.*] You ought to bring some flowers in the house.
Elizabeth. Oh! I forgot! I will tomorrow.
Proctor. It's winter in here yet. On Sunday let you come with me, and we'll walk the farm together; I never see such a load of flowers on the earth. [*With good feeling he goes and looks up at the sky through the open doorway.*] Lilacs have a purple smell. Lilac is the smell of nightfall, I think. Massachusetts is a beauty in the spring!
Elizabeth. Aye, it is.
  [*There is a pause. She is watching him from the table as he stands there absorbing the night. It is as though she would speak but cannot. Instead, now, she takes up his plate and glass and fork and goes with them to the basin. Her back is turned to him. He turns to her and watches her. A sense of their separation rises.*]
Proctor. I think you're sad again. Are you?
Elizabeth. [*She doesn't want friction, and yet she must.*] You come so late I thought you'd gone to Salem this afternoon.
Proctor. Why? I have no business in Salem.
Elizabeth. You did speak of going, earlier this week.
Proctor. [*He knows what she means.*] I thought better of it since.
Elizabeth. Mary Warren's there today.
Proctor. Why'd you let her? You heard me forbid her to go to Salem any more!

Elizabeth. I couldn't stop her.
Proctor. [*Holding back a full condemnation of her.*] It is a fault, it is a fault, Elizabeth—you're the mistress here, not Mary Warren.
Elizabeth. She frightened all my strength away.
Proctor. How may that mouse frighten you, Elizabeth? You——
Elizabeth. It is a mouse no more. I forbid her go, and she raises up her chin like the daughter of a prince and says to me, "I must go to Salem, Goody Proctor; I am an official of the court!"
Proctor. Court! What court?
Elizabeth. Aye, it is a proper court they have now. They've sent four judges out of Boston, she says, weighty magistrates of the General Court, and at the head sits the Deputy Governor of the Province.
Proctor. [*Astonished.*] Why, she's mad.
Elizabeth. I would to God she were. There be fourteen people in the jail now, she says. [PROCTOR *simply looks at her, unable to grasp it.*] And they'll be tried, and the court have power to hang them too, she says.
Proctor. [*Scoffing, but without conviction.*] Ah, they'd never hang——
Elizabeth. The Deputy Governor promise hangin' if they'll not confess, John. The town's gone wild, I think. She speak of Abigail, and I thought she were a saint, to hear her. Abigail brings the other girls into the court, and where she walks the crowd will part like the sea for Israel. And folks are brought before them, and if they scream and howl and fall to the floor—the person's clapped in the jail for bewitchin' them.
Proctor. [*Wide-eyed.*] Oh, it is a black mischief.
Elizabeth. I think you must go to Salem, John. [*He turns to her.*] I think so. You must tell them it is a fraud.
Proctor. [*Thinking beyond this.*] Aye, it is, it is surely.
Elizabeth. Let you go to Ezekiel Cheever —he knows you well. And tell him what she said to you last week in her uncle's house. She said it had naught to do with witchcraft, did she not?
Proctor. [*In thought.*] Aye, she did, she did. [*Now, a pause.*]
Elizabeth. [*Quietly, fearing to anger him by prodding.*] God forbid you keep that from the court, John. I think they must be told.
Proctor. [*Quietly, struggling with his thought.*] Aye, they must, they must. It is a wonder they do believe her.

Elizabeth. I would go to Salem now, John —let you go tonight.

Proctor. I'll think on it.

Elizabeth. [*With her courage now.*] You cannot keep it, John.

Proctor. [*Angering.*] I know I cannot keep it. I say I will think on it!

Elizabeth. [*Hurt, and very coldly.*] Good, then, let you think on it.

[*She stands and starts to walk out of the room.*]

Proctor. I am only wondering how I may prove what she told me, Elizabeth. If the girl's a saint now, I think it is not easy to prove she's fraud, and the town gone so silly. She told it to me in a room alone—I have no proof for it.

Elizabeth. You were alone with her?

Proctor. [*Stubbornly.*] For a moment alone, aye.

Elizabeth. Why, then, it is not as you told me.

Proctor. [*His anger rising.*] For a moment, I say. The others come in soon after.

Elizabeth. [*Quietly—she has suddenly lost all faith in him.*] Do as you wish, then.

[*She starts to turn.*]

Proctor. Woman. [*She turns to him.*] I'll not have your suspicion any more.

Elizabeth. [*A little loftily.*] I have no——

Proctor. I'll not have it!

Elizabeth. Then let you not earn it.

Proctor. [*With a violent undertone.*] You doubt me yet?

Elizabeth. [*With a smile, to keep her dignity.*] John, if it were not Abigail that you must go to hurt, would you falter now? I think not.

Proctor. Now look you——

Elizabeth. I see what I see, John.

Proctor. [*With solemn warning.*] You will not judge me more, Elizabeth. I have good reason to think before I charge fraud on Abigail, and I will think on it. Let you look to your own improvement before you go to judge your husband any more. I have forgot Abigail, and——

Elizabeth. And I.

Proctor. Spare me! You forget nothin' and forgive nothin'. Learn charity, woman. I have gone tiptoe in this house all seven month since she is gone. I have not moved from there to there without I think to please you, and still an everlasting funeral marches round your heart. I cannot speak but I am doubted, every moment judged for lies, as though I come into a court when I come into this house!

Elizabeth. John, you are not open with me. You saw her with a crowd, you said. Now you——

Proctor. I'll plead my honesty no more, Elizabeth.

Elizabeth. [*Now she would justify herself.*] John, I am only——

Proctor. No more! I should have roared you down when first you told me your suspicion. But I wilted, and, like a Christian, I confessed. Confessed! Some dream I had must have mistaken you for God that day. But you're not, you're not, and let you remember it! Let you look sometimes for the goodness in me, and judge me not.

Elizabeth. I do not judge you. The magistrate sits in your heart that judges you. I never thought you but a good man, John — [*With a smile.*] —only somewhat bewildered.

Proctor. [*Laughing bitterly.*] Oh, Elizabeth, your justice would freeze beer! [*He turns suddenly toward a sound outside. He starts for the door as* MARY WARREN *enters. As soon as he sees her, he goes directly to her and grabs her by her cloak, furious.*] How do you go to Salem when I forbid it? Do you mock me? [*Shaking her.*] I'll whip you if you dare leave this house again!

[*Strangely, she doesn't resist him, but hangs limply by his grip.*]

Mary Warren. I am sick, I am sick, Mr. Proctor. Pray, pray, hurt me not. [*Her strangeness throws him off, and her evident pallor and weakness. He frees her.*] My insides are all shuddery; I am in the proceedings all day, sir.

Proctor. [*With draining anger—his curiosity is draining it.*] And what of these proceedings here? When will you proceed to keep this house, as you are paid nine pound a year to do—and my wife not wholly well?

[*As though to compensate,* MARY WARREN *goes to* ELIZABETH *with a small rag doll.*]

Mary Warren. I made a gift for you today, Goody Proctor. I had to sit long hours in a chair, and passed the time with sewing.

Elizabeth. [*Perplexed, looking at the doll.*] Why, thank you, it's a fair poppet.

Mary Warren. [*With a trembling, decayed voice.*] We must all love each other now, Goody Proctor.

Elizabeth. [*Amazed at her strangeness.*] Aye, indeed we must.

Mary Warren. [*Glancing at the room.*] I'll get up early in the morning and clean the house. I must sleep now.

[*She turns and starts off.*]

Proctor. Mary. [*She halts.*] Is it true? There be fourteen women arrested?

Mary Warren. No, sir. There be thirty-nine now——

[*She suddenly breaks off and sobs and sits down, exhausted.*]

Elizabeth. Why, she's weepin'! What ails you, child?

Mary Warren. Goody Osburn—will hang! [*There is a shocked pause, while she sobs.*]

Proctor. Hang! [*He calls into her face.*] Hang, y'say?

Mary Warren. [*Through her weeping.*] Aye.

Proctor. The Deputy Governor will permit it?

Mary Warren. He sentenced her. He must. [*To ameliorate it.*] But not Sarah Good. For Sarah Good confessed, y'see.

Proctor. Confessed! To what?

Mary Warren. That she— [*In horror at the memory.*]—she sometimes made a compact with Lucifer, and wrote her name in his black book—with her blood—and bound herself to torment Christians till God's thrown down—and we all must worship Hell forevermore. [*Pause.*]

Proctor. But—surely you know what a jabberer she is. Did you tell them that?

Mary Warren. Mr. Proctor, in open court she near to choked us all to death.

Proctor. How, choked you?

Mary Warren. She sent her spirit out.

Elizabeth. Oh, Mary, Mary, surely you——

Mary Warren. [*With an indignant edge.*] She tried to kill me many times, Goody Proctor!

Elizabeth. Why, I never heard you mention that before.

Mary Warren. I never knew it before. I never knew anything before. When she come into the court I say to myself, I must not accuse this woman, for she sleep in ditches, and so very old and poor. But then—then she sit there, denying and denying, and I feel a misty coldness climbin' up my back, and the skin on my skull begin to creep, and I feel a clamp around my neck and I cannot breathe air; and then [*Entranced.*] I hear a voice, a screamin' voice, and it were my voice—and all at once I remembered everything she done to me!

Proctor. Why? What did she do to you?

Mary Warren. [*Like one awakened to a marvelous secret insight.*] So many time, Mr. Proctor, she come to this very door, beggin' bread and a cup of cider—and mark this: whenever I turned her away empty, she *mumbled.*

Elizabeth. Mumbled! She may mumble if she's hungry.

Mary Warren. But *what* does she mumble? You must remember, Goody Proctor. Last month—a Monday, I think—she walked away, and I thought my guts would burst for two days after. Do you remember it?

Elizabeth. Why—I do, I think, but——

Mary Warren. And so I told that to Judge Hathorne, and he asks her so. "Goody Osburn," says he, "what curse do you mumble that this girl must fall sick after turning you away?" And then she replies [*Mimicking an old crone.*] "Why, your excellence, no curse at all. I only say my commandments; I hope I may say my commandments," says she!

Elizabeth. And that's an upright answer.

Mary Warren. Aye, but then Judge Hathorne say, "Recite for us your commandments!" [*Leaning avidly toward them.*] and of all the ten she could not say a single one. She never knew no commandments, and they had her in a flat lie!

Proctor. And so condemned her?

Mary Warren. [*Now a little strained, seeing his stubborn doubt.*] Why, they must when she condemned herself.

Proctor. But the proof, the proof!

Mary Warren. [*With greater impatience with him.*] I told you the proof. It's hard proof, hard as rock, the judges said.

Proctor. [*Pauses an instant, then.*] You will not go to court again, Mary Warren.

Mary Warren. I must tell you, sir, I will be gone every day now. I am amazed you do not see what weighty work we do.

Proctor. What work you do! It's strange work for a Christian girl to hang old women!

Mary Warren. But, Mr. Proctor, they will not hang them if they confess. Sarah Good will only sit in jail some time [*Recalling.*] and here's a wonder for you; think on this. Goody Good is pregnant.

Elizabeth. Pregnant! Are they mad? The woman's near to sixty!

Mary Warren. They had Doctor Griggs examine her, and she's full to the brim. And smokin' a pipe all these years, and no husband either! But she's safe, thank God, for they'll not hurt the innocent child. But be that not a marvel? You must see it, sir, it's God's work we do. So I'll be gone every day for some time. I'm—I am an official of the court, they say, and I——

[*She has been edging toward offstage.*]

Proctor. I'll official you!

[*He strides to the mantel, takes down the whip hanging there.*]

Mary Warren. [*Terrified, but coming*

erect, striving for her authority.] I'll not stand whipping any more!

Elizabeth. [*Hurriedly, as* PROCTOR *approaches.*] Mary, promise now you'll stay at home——

Mary Warren. [*Backing from him, but keeping her erect posture, striving, striving for her way.*] The Devil's loose in Salem, Mr. Proctor; we must discover where he's hiding!

Proctor. I'll whip the Devil out of you! [*With whip raised he reaches out for her, and she streaks away and yells.*]

Mary Warren. [*Pointing at* ELIZABETH.] I saved her life today!

[*Silence. His whip comes down.*]

Elizabeth. [*Softly.*] I am accused?

Mary Warren. [*Quaking.*] Somewhat mentioned. But I said I never see no sign you ever sent your spirit out to hurt no one, and seeing I do live so closely with you, they dismissed it.

Elizabeth. Who accused me?

Mary Warren. I am bound by law, I cannot tell it. [*To* PROCTOR.] I only hope you'll not be so sarcastical no more. Four judges and the King's deputy sat to dinner with us but an hour ago. I—I would have you speak civilly to me, from this out.

Proctor. [*In horror, muttering in disgust at her.*] Go to bed.

Mary Warren. [*With a stamp of her foot.*] I'll not be ordered to bed no more, Mr. Proctor! I am eighteen and a woman, however single!

Proctor. Do you wish to sit up? Then sit up.

Mary Warren. I wish to go to bed!

Proctor. [*In anger.*] Good night, then!

Mary Warren. Good night.

[*Dissatisfied, uncertain of herself, she goes out. Wide-eyed, both,* PROCTOR *and* ELIZABETH *stand staring.*]

Elizabeth. [*Quietly.*] Oh, the noose, the noose is up!

Proctor. There'll be no noose.

Elizabeth. She wants me dead. I knew all week it would come to this!

Proctor. [*Without conviction.*] They dismissed it. You heard her say——

Elizabeth. And what of tomorrow? She will cry me out until they take me!

Proctor. Sit you down.

Elizabeth. She wants me dead, John, you know it!

Proctor. I say sit down! [*She sits, trembling. He speaks quietly, trying to keep his wits.*] Now we must be wise, Elizabeth.

Elizabeth. [*With sarcasm, and a sense of being lost.*] Oh, indeed, indeed!

Proctor. Fear nothing. I'll find Ezekiel Cheever. I'll tell him she said it were all sport.

Elizabeth. John, with so many in the jail, more than Cheever's help is needed now, I think. Would you favor me with this? Go to Abigail.

Proctor. [*His soul hardening as he senses . . .*] What have I to say to Abigail?

Elizabeth. [*Delicately.*] John—grant me this. You have a faulty understanding of young girls. There is a promise made in any bed——

Proctor. [*Striving against his anger.*] What promise!

Elizabeth. Spoke or silent, a promise is surely made. And she may dote on it now— I am sure she does—and thinks to kill me, then to take my place.

[PROCTOR'S *anger is rising; he cannot speak.*]

Elizabeth. It is her dearest hope, John, I know it. There be a thousand names; why does she call mine? There be a certain danger in calling such a name—I am no Goody Good that sleeps in ditches, nor Osburn, drunk and half-witted. She'd dare not call out such a farmer's wife but there be monstrous profit in it. She thinks to take my place, John.

Proctor. She cannot think it!

[*He knows it is true.*]

Elizabeth. ["*Reasonably.*"] John, have you ever shown her somewhat of contempt? She cannot pass you in the church but you will blush——

Proctor. I may blush for my sin.

Elizabeth. I think she sees another meaning in that blush.

Proctor. And what see you? What see you, Elizabeth?

Elizabeth. ["*Conceding.*"] I think you be somewhat ashamed, for I am there, and she so close.

Proctor. When will you know me, woman? Were I stone I would have cracked for shame this seven month!

Elizabeth. Then go and tell her she's a whore. Whatever promise she may sense— break it, John, break it.

Proctor. [*Between his teeth.*] Good, then. I'll go. [*He starts for his rifle.*]

Elizabeth. [*Trembling, fearfully.*] Oh, how unwillingly!

Proctor. [*Turning on her, rifle in hand.*] I will curse her hotter than the oldest cinder in hell. But pray, begrudge me not my anger!

Elizabeth. Your anger! I only ask you——

Proctor. Woman, am I so base? Do you truly think me base?

Elizabeth. I never called you base.

Proctor. Then how do you charge me with such a promise? The promise that a stallion gives a mare I gave that girl!

Elizabeth. Then why do you anger with me when I bid you break it?

Proctor. Because it speaks deceit, and I am honest! But I'll plead no more! I see now your spirit twists around the single error of my life, and I will never tear it free!

Elizabeth. [*Crying out.*] You'll tear it free—when you come to know that I will be your only wife, or no wife at all! She has an arrow in you yet, John Proctor, and you know it well!

[*Quite suddenly, as though from the air, a figure appears in the doorway. They start slightly. It is* MR. HALE. *He is different now—drawn a little, and there is a quality of deference, even of guilt, about his manner now.*]

Hale. Good evening.

Proctor. [*Still in his shock.*] Why, Mr. Hale! Good evening to you, sir. Come in, come in.

Hale. [*To* ELIZABETH.] I hope I do not startle you.

Elizabeth. No, no, it's only that I heard no horse——

Hale. You are Goodwife Proctor.

Proctor. Aye; Elizabeth.

Hale. [*Nods, then.*] I hope you're not off to bed yet.

Proctor. [*Setting down his gun.*] No, no. [HALE *comes further into the room. And* PROCTOR, *to explain his nervousness.*] We are not used to visitors after dark, but you're welcome here. Will you sit down, sir?

Hale. I will. [*He sits.*] Let you sit, Goodwife Proctor.

[*She does, never letting him out of her sight. There is a pause as* HALE *looks about the room.*]

Proctor. [*To break the silence.*] Will you drink cider, Mr. Hale?

Hale. No, it rebels my stomach; I have some further traveling yet tonight. Sit you down, sir. [PROCTOR *sits.*] I will not keep you long, but I have some business with you.

Proctor. Business of the court?

Hale. No—no, I come of my own, without the court's authority. Hear me. [*He wets his lips.*] I know not if you are aware, but your wife's name is—mentioned in the court.

Proctor. We know it, sir. Our Mary Warren told us. We are entirely amazed.

Hale. I am a stranger here, as you know.

And in my ignorance I find it hard to draw a clear opinion of them that come accused before the court. And so this afternoon, and now tonight, I go from house to house— I come from Rebecca Nurse's house and——

Elizabeth. [*Shocked.*] Rebecca's charged!

Hale. God forbid such a one be charged. She is, however—mentioned somewhat.

Elizabeth. [*With an attempt at a laugh.*] You will never believe, I hope, that Rebecca trafficked with the Devil.

Hale. Woman, it is possible.

Proctor. [*Taken aback.*] Surely you cannot think so.

Hale. This is a strange time, Mister. No man may longer doubt the powers of the dark are gathered in monstrous attack upon this village. There is too much evidence now to deny it. You will agree, sir?

Proctor. [*Evading.*] I—have no knowledge in that line. But it's hard to think so pious a woman be secretly a Devil's bitch after seventy year of such good prayer.

Hale. Aye. But the Devil is a wily one, you cannot deny it. However, she is far from accused, and I know she will not be. [*Pause.*] I thought, sir, to put some questions as to the Christian character of this house, if you'll permit me.

Proctor. [*Coldly, resentful.*] Why, we—have no fear of questions, sir.

Hale. Good, then. [*He makes himself more comfortable.*] In the book of record that Mr. Parris keeps, I note that you are rarely in the church on Sabbath Day.

Proctor. No sir, you are mistaken.

Hale. Twenty-six time in seventeen month, sir. I must call that rare. Will you tell me why you are so absent?

Proctor. Mr. Hale, I never knew I must account to that man for I come to church or stay at home. My wife were sick this winter.

Hale. So I am told. But you, Mister, why could you not come alone?

Proctor. I surely did come when I could, and when I could not I prayed in this house.

Hale. Mr. Proctor, your house is not a church; your theology must tell you that.

Proctor. It does, sir, it does; and it tells me that a minister may pray to God without he have golden candlesticks upon the altar.

Hale. What golden candlesticks?

Proctor. Since we built the church there were pewter candlesticks upon the altar; Francis Nurse made them, y'know, and a sweeter hand never touched the metal. But Parris came, and for twenty week he preach nothin' but golden candlesticks until he had them. I labor the earth from dawn of day to blink of night, and I tell you true, when I look to heaven and see my money glaring at his elbows—it hurt my prayer, sir, it hurt my prayer. I think, sometimes, the man dreams cathedrals, not clapboard meetin' houses.

Hale. [*Thinks, then.*] And yet, Mister, a Christian on Sabbath Day must be in church. [*Pause.*] Tell me—you have three children?

Proctor. Aye. Boys.

Hale. How comes it that only two are baptized?

Proctor. [*Starts to speak, then stops, then, as though unable to restrain this.*] I like it not that Mr. Parris should lay his hand upon my baby. I see no light of God in that man. I'll not conceal it.

Hale. I must say it, Mr. Proctor; that is not for you to decide. The man's ordained, therefore the light of God is in him.

Proctor. [*Flushed with resentment but trying to smile.*] What's your suspicion, Mr. Hale?

Hale. No, no, I have no——

Proctor. I nailed the roof upon the church, I hung the door——

Hale. Oh, did you! That's a good sign, then.

Proctor. It may be I have been too quick to bring the man to book, but you cannot think we ever desired the destruction of religion. I think that's in your mind, is it not?

Hale. [*Not altogether giving way.*] I—have—there is a softness in your record, sir, a softness.

Elizabeth. I think, maybe, we have been too hard with Mr. Parris. I think so. But sure we never loved the Devil here.

Hale. [*Nods, deliberating this. Then, with the voice of one administering a secret test.*] Do you know your Commandments, Elizabeth?

Elizabeth. [*Without hesitation, even eagerly.*] I surely do. There be no mark of blame upon my life, Mr. Hale. I am a covenanted Christian woman.

Hale. And you, Mister?

Proctor. [*A trifle unsteadily.*] I—am sure I do, sir.

Hale. [*Glances at her open face, then at* John, *then.*] Let you repeat them, if you will.

Proctor. The Commandments.

Hale. Aye.

Proctor. [*Looking off, beginning to sweat.*] Thou shalt not kill.

Hale. Aye.

Proctor. [*Counting on his fingers.*] Thou shalt not steal. Thou shalt not covet thy neighbor's goods, nor make unto thee any graven image. Thou shalt not take the name of the Lord in vain; thou shalt have no other gods before me. [*With some hesitation.*] Thou shalt remember the Sabbath Day and keep it holy. [*Pause. Then.*] Thou shalt honor thy father and mother. Thou shalt not bear false witness. [*He is stuck. He counts back on his fingers, knowing one is missing.*] Thou shalt not make unto thee any graven image.

Hale. You have said that twice, sir.

Proctor. [*Lost.*] Aye.

[*He is flailing for it.*]

Elizabeth. [*Delicately.*] Adultery, John.

Proctor. [*As though a secret arrow had pained his heart.*] Aye. [*Trying to grin it away—to* Hale.] You see, sir, between the two of us we do know them all. [Hale *only looks at* Proctor, *deep in his attempt to define this man.* Proctor *grows more uneasy.*] I think it be a small fault.

Hale. Theology, sir, is a fortress; no crack in a fortress may be accounted small.

[*He rises; he seems worried now. He paces a little, in deep thought.*]

Proctor. There be no love for Satan in this house, Mister.

Hale. I pray it, I pray it dearly. [*He looks to both of them, an attempt at a smile on his face, but his misgivings are clear.*] Well, then—I'll bid you good night.

Elizabeth. [*Unable to restrain herself.*] Mr. Hale. [*He turns.*] I do think you are suspecting me somewhat? Are you not?

Hale. [*Obviously disturbed—and evasive.*] Goody Proctor, I do not judge you. My duty is to add what I may to the godly wisdom of the court. I pray you both good health and good fortune. [*To* John.] Good night, sir. [*He starts out.*]

Elizabeth. [*With a note of desperation.*] I think you must tell him, John.

Hale. What's that?

Elizabeth. [*Restraining a call.*] Will you tell him?

[*Slight pause.* Hale *looks questioningly at* John.]

Proctor. [*With difficulty.*] I—I have no witness and cannot prove it, except my word be taken. But I know the children's sickness had naught to do with witchcraft.

Hale. [*Stopped, struck.*] Naught to do——?

Proctor. Mr. Parris discovered them sportin' in the woods. They were startled and took sick. [*Pause.*]

Hale. Who told you this?

Proctor. [*Hesitates, then.*] Abigail Williams.

Hale. Abigail!

Proctor. Aye.

Hale. [*His eyes wide.*] Abigail Williams told you it had naught to do with witchcraft!

Proctor. She told me the day you came, sir.

Hale. [*Suspiciously.*] Why—why did you keep this?

Proctor. I never knew until tonight that the world is gone daft with this nonsense.

Hale. Nonsense! Mister, I have myself examined Tituba, Sarah Good, and numerous others that have confessed to dealing with the Devil. They have *confessed* it.

Proctor. And why not, if they must hang for denyin' it? There are them that will swear to anything before they'll hang; have you never thought of that?

Hale. I have. I—I have indeed. [*It is his own suspicion, but he resists it. He glances at* ELIZABETH, *then at* JOHN.] And you—would you testify to this in court?

Proctor. I—had not reckoned with goin' into court. But if I must I will.

Hale. Do you falter here?

Proctor. I falter nothing, but I may wonder if my story will be credited in such a court. I do wonder on it, when such a steady-minded minister as you will suspicion such a woman that never lied, and cannot, and the world knows she cannot! I may falter somewhat, Mister; I am no fool.

Hale. [*Quietly—it has impressed him.*] Proctor, let you open with me now, for I have a rumor that troubles me. It's said you hold no belief that there may even be witches in the world. Is that true, sir?

Proctor. [*He knows this is critical, and is striving against his disgust with* HALE *and with himself for even answering.*] I know not what I have said, I may have said it. I have wondered if there be witches in the world—although I cannot believe they come among us now.

Hale. Then you do not believe——

Proctor. I have no knowledge of it; the Bible speaks of witches, and I will not deny them.

Hale. And you, woman?

Elizabeth. I—I cannot believe it.

Hale. [*Shocked.*] You cannot!

Proctor. Elizabeth, you bewilder him!

Elizabeth. [*To* HALE.] I cannot think the Devil may own a woman's soul, Mr. Hale, when she keeps an upright way, as I have. I am a good woman, I know it; and if you believe I may do only good work in the world, and yet be secretly bound to Satan, then I must tell you, sir, I do not believe it.

Hale. But, woman, you do believe there are witches in——

Elizabeth. If you think that I am one, then I say there are none.

Hale. You surely do not fly against the Gospel, the Gospel——

Proctor. She believe in the Gospel, every word!

Elizabeth. Question Abigail Williams about the Gospel, not myself!

[HALE *stares at her.*]

Proctor. She do not mean to doubt the Gospel, sir, you cannot think it. This be a Christian house, sir, a Christian house.

Hale. God keep you both; let the third child be quickly baptized, and go you without fail each Sunday in to Sabbath prayer; and keep a solemn, quiet way among you. I think——

[GILES COREY *appears in doorway.*]

Giles. John!

Proctor. Giles! What's the matter?

Giles. They take my wife.

[FRANCIS NURSE *enters.*]

Giles. And his Rebecca!

Proctor. [*To* FRANCIS.] Rebecca's in the jail!

Francis. Aye, Cheever come and take her in his wagon. We've only now come from the jail, and they'll not even let us in to see them.

Elizabeth. They've surely gone wild now, Mr. Hale!

Francis. [*Going to* HALE.] Reverend Hale! Can you not speak to the Deputy Governor? I'm sure he mistakes these people——

Hale. Pray calm yourself, Mr. Nurse.

Francis. My wife is the very brick and mortar of the church, Mr. Hale— [*Indicating* GILES.] —and Martha Corey, there cannot be a woman closer yet to God than Martha.

Hale. How is Rebecca charged, Mr. Nurse?

Francis. [*With a mocking, half-hearted laugh.*] For murder, she's charged! [*Mockingly quoting the warrant.*] "For the marvelous and supernatural murder of Goody Putnam's babies." What am I to do, Mr. Hale?

Hale. [*Turns from* FRANCIS, *deeply troubled, then.*] Believe me, Mr. Nurse, if Rebecca Nurse be tainted, then nothing's left to stop the whole green world from burning. Let you rest upon the justice of the court; the court will send her home, I know it.

Francis. You cannot mean she will be tried in court!

Hale. [*Pleading.*] Nurse, though our hearts break, we cannot flinch; these are new times, sir. There is a misty plot afoot so subtle we should be criminal to cling to old respects and ancient friendships. I have seen too many frightful proofs in court—the Devil is alive in Salem, and we dare not quail to follow wherever the accusing finger points!

Proctor. [*Angered.*] How may such a woman murder children?

Hale. [*In great pain.*] Man, remember, until an hour before the Devil fell, God thought him beautiful in Heaven.

Giles. I never said my wife were a witch, Mr. Hale; I only said she were reading books!

Hale. Mr. Corey, exactly what complaint were made on your wife?

Giles. That bloody mongrel Walcott charge her. Y'see, he buy a pig of my wife four or five year ago, and the pig died soon after. So he come dancin' in for his money back. So my Martha, she says to him, "Walcott, if you haven't the wit to feed a pig properly, you'll not live to own many," she says. Now he goes to court and claims that from that day to this he cannot keep a pig alive for more than four weeks because my Martha bewitch them with her books!

[*Enter* EZEKIEL CHEEVER. *A shocked silence.*]

Cheever. Good evening to you, Proctor.

Proctor. Why, Mr. Cheever. Good evening.

Cheever. Good evening, all. Good evening, Mr. Hale.

Proctor. I hope you come not on business of the court.

Cheever. I do, Proctor, aye. I am clerk of the court now, y'know.

[*Enter* MARSHAL HERRICK, *a man in his early thirties, who is somewhat shamefaced at the moment.*]

Giles. It's a pity, Ezekiel, an honest tailor that might have gone to Heaven must burn in Hell. You'll burn for this, do you know it?

Cheever. You know yourself I must do as I'm told. You surely know that, Giles. And I'd as lief you'd not be sending me to Hell. I like not the sound of it, I tell you; I like not the sound of it. [*He fears* PROCTOR, *but starts to reach inside his coat.*] Now believe me, Proctor, how heavy be the law, all its tonnage I do carry on my back tonight. [*He takes out a warrant.*] I have a warrant for your wife.

Proctor. [*To* HALE.] You said she were not charged!

Hale. I know nothin' of it. [*To* CHEEVER.] When were she charged?

Cheever. I am given sixteen warrant tonight, sir, and she is one.

Proctor. Who charged her?

Cheever. Why, Abigail Williams charge her.

Proctor. On what proof, what proof?

Cheever. [*Looking about the room.*] Mr. Proctor, I have little time. The court bid me search your house, but I like not to search a house. So will you hand me any poppets that your wife may keep here?

Proctor. Poppets?

Elizabeth. I never kept no poppets, not since I were a girl.

Cheever. [*Embarrassed, glancing toward the mantel where sits* MARY WARREN'S *poppet.*] I spy a poppet, Goody Proctor.

Elizabeth. Oh! [*Going for it.*] Why, this is Mary's.

Cheever. [*Shyly.*] Would you please to give it to me?

Elizabeth. [*Handing it to him, asks* HALE.] Has the court discovered a text in poppets now?

Cheever. [*Carefully holding the poppet.*] Do you keep any others in this house?

Proctor. No, nor this one either till tonight. What signifies a poppet?

Cheever. Why, a poppet— [*He gingerly turns the poppet over.*] a poppet may signify—— Now, woman, will you please to come with me?

Proctor. She will not! [*To* ELIZABETH.] Fetch Mary here.

Cheever. [*Ineptly reaching toward* ELIZABETH.] No, no, I am forbid to leave her from my sight.

Proctor. [*Pushing his arm away.*] You'll leave her out of sight and out of mind, Mister. Fetch Mary, Elizabeth.

[ELIZABETH *goes upstairs.*]

Hale. What signifies a poppet, Mr. Cheever?

Cheever. [*Turning the poppet over in his hands.*] Why, they say it may signify that she—— [*He has lifted the poppet's skirt, and his eyes widen in astonished fear.*] Why, this, this——

Proctor. [*Reaching for the poppet.*] What's there?

Cheever. Why— [*He draws out a long needle from the poppet.*] it is a needle! Herrick, Herrick, it is a needle!

[HERRICK *comes toward him.*]

Proctor. [*Angrily, bewildered.*] And what signifies a needle?

Cheever. [*His hands shaking.*] Why, this go hard with her, Proctor, this—I had my doubts, Proctor, I had my doubts, but here's calamity. [*To* HALE, *showing the needle.*] You see it, sir, it is a needle!

Hale. Why? What meanin' has it?

Cheever. [*Wide-eyed, trembling.*] The girl, the Williams girl, Abigail Williams, sir. She sat to dinner in Reverend Parris's house tonight, and without word nor warnin' she falls to the floor. Like a struck beast, he says, and screamed a scream that a bull would weep to hear. And he goes to save her, and, stuck two inches in the flesh of her belly, he draw a needle out. And demandin' of her how she come to be so stabbed, she [*To* PROCTOR *now.*] testify it were your wife's familiar spirit pushed it in.

Proctor. Why, she done it herself! [*To* HALE.] I hope you're not takin' this for proof, Mister!

[HALE, *struck by the proof, is silent.*]

Cheever. 'Tis hard proof! [*To* HALE.] I find here a poppet Goody Proctor keeps. I have found it, sir. And in the belly of the poppet a needle's stuck. I tell you true, Proctor, I never warranted to see such proof of Hell, and I bid you obstruct me not, for I——

[*Enter* ELIZABETH *with* MARY WARREN. PROCTOR, *seeing* MARY WARREN, *draws her by the arm to* HALE.]

Proctor. Here now! Mary, how did this poppet come into my house?

Mary Warren. [*Frightened for herself, her voice very small.*] What poppet's that, sir?

Proctor. [*Impatiently, pointing at the doll in* CHEEVER's *hand.*] This poppet, this poppet.

Mary Warren. [*Evasively, looking at it.*] Why, I—I think it is mine.

Proctor. It is your poppet, is it not?

Mary Warren. [*Not understanding the direction of this.*] It—is, sir.

Proctor. And how did it come into this house?

Mary Warren. [*Glancing about at the avid faces.*] Why—I made it in the court, sir, and—give it to Goody Proctor tonight.

Proctor. [*To* HALE.] Now, sir—do you have it?

Hale. Mary Warren, a needle have been found inside this poppet.

Mary Warren. [*Bewildered.*] Why, I mean no harm by it, sir.

Proctor. [*Quickly.*] You stuck that needle in yourself?

Mary Warren. I—I believe I did, sir, I——

Proctor. [*To* HALE.] What say you now?

Hale. [*Watching* MARY WARREN *closely.*]

Child, you are certain this be your natural memory? May it be, perhaps, that someone conjures you even now to say this?

Mary Warren. Conjures me? Why, no, sir, I am entirely myself, I think. Let you ask Susanna Walcott—she saw me sewin' it in court. *Or better still:* Ask Abby, Abby sat beside me when I made it.

Proctor. [*To* HALE, *of* CHEEVER.] Bid him begone. Your mind is surely settled now. Bid him out, Mr. Hale.

Elizabeth. What signifies a needle?

Hale. Mary—you charge a cold and cruel murder on Abigail.

Mary Warren. Murder! I charge no——

Hale. Abigail were stabbed tonight; a needle were found stuck into her belly——

Elizabeth. And she charges me?

Hale. Aye.

Elizabeth. [*Her breath knocked out.*] Why—! The girl is murder! She must be ripped out of the world!

Cheever. [*Pointing at* ELIZABETH.] You've heard that, sir! Ripped out of the world! Herrick, you heard it!

Proctor. [*Suddenly snatching the warrant out of* CHEEVER's *hands.*] Out with you.

Cheever. Proctor, you dare not touch the warrant.

Proctor. [*Ripping the warrant.*] Out with you!

Cheever. You've ripped the Deputy Governor's warrant, man!

Proctor. Damn the Deputy Governor! Out of my house!

Hale. Now, Proctor, Proctor!

Proctor. Get y'gone with them! You are a broken minister.

Hale. Proctor, if she is innocent, the court——

Proctor. If *she* is innocent! Why do you never wonder if Parris be innocent, or Abigail? Is the accuser always holy now? Were they born this morning as clean as God's fingers? I'll tell you what's walking Salem—vengeance is walking Salem. We are what we always were in Salem, but now the little crazy children are jangling the keys of the kingdom, and common vengeance writes the law! This warrant's vengeance! I'll not give my wife to vengeance!

Elizabeth. I'll go, John——

Proctor. You will not go!

Herrick. I have nine men outside. You cannot keep her. The law binds me, John, I cannot budge.

Proctor. [*To* HALE, *ready to break him.*] Will you see her taken?

Hale. Proctor, the court is just——

Proctor. Pontius Pilate! God will not let you wash your hands of this!

Elizabeth. John—I think I must go with them. [*He cannot bear to look at her.*] Mary, there is bread enough for the morning; you will bake, in the afternoon. Help Mr. Proctor as you were his daughter—you owe me that, and much more. [*She is fighting her weeping. To* PROCTOR.] When the children wake, speak nothing of witchcraft—it will frighten them.

[*She cannot go on.*]

Proctor. I will bring you home. I will bring you soon.

Elizabeth. Oh, John, bring me soon!

Proctor. I will fall like an ocean on that court! Fear nothing, Elizabeth.

Elizabeth. [*With great fear.*] I will fear nothing. [*She looks about the room, as though to fix it in her mind.*] Tell the children I have gone to visit someone sick.

[*She walks out the door,* HERRICK *and* CHEEVER *behind her. For a moment,* PROCTOR *watches from the doorway. The clank of chain is heard.*]

Proctor. Herrick! Herrick, don't chain her! [*He rushes out the door. From outside.*] Damn you, man, you will not chain her! Off with them! I'll not have it! I will not have her chained!

[*There are other men's voices against his.* HALE, *in a fever of guilt and uncertainty, turns from the door to avoid the sight;* MARY WARREN *bursts into tears and sits weeping.* GILES COREY *calls to* HALE.]

Giles. And yet silent, minister? It is fraud, you know it is fraud! What keeps you, man?

[PROCTOR *is half braced, half pushed into the room by two deputies and* HERRICK.]

Proctor. I'll pay you, Herrick, I will surely pay you!

Herrick. [*Panting.*] In God's name, John, I cannot help myself. I must chain them all. Now let you keep inside this house till I am gone!

[*He goes out with his deputies.*]

[PROCTOR *stands there, gulping air. Horses and a wagon creaking are heard.*]

Hale. [*In great uncertainty.*] Mr. Proctor——

Proctor. Out of my sight!

Hale. Charity, Proctor, charity. What I have heard in her favor, I will not fear to testify in court. God help me, I cannot judge her guilty or innocent—I know not. Only this consider: the world goes mad, and it profit nothing you should lay the cause to the vengeance of a little girl.

Proctor. You are a coward! Though you be ordained in God's own tears, you are a coward now!

Hale. Proctor, I cannot think God be provoked so grandly by such a petty cause. The jails are packed—our greatest judges sit in Salem now—and hangin's promised. Man, we must look to cause proportionate. Were there murder done, perhaps, and never brought to light? Abomination? Some secret blasphemy that stinks to Heaven? Think on cause, man, and let you help me to discover it. For there's your way, believe it, there is your only way, when such confusion strikes upon the world. [*He goes to* GILES *and* FRANCIS.] Let you counsel among yourselves; think on your village and what may have drawn from heaven such thundering wrath upon you all. I shall pray God open up our eyes. [HALE *goes out.*]

Francis. [*Struck by* HALE'S *mood.*] I never heard no murder done in Salem.

Proctor. [*He has been reached by* HALE'S *words.*] Leave me, Francis, leave me.

Giles. [*Shaken.*] John—tell me, are we lost?

Proctor. Go home now, Giles. We'll speak on it tomorrow.

Giles. Let you think on it. We'll come early, eh?

Proctor. Aye. Go now, Giles.

Giles. Good night, then.

[GILES COREY *goes out.*]

Mary Warren. [*After a moment, in a fearful squeak of a voice.*] Mr. Proctor, very likely they'll let her come home once they're given proper evidence.

Proctor. You're coming to the court with me, Mary. You will tell it in the court.

Mary Warren. I cannot charge murder on Abigail.

Proctor. [*Moving menacingly toward her.*] You will tell the court how that poppet come here and who stuck the needle in.

Mary Warren. She'll kill me for sayin' that! [PROCTOR *continues toward her.*] Abby'll charge lechery on you, Mr. Proctor!

Proctor. [*Halting.*] She's told you!

Mary Warren. I have known it, sir. She'll ruin you with it, I know she will.

Proctor. [*Hesitating, and with deep hatred of himself.*] Good. Then her saintliness is done with. [MARY *backs from him.*] We will slide together into our pit; you will tell the court what you know.

Mary Warren. [*In terror.*] I cannot, they'll turn on me——

[PROCTOR *strides and catches her, and she is repeating, "I cannot, I cannot!"*]

Proctor. My wife will never die for me! I will bring your guts into your mouth but that goodness will not die for me!

Mary Warren. [*Struggling to escape him.*] I cannot do it, I cannot!

Proctor. [*Grasping her by the throat as though he would strangle her.*] Make your peace with it! Now Hell and Heaven grapple on our backs, and all our old pretense is ripped away—make your peace! [*He throws her to the floor, where she sobs, "I cannot, I cannot . . ." And now, half to himself, staring, and turning to the open door.*] Peace. It is a providence, and no great change; we are only what we always were, but naked now. [*He walks as though toward a great horror, facing the open sky.*] Aye, naked! And the wind, God's icy wind, will blow!

[*And she is over and over again sobbing, "I cannot, I cannot, I cannot," as* THE CURTAIN FALLS]

ACT THREE

The vestry room of the Salem meeting house, now serving as the anteroom of the General Court.

As the curtain rises, the room is empty, but for sunlight pouring through two high windows in the back wall. The room is solemn, even forbidding. Heavy beams jut out, boards of random widths make up the walls. At the right are two doors leading into the meeting house proper, where the court is being held. At the left another door leads outside.

There is a plain bench at the left, and another at the right. In the center a rather long meeting table, with stools and a considerable armchair snugged up to it.

[*Through the partitioning wall at the right we hear a prosecutor's voice,* JUDGE HATHORNE'S, *asking a question; then a woman's voice,* MARTHA COREY'S, *replying.*]

Hathorne's Voice. Now, Martha Corey, there is abundant evidence in our hands to show that you have given yourself to the reading of fortunes. Do you deny it?

Martha Corey's Voice. I am innocent to a witch. I know not what a witch is.

Hathorne's Voice. How do you know, then, that you are not a witch?

Martha Corey's Voice. If I were, I would know it.

Hathorne's Voice. Why do you hurt these children?

Martha Corey's Voice. I do not hurt them. I scorn it!

Giles' Voice. [*Roaring.*] I have evidence for the court!

[*Voices of townspeople rise in excitement.*]

Danforth's Voice. You will keep your seat!

Giles' Voice. Thomas Putnam is reaching out for land!

Danforth's Voice. Remove that man, Marshal!

Giles' Voice. You're hearing lies, lies!

[*A roaring goes up from the people.*]

Hathorne's Voice. Arrest him, excellency!

Giles' Voice. I have evidence. Why will you not hear my evidence?

[*The door opens and* GILES *is half carried into the vestry room by* HERRICK.]

Giles. Hands off, damn you, let me go!

Herrick. Giles, Giles!

Giles. Out of my way, Herrick! I bring evidence——

Herrick. You cannot go in there, Giles; it's a court!

[*Enter* HALE *from the court, followed by* FRANCIS NURSE.]

Hale. Pray be calm a moment.

Giles. You, Mr. Hale, go in there and demand I speak.

Hale. A moment, sir, a moment.

Giles. They'll be hangin' my wife!

[JUDGE HATHORNE *enters. He is in his sixties, a bitter, remorseless Salem judge.*]

Hathorne. How do you dare come roarin' into this court! Are you gone daft, Corey?

Giles. You're not a Boston judge yet, Hathorne. You'll not call me daft!

[*Enter* DEPUTY GOVERNOR DANFORTH *and, behind him,* EZEKIEL CHEEVER *and* PARRIS. *On his appearance, silence falls.* DANFORTH *is a grave man in his sixties, of some humor and sophistication that does not, however, interfere with an exact loyalty to his position and his cause. He comes down to* GILES, *who awaits his wrath.*]

Danforth. [*Looking directly at* GILES.] Who is this man?

Parris. Giles Corey, sir, and a more contentious——

Giles. [*To* PARRIS.] I am asked the question, and I am old enough to answer it! [*To* DANFORTH, *who impresses him and to whom he smiles through his strain.*] My name is Corey, sir, Giles Corey. I have six hundred acres, and timber in addition. It is my wife you be condemning now.

[*He indicates the courtroom.*]

Danforth. And how do you imagine to help her cause with such contemptuous riot? Now be gone. Your old age alone keeps you out of jail for this.

Giles. [*Beginning to plead.*] They be tellin' lies about my wife, sir, I——

Danforth. Do you take it upon yourself to determine what this court shall believe and what it shall set aside?

Giles. Your Excellency, we mean no disrespect for——

Danforth. Disrespect indeed! It is disruption, Mister. This is the highest court of the supreme government of this province; do you know it?

Giles. [*Beginning to weep.*] Your Excellency, I only said she were readin' books, sir, and they come and take her out of my house for——

Danforth. [*Mystified.*] Books! What books?

Giles. [*Through helpless sobs.*] It is my third wife, sir; I never had no wife that be so taken with books, and I thought to find the cause of it, d'y'see, but it were no witch I blamed her for. [*He is openly weeping.*] I have broke charity with the woman, I have broke charity with her.

[*He covers his face, ashamed.* DANFORTH *is respectfully silent.*]

Hale. Excellency, he claims hard evidence for His wife's defense. I think that in all justice you must——

Danforth. Then let him submit his evidence in proper affidavit. You are certainly aware of our procedure here, Mr. Hale. [*To* HERRICK.] Clear this room.

Herrick. Come now, Giles.

[*He gently pushes* COREY *out.*]

Francis. We are desperate, sir; we come here three days now and cannot be heard.

Danforth. Who is this man?

Francis. Francis Nurse, Your Excellency.

Hale. His wife's Rebecca that were condemned this morning.

Danforth. Indeed! I am amazed to find you in such uproar. I have only good report of your character, Mr. Nurse.

Hathorne. I think they must both be arrested in contempt, sir.

Danforth. [*To* FRANCIS.] Let you write your plea, and in due time I will——

Francis. Excellency, we have proof for your eyes; God forbid you shut them to it. The girls, sir, the girls are frauds.

Danforth. What's that?

Francis. We have proof of it, sir. They are all deceiving you.

[DANFORTH *is shocked, but studying* FRANCIS.]

Hathorne. This is contempt, sir, contempt!

Danforth. Peace, Judge Hathorne. Do you know who I am, Mr. Nurse?

Francis. I surely do, sir, and I think you must be a wise judge to be what you are.

Danforth. And do you know that near to four hundred are in the jails from Marblehead to Lynn, and upon my signature?

Francis. I——

Danforth. And seventy-two condemned to hang by that signature?

Francis. Excellency, I never thought to say it to such a weighty judge, but you are deceived.

[*Enter* GILES COREY *from the left. All turn to see as he beckons in* MARY WARREN *with* PROCTOR. MARY *is keeping her eyes to the ground;* PROCTOR *has her elbow as though she were near collapse.*]

Parris. [*On seeing her, in shock.*] Mary Warren! [*He goes directly to bend close to her face.*] What are you about here?

Proctor. [*Pressing* PARRIS *away from her with a gentle but firm motion of protectiveness.*] She would speak with the Deputy Governor.

Danforth. [*Shocked by this, turns to* HERRICK.] Did you not tell me Mary Warren were sick in bed?

Herrick. She were, Your Honor. When I go to fetch her to the court last week, she said she were sick.

Giles. She has been strivin' with her soul all week, Your Honor; she comes now to tell the truth of this to you.

Danforth. Who is this?

Proctor. John Proctor, sir. Elizabeth Proctor is my wife.

Parris. Beware this man, Your Excellency, this man is mischief.

Hale. [*Excitedly.*] I think you must hear the girl, sir, she——

Danforth. [*Who has become very interested in* MARY WARREN *and only raises a hand toward* HALE.] Peace. What would you tell us, Mary Warren?

[PROCTOR *looks at her, but she cannot speak.*]

Proctor. She never saw no spirits, sir.

Danworth. [*With great alarm and surprise, to* MARY.] Never saw no spirits!

Giles. [*Eagerly.*] Never.

Proctor. [*Reaching into his jacket.*] She has signed a deposition, sir——

Danforth. [*Instantly.*] No, no, I accept no depositions. [*He is rapidly calculating this; he turns from her to* PROCTOR.] Tell me, Mr. Proctor, have you given out this story in the village?

Proctor. We have not.

Parris. They've come to overthrow the court, sir! This man is——

Danforth. I pray you, Mr. Parris. Do you know, Mr. Proctor, that the entire contention of the state in these trials is that the voice of Heaven is speaking through the children?

Proctor. I know that, sir.

Danforth. [*Thinks, staring at* PROCTOR, *then turns to* MARY WARREN.] And you, Mary Warren, how came you to cry out people for sending their spirits against you?

Mary Warren. It were pretense, sir.

Danforth. I cannot hear you.

Proctor. It were pretense, she says.

Danforth. Ah? And the other girls? Susanna Walcott, and—the others? They are also pretending?

Mary Warren. Aye, sir.

Danforth. [*Wide-eyed.*] Indeed.
[*Pause. He is baffled by this. He turns to study* PROCTOR's *face.*]

Parris. [*In a sweat.*] Excellency, you surely cannot think to let so vile a lie be spread in open court!

Danforth. Indeed not, but it strike hard upon me that she will dare come here with such a tale. Now, Mr. Proctor, before I decide whether I shall hear you or not, it is my duty to tell you this. We burn a hot fire here; it melts down all concealment.

Proctor. I know that, sir.

Danforth. Let me continue. I understand well, a husband's tenderness may drive him to extravagance in defense of a wife. Are you certain in your conscience, Mister, that your evidence is the truth?

Proctor. It is. And you will surely know it.

Danforth. And you thought to declare this revelation in the open court before the public?

Proctor. I thought I would, aye—with your permission.

Danforth. [*His eyes narrowing.*] Now, sir, what is your purpose in so doing?

Proctor. Why, I—I would free my wife, sir.

Danforth. There lurks nowhere in your heart, nor hidden in your spirit, any desire to undermine this court?

Proctor. [*With the faintest faltering.*] Why, no, sir.

Cheever. [*Clears his throat, awakening.*] I—Your Excellency.

Danforth. Mr. Cheever.

Cheever. I think it be my duty, sir— [*Kindly, to* PROCTOR.] You'll not deny it, John. [*To* DANFORTH.] When we come to take his wife, he damned the court and ripped your warrant.

Parris. Now you have it!

Danforth. He did that, Mr. Hale?

Hale. [*Takes a breath.*] Aye, he did.

Proctor. It were a temper, sir. I knew not what I did.

Danforth. [*Studying him.*] Mr. Proctor.

Proctor. Aye, sir.

Danforth. [*Straight into his eyes.*] Have you ever seen the Devil?

Proctor. No, sir.

Danworth. You are in all respects a Gospel Christian?

Proctor. I am, sir.

Parris. Such a Christian that will not come to church but once in a month!

Danforth. [*Restrained—he is curious.*] Not come to church?

Proctor. I—I have no love for Mr. Parris. It is no secret. But God I surely love.

Cheever. He plow on Sunday, sir.

Danforth. Plow on Sunday!

Cheever. [*Apologetically.*] I think it be evidence, John. I am an official of the court, I cannot keep it.

Proctor. I—I have once or twice plowed on Sunday. I have three children, sir, and until last year my land give little.

Giles. You'll find other Christians that do plow on Sunday if the truth be known.

Hale. Your Honor, I cannot think you may judge the man on such evidence.

Danforth. I judge nothing. [*Pause. He keeps watching* PROCTOR, *who tries to meet his gaze.*] I tell you straight, Mister—I have seen marvels in this court. I have seen people choked before my eyes by spirits; I have seen them stuck by pins and slashed by daggers. I have until this moment not the slightest reason to suspect that the children may be deceiving me. Do you understand my meaning?

Proctor. Excellency, does it not strike upon you that so many of these women have lived so long with such upright reputation, and——

Parris. Do you read the Gospel, Mr. Proctor?

Proctor. I read the Gospel.

Parris. I think not, or you should surely know that Cain were an upright man, and yet he did kill Abel.

Proctor. Aye, God tells us that. [*To* DANFORTH.] But who tells us Rebecca Nurse murdered seven babies by sending out her spirit on them? It is the children only, and this one will swear she lied to you.

[DANFORTH *considers, then beckons* HATHORNE *to him.* HATHORNE *leans in, and he speaks in his ear.* HATHORNE *nods.*]

Hathorne. Aye, she's the one.

Danforth. Mr. Proctor, this morning, your wife send me a claim in which she states that she is pregnant now.

Proctor. My wife pregnant!

Danforth. There be no sign of it—we have examined her body.

Proctor. But if she say she is pregnant, then she must be! That woman will never lie, Mr. Danforth.

Danforth. She will not?

Proctor. Never, sir, never.

Danforth. We have thought it too convenient to be credited. However, if I should tell you now that I will let her be kept another month; and if she begin to show her natural signs, you shall have her living yet another year until she is delivered—what say you to that? [JOHN PROCTOR *is struck silent.*] Come now. You say your only purpose is to save your wife. Good, then, she is saved at least this year, and a year is long. What say you, sir? It is done now. [*In conflict,* PROCTOR *glances at* FRANCIS *and* GILES.] Will you drop this charge?

Proctor. I—I think I cannot.

Danforth. [*Now an almost imperceptible hardness in his voice.*] Then your purpose is somewhat larger.

Parris. He's come to overthrow this court, Your Honor!

Proctor. These are my friends. Their wives are also accused——

Danforth. [*With a sudden briskness of manner.*] I judge you not, sir. I am ready to hear your evidence.

Proctor. I come not to hurt the court; I only——

Danforth. [*Cutting him off.*] Marshal, go into the court and bid Judge Stoughton and Judge Sewall declare recess for one hour. And let them go to the tavern, if they will. All witnesses and prisoners are to be kept in the building.

Herrick. Aye, sir. [*Very deferentially.*] If I may say it, sir, I know this man all my life. It is a good man, sir.

Danforth. [*It is the reflection on himself he resents.*] I am sure of it, Marshal. [HERRICK *nods, then goes out.*] Now, what deposition do you have for us, Mr. Proctor? And I beg you be clear, open as the sky, and honest.

Proctor. [*As he takes out several papers.*] I am no lawyer, so I'll——

Danforth. The pure in heart need no lawyers. Proceed as you will.

Proctor. [*Handing* DANFORTH *a paper.*] Will you read this first, sir? It's a sort of testament. The people signing it declare their good opinion of Rebecca, and my wife, and Martha Corey.

[DANFORTH *looks down at the paper.*]

Parris. [*To enlist* DANFORTH'S *sarcasm.*] Their good opinion!

[*But* DANFORTH *goes on reading, and* PROCTOR *is heartened.*]

Proctor. These are all landholding farmers, members of the church. [*Delicately, trying to point out a paragraph.*] If you'll notice, sir—they've known the women many years and never saw no sign they had dealings with the Devil.

[PARRIS *nervously moves over and reads over* DANFORTH'S *shoulder.*]

Danforth. [*Glancing down a long list.*] How many names are here?

Francis. Ninety-one, Your Excellency.

Parris. [*Sweating.*] These people should be summoned. [DANFORTH *looks up at him questioningly.*] For questioning.

Francis. [*Trembling with anger.*] Mr. Danforth, I gave them all my word no harm would come to them for signing this.

Parris. This is a clear attack upon the court!

Hale. [*To* PARRIS, *trying to contain himself.*] Is every defense an attack upon the court? Can no one——?

Parris. All innocent and Christian people are happy for the courts in Salem! These people are gloomy for it. [*To* DANFORTH *directly.*] And I think you will want to know, from each and every one of them, what discontents them with you!

Hathorne. I think they ought to be examined, sir.

Danforth. It is not necessarily an attack, I think. Yet——

Francis. These are all covenanted Christians, sir.

Danforth. Then I am sure they may have nothing to fear. [*Hands* CHEEVER *the paper.*] Mr. Cheever, have warrants drawn for all of these—arrest for examination. [*To*

PROCTOR.] Now, Mister, what other information do you have for us? [FRANCIS *is still standing, horrified.*] You may sit, Mr. Nurse.

Francis. I have brought trouble on these people; I have——

Danforth. No, old man, you have not hurt these people if they are of good conscience. But you must understand, sir, that a person is either with this court or he must be counted against it; there be no road between. This is a sharp time, now, a precise time—we live no longer in the dusky afternoon when evil mixed itself with good and befuddled the world. Now, by God's grace, the shining sun is up, and them that fear not light will surely praise it. I hope you will be one of those. [MARY WARREN *suddenly sobs.*] She's not hearty, I see.

Proctor. No, she's not, sir. [*To* MARY, *bending to her, holding her hand, quietly.*] Now remember what the angel Raphael said to the boy Tobias. Remember it.

Mary Warren. [*Hardly audible.*] Aye.

Proctor. "Do that which is good, and no harm shall come to thee."

Mary Warren. Aye.

Danforth. Come, man, we wait you.

[MARSHAL HERRICK *returns, and takes his post at the door.*]

Giles. John, my deposition, give him mine. other paper.] This is Mr. Corey's deposition.

Proctor. Aye. [*He hands* DANFORTH an-

Danforth. Oh?

[*He looks down at it. Now* HATHORNE *comes behind him and reads with him.*]

Hathorne. [*Suspiciously.*] What lawyer drew this, Corey?

Giles. You know I never hired a lawyer in my life, Hathorne.

Danforth. [*Finishing the reading.*] It is very well phrased. My compliments. Mr. Parris, if Mr. Putnam is in the court, will you bring him in? [HATHORNE *takes the deposition, and walks to the window with it.* PARRIS *goes into the court.*] You have no legal training, Mr. Corey?

Giles. [*Very pleased.*] I have the best, sir—I am thirty-three time in court in my life. And always plaintiff, too.

Danforth. Oh, then you're much put-upon.

Giles. I am never put-upon; I know my rights, sir, and I will have them. You know, your father tried a case of mine—might be thirty-five year ago, I think.

Danforth. Indeed.

Giles. He never spoke to you of it?

Danforth. No, I cannot recall it.

Giles. That's strange, he give me nine pound damages. He were a fair judge, your father. Y'see, I had a white mare that time, and this fellow come to borrow the mare— [*Enter* PARRIS *with* THOMAS PUTNAM. *When he sees* PUTNAM, GILES' *ease goes; he is hard.*] Aye, there he is.

Danforth. Mr. Putnam, I have here an accusation by Mr. Corey against you. He states that you coldly prompted your daughter to cry witchery upon George Jacobs that is now in jail.

Putnam. It is a lie.

Danforth. [*Turning to* GILES.] Mr. Putnam states your charge is a lie. What say you to that?

Giles. [*Furious, his fists clenched.*] A fart on Thomas Putnam, that is what I say to that!

Danforth. What proof do you submit for your charge, sir?

Giles. My proof is there! [*Pointing to the paper.*] If Jacobs hangs for a witch he forfeit up his property—that's law! And there is none but Putnam with the coin to buy so great a piece. This man is killing his neighbors for their land!

Danforth. But proof, sir, proof.

Giles. [*Pointing at his deposition.*] The proof is there! I have it from an honest man who heard Putnam say it! The day his daughter cried out on Jacobs, he said she'd given him a fair gift of land.

Hathorne. And the name of this man?

Giles. [*Taken aback.*] What name?

Hathorne. The man that give you this information.

Giles. [*Hesitates, then.*] Why, I—I cannot give you his name.

Hathorne. And why not?

Giles. [*Hesitates, then bursts out.*] You know well why not! He'll lay in jail if I give his name!

Hathorne. This is contempt of the court, Mr. Danforth!

Danforth. [*To avoid that.*] You will surely tell us the name.

Giles. I will not give you no name. I mentioned my wife's name once and I'll burn in hell long enough for that. I stand mute.

Danforth. In that case, I have no choice but to arrest you for contempt of this court, do you know that?

Giles. This is a hearing; you cannot clap me for contempt of a hearing.

Danforth. Oh, it is a proper lawyer! Do you wish me to declare the court in full session here? Or will you give me good reply?

Giles. [*Faltering.*] I cannot give you no name, sir, I cannot.

Danforth. You are a foolish old man. Mr. Cheever, begin the record. The court is now in session. I ask you, Mr. Corey——

Proctor. [*Breaking in.*] Your Honor—he has the story in confidence, sir, and he——

Parris. The Devil lives on such confidences! [*To* DANFORTH.] Without confidences there could be no conspiracy, Your Honor!

Hathorne. I think it must be broken, sir.

Danforth. [*To* GILES.] Old man, if your informant tells the truth let him come here openly like a decent man. But if he hide in anonymity I must know why. Now sir, the government and central church demand of you the name of him who reported Mr. Thomas Putnam a common murderer.

Hale. Excellency——

Danforth. Mr. Hale.

Hale. We cannot blink it more. There is a prodigious fear of this court in the country——

Danforth. Then there is a prodigious guilt in the country. Are *you* afraid to be questioned here?

Hale. I may only fear the Lord, sir, but there is fear in the country nevertheless.

Danforth. [*Angered now.*] Reproach me not with the fear in the country; there is fear in the country because there is a moving plot to topple Christ in the country!

Hale. But it does not follow that everyone accused is part of it.

Danforth. No uncorrupted man may fear this court, Mr. Hale! None! [*To* GILES.] You are under arrest in contempt of this court. Now sit down and take counsel with yourself, or you will be set in the jail until you decide to answer all questions.

[GILES COREY *makes a rush for* PUTNAM. PROCTOR *lunges and holds him.*]

Proctor. No, Giles!

Giles. [*Over* PROCTOR'S *shoulder at* PUTNAM.] I'll cut your throat, Putnam, I'll kill you yet!

Proctor. [*Forcing him into a chair.*] Peace, Giles, peace. [*Releasing him.*] We'll prove ourselves. Now we will.

[*He starts to turn to* DANFORTH.]

Giles. Say nothin' more, John. [*Pointing at* DANFORTH.] He's only playin' you! He means to hang us all!

[MARY WARREN *bursts into sobs.*]

Danforth. This is a court of law, Mister. I'll have no effrontery here!

Proctor. Forgive him, sir, for his old age. Peace, Giles, we'll prove it all now. [*He lifts up* MARY'S *chin.*] You cannot weep, Mary. Remember the angel, what he say to the boy. Hold to it, now; there is your

rock. [MARY *quiets. He takes out a paper, and turns to* DANFORTH.] This is Mary Warren's deposition. I—I would ask you remember, sir, while you read it, that until two week ago she were no different than the other children are today. [*He is speaking reasonably, restraining all his fears, his anger, his anxiety.*] You saw her scream, she howled, she swore familiar spirits choked her; she even testified that Satan, in the form of women now in jail, tried to win her soul away, and then when she refused——

Danforth. We know all this.

Proctor. Aye, sir. She swears now that she never saw Satan; nor any spirit, vague or clear, that Satan may have sent to hurt her. And she declares her friends are lying now.

[PROCTOR *starts to hand* DANFORTH *the deposition, and* HALE *comes up to* DANFORTH *in a trembling state.*]

Hale. Excellency, a moment. I think this goes to the heart of the matter.

Danforth. [*With deep misgivings.*] It surely does.

Hale. I cannot say he is an honest man; I know him little. But in all justice, sir, a claim so weighty cannot be argued by a farmer. In God's name, sir, stop here; send him home and let him come again with a lawyer——

Danforth. [*Patiently.*] Now look you, Mr. Hale——

Hale. Excellency, I have signed seventy-two death warrants; I am a minister of the Lord, and I dare not take a life without there be a proof so immaculate no slightest qualm of conscience may doubt it.

Danforth. Mr. Hale, you surely do not doubt my justice.

Hale. I have this morning signed away the soul of Rebecca Nurse, Your Honor. I'll not conceal it, my hand shakes yet as with a wound! I pray you, sir, *this* argument let lawyers present to you.

Danforth. Mr. Hale, believe me; for a man of such terrible learning you are most bewildered—I hope you will forgive me. I have been thirty-two year at the bar, sir, and I should be confounded were I called upon to defend these people. Let you consider, now—— [*To* PROCTOR *and the others.*] And I bid you all do likewise. In an ordinary crime, how does one defend the accused? One calls up witnesses to prove his innocence. But witchcraft is *ipso facto*, on its face and by its nature, an invisible crime, is it not? Therefore, who may possibly be witness to it? The witch and the victim. None other. Now we cannot hope the witch will accuse herself; granted? Therefore, we must rely upon her victims—and they do testify, the children certainly do testify. As for the witches, none will deny that we are most eager for all their confessions. Therefore, what is left for a lawyer to bring out? I think I have made my point. Have I not?

Hale. But this child claims the girls are not truthful, and if they are not——

Danforth. That is precisely what I am about to consider, sir. What more may you ask of me? Unless you doubt my probity?

Hale. [*Defeated.*] I surely do not, sir. Let you consider it, then.

Danforth. And let you put your heart to rest. Her deposition, Mr. Proctor.

[PROCTOR *hands it to him.* HATHORNE *rises, goes beside* DANFORTH, *and starts reading.* PARRIS *comes to his other side.* DANFORTH *looks at* JOHN PROCTOR, *then proceeds to read.* HALE *gets up, finds position near the judge, reads too.* PROCTOR *glances at* GILES. FRANCIS *prays silently, hands pressed together.* CHEEVER *waits placidly, the sublime official, dutiful.* MARY WARREN *sobs once.* JOHN PROCTOR *touches her head reassuringly.* Presently DANFORTH *lifts his eyes, stands up, takes out a kerchief and blows his nose. The others stand aside as he moves in thought toward the window.*]

Parris. [*Hardly able to contain his anger and fear.*] I should like to question——

Danforth. [*His first real outburst, in which his contempt for* PARRIS *is clear.*] Mr. Parris, I bid you be silent! [*He stands in silence, looking out the window. Now, having established that he will set the gait.*] Mr. Cheever, will you go into the court and bring the children here? [CHEEVER *gets up and goes out upstage.* DANFORTH *now turns to* MARY.] Mary Warren, how came you to this turnabout? Has Mr. Proctor threatened you for this deposition?

Mary Warren. No, sir.

Danforth. Has he ever threatened you?

Mary Warren. [*Weaker.*] No, sir.

Danforth. [*Sensing a weakening.*] Has he threatened you?

Mary Warren. No, sir.

Danforth. Then you tell me that you sat in my court, callously lying, when you knew that people would hang by your evidence? [*She does not answer.*] Answer me!

Mary Warren. [*Almost inaudibly.*] I did, sir.

Danforth. How were you instructed in your life? Do you not know that God damns all liars? [*She cannot speak.*] Or is it now that you lie?

Mary Warren. No, sir—I am with God now.

Danforth. You are with God now.

Mary Warren. Aye, sir.

Danforth. [*Containing himself.*] I will tell you this—you are either lying now, or you were lying in the court, and in either case you have committed perjury and you will go to jail for it. You cannot lightly say you lied, Mary. Do you know that?

Mary Warren. I cannot lie no more. I am with God, I am with God.

[*But she breaks into sobs at the thought of it, and the right door opens, and enter* SUSANNA WALCOTT, MERCY LEWIS, BETTY PARRIS, *and finally* ABIGAIL. CHEEVER *comes to* DANFORTH.]

Cheever. Ruth Putnam's not in the court, sir, nor the other children.

Danforth. These will be sufficient. Sit you down, children. [*Silently they sit.*] Your friend, Mary Warren, has given us a deposition. In which she swears that she never saw familiar spirits, apparitions, nor any manifest of the Devil. She claims as well that none of you have seen these things either. [*Slight pause.*] Now, children, this is a court of law. The law, based upon the Bible, and the Bible, writ by Almighty God, forbid the practice of witchcraft, and describe death as the penalty thereof. But likewise, children, the law and Bible damn all bearers of false witness. [*Slight pause.*] Now then. It does not escape me that this deposition may be devised to blind us; it may well be that Mary Warren has been conquered by Satan, who sends her here to distract our sacred purpose. If so, her neck will break for it. But if she speak true, I bid you now drop your guile and confess your pretense, for a quick confession will go easier with you. [*Pause.*] Abigail Williams, rise. [ABIGAIL *slowly rises.*] Is there any truth in this?

Abigail. No, sir.

Danforth. [*Thinks, glances at* MARY, *then back to* ABIGAIL.] Children, a very augur bit will now be turned into your souls until your honesty is proved. Will either of you change your positions now, or do you force me to hard questioning?

Abigail. I have naught to change, sir. She lies.

Danforth. [*To* MARY.] You would still go on with this?

Mary Warren. [*Faintly.*] Aye, sir.

Danforth. [*Turning to* ABIGAIL.] A poppet were discovered in Mr. Proctor's house, stabbed by a needle. Mary Warren claims that you sat beside her in the court when she made it, and that you saw her make it and witnessed how she herself stuck her needle into it for safe-keeping. What say you to that?

Abigail. [*With a slight note of indignation.*] It is a lie, sir.

Danforth. [*After a slight pause.*] While you worked for Mr. Proctor, did you see poppets in that house?

Abigail. Goody Proctor always kept poppets.

Proctor. Your Honor, my wife never kept no poppets. Mary Warren confesses it was her poppet.

Cheever. Your Excellency.

Danforth. Mr. Cheever.

Cheever. When I spoke with Goody Proctor in that house, she said she never kept no poppets. But she said she did keep poppets when she were a girl.

Proctor. She has not been a girl these fifteen years, Your Honor.

Hathorne. But a poppet will keep fifteen years, will it not?

Proctor. It will keep if it is kept, but Mary Warren swears she never saw no poppets in my house, nor anyone else.

Parris. Why could there not have been poppets hid where no one ever saw them?

Proctor. [*Furious.*] There might also be a dragon with five legs in my house, but no one has ever seen it.

Parris. We are here, Your Honor, precisely to discover what no one has ever seen.

Proctor. Mr. Danforth, what profit this girl to turn herself about? What may Mary Warren gain but hard questioning and worse?

Danforth. You are charging Abigail Williams with a marvelous cool plot to murder, do you understand that?

Proctor. I do, sir. I believe she means to murder.

Danforth. [*Pointing at* ABIGAIL, *incredulously.*] This child would murder your wife?

Proctor. It is not a child. Now hear me, sir. In the sight of the congregation she were twice this year put out of this meetin' house for laughter during prayer.

Danforth. [*Shocked, turning to* ABIGAIL.] What's this? Laughter during——!

Parris. Excellency, she were under Tituba's power at that time, but she is solemn now.

Giles. Aye, now she is solemn and goes to hang people!

Danforth. Quiet, man.

Hathorne. Surely it have no bearing on the question, sir. He charges contemplation of murder.

Danforth. Aye. [*He studies* ABIGAIL *for a moment, then.*] Continue, Mr. Proctor.

Proctor. Mary. Now tell the Governor how you danced in the woods.

Parris. [*Instantly.*] Excellency, since I come to Salem this man is blackening my name. He——

Danforth. In a moment, sir. [*To* MARY WARREN, *sternly, and surprised.*] What is this dancing?

Mary Warren. I—— [*She glances at* ABIGAIL, *who is staring down at her remorselessly. Then, appealing to* PROCTOR.] Mr. Proctor——

Proctor. [*Taking it right up.*] Abigail leads the girls to the woods, Your Honor, and they have danced there naked——

Parris. Your Honor, this——

Proctor. [*At once.*] Mr. Parris discovered them himself in the dead of night! There's the "child" she is!

Danforth. [*It is growing into a nightmare, and he turns, astonished, to* PARRIS.] Mr. Parris——

Parris. I can only say, sir, that I never found any of them naked, and this man is——

Danforth. But you discovered them dancing in the woods? [*Eyes on* PARRIS, *he points at* ABIGAIL.] Abigail?

Hale. Excellency, when I first arrived from Beverly, Mr. Parris told me that.

Danforth. Do you deny it, Mr. Parris?

Parris. I do not, sir, but I never saw any of them naked.

Danforth. But she have *danced?*

Parris. [*Unwillingly.*] Aye, sir.

[DANFORTH, *as though with new eyes, looks at* ABIGAIL.]

Hathorne. Excellency, will you permit me? [*He points at* MARY WARREN.]

Danforth. [*With great worry.*] Pray, proceed.

Hathorne. You say you never saw no spirits, Mary, were never threatened or afflicted by any manifest of the Devil or the Devil's agents.

Mary Warren. [*Very faintly.*] No, sir.

Hathorne. [*With a gleam of victory.*] And yet, when people accused of witchery confronted you in court, you would faint, saying their spirits came out of their bodies and choked you——

Mary Warren. That were pretense, sir.

Danforth. I cannot hear you.

Mary Warren. Pretense, sir.

Parris. But you did turn cold, did you not? I myself picked you up many times, and your skin were icy. Mr. Danforth, you——

Danforth. I saw that many times.

Proctor. She only pretended to faint, Your Excellency. They're all marvelous pretenders.

Hathorne. Then can she pretend to faint now?

Proctor. Now?

Parris. Why not? Now there are no spirits attacking her, for none in this room is accused of witchcraft. So let her turn herself cold now, let her pretend she is attacked now, let her faint. [*He turns to* MARY WARREN.] Faint!

Mary Warren. Faint?

Parris. Aye, faint. Prove to us how you pretended in the court so many times.

Mary Warren. [*Looking to* PROCTOR.] I—cannot faint now, sir.

Proctor. [*Alarmed, quietly.*] Can you not pretend it?

Mary Warren. I—— [*She looks about as though searching for the passion to faint.*] I —have no *sense* of it now, I——

Danforth. Why? What is lacking now?

Mary Warren. I—cannot tell, sir, I——

Danforth. Might it be that here we have no afflicting spirit loose, but in the court there were some?

Mary Warren. I never saw no spirits.

Parris. Then see no spirits now, and prove to us that you can faint by your own will, as you claim.

Mary Warren. [*Stares, searching for the emotion of it, and then shakes her head.*] I—cannot do it.

Parris. Then you will confess, will you not? It were attacking spirits made you faint!

Mary Warren. No, sir, I——

Parris. Your Excellency, this is a trick to blind the court!

Mary Warren. It's not a trick. [*She stands.*] I—I used to faint because I—I thought I saw spirits.

Danforth. *Thought* you saw them!

Mary Warren. But I did not, Your Honor.

Hathorne. How could you think you saw them unless you saw them?

Mary Warren. I—I cannot tell how, but I did. I—I heard the other girls screaming, and you, Your Honor, you seemed to believe them, and I—— It were only sport in the beginning, sir, but then the whole world cried spirits, spirits, and I—I promise you, Mr. Danforth, I only thought I saw them but I did not. [DANFORTH *peers at her.*]

Parris. [*Smiling, but nervous because* DANFORTH *seems to be struck by* MARY WARREN's *story.*] Surely Your Excellency is not taken by this simple lie.

Danforth. [*Turning worriedly to* ABIGAIL.] Abigail. I bid you now search your heart and tell me this—and beware of it, child, to God every soul is precious and His vengeance is terrible on them that take life without cause. Is it possible, child, that the spirits you have seen are illusion only, some deception that may cross your mind when——

Abigail. Why, this—this—is a base question, sir.

Danforth. Child, I would have you consider it——

Abigail. I have been hurt, Mr. Danforth; I have seen my blood runnin' out! I have been near to murdered every day because I done my duty pointing out the Devil's people—and this is my reward? To be mistrusted, denied, questioned like a——

Danforth. [*Weakening.*] Child, I do not mistrust you——

Abigail. [*In an open threat.*] Let *you* beware, Mr. Danforth. Think you to be so mighty that the power of Hell may not turn *your* wits? Beware of it! There is——

[*Suddenly, from an accusatory attitude, her face turns, looking into the air above —it is truly frightened.*]

Danforth. [*Apprehensively.*] What is it, child?

Abigail. [*Looking about in the air, clasping her arms around her as though cold.*] I—I know not. A wind, a cold wind, has come. [*Her eyes fall on* MARY WARREN.]

Mary Warren. [*Terrified, pleading.*] Abby!

Mercy Lewis. [*Shivering.*] Your Honor, I freeze!

Proctor. They're pretending!

Hathorne. [*Touching* ABIGAIL's *hand.*] She is cold, Your Honor, touch her.

Mercy Lewis. [*Through chattering teeth.*] Mary, do you send this shadow on me?

Mary Warren. Lord, save me!

Susanna Walcott. I freeze, I freeze!

Abigail. [*Shivering visibly.*] It is a wind, a wind!

Mary Warren. Abby, don't do that!

Danforth. [*Himself engaged and entered by* ABIGAIL.] Mary Warren, do you witch her? I say to you, do you send your spirit out?

[*With a hysterical cry* MARY WARREN *starts to run.* PROCTOR *catches her.*]

Mary Warren. [*Almost collapsing.*] Let me go, Mr. Proctor, I cannot, I cannot——

Abigail. [*Crying to Heaven.*] Oh, Heavenly Father, take away this shadow!

[*Without warning or hesitation,* PROCTOR *leaps at* ABIGAIL *and, grabbing her by the hair, pulls her to her feet. She screams in pain.* DANFORTH, *astonished, cries,* "*What are you about?*" *and* HATHORNE *and* PARRIS *call,* "*Take your hands off her!*" *and out of it all comes* PROCTOR'S *roaring voice.*]

Proctor. How do you call Heaven! Whore! Whore!

[HERRICK *breaks* PROCTOR *from her.*]

Herrick. John!

Danforth. Man! Man, what do you——

Proctor. [*Breathless and in agony.*] It is a whore!

Danforth. [*Dumfounded.*] You charge——?

Abigail. Mr. Danforth, he is lying!

Proctor. Mark her! Now she'll suck a scream to stab me with, but——

Danforth. You will prove this! This will not pass!

Proctor. [*Trembling, his life collapsing about him.*] I have known her, sir. I have known her.

Danforth. You—you are a lecher?

Francis. [*Horrified.*] John, you cannot say such a——

Proctor. Oh, Francis, I wish you had some evil in you that you might know me! [*To* DANFORTH.] A man will not cast away his good name. You surely know that.

Danforth. [*Dumfounded.*] In—in what time? In what place?

Proctor. [*His voice about to break, and his shame great.*] In the proper place— where my beasts are bedded. On the last night of my joy, some eight months past. She used to serve me in my house, sir. [*He has to clamp his jaw to keep from weeping.*] A man may think God sleeps, but God sees everything, I know it now. I beg you, sir, I beg you—see her what she is. My wife, my dear good wife, took this girl soon after, sir, and put her out on the highroad. And being what she is, a lump of vanity, sir—— [*He is being overcome.*] Excellency, forgive me, forgive me. [*Angrily against himself, he turns away from the* GOVERNOR *for a moment. Then, as though to cry out is his only means of speech left.*] She thinks to dance with me on my wife's grave! And well she might, for I thought of her softly. God help me, I lusted, and there *is* a promise in such sweat. But it is a whore's vengeance, and you must see it; I set myself entirely in your hands. I know you must see it now.

Danforth. [*Blanched, in horror, turning to* ABIGAIL.] You deny every scrap and tittle of this?

Abigail. If I must answer that, I will leave and I will not come back again!

[DANFORTH *seems unsteady.*]

Proctor. I have made a bell of my honor! I have rung the doom of my good name— you will believe me, Mr. Danforth! My wife is innocent, except she knew a whore when she saw one!

Abigail. [*Stepping up to* DANFORTH.] What look do you give me? [DANFORTH *cannot speak.*] I'll not have such looks!

[*She turns and starts for the door.*]

Danforth. You will remain where you are! [HERRICK *steps into her path. She comes up short, fire in her eyes.*] Mr. Parris, go into the court and bring Goodwife Proctor out.

Parris. [*Objecting.*] Your Honor, this is all a——

Danforth. [*Sharply to* PARRIS.] Bring her out! And tell her not one word of what's been spoken here. And let you knock before you enter. [PARRIS *goes out.*] Now we shall touch the bottom of this swamp. [*To* PROCTOR.] Your wife, you say, is an honest woman.

Proctor. In her life, sir, she have never lied. There are them that cannot sing, and them that cannot weep—my wife cannot lie. I have paid much to learn it, sir.

Danforth. And when she put this girl out of your house, she put her out for a harlot?

Proctor. Aye, sir.

Danforth. And knew her for a harlot?

Proctor. Aye, sir, she knew her for a harlot.

Danforth. Good then. [*To* ABIGAIL.] And if she tell me, child, it were for harlotry, may God spread His mercy on you! [*There is a knock. He calls to the door.*] Hold! [*To* ABIGAIL.] Turn your back. Turn your back. [*To* PROCTOR.] Do likewise. [*Both turn their backs—* ABIGAIL *with indignant slowness.*] Now let neither of you turn to face Goody Proctor. No one in this room is to speak one word, or raise a gesture aye or nay. [*He turns toward the door, calls.*] Enter! [*The door opens.* ELIZABETH *enters with* PARRIS. PARRIS *leaves her. She stands alone, her eyes looking for* PROCTOR.] Mr. Cheever, report this testimony in all exactness. Are you ready?

Cheever. Ready, sir.

Danforth. Come here, woman. [ELIZABETH *comes to him, glancing at* PROCTOR'S *back.*] Look at me only, not at your husband. In my eyes only.

Elizabeth. [*Faintly.*] Good, sir.

Danforth. We are given to understand that at one time you dismissed your servant, Abigail Williams.

Elizabeth. That is true, sir.

Danforth. For what cause did you dismiss her? [*Slight pause. Then* ELIZABETH *tries to glance at* PROCTOR.] You will look in my eyes only and not at your husband. The answer is in your memory and you need no help to give it to me. Why did you dismiss Abigail Williams?

Elizabeth. [*Not knowing what to say, sensing a situation, wetting her lips to stall for time.*] She—dissatisfied me. [*Pause.*] And my husband.

Danforth. In what way dissatisfied you?

Elizabeth. She were——

[*She glances at* PROCTOR *for a cue.*]

Danforth. Woman, look at me! [ELIZABETH *does.*] Were she slovenly? Lazy? What disturbance did she cause?

Elizabeth. Your Honor, I—In that time I were sick. And I—— My husband is a good and righteous man. He is never drunk as some are, nor wastin' his time at the shovel-board, but always at his work. But in my sickness—you see, sir, I were a long time sick after my last baby, and I thought I saw my husband somewhat turning from me. And this girl—— [*She turns to* ABIGAIL.]

Danforth. Look at me.

Elizabeth. Aye, sir. Abigail Williams——

[*She breaks off.*]

Danforth. What of Abigail Williams?

Elizabeth. I came to think he fancied her. And so one night I lost my wits, I think, and put her out on the highroad.

Danforth. Your husband—did he indeed turn from you?

Elizabeth. [*In agony.*] My husband—is a goodly man, sir.

Danforth. Then he did not turn from you.

Elizabeth. [*Starting to glance at* PROCTOR.] He——

Danforth. [*Reaches out and holds her face, then.*] Look at me! To your own knowledge, has John Proctor ever committed the crime of lechery? [*In a crisis of indecision she cannot speak.*] Answer my question! Is your husband a lecher!

Elizabeth. [*Faintly.*] No, sir.

Danforth. Remove her, Marshal.

Proctor. Elizabeth, tell the truth!

Danforth. She has spoken. Remove her!

Proctor. [*Crying out.*] Elizabeth, I have confessed it!

Elizabeth. Oh, God!

[*The door closes behind her.*]

Proctor. She only thought to save my name!

Hale. Excellency, it is a natural lie to tell; I beg you, stop now before another is condemned! I may shut my conscience to it no more—private vengeance is working through this testimony! From the beginning this man has struck me true. By my oath to Heaven, I believe him now, and I pray you call back his wife before we——

Danforth. She spoke nothing of lechery, and this man has lied!

Hale. I believe him! [*Pointing at* ABIGAIL.] This girl has always struck me false! She has——

[ABIGAIL, *with a weird, wild, chilling cry, screams up to the ceiling.*]

Abigail. You will not! Begone! Begone, I say!

Danforth. What is it, child? [*But* ABIGAIL, *pointing with fear, is now raising up her frightened eyes, her awed face, toward the ceiling—the* GIRLS *are doing the same—and now* HATHORNE, HALE, PUTNAM, CHEEVER, HERRICK, *and* DANFORTH *do the same.*] What's there? [*He lowers his eyes from the ceiling, and now he is frightened; there is real tension in his voice.*] Child! [*She is transfixed—with all the* GIRLS, *she is whimpering open-mouthed, agape at the ceiling.*] Girls! Why do you——?

Mercy Lewis. [*Pointing.*] It's on the beam! Behind the rafter!

Danforth. [*Looking up.*] Where!

Abigail. Why——? [*She gulps.*] Why do you come, yellow bird?

Proctor. Where's a bird? I see no bird!

Abigail. [*To the ceiling.*] My face? My face?

Proctor. Mr. Hale——

Danforth. Be quiet!

Proctor. [*To* HALE.] Do you see a bird?

Danforth. Be quiet!!

Abigail. [*To the ceiling, in a genuine conversation with the "bird," as though trying to talk it out of attacking her.*] But God made my face; you cannot want to tear my face. Envy is a deadly sin, Mary.

Mary Warren. [*On her feet with a spring, and horrified, pleading.*] Abby!

Abigail. [*Unperturbed, continuing to the "bird."*] Oh, Mary, this is a black art to change your shape. No, I cannot, I cannot stop my mouth; it's God work I do.

Mary Warren. Abby, I'm *here!*

Proctor. [*Frantically.*] They're pretending, Mr. Danforth!

Abigail. [*Now she takes a backward step, as though in fear the bird will swoop down momentarily.*] Oh, please, Mary! Don't come down.

Susanna Walcott. Her claws, she's stretching her claws!

Proctor. Lies, lies.

Abigail. [*Backing further, eyes still fixed above.*] Mary, please don't hurt me!

Mary Warren. [*To* DANFORTH.] I'm not hurting her!

Danforth. [*To* MARY WARREN.] Why does she see this vision?

Mary Warren. She sees nothin'!

Abigail. [*Now staring full front as though hypnotized, and mimicking the exact tone of* MARY WARREN'S *cry.*] She sees nothin'!

Mary Warren. [*Pleading.*] Abby, you mustn't!

Abigail and All the Girls. [*All transfixed.*] Abby, you mustn't!

Mary Warren. [*To all the* GIRLS.] I'm here, I'm here!

Girls. I'm here, I'm here!

Danforth. [*Horrified.*] Mary Warren! Draw back your spirit out of them!

Mary Warren. Mr. Danforth!

Girls. [*Cutting her off.*] Mr. Danforth!

Danforth. Have you compacted with the Devil? Have you?

Mary Warren. Never, never!

Girls. Never, never!

Danforth. [*Growing hysterical.*] Why can they only repeat you?

Proctor. Give me a whip—I'll stop it!

Mary Warren. They're sporting. They—!

Girls. They're sporting!

Mary Warren. [*Turning on them all hysterically and stamping her feet.*] Abby, stop it!

Girls. [*Stamping their feet.*] Abby, stop it!

Mary Warren. Stop it!

Girls. Stop it!

Mary Warren. [*Screaming it out at the top of her lungs, and raising her fists.*] Stop it!!

Girls. [*Raising their fists.*] Stop it!!

[MARY WARREN, *utterly confounded, and becoming overwhelmed by* ABIGAIL'S—*and the* GIRLS'—*utter conviction, starts to whimper, hands half raised, powerless, and all the* GIRLS *begin whimpering exactly as she does.*]

Danforth. A little while ago you were afflicted. Now it seems you afflict others; where did you find this power?

Mary Warren. [*Staring at* ABIGAIL.] I—have no power.

Girls. I have no power.

Proctor. They're gulling you, Mister!

Danforth. Why did you turn about this past two weeks? You have seen the Devil, have you not?

Hale. [*Indicating* ABIGAIL *and the* GIRLS.] You cannot believe them!

Mary Warren. I——

Proctor. [*Sensing her weakening.*] Mary, God damns all liars!

Danforth. [*Pounding it into her.*] You have seen the Devil, you have made compact with Lucifer, have you not?

Proctor. God damns liars, Mary!

[MARY *utters something unintelligible, staring at* ABIGAIL, *who keeps watching the "bird" above.*]

Danforth. I cannot hear you. What do you say? [MARY *utters again unintelligibly.*] You will confess yourself or you will hang! [*He turns her roughly to face him.*] Do you know who I am? I say you will hang if you do not open with me!

Proctor. Mary, remember the angel Raphael—do that which is good and——

Abigail. [*Pointing upward.*] The wings! Her wings are spreading! Mary, please, don't, don't——!

Hale. I see nothing, Your Honor!

Danforth. Do you confess this power! [*He is an inch from her face.*] Speak!

Abigail. She's going to come down! She's walking the beam!

Danforth. Will you speak!

Mary Warren. [*Staring in horror.*] I cannot!

Girls. I cannot!

Parris. Cast the Devil out! Look him in the face! Trample him! We'll save you, Mary, only stand fast against him and——

Abigail. [*Looking up.*] Look out! She's coming down!

[*She and all the* GIRLS *run to one wall, shielding their eyes. And now, as though cornered, they let out a gigantic scream, and* MARY, *as though infected, opens her mouth and screams with them. Gradually* ABIGAIL *and the* GIRLS *leave off, until only* MARY *is left there, staring up at the "bird," screaming madly. All watch her, horrified by this evident fit.* PROCTOR *strides to her.*]

Proctor. Mary, tell the Governor what they——

[*He has hardly got a word out, when, seeing him coming for her, she rushes out of his reach, screaming in horror.*]

Mary Warren. Don't touch me—don't touch me!

[*At which the* GIRLS *halt at the door.*]

Proctor. [*Astonished.*] Mary!

Mary Warren. [*Pointing at* PROCTOR.] You're the Devil's man!

[*He is stopped in his tracks.*]

Parris. Praise God!

Girls. Praise God!

Proctor. [*Numbed.*] Mary, how——?

Mary Warren. I'll not hang with you! I love God, I love God.

Danforth. [*To* Mary.] He bid you do the Devil's work?

Mary Warren. [*Hysterically, indicating* Proctor.] He come at me by night and every day to sign, to sign, to——

Danforth. Sign what?

Parris. The Devil's book? He come with a book?

Mary Warren. [*Hysterically, pointing at* Proctor, *fearful of him.*] My name, he want my name. "I'll murder you," he says, "if my wife hangs! We must go and over-throw the court," he says!

[Danforth's *head jerks toward* Proctor, *shock and horror in his face.*]

Proctor. [*Turning, appealing to* Hale.] Mr. Hale!

Mary Warren. [*Her sobs beginning.*] He wake me every night, his eyes were like coals and his fingers claw my neck, and I sign, I sign . . .

Hale. Excellency, this child's gone wild!

Proctor. [*As* Danforth's *wide eyes pour on him.*] Mary, Mary!

Mary Warren. [*Screaming at him.*] No, I love God; I go your way no more. I love God, I bless God. [*Sobbing, she rushes to* Abigail.] Abby, Abby, I'll never hurt you more!

[*They all watch, as* Abigail, *out of her infinite charity, reaches out and draws the sobbing* Mary *to her, and then looks up to* Danforth.]

Danforth. [*To* Proctor.] What are you? [Proctor *is beyond speech in his anger.*] You are combined with anti-Christ, are you not? I have seen your power; you will not deny it! What say you, Mister?

Hale. Excellency——

Danforth. I will have nothing from you Mr. Hale! [*To* Proctor.] Will you confess yourself befouled with Hell, or do you keep that black allegiance yet? What say you?

Proctor. [*His mind wild, breathless.*] I say—I say—God is dead!

Parris. Hear it, hear it!

Proctor. [*Laughs insanely, then.*] A fire, a fire is burning! I hear the boot of Lucifer, I see his filthy face! And it is my face, and yours, Danforth! For them that quail to bring men out of ignorance, as I have quailed, and as you quail now when you know in all your black hearts that this be fraud—God damns our kind especially, and we will burn, we will burn together!

Danforth. Marshal! Take him and Corey with him to the jail!

Hale. [*Starting across to the door.*] I denounce these proceedings!

Proctor. You are pulling Heaven down and raising up a whore!

Hale. I denounce these proceedings, I quit this court!

[*He slams the door to the outside behind him.*]

Danforth. [*Calling to him in a fury.*] Mr. Hale! Mr. Hale!

THE CURTAIN FALLS

ACT FOUR

A cell in Salem jail, that fall.

    At the back is a high barred window; near it, a great heavy door. Along the walls are two benches.

    The place is in darkness but for the moonlight seeping through the bars. It appears empty. Presently footsteps are heard coming down a corridor beyond the wall, keys rattle, and the door swings open. Marshal Herrick *enters with a lantern.*

    [*He is nearly drunk, and heavy-footed. He goes to a bench and nudges a bundle of rags lying on it.*]

Herrick. Sarah, wake up! Sarah Good!

    [*He then crosses to the other bench.*]

Sarah Good. [*Rising in her rags.*] Oh, Majesty! Comin', comin'! Tituba, he's here, His Majesty's come!

Herrick. Go to the north cell; this place is wanted now.

    [*He hangs his lantern on the wall.* Tituba *sits up.*]

Tituba. That don't look to me like his Majesty; look to me like the marshal.

Herrick. [*Taking out a flask.*] Get along with you now, clear this place.

    [*He drinks, and* Sarah Good *comes and peers up into his face.*]

Sarah Good. Oh, is it you, Marshal? I thought sure you be the devil comin' for us. Could I have a sip of cider for me goin'-away?

Herrick. [*Handing her the flask.*] And where are you off to, Sarah?

Tituba. [*As* SARAH *drinks.*] We goin' to Barbados, soon the Devil gits here with the feathers and the wings.

Herrick. Oh? A happy voyage to you.

Sarah Good. A pair of bluebirds wingin' southerly, the two of us! Oh, it be a grand transformation, Marshal!

[*She raises the flask to drink again.*]

Herrick. [*Taking the flask from her lips.*] You'd best give me that or you'll never rise off the ground. Come along now.

Tituba. I'll speak to him for you, if you desires to come along, Marshal.

Herrick. I'd not refuse it, Tituba; it's the proper morning to fly into Hell.

Tituba. Oh, it be no Hell in Barbados. Devil, him be pleasureman in Barbados, him be singin' and dancin' in Barbados. It's you folks—you riles him up 'round here; it be too cold 'round here for that Old Boy. He freeze his soul in Massachusetts, but in Barbados he just as sweet and—— [*A bellowing cow is heard, and* TITUBA *leaps up and calls to the window.*] Aye, sir! That's him, Sarah!

Sarah Good. I'm here, Majesty!

[*They hurriedly pick up their rags as* HOPKINS, *a guard, enters.*]

Hopkins. The Deputy Governor's arrived.

Herrick. [*Grabbing* TITUBA.] Come along, come along.

Tituba. [*Resisting him.*] No, he comin' for me. I goin' home!

Herrick. [*Pulling her to the door.*] That's not Satan, just a poor old cow with a hatful of milk. Come along now, out with you!

Tituba. [*Calling to the window.*] Take me home, Devil! Take me home!

Sarah Good. [*Following the shouting* TIBUTA *out.*] Tell him I'm goin', Tituba! Now you tell him Sarah Good is goin' too!

[*In the corridor outside* TITUBA *calls on* —"*Take me home, Devil; Devil take me home!*" *and* HOPKINS' *voice orders her to move on.* HERRICK *returns and begins to push old rags and straw into a corner. Hearing footsteps, he turns, and enter* DANFORTH *and* JUDGE HATHORNE. *They are in greatcoats and wear hats against the bitter cold. They are followed in by* CHEEVER, *who carries a dispatch case and a flat wooden box containing his writing materials.*]

Herrick. Good morning, Excellency.

Danforth. Where is Mr. Parris?

Herrick. I'll fetch him.

[*He starts for the door.*]

Danforth. Marshal. [HERRICK *stops.*] When did Reverend Hale arrive?

Herrick. It were toward midnight, I think.

Danforth. [*Suspiciously.*] What is he about here?

Herrick. He goes among them that will hang, sir. And he prays with them. He sits with Goody Nurse now. And Mr. Parris with him.

Danforth. Indeed. That man have no authority to enter here, Marshal. Why have you let him in?

Herrick. Why, Mr. Parris command me, sir. I cannot deny him.

Danforth. Are you drunk, Marshal?

Herrick. No, sir; it is a bitter night, and I have no fire here.

Danforth. [*Containing his anger.*] Fetch Mr. Parris.

Herrick. Aye, sir.

Danforth. There is a prodigious stench in this place.

Herrick. I have only now cleared the people out for you.

Danforth. Beware hard drink, Marshal.

Herrick. Aye, sir.

[*He waits an instant for further orders. But* DANFORTH, *in dissatisfaction, turns his back on him, and* HERRICK *goes out. There is a pause.* DANFORTH *stands in thought.*]

Hathorne. Let you question Hale, Excellency; I should not be surprised he have been preaching in Andover lately.

Danforth. We'll come to that; speak nothing of Andover. Parris prays with him. That's strange.

[*He blows on his hands, moves toward the window, and looks out.*]

Hathorne. Excellency, I wonder if it be wise to let Mr. Parris so continuously with the prisoners. [DANFORTH *turns to him, interested.*] I think, sometimes, the man has a mad look these days.

Danforth. Mad?

Hathorne. I met him yesterday coming out of his house, and I bid him good morning—and he wept and went his way. I think it is not well the village sees him so unsteady.

Danforth. Perhaps he have some sorrow.

Cheever. [*Stamping his feet against the cold.*] I think it be the cows, sir.

Danforth. Cows?

Cheever. There be so many cows wanderin' the highroads, now their masters are in the jails, and much disagreement who they will belong to now. I know Mr. Parris be arguin' with farmers all yesterday—there is great contention, sir, about the cows. Contention make him weep, sir; it were always a man that weep for contention.

[*He turns, as do* HATHORNE *and* DAN-FORTH, *hearing someone coming up the corridor.* DANFORTH *raises his head as* PARRIS *enters. He is gaunt, frightened, and sweating in his greatcoat.*]

Parris. [*To* DANFORTH, *instantly.*] Oh, good morning, sir, thank you for coming, I beg your pardon wakin' you so early. Good morning, Judge Hathorne.

Danforth. Reverend Hale have no right to enter this——

Parris. Excellency, a moment.

[*He hurries back and shuts the door.*]

Hathorne. Do you leave him alone with the prisoners?

Danforth. What's his business here?

Parris. [*Prayerfully holding up his hands.*] Excellency, hear me. It is a providence. Reverend Hale has returned to bring Rebecca Nurse to God.

Danforth. [*Surprised.*] He bids her confess?

Parris. [*Sitting.*] Hear me. Rebecca have not given me a word this three month since she came. Now she sits with him, and her sister and Martha Corey and two or three others, and he pleads with them, confess their crimes and save their lives.

Danforth. Why—this is indeed a providence. And they soften, they soften?

Parris. Not yet, not yet. But I thought to summon you, sir, that we might think on whether it be not wise, to— [*He dares not say it.*] I had thought to put a question, sir, and I hope you will not——

Danforth. Mr. Parris, be plain, what troubles you?

Parris. There is news, sir, that the court—the court must reckon with. My niece, sir, my niece—I believe she has vanished.

Danforth. Vanished!

Parris. I had thought to advise you of it earlier in the week, but——

Danforth. Why? How long is she gone?

Parris. This be the third night. You see, sir, she told me she would stay a night with Mercy Lewis. And next day, when she does not return, I send to Mr. Lewis to inquire. Mercy told him she would sleep in *my* house for a night.

Danforth. They are both gone?!

Parris. [*In fear of him.*] They are, sir.

Danforth. [*Alarmed.*] I will send a party for them. Where may they be?

Parris. Excellency, I think they be aboard a ship. [DANFORTH *stands agape.*] My daughter tells me how she heard them speak-ing of ships last week, and tonight I discover my—my strongbox is broke into.

[*He presses his fingers against his eyes to keep back tears.*]

Hathorne. [*Astonished.*] She have robbed you?

Parris. Thirty-one pound is gone. I am penniless.

[*He covers his face and sobs.*]

Danforth. Mr. Parris, you are a brainless man!

[*He walks in thought, deeply worried.*]

Parris. Excellency, it profit nothing you should blame me. I cannot think they would run off except they fear to keep in Salem any more. [*He is pleading.*] Mark it, sir, Abigail had close knowledge of the town, and since the news of Andover has broken here——

Danforth. Andover is remedied. The court returns there on Friday, and will resume examinations.

Parris. I am sure of it, sir. But the rumor here speaks rebellion in Andover, and it——

Danforth. There is no rebellion in Andover!

Parris. I tell you what is said here, sir. Andover have thrown out the court, they say, and will have no part of witchcraft. There be a faction here, feeding on that news, and I tell you true, sir, I feel there will be riot here.

Hathorne. Riot! Why, at every execution I have seen naught but high satisfaction in the town.

Parris. Judge Hathorne—it were another sort that hanged till now. Rebecca Nurse is no Bridget that lived three year with Bishop before she married him. John Proctor is not Isaac Ward that drank his family to ruin. [*To* DANFORTH.] I would to God it were not so, Excellency, but these people have great weight yet in the town. Let Rebecca stand upon the gibbet and send up some righteous prayer, and I fear she'll wake a vengeance on you.

Hathorne. Excellency, she is condemned a witch. The court have——

Danforth. [*In deep concern, raising a hand to* HATHORNE.] Pray you. [*To* PARRIS.] How do you propose, then?

Parris. Excellency, I would postpone these hangin's for a time.

Danforth. There will be no postponement.

Parris. Now Mr. Hale's returned, there is hope, I think—for if he bring even one of these to God, that confession surely damns the others in the public eye, and none may doubt more that they are all linked to Hell. This way, unconfessed and claiming innocence, doubts are multiplied, many honest people will weep for them, and our good purpose is lost in their tears.

Danforth. [*After thinking a moment, then going to* CHEEVER.] Give me the list.

[CHEEVER *opens the dispatch case, searches.*]

Parris. It cannot be forgot, sir, that when I summoned the congregation for John Proctor's excommunication there were hardly thirty people come to hear it. That speak a discontent, I think, and——

Danforth. [*Studying the list.*] There will be no postponement.

Parris. Excellency——

Danforth. Now, sir—which of these in your opinion may be brought to God? I will strive with him till dawn.

[*He hands the list to* PARRIS, *who merely glances at it.*]

Parris. There is not sufficient time till dawn.

Danforth. I shall do my utmost. Which of them do you have hope for?

Parris. [*Not even glancing at the list now, and in a quavering voice, quietly.*] Excellency—a dagger——

[*He chokes up.*]

Danforth. What do you say?

Parris. Tonight, when I open my door to leave my house—a dagger clattered to the ground. [*Silence.* DANFORTH *absorbs this. Now* PARRIS *cries out.*] You cannot hang this sort. There is danger for me. I dare not step outside at night!

[REVEREND HALE *enters. They look at him for an instant in silence. He is steeped in sorrow, exhausted, and more direct than he ever was.*]

Danforth. Accept my congratulations, Reverend Hale; we are gladdened to see you returned to your good work.

Hale. [*Coming to* DANFORTH *now.*] You must pardon them. They will not budge.

[HERRICK *enters, waits.*]

Danforth. [*Conciliatory.*] You misunderstand, sir; I cannot pardon these when twelve are already hanged for the same crime. It is not just.

Parris. [*With failing heart.*] Rebecca will not confess?

Hale. The sun will rise in a few minutes. Excellency, I must have more time.

Danforth. Now hear me, and beguile yourselves no more. I will not receive a single plea for pardon or postponement. Them that will not confess will hang. Twelve are already executed; the names of these seven are given out, and the village expects to see them die this morning. Postponement now speaks a floundering on my part; re-prieve or pardon must cast doubt upon the guilt of them that died till now. While I speak God's law, I will not crack its voice with whimpering. If retaliation is your fear, know this—I should hang ten thousand that dared to rise against the law, and an ocean of salt tears could not melt the resolution of the statutes. Now draw yourselves up like men and help me, as you are bound by Heaven to do. Have you spoken with them all, Mr. Hale?

Hale. All but Proctor. He is in the dungeon.

Danforth. [*To* HERRICK.] What's Proctor's way now?

Herrick. He sits like some great bird; you'd not know he lived except he will take food from time to time.

Danforth. [*After thinking a moment.*] His wife—his wife must be well on with child now.

Herrick. She is, sir.

Danforth. What think you, Mr. Parris? You have closer knowledge of this man; might her presence soften him?

Parris. It is possible, sir. He have not laid eyes on her these three months. I should summon her.

Danforth. [*To* HERRICK.] Is he yet adamant? Has he struck at you again?

Herrick. He cannot, sir, he is chained to the wall now.

Danforth. [*After thinking on it.*] Fetch Goody Proctor to me. Then let you bring him up.

Herrick. Aye, sir.

[HERRICK *goes. There is silence.*]

Hale. Excellency, if you postpone a week and publish to the town that you are striving for their confessions, that speak mercy on your part, not faltering.

Danforth. Mr. Hale, as God have not empowered me like Joshua to stop this sun from rising, so I cannot withhold from them the perfection of their punishment.

Hale. [*Harder now.*] If you think God wills you to raise rebellion, Mr. Danforth, you are mistaken!

Danforth. [*Instantly.*] You have heard rebellion spoken in the town?

Hale. Excellency, there are orphans wandering from house to house; abandoned cattle bellow on the highroads, the stink of rotting crops hangs everywhere, and no man knows when the harlots' cry will end his life—and you wonder yet if rebellion's spoke? Better you should marvel how they do not burn your province!

Danforth. Mr. Hale, have you preached in Andover this month?

Hale. Thank God they have no need for me in Andover.

Danforth. You baffle me, sir. Why have you returned here?

Hale. Why, it is all simple. I come to do the Devil's work. I come to counsel Christians they should belie themselves. [*His sarcasm collapses.*] There is blood on my head! Can you not see the blood on my head!!

Parris. Hush!

[*For he has heard footsteps. They all face the door.* HERRICK *enters with* ELIZABETH. *Her wrists are linked by a heavy chain, which* HERRICK *now removes. Her clothes are dirty; her face is pale and gaunt.* HERRICK *goes out.*]

Danforth. [*Very politely.*] Goody Proctor. [*She is silent.*] I hope you are hearty?

Elizabeth. [*As a warning reminder.*] I am yet six month before my time.

Danforth. Pray be at your ease, we come not for your life. We— [*Uncertain how to plead, for he is not accustomed to it.*] Mr. Hale, will you speak with the woman?

Hale. Goody Proctor, your husband is marked to hang this morning. [*Pause*]

Elizabeth. [*Quietly.*] I have heard it.

Hale. You know, do you not, that I have no connection with the court? [*She seems to doubt it.*] I come of my own, Goody Proctor. I would save your husband's life, for if he is taken I count myself his murderer. Do you understand me?

Elizabeth. What do you want of me?

Hale. Goody Proctor, I have gone this three month like our Lord into the wilderness. I have sought a Christian way, for damnation's doubled on a minister who counsels men to lie.

Hathorne. It is no lie, you cannot speak of lies.

Hale. It is a lie! They are innocent!

Danforth. I'll hear no more of that!

Hale. [*Continuing to* ELIZABETH.] Let you not mistake your duty as I mistook my own. I came into this village like a bridegroom to his beloved, bearing gifts of high religion; the very crowns of holy law I brought, and what I touched with my bright confidence, it died; and where I turned the eye of my great faith, blood flowed up. Beware, Goody Proctor—cleave to no faith when faith brings blood. It is mistaken law that leads you to sacrifice. Life, woman, life is God's most precious gift; no principle, however glorious, may justify the taking of it. I beg you, woman, prevail upon your husband to confess. Let him give his lie. Quail not before God's judgment in this,

for it may well be God damns a liar less than he that throws his life away for pride. Will you plead with him? I cannot think he will listen to another.

Elizabeth. [*Quietly.*] I think that be the Devil's argument.

Hale. [*With a climactic desperation.*] Woman, before the laws of God we are as swine! We cannot read His will!

Elizabeth. I cannot dispute with you, sir; I lack learning for it.

Danforth. [*Going to her.*] Goody Proctor, you are not summoned here for disputation. Be there no wifely tenderness within you? He will die with the sunrise. Your husband. Do you understand it? [*She only looks at him.*] What say you? Will you contend with him? [*She is silent.*] Are you stone? I tell you true, woman, had I no other proof of your unnatural life, your dry eyes now would be sufficient evidence that you delivered up your soul to Hell! A very ape would weep at such calamity! Have the devil dried up any tear of pity in you? [*She is silent.*] Take her out. It profit nothing she should speak to him!

Elizabeth. [*Quietly.*] Let me speak with him, Excellency.

Parris. [*With hope.*] You'll strive with him? [*She hesitates.*]

Danforth. Will you plead for his confession or will you not?

Elizabeth. I promise nothing. Let me speak with him.

[*A sound—the sibilance of dragging feet on stone. They turn. A pause.* HERRICK *enters with* JOHN PROCTOR. *His wrists are chained. He is another man, bearded, filthy, his eyes misty as though webs had overgrown them. He halts inside the doorway, his eye caught by the sight of* ELIZABETH. *The emotion flowing between them prevents anyone from speaking for an instant. Now* HALE, *visibly affected, goes to* DANFORTH *and speaks quietly.*]

Hale. Pray, leave them, Excellency.

Danforth. [*Pressing* HALE *impatiently aside.*] Mr. Proctor, you have been notified, have you not? [PROCTOR *is silent, staring at* ELIZABETH.] I see light in the sky, Mister; let you counsel with your wife, and may God help you turn your back on Hell.

[PROCTOR *is silent, staring at* ELIZABETH.]

Hale. [*Quietly.*] Excellency, let——

[DANFORTH *brushes past* HALE *and walks out.* HALE *follows.* CHEEVER *stands and follows,* HATHORNE *behind.* HERRICK *goes.*]

Parris. [*From a safe distance, offers.*] If you desire a cup of cider, Mr. Proctor, I am sure I— [PROCTOR *turns an icy stare at him, and he breaks off.* PARRIS *raises his palms toward* PROCTOR.] God lead you now.
[PARRIS *goes out.*]
[*Alone.* PROCTOR *walks to her, halts. It is as though they stood in a spinning world. It is beyond sorrow, above it. He reaches out his hand as though toward an embodiment not quite real, and as he touches her, a strange soft sound, half laughter, half amazement, comes from his throat. He pats her hand. She covers his hand with hers. And then, weak, he sits. Then she sits, facing him.*]

Proctor. The child?

Elizabeth. It grows.

Proctor. There is no word of the boys?

Elizabeth. They're well. Rebecca's Samuel keeps them.

Proctor. You have not seen them?

Elizabeth. I have not.
[*She catches a weakening in herself and downs it.*]

Proctor. You are a—marvel, Elizabeth.

Elizabeth. You—have been tortured?

Proctor. Aye. [*Pause. She will not let herself be drowned in the sea that threatens her.*] They come for my life now.

Elizabeth. I know it. [*Pause.*]

Proctor. None—have yet confessed?

Elizabeth. There be many confessed.

Proctor. Who are they?

Elizabeth. There be a hundred or more, they say. Goody Ballard is one; Isaiah Goodkind is one. There be many.

Proctor. Rebecca?

Elizabeth. Not Rebecca. She is one foot in Heaven now; naught may hurt her more.

Proctor. And Giles?

Elizabeth. You have not heard of it?

Proctor. I hear nothin', where I am kept.

Elizabeth. Giles is dead.
[*He looks at her incredulously.*]

Proctor. When were he hanged?

Elizabeth. [*Quietly, factually.*] He were not hanged. He would not answer aye or nay to his indictment; for if he denied the charge they'd hang him surely, and auction out his property. So he stand mute, and died Christian under the law. And so his sons will have his farm. It is the law, for he could not be condemned a wizard without he answer the indictment, aye or nay.

Proctor. Then how does he die?

Elizabeth. [*Gently.*] They press him, John.

Proctor. Press?

Elizabeth. Great stones they lay upon his chest until he plead aye or nay. [*With a tender smile for the old man.*] They say he give them but two words. "More weight," he says. And died.

Proctor. [*Numbed—a thread to weave into his agony.*] "More weight."

Elizabeth. Aye. It were a fearsome man, Giles Corey. [*Pause.*]

Proctor. [*With great force of will, but not quite looking at her.*] I have been thinking I would confess to them, Elizabeth. [*She shows nothing.*] What say you? If I give them that?

Elizabeth. I cannot judge you, John.
[*Pause.*]

Proctor. [*Simply—a pure question.*] What would you have me do?

Elizabeth. As you will, I would have it. [*Slight pause.*] I want you living, John. That's sure.

Proctor. [*Pauses, then with a flailing of hope.*] Giles' wife? Have she confessed?

Elizabeth. She will not. [*Pause.*]

Proctor. It is a pretense, Elizabeth.

Elizabeth. What is?

Proctor. I cannot mount the gibbet like a saint. It is a fraud. I am not that man. [*She is silent.*] My honesty is broke, Elizabeth; I am no good man. Nothing's spoiled by giving them this lie that were not rotten long before.

Elizabeth. And yet you've not confessed till now. That speak goodness in you.

Proctor. Spite only keeps me silent. It is hard to give a lie to dogs. [*Pause, for the first time he turns directly to her.*] I would have your forgiveness, Elizabeth.

Elizabeth. It is not for me to give, John, I am——

Proctor. I'd have you see some honesty in it. Let them that never lied die now to keep their souls. It is pretense for me, a vanity that will not blind God nor keep my children out of the wind. [*Pause.*] What say you?

Elizabeth. [*Upon a heaving sob that always threatens.*] John, it come to naught that I should forgive you, if you'll not forgive yourself. [*Now he turns away a little, in great agony.*] It is not my soul, John, it is yours. [*He stands, as though in physical pain, slowly rising to his feet with a great immortal longing to find his answer. It is difficult to say, and she is on the verge of tears.*] Only be sure of this, for I know it now: Whatever you will do, it is a good man does it. [*He turns his doubting, searching gaze upon her.*] I have read my heart this three month, John. [*Pause.*] I have sins of my own to count. It needs a cold wife to prompt lechery.

Proctor. [*In great pain.*] Enough, enough——

Elizabeth. [*Now pouring out her heart.*] Better you should know me!

Proctor. I will not hear it! I know you!

Elizabeth. You take my sins upon you, John——

Proctor. [*In agony.*] No, I take my own, my own!

Elizabeth. John, I counted myself so plain, so poorly made, no honest love could come to me! Suspicion kissed you when I did; I never knew how I should say my love. It were a cold house I kept!

[*In fright, she swerves, as* HATHORNE *enters.*]

Hathorne. What say you, Proctor? The sun is soon up.

[PROCTOR, *his chest heaving, stares, turns to* ELIZABETH. *She comes to him as though to plead, her voice quaking.*]

Elizabeth. Do what you will. But let none be your judge. There be no higher judge under Heaven than Proctor is! Forgive me, forgive me, John—I never knew such goodness in the world!

[*She covers her face, weeping.*]

[PROCTOR *turns from her to* HATHORNE; *he is off the earth, his voice hollow.*]

Proctor. I want my life.

Hathorne. [*Electrified, surprised.*] You'll confess yourself?

Proctor. I will have my life.

Hathorne. [*With a mystical tone.*] God be praised! It is a providence! [*He rushes out the door, and his voice is heard calling down the corridor.*] He will confess! Proctor will confess!

Proctor. [*With a cry, as he strides to the door.*] Why do you cry it? [*In great pain he turns back to her.*] It is evil, is it not? It is evil.

Elizabeth. [*In terror, weeping.*] I cannot judge you, John, I cannot!

Proctor. Then who will judge me? [*Suddenly clasping his hands.*] God in Heaven, what is John Proctor, what is John Proctor? [*He moves as an animal, and a fury is riding in him, a tantalized search.*] I think it is honest, I think so; I am no saint. [*As though she had denied this he calls angrily at her.*] Let Rebecca go like a saint; for me it is fraud!

[*Voices are heard in the hall, speaking together in suppressed excitement.*]

Elizabeth. I am not your judge, I cannot be. [*As though giving him release.*] Do as you will, do as you will!

Proctor. Would you give them such a lie? Say it. Would you ever give them this?

[*She cannot answer.*] You would not; if tongs of fire were singeing you you would not! It is evil. Good, then—it is evil, and I do it!

[HATHORNE *enters with* DANFORTH, *and, with them,* CHEEVER, PARRIS, *and* HALE. *It is a businesslike, rapid entrance, as though the ice had been broken.*]

Danforth. [*With great relief and gratitude.*] Praise to God, man, praise to God; you shall be blessed in Heaven for this. [CHEEVER *has hurried to the bench with pen, ink, and paper.* PROCTOR *watches him.*] Now then, let us have it. Are you ready, Mr. Cheever?

Proctor. [*With a cold, cold horror at their efficiency.*] Why must it be written?

Danforth. Why, for the good instruction of the village, Mister; this we shall post upon the church door! [*To* PARRIS, *urgently.*] Where is the marshal?

Parris. [*Runs to the door and calls down the corridor.*] Marshal! Hurry!

Danforth. Now, then, Mister, will you speak slowly, and directly to the point, for Mr. Cheever's sake. [*He is on record now, and is really dictating to* CHEEVER, *who writes.*] Mr. Proctor, have you seen the Devil in your life? [PROCTOR'S *jaws lock.*] Come man, there is light in the sky; the town waits at the scaffold; I would give out this news. Did you see the Devil?

Proctor. I did.

Parris. Praise God!

Danforth. And when he come to you, what were his demand? [PROCTOR *is silent.* DANFORTH *helps.*] Did he bid you to do his work upon the earth?

Proctor. He did.

Danforth. And you bound yourself to his service? [DANFORTH *turns, as* REBECCA NURSE *enters, with* HERRICK *helping to support her. She is barely able to walk.*] Come in, come in, woman!

Rebecca. [*Brightening as she sees* PROCTOR.] Ah, John! You are well, then, eh?

[PROCTOR *turns his face to the wall.*]

Danforth. Courage, man, courage—let her witness your good example that she may come to God herself. Now hear it, Goody Nurse! Say on, Mr. Proctor. Did you bind yourself to the Devil's service?

Rebecca. [*Astonished.*] Why, John!

Proctor. [*Through his teeth, his face turned from* REBECCA.] I did.

Danforth. Now, woman, you surely see it profit nothin' to keep this conspiracy any further. Will you confess yourself with him?

Rebecca. Oh, John—God send his mercy on you!

Danforth. I say, will you confess yourself, Goody Nurse?

Rebecca. Why, it is a lie, it is a lie; how may I damn myself? I cannot, I cannot.

Danforth. Mr. Proctor. When the Devil came to you did you see Rebecca Nurse in his company? [PROCTOR *is silent.*] Come, man, take courage—did you ever see her with the Devil?

Proctor. [*Almost inaudibly.*] No.

[DANFORTH, *now sensing trouble, glances at* JOHN *and goes to the table, and picks up a sheet—the list of condemned.*]

Danforth. Did you ever see her sister, Mary Easty, with the Devil?

Proctor. No, I did not.

Danforth. [*His eyes narrow on* PROCTOR.] Did you ever see Martha Corey with the Devil?

Proctor. I did not.

Danforth. [*Realizing, slowly putting the sheet down.*] Did you ever see anyone with the Devil?

Proctor. I did not.

Danforth. Proctor, you mistake me. I am not empowered to trade your life for a lie. You have most certainly seen some person with the Devil. [PROCTOR *is silent.*] Mr. Proctor, a score of people have already testified they saw this woman with the Devil.

Proctor. Then it is proved. Why must I say it?

Danforth. Why "must" you say it! Why, you should rejoice to say it if your soul is truly purged of any love for Hell!

Proctor. They think to go like saints. I like not to spoil their names.

Danforth. [*Inquiring, incredulous.*] Mr. Proctor, do you think they go like saints?

Proctor. [*Evading.*] This woman never thought she done the Devil's work.

Danforth. Look you, sir. I think you mistake your duty here. It matters nothing what she thought—she is convicted of the unnatural murder of children, and you for sending your spirit out upon Mary Warren. Your soul alone is the issue here, Mister, and you will prove its whiteness or you cannot live in a Christian country. Will you tell me now what persons conspired with you in the Devil's company? [PROCTOR *is silent.*] To your knowledge was Rebecca Nurse ever——

Proctor. I speak my own sins; I cannot judge another. [*Crying out, with hatred.*] I have no tongue for it.

Hale. [*Quickly to* DANFORTH.] Excellency, it is enough he confess himself. Let him sign it, let him sign it.

Parris. [*Feverishly.*] It is a great service, sir. It is a weighty name; it will strike the village that Proctor confess. I beg you, let him sign it. The sun is up, Excellency!

Danforth. [*Considers; then with dissatisfaction.*] Come, then, sign your testimony. [*To* CHEEVER.] Give it to him. [CHEEVER *goes to* PROCTOR, *the confession and a pen in hand.* PROCTOR *does not look at it.*] Come, man, sign it.

Proctor. [*After glancing at the confession.*] You have all witnessed it—it is enough.

Danforth. You will not sign it?

Proctor. You have all witnessed it; what more is needed?

Danforth. Do you sport with me? You will sign your name or it is no confession, Mister!

[*His breast heaving with agonized breathing,* PROCTOR *now lays the paper down and signs his name.*]

Parris. Praise be to the Lord!

[PROCTOR *has just finished signing when* DANFORTH *reaches for the paper. But* PROCTOR *snatches it up, and now a wild terror is rising in him, and a boundless anger.*]

Danforth. [*Perplexed, but politely extending his hand.*] If you please, sir.

Proctor. No.

Danforth. [*As though* PROCTOR *did not understand.*] Mr. Proctor, I must have——

Proctor. No, no. I have signed it. You have seen me. It is done! You have no need for this.

Parris. Proctor, the village must have proof that——

Proctor. Damn the village! I confess to God, and God has seen my name on this! It is enough!

Danforth. No, sir, it is——

Proctor. You came to save my soul, did you not? Here! I have confessed myself; it is enough!

Danforth. You have not con——

Proctor. I have confessed myself! Is there no good penitence but it be public? God does not need my name nailed upon the church! God sees my name; God knows how black my sins are! It is enough!

Danforth. Mr. Proctor——

Proctor. You will not use me! I am no Sarah Good or Tituba, I am John Proctor! You will not use me! It is no part of salvation that you should use me!

Danforth. I do not wish to——

Proctor. I have three children—how may I teach them to walk like men in the world, and I sold my friends?

Danforth. You have not sold your friends——

Proctor. Beguile me not! I blacken all of them when this is nailed to the church the very day they hang for silence!

Danforth. Mr. Proctor, I must have good and legal proof that you——

Proctor. You are the high court, your word is good enough! Tell them I confessed myself; say Proctor broke his knees and wept like a woman; say what you will, but my name cannot——

Danforth. [*With suspicion.*] It is the same, is it not? If I report it or you sign to it?

Proctor. [*He knows it is insane.*] No, it is not the same! What others say and what I sign to is not the same!

Danforth. Why? Do you mean to deny this confession when you are free?

Proctor. I mean to deny nothing!

Danforth. Then explain to me, Mr. Proctor, why you will not let——

Proctor. [*With a cry of his whole soul.*] Because it is my name! Because I cannot have another in my life! Because I lie and sign myself to lies! Because I am not worth the dust on the feet of them that hang! How may I live without my name? I have given you my soul; leave me my name!

Danforth. [*Pointing at the confession in* PROCTOR'S *hand.*] Is that document a lie? If it is a lie I will not accept it! What say you? I will not deal in lies, Mister! [PROCTOR *is motionless.*] You will give me your honest confession in my hand, or I cannot keep you from the rope. [PROCTOR *does not reply.*] Which way do you go, Mister?

[*His breast heaving, his eyes staring,* PROCTOR *tears the paper and crumples it, and he is weeping in fury, but erect.*]

Danforth. Marshal!

Parris. [*Hysterically, as though the tearing paper were his life.*] Proctor, Proctor!

Hale. Man, you will hang! You cannot!

Proctor. [*His eyes full of tears.*] I can. And there's your first marvel, that I can. You have made your magic now, for now I do think I see some shred of goodness in John Proctor. Not enough to weave a banner

with, but white enough to keep it from such dogs. [ELIZABETH, *in a burst of terror rushes to him and weeps against his hand.*] Give them no tear! Tears pleasure them! Show honor now, show a stony heart and sink them with it!

[*He has lifted her, and kisses her now with great passion.*]

Rebecca. Let you fear nothing! Another judgment waits us all!

Danforth. Hang them high over the town! Who weeps for these, weeps for corruption!

[*He sweeps out past them.* HERRICK *starts to lead* REBECCA, *who almost collapses, but* PROCTOR *catches her, and she glances up at him apologetically.*]

Rebecca. I've had no breakfast.

Herrick. Come, man.

[HERRICK *escorts them out,* HATHORNE *and* CHEEVER *behind them.* ELIZABETH *stands staring at the empty doorway.*]

Parris. [*In deadly fear, to* ELIZABETH.] Go to him, Goody Proctor! There is yet time!

[*From outside a drumroll strikes the air.* PARRIS *is startled.* ELIZABETH *jerks about toward the window.*]

Parris. Go to him! [*He rushes out the door, as though to hold back his fate.*] Proctor! Proctor!

[*Again, a short burst of drums.*]

Hale. Woman, plead with him! [*He starts to rush out the door, and then goes back to her.*] Woman! It is pride, it is vanity. [*She avoids his eyes, and moves to the window. He drops to his knees.*] Be his helper!—What profit him to bleed? Shall the dust praise him? Shall the worms declare his truth? Go to him, take his shame away!

Elizabeth. [*Supporting herself against collapse, grips the bars of the window, and with a cry.*] He have his goodness now! God forbid I take it from him!

[*The final drumroll crashes, then heightens violently.* HALE *weeps in frantic prayer, and the new sun is pouring in upon her face, and the drums rattle like bones in the morning air.*]

THE CURTAIN FALLS

ECHOES DOWN THE CORRIDOR

Not long after the fever died, Parris was voted from office, walked out on the highroad, and was never heard of again.

The legend has it that Abigail turned up later as a prostitute in Boston.

Twenty years after the last execution, the government awarded compensation to the victims still living, and to the families of the dead. However, it is evident that some people still were unwilling to admit their total guilt, and also that the factionalism was still alive, for some beneficiaries were actually not victims at all, but informers.

Elizabeth Proctor married again, four years after Proctor's death.

In solemn meeting, the congregation rescinded the excommunications—this in March 1712. But they did so upon orders of the government. The jury, however, wrote a statement praying forgiveness of all who had suffered.

Certain farms which had belonged to the victims were left to ruin, and for more than a century no one would buy them or live on them.

To all intents and purposes, the power of theocracy in Massachusetts was broken.

LOOK HOMEWARD, ANGEL*

By

KETTI FRINGS

A Play Based on the Novel by Thomas Wolfe

"HE ALWAYS HAD SO MANY WORDS left over from everything," wrote Mrs. Frings, recalling the difficulty of reducing Thomas Wolfe's proverbial eloquence as novelist to the crisp expression essential to a play. That she succeeded phenomenally in this respect, and even more tellingly in the selection of dramatically apt phrasing, was proven by popular acclaim, rave notices, and the Pulitzer and Dramatic Critics' Circle awards in 1958.

In fairness to the genius of this admittedly great American novelist, the first and most significant of whose fictionized autobiographical works is *Look Homeward, Angel,* the dramatizer would admit, we may be sure, that Wolfe's novel afforded her not only the plot, but, more impressively, the power and fascination of its stage success. In admiration and devotion she had assumed the task that no one since its publication in 1930 had dared to attempt: that of disentangling a dramatic sequence from Wolfe's enchanting jungle of life and golden words, which, as a critic once wrote, "sometimes swamped Wolfe's plots," even in the novels.

In his student days he had been eager to be a dramatist, enrolling under the foremost university teachers of playwriting, Frederick Koch of North Carolina and George Pierce Baker of Havard. But his stubborn indulgence in florid diction and his scorn for the conventional patterns of playmaking blocked his way to the stage. He wrote to Professor Baker, "I shall never express myself dramatically," and abandoned Baker's 47 Workshop for the career of university instructor. He did, however, rework his last student play, "Welcome to Our City," and offered it to the Neighborhood Playhouse and the New York Theatre Guild. It was declined by the Playhouse but was seriously considered by the Guild; but when cutting and other improvements were insisted on,

Wolfe characteristically refused to cooperate and gave up all hope of theatre success.

Years later, when applying for a Guggenheim fellowship for the completion of his novel, he could still write: "I loved the theatre, but I began to see I had to find a medium where I could satisfy my desire for fullness, intensity, and completeness." Clearly he was unwilling to renounce his instinctive "aim of free expression," or submit to "a hundred different people" of the stage demanding abbreviation. Resentment and petulance and Wolfe's supreme confidence in a self-directing genius also played a part.

Obviously Wolfe lacked and boldly decried the essentials of stage success: the talent to express a play's message by suggestion through action and dialogue, as Professor Baker tried to teach his hopefuls, rather than by explicitly descriptive dialogue. Wolfe's innate urge was the reverse—minutely to analyze and describe, now in blunt, now in poetic diction of great variety and beauty, as in the passage Mrs. Frings includes for Eugene to speak, beginning: "Even a cold one, standing in a station yard. . . ."

During his teaching career, Wolfe lost no opportunity to wander through Europe on meager savings, crystalizing his thoughts on the contrasting cultures of Europe and America. Travel increased his determination to reveal in novels his own experience as a searcher of the American mind. In 1928 he mentioned "twenty months" spent on his first, *O, Lost,* later to be known as *Look Homeward, Angel.* It had been begun in London and continued in New York. In both cities he had worked with great intensity and with a minimum of sensual indulgence so often linked with his name. He filled endless pages with notes greatly in excess of the resulting novel. But in 1930, thanks largely to the appreciative and sympathetic guidance of Scribner's editor, Maxwell Perkins, "swamping" words were reduced to 626 pages in the published form.

* Reprinted by permission of Edward C. Aswell and Ketti Frings.

To appreciate fully Mrs. Frings' technique, which Wolfe could not or would not have applied, one should read at least the last third of the novel, which, after strict elimination of characters and condensing of episodes, provided the scenario for the stage version. This ends with Eugene's (Wolfe's own) escape to the university at Chapel Hill from the vexations and family constraints of Altamount (Asheville)—the friction which, in the novel, extends much further. The escape is to mental liberty that is central in Wolfe's vague notion of a new American "myth" to replace the American dream of liberty, which was not liberating enough to satisfy a pathmaker in thought such as the youthful Wolfe believed himself to be. In a letter written in submitting *Mannerhouse*, a play begun at Harvard and later revised in vain for production in New York, Wolfe wrote that it had become "a mould for the expression of my secret life, of my own dark faith. . . . My play tries to express my passionate belief in all myth, in the necessity of defending and living not for truth—but for divine falsehood." In his *Story of a Novel* he declared: ". . . in the cultures of Europe and of the Orient the [American] artist can find no antecedent scheme . . . no body of tradition that can give his work the validity of truth. . . . he must make somehow a new tradition for himself, derived from his own life and from the enormous space and energy of American life." Such vague groping towards a traditional "myth" in the making underlies *Look Homeward, Angel* and the two subsequent novels, *Time and the River* and *The Web and the Rock*. Luckily it does not obtrude upon the vividly realistic persons and events of the story, but is merely the author's source of inspiration and epic intention, as apparent in this play as it is in O'Neill's *Long Day's Journey into Night*, a drama that also dissects biographically a discordant family held together by deeply buried but very real ties of affection and aspiration.

Symbolized in the title, Wolfe's structural design—which he called the "outward movement," or the characters' urge to escape, contrasted with a "downward movement" into the deteriorating family experience—is made dramatically poignant by Mrs. Frings in two scenes of the play that are largely her own invention: the meeting of the family group in W. O.'s shop presided over by the smiling Carrara angel, symbol of unattainable beauty and kindliness, and the scene at brother Ben's deathbed. In the former, the outward movement, described by Wolfe as "the effort for release, freedom, and loneliness," is brought to a climax in a *coup de théâtre* as Eliza tears up the bank check; and the downward movement, defined as "constant excavation into the buried life of a group of people" describing "the cyclic curve of a family's life—genesis, union, decay, and dissolution," reaches the depths. At Ben's bedside the same "movements" are more tragically defined, relieved by the indestructible bonds of family love.

In these passages and elsewhere Mrs. Frings has heightened the theatre values by a discerning selection of memorable bits of Wolfe's dialogue, as when Eugene's stammered prayer, only incidental in the novel, gains lingering beauty as the curtain falls upon Act II.

The brutal frankness with which the characters berate each other in this artistically depicted way of life—Wolfe's own—makes vigorous theatre as Mrs. Frings shrewdly adapts it to stage effect. Even Laura's deception of her cub lover—a kind of parody of the conventional love motive that centers most fiction and drama—refreshingly robs the book and play of sentimental unreality and heightens the meaning of Eugene's existential seeking of "release, freedom, and loneliness." Nevertheless, we must read with astonishment the very sincere "Note to the Publisher's Reader" that Wolfe submitted with his manuscript to Scribner's and other publishers. It reveals a strength of feeling hardly suspected as one reads the book or play. "To me who was joined so passionately with the people of this book, it seemed that they were the greatest people that I have ever known and the texture of their lives, the richest and strangest . . . If I could get my magnificent people on paper as they were . . . I believe no one would object to my 250,000 words." In her play version Mrs. Frings greatly helped to make these "magnificent" and strange people appear as Wolfe intended. To the same end the faultless acting of Jo Van Fleet as Eliza and Anthony Perkins as Eugene was outstanding in an exceptional cast. Similarly the symbolic but practical and realistic settings of designer Jo Mielziner were planned to underline the meaning of the play and to make effective Mrs. Frings' carefully visualized stage action, the complexity of which at the beginning of the play is not easy for a casual reader to follow, but which becomes perfectly lucid exposition to all who see it in the theatre.

KETTI (HARTLEY) FRINGS

Born 1916, Columbus, Ohio. Katharine Hartley.
Attended Principia College, St. Louis, Mo., for one year.
Free-lance writer of advertising matter and screen plays.
1938, Married Kurt Frings. Adopted name Ketti.
Lives in Southern California. Two children.

PLAYS

1942 *Mr. Sycamore.* 1957 *Look Homeward, Angel.* *You.* 1952 *Come Back, Little Sheba.* 1955 *The Shrike.*

SCREENWRITING

1941 *Hold Back the Dawn.* 1944 *God's Front Porch.* 1947 *Let the Devil Catch*

WRITINGS ON DRAMA

"O Lost! At Midnight," *Theatre Arts,* XLII (February 1958), 30 ff.

THOMAS WOLFE

Born 1900, Asheville, North Carolina; son of William Oliver Wolfe.
1920, A.B., University of North Carolina.
1920–1923, Graduate student at Harvard University. A.M., 1922, with distinction. Enrolled in Professor George Pierce Baker's playwriting course (47 Workshop).
1924–1930, Instructor of English at Washington Square College of New York University, broken by interruptions for European tours, and longer intervals after 1928 for travel and writing.
1930, *Look Homeward, Angel* published with immediate popular and critical success. Prolific writer of letters, short stories, and endless notes on life and travel, from which plays and novels, after much editing, were evolved.
Died 1938.

PLAYS

1924 *The Return of Buck Gavin* published, written earlier at U. of N.C. 1942 *Gentlemen of the Press.* 1948 *Mannerhouse* published, written 1923–24.

(Among other plays written in course *Niggertown,* later named *Welcome to Our City,* seriously considered for production by the New York Theatre Guild, but withdrawn by the author.)

LOOK HOMEWARD, ANGEL

PLACE AND TIME: *The Town of Altamont, North Carolina, in the fall of the year nineteen hundred and sixteen.*

ACT ONE

SCENE I

The Dixieland Boarding House is a flimsily constructed frame house of fifteen drafty, various-sized rooms. It has a gabled, unplanned and rambling appearance, and is painted a dirty yellow. Most of its furniture is badly worn and out of style. The beds are chipped enamel-covered iron. There are accordion hat trees, cracked mirrors, an occasional plant. On the typically southern veranda which embraces the front and one side of the house, there are chairs, rockers, and a wood box. There is a sign above the door, electrically lighted at night: Dixieland— Rooms and Board. In the center of the house, slightly raised, is a turntable on which all the bedroom scenes are played. At the back of the house a walk approaches the rear of the veranda. There is a side door and near it a circular yard seat. Also down front is a table and a chair.
The street itself has a feeling of great trees hanging over it. Occasionally during the play, the stillness is broken by the rustle of autumn leaves, and the poignant wail of a train whistle.
The curtain rises in darkness.
[After a moment we hear EUGENE's *voice coming from his room. Seated, his back to the audience, he is only partially glimpsed, writing, surrounded by books.]*

Eugene. [*Reading.*] "BEN, by Eugene Gant. . . .
My brother Ben's face is like a piece of slightly yellow ivory . . .
[Lights come up on the veranda where BEN GANT, *30, delicate and sensitive, the most refined of the Gants, and forever a stranger among them, is seated on the front steps reading a newspaper. He is sometimes scowling and surly, but*

he is the hero protector of those he loves, with quiet authority and a passion for home which is fundamental. At times he speaks to the side over his shoulder, in a peculiar mannerism of speech, as though he were addressing a familiar unseen presence.]
Eugene. His high, white forehead is knotted fiercely by an old man's scowl.
His mouth is like a knife.
His smile the flicker of light across the blade.
His face is like a blade, and a knife, and a flicker of light.
And when he fastens his hard white fingers
And his scowling eyes upon a thing he wants to fix,
He sniffs with sharp and private concentration.
[Lights reveal MARIE "FATTY" PERT, *43, seated near* BEN *in her rocker. She is a generous, somewhat boozy woman, knitting a pair of men's socks and tenderly regarding* BEN.]
Thus women looking, feel a well of tenderness
For his pointed, bumpy, always scowling face. . . ."
*[*EUGENE *continues writing.]*
Ben. Somebody's got to drive the Huns from the skies. Poor old England can't be expected to do it alone.
Mrs. Pert. It's their mess, isn't it?
Ben. It says here there's an American flying corps forming in Canada.
Mrs. Pert. Ben Gant, what are you thinking of?
Ben. All my life in this one little burg, Fatty! Besides getting away, I'd be doing my bit.
Mrs. Pert. Would they take you so old?
Ben. This article says eighteen to thirty-two.
Mrs. Pert. Aren't the physical standards pretty high?

537

Ben. Listen to her! I'm in good condition!

Mrs. Pert. You're twenty pounds underweight! I never saw anyone like you for not eating.

Ben. Maguire gave me a thorough checkup this spring!

Mrs. Pert. How would your family feel, if you went?

Ben. What family? The batty boarders? Apologies, Fatty. I never associate you with them. Except for Gene, nobody'd know I was gone. [*Looks up, dreamily.*] To fly up there in the wonderful world of the sky. Up with the angels.

[HELEN GANT BARTON *and her husband* HUGH *enter from the house.* HELEN *is gaunt, raw-boned, in her middle twenties, often nervous, intense, irritable, and abusive, though basically generous, the hysteria of excitement constantly lurking in her. It is a spiritual and physical necessity for her to exhaust herself in service to others, though her grievances, especially in her service to her mother, are many.*

HUGH *is a cash register salesman, simple, sweet, extremely warmhearted. He carries a tray with a coffee pot and cups and saucers which* HELEN *helps him set on a table. They have been arguing.*]

Hugh. We should never have agreed to live here for one day—that's the answer. You work yourself to the bone—for what?

Helen. Mrs. Pert, the other boarders have almost finished dinner!

Mrs. Pert. What's the dessert, Helen?

Helen. Charlotte Russe.

Hugh. They're like children with a tape worm.

Ben. Fatty, I told you you'd better get in there!

Mrs. Pert. I was trying to do without, but I'm afraid that calls me. See you later, Ben.

[*She leaves her knitting on the chair, exits inside.*]

Helen. Ben, where is Mama?

Ben. How should I know?

Helen. I've had to serve the entire dinner alone!

Hugh. Look at me, holes in my socks, a trouser button missing—and before I married you I had the reputation of being dapper.

Helen. I bet she's off somewhere with Uncle Will, and *I'm* left in the kitchen to slave for a crowd of old cheap boarders! That's her tactic!

Hugh. "Dapper Hugh Barton"—it said so in the newspaper when we were married.

Helen. [*To* BEN, *who pays no attention.*] You know that, don't you, *don't you?* And do I ever hear her say a word of thanks? Do I get—do I get as much as a go-to-hell for it? No. "Why, pshaw, child," she'll say, "I work more than anybody!" And most time, damn her, she does.

Boarders. [*Off stage, calling, ringing the service bell.*] Helen. Helen!

Helen. You come in, Hugh, and help me!

[HELEN *exits into the house.*]

Ben. How are the cash registers selling, Hugh?

Hugh. Putting the cigar box out of business. I got a good order in Raleigh last week. I've already put away nine hundred dollars toward our own little house.

Ben. You ought to have one, Hugh. You and Helen.

Hugh. [*Looking at part of the newspaper.*] I guess they don't have to advertise the good jobs, do they? The really big jobs . . . they wouldn't be here in the newspaper, would they?

Ben. Why?

Hugh. If there was something good here in town . . . not on the road so much . . . maybe then I could talk Helen into moving away. Ben, you hear things around the paper——

Helen. [*Off.*] Hugh! Hugh!

Ben. I'll keep my ears open, Hugh.

Hugh. Well, I guess I don't want to make Helen any madder at me. Thanks, Ben.

[*Exits inside. An automobile is heard off, driving up, stopping.* BEN *moves down to the yard seat, reads his newspaper. The car door slams.*]

Eliza. [*Off.*] I'll vow I never saw such a man. What little we have got, I've had to fight for tooth and nail, tooth and nail!

[ELIZA GANT *enters with* WILL PENTLAND, *her brother.* ELIZA, 57, *is of Scotch descent, with all the acquisitiveness and fancied premonitions of the Scotch. She is mercurial, with dauntless energy, greed, and love. She has an odd way of talking, pursing her lips, and she characteristically uses her right hand in a point-making gesture, fist enclosed, forefinger extended. These mannerisms are often imitated by those who hate and love her.* ELIZA *is carrying some fall leaves and a real-estate circular.* WILL *is punchy, successful, secure, a real-estate broker. They do not notice* BEN.]

Eliza. Like the fellow says, there's no fool like an old fool! Of course Mr. Gant's been a fool all his life. Pshaw! If I hadn't kept after him all these years we wouldn't have a stick to call our own.

Will. You had to have an *artistic* husband.

Eliza. Artistic. I have my opinion about that. Why, Will, the money that man squanders every year on liquor alone would buy all kinds of good downtown property, to say nothing of paying off this place. We could be well-to-do people now if we'd started at the very beginning.

Will. You've given him every opportunity.

Eliza. He always hated the idea of owning anything—couldn't bear it, he told me once —'cause of some bad trade he made when he was a young man up in Pennsylvania. If I'd been in the picture then, you can bet your bottom dollar there'd been no loss.

Will. [*Chuckling.*] Or the loss'd been on the other side.

Eliza. That's a *good* one! You know us Pentlands! Well, I'm going to get after Mr. Gant right today about that bank offer.

Will. Let me know when you've warmed him up enough for me to talk to him.

Eliza. It'll take a good deal of warming up, I can tell you. He's so blamed stubborn about that precious old marble yard, but I'll do it!

Will. Give me a jingle when you want to look at that farm property. I'll drive you out there.

Eliza. Thanks, Will! I appreciate it. [WILL *exits.* ELIZA *starts into the house, sees* BEN.] Ben! What are you doing home at this hour?

Ben. I'm working afternoons this week.

Eliza. Oh. [*Somewhat worriedly.*] Will you get dinner downtown?

Ben. I usually do.

Eliza. You always sound so short with me, Ben. Why is that? You don't even look at me. You know I can't stand not being looked at by the person I'm talking to. Don't you feel well?

Ben. I feel good.

[*A train whistle is heard in the distance.*]

Eliza. Oh, Pshaw, there's the midday train now! Has Eugene gone to the station?

Ben. How should I know?

Eliza. [*Calling up to* EUGENE's *room.*] Eugene, are you up in your room? Eugene? [EUGENE GANT, *hearing his mother's voice, rises from his chair, turns toward the window, but he doesn't answer, and* ELIZA *does not see him.* EUGENE *is 17, the youngest of the* GANTS, *tall, awkward, with a craving for*

knowledge and love. *During the following he leaves his room.*] Eugene! I'll vow, that boy. Just when I need him. . . . [*Notices* MRS. PERT's *knitting.*] Ben, I hope you haven't been lying around here wasting time with that Mrs. Pert again?

Ben. Listen to her! It's the nicest time I spend.

Eliza. I tell you what: it doesn't look right, Ben. What must the other boarders think? A woman her age . . . a drinking woman . . . married. Can't you find someone young and pretty and free to be with? I don't understand it. You're the best looking boy I've got.

Ben. [*More pleasantly.*] If it'll make you feel better, Mama, I'll look around.

[*Relieved by the change in his mood,* ELIZA *smiles. She also notices the sprawled newspaper.*]

Eliza. That's Mr. Clatt's newspaper. You know he's finicky about reading it first. Fold it up before you go.

[*During the above,* EUGENE *is seen coming down the stairs from his room. Now limping slightly, he starts to sneak out the side door, but* ELIZA *spots him.*]

Eliza. Eugene, where are you sneaking to? Come out here.

Eugene. [*Comes out.*] Yes, Mama?

Eliza. The train's just coming in. Now you hurry over to that depot.

Eugene. Today? I did it yesterday.

Eliza. Every day until every room is filled. The advertising cards are on the hall table. Go get them. [EUGENE, *disgruntled, goes into the entry hall to get the cards from a small stand.* ELIZA *strips some dead leaves off a plant.*] I declare, seventeen is an impossible age. I don't know why he complains. He hasn't anything else to do. Spending his time up there scribbling, dreaming.

Ben. The other boarding houses send their porters to the trains.

Eliza. Never you mind, Ben Gant, you used to do it. It's little enough I've ever asked of you boys. [*To* EUGENE *as he comes from the hall.*] Have you got the cards?

Eugene. In my pocket.

Eliza. [*Holding out her hand.*] Let me see them. Let me see them!

Eugene. [*Takes cards from pocket, reads.*] "Stay at Dixieland, Altamont's Homiest Boarding House."—It should be homeliest.

Eliza. Eugene!

Eugene. I hate drumming up trade! It's deceptive and it's begging.

Eliza. Oh my . . . my! Dreamer Eugene

Gant, what do you think the world is all about? We are all . . . all of us . . . selling something. Now you get over to the depot right this minute. And for heaven's sake, boy, spruce up, shoulders back! Look like you are somebody! [EUGENE *starts off.*] And smile! Look pleasant!

[EUGENE *grins, maniacally.*]

Ben. [*Suddenly, as he watches* EUGENE *limping.*] Gene! What are you walking like that for?

Eugene. Like what?

Ben. [*Rises.*] What are you limping for? My God, those are my shoes you've got on! I threw them out yesterday!

Eliza. They're practically brand new.

Ben. They're too small for *me;* they must be killing him.

Eugene. Ben, please!

Eliza. Maybe you can afford to throw out brand new shoes.

Ben. Mama, for God's sake, you ask him to walk straight, how can he? His toes must be like pretzels!

Eugene. They're all right. I'll get used to them.

Ben. [*Throwing down his paper.*] My God, it's a damned disgrace, sending him out on the streets like a hired man . . . Gene should be *on* that train, going to college!

Eliza. That's enough—that's just enough of that! You haven't a family to provide for like I have, Ben Gant. Now I don't want to hear another word about it! Gene will go to college when we can afford it. This year he can help his Papa at the shop.

Ben. I thought you were going to *warm up* Papa, so he'll sell the shop.

Eliza. Ben Gant, that wasn't intended for your ears. I'd appreciate it if you wouldn't mention it to Mr. Gant until I have. Hurry off now, son, get us a customer!

Eugene. Why should Papa sell his shop?

Eliza. Now you're too young to worry about my business. You tend to yours.

Eugene. What business do I have to attend to, Mama?

Eliza. Well, get busy, get busy! Help your Papa at the shop.

Eugene. I don't want to be a stonecutter.

Eliza. Well, go back to delivering newspapers. Work for Uncle Will in his real-estate office. But keep the ball rolling, child. Now hurry on or you'll be late!

[EUGENE *exits.*]

Helen. [*Entering.*] Mama, dinner's practically over! I'm no slave!

Eliza. I'll be right in, Helen. [HELEN *exits, slamming door.* ELIZA *sighs. For a moment, left alone with* BEN, *she becomes herself, a deeply troubled woman.*] What's the matter with him, Ben? What's wrong with that boy? What's the matter with all of you? I certainly don't know. I tell you what, sometimes I get frightened. Seems as if every one of you's at the end of something, dissatisfied, and wants something else. But it just can't be. A house divided against itself cannot stand. I'll vow, I don't know what we're all coming to. [*Approaches side door, pauses.*] If you like, this once, as long as you're home, why don't you eat here? I'm sure there's plenty left over.

Ben. No, thank you, Mama.

[*He starts off.*]

Eliza. A good hot meal!

Ben. I've got to get over there.

Eliza. Ben, are you sure you feel all right?

Ben. I feel fine.

Eliza. Well, have a nice day at the paper, son.

[BEN *exits.* ELIZA *looks after him, then hearing the voices of the boarders, exits into the house by the side door. The boarders, ushered by* HELEN, *enter through the front door. They are:* JAKE CLATT, *30, an insensitive boor;* MRS. CLATT, *60, Jake's mother, with a coarse smile and dyed hair; she is deaf and carries a cane;* FLORRY MANGLE, *29, wistful, humorless, interested in Jake;* MRS. SNOWDEN, *50, quiet, unobtrusive, lonely;* MISS BROWN, *36, prim on the surface, but with the marks of the amateur prostitute;* MR. FARREL, *60, a retired dancing master, new to* DIXIE-LAND.]

Mrs. Clatt. I ate too much again.

Helen. [*Loudly to* MRS. CLATT.] Help yourself to coffee, please, Mrs. Clatt. I'm short-handed today.

Mrs. Clatt. [*Brandishing her cane at* MR. FARREL, *who is about to sit.*] Not there, that's my chair! That one's free, since the school teacher left.

Miss Brown. You're a teacher too, aren't you, Mr. Farrel?

Mr. Farrel. Of the dance. Retired.

Miss Brown. I hope you'll stay with us for a while. Where are you from?

Mr. Farrel. Tampa.

Miss Brown. Do you know the Castle Walk, Mr. Farrel? I'd love to learn it!

[*They stroll down to the yard seat.*]

Mrs. Clatt. I don't know what Mrs. Gant makes this coffee of. There isn't a bean invented tastes like this.

Jake. Couldn't you make it for us sometime, Helen?

Helen. My mother always makes the coffee here.

[HUGH *and* MRS. PERT *enter. The others seat themselves.*]

Mrs. Pert. That was scrumptious dessert, but oh dear! [*Sits in her rocker.*]

Jake. Yes, it was good, if only the servings were bigger.

Mrs. Clatt. I'm told the best boarding house food in town is down the street at Mrs. Haskells'.

Jake. That's right, mother. That's what I heard.

Hugh. Then move in to Mrs. Haskell's!

Helen. [*With a shove.*] Hugh!

[*She exits.*]

Miss Mangle. I spent one season there, but I prefer it here. It's more informal and entertaining.

Jake. Not lately. It's been over a month since Mrs. Gant had to have Mr. Molasses Edwards and his two Dixie Ramblers evicted for not paying their rent. She certainly loves to see the police swarm around!

[LAURA JAMES, *23, carrying a suitcase and a* DIXIELAND *advertising card, enters. She is attractive, but not beautiful. She advances to the steps.*]

Miss Mangle. Don't you?

Jake. I like excitement—why shouldn't I?

Miss Mangle. Other people's excitement. Don't you ever want excitement of your own? I do.

[MRS. CLATT *sees* LAURA, *nudges her son into attention.*]

Laura. Good afternoon!

Hugh. [*Crosses to her.*] Good afternoon!

Laura. Is the proprietor here?

Hugh. I'll call her. [*Calls inside.*] Mrs. Gant! Customer! [*To* LAURA.] Please come right up.

Jake. [*Leaping to* LAURA.] Here, let me take that suitcase. It must be heavy for you.

Laura. Thank you.

[JAKE *takes* LAURA'S *suitcase. The other boarders look her over, whisper.* ELIZA, *wearing an apron, places the leaves in a vase on the hall table, enters. At first raking glance she doubts that* LAURA, *so young and different, is a true prospect.*]

Eliza. Yes?

Laura. Are you the proprietor?

Eliza. Mrs. Eliza Gant—that's right.

Laura. I found this card on the sidewalk.

Eliza. [*Takes card.*] On the sidewalk! And you're looking for a room?

Laura. If you have one for me.

Eliza. Of course I have, dear—a nice quiet room. You just sit down here and have yourself a cup of my *good* coffee, while I go and open it up, so I can show it to you. Hugh, you take care of the young lady. This is Mr. Barton, my son-in-law.

Laura. How do you do, Mr. Barton? I'm Laura James.

Eliza. Laura—why that's a *good* Scotch name. Are you Scotch?

Laura. On one side.

Eliza. Pshaw! I could have told you were Scotch the minute I laid eyes on you. I'm Scotch too. Well, isn't that nice? [*Makes introductions.*] Miss James, Mr. Clatt. . . . [*Each acknowledges the introduction according to his personality.*] . . . his mother, Mrs. Clatt, Mrs. Snowden, Miss Mangle, Mr. Farrel, [*Disapprovingly notices* MISS BROWN *with* MR. FARREL.] . . . Miss Brown . . . *Miss Brown!* And Mrs. Pert. Where do you come from, dear?

Laura. I live in Richmond.

[MISS BROWN *and* MR. FARREL *exit, practicing the Castle Walk, eventually reappear at the rear of the veranda.*]

Eliza. Richmond! Now that's a pleasant city—but hot! Not like it is here, cool and refreshing in these hills. You haven't come to Altamont for a cure, have you dear?

Laura. I'm healthy, if that's what you mean. But I've been working hard and I need a rest.

[HUGH *approaches with coffee.*]

Eliza. Here's your coffee.

Laura. [*Takes coffee.*] Thank you, Mr. Barton. What are your rates, Mrs. Gant?

Eugene. [*Off.*] Mama! Mama!

[EUGENE *runs up the back walk, around the veranda.*]

Eliza. Suppose I show you the room first.

Eugene. Mama!

Eliza. I declare, that child either crawls like a snail or speeds like a fire engine. . . .

Eugene. [*Pulls* ELIZA *away from the others.*] Can I speak to you, Mama?

Eliza. I don't see you limping *now*, when you're not trying to get sympathy. Don't think I don't know your little tricks to. . . .

Eugene. [*Urgently.*] Mama, Papa's been at Laughran's again. Doctor Maguire is trying to steer him home now.

Eliza. [*Momentarily stabbed.*] The doctor? Is he sick or is he drunk?

Eugene. He's rip-roaring! He's awful. He kicked Uncle Will again!

[*From offstage come the sounds of a small riot approaching. The occasional bull yell of* GANT, *children chanting "Old Man Gant came home drunk," a dog barking, etc.*]

Eliza. [*Weakly.*] I don't think I can stand it again. A *new* young lady, too. [EU-GENE *turns to see* LAURA, *who, with the other boarders, has heard the approaching* GANT.] Oh Eugene, why do they keep bringing him home? Take him to a state institution, throw him in the gutter, I don't care. I don't know what to do any more. What'll I do, child?

Eugene. At least it's been a month this time.

Gant. [*Off.*] Mountain Grills! Stay away from me!

Jake Clatt. My God, Mr. Gant's on the loose again!

Miss Mangle. Oh dear, oh dear——

Mrs. Clatt. What? What is it?

Jake Clatt. [*Shouting.*] The old boy's on the loose again!

Eugene. [*Crossing up to the boarders.*] Would you go inside, all of you, please?

Mrs. Clatt. I haven't finished my coffee.

Eugene. You can wait in the parlor. Please, just until we get him upstairs!

Jake Clatt. And miss the show?

Miss Brown. Come along, Mr. Farrel. Let's clear the deck for the old geezer.

Mr. Farrel. Perhaps there is some way I can help?

Miss Brown. I wouldn't recommend it, Mr. Farrel.

Jake Clatt. Look at him, he's really got a snootful this time!

[EUGENE *urges several of the boarders inside, where they cram in the hallway;* JAKE *and* MRS. CLATT *remain on the porch.* LAURA, *not knowing where to go, remains with* HUGH *outside.*]

Gant. [*Bellowing, off.*] Mountain Grills! Mountain Grills! Fiends, not friends! Don't push me! *Get away from me!*

Doctor Maguire. [*Off.*] All right then, Gant, if you can walk, walk!

[ELIZA *stands downstage, stiff and straight.* W. O. GANT, *60, clatters up the back steps, his arms flailing, his powerful frame staggering, reeling. At heart he is a far wanderer and a minstrel, but he has degraded his life with libertinism and drink. In him still, though, there is a monstrous fumbling for life. He is accompanied by* DR. MAGUIRE, *unkempt but kind, and by* TARKINGTON, *a disreputable crony, also drunk but navigating, and by* WILL PENTLAND.]

Dr. Maguire. Here we are, Gant, let's go in the back way.

[GANT *pushes the* DOCTOR *aside, plunges headlong along the veranda, scattering rockers, flower pots, etc.*]

Gant. Where are you? Where are you? The lowest of the low—boarding-house swine! Merciful God, what a travesty! That it should come to this!

Eugene. Papa, come on. Papa, please!

[EUGENE *tries to take* GANT *by the arm;* GANT *flings him aside.*]

Gant. [*With a sweeping gesture.*]
"Waken lords and ladies gay
On the mountain dawns the day——"
Don't let me disturb your little tete-a-tete. Go right ahead, help yourself! [MRS. CLATT *screams and dashes into the hall.*] Another helping of mashed potatoes, Mrs. Clatt? Put another tire around your middle——

[EUGENE *tries to catch his father's flailing arms, is flung into* MRS. PERT'S *rocker.*]

Eliza. Mr. Gant, I'd be ashamed. I'd be ashamed.

Gant. Who speaks?

Eliza. I thought you were sick.

Gant. I am not sick, madame, I am in a wild, blind fury. You're a Mountain Grill!

[*Raises a chair aloft, threatening* ELIZA. EUGENE *and the* DOCTOR *grab it away from him.*]

Eliza. Dr. Maguire, get him in the house.

Dr. Maguire. Come on, Gant, let me help you.

Gant. [*Plunging down the steps.*] Just one moment! You don't think I know my own home when I see it? This is not where I live. I reside at *92 Woodson Street.*

Dr. Maguire. That was some years ago. This is your home now, Gant.

Gant. This barn? This damnable, this awful, this murderous and bloody barn—home! Holy hell, what a travesty on nature!

Will. Why don't we carry him in?

Dr. Maguire. You keep out of this, Pentland. You're the one who enrages him.

Gant. Pentland—now that's a name for you! [*Pivots, searching for him.*] Where are you, Will Pentland? [*Sees him, staggers toward him.*] You're a Mountain Grill! Your father was a Mountain Grill and a horse thief, and he was hanged in the public square.

[*While* HUGH *holds* GANT, EUGENE *brings a cup of coffee.*]

Eugene. Papa, wouldn't you like some coffee? There's some right here.

Gant. Hah! Some of Mrs. Gant's *good* coffee? [*He kicks at the coffee cup.*] Ahh! I'll take some of that *good* bourbon, if you have it, son.

Dr. Maguire. Get him a drink! Maybe he'll pass out.

Gant. Drink!

[EUGENE *starts into the house.*]

Eliza. Gene! Dr. Maguire, you know there isn't a drop of alcohol in this house!

Laura. I have some. [*As all stare at her,* LAURA *quickly opens her handbag, takes from it a small vial, crosses to the doctor.*] I always carry it in case of a train accident.

Gant. Well, what are we waiting for, let's have it!

Dr. Maguire. [*Taking the vial.*] Good God, this won't fill one of his teeth.

Gant. [*Roars.*] Well, let's have it!

[LAURA *backs away in fear.* HELEN *enters, the joy of being needed shining on her face.*]

Dr. Maguire. You can have it, Gant, but you'll have to come up onto the veranda to drink it——

Gant. Mountain Grills! Vipers! Lowest of the low! I'll stand here until you take me home. *Isn't anybody going to take me home?*

Helen. Papa! Why have you been drinking again when you know what it does to you?

Gant. [*Weakens, leans against her.*] Helen—I have a pain right here.

Helen. Of course you do. Come with me now. I'll put you to bed, and bring you some soup.

[HELEN *takes the huge man's arm, leads him toward the veranda.* HELEN'S *success with* GANT *etches itself deeply into* ELIZA'S *face.*]

Gant. Got to sit down—— [*Sits on edge of veranda.*] Sit down, Helen, you and me. Sit and talk. Would you like to hear some Keats . . . beautiful Keats?

Eliza. [*Crossing up to veranda, angrily.*] He's got his audience now. That's all he wants.

Eugene. Mama, he's sick!

Eliza. Mr. Gant, if you feel so bad, why don't you act nice and go inside? The whole neighborhood's watching you.

Gant. [*Wildly sings.*] "Old Man Gant came home drunk. . . . [TARKINGTON *joins him.*] Old Man Gant came home drunk. . . ."

Tarkington. [*Singing, waving his arms.*] "Old Man Gant came home. . . ."

[*His joy fades as he sees* ELIZA *glaring at him.*]

Eliza. Were you drinking with him too, Mr. Tarkington?

Tarkington. Sev-everal of us were, Mrs. Gant, I regret to say.

Eliza. [*Pulling* TARKINGTON *to his feet.*] I'll have Tim Laughran thrown in jail for this.

Tarkington. He started out so peaceable like. . . .

Eliza. [*Pushing him toward rear exit of veranda.*] I've warned him for the last time.

Tarkington. Just on beer!

Eliza. Get off my premises!

[TARKINGTON *exits.* GANT *groans.*]

Helen. Dr. Maguire's here to give you something for your pain, Papa.

Gant. Doctors! Thieves and bloodsuckers! "The paths of glory lead but to the grave."—Gray's Elegy. Only four cents a letter on any tombstone you choose, by the master carver! Any orders? [*Groans, weak with pain.*] It's the devil's own pitchfork. Don't let them put me under the knife—promise me, daughter. Promise me! [HELEN *nods. With a giant effort,* GANT *pulls himself up.*] "Over the stones, rattle his bones! He's only a beggar that nobody owns."

Dr. Maguire. Good God, he's on his feet again!

Eugene. Hugh, let's get him in the house.

Gant. [*Throwing off* HUGH *and* EUGENE.] I see it! I see it! Do you see the Dark Man's shadow? There! There he stands—the Grim Reaper—as I always knew he would. So you've come at last to take the old man home? Jesus, have mercy on my soul!

[GANT *falls to the ground. There is an agonized silence.* EUGENE, *the* DOCTOR, *and* HUGH *rush to him.*]

Eliza. [*Anxiously.*] Dr. Maguire?

[DR. MAGUIRE *feels* GANT'S *heart.*]

Dr. Maguire. He's just passed out, Mrs. Gant. Men, let's carry him up!

[HUGH, WILL, MAGUIRE *and* EUGENE *lift the heavy body, quickly carry* GANT *inside.* HELEN *follows.* ELIZA, *saddened and miserable, starts to gather up the coffee cups.* LAURA *picks up her suitcase and starts off.* ELIZA *turns, sees her.*]

Eliza. Oh, Miss James. I was going to show you that room, wasn't I?

[*Seizes* LAURA'S *suitcase.*]

Laura. Hmmmmm?

Eliza. I think you'll enjoy it here. It's quiet and peaceful—oh, nobody pays any mind to Mr. Gant. I'll tell you what; we don't have occurrences like this every day.

Laura. Well, how much is it?

Eliza. Twenty—fifteen dollars a week. Three meals a day, and the use of electricity and the bath. Do you want me to show it to you?

Laura. No, I'm sure it will be all right.

Eliza. [*Starting in, turns back.*] That's in advance, that is.

[LAURA *opens her purse, takes out a roll of one dollar bills, puts them one by one into* ELIZA's *outstretched hand.*]

Laura. One, two, three—I always keep my money in one dollar bills—it feels like it's more.

Eliza. [*Almost cheerful again.*] Oh, I know what you mean.

[MR. FARREL *enters by the side door with his suitcase. He is hoping to sneak out.*]

Eliza. [*Sees him as the paying business continues.*] Mr. Farrel! Where are you going? Mr. Farrel, you've paid for a week in advance!

[MR. FARREL *wordlessly gestures that it's all too much for him, exits.*]

Eliza. Well, they come and they go. And you're here now, isn't that nice?

Laura. . . . Nine . . . ten. . . .

[BEN *enters from the other direction, hurriedly.*]

Ben. I heard about father—how is he?

Eliza. Drunk. Dr. Maguire's taking care of him now. Ben, this is Miss James . . . this is my son, Ben Gant.

Ben. [*Impressed by her looks, nods.*] Miss James.

Laura. [*Barely looking at* BEN, *nods.*] —fourteen, fifteen. There.

Eliza. [*Puts the money in bosom of her dress.*] Thank you dear. Miss James is going to stay with us a while, we hope! I'll take you up, dear. You'll be cozy and comfortable here. [*They start inside.*] I'll show you the rest of the house later.

Laura. [*Turning in doorway.*] Nice to have met you, Mr. Gant.

[ELIZA *and* LAURA *exit.*]

Ben. [*Imitating* LAURA's *disinterest, as he picks up cup of coffee.*] Nice to have met you, Mr. Gant.

[*Shrugs, drinks coffee.* WILL *enters from the house, still sweating.*]

Will. That father of yours. Do you know he kicked me? I don't want to tell you where. Why don't you watch out for him more, Ben? It's up to you boys, for your mother's sake—for Dixieland. I warned her about him . . . a born wanderer like he is, and a widower. But you can't advise women —not when it comes to love and sex. [*He starts off, stops.*] You might thank me for my help. No one else has.

Ben. Thank you, Uncle Will.

Will. Bunch of ungrateful Gants You're the only one of them who has any class.

[WILL *exits.* BEN *lights a cigarette.* EUGENE *enters.*]

Eugene. Did you hear about it, Ben?

Ben. There isn't a soul in town who hasn't.

Eugene. What's it all about? It doesn't make sense. Can you figure it out, Ben? Why does he do it?

Ben. How should I know? [*Drinks his coffee.*] Is Maguire almost through?

Eugene. [*Hurt, not understanding* BEN's *preoccupation.*] Ben, remember in the morning when we used to walk together and you were teaching me the paper route? We talked a lot then.

Ben. Listen to him! We're talking.

Eugene. If he hates it so much here, why does he stay?

Ben. You stupid little fool, it's like being caught in a photograph. Your face is there, and no matter how hard you try, how are you going to step out of a photograph? [DOCTOR MAGUIRE *enters.*] Shut up now, will you? Hello, Doc.

Dr. Maguire. Your sister sure can handle that old goat like a lamb! The funny thing though is that people like him. He's a good man, when sober.

Ben. Is he all right?

Dr. Maguire. He's going to be.

Ben. Can I speak to you a minute about me? If you have a minute.

Dr. Maguire. Shoot, Ben.

Ben. [*To* EUGENE.] Haven't you got something else to do?

Eugene. [*Seating himself.*] No.

Dr. Maguire. What's the matter—you got pyorrhea of the toenails, or is it something more private?

Ben. I'm tired of pushing daisies here. I want to push them somewhere else.

Dr. Maguire. What's that supposed to mean?

Ben. I suppose you've heard there's a war going on in Europe? I've decided to enlist in Canada.

Eugene. [*Rises.*] What do you want to do that for?

Ben. [*To* EUGENE.] You keep out of this.

Dr. Maguire. It is a good question, Ben. Do you want to save the world? This world?

Ben. In Christ's name, Maguire, you'll recommend me, won't you? You examined me just a couple of months ago.

Dr. Maguire. [*Puts down his bag.*] Well, let's see, for a war the requirements are somewhat different. Stick out your chest. [BEN *does so; the* DOCTOR *looks him over.*] Feet? Good arch, but pigeon-toed.

Ben. Since when do you need toes to shoot a gun?

Dr. Maguire. How're your teeth, son?

Ben. Aren't you overdoing it, Doc?

[BEN *draws back his lips and shows two rows of hard white grinders. Unexpectedly,* MAGUIRE *prods* BEN'S *solar plexus with a strong yellow finger and* BEN'S *distended chest collapses. He sinks to the veranda edge, coughing.*]

Eugene. What did you do that for?

Dr. Maguire. They'll have to save this world without you, Ben.

Ben. [*Rises, grabs the* DOCTOR.] What do you mean?

Dr. Maguire. That's all. That's all.

Ben. You're saying I'm not all right?

Dr. Maguire. Who said you weren't all right?

Ben. Quit your kidding.

Dr. Maguire. What's the rush? We may get into this war ourselves before too long. Wait a bit. [*To* EUGENE.] Isn't that right, son?

Ben. I want to know. Am I all right or not?

Dr. Maguire. Yes, Ben, you're all right. Why, you're one of the most all right people I know. [*Carefully, as he feels* BEN'S *arms.*] You're a little run down, that's all. You need some meat on those bones. [BEN *breaks from him, moves away.*] You can't exist with a cup of coffee in one hand and a cigarette in the other. Besides, the Altamont air is good for you. Stick around. Big breaths, Ben, big breaths.

[*Picks up his bag.*]

Ben. Thanks. As a doctor, you're a fine first baseman.

Dr. Maguire. Take it easy. Try not to care too much. [*Exits.*]

Eugene. He's right. You should try to look after yourself more, Ben.

[EUGENE *tries to comfort* BEN. BEN *avoids his touch, lurches away.*]

Ben. He doesn't have any spirit about this war, that's all that's the matter with him.

[BEN *recovers his coffee, drinks.* EUGENE *studies him.*]

Eugene. I didn't know you wanted to get away from here so badly.

Ben. [*Looks over at* EUGENE, *puts down coffee.*] Come here, you little bum. [EUGENE *approaches close.*] My God, haven't you got a clean shirt? [*He gets out some money.*] Here, take this and go get that damn long hair cut off, and get some shoes that fit, for God's sake. You look like a lousy tramp. . . .

Eugene. [*Backing away.*] Ben, I can't keep taking money from you.

Ben. What else have you got me for?

[*The brothers roughhouse playfully with the money,* EUGENE *giggling. Then, with sudden intense ferocity,* BEN *seizes* EUGENE'S *arms, shakes him.*] You listen to me. Listen to me. You go to college, understand? Don't settle for anyone or anything—learn your lesson from me! I'm a hack on a hick paper—I'll never be anything else. You can be. Get money out of them, anyway you can! Beg it, take it, steal it, but get it from them somehow. Get it and get away from them. To hell with them all! [BEN *coughs.* EUGENE *tries to help him.* BEN *escapes, sits tiredly on the veranda's edge.* EUGENE *disconsolately sinks into a nearby chair.*] Neither Luke, nor Stevie, nor I made it. But you can, Gene. I let her hold on and hold on until it was too late. Don't let that happen to you. And Gene, don't try to please everyone—please yourself. [BEN *studies* EUGENE, *realizes his confusion and depression. Then, noticing* LAURA'S *hat which she has left on the yard table, he points to it.*] Where's she from?

Eugene. [*Follows* BEN'S *gaze to* LAURA'S *hat, picks it up, sniffs it.*] I don't know. I don't even know her name.

Ben. Miss James. I'll have to announce her arrival in my society column. [*Takes hat from* EUGENE, *admires it.*] The firm young line of spring . . . budding, tender, virginal. "Like something swift, with wings, which hovers in a wood—among the feathery trees, suspected, but uncaught, unseen." Exquisite. [*Returns hat to table, rises.*] Want to walk downtown with me? I'll buy you a cup of mocha.

Eugene. Maybe I ought to stay here.

Ben. [*Ruffling* EUGENE'S *hair.*] With her around I don't blame you. I dream of elegant women myself, all the time.

Eugene. [*Rising.*] You do? But, Ben, if you dream of elegant women, how is it . . . well——

Ben. Mrs. Pert? Fatty's a happy woman —there's no pain in her she feels she has to unload onto someone else. Besides, she's as adorable as a duck. Don't you think so?

Eugene. I guess you're right. I like her— myself . . . sure.

Ben. Someday you'll find out what it means. I've got to get back to work.

Eugene. Ben, I'm glad they won't take you in Canada.

Ben. [*With that upward glance.*] Listen to him! I was crazy to think of going. I have to bring you up first, don't I?

[BEN *exits.* EUGENE *walks about restlessly, looks up at* LAURA'S *window.*

Miss Brown, *dressed for a stroll, carrying a parasol, enters from the house.*] *Miss Brown.* Gene! You haven't even said hello to me today.

Eugene. Hello, Miss Brown.

Miss Brown. My, everything's quiet again. Lovely warm day, isn't it?

[Miss Brown *sings and dances sensuously for* Eugene.]

"Pony boy, pony boy,
Won't you be my pony boy?
Don't say no, can't we go
Right across the plains?

[Miss Brown *approaches* Eugene; *he backs away from her, stumbling against the table.*]

Marry me, carry me
Far away with you!

[*She starts out through rear veranda.*]
Giddy-ap, giddy-ap, giddy-ap. Oh!
My pony boy!"

[Miss Brown *exits.* Eugene *sits on the yard seat, takes off one shoe and rubs his aching toes.* Laura *enters, picks up her hat, sees* Eugene. Eugene *hides his shoeless foot.*]

Miss Brown. [*Off stage, fainter.*]
"Pony boy, pony boy
Mmmm, mmm, mmmm—Mmmmm, mmmm, mmmm,
Marry me, carry me
Far away with you!
Giddy-ap, giddy-ap, giddy-ap. Oh!
My pony boy."

[*At the door,* Laura *looks again at* Eugene, *smiles, exits.*]

CURTAIN

ACT ONE

SCENE II

The Dixieland Boarding House. The night is sensuous, warm. A light storm is threatening. Long, swaying tree shadows project themselves on the house.
[*Seated on the side veranda are* Jake, Mrs. Clatt, Florry, Miss Brown, *and* Mrs. Snowden. Mrs. Pert *is seated in her rocker,* Ben *on the steps beside her. They are drinking beer.* Mrs. Pert *measures the socks she is knitting against* Ben's *shoe.* Jake Clatt *softly plays the ukelele and sings.* Eugene *is sitting on the side door steps, lonely, yearning.*]

Jake. [*Singing.*] "K-k-katy, K-k-katy" [etc.]

[*As* Jake *finishes,* Florry *gently applauds.* Jake *starts softly strumming something else.*]

Mrs. Pert. [*To* Ben, *quietly.*] I know you talked to the doctor today. What did he say? Tell Fatty.

Ben. I'm out before I'm in. Oh, I know you're pleased, but you don't know how it feels to be the weakling. All the other members of this family—they're steers, mountain goats, eagles. Except father, lately—unless he's drunk. Do you know, though, I still think of him as I thought of him as a little boy—a Titan! The house on Woodson Street that he built for Mama with his own hands,

the great armloads of food he carried home . . . the giant fires he used to build. The women he loved at Madame Elizabeth's. Two and three a night, I heard.

Mrs. Pert. It's nice for parents to have their children think of them as they were young. [*As* Ben *chuckles.*] I mean, that's the way I'd like my children to think of me. Oh, you know what I mean.

Ben. [*Laughs with his typical glance upward.*] Listen to her!

Mrs. Pert. Ben, who are you always talking to, like that?

[*Imitates* Ben *looking up over his shoulder.*]

Ben. Who, him? [*She nods.*] That's Grover, my twin. It was a habit I got into, while he was still alive.

Mrs. Pert. I wish you'd known me when I was young. I was some different.

Ben. I bet you weren't half as nice and warm and round as you are now.

Mrs. Pert. Ben, don't ever let your mother hear you say those things. What could she think?

Ben. Who cares what she thinks?

Mrs. Pert. Dear, I only hope when the right girl comes along you won't be sorry for the affection you've lavished on me.

Ben. I don't want the *right* girl. Like some more beer? I've got another bottle.

Mrs. Pert. Love some more, honey.

[Ben *rises, searches under the yard table for the bottle he has hidden, real-*

izes it's not there, suspiciously looks at EUGENE. EUGENE *innocently gestures, then reaches behind him and tosses the beer bottle to* BEN. BEN *and* FATTY *laugh.* BEN *returns with the beer to* FATTY *as* LAURA *enters from the house.*]
Jake. [*Rising expectantly.*] Good evening, Miss James.
Laura. Good evening.
Jake. Won't you sit down?
Mrs. Clatt. [*As* LAURA *seems about to choose a chair.*] That's Mr. Farrel's. Yours is back there!
Jake. [*Loudly.*] Mr. Farrel has left, Mother.
Mrs. Clatt. What?
Jake. Never mind. [*To* LAURA.] No sense in being formal. Won't you sing with me, Miss James?
Laura. I love music, but I have no talent for it.
[LAURA *moves toward rear of veranda, away from the others.*]
Florry. [*To* JAKE.] I love to sing.
[JAKE *ignores* FLORRY, *follows after* LAURA, FLORRY *tugging at* JAKE's *coat.*]
Mrs. Snowden. [*To* JAKE *as he passes.*] Do you know Indiana Lullaby? It's a lovely song. [JAKE *and* LAURA *exit.*]
Ben. I'm comfortable when I'm with you, Fatty.
Mrs. Pert. That's good, so'm I.
Ben. People don't understand. Jelly roll isn't everything, is it?
Mrs. Pert. Ben Gant, what kind of a vulgar phrase is that?
Ben. It's a Stumptown word. I used to deliver papers there. Sometimes those negro women don't have money to pay their bill, so they pay you in jelly roll.
Mrs. Pert. Ben—your little brother's right over there listening!
Ben. [*Glances toward* EUGENE.] Gene knows all about jelly roll, don't you? Where do you think he's been all his life—in Mama's front parlor?
Eugene. Oh, come on, Ben!
Ben. [*Laughs.*] There's another word I remember in the eighth grade. We had a thin, anxious looking teacher. The boys had a poem about her. [*Quotes.*]
"Old Miss Groody
Has good Toody."
Fatty. Ben, stop it!
[*They both laugh.* LAURA *has managed to lose* JAKE, *and has strolled around the back of the house. She enters to* EUGENE *from the side door.*]
Laura. Good evening.
Eugene. What!

Laura. I said good evening.
Eugene. [*Flustered.*] Goodyado.
Laura. I beg your pardon?
Eugene. I mean—I meant to say good evening, how do you do?
Laura. Goodyado! I like that much better. Goodyado! [*They shake hands,* LAURA *reacting to* EUGENE's *giant grip.*] Don't you think that's funny?
Eugene. [*Sits on yard seat.*] It's about as funny as most things I do.
Laura. May I sit down?
Eugene. [*Leaping up.*]. Please.
Laura. [*As they both sit.*] I'm Laura James.
Eugene. I know. My name's Eugene Gant.
Laura. You know, I've seen you before.
Eugene. Yes, earlier this afternoon.
Laura. I mean before that. I saw you throw those advertising cards in the gutter.
Eugene. You did?
Laura. I was coming from the station. You know where the train crosses the street? You were just standing there staring at it. I walked right by you and smiled at you. I never got such a snub before in my whole life. My, you must be crazy about trains.
Eugene. You stood right beside me? Where are you from?
Laura. Richmond, Virginia.
Eugene. Richmond! That's a big city, isn't it?
Laura. It's pretty big.
Eugene. How many people?
Laura. Oh, about a hundred and twenty thousand, I'd say.
Eugene. Are there a lot of pretty parks and boulevards?
Laura. Oh yes . . .
Eugene. And fine tall buildings, with elevators?
Laura. Yes, it's quite a metropolis.
Eugene. Theatres and things like that?
Laura. A lot of good shows come to Richmond. Are you interested in shows?
Eugene. You have a big library. Did you know it has over a hundred thousand books in it?
Laura. No, I didn't know that.
Eugene. Well, it does. I read that somewhere. It would take a long time to read a hundred thousand books, wouldn't it?
Laura. Yes, it would.
Eugene. I figure about twenty years. How many books do they let you take out at one time?
Laura. I really don't know.
Eugene. They only let you take out two here!

Laura. That's too bad.

Eugene. You have some great colleges in Virginia. Did you know that William and Mary is the second oldest college in the country?

Laura. Is it? What's the oldest?

Eugene. Harvard! I'd like to study there! First, Chapel Hill. That's our state university. Then Harvard. I'd like to study all over the world, learn all its languages. I love words, don't you?

Laura. Yes, yes, I do.

Eugene. Are you laughing at me?

Laura. Of course not.

Eugene. You are smiling a lot!

Laura. I'm smiling because I'm enjoying myself. I like talking to you.

Eugene. I like talking to you, too. I always talk better with older people.

Laura. Oh!

Eugene. They know so much more.

Laura. Like me?

Eugene. Yes. You're very interesting.

Laura. Am I?

Eugene. Oh yes! You're very interesting!

[JAKE CLATT *approaches,* FLORY MANGLE *hovering anxiously on the veranda.*]

Jake Clatt. Miss James?

Laura. Yes, Mr. Platt?

Jake Clatt. Clatt.

Laura. Clatt.

Jake Clatt. Jake Clatt! It's a lovely evening. Would you like to take a stroll?

Laura. It feels to me like it's going to rain.

Jake Clatt. [*Looking at the sky.*] Oh, I don't know.

Eugene. [*Rising, moving in between* LAURA *and* JAKE.] It's going to rain, all right.

Jake Clatt. Oh, I wouldn't be so sure!

Laura. Perhaps some other time, Mr. Clatt.

Jake Clatt. Certainly. Good night, Miss James. Good night, sonny.

[EUGENE *glares after* JAKE, *who returns to the veranda. The other boarders have disappeared.* JAKE *and* FLORRY *exit.* FATTY *and* BEN *still sit on the steps. A train whistle moans mournfully in the distance.* EUGENE *cocks an ear, listens.*]

Laura. You *do* like trains, don't you?

Eugene. Mama took us on one to St. Louis to the Fair, when I was only five. Have you ever touched one?

Laura. What?

Eugene. A locomotive. Have you put your hand on one? You have to feel things to fully understand them.

Laura. Aren't they rather hot?

Eugene. Even a cold one, standing in a station yard. You know what you feel? You feel the shining steel rails under it . . . and the rails send a message right into your hand—a message of all the mountains that engine ever passed—all the flowing rivers, the forests, the towns, all the houses, the people, the washlines flapping in the fresh cool breeze—the beauty of the people in the way they live and the way they work—a farmer waving from his field, a kid from the school yard—the faraway places it roars through at night, places you don't even know, can hardly imagine. Do you believe it? You feel the rhythm of a whole life, a whole country clicking through your hand.

Laura. [*Impressed.*] I'm not sure we all would. I believe *you* do.

[*There is a moment while* LAURA *looks at* EUGENE. BEN *moves up to the veranda and the phonograph, plays the record* "Genevieve." EUGENE *and* LAURA *speak simultaneously.*]

Eugene. How long do you plan to . . .

Laura. How old are you . . . ?

Eugene. I'm sorry—please.

[*Draws a chair close to* LAURA, *straddles it, facing her.*]

Laura. No, you.

Eugene. How long do you plan to stay, here, Miss James?

Laura. My name is Laura. I wish you'd call me that.

Eugene. Laura. It's a lovely name. Do you know what it means?

Laura. No.

Eugene. I read a book once on the meaning of names. Laura is the laurel. The Greek symbol of victory.

Laura. Victory. Maybe someday I'll live up to that! [*After a second.*] What does Eugene mean?

Eugene. Oh, I forget.

Laura. *You,* forget?

Eugene. It means "well born."

Laura. How old are you?

Eugene. Why?

Laura. I'm always curious about people's ages.

Eugene. So am I. How old are you?

Laura. I'm twenty-one. You?

Eugene. Nineteen. Will you be staying here long?

Laura. I don't know exactly.

Eugene. You're only twenty-one?

Laura. How old did you think I was?

Eugene. Oh, about that. About twenty-one, I'd say. That's not old at all!

Laura. [*Laughs.*] I don't feel it is!

Eugene. I was afraid you might think I was too young for you to waste time with like this!

Laura. I don't think nineteen is young at all!

Eugene. It isn't, really, is it?

Laura. Gene, if we keep rushing together like this, we're going to have a collision.

[LAURA *rises, moves away from* EUGENE. *He follows her. They sit together on the side steps, reaching with whispers toward each other. The turntable revolves, removing* EUGENE'S *room and revealing* GANT'S *room.*]

Fatty. Ben, what's your full name?

Ben. Benjamin Harrison Gant. Why?

Fatty. I thought Ben was short for benign.

Ben. Benign! Listen to her!

[*They laugh. The lights come up in* GANT'S *bedroom.* ELIZA, *carrying a pitcher and a glass, enters.* GANT *is in bed, turned away from her.*]

Gant. Helen?

Eliza. [*Bitterly.*] No, it's not Helen, Mr. Gant. [*Pours a glass of water.*]

Gant. [*Without turning.*] If that's water, take it away.

Eliza. Why aren't you asleep? Do you have any pain?

Gant. None but the everyday pain of thinking. You wouldn't know what that is.

Eliza. I wouldn't know?

[*She starts picking up* GANT'S *strewn clothing.*]

Gant. How could you? You're always so busy puttering.

Eliza. All the work I do around here, and you call it puttering?

Gant. Some people are doers, some are thinkers.

Eliza. Somebody has to *do,* Mr. Gant. Somebody has to. Oh! I know you look on yourself as some kind of artist fella—but personally, a man who has to be brought maudlin through the streets—screaming curses—if you call that artistic!

Gant. The hell hound is at it again. Shut up, woman!

Eliza. Mr. Gant, I came in here to see if there was something I could do for you. Only pity in my heart. Now will you please turn over and look at me when I talk to you? You know I can't stand being turned away from!

Gant. You're a bloody monster; you would drink my heart's blood!

Eliza. You don't mean that—we've come this far together, I guess we can continue to the end. You know I was thinking only this morning about the first day we met. Do

you realize it was thirty-one years ago, come July?

Gant. [*Groaning.*] Merciful God, thirty-one long miserable years.

Eliza. I can remember like it was yesterday. I'd just come down from Cousin Sally's and I passed by your shop and there you were. I'll vow you looked as big as one of your tombstones—and as dusty—with a wild and dangerous look in your eye. You were romantic in those days—like the fellow says, a regular courtin' fool—"Miss Pentland," you said, "you have come into this hot and grubby shop like a cooling, summer shower—like a cooling, summer shower." That's just what you said!

Gant. And you've been a wet blanket ever since.

Eliza. I forgive you your little jokes, Mr. Gant. I forgive your little jokes.

[*Sits beside him, finds needle and thread under her collar, mends his dressing gown.*]

Gant. Do you? [*Slowly turns and looks at her finally.*] Do you ever forgive me, Eliza? If I could make you understand something. I was such a strong man. I was dozing just now, dreaming of the past. The far past. The people and the place I came from. Those great barns of Pennsylvania. The order, the thrift, the plenty. It all started out so right, there. There I was a man who set out to get order and position in life. And what have I come to? Only rioting and confusion, searching and wandering. There was so much before, so much. Now it's all closing in. My God, Eliza, where has it all gone? Why am I here, now, at the rag end of my life? The years are all blotted and blurred—my youth a red waste—I've gotten old, an old man. But why here? Why here?

Eliza. You belong here, Mr. Gant, that's why! You belong here.

[*She touches his hand.*]

Gant. [*Throws away her hand.*] And as I get weaker and weaker, you get stronger and stronger!

Eliza. Pshaw! If you feel that way, it's because you have no position in life. If you'd ever listened to me once, things would have been different. You didn't believe me, did you, when I told you that little, old marble shop of yours would be worth a fortune someday? Will and I happened to be downtown this morning . . . [GANT *groans.*] . . . and old Mr. Beecham from the bank stopped us on the street and he said, "Mrs. Gant, the bank is looking for a site to build a big new office building, and do you know the one we have our eye on?" And I said, "No." "We have our eye on Mr. Gant's shop, and we're willing to pay twenty thousand dollars for it!" Now, what do you think of that?

Gant. And you came in here with only pity in your heart!

Eliza. Well, I'll tell you what, twenty thousand dollars is a lot of money! Like the fellow says, "It ain't hay!"

Gant. And my angel, my Carrara angel? You were going to sell her too?

Eliza. The angel, the angel, the angel. I'm so tired of hearing about that angel!

Gant. You always have been. Money dribbled from your honeyed lips, but never a word about my angel. I've started twenty pieces of marble trying to capture her. But my life's work doesn't interest you.

Eliza. If you haven't been able to do it in all these years, don't you think your gift as a stonecutter may be limited?

Gant. Yes, Mrs. Gant, it may be limited. It may be limited.

Eliza. Then why don't you sell the shop? We can pay off the mortgage at Dixieland and then just set back big as you please and live off the income from the boarders the rest of our lives!

Gant. [*Furious, he all but leaps from the bed.*] Oh holy hell! Wow-ee! The boarders! That parade of incognito pimps and prostitutes, calling themselves penniless dancing masters, pining widows, part-time teachers and God knows what all! Woman, have mercy! That shop is my last refuge on earth. I beg you—let me die in peace! You won't have long to wait. You can do what you please with it after I've gone. But give me a little comfort now. *And leave me my work.* At least my first wife understood what it meant to me. [*He sentimentally seeks the plump pillow.*] Cynthia, Cynthia . . .

Eliza. [*Coldly.*] You promised me you would never mention her name to me again. [*There is a long silence.* ELIZA *bites the sewing thread.*] Mr. Gant, I guess I never will understand you. I guess that's just the way it is. Good night. Try to get some sleep. [*She rises, tucks the bed clothes about him.*] I reckon it's like the fellow says, some people never get to understand each other—not in this life.

[ELIZA *exits, stands outside* GANT'S *door, trying to pull herself together.*]

Gant. [*Moans.*] Oh-h-h, I curse the day I was given life by that bloodthirsty monster up above. Oh-h-h, Jesus! I beg of you. I know I've been bad. Forgive me. Have

mercy and pity upon me. Give me another chance in Jesus' name. . . . Oh-h-h!

[*The turntable removes* GANT'S *room, replacing it with* EUGENE'S *room. Lights come up on the veranda.* LAURA *and* EUGENE *still sit on the side steps.* FATTY *and* BEN, *as earlier, seated, are softly laughing.* ELIZA, *bitterly warped by her scene with* GANT, *enters. She starts gathering up the boarders' coffee cups and saucers.*]

Mrs. Pert. [*A little giddy.*] Why, if it isn't Mrs. Gant! Why don't you sit down and join us for a while?

Eliza. [*Her sweeping glance takes in the beer glasses.*] I've told you before, Mrs. Pert, I don't tolerate drinking at Dixieland!

Ben. Oh, Mama, for God's sake . . .

Eliza. [*Angrily turns off the phonograph.*] You two can be heard all over the house with your carrying on.

Ben. Carrying on—listen to her!

Eliza. You're keeping the boarders awake.

Ben. They just went in!

Eliza. As I came past your door just now, Mrs. Pert, there was a light under it. If you're going to spend all night out here, there's no sense in wasting electricity.

Ben. The Lord said "Let there be light," even if it's only forty watts.

Eliza. Don't you get on your high horse with me, Ben Gant. You're not the one who has to pay the bills! If you did, you'd laugh out of the other side of your mouth. I don't like any such talk. You've squandered every penny you've ever earned because you've never known the value of a dollar!

Ben. The value of a dollar! [*Rises, goes into hall to get his jacket.*] Oh, what the hell's the use of it anyway? Come on, Fatty, let's go for a stroll.

Fatty. [*Rises.*] Whatever you say, Ben, old Fatty's willing.

Eliza. [*Attacking* MRS. PERT.] I don't want any butt-ins from you, do you understand? You're just a paying boarder here. That's all. You're not a member of my family, and never will be, no matter what low methods you try!

Eugene. [*Leaving* LAURA, *miserable.*] Mama, please!

Eliza. [*To* EUGENE.] I'm only trying to keep decency and order here, and this is the thanks I get! You should all get down on your knees and be grateful to me!

Ben. [*Coming out of hall, slamming the screen door.*] What am I supposed to be grateful for? For what?

Fatty. [*Trying to stop it.*] Ben, Ben, come on.

Ben. For selling the house that papa built with his own hands and moving us into this drafty barn where we share our roof, our food, our pleasures, our privacy so that you can be Queen Bee? Is that what I'm supposed to be grateful for?

Eliza. [*Picks up bottle and glasses.*] It's that vile liquor that's talking!

Eugene. Let's stop it! For God's sake, let's stop it! Mama, go to bed, please. Ben . . .

[EUGENE *sees that* LAURA *has exited into the house. He frantically looks after her.*]

Ben. Look at your kid there! You've had him out on the streets since he was eight years old—collecting bottles, selling papers—anything that would bring in a penny.

Eliza. Gene is old enough to earn his keep!

Ben. Then he's old enough for you to let go of him! But no, you'd rather hang on to him like a piece of property! Maybe he'll grow in value, you can turn a quick trade on him, make a profit on him. He isn't a son, he's an investment! You're so penny-mad that—

[*Shifting the bottles and glasses into one hand,* ELIZA *slaps* BEN. *There is a long silence. They stare at each other.*]

Ben. Come on, Fatty.

[BEN *exits, past* FATTY, *down the street.*]

Fatty. He didn't mean it, Mrs. Gant. [*She follows* BEN.] Ben? Ben, wait for Fatty! [*A moment's pause.*]

Eugene. [*Quietly, miserably.*] Mama. Mama. Mama!

Eliza. Well, she puts him up to it! He never used to talk to me like that. You stood right there and saw it. Now I'll just ask you: was it my fault? Well, was it?

Eugene. [*Looks after* LAURA.] Mama, Mama, in God's name go to bed, won't you? Just go to bed and forget about it, won't you?

Eliza. All of you. Every single one of you. Your father, then Ben, now you . . . you all blame me. And not one of you has any idea, any idea . . . you don't know what I've had to put up with all these years.

Eugene. Oh Mama, stop! Please stop!

Eliza. [*Sinking onto the steps.*] I've done the best I could. I've done the best I could. Your father's never given me a moment's peace. Nobody knows what I've been through with him. Nobody knows, child, nobody knows.

Eugene. [*Sits beside her.*] I know, Mama. I do know. Forget about it! It's all right!

Eliza. You just can't realize. You don't know what a day like this does to me. Ben and I used to be so close—especially after little Grover died. I don't think a mother and son were ever closer. You don't remember when he was a youngster, the little notes he was always writing me. I'd find them slipped under my door, when he got up early to go on his paper route . . . "Good morning, Mama!" . . . "Have a nice day, Mama . . ." We were so close . . .

Eugene. It's late. You're tired.

Eliza. [*Managing to pull herself together, rises.*] Well, like the fellow says, it's no use crying over *that* spilt milk. I have all those napkins and towels to iron for tomorrow.

Eugene. [*Rises, looking toward* LAURA'S *room.*] The boarders can get along without new napkins tomorrow, Mama. Why don't you get some sleep?

Eliza. Well, I tell you what: I'm not going to spend my life slaving away here for a bunch of boarders. They needn't think it. I'm going to sit back and take things as easy as any of them. One of these days you may just find us Gants living in a big house in Doak Park. I've got the lot—the best lot out there. I made the trade with old Mr. Doak himself the other day. What about that? [*She laughs.*] He said, "Mrs. Gant, I can't trust any of my agents with you. If I'm to make anything on this deal, I've got to look out. You're the sharpest trader in this town!" "Why, pshaw, Mr. Doak," I said (I never let on I believed him or anything), "all I want is a fair return on my investment. I believe in everyone making his profit and giving the other fellow a chance. Keep the ball a-rolling," I said, laughing as big as you please! [*She laughs again in recollection.*] "You're the sharpest trader in this town." That's exactly his words. Oh, dear. [EUGENE *joins her laughter.*] Well . . . I'd better get at those napkins. Are you coming in, child?

Eugene. [*Looks toward* LAURA'S *room.*] In a little while.

Eliza. Don't forget to turn off the sign. Goodnight, son. [EUGENE *returns to* ELIZA. *She kisses him.*] Get a *good* night's sleep, boy. You mustn't neglect your health.

[*She starts in.*]

Eugene. Don't work too late.

[EUGENE *starts toward the side door.*]

Eliza. Gene, you know where Sunset Terrace runs up the hill? At the top of the rise? Right above Dick Webster's place. That's my lot. You know where I mean, don't you?

Eugene. Yes, Mama.

Eliza. And that's where we'll build—right on the very top. I tell you what, though, in another five years that lot'll bring twice the value. You mark my words!

Eugene. Yes, Mama. Now, for God's sake, go and finish your work so you can get to sleep!

Eliza. No sir, they needn't think I'm going to slave away all my life. I've got plans, same as the next fellow! You'll see. [*Off stage, the church chimes start to sound the midnight hour.*] Well, good night, son.

Eugene. Good night, Mama . . . [ELIZA *exits.* EUGENE *calls with desperate softness.*] Laura . . . Laura!! [*Gives up, turns away.* LAURA *enters through the side door.* EUGENE *turns, sees her.*] Did you hear all that? I'm sorry, Laura.

Laura. What's there to be sorry about?

Eugene. Would you like to take a walk?

Laura. It's a lovely evening.

Eugene. It might rain.

Laura. I love the rain.

[EUGENE *and* LAURA *hold out their hands to each other.* EUGENE *approaches her, takes her hand. They go off together. For a moment the stage is silent.* ELIZA *enters with an envelope in her hand.*]

Eliza. See, looky here—I made a map of it. Sunset Terrace goes . . . [*She looks around.*] Gene? Eugene? [*She looks up towards* EUGENE'S *room.*] Gene, I asked you to turn out the sign! That boy. I don't know what I'm going to do with him. [ELIZA *goes into the hall, turns out the sign and stands for a moment. Offstage, a passerby is whistling "Genevieve."* ELIZA *comes down to the edge of the veranda and looks out into the night in the direction taken by* BEN *and* FATTY.] Ben? Ben?

SLOW CURTAIN

ACT TWO

SCENE I

Gant's marble yard and shop. A week later. Under a high, wide shed is the sign: W. O. GANT—STONE CARVER. *The shed is on a back street, behind the town square. In the distance can be seen the outline of Dixieland. Inside the shed are slabs of marble and granite and some finished monuments . . . an urn, a couchant lamb and several angels. The largest and most prominent monument is a delicately carved angel of a lustrous white Carrara marble, with an especially beautiful smiling countenance. There is a cutting area down stage right, protected from the sun by a shade, where* EUGENE, *wearing one of his father's aprons, is discovered operating a pedalled emery wheel. At the other side of the shed is an office with a grimy desk, a telephone, and a curtain into another room beyond. A sidewalk runs between the shed and a picket fence up stage. Near the office is a stone seat, bearing the inscription, "Rest here in peace."*

[ELIZA *enters from the street. The prim shabbiness of her dress is in contrast to her energetic mood and walk.*]

Eliza. [*Crosses to office, calls inside.*] Mr. Gant! Mr. Gant!

Eugene. [*Stops wheel, calls.*] Papa's not here now, Mama.

Eliza. [*Approaches* EUGENE *just as he accidentally blows some marble dust in her face.*] Where is he? Gene, you know I can't stand that marble dust—will you step out here where I can talk to you? [*As* EUGENE *ambles out to her.*] Besides, I can't stand not to see the face I'm talking to. My goodness, spruce up, boy—how many times do I have to tell you? Shoulders back—like you are somebody. And smile, look pleasant. [EUGENE *gives that idiotic grin.*] Oh pshaw! I hope your father's not over at you-know-where again.

Eugene. He went to buy a newspaper for the obituaries.

Eliza. How enterprising of him! But he won't follow up on it. Oh no, he says it's ghoulish to contact the bereaved ones right off. I declare, tombstones are no business anyway, anymore—in this day and age people die too slowly. [*Sinks onto stone seat, leans back, for a brief instant seems actually to rest.*] I tell you what, this feels good. I wish I had as much time as some folks and could sit outside and enjoy the air. [*Observes* EUGENE, *looking at her dress as he works lettering a marble slab.*] What are you looking at? I don't have a rent, do I?

Eugene. I was just noticing you have on your dealing and bargaining costume again.

Eliza. Eugene Gant, whatever do you mean by that? Don't I look all right? Heaven knows, I always try to look neatly respectable.

Eugene. Come on, Mama.

Eliza. What! I declare! I might have a better dress than this, but law's sake, there's some places it don't pay to advertise it! Oh, Gene, you're smart, smart, I tell you! You've got a future ahead of you, child.

Eugene. Mama, what kind of a future have I got if I can't get an education?

Eliza. Pshaw, boy, you'll get your education if my plans work out! I'll tell you what though—in the meantime, it wouldn't hurt you to work in Uncle Will's office, would it?

Eugene. I don't know anything about real estate, Mama.

Eliza. What do you have to know? Buying and selling is an instinct, and you've got it. You've got my eye for looking and seeing and remembering, and that's what's important. Why, there isn't a vital statistic about a soul in Altamont I don't carry right in my head. What they make, what they owe—what they're hiding, what they show! [*She laughs, enjoying her cleverness.*] You see, Eugene, I'm a poet, too—"a poet and I don't know it, but my feet show it—they're longfellows!" [*She leans back, chuckles.*] Oh dear, I can't get a smile out of you this morning. You've been so strange all this last week. [*Rises, slaps him on the back.*] Gene, stand with your shoulders back. If you go humped over, you'll get lung trouble sure as you're born. [*Moves upstage, looks toward the town center where she presumes* GANT *is.*] That's one thing about your papa: he always carried himself straight as a rod. Of course, he's not as straight now as he used to be—Gene, *what* in the world are you standing on one foot and then the other for? Do you have to go to the bathroom?

Eugene. Mama! Asking me that at my age!

Eliza. Then why are you fidgeting? It's not often we have a nice chance to chat like this.

Eugene. Papa's paying me thirty cents an hour!

Eliza. Paying you? How did you manage that?

Eugene. I told him I needed the money.

Eliza. For heaven's sake, what for? You've got your room and board.

Eugene. Don't you think I need new clothes, for one thing?

Eliza. Pshaw! The way you're still growing? It doesn't pay. [*She purses her lips, looks at him significantly.*] Has my baby gone and got himself a girl?

Eugene. What of it? What if it were true? Haven't I as much right as anyone?

Eliza. Pshaw! You're too young to think of girls, especially that Miss James. She's practically a mature woman compared to you. I don't think you realize how young you are, just because you're tall and read a lot of books. [*Sound of car.* ELIZA *looks off.*] Pshaw! That's your Uncle Will come for me. Say, how long does it take your father to buy a newspaper, anyway?

Eugene. He said he'd be right back. Is it something important?

Eliza. Oh, I've got plans, Gene, plans for him, plans for all of us. Well, tell him I'll be back. Second thought, don't tell him, I'll just catch him. I want you to be here too. Work hard, child!

[ELIZA *exits, the car leaves.* EUGENE *approaches the Carrara angel, touches the draped folds over her breast.* GANT *enters, watches, smiling. He has had a few beers, but he is not drunk.* EUGENE *becomes aware of his father's presence, starts guiltily.*]

Gant. I've done that myself many a time, son. Many a time. Well, what did your mother have to say?

Eugene. Did you see her?

Gant. I've been sitting over at Laughran's waiting for her to leave. What a longwinded bag!

Eugene. You promised the doctor you wouldn't go to Laughran's.

Gant. [*Putting on his apron.*] What difference does it make? A couple of beers won't hurt what I've got. Was that Will Pentland she went off with?

Eugene. Yes.

Gant. Aha! And she said she'd be back?

Eugene. Yes.

Gant. I have a mind what she's up to. She'll be back with freshly drawn-up papers tucked in her bosom. Yes, when you touch the breast of Miss Eliza, you feel the sharp crackle of bills of sale, not like the bosom of this angel. She begins to look better after a bath, doesn't she? I've been neglecting her lately. My, how she gleams!

Eugene. [*Sits below angel.*] Papa, you were young when you got married, weren't you?

Gant. What?

Eugene. When did you get married?

Gant. It was thirty-one bitter years ago when your mother first came wriggling around that corner at me like a snake on her belly. . . .

Eugene. I don't mean Mama. How old were you when you were first married? To Cynthia?

Gant. By God, you better not let your mother hear you say that name!

Eugene. I want to know . . . how old were you?

Gant. Well, I must have been twenty-eight. Ah, Cynthia, Cynthia.

Eugene. You loved her, didn't you, Papa?

Gant. She had a real glowing beauty. Sweet, noble, proud, and yet soft, soft—she died in her bloom.

Eugene. She was older than you, wasn't she?

Gant. Yes. Ten years.

Eugene. Ten years! But it didn't make any difference, did it?

Gant. [*Confidingly.*] She was a skinny, mean, tubercular old hag who nearly drove me out of my mind!

Eugene. [*Shocked.*] Then why do you talk about her the way you do? To Mama?

Gant. Because I'm a bastard, Gene. I'm a bastard! [LAURA *enters, carrying a picnic basket, her mood somewhat restless.*] Say, isn't this a pretty little somebody looking for you?

Eugene. Laura!

Laura. Hello, Mr. Gant.

Gant. Hello!

Laura. Hello, Gene. So this is your shop!

Gant. This is a real pleasure. It's not often I see *smiling* people around here. Haven't you got fed up with our little resort, young lady?

Laura. I'm really just beginning to enjoy it here.

Gant. What do you find to enjoy about it?

Laura. Oh, the countryside is beautiful. Gene and I have had lots of pleasant walks in the hills.

Gant. Oh, so it's Gene who makes it pleasant for you, hey?

Eugene. [*Taking off his apron.*] Papa!

Gant. You're fond of Gene, aren't you?

Laura. He's very nice and intelligent.

Gant. Gene's a good boy—our best.

Laura. [*Looking around.*] My, isn't this place interesting? How did you happen to become a stonecutter, Mr. Gant?

[EUGENE *studies* LAURA *during this, sensing her evasiveness.*]

Gant. Well, I guess you'd call it a passion with some people. When I was a boy Gene's age, I happened to pass a shop something like this. [*Of the angel.*] And this very angel was there. She's Carrara marble, from Italy. And as I looked at her smiling face, I felt more than anything in the world, I wanted to carve delicately with a chisel. It was as though, if I could do that, I could bring something of me out onto a piece of marble. Oh, the reminiscences of the old always bore the young.

Laura. No, they don't.

Gant. So I walked into that shop, and asked the stonecutter if I could become an apprentice. Well, I worked there for five years. When I left, I bought the angel. [*He looks at the angel with longing.*] I've hardly had her out of my sight since. I bet I've started twenty pieces of marble, but I've never been able to capture her. . . . I guess there's no use trying anymore. . . .

[*He becomes silent, morose. Sensitively,* EUGENE *touches his father's shoulder, looks at* LAURA].

Eugene. Would you like to look around, Laura?

Laura. I'm afraid I'm bothering you at your work.

Gant. [*Looks at* EUGENE, *coming out of his distant thought and mood.*] No, no. Show her about, Gene. [*Suddenly, decisive.*] I have some other things I must do . . . [*Starts toward office, pauses.*] —though some people find looking at tombstones depressing. Still, we all come to them in the end.   [GANT *exits.*]

Eugene. Why do you think you might be bothering me?

Laura. You are supposed to be working.

Eugene. You came here to see me. What's happened, Laura? Something's different today.

Laura. Oh, don't pay any attention to me. I just . . . I don't know.

Eugene. What's in the basket?

Laura. I asked Helen to pack us a picnic lunch.

Eugene. Good! Let's go!

Laura. [*Puts basket on marble slab.*] Not now.

Eugene. [*Puts his arm around her.*] What is it, Laura? What's the matter? Have I done something wrong?

Laura. [*Shakes her head.*] Gene, Helen knows about us! And your father too.

Eugene. I don't care—I want the whole world to know. [*Picks up basket.*] Here, let's go.

Laura. No. Let's not talk about it. [*Sits on stool, near slab.*] This is pretty marble. Where's it from?

Eugene. Laura, you don't give a damn where that marble came from!

Laura. [*Starts to cry.*] Oh, Gene, I'm so ashamed, so ashamed.

Eugene. [*Sits beside her on slab.*] Laura, my darling, what is it?

Laura. Gene, I lied to you—I'm twenty-three years old.

Eugene. Is that all?

Laura. You're not nineteen either. You're seventeen.

Eugene. I'm a thousand years old, all the love I've stored up for you.

[*Again puts his arms around her.*]

Laura. [*Struggling away.*] I'm an older woman. . . .

Eugene. In God's name, what does that have to do with us?

Laura. There have to be rules!

Eugene. Rules are made by jealous people. They make rules to love by so even those with no talent for it can at least pretend. We don't need rules. We don't have to pretend. Oh, Laura, my sweet, what we have is so beautiful, so rare . . . how often in life can you find it?

Laura. [*Escaping his arms, rises.*] Eugene, you're a young boy, a whole world just waiting for you.

Eugene. You are my world, Laura. You always will be. Don't let anything destroy us. Don't leave me alone. I've always been alone.

Laura. It's what you want, dear. It's what you'll always want. You couldn't stand anything else. You'd get so tired of me. You'll forget—you'll forget.

Eugene. I'll never forget. I won't live long enough. [*Takes her in his arms, kisses her.*] Will you forget?

Laura. [*As he holds her.*] Oh my darling, every word, every touch, how could I?

Eugene. Then nothing has changed. Has it? Has it?

Madame Elizabeth's Voice. [*Off.*] Good morning!

[MADAME ELIZABETH, *38, the town madame, enters along the street. She is well clad, carries herself stylishly. She sees* EUGENE *and* LAURA, *stops.* EUGENE *and* LAURA *break from each other.*]

Eugene. Good morning, Madame Elizabeth.

Madame Elizabeth. Is Mr. Gant here?

Eugene. He's inside.

Madame Elizabeth. Well, don't let me keep you from what you're doing. [*Approaches office, calls.*] Mr. Gant!

[LAURA *and* EUGENE *exit into yard.*

GANT, *changed into a better pair of trousers, tying his tie, enters.*]

Gant. Elizabeth, my dear Elizabeth! Well, this is a surprise!

[*Seizes her hands.*]

Madame Elizabeth. [*Sentimentally looking him over.*] Six years, W.O. Six years—except to nod to. Time, what a thief you are.

Gant. He hasn't stolen from you—you're still as handsome and stylish as ever. Won't you sit down?

Madame Elizabeth. Oh, W.O.—you and your gallant manners. But I'm no chicken any more, and no one knows it better than I do. If you only knew how often we talk about you up on Eagle Crescent. What a man you were! Wild! Bacchus himself. You remember the song you used to sing?

Gant. Life was many songs in those days, Elizabeth.

Madame Elizabeth. But when you got liquored up enough—don't you remember? Of course I can't boom it out like you do.

[*Sings, imitating* GANT. GANT *joins her.*]

"Up in that back room, boys,
Up in *that* back room,
All those kisses and those hugs,
Among the fleas and bugs.
In the evening's gloom, boys,
I pity your sad doom.
Up in that back room, boys,
Up in *that* back room."

[*They both laugh.* GANT *gives her an affectionate fanny-slap.*]

Gant. The loss of all that—that's the worst, Elizabeth.

Madame Elizabeth. [*Sitting on the bench.*] Oh, W.O., W.O.! We do miss you.

Gant. [*Joining her on the bench.*] How are all the girls, Elizabeth?

Madame Elizabeth. [*Suddenly distressed.*] That's what I came to see you about. I lost one of them last night.

[*Takes handkerchief from her pocket, quietly cries into it.*]

Gant. Oh. I'm sorry to hear that.

Madame Elizabeth. Sick only three days. I'd have done anything in the world for her. A doctor and two trained nurses by her all the time.

Gant. Too bad. Too bad. Which one was it?

Madame Elizabeth. Since your time, W.O. We called her Lily.

Gant. Tch . . . tch . . . tch. Lily.

Madame Elizabeth. I couldn't have loved her more if she had been my own daughter. Twenty-two, a child, a mere child. And not a relative who would do anything for her. Her mother died when she was thirteen, and her father is a mean old bastard who wouldn't even come to her deathbed.

Gant. He will be punished.

Madame Elizabeth. As sure as there's a God in heaven—the old bastard! I hope he rots! Such a fine girl, such a bright future for her. She had more opportunities than I ever had—and you know what I've done here. I'm a rich woman today, W.O. Why, not even your wife owns more property than I do. I beg your pardon—I hope you don't mind my speaking of her—— [GANT *gestures to go right ahead.*] Mrs. Gant and I both understand that property is what makes a person hold one's head up! And Lily could have had all that too. Poor Lily! No one knows how much I'll miss her.

[*A moment's quiet.* GANT *is respecting her grief.*]

Gant. I suppose you'll be wanting something for her grave? [*As* MADAME ELIZABETH *nods, he rises.*] Here's a sweet lamb . . . *couchant* lamb, it's called. *Couchant* means lying-down in French. That should be appropriate.

Madame Elizabeth. No, I've already made up my mind. . . . [*Rises, moves toward the Carrara angel.*] I want that angel.

Gant. You don't want *her,* Elizabeth. Why, she's a white elephant. Nobody can afford to buy her!

Madame Elizabeth. I can and I want her.

Gant. My dear Elizabeth, I have other fine angels. What about this one? My own carving.

Madame Elizabeth. No. Ever since I first saw that angel, I thought, when somebody who means something to me goes, she's going to be on the grave.

Gant. That angel's not for sale, Elizabeth.

Madame Elizabeth. Then why should you have her out here?

Gant. The truth is, I've promised her to someone.

Madame Elizabeth. I'll buy her from whoever you promised and give them a profit. Cash on the line. Who did you sell it to?

Gant. My dear Madame Elizabeth. Here is a nice expensive Egyptian urn. Your beloved Lily would like that.

Madame Elizabeth. Egyptian urns—pah! Pea pots! I want the angel!

Gant. [*With growing intensity.*] It's not for sale! Anything you like . . . *everything* you like . . . I'll give it to you. . . . I'll make you a present, for old times' sake. But not my angel!

Madame Elizabeth. Now let's not waste any more time over this. How much, W.O.?

Gant. She's Carrara marble from Italy, and too good for any whore! [*He calls.*] Eugene . . . Eugene!

Madame Elizabeth. [*Furious.*] Why you old libertine, how dare you speak to me like that?

Eugene. [*Entering, with* LAURA.] What is it, father? What's the matter?

Madame Elizabeth. Your father's a stubborn old nut, that's what!

Gant. [*Crosses toward office, turns.*] I'm sorry if I've offended you.

Madame Elizabeth. You have, W.O., deeply!

Gant. Gene, will you be so kind and see if you can wait upon the Madame?

[*Exits into the inner room of the office.*]

Madame Elizabeth. I've heard the trouble your mother has with the old terror—now I believe it! All I'm asking is that he sells me that angel—for one of my dear girls who's gone—a dear, young girl in the flower of her life . . . [*Of* LAURA.] . . . like this young girl here.

Eugene. Madame Elizabeth, I believe Papa is saving that angel for his own grave.

Madame Elizabeth. [*Sits on bench.*] Oh-h-h, why didn't he say so? Why didn't he tell me? Poor, poor W.O. Well, of course in that case. . . . [*She partially recovers. To* LAURA.] If you were to think of *your* death, dear—if you can, I mean, and we never know, we never know—is there something here that would appeal to you?

Laura. [*Looks around.*] I like the little lamb.

Madame Elizabeth. Lambs are for children, aren't they?

Eugene. [*Stoops behind lamb.*] Lambs are for anybody. Put your hand on it. Feel it. [*He takes* MADAME ELIZABETH'S *hand, strokes it across the lamb.*] Isn't it cool and content and restful? And you could have a poem engraved on the base.

Madame Elizabeth. A poem. . . .

Eugene. Let's see if we can find something you'd like. [*Picks up book.*] Here's a book of Fifty Fine Memorial Poems. [MADAME ELIZABETH *still strokes the lamb.* EUGENE *finds a poem.*] See if you like this. . . .

[*Reads.*]

"She went away in beauty's flower,
Before her youth was spent;
Ere life and love had lived their hour,
God called her and she went."

[MADAME ELIZABETH *sobs.*]

"Yet whispers faith upon the wind;
No grief to her was given.

She left your love and went to find
A greater one in heaven."
Madame Elizabeth. [*Quoting, through her heartfelt tears.*]
"She left *your* love and went to find
A greater one in heaven. . . ."
[*Rises, addresses* EUGENE.] I hope you never lose someone you love, boy. Well, let me know when the little lying-down lamb is ready.
[*She nods with majestic dignity to* LAURA, *exits.* WILL *and* ELIZA *enter, look off in the direction taken by* MADAME ELIZABETH.]
Eliza. Don't stare after her, Will! You know who that is. [*To* EUGENE.] Was that shameless woman here to see your father?
Eugene. One of the girls at Eagle Crescent died. She bought a monument.
Eliza. Oh she did! She bought one! Well, your father certainly has to deal with all kinds of people. Will, go in and tell Mr. Gant that we're here. [WILL *exits.* ELIZA *looks at* LAURA.] Oh, Miss James! It's five minutes to dinner time at Dixieland, and you know the rules about being late.
Eugene. [*Crosses to pick up basket.*] Laura and I are going on a picnic.
Eliza. Not now you're not. [*To* LAURA.] My dear, I want to talk privately to Mr. Gant—to Eugene, too, and I've asked Ben to join us.
Eugene. We've made plans, Mama.
Eliza. Son, this is a family conference.
Laura. Gene, please—I'll wait for you over at Woodruff's. Please.
[LAURA *and* EUGENE *stroll off, whispering.* WILL *enters from office, paring his nails.*]
Eliza. Is he in there?
Will. He's there. We've got him cornered.
[*They chuckle.* BEN, *looking feverish and ill, enters.*]
Ben. Hello, Uncle Will. Hello, Mama—you look like you just swallowed fifty or a hundred acres. What did you buy today?
Eliza. Now, Ben, it just happens that today we're selling—I hope we are anyway.
Ben. What's it all about?
Eliza. You just sit down there. I may not need you, but I want you to be here.
Ben. [*Sits beneath the angel.*] I hope it won't take long.
[GANT *enters. He wears a coat of carefully brushed black wool, a tie, and carries his hat, which he leaves just inside the office.*]
Gant. Good morning, Miss Eliza.

Eliza. My, how elegant! Aren't we burning a river this morning?
Gant. I heard you were out here, Miss Eliza. I so seldom have a visit from you!
[*He gestures the tribute.*]
Eliza. That's most gracious. You may all sit down now. Gene! Will! [EUGENE *enters, sits.* WILL *sits on office step.* GANT *moves a chair center.*] Now, Mr. Gant. . . .
Gant. [*As he sits.*] This isn't one of your temperance meetings?
Eliza. [*A bit surprised.*] Our private temperance problem—that's a part of it, yes. Mr. Gant, how old are you?
Gant. I've lost track.
Eliza. You're sixty years old in December. And if Dr. Maguire were here, he could tell you . . .
Gant. I've heard what Doc Maguire has to tell me. I shouldn't be lifting these marbles. I shouldn't be drinking liquor. I should take a nice, long rest.
Eliza. Then you save me a great deal of argument about that. Now, Gene . . .
Eugene. Yes, Mama?
Eliza. You want to go to college, don't you?
Eugene. Very much.
Eliza. Well, I figure that four years at Chapel Hill will cost thirty-four hundred dollars—but of course you'll have to wait on tables. Otherwise it would be forty-four hundred dollars, which is ridiculous—at the moment we don't even have thirty-four hundred dollars.
Gant. Oh, for God's sake, get to the point, Miss Eliza. Have you got the papers from the bank?
Eliza. [*Stands in front of him.*] Why, what do you mean, what papers?
Gant. You know what I mean. Fish for them, woman! [*Pointing to her bosom.*] Go ahead, fish for them.
[ELIZA *turns her back, from her bosom fishes out a large envelope.* GANT *laughs, a roaring bitter laugh, leaps up to* EUGENE, *who joins the laughter.*]
Eliza. [*Angrily.*] What in the world are you two hyenas laughing at?
Gant. Oh, as you would say, Miss Eliza, that's a good one, that's a *good* one.
Eliza. Well, I am glad to see you in a *good mood.*
Gant. So the bank wants this little old lot, here? That's what you told me, didn't you? Though I can't for the life of me see why.
Will. There's a new business street going through here in a few months.
Gant. Let me see the check.
Eliza. [*Takes check from envelope, hands*

it to him.] Well, it's for twenty thousand dollars. Will had to guarantee it personally for me to bring it here. Did you ever see anything like it. Two–zero–comma–zero–zero–zero–decimal–zero–zero!

Gant. W. O. Gant. It seems to be in good order all right.

Eliza. Well, it is—and Will's looked over this deed, and it's all in order too, isn't it, Will? [*Hands the deed to* GANT.] Give me your pen, Will.

Will. [*Hands* ELIZA *the pen.*] And I just had it filled.

Gant. [*Examining the deed.*] This fine print . . . I really do need glasses.

Eliza. [*Puts pen on work table.*] You can trust Will. He's been all over it, Mr. Gant!

Gant. [*Looks at angel.*] What about the marble stock and the monuments?

Eliza. They's not included.

Eugene. Papa—the years you've spent here . . . all your fine work. Please don't give it up!

Eliza. Now, Gene, your father knows what he's doing.

Eugene. But he's such a fine stonecutter!

Gant. You think my work is fine, son?

Eugene. Isn't it, Ben?

[GANT *crosses down right into the marble yard, looking about.*]

Eliza. Your father knows his duty to all of us—and to himself.

Eugene. There isn't a cemetery in the state that isn't filled with his work—you can always recognize it. Clean, and pure, and beautiful. Why should he give it up?

Eliza. Why, law, I don't say he should give it up entirely. He can have another little shop further out of town!

Eugene. But he's too old to transplant now, Mama. This is his street. Everyone knows him here. People pass by. Mr. Jannadeau's shop next door, and Woodruff's across the way—all the people and places Papa knows!

Gant. And Tim Laughran's down the block!

Eliza. [*Crosses down to* GANT.] Oh, yes. That's another reason for getting rid of this place. Put yourself out of temptation's way, Mr. Gant.

Gant. [*Sits on slab.*] I certainly do love it here.

Eugene. Don't give it up, Papa!

Ben. What do you want to do to him, Mama?

Eliza. Now looky here—you are a fine stonecutter—why, haven't I always said so?

But it's time you rested. You want to live a long time, don't you?

[*Sits beside him on slab.*]

Gant. Well, sometimes I'm not sure.

Eliza. Well, you do—and I want you to live a long time—we all want to! People can talk about a short but sweet life, but we all want to live! Look at me, I'm fifty-seven years old. I've borne nine children, raised six of them, and worked hard all my life. I'd like to back up and rest a little myself. And we can, Mr. Gant. If you'll just sign that little slip of paper. I guarantee, in a year from now, you'll have completely forgotten this dingy, crooked, dusty yard. Won't he, Ben? Won't he? Ben!

Ben. Some people have trouble forgetting some things, Mama.

Eliza. Why pshaw, I'm going to *see* to it that he forgets it. I'll have time to look after you. Won't I, Mr. Gant?

Gant. You're right about one thing, Miss Eliza, that I can't dispute. You have worked hard. [*Rises, moves to center work table.*]

Eugene. Papa, please, don't do it.

[GANT *sits at work table, signs the deed.* ELIZA *crosses to him, picks it up.*]

Eliza. Thank you, Mr. Gant. Now the check. You know what I'm going to do? I'm going to plan a great, glorious celebration. [*Gives the deed to* WILL, *speaks to* EUGENE.] We'll ask your brother Luke to come home, if the Navy will let him out. And we'll invite Stevie, and Daisy and her husband, too, except if she brings those whiny children of hers. [*Notices* GANT *just looking at the check.*] Turn it over, Mr. Gant. Sign it on the back.

Gant. Why do I have to sign it?

Eliza. Endorse it, that's all. W. O. Gant, like it's written on the front of check.

Gant. That can wait until I offer it, can't it?

Eliza. To clear the check, Mr. Gant!

Gant. I'm not used to these things. How do you clear it?

Eliza. You sign it—I'll deposit it in the Dixieland account, then we draw checks on it.

Gant. We?

Eliza. Yes. You draw what you want. I'll draw what we need for Gene's college—for Dixieland, and for anything else we need.

Gant. [*Rises, crosses to office.*] I think I'll wait to cash it until I get to Chapel Hill. The bank has a branch there, doesn't it, Will? [*Gives* WILL *his pen.*]

Eliza. Why would you want to cash it in Chapel Hill?

Gant. This is my check, isn't it? I'm the one who had the foresight to buy this little pie-cornered lot thirty-one years ago for four hundred dollars . . . money from the estate of Cynthia L. Gant, deceased. I guess I'm entitled to the profit.

Eliza. Now, Mr. Gant, if you're thinking to get my dander up . . .

Gant. [*Picks up hat, puts it on.*] Miss Eliza, I've been wanting to get away from here for a long time. I'm taking Gene with me. [*Crosses to* EUGENE.] I'm going to put him in that college there at Chapel Hill.

Eugene. Now?

Gant. Now! And then I'm going to travel . . . and when Gene's free in the summer, we'll travel together. [*Crosses back to* ELIZA.] And there's nothing in this whole wide world that you're going to do to stop me. And I can just see the word Dixieland forming on your cursed lips. What about Dixieland? Nothing for Dixieland? *No, not one God Damn red cent!* You've plenty of property of your own you can sell. If it's rest and comfort you really want, sell it, woman, sell it! But I think you like working hard, because then that makes us all feel sorry for you. And I do feel sorry for you too, from the bottom of my heart. [*Puts check in pocket.*] Well, Eugene?

Eugene. Papa, I can't go now.

Gant. Why not? You haven't got any better clothes . . . so you might as well go as you are. I guess we'll say our goodbyes. [*Addresses the angel.*] So long, dear Carrara angel. I'll arrange for us to be together again some day. [*Shakes hands with* BEN.] Goodbye, Ben—— Tell Helen—tell Helen I'll write to her.

Eliza. [*Leaping at* GANT.] I won't let you do this. I won't let you.

Eugene. Mama!

Eliza. [*Seizes check from* GANT'S *pocket, tears it up, flings it on the ground.*] All right, all right, all right! There's your check. I guess there's nothing to prevent you from going to the bank and trying to get another check, but it won't work because I'm going to put an injunction against you. I'll prove you're not responsible to sell this property, or even to own it. I'll get guardianship over you! Everyone knows the times you've been to the cure—the threats you've made to me . . . the times you've tried to kill me—I'll tell them. You're a madman, Mr. Gant, a madman. You're not going to get away with this. I'll fight you tooth and nail, tooth and nail. And I'll win.

[*Trembling, she picks up her handbag from the stone seat.*]

Gant. All the things you've said about me are true, Eliza. I've only brought you pain. Why don't you let me go?

Eliza. Because you're my husband, Mr. Gant! You're my husband. Thirty-one years together and we'll go on—we must go on. A house divided against itself cannot stand. We must try to understand and love each other. We must try. . . . [ELIZA *exits.*]

Gant. [*Quietly.*] Take her home, will you, Will?

[WILL *hurries after* ELIZA. *A long moment.* BEN, *weak and feverish, dries his forehead with his handkerchief.* GANT *sinks into a chair.*]

Gant. Eugene, go over to Laughran's and get me a bottle. You heard me.

Eugene. No, Papa.

Gant. Are you still padding along after your mother?

Ben. Leave Gene alone. If you want to get sick, do it yourself.

Gant. Ungrateful sons! Oh, the sad waste of years, the red wound of all our mistakes. [GANT *rises, exits.* EUGENE *looks after his father.*]

Ben. The fallen Titan. He might have succeeded if he hadn't tried to take you. He could still make it, but he won't try again.

Eugene. They loved each other once. They must have had one moment in time that was perfect. What happened? It frightens me, Ben. How can something so perfect turn into this torture?

Ben. They're strangers. They don't know each other. No one ever really comes to know anyone.

Eugene. That's not true. I know you— I know Laura.

Ben. Listen to him! No matter what arms may clasp us, what heart may warm us, what mouth may kiss us, we remain strangers. We never escape it. Never, never, never.

[*Closes eyes, leans back.*]

Eugene. Ben! Hey, Ben? [*Worriedly crosses down to* BEN, *feels his face.*] Ben, you're burning up! Come on . . . [*Tries to lift him.*] Put your arms around me. I'm going to take you home.

Ben. [*Sinks back.*] Can't. It's all right, I'm just tired.

Eugene. Why didn't you tell somebody you're sick, you crazy idiot!

[EUGENE *again tries to lift* BEN.]

Ben. To hell with them, Gene. To hell with them all. Don't give a damn for anything. Nothing gives a damn for you. There are a lot of bad days, there are a lot of good ones—— [EUGENE *rushes into the office, picks up the telephone.*] that's all there is

. . . a lot of days. . . . My God, is there no freedom on this earth?

Eugene. [*Into telephone.*] Get me Dr. Maguire quickly. *It's my brother Ben!*

Ben. [*Stirs, in anguish, looks up at the Carrara angel.*] And still you smile. . . .

CURTAIN

ACT TWO

SCENE II

The Dixieland Boarding House. It is the next night; a painful tenseness grips the house.

[LAURA *and* EUGENE *sit together on the yard seat.* MRS. PERT *sits motionless in her rocker near the front door.* HUGH *slowly walks about. The inside hall is lighted, as is* BEN'S *room, which we see for the first time. There* DR. MAGUIRE *and* HELEN *are hovering over* BEN'S *still body.* GANT *is at the hall telephone.*]

Gant. [*Shouting into telephone.*] Second class seaman, Luke Gant. G-A-N-T—Gant! [*Angrily.*] I don't know why you can't hear me.

Hugh. [*Crosses to door.*] W.O., you don't have to shout because it's long distance.

Gant. Shut up, Hugh, I know what I'm doing. [*Into telephone.*] Do what? I am standing back from the telephone. All right, all right. . . . [*Moves telephone away from him, lower.*] Can you hear me now? Of all the perversities. Very well, I will repeat. Yesterday I sent a telegram to my son, Luke Gant, to come home, that his brother Ben has pneumonia. Can you tell me if—oh, he did leave? Why didn't he let us know? All right! Thank you. Thank you very much.

[*Hangs up, joins the others on the veranda.*]

Hugh. They gave him leave?

Gant. If he made good connections he ought to be here by now.

Hugh. Ben'll be all right, W.O.

Gant. I remember when little Grover was ill in St. Louis, and Eliza sent for me. I didn't get there on time.

[*Sits on yard stool.* ELIZA *enters from the house.*]

Eliza. Did you reach him?

Gant. He's on his way.

Eliza. It's all nonsense, of course. Ben is far from dying. But you do like to dramatize, Mr. Gant. Still, it will be good to see Luke. . . .

Eugene. [*Crosses to* ELIZA.] Mama, when can I see Ben?

Eliza. When the doctor says. I'll tell you what: when you go in there, don't make out like Ben is sick. Just make a big joke of it—laugh as big as you please——

Eugene. [*Groans.*] Mama!

Eliza. Well, it's the sick one's frame of mind that counts. I remember when I was teaching school in Hominy township, I had pneumonia. Nobody expected me to live, but I did . . . I got through it somehow. I remember one day I was sitting down—I reckon I was convalescing, as the fella says. Old Doc Fletcher had been there—and as he left I saw him shake his head at my cousin Sally. "Why, Eliza, what on earth," she says, just as soon as he had gone, "he tells me you're spitting up blood every time you cough; you've got consumption as sure as you live!" "Pshaw!" I said. I remember I was just determined to make a big joke of it. "I don't believe a word of it," I said. "Not one single word." And it was because I didn't believe it that *I got well.*

Gant. [*Quietly.*] Eliza, don't run on so.

Helen. [*Appears on veranda.*] The doctor says Mama can come in for a few minutes, but no one else yet.

Eugene. How is he?

Helen. You know Dr. Maguire. If you can get anything out of him. . . .

[ELIZA *takes a big breath; she and* HELEN *go into house.*]

Gant. Oh God, I don't like the feel of it. I don't like the feel of it.

Ben. [*Weakly.*] Maguire, if you don't stop hanging over me I'll smother to death.

Maguire. [*To* ELIZA *and* HELEN *as they enter.*] With both of you in here soaking up oxygen, leave that door open.

[ELIZA *advances slowly to* BEN, *swallows a gasp at the sight of the tortured, wasted body.* BEN'S *eyes are closed.*]

Helen. Mama's here, Ben.

Eliza. [*Speaking as though to a baby.*] Why hello, son—did you think I wasn't ever coming in to see you?

Helen. [*After a pause.*] Ben, Mama's here.

Eliza. [*To* MAGUIRE.] Can't he talk? Why doesn't he look at me?

Maguire. Ben, you can hear what's going on, can't you?

Ben. [*Quietly, his eyes still closed.*] I wish you'd all get out and leave me alone.

Eliza. What kind of talk is that? You have to be looked after, son!

Ben. Then let Mrs. Pert look after me.

Helen. Ben!

Ben. Maguire, where's Fatty? I want to see Fatty.

Helen. Ben, how can you talk that way? Your mother and your sister! If it weren't for that woman you wouldn't be sick now. Drinking, carousing with her night after night——

Ben. [*Yells with dwindling strength.*] Fatty! Fatty!

[*On the veranda,* MRS. PERT *stands quickly, then enters house.*]

Helen. [*To* BEN.] You ought to be ashamed of yourself.

Dr. Maguire. Mrs. Gant, we need some more cold cloths. Why don't you . . .

Helen. [*Angrily to* MAGUIRE.] Fiend! Do you have to add to her misery? When you need something, ask me.

[ELIZA, *starting out of* BEN's *room, meets* MRS. PERT *in doorway.* MRS. PERT *hesitates.*]

Dr. Maguire. That's all right, Mrs. Pert.

Ben. [*Immediately turns toward her.*] Fatty?

Dr. Maguire. Ben seems to want you here, that's all I care about. [*To* HELEN.] You'll be called if you're needed.

Helen. This is the last time you come into this house, Dr. Maguire!

[HELEN *leaves the room. Outside* BEN's *door* ELIZA *hands some cold cloths to* HELEN. HELEN *reenters* BEN's *room, places them on the bureau.*]

Ben. Fatty, stay by me. Sing to me. "A Baby's Prayer at Twilight" . . .

Fatty. [*Sitting beside him.*] Sh-h-h, Ben. Be quiet, dear. Save yourself.

Ben. Hold my hand, Fatty.

Fatty. [*Takes his hand, sings.*]
"Just a baby's prayer at twilight
When lights are low
A baby's years
Are filled with tears
Hmmmm hmmmm hmmmm."

[*Hearing the voice,* EUGENE *stands, looks up toward* BEN's *room.* HELEN *and* ELIZA *appear on the veranda,* HELEN *comforting her mother.*]

Eugene. How does he seem, Mama?

Eliza. He couldn't stand to see me worrying. That's what it was, you know. He couldn't stand to see me worrying about him.

Gant. [*Groaning.*] Oh Jesus, it's fearful —that this should be put on me, old and sick as I am——

Helen. [*In blazing fury.*] You shut your mouth this minute, you damned old man. I've spent my life taking care of you! Everything's been done for you—everything —and you'll be here when we're all gone . . . so don't let us hear anything about your sickness, you selfish old man—it makes me furious!

Dr. Maguire. [*Appearing on veranda.*] If any of you are interested, Ben is a little better.

Eugene. Thank God!

Helen. Ben is better? Why didn't you say so before?

Eliza. I could have told you! I could have told you! I had a feeling all along!

Dr. Maguire. [*Crosses down steps.*] I'll be back in a little while.

Gant. Well! We can all relax now.

Dr. Maguire. [*Motions* EUGENE *away from the others.*] Eugene, it's both lungs now. I can't tell them. But see to it that they stay around. I'm going next door and phone for some oxygen. It may ease it a little for him. It won't be long.

[*He gives* EUGENE *a fond, strengthening touch, exits.*]

Gant. What about Luke? Luke'll be furious when he finds out he came all this way for nothing!

Eliza. For nothing? You call Ben's getting well "for nothing"?

Gant. Oh, you know what I mean, Miss Eliza. I'm going to take a little nap.

Eliza. You're going to take a little nip, that's what you mean.

Gant. You can come up and search my room if you don't believe me.

[*Exits into house.* EUGENE *stands, dazed and miserable. He forces himself during the following scene.* JAKE *and* FLORRY *enter from rear veranda.*]

Eliza. [*Excitedly.*] Mr. Clatt, Miss Mangle—did you hear? Ben is getting better! The crisis is past!

Jake. We're so happy for you, Mrs. Gant.

Eliza. I knew all along—something told me. Oh, not that he didn't have a very high fever—I admit that—but my second sense . . .

Luke. [*Off.*] Hello—o—o there!

Eliza. [*Peering off.*] Luke! [*Rushes down steps.*] Luke! Luke Gant!

[*The boarders melt into the background as* LUKE GANT, *wearing a Navy uniform, carrying a lightly packed duffle bag, enters. He is attractive, slight, lighted by an enormous love of humor and life, and adored by everyone. He is the son who got away early, but he still carries the marks of a distressing childhood; he stutters sometimes.*]

Luke. Mama, Mama!

[*Swings her around.*]

Hugh. Well, if it isn't the sailor himself! How are you?

Luke. [*Shaking hands with* HUGH.] I'm fine, Hugh! How goes it?

Eliza. Aren't you going to kiss your old mother?

Luke. Old? You're getting younger and stronger by the minute. [*Kisses her.*]

Eliza. I am, I am, son. I feel it—now that Ben's going to get well.

Luke. The old boy is better?

Helen. Luke!

Luke. Helen!

Helen. [*Leaps into his arms.*] How's my boy?

Luke. S-s-slick as a puppy's belly. I thought you all might need cheering up. I brought you some ice cream from Woodruff's!

[*Gives carton of ice cream to* HELEN.]

Helen. Naturally, you wouldn't be Luke Gant if you didn't!

Eugene. [*Crosses to* LUKE.] Welcome home, Luke!

Luke. [*They shake hands.*] My God, doesn't anybody buy you any clothes—and look at that hair. Mama, he looks like an orphan! Cut off those damn big feet of his, he'd go up in the air!

Eugene. How long have you got, Luke?

Luke. Can you s-s-stand me for twenty-four hours? [*Sees* LAURA.] Who's this?

Eliza. That's Miss James from Virginia. Laura, this is another of my sons, Luke Gant.

Laura. [*Shaking hands.*] How do you do, Mr. Gant?

Luke. How do you do?

Eliza. [*Drawing* LUKE *away.*] All right, just come along here, and behave yourself.

Helen. I'd better dish up the ice cream before it melts. [*Exits into house.*]

Luke. [*Calling after* HELEN.] Maybe Ben would like some. I got pistachio especially for him.

Eliza. Tell your father the admiral is here!

Luke. Can I see Ben, now?

Eliza. Well, the truth is, that Mrs. Pert is in there with him now.

Luke. Mrs. Pert is?

[*Looks at the others.*]

Hugh. I wouldn't go into it, Luke. It's a somewhat "fraught" subject.

Luke. Oh boy, oh boy, I know what that is! Still the same old happy household?

[LUKE *and* ELIZA *sit on the veranda edge.*]

Eliza. Nonsense. I have nothing against the woman except she's getting too many ideas that she's a fixture here. First thing in the morning I'm going to ask her to move.

Luke. Doesn't she pay her rent?

Eliza. Oh, she pays it.

Luke. [*Laughs.*] Then you're never going to ask her to move—don't kid me! The paying customers are what count around here! Aren't they, Mama?

Eliza. Luke Gant, there are certain standards I have to keep up, for the reputation of Dixieland!

Luke. [*Never unkindly.*] What kind of standards? The old dope fiend who hung himself in the same bedroom where Ben had to sleep for eight years after he cut him down? And all those amateur femme fatales who bask under your protection here, waylaying us in the hall, the bathroom—— Mama, we never had a s-s-safe moment! And people think you find out about life in the Navy!

Eliza. [*Playfully.*] I'm warning you, Luke! It's a good thing I know you're teasing.

[HELEN *enters with plates, dishes up ice cream.*]

Luke. Remember the early morning when Ben and Gene and I used to take the paper route together, remember, Gene? Old Ben used to make up stories for us about all the sleeping people in all the sleeping houses! He always used to throw the papers as lightly as he could because he hated to wake them. Remember, Gene?

Helen. And that book of baseball stories Ben used to read to us by the hour—what was it, Gene?

Eugene. [*In tears.*] *You know me, Al,* by Ring Lardner.

Eliza. [*Leaping to* EUGENE.] Eugene. Child, what is it? What is it!

[MRS. PERT *enters hurriedly.*]

Mrs. Pert. Mrs. Gant! Mrs. Gant!

Helen. What is it, Mrs. Pert?

Mrs. Pert. He can't get his breath!

Hugh. Gene, get the doctor!

[HELEN *and* ELIZA *follow* MRS. PERT *into the house.*]

Eliza. You ridiculous woman! The doctor said he was better.

[EUGENE *exits to get* MAGUIRE. GANT *enters through side door.*]

Gant. What the hell's all the commotion about? [*Sees* LUKE.] Luke! Welcome home!

Luke. [*As they shake hands.*] Papa—Ben's not doing so well.

Gant. Jesus, have mercy! That I should have to bear this in my old age. Not another one—first Grover, now Ben . . .

Luke. For God's sake, Papa, try to behave decently, for Ben's sake!

[EUGENE *and* DOC MAGUIRE *enter hurriedly.*]

Gant. [*Seizing the* DOCTOR.] Maguire, you got to save him—you got to save him.

[MAGUIRE *pushes past* GANT *into the house, enters* BEN'S *room where the three women are gathered,* MRS. PERT *standing nearest* BEN *at the head of the bed.*]

Maguire. You women step back, give him air. [*Bends over* BEN.]

Gant. [*Collapsing onto the steps.*] When the old die, no one cares. But the young . . . the young . . .

Eugene. [*Sits beside him.*] I would care, Papa.

Ben. It's one way—to step out of—the photograph—isn't it, Fatty?

Fatty. Hush, Ben, don't say that!

Helen. [*To the* DOCTOR.] There must be something you can do!

Maguire. [*Straightens up.*] Not all the king's horses, not all the doctors in the world can help him now.

Helen. Have you tried everything? Everything?

Maguire. My dear girl! He's drowning! Drowning!

Eliza. [*In deep pain.*] Mrs. Pert, you're standing in my place . . .

[MRS. PERT *moves away.* ELIZA *steps close to* BEN, *sits.*]

Eliza. Ben—son.

[*She reaches to touch him. His head turns toward her, drops. There is a last rattling, drowning sound.* BEN *dies.* MAGUIRE *checks his heart.*]

Maguire. It's over. It's all over.

[HELEN, *racked, exits toward the veranda.* MRS. PERT *puts the socks she has been knitting at* BEN'S *feet and exits upstairs.* HELEN *enters the veranda, tries to stifle her sobs.*]

Helen. He's gone. Ben's gone.

[HELEN *falls into* EUGENE'S *arms.* MAGUIRE, *carrying his doctor's bag, appears in the hall, puts a match to his chewed cigar.*]

Eugene. [*Crossing up to* DOCTOR.] Did he say anything? Did he say anything at the end?

Maguire. What were you expecting him to say?

Eugene. I don't know. I just wondered.

Maguire. If he found what he was looking for? I doubt that, Gene! At least he didn't say anything.

[EUGENE *leaves and goes into* BEN'S *room.* MAGUIRE *comes out onto the veranda.*]

Luke. How long have you known, Doc?

Maguire. For two days—from the beginning. Since I first saw him at three in the morning in the Uneeda Lunch with a cup of coffee in one hand and a cigarette in the other.

Gant. Was there nothing to be done?

Maguire. My dear, dear Gant, we can't turn back the days that have gone. We can't turn back to the hours when our lungs were sound, our blood hot, our bodies young. We are a flash of fire—a brain, a heart, a spirit. And we are three cents worth of lime and iron—which we cannot get back. [*He shakes his head.*] We can believe in the nothingness of life. We can believe in the nothingness of death, and of a life after death. But who can believe in the nothingness of Ben?

Helen. Come on, Papa, there's nothing more to sit up for. Let me put you to bed. Come along.

[*She takes the old man and leads him gently into the house, as the* DOCTOR *exits.* HUGH *and* LUKE *exit after* HELEN *and* GANT. *Only* LAURA *is left, still sitting on the yard seat.* EUGENE, *who has been standing in the corner in* BEN'S *room, goes to his mother, who is holding* BEN'S *hand tightly.*]

Eugene. Mama?

Eliza. He doesn't turn away from me any more.

Eugene. [*Takes her hand, tries gently to disengage* BEN'S.] Mama, you've got to let go. You've got to let go, Mama!

[ELIZA *shakes her head, her rough clasp tightening.* EUGENE *leaves the room, comes out to the veranda. There, slowly, he sinks to his knees, prays.* LAURA *watches him, her heart going out to him.*]

Eugene. Whoever You are, be good to Ben tonight. Whoever you are, be good to Ben tonight . . . Whoever You are . . . be good to Ben tonight . . . be good to Ben tonight. . . .

SLOW CURTAIN

ACT THREE

The Dixieland Boarding House. Two weeks later.

The house is seen in a soft early light. From offstage, a newsboy, whistling, throws four tightly wadded newspapers onto the veranda—plop—plop—plop—plop. The whistling and his steps fade away. The lights come up dimly in LAURA'S *room.*

[LAURA *is in bed in her nightgown.* EUGENE *is at the foot of the bed by the window, looking out. He takes his shirt from the bedpost, puts it on.*]

Laura. [*Stirring.*] Gene? What was that?

Eugene. Soaks Baker with the morning papers. Plop—plop—plop—plop—how I used to love that sound. Every time the heavy bag getting lighter. I'll always feel sorry for people who have to carry things. [*Sighs.*] It's getting light, it's nearly dawn.

Laura. Don't go yet.

[*Reaches for his hand.*]

Eugene. Do you think I want to on your last morning here? Mama gets up so early. Do you know that every morning before she cooks breakfast she visits Ben's grave?

[*Sits on bed, takes her in his arms.*]

Laura. Gene, Gene.

Eugene. Oh, Laura, I love you so. When I'm close to you like this, it's so natural. Are all men like me? Tell me.

Laura. I've told you I've never known anyone like you.

Eugene. But you have known men? It would be strange if you hadn't. A woman so beautiful, so loving. You make me feel like I only used to dream of feeling. I've hardly thought to daydream in weeks—except about us.

Laura. What did you use to dream?

Eugene. I always wanted to be the winner, the general, the spearhead of victory! Then, following that, I wanted to be loved. Victory and love! Unbeaten and beloved! And I am that now, truly! Laura, will you marry me?

Laura. [*Moving away.*] Oh darling!

Eugene. You knew I was going to ask you, didn't you? You knew I couldn't let you go even for a day.

Laura. Yes, I knew.

Eugene. You're happy with me. You know I make you happy. And I'm so complete with you. [*He draws her back into his arms.*] Do you know that three hundred dollars Ben left me? He would want me to use it for us. I'll go with you to Richmond today. I'll meet your parents, so they won't think I'm an irresponsible fool who's stolen you. That may be a little hard to prove— but there is a job I can get. Would you mind living in Altamont?

Laura. I don't care where I live. Just keep holding me.

Eugene. I am going to have to tell Mama first.

Laura. Let's not worry about that now. Tell me about us.

Eugene. All the treasures the world has in store for us? We'll see and know them all . . . All the things and the places I've read about. There isn't a state in this country you won't know. The great names of Arizona, Texas, Colorado, California—we'll ride the freights to get there if we have to. And we'll go to Europe, and beyond . . . the cool, green land of Shakespeare, the gloomy forests of Gaul, the great Assyrian plains where Alexander feasted . . . the crumbling walls of Babylon, the palaces of the kings of Egypt, the towering white crags of Switzerland . . . My God, Laura, there might not be time enough for all!

Laura. There will be time enough, darling.

[*They kiss longingly. From a far distance, they hear the whistle of a train as it passes.*]

Eugene. The Richmond train leaves at noon. I'll have to get packed.

Laura. You do love trains, don't you?

Eugene. I love only you. Will you have confidence in me, the unbeaten and beloved?

Laura. Yes, darling, I will have confidence in you.

Eugene. I'll never have to sneak out of this room again.

[EUGENE *rises, moves to the door.* LAURA, *on her knees, reaches toward him.*]

Laura. Eugene! [*He comes back to her.*] I will love you always.

[*They kiss.* EUGENE *exits.* LAURA *leaps from the bed, hurries after him.*]

Laura. Gene!

[ELIZA *has come out the side door. She takes flowers out of a bucket preparing to take them to* BEN'S *grave.* EUGENE *enters the hallway, lifts the phone receiver. He doesn't see* ELIZA. *Lights dim down on* LAURA'S *room as she dresses.*]

Eugene. [*Into telephone.*] Good morning. 3-2 please. Hello, Uncle Will? This is Eugene. Yes, I know how early it is . . .

You know that position you offered me? I've decided to take it.

Eliza. [*Pleased, to herself.*] Well, can you imagine!

Eugene. [*Into telephone.*] I've thought it over, and that's what I'd like to do, for a while anyway. That's right. That's fine . . . Well, you see, I'm getting married . . . [ELIZA *freezes in pain.*] Yes, married—to Miss James. We're going to Richmond for a few days. We're leaving on the noon train. Thanks, Uncle Will. Thanks a lot.

[EUGENE *hangs up. He starts to go back upstairs.*]

Eliza. Eugene!

Eugene. [*Coming out to her slowly.*] Well, now—with your second sense, I thought you would have guessed it, Mama.

Eliza. First Grover, then Ben, now you . . . Why didn't I know, why didn't I see?

Eugene. I'm sorry, Mama, but we couldn't wait any longer.

Eliza. Gene, child, don't make this mistake. She's so much older than you. Don't throw yourself away, boy!

Eugene. Mama, there's no use arguing. Nothing you can say will change my mind.

Eliza. [*Desperately.*] And my plans for you? What of my plans for you?

Eugene. Mama, I don't want your plans, I've got my own life to live!

Eliza. But you don't know! Gene, listen, you know that Stumptown property of mine? I sold it just yesterday so you could go to Chapel Hill—— You know I've always wanted you to have an education. You can have it now, child, you can have it.

Eugene. It's too late, Mama, it's too late!

Eliza. Why law, child, it's never too late for anything! It's what Ben wanted, you know.

Eugene. Laura and I are leaving, Mama. I'm going up to get packed.

[*He briefly kisses her, exits into house.*]

Eliza. Gene! [ELIZA *stands looking after him a moment, then quickly enters the hall, lifts the telephone receiver.*] Three-two, please.

[HELEN *enters from the kitchen with a broom. She sweeps the veranda.*]

Helen. What are you calling Uncle Will so early for?

Eliza. [*Into phone.*] Will? No, no, I know—I heard . . . Yes, I know it's early . . . Listen, Will, I want you to do something for me. You know my Stumptown property? I want you to sell it . . . Now, this morning. Will, don't argue with me— I don't care what it's worth. Call Cash Rankin, he's been after me for weeks to sell . . . Well, I know what I want to do— I'll explain it to you later—Just do what I say and let me know. [*She hangs up.*]

Helen. Well, it's never too early in the morning to turn a trade, is it? What are you selling?

Eliza. Some property I own.

Helen. Maybe you can put a little of that money into getting somebody else to help you at that altar of yours, the kitchen stove.

Eliza. Helen, get breakfast started, will you? I'll be in later. And if Gene comes down, keep him in there, will you?

Helen. Oh, all right. You let me know when I can let him out!

[*Exits into house.* ELIZA *appears at door of* LAURA'S *room.* LAURA *is dressed and is packing her suitcase.* ELIZA *knocks.*]

Laura. [*As* ELIZA *enters.*] Oh, Mrs. Gant. I've been expecting you. Come in.

Eliza. I should think you would.

Laura. Mrs. Gant, before you say anything . . .

Eliza. I'll vow, I can't believe a mature woman—at a time of trouble like this—would take advantage of a child, a mere child . . .

Laura. Mrs. Gant, will you please listen?

Eliza. I will listen to nothing. You just pack your things and get out of this house. I should have known what you were from the first minute I set eyes on you . . . "I'm looking for a room, Mrs. Gant . . ." Why, butter wouldn't melt in your mouth . . .

Laura. [*Slowly, distinctly.*] Mrs. Gant, I am not marrying Eugene. I'm not. I wish with all my heart I could.

Eliza. You can't lie out of it. Gene just told me.

Laura. I am engaged to be married to a young man in Richmond.

Eliza. What kind of a wicked game are you playing with my child?

Laura. Mrs. Gant, this isn't easy. I should have told Gene long ago . . . but I didn't. A girl about to get married suddenly finds herself facing responsibilities. I never liked responsibilities. Gene knows how I am. I like music, I like to walk in the woods, I like . . . to dream. I know I'm older than Gene, but in many ways I'm younger. The thought of marriage frightened me. I told my fiancé I needed time to think it over. I fell in love with Eugene. I found the kind of romance I'd never known before, but I've also found that it isn't the answer. Gene is a wonderful boy, Mrs. Gant. He must go to college. He must have room to expand and grow, to find himself. He mustn't be tied down at this point in his life. He needs the whole world to wander in—and I know now that I need a home, I need children—I need a husband. For people like me there are rules, very good rules for marriage and for happiness—and I've broken enough of them. I telephoned Philip last night. He's arriving at the depot on that early train. We're going on to Charleston together, and we'll be married there. He loves me, and I will love him too after a while. [*Takes note from desk.*] I left this note for Eugene. I couldn't just tell him. [*Gives it to* ELIZA.] Will you say goodbye to Mr. Gant for me, and tell him I hope he feels better? And my goodbyes to Mr. Clatt and the others? And to Helen. Especially to Helen. She works so hard. [*Looks around.*] Goodbye, little room. I've been happy here. [*Picks up suitcase, faces* ELIZA.] Some day you're going to have to let him go, too. Goodbye, Mrs. Gant.

[*She exits. During the above* HUGH *has entered the veranda, is seated, reading the newspaper.* LAURA *enters from the house, looks back lingeringly, then, hearing the approaching train, hurries off toward the station.* HELEN *enters, drinking coffee.*]

Helen. Mama? Now where on earth? Hugh, have you seen Mama?

Hugh. Umph.

Helen. Do you know she was on the phone just now selling some property? Imagine—at this hour! And she leaves me to slave in the kitchen . . . Do you know where she is?

Hugh. You know, they don't advertise the good jobs in here, not the really big ones.

Gant. [*Entering in his suspenders, sleepily rubbing his jaw.*] Isn't breakfast ready yet?

Helen. Papa, how many times has Mama told you, you wait until the boarders have had theirs! And don't you dare appear in front of them in your suspenders, do you hear?

Gant. Merciful God! What a way to greet the day! [*He exits.*]

Helen. [*Calling after* GANT.] Papa, do you know where Mama is?

[HELEN *exits after* GANT. EUGENE *enters down stairs, carrying his suitcase, stops at* LAURA's *door, knocks.* ELIZA *has just laid* LAURA's *letter on the bed.*]

Eugene. Laura? Laura? [EUGENE *enters to* ELIZA.] Mama! Where's Laura? Where is she?

Eliza. She's gone.

Eugene. Gone? Where?

Eliza. She just walked out on you, child. Just walked out on you. [*Shakes her finger at him.*] I could have told you, the minute I laid eyes on her——

Eugene. [*Seizing* ELIZA's *hand.*] You sent her away.

Eliza. I never did. She just walked out on you, child.

[EUGENE *breaks for the door.* ELIZA *picks up the letter, runs after him.*]

Eliza. Gene! Eugene! Wait!

Eugene. [*Runs down to the veranda.*] Laura . . . [*Looks up street.*] Laura . . . [*As* HUGH *points toward station, starts off that way.*] Laura . . .

Eliza. [*Entering, waving the letter.*] Wait! Wait! She left you this. Gene! [EUGENE *turns, sees the letter.*] She left you this. Read it, child.

[EUGENE *crosses to* ELIZA, *takes the letter, tears it open, reads it.*]

Eliza. You see, it's no use. It's no use.

[EUGENE *crosses slowly to the yard seat, sits.* ELIZA *watches him.* HELEN *enters through the front door.*]

Helen. Mama, there you are! Where have you been? We've got to start getting breakfast. [*As* ELIZA *waves her to silence.*] What's the matter?

Eliza. That Miss James. She and Eugene . . .

Helen. [*Laughs.*] Oh my God, Mama, have you just found out about that? What about it?

Eliza. She's gone.

Helen. What?

Eliza. She just walked out on him.

Helen. [*Crosses to* EUGENE.] Oh ho, so that's it, is it? Has your girl gone and left you, huh? Huh? [*Tickles his ribs. He turns, clasps her knees.*] Why, Gene, forget about it! You're only a kid yet. She's a grown woman.

Eliza. Helen's right. Why, child, I wouldn't let a girl get the best of me. She was just fooling you all the time, just leading you on, wasn't she, Helen?

Helen. You'll forget her in a week, Gene.

Eliza. Why, of course you will. Pshaw, this was just puppy love. Like the fellow says, there's plenty good fish in the sea as ever came out of it.

Helen. Cheer up, you're not the only man got fooled in his life!

Hugh. [*From behind his paper.*] By God, that's the truth!

[HELEN *and* ELIZA *glare at* HUGH.]

Eliza. Helen, go inside, I'll be in in a minute.

Helen. Oh, all right. Hugh, you come in and help me.

[HELEN *exits, followed by* HUGH.]

Eliza. [*Sits beside* EUGENE, *his back still turned to her.*] Gene. You know what I'd do if I were you? I'd just show her I was a good sport, that's what! I wouldn't let on to her that it affected me one bit. I'd write her just as big as you please and laugh about the whole thing.

Eugene. Oh, God, Mama, please, leave me alone, leave me alone!

Eliza. Why, I'd be ashamed to let any girl get my goat like that. When you get older, you'll just look back on this and laugh. You'll see. You'll be going to college next year, and you won't remember a thing about it. [EUGENE *turns, looks at her.*] I told you I'd sold that Stumptown property, and I have. This year's term has started already but next year . . .

Eugene. Mama, now! Now! I've wasted enough time!

Eliza. What are you talking about? Why you're a child yet, there's plenty of time yet . . .

Eugene. [*Rises, walks about her.*] Mama, Mama, what is it? What more do you want from me? Do you want to strangle and drown me completely? Do you want more string? Do you want me to collect more bottles? Tell me what you want! Do you want more property? Do you want the town? Is that it?

Eliza. Why, I don't know what you're talking about, boy. If I hadn't tried to accumulate a little something, none of you would have had a roof to call your own.

Eugene. A roof to call our own? Good God, I never had a bed to call my own! I never had a room to call my own! I never had a quilt to call my own that wasn't taken from me to warm the mob that rocks on that porch and grumbles.

Eliza. [*Rises, looking for an escape.*] Now you may sneer at the boarders if you like . . .

Eugene. No, I can't. There's not breath or strength enough in me to sneer at them all I like. Ever since I was this high, and you sent me to the store for the groceries, I used to think, this food is not for us—it's for them! Mama, making us wait until they've eaten, all these years—feeding us on *their* leftovers—do you know what it does to us—when it's you we wanted for us, *you* we needed for us. Why? Why?

Eliza. [*Trembling.*] They don't hurt me like the rest of you do—they wouldn't talk to me like you are, for one thing.

[*Starts toward side door.*]

Eugene. Because they don't care—they're strangers. They don't give a damn about you! They'll talk like this about you behind your back—I've heard them do that plenty!

Eliza. [*Turns.*] What? What? What kind of things do they say about me?

Eugene. What does it matter what they say—*they* say! Doesn't it matter to you what I say?

[*Takes her in his arms, holds her.*]

Eliza. [*Beginning to weep.*] I don't understand.

Eugene. [*Releases her, moves away.*] Oh it's easy to cry now, Mama, but it won't do you any good! I've done as much work for my wages as you deserve. I've given you fair value for your money, I thank you for nothing. [*Crosses up to veranda.*]

Eliza. What's that? What are you saying!

Eugene. I said I thank you for nothing, but I take that back. Yes, I have a great deal to be thankful for. I give thanks for every hour of loneliness I've had here, for every dirty cell you ever gave me to sleep in, for the ten million hours of indifference, and for these two minutes of cheap advice.

Eliza. You will be punished if there's a just God in Heaven.

Eugene. Oh, there is! I'm sure there is! Because I have been punished. By God, I shall spend the rest of my life getting my heart back, healing and forgetting every scar you put upon me when I was a child. The first move I ever made after the cradle was to crawl for the door. And every move I ever made since has been an effort to escape. And now, at last I am free from all of you. And I shall get me some order out of this chaos. I shall find my way out of it yet, though it takes me twenty years more—alone.

Eliza. Gene! Gene, you're not leaving?

Eugene. Ah, you were not looking, were you? I've already gone.

[EUGENE *exits into the house, into* LAURA'S *room, where he left his valise. He throws his body on the bed, stifles his crying.* ELIZA *sits on the veranda edge, stunned.* GANT, *wearing a vest over his suspenders, enters.*]

Gant. Now do you suppose I can get some breakfast? [ELIZA *doesn't answer.*] Well, do you mind if I make a fire in the fireplace? [*Goes to wood box, muttering.*] If I can't get any food to keep me alive, I can get a little warmth out of this drafty barn! [*Starts collecting wood from box.*] Some day I'm going to burn up this house—just pile in all the logs that old grate'll hold—and all the furniture—and all the wooden-headed people around here—and some kerosene—till this old barn takes off like a giant cinder blazing through the sky. That would show them—all fifteen miserable rooms—burning, blistering . . .

Eliza. I wish you would, Mr. Gant. I just wish you would.

Gant. You think I'm joking.

Eliza. No, I don't.

Gant. If I just get drunk enough, I will!

Eliza. [*Rises, faces house.*] Serve it right . . . miserable, unholy house!

Gant. Why, Miss Eliza!

Eliza. I'll do it myself— [*With demoniacal strength she shakes a newel post by the steps.*] I'll tear you down! I'll kill you, house, kill you! I'll shake you to pieces!

[*Picks up* MRS. PERT'S *rocker, crashes it.*]

Helen. [*Entering hurriedly.*] Eliza Gant, have you gone mad!

Gant. Let me help you, Mrs. Gant! [*Drops wood, starts tearing at the other post.*] God-damned barn! Thief! Travesty on nature!

Eliza. God-damned barn!

[*Kicks in latticed panels under the veranda.*]

Helen. [*Calls inside.*] Hugh, come out here!

Will. [*Entering from rear of veranda.*] My God, what are they doing?

Gant. [*Screaming up at house.*] Clatt— Mangle—Brown— Come out of there, you rats, all of you—come out, come out, wherever you are!

[THE BOARDERS *begin to yell and squeal from inside.*]

Eliza. [*Hysterically, imitating* GANT.] Come out, come out, wherever you are!

Hugh. [*Entering.*] What's going on?

Gant. [*Breaking off the newel post.*] We're tearing down this murderous trap, that's what. Hand me the hatchet, Hugh. It's in the wood box.

Hugh. Fine! Fine!

[*Dashes to woodbox, takes out hatchet.* THE BOARDERS *enter down the stairs in various stages of undress.*]

Miss Brown. Call the police.

Mrs. Clatt. Let's go to Mrs. Haskell's!

Jake. Gant's off his nut!

Gant. [*Chasing, threatening* THE BOARDERS.] Squeal, you croaking bastards. Croak and run! Run for your lives!

Boarders. [*Fleeing.*] The house is falling

down! It's a tornado! Ladies' Temperance Society, humph! Has anyone called the police?

Hugh. Here's the hatchet, W.O.

Gant. [*Leaping for it.*] Give it to me.

Will. Stop it, Gant—stop this! Have you all lost your minds?

Eliza. [*Throwing flower pot after* THE BOARDERS.] Go to Mrs. Haskell's!

Helen. Mama!

Gant. [*Brandishing hatchet at* JAKE *and* MRS. CLATT *as they exit.*] Look at 'em run! And they haven't even had breakfast. Run, scatterbrains, empty bellies!

Jake. I'll sue you for this, Gant, I'll sue you for this!   [*Exits.*]

[MRS. SNOWDEN *enters through front door.* GANT *whirls on her.*]

Gant. So you don't like the food here? So you don't like my wife's coffee!

[MRS. SNOWDEN, *screaming, hastily retreats.*]

Eliza. [*Lifting a chair to hurl after* THE BOARDERS.] Why, law, that's good coffee!

[HELEN *seizes* ELIZA'S *arms, stops her* ELIZA'S *sensibilities slowly return.*]

Gant. Look at 'em run! Oh, Miss Eliza what a woman you are!

[GANT, *roaring with laughter, crosses down to* ELIZA, *is about to embrace her sees her sober, shocked face.*]

Eliza. Mr. Gant, Mr. Gant, what have you done? What have you done?

Gant. What have I done? What have I— Merciful God, woman!

Eliza. Just look at this mess! And the boarders have all gone!

Helen. I don't know what got into you Papa.

Gant. Merciful God! What got into me. Didn't she just stand there herself and . .

Eliza. Helen, go get the boarders, tell them he's been drinking, tell them anything, but get them back!

Will. I never saw such an exhibition.

Eliza. Will, go with Helen. Tell them we all apologize. They'll listen to you. Hugh help me clean up this mess.

[HELEN *and* WILL *exit after* THE BOARDERS.]

Gant. Let them go, Miss Eliza. *Let the boarders go!*

[ELIZA *stands rigid.* GANT *waits anxiously.*]

Eliza. I just don't know what came over me.

Gant. [*Crosses, flings the hatchet in the woodbox.*] Merciful God!

[EUGENE *enters with his suitcase.*]

Gant. Where are you going?

Eugene. I'm going to school at Chapel Hill, Papa.

Gant. You are? [*He looks at* ELIZA.]

Eugene. Mama promised me the money. She sold her Stumptown property.

Gant. Oh? By God, maybe it isn't going to be such a god-damned miserable day, after all! Got any money, son?

Eugene. I've got Ben's money. Thanks, Papa.

Gant. [*Takes money from his pocket, tucks it into* EUGENE'S *pocket.*] Well go, Gene. Go for both of us. Keep right on going.

Eugene. I will, Papa. Goodbye.

Gant. [*As they shake hands.*] Goodbye, Gene. [*Starts into house, turns.*] You're going to bust loose, boy—you're going to bust loose, all over this dreary planet!

[GANT *exits.* ELIZA *starts picking up the debris.*]

Eliza. I reckon you've made up your mind all right.

Eugene. Yes, Mama, I have.

Eliza. Well, I'll deposit the money in the Chapel Hill Bank for you. I tell you what! It looks mighty funny, though, that you can't just stay a day or two more with Ben gone and all. It seems you'll do anything to get away from me. That's all right, I know your mind's made up and I'm not complaining! It seems all I've ever been fit for around here is to cook and sew. That's all the use any of you have ever had for me . . .

Eugene. Mama, don't think you can work on my feelings here at the last minute.

Eliza. It seems I've hardly laid eyes on you all summer long . . . [*Replacing wood in woodbox.*] Well, when you get up there, you want to look up your Uncle Emerson and Aunt Lucy. Your Aunt Lucy took a great liking to you when they were down here, and when you're in a strange town it's mighty good sometimes to have someone you know. And say, when you see your Uncle Emerson, you might just tell him not to be surprised to

see me any time now. [*She nods pertly at him.*] I reckon I can pick right up and light out the same as the next fellow when I get ready. I'm not going to spend all my days slaving away for a lot of boarders—it don't pay. If I can turn a couple of trades here this fall, I just may start out to see the world like I always intended to. I was talking to Cash Rankin the other day . . . he said, "Why Mrs. Gant," he said, "if I had your head for figures, I'd be a rich man in . . ." [*Her talk drifts off.* EUGENE *stands looking at her. There is another terrible silence between them. She points at him with her finger, finally—her old loose masculine gesture.*] Here's the thing I'm going to do. You know that lot of mine on Sunset Terrace, right above Dick Webster's place? Well, I been thinking. If we started to build there right away, we could be in our own house by spring. I've been thinking about it a lot lately . . . [*There is another silence.*] I hate to see you go, son.

Eugene. Goodbye, Mama.

Eliza. Try to be happy, child, try to be a little more happy . . .

[*She turns and, with unsteady step, starts into the house.*]

Eugene. MAMA! [*He drops the valise, takes the steps in a single bound, catching* ELIZA'S *rough hands which she has held clasped across her body, drawing them to his breast.*] GOODBYE . . . GOODBYE . . . GOODBYE . . . MAMA . . .

Eliza. [*Holding him.*] Poor child . . . poor child . . . poor child. [*Huskily, faintly.*] We must try to love one another. [*Finally,* EUGENE *moves from* ELIZA, *picks up the valise as the lights start dimming, holding a spot on her.* ELIZA *seems to recede in the distance as into his memory.*] Now for Heaven's sake, spruce up, boy, spruce up! Throw your shoulders back! And smile, look pleasant! Let them know up there that you *are* somebody!

[ELIZA'S *voice fades. The set is black. A spot holds on* EUGENE.]

EPILOGUE

Ben's Voice. So you're finally going, Gene?

Eugene. Ben? Is that you, Ben?

Ben's Voice. Who did you think it was, you little idiot? Do you know why you're going, or are you just taking a ride on a train?

Eugene. I know. Of course I know why I'm going. There's nothing here for me. Ben, what really happens? Everything is going. Everything changes and passes away. Can you remember some of the things I do? I've already forgotten the old faces. I forget the names of people I knew for years.

I get their faces mixed. I get their heads stuck on other people's bodies. I think one man has said what another said. And I forget. There is something I have lost and can't remember.

— *Ben's Voice.* The things you have forgotten and are trying to remember are the child that you were. He's gone, Gene, as I am gone. And will never return. No matter where you search for him, in a million streets, in a thousand cities.

Eugene. Then I'll search for an end to hunger, and the happy land!

— *Ben's Voice.* Ah, there is no happy land. There is no end to hunger!

Eugene. Ben, help me! You must have an answer. Help me, and I won't go searching for it.

— *Ben's Voice.* You little fool, what do you want to find out there?

Eugene. I want to find the world. Where *is the world?*

— *Ben's Voice.* [*Fading.*] The world is nowhere, Gene . . .

Eugene. Ben, wait! Answer me!

— *Ben's Voice.* The world is nowhere, no one, Gene. *You* are your world.

[*The train whistle sounds. Lights reveal Dixieland in dim silhouette.* EUGENE, *without looking back, exits.*]

CURTAIN

BIBLIOGRAPHY

Albright, H. D., and others, *Principles of Theatre Art*. 1955.
Altman, George, and others, *Theater Pictorial*. 1953.
Anderson, John, *The American Theatre*. 1938.
Anderson, Maxwell, *The Essence of Tragedy*. 1939.
Archer, William, *The Old Drama and the New*. 1923.
Bahr, Hermann, *Expressionism*. 1925.
Baker, Blanch M., *Theatre and Allied Arts*. 1952.
Baker, George Pierce, *Dramatic Technique*. 1918.
Beerbohm, Max, *Around Theatres*. 1928.
Bellinger, Martha F., *A Short History of the Drama*. 1927.
Bentley, Eric R., *In Search of Theater*. 1953.
———, *The Playwright as Thinker*. 1946.
Block, Anita, *The Changing World in Plays and Theatre*. 1939.
Blum, Daniel, *A Pictorial History of the American Theatre*. 1950.
———, *Great Stars of the American Stage*. 1951.
Boyle, Walden P., *Central and Flexible Staging*. 1956.
Bradshaw, Martha, ed., *Soviet Theaters 1917–1941*. 1954.
Braun, Hanns, *Theater in Germany*. 1952.
Brown, John Mason, *The Art of Playgoing*. 1936.
———, *The Modern Theatre in Revolt*. 1929.
Burris-Meyer, Homer, and Cole, Edward C., *Scenery for the Theatre*. 1938.
Chandler, Frank W., *Modern Continental Playwrights*. 1931.
Charques, Richard D., *Footnotes to the Theatre*. 1938.
Cheney, Sheldon, *Stage Decoration*. 1928.
———, *The Art Theatre*, 1925.
———, *The Theatre*. 1952.
Clark, Barrett H., *European Theories of the Drama*. 1929.
———, and Freedley, George, eds., *A History of Modern Drama*. 1947.
Clurman, Harold, *The Fervent Years*. 1945.
Craig, Edward Gordon, *On the Art of the Theatre*. 1911.
———, *The Theatre—Advancing*. 1925.
Dickinson, Thomas H., ed., *The Theatre in a Changing Europe*. 1937.
———, *An Outline of Contemporary Drama*. 1927.
Dolman, John, Jr., *The Art of Acting*. 1949.
———, *The Art of Play Production*. 1946.
Downer, Alan S., *Fifty Years of American Drama*. 1951.
Downs, Harold, ed., *Theatre and Stage*. 1934.
Drew, Elizabeth, *Discovering Drama*. 1937.
Eaton, Walter Prichard, *The Theatre Guild*. 1929.
Eliot, T. S., *Poetry and Drama*. 1951.
Ellis-Fermor, Una M., *The Irish Dramatic Movement*. 1939.
———, *Frontiers of Drama*. 1945.
Eustis, Morton, *Players at Work*. 1937.
Fay, William G., and Carswell, Catherine, *The Fays of the Abbey Theatre*. 1935.

Fergusson, Francis, *The Idea of the Theatre*. 1949.
Flanagan, Hallie, *Arena*. 1940.
Flexner, Eleanor, *American Playwrights, 1918–1938*. 1938.
Freedley, George, and Reeves, John A., *A History of the Theatre*. 1941.
Fuchs, Theodore, *Stage Lighting*. 1929.
Gagey, Edmond M., *Revolution in American Drama*. 1947.
Gassner, John, *Masters of the Drama*, 1954.
———, *The Theatre in Our Times*. 1954.
———, *Form and Idea in Modern Theatre*. 1956.
Granville-Barker, Harley, *Uses of the Drama*, 1945.
———, *The Study of Drama*. 1935.
Gregor, Joseph, and Fülöp-Miller, René, *The Russian Theatre*. 1930.
Gregory, Lady, *Journals*. 1946.
Harris, Mark, *The Case for Tragedy*. 1932.
Hartnoll, Phyllis, ed., *The Oxford Companion to the Theatre*. 1951.
Henn, T. R., *The Harvest of Tragedy*. 1956.
Hewitt, Barnard, *Art and Craft of Play Production*. 1940.
Houghton, Norris, *Advance from Broadway*, 1941.
———, *Moscow Rehearsals*. 1936.
Hughes, Glenn, *The Story of the Theatre*. 1929.
———, *A History of the American Theatre, 1700–1950*. 1951.
Hume, Samuel J., and Fuerst, Walter Rene, *XXth Century Stage Decoration*. 1929.
Isaacs, Edith J. R., ed., *Theatre*. 1927.
Jones, Robert Edmond, *The Dramatic Imagination*. 1956.
———, *Drawings for the Theatre*. 1925.
Komisarjevsky, Theodore, and Simonson, Lee, *Settings and Costumes of the Modern Stage*. 1933.
Kraft, Irma, *Plays, Players, Playhouses*. 1928.
Krutch, Joseph Wood, *The American Drama since 1918*. 1957.
———, *"Modernism" in Modern Drama*. 1953.
Lamm, Martin, *Modern Drama*, tr. Elliott. 1952.
Langner, Lawrence, *The Magic Curtain*. 1951.
Laver, James, *Drama, Its Costume and Decor*. 1951.
Lumley, Frederick, *Trends in 20th Century Drama*. 1956.
McCleery, Albert, and Glick, Carl, *Curtains Going Up*. 1939.
Macgowan, Kenneth, *Footlights across America*. 1929.
——— and Melnitz, William, *The Living Stage*. 1955.
Macleod, Joseph, *The New Soviet Theatre*. 1947.
———, *Soviet Theatre Sketch Book*. 1951.
Malone, Andrew E., *The Irish Drama*. 1929.
Mantle, Burns, *Contemporary American Playwrights*. 1938.
Marshall, Norman, *The Other Theatre*. 1947.
———, *The Producer and the Play*. 1957.

Miller, Anna Irene, *The Independent Theatre in Europe.* 1931.
Morehouse, Ward, *Matinee Tomorrow.* 1949.
Morris, Lloyd, *Curtain Time.* 1953.
Moses, Montrose J., and Brown, John Mason, *The American Theatre as Seen by its Critics, 1752–1934.* 1934.
Muller, Herbert J., *The Spirit of Tragedy.* 1956.
Nathan, George Jean, *The Theatre in the Fifties.* 1953.
Nemirovitch-Dantchenko, Vladimir I. *My Life in the Russian Theatre.* 1936.
Nicoll, Allardyce, *The Development of the Theatre.* 1948.
———, *The English Theatre.* 1936.
———, *Film and Theatre.* 1936.
———, *World Drama.* 1950.
Oenslager, Donald, *Scenery Then and Now.* 1936.
O'Hara, F. H., and Bro, M. H., *Invitation to the Theatre.* 1951.
Peacock, Ronald, *The Poet in the Theatre.* 1946.
———, *The Art of Drama.* 1956.
Prideaux, Tom, *World Theatre in Pictures.* 1953.
Quinn, Arthur H., *A History of American Drama.* 1943.
Reynolds, Ernest, *Modern English Drama.* 1949.
Robinson, Lennox, *Ireland's Abbey Theatre.* 1951.
Samachson, Dorothy and Joseph, *Let's Meet the Theatre.* 1954.
Sayler, Oliver M., *The Russian Theatre.* 1922.
———, *Revolt in the Arts.* 1930.
———, *Max Reinhardt and His Theatre.* 1924.

Shaw, George Bernard, *Our Theatres in the Nineties.* 1932.
Simonson, Lee, *The Art of Scenic Design.* 1950.
———, *Part of a Lifetime.* 1943.
———, *The Stage Is Set.* 1932.
Smith, Hugh A., *Main Currents of Modern French Drama.* 1925.
Stanislavsky on the Art of the Stage. 1950.
Strong, L. A. G., *Common Sense about Drama.* 1937.
Stuart, Donald C., *The Development of Dramatic Art.* 1928.
Thompson, Alan R., *The Anatomy of Drama.* 1942.
———, *The Dry Mock.* 1948.
Trewin, J. C., *Dramatists of Today.* 1953.
———, *The English Theatre.* 1948.
———, ed., *Theatre Programme.* 1954.
———, *The Theatre since 1900.* 1951.
Waxman, Samuel M., *Antoine and the Théâtre Libre.* 1926.
Whiting, Frank M., *An Introduction to the Theatre.* 1954.
Whitman, Willson, *Bread and Circuses, a Study of the Federal Theatre.* 1937.
Whitworth, Geoffrey A., *Theatre in Action.* 1938.
Williams, Raymond, *Drama from Ibsen to Eliot.* 1952.
———, *Drama in Performance.* 1954.
Wilson, A. E., *The Edwardian Theatre.* 1951.
Worsley, T. C., *The Fugitive Art.* 1952.
Young, Stark, *Theatre Practice.* 1926.

YEARBOOKS

Chapman, John, ed., *The Best Plays of 1947–48,* and subsequent years to *1951–52.*
———, ed., *Theatre '53,* and subsequent years.
——— and Sherwood, Garrison P., eds., *The Best Plays of 1894–99.*
Daniel Blum's Theatre World, 1944–1945, and subsequent years.
Kronenberger, Louis, ed., *The Best Plays of 1952–53* and subsequent years.

Mantle, Burns, ed., *The Best Plays of 1919–20* and subsequent years to *1946–47.*
——— and Sherwood, Garrison P., eds., *The Best Plays of 1899–1909,* and *The Best Plays of 1909–1919.*
Nathan, George Jean, *The Theatre Book of the Year 1942–1943* to *1950–1951.*
Stephens, Frances, ed., *Theatre World Annual, 1949–1950* and subsequent years.

INDIVIDUAL BIBLIOGRAPHIES

(Titles listed in the General Bibliography are not repeated under Individual Bibliographies, nor are writings listed under an author's Writings on Drama.)

ANTON P. CHEKHOV

Bentley, Eric, *What Is Theatre?* 1956.
Bruford, W. H., *Chekhov and His Russia.* 1947.
Chukovsky, K., *Chekhov the Man.* 1945.
Hingley, Ronald, *Chekhov.* 1950.
Magarshack, David, *Chekhov the Dramatist.* 1952.
Perry, Henry Ten Eyck, *Masters of Dramatic Comedy.* 1939.
Stanislavsky, K. S., *My Life in Art.* 1924.

THOMAS STEARNS ELIOT

Brooks, Cleanth, ed., *Tragic Themes in Western Literature.* 1955.
Fergusson, Francis, *The Human Image in Dramatic Literature.* 1957.
Gardner, Helen Louise, *The Art of T. S. Eliot.* 1949.
March, Richard, ed., *T. S. Eliot, a Symposium.* 1949.
Prior, Moody E., *The Language of Tragedy.* 1947.
Robins, Rossell Hope, *The T. S. Eliot Myth.* 1951.
Smith, Grover, Jr., *T. S. Eliot's Poetry and Plays.* 1956.
Unger, Leonard, ed., *T. S. Eliot, a Selected Critique.* 1948.
Wilson, Frank, *Six Essays on the Development of T. S. Eliot.* 1948.

HENRIK IBSEN

Bradbrook, M. C., *Ibsen the Norwegian.* 1946.
Downs, Brian W., *Ibsen: the Intellectual Background.* 1946.
———, *A Study of Six Plays by Ibsen.* 1950.
Jorgenson, Theodore, *Henrik Ibsen.* 1945.
Koht, Halvdan, *The Life of Ibsen.* 1931.
Northam, John, *Ibsen's Dramatic Method.* 1953.
Shaw, Bernard, *The Quintessence of Ibsenism.* 1913.
Tennant, P. F. D., *Ibsen's Dramatic Technique.* 1948.
Weigand, Hermann J., *The Modern Ibsen.* 1925.
Zucker, A. E., *Ibsen, the Master Builder.* 1929.

WILLIAM INGE

"Candidates for Prizes: Nine Younger Playwrights," *Vogue,* CXXIII (May 1, 1954), 134, 135.
"Picnic's Provider," *The New Yorker,* XXIX (April 4, 1953), 24, 25.

"Schizophrenic Wonder," *Theatre Arts,* XXXIV (May 1950), 32–33.

FEDERICO GARCÍA LORCA

Barea, Arturo, *Lorca, the Poet and His People.* 1949.
Campbell, Roy, *Lorca.* 1952.
Honig, Edwin, *García Lorca.* 1944.

ARTHUR MILLER

Bentley, Eric, *The Dramatic Event.* 1954.
Miller, Arthur, "The University of Michigan," *Holiday,* XIV (Dec. 1953), 68–71, 128–43.
Sievers, W. David, *Freud on Broadway.* 1955.
Tynan, Kenneth, "American Blues," *Encounter,* II (May 1954), 13–19.
Weales, Gerald, "Plays and Analysis," *The Commonweal,* LXVI (July 12, 1957), 382–83.

SEAN O'CASEY

Atkinson, Brooks, *Broadway Scrapbook.* 1947.
Byrne, Dawson, *The Story of Ireland's National Theatre.* 1929.
Koslow, Jules, *The Green and the Red; Sean O'Casey, the Man and His Plays.* 1950.
Robinson, Lennox, ed., *The Irish Theatre,* 1939.

EUGENE O'NEILL

Brown, John Mason, *Upstage.* 1930.
Clark, Barrett H., *Eugene O'Neill, the Man and His Plays.* 1947.
Dickinson, Thomas H., *Playwrights of the New American Theatre.* 1925.
Eaton, Walter P., *The Drama in English.* 1930.
Engel, Edwin A., *The Haunted Heroes of Eugene O'Neill.* 1953.
Falk, Doris V., *Eugene O'Neill and the Tragic Tension.* 1958.
Gelb, Arthur, "O'Neill's Hopeless Hope for a Giant Cycle," *The New York Times,* September 28, 1958, II.1.2.
Glaspell, Susan, *The Road to the Temple.* 1927.
Hamilton, Clayton, *Conversations on Contemporary Dramatists.* 1924.
Mickle, Alan D., *Studies on Six Plays of Eugene O'Neill.* 1929.
O'Hara, Frank H., *Today in American Drama.* 1939.
Sergeant, Elizabeth S., *Fire under the Andes.* 1927.
Skinner, Richard D., *Eugene O'Neill.* 1935.
Winther, Sophus K., *Eugene O'Neill.* 1934.

LUIGI PIRANDELLO

Livingston, Arthur, Prefaces to *Three Plays by Pirandello* and *Each in His Own Way and Other Plays.* 1922 and 1924.

MacClintock, Lander, *The Age of Pirandello.* 1951.
Palmer, John, *Studies in the Contemporary Theatre.* 1927.
Skinner, Richard D., *Our Changing Theatre.* 1931.
Starkie, Walter, *Luigi Pirandello.* 1937.
Vittorini, Domenico, *The Drama of Luigi Pirandello.* 1935.
———, *High Points in the History of Italian Literature.* 1958.

George Bernard Shaw

Bentley, Eric R., *Bernard Shaw.* 1947.
Chesterton, G. K., *George Bernard Shaw.* 1909.
Ellehauge, Martin, *The Position of Bernard Shaw in European Drama and Philosophy.* 1931.
Ervine, St. John G., *Bernard Shaw, His Life, Work, and Friends.* 1956.
Hamon, A., *The Twentieth-Century Molière: Bernard Shaw.* 1916.
Henderson, Archibald, *George Bernard Shaw, Man of the Century.* 1956.
———, ed., *Table Talk of G.B.S.* 1925.
Irvine, William, *The Universe of G.B.S.* 1949.
Joad, C. E. M., *Shaw.* 1949.
———, ed., *Shaw and Society.* 1953.
Kronenberger, Louis, ed., *George Bernard Shaw, a Critical Survey.* 1953.
MacCarthy, Desmond, *Shaw.* 1951.
Mander, Raymond, and Mitchenson, Joe, *Theatrical Companion to Shaw.* 1954.
Nethercot, Arthur H., *Men and Supermen.* 1954.
Patch, Blanch E., *Thirty Years with G.B.S.* 1951.
Pearson, Hesketh, *G.B.S., a Full-length Portrait.* 1942.
———, *G.B.S., a Postscript.* 1950.
Perry, Henry Ten Eyek, *Masters of Dramatic Comedy.* 1939.
Rattray, Robert F., *Bernard Shaw, a Chronicle.* 1951.
Shaw, Bernard, *16 Self Sketches.* 1949.
Ward, A. C., *Bernard Shaw.* 1951.
Winsten, S., ed., *G.B.S. 90.* 1946.

August Strindberg

Björkman, Edwin A., Prefaces to *Plays by August Strindberg.* 1912–1917.
Campbell, George A., *Strindberg.* 1933.
Dahlström, C. E. W. L., *Strindberg's Dramatic Expressionism.* 1930.
Henderson, Archibald, *European Dramatists.* 1916.
Huneker, James, *Iconoclasts.* 1928.
Lind-af-Hageby, Lizzy, *August Strindberg, the Spirit of Revolt.* 1913.
———, *August Strindberg.* 1928.
McGill, Vivian J., *August Strindberg, the Bedevilled Viking.* 1930.
Mortensen, B. M. E. and Downs, Brian W., *Strindberg.* 1949.

Sprigge, Elizabeth, *The Strange Life of August Strindberg.* 1949.
Uddgren, Carl G., *Strindberg the Man.* 1920.

J. M. Synge

Bickley, Francis L., *Synge and the Irish Dramatic Movement.* 1912.
Bourgeois, Maurice, *John Millington Synge and the Irish Theatre.* 1913.
Boyd, Ernest A., *The Contemporary Drama of Ireland.* 1917.
———, *Ireland's Literary Renaissance.* 1916.
Byrne, Dawson, *The Story of Ireland's National Theatre.* 1929.
Howe, P. P., *John Millington Synge.* 1912.
Masefield, John, *John M. Synge.* 1915.
Moore, George, *Hail and Farewell.* 1914.
Robinson, Lennox, ed., *The Irish Theatre.* 1939.
Synge, Samuel, *Letters to My Daughter.* 1932.
Yeats, W. B., *Synge and the Ireland of His Time.* 1911.
———, *Plays and Controversies.* 1923.
———, *Autobiography.* 1938.

Oscar Wilde

Mason, A. E. W., *Sir George Alexander and the St. James's Theatre.* 1935.
Pearson, Hesketh, *Oscar Wilde, His Life and Wit.* 1946.
Ransome, Arthur, *Oscar Wilde, a Critical Study.* 1923.
Wilde, Oscar, *The Importance of Being Earnest* (four-act version). 1956.
Winwar, Frances, *Oscar Wilde and the Yellow Nineties.* 1940.

Thornton Niven Wilder

Anon., "An Obliging Man," *Time,* LXI (Jan. 12, 1953), 44–49.
Atkinson, Brooks, *Broadway Scrapbook.* 1947.
Campbell, Joseph, and Robinson, Henry Morton, "The Skin of Whose Teeth?" *The Saturday Review of Literature,* XXV (Dec. 19, 1942), 3, 4; XXVI (Feb. 13, 1943), 16–19.
Fergusson, Francis, *The Human Image in Dramatic Literature.* 1957.
Firebaugh, Joseph J., "The Humanism of Thornton Wilder," *Pacific Spectator,* IV (Autumn 1950), 426–38.
Guthrie, Tyrone, "The World of Thornton Wilder," *The New York Times Magazine* (Nov. 27, 1955), 26–27, 64, 66–68.
Isaacs, Edith J. R., "Thornton Wilder in Person," *Theatre Arts,* XXVII (Jan. 1943), 21–30.
Kohler, Dayton, "Thornton Wilder," *The English Journal* (college edition), XXVIII (Jan. 1939), 1–11.
McCarthy, Mary, *Sights and Spectacles.* 1956.
Sievers, W. David, *Freud on Broadway.* 1955.
Wilson, Edmund, "The Antrobuses and the Earwickers," *The Nation,* CLVI (Jan. 30, 1943), 167–63.

Thomas Wolfe and Ketti Frings

Anon., "Pronounced Ket-tee," *The Saturday Evening Post*, CCXVI (Nov. 20, 1943), 4.

Muller, Herbert J., *Thomas Wolfe*. 1947.

Rubin, Louis D., *Thomas Wolfe, the Weather of His Youth*. 1955.

Watkins, Floyd C., *Thomas Wolfe's Characters*. 1957.